ONE WEEK LOAN

HANDBOOK OF
CONSUMER PSYCHOLOGY

Marketing and Consumer Psychology Series
Curtis P. Haugtvedt, Ohio State University
Series Editor

Curtis P. Haugtvedt, Paul M. Herr and Frank R. Kardes
Handbook of Consumer Psychology

Cele C. Otnes and Tina M. Lowrey
Contemporary Consumption Rituals: A Research Anthology

Gad Saad
The Evolutionary Bases of Consumption

Michel Wedel and Rik Pieters
Visual Marketing: From Attention to Action

HANDBOOK OF CONSUMER PSYCHOLOGY

EDITED BY
CURTIS P. HAUGTVEDT
PAUL M. HERR • FRANK R. KARDES

LEA Lawrence Erlbaum Associates
Taylor & Francis Group

New York   London

Psychology Press
Taylor & Francis Group
270 Madison Avenue
New York, NY 10016

Psychology Press
Taylor & Francis Group
27 Church Road
Hove, East Sussex BN3 2FA

© 2008 by Taylor & Francis Group, LLC

Printed in the United States of America on acid-free paper
10 9 8 7 6 5 4 3 2

International Standard Book Number-13: 978-0-8058-5603-3 (Hardcover)

Library of Congress Cataloging-in-Publication Data

Handbook of consumer psychology / edited by Curtis P. Haugtvedt, Paul M. Herr and Frank R. Kardes.
    p. cm. -- (Marketing and consumer psychology series ; 4)
    Includes bibliographical references and index.
    ISBN-13: 978-0-8058-5603-3 (acid free paper)
    ISBN-10: 0-8058-5603-X (acid free paper)
    1. Consumer behavior. 2. Decision making. 3. Marketing--Psychological aspects. 4.
Advertising--Psychological aspects. I. Haugtvedt, Curtis P., 1958- II. Herr, Paul, 1956- III. Kardes,
Frank R.

    HF5415.32.H363 2007
    658.8'342--dc22   2007017528

Visit the Taylor & Francis Web site at
http://www.taylorandfrancis.com

and the Psychology Press Web site at
http://www.psypress.com

Contents

Preface

This handbook contains a unique collection of chapters written by the world's leading researchers in the dynamic field of Consumer Psychology. Although these researchers are housed in different academic departments (i.e., marketing, psychology, advertising, communications), all have the common goal of attaining a better scientific understanding of cognitive, affective, and behavioral responses to products and services, the marketing of these products and services, and societal and ethical concerns associated with marketing processes. Consumer Psychology is a discipline at the interface of Marketing, Advertising, and Psychology. Work in Consumer Psychology integrates theories and methods from many different areas and many different approaches to research and practice. Consumer Psychology research focuses on fundamental psychological processes as well as on issues associated with the use of theoretical principles in applied contexts.

Our vision for the *Handbook of Consumer Psychology* was to bring together distinguished researchers from a variety of academic backgrounds to provide succinct summaries of state-of-the-art research as well as to provide a place for authors to speculate and provide suggestions for future research and practice. The chapters present theoretical frameworks that address a broad range of important well-established phenomena in addition to suggestions that will serve as a guide for future research on yet-to-be-discovered phenomena and practices. We were delighted that all of the researchers we contacted agreed that the discipline needed such a resource and that they were willing to write chapters for the *Handbook*.

The first chapter provides a history of the field of consumer psychology from 1895 to 1960. The remaining chapters are organized around seven themes. The first theme focuses on the dominant consumer information processing paradigm that specifies how product information is perceived, comprehended, interpreted, retained, and used. The second organizing theme centers on motivation, affect, and consumer decisions. These chapters focus on variables that energize consumers to buy and to consume. The next section examines the important topics of persuasion, attitudes, and social influence. These chapters describe principles that serve as the basis for understanding and influencing change in consumer beliefs, attitudes, and behaviors. The following theme, behavioral decision research, focuses on key factors that influence consumer choice. The next theme examines products, preferences, places, and people. This section covers topics such as aesthetics, branding, and retailing. The penultimate section focuses on consumer well-being, and the final section focuses on research methods. Together, these chapters provide a broad and integrative perspective on the field of consumer psychology.

While this edition of the *Handbook* covers many areas of research, it is by no means comprehensive or complete. Just as has been the case for the *Handbook of Social Psychology*, as new research, frameworks, and controversies develop, we plan on providing updates, revisions and extensions to the material in this *Handbook* in the coming years. We hope that the current *Handbook* contributions stimulate excitement and discussion about the topics and that the readers will contribute to the discipline of consumer psychology through their own teaching, research, and practice. This *Handbook* will be of interest to well-established academics and practitioners as well graduate students and individuals just beginning careers as academicians or practitioners. Consumer Psychology is truly an interdisciplinary field, and we are pleased to have the opportunity to provide a forum for the viewpoints of contributors to the discipline. It has been a pleasure to work with enthusiastic contributors and publishers!

Curtis P. Haugtvedt
Paul M. Herr
Frank R. Kardes

Contributors

Nidhi Agrawal
Department of Marketing
Northwestern University
Evanston, Illinois

Icek Ajzen
Department of Psychology
University of Massachusetts, Amherst
Amherst, Massachusetts

Joseph W. Alba
Department of Marketing
University of Florida
Gainesville, Florida

Chris T. Allen
Department of Marketing
University of Cincinnati
Cincinnati, Ohio

Eduardo B. Andrade
Department of Marketing
University of California, Berkeley
Berkeley, California

Lawrence W. Barsalou
Department of Psychology
Emory University
Atlanta, Georgia

Roy F. Baumeister
Department of Psychology
Florida State University
Tallahassee, Florida

Hans Baumgartner
Department of Marketing
Pennsylvania State University
University Park, Pennsylvania

James R. Bettman
Department of Marketing
Duke University
Durham, North Carolina

Eugene Borgida
Department of Psychology
University of Minnesota
Minneapolis, Minnesota

Susan M. Broniarczyk
Department of Marketing
University of Texas at Austin
Austin, Texas

James E. Burroughs
McIntire School of Commerce
University of Virginia
Charlottesville, Virginia

John T. Cacioppo
Department of Psychology
University of Chicago
Chicago, Illinois

Margaret C. Campbell
Department of Marketing
University of Colorado at Boulder
Boulder, Colorado

Terry L. Childers
Department of Marketing
University of Kentucky
Lexington, Kentucky

Robert B. Cialdini
Department of Psychology
Arizona State University
Tempe, Arizona

E. Gil Clary
Department of Psychology
College of St. Catherine
St. Paul, Minnesota

Joel B. Cohen
Department of Marketing
University of Florida
Gainesville, Florida

Catherine A. Cole
Department of Marketing
University of Iowa
Iowa City, Iowa

Maria L. Cronley
Department of Marketing
Miami University
Miami, Ohio

Vassilis Dalakas
Department of Marketing
Northern Kentucky University
Highland Heights, Kentucky

Edith Davidson
Department of Marketing
Auburn University
Auburn, Alabama

Ravi Dhar
Department of Marketing
Yale University
New Haven, Connecticut

Adam Duhachek
Department of Marketing
Indiana University
Bloomington, Indiana

Giovanna Egidi
Department of Psychology
University of Chicago
Chicago, Illinois

Eric M. Eisenstein
Department of Marketing
Cornell University
Ithaca, New York

Sevgin A. Eroglu
Department of Marketing
Georgia State University
Atlanta, Georgia

Ronald J. Faber
School of Journalism and Mass
     Communication
University of Minnesota
Minneapolis, Minnesota

Russell H. Fazio
Department of Psychology
Ohio State University
Columbus, Ohio

Ayelet Fishbach
Graduate School of Business
University of Chicago
Chicago, Illinois

Mark Forehand
Department of Marketing
University of Washington
Seattle, Washington

Susan Fournier
Department of Marketing
Boston University
Boston, Massachusetts

Marvin E. Goldberg
Department of Marketing
Pennsylvania State University
University Park, Pennsylvania

Anthony Greenwald
Department of Psychology
University of Washington
Seattle, Washington

Curtis P. Haugtvedt
Department of Marketing and Logistics
Ohio State University
Columbus, Ohio

Geraldine R. Henderson
Medill School
Northwestern University
Evanston, Illinois

Paul M. Herr
Department of Marketing
University of Colorado
Boulder, Colorado

James E. Heyman
Department of Marketing
University of St. Thomas
Saint Paul, Minnesota

JoAndrea Hoegg
Department of Marketing
University of British Columbia
Vancouver, British Columbia, Canada

Christopher K. Hsee
Graduate School of Business
University of Chicago
Chicago, Illinois

J. Wesley Hutchinson
Department of Marketing
University of Pennsylvania
Philadelphia, Pennsylvania

Alice M. Isen
Department of Psychology
Cornell University
Ithaca, New York

Chris Janiszewski
Department of Marketing
University of Florida
Gainesville, Florida

Timothy P. Johnson
Public Adminstration Program
University of Illinois at Chicago
Chicago, Illinois

Christopher Joiner
Department of Marketing
George Mason University
Fairfax, Virginia

Christopher R. M. Jones
Department of Psychology
Ohio State University
Columbus, Ohio

Lynn R. Kahle
Department of Marketing
University of Oregon
Eugene, Oregon

Frank R. Kardes
Department of Marketing
University of Cincinnati
Cincinnati, Ohio

Jeff A. Kasmer
Kasmer Associates
Los Angeles, California

James J. Kellaris
Department of Marketing
University of Cincinnati
Cincinnati, Ohio

Anita Kim
Department of Psychology
University of Minnesota
Minneapolis, Minnesota

Amna Kirmani
Department of Marketing
University of Maryland
College Park, Maryland

Angela Y. Lee
Department of Marketing
Northwestern University
Evanston, Illinois

Wei-Na Lee
Department of Advertising
University of Texas at Austin
Austin, Texas

Kaiya Liu
School of Communication
Ohio State University
Columbus, Ohio

Maggie Wenjing Liu
Rotman School of Management
University of Toronto
Ontario, Toronto, Canada

Barbara Loken
Department of Marketing
University of Minnesota
Minneapolis, Minnesota

Mary Frances Luce
Department of Marketing
Duke University
Durham, North Carolina

Karen A. Machleit
Department of Marketing
University of Cincinnati
Cincinnati, Ohio

Robert Madrigal
Department of Marketing
University of Oregon
Eugene, Oregon

Dominika Maison
Department of Psychology
University of Warsaw
Warsaw, Poland

Antonia Mantonakis
Graduate School of Business
University of Chicago
Chicago, Illinois

Barbara A. Mellers
Department of Marketing
University of California, Berkeley
Berkeley, California

Geeta Menon
Department of Marketing
New York University
New York, New York

David Glen Mick
McIntire School of Commerce
University of Virginia
Charlottesville, Virginia

Christopher Miller
Department of Psychology
University of Minnesota
Minneapolis, Minnesota

Felicia Miller
Department of Marketing
Marquette University
Milwaukee, Wisconsin

Kyeong Sam Min
Department of Marketing
University of South Dakota
Vermillion, South Dakota

C. Page Moreau
Department of Marketing
University of Colorado
Boulder, Colorado

Howard C. Nusbaum
Department of Psychology
University of Chicago
Chicago, Illinois

Thomas C. O'Guinn
Department of Marketing
University of Wisconsin
Madison, Wisconsin

John W. Payne
Department of Marketing
Duke University
Durham, North Carolina

Joann Peck
Department of Marketing
University of Wisconsin
Madison, Wisconsin

Andrew Perkins
Jones Graduate School of Management
Rice University
Houston, Texas

Petia K. Petrova
Tuck School of Business
Dartmouth College
Hanover, New Hampshire

Michel Tuan Pham
Department of Marketing
Columbia University
New York, New York

Rik Pieters
Department of Economics & Business
Tilburg University
Tilburg, the Netherlands

Steven S. Posavac
Department of Marketing
Vanderbilt University
Nashville, Tennessee

Priya Raghubir
Department of Marketing
University of California, Berkeley
Berkeley, California

Deborah Roedder John
Department of Marketing
University of Minnesota
Minneapolis, Minnesota

David W. Schumann
Department of Marketing
University of Tennessee
Knoxville, Tennessee

Norbert Schwarz
Department of Marketing
University of Michigan
Ann Arbor, Michigan

Sharon Shavitt
Department of Marketing
University of Illinois at Urbana-Champaign
Champaign, Illinois

Mark Snyder
Department of Psychology
University of Minnesota
Minneapolis, Minnesota

Dilip Soman
Rotman School of Management
University of Toronto
Toronto, Ontario, Canada

Emily N. Stark
Department of Psychology
University of Minnesota
Minneapolis, Minnesota

Arthur A. Stukas
School of Psychological Science
La Trobe University
Bundoora, Victoria, Australia

Dianne M. Tice
Department of Psychology
Florida State University
Tallahassee, Florida

Claire I. Tsai
Graduate School of Business
University of Chicago
Chicago, Illinois

Stijn M. J. van Osselaer
Department of Marketing
Erasmus University
Rotterdam, The Netherlands

Patrick T. Vargas
Department of Advertising
University of Illinois at Urbana-Champaign
Champaign, Illinois

Madhu Viswanathan
Department of Marketing
University of Illinois at Urbana-Champaign
Champaign, Illinois

Kathleen D. Vohs
Department of Marketing
University of Minnesota
Minneapolis, Minnesota

Kimberlee Weaver
Institute for Social Research
University of Michigan
Ann Arbor, Michigan

Bruce W. A. Whittlesea
Department of Psychology
Simon Fraser University
Burnaby, British Columbia, Canada

Jerome D. Williams
Department of Advertising
University of Texas at Austin
Austin, Texas

Robert S. Wyer, Jr.
Department of Marketing
Hong Kong University of Science and
    Technology
Kowloon Bay, Hong Kong

Guang-Xin Xie
Department of Marketing
University of Oregon
Eugene, Oregon

Carolyn Yoon
Department of Marketing
University of Michigan
Ann Arbor, Michigan

I

INTRODUCTION

1

History of Consumer Psychology

DAVID W. SCHUMANN

University of Tennessee

CURTIS P. HAUGTVEDT

Ohio State University

EDITH DAVIDSON

Auburn University

INTRODUCTION

The field of consumer psychology is alive and well. A review of recent issues of the *Journal of Consumer Research*, the *Journal of Consumer Psychology*, and other major publication outlets reveals continued high levels of interest and research activity on a widening array of basic and applied research topics. Contemporary consumer psychologists can be found in academic departments of advertising, marketing, psychology, human ecology, communications, sociology, anthropology, etc. Consumer psychologists can also be found government agencies, profit and non-profit businesses. Training for work in consumer psychology often consists of coursework and research in multiple areas (Haugtvedt, 2006).

As with most areas of study, the topical focus of contemporary research projects in consumer psychology are not all new. In this chapter, we trace the work of psychologists who can be characterized as pioneers in the field of consumer psychology. Our review is selective and not exhaustive. Our intention is to illustrate how the training, creativity, and motivation of early researchers provided a significant part of the foundation of the field as we know it today and as reflected by chapters in this volume.

Our review focuses on the years between 1895 and 1955. The activities in this time frame set the stage for two major events in the 1960s. One major event was the establishment of Consumer Psychology Division (Division 23) of the American Psychological Association in 1960. In the late 1950s, a conflict over ownership of the discipline took place within the American Psychological Association leading to the establishment of a society of practitioners and academics with sole interest in the psychological response of the consumer. A brief history of this conflict appears at the end of this chapter. The second major event was the publication of three widely recognized textbooks on the topic of consumer behavior. Books by Francesco Nicosia (1966), John Howard and Jagdish

Sheth (1965), and James Engel, David Kollat and Roger Blackwell (1968) each contained a comprehensive model of important constructs underlying consumer behavior.

Early pioneers of consumer psychology were influenced greatly by their training. Prominent perspectives included the mentalist approach (represented by experimental psychologists such as Wundt, James, and Titchener); the behavioral or mechanistic approach (represented by Watson and Thorndike); and the dynamic psychology approach (represented by Freud and McDougall). Early applied psychologists often had to hide their interest and research in consumer psychology from some of the leaders of the parent discipline because these leaders felt that the field of psychology had to mature before applications to the business world could be espoused. As will be reviewed, much of the work of these early consumer psychologists focused on responses to advertising. This, however, led to other concerns as consumer psychologists of the time were not well accepted by the professional advertising community. The practitioners viewed the psychologists as interfering in their work and felt that the scientific approaches were irrelevant. All of this changed in the early 1900s.

It is important to note that the label "consumer psychology" did not exist during this time period. Rather, work that explored the application of psychological principles to business activity was known simply as "applied psychology" and the proponents were "applied psychologists." The first contributions to what would be characterized as "consumer psychology" occurred within what was termed "scientific advertising," followed closely by the scientific study of personal selling. These early pioneers eventually established a home under the parent applied discipline of industrial psychology which became identified as Division 14 of the American Psychological Association. Use of the term "consumer psychology" did not appear until the late 1950s.

THE HISTORICAL CONTEXT LEADING TO THE
ADVENT OF COMSUMER PSYCHOLOGY

Our 65 year historical review of the study of consumer psychology begins in the last decade of the 19th century. The study of consumer psychology emerged from specific interest in advertising and how advertising influenced people. By the latter half of the 19th century, the advertising industry was well established in the United States. Its growth as an industry paralleled the industrial growth of this country. In the United States the first organized advertising appeared in colonial times and was enhanced through the advent of urban newspapers. As the country expanded, there was an obvious need to extend the reach of advertising. From 1850 to 1900, transportation and technology brought on a "new industrial age." An explosion in manufacturing productivity led to new factories, increased volume, greater diversity in consumer products, and the need for new markets (Oliver, 1956). Advertising became the critical vehicle for achieving growth. As new markets emerged reflecting new populations centers, so did the concept and practice of national advertising with the advent of large circulation magazines like *Atlantic Monthly, Colliers, Cosmopolitan, Harper's Monthly, Ladies Home Journal, McClure's,* and the *Saturday Evening Post* (Kuna, 1976).

The second half of the 1800s witnessed the advent and growth the advertising agent, the advertising copywriter, and, subsequently, the advertising agency. A new found need for professionalism resulted in numerous ad clubs, associations, trade journals, and codes of ethics (Wiebe, 1967). During this time period, two schools of advertising emerged (reflecting, but not to be confused with the dominant theoretical perspectives in economics and psychology). The first school was based on a rational view of man, the potential consumer who carefully paid attention to promotional messages before making product choices. The purpose of advertising was simply to inform the public that the item was available and what it could be used for. The public was viewed as skeptical and mostly incapable of being persuaded to act against their better judgment. This rational perspective followed classic economic theory that people are self-interested and naturally desire to maximize profits while valuing their time. Not surprisingly, the emphasis was therefore on reasonable price and basic selling points.

While the rational school was dominant during the 1890s and early 1900s, by 1910 it was supplanted by the non-rational perspective. Followers deemed it likely that the emotions of the public could be manipulated and that people could actually be persuaded to purchase goods. This school was much more open and receptive to a psychological approach to understanding audience response to advertising. Also contributing to the non-rational school was psychology's new emphasis on the unconscious and motivational states (e.g. Freud, 1924/1969), as well as on the mechanistic reinforcement of behavior (e.g., Watson, 1913).

EARLY ROOTS TO THE STUDY OF CONSUMER PSYCHOLOGY

As is the case with most all of experimental psychology, one must go back to Germany in the latter part of the 19th century to understand the roots of what was ultimately to become consumer psychology. These roots began in the laboratory of Wilhelm Wundt (1832–1920) in Leipzig in 1879. Of particular relevance to the study of consumer psychology was Wundt's focus on the topic of *attention* and his influence on a subset of students who would go on to become, much to Wundt's displeasure, the first applied, industrial/organizational psychologists in America. Wundt (as did James and Titchener) believed that psychology needed to first prove its worth and evolve as a pure science before it could adequately respond to problems of the applied world (Kuna, 1976).

During this same period of time, William James (1842–1910), trained as a philosopher, was bringing to light the new science of psychology in his laboratory at Harvard University. James promoted a mentalistic perspective for this new science. In his seminal book entitled *The Principles of Psychology*, he defined psychology as the "science of mental life, both of its phenomena and their conditions" and, like Wundt, professed that this young science needed to rely on introspective observation (James, 1890/1950).

The focus on this mentalistic approach to attention continued with Wundt's students, Edward Bradford Titchener (1867–1927) at Cornell and Hugo Munsterberg (1863–1916) at Harvard. While Titchener felt applied psychology was premature at best, Munsterberg became the first important voice in the promotion of applied psychology. Indeed, in the 1909 edition of *Psychological Bulletin*, he promoted founding of the department of applied psychology as part of the Harvard Psychological Laboratory (Munsterberg, 1909). In this announcement he calls for research on "psychotechnical studies, dealing with the psychological conditions in our technical civilization in business and commerce and industry…". (p. 49). He arguably was the first true industrial/organizational psychologist. Although he did little himself to contribute to knowledge regarding consumer related psychological topics, his promotion of applied psychology in business settings, in the face of the purists, provided significant professional support for those psychologists scientifically investigating applied business topics. Other students of Wundt's who reinforced the mentalistic focus but turned their interests toward the study of advertising, included Edward Wheeler Scripture at Yale, Harlow Gale at the University of Minnesota, and Walter Dill Scott at Northwestern University.

The most dominant belief of the mentalists was ideo-motor action. James (1890/1950) defined it this way:

> That every representation of a movement awakens in some degree the actual movement which is its object; and awakens it in a maximal degree whenever it is not kept from so doing by an antagonistic representation present simultaneously to the mind. (p. 526)

James viewed ideo-motor action as immediate, that the representations of the movement in the mind remain for a matter of seconds (or less) (James 1890/1950).

In the early part of the new century, the mentalistic approach had two challenges: behaviorism and dynamic psychology. The two pioneering advocates for behaviorism in America were Edward Lee Thorndike (1874–1949) and John Broadus Watson (1878–1958). Each attempted to discredit the mentalistic approach (as well as the functional approach) by advocating a mechanistic view of behavior.

Dynamic psychology, reflecting the dynamic (changing) nature of human behavior, prescribed that man was better understood through instinctive, unconscious, biologically driven actions (Watson and Evans, 1981). The two leading proponents were Sigmund Freud (1856–1939) and William McDougall (1981–1938). Freud was first formally introduced to American psychology in 1909 during his famous visit to Clark University at the invitation of G. Stanley Hall. Because behavior was in constant flux, dynamic psychologists viewed the conscious state as less important and less reliable than the unconscious state. McDougall (1912) was the first to propose that rather than being a study of consciousness, psychology was more accurately the study of behavior. He focused on the notion of innate instincts that drive men (and animals) towards goals. Both Freud and McDougall believed that tension reduction was at the root of all motivation and behavior. Their perspectives were reflected in the non-rational school of advertising emerging at the same time (Kuna, 1976). Their theories were obviously antithetical to both the mentalistic and the mechanistic perspectives. This established interesting conflicts and debates, both among "pure" psychologists as well as those psychologists seeking to focus on applied settings.

THE EARLY PIONEERS: 1895–1930

E. W. Scripture and Harlow Gale

Although Edward Wheeler Scripture (1864–1943) and Harlow Gale (1862–1945) are not considered by some to be true forefathers of consumer psychology (see Benjamin, 2004), they appear to be the first psychologists interested in consumer related issues, and specifically consumer response to advertising (Scripture, 1895; Gale, 1900). As such, their work is part of the history of consumer psychology. In perhaps the first discussion of psychology as it pertains to advertising, Scripture (1895), implicitly employing Wundt's notion of involuntary attention, denoted several psychological "laws" as they relate to advertising. For example, Scripture noted that "bigness" and the intensity of a sensation regulate attention to commercial promotion, noting the effectiveness of signage and lighting in stores and theaters. Scripture also considered feeling and expectations, proposing that "the degree of attention paid to an object depends on the intensity of the feeling aroused," and that the level of our expectations would determine the amount of attention paid to an object (Kuna 1976). Here Scripture hints at the notion of incongruity as attracting attention (e.g., putting notices upside down). Although Scripture discussed these psychological issues related to advertising and business, he left it up to others to do the scientific investigation.

Harlow Gale, an instructor at the University of Minnesota, picked up Scripture's call for greater scientific investigation. Gale (1900) conducted what many argue to be the first actual scientific studies of advertising and consumer behavior. He began with a qualitative survey mailed to advertising professionals where he posed a series of open-ended questions designed to provide practitioner opinions about the best means to attract attention and induce purchasing through advertising. The survey required significant effort and resulted in only a 10% response return. Gale then followed the survey with a series of experiments, employing the tachistoscope procedure learned from

Wundt. The attentional issues he examined included relevant versus irrelevant materials (words and advertising "cuts" or representative images), large versus small style of type, the side of the page first attended to, exposure levels, and colors used in advertising. As he moved from one study to another, he discovered potential confounds and attempted to correct for them in subsequent studies. Perhaps of interest at the time, but not surprising today, he found that gender moderated some of his effects.

It is interesting to note that Gale may have been the first to use the order-of-merit technique in determining the importance of message arguments. Gale would ask respondents to rank order brands based upon the information provided in advertisements. E. K. Strong Jr. (Strong will be discussed in depth in a subsequent section) first attributed this technique to James McKeen Cattell (Strong, 1911), but later reversed himself, giving credit for the method to Gale (Strong, 1938; see also Kuna, 1979). This method was widely used by subsequent researchers in advertising and business studies (but challenged by Adams, 1915, see further discussion later in this chapter). Gale confined his work to conducting studies within his classroom and was not willing to establish relationships with members of the advertising industry. He was more interested in giving his students practical experience with psychology.

Walter Dill Scott

At the turn of the century, the emphasis in psychology was transitioning from a mentalistic perspective, an ideational-cognitive explanation for unconscious phenomena, to the more dynamic notions of instinct and emotion. No more is this transition evidenced than in the long career of Walter Dill Scott (1869–1955). Scott is considered by many as America's first business psychologist and the first true applied psychologist (Jacobson, 1951). Unlike Gale, Scott actively promoted his findings to business and often served as a consultant. After his educational studies with both Wundt and Titchener, he began his academic career as a professor at Northwestern University, eventually serving as its president. Aside from studying advertising, he also published in the areas of salesmanship and classification of military personnel.

Scott was the first to actively promote the psychological study of advertising. He was very vocal in a series of 12 columns that appeared in *Mahin's Magazine* and challenged the thinking of those who rejected a scientific approach, then represented in *Printer's Ink* (Kuna, 1976, Watson and Evans, 1981). His first book, *The Theory of Advertising* (1903), was a compilation of those articles, and was written from a mentalist perspective, purporting that creating involuntary attention was the motive for advertising. This book, like his second, was filled mostly with advice for practitioners, although it did cite a few select studies. Like Scripture, Scott listed a number of "laws" and principles. These reflected numerous psychological dimensions and elements inherent in advertising as described in his chapters: apperception/attention, counter influences on attention, intensity of sensation, context effects, comprehension, repetition and rehearsal, mental imagery, laws of association, suggestion, perceptional illusions, and intensity of feeling (Scott, 1903). By 1905 Scott was deep into solving applied problems for business through various research methods. He was also authoring articles for other magazines including the *Atlantic Monthly, Business World*, and *Advertising World* (Kuna, 1976).

John Mahin asked Scott for more articles and Scott obliged with 21 more columns. This second set of articles formed his second and most famous book. *The Psychology of Advertising* (1908), while still maintaining a mentalist perspective, combined new irrational aspects of consumer behavior to include emotion and instinct, with the old focus on attention and suggestion. More studies were included that incorporated new methods: naturalistic observation, longitudinal study, order-of-merit, and memory value of advertising. His thoughts on suggestion in basic psychology became invited articles in the *Psychological Bulletin (1910–1916)*. Scott believed that humans were susceptible to suggestion and that the force of suggestion could lead to action. Effective advertising, according to Scott, should suggest a course of action in a manner that ruled out other contrary actions.

There are many examples of Scott's influence on advertising practitioners including his advice on the association of the advertising with the product (laws included repetition, recency, and vividness), direct commands embedded in advertising, and suggestion as how advertising works with couponing (Scott, 1916). He provided testimony from companies as to the success of his propositions. Of special note is the fact that Scott never published his studies in academic journals nor presented this work at academic conferences, even though he served as APA president.

Daniel Starch

One could say that Daniel Starch (1883–1979) followed in the footsteps of Walter Dill Scott, carrying on the mentalist tradition. Like Scott, Starch's applied research never appeared in an academic journal. During his time in academia, he chose to reinforce his reputation as an experimental psychologist, publishing on traditional topics including a series of review articles for Psychological Bulletin (1911–1916) on the topic of auditory space.

Yet Starch differed from Scott in that he attempted to bring an objective scientific view to all of his work. Rather than offering subjective opinions about the psychology of advertising, all of his contentions appear to be empirically supported. Starch reinforced the mentalist approach in his focus on attention, suggestion, and instinct, but he extended it by introducing the concept of consumer "interest," which he later labeled "appeals" (e.g., Starch, 1923).

Starch spent most of his relatively short academic life at the University of Wisconsin (1908–1919) and at Harvard (1920–1926). His first book titled *Principles of Advertising* (1910) consisted of two parts: attracting attention and securing action. While primarily focusing on the attention oriented topics of Scott, Starch did add the notion of primacy and recency of advertisements as attracting more attention in the mind of the consumer. While both Scott and Hollingworth mentioned the importance of optimal length of line in print advertising (as noted in Tinker & Paterson, 1928), Starch was the first to actually conduct studies on this important question (Starch, 1924, 1923).

Starch's second book was published in 1914. This book addressed not only the psychology of advertising, but also other non-psychological topics like advertising strategy and ethics. The book was again organized around attention and securing response. Several laws of attention were presented to include the laws of intensity, counter-attraction, and contrast. In securing a response, Starch focused on argumentation and suggestion. It was under the latter that Starch introduced the strategy of stimulating consumer interest. Interest was an extension of attention, a kind of involuntary prolonged attention to an object. It was assumed that a reader of an ad would be more likely to attend and respond if the stimuli presented in it reflected the reader's interests. He suggested that illustrations could be used to stimulate interests. This book became a standard for the advertising practitioner. It is important to note that for every topic, Starch went to significant lengths to support his contentions with empirical evidence from his own studies or the work of other psychologists or practitioners.

In 1924 while still at Harvard, Starch became heavily involved in supervising research for the American Association of Advertising Agencies. In 1932 Starch left academia altogether and started Daniel Starch & Staff, a marketing research company providing subscribing companies with data on the effectiveness of their ads. Starch became well known for his methodological innovations, including the Starch Recognition Procedure in 1922, which measured consumer reading habits, and the Buyometer in 1948, which isolated the influence of magazine advertising on sales (Kuna, 1976). He retired in 1968 at the age of 85.

BEHAVIORISM IN ADVERTISING RESEARCH

While the mentalistic approach was prevalent at the turn of the century, it was not without challenges. One of those challenges came from the faculty at Columbia University. James McKeen Cattell (1860–1944) had established multiple university laboratories for the study of psychology after returning from the tutelage of Wundt in Leipzig. He welcomed new faculty and students to Columbia in the early 1900s, especially those who had interests in applied psychology. Indeed, over time he recruited a remarkable group of faculty to include Robert Sessions Woodworth (1869–1962), Edward Lee Thorndike (1874–1949), Harry Levi Hollingworth (1880–1956), Edward Kellogg Strong Jr. (1884–1963), and Albert T. Poffenberger (1885–1977).

Thorndike (1911) had introduced laws of effect (i.e., the role of "satisfiers" and "annoyers" as reinforcing and inhibiting behavior) and exercise (i.e., connection of a response to a situation). In applying these laws to advertising, Hollingworth felt that, rather than focusing on whether an ad attracted someone's attention, the true measure of the effectiveness of an ad is ultimately reflected with the actual purchase behavior. Hollingworth held that research conducted by advertisers was by its very nature, flawed, as it didn't control for numerous extraneous variables (seasonal sales, competitor actions, amount of media, etc.). Hollingworth had advertisers send him ads to test in his lab. Interestingly, his lab tests were highly correlated with the actual sales figures related to each ad.

In several studies, Hollingworth (e.g., 1911) examined the same variables considered by Gale and Scott, (e.g., images, wording, size, color, position, and type style) but considered the variance of the response rather than introspection. As his studies progressed, he considered individual differences such as gender and socioeconomic differences. In some cases his results contradicted the results of Gale and Scott. Hollingworth even constructed a panel of New York City residents, the first systematic effort to track consumption behavior (Kuna, 1976). In 1913, *Advertising and Selling: Principles of Appeal and Responses* was published. Building on his earlier work but appearing to move away from behaviorism, his next book on the topic, *Advertising: Its Principles and Practice* (1915) captured four principle functions of advertising: securing attention, holding attention, establishing associations, and influencing conduct by making associations dynamic. Hollingworth's objectivity in his empirical methods clearly influenced other younger applied psychologists. One of these was Edward K. Strong Jr.

Thorndike's (1913) classic paper rejected ideo-motor action and promoted new laws of habit, effect, and exercise, Watson released his treatise on behaviorism (1913), and Hollingworth's (1913) book reflected aspects of this new wave of thought. Cattell had earlier challenged the claim that introspection was the most valid methodology for the study of psychology. His focus was on reducing qualitative responses into quantitative data. As an example, his version of the order-of-merit method was strictly objective, requiring subjects to order stimuli on some criterion (Kuna, 1976; 1979).

Strong and Hollingworth took a more "molar" view of behaviorism, with a focus on complex stimuli as opposed to discrete stimuli. Rather than being preoccupied with people's thoughts, they measured what they felt were surrogates for behavioral response to advertising stimuli. They employed the order-of-merit method as well as a refined recognition test that Strong (1914) developed in a reaction to the traditional mentalist recall measures. Strong believed that recognition was the best surrogate for actual purchase behavior and tested the influence of several presentation variables to include size and frequency, and repetition intervals (e.g., Strong, 1912, 1913, 1914).

One other behaviorist from this time period is worth considerable note. It is important to reflect on the contribution to consumer psychology of John Broadus Watson. His treatise on behaviorism in 1913 earned him great acclaim as a psychologist, as he informed the world that efforts based on psychology principles should lead to greater control and prediction of behavior. Watson's studies provided demonstrations of the influence of association and conditioning on behavioral responses (e.g., Watson and Raynor, 1920). He loudly and passionately disclaimed any reason for a mentalist perspective. He became the chair of the psychology department at Johns Hopkins University, editor of the *Psychological Review*, and served as a president of the American Psychological Association in 1915. However, a scandal led to his termination and exit from academic life, and a transition into a career in advertising. Stanley Resor, the "dean of American advertising," hired Watson to work for him at J. Walter Thompson in New York. Watson quickly found leverage for success in his psychological expertise. The business world embraced him and his leadership and philosophy resulted in numerous successful advertising campaigns. Resor showcased Watson in such a way that it legitimized the role of psychologists working in advertising.

ADVANCING AND APPLYING THE PSYCHOLOGICAL SCHOOLS OF THOUGHT

To understand how dynamicism eventually evolved from mentalistic and behavioralistic approaches, one needs to consider the influence that Freud had at the time. His influence was subtle. Although Gale, Scott, and Starch all brought forth such notions of the unconscious as instincts, emotions, and interests, they continued to offer explanations consistent with a mentalistic outlook. Thorndike (1911) explained instinct and motivation as an inherited response tendency, adhering to a behavioral explanation where the catalyst for the response was a stimulus, not a condition of the being. It was McDougall who took direct aim in differentiating his purposive psychology from Watsonian behavioral psychology as reflected in the following passage:

> The two principal alternative routes are (1) that of mechanistic science, which interprets all its processes as mechanical sequences of cause and effect, and (2) that of the sciences of mind, for which purposive striving is a fundamental category, which regard the process of purposive striving as radically different form mechanical sequence. (1923, p. vii)

Enter Robert S. Woodworth, a colleague of Thorndike and Hollingworth at Columbia. Woodworth is credited with putting the organism in the stimulus-organism-response (S-O-R) model and thus finding a home for the contribution of motivation and instinct to human behavior. In his book *Dynamic Psychology* (1918), he attempted to bring together (and even expand) the work of Freud and McDougall with mainstream psychology. It is important to note that the term "psychodynamic" as often describes Freud and his adherents' theories, is not viewed as the same as "dynamic psychology." While both referred to notions of the unconscious mind, the former term typically includes identification of certain emotional conflicts and the resolution of these conflicts with specific defense mechanisms. Dynamic psychology was focused upon the influence of basic motivational drives on behavior. McDougall spoke of "drives" as strong and persistent stimulation, as initiating goal-directed actions through selective excitation of response mechanisms related to particular goals (e.g., consumption behaviors). Hollingworth and Strong, as colleagues of Woodworth, were naturally exposed to his thinking and his ideas regarding drives and organism responses, even his early ideas on psychoanalysis. Indeed, Hollingworth earlier had occasion to meet Jung and be exposed to Freud's ideas.

Although Hollingworth and Strong were reticent to adopt the dynamic approach, Hollingworth challenged business leaders to better understand the role of motives, interests, and instincts (Kuna,

1976). Finally, in Hollingworth's multiple-authored book, *Advertising: Its Principles and Practice* (Tipper, Hollingworth, Hotchkiss, & Parsons, 1915), he provided a listing of a hierarchy of human needs (e.g., comfort, play, sociability, competition, shyness, revenge, and pride) as representative of the individual, not a specific stimulus. He also revised his functions of advertising from his previous book to now include tabulation of the fundamental needs of men and women, analysis of the satisfying power of the commodity in terms of the consumer's needs, establishing the association between need and commodity, and making the association dynamic. This was a remarkable transference. Strong too experienced this transference and by 1925 his thinking culminated in his book, *The Psychology of Selling and Advertising*.

While Strong provided leadership in the adoption of the dynamic approach to applied psychology, his eventual fame came from a different applied focus. Although he continued to conduct research in advertising, he also served on the committee on Classification of Personnel during World War I. In 1923, he published the Strong Vocational Interest Blank (SVIB) which became the most widely used career interest inventory in publication, a revision of which is still employed today in helping individuals understand their natural work propensities.

The influence of the work of Hollingworth and Strong on other psychologists was considerable. Another Columbia colleague, Joseph V. Breitwieser, made extensive reference to the work of both Hollingworth and Strong in his textbook *Psychological Advertising* (1915). Their work to adopt the order-of-merit method resulted in subsequent usage by many investigators. By 1923, Starch had conducted at least 34 studies using the method.

Henry Foster Adams and Dexter Kitson

In his book entitled *Advertising and Its Mental Laws* (1916a), Adams appears to be carrying on the mentalist tradition by specifically citing the work of those we've previously discussed: Gale, Scott, Hollingworth, Strong, and Starch. However, Adams himself conducted numerous empirical studies. Adams believed in testing factors in isolation applying a "mathematical exactness" in examining various elements found in advertising. Although he respected their contributions, Adams was especially critical of Hollingworth and Strong's use of the order-of-merit method (Adams, 1915). In *Advertising and Mental Laws* he repeats his criticism but also devotes one chapter on the use of statistical tools to examine response to advertising (correlation and variance), and another on experimentation in advertising.

One important contribution from Adams' book was his ordering of certain advertising stimulus factors, as he perceived them related to key response variables: attention, association, memory, perception, and aesthetics. Adams also considered the effectiveness of different media. He concluded the book with chapters on fusion (a nod to behaviorism) and action. The book, for the most part, was still a tribute to the mentalistic approach. His concluding chapter dealt with the empirical findings related to gender differences. He noted that women paid attention more to size, personal appeals and observed events while men attended more to successive presentations, pictures, industrial-job related, and recommendations of authorities. Of peculiar interest, he found that memory tests contradicted the attention effects. For example, women had better memory with successive presentations and pictures, while men had better memory based on size of ad and for trade names.

The comprehensive books by Adams and Starch, each promoting the importance of the empirical results to date, set the tone for much work to follow. In a short period of time following these books, numerous studies were reported. For example, Adams (1916b), still maintaining the mentalist approach, went on to study the relative memory for duplication and variation, and sizes of ads (Adams 1917), as well as the effect of order of presentation (Adams, 1920).

Henry Dexter Kitson helped set the stage for this focus on other aspects of the consumer in his book titled The *Mind of the Buyer*, published in 1921. His first chapter examines the "stream of thought" in a sale, prescribing six stages in a sale: attention, interest, desire, confidence, decision and action, and satisfaction. The book clearly takes an eclectic approach, citing researchers and theorists from all three schools of psychology: mentalist, behaviorist, and dynamic. Kitson contributed to the study of advertising as well, especially with his studies regarding illustrations within advertising (Kitson, 1921), and more specifically the use of color (Kitson, 1922a), various art forms (Kitson, 1922b), package illustrations (Kitson & Campbell, 1924), and illustrations containing people (Kitson & Allen, 1925). Indeed, in 1921, Kitson presented his "historical method of investigating problems in advertising." This appears to be the first documented use of content analysis methodology in advertising studies. In 1925, Kitson and Allen reported a trend in the usage of illustrations containing people in advertising, after analyzing 20 years of ads from *Saturday Evening Post*, *Literary Digest*, and *Women's Home Companion*. This continued focus on illustration is one of the first examples of programmatic research in consumer psychology.

Albert T. Poffenberger

Albert T. Poffenberger (1885–1977) studied at Columbia under Cattell and Woodworth. The influence of these associations are reflected in his lifelong interest in physiological psychology and objective response. His dissertation was titled *Reaction Time to Retinal Stimulation* (Wenzel, 1979). He never lost this interest and continued in this vane through much of his career. However, his strongest interest was in the area of applied psychology (see 1921 edition of *American Men in Science*). After conducting a number of studies, he published the book entitled *Psychology in Advertising* in 1925. This imposing tome is a remarkable recapitulation of all the conceptual and empirical work up to that time. Aside from a through review of traditional subjects like memory and attention, and some focus on methodology, statistics, measurement, and appeal, Poffenberger provided new reviews in comprehension, "feeling tone," attitude, human desires, and individual and group differences, among others. Poffenberger followed this book with *Applied Psychology: Its Principles and Methods* (1927, 1932). Here he defined applied psychology as "every situation in which human behavior is involved and where economy of human energy is of practical importance." In the section on Advertising and Selling, he explores the desires, habits, and logic of the consumer, and reviews the state of psychology as it has been applied to advertising and selling strategies to date. Poffenberger contributed heavily to the service of the discipline culminating in his election to the presidency of the APA in 1934.

OTHER CONTRIBUTORS DURING THIS TIME PERIOD

Others, notably Heller and Brown (1916) in their study on memory for street-car signage, Laslett (1918) in a study of relevance of illustrations, Hotchkiss and Franken (1920) in their study of attention factors, and Turner (1922) in his examination of testimonials used in advertising, continued the mentalist tradition. However, a number of applied researchers were beginning to employ more objective measures reflecting a clear leaning toward the behavioral approach. Poffenberger was arguably the most prolific examining face types (Poffenberger & Franken, 1923), return of coupon resulting from advertising (Poffenberger, 1923a), belief consistency with advertisement (1923b) and the value of lines used in advertising (Poffenberger & Barrows, 1924).

In what was to become a significant subject of study, as we shall see in the next section of this chapter, Nixon (1924, 1926) examined attention and interest in advertising and concluded that differences in attention between color ads and black and white ads lasted only briefly. He voiced concern over he reliability of differences in memory tests between the two types of ads, and designed and employed a method whereby researchers could observe where visual attention was focused. Up to this point, researchers from Gale forward suggested that more attention would be paid to relevant messages about products as opposed to irrelevant messages. Likewise Laslett (1918) found that relevant illustrations led to better recall. However, using Nixon's method of "visual fixation," irrelevant pictures paired with products garnered more attention than did relevant pictures.

As was noted above (and will be discussed in depth below), at this time psychologists began to consider other aspects of consumer behavior. For example, Geissler (1917) pointed out that consumers needed to be approached in more ways than just advertising and began to study processing that occurred in consideration of purchase. Heller (1919) studied the impact of package labels on purchasing, while Kitson (1923) authored a conceptual article examining the consumer's role in market strategy. Laird (1923) compared demographic and socioeconomic differences in the selection of toothpaste, and Hotchkiss and Franken (1923) considered the importance of brand familiarity.

James McKeen Cattell was eventually dismissed from Columbia because of his opposition to the draft. In 1921 he, along with Columbia colleagues Woodworth and Thorndike, formed the The Psychological Corporation in New York. They began by developing psychological tests and related materials that could be used in education, business, and government. In the following years, the company hired academics to run sponsored studies. As we shall see, a number of these research studies were eventually published in academic journals. It is interesting to note that through mergers and acquisitions, the corporate entity evolved and still exists today although under a different name (Harcourt Assessment).

THE POST-DEPRESSION ERA THROUGH WORLD WAR II: 1935–1945

The end of the Depression triggered significant research by economists studying product demand and usage. The *Journal of Marketing*, initiated in 1935, devoted a significant amount of journal space to articles authored by individuals trained in economics and measuring product demand and use. During this same period, applied psychologists were attempting to better understand consumer response to commercial product promotion. The decade following the depression was marked by the advent of a new media form—radio—that quickly found significant application for commercial advertising. As we shall address next in this section, there were numerous areas of consumer research that appeared to be focused on print and radio effectiveness (including comparative effectiveness); salesperson effectiveness; consumer preference, consumer motivation, and concern over research methods. We shall take each in turn and discuss how these applied psychologists addressed these various consumer related interests and issues. It is interesting to note that unlike the prolific work from key pioneers during the previous time period, this time period is marked with contributions from authors who published but a few articles reflecting consumer psychological topics. However, this work, in bulk, does demonstrate a significant level of progression forward in the discipline.

FOCUS ON MEDIA DIFFERENCES

Several applied psychologists approached the issue of comparing the effectiveness of visual versus spoken ads by mimicking the differences between print, posters, and radio media. This effort was initially reflected in a significant number of memory studies. Burtt and Dobell (1925) reported a series of studies that sought to replicate Ebbinghaus' (1885) notion of a forgetting curve, one that begins with a sharp decline flattening out over time. These researchers provided respondents with a long paired list of products and fictional brand names, two studies projected onto a screen, (over different time frames) and one provided by audio means. The results of all three studies reinforced the same type of forgetting curve, but the initial audio memory test yielded better results in both recall and recognition than did the projected pairs on a screen.

Noting that advertising posters seen on streets are also an important type of advertising, Brutt and Crockett (1928) studied memory for different types of posters. Their results reflected significant primacy and recency effects and that distance from the viewer makes a difference in memory for the add (reflecting the best visual angle). Stanton (1934) and Dewick (1935) conducted similar experiments where they provided a series of print advertisements and spoken advertisements in a counterbalanced study using common products. The brand names were mentioned three times in the script which lasted about 35 seconds. They then recorded recall scores for the product class and the brand name, employing both immediate and delayed recall tests. The findings of both studies revealed that there were no consistent differences upon immediate recall. After 5 to 7 days, there was the beginning of a favored auditory response, and in the Stanton study significant differences favoring auditory response were found for 21-day recall. In the Dewick study, recall of "ideas" mentioned in the advertisements were elicited, and while both visual and auditory memory decayed after 6 days, the visual decay in memory was significantly greater than the auditory. In hindsight, it would be interesting to know, in the delayed conditions, if individuals during their everyday normal experience, heard or read more ads for the products used in the study. If the former, that might explain the greater recall scores for auditory messages due to greater exposure to the brand name, product class, and advertising message. It is interesting to note that in the early 1930s William Stanton, while a PhD student at Ohio State, developed a forerunner of the radio and television rating audimeters, later developed for A.C. Nielsen by MIT. Stanton went on to become an executive with Columbia Broadcasting Company and an important pioneer in subsequent radio audience studies (Maloney, 1987, as cited in Kassarjian, 1994).

In perhaps what was a precursor to television and was reflected in the speaking movies of the time, Elliot (1936, 1937a, 1937b, 1937c) reviewed the literature on memory of visual and auditory stimuli dating back to Ebbinghaus and developed a series of studies comparing visual, auditory, and the combination of visual and auditory (termed "television" in one of his studies). In all cases, he found an advantage for the combination of the two as regards memory for an advertising message as well as a trade name. His studies also revealed certain gender effects but these effects were somewhat inconsistent across studies. In general, the difference of effectiveness of television over other modes was stronger for women than men.

A number of studies attempted to understand people's attitudes toward radio advertising in general (Cantril & Allport, 1935; Kornhauser & Lazarsfeld 1937; Sayre, 1939). Cantril and Allport, and Kornhauser and Lazarsfeld employed two measures (estimated time that commercials were heard, and amount of money willing to pay annually to remove advertisements) that they deemed reflective of possible positive or negative attitudes towards radio advertising. However, employing a Likert scale, Sayre found no correlation between a direct measure of attitude and the other two scales.

William Stanton, mentioned above, conducted radio studies under the guidance of Cantril and Allport at Princeton. The three were instrumental in bringing Paul Lazersfeld to the United States. Lazersfeld, a mathematics PhD from the University of Vienna, had established a radio research organization in Europe and conducted the first major study on radio audience listening. Lazersfeld soon left Princeton and founded what was to become the Bureau of Applied Social Research at Columbia University. Lazersfeld, in turn, was instrumental in bringing his Viennese students,

Ernest Dichter and Herta Herzog to the U.S. Dichter's contribution to consumer psychology will be discussed in a subsequent section (Maloney, 1987 as cited by Kassarjian, 1994).

Guest and Brown (1939) tested recall for radio advertising based on a number of variable differences. In a controlled study employing both ads and music programming for an hour, they found no differences for temporal position, whole versus part methods of presentation, nor for repetition. They did find an inverse relationship between recall and amount of material, less material presented led to better recall. In all cases, the average number of thought passages retained was small. Wolfe (1941) found a high correlation, .78, between women who could associate a product with a program. These strong results for early radio recall are intuitive given that each program was typically sponsored by only one product. Thus the repetition of the program with one sponsor likely led to a high level of rehearsal and retention. Fay and Middleton (1941) examined the gender of commercial announcers and found no differences in gender preference for announcers, but found that women tended to have a higher preference for announcers across both male and female products, then did males.

FOCUS ON MECHANICAL FEATURES OF PRINT AND POSTER ADVERTISEMENTS

Several important mechanical factors in print advertising were considered during this time period as they influenced reader response. The impact of color in advertising took center stage in the early 1930s along with an examination of positioning, type style, and amount of copy.

In the latter half of the 1920s and early 1930s, several studies pertaining to color, size and position in print advertising appeared. Nixon (1926, 1927) reported the first of several perceptual studies. These two studies compared color and black and white ads, using a measure of attention to the ad. He found no significant differences between color and black and white ads but did find that females tended to pay more attention to the ads than did males. Sumner (1932) studied the influence of color on legibility (blue print on a gray or white background scored highest however there were only 5 subjects. Dorcus (1932) examined people's habitual word associations with colors as they might be a factor in advertising (for a comprehensive review of studies on response to color going back 30 years, see Dorcus 1926). As noted in a 1932 edition of *Printer's Ink*, Starch, in an analysis of 5 million inquiries, studied 4 million returns from 3,349 advertisements. He found that "color ads brought 53% more returns per 100,000 than did black and white advertisements of similar size and character" (p. 65).

While still considering the effects of color, researchers also began to consider size and placement issues. In 1930, Cutler reported no recall differences for the same ad that appeared in magazines of different size. Ferguson (1934) supported Starch's findings by comparing position of magazine advertisements in the *Saturday Evening Post* (e.g., inside front cover, page opposite the table of contents, outside back cover), and found some differences for position, but also found that color typically out-performed black and white ads. Ferguson made an additional interesting contribution by noting potential differences in target readership: "those who buy *SEP* in order to read the articles and stories, 2) those who buy *SEP* for humor, and 3) those who buy *SEP* to mainly look at the ads." Ferguson (1934, 1935) concluded that contrary to belief, his findings revealed no relationship between the size of an advertisement and its attention value, no preferred positions, and no preference for right versus left hand pages, nor position on the page. Lucas (1937) employed a more sophisticated study as a follow up to Ferguson and found contradictory results. Specifically he found that the differential changes for the advertising by placement and size correlated strongly with recall and recognition, that women respond better to color than men, and that right- and left-hand page locations are of equal value for full-page ads, but right-hand position is better recalled for smaller ads. Guilford and Ewart (1940) examined the difference in reaction time resulting from the potential distraction of print ads that appeared in color or black and white. Listening and responding to the noise of the timer motor which was about the same decibel as the projector of the ads, they found that both types of ads served as significant distractors, but did not differ in reaction time. McNamara (1941) voiced the criticisms regarding previous attention and memory studies in the lab (see subsection on methodology below for these criticisms), and reported a study employing eye movement photography. He found no differences in attention to the prime positions (inside front, back, etc.), nor for right- versus left-hand pages, but did find differences favoring two-column ads found on the outside left page and ads that were found in the upper corners.

The continued investigation into typeface response was another mechanical feature of the early 1930's. In 1933, Davis and Smith, building on the earlier work of Poffenberger and Barrows (1924), considered emotional response to different forms of typeface. Respondents were asked to match typefaces with advertised products as well as emotions, revealing some differences based on such typeface characteristics as size, condensation, boldness, use of italics, etc. In a similar study, Schiller (1935) replicated the earlier study of Poffenberger and Franken (1923) examining the effectiveness of certain types of typefaces as representing certain products. However, in her study she also considered color of the typefaces.

In a follow up to Kitson's earlier content analysis on the use of illustrations, Klapp (1941) found that not only did advertisements without pictures decrease significantly over 4 decades (1900–1940), as did ads with pictures but not including people, but that ads with people, especially reflecting relevancy with the product, increased dramatically (1900—16.2%; 1915—34.7%; 1930—49%; 1940—67.1%).

One popular question of advertising effectiveness that still evokes research today is the issue of relative effectiveness of negative versus positive message appeals. Investigation of this question can be traced back to the historical content analysis work of Harry Kitson (reported in Lucas & Benson, 1929a). Kitson conclusion as well as Scott's was that in general, it was best to use positive appeals. Kitson based his opinion on the usage rate differences found in his content analysis favoring positive appeals. However, it is interesting to note that some practitioners of the day disagreed (Lucas & Benson, 1929b). Lucas and Benson undertook a program of research on this topic with a series of experiments. Reinforcing the practitioner opinion, across varied message appeals (negative versus positive) reflecting ads for several different product classes, these researchers found no differences in the amount of coupons returned based on the valance of appeal type (Lucas & Benson, 1929b), and no differences in recall among adults (Lucas & Benson, 1930a). However, they did find that among children, positive ads were recalled better than negative ads, especially among boys. They noted that as children age, differences between appeals and gender disappear. Lucas and Benson (1930b) also published *Psychology for Advertisers*, an extensive book that summarized advertising effectiveness research to date, and focused on the mechanics of print appeals and how these appeals could facilitate the effort of salespeople.

Focus on the amount and proximity of ads: In 1935, Fred McKinney designed a study to examine "retroactive inhibition." In earlier basic psychology studies, numerous results reflected "retroactive inhibition, distraction due to similar material that appears immediately subsequent to the targeted stimulus presentation. In his first study to apply retroactive inhibition to advertising, McKinney sought to discern how memory for parts of an ad (i.e., product name, slogan, headline, reading and picture content), are susceptible to subsequent reviewing of ads. McKinney found slight retroactive inhibition with slogans being the most affected and name of product the least affected. He does draw the obvious conclusion that placement of ads in relative isolation is the most effective for memory of the ad. Blankenship and Whitely (1941) focused on the effects of proactive inhibition to memory by providing both normal and similar preceding stimulus ads (containing a list of products and associated prices and comparing them to conditions containing a similar list of nonsense names and associated numbers. After subjects were asked to recall the inhibitory stimulus lists, they were then exposed to a regular ad with listed products and associated prices, and recall scores were taken. The results consistently demonstrated a proactive inhibition effect on memory. In a similar application, McNamara and Tiffen (1941), using the Purdue Eye Camera, found that ads adjacent to cartoons inhibited the time spent on the advertising.

Franzen (1940), in perhaps the first look at fatigue resulting from clutter, examined ad visibility reported in interviews comparing two magazines, one with 33% more advertising than the other. More fatigue was clearly present in the interview assessing memory for ads in the larger magazine.

FOCUS ON THE EFFECTIVENESS OF SALESPEOPLE

Salesperson effectiveness was viewed strictly as a "personnel" issue in the early part of the 20th century. Many applied psychologists developed theories as to what comprised a good salesperson (e.g., Link, 1932, 1938; Nixon, 1931, 1942; Snow, 1926; 1929). Indeed, Nixon's bibliography in his second edition of his Principles of Selling (1942) lists over a hundred books on the topic. Applied industrial psychologists had reported numerous studies correlating traits, interests, intelligence, and demographic factors with objective measures of performance like total sales (e.g., Freyd, 1922; Craig, 1933; Dodge 1938a, 1938b). An example of this type of study was conducted by the Psychological Corporation and reported by Schultz (1934). Schultz described results from a study in which sale personnel were measured on the traits of ascendance/submission (measured by Beckman's revision of the Allport Ascendance-Submission Test), and introversion/extroversion (measured by the Root Introversion-Extroversion Test). Intelligence, interests, and general demographic factors were also assessed. Level of ascendance and extroversion correlated with performance. Intelligence screened out "poor" performance but was not related to best or average performance. Age, education, experience, race, and length of service did not reveal any appreciable differences. Interestingly, the employment of E. K. Strong's Vocational Interest survey generated mixed performance results, identifying individuals that were among the best as well as the poorest performers.

In 1937, McKinney developed a strategy for rating sales messages. Developing two scripts of the sales "interview" partialed into message segments, student evaluators rated each segment as to their perceived value on a 10-point scale from "poor" to "excellent". Mitchell and Burtt (1938) extended McKinney's work by comparing four pairs of contrasting appeals: 1) demonstration versus oral elaboration; 2) presentation of facts versus short appeals; 3) a "breezy" versus a dignified approach; and 4) a domineering versus a friendly approach. Results favored the demonstration, presentation of facts, and a friendly approach. There was no difference between "breezy" and dignified approaches.

Arthur Dodge (1938a, 1938b) conducted studies testing multiple facets of personality against salesperson performance. Compared to poor salespeople, better salespeople tended to report themselves as less moody, more self-sufficient and self-confident, more aggressive and more willing to assume responsibility, less self-conscious, more social, less desirous of talking about self, less resentful of criticism or discipline, and more radical and unconventional. Hampton (1940) found similar results for small grocer retailers. While these studies suggested these personality variables reflected tendencies of salespeople, none boasted what would be termed "strong" differences.

FOCUS ON RESEARCH METHODS

Although by the mid 1920s there existed several methods in the study of response to advertising, two appeared to be most popular: recall and tests of association (recognition). Indeed, Poffenberger stated "as there are numerous brands of the commonly used articles that really differ little in quality, it is largely a matter of obeying the laws of recall that determines which particular brand shall be bought" (quoted in Lucas & Benson, 1930a, p. 219). Hotchkiss and Franken (1927), in their book entitled *The Measurement of Advertising Effects*, used tests of association and usage to demonstrate the public's familiarity with different brands of commodities. This work replicated the earlier work of Donovan (1924) by also examining the association of commodities with brands, and the subsequent work of Asher (1928) that revealed a correlation between newspaper advertising expenditures and recall of certain types of retail stores (e.g., drug stores, ladies' stores, real estate companies, automobile agencies) but not other stores (shoe stores, restaurants, music stores, jewelry stores). One of the benefits to practitioners derived from this method is the ability to focus on competitor influences.

Significant criticism of research methods arose during this period. Using a method of triple associates (as reported by Link, 1934), experiments were conducted by the Psychological Corporation employing 14,000 consumers and conducted by 60 examiners. Hathaway and Welch (1934) questioned the amount of guessing that occurred during this procedure. Link (1932 article cited in McNamara 1941) questioned whether advertisements tested under artificial conditions or with subjects who were arguably not the target of the product promotion provided a valid test. Earlier Poffenberger (1925) questioned whether studies were holding other factors constant like form of layout, quality, and such. Lucas (1937) questioned the inability to control for influence of past ads in present copy testing, suggesting that it was likely impossible to rule out the cumulative effects of similar copy. Gaudet & Zients (1932) suggested that content analyses conducted at certain intervals could not rule out cycling effects that might not be detected with a linear increase. During this time period, treatises began to appear on the types and combinations of questions to ask to ascertain psychological insights into marketing related behaviors (i.e., purchase rationale, advertising effectiveness, post-purchase evaluation) (Lazarsfeld 1934; Kornhauser & Lazarsfeld, 1935). Several individuals suggested improved methods for understanding the impact of radio advertising (Likert, 1936; Gaskill & Holcomb, 1936).

With these criticisms came other new methods of inquiry. Ruckmick (1939) found that respondents' arousal levels as a reflection of varied advertising, could be measured through detecting sweat gland activity. He found that 3-second exposures to print ads across a repeated series, revealed a relatively consistent pattern. Karslake (1940) presented a study employing a new technique called the Purdue Eye Camera. He compared results employing objective attention measures from the camera against reported results in surveys and found minimal correlation, contending that attention scores resulting from a camera are more accurate than self-reported attention scores.

D. B. Lucas (1940) voiced concern regarding the validity of examining recognition of specific advertisements apart from the context in which the advertising appears. Indeed, he noted the potential for false recognition rates based on a person's familiarity with other similar ads for the same product. Teaching at New York University, Lucas developed a continuing study of magazine readership of four weekly magazines and created a corrected recognition formula that accounted for false recognition scores. His method was based on exposing respondents to pre- and post-publication exposure advertising. As noted in this chapter, Lucas published multiple studies over the course of 2 decades and his research contributed significantly to knowledge of advertising response at that time. He became the first technical director for the Advertising Research Foundation (ARF).

Welch (1941) recommended that ad copy testing employ four known scales as a system of measurement rather than rely on any one scale. These four measures consisted of brand familiarity (Geissler 1917; Hotchkiss & Franken 1923, 1927), brand preference (Link 1932; Laird cited in Poffenberger 1932; Market Research Corporation of America 1935), theme familiarity (from Link's triple associates test (Link 1932, 1934), and theme credence (Link 1932; Market Research Corporation of America, 1937).

In 1941 and 1942 the *New York Times* ran split-run copy tests providing an opportunity to reply and obtain a free sample. Employing similar ads advertising "False Teeth" or "Dental Plate," in both cases "False Teeth" was slightly stronger in number of replies. Zubin and Peatman (1945), citing these studies, developed and tested a more statistically valid method for using split run copy testing data. They concluded by offering a number of important assumptions to include the randomness of the samples drawn from the population, equal numbers of potential buyers of the product, the availability and inclusion of the maximum size of the sample of potential buyers, and that clipping the coupon is a direct result of the advertisement and not some other factor.

FOCUS ON PREFERENCE

Several researchers during this period addressed how consumers were reacting to various packaging types, primarily as viewed in the size and shape of glass containers. In an earlier book published in 1928, Franken and Larrabee reviewed initial thoughts about packaging and a procedure to consider packaging preference. Employing an accepted method from Franken and Larrabee (1928), Hovde (1931) conducted a controlled field study to find the "best all-around" glass container. He employed multiple examples of caviar and herring containers representing two sizes, 4 oz. and 10 oz. The study was conducted in grocery stores in Philadelphia, beginning with 70 women and 30 men. It is interesting to note that Hovde kept adding groups of respondents to the initial sample until the results became consistent. Hovde began by instructing potential respondents as to the necessity of finding a container that allowed for complete extraction of what was contained inside. His first question sought to address attention value by inquiring as to "which container your attention is most forcibly drawn." Ranking every container employing an order of preference method, respondents were also asked for their reasons for their selection. A second question sought to uncover degree of identification by measuring which container could best be remembered if one forgot the trade name.

In one of the first studies on consumption and children, Guest (1942, 1944) surveyed over 800 school children from 3rd grade through the senior year in high school to assess degree of loyalty to brands versus product class. His results revealed that 1) brand loyalty was stronger than product class loyalty, 2) children form loyalty to brands at an early age, and 3) loyalty evolves and strengthens over time.

FOCUS ON MOTIVATION

The focus on consumer motives began to take hold in the United States with the hiring of Viennese psychologist Ernest Dichter by the Getchell agency in 1940 (see Allen 1941). Dichter sought clues into human motivation by questioning selected "indicator groups," individuals who would be proactive in providing insights into product usage. Dichter used this information to provide a "psychological inventory" of basic motives for specific product purchases. This information in turn, would help advertising creatives develop messages that would directly address the customer motives (a fuller description of Dichter's contribution appears in the next section).

In 1941, Allen authored an article that applied Allport's (1937) notion of functional autonomy to better understanding consumer motives. In this paper, Allen presents a list of "primary wants" that are more direct (e.g., appetizing food, comfortable surroundings, welfare of loved ones, social approval, play) and "secondary wants" that are more removed (e.g., health, convenience, cleanliness, style/beauty, dependability/quality). Allen provides examples of typical product/service appeals that would provide the linkage between product/service and motive.

In the years leading up to World War II, numerous European scholars like Lazersfeld, Dichter, and Politz (the European pollster) fled from their home countries to the United States and to American universities or industry. The nature of consumer research was also changing as former academics like George Gallup and Daniel Starch pioneered the profitable marketing research industry.

THE EARLY YEARS AFTER WORLD WAR II

During the final phase of this review (post-World War II–1960), we return to two major contributors to the discipline of consumer psychology and a number of smaller, but nonetheless, important players.

Ernest Dichter

Considered by many a founding father of motivational research, Ernest Dichter was born in Vienna in 1907 and lived across the street from Sigmund Freud's famous office. Dichter discovered early he had a strong interest in psychology. After completing his doctoral studies, he began his career as a practicing psychoanalyst. Indeed his dissertation topic was a "self-appraisal of one's own abilities." He soon found his way to work under Paul Lazarfeld's Vienna centre for industrial research. Dichter immigrated to New York in 1937 where he quickly found he was invited to consult with major companies about his insights into the psychology of the consumer.

Dichter was quite controversial. Denouncing all marketing research except his own as "nose-counting and "census-taking" (Fullerton & Stern, 1990, cited in Kassarjian, 1994), he became a highly vocal proponent of his own methodology which relied heavily on Freudian psychology (Stern, 2004). Indeed, his own mentor, Paul Lazersfeld became one of his harshest critics, along with researchers Gallup, Politz, and the Marketing discipline's Wroe Alderson (Ferber & Wales, 1958; Kassarjian, 1994)

To better understand human motivation, Dichter employed in-depth interviews and projective techniques to tap both conscious and subconscious states thought to guide the behavior of the consumer. He felt that his background in psychoanalysis provided him with insights into hidden motives behind purchasing behavior. From this understanding, he was able to work with advertisers to create impactful brand slogans— "Wash your troubles away" for Procter & Gamble's Ivory Soap. From 1943 to 1946 Dichter was employed by the Columbia Broadcasting System (CBS).

In 1946, Dichter founded his Institute for Motivational Research on the Hudson River just north of New York City. A *Harvard Business Review* article (Dichter 1947) reflected his belief that past methods only scratch the surface and that advertising and personal selling have dynamic effects on the consumer. He also pointed out the importance of multiple motives and reflects that Freud's multiple levels of consciousness provide reason for the importance of "modern" (qualitative) psychological methods. Dichter (1948) also employed multiple techniques (i.e., depth interviewing, role playing, sociometric maps) to discover what he termed the "real" reasons are behind brand purchasing.

Vance Packard's *The Hidden Persuaders* (1957) made Dichter a household name, suggesting that Dichter was the master manipulator of the consumer mind. Packard brought Dichter a significant amount of fame and fortune, creating a significant corporate demand for his consulting services. He published several books, with the *Handbook of Consumer Motivation* (1964) perhaps the most popular and most widely cited. It is important to note that Dichter's research went far beyond just the study of the consumer. His work also reflected the study of human motives behind topics like voter participation, religious tolerance, and racial prejudice. Dichter, always the business man, founded multiple research institutes in Europe as well the Hudson River Institute. Many of these are still active today.

George Katona

George Katona is considered to be the dean of behavioral economics. After an receiving a degree in law from the University of Budapest, he received his PhD in Germany under Georg Elias Nathanael Muller at Gottingen in 1921 following in the tradition of Wundt and Titchner. He came to the United States in 1933 and started employment as an investment counselor. In 1936, he began lecturing at the New School for Social Research and was heavily influenced by his colleague, the Gestalt psychologist Max Wertheimer. Wertheimer (and other gestalt psychologists), along with Watson's behaviorism and Freud's dynamic approach, had begun to successfully turn psychology away from the experimental work that followed the tradition of Wundt and Titchner (Boring, 1950). In 1945, Katona joined the faculty at the University of Michigan.

Katona, along with Likert, Campbell and others, founded Michigan's Business Survey Research Bureau, and he became the director of the economic behavioral program. His pioneering achievement was in the application of consumer psychology to economic forecasting. In contrast to existing economic theory that relied chiefly on factual demographic driven input (e.g., income, ability to buy), Katona believed that a consumer's willingness to buy, as denoted by the consumer's attitudes and expectations (his view of consumer psychology), was a critical economic indicator.

Katona authored numerous articles during his lifetime and published more than a dozen books including *The Powerful Consumer* (1960) and *The Mass Consumption Psychology* (1964). These books contained his caution to other economists as well as practitioners against stereotyping consumers as having simplistic motives and being easily manipulated. Perhaps Katona's most enduring legacy was his initiation of the Survey of Consumer Attitudes for the University of Michigan Institute for Social Research, today employed as a major indicator of economic stability of markets.

THE CONTRIBUTION OF OTHERS DURING THIS PERIOD

Immediately following the war came an emphasis on consumption by U.S. citizens who had just experienced several lean years of sacrifice. An explosion of manufacturing and new products led to new applied questions; for example, could the consumer discriminate in taste for food and drink. Pronko and Bowles reported three studies investigating whether drinkers of colas could discriminate between brands (Pronko & Bowles, 1948, 1949; Bowles & Pronko, 1948). It is not clear whether they gave respondents varied strategies for taste testing, but the results consistently reflected that there was no consistency in consumer discrimination of brands of cola.

Another important question that emerged during this time was based on the need to determine why consumers patronized certain retail stores. Heidingsfield (1949) surveyed patrons of downtown Philadelphia department stores to ascertain the motives for store selection. In rank order the factors included the nature of merchandise, prices, physical factors, and service. Blankertz (1949) reports a similar study by a group at his own university, but challenges both of these studies on issues of methodology. He provides several examples such as the notion that attitudes are relatively weak reflections of other important contributing factors like distance. He also argued against the wisdom of depending on attitude scores given their lack of ability to predict store expenditures, and the belief that reports of attitudes may reflect rationalization rather than other internal states (e.g., affect).

In 1950, Mason Haire published his famous article in the *Journal of Marketing* that called into question people's willingness to share their real responses. With the advent of instant coffee and consumers' reluctance to adopt it, studies suggested that taste was the reason. However, Haire was skeptical of this finding and designed a projective test to see if there were other underlying reasons. He employed two groups of homemakers, both of whom were provided with a shopping list. All the products on the list were held constant except that one list contained Nescafe Instant Coffee while the other contained "1 lb. Maxwell House Coffee (Drip Ground)." He then asked his two sample segments to describe a person who would be shopping for these products. The respondents with the Maxwell House Coffee on their list consistently described the person in more positive terms (e.g., housewife, concerned about what she served her family) than did those who received the list with Nescafe Instant Coffee (e.g., single woman living from one day to the next). There was no indication that taste was a factor. The real reason had much more to do with how a person using instant coffee would be perceived.

In 1952, Dik Twedt from Northwestern University conducted a survey study of 34 variables believed to be related to magazine readership scores. Prior to this, there were a number of individuals, including James D. Woolf, formerly the vice-president of the J. Walter Thompson advertising agency, claiming that content, rather than mechanical factors, were what pulled individuals to read ads (Woolf, 1951, see also earlier study by Ferguson, 1935). Using a popular trade magazine, Twedt's study actually revealed that a significant portion of explained variance for readership was due to three mechanical factors, size of advertisement, number of colors, and square inches of illustration. It is also of interest that Dik Twedt (1965) authored the first review of Consumer Psychology that appeared in the *Annual Review of Psychology*.

CONCLUSION: HOW CONSUMER PSYCHOLOGY HAS EVOLVED

This chapter sought to bring out two points of emphasis regarding the roots of consumer psychology. First, consumer psychology has evolved as the larger domain of general psychology has evolved. This is evident in the transition of schools of thought, from the early mentalist approach of Wundt and his students, to a rejection of mentalism in favor of behavioral and dynamic approaches. These schools are all important in the investigation of consumer behavior as we research it today. The second point of emphasis is the fact that these early psychologists built upon each other's work, and that many of the topics they studied are those that we're still engrossed with today and expect to be for many years to come.

It's hard to know what psychological discipline "owned" consumer psychology. In developing the sketches of these pioneers, it was apparent that they viewed themselves as "applied" psychologists. The words "industrial" and "organizational" psychologists rarely appeared. However, because the broader interests of individuals like Munsterberg, Scott, Strong, and Poffenberger, who, as a group, moved far beyond a singular focus on advertising and selling response, the study of the consumer was brought into the larger framework of the study of business. Thus consumer psychology for many years, certainly through the 1950s, was labeled a part of Industrial/Organizational Psychology.

In the late 1950s an informal group of applied psychologists known as the "headshrinkers" came into existence in Chicago (Kamen, 1995). The group consisted of applied psychologists primarily working for advertising agencies, polling companies, and marketing research firms. They met on a regular basis and before long they included academics in their meetings. Finally in 1959, they decided to approach the APA to initiate a new division and Division 23 of APA, the Division of Consumer Psychology, was born. Dik Twedt was the first President of the Division of Consumer Psychology and Clark Leavitt was the second President. Today, with a membership of over 600 and a sponsored scholarly periodical, the *Journal of Consumer Psychology*, the Society for Consumer Psychology symbolizes the independence of this growing discipline. Nevertheless, the history of consumer psychology will always be indebted to the early "applied psychologists."

REFERENCES

Adams, H. F. (1915). The adequacy of the laboratory test in advertising. *Psychological Review, 22*(September), 402–422.

Adams, H. F. (1916a). *Advertising and its mental laws.* New York: Macmillan.

Adams, H. F. (1916b). The relative memory values of duplication and variation in advertising. *Journal of Philosophy, Psychology and Scientific Methods, 18*, 141–152.

Adams, H. F. (1917). The memory value of mixed sizes of advertising. *Journal of Experimental Psychology, 2*, 448–465.

Adams, H. F. (1920). The effect of climax and anti-climax order of presentation on memory. *Journal of Applied Psychology, 4*, 330–338.

Allen, C. N. (1941) A psychology of motivation for advertisers. *Journal of Applied Psychology, 25*, 378–390.

Allport, G. W. (1937). *Personality.* New York: Holt.

Asher, E. J. (1928). The association test as a means of determining the relatively familiarity of retail stores. *Journal of Applied Psychology, 12*, 437–446.

Benjamin, L. T., Jr. (2004). Science for sale: Psychology's earliest adventures in American advertising. In J. Williams, W. Lee, & C. Haugtvedt (Eds.), *Diversity in advertising.* Mahwah, NJ: Lawrence Erlbaum.

Blankenship, A. B., & Whitely, P. L. (1941). Proactive inhibitions in the recall of advertising material. *Journal of Social Psychology, 13*, 311–322.

Blankertz, D. F. (1949). Motivation and rationalization in retail buying. *Public Opinion Quarterly, 13*, 659–668.

Bowles, J., Jr., & Pronko, N. (1948). Identification of cola beverages; II. A further study. *Journal of Applied Psychology, 32*, 559–564.

Breitwieser, J. V. (1915). *Psychological advertising.* Colorado Springs, CO: Apex Book.

Burett, H.. & Dobell, E. (1925). The curve of forgetting for advertising material. *Journal of Applied Psychology, 9*, 5–21.

Brutt, H., & Crockett, T. (1928). A technique for psychological study of poster board advertising and some preliminary results. *Journal of Applied Psychology, 12*, 43–55.

Cantril, H., & Allport, G. W. (1935) *The psychology of radio.* New York: Harper and Brothers.

Craig, D. R. (1933) The preference-interest questionnaire in selecting retail saleswomen, *Journal of Personnel Research, 3*(1924–1925), 366–374.

Cutler, T. (1930). The effectiveness of page size in magazine advertising. *Journal of Applied Psychology, 14*, 465–469.

Davis, R., & Smith, H. (1933). Determinants of feeling tone in type faces. *Journal of Applied Psychology, 17*, 742–764.

DeWick, H. (1935).The relative effectiveness of visual and auditory presentations of advertising material. *Journal of Applied Psychology, 19*, 245–264.

Dichter, E. (1947). Psychology in marketing research. *Harvard Business Review, 25*, 432–443

Dichter, E. (1948). These are the real reasons people buy. *Advertising and Selling, 41*, 33–40.

Dichter, E. (1949). A psychological view of advertising effectiveness. *Journal of Marketing, 12*, 61–66.

Dichter, E. (1964). *Handbook of consumer motivation: The psychology of the world of objects.* New York: McGraw-Hill.

Dodge, A. F. (1938a). Social dominance and sales personality. *Journal of Applied Psychology*, 22, 132–139

Dodge, A. F. (1938b) .What are the personality traits of the successful sales-person? *Journal of Applied Psychology*, 22, 229–238.

Donovan, H. (1924). *Advertising response*. Philadelphia: J. B. Lippincott.

Dorcus, R. (1932). Habitual word associations to colors as a possible factor in advertising. *Journal of Applied Psychology*, 16, 277–287

Dorcus, R. M. (1926). Color preferences and color associations, *Journal of Genetic Psychology*, 33, 399–434.

Elliott, F. (1936). Memory for visual, auditory and visual-auditory material. In R. Woodworth (Ed.), *Archives of Psychology* (p. 199). New York: Columbia University

Elliott, F. R. (1937a). Attention effects from poster, radio and poster radio advertising of an exhibit. *Journal of Applied Psychology*, 21, 365–371.

Elliott, F. R. (1937b). Memory effects from poster, radio, and television modes of advertising an exhibit. *Journal of Applied Psychology*, 21, 504–512.

Elliott, F. R. (1937c). Memory for trade names presented in screen, radio and television advertisements. *Journal of Applied Psychology*, 21, 653–667.

Engel, J. F., Kollat, D. T., & Blackwell, R. D. (1968). *Consumer behavior*. New York: Holt, Rinehart and Winston.

Fay, P. J., & Middleton, W. C. (1941). Indirect measurement of listeners' preferences of men and women commercial announcers. *Journal of Applied Psychology*, 25, 558–572.

Franken, R. B., & Larrabee, C. B. (1928). *Packages that sell*. New York: Harper & Brothers.

Ferber, R., & Wales, H. (Eds.). (1958). *Motivation and market behavior*. Homewood, IL: Richard D. Irwin.

Frazen, R. (1940). An examination of the effect of number of advertisements in a magazine upon the "visibility" of these advertisements. *Journal of Applied Psychology*, 24, 791–801.

Freud, S. (1924/1969). *A general introduction to psychoanalysis*. New York: Pocket Books.

Freyd, M. (1926–1927) Selection of Promotion Salesmen. *Journal of Personnel Resarch*, 5, 152–156.

Furguson, L. W. (1934). Preferred Positions of advertisements in the *Saturday Evening Post*. *Journal of Applied Psychology*, 18, 749–756.

Furguson, L. W. (1935). The importance of the mechanical features of an advertisement. *Journal of Applied Psychology*, 19, 521–526.

Gale, H. (1896). On the psychology of advertising. In H. Gale (Ed.), *Psychological studies*. Minneapolis: Author.

Gaskill, H. V., & Holcomb, R. L. (1936). The effectiveness of appeal in radio advertising: A technique with some typical results. *Journal of Applied Psychology*, 20, 325–339.

Gaudet, F. J., & Zients, S. B. (1932). The history of full-page advertisements. *Journal of Applied Psychology*, 16, 1932, 512–514.

Geissler, L. R. (1917). Association-reactions applied to ideas of commercial brands of familiar articles. *Journal of Applied Psychology*, 1, 275–290.

Goodrum, C., & Dalrymple, H. (1990). *Advertising in America: The first 200 years*. New York: Harry N. Abrams.

Guest, L. P., & Brown, R. H. (1939) A study of the recall of radio advertising material. *Journal of Psychology*, 89, 381–387.

Guest, L. P. (1942). The genesis of brand awareness. *Journal of Applied Psychology*, 26, 800–808.

Guest, L. P. (1944). The study of brand loyalty. *Journal of Applied Psychology*, 28, 16–27.

Guilford, J. P., & Ewart, E. (1940). Reaction-time during distraction of an indicator of attention-value. *American Journal of Psychology*, 53, 554–563.

Haire, M. (1950). Projective techniques in marketing research. *Journal of Marketing*, 14, 649.

Hampton, P. (1940) Personality and success in selling. *Personnel Journal*, 19, 108–115.

Haugtvedt, C. P. (2006). Consumer psychology. *Encyclopedia of social psychology*. Newbury Park, CA: Sage.

Hathaway, S. R., & Welch, A. C. (1934). Does guessing distort the results of the method of triple associates? *Journal of Applied Psychology*, 18, 793–798.

Heller, W. S. (1919). Analysis of package labels. *University of California Publications in Psychology*, 3(2), 61–72.

Heller, W. S., & Brown, W. (1916). Memory and association in the case of street-car advertising cards. *University of California Publications in Psychology*, 2(4), 267–275.

Heidingsfield, M. S. (1949). Why do people shop in downtown department stores? *Journal of Marketing, 13,* 510–512.

Hotchkiss, G. B., & Franken, R. B. (1920). *The attention value of advertisements in a leading periodical.* Report prepared for the New York University Bureau of Business Research.

Hotchkiss, G. B., & Franken, R. B. (1923). *The leadership of advertised brands.* New York: Doubleday, Page & Company.

Hotchkiss, G. B., & Franken, R. B. (1927) *The measurement of advertising effects.* New York, Harper & Brothers.

Hollingworth, H. L. (1911). Experimental studies in judgment: Judgments of the comic. *Psychological Review, 8*(March), 132–156.

Hollingworth, H. L. (1913). *Advertising and selling: Principles of appeals and responses.* New York: D. Appleton.

Hollingworth, H. L. (1916). *Vocational psychology.* New York: D. Appleton.

Hollingworth, H. L. (1920). *The psychology of functional neuroses.* New York: D. Appleton.

Hollingworth, H. L. (1929). *Vocational psychology and character analysis.* New York/London: D. Appleton.

Hollingworth, H. L. (1930). *Abnormal psychology.* New York: Ronald Press.

Hollingworth, H. L., & Poffenberger, A. T. (1917). *Applied psychology.* New York and London: D. Appleton.

Hollingworth, H. L., & Poffenberger, A. T. (1917). *Sense of taste.* New York: Maffat, Yard and Company.

Hovde, H. T. (1931) Consumer preferences for small glass containers. *Journal of Applied Psychology, 15,* 346–357.

Howard, J. A., & Sheth. J. N. (1969). *The theory of buyer behavior.* New York: Wiley.

Jacobson, J. A. (1951). *Scott of Northwestern.* Chicago: Louis Mariano.

James, W. (1890/1950). *The principles of psychology.* 2 volumes. New York: Dover.

Karslake, J. (1940). The Purdue Eye-Camera: A practical apparatus for studying the attention value of advertisements. *Journal of Applied Psychology, 24*(4) 417–440.

Kamen, J. (1995). The start of division 23 (consumer psychology) of the American Psychological Association. Unpublished article.

Kassarjian, H. (1994). Scholarly traditions and European roots of American consumer behavior," In G. Laurent, G. L. Lilien, & B. Pras (Eds.), *Research traditions in marketing* (pp. 265–279). Boston: Kluwer.

Katona, G. (1960). *The powerful consumer.* New York: McGraw-Hill Book.

Katona, G. (1964). *The mass consumption society.* New York: McGraw-Hill.

Kitson, H. D. (1921). Amount and rate of increase in the use of illustrations. *Journal of Applied Psychology, 5,* 12.

Kitson, H. D. (1921). The use of the historical method in investigating problems in advertising. *Journal of Applied Psychology,* 5–13.

Kitson, H. D. (1921). *The mind of the buyer: The psychology of selling.* New York: Macmillan.

Kitson, H. D. (1922a). Color in magazine advertising. *Journal of Applied Psychology, 6,* 64–66.

Kitson, H. D. (1922b). Minor studies in the psychology of advertising — Development of art forms in magazine advertising. *Journal of Applied Psychology, 6,* 59–64.

Kitson, H. D. (1923). Understanding the consumer's mind. *The Annals of the American academy of Political and Social Science, 110,* 131–138.

Kitson, H. D., & Campbell, J. J. (1924). The package as a feature in magazine advertising. *Journal of Applied Psychology, 8,* 444–445.

Kitson, H. D., & Allen, I. (1925). Pictures of people in magazine advertising. *Journal of Applied Psychology, 9,* 367–370.

Klapp, O. E. (1941) Imitation-value in advertising. *Journal of Applied Psychology, 25,* 243–250.

Kornhauser, A. W., & Lazarsfeld, P. F. (1935). The technique of marketing research from the standpoint of a psychologist, *Institute of Management Series #16.* New York, American Management Association,

Kuna, D. P. (1976). *The psychology of advertising, 1896–1916.* Dissertation, University of New Hampshire.

Kuna, D. P. (1979). Early advertising applications of the Gale-Cattell order-of-merit method. *Journal of History in Behavioral Science, 15*(1), 38–46.

Laird, D. A. (1923). The basis of tooth past sales in representative communities. *Journal of Applied Psychology, 2,* 173–177.

Laslett, H. R. (1918). The value of relevancy in advertisement illustrations. *Journal of Applied Psychology, 2,* 270–279.

Lazarsfeld, P. F. (1934). The psychological aspect of market research. *Harvard Business Review, 13,* 54–71.

Likert, R. (1936). A method for measuring the sales influence of a radio program. *Journal of Applied Psychology, 20,* 175–182.

Link, H. C. (1932) *The new psychology of selling and advertising.* New York: McMillan.

Link, H.C. (1934). A new method for testing advertising and a psychological sales barometer. *Journal of Applied Psychology, 18,* 1–26.

Link, H.C. (1938). *The new psychology of selling and advertising.* New York: Macmillan.

Lucas, D. B. (1937). The impression values of fixed advertising locations in the Saturday Evening Post. *Journal of Applied Psychology, 21,* 613–631.

Lucas, D. B., & Benson, C. E. (1929a) The historical trend of negative appeals in advertising. *Journal of Applied Psychology, 13,* 346–356.

Lucas, D. B., & Benson, C. E. (1929b) The relative values of positive and negative advertising appeals as measured by coupons returned. *Journal of Applied Psychology, 13,* 274–300.

Lucas, D. B., & Benson, C. E. (1930a) The recall values of positive and negative advertising appeals. *Journal of Applied Psychology, 14,* 218–238.

Lucas, D. B., & Benson, C. E. (1930b) *Psychology for advertisers.* New York: Harper.

Lucas, D. B. (1937) The impression values of fixed advertising locations in the *Saturday Evening Post. Journal of Applied Psychology, 19,* 613–631.

Lucas, D. (1940) A rigid technique for measuring the impression values of specific magazine advertisements. *Journal of Applied Psychology, 24,* 778–790.

Market Research Corporation (1935) Do we use the products we recall first and consider best? *Sales Management, 37,* 566–567, 607–609.

McDougall, W. (1912). *Psychology, the study of behaviour.* New York: H. Holt.

McDougall, W. (1923). *Outline of psychology.* New York: Scribner.

McKinney, F. (1935) Retroactive inhibitions in advertising. *Journal of Applied Psychology, 19,* 59–66.

McKinney, F. (1937) An empirical method of analyzing a sales interview. *Journal of Applied Psychology, 21,* 280–299.

McNamara, J. J. (1941). "A new method for testing advertising effectiveness through eye movement photography." *Psychological Record,* Vol. 4, 399–459.

McNamara, J. J., & Tiffin, J. (1941). The distracting effect of nearby cartoons on the attention holding power of advertisements. *Journal of Applied Psychology, 25,* 524–527.

Mitchell, G. E., & Burett, H. E. (1938). Psychological factors in the sales interview. *Journal of Applied Psychology, 22,* 17–31.

Muloney, J. C. (1987). "The First Eighty Years of Advertising Research," Paper presented at the Sixth Annual Advertising and Consumer Psychology Conference, Chicago.

Munsterberg, H. (1909). The field of applied psychology. *Psychological Bulletin, 6,* 49–50.

Nicosia, F. M. (1966). *Consumer decision process: Marketing and advertising implications.* Englewood Cliffs, NJ: Prentice Hall.

Nixon, H. K. (1924). Attention and interest in advertising. *Archives of Psychology, 72,* 5–67.

Nixon, H. K. (1926). *An investigation of attention to Advertisements.* New York, Columbia University Press.

Nixon, H. K. (1927). A study of perception of advertisements. *Journal of Applied Psychology, 11,* 135–142.

Nixon, H. K. (1931). *Principles of selling.* New York: McGraw-Hill.

Nixon, H. K. (1942). *Principles of selling* (2nd ed.). New York: McGraw-Hill Book Company.

Oliver, J. W. (1956). *History of American technology.* New York: Ronald Press.

Packard, V. (1957/1980). *Hidden persuaders.* New York: Washington Square Press

Poffenberger, A. T. (1923a). The return coupon as a measure of advertising efficiency. *Journal of Applied Psychology, 7*(3), 202–208.

Poffenberger, A. T. (1923b). The conditions of belief in advertising. *Journal of Applied Psychology, 7*(1), 1–9.

Poffenberger, A. T. (1925). *Psychology in advertising.* Chicago & New York: A. W. Shaw.

Poffenberger, A. T. (1927). *Applied psychology: Its principles and methods.* New York: D. Appleton.

Poffenberger, A. T. (1942). *Principles of applied psychology.* New York & London: D. Appleton-Century.

Poffenberger, A. T. (1957), Harry Levi Hollingworth: 1880–1956. *American Journal of Psychology, 70,* 138.

Poffenberger, A. T., & Barrows, B. E. (1924). The feeling value of lines. *Journal of Applied Psychology, 8,* 187–205.

Poffenberger, A. T., & Franken, R. B. (1923), A study of the appropriateness of type faces. *Journal of Applied Psychology, 7,* 312–329.

Pronko, N. H., & Bowles, J. W., Jr. (1948), Identification of cola beverages: I. First study. *Journal of Applied Psychology, 32,* 304–312.

Pronko, N. H., & Bowles, J. W., Jr. (1949). Identification of cola beverages. III. A final study. *Journal of Applied Psychology, 33,* 605–608.

Sayer, J. (1939) A comparison of three indices of attitude toward radio advertising. *Journal of Applied Psychology, 23,* 23–33.

Schiller, G (1935) An experimental Study of the appropriateness of color and type in advertising. *Journal of Applied Psychology, 19,* 652–664.

Schultz, R.S. (1935). Test-selected salesmen are successful. *Personnel Journal, 14,* 139–142.

Scripture, E. W. (1895). *Thinking, felling, doing.* New York: Flood and Vincent.

Scott, W. D. (1903). *Theory of advertising.* Boston: Small, Maynard, & Co.

Scott, W. D. (1908). *The psychology of advertising.* Boston: Small, Maynard, & Co.

Scott, W. D. (1908). A practical illuminator and its utility in a psychological laboratory. *Psychological Bulletin,* 5(February), 44.

Scott, W. D. (1910). Personal differences in suggestibility. *Psychological Review, 17*(March), 147–154.

Scott, W. D. (invited articles from 1910–1916). Suggestion. *Psychological Bulletin, 7* (November 1910): 369–372; *8* (September 1911): 309–311; *9* (July 1912): 269–271; *10* (July 1913): 269–270; *11* (July 1914): 250–252; *12* (June 1915): 225–226; *13* (July 1916): 266–268.

Scott, W. D. (1916). *The theory and practice of advertising.* Boston: Small, Maynard & Co.

Snow, A. J. (1926). *Psychology in personal selling.* New York: McGraw-Hill.

Snow, A. J. (1929). *Effective selling.* New York: McGraw-Hill.

Stanton, F. N. (1934). Memory for advertising copy presented visually vs. orally. *Journal of Applied Psychology, 18,* 45–64.

Starch, D. (1910). *Principles of advertising: A systematic syllabus.* Madison, WI: University Cooperative Co.

Starch, D. (invited articles from 1911–1916). Auditory Space. *Psychological Bulletin, 8* (July 1911: 232–233; *9* (July 1912): 254–255; *12* (June 1915): 213–214; *13* (July 1916): 264–265.

Starch, D. (1914). *Advertising: Its principles, practice and technique.* New York: D. Appleton.

Starch, D. (1923). *Principles of advertising.* Chicago: A.W. Shaw.

Strong, E. K., Jr. (1911). The relative merit of advertisements, *Columbia Contributions to Philosophy and Psychology* (vol. 19, no. 3, pp. 4–5). New York: The Science Press.

Strong, E. K., Jr. (1912). The effect of length of series upon recognition memory. *Psychological Review, 19,* 447–462.

Strong, E. K., Jr. (1913). The effect of time-interval upon recognition memory. *Psychological Review, 20*(September), 339–372.

Strong, E. K., Jr. (1914). The effect of size of advertisements and frequency of their presentation. *Psychological Review, 21*(March), 136–152.

Strong, E. K., Jr. (1925). *The psychology of selling and advertising.* New York: McGraw-Hill.

Strong, E. K., Jr. (1938). *Psychological aspects of business.* New York: McGraw-Hill.

Sumner, F. C. (1932). Influence of color on legibility of copy. *Journal of Applied Psychology, 16*(2), 201–204.

Thorndike, E. L. (1911). *Animal intelligence.* New York: Macmillan.

Thorndike, E. L. (1913). Ideo-motor action. *Psychological Review, 20*(March), 91–106.

Tipper, H., Hollingworth, H. L., Hotchkiss, G. B., & Parsons, F. A. (1915). *The principles of advertising.* New York: The Ronald Press Company.

Turner, E. M. (1922). The testimonial as an advertising appeal. *Journal of Applied Psychology, 6,* 192–197.

Twedt, D. (1952). A multiple factor analysis of advertising readership. *Journal of Applied Psychology, 36,* 207–215.

Twedt, D. W. (1965) Consumer psychology. *Annual Review of Psychology, 16,* 265–294.

Watson, J. B. (1913). Psychology as the behaviorist views it. *The Psychological Review, 10*(March). 158–177.

Watson, J. B., & Raynor, R. (1920). Conditioned emotional reactions. *Journal of Experimental Psychology, 3,* 1–14.

Watson, R. I., & Evans, R. B. (1981). *The great psychologists: A history of psychological thought,* 5th edition. New York: Harper Collins.

Welch, A. C. (1941) An analytic system of testing competitive advertising. *Journal of Applied Psychology, 25,* 176–190.

Wenzel, B. M. (1979). Albert T. Poffenberger (1885–1977). *American Psychologist, 34* (1), 88–90.

Wiebe, R. H. (1967). *The search for order, 1877–1920.* New York: Hill and Wang.

Wolfe, H. D. (1941) High rank correlation between radio listeners and product-program association. *Journal of Applied Psychology, 25,* 721 – 725.

Woodworth, R. S. (1918). *Dynamic psychology.* New York: Columbia University Press.

Zubin, J., & Peatman, J. G. (1945). Testing the pulling power of advertisements by the split-run copy method. *Journal of Applied Psychology, 29,* 40–57.

II

CONSUMER INFORMATION PROCESSING

2

The Role of Knowledge Accessibility in Cognition and Behavior

Implications for Consumer Information Processing

ROBERT S. WYER, JR.

Hong Kong University of Science and Technology

People's judgments and decisions are typically based on only a small subset of the knowledge they could potentially apply. Furthermore, when they receive new judgment-relevant information, they construe its implications without considering all of the alternative interpretations it might have. The concepts and knowledge they employ in each case are not necessarily either the most relevant or the most reliable, but rather, are the cognitions that come most easily to mind. This general tendency, which has been documented at all stages of information processing from the initial acquisition and comprehension of information to the generation of an overt response, is one of the most widely accepted phenomena to emerge in the past three decades of psychological research (Bargh, 1997; Higgins, 1996; Wyer, 2004). Nowhere is its importance greater than in the domain of consumer judgment and decision making. That is, purchase decisions, like judgments and behavior more generally, are often based on whatever criteria happen to be salient at the time.

Because of its pervasiveness, the role of knowledge accessibility is a central component of almost every theoretical formulation of social information processing to appear in the past three decades, ranging from general formulations of judgment and behavior (Bargh, 1997; Carlston, 1994; Smith, 1990; Wyer, 2004; Wyer & Srull, 1989) to more specific formulations of attitude formation and change (Chaiken, 1987; Petty & Cacioppo, 1986), attitude-behavior relations (Fazio, 1990), impression formation (Higgins, Rholes, & Jones, 1977; Srull & Wyer, 1979), stereotype activation and suppression (Bodenhausen & Macrae, 1998), the effects of the media on perceptions of social reality (Shrum, 2002), the impact of affect and subjective experience on judgments and decisions (Schwarz, 2004; Schwarz & Clore, 1996; Strack & Deutsch, 2004), goal-directed behavior (Chartrand & Bargh, 2002), cultural influences on behavioral decisions (Briley & Wyer, 2002; Hong, Morris, Chiu, & Benet-Martinez, 2000), and perspective effects in judgment (Adaval & Monroe, 2002). In the area of consumer research, the role of knowledge accessibility is implicit if not explicit in research on subliminal advertising (Moore, 1982, 1988; Trappey, 1996; see also Vargas, this volume), brand awareness (Kardes, Gurumurthy, Chandrashekaran, & Dronoff, 1993), pricing (Adaval & Monroe, 2002), and product evaluation more generally.

Extensive reviews of theory and research on knowledge accessibility are available elsewhere (Higgins, 1996; see also Bargh, 1994, 1997; Förster & Liberman, in press; Wyer, 2004), and we will not repeat this material unnecessarily. The first section of this chapter reviews alternative conceptualizations of knowledge accessibility phenomena, drawing largely from research and theory in cognitive and social psychology. Later sections provide examples of the role of knowledge accessibility at several different stages of information processing, including the attention to and comprehension of information, the representation of the information in memory, the computation of inferences on the basis of previously acquired knowledge, and behavior decisions. In the course of this discussion, we review representative research and theory in consumer judgment and decision-making in which differences in knowledge accessibility come into play.

GENERAL CONSIDERATIONS

Stages of Information Processing

The processing of information for the purpose of making a judgment or decision can occur in several stages. For example:

1. Attention—people pay differing amounts of attention to the various aspects of the information they receive.
2. Encoding and comprehension—people interpret individual pieces of information in terms of previously formed concepts that they exemplify, and may organize clusters of features with reference to a more general knowledge structure or "schema." Thus, they might interpret a $70 pair of jeans as expensive, or comprehend a temporally related sequence of events that occur at a restaurant in terms of a prototypic "restaurant script" (Schank & Abelson, 1977).
3. Inference—people often infer the likelihood that a statement or assertion is true, or the frequency with which a particular event has occurred. At the same time, they estimate the likelihood that an event will occur in the future, or that a certain state of affairs did or does exist. They sometimes infer that an object has a particular attribute, or might evaluate it as either favorable or unfavorable. In other cases, they make a comparative judgment of several objects or events along a given dimension, or might compute a preference for one alternative over another.
4. Response processes—people transform the implications of their subjective judgment into an overt response or behavioral decision.

Processing at each of these stages typically requires the activation and use of previously acquired concepts and knowledge. Therefore, it may depend in part on which of several potentially relevant subsets of this knowledge happens to be most accessible.

TYPES OF KNOWLEDGE REPRESENTATIONS

The knowledge that comes into play at these stages of processing can be of two general types. *Declarative* knowledge concerns the referents of everyday life experiences (persons, objects, events, attitudes and values, oneself, etc.). In contrast, *procedural* knowledge refers to the sequence of actions that one performs in pursuit of a particular goal (driving a car, using a word processor, etc.) Whereas declarative knowledge is reflected in the information we can recall about an entity or that we implicitly draw upon in the course of attaining a particular objective, procedural knowledge is reflected in the sequence of cognitive or motor acts that are performed in the pursuit of this objective. People can, of course, have declarative knowledge about how to attain a particular objective, and might sometimes consult this knowledge for use as a behavioral guide. Once the procedure is well learned, however, it may often be applied automatically, with little if any conscious cognitive mediation.

These automated procedures can be conceptualized as "productions" of the sort suggested by J. R. Anderson (1982, 1983; see also Smith, 1990, 1994). Thus, they may be metaphorically have the form of "If [X], then [Y]" rules in which [X] is a configuration of perceptual or cognitive stimulus features and [Y] is a sequence of cognitive or motor acts that are elicited automatically when the eliciting conditions are met. These productions, which are acquired through learning, are strengthened by repetition, and can ultimately be activated and applied with minimal cognitive mediation. The routines involved in driving a car (e.g., putting in the clutch, turning on the ignition, putting the car in gear, gradually releasing the clutch while stepping on the gas, etc.) initially require conscious thought. However, they ultimately come to be performed without consulting declarative knowledge about the sequence of steps involved, and require few if any cognitive resources (Schneider & Shiffrin, 1977). As Bargh (1997) argues, a very large amount of our social behavior is likely to involve the use of these automatically activated productions.

The influence of both declarative knowledge and procedural knowledge is apparent at all of the aforementioned stages of processing. Many effects that are attributed to the accessibility of declarative could be due to the accessibility of procedural knowledge instead. In this chapter, we focus primarily on the accessibility of declarative knowledge (Smith, 1990). Nevertheless, the accessibility of procedural knowledge is likely to have a particularly important impact on overt behavior as will be seen.

Declarative knowledge can consist of general semantic concepts (honest, woolen, etc.) or categories (lawyer, Irishman, high-tech, designer jeans, etc.) Alternatively, it could comprise a configuration of features that are organized temporally, spatially or causally and are stored in memory and later retrieved as a unit. These knowledge representations could pertain to a specific person or experience (e.g., George W. Bush, the 2004 Super Bowl game, my trip to Bermuda in 1985, last night's dinner at Jaspa's Restaurant) or a more general characterization that applies to several individuals or events (reactionary politicians, football games, vacation trips, restaurant visits).

Representations of a situation-specific sequence of events may constitute a story (Schank & Abelson, 1995). However, more generalized sequences of events can function as *implicit theories* that convey the antecedents and consequences of different types of experiences involving oneself or others (Dweck, 1991; Dweck, Chiu, & Hong, 1995; Ross, 1989; Wyer, 2004). These representations come into play in not only comprehending new experiences but also reconstructing past events and predicting future ones. Other generalized event sequences can constitute plans or procedures that are used as behavioral guides in attaining a particular goal.

The knowledge representations that people construct can be coded in different modalities. Although much of our knowledge is coded verbally, a very large portion of it (particularly the knowledge we acquire through direct experience) is nonverbal, consisting of mental images that have both visual and acoustic components (Wyer & Radvansky, 1998).

Finally, the knowledge we acquire can elicit subjective reactions (e.g., positive or negative affect) that, once experienced, can exert an influence on the processing of information at each of the stages listed earlier. These reactions, once elicited, can be a major source of the information people use as a basis for judgments and decisions (Schwarz & Clore, 1996; Strack & Deutsch, 2004). On the other hand, they can influence the interpretation of information (Adaval, 2003; Isbell & Wyer, 1999), and the weight that people attach to it when making a judgment (Adaval, 2001). Although affect, or subjective experience more generally, is not itself a part of the knowledge one stores in memory, it can be elicited by this knowledge (Wyer, Clore, & Isbell, 1998). Its influence can nevertheless be conceptualized in terms very similar to that of other aspects of knowledge that people have accessible at the time they receive information and make a judgment or decision.

Despite these differences in the content and structure of knowledge, the processes that govern its accessibility in memory are similar. In the next section, we propose a set of principles that describe these processes. These principles potentially apply at all stages of processing.

BASIC PRINCIPLES

Several theories of information processing purport to account for the determinants and effects of knowledge accessibility (e.g., Higgins, Bargh, & Lombardi, 1985; Smith, 1990; Wyer & Carlston, 1979; Wyer & Srull, 1989; Wyer, 2004). Although these theories often make different specific assumptions about the mechanisms that underlie memory storage and retrieval, they agree that the knowledge one retrieves and brings to bear on the processing of information is a function of its association with the thoughts and concepts that happen to be activated at the time the knowledge is sought. The cognitions that cue its retrieval can include aspects of the information to be processed and the situational context in which it is presented. They can also be internally generated. For example, people who wish to purchase a car may intentionally retrieve a set of attributes that characterize a high quality automobile and use the attributes as guides in construing the implications of information about a particular car they are considering. In many cases, however, thoughts that one has recently had for another, objectively irrelevant purpose can also cue the retrieval of knowledge from memory.

A fairly large number of concepts and knowledge representations can often be associated with a given set of retrieval cues, and people are usually neither able nor motivated to consider all of them. This observation leads to the most fundamental principle on which theory and research on knowledge accessibility is based:

> **Principle 1.** People rarely retrieve and use more knowledge than is necessary to attain the objective they are pursuing. When each of several knowledge representations is sufficient to attain this objective, the first representation that comes to mind is most likely to be applied.

This means that if two or more different concepts or knowledge representations can be used to attain a particular goal, the one that is identified and applied most quickly and easily will be employed. For example, suppose to attribute concepts, "tasty" and "unhealthy" are equally applicable for interpreting information that a drink has artificial sweeteners. In this case, the one that comes to mind first is most likely to be applied. Similarly, if several criteria (e.g., brand name, specific attributes) are potentially available for evaluating a product, the criteria that can be applied most easily are most likely to be considered.

Principle 1 does not necessarily imply that the first knowledge that comes to mind is the *only* knowledge to be employed. This is true only if it is deemed sufficient to attain the objective one is pursuing. Chaiken (1987; Chaiken, Liberman, & Eagly, 1989) assumed that people who process information for a particular purpose first invoke the criterion that they can apply most quickly and easily and evaluate their confidence that the results of applying it is sufficient to attain the objective they are pursuing. If their confidence is above a minimum threshold, they use it without further ado. If their confidence is below threshold, however, they apply the next most accessible criterion, and continue in this manner until their threshold is reached. The threshold that individuals apply in any given situation can increase with the importance of the goal to which the processing is relevant. It can also depend on the time and effort the person is able to devote to this activity. Therefore, the less motivated people are to engage in extensive cognitive processing, or the less time they have available, the more likely they are to use the first criterion they consider to the exclusion of others.

The sufficiency principle has broad applicability, and versions of it can be found in diverse theories of judgment, including the conception of satisficing (Simon, 1955) and the impact of affect on judgment (Schwarz & Clore, 1996). Its importance is apparent throughout this chapter.

DETERMINANTS OF KNOWLEDGE ACCESSIBILITY

Most theories agree on four determinants of knowledge accessibility: (1) the strength of association between the knowledge to be accessed and concepts that have already been activated in the situation at hand, (2) the recency with which knowledge has been acquired and used, (3) the frequency with which it has been employed, and (4) the amount of processing in which it has been directly or indirectly involved.

Strength of Association

As noted earlier, the accessibility of knowledge in memory at any given moment is determined in part by the strength of its association with situational, informational, or internally generated features that exist at the moment and, therefore, serve as implicit or explicit retrieval cues. These associations may be either semantic or experience-based. Thus, for example, the word "bread" might cue the retrieval of "butter," and a picture of a yellow double arch is likely to stimulate a concept of McDonald's. The retrieval of such associated cognitions may be a conditioned cognitive response to the stimulus concept or cognition that is acquired through learning in much the same way as other, noncognitive responses. In many instances, however, the features of a stimulus are associated to a similar extent with more than one concept or unit of knowledge. In this case, other factors come into play.

Recency and Frequency

When two concepts or knowledge units are equally useful in attaining a particular processing objective, the one that has been used more recently in the past is likely to be applied again. This effect was first identified in social psychology by Higgins, Rholes, and Jones (1977). They showed that unobtrusively exposing participants to a trait concept while they performed an ostensibly unrelated "priming" task* increased their use of this concept to interpret the information they later received about a fictitious target person and, consequently, influenced their liking for this person. These effects have been identified even when the concepts are primed subliminally (Bargh & Pietromonaco, 1982).

The accessibility of knowledge can also be determined by the frequency with which a unit of knowledge has been activated and used in the past (Higgins et al., 1985; Srull &Wyer, 1979). Frequently encountered concepts and knowledge can become *chronically* accessible in memory (Higgins, King, & Mavin, 1982) and, therefore, can have effects independently of situational factors that might activate them (Bargh, Bond, Lombardi, & Tota, 1986). The cognitive processes that theoretically underlie the effects of frequency of use and the effects of recency of use may differ (cf. Higgins et al., 1985; Wyer, 2004; Wyer & Srull, 1989). Consequently, these factors may contribute independently to their overall accessibility in memory (Bargh et al., 1986). However, although the

---

* In this chapter, we use the term "priming" to refer to an experimental procedure that is used to increase the accessibility of a unit of knowledge in memory, as distinct from the accessibility of the concept itself.

effects of recently activated concepts initially override the effects of frequency, they are short-lived. Consequently, the effect of frequency predominates after a period of time has elapsed (Higgins et al., 1985). To summarize:

> **Principle 2.** The accessibility of a unit of knowledge in memory is an increasing function of both the recency with which it has been activated in the past and the frequency with which it has been activated. The effect of recency decreases over time, whereas the effect of frequency persists.

The similar effects of recency and frequency of activation are of methodological importance. That is, hypotheses concerning the effects of chronically accessible concepts and knowledge can be confirmed indirectly by establishing the effects of recently activating them in a laboratory context. (For examples of the use of this strategy, see Schwarz & Strack, 1981; Shrum, Wyer, & O'Guinn, 1998; Wyer, Bodenhausen, & Gorman, 1985.)

Amount of Processing

The accessibility of knowledge in memory can also be influenced by the extent to which the knowledge was thought about at the time it was first acquired (Craik & Lockhart, 1972; Wyer & Hartwick, 1980). Several specific mechanisms could underlie these effects (Anderson, 1983), including the reconstructive processes outlined elsewhere in this handbook (Kronlund et al., this volume; for a specific empirical application of the role of reconstructive inference to brand memory, see Noel, 2006). In some cases, the impact of amount of processing might not be independent of the influence of frequency or alternatively, strength of association. That is, the greater the amount of cognitive activity that is devoted to a piece of information, the greater the number of cognitive elements with which is likely to become associated and the greater the number of knowledge units in which it is embedded. Nevertheless, its influence on knowledge accessibility is worth noting in its own right.

EFFECTS OF PRIOR JUDGMENTS ON SUBSEQUENT ONES

One manifestation of the effects of recency of knowledge activation is worth special consideration. Once an implicit or explicit judgment has been made on the basis of information received at one point in time, a representation of this judgment can often be stored in memory independently of the information that led to its construction. Consequently, the judgment may later be retrieved out of context and used as a basis for other judgments and decisions (Carlston, 1980; Higgins & Lurie, 1983; Sherman, Ahlm, Berman, & Lynn, 1978; for evidence in the consumer domain, see Kardes, 1986). This means that if situationally primed knowledge influences the representation that is formed of information and this representation is stored in memory, its influence is likely to persist over time.

As one example, participants in a study by Srull and Wyer (1980) first performed a sentence construction task in which a concept of hostility was activated. Then, they read a paragraph describing a target person whose behavior was ambiguous with respect to hostility with instructions to form an impression of the person and later judged the target with respect to this attribute. However, the time intervals between the sentence construction task, the target information, and judgments were varied. When trait concepts were primed 24 hours before the ambiguous target information was presented, they had little effect. When the concepts were primed immediately before participants received the target information, however, they had a positive effect on judgments. Furthermore, their effect was significantly greater 24 hours after the information was presented than it was immediately afterwards.

Principle 3. If people have interpreted information on the basis of recently activated concepts and knowledge, the effects of this interpretation on later judgments and decisions about its referent will persist over time.

A corollary of this principle is that once people have formed a mental representation of a stimulus, concepts that become accessible subsequently are likely to have little effect on the judgments they report later. In other conditions of Srull and Wyer's (1980) study, hostility-related concepts were primed immediately after participants had read the target description rather than beforehand. In this condition, participants presumably interpreted the target's behavior in terms of whatever concepts happened to be accessible and formed an impression on the basis of this interpretation. They later based their judgments on this impression, and concepts that were activated subsequent to its construction had no impact.

Darley and Gross (1983) reported analogous findings. That is, information about a child's socioeconomic background influenced participants' judgments of the child's ability if it was conveyed before the participants saw a videotape of the individual's performance on an exam. However, it had no impact on judgments if it was not conveyed until after the tape was viewed. Similarly, Yeung and Wyer (2004) found that if participants were induced to feel happy or unhappy before they encountered a picture of a product, they used their affective reactions as a basis for their initial impression of the product and this impression influenced their later evaluations of it independently of the attribute information they received subsequently. On the other hand, if participants' affective reactions were not induced until after they had seen the picture and formed an impression on the basis of it, the affect they were experiencing had no influence on their product evaluations.

It is nonetheless important to note that the interpretation of information in terms of recently activated trait concepts does not always occur spontaneously. Rather, it may only occur when people have a specific goal in mind that requires the application of these concepts (e.g., forming an impression of the object that the information describes). If people process the information with no particular goal in mind, they may not spontaneously engage in this cognitive activity (Wyer, 2004). In this case, the accessibility of concepts and knowledge at the time of judgment is more likely to exert an influence.

THE INFLUENCE OF AWARENESS ON THE IMPACT OF ACCESSIBLE KNOWLEDGE

People can be influenced by information that they do not know they have received. Bargh and his colleagues (for reviews, see Bargh, 1994, 1997) have identified these effects at several different stages of processing. For example, subliminally presented trait concepts can influence people's interpretation of information about a target person's behavior and, consequently, judgments of this person (Bargh & Pietromonaco, 1982); subliminally primed evaluative-toned concepts can affect the ease with which participants identify other words that are evaluative similar or dissimilar (Bargh, Chaiken, Raymond, & Hymens, 1996; Bargh, Chaiken, Govender, & Pratt, 1992). Subliminally priming high or low numbers can influence people's judgments of the expensiveness of a product they are later asked to evaluate (Adaval & Monroe, 2002), and subliminally exposing people to faces of a stereotyped group can influence the likelihood of behaving in ways that are characteristic of that group (Bargh, Chen, & Burrows, 1996).

Corrections for Bias

Even when people are exposed to information overtly, they may not be aware of its possible effect on their judgments in other, ostensibly unrelated situations. People are likely to assume that the concepts and knowledge that come to mind when they think about a stimulus are activated by this stimulus alone. Consequently, they are likely to consider the implications of these cognitions to be representative of the knowledge they have available about the stimulus and, therefore, to be an appropriate basis for judgments and decisions they might make concerning it. Only if they are aware that the knowledge that comes to mind might be biased, will they try to correct for this influence.

In such cases, they might discount implications of the knowledge entirely and search for alternative criteria to use. Lombardi, Higgins, and Bargh (1987), for example, found that when participants were able to recall the priming words to which they had been exposed (suggesting that they were aware of their possible influence), they were actually *less* likely to use the primed concepts to interpret the stimulus information than they otherwise would have been. In some instances, however, participants may believe that their interpretation of information might be biased but are either unmotivated or unable to correct for it. In a series of studies by Martin, Seta, and Celia (1990), for example, participants were clearly aware that the concepts they had employed in an ostensibly irrelevant task could influence their interpretation of the information they received subsequently. In these conditions, the primed concepts only had a positive influence on their judgments when participants were either unable to devote the cognitive effort required to identify and use a different concept (e.g., under high situational distraction) or, alternatively, were unmotivated to expend this effort (e.g., they were low in need for cognition, or felt little personal responsibility for the judgments to be made).

In a particularly intriguing demonstration of these contingencies, Martin (1986) primed trait concepts using procedures similar to those employed by Martin et al. (1990). However, some participants were ostensibly interrupted before they completed the priming task, whereas others were led to believe they had finished it. (In fact, all participants were exposed to the same number of primes, regardless of whether they were interrupted or not.) Participants who were interrupted apparently continued to ruminate about the task (Zeigarnik, 1938), and this cognitive activity prevented them from searching for alternative concepts to use in interpreting the target information they received subsequently. Thus, the primed concepts had a positive impact on the judgments they made on the basis of this information. When participants believed they had completed the priming task, however, they did not ruminate about it and devoted their cognitive resources to arrive at an unbiased interpretation of the target information. Consequently, the priming effects observed under interrupted-task conditions were not evident.

Rather than searching for alternative judgmental criteria to use, people who believe their judgments may be biased may sometimes find it easier to make a tentative judgment and then to adjust this judgment to compensate for the effects that the judgment-irrelevant knowledge is likely to have had. In this case, however, they may not know how much to adjust. If they do not adjust enough, the knowledge will continue to exert an influence. If they adjust too much, it could have a negative, contrast effect (Ottati & Isbell, 1986). Which effect occurs is likely to depend in part on individuals' implicit theories of the amount of bias produced by the external situational factors in question (Wegener & Petty, 1997; see also Strack, 1992).

Adjustment processes of particular relevance for consumer research were identified by Schwarz and Bless (1992; see also Strack et al., 1993). When people are exposed to items in an opinion survey, questions that occur at one point in the survey may activate concepts that are used as a basis for responses to later questions. However, if respondents are aware of this influence, they may try to correct for it. Indeed, they may believe that the questioner does not intend to ask the same question twice. In this case, they may use different criteria in responding to the questions even if the questions appear related.

Several other studies provide evidence of this effect. Strack, Martin, and Schwarz (1988; Strack & Martin, 1987), for example, asked participants to report their satisfaction with their marriage and also their satisfaction with life as a whole. When the questions appeared on separate pages of the questionnaire, responses to the questions were correlated .55. When the second question immediately followed the first, however, the correlation was reduced to .26. Respondents in the latter case apparently assumed they should use different criteria for evaluating their life as a whole than they used in responding to the first item, and consequently excluded their marriage from consideration.

Similarly, Ottati, Riggle, Wyer, Schwarz, and Kuklinski (1989) found that asking participants their opinions about the rights of a positive or negative social group (e.g., whether the American Civil Liberties Union or the American Nazi Party should be allowed to speak on campus) had a positive influence on their responses to a general question (whether people should be allowed to express their views in public) when the items were separated by six other, unrelated ones. When the group-specific item immediately preceded the general one, however, participants appeared to exclude the group from consideration in responding to the general question. As a result, the group-specific item had a negative, contrast effect on their responses.

The methodological implications of these findings are obvious. In much research on consumer behavior, multiple items are used to assess the same construct (e.g., liking for a product). This is done under the assumption that the use of several related provides a more reliable estimate of the construct of concern. In fact, however, by stimulating participants to use different criteria for responding to the items than they otherwise might, the procedure could often have precisely the opposite effect.

To summarize:

Principle 4. Knowledge that becomes accessible in memory for reasons that are unrelated to a judgment or decision will influence this judgment or decision if participants either are unaware of the conditions that activated the knowledge or, alternatively, are unaware of the relation between these conditions and the judgment or decision to be made. Even if people are aware of the biasing influence of judgment-irrelevant knowledge, they may not be motivated or able to correct for its influence or, alternatively, may not know how much they should adjust their response to compensate for its effect.

The contingencies implied by Principle 4 should not be overemphasized. As we noted earlier, people are unlikely to pay much attention to the extraneous situational factors that influence the knowledge they bring to bear on their judgments and decisions. Rather, they attribute the accessibility of this knowledge to the person or object they are judging. Consequently, the influence of extraneous determinants of knowledge accessibility may be quite pervasive.

The Effects of Thought Suppression on Knowledge Accessibility

People who consciously try to avoid the use of a concept or body of knowledge in interpreting information or making a judgment are often successful. However, active attempts to avoid using a judgmental criterion often require thinking about the criterion to be avoided. The effort expended in an attempt to suppress its use can actually increase its accessibility in memory relative to conditions in which this effort is not made. Consequently, once the restrictions on its use are lifted, the suppressed concept or knowledge may be more likely to be used than it otherwise would.

This possibility, which was identified empirically by Wegner (1994), was applied in an innovative series of studies by Macrae, Bodenhausen, and their colleagues (for a review, see Bodenhausen & Macrae, 1998). In one set of studies (Macrae, Bodenhausen, Milne, & Jetten, 1994), participants received a picture of a skinhead along with other verbal information and were told to form an impression of the person. However, some participants were told explicitly not to rely on a stereotype in arriving at their impression. Their judgments of the target indicated that the instructions were successful. Nevertheless, they responded more quickly than control participants to stereotype-related words in a subsequent word-identification task. Furthermore, they described a second skinhead more stereotypically once the restriction on the use of this stereotype was lifted, and avoided sitting close to a skinhead while waiting for a later part of the experiment. In short, the active suppression of a stereotype-related knowledge actually increased its accessibility in memory, and this knowledge influenced both later judgments and behavioral decisions once the sanctions against using it were removed.

The four principles summarized in this section typically apply independently of the type of knowledge involved and the type of judgment or decision to which this knowledge is applied. In the following sections, we review representative studies in both psychology and consumer research that bear on the effects of knowledge accessibility at different stages of processing. In this context, we note some additional considerations that arise in conceptualizing the effects at these stages.

ATTENTIONAL PROCESSES

Selective Information Seeking

Individual pieces of information are more likely to be identified and thought about if they can be interpreted in terms of concepts and knowledge that are easily accessible in memory. This may be true even if the other information available is equally relevant to the goal one is pursuing. The concepts that exert this bias could be activated either by the particular goal one is pursuing and by goal-irrelevant situational factors that happen to make these concepts come to mind.

The Effect of Goals on Selective Attention

The bias produced by goal-directed information seeking was demonstrated by Snyder, Swann, and their colleagues (Snyder, 1981; Snyder & Swann, 1978; Swann & Giuliano, 1987). Suppose people wish to decide if a person or object belongs to a certain category (e.g., extrovert, good secretary, high quality DVD player, etc.). To make this assessment, they are likely to activate a set of attributes that characterize members of this category and to search for information that can be encoded in terms of these attributes. At the same time, they may be disposed to ignore information that is not interpretable in terms of category-consistent features.

Thus, for example, people who want to determine if someone is an extravert may activate attribute concepts such as "talks a lot," "likes parties," "says hello to strangers on the street," etc.) and may search for information that can be interpreted in terms of these concepts. In doing so, they may ignore information that is interpretable in terms of attributes that might disconfirm the target's membership (e.g., "goes for long walks alone," "avoids large crowds," etc.) This selective search could produce a bias in the conclusions that are drawn.

Snyder and Swann (1978; see also Swann & Giuliano, 1987) gave some participants the opportunity to select questions to ask a person for the purpose of deciding if the person was an extravert, and gave others the opportunity to select questions to decide if (s)he was an introvert. Participants selected questions that presupposed the attribute they were attempting to evaluate (e.g., "What do you like about parties?") and, therefore, were likely to elicit answers that confirmed the person's membership in the category they were considering (Snyder & Swann, 1978). Alternatively, they selected questions, affirmative answers to which provided this confirmation (e.g., "Do you like parties?") (Swann & Giuliano, 1987).

In another study (Snyder & Cantor, 1979), participants read a paragraph about a person that contained equal amounts of extraverted and introverted behavioral descriptions with instructions either to decide if the person was an extravert or to decide if she was an introvert. They paid more attention to descriptions that confirmed the person's membership in the specific category they were considering, as inferred from both their judgments and the information they later identified as relevant to these judgments.

Initial preferences can operate in much the same way as hypotheses. Chernev (2001), for example, found that participants with an initial preference for a product tended to pay greater attention to information that confirmed their preference than to information that disconfirmed it, thus biasing the effects of the information in the direction of their initial attitude. Similarly, Yeung and Wyer (2004) found that consumers who had formed an initial impression of a product on the basis of a picture later recalled information about the product's specific attributes that was consistent with this impression rather than inconsistent with it.

A quite different demonstration of the impact of goal-directed processing on selective attention to information was provided by Ross, Lepper, Strack, and Steinmetz (1971). Participants read a clinical case study with instructions to explain either why the protagonist might have committed suicide after leaving therapy or, alternatively, why he might have donated a large sum of money to the Peace Corps. Later, they were asked to predict the likelihood that the protagonist engaged in a number of activities, including the one they had considered earlier. Participants were given convincing evidence that neither the experimenter nor anyone else actually knew what had happened to the protagonist after leaving therapy. Nevertheless, they predicted the outcome they had explained to be more likely than the outcomes they had not explained. Participants in generating their explanation selectively attended to features that were consistent with this explanation. Later, they used this selective subset of features as a basis for their prediction to the exclusion of other information that had been presented.

The Impact of Affect on Selective Attention

When people's processing objectives do not bias the information to which they attend, goal-irrelevant factors may have an impact. One such factor may be the affective reactions that people happen to be experiencing at the time the information is received. A study by Bower, Gilligan, and Monteiro (1981) is illustrative. Participants under hypnosis were instructed to recall a past experience that made them feel either happy or sad and then to maintain these feelings after they were brought out of their hypnotic state. Then they read a passage about two persons that described both happy events and unhappy events that occurred to them. Finally, they recalled the information they had read. Participants who had been induced to feel happy recalled a greater proportion of positively-valenced events, and a lower proportion of negatively-valenced events, than did participants who were induced to feel sad. It is unclear whether these effects were due to the affect that participants were experiencing per se or to the semantic concepts that were activated in the course of inducing these feelings (e.g., Niedenthal & Setterlund, 1994; Niedenthal, Halberstadt, & Setterlund, 1997; Wyer, Clore, & Isbell, 1999). Be that as it may, the study provides strong evidence that concepts activated by experiences of which participants were not consciously aware can bias the information they later identify and encode into memory.

In a study of greater relevance to consumer judgment (Adaval, 2001), participants who had been induced to feel happy or unhappy were later asked to judge an article of clothing that was described by an attribute that was either likely to be evaluated on the basis of subjective criteria (e.g., how it felt to wear it) or not. Participants weighted attributes more heavily in making their judgments if the affect they elicited was similar to the affect they were experiencing than if it was not. Thus, as in Bower et al.'s (1978) study, participants appeared to give more attention to information that was affectively congruent with the feelings they were experiencing for other, unrelated reasons, and so this information had more impact on the judgments they reported later.

The aforementioned studies converge on the conclusion that people with a specific subset of concepts accessible in memory (either because of a goal they are pursuing or for other, unrelated reasons) often give greater attention to aspects of information that can be easily encoded in terms of these concepts, and so the information has greater impact on judgments and decisions than it otherwise would. Selective attention to information that can be interpreted along an accessible dimension could occur as well. Evidence that persons interpret individual product attributes along dimensions that happen to be accessible in memory was obtained by Park, Yoon, Kim, and Wyer (2001) in a study to be described in more detail presently.

Categorical vs. Piecemeal Information Processing

The impact of affect on selective attention can result from other processes as well. Bless (2001)suggests that people who experience positive affect tend to use broader, categorical criteria for judgment than others do. This could result from a more general disposition to perceive the world as unproblematic and, therefore, to believe it is unnecessary to consider information in detail in order to make a judgment (Schwarz & Clore, 1990). In the consumer domain, this suggests a tendency for persons who experience positive affect to give more weight to global judgmental criteria (e.g., brand name, country of origin, etc.) than to specific attribute information. However, although this appears to be true, it is not for the reason that Schwarz and Clore's (1990) conceptualization suggests. Tesser (1978) suggests that people tend to evaluate a stimulus more extremely after thinking about it more extensively. If this is so, and if positive affect increases the attention to categorical bases for judgment, people may think about this information more extensively at the time it is presented and, therefore, may perceive its implications to be more extreme. This shift in the interpretation of the information could lead it to have greater impact independently of the weight attached to it at the time of judgment.

Adaval (2003) confirmed this possibility. She employed procedures developed by Anderson (1971, 1981) to distinguish between the scale values assigned to individual pieces of information (an indication of their evaluative implications) and the weight attached to them at the time of judgment. Inducing participants to experience positive affect at the time they received product information increased the extremity of the evaluative implications they attached to brand name without affecting the weight they attached to it. (That is, they evaluated favorable brands more favorably, and unfavorable brands more unfavorably, than control subjects did.) Moreover, once this interpretation was made, its impact persisted over time, as implied by Principle 3. Thus, participants who had received information about a product's brand name were asked 24 hours later to indicate their preference for this product and another that was normatively similar to it favorableness. Participants who had been happy at the time they considered the first product preferred it to the second product if the products' brand names were both normatively favorable. However, they preferred the second product to the first if the products' brand names were both unfavorable.

THE INTERPRETATION OF AMBIGUOUS INFORMATION

Several examples of the effect of attribute concept accessibility on the interpretation of ambiguous information were provided in our general discussion of knowledge accessibility earlier in this chapter (cf. Bargh & Pietromonaco, 1982; Higgins et al., 1977; Srull & Wyer, 1979) and do not need to be reiterated. However, some additional considerations warrant further consideration.

DIMENSIONAL VS. CATEGORY ACCESSIBILITY

Information can be ambiguous in terms of both the attribute dimension to which it pertains and the value it implies along this dimension (Higgins & Brendl, 1995). The attribute information "50% more banana flavoring," for example, has implications for both taste and healthfulness. Along a dimension of taste, however, it could be interpreted either favorably (as sweet) or unfavorably (as *too* sweet). The dimension along which the attribute description is interpreted may depend on whether health-related or taste-related concepts are more accessible in memory at the time.

An additional consideration arises, however. People are likely to interpret the aforementioned product description more favorably if concepts associated with good taste have been primed than if concepts associated with bad taste have been primed. However, the attribute's implications along a dimension of healthfulness are unambiguously negative. In this case, what effect does priming "healthy" have, as opposed to priming "unhealthy?"

Many bipolar attribute concepts ("bad" vs. "good,", "hot" vs. "cold, etc.) may be strongly associated in memory (Colombo & Williams, 1990). To this extent, priming one of these concepts may activate the second as well. In the present example, "healthy" and "unhealthy" might be strongly associated. If this is so, priming *both* concepts might increase the tendency to interpret the attribute described by "50% more banana flavoring" as unhealthy.

Park et al. (2001, Experiment 2) showed this to be true. Participants received materials that activated concepts associated with good taste, bad taste, good health, or bad health. Then, as part of an ostensibly unrelated experiment, they received an ad that contained a description of a milk product similar to that in the preceding example. That is, it had ambiguous implication for taste but clearly implied that the product was unhealthy. After seeing the ad, participants first generated an open-ended description of the product and then evaluated it. Participants who had been primed with a taste-related concept were more likely to describe the product in terms of this concept rather than its bipolar opposite. In contrast, participants who had been primed with a health-related concept were likely to describe the product as unhealthy regardless of whether good health or bad health was primed. Furthermore, their overall evaluations of the product were affected in the manner suggested by their open-ended attribute descriptions.

ASSIMILATION AND CONTRAST

Park et al's (2001) study provides an example of conditions in which activating a concept can have a contrast effect on the interpretation of information. (That is, priming "healthy" led participants to judge the product as more unhealthy, and to evaluate it more unfavorably, than they otherwise would.) However, contrast effects can also occur for other reasons. Herr (1986), for example, exposed participants to names of either moderately hostile individuals (e.g., Mohammed Ali) or extremely hostile persons (e.g., Adolf Hitler) before they evaluated a person whose behaviors were ambiguous with respect to hostility. Although priming moderately hostile exemplars had a positive impact on participants' judgments of the target's hostility, priming extremely hostile exemplars had a contrast effect.

There are two interpretations of these findings. First, when the implications of a concept are so extreme that the concept cannot be applied to stimulus information, it may be used as a standard of comparison. As a result, the stimulus might be assigned a lower value along the dimension of judgment than it would if the standard were more moderate. Second, standards of comparison are more likely to be used when the priming stimuli are people or objects of the same type as the target rather than general attribute concepts of the sort that were primed in the studies by Higgins and others (Moskowitz & Skurnik, 1999; Stapel & Koomen, 1997). In Herr's study, participants may have interpreted the target's behavior in terms of the attribute concepts activated by the priming stimuli in all conditions, regardless of the extremity of these stimuli. Once this interpretation was made, however, they may have spontaneously compared the target to the type of persons described in the priming task, and this effect may have overridden the effect of the primed concepts on the interpretation of the information at an earlier stage of processing.

DESCRIPTIVE VS. EVALUATIVE ENCODING

The criteria that people bring to bear on the interpretation of information can be either descriptive or evaluative. Thus, "stole a magazine from the newsstand" could be interpreted either as "dishonest" or, more generally, as "bad." Similarly, "60 miles per gallon," could be interpreted as either "fuel efficient" or "desirable." Normally, the concepts that are accessible at the time information is first interpreted are likely to influence evaluations only if they are descriptively applicable. In the aforementioned study by Higgins et al. (1977), for example, priming trait concepts such as adventurous or reckless affected the interpretation of information that a person wanted to cross the Atlantic in a sailboat, but priming evaluatively toned but descriptively inapplicable concepts ("kind," "hostile," etc.) did not.

There are two qualifications on this conclusion, however.

1. Once information about a stimulus is interpreted in terms of concepts that are accessible at the time, the stimulus may be attributed the characteristic implied by the interpretation. Once this occurs, the stimulus may be inferred to have other characteristics that are descriptively irrelevant to the primed concept but have become associated with this type of stimulus through learning. Thus, for example, priming a concept of hostility could affect the interpretation of a target person's behaviors that were ambiguous with respect to this particular attribute. If the target is inferred to be a "hostile person" on the basis of this interpretation, he may then be attributed other characteristics that have nothing to do with hostility per se but are stereotypically associated with individuals who possess this attribute (Srull & Wyer, 1979, 1980).
2. Traits with extreme evaluative implications may be spontaneously associated with a concept that summarizes these implications through learning. In these circumstances, priming the trait concept may spontaneously activate the evaluative concept that is associated with it as well. Thus, for example, "malevolent" may activate a negative evaluative concept ("bad"). The latter concept, once activated, could then influence the interpretation of information that is ambiguous with respect to other attributes that have evaluative implications (Stapel & Koomen, 2000).

GOAL-ACTIVATED PRIMING EFFECTS

To reiterate, people's goals at the time they receive information can activate concepts that are relevant to these goals. These concepts may influence not only which information they encode into memory, as noted in the preceding section (Snyder & Cantor, 1979) but also the interpretation of information to which the concepts apply. A study by Higgins and Rholes (1978) exemplifies these effects. Participants who had read a passage about a target person that was ambiguous with respect to the traits it implied were told to describe the person to another who either liked or disliked him. They communicated their description in terms that were evaluatively consistent with the attitude of the individual to whom they were communicating. As a consequence, both their own liking for the person and their memory for the original information were biased toward the implications of the communication they had prepared. This bias was not evident when participants anticipated writing a communication about the person but did not actually do so. Thus, their interpretation of the information in terms of goal-activated concepts was not spontaneous, but occurred only in the course of generating a goal-relevant message. Once this interpretation was made, however, it affected participants' own impression and evaluation of the target person, as implied by Principle 3.

It is interesting to speculate about the implications of these results for consumer judgments and decisions. For example, word-of-mouth communications about a product are often tailored to fit the expectations of the person to whom one is communicating (Grice, 1975; see also Higgins, 1981; Schwarz, 1994; Strack, 1994). As a result, they are likely to influence communicators' own interpretation of the information being transmitted and, perhaps, their evaluations of the product they are describing. For similar reasons, sales persons' own evaluations of the products may be influenced in a direction that is consistent with the communication they generate when extolling the product's virtues to their customers. (The tendency for people to change their attitudes to conform to implications of the communications they have generated is also predicted by cognitive dissonance theory, of course; see Festinger, 1957.) At the same time, the objective of selling the product is not sufficient to induce this change; the sales persons must actually deliver the communication for their underlying evaluations to be affected.

HIGHER ORDER COMPREHENSION PROCESSES

The preceding research focused on the effect of single concepts on the interpretation of single pieces of information. However, more complex bodies of knowledge can often influence the interpretation of new information. This knowledge might be chronically accessible as a result of its frequent use in the social environment in which one participates on a daily basis. On the other hand, situation-specific features that are contained in this knowledge could also activate it. Research in many areas exemplifies this possibility.

Chronic Accessibility of Knowledge

In an early study by Anderson, Reynolds, Schallert, and Goetz (1977), music education majors and physical education majors read a passage about a social interaction that could be interpreted as either a card game or the rehearsal of a woodwind ensemble (e.g., "…they couldn't decide exactly what to play. Jerry eventually took a stand and set things up…Karen's recorder filled the room with soft and pleasant music…finally, Mike said, 'Let's hear the score'…They listened carefully and commented on their performance.") After reading the passage, participants were asked what the protagonists had commented on. Responses indicated that music majors were significantly more likely to interpret the interaction as a music rehearsal than physical education majors were. Correspondingly, physical education majors were more likely than music education majors to interpret a second ambiguous passage as the description of a wrestling match rather than a jail break. Apparently, concepts that were chronically accessible as a result of their vocational and educational goals affected their interpretation of the story and, therefore, their responses to questions about it.

The knowledge that is necessary to comprehend information can often be called to mind by a single word or phrase. In a study by Bransford, Barclay, and Franks (1972), participants were asked to learn sentences such as "The haystack was important because the cloth would rip," "The notes were sour because the seam was split," etc. Their memory for these ostensibly anomalous sentences was typically very poor. However, participants' memory improved substantially when the sentences were preceded by with a single word ("parachute" and "bagpipes," in the preceding examples). The word apparently stimulated the activation of a complex body of knowledge that permitted participants to construct a mental representation of the situation described by the sentence that followed it, thus giving the sentence meaning and facilitating memory for it. In other research (Bransford & Johnson, 1972; Bransford & Stein, 1984), paragraphs containing a series of ostensibly unrelated sentences were given meaning, and therefore remembered better, by providing a title that allowed the sentences to be conceptually integrated.

Framing Effects

The importance of Bransford's work lies in its implication that simple words and phrases can prime quite diverse bodies of knowledge for use in interpreting information and construing its implications. These effects can be reflected in not only memory but also judgments. This is evidenced by Tversky and Kahneman's (1982; Kahneman & Tversky, 1982) research on decisions under uncertainty. To give a well-known example, imagine that 1,000 people are in danger of being infected with a deadly virus, that one serum, A, is definitely effective but in short supply, and that a second, B, is available to all but of uncertain effectiveness. Consider two possibilities:

1. If serum A is administered, 350 people will be saved. If serum B is administered, there is a 65% chance that everyone will be saved but a 35% chance that no one will be saved.
2. If serum A is administered, 650 people will die. If serum B is administered, there is a 35% chance that everyone will die but a 65% chance that no one will die.

Although the choice alternatives are identical, people are more likely to choose serum A in the first case, but serum B in the second. Presumably the first set of alternatives stimulates people to think about living, and so people choose the alternative that guarantees this positive outcome. However, the second set stimulates people to think about dying, and so they choose the alternative that has a chance of avoiding this negative fate.

MEMORY PROCESSES

The factors that influence the effect of knowledge accessibility on comprehension and judgment obviously exert this influence through their mediating effect on the concepts and cognitions that people retrieve from memory. In this section, we will restrict our discussion to research in which memory is the primary concern, independently of the effects that the remembered information has on judgments or decisions. In doing so, we focus on two memory phenomena: (1) the role of implicit theories on constructive and reconstructive memory, and (2) the interference of accessible knowledge representations on memory for the information on which these representations were based.

THE ROLE OF IMPLICIT THEORIES ON RECONSTRUCTIVE MEMORY

People may not pay equal attention to all details of an experience at the time it occurs. Moreover, unless the experience is particularly noteworthy, it may get "buried" among the large number of other experiences that people have in their daily lives. This is particularly true when the events that compose the experiences are rather commonplace. In many cases, people may interpret these experiences in terms of an implicit theory they have acquired about the type of events that occurred. If such a theory is frequently used, it may become more accessible in memory than the experiences that it is used to interpret (Principle 2). Consequently, if people are called upon to remember the experience, they may reconstruct it on the basis of this theory without searching memory for a representation of the experience itself.

Studies by Michael Ross (1989) support this contention. For example, women's recall of their mood swings during their most recent menstrual cycle were more highly correlated with their implicit theories of how they typically felt during their menstrual period than with the feelings they had actually reported at the time. In a second study (Conway & Ross, 1984), participants who received feedback about the results of a study skills training program recalled their pre-training ability to be lower if they believed that the training was effective than if they did not, independently of their actual improvement over the training period.

The role of implicit theories in memory is also suggested in a study by Bem and McConnell (1972). Participants whose attitudes toward a position had been assessed in an earlier experimental session were either asked to generate a counter-attitudinal communication voluntarily or told to do it without being given a choice. After generating their message, they were asked to recall the attitude they had reported in the earlier session. Participants recalled having more favorable attitudes toward the position advocated when they had generated the communication voluntarily than when they had not been given a choice. Participants apparently used their most recent behavior as a basis for inferring what their attitude must have been, based on an implicit theory that people who advocate a position voluntarily are likely to advocate it personally, without consulting their memory for the actual attitude they had reported.

INTERFERENCE OF ACCESSIBLE KNOWLEDGE ON MEMORY

According to Principle 3, mental representations that have been formed from information are typically more accessible in memory than the information on which they are based. Therefore, they tend to be used as a basis for reconstructing this information without recourse to the original material. In some cases, this can lead to memory errors. Schooler and Engstler-Schooler (1990) showed that people are less able to identify a face they have seen if they had described the face verbally at the time they first encountered it than if they had not. Adaval and Wyer (2004) obtained analogous effects in a situation more closely approximating those that occur outside the laboratory. Specifically, participants who had seen a movie about an interaction between a married couple were asked either to describe the sequence of events they had seen or to describe their impressions of the protagonists. Both writing tasks decreased participants' later recognition of things the protagonists had said during the interaction. Furthermore, describing the events that occurred decreased recognition of nonverbal behaviors as well. In this research, as in Schooler's, the mental representations that participants constructed in the course of writing the description, which were more abstract than the visual representation that they formed of the stimulus information at the time they encountered it, were later used as a basis for their recognition responses instead of this representation. Consequently, recognition accuracy decreased.

The representations that people construct as a result of post-information processing can not only interfere with the events they actually observe but also can produce intrusions. A classic study by Loftus and Palmer (1974) showed that asking participants questions about a traffic accident they had seen in a picture (e.g., "How fast was the car going when it smashed into the tree?") led them to reconstruct a memory of the accident in the course of generating an answer that contained features that they had not actually seen but were consistent with the implications of the question. Consequently, their later use of this reconstructed representation as a basis for recalling the picture's content produces intrusion errors. Other studies demonstrate the implications of reconstructive processes for the reliability of both "eye-witness" testimony (Loftus, 1975) and early childhood memories (Loftus, 2000).

Although the preceding examples pertain to the interference effects of recently constructed representations, recently *used* representations can have similar effects. Perhaps the best known examples of this influence are the part-list cueing effects identified by Slamecka (1968; Rundus, 1973). That is, when participants who have learned a series of stimulus items are given a subset of these items to use as retrieval cues, their memory for the remaining items in the list decreases. In a quite different paradigm, Macrae et al. (1995) found that when participants have been exposed to an Asian woman, they are subliminally primed with concepts pertaining to one of the two stereotypes that could be used to describe the person, the accessibility of concepts related to the other, unprimed stereotype (as inferred from response times in a lexical decision task) decreased.

Although the specific phenomena summarized in this section are somewhat remote from consumer behavior, their potential implications are nonetheless fairly clear. For example, people who have communicated about a product to others may not only choose to evaluate the product in a manner that is consistent with the communication they have generated as suggested in the previous section, but their memory for their actual experience with the product may be influenced correspondingly. Furthermore, their implicit theories about the quality of a product or service provider, if easily accessible in memory, could also bias their memory for their past experience independently of their actual reactions to the product or service at the time the experience occurred (Ross, 1989).

INFERENCE AND EVALUATION PROCESSES

Inferences are of many types. For example, people often infer the *likelihood* that a product has a certain attribute, that a statement is true, that an event will or did occur, or that a decision will have certain consequences. Second, they may estimate the *magnitude* of an attribute (the age of a bottle of wine, the price of a cashmere sweater). Third, they may *evaluate* a product as good or bad, or may have a *preference* for one alternative over another. In each case, however, the inference is unlikely to be based on an extensive analysis of all of the knowledge one has acquired that might be relevant, or a exhaustive construal of its implications (Principle 1). Rather, it is based on only a subset of relevant knowledge that happens to come to mind most easily. A complete discussion of these possibilities would far exceed the scope of this chapter. We therefore restrict our discussion to a few representative examples.

BELIEF ESTIMATION

Probability estimates can usually be viewed as *beliefs*. They can pertain to the occurrence of a past or future event (e.g., that Saddam Hussein had a stockpile of nuclear weapons, the United States will go to war with China before the end of the decade), or to the existence of a present state of affairs (e.g., Texas is bigger than Alaska, George W. Bush will receive the Nobel Peace Prize). Or, they could concern the causal relation between two events or states. More generally, beliefs are estimates of the likelihood that a proposition about an event, state or relation is true.

People who are asked their belief in a proposition may often search memory for previously acquired knowledge that bears on it. In some cases, this knowledge could itself be a semantically-coded proposition whose features are very similar to those of the proposition being evaluated. Alternatively, people may identify a second proposition that, if true, has implications for its validity. Finally, it could be an implicit theory that has implications for the validity of the proposition being judged.

A theory of comprehension by Wyer and Radvansky (1998; see Wyer, 2004) formalizes the first possibility. They assumed that to comprehend a piece of information, people form a mental representation of its features and search memory for a previously formed representation that contains these features. If similarity of the features of the new representation to those of an existing memorial representation is very high, people not only comprehend it but spontaneously identify it as true.

One implication of this conceptualization is that past experiences that lead a statement to be represented and stored in memory will increase the likelihood that people consider the statement to be true if they encounter it at a later point in time (Begg, Anus, & Farinacci, 1992). In a study by Hasher, Goldstein, and Toppin (1977; see also Hawkins & Hoch, 1992; Kelley & Lindsey, 1993), people completed a belief questionnaire in two different experimental sessions. Some items in the first questionnaire, which concerned obscure facts that few if any participants were likely to know, were repeated in the second. Participants typically judged these propositions as more likely to be true in the second session than they had initially. Exposure to the items in the first session apparently led them to seem more familiar in the second session, and so participants' belief in their validity increased. In a conceptually similar study, Jacoby, Kelley, Brown, and Jasechko (1989) found that exposing participants to fictitious names during an initial experimental session increased participants' beliefs that the names referred to well-known persons when they encountered the names 24 hours later.

These effects occur in part because the information to which people are exposed becomes dissociated from its source. If this is so, the information could have an effect on beliefs even when it is identified as invalid at the time it is first received. This possibility was demonstrated by Skurnik, Yoon, Park, and Schwarz (in press). Participants were exposed to statements about commercial products either one, two, or three times, in each case accompanied by an indication that the statement was not true. Participants, a short time after exposure to the statements, were less likely to believe the statements were true if they had been exposed to them three times than if they had been exposed to them only once. After a 3-day delay, however, older participants were *more* likely to believe the statements in the former case. (This was not true of college-age participants, suggesting that these subjects were less likely to dissociate the statements from their initial context than older subjects were.)

When a previously formed representation of a proposition does not easily come to mind, people are likely to search for other information that bears on its validity. (McGuire & McGuire, 1991).

Based on an earlier formulation of belief organization by McGuire (1960), Wyer and Hartwick (1980) proposed a conceptualization of conditional inference processes that recognize this possibility. That is, people who are asked to report their belief in a conclusion, C, search memory for an antecedent, A, that has implications for it, and estimate the likelihood that C would be true if A is or is not true . If these conditional beliefs differ, they average their implications, weighting each by their belief that A is and is not true, respectively. If the beliefs are in units of probability, this inference can be captured by the equation:

$$P(C) = P(A)P(C/A) + P(\sim A)P(C/\sim A), \tag{1}$$

where P(C) is the belief that C is true, P(A) and P(~A) are beliefs that A is and is not true, respectively, and P(C/A) and P(C/~A) are conditional beliefs that C is true if A is and is not true, respectively. If P(~A) = 1 − P(A), the effect of a communication changes beliefs in A by the amount ΔP(A) should theoretically induce a change in beliefs in C, ΔP(C), that is predictable from the equation:

$$\Delta P(C) = \Delta P(A)[P(C/A) - P(C/\sim A)]. \tag{2}$$

he difference between the two conditional beliefs is essentially an estimate of the perceived relevance of beliefs in A to beliefs in C.

The relevance of this conceptualization in the present context derives from its implication that people who estimate their belief in a proposition do not conduct an exhaustive search of memory for knowledge that has implications for its validity. Rather, they identify and use the first relevant "informational" proposition (A) that comes to mind. Therefore, when more than one such proposition exists in memory, the one that is most quickly and easily accessible is used. To give a specific example, the belief that drinking coffee is desirable (C) should be stronger if the proposition "Drinking coffee makes you alert" happens to be accessible in memory than if "Coffee gives you insomnia" is more accessible. Equation 1 can be a diagnostic tool for determining whether a particular proposition is used as a basis for beliefs in any given instance. That is, the equation should describe the relations among a set of beliefs associated with propositions A and C if A has been used as a basis for reporting beliefs in C than if it has not (Wyer, 1970; Wyer & Hartwick, 1980, 1984).

The effectiveness of advertisements could potentially be diagnosed in terms of this conceptualization. Suppose a commercial that asserts "Brand X has more energizing ingredients" (A) fails to change consumers' beliefs that they would purchase this product; that is, ΔP(C) = 0, as defined in Equation 2. This could occur for three reasons. First, the commercial might have been ineffective in changing beliefs that X has more energizing ingredients; that is, ΔP(A) = 0. Second, consumers' beliefs about X's energizing ingredients might be irrelevant to their belief that they would buy it, or P(C/A) = P(C/~A). Finally, the commercial might be effective in changing consumers' belief about the product, P(A), and this belief might potentially be relevant. However, consumers might have typically think about other judgmental criteria than A at the time they report their purchase intentions, as reflected in a discrepancy between obtained and predicted values of ΔP(C).

The third possibility raises an additional implication of the model that was initially proposed by McGuire (1960) and confirmed empirically by Rosen and Wyer (1972). That is, syllogistically related beliefs may sometimes be inconsistent because they have not recently been thought about in relation to one another. However, asking people to report these beliefs in temporal proximity may call attention to their inconsistency and, therefore, may stimulate attempts to eliminate it. As a result, the beliefs may become more consistent if they are reported again at a later point in time. This "Socratic" effect was demonstrated in consumer research by Kardes, Cronley, Pontes, and Houghton (2001), who also applied the model in diagnosing the influence of multiple sets of syllogistically related arguments and their impact on resistance to persuasion.

FREQUENCY ESTIMATION

Frequency estimates are conceptually related to probability estimates; the higher the frequency of an event's occurrence, the more likely it is. Nevertheless, the processes that underlie these two types of estimates can differ. The different strategies that people use to compute the incidence of an event, and the conditions in which they are applied, have been investigated by Menon (1993; Menon, Raghubir, & Schwarz,1995). When an event occurs regularly (as in eating breakfast, or tooth-brushing), for example, people are likely to estimate its incidence within a given time period by simply extrapolating, based on general knowledge of its frequency of occurrence over the course of a day or week. When an event occurs irregularly, however, people are more likely to search memory for specific instances of the event or attribute being judged. As implied by Principle 1, however, this search is unlikely to be exhaustive. Rather, people may base their judgment on how easily these instances come to mind.

This tendency, which was referred to by Tversky and Kahneman (1973) as the *availability heuristic*, may be a manifestation of a more general tendency to treat conditional rules of inference as biconditionals (Wyer & Srull, 1989). Thus, because people believe that things that occur frequently are likely to come to mind easily, they infer that things that come to mind easily are likely to occur frequently. As a result, objectively irrelevant factors that influence the accessibility of instances in memory can have an impact on frequency estimates.

One such factor, noted earlier, is simply the amount of thought that was devoted to these instances at the time they were first encountered. That is, the incidence of events and attributes that stimulate attention at the time they are encountered is likely to be overestimated. Hamilton and Gifford (1976), for example, found that people were more likely to overestimate the proportion of minority representatives in a fictitious group when the group was small in size (and, therefore, the number of minority members observed was correspondingly small) than when it was large.

A qualification on this conclusion was identified by Briley, Shrum, and Wyer (2006) in a study more directly relevant to consumer behavior. European Americans and African Americans were shown a series of clothing ads in which the number of Black (vs. White) models in the ads was systematically varied while holding the relative proportion of these models constant. Later, they were asked to estimate the number of models of each ethnicity that were contained in the ads and were also given a test of recognition memory for the specific models they had seen. European Americans overestimated the incidence of Black models when the frequency of their occurrence was low, but their accuracy increased as the number of models presented became larger. These participants apparently paid relatively more attention to the individual Black models at the time they were presented (as evidenced by the accuracy with which these models could later be recognized), and later used the ease of retrieving the models from memory as a basis for their frequency estimates. In contrast, African Americans, who had a personal interest in ensuring that their ethnic group was represented adequately, appeared to conduct an online count of the models at the time the models were encountered without paying attention to their individual features. Consequently, their ability to recognize the specific models presented was low. Nevertheless, their frequency estimates were quite accurate when only a few models were presented, but became less so as the number presented increased and were more difficult to keep track of.

Perceptions of Social Reality

When people are unmotivated to think extensively about the objects and events they encounter, an additional consideration arises. That is, people who simply comprehend information with no particular objective in mind may simply store the information in memory without attending to the context in which they encountered it. This information may later be retrieved out of context and used as a basis for judgment.

Shrum (2000) and his colleagues provide abundant evidence of this in research on the effects of watching television on perceptions of social reality. That is, people typically overestimate the incidence of objects and events in the real world when these entities occur frequently on television. Furthermore, the amount of this overestimation increases with the amount of television that people watch. Thus, heavy television viewers are more likely than light viewers to overestimate the incidence of crime, the numbers of lawyers and doctors, and the number of people who have swimming pools in their back yard (O'Guinn & Shrum, 1997). This "cultivation effect" (Gerbner, Gross, Morgan, & Signorielli, 1994) occurs independently of the educational and socioeconomic level of respondents. Rather, heavy television viewers are more likely to have instances of these stimuli easily accessible in memory and, therefore, estimate them to occur more frequently in the real world than light viewers do (O'Guinn & Shrum, 1997; Shrum, Wyer, & O'Guinn, 1998).

Additional Considerations

The ease of retrieving instances of an object or event should be distinguished from the actual number of instances that are retrieved. In fact, the effects of these variables can be opposite in direction. This possibility has been demonstrated in a number of innovative studies by Schwarz and his colleagues (for a review, see Schwarz, 1998, 2004). In one study, for example (Schwarz et al., 1991), people were asked to recall either 6 instances of assertive behavior or 12 such instances. Although 12 behaviors are likely to imply greater assertiveness than only six, participants judged themselves to be *less* assertive in the former condition than the latter. That is, participants who were asked to recall 12 assertive behaviors found it very difficult to do so. Consequently, they inferred that they actually did not have the attribute in question. Similar effects have been identified in other domains. For example, people who were asked to generate seven arguments in support of a position tended to report less favorable attitudes toward the position than those who were asked to generate only three (Wänke, Bless, & Biller, 1996), and individuals who generate many reasons why an event might not occur are more likely to believe that it did occur than are individuals who generate few such reasons (Sanna & Schwarz, 2003; Sanna, Schwarz, & Stocker, 2002).

Similar effects have been found in the consumer domain. For example, people report less favorable attitudes toward commercial products (e.g., a BMW) if they have listed many reasons for using the products than if they have listed only one (Wänke, Bohner, & Jurkowitsch, 1997). In a similar study, participants judged a computer they had seen advertised more favorably after being asked to recall two favorable features of the computer than after being asked to recall eight (Menon & Raghubir, 2003). Interestingly, this difference was reversed under conditions in which subjects were likely to attribute the ease of recalling these features to other, extraneous situational factors (i.e., distracting music).

MAGNITUDE ESTIMATES

People are often called upon to make judgments of magnitude. They might estimate the height of a mountain, the age of an antique, or the price of a product. These estimates are likely to be made with reference to a previously acquired body of knowledge about the type of stimulus being judged. The way in which this knowledge is used can depend on whether the estimate is in physical units (feet, years, dollars, etc.) or subjective ones (high or low, old or young, expensive or cheap, etc.). In each case, however, the estimate can depend on the particular subset of judgment-relevant knowledge that happens to be accessible at the time.

Estimates in Physical Stimulus Units

Consumers who consider the purchase of a particular product are likely to compare its features to those of other products they have encountered in the past. For example, they may evaluate a car's fuel efficiency in relation to the average miles per gallon of other automobiles they have seen. Or, the price they are willing to pay for the car could require an estimate of the price at which the product is typically available elsewhere. However, people may rarely have these quantities stored in memory, and consequently may consider a range of values to be plausible. This range may depend on the particular subset of past experiences that they use to compute it.

Strack and Mussweiler (1997) formalize this process and provide compelling evidence of its occurrence (Mussweiler & Strack, 1999, 2000a, 2000b; for a review, see Mussweiler, 2003). In their research, participants are typically asked to decide if a stimulus attribute is greater or less than either a high value (e.g., is the price of the average BMW greater or less than $100,000) or a very low one ($3,000). Having done so, they then make their own estimate of its value. In making their comparative judgment, participants theoretically activate concepts about a subset of stimuli whose values are close to the "anchor" value they are asked to consider. Then, they use these concepts to estimate the actual value when they are asked to report it later. Thus, in our example, participants estimate the average price of a BMW to be higher if they have been asked to compare this price to a higher value than if they have been asked to compare it to a lower value. This is true even when this value is implausible. In fact, it even occurs when participants believe that the "anchor" value was chosen at random and was objectively irrelevant to the stimulus being judged (Strack & Mussweiler, 1997).

Adaval and Wyer (2005) found that exposing participants to a high or low anchor price can affect their estimates of not only the average price of a product in the marketplace but also the price they are personally willing to pay for it. Nunes and Boatwright (2004) reported conceptually similar effects in field research and sowed that the effects can generalize over product domains. For example, passersby at a beachfront stand were willing to pay more money for a CD if the sweaters displayed at a nearby stand were on sale for a high price than if they were on sale for a low price.

This result should not be overgeneralized, however. Adaval and Wyer (2005) found that the impact of context prices on estimates of prices of products in other categories depends on the relevance of the thoughts activated by the comparative judgment task. Thus, making comparative judgments of clothing articles stimulated participants to think about the subjective reactions they might have to the use of these articles and to the shopping experience itself. Consequently, it influenced the price they were willing to pay for electronic products to which the (e.g., affect-related) concepts activated by these thoughts were also relevant. However, making comparative judgments of an electronic product stimulated participants to think about features that were specific to the type of product being judged. Consequently, it had little impact on the price they were willing to pay for clothing articles.

Subjective Magnitude Estimates

As the preceding considerations suggest, people frequently fail to remember the specific physical characteristics of a stimulus. (Consumers, for example, are unable to remember the price of a product they have purchased only seconds after they put in their shopping cart; see Dickson &

Sawyer, 1990.) Rather, they encode an object's physical units into subjective units at the time they encounter them and this encoding, once stored in memory, is later retrieved and used as a basis for later judgments and decisions.

The rules for transforming physical stimulus values into subjective values were described by Ostrom and Upshaw (1968; see also Parducci, 1965), and have been explicated in consumer research by Janiszewski and Lichtenstein (1999) and Lynch, Chakravarti, and Mitra (1991). According to Ostrom and Upshaw, people subjectively position the range of subjective values they have available to correspond to the range of physical stimulus values they consider to be relevant. Thus, the higher the range of physical stimulus values they consider, the lower the subjective value they assign to any given stimulus within this range. In some instances, the range of physical values they consider is determined by the type of stimuli being judged. For example, people might judge a baby as "big" but an apartment as "small" although few babies are as large as apartments. When the range of values that are relevant to a judgment are less clear, however, it may depend on the subset of physical stimulus values that happen to be accessible in memory at the time. Consequently, it may be influenced by factors of which they are unaware, and that are objectively irrelevant to the judgment to be made.

Adaval and Monroe (2002) confirmed this possibility. Participants were subliminally exposed to either high or low numbers in the course of performing an ostensibly unrelated perceptual task, and then were asked to judge a particular product on the basis of price and attribute information. Participants judged the product to be less expensive if they had been exposed to high numbers than if they had been exposed to low ones. Interestingly, they judged the product to be lower along other dimensions as well. Apparently, exposure to the numbers during the priming task affected the perspective that participants adopted in transforming objective stimulus values into subjective values regardless of the dimension to which the judgments pertained.

In summary, both physical stimulus estimates and subjective judgments can be influenced by the particular subset of knowledge that happens to be accessible at the time the judgments are made. However, the effects of this knowledge on the two types of judgments may be opposite in direction. For example, activating knowledge about high-priced products can increase participants' estimates of the average price of these products in the marketplace and the price they are willing to pay for them. On the other hand, this activated knowledge may also increase the range of values that compose the perspective that participants bring to bear on their subjective estimates to the product's cost. Thus, it may decrease their judgments of the product as expensive.

EVALUATIONS AND AFFECT-BASED JUDGMENTS

Evaluations that are reported along a good-bad dimension are essentially estimates of magnitude. However, they are distinguished from other magnitude estimates in two ways. First, they typically apply to a stimulus as a whole, and may reflect the combined implications of inferences about a number of more specific attributes (for discussions of these integration processes, see Anderson, 1971, 1981; Fishbein & Ajzen, 1975). Second, evaluations of a stimulus are often based on not only its descriptive features but also the affect that people happen to experience and attribute to their feelings about the stimulus. The possible use of affective reactions as bases for judgment, which was initially demonstrated by Schwarz and Clore (1983), is very well established both in consumer research (Pham, 1998, 2004; Yeung & Wyer, 2004, 2005) and more generally (Schwarz & Clore, 1996; Wyer, Clore, & Isbell, 1999).

Not all evaluations are based on affect, of course (Zanna & Rempel, 1988). Some products are typically evaluated on the basis of purely functional or utilitarian criteria. Consumers may consider their feelings to be irrelevant to their evaluation of these products and so the affect they are experiencing has little informational influence (Adaval, 2001; Pham, 1998, 2004; Yeung & Wyer, 2004). In other instances, both affective and nonaffective criteria may be employed. Then, because affective reactions to a stimulus typically occur spontaneously, without a detailed analysis of its specific features (Lazarus, 1982, 1991; Zajonc, 1980), they are likely to be highly accessible and, therefore, likely to be applied (for an exception, see Levine, Wyer, & Schwarz, 1994). Indeed, they may often be used to the exclusion of other information when people are unable or unmotivated to search for additional judgmental criteria (Schwarz & Clore, 1988; see also Forgas, 1995).

This contingency was demonstrated by Shiv and Fedorikhin (1999). Participants in the study were given a choice of eating either chocolate cake or fruit salad. In the absence of distraction, a large proportion of participants chose the fruit salad. When participants were required to keep a multiple-digit number in mind while making their decision, however, their preferences for the chocolate cake significantly increased. Apparently participants who were able to think about the implications of their decision based their choice on health-related criteria. In the presence of distraction, however, the cognitive deliberation required to make this choice was aborted, and preferences were based on hedonic (i.e., affective) criteria.

Further evidence that affect is more likely to come into play when participants are unable to think critically about their judgments was obtained by Albarracin and Wyer (2001). Participants in this study were first induced to feel either happy or unhappy by writing about a past experience. Then, they were exposed to a persuasive message containing either strong or weak arguments in favor of comprehensive examinations. When participants received the message in the absence of distraction, they based their attitudes toward the exams on the content of the message they received. When they were distracted, however, they based their attitudes on the affect that they were experiencing as a result of the past experience they had recalled, and the effect of the message content significantly decreased. Thus, as in Shiv and Fedorikhin's (1999) research, participants' affective reactions had a greater impact on judgments when other criteria could not easily be applied.

Effects of Extraneous Affect on Evaluations

Albaraccin and Wyer's (2001) results exemplify a more general phenomenon. That is, people often cannot easily distinguish between their affective reactions to a stimulus and the feelings they may be experiencing for other, unrelated reasons. Consequently, affect from sources that have nothing to do with the object being judged can have an impact on their evaluation of it. Thus, for example, people who have been thinking about a personal experience shortly before they are called upon to evaluate a product may evaluate the product more favorably if they feel happy as a result of these ruminations than if they feel sad.

Numerous situational factors can obviously influence the accessibility and use of affect as a basis for judgment, including the weather (Schwarz & Clore, 1983), a small gift (Isen, Shalker, Clark, & Karp, 1978), performance on an achievement test (Ottati & Isbell, 1996), and proprioceptive feedback (Strack, Martin, & Stepper, 1988). This research typically assumes that judgments are based on an integration of judgment-relevant criteria at the time the judgment is made. In many instances, however, people are likely to form an initial impression of an object before they receive information about its specific features. Once this initial impression is formed, it can later be recalled and used as a basis for judgment without construing the implications of information received subsequently (Principle 5). In this case, the feelings that people happen to be experiencing at the time their initial impression is formed may influence their impression and, as a result, may affect the judgments and decisions they report later. Furthermore, the impact of their feelings may be evident even after the feelings themselves have dissipated.

These considerations are particularly important in purchasing situations. Consumers often form a general impression of a product from seeing it in a store window or magazine. In such conditions, the affect they happen to be experiencing at the time they form this impression could influence their later evaluation of the product independently of any information about its specific features that they acquire later. Yeung and Wyer (2004) confirmed this possibility experimentally. Participants who saw an affect-eliciting picture of a product before they received information about its specific features formed an initial impression on the basis of this picture, and this impression influenced their later product evaluations independently of the specific attribute information they received later. Furthermore, the affect they were experiencing for unrelated reasons at the time the picture was presented had an impact on judgments through its mediating impact on this initial impression.

For affective reactions to have an impact, however, they must not only be accessible but also be relevant to the judgmental goal one is pursuing. Affective reactions influence product evaluations at the time of judgment only if the product is one that is typically based on hedonic rather than utilitarian criteria (Pham, 1998). Similarly, they influence people's initial impressions only if they are relevant to these impressions. Thus, in Yeung and Wyer's (2004) study, the feelings that participants were experiencing for extraneous reasons influenced their initial impressions only if the picture on which they based these impressions elicited affect; they had no influence when the picture conveyed functional characteristics of the product that were not themselves affect eliciting.

Responses to Affect-Congruent Information

A by-product of the use of affect as information may be its influence on the attention that is paid to the information that elicits this affect and, therefore, the weight that is attached to it in making a judgment. A formal statement of this possibility is provided by Adaval's (2001) affect-confirmation theory. She proposed that when information about a product's specific attributes elicits positive or negative affective reactions, the feelings that consumers are experiencing for other reasons can appear either to confirm or to disconfirm the implications of these reactions, making consumers more or less confident that they have assessed these implications correctly. Consequently, these feelings influence the weight they attach to the attribute information in making a judgment. Consistent with conclusions drawn by Pham (1998), however, this differential weighting only occurs when people consider their affective reactions to be a relevant basis for construing the information's evaluative implications. When the attribute information describes functional rather than hedonic qualities, the affect that people experience has no influence on the weight they attach to it.

A recent study by Förster (2004) is also worth noting in this context. He found that proprioceptive feedback (e.g., nodding or shaking the head) influenced participants' evaluations of a product, but only when the implications of the feedback were congruent with the intrinsic favorableness of the product being judged. That is, head nodding influenced evaluations of favorable products but not unfavorable ones, whereas head shaking affected evaluations of unfavorable products but not favorable ones. To the extent proprioceptive feedback elicits affect that is used as a basis for judgment (e.g., Strack, Martin, & Stepper, 1988), these results are consistent with Adaval's (2001) affect-confirmation theory. Other interpretations of these findings are possible, however, as noted later in this chapter.

Effects of Brand-Elicited Affect

The use of affect as a source of information plays a particularly important role in evaluations of brand extensions. It seems reasonable to suppose that the effect of a favorable brand name on evaluations of its extension is greater when the extension is physically or functionally similar to the parent brand category than when it is not (Aaker & Keller, 1990; Bottomley & Holden, 2001). However, Barone, Miniard, and Romeo (2000) found that stimulating participants to experience positive affect at the time they made similarity judgments led them to judge moderately similar extensions as more similar to the parent brand than they otherwise would and, therefore, more similar to the parent brand in favorableness. However, this effect occurs only when (a) participants estimate similarity before they evaluate the extension (Yeung & Wyer, 2005) and (b) are sufficiently motivated to take parent-extension similarity into account (Barone, 2005). When participants evaluate extensions without judging similarity, the affect they are experiencing has a direct, informational impact on judgments that is not mediated by its influence on similarity perceptions.

PREFERENCE JUDGMENTS

Purchase decisions are often comparative. That is, consumers decide which of several alternative products they prefer. In some cases, these decisions are likely to be determined by computing an overall evaluation of each choice alternative independently and comparing the magnitude of these separate evaluations. This process, however, requires cognitive effort. Consequently, if purchasers have not previously made overall evaluations of the products they are considering, they may resort to different strategies that are easier to apply.

For example, people may often perform a dimension-by-dimension comparison, choosing the product that is superior on the greatest number of dimensions. Or, when this procedure does not lead to a clear solution, they may resort to other, heuristic criteria. For example, suppose a product A is superior to B along one attribute dimension but is inferior to B along a second. Nevertheless, suppose consumers believe that A is superior to a third alternative but B is not. Then, they may consider this to be sufficient justification for choosing A despite the fact that a direct comparison of the products is not diagnostic (Shafir, Simonson, & Tversky, 1993; Simonson, 1989; but see Huber, Payne, & Puto, 1982, for a different interpretation). This criterion may only be applied, however, if independent evaluations of the products have not already been computed. If these evaluations have already been made and are easily accessible in memory at the time the products are compared, participants may base their preferences on these evaluations instead (Park & Kim, 2005).

Research on preference judgments has typically been based on the implicit assumption that these judgments are based primarily on the information that is provided in the experiment about the stimuli being judged. Consequently, the role of knowledge accessibility in these judgments has not been directly examined. Nevertheless, several phenomena identified in research in this area provide examples of its influence.

1. If the products described are encountered successively, people may focus their attention on the last alternative, which they have encountered more recently and is presumably more accessible in memory (Principle 2). Thus, they focus their attention on features of this product that the first does not have, and base their preference on the evaluative implications of these features while ignoring features of the first alternative that the second does not possess. Therefore, suppose both alternatives have unique positive features that are similar in favorableness. Then, people are likely to choose the second product they consider, as it has positive features that the first does not possess. In contrast, suppose the alternatives have unique negative features. In this case, people are likely to choose the first product they encountered, as the second has negative features that the first does not (Houston, Sherman, & Baker, 1989).

2. If two choice alternatives have common features and, therefore, are not diagnostic, consumers may ignore them and concentrate their attention on only those features that are unique to each option. Consequently, these latter features, which are processed more extensively, become more accessible in memory than others (Craik & Lockhart, 1972). Therefore, if consumers are later called upon to evaluate each alternative separately, the unique features are likely to be given relatively more weight than the shared features. Thus, for example, consumers who have compared two options that have unique favorable attributes and common unfavorable ones may mentally cancel the unfavorable attributes and consider only the favorable ones in making their choice. As a result, they should later evaluate both products more favorably than they would if the comparative judgment had not been made. Similarly, persons who compare products with common favorable and unique unfavorable features should later evaluate the products more unfavorably than they would otherwise (Houston & Sherman, 1995). This can even occur when persons are not explicitly asked to make these comparisons (Brunner & Wänke, 2006; but see Wang & Wyer, 2002, for contingencies in the occurrence of these effects).

BEHAVIORAL DECISIONS

Some of the most important demonstrations of the influence of knowledge accessibility have emerged in research on its impact on overt behavior. Persons who have unobtrusively been exposed to stimuli that are associated with aggressiveness (e.g., by waiting for the experiment in an office that contains ROTC equipment) are more likely to administer shocks to a confederate in a learning experiment (Berkowitz & LePage, 1967). Priming hostility-related concepts in a sentence-construction task (Srull & Wyer, 1979) can have similar effects (Carver, Ganellen, Froming, & Chambers, 1983).

A particularly compelling series of studies by Bargh, Chen, and Burrows (1996) provide more direct evidence that semantic concepts can have a direct impact on behavior that is not mediated by their influence on how the object of the behavior is interpreted. In one study, for example, participants were primed with concepts associated with rudeness in the course of performing a sentence construction task. These participants were more likely than control participants to interrupt an experimenter's conversation with a graduate student in order to return the questionnaire they had completed. However, their behavior was apparently not mediated by their interpretation of the experimenter's behavior as impolite; judgments of him were unaffected by the priming task.

In a second study, college-age participants completed a sentence construction task that required the use of concepts associated with the elderly. After leaving the experiment, these participants walked more slowly to the elevator than control subjects did. Finally, Caucasian participants who were subliminally exposed to faces of African Americans in the course of performing a boring perceptual task displayed more nonverbal indications of irritation than control participants upon being asked to perform the task a second time. Using similar priming techniques, Colcombe (reported in Wyer, 2004) found that subliminally priming African American faces decreased performance on a test of mathematics ability while increasing performance in tests of rhythm memory and basketball shooting. Numerous other examples are reviewed by Dijksterhuis, Smith, van Baaren, and Wigboldus (2005).

These effects could reflect the impact of "If [X], then [Y]" productions of the sort mentioned earlier in this chapter. That is, a configuration of stimulus features could, in combination, activate a sequence of behaviors that are performed spontaneously, with little if any cognitive deliberation. The configuration could include not only concepts activated by the situation in which the behavior occurs but also cognitions that happen to be accessible for other reasons. However, people need not be aware of all of the features of this configuration in order for the production to be activated. This possibility was demonstrated by Chartrand and Bargh (1996). They found that subliminally priming concepts associated with a goal-directed production can activate the production without conscious awareness of the goal to which it was relevant.

Although the evidence that behaviors can be influenced by subliminally primed concepts and cognitions is very clear, the cognitive mechanisms underlying these effects are less so (cf. Dijksterhuis et al., 2005; Janiszewski & van Osselaer, 2005; Strack & Deutsch, 2004). Why does priming a stereotype of the elderly, or of African American faces, influence the behavior of persons who are not themselves members of the stereotyped category? One possible answer is suggested by Prinz (1990), who postulated that in order to comprehend another's behavior, one must mentally simulate the performance of the behavior oneself. This process could establish a direct link between the representation of another's behavior and a representation of one's own, and the product activated by the latter representation, along with features of the situation itself, could elicit this behavior under conditions in which it is appropriate.

Another possibility is that priming a stereotype activates a general value (e.g., that people should not to taken advantage of, that academic achievement is unimportant, etc.) and that these values, once activated, have a mediating influence on people's behavior un the situation at hand. Thus, stimulating people to think about Nobel Prize winners leads them to perform better in a game of Trivial Pursuit (Dijksterhuis & van Knippenburg, 1998), and priming concepts associated with the elderly decreases college students' performance on a memory test (Dijksterhuis, Bargh, & Miedema, 2000). Colombe's finding that subliminally priming faces of African Americans led Caucasian participants to perform more poorly than control participants on a mathematics test, but better than controls in tests of rhythm memory and basketball shooting, is also consistent with this interpretation. That is, African Americans are stereotypically disinterested in intellectual achievement while valuing musical and athletic ability. Therefore, priming the stereotype activated these values, and the accessibility of these values affected the effort that participants expended on the task they were given to perform. Other findings confirm this view. For example, subliminally priming faces of Asians, who stereotypically attach high value to intellectual achievement, led participants to perform better on a mathematics test than control subjects (see Wyer, 2004). Furthermore, priming the stereotypes of a punk decreased performance on an analytical task but increased performance on a creativity task, whereas priming the stereotype of an engineer had the opposite effects (Förster, Friedman, Butterbach, & Sassenberg, 2005).

These findings clearly have implications for the effects of movies and television on both consumption and other behavior. They could also account for the effects of unobtrusively placing brands in the context of television shows to which they are objectively irrelevant. However, it is important to keep in mind that priming concepts in themselves are often not sufficient to activate behavior unless the behavior is appropriate in the situation at hand. Thus, activating concepts of African Americans doesn't lead people to express hostility unless the situation with which they are confronted is frustrating or in other ways conducive to the behavior. As Colombe's research shows, priming the same concepts in other situations can have quite different effects.

The situational cues that determine the activation of prime-related behavior may be internally generated. Strahan, Spencer, and Zanna (2002), for example, showed that subliminally priming thirst-related words led participants to drink more of a beverage they were provided during the course of a simulated taste test. However, this was only true when participants had gone without drinking for several hours prior to the experiment and, therefore, were thirsty at the time the priming occurred. A contingency in these effects may be the extent to which persons are generally sensitive to internal cues; DeMarree, Wheeler, and Petty (2005), for example, found that priming effects on behavior were less evident among high self-monitors, who typically focus their attention on external cues, than among low self-monitors.

Be that as it may, both Colcombe's and Strahan et al.'s studies both indicate that behavior is determined by both activated knowledge and situational features *in combination*. In considering the implications of this work for consumer behavior, therefore, it would be a mistake to assume that activating concepts and knowledge will stimulate purchase or consumption behavior in the absence of a stimulus situation in which these behaviors are appropriate.

EFFECTS OF BODILY FEEDBACK ON INFORMATION PROCESSING

One of the more interesting areas of research to emerge in recent years has concerned the impact of bodily feedback on judgments and behavior. Bodily movements (e.g., flexing or extending the arm, or shaking or nodding the head) can elicit proprioceptive feedback. This internally generated stimulation can serve as features of a cognitive production that, in combination with other stimulus features, spontaneously elicit a sequence of behavior. Furthermore, this can occur without conscious awareness.

Förster and Strack (1996), for example, showed that when participants were unobtrusively induced to nod or shake their heads while learning a list of positively-and negatively-valenced words, they had better memory for the words that were compatible with the implications of their head movements. Similarly, people were better able to generate names of liked celebrities when they were flexing their arms (a behavior associated with approach) than when they were extending them (a behavior associated with avoidance), but were better able to generate disliked celebrities in the latter condition than in the former (Förster & Strack, 1997, 1998). Analogous effects have been identified in research on consumption behavior. For example, people drink a larger amount of a positively flavored drink if their arms are flexed than if they are extended (Förster, 2003). The approach tendency that was associated with the bodily feedback was apparently restricted to positively valenced stimuli, however. Arm flexion or extension had no impact on drinking behavior when the drink was neutral in taste.

The influence of proprioceptive feedback is not restricted to the activation of cognitive productions, of course. It can also exert an influence behavior through its informational properties. For example, people who nod their head while engaging in cognitive activity may perceive themselves to approve of the activity and, as a result, may be more influenced by its implications. Brinol and Petty (2003) unobtrusively induced participants to nod or to shake their head while listening to a persuasive message that contained either strong or weak arguments. Participants were more inclined to agree with the position advocated in strong-argument messages if they nodded their head while listening to them. However, they were *less* inclined to agree with the position advocated in weak-argument messages in these conditions. Apparently, participants were disposed to elaborate the positive implications of strong arguments but to counterargue the implications of the weak arguments. The proprioceptive feedback associated with head nodding increased their confidence in the implications of these cognitive responses and, therefore, increased the use of these implications as a basis for judgments.

CHAMELEON EFFECTS

According to Prinz's (1990) conceptualization of observational learning, a direct link can often be established between others' motor behavior and one's own. This could occur even if the behavior in question is incidental. This possibility is suggested by the "chameleon effect," that is, a tendency to unconsciously imitate the nonverbal behavior and mannerisms of other persons in the situation with whom one interacts (Chartrand & Bargh, 1999; for a review, see Chartrand, Lakin, & Maddux, 1995). Thus, for example, participants in a group discussion are more likely to cross their legs or stroke their chin if others in the discussion are doing so. Similar effects have been investigated in consumer behavior research. Johnston (2002), for example, found that people ate more ice cream in the presence of a confederate who did likewise. Ferraro, Bettman, and Chartrand (cited in Chartrand, 2005) found that participants' choice of snacks was unconsciously influenced by another's choices in the same situation. There are undoubtedly analogous effects outside the laboratory. People at a party, for example, are more likely to eat or drink if others are doing so than if they are not. Similarly, people are more apt to make purchases if they are accompanied by other individuals who are on a shopping spree. Although there are obviously other explanations of these phenomena (e.g., bowing to social pressure), the role of nonconscious imitative behavior in a consumer context is worth examining.

IMPULSIVENESS

The role of accessible concepts and knowledge on the spontaneous activation of behavior is particularly important in conceptualizing the antecedents of impulsive consumption (Rook & Fisher, 1995). Several conceptualizations of impulsiveness have been proposed (Baumeister, 2002; Baumeister & Vohs, 2004; Carver, 2004; Strack & Deutsch, 2004). These conceptualizations have typically focused on the antecedents of behavioral self-regulation. In many instances, the behavior can be conceptualized in terms of individual and situational differences in the types of cognitive productions that are activated in the situations at hand.

In a conceptualization of impulsive eating behavior, Schachter (1968; Schachter & Rodin, 1974) identified individual differences obesity that were traceable to differences in the sensitivity to internal vs. external stimuli. Specifically, obese individuals' behavior is generally influenced by external stimulus features, whereas nonobese persons' behavior is more influenced by internal cues. Thus, for example, obese persons eating behavior is relatively more influenced by the physical attractiveness of the food, and by the time of day (as indicated by a clock on the wall), whereas nonobese individuals' eating is more influenced by knowledge of the food's nutritional value, or by how hungry they feel. These differences could be conceptualized in terms of individual differences in the sorts of cognitive productions that guide behavior in the situations in question.

Although an analysis of impulsive purchase behavior is beyond the scope of this chapter, it may be conceptualized in similar terms. That is, purchasing, like eating, may be governed by cognitive productions that are activated by a configuration of both external and internally generated stimulus features. Different configurations of situational features may activate different productions and, therefore, influence the occurrence of the behavior. Luo (2005), for example, found evidence in a scenario study that persons report a greater tendency to engage in impulsive buying in the presence of peers, but less tendency to do so in the presence of family members, than in other conditions. Moreover, this was particularly true when the purchasers were generally susceptible to social influence and the individuals they imagined accompanying them were cohesive. If participants' self-reported behavior in imagined purchasing situations reflects their actual purchasing dispositions, Luo's findings would be consistent with the possibility that different cognitive productions are spontaneously activated, and generate different sequences of behavior, depending on the specific individuals who happen to be present in the purchase situation.

GOALS AND MOTIVES

The influence of accessible knowledge on goal-directed behavior can be of two types. First, as noted in the previous section, goal-directed sequences of behavior may exist in memory in the form of cognitive productions that are activated spontaneously by a configuration of both situational features and other concepts and knowledge that happen to be accessible at the time. The latter concepts can be activated in any number of ways. Fitzsimons and Bargh (2003), for example, found that stimulating participants to think about their mother led them to try harder to succeed in a later achievement situation. Bargh et al. (2001) showed that goal-directed consumption activity could also be activated without awareness. In a particularly interesting study, Fitzsimons, Chartrand, and Fitzsimons (2005, cited in Chartrand, 2005), subliminally priming logos of Apple (a company associated with innovativeness), led individuals to generate more unusual uses of an object in a subsequent creativity test.

The assumption that these effects are mediated by cognitive productions should be qualified. As Bargh et al. (2001) note, a distinction may need to be made between the activation of a goal per se and the activation of other types of mental representation. As implied by Principle 2, the effects of activating most representations of knowledge decrease over time. In contrast, the salience of a goal may have increasing effects over time as long as the goal is not satisfied. Results reported by Bargh et al. (2001) and Chartrand, Huber, and Shiv (2005) suggest such increases. Therefore, the interpretation of such effects in terms of cognitive productions is not completely clear.

However, goals, and the sequence of steps required to attain them, are also part of declarative knowledge, and can exist as mental representations in memory. This possibility is implicit in Schank and Abelson's (1977) conception of a cognitive script and its relation to plans, goals and behavior. That is, prototypic sequences of events (e.g., the actions that occur when visiting a restaurant) could exist in memory and be used not only to predict and explain others' behavior but as guides to one's own goal-directed activity. Evidence of the existence of these representations has been obtained by Kruglanski et al. (2002). They found that subliminally priming concepts associated with a goal increases the accessibility of concepts associated with the means of attaining it. In addition, priming concepts associated with means increases the accessibility of concepts that are associated with goals to which they are relevant.

A goal can be viewed as a concept of a desirable state, along with a series of behavioral events that, if they occur, lead to the occurrence of this state (Shah, Kruglanski, & Friedman, 2003; Wyer & Srull, 1989). To this extent, concepts associated with the end state may activate a sequence of behaviors that could potentially attain it (Chartrand & Bargh, 2001). Furthermore, thoughts about the means of attaining a goal may activate concepts associated with the goal itself (Kruglanski et al., 2002), and these concepts, once activated, not only can facilitate goal-directed behavior to which they are relevant but also can interfere with goal-directed activity to which they are not relevant (Shah & Kruglanski, 2002, 2003).

Goals, and the behavior that facilitates their attainment, can be represented in memory at several levels of specificity (Vallacher & Wegner, 1987). Moreover, they may vary in their immediacy. In many instances, a plan-goal hierarchy may exist with more specific and immediate goals serving as means to the attainment of more general, long-range goals (Srull & Wyer, 1986). Thus, studying may be a means of attaining a good grade in calculus, which is a means of attaining the goal of getting into graduate school, which is a means of getting a well paying job, etc.

CULTURAL AND SOCIAL INFLUENCES ON REGULATORY FOCUS

At the most general level, behavior is likely to be governed by a desire to maximize pleasure and minimize pain. However, many behaviors have both costs and benefits, and so the behavior that potentially has the most desirable consequences can have undesirable consequences as well. Under these circumstances, a person's choice can depend on which set of consequences is more important.

The relative emphasis placed on positive vs. negative outcomes of a decision has been conceptualized in some detail by Higgins (1997, 1998). Specifically, people who are confronted with a decision may be *promotion* focused. That is, they may be motivated by the positive consequence of a decision while ignoring the negative consequences that might result. Others, however, may be *prevention* focused, or motivated by the desire to avoid negative consequences of a decision while giving relatively little weight to the positive effects it might have. Chronic individual differences in these motivational orientations may exist (Higgins et al., 2000). On the other hand, the motivational orientations can also be influenced by situational factors that make one or another set of criteria accessible in memory (for example, whether alternative outcomes are framed in terms of gains vs. nongains or losses vs. nonlosses; Idson, Liberman, & Higgins, 2000; Lee & Aaker, 2004; Monga & Zhu, 2005). Furthermore, once these orientations are activated, their effects may generalize over domains, affecting decisions in situations that are quite unrelated to the one that stimulated them (Briley & Wyer, 2002). A specification of these dispositions and the factors that activate them has obvious implications for an understanding of consumer decision making. Many products have both positive and negative features, and a decision to choose one product over another can often depend on which set of features is weighted more heavily.

Cultural Influences on Goal Accessibility

Chronic dispositions to emphasize the positive or negative consequences of a behavioral decision may be acquired through social learning. Asians, for example, are typically more concerned with negative consequences of their behavior than their North American counterparts (Aaker & Lee, 2001), a tendency that may be traceable to differences in early childhood socialization practices (Miller, Wiley, Fong, & Liang, 1997; for a discussion, see Wyer, 2004). If this is so, they may be relatively more inclined than Americans to focus on the avoidance of negative outcomes. Studies by Briley, Morris, and Simonson (2000, 2005), however, suggest that these different dispositions are often not apparent unless situational factors lead them to be activated. In one study, for example (Briley et al., 2000), Asian and European Americans were asked to choose between two products whose values along a given set of dimensions varied in the following pattern:

	Option A	Option B	Option C
Dimension 1	+3	−3	+1
Dimension 2	+3	−3	−1
Dimension 3	−3	+3	+1
Dimension 4	−3	+3	−1

In such a situation, participants who focus on the desirability of positive outcomes (or, in other words, are "promotion focused;" see Higgins, 1997) should choose either A or B, whereas those who focus on the avoidance of negative outcomes (or, alternatively, are "prevention focused") should choose C. In fact, the groups of participants did not differ in their preference of these alternatives when they were asked to make choices without much deliberation. When they were asked to give a reason for their choice, however, European Americans increased their preference for A and B, whereas Asians increased their preference for C.

These data are consistent with the conceptualization of culture proposed by Hong and Chiu (2001). They note that cultural values, like other concepts and knowledge, are not automatically applied in making judgments and decisions. Rather, these values may vary in their accessibility in memory, and their effects may be overridden by the effects of other more accessible dispositions unless participants are required to draw upon these values in order to justify their choices to others.

Differences in the accessibility of cultural norms may be particularly evident when individuals belong to a bicultural community in which different, often competing norms may be operating. In this case, situational factors may influence the specific norms that are most accessible and, therefore, are most likely to be applied (Hong, Morris, Chiu, & Benet-Martinez, 2000). In a second series of studies, Briley et al. (2005) asked bilingual Hong Kong students to make choices in the situation just described. Participants were more likely to choose the high reward alternative (A or B, in our example) when the experiment was conducted in English than when it was conducted in Chinese, suggesting that the language in which the study was conducted activated norms associated with this culture and consequently stimulated the use of decision criteria that were characteristic of it. Subsequent experiments by Briley et al. (2005) suggested that the language of the experiment activated different expectations for whether responses were socially desirable, and participants conformed to these expectations. Nevertheless, the results are consistent with the conjecture that situational factors influence the accessibility of promotion- and prevention-focused decision criteria.

Effects of Group Salience on Goal Accessibility

Cultural and social norms that are accessible in memory may influence behavior independently of whether people are aware of the factors that lead these norms to be activated. That is, Asians do not need to be aware of their identity as Asians, or Americans of their identity as Americans, for the norms that predominate in these cultures to have an impact. In fact, if participants are made aware of their cultural identity, it may have effects that override the impact of normative factors. Briley and Wyer (2002) found that participants who were led to believe that they were participating in the experiment as members of a group were more likely both (a) to endorse behaviors in an interpersonal situation that minimized inequalities among participants, and (b) to avoid the risk of negative consequences in an individual product choice situation. These data suggested that consciousness of group membership increased feelings of social responsibility and, therefore, the tendency to minimize risk of negative decision consequences in both interpersonal situations and product choices. This was true when this consciousness was induced both by having participants take part in a group activity before performing the decision tasks and by exposing them to cultural icons that made them aware of their cultural identity. (Thus, for example, both Chinese who were made aware of their identity as Chinese, and United States participants who were made aware of their identity as Americans, were more inclined than control participants to make choices that minimized the likelihood of negative consequences.)

In sum, the research by Briley and his colleagues provides evidence that once the motivational dispositions identified by Higgins are activated, they influence decision strategies that generalize over quite different types of choice situations that are unrelated to the conditions that led these dispositions to be activated. As noted earlier, however, cultural norms, or the salience of group membership, are only two of many factors that could activate a prevention or promotion focus and the decision strategies that are associated with them. The influence of these factors on product evaluation and purchase decisions is worthy of further investigation.

EFFECTS OF TERROR MANAGEMENT ON MATERIALISTIC MOTIVES

A quite different area of research on goal activation has direct relevance to consumer behavior and decision making. This research has largely been performed within the framework of terror management theory (Solomon, Greenberg, & Pyszczynski, 1991; for discussions of its implications for consumer behavior, see Arndt, Solomon, Kasser, & Sheldon, 2004a,b; Maheswaran & Agrawal, 2004; Rindfleisch & Burroughs, 2004). According to this theory, activating concepts associated with death increases concerns about one's personal mortality. This, in turn, increases the need to maintain self-esteem and to engage in consumption behavior that will enhance this esteem. Mandel and Heine (1999), for example, found that completing a measure concerning fear of death increased participants' attraction to high status products (e.g., Rolex watches) but had no effect on their liking for products that were not status-related.

Ironically, the effects of mortality-related concepts on consumption behavior are evident even if the consumption is deleterious to one's health and, therefore, potentially detrimental to one's longevity. Goldenberg, Arndt, and Brown (2004) found that women who had been primed with thoughts about death were less inclined to eat foods that were described as nutritious but likely to compromise the attractiveness of their figures. Similarly, priming mortality-related concepts increased participants' desire to purchase products that would increase their sun tan despite the fact that they would also increase the risk of skin cancer (Routledge, Arndt, & Goldenberg, 2003). Although the mortality-related concepts that produced these effects in the laboratory were situationally primed, it seems reasonable to assume that chronic concerns about death can give rise to a more general materialistic motive that influences consumption behavior in numerous situations outside the laboratory.

THE INFLUENCE OF AFFECT ON GOAL-DIRECTED ACTIVITY

The goals that people pursue, and the effort that they devote to their attainment, can be influenced by the affective reactions the happy to be experiencing at the time. Isen (1987) and her colleagues (Isen, Daubman, & Nowicki, 1987) found that happy individuals perform better on creativity tasks, suggesting that positive affect influences the ability and/or motivation to think innovatively. In many cases, however, the influence of affect on goal-directed behavior can result from its use as information about whether the behavior is effective. That is, people who are engaged in goal-directed activity may implicitly ask themselves if they feel that this activity is effective, and may use the affect they are experiencing as a basis for answering this question. Consequently, it may influence the extent to which they continue the activity or stop.

A series of studies by Martin, Ward, Achee, and Wyer (1993) provide evidence of this possibility. In one study, participants who had been induced to feel happy or sad were asked to form an impression of someone on the basis of a series of behaviors, each conveyed by a different card in a deck. In some conditions, they were told to turn over one card at a time and continue to do so until they felt they had formed a good impression. In other conditions, they were told to continue as long as they were enjoying themselves. In the first case, participants stopped sooner if they felt happy than if they did not, suggesting that they used the affect they were experiencing as a basis for deciding if the impression they had formed was good enough. In the second condition, however, participants spent longer on the task if they felt happy, suggesting that in this case, they used their feelings as a basis for deciding if they were enjoying what they were doing.

Similar results were obtained in a second study in which participants were asked to generate uses of a brick. That is, participants who had a performance goal generated fewer uses if they felt happy than if they did not, whereas participants who had an enjoyment goal generated more uses if they felt happy than they did otherwise. Results of numerous studies on the influence of affective reactions on goal-directed behavior can be interpreted in terms of the impact of these reactions on the evaluation of this behavior or its consequences (for reviews, see Wyer, 2004; Wyer et al., 1999). Its implications for consumer behavior are obvious. For example, people who go shopping for enjoyment are likely to spend more time in the activity if they are happy than if they are less so. In contrast, people who go shopping with the goal of buying a particular product are likely to spend *less* time in the activity if they are happy than if they are not.

CONCLUDING COMMENT

This chapter has covered a lot of ground. Yet, it has not begun to capture the number and diversity of phenomena that are directly and indirectly influenced by the concepts and knowledge that people happen to have accessible in memory at the time they are called upon to make a judgment or decision. Readers of this chapter will inevitably identify many important areas of research, in consumer behavior, and other areas, in which knowledge accessibility can play a role. The purpose of this chapter is primarily to call attention to the importance of taking into account both situational and individual differences in knowledge in conceptualizing the determinants of consumer judgment and decisions and the processes that underlie them.

The effect of knowledge accessibility on judgments and behavior is so well established that its existence can be taken as a given. In fact, as pointed out elsewhere (Wyer, 2004), the effect can often be used as a diagnostic tool in determining the causal relatedness of factors on judgments and behavior under conditions in which this relatedness is otherwise hard to establish. As Principle 1 implies, only a subset of the factors that influence a judgment or decision are likely to come into play at any given time. However, if a particular factor is among those that potentially affect a given behavior, increasing its accessibility in memory should increase the likelihood it is used as a basis for this behavior. If, on the other hand, the factor is *not* a determinant of the behavior, increasing its accessibility should have no effect. This strategy is of particular value in examining the determinants of behavior outside the laboratory.

This strategy was first employed by Schwarz and Strack (1981) to demonstrate the causal influence of a coercive government policy on people's willingness to sign petitions on a controversial social issue, and by Wyer, Bodenhausen, and Gorman (1985) in diagnosing the cognitive mediators of reactions to rape incidents. More recently, it was used by Shrum et al. (1998) to demonstrate the causal influence of television viewing on perceptions of social reality, and by Yeung and Wyer (2005) to confirm the impact of affective reactions to a brand name (as opposed to specific brand-related features) on evaluations of a brand extension. Knowledge activation techniques are likely to be useful in understanding a variety of relations among variables that are naturally confounded in every day life experience and cannot be directly manipulated. Their use in a consumer context may therefore be worthy of consideration.

ACKNOWLEDGMENT

The writing of this chapter, and some of the research discussed therein, was supported by grants HKUST6053/01H, HKUST6194/04H, and HKUST6192/04H from the Research Grants Council, Hong Kong. Appreciation is extended to Jens Förster and Frank Kardes for comments on an earlier draft of this chapter.

REFERENCES

Aaker, D. A., & Keller, K. L. (1990). Consumer evaluations of brand extensions. *Journal of Marketing, 54,* 27–41.

Aaker, J. L., & Lee, A. Y. (2001). "I" seek pleasures, "we" avoid pains: The role of self regulatory goals in information processing and persuasion. *Journal of Consumer Research, 28,* 33–49.

Aarts, H., & Dijksterhuis, A. (2003). The silence of the library: Environment, situational norm, and social behavior. *Journal of Personality and Social Psychology, 84,* 18–28.

Adaval, R. (2001). Sometimes it just feels right: The differential weighting of affect-consistent and affect-inconsistent product information. *Journal of Consumer Research, 7,* 207–245.

Adaval, R. (2003). How good gets better and bad gets worse: Understanding the impact of affect on evaluations of known brands. *Journal of Consumer Research, 30,* 352–367.

Adaval, R., & Monroe, K. B. (2002). Automatic construction and use of contextual information for product and price evaluations. *Journal of Consumer Research, 28,* 572–588.

Adaval, R., & Wyer, R. S. (1998). The role of narratives in consumer information processing. *Journal of Consumer Psychology, 7,* 207–245.

Adaval, R., & Wyer, R. S. (2004). Communicating about a social interaction: Effects on memory for protagonists' statements and nonverbal behaviors. *Journal of Experimental Social Psychology, 40,* 450–465.

Adaval, R., & Wyer, R. S. (2005). Exposure to price anchors from related and unrelated product categories: Implications for price perception and willingness to pay. Unpublished manuscript, Hong Kong University of Science and Technology.

Albarracin, D., & Wyer, R.S. (2001). Elaborative and nonelaborative processing of a behavior-related persuasive communication. *Personality and Social Psychology Bulletin,. 27,* 691–705.

Anderson, J. R. (1982). Acquisition of cognitive skill. *Psychological Review, 89,* 369–406.

Anderson, J. R. (1983). *The architecture of cognition.* Cambridge, MA: Harvard University Press.

Anderson, N. H. (1971). Integration theory and attitude change. *Psychological Review, 78,* 171–206.

Anderson, N. H. (1981). *Foundations of information integration theory.* New York: Academic Press.

Anderson, R C., Reynolds, R. E, Schallert, D. L., & Goetz, E. T. (1977). Frameworks for comprehending discourse. *American Educational Research Journal, 14,* 367–381.

Arndt, J., Solomon, S., Kasser, T., & Sheldon, K. M. (2004a). The urge to splurge: A terror management account of materialism and consumer behavior. *Journal of Consumer Psychology, 14,* 198–212.

Arndt, J., Solomon, S., Kasser, T., & Sheldon, K. M. (2004b). The urge to splurge revisited: Further reflections on applying terror management theory to materialism and consumer behavior. *Journal of Consumer Psychology, 14,* 225–229.

Bargh, J. A. (1994). The four horsemen of automaticity: Awareness, intention, efficiency, and control in social cognition. In R. S. Wyer & T. K. Srull (Eds.), *Handbook of social cognition* (2nd ed., Vol. 1, pp. 1–40). Hillsdale, NJ: Erlbaum.

Bargh, J. A. (1997). The automaticity of everyday life. In R. S. Wyer (Ed.), *Advances in social cognition* (Vol. 10, pp. 1–62). Mahwah, NJ: Erlbaum.

Bargh, J. A., Bond, R. N., Lombardi, W., & Tota, M. E. (1986). The additive nature of chronic and temporary sources of construct accessibility. *Journal of Personality and Social Psychology, 50,* 869–878.

Bargh, J. A., Chaiken, S., Govender, R., & Pratto, F. (1992). The generality of the automatic attitude activation effect. *Journal of Personality and Social Psychology, 62,* 893–912.

Bargh, J. A., Chaiken, S., Raymond, P., & Hymes, C. (1996). The automatic evaluation effect: Unconditionally automatic attitude activation in a pronunciation task. *Journal of Experimental Social Psychology, 32,* 104–120.

Bargh, J. A., Chen, M., & Burrows, L. (1996). Automaticity of social behavior: Direct effects of trait construct and stereotype activation on action. *Journal of Personality and Social Psychology, 71,* 230–244.

Bargh, J. A., Gollwitzer, P. M., Lee-Chai, A., Barndollar, K., & Troetsche, R. (2001). The automated will: Nonconscious activation and pursuit of behavioral goals. *Journal of Personality and Social Psychology, 81,* 1014–1027.

Bargh, J. A., & Pietromonaco, P. (1982). Automatic information processing and social perception: The influence of trait information presented outside of conscious awareness on impression formation. *Journal of Personality and Social Psychology, 43,* 437–449.

Barone, M. J. (2005). The interactive effects of mood and involvement on brand extension evaluations. *Journal of Consumer Psychology, 15,* 263–270.

Barone, M. J., Miniard, P.W., & Romeo, J. B. (2000). The influence of positive mood on brand extension evaluations. *Journal of Consumer Research, 26,* 386–400.

Baumeister, R. F. (2002). Yielding to temptation: Self-control failure, impulsive purchasing, and consumer behavior. *Journal of Consumer Research, 28,* 670–676.

Baumeister, R. F., & Vohs, K. D. (Eds.) (2004). *Handbook of self-regulation: Resarch, theory, and applications.* New York: Guilford.

Begg, I. M., Anas, A., & Farinacci, S. (1992). Dissociation of processes in belief: Source recollection, statement familiarity, and the illusion of truth. *Journal of Experimental Psychology: General, 121,* 446–458

Bem, D. J., & McConnell, H. K. (1970). Testing the self-perception explanation of dissonance phenomena: On the salience of premanipulation attitudes. *Journal of Personality and Social Psychology, 14,* 23–31.

Berkowitz, L., & LePage, A. (1967), Weapons as aggression-eliciting stimuli. *Journal of Personality & Social Psychology, 7,* 202–207.

Bless, H. (2001). Mood and the use of general knowledge structures. In L. L. Martin & G. L. Clore (Eds.), *Theories of mood and cognition: A user's guidebook* (pp. 9–26). Mahwah, NJ: Erlbaum.

Bodenhausen, G. V., & Macrae, C. N. (1998). Stereotype activation and inhibition. In R. S. Wyer (Ed.), *Advances in social cognition* (Vol. 11, pp. 1–52). Mahwah, NJ: Erlbaum.

Bottomley, P. A., & Holden, S. J. S. (2001). Do we really know how consumers evaluate brand extensions? Empirical generalizations based on secondary analyses of eight studies, *Journal of Marketing Research, 38,* 494–500.

Bower, G. H., Gilligan, S. G., & Monteiro, K. P. (1981). Selectivity of learning caused by affective states. *Journal of Experimental Psychology: General, 110,* 451–473.

Bransford, J. D., Barclay, J. R, & Franks, J. J. (1972). Sentence memory: A constructive versus interpretative approach. *Cognitive Psychology, 3,* 193–209.

Bransford, J. D., & Johnson, M. K. (1972). Contextual prerequisites for understanding: Some investigations of comprehension and recall. *Journal of Verbal Learning and Verbal Behavior, 11,* 717–726.

Bransford, J. D., & Stein, B. S. (1984). *The ideal problem solver: A guide to improving thinking, learning, and creativity.* New York: Freeman.

Briley, D. A., Morris, M., & Simonson, I. (2000). Reasons as carriers of culture: Dynamic versus dispositional models of cultural influence on decision making. *Journal of Consumer Research, 27,* 157–178.

Briley, D. A., Morris, M., & Simonson, I. (2005). Language triggers cultural frames: In bicultural Hong Kong consumers, English versus Chinese communication evokes divergent cultural patterns of decision making. *Journal of Consumer Psychology,*

Briley, D. A., Shrum, L. J., & Wyer, R. S. (2006). *Subjective impressions of minority group representation in the media: A comparison of majority and minority viewers' judgments and underlying processes.* Unpublished manuscript, Hong Kong University of Science and Technology.

Briley, D. A., & Wyer, R. S. (2001). Transitory determinants of values and decisions: The utility (or nonutility) of individualism and collectivism in understanding cultural differences. *Social cognition, 19,* 198–229.

Briley, D. A., & Wyer, R. S. (2002). The effect of group membership salience on the avoidance of negative outcomes: Implications for social and consumer decisions. *Journal of Consumer Research, 29,* 400–415

Brinol, P., & Petty, R. E. 2003). Overt head movements and persuasion: A self-validation analysis. *Journal of Personality and Social Psychology 84,* 1123–1139.

Brunner, T. A., & Wänke, M. (2006) The Reduced and Enhanced Impact of Shared Features on Individual Brand Evaluations. *Journal of Consumer Psychology, 16,* 101–111.

Carlston, D. E. (1980). Events, inferences and impression formation. In R. Hastie, T. Ostrom, E. Ebbesen, R. Wyer, D. Hamilton, & D. Carlston (Eds.), *Person memory: The cognitive basis of social perception* (pp. 89–119). Hillsdale, NJ: Erlbaum.

Carlston, D. E. (1994). Associated Systems Theory: A systematic approach to cognitive representations of persons. In R. S. Wyer (Ed.), *Advances in social cognition* (Vol. 7, pp. 1–78). Hillsdale, NJ: Erlbaum.

Carver, C. S. (2004). Self-regulation of action and affect. In R. F. Baumeister & K. D. Vohs (Eds.), *Handbook of self-regulation: Research, theory and applications* (pp. 13–39). New York: Guilford.

Carver, C. S., Ganellen, R. J., Froming, W. J., & Chambers, W. (1983). Modeling: An analysis in terms of category accessibility. *Journal of Experimental Social Psychology, 19,* 403–421.

Chaiken, S. (1987). The heuristic model of persuasion. In M. P. Zanna, J. M. Olson, & C. P. Herman (Eds.), *Social influence: The Ontario Symposium* (Vol. 5, pp. 3–39). Hillsdale, NJ: Erlbaum.

Chaiken, S., Liberman, A., & Eagly, A.H. (1989). Heuristic and systematic information processing within and beyond the persuasion context. In J. S. Uleman & J. A. Bargh (Eds.), *Unintended thought* (pp. 212–252). New York: Guilford.

Chartrand, T. L. (2005). The role of conscious awareness in consumer behavior. *Journal of Consumer Psychology, 15,* 203–210

Chartrand, T. L., & Bargh, J. A. (1996). Automatic activation of impression formation and memorization goals: Nonconscious goal priming reproduces effects of explicit task instructions. *Journal of Personality and Social Psychology, 71,* 464–478.

Chartrand, T. L., & Bargh, J. A. (1999). The chameleon effect: The perception-behavior link and social interaction. *Journal of Personality and Social Psychology, 76,* 893–910.

Chartrand, T. L., & Bargh, J. A. (2002). Nonconscious motivations: their activation, operation and consequences. In A. Tesser & D. Stapel (Eds.), *Self and motivation: Emerging psychological perspectives* (pp. 13–41). Washington, DC: American Psychological Association.

Chartrand, T. L., Huber, J., & Shiv, B. (2005). *Nonconscious value versus image goals and consumer choice behavior.* Unpublished manuscript, Duke University, Durham, NC.

Chernev, A. (2001). The impact of common features on consumer preferences: A case of confirmatory reasoning. *Journal of Consumer Research, 27,* 475–488.

Colombo, L., & Williams, J. (1990). Effects of word- and sentence-level contexts on word recognition. *Memory & Cognition, 18,* 153–163.

Conway, M., & Ross, M. (1984). Getting what you want by revising what you had. *Journal of Personality and Social Psychology, 47,* 738–748.

Craik, F. I. M., & Lockhart, R. S. (1972). Levels of processing: A framework for memory research. *Journal of Verbal Learning and Verbal Behavior, 11,* 671–684.

Darley, J. M., & Gross, P. H. (1983). A hypothesis confirming bias in labeling effects. *Journal of Personality and Social Psychology, 44,* 20–33.

DeMarree, K. G., Wheeler, S. C., & Petty, R.E. (2005). Priming a new identity: Self-monitoring moderates the effects of nonself primes on self-judgments and behavior. *Journal of Personality and Social Psychology, 89,* 657–671.

Dickson, P.R., & Sawyer, A. G. (1990). The price knowledge and search of supermarket shoppers. *Journal of Marketing, 54,* 42–53.

Dijksterhuis, A., Bargh, J. A., & Miedema, J.l (2000). Of men and mackerels: Attention and automatic behavior. In H. Bless & J. P. Forgas (Eds.), *Subjective experience in social cognition and behavior* (pp. 36–51). Philadelphia: Psychology Press.

Dijksterhuis, A., Smith, P, K., van Baaren, R. B., & Wigboldus, D. H. J. (2005). The unconscious consumer: Effects of environment on consumer behavior. *Journal of Consumer Psychology, 15,*

Dijksterhuis, A., & van Knippenberg, A. (1998). The relation between perception and behavior, or how to win a game of Trivial Pursuit. *Journal of Personality and Social Psychology, 74,* 865–877.

Dweck, C. S. (1991). Self-theories and goals: Their role in motivation, personality, and development. In R. Dienstbier (Ed.), *Nebraska Symposium on Motivation: Vol. 38. Perspectives on motivation* (pp. 199–235). Lincoln: University of Nebraska Press.

Dweck, C. S., Chiu, C., & Hong, Y. (1995). Implicit theories and their role in judgments and reactions: A world from two perspectives. *Psychological Inquiry, 6,* 267–285.

Fazio, R. H. (1990). Multiple processes by which attitudes guide behavior: The MODE model as an integrative framework. In M.P. Zanna (Ed.), *Advances in experimental social psychology* (Vol. 23, pp. 75–109). San Diego, CA: Academic Press.

Festinger, L.(1957).*A theory of cognitive dissonance.* Stanford, CA: Stanford University Press.

Fishbein, M., & Ajzen, I. (1975). *Belief, attitude, intention, and behavior: An introduction to theory and research.* Reading, MA: Addison-Wesley.

Fitzsimons, G. M., & Bargh, J. A. (2003). Thinking of you: Pursuit of interpersonal goals associated with relational partners. *Journal of Personality and Social Psychology, 84,* 148–164.

Fitzsimons, G. M., Chartrand, T. L., & Fitzsimons, G. J. (2005). Behavioral response to subliminal brand exposure. Unpublished manuscript.

Förster, J. (2003). The influence of approach and avoidance motor actions on food intake. *European Journal of Social Psychology, 33,* 339–350.

Förster, J. (2004). How body feedback influences consumers' evaluation of products. *Journal of Consumer Psychology, 14,* 415–425.

Förster, J., Friedman, R., Butterbach, E. M., & Sassenberg, K. (2005). Automatic effects of deviancy cues on creative cognition. *European Journal of Social Psychology,*

Förster, J., & Liberman, N. (in press). Knowledge activation. In A. Kruglanski & E. T. Higgins (Eds.), *Social psychology: Handbook of basic principles* (2nd ed.). New York: Guilford.

Förster, J., & Strack, F. (1996). The influence of overt head movements on memory for valenced words: A case of conceptual-motor compatibility. *Journal of Personality and Social Psychology, 71,* 21–430.

Förster, J., & Strack, F. (1997). Motor actions in retrieval of valenced information: A motor congruence effect. *Perceptual and Motor Skills, 85,* 1419–1427.

Förster, J., & Strack, F. (1998). Motor actions in retrieval of valenced information: II. Boundary conditions for motor congruency effects. *Perceptual and Motor Skills, 86,* 1423–1426.

Forgas, J. P. (1995). Mood and judgment: The affect infusion model (AIM). *Psychological Bulletin, 117,* 39–66.

Friedman, R., & Förster, J. (2000), The effects of approach and avoidance motor actions on the elements of creative insight. *Journal of Personality and Social Psychology, 79,* 477–492.

Gerbner, G., Gross, L., Morgan, M., & Signorielli, N. (1994). Growing up with television: the cultivation perspective. In J. Bryant & D. Zillmann (Eds.), *Media effects: Advances in theory and research* (pp. 17–41). Hillsdale, NJ: Erlbaum.

Goldenberg, J. L., Arndt, J., & Brown, M. (2004). Dying to be thin: The effects of mortality salience and body mass index on restricted eating among women. Unpublished manuscript, University of California, Davis.

Grice, H. P. (1975). Logic and conversation. In P. Cole & J. L. Morgan (Eds.), *Syntax and semantics: Speech acts* (pp. 41–58). New York: Academic Press.

Hamilton, D. L. & Gifford, R. K. (1976), Illusory correlation in interpersonal perception: A cognitive basis of stereotypic judgments, *Journal of Experimental Social Psychology, 12,* 392–407.

Hasher, L., Goldstein, D., & Toppin, T. (1977). Frequency and the conference of referential validity. *Journal of Verbal Learning and Verbal Behavior, 16,* 107–112.

Hawkins, S. A., & Hoch, S. J. (1992). Low-involvement learning: Memory without evaluation. *Journal of Consumer Research, 19,* 212–225.

Herr, P. M. (1986). Consequences of priming: Judgment and behavior. *Journal of Personality and Social Psychology, 51,* 1106–1115.

Higgins, E. T. (1981). The "communication game": Implications for social cognition and persuasion. In E. T. Higgins, C. P. Herman, & M. P. Zanna (Eds.), *Social cognition: The Ontario Symposium* (Vol. 1, pp. 342–392). Hillsdale, NJ: Erlbaum.

Higgins, E. T. (1996). Knowledge activation: Accessibility, applicability, and salience. In E. T. Higgins & A. Kruglanski (Eds.), *Social psychology: Handbook of basic principles* (pp. 133–168). New York: Guilford.

Higgins, E. T. (1997). Beyond pleasure and pain. *American Psychologist, 55,* 1217–1233.

Higgins, E. T. (1998). Promotion and prevention: Regulatory focus as a motivational principle. In M.P. Zanna (Ed.), *Advances in experimental social psychology* (Vol. 30, pp. 1–46). San Diego, CA: Academic Press.

Higgins, E. T., Bargh, J. A., & Lombardi, W. (1985). The nature of priming effects on categorization. *Journal of Experimental Psychology: Learning, Memory, and Cognition, 11,* 59–69.

Higgins, E T., & Brendl, C. M. (1995). Accessibility and applicabaility: Some "activation rules" influencing judgment. *Journal of Experimental Social Psychology, 31,* 218–243.

Higgins, E. T., Friedman, R. S., Harlow, R. E., Idson, L. C., Ayduk, O. N., & Taylor, A. (2000). Achievement orientations from subjective histories of success: promotion pride versus prevention pride. *European Journal of Social Psychology, 30,* 1–23.

Higgins, E. T., King, G.A., & Mavin, G. Hl. (1982). Individual construct accessibility and subjective impressions and recall. *Journal of Personality and Social Psychology, 43,* 35–47.

Higgins, E. T & Lurie, L. (1983). Context, categorization and recall: The "change-of-standard" effect. *Cognitive Psychology, 15,* 525–547.

Higgins, E. T., & Rholes, W. S. (1978). "Saying is believing": Effects of message modification on memory and liking for the person described. *Journal of Experimental Social Psychology, 14,* 363–378.

Higgins, E. T., Rholes, W. S., & Jones, C. R. (1977). Category accessibility and impression formation. *Journal of Experimental Social Psychology, 13,* 141–154.

Hong, Y. Y., & Chiu, C. Y. (2001). Toward a paradigm shift: From cross-cultural differences in social cognition to social-cognitive mediation of cultural differences. *Social Cognition, 19,* 181–196.

Hong, Y., Morris, M. W., Chiu, C., & Benet-Martinez, V. (2000). Multicultural minds: A dynamic constructivist approach to culture and cognition. *American Psychologist, 55,* 709–720.

Houston, D. A., & Sherman, S. J. (1995). Cancellation and focus: The role of shared and unique features in the choice process. *Journal of Experimental Social Psychology, 31,* 357–378.

Houston, D. A., Sherman, S. J., & Baker, S. M. (1989). The influence of unique features and direction of comparison on preferences. *Journal of Experimental Social Psychology, 25,* 121–141.

Huber, J., Payne, J. W., & Puto, C. (1982). Adding asymmetrically dominated alternatives: Violations of regularity and the similarity hypothesis: *Journal of Consumer Research, 9,* 90–98.

Idson, L. C., Liberman N., & Higgins, E. T. (2000). Distinguishing gains from nonlosses and losses from nongains: A regulatory focus perspective on hedonic intensity. *Journal of Experimental Social Psychology, 36,* 252–274.

Isbell, L. M., Clore, G. L., & Wyer, R. S. (1998). *Mood-mediated uses of stereotyping in impression formation.* Unpublished manuscript, University of Illinois at Urbana-Champaign.

Isbell, L. M., & Wyer, R. S. (1999). Correcting for mood-induced bias in the evaluation of political candidates. *Personality and Social Psychology Bulletin, 25,* 237–249.

Isen, A. M. (1987). Positive affect, cognitive processes, and social behavior. In L. Berkowitz (Ed.), *Advances in experimental social psychology* (Vol. 20, pp. 203–253). New York: Academic Press.

Isen, A. M., Daubman, L. A., & Nowicki, G. P. (1987). Positive affect facilitates creative problem solving. *Journal of Personality and Social Psychology, 52,* 1122–1131.

Isen, A. M., Shalker, T. E., Clark, M. S., & Karp, L. (1978). Affect, accessibility of material in memory and behavior: A cognitive loop? *Journal of Personality and Social Psychology, 36,* 1–12.

Jacoby, L. L., Kelley, C. M., Brown, J., & Jasechko, J. (1989). Becoming famous overnight: Limits on the ability to avoid unconscious influences of the past. *Journal of Personality and Social Psychology, 56,* 326–338.

Janiszewski, C., & Lichtenstein, D. R. (1999). A ranage theory account of price perception. *Journal of Consumer Research, 25,* 353–368.

Janiszewski, C. & van Osselaer, S. M. J. (2005). Behavior activation is not enough. *Journal of Consumer Psychology, 15,* 218–224.

Johnston, L. (2002). Behavioral mimicry and stigmatization. *Social Cognition, 20,* 18–35.

Kahneman, D., & Miller, D. T. (1986). Norm theory: Comparing reality to its alternatives. *Psychological Review, 93,* 136–153.

Kahneman, D., & Tversky, A. (1982). The simulation heuristic. In D. Kahneman, P. Slovic, & A. Tversky (Eds.), *Judgment under uncertainty: Heuristics and biases* (pp. 201–208). New York: Cambridge University Press.

Kardes, F. R. (1986). Effects of initial product judgments on subsequent memory-based judgments. *Journal of Consumer Research, 13,* 1–11.

Kardes, F. R., Cronley, M. L., Pontes, M. C., & Houghton, D. C. (2001). Down the garden path: The role of conditional inference processes in self-persuasion. *Journal of Consumer Psychology, 11,* 159–168.

Kardes, F. R., Gurumurthy, K., Chandrashekaran, M., & Dornoff, R. J. (1993). Brand retrieval, consideration set composition, consumer choice, and the pioneering advantage. *Journal of Consumer Research, 20,* 62–75.

Kelley, C. M., & Lindsay, D. S. (1993). Remembering mistaken for knowing: Ease of retrieval as a basis for confidence in answers to general knowledge questions. *Journal of Memory & Language, 32,* 1–24.

Kruglanski, A. W., Shah, J. Y., Fishbach, A., Friedman, R., Chun, W. Y., & Sleeth-Keppler, D. (2002). A theory of goal systems. In M. P. Zanna (Ed.), *Advances in experimental social psychology* (Vol. 34, pp. 331–378). San Diego, CA: Academic Press.

Lazarus, R. S. (1982). Thoughts on the relations between emotion and cognition. *American Psychologist, 37,* 1019–1024.

Lazarus, R. S. (1991). *Emotion and adaptation.* New York: Oxford University Press.

Lee, A. Y., & Aaker, J. A. (2004). Bringing the frame into focus: The influence of regulatory fit on processing fluency and persuasion. *Journal of Personality and Social Psychology, 86,* 205–218.

Lerner, M. J., Miller, D. T., & Holmes, J. G. (1976). Deserving and the emergence of forms of justice. In L. Berkowitz (Ed.), *Advances in experimental social psychology* (Vol. 9). New York: Academic Press.

Levine, S. R., Wyer, R. S., & Schwarz N. (1994). Are you what you feel? The affective and cognitive determinants of self-judgments. *Experimental Journal of Social Psychology, 24,* 63–77.

Loftus, E. F. (1975). Leading questions and the eyewitness report. *Cognitive Psychology, 7,* 560–572.

Loftus, E. F. (2000). Remembering what never happened. In E. Tulving (Ed.), *Memory, consciousness and the brain: the Tallinn conference* (pp. 106–118). Philadelphia, PA: Taylor & Francis.

Loftus, E. F., & Palmer, J. (1974). Reconstruction of automobile destruction. *Journal of Verbal Learning and Verbal Behavior, 2,* 467–471.

Lombardi, W. J., Higgins, E. T., & Bargh, J. A. (1987). The role of consciousness in priming effects on categorization. *Personality and Social Psychology Bulletin, 13,* 411–429.

Luo, X. (2005). How does shopping with others influence impulse purchasing? *Journal of Consumer Psychology, 15,* 288–294.

Lynch, J. G., Chakravarti, D., & Mitra, A. (1991). Contrast effects in consumer judgments: Changes in mental representations or in the anchoring of response scales? *Journal of Consumer Research, 18,* 284–297.

Macrae, C. N., Bodenhausen, G. V., & Milne, A. B. (1995). The dissection of selection in person perception: Inhibitory processes in social stereotyping. *Journal of Personality and Social Psychology, 69,* 397–407.

Macrae, C. N., Bodenhausen, G. V., Milne, A. B., & Jetten, J. (1994). Out of mind but hack in sight: Stereotypes on the rebound. *Journal of Personality and Social Psychology, 67,* 808–817.

Maheswaran, D. J., & Agraawal, N. (2004). Motivational and cultural variations in morality salience effects: Contemplations on terror management theory and consumer behavior. *Journal of Consumer Psychology, 14,* 213–218.

Mandel, N., & Heine, S. J. (1999). Terror management and marketing: He who dies with the most toys wins. *Advances in Consumer Research, 26,* 527–532.

Martin, L. L. (1986). Set/reset: Use and disuse of concepts in impression formation. *Journal of Personality and Social Psychology, 51,* 493–504.

Martin, L. L., Seta, J. J., & Crelia, R. A. (1990). Assimilation and contrast as a function of people's willingness and ability to expend effort in forming an impression. *Journal of Personality and Social Psychology, 59,* 27–37.

Martin L. L., Ward, D. W., Achee, J. W., & Wyer, R. S. (1993). Mood as input: People have to interpret the motivational implications of their moods. *Journal of Personality and Social Psychology, 64,* 317–326.

McGuire, W. J. (1960). A syllogistic analysis of cognitive relationships. In M. J. Rosenberg & C. I. Hovland (Eds.), *Attitude organization and change* (pp. 140–162). New Haven: Yale University Press

McGuire, W. J. (1981). The probabilogical model of cognitive structure and attitude change. In R. E. Petty, T. M. Ostrom, & T. C. Brock (Eds.), *Cognitive responses in persuasion* (pp. 291–307). Hillsdale, NJ: Erlbaum.

McGuire, W. J., & McGuire, C. V. (1988). Content and process in the experience of self. In L. Berkowitz (Ed.), *Advances in experimental social psychology* (Vol. 21, pp. 97–144). San Diego, CA: Academic Press.

McGuire, W. J., & McGuire, C. V. (1991). The content, structure and operation of thought systems. In R. S. Wyer & T. K. Srull (Eds.), *Advances in social cognition* (Vol. 4, pp.1–78). Hillsdale, NJ: Erlbaum.

Menon, G. (1993). The effects of accessibility of information in memory on judgments of behavioral frequencies. *Journal of Consumer Research, 20,* 431–440.

Menon, G., & Raghubir, P. (1998). When automatic accessibility meets conscious content: Implications for judgment formation. Unpublished manuscript, New York University.

Menon, G., & Raghubir, P. (2003). Ease of retrieval as an automatic input in judgments: A mere-accessibility framework? *Journal of Consumer Research, 30,* 230–243.

Menon, G., Raghubir, P., & Schwarz, N. (1995). Behavioral frequency judgments: An accessibility-diagnosticity framework, *Journal of Consumer Research, 22,* 212–228.

Miller, P. J., Wiley, A. R., Fung, H., & Liang, C. H. (1997). Personal storytelling as a medium of socialization in Chinese and American families. *Child Development, 68,* 557–568.

Monga, A., & Zhu, R (2005). Buyers versus sellers: How they differ in their responses to framed outcomes. *Journal of Consumer Psychology, 15,* 325–333.

Moore, T. E. (1982). Subliminal advertising: What you see is what you get. *Journal of Marketing, 46,* 38–47.

Moore, T. E. (1988). The case against subliminal manipulation. *Psychology & Marketing, 5,* 297–316.

Moskowitz, G. B., & Skurnik, I. W. (1999). Contrast effects as determined by the type of prime: Trait versus exemplar primes initiate processing strategies that differ in how accessible constructs are used. *Journal of Personality and Social Psychology, 76*, 911–927.

Mussweiler, T. (2003). Comparison processes in social judgment: Mechanisms and consequences. *Psychological Review,*

Mussweiler, T., & Strack, F. (1999a). Hypothesis-consistent testing and semantic priming in the anchoring paradigm: A selective accessibility model. *Journal of Experimental Social Psychology, 35*, 136–164.

Mussweiler, T., & Strack, F. (2000a). The use of category and exemplar knowledge in the solution of anchoring tasks. *Journal of Personality and Social Psychology, 78*, 1038–1052.

Mussweiler, T., & Strack, F. (2000b). The "relative self": Informational and judgmental consequences of comparative self-evaluation. *Journal of Personality and Social Psychology, 79*, 23–38.

Niedenthal, P.M., Halberstadt, J. B., & Setterlund, M. B. (1997). Being happy and seeing "happy": Emotional state mediates visual word recognition. *Cognition and Emotion, 11*, 403–432.

Niedenthal, P.M., & Setterlund, M. B. (1994). Emotion congruence in perception. *Personality and Social Psychology Bulletin, 20*, 401–411.

Noel, H. (2006). The spacing effect: Enhancing memory for repeated marketing stimuli. *Journal of Consumer Psychology, 16,*

Nunes, J. C., & Boatright, P. (2004). Incidental prices and their effect on willingness to pay. *Journal of Marketing Research, 41*, 457–466.

O'Guinn, T. C., & Shrum, L. J. (1997). The role of television in the construction of social reality. *Journal of Consumer Research, 23*, 278–294.

Ostrom, T. M., & Upshaw, H. S. (1968). Psychological perspective and attitude change. In A. G. Greenwald, T. M. Ostrom, & T. C. Brock (Eds.), *Psychological foundations of attitudes.* New York: Academic Press.

Ottati, V. C., & Isbell, L. M. (1996). Effects of mood during exposure to target information on subsequently reported judgments: An on-line model of assimilation and contrast. *Journal of Personality and Social Psychology, 71*, 39–53.

Ottati, V. C., Riggle, E. J., Wyer, R. S., Schwarz, N., & Kuklinski, J. (1989). The cognitive and affective bases of opinion survey responses. *Journal of Personality and Social Psychology, 57*, 404–415.

Parducci, A. (1965). Category judgment: A range-frequency model. *Psychological Review, 72*, 407–418.

Park, J. W., & Kim, J. K. (2005). The effects of decoys on preference shifts: The role of attractiveness and providing justification. *Journal of Consumer Psychology, 15,*

Park, J. W., Yoon, S. O., Kim, K. H., & Wyer, R. S. (2001). Effects of priming a bipolar attribute concept on dimension versus concept-specific accessibility of semantic memory. *Journal of Personality and Social Psychology, 81*, 405–420.

Petty, R. E., & Cacioppo, J. T. (1986) *Communication and persuasion: Central and peripheral routes to attitude change.* New York: Springer-Verlag.

Pham, M. T. (1998). Representativeness, relevance and the use of feelings in decision making. *Journal of Consumer Research, 25*, 144–159.

Pham, M. T. (2004). The logic of feeling. *Journal of Consumer Psychology, 14*, 360–369.

Prinz, W. (1990). On dynamic pertinence models. In H. G. Geissler & M. H. Miller (Eds.), *Psychophysical explorations of mental structures* (pp. 411–421). Kirkland, WA: Hofgrefe & Huber.

Rindfleisch, A., & Burroughs, J. E. (2004). Terrifying thoughts, terrible materialism? Contemplations on a terror management account of materialism and consumer behavior. *Journal of Consumer Psychology, 14*, 219–224.

Rook, D., & Fisher, R. (1995). Normative influences on impulsive buying behavior. *Journal of Consumer Research, 22*, 305–313.

Rosen, N. A., & Wyer, R. S. (1972). Some further evidence for the "Socratic effect" using a subjective probability model of cognitive organization. *Journal of Personality and Social Psychology, 24*, 420–424.

Ross, L., Lepper, M. R., Strack, F., & Steinmetz, J. (1977). Social explanation and social expectation: Effects of real and hypothetical explanations on subjective likelihood. *Journal of Personality and Social Psychology, 35*, 817–829.

Ross, M. (1989). Relation of implicit theories to the construction of personal histories. *Psychological Review, 96*, 341–357.

Routledge, C., Arndt, J., & Goldenberg, J. L. (2006). A time to tan: Proximal and distal effects of mortality salience on sun exposure intentions. *Personality and Social Psychology Bulletin, 30*, 1347–1358.

Rundus, D. (1973). Negative effects of using list items as retrieval cues. *Journal of Verbal Learning and Verbal Behavior, 12*, 43–50.

Sanna, L. J., & Schwarz, N. (2003). Debiasing hindsight: The role of accessibility experiences and attributions. *Journal of Experimental Social Psychology, 39*, 287–295.

Sanna, L. J., Schwarz, N., & Stocker, S. L. (2002). When debiasing backfires: Accessible content and accessibility experiences in debiasing hindsight. *Journal of Experimental Psychology: Learning, Memory, and Cognition, 28*, 497–502.

Schachter, S. (1968). Obesity and eating. *Science, 16*, 751–756.

Schachter, S., & Rodin, J. (1974). *Obese humans and rats.* Hillsdale, NJ: Erlbaum.

Schank, R. C., & Abelson, R. P. (1977). *Scripts, plans, goals and understanding.* Hillsdale, NJ: Erlbaum.

Schank, R. C., & Abelson, R. P. (1995). Knowledge and memory: The real story. In R. S. Wyer (Ed.), *Advances in social cognition* (Vol. 8, pp. 1–86). Mahwah, NJ: Erlbaum.

Schneider, W., & Shiffrin, R. M. (1977). Controlled and automatic human information processing: I. Detection, research and attention. *Psychological Review, 84*, 1–66.

Schooler, J.W., & Engstler-Schooler, T. Y. (1990). Verbal overshadowing of visual memories: Some things are better left unsaid. *Cognitive Psychology, 22*, 36–71.

Schwarz, N. (1990). Feelings as information: Informational and motivational functions of affective states. In E. T. Higgins & R. M. Sorrentino (Eds.), *Handbook of motivation and cognition: Foundations of social behavior* (Vol. 2, pp. 527–561). New York: Guilford.

Schwarz, N., & Bless, H. (1992). Constructing reality and its alternatives: An inclusion/exclusion model of assimilation and contrast effects in social judgment. In L. L. Martin & A. Tesser (Eds.), *The construction of social judgments* (pp. 217–245). Hillsdale, NJ: Erlbaum.

Schwarz, N. (1994). Judgment in a social context: Biases, shortcomings, and the logic of conversation. In M. P. Zanna (Ed.), *Advances in experimental social psychology* (Vol. 24, pp. 123–162). San Diego, CA: Academic Press.

Schwarz, N. (1998). Accessible content and accessibility experiences: The interplay of declarative and experiential information in judgment. *Personality and Social Psychology Review, 2*, 87–99.

Schwarz, N. (2004). Metacognitive experiences in consumer judgment and decision making. *Journal of Consumer Psychology, 14*, 332–348.

Schwarz, N., Bless, H., Strack, F., Klumpp, G., Rittenauer-Schatka, H., & Simons, A. (1991). Ease of retrieval as information: Another look at the availability heuristic. *Journal of Personality and Social Psychology, 61*, 195–202.

Schwarz, N., & Clore, G. L. (1983). Mood, misattribution, and judgments of well-being: Informative and directive functions of affective states. *Journal of Personality and Social Psychology, 45*, 513–523.

Schwarz, N., & Clore, G. L. (1988). How do I feel about it? Informative functions of affective states. In K. Fiedler & J. Forgas (Eds.), *Affect, cognition, and social behavior* (pp. 44–62). Toronto: Hofgrefe International.

Schwarz, N., & Clore, G. L. (1996). Feelings and phenomenal experiences. In E. T. Higgins & A. Kruglanski (Eds.), *Social psychology: A handbook of basic principles* (pp. 433–465). New York: Guilford.

Schwarz, N., & Strack, F. (1981). Manipulating salience: Causal assessment in natural settings. *Personality & Social Psychology Bulletin, 7*, 554–558.

Shafir, E., Simonson, I., & Tversky, A. (1993). Reason-based choice. *Cognition, 49*, 11–36.

Shah, J. Y., Friedman, R., & Kruglanski, A. W. (2002). Forgetting all else: On the antecedents and consequences of goal shielding. *Journal of Personality and Social Psychology, 83*, 1261–1280.

Shah, J. Y., & Kruglanski, A. W. (2002). Priming against your will: How goal pursuit is affected by accessible alternatives. *Journal of Experimental Social Psychology, 38*, 368–383.

Shah, J. Y., & Kruglanski, A. W. (2003). When opportunity knocks: Bottom-up priming of goals by means and its effects on self-regulation. *Journal of Personality & Social Psychology, 84*, 1109–1122.

Shah, J. Y., Kruglanski, A. W., & Friedman, R. (2003). Goal systems theory: Integrating the cognitive and motivational aspects of self-regulation. In Spencer, S. J. & Fein, S. (Eds.), *Motivated social perception: The Ontario symposium* (Vol. 9, pp. 247–275). Mahwah, NJ: Erlbaum.

Sherman, S. J., Ahlm, K., Berman, L., & Lynn, S. (1978). Contrast effects and the relationship to subsequent behavior. *Journal of Experimental Social Psychology, 14*, 340–350.

Shiv, B., & Fedorikhin, A. (1999). Heart and mind in conflict: The interplay of affect and cognition in consumer decision making. *Journal of Consumer Research, 26*, 278–292.

Shrum, L. J., Wyer, R. S., & O'Guinn, T. (1998).The effects of watching television on perceptions of social reality. *Journal of Consumer Research, 24*, 447–458.

Simon, H. (1955). A behavioral model of rational choice. *Quarterly Journal of Economics, 69*, 99–118.

Simonson, I. (1989). Choice based on reasons: The case of attraction and compromise effects. *Journal of Consumer Research, 16*, 158–174.

Simonson, I. (2005). In defense of consciousness: the role of conscious and unconscious inputs in consumer choice. *Journal of Consumer Psychology, 15*.

Simonson, I., & Tversky, A. (1992). Choice in context: Trade-off contrast and extremeness aversion. *Journal of Marketing Research, 29*, 281–295.

Skurnik, I., Yoon, C., Park, D. C., & Schwarz, N. (in press). How warnings about false claims become recommendations. *Journal of Consumer Research.*

Slamecka, N. J. (1968). An examination of trace storage in free recall. *Journal of Experimental Psychology, 76*, 504–513.

Smith, E. R. (1990). Content and process specificity I the effects of prior experiences. In T. K. Srull & R. S. Wyer (Eds.), *Advances in social cognition* (Vol. 3, pp. 1–59). Hillsdale, NJ: Erlbaum.

Smith, E. R. (1994). Procedural knowledge and processing strategies in social cognition. In R. S. Wyer &T. K. Srull (Eds.), *Handbook of social cognition* (2nd ed., Vol. 1, pp. 99–151). Hillsdale, NJ: Erlbaum.

Snyder, M., & Cantor, N. (1979). Testing hypotheses about other people: the use of historical knowledge. *Journal of Experimental Social Psychology, 15*, 330–342.

Solomon, S., Greenberg, J., & Pyszczynski, T. (1991). A terror management theory of social behavior: The psychological functions of self-esteem and cultural worldviews. In M. P. Zanna (Ed.), *Advances in experimental social psychology* (Vol. 24, pp. 93–159). New York: Academic Press.

Srull, T. K., & Wyer, R. S. (1979). The role of category accessibility in the interpretation of information about persons: Some determinants and implications. *Journal of Personality and Social Psychology, 37*, 1660–1672.

Srull, T. K., & Wyer, R. S. (1980). Category accessibility and social perception: Some implications for the study of person memory and interpersonal judgments. *Journal of Personality and Social Psychology, 38*, 841–856.

Srull, T. K., & Wyer, R.S. (1985). The role of chronic and temporary goals in social information processing. In E. T. Higgins & R. Sorrentino (Eds.), *Handbook of cognition and motivation* (pp. 503–549). New York: Guilford.

Stapel, D. A., & Koomen, W. (2000). How far do we go beyond the information given? The impact of knowledge activation on interpretation and inference. *Journal of Personality and Social Psychology, 78*, 19–37.

Stapel, D. A., Koomen, W., & van der Plight, J. (1997). Categories of category accessibility: The impact of trait concept versus exemplar priming on person judgments. *Journal of Experimental Social Psychology, 33*, 47–76.

Strack, F. (1992). The different routes to social judgments: Experiential versus informational strategies. In L. L. Martin & A. Tesser (Eds.), *The construction of social judgments* (pp. 249–275). Hillsdale, NJ: Erlbaum.

Strack, F. (1994). Response processes in social judgment. In R. S. Wyer & T. K. Srull (Eds.), *Handbook of social cognition* (2nd ed., Vol. 1, pp. 287–322). Hillsdale, NJ: Erlbaum.

Strack, F., & Deutsch, R. (2004). Reflective and impulsive determinants of social behavior. *Personality and Social Psychology Review, 8, 220–247.*

Strack, F., & Martin, L. L. (1987). Thinking, judging, and communicating: A process account of context effects in attitude surveys. In. H. J. Hippler, N. Schwarz, & S. Sudman (Eds.), *Cognitive aspects of survey methodology*. New York: Springer-Verlag.

Strack, F., Martin, L. L., & Schwarz, N. (1988). Priming and communication: Social determinants of information use in judgments of life satisfaction. *European Journal of Social Psychology, 18*, 429–442.

Strack, F., Martin, L. L., & Stepper, S. (1988). Inhibiting and facilitating conditions of the human smile: A nonobtrusive test of the facial feedback hypothesis. *Journal of Personality and Social Psychology, 54*, 768–777.

Strack, F., & Mussweiler, T. (1997). Explaining the enigmataic anchoring effect: Mechanisms of selective accessibility. *Journal of Personality and Social Psychology, 73*, 437–446.

Strahan, E. J., Spencer, S. J., & Zanna, M. P. (2002). Subliminal priming and persuasion: Striking while the iron is hot. *Journal of Experimental Social Psychology, 38*, 556–568.

Tesser, A. (1978). Self-generated attitude change. In L. Berkowitz (Ed.), *Advances in experimental social psychology* (Vol. 11, pp. 290–338). New York: Academic Press.

Trappey, C. (1996). A meta-analysis of consumer choice and subliminal advertising. *Psychology Marketing, 13,* 517–530.

Tversky, A., & Kahneman, D. (1973). Availability: A heuristic for judging frequency and probability. *Cognitive Psychology, 5,* 207–232.

Tversky, A., & Kahneman, D. (1982). Causal schemas in judgments under uncertainty. In D. Kahneman, P. Slovic, & A. Tversky (Eds.), *Judgment under uncertainty: Heuristics and biases* (pp. 117–128). New York: Cambridge University Press.

Wang, J., & Wyer, R. S. (2002). Comparative judgment processes: The effect of task objectives and time delay on product evaluations. *Journal of Consumer Psychology, 12,* 327–340.

Wänke, M., Bless, H., & Biller, B. (1996). Subjective experience versus content of information in the construction of attitude judgments. *Personality and Social Psychology Bulletin, 22,* 1105–1113.

Wänke, M., Bohner, G., & Jurkowitsch, A. (1997). There are many reasons to drive a BMW — Surely you know one: Ease of Argument Generation influences Brand Attitudes. *Journal of Consumer Research, 24,* 70–77.

Wegener, D. T., & Petty, R. E. (1997). The flexible correction model: The role of naïve theories of bias in bias correction. In M. P. Zanna (Ed.), *Advances in experimental social psychology* (Vol. 29, pp. 141–208). San Diego, CA: Academic Press.

Wegner, D. M. (1994). Ironic processes of mental control. *Psychological Review, 101,* 34–52.

Wyer, R. S. (1970). The quantitative prediction of belief and opinion change: A further test of a subjective probability model. *Journal of Personality and Social Psychology, 16,* 559–571.

Wyer, R. S. (2004). *Social comprehension and judgment: The role of situation models, narratives, and implicit theories.* Mahwah, NJ: Erlbaum.

Wyer, R. S., Adaval, R., & Colcombe, S. J. (2002). Narrative-based representations of social knowledge: Their construction and use in comprehension, memory and judgment. In M. P. Zanna (Ed.), *Advances in experimental social psychology* (Vol. 34, pp. 131–197). San Diego, CA: Academic Press.

Wyer, R. S., Bodenhausen, G. V., & Gorman, T. F. (1985). Cognitive mediators of reactions to rape. *Journal of Personality and Social Psychology, 48,* 324–338.

Wyer, R. S., & Carlston, D. E. (1979). *Social cognition, inference and attribution.* Hillsdale, NJ: Erlbaum

Wyer, R. S., Clore, G. L., & Isbell, L. M. (1999). Affect and information processing. In M. P. Zanna (Ed.), *Advances in experimental social psychology* (vol. 31, pp. 1–77). San Diego: Academic Press

Wyer, R. S., & Hartwick, J. (1980). The role of information retrieval and conditional inference processes in belief formation and change. In L. Berkowitz (Ed.), *Advances in experimental social psychology* (Vol. 13, pp. 241–284). New York: Academic Press.

Wyer, R. S., & Hartwick, J. (1984). The recall and use of belief statements as bases for judgments: Some determinants and implications. *Journal of Experimental Social Psychology, 20,* 65–85.

Wyer, R. S., & Radvansky, G. A. (1999). The comprehension and validation of social information. *Psychological Review, 106,* 89–118.

Wyer, R. S., & Srull, T. K. (1989). *Memory and cognition in its social context.* Hillsdale, NJ: Erlbaum.

Yeung, C. W. M., & Wyer, R. S. (2004). Affect, appraisal and consumer judgment. *Journal of Consumer Research, 31,* 412–424.

Yeung, C. W. M., & Wyer, R. S. (2005). Does loving a brand mean loving its products? The role of brand-elicited affect in brand extension evaluations. *Journal of Marketing Research, 42,* 495–506.

Zajonc, R. B. (1980). Feeling and thinking: Preferences need no inferences. *American Psychologist, 35,* 151–175.

Zanna, M., & Rempel, J. K. (1988). Attitudes: a new look at an old concept. In D. Bar-Tal & A. Kruglanski (Eds.), *The social psychology of knowledge* (pp. 315–334). Cambridge, UK: Cambridge University Press.

Zeigarnik, B. (1938). On finished and unfinished tasks. In W. D. Ellis (Ed.), *A sourcebook of gestalt psychology* (pp. 300–314). New York: Harcourt, Brace, & World.

Zillmann, D., & Bryant, J. (1982) Pornography, sexual callousness, and the trivialization of rape. *Journal of Communication, 32,* 10–21.

3

Consumer Memory, Fluency, and Familiarity

ANTONIA MANTONAKIS

University of Chicago

BRUCE W. A. WHITTLESEA

Simon Fraser University

CAROLYN YOON

University of Michigan

The systematic study of consumer behavior is heavily influenced by theories and paradigms from memory research, as the behavior of the consumer is largely influenced by prior experiences. The distinction is often drawn between memory-based, stimulus-based (all relevant information is physically present at the time of judgment or choice), and mixed (a combination of memory-based and stimulus-based) decisions (Lynch & Srull, 1982). However, purely stimulus-based decisions are relatively rare; most consumer decisions are necessarily dependent on memory and thereby range from the purely memory-based to mixed (Alba, Hutchinson, & Lynch, 1991).

Given the importance of memory in consumer research, it behooves us periodically to take stock of the contemporary theories of memory and consider their assumptions and implications. To that end, we aim in this chapter to provide a review of the dominant accounts of memory and the way they have shaped our understanding of consumer behavior in the past two decades. We discuss the advances that have been made as well as some areas of potential concern. Specifically, we frame the review and discussion vis-à-vis an alternative account of memory, the SCAPE framework, developed by Bruce Whittlesea and his colleagues (e.g., Whittlesea, 1997). In addition, we offer some suggestions and future directions for research on consumer memory.

MEMORY

Memory is the record of our personal past. As such, it is useful for remembering. But memory is also much more than that: it also involves the capacity to learn, to be influenced by prior experience, and to behave differently in the future as a consequence of an experience. Memory is the controller of all acquired human behavior, including speech, conceptual knowledge, skilled activities, social interactions, and consumer preferences. To achieve a true understanding of any aspect of human behavior, it is therefore essential to have an effective theory of memory.

During the 1970s, the notion of associative memory was introduced (Anderson & Bower, 1973). Following the assumption that elaboration is related to the creation of associative pathways in memory; the notion that elaboration could impact attitudes became an important research question. Elaborative processing became a heavily studied determinant of information accessibility (e.g., Kardes, 1994) and attitude formation (Kisielius & Sternthal, 1986; McGill & Anand, 1989). Such effects have been explained by a multiple-pathway explanation (cf. Anderson, 1983), although more recently explanations have favored the reconstruction hypothesis (e.g., Walker, 1986).

Despite the popularity of thinking about memory in terms of "construction" (e.g., Loftus & Palmer, 1974; Loftus, 1979), during the 1980s, "separate systems" approaches to memory became popular, and continue to be popular today. We will focus on these approaches: first outlining them in detail, and then contrasting them with the SCAPE framework.

SEPARATE SYSTEMS THEORIES

Three major dichotomies were proposed as the basic organization of memory, each pointing to some clear contrast in behavior. Each dichotomy is based on observations of various dissociations in performance on some tasks. For example, recognition performance has been found to be affected by varying levels of processing (Jacoby & Dallas, 1981) or delay of test (Tulving, Schacter, & Stark, 1982) while leaving identification performance unaffected. Amnesic patients demonstrate implicit learning (Knowlton & Squire, 1994) and respond to repetition priming (Warrington & Weiskrantz, 1970), despite poor recognition performance. These dissociations are taken as evidence of Nature's seams, the lines along which mind can be split and compartmentalized into convenient and independent sub-units, each of which can be studied without consideration of the other.

The *episodic/semantic* dichotomy of memory is arguably the most dominant of the three dichotomies. It distinguishes the preservation of detail and context of prior experiences from the preservation of context-free, abstract, summary properties of those experiences (e.g., Tulving, 1983, 1985). The former supports tasks such as recall and recognition; the latter supports tasks requiring perception, identification, and conceptual and categorical knowledge.

Also common is the *procedural/declarative* dichotomy which is based on the distinction between a declarative system, supporting tasks requiring conscious deliberation about the content and source of current knowledge, and a procedural system, supporting tasks requiring specific skills, or motoric ability (Cohen & Squire, 1980). The distinction is between intentional acquisition, storage, and retrieval of information versus non-reflective acquisition and application of prior experience, as evidenced by perceptual, cognitive, and sensorimotor performance on tasks demonstrating skill or involving repetition priming. *Skill* is considered to be a product of multiple prior experiences; *priming* is considered to be a product of a single prior experience. Evidence of either is measured by the observed savings or facilitation in performance, in the absence of conscious awareness, control, or volition.

The third dichotomy entails an *implicit/explicit* distinction that emphasizes the differential role of consciousness in performance, contrasting tasks such as recall and recognition, in which awareness of prior experience is important, versus tasks which measure repetition priming (Graf & Schacter, 1985). An implicit form of memory exists to account for effects of prior experience on current behavior in the absence of conscious awareness (e.g., effects observed in a priming task); an explicit form of memory exists to account for behavior accompanied by conscious awareness (e.g., effects observed in a remembering task).

These separate systems theories of memory are based on the assumption that the fundamental functions of mind are obvious: they consist of the capacity to perform each of the various activities that humans are faced with in the social world, such as recognition, knowing, and responding appropriately but unconsciously in skilled activities such as speech and dance. The important research question is thus not what the functions of mind are, but how they are performed. It has further been assumed that different functions of mind are served by separate dedicated mechanisms, and that the dissociated patterns of performance observed in performing various tasks is a consequence of the different principles by which the separate mechanisms work. Finally, because of this correspondence of mechanism with function, it has been assumed that each mechanism serves each function directly. Thus, for example, because recognition of a particular face or event requires differentiation among many others, that function is served by a specific retrieval mechanism; whereas classification of an object such as a dog in the street could benefit from experience of many similar beasts, and so instead relies on abstraction of knowledge across events and activation of a general concept node.

Applied to consumer memory, the separate systems distinctions have been useful for compartmentalizing consumer knowledge. For example, a "retrieval set" is distinguished from a "knowledge set" (e.g., Alba & Chattopadhyay, 1985), or a "consideration set" is distinguished from an "awareness set" (see Shapiro, MacInnis, & Heckler, 1997). In each example, the former is episodic in nature, the latter semantic. As such, the assumptions of the distinction are often used for hypothesis testing, and taken for granted. For example, many consumer researchers assume that activation of nodes in semantic memory is a necessary by-product of cueing to a brand category or feature (e.g., Cowley & Mitchell, 2003; Nedungadi, 1990; Shapiro, 1999), and often discuss "activation" as a causal mechanism, rather than a proposed theoretical construct.

This chapter argues that current major theories of memory are problematic, and instead favors an account of memory called SCAPE, which is an acronym for "Selective Construction And Preservation of Experiences" (Whittlesea, 1997). This account is a synthesis of ideas from the attribution theory of remembering (e.g., Jacoby & Dallas, 1981; Jacoby, Kelley, & Dywan, 1989; Whittlesea, 1993), the episodic-processing account of concept acquisition (e.g., Whittlesea & Dorken, 1993), instance theory (e.g., Brooks, 1978; Medin & Schaffer, 1978; Jacoby & Brooks, 1984), skill transfer (e.g., Kolers & Smythe, 1984), and transfer-appropriate processing (TAP; e.g., Morris, Bransford, & Franks, 1977; Roediger & Challis, 1992; Masson & MacLeod, 1992). In accordance with the SCAPE framework, we suggest that the functions of mind identified by separate systems (and most contemporary) theories are misleading: they are categories of mental performance that make sense from the point of view of the user of memory (one's conscious self), but do not correspond in any direct way with the fundamental principles of memory. We further argue that the real underlying mechanisms of memory are unitary and serve all of these user-defined functions; and moreover that they do so indirectly, such that the mechanism responsible for a certain behavior in no way resembles the behavior. Among other claims, we deny that remembering consists of retrieval; that spreading activation and inhibition are valid mental operations; that conscious and unconscious performance have different causal agents; and that controlled and automatic behavior differ in any meaningful way.

A FUNCTIONAL ANALYSIS

However obvious the contrasts between explicit and implicit performance, or between remembering and knowing, it will be argued in this chapter that none of those are fundamental functions of mind. Instead, they are emergent categories of behavior, useful in describing differences in a person's behavior from the outside, and perhaps in describing their current intentions, but not diagnostic of the underlying principles by which mind is organized. The problem, we assert, stems from a levels-of-analysis problem, confusing what a system achieves in operating on the world with the means by which that operation is attained. To take a simple example of the problem, in attempting a functional analysis of an automobile, one might perform an examination of the variety of things that cars are used for. Following such an examination, one might be tempted to say that a car's chief functions are transportation, ego projection, sport, and courtship. Certainly these are valid and separate categories of interaction with the world that cars enable us to achieve. However, they do not reveal anything about the underlying affordances that support these achievements (capacities such as steering, propulsion, shock absorption, and containment), and even less about the mechanisms that support these affordances (rack and pinion steering, disk brakes, Otto-cycle engine, and so on). That is, the functions of a system that are evident to and of value to the user of the system may not in any way resemble the basic principles by which the system operates. In consequence, arguing basic mechanism from dissociations among classes of activity that are important to the user is fraught with danger.

More important, we believe that Nature, in her subtlety, often arranges for behaviors that are of advantage to her offspring to come about in ways that are startlingly indirect. As an example, consider a well-known phenomenon: that of a sunflower's tendency to follow the path of the sun over the course of a day, known as *heliotropism*. A direct mechanism to bring about this correspondence would require, in addition to some mechanical means of twisting, (a) that the plant knows, at a given moment, where the sun is, (b) that it also knows the direction in which it is currently pointed, and (c) that it has some means of calculating the difference. Clearly, such a direct mechanism is wrong. In fact, the mechanism is indirect, having the *effect* of bringing about alignment with the sun without any computation of that alignment. The actual, more subtle, explanation of this behavior is that red and blue wavelengths of light respectively increase and reduce photosynthesis and the resulting uptake of water into the stem's cells. The gradient of blue light across the plant stem in full sunlight causes cells on the shady side of the stem to increase photosynthesis and water uptake, expanding their size, whereas photosynthesis in cells on the sunny side is reduced, leading these cells to shrink. This combination of effects causes the head of the plant to twist, bending toward the sun. That the plant faces the sun accurately is in some sense an accident, resulting from the ratio of swelling in cells on opposite sides of the stem; the real cause of that effect is that ancestral sunflowers that had better ratios of swelling, so that they followed the sun more precisely, out-competed those that did so less effectively. Thus, the success in sun-following, although vital to the plant, is better thought of as an incidental benefit or by-product of its fundamental architecture, rather than as an inherent function of that architecture.

These two examples illustrate the difficulty of functional analysis aimed at understanding the fundamental principles of a system that control that system's interactions with the world. We will propose a different dichotomy of functions of mind, of production versus evaluation, that is fundamental to the SCAPE framework of memory (Whittlesea, 1997). This dichotomy is much more abstract than any of those recounted earlier, and much less easily tied to any specific behavior that a person performs. However, we will argue that it provides a more thorough explanation of the variety of human performance than do any of the other so far mentioned accounts.

THE SCAPE FRAMEWORK

According to the SCAPE account, there is only one memory system, which contains only representations of the experience of processing the stimuli in various tasks and contexts. In any processing event, this memory system interacts with the environment; the environment constrains some activities and affords others (e.g., you can use a pencil as a weapon or to stir coffee, but cannot fly on it). The central function of memory is *construction*: memory never simply registers or records the environment, but instead imposes selection, organization, and meaning on it. It is this experience of construction that will be encoded in memory, and that will control performance on subsequent interactions involving stimuli, tasks, and contexts that are similar on relevant dimensions.

The construction function has two aspects: (1) the *production* of psychological events, controlled by the interaction of the stimulus, task, and context, with representations of previous processing experiences in memory; and (2) the *evaluation* of the significance of that production, given the stimulus, task, and context. The former leads to performance: the occurrence of all manner of perceptual, cognitive, and motoric events. The latter results in phenomenology: the subjective reaction to current processing that causes people to adopt the attitude that they are remembering, understanding, or identifying an object, either correctly or committing an error.

The production function begins by selecting some aspect of the current situation as a stimulus, or focus of attention, the rest as context. This selection depends on a variety of factors, including the prior history of memory with various aspects of the environment, each aspect's salience or apparent significance (threat, novelty, interest), and the preparedness of the system to perform some activity given how and what it has just been processing. This process continues on to construct a mental model of the event: of a percept of the stimulus, of its identity, class or covert properties, or of the detail of a past or future event involving that stimulus, depending on the task at hand and the affordances and cue properties of the stimulus and context.

Many accounts of memory involve (at least in part) assumptions that sound similar to those just stated. However, the SCAPE account makes two radical claims. The first is that current cognitive processing is always the product of a constructive act. One implication is that, although a prior episode can, in part, control the shape and ease of constructing a mental model of a current stimulus, that prior episode is not itself retrieved. That has major implications for understanding the nature of remembering, as documented below. A second departure is the account's insistence that the production function is always accompanied by the operation of the evaluation function, although that is often difficult to detect (see Kronlund & Whittlesea, 2005, for a demonstration of this point).

The evaluation function consists of chronic monitoring of the integrity and coherence of ongoing performance; it also makes inferences about unexpected successes or apparent failures of coherence. In the words of Marcel (1983), it consists of an attempt to "make sense of as much data as possible at the most functionally useful level" (p. 238). It is this act of inference which gives rise to the phenomenology accompanying performance. In attempting to make sense of apparent disparities between two aspects of a current stimulus, or between what is expected and what occurs, the evaluation function makes an attribution to some plausible source of influence. The apparent disparity may be resolved by an attribution to the stimulus, the situation, the person, or the past; these unconscious attributions give rise to conscious feelings such as desirability, impending danger, unusual mood, or familiarity.

THE CONSTRUCTIVE NATURE OF AWARENESS

According to separate systems accounts, explicit and declarative knowledge is thought to be accessed by retrieval. In contrast, the SCAPE account assumes that information is never retrieved, but constructed. This idea was originally proposed by Bartlett (1932), and with some exceptions (e.g., Janiszewski, Noel, & Sawyer, 2003; Braun-LaTour, LaTour, Pickrell, & Loftus, 2004),[1] it is hardly considered in the consumer literature. As an example, imagine that a recognition study begins with a study phase consisting of paired associates, such as onion-carrot, milk-cheese, bread-cake, etc. At test, when asked "Did you see MILK in the earlier list?", one subject may reply

"MILK…...oh yeah, CHEESE. Yes, I do remember seeing MILK." That performance seems to demonstrate that the person has used MILK as a cue to retrieve the episodic representation of the earlier experience, and that, in doing so, they have become aware of a prior experience. That description of the process is too simple, however. Another subject might respond "MILK, um, CHEESE, um, no, that's just a common associate. I don't remember MILK." That subject's initial performance duplicates that of the first subject's. However, although the content of the earlier experience comes to mind, this person has not become aware of the prior experience. Another subject might say, "MILK — oh right, DAIRY. Yes, I do remember seeing MILK." This person's performance is influenced by a source other than the specific prior experience, yet this person is experiencing awareness of encountering that item.

These examples demonstrate that becoming aware of a prior experience is caused by two interlinked processes: the production of a response, and an evaluation of the significance of that production. The coming-to-mind of an item in a remembering task is thus not one and the same as awareness of the prior event. Awareness of the source of the production comes about by an evaluation of the significance of that production, which results in an attribution to a source that seems most likely.

As another illustration of the difference between these two aspects of construction, Leboe and Whittlesea (2002) presented subjects with pairs of items: one-third contained two strong associates (e.g., LION-TIGER), one-third contained two unrelated words (e.g., ROAD-NAVY), and one-third contained one word and four Xs (e.g., TABLE-XXXX). Each associate in the former two cases occurred only once in the study phase, whereas XXXX occurred on many study trials. At test, subjects were provided with a word stem (e.g., LION-?) and were required to recall the item with which it was paired earlier, and provide a confidence rating about their performance. Subjects performed accurate recall on 48% of the trials involving strong associates, on only 13% of the trials involving unrelated words, and on 41% of the trials involving XXXXs. In contrast, subjects' confidence ratings for those trials were 78% for recall of the strong associates, 91% for recall of the unrelated words, and only 45% for recall of XXXXs.

Leboe and Whittlesea concluded that the differential rates of recall accuracy and confidence reflect the interaction of two operations: the coming-to-mind of a response (i.e., a strong associate, an unrelated word, or XXXX), and the subject's resulting evaluation of the significance of each of those types of responses coming to mind. For example, subjects were unimpressed with the coming-to-mind of XXXX, because they were aware that they could easily generate it because of their knowledge that one-third of studied items were paired with XXXX. Thus, they often produced XXXX correctly, but even when accurate, they were not convinced that they were actually recalling. In contrast, recall of an unrelated word was difficult, in part because the association formed during study would often be of low quality (e.g., the association between ROAD and NAVY). Consequently, accurate recall was low in this condition. However, when an unrelated word did come to mind, subjects were very impressed because they could think of no other reason why that word would come to mind other than that it had been presented in study. Such productions were thus experienced as accurate recall, and were associated with high confidence ratings.

Therefore, the conclusion that one is now aware of an aspect of the past is always a decision: an adoption of an attitude toward current processing. Awareness of the contents of previous experiences does not comprise direct access to a representation of the past. It is the product of a heuristic decision. People are chronically having to infer the nature of their past from the quality and content of their current processing. There are always multiple possible reasons why a particular mental event occurs: because it actually occurred in one's past, because one experienced a similar event with a different stimulus, because that event occurred in the life of someone else who has told you about it, or because one has experienced many similar events, which in parallel contribute to the ease of processing the current mental event.

This inferential relationship between awareness and experience is not limited to remembering. It is also true of knowledge in general. In the next section, we will demonstrate analogous performance in remembering and classification judgments, but that people claim awareness of the basis of their performance in the first but not the second. The difference appears to be only due to the adoption of an appropriate attitude and theory to understand their performance in the first case and a lack of doing so in the latter.[2]

SEPARATE SYSTEMS APPROACHES TO MEMORY

Separate-systems accounts of memory, including the episodic/semantic (Tulving, 1983, 1985), declarative/procedural (Cohen & Squire, 1980), and explicit/implicit (Graf & Schacter, 1985) dichotomies, are based on the notion that memory performance is sustained by distinct modules of memory. The modules support different functions of memory, each of which is based on specific types of knowledge, and thus have specific principles for acquiring and applying each type of knowledge. Each type of knowledge is also selectively cued by different types of tasks, and preserved in distinct stores. Evidence for such dichotomies in memory has come from dissociations that have been observed in both intact and amnesic subjects. We provide an in-depth description of the episodic/semantic and implicit/explicit dichotomies, as they have dominated how consumer researchers conceptualize memory.[3] We provide empirical evidence for each distinction, and examples of consumer behavior studies which have embraced or relied on each. We focus primarily on studies on consumer memory published since the review by Alba et al. (1991).

THE EPISODIC/SEMANTIC DICHOTOMY

According to this account, memory can be subdivided into an episodic system which preserves details of particular experiences and supports remembering tasks (i.e., recall and recognition), and a semantic system, which preserves conceptual and categorical knowledge and supports non-remembering activities (i.e., perception and identification). The semantic system thus preserves the abstract, context-free, summary properties of all prior experiences (Tulving, 1983, 1985). The fundamental distinction is between *remembering*, which depends on event-specific information, and *knowing*, which depends on the abstracted summary of prior experiences. Event-specific information can take on the form of tokens (Kanwisher, 1987); abstractions can take on the form of types (Anderson, 1980, 1983; Kanwisher, 1987), prototypes (Rosch, 1978), rules (Reber, 1989, 1993), or logogens (Paap & Noel, 1991). The process of acquiring knowledge occurs by automatic abstraction or implicit learning; the process of accessing knowledge is thought to be mediated by the principles of activation and inhibition.

Although not always made explicit, numerous consumer researchers appear to assume an episodic/semantic distinction of memory. A set of studies have examined how brand or product category schemas are formed and organized. For example, Meyvis and Janiszewski (2004) investigated how breadth of brand categories affects brand associations and perceptions of brand extensions (see also Gurhan-Canli, 2003); Wood and Lynch (2002) examined the effects of expertise or prior knowledge about products on learning of new information and subsequent memory; and Roedder-John and Sujan (1990) studied product information organization and categorization in young children.

The strength and extensiveness of information held in memory and how it affects consumers' judgments and decisions are almost always considered to be a direct or indirect function of person-related (e.g., motivation, ability), stimulus-related (e.g., distinctiveness, visual vs. verbal), and situational factors (e.g., time delay, usage situation). For example, Park and Hastak (1994) have examined how involvement affects product memory, and how the product memory affects judgments. Peracchio and Tybout (1996) have also investigated how product category schema affects product evaluations. In particular, they examined the effects of schema incongruity on product evaluations. Thus these consumer studies share commonalities with some aspects of the SCAPE framework. For instance, the production part of construction processes posited by the SCAPE assumes an interaction of stimulus, task, and context that is in line with the approach taken by consumer researchers. However, there is no accompanying acknowledgement in the studies that the significance of the production is, in turn, evaluated.

Other studies have also investigated the manner in which organization of brand information or prior knowledge affects how and what information is processed and remembered by consumers. The way that prior knowledge influences judgments or choice has been of interest to a number of consumer researchers (e.g., Crowley & Mitchell, 2003; Hutchinson, Raman, & Mantrala, 1994; Nedungadi, 1990). These studies, however, largely assume that "retrieval" occurs as the result of a spreading activation process. A threshold level of activation of a particular concept, such as a brand, is assumed to be facilitated through the use of cues such as attribute information. This in turn results in retrieval of the target brand. Spreading activation models have also been applied to models of brand equity (e.g., Aaker, 1991; Keller, 1993, 1998).

In the following sections we describe assumptions made by the episodic/semantic approach that separate principles are involved in remembering and knowing, that acquisition of knowledge occurs by automatic abstraction, and that access to knowledge structures is mediated by activation and inhibition. We consider further examples of consumer behavior studies which have embraced each assumption. We also provide predictions made by SCAPE for each observation discussed.

ACQUIRING KNOWLEDGE STRUCTURES

One observation that suggests the use of abstracted information is *implicit learning* (Dienes & Berry, 1997; Knowlton & Squire, 1994; Reber & Allen, 1978; Reber, 1989, 1993). As an example of what takes place during an implicit learning study, brand logos (e.g., the Hello Kitty picture) are shown to subjects in their regular and opposite orientations (e.g., Hello Kitty with a bow in her hair above her right ear instead of her left ear). Subjects are above chance at choosing the correct orientation, suggesting automatic, incidental learning of regularity in such stimuli (Kelly, Burton, Kato, & Akamatsu, 2001). Such results have also been found in controlled laboratory settings, where attention is directed to stimuli that follow a rule. At test, subjects are above chance at discriminating between legal and illegal items (i.e., they demonstrate sensitivity to the abstract structure of the domain) without having awareness of the rule (e.g., McGeorge & Burton, 1990).

Such performance is taken as evidence that the subjects must have abstracted information about the rule during the exposure phase. Because they are unaware of doing so, that abstraction must be automatic. The phenomenon of implicit learning is thus argued to demonstrate the existence in memory of an autonomous abstraction mechanism that proceeds independent of conscious intention or awareness, and supports performance in tasks such as classification and identification.

The suggestion of automatic abstraction has been criticized on the grounds that test items that are legal are highly similar to each previously encountered legal (studied) exemplar of the given class, therefore, if a subject simply memorizes one or more of the study items, and uses the perceived similarity of test items to those memorized instances as a basis for their decision, they will perform above chance (Brooks, 1978, 1987; Dulany, Carlson, & Dewey, 1984; Neal & Hesketh, 1997; Perruchet & Pacteau, 1991; Shanks & St. John, 1994; Vokey & Brooks, 1992). This provides a situation whereby the same processes that are involved in showing sensitivity to prior individual experiences (episodic) are also involved in showing sensitivity to general, abstract properties of classes (semantic). The SCAPE account is in agreement, but adds that memory preserves processing experiences, and the type of processing experience that occurred on a prior encounter with a stimulus will influence later processing of the same (or a similar) stimulus to the extent that later processing matches the earlier processing experience (i.e., transfer appropriate processing: henceforth TAP; Morris et al., 1977). The SCAPE account suggests that TAP will apply to both remembering and non-remembering tasks (Whittlesea & Dorken, 1993, 1997).

To demonstrate that TAP applies to non-remembering activities such as classification, Wright and Whittlesea (1998) developed a set of four-digit stimuli, each which followed the rule odd-even-odd-even (e.g., 3412, 8954, etc). They presented these items to subjects in a study phase, and encouraged them to read them as bigrams (e.g., "thirty-four, twelve," etc). At test, no studied items were shown, however, half corresponded to the odd-even-odd-even rule, half violated the rule (e.g., 4613, 8723, etc). Subjects were asked to discriminate legal from illegal items, and they accurately did so 68% of the time, although they were unable to state the rule. This type of finding is usually interpreted as providing evidence for automatic abstraction and subsequent use of a rule in semantic memory. In another study, the same study phase was used. At test, studied (e.g., 3412) and new (e.g., 1374) items were presented; subjects were asked to discriminate studied from unstudied items (i.e., they performed recognition); they accurately did so 71% of the time. This type of finding is usually interpreted as acquisition and use of episodic memory. In a subsequent study, half the subjects were given the identical study and instructions as outlined above (i.e., to read digits as bigrams), the other half were encouraged to read stimuli as individual digits (e.g., "three-four-one-two"). The bigram group classified legal from illegal test items with 70% accuracy, however the digit group had only 58% accuracy. This result demonstrates that representations of particular experiences are determined by the type of task used, and are preserved and demonstrate transfer to both recognition and classification tasks.

In their fourth experiment, they showed subjects digits in a study phase, and encouraged them to read them as bigrams. At test, subjects were able to discriminate legal (odd-even-odd-even) from illegal items at 65% accuracy, but could not state the rule, again suggesting automatic abstraction of the rule. In this study however, the study items all consisted of combinations of odd-odd or even-even bigrams with odd-even bigrams (e.g., 3714, 8432, 6897, etc). Thus, if subjects were abstracting a rule of some sort, it would be "either odd-odd or even-even as one of the two bigrams."

In this case, Wright and Whittlesea attempted to demonstrate that subjects could *appear* to show sensitivity to a rule (i.e., to a non-existent odd-even-odd-even rule). To achieve this end, they constructed the test items such that both bigrams in the "legal" test items (e.g., 1432) had occurred in several study items (e.g., in 3714, 8432, 7514, etc), whereas the bigrams of the "illegal" items (e.g., 3154) never occurred in any of the study items. Thus subjects could successfully classify the items if and only if they had encoded the instances from study rather than if they had automatically abstracted a rule. The ability of subjects to show above-chance performance at classifying according to the non-existent odd-even-odd-even rule demonstrates that subjects used the similarity of the test items to study instances to classify them.

The important lesson to be learned from these studies is about the nature of awareness. In the initial recognition study, when subjects were told about their above-chance scores, they were unimpressed: when asked for an explanation of their success, they said something like, "Well, I just remembered them, you know?" In contrast, subjects in the remaining studies were quite mystified when told about their above-chance success. Having not been told any rules, and having not consciously worked out any rules, they could think of no basis for above-chance success, and agreed that they must have learned the rules unconsciously. In fact, the set of experiments taken together suggest that the subjects performed on exactly the same basis in classification as they did in recognition. Why, then, should they not be aware of the basis of their success? We suggest that they adopted an inappropriate theory (as did the original investigators of this effect): that success in classifying according to a rule can occur only if one has the rule. This adoption of an inappropriate theory prevented the subjects from achieving awareness of the basis of their performance. In turn however, that conclusion changes the nature of what is meant by awareness. Rather than being aware or unaware of what we are doing, the question is whether we are aware or unaware of the effect of what we are doing now with respect to some unanticipated decision in the future. Viewed in that way, "awareness" is an attribution, based on an inference, about the significance of our current processing. Thought of in this way, "accessibility" and "diagnosticity" (Feldman & Lynch, 1988) are very complicated processes, which, according to the assumptions of SCAPE, may be based on a person's intuitive theories of cause and effect, the salient aspects of the current situation, and the current task, which selectively cues prior experiences, both individually and in parallel.

ACTIVATION

In the episodic/semantic view of memory, types, and prototypes are assumed to be stored as nodes in a network organization in memory (e.g., Anderson & Bower, 1973). The knowledge structures are assumed to be hierarchical (thus imposing cognitive economy and inheritance; e.g., Collins & Quillian, 1969; see also Nedungadi, 1990) or non-hierarchical (e.g., Collins & Loftus, 1975). Any prior exposure to an exemplar, associate, or conceptual feature of that node is thought to "activate" that node, adjacent nodes, and closely linked nodes within the network (e.g., Anderson, 1983; Collins & Loftus, 1975).[4]

The associative network model of memory is a common way that consumer researchers have conceptualized the organization of brands and brand-related information in memory. According to this perspective, consumer memory is represented in the form of episodic and semantic traces of the incoming information (e.g., source and content) that comprise schemas or knowledge structures. The fundamental assumption is that consumers hold knowledge structures or schemas that are related to specific consumer domains (e.g., Nedungadi, 1990). When a particular knowledge structure is accessed or "primed,"[5] the central node and related nodes are activated, and facilitation in processing is observed, either through a direct or indirect test. Basic reaction time measures are often used as the critical dependent measure demonstrating effects of prior experience (e.g., Jewell & Unnava, 2003), and are assumed to be advantageous over other measures (see Fitzsimons et al., 2002).

Instead of facilitation through activation, the SCAPE account argues for overlapping operations (e.g., Hughes & Whittlesea, 2003). No one can become aware of the entire content of their memory. However, it is often possible to be influenced by semantic relationships acquired in the past and to be aware of that influence in current experience. One example of this is the semantic priming effect. Originally explored by Meyer and Schvaneveldt (1971), the effect consists of the facilitation of performing a task, such as naming or lexical decision, when the test stimulus or probe (e.g., DOCTOR) is preceded by a meaningfully or associatively related stimulus, usually referred to as a "prime" (e.g., NURSE). One of the boundary conditions of the effect which has been regularly observed, and has been influential in theories about underlying mechanism, is that it is short-lived, both in terms of absolute time (stimulus onset asynchrony; SOA) and lag (number of unrelated items inserted between the prime and probe). The effect can disappear when the SOA is as little as 500 ms (Ratcliff & McKoon, 1988); facilitation of the probe is not observed if the presentation of the probe is delayed by more than two seconds (e.g., Neely, 1977, 1991). Further, any amount of lag eliminates the effect (e.g., Masson, 1995), although some investigators have observed priming occurring at a lag of one (e.g., Joordens & Besner, 1992; McNamara, 1992).

The finding of the initial boundary conditions led investigators (e.g., Anderson, 1976, 1983; Collins & Loftus, 1975) to propose spreading activation accounts of the effect. The proposed mechanism at the time was that presentation of the prime activates its node in a semantic network; that activation spreads along the linkages of the network to nodes of all related concepts. As a consequence, the nodes of all related concepts become partially activated, such that they can be stimulated above threshold more quickly than if not primed. By this account, the effect is short-lived because activation dies away quickly in the semantic network.

Whittlesea and Jacoby (1990) presented an alternative account of semantic priming, in which such a time course is not a central issue. This account was based on Kolers' (1973, 1976) idea of "remembering operations", by which any transfer is to be understood as resulting from recapitulating the specific processing operations a person learned to perform on a stimulus within a particular context on a previous occasion: to the extent that the later test involves the same operations as the earlier one, processing will be facilitated.

By Whittlesea and Jacoby's account, the direction of causation underlying semantic priming is from the probe back to the prime, the opposite of that assumed by activation theories. It assumes that processing the prime is a learning experience, like any other stimulus encounter. That experience establishes a resource for performing other, similar activities on other stimuli that are related on relevant dimensions. That explanation has been applied to long-term priming effects, including repetition priming (Scarborough, Cortese & Scarborough, 1977), form-based priming (Ruekl, 1990) and morphological priming (Bentin & Feldman, 1990). Whittlesea and Jacoby (1990) argued that it can also be applied to semantic priming.

In accord with Whittlesea and Jacoby's (1990) ideas, Becker, Moscovitch, Behrmann, and Joordens (1997) suggested that semantic priming is not observed outside the boundary conditions because the usual test tasks (naming or lexical decision) do not require extensive semantic processing (cf. Borowsky & Besner, 1993; Chumbley & Balota, 1984). By increasing the demands of the task (i.e., they used an animacy decision as the task), they were able to observe reliable semantic priming effects at up to 8 lags.

Hughes and Whittlesea (2003) modified these procedures by making the test task more challenging, but also different on every trial. For example, on prime trials, the subject would be asked to judge whether APPLE is a kind of FRUIT or MACHINE, or whether COBRA is a kind of BIRD or SNAKE. On probe trials, they could be given a primed target, such as ORANGE (a semantic associate of APPLE) and asked if it is a kind of FRUIT or JEWEL; or could be given an unprimed target such as CROW and asked if it is a kind of FRUIT or BIRD. Under these circumstances, they observed semantic priming effects of about 60–100 ms, enduring over a lag of 90 intervening questions and about a one-half hour interval. These long-term transfer effects demonstrate that semantic priming is not an inherently short-lived effect, but is so usually because of the extreme ease and non-distinctiveness of the prime and probe tasks (naming, lexical decision). Contrary to the idea of semantic priming illustrating a transient perturbation in an essentially stable system, these new observations suggest that it is a learning effect, occurring in much the same way that learning and recall or recognition occur in remembering tasks. Consistent with the data presented so far, these observations deny any strong distinction between processes conducted in "semantic" and "episodic" tasks.

Control studies revealed that these large and enduring semantic transfer effects depended both on performing a somewhat elaborate verification task on both the prime and probe trials, and that the decision for the prime and probe be the same (e.g., that the answers to both LION and TIGER both be ANIMAL). Further control studies revealed that the same size of priming effects occur not just with category verification, but also for the selection of categorical associates (e.g., PEAR – APPLE – CROW in the prime phase, and PEAR – ORANGE – COBRA in the probe phase) or of features (e.g., PEEL – APPLE – FEATHER in the prime phase, and PEEL – ORANGE – HISS in the probe phase). That is, semantic transfer was observed at three levels of abstractness: categorical membership of exemplars, association with other category exemplars, and features of particular exemplars. That might suggest to some readers that the semantic transfer observed was mediated by activation of knowledge about the category as a whole, perhaps through activation of some prototype representation of the category, giving primed access to all knowledge of the category at all levels of abstraction.

The authors tested this idea through cross-level priming, for example FRUIT – APPLE – BIRD in the prime phase and PEEL – ORANGE – HISS in the test, or alternatively PEEL – ORANGE – HISS in the prime phase and FRUIT – APPLE – BIRD in the test phase. In contradiction of the "categorical activation" hypothesis, no priming was seen in these cases. The authors concluded that, although the phenomenon occurs broadly across levels of abstraction, it occurs only when the same relationships are presented for both the prime and the probe. They thus further concluded that the phenomenon does not involve spreading activation in a semantic network, but instead reveals the importance of "overlapping operations," an idea introduced by Paul Kolers (1973, 1976). By this principle, any transfer is to be understood as resulting from recapitulating the specific processing operations a person learned to perform on a stimulus within a particular context on a previous occasion: to the extent that the later test involves the same operations as the earlier one, processing will be facilitated.

This concept of overlapping operations is central to the "production" function of the SCAPE framework. It explains all manner of transfer effects, when critical aspects of an earlier and later experience are specifically similar and distinctive, whether those aspects are of the nominal stimulus, the context, or the task. As illustrated in the "implicit learning" section provided above, it is not even necessary for the subject to be aware of the overlapping components to gain advantage from them.

Perhaps a more subtle point that is made in the Hughes and Whittlesea study is the importance of using a number of trials; each treated as a separate instance. Thus effects are less likely to be stimulus specific. While some consumer researchers examine effects of variables of interest on a significant number of brands (e.g., Morrin & Ratneshwar, 2003), other examine effects on only a limited number of brands (e.g., Jewell & Unnava, 2003; Krishnan & Shapiro, 1996; Nedungadi, 1990). Of special interest is the article by Nedungadi (1990). He argued that (a) indirectly cueing to a brand category will produce selective effect on "retrieval" and inclusion into the consideration set, in the absence of an effect on evaluation, and (b) that indirect "priming" (i.e., prior exposure to a related brand) selectively affects only the major brand in a minor subcategory of brands. That is, repeating Subway (minor brand in minor subcategory of fast-food places) three times increases "retrieval" of Joe's Deli (major brand in minor subcategory), however, repeating Wendy's (minor brand in major subcategory) three times *does not* increase "retrieval" of McDonald's (major brand in major subcategory)

A major limitation of Nedungadi's study is that he used only a select number of brand categories. Wagner and Kronlund (2005) performed a near-replication of Nedungadi's study, however they used 28 brand categories, and operationalized "priming" by having subjects read four brand names (e.g., Honda, GMC) and 14 associates (e.g., tire, gas, brakes) for each brand category. Critically, they never showed any major brands (e.g., Toyota). Unlike Nedungadi, they found consistently, subjects *falsely recognized* the major brand more often than any of the minor brands (or associates). That is, when subjects read "can, drink, soda…Pepsi, Sprite, Mountain Dew," they reported having seen Coke, but not Dr. Pepper.

In a subsequent study, they asked for subjects to report preference ratings for target brands after they had made their recognition decision. Subjects' preference ratings of the major brands were reliably higher than preference ratings for minor brands regardless of whether they were cued by their respective lists or not. Thus, preference ratings corresponded to remembering. Taken together, these results suggest that brand primes can indirectly shape brand remembering, but *only* for major brands. Further, influences on brand choice may not be independent of brand evaluation, as suggested by Nedungadi (1990). These findings provide us with the basis for using our stimulus set to assess the relationships between consideration set inclusion, brand evaluation, and choice. We have research currently underway that explores this possibility.

INHIBITION

Repeated practice in recalling some members of a category (e.g., apple, orange, pear; apple, orange, pear, etc.), impairs later recall of other members of that class (e.g., banana, strawberry, kiwi), but not members of other classes (e.g., dog, rabbit, giraffe). This observation is termed *retrieval induced forgetting* (RIF; Anderson, Bjork, & Bjork, 1994).[6] The notion is that repeated practice of some members of a class requires *inhibition* or suppression of unpracticed members of that category. Inhibition persists and prevents later recall of the unpracticed members. The result is that subjects are *less likely* to recall unpracticed items from practiced categories than items from non-practiced categories. Importantly, other categories are unaffected.

This idea once again assumes a network organization of memory that operates under principles of activation and inhibition. Such an inhibition account is dominant in other studies showing a decrement in performance, including studies on directed forgetting (Bjork, 1989; Bjork, Bjork, & Anderson, 1998), negative priming (e.g., Neill, 1977; Tipper, 1985; Tipper, Meegan, & Howard, 2002), and repetition blindness (Kanwisher, 1987, 1991; Kanwisher & Potter, 1990; Park & Kanwisher, 1994).

Such an inhibitory mechanism has been assumed by many investigators of consumer memory (e.g., Keller, 1991), although some use the terms "inhibition" or "suppression" and "interference" interchangeably (e.g., Burke & Srull, 1988; Jewell & Unnava, 2003; Kumar & Krishnan, 2004; Law, 2002; Unnava & Sirdeshmukh, 1994). The interference hypothesis however does not require the assumptions of a network organization. Rather, according to the interference hypothesis, performance in recalling category members will be facilitated to the extent that appropriate cues are available for accessing the traces, and will be impeded to the extent that the demands of the task are difficult. That is, while an inhibition account would predict that recall of unpracticed members are inaccessible; an interference account would predict that recall of unpracticed members are accessible, so long as the appropriate cues are provided during the test.

To demonstrate this point, Kronlund and Hughes (2005a) replicated the basic finding of RIF using eight categories.[7] After studying all eight category lists, half of the members from four of the categories were practiced; the other four categories were not practiced. We found that subjects were less likely to recall unpracticed items from the practiced categories than from the non-practiced categories.

The stimuli however, were chosen such that they could be subcategorized by a distinctive feature (e.g., red fruits vs. non-red fruits). In a subsequent study, the practiced members from the practiced categories were specifically grouped according to a feature (e.g., all non-red fruits were practiced). At test, we cued subjects with the feature (e.g., "Fruits that are red?") and were able to eliminate the effect: subjects were able to report unpracticed items from practiced categories. This finding suggests that the RIF effect is due to within-category interference.

To provide further evidence that the effect is not due to inhibition, in a subsequent study (Kronlund & Hughes, 2005b), we randomly assigned subjects to groups: one group was tested using the standard RIF procedures (i.e., all eight categories: four practiced, four unpracticed), a second group performed the procedure for six categories (three practiced categories, three unpracticed), and a third group performed the procedure for only four categories (two practiced categories, two unpracticed). Assignment of categories into conditions was randomly-determined, and was re-randomized for each subject. According to inhibition accounts, repeated practice of some members of a class requires inhibition of unpracticed members of that category, but not other categories. An inhibition account would predict that the amount of RIF found should not change as a function of the number of categories used. We found that the amount of RIF *decreased* as the number of categories tested decreased, suggesting between-category interference.

The results of Kronlund and Hughes (2005a, 2005b) demonstrate that a change in the way that stimuli are construed or characterized within the task can eliminate or enhance observed transfer. This point will be further demonstrated by the "mere exposure" studies described in the subsequent section. Kronlund and Hughes' results also highlight one final point: in contradiction of the neo-associationistic assumptions of accounts like the semantic/episodic distinction: the world does not consist of stable combinations of features that are available to be mapped into the mind of the prepared individual. Instead, consistent with the fundamental assumption of the SCAPE framework, the world consists of affordances and constraints; but is fundamentally ambiguous until the person supplies some particular organization of those features, based on past experience with similar stimuli, or the demands of the task, or the implications of the context.

THE IMPLICIT/EXPLICIT DICHOTOMY

Graf and Schacter (1985) proposed a distinction between implicit and explicit forms of memory as the fundamental dichotomy. The notion is that differential levels of consciousness are involved in performance, and that an implicit form of memory exists to account for effects of prior experience on current behavior in the absence of conscious awareness (e.g., effects observed in a priming task), whereas an explicit form of memory exists to account for behavior accompanied by conscious awareness (e.g., effects observed in a remembering task).

This dichotomy has been increasingly used as a theoretical framework by investigators of consumer memory (e.g., Krishnan & Shapiro, 1996; Lee, 2002). Lee (2002) introduced the implicit/explicit dichotomy as a means to evaluate exposure to brand names. She presented subjects with a list of brand names either in the context of a sentence (e.g., "He threw the case of Heineken in the truck of his car and drove off") or in isolation. After completing a distractor task, half of the subjects made a memory-based choice (i.e., subjects were presented with "beer" and asked which brand they would prefer be sold in a new store opening on campus) or a stimulus-based choice (i.e., they were asked to choose among two exemplars which brand of beer to stock). When presented in a sentence, the probability of brand choice for that brand was higher for the memory-based task than for the stimulus-based task, and the reverse occurred when the brand was presented in isolation. Lee concluded that such results demonstrate that "the effects of presentation context on conceptual and perceptual priming provide clear support that the two types of implicit memory are distinct constructs of memory" (p. 447), thus further subdividing implicit memory. She suggested that implicit memory tasks are superior to explicit tasks for measuring advertising effectiveness.

Another example of the use of the implicit-explicit dichotomy is in the *mere exposure effect* (Zajonc, 1968). The mere exposure effect is the observation that when pictures of the same category (e.g., chairs) are presented in rapid serial visual presentation (RSVP) format, recognition for items shown is at chance, but pleasantness ratings for items presented previously is above chance. This difference in awareness is thought to be due to different memory systems. The indirect test of preference is thought to be mediated by implicit memory; the direct test of recognition is thought to be mediated by explicit memory (Bornstein & D'Agostino, 1994; Schacter, 1990; Seamon, et al., 1995). The same applies to preference of brand names. "Mere exposure" to an ad or brand is thought to have an effect on fluency of processing of brands, such that brand choice and consideration-set membership can be affected (Nedungadi, 1990; Shapiro, 1999), and this is thought to be mediated by some form of automatic, spreading activation between hypothetical nodes in the brain, such that prior exposure of a brand or related brand facilitates processing of the target brand during brand choice or consideration-set.

FLUENCY AND THE MERE EXPOSURE EFFECT

In the case of the mere exposure effect, fluency of processing is thought to mediate increased ratings of liking, even in the absence of conscious recollection of the target stimulus (e.g., Bonnano & Stillings, 1986). The failure of reaching above chance levels in recognition is thought to be due to ineffective encoding of the stimuli caused by the rapid presentation of the items during the study phase (e.g., Bornstein & D'Agostino, 1994). However, a puzzle arises because fluency of processing also allows one to infer from the fluency of current performance to an earlier, perhaps in some cases hypothetical, experience of the stimulus and thus to make an effective remembering decision (Jacoby, Kelley, & Dywan, 1989). In fact, recognition memory results from either of two bases, *familiarity*, governed by fluent processing (e.g., Jacoby & Dallas, 1981), which is usually associated with the earlier global encoding of the stimulus, or *recollection*, governed by a remembering of details of a stimulus, which is associated with earlier, effective encoding of detailed elements of a stimulus (e.g., Mandler, 1991; see also Joordens & Hockley, 2000). Thus a paradox emerges: why is it that subjects are capable of using fluency as a basis for preference but not for recognition?

Whittlesea and Price (2001) attempted to disambiguate why the feeling of familiarity was not powerful enough to cause recognition ratings to be above chance in any previously examined mere exposure experiment. In their study, they first replicated the basic mere exposure effect. When subjects were asked to choose which of two items they preferred, they performed above chance in a preference judgment for items shown earlier, but were at chance on recognition for those items. They then performed two more experiments, one in which subjects were asked to choose which of two items globally resembled an item shown earlier, and one in which subjects were asked to choose which of two items they preferred and to justify their decision. In the former, subjects performed above chance at recognition, probably due to the non-analytical processing that they were required to do, which allowed them to experience and use fluency in their response. In the latter, subjects were at chance at preferring the old item, likely due to the now analytical processing that they were using, which prevented them from experiencing the fluency.

This demonstration shows the importance of thinking of memory not in terms of explicit and implicit systems, each only measurable by direct and indirect tests of performance, but rather as a unitary system, that uses different strategies which depend on the stimulus, task, and context. Memory uses the same set of knowledge and skill to perform a variety of tasks, including both remembering (recognition) and non-remembering (preference) tasks, using a variety of dimensions (e.g., analytic/non-analytic, specific/general, etc.). Whittlesea and Price's focus on types of processing used also explains mere exposure effects reported in the consumer literature (e.g., Nordhielm, 2002).

According to the separate systems account, awareness of the source of one's performance depends on the type of task one is performing, and the type of memory system (explicit or implicit) that that task accesses. In contrast, according to the SCAPE account, awareness of the source of performance is constructed through a process of generation, inference and attribution, in the same way that the performance itself is constructed. Explicit versus implicit is a description of the outcome of this process, not a description of the knowledge on which it is based or the process that controls performance and creates awareness. As illustrated in the next section, one consequence of this constructive process is that one can become aware of sources of performance that do not exist.

In the case of Lee (2002), the same applies. She highlighted the principles of elaboration and specificity. Her data reveal that the principle of TAP fully explains her data: the degree to which resources used for the given test match the resources used earlier (e.g., a memory-based task would rely on skills needed for generation, elaboration, and deeper processing—the same skills used when processing a brand in the context of a meaningful sentence as opposed to in isolation). There are yet other examples of dissociations that can be explained with the same principle (e.g., Janiszewski, 1993; Krishnan, 1999; Krishnan & Shapiro, 1996). Thus Lee's (2002) demonstration showed two dissociated *strategies*, not evidence for separate constructs of memory. This is often the case with research thought to provide test contexts which are believed to selectively tap into explicit and implicit memory systems. Those test contexts simply foster subjects in adopting different strategies which either facilitate or preclude them from experiencing priming. We submit that this is an important consideration for consumer researchers, who may simply be creating contexts which facilitate different processing strategies.

FLUENCY AND RECOGNITION

When subjects are able to experience fluency of processing, another problem arises when trying to interpret the meaning of the observation. Is it the absolute fluency of processing that is responsible for observable changes in performance? Or is it that subjects are responding to some type of perceived relative fluency? Said another way, are subjects able to form and use expectations about how fluent something ought to be? And then only if this expectation is met or exceeded respond a certain way?

The idea of fluency as a basis for recognition decisions was originally investigated by Jacoby and Dallas (1981). They performed a recognition experiment using low frequency (e.g., JANITOR) and high frequency (e.g., TABLE) words. At test, before making their recognition decision, subjects were required to make a tachistoscopic identification of each word; identification was used as an index of fluency of processing. Jacoby and Dallas observed that high-frequency words were processed more fluently than were low-frequency words. More importantly, prior experience enhanced the fluency of processing for the low-frequency words *more than* that of the high-frequency words. Further, they found that low-frequency words that were studied were more likely to be claimed "old" than high-frequency words which had been studied. Jacoby and Dallas suggested that subjects appeared to be impressed not by the absolute fluency of processing of a target item, but rather by the *relative* fluency of processing: subjects were impressed by the deviation between actual and expected fluency. Thus, relative fluency led to a feeling of familiarity.

Since Jacoby and Dallas' (1981) influential study, many investigators have observed similar effects of changes in fluency on recognition claims (e.g., Dewhurst & Hitch, 1997; Drummey & Newcombe, 1995; Higham & Vokey, 2000; Johnston, Hawley, & Elliott, 1991; Lindsay & Kelley,

1996; Luo, 1993; Masson & Macleod, 1996; Mayes & Gooding, 1997; Mulligan & Hirshman, 1995; Polson, Grabavac, & Parsons, 1997; Rajaram, 1993; Seamon, Luo, & Schwartz, 2002; Snodgrass, Hirshman, & Fan, 1996; Stark & McClelland, 2000; Ste-Marie, 1996; Verfaellie & Treadwell, 1993; Wippich & Mecklenbraeuker, 1994; Whittlesea & Leboe, 2000). The fluency-attribution idea has also been applied to understanding consumer behavior (e.g., Janiszewski, 1993; Janiszewski & Meyvis, 2001; Lee, 2002; Lee & Labroo, 2004).

There are two major problems with the above-mentioned studies as well as numerous other studies investigating fluency. First, unlike the procedure used by Jacoby and Dallas, the fluency manipulation in these studies was experimental: fluency was enhanced by some type of manipulation. The major disadvantage is that this minor procedural difference creates a confound: both absolute and relative fluency are enhanced, simultaneously, thus it is unclear which type of fluency is operating, and many investigators claim that it is the absolute type. Second, it seems illogical that the feeling of familiarity is created from absolute speed of processing. One's child, partner, friend, or even dog, although very fluently processed, never cause a feeling of "have I seen you before?" (Whittlesea & Williams, 1998).

This notion was investigated by Whittlesea and Williams (1998). They presented subjects with well-known words (e.g., TABLE), difficult to pronounce nonwords (e.g., LICTPUB) and easy to pronounce nonwords which were created from real words by changing one or more letters to create a nonword (e.g., HENSION). Each type of stimulus was studied for a memory test. During the test phase, subjects first named each word (to get an index of processing fluency) and then made a recognition decision on old and new stimuli of each category. The words (e.g., TABLE) were processed the most fluently (827ms), but were *not* associated with the most claims of "old." The HENSION items on the other hand, although processed less fluently than the words (988ms), produced the most false alarms (37% vs. 16% for the words).

Whittlesea and Williams (1998) reasoned that when reading the easy to pronounce nonwords surprise resulted from an unknown source that was wrongly attributed to the past. For example, when reading HENSION, subjects expected a meaningful word, but it was a nonword. It was the surprise associated with the mismatch between expectation and outcome which led to the feeling of familiarity. Said another way, the HENSION items were processed more fluently than could be expected for a nonword. This created the perception of discrepancy, leading to a feeling of familiarity. This study was replicated by Menon and Raghubir (2003) using the accessibility/ease of retrieval framework (see also Huber, 2004).

In this case, absolute fluency and relative fluency were not confounded, and though the regular words were processed more fluently than either of the nonwords, expected and actual fluency were matched. Whittlesea and Williams (2001a) proposed the *discrepancy-attribution hypothesis* which states that when there is a mismatch between expected and actual performance on a given stimulus in a given context (in this case, the test context), the perceived discrepancy is consciously experienced as the feeling of familiarity, and unconsciously attributed to a prior experience of that stimulus.

Whittlesea and Williams (2001a, 2001b) attempted to create and examine the perception of discrepancy using a different paradigm which consisted of probe items following a predictive sentence stem and a pause (e.g., "The stormy seas tossed the...BOAT"). Using this procedure during a test phase (targets in isolation during the study phase), subjects were more likely to claim "old" for probes following a predictive stem and pause as opposed to a predictive stem and no pause. In this case, the predictive stem was thought to create an expectation, the pause uncertainty, and the terminal word a surprising validation, similar to what occurs when waiting for the other shoe to drop.

When the subjects tried to identify the source of the surprise, their decision was based on the salient aspects of the stimulus (the semantic relationship of the stem and target), given the task and context. While subjects were focusing on the salient aspect of the task, they experienced the perception of discrepancy upon seeing the terminal probe. Knowing that they were in a recognition experiment, subjects unconsciously attributed the surprise to a prior experience of the target word, consciously experiencing the feeling of familiarity.

The perception of discrepancy occurs when outcomes either violate or validate expectations in a surprising way. Note that in the case of HENSION, a surprising violation occurred. Often this surprise occurs because the expectation is a constrained, indefinite one, so that the relationship between expectation and outcome is ambiguous (Whittlesea, 2002b). In support of this, Whittlesea and Williams (2001b) did not find increased false alarms for probes following a predictive stem and pause when subjects had to make recognition decisions on (a) probes that the subject generated as a completion to the stem, (b) probes following completely predictable stems (e.g., row, row, row, your GOAT), or (c) probes following completely predictable stems that are violated (e.g., row, row, row, your SHEEP).

This is not to say that absolute fluency, when unconfounded with relative fluency, is not associated with claims of familiarity. There are some cases in which people have been found to use absolute fluency to make judgments about self-alertness (Shimizu, Renaud & Whittlesea, 2006), aesthetic merit (Winkielman, Schwarz, Reber, & Fazendeiro, 2003), and nonwords (Whittlesea & Leboe, 2003).

Taken together, the evidence seems to suggest that people will only use the absolute fluency of performance to make remembering decisions when that is the only possible source of information, that is, when they cannot easily create and use expectations about the normative fluency for the target item. The evidence also seems to suggest that people invariably use the perception of discrepancy rather than absolute fluency for most decisions related to the feeling of familiarity.

A case in the consumer behavior literature whereby it is not clear whether subjects are responding to absolute or relative fluency was the study by Lee and Labroo (2004). They used Whittlesea's (1993) sentence stem paradigm to create conceptually fluent processing of words. They presented words in the context of predictive (e.g., the woman soaked the white sweater in some cold *water*) or non-predictive (e.g., the woman looked out of the window and saw the *water*) sentence stems. Another manipulation they used was presenting the target word as the same (water), related (drink), or unrelated word (house) immediately following the sentence. It was expected that the productiveness of the stem and the similarity of the target to the last word in the sentence that would both effect conceptual fluency, and that the repetition status would effect perceptual fluency. Results revealed that pleasantness ratings were higher for words in the predictive versus the non-predictive context and the related versus unrelated target words. This finding was the basis for later examining, and replicating, these effects with consumer products. It may be the relative fluency that is the basis of changes in attitudes or changes in pleasantness ratings in Lee and Labroo's (2004) study.

REMEMBERING

The above-chance pleasantness and recognition judgments observed in the "mere exposure" experiments reported earlier likely occurred because prior exposure caused the old member of test pairs to be processed with greater fluency than the novel member (i.e., repetition priming), at least when subjects performed nonanalytically. That is, these subjects appear to have used a simple decision heuristic such as "if fluent then old/pleasant" (cf., Jacoby & Whitehouse, 1989). However, the evaluation process that leads to a subjective reaction can be considerably more complex than that. Whittlesea and his colleagues (e.g., Kronlund & Whittlesea, 2005; Kronlund & Whittlesea, 2006;

Whittlesea, 2002b, 2004; Whittlesea & Leboe, 2003; Whittlesea & Williams, 2001a, 2001b) investigated the source of the feeling of familiarity. They concluded that people chronically examine their cognitive and perceptual processing at a variety of levels, attempting to integrate various aspects of that processing with other aspects (the "evaluation" function of mind described earlier). In doing so, they come to one of four primitive conclusions, or perceptions, about their current processing: *coherence* (well-formedness), *incongruity* (wrongness), *discrepancy* (strangeness), or *integrality* (predictability or unity). These primitive perceptions are not usually experienced consciously. Instead, they are further interpreted under some intuitive theory of cause and effect, and within the implications of salient aspects of the task, stimulus and context; this extended interpretation gives rise to some specific subjective reaction, such as a feeling of pleasantness, interest, or familiarity.

The perception of coherence occurs when all aspects of the current experience seem to fit well with others; the chief reaction to that perception is to accept the current processing event and move on. The perception of incongruity occurs when some aspect of current processing is clearly inconsistent with others, for example when a speech error is made or when stimulus elements conflict semantically or at some other level (e.g., on reading "The hunter sat quietly on the dog"). The chief reaction to the perception of incongruity is to stop processing the inflow of environmental stimuli and to focus on the source of the incongruity, resulting in error correction.

In contrast, the latter two perceptions can sponsor strong feelings of familiarity or remembering. The perception of discrepancy appears to occur when an indefinite expectation is surprisingly validated (Whittlesea & Williams, 2001b) The perception of discrepancy does not always cause illusory feelings of remembering, however; the errors committed by subjects experiencing this perception simply reveal the common mechanism whereby such feelings are aroused (i.e., the feelings contribute as much to hits as to false alarms); perception is probably primarily responsible for weak or powerful feelings of familiarity that occur without actually recalling the target event (i.e., without becoming aware of the distinctive context of the earlier event). Finally, the perception of integrality sponsors more extensive and specific claims of remembering. That perception, however, appears to occur when a *definite expectation* is validated by a consistent outcome (Kronlund & Whittlesea, 2006; Whittlesea, 2002a).

The conclusions that remembering occurs indirectly, through adopting an attitude to a production rather than directly through retrieval, and that the feelings of remembering that produce this attitude occur through a heuristic process of evaluation and inference, may seem extreme given the limited evidence presented here. However, both patterns of effects have been replicated repeatedly and subjected to all manner of convergent tests (cf. Kronlund, 2006; Kronlund & Whittlesea, 2006; Whittlesea & Williams, 1998, 2000; Leboe & Whittlesea, 2002; Whittlesea, 2002b, 2004). They suggest two quite different routes to a feeling of remembering, one based on surprise caused by the validation of an indefinite expectation aroused on the fly, the other based on the validation of a definite expectation laid down by prior specific experience. However, they share the same basic principles: in chronically evaluating their productions, people attempt to make what sense they can of the significance of apparent fit or lack of fit of the components of the current experience. They make inferences about the causes of the primitive perceptions aroused by different experiences, and make attributions to plausible sources.

CONCLUSIONS AND FUTURE DIRECTIONS

We have presented a small part of the data on which the SCAPE framework is based. However, the variety of evidence presented demonstrates that that account can make predictions about performance in both "episodic" and "semantic" tasks, through a single set of underlying principles: construction, with its corollary sub-functions of production and evaluation. This evidence is at least challenging for proponents of separate-systems accounts: it requires them to provide functional explanations at a deeper level than "there are two kinds of knowledge, and therefore two memory systems specialized to deal with them."

In re-evaluating their functional analysis, we would hope that researchers will listen to the wisdom of the user of memory. Such sensible statements as "I used to *know* his name, but I can't *remember* it now" reveal clearly some of the functional significance of such categories to the user: "know" means easy and fluent use of the past, with emphasis on *use* of the knowledge for some other purpose, rather than its accessibility; whereas "remember" means reflective use of the past, with focus on the act of making contact with the past. We submit that such functional analysis is essential, and cannot be replaced by neuropsychological investigations of correspondences between gross tasks and areas of brain activation. For example, Elliot and Dolan (1998) conducted a standard "mere exposure" study, and obtained the usual behavioral results (preference judgments biased toward old items, but recognition at chance). They also recorded brain activity via fMRI. They observed that the preference task was associated with right lateral prefrontal activity, whereas recognition was associated with left frontopolar and parietal activity. They concluded that that observation gave physiological support to the explicit/implicit memory dichotomy, indicating the anatomical distinctness of the subsystems responsible for the two behaviors. However, given the evidence above that the usual results of such studies come about through encouraging analytic versus non-analytic processing rather than two separate memory systems, the meaning of the fMRI data becomes much more difficult to interpret.

Our major point is thus simply this: one cannot *assume* that one knows the functions of memory; and no amount of physiological correlations will corroborate those assumptions. Instead, a more thorough task analysis is required, using convergent operations and broad examinations of dissociations and correspondences across widely different kinds of task.

Concepts of memory are continually molded and shaped by empirical findings and researchers' interpretations of those findings. Although the fundamental concepts of memory tend to change very slowly, conceptual changes do nonetheless occur. Almost no attention has been paid, however, to ensuring that we understand the similarities and differences among the terms, concepts, and assumptions related to memory. One frequent source of confusion lies in the use of one and the same term (e.g., priming) to refer to different concepts. Another common source of confusion is the use of different terms to refer to the same construct (e.g., fluency, accessibility, ease of retrieval[8]). It is our position that the lack of an effort by researchers to consider and weigh the conceptual similarities and differences among memory theories and studies has hampered our understanding of consumer memory. In this chapter, we elucidate some of the problems with the contemporary memory theories and the studies that implicitly or explicitly build on those theories. By doing so, we seek to encourage consumer researchers to place greater emphasis on conceptual clarity that will lead to meaningful advances in our understanding about consumer memory.

NOTES

1. A notable exception is the constructive view of consumer decision making posited by Bettman, Luce, and Payne (1998).
2. Note similarities between assumptions of SCAPE and Schwarz (2004), although see Huber (2004).
3. Readers interested in a critique of the procedural/declarative dichotomy may wish to examine Whittlesea (2002a).
4. Although distinct, the concept of activation is often used interchangeably with conceptual fluency (e.g., Lee, 2002; Lee & Labroo, 2004; Shapiro, 1999; see section on Fluency and Recognition below).
5. The term *priming* was originally used by Meyer & Schvaneveldt (1971) to describe facilitation in lexical decision of a word when that word is preceded by a meaningfully related word. The proposed mechanism for the effect at the time was "forward acting" spreading activation. We find that today, 35 years

later, people confuse mechanism with observation: facilitation in processing, however observed, can result from backward-acting TAP, through the use of matched resources, etc. (see the discussion of Whittlesea & Jacoby, 1990, and Hughes & Whittlesea, 2003, below).

6. Although this effect, and the notion of inhibition, has spurred further investigation by many psychologists since 1994, the effect itself, as well as the mechanism of inhibition, was actually discussed in 1985, by Alba and Chattopadhyay. They argued that both the retrieval practice, and the act of recall, cause inhibition. Their paper was not cited in 1994 by Anderson et al., or by any investigators who have cited Anderson's work. Interestingly, those who have cited Alba and Chattopadhyay's (1985) article since 1994 appear to not have cited the work of Anderson et al. (1994).

7. For the studies described here, Kronlund and Hughes (2005) used categories such as animals, fish, etc., however in other studies, they replicated their basic findings with brand name categories such as soda and shampoo.

8. A notable exception is Schwarz (2004) who distinguishes between fluency and accessibility and provides many consumer psychological examples. He also distinguishes between accessible content and accessibility experiences. Consistent with the implications of the SCAPE model, Schwarz (2004) emphasizes the importance of implicit theories for linking experiences and inferences.

REFERENCES

Aaker, D. A. (1991). *Managing brand equity: Capitalizing on the value of a brand name.* New York: The Free Press.

Alba, J. W., & Chattopadhyay, A. (1985). Effects of context and part-category cues on recall of competing brands. *Journal of Marketing Research, 22,* 340–349.

Alba, J. W., Hutchinson, J. W., & Lynch, Jr., J. G. (1991). Memory and decision making. In T. S. Robertson and H. H. Kassarjian (Eds.), *Handbook of Consumer Behavior* (pp. 1–49). Englewood Cliffs, NJ: Prentice-Hall.

Anderson, J. R. (1976). *Language, memory and thought.* Hillside, NJ: Erlbaum.

Anderson, J. R. (1980). *Cognitive psychology and its implications.* San Francisco, CA: W. H. Freeman.

Anderson, J. R. (1983). A spreading activation theory of memory. *Journal of Verbal Learning and Verbal Behavior, 22,* 261–295.

Anderson, J. R., & Bower, G. H. (1973). *Human associative memory.* Washington, DC: Winston & Sons.

Anderson, M. M. C., Bjork, R. A., & Bjork E. L. (1994). Remembering can cause forgetting: Retrieval dynamics in long-term memory. *Journal of Experimental Psychology: Learning, Memory, & Cognition, 20,* 1063–1087.

Bartlett, F. C. (1932). *Remembering.* Cambridge: Cambridge University Press.

Becker, S., Moscovitch, M., Behrmann, M., & Joordens, S. (1997). Long-term semantic priming: A computational account and empirical evidence. *Journal of Experimental Psychology: Learning, Memory, & Cognition, 23,* 1059–1082.

Bentin, S., & Feldman, L. (1990). The contribution of morphologic and semantic relatedness to repetition priming at short and long lags: Evidence from Hebrew. *Quarterly Journal of Experimental Psychology, 42A,* 693–711.

Bettman, J. R., Luce, M. F., & Payne, J. W. (1998). Constructive consumer choice processes. *Journal of Consumer Research, 25,* 187–217.

Bjork, R. A. (1989). Retrieval inhibition as an adaptive mechanism in human memory. In H. L. Roediger III & F. I. M. Craik (Eds.), *Varieties of memory and consciousness: Essays in honour of Endel Tulving* (pp. 309–330). Hillsdale, NJ: Erlbaum.

Bjork, E. L., Bjork, R. A., & Anderson, M. C. (1998). Varieties of goal-directed forgetting. In J. M. Golding & C. M. MacLeod (Eds.), *Intentional forgetting: Interdisciplinary approaches* (pp. 103–137). Mahwah, NJ: Erlbaum.

Bonnano, G. A., & Stillings, N. A. (1986). Preference, familiarity and recognition after repeated brief exposures to random geometric shapes. *American Journal of Psychology, 99,* 403–415.

Bornstein, R. F., & D'Agostino, P. R. (1994). The attribution and discounting of perceptual fluency: Preliminary tests of a perceptual fluency/attributional model of the mere exposure effect. *Social Cognition, 12,* 103–128.

Borowsky, R., & Besner, D. (1993). Visual word recognition: A multi-stage activation model. *Journal of Experimental Psychology: Learning, Memory, & Cognition, 19,* 813–840.

Braun-LaTour, K., LaTour, M. S., Pickrell, J. E., & Loftus, E. F. (2004). How and when advertising can influence memory for consumer experience. *Journal of Advertising, 33*, 7–25.

Brooks, L. R. (1978). Non-analytic concept formation and memory for instances. In E. H. Rosch & B. B. Lloyd (Eds.), *Cognition and categorization* (pp. 169–211). Hillsdale, NJ: Erlbaum.

Brooks, L. R. (1987). Decentralized control of categorization: The role of prior processing episodes. In U. Neisser (Ed.), *Concepts and conceptual development: Ecological and intellectual factors in categorization* (pp. 141–174). Cambridge: Cambridge University Press.

Burke, R. R., & Srull, T. K. (1988). Competitive interference and consumer memory for advertising, *Journal of Consumer Research, 15*, 55–68.

Chumbley, J. I., & Balota, D. A. (1984). A word's meaning affects the decision in lexical decision. *Memory & Cognition, 12*, 590–606.

Cohen, N. J., & Squire, L. R. (1980). Preserved learning and retention of pattern-analyzing skill in amnesia: Dissociation of knowing what and knowing how. *Science, 210*, 207–210.

Collins, A. M., & Loftus, E. F. (1975). A spreading-activation theory of semantic processing. *Psychological Review, 82*, 407–428.

Collins, A. M., & Quillian, M. R. (1969). Retrieval time from semantic memory. *Journal of Verbal Learning and Verbal Behavior, 8*, 240–247.

Crowley, E., & Mitchell, A. A. (2003). The moderating effect of product knowledge on the learning and organization of product information. *Journal of Consumer Research, 30*, 443–454.

Dewhurst, S. A., & Hitch, G. J. (1997). Illusions of familiarity caused by cohort activation. *Psychonomic Bulletin & Review, 4*, 566–571.

Dienes, Z., & Berry, D. (1997). Implicit learning: Below the subjective threshold. *Psychonomic Bulletin & Review, 4*, 1–23.

Drummey, A. B., & Newcombe, N. (1995). Remembering versus knowing the past: Children's explicit and implicit memories for pictures. *Journal of Experimental Child Psychology, 59*, 549–565.

Dulany, D. E., Carlson, R. A., & Dewey, G. I. (1984). A case of syntactical learning and judgment: How conscious and how abstract? *Journal of Experimental Psychology: General, 113*, 541–555.

Elliot, R. & Dolan, R. J. (1998). Neural response during preference and memory judgments for subliminally presented stimuli: a functional neuroimaging study. *Journal of Neuroscience, 18*, 4697–4704.

Feldman J. M., & Lynch, Jr., J. G. (1988). Self-generated validity and other effects of measurement on belief, attitude, intention and behavior. *Journal of Applied Psychology, 73*, 421–435.

Fitzsimons, G. J., Hutchinson, J. W., Williams, P, Alba, J. W., Huber, J., Kardes, F. R., Menon, G., Raghubir, P., Russo, J. E., Shiv, B., & Tavassoli, N. T. (2002). Non-conscious influences on consumer choice. *Marketing Letters, 13*, 269–279.

Graf, P., & Schacter, D. L. (1985). Implicit and explicit memory for new associations in normal and amnesic subjects. *Journal of Experimental Psychology: Learning, Memory, and Cognition, 11*, 501–518.

Gurhan-Canli, Z. (2003). The effect of expected variability of product quality and attribute uniqueness on family brand evaluations. *Journal of Consumer Research, 30*, 105–115.

Higham, P. A., & Vokey, J. R. (2000). Judgment heuristics and recognition memory: Prime identification and target-processing fluency. *Memory & Cognition, 28*, 575–584.

Huber, J. (2004). A comment on metacognitive experiences and consumer choice. *Journal of Consumer Psychology, 14*, 356–359.

Hughes, A. D., & Whittlesea, B. W. A. (2003). Long-term semantic transfer: An overlapping-operations account. *Memory & Cognition, 31*, 401–411.

Hutchinson, J. W., Kalyan R., & Mantrala, M. (1994). Finding choice alternatives in memory: Probability models of brand name recall. *Journal of Marketing Research, 31*, 441–461.

Jacoby, L. L., & Brooks, L. R. (1984). Nonanalytic cognition: Memory, perception and concept formation. *Psychology of Learning and Motivation, 18*, 1–47.

Jacoby, L. L., & Dallas, M. (1981). On the relationship between autobiographical memory and perceptual learning. *Journal of Experimental Psychology: General, 110*, 306–340.

Jacoby, L. L., Kelley, C. M., & Dywan, J. (1989). Memory attributions. In H. L. Roediger and F. I. M. Craik (Eds,), *Varieties of memory and consciousness: Essays in honor of Endel Tulving* (pp. 391–422). Hillsdale, NJ: Erlbaum.

Janiszewski, C. (1993). Preattentive mere exposure effects. *Journal of Consumer Research, 20*, 376–392.

Janiszewski, C., Noel, H., & Sawyer, A. G. (2003). A meta-analysis of the spacing effect in verbal learning: Implications for research on advertising repetition and consumer memory. *Journal of Consumer Research, 30*, 138–149.

Janiszewski, C., & Meyvis, T. (2001). Effects of brand logo complexity, repetition, and spacing on processing fluency and judgment. *Journal of Consumer Research, 28,* 18–32.

Jewell, R. D., & Unnava, H. R. (2003). When competitive interference can be beneficial. *Journal of Consumer Research, 30,* 283–291.

Johnston, W. A., Hawley, K. J., & Elliott, J. M. (1991). Contribution of perceptual fluency to recognition judgments. *Journal of Experimental Psychology: Learning, Memory, & Cognition, 17,* 210–223.

Joordens, S., & Besner, D. (1992). Priming effects that span an intervening unrelated word: Implications for models of memory representation and retrieval. *Journal of Experimental Psychology: Learning, Memory, & Cognition, 18,* 483–491.

Kanwisher, N. G. (1987). Repetition blindness: Type recognition without token individuation. *Cognition, 27,* 117–143.

Kanwisher, N. G. (1991). Repetition blindness and illusory conjunctions: Errors in binding visual types with visual tokens. *Journal of Experimental Psychology: Human Perception & Performance, 17,* 404–421.

Kanwisher, N. G., & Potter, M. C. (1990). Repetition blindness: Levels of processing. *Journal of Experimental Psychology: Human Perception & Performance, 16,* 30–47.

Kardes, F. R. (1994). Consumer judgment and decision processes. In R. S. Wyer, Jr. & T. K. Srull (Eds.), *Handbook of social cognition* (pp. 399–466). Hillside, NJ: Erlbaum.

Keller, K. L. (1993). Conceptualizing, measuring, and managing customer-based brand equity. *Journal of Marketing, 57,* 1–22.

Keller, K. L. (1998). Brand knowledge structures. In K. L. Keller (Ed.), *Strategic brand management: Building, measuring, and managing brand equity* (pp. 86–129). Upper Saddle River, NJ: Prentice Hall.

Kelly, S. W., Burton, A. M., Kato, T., & Akamatsu, S. (2001). Incidental learning of real-world regularities. *Psychological Science, 12,* 86–89.

Kisielius, J., & Sternthal, B. (1986). Examining the vividness controversy: An availability-valence interpretation. *Journal of Consumer Research, 12,* 418–431.

Kolers, P. A. (1973). Remembering operations. *Memory & Cognition, 1,* 347–355.

Kolers, P. A. (1976). Reading a year later. *Memory & Cognition, 2,* 554–565.

Kolers, P. A., & Smythe, W. E. (1984). Symbol manipulation: Alternatives to the computational view. *Journal of Verbal Learning and Verbal Behavior, 21,* 289–314.

Knowlton, B. J., & Squire, L. R. (1994). The information acquired during artificial grammar learning. *Journal of Experimental Psychology: Learning, Memory, and Cognition, 20,* 79–91.

Krishnan, H. S., & Shapiro, S. (1996). Comparing implicit and explicit memory for brand names from advertisements. *Journal of Experimental Psychology: Applied, 2,* 147–163.

Kronlund, A. (2006). *Remembering words and brand names after the perception of discrepancy.* Dissertation Abstracts International, Simon Fraser University.

Kronlund, A., & Hughes, A. D. (2005a). *Retrieval Induced Forgetting: Release from Interference.* Banff Annual Seminar in Cognitive Science, Banff, AB.

Kronlund, A., & Hughes, A. D. (2005b). *Retrieval Induced Forgetting: Release from Interference.* Northwest Cognition and Memory Conference, Bellingham, WA.

Kronlund, A., & Whittlesea, B. W. A. (2006). Remembering after a perception of discrepancy: Out with the old, in with the two. *Journal of Experimental Psychology: Learning, Memory, & Cognition, 32,* 1174–1184.

Kronlund, A., & Whittlesea, B. W. A. (2005). Seeing double: Levels of processing can cause false memory. *Canadian Journal of Experimental Psychology, 59,* 11–16.

Kumar, A., & Krishnan, S. (2004). Memory interference in advertising: A replication and extension. *Journal of Consumer Research, 30,* 602–611.

Law, S. (2002). Can repeating a brand claim lead to memory confusion? The effects of claim similarity and concurrent repetition. *Journal of Marketing Research, 39,* 366–378.

Leboe, J. P., & Whittlesea, B. W. A. (2002). The inferential basis of familiarity and recall: Evidence for a common underlying process. *Journal of Memory and Language, 46,* 804–829.

Lee, A. Y. (2002). Effects of implicit memory on memory-based versus stimulus-based brand choice. *Journal of Marketing Research, 39,* 440–454.

Lee, A. Y., & Labroo, A. (2004). Effects of conceptual and perceptual fluency on affective judgment. *Journal of Marketing Research, 41,* 151–165.

Lindsay, D. S., & Kelley, C. M. (1996). Creating illusions of familiarity in a cued recall remember/know paradigm. *Journal of Memory and Language, 35,* 197–211.

Loftus, E. F. (1979). The malleability of human memory. *American Scientist, 67,* 312–320.

Loftus, E. F., & Palmer, J. C. (1974). Reconstruction of automobile destruction: An example of the interaction between language and memory. *Journal of Verbal Learning & Verbal Behavior, 13*, 585–589.

Luo, C. R. (1993). Enhanced feeling of recognition: Effects of identifying and manipulating test items on recognition memory. *Journal of Experimental Psychology: Learning, Memory, and Cognition, 19*, 405–413.

Lynch, Jr., J. G., & Srull, T. (1982). Memory and attentional factors in consumer choice: Concepts and research methods. *Journal of Consumer Research, 9*, 18–37.

Marcel, A. J. (1983). Conscious and unconscious perception: An approach to the relations between phenomenal experience and perceptual processes. *Cognitive Psychology, 15*, 238–300.

Masson, M. E. J. (1995). A distributed memory model of semantic priming. *Journal of Experimental Psychology: Leaning, Memory, and Cognition, 21*, 3–23.

Masson, M. E. J., & MacLeod, C. M. (1992). Re-enacting the route to interpretation: Enhanced perceptual identification without prior perception. *Journal of Experimental Psychology: General, 121*, 145–176.

Masson, M. E. J., & Macleod, C. M. (1996). Contributions of processing fluency to repetition effects in masked word identification. *Canadian Journal of Experimental Psychology, 50*, 9–21.

Mayes, A. R., & Gooding, P. A. van E. (1997). A new theoretical framework for explicit and implicit memory. *Psyche: An Interdisciplinary Journal of Research on Consciousness, 3*. Available at http://psyche. cs.monash.edu.au/

McGeorge, P., & Burton, A. M. (1990). Semantic processing in an incidental learning task. *Quarterly Journal of Experimental Psychology: Human Experimental Psychology, 42*, 597–609.

McGill, A. L., & Anand, P. (1989). The effect of vivid attributes on the evaluation of alternatives: The role of differential attention and cognitive elaboration. *Journal of Consumer Research, 16*, 188–196.

McNamara, T. P. (1992). Theories of priming: I. Associative distance and lag. *Journal of Experimental Psychology: Learning, Memory, & Cognition, 18*, 1173–1190.

Medin, D. L., & Schaffer, M. M. (1978). Context theory of classification learning. *Psychological Review, 85*, 207–238.

Menon, G., & Raghubir, P. (2003). Ease-of-retrieval as an automatic input in judgments: A mere-accessibility framework? *Journal of Consumer Research, 30*, 230–243.

Meyer, D. E., & Schvaneveldt, R. W. (1971). Facilitation in recognizing pairs of words: Evidence of a dependence between retrieval operations. *Journal of Experimental Psychology, 90*, 227–234.

Meyvis, T., & Janiszewski, C. (2004).When are broader brands stronger brands? An accessibility perspective on the success of brand extensions. *Journal of Consumer Research, 31*, 346–357.

Morrin, M., & Ratneshwar, S. (2003). Does it make sense to use scents to enhance brand memory? *Journal of Marketing Research, 40*, 10–25.

Morris, C. D., Bransford, J. D., & Franks, J. J. (1977). Levels of processing versus transfer-appropriate processing. *Journal of Verbal Learning and Verbal Behavior, 16*, 519–533.

Mulligan, N., & Hirshman, E. (1995). Speed-accuracy trade-offs and the dual process model of recognition memory. *Journal of Memory & Language, 34*, 1–18.

Neal, A. & Hesketh, B. (1997). Episodic knowledge and implicit learning. *Psychonomic Bulletin & Review, 4*, 24–37.

Nedungadi, P. (1990). Recall and consumer consideration sets: Influencing choice without altering brand evaluations. *Journal of Consumer Research, 17*, 263–276.

Neely, J. H. (1977). Semantic priming and retrieval from lexical memory: Roles of inhibitionless spreading activation and limited capacity attention. *Journal of Experimental Psychology: General, 106*, 226–254.

Neely, J. H. (1991). Semantic priming effects in visual word recognition: A selective review of current findings and theories. In D. Besner & G. W. Humphreys (Eds.), *Basic processes in reading: Visual word recognition* (pp. 264–336). Hillside, NJ: Erlbaum.

Neill, W. T. (1977). Inhibitory and facilitatory processes in selective attention. *Journal of Experimental Psychology: Human Perception & Performance, 3*, 444–450.

Nordhielm, C. L. (2002). The influence of level of processing on advertising repetition effects. *Journal of Consumer Research, 29*, 371–382.

Paap, K. R., & Noel, R. W. (1991). Dual-route models of print to sound: Still a good horse-race. *Psychological Research, 53*, 13–24.

Park, J. W., & Hastak, M. (1994). Memory-based product judgments: Effects of involvement at encoding and retrieval. *Journal of Consumer Research, 21*, 534–547.

Park, J., & Kanwisher, N. G. (1994). Determinants of repetition blindness. *Journal of Experimental Psychology: Human Perception & Performance, 20*, 500–519.

Peracchio, L. A., & Tybout, A. M. (1996). The moderating role of prior knowledge in schema-based product evaluation. *Journal of Consumer Research, 23,* 177–192.

Perruchet, P., & Pacteau, C. (1991). Synthetic grammar learning: Implicit rule abstraction or explicit fragmentary knowledge? *Journal of Experimental Psychology: General, 119,* 264–275.

Polson, D. A. D., Grabavac, D. M., & Parsons, J. A. (1997). Intraverbal stimulus-response reversibility: Fluency, familiarity effects, and implications for stimulus equivalence. *Analysis of Verbal Behavior, 14,* 19–40.

Rajaram, S. (1993). Remembering and knowing: Two means of access to the personal past. *Memory & Cognition, 21,* 89–102.

Ratcliff, R., & McKoon, G. (1988). A retrieval theory of priming in memory. *Psychological Review, 95,* 385–408.

Reber, A. S. (1989). Implicit learning and tacit knowledge. *Journal of Experimental Psychology: General, 118,* 219–235.

Reber, A. S. (1993). *Implicit learning and tacit knowledge: An essay on the cognitive unconscious.* New York: Oxford University Press.

Reber, A. S. & Allen, R. (1978). Analogic and abstraction strategies in synthetic grammar learning: A functionalist interpretation. *Cognition, 6,* 193–221.

Roedder-John, D., & Sujan, M. (1990). Age differences in product categorization. *Journal of Consumer Research, 16,* 452–460.

Roediger, H. L., & Challis, B. H. (1992). Effects of exact repetition and conceptual repetition on free recall and primed word fragment completion. *Journal of Experimental Psychology: Learning, Memory, & Cognition, 18,* 3–14.

Rosch, E. H. (1978). Principles of categorization. In E. H. Rosch & B. B. Lloyd (Eds.), *Cognition and categorization* (pp. 27–48). Hillsdale, NJ: Erlbaum.

Ruekl, J. G. (1990). Similarity effects in word and pseudoword repetition priming, *Journal of Experimental Psychology: Learning, Memory, & Cognition, 16,* 374–391.

Scarborough, D. L., Cortese, C., & Scarborough, H. S. (1977). Frequency and repetition effects in lexical memory. *Journal of Experimental Psychology: Human Perception & Performance, 3,* 1–17.

Schacter, D. L. (1990). Perceptual representation systems and implicit memory: Toward a resolution of the multiple memory systems debate. In A. Diamond (Ed.), *Development and neural bases of higher cognitive functions. Annals of the New York Academy of Sciences, 608,* 543–571.

Schwarz, N. (2004). Metacognitive experiences in consumer judgment and decision making. *Journal of Consumer Psychology, 14,* 332–348.

Seamon, J. G., Luo, C. R., & Schwartz, M. A. (2002). Repetition can have similar or different effects on accurate and false recognition. *Journal of Memory & Language, 46,* 323–340.

Seamon, J. G., Williams, P. C., Crowley, M. J., Kim, I. J., Langer, S. A., Orne, P. J., & Wishengrad, D. L. (1995). The mere exposure effect is based on implicit memory: Effects of stimulus type, encoding conditions, and number of exposures on recognition and affect judgments. *Journal of Experimental Psychology: Learning, Memory and Cognition, 21,* 711–721.

Shanks, D. R., & St. John, M. F. (1994). Characteristics of dissociable human learning systems. *Behavioral and Brain Sciences, 17,* 367–395.

Shapiro, S. (1999). When an ad's influence is beyond our conscious control: Perceptual and conceptual fluency effects caused by incidental ad exposure. *Journal of Consumer Research, 26,* 16–36.

Shapiro, S., MacInnis, D. J., & Heckler, S. E. (1997). The effects of incidental ad exposure on the formation of consideration sets. *Journal of Consumer Research, 24,* 94–104.

Shimizu, Y., Renaud, M., & Whittlesea, B. W. A. (2006). *The attributional basis of judgments of self-alertness.* Unpublished manuscript.

Snodgrass, J. G., Hirshman, E., & Fan, J. (1996). The sensory match effect in recognition memory: Perceptual fluency or episodic trace? *Memory & Cognition, 24,* 367–383.

Stark, C. E. L., & McClelland, J. L. (2000). Repetition priming of words, pseudowords, and nonwords. *Journal of Experimental Psychology: Learning, Memory, & Cognition, 26,* 945–972.

Ste-Marie, D. M. (1996). International bias in gymnastic judging: Conscious or unconscious influences? *Perceptual & Motor Skills, 83,* 963–975.

Tipper, S. P. (1985). The negative priming effect: Inhibitory priming by ignored objects. *Quarterly Journal of Experimental Psychology: Human Experimental Psychology, 37,* 571–590,

Tipper, S. P., Meegan, D., & Howard, L. A. (2002). Action-centered negative priming: Evidence for reactive inhibition. *Visual Cognition, 9*, 591–614.

Tulving, E. (1983). *Elements of episodic memory.* Oxford: Clarendon Press.

Tulving, E. (1985). How many memory systems are there? *American Psychologist, 40*, 385–398.

Tulving, E., Schacter, D. L., & Stark, H. A. (1982). Priming effects in word-fragment completion are independent of recognition memory. *Journal of Experimental Psychology: Learning, Memory, & Cognition, 8*, 336–342.

Unnava, H. R., & Sirdeshmukh, D. (1994). Reducing competitive ad interference. *Journal of Marketing Research, 31*, 403–411.

Verfaellie, M., & Treadwell, J. R. (1993). Status of recognition memory in amnesia. *Neuropsychology, 7*, 5–13.

Vokey, J. R., & Brooks, L. R. (1992). The salience of item knowledge in learning artificial grammars. *Journal of Experimental Psychology: Learning, Memory, and Cognition, 18*, 328–344.

Wagner, L., & Kronlund, A. (2005). False memories of brand names. Northwest Cognition and Memory Conference, Bellingham, WA.

Walker, N. (1986). Direct retrieval from elaborated memory traces. *Memory & Cognition, 14*, 321–328.

Warrington, E. K., & Weiskrantz, L. (1970). The amnesic syndrome: consolidation or retrieval? *Nature, 228*, 628–630.

Whittlesea, B. W. A. (1993). Illusions of familiarity. *Journal of Experimental Psychology: Learning, Memory, and Cognition, 19*, 1235–1253.

Whittlesea, B. W. A. (1997). Production, evaluation and preservation of experiences: Constructive processing in remembering and performance tasks. In D. L. Medin (Ed.), *The Psychology of Learning and Motivation, 37*, 211–264. New York: Academic Press.

Whittlesea, B. W. A. (2002a). On the construction of behavior and subjective experience: The production and evaluation of performance. In J. Bowers & C. Marsolek (Eds.), *Rethinking Implicit Memory* (pp. 239–260). Oxford: Oxford University Press.

Whittlesea, B. W. A. (2002b). Two routes to remembering (and another to remembering not). *Journal of Experimental Psychology: General, 131*, 325–348.

Whittlesea, B. W. A., & Dorken, M. D. (1993). Incidentally, things in general are particularly determined: An episodic-processing account of implicit learning. *Journal of Experimental Psychology: General, 122*, 227–248.

Whittlesea, B. W. A., & Dorken, M. D. (1997). Implicit learning: Indirect, not unconscious. *Psychonomic Bulletin & Review, 4*, 63–67.

Whittlesea, B. W. A., & Jacoby, L. L. (1990). Interaction of prime repetition with visual degradation: Is priming a retrieval phenomenon? *Journal of Memory and Language, 29*, 546–565.

Whittlesea, B. W. A., & Leboe, J. P. (2000). The heuristic basis of remembering and classification: Fluency, generation and resemblance. *Journal of Experimental Psychology: General, 129*, 84–106.

Whittlesea, B. W. A., & Leboe, J. P. (2003). Two fluency heuristics (and how to tell them apart). *Journal of Memory and Language, 49*, 62–79.

Whittlesea, B. W. A., & Williams, L. D. (1998). Why do strangers feel familiar, but friends don't? A discrepancy-attribution account of feelings of familiarity. *Act Psychologica, 98*, 141–146.

Whittlesea, B. W. A., & Williams, L. D. (2001a). The discrepancy-attribution hypothesis I: The heuristic basis of feelings of familiarity. *Journal of Experimental Psychology: Learning, Memory, and Cognition, 27*, 3–13.

Whittlesea, B. W. A., & Williams, L. D. (2001b). The discrepancy-attribution hypothesis II: Expectation, uncertainty, surprise and feelings of familiarity. *Journal of Experimental Psychology: Learning, Memory, and Cognition, 27*, 14–33.

Winkielman, P., Schwarz, N., Reber, R., & Fazendeiro, T. A. (2003). Cognitive and affective consequences of visual fluency: When seeing is easy on the mind. In L. M. Scott & R. Batra (Eds.), *Persuasive Imagery: A Consumer Response Perspective* (pp. 75–89). Mahwah, NJ: Erlbaum.

Wippich, W., & Mecklenbraeuker, S. (1994). Perceptual fluency and recognition judgments in haptic information processing. *Perceptual & Motor Skills, 78*, 986–994.

Wood, S. L., & Lynch, Jr., J. G. (2002). Prior knowledge and complacency in new product learning. *Journal of Consumer Research, 29*, 416–426.

Wright, R., & Whittlesea, B. W. A. (1998). Implicit learning of complex structures: Active adaptation and selective processing in acquisition and application. *Memory & Cognition, 26*, 402–420.

Zajonc, R. B. (1968). Attitudinal effects of mere exposure. *Journal of Personality and Social Psychology, 9*, 1–27.

4

Consumer Learning and Expertise

J. Wesley Hutchinson

University of Pennsylvania

Eric M. Eisenstein

Cornell University

Consumer learning has been a central construct in models of consumer behavior since at least the 1960s (e.g., Howard & Sheth, 1969; Massy, Montgomery & Morrison, 1970). Research on consumer knowledge and expertise is more recent (e.g., Bettman & Park, 1980; Brucks, 1985; Alba & Hutchinson, 1987). In cognitive psychology, the topics of learning and expertise are more or less separate domains, or perhaps more accurately, expertise is a subfield that focuses on the highest levels of learning, where learning has occurred naturally over many years rather than in the laboratory as the result of experimental procedures (e.g., Chi, Glaser, & Farr, 1988; Shanteau, 1992). In consumer research, the topics have been more closely related and generally involve comparisons of more knowledgeable and less knowledgeable consumers without requiring that the more knowledgeable consumers be experts in the sense of representing the highest attainable levels of knowledge (e.g., grand masters in chess, professional judges of agricultural products, medical doctors, meteorologists, etc.). This focus on "relative" rather than "absolute" expertise is natural because many (arguably most) important problems in consumer behavior involve the very earliest stages of naturalistic learning (e.g., the adoption of innovations, transitions from trial to repeat purchases, differences between light and heavy users, etc.). Thus, in this chapter we emphasize the integration of learning and expertise and focus on the effects of relative differences in consumer knowledge across individuals.[1]

THE "PERFECT WORLD" PERSPECTIVE

To structure our review of research on consumer learning and expertise, it is useful to note a perspective that is seldom explicitly endorsed or rejected, but is lurking behind the scenes in the literature on consumer knowledge. In the normal course of everyday life, people have many experiences that involve products (i.e., goods and services), and they become increasingly familiar with those products. Also, over time people learn from these experiences and gain true expertise in a variety of product domains. Following Alba and Hutchinson (1987), we use the term *familiarity* to refer to the accumulated level of product-related experiences and *expertise* to refer to the ability to perform product-related tasks successfully. We will refer to the general hypothesis that increased familiarity leads to increases in expertise as *learning from experience* (H1). Also, it seems reasonable that as expertise increases, people become better and more efficient in their roles as consumers. We will refer to this general hypothesis as *inproved consumer welfare* (H2). As will become evident as we proceed, these hypotheses are not always supported, and sometimes opposite results obtain (i.e., increased familiarity leads to less expertise or increased expertise leads to lower welfare), but most people would agree that the world would be a better place if it worked according to H1 and H2. Hence, we have dubbed this pair of hypotheses the "perfect world" perspective.

Independent of whether the perfect world perspective is valid or not, one result of research in this area has been to show that the key constructs—product familiarity, consumer expertise, and consumer welfare—are multidimensional in nature (see Figure 4.1).

Product familiarity can arise from a wide variety of experiences, including information search, repeated decision making, repeated product usage and consumption, and deliberate practice. Each of these types of experience has been found to increase expertise in some cases, but not in others. However, high levels of expertise are seldom obtained without successful information search, or without clear and immediate feedback about the outcomes of decisions, usage, and consumption. In consumer domains that include competitive performance or creative expression, deliberate practice is often essential.

Similarly, there are a number of benefits that could arise from product familiarity through the development of consumer expertise. First, consumers could become more completely and perfectly informed because expertise allows consumers to comprehend, retain, recall, and infer more information with lower levels of error. Second, consumers could make more optimal decisions because they learn more successful strategies, rely less on simple heuristics, are able to reason further into the future and conform more to traditional conceptualizations of "rational," utility-maximizing behavior. Third, consumers could incur lower costs of information search, product usage, and consumption because they become faster and better at these activities or because they learn new, more efficient strategies and behaviors. These costs would include time, money, and mental and physical

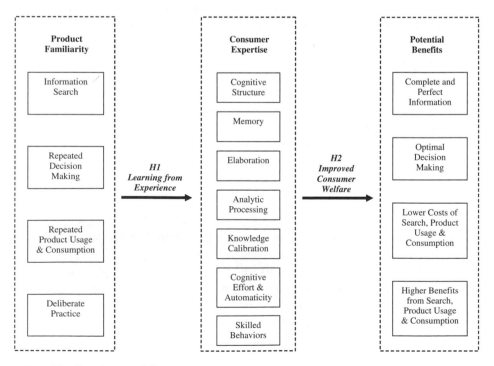

Figure 4.1 The "perfect world" perspective

effort. Finally, consumers could obtain more or better outcomes from information search, product usage, and consumption because the ultimate utilitarian and hedonic results of these activities are produced in part by consumers themselves, and expertise could create more effective production functions.

The multidimensionality of consumer expertise has been frequently noted (Alba & Hutchinson, 1987, 2000; Brucks, 1985). In the remainder of this section, we will specifically consider changes resulting from product familiarity in cognitive structure, memory, elaboration, analytic processing, knowledge calibration, cognitive effort/automaticity, and skilled behaviors, and the benefits that arise from these changes. For each dimension, we will summarize the status of learning from experience (H1) and improved consumer welfare (H2). Our discussions will highlight what we see as key results and ongoing issues and will refer readers to more comprehensive treatments of the topics. After this overview, we will continue assessing the perfect world perspective as we review theory and method in the area of consumer learning and expertise.

COGNITIVE STRUCTURE

Cognitive structure refers to the way in which factual knowledge is organized in memory. The most common forms of cognitive structures studied in consumer research are naturally occurring, taxonomic categories because the mappings onto the marketing concepts of product categories, brand families, and market niches are fairly direct. Several stylized facts from cognitive psychology are commonly adopted. First, most product categories exhibit the characteristics of basic level categories (e.g., objects are named at this level and processing is faster to identify objects as belonging to a basic level; Rosch, Mervis, Gray,. Johnson, & Boyes-Braem, 1976). The central claim about basic level categories is that within-category similarity and between-category dissimilarity are maximized at this level. It is easy to see how market forces make product categories the basic level insofar as product categories are defined as collections of substitutes that compete with each other to fulfill the same consumer needs. Moreover, as expertise increases, knowledge about subordinate categories increases and information at this level is processed as efficiently as (but not more efficiently than) at the basic level (Johnson & Mervis, 1997). Second, product categories exhibit a graded structure that can be indexed by measures of typicality (Medin & Smith, 1984; Rosch & Mervis, 1975). A central issue from the perspective of consumer research is the extent to which the most typical products are also the best products (in general or for specific consumers). Third, the ad hoc and goal-derived categories that consumers often use in shopping (e.g., things to by for a camping trip, my favorite restaurants, etc.) also exhibit graded structure (Barsalou, 1985).

Several researchers have confirmed that as product familiarity increases, especially from nonuser to user of a product, cognitive structure is acquired (e.g., Hutchinson, Raman, & Mantrala, 1994; Nedungadi & Hutchinson, 1985). Mitchell and Dacin (1996) provide a particularly thorough analysis of the cognitive structures found for motorcycles. They factor analyzed 10 measures related to product familiarity and expertise and found that subjective and objective measures of knowledge loaded on the same factor; however, number owned and magazines read formed a second factor and number owned by friends formed a third. In general, their results confirm the perfect world perspective, but there are some cautionary notes. Self-rated familiarity loaded on the same factor as measures of subjective and objective knowledge, supporting learning from experience (H1). However, the independence of number owned and magazines read (which clearly indexes the number of product-related experiences) from the knowledge measures does not support H1, or at least suggests that mere ownership does not lead to knowledge. Moreover, while the knowledge measures were strongly related to measures of the organization of knowledge, ownership was only weakly related, at best. Also, a separate experimental session assessed choices among hypothetical motorcycles for which there were objectively correct answers. The knowledge factor was strongly related to correct choices and correct reasons for the choices, supporting improved consumer welfare (H2). However, ownership was not predictive of choice, further weakening the simple view of familiarity leading to expertise leading to better decisions. These results suggest that not all types of product experiences increase learning and expertise. Interestingly, ownership of motorcycles by friends was also highly predictive of choice quality. This suggests a social dimension to consumer expertise that has not been explored in detail.

MEMORY

The hallmark of expertise in all domains is greater memory for domain facts. The classic studies of chess experts showed that grand masters could remember game configurations much better than novices, but only for configurations that were possible in real games (Chase & Simon, 1973). Memory for random configurations was the same for experts and novices. Similar results have been obtained in a wide variety of fields (see Vincente & Wang, 1998, for a discussion of theories that account for expert recall superiority). While little of this research has been called consumer research, many (arguably most) of the domains involve consumer markets (mainly for entertainment of various sorts) that become professions at the highest levels of expertise. Games (chess, bridge, and go), sports (baseball, basketball, football, figure skating, and field hockey), computer programming, and even medical diagnosis exhibit this type of continuum and have empirical evidence for expert recall superiority. Superior memory has also been found in explicitly consumer-oriented research (Mitchell & Dacin, 1996). Memory superiority, almost by definition, leads to more completely and perfectly informed consumers, and in that sense these results support both learning from experience (H1) and improved consumer welfare (H2).

In addition to greater recall, the cognitive structures that are acquired influence the recall of brands and attributes, which ones are recalled and in what order (Hutchinson, Raman, & Mantrala, 1994; Mitchell & Dacin, 1996; Nedungadi, Chattopadhyay, & Muthukrishnan, 2001; Ratneshwar, Peckman, & Shocker, 1996; Ratneshwar & Shocker, 1991). Cowley and Mitchell (2003) found that when novices were exposed to product information in the context of a specific usage situation, they could not reorganize that information in memory and successfully recall products appropriate for a different usage situation. Expert consumers were able to retain more information and better recall information that was appropriate for a new situation. Cowley and Janus (2004) found that high product familiarity consumers had better memory for a product experience and were more resistant to the biasing effects of misleading advertisements about that experience than were low familiarity consumers. Thus, in addition to information being more complete and perfect, there is evidence that decisions will be better (see also Mitchell & Dacin, 1996), supporting the perfect world perspective. In contrast, Wood and Lynch (2000) found that, compared to novices, experts were less likely to encode and remember new product information that made older information obsolete. However, experts did learn better than novices if they were cued that their knowledge might be out of date or if they were given incentives to carefully attend to all information about the new product.

ELABORATION

In addition to better organization and memory for information acquired directly from product experiences, experts sometimes exhibit higher levels of reasoning and problem solving in their domains of expertise. Alba and Hutchinson (1987) referred to these abilities as elaboration (i.e., new knowledge that is internally generated from old knowledge). Arguably the most frequent and important type of elaboration for consumers is the ability to infer the ultimate benefits and costs of a product based on its objective features and technical specifications and use these inferences to solve the problem of satisfying specific needs. For example, expert consumers in the domain of computer products can accurately assess the price, size, weight, CPU, RAM, cache, and I/O ports of various laptops, and choose the machine that best suits their need for out-of-office computing. Novices are less able to engage in this type of elaboration. However, novices are more likely to elaborate by simplification (e.g., many technical features are interpreted as implying performance superiority, regardless of the match between those features and their specific needs).

Evidence for accurate feature-to-benefit inferences by expert consumers and increased simplification by novices can be found in the results of an extensive experiment on mass customization conducted by Dellaert and Stremersch (2005). In this experiment a probability sample of consumers shopped for hypothetical computers using configurations of mass customization that varied in extent of customization, heterogeneity in levels of product attributes, pricing format, and presence and type of default option. These factors created large differences in the degree of success consumers had in constructing their most preferred computer (as measured by the rated utility of the final product design) and the amount of complexity they perceived in the customization process. Importantly, expertise was shown to reduce perceived complexity, increase product utility, and reduce the negative effect of complexity on product utility. These results are also supportive of the perfect world hypothesis.

ANALYTIC PROCESSING

A number of researchers in different areas of cognitive psychology have argued that there are two fundamentally different types of information processing and decision making (e.g., Hammond & Brehmer, 1973; Jacoby & Brooks, 1984; Sloman, 1996). One corresponds fairly closely to normative, logical reasoning. It is analytic and rule-based. A central characteristic of this type of thought is identifying and using only the information that is relevant and diagnostic, ignoring other information that may be salient but irrelevant. The second is associative, similarity-based, intuitive, and holistic in the sense that all salient information is integrated in some way to form an overall judgment or choose among options. Because this second type has been given so many different names and definitions, we will simply refer to it as non-analytic processing. In consumer research, this difference has been related to situational factors. Hutchinson and Alba (1991) found that intentional learning (e.g., deliberately trying to understand the product attributes that influence price) increased the likelihood of analytic information processing; however, incidental learning (e.g., learning about price when one's explicit goal is forming overall preferences), complexity, and memory load were all found to increase the likelihood of non-analytic processing factors. Importantly, several researchers have reported evidence that experts are more likely to engage in analytic processing than are novices (Alba & Hutchinson, 1987; Dillon, Madden, Kirmani, & Mukherjee, 2001; Spence & Brucks, 1997). Dillon et al. developed a psychometrically sophisticated model of brand ratings and found that the ratings of high experience consumers were more influenced by brand specific attributes and less influenced by general brand impressions than were the ratings of low experience consumers. Spence and Brucks compared professional appraisers (experts) to undergraduates (novices) in a task that required participants to estimate the market value of houses based on multi-attribute descriptions. They found that experts used fewer but more diagnostic attributes compared to novices. Both of these results are consistent with the hypothesis that processing shifts from holistic to analytic as product familiarity increases (i.e., H1, learning from experience).

KNOWLEDGE CALIBRATION

Knowledge calibration is the degree to which consumers accurately assess their knowledge about products and markets.[2] Typically, calibration is assessed by comparing confidence with accuracy (via a variety of methods which are discussed later). If people are high in confidence when their knowledge is accurate and low in confidence when it is errorful, then they are well-calibrated. Unfortunately, most research in marketing and psychology supports the stylized fact that people are overconfident (Alba & Hutchinson, 2000; however, see Juslin, Winman, & Olsson, 2000). They think they know more than they actually do.

Is overconfidence a bad thing? Generally speaking, the answer is yes, but there are exceptions (see Alba & Hutchinson, 2000). One obvious problem with consumer overconfidence about their level of knowledge, is that it is likely to lead to reduced information search and inattention to available information (consistent with the results of Wood & Lynch, 2002, which were discussed earlier). Also, confidence often exerts a direct influence on judgment and choice. If a consumer is overconfident that their knowledge is valid they will not appropriately factor their uncertainty into their decisions. For example, assume that a consumer is faced with a choice between Brands X and Y and believes that Brand X was rated higher than Y by *Consumer Reports*. Further assume that X is priced higher than Y, but the consumer is very confident that her belief is correct and therefore chooses X. To quantify these concepts, let's say that "very confident" means she believes her memory for what she reads in *Consumer Reports* is correct 95% of the time, the value to her for being rated higher is $10, and (to simplify things) there are no ties in the ratings. If she is perfectly calibrated, then the expected value of choosing X is $.95 \times \$10 + .05 \times (\$0) = \$9.50$. Thus, she should be willing to pay up to $9.50 more for Brand X. However, if she is overconfident about her beliefs and her memory is correct only 75% of the time, then the expected value of choosing X is only $.75 \times \$10 + .25 \times (\$0) = \$7.50$. If the price difference is between $7.50 and $9.50, then she will have chosen X when she should have chosen Y. This example shows that the overconfidence reduces consumer welfare when degree of confidence is a valid input for a decision, as is true for most decisions that require the valuation of all considered options. Some decisions, however, do not require such valuations. For example, if X and Y were priced the same, our hypothetical consumer should choose whichever brand is more likely to have been rated higher, and it does not matter whether the likelihood is 95% or 75% or even 55%. Any likelihood over 50% means X should be chosen over Y. In some cases, when valuation is not required, overconfidence may even be helpful if it leads to faster decisions or allows the consumer to worry less. Also, overconfidence may make consumers more resistant to misleading advertising and other persuasive marketing actions (e.g., see Bearden, Hardesty, & Rose, 2001; Obermiller & Spangenberg, 1998). Overall, however, we think such situations are rare, and we should regard miscalibration (i.e., over- or underconfidence) as lowering consumer welfare. The key question then is whether or not expertise increases calibration. If it does, then H2 of the perfect world perspective holds. If it does not, or if it instead increases overconfidence, then we have the somewhat ironic outcome that even though consumers learn from experience (H1), they are worse off as a result. Unfortunately, the evidence is mixed.

Classic studies of calibration require subjects to provide numerical estimates of the probability that each response they give is correct. Most studies have found domain experts to be as poorly calibrated as novices (Lichtenstein, Fischoff, & Phillips, 1982; Shanteau & Stewart, 1992). These results have been found for the domains of medicine, law, psychology, sports, and among undergraduates (assumed to be more expert in their major than other areas). The major exceptions have been the high level of calibration of professional meteorologists and world-class bridge players, leading some to speculate that large numbers of repetitions with immediate outcome feedback is necessary for calibration to be improved by experience; however, Koehler, Brenner, and Griffin (2002) provide a compelling, model-based alternative explanation. Interestingly, in contrast to the voluminous evidence of the poor calibration of physicians regarding a wide variety of medical events compared yoked physicians and their patients for predictions of surviving cancer. The physicians were well-calibrated, but patients were overconfident. It should be noted that in these studies, experts are often more accurate than novice even though they are equally overconfident. This suggests that learning from experience (H1) occurs, but experience is building confidence in that learning at an excessive rate.

A similar conclusion is suggested by Cowley (2004), who examined memory for product information and its subsequent effects on choice. She found that isolated brand evaluations improved both accuracy and confidence compared to brand comparisons. However, consumer knowledge of the product domain only affected confidence. Importantly, she also showed that confidence was a much stronger predictor of choice than was accuracy. Also, Muthukrishnan (1995) found that repeated product experience (that was devoid of new information by design) increased both decision confidence and an incumbent bias that resulted in increased choice of an objectively inferior product. Finally, we note that researchers have seldom examined confidence as a predictor of consumer preferences, but when they have strong effects have been observed (e.g., Brinol, Petty, & Tormala, 2004; Huang & Hutchinson, 2007; Petty, Brinol, & Tormala, 2002; see also Hutchinson & Alba, 1991).

Thus far, overconfidence seems to be a "necessary evil" that accompanies expertise, or at a minimum, expertise does little to reduce the overconfidence observed in most situations. Perhaps the most encouraging exceptions to this conclusion are the results of Sanbonmatsu, Kardes, and Herr (1992), who found that high levels of prior knowledge allowed subjects to spontaneously detect that important product information was missing, and appropriately lower both brand evaluations and decision confidence. Subjects with low and moderate levels of knowledge exhibited biases created by missing information. From a public policy perspective, we might be tempted conclude that benefits of expertise outweigh the costs with respect to calibration (supporting H2) because it sometimes reduces overconfidence and the biases it creates and even when confidence increases more rapidly than learning this makes consumer more self-assured about their preferences and more resistant to attempts by marketers to mislead and persuade. However, the dissociation of confidence from learning as product experience increases seems to us to be a cause for concern. This concern is probably greatest in the area of information search because overconfidence seems likely to slow the dissemination of new information and this effect will be magnified to the extent that novice consumers rely on identified expert consumers as a major source of their information.

COGNITIVE EFFORT, AUTOMATICITY, AND SKILLED BEHAVIOR

Although the definitions and theoretical explanations of automaticity vary across authors and domains of research (Bargh, 1994; Hasher & Zacks, 1979, 1984; Shiffrin & Schneider, 1977; Logan 1988, 2002), the term is generally applied to any mental process that (1) occurs in response to a specific internal or external event, (2) with little or no awareness or intentional control, and (3) requires little or no cognitive resources. Automatic processes also occur much more rapidly than similar non-automatic processes (i.e., responses to the same stimuli with the same goal that are conscious, effortful and intentionally controlled), and are unaffected by concurrent tasks that require cognitive resources. The types of process that are or can become automatic include associative recall, recognition, classification, rule learning, frequency counting, and a wide variety of verbal, quantitative, and motor skills. Almost all of these play a role in some aspect of consumer behavior (e.g.,

Alba & Hutchinson, 1987; Fitzsimons et al., 2002). Importantly for our present purpose, automatic processes are either "hard wired" (e.g., orienting responses, automatic frequency counting, etc.) or require extensive repetition of the same stimuli and responses. Thus, many processes that are conscious, effortful, and intentionally controlled for novices, are automatic for experts. Although there is considerable debate about the precise mechanisms that underlie the acquisition of automatic processes, most researchers agree that (1) repetition of any behavior leads to speedup and a reduction of cognitive effort almost immediately, and (2) after many repetitions there is a qualitative change from a controlled to an automatic process. Thus, the vast amount of research on cognitive effort and automaticity supports learning from experience (H1). Support for inproved consumer welfare (H2) is mixed. As nicely reviewed by Bargh and Chartrand (1999), automaticity can result (1) intentionally, when people have an intentional goal of acquiring a skill, and (2) unintentionally, when people repeatedly make the same choices in the same situation. The former type of acquisition seems to clearly increase consumer welfare. The latter, however, may sometimes be beneficial (e.g., automatic detection of a frequently purchased brand speeds up shopping) and sometimes harmful (e.g., automatic detection of a frequently purchased brand prevents consideration of new or lower priced brands).

Several other types of beneficial effects have recently been identified by Beilock and Carr and their co-researchers (Beilock & Carr, 2001; Beilock, Beilock, Benett, Bertenthal, McCoy, & Carr, 2004a; Beilock, Culp, Holt, & Carr, 2004b; Beilock, Wierenga, & Carr, 2002) who have shown that automaticity reduces or eliminates the problem of "choking" under pressure (e.g., due to incentives, peer pressure, social evaluation, and time pressure) in both higher order mental tasks (e.g., modular arithmetic) and motor skills (e.g., putting in golf). However, they find that for motor skills, if pressure increases self-monitoring, experts are hurt more than novices--presumably because it disrupts otherwise automatic processes. These deficits can be overcome by training. Analogs in consumer behavior are not hard to imagine. Many purchase situations require higher order reasoning and mathematical skills (e.g., financing a house) and consumers can be pressured by sales representatives, friends and family, or time pressures created by market conditions. Similarly, many product usage situations require automatized motor skills (e.g., driving a car) and are subject to similar pressures.

Additional negative effects of automaticity are suggested by the research of Bargh and his co-researchers (Bargh & Chartrand, 1999; Chartrand & Bargh, 1996; Kay et al., 2004) who have shown that specific goals can be automatically activated without the awareness of the decision maker. For example, Kay et al. (2004) showed that mundane objects (e.g., a briefcase or boardroom table) increased competition and reduced cooperation as perceived in social situations and as acted upon in economic games. Balancing competitive and cooperative tendencies is a key aspect of many aspects of information search and decision making, especially when some degree of negotiation is involved. The extent to which automatically accessed goals are beneficial or harmful will depend on the extent to which they are appropriate to the situation and consistent with the explicitly held goals of the decision maker.

THEORY

Expertise cannot occur without learning. Thus, there is a sense in which theories of learning and theories of expertise are necessarily unified through the assumption that expertise arises as the result of maximal amounts of learning. Despite the obvious truth of this necessary unification, the literatures on learning and expertise are surprisingly separate. To be sure, there are areas of overlap and common foundations, but in actuality most theories of learning have been designed to account for the early stages of knowledge development, typically explaining results of experiments in which subjects initially have none of the to-be-learned knowledge and acquire knowledge over relatively short periods of time (e.g., an hour to several days or weeks). In contrast, theories of expertise focus on the later phases of learning, identifying individuals who, over relatively long periods of time (usually years), have achieved levels of performance that surpass not just beginners, but others who have similarly large amounts of experience but have acquired less knowledge from that experience. Given this separation in the literature, we will review each area separately.

Models of Learning

The most straightforward way to organize models of learning is by the complexity of what is learned. As with overall theories of learning and expertise, distinct literatures have developed to account for the learning of simple and complex relationships among stimuli, response, and incentives in laboratory and real-world environments. At one end of this spectrum is the Pavlovian conditioning of a single stimulus to elicit a single response. In marketing, the conditioning of affective responses to brand names through exposures to advertising has been an important area of application. At the other end of the spectrum is the acquisition of an understanding of naturally occurring domains, including the logical and causal relationships among the elements of those domains. In marketing, information search and the development of differentiated brand concepts within (and across) product categories has been an important area of application. Although each end of this spectrum uses a rather different set of constructs, a shared foundation can be found in the principle most commonly called "the association of ideas." Aristotle noted that mental states came to be associated with each other if they were similar to each other, contrasted with each other, or occurred together in time or space. The variations of this principle have been many, and the differences between applications have not been small (e.g., behaviorists of the mid-20th century denied any theoretical status to mental states of any kind and worked strictly with associations between stimuli and responses). Nonetheless, there is a clear and common core that is nicely summarized by Young (1968), "The principle has aspects: (1) that complex mental phenomena are formed from simple elements derived ultimately from sensations and (2) that the mechanism by which these are formed depends on similarity and/or repeated juxtaposition of the simple elements in space and time. The association of ideas provides a mechanism for ordered change through experience which complements (and plays an analogous role to) the concept of attraction (or gravity) in the physico-chemical sciences."

Beginning with Chomsky's (1959) critique of Skinner's (1957) account of how language can be learned through conditioning, models of most human cognitive abilities have included more mechanisms than association (e.g., hypothesis testing, rule learning, production systems, etc.).[3] However, few models of learning deny any role for conditioning and association, and many propose some variation of a dual system model in which low-level associative learning (and decision making) combines in some way with higher level mechanisms. These two systems underlie not just learning, but reasoning and decision making as well. Thus, they constitute integrated models of cognition (for reviews of dual system models of cognition see Sloman, 1996). It is beyond the scope of this paper to review all of these models, so we focus on two types of learning models that have been widely used in consumer research and illustrate the trend toward integrated dual system models—conditioning and concept formation.

Conditioning and associative learning. Traditional descriptions of conditioning state that a previously neutral stimulus (called the conditioned stimulus, CS) can come to elicit the same response as another stimulus that has a pre-existing association with the response (and is called the unconditioned stimulus, US), if the CS repeatedly occurs immediately before or during the occurrence of the US. Rescorla (1998) has argued persuasively that this characterization oversimplifies current models and empirical results (especially for the animal learning literature). Nevertheless, this simple description has a natural and direct connection to advertising that has been investigated for some time and proved very useful (Allen & Janiszewski, 1989; Janiszewski & Warlop, 1993; Shimp, Stuart, & Engle, 1991; Stuart, Shimp, & Engle, 1987; van Osselaer & Janiszewski, 2001). Many types of advertising present a brand name (which initially has little or no affective response associated with it) together with content (pictures, music, words, etc.) that elicit positive affect based on pre-existing associations. The central thesis that has been studied is the extent to which that positive affect is learned as a conditioned response to the brand name. It is well-established that conditioning procedures using advertising in a laboratory setting result in increased brand attitudes. However, the explanation for these results has been controversial. The first explanation is direct transfer of affect. This is viewed as a Pavlovian conditioning mechanism that relies on simple associations and is a mechanism similar to those at work in the animal learning paradigms that dominate current research on conditioning (for reviews, including discussions of neural mechanisms, see Fanselow & Poulos, 2005; Staddon & Cerutti, 2003; Thompson, 2005). This type of learning should occur regardless of whether or not people are aware of the relationship between the conditioned and unconditioned stimuli (e.g., that Brand X always occurred with a picture of a cute kitten). The second explanation is inferential belief formation. This explanation asserts that people notice the relationship between the conditioned and unconditioned stimuli and make an inference about some attitude-relevant belief. For example, if kittens are used in advertising for facial tissue, consumers infer that the advertising is making a claim about superior softness, and their attitudes change to the extent that they value softness and believe the claim. Finally, several researchers have argued that the results for advertising may be due to demand artifacts (Darley & Lim, 1993; Kellaris & Cox, 1989). This too requires that people become aware of the relationship between conditioned and unconditioned stimuli, but reported attitudes change only because they deduce the goal of the experiment and desire to be cooperative. Kim, Allen, and Kardes (1996) report the results of several experiments that carefully rule out demand artifacts and show that both direct affect transfer and inferential belief contributed to attitude change; however, the awareness-dependent inferential mechanism was found to be the stronger component.

Concept formation. Concepts are the mental structures we use to represent our world. They can be discrete or continuous. Categories are discrete concepts (even if category membership is a matter of degree, as discussed earlier). For example, a mini-van is a type of automobile that can be distinguished from an SUV and a station wagon (even if some particular vehicles, like the Pontiac Aztec, are hard to classify). Among other things, consumers use discrete concepts to screen alternatives during the search phase of decision making. In contrast, choices among alternatives frequently involve continuous concepts like quality or market value. Both types of concepts must be learned over time so that new alternatives can be appropriately classified and evaluated. These components of consumer decision making closely parallel the major experimental paradigms in concept formation which present subjects with a multiattribute stimulus and require a discrete or a continuous response that reflects the subject is understanding some target concept.

The major theoretical models used to explain concept formation are of two primary types, typically labeled exemplar-based and rule-based models. Although there are many variations, exceptions, and nuances, exemplar-based models tend to postulate simple associative processes that can operate automatically and without significant cognitive resources. When some new thing is encountered, it recruits information from other concepts in memory that are similar to it and that information determines the response. If I see a new model of car that resembles a Dodge Caravan and a Honda Odyssey, I am likely to classify it as a minivan and believe it to have a price and quality level similar to those vehicles. As mentioned, this might occur very rapidly with little conscious thought; however, it might also occur through a very deliberate process of reasoning by analogy, and models of both types have been proposed. In contrast, rule-based models assume that each stimulus attribute contributes more or less independently through some rule of combination (frequently linear) to form an impression of how well the instance fits the concept. If it is a tall, boxy, cab-forward car with room for seven people, it is probably a minivan. Prototype models combine aspects of both exemplar-based and rule-based models. They are like exemplar-based models insofar as the prototype is essentially the "average" or most representative exemplar of the category. However, in these models it is the only exemplar that is recruited for comparison to the to-be-classified stimulus. In this sense, it is very much like an abstract rule.

In both psychology and in marketing, there has historically been a split between research on the learning of continuous and discrete functions of multiattribute stimuli. For example, in psychology there has been extensive research into modeling the learning process in categorization tasks. This research paradigm has concentrated on binary classification tasks (frequently based on binary attributes), and has primarily focused on testing specific models (e.g., rule-based vs. exemplar-based models, see Kruschke, 1992; Medin & Schaffer, 1978; Nosofsky, 1984). In marketing, there have been studies using the categorization paradigm that have investigated consumer learning of brand or category membership based on categorical cues (e.g., Huffman & Houston, 1993; Hutchinson & Alba, 1991; van Osselaer & Alba, 2000). In general, categorization research in marketing has placed greater emphasis on category definition, the categorization processes, and category structure than on the learning of categories (e.g., Alba & Hutchinson, 1987; Cohen & Basu, 1987; Moreau, Markman, & Lehmann, 2001; Park, Iyer, & Smith, 1989; Sujan, 1985; although Sujan & Bettman, 1989 examined adding new brands to an existing product category).

The learning of functional relationships between (usually abstract) continuous cues and a continuous criterion has been extensively pursued in psychology using the multiple-cue probability learning (MCPL) paradigm (Hammond, 1955). MCPL research has shown that a wide variety of functional relationships between cues and outcomes can be learned, given sufficient trials and appropriate feedback, but that some relationships are more difficult to learn than others (see Brehmer & Brehmer, 1988 for a review; see also Camerer, 1981; Mellers, 1980). In marketing, the MCPL paradigm has been used by a number of researchers. Meyer (1987) demonstrated that consumers could quickly learn positive attribute-quality relationships in a multiattribute setting. West (1996) used an agent learning task to demonstrate that veridical feedback eliminates the facilitative effects of initial preference similarity and that learners allocate more time to informative than uninformative feedback. Hutchinson and Alba (1997) demonstrated a framing effect in a budget allocation task where past allocations and their sales results served as the stimuli and feedback. Hoch and Schkade (1996) used a managerial credit-forecasting and learning task to investigate the design of decision support systems.

A number of researchers have recently noted that, although there are large literatures on categorization and multiple-cue judgment, they seldom reference each other, and the two experimental paradigms are seldom combined in the same study (DeLosh, Busemeyer, & McDaniel, 1997; Eisenstein, 2002; Eisenstein & Hutchinson, 2006; Juslin, Olsson, & Olsson, 2003). Also, there is a considerable amount of recent research directed at comparing the ability of exemplar-based and rule-based models to simultaneously account for results in classification and judgment tasks (Juslin et al., 2003; Eisenstein & Hutchinson, 2005; cf. Tversky, Sattath, & Slovic, 1988). In general, both types of model do surprising well accounting for the main results of the past 30 years of research on concept formation. Exemplar-based models are challenged by results showing strong prototype enhancement effects for discrete concepts and the robust ability of people to extrapolate beyond the set of exemplars they have encountered in making continuous judgments. Nonetheless, recent extensions of exemplar-based models perform admirably (Palmeri & Nosofsky, 2001). Rule-based models are challenged by observed patterns of errors that are hard to explain by any simple rule and by the ability of people to learn apparently complex relationships even though they cannot verbalize a rule that would predict their own behavior. To the extent that there is consensus across researchers, it is that (1) both classes of models do extremely well in accounting for most robust findings, (2) in certain "extreme" situations people seem to clearly use one or the other type of process, (3) hybrid models are therefore an "easy" solution, (4) there may be two separate systems that operate sometimes alone, sometimes sequentially, and sometimes in parallel, but (5) it is still possible that future research will yield a single unified model that relies on a single system (i.e., either rule-based or exemplar-based). Excellent reviews of the competing theories can be found in Ashby and Maddox (1998), Johansen and Palmeri (2002), Nosofsky, Palmeri, and McKinley (1994), and Palmeri, Wong, and Gauthier (2004).

Models of Expertise

Models of expertise have traditionally focused on explaining various aspects of skilled human performance. One question that arises is how experts are able to bring relevant information, inferential techniques, and other specialized skills to bear as quickly as they are observed to do. Given the slow computational speed of the human brain, it is somewhat surprising that experts are able to achieve high levels of performance as quickly as they do. In addition to the specific problem of skilled performance, we also discuss in this section an overarching theory of expert competence, with the goal of determining what characteristics of people and tasks are most likely to lead to the development of expertise. Finally, we examine attempts to model consumer expertise in a traditional economic framework.

Computation rate vs. knowledge base size. Experts are called upon to process complex decision inputs and to make accurate decisions quickly. There are two general ways to approach this problem: retrieval from memory and computational search. Retrieval from memory is a fast and relatively effortless process for humans; conditional on a match between the current situation and a past situation that has been stored in long term memory, retrieval is rapid and automatic (Ericsson & Kintsch, 1995). If it is discovered that there is no good match in memory, however, a slower computational search through the space of possible answers ensues to discover an appropriate course of action. Search is effortful and slower, but it is the foundation of general problem solving ability (Newell & Simon, 1972). The distinction between retrieval and search is analogous to the difference between knowing the answer and knowing how to compute the answer (e.g., most adults retrieve 5*6 = 30 from memory effortlessly, but need to laboriously compute 51*29 = 1,479). It is also analogous to the extensively discussed differences between declarative and procedural knowledge (e.g., Anderson, 1982; Cohen & Squire, 1980). There is an obvious tradeoff between knowledge and search. Building an extensive database of cases and committing them to memory is time intensive, though the costs can potentially be spread out over time. Learning procedural knowledge is frequently easier, but the actual computation is more effortful. The retrieval-search continuum represents the difference between the *cost of learning*, which is borne in the past, and the *cost of thinking*, which is incurred at the time of decision (cf., Eisenstein, 2002; Shugan, 1980).

Given the tradeoff between search and retrieval, it is reasonable to investigate the nature of isoperformance curves with respect to these two information processing mechanisms. The human brain is a slow information processor: it takes 5 to 10 seconds to store a chunk in long term memory

(Simon, 1974); the simplest operation of comparing two symbols in a memory search task takes about 40 ms (e.g., Sternberg, 1966); recognizing a letter takes approximately 10–20 ms (Sperling, 1963); and recognizing a familiar pattern or word takes about 200–400 ms (see Luce, 1986; Teichner & Krebs, 1974, for reviews). In addition, humans can only store and manipulate small numbers of items in short term working memory (Miller, 1956). These limitations imply two realities about expertise: first, expert performance is almost always based on retrieval rather than search; second, expertise is strongly tied to a given domain, because stored exemplars, case knowledge, and knowledge architectures are bound to domains. The clearest investigation of isoperformance between search and retrieval comes from studies of chess masters. In chess, human experts compete on nearly equal terms with computers that can search through nearly 200 million nodes per second (compared to humans, who can process approximately 1 node per second). Charness (1981) estimated the size of the knowledge base required to match computers' search capability at 50,000 to 100,000 stored positions. Although the order of magnitude of the number of stored exemplars may differ by domain, it is quite likely that similar effects would be revealed in many other areas of human expertise, from appraising collectables or houses to estimating the price of cars.

Given that expert performance is largely based on retrieval, a number of psychological questions arise. In particular, an expert's knowledge base must be accessible to be useful, but the larger the database, the slower we would expect the search for a given piece of information to be. However, experts are observed to make decisions faster than novices, leading to the question of how experts are able to marshal their knowledge quickly enough to be useful, given their large databases of knowledge. Several different knowledge structures have been proposed which demonstrate that, with appropriate architectures, search can be sufficiently fast. These architectures include symbolic processing models (e.g., Elementary Perceiver and Memorizer [EPAM], Feigenbaum & Simon, 1984), parallel distributed processing networks (e.g., McClelland & Rumelhart, 1988; McClelland & Rumelhart, 1981), and hybrid systems (e.g., Anderson's Adaptive Control of Thought [ACT] system, 1983; Hummel & Holyoak, 1997, LISA (Learning and Inference with Schemas and Analogies) analogical reasoning system; Newell, 1990, SOAR architecture). These models demonstrate that, although experts might be expected to have slightly slower access times than novices, such accessibility differences can be small if appropriate knowledge architectures are used to organize information, and therefore retrieval can remain the primary method relied upon by experts.

Shanteau's Theory of Expert Competence. Shanteau (1988a, 1988b) proposed the members of a given domain should set the standard for competent performance as well as indicating who are experts in the field. This proposal is a pragmatic means to avoid the thorny issue of an outsider determining objectively "good" performance in each domain. Conditional on the definitions of the relevant pool of people and the evaluative mechanism, Shanteau's theory proposes that expert competence is based on five factors: domain knowledge, psychological traits, cognitive skills, decision strategies, and task characteristics. From the point of view of marketing, these characteristics can be mapped onto typical situations faced by consumers to determine the likelihood of achieving expert level consumer performance.

Adequate *domain knowledge* is a prerequisite for expert performance. However, it is obvious that mere memorization of a laundry list of facts is not sufficient to guarantee expert-level decision making performance. This is because part of the domain knowledge that is needed comes from experience, which encompasses stored examples, anecdotes, and cases in long term memory, as well as the enrichment of the similarity metric that enables efficient matching of novel cases to stored examples. Shanteau (1988b) hypothesized that stored examples serve both as a mnemonic, so that experts remember rare possibilities, as well as a mechanism for experts to store large amounts of domain specific information.

Experts require specific *cognitive skills* in order to achieve high levels of performance. What these cognitive skills are depends on the specific task. For example, the task may require retrieving items from a large number of previously stored cases, the ability to perform well under pressure, or the ability to quickly recognize patterns, among other skills. Clearly, aspiring experts will have an advantage on tasks which load on these skills to the extent that their cognitive skills match the task requirements. In addition to cognitive skills, expertise requires mastery of specific *decision strategies,* which help experts overcome cognitive limitations. Most of these strategies are strongly domain dependent, but several are more generally applicable. Specifically, experts across many fields rely on decision aids to manage information, decompose complex problems into smaller sub-issues, prethink solutions to tough situations (when they are anticipatable), and make extensive use of feedback when it is provided (Shanteau, 1988a; Shanteau, 1992; Shanteau, 1988b).

Experts also possess certain *psychological traits,* such as "self-presentation — the creation and maintenance of a public image," (Shanteau, 1992; Shanteau, 1988b). Surprisingly, such traits may be highly relevant for consumer expertise. For example, most people have a friend or acquaintance who knows "everything" about cars, computers, stereos, food, stocks, or other common consumer goods, and one characteristic of such "consumer mavens" is that they are able to maintain the self-presentation of expertise. Consumer research has not extensively investigated the role of these consumer experts, except in thinking about them as early adopters in Bass and other diffusion frameworks.

Finally, the role of *task characteristics* are often overlooked in the study of expertise. Many have argued that characteristics of the task are critical in determining whether there will be any bona fide experts in the domain (e.g., Alba & Hutchinson, 1987; Blattberg & Hoch, 1990; Hoch & Schkade, 1996; Hutchinson & Alba, 1991; Klayman, 1988; Shanteau, 1988a). A common observation is that in some domains experts achieve at very high levels, but in other domains, performance is not significantly different from novices (Brehmer & Brehmer, 1988; Carroll, 1987; Chi et al., 1988; Ericsson, 1996; Grove & Meehl, 1996; Meehl, 1954; Oskamp, 1962). In general, task characteristics that predict good performance include repetitive tasks that are based on static, agreed-upon stimuli with timely, veridical, feedback available, and a stationary underlying model, in which the unmodelable error in the environment is low. Task characteristics that suggest poor performance with little evidence of objective expertise include dynamic stimuli, domains stimuli with little agreement about which are important, nonstationary underlying processes, cases where feedback is either unavailable, nonveridical, delayed, or ambiguous. The list above is nonexhaustive, but it should give a flavor of what types of tasks are likely to result in high levels of observed human performance—tasks such as weather forecasting, solving physics, math, or programming problems, some areas of medical diagnosis, and related fields are likely to result in high levels of performance. Other tasks, such as predicting recidivism rates among potential parolees, admissions officers, etc. are likely to result in lower levels of performance.

Applying the Theory of Expert Competence to consumer domains, we see that we should expect the development of expertise across a wide variety of consumer tasks. For example, many consumers buy "collectables." Some collectable purchases are priced using a typical retail take-it-or-leave-it formats. However, many collectables are sold at auction (e.g., on eBay) and others are sold at yard sales, flea markets, and other similar venues, which are not fixed price settings. Under such circumstances, we would expect that consumer expertise would develop, with some consumers able to accurately value objects within their domain of expertise. Similarly, experienced shoppers are likely to develop a reasonable sense of where to go for the cheapest product, if it is commonly purchased (though store choice is not usually determined by a single good). In other circumstances, it is unlikely that consumers will develop substantial expertise. For example, people infrequently negotiate over automobiles, little feedback is available to the consumer after the deal, and the relevant attributes change over time. Therefore, we would expect very little expertise to develop among ordinary consumers in this market.

Human capital. Human capital is defined as scarce knowledge, skills, or techniques that are acquired through investments in formal education, training, or experiential learning. Much of the important work in this area has been done by Gary Becker (for a comprehensive review, see Becker, 1993). The majority of the work in human capital has focused on those investments that would provide returns in the labor market. However, in marketing, Ratchford (2001) extended the original Stigler and Becker (1977) human capital model by adopting the original household production model and by further viewing the household as a producer of goods and services that it sells to itself.

The Ratchford theory of consumer human capital begins with the assumption that each household or consumer can be viewed as a small business that produces a positive, real-valued vector of activities, Z. Each activity, Z_i, is produced by using a combination of goods, X, time, T_i, and knowledge K, which represents the types of knowledge capital needed to produce Z_i. Experience is assumed to lead to at least some relevant knowledge consistent with H1, learning from experince. With appropriate constraints and assumptions on functional forms, consumers are assumed to maximize utility subject to constraints on time, income, and production functions for each activity. The fundamental insight is that knowledge changes the relative cost of producing goods, because for example, an expert chef will find the cost to produce a meal relatively cheaper than a novice. Furthermore, it is assumed (in keeping with the perfect world framework) that consumption events provide experience that automatically increases knowledge capital. It should be noted that increases in human capital will result in an increase in consumption of a given activity, but may result in either an increase or a decrease for the input goods and time required. The increase in the consumption of the activity follows from the fact that human capital decreases the true, or total, cost to produce it. Although consumption for the activity will increase, consumption of the component goods and time required to produce the activity may decrease because human capital may cut the amount of goods and time required per unit of the activity, essentially increasing efficiency (Ratchford, 2001). This is analogous to the standard economic analysis of income and substitution effects, and the net result will depend on the particulars of a given situation.

If the human capital model is true for consumer behavior, there are a number of consequences, which are detailed in Ratchford (2001). First, apparent heterogeneity of tastes may be due to differences in the full price of a good across households, which is due, in part, to heterogeneity in human capital. Second, if knowledge capital accumulates with mere experience, in accordance with H1, then decisions to invest in search should occur more frequently in the early stages of the product cycle, where returns are greatest. Furthermore, the full price of the activity should fall through the lifecycle if input prices and time are held constant, though most rapidly in the early stages of learning when returns are greatest. Third, brand-specific knowledge is likely to create brand loyalty because the brand specific knowledge reduces the costs associated with using it. In addition, if information about attributes and prices that were learned in the past can still be used in the current search, then the total amount of search will be reduced. Moreover, if there is learning about how to search, then search costs are effectively lower, and increased total search will result. Finally, if consumers are rational, then they will search more in categories in which search leads to information or skill capital (e.g., Internet shopping on different sites).

METHOD

Measuring Expertise as Individual Differences

It is obvious that novices are different from experts in a variety of ways. In particular, novices are likely to be less accurate than experts in predicting outcomes of interest, by definition in some cases. However, it is reasonable for us to ask whether there are certain judgment strategies that frequently underlie expert performance. As discussed previously, a large knowledge base that allows experts to draw on a larger store of memorized facts is one difference that explains a portion the expert-novice performance difference. A large knowledge base allows experts to employ a case-based judgment strategy. Case-based strategies rely on the impressive human ability to judge similarity between cases. Using such a strategy, an expert compares the attributes of the current case to those stored in long term memory, and makes a judgment in the current case that matches the judgment made in the stored case. This is a common strategy in fields such as law or medicine (Carroll, 1987), but it is also employed by chess masters (Charness, 1981), and is likely employed by experts in other domains as well (e.g., case studies are often used in MBA programs, and it is likely that business people use them as well). Case-based strategies are likely to be most useful and accurate in highly predictable environments because, in such environments, any individual case will be quite similar to other similar cases (Hoch & Schkade, 1996).[4] Using a case-based strategy, individual differences in the number of cases stored in long term memory and in the veridicality of the similarity metric will underlie differences in observed expertise. Importantly, there are two ways to learn the necessary case knowledge and similarity metric: experience and instruction.

Instruction is one of the most common ways that people become expert in a domain. For example, someone can take a course on computer programming and learn how to debug a program, or a doctor can attend medical school and become better than a novice at diagnosis. Instruction tends to be the primary path to skilled performance in most scientific and technical fields (Chi et al., 1988; Ericsson, 1996; Ericsson & Charness, 1994), which makes sense because these are fields in which "practice makes perfect" and in which there is an established base of facts and relationships to be mastered. Experience is another route to skilled performance, though the literature suggests that it is a much less successful path than instruction (Dawes, 1979; Eisenstein, 2002; Ericsson, 1996; Ericsson & Charness, 1994; Hoch, 2002; Klayman, 1988). Some people do appear to have learned complex rules that make them expert in a domain from experience. For example, Ceci and Liker (1986) showed that there exist experts at predicting the outcome of horse races (and their expertise extended to making money at it), and Einhorn (1974) showed that some pathologists used highly configural strategies in diagnosis. However, within both groups of experts, not all were accurate, and most were unable to articulate how they arrived at their predictions.

In fact, a robust finding is that many so-called experts (who may have substantial experience) are nonetheless inaccurate (Grove & Meehl, 1996; Meehl, 1954; Shanteau, 1988a). This appears to be most true when the environment of prediction has considerable unmodelable uncertainty in it, for example, when predicting the behavior of people (e.g., psychological or psychiatric diagnosis, financial forecasting). However, it is clear from numerous studies that mere experience is unlikely to lead to expert performance, contrary to H1 (learning from experience). As discussed earlier, the development of expertise is most likely when the task characteristics identified by Shanteau in his Theory of Expert Competence (Shanteau, 1988a; Shanteau, 1988b) are satisfied, and when the would-be expert has both the motivation and the ability to learn. Learning from experience is more difficult than learning by instruction, and the likelihood of developing expertise from experience is greatest when several conditions are satisfied. First, the outcome and the feedback relating to that outcome should be unambiguous. Second, the feedback about whether the expert's prediction was correct should be immediate (feedback that comes months or years later, as in many financial decisions, is not as helpful). Third, the number of experiences should be "large" (see Klayman, 1988, for a review). For example, learning how to appraise used cars is a skill that is likely to be learned from experience. But in order to learn the prices of used cars, the would-be expert must observe hundreds or even thousands of used car auctions, each time comparing his predicted price to the actual selling price, updating their knowledge base. Theory would predict that it would be much more difficult to learn medical diagnosis from experience, because outcomes are frequently ambiguous (or unknown), a critical input to the decision is probability, which is never directly observed, and when outcome feedback exists, it is temporally distant from decision making.

Amount of experience. Amount of experience is not a good predictor of performance (Ericsson & Charness, 1994; Grove & Meehl, 1996). This appears to be largely due to a subtlety in the definition of "experience." For most people, experience is the amount of time spent "doing" an activity. For example, if someone had played tennis for 20 years, they would say that they had 20 years of experience playing tennis. It appears that it is not really mere experience that leads to improved performance. What is necessary is the explicit comparison of one's performance with the correct outcomes. In the expertise literature, experience gained with the explicit goal of identifying discrepancies between one's mental model and the true state of the world is called *practice* (Charness, 1981; Ericsson & Charness, 1994). Practice is highly correlated with expertise.

Objective vs. Subjective Knowledge. Two separate paradigms exist for identifying experts: an objective test can be administered, and those who score high enough are termed experts; alternatively, people can be asked for a subjective opinion of how expert they are in a given field (e.g., compare Brucks, 1985; Mitchell & Dacin, 1996). Both techniques have advantages and disadvantages. Objective tests of knowledge are best when there is an obvious true/false quality to the questions under consideration, where the investigator can verify the correctness of the answer given, and where the costs of testing are reasonable. Subjective expertise is cheap, easy to collect, and generally involves no more than self-reported scale measures. Obviously another approach, pursued by both Brucks and Mitchell and Dacin, is to collect measures of expertise and compare their efficacy in predicting outcomes of interest. Numerous researchers have found that self-reported expertise is not a reliable predictor of accuracy (Brucks, 1985; Ceci & Liker, 1986; Grove & Meehl, 1996; Meehl, 1954; Spence & Brucks, 1997), although other studies have found consistencies between self-reports and objective measures (e.g., Mitchell & Dacin 1996). Other than comparing the task characteristics under investigation to Shanteau's Theory of Expert Competence (1988a), there does not appear to be a reliable method for predicting in which tasks self-reports will be a valid measure of expertise.

Experimental Paradigms

Given the breadth of what can be learned, and how people become expert, it should not be surprising that numerous different experimental methodologies have arisen. In this section, we provide an overview of the most important of them.

Test after Training. Perhaps the easiest paradigm for testing the acquisition of expertise is "test after training." In this type of experiment, novices are brought into the laboratory and are exposed to initial "training" stimuli. During the training phase, a stimulus is presented, the subject makes a response, and immediate veridical feedback is given. Based on the feedback, the subject updates his knowledge base, and the training continues. Training may continue until a fixed number of repetitions has been reached or until the subject is able to achieve a predetermined level of accuracy (training to a criterion). Regardless of how training ends, at some point there is a test phase.

During the test phase, stimuli are presented and subjects make responses, but no feedback is given. Under the assumption that the decision weights (and learning) obtained by the end of training do not change without feedback, the test phase is then a test of the acquired knowledge (e.g., Brehmer, 1987; Eisenstein & Hutchinson, 2006; Mellers, 1980; Meyer, 1987; West, 1996).

Intentional vs. Incidental Learning Goals. Most people think of learning as a deliberate process, but learning may proceed both intentionally or incidentally. When learning intentionally, people tend to actively test hypotheses to uncover rules or generalizations that hold across several examples (e.g., Bruner et al., 1956; Eisenstein & Hutchinson, 2006; Hoch & Deighton, 1989; Klayman & Ha, 1987; Wattenmaker, 1993; West, 1996). Incidental learning refers to the learning of complex information as a side-effect of performing some other activity. When such learning proceeds without awareness of what has been learned, it is termed implicit learning. In a series of seminal papers, Reber (1967, 1969), characterized implicit learning by two principles: (1) knowledge is not fully accessible to the conscious mind, so that subjects cannot provide a complete (or in some cases, any) description of what they have learned; and (2) the process gives rise to abstract knowledge, meaning that what is learned is more complex than a simple association or frequency count (both of which are frequently studied in the implicit memory literature, see Berry & Dienes, 1991). From the point of view of consumer research, incidental learning is important because consumers typically are not in a strategic problem solving or learning frame of mind when they are being exposed to potentially useful information.

In the psychological literature, incidental learning has been investigated in memory tasks, the control of complex systems, sequence learning, correlation assessment, MCPL function-learning, and in the learning of artificial grammars (e.g., Berry & Broadbent, 1987; Nisbett & Wilson, 1977; Reber, 1967; Reber, 1969; Seger, 1994; Wattenmaker, 1993). Artificial grammars were pioneered by Reber (1967, 1969). In these experiments, subjects typically study and memorize strings of 15–25 letters produced by an artificial grammar. After learning, subjects are asked to evaluate whether novel strings conform to the grammar, and they usually achieve accuracy levels of 60–80% (Reber, 1989). This type of stimulus is not usually encountered in marketing, although the demonstration that subjects notice regularities in seemingly meaningless strings may have implications for advertising and branding research. Another paradigm has subjects learn covariation between features within visual stimuli or between a visual stimulus and a verbal label. Although the covariations are usually simple, subjects do not explicitly detect them, perhaps because they are a priori improbable or because they involve small alterations. (such as a covariation between women's hair length and their personality, e.g., Lewicki, 1986; Lewicki et al., 1997). These studies typically use latency time ("efficiency") as the dependent variable to demonstrate that learning has occurred. For these studies, the link to consumer research is more obvious, because the entire process of branding involves the unconscious association of a meaningless stimulus (the brand name or logo) and an affective response. The demonstration that people unconsciously pick up on such associations is interesting, and the fact that they learn the associations incidentally to performing other tasks implies that H1 of the perfect world hypotheses may be more likely. Unfortunately, the correlations that are generally studied are considerably simpler than standard consumer-usage stimuli, and the incidental tasks are more focused, less noisy, and atypical of consumer behavior. MCPL function-learning represents the prototypical experiment in the MCPL stream in which subjects must learn the relationship between cues and a criterion from outcome feedback. Some subjects may intentionally learn these relationships, but evidence exists for substantial incidental learning (e.g., Eisenstein, 2002; Eisenstein & Hutchinson, 2006). Consumers may pick up incidental functions when learning prices in a market, or when learning attribute-quality relationships. Dynamic systems learning is similar to MCPL function-learning, as it requires subjects to control the value of an outcome variable by changing another variable. For example, in Berry and Broadbent's (1984) study, subjects had control over the size of the workforce in a sugar factory, which they used to control the amount of sugar output. Subjects who learned the dynamic system showed both explicit knowledge and implicit knowledge that was acquired incidentally, and their performance differed greatly from their explicit knowledge.

Overall, results from incidental learning experiments demonstrate that subjects can learn a substantial amount without being able to verbalize that knowledge, and that substantial amounts of expressible knowledge can be learned without deliberate attention to the learning process, supporting H1. Proponents of implicit learning argue that a counterintuitive characteristic of implicit learning has been robustly demonstrated: conscious attempts to discover and learn a pattern sometimes impede learning, at least when the pattern is not simple (see Howard & Howard, 2001). Lack of conscious awareness is typically demonstrated by subjects' inability to verbalize what they learned, or by a dissociation between confidence and accuracy such that subjects are (uncharacteristically) underconfident. However, there is considerable debate as to exactly what is being learned incidentally, how that knowledge is represented, and how transferable the knowledge is to new situations (e.g., see Dienes & Berry, 1997, and the antecedent articles). A reasonable integrative view would be that both intentional and incidental learning processes are likely to play a role in learning in many naturalistic environments.

In marketing, few studies have directly examined incidental or implicit learning. Typically, those studies that have been done have examined the learning a simple contingencies between two events or variables, such as attributes and price, or products and benefits. Most of the research has found that learning is successful, but only in some situations. For example, research on covariation assessment has found that consumers are able to learn contingencies between two variables such as price and quality (e.g., Bettman et al., 1986), but this learning is strongly biased by prior beliefs (Alloy & Tabachnik, 1984). Since simple contingencies are difficult to learn, more complex informational environments should present even greater problems. More complex stimuli introduce problems of selective attention and information overload (Eisenstein & Hutchinson, 2006; Hutton et al., 1986; Meyer, 1987), and the results in more complex domains depend critically on situational factors, including distracter stimuli, memory load, and learning goal (e.g., Hutchinson & Alba, 1991).

Feedback and Incentives. One of the necessary conditions for the development of expertise is receiving veridical feedback. We will follow the definition of Kluger and DeNisi (1996), and define feedback as "actions taken by an external agent to provide information regarding some aspect of one's performance on a task." Feedback is frequently combined with an incentive to get the answer correct. In the real world, such incentives take the form of arbitrage opportunities, promotions, or other payoffs for getting the answer right. In laboratory settings, incentives are typically structured by the investigator so that subjects are better off when they answer correctly. Contrary to popular wisdom, neither feedback nor incentives are sufficient to guarantee the development of expertise, and in some cases either may reduce the rate of learning.

Feedback can refer to outcomes or to the process used to arrive at those outcomes. For example, someone attempting to learn the link between attributes and product price at an auction could be given feedback about the actual transaction price for each product (outcome feedback) or they could be given information about how they weighted the input attributes to arrive at their answer (i.e., process feedback, possibly derived from a regression model of their judgments), or both. Both outcome and process feedback are frequently used in learning experiments (e.g., Brehmer, 1980; Eisenstein & Hutchinson, 2006; Hammond et al., 1973; Mellers, 1980; Meyer, 1987). Most people believe that feedback improves performance, and there is no shortage of studies to provide evidence for this position (e.g., Brehmer, 1987; see Klayman, 1988, for a review; Mellers, 1980). However, taken as a whole, improvements from feedback have been mixed, and the effect of feedback interventions (FI) has ranged from positive to negative. In their meta-analysis, Kluger and DeNisi (1996) found that, although the average Cohen's d for feedback interventions was .41, nearly 38% of all feedback interventions decreased performance (resulting in a negative d). They proposed a feedback intervention theory (FIT) to predict the effect of a feedback intervention based on: (1) the cues of the feedback message, (2) the nature of the task, and (3) situational and personality variables. Specifically, FIT proposes that feedback may interfere with learning for a number of reasons. First, feedback may direct attention away from some details of the task toward higher-level constructs (such as attention to self-esteem, general executive functions, or evaluation of performance, e.g., Vallacher & Wegner, 1987). Second, feedback may evoke a standard or evaluation criterion which changes the attentional allocation in the task, in which case improvement will result if attention is directed toward meaningful stimuli, or if increased attention allows bad hypotheses to be rejected, but negative effects result if attention is directed to nonproductive stimuli or hypotheses (Eisenstein & Hutchinson, 2006; cf., Kluger & DeNisi, 1996).

Economists love incentives, and typically assume that incentives will increase effort, motivation, and persistence. However, incentives are not universally helpful, and additional effort does not always result in improved performance. Like the effects of feedback, the effects of incentives are complex and vary depending on characteristics of the task and the learning environment (Bonner et al., 2000; Camerer & Hogarth, 1999; Hertwig & Ortmann, 2001, for reviews; see Jenkins et al., 1998). In general, incentives improve performance most in tasks where increased effort is likely to result in better performance, such as memory/recall tasks, MCPL, clerical tasks, and motor tasks (the latter two because they are otherwise boring, and incentives maintain effort). Incentives are likely to have no effect when intrinsic interest in the task is high (because motivation is already at a high level). And incentives are likely to hurt performance in tasks that require flexibility in mental models (e.g., Gestalt "set" and problem-representation tasks such as brain teasers) and when it would be better to rely on automatic processes (e.g., "choking" in sports, test anxiety). Task characteristics are important because it has been found that additional motivation to perform well is helpful mainly in tasks where little cognitive effort is required (see Ackerman, 1987 for a review), and increased motivation to perform can disrupt automaticity, causing decreases in performance (i.e., "choking" or similar performance anxiety, cf., Vallacher & Wegner, 1987). In addition, a seminal paper by Hogarth and Gibbs (1991) demonstrated that if the incentives are too "exacting," meaning that subjects are strongly penalized for errors, then incentives lowered overall performance.

Quantitative Modeling

Regression and Bootstrapping. Let us assume that we have an expert, and that this expert is more accurate than a novice at making a decision. One reasonable idea would be to try to capture the judgment strategy, or "policy," of the expert, so that others can derive the benefits of expert decision making without requiring input from the expert herself (e.g., Brehmer, 1987; Eisenstein & Hutchinson, 2006; Meehl, 1954; Meyer, 1987; Spence & Brucks, 1997; West, 1996). Policy capturing is the process of deriving a model of the expert's judgment. When the model of an expert is used to make predictions, rather than the expert herself, this is callrf "bootstrapping" (in the sense of "pulling oneself up by the bootstraps," Meehl, 1954). Usually, policy capturing uses regression to create a linear model of the expert by modeling the outcome as a linear combination of the inputs, which are called "cues." The first priority in capturing a policy is to define the judgment that is to be modeled in such a way that it is understood by the expert to be modeled, and so that the outcome, or "criterion," is properly operationalized. Most commonly, the criterion is operationalized as a rating on a continuous scale (i.e., a scale measure or a continuous prediction such as probability), although discrete choice tasks are also used. After defining the outcome or criterion, a prototypic procedure would be to have an expert make judgments for a large number of naturally occurring (i.e., "real") cases, and then to use the cues and judgments from these cases to form the dataset for the regression model. Of course, this procedure suffers from all of the standard limitations of an observational study, the most significant being the lack of control over cue leverage, outliers, and cue intercorrelations, all of which may distort the parameter estimates (Brehmer & Brehmer, 1988). These limitations suggest an alternative approach based on conjoint analysis, in which cues and distributions of levels of the cues are chosen, a series of profiles are created, and the expert judgments of these conjoint profiles are used to construct the regression model.

To begin with, the policy analyst must choose which cues to include. Frequently, the number of cues will have to be whittled down to a manageable number through interviews with experts in the domain of study (e.g., Hammond et al., 1977; Wind et al., 1989). The selection of cues is obviously a critical step, because omitted cues will introduce substantial bias into predictions and will further distort the task. Fortunately, experts tend to report using more cues than they actually do (Shanteau, 1992), so this procedure is more likely to include unimportant cues than to omit relevant ones. After choosing the cues, a context is defined, the cue distributions are developed, and cue intercorrelations are determined. The use of correlated cues is somewhat different than in a typical conjoint study, in which cues are frequently orthogonal, but the point is to try to match as closely as possible the actual environment to be modeled so as to avoid inadvertently slipping away from the expert's domain of competence. After setting up these prerequisites, the expert is exposed to multiple stimuli that consist of the cue profiles that have been defined, and she renders a judgment for each stimulus on the criterion scale. The policy analyst then regresses the criterion onto the cues to determine cue weights.

Although the conjoint-based approach to policy capturing may seem natural to consumer researchers, it has significant limitations (Brehmer & Brehmer, 1988). First, it is critical to keep both the task context and the output response mode (i.e., rating, ranking, choice) as close to that which the expert normally uses as is possible. This is because deviations in response mode or in presentation of the cues can disrupt various psychological processes that underlie expertise, including the retrieval of stored exemplars from memory, perceptual fluency in processing the cues, and overlearned or automatic cue integration procedures that experts normally use (imagine, for example, sitting on an admissions committee and evaluating candidates using unfamiliar scales for test scores and GPAs). These disruptions can cause experts to construct judgment rules on the fly, rather than using the previously stored policies that should be captured (see Brehmer & Brehmer, 1988, for a review; see also, Eisenstein, 2002; Eisenstein & Hutchinson, 2006). For the same reasons, the task should be designed to be as representative as possible. Other questions arise regarding the linearity of the model used by experts, whether to include interactions or not, and whether correlations or beta weights should be used as the reported outcome.

A frequent finding is that "bootstrap" models of an expert outperform the expert himself (Dawes, 1979; Grove & Meehl, 1996; Meehl, 1954). This is largely due to the fact that the model has no inconsistency in its predictions (see Camerer, 1981 for a comprehensive treatment).

Time-Series Analyses. Another way to model the development of expertise is to examine gains in expertise that accrue from training. One possibility is simply to look at people with different amounts of training, practice, or education in a domain, although this design suffers from the standard problems of cross-sectional analysis. Another approach is to do a longitudinal study of subjects as they progress through a training program. For example, Lehman, Lempert, and Nisbett

(1988) investigated the effects of graduate training on reasoning ability using both cross-sectional and longitudinal comparisons, and they found evidence that graduate training did increase reasoning ability, albeit differentially by field of study.

Longitudinal studies take a long time, and they suffer from other confounds as well. Another possibility is that researchers can bring otherwise naïve subjects into a laboratory, train them to perform some task, and can analyze the pre- and post-training data (e.g., Eisenstein & Hutchinson, 2006; Hoch & Schkade, 1996; Meyer, 1987; West, 1996). Frequently, training proceeds not just through a single pre- and post-test, but rather through a series of repeated study–test cycles. For example, a subject might receive feedback regarding his or her performance for an X trial study block, which could be followed by a Y trial test block in which stimuli were presented, but no feedback given (e.g., Meyer, 1987). The study–test cycle would then repeat a number of times, and the resulting data can be analyzed to generate a "learning curve," or a model of the rate of improvement.

Our intuitions and experience tell us that most tasks that we perform become faster with practice. What is surprising, however, is that the rate and shape of improvement appear to be common across many types of task. Specifically, learning curves demonstrate rapid improvement followed by diminishing marginal returns to further practice, which is a pattern than is usually modeled with a power function.[5] The widespread use of power functions to model learning curves has given rise to the phrase "the power law of practice." Power laws are ubiquitous, and have been demonstrated in physical tasks such as pressing buttons or rolling cigars (Newell & Rosenbloom, 1981), in mental tasks such as generating geometry proofs, writing books, mental arithmetic, and reading inverted text (Delaney et al., 1998; Newell & Rosenbloom, 1981; Ohlsson, 1992), and in myriad other tasks of both long and short duration (see, Heathcote et al., 2000, for a review). The ubiquity of learning curves has been noted for over 100 years, and it appears that multiple underlying processes explain their existence. For example, it has been proposed that learning curves arise from error correction (Ohlsson, 1992). Alternatively, learning curves could be explained by "horse race models," in which response time is a function of the fastest retrieval time among memory traces (e.g., Logan, 1988). ACT-R (Anderson, 1993) and SOAR (Newell, 1990) explain learning curves in different ways. ACT-R postulates that stored rules and memory traces are strengthened according to a power law, and applications of SOAR have explained the power law as arising out of hierarchical learning that begins with low-level, widely applicable actions and proceeds to learn larger, infrequently occurring patterns. Overall, learning curves represent one of the great triumphs of cognitive psychology. They provide substantial evidence that learning is ubiquitous, they provide a mathematical framework ("law") to use in modeling the rate of improvement, and the explanations above provide process explanations for why the mathematical structure should hold.

CONCLUSIONS

In this chapter, we have reviewed consumer learning and expertise from two complementary perspectives. First, we examined the evidence supporting and challenging a "perfect world" perspective in which (1) increases in familiarity lead to increases in expertise (i.e., learning from experience) and (2) as expertise increases, people become better and more efficient in their roles as consumers (i.e., inproved consumer welfare). The evidence is mixed, but it generally supports the conclusion that this perspective holds as a first approximation or stylized fact,. However, not all experience leads to expertise, and expertise sometimes has costs, many of which are due to overconfidence in and overgeneralization from one's knowledge. Second, we presented a "toolbox" of theories and methods that have been found useful in research on learning and expertise. Our toolbox is certainly not exhaustive, but it does cover a wide range of work in both areas. Thus, we hope the reader is now better prepared to address the what, why, and how of research on consumer learning and expertise in their own work.

NOTES

1. A more extensive treatment of this topic can be found in Hutchinson, Eisenstein, and Alba (2007).
2. Knowledge calibration is a form of metacognition, which is defined as a person's knowledge and beliefs about any type of cognitive process or mental activity. For a discussion of marketplace metacognition and social intelligence, see Wright (2002).
3. An interesting historical review and commentary on this divergence can be found in Bargh and Ferguson (2000).
4. To see this, imagine a world with an R2 = 1.0. Obviously, for any combination of X's, all that is necessary is to have a single observation with the same X values and the prediction will be exact. Furthermore, linear interpolation will also be zero-error.
5. See Heathcote, Brown, and Mewhort (2000), however, who claim that individual-level improvements are better modeled by an exponential, rather than a power function. The question of whether learning curves follow exponential or power functions is not devoid of theoretical content. If learning follows an exponential function, than learning is based on a fixed percentage of what remains to be learned, whereas if learning follows a power function, then the rate of learning slows down.

REFERENCES

Ackerman, P. L. (1987). Individual differences in skill learning: An integration of psychometric and information processing perspectives. *Psychological Bulletin, 102*(1), 3–27.

Alba, J. W., & Hutchinson, J. W. (1987). Dimensions of consumer expertise. *Journal of Consumer Research, 13* (March), 411–454.

Alba, J. W., & Hutchinson, J. W. (1991). Public policy implications of consumer knowledge. In Paul N. Bloom (Ed.), *Advances in marketing and public policy* (Vol. II, pp. 1–40). Greenwich, CT: JAI Press.

Alba, J. W., & Hutchinson, J. W. (2000). Knowledge calibration: What consumers know and what they think they know. *Journal of Consumer Research, 27* (September), 123–156.

Allen, C. T., & Janiszewski, C. A. (1989). Assessing the role of contingency awareness in attitudinal conditioning with implications for advertising research, *Journal of Marketing Research,* 26 (February), 30–43.

Alloy, B., & Tabachnik, N. (1984). Assessment of covariation by humans and animals: The joint influence of prior expectations and current situational information. *Psychological Review, 91*(1), 112–149.

Anderson, J. R. (1982). Acquisition of cognitive skill. *Psychological Review, 89*(4), 369–406.

Anderson, J. R. (1983). *The architecture of cognition.* Cambridge, MA: Harvard University Press.

Anderson, J. R. (1993). *Rules of the mind.* Hillsdale, NJ: Erlbaum.

Ashby, F. G., & Maddox, W. T. (1998). Stimulus categorization. In M. H. Birnbaum (Ed.), *Handbook of perception and cognition: Measurement, judgment, and decision making* (pp. 251–301). New York: Academic Press.

Bargh, J. A.(1994). The four horsemen of automaticity: Awareness, efficiency, intention, and control in social cognition. In R. S. Wyer, Jr. & T. K. Srull (Eds.), *Handbook of social sognition* (pp. 1–40). Hillsdale, NJ: Erlbaum.

Bargh, J. A., & Chartrand, T. L. (1999). The unbearable automaticity of being. *American Psychologist, 54* (July), 462–479.

Bargh, J. A. &. Ferguson, M. J. (2000). Beyond behaviorism: On the automaticity of higher mental processes. *Psychological Bulletin, 126*(6), 925–945.

Barsalou, L. W. (1985). Ideals, central tendency, and frequency of instantiation as determinants of graded structure. *Journal of Experimental Psychology: Learning, Memory, and Cognition, 11* (October), 629–654.

Bearden, W. O., Hardesty, D. M., &. Rose, R. L. (2001). Consumer self-confidence: Refinements in conceptualization and measurement., *Journal of Consumer Research, 28* (June), 121–134.

Beilock, S. L., & Carr, T. (2001). On the fragility of skilled performance: What governs choking under pressure? *Journal of Experimental Psychology: General, 130,* 701–725.

Beilock, S. L., Benett I., Bertenthal, A., McCoy, M., & Carr, T. (2004a). Haste does not always make waste: Expertise, direction of attention, and speed versus accuracy in performing sensorimotor skills. *Psychonomic Bulletin & Review, 11*(2), 373–379,

Beilock, S. L., Culp, C. A.,. Holt, L. E., & Carr, T. (2004b). More on the rragility of skilled performance: Choking under Pressure in Mathematical Problem Solving. *Journal of Experimental Psychology: General, 133*(4), 584–600.

Beilock, S. L., Wierenga, S. A., & Carr, T. H. (2002). Expertise, attention, and memory in sensorimotor skill execution: Impact of novel task constraints on dual-task performance and episodic memory. *Quarterly Journal of Experimental Psychology: Human Experimental Psychology, 55A*, 1211–1240.

Becker, G. (1993). *Human capital.* Chicago: University of Chicago Press.

Berry, D. C., & Broadbent, D. E. (1984). On the relationship between task performance and associated verbalizable knowledge. *Quarterly Journal of Experimental Psychology A: Human Experimental Psychology, 36A*(2), 209–231.

Berry, D. C., & Broadbent, D. E. (1987). The combination of explicit and implicit learning processes in task control. *Psychological Research, 49*(1), 7–15.

Berry, D. C., & Dienes, Z. (1991), The relationship between implicit memory and implicit learning.

Bettman, J. R., & Park, C. W. (1980). Effects of prior knowledge and experience and phase of the choice process on consumer decision processes: A protocol analysis. *Journal of Consumer Research, 7* (December), 234–248.

Bettman, J. R., D. R., & Scott, C. A. (1986). Covariation assessment by consumers. *Journal of Consumer Research, 13*(3), 316–326.

Blattberg, R. C., &. Hoch, S. J. (1990). Database models and managerial intuition: 50% model + 50% manager. *Management Science, 36*(8), 887–899.

Bonner, S. E., Hastie, R., Sprinkle, G. B., & Young, S. M. (2000). Financial incentives and performance in laboratory tasks: Implications for management accounting. *Journal of Management Accounting Research, 12*, 19–64.

Brehmer, B. (1980). Effect of cue validity on learning of complex rules in probabilistic inference tasks. *Acta Psychologica, 44*(2), 201–210.

Brehmer, B. (1987). Note on subjects' hypotheses in multiple-cue probability learning. *Organizational Behavior and Human Decision Processes, 40*(3), 323–329.

Brehmer, B., & Brehmer, A. (1988). What have we learned about human judgment from thirty years of policy capturing. In B. Brehmer & C. R. B. Joyce (Eds.), *Human judgment: The SJT view.* Amsterdam: North-Holland.

Brinol, P., Petty, R. E., & Tormala, Z. L. (2004). Self-validation of cognitive responses to advertisements.*Journal of Consumer Research, 30* (March), 559–573.

Brucks, M. (1985)..The effects of product class knowledge on information search behavior. *Journal of Consumer Research, 18* (June), 1–16.

Bruner, J. S., Goodnow, J., & Austin, G. (1956). *A study of thinking.* New York: Wiley.

Camerer, C. (1981). General conditions for the success of bootstrapping models. *Organizational Behavior and Human Performance, 27*(3): 411.

Camerer, C. F., & Hogarth, R. M. (1999). The effects of financial incentives in experiments: A review and capital-labor-production framework. *Journal of Risk and Uncertainty, 19*(1-3), 7–42.

Carroll, B. (1987). Expert systems for clinical diagnosis: Are they worth the effort? *Behavioral Science, 32*(4), 274–292.

Ceci, S. J. & Liker, J. (1986). A day at the races: IQ, expertise, and cognitive complexity. *Journal of Experimental Psychology: General,* 115, 255–266.

Charness, N. (1981). Search in chess: Age and skill differences. *Journal of Experimental Psychology: Human Perception and Performance, 7*, 467–476.

Chartrand, T. L., & Bargh, J. A. (1996). Automatic activation of impression formation and memorization goals: Nonconscious goal priming reproduces effects of explicit task instructions. *Journal of Personality and Social Psychology, 71*, 464–478.

Chase, W. G., & Simon, H. A. (1973). Perception in Chess. *Cognitive Psychology, 4*(1), 55–81.

Chi, M. T. H, Glaser, R., & Farr, M. J. (Eds.) (1988). *The nature of expertise.* Hillsdale, NJ: Erlbaum.

Chomsky, N. (1959). On certain formal properties of grammars. *Information and Control,* 1, 91–112.

Cohen, J. B., & Basu, K. (1987). Alternative models of categorization — Toward a contingent processing framework. *Journal of Consumer Research, 13*(4), 455–472.

Cohen, N., & Squire., L. R. (1980). Preserved learning and retention of pattern analyzing skill in amnesia: Dissociation of knowing how and knowing that. *Science, 210,* 207–209.

Cowley, E., & Janus, E. (2004). Not necessarily better but certainly different: A limit to the advertising misinformation effect on memory. *Journal of Consumer Research, 31,* 229–223.

Cowley, E., & Mitchell, A. A. (2003). The moderating effect of product knowledge on the learning and organization of product information. *Journal of Consumer Research, 30*(December) 443–454.

Delaney, P. F., Reder, L. M., Staszewski, J. J., & Ritter, F. R. (1998). The strategy-specific nature of improvement: The power law applies by strategy within task. *Psychological Science, 9*(1), 1.

Darley, W. K. & Lim, J. (1993). Assessing demand artifacts in consumer research: An alternative perspective. *Journal of Consumer Research, 20*(3), 489–495.

Dellaert, B. G. C., & Stremersch, S. (2005). Marketing mass-sustomized products: Striking a balance between utility and complexity. *Journal of Marketing Research, 52* (May) 219–227.

DeLosh, E. L., Busemeyer, J. R., & McDaniel, M. A. (1997). Extrapolation: The sine qua non for abstraction in function learning. *Journal of Experimental Psychology: Learning, Memory, and Cognition, 23*(4), 968–986.

Dienes, Z., & Berry, D. (1997). Implicit synthesis. *Psychonomic Bulletin and Review, 4*(1), 68–72.

Dillon, W. R., Madden, T. J., Kirmani, A., & Mukherjee, S. (2001). Understanding what's in a brand rating: A model for assessing brand and attribute effects and their relationship to brand equity. *Journal of Marketing Research, 38* (November), 415–429.

Eisenstein, E. M. (2002). Action-based reasoning: The cost of learning and the benefit of thinking less. *Dissertation Abstracts International.*

Eisenstein, E. M., Hutchinson, J. W. (2005). Action-based learning: Goals and attention in multiple feedback categorization. Working paper.

Eisenstein, E. M., & Hutchinson, J. W. (2006). Action-based learning: Goals and attention in the acquisition of market knowledge. *Journal of Marketing Research, 43*(May) 244–258.

Ericsson, K. A., & Charness, L. (1994). Expert performance: Its structure and acquisition. *American Psychologist, 49*(8), 7257–747.

Ericsson, K. A., & Kintsch, W. (1995). Longterm working memory. *Psychological Review, 102*(2), 211–245.

Ericsson, K., & Anders E.. (1996). *The road to excellence: the acquisition of expert performance in the arts and sciences, sports, and games.* Mahwah, NJ: Erlbaum.

Ericsson, K. A., Patel, V., & Kintsch, W. (2000). How experts' adaptations to representative task demands account for the expertise effect in memory recall: Comment on Vicente and Wang (1998). *Psychological Review, 107*(3), 578–592.

Fanselow M. S. & Poulos A.M. (2005). The neuroscience of mammalian associative learning. *Annual Review Psychology, 56,* 207–234.

Feigenbaum, E. A., & Simon, H. A. (1984). EPAM-like models of recognition and learning. *Cognitive Science, 8,* 305–306.

Fitzsimons, G. J., Hutchinson, J. W. Alba, J. W.,. Chartrand, T. L., Huber, J., Kardes, F. R., Geeta Menon, G. Priya Raghubir, Russo, J. E., Shiv, B., Tavassoli, N. T., &Williams, P. (2002). Non-conscious influences on consumer choice. *Marketing Letters, 13*(3), 267–277.

Grove, W. M., & Meehl, P. E. (1996). Comparative efficiency of informal (subjective, impressionistic) and formal (mechanical, algorithmic) prediction procedures: The clinical-statistical controversy. *Psychology, Public Policy, & Law, 2*(2), 293–323.

Hammond, K. R. (1955). Probabilistic functioning and the clinical method. *Psychological Review, 62,* 255–262.

Hammond, K. R., & Brehmer, B. (1973). Quasi-rationality and distrust: Implications for international conflict. In L. Rappoport & D. Summers (Eds.), *Human judgment and social interactions.* New York: Holt, Rineholt, & Winston.

Hammond, K. R., Summers, D. A., &. Deane, D. H. (1973). Negative effects of outcome-feedback in multiple-cue probability learning. *Organizational Behavior and Human Decision Processes, 9*(1), 30–34.

Hammond, K. R., Rohrbaugh, J., Mumpower, J., & Adelman, L. (1977). Social judgment theory: Applications in policy formation. In F. Kaplan & Schwartz, (Eds.), *Human judgment and decision processes in applied settings.* New York: Academic Press.

Hasher, L., & Zacks, R. T. (1979). Automatic and effortful processes in memory. *Journal of Experimental Psychology: General, 108,* 356–388.

Hasher, L., & Zacks, R. T. (1984). Automatic processing of fundamental information: The case of frequency of occurrence. *American Psychologist, 39,* 1372–1388.

Heathcote, A., Brown, S., & Mewhort, D. J. K. (2000),. The power law repealed: The case for an exponential law of practice. *Psychonomic Bulletin and Review, 7,* 185–207.

Hertwig, R., & Ortmann, A. (2001). Experimental practices in economics: A methodological challenge for psychologists? *Behavioral and Brain Sciences, 24,* 383–403.

Hoch, S. J. (2002). Product experience is seductive. *Journal of Consumer Research, 29*(3), 448–454.

Hoch, S. J., & Schkade, D. A. (1996). A psychological approach to decision support systems. *Management Science, 42*(1), 51–64.

Hoch, S. J., & Deighton, J. (1989). Managing what consumers learn from experience. *Journal of Marketing, 53.*

Hoch, S. J., & Ha, Y-W. (1986). Consumer learning: Advertising and the ambiguity of product experience. *Journal of Consumer Research, 13*(2), 221–233.

Hogarth, R. M., Gibbs, B. J., McKenzie, C. R., & Marquis, M. A. (1991). Learning from feedback: Exactingness and incentives. *Journal of Experimental Psychology: Learning, Memory, and Cognition, 17*(4), 734–752.

Howard, D. V., & Howard, J. W. Jr. (2001). When it does hurt to try: Adult age differences in the effects of instructions on implicit pattern learning. *Psychonomic Bulletin and Review, 8*(4), 798–805.

Howard, J. A., & Sheth, J. N. (1969). *The theory of buyer behavior.* New York: Wiley.

Huang, Y., & Hutchinson, J. W. (2006). An indirect approach to measuring cognitive responses to advertisements. Working paper.

Huffman, C., & M. J. (1993). Goal-oriented experiences and the development of knowledge. *Journal of Consumer Research, 20*(2), 190–207.

Hummel, J. E., &. Holyoak, K. J. (1997). Distributed representations of structure: A theory of analogical access and mapping. *Psychological Review, 104*(3), 427–466.

Hutchinson, J. W., & Alba, J. W. (1991). Ignoring irrelevant information: Situational determinants of consumer learning. *Journal of Consumer Research, 18*(December), 325–346.

Hutchinson, J. W., & Alba, J. W. (1997). Heuristics and biases in the 'eye-balling' of data: The effects of context on intuitive correlation assessment. *Journal of Experimental Psychology: Learning, Memory, and Cognition, 23* (May), 591–621.

Hutchinson, J. W., Eisenstein, E. M., & Alba, J. W. (2007). Consumer learning and expertise. Unpublished manuscript.

Hutchinson, J. W., Kalyan Raman, K, & Mantrala, M. (1994). Finding choice alternatives in memory: Probability models of brand name recall. *Journal of Marketing Research, 31*(November), 441–461.

Hutton, R. B., Mauser, G. A., Filiatrault, P., & Ahtola, O. T. (1986). Effects of cost-related feedback on consumer knowledge and consumption behavior: A field experimental approach. *Journal of Consumer Research, 13*(3), 327–336.

Jacoby, L. L., & Brooks, L. R. (1984). Nonanalytic cognition: Memory, perception, and concept learning. In G. H. Bower (Ed.), *The Psychology of Learning and Motivation* (Vol. 18, 379–421) . New York: Academic Press.

Janiszewski, C., & Luk, W. (1993). The influence of classical conditioning procedures on subsequent attention to the conditioned brand. *Journal of Consumer Research, 20*(September), 171–189.

Jenkins, G. D., Mitra, A., Gupta, N., & Shaw, J. D. (1998). Are financial incentives related to performance? A meta-analytic review of empirical research. *Journal of Applied Psychology, 83*(5), 777–787.

Johnson, K. E., & Mervis, C. B. (1997). Effects of varying levels of expertise on the basic level of categorization. *Journal of Experimental Psychology: General, 126,* 248–277.

Johansen, M. K., & Palmeri, T. J. (2002). Are there representational shifts during category. learning? *Cognitive Psychology, 45,* 482–553.

Juslin, P., Olsson, H., & Olsson, A. C. (2003). Exemplar effects in categorization and multiple-cue judgment. *Journal of Experimental Psychology: General, 132*(1), 133–156.

Juslin, P., Jones, S., Olsson, H., & Winman, A. (2003). Cue abstraction and exemplar memory in categorization. *Journal of Experimental Psychology: Learning, Memory, and Cognition, 29*(5), 924–941.

Kay, A. C., Wheeler, S. C., Bargh, J. A., & Rossa L. (2004). Material priming: The influence of mundane physical objects on situational construal and competitive behavioral choice. *Organizational Behavior and Human Decision Processes, 95*(1), 83–96.

Kellaris, J. J., & Cox, A. D. (1989). The effects of background music in advertising: A reassessment. *Journal of Consumer Research, 16*(1), 113–118.

Kim, J., Allen, C. T., & Kardes, F. R. (1996). An investigation of the mediational mechanisms underlying attitudinal conditioning. *Journal of Marketing Research, 33,* 318–328.

Klayman, J. (1988). On the how and why (not) of learning from outcomes. In Berndt Brehmer & C. R. B. Joyce (Eds.), *Human judgment: The SJT view.* North Holland: Elsevier.

Klayman, J.,& Ha, Y-H. (1987). Confirmation, disconfirmation, and information in hypothesis testing. *Psychological Review, 94*(2), 211–228.

Kluger, A. N., & DeNisi, A. (1996). The effects of feedback interventions on performance: A historical review, a meta-analysis, and a preliminary feedback intervention theory. *Psychological Bulletin, 119*(2), 254–284.

Koehler, D. J., Brenner, L. A., & Griffin, D. (2002). The calibration of expert judgment: Heuristics and biases beyond the laboratory. In T. Gilovich, D. Griffin, & D. Kahneman (Eds.), *Heuristics and biases: The psychology of intuitive judgment.* Cambridge: Cambridge University Press.

Kruschke, J. K. (1992). ALCOVE: An exemplar-based connectionist model of category learning. *Psychological Review, 99*(1), 22–44.

Lehman, D. R., Lempert, R. O., & Nisbett, R. E. (1988). The effects of graduate training on reasoning: Formal discipline and thinking about everyday-life events. *American Psychologist, 43*(6), 431–442.

Lewicki, P. (1986). Processing information about covariations that cannot be articulated. *Journal of Experimental Psychology: Learning, Memory, and Cognition, 12*(1), 135–146.

Lewicki, P., Hill, T., & Czyzewska, M. (1997). Hidden covariation detection: A fundamental and ubiquitous phenomenon. *Journal of Experimental Psychology: Learning, Memory, and Cognition, 23*(1), 221–228.

Lichtenstein, S., Fischoff, B., & Phillips, L. D. (1982). Calibration of probabilities: The state of the art to 1980. In D. Kahneman, P. Slovic, & A. Tversky (Eds.), *Judgement under uncertainty: Heuristics and biases* (pp. 306–334). Cambridge: Cambridge University Press.

Liker, J. & Ceci, S. J. (1987). IQ and complexity: The role of experience. *Journal of Experimental Psychology: General, 116,* 304–306.

Logan, G. D. (1988). Toward an instance theory of automatization. *Psychological Review, 95*(4), 492–527.

Logan, G. D. (2002). An instance theory of attention and memory. *Psychological Review, 109*(2) 376–400.

McClelland, J. L., & Rumelhart, D. E. (1981). An interactive activation model of context effects in letter perception: I. An account of basic findings. *Psychological Review, 88*(5), 375–407.

McClelland, J. L., &. Rumelhart, D. E. (1988). *Explorations in parallel distributed processing: A handbook of models, programs, and exercises.* Cambridge, MA: MIT Press.

Medin, D. L., & Schaffer, M. M. (1978). Context theory of classification learning," *Psychological Review, 85*(3), 207–238.

Medin, D. L., & Smith, E. E. (l984). Concepts and concept formation. *Annual Review of Psychology, 35,* 113–138.

Meehl, P. E. (1954). Clinical versus statistical prediction; a theoretical analysis and a review of the evidence. Minneapolis: University of Minnesota Press.

Mellers, B. A. (1980). Configurality in multiple-cue probability learning. *American Journal of Psychology, 93*(3), 429–443.

Meyer, R. J. (1987). The learning of multiattribute judgment policies. *Journal of Consumer Research, 14*(2), 155–173.

Miller, G. A. (1956). The magical number seven, plus or minus two: Some limits on our capacity for processing information. *Psychological Review.*

Mitchell, A. A., & Dacin, P .A. (1996). The assessment of alternative measures of consumer expertise. *Journal of Consumer Research, 23,* 219–239.

Moreau, C. P., Arthur B. Markman, A. B., &. Lehmann, D. R. (2001). 'What is it?' Categorization flexibility and consumers' responses to really new products. *Journal of Consumer Research, 27*(4), 489.

Muthukrishnan, A. V. (1995). Decision ambiguity and incumbent brand advantage. *Journal of Consumer Research, 22* (June), 98–109.

Nedungadi, P., Chattopadhyay, A., & Muthukrishnan, A. V. (2001). Category structure, recall, and choice. *International Journal of Research in Marketing, 18,* 191–202.

Nedungadi, P., & Hutchinson, J. W. (1985). The prototypicality of brands: Relationships with brand awareness, preference and usage. In E. Hirshunan & M. Holbrook (Eds.), *Advances in Consumer Research*, *12*, 498–503.

Newell, A. (1990). *Unified theories of cognition*. Cambridge, MA: Harvard University Press.

Newell, A., & Simon, H. A. (1972). *Human problem solving*. Englewood Cliffs, NJ: Prentice-Hall.

Newell, A., & Rosenbloom, P. S. (1981). Mechanisms of skill acquisition and the law of practice. In J. R. Anderson (Ed.), *Cognitive skills and their acquisition*. Hillsdale, NJ: Erlbaum.

Nisbett, R. E., & Wilson, T. D. (1977). Telling more than we can know: Verbal reports on mental processes. *Psychological Review, 84*(3), 231–259.

Nosofsky, R. M. (1984). Choice, similarity, and the context theory of classification. *Journal of Experimental Psychology: Learning, Memory, and Cognition, 10*(January), 104–114.

Nosofsky, R. M., Palmeri, T. J., & McKinley, S. C. (1994). Rule-plus-exception model of classification learning. *Psychological Review, 101*(1), 53–79.

Obermiller, C., & Spangenberg, E. R. (1998). Development of a scale to measure consumer skepticism toward advertising, *Journal of Consumer Psychology, 7*(2), 159–186.

Ohlsson, S. (1992). The learning curve for writing books: Evidence from Professor Asimov. *Psychological Science, 3*(6), 380–382.

Oskamp, S. (1962). The relation of clinical experience and training methods to several criteria of clinical prediction. *Psychological Monographs, 76*(28, Whole No. 547), 27.

Palmeri, T.J., Wong, A.C. N., & Gauthier, I. (2004). Computational approaches to the development of perceptual experience. *TRENDS in Cognitive Science, 8*, 378–386.

Park, C. W., E. S., & Smith, D. C. (1989). The effects of situational factors on in-store grocery shopping behavior: The role of store environment and time available for shopping. *Journal of Consumer Research, 15* (March), 422–433.

Park, C. W., Mothersbaugh, D. L., & Feick, L. (1994). Consumer knowledge assessment. *Journal of Consumer Research, 21*(June), 71–82.

Petty, R. E., Brinol, P., & Tormala, Z. L. (2002). Thought confidence as a determinant of persuasive: The self-validation hypothesis. *Journal of Personality and Social Psychology, 82*(May), 722–741.

Rangaswamy, A., Eliashberg, J., Burke, R. B., & Wind, J. (1989). Developing marketing expert systems: An application to international negotiations. *Journal of Marketing, 53*(4), 24–39.

Ratchford, B. T. (2001). The economics of consumer knowledge. *Journal of Consumer Research, 27*.

Ratneshwar, S., & Shocker, A. D. (1991). Substitution in use and the role of usage context in product category structures. *Journal of Marketing Research, 28*(August), 281–295.

Reber, A. S. (1967). Implicit learning of artificial grammars.

Reber, A. S. (1969), Transfer of syntactic structure in synthetic languages.

Reber, A. S. (1989). Implicit learning and tacit knowledge. *Journal of Experimental Psychology: General, 118*(3), 219–235.

Rescorla, R. A. (1998). Instrumental learning: Nature and persistence. In M. Sabourin, F. I. M. Craig, & M. Roberts (Eds.), *Proceedings of the XXVI International Congress of Psychology, Vol. 2. Advances in Psychological Science: Biological and Cognitive Aspects* (pp. 239–258). London: Psychology Press.

Rosch, E., & Mervis, C. B. (1975). Family resemblances: Studies in the internal structure of categories. *Cognitive Psychology, 7* (October), 573–605.

Rosch, E., Mervis, C. B., Gray, W. D., Johnson D. M., & Boyes-Braem, P. (1976).Basic objects in natural categories. *Cognitive Psychology, 8*(July), 382–439.

Seger, C. A. (1994). Implicit learning. *Psychological Bulletin, 115*(2), 163–196.

Sanbonmatsu, D. M., Kardes, F. R., & Herr, P. M. (1992). The role of prior knowledge and missing information in multiattribute evaluation. *Organizational Behavior and Human Decision Processes, 51*(February), 76–91.

Shanteau, J. (1988a). Competence in experts: The role of task characteristics. *Organizational Behavior and Human Decision Processes, 53*(2), 252–266.

Shanteau, J. (1988b). Psychological characteristics and strategies of expert decision makers. *Acta Psychologica, 68*, 203–215.

Shanteau, J. (1992). How much information does an expert use? Is it relevant? *Acta Psychologica, 81*(1), 75–86.

Shanteau, J., & Stewart, T. R. (1992). Why study expert decision making? Some historical perspectives and comments. *Organizational Behavior and Human Decision Processes, 53,* 95–106.

Shiffrin, R. M., & Schneider, W. (1977). Controlled and automatic human information processing: II. Perceptual learning, automatic attending, and a general theory. *Psychological Review, 84,* 127–190.

Shimp, T. A., Stuart, E. W., & Engle, R. W. (1991). A program of classical conditioning experiments testing variations in the conditioned stimulus and context. *Journal of Consumer Research, 18,* 1–12.

Shugan, S. M. (1980). The cost of thinking. *Journal of Consumer Research, 7*(2), 99.

Simon, Herbert A. (1974). How big is a chunk? *Science, 183,* 482–488.

Skinner, B. F. (1957). *Verbal learning.* New York: Appleton-Century-Crofts.

Sloman, Steven A. (1996). The empirical case for two reasoning systems. *Psychological Bulletin, 119*(1), 3–22.

Spence, M. T., & Brucks, M. (1996). The moderating effects of problem characteristics on experts' and novices' judgments. *Journal of Marketing Research, 34,* 233–247.

Sperling, G. (1963). A model for visual memory tasks. *Human Factors, 5,* 19–31.

Sternberg, S. (1966). High-speed scanning in human memory. *Science, 153,* 652–654.

Stigler, G., & Becker, G. (1977). De gustibus non est disputandum. *American Economic Review, 67* (March), 76–90.

Stuart, E. W., Shimp, T. A., & Engle, R. W. (1987). Classical conditioning of consumer attitudes: Four experiments in an advertising context. *Journal of Consumer Research, 14,* 334–349.

Sujan, M. (1985).Consumer knowledge — Effects on evaluation strategies mediating consumer judgments. *Journal of Consumer Research, 12*(1), 31–46.

Sujan, M., & Bettman, J. R. (1989). The effects of brand positioning strategies on consumers' brand and category perceptions: Some insights from schema research. *Journal of Marketing Research, 26*(4), 454–467.

Thompson, R. E. (2005). In search of memory traces. *Annual Review of Psychology, 56,* 1–23.

Tversky, A., Sattath, S., & Slovic, P. (1988). Contingent weighting in judgment and choice. *Psychological Review,* 95(3), 371–384.

Vallacher, R. R., & Wegner, D. M. (1987). What do people think they're doing? Action identification and human behavior. *Psychological Review, 94*(1), 3–15.

van Osselaer, S. J., & Alba, J. W. (2000). Consumer learning and brand equity. *Journal of Consumer Research,* 27(1), 1–16.

van Osselaer, S. M. J., & Janiszewski, C. (2001). Two ways of learning brand associations. *Journal of Consumer Research, 28,* 202–223.

Vicente, K. J., & Wang, J. H. (1998). An ecological theory of expertise effects in memory recall. *Psychological Review, 105,* 33–57.

Wattenmaker, W. D. (1993). Incidental concept learning, feature frequency, and correlated properties. *Journal of Experimental Psychology: Learning, Memory, and Cognition, 19*(1), 203–222.

West, P. M. (1996). Predicting preferences: An examination of agent learning. *Journal of Consumer Research,* 23(1), 68–80.

Wind, J., Green, P. E., Shifflet, D., & Scarbrough, M. (1989). Courtyard by Marriott: Designing a hotel facility with consumer-based marketing models. *Interfaces, 19,* 25–47.

Wood, S. L., & Lynch, J. G. Jr. (2002). Prior knowledge and complacency in new product learning. *Journal of Consumer Research,* 29 (December) 416–126.

Wright, P. (2002). Marketplace metacognition and social intelligence. *Journal of Consumer Research, 28* (March), 677–682.

Young, R. M. (1968). Association of ideas. In P. P. Wiener (Ed.), *Dictionary of the history of ideas* (vol. 1, pp. 111–118). New York: Scribner's.

5

Categorization Theory and Research in Consumer Psychology
Category Representation and Category-Based Inference

BARBARA LOKEN

University of Minnesota

LAWRENCE W. BARSALOU

Emory University

CHRISTOPHER JOINER

George Mason University

INTRODUCTION

To make sense of the myriad new and existing products and services in the marketplace, consumers construct and use categorical representations to classify, interpret, and understand information they receive about these products and services. We define a *consumer category* as a set of products, services, brands, or other marketing entities, states, or events that appear, to the consumer, related in some way. We define a *categorical representation* as information that becomes stored in the cognitive system for a consumer category, and that is later used to process it.[1] One important use of category representations is during *categorization*, when consumers use these representations to assign a particular product or service to a consumer category, so that they can understand and draw inferences about it. Consumers might classify a new product as an MP3 player on the basis of prior knowledge about physical or functional features of MP3 players, for example, that MP3 players store music efficiently, are small in size, and are rectangular in shape. Once the new product is categorized, prior categorical information about MP3 players may also be used to make inferences about unknown attributes or features of the new product, or to form an evaluation of the new product.

From a marketing perspective, a number of questions about categorization have been examined that have implications for marketing decision making. For example, how should a new product be positioned so that consumers can identify it as belonging to a particular product category? How can it be differentiated from competitors in the same category? How should the structural aspects of a product or consumer-relevant category be measured? What factors increase category flexibility and acceptance of new category members? If a new product is introduced with an existing brand name (e.g., Kraft microwave popcorn), how will the existing brand image (e.g., Kraft) affect its categorization? How will the image affect its acceptance? What contextual, environmental and individual difference variables influence acceptance of a new category member (e.g., a brand extension)? Will a brand (e.g., Kraft) be perceived differently if it includes a very different category (microwave popcorn) than prior existing members of the category (macaroni and cheese, cheese slices, etc.)?

Research in consumer psychology has studied categorization concepts by examining product categories (e.g., Herr, 1989; Loken & Ward, 1990; Meyers-Levy & Tybout, 1989; Sujan, 1985; Viswanathan & Childers, 1999), brand categories (e.g., Barone & Miniard, 2002; Boush & Loken, 1991; Boush et al., 1987; Cowley & Mitchell, 2003; Lee & Sternthal, 1999; Park, Milberg, & Lawson, 1991; Wanke, Bless, & Schwarz, 1998), goal-related categories (Ratneshwar, Barsalou, Pechmann, & Moore, 2001; Ratneshwar, Pechmann, & Shocker, 1996; Ratneshwar & Shocker, 1991), attribute-based categories (Hutchinson, Raman, & Mantrala, 1994), cultural categories (Aaker & Lee, 2001; Briley & Wyer, 2002), product user categories (Pechmann & Knight, 2002), and the self as a category (Sujan, Bettman, & Baumgartner, 1993; Aaker, 1999). In 1987, two decades ago, the categorization literature was reviewed in two seminal consumer psychology publications (Alba & Hutchinson, 1987; Cohen & Basu, 1987). At that time, the field of categorization research was relatively new to consumer psychology researchers. Both reviews included discussions of the major theories of categorization and empirical findings from publications in cognitive, social, and consumer psychology. Since that time, an upsurge of consumer research has occurred in the area of branding, an area that draws heavily from categorization theories. Consumer research has also shifted from an emphasis on brand and product benefits to an emphasis on consumer goals and contextual factors that impact the types of representations retrieved from memory (Loken, 2006). Research on consumer goals and contextual influences, like research on branding, draws heavily from categorization research.

In the present chapter, we build on the 1987 reviews by addressing theoretical and empirical research in consumer psychology in the subsequent two decades. The organization of this chapter uses a framework that reflects the structure of the basic science underlying the reviewed research, in particular addressing two general areas of study, *category representation* and *category-based inferences*. Within each of these sections, we discuss the types of consumer research questions that have been addressed. In the first general section, on category representation, we describe theory and research that addresses the nature, structure, and functional location of category representations. We provide a brief overview of the three prominent historical views of category representation, including the prototype, exemplar, and connectionist views (for more extensive discussion of these views, in cognitive psychology, see Barsalou, 2003a,b; Murphy, 2002; Smith & Medin, 1981; for further discussion of prototype and exemplar views in consumer psychology, see Cohen & Basu, 1987, Alba & Hutchinson, 1987).

Next we discuss the dual roles of category representations as both stable and flexible. Flexibility of category representations has been shown in recent literature of consumer psychology in the context of consumer goals and research on malleable self (and cultural) views. We also discuss consumer research that addresses the question of the conditions under which a specific category representation will be activated in a given context. Finally, we close the topic of category representations by addressing an emerging research direction within cognitive psychology on the functional location of category representations in consumers' memory. We introduce Barsalou's

(1999) proposition that representations reside in the brain's modality-specific systems. This work is important because the assumptions underlying the nature and neural location of category representations in Barsalou's theory departs significantly from the assumptions underlying previously-developed theories. We review consumer research that is consistent with this theory and call for future research that demonstrates and tests the theory in a variety of consumer contexts and across different sensory modalities.

In the second general section of this chapter we examine the role of category-based inferences in consumer judgments, particularly with respect to brand categories. Brand categorization research emerges as a prominent research direction of the prior two decades, with researchers studying the conditions under which category-based inferences are generated and used in judgments, particularly when a brand extension (a new category member) is introduced to the consumer. We examine the role of similarity (e.g., between a category and a new category member) in forming category inferences, together with when and how new instances of a category (e.g., new brand extensions) impact existing category representations and vice versa. Also in the context of brand categories, consumer researchers have examined factors that increase category expansion and acceptance of new category members, or flexibility in category structure. We demonstrate that factors that increase category expansion and flexibility often work through their impact on consumer perceptions of similarity. Building on research that addresses category structure and similiarity, we analyze the important relationship between prototypicality and affect, and alternative theoretical explanations for the conditions under which a positive relationship will be demonstrated.

Finally, we conclude this chapter by summarizing the methodologies and analytic techniques that categorization researchers in this area typically use, and then offer some final conclusions about research on category representations and category-based inferences.

HISTORICALLY SIGNIFICANT VIEWS OF CATEGORY REPRESENTATION

Prototype, exemplar, and connectionist theories represent three prominent accounts of how categories are represented in memory. The prototype view assumes that categories are represented by abstract composites, called prototypes, based on central tendency information. These summary representations are based on the most likely features of the category's instances, based on a person's experiences with category members (e.g., Rosch & Mervis, 1975). The features in a prototype need only be probable of the concept, not necessary and sufficient. Categories are assumed to have graded structure, such that some category members are more representative, or typical, of a category than other category members. For example, popcorn is more representative than yogurt of the snack food category. The brand iPod is more representative of MP3 players than the brand Rio Sport. Within brand categories, the product Diet Coke is more representative of the Coca-Cola brand than Vanilla Diet Coke. In general, greater feature overlap with common features of the category is presumed to increase a category member's prototypicality. A new stimulus is classified as a category member to the extent that it is more similar to the category prototype and less similar to competing category prototypes.

The exemplar view assumes that categories are represented by specific, stored instances of the category, rather than by general, abstracted prototypes. An exemplar is often viewed as a representation of a specific category instance (e.g., a specific MP3 player, such as iPod). Some exemplar theorists, however, assume that an exemplar can also be a subset of a category (e.g., sedans as a subset of automobiles), its representation consisting of other exemplars or a conceptualization of the subset's features. According to exemplar theorists, a new stimulus (e.g., an ad for a new MP3 player) acts as a retrieval cue to access similar exemplar representations (e.g., iPod) in memory. The stimulus is classified as a member in the category to which it has the most similar stored exemplar representation (Medin & Schaffer, 1978).

Finally, the connectionist approach (McClelland & Rumelhart, 1985) views categories as attractors in dynamic feature spaces. This view assumes that people establish correlations of features that co-occur for a category (e.g., MP3 players) by tuning associations between features in a network to represent these feature configurations. A new stimulus then activates the most similar feature configuration in the network (i.e., an attractor), which then captures the stimulus, and assigns it to the associated category.

STABILITY AND FLEXIBILITY IN CONSUMER CATEGORY REPRESENTATIONS

Regardless of the approach taken to representing categories, category representations must be both stable and flexible if they are to explain the information processing activity that underlies consumer behavior. The consumer environment is complex and ever changing. Thousands of new products are introduced in the marketplace each year. To keep up with these changes, consumers need two types of information processing capabilities. On the one hand, they need stable representations of products and brands in memory that relate veridically to their environment. These stable representations provide a foundation upon which consumer information processing can take place. They are important for recognizing, interpreting, and evaluating both objects and events in a wide variety of consumer environments. Simultaneously, however, these object and event representations require considerable flexibility, as consumers adapt them to an unlimited number of situations and unexpected changes in the environment. We address stability and flexibility further in turn.

Stability of Category Representations

Structure and stability of product categories. A number of consumer studies have sought to understand the determinants of prototypicality and the underlying structure of product categories. Some of these studies have assessed degree of prototypicality through analysis of a category's features or attributes, using measures such as *family resemblance* (Rosch & Mervis, 1975; in the consumer literature, Loken & Ward, 1990; Viswanathan & Childers, 1999), *ideals* (Barsalou, 1985; in the consumer literature, Loken & Ward, 1990; Viswanathan & Childers, 1999), *attribute structure* (Loken & Ward, 1987, 1990), and *fuzzy set-based* measures of category membership (Viswanathan & Childers, 1999; for a more complete discussion of these measures, see Barsalou, 1985; Loken & Ward, 1990; and Viswanathan & Childers, 1999.) Implementing these attribute-based measures often requires obtaining preliminary data to determine the attributes or ideals that are salient or accessible for a particular product category. Attribute-based measures are then correlated with various measures of prototypicality (e.g., Barsalou, 1985; Loken & Ward, 1987, 1990; Viswanathan & Childers, 1999). Across many studies, these attribute-based measures have been found to predict prototypicality measures well (Barsalou, 1985; Loken & Ward, 1990). For example, Loken and Ward (1990) found that a global typicality measure was significantly ($p < .05$) correlated with both an attribute structure measure ($r = .68$ for 8 subordinate and $r = .33$ for 8 superordinate product categories) and an ideals measure ($r = .64$ and $.51$, $p < .05$, for the same 8 subordinate and 8 superordinate categories). Viswanathan and Childers (1999), almost a decade later, made small modifications to the Loken and Ward (1990) attribute and exemplar lists, and recomputed the correlations for 8 of the original 16 categories with an updated sample. For categories at both the superordinate and subordinate levels, significant correlations again occurred between global typicality measures and attribute structure ($r = .47$ for the 4 subordinates, and $r = .42$ for the 4 superordinates); significant correlations also occurred between global typicality measures and ideals (r = .69 and .64, for the 4 subordinates and 4 superordinates, respectively). These correlations show that predictions with the ideals measure were very stable from 1990 to 1999. Prediction with the measure of attribute structure changed somewhat from the 1990 to the 1999 study, which may reflect expected changes over the course of a decade in category composition, or even in minor changes of attributes across the nine-year period. Viswanathan and Childers (1999) also found that two fuzzy-set measures that assessed representativeness at the attribute level also predicted typicality very well (reverse scored, with global typicality, r = .72 and .55 for the four superordinates and .75 and .93 for the four subordinates). As these results illustrate, the structure of product categories, both at the superordinate and subordinate levels, appears quite stable over time and across different product categories.

Structure and stability of emotion categories. One might expect emotion categories (e.g., anger) to be more unstable than other types of categories. However, research in consumer and social psychology suggests that even emotion responses exhibit stability. Over time, people provide reliable measures of emotion categories, as shown in Richins' (1997) review and development of scale descriptors for thirteen emotional states in consumption situations. Ruth (2001) further finds that when the description of an emotion in the tagline of an advertisement (e.g., affection) is congruent with a description of an emotion expressed in the ad (affection), people prefer the ad to one in which the emotions described are incongruent (affection and joy). Furthermore, emotionally-valenced product attributes that are bipolar opposites appear to be related in memory, such that priming one (e.g., healthy) can activate the other (unhealthy), as demonstrated through how product information is interpreted (e.g., "more sweeteners" is interpreted as unhealthy) and how it impacts brand evaluations (Park, Yoon, Kim, & Wyer, 2001). Together, these findings indicate that emotionally-valenced attributes of product and brand categories exhibit properties of stability.

Flexibility of Category Representations

Consumer goals and category flexibility. Research also supports the conclusion that category representations are flexible. Categories do not take the same form across different contexts or situations; the perceived structure of a category depends on goals that are salient at a particular time or in a particular context (Barsalou, 1982). Evidence in consumer psychology also supports this conclusion. For example, Ratneshwar and Shocker (1991) found that prototypical "snack foods" differed from prototypical "snacks that people might eat at a Friday evening party while drinking beer." The contextual information relevant in the latter judgment focused consumers selectively on goal-relevant attributes of the product (e.g., saltiness or convenience) that differed from attributes underlying snack food judgments more generally (e.g., saltiness, sweetness, portability, convenience). Data on brands and types of beverages (Hutchinson, Raman, & Mantrala, 1994) also support the need to consider consumer usage situations when asking consumers to recall relevant brands.

Barsalou (1983, 1985, 1987, 1989) argued that individuals actively construct cognitive representations toward achieving goals. Multiple goals associated with a category may coexist within a single individual (Sengupta & Johar, 2002). Ratneshwar, Pechmann, and Shocker (1996) found that when consumers could not meet the needs of two different goals that were salient with a single product, or when they experienced goal ambiguity, they were more likely to consider alternatives from different product categories. In other words, members of a goal-derived category crossed traditional product category boundaries (also, cf. Johnson's, 1989, research on noncomparable alternatives). In this study, consumers who experienced goal ambiguity chose consideration sets on the basis of brand names, whereas consumers who experienced goal conflict chose consideration sets on the basis of mixed categories to meet different goals (and postponed conflict resolution to a final stage). Ratneshwar, Barsalou, Pechmann, and Moore (2001) argued that similarity perceptions are influenced, not only by surface-level resemblances, but also by salient personal and situational goals. Although surface resemblance was important—for example, a granola bar was perceived as more similar to a candy bar than to fruit yogurt—goals were also important. Individuals for whom a personal health goal was salient rated the granola bar as more similar to fruit yogurt than to a candy bar, as long as other situational goals (convenience) were not also salient. Individuals for whom the situational goal of convenience was salient, and for whom a personal health goal was not salient, rated an apple as more similar to a donut than to an orange.

Contextual factors and category flexibility. Evaluations of category members also have been found to depend on contextual factors. Wanke, Bless, and Schwarz (1997, as reported in Wanke, Bless, & Schwarz, 1998) found that when consumers' task instructions encouraged them to place two disparate concepts (wine and lobster) in the same (versus different) category, the evaluations of these category members varied. For example, *wine* was rated more favorably when it was categorized together with *lobster* than when it was categorized separately.

When a really new product is introduced to the market, information from multiple categories may be relevant. Moreau, Markman, and Lehmann (2001) demonstrated that changing the salience of these categories influenced the extent to which they were used in making inferences about the new item. Information about the category that was encountered first, or cued by an ad, influenced consumers' categorizations, expectations, and preferences for the new product to a greater extent than category information encountered subsequently.

Flexible cultural and other self-views. A fundamental way of organizing information received from the environment is with respect to the self (Markus, 1977). The self category can be viewed as flexible or malleable (Aaker, 1999; Markus & Kunda, 1986). In consumer psychology, different self-views can be retrieved from memory and used in judgment, depending on situational cues. For example, an individual may view oneself as having several different personality traits, and when situational cues make a particular trait salient, brands that match the trait will be better liked (Aaker, 1999). Thus, different views of the self (see, also, Reed, 2004) can cue different categories, which are then used in subsequent processing.

When consumers are bicultural, they more easily retrieve and use both cultural views, as compared with monocultural consumers (Lau-Gesk, 2003). Situational cues can make different cultural views salient (e.g., independent versus interdependent views, Briley, Morris, & Simonson, 2000; Aaker & Lee, 2001) leading to different outcome effects (e.g., Forehand & Deshpande, 2001; Briley & Wyer, 2002; Mandel, 2003). For example, different views of the self (independent versus interdependent) have been found to vary in terms of category representations that are accessible for each. Interdependents, who were asked to describe their thoughts in response to an advertisement, listed more specific category exemplars than did independents (Ng & Houston, 2006). Situational cues can also make both cultural and subcultural schemas salient, which may conflict with one another even though they are both linked to the self (Brumbaugh, 2002).

Summary. In summary, research increasingly views categories as flexible representations. This flexibility has been demonstrated in research directed toward goal-derived categories, contextual influences on category structure, different self-views, and different cultural categories.

Activation of a Category Representation

Because much consumer knowledge can belong to multiple categories, it is important to understand factors that affect whether a specific category representation will be activated in a given situation.

When a consumer is exposed to information in an environment, a specific category representation may be activated, not activated, or even inhibited (see Macrae & Bodenhausen, 2000, for a more thorough discussion of activation of social categories). In the consumer psychology literature, evidence for accessibility generally includes measures of increased recall, increased use of the representation in subsequent judgments, and faster response times on either memory or judgment tasks. Priming of a category also increases its later use (Herr, 1989; Hoch & Ha, 1986; Yi, 1990), unless people are aware of the priming manipulation (Herr, 1989; Meyers-Levy & Sternthal, 1993).

In a branding context, Morrin (1999) analyzed whether exposing consumers to a hypothetical brand extension (e.g., Crest mouthwash) increased accessibility of the parent brand (e.g., Crest), as demonstrated by the speed with which the consumer indicated whether the parent brand was a member of the correct product category (e.g., toothpaste). The logic here is that if a person responds rapidly to a connection between Crest and toothpaste, then the brand extension (Crest mouthwash) also activates the parent brand (Crest) category. Morrin found that exposure to the brand extension increased accessibility of the parent brand, with the increase being less for typical than atypical brands in the category (e.g., Crest increasing less than Gleem in the toothpaste category). A prototypical brand (e.g., Crest) is already highly accessible in the context of its category (toothpaste), such that further increases in accessibility are unlikely to occur. In contrast, the atypical brand is not already accessible, such that exposure to it increased the parent brand's accessibility. Morrin also found that when the brand extension was a good fit for the brand category (e.g., breath mints, mouthwash, or dental floss), it increased the parent brand accessibility further (e.g., Gleem toothpaste), relative to when the brand extension was a poor fit (e.g., soft drinks, dishwashing liquid). Again, this facilitating effect occurred for the atypical brands (e.g., Gleem) more than for the typical brands (e.g., Crest). These effects replicate earlier consumer research indicating that prototypical category members are chronically more accessible than atypical category members (cf. Nedungadi & Hutchinson, 1985; Boush & Loken, 1991), and that priming a category increases its accessibility (Herr, 1989). In general, atypical category members stand to gain more from priming tasks.

A similar finding for accessibility and priming occurred in a different context, when ninth graders were primed with either cigarette ads or nonsmoking ads (Pechmann & Knight, 2002). Because most ninth graders have negative perceptions of smoking, anti-smoking beliefs should be chronically accessible whereas pro-smoking beliefs should not. Indeed, the authors found that priming pro-smoker beliefs (with cigarette ads) led to increases in pro-smoking responses (e.g., smoking intentions), whereas priming anti-smoker beliefs (with anti-smoking ads) led to no changes. Priming with both anti- and pro-smoking ads also led to no changes; the anti-smoking prime counteracted the pro-smoking one. Research in comparative advertising finds analogous effects. Specifically, comparative ads (showing a target brand along with a competitor) benefit an atypical brand such as Shasta cola, more than they benefit a typical brand such as Coke (e.g., see Grewal, Kavanoor, Fern, Costley, & Barnes, 1997), and a comparative ad between an atypical brand and leading brand may benefit the atypical brand more than no comparison at all (Hutchinson et al., 1994). Priming a category has also been found to influence the type of processing in which consumers engage. Priming category information increases relational processing, or the extent to which consumers elaborate on the relationships or similarities between the category and the target object, relative to processing specific attribute information of the target object alone (Malaviya, Meyers-Levy, & Sternthal, 1999).

Research also suggests that perceptions of a category as accessible (i.e., easy rather than difficult to recall) influence category use (Schwarz, 2004). When people are asked to recall few (versus many) exemplars of a category (e.g., behaviors that increase one's risk of heart disease), they experience the exemplars as easy (rather than difficult) to retrieve and infer that the exemplars are more typical (e.g., perceptions of heart disease risk increased, Rothman & Schwarz, 1998). Even imagined ease-of-retrieval influences judgments (Wanke, Bohner, & Jurkowitsch, 1997). In general, consumers utilize accessible experiences in evaluation and decision making, unless the relevance or information-value of these experiences is called into question (Schwarz, 2004). Consumer research on these meta-cognitive theories is increasing and provides an interesting focus for future research.

Modality-Specific Representations in Conceptual Processing: Where Do Categories Reside?

An important recent development in cognitive psychology is an increased empirical and theoretical interest in the interplay between cognitive systems (e.g., category representation) and the brain's modality-specific systems (e.g., for vision, action, affect) systems. In contrast to the traditional approach of viewing cognitive and modality-specific systems as functionally separate, recent research in cognitive psychology and cognitive neuroscience suggests that representations in modality-specific systems underlie conceptual knowledge (for reviews of relevant empirical findings, see Barsalou, 2003b; Barsalou, Niedenthal, Barbey, & Ruppert, 2003; Martin, 2001; Pecher & Zwaan, 2005). According to this view, the perceptions, actions, and mental states active while processing a category's members are captured in the respective modality-specific systems of the brain. For example, consumers' knowledge about colors is represented in their perceptual mechanisms that perceive and process colors; consumers' knowledge about sounds is represented in their perceptual systems that perceive and process sounds. Later, when representing a category in the absence of any members, the brain reenacts or "simulates" these perceptions, actions, and mental states. Barsalou (1999, 2003a) argues that these simulations can implement the central symbolic operations that underlie the human conceptual system, including categorical inference, the type-token distinction, predication, and conceptual combination. For example, in classifying a perceived category member, a simulation of the category is retrieved that is grounded in the modalities. In this way, the conceptual representation of a category (a modality-specific simulation) is similar to the perceived representation of the category, rather than being different (an amodal representation), thereby facilitating comparisons between them. Barsalou and Wiemer-Hastings (2005) further extend this approach to the representation of abstract concepts.

Prior consumer research. Consumer research is consistent with the view that modality-specific and conceptual systems are linked. Unnava, Agarwal, and Haugtvedt (1996) presented consumers with advertising information that was high in imagery-provoking ability (either high in visual imagery or high in auditory imagery) and then engaged them in a perceptual task involving either reading or listening to the information. They found that when mental images were activated, they competed with available cognitive resources if consumers were asked to perform perceptual processing in the same modality. The learning of visual information was reduced if the consumer read, rather than listened to, the information; the learning of auditory information was reduced if the consumer heard, rather than read, the information. Also, when information had high, rather than low, levels of visual imagery, it was learned better when it was presented auditorally, but less well when it was presented visually. These results provide support that imagery processing draws on the same mental resources as perceptual processing. Although imagery interferes with perceptual processing of the same modality (visual, auditory), generating visual imagery has been found to facilitate cognitive operations that are compatible with it. For example, visual images may serve as spatial representations (MacInnis & Price, 1987) that facilitate information processing. Along these lines, Keller and McGill (1994) found that visual imagery was effective when it was compatible with other aspects of the communication process. Attributes that were easy to imagine had more impact on judgments when consumers engaged in imagery processing than when they engaged in analytical processing.

Sometimes pictures can increase imagery and thereby spur processing. Information presented in a narrative format (e.g., stories) tends to be more effective than information presented in a disorganized list format, but only when accompanied by pictures or by instructions to image (Adaval & Wyer, 1998). Similarly, narrative information is easier to process when it is physically integrated with relevant picture information, rather than being placed below it (Peracchio & Meyers-Levy, 1997). It seems clear that pictorial information is processed both perceptually and conceptually (e.g., Kim, Allen, & Kardes, 1996; Mothersbaugh, Huhmann, & Franke, 2002; Scott, 1994; Unnava, Agarwal, & Haugtvedt, 1996). Languages that rely on pictures or symbolic figures (logographic script) have been found to rely more on visual processes than languages based on alphabetic script (Schmitt, Pan, & Tavassoli, 1994; Tavassoli, 1999, 2001; Tavassoli & Han, 2001).

Type of imaging also influences the perceptual or cognitive processing in which consumers engage. Imaging and thinking about one's past experiences tends to produce more contextual details than anticipatory thinking about future events (Krishnamurthy & Sujan, 1999). Yet, when consumers were asked for information relevant to designing new products, they produced more innovative and effective information when imaging new uses for the product (anticipatory) than when thinking about past experiences, which limited visualization to retrieved memories (Dahl, Chattopadhyay, & Gorn, 1999).

Summary and Future Research

Research on category representations is increasingly focused on the flexibility associated with goal-derived and other types of categories, and we anticipate this focus to continue in consumer research. Also, although the literature covers category activation rather extensively, category inhibition has been less thoroughly considered (e.g., Macrae & Bodenhausen, 2000). For example, the question of how consumers become cognizant of stereotypical (categorical) bias and then correct for it (e.g., stop unwanted thoughts) are both newer areas of research.

Finally, new research on the link between modality-specific and cognitive processing in categorical representations is a promising new direction for researchers. Consumer research shows a strong link between conceptual and modality-specific systems in the brain. Perception, imagery, and higher cognition, share representational mechanisms. Pictures tend to facilitate imagery as well as to facilitate cognitive processing. The quality of imagining (e.g., anticipating the future versus reflecting on past experiences) also influences the specific objects and events that are processed. Future research could examine the links between conceptual and modality-specific systems within particular modalities (e.g., touch, smell, taste, action) not previously examined in consumer psychology, and also in the context of different types of consumer categories (e.g., perception of brand categories and goal-derived consumer categories). Further research based on the nature of specific descriptive and affect-laden information associated with this link would also be worthwhile.

In addition to uncovering interesting findings about category representations in the previous two decades, consumer research on category-based inferences has also increased dramatically. In the next section, we examine this research, the second major topic addressed in this chapter.

SIMILARITY-BASED CATEGORY INFERENCES: THE INFLUENCE OF A CATEGORY ON A NEW CATEGORY MEMBER

A primary reason category information is useful to consumers is that it can be used in making judgments about new category members, which are traditionally referred to as *category inferences* or *inductions*. Much of the consumer research on category inferences has been performed with brand categories, examining the extent to which beliefs (and affect) associated with a brand category are used to draw inferences about a new brand extension. Although many other marketing categories are relevant, this focus on brand categories is understandable. Marketing practitioners often manage their companies' products as brand categories; many companies are organized by brands. Given the continuing popularity, for a variety of economic and strategic reasons, of brand leveraging strategies (e.g., brand and line extensions, licensing) the number of products associated with many brand names has continued to grow. As a result of this, it is common to see new products launched with existing brand names and increasingly, the promotion of the full range of products under a brand name in a single communication. In this environment, consumers will be more inclined to think about brands as categories when considering new products introduced with an existing brand name, when considering the specific image or evaluating a particular brand name (Loken, Joiner, & Peck, 2002), or when attending to marketing communications for an existing brand and product. In this literature, a typical research scenario is one that examines the extent to which brand category inferences extend from the original brand category (e.g., Lexus) to a new brand extension (e.g., Lexus Hybrid, usually a hypothetical extension of the brand). Measuring the extent to which the new extension is similar to the brand category is the most standard approach for determining whether these inferences will occur. For example, in learning about the new Lexus Hybrid, consumers may infer that it shares similarities with both the traditional Lexus (e.g., high performance, prestige, and leather seats) as well as other hybrid automobiles (e.g., good for the environment, high gas mileage, and expensive).

A key factor that determines whether category inferences are extended in this manner is the similarity or match between the representation of the brand category and the representation of the new brand extension. Consumers use prior knowledge about the category and the new category member to judge the relationship between them. When the relationship is perceived to be high, inferences are likely to be drawn from the category to the new member. When a new category member is viewed as dissimilar from the category, the relevance of category information is diminished, decreasing belief and the transfer of affect.

In the sections that follow, we review findings that affect the perceived similarity of two categories in the context of induction. In addition to the important role of prior knowledge about categories, we examine two other consumer psychological factors that affect perceived similarity: accessibility and relevance. Consumers selectively attend to only a subset of knowledge available about the category and the category extension, and this selective focus is influenced by: (a) the accessibility of information either retrieved from memory or in the environment, and (b) the relevance of information in achieving specific goals. In contexts that include both brand and product categories, researchers have also examined the alignability of attributes and the circumstances that increase contrast effects (rather than assimilation to the category). In the sections that follow, we review how these various factors affect category inferences.

Accessibility and Similarity-Based Inferences

Brand category accessibility and similarity-based inferences. The accessibility (or salience) of information pertains to the ease with which category information is retrieved from memory, or the ease with which it is perceived in the environment. A brand category, such as Snickers, can be viewed as consisting of a set of brand attributes (e.g., peanuts, chocolatey, tastes good), or as a set of exemplar products (e.g., Snickers candy bars, Snickers miniatures, Snickers ice cream bars), or both. In any given context, information about either brand attributes or exemplar products of a brand, or both, may vary widely in accessibility, with some being much more accessible than others (Loken,

Joiner, & Peck, 2002; Meyvis & Janiszewski, 2004). The highly accessible information for a new category member (e.g., Snickers ice cream topping) may include its product category (ice cream topping), its brand name (Snickers), its connection to the brand name (e.g., strong or weak connection), and/or its individuating attributes (e.g.,its texture when used as a topping for ice cream is creamy). Increasing the salience of specific attributes can have a very strong effect on category membership judgments and processing of new brands (Hutchinson & Alba, 1991). When accessible information about the brand category and accessible information about the brand extension are similar, category inferences are more likely to occur. An abundance of research supports the idea that the properties of the brand category (e.g., cognitions and affect regarding the brand Snickers) transfer to the properties of new exemplars (brand extensions such as"Snickers ice cream topping), to a greater extent as the perceived similarity between the brand category and the brand extension increases (Aaker & Keller, 1990; Bottomley & Holden, 2001; Boush & Loken, 1991; Boush et al., 1987; Hansen & Hem, 2004; Zhang & Sood, 2002).

Research also demonstrates that changing the focus of the similarity comparison often changes the perception of similarity between the two representations. Depending on what type of information is accessible and/or selectively attended to about the brand (brand image attributes; product categories of the brand) or about the extension (product category of the extension; individuating information; relationship-to-category information), similarity judgments can vary widely. For example, Lane (2000) found that when consumers were exposed repeatedly (five times) to information about a new brand extension, and that when the information focused on the extension's positive connection to the brand, people's perceptions of extension similarity increased relative to a single-exposure condition. The key mechanism that produced this change was an increase in positive thoughts about the extension as exposure increased. This effect even occurred when the exposure information included brand associations not strongly related to the brand. Just focusing on positive attributes of these peripheral associations was sufficient to trigger positive thoughts about the extension. In general, repeated exposure directed the focus of attention, the focus of elaboration, and consequently the inferences that consumers made about an extension, leading to an increasingly positive evaluation. Klink and Smith (2001) found, too, that multiple exposures (three versus one) increased the acceptance of a moderately dissimilar extension, in this case when only the brand name and extension category information were provided. Lane (2000) found, however, that when the extensions were highly dissimilar to the brand category, and when the ad evoked associations that were not strongly related to the brand, repeated exposure did not lead to more acceptance of the extensions.

Meyvis and Janiszewski (2004) found that properties of the brand category, specifically whether it included a narrow or broad array of products, influenced the type of information to which consumers selectively attended. They reasoned that narrow categories (e.g., a brand such as Campbell's, which makes mostly soups) will have accessible associations that include the product category (soup), more often than will broad categories (e.g., Healthy Choice, which makes a variety of products), for whom product category associations are more diffuse and weaker (cf. Boush & Loken, 1991). The product category associations of narrow (versus broad) brands (e.g., soup) are therefore stronger and more likely to compete and interfere with associations pertaining to brand image attributes (e.g., tastes good). When assessing new brand extensions, the narrow brand focus is more likely to include product category information (e.g., soup) as a basis for similarity perceptions, leading to greater acceptance of close category extensions (e.g., new soups) and lower acceptance of far category extensions. The broad brand, in contrast, for which product category associations are weaker and brand attribute associations are stronger, leads consumers to show less extreme responses to close and far extensions, and more acceptance as a function of whether the brand attributes are broadly similar (e.g., do the brand attributes transfer easily to the new extension?).

Finally, Klink and Smith (2001) found that when individuating attribute information is available, it can become the focus and reduce the emphasis on the parent brand category and on its relationship to the extension. Specifically, the effects of brand similarity on extension evaluations diminished when individuating information conveying novel features for the extension (e.g., Timex bicycle and a unique gear system) was accessible.

Brand name accessibility and similarity-based inferences. In the same way that narrow (versus broad) brands trigger specific (versus general) category associations, the *name* of a brand can vary in whether it triggers specific (or general) category associations and/or specific (or general) brand attribute associations. Keller, Heckler, and Houston (1998), for example, found that the name of a new extension was remembered better when it suggested superiority on a specific brand attribute (e.g., PicturePerfect televisions), than when it suggested superiority on a general attribute (e.g., Emporium). Focusing on a specific attribute of a brand can also diminish the emphasis placed by the consumer on the brand category (and its broad array of attributes), but it can also diminish consumers' acceptance of new brand extensions (van Osselaer & Alba, 2003). For example, the specific (versus general) name inhibited memory for brand attributes unrelated to the specific attributes.

Co-branding strategies and similarity-based inferences. When two brands are combined in a co-branding strategy (e.g., Slimfast chocolate cake mix by Godiva) or brand alliance (e.g., Northwest Airlines and Visa), associations of each brand category, as well as the relationship between the two brands, may be triggered. Park, Jun, and Shocker (1996) found that a co-branded extension (e.g., Slimfast chocolate cake mix by Godiva) led to more favorable attribute inferences when the header brand (Slimfast) was combined with a complementary brand (Godiva) than when combined with a noncomplementary brand (e.g., Haagen-Dazs). Complementary brands were those that contributed along attribute dimensions that the other brand lacked. Also, complementarity of brands was more effective in benefiting the co-branded extensions than simply combining two equally favorable brands. In addition, because a co-branded (versus monobranded) extension creates the perception of difference between a parent brand and the brand extension, countermoves made by a competitor in response to the extension are perceived less favorably (Kumar, 2005).

However, co-branding with two well-known brand names also increases consumers' expectations for the co-branded product. For example, ingredient branding using a well-known brand name weakened brand quality inferences because of overexpectations, an outcome described by van Osselaer and Janiszewski (2001) in terms of connectionist models of adaptive learning (also, van Osselaer & Alba, 2000).

When two brands are combined, and when consumers are more familiar with one than with the other, consumers' inferences from one brand to the other are unidirectional, from the familiar to the unfamiliar brand (Simonin & Ruth, 1998). Similarly, when two (hypothetical) restaurants are linked, and only one of the restaurants is well defined, the well-defined brand restaurant serves as a context for making inferences about the ambiguously-defined restaurant (Levin & Levin, 2000).

Relevance to a Specific Consumer Goal

As noted earlier, when a specific goal is salient, exemplars that accomplish the same goal will be perceived as more similar than exemplars that are physically similar but do not accomplish the same goal (Ratneshwar, Barsalou, Pechmann, & Moore, 2001). Furthermore, goal-relevant information is more likely than goal-irrelevant information to be used during comparison judgments when evaluating a new category exemplar. In the context of brand categories, consumers generate increasingly positive category inferences about a new brand extension as the perceived similarity between the extension and the parent brand on "image" and other goal-related attributes of the brand increases (e.g., Park, Milberg, & Lawson, 1991; see also Chakravarti, MacInnis, & Nakamoto, 1990; Herr, Farquhar, & Fazio, 1996; Keller & Aaker, 1992; Smith & Park, 1992). Consumers also generate more positive inferences as the perceived relevance of the brand's attributes to the new extension increases (Broniarczyk & Alba, 1994).

Broniarczyk and Alba (1994) found that even when an extension is in a dissimilar product category, it can be viewed as acceptable if the attributes of the brand category are relevant to the new extension. The Ralph Lauren brand image, for example, has transferred successfully to product categories that are low in physical similarity to its core product base of apparel (e.g., perfume, paint), but that share a prestige image of the brand. An extension that is physically similar to a parent brand product (e.g., Nike dress leather shoes), but that is incongruent with the brand category's goals, may not be successful. Martin and Stewart (2001) found that when an extension is moderately incongruent with the goals of the parent brand category, the attitudes toward the category have less impact on attitudes toward the brand extension (and purchase intent) than when the extension is congruent with the goals of the parent brand category. When the extension was extremely goal-incongruent, the attitudes toward the parent brand category had no impact on attitude toward the extension (or purchase intent). Further, when two products shared a set of goals, consumers' elaborations about those products were more detailed and focused on a link between attributes of the extension and the parent brand. When two products were less goal-congruent, consumers' elaborations about them were less detailed and focused on why the extension was not a good fit. Finally, Martin and Stewart (2001) found that when both product category similarity and brand attribute similarity reflected a common goal, they both predicted extension acceptance. If the consumer had multiple goals that were incongruent with one another, then other factors, such as a similarity heuristic, predicted extension acceptance (Martin & Stewart, 2001).

Similarity as a Heuristic

Using categorical information often simplifies judgment and decision-making, because consumers produce useful inferences by comparing current information about a perceived product to relevant category information. Similarity between a parent brand and an extension has also been viewed as a heuristic used in making extension-related judgments under certain conditions. For example, category inferences that simplify decision-making (e.g., evaluation-based inferences, similarity-based inferences, and correlational rules) are more likely to occur when cognitive resources are low, when people are unmotivated to process detailed information, when they lack the ability to do so, when the category information is sufficiently relevant and accessible for use, or when there is no sufficient justification for accuracy in judgment (e.g., Alba & Hutchinson, 1987; Alba, Broniarczyk, Shimp, & Urbany, 1994; Maheswaran 1994). In contrast, when resources, ability, and/or motivation are abundant, people are more likely to elaborate more on the details of the new category member and its idiosyncrasies.

In their research examining consumers' classification learning, Hutchinson and Alba (1991) distinguished between analytic and holistic processing. Analytic processing was operationalized as those categorization decisions that were based exclusively on features diagnostic of category membership (i.e., "criterial" attributes). Nonanalytic or "holistic" classification was operationalized as those involving membership decisions based on overall brand similarity. Hutchinson and Alba (1991) found that perceptual salience of attributes enhanced analytic learning if the attributes were criterial but inhibited learning if they were not. Both analytic and nonanalytic processing tended to be multiattribute in nature, but nonanalytic processing was limited to a smaller subset of available attribute information as compared with analytic processing.

Research further suggests that similarity is used as a heuristic when similarity information is accessible and when more relevant information is unavailable. For example, when the relationship between the category and the new category member is made accessible through repeated exposure, increased elaboration, or instructions to elaborate on relations between them, similarity will be more likely to be used as a heuristic (and when other information is not accessible). As noted earlier, similarity was used when product category information about the parent brand (Meyvis & Janiszewski, 2004), or product category information about the brand extension (Klink & Smith, 2001), was the only information available or accessible to the consumer. When individuating information about the brand extension was available, the individuating information, rather than a similarity heuristic, was used (Klink & Smith, 2001).

Alignability of Attributes

Another type of similarity-based comparison, generally studied outside the domain of brand categories, involves the alignability of attributes between the new category stimulus and the existing category representation in memory (Gentner & Markman, 1997; in the consumer literature, Gregan-Paxton, 2001; Moreau, Lehmann, & Markman, 2001; Roehm & Sternthal, 2001). Alignable differences focus on the structural properties of attributes and the degree to which attributes from one object can be "mapped onto" another object. Research finds that alignable differences (versus differences that are not alignable) are more accessible from memory (Zhang & Markman, 1998), are perceived as more useful inputs in judgments (Markman & Medin, 1995; Zhang & Fitzsimons, 1999), and increase brand evaluations in comparative advertising (Zhang, Kardes, & Cronley, 2002). When two different brands were paired in a comparative advertising setting, the more the attributes of the target brand could be mapped onto (or compared with) those of the comparison brand, the higher the target brand evaluations (Zhang, Kardes, & Cronley, 2002). When two brands were not alignable, the brands were more difficult to compare, and transfer of affect was less likely to occur.

Assimilation and Contrast in Consumer Contexts

The research on similarity-based inferences finds that the lower the similarity between the new category and an existing category, the lower the likelihood of category-based inferences. Assimilation and contrast theories in psychology (e.g., Herr, Sherman, & Fazio, 1983; Martin, 1986; Mussweiler, 2003; Schwarz & Bless, 1992) make a different set of predictions. They suggest that if, at encoding, the domains or categories for the context and target match (or are at least similar), assimilation will likely occur, and there will be a positive transfer of beliefs between the two. These theories suggest that the assimilation of information to a target results under conditions in which the information is included in a temporary representation of the target, whereas contrast effects result from exclusion of the information from the representation, and the use of the target as a standard of comparison from which to judge the information (Schwarz & Bless, 1992). When the similarity between the new instance and the existing category are high, an assimilation effect occurs, such that beliefs and affect are more likely to transfer to the new instance. But conditions that produce contrast effects show how the theories are different from theory and research discussed earlier that predict category-based inferences. In particular, under certain conditions, consumers' judgments show contrast effects for extremely dissimilar (atypical) category instances. In these cases, not only may beliefs fail to transfer from a familiar brand (Ralph Lauren) to an extremely atypical new brand extension (Ralph Lauren toaster oven), but contrast effects may produce a negative impact of the brand on the new product (evaluations and beliefs about the toaster oven may be *more* negative as a result of the brand name). Seemingly, category information should be viewed as irrelevant for judgments about a new category member that is extremely atypical, or when people are skeptical that an atypical instance is a category member. For example, a consumer may simply discount the Ralph Lauren toaster oven as an anomaly. If so, atypical instances should not affect category perceptions, and category knowledge should not be used to form inferences about the atypical instance (Fiske & Neuberg, 1990). As Wanke, Bless, and Schwarz (1998) suggest, however, if an atypical instance is perceived as excluded from the target category (the toaster oven is not included in the Ralph Lauren brand category), then judgments pertaining to it may reflect contrast effects (see, also, Stapel, Koomen, & Velthuijsen, 1998, for an alternative explanation for contrast effects).

Research finds some evidence for contrast effects. In the consumer domain, researchers have attempted to determine the conditions under which advertising information will be assimilated versus used as a standard of comparison and contrasted with the target category or representation. Assimilation effects, viewed as the default, occur more often than contrast effects, and are more likely to occur under conditions of category or domain similarity. Contrast effects are more likely under conditions of category or domain mismatch or dissimilarity (Hafner, 2004; Mussweiler, 2003). Contrast effects are also likely when substantial cognitive resources are available for processing comparison information (Meyers-Levy & Sternthal, 1993), when the individuals are high (versus low) in need for cognition (Meyers-Levy & Tybout, 1997), when remembered information is recounted analytically, rather than episodically (Bickart & Schwarz, 2001), and when situational cues include dissimilarities, rather than similarities (Hafner, 2004).

SUMMARY AND FUTURE RESEARCH

In sum, research shows that the degree to which inferences from a category are extended to a new category member reflects three factors: (1) What information is accessible? As information that triggers similarity associations between the brand category and new brand extension becomes more accessible, the greater the likelihood that category inferences are drawn (e.g., when product category information is the only information available; when the relationship between the brand category and new brand category member is salient; when attributes of the extension are the same as the category's attributes). (2) Is the accessible information appropriate? If accessible information pertains to the category in which an object is being judged, then that information will probably be viewed as relevant or appropriate. (3) What information is elaborated upon? To the extent that elaboration (e.g., due to repeated exposure to the extension) increases the perception that a connection exists between the category and extension, similarity-based inferences are more likely to occur.

Future research could analyze how similarity or typicality relations benefit from frequency (e.g., Barsalou, Huttenlocker, & Lamberts, 1998) apart from feature similarity. Future research could also examine how category inferences are influenced by the number and typicality of exemplars retrieved when a category judgment is made. In a context in which a larger number of exemplars, or a broader array of exemplars, is retrieved, consumers may be more confident in making inferences based on those exemplars than in a context in which a small number of exemplars, or a narrower array of exemplars, is retrieved. Individual differences may also exist in sampling exemplars from memory, such that some consumers retrieve more representative exemplars than other consumers, due to motivational, ability, and contextual factors.

A factor that could influence the perceived relevance of category information is the degree to which category information is stable or unstable for a given individual. When the same representations (e.g., prototypes, exemplars) are retrieved across multiple occasions and contexts (cf. Lord, Paulson, Sia, Thomas, & Lepper, 2004), the stability of these representations may facilitate category inferences that lead to more stable beliefs and attitudes, as compared with exemplars that are unstable or vary significantly across occasions and contexts. Also, when a consumer retrieves and uses unstable exemplars as bases for an attitude toward a category, that category attitude may be more vulnerable or susceptible to change. On the other hand, such attitudes, because they are based on unstable or changing exemplars, may be more flexible and less rigid in the face of disconfirming information.

THE INFLUENCE OF NEW CATEGORY MEMBERS ON EXISTING CATEGORY REPRESENTATIONS

Not only can category knowledge be used to make inferences about new category members, the reverse flow of influence can also occur. Information about new category members can influence existing category beliefs and attitudes, and thereby alter the representation of the existing category.

Brand Categories and New-Member Effects

In the consumer psychology literature, these new-member effects have been examined chiefly in the context of brand categories, where they can either have a positive (enhancement) effect or a negative (dilution) effect on people's general beliefs about the category. Loken and John (1993) examined whether information about a new inconsistent category member (brand extension) influenced beliefs about the brand category negatively. They found that, for the brand category Johnson & Johnson, negative information about a brand extension's gentleness rating influenced consumers' beliefs about both the extension and the general category, that is, the parent brand Johnson & Johnson.

John, Loken, and Joiner (1998) found that, in addition to affecting the parent brand category negatively, a moderately inconsistent brand extension can influence consumers' beliefs about prior existing products of the brand. For example, a new Johnson & Johnson brand extension (e.g., hand lotion) that was rated low on the gentleness attribute impacted consumers' beliefs about the parent brand, Johnson & Johnson, as well as beliefs about prior existing exemplars of the brand (e.g., Johnson & Johnson dental floss). Interestingly, Johnson & Johnson's flagship product, Johnson & Johnson baby shampoo, was most immune from dilution effects, presumably because gentleness beliefs about this product were firmly established and more resistant to change.

A key factor that determines extent of dilution is the similarity between the parent and new brand extension, or, alternatively, the perceived typicality of the new brand extension of the parent brand category. Milberg, Park, and McCarthy (1997) found that the more the brand extension was either inconsistent with the parent brand image or dissimilar from the parent brand's product categories, the greater the amount of dilution (i.e., negative transfer of association from the extension to the brand category). However, negative information had no effect on parent brand beliefs when the extension was viewed as extremely atypical and these atypical perceptions were salient (Loken & John, 1993), or when the extension was introduced using a sub-branding strategy (Milberg, Park, & McCarthy, 1997). These *modified* dilution effects are consistent with prior research in social categorization (Rothbart & Lewis, 1988). A moderately inconsistent brand extension (e.g., a Johnson

& Johnson facial tissue that was rated low on the gentleness attribute) was viewed as moderately atypical of the parent brand (Johnson & Johnson). An extremely inconsistent brand extension (e.g., a Johnson & Johnson facial tissue that was rated low on *both* gentleness and quality attributes) was viewed as extremely atypical of the parent brand. When these typicality judgments were made salient, consumers used them in forming judgments about the parent brand, such that moderately atypical extensions had a negative effect on the parent brand beliefs and extremely atypical extensions had no effect (cf. Rothbart & Lewis, 1988). Thus, people appear to discount inconsistent extension information when the extension is viewed as extremely inconsistent (versus moderately inconsistent) of the category and, importantly, the atypicality (or typicality) of the extension is salient (Loken & John, 1993). In a different applied domain, within U.S. culture, beliefs about social reality (e.g., occupational categories) have been shown to be caused in part by television viewing, especially among heavier viewers, who failed to discount TV-based exemplars in forming their beliefs (Shrum, Wyer, & O'Guinn, 1998), perhaps because these exemplars are moderately, but not extremely, inconsistent with prior category beliefs.

The dilution effects of Loken and John (1993), as well as positive extension effects on the brand (brand enhancement), were replicated by Gurhan-Canli and Maheswaran (1998) under conditions of high motivation, when people were more likely to use detailed, thoughtful processing to evaluate the brand category and its members. Under low motivation, the modified, heuristic-based dilution effects of Loken and John were replicated; that is, more (versus less) typical extensions diluted the parent brand evaluations. According to the authors, people used less analytical processing (Gurhan-Canli & Maheswaran, 1998), and the Rothbart and Lewis predictions applied.

In a follow-up study of brand enhancement and dilution, Ahluwalia and Gurhan-Canli (2000) predicted that negative information would be more diagnostic than positive information when evaluating close (typical) new brand extensions, but that positive information would be more diagnostic than negative information when evaluating far (atypical) brand extensions. Ahluwalia and Gurhan-Canli also predicted, however, that these effects would occur only when other relevant brand extension information was not accessible. Results of their research were supportive. When brand extension information was highly accessible, positive extension information created more positive parent brand category evaluations, and negative extension information created more negative parent brand category evaluations. When extension information was lower in accessibility, negative extension information induced dilution effects for close (but not far) categories, and positive information induced enhancement effects for far (but not close) categories, supporting the idea that negative information is more diagnostic for close (versus far) categories, whereas positive information is more diagnostic for far (versus close) categories.

The brand extension literature illustrates the conditions under which moderately typical but not extremely atypical extensions will impact parent brand beliefs. In these conditions, when typicality information is salient or accessible, extremely inconsistent brand extensions are viewed as implausible, or exceptions, and their information content is discounted.

Employees of a Firm and New-Member Effects

Folkes and Patrick (2003) reported analogous findings when the employees of a firm were the category members being evaluated. Negative information about a particular service employee was less diagnostic about other employees of the same firm when that service employee was viewed as atypical of the company overall. In these cases, information about the employee was discounted in evaluating the service category as a whole. Positive information about an atypical employee, however, did have an effect (and more effect than negative information) on evaluations of a related subgroup in the firm. Matta and Folkes (2005), too, demonstrate more discounting of information about atypical than typical employees of service providers, and further demonstrate that employing a positively-rated atypical provider increased brand differentiation (i.e., the perception that the firm was different from competing firms) compared with those employing a positively-rated typical provider.

Summary and Future Research

The literature on brand extensions has provided much insight into the possible influence a new category member can have on the overall category, and also on individual category exemplars. First, researchers have assessed when new category members will affect the category's representation. Empirical findings show that they affect it when they are viewed as at least somewhat typical of the category. If they are viewed as very atypical, then information about the new category member is discounted, and has no effect on the category. The diagnosticity of the atypical new category member varies depending on how related it is to the category, whether the information about the new category member is positive/negative, and the extent to which the information is accessible. Brand extension research has also demonstrated that a new category member can influence beliefs or evaluations of a particular existing category member, but that central category members (e.g., flagship products) are least vulnerable to change.

Additional areas to be examined in the future include developing a better understanding of the potential impact a new member has on individual category members. For example, what factors influence the diagnosticity of this information? Does diagnosticity reflect the characteristics of the existing category member (e.g., familiarity, strength of beliefs, linkage to the category) or of the new category member (e.g., plausibility of the information, confidence in the information, knowledge of the product category, salience of category membership) or of some other factor (e.g., availability of competitor information). Future research could also explore the conditions that make category membership appear relevant to the task. Does relevance depend on subjective experiences of the consumer, or on some form of meta-cognition?

Having considered the roles that similarity and related processes play in category-based inferences, we next turn to literature that addresses how similarity-based processes contribute to the flexibility of category structure described earlier.

FACTORS THAT INFLUENCE CATEGORY FLEXIBILITY AND EXPANSION

As described earlier, category representations are characterized by a degree of flexibility and expansiveness. In addition to the flexibility of category boundaries and category membership demonstrated through goal-derived category research, a number of motivational, ability, and contextual factors have been found to increase category expansiveness, usually by changing perceptions of category similarity. Emotional states, discussed next, are an example of motivational states that influence category flexibility.

Emotional States

A positive mood state has been found to increase category flexibility (Isen & Daubman, 1984). In the consumer psychology literature, researchers have found that people in a positive mood showed increased relational elaboration (elaborating on the interrelationship between items), which included greater clustering of brands by product category membership, greater recall of brand names when they were in the same categories as stimulus brands (Lee & Sternthal, 1999), increased categorization of nontypical items as belonging to a category, and increased optimism about the success of a stimulus product (Kahn & Isen, 1993).

Barone and Miniard (2002; Barone, Miniard, & Romeo, 2000) showed positive mood effects on category flexibility in the context of brand categories. Specifically, they suggested that increased flexibility might consist of rating moderately dissimilar extensions (e.g., Nike basketball nets) as more acceptable under certain affective conditions. When consumers were in a positive mood (relative to a negative mood), and when they received information about a new category member (brand extension), they were more likely to transfer positive evaluations from the category (parent brand) to the new category member (brand extension), even if the new category member (brand extension) was moderately dissimilar from the category (parent brand) attributes (Barone & Miniard, 2002; Barone et al., 2000). The categories of people in a negative mood were more rigid. These researchers also examined extensions in very similar and extremely dissimilar categories. The category flexibility of people in a positive mood did *not* occur when the membership of a category exemplar was viewed as implausible (e.g., for a distant, extremely dissimilar extension), and was not needed when the categories were highly similar (e.g., for near extensions).

Another motivational variable found to influence willingness to expand category boundaries is a person's feelings of commitment to the category. For example, a study done among South Korean homemakers (Park, Kim, & Kim, 2002) found that feeling trust and commitment toward a brand increased the acceptability of an extension when the attribute claims of the extension were atypical (versus typical) of the brand category, as long as the extension product category was not too dissimilar from the category.

Expertise

Expertise in a domain is an ability factor that has been found to increase flexibility in categorization. Cowley and Mitchell (2003) found that experts (relative to novices) were more likely to organize information by product subcategories, and to store information about alternatives in a way that increased flexibility when evaluating the same product across different usage occasions (Mitchell & Dacin, 1996), or when retrieving different brands for different usage occasions (Cowley & Mitchell, 2003). Owners (versus nonowners) of a brand were more likely to accept brand extensions that "stretch" a nonprestige brand's price line upward or downward, and that stretch prestige brands upward (e.g., American Express platinum card; Kirmani, Sood, & Bridges, 1999). Owners were less accepting of downward stretches of prestige brands (e.g., a new BMW for $11,990), because of owners' preferences for brand exclusivity, such that a sub-branding strategy (e.g., Ultra by BMW) was preferred.

Cognitive psychologists have argued further that, early during the development of expertise in a domain, conceptual knowledge increases the salience or importance of certain perceptual distinctions. Perceptual knowledge serves as the data to which conceptual theories originally pertain (Barsalou, 1999; Smith & Heise, 1992). As people's expertise increases, so does their ability to attend selectively to perceptual aspects that are relevant to precise categorization (Johnson & Mervis, 1997). In other words, experts are not simply able to think more abstractly conceptually. Their knowledge allows them to attentionally select increasingly subtle perceptual distinctions relevant to categorization (Johnson & Mervis, 1997).

Further research has found that teaching consumers strategies can increase their ability to process categories flexibly. For example, when consumers were taught decompositional strategies (e.g., unbundling credit card expenses into different subcategories), they exhibited both increased accessibility of information and reduced biases in memory and estimation (e.g., Menon, 1997; Srivastava & Raghubir, 2002).

Coverage/Diversity of Category Members

As noted earlier, brand names can be suggestive of broad or narrow categories. When an ingredient in a brand was branded (e.g., Tide with Irish Spring scent), and the change to the brand was relatively minor, consumers were more likely to accept the brand extension in the short-term. Using a new ingredient name (e.g., Tide with EverFresh scent), however, improved long-range expansion into new product categories (Desai & Keller, 2002). The exception to this effect is when the ingredient represented a significant attribute change. Under these conditions, the extension fares better when the ingredient is co-branded than when it has a new name, conceivably because the branded ingredient enables consumers to view the brand extension as a plausible extension (assuming that the brand connection to the ingredient is credible). In these cases, the branded ingredient provided additional associations that the existing brand did not originally possess (i.e., broadening the brand category), which proved beneficial in the new category. More diverse or broad categories (as compared to narrow categories) also have brand associations that allow for a broader range of new acceptable category exemplars to which parent category affect and associations can be assimilated (Boush & Loken 1991).

Brand diversity or coverage also explains why sequential brand strategies can increase brand acceptance over a nonsequential strategy (Dawar & Anderson, 1994; Keller & Aaker, 1992). Introducing new category members in a sequential strategy (i.e., moving from products that are more to less similar), increases the likelihood that extension categories will be viewed as moderately rather than extremely dissimilar, thereby increasing the chances of consumer acceptance. For example, if a brand category that makes only cameras moves into cell phones, consumers would view this product extension as more dissimilar to the brand than if the brand had instead initially introduced camera cell phones followed by regular cell phones. When Ralph Lauren expanded their product line to designer paints, they followed a sequential strategy that flowed from designer apparel to designer bedding (and home furnishings) to designer wall coverings (including paints), rather than moving directly from designer apparel to designer paints. A sequential expansion that progresses to more and more dissimilar categories slowly increases perceptions of brand coverage, which in turn increases perceptions of similarity and brand extension acceptance. A nonsequential strategy does not have these benefits, as the perception of similarity is too implausible for the perceiver, such that they reject the new extension. According to Osherson, Smith, Wilkie, Lopez, and Shafir's (1990) similarity-coverage model, premises from diverse categories that exhibit greater coverage lead to stronger arguments than premises from categories that are very similar to one another.

Diversity per se (i.e., having a greater number of products under the parent brand umbrella), however, does not translate into greater consumer confidence in the brand (Dacin & Smith, 1994). Sometimes diversity leads to uncertainty about category attributes. Folkes and Patrick (2003), for example, found that inferences from one category member to other category members were less likely to occur when the category members were heterogeneous than when they were homogeneous.

PROTOTYPICALITY AND AFFECT: HOW ARE THEY RELATED?

In addition to flexibility, another characteristic of categories that has been widely researched is the concept of graded membership. Many models of category representation suggest that membership is graded, with members ranging from very good (typical) members of the category to very poor (atypical) members of the category. One reason that this characteristic has been researched extensively in consumer psychology is because of its relationship to affect. For example, first movers in a consumer category are generally thought to have advantages of category prototypes such as being preferred to second or third movers in the category (Carpenter & Nakamoto, 1989).

In this section we present an overview of the relationship between prototypicality and affect, and we address the significance of this relationship in consumer research. Many studies in consumer psychology have reported a positive relationship between the prototypicality of a category member and the evaluation or attitude associated with it. For example, Loken and Ward (1990) found that, although the correlations between typicality and attitude ranged from .00 to .92 for 16 different product categories, it was positive and significant overall across the 16 categories (r = .58, p <. 01). More typical items were better liked. For instance, among fast food outlets, the more prototypical ones (e.g., McDonald's) tended to be more preferred or better liked relative to less typical ones (e.g., Church's Chicken or Taco Bell). Other research, too, supports a positive, linear relationship between prototypicality and attitude (Carpenter & Nakamoto, 1996; Folkes & Patrick, 2003; Simonin & Ruth, 1998; Veryzer & Hutchinson, 1998).

Several explanations have been offered for this linear relationship. One explanation is based on the concept of perceptual fluency. By this account, more typical members of a category also tend to have greater perceptual fluency, which is affectively pleasing (e.g., Schwarz, 2004). Perceptual fluency increases over time, as familiarity with a stimulus increases. A related concept is frequency of instantiation, or the frequency with which an item appears as an instance of the category (Barsalou, 1985). Researchers have found that both the extent to which a category member is instantiated, and also the person's perceived familiarity with the category member, are significant predictors of category member typicality, and also tend to predict attitudes toward the category (e.g., Barsalou, 1985; Loken & Ward, 1990; Viswanathan & Childers, 1999).

A second explanation for this linear relationship is that typical category members are more likely than atypical category members to have valued attributes, as the category has evolved over time (Loken & Ward, 1990). New category members tend to include attributes that are valued by consumers, and these attributes tend to overlap with attributes that are more common for typical than for atypical category members. If the value of attributes underlies this relationship, then categories with negatively valued attributes should show the opposite effect, and they do (Ward & Loken 1988). This explanation might also explain why earlier research on taxonomic categories did not find a positive relationship between typicality and attitude (Rosch, 1973). Because some categories had a positive relationship and other categories had a negative relationship, these patterns averaged to zero.

In the context of brand categories, as noted earlier, new category members (new brand extensions) are better liked when they are similar to, or typical of, the parent brand (Aaker & Keller, 1990; Boush & Loken, 1991; Boush et al., 1987; Broniarczyk & Alba, 1994; Zhang & Sood, 2002; see also, Chakravarti, MacInnis, & Nakamoto, 1990; Herr, Farquhar, & Fazio, 1996; Keller & Aaker, 1992; Park, Milberg, & Lawson, 1991; Smith & Park, 1992). Hence, in this context, too, greater typicality is related to more positive affect. While the nature of the criteria used for establishing similarity, typicality, or "fit" between the new extension and the parent brand varies for these studies, the conclusion is the same: In the absence of any relevant negative information about the brand extension, a greater fit contributes to more acceptance and stronger affect toward the new extension. In these studies, the brand categories examined were ones associated most with positive (rather than negative) features.

Aesthetic product design evaluations, in addition to being influenced by prototypicality, are also influenced by whether the visual elements of the design appear to belong together in a unified or Gestalt-like fashion (Veryzer & Hutchinson, 1998). In an advertising context, when the components of a communication process are congruent and seem to belong together, people's attitudes toward the brand increase (Kirmani & Shiv, 1998). Wanke, Bless, and Schwarz (1998) found that when the name of a sports car extension suggested continuation rather than discontinuation of prior models of the brand, people evaluated the new extension positively (as they would a typical sports car). Conversely, when the name suggested discontinuation, contrast effects occurred, particularly among nonexperts.

Research on alignable differences produces analogous effects as similarity and typicality. Alignable (versus nonalignable) differences have been found to increase brand evaluations in comparative ads (Zhang, Kardes, & Cronley, 2002).

A different research stream finds that the linear relationship between typicality and attitude breaks down in certain contexts, and shows that moderate levels of typicality induce more positive affect than low or high levels of typicality. According to this view, when consumers have abundant cognitive resources and are highly motivated to process information, the thought processes generated under a moderate level of incongruity are more pleasing than under a low level of incongruity. Meyers-Levy and Tybout (1989) argue, based on Mandler's (1982) moderate incongruity effect, that the process of resolving incongruity is pleasing, as long as people have the necessary resources and the incongruity is not too great. If the category is extremely similar, elaborative thought is less likely to be generated, resulting in more mildly positive affect. Meyers-Levy and Tybout found that the resulting positive affect deriving from the effort does indeed transfer to the target stimulus. Other research replicates the moderate incongruity effect (Meyers-Levy, Louie & Curren, 1994; Stayman, Alden & Smith, 1992). Peracchio and Tybout (1996), however, argue that for the moderate incongruity effect to occur, people need to have low prior knowledge of the category. Specifically, people with low prior knowledge will be more sensitive to category-inconsistent information, whereas people with high prior knowledge will be more likely to rely on their prior knowledge about salient category attributes. Peracchio and Tybout's findings support these predictions. Other research finds that the effect disappears under conditions of risk aversion (Campbell & Goodstein, 2001), or for people high in dogmatism (Meyers-Levy & Tybout, 1989).

Finally, under some circumstances, novelty and variety increase affect (Woll & Graesser, 1982). To the extent that a novel or unusual category member is more atypical of the category, typicality and affect are related negatively (Ward & Loken, 1988). In this case, the atypical members of the category are positively valued for their novel attributes. An area for future research is to investigate under what conditions these attributes are considered novel and positive, and under what conditions they appear atypical and less positive. In sum, however, most studies support a strong positive, linear relationship between typicality and affect, as long as the category has valued attributes. In more limited contexts, a nonlinear or even a negative relationship may exist.

METHODOLOGY AND ANALYTIC TECHNIQUES

In examining the extensive roles that category representation and category inference play in consumer information processing, researchers have had to draw on a diverse set of traditional methodologies, but have relied primarily on two. Many studies of category structure (e.g., category stability/flexibility and graded structure) have relied on correlational methods. As mentioned in an earlier section, various measures (ideals, attribute structure, fuzzy-set measures) are correlated with global measures of prototypicality (e.g., Barsalou, 1985, Loken & Ward, 1987, 1990; Ward

& Loken, 1986; Viswanathan & Childers, 1999). Similar correlational studies have been used in studying the roles that context and goals play in altering category representations (e.g., Barsalou 1982; Ratneshwar & Shocker 1991), and in altering the relationship between prototypicality and affect (Loken & Ward 1990; Ward & Loken 1988). One pertinent question is whether some of the measures discussed earlier (e.g., ideals, attribute structure, fuzzy set-based measures) can accommodate both taxonomic categories (which often have surface-level resemblances) and situational, goal-derived categories. The ideals measure captures the common goal(s) for both taxonomic and goal-derived categories (Barsalou, 1985; Loken & Ward, 1990). The attribute structure measure (Loken & Ward, 1990; Viswanathan & Childers, 1999) and fuzzy set measures (Viswanathan & Childers, 1999) capture the central tendency of categories, and feature elements can include both physical and nonphysical features of the category, as well as goals and/or image attributes. In the case of all three measures, the underlying attributes and goals are accessed via representations that are accessible for the category. Furthermore, because the attributes accessible in one context may differ from those accessible in another, the measures can accommodate and allow researchers to predict category fluctuations as a function of context.

The majority of the research in consumer categorization has relied not on correlational methods, but on experimental methods. When investigating category inferences in the context of brand categories and brand extensions, for example, researchers have typically presented consumers with information about a new category member (the extension) and then asked them to provide one of several conceptually relevant responses (e.g., choice, purchase intention, evaluation, beliefs, cognitive responses, see Aaker & Keller, 1990; Gurhan-Canli & Maheswaran, 1998; John, Loken, & Joiner, 1998; Lane, 2000; Loken & John, 1993; Meyvis & Janiszewski, 2004; Milberg, Park, & McCarthy, 1997). In these experiments, stimuli (extensions) and context information (brand category characteristics) are sampled or created such that the factors of interest that are being tested vary (e.g., presence of brand specific associations, Broniarczyk & Alba, 1994; brand breadth, Meyvis & Janiszewski, 2004; brand variability, Dacin & Smith, 1994; extension-category similarity Park, Milberg, & Lawson, 1991). Similar experimental methods have been used to examine the role of concepts in memory (e.g., Keller, Heckler, & Houston, 1998; Zhang & Markman, 1998) and inferences in induction (Levin & Levin, 2000; Park, Jun, & Shocker, 1996). Research on category expansion and flexibility has utilized measures of clustering and categorization/grouping as dependent variables (e.g., Isen & Daubman, 1984; Kahn & Isen, 1993; Lee & Sternthal, 1999), as has research on expertise and category structure (e.g., Cowley & Mitchell, 2003).

Finally, researchers who have focused on the question of category activation have used priming as a means of gaining insight into the relative accessibility of concepts for information processing. Morrin (1999), for example, used a priming and response time methodology to investigate what impact brand extensions had on the accessibility of parent brand associations (see also e.g., Pechmann & Knight, 2002; Grewal et al., 1997; Forehand & Deshpande, 2001).

An interesting question is whether a greater future focus on the modality-specific representation view of conceptual knowledge proposed by Barsalou (1999) will require a broadening of the methods used to examine concepts and categorization.

CONCLUSIONS

Consumer research that borrows from theories of categorization dates back to the mid-1980s. During the subsequent two decades, consumer researchers have identified applications beyond traditional product categories that include brand categories, goal-related categories, cultural categories, and service employee categories, among others. Research has found that the categories typically examined in consumer psychology have both stability and flexibility of structure, and that they are used across diverse environmental contexts. Also, consumers often adopt categories on the basis of goal-based criteria, rather than on more traditional structural and taxonomic criteria, and these goal-derived categories, as well as categories based upon one's self-view, are quite malleable and membership depends on the consumer context.

Research that further examines the roles of the brain's modality-specific systems in higher cognition is needed. Barsalou's (1999) conceptualization of categories as residing in these systems could be a fruitful direction for future research. Future research could aim to increase our understanding of how modality-specific processing and simulation affect consumers' perceptions of new category members, their representations of categories, and their inferences about new and existing category members.

Research has also furthered our understanding of factors that influence category inferences, specifically, inferences from category beliefs and attitudes to new category instances. Much of the work on category inferences has been conducted in the context of brand categories. Early research on the global construct of similarity gave way to more thoughtful analyses of the various dimensions of similarity relevant to understanding inferences from brand categories to new category members (e.g., similarity to the brand product categories, similarity to the brand's beliefs or image), along with important moderating variables (e.g., accessibility, diagnosticity) that increase perceived similarity and category inferences. Most research has examined category inferences pertaining to new category members (brand extensions), with relatively little research being conducted on factors that impact inferences between existing category members. For example how might advertising of Healthy Choice soups affect inferences about Healthy Choice frozen dinners? Or, if one branded product (say, Healthy Choice soups) increases in quality over time, how will this affect inferences about the quality of other branded products (e.g., Healthy Choice frozen dinners)?

Consumer research on inferences has also found that information about new category members (e.g., brand extension failures) can impact category beliefs, as long as the information about category members is accessible and relevant to the original category beliefs. Future research could also examine whether existing category members that are accessible and perceived negatively impact perceptions of the category as a whole. Also, the conditions under which representations of current category members are stable or unstable (e.g., if retrieved consistently across settings vs. inconsistently) may also influence the ability of category representations to resist change.

Consumer research has also examined conditions under which a new category member (typically a brand extension) is likely to be accepted as a category member of a favorably viewed category. Research that examines category expansion finds that certain motivational (e.g., positive mood), ability (e.g., product expertise), and contextual (e.g., category diversity) factors increase acceptance of new category members.

The extensive research on the relation between similarity (typicality) and affect generally shows a positive linear relationship between the two. Exceptions to this positive relationship occur, however, and a greater understanding of these contingencies would be useful. In particular, how prevalent and important are these exceptions? What is the impact of these exceptions on marketing decisions?

In conclusion, in the past two decades, consumer research on category representation and category inferences has yielded important theoretical and managerial insights. Consumer researchers have found categorization concepts useful for a variety of types of consumer-driven categories and for a variety of marketing applications. Consumer categorization research has used insights from cognitive and social psychology to further understand consumer applications such as branding and goal-derived categories. These findings, in turn, increase our basic understanding of how categories are represented, the nature of retrieval of category representations, the functional location of category representations, the conditions under which category inferences are generated, and contextual factors that influence flexibility of category boundaries.

ACKNOWLEDGMENTS

This work was supported by a McKnight-BER grant from the Carlson School of Management, University of Minnesota to Barbara Loken, and by National Science Foundation Grants SBR-9421326, SBR-9796200, and BCS-0212134 to Lawrence W. Barsalou.

NOTE

1. More generally, researchers in cognitive science define a *category* as a set of entities, states, or events that appear coherently related in some way. In turn, they define a *category representation* as the integrated knowledge acquired from experiencing the category's members, and also from reasoning about them (Barsalou, 2003a, 2003b; Murphy, 2002; Smith & Medin, 1981). The term *concept* is often used interchangeably with the term *category representation*, with both referring to mechanisms in the cognitive system that represent and process categories.

REFERENCES

Aaker, D. A., & Keller, K. L. (1990). Consumer evaluations of brand extensions. *Journal of Marketing*, 54 (Winter), 27–41.

Aaker, J. L. (1999). The malleable self: The role of self-expression in persuasion. *Journal of Marketing Research*, 36(1), 45–57.

Aaker, J. L., & Lee, A. Y. (2001). 'I' seek pleasures and 'We' avoid pains: The role of self-regulatory goals in information processing and persuasion. *Journal of Consumer Research*. 28(1), 33–50.

Adaval, R., & Wyer, R. S., Jr. (1998). The role of narratives in consumer information processing. *Journal of Consumer Psychology*, 7(3), 207–246.

Ahluwalia, R., & Gurhan-Canli, Z. (2000). The effects of extensions on the family brand name: An accessibility-diagnosticity perspective. *Journal of Consumer Research*, 27(3), 371–382.

Alba, J. W., Broniarczyk, S. M., Shimp, T. A., & Urbany, J. E. (1994). The influence of prior beliefs, frequency cues, and magnitude cues on consumers' perceptions of comparative price data. *Journal of Consumer Research*, 21(2), 219–236.

Alba, J. W., & Hutchinson, J. W. (1987). Dimensions of consumer expertise. *Journal of Consumer Research*, 13 (March), 411–454.

Barone, M. J., Miniard, P. W., & Romeo, J. (2000). The influence of positive mood on brand extension evaluations. *Journal of Consumer Research*, 26(4), 386–401.

Barone, M. J., & Miniard, P. W. (2002). Mood and brand extension judgments: Asymmetric effects for desirable versus undesirable brands. *Journal of Consumer Psychology*, 12(4), 283–291.

Barsalou, L. W. (1982). Context-independent and context-dependent information in concepts. *Memory & Cognition*, 10(1), 82–93.

Barsalou, L. W. (1983). Ad hoc categories. *Memory and Cognition*, 11, 211–227.

Barsalou, L. W. (1985). Ideals, central tendency, and frequency of instantiation as determinants of graded structure in categories. *Journal of Experimental Psychology: Learning, Memory, and Cognition*, 11, 629–654.

Barsalou, L.W. (1987). The instability of graded structure: Implications for the nature of concepts. In U. Neisser (Ed.), *Concepts and conceptual development: Ecological and intellectual factors in categorization* (pp. 101–140). Cambridge: Cambridge University Press.

Barsalou, L.W. (1989). Intraconcept similarity and its implications for interconcept similarity. In S. Vosniadou & A. Ortony (Eds.), *Similarity and analogical reasoning* (pp. 76–121). Cambridge: Cambridge University Press.

Barsalou, L. W. (1999). Perceptual symbol systems. *Behavioral and Brain Sciences*, 22, 577–660.

Barsalou, L. W. (2003a). Abstraction in perceptual symbol systems. *Philosophical Transactions of the Royal Society of London: Biological Sciences, 358*, 1177–1187.

Barsalou, L. W. (2003b). Situated simulation in the human conceptual system. *Language and Cognitive Processes, 18*, 513–562.

Barsalou, L. W., Huttenlocher, J., & Lamberts, K. (1998). Basing categorization on individuals and events. *Cognitive Psychology, 36*(3), 203–272.

Barsalou, L. W., Niedenthal, P. M., Barbey, A., & Ruppert, J. (2003). Social embodiment. In B. Ross (Ed.), *The psychology of learning and motivation* (pp. 43–92). San Diego, CA: Academic Press.

Barsalou, L. W., & Wiemer-Hastings, K. (2005). Situating abstract concepts. In D. Pecher & R. Zwaan (Eds.), *Grounding cognition: The role of perception and action in memory, language, and thought* (pp. 129–163). New York: Cambridge University Press.

Bickart, B., & Schwarz, N. (2001). Service experiences and satisfaction judgments: The use of affect and beliefs in judgment formation. *Journal of Consumer Psychology, 11*(1), 29–42.

Bottomley, P. A, & Holden, S. JS. (2001). Do we really know how consumers evaluate brand extensions? Empirical generalizations based on secondary analysis of eight studies. *Journal of Marketing Research, 38*(4), 494–500.

Boush, D., & Loken, B. (1991). A process-tracing study of brand extensions evaluations, *Journal of Marketing Research, 19*, 16–28.

Boush, D., Shipp, S., Loken, B., Gencturk, E., Crockett, S., Kennedy, E., Michall, B., Misurell, D., Rochford, L., & Strobel, J. (1987). Affect generalization to similar and dissimilar brand extensions. *Psychology and Markeitng, 4*(3), 225–237.

Briley, D. A., Morris, M. W., & Simonson, I. (2000). Reasons as carrier of culture: dynamic versus dispositional models of cultural influence on decision making. *Journal of Consumer Research, 27*(2), 157–179.

Briley, D. A., & Wyer, R. S. Jr. (2002). The effect of group membership salience on the avoidance of negative outcomes: Implications for social and consumer decisions. *Journal of Consumer Research, 29*(3), 400–415.

Broniarczyk, S. M., & Alba, J. W. (1994). The role of consumers' intuitions in inference making. *Journal of Consumer Research, 21*(3), 393–408.

Brumbaugh, A. M. (2002). Source and nonsource cues in advertising and their effects on the activation of cultural and subcultural knowledge on the route to persuasion. *Journal of Consumer Research, 29*(2), 258–270.

Campbell, M. C., & Goodstein, R. C. (2001). The moderating effect of perceived risk on consumers' evaluations of product incongruity: Preference for the norm. *Journal of Consumer Research, 28*(3), 439–449.

Carpenter, G. S., & Nakamoto, K. (1989). Consumer preference formation and pioneering advantage. *Journal of Marketing Research, 26* (August), 285–298.

Carpenter, G. S., & Nakamoto, K. (1996). Impact of consumer preference formation on marketing objectives and second mover strategies. *Journal of Consumer Psychology, 5*(4), 325–359.

Chakravarti, D., MacInnis, D. J., & Nakamoto, K. (1990). Product category perceptions, elaborative processing and brand name extension strategies. In M. E. Goldberg, G. Gorn, & R. W. Pollay (Eds.), *Advances in consumer research* (17, pp. 910–916), Provo, UT: Association for Consumer Research.

Cohen, J. B. & Basu, K. (1987). Alternative models of categorization: Toward a contingent processing framework. *Journal of Consumer Research, 13*(4), 455–473.

Cowley, E., & Mitchell, A. A. (2003). The moderating effect of product knowledge on the learning and organization of product information. *Journal of Consumer Research, 30* (December), 443–454.

Dacin, P. A., & Smith, D. C. (1994). The effect of brand portfolio characteristics on consumer evaluations of brand extensions. *Journal of Marketing Research*, 31(May), 229–242.

Dahl, D. W., Chattopadhyay, A., & Gorn, G. J. (1999). The use of visual mental imagery in new product design. *Journal of Marketing Research, 36*(1), 18–29.

Dawar, N., & Anderson, P. F. (1994). The effects of order and direction of multiple brand extensions. *Journal of Business Research, 30*(2), 119–129.

Desai, K. K., & Keller, K. L. (2002). The effects of ingredient branding strategies on host brand extendibility. *Journal of Marketing, 66*(1), 73–94.

Fiske, S., & Neuberg, S. L. (1990). A continuum of impression formation, from category-based to individuating processes: Influences of information and motivation on attention and interpretation. In M. P. Zanna (Ed.), *Advances in Experimental Social Psychology* (23, pp. 1–74). New York: Academic Press.

Folkes, V. S., & Patrick, V. M. (2003). The positivity effect in perceptions of services: Seen one, seen them all? *Journal of Consumer Research, 30*(1), 125–137.

Forehand, M. R., & Deshpande, R. (2001). What we see makes us who we are: Priming ethnic self-awareness and advertising response. *Journal of Marketing Research, 38*(3), 336–348.

Gentner, D., & Markman, A. B. (1997). Structure mapping in analogy and similarity. *American Psychologist, 52*(1), 45–56.

Gregan-Paxton, J. (2001). The role of abstract and specific knowledge in the formation of product judgments: An analogical learning perspective. *Journal of Consumer Psychology, 11*(3), 141–159.

Grewal, D., Kavanoor, S., Fern, E. F., Costley, C., & Barnes, J. (1997). Comparative versus noncomparative advertising: A meta-analysis. *Journal of Marketing, 61*(4), 1–15.

Gurhan-Canli, Z., & Maheswaran, D. (1998). The effects of extensions on brand name dilution and enhancement. *Journal of Marketing Research, 35*(4), 464–474.

Hafner, M. (2004). How dissimilar others may still resemble the self: Assimilation and contrast after social comparison. *Journal of Consumer Psychology, 14* (1-2), 187–196.

Hansen, H., & Hem, L. E. (2004). Brand extension evaluations: Effects of affective commitment, involvement, price consciousness and preference for bundling in the extension category. In B. E. Kahn & M. F. Luce (Eds.), *Advances in consumer research* (pp. 375–381). Valdosta, GA: Association for Consumer Research.

Herr, P. M. (1989), Priming price: Prior knowledge and context effects. Journal of Consumer Research, 16 (June), 67–75.

Herr, P. M., Farquhar, P. H., & Fazio, R. H. (1996). Impact of dominance and relatedness on brand extensions. *Journal of Consumer Psychology, 5*(2), 135–160.

Herr, P. M., Sherman, S. J., & Fazio, R. H. (1983). On the consequences of priming: Assimilation and contrast effects. *Journal of Experimental Social Psychology, 19*(4), 323–340.

Hoch, S. J., & Ha, Young-Won (1986). Consumer learning: Advertising and the ambiguity of product experience. *Journal of Consumer Research, 13*(September), 221–233.

Hutchinson, J. W., & Alba, J. W. (1991). Ignoring irrelevant information: Situational determinants of consumer learning. *Journal of Consumer Research, 18*(December), 325–344.

Hutchinson, J. W., Raman, K., & Mantrala, M. K. (1994). Finding choice alternatives in memory: Probability models of brand name recall. *Journal of Marketing Research, 31*(November), 441–461.

Isen, A. M., & Daubman, K. A. (1984). The influence of affect on categorization. *Journal of Personality & Social Psychology, 47*(6), 1206–1217.

John, D. R., Loken, B., & Joiner, C. (1998). The negative impact of extensions: Can flagship products be diluted? *Journal of Marketing, 62*, 19–32.

Johnson, K. E., & Mervis, C. B. (1997). Effects of varying levels of expertise on the basic level of categorization. *Journal of Experimental Psychology: General, 126*(3), 248–277.

Johnson, M. D. (1989). The differential processing of product category and noncomparable choice alternatives. *Journal of Consumer Research, 16*(3), 300–303.

Kahn, B. E., & Isen, A. M. (1993). The influence of positive affect on variety seeking among safe, enjoyable products. *Journal of Consumer Research, 20*(2), 257–271.

Keller, K. L., & Aaker, D. A. (1992). The effects of sequential introduction of brand extensions. *Journal of Marketing Research, 29*, 35–50.

Keller, K. L., Heckler, S. E., & Houston, M. J. (1998). The effects of brand name suggestiveness on advertising recall. *Journal of Marketing, 62*(1), 48–57.

Keller, P. A., & McGill, A. L. (1994). Differences in the relative influence of product attributes under alternative processing conditions: Attribute importance versus attribute ease of imagability. *Journal of Consumer Psychology, 3*(1), 29–49.

Kim, J., Allen, C. T., & Kardes, F. R (1996). An investigation of the mediational mechanisms underlying attitudinal conditioning. *Journal of Marketing Research, 33*(3), 318–328.

Kirmani, A., & Shiv, B. (1998). Effects of source congruity on brand attitudes and beliefs: The moderating role of issue-relevant elaboration. *Journal of Consumer Psychology, 7*(1), 25–47.

Kirmani, A., Sood, S., & Bridges, S. (1999). The ownership effect in consumer responses to brand line stretches. *Journal of Marketing, 63*(1), 88–101.

Klink, R. R., & Smith, D. C. (2001). Threats to the external validity of brand extension research. *Journal of Marketing Research, 38*(3), 326–336.

Krishnamurthy, P., & Sujan, M. (1999). Retrospection versus anticipation: The role of the ad under retrospective and anticipatory self-referencing. *Journal of Consumer Research, 26*(1), 55–69.

Kumar, P. (2005). The impact of cobranding on customer evaluation of brand counterextensions. *Journal of Marketing, 69* (July), 1–18.

Lane, V. R. (2000). The impact of ad repetition and ad content on consumer perceptions of incongruent extensions. *Journal of Marketing, 64*(2), 80–92.

Lau-Gesk, L. G. (2003). Activating culture through persuasion appeals: An examination of the bicultural consumer. *Journal of Consumer Psychology, 13*(3), 301–315.

Lee, A. Y., & Sternthal, B. (1999). The effects of positive mood on memory. *Journal of Consumer Research, 26*(2), 115–128.

Levin, I. P., & Levin, A. M. (2000). Modeling the role of brand alliances in the assimilation of product evaluations. *Journal of Consumer Psychology, 9*(1), 43–53.

Loken, B. (2006). Consumer Psychology: Categorization, Inference, Affect, and Persuasion. *Annual Review of Psychology, 57,* 453–485.

Loken, B., & John, D. R. (1993). Diluting brand beliefs: When do brand extensions have a negative impact? *Journal of Marketing, 57*(3), 71–85.

Loken, B., Joiner, C., & Peck, J. (2002). Category attitude measures: Exemplars as inputs. *Journal of Consumer Psychology, 12*(2), 149–161.

Loken, B., & Ward, J. (1987). Measures of attribute structure underlying product typicality. In M. Wallendorf & P. F. Anderson (Eds.), *Advances in consumer research* (14, pp. 22–28), Provo, UT: Association for Consumer Research.

Loken, B., & Ward, J. (1990). Alternative approaches to understanding the determinants of typicality. *Journal of Consumer Research, 17*(September), 111–126.

Lord, C. G., Paulson, R. M., Sia, T. L., Thomas, J. C., & Lepper, M. R. (2004). Houses built of sand: Effects of exemplar stability on susceptibility to attitude change. *Journal of Personality and Social Psychology, 87*(6), 733–749.

MacInnis, D. H., & Price, L. L. (1987). The role of imagery in information processing: Review and extensions. *Journal of Consumer Research, 13*(March), 473–491.

Macrae, C. N., & Bodenhausen, G. V. (2000). Social cognition: Thinking categorically about others. *Annual Review of Psychology, 51,* 93–120.

Maheswaran, D. (1994). Country of origin as a stereotype: Effects of consumer expertise and attribute strength on product evaluations. *Journal of Consumer Research, 21*(2), 354–366.

Malaviya, P., Meyers-Levy, J., & Sternthal, B. (1999). Ad repetition in a cluttered environment: The influence of type of processing. *Psychology & Marketing, 16*(2), 99–118.

Mandel, N. (2003). Shifting selves and decision making: The effects of self-construal priming on consumer risk-taking. *Journal of Consumer Research, 30*(June), 30–40.

Mandler, G. (1982). The structure of value: accounting for taste, in perception, cognition and development: Interactional analysis. In M. S. Clarke & S. T. Fiske (Eds.), *Affect and cognition: The seventeenth annual Carnegie symposium on cognition* (pp. 2–26). Hillsdale, NJ: Erlbaum.

Martin, A. (2001). Functional neuroimaging of semantic memory. In. R. Cabeza & A. Kingstone (Eds.), *Handbook of functional neuroimaging of cognition* (pp. 153–186). Cambridge, MA: MIT Press.

Markman, A. B., & Medin, D. L. (1995). Similarity and alignment in choice. *Organizational Behavior & Human Decision Processes, 63*(2), 117–130.

Markus, H. (1977). Self-schemata and processing information about the self. *Journal of Personality & Social Psychology, 35*(2), 63–78.

Markus, H., & Kunda, Z. (1986). Stability and malleability of the self-concept. *Journal of Personality & Social Psychology, 51*(4), 858–866.

Martin, I. M., & Stewart, D. W. (2001). The differential impact of goal congruency on attitudes, intentions, and the transfer of brand equity. *Journal of Marketing Research, 38*(November), 471–484.

Martin, L. L. (1986). Set/reset: Use and disuse of concepts in impression formation. *Journal of Personality and Social Psychology, 51,* 493–504.

Matta, S., & Folkes, V.S. (2005). Inferences about the brand from counterstereotypical service providers. *Journal of Consumer Research, 32*(2), 196–206.

McClelland, J. L., & Rumelhart, D. E. (1985). Distributed memory and the representation of general and specific information. *Journal of Experimental Psychology: General, 114,* 159–188.

Medin, D. L., & Schaffer, M. (1978). A context theory of classification learning. *Psychological Review, 85,* 207–239.

Menon, G. (1997). Are the parts better than the whole? The effects of decompositional questions on judgments of frequent behaviors. *Journal of Marketing Research, 34*(3), 335–346.

Meyers-Levy, J., Louie, T. A., & Curren, M. T. (1994). How does the congruity of brand names affect evaluations of brand name extensions? *Journal of Applied Psychology, 79*(1), 46–53.

Meyers-Levy, J., & Peracchio, L. A. (1996). Moderators of the impact of self-reference on persuasion. *Journal of Consumer Research, 22*(4), 408–424.

Meyers-Levy, J., & Tybout, A. M. (1989). Schema congruity as a basis for product evaluation. *Journal of Consumer Research, 16* (June), 39–54.

Meyers-Levy, J., & Tybout, A. M. (1997). Context effects at encoding and judgment in consumption settings: The role of cognitive resources. *Journal of Consumer Research, 24*(1), 1–15.

Meyers-Levy, J., & Sternthal, B. (1993). A two-factor explanation of assimilation and contrast effects. *Journal of Marketing Research, 30*(3), 359–368.

Meyvis, T., & Janiszewski, C. (2004). When are broader brands stronger brands? An accessibility perspective on the success of brand extensions. *Journal of Consumer Research, 31*(2), 346–357.

Milberg, S. J. Park, C. W., & McCarthy, M. S. (1997). Managing negative feedback effects associated with brand extensions: The impact of alternative branding strategies. *Journal of Consumer Psychology, 6*(2), 119–140.

Mitchell, A. A., & Dacin, P. A. (1996). The assessment of alternative measures of consumer expertise, *Journal of Consumer Research, 23* (December), 219–239.

Moreau, C. P., Lehmann, D. R., & Markman, A. B. (2001). Entrenched knowledge structures and consumer response to new products. *Journal of Marketing Research, 38* (1), 14–30.

Moreau, C. P., Markman, A. B., Lehmann, D. R. (2001). "What is it?" Categorization flexibility and consumers' responses to really new products. *Journal of Consumer Research, 27*(4), 489–498.

Morrin, M. (1999). The impact of brand extensions on parent brand memory structures and retrieval processes. *Journal of Marketing Research, 36*(4), 517–526.

Mothersbaugh, D. L., Huhmann, B. A., & Franke, G.R. (2002). Combinatory and separative effects of rhetorical figures on consumers' effort and focus in ad processing. *Journal of Consumer Research, 28*(4), 589–603.

Murphy, G. L. (2002). *The big book of concepts.* Cambridge, MA: MIT Press.

Mussweiler, T. (2003). Comparison processes in social judgment: Mechanisms and consequences. *Psychological Review, 110*(3), 472–489.

Nedungadi, P., & Hutchinson, J. W. (1985), The prototypicality of brands: Relationships with brand awareness, preference and usage. In E. C. Hirschman & M. Holbrook (Eds.), *Advances in consumer research* (12, pp. 498–503). Provo, UT: Association for Consumer Research.

Ng, S., & Houston, M. J. (2006). Exemplars or Beliefs? The impact of self-view on the nature and relative influence of brand associations. *Journal of Consumer Research, 32*(March), 519–529.

Osherson, D. N., Smith, E. E., Wilkie, O., Lopez, A., & Shafir, E. (1990). Category-based induction. *Psychological Review, 97*(2), 185–200.

Park, C. W., Jun, S. Y., & Shocker, A. D. (1996). Composite branding alliances: An investigation of extension and feedback effects. *Journal of Marketing Research, 33*(November), 453–466.

Park, C. W., Milberg, S., & Lawson, R. (1991). Evaluation of brand extensions: The role of product feature similarity and brand concept consistency. *Journal of Consumer Research, 18*(September), 185–193.

Park, J., Kim, K., & Kim, J. (2002). Acceptance of brand extensions: Interactive influences of product category similarity, typicality of claimed benefits, and brand relationship quality. In *Advances in consumer research* (29, pp. 190–198). Provo, UT: Association for Consumer Research.

Park, J., Yoon, S., Kim, K., & Wyer, R. S., Jr. (2001). Effects of priming a bipolar attribute concept on dimension versus concept-specific accessibility of semantic memory. *Journal of Personality & Social Psychology, 81*(3), 405–420.

Pecher, D., & Zwaan, R. (Eds.) (2005). *Grounding cognition: The role of perception and action in memory, language, and thought.* New York: Cambridge University Press.

Pechmann, C., & Knight, S. J. (2002). an experimental investigation of the joint effects of advertising and peers on adolescents' beliefs and intentions about cigarette consumption. *Journal of Consumer Research, 29*(1), 5–19.

Peracchio, L. A., & Meyers-Levy, J. (1997). Evaluating persuasion-enhancing techniques from a resource-matching perspective. *Journal of Consumer Research, 24*(2), 178–192.

Peracchio, L. A., & Tybout, A. M. (1996). The moderating role of prior knowledge in schema-based product evaluation. *Journal of Consumer Research, 23*(3), 177–193.

Ratneshwar, S., Barsalou, L. W., Pechmann, C., & Moore, M. (2001). Goal-derived categories: The role of personal and situational goals in category representations. *Journal of Consumer Psychology, 10*(3), 147–158.

Ratneshwar, S., Pechmann, C., & Shocker, A. D. (1996). Goal-derived categories and the antecedents of across-category consideration. *Journal of Consumer Research, 23*(December), 240–250.

Ratneshwar, S., & Shocker, A. D. (1991). substitution in use and the role of usage context in product category structures. *Journal of Marketing Research, 28*(August), 281–295.

Reed, A. II. (2004). Activating the self-importance of consumer selves: Exploring identity salience effects on judgments. *Journal of Consumer Research, 31*(2), 286–295.

Richins, M. L. (1997). Measuring emotions in the consumption experience. *Journal of Consumer Research, 24*(2), 127–146.

Roehm, M. L., & Sternthal, B. (2001). The moderating effect of knowledge and resources on the persuasive impact of analogies. *Journal of Consumer Research, 28*(2), 257–273.

Rosch, E. (1973). On the internal structure of perceptual and semantic categories. In T. E. Moore (Ed.), *Cognitive development and the acquisition of language* (pp. 111–144). New York: Academic Press.

Rosch, E., & Mervis, C. B. (1975). Family resemblances: Studies in the internal structure of categories, *Cognitive Psychology, 7*, 573–605.

Rothbart, M., & Lewis, S. (1988). Inferring category attributes from exemplar attributes: geometric shapes and social categories. *Journal of Personality and Social Psychology, 55*, 861–872.

Rothman, A. J., & Schwarz, N. (1998). Constructing perceptions of vulnerability: Personal relevance and the use of experiential information in health judgments. *Personality & Social Psychology Bulletin, 24*(10), 1053–1064.

Ruth, J. A. (2001). Promoting a brand's emotion benefits: The influence of emotion categorization processes on consumer evaluations. *Journal of Consumer Psychology, 11*(2), 99–114.

Schwarz, N. (2004). Metacognitive experiences in consumer judgment and decision making. *Journal of Consumer Psychology, 14*(4), 332–348.

Schwarz, N., & Bless, H. (1992). Constructing reality and its alternatives: Assimilation and contrast effects in social judgment. In L. L. Martin & A. Tesser (Eds.), *The construction of social judgment* (pp. 217–245). Hillsdale, NJ: Erlbaum.

Schmitt, B. H., Pan, Y., & Tavassoli, N. T. (1994). Language and consumer memory: The impact of linguistic differences between Chinese and English. *Journal of Consumer Research, 21*(3), 419–431.

Scott, L. M. (1994). Images in advertising: The need for a theory of visual rhetoric. *Journal of Consumer Research, 21*(2), 252–274.

Sengupta, J., & Johar, G. V. (2002). Effects of inconsistent attribute information on the predictive value of product attitudes: Toward a resolution of opposing perspectives. *Journal of Consumer Research, 29*(1), 39–56.

Shrum, L. J., Wyer, R. S., & O'Guinn, T. C. (1998). The effects of television consumption on social perceptions: The use of priming procedures to investigate psychological processes. *Journal of Consumer Research, 24*(4), 447–458.

Simonin, B. L., & Ruth, J. A. (1998). Is a company known by the company it keeps? Assessing the spillover effects of brand alliances on consumer brand attitudes. *Journal of Marketing Research, 35*(February), 30–42.

Smith, D. C., & Park, C. W. (1992). The effects of brand extensions on market share and advertising efficiency. *Journal of Marketing Research, 29*(3), 296–313.

Smith, E. E., & Medin, D. L. (1981). Categories and concepts. Cambridge, MA: Harvard University Press.

Smith, L. B., & Heise, D. (1992). Perceptual similarity and conceptual structure. In B. Burns (Ed.), *Percepts, concepts and categories: The representation and processing of information. Advances in psychology* (pp. 233–272). Oxford: North-Holland.

Srivastava, J., & Raghubir, P. (2002). Debiasing using decomposition: The case of memory-based credit card expense estimates. *Journal of Consumer Psychology, 12*(3), 253–264.

Stapel, D. A., Koomen, W., & Velthuijsen, A. S. (1998). Assimilation or contrast?: Comparison relevance, distinctness, and the impact of accessible information on consumer judgments. *Journal of Consumer Psychology, 7*(1), 1–24.

Stayman, D. M., Alden, D. L., & Smith, K. H. (1992). Some effects of schematic processing on consumer expectations and disconfirmation judgments. *Journal of Consumer Research, 19*(2), 240–255.

Strack, F., Schwarz, N., Bless, H., Kubler, A., & Wanke, M. (1993). Awareness of the influence as a determinant of assimilation versus contrast. *European Journal of Social Psychology, 23*, 53–62.

Sujan, M. (1985). Consumer knowledge: Effects on evaluation strategies mediating consumer judgments. *Journal of Consumer Research, 12*(June), 31–46.

Sujan, M., Bettman, J. R., & Baumgartner, H. (1993). Influencing consumer judgments using autobiographical memories: A self-referencing perspective. *Journal of Marketing Research, 30*(4), 422–436.

Tavassoli, N. T. (1999). Temporal and associative memory in Chinese and English. *Journal of Consumer Research, 26*(2), 170–181.

Tavassoli, N. T. (2001). Color memory and evaluations for alphabetical and logographic brand names. *Journal of Experimental Psychology: Applied, 7*(2), 104–111.

Tavassoli, N. T., & Han, J. K. (2001). Scripted thought: Processing Korean hancha and hangul in a multimedia context. *Journal of Consumer Research, 28*(3), 482–493.

Unnava H. R., Agarwal S., & Haugtvedt C. P. (1996). Interactive effects of presentation modality and message-generated imagery on recall of advertising information. *Journal of Consumer Research, 23*(1), 81–88.

van Osselaer, S. M. J., & Alba, J. W. (2000). Consumer learning and brand equity. *Journal of Consumer Research, 27*(1), 1–16.

van Osselaer, S. M. J., & Alba, J. W. (2003). Locus of equity and brand extension. *Journal of Consumer Research, 29*(4), 539–550.

van Osselaer, S. M. J., & Janiszewski, C. (2001). Two ways of learning brand associations. *Journal of Consumer Research, 28*(September), 202–223.

Veryzer, R. W., & Hutchinson, J. W. (1998). The influence of unity and prototypicality on aesthetic responses to new product designs. *Journal of Consumer Research, 24*(4), 374–393.

Viswanathan, M., & Childers, T. L. (1999). Understanding how product attributes influence product categorization: development and validation of fuzzy set-based measures of gradedness in product categories. *Journal of Marketing Research, 36*(1), 75–94.

Wanke, M., Bless, H., & Schwarz, N. (1998). Context effects in product line extensions: Context is note destiny. *Journal of Consumer Psychology, 7*(4), 299–322.

Wanke, M., Bohner, G., & Jurkowitsch, A. (1997). There are many reasons to drive a BMW: Does imagined ease of argument generation influence attitudes? *Journal of Consumer Research, 24*(2), 170–177.

Ward, J., & Loken, B. (1986). The quintessential snack food: Measurement of product prototypes. In R. J. Lutz (Ed.), *Advances in consumer research* (13, pp. 126–131). Provo, UT: Association for Consumer Research.

Ward, J., & Loken, B. (1988). The generality of typicality effects on preference and comparison: An exploratory test. In M. Houston (Ed.), *Advances in consumer research* (15, pp. 55–61). Provo, UT: Association for Consumer Research.

Woll, S. B., & Graesser, A. C. (1982). Memory discrimination for information typical or atypical of person schemata. *Social Cognition, 1*(4), 287–310.

Yi, Y. (1990). The effects of contextual priming in print advertisements. *Journal of Consumer Research, 17* (September), 215–222.

Zhang, S., & Fitzsimons, G. J. (1999). Choice-process satisfaction: The influence of attribute alignability and option limitation. *Organizational Behavior & Human Decision Processes, 77*(3), 192–214.

Zhang, S., Kardes, F. R., & Cronley, M. L. (2002). Comparative advertising: Effects of structural alignability on target brand evaluations. *Journal of Consumer Psychology, 12*(4), 303–311.

Zhang, S., & Markman, A. B. (1998). Overcoming the early entrant advantage: The role of alignable and non-alignable differences. *Journal of Marketing Research, 35*(4), 413–426.

Zhang, S., & Sood, S. (2002). "Deep" and "surface" cues: Brand extension evaluations by children and adults. *Journal of Consumer Research, 29*(1), 129–141.

6

Consumer Inference

Frank R. Kardes

University of Cincinnati

Steven S. Posavac

Vanderbilt University

Maria L. Cronley

Miami University

Paul M. Herr

University of Colorado

Consumers frequently make judgments and decisions based on limited or incomplete information. Secondhand sources of product information (e.g., information from advertising, promotion, or word-of-mouth communication) typically provide information about some product properties and characteristics (e.g., some attributes and benefits), but other properties and characteristics must be inferred by going beyond the information given (Bruner, 1957). To form inferences, consumers generate if-then linkages that associate information (e.g., cues, heuristics, arguments, knowledge) to conclusions in a subjectively logical fashion (Kardes, 1993; Kardes, Posavac, & Cronley, 2004; Kruglanski & Webster, 1996).

Subjective logic is based on perceptions of plausibility. People assess plausibility frequently and routinely, and plausibility judgments are so fundamental to reasoning that they are often formed without awareness or intention (Connell & Keane, 2004; Hirt, Kardes, & Markman, 2004). The primary determinant of plausibility is conceptual coherence, or the extent to which presented information matches or is consistent with prior knowledge stored in memory. That is, relationships between presented information and prior knowledge are explored, inferences implied by the presented information are formed, and the degree to which the implications of the presented information match the implications of prior knowledge determines the degree of plausibility of the presented information. Recent text comprehension research shows that different types of inferences influence plausibility to different extents: sentence pairs linked by causal inferences are rated highest, followed by missing attribute inferences, and lastly by temporal inferences (Connell & Keane, 2004). This chapter is organized in the following order: causal inferences are discussed first, followed by missing attribute inferences, and lastly by temporal inferences. Before discussing different types of inferences, however, we review methodologies for assessing spontaneous inference formation.

SPONTANEOUS INFERENCE FORMATION

To study inferences, researchers must ask participants questions about their inferences. However, questions about inferences are likely to encourage participants to form inferences that might not have occurred to them otherwise, in the absence of direct questioning. Hence, an important distinction must be drawn between spontaneous inferences that are formed naturally, and measurement-induced inferences that are formed as a result of direct questioning. This distinction is crucial because spontaneous inferences are more likely to generalize from the laboratory to the field (Kardes et al., 2004), are more accessible from memory (Kardes, 1988; Stayman & Kardes, 1992), are held with greater confidence (Levin, Johnson, & Chapman, 1988), and are more likely to influence other judgments and behavior (Fazio, 1995).

Spontaneous inferences are formed "in accordance with or resulting from natural feeling, temperament, or disposition, or from a native internal proneness, readiness, or tendency, without compulsion, constraint, or premeditation" (*Webster's New Universal Unabridged Dictionary*, 1983, p. 1756). Questions about inferences compel participants to form inferences that might not have been formed under more natural conditions. Consequently, nonspontaneous measurement-induced inferences are low in external validity because consumers who receive many questions about inferences in laboratory settings are less likely to receive the same questions in field settings. Fortunately, many procedures are available for distinguishing between spontaneous versus measurement-induced inferences—including response latency analysis, recognition confidence, cued recall, word stem completion, and relearning.

Response Latency Analysis

The speed with which participants can respond to questions about inferences (in milliseconds) provides useful information about the nature of the inferences (Fazio, 1990, 1995). If the inferences had been formed spontaneously prior to questioning, participants can simply retrieve these inferences from memory and respond relatively quickly. By contrast, if the inferences had not been formed prior to questioning, several time-consuming cognitive tasks must now be performed. First, participants must search memory for an appropriate response to the questions. If none exist, they must form new inferences that are relevant to the questions. This involves searching memory for inference-relevant information, integrating this information, and then, finally, responding to the questions. As a result, relatively slow response latencies are observed when spontaneous inferences had not been formed prior to questioning.

Kardes (1988b) manipulated the fear of invalidity (Kruglanski & Freund, 1983), or concern about committing an inferential error, to motivate consumers to draw conclusions about product benefits based on arguments embedded in an ad for a new compact disc player. In high fear of invalidity conditions, the header of the ad stated that compact disc players vary dramatically in quality and some are very good and some are very bad. This perceived variability manipulation was designed to encourage consumers to think carefully about the information presented in the ad. By contrast, in low fear of invalidity conditions, an uninformative header (i.e., Compact Disc Players) raising no concerns about inferential accuracy was presented. The text of the ad contained three sets of arguments implying three conclusions that were either presented in the ad (explicit conclusion conditions) or omitted (implicit conclusion conditions). It was hypothesized that omitting conclusions would enhance advertising effectiveness when consumers were motivated to draw their own conclusions, but not when they were unmotivated to do so.

Participants were asked to judge the validity of each conclusion and response latencies were measured for each judgment (conclusion latencies). Participants were also asked to indicate their overall evaluations of the advertised brand. Finally, response latencies for overall evaluations were measured (evaluation latencies). The results showed that conclusion latencies were slower in the low fear of invalidity/implicit conclusion condition than in the remaining three conditions. This pattern was observed because participants failed to draw their own conclusions spontaneously, prior to questioning. Because the target conclusions were omitted from the ad, participants failed to think about these conclusions until they were asked to do so. In response to these questions, participants had to construct an answer by recalling information that was presented in the ad and by construing its judgmental implications (a time-consuming computational process; Lichtenstein & Srull, 1985). In the remaining three conditions, participants could retrieve either a previously-perceived (in explicit conclusion conditions) or a previously-inferred (in implicit conclusion conditions) conclusion from memory (a relatively fast retrieval process; Lichtenstein & Srull, 1985). Hence, spontaneous inferences were formed when the fear of invalidity was high and when conclusions were implied but not presented explicitly.

Less favorable evaluations were formed in the low fear of invalidity/implicit conclusion condition than in the remaining three conditions. When explicit conclusions are omitted and consumers are unlikely to draw conclusions spontaneously, consumers miss the main point of the message and the ad is ineffective. In contrast, evaluation latencies were faster in the high fear of invalidity/implicit conclusion condition than in the remaining three conditions. This suggests that strong, more accessible attitudes are formed when consumers draw their own conclusions, rather than simply reading conclusions provided by the advertiser. Self-generated inferences are more accessible from memory (Moore, Reardon, & Durso, 1986), are held with greater confidence (Levin et al., 1988), and are less likely to encourage counterargumentation (Kardes, 1993), relative to information that is simply read.

A follow-up study conducted by Stayman and Kardes (1992) showed that spontaneous inference generation was also more likely when the need for cognition, or the extent to which people enjoy performing effortful cognitive activities (Cacioppo, Petty, Feinstein, & Jarvis, 1996), is high (vs. low). Conclusion latencies were slower in the low need for cognition/implicit conclusion condition than in the remaining three conditions. Although individuals who were high in the need for cognition were more likely to generate inferences spontaneously, these individuals were likely to use these inferences as inputs for attitude formation only when they were low (vs. high) in self-monitoring (Snyder, 1974). Individuals low (vs. high) in self-monitoring were more likely to use self-generated inferences because such individuals are more sensitive to information stored in memory. Because the need for cognition and self-monitoring were uncorrelated, and because spontaneous inference generation does not guarantee that inferences will be used as inputs for other judgments, stronger more accessible brand attitudes were formed by individuals who were both high in the need for cognition (and therefore more likely to generate inferences) and low in self-monitoring (and therefore more likely to utilize inferences).

Recognition Confidence

Following a brief delay, consumers often experience difficulty discriminating between implicit and explicit conclusions. Consequently, consumers often believe that their self-generated and spontaneously-inferred conclusions were actually presented explicitly in an ad or in a product description.

This type of memory confusion results in intrusions in measures of recognition memory. Kardes (1988a) presented arguments about product features that implied conclusions about product benefits. The arguments had the form: "Brand A has feature X," "if X then Y," therefore, "A has Y." For example, the arguments "Stresstabs contain B vitamins," and "B vitamins give you energy" imply the conclusion that "Stresstabs give you energy."

Forty-four randomly presented product claims were presented to participants who were asked to judge the plausibility of each claim. Conclusions were included in the set of product claims for half of the participants (explicit conclusion conditions) and were excluded for the remaining half (implicit conclusion conditions). Half of the claims were syllogistically related and half were not. Half of the product claims pertained to familiar brands and half pertained to unfamiliar brands. After rating the plausibility of each claim, participants were asked to perform an unexpected recognition confidence task in which they were asked to indicate how confident they were that each of 16 test conclusions were presented explicitly earlier during the plausibility judgment task.

Intrusions or high recognition confidence for conclusions that were implied but not presented (implicit conclusions) were of particular interest because prior research on source monitoring has shown that people experience difficulty in discriminating between perceived versus inferred conclusions when inferences are formed with relatively little processing effort (Johnson & Raye, 1981). Recognition confidence was higher when the product claims were syllogistically related (vs. unrelated). Even though the arguments were presented randomly, participants inferred implicit conclusions even though they were not asked to do so, and later, participants experienced difficulty determining whether these conclusions were presented or inferred. This pattern was observed for familiar and unfamiliar brands. A different pattern emerged for explicit conclusions: recognition confidence was higher for familiar brands, regardless of whether the conclusions were logically related to the premises. The results imply that syllogistic inferences are formed spontaneously, and memory intrusions (i.e., high recognition confidence for information that was not presented) provide a useful measure of spontaneous inference formation.

CUED RECALL

Cued recall procedures are based on the encoding specificity principle which suggests that, "specific encoding operations performed on what is perceived determine what is stored, and what is stored determines what retrieval cues are effective in providing access to what is stored" (Tulving & Thomson, 1973, p. 369). Memory performance is enhanced to the extent to which contextual cues present during encoding or learning match the contextual cues present later during retrieval. If consumers form spontaneous inferences while learning about a product, the inferences will be encoded along with the presented information, and later, the inferences will serve as effective retrieval cues. Winter and Uleman (1984) applied this procedure to the study of spontaneous trait inference. Participants were asked to memorize 18 sentences, each of which implied a different personality trait. For example, the sentence, "The reporter steps on his girlfriend's feet during the foxtrot," implies the trait, "clumsy." After a 2-minute distraction task designed to clear short-term memory, participants received a memory test. During the memory test, some sentences were cued by the implied trait, some were cued by a semantic associate of the actor (e.g., newspaper), and some received no cue (free recall). The results showed that memory performance was better when implied traits or semantic associates were used as recall cues than when no cues were provided. This pattern suggests that implied traits were inferred spontaneously during encoding. This pattern has been replicated many times (for a review, see Uleman, Newman, & Moskowitz, 1996).

This procedure could be applied to the study of spontaneous inferences about products and services. Sentences describing the attributes, features, or characteristics of products could be presented during the learning phase of an experiment. The sentences should imply a key benefit. For example, the sentence, "Automobile X has a sturdy frame," implies the benefit, "longlasting." Subsequently, the implied benefit (longlasting) should be an effective recall cue. It is also possible that a product claim might imply several different inferences. For example, a sturdy frame might imply "safe" or "low gas mileage" in addition to "longlasting." Presumably, each of these cues, if they were inferred spontaneously, should improve memory performance, relative to a no-cue control condition.

Many variations of the cued recall procedure are possible. For example, in one variation, participants were asked to memorize strings of digits (Winter, Uleman, & Cunniff, 1985). Each string was followed by a "distractor sentence" to read aloud and repeat from memory. After a two-minute anagram distractor task, participants received an unexpected cued recall test for the trait-implying "distractor sentences." Memory performance for the "distractor sentences" was greater for trait cues than for semantic cues, and greater for semantic cues than for no cues. This pattern suggests that spontaneous trait inferences were formed even though participants were not asked to memorize the "distractor sentences."

Word Stem Completion

Implicit memory measures can also be useful for distinguishing between spontaneous versus measurement-induced inferences. One such measure is word stem completion, in which participants read trait-implying sentences with comprehension instructions and later fill in the missing blanks for implied traits (e.g., CL _ _ _ _ for the implied trait "clumsy"). A target trait word is more likely to be completed if it was implied by the sentences than if it was not implied, and word stems (i.e., supplying the first two letters of a word) are more sensitive measures of spontaneous inference formation, relative to word fragments (i.e., supplying random letters instead of the first two letters; Uleman et al., 1996; Whitney, Waring, & Zingmark, 1992). The word stem completion procedure can be used as readily for implied product benefits as for implied personality traits. Exposure to product claims implying benefits such as safety or healthy should lead to greater completion rates for word stems such as SA _ _ _ _ or HE _ _ _ _ _, respectively.

Relearning

In a relearning paradigm, participants memorize information at Time 1, and then, at Time 2, memorize the same information again (old information) and new information. Memory performance is usually better for old information than for new information (Carlston & Skowronski, 1994; Uleman et al., 1996). For example, Carlston and Skowronski (1994) presented photographs of 29 people paired with self-descriptive trait-implying sentences (e.g., "I hate animals and I kicked a puppy" implies the trait "cruel"). Participants were instructed to either familiarize themselves with the information or to form impressions of each person. At Time 2, some old photograph-sentence pairs were presented again and some new photograph-sentence pairs were presented. Trait recall was greater for old pairs than for new pairs, regardless of the experimental instructions. This pattern suggests that spontaneous trait inferences were formed in familiarization conditions. The relearning paradigm can be used as readily for studying spontaneous benefit inferences as for spontaneous trait inferences. After presenting attribute-benefit pairs and brand-benefit pairs at Time 1, memory performance should be better for old pairs than for new pairs at Time 2.

The Automatic-Deliberative Processing Continuum

Inferences can be formed automatically (i.e., without awareness) or deliberatively (i.e., goal-directed inferences formed with awareness and intention). Automatic inferences are common in text comprehension. For example, when reading a passage stating that an actor pounded a nail into the wall, people automatically infer that the actor used a hammer (Bransford & Johnson, 1972). Less obvious inferences that require deliberation, however, are formed spontaneously only when consumers are sufficiently motivated (Kardes, 1988; Sawyer & Howard, 1991) and able (Maheswaran & Sternthal, 1990) to do so. The degree of motivation and ability required for spontaneous inference formation varies as a function of the strength of the evidence (e.g., a Rolls Royce is so luxurious that it is difficult not to infer that it is luxurious) and on consumers' goals (e.g., consumers interested in purchasing a luxury automobile are likely to evaluate all automobiles in terms of luxuriousness).

CAUSAL INFERENCES

A consumer walks into a shop and purchases a bottle of water. This is a rather common occurrence, of course, but why did the person exhibit this behavior? The first explanation that may come to mind is that the person was thirsty. But, what if the person's car had just overheated, or the person had a dog in their car that needed water? Drawing conclusions about why people do things or why events occur are the basis of causal inferences.

Everyday we observe and experience events that need explanation, and thus causal inferences. Like other inferences, causal inferences may be implicit or explicit. Seeing someone purchasing a package of cigarettes in a store leads us to infer that the person is a smoker. Such an inference may be almost automatic, and we may be unaware of such an inference. Causal analyses and inferences become explicit and intentional when unexpected, negative, or threatening events occur (Bohner, Bless, Schwarz, & Strack, 1988; Hastie, 1984; Wiener, 1980a, 1985) when a person feels a loss of control of a situation (Hastie, 1984; Pittman & Pittman, 1980), and when questions about cause-effect relationships in a given situation become salient (see Hastie, 1984; Silvera & Laufer, 2005, for a review).

At the heart of causal inference is attribution theory, a family of diverse ideas and theories which attempt to explain how and why people gather and process information in order to formulate causal explanations. The motivations underlying why people make causal attributions are to control their environment and predict the future, based on the assumption that understanding the cause of outcomes and events allows us to control and predict them (Heider, 1958; Jones & Davis, 1965; Kelley, 1967; Weiner, 1980a, 1985). Three foundational bodies of theoretical work, Jones and Davis's (1965) correspondent inference theory, Kelley's (1967, 1972a, 1972b, 1973) attribution contributions of the covariation model and causal schema theory, and Weiner's affect and control theories related to attribution (Weiner, 1979, 1980a, 1980b, 1982, 1985) have strongly influenced the area of causal inference.

Correspondent Inference Theory

Correspondent inference theory (Jones & Davis, 1965; Jones, 1990) concerns how people make inferences about another person's underlying dispositions by extrapolating from their observed behaviors. For example, observing a famous celebrity endorsing a product (e.g., Tiger Woods appearing in a Nike ad) leads us to infer that the celebrity likes and uses the product. Thus, the goal is to correspond behaviors to stable dispositions, with the assumption that knowing a person's internal dispositions allows us to ultimately predict their behavior.

Beyond simply looking at internal dispositional states in formulating causal explanations of other people's behaviors, people must also determine to what extent situational variables influence behaviors. This idea is reflected in the law of noncommon effects (Jones & Davis, 1965), which formalized the idea that when behavior occurs in the presence of strong situational factors, an observer should not assume the other's behavior is the result of just a natural, internal disposition (Gilbert & Malone, 1995). In other words, one should not discount the situation when attempting to explain another's behavior. Kelley (1967) later extended this idea to form the discounting principle (i.e., when one potential cause is discounted to the extent that other causes are possible), and Ross (1977) labeled the tendency to discount the situation as the Fundamental Attribution Error (see also Jones & Harris, 1967; Miller, Jones, & Hinkle, 1981).

The reality that many people do not adhere to the directives given in the law of noncommon effects, and often make the fundamental attribution error, is known as correspondence bias (Gilbert & Malone, 1995; Jones, 1979, 1986; Jones & Harris, 1967). In a classic study, Jones and Harris (1967) first investigated the phenomenon while doing work on correspondent and dispositional inferences. Participants were shown essays that reflected either a pro- or anti-position on Cuba's leader, Fidel Castro. Participants were told either that the essayist had been free to choose his written position or had been instructed by the debate coach to defend an assigned position. Participants then tried to infer the true attitudes of the essay writers. As expected, under the free choice condition, pro-Castro essay writers were seen as very pro-Castro and anti-Castro essay writers were seen as very anti-Castro. But surprisingly, in the assigned position condition, test participants still ascribed pro- or anti-Castro attitudes to the essayists in a similar manner, even though they knew the position was assigned.

More recently, correspondent inferences have been examined in the marketing context of product endorsers. This research suggests that correspondent inferences are positively associated with consumers' attitudes toward the advertisement, the product, the endorser, and to purchase intentions for the product (Cronley et al., 1999; Silvera, Grape, & Sørum, 2004; Sørum, Grape, & Silvera, 2003).

Kelley's Covariation Model

Kelley's (1967) attribution theory, called the covariation model, describes the types of information people should consider when trying to determine causality, and suggests that causes and effects should covary. Unlike correspondent inference theory, Kelley's theories encompass causal explanations based on situational factors, as well as on dispositional factors.

Causes come in two types: arising from a person and their behavior (i.e., dispositional), and arising from the situation (Heider, 1958). To determine which cause is the driver of the behavior, Kelley suggested that three types of information should be examined: consistency information (e.g., To what extent does a person's behavior toward an object generalize across situations?), distinctiveness information (e.g., To what extent does a person's behavior toward an object generalize across objects?), and consensus information (e.g., To what extent does the actor's behavior toward an object generalize across people?).

The covariation model describes how patterns observed among these three types of information have implications for judgment about the extent to which the actor's behavior is attributed to his or her personal traits and characteristics, as opposed to other factors, such as some situational variable. Consider this example: John criticizes a certain neighborhood grocery store as having terrible customer service. In attempting to figure why John is making this criticism, we should consider the following: (1) Does John repeatedly voice this complaint? (consistency information); (2) Does John only criticize this store and not all stores? (distinctiveness information); and (3) Do other people have a similar criticism of this store? (consensus information). High levels of each factor should lead us to attribute John's complaint to the fact that, indeed, the store has terrible customer service. Other combinations of the information may also yield relevant casual inferences. For example, high distinctiveness, low consistency, and low consensus would suggest a situation-driven attribution, specifically, that John is simply temporary upset about an isolated service experience, whereas low distinctiveness, high consistency, and low consensus would lead us to conclude that John is simply a complainer who is never satisfied.

Kelley's Causal Schemata

When consumers are unable to observe covariation patterns over time, they may form attributions from causal schemata based on prior knowledge. Based on our life experiences, we develop abstract and generalized cause-effect relationships (e.g., new products are improvements over old products), upon which we can draw when causal information is ambiguous or when confirmatory information is relatively uninformative (e.g., consumers expect an advertiser to say that its new product is the best).

Casual schemata are thought to be important to causal inferences for several reasons. First, they provide a type of inferential heuristic that allows us to make inferences quickly and easily. Second, causal schemata provide us with cause-effect "rules" that can be applied in a wide range of situations and provide us with a means to infer causality when information is incomplete, ambiguous, contradictory, and uninformative.

Weiner's Contributions to Casual Inference

Drawing on previous work by Kelley (1967) and others, Weiner (1979, 1980a, 1980b, 1982, 1985) combined locus of cause (dispositional vs. situational), stability (stable vs. temporary with regard to future occurrences), and a new factor of control (controllable vs. uncontrollable) into a model of casual inference. The controllability factor relates to a person's ability to control an outcome. For example, Mary has a poor dining experience in a restaurant. Is the cause of that experience within her control, such as she was in a bad mood and was rude to the wait staff, or is the cause beyond her control, such as there was a fire in the kitchen? Weiner's model also incorporates emotional processes and subsequent outcomes associated with each of the model's factors. For example, when negative outcomes result from stable (vs. temporary) causes, anger over the outcome is more likely.

While most of this work was conducted in situational contexts of personal achievement and helping behaviors, it has been applied in the marketing domain to areas of service recovery and customer satisfaction (e.g., Folkes, 1984; Folkes, Koletsky, & Graham, 1987).

The Role of Attributional Processes in Consumer Behavior

Attribution theory has had a central role in explaining a variety of important consumer behavior phenomena, in part because consumers typically make spontaneous (i.e., unintentional and without awareness) causal attributions to help them integrate incoming information, and form correct judgments and make satisfying choices (Hassin, Bargh, & Uleman, 2001). More specifically, researchers have observed that the manner in which consumers draw causal inferences affects their reactions to persuasive attempts (e.g., advertising, personal selling), evaluation of and responsiveness to comparative advertisements, satisfaction with products and services, response to service failure, perceptions of corporate cause sponsorship, and responsiveness to word-of-mouth (WOM) communication.

Friestad and Wright (1994) proposed a model of how individuals respond when they are the target of a persuasive attempt such as an advertisement. Persuasion knowledge, the knowledge of marketers' tactics and motivations, is accumulated with maturity as well as life experience. Although Friestad and Wright (1994) discuss a number of factors that influence the extent to which consumers will think systematically about a given advertisement, in general, a consumer who has developed high persuasion knowledge will be better able to resist marketers' influence in part because he or she will be able to make correct attributions for why marketers behave as they do (i.e., to facilitate sales; Campbell & Kirmani, 2000; see also, Campbell & Kirmani, in this volume).

Recent research has shown how attributional processes affect consumers' responses to comparative advertisements. Jain and Posavac (2004) empirically demonstrated that comparative ads vary in terms of whether the comparison is more positive ("The competing brand is good but ours is better") or negative ("The competing brand is bad but ours is good"). Generally, ads that feature more negative references to competition tend to provoke more counterarguing and less support arguments than positive comparative ads. Moreover, negative ads typically are less believable, and produce lower brand attitudes. All of these effects obtain because consumers attribute more nefarious motives to advertisers (e.g., that they are biased, manipulative, etc.) when they make negative versus positive comparisons.

Although advertising is a primary source of information for the consumer, the perspectives of family and friends may be weighted much more heavily because such individuals are typically perceived to be more much credible than are advertisers (Richins, 1983). However, as noted earlier, consumers often form causal inferences to help them understand the reasons underlying others' behavior. Laczniak, Decarlo, and Ramaswami (2001) investigated how causal attributions of the provider of negative WOM information affect consumers' brand evaluations. These authors exposed consumers to a negative WOM communication characterized by one of three combinations of Kelley's (1967) information dimensions: (1) high consensus, high distinctiveness, high consistency; (2) low consensus, low distinctiveness, high consistency; and (3) low consensus, high distinctiveness, low consistency. As predicted, consumers exposed to negative WOM configured as high consensus, high distinctiveness, and high consistency were more likely to form negative brand inferences than consumers exposed to either of the other configurations. In contrast, consumers exposed to negative WOM configured as low consensus, low distinctiveness, and high consistency were more likely to infer that the negativity of the message was due to the communicator than consumers exposed to either of the other configurations.

While these effects are quite consistent with core attribution theory predictions, Laczniak et al. (2001) also explored the potential of brand strength to attenuate these effects. Specifically, when consumers are exposed to negative WOM about a strong brand, they are less likely to attribute message negativity to the brand than if the brand is weak because the negative information is discounted (Sanbonmatsu, Kardes, & Gibson, 1989) in light of prior favorable brand perceptions (cf. Herr, Kardes, & Kim, 1991). Moreover, brand strength relates to inferences regarding the communicator; message negativity is more likely to be attributed to the communicator to the extent that a brand is strong. Both brand and communicator attributions, in turn, have implications for brand attitudes. Specifically, when strong brand attributions are made, brand evaluations are more negative. In contrast, when message negativity is attributed to the communicator, brand attitudes are more positive.

Another influence on consumers' brand preferences is their evaluation of the firm that manufactures the brand. Accordingly, firms have been expending increasing resources on sponsorships of events and social causes in an attempt to create more positive firm-level attitudes (Crimmins & Horn, 1996). Recent research has shown that consumers' attributions of the reasons underlying firms' sponsorship spending influence the extent to which firms will be successful in this endeavor. Rifon, Choi, Trimble, and Li (2004) demonstrated that the congruence, or goodness of fit, between a firm and the sponsored cause is a strong determinant of whether consumers will attribute the firms' sponsorship to either altruism or self-interest. To the extent that there is a good fit, consumers perceive the firm to have an altruistic motive, perceive the firm to be credible, and have favorable attitudes toward the firm. Moreover, these authors found that attributions were more favorable when a firm versus brand acted as a sponsor because the selling proposition is less obvious when a sponsorship occurs at the firm level.

A number of researchers have investigated how consumers' attributions of the reasons underlying service failures affect their perceptions and future behavior (Churchill & Surprenant, 1982; Folkes, Koletsky, & Graham, 1987). Folkes et al. (1987) for example, conducted a field study in an airport in which consumers who were booked on flights that were delayed were interviewed. Folkes et al. (1987) measured the extent to which consumers perceived that their flight was delayed due to factors controllable by the airline, and whether the cause of the delay was stable versus unstable. These attributional perceptions were strongly related to consumers' responses to the airline. To the extent that consumers inferred controllable and stable causes of the delay, they were angrier, and much less likely to repurchase tickets from the airline in the future. Controllability also affected consumers' propensity to complain; consumers who drew inferences that the delay was controllable were more likely to complain.

Recent research has focused more generally on the role of attributions in satisfaction. Weiner (2000) discussed the role of stability attributions in determining product satisfaction. When consumers experience a product outcome, they often engage in attributional thinking to inform their subsequent decision making. The intuitive attribution analysis is particularly likely when an experience is negative. To the extent that an outcome is stable versus unstable, consumers perceive that their experience will be predictive of future product satisfaction, and have an associated affective response (e.g., anger or fear in the event of a negative outcome). This expectation, then, guides future behavior (e.g., Will the consumer repurchase? What will the consumer tell friends about the product?).

Weiner (2000) also delineated how perceptions of responsibility (i.e., is the consumer or the company/brand responsible for the product experience), affect consumer behavior when a negative outcome is experienced. If the attributional search that follows a negative experience results in the inference that the company is responsible for the outcome, anger will typically result, and consumer responses such as failure to repurchase, complaining, and attempts to punish the company are likely. An internal attribution is unlikely to provoke such affective and behavioral responses.

Tsiros, Mittal, and Ross (2004) provided a more fine-grained analysis of the complex interactions attributional processes have in determining satisfaction. These authors explored the roles of responsibility and stability attributions when an expectation is disconfirmed. When a disconfirmation occurs and is perceived to be unstable, whether the company is judged to be responsible for the disconfirmation has no moderating role in satisfaction. However, when the disconfirmation is attributed to be stable, company responsibility plays a crucial role in determining satisfaction; to the extent that the company is responsible for a stable disconfirmation, positive disconfirmations result in particularly high satisfaction, whereas negative disconfirmations produce strong dissatisfaction.

MISSING ATTRIBUTE INFERENCES

Consumers often use implicit theories—or prior beliefs about the relationships among people, objects, and events—to link arguments and evidence to conclusions (Wyer, 2004). Many different implicit theories are possible—such as implicit theories about interattribute correlations, categories, accessibility experiences, and perceptual fluency. In each of these cases, implicit theories are used to reduce ambiguity by filling gaps in knowledge and by helping consumers to make predictions. Implicit theories can contain a single, simple if-then linkage (e.g., if a product is expensive, it must be good; Kardes, Cronley, Kellaris, & Posavac, 2004) or multiple sets of if-then linkages, such as those found in syllogisms or sets of syllogisms (e.g., Kardes, Cronley, Pontes, & Houghton, 2001).

If-then linkages can be idiosyncratic (e.g., if it is a Lynch Bages, it must be a good wine) or shared widely (e.g., if it is expensive, it must be good), and once consumers learn an if-then linkage, confusion of the inverse is likely. That is, if consumers believe one concept implies another (if X, then Y), they also believe that the second concept implies the first (if Y, then X; Wyer & Srull, 1989). Consequently, for implicit theories about interattribute correlations, if a product is expensive it is good (if X, then Y) implies that if a product is good it is expensive (if Y, then X). For implicit theories about categories, if a product is Japanese it is good (if X, then Y) implies that if a product is good it is Japanese (if Y, then X). For implicit theories about accessibility experiences, if a product is good it is easy to think of reasons for liking it (if X, then Y) implies that if it is easy to think of reasons for liking a product it is good (if Y, then X). For implicit theories about perceptual fluency, if a product claim is true it is familiar (if X, they Y) implies that if a product claim is familiar it is true (if Y, then X). Similarly, important ideas draw attention (if X, then Y) implies that attention-drawing ideas are important (Wyer & Srull, 1989). Confusion of the inverse is quite common in subjective logic and in inferential (if-then) reasoning.

Implicit Theories About Interattribute Correlations

The most widely studied inferences in consumer research are correlation-based inferences (for a review, see Kardes et al., 2004). Consumers often hold implicit theories that product quality is positively and strongly correlated with price, warranty, packaging, fit and finish, and other cues. To the extent that two variables are correlated, information about one variable enables consumers to draw inferences about the other. Many studies have shown that implicit theories or expectations about interattribute correlations dominate data-based judgments about interattribute correlations (e.g., Broniarczyk & Alba, 1994b, 1994c; Cronley, Posavac, Meyer, Kardes, & Kellaris, 2005; Kardes, Cronley, Kellaris, & Posavac, 2004).

Broniarczyk and Alba (1994c) presented price, quality, and advertising expenditure information for 25 brands of stereo speakers during the data-based learning phase of an experiment. Next, during the judgment phase, participants either judged the strength of the correlation between price and quality and between advertising and quality, or they predicted quality based on price or advertising. Correlation judgments were more accurate than predictive judgments even though, normatively, prediction is based on correlation. Moreover, participants overestimated the strength of the price-quality relationship and underestimated the strength of the advertising-quality relationship except when price and quality were uncorrelated or advertising and quality were perfectly correlated during the learning phase. This pattern of results suggests that consumers overestimate the strength of the relationship between two variables when the two variables are linked by an implicit theory (i.e., price and quality) and that consumers underestimate the strength of the relationship between two variables when the two variables are not linked by an implicit theory (i.e., advertising and quality), except when the data are very strong (i.e., correlations of zero or one).

Surprisingly, Broniarczyk and Alba (1994c) found no effects of information presentation format (i.e., rank ordered by quality vs. random) on judgment. Kardes et al. (2004) reasoned that format effects would emerge if cognitive load were sufficiently high and the motivation to search for information inconsistent with one's implicit theory were sufficiently low. To test this hypothesis, load was manipulated (i.e., price-quality data for 10 brands vs. 100 brands of wine) and the motivation to search for disconfirming evidence was manipulated by varying the need for cognitive closure—or the desire for a definite answer to a question or problem, any answer, as opposed to confusion and ambiguity (Kruglanski & Webster, 1996). Information presentation format (price-quality data rank ordered by quality or presented in a random order) should affect the ability to process information (rank ordered data are easier to process) as well as sensitivity to disconfirming evidence (randomly presented data increase sensitivity to disconfirming cases). These dual processes should produce opposite effects: a random format should reduce the ability to process information carefully and this should reduce judgmental accuracy. However, a random format should also increase the likelihood that consumers will encounter disconfirming cases by chance and this should enhance judgmental accuracy.

The results showed that format had a greater informational effect than an ability-to-process effect on judgment. Although a random format is more difficult to process, this format enhanced judgmental accuracy because it increased sensitivity to information that disconfirmed consumers' implicit theories about the price-quality relationship. This result is important because it suggests that consumer researchers should allocate greater attention to informational variables. The vast majority of studies of consumer inference and persuasion have focused on variables that influence the motivation and the ability to process information carefully at the expense of informational variables or environmental variables that influence consumers' learning structures (Hogarth, 2001; Kardes, 2006).

The results of four experiments using different manipulations of the need for cognitive closure and different product categories (digital cameras, interior house paints, boxed chocolates) show that the degree to which consumers use price as a basis for inferring quality is reduced when the need for cognitive closure is low, provided that they encounter a large amount of information presented randomly. The results support a selective information processing explanation of correlation-based inference: Consumers focus selectively on information that confirms their implicit theories, except when the need for cognitive closure is low, load is high, and the format is random.

More direct evidence for the critical role of implicit theories in correlation-based inference was provided by Cronley et al. (2005). Implicit theories about the price-quality relationship were measured by asking participants to indicate their assumptions about the strength of the relationship on a scale ranging from 0 (no relationship at all) to 10 (extremely strong relationship). This scale was administered before and after the learning phase of Experiment 4. The results showed that the learning phase changed participants' implicit theories in random format conditions, but not in rank ordered format conditions. Moreover, explicit instructions to focus on the presented information had no effects. The results suggest that a random format spontaneously increases learning, even though participants also indicated that learning is more difficult under these conditions.

Cronley et al. (2005) also ran mediational analyses on several experiments showing that sensitivity to disconfirming evidence mediates the effects of format, load, and the need for cognitive closure on price-quality inference. In their final experiment (Experiment 5), they showed that price-quality inference determines choice: When the need for cognitive closure was low, participants relied more heavily on price to infer quality and purchased more expensive wines when information was presented in a rank ordered format as opposed to a random format.

Of course, price is not the only cue used to infer quality. Consumers often assume that perceived advertising costs (Kirmani, 1990) and warranties (Boulding & Kirmani, 1993) are also correlated with quality. The accessibility-diagnosticity model (Feldman & Lynch, 1988; Lynch, Marmorstein, & Weigold, 1988) suggests that many different types of information can be used as inputs for judgment, and the inputs that are most accessible from memory and that are the most relevant or diagnostic are the inputs that are weighed the most heavily in judgment. Accessibility increases as salience, vividness, or elaborative processing increases, and diagnosticity increases as the perceived correlation between two variables increases. Research on warranty-quality inference shows that manufacturer reputation and retailer reputation influence the extent to which consumers use warranty information to infer quality (Purohit & Srivastava, 2001). Participants were given information pertaining to manufacturer reputation and retailer reputation and warranty coverage (4 months vs. 24 months) and were asked to evaluate a new computer (Purohit & Srivastava, 2001). When manufacturer or retailer reputation was favorable, warranty information was used to infer product quality, and better warranty coverage led to higher perceptions of quality. When manufacturer or retailer reputation was unfavorable, however, warranty information had no effect.

Dick, Chakravarti, and Biehal (1990) showed that accessibility-diagnosticity theory can be applied to other variables as well. When an accessible attribute is diagnostic because it is assumed to be correlated with a missing attribute, correlation-based inferences are formed. When diagnosticity is low because none of the accessible attributes are assumed to be correlated with a missing attribute, attitude-based inferences are formed (i.e., favorable [unfavorable] overall evaluations imply favorable [unfavorable] missing attributes). When correlations are low and attitudes are inaccessible or nondiagnostic, judgments are adjusted toward a more moderate position (Kardes & Sanbonmatsu, 1993).

Discounting and Slope Effects. Many studies of judgment based on missing information compare evaluations of products described on two attributes, A and B (e.g., price and quality), with evaluations of products described on one attribute, A or B. Products are evaluated less favorably when information about one attribute is missing than when this attribute is described as average for the product category (Huber & McCann, 1982; Jaccard & Wood, 1988; Johnson, 1987, 1989; Johnson & Levin, 1985; Lim, Olshavsky, & Kim, 1988; Meyer, 1981; Slovic & MacPhillamy, 1974; Yamagishi & Hill, 1981, 1983). At least three processes can lead to negative adjustment or discounting: (1) consumers may form correlation-based inferences with a negative adjustment (the correlation-based inference hypothesis), (2) consumers may treat missing information as a negative cue and this cue may be integrated separately with the evaluative implications of the presented information (the negative cue hypothesis), or (3) overall evaluations may be adjusted toward a more moderate position to correct for uncertainty caused by the detection of missing information (the inferential correction hypothesis of omission neglect theory).

In addition to discounting, many studies have observed a slope effect: In two-attribute contexts, the marginal effect of manipulations of the favorableness of the presented attribute on overall evaluations (i.e., the slope) is weaker when information about the other attribute is omitted as opposed to presented. Johnson and Levin's (1985) model of correlation-based inference captures the discounting effect and the slope effect. When attribute A is presented and attribute B is missing:

$$R = w_A s_A + w_B s'_B, \tag{1}$$

where R is the overall evaluation, s_A is the evaluation of A, s'_B is the inferred value of B, and the w's are weights that sum to one. The inferred value of B is:

$$s'_B = ms_A + k \, , \tag{2}$$

where m is the subjective correlation between A and B, and k is a constant that is often negative to reflect a penalty for missing information. When $m=0$ and k is negative, discounting is predicted. When m is negative and $k=0$, a slope reduction is predicted. When m is positive and $k=0$, a slope increase is predicted, but this effect has been observed in only a few studies (Johnson, 1989; Lim et al., 1988). Simmons and Lynch (1991) found discounting and slope effects without any evidence of correlation-based inference. Of course, correlation-based inference is just one type of inference process and other types are possible.

When people suspect that an initial judgment is invalid, they attempt to adjust this judgment to correct for perceived sources of bias using implicit theories about bias to guide the direction and the magnitude of the inferential correction (Gilbert, 2002; Johar & Simmons, 2000; Petty & Wegener, 1993; Wegener & Petty, 1995; Wilson, Centerbar, & Brekke, 2002). Judgment adjustment requires cognitive effort, and consequently, as cognitive load increases (due to time pressure, set size, simultaneous tasks, etc.), the amount of adjustment decreases. Hence, cognitive load manipulations provide a useful tool for separating initial and final judgments and for determining the direction and the amount of adjustment that is performed.

Omission Neglect. Consumers often use whatever information is readily available to them and neglect missing, unmentioned, or unknown information (Kardes & Sanbonmatsu, 2003). As a consequence, consumers often form extreme and confidently-held judgments on the basis of weak or limited evidence. Sensitivity to omissions increases and more moderate judgments are formed, however, when consumers are warned that information is missing (Sanbonmatsu, Kardes, & Herr, 1992), when consumers are highly knowledgeable about a product category and have well-articulated standards of comparison (Sanbonmatsu, Kardes, & Sansone, 1991; Sanbonmatsu et al., 1992), and when comparison processes make it painfully obvious that different products are described by different amounts of information (Muthukrishnan & Ramaswami, 1999; Kardes & Sanbonmatsu, 1993; Sanbonmatsu, Kardes, Houghton, Ho, & Posavac, 2003; Sanbonmatsu, Kardes, Posavac, & Houghton, 1997).

Although omissions are typically not salient, variables that increase the salience of omissions help consumers to recognize that their judgments are based on weak or limited evidence, and this encourages inferential correction toward a more moderate position. When information is weak or limited, moderate (vs. extreme) judgments are more accurate (Griffin & Tversky, 1992), more readily updated as new information becomes available (Cialdini, Levy, Herman, & Evenbeck, 1973), and are more justifiable to oneself and others (Lerner & Tetlock, 1999; Shafir, Simonson, & Tversky, 1993).

Contextual cues that prompt the recognition of specific omissions are more likely to be present in comparative (vs. singular) judgment contexts, and, consequently, set-size effects are more likely to be observed in comparative within-subject than in singular between-subject designs. However, even in within-subject designs, sensitivity to missing information is greater when the product described by the larger amount of information is presented second as opposed to first (Kardes & Sanbonmatsu, 1993) and when products are described on noncomparable attributes (Sanbonmatsu et al., 1997).

Comparative judgment contexts also reduce the tendency to overestimate the importance of the presented information (Sanbonmatsu et al., 2003). Half of the participants judged an automobile described by limited information (three noncomparable favorable attributes) singularly, and half judged this product in the context of another automobile described by a larger amount of information (six noncomparable favorable attributes). An open-ended measure of attribute importance was employed. Participants were asked to list at least four and not more than eight attributes that are important to consider in evaluating an automobile, and to explain why each listed attribute is important. One of three different sets of attributes was used to describe the target product, and for whichever set was used, the attributes describing (vs. not describing) the target product were more likely to be reported as important in the singular judgment context, but not in the comparative judgment context. Moreover, as the perceived importance of the information used to describe the target product increased, the perceived sufficiency of this information increased, and evaluation extremity increased.

Sensitivity to missing information is an important precursor to inference formation: Consumers are unlikely to infer values for missing attributes unless missing attributes are detected. Moreover, employing procedures that increase sensitivity to missing attributes—such as comparative judgment contexts, a priori criteria consideration and a priori rating of all relevant attributes (regardless of availability)—improve judgment by debiasing omission neglect (Kardes & Sanbonmatsu, 2003; Kardes et al., 2006).

Implicit Theories About Categories

Implicit theories about interattribute correlations are not the only basis for inference formation. Consumers also use implicit theories about categories to draw inferences about products. Categorical information includes product types (e.g., cars) and subtypes (e.g., sports cars), prototypes (e.g., abstract representations of the typical member of a category) and exemplars (e.g., concrete representations of specific members of a category), country of origin (e.g., all products made in Japan are high in quality) and brands (e.g., all products made by Sony are high in quality). In each of these examples, categorical reasoning involves generalization: A specific product is assumed to possess properties similar to those possessed by a category (e.g., product type, subtype, prototype, exemplars, country of origin, brand) to which the product is linked. Again, if-reasoning is involved (if it is a Sony, it is high in quality) and confusion of the inverse is common: If a product has features in common with a particular category, then it is a member of that category (if X, then Y); if a product is a member of a category, then it has features in common with that category (if Y, then X).

There are two major models of category-based inference: the Fiske and Pavelchak (1986) feature-matching model and the Brewer (1988) involvement model. Fiske and Pavelchak (1986) suggest that the features of a target object are compared to the features of a category, and if sufficient match or overlap exists, the object is assigned to the category and features typical of the category are assumed to be shared by the target object. If insufficient match or overlap exists, effortful piecemeal or attribute-based judgment occurs (e.g., Lynch, 1985). According to Brewer (1988), feature-matching is not as important or primary as involvement. When involvement is low, consumers attempt to assign a product to a category and category-based inference is likely. When involvement is high, effortful piecemeal or attribute-based judgment is likely.

Sujan (1985) conducted a study to delineate when individuals would engage in category versus piecemeal processing in a consumer context. She found that expert consumers, that is, those with well developed category knowledge, engaged in category-based processing when a target brand fits well with their knowledge of the relevant category. Specifically, they tended to arrive at evaluations of the brand quickly, and to consider more category information and less information specific to the singular brand. In contrast, when attributes of a brand did not match the category, expert consumers engaged in more analytical (i.e., piecemeal) processing of brand information that required more time than category-based processing, and arrived at final judgments of the brand that were based primarily on attributes of the brand versus the category.

This pattern did not hold for novice consumers, who have much less well developed category knowledge. While novices in Sujan's (1985) study were able to recognize when target brands matched versus did not match a given category, they typically made category-based inferences whether the target match matched the category or not. Rather than the normatively appropriate piecemeal processing strategy when a brand does not match its purported category, novices may be overly likely to use general feelings about a given category in evaluating a new brand claimed to belong to the category.

Sujan and Dekleva (1987) compared three ad types: (1) a noncomparative ad that introduced a new brand as belonging to a given product category (i.e., camera), (2) a noncomparative ad that introduced the new brand as belonging to a given subcategory (i.e., 35 mm SLR camera), and (3) an ad in which the new brand was compared to a well known competitor within the given product type. For both experts and novices, comparative ads that positioned a new product as belonging to a given product category, resulted in greater perceived ad informativeness, greater perceived similarity between the advertised brand and competitors, and greater perceived differences versus brands belonging to another category. For experts, but not novices, comparative ads were superior on these measures, relative to noncomparative ads that positioned a new product as belonging to a given product type. Ad-induced inferences were shown to mediate all of these effects.

Country-of-Origin Categories. Hong and Wyer (1989) asked participants to form an impression of a product or to judge the comprehensibility of the given information. Although country of origin (e.g., Japan or Mexico) typically had a direct influence on product evaluations, in the comprehension conditions it had the additional role of priming participants' interest in the product and increasing the care with which they processed attribute information. Attribute information, in turn, had a greater influence on product evaluations. In contrast, participants in the impression formation conditions always processed attribute information carefully.

Hong and Wyer (1990) replicated Hong and Wyer (1989) and demonstrated the importance of the timing of information presentation. Participants received country of origin information either before or after brand attribute information was presented, and these two sources of information were either presented sequentially or after a 24 hour delay. After receiving both sources of information participants completed brand evaluations, were asked to recall the information they received, and evaluate the favorableness of each brand attribute. Category-based (country-of-origin based) inference occurred in many experimental conditions, but different processes occurred depending on the timing of information presentation. When attributes were presented before country of origin, or country of origin was revealed immediately before attribute information, country of origin served as an ordinary attribute, and its evaluative implications were aggregated along with the evaluative implications of the other attributes. When country of origin was presented 24 hours before attribute information, however, country became a distinct concept that guided subsequent processing. Specifically, participants' perceptions of the country of origin directly affected overall evaluations, but additionally affected estimations of the favorableness of brand attributes such that ambiguous attributes were rated more favorably when the country of origin was reputed to make high versus low quality products.

Country of origin also affected the favorableness of unambiguously positive or negative attributes when there was a delay between the country of origin information and attribute ratings. Specifically, assimilation effects were evident such that when the country was reputed to make positive products, positive attributes were perceived more favorably, and when the country was reputed to make poor products, negative attributes were perceived less favorably. Contrast effects were also present. Specifically, when there was a mismatch between the reputation of the country and attribute valence (favorable country reputation paired with a negative attribute or an unfavorable country reputation paired with a positive attribute), the attribute was perceived more extremely in its initial direction. In cases of both match and mismatch between the reputation of the manufacturing country and attribute valence, learning the country in which a product was made led to more extreme perceptions of the unambiguous attributes.

Li and Wyer (1994) provided further insight into how a product's country of origin affects consumers' evaluations of it. In this study, country was particularly likely to serve as an independent attribute when context facilitated consumers' consideration of all available product information, specifically, when decision importance was high and when country of origin information was conveyed prior to other attribute information. Country of origin also was used in inference formation regarding missing attributes of a familiar product type (a wristwatch) when little product information was available. Finally, country of origin was shown to serve as a standard of comparison for product evaluations. When a consumer is familiar with a product described by a large amount of information, or is making an unimportant decision in which country information is encountered after attribute information is processed, contrast effects may emerge in which the product is perceived less favorably because of the lofty expectations regarding products made in that country.

Brand Categories. Extensive research has shown that when an unfamiliar new product is linked to a familiar brand category via brand extension (i.e., a shared brand name), the new product is assumed to have properties typical of the more general brand category (e.g., Aaker & Keller, 1990; Boush & Loken, 1991; Bridges, Keller, & Sood, 2000; Broniarczyk & Alba, 1994a; Chakravarti, MacInnis, & Nakamoto, 1990; Farquhar, Herr, & Fazio, 1990; Herr, Farquhar, & Fazio, 1996; Keller, 1993; Keller & Aaker, 1992; Park, Milberg, & Lawson, 1991). As implied by the Fiske and Pavelchak (1986) feature-matching model, the greater the match between a specific product and a more general brand category, the more likely it is that the product will be perceived as a member of that category. Consequently, properties typical of the brand category will be ascribed to the product. Several different matching procedures (e.g., similarity, fit, typicality, relatedness) have been investigated and when the match is high, brand category-based inference is likely. When the match is low, piecemeal or attribute-based judgment is likely.

Bridges et al. (2000) found evaluations of brand extensions were less favorable when the parent brand's dominant associations (i.e., those that define the brand within the marketplace along some positioning dimension; e.g., Volvo as "safe") were inconsistent with those of the extension brand. In this case, consistency was defined in terms of attribute-based vs. non-attribute-based dominant associations. Similarly, Park et al., (1991) found that product feature similarity determined extension evaluations but also found that product-level associations alone do not drive extension evaluations. The authors showed that consistency between parent and extension brands with respect to their brand-name-concepts (i.e., brand unique abstract meanings that are inferred from concrete brand features and are global in nature; e.g., Rolls Royce as "high social status") also influenced extension evaluations, with higher consistency resulting in more favorable evaluations of the extension. Herr et al. (1996) found that consumers' brand affect for category-dominant (e.g., Nike evokes the category of athletic shoes) brands transferred better to a proposed brand extension when the parent category and extension (target) category were closely (vs. distantly) related. Finally, Broniarczyk and Alba (1994a) argued that too much research attention has been allocated to similarity and too little to brand-specific associations. They found that salient brand-specific associations dominated brand affect and product category similarity in product evaluation.

Implicit Theories About Accessibility Experiences

Consumers have many implicit theories about how their minds work (metacognition) and about the implications of accessibility experiences—or experiences concerning the ease or difficulty with which information can be retrieved from memory or generated (Schwarz, 2004a, 2004b; Schwarz

& Vaughn, 2002). Many theories of consumer judgment (e.g., attribute-based judgment models, Lynch 1985; the accessibility-diagnosticity model, Feldman & Lynch, 1988; Lynch et al., 1988) focus on accessible content, or the specific pieces of information that come to mind. Schwarz (2004a, 2004b; Schwarz & Vaughn, 2002) argues that accessibility experiences, or the subjective ease or difficulty with which that content comes to mind, are equally important or even more important, in some situations.

For example, in a classic study, people were asked to recall either 6 or 12 examples of their own assertive or unassertive behavior (Schwarz, Bless, Strack, Klumpp, Rittenauer-Schatka, & Simons, 1991). Participants rated themselves as more assertive when they recalled few (6) rather than many (12) examples of assertive behavior. They also rated themselves as more unassertive when they recalled few (6) rather than many (12) examples of unassertive behavior. It is easier to recall few rather than many examples of a particular type of behavior, and consequently, more extreme trait inferences are formed when few rather than many examples are recalled. Similar results have been found for brand evaluations: Recalling 1 reason to drive a BMW is easier and results in more favorable brand evaluations than recalling 10 reasons (Wanke, Bohner, & Jurkowitsch, 1997). Ease of retrieval is informative in its own right, and ease dominates content when accessibility experiences are perceived to be diagnostic.

Different judgment tasks highlight different implicit theories about the implications of accessibility experiences. When it is easy to recall examples of a target event, people infer (a) that there are many examples when asked about frequency, (b) that the event happened recently when asked about timing, (c) that their memory is good when asked about memory clarity, (d) that the event is interesting or important when asked about interest or importance, (e) that the level of background noise is low when asked about distraction, and so on (Schwarz, 2004a). Schwarz (2004b) also found high levels of consensus for many different implicit theories about accessibility experiences, including "the more examples exist, the easier it is to bring some to mind; details of recent events are easier to recall than details of distant events; examples from categories that are well represented in memory are easier to recall than examples from categories that are poorly represented in memory; the more I know about something the easier it is to come up with examples; and things that are important to me are better represented in memory than things that are unimportant" (p. 370).

Schwarz (2004a) has shown that, over time, people might use different implicit theories, including implicit theories with opposite implications. For example, when asked to judge the quality of works of art, participants rated the work of art that took a long to complete (e.g., a year) as higher in quality than the work of art that took a short time to complete (e.g., a week). However, when asked to judge the talent of the artist, the artist that produced the work of art in a short period of time was rated as more talented than the artist that produced the work of art in a long period of time. Hence, the less talented artist produced the higher quality work of art.

Just as feelings of effort expenditure influence inferences about quality, so too do feelings of knowledge and ability. Consumers assume that if they spend a lot of time and effort thinking about an issue, they are likely to draw accurate conclusions. Similarly, if they have a lot of knowledge and experience regarding an issue, they assume that they are likely to draw accurate conclusions. However, the validity of consumers' inferences and conclusions depends not only on motivation, effort, knowledge, and ability, but also on the learning structure afforded by the environment (Hogarth, 2001). Wicked environments provide minimal, noisy, or delayed feedback, whereas kind environments provide ample and immediate feedback with a high signal-to-noise ratio. Although inferential validity increases with the friendliness of the learning environment, consumers believe that they learn a lot as motivation (Mantel & Kardes, 1999) or experience (Muthukrishnan & Kardes, 2001) increases, regardless of the friendliness of the learning environment. Consequently, confidently-held but invalid inferences are formed frequently in unfriendly learning environments (Kardes, 2006).

Several important moderators of the judgmental effects of accessibility experiences have been identified. People are more likely to use accessibility experiences when involvement or processing motivation is low, and are more likely to use accessible content when involvement or processing motivation is high (Schwarz, 2004a). Accessibility (accessibility-as-information; Schwarz, 2004a) and mood (mood-as-information; Schwarz, 2002) are both more likely to be used as heuristic cues when involvement is low. Both types of heuristic cues are also likely to be discounted when extraneous sources of feelings of accessibility or mood are salient. Accessibility experiences are also more likely to be used as inputs for judgment when accessibility is moderate rather than extremely low or high (Tybout, Sternthal, Malaviya, Bakamitsos, & Park, 2005). The use of accessibility experiences is also moderated by the need for cognitive closure (Hirt et al., 2004; Silvera, Kardes, Harvey, Cronley, & Houghton, 2005). For an unfamiliar judgment task involving the use of fault trees to diagnose reasons for system failure, accessibility experiences were used by high but not low need for cognitive closure individuals (Silvera et al., 2005). For a familiar judgment task involving generating reasons for predicting that a favored team will lose a key sporting event, accessibility experiences were used by low but not high need for closure individuals (Hirt et al., 2004).

Implicit Theories About Perceptual Fluency

Accessibility experiences pertain to memory-based judgments and the ease or difficulty with which information can be retrieved or generated. Perceptual fluency pertains to stimulus-based judgments and the ease or difficulty with which information can be perceived (Schwarz, 2004a). High figure-ground contrast, stimulus clarity, duration of presentation, and prior exposure (i.e., priming) increase perceptual fluency, and different theories about perceptual fluency have different implications for judgments of background noise, fame, familiarity, confidence, liking, and truth (for reviews, see Jacoby, Kelley, & Dywan, 1989; Kelley & Rhodes, 2002; Schwarz, 2004a). As perceptual fluency increases, judgments of background noise decrease and judgments of fame, familiarity, confidence, liking, and truth increase.

Familiar stimuli are easy to process (if X, then Y), and stimuli that are easy to process seem familiar (if Y, then X). Familiarity is often used as a heuristic cue for judging fame, confidence, liking, and truth. Consequently, even seemingly trivial manipulations of familiarity (e.g., priming, repetition, clarity, rhyming) can increase judgments of fame, confidence, liking, and truth. The truth effect is a particularly interesting case: simple repetition of a product claim increases ratings of the validity of the claim (Hawkins & Hoch, 1992; Hawkins, Hoch, & Meyers-Levy, 2001; Law, Hawkins, & Craik, 1998; Skurnik, Yoon, Park, & Schwarz, 2005). This effect is reduced as the motivation or ability to process information carefully increases or as extraneous sources of feelings of familiarity become more salient.

TEMPORAL INFERENCES

Considerable work has demonstrated the influence of time on people's judgments. A number of temporal biases have been identified, including confidence changes (people become less confident about their own performance ability with the approach of the performance; Nisan, 1972; Gilovich, Kerr, & Medvec, 1993), the planning fallacy (overly optimistic forecasts about the time required to complete a task, such as writing a chapter; Buehler, Griffin, & Ross, 1994; Kahneman & Tversky, 1979), impact bias (overestimating the duration or intensity of one's own emotional responses to an event (Gilbert, Pinel, Wilson, Blumberg, & Wheatley, 1998; Wilson & Gilbert, 2003), and hindsight bias (seeing a past outcome as inevitable, Fischhoff, 1975; Hawkins and Hastie, 1990). Sanna and Schwarz (2004) provide an integrative account of these phenomena. They find that the subjective ease or difficulty with which memory content comes to mind (accessibility experience, as described above) interacts with the thought content itself to determine the emergence of temporal biases. Specifically, the subjective experience of accessibility made generating few thoughts about success (failure) the same as generating many thoughts about failure (success).

Debiasing efforts (undoing the biased inference phenomena described above) also appear to be influenced by experiences of accessibility, bolstering our confidence in the centrality of experiences of accessibility as a key process in consumer inferences. Confidence changes were effectively eliminated by the thought-listing manipulation. Participants who experienced success-accessibility immediately before their performance showed no decrement in anticipated performance, and participants who experienced failure accessibility when making an initial performance prediction (28 days prior to performance) showed no increment in their anticipated performance. Likewise, the planning fallacy was also reduced when participants felt failure thoughts more easily than success thoughts at a time relatively distant from task completion, but was not completely eliminated when felt-accessibility of success thoughts was increased immediately prior to task completion. The impact bias was also eliminated for anticipated affective feelings about success (when felt-accessibility of failure thoughts was increased well before task performance), and for reactions to failure (when felt-accessibility of success thoughts was increased). Finally, Sanna and Schwarz (2004) eliminated the hindsight bias (with respect to the inevitability of past test performance) when the felt accessibility of thoughts incompatible with actual outcome (failure thoughts for successful performances, success thoughts for failure performances) was increased. Across all of these temporal biases, participants' ability to easily think about alternative outcomes essentially eliminated the bias.

According to Trope and Liberman's (2003) temporal construal theory, temporal inferences and biases are a consequence of different representations of events, depending on the time between the formation of the representation and the event itself. At relatively distant (pre-event) times, individuals' representations of the anticipated event are framed largely in terms of a few abstract features, conveying the perceived essence of the event (high level construals). As the event nears, this representation is dominated by more concrete and incidental details of the event. Trope and Liberman (2003) suggest that these differences in construal may lead to underweighting the feasibility of future decisions.

An intriguing possibility (noted by Schwarz, 2004a) is that the feelings of accessibility are given little (if any) effortful scrutiny by the individuals who hold them, and any resulting inferences are likely made automatically. The inferences themselves may then be used (and disused) deliberately (or automatically, if the decision is familiar and habitual) as inputs into other decisions, with the decision maker blissfully unaware that any feeling of accessibility signaled not the inherent rightness of the decision, but rather a natural (and biased) consequence of information processing.

The temporal inferences discussed here (and others) appear particularly informative for understanding consumer behavior. To the extent that consumer behavior is planned (e.g., planning a vacation, saving for college, gathering information for a future purchase of a consumer durable) any inference that changes solely with the passage of time is fair game for investigation. What may be disheartening to theorists who posit the ability of consumers to make informed, rational decisions (not to mention the consumers themselves) is the image of feelings of accessibility (likely induced by advertising and other tools under the control of marketers) undermining not only the appearance of a rational process, but the ability of consumers to learn from even failed consumption (e.g., the hindsight bias; "the product was bound to fail." Even if our focus is only on product-related inferences (e.g., the need for a product in the future), how long a product will last, the need for a product warranty, the ease of use (and construction) of a product) the potential impact of temporal inferences is wide ranging and profound, and ignored at the peril of both the marketer and consumer.

SUMMARY

Consumers frequently need to go beyond the information given to make sense of limited or incomplete information about products and services. Consumers use a wide variety of implicit theories to form if-then linkages that associate information (e.g., cues, heuristics, arguments, knowledge) to conclusions in a manner that seems logical or plausible. Plausibility judgments are influenced most heavily by causal inferences, followed by missing attribute inferences, and lastly by temporal inferences (Connell & Keane, 2004). Implicit theories have an important influence on all three types of inferences. Causal inferences depend on implicit theories about dispositions, motivation, ability, and control. Missing attribute inferences are determined by implicit theories about interattribute correlations (e.g., price-quality inference or inference based on presumed correlations between any two attributes), categories (e.g., categorical knowledge about the products produced by various countries or manufacturers), accessibility experiences (e.g., feelings of the ease with which relevant information can be retrieved from memory or constructed based on pieces of information stored in memory), and perceptual fluency (e.g., feelings of familiarity). Temporal inferences are also influenced by implicit theories about accessibility experiences, as well as by construal levels. Different implicit theories can lead to different conclusions, and, consequently, it is important for future research to identify the various implicit theories that are held by consumers and to specify the conditions under which each implicit theory is likely to be accessed and used. Future research should also make use of the response latency, recognition confidence, cued recall, word stem completion, and relearning procedures for measuring spontaneous inference formation to guard against drawing erroneous conclusions based on measurement-induced consumer inferences.

REFERENCES

Aaker, D. A., & Keller, K. L. (1990). Consumer evaluations of brand extensions. *Journal of Marketing, 54,* 27–41.

Bohner, G, Bless, H., Schwarz, N., & Strack, F. (1988). What triggers causal attributions? The impact of valence and subjective probability. *European Journal of Social Psychology, 18,* 335–345.

Boulding, W., & Kirmani, A. (1993). A consumer-side experimental examination of signaling theory: Do consumers perceive warranties of signals of quality? *Journal of Consumer Research, 20,* 111–123.

Boush, D. M., & Loken, B. (1991). A process tracing study of brand extension evaluations. *Journal of Marketing Research, 28,* 16–8.

Bransford, J. D., & Johnson, M. K. (1972). Contextual prerequisites for understanding: Some investigations of comprehension and recall. *Journal of Verbal Learning and Verbal Behavior, 11,* 717–726.

Brewer, M. (1988). A dual process model of impression formation. In T. K. Srull & R. S. Wyer (Eds.), *Advances in social cognition, Volume 1: A dual-process model of impression formation.* Hillsdale, NJ: Erlbaum.

Bridges, S., Keller, K. L., & Sood, S. (2000). Communication strategies for brand extension: Enhancing perceived fit by establishing explanatory links. *Journal of Advertising, 29,* 1–12.

Broniarczyk, S. M., & Alba, J. W. (1994a). The importance of the brand in brand extension. *Journal of Marketing Research, 31,* 214–28.

Broniarczyk, S. M., & Alba, J. W. (1994b). The role of consumers' intuitions in inference making. *Journal of Consumer Research, 21,* 393–407.

Broniarczyk, S. M., & Alba, J. W. (1994c). Theory versus data in prediction and correlation tasks. *Organizational Behavior and Human Decision Processes, 57,* 117–139.

Bruner, J. S. (1957). On perceptual readiness. *Psychological Review, 64,* 123–152.

Buehler, R., Griffin, D., & Ross, M. (1994). Exploring the "planning fallacy": Why people underestimate their task completion times. *Journal of Personality and Social Psychology, 67,* 366–381.

Cacioppo, J. T., Petty, R. E., Feinstein, J. A., & Jarvis, W. B. G. (1996). Dispositional differences in cognitive motivation: The life and times of individuals varying in the need for cognition. *Psychological Bulletin, 119,* 197–253.

Campbell, M. C., & Kirmani, A. (2000). Consumers' use of persuasion knowledge: The effects of accessibility and cognitive capacity on perceptions of an influence agent. *Journal of Consumer Research, 27,* 69–83.

Carlston, D. E., & Skowronski, J. J. (1994). Savings in the relearning of trait information as evidence for spontaneous inference generation. *Journal of Personality and Social Psychology, 69,* 420–436.

Chakravarti, D., MacInnis, D. J., & Nakamoto, K., (1990). Product category perceptions, elaborative processing, and brand name extension strategies. *Advances in Consumer Research, 17,* 910–916.

Churchill, G. A. & Surprenant, C. (1982). An investigation into the determinants of customer satisfaction. *Journal of Marketing Research, 19,* 491–504.

Cialdini, R. B., Levy, A., Herman, C. P., & Evenbeck, S. (1973). Attitudinal politics: The strategy of moderation. *Journal of Personality and Social Psychology, 25,* 100–108.

Connell, L., & Keane, M. T. (2004). What plausibly affects plausibility? Concept coherence and distributional word coherence as factors influencing plausibility judgments. *Memory & Cognition, 32,* 185–197.

Cronley, M. L., Houghton, D. C., Goddard, P., & Kardes, F. R., (1998). Endorsing products for the money: The role of the correspondence bias in celebrity advertising. In E. J. Arnould & L. Scott (Eds.), *Advances in consumer research* (Vol. 25, pp. 627–631). Provo, UT: Association for Consumer Research.

Cronley, M. L., Posavac, S. S., Meyer, T., Kardes, F. R., & Kellaris, J. J. (2005). A selective hypothesis testing perspective on price-quality inference and inference-based choice. *Journal of Consumer Psychology, 15,* 159–169.

Dick, A., Chakravarti, D., & Biehal, G. (1990). Memory-based inferences during choice. *Journal of Consumer Research, 17,* 82–93.

Farquhar, P. H., Herr, P. M., & Fazio, R. H., (1990). A relational model for category extensions of brands. *Advances in Consumer Research, 17,* 856–860.

Fazio, R. H. (1990). A practical guide to the use of response latencies in social psychological research. In C. Hendrick & M. S. Clard (Eds.), *Review of Personality and Social Psychology* (Vol. 11, pp. 74–97). Newbury Park, CA: Sage.

Fazio, R. H. (1995). Attitudes as object-evaluation associations: Determinants, consequences, and correlates of attitude accessibility. In R. E. Petty & J. A. Krosnick (Eds.), *Attitude strength: Antecedents and consequences* (pp. 247–282). Hillsdale, NJ: Erlbaum.

Feldman, J. M., & Lynch, J. G. (1988). Self-generated validity and other effects of measurement on belief, attitude, intention, and behavior," *Journal of Applied Psychology, 73,* 421–435.

Fischhoff, B. (1975). Hindsight ≠ foresight: The effect of outcome knowledge on judgment under uncertainty. *Journal of Experimental Psychology: Human Perception and Performance, 1,* 288–299.

Fiske, S. T., & Pavelchak, M. A. (1986). Category-based vs. piecemeal-based affective responses: Developments in schema-triggered affect. In R. M. Sorrentino & E. T. Higgins (Eds.), *Handbook of motivation and cognition.* New York: Guilford.

Folkes, V. S. (1984). Consumer reactions to product failure: An attributional approach. *Journal of Consumer Research, 10,* 398–409.

Folkes, V. S., Koletsky, S., & Graham, J. L. (1987). A field study of causal inferences and consumer Reaction: The view from the airport. *Journal of Consumer Research, 13,* 534–539.

Gilbert, D. T. (2002). Inferential correction. In T. Gilovich, D. Griffin, & D. Kahneman (Eds.), *Heuristics and biases: The psychology of intuitive judgment* (pp. 167–184). Cambridge: Cambridge University Press.

Gilbert D. T., & Malone, P. S. (1995). The correspondence bias. *Psychological Bulletin, 117,* 21–38.

Gilbert, D. T., Pinel, E. C., Wilson, T. D., Blumberg, S. J., & Wheatley, T. P. (1998). Immune neglect: A source of durability bias in affective forecasting. *Journal of Personality and Social Psychology Journal of Personality and Social Psychology, 59,* 617–638.

Gilovich, T., Kerr, M., & Medvec, V. H. (1993). Effect of temporal perspective on subjective confidence. *Journal of Personality and Social Psychology, 64,* 552–560.

Hastie, R. (1984). Causes and effects of causal attribution. *Journal of Personality and Social Psychology, 46,* 44–56.

Hassin, R. R., Bargh, J. A., & Uleman, J. S. (2001). Spontaneous causal inferences. *Journal of Experimental Social Psychology, 38*, 515–522.

Hawkins, S. A., & Hastie, R. (1990). Hindsight: Biased judgment of past events after the outcomes are known. *Psychological Bulletin, 107*, 311–327.

Hawkins, S. A., & Hoch, S. J. (1992). Low-involvement learning: Memory without evaluation. *Journal of Consumer Research, 19*, 212–225.

Hawkins, S. A., Hoch, S. J., & Meyers-Levy, J. (2001). Low-involvement learning: Repetition and coherence in familiarity and belief. *Journal of Consumer Psychology, 11*, 1–12.

Heider, F. (1958). *The psychology of interpersonal relations.* New York: Wiley.

Herr, P. M., Farquhar, P. H., & Fazio, R. H., (1996). Impact of dominance and relatedness on brand extensions. *Journal of Consumer Psychology, 5*, 135–159.

Herr, P. M., Kardes, F. R., & Kim, J. (1991). Effects of word-of-mouth and product attribute information on persuasion: An accessibility-diagnosticity perspective. *Journal of Consumer Research, 17*, 454–462.

Hirt, E. R., Kardes, F. R., & Markman, K. D. (2004). Activating a mental simulation mind-set through generation of alternatives: Implications for debiasing in related and unrelated domains. *Journal of Experimental Social Psychology, 40*, 374–383.

Hogarth, R. M. (2001). *Educating intuition.* Chicago: University of Chicago Press.

Hong, S. T., & Wyer, R. S. (1989). Effects of country-of-origin and product-attribute information on product evaluation: An information processing perspective. *Journal of Consumer Research, 16*, 175–187.

Hong, S. T., & Wyer, R. S. (1990). Determinants of product evaluation: Effects of the time interval between knowledge of a product's country of origin and information about its specific attributes. *Journal of Consumer Research, 17*, 277–288.

Huber, J., & McCann, J. W. (1982). The impact of inferential beliefs on product evaluations. *Journal of Marketing Research, 19*, 324–333.

Jaccard, J., & Wood, G. (1988). The effects of incomplete information on the formation of attitudes toward behavioral alternatives. *Journal of Personality and Social Psychology, 54*, 580–591.

Jacoby, L. L., Kelley, C. M., & Dywan, J. (1989). Memory attributions. In H. L. Roediger & F. I. M. Craik (Eds.), *Varieties of memory and consciousness: Essays in honor of Endel Tulving* (pp. 391–422). Hillsdale, NJ: Erlbaum.

Jain, S. P., & Posavac, S. S. (2004). Valenced comparisons. *Journal of Marketing Research, 46*, 46–58.

Johar, G. V., & Simmons, C. J. (2000). The use of concurrent disclosures to correct invalid inferences. Journal of Consumer Research, *26*, 307–322.

Johnson, R. D. (1987). Making judgments when information is missing: Inferences, biases, and framing effects. *Acta Psychologica, 66*, 69–82.

Johnson, R. D. (1989). Making decisions with incomplete information: The first complete test of the inference model. In T. K. Srull (Ed.), *Advances in consumer research* (Vol. 16, pp. 522–528). Provo, UT: Association for Consumer Research.

Johnson, R. D., & Levin, I. P. (1985). More than meets the eye: The effects of missing information on purchase evaluations. *Journal of Consumer Research, 12*, 169–177.

Johnson, M. K., & Raye, C. L. (1981). Reality monitoring. *Psychological Review, 88*, 67–85.

Jones, E. E. (1979). The rocky road from acts to dispositions. *American Psychologist, 34,* 107–117.

Jones, E. E. (1986). Interpreting interpersonal behavior: The effects of expectancies. *Science, 234,* 41–46.

Jones, E. E. (1990). *Interpersonal perception.* New York: Macmillan.

Jones, E. E., & Davis, K. E. (1965). From acts to dispositions: The attribution process in person perception. In L. Berkowitz (Ed.), *Advances in experimental social psychology* (Vol. 2, pp. 219–266). New York: Academic Press..

Jones, E. E., & Harris, V. A. (1967). The attribution of attitudes. *Journal of Experimental Social Psychology, 3,* 1–24.

Jones, E. E., Kanouse, D., Kelley, H. H., Nisbett, R., Valins, S., & Winer, B. (Eds.) (1987). *Attribution: Perceiving the causes of behavior.* Hillsdale, NJ: Erlbaum. (Originally published in 1971)

Kahneman, D., & Tversky, A. (1979). Intuitive prediction: Biases and corrective procedures. *Management Science, 12*, 313–327.

Kardes, F. R. (1988a). A nonreactive measure of inferential beliefs. *Psychology & Marketing, 5*, 273–286.

Kardes, F. R. (1988b). Spontaneous inference processes in advertising: The effects of conclusion omission and involvement on persuasion. *Journal of Consumer Research, 15*, 225–233.

Kardes, F. R. (1993). Consumer inference: Determinants, consequences, and implications for advertising. In A. A. Mitchell (Ed.), *Advertising exposure, memory and choice* (pp. 163–191). Hillsdale, NJ: Erlbaum.

Kardes, F. R. (2006). When should consumers and managers trust their intuition? *Journal of Consumer Psychology, 16*, 20–24.

Kardes, F. R., Cronley, M. L., Kellaris, J. J., & Posavac, S. S. (2004). The role of selective information processing in price-quality inference. *Journal of Consumer Research, 31*, 368–374.

Kardes, F. R., Cronley, M. L., Pontes, M. C., & Houghton, D. C. (2001). Down the garden path: The role of conditional inference processes in self-persuasion. *Journal of Consumer Psychology, 11*, 159–168.

Kardes, F. R., Kim, J., & Lim, J. S. (1994). Moderating effects of prior knowledge on the perceived diagnosticity of beliefs derived from implicit versus explicit product claims. *Journal of Business Research, 29*, 219–224.

Kardes, F. R., Posavac, S. S., & Cronley, M. L. (2004). Consumer inference: A review of processes, bases, and judgment contexts. *Journal of Consumer Psychology, 14*, 230–256.

Kardes, F. R., Posavac, S. S., Silvera, D. H., Cronley, M. L., Sanbonmatsu, D. M., Schertzer, S., Miller, F., Herr, P. M., & Chandrashekaran, M. (2006). Debiasing omission neglect. *Journal of Business Research, 59*, 786–792.

Kardes, F. R., & Sanbonmatsu, D. M. (1993). Direction of comparison, expected feature correlation, and the set-size effect in preference judgment. *Journal of Consumer Psychology, 2*, 39–54.

Kardes, F. R., & Sanbonmatsu, D. M. (2003). Omission neglect: The importance of missing information. *Skeptical Inquirer, 27*, 42–46.

Keller, K. L. (1993). Conceptualizing, measuring, and managing customer-based brand equity. *Journal of Marketing, 57*, 1–22.

Keller, K. L., & Aaker, D. A., (1992). The effects of sequential introduction of brand extension. *Journal of Marketing Research, 29*, 35–50.

Kelley, C. M., & Rhodes, M. G. (2002). Making sense and nonsense of experience: Attributions in memory and judgment. In B. H. Ross (Ed.), *The psychology of learning and motivation: Advances in research and theory* (Vol. 41, pp. 293–320). New York: Academic Press.

Kelley, H. H. (1967). Attribution theory in social psychology. In D. Levine (Ed.), *Nebraska symposium on motivation* (Vol. 15, pp. 192–240). Lincoln: University of Nebraska Press.

Kelley, H. H. (1972a). Attribution in social interaction. In E. E. Jones, D. E. Kanouse, H. H. Kelley, R. E. Nisbett, S. Valins, & B. Weiner (Eds.), *Attribution: Perceiving the causes of behavior* (pp. 1–26). Morristown, NJ: General Learning Press.

Kelley, H. H. (1972b). Causal schemata and the attribution process. In E. E. Jones, D. E. Kanouse, H. H. Kelley, R. E. Nisbett, S. Valins, & B. Weiner (Eds.), *Attribution: Perceiving the causes of behavior* (pp. 151–174). Morristown, NJ: General Learning Press.

Kelley, H. H. (1973). The process of causal attribution. *American Psychologist, 28*, 107–128.

Kirmani, A. (1990). The effect of perceived advertising costs on brand perceptions. *Journal of Consumer Research, 17*, 160–171.

Kruglanski, A. W., & Freund, T. (1983). The freezing and unfreezing of lay inferences: Effects on impressional primacy, ethnic stereotyping, and numerical anchoring. *Journal of Experimental Social Psychology, 19*, 448–468.

Kruglanski, A. W., & Webster, D. M. (1996). Motivated closing of the mind: "Seizing" and "freezing." *Psychological Review, 103*, 263–283.

Laczniak, R. N., Decarlo, T. E., & Ramaswami, S. N. (2001). Consumers' responses to negative word-of-mouth communication: An attribution theory perspective. *Journal of Consumer Psychology, 11*, 57–73.

Law, S., Hawkins, S. A., & Craik, F. I. M. (1998). Repetition-induced belief in the elderly: Rehabilitating age-related memory deficits. *Journal of Consumer Research, 25*, 91–107.

Lerner, J. E., & Tetlock, P. E. (1999). Accounting for the effects of accountability. *Psychological Bulletin, 125*, 255–275.

Levin, I. P., Johnson, R. D., & Chapman, D. P. (1988). Confidence in judgments based on incomplete information: An investigation using both hypothetical and real gambles. *Journal of Behavioral Decision Making, 1*, 29–41.

Li, W. K., & Wyer, R. S. (1994). The role of country of origin in product evaluations: Informational and standard-of-comparison effects. *Journal of Consumer Psychology, 3*, 187–212.

Lim, J. S., Olshavsky, R. W., & Kim, J. (1988). The impact of inferences on product evaluations: Replication and extension. *Journal of Marketing Research, 25*, 308–316.

Lynch, J. G. (1985). Uniqueness issues in the decompositional modeling of multiattribute overall evaluations: An information integration perspective. *Journal of Marketing Research, 22*, 1–19.

Lynch, J. G., Marmorstein, H., & Weigold, M. F. (1988). Choices from sets including remembered brands: Use of recalled attributes and prior overall evaluations. *Journal of Consumer Research, 15*, 169–184.

Maheswaran, D., & Sternthal, B. (1990). The effects of knowledge, motivation, and type of message on ad processing and product judgments. *Journal of Consumer Research, 17*, 66–73.

Mantel, S. P., & Kardes, F. R. (1999). The role of direction of comparison, attribute-based processing, and attitude-based processing in consumer preference. *Journal of Consumer Research, 25*, 335–352.

Meyer, R. J. (1981). A model of multiattribute judgments under attribute uncertainty and information constraint. *Journal of Marketing Research, 18*, 428–441.

Miller, A. G., Jones, E. E., & Hinkle, S. (1981). A robust attribution error in the personality domain. *Journal of Experimental Social Psychology, 17*, 587–600.

Mizerski, R. W., Golden, L., & Kernan, J. B. (1979). The attribution process in consumer decision making. *Journal of Consumer Research, 6*, 123–140.

Moore, D. J., Reardon, R., & Durso, F. T. (1986). The generation effect in advertising appeals. In R. J. Lutz (Ed.), *Advances in consumer research* (Vol. 13, pp. 117–120). Provo, UT: Association for Consumer Research.

Muthukrishnan, A. V., & Kardes, F. R. (2001). Persistent preferences for product attributes: The effects of the initial choice context and uninformative experience. *Journal of Consumer Research, 28*, 89–105.

Muthukrishnan, A. V., & Ramaswami, S. (1999). Contextual effects on the revision of evaluative judgments: An extension of the omission-detection framework. *Journal of Consumer Research, 26*, 70–84.

Nisan, M. (1972). Dimension of time in relation to choice behavior and achievement orientation. *Journal of Personality and Social Psychology, 21*, 175–182.

Park, C. W., Milberg, S., & Lawson, R., (1991). Evaluation of brand extensions: The role of product feature similarity and brand concept consistency. *Journal of Consumer Research, 18*, 185–193.

Petty, R. E., & Wegener, D. T. (1993). Flexible correction processes in social judgment: Correcting for context-induced contrast. *Journal of Experimental Social Psychology, 29*, 137–165.

Pittman, T. S., & Pittman, N. L. (1980). Deprivation of control and the attribution process. *Journal of Personality and Social Psychology, 39*, 377–389.

Purohit, D., & Srivastava, J. (2001). Effect of manufacturer reputation, retailer reputation, and product warranty on consumer judgments of product quality: A cue diagnosticity framework. *Journal of Consumer Psychology, 10*, 123–134.

Richins, M. L. (1983). Negative word-of-mouth by dissatisfied consumers: A pilot study. *Journal of Marketing, 47*, 68–78.

Rifon, N. J., Choi, S. M., Trimble, C. S., & Li, H. (2004). Congruence effects in sponsorship. *Journal of Advertising, 33*, 29–42.

Ross, L. (1977). The intuitive psychologist and his shortcomings: Distortions in the attribution process. In L. Berkowitz (Ed.), *Advances in experimental social psychology* (Vol. 10, pp. 174–221). New York: Academic Press.

Sanbonmatsu, D. M., Kardes, F. R., & Gibson, B. D. (1989). The impact of initial processing goals on memory-based brand comparisons. *Advances in Consumer Research, 16*, 429–432.

Sanbonmatsu, D. M., Kardes, F. R., & Herr, P. M. (1992). The role of prior knowledge and missing information in multiattribute evaluation. *Organizational Behavior and Human Decision Processes, 51*, 76–91.

Sanbonmatsu, D. M., Kardes, F. R., Houghton, D. C., Ho, E. A., & Posavac, S. S. (2003). Overestimating the importance of the given information in multiattribute consumer judgment. *Journal of Consumer Psychology, 13*, 289–300.

Sanbonmatsu, D. M., Kardes, F. R., Posavac, S. S., & Houghton, D. C. (1997). Contextual influences on judgment based on limited information. *Organizational Behavior and Human Decision Processes, 69*, 251–264.

Sanbonmatsu, D. M., Kardes, F. R., & Sansone, C. (1991). Remembering less and inferring more: The effects of the timing of judgment on inferences about unknown attributes. *Journal of Personality and Social Psychology, 61*, 546–554.

Sanbonmatsu, D. M., Shavitt, S., & Gibson, B. D. (1994). Salience, set size, and illusory correlation: Making moderate assumptions about extreme targets. *Journal of Personality and Social Psychology, 66,* 1020–1033.

Sanna, L. J., & Schwarz, N. (2004). Integrating temporal biases: The interplay of focal thoughts and accessibility experiences. *Psychological Science, 15,* 474–481.

Sawyer, A. G., & Howard, D. J. (1991). Effects of omitting conclusions in advertisements to involved and uninvolved audiences. *Journal of Marketing Research, 28,* 467–474.

Schwarz, N. (2002). Feelings as information: Moods influence judgments and processing strategies. In T. Gilovich, D. Griffin, & D. Kahneman (Eds.), *Heuristics and biases: The psychology of intuitive judgment* (pp. 534–547). Cambridge: Cambridge University Press.

Schwarz, N. (2004a). Metacognitive experiences in consumer judgment and decision making. *Journal of Consumer Psychology, 14,* 332–348.

Schwarz, N. (2004b). Metacognitive experiences: Response to commentaries. *Journal of Consumer Psychology, 14,* 370–373.

Schwarz, N., Bless, H., Strack, F., Klumpp, G., Rittenauer-Schatka, H., & Simons, A. (1991). Ease of retrieval as information: Another look at the availability heuristic. *Journal of Personality and Social Psychology, 61,* 195–202.

Schwarz, N., & Vaughn, L. A. (2002). The availability heuristic revisited: Ease of recall and content of recall as distinct sources of information. In T. Gilovich, D. Griffin, & D. Kahneman (Eds.), *Heuristics and biases: The psychology of intuitive judgment* (pp. 103–119). Cambridge: Cambridge University Press.

Shafir, E., Simonson, I., & Tversky, A. (1993). Reason-based choice. *Cognition, 49,* 11–36.

Silvera, D. H., Grape, K. M., & Sørum, K. A. (2004). *Correspondent inferences and their impact on endorser effectiveness in the United States and Norway.* Unpublished manuscript.

Silvera, D. H., Kardes, F. R., Harvey, N., Cronley, M. L., & Houghton, D. C. (2005). Contextual influences on omission neglect in the fault tree paradigm. *Journal of Consumer Psychology, 15,* 117–126.

Silvera, D. H., & Laufer, D. (2005). Recent developments in attribution research and their implications for consumer judgments and behavior. In F. R. Kardes, P. M. Herr, & J. Nantel (Eds.), *Applying social cognition to consumer-focused strategy* (pp. 53–77). Mahwah, NJ: Erlbaum.

Simmons, C. J., & Lynch, J. G. (1991). Inference effects without inference making? Effects of missing information on discounting and use of presented information. *Journal of Consumer Research, 17,* 477–491.

Skurnik, I., Yoon, C., Park, D. C., & Schwarz, N. (2005). How warnings about false claims become recommendations. *Journal of Consumer Research, 31,* 713–724.

Slovic, P., & MacPhillamy, D. (1974). Dimensional commensurability and cue utilization in comparative choice. *Organizational Behavior and Human Performance, 11,* 179–194.

Snyder, M. (1974). Self-monitoring of expressive behavior. *Journal of Personality and Social Psychology, 30,* 526–537.

Stayman, D. M., & Kardes, F. R. (1992). Spontaneous inference processes in advertising: Effects of need for cognition and self-monitoring on inference generation and utilization. *Journal of Consumer Psychology, 1,* 125–142.

Sujan, M. (1985). Consumer knowledge: Effects on evaluation processes mediating consumer judgments. *Journal of Consumer Research, 12,* 31–46.

Sujan, M., & Dekleva, C. (1987). Product categorization and inference making: Some implications for comparative advertising. *Journal of Consumer Research, 14,* 372–378.

Trope, Y., & Liberman, N. (2003). Temporal construal. *Psychological Review, 110,* 403–421.

Tsiros, M., Mittal, V., & Ross, W. T. (2004). The role of attributions in customer satisfaction: A reexamination. *Journal of Consumer Research, 31,* 476–483.

Tybout, A. M., Sternthal, B., Malaviya, P., Bakamitsos, G. A., & Park, S. B. (2005). Information accessibility as a moderator of judgments: The role of content versus retrieval ease. *Journal of Consumer Research, 32,* 76–85.

Uleman, J. S., Newman, L. S., & Moskowitz, G. B. (1996). People as flexible interpreters: Evidence and issues from spontaneous trait inference. In L. Berkowitz (Ed.), *Advances in experimental social psychology* (Vol. 28, pp. 211–279). New York: Academic Press.

Wanke, M., Bohner, G., & Jurkowitsch, A. (1997). There are many reasons to drive a BMW: Does imagined ease of argument generation influence attitudes? *Journal of Consumer Research, 24,* 170–177.

Webster's New Universal Unabridged Dictionary (1983). New York: Dorset & Baber.

Wegener, D. T., & Petty, R. E. (1995). Flexible correction processes in social judgment: The role of naïve theories in corrections for perceived bias. *Journal of Personality and Social Psychology, 68*, 36–51.

Weiner, B. (1979). A theory of motivation for some classroom experiences. *Journal of Educational Psychology, 71*, 3–25.

Weiner, B. (1980a). A cognitive (attribution)-emotion-action model of motivated behavior: An analysis of judgments of help-giving. *Journal of Personality and Social Psychology, 39*, 186–200.

Weiner, B. (1980b). *Human motivation*. New York: Holt, Rinehart, & Winston.

Weiner, B. (1982). The emotional consequence of causal attributions. In M. S. Clark & S. T. Fiske (Eds.), *Affect and cognition: The 17th annual Carnegie symposium on cognition* (pp. 185–210). Hillsdale, NJ: Erlbaum.

Weiner, B. (1985). An attributional theory of achievement motivation and emotion. *Psychological Review, 92*, 548–573.

Weiner, B. (2000). Attributional thoughts about consumer behavior. *Journal of Consumer Research, 27*, 382–387.

Whitney, P, Davis, P. A., & Zingmark, B. (1992). Task effects on the spontaneous activation of trait concepts. *Social Cognition, 10*, 377–396.

Wilson, T. D., Centerbar, D. B., & Brekke, N. (2002). Mental contamination and the debiasing problem. In T. Gilovich, D. Griffin, & D. Kahneman (Eds.), *Heuristics and biases: The psychology of intuitive judgment* (pp. 185–200). Cambridge: Cambridge University Press.

Wilson, T. D., & Gilbert, D. T. (2003). Affective forecasting. In M.P. Zanna (Ed.), *Advances in experimental social psychology* (Vol. 35, pp. 345–411). San Diego, CA: Academic Press.

Winter, L., & Uleman, J. S. (1984). When are social judgments made? Evidence for the spontaneousness of trait inferences. *Journal of Personality and Social Psychology, 47*, 237–252.

Winter, L., Uleman, J. S., & Cunniff, C. (1985). How automatic are social judgments? *Journal of Personality and Social Psychology, 49*, 904–917.

Wyer, R. S. (2004). *Social comprehension and judgment: The role of situation models, narratives, and implicit theories*. Mahwah, NJ: Erlbaum.

Wyer, R. S., & Srull, T. K. (1989). *Memory and cognition it its social context*. Hillsdale, NJ: Erlbaum.

7

Effects of Sensory Factors on Consumer Behavior

If It Tastes, Smells, Sounds, and Feels Like a Duck, Then It Must Be A ...

JOANN PECK

University of Wisconsin–Madison

TERRY L. CHILDERS

University of Kentucky

INTRODUCTION

As Colleen arrives at the entrance of the store, she scans the inside noticing the layout of merchandise, where the sales racks are located, and the table of sweaters just to the left of the entrance. She then hears the screaming of a baby in a stroller and the customer complaining to a sales person that a blouse she had purchased was the wrong size. At the same time, Colleen takes a sip of coffee from the Caribou store next door, notices the scent of flowers in the air, while she moves toward the table of sweaters. Picking up the pale blue sweater she strokes the collar and is impressed by the softness of the cashmere fabric. All of Colleen's impressions occur within seconds as she makes decisions about whether to remain in the store or move along to another shopping experience. Yet contained in those brief seconds was an integration of her "windows to the world" through her five senses. Our judgments about a store, its products, and even its personnel, are driven in part by the smells we encounter (our olfactory system), the things we hear (our auditory system), the objects we come into physical contact with (our tactile system), our taste experiences (the gustatory system), and what we see (the visual system).

Consumer research has approached the study of consumer behavior from a wide and varying set of perspectives. The chapters in this book provide a synthesis of these perspectives and the research that has followed. Among these perspectives is how information in the environment relates to the forms in which it is received and processed by individuals. Particularly for the latter, is how the perceptual system is organized to receive inputs in different forms or senses. The primary human senses consist of smell, taste, hearing, touch, and sight. Although each of these is a potentially important system for the processing of information, the sense of sight has perhaps received the greatest amount of attention and is discussed in a separate chapter (see Petrova & Cialdini, chapter 19 of this volume). In this chapter, we narrow our focus on the varied effects of the remaining four senses.

In psychology and the cognitive sciences, perception is the process of acquiring, interpreting, selecting, and organizing sensory information (Grohol, 2005). Perception is one of the oldest fields within scientific psychology. Many cognitive psychologists hold that, as we move about in the world, we create a model of how the world works. That is, we sense the objective world, but our sensations map to percepts, and these percepts are interpreted within the context of the environment we find ourselves in, such as the atmospherics of our store example. As we acquire this new information and consider it relative to the knowledge we have in memory from prior experiences, our perceptions shift as we select further pertinent information to aid our judgments and purchase decisions.

In this chapter, we examine research in the field of consumer behavior published over the past twenty five years on four of the senses. We first examine research on smell and the olfactory system, followed by a discussion of past research on the sense of taste (gustatory), then research on hearing, particularly music, (auditory), and finally research on touch (tactile and haptic system). We then discuss areas where future research might be directed, particularly in terms of implications for the study of individual differences, the role of mental imagery, the promise of more neurocognitive approaches, and the need for more consideration of the multi-sensory interactions of our senses on consumption behavior

METHODOLOGY

A search of articles concerning the senses of taste, hearing, smell and touch was performed through an examination of seven journals that are primarily, or in part, focused on the study of consumer behavior. A total of 81 articles were compiled from the *Journal of Consumer Research* (24 articles), the *Journal of Marketing Research* (15 articles), *Journal of Marketing* (9 articles), *Journal of Consumer Psychology* (10 articles), the *Journal of Business Research* (14 articles), the *Journal of Retailing* (7 articles) and *Psychology & Marketing* (2 articles). The most researched sense is the auditory sense (33 articles) with the majority of this research examining some form of music. Taste follows with 24 articles, smell with 14 and finally, touch with 10 articles. Interest in sensory research appears to be growing, with only 6 of the research articles published before 1980, 18 articles published in the 1980s, 29 in the 1990s and 28 articles in the last 5 years.

REVIEW OF PAST RESEARCH ON SENSORY FACTORS

Sense of Smell

The olfactory sense, or the sense of smell, has been the subject of study in several papers published in the marketing field. While some previous studies have looked at the scents of specific products (e.g., Schmitt & Shultz, 1995, men's fragrances; Schneider, 1977, package fragrance), research in the past ten years has focused on ambient scent. Ambient scent is defined as a scent that is present in the environment but not emanating from a particular object. In general, various scents have been classified by the affective quality of the scent (e.g., how pleasing the scent is), the arousal level of the scent (how likely it is to evoke a physiological response) and the intensity of the scent (e.g., how strong it is). Spangenberg, Crowley, and Henderson (1996) extensively pretested 26 individual scents and separated them into the affective dimension and the arousing or activating dimension and found that the affective dimension explained most of the variance. In this same paper, Spangenberg et al. (1996) manipulated the scent affect (neutral vs. pleasing) and scent intensity (low, medium, high) with an additional control group. The authors found that whether the scent was neutral or pleasing did not matter, nor did the intensity of the scent, compared to the control, no scent condition. Subjects in the scent condition perceived that they had spent less time in the store compared to the no scent condition. In addition, subjects in the no scent condition perceived having spent significantly more time in the store than they actually did. Subjects in the scented condition did not show this discrepancy. Evaluations of the store overall and of the store environment were more positive when the store was scented versus not scented. Authors found mixed evidence of scent on specific product evaluations and suggest that the congruency of product and scent may be an important dimension for further study.

This notion of congruency has been pursued by other researchers. Mitchell, Kahn, and Knasko (1995) manipulated whether the ambient odor was congruent with a product category. In the congruent conditions, a chocolate scent was paired with a candy assortment choice and a floral scent with a flower arrangement choice. When the odor was congruent with the product class, subjects spent more time processing the data, generated more self references, were more likely to make additional inferences and were more likely to exhibit variety seeking behavior. Interestingly, the researchers found no main effect of scent versus no scent. In general, cognitive elaboration was greater in the congruent conditions.

Scent and Music

In another variant of congruency, two studies concerning the interaction of scent and music have been conducted. Mattila and Wirz (2001) manipulated scent arousal (no scent, pleasant low arousal, and pleasant high arousal) and music arousal (no music, pleasant low and high arousal music) and examined whether scent and music were matched on arousal level or mismatched. When scent and music matched in terms of arousing qualities, consumers satisfaction with the shopping experience, approach behavior and impulse buying were significantly higher then in the mismatched conditions. This was true of both the high arousal match (scent of grapefruit and fast tempo music) and low arousal match (scent of lavender and slow tempo music). Spangenberg, Grohmann, and Sprott (forthcoming) also examined the effects of ambient scent and music by using a Christmas theme. They set up a lab experiment and manipulated scent (no scent vs. Christmas scent) and the type of music (non-Christmas music vs. Christmas music) in a mock retail store. Similar to previous research, they found that the matched condition of Christmas scent and Christmas music resulted in more favorable evaluations for the store, its merchandise, the store environment, and intentions to visit the store. When music and scent did not match, evaluation and behavior intentions were not affected, or, in some cases, negatively affected.

Scent and Other Moderators

Michon, Chebat, and Turley (2005), in the context of a field experiment varied scent along with retail density (how crowded the mall was) and examined shopper's perceptions of product quality, mall environment and positive affect. The authors found a u-shaped relationship in that the positive effect of ambient scent on shoppers' perceptions of the mall atmosphere was observed only at the medium retail density level. Further, a favorable perception of the retail environment influenced the perception of product quality. Shoppers' mood did not have a significant direct effect on the perceptions of product quality.

Morrin and Ratneshwar (2000, 2003) crossed ambient scent (unscented, pleasant) with brand familiarity (familiar, unfamiliar) and examined the evaluation, attention, and memory for familiar and unfamiliar brands. The authors (Morrin & Ratneshwar, 2000) found that a pleasant ambient scent improved evaluations for objects that were not as familiar or well liked. However, they were concerned about potential ceiling effects for the familiar brands as well as allowing only a 5-minute delay before the memory measures. In their subsequent research (Morrin & Ratneshwar, 2003), the authors examined the memory effects in more detail to determine if ambient scent influences memory of brands at encoding, retrieval, or both. In a two-phase experiment, 24 hours apart, the authors manipulated ambient scent (no scent, scent congruent to household cleaning products (geranium), scent incongruent to household cleaning products (clove)) and brand familiarity. In Study 1, the same scent was used at encoding and retrieval and it was found that ambient scent improved recall and recognition of familiar and unfamiliar brands. This was true whether or not the scent was congruent with the product category. In Study 2, the authors manipulated whether the scent was present at encoding or retrieval and found that the enhancement of brand memory was due to the presence of an ambient scent at encoding rather than retrieval. The ambient scent increased attention in terms of longer viewing times.

Process Explanations

Why does ambient scent influence consumer behavior? The two explanations most often used can be separated by whether scent primarily influences affect such as mood or whether a scent primarily influences cognition. In the area of retail atmospherics, Mehrabian and Russell (1974) discuss mood as a mediating factor between environmental cues and behavior. The environmental psychologists assert that shoppers react to environmental cues with approach (e.g., desire to stay in the environment, explore, etc.) or avoidance (e.g., desire to leave) behaviors and that mood mediates this relationship. However, in the marketing literature, this explanation has not received strong support. Bone and Ellen (1999), in a review article, found that only a small percentage of studies (16.1%) showed any influence of scent on mood. Another process explanation is that scent influences cognitive processes. Morrin and Ratneshwar (2003) found no effect of scent on mood, but found that scent increased attention to brands as measured by viewing times of various brands (Morrin & Ratneshwar, 2000, 2003). Mitchell et al. (1995) found that scent influenced the extent of information processing and cognitive elaborations. Chebat and Michon (2003) tested various process theories and concluded that cognitions pertaining to product quality and the shopping environment are influenced by scent, which in turn influenced the mood of the shopper. Hirsch (1995) examined the effects of ambient odors in a Las Vegas casino. While the specific odors used are not identified in the research, the author found that an ambient odor significantly increased slot-machine usage. The author suggests (but does not test) a cognitive process whereby the odor may have induced nostalgic recall of memories which enhanced the gambling mood. There seems to be more support for the influence of scent on cognitive processes but, given the interaction between cognition and affect, this is clearly a complicated question. Bone and Ellen (1999) suggest that accessibility and availability theories may be a more useful theoretical basis for understanding ambient scent research. We next turn to a discussion of past research in consumer behavior and marketing on the sense of taste.

Sense of Taste

Research on the sense of taste (or the gustatory sense) is quite varied and includes administration of taste tests, changes in taste as it relates to new product formulations, store-sampling, branding, packaging and taste as a form of direct product experience. Each of these topics will be discussed in turn.

Taste Discrimination

At the most basic level, some researchers have examined various methods of administering taste tests (e.g., Buchanan, Givon, & Goldman 1987). One of the key issues is to identify which type or method of taste test can best determine an individual's ability to discriminate between different tastes. This is important to marketing for several reasons. In some instances, a manufacturer may want to test the similarity of two alternative product formations to assess the consistency of taste from batch to batch of a product. Often, these tests involve in-house trained experts (Greenhalgh, 1966). Also, a taste test may be used to identify consumers who have greater ability to discriminate products by taste or to test alternative formulations. A common test, termed the triangle test asks consumers to identify the one sample of three that is different from the other two, which are identical. Researchers (Morrison, 1981; Moskowitz, Jacobs, & Firtle, 1980) have examined whether subjects who do well on this type of test are actually discriminating between the tastes or are simply guessing. The authors make statistical suggestions for improving the quality of the results of triangle tests.

Another common taste discrimination task involves consumers making several paired comparisons and noting their preferred choice following each comparison. Once subjects have completed several paired comparisons, the consistency of their choices is used to determine their discrimination ability. Finally, a preference rank procedure is used where subjects are given three taste samples, one different from the other two and are asked to rank the three from most to least preferred. A subject who ranks the different sample as most or least preferred is judged to have made a correct choice, regardless of the preference. A subject who ranks the odd sample as between the two identical samples is judged not to have discriminated. In an empirical investigation examining the three procedures, Buchanan et al. (1987) found that the repeated pair comparison method was the most sensitive discrimination task and preference ranking was the least sensitive. The researchers also found that the discrimination ability measured by triangle tests was significantly correlated with that measured by paired comparisons, which supports the validity of the tests.

In the area of product reformulations, Villani and Morrison (1976) investigated a method for estimating demand for a new product formulation and recommended that estimates for current users and non-users be made separately for more accuracy. In arguably the most famous product reformulation, the New Coke experience is discussed by Dubow and Childs (1998). These researchers explain the gradualist approach hypothesis which uses the perception and psychophysical concepts of just noticeable difference (when a consumer can just notice a change) and just unnoticeable difference (where the change is undetectable). In the gradualist approach to product reformulation, the manufacturers would change the taste of a product in a sequence of small, constant, just unnoticeable difference steps so that, at no point would tasters perceive the reformulation differences. Arguing against the gradualist approach hypothesis, the flavor balance hypothesis suggests that a gradualist approach is impossible in a multi-ingredient formula as unexpected interaction effects of various ingredients may be perceptible. Using New Coke and Coca-Cola Classic, Dubow and Childs (1998) conduct an empirical test which suggests that Coke may have been better off using a gradualist approach to reformulation and not announcing the product change.

Taste and Store Samples

The area of taste and sampling food items in stores has also been researched. Johnson, Sommer, and Matino (1985) unobtrusively observed consumer behavior at bulk food bins in fourteen supermarkets. The most frequent problem behaviors were consumers using their hands to retrieve products and consumers snacking on products. Not surprisingly, these two problem behaviors were correlated. Besides this unsanctioned behavior of snacking, stores often encourage taste by offering product samples. Steinberg and Yalch (1978) examined obese and nonobese shoppers in a supermarket, how hungry the shoppers were, and the effect of sales of other grocery items when shoppers were offered an in-store sample (a doughnut in the bakery section). For the nonobese, if a shopper was hungry, the food sample seemed to satisfy some of their hunger and they reduced their additional buying compared to the nonobese shoppers who were not hungry. For the obese shoppers, offering a food sample increased additional buying and this was only slightly moderated by their level of hunger. The authors conjecture that obese shoppers are not as sensitive to their internal cues of hunger so offering a sample may have increased further the salience of food and they purchased more.

Some research (Nowlis & Shiv, 2005; Shiv & Nowlis, 2004) looked at whether or not to distract shoppers as they tasted a food sample. Contrary to industry wisdom, these researchers found that distraction of the shopper increased subsequent choice for the sampled food. The authors explain these results using a two-component model in which the ultimate pleasure a shopper derives from tasting a food sample is a function of an informational and an affective component. The affective component involves the emotional responses of the shopper and is associated with relatively automatic processes. The informational component is a more objective feature of the tasting experience and related to aspects such as quality. This information component is comprised of more controlled processes. Distracting a consumer influences subsequent choice by increasing the impact of the affective component.

Taste and Branding

Another area of taste research concerns the relationship between and taste and brand name. In an early marketing study, Allison and Uhl (1964) found that, in a blind taste test, experienced beer drinkers (they drank beer at least three times per week) were unable to distinguish their preferred brand from other brands of beer. However, when the brands of beer were identified, these same beer drinkers rated the taste of their preferred brand significantly higher than in the blind taste test. Similarly, Bellizzi and Martin (1982) found that whether a brand was national or generic significantly influenced the taste of the product (national brands ranked higher). Sprott and Shimp (2004) examined the interaction of brand status (store brand, national brand) and quality of the tasting experience. They revealed that sampling a store brand substantially increased evaluation for the store brand compared to the group that did not have the opportunity to taste the product (juice) only if the sample store brand was high quality. No benefit was demonstrated with the national brand. The authors theorize two explanations that may be likely. When consumers make quality judgments, they base these judgments on inherent product features, or intrinsic cues and on extrinsic cues such as price and brand name. Intrinsic cues, such as taste, tend to dominate extrinsic cues when intrinsic cues can be evaluated with confidence at the time of purchase. When intrinsic cues cannot be evaluated (i.e., taste), consumers base their judgments more on extrinsic cues (i.e., brand name). By providing consumers with the opportunity to taste the store brand, an intrinsic cue was provided that influenced product perceptions.

The other theoretical explanation used is schema congruity theory (Mandler, 1982). Schema congruity theory asserts that affect for a particular brand will be most positive when a person perceives moderate incongruity between the product category schema compared to extreme congruity or incongruity. The expected schema for store brands is that they are lower quality compared to national brands. Participants who tasted the store brand learned that the juice was of high quality and consequently their store brand schema and their actual experience were moderately incongruent, thus resulting in more positive affect compared to the subjects who did not have the opportunity to taste.

LeClerc, Schmitt, and Dubé (1994) examined the effect of foreign branding (French) on product perception and attitudes. In Experiment 3, the authors crossed whether a participant could taste the product (yogurt) with whether the brand was foreign (English, French). They found that with no taste test, a French brand name generated higher ratings on the hedonic dimensions of the product (i.e., pleasantness, sweet, delicious, creamy) and lower ratings on the utilitarian dimension (healthy, wholesome, nutritious). Additionally, a French sounding brand name affected product perception and evaluation even after a taste test but only on the hedonic dimension.

The effect of brand awareness on sampling of brands and choice revealed that when subjects do not have any brand awareness, they tended to sample more brands and were more likely to select the high quality brand (Hoyer & Brown, 1990). If subjects were aware of one brand in a set (this study used brands of peanut butter), they tended to sample fewer brands and tended to choose the known brand even when it was lower quality than other brands in the sample. In a related area to branding, one study on product packaging and taste found that packaging influenced the taste of the product. McDaniel and Baker (1977) examined consumer reactions to identical potato chips placed in a wax coated potato chip bag or a "new" polyvinyl bag. In a blind taste test, subjects rated the chips as identical. However, when the taste test was conducted with the bags, even though the polyvinyl bags were extremely difficult to open (subjects had to use their teeth, stand on the bag and pull, etc.), the chips in the polyvinyl bags were viewed as crispier and tastier. The authors interpret the findings that a negative packaging attribute (hard to open) can enhance product quality perceptions since consumers infer other attributes such as crispier or fresher, even when no difference in the actual product quality exists.

Taste, Direct Experience, and Product Perceptions

Taste can be conceptualized as a form of direct product experience. Smith and Swinyard (1983) researched product trial (tasting a salted snack product) and attitude-behavior consistency. When attitudes were based on the taste of the product, the attitude-behavior correlation was much higher then without this tasting experience. The authors emphasize the information value of direct product experience. Scott and Yalch (1980), using Bayesian analysis, examined consumer acceptance of experiential information about a new product. Consumers who were given a reward for sampling a new product and who were encouraged to attribute their behavior to this situational factor (and thus discount their intrinsic interest in the product) were receptive to unfavorable product information and unreceptive to favorable information. The authors maintain that their research demonstrates a tendency for people to accept information consistent with their perceptions about the causes of their behavior and to reject information when it contradicts these attributions. Similarly, Roberts and Taylor (1975) demonstrate that even with a tasting experience, it is difficult to change consumer's previously held perceptions.

Some researchers consider that product trial through tasting can be diagnostic and influence perceptions and choice. Levin and Gaeth (1988) vary the temporal order of tasting a product (before or after reading a ground beef label) and the valence of the label information (positive, 75% lean; negative, 25% fat). The framing effect of the labeling was reduced when consumers sampled the product compared to when they did not. The authors note that product experience will have greater weight when it is unambiguous or diagnostic. Also, using diagnosticity, Pechmann and

Ratneshwar (1992) varied the diagnosticity of a taste test as well as the objective correlation of price and quality. Four samples of orange juice varying in quality were used.In one condition taste was perfectly correlated with price and in another the correlation was zero. Diagnosticity of the taste test was manipulated by either allowing participants to go back and forth between the four samples (high diagnosticity) or by presenting the samples sequentially with some time in between and no opportunity to go back to previous samples (low diagnosticity). It was found that prior beliefs biased judgments of the samples less when diagnosticity was high rather than low (Study 1). When subjects were allowed to use a memory aid (Study 2), they tended to be relatively accurate in their judgments, even though they had the same constraints as the low diagnosticity subjects in the first study. The authors conclude that the degree to which prior beliefs and actual direct taste experience are used depends on the diagnosticity of the mental representations of the taste experience. The higher the diagnosticity, the greater the impact of the actual taste experience relative to prior beliefs. The lower the diagnosticity, the greater the impact of prior beliefs relative to the actual taste experience.

Braun (1999) looked at a different aspect of taste and memory. She asked the question of whether advertising received after a direct product experience (tasting orange juice) altered how consumers remember their experience. This research found that consumer recall of a past direct experience with a product (tasting) was subject to distortions. Post-experience advertising made consumers think they had tasted a better tasting juice by altering their memories of the tasting experience through advertising. Altering the time between the tasting experience and the advertising exposure, this research revealed that the post experience is working at the memory reconstruction phase of recall rather than as a source confusion problem at encoding. Another study found that imagining a taste experience, even of a hedonic product (ice cream) may actually be a more affective experience than actually eating the product (Compeau, Grewal, & Monroe, 1998).

Taste as More Incidental

In some reach, the actual product tasting is not a key part of the research question yet product taste plays a role. Maison, Greenwald, and Bruin (2004) used a Coke-Pepsi taste test in a pretest to determine subjects who could identify each of the brands in a blind taste test. The primary focus of this research was to compare the predictive validity of implicit versus explicit preferences for brands. When separating subjects by their ability to identify Coke or Pepsi in a blind taste test, this research found that subjects who exhibited higher taste discrimination in the blind taste test had more extreme implicit preferences. This research suggests that implicit preference measures are more sensitive measures of preference than explicit preference measures.

Kahn and Isen (1993) did not include actual tasting in their study, but rather taste perceptions. They found that a positive affect manipulation increased variety seeking behavior relative to the control when unpleasant or negative features of the items were not made salient. However, when salient negative features were introduced into the choice set with the inclusion of products that potentially tasted bad (i.e., low salt and high fiber crackers—Experiments 1 and 2), or by alerting subjects to the negative health risks of familiar items (Experiment 3), there was no difference between positive affect and a control group on variety seeking behavior. We next turn to the discussion of research on hearing or auditory effects on consumer behavior.

Sense of Hearing

The auditory sense or hearing has been studied in marketing mostly in the context of background music in advertising and in retail stores. Researchers have examined the effects of music on consumers' moods, product evaluation and choice, fit with an ad or store, time perceptions, and as part of a retail store's atmosphere. A few studies have examined non-music elements such as voice pitch and the interaction between auditory information and visual information. First, the auditory sense as it relates to music in marketing will be discussed followed by studies concerning the interaction between audio and visual information.

Music and Mood

Bruner (1990), in a review article on music and mood, stressed the complexity of music and its influence on individual's moods. Bruner also provided a taxonomy of musical elements and the emotional expressions ascribed to each structural element. The three main structural features of music are tempo or time of the music (how fast or slow it is), pitch related characteristics (includes major, minor keys), and texture (includes volume, instrumentation). (Please see Bruner, 1990, Appendix, p. 102, for a more complete description of the elements.) Bruner stressed that people assign emotional meaning to music and experience affective reactions. For example, fast music is considered happier than slow music. Kellaris and Kent (1994) identify three basic musical properties similar to those of Bruner (1990) which are tempo (fast, moderate, slow), tonality (major, minor, atonal) and texture (classical, pop). These authors produced original compositions with digital sound technology to provide orthogonal manipulations of the three structural properties of music. They also identified three dimensions of response (pleasure, arousal, and surprise) that were elicited by the three properties of music. They call for a better understanding of the multidimensional nature of both musical stimuli and listener response. Similarly, Scott (1990) advocated using an interpretist approach in research to understand the complexity of consumer meaning and response to music.

In one study in marketing, Gorn (1982) used classical conditioning and illustrated that hearing liked music (music from the movie *Grease*) or disliked music (classical Indian music) while being exposed to a product (a pen) can directly affect product preferences as measured by product choice. Both Kellaris and Cox (1989) and Allen and Madden (1985) attempted to replicate Gorn (1992) but failed to do so. Kellaris and Kent (1994) note that Gorn (1992) did not control for the different structural properties of music. They argue that when fast tempo, upbeat music is used to operationalize the positive unconditioned stimulus, the valence of the music may have been confounded with the arousing quality of the music which may have altered the level of attention of participants. In classical conditioning, music is assumed to induce a mood which is directly transferred to the product.

The influence of music on mood states and new product evaluations was researched by Gorn, Goldberg, and Basu (1993). Mood was manipulated by music to induce either a good or a bad mood and subjects' awareness of the music as a source of their mood was also manipulated. When subjects were not aware of the source of their mood, their mood biased their evaluations of the product so that the product was evaluated more favorably when in a good mood than when in a bad mood. However, when subjects were made aware of the source of their mood (the music), there was no difference in product evaluations between those in a good or bad mood. The authors explained the results with a mood-based cognitive heuristic "How do I feel about it?" (Schwarz, 1990), which suggests that people observe their own feelings and draw conclusions from them. If a person is not aware of the source of their mood, they assume the feelings are information to be used in product evaluation.

Music was also used to induce either a pleasant or unpleasant affective state and examine its interaction with the affective tone of an advertisement (Gorn, Pham, & Sin, 2001). While controlling for arousal (Study 1), music was used to manipulate a pleasant or unpleasant affective state. In Study 2, both arousal and pleasure were manipulated with music. Results showed that the valence of a person's affective state influenced judgment in a mood congruent direction especially if an ad had an ambiguous affective tone. The arousal dimension, but not the valence dimension, influenced ad evaluations. Ad evaluations were more polarized in the direction of the ad's affective tone under high arousal than under low arousal.

Dubé and Morin (2001), in a field setting, examined the pleasure induced by music (measured, not manipulated) and its impact on store evaluations. No main effect of pleasure intensity induced by music on store evaluations was found and they explain that there was no support that mood induced by music directly influenced store perceptions. Instead, this is mediated by attitude toward the servicescape and attitude toward the sales personnel.

While the preceding studies focus on the influence of music on mood, some researchers have examined the cognitive processes resulting from background music. Olsen (1997) manipulated whether background music was present (2 levels, silence and music) and the amount of time between consecutive information presented in ads (0, 1, 2, 3, second) in two studies. Relative to silence, background music hindered recall when information was presented at 2 seconds or shorter but enhanced recall at 3 seconds. Using a resource matching explanation (cf. Anand & Sternthal, 1990), music had a detrimental effect on recall at shorter times because it distracted cognitive resources from the rehearsal of brand information thereby hindering attention. As cognitive resources increased to the point when those available matched those required, information was sufficiently processed and a higher level of recall was exhibited.

Music and Congruence

Park and Young (1986) examined the effect of music (present, absent) and three types of involvement (low involvement, cognitive involvement, affective involvement) on the formation of attitudes toward a brand in the context of TV commercials. Music increased the brand attitude for subjects in the low involvement condition but had a distracting effect for those in the cognitive involvement condition. Its effect for those in the affective involvement condition was not clear. They argue that music acted as a peripheral persuasion cue.

While the notion of fit was not specifically studied in Park and Young (1986), the music was selected since it was "best suited" for the commercial. MacInnis and Park (1991) examine two dimensions of music including its fit with the ad and the extent to which it arouses emotion laden memories. Fit was defined as a participant's perception of the music's relevance to the central advertising message. These two dimensions of music were fully crossed with two levels of involvement. The emotion laden quality of the music had similar effects on attention to the music and affective response for both high and low involvement participants. Yet, it had different effects on their message based processing. For low involvement participants, the emotion laden quality enhanced message processing while it seemed to distract high involvement participants from processing the message. Similarly, while fit had similar effects on high and low involvement participants by focusing attention on the music and the message, it created different effects on their affective responses. Lack of fit created more negative emotions for low than for high involvement participants. An unexpected finding of this research was the strong impact of fit on both positive emotions and attitude toward the ad.

Kellaris, Cox, and Cox (1993) examined the fit or congruency of music and the message (low, high) and the attention getting value of music (low, high) along with a no music control group. The dependent measures consisted of recall and recognition of brand names and message arguments in the context of a radio ad. This research found that when background music was congruent, attention getting music increased recall and recognition of brand names. When the music was attention getting and the message incongruent, it pulled listener's attention away from the message and negatively influenced recall. The no music ads performed as well or better than the musical ads in terms of recall and recognition.

The relationship between the fit of the mood induced music (happy/sad) and the purchase occasion (happy/sad) and its effect on purchase was studied by Alpert, Alpert, and Maltz (2005). While mood induced by music did not exhibit a main effect on purchase intentions, its interaction with fit was significant. The authors conclude that when music is used to evoke emotions congruent with the symbolic meaning of the product, the likelihood of purchase is increased.

Music and Tempo

Music is a key element in determining the atmosphere of a service or retail environment. Numerous studies have examined the role of music in these settings. Milliman (1982, 1986) researched the influence of background music tempo in a supermarket and in a restaurant. In the supermarket study, Milliman (1982) varied the tempo of classical music (fast, slow) and found that the pace of the in-store traffic was significantly slower with slow tempo music compared to fast tempo music. Also, higher sales volume was associated with slower tempo music and lower sales figures were associated with faster tempo music. Interestingly, when shoppers were asked about their awareness of background music, the majority of participants were not sure if music was in the background or they were incorrect. In the context of restaurant dining, Milliman (1986) varied the tempo of the background music (slow, fast) and found that with slower music, patrons stayed longer, ate about the same amount of food but consumed more alcoholic beverages. The author conjectured that the slower, more relaxing environment created a greater approach condition for the diners.

In the context of a travel agency service, participants viewed a video in which the four music conditions varied in the arousal quality through changes in tempo (Chebat, Chebat, & Vaillant, 2001). The classical music was pretested to be equally pleasurable. This research found that highly arousing music hampered cognitive activity and the authors argue that the "fit" between the highly arousing music and their context of the message from the travel agency was low. Similar to MacInnis and Park (1991), this study showed that when highly arousing music drew attention to itself, the effect was to reduce cognitive resources available for information processing and also reduce recall. In contrast, the slow tempo music did not attract attention to itself and did not interfere with the cognitive resources used to process the message. However, the authors caution that the deeper the cognitive activity, the more negative the attitude toward the employee and toward the visit.

Music and Atmospherics

Several studies have not simply manipulated an aspect of music but rather manipulated the image or atmosphere of a retail setting with music as an element. For example, Meyer (1981) manipulated the décor of a pizza restaurant and had an elaborate décor condition, which included live music, or plain décor condition with no music. The purpose of the research was not related to music but was to advance a model for the study of consumer evaluation of choice alternatives given uncertainty about the alternative and attributes.

Using videotape technology, Baker, Levy, and Grewal (1992) combined music and lighting to manipulate ambient cues in a retail environment. They found that ambient cues (low and high) interact with social cues (number and friendliness of employees) to influence shoppers' pleasure and subsequently their willingness to purchase. Again, music is confounded with lighting making the results from music alone impossible to interpret. Finally, while not the main focus of their study, Grewal, Baker, Levy, and Voss (2003) use classical music versus no classical music as one manipulation in the atmosphere of a jewelry store. (The number of store employees and the number of customers was also varied). Results found that classical music had a positive effect on store atmosphere and, in turn, intentions to shop at the store. The authors also point out that classical music "fit" with the jewelry store.

Schlosser (1998) manipulated music along with other components in order to operationalize a prestige and a discount condition. In the prestige condition, the store was described as having classical music, soft lighting, hardwood floors, and wide aisles; in the discount condition the music was top 40, the floors were linoleum, and the aisles were narrow. The primary conclusion from this research was that different types of products are differentially affected by the atmosphere of a store. Products were divided by whether they have a utilitarian function (more related to product performance) or a social identity function (more related to the expression of self-concept). Store atmosphere influenced perceptions of social identity products but not utilitarian products.

Music and Time Perceptions

Time perceptions are an active area of research in marketing. In the area of retail atmospherics Yalch and Spangenberg (2000) used a simulated shopping experiment and varied whether the music played was familiar or not. Participants reported shopping longer when exposed to familiar music but they actually shopped longer when exposed to unfamiliar music. The shorter actual shopping times in the familiar music condition were related to increased arousal. Emotional states were not directly related to the music manipulation.

Besides familiarity of music and time perceptions, researchers have looked at the valence of the music and time perceptions. Kellaris and Kent (1992) varied the tonality of the music (major, minor, atonal) and used a synthesizer so that other aspects of the music were equal. The music in a major key was positively valenced while the atonal music was negatively valenced. Results showed that perceived duration was the longest for participants exposed to positively valenced music and shortest for those exposed to negatively valenced music. They used Ornstein's (1969) storage size model to account for the findings. This model suggests that perceived time duration is a function of the amount of memory dedicated to storing stimulus information encountered during a given interval. Larger allocations of memory space are associated with longer perceived time durations. The relative pleasantness of the major key music motivated listeners to devote more attention to the music and allocate greater cognitive resources to processing it. This may have both reduced the allocation of processing to some internal clock used to judge the duration of an event and created the perception that more stimulus information was heard.

Hui, Dubé, and Chebat (1997) had people watch a video of a person waiting in line at a bank and varied the valence of the music. Results demonstrate that positively valenced music increased the perception of wait duration compared to negatively valenced music (similar to Kellaris and Kent, 1992) and compared to the no music condition. But, they note that the perceived wait time did not have a negative impact on attitude toward the service organization (the bank). In fact music, regardless of its valence, made the service environment seem more positive to customers waiting in lines. Related to this finding, Cameron, Baker, Peterson, and Braunsberger (2003) manipulated valence of music and found that while music likeability influenced both wait length evaluations and mood, only mood contributed to participants' evaluation of their overall experience. So, even though positively valenced music may influence wait length duration perceptions negatively, it also impacts mood positively and mood influences the overall evaluation of the experience.

In a field study concerning telephone wait times, music was used as one of the conditions to fill silence when people were waiting on a phone (Antonides, Verhoef, & VanAalst, 2002). Besides playing music, other conditions included wait duration information, queue information, or silence. Music had a significantly positive effect on the evaluation of the wait but did not influence the perceived duration of the wait.

Voice Characteristics Auditory Research

While the overwhelming majority of auditory studies in marketing involve music, there is some research examining other aspects of hearing. Both MacLachlan and Siegel (1980) and Chattopadhyay, Dahl, Ritchie, and Shahin (2003) investigated aspects of announcer speech. MacLachlan and Siegel (1980) found that a 25% time compression of TV commercials increased unaided and aided recall. However, they note that voice pitch was not changed with the compression. Chattopadhyay et al. (2003) varied three characteristics of announcer speech: voice pitch (high, low), syllable speed (normal, high), and pause length (normal, short). A voice with faster than normal syllable speed and low pitch produced less negative advertising directed cognitive responses and more favorable attitudes toward the ad and toward the brand. No significant results were found for pause length suggesting that participants had sufficient opportunity to process the information. Instead, the authors suggest that while the opportunity to process did not diminish with increased speed, the motivation to process did.

Auditory and Visual Processing

Using hemisphere specialization, Anand, Holbrook, and Stephens (1988) transmitted instrumental music to one ear of participants and verbal text in the other ear. Results showed that there was increased affect toward familiar stimuli and toward words transmitted to the right ear and music transmitted to the left ear. The authors argue that this evidence supports a cognitive affective model in which affective responses are formed with cognitive mediation rather than the independence of the affective and cognitive systems.

In the context of product placement, Russell (2002) examined the modality of presentation (auditory, visual) of the product placement as well as the connection between the plot of a show (more or less connected). An auditory placement refers to the brand being mentioned in the dialog of the show while a visual placement is the appearance of the brand on the screen. The author stated that since the auditory channel caries the plot of the show, it is inherently more meaningful than the visual channel in the context of product placement. Thus, a congruent modality/plot connection exists when either the product placement is audio and the product is integrated into the plot of the show or the product placement is visual and the connection to the plot is minor. A product/plot mismatch occurs when either the placement is audio and the product is not integrated into the plot or the placement is visual and the product is integrated into the plot. Memory improved when the modality and plot connection were incongruent but persuasion was enhanced by congruency. Incongruent placements adversely affected brand attitudes because they seemed out of place and were discounted.

The effects of presentation modality (audio, visual) along with the modality of imagery (audio, visual) and the influence on learning was researched by Unnava, Agarwal, and Haugtvedt (1996). Results showed that there was greater advertising recall when the presentation modality differed from the imagery modality. The cognitive resources that were used in the process of imaging were the same that were used in perceptual tasks of the same modality so mutual interference between imaging and perceptual tasks inhibited message learning. In a related study, Costley, Das, and Brucks (1997) asked the question of whether the modality of the retrieval cue (audio or visual) affects the recall of information originally presented in the same versus different modalities.

Support was found for a "modality match" hypothesis in which retrieval cues enhance recall better within modality rather than across modality. Results are explained using the encoding specificity principle (Tulving & Thomson, 1973). This principle states that the likelihood of recall improves as the features present in the environment when the memory is encoded match those present in the retrieval environment. Features can include aspects of the stimulus context such as the modality of the information presented.

Tavassoli and Lee (2003) examined auditory and visual elements in advertising in the context of Chinese logographs (which rely more on visual processing) and English works (which rely more on audio and sound based processing). Findings indicated that auditory elements interfered more with the learning of and cognitive responding to English ad copy than with Chinese copy and vice versa for visual elements. However, auditory elements are better retrieval cues for English than for Chinese copy and vice versa of visual elements. The authors concluded that non-verbal elements in advisements such as auditory cues can compete for cognitive resources during message encoding but can also serve as effective memory cues. While music was not the focus of this research, various forms of music were used throughout the three experiments.

In one study, preschoolers and school aged children were used to examine information presented using audio messages and visual messages (Macklin, 1994). Children that only heard the information and children who only saw the information performed equally well on learning (there was no visual superiority effect). However, presenting information both visually and by audio was the most effective. When incomplete visuals were presented, school aged children had the ability to imagine the remainder of the visual while preschool aged children could not. The author argues that a critical element in processing is the comprehensibility of the information rather than the modality.

Sense of Touch

The sense of touch, or haptics (touch with the hands) has historically been the least studied sense in marketing. Perhaps the rise of online and catalog shopping, and an inability to physically examine products prior to purchase has spurred this area of research. The primary categories of touch and haptic research include the differences in product attributes that encourage touch, individual differences in the motivation to touch, and situational influences that encourage touch. Finally, one research study examined the interaction between vision and touch and the elongation bias. Each of these areas will be discussed.

Touch and Product Differences

Products differ in whether consumers will be motivated to touch them prior to purchase. Touch excels at ascertaining what Klatzky and Lederman (e.g., Klatzky & Lederman, 1992; 1993) call material properties which include texture, softness, weight, and temperature. If a product category varies in a diagnostic way on one of or more of these attributes, consumers will be more motivated to touch the product prior to purchase. For example, clothing varies on texture and weight and will likely encourage pre-purchase touch more than books or CDs, which do not vary on material properties in a diagnostic manner. Since marketing uses many self-report measures, Peck and Childers (2004) asked the question of whether participants' verbal reports actually correspond to their behavior in the area of touch and product evaluation. They videotaped the hand movements of participants as they concurrently verbalized during product evaluations. They found that in the area of behavioral reports and actions, there was correspondence between what people say and what they do. Product categories that varied most in material properties (e.g., sweater, tennis racket), were touched longer than those that varied somewhat (e.g., calculator, cell phone) and these were touched longer than categories with no diagnostic material properties (e.g., cereal, toothpaste).

Another logical question to ask is whether consumers can be compensated for an inability to touch a product during evaluation. Holbrook (1983), when using sweaters as stimuli for study, noted the strong role played by tactile cues when participants were evaluating the product. He encouraged using, or at least being aware of using, actual products compared to visual representations of products such as pictures in research. McCabe, Brown, and Nowlis (2003) varied whether the products differed on material properties and whether participants had the actual product to evaluate, a picture of the product, a list of attributes, or some combination. The primary dependent variable was purchase likelihood. Results showed that product categories that vary in the diagnosticity of touch (e.g., bath towels, carpeting) were more likely to be preferred in shopping environments that allow physical inspection than in those where touch is unavailable. However, there was no difference in the preference of products across the shopping environments (touch, no touch) when a product category did not vary on material properties (e.g., videotape, rolls of film) since for these categories, vision was diagnostic. Results also found that the differences in preference between the two environments were reduced when the material properties of the products were verbally described. In effect, compensation for lack of touch was possible with a written description (see also, Peck & Childers, 2003a).

Touch and Individual Differences

Peck and Childers (2003a) also examined whether compensation for lack of touch was possible and considered the type of material properties to be compensated for as well as an individual difference in the preference for touch information. They conjectured that not all material properties create the same type of response in consumers. Specifically, the pleasant sensory feedback experienced when assessing softness may differentially influence the person touching compared to a more functional material property such as weight. In addition, they considered an individual difference in the preference for touch information. Peck and Childers (2003b) developed the Need for Touch scale (NFT) and tested the scale in seven studies. NFT is defined as a preference for the extraction and use of information obtained through touch. It includes two dimensions, an instrumental and an autotelic dimension. The instrumental dimension of NFT refers to those aspects of touch that reflect outcome directed touch with a salient purchase goal. The image of a consumer involved in instrumental touch is that of a problem solver consciously engaged in the goal directed activity of searching for information and arriving at a final judgment. The other dimension of NFT is the autotelic factor. Autotelic touch involves a consumer seeking fun, sensory stimulation and enjoyment with no purchase goal necessarily salient. The autotelic factor is defined as the enjoyment and affect of touch along with the compulsive or irresistible urge to explore via touch.

Peck and Childers (2003b) found that NFT moderated the relationship between direct experience and confidence in product judgments. For individuals higher in NFT, a lack of direct experience (an inability to touch) resulted in less confidence in the judgment. For low NFT individuals, confidence in judgment was unaffected by a barrier to touch provided there was a clear visual of the product. In a related study on compensation and an inability to touch products, Peck and Childers (2003a) found that high NFT participants were more confident and less frustrated when they could touch to evaluate products where low NFT subjects' confidence in judgment did not change on the basis of whether they could touch the product. The researchers also found that for individuals high in NFT, compensation for an inability to touch was possible. For more functional haptic information, such as weight, a written description compensated for the inability to touch. However, for a material property with pleasant sensory feedback (softness), a written description did not provide this compensation. In effect, there are certain types of product attributes for which there is no substitute for actual touch. Low NFT subjects required a visual cue and the authors conjecture that visual information compensated for actual haptic exploration.

Similar to the instrumental dimension of Need for Touch, Citrin, Stem, Spangenberg, and Clark (2003) developed an individual difference scale titled, "Need for Tactile Input," and found that it was negatively related to products purchased over the internet, especially those categories that vary with respect to material properties. They also found that women showed a higher Need for Tactile Input than men.

An individual difference in the preference for touch information has been found to moderate the time touching products to ascertain information (Peck & Childers, 2004). Specific stereotypical hand movements termed EPs (exploratory procedures) have been linked to the haptic perception of material properties. For example, when individuals need to assess texture, they engage in the lateral motion EP which consists of rubbing the fingers back and forth across the surface of the objects. Peck and Childers (2004) videotaped subject's hand movements as they were evaluating products. They found that for all material properties except texture, high NFT individuals spent less time exploring with their hands than did individuals low in NFT. The authors note that since touch information is more accessible for high NFT individuals, they are more efficient at extracting this information. Higher accessibility of haptic information for high NFT individuals was exhibited thorough a free recall exercise and through a timed response measure (Peck & Childers, 2003b). However, since texture provided a pleasant sensory feedback (a soft sweater), high NFT individuals spent a longer time assessing texture than their low NFT counterparts.

Touch and Situational Factors

While the forgoing research involved judgments related to actual products, some research on touch expands the use of touch in marketing. Peck and Wiggins (2006) examined touch completely unrelated to a product but in the context of a persuasive ad. They varied the valence of a touch element attached to a pamphlet (negative, neutral, and positive) as well as fit of the touch element with the ad. They found that adding a touch element that felt good, for example a feather on a pamphlet requesting donations to a local arboretum, increased persuasion measured as attitude toward the ad as well as the likelihood of donating time and/or money to the organization. An unexpected finding was that the fit of the touch element with the ad did not matter for those high in autotelic NFT. Any touch element was better than no touch element for the high autotelic NFT participants. However for people low in autotelic NFT, it was important that the touch element fit with the message or it had no influence on persuasion.

In another study, not related to product touch, Hornik (1992) examined touch as non-verbal communication in an interpersonal touch context. He found, in three field settings (Study 1, a bookstore; Study 2, a restaurant; Study 3, a supermarket) that an unobtrusive touch by an employee on the arm of a customer enhanced the positive feeling for the external stimuli (e.g., the bookstore) as well as the touching source (the employee). Customers touched by a requester tended to comply more than those customers that were not touched.

Peck and Childers (forthcoming) manipulated the environment in a study in a grocery store examining impulse purchase behavior and environmental stimuli encouraging touch. They varied point of purchase signs (either no sign or "feel the freshness" encouraging touch) and found that the sign encouraging touch resulted in more unplanned purchasing than the no sign condition. In addition, there was a main effect of the individual difference in autotelic NFT. Individuals high in autotelic NFT made more unplanned purchases than low autotelic NFT individuals.

Finally, Krishna (2006) investigated the elongation bias and shows that sensory modality (touch or vision) affects the extent and the direction of the elongation bias. The elongation bias predicts that with two containers of equal volume, the taller of the two is judged to have a larger volume. The author hypothesized that in a visual perception task, height is the salient dimension, thus the taller container appears larger. However, in another condition, when the participants had only haptic cues (they handled the objects blindfolded), width became the salient dimension and there was a reversal in the elongation bias (wide containers appeared bigger).

SUMMARY OF STUDIES

Research in the areas of olfactory, auditory, gustatory, and tactile senses can be grouped for the purposes of further discussion by whether the focus is on individual consumer factors, product or features of the stimuli, or on factors in the environment.

Individual Factors

Some research has looked at individual sensitivity to sensory input. In the area of haptics or touch research, researchers have delineated an individual difference in consumers' motivation to touch. Scales have been developed to measure this difference (Citrin et al., 2003, Peck & Childers, 2003b) and this individual difference has been found to have numerous effects. Consumers higher in their preference to touch have touch information more accessible in memory (Peck & Childers, 2003b), are not as likely to shop where they can't touch, such as on-line (Citrin et al., 2003, Peck & Childers, 2003b), are more difficult to compensate for an inability to touch (McCabe & Nowlis, 2003; Peck & Childers, 2003a), and are more likely to make impulse purchase decisions (Peck & Childers, 2003b; Peck & Childers, 2006).

In other areas of sensory research, an individual difference in the preference for information has not been as prevalent. In gustatory or taste research, taste discrimination has been an area of interest (Buchanan et al., 1987; Morrison, 1981; Moskowitz et al., 1980) and some individuals are better at discriminating various tastes compared to others. In fact, in the research on product reformulations, the goal may be to ensure that even the most taste sensitive individuals will not notice the taste change in a reformulation (Dubow & Childs, 1998). Individual differences in behavior have been the focus of some work in the taste area. In-store sampling was the context for the observation of obese and nonobese shoppers (Steinberg & Yalch, 1978) as well as consumer behavior around bulk food bins (Johnson, Sommer, & Martino, 1985). In some taste research, differential results have been found for different levels of users and non users of brands (Maison, Greenwald, & Bruin,. 2004) and researchers have called for a consideration of this individual difference in research (Villani & Morrison, 1976).

Similarly, a call has been made in the area of music to consider individual listener characteristics in response to different types of music (Bruner, 1990, Kellaris & Kent, 1994). Individual differences have been manipulated by manipulating involvement (MacInnis & Park, 1991; Park & Young, 1986) but, in general, individual responses to music or other auditory stimuli have not been examined in marketing.

Product or Stimuli Factors

Besides individual factors, some research focuses on the differences in products or stimuli and sensory research. Using real products versus pictures or sketches can produce differential product evaluations (Holbrook, 1983). This is at least partially due to information that is available through direct product experience versus another medium such as advertising (Smith & Swinyard, 1983). Both touch and taste are more directly related to specific products as compared to scent and music which may be ambient and may or may not be associated with a specific product. It can be argued that when judging physical products, touch and taste may give relatively more information about products when touch or taste is available compared to when it is not.

The sense of touch has been found to matter more for different types of product categories, those that vary on product attributes best determined by touch such as texture or weight (McCabe & Nowlis, 2003, Peck & Childers, 2003a). Tasting in the context of in-store sampling seems to be more critical for store versus national brands (Bellizzi & Martin,1982; Sprott & Shrimp, 2004) presumably because in these instances of touch and taste, sensory experience is diagnostic with respect to product quality. Yet, taste may be overridden by inferences regarding packaging (McDaniel & Baker, 1977) or brand name (LeClerc, Schmitt, & Dubé, 1994). Although it may be assumed that there is no substitute for direct product experience through taste or touch, the framing of the experience can influence customer perceptions (Levin & Gaeth, 1988). In fact, the memory of the actual experience can be altered through post experience advertising (Braun, 1999).

Products have also been examined in terms of familiarity of brands and sensory influences. An ambient scent had more impact on less familiar brands (Morrin & Ratneshwar, 2000; Spangenberg, Crowley, & Henderson, 1996), thereby providing an outcome similar to the research on taste influencing store or generic brands more than national brands (Bellizzi & Martin, 1982; Sprott & Shrimp, 2004). However, Morrin and Ratneshwar (2003), in a follow up study, found that ambient scent improved recall and recognition of both familiar and unfamiliar brands through an increase in attention.

In examining the product/stimuli factors, the idea of fit or congruence is a common theme. In general, the notion of fit has to do with a consumer's perception of the relevance of two elements. Whether the product class was congruent with the sensory element didn't matter as far as recall or recognition of brand names (Morrin & Ratneshwar, 2000, 2003), yet congruency encouraged more thorough decision making (Mitchell et al., 1995). In a background music study, Schlosser (1998) found that only social identity and not utilitarian product evaluations were influenced by retail atmospherics. Here, music was only one element of the retail atmosphere that fit with the other elements to convey either a prestige or a discount environment. Whether a sensory element fit with an advertisement has been manipulated with music (Kellaris, Cox, & Cox, 1993; McInnis & Park, 1991) and touch (Peck & Wiggins, forthcoming). Fit of the affective tone of an ad (Gorn et al., 2001) and purchase occasion (Alpert et al., 2005) with a person's mood evoked by music has also been examined. In general, a fit tends to facilitate processing.

Environmental Factors

While individual and product differences have been studied in consumer behavior, the majority of research involves manipulating elements of the environment to determine various consumer processing and behavior effects. Since scent and music are often ambient, it follows that an environmental manipulation is logical. Much of the research in scent and music falls into the retail atmospherics category and will be discussed first. Environmental factors associated with taste concern the opportunity to taste and in-store sampling. Similarly, the opportunity to touch has been manipulated, sometimes in the context of online versus in-store shopping environments. Finally, notions of fit or congruency of the environment and various sensory elements will be discussed.

In-store environments have been altered by sensory elements. Perceptions of the retail environment have been found to be influenced by scent (Chebat & Michon, 2003) and music (Dubé & Morin, 2001), which ultimately influenced the positive affect of the shopper. Sensory elements have been manipulated along with social cues and the density of the retail environment (scent, Michon et al., 2005) and the number of visible employees and customers (music, Baker et al., 1992). Music has also been shown to influence mood, which influences product choice (Gorn, 1982), especially when a shopper is not aware of the source of their mood (Gorn et al., 1993).

An active area of research concerns sensory stimuli in retail environments and actual time shopping or waiting as well as time perceptions (Antonides et al., 2002; Cameron et al., 2003; Hui et al., 1997; Kellaris & Kent, 1992, Milliman, 1982, 1986; Spangenberg et al., 1996; Yalch & Spangenberg, 2000). Research has examined actual time in an establishment (e.g., Milliman 1982 (music tempo), Spangenberg et al., 1996 (scent)) as well as perceived time (e.g., Yalch & Spangenberg, 2000). It is clear that sensory elements in the environment can alter time perceptions. For example, a positive scent (Spangenberg et al., 1996) and familiar music (Yalch & Spangenberg, 2000) resulted in shoppers thinking they had spent more time in the store then they actually did.

Similarly, pleasant music has shown to result in longer perceived wait times (Antonides et al., 2002; Hui et al., 1997; Kellaris & Kent, 1992), but a more positive evaluation of the service or retail establishment (Antonides et al., 2002; Cameron et al., 2003).

The opportunity to taste has been examined in the context of in-store sampling. The choice of a generic or store brand versus a national brand can be influenced by in-store sampling (Bellizzi & Martin, 1982; Sprott & Shrimp, 2004), but brand awareness can limit the choices sampled and the quality of the choice (Hoyer & Brown, 1990). An in-store distraction when tasting can also increase the purchase likelihood of the sampled food (Nowlis & Shiv, 2005; Shiv & Nowlis, 2004). In touch research, environmental salience of touch has been manipulated through a point of purchase sign encouraging touch (Peck & Childers, forthcoming). Increasing the environmental salience of touch increased impulse purchasing. The opportunity to touch has been manipulated, and researchers have examined types of compensation for when touch is unavailable (McCabe & Nowlis, 2003; Peck & Childers, 2003a). Hornik (1992) brings together taste and touch by examining the influence of interpersonal touch and in-store sampling (Study 3) and finds that unobtrusive interpersonal touch increased compliance behavior (larger number of people sampled).

Similar to product/stimuli factors, the notion of fit or congruency has been an active area of study. In some cases, the fit of the task to the particular sense has been examined. Krishna finds that the elongation bias is visual, and touch or haptic exploration reversed this bias. Russell (2002) noted that a congruency between type of product placement (audio or visual) and how embedded the placement is in the script differentially influenced memory and persuasion. While memory was enhanced for incongruity, persuasion was enhanced for congruency. Similarly, Unnava et al. (1996) found that a mismatch between sensory modality (audio or visual) and imagery modality increased recall for advertising information. Costley et al. (1997) investigated the nature of the modality of a retrieval cue (audio or visual) and found that recall was greatest when a modality match was present.

Other elements of fit or congruency that have been investigated concern the fit of scent and music (Mattila & Wirtz, 2001, Spangenberg et al. forthcoming), music and the retail store (Chebat et al., 2001; Grewal et al., 2003; Meyer 1981, Spangenberg et al., forthcoming), music with the advertising message (Gorn et al., 2001; MacInnis & Park, 1991), touch and the advertising message (Peck & Wiggins, 2006), music and purchase occasion (Alpert et al., 2005), and scent and product class (Mitchell et al., 1995). In general, positive effects of congruency or fit have been found. Following this synthesis of past research studies, we next consider some significant gaps that emerge from our review and discuss their potential for future research on sensory factors on consumer behavior.

FUTURE RESEARCH

Individual Differences—Ability and Preferences

An area for future investigation concerns whether an individual difference in sensory perception is a result of a differential ability or sensitivity of individuals to different types of sensory input or more of a motivation or preference for certain types of sensory information. The ability of individuals to obtain information refers to the capability of an individuals' sensory system. In the area of taste discrimination, it appears that some individuals may have greater sensitivity to variations in taste, or a greater ability to determine differences (e.g., Buchanan et al., 1987). However, in touch research, the focus has been on the motivation or preference for touch information by different individuals (e.g., Citrin et al., 2003; Peck & Childers, 2003b). Similarly, a preference for visual versus verbal information has been documented (Heckler, Childers, & Houston, 1993). Why do some individuals prefer different types of sensory information?

A logical step in sensory research would be to identify whether sensitivity to one type of sensory input translates to other types of sensory information. For example, women have been found to be more affected by scent (Bone & Ellen, 1999), music (Grewal et al., 2003), and touch (Citrin et al., 2003) compared to men. Do the individuals with a preference for a type of sensory information also have a greater ability or sensitivity to that type of information? Are people that are motivated to obtain one type of sensory input generally motivated to explore with their other senses as well? Perhaps taste and touch, being more direct senses are related more than smell and hearing. There are all unanswered questions in our literature.

Multi-Sensory Integration

Another major area in need of future research is the need to move from a more "sense by sense" perspective to investigations of the multi-sensory integration of sensory inputs. As Calvert, Spence, and Stein (2004, p. xi) note, "There can be no doubt that our senses are designed to function in *concert* and that our brains are organized to use the information they derive from their various sensory channels *cooperatively* in order to enhance the probability that objects and event will be detected rapidly, identified correctly, and responded to appropriately" (emphasis added). Ernst, Bulthoff, and Newell (2003; cited in Newell 2004) found that bimodal recognition was enhanced by 10% versus learning that occurred either visually or haptically. Recent research has examined how such cross modal interactions can affect the processing of texture perception (Lederman & Klatzky, 2004), recognition (Newell, 2004), as well as selective attention (Marks, 2004). For instance, Marks (2004) reviews studies on congruence across vision, audition, and tactile inputs. He distinguishes between cross modal interactions that facilitate versus interfere with judgments that can be differentiated by their perceptual (more semantic) versus stimulus similarities. Soto-Faraco, Lyons, Gazzaniga, Spence, and Kingstone (2002) found strong congruence effects for vision and hearing when the stimuli co-occurred temporally and spatially. One implication is that perceptual congruence rests on multi-sensory relativity within context, whereas stimulus congruence is more likely to be driven by the absolute values of the stimulus features. This research might bear additional insight on the perceptual versus conceptual effects of fluency on, for example, logos (Janiszewski & Meyvis, 2001). Likewise, Lederman and Klatzk (2004) conclude there is no sensory dominance of texture by vision and haptics, but rather processing is driven by the contextual emphasis of an object's surface (e.g., roughness or spatial density). These authors propose the modality appropriateness hypothesis, which focuses on the weights given sensory stimuli under unimodal performance when predicting the effects for multi-sensory integration judgments.

Multi-Sensory Mental Imagery

Mental imagery is a mental representation of something (esp. a visible object), not by direct perception, but by memory representation, i.e., a mental picture or impression, an idea, or conception (Richardson, 1999). This definition, like the work in consumer behavior, places much emphasis on visual mental imagery. However, imagery may be elicited by all of the senses and the papers reviewed in this chapter are conspicuous in the lack of attention directed toward gustatory, auditory, olfactory, and tactile imagery. How these images might affect consumer processing need to be investigated from both an individual differences perspective as well as how these forms of imagery would mediate the kinds of stimulus congruency, memory, attitude, and judgment effects summarized in this review. Some research suggests that tactile discrimination is mediated by visual imagery (Sathian, Zangaladze, Hoffman, & Grafton, 1997). Grunwald, Weiss, Krauss, Beyer, Rost, and Gutbertlet (2001) also report the involvement of visual areas of the brain in haptic object recognition and suggest a spatially-based integration of information (also see Kosslyn, Pascual-Leone, Felician, Camposano, Keenan, & Thompson, 1999). In her review, Newell (2004) concludes that visual imagery mediates, and is perhaps necessary, for tactile tasks, but given findings on cross modal facilitation it may be that other imaginal modalities may play a role as well. For instance, how might olfactory imagery affect gustatory cues in flavor perception (Dalton, Doolittle, Nagata, & Breslin, 2000).

Brain Imaging Techniques and Sensory Factors

Investigation of these effects across modalities also raises an opportunity for research in consumer behavior using alternative methodologies. Yoon, Gutchess, Feinberg, and Polk (forthcoming) used functional magnetic reasoning imaging (fMRI) to investigate whether judgments about products and persons share similar neural correlates. Their results show that human descriptor judgments are processed in the medial prefrontal cortex, whereas judgments about products occurred in the left inferior prefrontal cortex. The use of a variety of human imaging techniques, including EEG, MEG, PET, as well as fMRI, represent a significant challenge to researchers trained in more behaviorally based experimental paradigms, but the multi-sensory nature of consumption experiences represents a rich context for the application of these techniques. Using fMRI, Grill-Spector, Kushnir, Edelman, Itzchak, and Makach (1998) found that the lateral occipital complex (occipitotemporal areas) responds to visual objects defined by motion or texture. Amedi, Malach, Hendler, Peled, and Zohary (2001) also report activity in the same visual area for haptic based object identification. These results are also consistent with fMRI results reported by James, Humphrey, Gati, Servos, Menon, and Goodale (2002) for haptic priming on visual object recognition. One application of these techniques would be to support the validation efforts of psychometric assessments of new measures of individual difference scales, particularly in the area of multi-sensory imagery. Another would be a deeper understanding of how different specialty populations process sensory factors.

Sensory Interactions with Specialty Populations

To date, only a limited amount of consumer research has examined how disabled consumers fare in their consumption environment (cf., Kaufman-Scarborough, 1999). However, considerable research on brain plasticity (how neighboring cortical areas can remap as a result of sensory deprivation) suggests this population offers much potential for a deeper understanding of how sensory information is processed, stored, and utilized (for an indepth discussion, see sections VI and VII in Calvert, Spence, & Stein, 2004). Sadato, Pascual-Leone, Grafman, Ibanez, and Dold (1996) using PET found activation in primary visual areas of the brain in visually impaired individuals while reading Braille letters. However, no similar pattern of activation was found for sighted participants (see also, Kujala, Huotilainen, Sinkkonen, Ahonen, Alho, & Hamalainen, 1995) for auditory stimulation of the visual cortex). Similarly, visual stimulation has also increased activation of the auditory primary cortex for deaf, but not hearing-abled individuals (Finney, Fine, & Dobkins, 2001). These results raise interesting questions of how the visually impaired shop online using audio-based screen readers and how the addition of tactile-based graphics might affect their purchasing versus their sighted counterparts. Also, what effect would visual imagery instructions have on online visually impaired shoppers? Would resource consuming imagery overload these consumers as they are externally paced through a Web page through this assistive technology?

In addition to disabled consumers, sensitivity to sensory inputs likely varies by age. While one study with children has looked at the processing of audio and visual information (Macklin, 1994), it is clear that much more research could be done. The aging population also has implications for sensory exploration. In general, sensitivity to stimuli declines with age (c.f. touch, Thornbuy & Mistretta, 1981; Stevens & Patterson, 1995) so that it may take an increase in intensity of sensory stimuli to be perceived by older populations. For example, ambient scent may need to be more concentrated, and music may need to be louder. Beside a differential ability in perception, preferences are likely to differ by age, at least for some sensory stimuli, such as music.

Conscious Versus Nonconscious Sensory Processing

"When he (Freud) said that consciousness is the tip of the mental iceberg, he was short of the mark by quite a bit—it may be more the size of a snowball on top of that iceberg" (Wilson, 2002, p. 6). Does the individual have to be conscious of the sensory input in order for it to be influential? There seems to be some evidence that awareness may not be critical. Although not the focus of the studies, research in both scent (Hirsch, 1995; Morrin & Ratneshwar, 2000) and music (Milliman, 1982) has found that consumers may not even be aware of these environmental stimuli. Holland, Hendriks, and Aarts (2005) found that when individuals were exposed to citrus-scented cleaner, the accessibility of cleaning was increased (Studies 1 and 2) and cleaning behavior increased (Study 3). In addition, subjects were unaware of the influence of scent on both their memory accessibility and their behavior. The nonconscious processing of sensory information may be more likely for sensory stimuli present in the environment in which the consumer is passively surrounded with the sensory information (i.e., olfactory and auditory) compared to when direct physical contact is necessary for sensory input (i.e., gustatory and haptic).Given the rise in interest and knowledge of nonconscious processing and some evidence that individuals can be influenced without their awareness in various sensory domains, this area is worthy of further study.

In Conclusion, to Make a Full Turn: If It Tastes, Smells, Sounds, and Feels Like a Duck, Then It Must Be a … (Duck)

"Perhaps," would seem to be the best answer. Sensory stimuli can aid in our processing of information and sometimes can bias and mislead us in forming our impressions. This fascinating contradiction, however, makes the study of sensory factors in consumer behavior challenging and all the more rewarding as we further our investigations of how consumers make sense of their world.

REFERENCES

Allen, C. T., & Madden, T. J. (1985). A closer look at classical conditioning. *Journal of Consumer Research*, 12 (December), 301–315.

Allison, R. I., & Uhl, K. P. (1964). Influence of beer brand identification on taste perception. *Journal of Marketing Research*, 1(3), 36–39.

Alpert, M. I., Alpert, J. I., & Maltz, E. N. (2005). Purchase occasion influence on the role of music in advertising. *Journal of Business Research*, 58(3), 369–376.

Amedi, A., Malach, R., Hendler, Peled, S., & Zohary, E. (2001). Visuo-haptic object related activation in the ventral visual pathway. *Nature Neuroscience*, 4, 324–330.

Anand, P., Holbrook, M. B., & Stephens, D. (1988). The formation of affective judgments: The cognitive-affective model versus the independence hypothesis. *Journal of Consumer Research*, 15(3), 386–391.

Anand, P., & Sternthal, B. (1990). Ease of message processing as a moderator of repetition effects in advertising. *Journal of Marketing Research*, 27 (August), 345–353.

Antonides, G., Verhoef, P. C., & van Aalst, M. (2002). Consumer perception and evaluation of waiting time: A field experiment. *Journal of Consumer Psychology*, 12(3), 193–202.

Baker, J., Levy, M., & Grewal, D. (1992). An experimental approach to making retail store environmental decisions. *Journal of Retailing*, 68 (Winter), 445–460.

Bellizzi, J. A., & Martin, W. S. (1982). The influence of national versus generic branding on taste perceptions. *Journal of Business Research*, 10(3), 385–396.

Bone, P. F., & Ellen, P. S. (1999). Scents in the marketplace: Explaining a fraction of olfaction. *Journal of Retailing*, 75(2), 243–262.

Braun, K. A. (1999). Postexperience advertising effects on consumer memory. *Journal of Consumer Research*, 25(4), 319–334.

Bruner, G. C., II (1990). Music, mood, and marketing. *Journal of Marketing*, 54(4), 94–104.

Buchanan, B., Givon, M., & Goldman, A. (1987). Measurement of discrimination ability in taste tests: An empirical investigation. *Journal of Marketing Research*, 24(2), 154–163.

Calvert, G., Spence, C., & Stein, B. E. (2004). Introduction. In G. Calvert, C. Spence, & B. E. Stein (Eds.), *The handbook of multi-sensory processes* (pp. xi–xvii). Cambridge MA: The MIT Press,

Cameron, M. A., Baker, J., Peterson, M., & Braunsberger, K. (2003). The effects of music, wait-length evaluation, and mood on a low-cost wait experience. *Journal of Business Research*, 56, 421–430.

Chattopadhyay, A., Dahl, D. W., Ritchie, R. J. B., & Shahin, K. N. (2003). Hearing voices: The impact of announcer speech characteristics on consumer response to broadcast advertising. *Journal of Consumer Psychology*, 13(3), 198–204.

Chebat, J., Chebat, B. G., & Vaillant, D. (2001). Environmental background music and in-store selling. *Journal of Business Research*, 54, 115–123.

Chebat, J., & Michon, R. (2003). Impact of ambient odors on mall shoppers' emotions, cognition, and spending: A test of competitive causal theories. *Journal of Business Research*, 56, 529–539.

Citrin, A. V., Stem, D. E., Spangenberg, E. R., & Clark, M. J. (2003). Consumer need for tactile input: An internet retailing challenge. *Journal of Business Research*, 56(11), 915–922.

Compeau, L. D., Grewal, D., & Monroe, K. (1998). Role of prior affect and sensory cues on consumers' affective and cognitive responses and overall perceptions of quality. *Journal of Business Research*, 42(3), 295–308.

Costley, C., Das, S., & Brucks, M. (1997). Presentation medium and spontaneous imaging effects on consumer memory. *Journal of Consumer Psychology*, 6(3), 211–231.

Dalton, P., Doolittle, N., Nagata, H., & Breslin, P. A. S. (2000). The merging of the senses: Integration of subthreshold taste and smell. *Nature Neuroscience, 3*, 431–432.

Dubé, L., & Morin, S. (2001). Background music pleasure and store evaluation: Intensity effects and psychological mechanisms. *Journal of Business Research, 54*(2) 107–113.

Dubow, J. S., & Childs, N. M. (1998). New coke, mixture perception, and the flavor balance hypothesis. *Journal of Business Research, 43*(3), 147–155.

Finney, E. M., Fine, I., & Dobkins, K. R. (2001).Visual stimuli activate auditory cortex in the deaf. *Nature Neuroscience, 4*, 1171–1173.

Gorn, G. J. (1982). The effects of music in advertising on choice behavior: A classical conditioning approach. *Journal of Marketing, 46*(1), 94–101.

Gorn, G. J., Goldberg, M. E., & Basu, K. (1993). Mood, awareness, and product evaluation. *Journal of Consumer Psychology, 2*(3), 237–256.

Gorn, G. J., Pham, M. T., & Sin, L. Y. (2001). When arousal influences ad evaluation and valence does not (and vice versa). *Journal of Consumer Psychology, 11*(1), 43–55.

Greenhalgh, L. (1966). Some techniques and interesting results in discrimination testing. *Journal of the Market Research Society, 8* (October), 76–80.

Grewal, D., Baker, J., Levy, M., & Voss, G. B. (2003). The effects of wait expectations and store atmosphere on patronage intentions in service-intensive retail stores. *Journal of Retailing, 79*(4), 259–268.

Grill-Spector, K., Kushnir, T., Edelman, S., Itzchak, Y., & Makach, R. (1998). Cue invariant activation in object related areas of the human occipital lobe. *Neuron, 21*, 191–202.

Grohol, J. (2005) Perception. Available at http://psychcentral.com/psypsych/Perception.

Grunwald, M., Weiss, T., Krauss, W., Beyer, L., Rost, R., & Gutbertlet, I. (2001). Theta power in the EEG of humans during ongoing processing in a haptic object recognition task. *Cognitive Brain Research, 11*, 33–37.

Heckler, S., Childers, T., & Houston, M. (1993). On the contruct validity of the SOP scale. *Journal of Mental Imagery, 17*(4), 119–132.

Hirsch, A.R. (1995). Effects of ambient odors on slot-machine usage in a Las Vegas casino. *Psychology & Marketing, 12*(7), 585–594.

Holbrook, M. B. (1983). On the importance of using real products in research on marketing strategy. *Journal of Retailing, 59*(1), 4–23.

Holland, R. W., Hendriks, M., & Aarts, H. (2005). Smells like clean spirit: Non conscious effects of scent on cognition and behavior. *Psychological Science, 16*(9), 689–693.

Hornik, J. (1992). Tactile stimulation and consumer response. *Journal of Consumer Research, 19*(3), 449–458.

Hoyer, W. D., & Brown, S. P. (1990). Effects of brand awareness on choice for a common, repeat-purchase product. *Journal of Consumer Research, 17*(2), 141–148.

Hui, M. K., Dubé, L., & Chebat, J. (1997). The impact of music on consumers' reactions to waiting for services. *Journal of Retailing, 73*(Spring), 87–104.

James, T. W., Humphrey, G. K., Gati, J. S., Servos, P., Menon, R., & Goodale, M. A. (2002). Haptic study of three-dimensional objects activates extra striate visual areas. *Neuropsychologia, 40*, 1706–1714.

Janiszewski, C., & Meyvis, T. (2001). Effects of brand logo complexity, repetition, and spacing on processing fluency and judgment. *Journal of Consumer Research, 28*, 18–32.

Johnson, S. L., Sommer, R., & Martino, V. (1985). Consumer behavior at bulk food bins. *Journal of Consumer Research, 12*(1), 114–117.

Kahn, B. E. & Isen, A. M. (1993). The influence of positive affect on variety seeking among safe, enjoyable products. *Journal of Consumer Research, 20*(2), 257–270.

Kaufman-Scarborough, C. (1999). Reasonable access for mobility-disabled persons is more than widening the door. *Journal of Retailing, 75*, 479–508.

Kellaris, J. J. & Cox, A. D. (1989). The effects of background music in advertising: a reassessment. *Journal of Consumer Research, 16*(1), 113–118.

Kellaris, J. J, Cox, A. D., & Cox, D. (1993). The effect of background music on ad processing: A contingency explanation. *Journal of Marketing, 57*(4), 114–125.

Kellaris, J. J., & Kent, R. J. (1994). An exploratory investigation of responses elicited by music varying in tempo, tonality, and texture. *Journal of Consumer Psychology, 2*(4), 381–401.

Kellaris, J. J., & Kent, R. J. (1992). The influence of music on consumer's temporal perceptions: Does time fly when you're having fun? *Journal of Consumer Psychology, 1*(4), 365–376.

Klatzky, R. L., & Lederman, S. J. (1992). Stages of manual exploration in haptic object identification. *Perception & Psychophysics, 52*(6), 661–670.

Klatzky, R. L., & Lederman, S. J. (1993). Toward a computational model of constraint-driven exploration and haptic object identification. *Perception, 22*, 597–621.

Kosslyn, S. M., Pascual-Leone, A., Felician, O., Camposano, S., Keenan, J. P., & Thompson, W. L. (1999). The role of area 17 in visual imagery: convergent evidence from pet and rtms. *Science, 284*(5411), 167–170.

Krishna, A. (2006). Interaction of Senses: The Effect of Vision versus Touch on the Elongation Bias. *Journal of Consumer Research, 32* (March), 557–566.

Kujala, T., Huotilainen, J., Sinkkonen, A., Ahonen, I. Alho, K., & Hamalainen, M. S. (1995). Visual cortex activation in blind humans during sound discrimination. *Neuroscience Letters, 183*, 143–146.

LeClerc, F., Schmitt, B., & Dubé, L. (1994). Foreign branding and its effects on product perceptions and attitudes. *Journal of Marketing Research, 31*(2), 263–270.

Lederman, S. J., & Klatzky, R. L. (2004). Multisensory texture perception. In In G. Calvert, C. Spence, & B. E. Stein (Eds.), *The handbook of multi-sensory processes* (pp. 107–122). Cambridge MA: The MIT Press.

Levin, I. P., & Gaeth, G. J. (1988). How consumers are affected by the framing of attribute information before and after consuming the product. *Journal of Consumer Research, 15*(3), 374–378.

MacInnis, D. J., & Park, C. W. (1991). The differential role of characteristics of music on high- and low-involvement consumers' processing of ads. *Journal of Consumer Research, 18*(2), 161–173.

Macklin, M. C. (1994). The impact of audiovisual information on children's product-related recall. *Journal of Consumer Research, 21*(1), 154–164.

MacLachlan, J., & Siegel, M. H. (1980). Reducing the costs of TV commercials by use of time compressions. *Journal of Marketing Research, 17*(1), 52–57.

Maison, D., Greenwald, A. G., & Bruin, R. H. (2004). Predictive validity of the implicit association test in studies of brands, consumer attitudes, and behavior. *Journal of Consumer Psychology, 14*(4), 405–415.

Mandler, G. (1982). The structure of value: accounting for taste. In M. S. Clark & S. T. Fiske (Eds.), *Affect and cognition: The 17th annual symposium* (pp. 3–36). Hillsdale NJ: Erlbaum.

Marks, L. E. (2004). Cross-modal interactions in speeded classification. In In G. Calvert, C. Spence, & B. E. Stein (Eds.), *The handbook of multi-sensory processes* (pp. 85–105). Cambridge MA: The MIT Press.

Mattila, A. S., & Wirtz, J. (2001). Congruency of scent and music as a driver of in-store evaluations and behavior. *Journal of Retailing, 77*, 273–289.

McCabe, D. B., & Nowlis, S. M. (2003). The effect of examining actual products or product descriptions on consumer preference. *Journal of Consumer Psychology, 13*(4), 431–439.

McDaniel, C., & Baker, R. C. (1977). Convenience food packaging and the perception of product quality. *Journal of Marketing, 41*(4), 57.

Mehrabian, A., & Russell, J. (1974). *An approach to environmental psychology.* Cambridge, MA: MIT Press.

Meyer, R. J. (1981). A model of multiattribute judgments under attribute uncertainty and informational constraint. *Journal of Marketing Research, 18*(4), 428–441.

Michon, R., Chebat, J., & Turley, L. W. (2005). Mall atmospherics: the interaction effects of the mall environment on shopping behavior. *Journal of Business Research, 58*, 576–583.

Milliman, R. E. (1982). Using background music to affect the behavior of supermarket shoppers. *Journal of Marketing, 46*(3), 86–91.

Milliman, R. E. (1986). The influence of background music on the behavior of restaurant patrons. *Journal of Consumer Research, 13*(2), 286–289.

Mitchell, D. J., Kahn, B. E., & Knasko, S. C. (1995). There's something in the air: effects of congruent and incongruent ambient odor on consumer decision making. *Journal of Consumer Research, 22*(2), 229–238.

Morrin, M., & Ratneshwar, S. (2000). The impact of ambient scent on evaluation, attention, and memory for familiar and unfamiliar brands. *Journal of Business Research, 49*, 157–165.

Morrin, M., & Ratneshwar, S. (2003). Does it make sense to use scents to enhance brand memory? *Journal of Marketing Research, 15* (February), 10–25.

Morrison, D.G. (1981). Triangle taste tests: Are the subjects who respond correctly lucky or good? *Journal of Marketing, 45*(3), 111–118.

Moskowitz, H. R., Jacobs, B., & Firtle, N. (1980). Discrimination testing and product decisions. *Journal of Marketing Research, 17* (February), 84–90.

Newell, F. N. (2004). Cross-modal object recognition. In In G. Calvert, C. Spence, & B. E. Stein (Eds.), *The handbook of multi-sensory processes* (pp. 123–139). Cambridge, MA: The MIT Press.

Nowlis, S. M., & Shiv, B. (2005). The influence of consumer distractions on the effectiveness of food-sampling programs. *Journal of Marketing Research, 42*(2), 157.

Olsen, G. D. (1997). The impact of interstimulus interval and background silence on recall. *Journal of Consumer Research, 23*(4), 295–303.

Ornstein, R. E. (1969). *On the experience of time.* Harmondsworth: Penguin.

Peck, J., & Childers, T. L. (2003a). To have and to hold: The influence of haptic information on product judgments. *Journal of Marketing,* April *67*(2), 35–48.

Peck, J., & Childers, T. L. (2003b). Individual differences in haptic information processing: The 'need for touch' scale. *Journal of Consumer Research, 30*(3), 430–442.

Peck, J., & Childers, T. L. (2004). Self-report and behavioral measures in product evaluation and haptic information: Is what I say how I feel? *Association for Consumer Research* Working Paper Track.

Peck, J., & Childers, T. L. (2006). If I touch it I have to have it: Effects of need for touch on impulse purchasing. *Journal of Business Research, 59,* 765–769.

Peck, J., & Wiggins, J. (2006). It just feels good: Consumers' affective response to touch and its influence on persuasion. *Journal of Marketing, 70*(October), 56–69.

Park, C. W., & Young, S. M. (1986). Consumer response to television commercials: The impact of involvement and background music on brand attitude formation. *Journal of Marketing Research, 23*(1), 11–24.

Pechmann, C. & Ratneshwar, S. (1992). Consumer covariation judgments: Theory or data driven? *Journal of Consumer Research, 19*(3), 373–386.

Richardson, J. T. E. (1999). *Imagery.* East Sussex: Psychology Press.

Roberts, M. L., & Taylor, J. R. (1975). Analyzing proximity judgments in an experimental design. *Journal of Marketing Research, 12*(1), 68–72.

Russell, C. A. (2002). Investigating the effectiveness of product placements in television shows: The role of modality and plot connection congruence on brand memory and attitude. *Journal of Consumer Research, 29*(3), 306–318.

Sadato, N., Pascual-Leone, A., Grafman, J., Ibanez, V., & Dold, M. P. (1996). Activation of the primary visual cortex by braille reading in blind subjects. *Nature, 380*(6574), 526–528.

Sathian, K., Zangaladze, A., Hoffman, J. M., & Grafton, S. T. (1997). Feeling with the mind's eye. *NeuroReport, 8,* 3877–3881.

Schlosser, A. E. (1998). Applying the functional theory of attitudes to understanding the influence of store atmosphere on store inferences. *Journal of Consumer Psychology, 7*(4), 345–369.

Schmitt, B. H., & Shultz, C. J. II (1995). Situational effects on brand preferences for image products. *Psychology & Marketing, 12*(5), 433–446.

Schneider, K. C. (1977). Prevention of accidental poisoning through package and label design. *Journal of Consumer Research, 4*(2), 67–74.

Schwarz, N. T. (1990). Feelings as information: informational and motivational functions of affective states. In E. Tory Higgins & R. M. Sorretino (Eds.), *Handbook of motivation and cognition* (Vol. 2, 527–566). New York: Guilford.

Scott, L. M. (1990). Understanding jingles and needledrop: A rhetorical approach to music in advertising. *Journal of Consumer Research, 17*(2), 223–236.

Scott, C. A., & Yalch, R. F. (1980). Consumer response to initial product trial: A bayesian analysis. *Journal of Consumer Research, 7*(1), 32–41.

Shiv, B., & Nowlis, S. M. (2004). The effect of distractions while tasting a food sample: The interplay of informational and affective components in subsequent choice. *The Journal of Consumer Research, 31*(3), 599–608.

Smith, R. E., & Swinyard, W. R. (1983). Attitude-behavior consistency: The impact of product trial versus advertising. *Journal of Marketing Research, 20*(3), 257–267.

Soto-Faraco, S., Lyons, J., Gazzaniga, M., Spence, C. & Kingstone, A. (2002). The ventriloquist in motion: Illusory capture of dynamic information across sensory modalities. *Cognitive Brain Research, 14,* 139–146.

Spangenberg, E. R., Crowley, A. E., & Henderson, P. W. (1996). Improving the store environment: Do olfactory cues affect evaluations and behaviors? *Journal of Marketing, 60*(2), 67–80.

Spangenberg, E. R., Grohmann, B., & Sprott, D. E. It's beginning to smell a lot like Christmas: The interactive effects of ambient scent and music in a retail setting. *Journal of Business Research*, forthcoming.

Sprott, D. E., & Shimp, T. A. (2004). Using product sampling to augment the perceived quality of store brands. *Journal of Retailing, 80*, 305–315.

Steinberg, S. A. ,& Yalch, R. F. (1978). When eating begets buying: The effects of food samples on obese and nonobese shoppers. *Journal of Consumer Research, 4*(4), 243–246.

Stevens, J. C., & Patterson, M. Q. (1995). Dimensions of spatial acuity in the touch sense: Changes over the life span. *Somatosensory and Motor Research, 12*(1), 29–47.

Tavassoli, N. T., & Lee, Y. H. (2003). The differential interaction of auditory and visual advertising elements with Chinese and English. *Journal of Marketing Research, 15* (November), 468–480.

Thornbury, J. M., & Mistretta, C. M. (1981). Tactile sensitivity as a function of age. *Journal of Gerontology, 36*(1), 34–39.

Tulving, E., & Thomson, D. M. (1973). Encoding specificity and retrieval processes in episodic memory. *Psychological Review, 80*, 352–373.

Unnava, H. R., Agarwal, S., & Haugtvedt, C. P. (1996). Interactive effects of presentation modality and message-generated imagery on recall of advertising information. *Journal of Consumer Research, 23* (June), 81–88.

Wilson, T. D. (2002). *Strangers to ourselves: Discovering the adaptive unconscious.* Cambridge, MA: The Belknap Press of Harvard University Press.

Yalch, R. F. ,& Spangenberg, E. R. (2000). The effects of music in a retail setting on real and perceived shopping times. *Journal of Business Research, 49*, 139–147.

Yoon, C., Gutchess, A. H., Feinberg, F., & Polk, T. A. (in press). A functional magnetic resonance imaging study of neural dissociations between brand and person judgments. *Journal of Consumer Research.*

8

Stages of Consumer Socialization
The Development of Consumer Knowledge, Skills, and Values From Childhood to Adolescence

DEBORAH ROEDDER JOHN

University of Minnesota

Scholarly research examining children's consumer behavior dates back to the 1950s with a few publications on topics such as brand loyalty (Guest, 1955) and conspicuous consumption (Reisman & Roseborough, 1955). Further development took place in the 1960s, as the scope of inquiry expanded to include children's understanding of marketing and retail functions (McNeal, 1964), influence on parents in purchasing decisions (Berey & Pollay, 1968; Wells & LoSciuto, 1966), and relative influence of parents and peers on consumption patterns (Cateora, 1963). Interest in the topic exploded in the mid 1970s amidst vocal criticisms of advertising to young children, mounted by consumer activist groups such as Action for Children's Television (ACT) and government bodies such as the Federal Trade Commission. Emerging from this growing interest was a new field of academic study—consumer socialization—focusing on the acquisition of skills, knowledge, and values by children and adolescents as they prepared to take their role as consumers in the marketplace.

Thirty years later, an impressive body of research on children's consumer socialization has emerged. Researchers have explored a wide range of topics, including learning about products, brands, advertising, shopping, pricing, decision-making strategies, parental influence approaches, and consumption motives and values. Advertising effects have also been a popular topic, ranging from a large number of studies examining features of children's advertising that are more persuasive to a smaller number of studies examining the cumulative effective of advertising on children's values and consumption patterns. The undesirable consequences of marketing and advertising—such as underage drinking, cigarette smoking, and unhealthy diets—have also received attention throughout the years.

The purpose of this chapter is to merge findings from the last thirty years of research into a unified story of how consumer socialization occurs from childhood to adolescence. To provide an organizing theme, we focus on age-related developments in consumer socialization, with the objective of characterizing what children know and how they think as consumers at different ages. We acknowledge that important developments in consumer socialization take place in a social context, including family, peers, mass media, and marketing institutions. But, in order to provide the fullest picture of consumer socialization at different ages, we focus on age-related developments as the basis for our conceptualization.

We include research published in consumer behavior and marketing journals from 1975 to 2005. Findings reported earlier than 1975, or reported in journals outside consumer research, are included only to provide context or corroboration for more recent work by consumer researchers. Excluded from our discussion is research pertaining to children's consumption of products such as cigarettes, alcohol, and illegal drugs, which constitutes a vast body of literature reviewed elsewhere (for reviews, see U.S. Department of Health and Human Services, 1994, 1995). Also excluded is consumer research pertaining to children but outside the realm of consumer socialization, such as: (1) studies of the effects of advertising strategies, such as host selling or repetition, on children's responses to advertising; (2) content analyses of television commercials aimed at children; (3) surveys about parental views of advertising and marketing to children; and (4) discussions of specific public policy issues and regulatory debates (for reviews of these areas, see Adler et al., 1980; Young, 1990).

This chapter is divided into three parts. First, we provide a conceptual overview of consumer socialization, summarizing important theoretical views on cognitive and social development and developing a conceptual framework that describes stages of consumer socialization. These stage descriptions identify general characteristics of children's knowledge, skills, and reasoning at different ages. In the second part, we review research pertaining to the three stages of consumer socialization—perceptual, analytical, and reflective stage. Reviewed are findings about children's knowledge of advertising, products and brands, shopping, pricing, decision making, purchase influence strategies, and consumption motives and values. We conclude with a discussion of the challenges for future research addressing stages of consumer socialization.

STAGES OF CONSUMER SOCIALIZATION

Consumer socialization occurs in the context of dramatic cognitive and social developments, which take place from birth to adolescence. A common approach is to characterize these developments as a series of successive stages, with each stage describing children's thought, reasoning, and perspectives at particular ages. Below, we describe several frameworks most relevant for our subsequent discussion of consumer socialization.

Stages of Cognitive and Social Development

Cognitive Development. The most well known framework for characterizing developments in cognitive abilities is Piaget's theory, which proposes four main stages of cognitive development: sensorimotor (birth to 2 years), preoperational (2 to 7 years), concrete operational (7 to 11 years), and formal operational (11 through adulthood) (Ginsburg & Opper, 1988). Vast differences exist in the cognitive abilities of children at these stages, including the preoperational, concrete operational, and formal operational stages of most interest to consumer researchers. Preoperational children tend to be "perceptually-bound" to the readily-observable aspects of their environment, unlike concrete operational children, who do not accept perception as reality but can think about stimuli in their environment in a more thoughtful way. Preoperational children are also characterized by "centration," the tendency to focus on a single dimension. In contrast, the concrete operational child can consider several dimensions of a stimulus at a time and relate the dimensions in a thoughtful and relatively abstract way. Finally, in the formal operational stage, children progress to more adult-like thought patterns, capable of even more complex thought about concrete and hypothetical objects and situations.

Information processing theories of child development provide additional explanatory power for the types of cognitive abilities evidenced by children as they mature. Several formulations of information processing theory exist, but all share a focus on children's developing skills in the areas of acquisition, encoding, organization, and retrieval of information. In the consumer behavior literature, children have been characterized as belonging to one of three segments—strategic processors, cued processors, and limited processors—based on information processing skills they possess (Roedder, 1981). Strategic processors (age 12 and older) use a variety of strategies for storing and retrieving information, such as verbal labeling, rehearsal, and use of retrieval cues to guide memory search. Cued processors, ranging in age from 7 to 11 years, are able to use a similar set of strategies to enhance information storage and retrieval, but typically need to be aided by explicit prompts or cues. Finally, most children under the age of 7 years are limited processors, with processing skills that are not yet fully developed nor successfully utilized in learning situations, even when prompted to do so.

Social Development. The area of social development includes a wide variety of topics, such as moral development, altruism and pro-social development, impression formation, and social perspective taking. In terms of explaining aspects of consumer socialization, we consider social perspective taking and impression formation to be the most directly relevant for our consideration. Social perspective taking, involving the ability to see perspectives beyond one's own, is strongly related to purchase influence and negotiation skills. Impression formation, involving the ability to make social comparisons, is strongly related to understanding the social aspects of products and consumption.

Developments in social perspective taking are described well by Selman (1980). In the preschool and kindergarten years, the egocentric stage (ages 3–6), children are unaware of any perspective other than their own. As they enter the next phase, the social informational role taking stage (ages 6–8), children become aware that others may have different opinions or motives, but believe this is due to having different information rather than a different perspective on the situation. Thus, children in this stage do not exhibit the ability to actually think from another person's perspective. This ability surfaces in the self-reflective role taking stage (ages 8–10) as children understand that others may have different opinions, even if they have the same information. They can consider another person's viewpoint, but not simultaneously with their own, an ability that does not emerge until the fourth stage of mutual role taking (ages 10–12). This is a most important juncture as much social interaction, such as persuasion and negotiation, requires dual consideration of both parties' perspectives. The final stage, social and conventional system role taking (ages 12–15 and older), features an additional development, the ability to understand another person's perspective as it relates to the social group to which he (other person) belongs or the social system in which he (other person) operates.

Impression formation abilities also undergo dramatic development, as described by Barenboim (1981). Before the age of six, children describe other people in concrete or absolute terms, often mentioning physical appearances ("Nick is tall") or overt behaviors ("Elizabeth likes to skate"). However, these descriptions do not incorporate comparisons with other people. In Barenboim's first stage, the behavioral comparisons phase (ages 6–8), children do incorporate comparisons as a basis of their impressions, but the comparisons continue to be based on concrete attributes or behaviors ("Matthew runs faster than Sam"). In the second stage, which Barenboim calls the psychological constructs phase (ages 8–10), impressions are based on psychological or abstract attributes ("Rosemary is friendly"), but do include comparisons to others. Comparisons based on psychological or abstract attributes do not emerge until the psychological comparisons phase (11 or 12 years of age and older), which features more adult-like impressions of people ("Sara is more outgoing than Amy").

Stages of Consumer Socialization

We propose that consumer socialization be viewed as a developmental process occurring in a series of stages as children become socialized into their roles as consumers. Changes occur as children move through three stages of consumer socialization—the perceptual stage (ages 3–7), the analytical stage (ages 7–11), and the reflective stage (age 11–adult). The perceptual stage derives its name from the overwhelming emphasis that children in this stage place on perceptual as opposed to abstract or symbolic thought. The analytical stage is named for the vast improvements we see at this stage in children's abilities to approach matters in more detailed and analytical ways. Finally, the reflective stage derives its name from the ability of children of this age to reflect on the complex social contexts and meanings related to consumption. These stages are characterized along a number of dimensions that capture important shifts in knowledge development, decision-making skills, and influence strategies, as described below (see Table 8.1).

Perceptual Stage. The perceptual stage (ages 3–7) is characterized by a general orientation toward the immediate and readily observable perceptual features of the marketplace. Piaget's notion of "perceptual boundness" describes these children well, as does his idea of "centration" on single dimensions of objects and events. Children's consumer knowledge is based on perceptual features

Table 8.1   Consumer Socialization Stages

Characteristics	Perceptual stage, 3–7 years	Analytical stage, 7–11 years	Reflective stage, 11–16 years
Knowledge structures:			
Orientation	Concrete	Abstract	Abstract
Focus	Perceptual features	Functional/underlying features	Functional/underlying features
Complexity	Unidimensional Simple	Two or more dimensions Contingent ("if-then")	Multidimensional Contingent ("if-then")
Perspective	Egocentric (own perspective)	Dual perspectives (own + others)	Dual perspectives in social context
Decision-making and influence strategies:			
Orientation	Expedient	Thoughtful	Strategic
Focus	Perceptual features Salient features	Functional/underlying features Relevant features	Functional/underlying features Relevant features
Complexity	Single attributes Limited repertoire of strategies	Two or more attributes Expanded repertoire of strategies	Multiple attributes Complete repertoire of strategies
Adaptivity	Emerging	Moderate	Fully developed
Perspective	Egocentric	Dual perspectives	Dual perspectives in social context

and distinctions, often based on a single dimension or attribute, and represented in terms of concrete details from their own observations. These children exhibit familiarity with concepts in the marketplace, such as brands or retail stores, but rarely understand them beyond a surface level. Due to constraints in encoding and organizing information, individual objects or experiences are rarely integrated into more generalized knowledge structures with multiple dimensions, perspectives, and contingencies ("if-then" rules).

Many of these same characteristics hold true for consumer decision-making skills and influence strategies at the perceptual stage. The orientation here can best be described as simple, expedient, and egocentric. Decisions are often made on the basis of very limited information, often on the basis of a single attribute that is perceptually salient (e.g., size). This strategy is rarely modified to fit different choice tasks or situations. Limited adaptivity is also a feature of children's influence strategies. Children approach these situations from an egocentric perspective, unable to incorporate another person's perspective in using a strategy to influence or negotiate for desired items. Although they may be aware that parents have other views, children at this age have difficulty thinking about their own perspective and that of other person simultaneously.

Analytical Stage. Enormous changes take place, both cognitively and socially, as children move into the analytical stage (ages 7–11). This period contains some of the most important developments in terms of consumer knowledge, skills, and consumption motivations. The shift from perceptual thought to more symbolic thought noted by Piaget, along with dramatic increases in information processing abilities, results in a more sophisticated understanding of the marketplace, a more complex set of knowledge about concepts such as advertising and brands, and a new perspective that goes beyond their own feelings and motives. Concepts such as product categories or prices are thought of in terms of functional or underlying dimensions, products and brands are analyzed and discriminated on the basis of more than one dimension or attribute, and generalizations are drawn from one's experiences. Reasoning proceeds at a more abstract level, setting the stage for knowledge structures that include information about abstract concepts such as advertiser's motives as well as the notion of contingencies (e.g., sweetness is an appealing attribute for candy but not soup).

The ability to analyze stimuli on multiple dimensions and the acknowledgement of contingencies brings about vast changes in children's consumer decision-making skills and strategies. Now, children exhibit more thoughtfulness in their choices, considering more than just a single perceptually salient attribute and employing a decision strategy that makes sense given the task environment. As a result, children are more flexible in the approach they bring to making decisions, allowing them to be more adaptive. These tendencies also emerge in the way children try to influence and negotiate for desired items. The approach is more strategic, based on their newfound ability to think from the perspective of a parent or friend and adapt their influence strategy accordingly.

Reflective Stage. The reflective stage (ages 11–16) is characterized by further development in several dimensions of cognitive and social development. Knowledge about marketplace concepts such as branding and pricing becomes more mature and complex as children develop more sophisticated cognitive and social skills. Many of these changes are more a matter of degree than kind. More distinct is the shift in orientation to a more reflective way of thinking and reasoning, as children move into adolescence and become more focused on the social meanings and underpinnings of the consumer marketplace. A heightened awareness of other people's perspectives, along with a need to shape their own identity and conform to group expectations, results in more attention to the social aspects of being a consumer, making choices, and consuming brands. Consumer decisions are made in a more adaptive manner, depending on the situation and task. In a similar fashion, attempts to influence parents and friends reflect more social awareness as adolescents become more strategic, favoring strategies that they think will be better received than a simple direct approach.

Discussion. The consumer socialization stages being proposed here capture important changes in how children think, what they know, and how they express themselves as consumers. These stage descriptions, similar to other stage frameworks found in child psychology, have tremendous heuristic value. Yet, it is important to keep several caveats in mind. First, the ages associated with each stage are approximations based on the general tendencies of children in that age group. To constrain the number of stages to a reasonable number, some degree of variance among children in an age range was tolerated. For example, children 7 to 11 years of age are identified with the analytical stage, even though differences in degree clearly exist at the extremes. To deal with variations of this sort, we formulated our stage descriptions to be most representative of children in the middle to end of each age range and allowed the age ranges to overlap at transition points between stages. Second, we note that the nature of the task environment or marketing stimuli can alter the age at which certain knowledge or behaviors would occur. Tasks that are more complex, requiring consideration of more information or more in-depth knowledge, can be expected to increase the age at which children appear to have mastered a particular concept.

We turn now to a review of empirical findings pertaining to stages of consumer socialization. We begin our discussion by examining evidence about children's consumer knowledge, skills, and motivation for the first stage of consumer socialization—the perceptual stage.

PERCEPTUAL STAGE

Advertising and Persuasion Knowledge

Much of the concern about television advertising to children has been focused on children under the age of eight, who have been found to have a limited understanding of advertising. One of the few skills that emerge during this stage is the ability to identify television commercials and distinguish them from other forms of programming. By age five, almost all children have acquired the ability to pick out commercials from regular television programming (Blosser & Roberts, 1985; Butter, Popovich, Stackhouse, & Garner, 1981; Levin, Petros, & Petrella, 1982; Mallalieu, Palan, & Laczniak, 2005; Palmer & McDowell, 1979; Stephens & Stutts, 1982; Stutts, Vance, & Hudleson, 1981). Even 3- and 5-year-olds have been shown to discriminate commercials above chance levels (Butter, et al., 1981; Levin et al., 1982).

However, the ability to identify commercials does not necessarily translate into an understanding of the "true" difference between commercials and programs (entertainment vs. selling intent). Children under the age of six or seven usually describe the difference between commercials and programs using simple perceptual cues, such as "commercials are short" (Butter et al., 1981; Palmer & McDowell, 1979; Ward, 1972). Young children often view advertising as entertainment (e.g., "commercials are funny") or as a form of unbiased information (e.g., "commercials tell you about things you can buy"). Although preschool children may implicitly understand that commercials include mainly positive statements about advertised products (Pine & Veasey, 2003), explicit understanding of the selling intent of advertising does not emerge until many children are seven or eight years of age (Macklin, 1985; Ward, Wackman, & Wartella, 1977). For example, in a landmark study with first graders (6 to 7-year-olds), only 50% described the purpose of commercials as trying to sell something (Robertson & Rossiter, 1974).

Product and Brand Knowledge

In addition to advertising, products and brands are the most salient aspects of the marketplace for young consumers. Products and brands are advertised on television, displayed in stores, and found in the home. Even before they are able to read, children as young as two or three years of age can recognize familiar packages in the store and familiar characters on products such as toys and clothing (Derscheid, Kwon, & Fang, 1996; Haynes, Burts, Dukes, & Cloud, 1993). By preschool, children begin to recall brand names from seeing them advertised on television or featured on product packages, especially if the brand names are associated with salient visual cues such as colors, pictures, or cartoon characters (Macklin, 1996). By the time children reach first grade, most can recall at least one brand in popular child-oriented product categories, such as candy and fast food (Ward et al., 1977).

During this time, children develop a preference for particular brands. Children begin to express a preference for familiar branded items over generic offerings in the preschool years (Hite & Hite, 1995), with preference for branded items escalating further as children enter elementary school (Ward et al., 1977). In a clever study analyzing children's letters to Santa, Otnes, Kim, and Kim (1994) found that about 50% of children's gift requests were for specific branded (toy and game) items, with the vast majority of children (85%) mentioning at least one brand name in their letter to Santa.

Despite these developments, children's understanding of products and brands is limited by a focus on perceptual attributes that are visually dominant, such as shape, size, or color. Product categorization is a vivid illustration of this point. Although children learn to group or categorize products at an early age, young children rely on highly visible perceptual attributes to categorize products and discriminate brands (John & Lakshmi-Ratan, 1992; Klees, Olson, & Wilson, 1988). For example, in a study by John and Sujan (1990), preschoolers (ages 4–5) grouped beverage products together based on having similar packaging (e.g., cans vs. bottles), label colors (e.g., green vs. red), and size (e.g., 2-liter vs. 16 oz. bottles). Older children (ages 9–10) placed more emphasis on underlying attributes such as taste (e.g., cola vs. lemon-lime) or carbonation (e.g., orange juice vs. soft drink).

Shopping Knowledge and Skills

A major accomplishment at this stage is an understanding of money as a medium of exchange. Early childhood is a period of rapid development in abilities to understand where money comes from, to identify specific coins and bill values, and to carry out transactions with money involving simple addition and subtraction (Marshall, 1964; Marshall & MacGruder, 1960; Strauss, 1952). Significant jumps in knowledge occur between preschool and first and second grade, with most second graders having acquired many of the basic concepts for understanding the exchange of money for goods and services.

Also developing is an understanding of the basic sequence of events involved in the shopping process. Children acquire a vast amount of experience as an observer of the shopping process at very early ages, but these experiences do not result in an understanding of the basic shopping script until children reach the preschool or kindergarten years (Berti & Bombi, 1988; Karsten, 1996). Karsten (1996) illustrates this point in her study with kindergartners through fourth graders, who were asked to participate in a "shopping game." Each child was shown a small toy with a price tag and was given money to buy the item at a play store. A store area was set up nearby with a small cash register, containing visible amounts of coins and bills. Children were asked to show the interviewer how they would buy the toy in the store. Even the youngest children in the study enacted the basic shopping script. Kindergartners understood that one needed to select an item, check on the money available, place it on the cashier's counter, wait for the cashier offer change, and obtain a receipt.

Decision-Making Skills and Abilities

Children assume the role of consumer decision makers at a young age. During the period from preschool to early elementary school, one of the most important skills to emerge is the ability to adjust information search according to costs and benefits of additional search. Preschoolers can adjust their information search according to *either* costs or benefits (Davidson & Hudson, 1988, experiment 1), but adjusting information search in line with *both* costs and benefits emerges later as children move into elementary school. In a study with 4- to 7-year-olds, Gregan-Paxton and John (1995) found that 6- to 7-year-olds modified their search behavior in line with appropriate cost-benefit trade-offs, gathering the least amount of information in the condition with the least favorable cost-benefit profile (high cost, low benefit) and the most information in the condition with the most favorable cost-benefit profile (low cost, high benefit). Younger children (ages 4–5) were less discerning, however, gathering the most information for one of the conditions warranting a very modest degree of search (low cost, low benefit) and much less information for one of the conditions warranting the most extensive information search (low cost, high benefit).

The type of information gathered is often perceptual in nature, whether or not it is relevant for the decision at hand (Wartella, Wackman, Ward, Shamir, & Alexander, 1979). Once information is gathered, young children do not always utilize the information in an effective manner. Kindergarten children often rely on a single attribute or dimension in forming preferences, comparing products, or choosing one alternative from a set of options (Bahn, 1986; Capon & Kuhn, 1980; Ward et al., 1977; Wartella et al., 1979). The focus on perceptual data and single attributes is the hallmark of decision making in children at the perceptual stage.

Purchase Influence and Negotiation Strategies

Children influence purchases at a very young age. At this stage, children approach influence attempts from an egocentric perspective, with the goal of getting what they want instead of persuading parents who may have a different viewpoint on the purchase. Toddlers and preschool children exert their influence in a very direct way, often pointing to products and occasionally grabbing them off store shelves for deposit inside their parent's shopping cart (Rust, 1993). As children become more verbal, they ask for products by name, sometimes begging, screaming and whining to get what they want (McNeal, 1992). For frequently-purchased items, such as snack food and cereal, children are often able to exert their influence simply by asking (Isler, Popper, & Ward, 1987), due to parents who become more accepting of children's preferences for such items and more comfortable with the idea of occasionally yielding to those preferences.

Consumption Motives and Values

Consumer socialization involves more than the acquisition of knowledge and skills related to the consumer role. It also includes the adoption of motives and values pertaining to consumption activities. Researchers have addressed these developments by focusing on the adoption of social motivations for consumption, emphasizing consumption for social expression and status, and materialistic values, emphasizing the acquisition of material goods as a means of achieving personal happiness, success, and self-fulfillment.

Research suggests that children value material goods from a very young age, sometimes favoring them above all else. Goldberg and Gorn (1978) provide an interesting illustration in a study with 4- to 5-year-old boys. Children saw an ad for a new toy ("Ruckus Raisers") and were then given a choice between two hypothetical playmates: one described as "very nice" that did not own the new toy and one described as "not so nice" but owning the new toy. A majority of the children selected the boy with the new toy. Children also made choices from two hypothetical play situations: playing alone with the new toy or playing in a sandbox with friends (without the toy). Again, a majority of children selected the play situation with the new toy.

However, children's desires for material goods at this stage appear to be driven by rather simple considerations, such as novelty or quantity. Baker and Gentry (1996) provide an example in their study of collecting as a hobby among first and fifth graders. Children of all ages collected similar types of items—such as sports cards, dolls, and rocks—but did so for different reasons. First graders often compared their possessions to those of others in terms of quantity. Collecting appeared to be simply a way of getting more than someone else. Among fifth graders, however, the motivations for collecting had more social connotations. Collecting was appreciated as a way of socially expressing one's uniqueness and attaining a sense of personal achievement by having things that others do not. These findings are consistent with our descriptions of children in the perceptual stage, who value material goods on a perceptual dimension (quantity), and the analytical stage, who see things quite differently by virtue of their social comparison skills and perspective-taking abilities.

ANALYTICAL STAGE

Advertising and Persuasion Knowledge

A full understanding of advertising intent usually emerges by the time most children are 7 to 8 years old (Bever, Smith, Bengen, & Johnson, 1975; Blosser & Roberts, 1985; Lawlor & Prothero, 2003; Robertson & Rossiter, 1974; Rubin, 1974; Ward et al., 1977). Children see the persuasive intent of commercials quite clearly, coming to terms with the fact that advertisers are "trying to get people to buy something." In a study with first, third, and fifth grade boys, Robertson and Rossiter (1974) found that the understanding of persuasive intent increased dramatically from only 52.7% of first graders (6- to 7-year-olds) to 87.1% of third graders (8- to 9-year-olds) to 99% of fifth graders (10- to 11-year-olds). This trend supports our description of children in the analytical stage, who are capable of viewing advertising from a number of perspectives, the buyer's (assistive intent) and the advertiser's (persuasive intent).

Children in the analytical stage also recognize the existence of bias and deception in advertising. Children aged 8 years and older no longer believe that "commercials always tell the truth" (Bever et al., 1975; Robertson & Rossiter, 1974; Ward, 1972; Ward et al., 1977), with beliefs about the truthfulness of advertising becoming even more negative as children move toward adolescence (Bever et al., 1975; Robertson & Rossiter, 1974; Rossiter & Robertson, 1976; Ward, 1972; Ward et al., 1977). For example, Ward et al. (1977) report that the percentage of kindergartners, third graders, and sixth graders believing that advertising never or only sometimes tells the truth increases from 50% to 88% to 97%, respectively. Moreover, older children also understand why commercials are sometimes untruthful, connecting lying to persuasive intent (e.g., "they want to sell products to make money, so they have to make the product look better than it is").

Armed with an understanding of advertising's persuasive intent and skepticism about the truthfulness of advertising claims, children over the age of eight are often viewed as having a "cognitive defense" against advertising that shields them from being unfairly persuaded. Although this scenario seems straightforward, evidence regarding the extent to which children's general attitudes and beliefs about advertising function as cognitive defenses is quite mixed. Early survey research was successful in finding moderate links between children's knowledge of advertising's persuasive intent and their desire for advertised products (Robertson & Rossiter, 1974), but more recent experimental research finds that children's cognitive defenses have little or no effect on evaluations and preferences for advertised products (Christenson, 1982; Ross et al., 1984). For example, Christenson (1982) found that an educational segment on commercials was successful in increasing the awareness of advertising's persuasive intent and decreasing the perceived truthfulness of advertising, yet had little effect on younger (first–second graders) or older (fifth–sixth graders) children's evaluations of a subsequently advertised product. More recent research has provided an answer for this puzzle, finding that children's advertising knowledge serves as a cognitive defense only when that knowledge is accessed and used during commercial viewing (Brucks, Armstrong, & Goldberg, 1988).

Product and Brand Knowledge

Brand knowledge escalates from early to middle childhood. Children's awareness and recall of brand names increases with age, from early to middle childhood (Rossiter, 1976; Rubin, 1974; Ward et al., 1977). By the time children reach middle childhood, they can name multiple brands in most child-oriented product categories such as cereal, snacks, and toys (McNeal, 1992; Otnes et al., 1994; Rossiter, 1976; Rubin, 1974; Ward et al., 1977) and can name at least one brand in more adult-oriented product categories such as cameras and gasoline (Ward et al., 1977).

Between early and middle childhood, children also learn a great deal about the underlying structure of product categories. Children shift from using highly visible perceptual cues to more important underlying cues as a basis for categorizing and judging similarity among products (John & Sujan, 1990; John & Lakshmi-Ratan, 1992; Klees et al., 1988). By third or fourth grade, children are learning to group objects according to taxonomic relationships (e.g., belts and socks are items of clothing), attributes that indicate the relationship of categories to one another (e.g., fruit juices and soft drinks differ on the attribute of naturalness), and attributes inherent to the core concept of categories (e.g., taste, more than color, is central to the category of soft drinks). These are termed underlying, deep structure, or functional attributes because they convey the true meaning or function a category might serve. The shift to functional or underlying categorization cues around 8 to 10 years of age is consistent with symbolic thinking that characterizes children in the analytical stage.

Early to middle childhood is also a time of greater understanding of the symbolic meanings and status accorded to products. Nowhere is children's increasing understanding of the social significance of goods more in evidence than in studies of consumption symbolism (Belk, Bahn, & Mayer, 1982; Belk, Mayer, & Driscoll, 1984; Mayer & Belk, 1982). To illustrate, in the Belk et al. (1982) study, children in preschool through elementary school were shown pairs of pictures of automobiles or houses, which varied in size, age, or market value. For example, one pair included a Caprice (a large, traditional car) and a Chevette (a small economy car). Subjects were asked to pick the car that would be owned by different types of people (e.g., a doctor, a grandfather). Responses revealed that inferences based on ownership were minimal among preschoolers, emerging and evident in second graders, and almost fully developed in sixth graders. Thus, sometime between preschool and second grade, children begin to make inferences about people based on products they use (Belk et al., 1982; Mayer & Belk, 1982).

Shopping Knowledge and Skills

As children move into the analytical stage, they begin to understand more about the purpose and nature of retail establishments. The changes parallel those seen with understanding the purpose of advertising. At age 5, stores are seen as source for snacks or sweets, but children are unsure of why stores exist except to fulfill their own needs and wants. At age 9, however, there is an understanding that retail stores are owned by people selling goods at a profit. Thus, there is a considerable shift in understanding the purpose of retail establishments from the preschool years (an egocentric view of stores as fulfilling my wants) to the early elementary school years (a dual view of stores as profit centers that fulfill consumer wants) (McNeal, 1964). This shift is consistent with our description of children in the perceptual stage, where children have an egocentric perspective, versus those in the analytical stage, where children can take another person's perspective, such as retailers who have a profit motive.

Shopping scripts also undergo development as children gain more shopping experience and transform these experiences into more sophisticated scripts. John and Whitney (1986) illustrate these developments in a study with children ages 4–5, 6–7, and 9–10 years old. Children heard different stories about a boy or girl exchanging or returning a faulty product to a store. Amount of experience was manipulated by varying the number of stories read to children, resulting in low (1 story), medium (3 stories), or high (5 stories) levels of experience. After hearing the assigned number of stories, children were asked to describe how one would go about returning or exchanging a product.

As more information became available, 9- to 10-year-olds produced scripts that were generally more abstract and complex in terms of conditional events (if "x" happens, then do "y"). For example, children picked up the differences in return and exchange policies across stories and incorporated these contingencies into their scripts. The 6- to 7-year-olds also produced more sophisticated scripts with added experience, although this effect was limited to low versus moderate levels of experience (1 vs. 3 stories). In contrast, the scripts produced by 4- to 5-year-olds were similar across experience levels, with a relatively high percentage of episodic details and no conditional events. Older children have an advantage in encoding and organizing important information about their experiences, as well as retrieving information when needed (Peracchio, 1992, 1993).

Decision-Making Skills and Abilities

Some of the most important developments in decision-making skills surface in the analytical stage. Children gather information from a variety of sources (Ward et al., 1977), focus on more relevant information and ignore irrelevant information (Davidson, 1991b; Howse, Best, & Stone, 2003; Wartella et al., 1979), consider functional/performance attributes in addition to perceptual features (Ward et al., 1977), use more attributes and dimensions in forming preferences (Bahn, 1986; Capon & Kuhn, 1980; Ward et al., 1977), and more carefully consider these preferences in making choices (Roedder, Sternthal, & Calder, 1983).

Children also begin to use a variety of compensatory and noncompensatory choice strategies (Bereby-Meyer, Assor, & Katz, 2004; Howse, Best, & Stone, 2003). Wartella et al. (1979) provide a vivid example of these developments in a study with kindergartners and third graders. Children chose a gift for a friend from a set of candies described as having different amounts of various ingredients (e.g., chocolate, raisins). To provide attribute importance information, the ingredient preferences of the gift recipient were also described (e.g., loves chocolate and hates raisins). The choice alternatives (candies) and attribute importance information was designed in such a way that the chosen gift revealed the child's choice strategy: best single attribute (candy with the highest amount of the most important ingredient), variety of attributes (candy with the highest amount of different ingredients), lexicographic strategy (candy with the highest amount of the most important ingredient and, in the case of a tie, on the highest amount of the second most important ingredient), and a weighted adding strategy (candy with the highest amounts of ingredients multiplied by importance weights for ingredients).

Kindergartners chose candies with the most ingredients, regardless of their importance to the gift recipient. However, third graders used a variety of strategies, split between the single best attribute, variety of attributes, and lexicographic strategies. The weighted adding strategy, which is compensatory in nature, was used by only a small percentage of the older children. These trends, especially the use of the single best attribute and lexicographic strategies by older children, signal the use of noncompensatory strategies in children by the time they reach middle childhood.

Purchase Influence and Negotiation Strategies

Children exert more influence as they grow older (Atkin, 1978; Darley & Lim, 1986; Jenkins, 1979; Moschis & Mitchell, 1986; Nelson, 1979; Rust, 1993; Ward & Wackman, 1972; Swinyard & Sim, 1987; Ward et al., 1977). They have the most influence over purchases of child-relevant items (e.g., cereal, toys, clothes), a moderate degree of influence for family activities (e.g., vacations, restaurants), and the least influence for purchases of consumer durables and expensive items (Belch, Belch, & Ceresino, 1985; Corfman & Harlam, 1997; Foxman & Tansuhaj, 1988; Foxman, Tansuhaj, & Ekstrom, 1989; Isler et al., 1987; Swinyard & Sim, 1987).

Influence attempts also become more sophisticated at this stage. Bargaining, compromise, and persuasion enter the picture. Instead of simple purchase requests, which are then accepted or rejected by parents, interactions between parents and children of this age feature more mutual discussion and compromise (Rust, 1993). Discussion of this sort is made possible by the fact that children are developing greater abilities to see multiple points of view, such as theirs as well as their parents, simultaneously. As we have noted, this dual perspective is characteristic of older children in the analytical stage. Children are also primed to assume a more active role in purchase discussions after years of listening to their parents describe why certain requests can or cannot be honored (Palan & Wilkes, 1997; Popper, 1979), in effect learning to reason, persuade, and negotiate for what they want. Finally, it is also the case that extended discussions become more necessary as children shift purchase requests from inexpensive items such as candy and cereal to more expensive items, including sporting goods, clothes, and electronic goods (McNeal, 1992).

Consumption Motives and Values

As children approach adolescence, they begin to understand the social meanings and status attached to possessions. As a result, social motivations for consumption emerge. In Baker and Gentry's (1996) study, described earlier, the motivations of older children (ages 10–11) for collecting items included social ones, such as expressing their uniqueness or signaling an achievement.

Materialistic values also begin to surface during this period (Achenreiner, 1997; Goldberg, Gorn, Peracchio, & Bamossy, 2003). A greater understanding of the symbolic meanings and status accorded to possessions sets the stage for desiring material goods for instrumental reasons, such as happiness or popularity. For example, Goldberg et al. (2003) found evidence of materialism in a study of 9- to 14-year-olds. Children higher in materialism exhibited behaviors we have come to expect with materialistic values, such as shopping more, saving less, and being more responsive to advertising and marketing promotions.

REFLECTIVE STAGE

Knowledge of Advertising and Persuasion

In the reflective stage, advertising knowledge develops even further, especially in terms of understanding advertiser's selling tactics. Although younger children may have a general understanding of why commercials are sometimes untruthful, the ability to detect specific instances of bias and deception does not arrive until adolescence. For example, in a study with 7- to 12-year-olds, Bever et al. (1975) report that most of the 7- to 10-year-olds in their study could not detect misleading advertising and admitted to their difficulties: "'[Advertisers] can fake well,' they said, and 'you don't really know what's true until you've tried the product'" (p. 114). Eleven- to twelve-year-olds were more discriminating, using nuances of voice, manner, and language to detect misleading advertising. These children used clues such as "overstatements and the way they [the actors] talk," "when they use visual tricks or fake things," and when the commercial "goes on and on in too much detail" (p. 119). Clearly, developments in perspective taking that occur as children enter adolescence facilitate the ability to associate such nuances in advertising executions with deception or exaggeration.

Knowledge of advertising tactics and appeals becomes evident as children approach early adolescence (11–14 years of age) (Boush, Friestad, & Rose, 1994; Friestad & Wright, 1994; Paget, Kritt, & Bergemann, 1984). Although younger children may recognize that certain commercial features such as celebrity endorsers are meant to induce a positive reaction, they do not have an explicit understanding of how these features link to persuasion (Lawlor & Prothero, 2003) and underestimate the wide variety of commercial features (e.g., jingles, contests, animation) used by advertisers to persuade (Mallalieu, Palan, & Laczniak, 2005). To illustrate, Moore and Lutz (2000) found that younger children (ages 7–8) evaluated commercials based on their liking of the advertised product, whereas older children (ages 10–11) viewed advertisements in a more analytical nature, often focusing on creative content and execution (e.g., repetition and jingles).

Specific knowledge of advertising tactics and appeals continues to develop during adolescence, as documented in a study of sixth through eighth graders by Boush et al. (1994). Sixth through eighth graders were asked a series of questions about what advertisers are trying to accomplish when they use particular tactics, such as humor, celebrity endorsers, and product comparisons. Students were asked to rate eight possible effects (e.g., "grab your attention" and "help you learn about the product") for each tactic. The results indicate that knowledge of advertising tactics increases with age, becoming more adult-like as children enter their teenage years. This developmental path is consistent with our characterization of children in the reflective stage, who possess substantial perspective-taking skills that allow them to reason about different perspectives (advertiser and viewer) across different contexts or situations.

Thus, adolescents view advertising in a more skeptical, analytical, and discerning fashion. However, it is also the case that adolescents find advertising to be entertaining, interesting, and socially relevant. By virtue of their growing sophistication, older children and adolescents find entertainment in analyzing the creative strategy of many commercials and constructing theories for why certain elements are persuasive (Moore & Lutz, 2000). Advertisements are also valued as a device for social interaction, serving as a focus of conversations with peers, a means of belonging and group membership, and a conduit for transferring and conveying meaning in their daily lives (Ritson & Elliott, 1999).

Product and Brand Knowledge

Brand knowledge continues to develop as children move from middle childhood into adolescence. Awareness and recall of brand names continues to increase, for both child-oriented product categories as well as more adult-oriented ones (Keiser, 1975; Ward et al., 1977). This is to be expected as adult-oriented products—such as cars, computers, and cameras—become more relevant to older children who are potential consumers for these items.

More interesting, however, are the developments that occur in children's understanding of the symbolic meanings of products and brands. As discussed earlier, understanding of consumption symbolism begins to emerge by second grade, but is not well developed until sixth grade. This is especially true for understanding symbolic meanings attached to brands. Illustrative is a study with second graders, sixth graders, and high school students reported by Achenreiner and John (2003). Participants were shown ads for a pair of athletic shoes, which pictured an identical pair of shoes labeled as being either Nike (preferred brand) or Kmart (non-preferred brand), and gave their impressions of the owner of the athletic shoes. Second graders had similar impressions of the owners regardless of brand name. In contrast, sixth graders and high school students had impressions of the owner of the Nike shoes that were more positive (e.g., more popular, smarter) than those for the owner of the Kmart shoes.

Thus, by sixth grade, children are developing a keen sense of the social meaning and prestige associated with brands. Further, brands not only confer status to their owners, but also begin to symbolize group identity and a sense of belonging to certain groups (Jamison, 1996). These developments are consistent with our description of children in the reflective stage, who form impressions based on social comparisons of factors such as personality, social standing, and possessions.

Shopping Knowledge and Skills

Despite the fact that children understand many aspects of the shopping environment by middle childhood, they have relatively undeveloped notions about pricing until they reach adolescence. By the time children are 8 or 9 years old, they know that products have prices, know where to look for price information, and know that there are price variations among products and stores (McNeal & McDaniel, 1981). But, they have fairly simple notions of how these prices reflect supply and demand in the marketplace. Adults, for example, see prices as a reflection of the utility or function of the item to the consumer, the costs of inputs incurred by the manufacturer to make the item, and the relative scarcity of the item in the marketplace (Fox & Kehret-Ward, 1985).

Not until early adolescence do children perceive a full range of connections between price and value (Berti & Bombi, 1988; Fox & Kehret-Ward, 1985). A study by Fox and Kehret-Ward (1990), where children were asked to explain the basis of prices for selling a bicycle, provides a nice illustration. Preschoolers focused on a product's perceptual features, especially size, as the basis for pricing, but did not articulate a theory for why these features provide more value. Ten-year-olds linked price to perceptual features (size or fancy features), but reasoned that a higher price would be present due to the amount of production inputs required. Only 13-year-olds exhibited a more abstract level of reasoning, viewing prices as a function of the quality of the product's inputs and preferences of potential buyers.

Decision-Making Skills and Abilities

During the adolescent years, several changes occur in the use of information sources. Older adolescents seek out additional sources of information, generally favoring peers and friends over parents and mass media (Moore & Stephens, 1975; Moschis & Moore, 1979; Stephens & Moore, 1975; Tootelian & Gaedeke, 1992). They develop a greater ability to ignore irrelevant information, focus on more relevant information (Davidson, 1991b), use attribute information in forming preferences and making choices (Capon & Kuhn, 1980; Klayman, 1985; Nakajima & Hotta, 1989), and apply decision-making strategies more appropriately to make better choices (Bereby-Meyer, Assor, & Katz, 2004; Howse, Best, & Stone, 2003).

The most important development during adolescence is the ability to adapt decision-making strategies to more complex decision environments, which include more choice alternatives and more information per alternative. Adult decision makers adapt to more complex environments in several ways, including restricting search to a smaller percentage of the available information, focusing their search on more promising alternatives, and switching from compensatory choice strategies to noncompensatory ones that are less cognitively demanding (see Payne, Bettman, & Johnson, 1993). These adaptive responses develop in children as they approach adolescence, being consistently exhibited by the time children reach 11 or 12 years of age (Davidson, 1991a, 1991b; Gregan-Paxton & John, 1997; Klayman, 1985). Children's abilities undergo further refinement as they move into late adolescence, using a wider array of simplifying strategies in a more systematic manner (Nakajima & Hotta, 1989).

Illustrating these developments is a study by Davidson (1991a), conducted with second, fifth, and eighth graders. Children made choices from alternatives described on an information board. Four information boards varying in complexity were shown: 3 (alternatives) × 3 (dimensions), 3 × 6, 6 × 3, and 6 × 6. Information about each alternative was hidden from view by a card, but children were allowed to uncover as much information as they wanted prior to choice. As complexity increased, older children (fifth and eighth graders) were more efficient in gathering information, searched less exhaustively, and exhibited a greater use of noncompensatory strategies. In particular, these children appeared to be using conjunctive decision rules, consistent with Klayman's (1985) findings. In contrast, younger children (second graders) responded to increasing complexity by making smaller adjustments in their search strategies without using a consistent simplifying strategy such as the conjunctive rule.

Purchase Influence and Negotiation Strategies

By the time they reach early adolescence, children have an extended repertoire of influence strategies available to them (Kim, Lee, & Hall, 1991; Manchanda & Moore-Shay, 1996; Palan & Wilkes, 1997). These strategies are more sophisticated, appealing to parents in seemingly rational ways, and are used in a flexible manner to match the situation or answer the objection of a parent. Palan and Wilkes (1997) provide an illustration of this growing sophistication in a study conducted with 12- to 15-year-olds and their parents. Using interviews, the authors identified a diverse set of purchase influence strategies used by adolescents: (1) bargaining strategies, including reasoning and offers to pay for part of the purchase; (2) persuasion strategies, including expressions of opinions, persistent requesting, and begging; (3) request strategies, including straightforward requests and expressions of needs or wants; and (4) emotional strategies, including anger, pouting, guilt trips, and sweet talk.

Bargaining and persuasion were favorites among the group of adolescents, with emotional strategies favored least. Variations in frequency appear to be driven, in part, by which strategies adolescents perceive to be the most effective in obtaining desired items. Strategies such as reasoning and offers to pay for part of an item are seen as very effective; strategies such as begging and getting angry are seen as least effective. Adolescents also adapt the strategies they use depending on what they view as most effective in influencing parents. One way of doing so is by duplicating the strategies used by their parents for responding to their purchase requests. For example, adolescents perceived reasoning as the most effective influence strategy when they came from families where parents reported the frequent use of reasoning strategies. Also perceived as effective were influence strategies that had a logical connection with the objections parents raised to a purchase request. For example, in families where parents often refused purchase requests by stating the family could not afford the item, adolescents knew it was effective to use strategies that reduced the monetary outlay, such as offers to pay for part of the item.

Consumption Motives and Values

With a keen sense of the social meanings and status according to material possessions, teenagers are strongly motivated by social considerations in purchasing goods and services. Certain products and brand names not only confer status to their owners, but also begin to symbolize group identity and a sense of belonging to distinct social groups. Products such as clothing are particularly notable in this regard, as reported by Jamison (1996) in a study with children ages 11–12. Clothes are described as a means of fitting in and as a way to identify membership in a particular subgroup, such as the "preppies" and "hip-hops."

Chaplin and John (2005) provide an illustration of social motivations for consumption linked to self-identity in a study with 8-to 18-year-olds. Participants were asked to construct a collage, using a set of pictures and words, to answer the question, "Who Am I?" Provided were pictures and words referring to specific hobbies, sports, personality traits, TV/movie characters, and brand names. Results indicated that older children (ages 12–18) included more brands on their collages than did younger children (ages 8–9). In addition, teenagers explained these self-brand connections in social terms, describing how certain brands exuded their personality or group affiliation, whereas younger children made self-brand connections on a more concrete basis (e.g., owning an item with the brand). Thus, for teenagers, social motivations for owning brands are strong because brands are seen as reflecting one's self-concept.

Not surprisingly, social motivations for consumption are associated with higher levels of materialism. A recent study by Chaplin and John (2007) suggests that materialism increases as children move into their adolescent years. Children 8 to 18 years old were asked to construct a collage to answer the question, "What makes me happy?" For this purpose, participants were given a set of pictures and words, which included non-material themes (e.g., friends, good grades, hobbies) and material goods (e.g., money, computer games, brands). Children in the middle age group (ages 12–13) selected more material goods for their collages than either the youngest (ages 8–9) or oldest (ages 16–18) age groups. Given that happiness is an instrumental goal associated with materialism, these findings suggest that children just entering adolescence exhibit the strongest materialistic tendencies. Interestingly, these tendencies are somewhat abated in older adolescents, who begin to focus more on achievements (e.g., good grades, getting into a good college) than material goods as a means for achieving happiness.

CHALLENGES FOR FUTURE RESEARCH

Our framework views consumer socialization as progressing in a series of three stages—perceptual, analytical, and reflective—described by changes in children's knowledge and skills during childhood and adolescence. We have reviewed empirical evidence consistent with these stages, documenting children's growing sophistication about products, brands, advertising, shopping, pricing, decision-making strategies, influence approaches, and consumption motives and values (see Table 8.2). It is also the case, however, that significant gaps remain in our understanding of these stages of consumer socialization. These gaps, in topic areas as well as research methodologies, constitute challenges for future research.

Table 8.2   Summary of Findings by Consumer Socialization Stage

Topic	Perceptual stage, 3–7 years	Analytical stage, 7–11 years	Reflective stage, 11–16 years
Advertising knowledge	Can distinguish ads from programs based on perceptual features	Can distinguish ads from programs based on persuasive intent	Understand persuasive intent of ads as well as specific ad tactics and appeals
	Believe ads are truthful, funny, and interesting	Believe ads lie and contain bias and deception — but do not use these "cognitive defenses"	Believe ads lie and know how to spot specific instances of bias or deception in ads
	Positive attitudes toward ads	Negative attitudes toward ads	Skeptical attitudes toward ads
Product and brand knowledge	Can recognize brand names and beginning to associate them with product categories	Increasing brand awareness, especially for child-relevant product categories	Substantial brand awareness for adult-oriented as well as child-relevant product categories
	Perceptual cues used to identify product categories	Underlying or functional cues used to define product categories	Underlying or functional cues used to define product categories
	Beginning to understand symbolic aspects of consumption based on perceptual features	Increased understanding of symbolic aspects of consumption	Sophisticated understanding of consumption symbolism for product categories and brands
	Egocentric view of retail stores as a source of desired items	Understand retail stores are owned to sell goods and make a profit	Understanding and enthusiasm for retail stores
Shopping knowledge and skills	Understand sequence of events in the basic shopping script	Shopping scripts more complex, abstract, and with contingencies	Complex and contingent shopping scripts
	Value of products and prices based on perceptual features	Prices based on theories of value	Prices based on abstract reasoning, such as input variations and buyer preferences
Decision-making skills: Information search	Limited awareness of information sources	Increased awareness of personal and mass media sources	Contingent use of different information sources depending on product or situation
	Focus on perceptual attributes	Gather information of functional as well as perceptual attributes	Gather information on functional, perceptual, and social aspects
	Emerging ability to adapt to cost-benefit trade-offs	Able to adapt to cost-benefit trade-offs	Able to adapt to cost-benefit trade-offs

(Continued)

Table 8.2 Continued

Topic	Perceptual stage, 3–7 years	Analytical stage, 7–11 years	Reflective stage, 11–16 years
Product evaluation	Use of perceptually salient attribute information	Focus on important attribute information – functional and perceptual attributes	Focus on important attribute information – functional, perceptual, and social aspects
	Use of single attributes	Use two or more attributes	Use multiple attributes
Decision strategies	Limited repertoire of strategies	Increased repertoire of strategies, especially noncompensatory ones	Full repertoire of strategies
	Emerging ability to adapt strategies to tasks – usually need cues to adapt	Capable of adapting strategies to tasks	Capable of adapting strategies to tasks in adult-like manner
Purchase influence and negotiation strategies	Use direct requests and emotional appeals	Expanded repertoire of strategies, with bargaining and persuasion emerging	Full repertoire of strategies, with bargaining and persuasion as favorites
	Limited ability to adapt strategy to persons or situations	Developing abilities to adapt strategy to persons and situations	Capable of adapting strategies based on perceived effectiveness for persons or situations
Consumption motives and values	Value of possessions based on surface features, such as "having more" of something	Emerging understanding of value based on social meaning and significance	Fully developed understanding of value based on social meaning, significance, and scarcity

Consumer Socialization Topics

Advertising and Persuasion Knowledge. Due to concerns about advertising to young children, researchers have focused their attention on children under the age of twelve. We know a great deal about how an understanding of advertising develops in children prior to adolescence. However, we still have much to learn about developments during adolescence. The few studies including adolescents suggest that important developments occur during this period, such as a more sophisticated understanding of specific advertising tactics, types of bias, and social context. Further examination of these topics would contribute to our understanding of how persuasion knowledge develops, as well as providing insight for public policy concerns about adolescent response to advertising for products such as cigarettes and alcoholic beverages.

Further research would also be welcome to explore how advertising and persuasion knowledge is utilized in children's responses to persuasive communications (Wright, Friestad, & Boush, 2005). Existing research focuses on what children know or believe about advertising, assuming that once advertising knowledge is acquired, it will be used as a cognitive filter or defense when children are exposed to persuasive messages. Yet, the few studies that examine how advertising knowledge is actually used by children in viewing situations suggests that more attention should be paid to understanding when such knowledge is accessed and used. The evidence to date suggests that cognitive filters and defenses against advertising may emerge during early adolescence, providing yet another reason for more attention to developments during the reflective stage.

Product and Brand Knowledge. Perhaps the greatest challenge in this area is a better understanding of how children relate to brands at different stages. Consumption symbolism is an important topic, yet the few studies addressing this issue focus on products, not brands. Although few in number, studies of children's relationships with brands suggest that important changes occur with the approach of adolescence. Current research points to important qualitative changes in the way adolescents view brands, yet we lack descriptive detail about the nature of these changes. Brand relationship frameworks (Fournier, 1998) would be especially useful in describing how these relationships develop from adolescence to adulthood.

Shopping Skills. Despite the acknowledgement that children become enthusiastic shoppers at a young age, research is needed to understand the development of shopping skills, involving comparisons between prices, volumes, sizes, and the like. Surprisingly, we were unable to locate a single study focused on this topic within the last twenty years. Given the large body of research in child psychology on children's developing mathematical abilities and strategies (see Siegler & Jenkins, 1989), it would appear to be an opportune time to revisit issues related to shopping skills. A related topic, children's understanding of pricing and value, would also be a natural candidate for further research. Both topics would be welcome additions to our knowledge about the analytical stage, when mathematical abilities and abilities to integrate information converge, producing a situation conducive to major improvements in shopping skills.

Decision-Making Skills and Abilities. Perhaps the most noticeable gap in this literature is a basic understanding of what decision strategies children possess at different ages. Exploring the age at which children effectively utilize compensatory and noncompensatory strategies would be particularly important. Existing research provides some clues, but empirical data is particularly limited for younger children in the perceptual stage.

Also important would be research exploring decision-making goals. To date, research has proceeded as if children shared the same decision-making goals as adults, such as buying the "best" product or making a good decision with the least cognitive effort. It may well be that young children have quite different goals in mind, such as choosing a novel product, being surprised, or having fun. This may, in fact, provide a richer explanation for some of the findings regarding age differences in decision-making skills and behavior.

Purchase Influence and Negotiation Strategies. Investigations using in-depth interviews have provided vivid examples of the growing sophistication of older children and adolescents. Observational research, often conducted in grocery stores, has provided a picture of influence attempts for very young children accompanying their parents to the store. What is missing is research focused on children between these age groups, primarily children in the analytical stage between the ages of 7 and 11. As we have seen, much social development occurs during this period and it would be useful to track how changes in areas such as social perspective taking facilitate the development of purchase influence and negotiation strategies.

Also useful would be research looking at the connection between influence and negotiation strategies and other aspects of children's consumer knowledge and behavior. One example would be the relationship between purchase influence strategies and advertising knowledge. Although these areas have existed independently, they both deal with persuasion—how to persuade someone else or how someone tries to persuade you. Another example would be the relationship between purchase influence and negotiation strategies and parent–child conflict, sometimes viewed as a negative effect of advertising to children.

Consumption Motives and Values. Until recently, adolescents have been the focus of most research in this area. Studies including younger children are just beginning to emerge. As we have seen, perspective taking and impression formation undergo dramatic development from middle childhood to adolescence. These developments in social understanding are probably linked to important changes in views of consumption, yet we have little descriptive detail to identify the nature of these changes. Studies with children in the analytical stage (ages 7-11) would be useful in understanding the relationship between social and cognitive development and aspects of consumption motives and values.

Methodological Approaches

In addressing gaps in our knowledge, there are also challenges in designing appropriate methodologies for studying consumer socialization across a wide age range. Sample design, stimuli selection, and measurement design are issues common to researchers working with children of any age.

First, in terms of sample design, selecting the appropriate age groups can present difficulties. Often, researchers are addressing a specific question for the first time, without prior research to guide sample selection. Concerns about selecting age groups that will uncover developmental patterns, if they exist, are common. Questions about the youngest or oldest age group that should be included are often involved. Guidance on these issues is available by using the stages of consumer socialization described here. For example, if the socialization topic under inquiry involves abstract thinking or integration of multiple pieces of information, the sample should include children in the perceptual (ages 3–7) and analytical (ages 7–11) stages. If the socialization issue being addressed involves social awareness and impression formation, the sample should include children in the analytical (ages 7–11) and reflective (ages 11–16) stages.

Selection of experimental stimuli also requires careful consideration. Unless the age range being examined is quite narrow, the researcher will need to be aware of age differences in familiarity, relevance, and interest in stimuli such as advertisements, product categories, brands, choice situations, and tasks. Tailoring the stimuli to each age group will not work if the objective is to compare age groups. The best solution is to find stimuli that are familiar and appeal to children across age groups. If this is not possible, which is likely for studies spanning a wide age range, the next best solution is to find stimuli that are familiar and appealing to the youngest age group, while holding some appeal to the oldest age group. The selection is tipped in favor of younger children because it is usually this age group that is found to have a lower level of ability or skills than older children; therefore, it is important to rule out the possibility that unfamiliarity or disinterest with the stimuli contributed to younger children's poorer performance on a task. In situations where collections of stimuli are required, such as clothing brand names, a mixture of brands can be used that are of interest to younger children (e.g., Limited Too), older children (e.g., Express), and children of all ages (e.g., Nike).

Designing measures to assess consumer knowledge, skills, or values is perhaps the most pressing problem in moving research forward in this area. In the past, researchers have used a mixture of traditional techniques, with emphasis on rating scales, recall and recognition measures, and unstructured interview questions. Adjustments are often made to accommodate young children, but measurement concerns persist in using these techniques. Unstructured questions require greater verbalization abilities than many young children have at their disposal. Added to this is the fact that many of the unstructured questions are rather abstract, without the concreteness that dominates thinking for children under 8 years of age. For example, questions such as "What is the purpose of advertising?" are far too abstract for children in the perceptual stage.

Rating scales reduce problems with verbalization, but present a different set of issues. Even for simple evaluative scales, such as a 1–5 smiley face scale, there are concerns that young children use only the extreme scale points (Karsten & John, 1994). For more complex scales, researchers often design statements that can be easily misinterpreted by young children. For example, in measuring materialism, we might ask young children to agree or disagree with the following statement: "Money can buy happiness." Although similar statements are used to measure materialism in adults, the meaning is different for young children. Youngsters often take the statement quite literally, agreeing with the statement because money can buy many things they like, such as candy and toys. Oddly enough, rating scales can also be problematic at the other end of the age continuum. Here, the issue centers on social desirability bias among teenagers that are eager to present a positive face to interviewers. For examples, statements such as "Money can buy happiness" are quite transparent in intent, which may be more of a concern with adolescents who are eager to answer in a socially acceptable fashion.

In light of these difficulties, more attention needs to be given to developing new measures and measurement techniques for children and adolescents. First, when using rating scales, more careful attention needs to be paid to validating the scales across age groups. Examples of recent efforts in this vein can be found in areas such as children's attitudes toward advertising (Derbaix & Pecheux, 2003) and children's materialism (Goldberg et al., 2003). Second, newer measurement techniques need to be developed to supplement more traditional forms of questioning. For example, collages have been particularly useful in measuring constructs such as children's self-concepts and materialism (Chaplin & John, 2005, 2007). Young children are familiar with collages and can express themselves with modest amounts of verbalization; for older children, the collage task allows the researcher to be less transparent, diminishing social desirability bias. Finally, researchers need to seek out opportunities to assess children's consumer behavior in more naturalistic settings. Examples include studies of children's requests for Christmas presents (Otnes et al., 1994) and decision-making research using choice games and gift choices (Gregan-Paxton & John, 1995; Wartella et al., 1979).

These methodological challenges dictate a degree of creativity and attention to detail far beyond those ever encountered in research with adult consumers. However, the rewards are considerable. Understanding consumer socialization will continue to be a topic of importance for many reasons. No other area of consumer behavior research is so focused on the process and outcomes of consumer learning that evolve over time. No other consumer segment has changed as much in purchasing power and influence in the last decade than the children and teen segment. Finally, there is probably no topic in consumer research that holds as much interest from a public policy and societal perspective, especially given recent concerns over the consumption of alcohol, tobacco, and unhealthy foods. We look forward to meeting the challenges to produce a greater understanding of consumer socialization in the future.

REFERENCES

Achenreiner, G. B. (1997). Materialistic values and susceptibility to influence in children. In M. Brucks & D. J. MacInnis (Eds.), *Advances in consumer research* (Vol. 24, pp. 82–88). Provo, UT: Association for Consumer Research.

Achenreiner, G. B., & John, D. R. (2003). The meaning of brand names to children: A developmental investigation. *Journal of Consumer Psychology, 13,* 205–219.

Adler, R. P., Lesser, G. S., Meringoff, L., Robertson, T. S., Rossiter, J. R., & Ward, S. (Eds.) (1980). *Research on the effects of television advertising on children.* Lexington, MA: Lexington Books.

Atkin, C. K. (1978). Observation of parent–child interaction in supermarket decision-making. *Journal of Marketing, 42,* 41–45.

Bahn, K. D. (1986). How and when do brand perceptions and preferences first form? A cognitive developmental investigation. *Journal of Consumer Research, 13,* 382–393.

Baker, S. M., & Gentry, J. W. (1996). Kids as collectors: A phenomenological study of first and fifth graders. In K. P. Corfman & J. G. Lynch, Jr. (Eds.), *Advances in consumer research* (Vol. 23, pp. 132–137). Provo, UT: Association for Consumer Research.

Barenboim, C. (1981). The development of person perception in childhood and adolescence: From behavioral comparisons to psychological constructs to psychological comparisons. *Child Development, 52,*129–144.

Belch, G., Belch, M. A., & Ceresino, G. (1985). Parental and teenage influences in family decision making. *Journal of Business Research, 13,* 163–176.

Belk, R. W., Bahn, K. D., & Mayer, R. N. (1982). Developmental recognition of consumption symbolism. *Journal of Consumer Research, 9,* 4–17.

Belk, R. W., Mayer, R., & Driscoll, A. (1984). Children's recognition of consumption symbolism in children's products. *Journal of Consumer Research, 10,* 386–397.

Bereby-Meyer, Y., Assor, A., & Katz, I. (2004). Children's choice strategies: The effects of age and task demands. *Cognitive Development, 19,* 127–146.

Berey, L. A., & Pollay, R. W. (1968). The influencing role of the child in family decision making. *Journal of Marketing Research, 5,* 70–72.

Berti, A., & Bombi, A. (1988). *The child's construction of economics.* New York: Cambridge University Press.

Bever, T. G., Smith, M. L., Bengen, B., & Johnson, T. G. (1975). Young viewers' troubling response to TV ads. *Harvard Business Review, 53,* 109–120.

Blosser, B. J., & Roberts, D. F. (1985). Age differences in children's perceptions of message intent: Responses to TV news, commercials, educational spots, and public service announcements. *Communication Research, 12,* 455–484.

Boush, D. M., Friestad, & Rose, G. M. (1994). Adolescent skepticism toward TV advertising and knowledge of advertiser tactics. *Journal of Consumer Research, 21,* 165–175.

Brucks, M., Armstrong, G. M., & Goldberg, M. E. (1988). Children's use of cognitive defenses against television advertising: A cognitive response approach. *Journal of Consumer Research, 14,* 471–482.

Butter, E. J., Popovich, P. M., Stackhouse, R. H., & Garner, R. K. (1981). Discrimination of television programs and commercials by preschool children. *Journal of Advertising Research, 21,* 53–56.

Capon, N., & Kuhn, D. (1980). A developmental study of consumer information-processing strategies. *Journal of Consumer Research, 7,* 225–233.

Cateora, P. R. (1963). *An analysis of the teenage market.* Austin, TX: University of Texas Bureau of Business Research.

Chaplin, L. N., & John, D. R. (2005). The development of self-brand connections in children and adolescents. *Journal of Consumer Research, 32,* 119–129.

Chaplin, L. N., & John, D. R. (2007). Growing up in a material world: Age differences in materialism in children and adolescents. *Journal of Consumer Research, 34,* first published electronically June 12, 2007.

Christenson, P. G. (1982). Children's perceptions of TV commercials and products: The effects of PSAs. *Communication Research, 9,* 491–524.

Corfman, K., & Harlam, B. (1997). Relative influence of parent and child in the purchase of products for children. Working paper, Marketing Department, New York University, New York, NY.

Darley, W. F., & Lim, J. (1986). Family decision making in leisure-time activities: An exploratory analysis of the impact of locus of control, child age influence factor and parental type on perceived child influence. In R. J. Lutz (Ed.), *Advances in consumer research* (Vol. 13, pp. 370–374). Provo, UT: Association for Consumer Research.

Davidson, D. (1991a). Children's decision-making examined with an information-board procedure. *Cognitive Development, 6,* 77–90.

Davidson, D. (1991b). Developmental differences in children's search of predecisional information. *Journal of Experimental Child Psychology, 52,* 239–255.

Davidson, D., & Hudson, J. (1988). The effects of decision reversibility and decision importance on children's decision making. *Journal of Experimental Child Psychology, 46,* 35–40.

Derbaix, C., & Pecheux, C. (2003). A new scale to assess children's attitude toward TV advertising. *Journal of Advertising Research, 43,* 390–399.

Derscheid, L. E., Kwon, Y., & Fang, S. (1996). Preschoolers' socialization as consumers of clothing and recognition of symbolism. *Perceptual and Motor Skills, 82,* 1171–1181.

Fournier, S. (1998). Consumers and their brands: Developing relationship theory in consumer research. *Journal of Consumer Research, 24,* 343–373.

Fox, K. F.A., & Kehret-Ward, T. (1985). Theories of value and understanding of price: A developmental perspective. In E. C. Hirschman & M. B. Holbrook (Eds.), *Advances in consumer research* (Vol. 12, pp. 79–84). Provo, UT: Association for Consumer Research.

Fox, K. F.A., & Kehret-Ward, T. (1990). Naive theories of price: A developmental model. *Psychology & Marketing, 7,* 311–329.

Foxman, E. R., & Tansuhaj, P. S. (1988). Adolescents' and mothers' perceptions of relative influence in family purchase decisions: Patterns of agreement and disagreement. In M. J. Houston (Ed.), *Advances in consumer research* (Vol. 15, pp. 449–453). Provo, UT: Association for Consumer Research.

Foxman, E. R., Tansuhaj, P. S., & Ekstrom, K. (1989). Family members' perceptions of adolescents' influence in family decision making. *Journal of Consumer Research, 15,* 482–491.

Friestad, M., & Wright, P. (1994). The persuasion knowledge model: How people cope with persuasion attempts. *Journal of Consumer Research, 21,* 1–31.

Ginsburg, H. P., & Opper, S. (1988). *Piaget's theory of intellectual development.* Englewood Cliffs, NJ: Prentice-Hall.

Goldberg, M. E., & Gorn, G. J. (1978). Some unintended consequences of TV advertising to children. *Journal of Consumer Research, 5,* 22–29.

Goldberg, M. E., Gorn, G. J., Peracchio, L. A., & Bamossy, G. (2003). Understanding materialism among youth. *Journal of Consumer Psychology, 13,* 278–288.

Gregan-Paxton, J., & John, D. R. (1995). Are young children adaptive decision makers? A study of age differences in information search behavior. *Journal of Consumer Research, 21,* 567–580.

Gregan-Paxton, J., & John, D. R. (1997). The emergence of adaptive decision making in children. *Journal of Consumer Research, 24,* 43–56.

Guest, L. P. (1955). Brand loyalty—Twelve years later. *Journal of Applied Psychology, 39,* 405–408.

Haynes, J., Burts, D. C., Dukes, A., & Cloud. R. (1993). Consumer socialization of preschoolers and kindergartners as related to clothing consumption. *Psychology & Marketing, 10,* 151–166.

Hite, C. F., & Hite, R. E. (1995). Reliance on brand by young children. *Journal of the Market Research Society, 37,* 185–193.

Howse, R. B., Best, D. L., & Stone, E. R. (2003). Children's decision making: The effects of training, reinforcement, and memory aids. *Cognitive Development, 18,* 247–268.

Isler, L., Popper, E. T., & Ward, S. (1987). Children's purchase requests and parental responses: Results from a diary study. *Journal of Advertising Research, 27,* 28–39.

Jamison, D. J. (1996). Idols of the tribe: Brand veneration and group identity among pre-adolescent consumers. Working paper, Department of Marketing, University of Florida, Gainesville, FL.

Jenkins, R. L. (1979). The influence of children in family decision-making: Parents' perceptions. In W. L. Wilkie (Ed.), *Advances in consumer research* (Vol. 6, pp. 413–418). Ann Arbor, MI: Association for Consumer Research.

John, D. R., & Lakshmi-Ratan, R. (1992). Age differences in children's choice behavior: The impact of available alternatives. *Journal of Marketing Research, 29,* 216–226.

John, D. R., & Sujan, M. (1990). Age differences in product categorization. *Journal of Consumer Research, 16,* 452–460.

John, D. R., & Whitney, J. C., Jr. (1986). The development of consumer knowledge in children: A cognitive structure approach. *Journal of Consumer Research, 12,* 406–417.

Karsten, Y. M. C. (1996). *A dynamic systems approach to the development of consumer knowledge: Children's understanding of monetary knowledge.* Unpublished dissertation, University of Minnesota, Minneapolis, MN.

Karsten, Y. C., & John, D. R. (1994). Measuring young children's preferences: The use of behaviorally-anchored rating scales. Cambridge, MA: Marketing Science Institute.

Keiser, S. K. (1975). Awareness of brands and slogans. *Journal of Advertising Research, 15,* 37–43.

Kim, C., Lee, H., & Hall, K. (1991). A study of adolescents' power, influence strategy, and influence on family purchase decisions. In T. L. Childers (Ed.), *1991 AMA winter educators' conference proceedings* (pp. 37–45). Chicago: American Marketing Association.

Klayman, J. (1985). Children's decision strategies and their adaptation to task characteristics. *Organizational Behavior and Human Decision Processes, 35,* 179–201.

Klees, D. M., Olson, J., & Wilson, R. D. (1988). An analysis of the content and organization of children's knowledge structures. In M. J. Houston (Ed.), *Advances in consumer research* (Vol. 15, pp. 153–157). Provo, UT: Association for Consumer Research.

Lawlor, M., & Prothero, A. (2003). Children's understanding of television advertising intent. *Journal of Marketing Management, 19,* 411–431.

Levin, S. R., Petros, T. V., & Petrella, F. W. (1982). Preschoolers' awareness of television advertising. *Child Development, 53,* 933–937.

Macklin, M. C. (1985). Do young children understand the selling intent of commercials?" *Journal of Consumer Affairs, 19,* 293–304.

Macklin, M. C. (1996). Preschoolers' learning of brand names from visual cues. *Journal of Consumer Research, 23,* 251–261.

Mallalieu, L., Palan, K., & Laczniak, R. N. (2005). Understanding children's knowledge and beliefs about advertising: A global issue that spans generations. *Journal of Current Issues and Research in Advertising, 27,* 53–64.

Manchanda, R. V., & Moore-Shay, E. S. (1996). Mom, I want that! The effects of parental style, gender and materialism on children's choice of influence strategy. In E. A. Blair & W. A. Kamakura (Eds.), *1996 AMA winter educators' conference proceedings* (pp. 81–90). Chicago, IL: American Marketing Association.

Marshall, H. R. (1964). The relation of giving children an allowance to children's money knowledge and responsibility and to other practices of parents. *Journal of Genetic Psychology, 104,* 35–51.

Marshall, H. R., MacGruder, L. (1960). Relations between parent money education practices and children's knowledge and use of money. *Child Development, 31,* 253–284.

Mayer, R. N., & Belk, R. (1982). Acquisition of consumption stereotypes by children. *The Journal of Consumer Affairs, 16,* 307–321.

McNeal, J. U. (1964). *Children as consumers.* Austin, TX: Bureau of Business Research, University of Texas at Austin.

McNeal, J. U. (1992). *Kids as customers.* New York: Lexington Books.

McNeal, J. U., & McDaniel, S. W. (1981). Children's perceptions of retail stores: An exploratory study. *Akron Business and Economics Review, 12,* 39–42.

Moore, E. S., & Lutz, R. J. (2000). Children, advertising, and product experiences: A multi-method inquiry. *Journal of Consumer Research, 27,* 31–48.

Moore, R. L., & Stephens, L. F. (1975). Some communication and demographic determinants of adolescent consumer learning. *Journal of Consumer Research, 2,* 80–92.

Moschis, G. P., & Mitchell, L. G. (1986). Television advertising and interpersonal influences on teenagers' participation in family consumer decisions. In R. J. Lutz (Ed.), *Advances in consumer research* (Vol. 13, pp. 181–186). Provo, UT: Association for Consumer Research.

Moschis, G. P., & Moore, R. L. (1979). Decision making among the young: A socialization perspective. *Journal of Consumer Research, 6,* 101–112.

Nakajima, Y., & Hotta, M. (1989). A developmental study of cognitive processes in decision making: Information searching as a function of task complexity. *Psychological Reports, 64,* 67–79.

Nelson, J. E. (1979). Children as information sources in family decision to eat out. In W. L. Wilkie (Ed.), *Advances in consumer research* (Vol. 6, pp. 419–423). Ann Arbor, MI: Association for Consumer Research.

Otnes, C., Kim, Y. C., & Kim, K. (1994). All I want for Christmas: An analysis of children's brand requests to Santa Claus. *Journal of Popular Culture, 27,* 183–194.

Paget, K. F., Kritt, D., & Bergemann, L. (1984). Understanding strategic interactions in television commercials: A developmental study. *Journal of Applied Developmental Psychology, 5,* 145–161.

Palan, K. M., & Wilkes, R. E. (1997). Adolescent-parent interaction in family decision making. *Journal of Consumer Research, 24,* 159–169.

Palmer, E. L., & McDowell, C. N. (1979). Program/commercial separators in children's television programming. *Journal of Communication, 29,* 197–201.

Payne, J., Bettman, J. R., & Johnson, E. J. (1993). *The adaptive decision maker.* Cambridge: Cambridge University Press.

Peracchio, L. A. (1992). How do young children learn to be consumers? A script-processing approach. *Journal of Consumer Research, 18,* 425–440.

Peracchio, L. A. (1993). Young children's processing of a televised narrative: Is a picture really worth a thousand words? *Journal of Consumer Research, 20,* 281–293.

Pine, K. J., & Veasey, T. (2003). Conceptualising and assessing young children's knowledge of television advertising within a framework of implicit and explicit knowledge. *Journal of Marketing Management, 19,* 459–473.

Popper, E. T. (1979). Mothers mediation of children's purchase requests. In N. Beckwith, M. J. Houston, R. Mittelstaedt, K. B. Monroe, & S. Ward (Eds), *1979 AMA educators' proceedings* (pp. 645–648). Chicago: American Marketing Association.

Reisman, D., & Roseborough, H. (1955). Careers and consumer behavior. In L. Clark (Ed.), *Consumer behavior Vol. II, The life cycle and consumer behavior* (pp. 1–18). New York: New York University Press.

Ritson, M., & Elliott, R. (1999). The social uses of advertising: An ethnographic study of adolescent advertising audiences. *Journal of Consumer Research, 26,* 260–277.

Robertson, T. S., & Rossiter, J. R. (1974). Children and commercial persuasion: An attribution theory analysis. *Journal of Consumer Research, 1,* 13–20.

Roedder, D. L. (1981). Age differences in children's responses to television advertising: An information processing approach. *Journal of Consumer Research, 8,* 144–53.

Roedder, D. L., Sternthal, B., & Calder, B. J. (1983). Attitude-behavior consistency in children's responses to television advertising. *Journal of Marketing Research, 20,* 337–349.

Ross, R. P., Campbell, T., Wright, J. C., Huston, A. C., Rice, M. L., & Turk, P. (1984). When celebrities talk, children listen: An experimental analysis of children's responses to TV ads with celebrity endorsement. *Journal of Applied Developmental Psychology, 5,* 185–202.

Rossiter, J. R. (1976). Visual and verbal memory in children's product information utilization. In B. B. Anderson (Ed.), *Advances in consumer research,* (Vol. 3, pp. 572–576). Ann Arbor, MI: Association for Consumer Research.

Rossiter, J. R., & Robertson, T. S. (1976). Canonical analysis of developmental, social, and experiential factors in children's comprehension of television advertising. *Journal of Genetic Psychology, 129,* 317–327.

Rubin, R. S. (1974). The effects of cognitive development on children's responses to television advertising. *Journal of Business Research, 2,* 409–419.

Rust, L. (1993). Observations: Parents and children shopping together. *Journal of Advertising Research, 33,* 65–70.

Selman, R. L. (1980). *The growth of interpersonal understanding.* New York: Academic Press.

Siegler, R. S., & Jenkins, E. (1989). *How children discover new strategies.* Hillsdale, NJ: Erlbaum.

Stephens, L., & Moore, R. L. (1975). Price accuracy as a consumer skill. *Journal of Advertising Research, 15,* 27–34.

Stephens, N., & Stutts, M. A. (1982). Preschoolers' ability to distinguish between television programming and commercials. *Journal of Advertising, 11,* 16–26.

Strauss, A. (1952). The development and transformation of monetary meanings in the child. *American Sociological Review, 17,* 275–286.

Stutts, M. A., Vance, D., & Hudleson, S. (1981). Program-commercial separators in children's television: Do they help a child tell the difference between *Bugs Bunny* and the *Quick Rabbit? Journal of Advertising, 10,* 16–25.

Swinyard, W. R., & Sim, C. P. (1987). Perception of children's influence on family decision processes. *Journal of Consumer Marketing, 4,* 25–38.

Tootelian, D. H., & Gaedeke, R. M. (1992). The teen market: An exploratory analysis of income, spending, and shopping patterns. *The Journal of Consumer Marketing, 9,* 35–44.

U.S. Department of Health and Human Services (1995). *National Institute on Alcohol Abuse and Alcoholism, Monograph 28.* Bethesda, MD: National Institute on Alcohol Abuse and Alcoholism.

U.S. Department of Health and Human Services (1994). *Preventing tobacco use among young people: A report of the Surgeon General,* Atlanta, GA: U.S. Department of Health and Human Services, Public Health Service, Centers for Disease Control and Prevention, Office on Smoking and Health.

Ward, S. (1972). Children's reactions to commercials. *Journal of Advertising Research, 12,* 37–45.

Ward, S., & Wackman, D. B. (1972). Children's purchase influence attempts and parental yielding. *Journal of Marketing Research, 9,* 316–319.

Ward, S., Wackman, D. B., & Wartella, E. (1977). *How children learn to buy.* Beverly Hills, CA: Sage Publications.

Wartella, E., Wackman, D. B., Ward, S., Shamir, J., & Alexander, A. (1979). The young child as consumer. In E. Wartella (Ed.), *Children communicating: Media and development of thought, speech, understanding.* Beverly Hills, CA: Sage.

Wells, W. D., & LoSciuto, L. A. (1966). Direct observation of purchasing behavior. *Journal of Marketing Research, 3,* 227–233.

Wright, P., Friestad, M., & Boush, D. M. (2005). The development of marketplace persuasion knowledge in children, adolescents, and young adults. *Journal of Public Policy & Marketing, 24,* 222–233.

Young, B. M. (1990). *Television advertising and children.* New York: Oxford University Press.

9

Aging and Consumer Behavior

Carolyn Yoon

University of Michigan

Catherine A. Cole

University of Iowa

INTRODUCTION AND BACKGROUND

Until recently, most businesses and marketing researchers have virtually ignored the older market. Perhaps this neglect stemmed from inaccurate stereotypes about older consumers so that they were routinely written off as poor, overly frugal, or already set in their loyalty to brands. These stereotypes about older people, however, appear to be falling slowly by the wayside. For example, recent research conducted by the American Association of Retired Persons (AARP) suggests that for most products, the majority of older adults are not loyal to a single brand (AARP Report, 2002).

Increasingly, businesses, governmental agencies, and researchers are recognizing that older consumers comprise a segment that is generally substantial, identifiable, and accessible—key requirements for selecting target segments. For example, in the business area, the travel industry has found that compared to other age groups, senior travelers are an important target market because of their relative wealth, discretionary income, low consumer debt, and available free time (Littrel, Paige, & Song, 2004).

Today, there are about 35 million people over the age of 65; by 2010, this number is expected to reach 50 million. By the year 2020, one out of every six Americans will be 65 or older. Whereas the U.S. population used to be represented by a pyramid, with a broad young base that tapered off to a point at the top with extreme age, we have in more recent years seen a "rectangularization" of the age pyramid with greater life expectancy and lower birth rates (Long, 1998).

Not only is the size of the senior population increasing, its financial and health characteristics are improving. For example, the AARP reports that in the past decade, Americans aged 50 and over have seen their economic status improve where status is measured in terms of median inflation adjusted income and household financial assets. Additionally, in the same time period, the proportion of family budgets available for discretionary items has increased for the 50+ population overall (AARP Report, 2005).

Technological Changes

Contrary to stereotypes, older adults appear to be interested in using new technologies (Rogers & Fisk, 2000). However, learning to use new technological products may provide particular challenges to the elderly. Rogers, Meyer, Walker, and Fisk (1998) conducted a focus group study of healthy and active older adults (aged 65 to 88) in which they investigated the effects of changes in the environment and new technology. They found that the elderly faced a variety of challenges from new technologies; participants reported problems with a broad range of technologies including answering machines, home security systems, computerized telephone menus, multiple-line telephones, and computers.

For many years, marketing practitioners thought that older adults lagged behind younger adults in adopting new technologies. However, recent data suggest that this belief may be based on a negative stereotype rather than reality. Studies, investigating how age and attitudinal characteristics affect consumers' willingness to adopt new products, found that older consumers were as likely, or more likely, to adopt some new technological products (e.g., automatic bill payment, electronic funds transfer; Gilly & Zeithaml, 1985; Kolodinsky, Hogarth, & Hilgert, 2004). The studies concluded that like other consumers, seniors do purchase product innovations when they possess clear benefits and meet specific needs.

As older consumers encounter new technologies, they may be vulnerable to fraudulent marketing practices. On the one hand, older consumers may develop greater persuasion knowledge than younger adults through experience. Persuasion knowledge is knowledge about persuasion tactics and methods of resisting persuasion attempts (Friestad & Wright, 1994). With this rich knowledge base, older consumers should be able to resist persuasive efforts better than younger consumers. On the other hand, unlike younger adults, older consumers may not easily update their persuasion knowledge as technology changes. In addition, recent empirical work indicates that when cognitive capacity is constrained, younger consumers are less likely to recruit persuasion knowledge (Campbell & Kirmani, 2000). Thus, older adults, who may have more limited processing capacity than younger adults, may have difficulty using their persuasion knowledge, especially if the information is presented rapidly on a new technology (e.g., an advertisement on the Internet). As a result, new research is needed on the circumstances in which older adults can recruit relevant persuasion knowledge to resist persuasion efforts.

Hearings before the U.S. Senate's Special Committee on Aging (2000), which focused on Internet fraud and seniors, revealed that 59% of people aged 50 to 64, and 22% of those over 65, had become Internet users. Unfortunately, law enforcement agencies have witnessed a growth in reports of older adults being taken in by fraudulent online activities such as identify theft, "phishing" schemes in which criminals set up emails and websites designed to look like those of legitimate companies and financial institutions, nondelivery of merchandise, and investment fraud.

Heterogeneity of Older Adults

Older adults comprise a heterogeneous group. At a minimum, there are important cohort differences among seniors of different ages. For example, older adults who are currently in their mid-80s grew up during the Depression era, whereas those in their 60s and 70s reached adulthood during the post-World War II era, a period that was characterized by greater consumerism.

In the developmental psychology literature, researchers have distinguished among "young-old" (65 to about 75 years), "old-old" (75 to about 85) and "very-old" or "oldest-old" (over 85; e.g., Smith & Baltes, 1997). While most "young-old" people remain in relatively good health, physical decline usually becomes more evident in the "old-old" and may progress rapidly among the "very-old." These distinctions notwithstanding, there is no set agreement regarding the age at which a person is considered "old." Although in the consumer domain, an older person has been most commonly defined as someone over 65 years old, others have defined older adults as those over 60, and some have even begun considering those over 50 as senior consumers.

Segmentation schemes for the mature market might include age, income, education, personality and lifestyle variables. Along these lines, the Center for Mature Consumer Studies has developed a segmentation model known as "gerontographics" which segments the mature market based on aging processes and life circumstances (Moschis, 1996). Consumer behavior, such as patronization of specific food or grocery stores, has been found to vary across these gerontographic segments (Moschis, Curasi, & Bellenger, 2004).

Despite growing interest in the topic of older consumers, there are still relatively few studies that focus on aging and consumer behavior. In this chapter, we consider the aspects of aging that seem particularly relevant for consumer behavior and identify promising avenues for future research. In doing so, we provide a selective review of the literature that informs our understanding of older adults in consumer contexts. In particular, we discuss some physiological, cognitive, and socio-emotional changes that accompany aging and consider their implications for consumer decision making.

PHYSIOLOGICAL CHANGES

As people age, they experience physiological changes which, in turn, can affect the way they interact with the consumer environment. Problems with visual and auditory functions increase markedly with age, typically beginning in the fourth decade of life (Schieber & Baldwin, 1996; Willott, 1991). These changes can have dramatic effects on older adults' attention and cognition. In many cases, it may not be possible to fully restore visual and auditory functions to levels of younger adults through surgery or use of prostheses (e.g., contact lenses, eyeglasses, hearing aids). Motor control also declines in older adults. These declines include changes in the peripheral and central nervous system, and changes in control and coordination of motor functions that can lead to an array of behavioral decrements (Ketcham & Stelmach, 2003).

Vision

Approximately half of all adults over 65 years old have cataracts (Fozard & Gordon-Salant, 2001). As people age, size of the pupil declines and the lens becomes more opaque (Weale, 1961). The loss of transparency is particularly pronounced for short wavelengths (e.g., blue, green light) due to age-related yellowing of the lens. Moreover, age-related declines in visual acuity (an indicator of how well fine spatial detail can be recognized) become more severe when there is low luminance or the stimuli are low in contrast. However, color constancy mechanisms appear to remain relatively intact in older adults, possibly minimizing decrements on familiar real-world tasks performed in well-lighted conditions.

Age-related changes in vision suggest that the way in which information is presented or displayed can affect whether or not it is processed. For instance, messages and displays that appear clear, bright, and attractive to a younger person are likely to be fuzzy, dark, and unpleasant to an older one. In most cases, better illumination, higher contrasts, and reduced glare will help older consumers. Also because older adults tend to make less use of their peripheral fields than younger adults, managers may wish to place brands close to consumers' direct line of sight in retail environments.

Hearing

Older adults find it progressively more difficult to detect simple, low-intensity sounds, discriminate small changes in frequency or intensity, filter out background noise, and identify the source of a target noise in space (Schneider & Pichora-Fuller, 2000). Older adults in conversations also have more difficulty processing phonemes than syllables. These changes are not only likely to compromise listening, but they can negatively affect the ability to encode information in many consumer situations. It suggests that sound and sound clutter can be problematic for older adults in consumer environments over which they do not have control.

Motor Functions

Motor behavior refers to muscular actions performed to fulfill some objective of the performer (e.g., braking a car, pushing lawn mover, hitting a golf ball). Normally aging people are capable of performing many motor behaviors in everyday life well into their 80s. However, they have much slower reaction times, in some cases as much as 50% slower on complex tasks (Cerella, 1990; Salthouse, 1996).

Age-related changes in motor functions have important implications for product design and usability in consumer domains. For example, individual programming of devices becomes increasingly difficult due to declines in vision and poorer ability to handle very small objects. Use of a computer mouse has been found to pose a major impediment to computer usage among older adults (Walker, Philbin, & Fisk, 1997). It is thus important that there be development of more user-friendly means by which older adults can interface with smaller gadgets including items such as hearing aids and cell phones. A few studies have investigated the benefits of devices that improve the speed and accuracy of movements as well as coordination and balance in older adults (e.g., Maki et al., 1999). However, much work remains to be done in the design and development of assistive devices and technologies.

MEMORY

Another arena in which there is a great deal of age-related changes is memory processes. Although there is widespread agreement that aging negatively affects performance on most memory tasks, there is not as much consensus about when and why age-related differences in memory occur (Craik & Jennings, 1992; Kausler, 1994; Light, 1991; Schaie, 2005). Memory impairments that have been documented in the laboratory may not necessarily extend to everyday domains of behavior (Zacks, Hasher, & Li, 2000). In addition, not all aspects of memory are impaired (e.g., Rahhal, May, & Hasher, 2002; Schacter, Kihlstrom, Kaszniak, & Valdiserri, 1993). In this section we review the literature with respect to changes in memory.

Theoretical Perspectives

Three main theoretical perspectives have been advanced to account for age-related memory changes: speed of processing (e.g., Salthouse, 1996), reduced processing resources (e.g., Craik, 1986), and diminished inhibition (e.g., Hasher & Zacks, 1988). Although the theoretical accounts do share substantial conceptual overlap, they have tended to be discussed separately in the literature. Each is considered in turn, along with a discussion of empirical studies from psychology, neuroscience, and marketing that shed light on cognitive functioning of older adults.

Speed of processing

According to the speed of processing view, aging is accompanied by a general slowing of mental functioning (Cerella, 1985). There is substantial evidence that speed of working memory slows down across the lifespan (Salthouse, 1996). In particular, Salthouse argues that general processing speed serves as a mediator between age and cognitive performance on a variety of tasks. Although it is clear that older adults process information at a slower rate than younger adults, and that speed is an important explanatory variable, it is unlikely to provide a comprehensive theoretical account of cognitive aging. Factors other than speed (e.g., executive functions) frequently emerge as significant mediators of age-related differences in memory and fluid-intelligence tasks. For example, Hedden and Yoon (2006) found significant age differences in performance on tasks requiring critical executive functions such as shifting between relevant goals and/or updating representations in working memory.

Reduced processing resources

The reduced processing resources view arguably represents the most dominant theoretical account of age-related changes in memory performance (Craik, 1983, 1986). It suggests that reduced cognitive resources impair older adults' ability to engage in more cognitively demanding strategies such as deep, elaborate encoding operations which facilitate later memory retrieval (e.g., Cole & Houston, 1987; Craik & Byrd, 1982; Law, Hawkins, & Craik, 1998; Yoon, 1997).

A substantial proportion of the age-related decline in cognitive resources has been explained by deterioration in working memory (the ability to process small amounts of information for short periods of time while engaging in ongoing cognitive activities such as reading, listening, problem solving, reasoning or thinking) (Moscovitch & Winocur, 1992). In studies assessing span measures which are often taken as indicators of working memory capacity, older adults perform reliably worse than younger adults (Verhaeghen, Marcoen, & Goosens, 1993).

Age-related changes in working memory are associated with changes in executive functions (see West, 1996, for a review; Craik & Jennings 1992; Park et al., 1996). Executive functions of cognition are defined as the ability to schedule and optimize subsidiary processes. They include such mechanisms as shifting between active and inactive rules or task goals, updating the current contents of working memory to reflect task-relevance, and the inhibition or suppression of inappropriate or prepotent responses (Andrés 2003; Aron, Robbins, & Poldrack, 2004; Miyake et al., 2000). Recent neuroimaging evidence suggests that executive subcomponent mechanisms rely on distinct neural regions within a shared frontal-parietal network, the very same regions that are the most highly affected during the developmental processes of normal aging (see Hedden & Gabrieli, 2004, for a review).

A common finding is that across the adult lifespan, the prefrontal cortex exhibits volumetric declines that are larger than those in many connected regions, including parietal cortex and medial temporal structures such as the hippocampus and amygdala. Indeed, the largest age-related volume declines are in the lateral prefrontal cortex, which is functionally implicated in a variety of executive function tasks. Although the lateral prefrontal cortex is unlikely to be the sole site of executive processes, it is undoubtedly an important part of the neural circuits underlying several executive functions (Fuster, 2002). Supporting this interpretation, older adults display deficits in performance on a variety of neuropsychological tests of executive function (Bryan & Luszcz, 2000).

The similarity between the behavioral deficits exhibited by frontal patients with dysexecutive syndrome and those exhibited by healthy older adults led to the development of the frontal aging hypothesis (Moscovitch & Winocur, 1995; West, 1996). According to this hypothesis, age-related declines in prefrontal structures impair the ability of older adults to monitor and control processes subserved by other brain regions that may be less affected by normal aging (Hedden & Gabrieli, 2004). In support of this hypothesis, several neuroimaging studies have found that age-related changes in functional activity in the prefrontal cortex are associated with changes in activity in posterior and medial temporal regions during the performance of tasks of executive control in working memory and successful episodic encoding (Daselaar, Veltman, Rombouts, Raaijmakers, & Jonker, 2003; Grady, McIntosh, Bookstein, Horwitz, Rapoport, & Haxby, 1998; Gutchess et al., 2005).

Thus the neural and behavioral data appear to point to particular difficulties for older consumers on tasks that draw on the ability to maintain and manipulate information in working memory. For example, tracking and integrating new product information is likely to be challenging. Maintaining and manipulating multiple pieces of information in a noisy environments would also be more difficult for older than younger adults.

Interestingly, however, not all older adults exhibit marked declines in performance of executive function tasks. In fact, some older adults perform nearly as well as their younger counterparts (e.g., Hedden & Park, 2003). These "successful agers" tend to exhibit high performance on neuropsychological tasks thought to measure frontal functions (Glisky, Rubin, & Davidson, 2001). High performing older adults have been found to engage the prefrontal cortex regions bilaterally; and this has led to suggestions that high-performing older adults may counteract age-related neural decline by recruiting through a plastic reorganization of neurocognitive networks (Cabeza et al., 1997; Reuter-Lorenz et al., 2000).

Diminished inhibition

The third major theoretical account of age-related memory changes posits that inhibitory processing is impaired for older adults (Duchek, Balota, & Ferraro, 1995; Hasher & Zacks, 1988). The inhibitory framework assumes that the occurrence of familiar stimuli in the environment will activate the associated linkages including those irrelevant to the task at hand. Among those representations that have received some degree of activation, conscious awareness is assumed to be restricted to the most highly activated subset (cf. Cowan, 1988; 1993), which is referred to as the contents of working memory (Hasher, Zacks, & May, 1999).

Inhibitory mechanisms are critical for controlling the contents of working memory. They enable efficient on-line processing and subsequent successful retrieval of target information by preventing irrelevant information from entering working memory and deleting from working memory no longer relevant information. These two functions, access and deletion, minimize competition from distracting material during both encoding and retrieval, thus increasing the likelihood that items activated concurrently in working memory are relevant to one another, and that target information will be successfully processed and retrieved. Finally, inhibition operates to restrain strong responses from being emitted before their appropriateness can be evaluated. The restraint function of inhibition thus allows for the appraisal and rejection of dominant responses when they are undesirable, so that a less-probable but more suitable response can be produced.

There are direct consequences of diminished inhibition for cognition for older adults. For example, older individuals with impaired inhibitory functioning are susceptible to distracting, irrelevant information, whether that distraction is generated from external sources (e.g., from a radio program playing in the background) or internal sources (e.g., personal concerns) (Hartman & Hasher, 1991; Hamm & Hasher, 1992). This is particularly pronounced when people attempt to retrieve proper names (Maylor, 1990) and is consistent with other evidence indicating that name retrieval failure is a frequent subjective complaint by older adults.

In addition, the inability to clear away previously relevant but currently inappropriate information may lead to heightened interference between relevant and irrelevant information for poor inhibitors, resulting in difficulties in acquiring new material, comprehending questions, and retrieving stored memories. Poor inhibitors may also have difficulty disengaging from one line of thought or activity and switching to another, as well as in preventing the production of well-learned responses when those responses are inappropriate. Prior studies have also shown that older adults are more susceptible to interference than younger adults in a variety of domains including dual-task interference (Verhaeghen, Steitz, Sliwinski, & Cerella, 2003), global task switching (Verhaeghen & Cerella, 2002), retroactive interference (the effect of new material on memory for old) in working memory (Hedden & Park, 2001; 2003), and proactive interference (the effect of old material on memory for new) in working memory (Bowles & Salthouse, 2003; Lustig, May, & Hasher, 2001; May, Hasher, & Kane, 1999) as well as long-term memory (Jacoby, Debner, & Hay, 2001).

These direct impairments, produced by deficient inhibitory functioning, may lead to other indirect cognitive consequences. Since lack of control over working memory also ultimately reduces the efficiency of retrieval, diminished inhibition efficiency can further lead to an increased reliance on stereotypes and use of heuristics in decision making, even in situations where detailed, analytical processing may be more appropriate.

Automatic vs. Controlled Processing

Prior empirical work on memory and aging suggests that while some aspects of memory performance decline with increasing age, other aspects of performance are relatively spared. For instance, we know that whereas episodic recall and source memory become poorer with increasing age (e.g., Spencer & Raz, 1995), semantic memory for well-learned or familiar information remains more intact (e.g., Morrow, Leirer, & Altieri, 1992; Zacks et al., 2000). Further, information that is implicitly learned or processed tends to be relatively spared across the lifespan (Howard & Howard, 1989; Light & Singh, 1987).

A way in which these patterns of findings have been interpreted is by distinguishing between automatic and controlled processes (see Zacks & Hasher, 1979). Automatic processes are considered to require little cognitive capacity (e.g., event frequency, word meaning), to be independent of conscious control, and to occur without deliberate effort. For example, studies comparing experts in chess, aviation, typing, and piano playing report preservation of expert knowledge in older adults (e.g., Krampe & Ericsson, 1996). Automatic processes do not interfere with ongoing cognitive activity and are relatively immune to the effects of increased age (cf. Light & Zelinski, 1983). By contrast, controlled processes place a strain on processing resources because they are intentionally and consciously processed and require effort. Given that effortful processing requires cognitive capacity that is reduced with age, memory tasks involving deliberate, self-initiated processing (e.g., free recall) is negatively affected by age (Craik, 1986; Craik, Anderson, Kerr, & Li, 1995).

These two processes have also been considered central to the idea underlying dual process models of memory. Within the dual process theories, the processes are, however, more commonly referred to as recollection and familiarity. Whereas recollection is typically considered as conscious, intentional, or attention demanding, familiarity is regarded as unconscious with low attentional requirements. Light, Prull, La Voie, and Healy (2000) recently conducted a meta-analysis of the evidence relating to the dual process view of memory in older adults and reported two main results. They found larger priming effects for younger than older adults. In addition, they found that age differences in priming tasks were considerably smaller than in recall and recognition tasks. Hence the Light et al. findings are generally consistent with the dual process view of memory in older adults.

Contextual Perspectives and Moderators

Contextual factors can modulate the degree to which there are age-related memory decrements. This perspective reflects a more functional approach to understanding age-related memory impairments and is often considered in conjunction with the limited resources view (e.g., Craik, 1983; 1986). According to this viewpoint, memory performance is a function of the interaction of external and internal factors. The external factors represent the amount of environmental support available at encoding and retrieval. As such, environmental support is broadly construed and includes dimensions such as instructional guidance to engage in deeper processing at encoding, the availability of relevant information at encoding and retrieval, and the provision of external retrieval cues that might enhance direct access to memory traces. Greater environmental support might thus be represented by any factor that provides more processing resources for a given task.

Internal factors also affect the processing resources a person has available for encoding and retrieval. The presumed age-related reduction in processing resources means that older adults are less able than younger adults to perform effortful encoding and retrieval tasks. The resource-demanding operations include self-initiated processes such as generation of new connections among items in unfamiliar domains and free recall of unrelated items with poor retrieval cues. However, strong environmental support, in the form familiar tasks and availability of external cues can compensate for age-related impairments in self-initiated processing (Craik, 1983, 1986; Craik & Byrd, 1982; Craik & McDowd, 1987; Craik & Anderson, 1999). Other researchers have also suggested a contextualist perspective on memory and aging (e.g., Baltes, Cornelius, & Nesselroade, 1979; Sinnott, 1989). More recently, Hess (2005) has elegantly argued for an approach that accounts for a broader array of influences including goals and social contexts.

Picture memory

The contextual view is relevant for understanding picture memory as well. Picture memory is relatively spared with age perhaps because of the unique, contextually-supported nature of the information. Although highly perceptually or conceptually similar items will still be forgotten, pictures that are semantically meaningful and complex can be remembered equivalently by younger and older adults (Park, Puglisi, & Smith, 1986; Park, Royal, Dudley, & Morrell, 1988; Smith, Park, Cherry, & Berkovsky, 1990). These results suggest the importance of providing environmental support, such as semantically meaningful or vivid pictorial memory cues, in order to reduce the strain on limited processing resources in older adults (Craik, 1986; Craik & Jennings, 1992; Park, Smith, Morrell, Puglisi, & Dudley, 1990; Smith, Park, Earles, Shaw, & Whiting, 1998). Interestingly, the increased reliance of elderly adults on contextual cues suggests that they could be disproportionately influenced by contextual variables that may not affect the decisions of their younger counterparts.

Schemas and prior knowledge

Older adults appear to exhibit reliable biases in how they are influenced by preexisting knowledge and schemas (e.g., Hess, Flannagan, & Tate, 1993; Koutstaal & Schacter, 1997; Yoon, 1997). Schemas can sometimes contribute to distorted recollections of past events, even though they also perform important organizing functions in our cognitive lives (Mandler, 1979). However, schemas are important in guiding memory retrieval, promoting memory for schema-relevant information, and allowing us to develop accurate expectations of events that are likely to unfold in familiar settings on the basis of past experiences in those settings (Alba & Hasher, 1983).

Memory for schemas or gist may also be fundamental to such abilities as categorization and comprehension and may facilitate the development of transfer and generalization across tasks (Reyna & Brainerd, 1995). These benefits notwithstanding, false recall and recognition often occur when people remember the semantic or perceptual gist of an experience but do not recall specific details. Older adults are particularly prone to commit false recall and recognition and misattribute a memory to an incorrect time, place, or person (Norman & Schacter, 1997; Tun, Wingfield, Rosen, & Blanchard, 1998).

Presenting information using rich, meaningful materials and in ways that build on elderly adults' network of semantic knowledge will lead to better memory to support choices, particularly when the material can be recognized rather than recalled. Material presented verbally or in event-based scenarios, by contrast, should be more poorly remembered. Due to better autobiographical memory for periods before and during young adulthood and the early organization of semantic knowledge structures, older consumers may have the most knowledge of product categories and brands that were available at this earlier point in their lives. This suggests that older adults may have greater ability than younger adults to process information about established compared to newer product categories and brands.

Source memory and misattribution

People may correctly remember an item or fact from a past experience but misattribute the fact to an incorrect source. For instance, individuals sometimes recall encountering a bit of trivia in the newspaper that, in fact, they acquired from an experimenter in a study (Schacter, Harbluk, & McLachlan, 1984). Similarly, older adults also have greater problems remembering what they actually said or did versus merely imagining doing so (Cohen & Faulkner, 1989; Johnson et al., 1993). Source confusions of this kind can be particularly pronounced in older adults (McIntyre & Craik, 1987). For example, Schacter et al. (1997) found that older adults often confused whether they had seen an everyday action in a videotape or only in a photograph that they viewed several days later, whereas younger adults had little difficulty remembering the correct source. Further, older adults have greater difficulty remembering whether the speaker was male or female (Bayen & Murnane, 1996), and whether the items were presented auditorially or visually (e.g., Light et al., 1992).

Individuals sometimes misattribute a spontaneous thought or idea to their own imagination, when in fact they are retrieving it—without awareness of doing so—from a specific prior experience. This type of misattribution is characterized by an absence of any subjective experience of remembering. Older adults are especially susceptible to such misattributions (Dywan & Jacoby, 1990). In a recent study, Skurnik, Yoon, Park, and Schwarz (2005) found that telling people that a consumer claim is false can made them more likely to misremember it as true. In two experiments, older adults were especially susceptible to this "illusion of truth" effect. Repeatedly identifying a claim as false helped older adults remember it as false in the short term, but paradoxically made them more likely to remember it as true after a three-day delay. This unintended effect of repetition was due to increased familiarity with the claim itself, but decreased recollection of the claim's original context.

Socioemotional factors and meaningfulness

Recent studies support the idea that certain contexts acquire special significance with age. In a study by Rahhal et al. (2002), older adults exhibited the typical source memory impairments for which of two speakers, Mary or John, uttered a statement. However, when the information was presented in more social or emotional terms—whether the speaker was a liar or truth-teller (or "good" or "evil")—older adults' memory for the source was the same as that of the younger adults.

The findings by Rahhal et al. (2002) are consistent with research showing that memory for emotional information, and particularly so for positive emotions, is preserved with age (Mather, Knight, & McCaffrey, 2005). According to Carstensen's socioemotional selectivity theory (e.g., Carstensen, Isaacowitz, & Charles, 1999), older adults are likely to place emphasis on achieving emotional satisfaction and meaning through close social relationships. Recent studies suggest that as people age, they increasingly prefer persuasive messages with emotional rather than rational (Williams & Drolet, 2005) or knowledge-related appeals (Fung & Carstensen, 2003). Further, senior adults have better memory for messages with emotional than nonemotional content and are more likely than younger adults to be persuaded by messages with emotional content.

Work by Castel and Craik (2004) is consistent with the idea that information must be personally meaningful and relevant to the lives of older adults in order to be successfully remembered. They found that meaningful contexts support age-invariant memory ability, with intact recall of pricing information when prices reflected the market value but impaired memory when items were grossly over- or underpriced.

Because the elderly tend to engage in less self-initiated processing and rely heavily on environmental support, it is possible that they may be more influenced by contexts. This may argue for stability in the contexts in which information is presented and choices are made. Studies on expertise and personal relevance or meaningfulness of information are thus likely to continue to be important in distinguishing domains that draw on age-invariant memory abilities from those that rely on processes known to decline with aging. Such studies are needed as part of ongoing research efforts aimed at a systematic understanding of contextual factors leading to changes or stability of cognitive functioning with aging. Contextual factors that enable older adults to function particularly well may then lead to promising interventions and improvements in cognitive and behavioral outcomes.

Circadian arousal

A number of studies have found that the age differences in processing can be moderated by individual variation in circadian arousal patterns that is correlated with performance on a variety of cognitive tasks (e.g., May, Hasher, & Stoltzfus, 1993; Yoon, 1997). Specifically, performance tends to peak at certain level of circadian arousal when greater cognitive resources are presumably available, and this peak occurs, more or less regularly, at a specific point in the day. Hence, individual variation in circadian arousal patterns can significantly alter cognitive performance across time of day.

More directly relevant to the memory and aging is the finding that performance patterns across time of day are different for younger (typically university student participants) and older adults: younger adults' performance tends to improve as the day progresses, whereas older adults' performance peaks in the morning (during their optimal time of day) and then declines through the afternoon and evening (e.g., Adan, 1991; May et al., 1993). Normative data collected on over 2,200 college students (aged 18–23) and 1,200 older adults (aged 60–75) in North America indicate that roughly 40% of younger adults show eveningness tendencies, with less than 10% showing morningness tendencies. By contrast, less than 2% of older adults show eveningness tendencies, and the majority (~79%) are morning-types. Clearly, younger and older adults differ markedly in their circadian peaks over the day, and insofar as cognition follows circadian arousal patterns, the norms suggest that performance of many younger adults will improve across the day, while that of most older adults will deteriorate as the day progresses·

As one example of dramatic time of day differences in how younger and older adults live their daily lives, consider age differences in media use and shopping (Yoon, 1997). More than 80% of the older participants in that study indicated that they read newspapers early in the morning, while only 14 % of younger subjects reported doing so during early morning hours. Magazines, on the other hand, were read in the afternoon or evening by more than two-thirds of both younger and older adults. About half of the older people indicated a clear preference for shopping in the morning or early afternoon, whereas younger people tended to prefer the late afternoon or evening. Older people's preference for shopping in the morning is consistent with their tendency to be mentally alert and energetic in the morning.

Other studies have found intellectual and physical behavior to vary across age and time of day. For example, prospective memory (remembering to do something in the future) involving older adults' medication and appointment adherence was significantly greater in the morning than in the afternoon or evening (Leirer, Tanke, & Morrow, 1994). By contrast, Skinner (1985) reported that college students' grades were significantly lower in morning classes than in afternoon and evening classes. Although these studies did not collect MEQ-type measures, they suggest real intellectual and behavioral differences across time of day that are quite consistent with circadian patterns reported for these age groups (see May et al., 1993; Yoon, 1997).

There is mounting evidence that in studies of age-related changes in memory, it is important to account for the match between an individual's peak circadian arousal period and the time at which testing occurs, an influence referred to as the "synchrony effect" (May et al., 1993). The synchrony between circadian arousal periods and performance can have a major impact on a wide array of cognitive tasks, particularly on those with an inhibitory component (for a review, see Yoon, May, Goldstein, & Hasher, in press). Yoon (1997) found that the elderly at their optimal time of day (i.e., morning) are able to engage in levels of detailed processing that are equivalent to those of younger adults at their optimal time of day for some types of messages. At their nonoptimal time of day, however, older adults show a marked decline in cognitive performance. This is in contrast to younger adults who are able to process in detail even at their nonoptimal time of day.

Yoon, Lee, and Danziger (2007) further investigated whether this time of day effect also impacts persuasion processes performed under relatively high involvement. They find that the attitudes of older adults are more strongly affected by an easy to process criterion, picture-relatedness, at their nonoptimal time of day (afternoon) and by a more difficult to process criterion, argument strength, at their optimal time of day (morning). In contrast, the attitudes of younger adults are affected primarily by argument strength at both their optimal (afternoon) and nonoptimal (morning) times of day. The results accentuate the need for matching marketing communications to the processing styles and abilities of older adults.

Taken together, the evidence suggests that in investigations of aging, it is important to guard against any potential biases by controlling for individual and group differences in circadian arousal patterns. Insofar as we know that older adults tend to reach their mental peak in the morning while younger adults do so in the evening, studies failing to account for such differences in arousal patterns may otherwise produce results that reflect a systematic under- or overestimation of relationships between age and other variables of interest.

The set of contextual factors that we have discussed thus far are by no means exhaustive. They are, however, intended to underscore the importance of research aimed at integrating memory in broader cognitive, biological, and social contexts in order to continue to enhance our understanding of older adults.

DECISION-MAKING AND PROBLEM-SOLVING

Models of Consumer Decision Making

Most models of consumer decision making identify at least two types of decision making. The first involves deliberative decision making with the classic five stages: problem recognition, information search, alternative evaluation, purchase decision, and post-purchase behavior. Such decision making typically reflects systematic attribute-by-attribute processing and is characterized as conscious, analytical, reason-based, and relatively slow.

In contrast, the second type of decision making is affective/experiential, and involves intuitive, automatic, associative, and fast decisions. When consumers have limited processing resources, they may pass directly from problem recognition to purchase decision to the post-purchase phase, using affective feeling to direct their choice process. So, for example, in one recent experiment, consumers with limited processing resources were more likely to choose chocolate cake, an option that generates positive affect and negative cognitions about health, than to choose fruit salad, an option that generates negative affect and positive cognitions about health (Shiv & Fedorikhin, 1999). In this type of decision making, ambient mood can also affect how consumers evaluate an object through a "how do I feel about it heuristic." Consumers, using this heuristic, monitor their feelings to answer the question "how do I feel about it?" (Schwarz, 2001). They often end up mistaking their current mood state for their feeling toward a product (Pham, 1998).

Regarding age differences in use of deliberative and affective/experiential decision making, Hess, Rosenberg, and Waters (2001) have proposed a resource allocation hypothesis, which states that because older adults have limited cognitive resources, they tend to employ the latter affective/experiential information processing strategy in order to conserve their mental energy for important tasks. However, this hypothesis also suggests that older adults can, when necessary, employ deliberative information processing and decision making (a production deficiency). The frontal aging hypothesis, discussed earlier in the context of memory, suggests that age-related changes in frontal systems can favor affective/experiential type decision making (see Denburg, Tranel, & Bechara, 2005, for a discussion). This would tend to suggest that some older adults are unable to employ deliberative decision making (a processing deficiency).

A problem for consumer researchers has been defining what constitutes a good decision outcome. Some researchers have instructed consumers to use specific decision rules—generally the research indicates older adults are worse at applying specific decision rules (e.g., Cole & Gaeth, 1990). Other researchers have judged decision quality by focusing on satisfaction with choice. Research here reports that that not only does satisfaction level vary with age (Cole & Balasubramanian, 1993), but also that the relationship between satisfaction and consumer decision making varies with age (Lambert-Pandraud, Laurent, & Lapersonne, 2005). Finally, decision speed and decision efficiency are also used to judge the quality of decision outcomes. Interestingly, some decision researchers have argued that by engaging the experiential processing system more and/or reducing the analytic processing needed, younger consumers can be aided to make better (quicker and more efficient) decisions, which are more similar to those of older adults (Hibbard & Peters, 2003).

Although consumer decision-making research spans a broad range of topics, researchers studying age differences in consumer decision making have tended to focus on just a few topic areas. In this section, we review the empirical evidence for age differences in search for information, evaluation of alternatives, purchase decisions, and post-purchase behavior.

Search for information

Older consumers often search in different places and for less information than younger consumers. For example, when making investment decisions, older consumers, compared to younger consumers, are more likely to use television media and less likely to use the Internet for information about investments. In addition, older consumers spend less time searching for investment information than younger consumers (Lin & Lee, 2004). Similarly, a recent survey of automobile buyers found that older consumers searched for fewer brands, dealers, and models than younger consumers (Lambert-Pandraud, Laurent, & Lapersonne, 2005). Consistent findings have also been reported in the context of medical decisions (Ende, Kazis, Ash, & Moskowitz, 1989) and managerial decision making (Streufert, Pogash, Piaseck, & Post, 1990).

Another study investigated age differences in search behavior in a supermarket setting and in a computer laboratory (Cole & Balasubramanian, 1993). In the supermarket, shoppers inspected very few packages before making a choice, so no age differences emerged in how much people searched. However, when an observer intercepted shoppers and asked them to purchase a cereal that met certain nutritional criteria, younger adults engaged in more search than older adults who did not change how much they searched. In the laboratory, using a computer search program, older adults searched for less information about unfamiliar cereals than younger adults.

Whether or not age differences in search emerge, may depend on task characteristics. Age differences in search may not emerge when consumers perform simple, routine tasks such as grocery shopping because nobody searches very much in such situations. When engaging in familiar, but complex tasks, such as buying a new car, older adults may search less than younger adults because they use their years of shopping experience to design efficient search strategies. However, elderly consumers may restrict search when given a new search problem because of scarce information processing resources. For example, older consumers with diminished working memory capacity may not easily store information about alternatives in memory. As a result, they may not search for as much information as younger consumers.

Evaluation of alternatives and choice

There are three subissues explored here: (1) the types of information that people of different ages attend to, (2) how people of different ages combine information to form evaluations, and (3) whether or not there are systematic age differences in actual choices.

According to the socioemotional selectivity theory, age affects awareness of and use of emotional information (Carstensen et al., 1999). Older adults, who perceive their time horizon as limited, place greater emphasis on emotionally meaningful goals (goals related to feelings, such as balancing emotional states) than on knowledge-related goals (goals related to new information acquisitions). This age-related shift in goals could influence the type of information people use to make decisions (affective knowledge versus other types of information) (e.g., Fung & Carstensen, 2003).

Several researchers have suggested that older adults' extensive schema network, which have affective components tied to them, may allow them to easily use affective processing when making decisions (Myles-Worsley, Johnston, & Simons, 1988; Reyna, 2004). Investigators have found that adding affective category labels (poor, fair, good, excellent) alters age differences in decision making when participants are making choices about health plans (Peters, Slovic, & Hibbard, 2005). From a different perspective, a recent study examined framing effects in younger and older adults and found that when consumers used heuristic processing, older adults were more susceptible than younger adults to framing effects, but that the two groups did not differ when they were asked to justify their decisions or use more systematic processing (Kim, Goldstein, Hasher, & Zacks, 2005). This study also indicates that the types of information you present to consumers affects the size of age differences in decision making.

Regarding how people combine information, a recent study found that how people combined information to select a brand of financial services depended on both age and lifestyle variables (Lee & Marlowe, 2003). When selecting financial services, older singles were more likely to report using a disjunctive decision strategy (e.g., I chose the financial institution that I rated really good on at least one thing) than other life stage groups, whereas retired older couples were most likely to report using conjunctive decision strategies (e.g., I chose the financial institution that I did not rate poorly on anything). Another study found that older adults were more likely than younger adults to adopt a strategy of eliminating alternatives as soon as possible (Riggle & Johnson, 1996).

Regarding choices, research points to a tendency for older adults to avoid making decisions by postponing or delegating them. In medical decision making, older adults are more likely than younger adults to indicate that they would leave the medical decisions up to the doctors instead of making them themselves (Steginga & Occhipinti, 2002). In other everyday decisions, older adults preferred avoidant strategies, but younger adults preferred problem focused action. Interestingly, however, as the emotional contents of the problems increased, younger adults' strategies became more like those of older adults (Blanchard-Fields, Camp, & Casper Jahnke, 1995).

Retail decisions and post-purchase behavior

A recent study of patronage motives for consumers in the selection of food and grocery stores found that those 55 and over differed from those under 55 on the importance they attached to variables such as store location, availability of age-related discounts, availability of personnel to assist consumers, availability of special services, and recommendations by other people their age (Moschis et al., 2004).

Some self-report studies indicate that elderly adults say they favor retailers that offer senior citizen discounts; but other surveys show that older adults are reluctant to participate in such programs. Tepper (1994) conducted an experiment with three older age subgroups in order to determine whether or not older adults respond favorably to age-related discounts. In the experiment, consumers learned that a 10% discount was either a senior citizen discount offered to customers over a certain age or a privileged customer discount offered to special customers. Consumers' reactions to the discount varied by age subgroup. Respondents in the youngest age group (50–54) were the least likely to use a discount promoted with an age segmentation cue, and adults over the age of 65 were willing to use either of the 10% discounts. The middle of the older age group (55–64) was willing to use the senior discount even though they believed that others would not give senior citizen discount users much respect.

Another study examined how older adults dispose of favorite possessions (Price, Arnould, & Curasi, 2000). Through in-depth interviews they studied various aspects of disposition decisions including precipitating events, emotions associated with decision, meaning of possessions, and tactics for disposing of possessions. Of these, precipitating events seemed most sensitive to age differences, but it would be informative to have future research that conducts age-based comparisons across different possession or consumption domains.

Heuristic/Affective Decision Making

Age difference in one type of affect-based decision making—risky choices—has been extensively studied in psychology (e.g., Denburg et al., 2005; Kovalchik, Camerer, Grether, Plott, & Allman, 2004). For example, Denburg et al. studied neurologically and psychiatrically healthy older adults and younger adults, using the Iowa Gambling Task, which entails a series of 100 card selections from four decks. A monetary gain follows some card selections, but a monetary loss follows others. The decks with lower immediate rewards have lower long-term punishments and thus yield an overall net gain, but decks with higher immediate reward have higher long-term punishment. Participants do not know about the reward/punishment schedules. A subset of the older group manifested decision-making impairment on the gambling task, which Denburg et al. suggest may indicate impairment in the prefrontal region of the brain. Future research is needed linking performance on the gambling task to neurological changes.

Improving Consumer Decision Making

In general, the existing decision-making literature suggests that elderly consumers differ from younger consumers in important ways at each stage of the decision-making process. At the information search stage, the presence of age differences in the amount of search is not surprising because most of the consumer behavior research is based on extensive prior work in gerontology that suggests less search among older adults. At the alternative evaluation stage, a host of unresolved questions center on the decision rules and heuristics that different aged consumers use when evaluating alternatives. Some processes may differ across age groups because older consumers, with fewer cognitive resources than younger consumers, may perceive higher cognitive costs for certain strategies. Other processes may not differ, when consumers of all ages are able to use familiar and well-practiced heuristics.

We now discuss intervention programs such as decision aids, training programs and stimulus redesign.

Decision aids

A series of experiments used decision aids to reduce age differences in the correct use of the nutritional information contained on product labels (Cole & Gaeth, 1990). As discussed in the section on memory, older adults are known to be more susceptible to interference from the irrelevant components of a stimulus (or other environmental noise) than are younger adults. In the experiments, participants had to select a cereal that met certain criteria, but some participants first circled the relevant information before making a decision. Although both older and younger adults benefited from the simple aid, older consumers made fewer good nutritional choices than younger consumers. In a second experiment, the investigators put relevant information in a separate location on the label. This time, older adults with moderate, but not severe disembedding deficiencies, were helped, but the field independent younger individuals gained little from the aid. Given that the stated aim of nutritional labeling laws is to make nutritional information easy for all consumers to use, this study suggests that such information should be placed in the same spot on all labels.

In a different study, Cole and Balasubramanian (1993) tried to aid the use of nutritional information by encouraging older and younger adults to write information down as they acquired it from the computer. Using this decision aid, age differences in search intensity were greatly diminished.

Additional studies in the area of medicine suggest that by providing older adults with organizational charts and medication organizers, pharmacists can increase their patients' compliance with medication instructions (Park, Morell, Frieske, & Kincaid, 1992). Taken together, these studies suggest that decision aids may successfully improve consumer decision making. Circling, organizing, or writing down important information may especially help the elderly consumer focus on relevant information.

Training and education

Gaeth and Heath (1987) developed an interactive training program to reduce susceptibility to misleading advertising without increasing consumer suspicion of advertising claims. They found that the training: (1) reduced susceptibility to misleading statements in both age groups, (2) equated misleadingness between older trained adults and younger untrained adults, and (3) reduced the younger adult's ability to discriminate between nonmisleading and potentially misleading claims. Regarding knowledge, older adults appear to build up a knowledge system that they can deploy to aid in decision making. Some argue that knowledge systems become increasingly selective and domain-specific with age, so that older adults can draw on this knowledge system to make better decisions. For example, Kovalchik et al. (2004) reported that older subjects did somewhat better than younger subjects on a 20-item trivia multiple choice test. More important from a decision-making perspective, however, older subjects in the study were better calibrated (knew better what they knew and did not know) than younger subjects. They may have learned through experience to temper their overconfidence and thus look more like experts. Future research is needed to address the circumstances when older adults can and cannot recruit their knowledge base for decision making.

Modifying stimuli

Hibbard and Peters (2003) suggest a number of interesting ways that stimuli could be modified to improve decision making of all ages, including providing cues about the goodness of information (e.g., labels, stars), and presenting information in the form of narratives or stories about someone else's experience. In one recently reported study on Medicare health plan choices, older consumers who received both information with cues about goodness and narratives in addition to basic data made better choices than consumers who only obtained basic data (Hibbard, 2002).

Another series of study have examined whether providing information in a manner consistent with adult schemas improves decision making about medication (Morrow, Leirer, Andrassy, Tanke, & Stine-Morrow, 1996). Nonadherence to prescribed medication, a widespread health care problem, is more common among elderly adults because the numbers of medications that people take often increases with age. These authors found that providing information in a schema consistent manner improved recall of information for both older and younger adults. Future research is needed to investigate whether schema consistent instruction improves adherence or quality of consumer decisions about medicine. It could well be that older adults are more prone to falsely remember information that is inaccurate or incorrect but otherwise consistent with their schemas.

Summary

In summary, efforts to eliminate age differences with decision aids have not been entirely successful in equating older adults' performance with that of younger adults. Instead, training, stimulus redesign, and decision aids often help all age groups.

To develop a decision aid that differentially benefits the older consumer, researchers must first deconstruct the consumer's task. They then need to identify exactly why and where in the substeps age differences emerge. Perhaps age differences emerge at the information acquisition stage because of working memory differences, but at the alternative evaluation stage they emerge because of differential attention to affective information. Once researchers understand the source of age differences, effective aids can be designed.

However, researchers need to evaluate the effects of decision aids on both targeted and nontargeted groups. For example, when researchers trained study participants to discriminate between directly asserted and implied claims, they increased younger participants' skepticism of advertising. Similarly, an advertiser targeting older adults may increase learning among this audience by increasing the number of message repetitions. However, if younger adults also see the advertisements, the increased message repetitions may irritate them.

Additionally, the researchers need to think about designing a managerially relevant aid. For example, Cole and Gaeth (1990) suggested that older consumers highlight relevant information before making a decision. However, it is not practical to recommend that consumers take pens into the supermarket to highlight relevant information on product packages prior to purchase.

METHODOLOGICAL ISSUES IN AGING RESEARCH

The studies covered in this chapter are based primarily on experimental methods. Many compare well-educated healthy normal older adults (60+) with college undergraduates (18–22). Older adults' responses on many tasks are typically accompanied by greater variability than those of the relatively homogeneous college undergraduates.

The vast majority of experimental studies are based on cross-sectional designs. There are a handful of research labs that do collect longitudinal data (e.g., Seattle Longitudinal Study, Schaie, 2005; Berlin Aging Study, Baltes & Mayer, 1999). In addition, ICPSR (Inter-University Consortium for Political and Social Research) acts as a depository for a variety of longitudinal data sets primarily related to health and social status. Such data sets overcome some of the problems of cross-sectional design, but they are accompanied by their own unique problems such as sample selectivity and attrition.

In this section, we focus our discussion on issues that confront researchers conducting cross-sectional experimental studies on aging. First, recruiting older adults can be challenging compared to recruiting student participants. Researchers report difficulties finding sufficient numbers of older subjects to participate. Unlike younger college students, older adults, who are willing to participate in experimental studies, often must travel to the research laboratory and require substantially more compensation for their time. In addition, in cross-sectional research it is not possible to control for all the potential cohort differences. Nonetheless, researchers try to mitigate the effects of cohort differences by matching age groups in terms of health and educational status. However, even this matching can be problematic because quality of education varies between cohorts as does the length of time since education was completed. Most researchers screen participants for the ability to see and hear stimuli and administer vocabulary tests. Frequently, older adults score better on these vocabulary tests than college students.

In consumer studies, the stimuli may involve established brands or product categories, but because younger and older consumers often bring different product experience and knowledge to bear on consumer behavior, the stimuli may have different meaning to different age groups. Other variables are also hard to control for across age groups—e.g., a priori differences in motivation and arousal levels between younger and older study participants. Further, as discussed before, it may be important to control for synchrony effects; not doing so can systematically over-estimate or under-estimate the extent of age-related differences.

As Schwarz (2003) points out, much of the elderly data are collected via retrospective behavioral reports, and hence, there are likely to be systematic biases in responses to the extent that older adults have to rely on processes that are age sensitive—e.g., retrieve relevant information from memory, form a judgment online, and report the judgment to the researcher. In addition, telephone interviews are likely to be more difficult for older adults than written surveys containing self-paced questions. Age differences may therefore magnify with elicitation methods that require more cognitive effort.

Finally, we note that in experimental studies of aging, external validity tends to be sacrificed in favor of internal validity, with convergence of insights occurring over time via conceptual replications. We suggest that richer insights about older adults in more natural consumer contexts are likely to emerge and complement findings from experiments through greater use of alternative qualitative research methods (e.g., observation, ethnography).

FUTURE RESEARCH DIRECTIONS AND CONCLUSIONS

Over the life course, consumers' strategies for solving different consumption problems evolve to reflect their changing life experiences and abilities. Not only do consumers face new problems (e.g., buying a color TV in the 1960s vs. buying a laptop computer in 2007), but they also experience physiological and cognitive changes. There are a number of unanswered questions about how older consumers adjust their decision-making strategies to changing cognitive abilities, social roles, and to task and context demands.

We hypothesize that situations where older consumers are likely to run into difficulties are typically unfamiliar situations involving new products or services. For example, some older adults may encounter difficulties learning information about the side effects of new prescription drugs through advertising; similarly, they may run into problems using the information found on the drug label. In other familiar situations, such as buying a car, older consumers may make better (more efficient and quicker) decisions than their younger counterparts.

The consumer behavior literature has contributed to knowledge by showing that age differences found in the laboratory research often emerge in "real" world settings (John & Cole, 1986). We identify several avenues for future research. One direction would be to examine how and when the older consumers' considerable knowledge and experience moderates any age differences that emerge in memory performance or decision making. In addition, because age-related changes in cognitive ability do not occur at the same rate for everyone (nor do they occur in everyone), there is considerable heterogeneity in the older market. For example, an individual's health history and life style may attenuate the timing and size of changes. So, another important direction for future research is to investigate differences within the elderly market.

A fruitful area for more research is analyses of consumer task characteristics that may exacerbate or minimize age differences. For example, much of the consumer behavior literature points out memory deficiencies in older adults in comparison with younger adults (see Williams & Drolet, 2005, for a notable exception). However, the magnitude of memory deficits appears to vary with the task conditions of information processing and how information is placed into or recovered from memory. Parallel to this task analysis would be the development and testing of decision aids, training and stimulus redesign that can make decision making easier for all consumers by reducing the cognitive effort required to execute a particular strategy.

In summary, we suggest that a better understanding of the changes associated with aging and how they interact with intra-individual and contextual factors will benefit multiple audiences, including consumers, public policy makers, and marketing managers. If we are to aid older adults to successfully meet the challenges of a rapidly changing and increasingly complex consumer environment, greater insights are needed regarding age differences in consumer behavior. Toward that end, we have in this chapter briefly discussed many of these differences, and have highlighted particularly important areas for future research.

REFERENCES

AARP (2002). The truth about brand loyalty: Executive summary. Retrieved June 18, 2005, from http://www. aarp.org/press/statements/2002/st050702brdloyal.html.

AARP (2005). *The state of 50+ America.* Washington, DC: Consumer Affairs, American Association of Retired Persons.

Adan, A. (1991). Influence of morningness eveningness preference in the relationship between body temperature and performance: A diurnal study. *Personality and Individual Differences, 12,* 1159–1169.

Alba, J. W., & Hasher, L. (1983). Is memory schematic? *Psychological Bulletin, 93,* 203–231.

Andrés, P. (2003). Frontal cortex as the central executive of working memory: Time to revise our view. *Cortex, 39,* 871–895.

Aron, A. R., Robbins, T. W., & Poldrack, R. A. (2004). Inhibition and the right inferior frontal cortex. *Trends in Cognitive Sciences, 8,* 170–177.

Baltes, P. B., Cornelius, S. W., & Nesselroade, J. R. (1979). Cohort effects in developmental psychology. In J. R. Nesselroade & P. B. Baltes (Eds.), *Longitudinal research in the study of behavior and development* (pp. 61–87). New York: Academic Press.

Baltes, P. B., & Mayer, K. U. (1999). *The Berlin aging study: Aging from 70 to 100.* Cambridge: Cambridge University Press.

Bayen, U. J., & Murnane, K. (1996). Aging and the use of perceptual and temporal information in source memory tasks. *Psychology and Aging, 11,* 293–303.

Blanchard-Fields, F., Camp, C., & Casper Jahnke, H. (1995). Age differences in problem-solving style: The role of emotional salience. *Psychology and Aging, 10,* 173–180.

Bowles, R. P., & Salthouse, T. A. (2003). Assessing the age-related effects of proactive interference on working memory tasks using the Rasch model. *Psychology and Aging, 18,* 608–615.

Bryan, J., & Luszcz, M. A. (2000). Measurement of executive function: Consideration for detecting adult age differences. *Journal of Clinical and Experimental Neuropsychology, 22,* 40–55.

Cabeza, R., McIntosh, A. R., Tulving, E., Nyberg, L., & Grady C. L. (1997). Age-related differences in effective neural connectivity during encoding and recall. *NeuroReport, 8,* 3479–3483.

Campbell, M. C., & Kirmani, A. (2000). Consumers' use of persuasion knowledge: The effects of accessibility and cognitive capacity on perceptions of an influence agent. *Journal of Consumer Research, 10,* 69–83.

Carstensen, L. L., Isaacowitz, D. M., & Charles, S. T. (1999). Taking time seriously: A theory of socioemotional selectivity. *American Psychologist, 54,* 165–181.

Castel, A.D., & Craik, F. I. M. (2004). Memory for numerical information in younger and older adults: The role of schematic support. Poster session presented at the 10th Cognitive Aging Conference, Atlanta, Georgia.

Cerella, J. (1985). Information processing rates in the elderly. *Psychological Bulletin, 98,* 67–83.

Cerella, J. (1990). Aging and information-processing rate. In J. E. Birren & K. W. Schaie (Eds.), *The handbook of cognitive aging* (3rd ed., pp. 201–221). New York: Academic Press.

Cohen G., & Faulkner, D. (1989). Age differences in source forgetting: Effects on reality monitoring and on eyewitness testimony. *Psychology and Aging, 4,* 10–17.

Cole, C. A., & Balasubramanian, S. K. (1993). Age differences in consumers' search for information: Public policy implications. *Journal of Consumer Research, 20,* 157–169.

Cole, C. A., & Gaeth, G. A. (1990). Cognitive and age-related differences in the ability to use nutritional information in a complex environment. *Journal of Marketing Research, 17,* 175–184.

Cole, C. A., & Houston, M. J. (1987). Encoding and media effects on consumer learning deficiencies in the elderly. *Journal of Marketing Research, 24,* 55–63.

Cowan, N. (1988). Evolving conceptions of memory storage, selective attention, and their mutual constraints within the human information processing system. *Psychological Bulletin, 104,* 163–191.

Cowan, N. (1993). Activation, attention, and short-term memory. *Memory and Cognition, 21,* 162–167.

Craik, F. I. M. (1983). On the transfer of information from temporary to permanent memory source. *Philosophical transactions of the Royal Society of London, B302,* 341–359.

Craik, F. I. M. (1986). A functional account of age differences in memory. In F. Klix & H. Hagendorf (Eds.), *Human memory and cognitive capabilities, mechanisms and performances* (pp. 409–422). New York: Elsevier.

Craik, F. I. M., & Anderson, N. D. (1999). Applying cognitive research to problems of aging. In D. Gopher & A. Koriat (Eds.), *Attention and performance, XVII, cognitive regulation of performance: Interaction of theory and application* (pp. 583–615). Cambridge, MA: MIT Press.

Craik, F. I. M., Anderson, N. D., Kerr, S. A., & Li, K. Z. H. (1995). Memory changes in normal ageing. In A. D. Baddeley, B. A. Wilson, & F. N. Watts (Eds.), *Handbook of memory disorders* (pp. 211–241). New York: Wiley.

Craik, F. I. M., & Byrd, M. (1982). Aging and cognitive deficits: The role of attentional resources. In F. I. M. Craik & S. Trehub (Eds.), *Aging and cognitive processes* (pp. 191–211). New York: Plenum.

Craik, F. I. M., & Jennings, J. M. (1992). Human memory. In F. I. M. Craik & T. A. Salthouse (Eds.), *The handbook of aging and cognition,* (pp. 51–110). Hillsdale, NJ: Erlbaum.

Craik, F. I. M., & McDowd, J. M. (1987). Age differences in recall and recognition. *Journal of Experimental Psychology: Learning, Memory, and Cognition, 13,* 474–479.

Daselaar, S. M., Veltman, D. J., Rombouts, S. A. R. B., Raaijmakers, J. G. W., & Jonker, C. (2003). Neuroanatomical correlates of episodic encoding and retrieval in young and elderly subjects. *Brain, 126,* 43–56.

Denburg, N. L., Tranel, D., & Bechara, A. (2005). The ability to decide advantageously declines prematurely in some older persons. *Neuropsychologia, 43,* 1099–1106.

Duchek, J. M., Balota, D. A., & Ferraro, F. R. (1995). Inhibitory processes in young and older adults in a picture-word task. *Aging and Cognition, 2,* 156–167.

Dywan, J., & Jacoby, L. L. (1990). Effects of aging on source monitoring: Differences in susceptibility to false fame. *Psychology and Aging, 5,* 379–387.

Ende, J. Kazis, L., Ash, A., & Moskowitz, M. A. (1989). Measuring patients' desire for autonomy: Decision making and information-seeking preferences among medical patients. *Journal of General Internal Medicine, 4,* 23–30.

Fozard, J. L., & Gordon-Salant, S. (2001). Sensory and perceptual changes with aging. In J. E. Birren, & K. W. Schaie (Eds.), *Handbook of the psychology of aging* (5th ed., pp. 241–266). San Diego: Academic Press.

Friestad, M., & Wright, P. (1994). The persuasion knowledge model: How people cope with persuasion attempts. *Journal of Consumer Research, 21,* 1–31.

Fung, H. H., & Carstensen, L. L. (2003). Sending memorable messages to the old: Age differences in preferences and memory for advertisements. *Journal of Personality and Social Psychology, 85,* 163–178.

Fuster, J. M. (2002). Physiology of executive functions: The perception-action cycle. In D. T. Stuss & R. T. Knight (Eds.), *Principles of frontal lobe function* (pp. 96–108). New York: Oxford University Press.

Gaeth, G. A., & Heath, T. B. (1987). The cognitive processing of misleading advertising in young and old adults. *Journal of Consumer Research, 14,* 43–54.

Gilly, M. C., & Zeithaml, V. A. (1985). The elderly consumer and adoption of technologies. *Journal of Consumer Research, 12,* 353–357.

Glisky, E. L., Rubin, S. R., & Davidson, P. S. R. (2001). Source memory in older adults: An encoding or retrieval problem? *Journal of Experimental Psychology: Learning, Memory, and Cognition, 27,* 1131–1146.

Grady, C. L., McIntosh, A. R., Bookstein, F., Horwitz, B., Rapoport, S. I., & Haxby, J. V. (1998). Age-related changes in regional cerebral blood flow during working memory for faces. *Neuroimage, 8,* 409–425.

Gutchess, A. H., Welsh, R. C., Hedden, T., Bangert, A., Minear, M., Liu, L. L., & Park, D. C. (2005). Aging and the neural correlates of successful picture encoding: Frontal activations compensate for decreased medial-temporal activity. *Journal of Cognitive Neuroscience, 17,* 84–96.

Hamm V. P., Hasher L. (1992). Age and the availability of inferences. *Psychology and Aging, 7,* 56–64.

Hartman, M., & Hasher, L. (1991). Aging and suppression: Memory for previously relevant information. *Psychology and Aging, 6,* 587–594.

Hasher, L., & Zacks, R.T. (1988). Working memory, comprehension, and aging: A review and a new view. In G.H. Bower (Ed.), *The psychology of learning and motivation: Advances in research and theory* (Vol. 22, pp. 193–225). San Diego, CA: Academic Press.

Hasher, L., Zacks, R. T., & May, C. P. (1999). Inhibitory control, circadian arousal, and age. In D. Gopher & A. Koriat (Eds.), *Attention and performance, XVII, cognitive regulation of performance: Interaction of theory and application* (pp. 653–657). Cambridge, MA: MIT Press.

Hedden, T., & Gabrieli, J. D. E. (2004). Insights into the ageing mind: A view from cognitive neuroscience. *Nature Reviews Neuroscience, 5,* 87–96.

Hedden, T., & Park, D. C. (2001). Aging and interference in verbal working memory. *Psychology and Aging, 16,* 666–681.

Hedden, T., & Park, D. C. (2003). Contributions of source and inhibitory mechanisms to age-related retroactive interference in verbal working memory. *Journal of Experimental Psychology: General, 132,* 93–112.

Hedden, T., & Yoon, C. (2006). Individual differences in executive processing predict susceptibility to interference in verbal working memory. *Neuropsychology, 20,* 511–528.

Hess, T. M. (2005). Memory and aging in context. *Psychological Bulletin, 131,* 383–406.

Hess, T. M., Flannagan, D. A., & Tate, C. S. (1993). Aging and memory for schematically vs. taxonomically organized verbal materials. *Journal of Gerontology: Psychological Sciences, 48,* P37–P44.

Hess, T. M., Rosenberg, D. C., & Waters, S. J. (2001). Motivation and representational processes in adulthood: The effects of social accountability and information relevance. *Psychology and Aging, 16,* 629–642.

Hibbard, J. H. (2002). *Supporting informed consumer choices.* Presented at Who's in the Driver's Seat? Leading Efforts in Consumer-Centered Health Care. FACCT's ANNU Brief, 4th, Washington, DC.

Hibbard, J. H., & Peters, E. (2003). Supporting informed consumer health care decisions: Data presentation approaches that facilitate the use of information in choice. *Annual Review of Public Health, 24,* 413–433.

Howard, D. V., & Howard, J. H., Jr. (1989). Age differences in learning serial patterns: direct versus indirect measures. *Psychology and Aging, 4,* 357–364.

Jacoby, L. L., Debner, J. A., & Hay, J. F. (2001). Proactive interference, accessibility bias, and process dissociations: Valid subjective reports of memory. *Journal of Experimental Psychology: Learning, Memory and Cognition, 27,* 686–700.

John, D. R., & Cole, C.A. (1986). Age differences in information processing: Understanding deficits in young and elderly consumers. *Journal of Consumer Research, 13,* 297–315.

Johnson, M. K., Hashtroudi, S., & Lindsay, D. S. (1993). Source monitoring. *Psychological Bulletin, 114,* 3–28.

Kausler, D. H. (1994). *Learning and Memory in Normal Aging.* San Diego, CA: Academic Press.

Ketcham, C. J., & Stelmach, G. E. (2003). Movement control in the older adults. In R. W. Pew & S. B. Van Hemel (Eds.), *Technology for Adaptive Aging* (pp. 64–92). Washington, DC: National Academies Press.

Kim, S., Goldstein, D., Hasher, L., & Zacks, R. T. (2005). Framing effects in younger and older adults. *Journal of Gerontology: Psychological Sciences, 60B,* 215–218.

Kolodinsky, J. M., Hogarth, J. M., & Hilgert, M. A. (2004). The adoption of electronic banking technologies by US consumers. *The International Journal of Bank Marketing, 22,* 238–259.

Koutstaal, W., & Schacter, D. L. (1997). Gist-based false recognition of pictures in older and younger adults. *Journal of Memory and Language, 37,* 555–583.

Kovalchik, S., Camerer, C. F., Grether, D. M., Plott, C. R., & Allman, J. M. (2004). Aging and decision making: A comparison between neurologically healthy elderly and young individuals. *Journal of Economic Behavior and Organization.*

Krampe, R. T., & Ericsson, K. A. (1996). Maintaining excellence: deliberate practice and elite performance in young and older pianists. *Journal of Experimental Psychology: General, 125,* 331–359.

Lambert-Pandraud, R., Laurent, G., & Lapersonne, E. (2005). Repeat purchasing of new automobiles by older consumers: Empirical evidence and interpretations. *Journal of Marketing, 69,* 97–113.

Law, S., Hawkins, S. A., & Craik, F. I. M. (1998). Repetition-induced belief in the elderly: Rehabilitating age-related memory deficits. *Journal of Consumer Research, 25,* 91–107.

Lee, J., & Marlowe, J. (2003). How consumers choose a financial institution: Decision-making criteria and heuristics. *The International Journal of Bank Marketing, 21,* 53–71.

Leirer, V. O., Tanke, E. D., & Morrow, D. G. (1994). Time of day and naturalistic prospective memory. *Experimental Aging Research, 20,* 127–134.

Light, L. L. (1991). Memory and aging: Four hypotheses in search of data. *Annual Review of Psychology, 42,* 333–376.

Light, L. L., LaVoie, D. J., Valencia-Laver, D., Albertson Owens, S. A., & Mead, G. (1992). Direct and indirect measures for memory for modality in young and older adults. *Journal of Experimental Psychology: Learning, Memory, and Cognition, 18,* 1284–1297.

Light, L. L., Prull, M. W., La Voie, D J., & Healy, M. R. (2000). Dual-process theories of memory in old age. In T. J. Perfect & E. A. Maylor (Eds.), *Models of cognitive aging* (pp. 238–300). Oxford: Oxford University Press.

Light, L. L., & Singh, A. (1987). Implicit and explicit memory in young and older adults. *Journal of Experimental Psychology: Learning, Memory and Cognition, 13,* 531–541.

Light, L. L., & Zelinski, E. M. (1983). Memory for spatial information in young and old adults. *Developmental Psychology, 19*, 901–906.

Lin, Q., & Lee, J. (2004). Consumer information search when making investment decisions. *Financial Services Review, 13*, 319–332.

Littrel, M., Paige, R., & Song, K. (2004). Senior travelers: Tourism activities and shopping behaviours. *Journal of Vacation Marketing, 10*, 348–362.

Long, N. (1998). Broken down by age and sex—Exploring the ways we approach the elderly consumer. *Journal of the Market Research Society, 40*, 73–91.

Lustig, C., May, C. P., & Hasher, L. (2001). Working memory span and the role of *proactive interference*. *Journal of Experimental Psychology: General, 130*, 199–207.

Mandler, G. (1979). Organization and repetition: Organizational principles with special reference to rote learning. In L. G. Nilsson (Ed.), *Perspectives on Memory Research* (pp. 293–327). Hillsdale, NJ: Erlbaum.

Mather, M., Knight, M., & McCaffrey, M. (2005). The allure of the alignable: Younger and older adults' false memories of choice features. *Journal of Experimental Psychology: General, 134*, 38–51

May, C. P., Hasher, L., & Kane, M. J. (1999). The role of interference in memory span measures. *Memory and Cognition, 27*, 759–767.

May, C. P., Hasher, L., & Stoltzfus, E. R. (1993). Optimal time of day and the magnitude of age differences in memory. *Psychological Science, 4*, 326–330.

Maylor, E. A. (1990). Age and prospective memory. *Quarterly Journal of Experimental Psychology, 42A*, 471–493.

McIntyre, J. S., & Craik, F. I. M. (1987). Age differences in memory for item and source information. *Canadian Journal of Psychology, 41*, 175–192.

Miyake, A., Friedman, N. P., Emerson, M. J., Witzki, A. H., Howerter, A., & Wager, T. D. (2000). The unity and diversity of executive functions and their contributions to complex "frontal lobe" tasks: A latent variable analysis. *Cognitive Psychology, 41*, 49–100.

Morrow, D. G., Leirer, V. O., Andrassy, J., Tanke, E., & Stine-Morrow, E. (1996). Medication instruction design: Younger and older adults schemas for taking medication. *Human Factors, 38*, 556–573.

Morrow, D. G., Leirer, V. O., & Altieri, P. A. (1992). Aging, expertise, and narrative processing. *Psychology and Aging, 7*, 376–388.

Moschis, G. P. (1996). *Gerontographics*. Westport, CT: Quorom Books.

Moschis, G. P., Curasi, C., & Bellenger, D. (2004). Patronage motives of mature consumers in the selection of food and grocery stores. *Journal of Consumer Marketing, 21*, 123–133.

Moschis, G. P., Lee, E., Mathur, A., & Strautman, J. (2000). The *Maturing marketplace: Buying habits of baby boomers and their parents*. Westport, CT: Quorom Books.

Moscovitch, M., & Winocur, G. (1992). The neuropsychology of memory and aging. In F. I. M. Craik & T. A. Salthouse (Eds.), *The handbook of aging and cognition* (pp.315–372). Hillsdale, NJ: Erlbaum.

Moscovitch, M., & Winocur, G. (1995). Frontal lobes, memory, and aging. *Annals of the New York Academy of Sciences, 769*, 119–150.

Myles-Worsley, M., Johnston, W. A., & Simons, M. A. (1988). The influence of expertise on X-ray image processing. *Journal of Experimental Psychology: Learning, Memory and Cognition, 14*, 553–557.

Norman, K. A., & Schacter, D. L. (1997). False recognition in younger and older adults: Exploring the characteristics of illusory memories. *Memory & Cognition, 25*, 838–848.

Park, D. C., Morrell, R. W., Frieske, D., & Kincaid, D. (1992). Medication adherence behaviors in older adults: Effects of external cognitive supports. *Psychology and Aging, 7*, 252–256.

Park, D. C., Puglisi, T. J., & Smith, A. D. (1986). Memory for pictures: Does an age-related decline exist. *Psychology and Aging, 1*, 11–17.

Park, D. C., Royal, D., Dudley, W., & Morrell, R. (1988). Forgetting of pictures over a long retention interval in old & young adults. *Psychology and Aging, 3*, 94–95.

Park, D. C., Smith, A. D., Lautenschlager, G., Earles, J. L., Frieske, D., Zwahr, M., & Gaines, C. L. (1996). Mediators of long-term memory performance across the adult life span. *Psychology and Aging, 11*, 621–637.

Park, D. C., Smith, A. D., Morrell, R. W., Puglisi, J. T., & Dudley, W. N. (1990). Effects of contextual integration on recall of pictures in older adults. *Journal of Gerontology: Psychological Sciences, 45*, 52–58.

Peters, E., Hess, T. M., Auman, C., & Västfjäll, D. (2004). How do older adults decide?: Age differences in the impact of affect and deliberation on judgments and decisions. Decision Research and University of Oregon Working Paper.

Pham, M. T. (1998). Representativeness, relevance, and the use of feelings in decision making. *Journal of Consumer Research, 25*, 144–159.

Price, L. L., Arnould, E. J., & Curasi, C. F. (2000). Older Consumers' Disposition of Special Possessions. *Journal of Consumer Research, 27*, 179–201.

Rahhal, T. A., May, C. P., & Hasher, L. (2002). Aging, source memory and source significance. *Psychological Science, 13*, 101–105.

Reyna, V. F. (2004). How people make decisions that involve risk: A dual-processes approach. *Current Directions in Psychological Science, 13*, 60–66.

Reyna, V. F., & Brainerd, C. J. (1995). Fuzzy-trace theory: An interim synthesis. *Learning and Individual Differences, 7*, 1–75.

Reuter-Lorenz, P. A., Jonides, J., Smith, E. E., Hartley, A., Miller, A., Marshuetz, C., & Koeppe, R. A. (2000). Age differences in the frontal lateralization of verbal and spatial working memory revealed by PET. *Journal of Cognitive Neuroscience 12*, 174–187.

Riggle, E. D. B., & Johnson, M. M. S. (1996). Age differences in political decision making: Strategies for evaluating political candidates. *Political Behavior, 18*, 99–118.

Rogers, W. A., & Fisk, A. D. (2000). Human factors. In F. I. M. Craik & T. A. Salthhouse (Eds.), *The Handbook of Aging and Cognition* (2nd ed., pp. 559–591). Mahwah, NJ: Erlbaum.

Rogers, W. A., Meyer, B., Walker, N., & Fisk, A. D. (1998). Functional limitations to daily living tasks in the aged: a focus group analysis. *Human Factors, 40*, 111–125.

Salthouse, T. A. (1996). The processing-speed theory of adult age differences in cognition. *Psychological Review, 103*, 403–428.

Schacter, D. L., Harbluk, J. L., & McLachlan, D. R. (1984). Retrieval without recollection: An experimental analysis of source amnesia. *Journal of Verbal Learning and Verbal Behavior, 23*, 593–611.

Schacter, D. L., Kihlstrom, J. F., Kaszniak, A. W., & Valdiserri, M. (1993). Preserved and impaired memory functions in elderly adults. In J. Cerella, W. Hoyer, J. Rybash, & M. Commons (Eds.), *Adult information processing: Limits on loss* (pp. 327–350). New York: Academic Press.

Schacter D. L., Koutstaal, W., Johnson, M. K., Gross, M. S., & Angell, K. E. (1997). False recollection induced via photographs: A comparison of older and younger adults. *Psychology and Aging, 12*, 203–215.

Schaie, K.W. (2005). *Developmental influences on adult intelligence: The Seattle longitudinal study.* New York: Oxford University Press.

Schieber, F., & Baldwin, C. L. (1996). Vision, audition, and aging research. In F. Blanchard-Fields & T. M. Hess (Eds.), *Perspectives on cognitive change and adulthood and aging* (pp. 122–162). New York: McGraw-Hill.

Schneider, B. A., & Pichora-Fuller, M. K. (2000). Implications of perceptual deterioration for cognitive aging research. In F. I. M. Craik & T. A. Salthouse (Eds.), *The handbook of aging and cognition* (2nd ed., pp. 155–219). Mahwah, NJ: Erlbaum.

Schwarz, N. (2001). Feelings as information: implications for affective influences on information processing. In L. L. Martin & G. L. Clore (Eds.), *Theories of mood and cognition: A user's guidebook* (pp. 159–179). Mahwah, NJ: Erlbaum.

Schwarz, N. (2003). Self-reports in consumer research: The challenge of comparing cohorts and cultures. *Journal of Consumer Research, 29*, 588–594.

Shiv, B., & Fedorikhin, A. (1999). Heart and mind in conflict: The interplay of affect and cognition in consumer decision making. *Journal of Consumer Research, 26*, 278–292.

Sinnott, J. D. (1989). *Everyday problem solving: Theory and applications.* Westport, CT: Greenwood Publishing Group.

Skinner, N. F. (1985). University grades and time of day of instruction. *Bulletin of the Psychonomic Society, 23*, 67.

Skurnik, I., Yoon, C., Park, D. C., & Schwarz, N. (2005). How warnings become recommendations: paradoxical effects of warnings on beliefs of older consumers. *Journal of Consumer Research, 31*, 713–724.

Smith, A. D., Park, D. C., Cherry, K., & Berkovsky, K. (1990). Age differences in memory for concrete and abstract pictures. *Journal of Gerontology: Psychological Sciences, 45*, P205–P209.

Smith, A. D., Park, D. C., Earles, J. L. K., Shaw, R. J., & Whiting, W. L. (1998). Age differences in context integration in memory. *Psychology and Aging, 13*, 21–28

Smith, J., & Baltes, P. B. (1997). Profiles of psychology functioning in the old and oldest old. *Psychology and Aging, 12*, 458–472.

Special Committee on Aging (August, 2000). Hearings on Fraud Against Seniors, U.S. Senate, Washington, DC

Spencer, W.D., & Raz, N. (1994). Memory for facts, source, and context: Can frontal lobe dysfunction explain age-related differences? *Psychology and Aging, 9,* 149–159.

Spencer, W. D., & Raz, N. (1995). Differential effects of aging on memory for content and context: a meta-analysis. *Psychology and Aging, 10,* 527–539.

Steginga, S. K., & Occhipinti, A. (2002). Decision making about treatment of hypothetical prostate cancer: Is deferring a decision an expert-opinion heuristic? *Journal of Psychosocial Oncology, 20,* 69–84.

Streufert, S., Pogash, R., Piaseck, M., & Post, G. M. (1990). Age and management team performance. *Psychology and Aging, 5,* 551–559.

Tepper, K. (1994). The role of labeling processes in elderly consumers' responses to age segmentation cues. *Journal of Consumer Research, 20,* 503–519.

Tun P. A., Wingfield A., Rosen M. J., & Blanchard L. S. (1998). Response latencies for false memories: Association, discrimination, and normal aging. *Psychology and Aging, 14,* 230–241.

Verhaeghen, P., & Cerella, J. (2002). Aging, executive control, and attention: a review of meta-analyses. *Neuroscience and Biobehavioral Reviews, 26,* 849–857.

Verhaeghen, P., Marcoen, A., & Goosens, L. (1993). Facts and fiction about memory aging: A quantitative integration of research findings. *Journal of Gerontology: Psychological Sciences, 48,* P157–P171.

Verhaeghen, P., Steitz, D. W., Sliwinski, M. J., & Cerella, J. (2003). Aging and dual-task performance: A meta-analysis. *Psychology and Aging, 18,* 443–460.

Walker, N., Philbin, D. A., & Fisk, A. D. (1997). Age-related differences in movement control: Adjusting submovement structure to optimize performance. *Journal of Gerontology: Psychological Sciences, 52,* P40–52.

Weale, R. A. (1961). Notes on the photometric significance of the human crystalline lens. *Vision Research, 1,* 183–191.

West, R. L. (1996). An application of prefrontal cortex function theory to cognitive aging. *Psychological Bulletin, 120,* 272–292.

Williams, P., & Drolet, A. (2005). Age-related differences in responses to emotional advertisements. *Journal of Consumer Research, 32,* 343–354.

Willott, J. F. (1991). *Aging and the auditory system: Anatomy, physiology, and psychophysics.* San Diego, CA: Singular Publishing Group.

Yoon, C. (1997). Age differences in consumers' processing strategies: An investigation of moderating influences. *Journal of Consumer Research, 24,* 329–342.

Yoon, C., Lee, M., & Danziger, S. (2007). The effects of optimal time of day on persuasion processes in older adults. *Psychology and Marketing, 24,* 475–495.

Yoon, C., May, C. P., Goldstein, D., & Hasher, L. (in press). Aging, circadian arousal patterns and cognition. In D. C. Park & N. Schwarz (Eds.), *Cognitive aging: A primer* (2nd ed.). Philadelphia: Psychology Press.

Zacks, R.T., & Hasher, L. (1979). Automatic and effortful processes in memory. *Journal of Experimental Psychology: General, 108,* 356–388.

Zacks, R. T., Hasher, L., & Li, K, Z. H. (2000). Human memory. In F. I. M. Craik & T. A. Salthouse (Eds.), *The handbook of aging and cognition* (2nd ed., pp. 293–357). Mahwah, NJ: Erlbaum.

III

MOTIVATION, AFFECT, AND CONSUMER DECISIONS

10

Positive Affect and Decision Processes

Some Recent Theoretical Developments With Practical Implications

ALICE M. ISEN

Cornell University

In recent years, in a growing number of fields, both basic and applied, there has been a great deal of interest in the influence of affect on thinking, problem solving, and decision making (see Gardner, 1985, and Isen, 1984a, 1984b, 2000, for overviews of some of the earlier work, and Cohen, Pham, & Andrade, chapter 11, this volume, for further review and interesting statistics on how work on affect has burgeoned). Much of the work on affect's influence on thinking and decision making has been of a basic or theoretical nature, but it has found ready application in diverse applied fields, from consumer behavior and management to medical decision making and diagnosis, from clinical work and coping research to applied economics and health policy. And, happily, research in the applied fields has contributed to the basic work in ways that only applied fields can do, adding their practical perspectives along with rigorous methods, to advance both the applications and the basic work itself substantially (e.g., Aspinwall, 1998; Aspinwall & Taylor, 1997; Boush & Loken, 1991; Feldman & Lynch, 1988; Folkes & Matta, 2004; Friestad & Wright, 1995; Keller, Lipkus, & Rimer, 2003; Lurie, 2004; Lynch, Marmorstein, & Weigold, 1988; Posavac, Sanbonmatsu, Kardes, & Fitzsimons, 2004; Roehm & Sternthal, 2001; Staw & Barsade, 1993; Taylor & Aspinwall, 1996; Tybout, Sternthal, Malaviya, Bakamitsos, & Park, 2005; Weiss, Nicholas, & Daus, 1999, to name just a few of the many potential examples of excellent work from applied fields that contributes back to theory).

A recent paper in the *Journal of Consumer Psychology* discussed some of the affect findings and their potential applications (Isen, 2001). The purpose of the present chapter is to report on some more recent developments in the study of positive affect's influence on thinking and decision making, with an eye toward laying the groundwork for integrating these new developments into the applied fields, particularly consumer behavior. As noted by Cohen et al. (chapter 11, this volume), research in the area of emotion has increased dramatically. Thus, I could not hope to include all of the new developments in emotion in this chapter, and what I will cover will be only a portion of the interesting topics relating to affect that are currently under investigation that hold promise for contributing further to the field of consumer psychology. The topics I will address include the following: Focus of attention ("broad" versus "narrow" or "global" and "local"); distractibility; false memory; cognitive monitoring and the metacognition that follows from monitoring; and self-control. I have chosen these topics because, although there is growing activity relating to the effect of affect on those processes, and they are of clear potential importance to applied fields, the applied fields such as consumer behavior have not yet begun to investigate them extensively. Even within this circumscribed set of phenomena, space limitations preclude my conducting a complete review, as each one is a vast topic in itself. My goal in this chapter will be simply to point out some of the current work that is being done on these and related phenomena, work that has potential for contributing further to our understanding of the impact of positive affect on consumers' thought and decision processes.

FOCUS OF ATTENTION

Some of the recent theoretical developments regarding affect have centered on the question of the influence that affect has on focus of attention. I begin with a brief historical digression, for the purpose of providing context: Affect and focus of attention has been a question of interest for decades, but the form that it took historically was somewhat different from what is being investigated currently. For example, in the 1950s Easterbrook (1959) proposed that arousal or anxiety, called "emotion," narrowed the focus of attention and reduced cue utilization. That view was quite compatible with a line of thinking emerging from the decades preceding it that conceptualized high motivation or "Drive" (D) or arousal as reducing cue utilization (e.g., Bruner, Matter, & Papanek, 1955) and thus potentially interfering with performance. This interest itself stemmed from the even earlier suggestion that too high motivation or arousal—later to be thought of, often, as the emotion of anxiety—resulted in impaired performance (Yerkes & Dodson, 1908). In the early and middle part of the last century, scientific consideration was given to "arousal" as a factor in behavior, thinking or learning, and performance, but it was not entirely clear how arousal should be conceptualized. Based on theories prevalent at that time, it was demonstrated, primarily in animal learning studies, that arousal or high D (motivation) facilitated the dominant response in the organism's repertoire (see Hilgard & Bower, 1966, and Woodworth & Schlosberg, 1954, for consideration of the role of arousal or "Drive" in various theories of learning, of the time). This, then, later also fit with the idea that arousal ("emotion") would narrow focus and reduce cue utilization of peripheral or secondary cues as demonstrated by authors such as Bruner et al. (1955) and Easterbrook, (1959).

It seems that affect (emotion) and arousal were often thought to be synonymous, and co-mixed with motivation. At least one theorist held the position specifically that affect and arousal were synonymous and that there was no real role for emotion apart from motivation in the form of arousal (Duffy, 1934, 1941). Arousal was seen in most of these formulations as necessary to motivate behavior, but generally disruptive beyond the basic level needed to energize behavior (e.g., Yerkes & Dodson, 1908). Possibly as a result of this legacy, somewhat later views that included emotion as separate from arousal or motivation also tended to see it as disruptive (e.g., Simon, 1967). But none of these views, over all of those decades, considered emotion to be anything other than negative in tone, perhaps stemming from its earlier conceptualization as too-high arousal.

Gradually affect, arousal, and motivation have been distinguished and studied separately, although there continues to be some confusion among them. For example, in common usage, anxiety, a negative affective state, is sometimes labeled "arousal" (also called "stress"), and it is often assumed that high arousal is negative in feeling tone. There are models of emotion that distinguish between affect and arousal (see, e.g., Russell & Carroll, 1999; Watson & Tellegen, 1999, for discussions of these models), and some research has investigated valence and arousal separately (e.g., Lewinsohn & Mano, 1993; Mano, 1994; Sanbonmatsu & Kardes, 1988), or has contrasted effects of positive affect, negative affect, and affectless arousal in the form of increased heart rate raised by physical movement such as stepping up and down (e.g., Isen & Daubman, 1984; Isen, Daubman, & Nowicki, 1987); but people still often slip into thinking of arousal as negative affect.

An important development in the past 30 years has been the recognition that positive and negative affect are separate phenomena, and that positive affect has clear and strong effects, often beneficial ones, on thinking and behavior—from generosity, helping, and social behavior, to problem solving, decision making, and basic cognitive processes (see, e.g., a review by Isen, 2004). Now that positive affect has been recognized as a process, or processes, of its own, with effects that are separate from those of arousal, negative affect, or motivation, the stage has been set for a fuller consideration of a range of influences of emotions on basic thought and behavioral processes.

In this context, the current work on affect and focus of attention builds on that earlier work that suggested that negative affect narrows the focus of attention, as was proposed by Easterbrook (1959) and others, but extends it now beyond negative emotion. More recently, people have begun looking at the effect that *positive* affect might have on focus of attention, with the idea that it might broaden the focus of attention. This was originally suggested based on an unexpected finding in a study of affect's influence on helping behavior (Isen, 1970; see Isen, 1990, for discussion). Participants were asked a set of questions about a person and activities that had unexpectedly occurred in the room where they were waiting for the experimenter to return. The results showed that not only did people in a negative affect condition (created by report of failure on a task) do more poorly on the surprise question about the surrounding conditions, but those in whom positive affect had been induced (by report of success on the task) did not have narrowed attention like people in the negative-affect condition, but reported more correct information about what had happened around them.

Effects of negative and positive affect compatible with those just described were reported more recently by Derryberry (1993), using a different task and materials. He found that success resulted in the ability to attend to low-value targets without missing high-value targets, whereas failure reduced the ability to attend to the low-value targets while attending to the high-value targets. Thus, it appears that positive affect (success) facilitates broader deployment of attention with no loss of accuracy or speed of processing, and negative affect (failure) reduces breadth of attention in order to remain accurate on a subset of the items. Derryberry (1993) summarizes the work on this effect as best described as showing that stressful states "narrow" focus rather than "concentrating" it, because they impair secondary information without facilitating primary information or causing improved performance on the primary items. With regard to positive affect, he concludes that attention may broaden but this broadening is not accompanied by dilution of resources devoted to the primary focus (p. 84).

More recently, other authors have begun to investigate the question of focus of attention (often referred to as "global" versus "local" processing) during positive and negative affect, looking at matters such as literally whether people first tend to use broad features of a display or more narrowly focused features to understand what they are seeing (e.g., Derryberry & Reed, 1998; Friedman & Forster, 2005; Gasper & Clore, 2002). For example, several studies use a task similar to the one developed by Navon (1977) or Kimchi & Palmer (1982), in which a stimulus is presented to participants that is a shape constructed out of smaller building blocks of another shape (for example, a square made out of smaller triangles), or one letter (say, F) made up of another letter (say, small Ls), with the stimulus thus being small Ls that form the shape of an F. In such studies people are asked, for example, to identify the shape or letter that is presented (responding "a square" or "F," in the two examples above, would indicate a global focus, whereas saying "triangle" or "L" would indicate local focus). According to Navon (1977) and Kimchi and Palmer (1982), most people respond based on the broader focus, indicating hierarchical organization of perception; but the point of the research on affect and focus has been to see whether positive and negative affect influence focus of attention, using that type of task. That research has reported that people in positive affect show a tendency to process the broader dimensions of the display, at least initially. Some researchers assume that this means that people in positive affect can *only* process broadly, that they cannot focus narrowly or would have difficulty, or show impaired processing and distractibility (more on this later), when required to focus narrowly.

A recent paper (Baumann & Kuhl, 2005) addressed this question specifically, using a task similar to one used in the research by Gasper and Clore (2002), by having the experimental participants solving a problem that required using the broader dimension and the narrower dimension in order to obtain the correct solution. The data in that paper show that people in positive affect were at least as capable of using the narrow focus if there was a reason to do so: When it was necessary for solving the problem, they opted for the narrow focus and performed well, as reflected by both reaction time and error rates (Baumann & Kuhl, 2005). This, then, supports the view that positive affect enables flexible deployment of attention (e.g., Isen, 2000a), rather than merely broadening attention or limiting people to the one, albeit broad, perspective. It is, thus, also compatible with the work reported by Derryberry (1993), described earlier, showing that positive affect leads to broader focus or perception (attention to secondary targets), but not at the cost of processing of valuable targets—that is, it leads to broader focus and success on low-value targets, but no dilution of resources devoted to the primary focus, and unimpaired success on high-value targets.

It must be noted that in the paper by Gasper and Clore (2002) what was actually found was that the positive-affect and the control condition did not differ, and that it was the negative-affect condition that was more narrowly focused than the controls. Although in places those authors were careful to state the difference between the positive and negative conditions in terms of negative affect causing a narrower focus, they did imply that their results indicate that positive mood fosters a global focus. Further, they again raise the points, made in more detail elsewhere, that positive affect is often assumed to prompt less extensive than usual thinking (which, they believe, would correspond to the more global focus), and that negative affect is often assumed to foster more extensive processing (which they argue would correspond to the more local focus). They acknowledge that their findings are not supportive of such views, in several ways; however, repetition of those contra-indicated views, after such acknowledgment, contributes to sustaining these misconceptions in the literature.

Thus, it is useful to consider the findings of other authors, such as those presented above—Baumann and Kuhl (2005) and Derryberry (1993), and others—to provide more context for the findings of Gasper and Clore (2002). As suggested by Derryberry and colleagues (e.g., Derryberry, 1993; Derryberry & Reed, 1998), narrow focus may not indicate more extensive processing, and the broad focus shown by the positive-feedback group in his studies corresponds to more, not less, extensive and effective processing.

Another program of research dealing with the question of focus, but in a different way, is that of Fredrickson, who postulates that people in positive affect "broaden and build" their skills, knowledge, and resources and then can use them in multiple ways, and describes upward spirals of well-being as resulting from positive feelings (e.g., Fredrickson, 1998; Fredrickson & Branigan, 2005). That is, not only do people in positive affect look at the bigger picture, but they build their resources as they do so. They look at the bigger picture not just literally or in perception, but they take in the context of a stimulus or event and learn about the whole stimulus or experience. This work would be compatible with the interpretation, and findings described above, that people in positive affect are not *limited* to the wider perspective, even though they may be able to access it and use it more readily than those in comparison affect states.

THE FLEXIBILITY HYPOTHESIS

Fredrickson's view is also compatible with the flexibility hypothesis (e.g., Isen, 1984b, 1990, 2000a), which holds that people in positive affect are more flexible than others, and can see things both ways or change between broad and narrow focus, or typical and non-typical views, as appropriate in the situation. For example, in three studies investigating positive affect's influence on the unusualness, and range, of word associations to common, neutral words, it was found that people in positive affect did not lose the more common associates when they showed more unusual associates, and a broader range of first associates, to neutral words (Isen et al., 1985). Similarly, in two studies extending this work to investigate the influence of positive affect on the range of consumers' consideration sets (Kahn & Isen, 1993), people in the positive affect condition did not stop categorizing typical snacks as snacks, just because they broadened their consideration sets to include less typical foods in the snack category. Results compatible with these had also been reported in the categorization studies of Isen & Daubman (1984), which showed that, even though people in the positive-affect condition rated nontypical vehicles such as "camel" and "elevator" as better examples of the category "vehicle" than did controls, they still rated vehicles such as "car," "truck," and "bus" as better examples of the category than "elevator" and "camel" (and did not differ from controls in their ratings of the typical vehicles). Likewise, in studying categorization of social stimuli, Isen, Niedenthal, & Cantor (1992) reported that people in positive affect rated nontypical examples of the category "nurturant people" (e.g., bartender) as possible members of that category to a greater extent than did people in a control condition. At the same time, however, typical examples of the category such as "grandmother" were rated higher than the less typical exemplars by participants in both affect conditions, and to the same extent. Another set of studies that show flexibility in conjunction with positive affect are those reported by Murray, Sujan, Hirt, & Sujan (1990), who also found that people in positive affect showed more flexibility in categorizing stimuli.

Relating this flexibility to the topic of broad and narrow focus, this kind of flexibility is proposed to characterize people who are in a mild positive affective state, so that the fact that they may tend to look at the larger picture first, or broaden their view, or integrate context into their conceptualization, does not mean that they cannot focus or are limited to only the broad level of focus. Some of this work relates this ability, further, to a change in cognitive organization, wherein people are able to be flexible in the way they view and interpret situations and sets of stimuli, able to see and interpret them in multiple ways and reorganize and integrate their elements in multiple ways, often depending on the context or task that needs to be done (e.g., Isen, Daubman, & Nowicki, 1987; see, e.g., Isen, 1984b, 1993; Isen, Daubman, & Gorgoglione, 1987, for discussion). Thus, this view, compatibly with Fredrickson's and the results such as those reported above, suggests that people who are feeling happy not only have a broad perspective perceptually, but also have a broad perspective cognitively, can conceptualize and integrate more material and see it in more different ways (e.g., Isen, 1990, 1993a, 1993b). As we have seen, the evidence for this kind of increased flexibility has been obtained not only in the influence of positive affect on people's preference for variety, consideration sets in product choice, acceptance of unusual and nontypical associates to words and other stimuli, and ways of categorizing both social and non-social stimuli, but also in their problem-solving ability and innovation and creativity (e.g., Greene & Noice, 1988; Isen et al., 1987; Isen, 1993a;

Staw & Barsade, 1993). It has also been supported in work on coping, and in clinical and neuroscience studies of the influence of affect (e.g., Aspinwall, 1998; Compton, Wirtz, Pajoumand, Claus, & Heller, 2004; Taylor & Aspinwall, 1996; to name just a few).

Work on focus of attention has several potential applications to consumer behavior and understanding the decision processes of consumers. The consumer literature has started to investigate some of these topics, especially those stemming from the earlier work on flexibility in processing and categorization For example, building on a similar line of thought—that positive affect may lead consumers to think more broadly about brands—consumer researchers have investigated the influence of affect on acceptability of brand extensions (e.g., Barone & Miniard, 2002; Barone, Miniard, & Romeo, 2000; Yeung & Wyer, 2005). One series of studies found that people in positive affect evaluated moderately incongruent extensions of favorably-evaluated brands, but not of unfavorably evaluated brands, as more acceptable than did controls (e.g., Barone & Miniard, 2002; Barone et al., 2000). Further exploration has addressed differences that may result when the affect in the situation arises not from extraneous sources but out of the brand itself (Yeung & Wyer, 2005).

ASYMMETRY OF EFFECTS ON POSITIVE AND NEGATIVE MATERIAL

The finding reported by Barone and Miniard (2002) of asymmetry in the effects of positive affect on positive stimuli and negative stimuli is an example of a phenomenon that has been found repeatedly in the affect literature and has very important implications for understanding the processes associated with positive affect. For example, although the term "mood congruency" seemed to catch on years ago, there was little support, from the very beginning, for the general, across-the-board idea of "mood congruency," wherein any mood would be expected to cue material of the same affective tone and influence the evaluation of any material considered. In actuality, positive affect was found to be an effective cue for positive material, but negative affect, especially sadness, was not found to cue negative material or was found to do so to a much lesser extent than positive affect; similarly, the effect of positive affect on behavior such as helping and generosity was more clear than the effect of negative affect, which did not simply produce the opposite effects (see Isen, 1984b, 1990, for discussions).

More important and intriguing for the present discussion, however, is the fact that there were also asymmetries observed of the kind reported by Barone & Miniard (2002), wherein positive affect was found to have an impact on some kinds of stimuli but not others, or to operate in some situations but not others. For example, positive affect was found to influence the evaluation of neutral pictures but not positive or negative pictures, neutral facial expressions but not positive or negative facial expressions, and so on; and in terms of positive affect's other kinds of effects, similarly, positive affect was demonstrated to influence the categorization of neutral-to-positive words, person types, and products, but not negative words, person types, or products (see, e.g., Isen, 1990, 2000, for discussion). Some of these findings have already been described above in greater detail.

These kinds of asymmetries indicate that there are different, and more complex, processes going on than mere mood-matching, or mood acting as a lens or filter, coloring everything rosy or making everything seem more similar and more acceptable. Rather, they suggest that affect's influence depends on what the person is trying to accomplish and how the person interprets the situation, often in light of his or her goals. It is important to keep these kinds of findings in mind when considering the effects that are to be expected of positive affect.

Returning to consideration of the topic of the potential importance of positive affect's influence on focus of attention, it seems, then, that the figurative effects of altered focus of attention have already begun to receive some attention in the field of consumer behavior. That work would include studies stemming from the effects of affect on focus in the sense of flexibility (for example, broadening—or narrowing, when that is appropriate—in the use of categories in size or scope, reorganization of material, integration of context; and so forth). The research described above on affect's influence on reactions to brand extensions is an example of such work. Still, there remain many more potential applications to be addressed, such as integration of context and/or meaning, as well as further development of some that have been begun—as is evident from some of the most recent work on brand extension, for only one example.

Beyond that, however, the idea of focus of attention also has additional potential applications that might be fruitfully explored in consumer behavior, and the newer work focusing more directly on global versus local processing highlights some additional areas that may be useful to investigate. First, regardless of the fact that ultimately people in positive affect are flexible, not limited to the broad perspective, it is noteworthy that they may focus first on the broader picture or its implications and associates, or notice more about the entire setting of the presentation or notice peripheral aspects of displays or situations. Perhaps this is a figurative statement as well as a literal one, as has been discussed, and it is likely that people in positive affect may see multiple interpretations or applications of displays, products, companies, and/or what they discern are strategies by manufacturers. This suggests several lines of investigation as important consumer topics, drawing out both the figurative implications of broadened perspective and the literal. Practitioners and researchers trying to understand and accommodate to the preferred processing style of consumers who are in a positive affect state might benefit from knowing that people who are feeling mildly happy may notice more aspects of situations and displays, or that they may notice the broader, integrative ones first, or that they may integrate more thoughts and interpretations about an ad or a display or a product line, or that they may respond first to the implications or meaning of a display or ad or promotion experience. They may also integrate the context with the product more—which can result in a product's advantage, or disadvantage. These are just some of the potential applications of the current findings that would be intriguing topics for continued consumer research.

Although I am focusing on positive affect in this chapter, it seems appropriate to consider, in the context of focus of attention, the effect of negative affect or stress on attentional focus. This is because the findings relating negative affect and narrowed focus are so clear and strong and go back decades, if not a century. As reviewed above, here the evidence suggests clearly that stress causes people to focus in narrowly and to miss peripheral, global, or secondary aspects of situations or displays. Findings compatible with this statement have been obtained for decades, but the more recent ones are even more clear because they attempt to distinguish between arousal and affect and between negative and positive affect. In sum, regardless of how ideal it would be, especially for over-simplified versions of evolutionary accounts, if negative affect caused improved performance or had some direct, simple compensatory benefit associated with the limited range of focus that has been found to result from it, what has been found repeatedly in studies on the topic of affect-and-focus is that negative affect narrows focus (not "concentrates" it, as pointed out by Derryberry, 1993, for example) and limits what people attend to and how they interpret material.

Although marketers do not usually try to induce negative affect in consumers,[1] still there may be times when consumers will be in a negative state when shopping, or when considering ads or products. For example, when people are tired or in a hurry, or have to cope with tired, bored children who are with them, but still must shop or consider a purchase, and so forth, they may be stressed or in a negative state. Therefore, consumer researchers may find it of interest to investigate what kinds of displays or presentations would be most effective for such circumstances. One approach may be to try to make the consumer feel better, and perhaps this can be done with a broader display and playful peripheral, secondary material; however, one has to accept the possibility that the tired, harassed shopper or ad viewer may miss the secondary material (and note that removing negative affect is a complex issue; see Isen, 1989, for discussion). Thus, another approach might be the time-honored, KIS ("Keep It Simple"). But these issues require research.

There are several implications to the various types of focus that have been described above, all of which require research to understand and implement correctly. First, there is the matter of actual focus—on the broader or more global stimulus or configuration of stimuli or materials that are present in a display. For only one example, marketers, especially when using positive-affect-inducing materials (e.g., ads, promotions, the products themselves) may want to use this knowledge to create displays they think might be favorable to their products, for example, with features they want to highlight portrayed more broadly or placed around the display in multiple locations to create the main theme so that they will be noticed first. The overall effect, or its implications, may be more important—especially initially—than the details. This would not be because people in positive affect are limited in their resources or motivation, nor because they cannot process the details, as has sometimes been suggested, but because they are taking in the whole picture, its context, and its meaning, and they may prefer experiencing more varied materials, materials with secondary themes as well as primary. However, before such strategies are implemented, additional research on the topic, using complex materials and settings would be called for.

Second, as has become evident from our consideration of the evidence here, the effect of positive affect is really one of attentional flexibility, not breadth per se, and therefore having secondary themes that can be discerned and integrated with the larger theme might be especially attractive to people who are feeling happy. In fact, one way to accommodate tired or time-pressed consumers at the same time as those who are enjoying the experience may be to have a simple focal message within a larger or broader context that offers the variety and secondary themes that may be attractive and can be selected and attended to by those who are in positive affect.

Third, the research reviewed suggests that people in positive affect may integrate disparate aspects of displays or products and see or construct more different meanings and applications of the materials or products. This possibility was actually discussed also in an earlier consideration of the effect of positive affect on cognitive organization (e.g., Isen, 1993a, 1993b), but now we know more about how such effects may occur and the factors that may influence them, and additional research on these topics could be very helpful.

DISTRACTIBILITY

As has been pointed out already in this chapter and elsewhere, it is well established that positive affect leads to flexibility in thinking and problem solving. This capability is evident in people's ratings, choices, categorizations, word associations, innovation, problem solving, and other thought processes, measured in many different ways (see, e.g., Isen, 2000a, for illustration and discussion). A growing body of evidence suggests that this flexibility means that people can deploy their attention to multiple targets, can change attention, set, goals, or interpretation, can integrate ideas and use that integration to help solve problems, and so forth (e.g., Derryberry, 1993; Isen et al., 1987; see Isen, 2000a, for discussion). This increased flexibility does not mean that their thinking is "loose" or unhinged or wanders, or *must* move from topic to topic, but rather that they can deploy their attention to multiple targets or change set, when they choose to do so.

Nonetheless, some authors have reasoned that flexibility implies distractibility, as if attentional focus cannot be maintained, or is more difficult to maintain, in cases where flexibility is present (e.g., Dreisbach & Goschke, 2004). Thus, Dreisbach and Goschke (2004) have argued that people in positive affect will be less susceptible to perseveration (i.e., the inability to change set, focus, or goal when the problem changes), but more susceptible to distraction (the inability to stay on target), because, they reason, there is a reciprocal relationship between perseveration and distractibility (e.g., Dreisbach & Goschke, 2004). In other words, they assume that an influence that leads people to be more flexible, and not constrained to keep thinking about or responding to the same stimulus in the same way, will also lead people to be more easily distracted or unable to stay on target; and they predict that this will be the case for people in positive affect. In its simplest form, the argument would be something like saying that, because positive affect increases flexibility, and broadens perspective and/or focus of attention, it will carry a benefit when people need to change focus, but a cost when people need to stay on target. Those authors present data showing that positive affect does decrease perseveration (decreases the tendency to stay on a given task or target or response set when it is no longer appropriate) but that it also does increase distractibility, in the form of reaction time (though not errors) on a target stimulus, when the distractor stimulus consists of items that were previously correct but no longer represent correct answers (a failure of what they call "learned irrelevance"), or when the distractor is novel. Their definition of distractibility, however, is not what one would expect—it is not the simple inability to stay on target or keep the same frame of reference—but rather bears a complex relationship to the nature of the interfering stimulus. (In some ways it even seems to be like perseveration, because it involves the "failure of learned irrelevance," which would seem to imply a perseveration of the idea that the old stimulus is still relevant. However, those authors distinguish between perseveration and this kind of distractibility.)

Leaving that aside, the argument is an interesting one that raises several interesting issues, from whether those two processes (perseveration and distractibility) are reciprocally related, to whether additional processes (such as inhibition, cognitive monitoring, or other response factors) might not come into play to moderate the ultimate outcome, and need to be added to the mix in order to understand the role that affect will play in attentive processes. In fact, other authors have reported data that would not support Dreisbach and Goschke's (2004) interpretation of their data. For example, if one relates Dreisbach and Goschke's (2004) reasoning to the findings on focus of attention, described earlier, the argument would be that a broader focus of attention and ability to monitor secondary targets would imply an inability to stay on target and perform as well on the main targets. But, as discussed above, this is not what was found by, for example, Derryberry (1993). Rather, what was found was that positive affect led people to be able to perform well on secondary targets while at the same time showing no diminution in performance on the main targets.

In addition, other authors have also found results that suggest that more is going on than a simple reciprocal relationship between flexibility and distractibility. For example, Kuhl and Kazen (1999) studied the influence of positive affect on Stroop interference. The Stroop task is one in which a person is shown a stimulus that consists of a word that is the name of a color, but the word is written in a different color ink; and the person's task is to report the color of the ink in which the word is written. Therefore, in that task, two conflicting tendencies are activated, the tendency to report the color that the word is written in, and the tendency to read the word, which is the name of a different color (and which would produce an incorrect response). In order to respond correctly, the person must suppress the tendency to read the word, which is the dominant response, and which would produce the wrong answer. Reaction times to giving the correct response are measured in order to gauge amount of interference, called "Stroop interference," arising from that dominant tendency. Kuhl and Kazen (1999) reported that positive affect improves performance (reaction time) on this task and removes Stroop interference. Another program of research, by Friedman and Forster (e.g., 2005), also reports, compatibly with this work, that approach motivation—a concept that may relate to positive affect (see Carver, Sutton, & Scheier, 2000)—improves performance on the Stroop task and facilitates attentional flexibility.

Another recent series of three studies also finds that positive affect induced in two additional ways (receipt of a small bag of 10 wrapped hard candies, and viewing a few minutes of a non-sexual, non-aggressive amusing film) leads people to perform better on tasks requiring divided attention or incidental learning, while not impairing performance on the main task (Isen & Shmidt, 2007). This held true whether the potentially interfering stimuli were novel or previously correct (now incorrect) responses.

The results reported by Kuhl and Kazen (1999) and Kazen and Kuhl (2005), and other authors, indicate that positive affect facilitates the processes that underlie improved performance on tasks such as the Stroop task—which include maintaining a difficult intention and inhibiting an unwanted response. This means that with positive affect, a difficult intention can be carried out, in the presence of an otherwise dominant response, with less increase in reaction time than is observed in the control group. This suggests that, when the context of the whole task is taken into account, positive affect, rather than causing distractibility, enables control. The authors' interpretation of their finding included the point that positive affect facilitates the processes that allow the correct (intended) process to be activated, when two processes are in competition, and then to be performed at the appropriate time. Thus, in tasks involving distraction and perseveration, it seems that processes of inhibition, activation, maintenance, monitoring, and intention must also be considered.

To summarize this matter, then, the evidence with regard to positive affect's influence on distractibility is mixed: Some evidence suggests that positive affect, while decreasing perseveration, may increase distractibility, as measured by reaction time to irrelevant stimuli that previously were relevant. But there is also countervailing evidence suggesting that positive affect allows deployment of attention to additional targets without interfering with performance on the primary targets. And there is also evidence suggesting that positive affect, compared with a control condition, removes Stroop interference, which indicates that people in positive affect are better than controls at maintaining a difficult intention and inhibiting unwanted responses. More research is needed on this topic, but it is an area that relates to what is called "executive" attention or processing, and the topic of affect's influence on executive processing is the focus of much current research.

Similarly, this seems to be an issue that could be of substantial interest to consumer researchers and seems worth pursuing in a consumer context. Not only would it be important for consumer researchers to know whether positive affect increases distractibility, and if so how that plays out in a complex consumer context, but this seems to be one of those situations in which the rich stimulus context provided by realistic consumer tasks, stimuli, and settings might add to the theoretical understanding of the fundamental issue, as well.

That is, it may be that in the abstract, or with a tedious task or meaningless distinction between two barely distinguishable stimuli, people in positive affect may appear to be distractible, because they may take a few additional milliseconds to respond (however, the contradictory evidence reported by other authors should also be kept in mind). But in such a setting one cannot know the reason for the person's increased response time—were they unable to respond more quickly, or did they take a few milliseconds to think about something more interesting, because they didn't think it would matter? While it may be possible to argue that something like this is the meaning of "distractible," it seems more likely that such a context-induced effect would not be what most people would mean when they say that a person is distractible. (Distractibility might more usually be thought of as akin to impulsiveness or failure to inhibit response to the distracting stimulus—in fact, Dreisbach & Goschke, 2004, make this connection.) Further, motivational differences between affect and control conditions may exist in such a context. We do know that people in positive affect are more likely to do what they prefer to do (e.g., see Isen & Reeve, 2005, for discussion), and the apparent "distractibility" could simply be a reflection of that greater freedom to behave as one wishes or this alternative motive that is introduced by positive affect in that context.

Still, the more general point to be made is that the question of whether positive affect influences distractibility seems an important topic for investigation. In addition, given several of the findings that have been discussed thus far, one might also ask whether negative affect influences distractibility. To progress, some agreement will have to be achieved on the best way to define and measure distractibility, and distinctions among the existing ways should be considered (perhaps some ways are more appropriate for certain purposes, whereas other ways will be more appropriate for others). In addition, the question of whether distractibility involves impulsiveness also needs to be considered. Most likely distinctions will need to be drawn here, especially given the findings in the affect-and-risk literature, which call into question the idea that people in positive affect are careless, impulsive risk-takers (see, e.g., Isen, 2000b, for discussion), and also question the assumption that people in negative affect are careful in risky situations. Finally, distinctions among stimuli and settings may need to be considered as well, in coming to predictions about how distractible people in various affective states will be. All of this suggests that consumer research on the topic would be welcome and needed.

FALSE MEMORY

Another current line of investigation that follows from one possible extrapolation of the affect-flexibility link is the proposition that positive affect will lead to false memory. False memory has been studied using what is called the Deese-Roediger-McDermott (DRM) paradigm (Deese, 1959; Roediger & McDermott, 1995). In this procedure, participants are presented with multiple lists of semantically associated words (e.g., "snow," "winter," "ice," and so on) that are related also to a critical item (e.g., "cold") that is not presented. Then they are given a recognition test, that presents words that were previously presented and words that were not previously presented, including the critical word (the one that is related to the theme of the presented words but was not itself presented), and asks participants to say whether each word in the test was presented before or not. The test for "false memory" is whether the critical word is erroneously identified as having been presented previously. Results in the cognitive psychology literature indicate that false memory measured in this way is very common, with people generally making this error as frequently as they correctly identify words that had been presented (see Roediger, McDermott, & Robinson, 1998, for review).

It has been reported that positive affect leads to better recall of schematic material—that is, material that is related to a given schema or theme (e.g., Bless et al., 1996). Thus, in a recent paper, Storbeck and Clore (2005) used a procedure based on the DRM paradigm (not exactly following the DRM paradigm, a difference that will be discussed later), and proposed that positive affect would lead to an increase in false memory. Those authors apparently reasoned that because people in positive affect could think of more related words than controls, or perhaps because they would just be more likely to think of related words than controls would, people in positive affect would also have a greater rate of false memory. However, that is not what happened.

The title of the article by Storbeck and Clore (2005) ("With sadness comes accuracy, with happiness, false memory") suggests that positive affect does lead to more false memory, but in actuality, what those authors found was that positive affect did not increase false memory above the level of the control group. They also had a negative-affect group in their study, and they reported a difference between the negative-affect group on the one hand, and the control group and positive affect group on the other, with the latter two not differing from each other, and the negative-affect group lower than both of the comparison groups. Thus, it seems that the effect of positive affect on false memory was not obtained, but it also seems that an interesting effect of negative affect may have been obtained, because negative affect appeared to reduce false memory compared with the control group.

However, it is not clear that the effect of negative affect was actually an effect on false memory. To understand these results fully, it should be noted that Storbeck and Clore (2005) did not use a recognition test to assess false memory, but rather instructed participants to indicate all of the thoughts they had during the presentation of the initial word list, including any related thoughts. Thus, they used a procedure that simply asked people to indicate all of the thoughts they had, and did not allow or request any role for monitoring or checking. That is, if people usually monitor and check their thoughts and answers to questions about what had been presented previously and what had not, or if they could do so if requested to do so, or if alerted to the need to do so in order to avoid errors, and if monitoring and checking play a crucial role in whether or not false memory occurs, when people are asked to distinguish between words that had been presented and those that had not been presented, the effect of any such process would not be apparent using the procedure used by Storbeck and Clore (2005). That is, if there is more to false memory than just having associates to presented words, then false memory would not be assessed by the technique used by Storbeck and Clore (2005).

In fact, it would seem that false memory involves not just associated words coming to mind, but also a failure of monitoring, a failure to differentiate between words that come to mind and words that were previously presented. For a person to have a false memory, he or she must fail to realize that the word that came to mind was not a previously presented word, and the person must incorrectly report that the word had been presented previously. Therefore, the occurrence of false memory depends, not just on having associated or schematically related thoughts and words to the presented words, but also on a failure of monitoring so as not to be able to know that those words were not previously presented. Perhaps having more associates to a given idea or event may indeed play a role, as hypothesized by Storbeck and Clore (2005), but it would seem important also to assess the critical process of monitoring as well, in order to determine whether false memory should occur.

Further, if there is reason to believe that affect differentially influences monitoring or checking, and in particular that positive affect improves or increases the tendency to engage in such monitoring processes, then it is apparent that any such beneficial influence would be obscured in the research by Storbeck and Clore (2005). In fact, there is evidence in the literature that positive affect does facilitate monitoring and checking. Although some researchers have argued that positive affect leads to superficial or sloppy or impulsive processing, there is a great deal of evidence in the affect-and-problem-solving literature, the affect-and-risk literature, and other studies of positive affect, that points to careful, thorough thinking by people in positive affect (see Isen, 2000a, for review and discussion of this issue).

Compatibly with this suggestion, increased monitoring and decreased false memory were indeed found in a recent pair of studies investigating the influence of positive affect on false memory using the DRM paradigm including a recognition test (Yang, Ceci, & Isen, 2006). In these studies, in Study 1, it was found, again, that the positive affect and control conditions did not differ in false memory, but in Study 2, in which participants were told about the nature of the false-memory effect and encouraged not to fall prey to such errors, people in the positive-affect condition showed significantly less false memory than controls. The authors attributed this effect to better monitoring on the part of the positive-affect participants.

This finding, indicating that people in positive affect are more likely to engage in monitoring or checking of their thinking or behavior, is quite compatible with many other findings in the affect literature. For example, one study that illustrates this greater tendency to check was conducted in a medical setting and involved physicians asked to make a diagnosis of a hypothetical patient. Those in the positive-affect condition, even though they were quicker to make a connection between the relevant disease area and the described symptoms, were also more likely than those in the control condition to stay open to the possibility that their initial hypothesis might be wrong, and to check their answers and hypotheses against additional information before giving a final answer to the diagnostic problem (Estrada, Isen, & Young, 1997). A similar finding was obtained in a study of fourth-year medical students who were asked to solve a problem that involved identifying which of several hypothetical patients was most likely to have a certain disease, given various sets of signs and symptoms. In that study, the clinicians in the positive affect condition, even though they came up with the correct answer earlier in their protocols, did not stop working with the materials and were significantly more likely than controls to go beyond the assigned task and do more, checking on the rest of the cases to make sure that each was not likely to have the target disease (see Isen, 2000a, for discussion).

As a final example of this tendency, consider the effects that have been observed in the affect-and-risk literature. There, it has been found repeatedly that people in whom positive affect is induced, and who are facing the possibility of a real and meaningful loss, display more caution and are risk-averse compared with controls—are significantly less likely than those in control groups to bet, or bet significantly less. In one of those studies that included a thought-listing task, it was also found, specifically, that participants in the positive-affect group listed more thoughts about the potential loss, which relates to increased checking and monitoring and may help to explain their increased caution (Isen & Geva, 1987).

False memory, especially as it has been defined in the research literature, actually involves confusion among stimuli that are thematically related. This is a topic that would naturally be of interest to researchers and practitioners in consumer psychology. Confusion among brands, product categories, product attributes, product benefits, advertisements, manufacturers, and the like is a serious potential problem in marketing and in every phase of dealing with consumers. As noted, in the psychology literature, it has been demonstrated that false memory is quite prevalent in general, indicating that it may be a problem wherever people want to induce the ability to differentiate among items or reasons or concepts of any kind. It is a problem in marketing, just as it is a general problem—perhaps even more-so, because marketing is concerned with persuasion and presentation and differentiation of options. Therefore, if research suggests something that could reduce the effects of the false-memory process, that would be important to investigate further.

Especially if there is reason to believe that affect can make false memory more likely, or less likely—or if it would be possible to determine circumstances under which each of these possibilities is likely to be true—this would be very useful to study in a consumer context. Even more important, research suggesting that positive affect can reduce false memory would be crucial to pursue—in part because marketing and product presentation depend heavily on developing positive affect among one's customers. And at the same time, differentiation of one's product is a constant concern and goal. Thus, this phenomenon might be investigated in the context of marketing stimuli, using products and brands or attributes or benefits, and so on, instead of just neutral, common words. Beyond that, studies might focus on ways to develop strategies to overcome this ubiquitous problem. (If it does turn out that negative affect reduces false memory—which is not yet clear—still it might not be wise to adopt a strategy of putting consumers into negative affect for that purpose.)

One caveat should be raised, before leaving this topic, and that has to do with the factors that would lead someone to monitor carefully, and specifically the factors that might lead someone in a mild positive affective state to monitor carefully. In the study reported by Yang et al., 2006, it was found that people in positive affect did monitor more carefully than controls, when participants were told about the phenomenon of possible intrusions of schematically related words. It had been found previously that people generally show substantially reduced error rates when given such warnings and encouragement to avoid those kinds of errors (e.g., Gallo, Roediger, & McDermott, 2001; McCabe & Anderson, 2002). And the study by Yang et al., 2006, found that this is even more true among people who were feeling mildly happy. Still one might wonder whether people will make the effort to monitor carefully in an everyday consumer situation (shopping, reading or viewing ads, seeing promotional material, and so forth), especially if the product is a low-involvement product, or the situation is one in which people might not want to put forth the effort to distinguish among ads or features or brands, or any kind of stimulus materials shown to them. And one might wonder, equally, whether the advantage of people in positive affect in monitoring and distinguishing among stimuli would be obtained in settings related to purchases.

Of course, different kinds of purchases may evoke different strategies and willingness to exert effort. For some kinds of purchases consumers may be willing to put forth a lot of effort to understand the purchase landscape; and there perhaps one would see the advantage to people in positive affect that was observed in the work by Yang et al., 2006. Or there may be factors in the way the message or product or promotion is presented that can lead consumers to be willing to differentiate or monitor differences, for example, among products or features of products. These are primarily empirical questions, and ones that would be exciting research topics in consumer behavior.

COGNITIVE MONITORING AND METACOGNITION

The work on false memory, showing that positive affect reduces false memory when people are warned that such intrusion effects often occur, calls attention to the role of fundamental cognitive processes such as encoding strategies, cognitive monitoring, and metacognition (i.e., awareness of one's own knowledge or lack of it) in people's processing of information.[2] However, even more interestingly, that work also implicates positive affect as a factor in these processes of monitoring and metacognition—and it suggests that people can exert control over such fundamental processes that determine many aspects of thinking and functioning. In the recent studies by Yang et al. (2006), it was reported that people in positive affect had a more correct sense of whether a word had actually been presented or just "felt" like it had been presented ("remember" versus "know" judgments), which is often related to metacognition (see, Nelson, 1996, for discussion of this and related topics). In the second study, importantly, people in the positive affect condition took better advantage of a warning about the possibility of intrusions arising from conceptually related material, possibly indicating improved monitoring of their knowledge.

Similarly, several studies of problem solving and decision making have shown that people in positive affect are more careful and controlled in the way they go about thinking about a problem: they tend to elaborate on ideas and stimulus materials presented and have more thoughts about them, check more, remain open to alternative hypotheses, decline to bet, or bet less, in a risky, real gambling situation, have more thoughts about potential dangers in a dangerous situation, and so forth (e.g., Estrada et al., 1997; Isen, Daubman, & Nowicki, 1987; Isen & Geva, 1987; Isen et al., 1991; see Isen, 2000a for discussion).

Thus, it may be instructive to investigate this question specifically, and especially in a consumer context. These findings relating to monitoring have not yet been fully developed or extensively researched in the context of affect's influence or contribution to them, but the topic area would seem to provide a set of possibilities for research that consumer researchers might find especially interesting.

THE DOPAMINE HYPOTHESIS

These findings and suggestions regarding monitoring and metacognition are also compatible with the dopamine hypothesis regarding positive affect's influence on cognitive processes, which is a theory that can help in understanding positive affect's facilitative effect on thinking processes (e.g., Isen, 2000a). It has been proposed that positive affect is associated with release of brain dopamine, which activates regions of the brain such as frontal areas that are known to be related to thinking, working memory, attentional flexibility, and other related cognitive processes (Ashby, Isen, & Turken, 1999). The growing body of work on social cognitive neuroscience is beyond the scope of this chapter; however, it is important to mention at least the dopamine hypothesis in the context of these ideas about positive affect's improving processes such as monitoring. Activation of frontal brain regions may account for participants' improved ability to consider multiple factors in the situation, including long-term welfare and not just immediate pleasant feelings, ability to monitor and keep track of several factors in the situation at the same time, and other indications of more complex cognitive processing. Despite the fact that space limitations prelude discussion of the social cognitive neuroscience area, this is surely an area that would be an exciting addition to the consumer research literature.

The findings regarding metacognition and monitoring may relate to matters of self-control, as well. Self-control is usually assumed to relate to refraining from some tempting action, such as eating rich food when one is trying to limit indulgence in such consumption, or lashing out in anger (note) at someone who has been offensive, and it is often studied in such a context—refraining from some action. It can also be conceptualized as relating to staying at a task that is difficult or unpleasant or competing with some more attractive task—staying at work studying when a friend calls and suggests going to a movie, for example. But self-control can also involve keeping one's mental focus, organizing cognitive material according to a strategy for remembering it or working with it, monitoring the occurrence of intruding but misleading cognitions, checking to make sure that one is staying on target or on task. Thus, the processes of metacognition and/or monitoring and checking may relate to self-control of a kind. Even though this kind of self-control may be seen as different from prototypic resistance to temptation, still it is possible to see the similarities and connections. Thus, based on the kinds of findings discussed above in the literature on focus, false memory, intention, intention-memory (e.g., Kuhl & Kazen, 1999), and the like, there may also be reason to expect a link between positive affect and self-control (and between some kinds of negative affect and lack of self-control), based on processes such as monitoring.

SELF-CONTROL

Self-control is a topic that has always been of interest, at least indirectly, among researchers in consumer psychology, and similarly there has been a huge amount of research on self-control in the theoretical literature. A review of either of these bodies of research is beyond the scope of this chapter, but what I want to focus on in this section are two kinds of relatively recent lines of work on self-control that may provide additional opportunities for interesting consumer research, especially when integrated with work on affect. These involve self-regulation (including affect-regulation), and motivation, including the processes by which affect influences motivation.

The work described throughout this chapter—on affect's influence on flexibility in focus of attention, distractibility, false memory, meta-memory, and monitoring processes—also has implications for the influence of affect on self-control, at least one type of self-control. Take, for example, the findings reported with regard to false memory. As we have seen, they indicate that people in positive affect may have better monitoring functions and better meta-memory or awareness of their own memory or thought processes (Yang et al., 2006). But, as noted above, in addition, those results also suggest that people in positive affect may have more self-control, because they were more successful at making use of the information that intrusions were likely in the situation, and they were better at refraining from falling prey to misleading intrusions. That is, the literature indicates, and the study by Yang et al. (2006) confirmed again, that error rates in general go down substantially when people are warned about the possibility of intrusions—indicating that people can monitor and decrease their likelihood of error in that situation. However, that study showed that people in positive affect benefited more than controls from having been made aware of that potential for errors. This suggests that people in the positive-affect group are better able to exert the control over their thought processes that enables them to keep straight which words were seen previously and which were not. (It should be noted that other aspects of the results reported by Yang et al., 2006, indicate that this effect cannot be attributed to increased motivation in the form of simply trying harder, because the conditions did not differ in overall levels of correct recognition.) The idea that monitoring ability is crucial to self-control is compatible with Carver's (e.g., 2004) model of the self-regulation process, though perhaps in a slightly different way.

Two programs of research that have stimulated a great deal of work focusing on self-regulation have been that of Baumeister, Tice, Vohs, and their colleagues (e.g., Baumeister et al., 1998), and that of Carver and Scheier and their colleagues (e.g., Carver, 2004; Carver & Scheier, 1998). The work of Baumeiester and colleagues has centered on the idea that exerting self-control causes depletion of what is thought to be a limited self-control resource and therefore makes continued self-control, even in unrelated domains, less likely (if not impossible). The work of Carver and colleagues also relates to self-regulation, but takes a different focus, proposing a model involving a discrepancy-reducing feedback process that implicates resource monitoring in the process of control of both behavior and affect.

Of course, these descriptions of these two extensive lines of research are over-simplifications, but they serve to highlight two relatively new foci for a topic that has long been of interest in consumer behavior. Additional work relating these conceptualizations and lines of investigation to the consumer research area would be of substantial interest. In fact, some research in the consumer literature on these and related topics is already under way (e.g., Wan, Isen, & Sternthal, 2006; Wan & Sternthal, 2005). It is also interesting that Baumeister has directed some of his work recently to the consumer research domain (Baumeister, 2002).

Other lines of work on self-control, and particularly affect and self-control also offer promise of interesting development by consumer researchers. For example, Trope's model of "mood as a resource" suggests that positive affect increases the resources available to a person, and the additional resource enables a person to take a more future-oriented view or to consider his or her long-term welfare rather than simply opting for immediate affect maintenance (e.g., Gervey, Igou, & Trope, 2005; Trope & Pomerantz, 1998). In a recent paper, Raghunathan and Trope (2002) suggested a way to differentiate among three kinds of effects of positive affect that have been observed in the literature: affect as information (indicating whether it is important to process carefully), affect as a goal (i.e., affect-maintenance), and positive affect as providing additional resources that can be used during decision making or problem solving (e.g., Raghunathan & Trope, 2002). The authors suggest conditions under which each kind of effect might be expected. This differentiation suggests some interesting topics for continued research. It would also be important, however, to investigate the source and nature of the additional resources that affect provides.

Other authors have also emphasized that positive affect fosters taking one's long-term welfare into account rather than focusing only on immediate affect-maintenance (e.g., Aspinwall, 1998; Aspinwall & Brunhart, 1996; Aspinwall & Taylor, 1997; Isen & Geva, 1997; Isen & Reeve, 2005;

Reed & Aspinwall, 1998; Staw & Barsade, 1993; see also, Isen, 1993a, 1993b, 2000b, for discussion). They take the view that the broader perspective, greater flexibility, and capacity for utilizing and integrating more information, which is promoted by positive affect and positive states such as optimism or positive affectivity, enables the ability to take the long-term view or to realize what is most important in the situation (see, e.g., Isen, 2000a, 2007, for discussion). In other words, the flexibility fostered by positive affect enables the person to see several options, short-term and long-term, several aspects of situations, and to integrate them in deciding what to do. As discussed in this chapter, a substantial body of work supports the idea that positive affect promotes flexibility, the tendency to integrate more material and aspects of situations into decisions, to monitor situations more carefully, and so forth. Thus, those cognitive processes that are fostered by positive affect are the kind that contribute to the likelihood that the person will base his or her actions and decisions on a fuller consideration of the situation, including longer-term welfare where that is relevant.

These views are also compatible with the dopamine hypothesis regarding positive affect's influence on cognitive processes, mentioned in the previous section. As noted there, release of dopamine into frontal brain regions that foster processes that allow cognitive flexibility and complex cognitive processes, including working memory, monitoring processes, attentional flexibility, and the like, may play a role in positive affect's facilitation of complex cognitive processing. It thus may well play a role in enabling people to take their long-term welfare into account, as they think about more factors of many kinds in the situation (e.g., see Isen, 2000a). It may also be useful to consider the dopamine hypothesis in the context of any theories or models that propose that positive affect provides additional resources, because activation of brain areas that enable careful and effective thinking might well feel as though one had acquired additional resources, and it could account for participants' improved ability to consider multiple factors in the situation, including long-term welfare and not just immediate pleasant feelings.

The context of these theories about the role of flexibility and/or additional resources suggests the point that it is important to recognize that positive affect undoubtedly fosters more than one process at a time, and researchers need to take several of these into account at once when making predictions about what effect positive affect will have. It is especially important to take affect's influence on flexibility into account in making any prediction involving positive affect.

A problem has resulted from not taking this complexity into account, and unfortunately it has led to confusion in the literature on the effects of affect on cognitive processing. For example, starting with the proposition that positive affect, for example, has been found to have a certain effect, say, cueing positive material, or desire to maintain a positive state, some researchers have then assumed that this one effect drives the situation and can be followed to its logical conclusion in isolation from the rest of the factors in the situation and, importantly, in isolation from the other effects that are known to result from positive affect (most notably, flexibility). The reasoning in the research article might be something like the following: Positive affect cues positive material; therefore, if affect will play a role in the situation under consideration, it will be to trigger improved evaluations, and therefore everything will be more highly evaluated. As discussed earlier, the data have shown repeatedly that that is not the case. Negative or dangerous events or materials are not evaluated more favorably when one is feeling happy; no simple, blind bias or rosy filter appears.

Or another example might be to assume that because positive affect has been shown to engender a tendency to preserve the positive state, that people who are feeling happy will engage in affect-maintenance above all else (as some authors have caricatured the findings) and not consider negative material, even when that would be beneficial and informative for them. Over the years, again, the data have shown us that positive affect does not exert such a simple influence or produce such narrow effects (see, e.g., Isen, 1993b, 2000a, 2007, for discussion). Thus, an important proposition to keep in mind when dealing with affect and trying to understand or predict its effects, is that the several effects of an affective state must be considered simultaneously and as an integrated whole, rather than developing hypotheses based on only one effect at a time.

Another point that needs to be made in this context is the general one that applies to most common situations, and that is that behavior is multi-determined: There is not just one motive operating at a time.[3] This principle is not just applicable to situations involving affect, but is a constant in understanding people's experience, choices, and behavior. Thus, it is not only in situations of positive affect, but in all normal life situations, that researchers must be mindful of multiple motives influencing people at the same time. The work demonstrating that certain motives, such as affect maintenance, are active during a positive-affect state only serve to help delineate some of the motives that are likely to be present and that may be exerting an influence. The identification that a certain specific one is likely to be more active during a given state, such as positive affect, does not mean that that motive will be the only one or even the most dominant one. Other cognitive factors will play a role, as noted above, and other motives will also exert influence. The combination of those cognitive and motivational factors is what will determine what the person will do or prefer in the situation, as the person chooses among the options and courses of action he or she sees as potential resolutions in the situation.

The final type of work on self-control or self-regulation that I would like to raise here is work showing that positive affect influences motivational processes that involve choice of behavior and expectation of outcome, and do so in some specific ways that depend on the opportunities and realities of the situation, not the person's affect alone. There are two lines of work of this kind that I will discuss, work on positive affect and intrinsic and extrinsic motivation, and work investigating the influence of positive affect on the components of expectancy motivation. Both of these lines of work show that positive affect fosters detailed, realistic consideration of the whole situation, including others' needs as well as one's own.

INTRINSIC MOTIVATION

In one series of studies, it was found that people in whom positive affect had been induced showed more intrinsic motivation than controls, but also responded well to extrinsic motivation when the work-task needed to be done (Isen & Reeve, 2005). Intrinsic motivation was measured in a free-choice situation by (1) choice of a more interesting task, over a dull task that had a very small chance of paying a small amount of money; and (2) increased amount of reported enjoyment of the enjoyable task (but not the dull task). These are standard measures used in the intrinsic motivation literature (e.g., Deci & Ryan, 1985). However, when participants were informed that there was some work that needed to be done (no money was involved this time), and again they had the choice of what activity to do during the 20-minute time period, they chose to do the work that needed to be done, but spent the rest of their time with the more enjoyable task, and thus spent more time than controls on the interesting task (even though they got their work done and did not make any more errors than the control group—both had very low error rates). They again liked the enjoyable task more than controls, but showed no difference from controls on the dull work task. Thus, they displayed self-control in the sense that that term is normally used—they did not like the work task as much as the puzzle task, but they engaged it as much as was necessary.

EXPECTANCY MOTIVATION

The other set of studies on motivation that relates to self-control that I want to mention are two showing that positive affect influences the three components of expectancy motivation (see, e.g.,

Ilgen, Nebeker, & Pritchard, 1981; Kanfer, 1990, for discussions of the theory of expectancy motivation). In a moderate range of performance (but not at extremely high or extremely low performance levels), people in positive affect saw more connection between how hard they tried and how well they would do, resulting in greater motivation that is based on their realistic expectations in the situation (see Erez & Isen, 2002 for more detail and discussion). This is not just a matter of motivation in the sense of "trying harder," but reflects how effective the person expects to be if he or she tries moderately hard. The results indicate that people in the positive-affect condition have greater expectation that their effort will pay off (where it is likely to pay off, but not where it is not), and this is the source of trying. This is important for self-control, because it prompts people to put forth effort and stay at tasks, in the expectation that trying will lead to success and the desired outcome.

OMISSION DETECTION

Another matter of very great theoretical importance is omission detection, which of course has been investigated extensively in the consumer literature (e.g., Kim et al., 1996; Sanbonmatsu, Kardes, Houghton, Ho, & Posavac, 2003). I did not mention this topic as a focus within this chapter at the outset precisely because it *has* been investigated extensively within the field of consumer behavior, and in fact many of the most important advances in understanding its determinants and effects have been explored in those contexts. It is also investigated in the theoretical Psychology literature, most recently by Dunning and his students and colleagues (e.g., Caputo & Dunning, 2005), who have pointed out the damaging and problematic consequences of not realizing what we do not know. However, I do want to bring the topic of omission detection up in this chapter, because based on much of the discussion in this chapter, it seems possible for positive affect to play a role in enabling people to see what is missing, what they are not considering, and thus for positive affect to link these two streams of research (e.g., Mantel et al., 2006).

That is, if positive affect leads people to be more flexible thinkers, as has been widely demonstrated in the literature—to solve problems requiring a creative or innovative approach to looking at the functions or aspects of stimulus elements available for solving the problem; to think of unusual associates to stimuli; to categorize more flexibly; to understand and welcome mildly unusual brand extensions—as well as the newer effects that have been proposed to result from such flexibility and discussed in this chapter (broad focus of attention, broadened and built-up approaches, resources, and skills; improved incidental learning and ability to divide attention among tasks; and increased cognitive monitoring ability and tendency to check)—then it also seems likely that positive affect could lead people to notice missing information or material that they are not considering that they should be considering. This link has not yet been explicitly made between these two streams of research.

However, the role of affect in influencing omission detection has recently begun to be studied (e.g., Mantel et al., 2006). It is clear, from the foregoing discussions of the critical predictions for each of the phenomena described so far that follow from the findings on positive affect, that positive affect should improve omission detection. That is, the flexibility that has been demonstrated to result from positive affect should lead to noticing when one is not considering all of the important relevant aspects of a situation or problem. A recent series of studies is offering indication that, indeed, positive affect may help to reduce the problem, in judgment and decision making, of not realizing that there is important information that is missing (Mantel et al., 2006). In one study, those authors have found that people in positive affect, when given only a small number of product attributes as a product description for a product they are asked to evaluate, are more likely than controls to ask for additional information, and without the additional information, are less extreme in their evaluations of the product. A second study, based on the Ellsberg (1961) paradox, found that where the risk in the situation was undeclared, people in the positive affect condition were less likely than controls to take the risky option. As noted earlier, we know from previous research that people in positive affect are less likely to take a risk if the risk is high and real (e.g., Isen & Patrick, 1983; Isen & Geva, 1987). But in the case under discussion, the results indicate that they are less likely to take the risky option when the risk is unspecified. Together, these results suggest that people in positive affect are more likely to notice when important information is missing from a decision situation. This line of work is just beginning, and much more needs to be done, but it is an exciting area for development, because the ability to notice missing information has so many important implications, both theoretically and in understanding the choices and behavior of consumers.

CONCLUSION

It is well-known that theoretical issues can have important practical implications, which is as it should be. Such implications have been discovered in the area of affect and cognition, where basic findings regarding affect's influence on thought processes have been explored in applied contexts such as consumer behavior, managerial decision making, and medical decision making, and found to contribute to our understanding of the processes that underlie important phenomena in applied domains. For example, the finding that positive affect leads people to consider more aspects of situations and integrate that material is relevant for many fields, from consumer decision making to managerial decision making to physician diagnostic processes. Current developments in theoretical research domains offer exciting new directions for applied work relating basic processes to consumers' behavior and decision processes, and we can look forward to continued new applications of this and other work. At the same time, the applied research has a history of contributing back to theoretical development itself, in part because the richness of the contexts in which the applied work takes place offers the opportunity to add shadings, detail, nuances, and specifics that help to expand and refine the theoretical work. We can all look forward to these developments as well.

ACKNOWLEDGMENT

Thank go to Frank Kardes for helpful comments on an earlier draft of this chapter.

NOTES

1. A few exceptions to this general statement can be found, for example, in advertising, in which we sometimes see fear appeals or annoying, repetitive ads that probably induce negative affect in consumers.
2. There is a substantial body of interesting work in consumer psychology developing on topics related to *fluency* as a meta-cognitive cue influencing affective and cognitive judgments (see, e.g., Pham, 2004; Schwarz et al., 1991). In the present context, I am considering the inverse—the influence of affect on the tendency to know what one knows (see, e.g., Nelson, 1996).
3. Of course, in extreme or emergency situations that will not be true, as one motive will take precedence; but such situations are not the focus of much of the needed research that is done on human decision making, choice, and behavior, and are not the common, everyday situations that are so in need of clarification.

REFERENCES

Aspinwall, L .G. (1998). Rethinking the role of positive affect in self-regulation. *Motivation and Emotion, 22,* 1–32.

Aspinwall, L. G., & Brunhart, S. M. (1996). Distinguishing optimism from denial: Optimistic beliefs predict attention to health threats. *Personality and Social Psychology Bulletin, 22,* 993–1003.

Aspinwall, L. G., & Taylor, S. E. (1997). A stitch in time: Self-regulation and proactive coping. *Psychological Bulletin, 121,* 417–436.

Barone, M .J., & Miniard, P. W. (2002). Mood and brand extension judgments: Asymmetric effects for desirable versus undesirable brands. *Journal of Consumer Psychology, 12,* 283–290.

Barone, M. J., Miniard, P. W., & Romeo, J. B. (2000). The influence of positive mood on brand extension evaluations. *Journal of Consumer Research, 26*(4), 386–400.

Baumeister, R. F. (2002). Yielding to temptation: Self-control failure, impulsive purchasing, and consumer behavior. *Journal of Consumer Research, 28,* 670–676.

Baumeister, R. F., Bratslavsky, E., Muraven, M., & Tice, D. M. (1998). Ego depletion: Is the active self a limited resource?" *Journal of Personality and Social Psychology, 74,* 1252–1265.

Boush, D. M., & Loken, B. (1991). A process-tracing study of brand extension evaluation. *Journal of Marketing Research, 28,* 16–28.

Baumann, N., & Kuhl, J. (2005). Positive affect and flexibility: Overcoming the precedence of global over local processing of visual information. *Motivation and Emotion, 29,* 123–134.

Bruner, J. S., Matter, J., & Papanek, M. L. (1955). Breadth of learning as a function of drive level and mechanization. *Psychological Review, 62,* 1–10.

Caputo, D., & Dunning, D. A. (2005). What you don't know: The role played by errors of omission in imperfect self-assessments, *Journal of Experimental Social Psychology, 41*(5), 488–505.

Carver, C. S. (2004), "Self-Regulation of Action and Affect" In R. F. Baumeister & K. D. Vohs (Eds.), *Handbook of self-regulation: Research, theory and applications* (pp. 13–39). New York: Guilford.

Carver, C. S., & Scheier, M. F. (1998). Discrepancy-reducing feedback processes in behavior. In C. S. Carver & M. F. Scheier (Eds.), *On the self-regulation of behavior* (pp. 29–47). New York: Cambridge University Press.

Carver, C. S., Sutton, S. K., & Scheier, M. F. (2000). Action, emotion, and personality: Emerging and conceptual integration. *Personality and Social Psychology Bulletin, 26,* 741–751.

Compton, R. J., Wirtz, D., Pajoumand, G., Claus, E., & Heller, W. (2004). Association between positive affect and attentional shifting. *Cognitive Therapy and Research, 28,* 733–744.

Deci, E. L., & Ryan, R. M. (1985). *Intrinsic motivation and self-determination in human behavior.* New York: Plenum.

Deese, J. (1959). On the prediction of occurrence of particular verbal intrusions on immediate recall. *Journal of Experimental Psychology, 58,* 17–22.

Derryberry, D. (1993). Attentional consequences of outcome-related motivational states: Congruent, incongruent, and focusing effects. *Motivation and Emotion, 17,* 65–89.

Derryberry, D., & Reed, M. A. (1998). Anxiety and attentional focusing: Trait, state, and hemispheric influences. *Personality and Individual Differences, 25,* 745–761.

Dreisbach, G., & Goschke, T. (2004). How positive affect modulates cognitive control: Reduced perseveration at the cost of increased distractibility. *Journal of Experimental Psychology: Learning, Memory, and Cognition, 30,* 343–353

Duffy, E. (1934). Emotion: An example of the need for reorientation in psychology. *Psychological Review, 41,* 184–198.

Duffy, E. (1941). An explanation of "emotional" phenomena without the use of the concept of "emotion." *Journal of General Psychology, 25,* 282–293.

Easterbrook, J. A. (1959).The effect of emotion on cue utilization and the organization of behavior. *Psychological Review, 66*(3), 183–201.

Ellsberg, Daniel (1961).Risk, Ambiguity, and the Savage Axioms. *Quarterly Journal of Economics, 75,* 643–669.

Erez, A., & Isen, A. M. (2002). The influence of positive affect on the components of expectancy motivation. *Journal of Applied Psychology, 87,* 1055–1067.

Estrada, C. A., Isen, A. M., & Young, M. J. (1997). Positive affect facilitates integration of information and decreases anchoring in reasoning among physicians. *Organizational Behavior and Human Decision Processes, 72* 117–135.

Feldman, J. M., & Lynch, Jr., J. G. (1988). Self-generated validity and other effects of measurement on belief, attitude, intention, and behavior. *Journal of Applied Psychology, 73,* 421–435.

Folkes, V. S., & Matta, S. (2004). The effect of package shape on consumers' judgments of product volume: Attention as a mental contaminant. *Journal of Consumer Research, 31* (September), 390–401.

Forest, D., Clark, M. S., Mills, J., & Isen, A. M. (1979). Helping as a function of feeling state and nature of the helping behavior. *Motivation and Emotion, 3*(2), 161–169.

Fredrickson, B. L. (1998). What good are positive emotions? *Review of General Psychology, 2,* 300–319.

Fredrickson, B. L., & Branigan, C. (2005). Positive emotions broaden the scope of attention and thought-action repertoires. *Cognition and Emotion, 19,* 313–332.,

Fredrickson, B. L., & Joiner, T. (2002). Positive emotions trigger upward spirals toward emotional well-being. *Psychological Science, 13,* 172–175.

Friedman, R. S., & Forster, S. (2005). The influence of approach and avoidance cues on attentional flexibility. *Motivation and Emotion, 29,* 69–81.

Friestad, M., & Wright, P. (2004). Persuasion knowledge: Lay people's and researchers' beliefs about the psychology of advertising. *Journal of Consumer Research, 22* (June), 62–74.

Gallo, D. A., Roediger, H. L., III, & McDermott, K. (2001). Associative false recognition occurs without strategic criterion shifts. *Psychonomic Bulletin and Review, 8,* 579–586.

Gardner, M. P. (1985). Mood states and consumer-behavior: A critical-review. *Journal of Consumer Research, 12*(3), 281–300.

Gasper, K., & Clore, G. L. (2002). Attending to the big picture: Mood and global versus local processing of visual information. *Psychological Science, 13,* 34–40.

Gervey, B., Igou, E. R., & Trope, Y. (2005). Positive mood and future-oriented self-evaluation. *Motivation and Emotion, 29,* 267–294.

Greene, T. R., & Noice, H. (1988). Influence of positive affect upon creative thinking and problem solving in children. *Psychological Reports, 63*(3), 895–898.

Hilgard, E. R., & Bower, G. H. (1966) *Theories of learning* (3rd ed.). New York: Appleton-Century-Crofts.

Ilgen, D. R., Nebeker, D. M., & Pritchard, R. D. (1981). Expectancy theory: An empirical comparison in an experimental situation. *Organizational Behavior and Human Performance, 28,* 189–223.

Isen, A. M. (1970). Success, failure, attention, and reactions to others: The warm glow of success. *Journal of Personality and Social Psychology, 15,* 294–301.

Isen, A. M. (1984a). The influence of positive affect on decision making and cognitive organization. In T. Kinnear (Ed.), *Advances in consumer research* (Vol. 11, pp. 530–533). Provo, UT: Association for Consumer Research.

Isen, A. M. (1984b). Toward understanding the role of affect in cognition. In R. S. Wyer & T. K. Srull (Eds.), *Handbook of social cognition* (Vol. 3, pp. 179–236). Hillsdale, NJ: Erlbaum.

Isen, A. M. (1989). Some ways in which affect influences cognitive processes: Implications for advertising and consumer behavior. In P. Cafferata & A.M. Tybout (Eds.), *Cognitive and affective responses to advertising* (pp. 91–118). Lexington, MA: Lexington Books.

Isen, A. M. (1990). The influence of positive and negative affect on cognitive organization: Some implications for development. In N. Stein, B. Leventhal, & T. Trabasso (Eds.), *Psychological and biological approaches to emotion* (pp. 75–94). Hillsdale, NJ: Erlbaum.

Isen, A. M. (1993a) Positive affect and decision making. In M. Lewis & J. Haviland (Eds), *Handbook of emotions* (pp. 261–273). New York: Guilford.

Isen, A. M. (1993b) The influence of positive affect on cognitive organization: Some implications for consumer decision making in response to advertising. In A. Mitchell (Ed.), *Advertising exposure, memory, and choice.* Hillsdale, NJ: Erlbaum.

Isen, A. M. (2000a). Positive affect and decision making. In M. Lewis & J. Haviland-Jones (Eds.) *Handbook of emotions* (2nd ed., pp. 417–435). New York: Guilford.

Isen, A. M. (2000b). Some perspectives on positive affect and self-regulation. *Psychological Inquiry, 11,* 111–115.

Isen, A. M. (2001). An influence of positive affect on decision making in complex situations: Theoretical issues with practical implications. *Journal of Consumer Psychology, 11*(2), 75–85.

Isen, A. M. (2007). Positive affect, cognitive flexibility, and self-control. In X. Shoda, D. Cervone, & G. Downey (Eds.), *Persons in context* (pp. 130–147). New York: Guilford.

Isen, A. M., & Daubman, K. A. (1984). The influence of affect on categorization. *Journal of Personality and Social Psychology, 47*(6), 1206–1217.

Isen, A. M., Daubman, K. A., & Nowicki, G. P. (1987). Positive affect facilitates creative problem solving. *Journal of Personality and Social Psychology, 52*(6), 1122–1131.

Isen, A. M., & Geva, N. (1987). The influence of positive affect on acceptable level of risk: The person with a large canoe has a large worry. *Organizational Behavior and Human Decision Processes, 39*(2), 145–154.

Isen, A. M., Johnson, M. M. S., Mertz, E., & Robinson, F. G. (1985). The influence of positive affect on the unusualness of word associations. *Journal of Personality and Social Psychology,48,* 1–14.

Isen, A. M., & Patrick, R. (1983). The effect of positive feelings on risk-taking: When the chips are down. *Organizational Behavior and Human Performance, 31,* 194–202.

Isen, A. M., & Reeve, J. (2005). The influence of positive affect on Intrinsic and extrinsic motivation: Facilitating enjoyment of play, responsible work behavior, and self-control. *Motivation and Emotion, 29,* 297–325.

Isen, A. M., & Schmidt, E. (2007, January). Positive affect facilitates incidental learning and divided attention while not impairing performance on a focal task. Paper presented at the Emotion pre-conference to the meeting of the Society for Personality and Social Psychology, Memphis, TN.

Johnson, K. J., & Fredrickson, B. L. (2005). "We all look the same to me": Positive emotions eliminate the own-race bias in face recognition. *Psychological Science, 16,* 875–881.

Kahn, B. E., & Isen, A. M. (1993). The influence of positive affect on variety seeking among safe, enjoyable products. *Journal of Consumer Research, 20*(2), 257–270.

Kanfer, R. (1990). Motivation theory and industrial and organizational psychology. In M. D. Dunnette & L. M. Hough (Eds.), *Handbook of industrial and organizational psychology* (Vol. 1, pp. 75–170). Palo Alto, CA: Consulting Psychologists Press.

Kazen, M., & Kuhl, J. (2005). Intention memory and achievement motivation: Volitional facilitation and inhibition as a function of affective contents of need-related stimuli. *Journal of Personality and Social Psychology, 39,* 426–448.

Keller, P. A., Lipkus, I. M., & Rimer, B. K. (2003). Affect, framing, and persuasion. *Journal of Marketing Research, 40*(1), 54–64.

Kim, J., Allen, C. T., & Kardes, F. R. (1996). An investigation of the mediational mechanisms underlying attitudinal conditioning. *Journal of Marketing Research, 33,* 318–328.

Kimchi, R., & Palmer, S. E. (1982). Form and texture in hierarchically constructed patterns. *Journal of Experimental Psychology: Human Perception and Performance, 8,* 521–535.

Kuhl, J., & Kazen, M. (1999). Volitional facilitation of difficult intentions: Joint activation of intention memory and positive affect removes Stroop interference. *Journal of Experimental Psychology: General, 128,* 382–399.

Lee, A. Y., & Sternthal, B. (1999). The effects of positive mood on memory. *Journal of Consumer Research, 26,* 115–127.

Lewinsohn, S., & Mano, H. (1993). Multiattribute choice and affect: The influence of naturally occurring and manipulated moods on choice processes. *Journal of Behavioral Decision Making, 6,* 33–51.

Lurie, N. (2004). Decision making in information-rich environments: The role of information structure. *Journal of Consumer Research, 30,* 473–486.

Lynch, Jr., J. G., Marmorstein, H., & Weigold, M. F. (1988). Choices from sets including rememebered brands: Use of recalled attributes and prior overall evaluation. *Journal of Consumer Research, 15,* 169–184.

Mano, H. (1994). Risk taking, framing effects, and affect. *Organizational Behavior and Human Decision Processes, 57,* 38–58.

Mano, H. (1997). Affect and persuasion: The influence of pleasantness and arousal on attitude formation and message elaboration. *Psychology and Marketing, 14,* 315–335.

Mantel, S., Kardes, F. R., Isen, A. M., & Herr, P. (2006). Effects of positive affect on omission neglect in the multiattribute evaluation and Ellsberg paradigms. Manuscript. University of Indiana.

Muraven, M., & Baumeister, R. F. (2000). Self-regulation and depletion of limited resources: Does self-control resemble a muscle? *Psychological Bulletin, 126,* 247–259.

McCabe, D. P., & Anderson, S. D. (2002). The effect of warnings on false memories in young and older adults. *Memory and Cognition. 30,* 1065–1077.

Murray, N., Sujan, H., Hirt, E. R., & Sujan, M (1990). The influence of mood on categorization: A cognitive flexibility interpretation. *Journal of Personality and Social Psychology, 59,* 411–425.

Navon, D. (1977). Forest before trees: The precedence of global features in visual perception. *Cognitive Psychology, 9,* 353–383.

Nelson, T. O. (1996). Consciousness and metacognition. *American Psychologist, 51,* 102–116.

Pham, M. T. (2004). The logic of feeling. *Journal of Consumer Psychology, 14,* 360–369.

Posavac, S. S., Sanbonmatsu, D. M., Kardes, F. R., & Fitzsimons, G. J. (2004). The brand positivity effect: when evaluation confers preference. *Journal of Consumer Research, 31* (Dec.), 643–651.

Raghunathan, R., & Trope, Y. (2002). Walking the tightrope between feeling good and being accurate: Mood as a resource in processing persuasive messages. *Journal of Personality and Social Psychology, 83,* 510–525.

Reed, M. B., & Aspinwall, L. G. (1998). Self-affirmation reduces biased processing of health-risk information. *Motivation and Emotion, 22,* 99–132.

Roediger, H. L., III, & McDermott, K. B. (1995). Creating false memories: Remembering words not presented in lists. *Journal of Experimental Psychology: Learning, Memory, and Cognition, 21,* 803–814.

Roediger, H. L., III, McDermott, K. B., & Robinson, K. J. (1998). The role of associative process in creating false memories. In M. A. Conway, S. E. Gathercole, & C. Cornoldi (Eds.), *Theories of memory II* (pp. 187–245). Hove: Psychological Press.

Russell, J. A., & Carroll, J. M. (1999). On the bipolarity of positive and negative affect. *Psychological Bulletin, 125*(1), 3–30.

Sanbonmatsu, D. M., & Kardes, F. R. (1988). The effects of physiological arousal on information processing and persuasion. *Journal of Consumer Research, 15,* 379–385.

Schwarz, N., Bless, H., Strack, F., Klumpp, G. Rittenauerschatka, H., & Simons, A. (1991). Ease of retrieval as information: Another look at the availability heuristic. *Journal of Personality and Social Psychology, 61,* 195–202.

Simon, H. A. (1967). Motivational and emotional controls of cognition. *Psychological Review, 74*(1), 29–39.

Staw, B. M., & Barsade, S. Y. (1993). Affect and managerial performance: A test of the sadder-but-wiser vs happier-and-smarter hypotheses. *Administrative Science Quarterly, 38,* 304–331.

Storbeck, H. A., & Clore, G. L. (2005). With sadness comes accuracy, with happiness, false memory: Mood and the false memory effect. *Psychological Science, 16,* 785–791.

Taylor, S. E., & Aspinwall, L. G. (1996). Mediating and moderating processes in psychosocial stress: Appraisal, coping, resistance and vulnerability. In H. B. Kaplan (Ed.), *Psychosocial stress: Perspectives on structure, theory, life-course, and methods* (pp. 71–110). San Diego, CA: Academic.

Trope, Y., & Pomerantz, E. M. (1998). Resolving conflicts among self-evaluative motives: Positive experiences as a resource for overcoming defensiveness. *Motivation and Emotion, 22,* 53–72.

Tybout, A. M., Sternthal, B., Malaviya, P., Bakamitsos, G. A., & Park, S-B. (2005). Information accessibility as a moderator of judgments: The role of content versus retrieval ease. *Journal of Consumer Research, 32,* 76–85.

Vohs, K., & Schmeichel, B. J. (2003). Self-regulation and the extended now: Controlling the self alters the subjective experience of time. *Journal of Personality and Social Psychology, 85,* 217–230.

Wan, W., Isen, A. M., & Sternthal, B. (2006, September). The influence of positive affect on regulatory depletion. Paper presented at the meeting of the Association for Consumer Research, Orlando, FL.

Wan, W., & Sternthal, B. (2005, October). Eliminating depletion effects. Paper presented at the meeting of the Association for Consumer Research, San Antonio, TX.

Watson, D., & Tellegen, A. (1999). Issues in the dimensional structure of affect: Effects of descriptors, measurement error, and response formats: Comment on Russell and Carroll (1999). *Psychological Bulletin, 125*(5), 601–610.

Woodworth, R. S., & Schlosberg, H. (1954). *Experimental Psychology* (rev. ed.). New York: Holt, Rinehart, and Winston.

Yang, H., Ceci, S., & Isen, A. M. (2006, January). Positive affect increases monitoring and does not increase false memory. Poster presented at the meeting of the Society for Personality and Social Psychology, Palm Springs, CA.

Yerkes, R. M., & Dodson, J. D. (1908). The relationship of strength of stimulus to rapidity of habit formation. *Journal of Comparative and Neurological Psychology, 18,* 459–482.

Yeung, C. W. M., & Wyer, Jr., R. S. (2005). Does loving a brand mean loving its products? The role of brand-elicited affect in brand extension evaluations. *Journal of Marketing Research, 42,* 495–506.

11

The Nature and Role of Affect in Consumer Behavior

JOEL B. COHEN

University of Florida

MICHEL TUAN PHAM

Columbia University

EDUARDO B. ANDRADE

University of California, Berkeley

In the intervening years since publication of the chapter "Affect and Consumer Behavior" (Cohen & Areni, 1991) in the *Handbook of Consumer Behavior* (Kassarjian & Robertson, 1991), research in consumer behavior dealing with affect has exploded, making it one of the field's central research topics. Within psychology more generally, Schimmack and Crites (2005) located 923 references to affect between 1960 and 1980 and 4,170 between 1980 and 2000. Since research on affect has become more specialized, this chapter will concentrate on the various ways affect influences judgment and choice rather than on broader and historical perspectives. These will include the role of affect in information retrieval, differential processing of affectively colored information (including the role of affect in strengthening mental associations and memory consolidation), how and when affect provides information that influences judgments and decisions, and the motivational role of affect in guiding behavior and signaling the need for changes in vigilance, intensity, and direction. We begin, however, with some essential definitions.

THE NATURE AND STRUCTURE OF AFFECT

On Affect: Feelings, Emotions, and Moods

What affect means

There is still some carryover from the use of the term "affect" to also refer to what is, in essence, the evaluative aspect of attitudes. This stems from the classic tri-partite depiction of attitudes: cognitive, affective, and conative (see Eagly & Chaiken, 1993) and a failure to adequately differentiate between evaluative measures (e.g., favorable/unfavorable) and antecedent or subsequent processes, which might be feeling-based. Consistent with most recent scholarly discussions, we reserve the term "affect" to describe an internal feeling state. One's explicit or implicit "liking" for some object, person, or position is viewed as an evaluative judgment rather than an internal feeling state. As Russell and Carroll (1999a) put it:

> By *affect,* we have in mind genuine subjective feelings and moods (as when someone says, 'I'm feeling sad'), rather than thoughts about specific objects or events (as when someone calmly says, 'The crusades were a sad chapter in human history'). (pp. 3–4)

This chapter maintains the separation of affect as a feeling state that is distinct from either liking or purely descriptive cognition. So when we use the term "affect" to describe stimuli, internal and overt responses, it is only in relation to evoked feeling states. Imagine, in contrast, an advertisement whose words or images connote a happy (i.e., successful) outcome. Affective processes cannot merely be assumed. Alternative explanations (e.g., the advertised product seems likely to produce favorable outcomes) for so-called "affective" influences on subsequent evaluations and behavior must be ruled out before implicating affect. These include semantically associated changes in object meaning or construct accessibility.

This definition also raises both philosophical and empirical questions about whether such a feeling state must be consciously experienced or whether we can be unaware that we are experiencing affect. Research where subliminally presented smiling or frowning faces were used to prime affect (outside of awareness) and bring about subsequent evaluative responses (Winkielman, Zajonc, & Schwarz, 1997), is a case in point. Affective experience in the absence of an identified basis for that experience has been a staple of psychological research since Zajonc's (1980) early work on "mere exposure." In that program of research, repeated subliminal exposure to unfamiliar stimuli having neutral valence such as Chinese ideographs has been shown to generate some degree of liking for the stimuli, possibly as a result of a primitive reward mechanism associated with increasing familiarity or a reduction in uncertainty. Another standard paradigm for investigating precognitive affective processes is to present (outside of awareness) a stimulus known to evoke either a negative or positive affective response (e.g., a sad face). Following that exposure, people are asked to indicate how they are feeling (to rule out more conscious affective responses including inferences) and to rate the emotional quality of a semantically unrelated object, such as a piece of music. Using such a procedure, for example, Strahan, Spencer, and Zanna (2002) found that affective stimuli can influence positive/negative assessments even without producing a measurable effect on people's affective experiences (i.e., reported feelings). In a particularly sophisticated study (Schimmack, 2004), subjects received masked subliminal presentations of pleasant and unpleasant pictures, followed by supraliminal presentations of an identical picture (the target) paired with a foil whose valence was either the same as the target or opposite. If the initial subliminal target exposure produced a spontaneous affective experience, participants should be better able—and they were—to discriminate the target from the foil when they had a different valence because only one object should match the originally experienced affect. Different results have frequently been observed for pictures and words when used as subliminal stimuli (Schimmack & Crites, 2005). Words have been found to elicit a skin-conductance response under conditions of very short exposure (suggesting affective experience), whereas pictures have not. However, this finding may also be due to the greater inherent polarity of the selected words relative to pictures, since the interpretation of pictures may require more cognitive resources than words having relatively fixed affective associations.

Most consumer research on affect deals with moods (e.g., Barone, Miniard, & Romeo, 2000; Cohen & Andrade, 2004; Gorn, Goldberg, & Basu, 1993; Pham, 1998), although there has been growing interest in the study of specific emotions (e.g., Lerner, Small, & Loewenstein, 2004; Raghunathan & Pham, 1999; Raghunathan, Pham, & Corfman, 2006). Moods are usually thought of as low intensity and diffuse affective states that generally lack source identification.[1] The individual, prompted either by physiological or hormonal/chemical activity (such as changes in levels of serotonin and dopamine) or by external stimuli (music, weather, exposure to happy versus sad information), experiences a vague sense of feeling good or bad without necessarily knowing quite why. Some days or after certain experiences, we are aware of feeling good or bad, optimistic or pessimistic, up or down, relaxed or restless, alert or drowsy. Mood states also track our bodily energy levels (e.g., blood glucose levels), our daily circadian rhythm, and our general wellness or illness, thereby guiding relatively automatic self-regulatory responses as well as more conscious decisions, as we shall discuss later on. Emotions, on the other hand, are much more differentiated and hence provide more attitude- and behavior-specific information. Feeling anger, for example, will often lead to target and context-specific responses rather than more general displays of unhappiness (Bushman & Baumeister, 1998). It should be noted, however, that specific emotions can produce mood-like effects (e.g., being angry or sad can affect a pattern of behavior) often without realizing that one has transferred the emotional response (to an identified target) to unrelated behaviors. Recent studies show that the degree of transfer will be a function of two factors: (1) the salience of the source of the emotional state—transfer is more likely when the actual source of the affect is not salient; and (2) the domain similarity between the actual source of the affective state and the objectively unrelated behavior (Raghunathan, Pham, & Corfman, 2006).

Moods have been shown to be easily manipulated through exposure to affectively charged stimuli such as music, videos, and pictures, or through the recall of emotionally involving experiences (e.g., Cohen & Andrade, 2004). Note that the use of low intensity emotion manipulations, such as sadness, displeasure, or happiness, to create positive or negative mood states tends to blur the line between emotions and moods, especially when the source is made salient.

Because affect is often used as information (Schwarz, 1990; Schwarz & Clore, 1983), the misattribution of incidental affect may play a powerful role in everyday life. Even experimentally-induced proprioceptive feedback of head nodding or shaking can lead a person to conclude that message-related thoughts are positive or negative (Brinol & Petty, 2003). The duration of mood changes is typically assumed to be short, from a few minutes to a couple of hours (Isbell & Wyer, 1999), although this duration probably varies with the method of instigation (Ehrlichman & Halpern, 1988; Isen, Clark, & Schwartz, 1976).

Experimental manipulation of affective states

Multiple techniques have been used to manipulate individuals' transient affective states. In most experiments, participants are exposed to a sequence of ostensibly unrelated studies, where the first study is meant to manipulate people's feelings while the second assesses the dependent variables of interest. In the first study, participants might be exposed, for instance, to false positive or negative performance feedback (Barone, Miniard, & Romeo, 2000; Swinyard, 1993), cheerful or depressing movies (Andrade, 2005; Cohen & Andrade, 2004), pleasant or unpleasant music (Gorn, Goldberg, & Basu, 1993), or positive or negative affective self-referential statements such as the Velten procedure (Velten, 1968), unexpected gifts (Barone, Miniard, & Romeo, 2000; Isen & Simmonds, 1978). Alternatively, participants may be asked to recall and describe an affectively-charged experience in writing (Pham, 1998). Due to their transient and mild, hence, short-lived nature, experimentally induced moods may dissipate relatively fast (see Isen, Clark, & Schwartz, 1976). Therefore, regardless of the mood induction procedure, the dependent measure usually is collected not long after the manipulation. Sometimes the mood manipulation and dependent measures co-occur. Mood manipulations using background music or physical ambience, like scent, for instance, allow for a simultaneous assessment of dependent variables (Grunberg & Straub, 1992; Schwarz, Strack, Kommer, & Wagner, 1987).

There is no single best option among all potential techniques. Different techniques raise different issues in terms of potential confounds, control for intensity levels, reliability, demand characteristics, and motivational requirements. For instance, receiving an unexpected gift, a common manipulation of positive mood (Isen, Shalker, Clark, & Karp, 1978; Kahn & Isen, 1993), can activate norms of reciprocity independently of affective changes (e.g., "The experimenter was nice to me, I'll be nice to him/her"). Similarly, false performance feedback can influence self-esteem or self-efficacy along with desired changes in affective states (Hill & Ward, 1989). Such unwanted effects might be confounded with the affect manipulation depending on the research question and other aspects of the procedure.

Asking participants to report an affectively charged personal experience can avoid some of the above-mentioned concerns. A major advantage of this method is that because each participant recruits his or her own personal experience, there is a lesser chance of confounding with the *content* of the affect-inducing event. Content-related confounds are much more likely with manipulations that involve exposure to a *common* affect-inducing stimulus across participants, such as watching a happy or sad movie. On the other hand, the personal experience method requires relatively high participant motivation; otherwise, the manipulation tends to be weakened. A second drawback of this method is that participants usually are explicitly directed to write about experiences that lead them to feel good or bad, which may enhance the likelihood of hypothesis guessing and demand artifacts. This concern is heightened if a salient mood manipulation check is administered before the dependent measures are collected. In addition, there may be extra variability in emotional states induced—hence higher experimental error—because participants may have different interpretations of the type of experience they are supposed to report. Some respondents may interpret "an event that made you feel bad" as one that made them feel angry, whereas others may interpret it as one that made them feel sad. It is therefore important that the instructions be very precise when using this manipulation.

Music does not require highly motivated participants, does not direct participants to specific feelings, and has been shown to produce significant effects on judgment and behavioral measures (Gorn, Goldberg, & Basu, 1993; Gorn, Pham, & Sin, 2001). However, there is significant variance in the population when it comes to music tastes, which can compromise reliability. Exposure to affectively charged videos has proven to be quite successful due to the general appeal of these stimuli (low motivation required), their easy-to-determine valence, and their higher intensity, compared to written or audio stimuli. However, as mentioned before, using a common video across participants within a given mood condition raises the possibility of confounding between affective experience and the semantic or episodic content of the video. To try to mitigate this problem, one can consider using different stimulus replicates across conditions or experiments. Another potential drawback of video-based inductions is that, compared to other procedures, exposure to videos may also facilitate hypothesis guessing and, consequently, demand artifacts. To avoid such concern, the cover story must be convincing and, also importantly, the affect manipulation check disguised. For example, Cohen and Andrade (2004) used a combined technique of video plus personal experience, in which participants were informed that the university, in order to augment its web-based teaching environment, attempted to assess the impact of audio and video stimuli transmitted through the web. Students were informed that they would watch five minutes of a video and then would perform memory and judgment recall tasks. After the video, the "memory task" instructed them to write a personal story related to the scenes watched in the clip. After the "memory task," a "judgment task" (in fact, the manipulation check) asked participants to assess ten items related to the video. Only three of them were affect-related. The other items were in line with the general cover story. This manipulation has shown strong and reliable effects on people's feelings and, importantly, very low incidence of hypothesis guessing (see also Andrade, 2005).

Videos have also been used to manipulate specific emotional states, such as anger (Andrade & Ariely, 2007; Phillipot, 1993) sadness and disgust (Lerner, Small, & Loewenstein, 2004), and fear (Andrade & Cohen, 2007b). Restricting the effect to one specific emotion may be challenging; some video manipulations can enhance more than one specific affective state at the same time. For instance, Gross and Levenson (1995) showed that an anger manipulation tended to increase disgust levels as well. As they pointed out, "With films, it appears that there is a natural tendency for anger to co-occur with other negative emotions" (p. 104). Still, videos and some combined techniques (video and personal story writing) are relatively successful affect manipulations (Westermann, Spies, Stahl, & Hesse, 1996).

Physiological and cognitive antecedents of emotion

The influential James-Lange theory (James, 1884) held that emotional stimuli elicited bodily responses, that is, peripheral activity such as changes in heart rate, blood pressure, and skin conductance, and that these bodily responses were translated fairly directly into conscious differences in emotional experience (e.g., fear versus anger). While there was modest success relating "energetic" physiological responses to higher arousal negative affect (compared to lower arousal states such as sadness and guilt), there was no consistent translation of bodily responses into differential positive affect. More generally, such physiological measures do not appear to reflect essential differences in the valence of emotion (Bradley, Cuthbert, & Lang, 1993; Schimmack & Crites, 2005). One response to the failure to support the James-Lange theory was to search for other, more sensitive indicants of emotional response that could then be interpreted as particular types of emotion. Facial feedback theories identified patterns that corresponded to happiness, surprise, sadness, fear, anger, and disgust (Ekman, 1973; Izard, 1977; Kleinke, Peterson, & Rutledge, 1998). However, a meta-analysis of these studies (including those where participants were induced to adopt musculature associated with smiling and frowning) indicated that these effects were too weak to perform the central function ascribed to bodily responses in the James-Lange theory (Matsumoto, 1987).

A more basic challenge to the original theory was to question the central role of bodily response to subsequent emotional experience. Schachter and Singer (1962) made significant inroads by showing (via injections of either epinephrine or a placebo) that peripheral arousal only differentiated an emotional response from merely cognitive responses. In their two-factor theory, cognitive processes played the decisive role in interpreting the arousal that was being experienced. A substantial challenge to the bodily arousal component of this theory can be seen in other research conducted at about the same time. Lazarus and Alfert (1964) asked people to watch a film depicting a tribal ritual involving what appeared to be genital mutilation. However, half of those watching were given misinformation that the experience was actually not painful and that adolescents looked forward to this initiation into manhood, and significant cognitive control over arousal was observed. Subsequent research on spinal cord injured patients best supports the view that peripheral arousal is not necessary to the experience of emotion, but can intensify it (Mezzacappa, Katkin, & Palmer, 1999). However, the importance of emotional intensification should not be minimized. Recent research on memory, for example, demonstrates the importance of such emotional experience to memory consolidation, and is, thus, consistent with evolutionary underpinnings of classical conditioning (Cahill & McGaugh, 1998). More generally, emotional response was shown to be far more under cognitive control and appraisals of experience than had been imagined.

Since then, cognitive appraisal theories have dominated research on emotion (see Scherer, Schorr, & Johnstone, 2001, for current theoretical perspectives). While emotional underpinnings may be somatic, and in that sense have significant evolutionary value in predisposing the body toward approach/appetitive or avoidance/inhibitory action, modern theories point to relatively few hardwired connections to discrete emotional states (Oatley & Johnson-Laird, 1987; Ortony, Clore, & Collins, 1988). Instead, such theories stress the involvement of cognitive appraisal (Scherer, Schorr, & Johnstone, 2001). These appraisal processes assign evaluative meaning to objects and events (i.e., desirable versus undesirable) and facilitate causal attributions to sources either in the external world, such as another person's actions or in our own behavior or thoughts. The combination of evaluative meaning, assessment of internal versus external causation and responsibility, and temporal perspective is then assumed to produce such highly differentiated emotions as happiness, pride, envy, disgust, sadness, anger, and fear (see Lazarus, 1991). While research supports the role of arousal in the experience of relatively intense emotions, cognitive processes (e.g., telling someone that an experience is/is not painful) play a major role and have been shown to alter the experience even when assessed by heart rate and skin conductance.

Building on earlier work by Leventhal (1980), Buck (1985), and Hoffman (1986), Cohen and Areni (1991) advanced a three-phase dynamic model in which activation of a mental concept (e.g., identification of a flashing red light) produces a largely unconscious and very rapid, sensory-level affective response. Some such responses may be largely innate (e.g., surprise) or at least potentiated by evolutionary processes (e.g., responses to taste; Steiner, Glaser, Hawilo, & Berridge, 2001). Others require very little learning beyond simple association to become generalized tendencies, such as preferences for smiling and familiar faces. These phase-one emotional responses interrupt other cognitive processes, orient attention, and bring resources to bear on the instigating stimulus. In phase two, the cognitive system attaches somewhat greater meaning to the stimulus by automatically extracting easily processed stimulus information and associating it with experienced pleasantness/unpleasantness and arousal. Thus, the second-phase affective response becomes more differentiated through the operation of associational, rather than reasoning processes. In phase three, affective experience results from cognitive elaboration, thereby taking into account context and previous experience. At stage two, and to a much greater degree at stage three, cognitive appraisal can enhance or suppress arousal (Lazarus & Alfert, 1964) as well as create more nuanced feeling states, such as disgust rather than sadness.

Memory for affective experiences

There is considerable evidence that the arousal intensity of an affective experience increases people's immediate and long-term memory for this experience (Bradley, Greenwald, Petry, & Lang, 1992; Kroeber-Riel, 1979; Thorson & Friestad, 1989), especially with respect to the central elements of this experience (Christianson, Loftus, Hoffman, & Loftus, 1991). This appears to be the case even when the source of arousal is unrelated to the material to be learned and comes after the learning has taken place, which suggests that the phenomenon may be due, in part, to a better consolidation of memory traces under high emotional arousal (Nielson, Yee, & Erickson, 2005). Emotional intensity is no guarantee of memory accuracy, however. Biases due to changes in cognitive appraisals of the events or revised standards of judgment (e.g., looking back, a person may have a different perspective on the emotion-eliciting event) as well as a desire to see things differently (e.g., when anticipating a recurrent experience such as childbirth) may intrude on people's memory (Levine, 1997; Levine, Prohaska, Burgess, Rice, & Laulhere, 2001). Retrospective assessments of affective experiences also seem to be more impacted by intensity at both the peak and the end of the experience, with duration playing a less significant role (Ariely & Loewenstein, 2000; Fredrickson & Kahneman, 1993; Kahneman, Fredrickson, Schreiber, & Redelmeier, 1993).

The Structure and Assessment of Affect

There are two separate research traditions among those whose work involves the assessment of affect. The first is to identify the underlying dimensions of affect by analyses of judged similarities and semantic differential ratings of mood terms, as well as facial and vocal emotional expressions. The second combines a more functional/motivational analysis with evidence from studies of neurophysiological and hormonal processes.

The first body of work supports the existence of two general dimensions: pleasantness versus unpleasantness and activation/arousal/engagement (see Remington, Fabrigar, & Visser, 2000; Russell & Carroll, 1999a; see Russell & Carroll, 1999b; Watson, Wiese, Vaidya, & Tellegen, 1999). Research in this tradition is heavily measurement-based and has been extended into several practical domains to classify affective responses to stimuli of interest, such as pictures and advertisements, as well as to provide a more general basis for delineating categories of emotional response (Watson & Tellegen, 1985).

Affect taxonomies in consumer research

Researchers with a primary interest in affective aspects of stimuli, such as advertisements and how people describe their affective responses to them, have been less interested in the underlying dimensionality of affect and often prefer to think in terms of affect taxonomies that correspond to more macro-level constellations or prototypes (Shaver, Schwartz, Kirson, & Oconnor, 1987). They rely on specially constructed inventories of mood and emotion terms, as well as scales that have been developed for other purposes (e.g., to represent appetitive and aversive motivational systems). In research on advertising, for example, Holbrook and Batra (1987) began with over 90 items that combined emotional responses and evaluative reactions to advertising content, and Edell and Burke (1987) used a 69-item inventory of feelings. In such research, investigators typically attempt to reduce the individual items to distinct clusters using techniques such as factor analysis and hierarchical cluster analysis (Shaver, Schwartz, Kirson, & Oconnor, 1987). At times, claims are made about underlying structure, but the generality of such claims is questionable because of the arbitrary selection of items and stimuli, the ambiguity of hierarchical configurations of emotion terms, as well as measurement issues to be discussed below (see also Mano, 1991; Schimmack & Crites, 2005). Nevertheless, such research may serve the investigator's needs in differentiating between types of affective responses to content and situations (e.g., store settings) of particular interest. Much of the earlier affect taxonomy research in consumer behavior, at least through 1990, was reviewed by Cohen and Areni (1991), and so it will not receive explicit attention here.

An extremely comprehensive analysis of many of the emotion measures used in consumer research was carried out by Richins (1997), who identified shortcomings in their ability to address a greater variety of consumption experiences. These included the contemplation, purchase, use, and subsequent reactions to a broad variety of products and services from the mundane to the important and sentimental (see also Derbaix & Pham, 1991). She identified a list of 175 emotion terms that had been used in consumer research and that satisfied criteria developed by Ortony, Clore, and Collins (1988) to screen out nonemotion terms focusing on bodily states such as "sleepy," subjective evaluations such as "feeling confident," behaviors and action tendencies such as "crying" and "hesitant," and cognitive states such as "interested." She supplemented this list by prompting open-ended self reports of positive and negative feelings (most commonly, the positive affective terms "happiness," "relief," and "excitement," but also "worry," "sadness," and "guilt") to a variety of consumption experiences. Although the underlying dimensionality of the resulting "Consumption Emotion Set" (CES) is somewhat ambiguous (beyond the traditional positive-negative axis), the instrument appears to be quite useful for those who wish to assess consumers' affective responses to a more comprehensive set of consumption experiences.

Underlying dimensions: The bipolarity of affect

More basic research on the structure of affect attempts to identify relationships among two primary components of affect, pleasantness, and arousal/activation. Russell (1980) originally proposed that these two dimensions be viewed as a circumplex, that is, a model in which individual mood and emotion descriptors are systematically arranged around the perimeter of a circle. Data from Russell and Barrett (1999) indicate that affective structure actually falls somewhere between a classic simple structure in which the variables cluster in dense groups around labeled axes and a true circumplex, as in Figure 11.1, in which the variables are more evenly spaced and define a complete circle.

Within this measurement tradition, there has been a debate over the bipolarity versus independence of positive and negative affect. When people experience and report high negative affect, does that mean that positive affect is low (i.e., bipolarity)? When thinking about implications of bipolarity, it is important to differentiate between "core affect" (Russell & Barrett, 1999) and evaluative outcomes of affective processes. The latter are the result of cognitive appraisals and clearly allow for mixed assessments (i.e., positive in some respects and negative in others). Core affect, on the

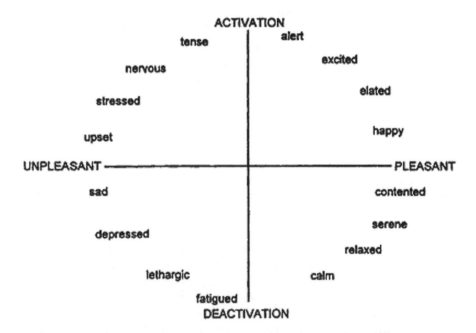

Figure 11.1 The circumplex model of affect. The circumplex model describes affect in terms of the two orthogonal dimensions of valence and activation. From "The structure of currect affect: Controversies and emerging consensus," by L. Feldman Barrett and J. A. Russell, 1999, *Current Directions in Psychological Sciences, 8*, 11. Copyright 1999 by the American Psychological Society. Reprinted with permission.

other hand, refers to how a person is feeling emotionally at a point in time. Also, when the analysis is performed at an aggregate-level across emotional experiences over time, bipolarity assumptions do not necessarily predict independence. People who are asked to report emotional states using experience sampling diaries are just as likely to have self reports indicating high average negative (positive) affect, regardless of their average levels of positive (negative) affect (Diener & Irannejad, 1986; Diener, Smith, & Fujita, 1995).

A general consensus has emerged that a bipolar structure dominates (see Russell & Carroll, 1999a), as acknowledged even by original proponents of the independence assumption (see Watson & Clark, 1997; Watson, Wiese, Vaidya, & Tellegen, 1999). While interested readers should consult the extensive literature directly, several key issues must be noted. First, tests of independence versus bipolarity require truly independent measures of positive and negative affect. Using bipolar items (e.g., –3 = sad, 0 = neutral, +3 = happy) artificially promotes bipolarity. On the other hand, using unipolar items often leaves the lower endpoint of the scale ambiguous. For example, if respondents are asked to rate their happiness on a 1–5 scale going from "not at all" to "extremely," does a "1" mean a mere absence of happiness or an opposite state such as sadness? In addition, where does neutrality lie in such a scale? Such measurement issues can have major influences on the factor structure of the resulting scale.

Even assuming independent measurement of positive and negative affect, the bipolarity of specified circumplex axes (corresponding to particular affective states shown in Figure 11.1 and measured by various scales) has proven to be far more problematic. A primary reason is the confounding caused by variations in arousal/engagement that prevent the semantic opposites in Figure 11.1 from lying along a 180° angle. Across a number of such studies, positive and negative affect have been found to be moderately negatively correlated (typically around r = –.44) rather than nearly perfectly negatively correlated, implying bipolarity, or nearly perfectly uncorrelated, implying independence (Diener, Smith, & Fujita, 1995; Watson, Clark, & Tellegen, 1988; Watson, Wiese, Vaidya, & Tellegen, 1999). However, the correlation increases dramatically when people report affect in the presence of strong, intense emotion (Diener & Irannejad, 1986), demonstrating the bipolarity of strong emotional states. On the other hand, feelings originally characterized as low positive affect (hence low in activation/arousal) and that correspond to quietude and calmness are not far removed from low negative affect states (e.g., sluggish) characteristic of mild depression. Consider a person who views himself as experiencing a lack (or loss) of pleasure or lack of response to pleasurable stimuli. At low levels, then, self reports of positive and negative affect can be positively correlated (Watson, Wiese, Vaidya, & Tellegen, 1999), suggesting independence.

Underlying neurophysiological processes clearly register and potentiate positive and negative affect simultaneously. Though conflict and/or ambivalence would seem to be logical consequences of events and stimuli that simultaneously prompt fear and excitement, making effective reactions difficult, emotional paralysis in not the norm. A great deal of current research beyond the scope of this chapter is providing substantial insight about how these underlying neurophysiological processes translate into more molar responses. We will discuss some relevant work on "mixed emotions" a bit later.

The PANAS scales: Combining valence and activation

Consumer researchers rely heavily on the positive and negative affect scales of the PANAS (Watson, Clark, & Tellegen, 1988). The positive cluster consists of active, alert, attentive, determined, enthusiastic, excited, inspired, interested, proud, and strong. The negative cluster consists of afraid, ashamed, distressed, guilty, hostile, irritable, jittery, nervous, scared, and upset. While this instrument has proven to be useful in many studies, there are two significant issues that consumer researchers should consider. First, the two scales do not cover the full range of positive and negative affect. Pleasant states of low to moderate activation (e.g., happy, positive, satisfied, serene, pleased) are missing from the positive affect (PA) scale where high activation states (e.g., active, alert, attentive, excited) predominate. Unpleasant states of low to moderate activation (e.g., unhappy, negative, depressed, sad) are also missing from the negative affect (NA) scale where high activation states (distressed, jittery, upset) predominate. This is not an oversight, though perhaps an inartful choice of labels. Watson and colleagues were clear at the outset that they wished to capture a combination of positive affect *and* activation (and the same enhanced activation on the negative side). In effect, Watson and Tellegen (1985) rotated the axes 45° to attempt to focus on two orthogonal dimensions that they now term positive activation and negative activation (Watson, Wiese, Vaidya, & Tellegen, 1999).

The functional significance of these two dimensions was recognized by Fowles (1994). PA corresponds to affect that energizes and facilitates approach behavior and reward seeking; whereas NA corresponds to affect that inhibits similar behavior and leads instead to avoidance—a "stop, look and listen" response to the environment. Considerable research in neurophysiology is being directed to understanding the processes responsible for these appetitive and aversive effects, but that is beyond the scope of this chapter (for a review, see Lang, 1995).

Most recently, then, affect researchers have been redefining the PANAS instrument to more appropriately recognize its measurement of positive activation and negative activation (J. T. Larsen, McGraw, & Cacioppo, 2001; Schimmack & Crites, 2005). The second and related problem with the PANAS instrument is that it violates the semantic-opposites requirement listed earlier for a test of bipolarity. Only positive affective states of high activation are semantically opposite (180° away) of negative affective states of low activation. Russell and Carroll (1999a) note that the negative set includes none of the semantic opposites of the positive set because the opposite of positive activation is not negative activation, but a state combining negative affect and low arousal. Accordingly, PANAS does not have psychometric properties that allow it to be used to investigate questions involving the independence of positive and negative affect.

In a reanalysis of available data, Russell and Carroll (1999a) identified three clusters of positive items that could alternatively be viewed as varying continuously in arousal. The first cluster involves positive affective states of high activation such as being enthused, ebullient, excited, and energetic. A second cluster involves positive affective states of moderate activation such as being happy, gratified, pleased and content. A third cluster involves positive affective states of low activation such as being calm, serene, tranquil and relaxed. A parallel clustering was uncovered on the negative affect side: (1) negative affective states of high activation such as being tense, upset, jittery, and nervous; (2) negative affective states of moderate activation such as being unhappy, miserable, discontent and troubled; and (3) negative affective states of low activation such as being depressed, bored, lethargic, and glum.

Mixed emotions

A person can feel sad and guilty *or* happy and proud at the same time. But is it possible to feel guilty and proud (or any other combination of oppositely valenced emotions) at the same time? Imagine, for example, being very successful in a negotiation in a third-world country that deprived the seller of money that had significantly greater value to her than to you. You might feel pride at your skill (particularly if others in your group did less well in similar negotiations), but you also may experience guilt. Do we simply shift back and forth in such emotional quandaries (alternating between positive and negative feelings), or can we actually be happy and sad at the same time? Note that this is a different issue from an evaluation of one's behavior (which might be tempered because of oppositely-valenced emotions) or how a person would translate mixed emotions in responding to a sad-happy scale, since a person would need to resolve that conflict in order to make such judgments. Russell and Carroll (1999a) argue that the bipolarity of emotional experience implies that when you are happy, you are not sad, just as when you are hot, you are not cold. Strictly speaking, that claim is very strong since being at one point on the abscissa of an affect distribution precludes being at any other point. As Larsen et al. (2001) point out, bipolarity implies a linear relationship, and thus a correlation close to -1. Mutual exclusivity of positive and negative affect, on the other hand, would produce intermediate degrees of independence. But does any level of correlation between measures of positive and negative affect imply that any (even low) levels of happiness preclude *experiencing* sadness? Watson and Tellegen (1999) maintained that sadness decreases as happiness increases. In that sense, happiness and sadness regularly co-occur and are only mutually exclusive when people are maximally happy or maximally sad.

Williams and Aaker (2002) employed either happy, sad, or mixed emotional appeals by combining the same picture with different characterizations of it. They found that the acceptance of the duality of emotions (via mixed emotional appeals) was greater among Asian American than Anglo Americans (who actually reported discomfort), although both groups reported experiencing a combination of happiness and sadness when given the mixed emotional appeal. Such self reports are ambiguous since it is difficult to know whether people assume they should be experiencing mixed emotions when confronted with a stimulus presenting a happy *and* sad event or could be translating their "somewhat sad" (or somewhat happy) feelings on to scales that allow them to report mixed emotions.

A well-known demonstration of mixed emotions was carried out by Larsen et al. (2001). They exposed people to a mixture of happy and sad events in the movie *Life is Beautiful* in which a father seeks to keep his child's spirits up while they are in a concentration camp. Viewers reported mixed feelings of happiness and sadness. Since people may well have alternated back and forth, in a subsequent study, Larsen et al. (2004) created a gambling context which led to disappointing wins (because people expected more favorable outcomes) and relieving losses (because people expected even worse outcomes). A button-pressing task suggested that people, in fact, experienced mixed emotions simultaneously. Note, however, that these are unlikely to be extremely positive *and* extremely negative feelings—a combination that seems difficult to imagine. So, another possibility is that people subjectively interpreted these more moderate feelings as though they were part positive and part negative in light of the information they were given. Such findings raise important questions about the nature of affective experience.

Evidence supporting mixed emotions has also shed new light into the potential processes underlying the consumption of products and services that—at least from an outside observer's point of view—are expected to produce negative feelings (e.g., watch horror movies, practice dangerous sports, etc). Andrade and Cohen (2007b) point out that previous theories tended to rely on the assumption that positive and negative feelings cannot be experienced at the same time. As a result, people who deliberately exposed themselves to apparent sources of negative feelings either do not experience much negative affect (Fenz & Epstein, 1967; Zuckerman, 1996) or focus on its relieving consequences—after removal of the aversive stimuli (Solomon & Corbit, 1974; Zillmann, 1980). Andrade and Cohen showed the importance of relaxing the single affective valence assumption in order to provide a more complete understanding of the phenomenon. In a series of four studies, it was shown that after exposing participants to horrifying scenes of a film clip (scenes from *The Exorcist*), fear approach (horror movie watchers) and fear avoidance (non-horror movie watchers) consumers displayed strikingly similar levels and patterns of negative affect. However, fear approach consumers also showed increased levels of positive affect, whereas fear avoidance consumers showed no signs of positive experiences. Also importantly, the authors demonstrated that mixed feelings are more likely when individuals are able to place themselves within a protective (detachment) frame: "An ideal detachment frame gives people the ability to increase psychological distance from the main actors of the movie, while still absorbing the impact of the scenes" (p. 32). When presented with the actors' biography prior to the movie, and the actors' "regular" pictures next to the video during the scenes, which was supposed to remind the audience that these were simply actors playing a role, fear-avoidance and fear-approach participants reacted similarly, both displaying increased levels of positive or negative affective states during the movie. People tend to deliberately choose to expose themselves to sources of negative affect when a psychological protective frame is present, as it allows for the co-activation of positive and negative affect. A similar rationale has been adopted to show the presence of mixed feelings of disgust and amusement as a result of video exposure (Hemenover & Schimmack, 2004).

THE ROLE OF AFFECT IN CONSUMER JUDGMENT AND DECISION MAKING

It is useful to distinguish three types of affect in consumer judgment and decision making. *Integral affect* refers to affective responses that are genuinely experienced and directly linked to the object of judgment or decision.[2] Integral affective responses include momentary feelings experienced through direct exposure to the object itself (such as the pleasant feeling of tasting a fine wine) and those experienced in response to some representation of the object—a representation that may be externally provided (e.g., a TV commercial for a product) or internally generated (e.g., thinking about a product). These affective responses are integral to the extent that they are elicited by *features* of the object, whether these features are real, perceived, or only imagined.

Incidental affect refers to affective experiences whose source is clearly unconnected to the object to be evaluated. Most of the literature on mood effects on consumer behavior (e.g., Gardner, 1985; e.g., Kahn & Isen, 1993; Lee & Sternthal, 1999) deals with incidental affect in that the source of the mood is typically unrelated to the judgment or decision being made. In addition to a person's current mood, incidental affect may also come from a person's emotional dispositions (such as chronic anxiety or depression) and temperament (such as general optimism or pessimism), or from any contextual stimuli associated with integral affect (such as background music, pleasant scent, etc.).

Task-related affect lies somewhere between integral and incidental affect. It refers to affective responses that are elicited by the task or process of making judgments and decisions, as opposed to direct, integral responses to features of the target objects or purely incidental feelings. For example, the emotional stress of having to choose between two very attractive offers would be considered task-induced in that it is the *process* of having to choose between these two offers that is stressful, not the offers themselves. Indeed, decisions may trigger unpleasant task-related affect even when the options are associated with pleasant integral affect, for example, a choice between two vacation destinations. In the above example, the emotional stress experienced would not be incidental either because, by definition, it would not have arisen had a judgment or decision not been required. Each type of affect will be discussed separately in relation to consumer judgment and decision making.

Integral Affect in Judgment and Decision Making

The influence of integral affect on target evaluation

Numerous studies across various disciplines show that integral affective responses to a target object—whether the object is a product, a person, or a company—are often incorporated into a summary evaluation of the object. In general, though not always, objects that elicit pleasant feelings, such as a beautiful symphony, a sweet dessert, or an attractive singer, are evaluated more favorably, and objects that elicit unpleasant feelings, such as a noisy apartment, a sour tasting dish or a rude salesperson, are evaluated less favorably. The relation between integral affective responses and object evaluation is so strong that, for a long time, affect and evaluation (or attitude) were considered to be synonymous (e.g., Fishbein & Azjen, 1975). Nevertheless, despite the generally strong positive correlation between measures of integral affective responses and measures of overall evaluation, there is growing consensus that the two constructs are theoretically and empirically distinct, with integral affective responses generally conceived as one of several potential antecedents or determinants of overall evaluation or attitude (see Breckler & Wiggins, 1989; Crites, Fabrigar, & Petty, 1994; Pham, Cohen, Pracejus, & Hughes, 2001; Wyer, Clore, & Isbell, 1999; Zanna & Rempel, 1988).

In an early demonstration of the influence of integral affective responses on summary evaluations, Abelson, Kinder, Peters, and Fiske (1982) documented in two large surveys that people's emotional responses to prominent politicians (notably, Jimmy Carter, Gerald Ford, and Ronald Reagan) were highly predictive of their overall attitudes and preferences toward these politicians. Importantly, people's emotional responses predicted their attitudes *over and above* their own party affiliation and their assessments of the politicians' traits and behaviors. A major theme of research in social psychology and consumer research during the 1980s and 1990s was that integral affective responses to various target objects may predict judgment, choice, and behavior toward these objects over and above assessments based on more descriptive or "cognitive" bases of judgments such as beliefs, stereotypes, base-rates, prior attitudes, etc. In marketing and consumer research, this theme was pursued most extensively in the advertising domain. A large number of studies have indicated that affective responses to advertisements have direct effects on consumers' attitudes toward the ad (A_{ad}) and at least indirect effects on consumers' attitudes toward the brand (A_b) through the effects on A_{ad} (cf. Aaker, Stayman, & Hagerty, 1986; Batra & Ray, 1986; Brown, Homer, & Inman, 1998; Brown & Stayman, 1992; Edell & Burke, 1987; Holbrook & Batra, 1987). Some studies indicate that ad-induced affective responses may also influence A_b directly, independently of A_{ad}. (e.g., Burke & Edell, 1989; C. M. Derbaix, 1995; Morris, Woo, Geason, & Kim, 2002; Stayman & Aaker, 1988) However, the findings probably deserve further analysis because, at the time, less attention was paid to separating actual affective responses to the ad from sheer liking of the ad. In addition, the mechanisms explaining how affect was transferred from the ad to the brand were not closely examined.

Conceptually related results have been obtained across a variety of other domains of judgment, choice, and behavior. For instance, Bodur, Brinberg, and Coupey (2000) indicated that affect toward various AIDS prevention behaviors such as abstinence or condom usage predicted attitudes and intentions toward these behaviors over and above personal beliefs about these behaviors. Similarly, Allen, Machleit, and Kleine (1992) reported that emotional responses to past blood donations predicted future donation behavior over and above expressed attitudes toward donation. Likewise, Oliver (1993) indicated that affective responses to products such as cars and a college class predicted overall satisfaction with these products over and above one's satisfaction with the products' specific attributes. In the investment domain, MacGregor, Slovic, Dreman, and Berry (2000) found that investment banking students' feelings toward various industry sectors (electronics, managed healthcare, etc.) were strongly predictive of their intentions to invest in these sectors, independent of the sectors' financial fundamentals. In summary, the literature indicates that integral affective responses to a variety of target objects influence consumers' overall evaluations of and behaviors toward these objects beyond more descriptive bases of object evaluation such as beliefs, stereotypes, prior attitude, etc. However, as noted above, some caution may be called for because some of the studies in this line of research may not adequately distinguish actual feeling states from overall liking responses.

Underlying processes

Three mechanisms may explain why integral feelings have a direct influence on overall evaluation and behavior independent of one's descriptive knowledge about the target. The first two mechanisms both imply a noninferential, "automatic" influence of integral feelings on target evaluation. The first possibility is that integral feelings enter evaluations directly through simple evaluative conditioning. Evaluative conditioning refers to the transfer of evaluative meaning across stimuli that are presented simultaneously (see Staats & Staats, 1957); it differs from classical (Pavlovian) conditioning in that one stimulus does not serve as a signal of another (see De Houwer, Thomas, & Baeyens, 2001). A close proximity between a target and an integral feeling experience may result in the evaluative meaning of the feelings (mostly their valence) being carried over to the target—a mechanism sometimes called "affect transfer" in consumer research and marketing (e.g., Mackenzie, Lutz, & Belch, 1986). A second possibility builds on the idea that affective experiences are associated with particular action tendencies such as approach, avoidance, withdrawal, or confrontation (see Frijda, Kuipers, & Terschure, 1989). These action tendencies may not only carry over to actual behavior, but also be translated spontaneously into proxies of behavior such as evaluations and intentions. This mechanism would be consistent with the emerging view of affect as an embodied mode of evaluation (e.g., Clore & Schnall, 2005; Damasio, 1994; Forster, 2004; Zajonc & Markus, 1982).

A third mechanism is based on the hypothesis that integral affective responses are often viewed as sources of information during object evaluation (Schwarz, 1990; Schwarz & Clore, 1996). To evaluate a target, people may consciously inspect their feelings to see "how they feel" about it. Pleasant feelings would be interpreted as evidence of liking, satisfaction, well-being, and so on; unpleasant feelings would be interpreted as evidence of disliking, dissatisfaction, misery, and so on. This process is known as the "how-do-I feel-about-it?" heuristic (Schwarz & Clore, 1988). Numerous studies have documented the existence and operation of this heuristic both in psychology (e.g., Schwarz & Clore, 1983; see Schwarz & Clore 1996, for a review) and in consumer research (e.g., Gorn, Goldberg, & Basu, 1993; Pham, 1998; Pham, Cohen, Pracejus, & Hughes, 2001). Although the heuristic was originally proposed as an explanation of incidental mood effects on judgment (Schwarz & Clore, 1983, 1988; see the discussion of incidental affect below), there is growing evidence that the heuristic is used with integral feelings as well (Pham et al., 2001). In fact, the primary application of this heuristic—its raison d'être—is in relation to integral affective feelings (see Pham, 2004, for a discussion). Some research indicates that the heuristic is also used *anticipatorily* in consumer decision making. Sometimes consumers appear to construct "mental pictures" of the alternatives and assess how they feel as they hold these pictures in their minds (Pham, 1998).[3] (See also Gilbert, Gill, & Wilson, 2002, for conceptually related results). These pictures appear to be concrete, which explains why the reliance on momentary feelings in decision making has been found to be more pronounced among people with high imagery ability (Pham, 1998). Unlike the first two mechanisms, the "how-do-I-feel-about-it?" heuristic is assumed to be inferential, as opposed to purely associationistic or mechanistic. That is, people are assumed to *reflect* on what their integral feelings mean for the judgment to be made; they do not rely on these feelings automatically (see Avnet & Pham, 2004, for evidence consistent with this interpretation).

The three mechanisms described above all predict a direct effect of integral affective responses on evaluations. A fourth mechanism posits an *indirect* effect. It has been suggested that integral affective responses enter evaluations only indirectly by changing the person's perceptions or beliefs about the target (e.g., Fishbein & Middlestadt, 1995). For instance, feelings of frustration toward a service provider might reinforce perceptions that "they are not reliable" or trigger beliefs that "they don't care about the customer." It is these perceptions and beliefs—not the feelings that triggered them—that are then summarized and integrated into the overall evaluation. Consistent with this mechanism, some studies indicate that affective responses to advertisements may also influence brand attitudes by changing brand beliefs (see Brown & Stayman, 1992; Mackenzie, Lutz, & Belch, 1986). This mechanism is also consistent with a major explanation of incidental mood-congruency effects on evaluations (discussed further below). According to this explanation, evaluations tend to be assimilated toward incidental mood states because these states cue mood-consistent materials in memory, which then color perceptions of the target (Isen, Shalker, Clark, & Karp, 1978).

Properties of evaluations and decisions based on integral affect

It is widely accepted that, in general, judgments and decisions based on integral feelings are *reached more rapidly* than are comparable judgments and decisions based on descriptive inputs. Although this property was originally assumed mostly on theoretical grounds (e.g., Epstein, 1990; Zajonc, 1980), it has since been documented empirically both with stimulus-based evaluations (Pham, Cohen, Pracejus, & Hughes, 2001) and with memory-based evaluations (Verplanken, Hofstee, & Janssen, 1998). This property should logically extend to decisions and choices as well, although this prediction remains to be tested. Three factors account for the generally greater speed of judgments and decisions based on integral affect. First, integral affect often arises very rapidly (e.g., LeDoux, 1996; Zajonc, 1980). Second, integral affective responses often enter evaluations through simple associations. Finally, even if integral affective responses have to be interpreted, as they do in the "how-do-I-feel-about-it?" heuristic, their interpretation is generally very clear (Strack, 1992).

It is also widely accepted that judgments and decisions based on integral affect generally *require less processing resources* (e.g., Epstein, 1990). As a result, any constraint on processing resources (time pressure, distraction, cognitive load, etc.) tends to increase the reliance on integral affective responses both in evaluative judgments (Pham et al., 2001) and in choices (Nowlis & Shiv, 2005; Shiv & Fedorikhin, 1999). For example, when given a choice between a tempting piece of chocolate cake (an affectively attractive option) and a healthier fruit salad (a "cognitively" attractive option), consumers whose cognitive resources were not constrained tended to choose the healthier fruit salad. However, when cognitive resources were constrained, consumers tended to choose the more tempting cake, presumably because affective drivers of preference still operated while the more cognitive drivers could not (Shiv & Fedorikhin, 1999). Similarly, Nowlis, and Shiv (2005) found that distracting consumers while they are sampling a pleasant-tasting but relatively unknown brand of chocolate increases the likelihood that they will subsequently choose the sampled brand over a better-known brand of chocolate. Again, this is presumably because distraction increases the relative weight attached to the pleasant integral feelings associated with the sampling experience.

Evaluations and decisions based on integral affect also tend to be *myopic*. Immediate affective rewards and punishments tend to be weighted too heavily, whereas delayed consequences are not weighted sufficiently (see Loewenstein, 1996). This property is very salient in impulse control situations where people have to trade off the immediate hedonic consequences of an option (such as the pleasure of eating junk food or the pain of visiting the dentist) against its long-term consequences (high cholesterol and obesity; healthy teeth and gums). According to Loewenstein (1996), the myopia of affect-based judgments and decisions is caused by the differential accessibility of current and delayed affective states. Whereas the experience of immediate integral affect has strong drive properties (e.g., the cathartic anger release of yelling at an uncooperative salesclerk), it is more difficult to anticipate and vividly picture future affective states (e.g., the embarrassment of being escorted out of the store). As a result, a reliance on affect tends to yield preferences for options that are more rewarding (or less painful) in the short term even if these options are less desirable in the long run. Consistent with this proposition, recent brain imaging studies indicate that preferences for immediate rewards are associated with greater activation in parts of the limbic system that are associated with affect (McClure, Laibson, Loewenstein, & Cohen, 2004). Affective responses, it seems, are part of a decision-making system of the present (Pham, 2004).

A lesser-known property of evaluations based on integral affect is that they *can exhibit relatively high consensus.* Contrary to popular beliefs that affect is highly subjective, a growing body of evidence suggests that affective judgments are, in fact, quite consensual, sometimes even more so than cognitive judgments. For instance, judgments of physical attractiveness, long thought to be purely subjective ("beauty is in the eye of the beholder") have recently been shown to be largely universal (Etcoff, 1999). Similarly, emotional responses to music have been shown to be largely shared (Peretz, Gagnon, & Bouchard, 1998). It has also been observed that, although juries may disagree widely on the amount of punitive damages they are willing to award in legal cases, they tend to agree strongly on how outraged they feel in response to each case (Kahneman, Schkade, & Sunstein, 1998). In fact, for a variety of everyday stimuli, people seem to agree more on how they feel toward the stimuli than on how they would cognitively assess these stimuli (Pham, Cohen, Pracejus, & Hughes, 2001). According to Pham et al. (2001), affect-based judgments will be most consensual when the integral affective responses are triggered through hardwired programs involved in bioregulation (such as the pleasure experience of eating ice cream) or through emotional schemata acquired through conditioning and socialization (e.g., the outrage elicited by an unprovoked insult). Affect-based judgments will be less consensual when based on integral affective responses arising through controlled appraisal processes such as the guilt experienced when attributing one's failure to a lack of effort.

Evaluations and decisions based on integral affect additionally tend to be *sensitive to the presence or absence of affect-producing stimuli but relatively insensitive to further variations in the magnitude of these stimuli.* This property was recently demonstrated in an interesting series of studies by Hsee and Rottenstreich (2004). In one study, respondents were asked to assess how much they would pay for a used collection of either 5 or 10 Madonna CDs. One group of respondents was primed to make their assessments based on how they felt toward the target (Madonna and her music); the others were primed to make their assessment in a calculating fashion. Consistent with the researchers' predictions, respondents' willingness to pay for the CD collection was much more sensitive to the size of the collection among respondents who had had been primed to rely on calculation than among respondents who had been primed to rely on their feelings. In another study, respondents were asked to assess how much they would be willing to donate for a rescue effort that would save either one or four pandas' lives. For one group of respondents the number of pandas saved was simply represented by one or four dots. For the other group, the number of pandas saved was represented by one or four cute pictures of pandas, which was expected to trigger a more affective mode of evaluation. Again, as predicted, respondents' donations were much more sensitive to the number of pandas saved in the affect-poor (dot) condition than in the affect-rich (picture) condition. Hsee and Rottenstreich (2004) explain this phenomenon as follows. Affect-based evaluations are often based on concrete mental images of the target (see Pham, 1998). Because these images are discrete, usually consisting of prototypical representations of the target (a lovely panda, a popular Madonna song), continuous quantitative information tends to be lost (Kahneman, Ritov, & Schkade, 1999).

Similarly, evaluations and decisions based on integral affect are *relatively insensitive to probabilities,* except for the presence or absence of uncertainty (Loewenstein, Weber, Hsee, & Welch,

2001; Rottenstreich & Hsee, 2001). In a telling demonstration of this phenomenon, Rottenstreich & Hsee (2001) asked respondents how much they would be willing to pay to avoid two types of negative outcomes, either losing $20 or receiving a painful but harmless electric shock, with an either 1% or 99% probability of occurrence. Consistent with standard economic theory, respondents were willing to pay much more to avoid a 99% probability of losing $20 (Mean = $18) than to avoid a 1% probability of losing $20 (Mean = $1). However, when the decision was about receiving an electric shock, a prospect rich in negative affect, respondents were not willing to pay much more to avoid a 99% probability of shock (Mean = $10) than to avoid a 1% probability of shock (Mean = $7). According to Loewenstein et al. (2001), this phenomenon again arises because affective decisions and evaluations often involve anticipatory affective responses to discrete images of the options that do not incorporate probabilities. However, affect-based decisions and evaluations are sensitive to deviations from absolute certainty (i.e., from impossibility to small probability and vise versa). For example, many consumers grossly overpay to turn zero probabilities of winning in big lotteries (a prospect rich in affect) into probabilities that are infinitesimal. Similarly, most consumers would be willing to pay large insurance or security premiums to convert minute probabilities of catastrophic events (prospects rich in affect) into zero probabilities. Loewenstein and colleagues (2001) argue that anticipatory affective responses such as dread (of negative outcomes) or hope (of positive outcomes) are sensitive to *possibility* (i.e., deviations from certainty) rather than actual probability (see also Slovic, Finucane, Peters, & MacGregor, 2002).

Finally, evaluations and decisions based on integral affect tend to have a *high degree of internal coherence* (Pham, 2004). This is because integral affective responses to a target, which are often immediate and highly accessible, often trigger a confirmatory search for information that supports or helps explain these initial feelings (Pham, Cohen, Pracejus, & Hughes, 2001; Yeung & Wyer, 2004). This confirmatory search results in a strong correlation between the immediate affective response elicited by a target and the spontaneous thoughts that people associate with the target.[4] This strong correlation in turn results in more polarized evaluations (Adaval, 2003). Consistent with this proposition, Pham et al. (2001) found, for instance, that affective feelings toward a variety of stimuli (magazine pictures, TV commercials, etc.) are almost perfect predictors of the thoughts generated spontaneously by the stimuli. Similarly, Yeung and Wyer, (2004) found that that consumers' initial affective responses to a product's appearance make them more likely to attend and weigh product attribute information that is evaluatively consistent with the valence of the initial affective responses. A review of neurophysiological evidence led Damasio (1994) to a similar proposition: "Somatic states, negative or positive, caused by the appearance of a given representation, operate not only as a marker for the value of what is represented, but also as a booster for continued working memory and attention" (p. 198). That immediate integral affect directs subsequent thoughts may partly explain why personal impressions based on very limited samples of expressive behavior (watching a 30-second video clip of an instructor teaching) are surprisingly predictive of long-term evaluations (the instructor's end-of-semester student evaluations) (see Ambady & Rosenthal, 1992). Pham (2004) speculates that the internal coherence of affect-based judgments and decisions may have had the evolutionary purpose of promoting faster and more efficient behavioral responses to the environment by increasing the intrapsychic consistency of the signals that the person receives.

Determinants of reliance on integral affect

A number of factors have been found to increase people's reliance on integral affective responses in judgment and decision making. Although some of these factors were actually identified in studies of incidental affect, they are discussed here to the extent that they apply to integral affect as well.

Because integral affective responses are easy to access, monitor, and interpret (e.g., Pham, Cohen, Pracejus, & Hughes, 2001; Wyer, Clore, & Isbell, 1999), consumers tend to rely on integral affect more when (a) their motivation to process information is low (e.g., Miniard, Bhatla, Lord, Dickson, & Unnava, 1991; Petty, Schumann, Richman, & Strathman, 1993), (b) they are distracted, cognitively constrained, or under time pressure (e.g., Albarracin & Wyer, 2001; Pham, Cohen, Pracejus, & Hughes, 2001; Shiv & Fedorikhin, 1999), (c) other bases of evaluation are ambiguous (e.g., Gorn, Pham, & Sin, 2001; e.g., Isen & Shalker, 1982; Miniard, Bhatla, & Sirdeshmukh, 1992), or (d) they lack expertise in the target domain (Ottati & Isbell, 1996; Srull, 1987). These types of results have led some authors to theorize that the reliance on feelings in judgment and decision making is primarily a low-involvement, simplifying strategy (e.g., Clore, Schwarz, & Conway, 1994; Forgas, 1995; Petty, Schumann, Richman, & Strathman, 1993). However, the reliance on feelings is not always a low-involvement heuristic. Certain high-involvement decisions, such as who to marry or which house to buy, often seem based on affect (e.g., P. R. Darke, Chattopadhyay, & Ashworth, 2006). Sometimes, integral affective responses are considered to be very relevant for the judgment or decision to be made, even if the judgment or decision is highly involving (Pham, 1998).

Several factors have been found to influence the perceived relevance of affective responses in judgments and decisions. Affective responses to the target are perceived to be more relevant (hence, are relied upon more) under the following conditions: (a) when the consumer has experiential motives (e.g., evaluating a book as a potential beach read), as opposed to instrumental motives (e.g., evaluating a tax manual as potential help for a tax return) (Pham, 1998); (b) when the judgment or decision is inherently affective, e.g., evaluating one's satisfaction (Clore, Schwarz, & Conway, 1994; Wyer, Clore, & Isbell, 1999); (c) when the consumer makes the decision for himself or herself as opposed to someone else (Raghunathan & Pham, 1999); (d) when the consumer is promotion-focused (an inclination to use approach strategies in goal pursuit) as opposed to prevention-focused (an inclination to use avoidance strategies in goal pursuit) (Pham & Avnet, 2004); and (d) when the consumer generally trusts his or her feelings (Avnet & Pham, 2007). Overall, it appears that consumers are much more flexible in their reliance on feelings than previously thought (Pham, 2004).

Emerging research on anticipatory and anticipated integral affect

As demonstrated by Pham's (1998) research on the use of the "how-do-I-feel-about-it?" heuristics in consumer decision making, consumers often make decisions based on feelings that they experience *anticipatorily* while holding a mental representation of the target in their minds (see also Gilbert, Gill, & Wilson, 2002 for conceptually related results). These anticipatory feelings function as valuation proxies for the anticipated consequences of alternative courses of actions (Pham, 2004).

Although the two notions are often confused, the notion of *anticipatory* feelings should be differentiated from the notion of *anticipated* or *expected* affect. Anticipatory feelings refer to actual feeling experiences that arise during the decision process in the course of evaluating a target object (Bechara, Damasio, Tranel, & Damasio, 1997; Pham, 1998). Although anticipatory feelings may be subtle, they are genuine feelings with a distinct emotional quality (see Pham, 1998, Experiment 3). In contrast, anticipated or expected affect refers to *predictions* about potential affective consequences of the decision (see Loewenstein & Lerner, 2003). For example, in order to make a choice between two houses, a consumer may try to predict how happy she and her family would be in each house. This type of affect, sometimes called "predicted utility" by decision theorists (Kahneman & Snell, 1990), is central to the standard economic theory of choice, where people are posited to make choices based on the predicted hedonic consequences of the various options. These predictions appear to be strong determinants of risky choice in gambling tasks (Mellers, Schwartz,

Ho, & Ritov, 1997; Mellers, Schwartz, & Ritov, 1999). As shall be discussed later in the section on affect and motivation, expected affect also plays an important role in affect regulation where options and behaviors are chosen specifically in terms of their affect-changing or affect-maintaining consequences. However, these predictions are affective *beliefs* (i.e., cognitions), not genuine visceral feelings. Although anticipatory feelings and affective beliefs (expected affect) will naturally be correlated when the former informs the latter, there can be substantial dissociation between the two (Pham & Raghunathan, 2007; Robinson & Clore, 2002). For example, whereas genuine feelings of anxiety tend to push decision makers toward low-risk/low-reward options and genuine feelings of sadness tend to push decision makers toward high-risk/high-reward options, affective beliefs about anxiety or sadness do not have the same influences (Pham & Raghunathan, 2007). As Pham (2004) recently pointed out, the distinction between genuine anticipatory feelings and mere affective beliefs has important methodological implications. Certain methodologies such as survey questionnaires about future behavior (commonly used in attitude research) and hypothetical scenarios (commonly used in decision research) may tap into people's affective beliefs (and the intuitive theories that guide these beliefs) rather than genuine integral feelings.

An important type of anticipatory feeling is the fear response. Although such responses were examined many years ago in connection with fear appeals in persuasion (Dollard & Miller, 1950; see Eagly & Chaiken, 1993), they remain important in understanding the reluctance of people to depart from the status quo and to take action when pathways to successful outcomes are uncertain and risky. Leventhal (1970) argued that threat-related cues instigated both a problem-solving process ("danger control") and a process that focused on threat avoidance ("fear control"). To the extent the latter dominates, people may minimize or rationalize the threat and fail to take effective action. This parallel-response model influenced the development of protection motivation theory (Rogers, 1975) and the health-belief model (Janz & Becker, 1984) in which perceived vulnerability and response efficacy are key elements of coping behavior. Consistent with the affect-as-information perspective (Schwarz & Clore, 1996), a growing body of evidence suggests that subjective estimates of risks are largely based on anticipatory feelings elicited by the threat—a proposition known as the "risk-as-feelings" hypothesis (Loewenstein, Weber, Hsee, & Welch, 2001).

Incidental Affect in Judgment and Decision Making

Although integral affect appears to play a major role in consumers' judgments and decisions, social and consumer psychologists have generally focused instead on incidental affect, especially mood states.

Congruency effects of mood and other forms of incidental affect

Numerous studies have shown that mood states and other forms of incidental affect generally have assimilative (i.e., affect-congruent) influences on evaluations, decisions, and behaviors. Objects are typically evaluated more favorably when the evaluator is in a good mood than when the evaluator is in a bad mood (for reviews, see Forgas, 1995; Gardner, 1985), and more generally when the objects are evaluated in the context of pleasant stimuli than when they are evaluated in the context of unpleasant stimuli. In fact, some of the earliest demonstrations of this phenomenon appeared in marketing. In a pioneering study, Axelrod (1963) observed that, after viewing a depressing television documentary, consumers evaluated a variety of products more negatively than they did before they saw the documentary. These shifts in evaluation were found to be directly related to changes in participants' moods. In another early study, Dommermuth and Millard (1967) found that consumers, who one week earlier had watched a pleasant movie after tasting a soft drink, evaluated the drink more favorably than consumers who had watched an unpleasant movie. Still, the most widely-cited demonstration of mood-congruency effects is the one published more than 10 years later by Isen, Shalker, Clark, and Karp (1978), who observed that people who were put in a good mood through a small gift were more willing to participate in a survey and evaluated products more favorably than control subjects who did not receive a gift. In a debated study, Gorn (1982) also observed that people who had seen a pen advertised while pleasant music was playing in the background were more likely to choose this pen than people who had seen the same pen advertised with unpleasant music playing in the background. Similar congruency effects of incidental affect have been observed on a variety of other evaluative and behavioral responses, including judgments of life satisfaction (e.g., Schwarz & Clore, 1983), evaluations of brand extensions (Barone, 2005; Barone, Miniard, & Romeo, 2000; Yeung & Wyer, 2005), evaluations of political candidates (Isbell & Wyer, 1999), judgments of perceived risks (Johnson & Tversky, 1983), and decisions about future consumption episodes (e.g., Gilbert, Gill, & Wilson, 2002; Pham, 1998).

Much of the early evidence about this phenomenon was reviewed 20 years ago by Gardner (1985). Two main types of developments have emerged since. Substantive-oriented investigations have focused on how various aspects of the marketplace can trigger incidental affect that influences evaluations in a congruent fashion. A number of studies have shown that incidental affect elicited by the media context of an ad (TV program or magazine) generally has a congruent influence on consumers' evaluations of the ad but less influence on their evaluations of the advertised brand (e.g., Gardner & Wilhelm, 1987; Goldberg & Gorn, 1987; Mathur & Chattopadhyay, 1991; Murry & Dacin, 1996; Yi, 1990; but see Kamins, Marks, & Skinner, 1991 for different findings). Gift wrapping can also enhance the recipient's evaluation of the gift by elevating the recipient's mood (Howard, 1992). Even the mere action of browsing a series of attractive options may elevate a consumer's mood and result in assimilative effects on subsequent evaluations (Raghunathan & Irwin, 2001). Incidental affect can "transfer" to the target object very rapidly. Morales and Fitzsimons (2007) recently found that a mere physical contact between a new, factory-sealed pack of sanitary napkins (a product many male consumers find disgusting) and another factory-sealed product is sufficient to decrease consumers' intention to try the latter product even though there is no chance of real contamination by the former. An important question is whether this type of spontaneous incidental affect transfer is limited to disgust—as Morales and Fitzsimons (2007) propose—or whether it applies to other types of incidental affect as well (e.g., pride, anger, joy).

More theoretically-oriented investigations have focused on clarifying the process (or processes) that underlie the phenomenon and identifying its boundary conditions. The best-known explanation for the congruency effects of incidental affective states attributes the phenomenon to a differential accessibility of valenced materials in memory under positive versus negative affective states (Isen, Shalker, Clark, & Karp, 1978). Consistent with other research on the effects and representation of mood states in memory (Bower, 1981), Isen and her colleagues (1978) proposed that positive moods enhance target evaluations by making positive thoughts about the target object more accessible in memory. Consistent with this explanation, they found that participants who were put in a good mood through false success feedback had better memory for pleasant words studied earlier than did participants who were put in a bad mood through false failure feedback. Interestingly, however, there was no difference between the two groups in their memory for unpleasant words, suggesting that the proposed explanation may not equally account for negative mood congruency effects.

Building on the idea that affect is often seen as having information value—an idea known as the "affect-as-information" hypothesis, Schwarz and Clore (1983) proposed a different explanation. They argued that positive and negative affective states have congruent effects on evaluations because, in the course of evaluating objects, people are often inclined to inspect how they feel about these objects—a process known as the "how-do-I-feel-about-it?" heuristic (Schwarz & Clore, 1988; see also Pham, 1998). When relying on this heuristic, people may not always realize that the feelings they experience while evaluating an object may have been affected by preexisting affective states, resulting in assimilation effects. Consistent with this interpretation, Schwarz and Clore (1983) found that respondents, who were in a good mood as a result of being interviewed on a sunny day, reported higher levels of life satisfaction than respondents who were in a bad mood as a result of being interviewed on a rainy day. Importantly, this mood congruency effect disappeared when respondents were made aware of the actual source of their affective state (i.e., the weather). This contingency—known as the *representativeness* principle (Pham, 1998; Strack, 1992)—supports the interpretation that incidental feelings influence evaluations only to the extent that they are perceived to provide information pertaining to the target. In a related study in a consumer context (Gorn, Goldberg, & Basu, 1993), respondents were asked to evaluate a pair of speakers through which music was being played. Incidental affect was manipulated by varying the music being played to be either pleasant or unpleasant. Awareness of the actual source of the feelings was manipulated by asking respondent to rate the music either before they evaluated the speakers (high awareness) or after they had evaluated the speakers (low awareness). As predicted, respondents in the low awareness condition evaluated the speakers more favorably when the music was pleasant than when it was unpleasant—a classic affect congruency effect. In contrast, respondents in the high awareness condition evaluated the speakers equally whether the music was pleasant or unpleasant—consistent with the idea that the congruency effect was driven by the perceived informativeness of the music-induced feelings.

According to the integrative "affect-infusion" model (Forgas, 1995), the two accounts—differential memory accessibility and mood-as-information—are not inconsistent; instead, they operate under different conditions. The differential memory accessibility account is more likely when the person engages in extensive substantive processing such as full and open search in memory, which presumes a certain level of involvement. The mood-as-information account is more likely when the person engages in heuristic processing, which is more common under conditions of low involvement. Consistent with this proposition, it has been found that positive moods have two separate effects in persuasion (Batra & Stayman, 1990; Petty, Schumann, Richman, & Strathman, 1993). Under conditions favoring low elaboration, positive moods have direct assimilative effects on attitudes—a finding consistent with a mood-as-information process. Under conditions favoring high elaboration, the assimilative effects of positive moods on attitudes appear to be mediated by the valence of target-related thoughts during message exposure—a finding consistent with a differential memory accessibility explanation.

Within the mood-as-information account, there is still uncertainty as to the exact locus of the process. In conventional interpretations of the process, feelings are assumed to enter judgments during the formal evaluation stage (Schwarz & Clore, 1988, 1996). However, recent findings suggest that the informative influence of incidental feelings may take place earlier in the process, during an initial appraisal of the object (Yeung & Wyer, 2004).

Moderators of congruency effects of incidental affective states

Factors that increase the reliance on integral feelings in evaluations generally also increase the influence of incidental affect on evaluations. Incidental moods are generally found to have stronger assimilative influences on evaluations when motivation to process information is low (e.g.,

Miniard, Bhatla, Lord, Dickson, & Unnava, 1991; Petty, Schumann, Richman, & Strathman, 1993) and when processing resources are constrained such as under distraction (e.g., Albarracin & Wyer, 2001) or under time pressure (Siemer & Reisenzein, 1998). However, recent studies suggest that higher levels of motivation and ability to process information do not necessarily result in a monotonic decrease of the influence of incidental mood on evaluations. The relationship may sometimes be curvilinear, with stronger influence of incidental mood under moderate levels of motivation and ability (Albarracin & Kumkale, 2003). This is because when motivation and ability to process information are very high, people are likely to recognize that their feelings are incidental and therefore irrelevant for the judgment at hand. Incidental feelings would therefore be discounted. However, when people's motivation and ability to process information is extremely low, they may fail to even notice their incidental feelings. Incidental feelings would therefore not have any influence. There is also consistent evidence that incidental affective states have stronger affect-congruent influences on evaluations when other bases of evaluation are ambiguous (e.g., Bakamitsos, 2006; Gorn, Pham, & Sin, 2001; e.g., Isen & Shalker, 1982; Miniard, Bhatla, & Sirdeshmukh, 1992), or when people lack expertise with the target domain (Ottati & Isbell, 1996; Srull, 1987).

The affect-as-information hypothesis implies two additional moderators. Consistent with the principle of representativeness mentioned earlier, incidental affective states tend to be more influential when their actual source is not salient (Gorn, Goldberg, & Basu, 1993; Raghunathan, Pham, & Corfman, 2006; Schwarz & Clore, 1983; Siemer & Reisenzein, 1998). This is because, when the actual source of the affective state is salient, people recognize that the affective state is unrelated to (i.e., not representative of) the target and therefore noninformative. Further evidence of a representativeness interpretation of this contingency comes from the finding that, *even when their actual source is salient*, incidental affective states may still influence objectively unrelated judgments and decisions provided that there is a superficial domain similarity between the judgment or decision and the salient origin of the affective state (Raghunathan, Pham, & Corfman, 2006). Inferences of representativeness, we know, are very sensitive to surface similarity (Gilovich, 1981).

Also consistent with the logic of affect-as-information is the findings that, even when people do not recognize that their feelings are truly incidental—that is, even when they assume that their feelings are representative—they do not seem to use them unless they perceive their feelings to be a relevant basis for a specific judgment or decision—a contingency known as the *relevance* principle (Pham, 1998). For example, people are more influenced by their mood when making decisions guided by experiential motives, such as assessing a movie for an evening out, than when making decisions guided by instrumental motives, e.g., assessing the same movie as material for a school project (Pham, 1998). As a result, they are typically more influenced by their moods in decisions involving hedonic products than in decisions involving utilitarian products (Adaval, 2001; Yeung & Wyer, 2004). Mood states have also been found to have greater influence on global judgments of well-being than on more specific judgments such as satisfaction with one's work or housing (Schwarz, Strack, Kommer, & Wagner, 1987). In addition, incidental affective states have been found to be more influential when people make decisions for themselves as opposed to for someone else (Raghunathan & Pham, 1999). Avnet and Pham (2007) recently suggested the idea and found evidence that the reliance on feelings in judgments and decisions may involve a meta-cognitive stage in which people assess whether they *should* use their feelings in a given judgment or decision, and found evidence consistent with this proposition. This meta-cognitive assessment appears to require significant cognitive resources; when resources are insufficient, incidental and integral feelings influence judgments and decisions more indiscriminately. The dual-process, meta-cognitive model proposed by Avnet and Pham (2007) appears to account for a wide variety of findings about the moderators of incidental and integral affect in judgments and decisions.

According to Forgas's (1995) affect-infusion model, incidental affective states have greater assimilative influences on evaluations when the person engages in constructive processing. Evaluations based on nonconstructive processes, such as the retrieval of prior attitudes, are less amenable to affect infusion. For example, Fedorikhin and Cole (2004) found that respondents exposed to a mood-inducing video *prior* to being exposed to a commercial were more influenced by their mood in their evaluation of the advertised product than were respondents exposed to the mood-inducing video *after* viewing the same commercial and forming an initial evaluation of the product. This is presumably because respondents in the mood-before condition had to form their product evaluations "from scratch," which required constructive processing, whereas respondents in the mood-after condition could simply retrieve their previously-formed initial evaluations. More generally, Srull (1987) showed, in a very compelling series of studies, that mood congruent evaluation effects generally require that the incidental mood be experienced at the same time the evaluation is constructed.

Beyond simple valence congruency

Recent findings suggest that incidental mood states do not always influence evaluations in a mood-congruent fashion (i.e., higher evaluations under positive moods than under negative moods). Sometimes, incidental mood states *interact* with the target object to produce evaluations that are *configural*—hence, judgment-specific—rather than strictly mood-congruent. Martin, Abend, Sedikides, and Green (1997) observed that, when asked to evaluate a story that was meant to be happy, participants in a happy mood reported more favorable evaluations than participants in a sad mood. However, when asked to evaluate a story that was meant to be sad, participants in a sad mood reported more favorable evaluations than participants in a happy mood. This finding suggests that people do not literally interpret the valence of their feelings as meaning "goodness" versus "badness." Instead, they interpret the valence of their feelings in light of salient goals and judgment criteria (Pham, 2004). If the criterion is "Is this a good happy story?", feelings of happiness will mean "Yes" and feelings of sadness will mean "No." On the other hand, if the criterion is "Is this a good sad story?", feelings of happiness will mean "No" and feelings of sadness will mean "Yes." Similar configural effects were obtained by Kamins, Marks, and Skinner (1991) who observed that a happy commercial was evaluated more favorably and elicited stronger purchase intentions when presented after a happy TV program than when presented after a sad TV program. In contrast, a sad commercial was evaluated more favorably when presented after a sad program than when presented after a happy program. Somewhat related to the idea of configurality, some findings suggest that mood states increase the weight attached to information that is evaluatively consistent with the mood in product evaluations (Adaval, 2001). According to Adaval (2001), when there is a match between the consumer's affective state and the valence of a piece of information, this information "feels right" and is therefore relied upon with greater confidence.

A growing body of research suggests that incidental affective states also influence target evaluations when the valence of the affective state is held constant. Two main types of findings have been uncovered in this regard. The first set of findings pertain to the effects of incidental emotional arousal. The second set of findings pertain to the differential influence of qualitatively distinct emotional states.

A large number of studies show that, holding valence constant, the arousal component of incidental affective states tends to polarize the evaluation of objects. Evaluations of target objects are usually more extreme under incidental states of high arousal than under incidental states of low arousal (Dutton & Aron, 1974; Foster, Witcher, Campbell, & Green, 1998; Gorn, Pham, & Sin, 2001;

Mattes & Cantor, 1982; White, Fishbein, & Rutsein, 1981; Zillmann, 1971). For example, individuals aroused by contextual factors such as a roller-coaster ride or crossing a high suspension bridge have been found to be more attracted to good-looking individuals of the opposite sex and less attracted to individuals of the same sex (Dienstbier, 1979; Dutton & Aron, 1974; White, Fishbein, & Rutsein, 1981). Similarly, Gorn, Pham, and Sin (2001) observed that consumers who had recently listened to an arousing piece of music (in a supposedly unrelated study) reported more polarized evaluations of an advertisement than consumers who had listened to a less arousing piece of music. Compared to consumers in the low arousal conditions, consumers in the high arousal condition reported more favorable ad evaluations when the ad's affective tone was positive and more unfavorable evaluations when the ad's affective tone was negative. Therefore, incidental states of arousal seem to amplify people's inherent affective and evaluative responses to a target.

Three main explanations have been offered for this phenomenon. According to the cognitive-complexity hypothesis (Paulhus & Lim, 1994), under high arousal, people's representations of target objects become simpler. As a result, the evaluative dimension becomes relatively more salient, causing more polarized judgments. This explanation is consistent with the finding that high arousal induces a selective reliance on information perceived to be more diagnostic in judgment (Pham, 1996). A second explanation is that states of high arousal encourage dominant responses in judgment and behavior (Zajonc, 1965). Because evaluative responses tend to be dominant, high arousal induces polarization (e.g., Allen, Kenrick, Linder, & McCall, 1989). A third explanation, consistent with the affect-as-information hypothesis, is that individuals misattribute their incidental arousal as indicating the strength of their integral affective response to the target, which again results in more polarized evaluations (Pham, 2004). Overall, it seems that all three explanations are viable and may be differentially operative in different situations. For instance, Gorn, Pham, and Sin (2001) suggest that the cognitive-complexity may be more valid under conditions of very strong arousal, whereas the misattribution explanation may be more applicable under conditions of milder arousal. This is because strong arousal states are known to narrow people's focus of attention (Easterbrook, 1959) but are unlikely to be misattributed, whereas milder arousal states may not narrow people's attention but are more likely to be misattributed.

More recent demonstrations of the importance of studying incidental affective states beyond their valence come from the growing body research on the differential effects of distinct emotional states (Lerner & Keltner, 2000, 2001; Lerner, Small, & Loewenstein, 2004; Raghunathan & Pham, 1999; Raghunathan, Pham, & Corfman, 2006; Tiedens & Linton, 2001). In one of the earliest demonstrations, Raghunathan and Pham (1999) found that, in choices between high-risk/high-reward and low-risk/low-reward options, sad individuals consistently favor the former, whereas anxious individuals consistently favor the latter. This is presumably because, even though their states are incidental, sad individuals tend to infer that they have lost something of value (a typical cause of sadness), which activates a goal of reward acquisition that shifts preferences toward high-reward options. In contrast, anxious individuals tend to infer that the situation is uncertain and beyond control (typical causes of anxiety), which activates a goal of risk avoidance that shifts preferences toward low-risk options. Similarly, Lerner, Small, and Loewenstein (2004) found that incidental states of sadness reverse the classic endowment effect, that is, the tendency to place a higher value on objects that are already in our possession compared to identical objects that not in our possession. In contrast, incidental states of disgust eliminate the endowment effect. According to the authors, this is because sadness creates a motivation to change the current situation, which increases the willingness to pay for objects that are not in our possession (higher purchase prices) and also increases the willingness to sell objects that currently are (lower selling prices). In contrast, disgust triggers an impulse to get rid of objects that are currently in our possession (lower selling prices) without necessarily distorting the value of objects that are not in our possession (unchanged purchase prices). Tiedens and Linton (2001) also observed that respondents made predictions with greater confidence when under states of disgust or happiness than when under states of fear or hopefulness. This is presumably because both disgust and happiness typically arise in situations appraised as certain (e.g., witnessing something repulsive or receiving very good news), whereas fear and hope typically arise in situations appraised as uncertain (e.g., going up for tenure). These findings are generally consistent with an affect-as-information process in which the information conveyed by affective states comes from the typical appraisal content of these affective states (Pham, 2004). Further evidence that these effects are driven by an affect-as-information process comes from the finding that they tend to disappear when the true source of the affective state is made salient (Raghunathan et al. 2006, Experiment 1), unless there is a surface domain resemblance between the source of the incidental affective state and the target decision (Raghunathan et al., 2006, Experiment 2).

Effects of incidental affect on judgment and decision processes

In addition to shaping the *content* of consumer's judgments and decisions, incidental affective states can also influence the *process* through which these judgments and decisions are made. The nature of these influences seems to depend on (a) the intensity of the affective state, (b) the valence of the affective state, and (c) the appraisal content of the emotional state.

Because high arousal is known to impair working memory capacity (S. Darke, 1988a; Humphreys & Revelle, 1984), it is generally believed and often observed that states of high emotional arousal interfere with people's ability to reason and make judgments and decisions. For example, compared to nonanxious participants, anxious participants have been observed to (a) take longer to verify logical inferences (S. Darke, 1988b), (b) scan alternatives in a more haphazard fashion and select options without considering every alternative (Keinan, 1987), (c) commit more errors in analogical problems (Keinan, 1987; Leon & Revelle, 1985), and (d) process persuasion arguments less thoroughly (Sanbonmatsu & Kardes, 1988; but see Pham, 1996 for a different interpretation) It should be noted, however, that most of these findings pertain to the effects of high anxiety. It is therefore not clear whether they generalize to other types of emotional arousal such as intense joy, anger, or pride. It should also be noted that states of intense emotional arousal can benefit judgment processes in at least one respect. Compared to states of lower arousal, states of high emotional arousal seem to increase the selective relative reliance on diagnostic information in persuasion and judgment in general (Pham, 1996). This explains the finding that incidental states of high anxiety do not decrease message elaboration when the message is related to the source of anxiety (Sengupta & Johar, 2001).

Interestingly, acute emotional states characterized by low arousal also appear to interfere with people's judgment abilities. A number of studies indicate that chronic depression interferes with people's reasoning and ability to engage in effortful processing in judgment (Conway & Giannopoulos, 1993; Hartlage, Alloy, Vazquez, & Dykman, 1993; Silberman, Weingartner, & Post, 1983). Overall, it appears that intense emotional states, regardless of their associated level of arousal, generally interfere with people's reasoning and judgment processes. One exception, however, relates to the ability to prioritize diagnostic versus nondiagnostic information, which seems to increase under states of high emotional arousal (Pham, 1996).

Milder incidental affective states, such as moods, can also influence people's judgmental processes. Compared to individuals in a neutral mood, individuals in a good mood have been found to (a) categorize objects more broadly (Isen & Daubman, 1984; Isen, Niedenthal, & Cantor, 1992), (b) generate more creative answers in response-generation tasks (Greene & Noice, 1988; Hirt, Melton, McDonald, & Harackiewicz, 1996), (c) perform better in problem-solving tasks that require ingenuity (Greene & Noice, 1988; Isen, Daubman, & Nowicki, 1987), and (d) solve a multi-attribute decision problem more efficiently (Isen & Means, 1983). These and other findings have been interpreted as showing that positive moods have generally beneficial effects on reasoning, problem solving, judgment, and decision making (Isen, 2001).

However, a number of studies suggest that positive moods lead to poorer reasoning performance in a variety of respects. Positive mood individuals are more likely to commit the "fundamental attribution error" of overestimating the degree to which others' behaviors are driven by their personal disposition as opposed to by situational factors (Forgas, 1998). Positive mood participants have also been found to perform more poorly in deductive reasoning tasks (Oaksford, Morris, Grainger, & Williams, 1996) and exhibit more intransitive preferences (Fiedler, 1988). Numerous studies also indicate that positive moods generally decrease the depth with which people process substantive information in persuasion and attitude formation (Batra & Stayman, 1990; Bless, Bohner, Schwarz, & Strack, 1990; Bless, Mackie, & Schwarz, 1992; Mackie & Worth, 1989; Worth & Mackie, 1987). Positive mood individuals seem to rely instead on global knowledge structures and internal cues including scripts (Bless, Schwarz, Clore, Golisano, & Rabe, 1996), stereotypes (Bodenhausen, Kramer, & Suesser, 1994), and judgmental heuristics such as the ease of retrieval (Ruder & Bless, 2003). Overall, positive moods seem to have mixed effects on people's reasoning and judgment processes. On the one hand, they seem to promote greater flexibility and creativity in problem solving; on the other hand, they seem to promote a more top-down, less data-driven, and less thorough mode of processing. Recent studies by Adaval (2003) suggest that one consequence of this more top-down form of processing is that positive moods polarize the evaluative impact of judgment inputs involving preexisting knowledge structures (e.g., schemata, stereotypes, categories, brands, etc.). Adaval's (2003) studies show that, under positive mood, brand names (and their associated knowledge structures) have greater influence on product evaluations than under negative mood. Specifically, products from popular brands are evaluated more favorably under positive mood than under negative mood, whereas products from unpopular brands are evaluated less favorably under positive mood than under negative mood.

Negative moods, especially those of sad nature, have generally been found to have effects that mirror those described above. Compared to neutral and pleasant moods, sad moods have been found to increase the care with which people process substantive information in persuasion (Bless, Bohner, Schwarz, & Strack, 1990; Sinclair, Mark, & Clore, 1994), decrease the reliance on general knowledge structures such as scripts and stereotypes (Bless, Schwarz, Clore, Golisano, & Rabe, 1996; Bodenhausen, Kramer, & Suesser, 1994), increase the ability to estimate covariation from scatter plot data (Sinclair & Mark, 1995), reduce the susceptibility to halo effects (Sinclair, 1988), reduce fundamental attribution errors (Forgas, 1998), and increase the transitivity of preferences (Fiedler, 1988). Overall, temporary sad moods seem to trigger a more systematic, data-driven, and analytical form of reasoning. One possible explanation, also based on the affect-as-information hypothesis, is that sad moods signal to the individual that the situation is problematic and therefore requires a more vigilant form of processing, whereas good moods signal that the situation is benign and allows a more nonchalant form of processing (Schwarz, 2002).

It should be noted, however, that not all negative moods trigger a vigilant form of processing. States of anger or disgust seem to *decrease* the depth of processing and increase the reliance on stereotyping and other heuristic cues, apparently because these states trigger a sense of certainty (Bodenhausen, Sheppard, & Kramer, 1994; Tiedens & Linton, 2001).

It should also be noted that negative moods do not always increase task effort and positive moods always decrease it. Martin, Ward, Achee, and Wyer (1993) asked respondents in a positive or negative mood to perform various tasks under one of two sets of instructions. One group was asked to keep working until they were satisfied with their performance. The other group was asked to keep working until they no longer enjoyed the task. When instructed to keep working until they were satisfied with their performance, respondents in a negative mood worked longer than those in a positive mood (a result consistent with the typical finding that negative mood leads to more careful processing compared to positive mood). However, when instructed to keep working until they no longer enjoyed the task, the effect reversed: respondents in a negative mood stopped *sooner* than those in a positive mood. Apparently, when the instruction was to keep working until satisfied with the performance, a negative mood was construed as dissatisfaction with one's effort, producing greater perseverance, whereas a positive mood was construed as satisfaction with one's effort, triggering an early stop. In contrast, when the instruction was to keep working until the task was no longer enjoyed, a negative mood was construed as the task being not fun, producing an early stop, whereas a positive mood was construed as the task being fun, producing perseverance. This interpretation, known as the "mood-as-input" hypothesis (Martin, Ward, Achee, & Wyer, 1993), illustrates a broader principle about the informative role of feelings in judgments. The same feelings can have very different interpretations depending on the question that people are asking themselves (Pham, 2004). The information value of the feelings lies not so much in the feelings themselves as in the interaction between these feelings and the questions that people are trying to answer when consulting their feelings, which depends on situational demands and more generally on the person's currently active goals.

Effects of mood states on risk-taking

A number of studies indicate that, compared to neutral moods, positive moods promote risk-taking when the stakes and chances of loss are low but risk-avoidance when the stakes and chances of loss are high (Arkes, Herren, & Isen, 1988; Dunegan, Duchon, & Barton, 1992; Isen & Geva, 1987; Isen, Nygren, & Ashby, 1988; Kahn & Isen, 1993; Nygren, Isen, Taylor, & Dulin, 1996). For example, Arkes, Herren, and Isen (1988) observed that, compared to control participants, participants who received a small gift were willing to pay more for lottery tickets, especially when the prize level and probability of winning were high—indicating greater risk-seeking under positive mood in situations with only upsides. However, participants who received a small gift were also more willing to pay more to insure against a variety of losses, especially when potential losses were high—indicating greater risk-aversion under positive mood in situations characterized by downsides. Kahn and Isen (1993) observed a similar pattern in the effects of positive mood on variety-seeking. They found that, compared to control participants, participants who were in a good mood sampled a greater variety of products such as crackers, soups, and chips, unless the choice set included items expected to taste poorly. Again, positive mood appeared to promote risk-seeking in benign settings and risk-avoidance in settings involving potential risk. According to Isen and her colleagues, when the decisions entail low risks and stakes, positive mood individuals tend to have more optimistic (mood-congruent) expectations about the outcomes and, therefore, take greater risks compared to neutral mood individuals. However, when the stakes are high and the potential for losses significant, positive mood individuals become risk-averse because they want to maintain their positive affective state, which a loss would disrupt (e.g., Isen, Nygren, & Ashby, 1988; Kahn & Isen, 1993) as will be discussed further in the section on affect regulation.

The effects of negative affective states on risk-risking are not as clear. Several studies indicate that negative emotional states accompanied by strong arousal increase risk-seeking (Fessler, Pillsworth, & Flamson, 2004; Leith & Baumeister, 1996; Mano, 1992, 1994). For example, Leith and Baumeister (1996) found that angry participants and participants anticipating impending embarrassment were more likely to choose an economically inferior "long-shot" gamble with a low probability of obtaining a larger amount of money and a high complementary probability of enduring some stressful noise, over a superior "safe-bet" gamble with a higher probability of obtaining a smaller amount of money with a low probability of enduring the stressful noise. Sad participants, however, did not exhibit this bias. Fessler, Pillsworth, and Flamson (2004) also found that anger triggered more risk-seeking in gambling, especially among men. Similarly, Mano (1994) found that intense emotional arousal increased people's willingness to pay for lotteries and decreased their willingness to pay for insurance; that is, increased risk-taking for both potential gains and potential losses.

However, other findings indicate that people's attitude toward risk under negative affective states is not just a function of the level of arousal associated with the affective state, but also a function of the appraisal content of the affective state (Lerner & Keltner, 2001; Raghunathan & Pham, 1999). For example, as mentioned previously, in choices between low-risk/low-reward and high-risk/high-reward options, anxious individuals tend to prefer the former, whereas sad individuals tend to prefer the latter (Raghunathan & Pham, 1999; Raghunathan, Pham, & Corfman, 2006). The consistent risk-aversion exhibited by anxious individuals in these studies seems inconsistent with Leith and Baumeister's (1996) proposition that high-arousal emotion lead to risk-seeking. In fact, other studies show that, when the level of arousal is held constant, anxiety *reduces* risk-seeking (Mano, 1992, 1994). According to Raghunathan and Pham (1999), this is because anxiety, which is typically associated with situations of low control and high uncertainty, activates a goal of risk and uncertainty minimization, whereas sadness, which is typically experienced in response to the loss of a source of reward, activates a goal of reward maximization. Similarly, Lerner and Keltner (2001) observed that, even though fear and anger are both high-arousal negative emotions, fear tends to trigger risk-aversion, whereas anger tends to trigger risk-seeking. This is apparently because fear is typically associated with situations of uncertainty and low control, whereas anger is typically associated with situations of certainty and high control. It has also been found that disgust, another high arousal emotion, decreases risk-seeking in gambling among women (Fessler, Pillsworth, & Flamson, 2004).

In summary, it appears that intense negative emotions do not have a uniformly positive effect on risk-seeking. High emotional arousal seems neither necessary, nor sufficient to explain risk-seeking under negative emotions. The effects of negative emotions on risk-seeking appear to depend not only on the level of arousal associated with the emotional state, but also on complex interactions between the goals activated by the emotional state and the nature of the risks to be taken. This may partly explain why a meta-analysis of published studies relating chronic states of anger, sadness, and anxiety to risky sexual behavior (Crepaz & Marks, 2001) found virtually no correlation (r = .05).[5]

Task-Related Affect in Judgment and Decision Making

The *process* of making judgments or decisions may *itself* induce feelings and emotions. We call this type of affect *task-related affect*. A common task-related affect is the unpleasant feelings that consumers often experience when they have to trade off important attributes whose values are negatively correlated across choice options. Consider a choice between prospective apartments. Apartment A is much roomier, but is located in a bad neighborhood; whereas Apartment B is much smaller, but located in a great neighborhood. It has been found that the aversive emotional experience of having to make trade-offs across important attributes often leads consumers to prefer avoidant options such as choosing the status quo or deferring the choice (Luce, 1998). This avoidant behavior seems to be a deliberate attempt by the consumer to mitigate the unpleasant feelings by eschewing the trade-offs altogether. This avoidant behavior is attenuated under situations of cognitive load, which reduces the aversiveness of the trade-offs by making them less apparent (Drolet & Luce, 2004). Another way in which consumers attempt to deal with the emotional aversiveness of difficult decisions is to resort to simpler, heuristic decision strategies such as processing attribute-by-attribute (as opposed to alternative-by-alternative) and invoking dominance relations (Luce, 1998; Luce, Bettman, & Payne, 1997). It has also been found that, when trade-offs are emotional, consumers tend to place greater weight on the relative quality of the options, such as the relative safety of two cars, rather than on their relative resource requirements, e.g., the relative price of the cars (Luce, Payne, & Bettman, 1999).

Task-related affect, in the form of stress, can also be induced by giving decision makers some time pressure and the impression of being monitored during the decision (Stone & Kadous, 1997). Unlike the manipulations based on trade-off difficulty mentioned above, this method presents the advantage of holding information about the options constant. Stone and Kadous (1997) found that, under task-related stress, decision makers tend to use a "scanning" strategy of quickly but indiscriminately examining available information, which may increase choice accuracy in easy choice environments but decrease choice accuracy in difficult choice environments.

Another common type of task-related affect in decision making is the unpleasant feeling of having to forego attractive options. In a choice among a Mercedes-Benz S550, a BWM 750i, and an Audi A8, for example, choosing the Mercedes-Benz also means forfeiting the BMW and the Audi—a classic approach, approach conflict that may be emotionally stressful. Dhar and Wertenbroch (2000) found that the emotional discomfort of forgoing an option is greater when the option is primarily hedonic, such as a fun sports car, than when the option is primarily utilitarian, such as a functional minivan. It has also been found that the more consumers deliberate about their choices, the more they become emotionally attached to the options, which leads to decision-related discomfort (or cognitive dissonance) once one option has been chosen (Carmon, Wertenbroch, & Zeelenberg, 2003).

A particularly important outcome of task-related affect is the transfer of that affect onto the valuation of the chosen alternative. Just like incidental affective states, task-related affective responses may be misconstrued as reflecting genuine integral affective responses to one of the options—a phenomenon again broadly consistent with the affect-as-information framework (Schwarz, 1990; see also Pham [2004] for a review). For example, Garbarino and Edell (1997) found that reducing the effort involved in selecting an alternative (i.e., making a task less unpleasant) can increase the price respondents are willing to pay for that alternative. The transfer of task-related affect onto the valuation of alternatives underlies a growing body of research on the "value-from-fit" hypothesis (Higgins, 2000). According to this hypothesis, a fit between the manner in which a decision is made and the current orientation of the decision maker can produce pleasant task-related feelings of "being right," which can then be (mis)attributed to a chosen object, enhancing its perceived value (e.g., Avnet & Higgins, 2003, 2006; Higgins, Idson, Freitas, Spiegel, & Molden, 2003). This finding also illustrates the close connection between affect and motivation, discussed next.

AFFECT AND MOTIVATION

The study of affect and the study of motivation have traditionally been interrelated (Young, 1961). Motivation and emotion share the same Latin root, *movere*, which means "to move." Affective states are said to stimulate action tendencies (Elster, 1999; Lazarus, 1991), action readiness (Frijda,

1986; Lang, 1995), and goal shifts (Oatley, 1992; Simon, 1967). Some researchers argue that affective states function as part of a superordinate program that directs motivational priorities and goal choice (Cosmides & Tooby, 2000) and motivates individuals to pursue specific goals. The interaction between motivation and affect is bidirectional: (1) affective states activate goals; and (2) goal pursuit (achievement, blockage, progress rate, etc.) triggers specific affective reactions (Carver, Lawrence, & Scheier, 1996). Although both directions of influence are of substantial theoretical interest, in this chapter we focus on the affect-to-motivation direction because the motivational consequences of affect have been studied more extensively.

In general, affective motivation relies on affect's informational role. As previously described, Schwarz and Clore's (1983) seminal work represents the cornerstone of the informational tradition associated with experienced affective states. When asked to assess their life satisfaction, many respondents in this study misattributed their weather-induced feelings to the unrelated judgment at hand. Usually overlooked in the literature is the fact that the study also asked individuals to assess their "desire to change." When asked this question on a rainy (versus sunny) day, individuals reported a stronger desire—hence, a stronger motivation—to change. Schwarz and Clore's (1983) findings thus demonstrate not only the informational role of affect, but also its *motivational* consequences.

Strength of the Signal, Approach, and Avoidance

When affect deviates from a homeostatic range, this signals that something has altered the actual or anticipated state of the environment, thus increasing the likelihood of unanticipated negative or positive consequences, such as those related to threats or safety. The strength of this signal is a direct function of how much affect deviates from its normal homeostatic range. However, the relation is not symmetric. Cacioppo, Gardner, and Berntson (1999) suggest that when the affective signal is at zero (in terms of motivational input), there is a weakly positive approach tendency (in terms of motivational output)—a phenomenon, the authors call the "positivity offset." In other words, at very low levels of affective activation, the motivation to approach is stronger than the motivation to avoid. Cacioppo, Gardner, and Berntson (1999) further suggest that the evolutionary function of the positivity offset is to increase the organism's tendency to approach novel objects and stimuli in neutral environments. In the absence of such a motivation to explore, organisms would learn little about novel or neutral-appearing environments and their potential reward value.

However, there is also a well documented negativity bias in human behavior (Baumeister, Bratslavsky, Finkenauer, & Vohs, 2001), which cannot be fully explained by the greater diagnosticity (e.g., reduced frequency and greater information value) of negative information (Skowronski & Carlston, 1989). Ito, Cacioppo, and Lang (1998) analyzed affective responses to hundreds of slides from the International Affective Picture System (Lang, Bradley, & Cuthbert, 1997). In one analysis, subjective ratings of positivity of the mostly pleasant slides, and subjective ratings of negativity of the mostly unpleasant slides, were modeled as a function of the level of arousal elicited by each slide. Not surprisingly, both relationships were positive: pleasant slides were rated more positively as they arousal levels increased; and unpleasant slides were rated more negatively as they arousal levels increased. More importantly, ratings of positivity had a *higher intercept* than ratings of negativity. When arousal was very low, pleasant slides were rated more positively than unpleasant slides were rated negatively—a finding consistent with a positivity offset. On the other hand, the slope of the negativity ratings was steeper than that of the positivity ratings—a finding consistent with the negativity bias. Therefore, at low levels of activation, positive stimuli have a greater impact on affective responses (and presumably behavior) than negative stimuli do. However, at higher levels of activation, negative stimuli have greater impact than positive stimuli do. (See Crites, Fabrigar, & Petty, 1994; Taylor, 1991; Wojciszke, Brycz, & Borkenau, 1993 for supportive findings.) A recent study by Dijksterhuis and Aarts (2003) provides additional support for these propositions. Respondents were exposed subliminally to both positive and negative words and asked to guess whether the words were positive or negative. Performance was better than chance for negative words, but not for positive words. This finding suggests a lower threshold for unconscious negative affect to become accessible. According to Cacioppo, Gardner, and Bernsten (1999), the positivity offset fosters useful exploratory behavior. However, because exploration can also have aversive consequences, and it is more difficult to reverse adverse consequences, natural selection may have favored a capacity to respond more strongly to, and withdraw from, proximate negative stimuli. This duality of function may have contributed to distinguishable approach and avoidance mechanisms mobilizing the individual toward immediate action.

A similar analysis by Lang and his colleagues (Lang, Bradley, & Cuthbert, 1990, 1992) supports the distinction between an aversive/defensive/withdrawal system and an appetitive/approach system, each with distinct patterns of neural activity. The greater the appetitive input, the stronger the activation of positivity and approach forces; the greater the aversive input, the stronger the activation of negativity and avoidance forces. Cacioppo & Berntson's (1994) evaluative space formulation allows for a co-activation of both systems, resulting in either directional action (approach or avoidance), indifference (low activation of both positivity and negativity), or ambivalence (high activation of both positivity and negativity).

However, physical behavior is facilitated by integrating the output of these dual processes and resolving any co-activation of opposing forces to express the dominant tendency and inhibit the weaker tendency. This is evident in postural support reactions, balance, and dynamic motor adjustments and implies a neurological substrate for central bivariate control (i.e., coactivity) of flexors and extensors despite the fact that outcomes are physically constrained into bipolar molar responses. Co-activation is also consistent with findings indicating that central mechanisms for reward and aversion can be independently manipulated, since this implies a fundamental dissociability of related brain systems. Furhter research should examine whether this separability can help explain why initiatives designed to produce positive affective responses do not necessarily overcome negative biases and so-called "implicit attitudes" (see Sarason et al., 1993; Schofield, 1991). One important implication of co-activation is that an increase in the intensity of either positive or negative valence can transform inaction into action, perhaps leading a person to take risks that had restrained behavior, as when fear of unsafe sex or cigarette addiction are overcome by either added momentary attractiveness or the perception of reduced likelihood or severity of consequences (Bolton, Cohen, & Bloom, 2006).

Broadly speaking, then, affective signals direct attention to both environmental and personal factors (particular current actions) that seem likely to alter consequences. This also fosters, or mitigates, energy and resource expenditure for both mental and behavioral activity. This "effort to perform" response is one of the accounts used to explain why people may devote more time or higher levels of thought in scrutinizing the information available (versus relying on heuristics) when experiencing a negative (versus positive) affective state (Schwarz, 2002).

While goal achievement and harm avoidance are particularly responsive to affective signals, hedonism (the emphasis on feeling good) can be a default goal. For example, psychological theories have traditionally stressed the dynamic tension between task success and accuracy motivations, on the one hand, and ego-bolstering and feeling good on the other (e.g., Lazarus & Folkman, 1984). Of particular interest in research on affect is the notion that a currently negative affective state can motivate individuals to pursue a short-term hedonistic objective, whereas a positive affective state can motivate individuals to protect the current given state. People are not necessarily spending more effort in order to perform well, but are selectively choosing the stimuli that will regulate their current affective states.

Affect Regulation

In the last two decades, affect regulation has received special attention in the literature (Forgas, Johnson, & Ciarrochi, 1998; Gross, 1998; Larsen, 2000; Zillmann, 1988a, 1988b). For our purposes, affect regulation corresponds to people's spontaneous (conscious or unconscious) attempt to intensify, attenuate, or maintain a given affective state, usually in the short-term. It incorporates related constructs, such as mood regulation (Erber & Erber, 2001; Larsen, 2000), negative state relief (Cialdini, Darby, & Vincent, 1973), mood management (Forgas, Johnson, & Ciarrochi, 1998; Wegener & Petty, 1994; Zillmann, 1988b), mood maintenance (Clark & Isen, 1982; Isen, 1984), emotion regulation (Gross, 1998), and coping (Lazarus, 1991). Although biological drives such as hunger and thirst (Buck, 1999) could also be incorporated within the affect regulation umbrella (Gross, 1998), they are beyond our scope of analysis.

As a basic psychological mechanism, Andrade (2005) proposes that affect regulation rests on three principles: dynamic affect, conditional hedonism, and affective signaling (see also Cohen & Andrade, 2004). *Dynamic affect* represents individuals' projected discrepancy between feelings at two points in time, that is, what they feel now and what they could feel in the future as a result of the cognitive or behavioral activity. This gap captures the motivational property of affect in guiding information processing, judgment, and decision making. Coupled with a basic hedonistic assumption, when no contingencies are available in the environment, affect regulation predicts that people in negative affective states will be the most likely to engage in cognitive or behavioral activities in anticipation of the mood-lifting consequences of such enterprises, whereas people in a positive mood will be the most likely to avoid thoughts and actions in anticipation of the mood-threatening consequences associated with them. In short, as a result of a dynamic analysis, people are likely to move toward the goal of a more positive affective state when they feel bad, as well as to protect a current affective state when they feel good. At the core of the dynamic affect principle is the idea that people's intuitive theories about the affective changing properties of the forward-looking cognitions or behaviors are critical determinants of the impact of affect regulation. For affect regulation to guide responses, people must intuitively believe that the forthcoming thoughts and/or actions will regulate a current state upward or downward (e.g., Manucia, Baumann, & Cialdini, 1984; Tice, Bratslavsky, & Baumeister, 2001).

Although individuals are predisposed to improve a negative affective state and/or protect a current positive affective state, there are circumstances in which internal or environmental contingencies convince them to follow a different route (e.g., Erber, Wegner, & Therriault, 1996). *Conditional hedonism*, therefore, implies that both upward and downward affect regulation, and negative and positive mood maintenance, represent potential affect regulation strategies, depending on competing goals available in the environment. If a performance goal overcomes a short-term hedonistic goal, the former may be preferred (e.g., Cohen & Andrade, 2004).

Finally, stronger, more accessible affective signals lead to clearer assessment of the discrepancy between current and expected affective states and the appropriateness of the actual state. As polarized affective states produce stronger signals compared to more neutral feelings, affect regulation should lead to stronger impacts when people experience positive or negative affect versus neutrality (e.g., Cohen & Andrade, 2004; Wegener & Petty, 1994). If one's current affective state is not salient, a discrepancy is less likely to be identified, minimizing the impact of affect regulation on thoughts and behavior. Not only accessibility, but also diagnosticity should play a role. Consistent with the affect-as-information hypothesis (Schwarz & Clore, 1983; Pham, 1998, 2004), calling for the diagnosticity of the current affective state into question can undo efforts to regulate affect. For example, if sad consumers suddenly realize that they are buying comfort food in a supermarket in an attempt to regulate theirr current negative feelings, having them properly attribute their feelings may mitigate their affect-regulation-driven impulse-buying motives, unless the comfort food seems somewhat related to the cause of sadness (Raghunathan, Pham, & Corfman, 2006). However, at least two other aspects must be considered. First, a normative assessment of the affect-behavior relationship is required. One must believe that the ongoing/forthcoming cognitive or behavioral activity that results from the transient feeling state is *inappropriate* (e.g., "I shouldn't be buying that much just because I feel sad today"). This may not be always the case. For instance, many consumers report going shopping in a *deliberate* attempt at affect regulation (Babin, Darden, & Griffin, 1994; Mick & Demoss, 1990). Trying to regulate current negative feelings through a shopping experience may sometimes be perceived as an appropriate and effective reaction. In that case, to highlight negative affect as a potential cause for the behavior may intensify rather than mitigate the impact of affect regulation on behavior. Second, the consumer must have the *skills* to stop the ongoing action or avoid the forthcoming action. Behavioral reactions driven by current affective states are sometimes much more difficult to control than one would expect, even when the person consciously knows that his/her behavior is inappropriate (e.g., "I shouldn't be doing this, but I can't control myself"; Loewenstein, 1996). How perceived appropriateness and skills moderate affect regulation motives is an important issue that remains to be examined in this literature.

Affect Regulation Effects on Information Processing

Affective states have been shown to produce changes in attention, recall, and processing style via affect regulation. Most research has so far been conducted in the psychology literature (for a review, see Gross, 1998), although consumer researchers have demonstrated growing interest in the topic (e.g., Keller, Lipkus, & Rimer, 2003; Meloy, 2000).

Attention

Standard information processing theory assumes limited cognitive resources and therefore selective processing. Thus, at the perceptual level, decisions have to be made as to what pieces of information one attends to. Incidental (dispositional or situational) and integral affect have both been shown to influence such perceptual decision processes via affect regulation (Krohne, 2003). First, one can simply avoid the threatening stimulus when there is no reason to pay attention to it. For instance, MacLeod and Mathews (1988) observed that states of high anxiety (as assessed 1 week before a exam) shifted attention toward exam-relevant threat words, suggesting vigilance, whereas, states of low anxiety (as assessed 12 weeks before the exam) shifted attention away from exam-relevant threat words, suggesting avoidance. Second, recent evidence suggests that negative stimuli not only capture but also hold people's attention (Fox, Russo, Bowles, & Dutton, 2001; Putman, Hermans, & van Honk, 2004). Thus, those who display stronger upward affect regulation tendencies should demonstrate faster disengagement skills. Mather and Carstensen (2003) adopted such a rationale to provide further evidence that upward affect regulation skills improve with age. After being presented with pairs of negative and neutral faces, older adults responded faster to a subsequent dot probe that appeared on the opposite side of the negative (versus neutral) face. This attentional bias did not emerge among younger adults. Finally, it has been suggested that affect regulation directs people's attention not only away from negativity, but also toward relieving cues (Derryberry & Tucker, 1994).

Memory

Feelings not only influence what individuals encode but also how much they store and retrieve (Blaney, 1986). Initial evidence supported mood congruent recall. However, as data accumulated, the phenomenon has been shown to be more robust on the positive side of the affective spectrum— i.e., people in a positive mood were more likely to recall positive events than those in a negative mood were to recall negative events (Bower & Forgas, 2000). Isen (1984) suggested that affect regulation could explain this asymmetry. Negative feelings can sometimes encourage the recall of positive information because people are naturally motivated to feel better. Considerable evidence supports Isen's initial proposition (Erber & Erber, 1994; McFarland & Buehler, 1997,1998; Parrott & Sabini, 1990; Rusting & DeHart, 2000; Sedikides, 1994; Smith & Petty, 1995). However, boundary conditions do exist. The impact of upward affect regulation is weaker among chronically sad individuals. Josephson and colleagues (1996) found that whereas a negative affect manipulation increased mood-incongruent recall among nondysphoric individuals, the effect dissipated among chronically dysphoric participants. Moreover, further evidence showed that when explicitly asked to recall more positive autobiographical memories, nondysphoric and dysphoric participants were equally capable of accomplishing the task. However, only nondysphoric participants felt better afterwards (Joormann & Siemer, 2004). These results suggest that recall of positive memories is reduced among dysphoric individuals, not because of cognitive inability but probably because such memories are not be perceived as an affect regulation opportunity within this group. Consistent with the *dynamic affect* assumption described above, if the cognitive or behavioral activity is not perceived as mood-lifting, or mood-threatening, affect regulation will be less likely to influence information processing.

Whereas the impact of mood incongruent recall has been more consistently explored within the negative affect realm, there has been some evidence suggesting that positive affect can also trigger affect regulation and biased recall. Parrott and Sabini (1990) showed in natural (Studies 1 and 2) and laboratory (Studies 3 and 4) settings that not only did subjects in a negative mood recall more positive events, but that subjects in a positive mood were also more likely to recall negative events. The authors do not make strong claims as to the reason for mood incongruent recall but speculate that people may be engaging in spontaneous, and probably unconscious, downward mood regulation. According to the *conditional hedonism* assumption described above, positive mood attenuation is possible. However, this usually happens when competing goals—including the need for accuracy and objectivity—are made available. In this case, individuals have a reason to give up their short-term happiness in exchange for better task performance and subsequent pleasantness (e.g., Cohen & Andrade, 2004; Erber, Wegner, & Therriault, 1996).

Affect regulation motivates people to protect positive affect sometimes at the expense of performance. However, when the task at hand produces harmful effects in the long run, performance becomes a major concern (a stronger competing goal) and positive affect can serve as a psychological buffer to help individuals cope with the negativity in the environment. That is the rationale behind Trope and colleagues' mood-as-resource hypothesis and findings (Raghunathan & Trope, 2002; Trope & Neter, 1994; Trope & Pomerantz, 1998). They showed that when information is highly self-relevant, those in a positive, hence bolstered, mood were more likely to select and/or recall negative information. For example, heavy consumers of caffeine in a positive (versus negative) mood recalled more pieces of negative information, as compared to positive information, about caffeine consumption. However, a positive mood did not enhance the recall of the negative information for light consumers of caffeine. Although it is not clear whether this effect is mediated solely by motivation (i.e., goal shift from happiness in the short-term to happiness in the long-term) or also by skill (i.e., higher cognitive capacity to deal with information), the mood-as-a-resource hypothesis can, under certain circumstances, account for mood incongruent recall by people experiencing positive affect.

Processing style

Some authors have suggested that the motivational influence of affect may not only represent a stronger or weaker desire to process the information per se, but also corresponds to a deliberate attempt at affect regulation (Ambady & Gray, 2002; Forgas, 1998). People experiencing negative affect may be pursuing more systematic and effortful processing in an attempt to improve their negative affective state (Clark & Isen, 1982; Forgas, 1991a, 1991b; Sedikides, 1994), whereas those in a good mood may spend less effort in an attempt to protect their current affective state (Clark & Isen, 1982; Isen, 1984). According to the main implication of the *dynamic affect* principle, the impact of affect regulation on the quantity and quality of information processing is highly contingent on the expected affective changes associated with the task (i.e., its mood-lifting or mood-threatening characteristics). For instance, if people's unbiased assessment of the attitude object when in a bad mood represents an effective mood-lifting opportunity (e.g., "I will feel happier if I do not rely on stereotypes"), sad people should be less likely to rely on such heuristics. Similarly, if the effort spent processing the information represents a mood-threatening experience (e.g., "If I think too much about it, I will feel bad"), happy people should be more likely to rely on heuristics. Although plausible, one of the major challenges in this line of research is to isolate the impact of the affect regulation motive from other mediating processes, such as affect-as-information and the role of confidence. For instance, when a sad person processes a message more carefully than a happy person, is it due to (1) a basic inner signal ("Threatening environment, be careful!"), (2) a lower level of confidence about his/her level of accuracy ("I'm not yet ready to make up my mind."), and/or (3) an affect regulation strategy ("If I accomplish this task accurately, I will feel much better!")? Moreover, these accounts may overlap, which makes claims about affect regulation effects on information processing even more challenging. For affect regulation to operate and bias thought and behavior, individuals must perceive the usually short-term, mood-lifting or mood-threatening cues associated with the upcoming activity. In the information processing world, people have to recognize that the *effort or performance consequences* will regulate their affective state upwards when they feel bad; whereas it will attenuate their affective state when they feel good. Further research is needed to tackle this issue.

Affect Regulation in Judgment and Decision Making

The impact of affect regulation on decision making has drawn increasing attention. Consumers often take the affective consequences of decisions (buy vs. not buy; shop vs. not shop; buy product A vs. B) into account. In the past 25 years, the results converge with the affect regulation principles described above.

Negative affect and affect regulation

An overview of different research streams shows that people experiencing negative affect are more willing to make behavioral choices that will lead to more positive feelings. Thus, they will engage in a wide variety of behaviors in an attempt to change the current feelings. Documented regulation behaviors include watching comedies (Weaver & Laird, 1995; Zillmann, 1988a, 1988b), listening to uplifting music (Cohen & Andrade, 2004; Knobloch & Zillmann, 2002), eating (Grunberg & Straub, 1992; Tice, Bratslavsky, & Baumeister, 2001), exercising (Hsiao & Thayer, 1998), acting in an aggressive way toward others (Bushman, Baumeister, & Phillips, 2001), reading uplifting news (R. Erber, Wegner, & Therriault, 1996), purchasing gifts for themselves (Luomala & Laaksonen, 1997; Mick & Demoss, 1990), helping others (Bagozzi & Moore, 1994; Cialdini, Darby, & Vincent, 1973), taking greater risks for greater rewards (Raghunathan & Pham, 1999), buying impulsively (Rook & Gardner, 1993), selling unwanted items (Lerner, Small, & Loewenstein, 2004), choosing the status-quo option (Luce, 1998), or simply procrastinating (Tice, Bratslavsky, & Baumeister, 2001).

Under the affect regulation umbrella, these examples all represent mood-lifting alternatives pursued in an attempt to restore or achieve the desired affective state (i.e., to close the gap between current and ideal affect). At the core of the dynamic affect principle is the implication that affect regulation is contingent on one's intuitive theories about the affective changing properties of the forward-looking cognitions and behavior. Thus, for affect regulation to fully operate, sad people must expect the behavioral activity to improve their current affective state. If that expectation is not present, the effect disappears. Several experiments have intrinsically or extrinsically controlled for the mood-changing properties associated with the behavioral activity. For example, helping is usually perceived as a mood-lifting opportunity because most people have learned the self-satisfying, and therefore uplifting, benefits associated with altruistic acts. This explains why, when experiencing negative affect, teenagers and adults are more willing to help compared to children who have yet to learn these associations (Cialdini & Kenrick, 1976). Food items, such as chocolate, have also been shown to present different mood-lifting expectations. Affect regulation via chocolate has a greater influence on women, who are more likely to perceive chocolate as a mood-lifting opportunity (Andrade, 2005; Grunberg & Straub, 1992). Similarly, sad participants are more willing to snack as long as they believe the action will regulate their affective states. Chronic tendencies such as general low expectations about affect regulation dampen many such effects (Tice, Bratslavsky, & Baumeister, 2001). Also, when people are led to believe their affective states are going to be temporarily frozen (i.e., the "mood-freezing pill" technique), attempts at upward affect regulation via aggression (Bushman, Baumeister, & Phillips, 2001) or helping (Manucia, Baumann, & Cialdini, 1984) also dissipate. Finally, specific emotions can alter the perceived mood-lifting opportunity of a given behavioral activity. As mentioned previously, anxious people take fewer risks than sad individuals (Raghunathan & Pham, 1999). Since anxiety stems from feelings of uncertainty, a risky choice may not represent an effective mood-lifting opportunity. Also, disgust has been shown to increase people's willingness to sell (Lerner, Small, & Loewenstein, 2004) probably because they have learned that "getting rid of" something when experiencing disgust will make them feel better.

Attempts at upward affect regulation can also be mitigated by competing goals. The principle of *conditional hedonism* implies that goals other than feeling better may lead individuals to give up a short-term pleasant opportunity (Erber, Wegner, & Therriault, 1996) or even to pursue an unpleasant path to achieve a competing goal, to improve performance, for example. Cohen and Andrade (2004) found that when people were expecting a task that required control over impulse buying, participants experiencing either positive or negative affect preferred to listen to mood incongruent songs in an attempt to neutralize stronger affective states prior to the task.

Positive affect and affect regulation

There is also evidence suggesting that people experiencing positive affect can, under certain circumstances, be less willing to take risks (Arkes, Herren, & Isen, 1988; Isen & Geva, 1987), to help others (Forest, Clark, Mills, & Isen, 1979; Isen & Simmonds, 1978), or to seek variety (Kahn & Isen, 1993). Isen and Simmonds (1978) found that when the helping scenario displayed situational cues that threatened participants' current positive feelings, participants were less willing to help compared to a control (neutral affect) condition. Similarly, Kahn and Isen (1993) showed that the increase in variety-seeking behavior for happy subjects disappeared as soon as a product's negative features were included or made salient in the search context. In other words, as mood-threatening cues become salient, happy subjects—who have more to lose—anticipate negative affect, which triggers a strong self-protective regulatory mechanism.

Mood-threatening stimuli may also be more persuasive when the message attempts to convince people of the risks associated with a particular activity. Keller, Lipkus, and Rimer (2003) showed that a loss-framed (vs. gain-framed) message was more persuasive when people were experiencing positive affect, *increasing* the perceived risk associated with breast cancer as well as the participant's intentions to get a mammogram. In other words, as the consequences seemed more threatening, the message became more influential. The opposite was true for those experiencing negative affect, where the gain-framed message was more persuasive, probably as a result of its mood-lifting cues.

It has also been suggested that people may be more willing to take actions that will help them to maintain the current affective state. So, people would not only avoid what is bad in order to protect their current positive state but also approach what is good in order to maintain it (Clark & Isen, 1982). However, claims about mood maintenance effects must rule out people's willingness to act as a result of a more positive assessment of the environment (affect-as-information and/or mood congruency effects) rather than a deliberate attempt to "fuel" current positive feelings. Moreover, there is evidence inconsistent with the "mood fueling" proposition. First, whereas negative affect increases helping among adults but not among children (Cialdini & Kenrick, 1976), positive affect increases helping across both groups (Barden, Garber, Duncan, & Masters, 1981; Rosenhan, Underwood, & Moore, 1974). If children are less likely to perceive helping as a mood-lifting alternative, why would they be more willing to help? Similarly, Manucia, Baumann, and Cialdini (1984) showed that positive and negative mood increased helping. However, after a mood-freezing pill was administered, the effect of mood on helping disappeared in the sad mood condition *only*. Finally, Andrade (2005) showed that positive affect increased intentions toward chocolate tasting even among those who reported not perceiving chocolate as a mood-lifting alternative—in that case, most of the male participants. However, intentions toward tasting the product decreased for those in a bad mood who did not perceive chocolate as mood-lifting.

In short, when it comes to the impact of positive affect on behavior via affect regulation, it is important to make salient two distinguishable propositions. First, there are the *mood protection effects*, in which positive affect makes people more sensitive to mood-*threatening* cues, and less likely to take risks, help, or seek variety in order to preserve a current state (Andrade, 2005; Arkes, Herren, & Isen, 1988; Forest, Clark, Mills, & Isen, 1979; Isen & Geva, 1987; Isen & Simmonds, 1978; Kahn & Isen, 1993). Second, there are potentially *mood fueling effects* in which positive affect makes people more sensitive to mood-*lifting* cues, and, as a result, more likely to act in order to fuel an otherwise decaying positive feeling. However, direct evidence to support the latter proposition is still scant. The "fueling"-like effects have usually been explained by evaluation (affect-as-information and/or mood-congruency) rather than regulation mechanisms (Andrade, 2005; Manucia, Baumann, & Cialdini, 1984). Future research should address circumstances in which mood fueling effects are likely, independently of evaluation biases.

Our review suggests that from the more basic (perceptual) to the highest (decision making) cognitive levels, affective states can shape responses. In many circumstances, affect regulation seems to represent an important mechanism driving the effects. Changes in the perceived mood-altering consequences of the cognitive or behavioral activity, the quantity and quality of the competing goals, and the strength of the affective signals will influence the impact of affect regulation on attention, retrieval, processing style, judgments, and decision making. However, many issues deserve further exploration. As described above, the role of perceived appropriateness and correction skills are important research avenues. Also, the impact of affect in judgment and decision making cannot be well understood without placing it in a more multifaceted context. For example, people could be led to discount or heighten the relevance of affect for a decision (in relation to other informational inputs or goals). So, a person with an eating disorder may be led to realize that s/he is eating too much, not because of hunger or even especially good-tasting food, but because of a mood repair need. One could, however, speculate that certain types of advertising for fattening food might engage mood repair needs. In that case, focusing on feelings may foster consumption.

We know relatively little about how affect regulation interacts with the other mechanisms (e.g., affect-as-information/mood congruency) also known to mediate the impact of affect on information processing and decision making. Direct evidence of the interaction of these mechanisms on both sides of the affective spectrum is still scant (Andrade, 2005; Manucia, Baumann, & Cialdini, 1984). Based on evidence from three largely unrelated research streams (helping, risk-taking, and eating), Andrade and Cohen (2007a) showed how a merger of the *affective evaluation* (affect-as-information and/or mood-congruency) and the *affect regulation* mechanisms can be critical to a more complete understanding of the affect-behavior relationship.

CONCLUSION

In the past 15 years, consumer research as a field has greatly matured in its understanding of the important role of affect in consumer behavior. The field has moved away from its original emphasis on mood states as "just another" source of contextual influence on consumer behavior and ad-induced feelings as "just another" determinant of brand attitudes. The field has moved toward a richer analysis of the very central role that affect—in its different forms: integral, incidental, task-related—plays in consumers' experiences, decisions, motives, and actions. Yet, while our understanding of the role of affect in consumer behavior may be growing rapidly, the subject is barely in its adolescence. As illustrated by this review, so many important questions remained to be answered. For example, an important avenue for future research would be to analyze to what extent emotional experiences have lasting influences on consumer judgment, decision, and behavior—influences that persevere after the feeling state has dissipated. Some preliminary evidence suggests certain cascading mechanisms contribute to such lasting influences (Andrade & Ariely, 2007). It has also been noted that feelings seem to be interpreted differently depending on the questions that people are asking themselves when inspecting their feelings (Pham, 2004). These questions seem to function as lenses through which feelings are read and understood. Another important research avenue would be to better understand the types of questions that feelings are meant to answer. Our purpose in writing this chapter is to stimulate readers to tackle these and many other important issues we have surveyed, so that even greater progress can be seen when the chapter's successor is written.

NOTES

1. As will be discussed later, more recent research suggests that incidental mood states may be more differentiated and have greater content specificity than previously thought (e.g., Lerner & Keltner, 2000, , 2001; Raghunathan & Pham, 1999; Tiedens & Linton, 2001).

2. The distinction between integral and incidental affect was first introduced by Bodenhausen (1993). We elaborate on this distinction by identifying a third type of judgment and decision-relevant affect: task affect.
3. This anticipatory use of the "how-do-I feel-about-it?" heuristic should be distinguished from the notion of anticipated or expected affect to be discussed further below. When relying on this heuristic anticipatorily, consumers appear to experience genuine momentary affective responses at the time of the decision (see Pham, 1998, Experiment 3). These momentary affective responses, which can be called *anticipatory* affective responses, are not merely affective beliefs unlike typical anticipated or expected affect.
4. These spontaneous thoughts should not be confused with the thoughts elicited by explicit requests to analyze reasons in judgments and decisions. As Wilson and his colleagues have repeatedly demonstrated, explicit requests to analyze reasons in judgments and decisions often trigger thoughts and reasons that are unrelated to the ones that people would otherwise generate and rely on spontaneously (e.g., Wilson, Dunn, Kraft, & Lisle, 1989; Wilson & Schooler, 1991).
5. Another explanation could be that chronic emotional states have lesser effects on risk-taking than momentary states.

REFERENCES

Aaker, D. A., Stayman, D. M., & Hagerty, M. R. (1986). Warmth in advertising — Measurement, impact, and sequence effects. *Journal of Consumer Research, 12*(4), 365–381.

Abelson, R. P., Kinder, D. R., Peters, M. D., & Fiske, S. T. (1982). Affective and semantic components in political person perception. *Journal of Personality and Social Psychology, 42*(4), 619–630.

Adaval, R. (2001). Sometimes it just feels right: The differential weighting of affect-consistent and affect-inconsistent product information. *Journal of Consumer Research, 28*(1), 1–17.

Adaval, R. (2003). How good gets better and bad gets worse: Understanding the impact of affect on evaluations of known brands. *Journal of Consumer Research, 30*(3), 352–367.

Albarracin, D., & Kumkale, G. T. (2003). Affect as information in persuasion: A model of affect identification and discounting. *Journal of Personality and Social Psychology, 84*(3), 453–469.

Albarracin, D., & Wyer, R. S. (2001). Elaborative and nonelaborative processing of a behavior-related communication. *Personality and Social Psychology Bulletin, 27*(6), 691–705.

Allen, C. T., Machleit, K. A., & Kleine, S. S. (1992). A comparison of attitudes and emotions as predictors of behavior at diverseLevels of behavioral experience. *Journal of Consumer Research, 18*(4), 493–504.

Allen, J. B., Kenrick, D. T., Linder, D. E., & McCall, M. A. (1989). Arousal and attraction: A response-facilitation alternative to misattribution and negative-reinforcement models. *Journal of Personality and Social Psychology, 57*(2), 261.

Ambady, N., & Gray, H. M. (2002). On being sad and mistaken: Mood effects on the accuracy of thin-slice judgments. *Journal of Personality and Social Psychology, 83*(4), 947–961.

Ambady, N., & Rosenthal, R. (1992). Thin Slices of Expressive Behavior as Predictors of Interpersonal Consequences — A Metaanalysis. *Psychological Bulletin, 111*(2), 256–274.

Andrade, E. B. (2005). Behavioral consequences of affect: Combining evaluative and regulatory mechanisms. *Journal of Consumer Research, 32*(3), 355–362.

Andrade, E. B., & Ariely, D. (2006). Short and long-term consequences of emotions in decision making. Unpublished manuscript, University of California-Berkeley.

Andrade, E .B., & Cohen, J.B. (2007a). Affect-based evaluation and regulation as mediators of behavior: The role of affect in risk taking, helping and eating patterns. In K.D. Vohs, R.F, Baumeister, & G. Loewenstein (Eds.), *Do emotions help or hurt decision making? A hedgefoxian perspectives*. New York: Russell Sage, forthcoming.

Andrade, E. B., & Cohen, J. B. (2007b). On the consumption of negative feelings. *Journal of Consumer Research*, October, forthcoming.

Ariely, D., & Loewenstein, G. (2000). When does duration matter in judgment and decision making? *Journal of Experimental Psychology-General, 129*(4), 508–523.

Arkes, H. R., Herren, L. T., & Isen, A. M. (1988). The role of potential loss in the influence of affect on risk-taking behavior. *Organizational Behavior and Human Decision Processes, 42*(2), 181–193.

Avnet, T., & Higgins, E. T. (2003). Locomotion, assessment, and regulatory fit: Value transfer from "how" to "what". *Journal of Experimental Social Psychology, 39*(5), 525–530.

Avnet, T., & Higgins, E. T. (2006). How regulatory fit affects value in consumer choices and opinions. *Journal of Marketing Research, 43*(1), 1–10.

Avnet, T., & Pham, M. T. (2007). Metacognitive and non-metacognitive reliance on affect-as-information in judgment. Unpublished manuscript, Columbia University.

Axelrod, J. N. (1963). Induced Moods and Attitudes toward Products. *Journal of Advertising Research, 3*(2), 19–24.

Babin, B. J., Darden, W. R., & Griffin, M. (1994). Work and or fun — Measuring hedonic and utilitarian shopping value. *Journal of Consumer Research, 20*(4), 644–656.

Bagozzi, R. P., & Moore, D. J. (1994). Public-service advertisements — Emotions and empathy guide prosocial behavior. *Journal of Marketing, 58*(1), 56–70.

Bakamitsos, G. A. (2006). A cue alone or a probe to think? The dual role of affect in product evaluations. *Journal of Consumer Research, 33*(3).

Barden, R. C., Garber, J., Duncan, S. W., & Masters, J. C. (1981). Cumulative effects of induced affective states in children — Accentuation, Inoculation, and Remediation. *Journal of Personality and Social Psychology, 40*(4), 750–760.

Barone, M. J. (2005). The interactive effects of mood and involvement on brand extension evaluations. *Journal of Consumer Psychology, 15*(3), 263–270.

Barone, M. J., Miniard, P. W., & Romeo, J. B. (2000). The influence of positive mood on brand extension evaluations. *Journal of Consumer Research, 26*(4), 386–400.

Batra, R., & Ray, M. L. (1986). Affective responses mediating acceptance of advertising. *Journal of Consumer Research, 13*(2), 234–249.

Batra, R., & Stayman, D. M. (1990). The role of mood in advertising effectiveness. *Journal of Consumer Research, 17*(2), 203–214.

Baumeister, R. F., Bratslavsky, E., Finkenauer, C., & Vohs, K. D. (2001). Bad is stronger than good. *Review of General Psychology, 5*(4), 323–370.

Bechara, A., Damasio, H., Tranel, D., & Damasio, A. R. (1997). Deciding advantageously before knowing the advantageous strategy. *Science, 275*(5304), 1293–1295.

Blaney, P. H. (1986). Affect and memory — A review. *Psychological Bulletin, 99*(2), 229–246.

Bless, H., Bohner, G., Schwarz, N., & Strack, F. (1990). Mood and persuasion — A cognitive response analysis. *Personality and Social Psychology Bulletin, 16*(2), 331–345.

Bless, H., Mackie, D. M., & Schwarz, N. (1992). Mood effects on attitude judgments — Independent effects of mood before and after message elaboration. *Journal of Personality and Social Psychology, 63*(4), 585–595.

Bless, H., Schwarz, N., Clore, G. L., Golisano, V., & Rabe, C. (1996). Mood and the use of scripts: Does a happy mood really lead to mindlessness? *Journal of Personality and Social Psychology, 71*(4), 665–679.

Bodenhausen, G. V. (1993). Emotions, arousal, and stereotype-based discrimination: A heuristic model of affect and stereotyping. In D. M. Mackie & D. L. Hamilton (Eds.), *Affect, cognition, and stereotyping* (pp. 13–37). San Diego, CA: Academic Press.

Bodenhausen, G. V., Kramer, G. P., & Suesser, K. (1994). Happiness and stereotypic thinking in social judgment. *Journal of Personality & Social Psychology, 66*(4), 621–632.

Bodenhausen, G. V., Sheppard, L. A., & Kramer, G. P. (1994). Negative affect and social judgment — The differential Impact of anger and sadness. *European Journal of Social Psychology, 24*(1), 45–62.

Bodur, H. O., Brinberg, D., & Coupey, E. (2000). Belief, affect, and attitude: Alternative models of the determinants of attitude. *Journal of Consumer Psychology, 9*(1), 17–28.

Bolton, L. E., Cohen, J. B., & Bloom, P. N. (2006). Does marketing products as remedies create "Get Out of Jail Free Cards"? *Journal of Consumer Research, 33*(1).

Bower, G. H. (1981). Mood and memory. *American Psychologist, 36*(2), 129–148.

Bower, G. H., & Forgas, J. P. (2000). Affect, memory, and social cognition.

Bradley, M. M., Cuthbert, B. N., & Lang, P. J. (1993). Pictures as prepulse — Attention and emotion in startle modification. *Psychophysiology, 30*(5), 541–545.

Bradley, M. M., Greenwald, M. K., Petry, M. C., & Lang, P. L. (1992). Remembering pictures — Pleasure and arousal in memory. *Journal of Experimental Psychology-Learning Memory and Cognition, 18*(2), 379–390.

Breckler, S. J., & Wiggins, E. C. (1989). Affect versus evaluation in the structure of attitudes. *Journal of Experimental Social Psychology, 25*(3), 253–271.

Brinol, P., & Petty, R. E. (2003). Overt head movements and persuasion: A self-validation analysis. *Journal of Personality and Social Psychology, 84*(6), 1123–1139.

Brown, S. P., Homer, P. M., & Inman, J. J. (1998). A meta-analysis of relationships between Ad-evoked feelings and advertising responses. *Journal of Marketing Research, 35*(1), 114–126.

Brown, S. P., & Stayman, D. M. (1992). Antecedents and consequences of attitude toward the ad — A meta-analysis. *Journal of Consumer Research, 19*(1), 34–51.

Buck, R. (1985). Prime theory — An integrated view of motivation and emotion. *Psychological Review, 92*(3), 389–413.

Buck, R. (1999). The biological affects: A typology. *Psychological Review, 106*(2), 301–336.

Burke, M. C., & Edell, J. A. (1989). The impact of feelings on ad-based affect and cognition. *Journal of Marketing Research, 26*(1), 69–83.

Bushman, B. J., & Baumeister, R. F. (1999). Threatened egotism, narcissism, self-esteem, and directed and displaced aggression: Does self-love or self-hate lead to violence? *Journal of Personality and Social Psychology, 75*, 219–229.

Bushman, B. J., Baumeister, R. F., & Phillips, C. M. (2001). Do people aggress to improve their mood? Catharsis beliefs, affect regulation opportunity, and aggressive responding. *Journal of Personality and Social Psychology, 81*(1), 17–32.

Cacioppo, J. T., & Berntson, G. G. (1994). Relationship between attitudes and evaluative space — A critical-review, with emphasis on the separability of positive and negative Substrates. *Psychological Bulletin, 115*(3), 401–423.

Cacioppo, J. T., Gardner, W. L., & Berntson, G. G. (1999). The affect system has parallel and integrative processing components: Form follows function. *Journal of Personality and Social Psychology, 76*(5), 839–855.

Cahill, L., & McGaugh, J. L. (1998). Mechanisms of emotional arousal and lasting declarative memory. *Trends in Neurosciences, 21*(7), 294–299.

Carmon, Z., Wertenbroch, K., & Zeelenberg, M. (2003). Option attachment: When deliberating makes choosing feel like losing. *Journal of Consumer Research, 30*(1), 15–29.

Carver, C. S., Lawrence, J. W., & Scheier, M. F. (1996). A control-process perspective on the origins of affect. In L. L. Martin & A. Tesser (Eds.), *Striving and feeling: Interactions among goals, affect, and self-regulation* (pp. 11–52). Mahwah, NJ: Erlbaum.

Christianson, S.-A., Loftus, E. F., Hoffman, H., & Loftus, G. R. (1991). Eye fixations and memory for emotional events. *Journal of Experimental Psychology-Learning Memory and Cognition, 17*(4), 693–701.

Cialdini, R. B., Darby, B. L., & Vincent, J. E. (1973). Transgression and altruism — case for hedonism. *Journal of Experimental Psychology, 9*(6), 502–516.

Cialdini, R. B., & Kenrick, D. T. (1976). Altruism as hedonism — Aocial-development perspective on relationship of negative mood state and helping. *Journal of Personality and Social Psychology, 34*(5), 907–914.

Clark, M. S., & Isen, A. M. (1982). Toward understanding the relationship between feeling states and social behavior. In L. Berkowitz (Ed.), *Cognitive psychology* (pp. 73–108). New York: Elsevier/North-Holland.

Clore, G. L., & Schnall, S. (2005). The influence of affect on attitude. In D. Albarracin, B. T. Johnson & M. P. Zanna (Eds.), *The handbook of attitudes* (pp. 437–489). Hillsdale, NJ: Erlbaum.

Clore, G. L., Schwarz, N., & Conway, M. (1994). Affective causes and consequences of social information processing. In R. S. Wyer & T. K. Srull (Eds.), *Handbook of social cognition* (2nd ed., pp. 323–417). Hillsdale, NJ Erlbaum.

Cohen, J. B., & Andrade, E. B. (2004). Affective intuition and task-contingent affect regulation. *Journal of Consumer Research, 31*(2), 358–367.

Cohen, J. B., & Areni, C. S. (1991). Affect and consumer behavior. In T. S. Robertson & H. H. Kassarjian (Eds.), *Handbook of consumer behavior* (pp. 188–240). Englewood Cliffs, NJ: Prentice Hall.

Conway, M., & Giannopoulos, C. (1993). Dysphoria and decision-making — limited information use for evaluations of multiattribute targets. *Journal of Personality and Social Psychology, 64*(4), 613–623.

Cosmides, L., & Tooby, J. (2000). Evolutionary psychology and the emotions. *Handbook of emotions.*

Crepaz, N., & Marks, G. (2001). Are negative affective states associated with HIV sexual risk behaviors? A meta-analytic review. *Health Psychology, 20*(4), 291–299.

Crites, S. L., Fabrigar, L. R., & Petty, R. E. (1994). Measuring the affective and cognitive properties of attitudes — Conceptual and methodological issues. *Personality and Social Psychology Bulletin, 20*(6), 619–634.

Damasio, A. R. (1994). *Descartes' error: Emotion, reason, and the human brain.* New York: Putnam.

Darke, P. R., Chattopadhyay, A., & Ashworth, L. (2006). Going with your "gut feeling": The importance and functional significance of discrete affect in consumer choice. *Journal of Consumer Research*(December).

Darke, S. (1988a). Anxiety and working memory capacity. *Cognition and Emotion, 2*(2), 145–154.

Darke, S. (1988b). Effects of anxiety on inferential reasoning task-performance. *Journal of Personality and Social Psychology, 55*(3), 499–505.

De Houwer, J., Thomas, S., & Baeyens, F. (2001). Associative learning of likes and dislikes: A review of 25 years of research on human evaluative conditioning. *Psychological Bulletin, 127*(6), 853–869.

Derbaix, C., & Pham, M. T. (1991). Affective reactions to consumption situations — A Pilot Investigation. *Journal of Economic Psychology, 12*(2), 325–355.

Derbaix, C. M. (1995). The impact of affective reactions on attitudes toward the advertisement and the brand — A step toward ecological validity. *Journal of Marketing Research, 32*(4), 470–479.

Derryberry, D., & Tucker, D. M. (1994). Motivating the focus of attention. In P. M. Niedenthal & S. Kiayama (Eds.), *The heart's eye* (pp. 167–196). New York: Academic Press.

Dhar, R., & Wertenbroch, K. (2000). Consumer choice between hedonic and utilitarian goods. *Journal of Marketing Research, 37*(1), 60–71.

Diener, E., & Irannejad, A. (1986). The relationship in experience between various types of affect. *Journal of Personality and Social Psychology, 50*(5), 1031–1038.

Diener, E., Smith, H., & Fujita, F. (1995). The personality structure of affect. *Journal of Personality and Social Psychology, 69*(1), 130–141.

Dijksterhuis, A., & Aarts, H. (2003). On wildebeests and humans: The preferential detection of negative stimuli. *Psychological Science, 14*(1), 14–18.

Dollard, J., & Miller, N. E. (1950). *Personality and psychotherapy.* New York: McGraw-Hill.

Dommermuth, W. P., & Millard, W. J. (1967). Consumption coincidence in product evaluation. *Journal of Marketing Research, 4*(4), 388–390.

Drolet, A., & Luce, M. F. (2004). The rationalizing effects of cognitive load on emotion-based trade-off avoidance. *Journal of Consumer Research, 31*(1), 63–77.

Dunegan, K. J., Duchon, D., & Barton, S. L. (1992). Affect, risk, and decision criticality — Replication and extension in a business setting. *Organizational Behavior and Human Decision Processes, 53*(3), 335–351.

Dutton, D. G., & Aron, A. P. (1974). Some evidence for heightened sexual attraction under conditions of high anxiety. *Journal of Personality and Social Psychology, 30*(4), 510–517.

Eagly, A. H., & Chaiken, S. (1993). *The psychology of attitudes.* Orlando, FL: Harcourt Brace Jovanovich.

Easterbrook, J. A. (1959). The effect of emotion on cue utilization and the organization of behavior. *Psychological Review, 66*(3), 183–201.

Edell, J. A., & Burke, M. C. (1987). The power of feelings in understanding advertising effects. *Journal of Consumer Research, 14*(3), 421–433.

Ehrlichman, H., & Halpern, J. N. (1988). Affect and memory — Effects of pleasant and unpleasant odors on retrieval of happy and unhappy memories. *Journal of Personality and Social Psychology, 55*(5), 769–779.

Ekman, P. (1973). Universal facial expressions in emotion. *Studia Psychologica, 15*(2), 140–147.

Elster, J. (1999). *Alchemies of the mind: Rationality and the emotions.* Cambridge: Cambridge University Press.

Epstein, S. (1990). Cognitive-experiential self-theory. In L. A. Pervin (Ed.), *Handbook of personality: Theory and research* (pp. 165–192). New York: Guilford.

Erber, M. W., & Erber, R. (2001). The role of motivated social cognition in the regulation of affective states. In J. P. Forgas (Ed.), *Affect and social cognition* (pp. 275–289). Mahwah, NJ: Erlbaum.

Erber, R., & Erber, M. W. (1994). Beyond mood and social judgment — Mood-incongruent recall and mood regulation. *European Journal of Social Psychology, 24*(1), 79–88.

Erber, R., Wegner, D. M., & Therriault, N. (1996). On being cool and collected: Mood regulation in anticipation of social interaction. *Journal of Personality and Social Psychology, 70*(4), 757–766.

Etcoff, N. (1999). *Survival of the prettiest.* New York: Doubleday.

Fedorikhin, A., & Cole, C. A. (2004). Mood effects on attitudes, perceived risk and choice: Moderators and mediators. *Journal of Consumer Psychology, 14*(1–2), 2–12.

Fenz, W. D., & Epstein, S. (1967). Gradients of physiological arousal in parachutists as a function of an approaching jump. *Psychosomatic Medicine, 29*, 33–52.

Fessler, D. M. T., Pillsworth, E. G., & Flamson, T. J. (2004). Angry men and disgusted women: An evolutionary approach to the influence of emotions on risk taking. *Organizational Behavior and Human Decision Processes, 95*(1), 107–123.

Fiedler, K. (1988). Emotional mood, cognitive style, and behavior regulation. In K. Fiedler & J. Forgas (Eds.), *Affect, Cognition and Social Behavior* (pp. 100–119). Toronto: C.J. Hogrefe.

Fishbein, M., & Azjen, I. (1975). *Belief, attitude, intention, and behavior: An introduction to theory and research*

Fishbein, M., & Middlestadt, S. (1995). Noncognitive effects on attitude formation and change: Fact or artifact? *Journal of Consumer Psychology, 4*(2), 181–202.

Forest, D., Clark, M. S., Mills, J., & Isen, A. M. (1979). Helping as a function of feeling state and nature of the helping behavior. *Motivation and Emotion, 3*(2), 161–169.

Forgas, J. P. (1991a). Affective influences on partner choice — Role of mood in social decisions. *Journal of Personality and Social Psychology, 61*(5), 708–720.

Forgas, J. P. (1991b). *Emotions and social judgments.* Oxford: Pergamon

Forgas, J. P. (1995). Mood and judgement: The affect infusion model (AIM). *Psychological Bulletin, 117*(1), 39.

Forgas, J. P. (1998). On being happy and mistaken: Mood effects on the fundamental attribution error. *Journal of Personality and Social Psychology, 75*(2), 318–331.

Forgas, J. P., Johnson, R., & Ciarrochi, J. V. (1998). Mood management: The role of processing strategies in affect control and affect infusion. In M. Kofta, G. Weary & G. Sedek (Eds.), *Personal control in action: Cognitive and motivational mechanisms* (pp. 155–189). New York: Plenum Press.

Forster, J. (2004). How body feedback influences consumers' evaluation of products. *Journal of Consumer Psychology, 14*(4), 416–426.

Foster, C. A., Witcher, B. S., Campbell, W. K., & Green, J. D. (1998). Arousal and attraction: Evidence for automatic and controlled processes. *Journal of Personality and Social Psychology, 74*(1), 86–101.

Fowles, D. C. (1994). A motivational theory of psychopathology. In W. D. Spaulding (Ed.), *Nebraska symposium on motivation: Integrated views of motivation, cognition and emotion* (Vol. 41, pp. 181–238). Lincoln, NE.

Fox, E., Russo, R., Bowles, R., & Dutton, K. (2001). Do threatening stimuli draw or hold visual attention in subclinical anxiety? *Journal of Experimental Psychology-General, 130*(4), 681–700.

Fredrickson, B. L., & Kahneman, D. (1993). Duration neglect in retrospective evaluations of affective episodes. *Journal of Personality and Social Psychology, 65*(1), 45–55.

Frijda, N. H. (1986). *The emotions.* Cambridge, UK: Cambridge University Press.

Frijda, N. H., Kuipers, P., & Terschure, E. (1989). Relations among emotion, appraisal, and emotional action readiness. *Journal of Personality and Social Psychology, 57*(2), 212–228.

Gardner, M. P. (1985). Mood states and consumer-behavior — A critical-review. *Journal of Consumer Research, 12*(3), 281–300.

Gardner, M. P., & Wilhelm, F. O. (1987). Consumer responses to ads with positive vs. negative appeals: Some mediating effects of content-induced mood and congruency between context and ad. *Current Issues and Research in Advertising, 10*(1), 81–98.

Gilbert, D. T., Gill, M. J., & Wilson, T. D. (2002). The future is now: Temporal correction in affective forecasting. *Organizational Behavior and Human Decision Processes, 88*(1), 430–444.

Gilovich, T. (1981). Seeing the past in the present — the effect of associations to familiar events on judgments and decisions. *Journal of Personality and Social Psychology, 40*(5), 797–808.

Goldberg, M. E., & Gorn, G. J. (1987). Happy and sad Tv Programs — How they affect reactions to commercials. *Journal of Consumer Research, 14*(3), 387–403.

Gorn, G. J. (1982). The effects of music in advertising on choice behavior: A classical conditioning approach. *Journal of Marketing, 46*(1), 94–101.

Gorn, G. J., Goldberg, M. E., & Basu, K. (1993). Mood, awareness and product evaluation. *Journal of Consumer Psychology, 2*(3), 237–256.

Gorn, G. J., Pham, M. T., & Sin, L. Y. (2001). When arousal influences ad evaluation and valence does not (and vice versa). *Journal of Consumer Psychology, 11*(1), 43–55.

Greene, T. R., & Noice, H. (1988). Influence of positive affect upon creative-thinking and problem-solving in children. *Psychological Reports, 63*(3), 895–898.

Gross, J. J. (1998). The emerging field of emotion regulation: An integrative Review. *Review of General Psychology, 2*(3), 271–299.

Gross, J. J., & Levenson, R. W. (1995). Emotion elicitation using films. *Cognition and Emotion, 9,* 87–108.

Grunberg, N. E., & Straub, R. O. (1992). The role of gender and taste class in the effects of stress on eating. *Health Psychology, 11,* 97–100.

Hartlage, S., Alloy, L. B., Vazquez, C., & Dykman, B. (1993). Automatic and effortful processing in depression. *Psychological Bulletin, 113*(2), 247–278.

Hemenover, S. H., & Schimmack, U. (2004). Mixed feelings of amusement and disgust.

Higgins, E. T. (2000). Making a good decision: Value from fit. *American Psychologist, 55*(11), 1217–1230.

Higgins, E. T., Idson, L. C., Freitas, A. L., Spiegel, S., & Molden, D. C. (2003). Transfer of value from fit. *Journal of Personality and Social Psychology, 84*(6), 1140–1153.

Hill, R. P., & Ward, J. C. (1989). Mood manipulation in marketing research: An examination of potential confounding effects. *Journal of Marketing Research, 26,* 97–104.

Hirt, E. R., Melton, R. J., McDonald, H. E., & Harackiewicz, J. M. (1996). Processing goals, task interest, and the mood-performance relationship: A mediational analysis. *Journal of Personality and Social Psychology, 71*(2), 245–261.

Hoffmann, M. L. (1986). Affect, Cognition, and Motivation. In R. M. Sorrentino & E. T. Higgins (Eds.), *The handbook of aotivation and cognition.* New York: Guilford.

Holbrook, M. B., & Batra, R. (1987). Assessing the role of emotions as mediators of consumer responses to advertising. *Journal of Consumer Research, 14*(3), 404–420.

Howard, D. J. (1992). Gift-wrapping effects on product sttitudes: A mood-biasing explanation. *Journal of Consumer Psychology, 1*(3), 197–223.

Hsee, C. K., & Rottenstreich, Y. (2004). Music, pandas, and muggers: On the affective psychology of value. *Journal of Experimental Psychology-General, 133*(1), 23–30.

Hsiao, E. T., & Thayer, R. E. (1998). Exercising for mood regulation: The importance of experience. *Personality and Individual Differences, 24*(6), 829–836.

Humphreys, M. S., & Revelle, W. (1984). Personality, motivation, and performance — A theory of the relationship between individual-differences and information-processing. *Psychological Review, 91*(2), 153–184.

Isbell, L. M., & Wyer, R. S. (1999). Correcting for mood-induced bias in the evaluation of political candidates: The roles of intrinsic and extrinsic motivation. *Personality and Social Psychology Bulletin, 25*(2), 237–249.

Isen, A. M. (1984). Toward understanding the role of affect in cognition. In R. S. Wyer & T. K. Srull (Eds.), *Handbook of social cognition* (Vol. 3, pp. 179–236). Hillsdale, NJ: Erlbaum.

Isen, A. M. (2001). An influence of positive affect on decision making in complex situations: Theoretical issues with practical implications. *Journal of Consumer Psychology, 11*(2), 75–85.

Isen, A. M., Clark, M. S., & Schwartz, M. F. (1976). Duration of the effect of good mood on helping: "Footprints on the Sands of Time". *Journal of Personality and Social Psychology, 34*(3), 385–393.

Isen, A. M., & Daubman, K. A. (1984). The influence of affect on categorization. *Journal of Personality and Social Psychology, 47*(6), 1206–1217.

Isen, A. M., Daubman, K. A., & Nowicki, G. P. (1987). Positive affect facilitates creative problem-solving. *Journal of Personality and Social Psychology, 52*(6), 1122–1131.

Isen, A. M., & Geva, N. (1987). The influence of positive affect on acceptable level of risk — The person with a large canoe has a large worry. *Organizational Behavior and Human Decision Processes, 39*(2), 145–154.

Isen, A. M., & Means, B. (1983). The influence of positive affect on decision-making strategy. *Social Cognition, 2*(1), 18–31.

Isen, A. M., Niedenthal, P. M., & Cantor, N. (1992). An influence of positive affect on social categorization. *Motivation and Emotion, 16*(1), 65–78.

Isen, A. M., Nygren, T. E., & Ashby, F. G. (1988). Influence of positive affect on the subjective utility of gains and losses — It is just not worth the risk. *Journal of Personality and Social Psychology, 55*(5), 710–717.

Isen, A. M., & Shalker, T. E. (1982). The effect of feeling state on evaluation of positive, neutral, and negative stimuli — When you accentuate the positive, do you eliminate the negative. *Social Psychology Quarterly, 45*(1), 58–63.

Isen, A. M., Shalker, T. E., Clark, M., & Karp, L. (1978). Affect, accessibility of material in memory, and behavior — Cognitive loop. *Journal of Personality and Social Psychology, 36*(1), 1–12.

Isen, A. M., & Simmonds, S. F. (1978). The effect of feeling good on a helping task that is incompatible with good mood. *Social Psychology, 41*(4), 346–349.

Ito, T. A., Cacioppo, J. T., & Lang, P. J. (1998). Eliciting affect using the international affective picture system: Trajectories through evaluative space. *Personality and Social Psychology Bulletin, 24*(8), 855–879.

Izard, C. E. (1977). *Human emotions.* New York: Plenum.

James, W. (1884). What is an emotion? *Mind, 9,* 188–205.

Janz, N. K., & Becker, M. H. (1984). The health belief model — A decade later. *Health Education Quarterly, 11*(1), 1–47.

Johnson, E. J., & Tversky, A. (1983). Affect, generalization, and the perception of risk. *Journal of Personality and Social Psychology, 45*(1), 20–31.

Joormann, J., & Siemer, M. (2004). Memory accessibility, mood regulation, and dysphoria: Difficulties in repairing sad mood with happy memories? *Journal of Abnormal Psychology, 113*(2), 179–188.

Josephson, B. R., Singer, J. A., & Salovey, P. (1996). Mood regulation and memory: Repairing sad moods with happy memories. *Cognition & Emotion, 10*(4), 437–444.

Kahn, B., & Isen, A. M. (1993). The influence of positive affect on variety seeking among safe, enjoyable products. *Journal of Consumer Research, 20*(2), 257–270.

Kahneman, D., Fredrickson, B. L., Schreiber, C. A., & Redelmeier, D. A. (1993). When more pain is preferred to less — Adding a better end. *Psychological Science, 4*(6), 401–405.

Kahneman, D., Ritov, I., & Schkade, D. (1999). Economic preferences or attitude expressions? An analysis of dollar responses to public issues. *Journal of Risk and Uncertainty, 19*(1-3), 203–235.

Kahneman, D., Schkade, D., & Sunstein, C. R. (1998). Shared outrage and erratic awards: The psychology of punitive damages. *Journal of Risk and Uncertainty, 16*(1), 49–86.

Kahneman, D., & Snell, J. (1990). Predicting utility. In R. M. Hogarth (Ed.), *Insights in decision making — A tribute to Hillel. J. Einhorn* (pp. 295–342). Chicago: The University of Chicago Press.

Kamins, M. A., Marks, L. J., & Skinner, D. (1991). Television commercial evaluation in the context of program induced mood — Congruency versus consistency effects. *Journal of Advertising, 20*(2), 1–14.

Kassarjian, H. H., & Robertson, T. S. (1991). *1991 Handbook of consumer behavior.* Englewood Cliffs, N.J.: Prentice-Hall.

Keinan, G. (1987). Decision-making under stress — Scanning of alternatives under controllable and uncontrollable threats. *Journal of Personality and Social Psychology, 52*(3), 639–644.

Keller, P. A., Lipkus, I. M., & Rimer, B. K. (2003). Affect, framing, and persuasion. *Journal of Marketing Research, 40*(1), 54–64.

Kleinke, C. L., Peterson, T. R., & Rutledge, T. R. (1998). Effects of self-generated facial expressions on mood. *Journal of Personality and Social Psychology, 74*(1), 272–279.

Knobloch, S., & Zillmann, D. (2002). Mood management via the digital Jukebox. *Journal of Communication, 52*(June), 351–366.

Kroeber-Riel, W. (1979). Activation research — Psychobiological approaches in consumer research. *Journal of Consumer Research, 5*(4), 240–250.

Krohne, H. (2003). Individual differences in emotional reactions and coping. In R. J. Davidson, K. R. Scherer & H. H. Goldsmith (Eds.), *Handbook of affective sciences* (pp. 698–725). New York: Oxford University.

Lang, P. J. (1995). The emotion probe — Studies of motivation and attention. *American Psychologist, 50*(5), 372–385.

Lang, P. J., Bradley, M. M., & Cuthbert, B. N. (1990). Emotion, attention, and the startle reflex. *Psychological Review, 97*(3), 377–395.

Lang, P. J., Bradley, M. M., & Cuthbert, B. N. (1992). A motivational analysis of emotion — Reflex cortex connections. *Psychological Science, 3*(1), 44–49.

Lang, P. J., Bradley, M. M., & Cuthbert, B. N. (1997). *International affective picture system (IAPS): Technical manual and affective ratings.* Gainesville, FL: NIMH Center for the Study of Emotion and Attention, University of Florida.

Larsen, J. T., McGraw, P. A., & Cacioppo, J. T. (2001). Can people feel happy and sad at the same time? *Journal of Personality and Social Psychology, 81*(4), 684–696.

Larsen, J. T., McGraw, P. A., Mellers, B. A., & Cacioppo, J. T. (2004). The agony of victory and thrill of defeat. *Psychological Science, 15*(5), 325–330.

Larsen, R. J. (2000). Toward a science of mood regulation. *Psychological Inquiry, 11*(3), 129–141.

Lazarus, R. S. (1991). *Emotion and adaptation.* New York: Oxford University Press.

Lazarus, R. S., & Alfert, E. (1964). Short-circuiting of threat by experimentally altering cognitive appraisal. *Journal of Abnormal and Social Psychology, 69*(2), 195–205.

Lazarus, R. S., & Folkman, S. (1984). The concept of coping. In R. S. Lazarus & S. Folkman (Eds.), *Stress, appraisal, and coping* (pp. 117–180). New York: Springer.

LeDoux, J. E. (1996). *The emotional brain: The mysterious underpinnings of emotional life.* New York: Simon & Schuster.

Lee, A. Y., & Sternthal, B. (1999). The effects of positive mood on memory. *Journal of Consumer Research, 26*(2), 115–127.

Leith, K. P., & Baumeister, R. F. (1996). Why do bad moods increase self-defeating behavior? Emotion, risk taking, and self-regulation. *Journal of Personality and Social Psychology, 71*(6), 1250–1267.

Leon, M. R., & Revelle, W. (1985). Effects of anxiety on analogical reasoning — A Test of 3 Theoretical-Models. *Journal of Personality and Social Psychology, 49*(5), 1302–1315.

Lerner, J. S., & Keltner, D. (2000). Beyond valence: Toward a model of emotion-specific influences on judgement and choice. *Cognition & Emotion, 14*(4), 473–493.

Lerner, J. S., & Keltner, D. (2001). Fear, anger, and risk. *Journal of Personality & Social Psychology, 81*(1), 146–159.

Lerner, J. S., Small, D. A., & Loewenstein, G. (2004). Heart strings and purse strings: Carryover effects of emotions on economic decisions. *Psychological Science, 15*(5), 337–341.

Leventhal, H. (1970). Findings and theory in the study of fear communications. In L. Berkowitz (Ed.), *Advances in experimental social psychology* (Vol. 5, pp. 119–186). San Diego, CA: Academic Press.

Leventhal, H. (1980). Toward a comprehensive theory of emotion. *Advances in Experimental Social Psychology,* 149–207.

Levine, L. J. (1997). Reconstructing memory for emotions. *Journal of Experimental Psychology-General, 126*(2), 165–177.

Levine, L. J., Prohaska, V., Burgess, S. L., Rice, J. A., & Laulhere, T. M. (2001). Remembering past emotions: The role of current appraisals. *Cognition & Emotion, 15*(4), 393–417.

Loewenstein, G. (1996). Out of control: Visceral influences on behavior. *Organizational Behavior and Human Decision Processes, 65*(3), 272–292.

Loewenstein, G., & Lerner, J. S. (2003). The role of affect in decision making. In R. J. Davidson, K. R. Scherer & H. H. Goldsmith (Eds.), *Handbook of affective sciences* (pp. 619–642). Oxford: Oxford University Press.

Loewenstein, G., Weber, E. U., Hsee, C. K., & Welch, N. (2001). Risk as feelings. *Psychological Bulletin, 127*(2), 267–286.

Luce, M. F. (1998). Choosing to avoid: Coping with negatively emotion-laden consumer decisions. *Journal of Consumer Research, 24*(4), 409–433.

Luce, M. F., Bettman, J. R., & Payne, J. W. (1997). Choice processing in emotionally difficult decisions. *Journal of Experimental Psychology-Learning Memory and Cognition, 23*(2), 384–405.

Luce, M. F., Payne, J. W., & Bettman, J. R. (1999). Emotional trade-off difficulty and choice. *Journal of Marketing Research, 36*(2), 143–159.

Luomala, H. T., & Laaksonen, M. (1997). Mood-regulatory self-gifts: Development of a conceptual framework. *Journal of Economic Psychology, 18*(4), 407–434.

MacGregor, D. G., Slovic, P., Dreman, D., & Berry, M. (2000). Imagery, affect, and financial judgment. *The Journal of Psychology and Financial Markets, 1*(2), 104–110.

Mackenzie, S. B., Lutz, R. J., & Belch, G. E. (1986). The Role of attitude toward the ad as a aediator of advertising effectiveness — A test of competing explanations. *Journal of Marketing Research, 23*(2), 130–143.

Mackie, D. M., & Worth, L. T. (1989). Processing deficits and the mediation of positive affect in persuasion. *Journal of Personality and Social Psychology, 57*(1), 27–40.

MacLeod, C., & Mathews, A. (1988). Anxiety and the allocation of attention to threat. *The Quarterly journal of experimental psychology, 40*(4), 653–670.

Mano, H. (1991). The structure and intensity of emotional experiences — Method and context convergence. *Multivariate Behavioral Research, 26*(3), 389–411.

Mano, H. (1992). Judgments under distress — Assessing the role of unpleasantness and arousal in judgment formation. *Organizational Behavior and Human Decision Processes, 52*(2), 216–245.

Mano, H. (1994). Risk-taking, framing effects, and affect. *Organizational Behavior and Human Decision Processes, 57*(1), 38–58.

Manucia, G. K., Baumann, D. J., & Cialdini, R. B. (1984). Mood influences on helping — Direct effects or side-Effects. *Journal of Personality and Social Psychology, 46*(2), 357–364.

Martin, L. L., Abend, T., Sedikides, C., & Green, J. D. (1997). How would it feel if...? Mood as input to a role fulfillment evaluation process. *Journal of Personality & Social Psychology, 73*(2), 242–253.

Martin, L. L., Ward, D. W., Achee, J. W., & Wyer, R. S. (1993). Mood as input — People have to interpret the motivational implications of their moods. *Journal of Personality and Social Psychology, 64*(3), 317–326.

Mather, M., & Carstensen, L. L. (2003). Aging and attentional biases for emotional faces. *Psychological Science, 14*(5), 409–415.

Mathur, M., & Chattopadhyay, A. (1991). The impact of moods generated by television programs on responses to advertising. *Psychology & Marketing, 8*(1), 59–77.

Matsumoto, D. (1987). The role of facial response in the experience of emotion — more methodological problems and a metaanalysis. *Journal of Personality and Social Psychology, 52*(4), 769–774.

Mattes, J., & Cantor, J. (1982). Enhancing responses to television advertisements via the transfer of residual arousal from prior programming. *Journal of Broadcasting, 26*(4), 553–566.

McClure, S. M., Laibson, D. I., Loewenstein, G., & Cohen, J. D. (2004). Separate neural systems value immediate and delayed monetary rewards. *Science, 306*(5695), 503–507.

McFarland, C., & Buehler, R. (1997). Negative affective states and the motivated retrieval of positive life events: The role of affect acknowledgment. *Journal of Personality and Social Psychology, 73*(1), 200–214.

McFarland, C., & Buehler, R. (1998). The impact of negative affect on autobiographical memory: The role of self-focused attention to moods. *Journal of Personality and Social Psychology, 75*(6), 1424–1440.

Mellers, B. A., Schwartz, A., Ho, K., & Ritov, I. (1997). Decision affect theory: Emotional reactions to the outcomes of risky options. *Psychological Science, 8*(6), 423–429.

Mellers, B. A., Schwartz, A., & Ritov, I. (1999). Emotion-based choice. *Journal of Experimental Psychology-General, 128*(3), 332–345.

Meloy, M. G. (2000). Mood-driven distortion of product information. *Journal of Consumer Research, 27*(3), 345–359.

Mezzacappa, E. S., Katkin, E. S., & Palmer, S. N. (1999). Epinephrine, arousal, and emotion: A new look at two-factor theory. *Cognition & Emotion, 13*(2), 181–199.

Mick, D. G., & Demoss, M. (1990). Self-gifts — Phenomenological insights from 4 contexts. *Journal of Consumer Research, 17*(3), 322–332.

Miniard, P. W., Bhatla, S., Lord, K. R., Dickson, P. R., & Unnava, H. R. (1991). Picture-based persuasion processes and the moderating role of involvement. *Journal of Consumer Research, 18*(1), 92–107.

Miniard, P. W., Bhatla, S., & Sirdeshmukh, D. (1992). Mood as a determinant of postconsumption product evaluations. *Journal of Consumer Psychology, 1*(2), 173–195.

Morales, A. C., & Fitzsimons, G. J. (2007). Product contagion: Changing consumer evaluations through physical contact with "disgusting" products. *Journal of Marketing Research, 44*(2), 282–283.

Morris, J. D., Woo, C., Geason, J. A., & Kim, J. (2002). The power of affect: Predicting intention. *Journal of Advertising Research, 42*(3), 7–17.

Murry, J. P., & Dacin, P. A. (1996). Cognitive moderators of negative-emotion effects: Implications for understanding media context. *Journal of Consumer Research, 22*(4), 439–447.

Nielson, K. A., Yee, D., & Erickson, K. I. (2005). Memory enhancement by a semantically unrelated emotional arousal source induced after learning. *Neurobiology of Learning and Memory, 84*(1), 49–56.

Nowlis, S. M., & Shiv, B. (2005). The influence of consumer distractions on the effectiveness of food-sampling programs. *Journal of Marketing Research, 42*(2), 157–168.

Nygren, T. E., Isen, A. M., Taylor, P. J., & Dulin, J. (1996). The influence of positive affect on the decision rule in risk situations: Focus on outcome (and especially avoidance of loss) rather than probability. *Organizational Behavior and Human Decision Processes, 66*(1), 59–72.

Oaksford, M., Morris, F., Grainger, B., & Williams, J. M. G. (1996). Mood, reasoning, and central executive processes. *Journal of Experimental Psychology-Learning Memory and Cognition, 22*(2), 476–492.

Oatley, K. (1992). *Best laid schemes: The psychology of emotions*: Cambridge University.

Oatley, K., & Johnson-Laird, P. N. (1987). Towards a cognitive theory of emotions. *Cognition and Emotion, 1*, 29–50.

Oliver, R. L. (1993). Cognitive, affective, and attribute bases of the satisfaction response. *Journal of Consumer Research, 20*(3), 418–430.

Ortony, A., Clore, G. L., & Collins, A. (1988). *The cognitive structure of emotions*. Cambridge: Cambridge University Press

Ottati, V. C., & Isbell, L. M. (1996). Effects of mood during exposure to target information on subsequently reported judgments: An on-line model of misattribution and correction. *Journal of Personality and Social Psychology, 71*(1), 39–53.

Parrott, W. G., & Sabini, J. (1990). Mood and memory under natural conditions — Evidence for mood incongruent recall. *Journal of Personality and Social Psychology, 59*(2), 321–336.

Paulhus, D. L., & Lim, D. T. K. (1994). Arousal and evaluative extremity in social judgments — A dynamic complexity model. *European Journal of Social Psychology, 24*(1), 89–99.

Peretz, I., Gagnon, L., & Bouchard, B. (1998). Music and emotion: Perceptual determinants, immediacy, and isolation after brain damage. *Cognition, 68*(2), 111–141.

Petty, R. E., Schumann, D. W., Richman, S. A., & Strathman, A. J. (1993). Positive mood and persuasion: Different roles for affect under high- and low-elaboration conditions. *Journal of Personality and Social Psychology, 64*(1), 5.

Pham, M. T. (1996). Cue representation and selection effects of arousal on persuasion. *Journal of Consumer Research, 22*(4), 373–387.

Pham, M. T. (1998). Representativeness, relevance, and the use of feelings in decision making. *Journal of Consumer Research, 25*(2), 144–159.

Pham, M. T. (2004). The logic of feeling. *Journal of Consumer Psychology, 14*(4).

Pham, M. T., & Avnet, T. (2004). Regulatory focus and the use of feelings in judgment. Unpublished manuscript, Columbia University, New York.

Pham, M. T., Cohen, J. B., Pracejus, J. W., & Hughes, G. D. (2001). Affect monitoring and the primacy of feelings in judgment. *Journal of Consumer Research, 28*(2), 167–188.

Pham, M. T., & Raghunathan, R. (2007). On the distinction between feelings and affective beliefs in decision making: The case of anxiety vs. sadness Unpublished manuscript, Columbia University, New York.

Phillipot, P. (1993). Inducing and assesing differentiated emotion-feeling states in the laboratory. *Cognition and Emotion, 7*, 171–193.

Putman, P., Hermans, E., & van Honk, J. (2004). Emotional Stroop performance for masked angry faces: It's BAS, not BIS. *Emotion, 4*(3), 305–311.

Raghunathan, R., & Irwin, J. R. (2001). Walking the hedonic product treadmill: Default contrast and moodbased assimilation in judgments of predicted happiness with a target product. *Journal of Consumer Research, 28*(3), 355–368.

Raghunathan, R., & Pham, M. T. (1999). All negative moods are not equal: Motivational influences of anxiety and sadness on decision making. *Organizational Behavior and Human Decision Processes, 79*(1), 56–77.

Raghunathan, R., Pham, M. T., & Corfman, K. P. (2006). Informational properties of anxiety and sadness, and displaced coping. *Journal of Consumer Research, 32*(4).

Raghunathan, R., & Trope, Y. (2002). Walking the tightrope between feeling good and being accurate: Mood as a resource in processing persuasive messages. *Journal of Personality and Social Psychology, 83*(3), 510–525.

Remington, N. A., Fabrigar, L. R., & Visser, P. S. (2000). Reexamining the circumplex model of affect. *Journal of Personality and Social Psychology, 79*(2), 286–300.

Richins, M. L. (1997). Measuring emotions in the consumption experience. *Journal of Consumer Research, 24*(2), 127–146.

Robinson, M. D., & Clore, G. L. (2002). Belief and feeling: Evidence for an accessibility model of emotional self-report. *Psychological Bulletin, 128*(6), 934–960.

Rogers, R. W. (1975). Protection motivation theory of fear appeals and attitude-change. *Journal of Psychology, 91*(1), 93–114.

Rook, D. W., & Gardner, M. P. (1993). In the mood: Impulse buying's affective antecedents. *Research in Consumer Behavior, 6*, 1–26.

Rosenhan, D. L., Underwood, B., & Moore, B. S. (1974). Affect moderates self-gratification and altruism. *Journal of Personality and Social Psychology, 30*(4), 546–552.

Rottenstreich, Y., & Hsee, C. K. (2001). Money, kisses, and electric shocks: On the affective psychology of risk. *Psychological Science, 12*(3), 185–190.

Ruder, M., & Bless, H. (2003). Mood and the reliance on the ease of retrieval heuristic. *Journal of Personality and Social Psychology, 85*(1), 20–32.

Russell, J. A. (1980). A circumplex model of affect. *Journal of Personality and Social Psychology, 39*(6), 1161–1178.

Russell, J. A., & Barrett, L. F. (1999). Core affect, prototypical emotional episodes, and other things called Emotion: Dissecting the elephant. *Journal of Personality and Social Psychology, 76*(5), 805–819.

Russell, J. A., & Carroll, J. M. (1999a). On the bipolarity of positive and negative affect. *Psychological Bulletin, 125*(1), 3–30.

Russell, J. A., & Carroll, J. M. (1999b). The phoenix of bipolarity: Reply to Watson and Tellegen (1999). *Psychological Bulletin, 125*(5), 611–617.

Rusting, C. L., & DeHart, T. (2000). Retrieving positive memories to regulate negative mood: Consequences for mood-congruent memory. *Journal of Personality and Social Psychology, 78*(4), 737–752.

Sanbonmatsu, D. M., & Kardes, F. R. (1988). The effects of physiological arousal on information-processing and persuasion. *Journal of Consumer Research, 15*(3), 379–385.

Sarason, I. G., Sarason, B. R., Slichter, S. J., Beatty, P. G., Meyer, D. M., & Bolgiano, D. C. (1993). Increasing participation of blood-donors in a bone-marrow registry. *Health Psychology, 12*(4), 272–276.

Scherer, K. R., Schorr, A., & Johnstone, T. (2001). *Appraisal processes in emotion: Theory, methods, eesearch.* New York: Oxford University Press.

Schimmack, U. (2005). Respons latencies of pleasure and displeasure ratings: Further evidence for mixed feelings. *Cognition and Emotion, 19*, 671–691..

Schimmack, U., & Crites, S. L. (2005). The stucture of affect. In D. Albarracin, B. T. Johnson & M. P. Zanna (Eds.), *The handbook of attitudes* (pp. 397–435). Hillsdale, NJ: Erlbaum.

Schofield, J. W. (1991). School desegration and intergroup relations. In G. Grant (Ed.), *Review of research in education* (Vol. 17, pp. 335–409). Washington, D.C.: American Educational Research Association.

Schwarz, N. (1990). Feelings as information: Informational and motivational functions of affective states. In R. M. Sorrentino & E. T. Higgins (Eds.), *Handbook of motivation and cognition* (Vol. 2, pp. 521–561). New York: Guilford.

Schwarz, N. (2002). Situated cognition and the wisdom of feelings: Cognitive tuning. In L. F. Barrett & P. Salovey (Eds.), *The wisdom in feelings: Psychological processes in emotional intelligence* (pp. 144–166). New York: Guilford.

Schwarz, N., & Clore, G. L. (1983). Mood, misattribution, and judgments of well-being — Informative and directive functions of affective states. *Journal of Personality and Social Psychology, 45*(3), 513–523.

Schwarz, N., & Clore, G. L. (1988). How do I feel about it? The information function of affective states. In K. Fiedler & J. Forgas (Eds.), *Affect, cognition and social behavior: New evidence and integrative attempts* (pp. 44–63). Toronto: C.J. Hogrefe.

Schwarz, N., & Clore, G. L. (1996). Feelings and phenomenal experiences. In E. T. Higgins & A. W. Kruglanski (Eds.), *Social psychology: Handbook of basic principles* (pp. 433–465). New York: Guilford.

Schwarz, N., Strack, F., Kommer, D., & Wagner, D. (1987). Soccer, rooms, and the quality of your life — Mood effects on judgments of satisfaction with life in general and with specific domains. *European Journal of Social Psychology, 17*(1), 69–79.

Sedikides, C. (1994). Incongruent effects of sad mood on self-conception valence: Its a matter of time. *European Journal of Social Psychology, 24*(1), 161–172.

Sengupta, J., & Johar, G. V. (2001). Contingent effects of anxiety on message elaboration and persuasion. *Personality and Social Psychology Bulletin, 27*(2), 139–150.

Shaver, P., Schwartz, J., Kirson, D., & Oconnor, C. (1987). Emotion knowledge — Further exploration of a prototype approach. *Journal of Personality and Social Psychology, 52*(6), 1061–1086.

Shiv, B., & Fedorikhin, A. (1999). Heart and mind in conflict: The interplay of affect and cognition in consumer decision making. *Journal of Consumer Research, 26*(3), 278–292.

Siemer, M., & Reisenzein, R. (1998). Effects of mood on evaluative judgements: Influence of reduced processing capacity and mood salience. *Cognition & Emotion, 12*(6), 783–805.

Silberman, E. K., Weingartner, H., & Post, R. M. (1983). Thinking disorder in depression — Logic and strategy in an abstract reasoning task. *Archives of General Psychiatry, 40*(7), 775–780.

Simon, H. A. (1967). Motivational and emotional controls of cognition. *Psychological Review, 74*(1), 29-39.

Sinclair, R. C. (1988). Mood, categorization breadth, and performance-appraisal — The effects of order of information acquisition and affective atate on halo, accuracy, information-retrieval, and evaluations. *Organizational Behavior and Human Decision Processes, 42*(1), 22–46.

Sinclair, R. C., & Mark, M. M. (1995). The effects of mood state on judgmental accuracy — Processing strategy as a mechanism. *Cognition & Emotion, 9*(5), 417–438.

Sinclair, R. C., Mark, M. M., & Clore, G. L. (1994). Mood-related persuasion depends on (mis)attributions. *Social Cognition, 12*(4), 309–326.

Skowronski, J. J., & Carlston, D. E. (1989). Negativity and extremity biases in impression-formation — A review of explanations. *Psychological Bulletin, 105*(1), 131–142.

Slovic, P., Finucane, M., Peters, E., & MacGregor, D. G. (2002). The affect heuristic. In T. Gilovich, D. Griffin, & D. Kahneman (Eds.), *Heuristics and biases: The psychology of intuitive judgment* (pp. 397–420). New York: Cambridge University Press.

Smith, S. M., & Petty, R. E. (1995). Personality moderators of mood congruency effects on cognition — The role of self-esteem and negative mood regulation. *Journal of Personality and Social Psychology, 68*(6), 1092–1107.

Solomon, R. L., & Corbit, J. D. (1974). Opponent-process theory of motivation: 1. Temporal dynamics of affect. *Psychological Review, 81*(2), 119–145.

Srull, T. K. (1987). Memory, mood, and consumer judgment. *Advances in Consumer Research, 14,* 404–407.

Staats, C. K., & Staats, A. W. (1957). Meaning established by classical-conditioning. *Journal of Experimental Psychology, 54*(1), 74–80.

Stayman, D. M., & Aaker, D. A. (1988). Are all the effects of ad-induced feelings mediated by ad. *Journal of Consumer Research, 15*(3), 368–373.

Steiner, J. E., Glaser, D., Hawilo, M. E., & Berridge, K. C. (2001). Comparative expression of hedonic impact: affective reactions to taste by human infants and other primates. *Neuroscience and Biobehavioral Reviews, 25*(1), 53–74.

Stone, D. N., & Kadous, K. (1997). The joint effects of task-related negative affect and task difficulty in multiattribute choice. *Organizational Behavior and Human Decision Processes, 70*(2), 159–174.

Strack, F. (1992). The different routes to social judgements: Experiential versus informational strategies. In L. L. M. A. Tesser (Ed.), *The construction of social judgements* (pp. 249–275). Hillsdale, NJ: Erlbawm.

Strahan, E. J., Spencer, S. J., & Zanna, M. P. (2002). Subliminal priming and persuasion: Striking while the iron is hot. *Journal of Consumer Research, 20,* 271–280.

Swinyard, W. R. (1993). The effects of mood, involvement, and quality of store experience on shopping intentions. *Journal of Consumer Research, 20*(2), 271–280.

Taylor, S. E. (1991). Asymmetrical effects of positive and negative events — The mobilization minimization hypothesis. *Psychological Bulletin, 110*(1), 67–85.

Thorson, E., & Friestad, M. (1989). The effects of emotion on episodic memory for television commercials. In P. Cafferata & A. M. Tybout (Eds.), *Cognitive and affective responses to advertising* (pp. 305–325). Lexington, MA: D.C. Heath and Company.

Tice, D. M., Bratslavsky, E., & Baumeister, R. F. (2001). Emotional distress regulation takes precedence over impulse control: If you feel bad, do it! *Journal of Personality and Social Psychology, 80*(1), 53–67.

Tiedens, L. Z., & Linton, S. (2001). Judgment under emotional certainty and uncertainty: The effects of specific emotions on information processing. *Journal of Personality and Social Psychology, 81*(6), 973–988.

Trope, Y., & Neter, E. (1994). Reconciling competing motives in self-evaluation — The role of self-control in feedback seeking. *Journal of Personality and Social Psychology, 66*(4), 646–657.

Trope, Y., & Pomerantz, E. M. (1998). Resolving conflicts among self-evaluative motives: Positive experiences as a resource for overcoming defensiveness. *Motivation and Emotion, 22*(1), 53–72.

Velten, E. (1968). A laboratory task for induction of mood states. *Behaviour Research and Therapy, 6*(4), 473–482.

Verplanken, B., Hofstee, G., & Janssen, H. J. W. (1998). Accessibility of effective versus cognitive components of attitudes. *European Journal of Social Psychology, 28*(1), 23–35.

Watson, D., & Clark, L. A. (1997). Measurement and mismeasurement of mood: Recurrent and emergent issues. *Journal of Personality Assessment, 68*(2), 267–296.

Watson, D., Clark, L. A., & Tellegen, A. (1988). Development and validation of brief measures of positive and negative affect — The PANAS scales. *Journal of Personality and Social Psychology, 54*(6), 1063–1070.

Watson, D., & Tellegen, A. (1985). Toward a consensual structure of mood. *Psychological Bulletin, 98*(2), 219–235.

Watson, D., & Tellegen, A. (1999). Issues in the dimensional structure of affect — Effects of descriptors, measurement error, and response formats: Comment on Russell and Carroll (1999). *Psychological Bulletin, 125*(5), 601–610.

Watson, D., Wiese, D., Vaidya, J., & Tellegen, A. (1999). The two general activation systems of affect: Structural findings, evolutionary considerations, and psychobiological evidence. *Journal of Personality and Social Psychology, 76*(5), 820–838.

Weaver, J. B., & Laird, E. A. (1995). Mood management during the menstrual-cycle through selective exposure to television. *Journalism & Mass Communication Quarterly, 72*(1), 139–146.

Wegener, D., & Petty, R. E. (1994). Mood management across affective states — The hedonic contingency hypothesis. *Journal of Personality and Social Psychology, 66*(6), 1034–1048.

Westermann, R., Spies, K., Stahl, G., & Hesse, F. W. (1996). Relative effectiveness and validity of mood induction procedures: A meta-analysis. *European Journal of Social Psychology, 26*(4), 557–580.

White, G. L., Fishbein, S., & Rutsein, J. (1981). Passionate love and the misattribution of arousal. *Journal of Personality & Social Psychology, 41*(1), 56–62.

Williams, P., & Aaker, J. L. (2002). Can mixed emotions peacefully coexist? *Journal of Consumer Research, 28*(4), 636–649.

Wilson, T. D., Dunn, D. S., Kraft, D., & Lisle, D. J. (1989). Introspection, attitude change, and attitude-behavior consistency: The disruptive effects of explaining why we feel the way we do. *Advances in Experimental Social Psychology, 22*, 287–343.

Wilson, T. D., & Schooler, J. W. (1991). Thinking too much — Introspection can reduce the quality of preferences and decisions. *Journal of Personality and Social Psychology, 60*(2), 181–192.

Winkielman, P., Zajonc, R. B., & Schwarz, N. (1997). Subliminal affective priming resists attributional interventions. *Cognition & Emotion, 11*(4), 433–465.

Wojciszke, B., Brycz, H., & Borkenau, P. (1993). Effects of information-content and evaluative extremity on positivity and negativity biases. *Journal of Personality and Social Psychology, 64*(3), 327–335.

Worth, L. T., & Mackie, D. M. (1987). Cognitive mediation of positive affect in persuasion. *Social Cognition, 5*(1), 76–94.

Wyer, R. S., Clore, G. L., & Isbell, L. M. (1999). Affect and information processing. In M. P. Zanna (Ed.), *Advances in experimental social psychology* (Vol. 31, pp 1–77) .

Yeung, C. W. M., & Wyer, R. S. (2004). Affect, appraisal, and consumer judgment. *Journal of Consumer Research, 31*(2), 412–424.

Yeung, C. W. M., & Wyer, R. S. (2005). Does loving a brand mean loving its products? The role of brand-elicited affect in brand extension evaluations. *Journal of Marketing Research, 42*(4), 495–506.

Yi, Y. (1990). Cognitive and affective priming effects of the context for print advertisements. *Journal of Advertising, 19*(2), 40–48.

Young, P. T. (1961). *Motivation and emotion: A survey of the determinants of human and animal activity.* New York: Wiley.

Zajonc, R. B. (1965). Social facilitation. *Science, 149*, 269–274.

Zajonc, R. B. (1980). Feeling and thinking — Preferences need no inferences. *American Psychologist, 35*(2), 151–175.

Zajonc, R. B., & Markus, H. (1982). Affective and cognitive-factors in preferences. *Journal of Consumer Research, 9*(2), 123–131.

Zanna, M. P., & Rempel, J. K. (1988). Attitudes: A new look at an old concept. In D. Bar-Tal & A. W. Kruglanski (Eds.), *The social psychology of knowledge* (pp. 315–334). Cambridge: Cambridge University Press.

Zillmann, D. (1971). Excitation transfer in communication-mediated aggressive behavior. *Journal of Experimental Social Psychology, 7*(4), 419–&.

Zillmann, D. (1980). The anatomy of suspense. In P. H. Tannenbaum (Ed.), *The entertainment function of television* (pp. 133–163). Hillsdale, NJ: Erlbaum.

Zillmann, D. (1988a). Mood management through communication choices. *American Behavioral Scientist, 31*(3), 327–340.

Zillmann, D. (1988b). Mood management: Using entertainment to full advantage. In L. Donohew, H. E. Sypher, & E. T. Higgins (Eds.), *Communication, social cognition, and affect* (pp. 147–171). Hillsdale, NJ: Erlbaum.

Zuckerman, M. (1996). Sensation seeking and the taste of vicarious horror. In J. B. Weaver III & R. Tamborini (Eds.), *Horror films: Current research on audience preferences and reactions* (pp. 147–59). Mahwah, NJ: Erlbaum.

12

Self-Regulation
Goals, Consumption, and Choices

KATHLEEN D. VOHS

University of Minnesota

ROY F. BAUMEISTER AND DIANNE M. TICE

Florida State University

Modern, economic society depends on consumers and their consumption, and, in some ways, the more they consume, the more successful the economy. But few consumers can really have all they might want. They have to curb their appetites to live within their financial means (or, if not within the limits of how much money they have, at least within the limits of how much they can borrow). They must restrain their consumption of some goods (such as cigarettes, fattening foods, and alcohol) that are bad for their health if consumed to excess. They have to restrain their consumption of goods (such as violent video games or pornography) that they perceive as a moral threat. They must restrain their consumption of goods (such as illegal drugs) that are illegal.

In short, the consumer's life is one of restrained consumption. In this chapter, our focus is on those restraints. Self-regulation is the inner psychological process by which people alter their responses to bring them into line with various rules and standards. In this way, it is also the crucial mechanism by which people curb their impulses to consume and keep their consumption within acceptable limits and parameters.

Overviews of the nature of consumer behavior note that setting goals and engaging in actions to attain them are the cornerstone of purposive consumer behavior (Bagozzi & Dholakia, 1999). For instance, investment and savings goals direct consumer spending (e.g., Shefrin & Thaler, 1988) and health goals, such as dieting, lead people to make different choices about caloric intake (Bagozzi & Edwards, 2000).

In this chapter, we detail how the study of self-regulation can explain and predict consumer behavior. Starting with the observation that self-regulation is needed when people deviate or want to deviate from rationality, next we will detail self-regulatory theory by specifying three ingredients of (a) standards, (b) the operation of moving oneself from current to desired state, and (c) monitoring one's progress along the way. Then we move from the basics to applications to consumer matters. Issues closely relevant to consumer behavior that have been linked to self-regulation are: impulsive and compulsive spending, vulnerability to persuasion, the effects of making choices on regulatory behavior, and self-regulation's role in making good decisions. Please note at the outset that this overview of research on self-regulation will focus only on conscious self-regulation; we do not discuss the increasingly important effects of nonconscious regulatory processes on consumption. This chapter thus provides an understanding of the crucial role of self-regulation in consumer behavior. The relevance of self-regulation lies at the heart of marketing by understanding consumption in order to increase consumer welfare.

DEFINITIONAL ISSUES

Self-regulation can be understood as the process by which one response is overridden, allowing for a different response to take its place. To regulate something is to bring it under the control of rules or laws, and in the process to change it, and so self-regulation is a matter of bringing one's own behavior into line with standards such as laws, goals, morals, ideals, or rules. Essentially, the person's initial impulse may be to act, feel, or think in a particular way that goes against these personal or social standards, and so self-regulation enables the person to resist that impulse so as to respond in a more appropriate or desirable manner.

Self-regulation is most commonly seen in the struggle between impulses and restraints (cf. Hoch & Loewenstein, 1991). Oftentimes, a person will have a goal that requires inhibiting one response and perhaps replacing it with another. Situations that require self-control are those in which an urge that goes against the person's overarching goal is stimulated and therefore restraints to change, modify, or otherwise alter the impulse are required.

We use the terms "self-regulation" and "self-control" interchangeably, although other authors may use them to refer to different constructs. The main distinction that is sometimes made is to equate self-control with conscious, effortful processes, whereas self-regulation is a broader term that also encompasses nonconscious regulating processes such as how the body maintains a constant temperature or heartbeat. Our focus in this chapter will be exclusively on the conscious, effortful processes by which the self exerts control over its responses, and hence any distinction between conscious self-control and nonconscious self-regulation is irrelevant to this discussion.

The word "self" in self-control refers both to the fact that it is the self (the "I") that is doing the operating and that the self is what is being operated upon (the "me"). Impulses and urges are two terms also used interchangeably and they refer to a state that arises typically from the interaction between an underlying motivation (e.g., to increase good feelings) and a stimulus in the environment (e.g., a shiny piece of jewelry that is available for purchase). There are four broad domains in which self-control can be exercised (Vohs & Baumeister, 2004a). Mental control encompasses regulating cognitive processes, ranging from controlling attention (e.g., trying to concentrate) to suppressing unwanted thoughts (e.g., Wegner, 1994) and even guiding one's reasoning process toward a desired conclusion (Baumeister & Newman, 1994). Emotion control is essentially the effort to induce, suppress, or prolong an emotional state. Impulse control typically involves keeping oneself from acting on desires or appetites deemed unsuitable, whether these be food cravings, addictive yearnings, sexual or violent inclinations, or other temptations. Last, performance management encompasses the attempt to perform at a certain (usually high) level, such as persistence in the face of failure or fatigue, speed/accuracy tradeoffs, or trying not to choke under pressure.

We start with an example that illustrates the ingredients of self-regulation. A young man wants to buy a pickup truck but cannot afford it. He assesses how much money he has and how much money he needs to buy the truck, which indicates how much more money he needs to have. Accordingly, he forms a plan to save some money from his weekly paycheck, which will enable him to afford the truck in time for, say, a planned camping trip next summer. Along the way, however, he may have to resist temptations to spend his income on a new stereo system. His success depends on monitoring his progress at saving money while also resisting these intervening temptations.

The example of saving up to buy includes the four main ingredients of self-regulation. First, one has to have a goal, in this case to save enough money to buy the truck. Second, one has to be motivated to reach the goal: the more he wants the truck, the more likely he is to be willing to make the efforts and sacrifices required to save. Third, he has to monitor progress toward the goal, rather than just vaguely stuffing a few bucks into various envelopes scattered in his desk and sock drawer now and then. (In particular, he has to keep track of how much he has saved and how much he needs, plus ideally whether he is on schedule of saving enough to get the truck in time for the camping trip.) Last, he will need the willpower to resist other temptations in order to keep saving toward his goal.

STANDARDS

Standards are the ideals, norms, goals, or other rules or guidelines that provide the endpoint of the regulatory chain. Akin to the idea that the first step in the buyer's decision process involves consumers recognizing that they have an unmet need, self-regulators' first step is to recognize that there exists a standard that they want to meet. Typically, this step is accompanied by an almost-immediate comparison to see where one is located with respect to the standard. (We return to the idea of monitoring in a subsequent section.) Assuming there exists a difference between current and goal states, the person needs self-control. If there is no discrepancy, there is no need for self-control. Much of the strain on self-regulation can sometimes be alleviated by modifying standards. For example, whereas many people struggle to lose weight so as to conform to social standards of fashionable thinness, some instead join the so-called size-acceptance movements that essentially say it is okay to be fat. In the same vein, recent decades have witnessed a marked reduction in the social stigma associated with bankruptcy and with out-of-wedlock reproduction, thereby reducing the demand on people to regulate their behavior as tightly as they may have in past decades to avoid those outcomes.

The more specific the standard, the better able people are to reach the goal. Specificity in setting the goal helps at two levels. One, being specific about the goal reduces the goal's abstractness, which clarifies the steps needed to reach the goal (see Gollwitzer, 1999; Gollwitzer & Brandstätter, 1997). Instead of trying to reach the abstract goal to "save money," the consumer who sets the more concrete goal of "forgoing a latte three times a week" is better positioned to reach the ultimate goal of saving more money.

Two, specific goals (or the creation of subgoals) allow for better monitoring of progression toward the goal. With a precise endpoint, one can see how to measure current states and distance to the goal. Grocery shopping with a list makes it easy to see which foods still need to be acquired by looking at which foods are already in the cart. In addition to having a specified goal, having only one goal makes self-regulation more successful than when people have two or more conflicting goals. Research on children similarly shows that when adults give different and inconsistent rules to children, the children behave inconsistently (Maphet & Miller, 1982).

In general, having clear standards is a benefit to goal attainment, but new research suggests that holding highly rigid standards can at times lead to worse self-regulation. Research by Soman and Cheema (2004) found that when people violated a standard they had set for themselves, their subsequent goal-directed behavior faltered—with the result being even worse than the performance of people who held no performance standards. The researchers found that a feeling of failure from the violation of standards was key, especially when goals were perceived as being "all of none." This deleterious outcome is best avoided by choosing moderate standards: Standards that are too low may not motivate people, but those that are too high may demotivate people via the potential for perceptions of standard violations and concomitant feelings of failure. Baumeister, Heatherton, and Tice (1994) compared the stringent, so-called "zero tolerance" standards to a military tactic of putting all one's troops on the front line. It offers the best chance of preventing any breach, but it leaves nothing in reserve to cope when a breach does occur. They suggested, for example, that the zero tolerance approaches help explain the seeming paradox that the United States has relatively high rates of both teetotalers and alcoholics, in contrast to other cultures that emphasize controlled drinking as the standard.

One motivational theory that has had widespread success in predicting consumer behavior centers on differences in behavioral guides. *Promotion* behavior pursues positive outcomes, whereas *prevention* behavior avoids negative outcomes (Higgins, 1997). Promotion behavior is aimed at achieving ideal standards, such as hopes, wishes, and dreams. Prevention behavior is geared toward goals that people feel obligated to achieve, such as duties and responsibilities. Research has shown that when people are in a promotion mode and geared toward goal attainment, their actions are best described as eager, whereas when people are in a prevention mode, vigilance is the best descriptor of behavior.

Moreover, if a situation calls for a strategy that contrasts with the type of goal being pursued (e.g., a promotion goal that is pursued by being vigilant), people fail to achieve their goals more often than when goal types and behavioral strategies are matched. Recent research suggests that promotion and prevention may not only be suited for certain strategies, but for information processing routes as well. Research by Pham and Avnet (2004) revealed that ideal standards bias people's reactions in terms the emotions evoked by incoming information, whereas ought standards lead to processing a message based on its content. That different standards activate different psychological systems (affect vs. cognition) has broad implications for behavioral change strategies. This finding, in addition to providing information such as knowing whether a woman seeks to lose weight because of her dreams of fitting into a shapely swimsuit or because her partner told her to do so, will help predict whether her diet will be upset by a distressing incident versus new findings indicating that weight is more genetic than people once thought (i.e., emotional vs. cognitive information-processing styles).

One type of goal conflict occurs when people come up against a seemingly unattainable goal. Outside the laboratory, it is often difficult to know whether one's goals are unattainable or unrealistic. A lack of progress toward the goal may be the first sign, but such signs are hard to read. For example, consider the thousands upon thousand of young men who sacrifice years of their lives, plus their best educational opportunities, plus their physical well-being in pursuing the goal of becoming a professional athlete. The immense rewards associated with such success make the dream appealing, and the young men can see exemplars who have achieved that level of success on television any time. But far more than 99% of those who pursue the dream will fail, and it may take a very long time (often until one has spent 5 years in college, with no degree) to realize that one is never going to succeed at that level.

Wrosch et al. (2003) showed that people who disengage from seemingly impossible goals are mentally healthier than those who stay entrapped in the pursuit of this type of goals. In this case, the goal of using one's limited effort and time effectively conflicts with trying to achieve the impossible, and the healthiest strategy is to drop the frustrating goal. Although little is known about when people consciously decide to abandon a goal (cf. Shah, Bodmann, & Hall, 2005), this line of research has much theoretical and practical importance.

Another type of goal conflict is probably endemic to consumer behavior, because almost all consumers face a variety of tradeoffs in which they want incompatible things. Most fundamentally, perhaps, consumers want to save their money but also to acquire goods and services. And even if they are determined to purchase, there are endless further tradeoffs: higher quality versus lower price; sensible comfort versus fashionable looks; name brand reputation versus more immediate availability; higher safety rating versus better gas mileage; less filling or great taste. Rational choice is supposedly the human cognitive tool for making such choices, but recent evidence suggests that requires effort and consumes some of the same resources required for self-regulation, as we will explain shortly.

MOTIVATION AND COMMITMENT; OR, THE "GUN TO THE HEAD" TEST

Having standards does not mean that good self-regulation will necessarily follow. Recall that people may have standards but perceive that their behavior already meets these standards. Others may see that they fall short of standards but not care. People must be motivated to enact a behavioral change. The motivation to self-regulate is probably crucial to its success, although it is probably the least studied of the four basic ingredients.

How common are irresistible impulses? Some people claim—and some legal institutions condone—that under some circumstances, impulsive actions may not be controllable due to either strong emotional states or other internal breakdowns of will. Self-regulatory researchers generally find these claims dubious. Suppose, for example, that a compulsive gambler was truly unable to resist the temptation to gamble. Taken to an extreme, this would mean that if a gun was held to the head of the person who was about to lay down another bet at the blackjack table, he or she could not help but place that bet. Yet, this rarely (if ever) happens: People, if they really want, are able to avoid giving into all kinds of impulses (Baumeister & Heatherton, 1996). One of the FBI's foremost experts on serial killers observed that although the killers sometimes claimed that their homicidal impulses were irresistible, not one of the thousands of murderers documented by this group had been committed in the presence of a police or security officer (Douglas, 1996). Apparently, the irresistible impulses could be resisted if the chances of getting caught right away were high.

Considering the truly irresistible impulses is a good way to appreciate the contrast. A person cannot remain standing forever, and sooner or later will sit, lie, or fall down, even if threatened at gunpoint to remain standing or else. People cannot hold their breaths indefinitely, and even if the willpower is sufficient to keep them from breathing for a long time, they will pass out and start breathing. They cannot remain awake indefinitely, and some people die because of falling asleep on sentry duty or while driving. There are of course a few other bodily functions that are likewise truly irresistible, and it is appropriate to refrain from blaming people who break down under such circumstances. In contrast, the spouse who ruins the family's monthly budget by spending an inordinate amount on a new jacket, and who seeks to justify the act by saying "I couldn't resist," is almost certainly speaking merely figuratively (which is to say lying).

For consumer behavior, the important implication is that purchasing impulses are in fact almost always resistible. But consumers may prefer to conceal that fact from themselves and their families. "I had to have it, I couldn't help myself" is much preferred over the more realistic "I deliberately chose to blow a lot of our money on selfish gratification for myself."

People may get the motivation to control themselves from the situation; the crime examples illustrate the power of external punishments. Or rewards may drive the motivation to control oneself. Some empirical work has found that even when the ability to engage in self-regulation is significantly impaired, people can nevertheless control themselves when an incentive is offered, such as money or believing that one's self-control efforts will be a benefit to oneself or a vulnerable group (Alzheimer's patients) (Muraven & Slessareva, 2003).

The outcome of the self-control endeavor may be a sufficient enough prize to encourage controlling oneself. A model of self-regulation from the health domain (Rothman, 2000) describes the desire to initiate a behavioral change as stemming from the positivity of the outcome. Thus, most people believe that smoking cigarettes is bad for them, and many have quit smoking in order to improve their odds of avoiding lung cancer in later life, but others may not value that outcome. Teenagers who disdain old-age health issues as absurdly remote, soldiers in combat zones who doubt their chances of surviving the war, prisoners serving life sentences, and AIDS sufferers, among others, may not find the increased chance of escaping lung cancer in the distant future a sufficient reason to give up the pleasure of smoking.

Motivation may come from perceptions of the difficulty (or possibility) that the goal can be attained. One model that focuses on outcomes derived from consumption (Bagozzi & Dholakia 1999) places self-efficacy at center stage, such that people's beliefs about the skills they possess to achieve their goals is crucial to their willingness to self-regulate. This model emphasizes self-efficacy as key to whether and how the consumer will approach the self-control task. Self-efficacy is particularly related to the means chosen to reach the goal. Thus, if a person considering a diet thinks, "If I am offered cake at parties, I am confident that I can refuse and instead I eat fruit," he or she is displaying self-efficacy and its aid in selecting suitable means to attain the larger goal of limiting caloric intake.

Research on the overconsumption of food (binge eating) supports the importance of self-beliefs in motivating people to self-regulate—as well as the demotivating effects of not believing in oneself. This research shows that women who hold high standards for thinness but believe that they are overweight have high binge eating tendencies—but only if they also doubt their ability to reach their goal (Vohs et al., 1999, 2001). Women who believe that they close the gap between their current (perceived) body image and their desired body image do not overeat.

Last, motivation may also depend on beliefs about how self-control works. Recent work suggests that laypersons have personal beliefs about how self-control operates (Mukhopadhyay & Johar, 2005). Moreover, personal theories about self-control can help predict variance in goal attainment, presumably because they influence commitment to self-regulatory goals and subsequent motivation.

MONITORING AND FEEDBACK LOOPS

Monitoring involves being aware of the self's behavior or responses and comparing them to a standard. Breakdowns in the monitoring aspect of self-regulation are not as well understood as are breakdowns in the other ingredients, but nevertheless breakdowns in monitoring are a key reason that goals are not met. Monitoring is perhaps more central to understanding consumption than other aspects of goal attainment, which suggests that more work could be done to underscore its value in consumer behavior.

The study of monitoring is also worth pursuing for practical reasons. Baumeister et al. (1994) proposed that monitoring is the aspect of self-regulation that is most readily susceptible to improvement, and so whenever one desires to improve self-control, improving monitoring generally offers the most promising opportunity for substantial (and immediate) improvement. Thus, if someone has money problems, it may be difficult to increase income or willpower, and revising standards downward (to accept being on the verge of bankruptcy) may be problematic. Nonetheless, keeping close tabs on one's income and expenses, such as by keeping a daily written record of spending, is often both viable and effective. Likewise, it is no accident that successful dieters count calories and otherwise carefully monitor what they eat, and that the cessation of monitoring often undermines dietary efforts.

One reason (and there are many) for the difficulty of self-control is that effective self-control necessitates that people monitor their behavior, but the act of monitoring means a focus on the present time (Vohs & Schmeichel, 2003). This "extended-now" state renders people vulnerable to incoming urges and impulses and makes long-term goals seem less pressing. This extended-now theory of self-regulation is supported by studies showing that self-regulation changes time perception, such that self-regulators feel that time is moving more slowly as compared to non-regulators (and as compared to veridical durations). Monitoring one's progress, although being an integral part of goal strivings, may, unfortunately, bring about perceptions that time is moving slowly, which in turn reduces self-regulatory efforts (Vohs & Schmeichel, 2003).

Classic work on chronic dieters demonstrates that not only the reliability or strength of the signal is important in monitoring, but also the interpretation of the feedback. Research on dieting versus nondieting[1] shoppers shows that dieters buy less when they have not recently eaten than when they have recently eaten, whereas the opposite pattern holds with nondieters (Nisbett & Kanouse, 1969). Why would dieters buy less when they are hungrier? The idea is that the bodily signals that one has not eaten in a while is a positive, reinforcing signal that the goal of limiting caloric intake is being met. Therefore, dieters—who have the goal of restricting caloric intake—buy less food when they get feedback that they are meeting their dieting goals.

As another example of how interpretation can undermine monitoring, Gilovich (1983) addressed the seeming paradox that many gamblers continue to gamble and even seem to remain optimistic, even though most lose more than they win, and, in fact, long-term net losses are almost guaranteed by the structure of the gambling system (by which, for example, the casino or indeed the state government must make a net profit, so it pays out less in winnings than it takes in). Accurate monitoring would have to reveal to gamblers that they had lost more often than won. But Gilovich (1990) found that gamblers discounted some losses as "near wins" and so felt encouraged despite losing. They were much less likely to discount their wins as "near losses." By taking credit for all successes and discounting some wins, they were able to transform the objective feedback of overall loss into the subjective impression of efficacy and confidence at "continued" success.

Monitoring allows people to assess distance to the goal. This can be done by looking back at how far one has come or how much more has to be done. A new study suggests that seeing how far one has come may be more effective in promoting self-regulation than how much more work is ahead. Nunes and Dreze (in press) gave loyalty cards to customers at a professional car wash. Some customers were given a card that required 10 car wash purchases before one free car wash was earned, whereas others were given a loyalty card that required 8 car wash purchases before the reward. However, those in the 10 car wash condition were given their card with two "free" stamps already affixed to it, making the amount of effort needed to reach the goal equivalent. Perceptions of progress mattered, though—34% of customers filled their card and earned a free car wash in the 10 washes-but-2-free condition, whereas only 19% did in the 8 washes condition. Moreover, the goal gradient was steeper for those in the 10-but-2 condition, such that after receiving the loyalty card, they came to the car wash more often than did the 8 wash condition customers. Believing that one has come a long way apparently increases commitment to the goal, thereby leading to heightened efforts to reach it.

OPERATIONS: USING SELF-REGULATORY STRENGTH TO MOVE ONESELF TO THE GOAL

Even if a consumer has clear, unconflicting, and appropriate standards and monitors his or her behaviors, the goal will not necessarily be met. Without the capacity to move oneself from current to goal state, the best laid plans and all the monitoring in the world will not be good enough. The strength model of self-control has been the most comprehensive model in terms of specifying what allows people to move toward a goal. Self-regulation, from this perspective, is governed by a finite supply of energy that is used in all controlled responses and actions (Baumeister & Heatherton, 1996; Baumeister et al., 1994; Vohs & Baumeister, 2004b).

The strength model depicts the ability to get oneself to the goal as a function of the amount of self-regulatory resources available when exhibiting the response. Because self-regulatory resources are put toward all acts of self-control, the supply is rather fragile and precious and, according to the model, can diminish to a point where impaired self-control can be observed. Therefore, laboratory experiments testing the strength model of self-control typically have used a two-task paradigm. The first task varies on its self-control demands such that some participants are given a task that is thought to require expending self-regulatory resources, whereas others are given a neutral task that does not require self-regulatory resources. The second task, then, is the measure of self-control ability. To test the strength model, the hypothesis put forth is that differences in the second task reveal that the experimental condition in the first task was indeed an act of self-control that presumably depleted the self's resources. Indeed, the work of over 30 published experiments (e.g., Baumeister et al., 1998; Muraven et al., 1998; Schmeichel, Vohs, & Baumeister, 2003; Vohs, Baumeister, & Ciarocco, 2005; Vohs & Heatherton, 2000) supports the idea that the "operate" component of self-regulation can be modeled as a stock of energy that becomes temporarily reduced with use, with the consequence being disrupted self-control. Several extensions of the model that are particularly applicable to understanding consumer behavior are discussed hereafter.

Early investigations of the model focused on confirming basic tenets. Here, researchers took core self-control tasks, such as persisting at a different task, controlling one's emotions or suppressing thoughts and tested whether engaging in these activities left people with less ability to engage in another self-control act. For instance, Baumeister et al. (1998) asked participants to control either emotions to an emotional film, or to watch the film naturally (without instructions). Subsequently, they were given a set of difficult anagrams to solve. In line with expectations from the strength model, participants who had to modify their emotions solved fewer anagrams. Notably, both a happy and sad film were used and type of film did not affect anagram performance; only being in a condition that required emotional modification mattered.

Manipulations of thought suppression complemented these findings. One experiment, which asked participants to suppress thoughts of a white bear (Wegner, Schneider, Carter, & White, 1987) versus complete simple mathematical problems, showed that the former group was less able to control their emotions later when asked to do so (Muraven et al., 1998; Study 3). A host of similar studies confirmed the basic tenets of the model using a variety of different manipulations and dependent measures. Therefore, we have concluded that self-regulation relies on a precious, but finite, resource that is taxed when self-control is needed. The term "regulatory resource depletion" is now used to suggest phenomena when one does not have the strength to exert proper control over one's actions.

An important extension of the regulatory resource model indicates that the same resource is used for making choices. A series of studies by Vohs, Baumeister, Twenge, Schmeichel, and Tice (2005/under review) showed that after people make a series of choices, their self-control falters and fails just as it does following prior exertions of self-control (see also Baumeister et al., 1998). In particular, participants in several studies were asked to make a series of binary choices between various consumer items (e.g., would you rather have a red or a blue t-shirt? Would you rather have a vanilla scented candle or an almond scented candle?). Others simply rated the same items on various dimensions, including whether they had used them in the past 6 months. Those who made choices were subsequently poorer at self-control on a variety of measures, including holding one's hand in ice water or making oneself consume a healthy but bad-tasting beverage.

Because the same resource appears to be used for both decision making and for self-regulation, Baumeister et al. (1998) introduced the term "ego depletion" to refer to the state of diminished resources. The term "ego" was adopted in a deliberate homage to Freud, who was one of the only psychologists to speak (albeit rather vaguely) of the self as an energy system.

For consumer psychology, the implication is that two perennially central issues in consumer behavior—namely decision making and self-control—rely on a common resource that becomes depleted when one engages in either activity. Hence either activity can have an adverse effect on the other. Making effortful decisions is likely to impair subsequent self-control, and, conversely, exertions of self-control may reduce the care and effort that people put into their subsequent choices. Examples of both patterns will be covered below.

APPLYING THE STRENGTH MODEL TO CONSUMER ISSUES

Overeating

Eating is one of the most fundamental consumption acts. People must eat to survive, and yet society, dietary, and health reasons prompt many people to regulate their caloric intake at some point in their lives. However, the outlook for people wanting to lose weight and maintain their slimmer size is dim: comprehensive long-term research (Kramer, Jeffery, Forster, & Snell, 1989) revealed that fewer than 3% of all dieters will manage to keep the weight off, and, by 5 years after their weight loss, most will weigh more than they did when they began dieting.

Thus, the concept of limiting food intake is a tantalizing topic for self-control theorizing because, unlike other consumption domains such as drinking alcohol, smoking cigarettes, or even having sex, people need to take in calories to live. Consequently, achieving the goal of losing weight by cutting caloric intake cannot be met using the same strategies as could be used to limit alcohol intake, namely refraining from consumption altogether.

Thus neither the advantages nor the inherent problems (see above) of zero tolerance self-regulation policies are relevant to eating, and controlled moderation is the only viable strategy for controlling food intake. Stopping oneself from taking in any calories is a route that no one can take without landing in the hospital, which therefore means that people wanting to control their food consumption must use other strategies. Consequently, the intricacies of dieting make it one of the most perplexing and difficult regulatory tasks that one may take on.

Being exposed to forbidden foods is a situation that many dieters face and if they intend to stick to their diet, they must override their desire to eat the tempting food. Baumeister et al. (1989) recruited a sample of hungry undergraduates (but who were not selected because they were dieters) and created a situation to mimic the forbidden-food situation that dieters often face. Participants were seated in front of a tray of chocolate chip cookies that had been freshly baked in the laboratory (with the aroma of warm chocolate wafting throughout the room for everyone to smell), chocolate candies, and a rather large bowl of radishes. Some participants were told they could eat as many of the cookies and candies as they wanted, whereas participants in the forbidden-food condition were told that their task was to eat the radishes. (There was also a no-food condition.) After 5 minutes of privacy with the foods, participants were given a geometric puzzle to solve, which was unsolvable, although, of course, they did not know this. Persistence in the face of frustration and disappointing failure is one standard measure of self-regulation, because the vexing failures presumably create the desire to quit so as to do something else instead, and, in order to persist, the performer must override this urge to quit. Participants in the forbidden-food condition were less persistent at the puzzle as compared to participants in either of the other two conditions. Being tempted by the chocolates but not being able to indulge presumably taxed the resources of those participants, which therefore impaired their ability to continue on the difficult cognitive task.

Another set of studies examined the effects of self-regulatory resource depletion in a context in which people have pre-established consumption goals. In these studies, chronic dieters were the main focus, and the hypothesis was that underlying differences in long-term goals render people differentially affected by the same situational self-control demands. Vohs and Heatherton (2000) asked dieters and nondieters to watch a boring video on Bighorn sheep while being seated either next to or far away from a tempting bowl of M&M candies. This formed the temptation factor, which was combined with instructions that the candies were available to be eaten ("go ahead, help yourself") or that the candies were needed later in the day, and therefore "please don't touch" them. After watching the boring video for 10 minutes, participants were moved to a different room to "taste and rate" three flavors of ice cream. Ice cream consumption was the measure of self-control.

Given that nondieters do not (by definition) control their caloric consumption, they would not have to override the temptation (and hence become depleted) to eat the yummy chocolates. (That said, it was not the case that the nondieters consumed many M&Ms—only five nondieters ate the snacks and even they did so minimally.) Hence, nondieters' ice cream intake was predicted to be relatively unaffected by the two factors of temptation and allowance to eat the snacks. For dieters, however, the urge to eat the chocolates must be acted on. Therefore, Vohs and Heatherton expected that only dieters would expend regulatory resources in the presence of tempting snacks. However, if an external force prevented them from having to exert *self*-control to not eat the candies—such as a caution from the experimenter to not partake in the snacks—then their supply of self-regulatory resources would be spared. As a result, the researchers predicted that ice cream consumption would be highest among dieters who sat close to the snacks and were allowed to eat them.

The predictions were confirmed. Dieters ate significantly more when they were highly tempted by sitting next to the M&M candies and were told the candies were available to be eaten. Notably, however, dieters ate the least when they were seated far from the chocolates and were told they could indulge in them (which, being dieters, they did not). This pattern may represent an inoculation effect, which would be an intriguing idea for future depletion research. And as expected, nondieters' ice cream eating was not determined by whether they had sat near or far from the M&Ms nor whether they were allowed to eat the candies.

A second study replicated the loss of self-control among dieters after having engaged in emotion regulation (Vohs & Heatherton, 2000). In this experiment, dieters watched a sad movie about a woman on her deathbed saying good-bye to her husband, two sons, and mother. Participants were asked either to suppress their emotions or to watch the movie naturally. Ice cream eating again represented self-regulatory ability. As expected, asking these women to engage in emotion regulation, as opposed to being able to watch the same movie but without having to suppress sad feelings, led them to eat more ice cream later. Both groups reported similarly negative feelings after the movie, meaning that differences in mood did not account for eating differences, but having to stifle those feelings led to a depletion of the resource that later would have helped them control their ice cream consumption.

A third study showed that persistence drops after dieters have had to overcome the temptation of forbidden foods. In this study, being highly tempted by an array of snack foods led subsequent persistence on an embedded-figures task to be impaired, relative to persistence among dieters who watch the same boring film and looked at the same snack foods but who did so from across the room.

Thus, regulating the consumption of food determines and is determined by the availability of self-regulatory resources—but only among people for whom caloric regimens were highly important and thus demanded much regulation. Moreover, having to defeat the desire to eat a tempting, but forbidden, food in order to make oneself eat a less appealing, but healthier, food also takes away from the capacity to later bring one's performance in line with standards.

Overspending: Impulsive Purchases

Just as controlling one's eating represents a special kind of self-control problem, so does spending. If one includes the paid consumption of energy and utilities such as water, the typical modern citizen spends money every day. Much spending is fairly inevitable, and other spending is appropriate and judicious. Still, some money is spent impulsively and in ways that the consumer may later regret. Vohs and Faber (2005) turned to the self-regulatory resource model to help explain why people spend money impulsively.

Impulsive buying is defined purchases that result from an urge that arises spontaneously within the consumer to buy. In impulsive purchasing, the desire to purchase is unreflective (Strack, Werth, & Deutsch, in press) and not based on any careful considerations of why the product should be acquired (Rook & Fisher 1995). Vohs and Faber surmised that impulses to buy would arise and be acted upon more often when people's self-regulatory capacity is reduced than when it is fully intact. The results of empirical work support this idea.

Two studies manipulated attentional control demands as a way to alter self-regulatory ability. Participants watched an audioless video of a woman being interviewed that, at the same time, showed irrelevant words appearing at the bottom of the screen every 30 seconds. Some participants were not told anything about the irrelevant words, whereas those in the depletion condition were told not to look at the words and if they found themselves orienting toward the words to revert their eyes back to the interviewee. In one study, participants were then given a scale to measure immediate buying impulses; in another study, participants were shown high-end products (e.g., watches, appliances) and asked to state the price at which they would be willing to purchase the item. Both studies showed an effect of self-regulatory resource availability on impulsive spending tendencies: participants who had earlier used their resources to orient their attention away from a distracting stimulus later reported stronger urges to spend impulsively (Study 1) and gave higher willingness-to-pay rates (Study 2), as compared to participants who did not engage in attention control. Feeling a spontaneous urge to buy is, as we saw earlier, the root of impulsive spending, and one way to control that urge is to believe a product is not worth its monetary price (Rook & Fisher, 1995). That self-regulatory resource depletion affected impulsive spending tendencies both at the level of the impulse and the cognitive strategies to rein in that impulse is noteworthy.

Moreover, this research found that actual impulsive spending was affected by resource availability. One of these studies asked participants in the resource depletion condition to suppress thoughts of a white bear; the other study asked participants to read aloud a boring text with emotion. Subsequently, participants were given the opportunity to buy in a spontaneous, ad hoc purchasing situation in a mock store. As predicted, participants whose resources had been depleted spent more impulsive than did participants who had not expended their resources. This effect was found in terms of purchases of bookstore-like products, such as school insignia pens, coffee mugs, and decks of playing cards (Study 3) as well as grocery store items, such as cookies, pretzels, and potato chips (Study 4).

Moreover, the latter two studies incorporated the idea of underlying tendencies toward a certain type of self-control failure, in a similar manner as was done in the work on chronic dieters (Vohs & Heatherton, 2000). In this work, however, generalized tendencies to want to spend money impulsively were measured prior to the experimental manipulation of self-regulatory demands. Similar to the findings on dieters, Vohs and Faber (2005) also found that the effect of self-regulatory resource depletion was exacerbated among people who normally feel strong desires to buy impulsively. In contrast to the work on dieters versus nondieters, however, was the fact that even participants who were low in general impulsive spending tendencies showed heightened purchasing behavior when depleted. This effect is probably due to the idea that nondieters and nonimpulsive spenders differ in that almost everyone needs to control their spending at some level, irrespective of whether buying impulsively is generally a problem, whereas nondieters are presumably not controlling their eating to the same extent.

Hence, spontaneous urges to buy something too are affected by self-regulatory resources (Vohs & Faber, 2005). Whether from regulating attention, stifling thoughts, or modifying one's behavior to appear unemotional, people who had engaged in self-control earlier were more likely to buy impulsively. Perhaps the most intriguing result of this line of research is that decreases in the self's controlled processes strengthen the feeling to buy impulsively. Theoretically, the strength of the urge and inhibitions on that urge have been considered to be orthogonal, but to detect a change in the potency of the impulse with depletion suggests that empirically the two core components of self-control may be intricately related. Research at the intersection of the urge and the self's regulatory resources (Vohs & Mead, in preparation) presents an exciting new avenue of study.

Thus far we have discussed about impulsive consumption in the context of purchasing. Impulses may also affect what people consume in another fashion, namely watching movies. The core idea behind this research (Novemsky & Baumeister, 2005) was that, at times, choosing a more virtuous option may require overriding an impulse to do something nonvirtuous, and so self-regulation is required for choosing the path of virtue. In one study, Novemsky and Baumeister (2005) offered students a choice of a movie to watch (for later, not immediate viewing). The options contained either intellectually edifying fare and low-brow sleaze. These options were presented either before or after an intensive study session, which was assumed to be somewhat depleting. Different levels of depletion were inferred based on study time in the library (i.e. by having students make the choice as they first approached the library to begin the evening's studying, or as they departed after several hours of work) or were experimentally manipulated by having participants make a brief series of choices and decisions (e.g., Vohs et al., 2005). Sure enough, when students were fresh and their resources were not depleted from studying, they exhibited a marked preference for the highbrow films. After a study session, however, they shifted heavily toward the lowbrow fare.

The implication is that some consumer decisions present a challenge between higher and lower impulses. Self-regulation enables human beings to override the latter sort of impulse in order to pursue the former. But when self-regulatory resources have been depleted, preferences shift toward the less virtuous product.

Making Intelligent Decisions

The ability to make the right decision should (by definition) free consumers from a great deal of regret. However, because the "right" option is not always readily apparent when one faces a decision, the human psyche has developed highly intelligent methods for determining the best answer, such as cost-benefit analyses. For instance, consumer theorists recognize that consumers' attempts to control consumption frequently entail assessing a decision's economic costs (Hoch & Loewenstein, 1991). As we have already said, both decision making and self-regulation are crucial aspects of the self's executive function, and both seem to consume the same resource (Baumeister, 1998). The agentic self must oversee the active parts of the decision making process, such as problem solving, but it is not involved in automatic information processing actions such as categorization. Indeed, one review of the problem solving literature (Crinella & Yu, 2000) concluded that almost all problem solving requires executive functioning. On that basis, Schmeichel, Vohs, and Baumeister (2003) proposed that the logical style of problem solving, with its inefficient manner but high-quality output, would be deeply related to self-regulatory resources. The fewer resources people have, they predicted, the worse they would be able to solve problems.

The first test of the hypothesis involved a standard attention control task in which participants' attentional abilities were challenged by having to ignore distracting words during a video they were to be watching or being allowed to gaze at the distractors as much as they wished (similar to the method described earlier). Next, participants solved problems from the analytical section of the Graduate Record Examination (GRE), an entrance exam required to apply to most graduate studies programs. The results showed clear support for the hypothesis, in that participants who had earlier controlled their attention completed fewer GRE problems, got fewer problems correct, and achieved a worse effort/speed trade off quotient overall as compared to participants whose earlier task did not involve self-control (Schmeichel et al., 2003).

Another experiment tested the idea that only higher-order, intelligent processing would be interrupted by self-regulatory resource depletion by including a task that required a rudimentary mental task as well one that needed more advanced thinking. In this study, the manipulation of self-regulatory resources was followed by the reading comprehension section of the GRE and a nonsense syllable task, which is used often in cognitive science as a working memory task (note that the tasks were counterbalanced in order). In the former task, participants read a passage about Toni Morrison's writings and her identity as a black, female author and, in the latter, participants were asked to read a list of 15 nonsense words and memorize them in the space of 60 seconds. As expected, self-regulatory resource depletion condition related to ability to correctly work out the answers to the reading comprehension questions but was unrelated to memorization skills.

Thus far we have presented evidence that depletion impairs intelligent thought. But does it actually alter decision making? A series of studies by Amir, Dhar, and Baumeister (2005/unpublished) had participants first undergo a brief depletion manipulation and then confront one of several standard decision problems. The results suggested that ego depletion brought on by brief acts of self-control can shift decision making toward simpler, lazier, and more superficial styles of decision making. Several such patterns were observed. First, depleted participants seem less inclined to face up to tradeoffs in a cognitively complex, integrative manner. Simonson (1989) proposed that choosing a compromise option requires more cognitive work than simply choosing an extreme one, because the compromise requires the person to process multiple, conflicting criteria and trade some degree of one for some measure of the other. Amir et al. (2005) found that depleted participants were more likely to choose extreme options over compromise ones, as compared to non-depleted participants.

Second, depleted participants showed a stronger version of the asymmetric dominance effect (also called the attraction effect; Huber, Payne, & Puto, 1982). This effect can be understood in the context of a decision problem that has both an easy and more difficult choice. That is, it is a choice between three options, two of which are quite different in specific attributes but similar in overall quality (hence the difficult choice), and the third is a decoy that is clearly inferior to one of the other options on all attributes (the easy choice). Depleted participants avoided the difficult choice by letting the easy decision stand in for the difficult one as well. In other words, depleted participants were more likely than others to pick the item that was superior to the decoy.

Third, depleted participants were more likely than others to choose to do nothing. In this pair of studies, participants were asked to choose between two products (e.g., two cell phones) but also had the option of taking neither and "going to another Web site." Whereas nondepleted participants would often make a selection from what was offered, depleted ones tended to avoid the choice.

The bottom line is that making decisions can be an effortful, thoughtful task in which the various product options and attributes are carefully weighed and compared—but this sort of decision process requires considerable resources. When people's resources have been depleted by prior acts of self-control, people shift toward more simplistic and less effortful styles of choosing. They become more prone to biases, and they also become more prone to choose not to choose anything.

In short, consumers' ability to make good decisions depends on the extent to which they have previously engaged in self-control. When consumers inhibit impulses or force themselves to do what they do not want to do, they will be less prepared to make rational decisions, especially under circumstances of complex layers of information. Decision making, then, is more than a function of opportunity or willingness, this research implies, but also executive functioning ability.

DECISION MAKING MAKES CONSUMERS VULNERABLE TO A LOSS OF SELF-CONTROL

In the previous section, we examined rational decision making as an outcome of self-regulatory resource depletion. In the current section, we look at the opposite side of that equation, whether making choices affects subsequent self-control.

Recall that we described the relationship between decision making and self-regulation as related to their constituency as components of executive control. To be clear, by decision making we mean the type of active, option-weighing, high-level processing that was studied in the work by Schmeichel et al. (2003). Willfully engaging in control over oneself would seem to naturally relate to exerting control over the environment in the form of making choices.

Extant findings suggest that although people generally like the idea that they have control over their life outcomes, at the time same people may find making choices onerous. Consider, for example, the coffee company Starbucks. In 2003 Starbucks boasted that each store offered consumers over 19,000 beverage "possibilities" and that the number was growing with the introduction of their new superheated option. Contrast Starbucks' underlying assumption (that more options are good) with the now-seminal work by Iyengar and Lepper (2000) who showed that shoppers who were given 24 varieties of jam, as opposed to six varieties, were less likely to buy jam at all and were more dissatisfied when they did make a purchase. The rational choice model would likely say that having more options is better for consumers because each option increases the potential for preference-matching. Although this may be true relative to conditions under which no options are available, more likely is that people today view the proliferation of choice with distress, resulting in what Schwartz (2000) refers to as "the tyranny of freedom." Hence, Vohs and colleagues set out to test whether active decision making renders ensuing self-control less successful due its debilitating effect on ego resources. Their research included eight studies that converged on the conclusion that making choices depletes self-regulatory resources.

In one study participants made a series of binary choices between different versions of household products. For instance, participants in the choice condition were asked to choose between different colors of t-shirts, different colors of socks, and differently-scented candles. Participants in the no-choice condition were asked to give their opinions on eight advertisements taken from popular magazines. Thus, participants in both conditions were asked to evaluate the stimuli and engage in detailed thought processing, but only in the binary choice condition did participants render a decision. For the second task, participants were taken to a second room with a new experimenter and asked to hold their arm in a tank of freezing cold water for as long as they could (the cold pressor task). As would be predicted on the basis of a limited-resource model of self-control, participants who had previously made decisions were less able than were participants who had not had to make choices to keep their arm submersed in icy cold water. A second experiment that also used this manipulation found that participants in the choice condition, as opposed to no-choice condition, procrastinated longer when they could have been studying for an upcoming intelligence test.

In two additional studies, participants made decisions about the course in which they were currently enrolled, or they simply evaluated similar aspects of the course. Afterwards, they attempted to solve unsolvable puzzles (in one study) or were asked to perform mathematic problems (in another study). In line with the previous findings, these experiments showed that participants who made decisions about how the course should be run persisted less at the subsequent puzzle, as well as attempted fewer math problems and got fewer correct, as compared to participants who only evaluated aspects of the course.

There were several confounds with the laboratory experiments, namely the idea that being in the choice condition primed the idea of choices, which led to participants in that condition being more aware of their ability to choose to stop the second task. To get around that alternate explanation, Vohs et al. went to a local mall and asked shoppers to complete a questionnaire about how much they had made choices throughout their shopping trip that day. Then they asked the same shoppers to complete as many 3 digit + 3 digit addition problems as they could. A second experimenter surreptitiously recorded the length of time spent on the math problems, and this measure in addition to number of problems attempted was the indicator of self-control ability. As expected, shoppers who said that they had made many active choices were less persistent at the math problems, both in terms of number of problems attempted and duration, than were shoppers who said they had made fewer choices. This effect held even when statistically controlling for amount of time spent shopping and other pertinent variables such as age and gender. Given that all shoppers were exposed to the same scale that would have primed them with the same choice-related concepts, it is unlikely that a simple priming effect could explain the naturalistic experiment. In other words, this field study showed that compared to consumers who had consumers who had made fewer choices during their shopping trip, those who had made multiple choices were less able to engage in the self-control needed to persevere at tedious math problems in the middle of a shopping mall.

In short, because the executive aspect of the self is involved in both decision making and controlled processes, the two functions are intimately related. This interrelation means that when one is engaged, the other is later impaired. The assumption is that self-regulatory resources grease the wheel for both decision-making processes and controlled processes to operate smoothly. If there are fewer self-regulatory resources due to decision making, self-regulation will be crippled; and, as we saw earlier, if there are fewer self-regulatory resources because of more basic acts of self-control, decision making will be poorer. Studies showing how easily goal attainment can be thwarted hint at the preciousness and fragility of self-regulatory resources.

SUMMARY

Setting standards or goals is the first important step in self-regulation. If people see that their current state is discrepant from their desired goal state, they may engage in behavior to try to meet their goal. In order to be effective at producing behavior change, goals should be specific, consistent, and attainable. People need to be motivated to change, and see themselves as capable of changing, in order for effective self-regulation to occur.

Not only does one need to have standards for self-regulation, one needs to monitor one's progress toward meeting those standards. Monitoring involves being aware of the self's behavior or responses and comparing them to the standard. Keeping track of one's purchases by keeping a running total of the dollar amount spent is an example of monitoring one's consumer spending. Monitoring allows people to assess distance to the goal. Effective monitoring requires accurate and reliable feedback about one's progress toward the goal. A breakdown in monitoring is a key reason why goals are not met, and improved monitoring is one of the best ways to improve self-control in all spheres.

Even if a consumer has specific, consistent, and appropriate standards and monitors his or her behaviors, the goal will not necessarily be met. Willpower or self-control strength is necessary to bring behavior in line with the standard. Self-control functions like a muscle that can be depleted with use but strengthened over time. Self-regulation is governed and limited by a finite supply of energy or strength that is used for all controlled responses and actions (as well as for other executive functions, such as making choices). Engaging in one self-control task leaves less energy available for subsequent self-control tasks.

Self-control can affect consumers in areas as varied as eating, spending, and making choices and decisions (including purchasing decisions). If people have to restrain their eating when they are hungry for dietary or other reasons, they use some of their self-control energy and thus have less of this resource available subsequently to engage in other self-control tasks. Likewise, people who engage in initial acts of self-control may be less able to control their eating. People whose self-regulatory capacity is reduced by engaging in self-control tasks of various kinds are more likely to make subsequent impulsive purchases and to choose self-indulgent products than people whose self-control was not depleted.

Self-regulatory resource depletion brought on by brief acts of self-control was found to impair intelligent thought and shift decisions toward simpler, lazier, and more superficial styles of decision making. This research implies that decision making is more than just a function of opportunity or willingness; decision making is also executive functioning ability. Not only does engaging in self-control affect subsequent decision making, but decision making can affect self-control as well. Active decision making can render subsequent self-control less successful due to its depleting effect on self-regulatory resources. Self-regulatory resources provide the energy for both active decision making and a wide variety of self-control tasks.

NOTES

1. Although the original research compared obese versus nonobese consumers, Herman, Olmstead, and Polivy (1983) revolutionized research on eating with their insight and empirical data showing that chronic dieting is the driver of most of the effects found between obese and nonobese participants, due to the fact that the obese people were very often chronically dieting. When the analyses were conducted using restrained eaters (the technical term for chronic dieters) versus nonrestrained eaters, this distinction captured the lion's share of the variance in terms of past research on obese versus nonobese participants.

REFERENCES

Bagozzi, R. P., & Edwards, E.A. (2000). Goal-striving and the implementation of goal intentions in the relation of body weight. *Psychology and Health, 15,* 255–270.

Bagozzi, R. P., & Dholakia U. (1999). Goal-setting and goal-striving in consumer behavior. *Journal of Marketing, 63,* 19–32.

Baumeister, R. F. (1998). The self. In D. T. Gilbert, S. T. Fiske, & G. Lindzey (Eds.), *Handbook of social psychology* (4th ed., pp. 680–740). New York: McGraw-Hill.

Baumeister, R. F., & Heatherton, T. F. (1996). Self-regulation failure: An overview. *Psychological Inquiry, 7,* 1–15

Baumeister, R. F., & Newman, L. S. (1994). Self-regulation of cognitive inference and decision processes. *Personality and Social Psychology Bulletin, 20,* 3–19.

Baumeister, R. F., Bratslavsky, E., Muraven, M., & Tice, D. M. (1998). Ego depletion: Is the active self a limited resource? *Journal of Personality and Social Psychology, 74,* 1252–1265.

Baumeister, R. F., Heatherton, T. F., & Tice, D. M. (1994). *Losing control: How and why people fail at self-regulation.* San Diego, CA: Academic Press.

Crinella, F. M., & Yu, J. (2000). Brain mechanisms and intelligence: Psychometric *g* and executive function. *Intelligence, 27*, 299–327.

Douglas, J. E. (1996). *Mindhunter: Inside the FBI's elite serial crime unit.* New York: Pocket Books.

Gilovich, T. (1983). Biased evaluation and persistence in gambling. *Journal of Personality and Social Psychology, 55*, 1110–1126.

Gilovich, T. (1990). The cognitive psychology of gambling, *Journal of Gambling Studies, 6*, 31–42.

Gollwitzer, P. M. (1999). Implementation intentions: Strong effects of simple plans. *American Psychologist, 54*, 493–503.

Gollwitzer, P. M., & Brandstätter, V. (1997). Implementation intentions and effective goal pursuit. *Journal of Personality and Social Psychology, 73*, 186–199.

Herman, C. P., Olmstead, M. P., & Polivy, J. (1983). Obesity, externality, and susceptibility to social influence: An integrated analysis. *Journal of Personality and Social Psychology, 45*, 926–934.

Higgins, E. T. (1997). Beyond pleasure and pain. *American Psychologist, 52*, 1280–1300.

Hoch, S. J., & Loewenstein, G. F. (1991). Time-inconsistent preferences and consumer self-control. *Journal of Consumer Research, 17*, 492–507.

Huber, J., Payne, J. W., & Puto, C. (1982). Adding asymmetrically dominated alternatives: Violations of regularity and the similarity hypothesis. *Journal of Consumer Research, 9*, 90–98.

Iyengar, S. S., & Lepper, M. R. (2000). When choice is demotivating: Can one desire too much of a good thing? *Journal of Personality and Social Psychology, 79*, 995–1006.

Kramer, F. M., Jeffery, R. W., Forster, J. L., & Snell, M. K. (1989). Long-term follow-up of behavioral treatment for obesity: Patterns of weight regain among men and women. *International Journal of Obesity, 13*, 123–136.

Maphet, H. W. & Miller, A. L. (1982). Compliance, temptation, and conflicting instructions. *Journal of Personality and Social Psychology, 42*, 137–144.

Mukhopadhyay, A., & Johar. G. (2005). Where there is a will, is there a way? The effects of consumers' lay theories of self-control on setting and keeping resolutions. *Journal of Consumer Research, 31*, 779–786.

Muraven, M., & Slessareva, E. (2003). Mechanisms of self-control failure: Motivation and limited resources. *Personality and Social Psychology Bulletin, 29*, 894–906.

Muraven, M., Tice, D. M., & Baumeister, R. F. (1998). Self-control as a limited resource: Regulatory depletion patterns. *Journal of Personality and Social Psychology, 74*,774–789

Nisbett, R. E., & Kanouse, D. E. (1969). Obesity, food deprivation, and supermarket shopping behavior. *Journal of Personality and Social Psychology, 12*, 289–294.

Nunes, J. C., & Dreze, X. (2006). The endowed progress effect: How artificial advancement increases effort. *Journal of Consumer Research, 32*, 504–512.

Pham, M., & Avnet, T. (2004). Self-regulation and affect versus substance. *Journal of Consumer Research, 30*, 503–518.

Rook, D.W., & Fisher, R.J. (1995), Normative influences on impulsive buying behavior. *Journal of Consumer Research, 22*, 305–313.

Rothman, A.J. (2000). Toward a theory-based analysis of behavioral maintenance. *Health Psychology, 19*, 64–69.

Schmeichel, B. J., Vohs, K. D., & Baumeister, R. F. (2003). Intellectual performance and ego depletion: Role of the self in logical reasoning and other information processing. *Journal of Personality and Social Psychology, 85*, 33–46.

Schwartz, B. (2000). Self-determination: The tyranny of freedom. *American Psychologist, 55*, 79–88.

Shah, J.Y., & Bodmann, S., & Hall, D. (2005). *Automatic and deliberate goal management.* Presentation at Society for Social and Personality Psychology Annual Conference, Palm Springs, CA.

Shefrin, H. M., & Thaler, R. H. (1988). The behavioral life cycle hypothesis. *Economic Inquiry, 26*, 609–643

Simonson, I. (1989). Choice based on reasons: The case of attraction and compromise effects. *Journal of ConsumerResearch, 16*, 158–174.

Soman, D., & Cheema, A. (2004). When goals are counter-productive: The effects of violation of a behavioral goal on subsequent performance. *Journal of Consumer Research, 31*, 52–62.

Strack, F., Werth, L., & Deutsch R. (in press). Reflective and impulsive determinants of consumer behavior. *Journal of Consumer Research.*

Vohs, K. D., Bardone, A. M., Joiner, T. E., Jr., Abramson, L.Y., & Heatherton, T. F. (1999). Perfectionism, perceived weight status, and self-esteem interact to predict bulimic symptoms: A model of bulimic symptom development. *Journal of Abnormal Psychology, 108*, 695–700.

Vohs, K. D., & Baumeister, R.F. (2004a). Understanding self-regulation: An introduction. In R. F. Baumeister & K. D. Vohs (Eds.), *Handbook of self-regulation: Research, theory, and applications* (pp. 1–9). New York: Guilford.

Vohs, K. D., & Baumeister, R.F. (2004b). Ego-depletion, self-control, and choice. In J. Greenberg, S. L. Koole, & T. Pyszczynski (Eds.), *Handbook of experimental existential psychology* (pp. 398–410). New York: Guilford.

Vohs, K. D., Baumeister, R. F., & Ciarocco, N. J. (2005). Self-regulation and self-presentation: Regulatory resource depletion impairs impression management and effortful self-representation depletes regulatory resources. *Journal of Personality and Social Psychology, 88*, 632–657.

Vohs, K. D., Baumeister, R. F., Twenge, J. M., Schmeichel, B. J. & Tice, D. M. (2005). Decision fatigue exhausts self-regulatory resources. Unpublished manuscript. University of Minnesota, Minneapolis.

Vohs, K. D., & Faber, R.J. (2005). Spent resources: Self-regulatory resource availability impulse buying. Unpublished manuscript. University of Minnesota, Minneapolis.

Vohs, K. D., & Heatherton, T. F. (2000). Self-regulatory failure: A resource-depletion approach. *Psychological Science, 11*, 249–254.

Vohs, K. D., & Schmeichel, B. J. (2003). Self-regulation and the extended now: Controlling the self alters the subjective experience of time. *Journal of Personality and Social Psychology, 85*, 217–230.

Vohs, K. D., Voelz, Z. R., Pettit, J. W., Bardone, A. M., Katz, J., Abramson, L. Y., Heatherton, T. F., & Joiner, T. E., Jr. (2001). Perfectionism, body dissatisfaction, and self-esteem: An interactive model of bulimic symptom development. *Journal of Social and Clinical Psychology, 20*, 476–497.

Wegner, D. M. (1994). Ironic processes of mental control. *Psychological Review, 101*, 34–52.

Wegner, D. M., Schneider, D. J., Carter, S. R., & White, T. L. (1987). Paradoxical effects of thought suppression. *Journal of Personality and Social Psychology, 53*, 5–13.

Wrosch, C., Scheier, M. F., Miller, G. E., Schulz, R., & Carver, C. S. (2003). Adaptive self-regulation of unattainable goals: Goal disengagement, goal re-engagement, and subjective well-being. *Personality and Social Psychology Bulletin, 29*, 1494–1508.

13

Goal-Directed Consumer Behavior
Motivation, Volition, and Affect

HANS BAUMGARTNER

Pennsylvania State University

RIK PIETERS

Tilburg University

Consumer behavior, like other human endeavors, is unmistakably goal-directed. As Aristotle (1953, p. 3) said, "every act and every investigation, and similarly every action and pursuit, is considered to aim to some good," with the final aim of goal-directed behavior being happiness. "Happiness, then, is found to be something perfect and self-sufficient, being the end to which our actions are directed" (Aristotle, 1953, p. 15). Yet, between the daily activities of consumers and the ultimate ends to which they aspire there is a vast terrain in which more specific and mundane goals and affect provide direction and energy to behavior. It is this terrain that the present chapter explores. That is, we focus on the motivational and volitional properties of goals and the interplay between goals and affect in consumer behavior.

Proposing that consumer behavior is goal-directed seems like arguing that water is wet. Surprisingly, however, even though motivational and volitional concepts abound in the marketing literature, systematic research on goal-directed consumer behavior has been lacking. To be sure, researchers have investigated issues related to consumers' pursuit of goals. For example, both abstract goals such as values (Kahle, Beatty, & Homer, 1986; Kamakura & Novak, 1992) and concrete goals important in decision making and information processing (Bettman, 1979; Bettman, Luce, & Payne, 1998; Keller, 1987; see also Fishbach & Dhar, this volume) have been examined. If behaviors such as the purchase of routine products are thought of as the pursuit of simple, unproblematic goals, then attitude-behavior models may be interpreted as models of goal-directed behavior. In fact, these models have often been applied to situations in which the behavior is actually a more long-term, complex goal, such as losing weight (see the review by Sheppard, Hartwick, & Warshaw, 1988). In general, however, understanding goal-directed consumer behavior has not been emphasized in consumer research.

Research on affect has a longer tradition in the study of consumer behavior (Bagozzi, Gopinath, & Nyer, 1999; Cohen, Pham, & Andrade, chapter 11, this volume). However, despite the clear linkages between the goals of consumers and the affect they experience, there is little literature on the interface between affect and goal-directed behavior (Bagozzi et al., 2001).

In this chapter, we attempt to integrate research on goal-directed consumer behavior with relevant work on affect, and offer a model of goal pursuit and the functions that affect plays in goal setting and goal striving. The chapter focuses on goals that are selected in a reflective manner and pursued consciously, although we acknowledge that there are important and frequent automatic, nonconscious influences on goal pursuit (Chartrand & Bargh, 2002; see also Fishbach & Dhar, chapter 24, this volume). We start with a discussion of important issues related to goals and goal-directed behavior in general. We then turn to affect, distinguishing between endogenous (integral, task-relevant) and exogenous (incidental, ambient) affective influences and considering various functions of affect in goal pursuit.

GOAL STRUCTURE

Goals are internal representations of desirable states that people try to attain and undesirable states that they try to avoid. Goals differ from other motivational constructs, such as needs and drives, because they tend to be more concrete and domain-specific, thus exerting a stronger influence on particular consumer behaviors. Although, in the final analysis, high-level goals, such as trying to be independent, converge with terminal values, such as the importance of freedom, goals normally differ from values because they direct and energize behavior actively, rather than merely providing abstract evaluative criteria for appraising objects, events, or actions. Goals are relevant if an attempt to attain a desirable state can fail, or if consumers need to sacrifice something in order to get what they want. Turning off the air conditioner is usually not a goal but an act, but it becomes a goal when it is steaming hot outside and the consumer desires to be environmentally friendly. Following other goal theories, we assume that many of the interesting consumer behaviors are organized around the pursuit of goals, that goals are hierarchically structured from lower to higher levels, that goal-directed behavior is characterized by effort expenditure and persistence in the face of temptations and interruptions, and that goals are accessible to conscious awareness, although they need not always be top-of-mind during goal pursuit (Austin & Vancouver, 1996; Emmons, 1996; Locke & Latham, 1990). Before discussing how goal pursuit takes place, we examine goal features and goal structure. First, we discuss several goal features that characterize and distinguish the goals that consumers pursue. Second, since goal-directed behavior usually involves many different goals at varying levels, we describe how goals are organized.

Features of Goals

Individual goals have several features that give them meaning and account for their influence on behavior, and also distinguish them from each other (Austin & Vancouver, 1996; Emmons, 1989; Little, 1983; Winell, 1987). We will briefly discuss the features of goal content, desirability, importance, and feasibility.

Goal content. Goal content refers to what it is that consumers pursue. Several classifications of general or domain-specific goals or goal categories have been proposed, the only restriction being an author's creativity and drive toward completeness or generality. Winell (1987), for instance, distinguishes goals related to different life domains such as career, family, social/community, leisure, and material/environment. Emmons (1996) lists 12 general categories of goals, including achievement, affiliation/intimacy, power, independence, and self-presentation. Kasser and Ryan (1993, 1996) identify intrinsic (e.g., affiliation and personal growth) and extrinsic (e.g., power, materialism) goal orientations that are reflected in more specific goals. In the most general sense, goals may be approach-oriented (e.g., start an investment program) or avoidance-oriented (e.g., stop smoking).

Goal desirability. Because goals are internal representations of desired states to be attained or undesirable states to be avoided, the desirability of a goal is an important motivational dimension. Although avoidance goals focus on undesirable states, successful pursuit of these goals can be highly desirable, and some goals are more desirable than others. In expectancy-value theories of motivation (Heckhausen, 1977; Kuhl, 1982), value, utility, valence, or incentive are often used to capture a goal's desirability. The affect associated with a goal is an important determinant of goal desirability, and this issue will be discussed in greater detail below.

Goal importance. Goal importance is a related but different dimension. That is, goals may be highly desirable, such as having the right salad dressing, but not very important in the larger scheme of things. The distinction between goal desirability and importance is analogous to the distinction between the valence and strength dimensions of attitudes (Petty & Krosnick, 1995). Goal importance and the closely related notion of commitment are considered to be antecedents of the amount of effort expended on goal pursuit and the persistence of goal-directed behavior, and they have been linked to consumer involvement (Celsi & Olson, 1988), defined as the personal relevance or importance of a situation or task to a consumer's goals. One way to conceptualize importance is as the discrepancy between the current state of affairs and a desired state. The greater the discrepancy is perceived to be, the more important the goal is expected to be to the person. Commitment to the goal is particularly important when people do not freely choose their goals, but the goals are assigned to them (e.g., in work settings), and when goal pursuit is difficult and takes place over extended periods of time (e.g., losing weight or saving money for a new home).

Goal feasibility. In general, feasibility is a consumer's perception of control over whether or not a goal can be achieved (see Skinner, 1996). Constructs subsumed under this term include various forms of expectancies, probability of success, confidence, self-efficacy, controllability, and ease or difficulty of goal achievement.

Skinner (1996) proposed a useful distinction between agents (the person exerting control), means (pathways through which control is exerted), and ends (outcomes over which control is exerted) of control, and classifies the various control constructs found in the literature by whether they refer to agent-means, agent-ends, or means-ends relations. Agent-means relations are beliefs held by agents that they can use certain means. Examples of these beliefs are Bandura's (1977) self-efficacy expectations, Vroom's (1964) expectancies, Heckhausen's (1977) action-outcome expectancies, and Ford's (1992) capability-based personal agency beliefs. Agent-ends relations are beliefs held by agents that they can attain desired and avoid undesired outcomes. Evaluations of the probability of goal success and goal failure, the perceived ease or difficulty of goal attainment, and confidence in one's ability to attain a particular goal belong in this category. Skinner also argues that Bandura's later writings on self-efficacy (Bandura, 1989) place the construct in this group. Finally, means-ends relations are beliefs that certain causes (internal vs. external causes, actions vs. attributes of agents, etc.) will lead to desired or undesired outcomes. Rotter's (1966) locus of control, Vroom's (1964) instrumentalities, Bandura's (1989) response-outcome expectations, Heckhausen's (1977) outcome-consequence expectancies, and Ford's (1992) context-based personal agency beliefs are examples that fit this description.

Organization of Goals

Goals are organized in semantic networks, with goals and their means as nodes and the relationships between them as linkages. Although goal structures are latent, hypothetical constructs, we can distinguish horizontal and vertical dimensions in them. The horizontal dimension in goal structures represents the degree of similarity, relatedness or conceptual overlap between goals, based on goal content. Thus, related goals will tend to be closer together, because they share similar higher-level goals and lower-level means. The vertical dimension reflects the hierarchical organization of goals. The idea is that goals are hierarchically organized from lower-level, subordinate, more concrete means to higher-level, superordinate, more abstract ends (Bandura, 1989; Carver & Scheier, 2000; Hacker, 1985; Little, 1989; Locke, 1991; Powers, 1973; Vallacher & Wegner, 1985). The vertical location of goals in the hierarchy relative to other goals reflects their abstractness or specification level.

Goal abstractness. Concrete goals are generally more perceptual, observable in nature, referring to specific ways in which a desired state can be accomplished. An example would be the goal of eating smaller portions at lunch and dinner as part of a dieting plan. Abstract goals embody high-level motivational concerns that do not provide specific guides to behavior but indicate what the individual wants to be. The most abstract goals are not restricted to a particular domain and have motivational relevance for many different behaviors. Values are prime examples of abstract goals. The consumer behavior literature has explored low-level, domain-specific goals for advertising processing and decision-making and high-level goals such as values that guide consumption decisions in an abstract way.

In advertising, Pieters and Wedel (2007) distinguish four categories of processing goals that may be active during ad exposure, depending on the goal target (brand vs. ad) and goal content (learning vs. evaluation), based on the work of Keller (1987) and Dweck and Leggett (1988). They point out that most advertising theory is devoted to brand evaluation goals (as in dual process models such as the elaboration likelihood model), which cover a single quadrant of their conceptual model, and they show that once activated each of the goal categories rapidly affects advertising processing in systematically different ways.

In decision making, Bettman, Luce, and Payne (1998) consider four decision-making goals underlying choice processing: maximizing decision accuracy; minimizing decision effort; minimizing negative emotions during decision making; and maximizing the ease of justification of a decision. In attitude research, it is all too frequently assumed that people are motivated to hold accurate attitudes, although more recently other goals have been considered as well, such as the goal to hold attitudes that are congruent with core aspects of the self-concept (defense motivation) or the goal to express attitudes that have desirable interpersonal consequences (impression motivation) (see Chaiken, Wood, & Eagly, 1996). These decision-making goals may govern decisions independently of the specific life goals that consumer pursue. That is, during goal pursuit consumers need to make decisions between alternative courses of action, which may be influenced by various decision-making goals, in order to attain particular, more abstract life goals. However, it is clear that decision-making goals are at a relatively low level of abstraction in the goal hierarchy, particularly if one considers how they have been studied in empirical research (e.g., choosing among three cars described with numerical ratings on two attributes, ride quality, and miles per gallon).

In contrast, research on values can be viewed as investigating goals at a very high level of abstraction (Kahle et al., 1986; Kamakura & Novak, 1992). Much work on values has been concerned with investigating the structure of values, and the studies that have tried to relate values to actual behavior have generally shown very modest success. However, it should not be too surprising that goals at the highest level will not predict specific consumption behaviors very well, and means-end chain theory (Reynolds & Olson, 2001) was developed to make the linkages between values and consumption behaviors (in the form of preferences for certain product attributes) more explicit.

Three fundamental goal levels. The abstractness or specification level of a goal can be considered as a continuous characteristic, and goal research has applied quantitative measures to assess abstractness in goal structures (Pieters, Baumgartner, & Allen, 1995). Qualitative differences in the role and meaning of various levels of goals have been proposed as well.

For instance, Huffman, Ratneshwar, and Mick (2000) developed a hierarchical model of consumer goal structure that ranges from the most abstract goals such as life themes and values via life projects, current concerns, consumption intentions, and benefits-sought to feature preferences. As stated by these authors (p. 20), "we [as consumers] *acquire* possessions to *perform* actions that move us closer to *realizing* our values and ideal selves." In this way, the levels in the hierarchy link "having" to "doing" and ultimately to "being" goals.

We have found a different conceptualization of consumer goal structures useful (Pieters, 1993; Pieters, Allen, & Baumgartner, 2001; Pieters, Baumgartner, & Allen, 1995). Our framework is most closely related to Little's (1983, 1989) work on personal projects, Emmons' (1996) research on personal strivings, and Vallacher and Wegner's (1985) action identification theory. We distinguish three levels of goal-directed behavior: the "what" or identification level; the "why" or motivation level; and the "how" or operation level (see the left panel of Figure 13.1). The "what" level is the level at which goal pursuit is initially considered and it is the level at which a goal is set or a goal intention is formed. It is the basic level in the goal hierarchy, that is, the specific goal a consumer is currently pursuing. For example, in the domain of weight control, the "what" level generally involves the decision to lose body weight. Deciding to lose weight might entail more specific deliberations about how much weight to lose within a certain time frame, but the essence of goal setting is the formation of an intention to lose weight. The goal at the "what" level coordinates the execution of the lower-level goals at the operation level, whose attainment is needed to achieve the basic-level goal, and it is itself motivated by higher-level goals, which provide the ultimate meaning for why the goal is pursued.

Goals below the identification level may be called "how" goals because they indicate what has to be done in order to achieve the basic-level goal. With very simple behaviors aimed at relatively low basic-level goals, the operation level may be relatively undifferentiated or not even reach conscious

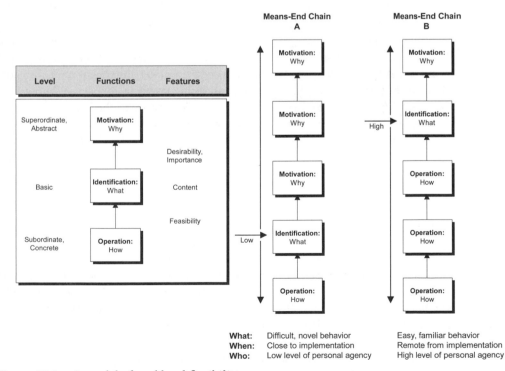

Figure 13.1   A model of goal level flexibility

levels of awareness, but in other cases it will consist of potentially many levels, at each of which distinct goal setting and goal striving processes take place. For example, in order to lose weight consumers can diet or exercise, and many specific decisions are involved in deciding how to diet or how to exercise.

Following action identification theory, we argue that there is an optimal level at which goal-directed behavior is identified, and that the level at which goal-directed behavior is identified may change depending on various factors such as the novelty and difficulty of the action, the time to goal implementation, and individual differences (see Vallacher & Wegner, 1989, on "levels of personal agency," and Emmons, 1996, on low-level versus high-level strivers). For example, the more difficult and novel the action is, and the closer the person is to goal implementation, the lower the abstraction level at which the action is identified. On the other hand, the more remote, easy and familiar the action, the higher the abstraction level. Furthermore, since lower-level behaviors can be components of many different higher-level actions, an initial move to a lower level (e.g., due to difficulties encountered during the enactment of a certain behavior) and a subsequent return to a higher level (because people attempt to control their behavior at the highest possible level) may lead to the emergence of entirely new actions (Vallacher & Wegner, 1987). In practice, it is not clear how often this will actually occur, and even though conscious control of behavior may shift to lower levels when difficulties are encountered, our framework assumes that the stream of goal-directed behaviors is ultimately controlled by the basic-level goal. Of course, the basic-level goal need not always be top-of-mind, and sometimes it will be nonconscious.

Goals above the identification level are "why" goals because they usually provide the motivation for pursuing the basic-level goal. Sometimes, when the basic-level goal is intrinsically motivating (e.g., spending a fun afternoon at the amusement park), there is little reason for studying superordinate goals, and such goal-directed behavior could be called consummatory rather than instrumental, since its execution is the only goal. However, frequently basic-level goals acquire their motivating potential through their association with higher-level goals. For example, losing weight is unlikely to be an intrinsically desirable goal. People desire to lose weight because they want to lead a long and healthy life, because they want to feel good about themselves, or because they want to be attractive and socially accepted by others. Thus, in order to understand what motivates goal pursuit and ultimately leads to a decision to try to attain the basic-level goal, one has to know what the "why" goals underlying a "what" goal are and how desirable they are to the consumer. In this sense, "why" goals endow goal-directed activities with meaning.

The idea of a three-layered goal hierarchy clarifies the goal features of desirability, importance and feasibility, because goal desirability and importance derive from the linkages of the basic-level goal to the superordinate goals at the motivational level, while feasibility derives from the linkages of the basic-level goal to the subordinate goals at the operation level.

The proposed three-layered goal hierarchy also emphasizes the crucial importance of goal identification because the motivation and operation of goal-directed behavior depend on how the goal is identified. In other words, "why" and "how" consumers do what they do depends on "what" they are doing. Consumers who "try to be environmentally friendly" (identification) may do so by "buying environmentally products" (operation) in order to "be good citizens" (motivation). On the other hand, consumers who "try to be good citizens" (identification) may do so by "being environmentally friendly" (operation) in order to "feel good about themselves" (motivation). This shows that the three goal levels are mutually dependent because motivation for one consumer or situation may be identification for another, as the right panel of Figure 13.1 indicates.

Means-end linkages. The hierarchical organization of goal structures in terms of the three goal levels, and the abstractness of the individual goals in the structure, are due to specific relationships between goals and behaviors, so-called means-end linkages, which form the fabric of goal structures. We distinguish several such linkages (see Emmons, 1996; Pieters, 1993; Pieters et al., 2001; Shah, Kruglanski, & Friedman, 2003). First, there can be vertical relations between goals at different levels in the hierarchy. For example, a consumer may want to lose weight in order to look more attractive, or exercise because of the belief that this is an efficient means of losing weight. We call such means-end linkages *instrumentalities*, because elements at lower levels in the hierarchy serve as means to achieve elements at higher levels as ends. If a single lower-level goal is connected to a single higher-level goal, ordinary instrumentality is present. Since consumers can also do different things simultaneously, each behavior for its own reasons, it is possible that several ordinary instrumentalities co-exist, a form of *parallel finality*. This occurs, for instance, when consumers entertain friends while cooking, shop while baby-sitting their neighbors' children, or eat while reading. Commonly, a given lower-level goal is associated with multiple higher-level goals, or several lower-level goals all lead to a single higher-level goal. In the former case we speak of *multifinality*, in the latter case of *equifinality*. For example, a consumer who sees physical appearance as instrumental to both personal confidence and social acceptance illustrates multifinality. In contrast, a consumer who pursues both dieting and exercising in order to lose weight exemplifies equifinality. When the multiple outcomes of an act are dissonant, rather than consonant as in multifinality, goal conflicts arise, as discussed later.

Second, there can be horizontal relations between goals at the same level of the hierarchy. For example, buying a washing machine may involve a sequential process in which information on various brands and their attributes is collected first, some decision rule is used to make a choice, and then the chosen brand is actually purchased at some store. Although one could argue that all three behaviors are instrumental for attaining the purchase goal, the difference is that each step is conditional on the previous step. Furthermore, it is probably more natural to think of the three behaviors as occupying the same level in the goal hierarchy. One might refer to such relations as *sequential finality*. Sequential finality introduces time and sequences of behavior (scripts and programs) that need to be executed in some order or combination as an explicit influence on goal pursuit. Goal structures represent consumers' knowledge of how and why to attain specific goals (Shah, Kruglanski, & Friedman, 2003), containing specific as well as more generalized knowledge of goal attainment, such as generalized scripts, which are typically comprised of sequential finality components. Bettman (1979) was one of the first to extensively discuss and use goal hierarchies in his information processing theory of consumer choice. For example, he considered how lower-level goals such as buying a washing machine can be broken down into more specific subgoals that are accomplished sequentially over time in pursuit of the overarching goal.

The five means-end linkages, shown graphically in Figure 13.2, jointly form the building blocks of goal structures. In the case of (simple) instrumentality, there is a single means-end linkage without branching. In the case of equifinality and sequential finality, there is a single goal and multiple means, and, in the case of multifinality and parallel finality, there are multiple goals and one or more means. Goal structures become activated during goal pursuit, as explained next.

GOAL PURSUIT

Goal pursuit unfolds over time and space. Following several comprehensive models of the processes involved in goal pursuit (Carver & Scheier, 2000; Gollwitzer, 1990; Heckhausen, 1991; Locke & Latham, 1990), we distinguish between two subprocesses: goal setting and goal striving. Goal setting is a motivational process during which a consumer has to decide whether or not to pursue a given goal, or chooses between conflicting goals. Goal striving is a volitional process concerned

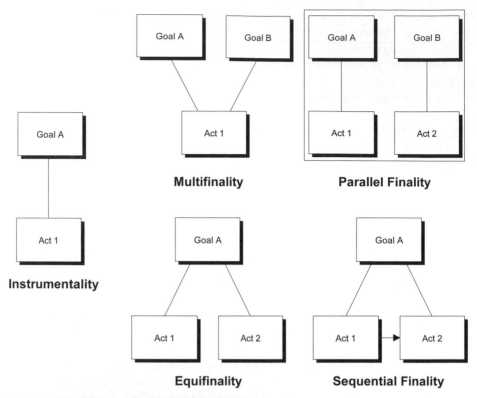

Figure 13.2   Components of goal structures

with working toward the chosen goal (Heckhausen, 1991). The distinction is old (Lewin, Dembo, Festinger, & Sears, 1944), but has been found useful by many authors over the years (see Bagozzi & Dholakia, 1999; Gollwitzer, 1990; Heckhausen, 1991; Oettingen & Gollwitzer, 2004). Table 13.1 summarizes goal setting and goal striving processes, and the specific activities involved in each.

Goal setting and goal striving processes occur at different levels in the goal hierarchy, and goal setting determines but is also determined by goal striving. For example, a consumer who has decided to lose weight and is working toward this goal has to make further decisions about whether to diet or exercise. If she decides to focus her efforts on exercising, still further decisions have to be made about which exercise regimen to adopt. Thus, it may seem difficult to separate the two processes since they are so heavily intertwined. To some extent this is the case. However, it is also true that the psychological problems involved in goal setting and goal striving are quite distinct (making a decision to pursue a certain goal and choosing between alternative goals in the case of goal setting versus planning, initiating action, monitoring progress, dealing with obstacles, and evaluating goal achievement in the case of goal striving). Furthermore, goal setting is presumably most important when a consumer makes the initial decision to pursue a particular goal, which we call the basic or identification level of goal pursuit, and our discussion of goal setting is mostly focused on this issue.

Goal Setting

Setting a goal refers to the processes involved in representing a desired state internally with the intention of reaching this state, including selecting a goal from among its alternatives (dieting vs.

Table 13.1 Goal Pursuit and Functions of Affect

Stage	Focus	Goal pursuit activities	Functions of affect
Goal Setting	Motivational: Why & what	a. Select goal b. Set goal level	a. Endogenous affective influence • Affect-as-goal • Affect-as-motivation b. Exogenous affective influence • Affect-as-filter c. Affective externality • Affect-as-hedonic spillover
Goal Striving	Volitional: How & when	a. Plan b. Implement plan c. Monitor progress d. *If goal is attained*: • Terminate e. *If goal is not attained*: • Continue striving • Revise plan • Postpone & reinstate plan • Abandon plan	a. Endogenous affective influence • Affect-as-feedback • Affect-as-volition b. Exogenous affective influence • Affect-as-volition • Affect-as-input c. Affective output • Affect-as-output

reducing debt), as well as committing oneself to a specific level to attain (lose 10 lbs. in the next 6 months or 4 lbs. in the next 4 weeks). The outcome of the goal-setting process is a goal intention, a self-instruction to strive toward attaining the desired state, which provides overall direction to goal pursuit and commits the person to trying to attain the desired state (Gollwitzer, 1990). But how does a consumer decide to pursue a particular goal?

As a first step, let us distinguish between external and internal goals (Austin & Vancouver, 1996). Although all goals are ultimately internally represented, some goals are motivated by external factors and other goals by internal ones. The prototypes of external goals are assigned goals, which have been studied extensively by industrial psychologists (Locke & Latham, 1990). Examples in a consumer behavior setting are buying "commissioned gifts" for weddings or similar occasions, dieting on the advice of the doctor, buying groceries with someone else's list, and so forth. We focus on internal goals (i.e., goals that are pursued primarily for personal reasons), but acknowledge that external factors can have a significant influence on goal pursuit (Fishbein & Ajzen, 1975). We also emphasize deliberate goal-setting processes, although goals may become activated incidentally, for example during exposure to means with strong linkages to higher-level desirable goals (such as when exposure to an ad for a low-fat product primes a weight loss goal). Such bottom-up goal priming effects have obvious relevance for consumer behavior (see Fishbach & Dhar, chapter 24, this volume).

Expectancy-value theories of goal setting. Consumers usually face a multitude of wishes that cannot all be enacted. One source of these wishes is the marketing environment, which is designed to arouse desires in consumers and encourage wish fulfillment. How do some wishes get transformed into goals that the consumer wants to attain (buying a Ford), while others remain mere fantasies (driving around in a Ferrari)? The general principle of expectancy-value theories is that the more desirable the goal, the higher the likelihood that it will be chosen, but the consumer also has to believe that goal achievement is feasible. There is a long tradition of expectancy-value models of motivation, starting with the work on level of aspiration (see Lewin et al., 1944, for a review), but the models that have had the greatest influence on the consumer behavior literature are two attitudinal theories, the theory of reasoned action (Fishbein & Ajzen, 1975) and the theory of planned behavior (Ajzen, 1985).

The theory of reasoned action (TRA) was originally designed to explain and predict volitional behaviors (e.g., using birth control pills or donating blood), which may be thought of as very simple goals, in the sense that goal pursuit is not problematic. However, the theory has often been applied to goals rather than behaviors (e.g., losing weight). TRA can be regarded as a theory of goal setting because the essence of the model is how people form intentions to engage in a behavior or pursue a goal. According to TRA, behavioral intentions are a function of a personal factor, attitude toward the behavior, and a social factor, subjective norms. Attitudes are conceptualized as the summation of a person's evaluation of the consequences of engaging in the behavior weighted by his or her beliefs that the behavior will lead to these consequences. The consequences have generally been rather cognitive in nature, although they could include affective experiences (e.g., guilty feelings or increased sexual pleasure as consequences of using birth control pills, as in Jaccard & Davidson, 1972), and they are usually rated on semantic differential scales such as good–bad. In the terminology used earlier, the belief strength ratings are similar to instrumentalities or outcome-consequence expectancies, and the evaluations measure the desirability of the consequences associated with the behavior.

Ajzen (1985, 1991) proposed the theory of planned behavior (TPB) as an extension of TRA to deal with situations in which a person does not have complete volitional control over the behavior (i.e., a person cannot decided at will whether or not to perform the behavior). Ajzen argues that in such cases perceived behavioral control (i.e., the perceived ease or difficulty of performing the behavior, which reflects goal feasibility) serves as an additional determinant of intentions and possibly behavior. Research shows that the inclusion of perceived behavioral control generally improves the explanation of intentions and actual behavior and that perceived behavioral control has unmediated effects on behavior when perceptions of control are low (Ajzen, 1991; Madden, Scholder-Ellen, & Ajzen, 1992). Ajzen (1991) argues that perceived behavioral control closely corresponds to self-efficacy beliefs, but the empirical measurement of this construct frequently includes aspects of situation-outcome expectancies as well (e.g., the number of events outside people's control which could prevent them from engaging in the behavior are numerous or few).

Bagozzi and Warshaw (1990) proposed a theory of trying (TT), which describes the determinants of consumers' attempts at goal attainment. The theory is similar to Ajzen's (1985) model but includes influences of past behavior (frequency and recency), although this aspect of the theory is less relevant here. Bagozzi and Warshaw argue that when behaviors are not under complete volitional control, the relevant dependent variable is not behavior but attempts to achieve the goal (i.e., trying). Trying is a function of intention to try (as well as the frequency and recency of past trying), which in turn depends on attitude toward trying and social norm toward trying (as well as the frequency of past trying). Attitude toward trying is determined by attitude toward success, weighted by expectation of success, attitude toward failure, weighted by expectation of failure, and attitude toward the process of trying. Attitudes toward success, failure and process are specified as multiplicative functions of the likelihood of various consequences and their evaluation. The findings of a study on weight loss supported the model, except that attitude toward failure and expectations of failure did not influence attitude toward trying. Note that expectations of success and failure are meant to represent self-efficacy beliefs by Bagozzi and Warshaw.

Although the theories of reasoned action and planned behavior have been extremely popular as models for explaining and predicting behavior and have frequently been applied to goals, they were not designed to be goal-setting models. The theory of trying was explicitly proposed to deal with goals, but empirical tests have been limited. In general, conceptualizations of the desirability of behaviors and goals have been based on an expectancy-value model, but in empirical applications researchers have left it to the participants to determine whatever outcomes or consequences are relevant to the behavior in question. Furthermore, feasibility considerations have only been incorporated into these models in a very rudimentary way, for instance as perceived behavioral control. Verhallen and Pieters (1984) proposed to include the mental, physical and time costs of goal pursuit in attitude models of goal-directed behavior, in order to more fully capture the feasibility of goal attainment.

Goal conflict. Expectancy-value models of motivation assume that in case of multiple goals, the desirability and feasibility of each is determined, and that the highest scoring goal will be implemented in a "winner takes all" approach. Yet, consumers frequently experience goal conflicts (Baumeister, Heatherton, & Tice, 1994; Emmons, 1996), either due to ambivalence or goal incompatibility. First, ambivalence may be experienced in case of an approach-avoidance conflict, when a goal simultaneously combines desirable and undesirable outcomes, such as when a person strives to lose weight during a Sunday BBQ at the lakeside. Second, two highly desirable goals may compete for the same resources, leading to an approach-approach conflict. For example, a consumer may want to take a year-long world cruise but also build a house. Similarly, two desirable goals may be intrinsically conflicting, leading to an approach-approach conflict due to a value restriction. For example, consumers' religious values calling for a life of material simplicity may conflict with their material values (Burroughs & Rindfleisch, 2002). Comparatively little is known about the frequency, determinants and consequences of goal conflicts, and how consumers resolve them.

Goal Striving

Once a decision has been made to pursue a goal (i.e., a goal intention has been formed), the consumer has to consider the implementation of the chosen goal: possible courses of action have to be planned, actual goal-directed behaviors have to be initiated and maintained, progress has to be monitored and possible adjustments have to be made, obstacles have to be dealt with, and, finally, goal achievement has to be evaluated. Almost no research on these issues is available in the consumer behavior literature, and even in psychology literature, relevant research is of fairly recent origin. We will provide a brief overview of this work.

Planning. Planning means deliberating what has to be done in order to enact the chosen goal. As observed by Aristotle (1953, p. 58), "we deliberate not about ends but about means ... [people] first set some end before themselves and then consider how and by what means it can be attained. If it appears that it can be attained by several means, they further consider by which it can be attained best and most easily." Planning thus involves thinking about how, where and when to act with the purpose of reaching the goal. Mental simulation about future outcomes and the courses of action to attain them yield plans that encourage goal achievement. Taylor and Pham (1996) distinguish outcome simulations (where only desired results are imagined) from process simulations (during which people imagine the steps involved in achieving a certain outcome) and show that the latter are more likely to lead to goal attainment.

An idea somewhat similar to mental simulation is Gollwitzer's notion of implementation intention (Gollwitzer, 1993, 1996; Gollwitzer, Fujita, & Oettingen, 2004). Gollwitzer argues that when goals are simple and enactment has been habitualized, goal intentions may be sufficient to bring about successful goal achievement. However, when implementation is not a matter of routine and the person is having difficulties getting started, implementation intentions may have beneficial effects. An implementation intention is a self-instruction to execute a particular goal-directed behavior "automatically" when a certain situation is encountered (i.e., I will do x when situation y arises). Implementation intentions are expected to promote successful goal pursuit for two reasons. First, they heighten the salience of the critical situation with which goal-directed behavior is associated. Second, they automate the execution of the relevant behavior when the critical situation is encountered. A recent field experiment by Kardes, Cronley, and Posavac (2005) in a marketing context illustrates these benefits. All study participants received a free sample of a household liquid cleaning product to take home. Half of the participants (those in the implementation intention condition) were asked to indicate the exact dates and times that they intended to use the product and the specific uses they had in mind, whereas the other half (those in the control condition) were only asked to indicate their intentions to use the product. An unexpected follow-up survey 2 weeks later revealed that participants used more of the product in a greater variety of different situations and formed more favorable attitudes and purchase intentions in the implementation intention condition than in the control condition.

Research so far has (a) shown that implementation intentions promote successful goal pursuit; (b) provided support for the processes assumed to underlie their volitional benefits, and (c) identified important moderators of their usefulness (e.g., goal difficulty, plan detail level). However, as acknowledged by Gollwitzer, in all of these studies participants were explicitly instructed to form implementation intentions, and we know little about if and when implementations are formed under self-generated goals. Furthermore, implementation intentions have usually been studied in contexts in which the goal was concrete rather than abstract, and we need to know more about intention formation and implementation in this latter, more realistic case. Moreover, overly specific plans and implementation intentions may backfire. For example, when a behavior is identified at a very low level and a person is focused on the operation (how) of the behavior rather than the attainment of the final goal (why), there may be little room for free choice and flexibility in the case of interruptions. In support of this, research (reported in Baumeister et al., 1994) shows that students who were instructed to formulate global, monthly plans for improving their study skills performed better and more persistently than students with detailed, daily plans.

Initiation and maintenance of goal-directed behaviors. Goal-directed behavior can be spontaneously triggered by the situational context (either because of previous experiences in which particular instrumental responses have been linked to certain environmental cues or because of previously formed implementation intentions) or deliberatively initiated by the person. In the latter case, if the behavior is entirely under volitional control, goal pursuit is unproblematic. However, often one has to wait for an opportune moment to initiate action and maintain goal-directed behavior until it is completed. It has been proposed that a so-called implemental mindset, in which the focus of thought is on doing rather than on thinking, may help with this phase of goal pursuit (Gollwitzer, 1996; Gollwitzer et al., 2004). That is, after people have committed themselves to pursuing a given goal, they are presumably focused on information that is relevant to goal achievement and will tune out distracting information. Furthermore, information about the desirability and feasibility of the chosen goal will be processed in a biased fashion so as to favor continued commitment and persistent goal pursuit.

Another important contribution to the literature on how people deal with difficulties in enacting goal intentions is Kuhl's (1984) work on action control. A central aspect of his theory is how the focal intention can be shielded from competing behavioral tendencies. The model assumes that action control motivation will increase when enactment difficulties are encountered, either due to internal reasons (competing action tendencies) or external reasons (situational features that are incompatible with the goal intention). A variety of action control processes are specified. First, selective attention directs processing to information favoring the goal intention, and encoding control leads to a focus on intention-relevant aspects of the stimulus. Second, emotion control involves regulating one's emotions such that they are conducive to action implementation. Third, motivation control deals with biased processing of desirability and feasibility information. Fourth, environmental control means structuring the environment in such as way as to make it supportive of goal enactment. Finally, parsimonious information processing refers to limiting continued deliberation about action alternatives and initiating action execution. Kuhl has also proposed a personality variable called action- vs. state-orientation, which reflects whether or not a person is generally in an action-oriented mode of control, which favors the implementation of intentions, or a state-oriented mode, which favors reflection and deliberation.

Monitoring of progress. According to control theory (Carver, Lawrence, & Scheier, 1996; Powers, 1973), goal progress is monitored by feedback loops in which the consumer's current situation is compared to a reference standard (i.e., a goal). The implications of this comparison depend on the type of feedback loop. In a negative feedback loop, the goal is something to be approached. Therefore, a perceived discrepancy between the current situation and the goal requires adjustments to the current state. In contrast, in a positive feedback loop, where the goal is something to be avoided, the system is designed to enlarge the discrepancy between the current state and the avoidance goal. Carver and Scheier argue that positive feedback loops are generally unstable and are often constrained by negative feedback loops, such that a person trying to avoid an undesirable state eventually gravitates toward a more desirable state.

During reasonably complex goal pursuits many different goals at different levels of abstraction have to be monitored. Feedback loops can be specified at various levels of the goal hierarchy. The result of the comparison between the current state and a goal can be posited to serve as input to the establishment of a reference value (i.e., a goal) at a lower level of the hierarchy. In this way, an integrated monitoring system for the entire process of goal pursuit can be achieved.

Evaluation of goal achievement. People may hold outcome and process goals (Austin & Vancouver, 1996). With an outcome goal, goal pursuit is terminated when the goal has been reached (e.g., buying a car). With a process goal, goal pursuit is continuous since attaining the goal is not a discrete event and discrepancies are always possible (e.g., avoid making impulse purchases). In the latter case, successful goal pursuit does not lead to the termination of goal striving but attempts to maintain progress.

We distinguish four general coping strategies when evaluations of goal attainment are unfavorable (see Table 13.1). First, consumers can continue striving, working harder or longer (Baumeister et al., 1994). Second, an initial plan can be revised when assumptions made during planning turn out to be untenable or unforeseen circumstances occur. In this case, a new planning cycle starts that takes into account the new contingencies. Third, a goal can be postponed or tabled (Austin & Vancouver, 1996; Ford, 1992). Tabling means that the goal is temporarily put aside because of a preoccupation with a different goal favored by current circumstances. When this occurs, the question arises whether and under what conditions the original goal will be reinstated. Fourth, a goal can be abandoned when the likelihood of successful goal achievement is deemed too small. Stein, Trabasso, and Liwag (1993) and Oatley and Johnson-Laird (1996) have stressed the role of emotions in alerting people to aspects of goal pursuit that need attention and in orienting them toward possible courses of action. These issues are discussed in further detail below.

AFFECT AND GOAL SETTING

We use the term "affect" to refer to any type of valenced state, including emotions and moods, having experiential (thoughts, feelings), expressive (automatic and controlled) and arousal (autonomic nervous system) components (Frijda, 1986; Gross, 1998). We propose three functions of affect in goal setting. First, the goal itself can be an affective experience, or the consequences resulting from goal achievement may be affectively charged. We call the former affect-as-goal and the latter affect-as-motivation. Both of these reflect endogenous affective influences. Second, the affect that is incidentally experienced at the time goal pursuit is deliberated may have an impact on goal setting. The nature of the affective influence is exogenous in this case, and we call it affect-as-filter. Third, setting certain types of goals can have implications for subjective well-being, which is a type of affective externality, and we call this affect-as-hedonic spillover. Thus, affect can be an integral part of goal setting (i.e., endogenous), it can be incidental to goal setting but influence it nonetheless (i.e., exogenous), or it may be an unintended consequence of goal setting (i.e., an externality). The third column of Table 13.1 summarizes these functions.

Influence of Endogenous Affect on Goal Setting

The most direct way in which affect can impact goal setting is when the goal itself is an affective experience (i.e., the desired outcome of goal-directed behavior is affective in nature or the process of goal pursuit is intrinsically pleasurable): *affect-as-goal*. Pervin's (1989, p. 474) definition of a goal, "a mental image or other end point representation associated with affect toward which action may be directed," makes this point very well. For example, a person might be guided by values of hedonism and stimulation and generally pursue experiences that are pleasurable and exciting (Schwartz, 1992). Less abstract goals might include spending a fun afternoon at an amusement park or watching a romantic comedy in a movie theater. These goals may be called consummatory (as opposed to instrumental), and research has confirmed that affect plays an important role in these types of decisions (e.g., Pham, 1998). Research also indicates that, in situations where affective and cognitive considerations are in conflict (e.g., a chocolate cake may be more affectively appealing than a fruit salad, but the cognitive consequences may be less favorable), choices are based on immediate affect when processing resourced are limited, at least under certain conditions (Shiv & Fedorikhin, 1999; also see the chapter by Cohen et al., chapter 11, this volume, on the speed of affective processing).

Often, the process of goal pursuit it not pleasurable and even the goal itself is not intrinsically associated with affect. Nevertheless, a person may decide to pursue the goal because the act of goal achievement induces affect, or goal achievement is instrumental in reaching desired higher-level goals, which may be affectively charged. The affect experienced is not the goal per se, but the affective charge of attaining the goal influences goal setting, hence *affect-as-motivation*. Expectancy-value theories of motivation illustrate this perspective in a general sense, although they usually do not deal with affect directly. Goal choice in these models depends on the multiplicative combination of incentive (value) and likelihood of occurrence (expectancy or instrumentality). Although the incentive component may include affective experiences, any kind of outcome or consequence associated with the goal can have incentive value. For example, Heckhausen (1977) argues that self-evaluations such as feelings of pride and shame may serve as incentives for behavior.

Several attempts have been made to explicitly incorporate (anticipated) affect into expectancy-value models of behavior (see van der Pligt et al., 1998). The basic idea is that conventional models (e.g., the theories of reasoned action and planned behavior) only study evaluative responses based on beliefs associated with the behavior, but that people may also have anticipated affective reactions to the behavior or process (e.g., they may enjoy eating junk food) as well as anticipated postbehavioral affective responses (e.g., they may anticipate feeling bad after having eaten a lot of junk food). Thus, anticipated affect enters the goal setting stage in a way similar to mental simulation (Taylor & Pham, 1996). In an illustrative study, Richard, van der Pligt, and de Vries (1996) assessed evaluations, affective reactions, and anticipated postbehavioral affective responses for four behaviors (eating junk food, using soft drugs, drinking alcohol, and studying hard) using the same semantic differential scales (pleasant-unpleasant, nice-awful, good-bad). They found that while evaluations and affective reactions toward the behavior were not empirically distinct, anticipated postbehavioral affective responses differed from both evaluations and affective reactions and had a unique influence on behavioral expectations, controlling for attitudes, subjective norms, and perceived behavioral control. Richard, van der Pligt, and de Vries (1995) obtained a similar finding for a more specific measure of anticipated postbehavioral negative emotions (worry, regret, and tension) in the context of behavioral expectations about HIV preventive behaviors. These findings illustrate the function of affect-as-motivation in goal setting.

A similar but more explicitly goal-based model was proposed by Baumgartner, Pieters, and Bagozzi (forthcoming). They draw a distinction between two types of future-oriented emotions, anticipatory emotions and anticipated emotions (see also Loewenstein et al., 2001; Loewenstein & Lerner, 2003). Anticipatory emotions are emotions that are currently experienced due to the prospect of a desired or undesired future event. The prototypes of these emotions are anticipatory excitement or hope in the case of positive future events and anticipatory worry or fear in the case of negative future events. Anticipated emotions, on the other hand, are based on imagining that certain desired or undesired events have already happened (possibly because of what one has or has not done) and then experiencing actual or imaginary emotions in anticipation of these simulated events.

There are several important differences between these two types of emotions. First, anticipatory emotions are currently experienced, veridical affective responses to possible future events that have positive or negative implications for the self, whereas anticipated emotions are based on pre-factual thinking about a future positive or negative event. They could be real emotional experiences, but may also function like affective forecasts (Gilbert et al., 1998). Second, anticipatory emotions are a subset of the complete range of discrete emotions that people can experience, namely, those related to the possible occurrence of future desired or undesired outcomes (i.e., hope and fear). Furthermore, the experienced emotion is generally either a positive or negative emotion, depending on the valence of the future event (unless the event is emotionally ambiguous). In contrast, any discrete emotion that can be experienced may be anticipated in advance, based on a mental simulation of future outcomes, and the anticipation of positive and negative future events can lead to the simultaneous experience of both positive and negative affective states. Third, since anticipatory emotions are current affective responses to the *prospect* of future events that have positive or negative consequences, uncertainty about what is going to happen constitutes part of the meaning of the emotion and is inseparable from the emotion (e.g., anticipatory hope in the case of desired events and anticipatory worry in the case of undesired events). In contrast, the likelihood of the focal event happening is a mental event distinct from anticipated emotions related to the event.

In a study dealing with the millennium transition (i.e., the so-called Y2K problem), Baumgartner et al. showed that positively and negatively valenced anticipatory and anticipated emotions were empirically distinct and that people who were fearful and experienced positive and negative anticipated emotions more intensely were more likely to form behavioral intentions aimed at averting possible negative consequences of the millennium change. Although goal intentions were not directly assessed in the study, intentions for a wide variety of behaviors were collected so that the measure is interpretable as the intensity of a person's goal to avoid or limit the expected problems caused by the millennium problem. This demonstrates how anticipatory and anticipated emotions can influence goal intentions, expressing the affect-as-motivation function. In Baumgartner et al.'s study, anticipated emotions were assessed as people's affective experiences to simulated goal success and goal failure. However, more generally one might investigate how affect associated with the outcomes or consequences of the focal goal influences the desirability of the focal goal.

A related literature in decision making has focused on the emotions of regret and, to a lesser extent, disappointment (Zeelenberg et al., 2000). In an early study, Simonson (1992) showed that when consumers were reminded that they might later regret a bad decision, they were more likely to choose a higher-priced, brand-name product, presumably because this was expected to shield them from possible future regret. More recently, Mellers and her associates (e.g., Mellers & McGraw, 2001) developed a comprehensive framework for considering the effects of anticipated emotions on choice called subjective expected pleasure theory (see Heyman & Mellers, chapter 27, this volume).

Influence of Exogenous Affect on Goal Setting

Exogenous moods and emotions, which originate outside current goal pursuit, can have both direct and indirect effects on goal setting. With regard to direct effects, it has been known for quite some time that incidental positive mood (induced by a small gift, for example) tends to increase the likelihood of pro-social behaviors (see Cohen et al., chapter 11, this volume).

More recently, researchers have become interested in the effects of specific exogenous moods and emotions on behavior and goal pursuit. As a case in point, Raghunatham and Pham (1999) contrasted the effects of sadness and anxiety. They argue that since sadness is associated with appraisals of loss, sad individuals will be motivated to replace their loss with something else that is rewarding, leading to an implicit goal of reward acquisition. In contrast, fear is associated with appraisals of uncertainty and lack of control, which may prompt a goal of uncertainty reduction. Consistent with expectations, sad individuals had a greater preference for high-risk/high-reward options, whereas the opposite was true for anxious individuals.

Exogenous affect can also influence goal-directed behavior indirectly by impacting judgments of the desirability and feasibility of goals. A well-established finding in the mood literature is that moods tend to bias evaluations in mood-congruent directions (see Cohen et al., chapter 11, this volume). This suggests that a goal, or the outcomes and consequences associated with the goal, may be evaluated more positively when a person is in a good mood and more negatively when the person is in a bad mood. Exogenous mood can also influence estimates of the likelihood that particular events will occur, thus affecting feasibility. For example, Johnson and Tversky (1983) found that people who read happy newspaper articles provided more optimistic risk judgments than people who read sad articles. Recent research has qualified and extended these findings by arguing that judgments may be sensitive to the particular exogenous affect experienced. For example, Lerner and Keltner (2000, 2001) proposed the so-called appraisal-tendency hypothesis, according to which the appraisal dimensions that caused an emotion also influence people's evaluation of objects and events that are encountered while they experience the emotion in question. Lerner and Keltner apply their model to fear and anger, and reason that since fear is characterized by uncertainty and situational control, it should lead to higher risk perceptions, whereas anger should lead to lower risk perceptions since it is characterized by certainty and personal control. The authors find support for these predictions not only for dispositional fear and anger (measured with personality variables) but also experimentally manipulated exogenous sources of fear and anger. Such findings reflect what we call the *affect-as-filter* function in goal setting (see Table 13.1), where the perception of incoming information is biased toward the currently experienced affect and its appraisal dimensions.

Goal Setting Influence on Affect

So far we have examined how affect influences goal setting. However, the goals that people set may have affective implications (i.e., externalities) that are independent of the specific outcomes of goal pursuit. We call these influences *hedonic spillover* (see Table 13.1). We distinguish two types of spillover here. First, there is evidence that certain goal orientations (i.e., individual differences in how goals are represented mentally) have characteristic effects on subjective well-being such as life satisfaction and the frequency with which positive and negative affective states are experienced. Second, goal content seems to have important ramifications for well-being. Specifically, extrinsic goals such as those related to financial success and materialism have generally been linked with lower well-being.

The first goal orientation is abstractness or level of goal specification. This goal dimension refers to whether people tend to frame their goals in concrete or abstract ways. For the present purposes, it suffices that there appear to be reliable individual differences in the extent to which people identify their goals and behaviors in superordinate or subordinate terms (i.e., "level of personal agency" in action identification theory). For example, high-level agents may identify the act of eating as getting nutrition, whereas low-level agents might think of it as chewing and swallowing.

Emmons (1992) investigated the relationship between level of goal specification and psychological and physical well-being. He asked three different sets of participants to generate 15 personal strivings (i.e., goals that they were typically trying to attain) and had coders rate a person's strivings as either relatively concrete, specific and more behavioral in nature, or as abstract, reflective, and involving greater self-scrutiny. Emmons also collected reports of daily moods, ratings of life satisfaction, and other measures of psychological well-being (e.g., depression, anxiety), as well as various indices of physical well-being (e.g., health center visits). Interestingly, high-level strivings tended to be associated with certain indicators of lower psychological well-being but fewer symptoms of physical illness. Emmons (1992) argues that it is more difficult to attain and monitor progress toward abstract goals, which leads to negative affect for high-level strivers. On the other hand, low-level strivers may be more prone to repress stressful experiences and as a consequence suffer physical illnesses.

Psychological and physical well-being have also been linked to another goal orientation, namely, whether people frame their goals as approach or avoidance goals. Approach goals are desired states that one wants to attain (e.g., spending time with others), whereas avoidance goals are aversive states that one wants to avoid (e.g., being lonely). Emmons and Kaiser (1996) coded the personal strivings elicited from four sets of respondents into approach and avoidance strivings and then correlated the proportion of avoidance strivings (which ranged from 9 to 15% overall) with measures of psychological and physical well-being (similar to those used in Emmons, 1992). People with a relatively high proportion of avoidance strivings tended to experience less positive affect, lower life satisfaction, and more anxiety. In addition, they reported more symptoms of physical illness. One reason for these differences might be that, compared to avoidance strivings, approach goals were rated as more desirable and important, success was seen as more likely, and goal pursuit was based more on intrinsic reasons.

A third goal orientation is goal conflict, which we introduced earlier. In Emmons' work on personal strivings, ambivalence (approach-avoidance conflict) is assessed as the degree of unhappiness one would feel about succeeding at the striving, whereas goal incompatibility is measured as the extent to which success at one striving has helpful or harmful effects on another striving (averaged across all possible pairs of strivings). Both ambivalence and incompatibility have been associated with lower psychological well-being and various physical symptoms, including more frequent health center visits (Emmons & King, 1988).

The final goal orientation is goal differentiation. Emmons and King (1989) define differentiation as the degree to which different goals (i.e., personal strivings in their study) are independent rather than interdependent. For example, one operationalization of this construct is the rated dissimilarity between a person's strivings. Emmons and King argue that striving differentiation should be associated with greater affective reactivity, and in two studies they find support for this hypothesis for both a measure of affective intensity (i.e., the intensity of experiencing positive and negative moods over a period of time) and affective variability.

The second approach to studying the relationship between goals and subjective well-being is based on the notion that well-being is not only a function of structural characteristics of goals, such as their level of differentiation, but also the content of goals. Of particular importance to consumer behavior is the finding that extrinsic goals such as financial success, social recognition, and appearance can have a detrimental effect on well-being (although the direction of causality is not always clear from the existing studies, the findings are usually interpreted in this way). For example, Kasser and Ryan (1993, 1996) established that people who assigned greater importance to aspirations such as self-acceptance (concern with growth, autonomy, and self-regard), affiliation, community feeling, and physical fitness, and thought they could attain these goals in the future, rated more highly on a variety of indices of well-being (including diary measures of experienced positive affect and depression and anxiety), whereas people who endorsed values relating to financial success, appearance and social recognition had lower well-being scores.

There is generally good support for a negative effect of materialism on well-being, but there also seem to be important boundary conditions. Burroughs and Rindfleisch (2002) propose that materialism will lead to stress and lower well-being when it conflicts with collective-oriented values. In two studies (a large-scale survey with a representative sample of American adults and an experiment with students) they find support for this notion for two of the three collective-oriented values studied, namely, religious and family values, although not for community values. The foregoing results show mostly negative affective implications of particular goals and goal setting situations, and more research about potential positive implications would be welcome.

AFFECT AND GOAL STRIVING

Affect has different functions in goal striving as well. First, affect experienced during goal striving provides information about goal progress, and directs and energizes future goal striving (endogenous affective influence). Second, affect that is unrelated to the process of goal pursuit can influence future goal striving (exogenous affective influence). Third, goal striving may be successful or unsuccessful, thus inducing positive or negative affective states as a function of the goal outcome (affective output). Table 13.1 (third column) summarizes these functions in our model. We focus on the first two functions because they exert an important influence on current goal pursuit, and also because affect-as-output has been documented in detail by emotion theorists in psychology and marketing (Bagozzi, Gopinath, & Nyer, 1999; Frijda, 1986; Gross, 1998).

Influence of Endogenous Affect on Goal Striving

Affect arises when goal progress is thwarted or facilitated. The cause and effect functions of such endogenous affect are closely intertwined because affect, on the one hand, provides feedback about current and past goal striving (*affect-as-feedback*) and, on the other, directs future goal striving (*affect-as-volition*). But how does affect arise during goal striving, which types of affect are generated, and how does affect influence goal striving?

Theories of affect are often not very precise about how goal progress leads to affect (Frijda, 1986; Lazarus, 1991; Roseman, Antoniou, & Jose, 1996; Stein, Trabasso, & Liwag, 1993). One prominent exception is Carver and Scheier's control theory of affect (Carver, Lawrence, & Scheier, 1996). The theory argues that progress at a rate higher than some standard generates positive affect. This implies that somebody might be making progress toward a goal, but if the progress is slower than expected, the affect experienced could still be negative.

There are at least three possibilities about how goal progress or lack thereof can induce affect (Carver et al., 1996). For simplicity, we frame the three ways in terms of positive affect. First, the absolute rate of progress may elicit affect such that any movement toward (away from) an approach (avoidance) goal leads to positive affect. Second, the relative rate of progress may elicit affect: the faster one moves toward (away from) an approach (avoidance) goal, the more likely the experience of positive affect and the greater its intensity. Alternatively, the movement may be compared to an expected, acceptable, or desired rate of movement, and the nature and intensity of affect depends on the speed of movement relative to the chosen standard. Third, changes in the rate of progress may elicit affect such that if the movement toward (away from) an approach (avoidance) goal accelerates over time, positive affect will be generated. Hsee and Abelson (1991) and Hsee, Salovey, and Abelson (1994) have provided support for the affective implications of all three aspects of goal progress using satisfaction with various outcomes as the criterion. Boldero and Francis (2002) speculate that in the case of what they call standards (i.e., desired states in the present), the magnitude of the discrepancy with the standard matters, whereas with goals (i.e., desired states in the future) the rate of discrepancy reduction relative to an expected rate is critical for emotional experience.

Initially, the focus in goal theory was on the overall valence of the affective state, either positive or negative (Carver, Lawrence, & Scheier, 1996). More recently, specific affective states have been considered in detail. As a case in point, regulatory focus theory (Higgins, 1997) specifies that if people are doing well in their approach strivings (e.g., achievement goals), they will feel cheerful, excited, and elated, whereas when they are doing poorly they will feel dejected, sad, and depressed. In contrast, when people are doing well in their avoidance strivings (e.g., protection goals), they will feel quiescent, relieved, and calm, whereas when they are doing poorly they will feel agitated, anxious, and nervous (see also Carver, Sutton, & Scheier, 2000).

The affect-as-feedback function is essentially retrospective, whereas the affect-as-volition function is prospective. This is because the experience of specific affect does not only comprise thoughts and feelings but also so-called emotivational goals and action tendencies (Frijda, 1986; Roseman, Antoniou, & Jose, 1996). For example, the experience of regret activates a person to try to undo a behavior or its undesirable outcomes.

The affect-as-feedback and affect-as-volition functions in goal striving are integrated in the work of Stein (Stein, Liwag, & Wade, 1996; Stein, Trabasso, & Liwag, 1993) on the unfolding of emotional experiences over time. The theory proposes a limited number of goal-outcome-goal-revision combinations, each with a distinct corresponding emotion. A precipitating event that is seen as facilitating or obstructing a goal, along with an evaluation of certainty of goal success or goal failure, causes an emotion. Specifically, being certain about attaining something desirable or not attaining something undesirable leads to happiness; not attaining something desirable or experiencing something undesirable lead to sadness and anger; and not wanting an undesirable uncertain outcome or wanting a desirable uncertain outcome leads to fear. Depending on the emotion, a goal to attain, maintain, reinstate or avoid is generated, or the goal is substituted or abandoned. If no plan is available, the original goal is forfeited or it is replaced with a new goal if this course is acceptable (which is often the case in sadness), otherwise the person redoubles efforts to find a plan. If a plan *is* available, it is enacted in an effort to reinstate the original goal (e.g., in anger attempts are usually made to remove the goal blockage) or to prevent an undesirable state (e.g., in the case of fear). Subsequently, the outcome is monitored, and a new goal-outcome-goal-revision cycle is initiated.

In line with this, Bougie, Pieters, and Zeelenberg (2003) found that consumers who were angry due to a service provider's wrong-doing experienced emotivational goals such as trying to get back at someone and wanting to hurt someone, and action tendencies such as feeling like behaving aggressively and feeling like letting oneself go. They also found that, independent of the level of dissatisfaction with the service, higher levels of anger increased the likelihood that consumers would complain to the service provider, which reflects attempts to attain the original goal of the service encounter, rather than abandoning it.

A related framework is the communicative theory of emotions (Oatley & Johnson-Laird, 1996), which is also based on the idea that emotions are caused by perceived changes in the likely success of plans. Emotions alert people to those parts of the goal structure that require attention and lead to evaluations of what can be done about the situation. For example, the theory suggests that the behavioral consequences of happiness are to continue with the plan; of sadness to disengage from the goal; of fear to stop, attend to the environment, or escape; and of anger to try harder or aggress.

Bagozzi, Baumgartner, and Pieters' (1998) research on goal-directed emotions is also relevant to goal striving. They assume that people can anticipate how they would feel if they achieved their goal and how they would feel if they failed to achieve their goals. These anticipated emotions initiate volitional processes in which intentions and plans about how to enact the chosen goal are formed and decisions about effort expenditure are made. Instrumental behaviors aimed at goal attainment are then executed, goal attainment is evaluated, and goal-outcome emotions are experienced. Bagozzi et al. tested these ideas in a longitudinal study of weight control, using data from 406 adults who already had a weight loss or weight maintenance goal. The findings showed that positive and negative anticipated emotions influenced both dieting and exercising volitions, which in turn impacted dieting and exercising behaviors. For men, perceived goal attainment was a function of exercising, whereas for women it was a function of dieting. Furthermore, greater goal attainment led to more positive and less negative goal-outcome emotions.

Finally, decision-making research on the behavioral effects of currently experienced specific emotions such as regret and disappointment has implications for goal striving. For example, Zeelenberg et al. (2000) argue that experienced regret leads to a focus on nonattained goals and encourages persistence in goal pursuit, whereas disappointment promotes goal abandonment. In a services context, Zeelenberg and Pieters (1999) showed that regret had a direct effect (unmediated by dissatisfaction) on switching, whereas disappointment had a direct effect (unmediated by dissatisfaction) on negative word-of-mouth.

Influence of Exogenous Affect on Goal Striving

During goal striving, consumer may experience affect that is unrelated to goal pursuit, which may nonetheless influence goal pursuit. As suggested by Seo, Feldman, Barrett, and Bartunek (2004), who discuss the role of affective experience in work settings, such exogenous affect can influence the amount of effort expended on goal pursuit as well as the persistence of goal striving directly or indirectly through judgments of goal progress (*affect-as-volition*). With regard to direct effects, they propose that activated affective states may result in greater effort expenditure and that processes of mood maintenance and mood repair may encourage the continuation of a current activity or lead to a change in plans. With regard to indirect effects, they rely on research which shows that good (bad) mood induces more heuristic (systematic) processing of information to argue that people in a good (bad) mood will monitor progress toward a goal less (more) frequently, less (more) thoroughly, and more (less) favorably.

Martin (e.g., Martin et al., 1993; Martin et al., 1997) argues that the valence of a person's mood by itself does not have clear motivational implications. Rather, moods have to be interpreted and depending on the meaning ascribed to one's mood, a given mood may have very different motivational effects (*affect-as-input*). For example, in Martin et al. (1993) the effect of "stop rules" on behavior was investigated, that is, when to terminate goal pursuit. Participants engaged in a task with instructions that encouraged them to stop when they had reached their goal (goal attainment) or to stop when they no longer enjoyed the task (task enjoyment). Thus, the goal attainment instruction induced an (external) outcome or performance goal, whereas the task enjoyment instruction promoted an (internal) process or learning goal (Dweck & Leggett, 1988). With goal attainment instructions, participants in the positive exogenous mood condition stopped earlier than participants in the negative exogenous mood condition, presumably because a positive mood implies doing well on a task or at least making progress toward the goal. The opposite was true with the task enjoyment instructions, because in this case a positive mood should promote maintenance of the behavior.

Although it does not deal directly with goal striving, the work of Bosmans and Baumgartner (2005) on goal-relevant emotional information is relevant here as well. These authors induced different exogenous emotions in participants and exposed them to ads that appealed either to achievement or protection motives. When the ad made achievement goals salient (e.g., increasing one's energy by eating organically grown apples), participants evaluated the product (i.e., the brand of apples) more favorably when participants happened to feel cheerful rather than dejected, but there was no difference in brand evaluations for participants who felt quiescent versus agitated. In contrast, when the ad made protection goals salient (e.g., preventing fatigue by eating organically grown apples), participants who felt quiescent provided higher brand evaluations than participants who felt agitated; there was not difference between participants who felt cheerful or dejected.

CONCLUDING THOUGHTS

Based on a review of the literature, this chapter developed a framework describing the interplay of goals, action, and affect in goal-directed consumer behavior. The framework is based on the idea that goals are organized in hierarchical structures, and that goals derive their meaning from relationships with goals at the same level of the hierarchy and goals lower and higher in the hierarchy. Based on the notion of goal hierarchies, we indicated the relevance of the abstractness or specification level of goals, and noted that consumers can flexibly adapt their level of goal identification (i.e., what they are pursuing) depending on the demands and novelty of the task, the distance to goal implementation, and individual differences. Next, we described goal setting and goal striving as separate but related processes in consumers' goal pursuit, and discussed the role played by affect in goal pursuit. Our framework assumes that in most circumstances affect serves goal-directed consumer behavior in multiple ways. Specifically, affect was shown to function as a goal, filter, feedback, and source of motivation and volition, among others. With regard to goal setting, some goals are affective in nature, in which case affect is an intrinsic motivator (affect-as-goal), whereas other goals derive motivational potential from anticipatory and anticipated affective reactions associated with goal achievement (affect-as-motivation). Affect unrelated to goal setting may also color consumers' perception of goal-relevant information (affect-as-filter), and affect can result as a function of the types of goals consumers set (affect-as-hedonic spillover). With regard to goal striving, affect provides feedback about goal progress (affect-as-feedback) and the affect generated in turn directs future behavior (affect-as-volition). In the control loops that occur during goal pursuit these various functions of endogenous affect are intertwined, and more research is needed to understand when and how these antecedent and consequent functions of affect promote successful goal pursuit. In addition, exogenous affect emanating from outside the specific goal pursuit may influence goal striving as in affect-as-input. Finally, after all is said and done, and goal pursuit has been successful or unsuccessful, affect serves as hedonic output. Then, consumers are happy with their flat tummy, relieved to be without debt, proud to have bought the best computer for less, and so forth.

As always, further research is needed and we have raised possible avenues at various places in the chapter. As mentioned at the beginning of the chapter, it is surprising that consumer researchers have paid so little attention to goal-directed consumer behavior because much of what consumers do involves goal pursuit, not only when they are trying to keep to their diet, but also when they are saving money, trying to stay out of debt, planning their holidays, raising their kids without buying them too much or too little, and so forth. Amazingly, we know very little about such patterns of behavior over time, where consumers try to attain or maintain long-term and abstract goals, and what functions affect has in goal pursuit. And we know even less about how consumers deal with multiple goals over time, without breaking down. Researchers have generally emphasized breakdowns of control, such as when people overeat, drink too much, or consume compulsively, but one should probably be more amazed by the fact that most consumers do a fairly good job at juggling a multitude of goals at the same time. It would be interesting to find out how they accomplish this.

REFERENCES

Ajzen, I. (1985). From intentions to actions: A theory of planned behavior. In J. Kuhl & J. Beckmann (Eds.), *Action control: From cognition to behavior* (pp. 11–39). New York: Springer.

Ajzen, I. (1991). The theory of planned behavior. *Organizational Behavior and Human Decision Processes, 50*, 179–210.

Aristotle (1953), *Nichomachean ethics* (J. A. K Thomas, trans.). London: Penguin Classics.

Austin, J. T., & Vancouver, J. B. (1996). Goal constructs in psychology: Structure, process, and content. *Psychological Bulletin, 120*, 338–375.

Bagozzi, R. P., Baumgartner, H., Pieters, R., & Zeelenberg, M. (2001). The role of emotions in goal-directed behavior. In C. Huffman, R. Ratneshwar, & D. Mick (Eds.), *The why of consumption: Perspectives on consumer motives, goals, and desires* (pp. 36–58). London: Routledge.

Bagozzi, R. P., & Dholakia, U. (1999). Goal setting and goal striving in consumer behavior. *Journal of Marketing, 63* (Special issue), 19–32.

Bagozzi, R. P., & Warshaw. P. R. (1990). Trying to consume. *Journal of Consumer Research, 17*, 127–140.

Bagozzi, R. P., Baumgartner, H., & Pieters, R. (1998). Goal-directed emotions. *Cognition and Emotion, 12*, 1–26.

Bagozzi, R. P., Gopinath, M., & Nyer, P. U. (1999). The role of emotions in marketing. *Journal of the Academy of Marketing Science, 27*, 184–206.

Bandura, A. (1977). Self-efficacy: Toward a unifying theory of behavioral change. *Psychological Review, 84*, 191–215.

Bandura, A. (1989). Human agency in social cognitive theory. *American Psychologist, 44*, 1175–1184.

Baumeister, R. F., Heatherton, T. F., & Tice, T. M. (1994). *Losing control: How and why people fail at self-regulation*. San Diego, CA: Academic Press.

Baumgartner, H., Pieters, R., & Bagozzi, R. P. (forthcoming). Future-oriented emotions: Conceptualization and measurement. *European Journal of Social Psychology*.

Bettman, J. R. (1979). *An information processing theory of consumer choice*. Reading, MA: Addison-Wesley.

Bettman, J. R., Luce, M. F., & Payne, J. W. (1998). Constructive consumer choice processes. *Journal of Consumer Research, 25,* 187–217.

Boldero, J., & Francis, J. (2002). Goals, standards, and the self: Reference values serving different functions. *Personality and Social Psychology Review, 6,* 232–241.

Bosmans, A., & Baumgartner, H. (2005). Goal-relevant emotional information: When extraneous affect leads to persuasion and when it does not. *Journal of Consumer Research, 32,* 424–434

Bougie, R., R. Pieters, & M. Zeelenberg (2003). Angry customers don't come back, they get back: The experience and behavioral implications of anger and dissatisfaction in services. *Journal of the Academy of Marketing Science, 31,* 377–391.

Burroughs, J. E., & Rindfleisch, A. (2002). Materialism and well-being: A conflicting values perspective. *Journal of Consumer Research, 29,* 348–370.

Carver, C. S., & Scheier, M.,F. (2000). On the structure of behavioral self-regulation. In M. Boekaerts, P. R. Pintrich, & M. Zeidner (Eds.), *Handbook of self-regulation* (pp. 41–84). San Diego, CA: Academic Press.

Carver, C. S., Lawrence, J. W., & Scheier, M. F. (1996). A control-process perspective on the origins of affect. In L. L. Martin & A. Tesser (Eds.), *Striving and feeling: Interactions among goals, affect, and self-regulation* (pp. 11–52). Mahwah, NJ: Erlbaum.

Carver, C. S., Sutton, S. K., & Scheier, M. F. (2000). Action, emotion, and personality: Emerging conceptual integration. *Personality and Social Psychology Bulletin, 26,* 741–751.

Celsi, R. L., & Olson, J. C. (1988). The role of involvement in attention and comprehension processes. *Journal of Consumer Research, 15,* 210–224.

Chaiken, S., Wood, W., & Eagly, A. H. (1996). Principles of persuasion. In E. T. Higgins & A. W. Kruglanski (Eds.), *Social psychology: Handbook of basic principles* (pp. 702–742). New York: Guilford.

Chartrand, T. L., & Bargh, J. A. (2002). Nonconscious motivations: Their activation, operation, and consequences. In A. Tesser, D. A. Stapel, & J. V. Wood (Eds.), *Self and motivation: Emerging psychological perspectives* (pp. 13–41). Washington, DC: American Psychological Association.

Dweck, C. S., & E. L. Leggett (1988). A social-cognitive approach to motivation and personality. *Psychological Review, 95*(2), 256–73.

Emmons, R. A. (1989). The personal striving approach to personality. In L. A. Pervin (Ed.), *Goal concepts in personality and social psychology* (pp. 87–126). Hillsdale, NJ: Erlbaum.

Emmons, R. A. (1992). Abstract versus concrete goals: Personal striving level, physical illness, and psychological well-being. *Journal of Personality and Social Psychology, 62,* 292–300.

Emmons, R. A. (1996). Striving and feeling: Personal goals and subjective well-being. In P. M. Gollwitzer & J. A. Bargh (Eds.), *The psychology of action* (pp. 313–337). New York: Guilford

Emmons, R. A., & Kaiser, H. A. (1996). Goal orientation and emotional well-being: Linking goals and affect through the self. In L. L. Martin & A. Tesser (Eds.), *Striving and feeling: Interactions among goals, affect, and self-regulation* (pp. 79–98). Mahwah, NJ: Erlbaum.

Emmons, R. A., & King, L. A. (1988). Conflict among personal strivings: Immediate and long-term implications for psychological and physical well-being. *Journal of Personality and Social Psychology, 54,* 1040–1048.

Emmons, R. A., & King, L. A. (1989). Personal striving differentiation and affective reactivity. *Journal of Personality and Social Psychology, 56,* 478–484.

Fishbein, M., & Ajzen, I. (1975). *Belief, attitude, intention, and behavior: An introduction to theory and research.* Reading, MA: Addison-Wesley.

Ford, M. E. (1992). *Motivation humans: Goals, emotions, and personal agency beliefs.* Newbury Park, CA: Sage.

Frijda, N. H. (1986). *The emotions.* Cambridge: Cambridge University Press.

Gilbert, D. T., Pinel, E. C., Wilson, T. D., Blumberg, S. J., & Wheatley. T. P. (1998). Immune neglect: A source of durability bias in affective forecasting. *Journal of Personality and Social Psychology, 75*(3), 617–638.

Gollwitzer, P.M. (1990). Action phases and mind sets. In E. T. Higgins & R. M. Sorrentino (Eds.), *Handbook of motivation and cognition* (Vol. 2, pp. 53–92). New York: Guilford.

Gollwitzer, P. M. (1993). Goal achievement: The role of intentions. In W. Stroebe & M. Hewstone (Eds.), *European review of social psychology* (Vol. 4, pp. 141–185). Chicheste: John Wiley.

Gollwitzer, P. M. (1996). The volitional benefits of planning. In P. M. Gollwitzer & J. A. Bargh (Eds.), *The psychology of action* (pp. 287–312). New York: Guilford.

Gollwitzer, P. M., Fujita, K., & Oettingen, G. (2004). Planning and the implementation of goals. In R. F. Baumeister & K. D. Vohs (Eds.), *Handbook of self-regulation: Research, theory, and applications* (pp. 211–228). New York: Guilford.

Gross, J. J. (1998). The emerging field of emotion regulation: An integrative review. *Review of General Psychology, 2*, 271–299.

Hacker, W. (1985), Activity: A fruitful concept in industrial psychology. In M. Frese & J. Sabini (Eds.), *Goal-directed behavior: The concept of action in psychology* (pp. 262–283). Hillsdale, NJ: Erlbaum.

Heckhausen, H. (1977). Achievement motivation and its constructs: A cognitive model. *Motivation and Emotion, 1*, 283–329.

Heckhausen, H. (1991). *Motivation and action* (2nd ed.). Berlin: Springer.

Higgins, E. T. (1997). Beyond pleasure and pain. *American Psychologist, 52*, 1280–1300.

Hsee, C. K., & Abelson, R. P. (1991). Velocity relation: Satisfaction as a function of the first derivative of outcome over time. *Journal of Personality and Social Psychology, 60*, 341–347.

Hsee, C. K., Salovey, P., & Abelson, R. P. (1994). The quasi-acceleration relation: Satisfaction as a function of the change of velocity of outcome over time. *Journal of Experimental Social Psychology, 30*, 96–111.

Huffman, C., Ratneshwar, S., & Mick, D. G. (2000). Consumer goal structures and goal- determination processes. In C. Huffman, R. Ratneshwar, & D. Mick (Eds.), *The why of consumption: Perspectives on consumer motives, goals, and desires* (pp. 9–35). London: Routledge.

Jaccard, J. J., & Davidson, A.,R. (1972). Toward an understanding of family planning behaviors: An initial investigation. *Journal of Applied Social Psychology, 2*, 228–235.

Johnson, E. J., & Tversky, A. (1983). Affect, generalization, and the perception of risk. *Journal of Personality and Social Psychology, 45*, 20–31.

Kahle, L. R., Beatty, S. E., & Homer, P. (1986). Alternative measurement approaches to consumer values: The list of values (LOV) and values and life style (VALS). *Journal of Consumer Research, 13*, 405–409.

Kamakura, W. A., & Novak, T. P. (1992). Value-system segmentation: Exploring the meaning of LOV. *Journal of Consumer Research, 19*, 119–132.

Kardes, F. R., Cronley, M. L., & Posavac, S. S. (2005). Using implementation intentions to increase new product consumption: A field experiment. In F. R. Kardes, P. M. Herr, & J. Nantel (Eds.), *Applying social cognition to consumer-focused strategy* (pp. 219–233). Mahwah, NJ: Erlbaum.

Kasser, T., & Ryan, R. M. (1993). A dark side of the American dream: Correlates of financial success as a central life aspiration. *Journal of Personality and Social Psychology, 65*, 410–422.

Kasser, T., & Ryan, R. M. (1996). Further examining the American dream: Differential correlates of intrinsic and extrinsic goals. *Personality and Social Psychology Bulletin, 22*, 280–287.

Keller, K. L. (1987). Memory factors in advertising: The effect of advertising retrieval cues on brand evaluations. *Journal of Consumer Research, 14*, 316–333.

Kuhl, J. (1982). The expectancy-value approach within the theory of social motivation: Elaboration, extensions, critique. In N. T. Feather (Ed.), *Expectations and action: Expectancy-value models in psychology* (pp. 125–160). Hillsdale, NJ: Erlbaum.

Kuhl, J. (1984). Volitional aspects of achievement motivation and learned helplessness: Toward a comprehensive theory of action control. In B. A. Maher & W. B. Maher (Eds.), *Progress in experimental personality research* (Vol. 13, pp. 99–171). Orlando, FL: Academic Press.

Lazarus, R. S. (1991), *Emotion and adaptation*. New York: Oxford University Press.

Lerner, J. S., & Keltner, D. (2000). Beyond valence: Toward a model of emotion-specific influences on judgment and choice. *Cognition and Emotion, 14*, 473–493.

Lerner, J. S., & Keltner, D. (2001). Fear, anger, and risk. *Journal of Personality and Social Psychology, 81*, 146–159.

Lewin, K., Dembo, T. Festinger, L., & Sears, P. S. (1944). Level of aspiration. In J. M. Hunt (Ed.), *Personality and the Behavior Disorders* (pp. 333–378). New York: Ronald Press.

Little, B. R. (1983). Personal projects: A rationale and method for investigation. *Environment and Behavior, 15*, 273–309.

Little, B. R. (1989). Personal projects analysis: Trivial pursuits, magnificent obsessions, and the search for coherence. In D. M. Buss & N. Cantor (Eds.), *Personality psychology: Recent trends and emerging directions*. New York: Springer.

Locke, E. A. (1991). Goal theory vs. control theory: Contrasting approaches to understanding work motivation. *Motivation and Emotion, 15*, 9–27.

Locke, E. A., & Latham, G. P. (1990). *A theory of goal setting and task performance.* Englewood Cliffs, NJ: Prentice-Hall.

Loewenstein, G., & Lerner, J. S. (2003). The role of affect in decision making. In R. J. Davidson. K. R. Scherer, & H. H. Goldsmith (Eds.), *Handbook of affective sciences* (pp. 619–642). Oxford: Oxford University Press.

Loewenstein, G. F., Weber, E. U., Hsee, C. K., & Welch, N. (2001). Risk as feelings. *Psychological Bulletin, 127,* 267–286.

Madden, T. J., Scholder-Ellen, P., & Ajzen, I. (1992). A comparison the theory of planned behavior and the theory of reasoned action. *Personality and Social Psychology Bulletin, 18,* 3–9.

Martin, L. L., Abend, T., Sedikides, C., & Green, J. D. (1997). How would I feel if …? Mood as input to a role fulfillment evaluation process. *Journal of Personality and Social Psychology, 73,* 242–253.

Martin, L. L., Ward, D.W., Achee, J. W., & Wyer, R. S. (1993). Mood as input: People have to interpret the motivational implications of their moods. *Journal of Personality and Social Psychology, 64,* 317–326.

Mellers, B. A., & McGraw, A. P. (2001). Anticipated emotions as guides to choice. *Current Directions in Psychological Science, 10,* 210–214.

Oatley, K., & Johnson-Laird, P. N. (1996). The communicative theory of emotions: Empirical tests, mental models, and implications for social interaction. In L. L. Martin & A. Tesser (Eds.), *Striving and feeling: Interactions among goals, affect, and self-regulation.* Mahwah, NJ: Erlbaum.

Oettingen, G., & Gollwtizer, P.M. (2004). Goal setting and goal striving. In M. B. Brewer & M. Hewstone (Eds.), *Emotion and motivation* (pp. 165–183). Malden, MA: Blackwell.

Pervin, L. A. (1989). Goal concepts in personality and social psychology: A historical perspective. In L. A. Pervin (Ed.), *Goal concepts in personality and social psychology* (pp. 1–17). Hillsdale, NJ: Erlbaum.

Petty, R. E., & Krosnick, J. A. (1995). *Attitude Strength: Antecedents and Consequences.* Mahwah, NJ: Erlbaum.

Pham, M. T. (1998). Representativeness, relevance, and the use of feelings in decision making. *Journal of Consumer Research, 25,* 144–159.

Pieters, R. G. M. (1993). A control view on the behavior of consumers: Turning the triangle. In G. J. Bamossy & W. F. van Raaij (Eds.), *European advances in consumer research, 1,* 507–512.

Pieters, R., Allen, D., & Baumgartner, H. (2001). A means-end conceptualization of goal-directed consumer behavior. In T. J. Reynolds & J. C. Olson (Eds.), *Understanding consumer decision making: The means-end approach to marketing and advertising Strategy* (pp. 413–433). Mahway, NJ: Erlbaum.

Pieters, R. G. M., Baumgartner, H., & Allen, D. (1995). A means-end chain approach to consumer goal structures. *International Journal of Research in Marketing, 12,* 227–244.

Pieters, R. G. M., & M. Wedel (2007). Goal control of attention to advertising: The Yarbus implication. *Journal of Consumer Research, 34,* 224–233.

Powers, W. T. (1973). *Behavior: The control of perception.* Chicago, IL: Aldine.

Raghunathan, R., & Pham, M. T. (1999). All negative moods are not equal: Motivational influences of anxiety and sadness on decision making. *Organization Behavior and Human Decision Processes, 79,* 56–77.

Richard, R., van der Pligt, J., & de Vries, N. (1995). Anticipated affective reactions and prevention of AIDS. *British Journal of Social Psychology, 34,* 9–21.

Richard, R., van der Pligt, J., & de Vries, N. (1996). Anticipated affect and behavioral choice. *Basic and Applied Social Psychology, 18,* 111–129.

Reynolds, T. J., & Olson, J. C. (Eds.). (2001). *Understanding consumer decision making: The means-end approach to marketing and advertising strategy.* Mahway, NJ: Erlbaum.

Roseman, I. J., Antoniou, A. A., & Jose, P. E. (1996). Appraisal determinants of emotions: Constructing a more accurate and comprehensive theory. *Cognition and Emotion, 10,* 241–277.

Rotter, J. B. (1966). Generalized expectancies for internal versus external control of reinforcement. *Psychological Monographs, 80* (1, Whole No. 609), 1–28.

Schwartz, S. H. (1992). Universals in the content and structure of values: Theoretical and empirical tests in 20 countries. In M. Zanna (Ed.), *Advances in experimental social psychology* (Vol. 25, pp. 1–65). New York: Academic Press.

Seo, M.-G., Feldman Barrett, L., & Bartunek, J. M. (2004). The role of affective experience in work motivation. *Academy of Management Review, 29,* 423–439.

Shah, J. Y., Kruglanski, A. W., & Friedman, R. (2003). Goal systems theory: Integrating the cognitive and motivational aspects of self-regulation. In S. J. Spencer, S. Fein, M. P. Zanna, & J. M. Olson (Eds.), *Motivated social perception: The Ontario Symposium* (Vol. 9, pp. 247–275). Mahwah, NJ: Erlbaum.

Sheppard, B. H., Hartwick, J., & Warshaw, P. R. (1988). The theory of reasoned action: A meta-analysis of past research with recommendations for modifications and future research. *Journal of Consumer Research*, *15*, 325–343.

Shiv, B., & Fedorikhin, A. (1999). Heart and mind in conflict: the interplay of affect and cognition in consumer decision making. *Journal of Consumer Research*, *26*, 278–292.

Simonson, I. (1992). The influence of anticipating regret and responsibility on purchase decisions. *Journal of Consumer Research*, *19*, 105–118.

Skinner, E. A. (1996). A guide to constructs of control. *Journal of Personality and Social Psychology*, *71*, 549–570.

Stein, N. L., M. D. Liwag, & E. Wade (1996). A goal-based approach to memory for emotional events: Implications for theories of understanding and socialization. In R. D. Kavanaugh, B. Zimmerberg, & S. Fein (Eds.), *Emotion: Interdisciplinary perspectives* (pp. 91–118). Mahway, NJ: Erlbaum.

Stein, N. L., Trabasso, T., & Liwag, M. (1993). The representation and organization of emotional experience: Unfolding the emotion episode. In M. Lewis & J. M. Haviland (Eds.), *Handbook of emotions* (pp. 279–300). New York: Guilford.

Taylor, S. E., & Pham, L. B. (1996). Mental simulation, motivation, and action. In P. M. Gollwitzer & J.A. Bargh (Eds.), *The psychology of action: Linking cognition and motivation to behavior* (pp. 219–235). New York: Guilford.

Vallacher, R. R., & Wegner, D. M. (1985). *A theory of action identification*. Hillsdale, NJ: Erlbaum.

Vallacher, R. R., & Wegner, D. M. (1987). What do people think they're doing? Action identification and human behavior. *Psychological Review*, *94*, 3–15.

Vallacher, R. R., & Wegner, D. M. (1989). Levels of personal agency: Individual variation in action identification. *Journal of Personality and Social Psychology*, *57*, 660–671.

van der Pligt, J., Zeelenberg, M., van Dijk, W.W., de Vries, N. K., & Richard, R. (1998). Affect, attitudes and decisions: Let's be more specific. In W. Stroebe & M. Hewstone (Eds.), *European review of social psychology* (Vol. 8, pp. 34–66). Chichester: Wiley.

Verhallen, T. M. M., & Pieters, R.G. M. (1984). Attitude theory and behavioral costs. *Journal of Economic Psychology*, *5*, 223–249.

Vroom, V. H. (1964). *Work and motivation*. New York: Wiley.

Winell, M. (1987). Personal goals: The key to self-direction in adulthood. In M. E. Ford & D. H. Ford (Eds.), *Humans as self-constructing living systems: Putting the framework to work* (pp. 261–287). Hillsdale, NJ: Erlbaum.

Zeelenberg, M., & Pieters, R. (1999). Comparing service delivery to what might have been: Behavioral responses to regret and disappointment. *Journal of Service Research*, *2*, 86–97.

Zeelenberg, M., van Dijk, W. W., Manstead, A.,S. R., & van der Pligt, J. (2000). On bad decisions and disconfirmed expectancies: The psychology of regret and disappointment. *Cognition and Emotion*, *14*, 521–541.

14

Goal-Directed Perception

CHRIS JANISZEWSKI

University of Florida

The study of perception is guided by metaphors of the mind and the role perception plays within the context of the metaphor. For example, consider the metaphor that the mind is a machine or that the mind operates like a computer program. In this metaphor, perception is an act that allows the system to represent the environment as a series of symbolic concepts that can be input into higher order processes (i.e., it is a decoder). Consistent with the computer program metaphor, an identical input should be perceived in a constant fashion (1) by the same person on different occasions or (2) by different people on the same occasion. The assumption of *perceptual invariance* allows researchers to make inferences about higher order processes that manipulate these perceptual inputs, without worrying about the variability of the inputs. The computer metaphor also directs the research of those that focus on the act of perception. If cognition depends on software, then the goal of perceptual research should be to discover fundamental subroutines (i.e., decipher the programming code). Research on feature identification, feature integration, and visual search all seek to discover how a perception is constructed.

An alternative metaphor of the mind is the neural metaphor. In this metaphor, the mind is composed of neurons that must learn to execute motor and, subsequently, conceptual acts. To execute any one simple act, a considerable amount of parallel processing and coordination must occur. In this metaphor, perception is the act of isolating and assigning meaning to the neural activation that was responsible for the execution of motor and conceptual acts. As the individual develops a larger array of motor and cognitive abilities, perceptual processes are used to (1) identify patterns of neural stimulation that are useful for goal achievement and (2) identify the differentiating characteristics of neural activation that lead to unexpected, but relevant outcomes. In this type of model, systems for initiating motor acts, representing sequences of neural activation, and assigning the cognitive concepts to these sequences, are all related through their overlapping neural activation. If perception is a consequence of the selection of a neural array, then the goal of perceptual research should be to discover how meaning is created at any given moment, how meaning motivates behavior, and how verbal, motor, and affective responses interact owing to their common source of initiation (i.e., perception).

The goal of this chapter is the provide insight into the content and consequences of perception (the neural metaphor) as opposed to the processes used to generate or use a perception (the computer metaphor). The review begins with a historical account of the many metaphors that have been used to account for perceptual processes. This review is meant to illustrate two points. First, privileged metaphors are inevitably replaced when they are no longer able to offer any additional insights. Second, there are recurrent themes that permeate the history of perceptual research. The review continues with a discussion of two recent accounts of perception, proposed by Anthony Marcel and Michael Tomasello, that are consistent with the neural metaphor. These accounts of perception are used as a foundation for a model of goal directed perception. The model is used to provide insight into a number of intriguing findings within the perceptual, cognitive, social, and consumer literatures.

HISTORY OF PERCEPTUAL THEORY

Early Perceptual Research

The study of perception has been an ongoing topic of inquiry for over 2,000 years. Many of the early theories of vision and perception incorporated emission (i.e., light emitted by eyes), reception (i.e., light reflected by objects and received by eyes), or a combination of the two (see Wade 2001 for discussion). Democritus (460–370 B.C.) hypothesized that objects emit moving atoms that displace air and leave an imprint on the eye. Plato (427–347 B.C.) proposed that both the object and the eyes emit light and that vision occurs when the two streams of light intersect in space. Aristotle (384–322 B.C.) rejected the emission assumption, owing to the inability of people to see in the dark, and argued that objects reflect light that displace the medium (e.g., air) between the object and the viewer. Euclid (365–275 B.C.) proposed that the eyes emit visual rays at varying densities within the visual field. Euclid used his approach to deduce important principles in visual acuity, foveal and parafoveal vision, and spatial perception. Ptolemy (85–165 A.D.) advanced Euclid's ideas by arguing that both eyes emitted continuous light rays and that the differences in object displacement for each eye were the source of depth perception. Kepler (1571–1631) was the first to discuss a reception theory that incorporated the optics of the eye, arguing that the retina acted like a camera obscura and that vision was the recording of an image.

The 17th Through 19th Centuries

Perceptual research in the 17th through 19th centuries represents an initial appreciation for the perceptual content versus perceptual process distinction. Rationalists, including Descartes (1595–1650), Spinoza (1632–1677), and Leibniz (1646–1716) argued that meaning was derived through reasoning, logic, and mathematical principles. The goal of perceptual research should be an understanding of these processes (i.e., the innate laws of perception). Empiricists,[1] including Locke (1632–1704), Berkeley (1685–1783), and Hume (1711–1776), argued the laws and knowledge used to assign meaning were initiated, refined, and generalized through experience (i.e., perception, and by extension knowledge, is subjective). Locke solved the subjective content problem by arguing that the study of perception should be limited to the objective qualities of objects (e.g., shape, size, quantity, and movement), forsaking the more subjective qualities (e.g., color, taste, and temperature). Berkeley adopted the more radical position that all perceptual experience is subjective and that there was no way to have true knowledge about the state of the world, and by extension, the laws of perception.

The work of Weber (1795–1878) and Fechner (1801–1887) was a direct response to the claim that the discipline of psychology could not be scientific owing to the subjective nature of perception (Ballantyne, 2003). Weber showed that the just noticeable difference in stimulus intensity (i.e., touch sensation) was proportionate to the current intensity of the stimulus and that the proportion was constant across levels of stimulus intensity ($k = \Delta I / I$). Weber further found that just noticeable differences varied by the location of the receptors (e.g., tongue, arm, back) and that active discrimination (i.e., lifting weights) is more sensitive than passive discrimination (i.e., holding weights).

Fechner described the empirical laws of subjective perception in mathematical terms (e.g., Sensation = K log R; where R = stimulus value), setting the foundation for modern psychophysics. By demonstrating that subjective perception behaved in a systematic and predictable way (i.e., focusing on process), Fechner countered Berkeley's claim that the study of perception was inherently nonscientific.

Helmholtz (1821–1894) took an alternative approach to Berkeley's criticism and theorized about the source of perceptual content. For example, Helmholtz adopted a reductionist position and proposed that sensations from external stimuli (elemental units) were impoverished. To achieve meaning, these sensations were combined with learned unconscious associations. Helmholtz argued that perception did not have to be an accurate representation of the sensory data because the unconscious associations encouraged the most likely representation (i.e., the likelihood principle). In effect, the perceiver was a problem solver that used subsets of the sensory data to generate hypotheses and then selected the hypothesis that had the best goodness of fit with the data. These hypotheses were learned, confirmed, and updated with experience (i.e., empiricism assumption). Helmholtz's approach was especially appealing because it offered a solution to the vexing problem of object constancy—i.e., the fact that perception is not sensitive to changes in the size, brightness, and shape of the retinal image that occur when an object is manipulated in space and/or the viewer moves in space. In summary, Helmholtz was the first prominent researcher to theorize about the contents of perception.

The reminder of the 19th century perception research focused on what were, and were not, appropriate areas of psychological study. Wundt (1832–1920) argued that there was a set of basic processes (e.g., sensation, perception, reaction time) that were observable through a scientific method and a set of higher order processes (e.g., meaning, memory, language, intention) that could not be observed owing to the reactivity inherent in self-reports (i.e., the subjectivity of perception). The defining feature of basic processes was that they were simple and could be evoked by external stimuli, hence responses to changes in the characteristics of these external stimuli could be mapped. Yet, Wundt did not see perceptual processes as elemental, arguing that a series of tones could make a chord and that perception of each tone was not necessary to appreciate the chord. This holistic perceptual process, called creative synthesis, was also supported by the finding that reaction times to letters and words were equivalent and that the number of flashed letters or words people can remember averages four to six units. In contrast, Titchener (1867–1927) adopted a more reductive position than Helmholtz and argued that all cognition was elemental. Perceptions were created by combining sensory elements and higher order processes were combinations of these perceptions. Külpe (1862–1915) offered a third view, arguing that higher order processes were a relevant topic of inquiry and that there were meaningful and persistent relationships between task instructions and behavioral responses. Thus, Külpe adopted a much more molar level of analysis, assuming perceptions were inputs into higher order processes, but not worrying about their source.

Direct Perception

James J. Gibson and Eleanor J. Gibson (E. J. Gibson, 1969; J. J. Gibson, 1966, 1979) made the next significant contribution in the conceptualization of the contents of perception.[2] Prior to the Gibsons' critique, it was assumed that the role of the visual system, and the sensory system in general, was to gather information for subsequent interpretation. The visual sensory system was passive, recording stimulation, in a manner similar to a video camera.[3] The Gibsons' insight was that the sensory system is part of an active system that must accomplish goals by navigating the environment. If this is so, the unit of analysis should not be the retinal image of an isolated object, but the array of ambient light reflected in a dynamically changing environment. The study of perception should not focus on the construction of meaning from the integration of elemental units, but the differentiation of events within the overly rich environment so as to make them useful during current and future goal pursuit. In effect, the Gibsons' reversed the Helmholtzian perspective, arguing that the environment was too rich, not too impoverished, to be useful without additional processing. In an overly rich environment, a person cannot possibly perceive each individual element and then integrate the elements, so it must be the case that people discriminate patterns among the stimulation.[4]

J. J. Gibson viewed visual perception as the act of identifying structure in the light reflected by an environment (i.e., a perception is selected, not constructed). Gibson observed that light reflects off surfaces in a lawful manner. Therefore, each point of ambient light within the visual array provides information about the reflecting surfaces facing that point. Through experience, a person learns to interpret the relationships among the points of light (i.e., assign meaning to the structure in the array). This ability to isolate structure in the visual array of light is useful when combining information from each eye or when attempting to maintain object constancy. The person also learns how to combine this information about ambient light with kinetic information, so that the perceptual representation is of the perceiver in the environment (i.e., one could not catch a ball if the ball and the hand could not be represented in perceptual space). Repeated sampling of the environment, and sensitivity to invariants (e.g., ambient light related to contours and texture), allows the perceiver to perceive certain items as stationary and others as moving within the environment, even when the perceiver is moving. Gibson also argued that perception is defined by the organism's goals in its current environment. Representation consists of the acts that can be performed with an object, "what it provides or furnishes, either for good or ill" (Gibson, 1979). This insight explains the diversity of visual systems among species and the variance of perceptual responses to common environments among different people and cultures.

Present Day Perceptual Research

The historical review of perceptual research is meant to illustrate that both content and process have been important topics in the investigation into the act of perception. Yet, if one were to review the past 50 years of perceptual research, a large majority of the effort has focused on process, as opposed to content. Major process contributions include feature detection theory (Julesz, 1971), feature integration theory (Treisman & Gelade, 1980), pattern matching (cf. Geisler & Super, 2000), object perception (cf. Kersten, Mamassian, & Yuille 2004), visual search behavior (Posner, 1980; but see Vecera & Farah, 1994), and enumeration (cf. Trick & Pylyshyn, 1994). This conclusion extends to consumer research. A large majority of consumer researchers assume perception is a process that generates an output to be used in higher order information processes (Greenwald & Leavitt, 1984). The primary exceptions to this conclusion are research on semiotics (e.g., McQuarrie & Mick, 2003; Mick & Buhl, 1992), literary criticism (e.g., Stern, 1993), and volume, size, and distance perception (e.g., Brooks, Kaufmann, & Lichtenstein, 2004; Raghubir & Krishna, 1996, 1999).

In the next section, I discuss two relatively modern theories of perceptual content. Anthony Marcel exemplifies the elemental, constructive, mediated approach to perception first proposed by Helmholtz. Michael Tomasello exemplifies and the selective, differentiating, direct approach to perception first proposed by the Gibsons. These theories are interesting because they differ considerably in orientation, but attempt to address the perceptual variance problem that has plagued perception research since its inception. Perceptual variance refers to the idea that the same stimulus can have different meanings in different contexts. Marcel emphasizes perceptual experience and attempts to explain *how* a perception is generated. Tomasello emphasizes goal-directed behavior and attempts to explain *why* a perception is generated.

THE VARIANCE OF PERCEPTUAL CONTENT

Anthony Marcel

Anthony Marcel's (1983b) theory of perception addresses the issue of perceptual variance by advocating a role for the subconscious in perception. Marcel defines his theory by challenging the assumptions common to mainstream perceptual research. First, Marcel rejects the assumption that cognition and conscious experience are one in the same (i.e., the Identity Assumption). Second, Marcel rejects the assumption that behavior can only be directed by the contents of conscious experience (i.e., Directed Thought Assumption). Third, Marcel rejects the assumption that external stimuli engage the perceptual system as a series of discrete events (i.e., Discrete Sampling Assumption). Of these assumptions, the first two directly address the issue of perceptual variance. By allowing for cognition and conscious experience to be dissociated, Marcel allows for perceptual invariance at the subconscious level, but perceptual variance at the conscious level. In this way, subconscious perception can direct behavior, whereas conscious experience can only provide an account of the behavior.

Marcel (1983a) provides an interesting empirical demonstration to support his position. Marcel presented masked stimuli for very short periods of time and asked viewers to indicate (1) whether or not they saw a stimulus (presence/absence judgment), (2) which of a pair of stimuli had more graphic similarity to the presented stimulus (graphemic similarity), and (3) which of a pair of stimuli had more semantic similarity to the presented stimulus (semantic similarity). Although one might expect that reduced presentation times will impact semantic judgments prior to graphemic judgments prior to presence/absence judgments, the opposite pattern of results was observed. That is, for a given presentation duration, people were quite accurate (e.g., over 90%) at making semantic judgments even though they were fairly inaccurate (e.g., 55%) at making presence/absence judgments. The implication is that the subconscious can respond to the environment before conscious, subjective experience has an opportunity to exist. Marcel argued that this demonstration was inconsistent with the identity and directed thought assumptions because conscious thought did not direct responses in the semantic similarity judgments. Marcel further argued that any of a number of conscious experiences could be produced from the same array of subconscious activation.

Marcel was not the first to claim a dissociation between the "sources of behavior" and conscious thought (e.g., Freud, 1856–1939; the behaviorist movement in the first half of the 20th century), even within the standard information processing paradigm (e.g., Nisbett & Wilson, 1977). Yet, Marcel was one of the first to describe a perceptual processing system in which the determinants of behavior were independent of conscious experience. Marcel proposed that subconscious perception depended on distributed processing in that all sensory stimulation is analyzed, transformed, and redescribed into all possible forms of representation automatically and independently of consciousness (all perceptual variants exist in the subconscious). These moment-to-moment representations are both temporary (called a *result*) and sustained (called a *record*). Results are subconscious perceptions that can be used as input into other processes, to direct behavior, to prime related concepts, and to suggest candidate hypotheses for conscious experience. Because conscious experience is a slow process, these candidate hypotheses are then fit to records, the more permanent trace of the moment-to-moment representations. Thus, Marcel believes conscious experience is a behavior produced by the subconscious that does not have special status relative to other behaviors (e.g., motor responses, affective responses, language) produced by the subconscious.

Perceptual variance occurs because of the way in which conscious percepts are fit to records. Marcel argues that the constructive act of generating a conscious experience depends on expectancy, frequency, and a tendency to have experiences corresponding to the highest or most functional level of representation. This means that the selection of a conscious experience is sensitive to recent experiences and the constraints of the current processing goal (i.e., consciousness is context specific). The perception of an object is variable because the object is encountered in different contexts. These contexts can be prior thoughts, the environment, or task objectives.

Critique. Marcel's theory represents a departure from traditional perceptual theories because it minimizes the role of conscious experiences in directing behavior. The strength of Marcel's theory is that it provides a detailed account of how a person can use the subconscious to respond to the environment, from mundane postural adjustments to more meaningful choice behavior. Marcel's theory also provides insight as to why conscious experience is variable and why this variance need not limit research into cognition. The weaknesses of Marcel's theory is it (1) does not specify how subconscious records come to motivate behavior, (2) why any one record should be more influential than another, (3) how goals are integrated into the perception/behavior system, (4) how people generate creative behavior and thought, and (5) why consciousness exists and/or when it might exert an influence on behavior.

Michael Tomasello

Michael Tomasello (1999) adopts a cultural, evolutionary perspective on perceptual development, thus addressing the issue of perceptual variance from a functional perspective. Tomasello argues that perceptual processes cannot be understood unless one understands the role these processes play in development (i.e., why they exist). Tomasello remarks that human infants are born without the ability to survive. In order to survive, infants must learn how to achieve goals through the efforts of others. Owing to their dependence on others, infants develop a communication system, both verbal and nonverbal. In effect, children and caregivers develop a communication system that allows each of them to understand the needs of the child. Perception supports the communication system and, ultimately, must support goal identification and achievement.

Tomasello (1999) contends that the human communication system is unique among all species because humans have a special capacity to understand that their behavior, and *the behavior of others*, is intentional. Humans do not mentally represent others' behaviors as static outcomes. Humans represent the intent of others behaviors (e.g., a "moving person" can be running, chasing, or fleeing). Likewise, humans do not represent objects, but the intent associated with the use of the objects (e.g., a block of wood can be a paperweight, building material, or a weapon). Thus, perceptual processes operate in a system that is trying to understand why others behave as they do, help identify and represent the causes of these behaviors, and, as the individual develops, do the same with respect to achieving goals in a multitude of environments.

One of the critical assumptions of Tomasello's theory is that humans can take the attentional perspective of others. This ability is useful at all stages of development. For infants, behavioral modeling requires that the child understand the parent is trying to demonstrate a skill that helps achieve a goal. For example, by the age of 9 months, a child can be selective in its mimicry because it understands that only a subset of the observed behavior is necessary for goal achievement. This subset of behaviors must be differentiated relative to the host of available behaviors. This differentiation is a perceptual process. Likewise, language can be used to represent causes and effects associated with goal achievement. Between the ages of 18 and 24 months, the child becomes sensitive to the parent's use of common and novel communication symbols and can assign novel language symbols to novel objects. This creation of a communication system is also a perceptual process. Novel language symbols are also assigned to novel objects used in intentional acts, but not to novel objects used in unintentional acts. This implies that language (and all its labels) exists because it allows a person to represent and communicate about intentional behavior.

Tomasello's theory incorporates many of the ideas advanced by the Gibsons, but adds insight as to the motivation for development of perceptual skills and the growth of a representational system. Perception is a dynamic and selective act, as opposed to static process, that relies on successes and failures in goal-directed behavior to determine what is worthy of representation and what is not. People use the environment, in combination with their personal perspective and/or the perspectives of others, to generate meanings associated with objects that are used in intentional behavior. These objects can be gestures, physical objects, symbols (e.g., words), or concepts. In this perspective, memory supports the creation of novel representations because it allows a person to note differences between prior and current activation.

Tomasello's theory of perception has three important implications. First, knowledge and meaning are goal-based. The meanings people assign to words, objects, behaviors, and situations are a consequence of the "uses" of these stimuli. Second, perception is perspectival in that the experienced meaning depends on a shared perspective. The same object, word, or gesture can have very different meanings depending on assumptions about the intent of the communicator. It is only in the absence of contextual information that signals intent that an object, word, or gesture will be represented consistent with its most common intent (i.e., the likelihood principle). Third, perception and behavior are symbiotic in their representation. If the purpose of perception is to understand intent, and meaning is intentional, then it should not be surprising that any ongoing behavior can influence perception (e.g., smiling while perceiving an event can influence perception of the event) or that perception can initiate behavior (e.g., mimicry).

GOAL-DIRECTED PERCEPTION

The work of Marcel and Tomasello represent the contrast in a Helmholtzean and a Gibsonian approach to perception. Despite this difference in approaches, each theorist addresses the issue of perceptual variance in an insightful way that, surprisingly, does not contradict the view of the other. Marcel accounts for perceptual variance by arguing subconscious perception is invariant, but that many possible conscious experiences can be assigned to representations available at the subconscious level. Tomasello accounts for perceptual variance by arguing that an item is assigned meaning according to the person's goals, prior experiences, and the item's function in the environment. The views of Marcel and Tomasello can be combined to create a hybrid model of perception that is consistent with the goal-directed view of Tomasello, but borrows some of the subconscious processing ideas advanced by Marcel.

First, let's begin with the assumption that perception depends on a distributed memory system (Fiedler, 2000; McClelland & Rumelhart, 1985). In this system, *concepts* are represented as a distribution of binary units that can be thought of as *feature codes*, as illustrated in Figure 14.1.[5] For example, a dog has four legs, fur, a bark, a gait, etc., that can thought of as feature codes. The array of feature codes that define a concept can come from any combination of sensory systems (e.g., visual, aural, motor, proprioceptive) and need no have a corresponding verbal label. Concepts are created through a process of discrimination learning (i.e., each new concept includes the distribution of an old concept plus / less additional differentiating units). New concepts develop because previous concepts are insufficiently predictive, hence differentiating a concept is adaptively valuable. The act of perception is the act of selecting an existing concept(s) as pertinent to an ongoing

Stimulation is mapped onto feature codes.

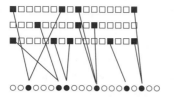

Visual Stimulation
Audio Stimulation
Tactile Stimulation

Patterns of feature codes represent concepts

○○●●○○●○○○○●●○○●○●○○   Concept 1
○○●●●●○●○○○○○○●○○●○○   Concept 2
○○●●●●○●○○○○●●○●○○○○○   Concept 3
○○○○○○○●○○○○●●○●○○○●○○   Concept 4
●●●●●○●○○●○●●○●○○●○○   Concept 5

Figure 14.1 Illustration of distributed memory (adapted from Fiedler, 2000)

set of goals. Concepts can be communicative, emotional, or behavioral. More than one concept can be selected concurrently (i.e., a person can be talking while engaging in behavior). Meaning is inherent in all concepts, hence there is no need to propose a underlying semantic-concept system, although it may be easier to think in these terms.

The process of perception is noisy and imprecise for a number of reasons, including (1) there is a large amount of neural activation available at any one moment, owing to the complexity of the environment and the continuous nature of this activation; (2) an array of neural activation can support many concepts; (3) it is uncommon that any one concept will be uniquely represented in the array of neural activation (i.e., competing concepts can be activated by different subsets of the stimulation); (4) the selection of one concept can inhibit the simultaneous selection of other concepts that are based in the same response system; (5) the selection of a concept can prime the selection of related concepts in subsequent perceptions, and (6) inhibited concepts are less likely to be selected in subsequent perceptions. The process of perception is complex because multiple concepts (e.g., those supporting motor responses, emotional experiences, language) can be generated from the same pattern of neural activation. The process is also complex because the sensory system "observes" ongoing behavior (i.e., a person observes his behavior), hence overt responses become part of the array of neural activation for future perception (Welch, 1986).

The second assumption is that perception is goal-based (Allport, 1987; Hommel, Müsseler, Aschersleben, & Prinz, 2001). The term "goal" is used broadly in that the cognitive system is designed to allow the individual to accomplish acts. Thus, a pattern of neural activation can activate goals (i.e., one type of concept) and these goals can encourage the selection of concepts that are consistent with the achievement of the goal. Goals are represented as distributions of feature codes and these feature codes are part of many of the concepts represented in memory. Hence, overlap in the activation of the feature codes that define a goal concept and the feature codes that define other concepts can guide perception (i.e., the selection of communicative, emotional, or behavioral concept). In other words, once a goal becomes active owing to its perception, people become more likely to select concepts (i.e., generate perceptions) that include the neural activation that supported the generation of the goal. The Theory of Event Coding (Hommel, Müsseler, Aschersleben, & Prinz, 2001) provides a detailed analysis of how distributions of feature codes come to have meaning and how the activation associated with a goal can encourage the selection of specific feature codes (e.g., features) for integration into a more complete concept. In effect, this allows for a hierarchical structure in the perception of concepts that support perception, although it does not imply that concepts are learned hierarchically.

The third assumption is that language/conscious experience is a type of concept in the perceptual system, but it is not *the* concept that guides behavior (i.e., conscious experience is not causal cognition). Still, conscious thought, language production, and motor acts are observed by the sensory system and are a source of subsequent neural activation. Hence, the cognitive system has the interesting property of being able to generate a conscious commentary that does not guide current behavior, yet being able to incorporate this conscious commentary into the concepts that guide future behavior.

Given these assumptions, I propose that perception has the following properties.

1. *Nonconscious.* Perception is an inherently nonconscious process. People may have concepts that support conscious experience, but this conscious experience is not the cognition that directs behavior.
2. *Act-based representation.* Object /environments acquire meaning from the acts they afford. People learn neural/cognitive representations (concepts) because they are useful in achieving goals. There is no incentive to parse the world into concepts other than those that help achieve (avoid) beneficial (harmful) outcomes. Meaning is an inherent property of any concept (i.e., the concept exists because it is useful), but there is no semantic network that is a fundamental basis for all concepts.
3. *Goal-directed.* People generate perceptions to help accomplish current goals. People only perceive the events in the environment that are instrumental to an ongoing task, failing to perceive that which is currently irrelevant. It is only in those instances where there are few active goals that people perceive events as the events have been commonly perceived in the past (i.e., rely on the likelihood principle) when selecting a concept. In other words, the recency and frequency of prior perceptual experience represents a default for current perceptual experience, but is often overridden by the perceptions necessary to accomplish currently active goals.
4. *Perceptual variance.* The same "stimulus" can afford a variety of concepts. The number and variety of concepts is influenced by the ambiguity of the environment and recently available concepts. As such, there can be multiple ways to perceive a stimulus (perceptual variance) and multiple actions initiated by the stimulus (i.e., automatic goal activation of multiple goals).
5. *Perception-act equivalence.* The perception of an act and the production of an act rely on common subset of neural activation or feature codes (cf. Hommel, Müsseler, Aschersleben, & Prinz, 2001; Kohler et al., 2002). The implication is that the act of perception can prepare the individual for behavior.
6. *Multi-process.* Perceptual learning implies both the creation of meaning and the assignment of meaning. The goal of the perceptual system is to differentiate the environment so as to become more effective at achieving goals. An adaptive perceptual system is always prepared to engage in the process of discrimination. The ability to discriminate depends on the ability to know what is old (i.e., a concept) and to create something new (i.e., isolate

a novel set of feature codes as a new concept). Thus, new concepts are defined because they are useful.

7. *Resource dependent learning.* People must differentiate the patterns and sequences of feature codes/concepts that lead to novel consequences in order to enable perception of these events in the future. In discrimination learning, a person must isolate the new pattern and receive feedback, directly or indirectly, on whether this differentiation is useful. Attention is necessary for the execution of the discrimination learning (i.e., attention is necessary to differentiate the new from the old). In humans, the isolation of the novel set of feature codes is accompanied by an experience of novelty and, for noninfants, a cognitive representation. The acts of discrimination, cognitive representation, and association formation between communication, emotion, and behavioral concepts contribute to the creation of meaning for the novel event.

The usefulness of the goal-directed view of perception depends on the ability of the perspective to account for findings that are not easily explained by more traditional models of perception. Below, I discuss a range of interesting and unusual findings and an effort to show the explanatory power of the goal-directed view of perception. The discussion will focus on demonstrations that (1) people exhibit perceptual "blindness," (2) people initiate behavior nonconsciously, and (3) the conscious consideration of behavior alters behavior.

Perceptual Blindness

Inattentional Blindness. Simons and Chabris (1999) provide a popular demonstration that people can fail to perceive obvious events in their environment.[6] Simons and Chabris ask participants to view a 75-second video of two three-player teams tossing basketballs. The participant's goal is to keep separate counts of the number of bounce and aerial passes by the team wearing white (black) shirts, ignoring passes by the team wearing black (white) shirts. Forty-five seconds into the video, a woman in a gorilla suit or a woman holding an umbrella walks through the group of ball players. Afterwards, only 54% of the participants report having seen the gorilla and only 70% of the participants report seeing the woman with the umbrella. When the counting task is made easier (i.e., count the total number of passes), perception of the gorilla increases to 62% and perception of the woman with umbrella increases to 79%.[7]

Simons and Chabris' demonstration is a compelling example of a phenomenon Mack and Rock (1998) call inattentional blindness. Mack and Rock report a large number of studies that use a common experimental procedure. Participants watch presentations of a cross on a screen and judge which of the two arms is longer. During the fourth trial, a secondary object (e.g., brightly colored rectangle) appears on the screen. When the cross is in the foveal visual field and the secondary object is in the parafoveal visual field, approximately 25% of the participants fail to notice the secondary object. When the secondary object is in the foveal visual field and the cross is in the parafoveal visual field (i.e., the cross changes locations relative to earlier trials), approximately 75% of the participants fail to notice the secondary object. Yet, when participants are informed that another object might appear, or are directly informed to watch for a secondary object, it is always noticed. The secondary object is also noticed when it is relevant to the individual (e.g., their name, a smiley face), but features that are thought to be preattentively hardwired to create attention (e.g., contrasting color, contrasting orientation) do not increase the likelihood of seeing the secondary object. For example, when the distracter item was a red circle in a field of green circles, only 33% of the participants saw the secondary object.

Demonstrations of perceptual inattention are consistent with the claim that perception is goal-directed. People fail to perceive events that are irrelevant to their current goals, unless those events hold some significance for chronically active goals (e.g., a person's name in the Mack and Rock studies). Even more interesting is the failure of what was previously believed to be a perceptual universal—the ability of unique objects to "pop-out" of a visual display (cf. Treisman, 1988). Pop-out effects have been assumed to be automatic because pop-out is insensitive to the number of distracter items (e.g., a red circle is noticed among a group of green circles independent of the number of green circles). The Mack and Rock studies show items only pop-out if they are relevant to current processing goals. People are often blind to that which is irrelevant for current processing goals. It is this perceptual irrelevance that often leads to failures in perception, as is the case when a motorist fails to see a pedestrian, bicyclist, or an animal prior to a traffic accident.

Change Blindness. Change blindness is the inability of a person to notice a change in a scene if the change occurs while there is a visual disruption (e.g., camera pan, eye blink, saccadic eye movement) (Simons & Levin, 1997). In one of the more compelling examples of change blindness, people are approached by a confederate and asked for directions (Simons & Levin, 1998). During the conversation, two confederates carry a door between the respondent and the original confederate is replaced by a different person (i.e., one of the people behind the door switches places with the confederate). Subsequently, only 47% of the respondents notice the confederate has changed. In a second experiment, Simons and Levin find that only 35% of the respondents notice their conversation partner has changed if the confederates are from a different social group than the respondent. Other demonstrations involve trying to detect changes in a scene that changes slowly over a 20 to 30 second period. People show a remarkable inability to notice changes including adding or deleting a building from a street scene, adding or deleting a road from a corn field, or changing the color of one of four people's shirts (Simons, Franconeri, & Reimer, 2000).

Change blindness is often attributed to a person's inability to notice important details about the initial actor or scene (Simons, Reimer, & Franconeri, 2000). What is missing from this explanation is why some people perceive detail and others do not. It may be the case that the detail of perception is sensitive to the goals accompanying the perceptual experience. For example, when a person is stopped and asked for directions, the enquirer is often perceived at a general level (e.g., a white, male, college-aged stranger). This classification might rely on additional details (e.g., age, hair length, type of clothing), although these details need not be perceived directly (i.e., a classification of a college student relies on a perception of t-shirt, though not a specific type of t-shirt). As long as these features remain consistent for a level of classification (i.e., ethnicity, gender do not change), people will not notice a change in the conversation partner. In contrast, if an enquirer is an attractive person of the opposite sex, the perception may be more detailed owing to goals associated with social interaction, and changes in the conversation partner may be more easily noticed. In other words, if the change in the person or scene does not violate the feature codes and concepts used to generate the perception, a reality determined by the person's processing goals, the change will not be noticed.

The literature on inattentional blindness and change blindness implicitly assumes that a person must be consciously aware of an event if it is going to have an influence on their behavior. Recall that Marcel referred to this as the fallacy of the identity assumption (i.e., cognition and conscious experience are not one in the same). It may be more reasonable to assume that perception is a subconscious act which may, or may not, lead to a conscious experience. Thus, the demonstrations of perceptual blindness could be interpreted as evidence that many types of subconscious concepts are being generated (e.g., "gorilla concept"), but that concepts irrelevant to the task are not used to guide behavior or conscious experience. When subsequent questions are asked about these "ignored" concepts, they are not fluent and the person does not experience a feeling of memory (Whittlesea & Leboe, 2000). Admittedly, this is evidence of a null effect of perception on conscious experience. Yet, the evidence is interesting because most people claim they would be aware of the changes in their environment (cf. Levin, Momen, Drivdahl, & Simons, 2000) and, in fact, might have been if they had different processing goals. In fact, it is a person's failure to understand that processing goals influence perception that results in a person's disbelief that they could be susceptible to change blindness.

Consumer Applications. Demonstrations of perceptual blindness could be viewed as cute, anomalies in human perception. Yet, these same perceptual principles are prevalent in consumer behavior. For example, consider the finding that people are quite sensitive to price changes (Greenleaf 1995; Kalyanaram & Winer, 1995), yet cannot report the price of an item immediately after viewing it (Dickson & Sawyer, 1990). One explanation for these findings is that the goal of the price checking task is a comparison of the list price relative to a memory-based or context-based price standard. Hence, the perception of the price is more likely to consist of a perception of *higher than*, *lower than*, or *the same as* the list price. Also, consider the finding that increasing the size of an ad is effective in yellow page advertising (the claim is a standard part of the yellow page sales force support materials), but is fairly ineffective in feature advertising (Pieters, Wedel, & Zhang, 2005). In yellow page advertising, the reader's goals are consistent with the perception of all of the ads on a page, hence a larger ad draws initial attention and the ad is perceived. In feature advertising, the perceptual goals of most readers are inconsistent with the content of an ad. An ad will not be perceived even if it does receive a limited amount of attention owing to its size. Hence, the impact of ad size and other attention drawing factors is dependent on the goals of the viewer.

Nonconsciously Mediated Behavior

Volitional Behavior. There is considerable evidence that postural adjustment, proprioception (i.e., knowledge of body's location in space), athletic movements, etc., can occur without the participation of conscious experience. These events are often regarded as over learned behaviors that have become automatic. Rarer are demonstrations that people can engage in volitional behavior without the participation of any conscious experience. Yet, these demonstrations do exist. For example, the Titchener illusion occurs when people perceive a constant-sized disk to be larger when surrounded by small disks as compared to large disks. Despite the perceptual illusion associated with the two presentation formats, grip size is constant when people attempt to grasp the disk (Aglioti, DeSouza, & Goodale, 1995; cf. Glover, 2002). Similarly, if a to-be-touched object is moved while the eyes are in saccade, the hand is redirected to complete the touch, even though the person is not consciously aware of the new location (i.e., does not know the object has moved) (Bridgman, Lewis, Heit, & Nagle, 1979). The implication is that conscious experience is not being used to actively guide motor behavior. Instead, motor control systems are responding to nonconscious perceptions concerning the object.

What is interesting about the demonstrations involving the Titchener illusion and in-saccade object perception is that the concept that guides behavior has the potential to compete with the concept that supports the conscious experience, yet it does not. This lack of interference between the two concepts may be a consequence of the two concepts supporting different goals. The perception associated with the motor act supports the goal of picking up the disk. The perception associated with conscious experience supports the goal of communicating with others. To the extent that all people experience illusions in a similar manner, it is reasonable that the conscious experience associated with the task should be illusionary. In other words, people see and accept the illusion because they expect others will have the same experience.

Mimicry. Chartrand and Bargh (1999) show that people mirror the behaviors of others. For example, Chartrand and Bargh have a confederate engage in face rubbing or foot shaking and show that interaction partners are prone to mimic these behaviors. Chartrand and Bargh argue that there is a perception-behavior link in that the perception of a behavior also primes the motor representation of that behavior. As a consequence, the behavior becomes more likely to be initiated at some time in the near future. Chartrand and Bargh later show that these mimicking behaviors lead to greater liking of the mimicker by the mimickee and propose that mimicry acts like a social glue that promotes communication. What is critical across all of their studies is that participants have no conscious intent to mimic.

Mimicry has also been observed in infants. Children as young as 6-weeks-old can mimic the tongue protrusions, mouth openings, and head movements of their caregivers (Meltzoff & Moore, 1989, 1994; cf. Anisfeld, 1996). Interestingly, infants only mimic behaviors that already exist in their behavioral repertoire. It has been claimed that this mimicry occurs because of mirror neurons, neurons that are common to the perception and execution of a behavior.[8] Mirror neurons have been shown to be involved in the mimicking behavior of macaque monkeys (Rizzolatti & Arbib, 1998) and infants (Buccion, Binkofski, & Riggio, 2004). Mirror neurons have also been shown to allow for the coordinated representation of perceived movement, executed movement, and sounds accompanying the movement (Kohler et al., 2002), the implication being that the cognitive system can execute acts in response to a verbal cue without the participation of conscious experience.

It is important to recognize that mimicry is selective. For example, participants in the Chartrand and Bargh (1999) studies do not mimic the positioning of a confederate's feet or hands. It is also unlikely that the participants would mimic the confederate's direction of gaze, posture in the chair, or method of pointing, unless these acts were communicatively relevant. In fact, the majority of the confederate's behaviors are not even perceived because they are irrelevant to the goals of the conversation. In other words, the participant's interaction with the confederate provides an opportunity to isolate a large number of concepts, of which only a small number will be selected by the participant. Selected concepts do become more likely to guide future behavior, although the reasons for this mimicry are debatable (cf. Dijksterhuis, Smith, van Baaren, & Wigboldus, 2005; Janiszewski & van Osselaer, 2005).

Subliminally Primed Perception. One of the more robust findings in perception is the influence of expectations on perception (Stroop, 1935). For example, people that have been primed to perceive letters (numbers) will name an ambiguous stimulus (e.g., 13) as a letter (number) (Bruner & Minturn, 1955). The implication being that recent perceptions can influence current perceptions. This principle is often apparent in demonstrations of subliminal priming. For example, Bargh and Pietromonaco (1982) found that people subliminally primed with hostile words judge an ambiguously described person to be more hostile than people subliminally primed with neutral words. Subliminal priming can also influence perceptions of seemingly unrelated events. For example, Bargh, Chen, and Burroughs (1996) use a computer to subliminally present a picture of a either a young African American or young Caucasian face prior to each of 130 trials in a boring classification task. On the 130th trial, the program fails and the experimenter informs the participant that the task will have to be repeated. Participants exposed to the African American prime react with greater hostility to the computer failure. These findings, and others (cf. Dagenbach, Carr, & Wilhelmsen, 1989; Draine & Greenwald, 1998), have been interpreted as evidence that subliminal stimuli can prime memory and bias subsequent judgments.

Recent research on subliminal priming suggests the process of subliminal priming is much more complex than previously believed. It may be the case that subliminal primes encourage the creation of nonconscious perceptions and these perceptions then bias subsequent perceptions. To appreciate this distinction, consider the recent findings of Abrams and Greenwald (2000). Abrams and Greenwald had participants classify 12 unambiguously pleasant (e.g., virture, cheer, angel, warm) and 12 unambiguously unpleasant words (e.g., bile, smut, fraud, death) as "positive" or "negative" using a speeded classification task. After 192 practice classification trials, participants engage in 288 priming trials in which a one of the 24 parent words subliminally precedes one of the other parent words. Finally, participants engage in 288 hybrid priming trials in which a hybrid of the pleasant (e.g., virtue + cheer = *virer*) or unpleasant (e.g., bile + smut = *biut*) words subliminally precedes one of the 24 target words. As expected, Abrams and Greenwald find that participants make classification errors when a subliminal prime and a target word are inconsistent in valence. More interestingly, participants continue to make these classification errors when the primes are hybrids (e.g., *biut* prime encourages the classification of a pleasant word as negative). A subsequent study shows that people are sensitive to the original valence of the words from which the hybrid was constructed, not the meaning of the hybrid. For example, if *smut* and *bile* are combined to create *smile*, the prime behaves as a negative, not as a positive, prime. A final study shows that primes only exert an influence if they are classified in the initial practice trials.

Abrams and Greenwald (2000) provide a number of findings consistent with the claim of goal-directed perception. First, processing goals (e.g., classify a word as positive or negative) can encourage a person to generate a perception (e.g., a valenced classification) that is independent of the default perception (e.g., semantic meaning associated with the more common use of the stimulus) as determined by the likelihood principle. Second, people can learn to use parts of words to make valenced classifications, much in the same way they use parts of words to make inferences about the identity and/or meaning of the word (e.g., Kouider & Dupoux, 2004). Since perception is the induction of meaning from a neural activation pattern, parts of the pattern have the potential to generate the same meaning as the entire pattern, assuming the parts are unique. Third, people are most sensitive to their most recent perceptual act. In Abrams and Greenwald (2000), people practice classifying the parent words as positive or negative on eight occasions prior to the whole-word and hybrid priming trials. Thus, the subconscious perception of the prime is likely to be its classification, not its semantic meaning. Fourth, the valenced subconscious perceptions can only bias judgments for which these perceptions have relevance. When people have not been trained to classify the valenced word in the training trials, the nonconscious perception is likely to be semantic. The semantic perception has little influence on the subsequent perception that supports the valence classification of the target word, so it exerts no influence.

There are other curious findings in the semantic priming literature that are consistent with the goal-directed perception perspective. First, subliminal priming effects are sometimes limited to situations where the participant is aware that there are subliminal primes. For example, Kouider and Dupoux (2004) observe a Stroop priming effect only when respondents are aware that there is a subliminal priming procedure. Thus, it may be that subliminal perceptions do not exert an influence on judgments and behavior unless the goals of the processing task dictate their usage. Second, subliminal priming effects are sometimes limited to situations where the prime is consistent with the motivations of the individual. For example, Strahan, Spencer, and Zanna (2002) show that thirst related subliminal primes enhance the consumption of beverages for people that are thirsty, but not for people that are not thirsty. Again, it appears as if the prime must be consistent with the goal if it is going to influence a behavior (i.e., more consumption) or experience (i.e., experiencing the beverage as thirst quenching).

Implicit Learning. There is a fair amount of evidence that people can execute behaviors without an accompanying verbal commentary. Automatically learned responses comprise a large portion of these behaviors (cf. Bargh & Chartland, 1999; Shiffrin & Schneider, 1977). There are also automatic responses that are either learned incidentally (i.e., without the conscious awareness of the rule) or learned better incidentally. For example, people can learn to predict more preferable outcomes without knowing the reason for their prediction. Bechara et al. (1997) had people pick monetary outcomes from four decks of cards, with decks A and B providing high variance outcomes that had a negative mean value and decks C and D providing low variance outcomes that have a positive mean value. People learned to favor the C and D decks, but were not aware of their preference. People were also unaware that they had heightened skin conductance responses to decks A and B (i.e., a somatic marker), a nonconscious signal to avoid these decks (but see Tomb et al., 2002). People can also learn procedural knowledge and artificial grammars without being aware of the rules governing these patterns (e.g., Lewicki, Hill, & Bizot, 1988; Reber, 1967, 1989; cf. Gomez & Schvaneveldt, 1994). In fact, instructions to actively use conscious processes to learn procedural knowledge and artificial grammars reduces the effectiveness of learning (Reber, 1976).

Consumer Applications. The key insight from these findings is not that consciousness plays a limited role in directing behavior, but that currently active goals combine with the activation initiated by the environment to direct behavior. For example, consider the large number of demonstrations of framing effects (Kahneman & Tversky, 1979; Levin, Schneider, & Gaeth, 1998). Framing effects are interesting because they seem to violate the assumption that there should be a context-free representation of information. Yet, it is odd that researchers would expect a context-free representation. Contextual effects on perception form the foundation of many theories of cognitive and social judgment (e.g., range theory, adaptation level theory, assimilation-contrast theory). In fact, Kahneman (2002) argues that framing effects are robust because they are perceptual. People generate a perception that is consistent with a frame, and fail to generate an alternative perception, because perception is sensitive to the information in the environment.

Consciously Mediated Behavior

The Illusion of Conscious Will. Daniel Wegner (2002) argues that many behaviors feel like they are determined by conscious will, but are not. People have the illusion of the conscious control over behavior because they make causal inferences by attending to the contingency between the act of doing and the conscious experience of doing. What people fail to realize is that there are situations in which they behave, but have no conscious experience of doing (e.g., automatic behaviors) and there are situations in which they have a conscious experience of doing, but are not actually in control of their behavior. People tend to ignore these later classes of behavior, thus perceive there to be a perfect correlation between the conscious experience of doing and the act of doing. In fact, this correlation is spurious. The real causal agents responsible for the conscious experience of doing and the act of doing are nonconscious perceptions.

Evidence that people mistakenly believe they are in control of their behavior is sparse because it is uncommon to look for such evidence. Still, there is some support for the hypothesis. For example, Brasil-Neto et al. (1992) asked respondents to move their left or right forefinger when they heard a click. During this task, magnets were turned on and off over motor areas on the left/right side of the brain. Although the magnets determined which finger was moved in response to the click, subjects claimed to voluntarily select the finger to be moved. Wegner observes that people make similar mistakes about systems outside of their body. Many people believe they can influence a random system (i.e., exhibit skill in a game of chance), a stable system (i.e., will a car to start), or an independent event (i.e., influence the outcome of a sporting contest).

Conscious Thought and Behavior. People often try to introspect in order to understand the reasons for their behavior. In many cases, introspection provides no insight into the reasons for behavior, except to the extent that the prior culturally-based explanations of behavior help a person to generate potential causes (Nisbett & Wilson, 1977; Wilson, 2002). To support this claim, consider the infant that attempts to "explain" its discomfort owing to a warm room, teething, or a diaper rash. If the child cannot yet perceive these causes as distinct perceptual events, they cannot be perceived as causes of the discomfort. As the child matures, it is taught reasons for its behavior, some accurate and some not (Nisbett & Wilson, 1977). Nonetheless, the causes and responses to the environment exist long before the child can understand their relationship. This failure to understand cause-behavior relationships persists into adulthood, where people make a variety of misattributions about the causes of their behavior (Ross & Nisbett, 1991).

Wilson and colleagues (cf. Wilson 2002; Wilson & Dunn 2004) have argued that the failure of introspection is apparent in people's inability to state the reasons for their behavior. In fact, stating reasons for behavior often alters behavior. For example, analyzing reasons for behavior lowers the correlation between a person's feelings and actual behavior (Wilson & Dunn, 1986), predicted and actual behavior (Wilson & LaFleur, 1995), and satisfaction with his/her choices (Wilson et al., 1993). Thus, it may be the case that conscious experience can be used to activate goals that guide decisions about behavior, but these rule-based behaviors may not be equivalent to the behavior that would have been initiated by the more basic associative system that guides most behaviors.

The work of Wilson and colleagues suggests that conscious thoughts can create a bias. In some ways, this is the equivalent of stating that a secondary task interferes with primary task completion, an obvious point. Yet, what is interesting about Wilson's evidence is the derogating conscious experiences were related to the task being performed. There is similar evidence that conscious monitoring can inhibit athletic performance (Hefferline, Keenan, & Halford, 1959), reduce the fluency of spoken language (Woods, Miltenberger, & Flach, 1996), and impair the performance of any over-learned behavior (Baumeister, 1984). It may be that conscious experience primes other feature codes and concepts that somehow get incorporated into the behavioral responses that might have naturally occurred. These additional feature codes and concepts make performance different and in many cases worse. In this type of system, consciousness has no special status in directing behavior, except that it can make certain feature codes and concepts more available and increase the likelihood that they are used in perception.

Motor Responses and Behavior. Two of the assumptions of the goal-directed model of perception are that the perceptual system uses stimulation from all sensory systems to generate perceptions and that observation of one's personal behavior creates neural activation (i.e., feature codes and concepts) for subsequent perceptions. Both of these assumptions are apparent in the influence of motor acts on judgment. For example, Strack, Martin, and Stepper (1988) have respondents hold a pen between their teeth (simulating smiling) or between their lips (inhibiting smiling) while judging the humor of cartoons. Smiling respondents judge the cartoons to be funnier. Similarly, Zajonc, Murphy, and Inglehart (1989) find that reading a script containing many words with the vowel "e" (facilitating smiling) led to a more enjoyable experience than reading a script containing many words with the vowel "ü" (inhibiting smiling). Smiling, or not, has also been shown to influence judgments of perceived guilt (Bodenhausen, Kramer, & Süsser, 1994) and an ambiguous social situation (Martin, Harlow, & Strack, 1992). In each of these cases, the act of smiling or not generates stimulation that is incorporated into subsequent perceptions.

There are numerous other demonstrations of the influence of motor movements on subsequent behavior that suggest interesting interactions among "cognitive systems." For example, in the realm of memory, moving one's head vertically (i.e., nodding yes) while viewing positive and negative words enhances memory for the positive words, whereas moving one's head horizontally (i.e., nodding no) enhances memory for the negative words (Förster & Strack, 1996). In the realm of reflexive eye blinks, eye blinks are slower when a startle response is to a positive picture than a negative picture (Lang, Bradley, & Cuthbert, 1990). In the realm of experiences, furrowing the brow induces feelings of mental effort (Strepper & Strack, 1993) and receiving positive feedback while sitting upright, as opposed to slumped, increases feelings of pride (Strepper & Strack, 1993). All of these demonstrations suggest the execution of a motor behavior provides neural activation that is used to generate perceptions that support future behavior and experience.

Impulsive Behavior. Research on impulsive behavior suggests there are two classes of behavior: impulsive behaviors that are gratifying, easily executed, and detrimental to our long term well-being (overeating, overspending, excessive drinking) and countervailing control behaviors that are difficult to monitor and execute (e.g., responsible eating, spending, and drinking). Impulsive behaviors are often claimed to "result from the encounter between a motivation and some activating stimulus" and to "occur without intention or plan" (Baumeister, 2002, p. 670). Impulsive behaviors are automatically initiated by a variety of stimulus cues, some that are novel, and control behaviors can only override the impulsive behaviors provided there are enough resources available to execute the control (Baumeister et al., 1998).

The goal-directed perspective on perception can be used to explain two events that are inconsistent with this currently popular explanation of impulsive behavior. First, available stimuli do not always result in impulsive behavior, even in the absence of conscious control. People do not overindulge every time they are in the presence of stimuli that have been inviting in the past, yet do occasionally overindulge in the presence of a novel stimulus. This apparently inconsistent behavior may be attributed to the fact that perception relies on currently active goals. For example, consider an overeater in the context of a party. If the overeater is actively involved in a conversation, goals associated with the conversation may preclude the person from perceiving the inviting food on an adjacent buffet. The conversation goals are more accessible relative to the oral gratification goals, thus perception is driven by these conversation goals. Yet, if the conversation wanes, the oral gratification goals may become more accessible, owing to feature codes associated with the food prime, and the food on the buffet becomes more likely to be perceived and eaten. Alternatively, in the absence of any motivating goal (i.e., boredom), people perceive the most practiced meanings in their environment owing to the likelihood principle. Perception of the food can activate the oral gratification goal and promote eating.

Second, Baumeister also claims that conscious control can limit indulgence. For example, suppose that a person perceives food in the environment and becomes more likely to indulge owing to active oral gratification goals. Also assume that the perception of food activates the language concept of "don't eat," a conscious description associated with prior instances of overindulgence. If the language concept is tied to self-presentation and health goals, then thoughts of not eating can prime goals that make other, nonindulgent behaviors more valued. For example, a person with active oral gratification and health goals may choose a healthier snack from the buffet.

Consumer Applications. The literature on consciously mediated behavior suggests that people have a difficult time explaining why they behave the way they do and that attempts at explanation and/or monitoring can alter behavior. If this is so, there should be a premium placed on investigations that focus on behavior, as opposed to the measurement of constructs that are hypothesized to influence behavior (unless the verbal behavior is meaningful in its own right). Second, there should be a premium on investigations that show mediation by experimentally manipulating a process, as opposed to measuring the process. Third, it may be interesting to consider the potential research agenda that might follow from the conclusions that conscious thought does not cause behavior, except through its ability to prime subsequent subconscious perceptions. This viewpoint implies that thought is an experience similar to an emotional experience. Value can be conceptualized as the premiums people place on different types of thought experiences. Marketers are successful because they can link their products, or the consumption of their products, to valuable thought experiences. The recent movement toward visual, image-based advertising, and away from benefit advertisement (cf. McQuarrie & Mick, 2003) is consistent with this perspective. McQuarrie and Mick (2003) suggest that advertising uses imagery to teach consumers about product meaning and the appropriate conscious experiences that should accompany consumption.

Similarly, consider the interest in hot cognition and its influence on thought (Dai & Sternberg, 2004; Mayer, Salovey, & Caruso, 2004), product appraisal (Yeung & Wyer, 2004), and decision making (Allen, 2002). Researchers who work in these paradigms have a difficult time quantifying causal agents because people cannot always communicate about hot perceptions. Yet, these perceptions certainly do influence behavior. In these situations, language, and in all likelihood conscious experience, may not be diagnostic of the nonconscious perceptions that are guiding behavior. The difficulty people have when trying to articulate the meaning of emotional decisions or possessions is apparent in their protocols about these events (e.g., Allen 2002; Price, Arnold, & Curasi, 2000).

CONCLUDING THOUGHTS

The objective of this chapter has been to encourage consumer researchers to embrace the variance of perceptual experience as a potential source of insight into consumer behavior, as opposed to unwanted error. Although the higher order processes that manipulate "perceptual outputs" are interesting and worthy of the extensive study they have received, the factors that lead to the selection of a single perception, or a collection of related perceptions, are also worthy of study. I anticipate that there are a number of areas that could benefit from incorporating the perspective of perceptual variance. I discuss two mainstream areas in an effort to illustrate how the ideas discussed in this chapter might be implemented.

Brand Relationships

Fourier (1998) discusses the importance of the relationships consumers develop with brands. Fournier's work is some of the most highly cited over the past 5 years, yet it has not yet been embraced by many mainstream information processing researchers. Perhaps this is because these researchers do not have relationships with brands, using the more formal definition of an interpersonal relationship (i.e., reciprocity). Yet, in some way, this misses the key conceptual insight of Fournier's contribution. An interpersonal relationship is defined by a series of interactions, all of them unique. A brand or product relationship can also be defined by a series of consumption experiences, all of them unique. These consumption experiences with a brand or product can vary, even though the product is standardized owing to mass production. The consumption experiences are supported by subconscious feature codes and concepts. It is the variety and use of these concepts that creates the relationship.

The second conceptual insight afforded by Fournier's analysis is that it is the perceptual variance at the conscious level, not the perceptual invariance at the subconscious level, that defines the consumer's relationship with the brand. A relationship is not simply summation of satisfactory and dissatisfactory experiences. It is the rich collection of varied conscious experiences (supported by subconscious concepts). In the absence of a conceptualization of perceptual variance, Fournier develops summary terms for the collection of conception experiences. The next major advance in the brand (product) relationship literature will come when marketers learn how to manage these consumption experiences. The key will not be "having a conversation with the consumer," as some have suggested. Instead, it will be learning how to encourage the consumer to have the experiences that make the product an integral part of their lives. Such an understanding will allow marketers to encourage consumers to be loyal to a product (e.g., Coke), a product category (e.g., seafood), an activity (e.g., mountain biking), or a belief (e.g., conservatism). Although these ideas are certainly a part of our history of research in consumer behavior (e.g., Holt, 2002; Levy, 1981), they have largely been ignored by researchers with a more cognitive, positivist orientation to their research program.

Customer-Based Brand Equity

Customer-based brand equity may be another area of inquiry that could benefit from the concept of perceptual variance. Consider the conventional wisdom about the source of customer-based brand equity. More positive experiences lead to more brand equity (Janiszewski & van Osselaer, 2000; Keller, 1993). Yet, the number of positive experiences may not be the sole source of brand equity. The variability in positive experiences may also contribute to brand equity. Although Keller (1993) refers to this variability of experience, he uses the variability of experience to support enhanced recall of the brand name, an increased likelihood of judging the brand appropriate for different consumption situations, and an increased differentiation of the brand. Yet, there are more consequences of variability than memory, contextual appropriateness, and differentiation effects. For example, soft drinks and deodorants both offer variability in experience, but successful soft drink brands have more equity on a per customer basis than successful deodorant brands. The difference between the variability of the experiences among these two brands is that the soft drink experiences are more varied over time (i.e., more complex). In a Gibsonian sense, the perception must be culled from an internal and external environment that is more information rich. This may be why ritual consumption often involves products that provide an opportunity for many motor acts during preparation and consumption. This complex consumption process allows for a highly nuanced experience. It is this interplay between motor behavior and conscious experience that give the experiences, and by extension the product, a richer meaning.[9] This richer meaning is the source of equity. More importantly, it is likely that certain mixtures of positive experiences (e.g., thoughtful, extended, affectively mixed, etc.) may lead to more equity than a simple stream of consistently uniform positive experiences.

Summary

The discussion of the potential opportunities to explore the consequences of perceptual variance might be interpreted as a call for more research in the domains traditionally associated with consumer culture theory (Arnold & Thompson, 2005). To some extent it is, but with three caveats. First, there is no reason that the study meaning should be relegated to the methodological techniques commonly used to investigate consumer culture theory. Experimental techniques can be effective at providing insight into meaning creation, as has been illustrated in the priming literature. Second, to some extent, much of consumer culture theory has focused on common meanings that are shared among individuals, not on the diversity of meanings experienced by a single individual or group of individuals. Although looking for commmonalities in the diversity of experiences among people may seem like a monumental task, there are certainly exemplars of these types of investigations in consumer research (e.g., Muniz & O'Guinn, 2001; Sirsi, Ward, & Reingen, 1996). Third, since perception and behavior may be inherently linked, there is an opportunity to assess how meaning evolves with consumption and brand communication. Consumption and communication experiences contribute to the meaning of the brand. Hence, research that investigates the influence of consumption (and communication) context, ritual, variability, and experience on meaning is needed. Given the inherent difficulty of self-reports, my hope is that this research will involve the manipulation of consumption and communication episodes in an effort to understand how these factors influence meaning.

NOTES

1. Empirism refers to the doctrine that abilities are learned through experience. Empiricism refers to the claim that knowledge should be generated from observation (data) as opposed to through reason.
2. Pomerantz and Kubovy (1986) offer an excellent review of the Gestalt approach to perception. The Gestalt view assumes perceptual organization relies on the innate structure of the brain and that the goal of perceptual research is to document perceptual laws. The gestalt approach to perception is not included in this review.
3. William James is the notable exception to this generalization. James felt some perceptual experiences were hard-wired (e.g., emotions) and other perceptual experiences were mental events that aided the survival of the species.
4. Wilson (2002) observes that the visual system sends 10 million pieces of information to our brain per second, but that our brain can only perform 40 active operations per second. If the perceptual system is integrating elements, it would take 70 hours to generate a perception. Although automaticity could be used to solve this integration problem, automaticity cannot account for perception among infants or perception in novel environments.
5. Connectionist models use weights to define the relationship between the receptors that are activated owing to stimulation of the senses and the binary units that represent a concept. The connection weights, not the physical pattern of the distribution, are the concepts. This additional complexity is not pertinent to the arguments made in this chapter.
6. For prior demonstrations of perceptual blindness, see Becklen and Cervone (1983) and Neisser and Becklen (1975).
7. Videotapes of stimuli used to study inattentional blindness and change blindness can be found at http://viscog.beckman.uiuc.edu/djs_lab/demos.html.
8. See http://www.pbs.org/wgbh/nova/sciencenow/3204/01.html for a 14-minute discussion of mirror neurons.
9. Again, it is the feature codes and concept that support conscious experience, not the experience itself, that are the causal agents.

REFERENCES

Abrams, R. L., & Greenwald, A. G. (2000). Parts outweigh the whole (word) in unconscious analysis of meaning. *Psychological Science, 11*(March), 118124.
Aglioti, S., DeSouza, J. F. X., & Goodale, M. A. (1995).. Size-contrast illusions deceive the eye but not the hand. *Current Biology, 5*(June), 679–685.
Allen, D. E. (2002). Toward a theory of consumer choice as sociohistorically shaped practical experience: The fits-like-a-glove (FLAG) Framework. *Journal of Consumer Research, 28*(March), 515–532.
Allport, D. A. (1987). Selection for action: Some behavioral and neuropsychological considerations of attention and action. In H. Heuer & A. F. Sanders (Eds.), *Perspectives on perception and attention*, (pp. 395–419). Hillsdale, NJ: Erlbaum.
Andrew, N., & Moore, K. M. (1989). Imitation in newborn infants: Exploring the range of gestures imitated and underlying mechanisms. *Developmental Psychology, 25*(November), 954–962.

Anisfeld, M. (1996). Only tongue protrusion modeling is matched by neonates. *Developmental Review, 16* (June), 149–161.

Arnould, E. J, & Thompson, C. (2005). Consumer culture theory (CCT): Twenty years of research. *Journal of Consumer Research, 31*(March), 868–882.

Ballantyne, P. F. (2003). *History of psychology,* http://www.comnet.ca/~pballan/HistPsyc(Intro).htm

Bargh, J. A., & Chartland, T. L. (1999). The unbearable automaticity of being. *American Psychologist, 54*(July), 462–479.

Bargh, J. A., Chen, M., & Burrows, L. (1996). Automaticity of social behavior: Direct effects of trait construct and stereotype activation on action. *Journal of Personality and Social Psychology, 71*(August), 230–244.

Baumeister, R. F. (1984). Choking under pressure: Self-consciousness and paradoxical effects of incentives on skillful performance. *Journal of Personality & Social Psychology, 46*(March), 610–620.

Baumeister, R. F. (2002). Yielding to temptation: Self-control failure, impulsive purchasing, and consumer behavior. *Journal of Consumer Research, 28*(March), 670–676.

Baumeister, R. F., Bratslavsky, E., Muraven, M., & Tice, D. M. (1998). Ego depletion: Is the active self a limited resource? *Journal of Experimental Social Psychology, 74*(May), 1252–1264.

Bechara, A., Damasio, H., Tranel, D., & Damasio, A. R. (1997). Deciding advantageously before knowing the advantageous strategy. *Science, 275*(5304), (February), 1293–1294.

Becklen, R., & Cervone, D. (1983). Selective looking and the noticing of unexpected events. *Memory and Cognition, 11*(November), 601–608.

Bodenhausen, G. V., Kramer, G. P., & Süsser, K. (1994). Happiness and stereotypic thinking in social judgment. *Journal of Personality and Social Psychology, 66*(April), 621–632.

Brasil-Neto, J. P. Pascual-Leone, A., Valls-Sole, J., Cohen, L. G., & Hallet, M. (1992). Focal transcranial magnetic stimulation and response bias in a forced-choice task. *Journal of Neurology, Neurosurgery & Psychiatry, 55*(October), 964–966.

Broadbent, D. E. (1958), *Perception and communication.* New York: Pergamon Press.

Brooks, C. M., Patrick J. Kaufmann, P. J., & Lichtenstein, D. R. (2004). Travel configuration on consumer tripchained store choice. *Journal of Consumer Research, 31*(September), 241–248.

Buccion, G., Binkofski, F., & Riggio, L. (2004). The mirror neuron system and action recognition. *Brain & Language, 89* (May), 370–376.

Bruner, J. S., &. Minturn, A. L. (1955). Perceptual identification and perceptual organization. *Journal of General Psychology, 53,* 21–28.

Chartrand, T. L., & Bargh, J. A. (1999). The chameleon effect: The perception-behavior link and social interaction. *Journal of Personality and Social Psychology, 76* (June), 893–910.

Dagenbach, D., Carr, T. H., & Wilhelmsen, A. L. (1989). Task-induced strategies and near-threshold priming: Conscious influences on unconscious perception. *Journal of Memory and Language, 28*(August), 412–443.

Dai, D. Y., & Sternberg, R. J. (2004). *Motivation, emotion, and cognition: Integrative perspectives on intellectual functioning and development.* Mahwah, NJ: Erlbaum.

Dickson, P. R., & Sawyer, A. G. (1990). The price knowledge and search of supermarket shoppers. *Journal of Marketing, 54*(July), 42–53.

Dijksterhuis, A., Smith, P. K., van Baaren, R. B., &. Wigboldus, D. H, G. (2005). The unconscious consumer: Effects of environment and consumer behavior. *Journal of Consumer Psychology, 15*(3), 195–202.

Draine, S. C., & Greenwald, A. G. (1998). Replicable unconscious semantic priming. *Journal of Experimental Psychology: General, 127*(September), 286–303.

Fiedler, K. (2000). On mere considering: The subjective experience of truth. In H. Bless & J. P. Forgas (Eds.), *The message within: Subjective experiences and social cognition* (pp. 13–36). Philadelphia: Psychology Press.

Fournier, S. (1998). Consumers and their brands: Developing relationship theory in consumer research. *Journal of Consumer Research, 24* (March), 343–373.

Förster, J., & Strack, F. (1996). The influence of overt head movements on memory for valenced words: A case of conceptual motor compatibility. *Journal of Personality and Social Psychology, 71*(September), 421–430.

Geisler, W. S., &. Super, B. J. (2000). Perceptual organization of two–dimensional patterns. *Psychological Review, 107*(October), 677–708.

Gibson, E. J. (1969). *Principles of perceptual learning and development.* New York: Appleton-Century-Crofts.

Gibson, J. J. (1966). *The senses considered as perceptual systems*. Boston, MA: Houghton Mifflin.

Gibson, J. J. (1979). *The ecological approach to visual perception*. Boston, MA: Haughton-Mifflin.

Glover, S. (2002). Visual illusions affect planning but not control. *Trends in Cognitive Sciences*, 6(July), 288–292.

Gomez, R. L., & Schvaneveldt, R. W. (1994). What is learned from artificial grammars? Transfer tests of simple association. *Journal of Experimental Psychology: Learning, Memory, & Cognition*, 20(March), 396–410.

Greenleaf, E. A. (1995). The relative impact of reference price effects on the profitability of price promotions. *Marketing Science*, 14(Winter), 82–104.

Greenwald, A. G., & Leavitt, C. (1984). Audience involvement in advertising: Four levels. *Journal of Consumer Research*, 11(June), 581–592.

Hefferline, R. F., Keenan, B., & Harford, R. A. (1959). Escape and avoidance conditioning in human subjects without their observation of the response. *Science*, 130, 1338–1339.

Hommel, B., Müsseler, J., Aschersleben, G., & Prinz, W. (2001). The theory of event coding (TEC): A framework for perception and action planning. *Behavioral and Brain Sciences*, 24(October), 849–937.

Holt, D. B. (2002). Why do brands cause trouble? A dialectical theory of consumer culture and branding. *Journal of Consumer Research*, 29(June), 70–90.

Janiszewski, C., &. van Osselaer, S. M. J. (2005). Behavior activation is not enough. *Journal of Consumer Psychology*, 15(3), 218–224.

Janiszewski, C., & van Osselaer, S. M. J. (2000). A connectionist model of brand-quality associations. *Journal of Marketing Research*, 37(August), 331–350.

Julez, B. (1971). *Foundations of cyclopean perception*. Chicago: University of Chicago Press.

Kahneman, D. (2002). *Maps of bounded rationality: A perspective on intuitive judgment and choice*. Nobel Prize lecture, December 8, 2002.

Kahneman, D., & Tversky, A. (1979). Prospect theory. An analysis of decision under risk. *Econometrica*, 47(2), 263–291.

Kalyanaram, G., & Winer, R. S. (1995). Empirical generalizations from reference price research. *Marketing Science*, 14(3), G161–G169.

Keller, K. L. (1993). Conceptualizing, measuring, and managing customer-based brand equity. *Journal of Marketing*, 57 (January), 1–22.

Kersten, D., Mamassian, P., & Yuille, A. (2004). Object perception as Bayesian inference. *Annual Review of Psychology*, 55, 271–304.

Kohler, E., Keysers, C., Umilta, M. A., Fogassi, L., Gallese, V., & Rizzolatti, G. (2002). Hearing sounds, understanding actions: Action representation in mirror neurons. *Science*, 297(August), 846–848.

Kouider, S., & Dupoux, E. (2004). Partial awareness creates the "illusion" of subliminal semantic priming. *Psychological Science*, 15(February), 75–81.

Lang, P. J., Bradley, M. M., & Cuthbert, B. N. (1990). Emotion, attention, and the startle reflex. *Psychological Review*, 97(July), 377–395.

Levin, D. T., Momen, N., Drivdahl, S. B., & Simons, D. J. (2002). Change blindness blindness: The metacognitive error of overestimating change-detection ability. *Visual Cognition*, 7(Jan–Mar), 397–412.

Levin, I. P., Schneider, S. L., &. Gaeth, G. J. (1998). All frames are not created equal: A typology and critical analysis of framing effects. *Organizational Behavior and Human Decision Processes*, 76(November), 149–188.

Levy, S. J. (1981). Interpreting consumer mythology: A structural approach to consumer behavior. *Journal of Marketing*, 45(Summer), 49–61.

Lewicki, P., Hill, T., & Bizot, E. (1988). Acquisition of procedural knowledge about a pattern of stimuli that cannot be articulated. *Cognitive Psychology*, 20(January), 24–37.

Mack, A., & Rock, I. (1998). *Inattentional blindness*. Boston: MIT Press.

Marcel, A. J. (1983a). Conscious and unconscious perception: Experiments on visual masking and word recognition. *Cognitive Psychology*, 15(April), 197–237.

Marcel, A. J (1983b). Conscious and unconscious perception: An approach to the relations between phenomenal experience and perceptual processes. *Cognitive Psychology*, 15(April), 238–300.

Martin, L. L., Harlow, T. F., & Strack, F. (1992). The role of bodily sensations in the evaluation of social events. *Personality and Social Psychology Bulletin*, 18(August), 412–419.

Mayer, J. D., Salovey, P. , & Caruso, D. R. (2004). Emotional intelligence: Theory, findings, and implications. *Psychological Inquiry, 15*(3), 197–215.

McClelland, J. L., & Rumelhart, D. E. (1985). Distributed memory and the representation of general and specific information. *Journal of Experimental Psychology: General, 114*(June), 159–188.

McQuarrie, E. F., & Mick, D. G. (2003). The contribution of semiotic and rhetorical Perspectives to the explanation of visual persuasion in advertising. In Linda M. Scott & Rajeev Batra (Eds.), *Persuasive imagery: A consumer response perspective* (pp. 191–221). Mahwah, NJ: Erlbaum.

Meltzoff, A. N., Moore, K. M. (1994. Imitation, memory, and the representation of persons. *Infant Behavior and Development, 17*(Jan–Mar), 83–99.

Mick, D. G., & Buhl, C. (1992). A meaning-based model of advertising experiences. *Journal of Consumer Research, 19*(December), 317–338.

Muniz, A. M., Jr., & O'Guinn, T. C. (2001). Brand community. *Journal of Consumer Research, 27*(March), 412–432.

Neisser, U., & Becklen, R. (1975). Selective looking: Attending to visually specified events. *Cognitive Psychology, 7*(October), 480–494.

Nisbett, R. E., & Wilson, T. D. (1977). Telling more than we can know, verbal reports on mental processes. *Psychological Review, 84*(March), 231–259.

Pieters, R., Wedel, M., & Zhang, J. (2005). *Sales effects of attention to feature ads*. Working paper, University of Michigan.

Pomerantz, J. R., & Kubovy, M. (1986). Theoretical approaches to perceptual organization. In K. R. Boff & L. Kaufman (Eds.), *Handbook of Perception and Human Performance, Vol. 2: Cognitive Processes and Performance* (pp. 1–46). Oxford: John Wiley.

Posner, M. I. (1980). Orienting of attention. *Quarterly Journal of Experimental Psychology, 32*(February), 3–25.

Price, L. L., Arnould, E. J., & Curasi, C. F. (2000). Older consumers' disposition of special possessions. *Journal of Consumer Research, 27*(September), 179–201.

Raghubir, P., & Krishna, A. (1996). As the crow flies: Bias in consumers' map-based distance judgments. *Journal of Consumer Research, 23*(June), 26–39.

Raghubir, P., & Krishna, A. (1999). Vital dimensions in volume perception: Can the eye fool the stomach?," *Journal of Marketing Research, 36*(August), 313–326.

Reber, A. S. (1976). Implicit learning of synthetic languages: The role of instructional set. *Journal of Experimental Psychology: Human Learning & Memory, 2*(January), 88–94.

Reber, A. S. (1989). Implicit learning and tacit knowledge. *Journal of Experimental Psychology: General, 118* (September), 219–235.

Rizzolatti, G., & Arbib, M. A. (1998). Language within our grasp. *Trends in Neurosciences*, (May), 188–194.

Ross, L., & Nisbett, R. E. (1991). *The person and the situation: Perspectives of social psychology*. Philadelphia: Temple University Press.

Shiffrin, R. M., & Schneider, W. (1977). Controlled and automatic human information processing: II. Perceptual learning, automatic attending, and a general theory. *Psychological Review, 84*(March), 127–190.

Simons, D. J., & Chabris, C. F. (1999). Gorillas in our midst: Sustained inattentional blindness for dynamic events. *Perception, 28*(9), 1059–1074.

Simons, D. J., Franconeri, S. L., & Reimer, R. L. (2000). Change blindness in the absence of visual disruption. *Perception, 29*(10), 1143–1154.

Simons, D. J., & Levin, D. T. (1997). Change blindness. *Trends in Cognitive Science, 1,* 261–267.

Simons, D. J., & Levin, D. T. (1998). Failure to detect changes to people in real-world interactions. *Psychonomic Bulletin and Review, 5*(December), 644–649.

Sirsi, A. K.,.Ward, J. C., & Reingen, P. H. (1996). Microcultural analysis of variation in sharing of casual reasoning about behavior. *Journal of Consumer Research, 22*(March), 345–372.

Stern, B. B. (1993). Feminist literary criticism and the deconstruction of ads: A postmodern view of advertising and consumer responses. *Journal of Consumer Research, 19*(March), 556–566.

Strack, F., Martin, L., & Stepper, S. (1988). Inhibiting and facilitating conditions of the human smile: A nonobtrusive test of the facial feedback hypothesis. *Journal of Personality and Social Psychology, 54*(May), 768–777.

Strahan, E. J., Spencer, S. J., & Zanna, M. P. (2002). Subliminal priming and persuasion: Striking while the iron is hot. *Journal of Experimental Social Psychology, 38*(November), 556–568.

Stepper, S., & Strack, F. (1993). Proprioceptive determinants of emotional and nonemotional feelings. *Journal of Personality and Social Psychology, 64*(February), 211–220.

Stroop, J. R. (1935). Studies of interference in serial verbal interaction. *Journal of Experimental Psychology, 18*, 643–662.

Tomasello, M. (1999). *The cultural origins of human cognition.* Cambridge, MA: Harvard University Press.

Treisman, A.M., & Gelade, G. (1980). A feature integration theory of attention. *Cognitive Psychology, 12* January), 97–136.

Treisman, A. (1988). Features and objects: The fourteenth Bartlett memorial lecture. *The Quarterly Journal of Experimental Psychology, 40A*(May), 201–237.

Trick, L. M., & Pylshyn, Z. W. (1994). Why are small and large numbers enumerate differently? A limited-capacity preattentive stage of vision. *Psychological Review,* 80–102.

Vecera, S. P., & Farah, M. J. (1994). Does visual attention select objects or locations. *Journal of Experimental Psychology: General, 123*(June), 146–160.

Wade, N. (2001). *Visual perception: An introduction.* Philadelphia: Psychology Press.

Wegner, D. (2002). *The illusion of conscious will.* Cambridge, MA: MIT Press.

Welch, R. B. (1986). Adaptation of space perceptions. In K. R. Boff, L. Kaufman, & J. P. Thomas (Eds.), *Handbook of perception and human performance: Vol. 1* (pp, 1–24). Oxford: Wiley.

Whittlesea, B. W. A., & Leboe, J. P. (2000). The heuristic basis of remembering and classification: Fluency, generation, and resemblance. *Journal of Experimental Psychology: General, 129*(March), 84–106.

Wilson, T. D. (2002). *Strangers to ourselves.* Cambridge, MA: Belknap Press of Harvard University Press.

Wilson, T. D., & Dunn, D. S. (1986). Effects of introspection on attitude-behavior consistency: Analyzing reasons versus focusing on feelings. *Journal of Experimental Social Psychology, 47*(May), 5–16.

Wilson, T. D., & Dunn, E. W. (2004). Self knowledge: Its limits, value, and potential for improvement. *Annual Review of Psychology, 55,* 493–518.

Wilson, T. D., & LaFleur, S. J. (1995). Knowing what you'll do: Effects of analyzing reasons on self-prediction. *Journal of Personality and Social Psychology, 68*(January), 21–35.

Wilson, T. D., Lisle, D. L., Schooler, J. H., Hodges, S. D., Klaaren, K. J., & LaFleur, S. J. (1993). Introspecting about reasons can reduce post-choice satisfaction. *Personality and Social Psychology Bulletin, 19*(June), 331–339.

Woods, D. W., Miltenberger, R. G., & Flach, A. D. (1996). Habits, tics, and stuttering: Prevalence and relation to anxiety and somatic awareness. *Behavior Modification, 20*(April), 216–225.

Yeung, C. W. M., & Wyer, Jr., R. S. (2004). Affect, appraisal, and consumer judgment. *Journal of Consumer Research, 31*(September), 412–424.

Zajonc, R. B., Murphy, S. T., & Inglehart, M. (1989). Feeling and facial efference: Implications of the vascular theory of emotion. *Psychological Review, 96*(July), 395–416.

IV

PERSUASION, ATTITUDES, AND SOCIAL INFLUENCE

15

Attitude Change and Persuasion

Curtis P. Haugtvedt

Ohio State University

Jeff A. Kasmer

Kasmer Associates

Allport (1935, p. 798) characterized attitude as "...probably the most distinctive and indispensable concept in ... social psychology." Allport and other theorists viewed attitudes as a fundamental contributor to how persons deal with the world around them. Thomas and Znaniecki (1918) describe social psychology as the scientific study of attitudes. Contemporary researchers and theorists share the view that attitudes have very important influences on perceptions, thoughts, and behavior at individual, social, and cultural levels (e.g., Eagly & Chaiken, 1993; Greenwald, 1968, 1989). The ways in which attitudes are formed, changed, stored, activated, and used has been the focus of a tremendous amount of research activity in the past 90 years. Our goal in this chapter is to briefly outline the history of research and thinking with regard to attitudes, attitude change, and persuasion. We then discuss selected studies that have advanced and/or challenged theoretical perspectives. We end our chapter with a brief summary of some exciting new developments in the study of attitudes, attitude change, and persuasion in social and consumer psychology.

ATTITUDE AND ATTITUDE MEASUREMENT

A commonly used definition is that attitudes are general evaluations of objects, issues, or people (Petty & Cacioppo, 1981); Fazio views attitudes as object-evaluation associations (chapter 16, this volume). Attitudes are contrasted with other constructs such as "affect" (see chapters 10, 11, and 43, this volume; Petty, Cacioppo, & Kasmer, 1988). Fleming (1967) provides an historical view of the term "attitude." Attitude formation and attitude change (e.g., Palmerino, Langer, & McGillis, 1984; Petty & Cacioppo, 1986a) can be thought of as points along a continuum. Consistent with other writing, for our purposes, the terms will be used interchangeably (cf., Crano & Prislin, 2006; Petty, Schumann, Richman, & Strathman 1993; Petty & Wegener, 1999).

Prompted by issues raised by psychologist Floyd Allport, L. L. Thurstone boldly titled his (1928) paper: "Attitudes can be measured." In the paper and other work, he described the extensive psychometric methods that could be used to measure the construct of attitude. In part, because of the time and effort needed to construct a Thurstone scale, it is rarely used. Over the years, researchers have employed many techniques to assess attitudes (see Petty & Cacioppo, 1981; Krosnick, Judd, & Wittenbrink, 2005, for descriptions).

In contemporary research, popular methods to assess attitudes in experimental studies are the Likert scale and the semantic differential. Thus, for example, Petty, Cacioppo, and Goldman (1981, p. 850) assessed attitudes toward comprehensive exams with "four 9-point semantic differential scales (good/bad, beneficial/harmful, foolish/wise, and favorable/unfavorable). Next, on an 11-point scale anchored by 1-"do not agree at all," and 11-"agree completely," subjects rated the extent to which they agreed with the proposal requiring seniors to take a comprehensive exam before graduating." The scores were then standardized and averaged to form a single measure for attitude toward senior comprehensive examinations. Similarly, Petty, Cacioppo, and Schumann (1983, p. 140) assessed attitudes toward a product with "three nine point semantic differential scales anchored at –4 and +4 (bad–good, unsatisfactory–satisfactory, and unfavorable–favorable)." Petty et al. (1983) combined the attitude data across the three scales to assess the attitudes toward the product. Reviewing details of the advantages and disadvantages of various measurement techniques are beyond the scope of this chapter; readers interested in learning more about the topic are referred to Krosnick, Judd, and Wittenbrink (2005) for a review of the importance of attitude measurement issues in contemporary research.

Although many dimensions of attitudes were mentioned in early theorizing and research, changes in technology and measurement methods have ignited interesting discussions regarding the difference between indirect (implicit) and direct (explicit) measures of attitudes. These methods are detailed in chapters by Jones and Fazio (chapter 11, this volume), Vargas (chapter 18, this volume) and Perkins, Forehand, Greewald, and Maison (chapter 17, this volume). Continued research on classic issues and the development of new perspectives that build on and challenge existing empirical research and theoretical frameworks keep the topic of attitude change and persuasion on the center stage of social and consumer psychology research.

ATTITUDE CHANGE AND PERSUASION

Carl Hovland and his colleagues at Yale were instrumental in developing the first set of systematic studies on variables relevant to attitude change (e.g., Hovland, Janis, & Kelley, 1953; Hovland & Weiss, 1951). One of the milestones in the attitude change and persuasion literature was the evolution of the Yale message learning approach to the cognitive response approach developed and advocated by Timothy Brock (a student of Carl Hovland) and his colleagues at Ohio State University (e.g., Greenwald, 1968; Petty, Ostrom, & Brock, 1981). Richard Petty (1977; Petty & Cacioppo, 1981) extended and qualified the cognitive response approach with the Elaboration Likelihood Model. While the cognitive response approach viewed all attitude changes as requiring a relatively high degree of elaboration, Petty and Cacioppo postulated that attitude change could also take place with relatively little elaboration of message content. Their 1981 book focused on describing where various theoretical perspectives and interpretations of empirical studies might fall on an elaboration continuum. The final chapter of their book contains a description of their model. Petty's 1977 dissertation contains a schematic and description of the model. A book by Petty and Cacioppo (1986a) and a chapter ("Advances in Experimental Social Psychology," Petty and Cacioppo, 1986b) provide detailed postulates of the Elaboration Likelihood Model (ELM). See also Petty, Priester, and Wegener (1994) for a more recent summary of research on cognitive processes in the ELM.

Contemporary research on attitude change and persuasion has been dominated by dual route perspectives (e.g., Petty & Cacioppo, 1981, 1986a; Chaiken, 1987). Dual route models and their implications will be discussed in more detail later in this chapter.

Research on attitudes and persuasion played a central role for the relatively young field of consumer psychology (see chapter 1, this volume). Reviews of much of this work can be found in consumer psychology chapters appearing in the Annual Review of Psychology approximately every 3 to 4 years (e.g., Kassarjian, 1982; Bettman, 1986; Loken, 2006). Reviews of social influence (Cialdini & Goldstein, 2004) and attitude change (Crano & Prislin, 2006) will also be of interest to consumer psychologists.

Contemporary research and theorizing still draws heavily on the fundamental measurement and methodological issues addressed in pioneering work in attitude change and persuasion. Petty (1997) provides a review on how research on attitude change and persuasion evolved from single-effect and single-process assumptions to contemporary views of multiple effect and multiple process models. Models such as the Elaboration Likelihood Model (ELM) and Heuistic Systematic Model (HSM) have generated a great deal of research in the past 30 years. In the following sections, we highlight just a few of the areas of research. In addition, we review some of the debates that have emerged in the literature that have been stimulated by the development of models like the ELM. Readers unfamiliar with the attitude change and persuasion literature are encouraged to review Petty and Cacioppo (1981) and Chaiken and Eagly (1993).

CONSEQUENCES OF ATTITUDE CHANGE PROCESSES

Consumer and social psychologists share the goal of developing persuasive campaigns, interventions, and strategies that increase the likelihood of desired outcomes. In most cases, this means a change in behavior. As other chapters in this handbook and other sources describe (e.g., Petty & Krosnick, 1995; Ajzen, chapter 20, this volume), there are many factors to consider with regard to the abilities of attitudes to predict behavior. In this section, we focus on how aspects of the attitude change process are hypothesized to lead to newly formed or changed attitudes relatively more persistent (decay less over time), relatively more resistant (change less in the face of attack) and lead to greater degrees of attitude-behavior consistency.

Petty, Haugtvedt, and Smith (1995) provide a detailed review of an ELM perspective on the consequences of attitude change processes. As they note, the ELM was initially proposed as a means of understanding why in some studies attitude changes could be characterized as relatively strong (e.g., persistent), whereas in other studies the attitude changes could be characterized as weak (not persistent). According to the ELM, persuasion that occurs via the central route to persuasion versus persuasion that occurs via the peripheral route to persuasion can initially lead to equivalently positive or negative (equally extreme) attitudes. Nevertheless, the model specifies that newly formed or changed attitudes as result of central route persuasion should be stronger (e.g., more persistent, resistant, and predictive of behavior; Petty, 1977; Petty & Cacioppo, 1981, 1986a). Central route attitude changes are characterized as resulting in more extensive and integrated structures, whereas peripheral route attitude changes are characterized as resulting in fewer and weaker linkages.

To examine the ELM's attitude elaboration-persistence hypothesis, Haugtvedt and Petty (1992) used the individual difference variable of Need for Cognition (NFC; Cacioppo, Petty, & Morris, 1983) to operationalize motivation to process. While viewing a television program, individuals high and low in Need for Cognition were exposed to a television advertisement for a telephone answering machine in the context of other ads. Importantly, the critical advertisement was pretested to contain strong arguments and variables that could serve as positive peripheral cues so that initially comparable attitudes could be developed in both the high and low need for cognition groups. Participants completed product attitude assessments and other questions immediately after viewing the show. Two days later, participants returned to the lab expecting to view and rate another TV show. During this second session, participants completed another attitude assessment and listed their thoughts about the target product. As expected, both high and low need for cognition groups formed equally positive attitudes toward the product in the immediate setting, but the attitudes of the low need for cognition participants showed significant decay over the 2-day period. That is, consistent with predictions, attitudes of high need for cognition participants were relatively more persistent than those of the low need for cognition participants. In general, high Need for Cognition (HNC) participants should elaborate more on message content when exposed to the initial message, whereas low Need for Cognition (LNC) participants would rely on other factors (such as the number of arguments) to form their attitudes.

In a second study, Haugtvedt and Petty (1992) examined the degree to which newly changed attitudes of high versus low need for cognition participants were able to resist change in the face of a weak attack. Participants were exposed to an initial message about the safety of a well-known food additive. The initial message was pre-tested to contain strong arguments from an expert source. Attitudes were assessed after exposure to the message. Participants were then exposed to an opposing message that contained weaker arguments from a different expert source. Attitudes were again assessed, along with cognitive responses. Because of methodological concerns, cognitive responses were not assessed until after attitude assessment and only after exposure to the second message. Based on pre-testing and prior research, attitudes of HNC participants were expected to be based on elaboration of the initial message content, whereas the attitudes of LNC participants were expected to be based on perceptions on schemata source expertise. Consistent with predictions, although equivalent after the first message, Haugtvedt and Petty (1992) found that attitudes of LNC individuals changed more after exposure to the opposing message than did the attitudes of the HNC participants. Additional analyses provided support for the ELM based process explanation of active resistance by the HNC participants and greater influence of source expertise on attitudes by the LNC participants. A recent study by Wheeler, Petty, and Bizer (2005) suggests that similar processes may be invoked by messages that match self-schema. Because messages that match self-schemata tend to lead to greater elaboration, such attitudes should also exhibit greater resistance to later, opposing messages.

Further support for the elaboration-resistance hypotheses is found in studies by Haugtvedt and Wegener (1994). Using a situational manipulation of the personal relevance of topics in a message order effect paradigm, studies by Haugtvedt and Wegener (1994) showed that participants exposed to an initial message under high relevance were more resistant to an equally strong, opposing, second message.

Studies by Haugtvedt, Schumann, Schneier, and Warren (1994) provided support for the ELM's notion that persistent attitudes can be based on strong cue associations but that such attitudes are likely to change in the face of challenges. Using an advertising repetition paradigm of substantively or cosmetically varied ads developed by Schumman, Petty, and Clemons (1990), Haugtvedt, Schuman, et al. (1994) showed that three exposures to cosmetically varied ads or three exposures to substantively varied ads could lead to equally positive and equally persistent attitudes over a two day period. Nevertheless, when faced with challenges in the delayed setting, attitudes developed from exposure to substantively varied ads were relatively more resistant to change. In sum, equally persistent attitudes can otherwise differ on other important dimensions.

Petty, Haugtvedt, and Smith (1995) note that most studies of attitude-behavior consistency assess the extent to which pre-existing attitudes predict behavior (cf., chapter 20, this volume). Results of such studies can be interpreted as supportive of the ELM's elaboration-consistency hypothesis. Attitudes based on the relatively greater operation of central route to persuasion processes should be based on more elaboration and therefore should be more predictive of behavior than attitudes based on the relative operation of peripheral route to persuasion processes. Petty, Haugtvedt, and Smith (1995) also review studies that focus on how characteristics of persons are associated with greater attitude-behavior consistency (e.g., NFC, self-monitoring etc.).

Importantly, studies can also be interpreted as consistent with the ELM's proposition that newly formed attitudes based on greater elaboration should be more predictive of behavior. For example, data analyses of Petty, Cacioppo, and Schumann (1983) showed that the post advertising exposure attitudes of persons randomly assigned to the high relevance condition were significantly more predictive of purchase intentions than persons randomly assigned to the low relevance condition. Similarly, data from a study on self-relevance and attitude behavior consistency by Leippe and Elkin (1987) showed that the contents of essays written by participants after exposure to a message under high relevance conditions were more consistent with attitudes than persons who had been exposed to the message under conditions of low relevance.

Research on attitude strength consequences such as persistence, resistance, and attitude-behavior consistency have been topics of long-standing interest and research by social psychologists and others (see Petty et al., 1995, for a review). Research guided by the ELM, however, has typically employed manipulations and measures that provide a clearer understanding of the mechanisms underlying the consequences.

Perhaps, in part, because Petty and his colleagues have used extensive literature reviews that include reinterpretations and inferences regarding underlying processes in existing studies, some researchers (and reviewers!) sometimes view the findings of the new studies as "already well-known or well-established." Of course, although inferences about process and reinterpretations of past studies have been used as advocacy for a theory, it remains important for consumer and other researchers to conduct original studies that include measures designed to assess the hypothesized underlying processes. It is also important for consumer psychology researchers to understand the boundary conditions for the various processes and mechanisms (McGuire, 1985). In sum, there are many remaining profitable avenues of inquiry surrounding the important issue of understanding and predicting consequences of attitude change processes. Once established, various research paradigms may be integrated with newer theoretical formulations to better understand the multiple processes by which attitudes may or may not be persistent, resistant, or predictive of behavior (cf., Wegener, Downing, Krosnick, & Petty, 1995; Haugtvedt, Shakarchi, Samuelson, & Liu, 2004).

MULTIPLE ROLES FOR VARIABLES

In the preceding section, we briefly reviewed studies supportive of some of the ELM's postulates related to the consequences of attitude change processes. These consequences are especially important and relevant to consumer researchers and policy makers. Basic descriptions of the ELM can be found in most contemporary consumer behavior textbooks. The Petty, Cacioppo, and Schumann (1983) study is one of the most frequently cited papers from the *Journal of Consumer Research*. Despite the high awareness levels of the basic ELM framework among consumer psychologists, many researchers are often unaware of the more intricate aspects of the model. As an approach to research, the ELM is a good example of a programmatic approach as advocated by William McGuire (McGuire, 1985). As noted earlier, the ELM evolved, in part, out of a critique of the cognitive response tradition of persuasion research. Richard Petty and John Cacioppo, trained as experimental social psychologists, understood the value of standardized research paradigms and a standardized toolbox of messages and measures for initial basic studies. Their initial research challenged existing paradigms and thinking and suggested boundary conditions for prominent theoretical frameworks and established phenomena (e.g., Petty & Cacioppo, 1979) by adding new manipulations and measures. They drew on classic issues in social psychology as a source of materials and utilized newer psychophysiological techniques to assess hypothesized underlying processes (e.g., Cacioppo & Petty, 1983). Building on these ideas, Sanbonmatsu and Kardes (1988) used a manipulation of physiological arousal to find that a source's celebrity or noncelebrity status was a more important determinant of brand attitudes under high arousal. The postulates of the ELM and the research methods used in ELM studies provide basic and applied researchers with useful guides when developing and assessing persuasion attempts in advertising and other contexts (Haugtvedt & Priester, 1997).

With the general foundation of basic processes and measures established in both the social and consumer psychology research domains, some of the most interesting work using the ELM framework remains to be conducted. Some of this work, in our view, focuses on the issue of multiple roles for variables. In the following pages, we outline some of the initial work that can be seen as supportive of the ELM's multiple roles principles. In addition, we encourage consumer psychologists to consider how the many important variables in the marketplace can and should be examined from a multiple roles perspective. Understanding the roles a variable does or can play has important implications for marketing strategy and advertising decisions (cf., Haugtvedt, Leavitt, & Schneier, 1993; Haugtvedt & Priester, 1997).

Petty, Cacioppo, and Schumann (1983) introduced the ELM to the consumer researchers with an experimental laboratory study that used manipulations of three important components: a manipulation that was designed to influence the motivation of participants (personally relevant vs. less personally relevant), a manipulation of product attribute or argument quality to assess the degree of elaboration (strong vs. weak arguments), and a manipulation of source factors (celebrity vs. noncelebrity sources). Each of these factors was carefully pre-tested before they were combined in the final study. Results of the study showed, consistent with predictions, that the situational manipulation of motivation moderated the extent to which participants elaborated on message content (as assessed by final attitudes) and the extent to which participants relied on celebrity status as a peripheral cue in attitude change. The basic ELM laboratory paradigm illustrated by the Petty et al. (1983) study has been used in numerous attitude change and persuasion studies.

When first exposed to the ELM models and studies, students and researchers sometimes assume that there should be a taxonomy of variables that nicely fit into the various categories of motivation, ability, arguments, and cues. Based on theoretical reasoning, the ELM authors have not endorsed an arbitrary categorization of variables. An important aspect of the ELM is the idea of an elaboration continuum (Petty & Cacioppo, 1986a). The more motivated and able consumers are to assess the central merits of an attitude object, the more likely they are to employ effortful processes and consider all available information. The less motivated and able consumers are to assess central merits of an attitude object, the more they may rely on processes that do not require much effort to arrive at a judgment. Petty and Wegener (1998) describe these processes in detail.

Most relevant for our current discussion is the idea that the ELM does not hold that a given variable will always serve the same role in different persuasion settings. From early descriptions of the ELM, Petty and Cacioppo (1986a) specifically note that any given variable has the potential to influence attitudes by serving as a peripheral cue, an inducement to process, an argument, or a factor that might bias information processing given a specific combination of other factors. Importantly, the role for a specific variable can be specified in advance. In addition, research using the ELM research paradigm can be employed to assess the role that a given variable typically plays for a given group of consumers at a specific time. For example, although some consumer research studies show that brand name can serve as a peripheral cue (see Maheshwaran, Mackie, & Chaiken, 1992), brand name has the potential to be much more than a peripheral cue (Haugtvedt & Rucker, 2002; Haugtvedt & Rucker, 2007). In other circumstances, brand name may induce greater elaboration of message content, or biased elaboration of message content. In other situations, brand name also has the potential to serve as an argument. Importantly, and especially relevant for consumer psychology research, is the likely possibility that the role a brand name plays for a consumer changes over time (based on factors such as greater knowledge, product usage experience, effects of advertising and other marketing communications, discussions with others, integration of affect, etc.). In addition, ELM research paradigms can be used to assess the role that brand name or other marketing factors play in the development or change of consumer attitudes (cf., Haugtvedt, Leavitt, & Warren, 1993; Haugtvedt et al., 1994; Haugtvedt & Priester, 1997). For reviews of and responses to misunderstandings of the ELM's multiple roles postulate and responses to critics of the ELM, readers are referred to Petty, Kasmer, Haugtvedt, and Cacioppo (1987); Petty, Cacioppo, Kasmer, and Haugtvedt (1987); Petty, Wegener, Fabrigar, Priester, and Cacioppo (1993); Petty and Wegener (1999).

In the following pages, we provide a few examples of empirical research that provides support for the ELM's multiple roles perspective. As noted in the previous section, we see many opportunities for consumer psychology researchers to re-examine previous conceptualizations and categorizations of variables when considered in light of the multiple roles perspective.

Petty, Kasmer, Haugtvedt, and Cacioppo (1987) review the results of the Moore, Hausknecht, and Thamodaran's study (1986) and interpret the results as consistent with a multiple roles approach. In their study, Moore et al. (1986) manipulated elaboration likelihood by changing the speed of radio commercials. Results of their study show that the source of the commercial served as a peripheral cue under low elaboration, but as a message argument under high elaboration. Under moderate levels of elaboration likelihood, the source served as a motivator of thinking about the message arguments.

Research has also supported the view that affect can serve in multiple roles (Petty, Cacioppo, & Kasmer, 1988). For example, Petty, Schumann, Richman, and Strathman (1993) measured attitudes toward a pen under conditions of low or high elaboration likelihood. Under conditions of a pleasant TV show context (in contrast to a neutral TV show context), when participants were motivated to think more carefully about the advertisement for the pen because they would have to choose a pen to take home, positive cognitive responses increased as did their positive attitude change toward the pen. On the other hand, when participants were under low elaboration likelihood, they also experienced the positive attitude change, but their positive cognitive responses showed no increase. Relevant to the ELM multiple roles perspective, mood affected attitudes through influencing issue-relevant thoughts under high motivation but had a direct influence on attitudes under low motivation. In a recent publication, Bakamitsos (2006) also provides evidence that affect can serve either as a peripheral cue or as stimulus to thinking.

Comparative advertising formats have also been shown to influence attitude change processes in different ways depending on the nature of participant motivation. In a study designed to examine the influence of comparative versus noncomparative advertising formats, Pechmann and Esteban (1994) were able to create three distinct levels of participant motivation. Using an argument quality manipulation to assess the degree of message content elaboration, Pechmann and Esteban (1994) showed that under low levels of motivation, a direct comparative advertising format served as a peripheral cue; under moderate levels of motivation, a direct comparative format led to greater elaboration of message content; under high motivation, a comparative format did not differentially influence attitudes toward the product.

How an information source or endorser influences the persuasion process has been of long-standing interest. Research by Priester and Petty (1995) and Kang and Herr (2006) provide evidence that aspects of message sources can take on different roles in the persuasion process. Priester and Petty (1995) demonstrated that expectations of source trustworthiness can result in greater or lesser elaboration of message content. Similarly, Kang and Herr (2006) demonstrated that when source attractiveness is related to the nature of the product, attractiveness can serve as an argument but when attractiveness is unrelated to the nature of the product, source attractiveness serves as a peripheral cue.

While other studies can also be interpreted as consistent with the ELM's multiple roles for variables perspective (see Petty & Wegener, 1998), future research showing multiple roles for the same variable in the context of a single study (along with process measures) would be an important and valuable contribution to basic research as well as provide useful advice for practitioners in a wide variety of domains.

CHALLENGES AND CONTROVERSIES

Dual route models support the view that attitude change can take place by direct influences of factors such as emotional reactions (e.g., classical conditioning) as well as automatic influences of variables serving as heuristics or peripheral cues. Importantly, dual route models are "moderated mediation" models (Petty, 1997). In his presidential address to the Society for Consumer Psychology, Martin Fishbein challenged the validity and usefulness of dual route perspectives to attitude change. Fishbein and Middlestadt (1995) state that all attitude change is cognitive and is accounted for by the expectancy-value theories perspectives on attitude change processes and that studies that purport to show otherwise are methodologically flawed. Fishbein and Middlestadt's provocative address and subsequent article resulted in a series of responses appearing in the *Journal of Consumer Psychology* (Herr, 1995; Haugtvedt, 1997; Priester & Fleming, 1997; Miniard & Barone, 1997; Schwarz, 1997). Fishbein and Middlestadt (1997) provide a response to the commentaries. Chapters 17 and 20 of this volume offer perspectives that also address the views of Fishbein and Middlestadt.

Fishbein's perspective can be characterized as a single process model. In a similar manner, Kruglanski and his colleagues (1999, 2006a, 2006b) use his Lay Epistemic Theory to reinterpret many areas related to social psychology including attitude change and persuasion. Kruglanski and colleagues (Kruglanski & Thompson, 1999, Kruglanski et al., 2006a, Kruglanski, Erb, Pierro, Mannetti, & Chun, 2006b) believe that their "unimodel" provides a more parsimonious approach than dual process models such as the ELM and HSM. Kruglanski's view has stimulated a great deal of commentary and debate. Responses by Petty, Wheeler, and Bizer (1999) and Petty and Brinol (2006) address Kruglanski's misinterpretation of the ELM. Wyer (2006) and Pryor and Reeder (2006) also provide critiques of the unimodel.

CURRENT RESEARCH DIRECTIONS

Research on the attitude construct, attitude structure, and attitude change continues to address classic questions raised in the early literature. An examination of recent literatures in psychology and other disciplines clearly shows reciprocal influences of theories and research methods from diverse areas. As the range of chapters in this *Handbook* illustrates, many similar predictions and process level explanations can be derived from seemingly different areas of inquiry. In this section, we provide a brief overview of evolving areas of research in consumer and social psychology as they relate to attitudes and attitude change processes.

Attitude Structure

Inherent in the discussion of attitudes and attitude change are issues associated with attitude structure and properties of attitudes. An overview and detailed discussion of attitude structure concepts, as well as the larger context of various debates and research topics can be found in Fabrigar, Macdonald, and Wegener (2005) as well as other chapters in *The Handbook of Attitudes* (Albarricin, Johnson, & Zanna, 2005). Attitude structure properties include the accessibility of attitudes (e.g., Fazio, Sanbonmatsu, Powell, & Kardes, 1986); the affective, cognitive and behavioral bases of attitudes (e.g., Ostrom, 1969); the functional nature of attitudes (e.g., Katz & Stotland, 1959); working knowledge (e.g., Wood, Rhodes, & Biek, 1995); complexity of knowledge (e.g., Scott, 1969; Tetlock, 1989); attitudinal ambivalence (e.g., Priester & Petty, 1996; Priester & Petty, 2001; Priester, Petty, & Park, in press; Thompson, Zanna, & Griffin, 1995); attitude systems (e.g., Judd, Drake, Downing, & Krosnick, 1991); and dual attitude structure (e.g., Wilson, Lindsey, & Schooler, 2000; Petty, Tormala, Brinol, & Jarvis, 2006).

Much of the work on attitude change and persuasion assumes that attitudes exist in memory and that aspects of the attitudes as well as situational factors make it more or less likely that persons will use the pre-existing evaluations. Some researchers and theorists (e.g., Schwarz & Bohner, 2001) challenge this view. While there are numerous sources to review concerning the debates concerning a constructivist view of attitudes, a set of papers in the *Journal of Consumer Research* highlights many issues for consideration and clarification in future work related to the attitude construct and persuasion process in consumer psychology (e.g., Cohen & Reed, 2006a, 2006b; Johar, Maheshwaran, & Perrachio, 2006; Park & MacInnis, 2006; Petty, 2006; Schwarz, 2006).

Metacognitive Processes

Although understanding thought processes is a long-standing issue of interest in psychology (e.g., James 1890), research and theory development on the topic of social cognition (e.g., Fiske & Taylor, 1991) has highlighted the importance of thought processes in specific domains such as social judgment (cf., Petty, Brinol, Tormala, & Wegener, in press). Recent theoretical frameworks have focused on the issue of "thoughts about thoughts." As noted in our earlier discussion of attitude change processes, the role of primary thoughts in attitude change processes could range from elaborate, effortful, and complex or simple, less effortful inferences. Petty and his colleagues have begun to systematically examine how aspects of an individual's thoughts about thoughts underlying personal attitudes influence issues such as attitude confidence and certainty and the role of such thoughts in resistance to attitude change (cf., Petty, 2006). This metacognitive perspective has led to new insights regarding various phenomena associated with attitude change and persuasion. For example, Tormala and Petty (2002) demonstrated that when participants perceive themselves resisting persuasion they can become more certain of their initial attitudes. In a subsequent study, Tormala and Petty (2004) showed that participants became more certain of their attitudes only when they resisted a message that came from a high expertise source. They were also able to show that the correspondence between attitudes and behavioral intentions was higher in conditions where attitudes were held with greater certainty.

Another interesting area of metacognitive guided insights comes from research on the ease of retrieval. Ease of retrieval research has generally shown that how easy something comes to mind is an indicator of the validity of the information. Tormala, Brinol, and Petty (2002) suggested that ease of retrieval effects can be mediated by feelings of confidence or validity associated with the particular thoughts. Building on this research, Brinol, Petty, and Tormala (2006) found that the typical effect was replicated when they told participants that ease of retrieval was a sign of positive mental functioning. Interestingly, the typical finding was reversed when they told participants that ease of retrieval was a sign of negative mental functioning.

Petty, Tormala, Brinol, and Wegener (in press) discuss their metacognitive view of attitudes and social judgment and they provide a set of postulates to help provide an organizational framework for knowledge in this area. Campbell and Kirmani (chapter 21, this volume) provide examples of metacognitive processes based on Friestad and Wright's (1995) Persuasion Knowledge Model. We anticipate much more work will be done on the topic of metacognition in consumer psychology related to attitudes and attitude change as well as other areas in the coming years. Research on this topic may also be a fruitful point for collaboration between behavioral decision researchers and researchers interested in persuasion processes.

IMPLICIT AND EXPLICIT ATTITUDES AND ATTITUDE CHANGE PROCESSES

The topics of implicit attitudes and implicit social cognition are discussed in detail by Perkins et al. (chapter 17, this volume). The topic is also addressed by Vargas (chapter 18, this volume) and Fazio and Olson (2003). Systematic research on the nature and influence of implicit attitude change processes are in early stages of development. Related to the attitude strength focus in part of this chapter, findings in a recent study by Karpinski, Steinman, and Hilton (2005) are of particular interest. Using Fazio's MODE (Jones & Fazio, this volume) model as a theoretical guide, Karpinski and Steinman (2005) found that attitude importance served as a moderator of the relationship between Implicit Association Test (IAT) scores and explicit measures of attitudes. Stronger relationships between IAT scores and explicit attitudes were observed under high attitude importance for the topics such as presidential politics as well as attitudes toward consumer products such as Coke and Pepsi. Explicit attitudes were better predictors of deliberative behaviors than were IAT scores for both sets of topics. In their third study, the authors provided data that supported the hypothesis that increased elaboration was a mechanism by which attitude importance moderated IAT-explicit attitude correlations.

Rydell and McConnell (2006) offer a "systems of reasoning analysis" of implicit and explicit attitude change. They suggest that explicit attitude change is based on a fast learning system requiring some degree of cognitive resources. Implicit attitude change, they suggest, is based an associative system that is characterized by slower processes of repeated pairings between an attitude object and evaluations. In series of five studies, they show that explicit attitudes are affected by explicit processing goals and were better predictors of deliberative behavioral intentions. In contrast, implicit attitudes were unaffected by explicit processing goals and were better predictors of spontaneous behaviors.

The research findings by Karpinski and Steinman (2005) and Rydell and McConnell (2006) seem to be in conflict. Are the same underlying mechanisms operative in both situations? Are implicit attitudes based on a different cognitive system or process or are they simply efficient storage and access mechanism for attitudes that were initially developed in different ways? In addition, what happens in the attitude change process? Do attitudes that are formed and changed via explicit processes eventually become implicit attitudes? If so, what speeds up or slows down these processes? Does having greater agreement between explicit and implicit attitudes lead to greater satisfaction with a product or service? Why are the attitudes of subgroups influenced by both subtle and powerful factors in the assessment situation?

Research on the relationship between implicit and explicit attitudes and attitude change processes is needed to understand how the properties and processes associated with explicit attitude change compare with properties and processes associated with implicit attitude change. We anticipate that much of this research will be conducted by consumer psychologists. Similar to other areas of research, we anticipate that the initial confusion will lead to the development of overarching frameworks that help researchers and practitioners better able to predict when particular processes are more or less likely to occur. In the remainder of this chapter, we review some of the newest theoretical formulations and perspectives that have been offered in attempts to reconcile and integrate past theory and research findings with newer perspectives in cognitive psychology.

Future Directions

Cohen and Reed (2006a) offer the Multiple Pathway Anchoring and Adjustment model (MPAA). The MPPA, based on traditional theories of attitudes, attempts to account for implicit and explicit attitude change as well as factors that influence attitude activation and expression. Schwarz and Bohner (2001) argue that knowledge structures are used to construct new evaluations as demanded by situations. In this constructivist view, attitudes do not exist as stored evaluations in memory. Rather, components of knowledge that influence evaluation come together when needed for evaluative expression and decision making (e.g., Schwarz & Bohner, 2001). In contrast to the constructivist view, Cohen and Reed (2006) argue that many attitudes undergo an anchoring and adjustment process at the point of expression or decision making. Using various research findings and theoretical frameworks from attitude strength and accessibility/diagnosticity perspectives, Cohen and Reed discuss the possibility that attitudes have characteristics of representational and functional sufficiency. Representational sufficiency of an attitude relates to the existence of a clear and understandable position toward a given attitude object. Functional sufficiency focuses on the idea as to whether or not the attitude is a good basis for a particular behavior—providing a mechanism for connecting attitudes to behavior (c.f., Fabrigar, Petty, Smith, & Crites, 2006). In cases when an attitude does not provide a good basis for behavior, Cohen and Reed (2006) suggest that other processes may come into play. Another important consideration according to the MPAA is the idea that attitude research needs to give greater consideration of role attitudes play in self-identity (cf., Shavitt, 1990; Shavitt & Nelson, 2000).

In recent years, discussions have focused on the possibility of dual attitudes (Wilson, Lindsey, & Schooler, 2000). In this view, some responses to an attitude object may be based on implicit attitudes; whereas others are based on explicit attitudes. In some cases, an automatic override mechanism is utilized. Cohen and Reed (2006) suggest that multiple attitudes may exist for the same attitude object. They suggest that the multiple attitudes may exist independently. In their view, some attitudes are more appropriate for some situations than others.

The Associative-Propositional Model (Gawronski & Bodenhausen, 2006, in press) focuses on how sometimes automatic associative processes (e.g., automatic affective reactions) influence attitude formation and change, whereas in other situations, a deliberate propositional process (e.g., evaluations based on syllogistic inferences) occur in attitude formation and change. The former refers to implicit processes which might be assessed with the IAT or evaluative priming (see chapter 16, this volume), whereas the latter refers to explicit processes which might be assessed with the semantic differential. Similar to Deutsch and Strack's (2006a, 2006b) RIM model discussion of the reflective and impulsive components, both of these processes are assumed to be independent (cf., Sherman's, 2006a; 2006b Quad model).

In yet another model related to the ideas noted above, Petty's metacognitive view of attitudes (MCM; e.g., Petty, 2006: Petty, Brinol, Tormala, & Wegener, in press; Petty, Tormala, Brinol, & Jarvis, 2006) includes the PAST Model. In the Past Attitudes are Still There (PAST) model, the old attitude is tagged with a label indicating that it is held with lessened confidence, however, the old attitude still exists and can be activated in certain situations. According to the PAST model, two attitudes relevant to the same object can be activated at the same time. In some cases, the activated attitudes might have different valences. (cf., Cacioppo, Gardner, & Berntson, 1997). From the perspective of the MCM, persons will sometimes actively assess the validity of their reactions to an attitude object, and at other times this process will be more automatic. These assessment processes will sometimes cause a tension or ambivalence in the attitudes and may change the nature of the attitude representations.

SUMMARY

As we stated at the outset of this final discussion, much of the research in the area of the relationship between implicit and explicit attitudes and attitude change processes is in the early stages of development. The principles of attitude change processes that have been researched and supported in the past thirty years are likely to stand the test of time, but we look forward to new insights gained about the way in which implicit attitudes are formed and changed. Advances in the past thirty years have in part been made possible by programmatic approaches to research in which initial phenomena are reliability created in standardized laboratory settings. Systematic manipulation of variables designed to assess underlying processes the boundary conditions have built on the foundation of the early research. We hope that the work on the new areas follows the trend of programmatic approaches to the research.

REFERENCES

Albarracin, D., Johnson, B. T., & Zanna, M .P. (Eds.). (2005). *The handbook of attitudes*. Mahwah, NJ: Erlbaum.

Allport, G. W. (1935). Attitudes. In C. Murchison (Ed.), *Handbook of social psychology* (Vol. 2, pp. 798–884). Worcester, MA: Clark University Press.

Bakamitsos, G. A. (2006). A cue alone or a probe to think? The dual role of affect in product evaluations. *Journal of Consumer Research, 33*(3) (December). 403–412.

Bettman, J. R. (1986). Consumer psychology. *Annual Review of Psychology, 37*, 257–289.

Briñol, P., Petty, R. E., & Tormala, Z. L. (2004). Self-validation of cognitive responses to advertisements. *Journal of Consumer Research, 30*, 559–573.

Briñol, P., Petty, R. E., & Tormala, Z. L. (2006). The malleable meaning of subjective ease. *Psychological Science, 17*, 200–206.

Cacioppo, J. T., Gardner, W. L., & Berntson, G. G. (1997). Beyond bipolar conceptualizations and measures: The case of attitudes in evaluating space. *Personality and Social Psychology Review, 1*(1), 3–25.

Cacioppo, J. T., & Petty, R. E. (Eds.). (1983). *Social psychophysiology: A sourcebook*. New York: Guilford.

Chaiken, S. (1987). The heuristic model of persuasion. In M. P. Zanna, J. M. Olson, & C. P. Herman (Eds.),*Social influence: The Ontario Symposium* (Vol. 5, pp. 3–39). Hillsdale, NJ: Erlbaum.

Chaiken, S., Liberman, A., & Eagly, A. H. (1989). Heuristic and systematic information processing within and beyond the persuasion context. In J. S. Uleman & J. A. Bargh (Eds.), *Unintended thought* (pp. 212–252). New York: Guilford.

Cialdini, R. B., & Goldstein, N .J. (2004). Social influence: compliance and conformity. *Annual Review of Psychology, 55*, 591–621

Cohen, J. B., & Reed, A. (2006a) A Multiple Pathway Anchoring and Adjustment (MPAA) model of attitude generation and recruitment. *Journal of Consumer Research, 33*(1), 1–15.

Cohen, J. B., & Reed, A. (2006b). Perspectives on parsimony: How long is the coast of England? A reply to Park and MacInnis; Schwarz; Petty; and Lynch. *Journal of Consumer Research, 33*(1), 28–30.

Crano, W. D., & Prislin, R. (2006). Attitude change and persuasion. *Annual Review of Psychology, 57*, 345–374.

Deutsch, R., & Strack, F. (2006a). Duality models in social psychology: From dual processes to interacting systems. *Psychological Inquiry, 17*(3), 166–172.

Deutsch, R., & Strack, F. (2006b). Duality models in social psychology: Response to commentaries. *Psychological Inquiry, 17*(3), 265–268.

Eagly, A. H., & Chaiken, S. (1993). *The psychology of attitudes.* Orlando, FL: Harcourt Brace Jovanovich College Publishers.

Fabrigar, L.R., MacDonald, T. K., & Wegener, D. T. (2005). The structure of attitudes. In D. Albarracin, B. T. Johnson, & M. P. Zanna (Eds.), *The handbook of attitudes* (pp. 79–124). Mahwah, NJ: Erlbaum.

Fabrigar, L., Petty, R. E., Smith, S. M., & Crites, S. L. (2006). Understanding knowledge effects on attitude-behavior consistency: The role of relevance, complexity, and amount of knowledge. *Journal of Personality and Social Psychology, 90,* 556–577.

Fazio, R. H., & Olson, M. A. (2003). Implicit measures in social cognition research: Their meaning and use. *Annual review of psychology, 54,* 297–327.

Fazio, R. H., Sanbonmatsu, D. M., Powell, M. C., & Kardes, F .R. (1986). On the automatic activation of attitudes. *Journal of Personality and Social Psychology, 50,* 229–238.

Fishbein, M., & Middlestadt, S. E. (1995) Noncognitive effects on attitude formation and change: Fact or artifact? *Journal of Consumer Psychology, 4*(2), 181–202.

Fishbein, M., & Middlestadt, S.E. (1997) A striking lack of evidence for nonbelief-based attitude formation and change: A response to five commentaries. *Journal of Consumer Psychology, 6,* 107–115.

Fiske, S. T., & Taylor, S. E. (1991). *Social cognition* (2nd ed.). New York: McGraw-Hill.

Fleming, D. (1967). Attitude: The history of a concept. In D. Fleming, & B. Bailyn, (Eds.), *Perspectives in American history* (Vol. 1). Cambridge, MA: Charles Warren Center for Studies in American History.

Gawronski, B., & Bodenhausen, G. V. (2006). Associative and propositional processes in evaluation: An integrative review of implicit and explicit attitude change. *Psychological Bulletin, 132*(5) 692–731.

Gawronski, B., & Bodenhausen, G. V. (in press). Unraveling the processes underlying evaluation: Attitudes from the perspective of the APE Model. Social Cogniton.

Greenwald, A. G. (1968). Cognitive learning, cognitive response to persuasion, and attitude change. In A. G. Greenwald, T. C. Brock, & T. M. Ostrom (Eds.), *Psychological foundations of attitudes* (pp. 147–170). New York: Academic Press.

Greenwald, A. G. (1989). Why are attitudes important? In A. R. Pratkanis, S. J. Breckler, & A. G. Greenwald (Eds.), *Attitude structure and function* (pp. 1–10). Hillsdale, NJ: Erlbaum.

Haugtvedt, C. P., Leavitt, C., & Schneier, W. (1993), Cognitive strength of established brands: Memory, attitudinal, and structural approaches. In D. Aaker & A. Biel (Eds.), *Brand equity and advertising* (pp. 247–261). Hillsdale, NJ: Erlbaum.

Haugtvedt, C. P., (1997). Beyond fact or artifact: An assessment of Fishbein and Middlestadt's perspectives on attitude change processes. *Journal of Consumer Psychology, 6,* 99–106.

Haugtvedt, C. P., & Petty, R. E. (1989). Need for cognition and attitude persistence. *Advances in Consumer Research, 16,* 33–36.

Haugtvedt, C. P., & Petty, R. E. (1992). Personality and persuasion: Need for cognition moderates the persistence and resistance of attitude changes. *Journal of Personality and Social Psychology, 63,* 308–319.

Haugtvedt, C. P., Petty, R. E., & Cacioppo, J. T. (1992). Need for cognition and advertising: Understanding the role of personality variables in consumer behavior. *Journal of Consumer Psychology, 1,* 239–260.

Haugtvedt, C. P., & Priester, J. R. (1997). Conceptual and methodological issues in advertising effectiveness: An attitude strength perspective. In W. Wells (Ed.), *Measuring advertising effectiveness* (pp. 79–93). Hillsdale, NJ: Erlbaum.

Haugtvedt, C. P., & Rucker, D. (June 2003). Brand name and elaboration, Midwest Marketing Camp, Columbus, OH.

Haugtvedt, C. P., & Rucker, D. (2007). *Multiple roles for brand name.* Working paper, Fisher College of Business, Ohio State University.

Haugtvedt, C. P., Schumann, D. W., Schneier, W., & Warren, W. (1994). Advertising repetition and variation strategies: Implications for understanding attitude strength. *Journal of Consumer Research, 21,* 176–189.

Haugtvedt, C. P., Shakarchi, R. J., Samuelson, B. M., & Liu, K, (2004). Consumer psychology and attitude change. In E. Knowles & J. A. Linn (Eds.), *Resistance and persuasion* (pp. 283–297). Mahwah, NJ: Erlbaum.

Haugtvedt, C. P., & Wegener, D. T. (1994). Message order effects in persuasion: An attitude strength perspective. *Journal of Consumer Research, 21,* 205–218.

Herr, P.M. (1995). Whither fact, artifact, and attitude: Reflections on the theory of reasoned action. *Journal of Consumer Psychology, 4*(4), 371–380.

Hovland, C. I., Janis, I., & Kelley, H. H. (1953). *Communication and persuasion.* New Haven, CT: Yale University Press.

Hovland, C. I., & Weiss, W. (1951). The influence of source credibility on communication effectiveness. *Public Opinion Quarterly, 15,* 635–650.

James, W. (1890) *Principles of psychology.* New York: Dover.

Johar, G. V., Maheswaran, D., & Perracchio, L. A. (2006). MAPPing the frontiers: Theoretical advances in consumer research on memory, affect, and persuasion. *Journal of Consumer Research, 33*(June), 139–150.

Judd, C. M., Drake, R. A., Downing, J. W., & Krosnick, J. A. (1991). Some dynamic properties of attitude structures: Context-induced response facilitation and polarization. *Journal of Personality and Social Psychology, 60,* 193–202.

Kang, Y., & Herr, P. (2006). Beauty and the beholder: Toward an integrative model of communication source effects, *Journal of Consumer Research, 33*(June), 123–130.

Karpinski, A., Steinman, R. B., & Hilton, J. L. (2005). Attitude importance as a moderator of the relationship between implicit and explicit attitude measures. *Personality and Social Psychology Bulletin, 31*(7), 949–962.

Kassarjian, H. (1982). Consumer psychology. *Annual Review of Psychology, 33,* 619–649.

Katz, D., & Stotland, E. (1959). A preliminary statement to a theory of attitude structure and change. In S. Koch (Ed.), *Psychology: A study of a science: Vol. 3 Formulations of the person and the social context* (pp. 423–475). New York: McGraw-Hill.

Krosnick, J. A., Judd, C. M., & Wittenbrink, B. (2005). The measurement of attitudes. In D. Albarracin, B. T. Johnson, & M. P. Zanna (Eds.), *The handbook of attitudes* (pp. 21–76). Mahwah, NJ: Erlbaum.

Kruglanski, A. W., Dechesne, M., Erb, H., Pierro, A., Mannetti, L., & Chun, W. Y. (2006a). Modes, systems, and the sirens of specificity: The issues in gist. *Psychological Inquiry, 17*(3), 265–268.

Kruglanski, A. W., Erb., H., Pierro, A., Mannetti, L., & Chun, W. Y. (2006b). On parametric continuities in the world of binary either ors. *Psychological Inquiry, 17*(3), 153–165.

Kruglanski, A. W., & Thompson, E. P. (1999). Persuasion by the single route: A view from the unimodel. *Psychological Inquiry, 10,* 83–109.

Lieppe, M. R., & Elkin, R. A. (1987) When motives clash: Issue involvement and response involvement as determinants of persuasion. *Journal of Personality and Social Psychology, 52,* 269–278.

Loken, B. (2006). Consumer psychology: Categorization, inferences, affect, and persuasion. *Annual Review of Psychology, 57,* 453–485.

Lynch, J. G. (2006) Accessiblity-Diagnosticity and the Multiple Pathway Anchoring and Adjustment Model, *Journal of Consumer Research, 33*(1), 25–27.

Maheshwaran, D., Mackie, D. M., & Chaiken, S. (1992). Brand name as a heuristic cue: The effects of task importance and expectancy confirmation on consumer judgments. *Journal of Consumer Psychology, 1,* 317–333.

McGuire, W. J. (1985). Attitudes and attitude change. In G. Lindzey & E. Aronson (Eds.), *Handbook of social psychology* (Vol. 2, pp. 233–346). New York: Random House.

Miniard P. W., & Barone M. J. (1997). The case for noncognitive determinants of attitude: A critique of Fishebein and Middlestadt. *Journal of Consumer Research, 6,* 77–91.

Moore, D. L., Hausknecht, D., Thamodaran, K. (1986). Time compression, response opportunity, and persuasion. *Journal of Consumer Research, 13,* 85–99.

Ostrom, T. M. (1969). The relationship between the affective, behavioral, and cognitive components of attitude. *Journal of Experimental Social Psychology, 5,* 12–30.

Palmerino, M., Langer, E., & McGillis, D. (1984) Attitudes and attitude change: Mindlessness-mindfulness perspective. In J. R. Eiser (Ed.) *Attitude judgment.* New York, New York: Springer-Verlag.

Park, C. W., & MacInes, D. (2006). What's In and What's Out: Questions on the boundaries on the attitude construct. *Journal of Consumer Research, 33*(1), 16–18.

Pechmann, C., & Esteban, G. (1994). Persuasion processes associated with direct comparative and noncomparative advertising and implications for advertising effectiveness. *Journal of Consumer Psychology, 2*(4), 404–432.

Petty, R. E. (1977a). *A cognitive response analysis of the temporal persistence of attitudes induced by persuasive communication.* Unpublished Doctoral Dissertation, The Ohio State University.

Petty, R. E. (1997). The evolution of theory and research in social psychology: From single to multiple effect and process models. In C. McGarty & S. A. Haslam (Eds.), *The message of social psychology: Perspectives on mind in society* (pp. 268–290). Oxford: Blackwell.

Petty, R. E. (2006). A metacognitive model of attitudes. *Journal of Consumer Research, 33*(1), 22–24

Petty, R. E., & Briñol, P. (2006b). Understanding social judgment: Multiple systems *and* proceses. *Psychological Inquiry, 17,* 217–223

Petty, R. E., Briñol, P., & Tormala, Z. L. (2002). Thought confidence as a determinant of persuasion: The self-validation hypothesis. *Journal of Personality and Social Psychology, 82,* 722–741.

Petty, R. E., Briñol, P., Tormala, Z. L., & Wegener, D. T. (in press). The role of meta-cognition in social judgment. In E. T. Higgins & A. Kruglanski (Eds.), *Handbook of social psychology: Handbook of basic principles,* (2nd ed., pp.). New York: Guilford.

Petty, R. E., & Cacioppo, J. T., (1979). Issue involvement can increase or decrease persuasion by enhancing message-relevant cognitive responses. *Journal of Personality and Social Psychology, 37,* 1915–1926,

Petty, R. E., & Cacioppo, J. T. (1981). *Attitudes and persuasion: Classic and contemporary approaches.* Dubuque, IA: Wm. C. Brown.

Petty, R. E., & Cacioppo, J. T. (1986a). *Communication and persuasion: Central and peripheral routes to attitude change.* New York: Springer/Verlag.

Petty, R.E., & Cacioppo, J. T. (1986b). The elaboration likelihood model of persuasion. In L. Berkowitz (Ed.), *Advances in expeimental social psychology* (Vol. 19, pp. 123–205). New York: Academic Press

Petty, R. E., Cacioppo, J. T., & Goldman, R. (1981). Personal involvement as a determinant of argument-based persuasion. *Journal of Personality and Social Psychology, 41,* 847–855.

Petty, R. E., Cacioppo, J. T., & Kasmer, J. A. (1988). The role of affect in the Elaboration Likelihood Model of persuasion. In L. Donohew, H. Sypher, & E. T. Higgins (Eds.), *Communication, social cognition, and affect* (pp. 117–146). Hillsdale, NJ: Erlbaum.

Petty, R. E., Cacioppo, J. T., Kasmer, J. A., & Haugtvedt, C. P. (1987). A reply to Stiff and Boster. *Communication Monographs, 54,* 257–263.

Petty, R. E., Cacioppo, J. T., & Schumann, D. (1983). Central and Peripheral Routes to Advertising Effectiveness: The Moderating Role of Involvement. *Journal of Consumer Research, 10*(2), 135–146.

Petty, R. E., Haugtvedt, C. T., & Smith, S. M. (1995). Elaboration as a determinant of attitude strength: Creating attitudes that are persistent, resistant, and predictive of behavior. In R. E. Petty & J. A. Krosnick (Eds.), *Attitude strength: Antecedents and Consequences* (pp. 93–130). Mahwah, NJ: Erlbaum.

Petty, R. E., Kasmer, J. A., Haugtvedt, C. P., & Cacioppo, J. T. (1987). Source and message factors in persuasion: A reply to Stiff's critique of the Elaboration Likelihood Model. *Communication Monographs, 54,* 233–249.

Petty, R. E., & Krosnick, E. J. (1995). *Attitude strength: Antecedents and consequences.* Mahwah, NJ: Erlbaum.

Petty, R. E., Ostrom, T. M., & Brock, T. C. (1981). In R. E. Petty, T. M. Ostrom, & T. C. Brock (Eds.), *Cognitive responses in persuasion.* Hillsdale, NJ: Erlbaum.

Petty, R. E., Priester, J. R., & Wegener, D. T. (1994). Cognitive processes in attitude change. In R. S. Wyer & T. K. Srull (Eds.), *Handbook of social cognition* (2nd ed., Vol. 2, pp. 69–142). Hillsdale, NJ: Erlbaum.

Petty, R. E., Schumann, D. W., Richman, S. A., & Strathman, A. J. (1993). Positive mood and persuasion: Different roles for affect under high- and low-elaboration conditions. *Journal of Personality and Social Psychology, 64,* 5–20.

Petty, R. E., Tormala, Z. L., Briñol, P., & Jarvis, W. B. G. (2006). Implicit ambivalence from attitude change: An exploration of the PAST model. *Journal of Personality and Social Psychology, 90,* 21–41.

Petty, R. E., & Wegener, D. T. (1998). Attitude change: Multiple roles for persuasion variables. In D. Gilbert, S. Fiske, & G. Lindzey (Eds.), *The handbook of social psychology* (4th ed., Vol. 1, pp. 323–390). New York: McGraw-Hill.

Petty, R. E., & Wegener, D. T. (1999). The elaboration likelihood model: Current status and controversies. In S. Chaiken & Y. Trope (Eds.), *Dual process theories in social psychology* (pp. 41–72). New York: Guilford.

Petty, R. E., Wegener, D. T., Fabrigar, L. R., Priester, J. R., & Cacioppo, J. T. (1993). Conceptual and methodological issues in the Elaboration Likelihood Model of persuasion: A reply to the Michigan State critics. *Communication Theory, 3,* 336–362.

Petty, R. E., Wheeler, S. C., & Bizer, G. Y. (1999). Is there one persuasion process or more? Lumping versus splitting in attitude change theories. *Psychological Inquiry, 10,* 156–163

Pratkanis, A. R., Breckler, S. J., & Greenwald, A.G. (Eds.). (1989). *Attitude structure and function.* Hillsdale, NJ: Erlbaum

Priester, J. R., & Fleming, M. A. (1997). Artifact or meaningful theoretical constructs?: Evidence for nonbelief-and belief-based attitude change processes. *Journal of Consumer Psychology, 6*(1), 67–76.

Priester, J. R., & Petty, R. E. (1995). Source attributions and persuasion: Perceived honesty as a determinant of message scrutiny. *Personality and Social Psychology Bulletin, 21,* 637–654.

Priester, J. R., & Petty, R. E. (1996). The gradual threshold model of ambivalence: Relating the positive and negative bases of attitudes to subjective ambivalence. *Journal of Personality and Social Psychology, 71,* 431–449.

Priester, J. R., & Petty, R. E. (2001). Extending the bases of subjective attitudinal ambivalence: Interpersonal and intrapersonal antecedents of evaluative tension. *Journal of Personality and Social Psychology, 80,* 19–34.

Priester, J. R., Petty, R. E., & Park, K. (in press). Whence univalent ambivalence? From the anticipation of conflicting reactions. *Journal of Consumer Research, 34*(1) (June).

Pryor, J. B., & Reeder, G.D. (2006). A critique of three dueling models of dual processes. *Psychological Inquiry, 17*(3), 231–236.

Rydell, R. J., & McConnell, A. R. (2006). Understanding implicit and explicit attitude change: A systems of reasoning analysis. *Journal of Personality and Social Psychology, 91,* 995–1008.

Sanbonmatsu, D. M., & Kardes, F. R. (1988). The effects of physiological arousal on information processing and persuasion. *Journal of Consumer Research, 15,* 379–385.

Schwarz, N. (1997). Moods and attitude judgments: A comment on Fishbein and Middlestadt. *Journal of Consumer Psychology, 6,* 93–98.

Schwarz, N. (2006) Attitude research between Ockham's razor and the fundamental attribution error. *Journal of Consumer Research, 33*(1), 19–21.

Schwarz, N., & Bohner, G. (2001). The construction of attitudes. In A. Tesser & N. Schwarz (Eds.), *Blackwell handbook of social psychology: Intrapersonal processes* (436–457). Oxford: Blackwell

Schumann, D. W., Petty, R. E., & Clemons, D. S. (1990). Predicting the effectiveness of different strategies of advertising variation: A test of the repetition-variation hypotheses. *Journal of Consumer Research, 17,* 192–202.

Scott, W. A. (1969). Structure of natural cognitions. *Journal of Personality and Social Psychology, 12,* 261–278.

Shavitt, S. (1990). The role of attitude objects in attitude functions. *Journal of Experimental Social Psychology, 26*(2), 124–148.

Shavitt, S., & Nelson, M. R. (2000). The social-identity function in person perception: Communicated meanings of product preferences. In G. Maio & J. M. Olson (Eds.), *Why we evaluate: Functions of attitudes* (pp. 37–57). Mahwah, NJ: Erlbaum.

Sherman, J. W. (2006a). On building a better process model: It's not only how many, but which ones and by which means? *Psychological Inquiry, 17*(3), 173–184.

Sherman, J. W. (2006b). Clearing up some misconceptions about the quad model *Psychological Inquiry,* 17(3), 269–276.

Tetlock, P. E. (1989). Structure and function of political belief systems. In A. R. Pratkanis, S. J. Brecker, & A. G. Greenwald (Eds.), *Attitude structure and function* (pp. 129–151). Hillsdale, NJ: Erlbaum.

Thomas, W. I., & Znaniecki, F. (1918) *The Polish peasant in Europe and America.* Chicago: University of Chicago Press.

Thompson, M. M., Zanna, M. P., & Griffin, D. W. (1995). Let's not be indifferent about attitudinal ambivalence. In R. E. Petty & J. A. Krosnick (Eds.), *Attitude strength: Antecedents and consequences* (pp. 361–386). Mahwah, NJ: Erlbaum.

Thurstone, L. L. (1928). Attitudes can be measured. *American Journal of Sociology, 33,* 529–544.

Tormala, Z. L., Briñol, P., & Petty, R. E. (2006). When credibility attacks: The reverse impact of source credibility on persuasion. *Journal of Experimental Social Psychology, 42,* 684–691.

Tormala, Z. L., & Petty, R. E. (2002). What doesn't kill me makes me stronger: The effects of resisting persuasion on attitude certainty. *Journal of Personality and Social Psychology, 83,* 1298–1313.

Tormala, Z. L., & Petty, R. E. (2004). Source credibility and attitude certainty: A meta-cognitive analysis of resistance to persuasion. *Journal of Consumer Psychology, 14,* 426–441.

Tormala, Z. L., Petty, R. E., & Briñol, P. (2002). Ease of retrieval effects in persuasion: A self-validation analysis. *Personality and Social Psychology Bulletin, 28,* 1700–1712.

Wegener, D. T., Downing, J., Krosnick, J. A., & Petty, R. E. (1995). Measures and manipulations of strength related properties of attitudes: Current practice and future directions. In R. E. Petty & J. A. Krosnick (Eds.), *Attitude strength: Antecedents and Consequences* (pp. 455–488). Mahwah, NJ: Erlbaum.

Wheeler, S. C., Petty, R. E., & Bizer, G. Y. (2005). Self-schema matching and attitude change: Situational and dispositional determinants of message elaboration. *Journal of Consumer Research, 31,* 787–797.

Wilson, T. D., & Hodges, S. D. (1992). Attitudes as temporary constructions: In L. L. Martin & A. Tesser (Eds.), *The construction of social judgments* (pp. 37–65). Hillsdale, New Jersey: Erlbaum.

Wilson, T. D., Lindsey, S. & Schooler, T. (2000). A model of dual attitudes. *Psychological Review, 107*(January), 101–126.

Wood, W., Rhodes, N., & Biek, M. (1995). Working knowledge and attitude strength: An information processing analysis. In R. E. Petty & J. A. Krosnick (Eds.), *Attitude strength: Antecedents and consequences* (pp. 283–313). Mahwah, NJ: Erlbaum.

Wyer, R. S. (2006). Three models of information processing: An evaluation and conceptual integration. *Psychological Inquiry, 17*(3), 185–194.

16

Associative Strength and Consumer Choice Behavior

CHRISTOPHER R. M. JONES

RUSSELL H. FAZIO

Ohio State University

INTRODUCTION

The practice of advertising is predicated on the assumption that consumer choice behavior is at least partially determined by representations of the product or brand in memory. Rather than entering a choice situation as a "blank slate" and assessing alternatives completely on-the-spot, individuals virtually always have some knowledge of the type or category of product in question and often about specific brands as well. According to associative network theories of cognition (e.g., Anderson & Bower, 1973), these representations are not isolated but linked in memory by connections that vary in strength. This chapter will consider how concepts like brands and categories of products can be related to other representations in memory and the implications for consumer behavior.

We begin with the assumption that these consumer-related concepts can be uniquely represented in memory and associated to varying degrees with other mental representations. This variation, the strength of the association between two representations, determines the likelihood that activating one concept will result in the activation of the associated concept. Obviously, the nature of the associates of, for example, the representation of a brand will largely determine how an individual thinks about that brand and whether they might choose to purchase it. Further, not all associations are created equal. A representation strongly associated with a brand is more likely than a representation weakly associated with a brand to ultimately influence behavior. Predicting consumer choice thus entails having some idea about both the content of associated representations and on the strength of those associations.

Many different kinds of associations in memory may prove relevant to consumer behavior. A brand, for instance, might be associated with usage situations, particular attributes, previous experiences, and so on. We will focus on two kinds of associated representation: *attitudes*, which can be conceptualized as associations between an object and a summary evaluation of that object, and *category-exemplar* associations, associations between an object and a superordinate classification. The goal of this chapter is to describe some differences and commonalities between these two types of associations, both of which we believe to be important for understanding consumer choice behavior. The chapter will present some broad guidelines for identifying situations and product classes for which each type of association is likely to be particularly relevant. We will first focus on the determinants and consequences of attitudinal associative strength. We then will turn to category-exemplar associations, and then finally we will discuss some contextual factors that moderate the role of associative strength in consumer choice situations.

ATTITUDES: OBJECT-EVALUATION ASSOCIATIONS

Attitudes can be viewed as associations in memory between an object and one's summary evaluation of that object (Fazio, Chen, McDonel, & Sherman, 1982). When individuals encounter or consider an attitude object, the associated evaluation can be activated. The likelihood that an evaluation is activated contingently by the attitude object is the attitude's *accessibility*, and it is determined by the strength of the association between the object and evaluation. Since the proposal of this theoretical perspective, considerable research has examined the consequences, determinants, and correlates of attitude accessibility and its role in the attitude-to-behavior process (see Fazio, 1995, for a review). This section will review these findings with attention to the implications for how attitudes function in object-appraisal and decision-making processes of interest to consumer psychology.

Before proceeding, it will be useful to clarify what is intended when describing attitudes as object-evaluation associations in memory that vary in strength. Both object and evaluation are meant broadly. Individuals may not only store evaluations of physical objects, but also of concepts of all levels of abstraction. These evaluations associated with objects have various bases that range from "hot" affective responses to "cold" analytical beliefs concerning attributes of the object. Regardless of the precise nature of the object and evaluation, the strength of the association between the two will influence the likelihood of its use. This structural approach to attitude strength and to attitudes in general has the advantage of operating at an information processing level of analysis, allowing for specificity in the treatment of the concept and integration thereof into broader models of cognition and behavior (e.g., Fazio, 1990; Herr & Fazio, 1993).

Accessibility

The crux of the conceptualization of attitudes as object-evaluation associations is that the strength of this association influences attitude accessibility, the likelihood that the attitude will be activated from memory automatically when the object is encountered. Here, the term "automatic" refers to the attitude being activated "whenever a given set of external initiating stimuli are present, regardless of a subject's attempt to ignore or bypass the distraction" (Shiffrin & Dumais, 1981, p. 117). This begs the question of how associations attain such strength. According to associative network theories of mental representation, associations in memory will be strengthened to the extent that the representations they link are experienced or thought about together; this strength changes only slowly over time (Smith & Queller, 2001). Attitude accessibility can be measured by the latency of response to a direct attitudinal inquiry. Relatively high accessibility may be chronic, reflecting high associative strength, or it may be temporarily enhanced by recency of use (Higgins, 1996).

Empirical support regarding the automatic activation of attitudes was gathered using priming procedures (Fazio, Sanbonmatsu, Powell, & Kardes, 1986). The evidence concerns the effect of semantic primes on the latency with which individuals are able to identify the connotation of target adjectives (e.g., attractive, disgusting) as positive or negative. These primes were positive or negative words selected idiosyncratically for each participant. For each participant, attitudes towards the objects were categorized as accessible or inaccessible according to the latency of response required to evaluate them. Priming with these items, which were presented to participants as distracting "memory words," facilitated performance in the adjective connotation task when the valence of the primed object was the same as the valence of the target adjective. That is, responding was faster. On the other hand, when the valence of the prime and target were incongruent, it took longer to identify the target adjective as positive or negative. So, participants were able to classify a positive adjective more quickly when it was preceded by a positively valued object. Importantly, the facilitation and inhibition effects of the primes were more pronounced for objects towards which participants held accessible attitudes.

Similar automatic attitude activation has been demonstrated in research employing brand names as primes (Sanbonmatsu & Fazio, 1986). Accessible attitudes towards brand names influenced how quickly individuals could categorize the target adjectives that followed them as positive or negative.

A notable characteristic of the priming procedure is that accessible attitudes towards the prime words influenced evaluative categorization even though participants were aware that the prime itself was irrelevant to their goals in the task, providing preliminary evidence that the influence of the primes was spontaneous and uncontrollable. Further evidence of the validity of automatic attitude activation is that it also occurs when participants are engaged in a task that is not dependent on any evaluative intent (e.g., Bargh, Chaiken, Raymond, & Hymes, 1996).

The findings regarding the moderating role of associative strength on automatic attitude activation relate to an important conceptual distinction offered by Converse (1970). Noting that a person may respond to an evaluative item on a survey even though that person had never previously encountered or considered the item's referent, Converse (1970) distinguished between attitudes and nonattitudes. Based on the finding that attitude accessibility varies as a function of associative strength, it has been suggested that the distinction between attitudes and nonattitudes may be more usefully considered a continuum (Fazio, Sanbonmatsu, Powell, & Kardes, 1986). At the nonattitude end of the continuum is the case in which no appropriate a priori evaluation is available in memory and evaluative assessment must occur in an on-line fashion. Approaching the upper end of the continuum, well-learned object-evaluation associations are increasingly capable of being activated automatically from memory. This does not mean that only highly accessible attitudes are available in memory. Attitudes that are low in accessibility may also be activated, but this is more likely to require motivated efforts to retrieve information about the attitude-object.

The potential for automatic activation provides much of the functional value of attitudes. Accessible attitudes can be activated instantly upon encountering an attitude-object and help individuals understand and react to the world around them. The basic value of attitudes is this object-appraisal function (Smith, Bruner, & White, 1956) and automatic activation allows the rapid initiation of approach or avoidance behavior based on these object-appraisals. The following sections will discuss the consequences of attitude accessibility, which determines the functional role of attitudes in guiding thought and behavior.

Manipulating Associative Strength

A number of manipulations have been used to increase the strength of the association between attitude-objects and evaluations (thus increasing attitude accessibility) in the laboratory. Always, participants are one way or another induced to note and rehearse their attitudes by repeatedly expressing them. For instance, this has been achieved by requesting that participants copy their attitudinal ratings onto multiple forms (Fazio et al., 1982, Experiment 3). Other studies (e.g., Powell

& Fazio, 1984) varied the number of times that a particular attitude-object appeared on a question-naire, in each instance followed by a different (but always evaluative) semantic differential scale. Another variation of this manipulation has the advantage of distinguishing the effects of attitude accessibility from mere object accessibility (e.g., Fazio et al., 1986, Experiment 3; Roskos-Ewold-sen & Fazio, 1992, Experiment 2). In these experiments, each attitude-object was presented an equivalent number of times, but how often the attitude-object was paired with an evaluative ques-tion versus some control question (e.g., "Is this object animate or inanimate?") varied. Increasing attitudinal associative strength through repeated expression increases automatic attitude activa-tion, measured by the extent to which that attitude-object facilitates the evaluative categorization of items of congruent valence and inhibits the evaluative categorization of items of incongruent valence (Fazio et al., 1986). As we describe the ways in which attitudes ultimately exert an influence on behavior in the following sections, it should be remembered that such effects should only be expected when object-evaluation associations are sufficiently strong, either due to a manipulation of associative strength or the pre-existing strength of associations held by individuals.

CONSEQUENCES OF ATTITUDE ACCESSIBILITY

An interaction with a physical object often begins with a perception and ends in behavior. We will first review evidence suggesting that attitudes can bias individuals' basic perceptions of visual stimuli. In subsequent sections, we will explore other consequences of the associative strength of attitudes—ones that serve as further mechanisms through which attitudes ultimately shape behavior.

Perception

Higher-order cognitive and motivational processes can influence perception in a top-down fash-ion. For example, it has been demonstrated that individuals perceive a briefly presented ambiguous figure (it could be construed as either the letter "B" or the number "13") in the manner consistent with their desired outcome (Balcetis & Dunning, 2006). Participants were informed that a number or letter would appear on a computer screen, indicating into which experimental condition they would be assigned. Participants were more likely to perceive the stimulus in a way that would indicate that they would be in the condition requiring that they drink orange juice rather than a disgusting, viscous "health drink." This type of motivation, described by Balcetis and Dunning as "wishful thinking" extends previous research documenting similar perceptual effects caused by motivation from biological drives. For example, Changizi and Hall (2001) found that when indi-viduals were thirsty, they displayed a greater tendency to perceive a concept associated with water, transparency, in ambiguous visual stimuli varying in opacity.

Research by Powell and Fazio (summarized in Fazio, Roskos-Ewoldsen, & Powell, 1994) exam-ined the influence of attitudinal biases on perception in an informationally sparse visual environ-ment. Participants were required to observe a computerized tennis game in which flashes of light appeared in a rectangle divided by a vertical line, representing a tennis court. The flashes of light represented the location of shots landed by either the computer or (supposedly) a confederate who had previously behaved in such a way that he/she would be liked or disliked by the participant. On target trials, flashes of light appeared within 5 pixels of the end line, making the participants' task, judging whether the shot landed "in" or "out," difficult. Despite being informed that their judg-ments (indicated with a key press) were solicited only to test the quality of the game's visual display and that the computer would accurately judge and tally the score, participants displayed patterns of errors that were influenced by their liking of the confederate. Participants who had been led to like the confederate called more balls hit by the confederate "in" when they were truly "out" and balls hit by the computer "out" when they were truly "in" than errors which would have been in the computer's favor. The opposite pattern of results was observed when participants had been led to dislike the confederate.

Attention

An important aspect of the influence of associative strength on basic perceptual processes is the potential for objects associated with highly accessible attitudes to attract visual attention when the object enters the visual field. Roskos-Ewoldsen and Fazio (1992) assessed recall for stimulus items presented briefly in groups of six in a circular visual array. Participants were more likely to notice and report objects for which they held more accessible attitudes. This was the case both when attitude accessibility had been previously measured by latency of response and when it was manipulated through attitude rehearsal. In another experiment in the series, participants noticed the more attitude-evoking objects incidentally, i.e., even when their task was to categorize a stimulus that appeared in the center of the visual array of objects as either a number or a letter. In a final experiment, performance on a visual search task was shown to be disrupted by the presence of more attitude-evoking objects as distractors. Attitude accessibility predicted the extent to which these distracters interfered with performance on the visual search task. Thus, the influence of attitude accessibility on selective attention appears to be automatic not only in that it is spontaneous, but also in that it occurs regardless of intentional efforts to ignore the attitude-object.

Roskos-Ewoldsen and Fazio (1992) argued that attitudes provide an adaptive, orienting function towards objects that have hedonic value, allowing them to be rapidly approached or avoided. These findings may be of particular relevance to consumer psychologists. In any environment, multiple stimuli are likely to be present that may attract an individual's attention. Indeed, in environments such as supermarkets, many objects are specifically designed to attract attention and are intended to compete in this respect with one another. One strategy to ensure that a product draws attention is through manipulating properties of the object itself, usually by carefully designing its appearance. Another approach is to depend on the accessibility of consumers' attitudes towards the brand to guide attention. Sometimes, it may be easier or more effective to influence consumers' mental representation of the product than to enhance the relative attention-drawing capacity of the object itself.

Categorization

All objects are multiply categorizable and the particular category or categories activated depend not only on properties of the object, but also on those of the observer. Another consequence of the associative strength of an attitude is its capacity to determine which of multiple suitable categories is actually applied to the object (Smith, Fazio, & Cejka, 1996). For instance, at any moment in time a given individual might construe a cup of yogurt as a "snack" or as a "dairy product." For a person with lactose-intolerance, the category dairy product is likely to be strongly associated with a negative evaluation. This associative strength makes the category more attitude-evoking, more likely to attract attention, and, hence, more likely to dominate construal of the yogurt. That is, the individual is more likely to categorize yogurt as a dairy product than a snack. Across a series of experiments, Smith et al. (1996) obtained empirical support for the notion that highly accessible attitudes towards categories determine which categories will be preferentially applied to multiply categorizable stimuli. An attitude rehearsal manipulation increased the accessibility of attitudes toward one of two potential categorizations for each item in a series of objects. When these objects were later presented as a cue, the category for which attitudes had been rendered more accessible was more likely to be evoked. In addition, individuals could more quickly verify that the category applied to the object. Thus, accessible attitudes shape basic categorization processes and facilitate construals that are hedonically meaningful.

Information Processing

Relatedly, yet another well-known consequence of attitudes is their potential to shape the manner in which individuals interpret information. As a function of their personal biases, individuals may view and describe the same event in radically different ways (e.g., Hastorf & Cantril, 1954). In a classic experiment, Lord, Ross, and Lepper (1979) found that individuals who held strong opinions toward the death penalty examined relevant empirical evidence in a biased manner. College students who either supported or opposed capital punishment were exposed to two fabricated studies, one that seemingly provided evidence supporting the efficacy of the death penalty as a deterrent to crime and one that denied it. Participants rated not the conclusions but the actual methodology of the studies as being more valid when the study reached conclusions consistent with their own attitudes. Participants actually endorsed their initial opinions more strongly after reading the conflicting accounts, even though the quality of the messages themselves was essentially equal.

Houston and Fazio (1989) examined the influence of attitude accessibility on such information processing. Because the participants in the research by Lord and colleagues (1979) were selected on the basis of their strong pre-existing attitudes toward the topic, Houston and Fazio reasoned that these participants likely had highly accessible attitudes toward capital punishment and that the biased processing effect might be less general and not occur for participants who did not have such accessible attitudes—an attitude will not bias processing if it is not activated. Attitude accessibility was measured in one study via latency of response to a direct attitudinal query and experimentally manipulated via repeated attitudinal expression in another. In both cases, the strength of the object-evaluation association predicted the degree of correspondence between attitudes toward capital punishment and ratings of the scientific quality of the studies. The correlations were rather meager among the participants whose attitudes were relatively low in accessibility (r's < .18), but accounted for much more variance among those with greater attitude accessibility (r's .44–.58). Attitudes had a much stronger biasing influence as the strength of the object-evaluation association increased.

That accessible attitudes bias the processing of incoming information is consistent with the finding that the impact of a persuasive communication is attenuated when an individual can rapidly retrieve attitudinal beliefs about the message topic from memory (Wood, 1982). For this reason, another consequence of attitudinal associative strength may be stability, insofar as highly accessible attitudes are relatively resistant to change. Holding accessible attitudes towards a product or brand, then, will influence the processing of relevant information. A positive attitude, if activated, can attenuate the impact of all manner of negative information, be it unfavorable nutritional information or a communicated negative reaction from a friend, acquaintance, or even an expert, as suggested by the supposed origin of the capital punishment arguments in the above studies. Of course, negative attitudes, exert a similar biasing influence, suggesting that, for example, advertisers may have great difficulty in modifying highly accessible negative attitudes and that attempts to "re-position" the brand as a new product may be a more successful alternative (Herr & Fazio, 1993).

Ease of Decision Making

Attitudes allow individuals to access stored evaluations from memory based on previous experience with an attitude-object rather than being forced to effortfully generate immediate appraisals of an object on every instance on which it is encountered, a process that is dependent on the availability of cognitive resources and is comparatively slow. For this reason, attitudes should influence the decision making process not only by biasing it, but also by easing it. Research in psychophysiology has established that "patterns of enhanced autonomic, especially cardiovascular, reactivity are associated with psychologically effortful or challenging situations involving decision making and other types of cognitive activities" (Blascovich, Ernst, Tomaka, Kelsey, Salomon, & Fazio, 1993, p. 165). A series of experiments exploited these biological hallmarks of effort to test the hypothesis that accessible attitudes ease decision making by using physiological measures (Blascovich et al., 1993; Fazio, Blascovich, & Driscoll, 1992). Sharing a common paradigm, these experiments required participants to make preference judgments between pairs of abstract paintings under significant time pressure. Before this pairwise preference task, some participants repeatedly reported their liking for each painting while others merely announced the predominant color appearing in each painting, allowing the experimenters to control for the familiarity of the stimuli while manipulating their position on the attitude-nonattitude continuum. When making their pairwise preference decisions, participants in the attitude-rehearsal condition displayed less reactivity on a variety of cardiovascular and skin conductance measures. Accessible attitudes, importantly, reduce the resource-dependence of decision making both cognitively and physically (see Fazio & Powell, 1997, for consideration of the long-term implications of such attitudinal functionality for adjustment and well-being).

The MODE Model

Attitudes are generally of interest because of their potential to guide behavior. However, human behavior is multiply determined, and the specific role of attitudes in provoking behavior has been a subject of some controversy (see Zanna & Fazio, 1982, for a historical review). Much of the research program discussed so far grew out of an investigation of the problem of attitude-behavior consistency. That is, sometimes attitudes have been noted to be very poor predictors of actual behavior (e.g., see LaPiere, 1934, for a famous albeit not methodologically rigorous instance; or Wicker, 1969, for an influential review). There are obvious reasons why this could be the case. As a determinant of behavior, attitudes sometimes compete against impulses derived from individuals' immediate construal of their situation that may dictate a different behavior than would be predicted from an attitude measure. Behavioral norms, for instance, have a moderating influence on attitude-behavior consistency (Ajzen & Fishbein, 1973). Also, as individuals experience the world they encounter actual, unique exemplars of attitude-objects. Deliberative evaluations of these objects in the context in which they appear may bear little resemblance to a stored evaluation of a prototype (Lord & Lepper, 1999; Lord, Lepper, & Mackie, 1984).

The MODE model (Fazio, 1990) of attitude-behavior consistency outlines the general conditions under which object-evaluation associations can be predicted to guide behavior. Attitudes can be activated automatically and influence behavior in a relatively spontaneous manner. By coloring one's appraisal of an object in the immediate situation, attitudes can promote approach or avoidance behavior, even without the individual reflecting upon the behavioral action. However, individuals also may determine a situationally appropriate course of action through thoughtful analysis of its costs and benefits (see Ajzen & Fishbein, 1980). The MODE model postulates that

*M*otivation and *O*pportunity are *D*eterminants of which mode of evaluative processing, spontaneous or deliberative, is likely to occur in a given situation. First, deliberative processing is contingent on an individual's *M*otivation to undergo thoughtful reflection regarding a behavioral decision. The MODE model may be viewed as an extension of Kruglanski's (1989) theory of lay epistemology to the question of the attitude-behavior relation. Kruglanski (1989) described general processes and motivating variables relevant to the acquisition of knowledge. When individuals are motivated to avoid reaching an invalid conclusion due to its perceived consequences, they are said to have "fear of invalidity," and are likely to carefully deliberate concerning the relevant judgment or action. Applying these ideas to the attitude-behavior relation, when individuals are motivated by "fear of invalidity" to expend cognitive effort, behavioral decisions (which may or may not appear consistent with one's attitudes) will be reached through effortful deliberation.

While motivational factors may initiate deliberative processing, it must also be considered that even when such deliberation is desirable, it may not always be possible. Thus, *O*pportunity is the second element of the MODE acronym, because situations will occur in which time pressure or resource depletion precludes the possibility of sufficient cognitive effort. By virtue of their capacity for automatic activation, attitudes may guide behavior by default in these circumstances. In the case of a more spontaneous attitude-behavior relation, accessibility will play a moderating role. Even if motivation and opportunity are lacking, attitudes will only determine behavior if they are activated from memory. If stored attitudes are not retrieved, an individual's behavior must depend on their immediate appraisal of the situation, regardless of any insufficiency in motivation or opportunity for satisfactory deliberation on it.

MODE's acronymic assumption that motivation and opportunity are determinants of processing type has been tested in a laboratory experiment using consumer choice scenarios. Sanbonmatsu and Fazio (1990) presented participants with a series of statements about two department stores that described qualities of the various departments of each. The hypothetical department store "Smith's" was generally presented in favorable terms whereas "Brown's" was generally described in unfavorable ones. Consistent with their instructions to form a general evaluation of the two stores, participants did come to view Smith's much more favorably than Brown's. However, contrary to the general evaluation thus formed, the camera department of each store was described in the opposite fashion—as unfavorable at Smith's but as favorable at Brown's. This resulted in particular attribute information in opposition to the valence of the summary evaluation associated with each store. Later, participants were asked to imagine which store they would prefer to buy a camera from. Choosing Smith's would suggest that participants relied on their attitudes toward the department stores themselves without any further considerations, indicating relatively effortless processing. On the other hand, a choice of Brown's would suggest that participants underwent the deliberative process of retrieving relevant information, comparing specific attribute information, and disregarding the general preference for Smith's relative to Brown's.

The conditions under which the decision was made were manipulated with respect to both the motivation and the opportunity participants would have to deliberate upon it. The opportunity to deliberate was determined by allowing some participants only 15 seconds to decide while others were not subject to time constraints. Crossed with the manipulation of opportunity for deliberation, half of the participants were motivated to make an accurate decision by the expectation that they would later have to justify their choice to other participants and the experimenter, while others would have no reason to perceive their choice as having any repercussions whatsoever. The results conformed to predictions from the MODE model. Participants who were motivated to make an accurate decision and had unlimited time to do so were more likely to make a choice indicative of deliberative processing (choosing the store with the better camera department) than participants in any of the other three conditions. The latter relied on their general attitudes toward the two stores.

The specific role of attitude accessibility in the MODE model was tested in a field experiment investigating the 1984 presidential election (Fazio & Williams, 1986). Attitude accessibility towards the Republican and Democratic presidential candidates, Ronald Reagan and Walter Mondale, was measured in a large sample of individuals approached at a shopping mall. Latency of response to attitudinal queries regarding each candidate moderated the degree to which those attitudes predicted (1) participants' judgments of the quality of performance by each candidate during a subsequent televised debate, and (2) participants' actual voting behavior several months later. That those with highly accessible attitudes towards the candidates judged the performances in the presidential debates in accordance with those attitudes supports the assertion that one's attitudes can color judgments about complex social stimuli, likely due to the various perceptual, attentional, and biased-processing consequences of attitude function described above. Moreover, such attitudinally-driven biases increase as the strength of the object-evaluation association increases. The finding regarding voting behavior illustrates the persistence of more accessible attitudes over time and, hence, their greater likelihood of influencing subsequent behavior, in this case months later.

The basic finding from the election study supporting the prediction that attitude accessibility moderates the attitude-behavior relation was replicated in the laboratory using consumer products as attitude-objects (Fazio, Powell, & Williams, 1989). Following the usual latency measure of the accessibility of attitudes towards 100 products, participants were given the opportunity to select five products from a set of 10 alternatives that were arranged into two rows of five and presented on a table. Two observed relationships were moderated by attitude accessibility. First, attitude accessibility moderated the consistency between attitudes and the subsequent product selection measure such that attitudes had greater predictive utility when they were more accessible for a given individual. Also, as attitude accessibility increased, the extent to which participants tended to exhibit a preference for products from the first row decreased. This position effect was irrelevant to the quality of the randomly ordered products, and it was less evident when participants possessed accessible attitudes to guide behavior. Yet, among those with less accessible attitudes, the salience afforded a product by virtue of its positioning in the first row increased the likelihood of its being selected. When people lack strong evaluative associations to an object, their immediate appraisals of the object must be constructed as part of the decision process. In such cases, the immediate appraisals are subject to the influence of momentarily salient, and potentially extraneous, considerations.

Implications for Consumer Behavior

Herr and Fazio (1993) have articulated the relevance of the MODE model to the domain of consumer behavior. The model offers a perspective on when and how attitudes towards products are likely to influence consumer behavior (see Herr & Fazio, 1993, for a much fuller description of the approach, as well as additional implications for advertisers). Most centrally, the model serves to highlight that different marketing strategies may be more appropriate for particular classes of products. Decisions regarding "big ticket" items, which are expensive and/or important purchases, are more likely to be executed in a deliberative fashion than routine purchases (Herr & Fazio, 1993). Even an extremely positive, accessible attitude is irrelevant if an individual has reasoned that they cannot afford the product. Moreover, the importance of the decision is likely to lead to additional review and consideration of the available attribute information, instead of reliance on the pre-existing attitude. Accessible attitudes may color the sampling and evaluation of the relevant data.

So, it is not that attitudes are irrelevant. However, fear of invalidity is likely to promote a return to the data—a bottom-up process instead of a top-down, attitudinally driven process.

In the case of routine purchases, on the other hand, behavior is more likely to be determined by spontaneous processes resulting from automatic attitude activation. With such minor purchases, the potential for normative concerns or fear of invalidity is reduced. The multiple consequences of attitude accessibility and its moderating role in the attitude-behavior relation suggest that, especially with respect to routinely purchased products, attitude accessibility is a variable that marketers have a vested interest in fostering, presuming that the product is good and attitudes are generally positive. Hence, we now turn to what is known about the determinants of associative strength and specific strategies for strengthening object-evaluation associations through advertising.

DETERMINANTS OF ASSOCIATIVE STRENGTH

Rehearsal

As seen in the research on attitude accessibility, the strength of object-evaluation associations can be increased through repetition. Repetition refers to any instance in which the attitude object and the evaluation co-occur, whether solely in one's mind or in the environment. One of the basic assumptions of associative network theories in cognition is that links are strengthened to the extent the objects they link are experienced or thought about together and that strength changes only slowly over time (Smith & Queller, 2001). Noting these co-occurrences may function as trials of associative learning whether the attitude-object is actually present and being evaluated or not. Repetitions may not only take the form of passive observation of co-occurrences, but also may involve actively relating the associated concepts. Repeatedly rehearsing an attitude by expressing it seems to be particularly effective in increasing attitude accessibility, though initial rehearsals will increase attitude accessibility more than subsequent ones when they occur within a short span of time (Powell & Fazio, 1984).

Repetitions of advertisements or other product-related messages obviously have the potential to increase associative strength. Indeed, Berger and Mitchell (1989) found that although four repetitions of an entire advertisement did not enhance the favorability of participants' attitudes toward the target products relative to one presentation of the ad, four exposures did increase the likelihood that their brand selections would be consistent with those attitudes. Presumably, the multiple exposures functioned as instances of attitude rehearsal, which enhanced attitude accessibility and, hence, the likelihood of attitudinally-congruent subsequent behavior.

Evaluative Conditioning

Repeated attitudinal expression involves an individual's noting and rehearsing object-evaluation associations. However, as implied earlier, more passive processes also may promote the development of relevant associations in memory. Mere co-occurrence can be consequential. When two objects are experienced together, a cognitive association between the two will form or strengthen. In addition to strengthening object-object associations, mere co-occurrence may affect other associations. Sometimes when two objects are experienced in conjunction an object-evaluation association of one object becomes closer in valence to that of the other, even in the absence of a causal or otherwise meaningful relationship between the two that would explain and justify such changes in attitude. This phenomenon has been termed "evaluative conditioning" (EC) and is believed to be a distinct form of Pavlovian conditioning. Hence, researchers in this domain have adopted the terminology of classical conditioning research.

According to evaluative learning theory (De Houwer, Thomas, & Baeyens, 2001), the mere spatio-temporal co-occurrence of a positively or negatively valenced unconditioned stimulus (US) and a relatively neutral conditioned stimulus (CS) is sufficient to elicit an affective transfer from the US to the CS. For example, in the implicit learning procedure developed by Olson and Fazio (2001), participants are presented with a rapid, non-rhythmic stream of images on a computer screen. Participants are instructed to attend for particular target cartoons within this stream of images and to respond to them with a button-press. Embedded at intervals within this stream of images are CS-US pairs composed of a different type of relatively neutral cartoon and a moderately positive or negative word or image. One cartoon is paired with positive words or images a total of 20 times, and another is paired with negative words or images 20 times. Olson and Fazio (2001) found that on both an implicit and an explicit attitude measure, participants expressed greater liking for the cartoon that had appeared with positive stimuli than for the cartoon that appeared with negative stimuli, even though these participants did not demonstrate awareness of the CS-US contingencies on a subsequent recall task. Merely presenting the pairs contiguously while participants performed an unrelated task influenced individuals' attitudes toward the CS.

EC is of obvious interest to advertisers and marketers as a method of creating and strengthening positive attitudes. Some of its characteristics serve to further heighten its utility. In addition to potentially occurring without an individual's explicit awareness, EC is a notable attitude-forming process because its effects are more resistant to extinction than signal or expectancy-learning forms of Pavlovian conditioning (Baeyens, Crombez, Van den Bergh, & Eelen, 1988). Presenting the CS without the US after an *evaluative* conditioning procedure does not generally result in "extinction." That is, the attitude towards the object typically does not revert to its prior valence. Another characteristic suggestive of its practical utility is that some studies have successfully demonstrated evaluative conditioning with few conditioning trials, though increasing the number of pairings generally increases evaluative conditioning (De Houwer, Thomas, & Baeyens, 2001). Evaluative conditioning can also occur subliminally (see Dijksterhuis, Aarts, & Smith, 2005, for implications for practical, commercial, and political usage). Dijksterhuis (2004) demonstrated the procedural flexibility of subliminal EC in a series of experiments testing whether implicitly-measured self-esteem could be enhanced by presenting self-related words with positive nouns and adjectives. Such enhancement was obtained not only when the self-related words were presented subliminally (Experiments 1–2), but also when both the CS and US were presented subliminally (Experiments 3–5b). Finally, EC effects can be mediated both by a direct transfer of affect from the US to the CS, or they can be cognitively mediated when the US causes the formation of inferential beliefs about the CS (Kim, Allen, & Kardes, 1996; Kim, Lim, & Bhargava, 1998). The latter cognitive route, however, appears more dependent upon conditions of high involvement and individual need for cognition, as well as upon the awareness of CS-US contingencies (Priluck & Till, 2004).

Some EC research has been conducted in the domain of consumer psychology, though much further research will be necessary to fully explore its role in the formation of attitudes toward brands and products and its potential as a tool for influencing them. The earliest work in consumer psychology related to EC described an associative transfer called "affect referral" as an antecedent of consumer purchases (e.g., Wright, 1975). Shimp and colleagues have most thoroughly examined the role of associative learning in an advertising/consumer behavior context. Gresham and Shimp (1985) attempted to evaluate a classical-conditioning model of advertising by treating affectively valenced commercials as US. Results were mixed. Responses to only 3 of 10 advertisements provided support for the hypothesis that attitudes toward the advertisement would affect attitudes toward the product. Using hypothetical brand names as CS and pleasant images of natural scenes as

US, Stuart, Shimp, and Engle (1987) were more successful in demonstrating a robust conditioning effect on consumer attitudes and replicated some well-known effects in the conditioning literature (e.g., that forward conditioning is superior to backward conditioning), in the consumer domain. A series of 21 experiments tested the effectiveness of evaluative conditioning for various brands of cola (Shimp, Stuart, & Engle, 1991). This research supplied further evidence for EC in the consumer domain and identified a noteworthy moderator. Evidence for EC was only obtained for brands low and moderate in familiarity (see also Cacioppo, Marshall-Goodell, Tassinary, & Petty, 1992).

Another moderator of EC of practical interest is mood. Theories of mood agree that happy moods tend to elicit top-down, concept-driven information processing while sad moods elicit bottom-up, stimulus-driven processing (Forgas, 2002; Schwarz & Clore, 2003). This suggests that sad moods might induce modes of information processing that tend to result in stronger cognitive associations between objects that enter individuals' perceptual fields. The finding that sad moods increase implicit covariation detection (Braverman, 2005), provides some evidence for this hypothesis. Walther and Grigoriadis (2004) found that individuals in sad moods showed greater evidence of both positive and negative evaluative conditioning for consumer attitudes. In their experiment, liked and disliked faces presented with the CS (various images of shoes) had a greater influence on attitudes after watching a sad film clip. More research would also be useful to identify further moderators that determine when evaluative conditioning will prove effective in influencing attitudes towards what products.

PERCEIVED DIAGNOSTICITY

The strength of object-evaluation associations has been found to be influenced by factors in addition to rehearsal and co-occurrence. The perceived diagnosticity of the information on which the attitude is based also plays a role. Attitudinal evaluations may be based on a variety of sources including the emotional reactions evoked by the object, beliefs about the object's attributes and significance, and prior behavior towards that object. Fazio (1995) argued that individuals are sensitive to attitudinal diagnosticity, the perception of the evidentiary base upon which an evaluation is relying, and may view some classes of information as more reliable than other classes of information. As a consequence of individuals' tendency to view particular classes of information as especially diagnostic of their attitudes, individuals may be more likely to note them and to form stronger object-evaluations.

Attitudes are perceived as more diagnostic if they are based on one's own direct experience with the attitude object. Consequently, such attitudes tend to be more accessible from memory (Fazio et al., 1982; Fazio, Powell, & Herr, 1983) and more likely to influence subsequent behavior (see Fazio & Zanna, 1981, for a review). Similar effects of direct experience have been observed in the consumer domain. Smith and Swinyard (1983) found that attitudes towards various snack foods were more consistent with behavior when they were based on a product trial (direct experience) rather than advertising (see Wu & Shaffer, 1987; Berger & Mitchell, 1989, for related findings).

A reason attitudes based on first-hand experience are perceived as diagnostic derives from Bem's self-perception theory. One's own freely chosen behavior is viewed as diagnostic of one's internal states (Bem, 1972). Fazio, Herr, and Olney (1982) found that inducing individuals to recall voluntary behaviors relevant to a given attitude domain increased the strength of the object-evaluation association more so than having individuals review the same class of behaviors in circumstances in which the behavior occurred under coercion.

Emotional reactions to an object also may be viewed as especially diagnostic of one's attitudes toward the object. One's emotional experiences are very much one's own, and, hence, thought to be revealing. Some relevant evidence is provided by Fazio, Zanna, and Cooper (1978), who presented participants with video clips of an actor working on various novel intellectual puzzles. Participants were instructed either to "just listen and watch carefully" or to "imagine how you would feel if you were working the examples." Focusing on the feelings that the puzzles generated led to greater correspondence between the attitudes that participants developed and their behavior during a subsequent "free play" period. In contrast, an extensive research program by Wilson and his colleagues has demonstrated that analyzing the reasons (cognitive bases) for one's attitudes, especially in domains in which it is difficult to verbalize the basis for liking or disliking an object, can weaken attitude-behavior correspondence. Focusing on the presumed reasons underlying one's attitudes can lead to a momentary emphasis on salient and easily verbalizable features that do not necessarily correspond to the factors that determine behavior, or if they do, that determine post-choice satisfaction (Wilson et al., 1989, 1993).

This is not to say that analytical thought cannot provide a useful and valid basis for attitudes. In domains not marked by difficulty in noting and verbalizing significant features, more extensive thought has been shown to enhance attitude strength. For example, attitudes formed through the careful consideration of the arguments contained in a persuasive message (central processing) are generally more accessible than those formed through peripheral processing (Petty, Haugtvedt, & Smith, 1995).

CATEGORY-EXEMPLAR ASSOCIATIONS

Structure

To this point, we have focused exclusively on the strength of object-evaluation associations. However, a second kind of association is also very relevant to consumer choice behavior — that between the representation of a category and an exemplar or instance of the category. These category-exemplar associations also vary in strength such that activation of the category can automatically activate particular exemplars and vice versa. For example, the category "U.S. Presidents" will cause many people to automatically retrieve exemplars such as George Washington and George W. Bush. These individuals have not only often been thought of frequently, but also have been frequently thought of *as Presidents*, whereas other exemplars (e.g., Rutherford B. Hayes) may be more weakly associated with the category and are not as likely to be activated automatically by the relevant category.

One property of category-exemplar associations that distinguishes them from attitude-object associations is their bidirectionality. The likelihood that an exemplar automatically activates a category may differ from the likelihood that that category automatically activates that exemplar. To use the previous example, the likelihood that the category "U.S. Presidents" will automatically activate Rutherford B. Hayes may be low for most people. However, mentioning Rutherford B. Hayes to many people will often automatically activate the category "U.S. Presidents" (and perhaps little else). This bidirectionality is less relevant to attitudes. Encountering attitude objects can automatically activate associated evaluations, but individuals don't generally encounter evaluations that activate specific attitude objects. The more useful variable tends to be the likelihood that objects automatically activate evaluations, not the other way around.

With category-exemplar associations, however, the likelihood that the category will evoke the exemplar and the likelihood that the exemplar will evoke the category are often both of interest. Additionally, it is possible for an exemplar and category to be strongly associated in both directions such that a "unit relation" exists in which the pair has all-or-none storage and retrieval properties (Anderson, 1980). In this case, the category and exemplar will each always automatically activate the other. Consumer psychologists have recognized that it is important to consider the bi-directionality of associations between brands (exemplars) and the relevant product category (see Farquhar & Herr, 1993). The terms "category dominance" and "instance dominance" have been used to describe, respectively, the strength of the category-to-brand association and the strength of the brand-to-category association.

Category Dominance

Regarding category dominance, a brand has a relative advantage if for many individuals that brand is activated automatically from memory upon consideration of a relevant product category. This "top-of-mind awareness" has been posited as a key link between media advertising and purchase behavior (Krugman, 1965; Sutherland & Galloway, 1981). It is easy to imagine situations in which retrieving a brand from memory is a prerequisite to initiating purchase behavior, and research does indicate that brand retrieval is a predictor of choice (Nedungadi, 1990). As this would suggest, the first brand listed upon presentation of a product category is both a reliable and valid measure of repeat purchases (Axelrod, 1968). As an example, imagine that an individual has decided to order a pizza. The first brands activated in consideration of the category "pizza" have an enormous advantage. The first pizza considered, if it "sounds good" and is practical, is ordered post haste.

Indeed, consumer studies have observed that only the first brands recalled are likely to be part of a consideration set. If the first option considered is deemed desirable, actions toward acquiring that brand rather than a competitor are undertaken without further consideration, preempting the choice process (Nedungadi, 1990). This seems especially likely if the steps required to make a purchase are clear and convenient, for example if the necessary phone number is known or easily locatable and so on. Sometimes this occurs to the detriment of satisfaction with a purchase or other choice. Had the individual recalled more pizza purveyors, it is possible that another would have seemed even better, but the advantage of accessibility is such that sometimes highly accessible exemplars can be chosen even if ultimately not preferable given the full set of potential options. Category dominance, the strength of the category-to-brand association, appears to be an important determinant of consumer choice that advertisers and marketers would want to foster unconditionally.

Instance Dominance

Sometimes it may also be beneficial for advertisers and marketers to consider instance dominance, the strength of the brand-to-category association. Instance dominance is a fundamental aspect of "brand meaning" along with other brand associates like usage situations, product attributes, or customer benefits (Herr, Farquhar, & Fazio, 1996). Instance dominance for a particular brand may apply to various specific categories and also to more general categories. For example, some individuals might associate the brand Johnson's® most strongly with baby shampoo, others with baby powder, and still others, more generally, with personal care products. These associations will influence what comes to mind upon consideration of the brand and how information about the brand will be interpreted.

Instance dominance has interesting implications for automatic attitude activation. As already mentioned, encountering an object that is an exemplar of a category may result in activation of an attitude associated with that object. Additionally, though, it has been observed that exemplars can automatically activate attitudes associated with the *category* (e.g., Fiske & Pavelchak, 1986; Castelli,

Zogmaister, Smith, & Arcuri, 2004). Presumably, this spreading activation is dependent on the strength of the exemplar-to-category association. So, consideration of a product or brand is likely to automatically activate attitudes associated with categories strongly associated with that product or brand.

This process has some interesting implications for marketers. It may be desirable for pragmatic reasons for businesses to attempt to create positive attitudes specifically towards a product category rather than a brand, even when the primary goal is in service of a particular brand. One such reason is that it may be easier to influence attitudes subtly at the category level. Social influence attempts often evoke psychological reactance (Brehm, 1966), a motivation to assert autonomy and defy another's prescription for one's behavior. The awareness that one is targeted for a persuasive message can reduce the efficacy of that message (e.g., Petty & Cacioppo, 1979). In modern society, individuals are bombarded with advertisements and consumer psychologists have recognized that consumer cynicism can be problematic (Kanter, 1989). Attempts to influence attitudes towards categories of products may be inherently more subtle because of the absence of conspicuous focus on particular brands, often an obvious cue that one is currently a target of persuasive efforts. Often when advertisements influencing attitudes at a category level are actually observed it is because businesses not representing particular brands but having a vested interest in the successful marketing of a product category are responsible, as when the National Cattlemen's Beef Association informs, "Beef—It's what's for dinner." Research demonstrating that exemplars automatically activate attitudes associated with superordinate categories provides some empirical evidence suggesting that such efforts should have the effect of influencing attitudes towards particular brands, presuming that brand-to-category associations are strong and that the fit between the object of the advertisement and the categorical mental representation of the brand is good. Upon encountering an actual product, attitudes toward the category can be as or more important than attitudes towards the brand.

Brand Extensions

It has been argued that advertisers and marketers should consider the bi-directionality of category-exemplar associations and that failure to take them into account (as when symmetry is assumed) can result in mistaken predictions about consumer choice behavior (Farquhar & Herr, 1993). The issue of brand extensions, the transfer of brand-related associations to new product categories, illustrates the necessity of considering category and instance dominance. Brand extensions are desirable because they allow new products to be accompanied by immediate brand recognition and because individuals may infer that positive aspects of brand's known product will generalize to the new extension.

Herr et al. (1996) investigated the impact of category dominance and intercategory relatedness on the transfer of associations to hypothetical brand extensions. Relatedness refers to the strength of association between the brand's parent category and the target extension category. For example, a soda company extending their brand to bottled water would have greater relatedness between the parent and target extension categories than if that soda company introduced potato chips (or swimwear). This associative strength is determined by factors including but not limited to the similarity of common features. Herr et al. (1996, Experiment 2) showed that the transfer of associations was facilitated for closely related categories relative to distantly related categories. Participants were presented with lists of 16 hypothetical extensions to real brands that varied in the relatedness of the target category to the parent category and in the strength of the category-to-brand association of the parent category. Following a distractor task, participants' recall of the extension was measured as were liking for and intention to purchase each extension. Regarding the mental representations held by consumers, the success of a brand extension should depend, at least, on both the ease of learning the new brand-category pairing and on the transfer of affect to the extension. Participants were very successful in learning extensions when the target category was closely related to the parent category. Also, participants displayed somewhat better recall for extensions of highly category dominant brands regardless of relatedness. Affective associations also transferred more easily to extensions (according to the liking and intention to purchase measures) when intercategory relatedness was high and when the brand was highly category dominant. Furthermore, an interaction emerged such that brand extensions were viewed *most* favorably when category dominance was strong and the categories were highly related.

On the other hand, it is likely that instance dominance is a limiting factor of the extent to which brands might be stretched to other categories. A strongly instance dominant association defines a brand specifically and is likely to inhibit learning of the extension and its subsequent inclusion in consideration sets. This seems especially likely in the case of distantly related parent and target categories, in which extensions to far-flung categories may seem jarring or inappropriate given the strength with which the brand is associated with a very different class of product. Research has not fully addressed the role of instance dominance in brand extensions, and more research is required to test this reasoning. Regardless, category and instance dominance probably have different impacts on the feasibility of brand extensions, demonstrating that sometimes the nuances of associative structure are necessary considerations when predicting choice.

Determinants of Category-Exemplar Associations

The basic principles of associative strength that applied to strengthening attitudes again apply to category-exemplar associations. Various forms of repetition and rehearsal of the pairing of category and exemplar will form and strengthen connections between the two (Smith & Queller, 2001). Advertisements can be specifically designed to promote strong category-exemplar associations between product categories and brands. One form of commercial, for example, has been shown to be effective in increasing the strength of category-brand associations. *Mystery ads* leave the identity of the brand being advertised unclear until the very end of the ad, despite well-established benefits of early brand identification on message recall (Stewart & Furse, 1986). Mystery ads are intended to induce some curiosity about the subject of the ad. The technique used to achieve this can vary. A dramatic narrative might create suspense about the product's identity. Surreal or absurd commercials sometimes seem to be largely intended to provoke the question "What is this a commercial for, anyway?" Fazio, Herr, and Powell (1992) argued that mystery ads create a "readiness to categorize" the product when it is finally revealed by inducing viewers to ask "What is it?" questions. In their study, participants viewed television commercials in either their original, mystery forms, or in professionally edited non-mystery versions in which everything was identical except the identification of the brand having been moved from the end of the ad to the beginning.

Afterwards, the strength of category-brand associations was measured by the latency of response required to correctly identify the brands as belonging to their product category. The results indicated that mystery ads were more effective than traditional ads in strengthening category-brand associations. However, this effect was only observed for novel brands, ones that were promoting brands unavailable in the United States. For familiar brands, mystery ads were no more effective than traditional ads in influencing category-brand associations. Thus, it appears that mystery ads are an effective means of introducing a new brand to a product category.

FURTHER IMPLICATIONS FOR CONSUMER PSYCHOLOGY

We have argued that object-evaluation associations and category-exemplar associations are important for understanding consumer behavior at an information processing level. The previous sections described various consequences and determinants of object-evaluation and category-exemplar associations. The applied focus has been on methods of strengthening the cognitive associations that are involved in consumer choice. Advertisers and marketers may wish to devise explicit strategies for fostering particular types of associations depending on the nature of the product and brand. To do so, however, requires some understanding of when object-evaluation associative strength versus category-exemplar associative strength is more likely to matter. When is one more likely to predict consumer behavior than the other?

Which Associations Matter?

Generally, no single type of association will be important to the exclusion of all others, but sometimes it will be more strategically valuable to focus efforts on creating or strengthening specific associations in memory. Posavac, Sanbonmatsu, and Fazio (1997) investigated the impact of whether decision alternatives are self-generated or presented externally to the decision-maker. In a series of two session experiments, participants first generated a list of worthwhile charities (along with several other lists to obscure its significance) and were later asked in a second session unexpectedly to choose a charity to receive a small donation. This choice occurred under one of two conditions. Participants were either required to write their choice on a blank piece of paper or were first provided with a list of charities by the experimenter. Studies 1 and 2 showed that when alternatives were provided to participants, the charity chosen was highly consistent with their self-reported attitudes, but when alternatives had to be self-generated, decisions were less consistent with attitudes. Instead, choice was better predicted by the order in which participants generated charities during the first session—an indicator of category-exemplar accessibility. In Study 3, participants were not presented with a list of charities when they made their decisions. During the first session, participants either did or did not repeatedly rehearse the *category membership* of several charities. Notably, when the accessibility of several charities had been increased, the decisions again were highly consistent with attitudes. Thus, when several strong category-exemplar associations were available and a larger set of exemplars readily came to mind in response to the category consideration, participants comparatively evaluated the favorability of the alternatives on the basis of their attitudes, much as they did when the alternatives had been presented by an experimenter.

Attitudes are generally more likely to guide behavior when alternatives are salient, whether in memory or the environment. After all, attitudes involving strong object-evaluations are automatically activated as a response to the object being encountered. Some cue must be present for the evaluation to be activated. When behavioral alternatives must be self-generated, category-exemplar associations necessarily play an important role. Only accessible exemplars can be included in a consideration set. The research findings highlight the role of influencing attitudes as the major goal of advertisement for the many products that are typically encountered in consumer situations involving environmentally salient alternatives. When a brand appears in a supermarket, for example, surrounded by eye-catching, competitive alternatives, category-brand associations are rendered largely irrelevant. On the other hand, when decisions are made in the absence of salient alternatives, the most favorably evaluated option may not be chosen. The example of ordering pizza again comes to mind. Regarding an individual, perhaps sitting on a couch, wondering from where to order pizza, category-brand accessibility is paramount.

However, a point made previously bears repeating in this context. The impact of associative strength and accessibility on consumer judgment is greatest when individuals are not motivated to recall or seek out many choice alternatives and are not motivated to effortfully reevaluate the merits of the relevant product rather than relying on preexisting attitudes. Thus, the role of associative strength will generally be more important for routine, inexpensive purchases rather than purchases which elicit some fear of choosing poorly. Also, associative strength will also play a greater role in situations in which the opportunity to deliberate or seek out alternatives is low, as when decisions occur under time pressure.

Situational Cues

Associative strength and accessibility have been thus far presented as susceptible to social influence (e.g., advertising) but basically as fixed characteristics that the consumer essentially brings to the choice situation. So, individuals enter a consumer situation with some pre-existing associative structure of mental representation pertinent to the purchase decision which determines what concepts will be activated as objects are encountered in the environment. Though this is often what happens, it is also possible for environmental cues to activate associative representations in memory or elicit the formation of new associations, rendering irrelevant their chronically low accessibility or absence. Through point-of-purchase displays and other techniques, it is possible to increase the likelihood that desirable attitudes or category-exemplar associations are activated—ones that may promote the desired consumer behaviors.

An example of how cues can be used to form or activate desired associations comes from an experiment by Snyder and Kendzierski (1982). These researchers demonstrated that attitude-behavior consistency can be increased by exposing individuals to an attitudinal cue just before a choice is required. In their study, participants' attitudes toward psychological research had been previously measured and all selected participants had positive attitudes toward psychological research. Upon arriving for the experimental session, participants encountered two confederates reading a notice posted on the wall. The notice requested that participants sign-up to return for two future sessions for a small compensation. Two confederates were always present. One read the notice aloud and asked, "I don't know whether I should volunteer or if I shouldn't volunteer. What do you think?" In the control condition, the other confederate replied "Beats me—It's up to you." Or, the second confederate replied "Well, I guess whether you do or don't is really a question of how worthwhile you think experiments are." When a situational cue provoked participants to assess their attitudes toward psychological research, the percentage of participants who signed up for further participation more than doubled, reflecting greater attitude-behavior consistency given that all the selected participants believed psychological research to be meritorious. In such a manner, an appropriate situational cue can induce individuals to activate or construct associations that would have otherwise not influenced behavior, enhancing attitude-behavior consistency.

Measurement

Having hopefully made a case for the importance of the strength of association between various representations as determinants of consumer behavior, we will conclude with some comments for those who may be interested in measuring associative strength. Fazio, Williams, and Powell (2000) investigated the validity of three methods of assessing the strength of category-brand associations. The researchers identified one particular method as providing essentially a "gold standard" measure of category-exemplar associations. The procedure involves presentation of a category label as a prime, followed by presentation of a visually degraded exemplar that gradually becomes less obscured. The degree to which the category prime facilitates recognition of the exemplar is the most direct indicant of the extent to which the exemplar is spontaneously activated when the category is considered. This measure minimizes the potential role of individuals' immediate goals and conscious retrieval strategies. When feasible, this method is recommended, but each of the two other methods that were examined was substantially correlated with the facilitation measure. One such procedure involves latency to a direct query, which was employed in many of the experiments summarized in this chapter. The latency required for individuals to correctly categorize exemplars as members or non-members of a specific category can be used to measure the strength of category-exemplary associations. Both the priming measure and the direct query measure require the electronic measurement of latencies. A far easier method of assessment was also found to be valid, corroborating previous research (Axelrod, 1968). The order in which participants listed brands following a category cue also reflects associative strength. This simple order-of-output measure is especially well-suited to field research methodologies requiring easily-administered, paper-and-pencil assessments.

Many readers will be aware that there has been a surge in the development and use of indirect or implicit measures of attitude in recent years (see Fazio & Olson, 2003, for a review). A proper discussion of the merits of various measures and their appropriateness for particular research problems is beyond the scope of this chapter. Nevertheless, a few brief comments are in order, for the implicit measures hold the potential for providing important insights. The most frequently used implicit measures of attitude, affective priming (Fazio, Jackson, Dunton, & Williams, 1995) and the Implicit Association Test (IAT, Greenwald, McGhee, & Schwarz, 1998), are especially pertinent in this context because they involve inferring attitudes from the latencies with which participants categorize objects. The priming measure is based on the paradigm described earlier for investigating automatic attitude activation; attitudes are inferred from the extent to which a given prime facilitates identification of the connotation of positive versus negative evaluative adjectives. The IAT assesses the ease with which participants can associate the dual meanings of a given response key. Is performance better when the presentation of a given type of object is to lead to responding with the same key that signifies "good" or when the response to that object is mapped onto the key that also represents "bad?" In other words, these methods reflect associative strength rather than deliberative evaluations. Individuals may not realize that their attitudes are being assessed during these procedures (more true, in our view, of the priming procedure). Or, if they do come to such a realization, it is difficult for individuals to misrepresent one's attitudes, provided they follow the task instructions (more true, in our view, of the IAT). Another difference between IAT measures and affective priming ones is that IAT measures seem to primarily reflect the associations between the category labels and their evaluations, whereas affective priming measures reflect the associations between the particular exemplars used and their evaluations (see Fazio & Olson, 2003). Researchers in consumer psychology should consider this distinction when choosing what kind of implicit attitude measure is most appropriate for the task at hand.

For research involving certain types of attitudes, for instance those probing for prejudicial attitudes, implicit measures of attitude are almost a necessity due to concerns about the truthfulness of responses and social desirability effects. Though individuals generally have little motivation to misrepresent their attitudes in most consumer studies, implicit measures may be nevertheless desirable at times. For example, participants who believe (accurately or not) that the experimenter wishes them to express (dis)liking for a particular brand over another may do so regardless of their actual attitudes.

Some evidence has been offered in the domain of consumer psychology for the IAT's validity and predictive utility (Brunel, Tietje, & Greenwald, 2004; Maison, Greenwald, & Bruin, 2004). Morever, an experiment conducted by Brunel et al. (2004, Study 2) demonstrates the potential for divergence between implicit and explicit measures of attitude within an advertising context. Participants viewed multiple ads for sneakers. Each ad consisted of a spokesperson and a brand logo. Attitudes toward the ad itself were assessed by explicit measures and the IAT. The critical manipulation was whether the spokesperson was White or Black. On explicit, semantic differential measures, white participants professed equally positive attitudes toward the ads with Black and White spokespeople. On the IAT, however, white participants showed an implicit preference for the ads with White spokespeople. Regardless of the specific interpretation of these findings and their relation to individuals' "true" attitudes, this type of divergent finding is worthy of consideration. Consumer psychologists should be aware that implicit measures of attitude can suggest different inferences than those revealed by explicit measures. In accord with Fazio and Olson (2003), we believe that as more is learned about the mechanisms that underlie implicit measures, and the appropriate inferences to be drawn from them, they will become increasingly valuable tools for understanding choice behavior.

REFERENCES

Ajzen, I., & Fishbein, M. (1973). Attitudinal and normative variables as predictors of specific behaviors. *Journal of Personality and Social Psychology, 27,* 41–47.

Ajzen, I., & Fishbein, M. (1980). *Understanding attitudes and predicting social behavior.* Englewood Cliffs, NJ: Prentice-Hall.

Anderson, J. R. (1980). Concepts, propositions, and schemata: What are cognitive units? In J. H. Flowers (Ed.), *Nebraska symposium on motivation: Cognitive processes* (pp. 121–162). Lincoln: University of Nebraska Press.

Anderson, J. R., & Bower, G. H. (1973). *Human associative memory.* New York: Wiley.

Axelrod, J. N. (1968). Advertising measures that predict purchase. *Journal of Advertising Research, 8,* 3–17.

Baeyens, F., Crombez, G., Van Den Bergh, O., & Eelen, P. (1988). Once in contact always in contact: Evaluative conditioning is resistant to extinction. *Advances in Behaviour Research and Therapy, 10,* 179–199.

Balcetis, E. & Dunning, D. (2006). See what you want to see: Motivational influences on visual perception. *Journal of Personality and Social Psychology, 91,* 612–625.

Bargh, J. A., Chaiken, S., Raymond, P., & Hymes, C. (1996). The automatic evaluation effect: Unconditional automatic attitude activation with a pronunciation task. *Journal of Personality and Social Psychology, 32,* 104–128.

Berger, I. E., & Mitchell, A. A. (1989). The effect of advertising on attitude accessibility, attitude confidence, and the attitude-behavior relationship. *Journal of Consumer Research, 16,* 269–279.

Bem, D. J. (1972). Self-perception theory. In L. Berkowitz (Ed.). *Advances in experimental social psychology* (Vol. 6, pp. 1–62). New York: Academic.

Blascovich, J., Ernst, J. M., Tomaka, J., Kelsey, R. M., Salomon, K. L., & Fazio, R. H. (1993). Attitude accessibility as a moderator of autonomic reactivity during decision making. *Journal of Personality and Social Psychology, 64,* 165–176.

Braverman, J. (2005). The effect of mood on detection of covariation. *Personality and Social Psychology Bulletin, 31,* 1487–1497.

Bourne, F. S. (1963). Different kinds of decision and reference-group influence. In P. Bliss (Ed.), *Marketing and the behavioral sciences* (pp. 247–255). Boston: Allyn & Bacon.

Brehm, J. W. (1966). *A theory of psychological reactance.* New York: Academic Press.

Brunel, F. F., Tietje, B. C., & Greenwald, A. G. (2004). Is the Implicit Association Test a valid and valuable measure of implicit consumer cognition? *Journal of Consumer Psychology, 14*, 385–404.

Cacioppo, J. T., Marshall-Goodell, B. S., Tassinary, L. G., & Petty, R. E. (1992). Rudimentary determinants of attitudes: Classical conditioning is more effective when prior knowledge about the attitude stimulus is low than high. *Journal of Experimental Social Psychology, 28*, 207–233.

Castelli, L., Zogmaister, C., Smith, E. R., & Arcuri, L. (2004). On the automatic evaluation of social exemplars. *Journal of Personality and Social Psychology, 86*, 373–387.

Changizi, M. A., & Hall, W. G. (2001). Thirst modulates a perception. *Perception, 30*, 1489–1497.

Converse, P. E. (1970). Attitudes and non-attitudes: Continuation of a dialogue. In E. Rufte (Ed.), *The quantitative analysis of social problems* (pp. 168–189). Reading, MA: Addison-Wesley.

De Houwer, J., Thomas, S., & Baeyens, F. (2001). Associative learning of likes and dislikes: A review of 25 years of research on human evaluative conditioning. *Psychological Bulletin, 127*, 853–869.

Dijksterhuis, A. (2004). I like myself but I don't know why: Enhancing implicit self-esteem by subliminal evaluative conditioning. *Journal of Personality and Social Psychology, 86*, 345–355.

Dijksterhuis, A., Aarts, H., & Smith, P. K. (2005). The power of the subliminal: Subliminal persuasion and other potential applications. In R. Hassin, J. Ulemann, & J. Bargh (Eds.), *The new unconscious.* New York: Oxford University Press.

Farquhar, P. H., & Herr, P. M. (1993). The dual structure of brand associations. In D. Aaker & A. L. Biel (Eds.), *Brand equity and advertising: Advertising's role in building strong brands* (pp. 263–277). Hillsdale, NJ: Erlbaum.

Fazio, R. H. (1990). Multiple processes by which attitudes guide behavior: The MODE model as an integrative framework. In M. P. Zanna (Ed.), *Advances in experimental social psychology* (Vol. 23, pp. 75–109). New York: Academic.

Fazio, R. H. (1995). Attitudes as object-evaluation associations: Determinants, consequences, and correlates of attitude accessibility. In R. E. Petty & Krosnick, J. A. (Eds.), *Attitude strength: Antecedents and consequences.* Hillsdale, NJ: Erlbaum.

Fazio, R. H., Blascovich, J., & Driscoll, D. M. (1992). On the functional value of attitudes: The influence of accessible attitudes upon the ease and quality of decision making. *Personality and Social Psychology Bulletin, 18*, 388–401.

Fazio, R. H., Chen, J., McDonel, E. C., & Sherman, S. J. (1982). Attitude accessibility, attitude-behavior consistency, and the strength of the object-evaluation association. *Journal of Experimental Social Psychology, 18*, 339–357.

Fazio, R. H., Herr, P. M., & Olney, T. J. (1984). Attitude accessibility following a self-perception process. *Journal of Personality and Social Psychology, 47*, 277–286.

Fazio, R. H., Herr, P. M., & Powell, M. C. (1992). On the development and strength of category-brand associations in memory: The case of mystery ads. *Journal of Consumer Psychology, 1*, 1–14.

Fazio, R. H., Jackson, J. R., Dunton, B. C., & Williams, C. J. (1995). Variability in automatic activation as an unobtrusive measure of racial attitudes: A bona fide pipeline? *Journal of Personality and Social Psychology, 69*, 1013–1027.

Fazio, R. H., & Olson, M. A. (2003). Implicit measures in social cognition research: Their meaning and use. *Annual Review of Psychology, 54*, 297–327.

Fazio, R. H., & Powell, M. C. (1997). On the value of knowing one's likes and dislikes: Attitude accessibility, stress, and health in college. *Psychological Science, 8*, 430–436.

Fazio, R. H., Powell, M. C., & Herr, P. M. (1983). Toward a process model of the attitude-behavior relation: Accessing one's attitude upon mere observation of the attitude object. *Journal of Personality and Social Psychology, 44*, 723–735.

Fazio, R. H., Powell, M. C., & Williams, C. J. (1989). The role of attitude accessibility in the attitude-to-behavior process. *Journal of Consumer Research, 16*, 280–288.

Fazio, R. H., Roskos-Ewoldsen, D. R., & Powell, M. C. (1994). Attitudes, perception, and attention. In P. M. Niedenthal & S. Kitayama (Eds.), *The Heart's Eye: Emotional influences in perception and attention* (pp. 197–216). New York: Academic.

Fazio, R. H., Sanbonmatsu, D. M., Powell, M. C., & Kardes, F. R. (1986). On the automatic activation of attitudes. *Journal of Personality and Social Psychology, 50*, 229–238.

Fazio, R. H., & Williams, C. J. (1986). Attitude accessibility as a moderator of the attitude-perception and attitude-behavior relations: An investigation of the 1984 presidential election. *Journal of Personality and Social Psychology, 51*, 505–514.

Fazio, R. H., Williams, C. J., & Powell, M. C. (2000). Measuring associative strength: Category-item associations and their activation from memory. *Political Psychology, 21*, 7–25.

Fazio, R. H., & Zanna, M. P. (1981). Direct experience and attitude-behavior consistency. In L. Berkowitz (Ed.), *Advances in Experimental Social Psychology* (Vol. 14, pp. 161–202). New York: Academic.

Fazio, R. H., Zanna, M. P., & Cooper, J. (1978). Direct experience and attitude-behavior consistency: An information processing analysis. *Personality and Social Psychology Bulletin, 4*, 48–51.

Fiske, S. T., & Pavelchak, M. A. (1986). Category-based versus piecemeal-based affective responses: Development in schema-triggered affect. In R. M. Sorrentino & E. T. Higgins (Eds.), *Handbook of motivation and cognition: Foundations of social behavior* (pp. 167–203). New York: Guilford.

Forgas, J. P. (2002). Toward understanding the role of affect in social thinking and behavior. *Psychological Inquiry, 13*, 90–102.

Gresham, L. G., & Shimp, T. A. (1985). Attitude toward the advertisement and brand attitudes. *Journal of Advertising, 14*, 10–17.

Greenwald, A. G., McGhee, D. E., & Schwarz, J. (1998). Measuring individual differences in implicit social cognition: The Implicit Association Test. *Journal of Personality and Social Psychology, 74*, 1464–1480.

Hastorf, A. H., & Cantril, H. (1954). They saw a game: A case study. *Journal of Abnormal and Social Psychology, 49*, 129–134.

Herr, P. M., Farquhar, P. H., & Fazio, R. H. (1996). Impact of dominance and relatedness on brand extensions. *Journal of Consumer Psychology, 5*, 135–159.

Herr, P. M., & Fazio, R. H. (1993). The attitude-to-behavior process: Implications for consumer behavior. In A. A. Mitchell (Ed.), *Advertising exposure, memory, and choice*. Hillsdale, NJ: Erlbaum.

Higgins, E. T. (1996). Knowledge activation: Accessibility, applicability, and salience. In E. T. Higgins & A. Kruglanski (Eds.), *Social psychology: Handbook of basic principles* (pp. 133–168). New York: Guilford.

Houston, D. A., & Fazio, R. H. (1989). Biased processing as a function `of attitude accessibility: Making objective judgments subjectively. *Social Cognition, 7*, 51–66

Kanter, D. L. (1989). Cynical marketers at work. *Journal of Advertising Research, 28*, 28–34.

Kim, J., Allen, C. T., & Kardes, F. R. (1996). An investigation of the mediational mechanisms underlying attitudinal conditioning. *Journal of Marketing Research, 33*, 318–328.

Kim, J., Lim, J., & Bhargava, M. (1998). The role of affect in attitude formation: A classical conditioning approach. *Journal of the Academy of Marketing Science, 26*, 143–152.

Kruglanski, A. W. (1989). *Lay epistemics and human knowledge*. New York: Penguin.

Krugman, H. E. (1965). The impact of television advertising: Learning without involvement. *Public Opinion Quarterly, 29*, 349–356.

La Piere, R. (1934). Attitudes and actions. *Social Forces, 13*, 230–237.

Lord, C. G., & Lepper, M. R. (1999). Attitude representation theory. In M. P. Zanna (Ed.), *Advances in experimental social psychology* (Vol. 31, pp. 265–343). San Diego, CA: Academic Press.

Lord, C. G., Lepper, M. R., & Mackie, D. (1984). Attitude prototypes as determinants of attitude-behavior consistency. *Journal of Personality and Social Psychology, 46*, 1254–1266.

Lord, C. G., Ross, L., & Lepper, M. R. (1979). Biased assimilation and attitude polarization: The effects of prior theories on subsequently considered evidence. *Journal of Personality and Social Psychology, 37*, 2098–2109.

Maison, D., Greenwald, A. G., & Bruin, R. H. (2004). Predictive validity of the Implicit Association Test in studies of brands, consumer attitudes, and behavior. *Journal of Consumer Psychology, 14*, 405–415.

Nedungadi, P. (1990). Recall and consumer consideration sets: Influencing choice without altering brand evaluations. *Journal of Consumer Psychology, 17*, 263–276.

Olson, M. A., & Fazio, R. H. (2001). Implicit attitude formation through classical conditioning. *Psychological Science, 12*, 413–417.

Petty, R. E., & Cacioppo, J. T. (1979). Effects of forewarning of persuasive intent and involvement on cognitive responses and persuasion. *Personality and Social Psychology Bulletin, 5*, 173–176.

Petty, R. E., Haugtvedt, C. P., & Smith, S. M. (1995). Elaboration as a determinant of attitude strength: Creating attitudes that are persistent, resistant, and predictive of behavior. In R. E. Petty & Krosnick, J. A. (Eds.), *Attitude strength: Antecedents and consequences*. Hillsdale, NJ: Erlbaum.

Powell, M. C., & Fazio, R. H. (1984). Attitude accessibility as a function of repeated attitudinal expression. *Personality and Social Psychology Bulletin, 10*, 139–148.

Priluck, R., & Till, B. D. (2004). The role of contingency awareness, involvement, and need for cognition in attitude formation. *Journal of the Academy of Marketing Science, 32*, 329–344.

Roskos-Ewoldsen, D. R., & Fazio, R. H. (1992). On the orienting value of attitudes: Attitude accessibility as a determinant of an object's attraction of visual attention. *Journal of Personality and Social Psychology, 63*, 198–211.

Sanbonmatsu, D. M., & Fazio, R. H. (1986, October). The automatic activation of attitudes towards products. Paper presented at the meeting of the Association for Consumer Research, Toronto.

Sanbonmatsu, D. M., & Fazio, R. H. (1990). The role of attitudes in memory-based decision making. *Journal of Personality and Social Psychology, 59*, 614–622.

Schwarz, N., & Clore, G. L. (2003). Mood as information: 20 years later. *Psychological Inquiry, 14*, 296–303.

Shiffrin, R. M., & Dumais, S. T. (1981). The development of automatism. In J. R. Anderson (Ed.), *Cognitive skills and their acquisition.* Hillsdale, NJ: Erlbaum.

Shimp, T. A., Stuart, E. W., & Engle, R. W. (1991). A program of classical conditioning experiments testing variations in the conditioned stimulus and context. *Journal of Consumer Psychology, 18*, 1–12.

Smith, E. R., Fazio, R. H., & Cejka, M. A. (1996). Accessible attitudes influence categorization of multiply categorizable objects. *Journal of Personality and Social Psychology, 71*, 888–898.

Smith, E. R., & Queller, S. (2001). Mental representations. In A. Tesser & N. Schwarz (Eds.) *Blackwell handbook in social psychology* (Vol. 1, pp. 111–133). Oxford: Blackwell.

Smith, M. B., Bruner, J. S., & White, R. W. (1956). *Opinions and personality.* New York: Wiley.

Smith, R. E., & Swinyard, W. R. (1983). Attitude-behavior consistency: The impact of product trials vs. advertising. *Journal of Marketing Research, 20*, 256–267.

Snyder, M., & Kendzierski, D. (1982). Acting on one's attitude: Procedures for linking attitude and behavior. *Journal of Experimental Social Psychology, 18*, 165–183.

Sutherland, M., & Galloway, J. (1981). Role of advertising: Persuasion or agenda setting? *Journal of Advertising Research, 25*, 25–29.

Stewart, D. W., & Furse, D. H. (1986). *Effective television advertising.* Lexington, MA: Heath.

Stuart, E. W., Shimp, T. A., & Engle, R. W. (1987). Classical conditioning of consumer attitudes: Four experiments in an advertising context. *Journal of Consumer Research, 14*, 334–349.

Walther, E., & Grigoriadis, S. (2004). Why sad people like shoes better: The influence of mood on the classical conditioning of consumer attitudes. *Psychology & Marketing, 21*, 755–733.

Wicker, A. W. (1969). Attitudes versus actions: The relationship of verbal and overt behavioral responses to attitude objects. *Journal of Social Issues, 25*, 41–78.

Wilson, T. D., Dunn, D. S., Kraft, D., & Lisle, D. J. (1989). Introspection, attitude change, and attitude-behavior consistency: The disruptive effects of explaining why we feel the way we do. In L. Berkowitz (Ed.), *Advances in experimental social psychology* (Vol. 22, pp. 287–343). San Diego: Academic Press.

Wilson, T. D., Lisle, D. J., Schooler, J. W., Hodges, S. D., Klaaren, K. J., & Lafleur, S. J. (1993). Introspecting about reasons can reduce post-choice satisfaction. *Personality and Social Psychology Bulletin, 19*, 331–339.

Wood, W. (1982). Retrieval of attitude-relevant information from memory: Effects on susceptibility to persuasion and on intrinsic motivation. *Journal of Personality and Social Psychology, 42*, 798–810.

Wright, P. (1975). Consumer choice strategies: Simplifying vs. optimizing. *Journal of Marketing Research, 12*, 60–67.

Wu, C., & Shaffer, D. R. (1987). Susceptibility to persuasive appeals as a function of source credibility and prior experience with the attitude object. *Journal of Personality and Social Psychology, 52*, 677–688.

Zanna, M. P., & Fazio, R. H. (1982). The attitude-behavior relation: Moving toward a third generation of research. In M. P. Zanna, E. T. Higgins, & C. P. Herman (Eds.), *Consistency in social behavior: The Ontario symposium* (Vol. 2, pp. 283–301). Hillsdale, NJ: Erlbaum.

17

Measuring the Nonconscious
Implicit Social Cognition in Consumer Behavior

ANDREW PERKINS

Rice University

MARK FOREHAND

ANTHONY GREENWALD

University of Washington

DOMINIKA MAISON

University of Warsaw

INTRODUCTION

Current research in psychology suggests that much of human behavior is influenced by uncontrolled, unobserved processes in memory (Bargh, 2002; Greenwald et al., 2002). Despite this increased attention to nonconscious processes within academic psychology, consumer research has largely neglected this nascent field: reviews of the last fifteen years of consumer behavior research report a focus on research methodologies that directly tap conscious beliefs, but which provide little insight into underlying implicit processes (Cohen & Chakravarti, 1990; Jacoby, Johar, & Morrin, 1998; Simonson Carmon, Dhar, Drolet, & Nowlis, 2001). As an example, research into the structure and function of attitudes has relied almost exclusively on explicit measures, encouraging the development of theories dependent on conscious evaluation and deliberation. Although these theories are essential to the advancement of the field, they often neglect the potential role of nonconscious processes. Moreover, the validity of explicit measures is threatened if subjects do not possess an attitude prior to measurement, are unable to access an attitude in memory, or are unwilling to share that information (Dholakia & Morwitz, 2002; Dovidio & Fazio, 1992; Fazio, 1986; Fazio & Williams, 1986; Gur & Sackeim, 1979; Hawkins & Coney, 1981; Louie, Curren, & Harich, 2000; Orne, 1962; Taylor & Brown, 1994). In sum, explicit measures are an important component of any behavioral research program, but they often illuminate only a partial picture of consumers' underlying cognitions.

INTEREST IN IMPLICIT MEASURES OF SOCIAL COGNITION

Interest in what are now identified as "implicit" measures of social cognition has increased as the limitations of self-report measures have become more apparent. The most recent, well-established, and popular of these new measures is the Implicit Association Test, or IAT (Greenwald, Mcghee, & Schwartz, 1998). The IAT is a computer-based categorization task designed to measure relative strengths of association among concepts in memory without requiring introspection on the part of the subject. The IAT is easy to implement, generates large effects sizes, and possesses good reliability (Greenwald & Nosek, 2001). While initial applications of the IAT focused on implicit attitude measurement (Greenwald, Mcghee, & Schwartz, 1998; Greenwald & Nosek, 2001), researchers have expanded its usage to include measures of self-concept (Farnham, Greenwald, & Banaji, 1999; Greenwald et al., 2002; Greenwald & Farnham, 2000; Perkins, Forehand, & Greenwald, 2005; Perkins, Forehand, & Greenwald, 2006; Spalding & Hardin, 1999), stereotypes (Greenwald et al., 2002; Nosek, Banaji, & Greenwald, 2004; Rudman, Greenwald, & Mcghee, 2001), self-esteem (Farnham, Greenwald, & Banaji, 1999; Greenwald et al., 2002), implicit egotism (Jones, Pelham, Mirenberg, & Hetts, 2002; Pelham, Mirenberg, & Jones, 2002), and implicit partisanship (Greenwald, Pickrell, & Farnham, 2002; Perkins et al., 2006). As many of these concepts appear regularly in consumer behavior research, application of the IAT in consumer psychology seems like an obvious and viable opportunity.

AN EXPLANATION OF THE IAT METHODOLOGY

The IAT (Greenwald, McGhee, & Schwartz 1998) is an indirect measure of relative strength of association between concepts or objects in memory. The IAT procedure requires subjects to quickly map items representing four different categories onto two responses on a computer keyboard (e.g., pressing two prespecified keys such as "D" and "K"). Following the appearance of a category exemplar on the computer screen, a respondent categorizes the item as quickly as possible by pressing the response key that represents its appropriate category. The ease or difficulty with which a subject is able to assign the same response to distinct concepts is taken as a measure of strength of the association between them in memory. The following discussion is meant to familiarize the audience with the IAT method: several recent reviews (Brunel, Tietje, & Greenwald, 2004; Nosek, Greenwald, & Banaji, 2005) examine related methodological and psychometric issues.

Consider a *brand attitude* IAT designed to assess relative attitudes toward Coke and Pepsi. This attitude IAT requires the use of four categories, each having multiple exemplars. The two brand categories (Coke and Pepsi) are referred to as *target concepts*. The remaining two categories are the *attributes* that may be variably associated with the target concepts. In an attitude IAT, the attribute categories are *pleasant* and *unpleasant*. Typical target concept and attribute categories include between three and six stimulus items (category exemplars), although IATs with as few as two items per category have been effective (Nosek, Greenwald, & Banaji, 2004). Exemplar items for a target concept or attribute category can include images, brand logos, and/or words.

A typical IAT has a sequence of five *discrimination tasks*. Each task serves either to train the respondent in the appropriate responses to a given set of stimuli, or to measure the speed with which the subject can categorize concepts and attributes when they share a response key. The initial discrimination task involves distinguishing items of the two target concept categories, for example, images representing Coke versus Pepsi. Often, the number of initial training trials varies with the number of stimulus items, such that each stimulus item is viewed twice, in random order. The second discrimination task parallels the first, using the attribute category stimulus items (e.g., words for *pleasant* vs. *unpleasant*).

In the third discrimination task, or *initial combined task*, subjects categorize a series of items drawn from both target concept categories and both attribute categories. During this task, a target concept category and an attribute category are assigned a shared response key. For example, subjects press a specified response key with one hand (e.g., the "D" key with left hand) as quickly as possible whenever a Coke category item or a pleasant attribute appears on the screen. Whenever a Pepsi category item or an unpleasant attribute item is presented, the subject would press the alternate response key (e.g., the "K" key with right hand). Stimulus items are presented alternately from the two target concept and the two attribute categories, with the particular stimulus item being randomly chosen from the available set of exemplars.

The final two discrimination tasks reverse the appropriate response for the target concepts and thereby create a task that can be directly compared to the initial combined task. In the fourth discrimination task, the *reversed target concept discrimination*, subjects practice categorizing the Coke and Pepsi target concept items with the response keys previously used for the other. If the initial target concept discrimination assigned the Coke category to the "D" key and the Pepsi category to the "K" key, the *reversed* discrimination task would assign Pepsi to the "D" key and Coke to the "K" key. This reversal serves two purposes: it allows subjects to unlearn the category-response key associations acquired during the first and third discrimination tasks, and it sets up the fifth discrimination task, or *reversed combined task*. This final task is identical to the initial combined task, with the target concept categories reversed. The critical response latency data are captured in tasks three and five.

SCORING THE IAT

The IAT measure is computed as a function of the difference in average response speed between the *initial combined task* and the *reversed combined task*. After transformation of these aggregated response times (discussed below), the difference in performance speed between the initial and reverse combined tasks provides the basis for the IAT measure. Greenwald, McGhee, and Schwartz (1998) provided a *conventional* scoring algorithm that provides detailed procedures for data reduction, difference score calculation, and IAT effect assessment. This algorithm was chosen over alternative latency-based scoring algorithms because it produced the largest statistical effects sizes. Although effective, the conventional algorithm was selected over other latency measure scoring methods based upon the effect sizes it produced rather than any theoretical reasoning (Greenwald & Nosek, 2001). To establish a psychometrically preferable measure, a new scoring algorithm was developed: the *D* measure (Greenwald, Nosek, & Banaji, 2003). The *D* measure differs in several ways from the conventional scoring procedure. The *D* measure is computed by dividing the difference between the congruent and incongruent test blocks by the standard deviation of the aggregate test-block latencies. This was justified because the magnitudes of differences between experimental treatment means are often correlated with the variability of the data from which the means are computed. Using the standard deviation as the devisor adjusts differences between means for this effect of underlying variability (Greenwald, Nosek, & Banaji, 2003). As a result, the *D* measure is similar to Cohen's *d* (Cohen, 1977) and may be interpreted as an effect size. However, where Cohen's *d* uses the pooled standard deviation *within treatment* as the divisor, the *D* measure computes an *inclusive* standard deviation from all latencies in the two combined tasks of the IAT (Greenwald, Nosek, & Banaji, 2003). Further, the *D* measure includes data from both practice and test blocks as well as the data from the first two trials in test blocks (these data are dropped in the conventional scoring procedure due to typically lengthened latencies). The inclusion of these additional trials improves the stability of the measure and increases correlations with explicit measures.

Overall, recent analysis suggests that the D measure is a superior measure to the conventional scoring procedure as it increases the magnitude of effects measured using the IAT, leads to higher correlations between the IAT and explicit measures, and increases the predictive validity of IAT scores on behavioral dependent variables (Perugini, 2004). A full discussion of the D measure may be found at http://faculty.washington.edu/agg/, where one can download analysis scripts that calculate the conventional and the improved D measure (as well as other measures discussed in Greenwald et al. (2003)). The current authors recommend using the D measure, not only because it has been shown to be a superior measure to the conventional scoring procedure, but also because its use will increase the interpretability and comparability of results across disciplines and experiments by providing an effect size-like statistic.

APPLICATIONS OF THE IAT IN CONSUMER BEHAVIOR

Implicit Attitude Measurement

Starting with Allport's declaration that attitude is "social psychology's most indispensable concept" (Allport, 1935), the psychological definition of *attitude* has evolved. In general, attitude has been defined as inclination toward evaluation, whether it be "a disposition to react favorably or unfavorably to a class of objects" (Sarnof, 1960) or "an individual's disposition to respond favorably or unfavorably to an object, person, institution, or event, or to any other discriminable aspect of the individual's world" (Greenwald, 1989). To say that attitude measurement is a cornerstone of social psychology historically and consumer behavior more recently is not hyperbole. Surveys of recent developments in consumer research (Cohen & Chakravarti, 1990; Jacoby, Johar, & Morrin, 1998; Simonson et al., 2001) are replete with a staggering array of models that describe people as creatures of conscious, careful, analytical decision making. Consumers are thought to be active, rational processors of the vibrant stimuli in their environment, consciously parsing information, deciding about what to attend to, discarding irrelevant or extraneous information, and weighing what is left over in order to optimize value and facilitate attitude creation. This social cognition paradigm is epitomized by the development of two related models of persuasion: the elaboration likelihood model (ELM) (Petty, Cacioppo, & Schumann, 1983) and the heuristic-systematic model (HSM) (Chaiken, 1987). These theories provide a foundation for models of advertising effectiveness, purchase decisions, and brand and product attitude development. Interestingly, while the focus of ELM and HSM is clearly conscious and cognitive, both models propose that consumers may be influenced by inputs that are not consciously analyzed. By incorporating nondeliberative judgment into the process, these theories are the precursors to newer theories that advocate attitude development in the absence of overt cognition.

The notion that attitudes might develop as a byproduct of nonconscious, automatic, or implicit process gained momentum in the early 1990s (Bargh, Chaiken, Govender, & Pratto, 1992; Bargh, Chaiken, Raymond, & Hymes, 1996; Bargh, Chen, & Burrows, 1996; Fazio, Powell, & Williams, 1989), spawning the notion of *implicit* attitudes—"introspectively unidentified (or inaccurately identified) traces of past experience that mediate favorable or unfavorable feeling, thought, or action toward social objects" (Greenwald & Banaji, 1995). Implicit attitudes are thought to be more strongly influenced by nonconscious processing due to their independence from conscious adjustment and evaluation. Thus, it is common to observe dissociation between explicitly self-reported attitudes and implicit attitudes measured by nontraditional methodologies like the IAT. Initially, these disassociations prompted theorizing that implicit and explicitly stated attitudes may be independent constructs (Devine, 1989; Greenwald & Banaji, 1995), while more recent theorizing suggests that implicit and explicit measures assess related but distinct constructs in memory (Nosek & Smyth, 2005). However, interpretations of IAT results have generally not been committed to a theoretical position on the question of whether implicit and explicit measures of attitude tap two types of indicator of a common construct (single-process theories), tap two distinct constructions (dual-process theories), or represent general cultural knowledge versus personal attitudes (Greenwald & Nosek, 2007).

USING THE IAT TO ASSESS IMPLICIT CONSUMER ATTITUDES

Within consumer research, there are many domains in which similar disassociations between explicit and implicit attitudes may occur. Constructs that have relied on self-report measures for description such as vanity (Netemeyer, Burton, & Lichtenstein, 1995), stigmatized behaviors (Mowen & Spears, 1999; Swanson, Rudman, & Greenwald, 2001), or the exploration of "dark side behaviors" such as drug and alcohol use (Mick, 1996) may be affected by subject unwillingness to accurately report due to social desirability biases. One of the first examples of the IAT being applied to problems of this sort examined behavioral and attitudinal responses to spokesperson race in print advertising (Brunel, Tietje, & Greenwald, 2004). Prior research revealed low correlations between explicit and implicit measures when the focus of attitudinal measurement is related to race, suggesting that explicit measures are consciously modified as a result of self-presentation bias or reluctance to report true feelings (Dasgupta et al., 2000; Greenwald, Mcghee, & Schwartz, 1998). Thus, the question of interest was whether the IAT would pick up negative attitudes related to the race of celebrity spokespersons. To this end, advertisements were created that paired brand information with athletes, and which manipulated the race of the celebrity sportsperson. Interestingly, White respondents exhibited a significant "pro-White" preference when measured with the IAT, but did not reveal a significant preference on self-report measures. On the other hand, Black respondents indicated a preference for advertisements with Black spokespersons on self-report measures, but no significant implicit preference. Further, the magnitude of implicit preference for advertisements that included White spokespersons was significantly greater for White respondents than for Black respondents, whereas the opposite was true for the self-report measures. Further analysis confirmed a significant interaction of ethnicity and measurement method on the revealed preference for advertisements with spokespersons of one's own ethnicity.

A number of other researchers have used the IAT to explore the effects of implicit attitudes on judgments as well. For example, Forehand and Perkins (2005) found that favorable attitude toward a celebrity positively influenced response to advertising utilizing that celebrity's voice, but only when the subject was unable to identify the celebrity behind the voice. This influence reversed if the subject could correctly identify the celebrity, was motivated to eliminate irrelevant influences, *and* was able to consciously adjust response (an adjustment that was only possible on explicit measures). Using set/reset theory (Martin, 1986), the authors argued that this reversal on explicit measures was due to *resetting*, a correction of the perceived influence of the celebrity cue due to its logical irrelevance. The disassociation between the explicit and implicit results suggested that resetting requires explicit evaluation. This experiment also demonstrates that the IAT can be used to discern the underlying processes that produce effects traditionally observed on explicit measures.

Maison and colleagues (Maison, Greenwald, & Bruin, 2001) conducted a number of experiments exploring domains where one might expect dissociation between explicit and implicitly measured attitudes. One of these studies explored attitudes toward high- and low-calorie products. For these products, it was hypothesized that consumers (young women) hold ambivalent attitudes, perceiving high-calorie products as good in taste, but bad for their health and perceiving low-calorie products as bad in taste, but good for their health. When attitudes toward these food products were measured using traditional explicit measures, results suggested that young women preferred high calorie products on some dimensions (e.g., taste). However, implicit attitude measures revealed that young women had more positive attitudes toward low calorie products. Moreover, favorable implicit attitudes toward low calorie products predicted dieting activities.

Another set of experiments investigated consumer ethnocentrism. Consumer ethnocentrism is defined as a conscious preference for one's own native products (e.g., products produced within your country or region) compared to foreign products (Verlegh & Steenkamp, 1999; Watson & Wright, 2000). Consumer ethnocentrism may result from any number of different mental processes: cognitive (people believe that products produced in their own country are better), affective (people have a positive affective reaction toward native products), or ideological or normative (people believe that it is appropriate to purchase products manufactured in their own country). Until recently, consumer ethnocentrism was studied in developed countries using explicit measures and this typically revealed a bias in favor of products produced in the subject's native country. However, in less economically developed countries this domestic preference is often not observed. This is thought to be the result of experience with poorer-quality native products compared to foreign brands. Maison and colleagues predicted that this situation can lead to dissociation between implicit and explicit attitudes and could produce internal conflict between automatic preference based on emotions and rational judgment based on observation and experience.

Thus, two experiments were conducted to explore explicitly and implicitly measured preferences toward foreign versus local products and their relationship to behavior. The first study measured attitude toward Polish versus foreign brands of cigarettes, on the assumption that Polish cigarettes were considered to be lower quality than foreign brands of cigarettes. Subjects completed an attitude IAT that incorporated Polish (e.g., Sobieskie, Carmen) and American (e.g., Marlboro, Camel) cigarettes brands and filled out a survey measuring their opinions and attitudes toward these brands. Interestingly, the explicit measures revealed that the subjects preferred foreign brands, while attitude IAT suggested that the subjects preferred the Polish cigarette brands. This dissociation was stronger among nonsmokers than among smokers, while smokers smoked foreign brands and reported a preference for the foreign brands of cigarettes but still revealed a slight preference for Polish brands using the IAT. A second experiment replicated these findings across a number of product categories.

The IAT has been used to explore other types of associations in memory beyond attitude. For example, recent research into the processing and understanding of brand slogans suggests that a significant component of the understanding of brand slogans may be implicit in nature (Dimofte & Yalch, 2004). Brand slogans may have implicit influence on belief to the extent that they are *polysemous* (i.e., the extent they possess both a literal and figurative meaning). For example, Hoover's brand slogan is "Deep down you want Hoover," a statement that implies both cleaning power and consumer's inner desire for the brand. Dimofte and Yalch suggest that polysemous advertising slogans (those that include both literal and figurative meanings) may be processed differently by consumers, according to ability to access meanings. Dimofte and Yalch argued that, in the case where a polysemous slogan incorporates literal and secondary slogans that potentially differ in valence, one would expect differential responses to those slogans to the extent that the viewer of those slogans was able to discern both meanings.

To test these hypotheses, three versions of an experimental advertisement were created using two well-known automobile brands: Lexus and Mercedes-Benz. The advertisements were identical in their presentation of comfort and performance attributes, but differed in the slogans that were included in the advertisements: "Unlike any other" (literal positive), "No one comes close" (polysemous mixed, such that the secondary negative reading suggests that it is too expensive and thus unattainable for the vast majority of automobile buyers) and "For the few who can afford it" (literal negative). The IAT was used to measure subjects' automobile brand associations with attributes related to "expensive" versus "affordable." Consistent with expectations, Dimofte and Yalch found that subjects who were better able to access multiple meanings of the slogans exhibited a significant "Mercedes + Expensive" association suggesting that these subjects implicitly understood the secondary slogan meanings. On the other hand, subjects who were unable to access the multiple meanings of the slogans did not appear to process the secondary, implicit meaning of the slogan, suggesting that different cognitive processes were occurring between the groups.

A follow-up experiment by Dimofte and colleagues (Dimofte, Yalch, & Greenwald, 2003) suggested that incidental exposure to an object could produce novel implicit associations with that object. A particular brand name (Trojan) that could both represent a "party"-related product and the mascot of a major American university was chosen as a stimulus item. After incidental exposure to the brand name and logo, subsequent implicit associations of that specific university and the concept of "party" emerged robustly among subjects familiar with both categories. Further, the strength of this novel implicit association was enough to reverse perceptions of the target university when compared to another, comparable university that was explicitly considered more of a "party" school (UCLA). A similar result was obtained using a different brand name that could trigger positive or negative valence depending on the context. To the extent that the context primed either positive or negative valence, subsequent implicit measures of brand attitude revealed valence-consistent associations with the brand in question.

PREDICTING CONSUMER BEHAVIOR WITH THE IAT

Previous research suggests that the ability of the IAT to predict behavior is somewhat inconsistent, with some projects finding adequate predictive ability (Greenwald & Farnham, 2000; Mcconnell & Leibold, 2001; Rudman & Glick, 2001) and others not (Karpinski & Hilton, 2001). A recent meta-analysis (Poehlman et al., 2006) of IAT research in psychology (including 14 consumer behavior studies) found that both IAT and explicit measures reliably predicted behavior, and that implicit measures were superior in predicting stereotyping and prejudicial behaviors. Explicit measures were better predictors of behavior only when predictions by both implicit and explicit measures were both relatively strong.

Recent consumer behavior studies incorporating the IAT have found that the IAT does predict behavior. For example, purchase intention, brand preference, and perceived brand superiority were all predicted by implicitly measured self-brand association (Perkins, 2005). Further, these relationships were completely mediated by implicit attitude toward the brand. These results are consistent with the notion that self-concept association with objects directly influences attitude formation and behavior (Bargh & Chartrand, 1999; Greenwald & Banaji, 1995; Perkins, Forehand, & Greenwald, 2005; Perkins et al., 2006).

Interestingly, explicit and implicit measures of brand attitude predict brand choice differentially. When under time constraints, consumer brand choice was significantly influenced by prior implicit attitude, while explicitly reported attitudes were more diagnostic when consumers had more time available (Wanke, Plessner, & Friese, 2002). Similarly, Plessner and colleagues (Plessner, Wanke, Harr, & Friese, 2004) looked at the effect of time pressure on product choice of recycled versus nonrecycled writing pads, finding that implicit attitudes toward recycled versus nonrecycled paper predicted product choice only when subjects were required to make the product choice within a 5-second response window, while explicit measures predicted product choice when there was no response window limitation. Taken together, these findings suggest that cognitive resource limitations may lead people to base choices on implicit associations in memory, since they lack the cognitive resources to go through conscious deliberation. While exploring consumer behavioral situations where a dissociation between explicit and implicit attitudes might occur, Vantomme and colleagues (Vantomme, Geuens, De Houwer, & De Pelsmacker, 2004) suggested that implicit measures of negative attitudes toward "green" or ecologically friendly products should be both dissociated from explicit measures of attitude toward green products, and be less likely to predict product choice, because it was thought that negative implicit attitudes toward green products should be consciously modified by subjects. Interestingly, the reverse was true: implicit attitudes were found to be extremely positive toward green products, and predicted green product choice.

THE SELF-CONCEPT IN CONSUMER BEHAVIOR

Recent research suggests that many cognitive processes related to the self-concept and its effect on behavior may be unconscious or beyond active control (Bargh, Mckenna, & Fitzsimons, 2002; Farnham, Greenwald, & Banaji, 1999; Greenwald et al., 2002; Greenwald & Farnham, 2000; Hetts, Sakuma, & Pelham, 1999; Spalding & Hardin, 1999). This differs from previous theorizing about the self-concept, which suggests that self-related cognitions tended to be conscious, active processes (Higgins, 1987; Higgins, Klein, & Strauman, 1985; Markus, 1983; Markus & Nurius, 1986; Markus & Nurius, 1987; Meyers-Levy & Peracchio, 1996). The idea that cognitive processes related to the self-concept may unconsciously influence behavior builds from prior research that suggests that people process social information at both an explicit and implicit level (Bargh et al., 1992; Devine, 1989; Fazio et al., 1986; Greenwald & Banaji, 1995). For example, automatic or implicit process have been observed in stereotype activation and resultant behavior (Bargh, Chen, & Burrows, 1996), automatic attitude formation (Greenwald & Banaji, 1995), self-esteem development (Farnham, Greenwald, & Banaji, 1999; Greenwald et al., 2002), implicit egotism (Jones et al., 2002; Pelham, Mirenberg, & Jones, 2002), implicit partisanship (Greenwald, Pickrell, & Farnham, 2002; Perkins et al., 2006), and self-concept organization (Perkins, Forehand, & Greenwald, 2006).

The influence of the implicit self-concept has been explored in a number of domains. For example, people exhibit automatic minimal group bias, but were unaware of the bias at an explicit level (Ashburn-Nardo, Voils, & Monteith, 2001). Greenwald and Farnham (2000) found low correlations between implicitly and explicitly measured self-esteem and self-concept, suggesting differences in the constructs tapped by each measurement technique. Further, implicitly measured self-esteem predicted expected mental buffering following manipulations of success versus failure. Spalding and Hardin (1999) found that implicit self-esteem predicted anxiety during an interview. Swanson, Rudman, and Greenwald (2001) reported inconsistent attitude-behavior relationships for smokers using both implicit and explicit measures. Overall, there seems to be evidence that the self-concept operates at an implicit level, and that the implicit self-concept may reveal different associations and attitudes compared to the explicit self-concept.

One of the newest areas of exploration that leverages much of the methodological development of the IAT is a project by Perkins, Forehand, and Greenwald (under review). The authors introduce the notion of *implicit self referencing*, or the automatic self-association of objects encountered in the environment and subsequent generation of a positive implicit attitude toward those objects. Recent research (Greenwald et al., 2002), in the tradition of cognitive consistency theory (Festinger, 1957; Heider, 1958; Osgood & Tannenbaum, 1955), suggests that self-object relationships are tied to implicit identities (self-group associations). Greenwald et al. (2002) theorized interrelations among triads composed of the following components: the *self*, a *group*, and an attribute such as *valence*.

Thus, a linkage between the self-concept and valence is interpreted as *implicit self-esteem*, (Farnham, Greenwald, & Banaji, 1999; Greenwald & Farnham, 2000), an association between an object and valence is interpreted as an *implicit attitude* (Greenwald et al., 2002) and an association between a group or object and the self-concept is interpreted as an implicit *identity* (Rudman, Greenwald, & Mcghee, 2001). Although the research cited here focuses primarily on self-group interactions and notions of identity, a long tradition in social psychology and consumer behavior has argued that objects (in the form of gifts, products, or brands) may help define identity as well (Aaker, 1999; Belk, 1988; James, 1890; Kleine, Kleine, & Kernan, 1993; Tietje & Brunel, 2005; Wicklund & Gollwitzer, 1982). Tietje and Brunel (2005) applied these theories to establish a unified brand theory framework and experimental results that examine the existence and influence of these existing triads in memory. The authors' previous research (Brunel, Tietje, & Greenwald, 2004) provides initial support for the unified theory framework, finding that Macintosh users revealed stronger self-Macintosh association than PC users revealed self-PC association. They suggested that Macintosh users identify with Macintosh due to the minority status of Macintosh in the marketplace, the strong sense of community that surrounds Macintosh users, and the notion that, while PC users are generally compelled to use PCs due to work availability, Macintosh users must actively choose the brand, usually incurring social and professional difficulties. Tietje and Brunel (2005) propose a theoretical framework that incorporates self-esteem, attitudes, stereotypes, and self-concept similar to Greenwald and colleagues (2002) framework.

Perkins and colleagues have extended these theoretical and experimental findings to the creation of new attitudes toward novel stimuli items, such as brands. Greenwald and Banaji (1995) define *implicit self-esteem* as "the introspectively unidentified (or inaccurately identified) effect of the self-attitude on evaluation of self-associated and self dissociated objects" (p. 11). Numerous studies (Taylor & Brown, 1994) have established that the majority of people report favorable self-descriptions and self-evaluations, suggesting that a link in memory exists between the self-concept and a cognitive representation of positive valence. To the extent that a new link is created between the self and some object in the environment, perhaps due to environmental exposure, one would expect a new link to form between that object and a positive valence representation (i.e., forming or increasing a positive attitude). This should occur not require either conscious input or awareness of attitude formation by the subject.

Two experiments bear this out. In the first experiment, subjects were randomly assigned to perform a categorization task that created a trivial link between their own self-concepts and an innocuous object, in this case either *analog* or *digital clocks*. These target concept categories were extensively pretested to ensure that pre-experimental implicit attitudes toward the two categories were, on average, approximately equal. The categorization task required subjects to categorize target concepts (images of either *analog* or *digital clocks*) and attribute items (words representing the concepts of "self" and "other") in specific pairs. For example, subjects who were randomly assigned to associate self with *analog clocks* did a categorization task that required the same response (pressing the computer's "D" key) when items that represent *self* or *analog clocks* appeared on the screen, and required a different response (pressing the "K" key) when items that represent the concept *other* (opposite of self) or images of *analog* clocks appeared on the screen. No specific explanation of this purpose of the categorization task was provided. Phase 1 required subjects to complete two blocks of 36 trials each categorizing *digital* and *analog* clock images with the attributes *self* and *other*. The response key ("D" or "K") was reversed for both contrasts in the second categorization task to avoid associating any concept with a specific key response.

After this associative practice, subjects completed an IAT that measured implicit attitudes toward the target concepts. It was hypothesized that the association practice would create a new link in memory between the self and one of the target concept categories, indirectly producing an association of positive valence with that concept. This was precisely what was found: subjects who (for example) associated self with analog clocks subsequently showed IAT-measured positive implicit attitudes toward analog clocks.

Experiment 2 replicated Experiment 1, but added a twist: instead of a self-association task designed to create a link between the self-concept and a known but previously unlinked object category in memory (clocks), Experiment 2 incorporated invented brand names that were unknown to the subjects. Again, the brand names were pretested to make sure that the subjects did not prefer one of the brand name sets (ACE and STAR, each with four invented model names) prior to the manipulation. In order to facilitate the learning of the new brand names, subjects were presented with a static list of the brand names for 30 seconds prior to the self-categorization task. Following the self-categorization task, subjects again completed attitude IAT. The same results as Experiment 1 obtained: Subjects who self-associated with the ACE brand, for example, automatically generated a positive implicit attitude toward the ACE brand relative to the STAR brand. Taken together, these results suggest that attitudes may be automatically generated toward objects as a result of merely self-associating that object. The research question is now whether we can pin down automatic self-association.

An extension of this implicit self-referencing project examined the possibility that implicit attitudes may be spontaneously formed as a result of a self-group association. Previous research suggests that simply learning the names of randomly assigned team members leads a subject to associate self with that team (Greenwald, Pickrell, & Farnham, 2002). This automatic self-group association has been shown in related research as well. Pinter and Greenwald (2004) found that automatic self-group association led to differential resource allocation amongst competing teams. Perkins and colleagues (Perkins et al., 2006) sought to further understand mere group membership by looking at its effects on brand attitude formation in two experiments.

Under the guise of a scavenger hunt, subjects were instructed that they would be randomly assigned to one of two fictitious groups, named "circle" or "triangle." In order to learn their group membership, subjects were first exposed to a list of names either of members of the subject's or another, competing group. Following this exposure, subjects practiced categorizing the names of their own and the competing team to become familiar with the names and the group memberships. The subject's group included four names, and the word "myself" representing the subject's membership in that category, while the opponent group included five names.

Subjects were next instructed to learn a set of objects pretested to assure that they were, on average, initially equivalent in evaluation: *analog* or *digital clocks* (Study 1) or fictitious automobile brand names Ace or Star (Study 2; the experimental design differed only with regard to the stimuli employed between the two studies). These objects were to be the target of a fictitious scavenger hunt on the campus where the experiments were run. However, the categorization task required here was different from the task employed in the implicit self-referencing project described above. Subjects categorized their team members' names and one of the target objects using the same response key. For example, if the subject was on the circle team, and was assigned to find the Ace automobile brand names, then the categorization task required giving the same response when either circle team names or Ace brand names were presented, and a different response when triangle team names or Star brand names were presented. For this categorization task, only four names from each team were used, allowing omission of "yourself" stimuli. Thus, during the second categorization task, the subject never categorized any explicitly self-identified stimuli with the target objects. Following these tasks, subjects completed a self-target object IAT (either clocks or brands) and a parallel attitude IAT for the target objects.

The results revealed that subjects spontaneously generated positive implicit self-associations as well as positive implicit attitudes toward the target objects that were sorted together with the names of their group's members during the experimental treatments. Specifically, subjects in the circle group, who categorized their group members with the Ace brand model names, subsequently self-associated with and generated a positive implicit attitude toward the Ace brand, even though there was no direct linkage of self with the Ace brand during the experiment. These results extend the implicit self-referencing experiments described above: instead of examining the spontaneous creation of an implicit attitude that is the direct result of implicit self-association, these two experiments revealed a positive implicit attitude resulting from merely being associated with a group that was in turn associated with the arbitrarily assigned target object.

Finally, Forehand and colleagues (Forehand, Perkins, & Reed II, 2003) explored self-identity and responses to advertising stimuli in three experiments. Prior research demonstrates that accessible and self-important social identities affect judgments in predictable ways, and has identified three main classes of variables that may influence identity accessibility—enduring traits such as strength of identification with a specific identity, aspects of the social context in which a consumer resides, and contextual primes that can activate or prompt identity-based processing (Forehand et al., 2003). In these two experiments, consumer sensitivity to situational manipulations of distinctiveness (Mcguire, McGuire, Child, & Fujioka, 1978) was assessed using standard explicit self-report measures and IATs. The IATs measured the degree to which each subject associated specific self components (gender and ethnicity) with identity-related concepts and thereby provided implicit measures of identity accessibility. During a preliminary phase of the first two experiments, subjects completed a battery of demographic items, personality scale items, and implicit identity IATs to provide baseline measures of their prevailing identity accessibility. Several weeks after this initial measurement, the subjects participated in an ostensibly unrelated experiment in which the composition of the subject's immediate social environment was either measured (Experiment 1) or manipulated (Experiment 2). It was hypothesized that identity accessibility during this second session would be influenced not only by the subject's distinctiveness within their immediate social context, but also by general sensitivity to such social information (as measured using Snyder's self-monitoring scale). Forehand and colleagues found that social distinctiveness did influence both explicit and implicit identity accessibility, and that the influence of distinctiveness on identity accessibility was moderated by the subject's predisposition toward self-monitoring, such that high self-monitors were influenced by social cues to a greater extent than were low-self monitors. This pattern of results was observed on both explicit and implicit measures of identity accessibility.

Forehand et al.'s (2003) third experiment assessed the degree to which the expression of an identity-based preference reinforces identity accessibility. It was hypothesized that the use of one's identity as an informational cue in attitude expression reinforces the accessibility of that identity and thereby increases the likelihood that the identity will be used in subsequent judgments. To test this hypothesis, college-age subjects evaluated advertisements for vitamins intended for children, young adults, or seniors and then completed an Implicit Association Test designed to measure self-association with youth versus aged. Compared to subjects who evaluated the young adult version of the ad (the control condition), subjects who evaluated the children-focused ad or the senior-focused ad demonstrated stronger self-youth associations. This finding suggests that the use of an identity dimension in an evaluation activates preexisting identity associations. Since the majority of consumers possess preexisting strong associations between the self and youth (Nosek, Banaji, & Greenwald, 2002), this identity activation increased the self-youth association.

CONCLUDING REMARKS

Since its introduction, the IAT has exploded in popularity and usage. While previous reviews (Brunel, Tietje, & Greenwald, 2004; Nosek, Greenwald, & Banaji, 2005) have explored various psychometric and methodological issues, the purpose of this chapter is to review the most recent examples of IAT usage in consumer behavior research. It is hoped that this review will serve as a launching pad for marketing researchers to become familiar with current research streams and to start exploring the unconscious or implicit processes that most of us believe underlie much consumer behavior. The current state of theoretical development, methodology, and areas of application form a "perfect storm" of exciting, valuable, and rewarding research, and the opportunity to incorporate what seems to be a major component of social cognition—the nonconscious role of implicit cognitive processes in consumer decision making and behavior.

NOTES

1. Steps 4 and 5 are reversed here as a result in a change in the scoring algorithm following publication of Greenwald et al. (2003). The published algorithm requires the calculation of standard deviation prior to error trial replacement. The description here (error trial replacement followed by standard deviation calculation) is corrected.

REFERENCES

Aaker, J. L. (1999). The malleable self: The role of self-expression in persuasion. *Journal of Marketing Research, 36*(1), 45–57.

Allport, G. W. (1935). Attitudes. In C. Murchison (Ed.), *A handbook of social psychology* (pp. 798–844). Worcester, MA: Clark University Press.

Ashburn-Nardo, L., Voils, C. I., & Monteith, M. J. (2001). Implicit associations as the seeds of intergroup bias: how easily do they take root? *Journal of Personality and Social Psychology, 81*(5), 789–799.

Bargh, J. (2002). Losing Consciousness: Automatic influences on consumer judgment, behavior, and motivation. *Journal of Consumer Research, 29,* 280–285.

Bargh, J. A., Chaiken, S., Govender, R., & Pratto, F. (1992). The generality of the automatic attitude activation effect. *Journal of Personality and Social Psychology, 62*(6), 893–912.

Bargh, J. A., Chaiken, S., Raymond, P., & Hymes, C. (1996). The automatic evaluation effect: Unconditional automatic attitude activation with a pronunciation task. *Journal of Experimental Social Psychology, 32*(1), 104–128.

Bargh, J. A., & Chartrand, T. L. (1999). The unbearable automaticity of being. *American Psychologist, 54*(7), 462–479.

Bargh, J. A., Chen, M., & Burrows, L. (1996). Automaticity of social behavior: Direct effects of trait construct and stereotype activation on action. *Journal of Personality and Social Psychology, 71*(2), 230–244.

Bargh, J. A., McKenna, K. Y. A., & Fitzsimons, G. M. (2002). Can you see the real me? Activation and expression of the "true self" on the Internet. *Journal of Social Issues, 58*(1), 33–48.

Belk, R. W. (1988). Possessions and the extended self. *Journal of Consumer Research, 15*(2), 139–168.

Brunel, F., Tietje, B., & Greenwald, A. G. (2004). Is the Implicit Association Test a valid and valuable measure of implicit consumer social cognition? *Journal of Consumer Psychology, 14*(4), 385–404.

Chaiken, S. (1987). The heuristic model of persuasion. In M. P. Zanna & J. M. Olson (Eds.), *Social influence: The Ontario symposium on personality and social psychology* (Vol. 5, pp. 3–39). Hillsdale, NJ: Erlbaum.

Cohen, J. (1977). *Statistical power analysis for the behavioral sciences* (Ref. ed.). New York: Academic Press.

Cohen, J. B., & Chakravarti, D. (1990). Consumer Psychology. *Annual Review of Psychology, 41,* 243–288.

Dasgupta, N., McGhee, D. E., Greenwald, A. G., & Banaji, M. R. (2000). Automatic preference for White Americans: Eliminating the familiarity explanation. *Journal of Experimental Social Psychology, 36*(3), 316–328.

Devine, P. G. (1989). Stereotypes and prejudice: Their automatic and controlled components. *Journal of Personality and Social Psychology, 56*(1), 5–18.

Dholakia, U. M., & Morwitz, V. G. (2002). The scope and persistence of mere-measurement effects: Evidence for a field study of customer satisfaction measurement. *Journal of Consumer Research, 29*(3), 159–167.

Dimofte, C., & Yalch, R. (2004). A rose by any other name would not always smell as sweet: Assessing consumer access to meaning and response to polysemous brand slogans. Unpublished manuscript.

Dimofte, C., Yalch, R., & Greenwald, A. G. (2003). *Brand names as sources and targets of tangential implicit associations.* Paper presented at the Association for Consumer Research, Toronto, Canada.

Dovidio, J. F., & Fazio, R. H. (1992). New technologies for the direct and indirect assessment of attitudes. In J. M. Tanur (Ed.), *Questions about questions: Inquiries into the cognitive bases of surveys* (Vol. 21, pp. 204–237). New York: Russell Sage Foundation.

Farnham, S. D., Greenwald, A. G., & Banaji, M. R. (1999). Implicit self-esteem. In D. Abrams & M. A. Hogg (Eds.), *Social identity and social cognition* (Vol. xvii, pp. 230–248). Malden, MA: Blackwell Publishers.

Fazio, R. H. (1986). How do attitudes guide behavior? In R. M. Sorrentino & E. T. Higgins (Eds.), *Handbook of motivation and cognition: Foundations of social behavior* (Vol. x, pp. 204–243). New York: Guilford.

Fazio, R. H., Powell, M. C., & Williams, C. J. (1989). The role of attitude accessibility in the attitude-to-behavior process. *Journal of Consumer Research, 16*(3), 280–288.

Fazio, R. H., Sanbonmatsu, D. M., Powell, M. C., & Kardes, F. R. (1986). On the automatic activation of attitudes. *Journal of Personality and Social Psychology, 50*(2), 229–238.

Fazio, R. H., & Williams, C. J. (1986). Attitude accessibility as a moderator of the attitude-perception and attitude-behavior relations: An investigation of the 1984 presidential election. *Journal of Personality and Social Psychology, 51*(3), 505–514.

Festinger, L. (1957). *A theory of cognitive dissonance.* Palo Alto, CA: Stanford University Press.

Forehand, M. R., Perkins, A. W., & Reed II, A. (2003). Identity reinforcement: The dynamic effects of evaluation on implicit self-concept. Paper presented at the Association of Consumer Researchers.

Greenwald, A. G. (1989). Why are attitudes important? In A. R. Pratkanis & S. J. Breckler (Eds.), *Attitude structure and function. The third Ohio State University volume on attitudes and persuasion* (pp. 1–10). Hillsdale, NJ: Erlbaum.

Greenwald, A. G., & Banaji, M. R. (1995). Implicit social cognition: Attitudes, self-esteem, and stereotypes. *Psychological Review, 102*(1), 4–27.

Greenwald, A. G., & Farnham, S. D. (2000). Using the Implicit Association Test to measure self-esteem and self-concept. *Journal of Personality and Social Psychology, 79*(6), 1022–1038.

Greenwald, A. G., & Nosek, B. A. (2001). Health of the Implicit Association Test at age 3. *Zeitschrift fuer Experimentelle Psychologie, 48*(2), 85–93.

Greenwald, A. G., & Nosek, B. A. (2007). Attitudinal dissociation: What does it mean? In R. E. Petty, R. H. Fazio & P. Brinol (Eds.), *Attitudes: Insights from the new implicit measures.* Hillsdale, NJ: Erlbaum.

Greenwald, A. G., Nosek, B. A., & Banaji, M. R. (2003). Understanding and using the implicit association test: I. An improved scoring algorithm. *Journal of Personality and Social Psychology, 85*(2), 197–216.

Greenwald, A. G., McGhee, D. E., & Schwartz, J. L. K. (1998). Measuring individual differences in implicit cognition: The implicit association test. *Journal of Personality and Social Psychology, 74*(6), 1464–1480.

Greenwald, A. G., Pickrell, J. E., & Farnham, S. D. (2002). Implicit partisanship: Taking sides for no reason. *Journal of Personality and Social Psychology, 83*(2), 367–379.

Greenwald, A. G., Banaji, M. R., Rudman, L. A., Farnham, S. D., Nosek, B. A., & Mellott, D. S. (2002). A unified theory of implicit attitudes, stereotypes, self-esteem, and self-concept. *Psychological Review, 109*(1), 3–25.

Gur, R. C., & Sackeim, H. A. (1979). Self-deception: A concept in search of a phenomenon. *Journal of Personality and Social Psychology, 37*(2), 147–169.

Hawkins, D. I., & Coney, K. A. (1981). Uninformed response error in survey research. *Journal of Marketing Research, 18*(3), 370–374.

Heider, F. (1958). *The psychology of interpersonal relations.* New York: Wiley.

Hetts, J. J., Sakuma, M., & Pelham, B. W. (1999). Two roads to positive regard: Implicit and explicit self-evaluation and culture. *Journal of Experimental Social Psychology, 35*(6), 512–559.

Higgins, E. T. (1987). Self-discrepancy: A theory relating self and affect. *Psychological Review, 94*(3), 319–340.

Higgins, E. T., Klein, R., & Strauman, T. (1985). Self-concept discrepancy theory: A psychological model for distinguishing among different aspects of depression and anxiety. *Social Cognition, 3*(1), 51–76.

Jacoby, J., Johar, G. V., & Morrin, M. (1998). Consumer behavior: A auadrennium. *Annual Review of Psychology, 49*, 319–344.

James, W. (1890). *The principles of psychology*. New York: Holt.

Jones, J. T., Pelham, B. W., Mirenberg, M. C., & Hetts, J. J. (2002). Name letter preferences are not merely mere exposure: Implicit egotism as self-regulation. *Journal of Experimental Social Psychology, 38*(2), 170–177.

Karpinski, A., & Hilton, J. L. (2001). Attitudes and the Implicit Association Test. *Journal of Personality and Social Psychology, 81*(5), 774–788.

Kleine, R. E., Kleine, S. S., & Kernan, J. B. (1993). Mundane consumption and the self: A social-identity perspective. *Journal of Consumer Psychology, 2*(3), 209–235.

Louie, T. A., Curren, M. T., & Harich, K. R. (2000). "I knew we would win": Hindsight bias for favorable and unfavorable team decision outcomes. *Journal of Applied Psychology, 85*(2), 264–272.

Maison, D., Greenwald, A. G., & Bruin, R. (2001). The Implicit Association Test as a measure of implicit consumer attitudes. *Polish Psychological Bulletin, 32*(1), 61–69.

Markus, H. R. (1983). Self-knowledge: and expanded view. *Journal of Personality, 51*(3), 543–565.

Markus, H. R., & Nurius, P. (1986). Possible selves. *American Psychologist, 41*(9), 954–969.

Markus, H. R., & Nurius, P. (1987). Possible selves: The interface between motivation and the self-concept. In K. Yardley & T. Honess (Eds.), *Self and identity: Psychosocial perspectives* (pp. 157–172).

Martin, L. L. (1986). Set/reset: Use and disuse of concepts in impression formation. *Journal of Personality and Social Psychology, 51*(3), 493–504.

McConnell, A. R., & Leibold, J. M. (2001). Relations among the Implicit Association Test, discriminatory behavior, and explicit measures of racial attitudes. *Journal of Experimental Social Psychology, 37*(5), 435–442.

McGuire, W. J., McGuire, C. V., Child, P., & Fujioka, T. (1978). Salience of ethnicity in the spontaneous self-concept as a function of one's ethnic distinctiveness in the social environment. *Journal of Personality and Social Psychology, 36*(5), 511–520.

Meyers-Levy, J., & Peracchio, L. A. (1996). Moderators of the impact of self-reference on persuasion. *Journal of Consumer Research, 22*(March), 408–423.

Mick, D. G. (1996). Are studies of dark side variables confounded by socially desirable responding? The case of materialism. *Journal of Consumer Research, 23*(2), 106–119.

Mowen, J. C., & Spears, N. (1999). Understanding compulsive buying among college students: A hierarchical approach. *Journal of Consumer Psychology, 8*(4), 407–430.

Netemeyer, R. G., Burton, S., & Lichtenstein, D. R. (1995). Trait aspects of vanity: Measurement and relevance to consumer behavior. *Journal of Consumer Research, 21*(4), 612–626.

Nosek, B. A., Banaji, M. R., & Greenwald, A. G. (2002). Harvesting implicit group attitudes and beliefs from a demonstration web site. *Group Dynamics, 6*(1), 101–115.

Nosek, B. A., Banaji, M. R., & Greenwald, A. G. (2004). Math – Male, M = Female, therefore Math does not equal Me. *Journal of Personality and Social Psychology, 83*(1), 44–59.

Nosek, B. A., Greenwald, A. G., & Banaji, M. R. (2004). *Understanding and using the Implicit Association Test: II. Methodological issues.* Working Paper.

Nosek, B. A., Greenwald, A. G., & Banaji, M. R. (2005). The Implicit Association Test at age 7: A methodological and conceptual review. In J. A. Bargh (Ed.), *Automatic processes in social thinking and behavior*: Psychology Press.

Nosek, B. A., & Smyth, F. L. (2005). A multitrait-multimethod validation of the Implicit Association Test: Implicit and explicit attitudes are related but distinct constructs.Unpublished manuscript.

Orne, M. T. (1962). On the social psychology of the psychological experiment: With particular reference to demand characteristics and their implications. *American Psychologist, 17*(10), 776–783.

Osgood, C. E., & Tannenbaum, P. H. (1955). The principle of congruity in the prediction of attitude change. *Psychological Review, 62*, 42–55.

Pelham, B. W., Mirenberg, M. C., & Jones, J. T. (2002). Why Susie sells seashells by the seashore: Implicit egotism and major life decisions. *Journal of Personality and Social Psychology, 82*(4), 469–487.

Perkins, A. W. (2005). Implicit attitudes mediate the implicit self association-behavior link. Unpublished manuscript, Rice University, Houston, TX.

Perkins, A. W., Forehand, M. R., & Greenwald, A. G. (2005). Implicit self-referencing: The self-concept as a source of implicit attitude formation. Unpublished manuscript, Rice University, Houston, TX.

Perkins, A. W., Forehand, M. R., & Greenwald, A. G. (2006). Decomposing the Implicit Self-Concept: The relative influence of semantic meaning and valence on attribute self-association. *Social Cognition, 24*(4), 387–408.

Perkins, A. W., Pinter, B., Forehand, M. R., & Greenwald, A. G. (2006). "Gentlemen and ladies, lend be your attitudes": Implicit attitudes resulting from mere group association. Unpublished manuscript, Rice University, Houston, TX.

Perugini, M. (2004). Predictive models of implicit and explicit attitudes. *British Journal of Social Psychology* (in press).

Petty, R. E., Cacioppo, J. T., & Schumann, D. (1983). Central and peripheral routes to advertising effectiveness: The moderating role involvement. *Journal of Consumer Research, 10*, 135–146.

Pinter, B., & Greenwald, A. G. (2004). Exploring implicit partisanship: Enigmatic (but genuine) group identification and attraction. *Group Processes and Intergroup Relations, 7*, 283–296.

Plessner, H., Wanke, M., Harr, T., & Friese, M. (2004). Implicit consumer attitudes and their influence on brand choice. Unpublished manuscript.

Poehlman, T. A., Uhlmann, E., Greenwald, A. G., & Banaji, M. R. (2006). Understanding and using the Implicit Association Test: III. Meta-analysis of predictive validity. Submitted for publication.

Rudman, L. A., & Glick, P. (2001). Prescriptive gender stereotypes and backlash toward agentic women. *Journal of Social Issues, 57*, 743–762.

Rudman, L. A., Greenwald, A. G., & McGhee, D. E. (2001). Implicit self-concept and evaluative implicit gender stereotypes: Self and ingroup share desirable traits. *Personality and Social Psychology Bulletin, 27*(9), 1164–1178.

Sarnof, I. (1960). Psychoanalytic theory and social attitudes. *Public Opinion Quarterly, 24*, 251–279.

Simonson, I., Carmon, Z., Dhar, R., Drolet, A., & Nowlis, S. M. (2001). Consumer research: In search of identity. *Annual Review of Psychology, 52*, 249–275.

Spalding, L. R., & Hardin, C. D. (1999). Unconscious unease and self-handicapping: Behavioral consequences of individual differences in implicit and explicit self-esteem. *Psychological Science, 10*(6), 207–230.

Swanson, J. E., Rudman, L. A., & Greenwald, A. G. (2001). Using the Implicit Association Test to investigate attitude-behaviour consistency for stigmatised behaviour. *Cognition and Emotion, 15*(2), 207–230.

Taylor, S. E., & Brown, J. D. (1994). Positive illusions and well-being revisited: Separating fact from fiction. *Psychological Bulletin, 116*(1), 21–27.

Tietje, B., & Brunel, F. (2005). Towards a unified theory of implicit consumer brand cognitions. In F. R. Kardes, P. M. Herr & J. Natel (Eds.), *Applying social cognition to consumer-focused strategy*. Mahwah, NJ: Erlbaum.

Vantomme, D., Geuens, M., De Houwer, J., & De Pelsmacker, P. (2004). Implicit attitudes toward green consumer behavior. Unpublished manuscript.

Verlegh, P. W. J., & Steenkamp, J.-B. E. M. (1999). A review and meta-analysis of country-of-origin research. *Journal of Economic Psychology, 20*(5), 521–546.

Wanke, M., Plessner, H., & Friese, M. (2002). *When implicit attitudes predict brand-choice and when they don't*. Paper presented at the Asia Pacific Advances in Consumer Research.

Watson, J. J., & Wright, K. (2000). Consumer ethnocentrism and attitudes toward domestic and foreign products. *European Journal of Marketing, 34*(9–10), 1149–1166.

Wicklund, R. A., & Gollwitzer, P. M. (1982). *Symbolic self-completion*. Hillsdale, NJ: Erlbaum.

18

Implicit Consumer Cognition

Patrick T. Vargas

University of Illinois at Urbana-Champaign

The ubiquity of advertising in daily life was bad enough for consumers in September of 1957. But the thought that advertisers were scheming to deprive consumers of their free will by advertising to the subconscious was just too much to bear. James M. Vicary and Francis Thayer had announced that they presented messages such as "Eat popcorn" and "Drink Coca-Cola" for a duration of 1/3000th of a second, well below the threshold for conscious perception, during movie screenings. According to Vicary and Thayer, this subliminal persuasion technique increased popcorn sales 57.5% and cola sales 18.1%. Some unseen stimulus allegedly influenced consumers to buy more snacks at the movies. The implications were staggering: politicians could use subliminal advertising to get elected; anyone who had enough money to subliminally advertise on television could make an unsuspecting public do their bidding. Even a suspecting public might be susceptible to subliminal advertising, since there would be no way know whether advertisements were being played.

Outraged letters and editorials appeared in major magazines and newspapers; both the U.S. Congress and the Federal Communications Commission debated the legal and ethical implications of subliminal advertising. In June, 1958, American networks and the National Association of Broadcasters banned subliminal advertising. The best available evidence, however, suggested that subliminal advertising simply did not work. Vicary's attempts to duplicate his claims under controlled conditions were unsuccessful, at best. In a June, 1962, interview in *Advertising Age,* Vicary admitted that his claim was fraudulent.

No advertising- or consumer-related claim has captured the public imagination quite like the notion that consumers can be persuaded *outside of their conscious awareness* to buy. Vance Packard's (1957) best seller, *The Hidden Persuaders,* described nefarious tricks used by marketing and advertising professionals designed to appeal to consumers' unconscious needs and desires. Published only two years later, Haber's (1959) survey of 324 San Fransiscans revealed that 41% were aware of subliminal advertising, and 50% believed it to be unethical. Still, two-thirds of them were willing to watch a television program even if they knew that subliminal advertising was used in the commercials.

Surveys conducted more recently (Rogers & Smith, 1993; Synodinos, 1988; Zanot, Pincus, & Lamp, 1983) reveal that the public has substantially greater familiarity with subliminal advertising today. Between 74 and 82% of respondents (depending on the survey) claimed to have heard of subliminal advertising. Of those respondents who have heard of subliminal advertising, more than 99% believe that subliminal advertising is actually used and 44 to 48% of respondents believe that they may be susceptible to subliminal advertising. The threat of subliminal advertising has not abated; instead, in the past 50 years the general public has become more aware and more suspicious of subliminal advertising. As described in greater depth later in this chapter, public concern over the power of subliminal advertising is likely quite unfounded. Subliminal advertising is, at best, a very weak force.

However, there *is* evidence that subliminally presented stimuli can influence affect, behavior, and cognition. And subliminal stimulation is not the only way in which we can be influenced without awareness. Consumer-related affect, behavior, and cognition can be, and often is, driven by forces that are at entirely outside of conscious awareness.

IMPLICIT (CONSUMER) COGNITION

The concept of subliminal advertising is but one example of a broader class of phenomena that may be grouped under the label implicit consumer cognition. Before addressing the more specific implicit consumer cognition, consider first implicit cognition, more generally. Implicit cognition is evidenced by the influence of past experience on some task, without conscious recollection or awareness of the influencing experience (e.g., Greenwald & Banaji, 1995; Khilstrom, 1990, 1999; Roediger, 1990; Schacter, 1987).

A classic example of implicit cognition may be found in the study of memory. When presented with a list of words to memorize, amnesiacs show very poor performance on recall and recognition tasks compared to nonamnesiac control subjects. Amnesiacs do not seem to have introspective access to memory. However, when presented with an identical list of words and later asked to complete a series of word fragments or word stems (e.g., c_k_ or pep_ _), the amnesiacs produce previously seen words at essentially the same rate as nonamnesiacs. That is, amnesiacs' past experiences have an influence on subsequent performance that is nearly identical to nonamnesiacs; their implicit memory is every bit as good as unimpaired control subjects (Warrington & Weiskrantz, 1970).

In recent years research on implicit cognition has moved well beyond memory, to the study of social cognition (e.g., attitudes, stereotyping, self-esteem; Greenwald & Banaji, 1995) and, by natural extension, to the study of consumer cognition. Implicit consumer cognition is the unacknowledged or misidentified influence of past experience on consumer-related judgment and behavior. Consumer cognition may be implicit in different ways: Consumers may be unaware of some biasing stimulus (as in the subliminal advertising example); they may be unaware of cognitive processes mediating the relationship between some stimulus and an outcome, or they may be unaware of the actual outcome (Chartrand, 2005). To what extent, though, is consumer behavior driven by influences and processes of which we are unaware?

Decades of research have shown a reliable impact of explicit cognition on consumer behavior. Different models of human cognition have portrayed people as naïve scientists (engaging in careful, semiscientific attempts to understand the world around them), cognitive misers (of limited cognitive capacity, and generally unwilling to expend full cognitive effort), and motivated tacticians (possessing multiple processing strategies and using them according to motivation and ability) (Fiske & Taylor, 1991). Despite numerous differences, all of these models clearly posit the utility of explicit cognition. People process information intentionally and effortfully, and doing so often leads them to correct decisions. In studies of attitude change, for example, people who are both motivated and able to carefully process persuasive information generally come to accept high-quality arguments, and reject low-quality arguments (e.g., Petty & Cacioppo, 1986). Of course, persuasion need not involve extensive cognitive elaboration. People can also be persuaded by lightly processing peripheral cues (e.g., an attractive model may engender positive feelings toward a brand) or by evoking heuristics (e.g., a highly credible source would only endorse a good product).

But given our limited cognitive resources, and the volume of stimuli we encounter each day, it is surely impossible to devote even small amounts of our cognitive resources to *all* of the stimuli we encounter each day. Clearly we cannot always engage in thoughtful, systematic information processing (Bargh, 1997; Kahneman & Triesman, 1984; Posner & Snyder, 1975; Schneider & Shiffrin, 1977). Sometimes our performance is improved when we devote less attention, or fewer cognitive resources, to decisions (e.g., Ambady, Hallahan, & Conner, 1999; Ambady & Rosenthal, 1992, 1993; Dijksterhuis, 2004). Indeed, our frequent inability to correctly explain our own behavior (Nisbett & Wilson, 1977) speaks directly to the notion that we lack conscious awareness of many basic cognitive processes. If we were consciously aware of how and why we do things, we ought to be able to coherently explain how and why we do them. In fact, we are so bad at explaining our own behavior that attempting to do so often fouls up the behavior we are trying to explain (Wilson & Kraft, 1993; Wilson & Schooler, 1991; Schooler, 2002; Schooler, Ohlsson, & Brooks, 1993).

In a remarkably compelling (if somewhat inhumane) example of our inability to make accurate attributions about our behavior, a nonstuttering research participant was induced to stutter via negative reinforcement (Goldiamond, 1965). He was given electric shock while reading aloud, and the shock was stopped only when the participant stuttered. At the end of the session, his rate of stuttering was so high that he received no shocks at all. Two days later he came back to the lab and stuttered so frequently that he was shocked only twice. When asked about his stuttering, he attributed it to his anxiety. When asked directly whether the electric shock could have impacted his stuttering, he claimed that shock had nothing at all to do with his stuttering. Sometimes cognition occurs outside of conscious awareness (in this example, an awareness of the stuttering-shock contingency), and this cognition can have important implications for our behavior, including consumer behavior.

A contemporary explosion of research on implicit cognition continues to reveal ways in which mental processes that occur outside of conscious awareness can have a profound impact on judgment and behavior. This chapter is a review of research and theory on implicit cognition as it applies to consumer behavior, organized into two main sections. The first section addresses implicit measures of attitudes (other than the Implicit Association Test, see chapter 17, this volume), affect, memory, and personality. The second section is devoted to implicit processes and effects, including subliminal persuasion and priming, consumer decision-making, and verbal overshadowing.

IMPLICIT MEASURES

Explicit measures are those that require the respondent to intentionally retrieve some stored information about him- or herself. Explicit attitude measures, such as Likert, Thurstone, or semantic differential measures, require respondents to retrieve stored evaluative information about a particular attitude object. Explicit measures of personality require respondents to indicate the extent to which different trait words, or behaviors, accurately describe them. According to accepted wisdom explicit measures are best used when respondents are willing and able to report on their psychological states. Explicit measures ought to work fine when used to assess attitudes or personality traits of which respondents are consciously aware, and are not wrought with social desirability concerns. On the other hand, explicit measures are thought to be of quite limited utility when the object under consideration is socially undesirable (e.g., prejudice [Crosby, Bromley, & Saxe, 1980], attitudes toward cheating [Corey, 1937]). When people are either unwilling or unable to report their true attitudes, conventional wisdom would advocate the use of implicit, or indirect measures.

Implicit measures also assess stored information about the respondents, but they do not require the respondent to intentionally retrieve the information. Instead, information about the respondent is inferred from the responses to tasks or questions that ostensibly have nothing to do with the respondents' psychological state (attitude, trait, etc.). A classic example of implicit measures is the Thematic Apperception Test (TAT; Morgan & Murray, 1935). The TAT is a projective measure, in which respondents are shown a series of ambiguous images, and asked to write a brief story about each image. Trained coders then rate the story according to prespecified criteria, giving the respondent a score on the dimension of interest (e.g., Need for Affiliation [Winter et al., 1998], attitudes toward union labor [Proshansky, 1948]). Projective implicit measures have fallen out of favor due to perceptions about poor validity and reliability (Lemon, 1973; but see Lundy, 1985; Winter & Stewart, 1977). Contemporary implicit measures rely more on the speed with which respondents can perform certain tasks, such as word categorization; or make word-non-word judgments (e.g., Dovidio, Kawakami, Johnson, Johnson, & Howard, 1997; Fazio, Jackson, Dunton, & Williams, 1995; Greenwald, McGhee, & Schwartz, 1998). The Implicit Association Test (see Perkins, chapter 17, this volume) and the evaluative priming paradigm (Fazio et al., 1995; Wittenbrink, in press) are two such measures. Although both response-time based measures and projective-type measures can be implicit, they seem fundamentally different in terms of the type of information processing each requires.

Different Classes of Measures

In 1964 Cook and Selltiz published an article describing a basic taxonomy of attitude measures. What is remarkable about their taxonomy is the fact that, over 40 years since its publication, it continues to hold up well enough to account for all extant attitude measures. Further, although their analysis was intended to address attitude measures, only, the five classes of measures they identified are more broadly applicable to measures of other constructs such as personality, affect, self-esteem, and so forth.

The first class of measures identified by Cook and Selltiz was self-report measures, now known as explicit measures, in which respondents simply report their attitudes by responding to direct questions. Self-report measures are of obvious importance and utility, but they are not the primary concern here. The second class was behavioral measures, in which attitudes were inferred based on the observation of behavior (e.g., Byrne, Ervin, & Lamberth, 1970; Milgram, Mann, & Harter, 1965; Webb, Campbell, Schwartz, Sechrest, & Grove, 1981). Today behavior is considered more of an attitudinal outcome than an attitude measure (but see Albarracin & Wyer, 2000, Ouellette & Wood, 1998). A third class was comprised of physiological measures. At the time, physiological measures included galvanic skin response, pupillary response, and the like; contemporary physiological measures are far more sophisticated and require expensive and sophisticated equipment (e.g., Cacioppo, Crites, Berntson, & Coles, 1993; Ito & Cacioppo, 2007). The fourth and fifth classes described by Cook and Selltiz are of greatest interest for the present chapter because they are implicit measures, and they have important implications for measurement, predictive ability, and even our understanding of the broader constructs that we are attempting to measure—attitudes, personality, and so forth.

The fourth class of measures identified by Cook and Selltiz (1964) was labeled partially structured (PS) measures. Use of these measures involves presenting respondents with ambiguous stimuli: "while there may be no attempt to disguise the reference to the attitudinal object, the subject is not asked to state his own reactions directly; he is ostensibly describing a scene, a character, or the behavior of a third person" (p. 47). Thus, projective tests fall into this category. Attitude researchers have used projective tests to differentiate between known groups (Proshansky, 1943), and consumer researchers have used such measures to assess attitudes toward different products.

Haire (1950) presented consumers with 7-item shopping lists that were identical except for the type of coffee: half of the respondents read a list that contained Maxwell House drip, and half read a list that contained Nescafe instant. Participants were asked to make judgments about the woman who made the list. They were more likely to describe the woman who used Nescafe as "lazy," "a poor planner," and a "bad wife," suggesting quite negative attitudes toward instant coffee. These classic measures are no longer frequently used, but attitude researchers continue to develop new PS measures.

The Affective Misattribution Paradigm (AMP; Payne, Cheng, Govorun, & Stewart, 2005) fits the profile of PS measures perfectly. The AMP is a computer-mediated task that simply requires participants to evaluate previously unseen, ambiguous Chinese ideographs. The ambiguous ideograph rating task is preceded by the brief (supraliminal) presentation of "real life" images (i.e., attitude objects under consideration, such as African American or Caucasian faces, or images of two competing brands). Participants' ratings of the ideographs are assimilated to their spontaneous, unintentional evaluative responses to the real life images. For example, a Dallas Cowboys fan's ratings of ideographs preceded by Dallas Cowboys imagery would be more positive than those preceded by Pittsburgh Steelers imagery, whereas the opposite would be true for the Steelers fan. Remarkably, participants are given instructions explicitly warning them against being influenced by the real life images, yet evaluative responses to the attitude objects reliably influence ratings of the ideographs. AMP scores reliably correlate with explicit attitude measures, and with self-reported behavioral intentions (i.e., voting intentions; Payne et al., 2005, Study 5). Other types of PS measures have been used to predict behavior in domains with, and without, social desirability concerns.

Vargas, von Hippel, and Petty (2004) developed a measure based on respondents' tendency to contrast information away from their own attitudes (see also Edwards & Smith, 1996; Lord, Ross, & Lepper, 1979). Participants were presented with a series of vignettes describing different characters engaged in ambiguously conflicting behavior. For example, one of the vignettes designed to assess attitudes toward religion was about a character who described herself as "very religious" but who had not attended church services in several years. Instead, she occasionally watched religious programming on television. Following each vignette respondents were asked to indicate how religious they thought each character was (using a pair of 11-point semantic-differential type scales). As expected, religious respondents tended to describe the character as not very religious, and atheistic respondents tended to describe the character as quite religious. Participants' judgments of the targets' religiosity were treated as an implicit (PS) measure of their religious attitudes. This PS measure reliably predicted unique variance in participants' self-reported religious behavior, beyond that predicted by traditional, explicit measures. Similar effects obtained with different vignettes assessing attitudes toward dishonesty, and toward political liberalism and conservatism (Vargas et al., 2004). This measure may be adapted to assess brand attitudes by creating vignettes featuring characters behaving in both positive and negative ways toward a particular brand (e.g., he traveled far to buy a pair of Timberland boots, but he has never worn them outside of his house). It may also be adapted to assess attitudes toward shopping, materialism, or advertising in general. The unique predictive ability of PS measures is important, and we shall return to address this issue shortly. However, it is also important to note that PS measures are not limited to attitudinal studies.

PS measures have also been used to assess prejudice, and predict prejudiced behavior (von Hippel et al., 1995; 1997; Sekaquaptewa et al., 2003; Sekaquaptewa & Espinoza, 2004; Vargas, Sekaquaptewa, & von Hippel, 2004). One such PS measure, called the stereotypic explanatory bias (SEB), relies on Hastie's (1984) finding that people tend to spontaneously explain mildly surprising events (see also Stangor & McMillan, 1992). The SEB measure presents respondents with mildly stereotype-congruent (e.g., Mary asked for help getting home) and -incongruent (e.g., Jenny confronted the man) sentence beginnings, and simply asks respondents to complete the sentences in any way they see fit, so long as they are grammatically correct. High-prejudice respondents are more likely than low-prejudice respondents to explain the stereotype-incongruent sentence beginnings. The SEB measure reliably predicted the tendency to ask sexist questions to a female (Vargas et al., 2004), and stereotypic questions to an African American female (Sekaqupatewa et al., 3002). The SEB seems to emerge more when members of low-status, compared to high-status, groups behave in stereotype-incongruent ways (Sekaquaptewa & Espinoza, 2004). Finally, the SEB measure reliably correlated with a conceptually related, but different PS measure of prejudice (von Hippel et al., 1997).

One might imagine applying the SEB to consumer related research as an implicit measure of country-of-origin (COO) attitudes (see, for example, Liu & Johnson, 2005). Consider a very rough example: Respondents may be presented with sentence beginnings such as, "Paul's Hyundai broke down…" or "The odometer on Cindy's Kia rolled past 100,000 miles…" and researchers would code for continuations or explanations. Individuals with negative attitudes toward Korean automobiles would be more likely to continue the first sentence, e.g., "…for the fifth time that month," and more likely to explain the second sentence, e.g., "…because she religiously followed the maintenance schedule." Individuals with positive attitudes toward Korean automobiles would be more likely to continue the first sentence, and explain the second.

Another PS measure relies on the linguistic intergroup bias (LIB; Maass et al., 1995; Maass et al., 1996), the tendency for people to describe stereotype-congruent events more abstractly than stereotype-incongruent events. In this measure respondents are presented with ersatz newspaper articles written to be either stereotype-congruent (e.g., an article about an African American high school basketball star) or -incongruent (e.g., an article about a Jewish inner-city drug dealer), and asked to indicate the extent to which each of four descriptions, ranging from very concrete to very abstract, accurately convey the main point of each article. Greater prejudice is indicated by the tendency to endorse abstract descriptions ("Washington is athletic") of stereotype-congruent, and concrete descriptions ("Rosenberg sold drugs") of stereotype-incongruent articles. The LIB measure predicted the tendency to evaluate an African American asking for change as threatening (von Hippel et al., 1997).

An LIB measure could also be easily adapted to assess COO effects, and brand attitudes. Respondents might be asked to read favorable or unfavorable stories about specific brands (e.g., a story about a man who has driven his Volvo over one million miles; a story about a man who bought a Saab that broke down as he was leaving the dealer's lot) and asked to indicate the extent to which concrete and abstract descriptions accurately describe the main point of the story. Swedish car aficionados would likely prefer abstract descriptions of the positive stories (e.g., Volvos are reliable), but concrete descriptions of the negative stories (e.g., the Saab broke down quickly); people who dislike Swedish cars would prefer concrete descriptions of the positive stories (the Volvo has been driven far), but abstract descriptions of the negative stories (Saabs are unreliable).

Personality theorists have also made use of PS measures. In administering the TAT measure, respondents are presented with a series of different images, instructions to be creative, and a set of four questions to guide them in writing stories about each of the images (Murray, 1965). As with other implicit measures, there is no mention of the true topic under consideration. Respondents' stories are then coded for the extent to which various motives (e.g., affiliation, achievement, power) are present. For example, David McClelland and colleagues (McClelland, 1985; McClelland, Koestner, & Weinberger, 1989) have used projective measures of individuals' need for achievement to predict long-term behavioral trends and outcomes. Such measures of need for achievement have reliably predicted entrepreneurial activity in the United States (McClelland, 1965) and in India (McClelland, 1987). Similarly, a PS measure of the inhibited power motive predicted managerial success over 16 years (McClelland & Boyatzis, 1982), and elevated blood pressure over 20 years (McClelland, 1979).

Finally, consider measures described earlier assessing implicit memory in amnesiacs. These measures would also be included in Cook and Selltiz's PS category: the extent to which individuals can identify (previously viewed) words presented in a degraded form, or complete words when presented with fragments (e.g., Vi_____ for Viagra; Warrington & Weiskrantz, 1970). Similar word production-type measures have been used to assess affect: ambiguous word fragments may be presented that can be completed with positively- or negatively-valenced words. In a word association task, respondents may be presented with words and asked to generate associates; affective valence of the words, or proportion of emotion-related words, may then be coded. Participants may be given unfamiliar words and asked to rate the valence of those words (Tesser, Millar, & Moore, 1988). In another technique, participants may be told that they had been subliminally presented with a word and asked to select the word they believe was presented from a list. The list from which participants are asked to choose contains an emotion-laden word and some similar-sounding, but affectively neutral foils (Twenge, Catanese, & Baumeister, 2003). Participants tend to select words congruent with their current affective states. Certainly such measures may be used to tap implicit responses to advertising.

Cook and Selltiz's (1964) fifth class of measures was identified as measures of performance on objective tasks (OT). When using these types of measures respondents are presented with, "specific tasks to be performed; they are presented as tests of information or ability, or simply as jobs that need to be done" (p. 50). Classic attitudinal measures of this type include Hammond's (1948) error choice method, in which respondents were presented with an "information test." Items in the test were of two types: the first provided response options that were equidistant and in opposite directions to the truth. For example, "A hypothetical Wal-Mart store employing 200 people would cost local taxpayers *[a] $220,750 or [b] $620,750* per year because of Wal-Mart's low wages and poor benefits packages." The respondent's answer was believed to be influenced by her attitude, such that individuals with positive attitudes toward Wal-Mart would select option a, and those with negative attitudes option b. The second type of question also presented two response options, but the true answer to the question was indeterminate. For example, "Wal-Mart's relationship with the general public could be characterized as *[a] benevolent or [b] malevolent.*" Again, responses to this question should be influenced by attitudes toward the object under consideration. Other classic OT measures include respondents' ability to judge the validity of logically flawed but emotionally charged arguments. In one such study, students from Northern colleges were more likely to accept as true logically flawed arguments in favor of integration, and against segregation; students from Southern colleges tended to show the opposite pattern (Thistlethwaite, 1950; see also Selltiz & Cook, 1966; Waly & Cook, 1965).

Contemporary versions of the "objective tasks" category include the IAT (Greenwald et al., 1998) evaluative priming procedures (Fazio et al., 1995), the affective Simon paradigm (De Houwer & Eelen, 1998), the Go/No-Go Association Task (Nosek & Banaji, 2001), and the emotional Stroop task (Williams, Matthews, & MacLeod, 1996). None of these contemporary measures requires the obfuscation of the attitude object under consideration, and all are presented as tasks to be preformed. Respondents are asked simply to categorize words, make word-nonword judgments, or identify words. Further, contemporary OT measures are quite flexible, and have been used to measure attitudes toward a wide variety of objects, including prejudice, self-esteem, and so forth. The IAT has emerged as the preeminent OT implicit measure, and is covered in depth in this volume (Perkins et al.). Here it may be useful simply to note the existence some other OT implicit measures. As with PS measures, though, OT measures are not limited to attitudes.

The use of implicit measures began with an OT measure of memory. Ebbinghaus (1885/1964) developed a method for studying the effect of consciously inaccessible prior experience on current thought and/or behavior. This first implicit memory measure, called savings, involved a simple procedure. Respondents learned some material, were induced to forget the material via interference, time, etc., and were then asked to relearn the (apparently novel) material. The savings, or difference in speed with which respondents were able to learn the material the second time, serves as a marker of implicit memory. (Of course, the savings paradigm may be used to measure memory whether the material is consciously accessible or not, but it would seem to be particularly useful when material is not consciously accessible.)

An OT measure of affect was developed by Mayer and Hanson (1995). This measure was presented as an "association and reasoning scale" and required participants to respond to different types of questions. One type of question asked participants to indicate "How many thoughts, images, and associations are brought to mind by the word:" and presented positive and negative words (e.g., peace, disappoint). Another type of question asked respondents to indicate the probability of different positive and negative events occurring (e.g., getting a divorce within five years of marriage, the economy will improve within five years). The final type of question was determinant choice, asking participants to select "typical" objects from categories (e.g., types of workers). The response options were positive and negative (e.g., conscientious, lazy, honest). This affect measure correlated .3 to .5 with self-report mood measures.

The description of different types of measures above is not intended to be an exhaustive compendium of all possible implicit measures. Such a task is well beyond the scope of this chapter, especially since new implicit measures seem to be introduced at a very rapid pace. The critical point is that contemporary and classic implicit measures still fit into a distinction between PS and OT that was first suggested over 40 years ago. But it may not be wise to remain content with a categorization scheme simply because it has longevity. Just as there are numerous ways to parse knowledge and information processing (e.g., semantic vs. episodic, procedural vs. declarative, heuristic vs. systematic, etc.) there may be different ways to parse implicit measures.

A Different Classification Scheme

From an information processing perspective Cook and Selltiz's (1964) PS and OT measures have more common ground than differences with one another. It is certainly true that some implicit measures involve the presentation of highly ambiguous stimuli, and others have more of an "objective" feel. However, both types of measures rely on the tendency for some characteristic of the individual (e.g., attitudes, personality, mood) to influence they way in which relevant stimuli are responded to. As noted by Cook and Selltiz, PS measures rely on the notion that "perception of stimuli that are not clearly structured is influenced by the perceiver's own needs and dispositions… the expressed response corresponds directly to the individual's attitude" (pp. 47–48). Similarly, OT measures rely on the notion that, "performance may be influenced by attitude, and that a systematic bias in performance reflects the influence of the attitude" (p. 50). These analyses of the mechanisms underlying PS and OT measures may easily be applied to implicit measures in other domains, as well. Thus, the distinction between PS and OT measures is based more on the differences in the types of stimuli presented to respondents than on the differences in the process underlying responses to the measures. From an information processing perspective, PS and OT measures are quite similar to one another, and yet not all implicit measures are created equal.

We know that some implicit measures differ from others in terms of what aspects of the individual they are tapping. In an excellent demonstration of these differences Smith and Branscombe (1988) had participants either study 24 trait words, or generate those words from behavioral instances and the first letter of the target word (e.g., attended church three times a week = r_____). Next, participants were given one of three memory measures. Two of the memory measures were implicit (category accessibility or word-fragment completion), and the third was explicit (free-recall). Performance on the memory measures was dependent on the type of studying done. Among participants who received the free-recall explicit test, those who generated the words did better than those who read them. Participants who received the word-fragment completion implicit measure showed the opposite pattern: those who read the words did better than those who generated them. But participants who received the category accessibility implicit measure performed more like those who had received the explicit measure: those who generated the words did better than those who read the words. Why would two implicit measures obtain such different patterns of results?

Implicit memory measures may be dissociated from one another because they tap different aspects of learning. The word-fragment completion measure was more sensitive to visual features of the written words, and the reading study condition allowed respondents to focus on similar aspects at study. Respondents who read the words were able to focus on how the words appeared on the printed page, and the word-fragment completion measure similarly taps perceptual information processing. The category accessibility measure was more sensitive to conceptual features of the words, and the generation study condition allowed respondents to focus on the meaning of the words. Test performance was dependent on the degree of match between type of information processing at study and testing phases. Lee (2002) presented very similar results from a set of studies where respondents read brand names in sentences or in isolation, and were given either a word-fragment completion task (perceptual processing) or a "list brands belonging to a particular product category" task (conceptual processing). Participants who read brands in sentences showed better performance on the implicit measure tapping conceptual processing, and those who read brands in isolation showed better performance on the implicit measure tapping perceptual processing. The type of information processing required by an implicit measure might thus be a valuable way to differentiate implicit measures (see also DeCoster, Banner, Smith, & Semin, 2006; Bassili & Brown, 2005).

Each implicit measure likely taps aspects of the individual that are untapped by other implicit measures. So there may be as many ways to differentiate implicit measures as there are measures. However, we may easily differentiate many contemporary implicit measures that rely on response time, and the speed with which respondents can perform tasks, from those that require more careful, deliberative information processing, such as the TAT. Implicit measures may be differentiated by the type, or level, of cognitive processing required to complete the measure. Implicit measures that rely on response times may be categorized as spontaneous; implicit measures that rely on more extensive cognitive processing may be categorized as deliberative; however, this distinction should not be considered a dichotomous split.

No implicit measure may be said to be "process-pure." That is, implicit (and explicit) measures likely involve some aspects of both spontaneous and deliberative information processing (Bassili & Brown, 2005). Even a measure such as the IAT requires respondents to consciously focus on the task at hand, intentionally select one from the different categories to which a target word may belong, and dutifully press a button corresponding to that category. That said, it is clear that some measures rely more on spontaneous information processing, and others rely more on deliberative information processing. The labels spontaneous and deliberative may best be considered anchors at opposite ends of a continuum of information processing. Response time-based measures tend to fall toward the spontaneous end of the continuum, and other implicit measures may be scattered along the remainder of the continuum.

Why Type of Processing Should Matter

There are several interrelated reasons to expect that type of information processing should be a meaningful way to parse implicit attitude measures. First, the type of information processing tapped by a measure might be directly related to the type of behavior one can predict with the measure (Blaxton, 1989; Morris, Bransford, & Franks, 1977; Roediger, 1990). Behaviors, like implicit measures, lie along a continuum ranging from spontaneous to deliberative. Following Fazio's (1990; Fazio & Towles-Schwen, 1999) MODE model of attitude-behavior relations, we might expect that some behaviors are driven by spontaneously activated attitudes, and other behaviors are driven by more carefully thought-out attitudes (see also Ajzen & Fishbein, 1977; Vargas, 2004). To the extent that a measure taps spontaneous processing, it might be expected to predict more spontaneous behavior.

Response time-based implicit attitude measures have reliably predicted some spontaneous behaviors such as nonverbal friendliness toward African American confederates (Dovidio et al., 1997), and condom use with casual partners (Marsh et al., 2001), but they have also been shown to predict somewhat more deliberative behaviors such as smoking, vegetarianism (Swanson, Rudman, & Greenwald, 2001), and consumer choices (Maison, Greenwald, & Bruin, 2004; Wänke, Plessner, & Friese, 2002). Response time-based attitude measures seem to occasionally predict both spontaneous and more deliberative behaviors. However, a case might be made that smoking, vegetarianism, and consumer brand choices may be habitual, automatic behaviors that require little deliberative processing. Vegetarians likely do not think carefully about choosing steak or broccoli; smokers often light up without any awareness of having done so (indeed, many smokers can recall a time they have found themselves facing one lit cigarette in hand, and another in a nearby ashtray); heavy users of Diet Coke do not seem to deliberate over whether to buy Diet Pepsi or Diet Coke. Nevertheless, the data do not match the theory perfectly. The likely cause of this discrepancy between theory and data is the fact that neither implicit measures nor behaviors are process-pure; however, it remains plausible that measures tapping more spontaneous (deliberative) information processing are more likely to be related to behaviors that are more spontaneous (deliberative).

Explicit and implicit measures of personality have also been hypothesized to predict different types of behavior. McClelland, Koestner, and Weinberger (1989) have suggested that implicit measures tap a "more primitive motivational system derived from affective experiences" (p. 690), whereas explicit measures tap "a relatively well-developed concept off the self… and some ideas acquired during socialization as to what is valuable" (p. 697). They have provided evidence for the notion that implicit measures of personality are more closely related to long-term behavioral tendencies where pleasure is derived from the behavior, itself. Explicit measures of personality, on the other hand, are more closely related to immediate behavioral choices where pleasure is derived more from social reinforcement of the behavior.

The second reason to expect that type of information processing should matter has to do with the different aspects of the attitude (trait, mood, etc.) that are tapped by the different measures. Spontaneous implicit measures rely heavily on the automatic accessibility of psychological constructs. For example, both the IAT and the evaluative priming paradigm rely on the automatic activation of attitudes from memory. Thus, one would expect such measures to be particularly likely to predict behaviors that also rely on the automatic activation of attitudes. These behaviors need not be spontaneous behaviors, but they are likely to be behaviors driven primarily by automatically accessed attitudes. More deliberative measures may tap different aspects of the constructs under consideration, and predict different types of behaviors.

PS attitude measures, for example, present respondents with ambiguous stimuli and rely on the tendency for attitudes to influence the perception of that information. Many of the more deliberative OT measures operate on a similar principle. The idea is akin to the classic Hastorf and Cantril (1954) "They saw a game" study. In this study students from Dartmouth and Princeton were shown a film of a football game between the two schools. The students tended to see more fouls and examples of unfair play committed by the rival school than by their own. Their favorable attitudes toward their own schools biased the way they perceived the game (see also Lord, Ross, & Lepper, 1979; Vallone, Ross, & Lepper, 1985).

Consider another example in which one encounters an apparently unattended backpack sitting near a gate at the airport. The bag could be perceived as a place-marker for someone saving a seat in a crowded area, a lost item that ought to be turned in to lost and found, a "finders keepers" opportunity that ought to be picked up and relieved of valuables, or the container of a dangerous explosive that must be reported to the authorities. One's perception of the backpack is likely to predict behavioral response: whether one ignores, turns in, takes, or reports it. While one's evaluative feelings and beliefs (i.e., attitude) about backpacks might play some role in driving these different perceptions and behavioral responses, they are unlikely to account for the lion's share of behavioral variance. Indeed, the different behaviors are unlikely to be predicted by either an explicit attitude measure, or a measure that taps attitude accessibility. A measure that taps perceptions of ambiguous stimuli is most likely to predict behavior in an ambiguous context. Thus, measures that tap different aspects of the construct under consideration are likely to be predictive of corresponding behaviors. This analysis is not intended to imply that one should seek different attitude measures corresponding to different types of behaviors. As noted above, it is unlikely that one would find direct correspondence between the type of processes tapped by a particular attitude measure, and those processes recruited in completing some behavior. Instead, the use of multiple measures would seem most effective (Campbell & Fiske, 1959). Indeed, to the extent that each measure taps a different aspect of the critical construct that measure is likely to add unique predictive ability to a behavior or set of behaviors.

Clearly, behaviors are influenced by multiple factors (Albarracin et al., 2001; Ajzen & Fishbein, 1972; Wicker, 1969, 1971). And since different implicit measures likely tap different aspects of attitudes, it makes sense to use multiple measures in the prediction of behavior. As suggested by the need for affiliation and attitudes toward union labor examples presented above, implicit measures may have utility beyond the assessment of socially undesirable information.

Sometimes different measures will add unique predictive power, such as in Vargas et al. (2004). In a series of four studies, respondents were administered explicit and implicit measures assessing their attitudes toward dishonesty (Study 1), political liberalism and conservatism (Study 2), and religion (Studies 3 and 4). The PS measure used in these studies was described above. In simultaneous multiple regression analyses, the PS measure reliably accounted for significant amounts of unique variance, beyond that predicted by explicit measures, in both self reported behavior (all studies) and actual behavior (Studies 1 and 2). The addition of implicit measures may thus be used to add predictive ability beyond what can be obtained with explicit measures, even when social desirability concerns are not paramount.

Other studies have shown that implicit measures may interact with explicit measures to predict behavior. Constantitian (1981; cited in McClelland, 1985) obtained explicit measures of the extent to which individuals preferred affiliation versus solitude, as well as an implicit TAT measure of the need for affiliation. There were two critical dependent measures: ratings of how much respondents would like taking a country walk with friends, and the proportion of respondents who were found to be writing letters when beeped (participants wore beepers, were beeped seven times a day, and asked to write down their activities when they were beeped). Only individuals who were high on both implicit and explicit affiliation measures were significantly more favorable toward going on a walk with friends. People who had high explicit and implicit needs for affiliation liked an overtly affiliative act. However, individuals who were high on implicit need for affiliation, but low on explicit need for affiliation were most likely to be writing letters when beeped. People who had high implicit but low explicit need for affiliation were most likely to be engaged in an affiliative act that could be performed in solitude.

A pair of longitudinal studies by Winter et al. (1998) also involved the collection of implicit TAT measures of affiliation when the women were of college age, and an explicit measure of extraversion when the women were in their forties. Critical dependent measures in these studies included volunteer work, the tendency to be involved in both work and family roles, marriage and divorce, and dissatisfaction in intimate relationships. There is remarkable consistency in the results: women who showed implicit-explicit consistency (i.e., were high on implicit need for affiliation and high on extraversion, or low on both measures) fared better than their counterparts who showed implicit-explicit inconsistency (i.e., were high on implicit need for affiliation but introverted, or low on implicit need for affiliation but extraverted). Clearly, different implicit measures have utility beyond the assessment of constructs that are socially undesirable.

Implicit measures should not be considered to be secondary to explicit measures, to be used only when explicit measures are expected to be distorted due to social desirability concerns. Implicit measures can and should be used to tap different aspects of attitudes, personality, affect, and so forth, that can contribute to the prediction of behavior. By re-evaluating the utility of implicit measures we may also re-evaluate the constructs we are measuring. Consider attitudes by way of example.

Since Allport's (1935) crowning of attitude as the "most distinctive and indispensable concept in contemporary social psychology" (p. 798), the construct has gone through a number of conceptual or definitional changes. Early definitions of the attitude construct were quite broad: Allport, himself, referred to attitude as, "a mental and neural state of readiness, organized through experience, exerting a directive or dynamic influence upon the individual's response to all objects and situations with which it is related" (1935, p. 810). Krech and Crutchfield (1948) defined attitude as, "an enduring organization of motivational, emotional, perceptual, and cognitive processes with respect to some aspect of the individual's world" (p. 152). Smith, Bruner, and White (1956) defined attitude as, "a predisposition to experience a class of objects in certain ways, with characteristic affect; to be motivated by this class of objects in characteristic ways; and to act with respect to these objects in characteristic fashion" (p. 33). These older definitions of attitude contrast sharply with more limited, contemporary definitions of attitude, such as Eagly and Chaiken's (1993) widely cited definition, "a psychological tendency that is expressed by evaluating a particular entity with some degree of favor or disfavor" (p. 1). The more recent definition likely reflects the tendency in recent decades to measure attitudes with unipolar or bipolar evaluative scales (e.g., Likert, Thurstone, and semantic differential-type measures).

As implicit measures have become more common, more useful, and better understood, it seems worth re-evaluating classic definitions of the attitude construct. The relationship between measurement and theory has been well documented, as both influence one another (Ostrom, 1988). As noted above, personality researchers have come some way in integrating trait theory (typically assessed via explicit measures) and motive theory (typically assessed via implicit measures). It is time for other areas to follow suit, integrating implicit and explicit measures of different constructs. The implicit measures described herein tap much more than evaluative tendencies, and in so doing allow us to think of attitudes as less a static collection of stored evaluative thoughts, and more an expansive, dynamic construct with many different dimensions, influencing affect, cognition, and behavior.

IMPLICIT PROCESSES: DOING WITHOUT UNDERSTANDING

In this section the focus is on the applications of implicit cognition to consumer psychology. The structure of this section is loosely based on Chartrand's (2005) model of automatic processes. According to the model, actors can lack awareness of (a) environmental stimuli that could influence their behavior, (b) automatic processes that mediate behavior, or (c) the outcome, including "behavior, motivation, judgments, decisions, and emotions" (p. 203). We begin with a review of research on environmental influences of which people are unaware (e.g., subliminal influences). Next is a discussion of automatic processes, followed by a few notes on awareness of outcomes. As in the above section, the intent is not to catalog all studies involving implicit processes and/or effects, but rather to provide an overview of the theoretical and empirical work being done in the various research areas.

Subliminal Presentation of Stimuli, and More Overt Priming Effects

Although there is little scientific doubt about the existence of unconscious mental activity, there remain serious questions about subliminal perception and the types of effects it can have. There are a variety of different problems with research involving the presentation of subliminal stimuli, but it is perhaps best to begin with definitional problems, and different usages of the term. Stimuli (visual, auditory, tactile) are said to be subliminal when they are presented in a way that evokes no sensation in a respondent. Pratkanis and Greenwald (1988) defined four categories of subliminal: subthreshold stimuli, or stimuli presented at energy levels too low to be detectable; masked stimuli, or stimuli presented very rapidly and immediately followed by another meaningless stimulus intended to interfere with perception; unattended stimuli, where attention is drawn away from the critical stimulus; and figurally transformed stimuli, including items that are blurred, decomposed, or otherwise rendered unrecognizable, even when attended to. The first two categories fit a psychological definition of subliminal because they evoke the limen.

The threshold, or limen, is the point at which a stimulus evokes a sensation. The concept of an absolute threshold, unfortunately, is essentially like the concept of the Easter Bunny. Thresholds vary both inter- and intrapersonally (Stevens, 1951), and tend to be normally distributed along a continuum. Operationally the threshold may be set by presenting respondents with a large number of trials and finding the central tendency. Items falling below this line are consciously perceived less than 50% of the time, and may be called subliminal. Note that this does not fit the limen "all-or-none" concept of threshold, making true subliminal perception a rather difficult concept to pin down. Synodinos (1988) has recommended a signal detection theory approach to identifying subliminal perception, when d' = 0. These approaches to operationalizing the subliminal presentation of stimuli are objective, and may be contrasted with more subjective approaches.

The emergent consensus on the most appropriate way to identify subliminal perception is to simply ask participants whether they noticed the presentation of a stimulus (Cheesman & Merikle, 1986; Fowler, 1986; Greenwald, 1992; Kihlstrom, 1987; Merikle, 1988). Analogous to the distinction between implicit and explicit memory, Kihlstrom (1999) suggested a distinction between explicit and implicit perception. Explicit perception refers to the conscious awareness of some element in the environment, and the ability to report on that element. Implicit perception is perception without awareness, and may include perceptions of stimuli that are subliminal, or supraliminal. The critical aspect of implicit perception is the inability to consciously report on the presence of the stimuli. If respondents claim to be unable to see the stimulus, then it may be called subliminal. As Kihlstrom notes, this conceptualization also has the advantage of obviating another problem with defining subliminal perception, viz., the limen. Of course, with this approach one still has to worry about respondents being truthful, but incentives may be used to increase respondents' motivation to be truthful. Next is a brief review of research on subliminal persuasion—attempts to influence consumer behavior via the subliminal presentation of stimuli.

In general, the evidence for subliminal persuasion is quite weak. Even early studies with questionable threshold operationalizations failed to obtain reliable effects following presentation of "subliminal" stimuli. In one such study (Champion & Turner, 1959), participants were exposed to either a slide that pictured a spoon full of rice and the words "Wonder Rice" or (as a control) four lines on a black background. The exposure time, aperture opening, and slide construction were manipulated so that the experimenters could no longer detect the presence of a slide, and this was designated subliminal. Evidently, the participants were unable to detect the stimuli, either; the authors concluded that, "subliminal presentation had no effect on the responses of Ss in recognizing the stimulus figure or of associating the brand name with the stimulus figure" (p. 383). Other researchers conducted an on-air study with subliminal advertisements (as above, subliminal was operationalized by the experimenters' inability to detect the stimulus), and before-and-after measures of sales and found no effect at all (DeFleur & Petranoff, 1959). One study that did find an effect (Hawkins, 1970), was replicated only to find no effect (Beatty & Hawkins, 1989). Other studies made more careful efforts to insure that the stimuli were subliminal (George & Jennings, 1975) and still found no effect of presenting the words "Hershey's Chocolate" to experimental participants. A study of a more direct command ("choose this") similarly found no effect on respondents' intention to purchase, use, etc. (Smith & Rogers, 1994).

Many of the critiques of subliminal persuasion studies rest on methodological issues of properly setting stimuli to be subliminal[1]. Moore (1982, 1988) reviewed a number of different studies, pointing out methodological shortcomings ranging from flawed operationalizations of subliminal (e.g., Cupterfain & Clarke, 1985), to logical inconsistencies in what may be expected of subliminal perception even under the best of circumstances (e.g., Kaser, 1986). Evidence for effects of subliminal auditory messages has been similarly weak to nonexistent (Greenwald, Spangenberg, Pratkinis, & Eskenazi, 1991; Merikle, 1988; Pratkanis, Eskenazi, & Grenwald, 1994; Vokey & Read, 1985), until very recently. Kouider & Dupoux (2005) found evidence for unconscious lexical repetition priming, but no evidence of unconscious semantic priming; thus, these effects are not of obvious use to consumer psychology.

In a remarkably comprehensive effort, Pratkanis and Aronson (1992) reviewed over 150 mass media articles and over 200 academic papers and found no clear evidence in support of subliminal persuasion. Pratkanis (1992) listed failures of subliminal persuasion research, "the failure to control for subject expectancy and experimenter bias effects, selective reporting of positive over negative findings, lack of appropriate control treatments, internally inconsistent results, unreliable dependent measures, presentation of stimuli in a matter that is not truly subliminal, and multiple experimental confounds specific to each study" (p. 263).

Other reviews of subliminal persuasion have been more charitable, but still pessimistic about the ultimate value of subliminal advertising. Theus (1994) concludes that there is little evidence for effects of subliminal advertising on brand choice behavior, but suggests that other applications may be more fruitful. She suggests additional research on the use of visual imagery as stimuli, recipient characteristics (e.g., using messages relevant to the audience's needs, hopes, and desires), and repetition of subliminal stimuli. Trappey (1996) conducted a meta-analysis of 23 studies on consumer choice and subliminal advertising and found an average effect size of r = 0.0585. This effect, while certainly small, is not unremarkable—it is larger than the effect of aspirin on heart attacks. However, Trappey did not eliminate studies based on methodological concerns or weaknesses, and he included studies that identified embedded objects as subliminal. So this datum supporting a small effect of subliminal advertising on consumer choice must be considered generous, at best.

Despite the lack of evidence in favor of subliminal persuasion, there is a good deal of evidence demonstrating that the subliminal presentation of stimuli can have some impact on affect, cognition, and behavior. Word-nonword judgments can be speeded following subliminal presentation of a semantically related prime (e.g., priming bread facilitates recognition of butter; Balota, 1983; Fowler, Wolford, Slade, & Tassinary, 1981; Marcel, 1983). Similarly, judgments of word valence can be facilitated by the subliminal presentation of evaluatively congruent primes (Greenwald, Klinger, & Liu, 1989). Social judgments, too, can be impacted by the subliminal priming of trait words. Bargh and Pietromonaco (1982) had participants engage in a "vigilance task" in which words were presented subliminally. Either zero, 20%, or 80% of the words were related to the concept of hostility. Following the vigilance task, participants read an ambiguous paragraph about a fictional character named Donald, and rated him on a variety of dimensions. The greater percentage of hostile words they had been exposed to, the more negatively they rated Donald (see also Chen & Bargh, 1997; Erdley & D'Agostino, 1988). Finally, we know that subliminally presented stimuli can also impact attitudes.

The mere exposure effect (Zajonc, 1968) posits greater liking of a stimulus as a result of greater exposure to the stimulus. Kunst-Wilson and Zajonc (1980) subliminally presented polygons to participants via tachistoscope, and found that the more times a stimulus had been presented the better it was liked (see also Bornstein, 1992). A similar effect has also been demonstrated with the subliminal presentation of human faces (Bornstein, Leone, & Galley, 1987). Although not strictly subliminal in the subthreshold or masked sense of the term (Pratkanis & Greenwald, 1988), a similar effect was obtained with aurally presented information in a dichotic listening task (Anand & Sternthal, 1991). Further, some research has demonstrated that subliminal exposure to stimuli can also increase disliking of those stimuli (Mandler, Nakamura, & Van Zandt, 1987; Seamon, McKenna, & Binder, 1998). Subliminal primes can also be used in a value-transfer procedure. Murphy and Zajonc (1993) found that unfamiliar Chinese ideographs preceded by subliminal presentation of smiling faces were liked more than those subliminally preceded by scowling faces. And Krosnick, Betz, Jussim, and Lynn (1992) demonstrated a subliminal version of classical conditioning—preceding some faces with subliminal presentation of positive images, and others with negative images caused liking and disliking, respectively (see also De Houwer, Hendrickx, & Baeyens, 1997). The applications to advertising and consumer psychology are obvious, but inducing liking is a long way from making people get out of their seats at the movies to buy more popcorn and soda.

Other lines of research have demonstrated reliable effects of subliminal priming on judgments about the self and on behavior. For example, subliminal presentation of threatening stimuli has been shown to increase self-reported anxiety (Robles, Smith, Carver, & Wellens, 1987). A number of studies have subliminally activated stereotypes and demonstrated behavioral assimilation to those stereotypes. Elderly participants subliminally exposed to words reflecting positive aspects of the elderly stereotype (e.g., wise) have been shown to walk faster (Hausdorff, Levy, & Wei, 1999) and show improved memory (Levy, 1996); but elderly participants exposed to negative aspects of the elderly stereotype (e.g., senile) show worsened memory (Levy, 1996). Caucasian male undergraduates subliminally presented with African American faces became more hostile in the face of frustration (Bargh, Chen, & Burrows, 1996). Wyer (chapter 2, this volume) reviews additional research along these lines.

Two recent studies have shown effects of subliminally priming motives or goals on behavior, and on responses to advertising. Cooper and Cooper (2002) had participants watch an episode of *The Simpsons* and subliminally presented experimental participants with words and images pertaining to thirst, while control participants were subliminally presented with blank slides. Participants in the experimental condition subsequently rated themselves as thirstier than those in the control condition. Strahan, Spencer, and Zanna (2002) likewise subliminally primed people with either thirst-related or neutral words (Study 1) and found no effect on self-reported thirst; however, thirst-primed respondents drank significantly more liquid than neutral-primed participants. In a follow-up study, thirst-primed participants were more favorable than neutral-primed participants toward an advertisement for a thirst-quenching sports drink, but no difference emerged for an advertisement for an electrolyte-restoring sports drink. Conceptually similar results emerged in a third study, where subliminally presented sad-face primes caused respondents who expected to interact with another to prefer a mood-restoring music CD, and to choose to listen to more songs from the mood-restoring CD.

Subliminally presented stimuli can also have an impact on persuasion, but in a rather indirect fashion. Weisbuch, Mackie, and Garcia-Marques (2003) examined the effects of prior source exposure on persuasion. In two studies participants were either not exposed, subliminally exposed, or explicitly exposed to a face, and then presented with persuasive arguments ostensibly made by the same person. In both studies subliminal exposure to the source increased agreement with the arguments. The authors suggested that this effect was due to positive affect toward the source being misattributed to the persuasive arguments.

Before concluding this section it is worth briefly noting some studies that examined the effects of "subliminal" embeds on consumer response (Although, as noted above, embedded figures may more accurately be described as unattended stimuli [Pratkanis & Greenwald, 1988]). Research on sexually embedded stimuli is mixed: Two studies (Caccavale, Wanty, & Edell, 1989; Gable, Wilkins, Harris, & Feinberg, 1987) report no effect on consumer attitudes, but Aylesworth, Goodstein, and Kalra (1999) report an effect of increased upbeat feelings reported by men (but not women), and an effect of increased negativity by both men and women. Bagley and Dunlap (1980, cited in Aylesworth et al., 1999) report that sexual embeds led respondents to report feeling "turned on." Kilbourne, Painton, and Ridley (1985) report an effect of sexual embeds on favorable attitudes toward a liquor ad, but not a cigarette ad. In a second (within subjects) study respondents showed increased GSR when shown embedded versions of the ads. The data addressing the efficacy of sexual embeds is equivocal, at best, contrary to sensationalistic claims by Packard (1957) and Key (1973, 1976, 1980).

Subliminal persuasion is, simply put, unlikely; and the effects of subliminal advertising are certainly nowhere near those suggested by Vicary. But subliminally presented stimuli can influence semantic, evaluative, and social judgments, as well as attitudes, behavior, and the processing of ostensibly unrelated information. In short, the evidence collected to date suggests that subliminal stimuli can be used to evoke abstract concepts and affect, and can influence related judgments and behaviors where the primed concepts can reasonably be availed (e.g., increase hostility in an already frustrating situation, walk more slowly when asked to walk down a hall, drink more of a beverage when thirsty). But subliminal stimuli cannot be used to directly persuade or dictate behavior (i.e., cause hostile outbursts without provocation, get up and walk down the hallway, go to the soda machine and buy a beverage). Increasing accessibility via subliminal priming is possible, and it can affect behavior to the extent that the newly accessible primes are applicable to the current situation.

An important note about the research described in this section: many of the effects described herein resulting from subliminal presentation of stimuli can also be achieved with supraliminal primes. Interested readers should consult Wyer (chapter 2, this volume) for a thorough review of accessibility effects on judgment and behavior.

At this point we consider situations in which consumers lack introspective access to their own cognitive processes. Individuals may be aware of potentially influential stimuli, and some outcome, but not of the mediating cognitive processes. The process by which supraliminal primes affect judgment, behavior, attitudes, and so forth, is outside of conscious awareness (Chartrand, 2005). Indeed, when respondents become aware of the prime's relationship with the critical dependent variable supraliminal primes tend to be ineffective (see Bornstein, 1992), or cause contrast effects, instead of assimilative tendencies. In these cases participants show reactance, or more conscious and deliberative correction strategies (see Wegener & Petty, 1995). Somewhat strangely, supraliminal primes can also cause contrast effects when participants are unaware of the prime's relationship with the dependent variable (see Wheeler & Petty, 2001). The extent to which primes can evoke contrast effects is one of many unanswered questions awaiting future research.

Aware of the Stimulus, but Unaware of the Cognitive Processes

One area where surprisingly little research has been conducted is that of actual purchasing behavior. Certainly a great deal of buying is done purposefully, intentionally, and deliberatively; however, there may be innumerable forces acting outside of conscious awareness that influence what, when, and how we buy (Simonson, 2005). Morwitz, Fitzsimons, and colleagues have done a great deal of work on the mere-measurement effect (Fitzsimons & Morwitz, 1996; Fitzsimons & Shiv, 2001; Fitzsimons & Williams, 2000; Morwitz & Fitzsimons, 2004; Morwitz, Johnson, & Schmittlein, 1993; Williams, Fitzsimons, & Block, 2004). In a series of studies, these researchers have shown that simply asking consumers about their purchase intentions can increase the likelihood of purchase. Asking general, category-level questions (e.g., how likely are you to purchase an automobile?) increases the likelihood of purchase in that product category. Asking category-level questions to regular users of a brand causes greater likelihood of specific brand repurchase, and asking category-level questions to nonusers causes greater likelihood of category leader purchase.

The mere-measurement effect seems to emerge because asking intention questions increases the accessibility of attitudes toward specific members of the product category. Further, the effect seems to dissipate when respondents recognize the intention questions as persuasion attempts. Clearly, participants in these studies are aware of the environmental stimulus (i.e., a direct question about purchase intentions), but they are unaware of the automatic processes evoked by the question (increased attitude accessibility). This general idea is a familiar one: people often lack awareness of, and introspective access to, the cognitive processes mediating their behavior (Bargh, 1997; Hefferline, Keenan, & Harford, 1958; Kahneman, 2003; Langer, 1978; Lowenstein, 2001; Nisbett & Wilson, 1977).

Although Theus's (1994) suggestions for further research have been largely addressed, there are numerous unanswered questions, particularly those pertaining to the specific mechanisms by which (subliminal) priming has its effects, and the extent to which priming techniques can usefully (and ethically) be applied to consumer decisions making and behavior. Greenwald, Draine, and Abrams (1996) suggested that semantic and evaluative priming may be due to spreading activation processes; Klinger, Burton, and Pitts (2000) argued for a response competition account of the same effects. Wheeler and Petty (2001) suggested that behavioral effects of priming stereotypes may be due to either hot (stereotype-threat) or cold (ideomotor) cognitive processes. Janiszeski and van Osselaer (2005) proposed a nonconscious behavioral choice model wherein multiple behavioral outcomes are aroused by a prime, and the emergent behavior is selected on the basis of activation and evaluation of multiple possible behaviors. Dijksterhuis, Smith, van Baaren, and Wigboldus (2005) described low and high roads to priming effects on behavior. The low road is a simple ideomotor (mimicry) process, hard-wired in mirror-neurons found in both humans and monkeys (see Iacoboni, Woods, Brass, Bekkering, Mazziotta, & Rizzolatti, 1999); the high road is more like a spreading activation process, in which abstract concepts are activated (e.g., stereotypes, traits, goals) and concept-relevant behavior emerges, given the appropriate opportunity. Mirror neurons may be involved in concept (high road) priming, as well. Recent research suggests that mirror neurons are sensitive to contextual cues, and behavioral intentions (Iacoboni, Molnar-Szakacs, Gallese, Buccino, Mazziotta, & Rizzolati, 2005).

In the consumer domain, it seems possible that different processes could mediate the effects of priming on subsequent tasks. Priming motives or goals may initiate hot cognition, and priming less personally involving concepts may initiate cold, ideomotor cognition. Developing a methodology to test hypotheses about mediating cognitive processes will represent a major step toward improving our understanding of priming. Since most of the work on implicit cognition—including subliminal perception—has been conducted by cognitive psychologists, we are only now beginning to scratch the surface of social and consumer-related applications.

A different line of work wherein people appear to have very limited introspective access to their own cognitive processes is in the use of "thin-slices" of behavior to make judgments. Ambady and colleagues have demonstrated that people can make surprisingly accurate and reliable assessments of easily observable personality traits, interpersonal motives, and job performance based on very limited amounts of information. Less observable traits (e.g., intelligence, analytic abilities) can also be assessed, but not with the same degree of reliability. In a typical study, naïve participants were exposed to three 10-second video clips of university teachers, and were asked to rate the targets on a series of 15 different personality traits (e.g., accepting, confident, honest, etc.). The participants' ratings were significantly correlated with teaching evaluations made by students in the classes from which the videotaped information was taken. A total of 30 seconds worth of dynamic information enabled naïve perceivers to make effectiveness ratings that corresponded with students who had a full semester's worth of information on which they could base their evaluations (Ambady & Rosenthal, 1993).

In a more direct application to consumer research, Ambady, Krabbenhoft, and Hogan (2006) demonstrated that naïve raters could accurately judge the effectiveness of salespeople based on three 20-second audio clips—with the semantic content filtered out. Participants listened to a total of 60 seconds worth of audio clips for each salesperson that effectively conveyed just the tone of the speaker's voice. Based on this information, participants rated the salespeople on 19 traits (e.g., achievement-oriented, empathic, supportive, etc.). The traits were grouped into three composite variables—interpersonal, task-oriented, and anxious, and these composites were correlated with managers' ratings of the salespeople. Participants' interpersonal and anxiety ratings were significantly correlated (r's > .50) with managers' assessments of the salespeople's effectiveness. In a second study, the content of the speech was retained in the 20-second audio clips. This time only participants' interpersonal ratings were correlated with managers' ratings of the sales people. Having more information (i.e., knowing *what* was said in study two, as opposed to knowing only *how* something was said in study one) actually impaired naïve judges' ability to accurately evaluate the salespeople.

A good deal of research suggests that the ability to read thin slices of behavior is largely automatic (see Ambady, Bernieri, & Richeson, 2000). First, participants in thin slicing studies are unable to articulate (i.e., tend to be unaware of) the criteria they use to make judgments (Smith, Archer, & Costanzo, 1991); and asking participants explain the reasons for their judgments causes poorer performance (Ambady & Gray, 2002). Second, adding a cognitive load manipulation, which tends to disrupt controlled information processing, does not affect the accuracy of judgments based on thin slices of behavior (Ambady & Gray, 2002). Finally, increased effort, in the form of incentives, does not seem to improve performance (Bernieri & Gillis, 1995). Thus, the processes by which people make judgments based on thin slices of behavior tend to be consciously inaccessible and remain unaffected by attempts at either disruption or enhancement.

Because the participants in these studies seem to be unable to tell researchers how they make these judgments, the causal mechanism(s) underlying thin slice effects remain open to question. Ambady et al. (2000) have suggested that people are essentially relying on their stereotypes to make thin slice judgments. Consistent with the stereotyping account, Alba (2006) has suggested that halo effects may be at least partially behind the findings. People may be responding to physical features of the target, such as attractiveness, or baby-facedness (see Hassin & Trope, 2000). Peracchio and Luna (2006) suggest that affective responses might be driving thin slice effects. People may make judgments by relying on positive or negative feelings aroused by the thin slices of information (see Pham, Cohen, Pracejus, & Hughes, 2001; Pham & Avnet, 2005, for similar accounts of persuasion processes).

Another open question concerns conditions under which judgments based on thin slices are effective. Kardes (2006) applied Hogarth's (2001, 2005) learning structure model to analyze this problem, and suggested that thin slice judgments are most trustworthy when feedback quality is high (i.e., "frequent, prompt, and diagnostic," [p. 21]), and errors are consequential. These conditions enable people to learn very effectively, and make accurate judgments based on experience. When feedback quality is low, or when errors are relatively inconsequential, judgments based on thin slices of information are less likely to be accurate. This analysis, as well as further applications of the thin slicing research paradigm to consumer psychology, await empirical testing.

The thin slice paradigm presented by Ambady et al. (2006) may be useful for employers seeking to hire salespeople, but the general technique of thin slicing may be of use to others, as well, once boundary conditions are better understood. Spokespeople and product endorsers may be judged for credibility and trustworthiness using the thin slice technique (Ambady et al., 2006). Consumers and consumer researchers may use the technique to evaluate salespeople, lawyers, physicians, politicians, Web sites, brands, advertisements, customer service interactions, and so forth (Alba, 2006; Peracchio & Luna, 2006).

Applications of Implicit Memory. The literature on implicit memory, as it pertains to consumer psychology, is substantially smaller than that on subliminal perception and priming effects. Most of the implicit memory research in consumer psychology focuses on dissociations between implicit and explicit memory (with the notable exception of Lee, 2002, above), suggesting that explicit memory tests may not tell the full story with regard to brand awareness, or advertising efficacy.

A good example of implicit-explicit memory dissociation is in Jacoby, Kelley, Brown, and Jasechko's (1989) "false fame" effect. In the false fame effect, nonfamous names presented at time one are likely to be mistakenly identified as famous at time two, 24 hours later. Participants have no explicit recollection of the names, but their sense of familiarity with the previously presented nonfamous names leads them to attribute false fame. The same effect can emerge among brand names (Holden & Vanheule, 1999). Participants have no explicit awareness of having seen brand names previously, but are likely to identify them as "real" brands. In a somewhat related vein, Butler and Berry (2001) found that previously shown brand names were more likely to be selected at time two, even when the product was different (e.g., brand X peaches at time one, brand X tomato sauce at time two). Importantly, this effect emerged among participants who showed no awareness of the primary aims of the study.

When examining memory for brands, Krishnan and Shapiro (1996) found that high-frequency brand names (e.g., Apple) are more likely to appear on word-stem completion measures than low-frequency brand names (e.g., Zenith). Further, semantic elaboration of brand names improved explicit memory over sensory elaboration, but showed no effect on implicit measures. Law and Braun (2000) used explicit and implicit measures to assess the impact of product placement on consumer memory and choice behavior. The explicit measures in this study were recognition and recall of products in a television show; the implicit measure was simply whether respondents chose a brand or not. Respondents showed better explicit memory for products that were central to the show, but centrality had little impact on the implicit choice measure. Also, products that were seen-only (as opposed to heard-only, and seen/heard) were most likely to be chosen on the implicit measure, but were the least likely to be recalled.

Acting Without Knowing: Awareness of Outcomes

Although there is a great deal of psychological research on behavior without awareness, the work on consumer behavior without awareness is limited, to say the least. The scientific study of behavior without awareness is a tricky business largely because conceptual and operational definitions of behavior without awareness are many and varied (see Adams, 1957; Frensch & Rünger, 2003). People may be unaware of the behavior, itself (e.g., the may not realize they are tapping their foot). People may be unaware of some behavior's relation to a contingent event (e.g., greater likelihood of buying as a function of having been asked a question about a product category). They may be unaware of physiological responses to stimuli (e.g., pupillary response, GSR). They may be unaware of goal activation, learning, and so forth.

It is clear enough that people cannot be aware of differential behavior as a function of subliminally presented stimuli. And it is generally assumed that people are unaware of subtle changes in their behavior as a result of priming manipulations. As noted above, when people become aware of these contingencies they tend to react against the primes. Still, it is uncertain whether people are consciously aware of their own tendencies toward reactance. The reactance, itself, could be operating automatically, outside of conscious awareness. A fuller discussion of implicit outcomes is beyond the scope of the present chapter, more deserving of a separate chapter. But it is also certainly an area ripe for future study.

CONCLUSIONS

Another unanswered research question is the extent to which implicit processes actually drive consumer behavior. Simonson (2005) argued that implicit cognition is unlikely to account for much of the variance in consumer choice and decision-making because most shopping environments are so cluttered with potentially priming stimuli that all primes would effectively wash one another out. Further, he argues that models of conscious, deliberative information processing and consumer choice (e.g., Bettman, Luce, & Payne, chapter 23, this volume) do a very good job of predicting behavior. He notes, "at this point it appears highly unlikely that the explanatory power offered by an analysis of unconscious influences will approach that provided by the assumption that choices are largely determined by conscious processing of task-relevant inputs" (p. 214).

While Simonson (2005) does not go so far as to suggest abandoning research on implicit consumer cognition (on the contrary, he is very encouraging), his comments are somewhat reminiscent of Mischel's (1968) assessment of personality research, and Wicker's (1969, 1971) critique of the attitude construct. Wicker's suggestion to consider abandoning the attitude construct for more fruitful areas of research was followed by a decade of enormous strides in understanding the relationship between attitudes and behavior (e.g., Ajzen & Fishbein, 1977; Fazio, Zanna, & Cooper, 1978; Fishbein, 1980; Fishbein & Ajzen, 1974). Now, over 35 years later, we are faced with a similar opportunity to conduct watershed research enabling a greater understanding of introspectively inaccessible cognitions and their influence on (consumer) behavior.

NOTE

1. An early criticism of the Vicary movie theater "study" was the claim that stimuli were presented at 1/3000 second. McConnell, Cutler, and McNeil (1958) expressed skepticism that 1/3000 second was "far faster than any previously reported stimulation" (p. 230).

REFERENCES

Adams, J. K. (1957). Laboratory studies of behavior without awareness. *Psychological Bulletin, 54,* 383–405.

Aizen, I., & Fishbein, M. (1977). Attitude-behavior relations: A theoretical analysis and review of empirical research. *Psychological Bulletin, 84,* 888–918.

Alba, J. W. (2006). Let the clips fall where they may. *Journal of Consumer Psychology, 16,* 14–19.

Albarracin, D., Johnson, B. T., Fishbein, M., & Muellerleile, P. A. (2001). Theories of reasoned action and planned behavior as models of condom use: A meta-analysis. *Psychological Bulletin, 127,* 142–161.

Albarracin, D., & Wyer. (2000). The cognitive impact of past behavior: influences on belief, attitudes, and future behavioral decisions. *Journal of Personality and Social Psychology, 79,* 5-22.

Allport, G. W. (1935). Attitudes. In C. Murchison (Ed.), *Handbook of social psychology* (pp. 798–884). Worcester, MA: Clark University Press.

Ambady, N., Bernieri, F. J., & Richeson, J. A. (2000). Toward a histology of social behavior: Judgmental accuracy from thin slices of the behavioral stream. In M. P. Zanna (Ed.), *Advances in experimental social psychology* (Vol. 32, pp. 201–271). San Diego, CA: Academic Press.

Ambady, N., & Gray, H. (2002). On being sad and mistaken: Mood effects on the accuracy of thin slice judgments. *Journal of Personality and Social Psychology, 83,* 947–961.

Ambady, N., & Hallahan, M. & Conner, B. (1999). Accuracy of judgments of sexual orientation from thin slices of behavior. *Journal of Personality and Social Psychology, 77,* 538–547.

Ambady, N., Krabbenhoft, M. A., & Hogan, D. (2006). The 30-sec scale: Using thin-slice judgments to evaluate sales effectiveness. *Journal of Consumer Psychology, 16,* 4–13.

Ambady, N., & Rosenthal, R. (1993). Half a minute: Predicting teacher evaluations from thin slices of nonverbal behavior and physical attractiveness. *Journal of Personality and Social Psychology, 64,* 431–441.

Ambady, N., & Rosenthal, R. (1992). Thin slices of expressive behavior as predictors of interpersonal consequences: A meta-analysis. *Psychological Bulletin, 111,* 256–274.

Anand, P., & Sternthal, B. (1991). Perceptual fluency and affect without recognition. *Memory & Cognition, 19,* 293–300.

Aylesworth, A. B., Goodstein, R. C., & Kalra, A. (1999). Effect of archetypal embeds on feelings: An indirect route to affecting attitudes? *Journal of Advertising, 28,* 73–81.

Balota, D. A. (1983). Automatic semantic activation and episodic memory. *Journal of Verbal Learning and Verbal Behavior, 22,* 88–104.

Bargh, J. A. (1997). The automaticity of everyday life. In R. S. Wyer (Ed.), *Advances in Social Cognition* (Vol. 10, pp. 1–61). Mahwah, NJ: Erlbaum.

Bargh, J. A., & Pietromonaco, P. (1982). Automatic information processing and social perception: The influence of trait information presented outside of conscious awareness on impression formation. *Journal of Personality and Social Psychology, 43,* 437–449.

Bargh, J. A., Chen, M., & Burrows, L. (1996). Automaticity of social behavior: Direct effects of trait construct and stereotype activation on action. *Journal of Personality and Social Psychology, 71*(2), 230–244.

Bassili, J. N., & Brown, R. (2005). Implicit and explicit attitudes: Research, challenges and theory. In D. Albarracín, B. T. Johnson, & M. P. Zanna (Eds.), *Handbook of attitudes and attitude change*. Mahwah, NJ: Erlbaum.

Beatty, S. E., & Hawkins, D. I. (1989). Subliminal stimulation: Some new data and interpretation. *Journal of Advertising, 18*, 4–8.

Bernieri, F. J., & Gillis, J. S. (1995). Personality correlates of accuracy in a social perception task. *Perceptual and Motor Skills, 81*(1), 168–170.

Blaxton, T. A. (1989). Investigating dissociations among memory measures: Support for a transfer appropriate processing framework. *Journal of Experimental Psychology: Learning, Memory, and Cognition, 15*, 657–668.

Bornstein, R. F. (1992). Subliminal mere exposure effects. In R. F. Bornstein & T. S. Pittman (Eds.), *Perception without awareness* (pp. 191–210). New York: Guilford.

Bornstein, R. F. (1992). Critical importance of stimulus unawareness for the production of subliminal psychodynamic activation effects: An attributional model. *Journal of Nervous and Mental Disease, 180*(2), 69–76.

Bornstein, R. F., Leone, D. R., & Galley, D. J. (1987). The generalizability of subliminal mere exposure effects: Influence of stimuli perceived without awareness on social behavior. *Journal of Personality and Social Psychology, 53*, 1070–1079.

Byrne, D., Ervin, C. R., & Lambert, J. (1970). Continuity between the experimental study of attraction and real-life computer dating. *Journal of Personality and Social Psychology, 16*, 157–165.

Butler, L. T., & Berry, D. C. (2001). Transfer effects in implicit memory and consumer choice. *Applied Cognitive Psychology, 15*, 587–601.

Caccavale, J. G., Wanty, T. C., III, & Edell, J. A. (1979). Subliminal implants in advertisements: An experiment. *Association for Consumer Research Proceedings, 9*, 418–423.

Cacciopo, J. T., Crites, S. L., Bernston, G. G., & Coles, M. G. (1993). If attitudes affect how stimuli are processed, should not they affect the event-related brain potential? *Psychological Science, 4*, 108–112.

Campbell, D. T., & Fiske, D. W. (1959). Convergent and discriminant validation by the multitrait-multimethod matrix. *Psychological Bulletin, 56*, 81–105.

Champion, J. M., & Turner, W. W. (1959). An experimental investigation of subliminal perception. *Journal of Applied Psychology, 43*, 382–384.

Chartrand, T. L. (2005). The role of conscious awareness in consumer behavior. *Journal of Consumer Psychology, 15*(3), 203–210.

Cheesman, J., & Merikle, P. M. (1986). Distinguishing conscious from unconscious perception. *Canadian Journal of Psychophysics, 40*, 343–367.

Chen, M., & Bargh, J. A. (1997). Nonconscious behavioral confirmation processes: The self-fulfilling consequences of automatic stereotype activation. *Journal of Experimental Social Psychology, 33*, 541–560.

Coates, S. L., Butler, L. T., & Berry, D. C. (2004). Implicit memory: A prime example for brand consideration and choice. *Applied Cognitive Psychology, 18*(9), 1195–1211.

Cooper, J., & Cooper, G. (2002). Subliminal motivation: A story revisited. *Journal of Applied Social Psychology, 32*, 2213–2227.

Cook, S. W., & Selltiz, C. (1964). A multiple-indicator approach to attitude measurement. *Psychological Bulletin, 62*, 36–55.

Constantian, C. A. (1981). Attitudes, beliefs, and behavior in regard to spending time alone. Unpublished doctoral dissertation, Harvard University, Cambridge, MA.

Corey, S. M. (1937). Professed attitudes and actual behavior. *Journal of Educational Psychology, 28*, 217–280.

Crosby, E., Bromley, S., & Saxe, L. (1980). Recent unobtrusive studies of Black and White discrimination and prejudice: A literature review. *Psychological Bulletin, 87*, 546–563.

Cuperfain, R., & Clarke, T. K. (1985). A new perspective of subliminal perception. *Journal of Advertising, 14*, 36–41.

DeCoster, J., Banner, M. J., Smith, E. R., & Semin, G. R. (2006). On the inexplicability of the implicit: Differences in the information provided by implicit and explicit tests. *Social Cognition, 24*, 5–21.

DeFleur, M. L. & Petranoff, R. M. (1959). A televised test of subliminal persuasion. *Public Opinion Quarterly, 23*, 168–180.

De Houwer, J., & Eelen, P. (1998). An affective variant of the Simon paradigm. *Cognition and Emotion, 12*, 45–61.

De Houwer, J., Hendrickx, H., & Baeyens, F. (1997). Evaluative learning with "subliminally" presented stimuli. *Consciousness and Cognition, 6,* 87–107.

Dijksterhuis, A. (2004). Think different: The merits of unconscious thought in preference development and decision making. *Journal of Personality and Social Psychology, 87,* 586–598.

Dijksterhuis, A., Aarts, H., Bargh, J. A., & van Knippenberg, A. (2000). On the relation between associative strength and automatic behavior. *Journal of Experimental Social Psychology, 36*(5), 531–544.

Dijksterhuis, A., & Smith, P. K. (2005). What do we do unconsciously? And how? *Journal of Consumer Psychology, 15*(3), 225–229.

Dijksterhuis, A., Smith, P. K., van Baaren, R. B., & Wigboldus, D. H. J. (2005). The unconscious consumer: Effects of environment on consumer behavior. *Journal of Consumer Psychology, 15*(3), 193–202.

Dovidio, J., Kawakami, K., Johnson, C., Johnson, B., & Howard, A. (1997). The nature of prejudice: Automatic and controlled processes. *Journal of Experimental Social Psychology, 33,* 510–540.

Eagly, A. H., & Chaiken, S. (1993). *The psychology of attitudes.* Fort Worth, TX: Harcourt Brace.

Ebbinghaus, H. (1964). *Memory: A contribution to experimental psychology.* New York: Dover. (Original work published in 1885; translated 1913)

Erdley, C. A., & D'Agostino, P. R. (1988). Cognitive and affective components of automatic priming effects. *Journal of Personality and Social Psychology, 54,* 741–747.

Edwards, K., & Smith, E. E. (1996). A disconfirmation bias in the evaluation of arguments. *Journal of Personality and Social Psychology, 71,* 5–24.

Fazio, R. H. (1990). Multiple processes by which attitudes guide behavior: The MODE model as an integrative framework. In M. P. Zanna (Ed.), *Advances in experimental social psychology* (Vol. 23, pp. 75–109). San Francisco: Academic Press.

Fazio, R. H., & Towles-Schwen, T. (1999). The MODE model of attitude-behavior processes. In S. Chaiken & Trope, Y. (Eds.), *Dual-process theories in social psychology* (pp. 97–116). New York: Guilford.

Fazio, R. H., Jackson, J. R., Dunton, B. C., & Williams, C. J. (1995). Variability in automatic activation as an unobstrusive measure of racial attitudes: A bona fide pipeline? *Journal of Personality and Social Psychology, 69,* 1013–1027.

Fazio, R. H., Zanna, M. P., & Cooper, J. (1978). Direct experience and attitude-behavior consistency: An information processing analysis. *Personality and Social Psychology Bulletin, 4,* 48–51.

Fiske, S. T., & Taylor, S. E. (1991). *Social cognition* (2nd ed.). New York: McGraw Hill.

Fishbein, M. (1980). A theory of reasoned action: Some applications and implications. In H. Howe & M. Page (Eds.), *Nebraska symposium on motivation* (Vol. 27, pp. 65–116). Lincoln: University of Nebraska Press.

Fishbein, M., & Ajzen, I. (1974). Attitudes toward objects as predictors of single and multiple behavioral criteria. *Psychological Review, 81,* 59–74.

Fitzsimons, G. J., & Morwitz, V. G. (1996). The effect of measuring intent on brand-level purchase behavior. *Journal of Consumer Research, 23,* 1–11.

Fitzsimons, G. J., & Shiv, B. (2001). Nonconscious and contaminative effects of hypothetical questions on subsequent decision making. *Journal of Consumer Research, 28,* 224–238.

Fitzsimons, G. J., & Williams, P. (2000). Asking questions can change choice behavior: Does it do so automatically or effortfully? *Journal of Experimental Psychology: Applied, 6,* 195–206.

Fowler, C. A., Wolford, G., Slade, R., & Tassinary, L. (1981). Lexical access with and without awareness. *Journal of Experimental Psychology: General, 110,* 341–362.

Frensch, P. A., & Rünger, D. (2003). Implicit learning. *Current Directions in Psychological Science, 12,* 13–18.

Gable, M., Wilkens, H. T., Harris, L., & Feinberg, R. (1987). An evaluation of subliminally embedded sexual stimuli in graphics. *Journal of Advertising, 16,* 26–31.

George, S. G., & Jennings, L. B. (1975). Effect of subliminal stimuli on consumer behavior: Negative evidence. *Perceptual and Motor Skills, 41,* 847–854.

Goldiamond, I. (1965). Stuttering as manipulatable operant response classes. In L. Krasner & L. P. Ullman (Eds.), *Research in behavior modification* (pp. 106–156). New York: Holt, Rinehart & Winston.

Greenwald, A. G. (1992). New look 3: Unconscious cognition reclaimed. *American Psychologist, 47,* 766–779.

Greenwald, A. G., & Banaji, M. R. (1995). Implicit social cognition: Attitudes, self-esteem, and stereotypes. *Psychological Review, 102,* 4–27.

Greenwald, A. G., Draine, S. C., & Abrams, R. L. (1996). Three cognitive markers of unconscious semantic activation. *Science, 273,* 1699–1702.

Greenwald, A. G., Klinger, M. R., & Liu, T. J. (1989). Unconscious processing of dichoptically masked words. *Memory and Cognition, 17,* 35–47.

Greenwald, A. G., McGhee, D. E., & Schwartz, J. L. K. (1998). Measuring individual differences in implicit social cognition: The implicit association test. *Journal of Personality and Social Psychology, 74,* 1464–1480.

Greenwald, A. G., Spangenberg, E. R., Pratkanis, A. R., & Eskanazi, J. (1991). Double-blind tests of subliminal self-help audiotapes. *Psychological Science, 2,* 119–122.

Hammond, K. R. (1948). Measuring attitudes by error choice: An indirect method. *Journal of Abnormal and Social Psychology, 43,* 38–48.

Hastie, R. (1984). Causes and effects of causal attribution. *Journal of Personality and Social Psychology, 46,* 44–56.

Hassin, R., & Trope, Y. (2000). Facing faces: Studies on the cognitive aspects of physiognomy. *Journal of Personality and Social Psychology, 78,* 837–852.

Hastorf, A. H., & Cantril, H. (1954). They saw a game; a case study. *Journal of Abnormal and Social Psychology, 49,* 129–134.

Hausdorff, J. M., Levy, B. R., & Wei, J. Y. (1999). The power of ageism on physical function of older persons: Reversibility of age-related gait changes. *Journal of the American Geriatrics Society, 47*(11), 1346–1349.

Hawkins, D. (1970). The effects of subliminal stimulation on drive level and brand preference. *Journal of Marketing Research, 7,* 322–326.

Hefferline, R. F., Keenan, B., & Harford, R. A. (1958). Escape and avoidance conditioning in human subjects without their observation of the response. *Science, 130,* 1338–1339.

Hogarth, R. M. (2001). *Educating intuition.* Chicago: University of Chicago Press.

Hogarth, R. M. (2005). Deciding analytically or trusting your intuition? The advantages and disadvantages of analytic and intuitive thought. In T. Betsch & S. Haberstroh (Eds.), *The routines of decision making* (pp. 67–82). Mahwah, NJ: Erlbaum.

Holden, S. J. S., & Vanheule, M. (1999). Know the name, forget the exposure: Brand familiarity versus memory of exposure context. *Psychology and Marketing, 16,* 479–496.

Iacoboni, M., Woods, R. P., Brass, M., Bekkering, H., Mazziotta, J. C., & Rizzolatti, G. (1999). Cortical mechanisms of human imitation. *Science, 286*(5449), 2526–2528.

Iacoboni, M., Molnar-Szakacs, I., Gallese, V., Buccino, G., Mazziotta, J. C., & Rizzolati, G. (2005). Grasping the intentions of others with one's own mirror neuron system. *PLoS Biology, 3*(3): e79

Ito, T. A., & Cacciopo, J. T. (2007). Physiological measures of implicit attitudes. In B. Wittenbrink & N. Schwarz (Eds.), *Implicit measures of attitudes.* New York: Guilford.

Jacoby, L. L., Kelley, C., Brown, J., & Jasechko, J. (1989). Becoming famous overnight: Limits on the ability to avoid unconscious influences of the past. *Journal of Personality and Social Psychology, 56,* 326–338.

Janiszewski, C., & van Osselaer, S. M. J. (2005). Behavior activation is not enough. *Journal of Consumer Psychology, 15*(3), 218–224.

Kahneman, D. (2003). A perspective on judgment and choice. *American Psychologist, 58,* 697–720.

Kahneman, D., & Triesman, A. (1984). Changing views of attention and automaticity. In R. Parasuraman & D. R. Davies (Eds.), *Varieties of attention* (pp. 29–61). New York: Academic Press.

Kardes, F. R. (2006). When should consumers and managers trust their intuition? *Journal of Consumer Psychology, 16,* 20–24.

Kaser, V. A. (1986). The effects of an auditory subliminal message upon the production of images and dreams. *Journal of Nervous and Mental Disease, 174*(7), 397–407.

Key, W. B. (1973). *Subliminal seduction: Ad media's manipulation of a not so innocent America.* Englewood Cliffs, NJ: Prentice-Hall.

Key, W. B. (1976). *Media sexploitation.* Englewood Cliffs, NJ: Prentice-Hall.

Key, W. B. (1980). *The clam-plate orgy: And other subliminals the media use to manipulate your behavior.* Englewood Cliffs, NJ: Prentice-Hall.

Kihlstrom, J. F. (1987). The cognitive unconscious. *Science, 237,* 1445–1452.

Kihlstrom, J. F. (1999). The psychological unconscious. In Pervin, L. A. Pervin & O. P John (Eds), *Handbook of personality: Theory and research* (pp. 424–442). New York: Guilford.

Kilbourne, W. E., Painton, S., & Ridley, D. (1985). The effect of sexual embedding on responses to magazine advertisements. *Journal of Advertising, 14,* 48–55.

Klinger, M. R., Burton, P. C., & Pitts, G. S. (2000). Mechanisms of unconscious priming: I. Response competition, not spreading activation. *Journal of Experimental Psychology: Learning, Memory, and Cognition, 26*, 441–455.

Kouider, S., & Dupoux, E. (2005). Subliminal speech priming. *Psychological Science, 16*, 617–625.

Krech, D., & Crutchfield, R. (1948). *Theory and problems of social psychology.* New York: McGraw-Hill.

Krishnan, H. S., & Shapiro, S. (1996). Comparing implicit and explicit memory for brand names from advertisements. *Journal of Experimental Psychology: Applied, 2*, 147–163.

Krosnick, J. A., Betz, A. L., Jussim, L. J., & Lynn, A. R. (1992). Subliminal conditioning of attitudes. *Personality and Social Psychology Bulletin, 18*(2), 152–162.

Kunst-Wilson, W. R., & Zajonc, R. B. (1980). Affective discrimination of stimuli that cannot be recognized. *Science, 207*, 557–558.

Langer, E. J. (1978). Rethinking the role of thought in social interaction. In J. H. Harvey, W. Ickes, & R. F. Kidd (Eds.), *New directions in attribution research* (Vol. 2, pp. 35–58). Hillsdale, NJ: Erlbaum.

Law, S., & Braun, K. A. (2000). I'll have what she's having: Gauging the impact of product placements on viewers. *Psychology and Marketing, 17*, 1059–1075.

Liu, S. S., & Johnson, K. F. (2005). The automatic country-of-origin effects on brand judgments. *Journal of Advertising, 34*, 87–97.

Lee, A. Y. (2002). Effects of implicit memory on memory-based versus stimulus-based brand choice. *Journal of Marketing Research, 39*, 440–454.

Levy, B. (1996). Improving memory in old age by implicit self-stereotyping. *Journal of Personality and Social Psychology, 71*, 1092–1107.

Lord, C. G., Ross, L., & Lepper, M. (1979). Biased assimilation and attitude polarization: The effects of prior theories on subsequently considered evidence. *Journal of Personality and Social Psychology, 37*, 2098–2109.

Lowenstein, G. (2001). The creative destruction of decision research. *Journal of Consumer Research, 28*, 499–505.

Lundy, A. (1985). The reliability of the Thematic Apperception Test. *Journal of Personality Assessment, 49*, 141–145.

Maass, A., Ceccarelli, R., & Rudin, S. (1996). Linguistic intergroup bias: Evidence for in-group-protective motivation. *Journal of Personality and Social Psychology, 71*, 512–526.

Maass, A., Milesi, A., Zabbini, S., & Stahlberg, D. (1995). Linguistic intergroup bias: Differential expectancies or in-group protection? *Journal of Personality and Social Psychology, 68*, 116–126.

Maison, D., Greenwald, A. G., & Bruin, R. H. (2004). Predictive validity of the implicit association test in studies of brands, consumer attitudes, and behavior. *Journal of Consumer Psychology, 14*(4), 405–415.

Mandler, G., Nakamura, Y., & Van Zandt, B. J. (1987). Nonspecific effects of exposure on stimuli that cannot be recognized. *Journal of Experimental Psychology: Learning, Memory, and Cognition, 13*(4), 646–648.

Marcel, A. J. (1983). Conscious and unconscious perception: Experiments on visual masking and word recognition. *Cognitive Psychology, 15*, 197–237.

Marsh, K. L., Johnson, B. T., & Scott-Sheldon, L. A. (2001). Heart versus reason in condom use: Implicit versus explicit attitudinal predictors of sexual behavior. *Zeitschrift für Experimentelle Psychologie, 48*(2), 161–175.

Mayer, J. D., & Hanson, E. (1995). Mood-congruent judgment over time. *Personality and Social Psychology Bulletin, 21*, 237–244.

Mischel, W. (1968). *Personality and assessment.* New York: Wiley.

McClelland, D. C. (1987). Characteristics of successful entrepreneurs. *Journal of Creative Behavior, 21*, 219–233.

McClelland, D. C. (1985). How motives, skills, and values determine what people do. *American Psychologist, 40*, 812–825.

McClelland, D. C. (1979). Inhibited power motivation and high blood pressure in men. *Journal of Abnormal Psychology, 88*, 182–190.

McClelland, D.C. (1965). Achievement motivation can be developed. *Harvard Business Review, 43*, 6–24.

McClelland, D. C., & Boyatzis, R.E. (1982). Leadership motive pattern and long term success in management. *Journal of Applied Psychology, 67*(6), 737–743.

McClelland, D. C., Koestner, R., & Weinberger, J. (1989). How do self-attributed and implicit motives differ? *Psychological Review, 96*, 690–702.

McConnell, J. V., Cutler, R. L., & McNeil, E. B. (1958). Subliminal stimulation: An overview. *American Psychologist, 13,* 229–242.

Merikle, P. M. (1988). Subliminal auditory messages: An evaluation. *Psychology and Marketing, 5*(4), 355–372.

Milgram, S. L., Mann, L., & Harter, S. (1965). The lost-letter technique: A tool of social science research. *Public Opinion Quarterly, 29,* 437–438.

Moore, T. E. (1982). Subliminal advertising: What you see is what you get. *Journal of Marketing, 46,* 38–47.

Moore, T. E. (1988). The case against subliminal manipulation. *Psychology and Marketing, 5,* 297–316.

Morgan, C. D., & Murray, H. A. (1935). A method for investigating fantasies: The Thematic Appreciation Test. *Archives of Neurology and Psychiatry, 34,* 298–306.

Morris, C. D., Bransford, J. D., & Franks, J. J. (1977). Levels of processing versus transfer appropriate processing. *Journal of Verbal Learning and Verbal Behavior, 16,* 519–533.

Morwitz, V. G., Johnson, E., & Schmittlein, D. (1993). Does measuring intent change behavior? *Journal of Consumer Research, 20*(1), 46–61.

Morwitz, V. G., & Fitzsimons, G. J. (2004). The mere-measurement effect: Why does measuring intentions change actual behavior? *Journal of Consumer Psychology, 14,* 64–74.

Murphy, S. T., & Zajonc, R. B. (1993). Affect, cognition, and awareness: Affective priming with optimal and suboptimal stimulus exposures. *Journal of Personality and Social Psychology, 64,* 723–739.

Nisbett, R. E., & Wilson, T. D. (1977). Telling more than we can know: Verbal reports on mental process. *Psychological Review, 84,* 231–259.

Nosek, B. A., & Banaji, M. R. (2001). The Go/No-go Association Task. *Social Cognition, 19,* 625–666.

Ostrom, T. M. (1988). Interdependence of attitude theory and measurement. In A.R. Pratkanis, S.J. Breckler, & A.G. Greenwald (Eds.), *Attitude structure and function* (pp. 11–36). Hillsdale, NJ: Erlbaum.

Ouelette, J. A., & Wood, W. (1998). Habit and intention in everyday life: The multiple processes by which past behavior predicts future behavior. *Psychological Bulletin, 124,* 54–74.

Packard, V. O. (1957). *The hidden persuaders.* New York: D. McKay Co.

Payne, B. K., Cheng, C. M., Govorun, O., & Stewart, B. D. (2005). An inkblot for attitudes: Affect misattribution as implicit measurement. *Journal of Personality and Social Psychology, 89*(3), 277–293.

Peracchio, L. A., & Luna, D. (2006). The role of thin-slice judgments in consumer psychology. *Journal of Consumer Psychology, 16,* 25–32.

Petty, R. E., & Cacioppo, J. T. (1986). *Communication and persuasion: Central and peripheral routes to attitude change.* New York: Springer-Verlag.

Pham, M. T., & Avnet, T. (2005). Ideals and oughts and the reliance on affect versus substance in persuasion. *Journal of Consumer Research, 30,* 503–518.

Pham, M. T., Cohen, J. B., Pracejus, J. W., & Hughes, G. D. (2001). Affect monitoring and the primacy of feelings in judgment. *Journal of Consumer Research, 23,* 167–188.

Posner, M. I., & Snyder, C. R. R. (1975). Attention and cognitive control. In R. L. Solso (Ed.), *Information processing and cognition: The Loyola symposium* (pp. 55–85). Hillsdale, NJ: Erlbaum.

Pratkanis, A. R. (1992). The cargo-cult science of subliminal persuasion. *Skeptical Inquirer, 16,* 260–272.

Pratkanis, A. R., & Aronson, E. (1992). *Age of propaganda: The everyday use and abuse of persuasion.* New York: W. H. Freeman/Times Books/ Henry Holt & Co.

Pratkanis, A. R., & Greenwald, A. G. (1988). Recent perspectives on unconscious processing: Still no marketing applications. *Psychology and Marketing, 5,* 337–353.

Pratkanis, A. R., Eskenazi, J., & Greenwald, A. G. (1994). What you expect is what you believe (but not necessarily what you get): A test of the effectiveness of subliminal self-help audiotapes. *Basic and Applied Social Psychology, 15*(3), 251–276.

Proshansky, H. M. (1943). A projective method for the study of attitudes. *Journal of Abnormal and Social Psychology, 38,* 393–395.

Robles, R., Smith, R., Carver, C. S., & Wellens, A. R. (1987). Influence of subliminal visual images on the experience of anxiety. *Personality and Social Psychology Bulletin, 13,* 399–410.

Roediger, H. L. (1990). Implicit memory: Retention without remembering. *American Psychologist, 45,* 1043–1056.

Rogers, M., & Smith, K. H. (1993). Public perceptions of subliminal advertising: Why practitioners shouldn't ignore this issue. *Journal of Advertising Research, 33,* 10–18.

Schneider, W., & Shiffrin, R. M. (1977). Controlled and automatic human information processing: I. Detection, search, and attention. *Psychological Review, 84,* 1–66.

Schooler, J. W. (2002). Verbalization produces a transfer inappropriate processing shift. *Applied Cognitive Psychology, 16,* 989–997.

Schooler, J. W., & Ohlsson, S. & Brooks, K. (1993). Thoughts beyond words: When language overshadows insight. *Journal of Experimental Psychology: General, 122,* 166–183.

Seamon, J. G., McKenna, P. A., & Binder, N. (1998). The mere exposure effect is differentially sensitive to different judgment tasks. *Consciousness and Cognition, 7*(1), 85–102.

Sekaquaptewa, D., & Espinoza, P. (2004). Biased processing of stereotype-incongruency is greater for low than high status groups. *Journal of Experimental Social Psychology, 40,* 128–135.

Sekaquaptewa, D., Espinoza, P., Thompson, M., Vargas, P., & von Hippel, W. (2003). Implicit stereotyping as a predictor of discrimination. *Journal of Experimental Social Psychology, 39,* 75–82.

Selltiz, C., & Cook, S. W. (1966). Racial attitude as a determinant of judgments of plausibility. *Journal of Social Psychology, 70,* 139–147.

Simonson, I. (2005). In defense of consciousness: The role of conscious and unconscious inputs in consumer choice. *Journal of Consumer Psychology, 15*(3), 211–217.

Smith, E. R., & Branscombe, N. R. (1988). Category accessibility as implicit memory. *Journal of Experimental Social Psychology, 24,* 490–504.

Smith, H. J., Archer, D., & Constanzo, M. (1991). "Just a hunch": Accuracy and awareness in person perception. *Journal of Nonverbal Behavior, 15,* 3–18.

Smith, K. H., & Rogers, M. (1994). Effectiveness of subliminal messages in television commercials: Two experiments. *Journal of Applied Psychology, 79,* 866–874.

Smith, M. B., Bruner, J. S., & White, R. W. (1956). *Opinions and personality.* New York: Wiley.

Stangor, C., & McMillan, D. (1992). Memory for expectancy-congruent and expectancy-incongruent information: A review of the social and development literatures. *Psychology Bulletin, 111,* 42–61.

Strahan, E. J., Spencer, S. J., & Zanna, M. P. (2002). Subliminal priming and persuasion: Striking while the iron is hot. *Journal of Experimental Social Psychology, 38,* 556–568.

Stevens, S. S. (1951). *Handbook of experimental psychology.* Oxford: Wiley.

Swanson, J. E., Rudman, L. A., & Greenwald, A. G. (2001). Using the Implicit Association Test to investigate attitude-behavior consistency for stigmatized behavior. *Cognition and Emotion, 15,* 207–230.

Synodinos, N. E. (1988). Review and appraisal of subliminal perception within the context of signal detection theory. *Psychology and Marketing, 5*(4), 317–336.

Tesser, A., Millar, M., & Moore, J. (1998). Some affective consequences of social comparison and reflection processes: The pain and pleasure of being close. *Journal of Personality and Social Psychology, 54*(1), 49–61.

Theus, K. T. (1994). Subliminal advertising and the psychology of processing unconscious stimuli: A review of research. *Psychology and Marketing, 11,* 271–290.

Thistlethwaite, D. L. (1950). Attitude and structure as factors in the distortion in reasoning. *Journal of Abnormal and Social Psychology, 45,* 442–458.

Trappey, C. (1996). A meta-analysis of consumer choice and subliminal advertising. *Psychology and Marketing, 13,* 517–530.

Twenge, J. M., Catanese, K. R., & Baumeister, R. F. (2003). Social exclusion and the deconstructed state: Time perception, meaninglessness, lethargy, lack of emotion, and self-awareness. *Journal of Personality and Social Psychology, 85*(3), 409–423.

Vallone, R. P., Ross, L., & Lepper, M. R. (1985). The hostile media phenomenon: Biased perception and perceptions of media bias in coverage of the Beirut massacre. *Journal of Personality and Social Psychology, 49,* 577–585.

Vargas, P. T. (2004). On the relations among implicit and explicit attitude measures, and behavior: A 2 x 2 typology of attitude measures. G. Haddock & G. R. O. Maio (Eds.), *Contemporary perspectives on the psychology of attitudes.* London: Psychology Press.

Vargas, P. T., von Hippel, W., & Petty, R. E. (2004). Using "partially structured" attitude measures to enhance the attitude-behavior relationship. *Personality and Social Psychology Bulletin, 30,* 197–211.

Vargas, P. T., Sekaquaptewa, D., & von Hippel, W. (2004). It's not just what you think, it's also how you think: Prejudice as biased information processing. *Diversity in advertising.* Mahwah, NJ: Erlbaum.

Vokey, J. R., & Read, J. D. (1985). Subliminal messages: Between the devil and the media. *American Psychologist, 40*, 1231–1239.

von Hippel, W., Sekaquaptewa, D., & Vargas, P. (1995). On the role of encoding processes in stereotype maintenance. In M. P. Zanna (Ed.), *Advances in Experimental Social Psychology, 27*, 177–254.

von Hippel, W., Sekaquaptewa, D., & Vargas, P. (1997). The linguistic intergroup bias as an implicit indicator of prejudice. *Journal of Experimental Social Psychology, 33*, 490–509.

Waly, P., & Cook, S. W. (1965). Effect of attitude on judgments of plausibility. *Journal of Personality and Social Psychology, 2*, 745–749.

Wänke, M., Plessner, H., & Friese, M. (2002). *When implicit attitude measures predict brand choice — and when they don't.* Special session: Predicting consumer behavior by implicit attitudes, at the annual convention of the Association for Consumer Research Asia-Pacific conference, Beijing, China.

Warrington, E. K., & Weiskrantz, L. (1970). Amnesia: Consolidation or retrieval? *Nature, 228*, 628–630.

Webb, E. J., Campbell, D. T., Schwartz, R. D., Sechrest, L., & Grove, J. B. (1981). *Nonreactive measures in the social science.* Boston: Houghton Mifflin.

Wegener, D. T., & Petty, R. E. (1995). Flexible correction processes in social judgment: The role of naive theories in corrections for perceived bias. *Journal of Personality and Social Psychology, 68*(1), 36–51.

Weisbuch, M., Mackie, D. M., & Garcia-Marques, T. (2003). Prior source exposure and persuasion: Further evidence for misattributional processes. *Personality and Social Psychology Bulletin, 29*, 691–700.

Wheeler, S. C., & Petty, R. E. (2001). The effects of stereotype activation on behavior: A review of possible mechanisms. *Psychological Bulletin, 127*, 797–826.

Wicker, A. W. (1969). Attitudes vs. actions: The relationship of verbal and overt behavioral responses to attitude objects. *Journal of Social Issues, 25*, 41–78.

Wicker, A. W. (1971). An examination of the "other variables" explanation of attitude-behavior inconsistency. *Journal of Personality and Social Psychology, 19*, 18–30.

Williams, P., Fitzsimons, G. J., & Block, L. G. (2004). When consumers do not recognize "benign" intention questions as persuasion attempts. *Journal of Consumer Research, 31*, 540–550.

Williams, J. M. Mathews, A., & MacLeod, C. (1996). The emotional Stroop task and psychopathology. *Psychological Bulletin, 120*, 3–24.

Wilson, T. D., & Kraft, D. (1993). Why do I love thee? Effects of repeated introspections about a dating relationship on attitudes toward the relationship. *Personality and Social Psychology Bulletin, 19*, 409–418.

Wilson, T. D., & Schooler, J. W. (1991). Thinking too much: Introspection can reduce the quality of preferences and decisions. *Journal of Personality and Social Psychology, 60*, 181–192.

Winter, D. G., & Stewart, A. J. (1977). Power motivation as a function of retest instructions. *Journal of Consulting and Clinical Psychology, 45*, 436–440.

Winter, D. G., John, O. P., Stewart, A. J., Klohnen, E. C., & Duncan, L. E. (1998). Traits and motives: Toward an integration of two traditions in personality research. *Psychological Review, 105*, 230–250.

Wittenbrink, B. (2007). Measuring attitudes through priming. In B. Wittenbrink & N. Schwarz (Eds.). *Implicit measures of attitudes* New York: Guilford.

Zajonc, R. B. (1968). Attitudinal effects of mere exposure. *Journal of Personality and Social Psychology, 9*(2), 1–27.

Zanot, E. J., Pincus, J. D., & Lamp, E. J. (1983). Public perceptions of subliminal advertising. *Journal of Advertising, 12*, 39–45.

19

Evoking the Imagination as a Strategy of Influence

PETIA K. PETROVA

Dartmouth College

ROBERT B. CIALDINI

Arizona State University

The human race is governed by its imagination.

Napoleon Bonaparte

Browse the pages of any popular magazine, and you will be invited to imagine yourself experiencing various products. To evoke consumption imagery, advertisers often use appeals such as "imagine yourself in a Mercury," "find yourself here," or "imagine your perfect home." 3D advertising and virtual realities encourage consumers to interact with the product and visualize the consumption experience (Griffth & Chen, 2004; Grigirivici, 2003; Li, Daugherty, & Biocca, 2002; Schlosser, 2003; Sheridan, 1992). Imagery is a central component of narrative stories (Green & Brock, 2000; Mandel, Petrova, & Cialdini, 2006), drama ads (Deighton, Romer, & McQueen, 1989; Stern, 1994), slice-of-life ads (Mick, 1987), and transformational ads (Puto & Wells, 1984). Consumer researchers define imagery as a process by which sensory information is represented in working memory (MacInnis & Price, 1987). Imagery has been distinguished from discursive, analytical processing of information such as verbal encoding, cognitive responding, counterarguing, and formulation of choice rules. Whereas discursive processing involves abstract symbols, words, and numbers (MacInnis & Price, 1987), imagery involves encoding in the form of nonverbal concrete sensory representations (Childers, Houston, & Heckler, 1985; Epstein, 1994).

The existing evidence suggests that imagery can have powerful effects on consumers' behavior. It has been shown to enhance memory (Lord, 1980; Slee, 1978; Swann & Miller, 1982), even to create false memories (Garry & Polaschek, 2000; Gonzalves et al., 2004; Schlosser, 2006), and to increase the perceived likelihood of an event (Carroll, 1978; Cialdini, 2001; Gregory, Cialdini, & Carpenter, 1982; Sherman, Cialdini, Schwartzman, & Reynolds, 1985). For example, imagining a political candidate winning the election can increase the perceived likelihood of the candidate's victory (Carroll, 1978), and imagining winning the lottery can increase the perceived chance of winning (Gregory et al., 1982). Imagery has also been demonstrated to increase the intentions to perform a behavior (Anderson, 1983; Cialdini, 2001; Gregory et al., 1982). Imagining taking a trip, starting a new job, or donating blood increased intentions to engage in these activities (Anderson, 1983).

Of course, of specific interest to consumer researchers are the effects of product imagery. Research in this direction reveals that instructing individuals to use their imagination while processing the product information (Keller & Block, 1997; Keller & McGill, 1994; Krishnamurthy & Sujan, 1999; McGill & Anand, 1989) or incorporating imagery appeals in an ad (Babin & Burns, 1997; Bone & Ellen, 1992; Escalas, 2004) can enhance product evaluations and the likelihood of purchasing the product. For example, in one of the first studies on the effects of imagination in a consumer context (Gregory et al., 1982), half of the residents in a neighborhood were given information about the features of a cable service. The other half of the residents were asked to imagine themselves utilizing the features of the cable service. Several weeks later, representatives from the cable company solicited these residents' orders for cable service. The results revealed that 19.5% of the residents who had only heard the features of the product subscribed to the service. However, among those that imagined having the cable TV service, the subscription rate was 47.4%. Simply asking consumers to imagine having the product doubled the sales.

Given the evidence for the effects of imagery on consumers' judgments and behavior, it is important to understand the mechanisms through which such effects occur. Researchers have suggested several mechanisms, yet how imagery changes consumers' preferences and behavior is not fully understood. Hoping to spur more research in this direction, we review the existing evidence for the processes underlying the effects of imagery and suggest unexplored possibilities. We also review variables moderating these effects and outline conditions under which asking consumers to imagine their experience with the product can be particularly effective or, alternatively, can decrease the likelihood of purchasing the product. Our goal is twofold: to provide an integrative view of the different approaches toward the use of imagery as a strategy of influence, and to inspire new ideas in this fascinating domain of consumer psychology.

PROCESSES UNDERLYING THE EFFECTS OF IMAGERY

> Visualizing is a way of knowing: it is a mode of generating knowledge.... How we see determines what we see; and how we see is embodied in our mental images. By virtue of their condensing impulse, images have a kind of power that abstract ideas can never have.
>
> **Mervyn Nicholson,** *13 Ways of Looking at Images*

Traditional Approaches

Traditional approaches in persuasion research have focused on processes such as affect, consideration of arguments, and recall. Such approaches have been applied to the effects of imagery as well. For example, studies suggest that because of the affective responses it evokes, imagery can enhance product evaluations (Bolls, 2002; Goossens, 1994, 2000; Mani & MacInnis, 2001; Oliver, Thomas, & Mitchell, 1993; Strack, Schwarz, & Gschneidinger, 1985). Research also reveals that information processed using imagery is stored in both a sensory code and a semantic code; thus imagery has multiple linkages in memory (Childers & Houston, 1984; Kieras, 1978) and is more easily retrieved than information stored in a semantic code only (Houston, Childers, & Heckler, 1987; Pavio, 1971). Given the role of information accessibility, it has also been suggested that vivid information or instructions to imagine the product are likely to influence product preferences by increasing the accessibility of favorable product-related information (Kisielius & Sternthal, 1984, 1986). This proposition, known as the *availability-valence hypothesis,* further suggests that because imagery can increase cognitive elaboration, it can increase or decrease product preferences according to the valence of the product information made accessible. That is, imagery can increase the accessibility of not only favorable but also unfavorable product information. In such cases, asking consumers to imagine the product experience can decrease product preferences.

Despite the evidence in support of these processes, more recent research suggests that there are additional processes taking place when consumers imagine the product experience. For example, Mani and MacInnis (2001) and Escalas (2004) reported that imagining the consumption experience influenced consumers' affective responses. In both studies, however, imagery had a positive effect on product preferences even when controlling for affect, suggesting that affect alone cannot account for the positive effects of the imagery on product evaluations. Furthermore, positive affect would not account for the effects of imagery on estimates of the likelihood of negative events such as being arrested for armed robbery (Gregory et al., 1982) or the effects of imagery on the likelihood of performing behaviors evoking negative affect (e.g., blood donation; Anderson, 1983).

Similarly, imagery appeals may engage processes that are different from those evoked by simply presenting individuals with a pictorial product depiction. A recent set of studies revealed that, consistent with the availability-valence hypothesis, increasing the vividness of the product depiction resulted in a greater number of product-relevant thoughts and greater recall of the product information (Petrova & Cialdini, 2005). However, these effects were not observed with regard to imagery appeals. In fact, instructing participants to process the information using their imagination decreased product-related thoughts, thoughts about specific product attributes, and recall of the product attributes. It has also been demonstrated that imagining the process of using the product can make consumers less sensitive to the strength of the arguments in the ad (Escalas & Luce, 2003, 2004). Furthermore, the effects of imagery were not mediated by cognitive elaboration (Schlosser, 2003); neither were they moderated by the individuals' dispositional tendency to spontaneously elaborate on information (measured with the Need for Cognition Scale; Cacioppo, Petty, & Kao, 1984; Green & Brock, 2000; Schlosser, 2003). According to these findings, imagery may not necessarily increase consideration of the positive and negative features of the product and in some cases may even decrease elaboration on the message arguments. Thus, additional processes may be taking place when consumers imagine their future experience with the product. Recent investigations provide some insight into this possibility.

New Approaches

Transportation and reduced counterarguing. Contemporary investigations reveal conceptually new processes that may be taking place when consumers engage in imagining the product experience. One such approach stems from findings in the area of narrative transportation. As research on the persuasiveness of narratives reveals, narratives are effective in changing attitudes and beliefs because they transport individuals into a different reality, thus reducing consideration of the positive and negative aspects of the message (Green & Brock, 2000). The process of transportation has been described as "immersion into a text," and being "lost" in a story (Green & Brock, 2000, p. 702). "A person engaged in elaboration might be accessing his or her own opinions, previous knowledge, or other thoughts and experiences in order to evaluate the message at hand. Under high elaboration, connections are established to an individual's other schemas and experiences. In contrast, under high transportation, the individual may be distanced temporarily from current and previous schemas and experiences" (p. 702). Imagery may influence product evaluations through a similar mechanism, by transporting consumers into a distant reality and *reducing* their attention to the favorability of the product information (Escalas, 2004, 2007). When individuals are transported into an imagined world, they may not be motivated to correct for their initial beliefs and expectations, because (a) they may not believe that the imagery had an effect on them, and (b) interrupting the imagery to counterargue the information can make the experience less enjoyable. Moreover, because experiencing the imagery is likely to occupy considerable mental resources, individuals may not be able to correct for the initial effects of the imagery on their evaluations. Indeed, recent research suggests that when consumers imagine their experience with the product they are less likely to evaluate the specific product attributes and counterargue the message arguments. For example, argument strength had an impact on the evaluation of the brand when individuals were not asked to imagine their experience with the product, but it did not have an impact when participants engaged in imagery (Escalas, 2004, 2007). Furthermore, when the product was described in a narrative, the inclusion of undesirable product features in the presentation did not affect product evaluations, although this information did undermine evaluations when the product features were presented in a list format (Adaval & Wyer, 1998). When presented with the narrative description of the product, participants processed the information in a holistic manner and were less likely to draw inferences based on the specific attributes presented in the ad. Such findings are consistent with research examining the effects of imagery on comparative advertising, which demonstrates that advertisements comparing the product to its competitor are effective under analytical processing but not under imagery processing (Thompson & Hamilton, 2006). Again, these findings suggest that when individuals process product information using their imagination, they are not likely to consider the positive and negative aspects of the presented information, but rather they adopt a more holistic approach, transporting themselves into a fictitious reality.

The imagery accessibility account. Another general area of research that has spurred new investigations into the processes underlying the effects of imagery focuses on consumers' subjective experiences of fluency. A considerable amount of evidence has been accumulated to demonstrate that when forming attitudes, opinions, and judgments, individuals are likely to take into account not only the content of the information with which they are presented, but also the ease with which this information comes to mind (Schwarz, 1998, 2004). For instance, consumers may not necessarily base their product evaluations on the content of the product information with which they are presented; they may base their evaluations instead on the fluency with which they can process this information (Lee & Labroo, 2004). Furthermore, consumers often base their product preferences not on the number of arguments for purchasing the product that they can generate, but rather on the subjective accessibility of these arguments (Menon & Raghubir, 2003; Wänke, Bohner, & Jurkowitsch, 1997).

Based on this approach, in contrast to examining the impact of imagery on consumers' elaboration on the message arguments, the imagery accessibility account focuses on the metacognitive experiences involved in processing product information using imagery. For example, when purchasing a house, consumers may consider how easily they see themselves living in this house. Typically, individuals can easily imagine having products that are suitable for them, that they intend to purchase, or that they desire; therefore, simulating the product experience can be an efficient decision-making strategy. However, the ease with which consumers can imagine themselves with the product can also be influenced by factors irrelevant to their intentions or the merits of the product. For example, when a consumer is deciding on a vacation destination, an image of a vacation in Hawaii might come to mind easily if the individual has previously been provided with imagery-evoking information in brochures or movies. Engaging consumers in product imagery through use of such commercial images of the consumption experience can create readily accessible mental representations of having the product and can increase the ease with which such representations will spring to mind during the decision-making process.

Indeed, research suggests that we tend to use the ease with which we create a mental representation of an event to estimate the likelihood of an event (Sherman et al., 1985). Furthermore, the ease of imagery generation has been found to influence not only the perceived likelihood of external events but also product evaluations and purchase intentions (Dahl & Hoeffler, 2004; Petrova & Cialdini, 2005; Zhao, Hoeffler, & Dahl, 2007). Further evidence about the role of imagery accessibility comes from research on the effect of hypothetical questions. As a number of studies in this area have demonstrated, simply asking individuals about the likelihood that they will engage in a behavior could make them actually perform the behavior (Fitzsimons & Morwitz, 1996; Greenwald, Carnot, Beach, & Young, 1987; Morwitz, Johnson, & Schmittlein, 1993). More recent research, however, reveals that this effect is moderated by the ease with which individuals can generate a mental representation of the behavior (Levav & Fitzsimons, 2006). That is, when asked a hypothetical question about engaging in an activity, individuals spontaneously engage in generating a mental representation of the behavior. Subsequently, they base their intentions to actually perform the behavior on the ease with which a mental representation of the behavior was generated.

These findings suggest that when considering buying a product, individuals may spontaneously attempt to create a mental representation of the product experience. By increasing the accessibility of such representations, imagery appeals can increase the likelihood of purchasing the product.

Imagination-behavior link. A third source of new insight into the effects of imagination comes from research on automatic processes. According to the principle of ideomotor action (James, 1980), the mere act of thinking about a behavior may increase the tendency to engage in that behavior. "We may lay it down for certain that every representation of a movement awakens in some degree the actual movement which is its object" (p. 526). According to James's proposition, activating a representation of the behavior through imagining may increase the likelihood of activating the behavior itself. Contemporary investigations provide findings consistent with this idea. Research on the perception-behavior link suggests that the activation of a perceptual representation may lead to the corresponding behavior (Bargh, Chen, & Burrows, 1996; Bargh, Gollwitzer, Lee-Chai, Barndollar, & Trörschel, 2001; Chartrand, Maddux, & Lakin, 2005; Dijksterhuis & Van Knippenberg, 1998). Research on ironic processes has also demonstrated that under conditions of limited attentional resources "the mere act of thinking about a behavior causes the behavior, even when the thought involved is meant to help prevent that behavior" (Ansfield & Wegner, 1996; Wegner, 1994). Because imagery and perception involve similar mental processes (Segal & Fusella, 1970; Unnava, Agarwal, & Haugtvedt, 1996), we may expect that—by activating a mental representation of consuming the product—imagery may evoke the actual consumption.

Neurophysiological research also suggests an automatic link between imagination and behavior (Decety, Jeannerod, Germain, & Pastene, 1991; Jeannerod, 1994, 1997; Paus, Petrides, Evans, & Myer, 1993; Pulvermuller, Harle, & Hummel, 2001; Rizzolatti & Arbib, 1998). A growing body of functional imaging research suggests that imagining an action and the actual production of the action rely upon common neural structures. For example, thinking about a word or gesture leads to the same activation in the anterior cingulated cortex as actually uttering the word or making the gesture (Paus et al., 1993). Similarly, imagining performing actions such as finger and toe flexion and extension and simultaneous horizontal movements of the tongue activated specific somatosensory and motor areas activated during actual motor execution that were also activated during actual performance of these movements (Ehrsson, Geyer, & Naito, 2003). In another study, participants were asked to perform, imagine, or prepare for specific hand movements while undergoing functional MRI scanning. The results revealed that the actual hand movements activated components of the motor system, including the primary motor and somatosensory cortex, the supplementary motor area (SMA), the thalamus, and the cerebellum. When participants imagined these movements or prepared to perform them, the primary motor cortex, the SMA, and the thalamus were activated (Michelon, 2005). Similar results have been reported with imagining more complex actions such as running, rowing, or weightlifting. Imagining such behaviors triggered neurophysiological activities comparable to those generated by actually engaging in these behaviors (Decety et al., 1991; Jeannerod, 1994, 1997).

These findings suggest that imagination and behavior may share the same motor representations, which may be triggered during mental simulation as well as by action preparation, execution, or observation. By activating a picture in front of the mind's eye, imagery may simultaneously activate the corresponding action. Despite this initial evidence, the automatic link between imagination and behavior in the context of more complex actions—including purchase behavior—is yet to be examined. As the integration of neuroscience and consumer research has proved fruitful in other domains (Yoon, Gutchess, Feinberg, & Polk, 2006), the use of neuroimaging to test the automatic link between imagination and purchase behavior is likely to be a worthy endeavor.

VARIABLES MODERATING THE EFFECTS OF IMAGERY

The only limit of imagethinking is the unimaginable.

Mervyn Nicholson, *13 Ways of Looking at Images*

Vividness of the Product Information

For imagery processing to occur, it is important that consumers be provided with sufficient knowledge and concrete cues (Pavio & Csapo, 1973; Richardson, 1983; Wright & Rip, 1980). Often, however, consumers are invited to imagine the product experience without being provided with such cues. For example, suppose you receive the following e-mail:

> Earn up to 32,500 bonus points with American Express! Take a moment to consider all the rewards you can earn with Hilton HHonors points. Now, picture earning more points everyday for even greater travel rewards. American Express is providing you with a limited time opportunity to turn the best Hilton HHonors rewards you can imagine into a valuable reality!

Without a vivid description of the offered rewards, you would probably find it difficult to imagine yourself earning these rewards as suggested in the message. How would that influence the likelihood that you would enroll in the promoted program?

Research examining the use of vivid information as an imagery-eliciting strategy has employed various ways to manipulate vividness; these include presence versus absence of pictures (Keller & Block, 1997; Kiseilius & Sternthal, 1984), concrete versus abstract pictures (Babin & Burns, 1997; Mitchell & Olson, 1981), concrete versus abstract words (Robertson, 1987; Rook, 1987), narrative versus statistical information (Keller & Block, 1997), and detailed product description versus expert ratings (Petrova & Cialdini, 2005). Based on the premise that concrete words can stimulate greater generation of imagery (MacInnis & Price, 1987; Pavio & Csapo, 1973; Pavio & Foth, 1970; Pavio, Yuille, & Madigan, 1968; Richardson, 1980), research demonstrates that messages using concrete wording are more persuasive than those using abstract wording (Adaval & Wyer, 1998; Robertson, 1987; Rook, 1987). Studies manipulating the vividness of the information through the use of pictures further indicate the capacity of pictures to evoke imagery (Bugelski, 1983; Finke, 1980; Pavio, 1971; Shepard, 1967; Singer, 1978) and influence product evaluations (Childers & Houston, 1984; Lutz & Lutz, 1977, 1978; Macinnis & Price, 1987; Mitchell, 1986).

The vividness of the product depiction has a special role in the effect of imagery appeals. Vivid product attributes have a disproportionate influence on product preferences when consumers process the product information using imagery (Keller & McGill, 1994; McGill & Anand, 1989). Moreover, because consumers are likely to base their purchase intentions on the ease with which they can imagine the product experience, asking consumers to imagine the product experience in the absence of vivid product information may not only be inefficient but may actually decrease the likelihood of purchasing the product (Petrova & Cialdini, 2005). For example, when the photograph in a vacation ad was modified to resemble an abstract painting, incorporating imagery appeals in the ad decreased its persuasiveness in comparison to that of an ad that lacked such appeals. Similarly, when a restaurant was described with highly positive numerical expert ratings, asking individuals to process the information using their imagination decreased the likelihood of their purchasing the product. On the other hand, imagery appeals increased product choice when the abstract information was replaced with a vivid, imagery-evoking description (e.g., the dining room, with its old wooden floor and peach color walls, basks in a soft gentle light . . . the meat is so tender that you can feel it melt on your tongue). Importantly, these effects were observed despite the fact that the vivid and the nonvivid product depictions were equally persuasive in the absence of imagery appeals (Petrova & Cialdini, 2005). According to these findings, the type of processing strategy that consumers engage in determines whether vivid information is more persuasive than abstract, nonexperiential information. In fact, when individuals are motivated to process the information analytically and to make a logical decision, describing the product with vivid, imagery-evoking information decreased the likelihood of choosing the product (Petrova & Cialdini, 2005). Yet, presenting a vivid product depiction is crucial when consumers are asked to imagine their future experience with the product. Without a vivid product depiction, imagery appeals may not only be ineffective, they can decrease the persuasiveness of the message.

Cognitive Load

In order for consumers to imagine their future experience with the product, they should not only be provided with the appropriate information; they should also have the cognitive capacity to do so. Because imagery is a resource-demanding process (MacInnis & Price, 1987; McGill & Anand, 1989; Unnava et al., 1996) allocating resources to another cognitive task may undermine its effects. For example, in a study by Shiv and Huber (2000), cognitive load was manipulated by asking participants to memorize a nine-digit number that prevented them from engaging in mental imagery. This diminished the otherwise observed shift in preferences between anticipated-satisfaction judgments and choice. Increased cognitive load may also result from considering factual information simultaneously with constructing the suggested mental image. For example, along with imagery-evoking information, product depictions are frequently accompanied by nonexperiential information such as numerical ratings, technical specifications, or attribute comparisons. A potential drawback of such an approach is that consumers may experience difficulty in simultaneously processing these two types of information. For instance, adding numerical expert ratings to a vivid product depiction undermined the effects of imagining instructions despite the fact that the numerical ratings enhanced product preferences when participants were processing the information analytically (Petrova & Cialdini, 2005). In another study, adding statistical information to a story of success diminished the otherwise positive effect of the story on participants' expectations for their own success (Mandel, Petrova, & Cialdini, 2006). Comparative information can have similar effects. For example, adding attribute comparison between the advertised brand and the competitor undermined brand preferences under imagery processing. This effect was observed despite the fact that the comparative information had a positive effect on brand attitudes when participants engaged in analytical processing (Thompson & Hamilton, 2006).

According to these findings, when consumers engage in imagery, adding nonexperiential information will not only fail to increase the persuasiveness of the message but can undermine the effects of imagery appeals. That is, imagery instructions are likely to be effective only when the vivid information is the only information that the consumer considers. Further research is needed to examine the effects of cognitive load on imagery. This research would benefit from examining the impact of other factors that can undermine consumers' cognitive capacity to generate the suggested imagery (e.g., time pressure, distractions in the environment). Along with its practical implications, such research would provide better light into the cognitive processes involved in the effects of imagery on product preferences.

Self-Relevant Versus Other-Relevant Imagery

Engaging in imagery may have different effects on subsequent evaluations and behavior, according to whether consumers imagine themselves or another person. A number of studies demonstrate that visualization has stronger effects on one's intentions if it involves the self, rather than another person (Anderson, 1983; Bone & Ellen, 1992; West, Huber, & Min, 2004). For example, in a set of studies by Bone and Ellen (1992), participants heard a popcorn radio ad in which they were asked to imagine either themselves or an eccentric chemistry professor consuming the advertised product. Those who imagined themselves reported greater imagery generation, more positive attitudes toward the brand, and greater likelihood of purchasing the product than those who imagined another person (in this case, the chemistry professor). Research examining the effects of self- versus other-relevant imagery evoked by reading a narrative story about another person revealed consistent results. Reading about someone else's success increased participants' luxury brand preferences and expectations for their own success, but only when participants could easily imagine themselves in the story. When the story described the success of someone who was quite different from the participants, it had a negative effect on their expectations for success (Mandel, Petrova, & Cialdini, 2006).

Neuroimaging research has further revealed that imagining the self and imagining another person are related to somewhat different brain activities. For example, participants in a study by Ruby and Decety (2001) were trained to imagine either themselves or another individual performing a series of actions. Both self-relevant and other-relevant imagery activated common clusters in the SMA, the precentral gyrus, and the precuneus. However, some differences in the activated areas when imagining oneself or another person were also observed. While imagining the self was specifically associated with increased activity in the left inferior parietal lobule and the left somatosensory cortex, imagining another person activated the right inferior parietal lobule, the posterior cingulate, and the fronto-polar cortex (Ruby & Decety, 2001). The effects of self- versus other-relevant imagery have also been studied in the experience of pain. Both imagining oneself and imagining another individual in pain have been found to activate the neural network involved in pain processing, including the parietal operculum, ACC, and anterior insula (Jackson et al., 2005). However, imagining the self in pain resulted in higher pain ratings and involved the pain matrix more extensively in the secondary somatosensory cortex, the posterior part of the anterior cingulate cortex, and the insula proper.

These results suggest that consumers are more likely to purchase a product when they imagine themselves using the product rather than another person. However, there is a notable exception to this conclusion. Under some circumstances, instead of asking consumers to imagine themselves with the product, marketers would be better advised to ask consumers to imagine a broader audience. That is, when imagining their experience with a product, consumers usually rely on past experience with similar products. However, when it comes to novel, innovative products that allow consumers to do something they have never been able to do before (Robertson, 1971; Ulrich & Eppinger, 2000), consumers could no longer rely on their own past experiences. In this case it is more effective to encourage more abstract imagery (e.g., imagine how *a consumer* can use this notepad to transfer handwritten notes to a digital file; Dahl & Hoeffler, 2004). Although further research is needed to examine the processes involved when consumers imagine really new products, these findings suggest that under some conditions, other-relevant visualization may result in more positive evaluations of the product than self-relevant visualization.

Process-Oriented Versus Outcome-Oriented Imagery

Recent research distinguishes between process- versus outcome-based mental simulation (Escalas & Luce 2003, 2004; Oettingen & Mayer, 2002; Pham & Taylor, 1999; Rivkin & Taylor, 1999; Taylor, Rivkin, & Armor, 1998). Process-focused imagery emphasizes the actions necessary to achieve an outcome. It encourages plan formation by creating a step-by-step story or narrative. Outcome-focused imagery, on the other hand, emphasizes the end of the story, such as the positive benefits of consuming the product. Escalas and Luce (2004) found different mechanisms involved in the two types of imagery. In outcome-focused imagery, individuals' sensitivity to argument strength increased when participants were explicitly asked to pay attention to the information in the ad. This finding is consistent with the elaboration likelihood model of persuasion (Chaiken & Trope, 1999; Petty & Cacioppo, 1986) and with the availability-valence paradigm (Kissielius & Sternthal, 1984). However, Escalas and Luce found that under process-focused imagery, asking participants to pay attention to the ad decreased their sensitivity to argument strength. This finding is consistent with the transportation and reduced counterarguing explanation of the effects of imagery (Escalas, 2004; Green & Brock, 2000) as well as with the imagery accessibility account (Petrova & Cialdini, 2005).

One variable that may influence whether individuals will engage in process- or outcome-focused imagery is the temporal distance of the imagined event. According to the construal level theory (Liberman & Trope, 1998; Trope & Liberman, 2000, 2003), the temporal distance of an event changes the way in which that event is mentally represented. When consumers think of near-future events, they tend to focus on concrete aspects such as the product feasibility. On the other hand, when making a decision about consequences in the distant future, consumers are more likely to think of abstract features of the product such as its desirability. It is possible, therefore, that consumers will be more likely to engage in process-oriented simulation when imagining a near future event and more likely to engage in outcome-oriented simulation when imagining a distant future event. If that is the case, marketers should be highlighting different features of the product depending on the temporal distance of the imagined event. Moreover, messages that are relevant to near future consumption and distant future consumption should be structured in a way that facilitates the type of mental simulation in which consumers are likely to engage. Marketers should also be aware that focusing on different features according to the temporal distance of an event can lead to inconsistency of preferences over time (Liberman & Trope, 1998). That is, when considering a purchase in the distant future, consumers may choose the option that is more desirable. However, when the time for making the purchase approaches, consumers may shift their preferences toward the more feasible option. One way to prevent such shift in preferences is to engage consumers who consider a distant future purchase in process-oriented mental simulation and thus increase feasibility-related considerations. As a result, consumers will be more consistent in their preferences at the time of making the initial decision and the time of purchase (Zhao, Hoeffler, & Zauberman, 2007).

Individual Differences

Dispositional imagery vividness. Individuals' ability to generate vivid mental images has been shown to be a stable dispositional characteristic. Several scales exist to measure dispositional imagery abilities. For example, Betts's Questionnaire Upon Mental Imagery (QMI) assesses individual differences in imagery vividness in regard to visual, auditory, cutaneous, kinesthetic, gustatory, olfactory, and organic modalities (Betts, 1909; Sheenan, 1967). Another scale, the Vividness of Visual Imagery Questionnaire (VVIQ; Marks, 1973), assesses imagery abilities in regard to visual images only. Research using measures of imagery abilities has demonstrated the impact of dispositional imagery vividness on a variety of psychological processes; these include hypnotizability (Crawford, 1982), creativity (Shaw & Belmore, 1982), and information processing (Hiscock, 1976; Marks, 1973; Pham, Meyvis, & Zhou, 2001; Swann & Miller, 1982).

The individual's ability to generate mental images can also influence the effect of imagining instructions. For example, individuals high in dispositional imagery vividness were better able to memorize a sentence when they were instructed to create a mental image of the situation in the sentence rather than repeat the sentence to themselves. For low imagers, however, both strategies were equally effective in memorizing the target sentences (Slee, 1978). Similarly, in a study by Bone and Ellen (1992), participants' imagery ability had an effect on (1) the reported vividness of the image of consuming the advertised brand and (2) the subjectively perceived ease of imagining experiencing the product. These two variables, in turn, had a significant impact on the attitudes toward the advertised brand. Differences in imagery abilities can even reverse the effects of imagery appeals. Consistent with the imagery accessibility account, imagery appeals enhanced attitudes and purchase intentions for high imagers, whereas among low imagers, difficulties in creating the suggested mental image decreased subsequent product evaluations (Petrova & Cialdini, 2005).

Internal focus. Because imagery involves processing information by generating an internal sensory representation of the perceived information, individuals who tend to focus on their internal representations and experiences are likely to be influenced by imagery processes to a greater extent. The tendency of individuals to pay attention to their internal experiences has been well documented as a stable dispositional variable (Fenigstein, Scheier, & Buss, 1975). To measure the general tendency toward self-focused attention, Fenigstein et al. constructed the Self-Consciousness Scale, which has two factors: public self-consciousness and private self-consciousness. The public self-consciousness factor measures awareness of oneself as a social object; the private self-consciousness factor measures awareness of one's inner thoughts, feelings, and experiences. For example some of the items from the private self-consciousness scale include "I reflect about myself a lot" and "I'm generally attentive to my inner feelings."

Research using the private self-consciousness scale as a measure of dispositional internal focus has demonstrated stronger effects of imagery for individuals high in internal focus (Petrova & Cialdini, 2005). However, more research is needed to examine the relationship between the effects of imagery and internal focus and to investigate other variables that can influence self-focused attention and consequently the effects of imagery appeals. For example, manipulations of internal focus through the use of a mirror have demonstrated effects similar to the effects of private self-consciousness (Carver & Scheier, 1978). On the other hand, it has also been suggested that chronic differences in internal focus and situational manipulations may have different effects (Hull, Slone, Meteyer, & Matthews, 2002). Thus, future research needs to examine the possible differential effects of dispositional and situationally manipulated internal focus in regard to imagery. Future research may also examine novel variables that may influence internal focus and consequently moderate the effects of imagery.

CONCLUSIONS AND DIRECTIONS FOR FUTURE RESEARCH

Imagination is more important than knowledge.

Albert Einstein

We reviewed evidence for a strategy of influencing consumers that, rather than providing logical arguments, draws consumers into an imagined reality that includes the product. Although imagery has long been recognized and used as a strategy of influence, consumer researchers have only recently started to systematically investigate the psychological mechanisms underlying its effects. The research discussed in this chapter provides important insights into the powerful effects of visualization on consumers' preferences and behavior. Moreover, it suggests processes that are conceptually different from the psychological mechanisms traditionally studied by influence and persuasion researchers. Yet, more research is needed to uncover the processes through which imagery influences consumers and the conditions under which such effects occur. In the following sections we examine some possibilities for research in these directions.

What Are the Mechanisms Through Which Imagery Influences Consumers?

We reviewed several processes that are suggested to underlie the effects of imagery. As proposed by the availability-valence hypothesis (Kissielius & Sternthal, 1984), when asked to imagine their experience with the product, consumers are more likely to elaborate on the product information as well as to bring to mind relevant positive or negative product information. Depending on the favorability of the information made accessible, imagery can increase or decrease product evaluations. The availability-valence hypothesis is consistent with many theories of consumer judgment according to which consumers make judgments by examining the implications of each piece of product information that they have available.

More recent research, however, proposes an alternative view. For example, the transportation account suggests that when consumers imagine their experience with the product, they process the information holistically. Consequently, they are less likely to be influenced by the favorability of the presented information (Adaval & Wyer, 1998) and the strength of the presented arguments (Escalas, 2004). The imagery accessibility account (Petrova & Cialdini, 2005) further suggests that imagery creates a readily available mental image of the consumption experience. Instead of examining the favorability of the product information, consumers may base their decisions on the ease with which a mental image of having the product comes to mind. Imagery also has an effect on consumers' affective responses to the ad and the product. And finally, there might be more direct effects of mental images through an automatic link between perception and behavior.

Future research should shed more light on the processes through which imagery influences consumers' judgments and behavior. Future research should also examine how these processes interact and what are the direct outcomes that each of the processes is likely to influence. For example, the emotional response to the message and the valence of the accessible information may directly influence brand attitudes (Bone & Ellen, 1992). On the other hand, if the effects of imagery are mediated by (a) the increased accessibility of the consumption images or (b) a direct automatic link between imagination and behavior, then imagery should have a more direct effect on purchase intentions (Gregory et al., 1982; Schlosser, 2003). Some evidence for such independent effects of imagery on behavioral intentions comes from research by Schlosser (2003), in which participants viewed a Web site that had either passive or interactive information about Kodak cameras. While product interactivity increased brand attitudes among participants instructed to have fun and look at whatever they considered interesting, participants who were instructed to search the Web site with the goal of finding something specific held less favorable brand attitudes when looking at the interactive site than after looking at the passive site. However, regardless of whether participants were searching for specific information or browsing the Web site for fun, they had stronger purchase intentions after viewing the interactive Web site. Imagery, evoked by object interactivity, had a positive effect on intentions even when it resulted in more negative attitudes. These findings suggest that, depending on the cognitive processes taking place, imagery may influence brand attitudes or have a direct effect on intentions.

Future research should examine the circumstances under which the different processes are likely to take place. A promising direction for such research is the distinction between process- versus outcome-based mental simulation (Escalas & Luce, 2003, 2004) which suggests that a different set of psychological processes will be activated according to whether consumers imagine the process or the outcome of using the product.

Another fruitful direction for research is to examine the role of imagery in other processes through which consumers form their preferences. Incorporating research on imagery in other domains may prove useful in understanding phenomena such as narrative persuasion, media effects, and social comparison processes. For instance, research on the effects of social comparison (Festinger, 1954) established that individuals tend to evaluate their own opinions and abilities by comparing themselves to others (Lockwood, 2002; Mills, Polivy, Herman, & Tiggemann, 2002; Mussweiler, 2003; Richins, 1991). This research has further revealed that social comparison can result in contrast effects (in which individuals alter their judgments and expectations in a direction opposite of the comparison target) or assimilation effects (in which individuals changed their judgments in a direction toward the comparison target). Little is known, however, about the cognitive processes underlying these effects (Mussweiler, 2003). Taking the role of imagery into account can bring valuable insights in this regard. When exposed to a comparison target, individuals may spontaneously attempt to imagine themselves in the same position. To the extent that they can easily imagine themselves in the place of the comparison target, an assimilation effect is likely to occur. On the other hand, when individuals experience difficulty imagining themselves in the place of the comparison target, a contrast effect is likely to occur. Evidence for this possibility was provided in a series of studies (Mandel, Petrova, & Cialdini, 2006) in which business students increased their expectations for success and their luxury brand preferences when they compared themselves to a successful business student. However, they found it difficult to imagine themselves in the place of a successful biology major, and trying to do so reduced their expectations for success in the future.

When Does Imagery Influence Consumers' Judgments?

Although imagery processing can have powerful effects on product evaluations, our review of the existing literature reveals that such effects are likely to occur only under specific circumstances. We reviewed several factors that can undermine the effects of imagery: (a) individual differences that reduce imagery vividness and internal focus, (b) low vividness of the product information, (c) high cognitive load, and (d) low relevance of the imagined scenario to the self. Moreover, we reviewed evidence suggesting that when individuals experience difficulty generating the suggested mental image as a result of any of these factors, imagery appeals can not only be ineffective but can decrease the likelihood of purchasing the product. When implementing imagery appeals as a strategy of persuasion, therefore, marketers should be aware of the possibility that under some circumstances, encouraging imagining may decrease the persuasiveness of the ad.

Future research is needed to examine the circumstances under which the experience of ease or difficulty in imagining the product experience is likely to influence consumers' judgments. One variable that has been demonstrated to moderate these effects is the extent to which consumers are likely to focus on their internal experiences. For example, although imagery fluency had an impact on product choice for participants high in private self-consciousness, those low in private self-consciousness were equally likely to choose the product regardless of whether it was easy or difficult for them to imagine the product experience (Petrova & Cialdini, 2005). Future research should examine the potential moderating role of other variables related to individuals' focus on their subjective experiences. For example, Pacini and Epstein (1999) identified stable dispositional differences in the extent to which individuals process information experientially or analytically. Because individuals who tend to process information experientially are sensitive to their intuitions and subjective experiences (Danziger, Moran, & Rafaely, 2006; Pacini & Epstein, 1999), it seems likely that these would be the consumers who would be most influenced by imagery evoking information. The specific effects of individuals' tendency toward an experiential or analytical style of processing, as well as the effects of situational factors that prime one or the other processing style, are yet to be examined.

It is also important for future research to examine the conditions under which the experience of ease or difficulty of imagining the product experience is likely to be perceived as diagnostic (Tybout, Sternthal, Malaviya, Bakamitsos, & Park, 2005; Zhao, Hoeffler, & Dahl, 2007). For example, consumers may not be influenced by the experience of difficulty imagining the product experience for product categories that are generally difficult to imagine. Furthermore, whether imagery fluency will increase or decrease purchase intentions depends on consumers' interpretation of the fluency experience (Brinol, Petty, & Tormala, 2006; Unkelbach, 2006). Thus, there may be circumstances in which the ease of imagining the product experience will have a negative effect on judgments.

It will also be fruitful for future research to examine the effects of imagery for different types of products. The existing findings converge across a variety of products, such as automobiles (Burns, Biswas, & Babin, 1993; McGill & Anand, 1989), beer (Rossiter & Percy, 1978), apartments (Keller & McGill, 1994; McGill & Anand, 1989), restaurants (Petrova & Cialdini, 2005), cameras (Schlosser, 2003), and vacations (Adval & Wyer, 1998; Krisnamurty & Sujan, 1999; Petrova & Cialdini, 2005). However, all of these product categories have an experiential component, and the product use has been associated with positive affect. Although there is evidence for the effects of imagination on products with a greater utilitarian component, such as computers (Zhao, Hoeffler, & Dahl, 2007), further research is needed to examine possible differences in the effects of imagery on different types of products. For example, imagery may have a different effect with products associated with extraordinary experiences—such as skydiving, rock climbing, or river rafting—in which consumers are looking for something beyond their imagination and some of the value of the experience comes from its unpredictable nature (Abrahams, 1968; Arnould & Price, 1993). Furthermore, research suggests that imagery appeals may have different effects on evaluations of new products, especially innovative products that define a novel product category. Because it is typically difficult for consumers to imagine the use of such products, marketers may need to use different ways to engage the consumers' imagery when introducing really new products (Dahl & Hoeffler, 2004; Zhao, Hoeffler, & Dahl, 2007).

As is the case with most persuasion research, the majority of the studies reviewed in this chapter examined the effects of imagery directly after the presentation of the message. There have been notable exceptions. For example, Gregory et al. (1982) suggested that imagining the product experience can impact purchase intentions even weeks later. Furthermore, as research by Anderson (1983) demonstrates, repeatedly imagining a scenario can increase the likelihood of performing the imagined behavior. Nevertheless, future research can examine the temporal effects of imagery, especially regarding imagining consumption experiences. Future research should also examine how imagery-processed information influences not only consumers' judgments and purchases but also other aspects of the consumption process, such as decision confidence (Thompson, Hamilton, & Petrova, 2007), satisfaction (MacInnis & Price, 1990; Shiv & Huber, 2000), and word-of-mouth (Petrova, 2007).

REFERENCES

Abrahams, R. D. (1986). Ordinary and extraordinary experience. In V. W. Turner & E. M. Bruner (Eds.), *The anthropology of experience* (pp. 45–73). Urbana: University of Illinois Press.

Adaval, R., & Wyer, R. S. (1998). The role of narratives in consumer information processing. *Journal of Consumer Psychology, 7*(3), 207–245.

Anderson, C. A. (1983). Imagination and expectation: The effect of imagining behavioral scripts on personal intentions. *Journal of Personality and Social Psychology, 45*(2), 293–305.

Ansfield, M., & Wegner, D. (1996). The feeling of doing. In P. M. Gollwitzer & J. A. Bargh (Eds.), *The psychology of action* (pp. 482–506). New York: Guilford.

Arnould, E. J., & Price, L. L. (1993). River magic: Extraordinary experience and the extended service encounter. *Journal of Consumer Research, 20* (June), 24–45.

Babin, L. A., & Burns, A. C. (1997). Effects of print ad pictures and copy containing instructions to imagine on mental imagery that mediates attitudes. *Journal of Advertising, 26,* 3.

Bargh, J. A., Chen, M., & Burrows, L. (1996). Automaticity of social behavior: Direct effects of trait construct and stereotype activation on action. *Journal of Personality and Social Psychology, 71*(2), 230–244.

Bargh, J. A., Gollwitzer, P. M., Lee-Chai, A., Barndollar, K., & Trörschel, R. (2001). The automated will: Nonconcious activation and pursuit of behavioral goals. *Journal of Personality and Social Psychology, 81*(6), 1014-1027.

Betts, G. H. (1909). *The distribution and function of mental imagery.* New York: Columbia University Press.

Bolls, P. D. (2002). I can hear you, but can I see you? The use of visual cognition during exposure to high-imagery radio advertisements. *Communication Research, 29*(5), 537–563.

Bone, P. F., & Ellen, P. S. (1992). The generation and consequences of communication-evoked imagery. *Journal of Consumer Research, 19*(1), 93–103.

Brinol, P., Petty, R., & Tormala, Z. L. (2006). The meaning of subjective ease and its malleability. *Psychological Science, 17,* 200–205.

Bugelski, B. R. (1983). Imagery and the thought process. In A. Sheikh (Ed.), *Imagery: Current theory, research and application* (pp. 72–95). New York: Wiley.

Burns, A. I., Biswas, A., & Babin, L. L. (1993). The operation of mental imagery as a mediator of advertising effects. *Journal of Advertising, 22*(2), 71–85.

Cacioppo, J. T., Petty, R. E., & Kao, C. F. (1984). The efficient assessment of need for cognition. *Journal of Personality Assessment, 48* (June), 306–307.

Carroll, J. S. (1978). The effect of imagining an event on expectations for the event: An interpretation in terms of the availability heuristic. *Journal of Experimental Social Psychology, 14,* 88–96.

Chaiken, S., & Trope, Y. (1999). *Dual-process theories in social psychology.* Guilford.

Chartrand, T. L., Maddux, W. W., & Lakin, L. J. (2005). Beyond the perception-behavior link: the ubiquitous utility and motivational moderators of nonconscious mimicry. In R. R. Hassin, J. S. Uleman & J. A. Bargh (Eds.), *The new unconscious* (pp. 334–361). New York: Oxford Univiversity Press.

Childers, T. L., & Houston, M. J. (1984). Conditions for a picture-superiority effect on consumer memory. *Journal of Consumer Research, 11*(2), 643–654.

Childers, T. L., Houston, M. J., & Heckler, S. H. (1985). Measurement of individual differences in visual versus verbal information processing. *Journal of Consumer Research, 12*(2), 125–134.

Cialdini, R. B. (2001). Systematic opportunism: An approach to the study of tactical social influence. In P. J. Forgas & K. D. Williams (Eds.), *Social influence: direct and indirect processes.* Philadelphia: Psychology Press.

Crawford, H. J. (1982). Hypnotizability, daydreams styles, imagery vividness and absorption: A multidimensional study. *Journal of Personality and Social Psychology, 42*(5), 915–926.

Dahl, D. W., & Hoeffler, S. (2004). Visualizing the self: Exploring the potential benefits and drawbacks for new product evaluation. *Journal of Product Innovation Management, 21* (July), 259–267.

Danziger, S., Moran, S., & Rafley, V. (2006). The influence of ease of retrieval on judgment as a function of attention to subjective experience. *Journal of Consumer Psychology, 16*(2), 191–195.

Decety, J., Jeannerod, M., Germain, M., & Pastene, J. (1991). Vegetative response during imagined movements is proportional to mental effort. *Behavioral Brain Research, 42*, 1–5.

Deighton, J., R., D., & McQueen, J. (1989). Using drama to persuade. *Journal of Consumer Research, 16*(December), 335–343.

Dijksterius, A. P., & Bargh, J. A. (2001). The perception-behavior expressway: Automatic effects of social perception on social behavior. *Advances in Experimental Social Psychology, 33*, 1–40.

Dijksterius, A. P., & Knippenberg, A. (1998). The relation between perception and behavior, or how to win a game of trivial pursuit. *Journal of Personality and Social Psychology, 74*(4), 865–877.

Ehrsson, H. H., Geyer, S., & Naito, E. (2003). Imagery of voluntary movement of fingers, toes and tongue activates corresponding body-part-specific motor representations. *Journal of Neurophysiology, 90*, 3304–3316.

Epstein, S. (1994). Integration of the cognitive and the psychodynamic unconscious. *American Psychologist, 49* (August), 709–724.

Escalas, J. E. (2004). Imagine yourself in the product. *Journal of Advertising, 33*, 2.

Escalas, J. E. (2007). Self-referencing and persuasion: Narrative transportation versus analytical elaboration. *Journal of Consumer Research, 33*(4), 421–429.

Escalas, J. E., & Luce, M. F. (2003). Process versus outcome thought focus and advertising. *Journal of Consumer Psychology, 13*(3), 246–254.

Escalas, J. E., & Luce, M. F. (2004). Understanding the effects of process-focused versus outcome-focused thought in response to advertising. *Journal of Consumer Research, 31*(September), 274–285.

Fenigstein, A., Scheier, M. F., & Buss, A. H. (1975). Public and private self-consciousness — assessment and theory. *Journal of Consulting and Clinical Psychology, 43*(4), 522–527.

Festinger, L. (1954). A theory of social comparison processes. *Human Relations, 7*, 117–140.

Finke, R. A. (1980). Levels of equivalence in imagery and perception. *Psychological Review, 87*(March), 113–132.

Fitzsimons, G. J., & Morwitz, V. M. (1996). The effect of measuring intent on brand level purchase behavior. *Journal of Consumer Research, 23*, 1–11.

Garry, M., & Polaschek, D. L. (2000). Imagination and memory. *Current Directions in Psychological Science, 9*, 1.

Gonzalves, B., Reber, P. J., Gitelman, D. R., Parrish, T. B., Mesulam, M. M., & Paller, K. A. (2004). Neural evidence that vivid imagining can lead to false remembering. *Psychological Science, (15)*, 10.

Goossens, C. (1994). Enactive Imagery: Information processing, emotional responses, and behavioral intentions. *Journal of Mental Imagery, 18*(3–4), 119–150.

Goossens, C. (2000). Tourism information and pleasure motivation. *Annals of Tourism Research, 27*(2), 301–322.

Green, M. C., & Brock, T. C. (2000). The role of transportation in the persuasiveness of public narratives. *Journal of Personality and Social Psychology, 79*, 701–721.

Greenwald, A. G., Carnot, C. G., Beach, R., & Young, B. (1987). Increasing voting behavior by asking people if they expect to vote. *Journal of Applied Psychology, 72*, 315–318.

Gregory, L. W., Cialdini, R. B., & Carpenter, K. M. (1982). Self-Relevant scenarios as mediators of likelihood estimates and compliance: Does imagining make it so? *Journal of Personality and Social Psychology, 43*(1), 89–99.

Grèzes, & Decety. (2001). Functional anatomy of execution, mental simulation, observation and verb generation of actions: a meta-analysis. *Human Brain Mapping, 12*(1–19.).

Griffth, D. A., & Chen, Q. (2004). The influence of virtual direct experience VDE on on-line ad message effectiveness. *Journal of Advertising, 3*(Spring).

Grigorovici, D. (2003). Persuasive effects of presence in immersive virtual environments. In F. R. Davide, G. (Ed.), *Being there: Concepts, effects and measurements of user presence in synthetic environments* (pp. 191–207). Amsterdam: IOS Press.

Hiscock, M. (1976). Effects of adjective imagery on recall from prose. *Journal of General Psychology, 94*(2), 295–299.

Houston, M., Childers, T. L., & Heckler, S. E. (1987). Picture-word consistency and the elaborative processing of advertisements. *Journal of Marketing Research, 24*(4), 359–369.

Hull, J. G., Slone, L. B., Meteyer, K. B., & Matthews, A. R. (2002). The nonconsciousness of self-consciousness. *Journal of Personality and Social Psychology Review, 83*(2), 406–424.

Jackson, P. L., Brunet, E., Meltzoff, A. N., & Decety, J. (2006). Empathy examined through the neural mechanisms involved in imagining how I feel versus how you feel pain. *Neuropsychologia, 44*(5), 752.

James, W. (1980). *Principles of psychology*. New York: Holt.

Jeannerod, M. (1994). The representing brain: Neural correlates of motor intention and imagery. *Behavioral and Brain Sciences, 17*, 187–245.

Jeannerod, M. (1997). *The cognitive neuroscience of action*. Blackwell.

Keller, P. A., & Block, L. G. (1997). Vividness effects: A resource-matching perspective. *Journal of Consumer Psychology, 24*(December).

Keller, P. A., & McGill, A. L. (1994). Differences in the relative influence of product attributes under alternative processing conditions: Attribute importance versus attribute ease of imagebility. *Journal of Consumer Psychology, 3*(1), 29–49.

Kieras, D. (1978). Beyond pictures and words: Alternative information processing models for imagery effects in verbal memory. *Psychological Bulletin, 85*, 532–544.

Kisielius, J., & Sternthal, B. (1984). Detecting and explaining vividness effects in attitudinal judgments. *Journal of Marketing Research, 21*(February), 54–64.

Kisielius, J., & Sternthal, B. (1986). Examining the vividness controversy: An availability-valence interpretation. *Journal of Consumer Research, 12*, 418–431.

Krishnamurthy, P., & Sujan, M. (1999). Retrospection versus anticipation: The role of the ad under retrospective and anticipatory self-referencing. *Journal of Consumer Research, 26*(June), 55–69.

Lee, A. Y., & Labroo, A. A. (2004). The effect of conceptual and perceptual fluency on Brand Evaluation. *Journal of Marketing Research, 41*(May), 151–165.

Levav, J., & Fitzsimons, G. (2006). When questions change behavior: The role of ease of representation. *Psychological Science, 17*(3), 3.

Li, H., Daugherty, T., & Biocca, F. (2002). Impact of 3-D advertising on product knowledge, brand attitude, and purchase intention: The mediating role of presence. *Journal of Advertising, 31*(3), 43–75.

Liberman, N., & Trope, Y. (1998). The role of feasibility and desirability considerations in near and distant future decisions: A test of temporal construal theory. *Journal of Personality and Social Psychology, 75*(1), 5–18.

Lockwood, P. (2002). Could it happen to you? Predicting the impact of downward comparisons on the self. *Journal of Personality and Social Psychology, 82*(3), 343–358.

Lord, C. G. (1980). Schemas and images as memory aids: Two modes of processing social information. *Journal of Personality and Social Psychology, 38*(2), 257–269.

Lutz, K., & Lutz, R. (1977). Effects of interactive imagery on learning: Application to advertising. *Journal of Applied Psychology, 62*(4), 493–498.

Lutz, K., & Lutz, R. (1978). Imagery-eliciting strategies: Review and implications of research. In H. K. Hunt (Ed.), *Advances in consumer research* (Vol. 5, pp. 611–620). Ann Arbor, MI: Association for Consumer Research.

MacInnis, D., & Price, L. (1987). The role of imagery in information processing: Review and extensions. *Journal of Consumer Research, 13*(March), 473–491.

MacInnis, D., & Price, L. (1990). An exploratory study of the effects of imagery processing and consumer experience on expectations and satisfaction. In R. Holman & M. Solomon (Eds.), *Advances in consumer research* (pp. 41–47). Provo, UT: Association for Consumer Research.

MacInnis, D. J., Shapiro, S., & Mani, G. (1999). Enhancing brand awareness through brand symbols. *Advances in Consumer Research, 26*, 601–608.

Mandel, N., Petrova, P. K., & Cialdini, R. B. (2006). Images of success and the preference for luxury brands. *Journal of Consumer Psychology, 16* (January), 57–69.

Mani, G., & MacInnis, D. J. (2001). Imagery instructions, imagery processes and visual persuasion. In R. Batra & L. L. Scott (Eds.), *Advertising and consumer psychology*.

Marks, D. F. (1973). Visual imagery differences in the recall of pictures. *British Journal of Psychology, 64*(1), 17–24.

McGill, A. L., & Anand, P. (1989). The effect of vivid attributes on the evaluation of alternatives: The role of differential attention and cognitive elaboration. *Journal of Consumer Research, 16* (September), 188–196.

Menon, G., & Raghubir, P. (2003). Ease-of-retrieval as an automatic input in judgments: A mere-accessibility framework? *Journal of Consumer Research, 30,* 230–243.

Michelon, P., Vettel, J. M., & Zacks, J. M. (2005). Lateral somatotopic organization during imagined and prepared movements. *Journal of Neurophysiology, 95,* 811–822.

Mick, D. G. (1987). Toward a semiotic of advertising story grammars. In J. Umiker-Sebeok (Ed.), *Marketing and semioyics: New directions in the study of signs for sale* (pp. 249–278). Berlin: Walter de Gruyter.

Mills, J. S., Polivy, J. C., Herman, P., & Tiggemann, M. (2002). Effects of exposure to thin media images: Evidence of self-enhancement among restrained eaters. *Personality and Social Psychology Bulletin, 28* (December), 1687–1699.

Mitchell, A. A. (1986). The effect of verbal and visual components of advertisements on brand attitudes and attitude toward the advertisement. *Journal of Consumer Research, 13*(1), 12–24.

Mitchell, A. A., & Olson, J. C. (1981). Are product attribute beliefs the only mediator of advertising effects on brand attitude. *Journal of Marketing Research, 18*(3), 318–332.

Morwitz, V. G., & Fitzsimons, G. J. (2004). The mere-measurement effect: Why does measuring intentions change actual behavior? *Journal of Consumer Psychology*(14), 64–73.

Mussweiler, T. (2003). Comparison processes in social judgment: Mechanisms and consequences. *Psychological Review, 110,* 472–489.

Nicholson, M. (2003). *13 ways of looking at images: The logic of visualization in literature and society.* Beverly Hills, CA: Red Heifer Press.

Oettingen, G., & Mayer, D. (2002). The motivating function of thinking about the future: Expectations versus fantasies. *Journal of Personality and Social Psychology, 83*(5), 1198–1212.

Oliver, R. L., Thomas, S. R., & Mitchell, D. J. (1993). Imagining and analyzing in response to new product advertising. *Journal of Advertising, 22*(4), 35–50.

Pacini, R., & Epstein, S. (1999). The relation of rational and experiential information processing styles to personality, basic beliefs, and the ratio-bias phenomenon. *Journal of Personality and Social Psychology, 76*(6), 972–987.

Paus, T., Petrides, M., Evans, A. C., & Myer, E. (1993). Role of human anterior cingaluate cortex in the control of oculomotor, manual and speech responses: A positron tomography study. *Journal of Neurophysiology, 70,* 453–469.

Pavio, A. (1971). *Imagery and verbal processes.* New York: Holt, Rinehart, & Winston.

Pavio, A., & Csapo, K. (1973). Picture superiority in free recall: Imagery or dual coding. *Cognitive Psychology, 5,* 176–206.

Pavio, A., & Foth, D. (1970). Imaginal and verbal mediators and noun concreteness in paired associate learning: The elusive interaction. *Journal of Verbal Learning and Behavior, 9,* 384–390.

Pavio, A., Yuille, C., J., & Madigan, S. A. (1968). Concreteness, imagery and meaningfulness values for 925 nouns. *Journal of Experimental Psychology, 76,* 1–25.

Petrova, P. K., & Cialdini, R. B. (2005). Fluency of consumption imagery and the backfire effects of imagery appeals. *Journal of Consumer Research, 32* (December), 442–452.

Petrova, P. K. (2007). Effects of communicating information on consumers' judgments. Working paper.

Petty, R. E., & Cacioppo, J.T. (1986). *Communication and persuasion: Central and peripheral routes to attitude change.* New York: Springer-Verlag.

Pham, L., & Taylor, S. (1999). From thought to action: Effects of process-versus outcome-based mental simulations on performance. *Personality and Social Psychology Bulletin, 25*(February), 250–260.

Pham, M. T., Meyvis, T., & Zhou, R. (2001). Beyond the obvious: Chronic vividness of imagery and the use of information in decision-making. *Organizational Behavior and Human Decision Processes, 84*(2), 226–253.

Pulvermuller, F., Härl, M., & Hummel, F. (2001). Walking or talking? Behavioral and neuropsychological correlates of action verb processing. *Brain and Language, 78,* 143–198.

Puto, C., & Wells, W. (1984). Informational and transformational advertising: The differential effects of time. In T. C. Kinnear (Ed.), *Advances in Consumer Research* (Vol. 11, pp. 572–576). Provo, UT: Association for Consumer Research.

Richardson, A. (1969). *Mental imagery.* London: Routledge and Kegan Paul.

Richardson, A. (1983). Imagery: Definition and types. In A. A. Sheikh (Ed.), *Imagery: current theory, research, and application* (pp. 3–42). New York:Wiley.

Richins, M. (1991). Social comparison and the idealized images of advertising. *Journal of Consumer Research, 19*(June), 71–83.

Rivkin, I. D., & Taylor, S. E. (1999). The effects of mental simulation on coping with controllable stressful events. *Personality and Social Psychology Bulletin, 25*(12), 1451–1462.

Rizzolatti, G., & Arbib, M. A. (1998). Language within our grasp. *Trends in Neuroscience, 21*, 188–194.

Robertson, K. R. (1987). Recall and recognition effects of brand name imagery. *Psychology and Marketing, 4*, 3–15.

Robertson, T. S. (1971). *Innovative behavior and communication.* New York: Holt.

Rook, D. W. (1987). The buying impulse, *Journal of Consumer Research, 14*(2), 189–199.

Rossiter, J., & Percy, L. (1978). Visual imaging ability as a mediator of advertising response. In H. K. Hunt (Ed.), *Advances in consumer research* (Vol. 5, pp. 621–629). Ann Arbor, MI: Association for Consumer Research.

Ruby, P., & Decety, J. (2001). Effect of subjective perspective taking during simulation of action: a PET investigation of agency. *Natural Neuroscience, 4*, 546–550.

Scheier, M., & Carver, C. (1978). Self-focusing effects of dispositional self-consciousness, mirror presence, and audience presence. *Journal of Personality and Social Psychology, 36*(3), 324–332.

Schlosser, A. E. (2003). Experiencing products in a virtual world: The role of goals and imagery in influencing attitudes versus intentions. *Journal of Consumer Research, 30*(September), 184–196.

Schlosser, A. E. (2006). Learning through virtual product experience: The role of imagery on true versus false memories. *Journal of Consumer Research, 33*(3), 370–376.

Schwarz, N. (1998). Accessible content and accessibility experiences: The interplay of declarative and experiential information in judgment. *Journal of Personality and Social Psychology Review, 2*(2), 87–99.

Schwarz, N. (2004). Metacognitive experiences in consumer judgment and decision making. *Journal of Consumer Psychology, 14*(4), 332–348.

Segal, S. J., & Fusella, V. (1970). Influence of imaged pictures and sounds on detection of visual and auditory signals. *Journal of Experimental Psychology, 83*(March), 458–464.

Shaw, G. A., & Belmore, S. M. (1982). The relationship between imagery and creativity. *Imagination, Cognition and Personality, 2*(2), 115–123.

Shepard, R. N. (1967). Recognition memory for words, sentences, and pictures. *Journal of Verbal Learning and Verbal Behavior, 6*, 156–163.

Sherman, S., Cialdini, R. B., Schwartzman, D. F., & Reynolds, K. D. (1985). Imagining can heighten or lower the perceived likelihood of contracting a disease: The mediating effect of ease of imagery. *Personality and Social Psychology Bulletin, 11*, 118–127.

Shiv, B., & Huber, J. (2000). The impact of anticipating satisfaction on consumer choice. *Journal of Consumer Research, 27*, 202–216.

Singer, J. (1978). Experimental studies of daydreaming and the stream of thought. In K. Pope & J. Singer (Eds.), *The stream of conciousness: Scientific investigations into the flow of human experience.* New York: Plenum.

Singer, T., Seymour, B., O'Doherty, J., Kaube, H., Dolan, R. J., & Frith, C. D. (2004). Empathy for pain involves the affective but not sensory components of pain. *Science, 303*, 1157–1161.

Slee, J. (1978). The consistency of different manipulations of visual imagery: A methodological study. *Australian Journal of Psychology, 30*, 7–20.

Stern, B. B. (1994). Classical and vignette television advertising dramas: Structural models, formal analysis, and consumer effects. *Journal of Consumer Research, 20*(4), 601–615.

Strack, F., Schwarz, N., & Gschneidinger, E. (1985). Happiness and reminiscing: The role of time perspective, mood, and mode of thinking. *Journal of Personality and Social Psychology, 49*, 1460–1469.

Swann, W. B., & Miller, L. C. (1982). Why never forgetting a face maters: Visual imagery and social memory. *Journal of Personality and Social Psychology, 43*(3), 457–480.

Taylor, Rivkin, I., & Armor, D. (1998). Harnessing the imagination: Mental simulation, self-regulation and coping. *American Psychologist, 53*(April), 429–439.

Thompson, D. V., & Hamilton, R. W.. (2006). The effects of information processing mode on consumers' responses to comparative advertising. *Journal of Consumer Research, 32*(March), 530–540.

Thomson, D. V., Hamilton, R. W., & Petrova, P. K. (2008). Process vs. outcome oriented mental simulation and choice difficulty. In A. Y. Lee & D. Soman (Eds.), *Advances in consumer research* (Vol. 95). Chicago: Association for Consumer Research.

Trope, Y., & Liberman, N. (2000). Temporal construal and time-dependent changes in preference. *Journal of Personality and Social Psychology, 79*(6), 876–889.

Tybout, A. M., Sternthal, B., Malaviya, P., Bakamitsos, G. A., & Park, S. (2005). Information accessibility as a moderator of judgments. *Journal of Consumer Research, 32*(June), 76–85.

Ulrich, K. T., & Eppinger, S. D. (2000). *Product design and development.* Toronto, Canada: McGraw-Hill Higher Education.

Unkelbach, C. (2006). The learned interpretation of cognitive fluency. *Psychological Science, 17*(4), 339–345.

Unnava, R. H., Agarwal, S., & Haugtvedt, C. P. (1996). Interactive effects of presentation modality and message-generated imagery on recall of advertising information. *Journal of Consumer Research, 23*(June), 81–89.

Wänke, M., Bohner, G., & Jurkowitsch, A. (1997). There are many reasons to drive a BMW: Does imagined ease of argument generation influence attitudes? *Journal of Consumer Research, 24,* (170–177.).

Wegner, D. M. (1994). Ironic processes of mental control. *Psychological Review, 101,* 34–52.

West, P. M., Huber, J., & Min, K. S. (2004). Altering experienced utility: The impact of story writing and self-referencing on preferences. *Journal of Consumer Research, 31*(December), 623–630.

Wright, P., & Rip, P. D. (1980). Product class advertising effects on 1st-time buyers decision Strategies. *Journal of Consumer Research, 7*(2), 176–188.

Yoon, C., Gutchess, A. H., Feinberg, F., & Polk, T. A. (2006). A functional magnetic resonance imaging study of neural dissociations between brand and person judgments. *Journal of Consumer Research, 33*(1), 31–40.

Zhao, M., Hoeffler, S., & Dahl, D. (2007). Visualization and new product evaluation: The role of memory-and imagination-focused visualization. In G. J Fitzsimons & V. G. Morwitz (Eds.), *Advances in consumer research* (Vol. 34, pp. 235–237). Chicago: Association for Consumer Research.

Zhao, M., Hoeffler, S., & Zauberman, G. (2007). Mental simulation and preference consistency over Time: The role of process- versus outcome-focused thoughts. *Journal of Marketing Research, 44*(3), 379–388.

20

Consumer Attitudes and Behavior

Icek Ajzen

University of Massachusetts–Amherst

Consumers are ordinary human beings who happen to be engaged in activities related to the purchase of products or services. It should come as no surprise, therefore, that the psychology of the consumer deals with the same kinds of issues as psychology in general: memory and cognition, affect and emotion, judgment and decision making, group dynamics, and the myriad of other topics covered in the psychological literature. As is evident in this volume, consumer psychologists employ the concepts, theories, and findings of psychology—and in particular of social psychology—to explain the behavior of the consumer (see Bagozzi, Gürhan-Canli, & Priester, 2002; Simonson, Carmon, Dhar, Drolet, & Nowlis, 2000). In the present chapter, I examine social psychological theory and research on the attitude-behavior relation as it applies to consumer behavior.

CONSUMER BEHAVIOR

There is general agreement that consumer behavior refers first and foremost to the act of buying a certain product or service. This, however, is by no means the only behavior of interest to consumer psychologists. At issue as well are search of information relevant to a purchase decision, selection of retail outlet or service provider, and other actions performed prior to, and in the service of, a purchase. Consider, for example, the act of buying a washing machine. Prior to the purchase, consumers may search for relevant information on the Web, consult friends and coworkers, read consumer magazines, and discuss the options with a spouse or partner. The information obtained may narrow the decision to a small number of manufacturers and brands. At this point, the consumer may well visit one or more local showrooms to view the different brands and consult sales representatives about prices, warranty, installation, delivery times, removal of the existing washing machine, and so forth. Finally, the consumer decides on a particular brand and places an order.

Consumer psychology is concerned with all aspects of the consumer's purchase decision, but in any given investigation we must, for practical reasons, limit our focus. We will usually select a behavior of particular interest and examine the determinants of the behavior in question. Although not always clearly recognized, every behavior involves a choice, even if the alternative is taking no action and thus maintaining the status quo (Ajzen, 1996; Ajzen & Fishbein, 1980). Nevertheless, it is useful to distinguish between behaviors that focus on a single option and behaviors that involve a choice among two or more distinct alternatives. As the washing machine example illustrates, most purchase decisions involve both types of behavior: the decision to buy or not to buy a new washing machine focuses on a single option whereas the decision to buy one brand of washing machine rather than another is a choice among multiple alternatives. However, in the final analysis, even behaviors involving multiple alternatives are ultimately reduced to a single-option decision. After going through the preliminary stages, the consumer either buys or does not buy a particular brand of washing machine. My discussion will therefore first focus on single-option behaviors, the basic unit of analysis, and then consider additional issues related to the prediction and understanding of purchase decisions that involve multiple options.

SINGLE-OPTION BEHAVIORS

Any single instance of a behavior is an observable event that takes place in a certain context and at a given point in time. In addition, purchase behaviors are also directed at some target, usually a product or brand. It is therefore useful to think of purchase behavior as comprised of four elements: the *action* performed (buying, searching for information), the *target* at which the action is directed (the product category or brand), the *context* in which it is performed (Sears, online retailer), and the *time* at which it is performed (Ajzen, 1988; Ajzen & Fishbein, 1980). Each of a purchase behavior's four elements can be defined at varying levels of generality or specificity. If we decided to collect data about the extent to which people search for information (action) about a particular model of Sony flat-screen TV (target) online (context) on a particular weekend (time), all elements would be defined at a very high level of specificity. In this case, the behavior is so narrowly defined as to be of little practical or theoretical significance. A more meaningful criterion might focus on, say, searching online for information about any kind of product in the next two weeks. Here, the action element (searching for information) and the context element (online) remain quite specific, the time element has been expanded to a two-week period, and the target elements have been greatly generalized to include all product categories. Alternatively, we might be interested in searching for information about automobiles in the next 6 months. In this example we are still interested in the same action (information search), but now the target is more narrowly defined as automobiles; the context is not limited to online search but could include visits to showrooms, consulting *Consumer Reports*, or reading automotive magazines; and the time element has been expanded to 6 months.

The important point to be made is that observed behavior may differ depending on the particular definition we adopt. Thus, consumers may act differently when they search for automobiles as opposed to life insurance policies; and different patterns of information search may occur 6 months compared to 1 week prior to a purchase decision. Moreover, to study a broad category of behaviors, such as information search in general, we have to obtain data that generalizes the target, context, and time elements. This requires that we observe—or obtain self-reports—of information search with respect to different kinds of products, using different media, over an extended period of time. (For discussions of the logic of behavioral aggregation, see Ajzen, 1988; Epstein, 1979.)

Choice Behaviors

We have seen that single-option behaviors can be studied at a high level of generality. In fact, questions of theoretical significance are usually formulated at a fairly general level, whether they have to do with the decision to buy (or not to buy) a product, such as a new automobile, or with the determinants of such consumer behaviors as buying life insurance, putting money in a pension plan, using credit cards, and so forth. By comparison, questions about behaviors that involve a choice among two or more options are usually studied at a lower level of generality. Thus, we may be interested to know why people buy one brand of automobile rather than another, why they choose one type of medical treatment over another, or why they fly one airline rather than another. Here too, however, we must clearly define the action, target, context, and time elements of the behavioral alternatives. The decision to buy tickets on one airline rather than another can be affected by the destination (target element): A person may prefer one airline for overseas flights but another for domestic flights. Similarly, choice of insurance company may vary depending on whether we buy life insurance, automobile insurance, or property insurance.

DETERMINANTS OF CONSUMER BEHAVIOR

A purchase decision confronts the consumer with a host of potential challenges. Most important, perhaps, is the problem structuring that occurs prior to making a decision: becoming aware of the need for, or availability of, a new product or service; collecting information about the alternatives; identifying likely future events and other circumstances relevant to the purchase decision; and considering possible outcomes contingent on the decision (Albert, Aschenbrenner, & Schmalhofer, 1989; Peter & Olson, 1993; Slovic, Lichtenstein, & Fischhoff, 1988). After structuring the problem, the consumer needs to process the obtained information, choose a preferred course of action, and implement the decision at an appropriate opportunity. Finally, consumers can use feedback resulting from a purchase to reevaluate their decision, perhaps reversing it by returning a purchased product to the store. This information can also prove valuable for future purchase decisions.

MULTIATTRIBUTE DECISION MODELS

One approach to consumer behavior is grounded in behavioral decision theory (for reviews of this literature, see Goldstein & Hogarth, 1997; Shafir & LeBoeuf, 2002; Slovic et al., 1988). With its roots in economics and statistics, the starting point of this approach is a rational model of choice behavior. The decision maker is likened to an intuitive statistician who carefully considers the alternatives and makes full use of all available information in accordance with normative principles of probability and logic (Peterson & Beach, 1967). When faced with a choice among competing brands or products, consumers are assumed to first identify the attribute dimensions relevant to the decision. Each option is then evaluated on these attributes to reach a decision.

Consider, for example, consumers trying to decide whether to buy a picture tube (CRT) or a flat panel (LCD) television set. Certain attributes, such as the dimensions of the display, warranty period, and location of dealer may be irrelevant as they are the same for the two products. The comparison may therefore rest primarily on such attributes as picture quality, price, reliability, and visual appeal. Imagine that in a particular consumer's eyes, CRT sets are relatively inexpensive with proven reliability, moderate picture quality, and low visual appeal whereas LCD sets are expensive and without proven reliability, but have high picture quality and high visual appeal. To make a decision, the consumer must derive an overall evaluation of each product category in terms of the combination of attributes that characterize it. In the basic multiattribute model, this overall evaluation is assumed to be a weighted average of the subjective values or *utilities* associated with the individual attributes. That is, each attribute dimension is given a weight representing its subjective importance to the decision (with the restriction that weights add to one) and the product is given a value for each attribute.[1] The subjective utility of each product is obtained by summing the weighted attribute values for that product, and the product with the highest subjective utility is chosen (see W. Edwards & Fasolo, 2001).

Decisions Under Uncertainty

In the above example, the attributes of each product were assumed to be known with certainty. Thus, the consumers knew the price, picture quality, reliability, and visual appeal of each product type. All they needed to do was to assign importance weights and subjective values to these attributes and then derive a weighted average. In many situations, however, the attributes or outcomes of choice alternatives are not known with certainty ahead of time. Often, the outcomes produced by a decision depend on the "state of the world" at the time the decision is made. For example, an LCD television can produce a high-definition picture only if the service providers transmit high-definition programs. To take this uncertainty into account, the consumer has to judge not only the value of a high-definition display but also the likelihood that this attribute will be available. Perhaps more readily recognized are the risks and uncertainties inherent in investment decisions. The outcomes of a decision to invest $10,000 in a fixed-interest certificate of deposit or a stock market mutual fund depend on future market conditions. Whereas the CD produces a known payoff over a given time period, the amount and probability of possible gains or losses to be expected of the mutual fund can only be estimated.

Perhaps the most popular approach to the analysis of decisions under conditions of uncertainty is the subjective expected model (SEU) model (Edwards, 1954, 1955). The subjective expected utility of a Product P is defined in Equation 1, where SP_i is the subjective probability that Product P will produce attribute or outcome i, U_i is the subjective utility of the attribute or outcome i, and the sum is taken over the n attributes or outcomes of Product P. The decision situation is formulated such that the available alternatives are mutually exclusive and the subjective probabilities of outcomes associated with a given product sum to one. It is assumed that a subjective expected utility is produced for each alternative product and that decision makers choose the product with the highest SEU.

$$SEU \ (P) = \sum_{i=1}^{n} SP_i \ U_i \qquad (1)$$

Revealed Preferences

Of course, individuals are not expected actually to perform the mental calculations described by multi-attribute models every time they make a decision. These models are taken not as accurate descriptions of the way in which decisions are made, but rather as ideal or normative models against which actual judgments and decisions can be compared. It is assumed that consumer decisions, like decisions in any domain, can be modeled as if the consumer were performing the stipulated calculations.

Consistent with economists' mistrust of self-reports and reliance on revealed preferences, much work on behavioral decision theory involves attempts to infer the decision process from choices among specified alternatives. Indeed, importance weights, subjective probabilities, and utilities are rarely, if ever, assessed in research with these models (Coombs, Bezembinder, & Goode, 1967).[2] Applications of multiattribute decision models typically confront participants with a choice involving certain options and their possible outcomes. The decisions made are then evaluated as to whether they conform to the model's implications. For example, in their well-known work on framing and risk aversion, Tversky and Kahneman (1981, p. 453) posed the following decision dilemma in a positive (lives to be saved) frame.

> Imagine that the U.S. is preparing for the outbreak of an unusual Asian disease, which is expected to kill 600 people. Two alternative programs to combat the disease have been proposed. Assume that the exact scientific estimates of the consequences of the programs are as follows:
>
> If Program A is adopted, 200 people will be saved. [72%]
> If Program B is adopted, there is 1/3 probability that 600 people will be saved, and 2/3 probability that no people will be saved.

In the negative (lives to be lost) frame, the same cover story was used to offer the following options.

> If Program C is adopted, 400 people will die.
> If Program D is adopted, there is 1/3 probability that nobody will die, and 2/3 probability that 600 people will die. [78%]

The values in parentheses show the percentage of participants who chose the more popular option. No attempt was made to assess the subjective probabilities or values of the different possible outcomes. The different results for the two frames were interpreted as risk aversion in the case of a positive frame and risk seeking in the case of a negative frame.

A great deal of research in the past 25 years has shown that real-life decisions fall far short of the ideal assumed in the normative multi-attribute decision models. Due presumably to cognitive limitations of the human decision maker (Simon, 1955), subjective probability estimates are biased in numerous ways, deviating systematically from normative values (Kahneman, Slovic, & Tversky, 1982; Nisbett & Ross, 1980; Zwick, Pieters, & Baumgartner, 1995), and decisions often seem to follow rules that are incompatible with utility maximization (Coombs, 1975; Corfman, Lehmann, & Narayanan, 1991; Foxall, Oliveira-Castro, & Schrezenmaier, 2004; Kahneman & Tversky, 1979; Tversky, 1969). It is beyond the scope of this chapter to review the voluminous research related to models of this kind. Suffice it to say that many of the conclusions derived in the general judgment and decision-making literature—conclusions regarding hindsight biases, the effects of construct availability and accessibility, preference reversals, framing effects, and so forth—have also been shown to apply to the decisions of consumers (see Bettman, 1986 for reviews; Cohen & Chakravarti, 1990).

As is true of research on human judgment and decision making in general, many studies on consumer behavior employ simple decision situations involving known outcomes (e.g., Carmon & Simonson, 1998; Coupey, Irwin, & Payne, 1998; Dhar & Nowlis, 1999; Hsee & Leclerc, 1998). For example, in the first of a series of studies on the relative attractiveness of products presented together or in isolation (Hsee & Leclerc, 1998), cordless telephones were described in terms of two attribute dimensions: Model A was said to have a maximum range of 150 feet and a 2-day battery life per recharge whereas Model B had a maximum range of 60 feet and the charge lasted for 10 days. Participants were asked to decide which of the two models they would buy. Similarly, in a program of research on choice deferral due to time pressure (Dhar & Nowlis, 1999), participants were given, among other hypothetical scenarios, a choice between two brands of binoculars, as follows.

Brand name: JASON	Brand name: NIKON
Somewhat sturdy design	Extremely sturdy design
14X magnification	7X magnification
Black case	Black case
Price: $44	Price: $69

Under conditions of time pressure or no time pressure, participants were asked to indicate which of these two pairs of binoculars they would buy, and they were also given the option of buying neither and continuing their search. Whether time pressure influenced choice deferral was found to depend on the relative overall attractiveness of the options and on the extent to which the options shared common attributes.

Clearly, the revealed preferences approach can provide valuable information about the decision-making process in general, as well as about decisions of particular relevance to consumer behavior. However, this approach also imposes severe limitations on the amount and kind of information obtained. The hypothetical decision scenarios are structured in artificial ways to enable testing of specific hypotheses about the underlying process. Attributes describing the available options are typically selected by the investigator because of their suitability for hypothesis testing, not because they realistically describe actual decisions confronting consumers. Participants are assumed to base their decisions on the information about the products provided by the investigator, and only on that information—an assumption that is highly unrealistic as consumers are likely to go beyond the information given (Bruner, 1973) to infer unmentioned attributes as well. In the above example, the particular attributes selected by the investigator may not be a representative set of attributes considered by consumers in actual purchase decisions. Moreover, participants in the experiment may have gone beyond the attributes provided to infer, for example, that because of their less than sturdy design, Jason binoculars are unsuitable for hiking. It stands to reason that the final decision will be based on all attributes the consumer associates with the available alternatives, not only those attributes originally listed by the investigator.[3] The revealed preferences approach thus can provide information about general principles of consumer decision making, but it is not particularly useful for learning about the considerations that guide actual decisions with respect to the purchase of real-life consumer products.

Another related limitation of the revealed preferences approach to consumer decision making is that the decision situations typically involve choice among two or a small number of alternative brands described in terms of the same attribute dimensions. Real consumer decisions, however, often focus on a single alternative—for example, whether or not to buy a new television set—or involve a choice between alternatives with noncompatible attribute dimension, such as a choice between buying a new television set or a new dishwasher. A different approach is needed to investigate consumer behavior in these kinds of situations.

ATTITUDES

As is true for the field of social psychology (Allport, 1968), the attitude construct occupies a central role in theories and research regarding consumer behavior. This construct, and in particular the expectancy–value model of attitude, offer an alternative to reliance on revealed preferences. A great deal of research in the area of consumer behavior has focused on the structure and determinants of brand attitudes or evaluations, and on persuasion and other techniques designed to change these attitudes (for a few recent examples, see Brunel, Tietje, & Greenwald, 2004; Coulter & Punj, 2004; Sengupta & Fitzsimons, 2004). Much of this work is based on the assumption that consumers' attitudes toward competing brands are important determinants of their buying decisions. Before considering this proposition, however, we must examine several issues related to attitude theory and measurement.

THE EXPECTANCY–VALUE MODEL

Although formal definitions vary, most theorists today agree that attitude is the tendency to respond to an object with some degree of favorableness or unfavorableness (e.g., Eagly & Chaiken, 1993; Fishbein & Ajzen, 1975; Osgood, Suci, & Tannenbaum, 1957; Petty & Cacioppo, 1986). It is the evaluative reaction to the attitude object that is considered to be at the core of a person's attitude. Consistent with the cognitive tenor of most current theorizing in social psychology, this evaluative reaction is generally thought to be based on the person's expectations or beliefs concerning the attitude object. Similar to multiattribute utility models in work on judgment and decision making, the most widely accepted theory of attitude formation describes the relation between beliefs about an object and attitude toward the object in terms of an expectancy–value (EV) model (see Dabholkar, 1999; Feather, 1959, 1982).

One of the first and most complete statements of the EV model can be found in Fishbein's (1963; Fishbein, 1967b) summation theory of attitude, although somewhat narrower versions were proposed earlier (Carlson, 1956; Peak, 1955; Rosenberg, 1956). In Fishbein's theory, people's evaluations of, or attitudes toward, an object are determined by their beliefs about the object, where a belief is defined as the subjective probability that the object has a certain attribute (Fishbein & Ajzen, 1975). The terms "object" and "attribute" are used in the generic sense and they refer to any discriminable aspect of an individual's world. For example, a person may believe that Apple iPod media players (the attitude object) are popular with young people (the attribute).

Each belief thus associates the object with a certain attribute. According to the expectancy–value model, a person's overall attitude toward an object, such as a product, is determined by the subjective values or evaluations of the attributes associated with the product and by the strength of these associations. Specifically, the evaluation of each attribute contributes to the attitude in direct proportion to the person's subjective probability that the product possesses the attribute in question. The basic structure of the model is shown in Equation 2, where A is the attitude toward the product, b_i is the strength of the belief that the product has attribute i, e_i is the evaluation of attribute i, and n is the number of accessible attributes (see Fishbein & Ajzen, 1975).

$$A \propto \sum_{i=1}^{n} b_i e_i \qquad (2)$$

People can, of course, form many different beliefs about a product or any other object, but it is assumed that only a relatively small number influence attitude at any given moment. It is these *accessible* beliefs that are considered to be the prevailing determinants of a person's attitude. Some correlational evidence is available to support the importance of belief accessibility. The subjective probability associated with a given belief, i.e., its strength, correlates with the frequency with which the belief is emitted spontaneously in a sample of respondents, i.e., with its accessibility (Fishbein, 1963) as well as with order of belief emission (Kaplan & Fishbein, 1969); and highly accessible beliefs tend to correlate more strongly with an independent measure of attitude than do less accessible beliefs (Petkova, Ajzen, & Driver, 1995; Van der Pligt & Eiser, 1984). Furthermore, the likelihood that a given belief will be emitted in a free-response format is found to correspond to its accessibility as measured by response latency (Ajzen, Nichols, & Driver, 1995).

Despite its apparent similarity to the SEU model, the EV model of attitude differs substantially from multiattribute utility maximization models in a number of important ways. One fundamental difference is that unlike formal decision theory, the attitude model makes no assumptions about rationality. Instead, it relies on the much weaker requirement of internal consistency. Attitudes are assumed to follow reasonably from beliefs about the attitude object, as described by the expectancy–value model. The more positive the beliefs, and the more strongly they are held, the more favorable should be the attitude. The source of the beliefs, and their veridicality, are immaterial in this model. Whether true or false, biased or unbiased, beliefs represent the subjectively held information upon which attitudes are based. People may hold beliefs about many objects and issues that are derived not from a logical process of reasoning but instead are biased by emotions or desires and may serve a variety of personal needs. The documentation of biases and errors in human judgments mentioned earlier lends support to this view. It follows that attitudes which are assumed to be based on beliefs will be similarly subjective and potentially biased. This view of attitudes can be seen clearly in work on such topics as prejudice and stereotypes (Allport, 1954), cognitive dissonance theory (Festinger, 1957), self-serving attributions (Kunda, 1987; Miller & Ross, 1975), and social judgment theory in persuasion (Hovland & Sherif, 1952; Sherif & Hovland, 1961).

Measuring Beliefs and Attitudes

In contrast to the revealed preference approach, work with the EV model assumes that attitudes toward products or brands (i.e., their expected utilities), as well as the beliefs on which they are assumed to be based, can be directly assessed. Any standard attitude scaling procedure (e.g., Likert or Thurstone scaling, the semantic differential, see A. L. Edwards, 1957; Fishbein & Ajzen, 1975; Green, 1954) can be used to measure a consumer's general evaluation of a brand or product. Due largely to its ease of construction, the semantic differential (Osgood et al., 1957) is often the preferred method (e.g., Batra & Ray, 1986; Lutz, 1977; Madden & Ajzen, 1991; Mitchell & Olson, 1981). To illustrate, in a study on the effects of advertising on attitudes toward a fictitious brand of clothing (Coulter & Punj, 2004), brand attitudes were assessed by means of four 7-point evaluative semantic differential scales: *like - dislike, good - bad, positive - negative,* and *favorable - unfavorable.* The scale formed by the unweighted sum of these four evaluative scales served as a measure of attitude toward the fictitious brand of clothing, with a reliability coefficient alpha of .92 .

Numerous studies have shown that attitudes towards products or services and toward other aspects of consumer behavior, such as attitudes toward ads or toward retailers, can easily and reliably be assessed in this manner. To understand the basis for these attitudes, however, we must—according to the expectancy–value model—examine the beliefs consumer hold about the product or service of interest. Many investigators rely on their own familiarity with the product or on prior research to select a set of attributes for investigation, under the assumption that these attributes are important determinants of attitudes or purchase decisions (for a few recent examples, see Batra & Homer, 2004; Hui & Zhou, 2003; Stoel, Wickliffe, & Lee, 2004). Thus, in a study on the effects of a product's country of origin on beliefs and attitudes about the product (Hui & Zhou, 2003), college students were asked to rate, on 7-point scales, the standing of two brands of digital cassette players (Sony and Sanyo) on three attribute dimensions: reliability, workmanship, and durability. These attribute dimensions were selected because they were said to be commonly used in research on durable goods. In addition, the investigators also assessed overall attitudes toward the two brands by means of a three-item evaluative semantic differential scale. Country of manufacture was found to influence both brand beliefs and overall attitudes. The correlation between beliefs and attitudes was not reported, but structural equation analyses revealed significant path from beliefs about the three product attributes to overall attitudes.

Use of the expectancy–value model requires a more systematic approach to the identification of accessible brand or product attributes. One popular approach, pioneered by marketing researchers but now popular in other social sciences as well (see Kahan, 2001; Kleiber, 2004), is the use of focus groups. Potential consumers of a product are brought together in small groups and, in a permissive atmosphere under the guidance of a moderator, discuss various aspects of the product or brand in question.[4] The protocols from these discussions can be used, among other things, to identify product attributes that may guide consumer attitudes and buying decisions (Calder, 1977; Greenbaum, 1998). Consider, for example, a study on beliefs and attitudes regarding genetically modified (GM) food conducted in Belgium (Verdurme & Viaene, 2003). Two focus groups, consisting of eight to nine female participants varying in age and education but of similar cultural background, each discussed what the term genetically modified food evokes, their beliefs and attitudes with regard to GM food products and with respect to organic food, the benefits of GM food, as well as various other questions related to food consumption in general and to GM food in particular. A wealth of data was produced. Most relevant for our purposes, several beliefs about GM food were identified, including the belief that GM food has been genetically tampered with, is artificial or unnatural, involves cloning, is uncontrollable, is good for the Third World, and yields higher crops.

The open discussion format of focus groups allows the investigator to identify various beliefs and feelings about a product or other consumer-related issue, to follow-up on thoughts expressed by groups members, and thus to obtain a comprehensive picture of the way consumers relate to a product of interest. It is then up to the investigator to distill the different ideas expressed and to extract from them the information relevant to a particular research question, such as identifica-tion of beliefs about a product's most important attributes. The interactive nature of focus groups has, however, also serious potential drawbacks. Discussion participants are likely to influence each other (Bristol & Fern, 2003), with dominant individuals perhaps channeling and biasing the discussion in a particular direction; and self-presentational concerns can bias views expressed by participants (Wooten & Reed, 2000). An alternative individualistic belief elicitation approach has been used in the context of work with the expectancy–value model of attitude. This approach was specifically designed to identify attributes people associate with a given attitude object, such as a brand or product (see Fishbein, 1963; Fishbein & Ajzen, 1975). In formative research, partici-pants—usually in groups but working by themselves—are given a few minutes to list the positive and negative characteristics, qualities, and attributes of a brand or product. It is assumed that only attributes highly accessible in memory are likely to be emitted.

Whether obtained by means of focus groups, individual interviews, or belief elicitation, a con-tent analysis can be performed to identify the most frequently mentioned attributes, and these attributes are then used in subsequent research (see Ajzen & Fishbein, 1980). With respect to each attribute, respondents are asked to indicate the likelihood that the attitude object possesses the attribute and to provide an evaluation of the attribute. In accordance with the expectancy–value model, the evaluations are multiplied by the likelihood ratings and the resulting products are summed (see Equation 2). Correlations of this belief-based estimate of attitude with a direct measure have generally provided good support for the EV model (Ajzen, 1974; Fishbein, 1963, see Eagly, 1993). Although also popular in the area of consumer research (Bagozzi et al., 2002), complete tests of the model in this domain have been relatively rare (but see Lutz, 1977; Mitchell & Olson, 1981). As indicated earlier, investigators often select a few product attributes in a non-systematic manner and assume that these attributes are important determinants of consumer attitudes and behavior.

That selective choice of attribute beliefs can result in misleading conclusions was shown in a study of the relative impact of attitude toward the ad and brand beliefs on brand attitudes (Mit-tal, 1990). It was argued that prior studies (e.g., Mitchell & Olson, 1981) had focused primarily on a brand's utilitarian aspects to the exclusion of image-related beliefs, and that this resulted in an overestimation of the importance of attitudes toward the ad. Pilot work was conducted to elicit accessible beliefs about shampoos and wines. Image-related attributes (e.g., looks prestigious, will impress people) as well as utilitarian attributes (e.g., gets rid of dandruff, is made from good qual-ity grapes) were elicited. In the main study, participants saw print ads for a fictitious new brand of shampoo and for a new brand of wine, they expressed their beliefs that the two brands pos-sessed each of the utilitarian and image attributes, they rated each attribute on an evaluative scale, and they expressed their overall attitude toward the two brands and toward the ads on three-item evaluative semantic differential scales. The results showed that the direct relation between attitudes toward the ad and toward the brand was greatly attenuated when not only utilitarian but also image-related brand beliefs were included in the regression analysis.

PREDICTION OF CONSUMER BEHAVIOR

Up to this point we have focused on attitudes toward brands, products, services, or other aspects of consumer behavior. In our multiattribute and expectancy–value models it is postulated that these attitudes derive from underlying beliefs about the product's attributes together with the subjective values of these attributes. The main focus of the present chapter, however, is the effect of consumer attitudes on actual behavior. As a general rule, it is assumed that attitudes toward available options—whether inferred from choices in the revealed preferences paradigm or measured directly—determine consumer decisions. When confronted with a choice between alternative brands or services, consumers presumably select the alternative toward which they hold the most favorable overall attitude.[5] Because this assumption is virtually an article of faith, it is rarely questioned or empirically validated. The focus instead is on such factors as advertising that can influence beliefs and attitudes, and should thus have an effect on behavior. The criterion in many studies is a (hypothetical) choice between products, often fictitious, or an indication of willingness to perform a given behavior (for a few recent examples, see Arvola, Lähteenmäki, & Tuorila, 1999; Litvin & MacLaurin, 2001; Madrigal, 2001).

ATTITUDES VERSUS BEHAVIOR

Although intuitively reasonable, the assumption that consumer attitudes are predictive of behavior must be regarded with caution in light of extensive research on the attitude-behavior relation conducted over the past 40 years (see Ajzen & Fishbein, 2005; Eagly & Chaiken, 1993). Consider, for example, attempts to understand environmentally responsible consumer behavior. The predominant explanatory construct in this domain is an attitudinal indication of environmental concern. Unfortunately, measures of environmental concern are usually poor predictors of such environmentally responsible consumer behaviors as buying fewer packaged products, using less detergent, and using returnable containers (Balderjahn, 1988; see Gill, Crosby, & Taylor, 1986; Hines, Hungerford, & Tomera, 1987).

The Principle of Compatibility

To anybody familiar with current theory and research regarding the attitude-behavior relation, these negative findings come as no surprise. It is well known that attitudes can be expected to correlate with behavior only to the extent that the predictor and criterion are measured at compatible levels of generality or specificity in terms of their target, action, context, and time elements (Ajzen, 1988; Ajzen & Fishbein, 1977, 2005). General attitudes cannot be expected to be good predictors of specific actions directed at the attitude object. In the case of environmental concern—a very general attitude that specifies only a broad set of behaviors (protection) with respect to a global target (the environment)—the behavioral criterion would have to be assessed at an equally general level by aggregating over the many different actions in this behavioral category (Fishbein & Ajzen, 1974). In fact, the case for this argument in the domain of environmental behavior was made some time ago by Weigel and Newman (1976). The investigators used a multi-item scale designed to measure attitudes toward environmental quality and, 3 to 8 months later, observed 14 behaviors related to the environment. The behaviors involved signing and circulating three different petitions concerning environmental issues, participating in a litter pick-up program, and participating in a recycling program on eight separate occasions. In addition to these 14 single-act, single-observation criteria, Weigel and Newman constructed four behavioral aggregates: one based on petition-signing behaviors, one on litter pick-ups, one on recycling, and one overall index based on all 14 observations. Prediction of each single observation from the general attitude measure was quite weak; the average correlation was .29 and not significant. The aggregates over occasions, based on multiple observations of single actions, showed a mean correlation of moderate magnitude with the general attitude (r = .42), while the multiple-act index over all 14 observations correlated .62 with the same attitude measure.

Although Weigel and Newman examined behaviors unrelated to the purchase and consumption of products, the same argument can be made with respect to the prediction of consumer behavior. Concern for the environment should predict a measure of environmentally responsible consumer behaviors that aggregates across many different kinds of actions but not necessarily any particular action. In most consumer decision situations, however, we are interested not in understanding broad patterns of behavior but rather the purchase or use of a particular product or service, choice of one particular retailer over another, and so forth. These are relatively specific behaviors involving particular target and action elements, and sometimes context and time elements as well. While the principle of compatibility argues against reliance on general attitudes to predict specific behaviors of this kind, many investigators continue to be interested in broad attitudinal dispositions and their possible effects on specific behaviors (see Eagly & Chaiken, 1993).

The MODE Model

The most direct and sophisticated attempt to deal with the processes whereby general attitudes may influence performance of specific behavior was provided by Fazio (1986, 1990; Fazio, 1995; Fazio & Towles-Schwen, 1999) in his MODE model. Consistent with past work on the effects of attitudes on perceptions and judgments (see Eagly & Chaiken, 1998, for a review), the model assumes that general attitudes can influence or bias perception and judgment of information relevant to the attitude object, a bias that is congruent with the valence of the attitude. However, for this bias to occur the attitude must first be "activated." Consistent with the logic of other dual-mode processing theories (see Chaiken & Trope, 1999) the MODE model posits that attitudes can be activated in one of two ways: in a controlled or deliberative fashion and in an automatic or spontaneous fashion. The acronym MODE is used to suggest that "*m*otivation and *o*pportunity act as *de*terminants of spontaneous versus deliberative attitude-to-behavior processes" (Fazio, 1995, p. 257). When people are sufficiently motivated and have the cognitive capacity to do so, they can retrieve or construct their attitudes toward an object in an effortful manner. When motivation or cognitive capacity is low, attitudes can become available only if they are automatically activated. According to the MODE model, such automatic or spontaneous activation is reserved for strong attitudes. The stronger the attitude, the more likely it is that it will be automatically activated and hence be chronically accessible from memory.

Whether activated automatically or retrieved effortfully, the general attitude is available and can then bias processing of information. Individuals who hold favorable attitudes are likely to notice, attend to, and process primarily the object's positive attributes whereas individuals with unfavorable attitudes toward the object are likely to direct attention to its negative qualities. Such automatic biasing of information processing and judgments is more likely to be the case for strong, highly accessible attitudes than for weak attitudes. As a result, readily accessible, automatically activated attitudes are more likely than relatively inaccessible attitudes to bias the definition of the event and hence to guide performance of specific behaviors with respect to the attitude object.

Studies that were designed to test the MODE model's predictions concerning the attitude-to-behavior process (Berger & Mitchell, 1989; Fazio, Chen, McDonel, & Sherman, 1982; Fazio, Powell, & Williams, 1989; Fazio & Williams, 1986; Kokkinaki & Lunt, 1997) have focused on behavior in a deliberative processing mode. The results of these studies are generally consistent with the model. For example, in a study of consumer behavior (Fazio et al., 1989), participants seated at a computer first expressed their attitudes toward 100 commonly available products by pressing one of two keys labeled "like" and "dislike." They were instructed to respond as quickly and as accurately as possible. The response latencies constituted a measure of attitude accessibility in memory. Participants then completed a questionnaire which assessed their attitudes toward the same 100 products on a 7-point evaluative scale (*extremely bad–extremely good*). Finally, they were shown 10 of the 100 products (a Snickers candy bar, a can of Dr. Pepper, a box of Cracker Jacks, etc.) and asked to choose five to take as a present. As expected, prediction of product choice from the 7-point attitude measure was significantly better for participants with highly accessible (low latency) attitudes toward the products ($r = .62$) than for participants with moderately accessible attitudes ($r = .54$) or relatively inaccessible attitudes ($r = .51$).

The MODE model provides an elegant account of the processes and conditions under which general attitudes toward objects will or will not guide the performance of specific behaviors. Nevertheless, several important issues have been raised in regard to this approach.

First, the assumption that only strong attitudes are activated automatically by mere observation of the attitude object has been challenged in priming research where it was found that all attitudes are activated automatically, irrespective of their strength or accessibility (Bargh, Chaiken, Govender, & Pratto, 1992; Bargh, Chaiken, Raymond, & Hymes, 1996). In his rebuttal, Fazio (1993) reexamined the priming results and concluded that they are not inconsistent with the idea that highly accessible attitudes are more likely to be automatically activated. The MODE model's implications for attitude-behavior consistency, however, do not depend on the assumption that only strong attitudes are automatically activated. All we need to assume is that readily accessible or strong attitudes are more likely than less accessible attitudes to bias perceptions and judgments.

Related to this issue, it has been suggested that the magnitude of the attitude-behavior relation may be moderated not by attitude accessibility but by other correlated factors such as certainty, amount of knowledge, or the attitude's temporal stability. Support for the superior predictive validity of stable attitudes was provided by Doll and Ajzen (1992). Compared to second-hand information, direct experience with different video games was found to raise the accessibility of attitudes toward playing those games and to increase the temporal stability of the attitudes. The superior predictive validity of the attitude measures following direct as apposed to indirect experience could be explained better by their greater stability than by their higher level of accessibility.

REASONED ACTION

The SEU model of behavioral decision theory and the EV model of attitude theory both make the assumption that consumer decisions are based on the relative attractiveness of available alternatives. Although this approach to consumer behavior can produce valuable insights, it tends to lack ecological validity. We saw earlier that research relying on revealed preferences to infer decision-making processes typically confronts participants with artificial decisions among hypothetical products or services defined in terms of a selective set of attribute dimensions. Little information is gained about the specific considerations that actually guide the consumer's behavior. Elicitation of accessible beliefs in investigations of attitudes toward brands, products, or services can provide ecologically valid information about perceived product attributes, and these beliefs may help explain consumer decisions. However, here too the decision-making situation is contextually impoverished. It is assumed that consumers consider the attributes of alternative products and base their decisions only on the relative advantages and disadvantages of the products in terms of these attributes. This approach fails to take into account other potentially important considerations associated with the consumer's behavior, considerations that have to do with the social context in which the behavior occurs as well as potential situational constraints.

An alternative approach to the prediction of consumer behavior has been gaining ground in recent years. Instead of focusing on general attitudes toward products or services, it is possible to focus instead on the specific consumer behaviors of interest. The principle of compatibility would suggest that the most relevant antecedents of a particular consumer behavior are identical to the behavior in terms of action, context, target, and time elements. Consider, for example, the purchase (action) of a Sony television set (target) in the next 6 months (time). In this example, the context element is left unspecified, perhaps because the investigator has no interest in studying where the product is purchased. Arguably the most immediate direct antecedent of this action is the *intention* to buy a Sony television set in the next 6 months. In fact, we saw earlier that measures of intention to buy or use a specified product are often used as substitutes of behavioral measures, presumably under the assumption that people's intentions are good indications of what they actually do. Many studies have indeed substantiated the predictive validity of behavioral intentions. When appropriately measured, behavioral intentions account for an appreciable proportion of variance in actual behavior. Meta-analyses covering diverse behavioral domains have reported mean intention-behavior correlations of .47 (Armitage & Conner, 2001; Notani, 1998), .53 (Sheppard, Hartwick, & Warshaw, 1988), .45 (Randall & Wolff, 1994), and .62 (van den Putte, 1993). Studies in specific behavioral domains, such as condom use and exercise, have produced similar results, with intention-behavior correlations ranging from .44 to .56 (Albarracin, Johnson, Fishbein, & Muellerleile, 2001; Godin & Kok, 1996; Hausenblas, Carron, & Mack, 1997; Sheeran & Orbell, 1998). In a meta-analysis of these and other meta-analyses, Sheeran (2002) reported an overall correlation of .53 between intention and behavior.

Consider just one example from the consumer behavior domain (East, 1993). The study was conducted in 1990 in the United Kingdom when the British Government sold shares to the public in 12 regional electric companies. Participants in the study indicated their intentions to apply for shares and—after the application period was closed—they reported whether they had actually applied. The correlation between intention and behavior was found to be .82.

The Theory of Planned Behavior

The intention to adopt a certain course of action logically precedes actual performance of the behavior. Consistent with this reasoning, social psychologists tend to view intentions as mediating between attitudes and actions (e.g., Bagozzi & Warshaw, 1990; Bentler & Speckart, 1979; Fishbein & Ajzen, 1975; Fisher & Fisher, 1992; Gollwitzer, 1993; Kuhl, 1985; Locke & Latham, 1990; Triandis, 1977). In research on consumer behavior, investigators have conceptualized this causal sequence as the belief-attitude-intention hierarchy (e.g., Follows & Jobber, 2000; Madrigal, 2001; Ogle, Hyllegard, & Dunbar, 2004). Undoubtedly the most popular models in this domain are the *theory of reasoned action* (Ajzen & Fishbein, 1973, 1980; Fishbein, 1967a; Fishbein & Ajzen, 1975) and its successor, the *theory of planned behavior* (Ajzen, 1988, 1991). Briefly, according to the theory of planned behavior, intentions to perform a given behavior are influenced by three major factors: a favorable or unfavorable evaluation of the behavior (attitude toward the behavior), perceived social pressure to perform or not perform the behavior (subjective norm), and self-efficacy in relation to the behavior (perceived behavioral control). In combination, attitude toward the behavior, subjective norm, and perception of behavioral control lead to the formation of a behavioral intention. As a general rule, the more favorable the attitude and subjective norm, and the greater the perceived behavioral control, the stronger should be the person's intention to perform the behavior in question. Finally, given a sufficient degree of actual control over the behavior, people are expected to carry out their intentions when the opportunity arises. Intention is thus assumed to be an immediate antecedent of behavior. However, because many behaviors pose difficulties of execution that may limit volitional control, it is useful to consider perceived behavioral control in addition to intention. To the extent that people are realistic in their judgments of a behavior's difficulty, a measure of perceived behavioral control can serve as a proxy for actual control and contribute to the prediction of the behavior in question (see Ajzen, 1991). A schematic representation of the theory is shown in Figure 20.1.

When applied to consumer behavior, the intention of interest may be the intention to purchase a given product or service. The three major determinants of this behavior—attitudes toward buying the product, subjective norms, and perceptions of behavioral control—are traced to corresponding sets of behavior-relevant beliefs. Consistent with the expectancy–value model discussed earlier, attitude toward buying a product is assumed to be determined by accessible beliefs about the consequences of doing so, each belief weighted by the subjective value of the consequence in question. A similar logic applies to the relation between accessible normative beliefs and subjective norm, and the relation between accessible control beliefs and perceived behavioral control. Normative beliefs refer to the perceived behavioral expectations of such important referent individuals or groups as the person's family, friends, and coworkers. These normative beliefs—in combination with the person's motivation to comply with the different referents—determine the prevailing subjective norm regarding the purchase. Finally, control beliefs have to do with the perceived presence of factors that can facilitate or impede performance of a behavior. It is assumed that the perceived power of each control factor to impede or facilitate a purchase contributes to perceived control over this behavior in direct proportion to the person's subjective probability that the control factor is present. In the case of a purchase decision, issues of control may be related to financial constraints or a product's availability. It can be seen that the theory of planned behavior represents a "reasoned action" approach to consumer behavior because it assumes that intentions and behavior in this domain follow reasonably from the behavioral, normative, and control beliefs people hold about the behavior.

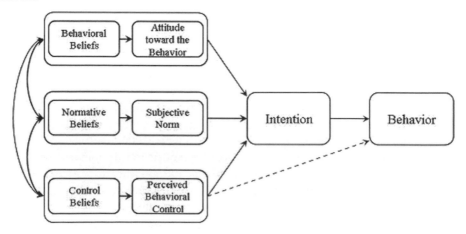

Figure 20.1   Theory of planned behavior

Virtually hundreds of studies have been conducted over the past 35 years, applying the theories of reasoned action and planned behavior in a variety of different domains. In the domain of consumer behavior, investigators have used these models to explore the purchase of familiar versus unfamiliar products (Arvola et al., 1999), environmentally responsible purchases in different cultures (Chan & Lau, 2001), clipping coupons online (Fortin, 2000), patronage of a particular retail environment (Ogle et al., 2004), mail-order purchases of apparel (Shim & Drake, 1990), shoplifting (Tonglet, 2002), and a host of other consumer behaviors. We saw earlier that intentions are generally found to be good predictors of behavior. In addition, a great number of studies conducted in the context of Bandura's (1977) social cognitive theory have documented that self-efficacy is a good predictor of behavior (e.g., Garcia & King, 1991; Longo, Lent, & Brown, 1922; Sadri & Robertson, 1993). Further, measures of perceived behavioral control are often found to improve prediction over and above intention (Armitage & Conner, 2001; Cheung & Chan, 2000), and this is particularly true when the behavior is not under complete volitional control (Madden, Ellen, & Ajzen, 1992).

Several meta-analyses of the empirical literature have provided evidence to show that intentions can be predicted with considerable accuracy from measures of attitudes toward the behavior, subjective norms, and perceived behavioral control (Albarracin et al., 2001; Armitage & Conner, 2001; Godin & Kok, 1996; Hagger, Chatzisarantis, & Biddle, 2002; Sheeran & Taylor, 1999; Shepperd et al., 1988; van den Putte, 1993). For a wide range of behaviors, attitudes are found to correlate well with intentions; across the different meta-analyses, the mean correlations range from .45 to .60. For the prediction of intentions from subjective norms, these correlations range from .34 to .42, and for the prediction of intention from perceived behavioral control, the range is .35 to .46. Finally, the multiple correlations for predicting intentions from attitudes, subjective norms, and perceived behavioral control ranged from .63 to .71.

CONCLUDING COMMENTS

The two major conceptual and research paradigms in consumer behavior—behavioral decision theory and the theories or reasoned action and planned behavior—may both seem to imply that consumers are assumed to be rational in their decisions and actions. This would, however, be an inaccurate reading of either approach. Although behavioral decision theory takes rational, normative models as its starting point, it recognizes that human decision making can be biased in a variety of ways and is best described as observing "bounded rationality" (Simon, 1955). In fact, the nature of biases in judgment and decision making has been at the center of research over the past 30 years.

Similarly, the theory of planned behavior also does not assume a rational decision process. Human social behavior is said to be reasoned, controlled, or planned in the sense that it takes account of the behavior's likely consequences, the normative expectations of important referents, and factors that may impede performance. As noted in the discussion of the expectancy–value model of attitudes, the beliefs people hold may be unfounded, inaccurate, biased, or even irrational. However, their attitudes, subjective norms, and perceptions of behavioral control are thought to follow spontaneously and reasonably from these beliefs, produce a corresponding behavioral intention, and ultimately result in behavior that is consistent with the overall tenor of the beliefs. It should be noted, however, that this does not necessarily imply a deliberate, effortful retrieval of information and construction of attitudes prior to every behavior. Attitudes, subjective norms, and perceived behavioral control are assumed to be available automatically as performance of a behavior is being considered (Ajzen & Fishbein, 2000).

These ideas may help us understand several issues relevant to consumer behavior: brand loyalty, the importance of brand image, the purchase of luxury goods, and impulse buying. Brand loyalty refers to the tendency to purchase a particular brand repeatedly, to stay with a familiar brand used in the past rather than switch to a new brand, or to psychological commitment to a brand (Jacoby, 1971; Odin, Odin, & Valette-Florence, 2001; Olson & Jacoby, 1971). This tendency may appear to be unreasonable, especially when a new brand offers potential advantages, and various attempts have been made to study the determinants and consequences of brand loyalty (for recent examples, see Chaudhuri & Holbrook, 2001; Danaher, Wilson, & Davis, 2003; Kim, Han, & Park, 2001; Yi & Jeon, 2003). A related issue has been raised in work with the theory of planned behavior where it is often found that frequency of past behavior has an effect on later behavior that is often not fully mediated by the predictors in the theory of planned behavior (Ajzen, 1991; Albarracin et al., 2001; Bagozzi, 1981; Bentler & Speckart, 1979; for reviews, see Conner & Armitage, 1998; Fredricks & Dossett, 1983; Ouellette & Wood, 1998). Although various explanations for this effect can be offered (see Ajzen, 2002), the possibility cannot be ruled out that repeated purchase of a given product produces a habit or routine such that on future occasions the product is chosen almost automatically with only minimal cognitive control.

A great deal of research has been devoted to the role of brand image in consumer behavior (for recent examples, see Batra & Homer, 2004; Jo, Nakamoto, & Nelson, 2003; Martinez & de Chernatony, 2004). At first glance, it might appear unreasonable for consumers to prefer brand-name products over unknown or generic products with the same qualities. However, the theory of planned behavior assumes that people's intentions and actions are guided by their *beliefs* about buying a product, not by the objective attributes of the product. Advertising and other exposures to a brand can provide an advantage by associating the brand with favorable attributes, resulting in a positive brand image not available to unfamiliar brands. If, for example, consumers believe that Bayer aspirin is a more effective pain reliever than a generic brand of aspirin, it is reasonable for them to develop a more favorable attitude toward buying the Bayer brand.

Similar arguments apply to the purchase of "luxury goods," i.e., goods that command a premium price because of the manufacturer's reputation. It might be argued that it makes no sense to buy a $2,000 Rolex watch when equally accurate, durable, and attractive watches are available for a fraction of the price. This does not, however, contradict the logic of the theory of planned behavior which only assumes that the purchase of a Rolex watch is reasonable in light of the consumer's own subjective beliefs and values associated with the purchase. Consumers may well believe that owning a Rolex watch confers high status or otherwise reflects positively on them. If they place high value on these consequences, their purchase of a Rolex watch would be quite reasonable. Alternatively, they may believe that important others think they should buy an expensive watch or that in their circle of friends this is a common purchase, and the resulting subjective norm could be an important motivating factor.

Finally, buying on impulse is also an apparently unreasoned action that has attracted considerable attention (e.g., Beatty & Ferrell, 1998; Hausman, 2000; Jones, Reynolds, Weun, & Beatty, 2003; Verplanken & Herabadi, 2001). Fast, immediate reactions to the requirements of a situation are, of course, not inconsistent with a reasoned action approach. Well-established beliefs and attitudes are activated spontaneously and thus guide behavior without much cognitive effort. However, impulse buying appears to bypass reasoning, to be based more on emotions than on rational factors. Indeed, it is often argued that the theories of reasoned action and planned behavior are too rational, failing to take into account emotions, compulsions, and other noncognitive or irrational determinants of human behavior (e.g., Armitage, Conner, & Norman, 1999; Gibbons, Gerrard, Blanton, & Russell, 1998; Ingham, 1994; Morojele & Stephenson, 1994; van der Pligt & de Vries, 1998; Verplanken &

Herabadi, 2001). To be sure, much of the research conducted in the framework of these theories has devoted little attention to the role of emotion in the prediction of intentions and actions. This is not to say, however, that emotions have no place in theories of this kind. It is well known that general moods and emotions can have systematic effects on beliefs and evaluations: People in a positive mood tend to evaluate events more favorably and to judge favorable events as more likely than people in a negative mood (Forgas, Bower, & Krantz, 1984; Johnson & Tversky, 1983; Robles, Smith, Carver, & Wellens, 1987; Schaller & Cialdini, 1990). In a reasoned action approach, such effects would be expected to influence attitudes and intentions and thus to have an impact on behavior.

SUMMARY

Two major paradigms have provided much of the impetus for the study of consumer behavior. Choices among alternative brands, products, or services are in many ways no different from other kinds of decisions, and the methods of behavioral decision theory have thus proven valuable to the study of consumer behavior. Multiattribute decision models emphasize the importance of expected values derived from a product's perceived attributes. However, as in other kinds of decisions, judgments underlying consumer choices are found to deviate in systematic ways from normative prescriptions.

One limitation of the revealed preferences approach adopted in work on multiattribute decisions is that it provides no direct information about consumers' beliefs and attitudes regarding real-life products or services. A more fruitful approach in this regard is found in the expectancy–value model of attitude. In work with this model, accessible beliefs about a product are elicited in a free-response format and attitudes toward the product are directly assessed. This approach makes it possible for the investigator to identify important attribute characteristics that guide consumer attitudes and behavior.

In a related fashion, the theory of planned behavior provides a conceptual framework that focuses on the specific behaviors performed by consumers, be they buying a given brand or product, searching for information about a product, or shopping at a given retail outlet. According to the theory, the immediate antecedent of such behaviors is the intention to perform the behavior in question. Intentions, in turn, are determined by attitudes toward the behavior, subjective norms, and perceived behavioral control. Behavioral, normative, and control beliefs, respectively, provide the basis for the formation of attitudes, subjective norms, and perceptions of behavioral control. As in many other behavioral domains, the theory of planned behavior has proven to be a useful conceptual and methodological framework for the study of consumer behavior.

NOTES

1. Attribute values can interact with each other, requiring separate evaluation of each possible combination of attributes. This complication is usually disregarded because it seems to make little difference to the results (W. Edwards & Fasolo, 2001).
2. A notable exception are process tracing methods, such as think-aloud protocols developed for the study of problem solving (see Ericsson & Simon, 1980; Payne, 1994), which have also been applied to consumer decision making (e.g., Backlund, Skavér, Montgomery, Bring, & Strender, 2003).
3. See Ajzen (1977) for a similar argument in relation to research on interpersonal attraction.
4. It is now also possible to conduct focus groups online, by involving computer users in a simultaneous online discussion, or letting them contribute to the discussion sequentially over a period of time (see Sweet, 2001).
5. Framing and other situational variations affect choices presumably because they influence beliefs about and evaluations of the available alternatives.

REFERENCES

Ajzen, I. (1974). Effects of information on interpersonal attraction: Similarity versus affective value. *Journal of Personality and Social Psychology, 29*, 374–380.

Ajzen, I. (1977). Information processing approaches to interpersonal attraction. In S. Duck (Ed.), *Theory and practice in interpersonal attraction* (pp. 51–77). London: Academic Press.

Ajzen, I. (1988). *Attitudes, personality, and behavior.* Chicago: Dorsey Press.

Ajzen, I. (1991). The theory of planned behavior. *Organizational Behavior and Human Decision Processes, 50*, 179–211.

Ajzen, I. (1996). The social psychology of decision making. In E. T. Higgins & A. W. Kruglanski (Eds.), *Social psychology: Handbook of basic principles* (pp. 297–325). New York: Guilford..

Ajzen, I. (2002). Residual effects of past on later behavior: Habituation and reasoned action perspectives. *Personality and Social Psychology Review, 6*, 107–122.

Ajzen, I., & Fishbein, M. (1973). Attitudinal and normative variables as predictors of specific behavior. *Journal of Personality and Social Psychology, 27*, 41–57.

Ajzen, I., & Fishbein, M. (1977). Attitude-behavior relations: A theoretical analysis and review of empirical research. *Psychological Bulletin, 84*, 888–918.

Ajzen, I., & Fishbein, M. (1980). *Understanding attitudes and predicting social behavior.* Englewood-Cliffs, NJ: Prentice-Hall.

Ajzen, I., & Fishbein, M. (2000). Attitudes and the attitude-behavior relation: Reasoned and automatic processes. In W. Stroebe & M. Hewstone (Eds.), *European review of social psychology* (Vol. 11, pp. 1–33). Chichester, England: Wiley.

Ajzen, I., & Fishbein, M. (2005). The influence of attitudes on behavior. In D. Albarracín, B. T. Johnson & M. P. Zanna (Eds.), *Handbook of attitudes and attitude change: Basic principles* (pp. 173–221). Mahwah, NJ: Erlbaum.

Ajzen, I., Nichols, A. J., & Driver, B. L. (1995). Identifying salient beliefs about leisure activities: Frequency of elicitation versus response latency. *Journal of Applied Social Psychology, 25*, 1391–1410.

Albarracin, D., Johnson, B. T., Fishbein, M., & Muellerleile, P. A. (2001). Theories of reasoned action and planned behavior as models of condom use: A meta-analysis. *Psychological Bulletin, 127*, 142–161.

Albert, D., Aschenbrenner, K. M., & Schmalhofer, F. (1989). Cognitive choice processes and the attitude–behavior relation. In A. Upmeyer (Ed.), *Attitudes and behavioral decisions* (pp. 61–99). New York: Springer–Verlag.

Allport, G. W. (1954). *The nature of prejudice.* Oxford: Addison-Wesley.

Allport, G. W. (1968). The historical background of modern social psychology. In G. Lindzey & E. Aronson (Eds.), *Handbook of social psychology* (Vol. 1, pp. 1–80). Reading, MA: Addison-Wesley.

Armitage, C. J., & Conner, M. (2001). Efficacy of the theory of planned behavior: A meta-analytic review. *British Journal of Social Psychology, 40*, 471–499.

Armitage, C. J., Conner, M., & Norman, P. (1999). Differential effects of mood on information processing: Evidence from the theories of reasoned action and planned behaviour. *European Journal of Social Psychology, 29*, 419–433.

Arvola, A., Lähteenmäki, L., & Tuorila, H. (1999). Predicting the intent to purchase unfamiliar and familiar cheeses: The effects of attitudes, expected liking and food neophobia. *Appetite* (Vol. 32, pp. 113–126): Elsevier Science.

Backlund, L., Skavér, Y., Montgomery, H., Bring, J., & Strender, L.-E. (2003). Doctors' decision processes in a drug-prescription task: The validity of rating scales and think-aloud reports. *Organizational Behavior & Human Decision Processes, 91*, 108–117.

Bagozzi, R. P. (1981). An examination of the validity of two models of attitude. *Multivariate Behavioral Research, 16*, 323–359.

Bagozzi, R. P., Gürhan-Canli, Z., & Priester, J. T. (2002). *The social psychology of consumer behaviour.* Buckingham: Open University Press.

Bagozzi, R. P., & Warshaw, P. R. (1990). Trying to consume. *Journal of Consumer Research, 17*, 127–140.

Balderjahn, I. (1988). Personality variables and environmental attitudes as predictors of ecologically responsible consumption patterns. *Journal of Business Research, 17*, 51–56.

Bandura, A. (1977). Self-efficacy: Toward a unifying theory of behavioral change. *Psychological Review, 84*, 191–215.

Bargh, J. A., Chaiken, S., Govender, R., & Pratto, F. (1992). The generality of the automatic attitude activation effect. *Journal of Personality and Social Psychology, 62*, 893–912.

Bargh, J. A., Chaiken, S., Raymond, P., & Hymes, C. (1996). The automatic evaluation effect: Unconditional automatic attitude activation with a pronunciation task. *Journal of Experimental Social Psychology, 32*, 104–128.

Batra, R., & Homer, P. M. (2004). The situational impact of brand image beliefs. *Journal of Consumer Psychology, 14*, 318–330.

Batra, R., & Ray, M. L. (1986). Situational effects of advertising repetition: The moderating influence of motivation, ability, and opportunity to respond. *Journal of Consumer Research, 12*, 432–445.

Beatty, S. E., & Ferrell, M. E. (1998). Impulse buying: Modeling its precursors. *Journal of Retailing, 74*, 169–191.

Bentler, P. M., & Speckart, G. (1979). Models of attitude-behavior relations. *Psychological Review, 86*, 452–464.

Berger, I. E., & Mitchell, A. A. (1989). The effect of advertising on attitude accessibility, attitude confidence, and the attitude-behavior relationship. *Journal of Consumer Research, 16*, 269–279.

Bettman, J. R. (1986). Consumer psychology. *Annual Review of Psychology* (Vol. 37, pp. 257–289). Annual Reviews Inc.

Bristol, T., & Fern, E. F. (2003). The effects of interaction on consumers' attitudes in focus groups. *Psychology and Marketing, 20*, 433–454.

Brunel, F. d. r. F., Tietje, B. C., & Greenwald, A. G. (2004). Is the Implicit Association Test a valid and valuable measure of implicit consumer social cognition? *Journal of Consumer Psychology* (Vol. 14, pp. 385–404). Mahwah, NJ: Erlbaum.

Bruner, J. S. (1973). *Beyond the information given: Studies in the psychology of knowing*. New York: W. W. Norton.

Calder, B. J. (1977). Focus groups and the nature of qualitative marketing research. Journal of Marketing Research, 14, 353–364.

Carlson, E. R. (1956). Attitude change through modification of attitude structure. *Journal of Abnormal & Social Psychology, 52*, 256–261.

Carmon, Z., & Simonson, I. (1998). Price-quality trade-offs in choice versus matching: New insights into the prominence effect. *Journal of Consumer Psychology, 7*, 323–343.

Chaiken, S., & Trope, Y. (Eds.). (1999). *Dual-process theories in social psychology*. New York: Guilford.

Chan, R. Y. K., & Lau, L. B. Y. (2001). Explaining green purchasing behavior: A cross-cultural study on American and Chinese consumers. *Journal of International Consumer Marketing* (Vol. 14, pp. 9–40). Haworth Press.

Chaudhuri, A., & Holbrook, M. B. (2001). The chain of effects from brand trust and brand affect to brand performance: The role of brand loyalty. *Journal of Marketing, 65*, 81–93.

Cheung, S.-F., & Chan, D. K.-S. (2000). *The role of perceived behavioral control in predicting human behavior: A meta-analytic review of studies on the theory of planned behavior*. Unpublished manuscript, Chinese University of Hong Kong.

Cohen, J. B., & Chakravarti, D. (1990). Consumer psychology. *Annual Review of Psychology* (Vol. 41, pp. 243). Annual Reviews Inc.

Conner, M., & Armitage, C. J. (1998). Extending the theory of planned behavior: A review and avenues for further research. *Journal of Applied Social Psychology, 28*, 1429–1464.

Coombs, C. H. (1975). Portfolio theory and the measurement of risk. In M. F. Kaplan & S. Schwartz (Eds.), *Human judgment and decision processes* (pp. 63–85). New York: Academic Press.

Coombs, C. H., Bezembinder, T. G., & Goode, F. M. (1967). Testing expectation theories of decision making without measuring utility or subjective probability. *Journal of Mathematical Psychology, 4*, 72–103.

Corfman, K. P., Lehmann, D. R., & Narayanan, S. (1991). Values, utility, and ownership: Modeling the relationships for consumer durables. *Journal of Retailing, 67*, 184–204.

Coulter, K. S., & Punj, G. N. (2004). The effects of cognitive resource requirements, availability, and argument quality on brand attitudes: A melding of elaboration likelihood and cognitive resource matching theories. *Journal of Advertising, 33*, 53–64.

Coupey, E., Irwin, J. R., & Payne, J. W. (1998). Product category familiarity and preference construction. *Journal of Consumer Research, 24*, 459–468.

Dabholkar, P. A. (1999). Expectancy-value models. In P. E. Earl & S. Kemp (Eds.), *The elgar companion to consumer research and economic psychology*. Cheltenham: Edward Elgar.

Danaher, P. J., Wilson, I. W., & Davis, R. A. (2003). A comparison of online and offline consumer brand loyalty. *Marketing Science, 22*, 461–476.

Dhar, R., & Nowlis, S. M. (1999). The effect of time pressure on consumer choice deferral. *Journal of Consumer Research, 25*, 369–384.

Doll, J., & Ajzen, I. (1992). Accessibility and stability of predictors in the theory of planned behavior. *Journal of Personality and Social Psychology, 63*, 754–765.

Eagly, A. H., & Chaiken, S. (1993). *The psychology of attitudes*. Fort Worth, TX: Harcourt Brace.

Eagly, A. H., & Chaiken, S. (1998). Attitude structure and function. In D. T. Gilbert & S. T. Fiske (Eds.), *The handbook of social psychology* (4th ed., Vol. 1, pp. 269–322). Boston, MA: McGraw-Hill.

East, R. (1993). Investment decisions and the theory of planned behavior. *Journal of Economic Psychology, 14*, 337–375.

Edwards, A. L. (1957). *Techniques of attitude scale construction*. East Norwalk, CT: Appleton-Century-Crofts.

Edwards, W. (1954). The theory of decision making. *Psychological Bulletin, 51*, 380–417.

Edwards, W. (1955). The prediction of decisions among bets. *Journal of Experimental Psychology* (Vol. 50, pp. 201–214).

Edwards, W., & Fasolo, B. (2001). Decision technology. *Annual Review of Psychology, 52*, 581–606.

Epstein, S. (1979). The stability of behavior: I. On predicting most of the people much of the time. *Journal of Personality and Social Psychology, 37*, 1097–1126.

Ericsson, K. A., & Simon, H. A. (1980). Verbal reports as data., *Psychological Review* (Vol. 87, pp. 215–251). Washington, DC: American Psychological Association.

Fazio, R. H. (1986). How do attitudes guide behavior? In R. M. H. Sorrentino & E. Tory (Eds.), *Handbook of motivation and cognition: Foundations of social behavior* (pp. 204–243). New York: Guilford.

Fazio, R. H. (1990). Multiple processes by which attitudes guide behavior: The MODE model as an integrative framework. In M. P. Zanna (Ed.), *Advances in experimental social psychology* (Vol. 23, pp. 75–109). San Diego, CA: Academic Press.

Fazio, R. H. (1993). Variability in the likelihood of automatic attitude activation: Data reanalysis and commentary on Bargh, Chaiken, Govender, & Pratto (1992). *Journal of Personality and Social Psychology, 64*, 753–758.

Fazio, R. H. (1995). Attitudes as object-evaluation associations: Determinants, consequences, and correlates of attitude accessibility. In R. E. Petty & J. A. Krosnick (Eds.), *Attitude strength: Antecedents and consequences* (pp. 247–282). Mahwah, NJ: Erlbaum.

Fazio, R. H., Chen, J., McDonel, E. C., & Sherman, S. J. (1982). Attitude accessibility, attitude-behavior consistency, and the strength of the object-evaluation association. *Journal of Experimantal Social Psychology, 18*, 339–357.

Fazio, R. H., Powell, M. C., & Williams, C. J. (1989). The role of attitude accessibility in the attitude-to-behavior process. *Journal of Consumer Research, 16*, 280–288.

Fazio, R. H., & Towles-Schwen, T. (1999). The MODE model of attitude-behavior processes. In S. Chaiken & Y. Trope (Eds.), *Dual-process theories in social psychology* (pp. 97–116). New York: Guilford.

Fazio, R. H., & Williams, C. J. (1986). Attitude accessibility as a moderator of the attitude-perception and attitude-behavior relations: An investigation of the 1984 presidential election. *Journal of Personality and Social Psychology, 51*, 505–514.

Feather, N. T. (1959). Subjective probability and decision under uncertainty. *Psychological Review, 66*, 150–164.

Feather, N. T. (Ed.). (1982). *Expectations and actions: Expectancy–value models in psychology*. Hillsdale, NJ: Erlbaum.

Festinger, L. (1957). *A theory of cognitive dissonance*. Oxford: Row, Peterson.

Fishbein, M. (1963). An investigation of the relationships between beliefs about an object and the attitude toward that object. *Human Relations, 16*, 233–240.

Fishbein, M. (1967a). Attitude and the prediction of behavior. In M. Fishbein (Ed.), *Readings in attitude theory and measurement* (pp. 477–492). New York: Wiley.

Fishbein, M. (1967b). A consideration of beliefs and their role in attitude measurement. In M. Fishbein (Ed.), *Readings in attitude theory and measurement* (pp. 257–266). New York: Wiley.

Fishbein, M., & Ajzen, I. (1974). Attitudes towards objects as predictors of single and multiple behavioral criteria. *Psychological Review, 81,* 59–74.

Fishbein, M., & Ajzen, I. (1975). *Belief, attitude, intention, and behavior: An introduction to theory and research.* Reading, MA: Addison-Wesley.

Fisher, J. D., & Fisher, W. A. (1992). Changing AIDS-risk behavior. *Psychological Bulletin, 111,* 455–474.

Follows, S. B., & Jobber, D. (2000). Environmentally responsible purchase behaviour: A test of a consumer model. *European Journal of Marketing, 34,* 723–746.

Forgas, J. P., Bower, G. H., & Krantz, S. E. (1984). The influence of mood on perceptions of social interactions. *Journal of Experimental Social Psychology, 20,* 497–513.

Fortin, D. R. (2000). Clipping coupons in cyberspace: A proposed model of behavior for deal-prone consumers. *Psychology and Marketing, 17,* 515–534.

Foxall, G. R., Oliveira-Castro, J. M., & Schrezenmaier, T. C. (2004). The behavioral economics of consumer brand choice: Patterns of reinforcement and utility maximization. *Behavioural Processes, 66,* 235–260.

Fredricks, A. J., & Dossett, D. L. (1983). Attitude-behavior relations: A comparison of the Fishbein-Ajzen and the Bentler-Speckart models. *Journal of Personality and Social Psychology, 45,* 501–512.

Garcia, A. W., & King, A. C. (1991). Predicting long-term adherence to aerobic exercise: A comparison of two models. *Journal of Sport and Exercise Psychology, 13,* 394–410.

Gibbons, F. X., Gerrard, M., Blanton, H., & Russell, D. W. (1998). Reasoned action and social reaction: Willingness and intention as independent predictors of health risk. *Journal of Personality and Social Psychology, 74,* 1164–1180.

Gill, J. D., Crosby, L. A., & Taylor, J. R. (1986). Ecological concern, attitudes, and social norms in voting behavior. *Public Opinion Quarterly, 50,* 537–554.

Godin, G., & Kok, G. (1996). The theory of planned behavior: A review of its applications to health-related behaviors. *American Journal of Health Promotion, 11,* 87–98.

Goldstein, W. M., & Hogarth, R. M. (1997). Judgment and decision research: Some historical context. In W. M. Goldstein & R. M. Hogarth (Eds.), *Research on judgment and decision making: Currents, connectionc, and controversies.* Cambridge: Cambridge University Press.

Gollwitzer, P. M. (1993). Goal achievement: The role of intentions. In W. Stroebe & M. Hewstone (Eds.), *European Review of Social Psychology* (Vol. 4, pp. 141–185). Chichester: Wiley.

Green, B. F. (1954). Attitude measurement. In G. Lindzey (Ed.), *Handbood of social psychology* (Vol. 1, pp. 335–369). Reading, MA: Addison-Wesley.

Greenbaum, T. L. (1998). *The handbook for focus group research* (2nd ed.). Sage.

Hagger, M. S., Chatzisarantis, N. L. D., & Biddle, S. J. H. (2002). A meta-analytic review of the theories of reasoned action and planned behavior in physical activity: Predictive validity and the contribution of additional variables. *Journal of Sport and Exercise Psychology, 24,* 3–32.

Hausenblas, H. A., Carron, A. V., & Mack, D. E. (1997). Application of the theories of reasoned action and planned behavior to exercise behavior: A meta-analysis. *Journal of Sport and Exercise Psychology, 19,* 36–51.

Hausman, A. (2000). A multi-method investigation of consumer motivations in impulse buying behavior. *Journal of Consumer Marketing, 17,* 403–419.

Hines, J., Hungerford, H., & Tomera, A. (1987). Analysis and synthesis or research on environmental behaviour: a meta-analysis. *Journal of Environmental Education, 18,* 1–8.

Hovland, C. I., & Sherif, M. (1952). Judgmental phenomena and scales of attitude measurement: Item displacement in Thurstone scales. *Journal of Abnormal & Social Psychology, 47,* 822–832.

Hsee, C. K., & Leclerc, F. (1998). Will products look more attractive when presented separately or together? *Journal of Consumer Research, 25,* 175–186.

Hui, M. K., & Zhou, L. (2003). Country-of-manufacture effects for known brands. *European Journal of Marketing, 37,* 133–153.

Ingham, R. (1994). Some speculations on the concept of rationality. Advances *in Medical Sociology, 4,* 89–111.

Jacoby, J. (1971). Brand loyalty: A conceptual definition. *Proceedings of the Annual Convention of the American Psychological Association,* Vol. 6, 655–656.

Jo, M.-S., Nakamoto, K., & Nelson, J. E. (2003). The shielding effects of brand image against lower quality countries-of-origin in global manufacturing. *Journal of Business Research, 56,* 637–646.

Johnson, E. J., & Tversky, A. (1983). Affect, generalization, and the perception of risk. *Journal of Personality & Social Psychology, 45*, 20–31.

Jones, M. A., Reynolds, K. E., Weun, S., & Beatty, S. E. (2003). The product-specific nature of impulse buying tendency. *Journal of Business Research, 56*, 505–511.

Kahan, J. P. (2001). Focus groups as a tool for policy analysis. *Analyses of Social Issues & Public Policy (ASAP), 1*, 129–146.

Kahneman, D., Slovic, P., & Tversky, A. (Eds.). (1982). *Judgments under uncertainty: Heuristics and biases.* New York: Cambridge University Press.

Kahneman, D., & Tversky, A. (1979). Prospect theory: An analysis of decision under risk. *Econometrica, 47*, 263–291.

Kaplan, K. J., & Fishbein, M. (1969). The source of beliefs, their saliency, and prediction of attitude. *Journal of Social Psychology, 78*, 63–74.

Kim, C. K., Han, D., & Park, S.-B. (2001). The effect of brand personality and brand identification on brand loyalty: Applying the theory of social identification. *Japanese Psychological Research, 43*, 195–206.

Kleiber, P. B. (2004). Focus groups: More than a method of qualitative inquiry. In A & A (Eds.), *Foundations for research: Methods of inquiry in education and the social sciences.* (pp. 87–102) Mahwah, NJ: Erlbaum.

Kokkinaki, F., & Lunt, P. (1997). The relationship between involvement, attitude accessibility and attitude-behaviour consistency. *British Journal of Social Psychology, 36*, 497–509.

Kuhl, J. (1985). Volitional aspects of achievement motivation and learned helplessness: Toward a comprehensive theory of action control. In B. A. Maher (Ed.), *Progress in experimental personality research* (Vol. 13, pp. 99–171). San Diego: Academic Press.

Kunda, Z. (1987). Motivated inference: Self-serving generation and evaluation of causal theories. *Journal of Personality & Social Psychology, 53*, 636–647.

Litvin, S. W., & MacLaurin, D. J. (2001). Consumer attitude and behavior. *Annals of tourism research* (Vol. 28, pp. 821–823). Elsevier Science.

Locke, E. A., & Latham, G. P. (1990). *A theory of goal setting and task performance.* Englewood Cliffs, NJ: Prentice-Hall.

Longo, D. A., Lent, R. W., & Brown, S. D. (1922). Social cognitive variables in the prediction of client motivation and attrition. *Journal of Counseling Psychology, 39*, 447–452.

Lutz, R. J. (1977). An experimental investigation of causal relations among cognitions, affect, and behavioral intention. *Journal of Consumer Research, 3*, 197–208.

Madden, T. J., & Ajzen, I. (1991). Affective cues in persuasion: An assessment of causal mediation. *Advertising Letters, 2*, 359–366.

Madden, T. J., Ellen, P. S., & Ajzen, I. (1992). A comparison of the theory of planned behavior and the theory of reasoned action. *Personality and Social Psychology Bulletin, 18*, 3–9.

Madrigal, R. (2001). Social identity effects in a belief-attitude-intentions hierarchy: Implications for corporate sponsorship. *Psychology & marketing* (Vol. 18, pp. 145–165). New York: Wiley.

Martinez, E., & de Chernatony, L. (2004). The effect of brand extension strategies upon brand image. *Journal of Consumer Marketing, 21*, 39–50.

Miller, D. T., & Ross, M. (1975). Self-serving biases in the attribution of causality: Fact or fiction? *Psychological Bulletin, 82*, 213–225.

Mitchell, A. A., & Olson, J. C. (1981). Are product attribute beliefs the only mediator of advertising effects on brand attitude? *Journal of Marketing Research, 18*, 318–332.

Mittal, B. (1990). The relative roles of brand beliefs and attitude toward the ad as mediators of brand attitude: A second look. *Journal of Marketing Research, 27*, 209–219.

Morojele, N. K., & Stephenson, G. M. (1994). Addictive behaviours: Predictors of abstinence intentions and expectations in the Theory of Planned Behaviour. In D. R. Rutter & L. Quine (Eds.), *Social psychology and health: European perspectives* (pp. 47–70). Aldershot: Avebury/Ashgate Publishing Co.

Nisbett, R., & Ross, L. (1980). Human inference: Strategies and shortcomings of social judgment. Englewood Cliffs, NJ: Prenctice-Hall.

Notani, A. S. (1998). Moderators of perceived behavioral control's predictiveness in the theory of planned behavior: A meta-analysis. *Journal of Consumer Psychology, 7*, 247–271.

Odin, Y., Odin, N., & Valette-Florence, P. (2001). Conceptual and operational aspects of brand loyalty: An empirical investigation. *Journal of Business Research, 53*, 75–84.

Ogle, J. P., Hyllegard, K. H., & Dunbar, B. H. (2004). Predicting Patronage Behaviors in a Sustainable Retail Environment: Adding Retail Characteristics and Consumer Lifestyle Orientation to the Belief-Attitude-Behavior Intention Model. *Environment and Behavior, 36*, 717–741.

Olson, J. C., & Jacoby, J. (1971). A construct validation study of brand loyalty. *Proceedings of the Annual Convention of the American Psychological Association* (Vol. 6, pp. 657–658).

Osgood, C. E., Suci, G. J., & Tannenbaum, P. H. (1957). *The measurement of meaning.* Urbana: University of Illinois Press.

Ouellette, J. A., & Wood, W. (1998). Habit and intention in everyday life: The multiple processes by which past behavior predicts future behavior. *Psychological Bulletin, 124*, 54–74.

Payne, J. W. (1994). Thinking aloud: Insights into information processing. *Psychological Science, 5*, 241, 245–248.

Peak, H. (1955). Attitude and motivation. In M. R. Jones (Ed.), *Nebraska symposium on motivation* (Vol. 3, pp. 149–188). Lincoln: University of Nebraska Press.

Peter, J. P., & Olson, J. C. (1993). Consumer behaviora and marketing strategy (3rd ed.). Homewood, IL: Richard D. Erwin, Inc.

Peterson, C. R., & Beach, L. R. (1967). Man as an intuitive statistician. *Psychological Bulletin, 68*, 29–46.

Petkova, K. G., Ajzen, I., & Driver, B. L. (1995). Salience of anti-abortion beliefs and commitment to an attitudinal position: On the strength, structure, and predictive validity of anti-abortion attitudes. *Journal of Applied Social Psychology, 25*, 463–483.

Petty, R. E., & Cacioppo, J. T. (1986). The elaboration likelihood model of persuasion. In L. Berkowitz (Ed.), *Advances in experimental social psychology* (Vol. 19, pp. 123–205). New York: Academic Press.

Randall, D. M., & Wolff, J. A. (1994). The time interval in the intention-behaviour relationship: Meta-analysis. *British Journal of Social Psychology, 33*, 405–418.

Robles, R., Smith, R., Carver, C. S., & Wellens, A. R. (1987). Influence of subliminal visual images on the experience of anxiety. *Personality and Social Psychology Bulletin, 13*, 399–410.

Rosenberg, M. J. (1956). Cognitive structure and attitudinal affect. *Journal of Abnormal and Social Psychology, 53*, 367–372.

Sadri, G., & Robertson, I. T. (1993). Self-efficacy and work-related behavior: A review and meta-analysis. *Applied Psychology, 42*, 139–152.

Schaller, M., & Cialdini, R. B. (1990). Happiness, sadness, and helping: A motivational integration. In E. T. Higgins & R. M. Sorrentino (Eds.), *Handbook of motivation and cognition: Foundations of social behavior* (Vol. 2, pp. 265–296). New York: Guilford.

Sengupta, J., & Fitzsimons, G. J. (2004). The effect of analyzing reasons on the stability of brand attitudes: A reconciliation of opposing predictions. *Journal of Consumer Research* (Vol. 31, pp. 705–711). Chicago: University of Chicago Press.

Shafir, E., & LeBoeuf, R. A. (2002). Rationality. *Annual Review of Psychology, 53*, 491–517.

Sheeran, P. (2002). Intention-behavior relations: A conceptual and empirical review. In W. Stroebe & M. Hewstone (Eds.), *European review of social psychology* (Vol. 12, pp. 1–36). Chichester: Wiley.

Sheeran, P., & Orbell, S. (1998). Do intentions predict condom use? Meta-analysis and examination of six moderator variables. *British Journal of Social Psychology, 37*, 231–250.

Sheeran, P., & Taylor, S. (1999). Predicting intentions to use condoms: A meta-analysis and comparison of the theories of reasoned action and planned behavior. *Journal of Applied Social Psychology, 29*, 1624–1675.

Sheppard, B. H., Hartwick, J., & Warshaw, P. R. (1988). The theory of reasoned action: A meta-analysis of past research with recommendations for modifications and future research. *Journal of Consumer Research, 15*, 325–342.

Sherif, M., & Hovland, C. I. (1961). *Social judgment: Assimilation and contrast effects in communication and attitude change.* New Haven, CT: Yale University Press.

Shim, S., & Drake, M. F. (1990). Consumer intention to purchase apparel by mail order: Beliefs, attitude, and decision process variables. *Clothing and Textiles Research Journal, 9*, 18–26. International Textile & Apparel Assn.

Simon, H. A. (1955). A behavioral model of rational choice. *Quarterly Journal of Economics, 69*, 99–118.

Simonson, I., Carmon, Z., Dhar, R., Drolet, A., & Nowlis, S. M. (2000). Consumer research: In search of identity. *Annual Review of Psychology, 52*, 249–275.

Slovic, P., Lichtenstein, S., & Fischhoff, B. (1988). Decision making. In R. C. Atkinson, R. J. Hernstein, G. Lindzey, & R. Duncan Luce (Eds.), *Stevens' handbook of experimental psychology* (2nd ed., Vol. 2, pp. 673–738). New York: Wiley.

Stoel, L., Wickliffe, V., & Lee, K. H. (2004). Attribute beliefs and spending as antecedents to shopping value. *Journal of Business Research, 57.*

Sweet, C. (2001). Designing and conducting virtual focus groups. *Qualitative Market Research: An International Journal,* 4, 130–135.

Tonglet, M. (2002). Consumer misbehaviour: An exploratory study of shoplifting. *Journal of Consumer Behaviour, 1,* 336–354.

Triandis, H. C. (1977). *Interpersonal behavior.* Monterey, CA: Brooks/Cole.

Tversky, A. (1969). Intransitivity of preferences. *Psychological Review, 76,* 31–48.

Tversky, A., & Kahneman, D. (1981). The framing of decisions and the psychology of choice. *Science, 211,* 453–458.

van den Putte, B. (1993). *On the theory of reasoned action.* Unpublished Dissertation, University of Amsterdam, The Netherlands.

van der Pligt, J., & de Vries, N. K. (1998). Expectancy-value models of health behavior: The role of salience and anticipated regret. *Psychology and Health, 13,* 289–305.

Van der Pligt, J., & Eiser, J. R. (1984). Dimensional salience, judgment, and attitudes. In J. R. Eiser (Ed.), *Attitudinal judgment* (pp. 161–177). New York: Springer-Verlag.

Verdurme, A., & Viaene, J. (2003). Exploring and modelling consumer attitudes towards genetically modified food. *Qualitative Market Research: An International Journal, 6,* 95–110.

Verplanken, B., & Herabadi, A. (2001). Individual differences in impulse buying tendency: Feeling and no thinking. *European Journal of Personality, 15,* S71–S83.

Weigel, R. H., & Newman, L. S. (1976). Increasing attitude-behavior correspondence by broadening the scope of the behavioral measure. *Journal of Personality and Social Psychology, 33,* 793–802.

Wooten, D. B., & Reed, A. I. (2000). A conceptual overview of the self-presentational concerns and response tendencies of focus group participants. *Journal of Consumer Psychology, 9,* 141–153.

Yi, Y., & Jeon, H. (2003). Effects of loyalty programs on value perception, program loyalty, and brand loyalty. *Journal of the Academy of Marketing Science, 31,* 229–240.

Zwick, R., Pieters, R., & Baumgartner, H. (1995). On the practical significance of hindsight bias: The case of the expectancy-disconfirmation model of consumer satisfaction. *Organizational Behavior & Human Decision Processes, 64,* 103–117.

21

I Know What You're Doing and Why You're Doing It

The Use of Persuasion Knowledge Model in Consumer Research

Margaret C. Campbell

University of Colorado at Boulder

Amna Kirmani

University of Maryland

A consumer is shopping for a suit for an upcoming job interview. When he tries on one suit, a salesperson mentions how good it looks on him. What does the consumer think of the salesperson? A teenager is eagerly watching *American Idol* and notices a can of Coke on the judge's table. What is the teenager's response toward Coke? A shopper on a Web site sees that the default option on the computer system she is putting together is the most expensive option. Is she more or less likely to choose the default?

The answers to these questions depend on the extent to which consumers activate and use their persuasion knowledge, i.e., theories and beliefs about how marketers try to influence them. The extent that a consumer imputes an ulterior persuasion motive to the salesperson's comment, the product placement, or the default option, is likely to affect the consumer's response. If these tactics are considered inappropriate, unfair, or manipulative, the consumer is likely to respond by discounting the salesperson's comments, reducing his or her attitude toward Coke, and steering away from the default option. Hence, an understanding of marketplace interactions is often dependent upon understanding the consumer's use of knowledge about marketplace persuasion. However, the role of consumers' persuasion knowledge and the interaction of consumer and marketing agent within a persuasion episode have received direct research attention only in the last few years.

The impetus for research on persuasion knowledge was Peter Wright's 1985 ACR Presidential Address, which introduced the concept of "schemer schema" to capture the idea that consumers have knowledge about persuasion that they sometimes use in interpreting marketers' persuasion attempts (Wright, 1986). Wright argued that consumer researchers were more focused on the persuasion agent than the persuasion target, and that our role as consumer researchers suggested that we should focus on the consumer, i.e., the target of persuasion. Focusing on the consumer and, particularly, on consumers' knowledge about persuasion, could provide greater insight into how consumers interpret and respond to marketers' persuasion attempts.

These ideas were formalized into the Persuasion Knowledge Model or PKM (Friestad & Wright, 1994). Drawing from work on persuasion schemata (Rule, Bisanz, & Kohn, 1985), the PKM proposes that consumers develop knowledge about persuasion and others' persuasion attempts and delineates how people develop and use this knowledge. The PKM significantly contributes to the fields of consumer behavior and marketing by focusing on the central role that consumers' knowledge about persuasion plays in persuasion episodes. The PKM (see Figure 21.1) depicts consumers as bringing three types of knowledge to a persuasion interaction: topic knowledge, agent knowledge, and persuasion knowledge. These three types of knowledge interact to influence consumers' persuasion "coping" behaviors, i.e., their personal responses to a persuasion attempt. On the other side, persuasion agents also have topic, target, and persuasion knowledge that interact to influence

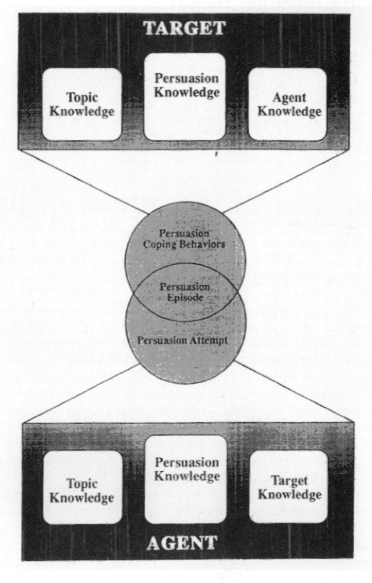

Figure 21.1   Reproduced from Friestad and Wright (1994)

their persuasion attempts. Together, the consumer target's persuasion coping behaviors and the marketing agent's persuasion attempts comprise a persuasion episode. The PKM points out that consumers' persuasion knowledge is critical to how consumers respond to marketing efforts and can be used in a variety of ways to help consumers to achieve their own goals within the situation.

In this chapter we provide an overview of the status of current research related to persuasion knowledge and the Persuasion Knowledge Model. Friestad and Wright (1994) provide a detailed discussion and delineation of the PKM itself as well as an excellent review of related research published prior to their article. Thus, the focus of this chapter is on persuasion-knowledge-related research generated since the publication of the Persuasion Knowledge Model. Our hope is to create a sense of where we have come since 1994 in terms of understanding important issues of consumers' persuasion knowledge and identifying gaps or opportunities in our understanding of the PKM. The chapter outlines directions for a future research agenda to further develop understanding of the PKM, consumers' persuasion knowledge, and its role in consumer behavior and marketplace interactions.

A basic thesis is that research thus far has captured only a small portion of the potential of the PKM. The extant research primarily focuses on persuasion knowledge (as opposed to other aspects of the PKM). The research on persuasion knowledge spans a variety of contexts, including advertising, sponsorship, interpersonal persuasion, cause-related marketing, retailing and decision-making. However, this research is only the tip of the iceberg. Much more remains to be done within the framework of the PKM, both in terms of other components of the model and in terms of furthering development of the model itself. Therefore, in the final section of the chapter, we offer some prescriptions for future research.

The rest of the chapter is organized as follows. We first discuss research on the three target knowledge structures proposed by the PKM. This is followed by a discussion of the content of persuasion knowledge, antecedents to the use of persuasion knowledge, consequences of persuasion knowledge, and target-agent interplay. We then consider research on the development of persuasion knowledge. We conclude by presenting research that addresses issues of measurement of persuasion knowledge. We conclude with prescriptions for future research.

THREE TYPES OF KNOWLEDGE

The PKM proposes that there are three types of knowledge—specifically, persuasion, agent, and topic—that influence responses and outcomes to persuasion attempts. Consumers' persuasion knowledge includes beliefs about marketers' motives, strategies, and tactics; causality in persuasion; the effects of persuasion tactics; appropriateness of tactic use; psychological mediators of persuasion; and strategies to respond to others' influence attempts. Thus, persuasion knowledge includes implicit theories about the persuasion context, as well as causal inferences drawn about motives (Kardes et al., chapter 6, this volume). After discussing agent and topic knowledge, we describe the content of persuasion knowledge in more detail in the next section.

Agent knowledge includes beliefs about the "traits, competencies, and goals of the persuasion agent" (Friestad & Wright, 1994, p. 3). Agent knowledge can include general knowledge or schemas about marketing agents, such as salespeople, companies, or brands. For example, a consumer could have a general stereotype about salespeople (e.g., Sujan, Bettman, & Sujan, 1986) or a general belief about brands, e.g., well-known brands provide better products. Agent knowledge could also include knowledge about a specific salesperson, company, or brand. For instance, a consumer who sees the same salesperson every time he visits Nordstrom is likely to have specific agent knowledge. This might include impressions about the agent's credibility, product knowledge, likeability, or dependability. A variety of research streams explore the role of agent knowledge. For example, the literature on source effects gives insight into some ways that agent knowledge affects consumer behavior (e.g., Dholakia & Sternthal, 1977). Likewise, research on brand or company familiarity can be applied to agent knowledge (Campbell & Keller, 2003). Perhaps because of these literatures, thus far little PKM-inspired research specifically focuses on agent knowledge.

Topic knowledge refers to the consumer's knowledge about the topic, or content, of the persuasion attempt. Thus, product or issue expertise would be part of topic knowledge, with experts displaying higher topic knowledge than novices. For example, when the consumer above visits Nordstrom, he is likely to have some knowledge about the product under consideration. If shopping for home accessories, he may have some knowledge about bedding, such as that higher thread counts indicate higher quality sheets. When the consumer interacts with the salesperson, the consumer's topic knowledge is likely to be accessed in the interaction. Research from streams other than PKM emphasizes the important role of topic knowledge in consumer behavior (see, for example, Alba & Hutchinson, 1987, 2000). However, much of this work looks at the role of expertise for product acceptance (e.g., Moreau, Lehmann, & Markman, 2001), less examines topic knowledge in terms of persuasion. Thus, there is an opportunity for research that examines the role that topic knowledge plays directly within persuasion episodes.

The line between persuasion, agent, and topic knowledge is sometimes blurred, suggesting that they are not as independent as depicted in the PKM. For example, if a consumer in a marketplace interaction infers the persuasion agent's motive or goals, is the consumer drawing upon persuasion, agent or both types of knowledge? If the consumer interprets a car salesperson's statement that the car of interest has been selling quickly as a persuasion tactic, is this because the consumer has agent knowledge that car salespeople use this tactic to increase consumer interest or persuasion knowledge that allows understanding of persuasion tactics? Similarly, does the consumer who knows a good deal about how promotions work have high persuasion knowledge or topic knowledge?

There are two approaches to dealing with these unclear lines. The first is that rather than trying to create artificial distinctions between these three types of knowledge, the knowledge structures be viewed as partially overlapping. The overlap between persuasion and agent knowledge consists of persuasion-related beliefs about the traits and goals of marketing agents. Similarly, the overlap between persuasion and topic knowledge contains persuasion-related topic information. Aside from these overlaps, persuasion, topic and agent knowledge also have independent (nonoverlapping) components.

The second approach, which we follow, is to use the terms to definitionally delineate and specify independent, nonoverlapping, types of knowledge. Thus, persuasion knowledge is defined as all knowledge related to persuasion, including persuasion-related knowledge of an agent or topic. Agent knowledge includes all non-persuasion-related knowledge having to do with characteristics of the agent. Likewise, topic knowledge includes all non-persuasion-related knowledge about the topic or content of the persuasion attempt. Thus, the terms are defined as separable constructs. The advantage of this approach is that it allows for distinctions and enables research to more clearly focus on each type of knowledge, as well as on interactions among levels of the three types of knowledge.

Consumers' persuasion knowledge is proposed to interact with their (nonpersuasion) agent knowledge and topic knowledge to shape persuasion interactions and influence the consumer's responses to persuasion attempts. For example, imagine Frank is shopping for a new car and goes to the closest Audi dealership. Frank likes cars and occasionally buys *Car and Driver* magazine. He has read some background information and seen ads from which he has gained some topic knowledge about the Audi A4. He has bought cars before and certainly knows the societal stereotype of car dealers; thus, Frank has some agent knowledge about car salespeople in general. His wife purchased a car from the same dealer the previous year, so Frank even has some specific agent knowledge about Audi salespeople, including the person helping him at this time. Based on a combination of societal information and past experience, Frank also has some persuasion knowledge about the strategies and tactics the car salesperson (this particular one or car salespeople in general) may use to persuade him to purchase the Audi A4 Wagon. All of these types of knowledge may be brought to bear upon Frank's interactions at the dealership.

To date, most research that builds upon the PKM has focused on persuasion knowledge. Only a few studies have examined the interactions among the three different knowledge structures; for instance, Brown and Krishna (2004) show that the effects of topic knowledge are influenced by persuasion knowledge. They distinguish between persuasion knowledge and topic knowledge (note that they call these "marketplace metacognition" and "category expertise," respectively) and explore differences in the effects of topic knowledge on response to default levels, depending on the level of persuasion knowledge. They found no effect of topic knowledge (product category expert vs. novice) when there was low persuasion knowledge, but an effect of topic knowledge when persuasion knowledge was high. Specifically, for people with high levels of persuasion knowledge, novices responded more favorably to low default options, whereas experts responded more favorably to high default options (Brown & Krishna, 2004).

In a second example of exploration of interactions between knowledge types, Ahluwalia and Burnkrant (2004) show that persuasion knowledge interacts with agent knowledge to affect message persuasion. Using the PKM, they hypothesized that when rhetorical questions become salient, consumers may focus on why the persuasion agent is using a rhetorical. Consumers may use existing agent knowledge, specifically, attitudes toward the agent, to interpret the use of rhetorical questions in advertising. When individuals have high persuasion knowledge, positive prior attitudes toward the agent enhance message persuasion, while negative prior attitudes toward the agent diminish message persuasion. However, low PK individuals are not sensitive to the source of the rhetorical questions. Thus, for high PK individuals, prior attitude toward the source determines whether the rhetorical is interpreted positively or negatively, but low PK individuals do not use their agent knowledge in their responses to rhetorical questions. Similarly, Hardesty, Carlson, and Bearden (2002) find an interaction between skepticism (persuasion knowledge) and brand familiarity (agent knowledge) in the context of reference price advertising.

These papers indicate the value in considering persuasion, agent, and topic knowledge as three different structures. The results support the interaction of different knowledge structures as proposed by the PKM and demonstrate the need for further research in this area. It is clear that there are many questions remaining about these three types of knowledge and their inter-relationships. For example, can some generalizations be drawn about when persuasion knowledge will be used more than (or instead of) agent or topic knowledge? What is required for the use of each and when and why are they likely to interact?

THE CONTENT OF PERSUASION KNOWLEDGE

Figure 21.2 depicts what research has shown thus far about the content of persuasion knowledge, its antecedents, and its consequences. In this section, we will examine in detail the research on the content of persuasion knowledge. In the next section we will discuss antecedents, followed by a section on consequences.

Friestad and Wright (1994) indicate that persuasion knowledge involves beliefs about motives, tactics, appropriateness of motives and tactics, and how persuasion works. Most research on

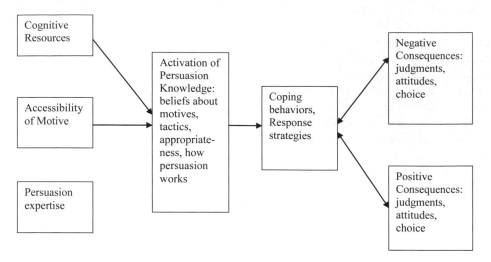

Figure 21.2   Antecedents and consequences of persuasion knowledge

persuasion knowledge focuses on one of these categories. That is, the bulk of PKM research focuses on one of these types of persuasion knowledge. Prior to discussing each category, we distinguish between persuasion knowledge and marketplace metacognition.

Persuasion Knowledge vs. Marketplace Metacognition

Just as "schemer schema" was a precursor to persuasion knowledge, "marketplace metacognition" appears to be a further step in Wright's (2002) thinking about consumers' knowledge of the marketplace. Marketplace metacognition is defined as "everyday individuals' thinking about market-related thinking" (Wright, 2002, p. 677). It includes people's beliefs about their own mental states and about the states of others, as well as about processes, strategies, and intentions as these relate to the social domain of marketplace interactions. Thus, marketplace metacognition is knowledge and thinking about one's own knowledge about the marketplace and interactions between market players.

Is marketplace metacognition just another term for persuasion knowledge or is it a different construct? Persuasion knowledge focuses on knowledge and beliefs about how persuasion "works," how people persuade, and how to effectively respond to persuasion. Persuasion knowledge may be either a chronic, individual difference variable (Bearden, Hardesty & Rose, 2001) or a situationally induced variable that can be accessed in a variety of persuasion interactions. Persuasion knowledge spans both marketing and nonmarketing persuasion situations. For instance, a consumer may have knowledge about how a marketer is likely to persuade a consumer as well as knowledge about how a husband is likely to persuade a wife or how friends persuade each other. Moreover, persuasion knowledge is focused on coping with persuasion and does not necessarily involve the consumer's thoughts about the non-persuasion-based marketplace.

Marketplace metacognition, on the other hand, is somewhat different in terms of topics and agents to which it applies. Marketplace metacognition focuses solely on marketplace agents and includes both persuasion and non-persuasion contexts. Marketplace metacognition centers on consumers' thinking about their knowledge about procedures, strategies and tactics for marketplace interaction and exchange. While persuasion is clearly one important component of the marketplace, more than persuasion is involved. Marketplace metacognition could include beliefs about the meaning of prices and price changes, reactions to different distribution channels, thoughts about a product and product attributes, and so forth.

In short, persuasion knowledge and marketplace metacognition clearly overlap in terms of consumers' beliefs about own and others' strategies and intentions about marketplace persuasion. However, they have distinct components as well. This chapter will primarily address issues of consumers' knowledge about persuasion in the marketplace, that is, topics that fall in the overlap between persuasion knowledge and marketplace metacognition. Consistent with the PKM, we will use the term "persuasion knowledge" to refer to consumers' thoughts and beliefs about marketplace persuasion, reserving the term "marketplace metacognition" for consumers thinking about their marketplace-related thinking.

Consideration of Motives

Beliefs about marketers' motives are a centerpiece of persuasion knowledge. In fact, a consumer's consideration of a marketer's motives can be measured as an indicator of whether persuasion knowledge has been activated. Following research on suspicion in the person perception literature (e.g., Fein, 1996), Campbell and Kirmani (2000) suggested that use of persuasion knowledge can involve consideration of whether persuasion agents have ulterior motives. In other words, in order to use persuasion knowledge within a particular interaction, the consumer must recognize the potential for persuasion. This entails consideration of whether there is a persuasion motive, as opposed to some nonpersuasion motive, behind the action(s) to which the consumer is responding. If the consumer does not think about the possibility of persuasion, she does not use persuasion knowledge. If the consumer infers that there is no persuasion motive, she is likely to curtail use of persuasion knowledge because it does not usefully apply to the situation (although some other knowledge structure may be used). If the consumer infers that there is a persuasion motive, she is likely to continue to use persuasion knowledge in coping with the interaction.

Thus far, a large proportion of research that directly relates to persuasion knowledge focuses on inferences of motive as an indicator of a consumer's use of persuasion knowledge. Acknowledging that consumers will not always draw inferences about the motives and/or trustworthiness of a source and, in fact, consumers often assume that a source is cooperative (cf., Schwarz, 1994), this research has examined factors that influence such inference making. Research has shown that suspicion[1] of firms' motives may be raised by a variety of marketing stimuli, including flattery (Campbell & Kirmani, 2000), the use of rhetorical questions (Ahluwalia & Burnkrant, 2004), incongruent placement of brands in television shows (Russell, 2002), advocacy advertising (Menon & Kahn, 2003), cause-related marketing (Szykman, Bloom, & Blazing, 2004), negative ad comparisons (Jain & Posavac, 2004), partially comparative pricing (Barone, Manning, & Miniard, 2004), biased sources (Williams, Fitzsimons, & Block, 2004), and expensive default options (Brown & Krishna, 2004). The presence of these tactics is likely to trigger persuasion knowledge by making consumers consider the marketer's ulterior motives. In turn, use of persuasion knowledge is seen to lead to negative evaluations of marketers and/or marketing agents. This will be discussed further in the section on consequences.

In short, research strongly supports consideration of persuasion motive as a critical type of persuasion knowledge use. Consumers appear to make positive or negative attributions about marketers' motives in different situations, and these attributions affect how they respond to the marketer's actions. However, consideration of motives is not the only demonstration of persuasion knowledge activation. As discussed next, persuasion knowledge is also activated when consumers consider the marketer's behavior as a persuasion tactic.

Beliefs About Tactics and How Persuasion Works

An important component of persuasion knowledge is knowledge or beliefs that a person holds about others' persuasion tactics. It makes sense that consumers think about the methods that marketers have for achieving their marketplace persuasion goals. In order for a marketer's behavior (e.g., advertising approach, promotional reward, product positioning) to be thought of as a tactic, i.e., a means for achieving a goal, as opposed to merely an action, there must be a "change of meaning" (Friestad & Wright, 1994). A change of meaning occurs when a consumer conceives of an action that previously was not assigned any particular meaning as being a tactic used to persuade the target. The notion that an action is a tactic is based on the idea that the action can give rise to some psychological reaction that is believed to create persuasion. That is, belief in an action as a persuasion tactic rests on the consumer's lay theory about how persuasion occurs, or at the very least, the consumer's theory of how marketers believe that persuasion occurs. Once an action is identified as a tactic, in addition to considering the effectiveness of the tactic, consumers may begin to think about the appropriateness of the marketer's motive and specific tactic use. There is some research that addresses each of these, namely, consumers' beliefs about tactics, consumers' theories of causality in persuasion, change of meaning, and appropriateness of tactics and motives.

Beliefs About Tactics. Some research has directly explored beliefs that consumers have about marketing tactics. While the majority of studies in this area provide respondents with a list of tactics and ask them to indicate what they believe is the goal of each tactic, there are a few studies that examine consumers' own identification of persuasion tactics. Tactics that respondents have identified on their own include: borrowed interest appeals, i.e., an advertiser's use of something for which the audience has inherent interest, e.g., a cute puppy or sexy woman (Campbell, 1995); amount of money spent on advertising (Kirmani, 1997); advertising repetition (Campbell & Keller, 2003; Kirmani, 1997); context effect of the other alternatives presented with an item (Hamilton, 2003); intention questions (Williams et al., 2004); rhetoricals (Ahluwalia & Burnkrant, 2004); and guilt appeals (Cotte, Coulter, & Moore, 2005). Research indicates that consumers sometimes recognize, think about, and respond to these actions as persuasion tactics.

Beliefs About How Persuasion Works. The idea that an action is a persuasion tactic must rest on some type of conceptualization of how persuasion occurs. Researchers have uncovered some consumer beliefs about causality in persuasion. Bousch, Friestad, and Rose (1994) examined adolescents' beliefs about why advertisers use particular tactics. This research shows that adolescents have theories about advertisers' intentions and how persuasion works and that these theories become more similar to those of adults as adolescents get older. Examination of adult consumers' beliefs about the psychology of advertising persuasion reveals that adults likewise have ideas about how advertising tactics affect persuasion (Friestad & Wright 1995). Friestad and Wright collected data on consumers' beliefs about the various roles 13 different psychological events play in advertising persuasion. Consumers believe that psychological events are important to the persuasion process and believe that different events have different roles. Importantly, there is evidence of folk knowledge about advertising persuasion based on shared beliefs about the roles that different psychological events play in persuasion (Friestad & Wright, 1995). Consumers have ideas about the difficulty of eliciting a variety of psychological events (e.g., attention, feeling emotion, connecting, etc.), as well as of the importance of these psychological events to advertising effectiveness.

Change of Meaning. Surprisingly little research has examined change of meaning, i.e., the transformation of a consumer's understanding of a particular action as a persuasion tactic. It is important to note, however, that there is some evidence that consumers can be "taught" that an action is a tactic. In other words, a change of meaning in which an action becomes understood as a tactic can occur because of external influence. Providing information on marketers' actions as tactics and/or their appropriate usage can help consumers think of the action as a persuasion tactic. After being exposed to this information, respondents are more likely to respond to the marketers' actions as persuasion tactics, becoming more resistant and thus, exhibiting less change in response to the actions than when they are not exposed to the information on the tactical nature and effects of the marketers' actions (Sagarin, Cialdini, Rice, & Serna 2002; Williams, Fitzsimons, & Bloch 2004). For example, by providing some respondents with an article describing the mere-measurement effect, Williams et al. (2004) elicited a change of meaning such that those respondents exposed to the article responded to an intention question from a biased source as if it were a persuasion tactic, whereas respondents who did not see the article, did not.

While there is evidence that change of meaning can be externally prompted, there is less understanding about the internal process by which changes of meaning "naturally" occur. There are a variety of questions that still need answers. For example, what is the process by which change of meaning occurs? What factors influence the process? When is a change of meaning likely to arise? Are there developmental stages at which changes of meaning are more or less likely to occur? Are there aspects of marketplace actions that make it more or less likely that a consumer will experience a change of meaning, identifying the actions as persuasion tactics? How does a consumer respond at the time that he or she first comes to believe that an action is a persuasion tactic? Examination of the process by which consumers begin to identify marketplace actions as persuasion tactics is necessary to develop better understanding of how consumers respond within the marketplace and factors that affect likely responses.

Beliefs About Appropriateness. Once a consumer is using persuasion knowledge to consider a marketer's actions, she may begin to think about the appropriateness of the marketer's motives and tactics. Appropriateness differs from effectiveness in that appropriateness has to do with the consumer's belief that it is right or wrong to use the tactic, regardless of whether the tactic works. Evaluations of appropriateness are quite important to consumer exchange because consumers sometimes respond negatively to "punish" what they perceive to be inappropriate behavior. Consideration of motive and/or tactic appropriateness can be elicited by borrowed interest advertising appeals (Campbell, 1995), negative framing (Shiv, Edell, & Payne, 1997); negative comparative advertising (Jain & Posavac, 2004), pricing practices (Campbell, 1999); and guilt appeals (Cotte et al., 2005). There are undoubtedly other important marketplace variables that could likewise be perceived as inappropriate.

A consumer's perception that a marketer's persuasion attempt is inappropriate can result in inferences of manipulative intent (Campbell, 1995; Cotte et al., 2005), perceived unfairness (Campbell, 1999; Shiv et al., 1997) and negative attitudes (Jain & Posavac, 2004). While all of these negative outcomes are important, recently there has been strong interest in perceptions of (un)fairness, particularly price (un)fairness, so much so that perceptions of price (un)fairness are a topic of exploration in their own right. Campbell (1999) drew from both the economic and the persuasion knowledge literatures, showing that consumers make inferences about the firm's motive for changing a price and that the inferred motive influences perceptions of (un)fairness above and beyond the influence of the firm's profits. Since this research, a variety of factors have been found to give rise to perceptions of unfairness, including several that appear to be based in consumers' persuasion, agent, and topic knowledge. For instance, attributions about the salesperson (Vaidyanathan & Aggarwal, 2003), comparisons to what other consumers receive (Feinberg, Krishna, & Zhang, 2002), the source of the price change information (Campbell, 2005), and external reference prices and consumer skepticism (Hardesty et al., 2002) all can influence consumer perceptions of price fairness.

The research discussed above finds instances when consumers perceive particular marketer motives and tactics to be inappropriate. Warlop and Alba (2004) suggested that consumers would perceive the blatant copying of market leaders' trade dress to be inappropriate. However, while respondents' unfavorable responses to national or high-priced brands that copied the marketer leaders' trade dress indicated some perceived inappropriateness, respondents did not penalize follower brands (store or low-priced brands) for blatantly copying market leaders' trade dress. These results suggest that consumers may believe that there are conditions under which visual similarity is an acceptable, rather than deceptive or inappropriate, persuasion tactic. Important questions remain as to when consumers are likely to judge tactic use as appropriate versus inappropriate.

Summary

Persuasion knowledge consists of a variety of components, including consideration of motives, beliefs about tactics, appropriateness of tactics, and how persuasion works. While research provides preliminary insight into each of these areas, there are still unaddressed questions that remain to be researched. Some research covers each of these areas, however, the largest amount of research has focused on consideration of motives. Many other aspects and components of persuasion knowledge can add richness to our understanding of consumers' interactions with marketers.

ANTECEDENTS TO THE USE OF PERSUASION KNOWLEDGE

A more complete development of the PKM requires understanding of when consumers are more or less likely to use their persuasion knowledge. That is, in any given persuasion episode, how likely is it that a consumer will access and utilize personal knowledge about persuasion? What factors influence the use of persuasion knowledge? Although the PKM discusses some possible issues surrounding use of persuasion knowledge, it does not delineate conditions that evoke or suppress persuasion knowledge. Recent research has identified three antecedents of persuasion knowledge: cognitive resources, accessibility of motives, and persuasion expertise.

Cognitive Resources

Friestad and Wright (1994) state that persuasion knowledge "is a resource to which people must have immediate access during any interaction in which the need may arise to recognize and manage, or to construct and deliver, a persuasion attempt. In short, for consumers it is a necessary resource in virtually all interactions with marketers" (p. 3). Thus, one reasonable proposition is that persuasion knowledge can be fairly automatically applied to any interaction in which persuasion may play a role. However, a plausible alternative hypothesis is that persuasion knowledge is not accessed automatically, and instead may require more effortful, higher-order processing. For example, tactic-related cognitions appear to be more effortful than claims-related cognitions, such that tactic-related cognitions have greater influence when processing resources are unconstrained (Shiv et al., 1997). In fact, Campbell and Kirmani (2000) proposed that activation and use of persuasion knowledge requires cognitive resources. In a series of studies of interpersonal persuasion between a salesperson and a consumer, they conceptualized activation of persuasion knowledge as consideration of ulterior motives. They suggested that cognitive resources were necessary to use persuasion knowledge because inferences of motives require higher order, attributional thinking. Using multiple manipulations of cognitive resources, the research demonstrated that consumers are less likely to use persuasion knowledge within a marketplace interaction when processing resources are constrained than when resources are unconstrained.

The determining role of cognitive resources in the use of persuasion knowledge was replicated in research on the mere measurement effect (Williams et al., 2004). Using a blink counting distraction task to manipulate cognitive capacity, this research showed that consumers were less likely to use persuasion knowledge to interpret a marketer's intention question when cognitive capacity was constrained and more likely when capacity was unconstrained. Consistent with the flexible correction model (Wegener & Petty, 1997), when consumers had sufficient capacity, they used persuasion knowledge to consider whether a source of an intention question was biased. When the source was perceived as biased, respondents used their persuasion knowledge to correct for the effect of an intention question on their behavior. However, when cognitive capacity was constrained, correction of the mere measurement effect did not occur (Williams et al.). In short, cognitive capacity appears to be an important antecedent of persuasion knowledge use.

Accessibility of Motives

In addition to the critical role of cognitive capacity, accessibility of persuasion motives is an important antecedent for the use of persuasion knowledge. Research shows that consumers are more likely to use persuasion knowledge within a persuasion episode when ulterior motives are highly accessible, but unlikely to use persuasion knowledge when ulterior motives are less accessible (Brown & Krishna, 2004; Campbell & Kirmani, 2000). Accessibility of ulterior motives may be increased with information about the status of the firm's business (Brown & Krishna, 2004), priming of motives or tactics (Campbell & Kirmani, 2000; Morales, 2005), blatancy of persuasion tactics (Campbell & Kirmani, 2000), agent knowledge (e.g., priors about car salespeople), and consumer goals. Accessibility of motives has been shown to interact with cognitive resources to affect use of persuasion knowledge (Campbell & Kirmani, 2000). High accessibility may make consumers likely to use persuasion knowledge even when cognitive resources are low. For instance, cognitively busy targets may be able to see through blatant persuasion tactics, such as ingratiation, because of high levels of motive accessibility.

Persuasion Expertise

The third antecedent of use of persuasion knowledge that has thus far been identified is the individual's persuasion expertise. Whereas persuasion knowledge has often been conceptualized as a situational variable (i.e., activated when cognitive resources or accessibility of motives are high), it could also be a chronic, individual difference variable. Differential experience with persuasion might lead individuals to have higher or lower levels of persuasion expertise. As noted above, Friestad and Wright (1994) suggested that experience would be important for the development of persuasion knowledge. In support of this, research has found that older adults (over 30 years of age), who typically have more persuasion experience, demonstrate more sophisticated use of persuasion knowledge than younger adults (Kirmani & Campbell, 2004). Experience is likely to lead to individual differences in the quantity and content of persuasion knowledge.

The notion of an individual difference in the use of persuasion knowledge led to the development of an individual difference scale that measures persuasion knowledge as a subcomponent of consumer self-confidence (Bearden et al., 2001). This scale has been used to divide people into high and low PKs, with clear behavioral differences between the two groups (Ahluwalia & Burnkrant, 2004; Brown & Krishna, 2004). Thus, research shows that persuasion knowledge may be situationally or chronically activated. More research into both situational and individual differences in use of persuasion knowledge is needed at this time.

Summary

Several studies have explored when consumers are more or less likely to utilize persuasion knowledge within a particular persuasion episode. Cognitive capacity, motive accessibility, and persuasion expertise all influence the extent to which persuasion knowledge is used. Overall, consumers are more likely to use persuasion knowledge when they have high motivation, ability and opportunity to elaborate about marketers' intentions. This fits nicely with other theories of consumer behavior. At this time, research opportunities exist to identify and explore additional factors that increase or suppress the use of persuasion knowledge. It is highly likely that there are other, unexplored antecedents of persuasion knowledge use. For instance, since consumers are goal-directed (Friestad & Wright, 1994), a consumer's goals are likely to influence the extent to which s/he activates persuasion knowledge. Consumers may have persuasion-related goals, such as not succumbing to persuasion or getting the best deal, which might increase the likelihood of using persuasion knowledge. The effect of goals on persuasion knowledge is largely unexplored. Likewise, it would be useful to identify factors that are antecedents to the combined use of persuasion knowledge with either topic or agent knowledge.

CONSEQUENCES OF PERSUASION KNOWLEDGE ACTIVATION

What are the outcomes of the use of persuasion knowledge and where do they appear in the PKM? One important type of outcome of persuasion knowledge use is persuasion coping behaviors, which refers to the target's "cognitive and physical actions" before, during, and after a persuasion episode (Friestad & Wright, 1994, p. 3). Other, more "terminal" outcomes are beliefs, attitudes, and choices. The PKM depicts the persuasion episode as the combination of the target's coping responses with the part of the marketing agent's persuasion attempt that the consumer is able to observe directly. Following the model, the consequences of persuasion knowledge activation and use would thus appear to be found in the persuasion episode (see Figure 21.1).

Several types of consequences of persuasion knowledge have been studied empirically, including consumers' coping behaviors and response strategies, beliefs, attitudes, and choices. Since the persuasion episode is the overlap of the marketer's persuasion attempts and the target's coping responses, there will be back-and-forth give-and-take among the coping responses and other outcomes. That is, we expect that the consumer's use of persuasion knowledge will allow him or her to consider the marketer's motives and tactics. The consumer is likely to form beliefs about what the marketer is doing and then engage in some response. The marketer is likely to also engage in further behaviors, which may change the consumer's beliefs, attitudes, etc. Thus, while coping behaviors and response strategies can be thought of as precursors to more "terminal" outcomes of beliefs, attitudes, and choices, it is clear that persuasion response and outcomes involve a recursive process and that all are outcomes of the use of persuasion knowledge. We first address coping responses that result from the use of persuasion knowledge and then outcomes of beliefs, attitudes and choices. While the majority of research has found that activation of persuasion knowledge leads to negative outcomes in terms of persuasion, research does find positive consequences of persuasion knowledge usage. Thus, we discuss negative and positive outcomes in turn.

Target Coping Response Behaviors

Persuasion coping behaviors arise when the consumer target's topic, persuasion, and agent knowledge come together in interpreting and responding to the marketer. As noted above, persuasion coping behaviors are consequences of persuasion knowledge activation as well as antecedents to the "terminal" outcomes of attitudes, choices, etc. The PKM proposes that consumers' coping responses are central to their marketplace behavior (Friestad & Wright 1994). Thus, it is surprising that thus far, little research has directly examined responses strategies that consumers use to cope with marketplace influence.

One exception to this uses both qualitative and experimental methodologies to explore and identify strategies that consumers use to respond to marketers (Kirmani & Campbell 2004). This research identified 15 strategies by which consumers respond to persuasion attempts and conditions under which the strategies are used. Importantly, the research revealed that consumers have two general modes of response: consumers act as "persuasion sentries," guarding against unwanted persuasion, and they also act as "goal seekers," using persuasion agents to achieve their own marketplace goals (Kirmani & Campbell). Whereas persuasion sentries exhibit negative response strategies (e.g., resistance, withdrawal to avoid persuasion), goal seekers exhibit positive response strategies (e.g., directing the agent to best fulfill the consumer's needs, establishing a relationship with the agent to get better deals). Although some of the resistance-related strategies have been considered in work in psychology on resistance to persuasion (e.g., Knowles & Linn 2004), the positive response strategies follow uniquely from the PKM perspective. The findings support the proposition of the PKM that consumers strive to achieve their own goals within marketplace interactions. At this time, it would be beneficial to further understand consumers' response strategies and, importantly, conditions and moderators that affect their use.

Negative Consequences of Persuasion Knowledge Activation

Most of the work that draws upon the PKM proposes and finds negative persuasion outcomes arising from the consumer's use of persuasion knowledge. In particular, research on suspicion of ulterior motives finds that when consumers infer that a marketer's action is driven by a self-serving ulterior motive, there is greater resistance to persuasion. For instance, the use of persuasion knowledge has been shown to lead to less favorable perceptions of a sales agent's sincerity (Campbell & Kirmani, 2000), less favorable perceptions of corporate social responsibility (Menon & Kahn, 2003), less favorable attitudes toward the brand or firm (Ahluwalia & Burnkrant, 2004; Campbell, 1995; Forehand & Grier, 2003; Jain & Posavac, 2004; Russell, 2002), higher perceptions of unfairness (Campbell, 1999; Hardesty, Carlson, & Bearden, 2002), increased skepticism, even in the face of honest claims (Koslow, 2000), lower willingness to pay (Morales, 2005), lower purchase intention (Barone, Manning, & Miniard, 2004), and lower choice (Brown & Krishna, 2004; Williams et al., 2004) relative to when persuasion knowledge is not used. It is likely that many outcomes of the use of persuasion knowledge are negative because of reactance that arises in response to believing that someone else is trying to persuade, and thereby control, the self (e.g., Brehm, 1966). Because of this, the majority of research to date has examined negative reactions.

However, the outcomes of persuasion knowledge use do not have to be negative. As noted earlier, consumers often assume that communicators are cooperative, rather than competitive (e.g., Schwarz, 1994). Consumers may use their knowledge to achieve their own goals; goal attainment will not always involve resisting marketers' persuasion. A few studies demonstrate situations in which people do not display reactance when they know that an ulterior motive is present. Examining context effects in decision-making, Hamilton (2003) finds that people intuitively understand how to use context effects to influence others' decisions, e.g., by creating a choice environment that will lead others' to select a particular outcome. Despite this knowledge, however, people are still influenced by others' menu creation even when they realize that the other person has an ulterior motive (Hamilton, 2003). That is, even though the respondent appears to consider the persuader's ulterior motive, the respondent in positively influenced by the persuasion attempt. In this case, we do not see a negative persuasion outcome.

Recent research specifically examines when suspicion of a self-serving motive does and does not lead to negative consumer response (Forehand & Grier, 2003). This suggests that consumer inference of self-serving ulterior motive gives rise to negative responses to marketplace persuasion only when there is a consumer perception of firm deception or dishonesty about the firm's motives. When a firm only states that it is engaging in cause-related marketing in order to help others, but the situation suggests to consumers that the cause-related behavior will also help the firm, consumers are seen to respond more negatively. However, when the firm expresses that the cause-related marketing will help others and help themselves, consumers do not appear to respond negatively to the firm (Forehand & Grier, 2003). This research suggests that in some cases, consumers have sophisticated, conditionally based concepts of persuasion appropriateness that influence important responses to persuasion.

Positive Consequences of Persuasion Knowledge Activation

Thus far, we have shown that persuasion knowledge use can lead either to negative outcomes or does not affect outcomes. Can persuasion knowledge activation lead to positive outcomes, such that people respond more positively to the marketer who is trying to persuade them? There is little research that shows positive outcomes of persuasion knowledge. An exception is Kirmani and Campbell (2004), who investigated consumers' response strategies when interacting with interpersonal marketing agents (e.g., salespeople and service personnel). As discussed above, this research shows that consumers have both negative, persuasion-sentry response strategies, and positive, goal-seeker strategies. Consumers do not merely react against marketers, they use persuasion coping behaviors to both positively and negatively respond to marketers in order to attain their own goals. An important aspect of this research is that the findings demonstrate that consumer use of persuasion knowledge does not necessarily result in negative responses to marketing agents.

Persuasion knowledge may also lead to positive outcomes when consumers are able to understand firms' incentives, such as the incentive to signal product quality. Thus, consumers may attribute higher product quality to firms that exert greater effort in advertising (Kirmani, 1997) and offer more extensive warranties (Boulding & Kirmani, 1993). In order for this type of attribution to occur, consumers need to believe that firms that spend more on advertising or offer higher warranties could not do so if the quality of the product was so bad that these expenditures could not be recouped by a large number of sales. This type of persuasion knowledge can lead to positive firm evaluations.

Summary

There is nothing within the Persuasion Knowledge Model that suggests that persuasion knowledge will always result in less positive outcomes for the persuasion agent than when persuasion knowledge is not used. However, much more research depicts negative than positive consequences of the use of persuasion knowledge. Clearly, the activation of persuasion knowledge may make consumers suspicious, leading to less favorable marketer perceptions, and thus allowing consumers to avoid being persuaded unnecessarily. However, consumers may also use persuasion knowledge to more positively achieve their goals. More research is needed into conditions under which the use of persuasion knowledge may lead to positive outcomes. Future research will contribute to a more complete theory of persuasion by examining positive, as well as negative effects of consumer use of persuasion knowledge and by developing a more nuanced understanding of the components, interplay, and processes involved within the persuasion episode.

TARGET AND AGENT INTERPLAY

Examination of Figure 21.1 shows that the PKM is a general model about how targets and agents interact (Friestad & Wright, 1994). As we have discussed, targets use multiple types of knowledge to develop, select, and use persuasion coping behaviors. Agents similarly use persuasion, topic, and target knowledge in the development, selection, and use of persuasion attempts. As noted earlier, one of the real contributions of the PKM was its emphasis on the active role of the target. Because of this, by far the majority of PKM-related research focuses on better understanding the target. However, it is also important to understand the agent in terms of the agent's knowledge about the target, beliefs about the target's knowledge, and interactions with the target. A more complete development of the PKM will include research on the back-and-forth interplay between the target and agent. In other words, what do targets know about agents, what do targets believe that agents know about targets, and so on?

For instance, Moreau et al. (2001) examine both consumer knowledge about promotion actions and manufacturer and retailer beliefs about consumers' perceptions of promotions. That is, they study consumer topic and persuasion knowledge as well as marketing agent target knowledge. On the consumer side, their data show that consumers think both about *what* types of promotional activities occur in the grocery retail environment, and also about *why* marketers choose these actions. Overall, it appears that consumers not only have some ideas about how and why products are promoted, but that their knowledge is fairly accurate. On the marketer side, the data on the manufacturers' and retailers' beliefs about consumers' thoughts about promotions show that these channel members' beliefs about consumers' beliefs are similar to each other. Interesting, both the manufacturers and the retailers consistently underestimate consumers' understanding of promotions, although they both are reasonably accurate at predicting consumers' beliefs about marketers' motivations for promotions. In sum, the concurrent examination of target and agent knowledge reveals that, in this context, consumers have some fairly accurate persuasion knowledge but that marketers' target knowledge is surprisingly inaccurate.

Another stream of research, stemming from game theory, examines whether consumers understand the signals that firms are trying to send. Analytic information economics models assume a give and take between the agent and the target; specifically, firms send signals of quality and expect consumers to interpret these signals as intended. Correct interpretation of signals requires consumers' understanding of firms' incentives and the conditions under which the signals might be true or false. This research is interested in the sophistication of consumers' beliefs about why marketers engage in particular marketplace behaviors and how these beliefs affect their responses. Thus, the firm (agent) sends a signal to the consumer (target), the target receives the signal and assesses its veracity, and the target responds accordingly. This requires the firm to know what consumers know about firms and for consumers to know what makes firms act in certain ways.

In most of the behavioral studies testing information economics predictions, consumers' firm-related attributions have been inferred from the firm's marketplace decisions (Kirmani, 1990; Kirmani & Wright, 1989; Boulding & Kirmani, 1993). For instance, in Boulding and Kirmani, consumers inferred high product quality when a company with a high reputation offered a high warranty, but not when a low reputation company offered a high warranty. This suggests that consumers believe that the high reputation company has more at stake, since it is putting its reputation on the line. In contrast, the low reputation company may be fly-by-night, never intending to honor the warranty. This outcome suggests fairly sophisticated reasoning on the part of consumers.

However, there appear to be some limitations on how far consumers go in terms of thinking about firms' incentives. In a study on consumers' understanding of collusion on price-matching guarantees (PMGs), consumers failed to suspect collusion in price-matching offers, suggesting that they are not as sophisticated in their reasoning about firms' motives as information economics assumes (Chatterjee, Heath, & Basuroy, 2003). Even consumers with more cognitive resources (e.g., those with high need for cognition) did not suspect collusion. Overall, this suggests the need for research on how much consumers can spontaneously infer from marketing actions, and how much might be the function of other variables in the situation, such as accessibility of motives. In general, we need to know more about motives that consumers infer on the basis of marketers' actions.

Summary

The research identified in this section represents one step toward understanding the interplay of the marketer's target and persuasion knowledge and the knowledge of the target about the agent and persuasion. However, there are many questions about these interactions that have not been examined. It will be important for future research to continue to delve into marketer and consumer "schemer schemas" to develop more complete knowledge about the balance and interaction between consumers and marketers.

DEVELOPMENT OF PERSUASION KNOWLEDGE

One of the important issues raised by the PKM is how persuasion knowledge develops. It is important to understand the extent to which children have persuasion knowledge, when and how individuals develop persuasion knowledge, as well as how, or whether, this knowledge continues to develop during a consumer's life span. Friestad & Wright (1994) propose that development of persuasion knowledge is contingent upon: (1) cognitive skills, (2) experience, and (3) vicarious learning (e.g., from other consumers, friends and family, educational environments, media discussion, etc.).

Some earlier research shows that young children do not have a real concept of persuasive intent, but that understanding of persuasive intent begins to develop by age 8 (e.g., Robertson & Rossiter, 1974; Ward, 1972; see Roedder, 1999 for a review). However, only a few pieces of research have directly examined the development of persuasion knowledge past this age. Younger children (e.g., second graders, 7–8 years old) show less sophisticated processing of advertising and product experience than do older (fifth grade, 10–11 years old) children (Moore & Lutz, 2000). A longitudinal study examined how children in U.S. middle school (grades 6–8, typically ages 11–14) think about television advertising and advertisers' tactics (Boush et al., 1994). This study shows that knowledge about advertisers' tactics increases over the studied time period. This also provides some evidence that distrust of advertising claims also increases. Overall, this research contributes support for the notion that persuasion knowledge is developmentally contingent and that understanding of persuasion tactics continues to develop past the understanding of persuasive intent that develops in the first 8 years of childhood.

Kirmani and Campbell (2004) add to understanding of the development of persuasion knowledge by examining adult consumers of a variety of ages. This research followed up on the PKM notion that experience with certain types of marketplace persuasion is less likely to occur until young adults begin making a wide range of purchase decisions. Examination of strategies adults use in response to interpersonal persuasion by marketers indicates that the number and quality of response strategies used increases with age. Younger adult consumers (in their early 20s) tended to use fewer response strategies, and to use them less successfully, than did middle adult consumers, between 30 and 60 years of age. Interestingly, elderly adult consumers (over 65), who might have the greatest experience with persuasion, were likely to use fewer response strategies than middle adults, suggesting that response strategy usage is at its highest in middle adulthood. More research on elderly consumers' use of persuasion strategies is needed to understand this result. Overall, this research shows that middle adults have better developed persuasion knowledge than younger adults, indicating that persuasion knowledge continues to develop in adulthood.

Another piece of research following the PKM framework examined adult consumers' beliefs about advertising tactics and how advertising persuasion works (Friestad & Wright, 1995). Interestingly, the beliefs of adult consumers were compared to those of consumer researchers. There were both similarities and differences between consumers' and researchers' beliefs about advertising effects. In general, consumers' and researchers' views were similar about topics that have been studied for some time (e.g., understanding and attitudes) but dissimilar about topics that are currently under study (e.g., imagining, remembering and emotion). While this research does not directly examine the development of persuasion knowledge, the similarities and differences between adult consumers and researchers suggests: (1) that understanding of persuasion and tactics can continue to develop in adulthood, and (2) that consumers may learn from the media and others' experiences.

Summary

Overall, there is some support for the propositions of the PKM about development of persuasion knowledge. A great deal of research demonstrates that understanding of persuasive intent is contingent upon the development of cognitive skills during early childhood (by 8 years). However, there is still debate—and room for research—about the underlying cause of the skill development (e.g., neurological, experiential, or structural). Less research examines the other two propositions, that is, that persuasion knowledge development is driven by experience and vicarious learning. The existing research provides some support for these, but future research should continue to examine the development of persuasion knowledge throughout later childhood and different stages of adulthood and the roles that experience and vicarious learning play in persuasion knowledge development. In particular, additional research on the extent to which children, young adults, and older adults can be taught to identify and successfully respond to marketplace persuasion will be helpful to consumers, educators, and public policy.

THE MEASUREMENT OF PERSUASION KNOWLEDGE

An important issue in research on persuasion knowledge is how to determine whether persuasion knowledge has been activated. Given that persuasion knowledge is multidimensional and covers a variety of beliefs and behaviors, there is no single method of measuring persuasion knowledge or persuasion knowledge activation. Instead, researchers have come up with their own measures, and these measures depend on which component of persuasion knowledge is being considered. We focus on studies that directly measure persuasion knowledge rather than those in which activation of persuasion knowledge is inferred from outcomes (e.g., Chatterjee et al., 2003; Warlop & Alba, 2004). Direct measures of assessing persuasion knowledge include ratings, cognitive responses, depth interviews, individual difference measures, and response times.

Ratings

Perhaps the most common method is to ask respondents about their persuasion-related beliefs through written questionnaires (e.g., Friestad & Wright, 2005; Bousch et al., 1994). For instance, Friestad and Wright asked respondents to rate different psychological mediators (e.g., attention) on multiple dimensions, such as difficulty of eliciting and awareness. Ratings have also been used to assess consumers' beliefs about how others are trying to influence them. Respondents have been asked to rate whether a marketer has a specific motive (Campbell & Kirmani, 2000) or manipulative intent (Campbell, 1995; Williams et al., 2004); to rate companies on dimensions such as dishonest, manipulative (Jain & Posavac, 2004), and collusive (Chatterjee et al., 2003); and to assess how much others had tried to influence them (Hamilton, 2003).

Ratings are appropriate to measure beliefs that consumers are aware of and can clearly articulate. They may not be a good measure of persuasion effects that consumers are unaware of as well as beliefs about what influences consumers, since consumers may not have a good sense of what influences them. Ratings have the disadvantage of reactivity, i.e., the rating itself may make salient a particular construct.

Cognitive Responses

Another common method of measuring persuasion knowledge activation is to code open-ended responses, either to specific questions (e.g., why is the advertiser using this tactic?) or general cognitive responses (please write down the thoughts that went through your head). Because it minimizes reactivity, this technique has been particularly useful in uncovering suspicion (Barone et al., 2004; Campbell & Kirmani, 2000) and ulterior motives (Forehand & Grier, 2003; Szykman, Bloom, & Blazing, 2004). Cognitive responses must be used cautiously to make sure they capture persuasion knowledge rather than simply non-persuasion related counterarguments. Finally, cognitive responses capture only those beliefs that consumers are aware of and can articulate. Unconscious beliefs will not be captured by either cognitive responses or ratings.

Depth Interviews

Relatively little research has used qualitative research methods in efforts to measure use or content of persuasion knowledge, even though such methods seem particularly appropriate for capturing some aspects of persuasion knowledge. The research that has used depth interviews has successfully identified response tactics and coping strategies. For instance, Kirmani and Campbell (2004) conducted depth interviews to develop a taxonomy of tactics used by consumers to respond to interpersonal persuasion attempts by marketing agents (e.g., salespeople, service agents). Trocchia (2004) also used depth interviews to reveal consumers' coping strategies in an auto-buying context. Depth interviews may be a good way to uncover beliefs and behaviors of which consumers may not be consciously aware. Further exploration of ethnographic methods for understanding persuasion and agent knowledge may be quite useful.

Response Times

Response latencies have been used as an indirect measure of persuasion knowledge activation. Williams et al. (2004) asked respondents to indicate whether a word was good or bad by pressing different computer keys. Speed of response to the words "suspicious," "manipulate," and "coerce" were measures of persuasion knowledge. These words were interspersed with seven other words. Such techniques should be further used. Response times have the advantage of being nonreactive and being able to uncover unconscious beliefs and automatic processes.

Individual Difference Variables

Whereas the previous measures assess persuasion knowledge activation in specific situations, two scales have been developed that may be used to capture individual differences in persuasion knowledge. Bearden et al. (2001) developed a six-item individual difference measure of persuasion knowledge (PK) as part of a broader scale of consumer self-confidence. The PK scale assesses consumers' confidence in their knowledge of marketing persuasion tactics and of their ability to cope with marketers' tactics. It contains the following items: I know when an offer is "too good to be true"; I can tell when an offer has strings attached; I have no trouble understanding the bargaining tactics used by salespersons; I know when a marketer is pressuring me to buy; I can see through sales gimmicks used to get consumers to buy; I can separate fact from fantasy in advertising. The PK scale has been used as a moderator to divide individuals into those with high and low persuasion knowledge and to demonstrate that behavior differs across the two levels (Ahluwalia & Burnkrant, 2004; Brown & Krishna, 2004).

Another individual difference scale that is related to persuasion knowledge is the advertising skepticism scale (SKEP; Obermiller & Spangenberg, 1998). The nine-item scale measures consumers' general disbelief about advertising claims, and could be considered a part of persuasion knowledge. Although the SKEP scale is likely to be related to the PK scale, they do measure different constructs. Whereas SKEP covers general distrust of advertising, the PK scale assesses knowledge about persuasion tactics.

Although persuasion knowledge includes many different aspects, these scales each focus on one particular domain of persuasion knowledge. They may not capture consumers' sensitivity to ulterior motives, suspicion, or appropriateness of tactics. For instance, there may be some opportunity to develop a scale that captures the ability to infer ulterior motives, or the ability to assess the effectiveness of different tactics, and so on.

Summary

Different dimensions of persuasion knowledge have been measured using rating scales, cognitive responses, depth interviews, response times, and individual difference scales. An area for future research is the use of implicit measures of persuasion knowledge. These are likely to be beneficial in capturing automatic activation of persuasion knowledge and to capture nonconscious processes. Ultimately, the method must suit the inquiry, and the best approach may be to use multiple methods to capture persuasion knowledge and its use.

A PRESCRIPTION FOR THE FUTURE

One of the themes of this chapter has been that persuasion knowledge is multidimensional and contains many different components, such as beliefs about motives, tactics, and appropriateness of tactics. Another theme has been that persuasion knowledge is but one component of the PKM. Thus, there are opportunities to conduct research on a variety of topics related to persuasion knowledge and the PKM. As researchers continue to build upon the PKM, it will be important to draw carefully from existing research. For example, it is important to resist the temptation to spawn new terminology; researchers should carefully consider whether an existing term captures the construct of interest before suggesting a new one. If a new one is necessary, it is essential that differences between related constructs are delineated. Carefully defined terms will help to not only improve understanding, but they will also enable research in this domain to make a clearer and stronger contribution to the persuasion literature. Some general guidelines for future research in the exciting domain of the PKM are offered below.

First, we need more theoretical research about persuasion knowledge and the PKM. Most of the empirical work applies the PKM to a particular context, such as advertising, pricing or promotions. We often learn more about the substantive domain than we do about persuasion knowledge per se. There is little research that pushes theory development. Thus, we see the opportunity to conduct more theoretical research on the antecedents of persuasion knowledge; the interaction of persuasion, target and agent knowledge; the interplay between target and agent; and the consequences of persuasion knowledge. Research that enables a richer depiction of Figure 21.2 would be useful in enhancing our understanding about persuasion knowledge. Likewise, it is important to build our knowledge of when persuasion knowledge is a mediator and when it is a moderator of effects.

Second, there is virtually no research on the emotional consequences of persuasion knowledge usage. Although the PKM is a model about knowledge rather than emotions, the activation of persuasion, agent and even topic knowledge is also likely to affect emotions. The only paper that we found that directly examines emotions in the context of the PKM is Morales (2005); her research shows that when firms are perceived as having an ulterior motive, consumers do not feel gratitude toward the firm. There are many other intriguing questions about persuasion knowledge and affect. Besides the obvious negative emotions that may arise from being the recipient of a persuasion attempt, can the use of persuasion knowledge make people happy? For instance, a consumer may feel elation if he is able to successfully achieve his goals in dealing with a car salespeople. Successful negotiation of a persuasion attempt may lead to feelings of self-efficacy and thus happiness.

Third, there is little research on cross cultural persuasion knowledge. How does knowledge about persuasion differ across cultures? Do people have more sophisticated persuasion knowledge in bargaining cultures, such as those in the Middle East and Asia? Or is it just a different type of persuasion knowledge in other cultures? It is possible that the persuasion knowledge of people in collective cultures would be different from that of people in individualistic cultures? As one possibility, collective or interdependent cultures may rely more on cooperative relationship building than do individual or independent cultures.

In summary, the study of the PKM is only a decade old. The fairly large amount of research that has been generated following aspects of the PKM speaks to the importance of this model. Particularly, we see the contribution that the idea of the consumer as an active, knowledgeable, participant in marketplace persuasion interactions has made to furthering understanding of aspects of consumer behavior. As we have shown in this chapter, researchers have begun to get a sense of what persuasion knowledge is, what precedes it, what follows it, how it develops and how it is measured. However, much more needs to be done in order to enhance our understanding of consumers' beliefs about marketplace persuasion and how these beliefs affect consumers' responses to persuasion attempts. It is time for research to not only further develop our understanding of persuasion knowledge, but to go beyond persuasion knowledge. It is essential that we continue to identify specific implicit theories that consumers have about marketplace persuasion. At this time, research is needed to more completely develop the entire Persuasion Knowledge Model and use this to gain better understanding of consumers' implicit theories about marketplace persuasion.

NOTES

1. Note that suspicion and skepticism have sometimes been used interchangeably and sometimes to refer to different constructs; we follow the latter convention. Suspicion is defined in terms of a psychological state in which the consumer considers whether the agent has an ulterior motive. Skepticism is a dispositional or state doubt in the truthfulness of various forms of marketing communication and the marketer's motives (e.g., Forehand & Grier, 2003).

REFERENCES

Ahluwalia, R., & Burnkrant, R. E. (2004). Answering questions about questions: A persuasion knowledge perspective for understanding the effects of rhetorical questions. *Journal of Consumer Research, 31*, 26–42.

Alba, J. W., & Hutchinson, J. W. (1987). Dimensions of consumer expertise. *Journal of Consumer Research, 13*, 411–454.

Alba, J. W., & Hutchinson, J. W. (2000). Knowledge calibration: What consumers know and what they think they know. *Journal of Consumer Research, 27*, 123–156.

Barone, M. J., Manning, K. C., & Miniard, P. W. (2004). Consumer response to retailers' use of partially comparative pricing. *Journal of Marketing, 68*, 37–47.

Bearden, W. O., Hardesty, D. M., & Rose, R. L. (2001). Consumer self-confidence: Refinements in conceptualization and measurement. *Journal of Consumer Research, 28*, 121–134.

Boulding, W., & Kirmani, A. (1993). A consumer-side experimental examination of signalling theory. *Journal of Consumer Research, 20*, 111–123.

Boush, D. M., Friestad, M., & Rose, G. M. (1994). Adolescent skepticism toward TV advertising and knowledge of advertiser tactics. *Journal of Consumer Research, 21*, 165–175.

Brehm J. W. (1966). *Theory of Psychological Reactance.* New York: Academic Press.

Brown, C. L., & Krishna, A. (2004). The skeptical shopper: A metacognitive account for the effects of default options on choice. *Journal of Consumer Research, 31*, 529–539.

Campbell, M.C. (1995). When attention-getting advertising tactics elicit consumer inferences of manipulative intent: the importance of balancing benefits and investments. *Journal of Consumer Psychology, 4*, 225–254.

Campbell, M. C. (1999). Perceptions of price unfairness: Antecedents and consequences. *Journal of Marketing Research, 36*, 187–199.

Campbell, M. C., & Keller, K. L. (2003). Brand familiarity and advertising repetition effects. *Journal of Consumer Research, 30*, 292–304.

Campbell, M. C., & Kirmani, A. (2000). Consumers' use of persuasion knowledge: The effects of accessibility and cognitive capacity on perceptions of an influence agent. *Journal of Consumer Research, 27*, 69–83.

Chatterjee, S., Heath, T. B., & Basuroy, S. (2003). Failing to suspect collusion in price-matching guarantees: Consumer limitations in game-theoretic reasoning. *Journal of Consumer Psychology, 13*, 255–267.

Cotte, J., Coulter, R. A., & Moore, M. (2005). Enhancing or disrupting guilt: The role of ad credibility and perceived manipulative intent. *Journal of Business Research, 58*, 361–368.

Dholakia, R. R., & Sternthal, B. (1977). Highly credible sources: Persuasive facilitators or persuasive liabilities? *Journal of Consumer Research, 3*, 223–232.

Fein, S. (1996). Effects of suspicion on attributional thinking and the correspondence bias. *Journal of Personality & Social Psychology, 70*, 1164–1184.

Feinberg, F., Krishna, A., & Zhang (2002). Do we care what others get? A behaviorist approach to targeted promotions. *Journal of Marketing Research, 39*, 277–291.

Forehand, M. R., & Grier, S. (2003). When is honesty the best policy? The effect of stated company intent on consumer skepticism. *Journal of Consumer Psychology, 13*, 349–356.

Friedstad, M., & Wright, P. (1994). The persuasion knowledge model: How people cope with persuasion attempts. *Journal of Consumer Research, 21*, 1–31.

Friestad, M., & Wright, P. (1995). Persuasion knowledge: Lay people's and researchers' beliefs about the psychology of advertising. *Journal of Consumer Research, 21*, 1–31.

Hamilton, R. W. (2003). Why do people suggest what they do not want? Using context effects to influence others' choices. *Journal of Consumer Research, 29*, 492–506.

Hardesty, D. M., Carlson, J. P., & Bearden, W. O. (2002). Brand familiarity and invoice price effects on consumer evaluations: The moderating role of skepticism toward advertising. *Journal of Advertising, 31*, 1–15.

Jain, S. P., & Posavac, S. S. (2004). Valenced comparisons. *Journal of Marketing Research, 41*, 46–58.

Kirmani, A. (1990). The effect of perceived advertising costs on brand perceptions. *Journal of Consumer Research, 17*, 160–171.

Kirmani, A. (1997). Advertising repetition as a signal of quality: If it's advertised so often, something must be wrong. *Journal of Advertising, 26*, 77–86.

Kirmani, A., & Campbell, M. C. (2004). Goal seeker and persuasion sentry: How consumer targets respond to interpersonal marketing persuasion. *Journal of Consumer Research, 31,* 573–582.

Kirmani, A., & Wright, P. (1989). Money talks: Perceived advertising expense and expected product quality. *Journal of Consumer Research, 16,* 344–353.

Knowles. E. S. & Linn, J. A. (Eds.). (2004). *Resistance and persuasion.* Mahwah, NJ: Erlbaum.

Koslow, S. (2000). Can the truth hurt? How honest and persuasive advertising can unintentionally lead to increased consumer skepticism. *Journal of Consumer Affairs, 34,* 245–269.

Menon, S., & Kahn, B. (2003). Corporate sponsorships of philanthropic activities: When do they impact perception of sponsor brand? *Journal of Consumer Psychology,* 316–327.

Moore, E. S., & Lutz, R. J. (2000). Children, advertising, and product experiences: A multimethod inquiry. *Journal of Consumer Research, 27,* 31–48.

Morales, A. C. (2005). Giving firms an 'E' for effort: Consumer responses to high-effort firms. *Journal of Consumer Research, 31,* 806–812.

Moreau, C. P., Lehmann, D., & Markman, A. (2001). Entrenched knowledge structures and consumer response to new products. *Journal of Marketing Research,* 14–29.

Moreau, P., Krishna, A., & Harlam, B. (2001). The manufacturer-retailer-consumer triad: Differing perceptions regarding price promotions. *Journal of Retailing, 77,* 547–569.

Obermiller, C., & Spangenberg, E. R. (1998). Development of a scale to measure consumer skepticism toward advertising. *Journal of Consumer Psychology, 7,* 159–186.

Robertson, T., & Rossiter, J. R. (1974). Children and commercial persuasion: An attribution theory analysis. *Journal of Consumer Research, 1,* 13–20.

Roedder, J. D. (1999). Consumer socialization of children: A retrospective look at twenty-five years of research. *Journal of Consumer Research, 26,* 183–213.

Rule, B. G., Bisanz, G. L., & Kohn, M. (1985). Anatomy of a persuasion schema: Targets, goals, and strategies. *Journal of Personality and Social Psychology, 48,* 1127–1140.

Russell, C. (2002). Investigating the effectiveness of product placements in television shows: The role of modality and plot connection congruence on brand memory and attitude. *Journal of Consumer Research, 29,* 306–318.

Sagarin, B. J., Cialdini, R. B., Rice, W. E., & Serna, S. B. (2002). Dispelling the illusion of invulnerability: The motivations and mechanisms of resistance to persuasion. *Journal of Personality and Social Psychology, 83,* 526–541.

Schwarz, N. (1994). Judgment in a social context: Biases, shortcomings, and the logic of conversation. In M. P. Zanna (Ed.), *Advances in experimental social psychology* (Vol. 26, pp. 123–162), San Diego, CA: Academic Press.

Shiv, B., Edell, J. A., & Payne, J. W. (1997). Factors affecting the impact of negatively and positively framed ad messages. *Journal of Consumer Research, 24,* 285–294.

Sujan, M., Bettman, J., & Sujan, H. (1986). Effects of consumer expectations on information processing in selling encounters. *Journal of Marketing Research, 23,* 346–353.

Szykman, L. R., Bloom, P. N., & Blazing, J. (2004). Does corporate sponsorship of a socially-oriented message make a difference? An investigation of the effects of sponsorship identity on responses to an anti-drinking and driving message. *Journal of Consumer Psychology, 14,* 13–20.

Trocchia, J. (2004). Caving, role playing, and staying home: Shopper coping strategies in a negotiated pricing environment. *Psychology & Marketing, 52,* 823–853.

Vaidyanathan R., & Aggarwal, P. (2003). Who is the fairest of them all? An attributional approach to price fairness perceptions. *Journal of Business Research, 56,* 453–463.

Ward, S. (1972). Children's reactions to commercial. *Journal of Advertising Research, 12,* 37–45.

Warlop, L., & Alba, J. W. (2004). Sincere flattery: Trade-dress imitation and consumer choice. *Journal of Consumer Psychology, 14,* 21–27.

Wegener, D. T., & Petty, R. E. (1997). The flexible correction model: The role of naive theories of bias in bias correction. In M. P. Zanna (Ed.), *Advances in experimental social psychology* (Vol. 29, pp. 141–208). Mahwah, NJ: Erlbaum.

Williams, P., Fitzimons, G. J., & Block, L. G. (2004). When consumers do not recognize 'benign' intention questions as persuasion attempts. *Journal of Consumer Research, 31,* 540–550.

Wright, P. (1986). Schemer schema: Consumers' intuitive theories about marketers' influence tactics. In R. L. Lutz (Ed.), *Advances in Consumer Research* (Vol. 13, pp. 1–3). Provo, UT: Association for Consumer Research.

Wright, P. (2002). Marketplace metacognition and social intelligence. *Journal of Consumer Research, 28.*

22

Social Values in Consumer Psychology

Lynn R. Kahle

Guang-Xin Xie

University of Oregon

Milton Rokeach (1973) described social values as the single most important construct in social science. He argued that social values are the building blocks from which the rest of social science expands. Although Rokeach only dealt with consumer behavior once in his seminal 1973 book—in a section headed "Inconsequential Findings" (referring to the purchase of a car)—his perspective as applied to consumer psychology seems well founded because research on consumer means-end chains (e.g., Gutman, 1982; Reynolds, 1985) consistently finds that often the core reason consumers choose products is value fulfillment. Research shows that consumers select products with attributes that deliver consequences, which in turn contribute to value fulfillment; however, the assumed causal sequence flows from value fulfillment to consequences to brand attribute selection. We can expect useful understandings of consumer choices when we understand each of these elements (Homer & Kahle, 1988). Ultimately, most products that do not contribute to value fulfillment one way or another will fall from favor.

Social values summarize the most important goals that people have in life, thus fueling their decisions in life about such topics as product choice. Not all consumer choices relate to values, but often an understanding of a person's values will help researchers to understand a person's relation to a particular brand or product above and beyond what can be learned only from other demographic and lifestyle information. Since different people have consistent different choice patterns, value groups can be an effective basis for segmentation. People with one value will expect different product features, distribution, perhaps pricing, and certainly communication (e.g., Cho, Kwon, Gentry, Jun, & Kropp, 1999) regarding a product. For many brands effectively reaching people in different value segments will be an important component of marketing success (Frank, Andreas, & Robert, 2001; Kropp, Lavack, & Holden, 1999; Raval, & Subramanian, 2004).

Pitts, Canty, and Tsalikis (1985; Alwitt & Pitts, 1996) provided an important experiment to demonstrate the effectiveness of linking values to consumer choice. In this study, Pitts and colleagues showed that consumers increased their purchase intentions following exposure to a value-consistent ad versus a value-inconsistent ad. When consumers perceive a particular product or brand as appropriate to their value fulfillment, they will in general find that product or brand more attractive. Marketing communication that establishes the link between personal values and brands can resonate with consumers (Kim, Boush, Marquardt, & Kahle, 2006).

THEORIES OF VALUES

No one theoretical approach dominates the study of values, although several have been proposed. Some of these theories include Maslow's (1970) hierarchy, cognitive consistency (Rokeach, 1973), social adaptation (Kahle, 1983, 1996; Kahle, Kulka, & Klingel, 1980), and functional theory (Kelman, 1974; Kahle, Kambara, & Rose, 1996; Sheth, Newman, & Gross, 1991; Sheth, Stern, & Gross, 1991). Contributions come from both psychology (Maio, Olson, Bernard, & Luke, 2003) and sociology (Hitlin & Piliavin, 2004).

Maslow's theory is widely studied in undergraduate classes. It assumes that individuals developmentally progress through a hierarchical transition of values (or *needs*, a term Maslow uses interchangeably with *values*), progressing from the physiological to the safety to the social to the esteem finally to the self-actualization stage. Each stage requires that previous stages be mastered, and each higher stage is theoretically more sophisticated than the previous one. The values or stages that Maslow describes are certainly valid and useful in consumer psychology, but his presumed hierarchical perspective is highly questionable from an empirical perspective (Hilles & Kahle, 1985; Kahle, Homer, O'Brien, & Boush, 1997; Kahle, Kulka, & Klingel, 1980).

Rokeach (1973) believes that the principles of cognitive consistency apply equally well to values as with other cognitions. Values form and change, in his view, according the same principles as other cognitions. A slightly different take on this perspective assumes that values are cognitions used to develop adaptive abstractions about adaptation to social environments. In this view values function and change via the same processes of adaptation and accommodation that characterize other cognitive changes in Piagetian theory (e.g., Piaget, 1952).

Schwartz and Bilsky (1987) developed a similar viewpoint. They view values as cognitive representations of biological needs, interaction needs, and societal demands for welfare and survival. Schwartz (1996) elaborated their perspective into a comprehensive perspective on integrated value systems (Schwartz, 1996).

Functional theory (e.g., Kahle, Kambara, & Rose, 1996; Kelman, 1974; Sheth, Newman, & Gross, 1991; Sheth, Stern, & Gross, 1991) emphasizes attitudes rather than values. It implies that values only matter some of the time. The assumption is that some attitudes develop and change based on rewards and punishments rather than values (Beldona, Kline, & Morrison, 2004), and other attitudes develop and change based on psychoanalytic and psychosexual tension rather than based on values. Some attitudes, however, do indeed form, change, and function to fulfill values. In this view the relevance of values depends on the function of the attitudes currently activated.

CRITICAL ISSUES IN CONSUMER VALUES RESEARCH

A number of critical issues in value theory remain unresolved.

1. We need to revisit the concepts of *values, motivation, goal*, and *personality* to understand the exact relations between these conceptual definitions, which deserves attention.
2. We need to understand better the origins and changing conditions of consumer values.
3. We need to examine the concerns that linger in measuring values.
4. A great deal of discussion has occurred regarding the value-attitude-behavior linkage, and much more remains to be learned.
5. What can we learn about values from cross-cultural studies, and what can values teach us about cultures?

6. In most substantive areas, applications add complexities to our ability to understand phenomena. Applications of consumer values are no different. What are the lessons from applying values theory?

7. Postmodernism has proposed many challenges to the field of consumer behavior as a whole. The postmodern approach in consumer values research is yet another example of such an area of discussion. We will discuss each of these seven topics sequentially.

Revisiting Concepts: Value, Motivation, Goal, and Personality

Rokeach (1973) provided perhaps the most frequently cited definition of *value* as a psychological construct as an "enduring belief that a specific mode of conduct or end-state of existence is personally or socially preferable to an opposite or converse mode of conduct or end-state of existence" (p. 5). He further argued that individual values integrate into a system as an enduring belief organization of preferences in models of conduct or end-states of existence. Consumer researchers in contrast view *value* as an abstract type of social cognition that consumers use to store and guide general responses to classes of marketing stimuli (Kahle, 1996).

Murray's theory of *motivation* (1951) suggests that motivations are driven by needs. *Value*, widely shared among researchers (Beatty, Kahle, Homer, & Misra, 1985; Corfman, Lehmann, & Narayanan, 1991; Grunert & Scherhorn, 1990; Gutman, 1982; Kahle, 1996; Kahle, Beatty, & Homer, 1986; Kahle & Kennedy, 1989; Spiggle, 1986; Vriens & Hofstede, 2000), represents social discourse and gives expressions to human needs. Personal *goal* differs from *value* in that people's goals are concerned exclusively about specific objectives, ends or aspirations. Alain and Gary (1997) argued that the lack of clear-cut conceptual distinctions between motivations, goals, and values in the literature leads to a certain confusion in explanation and theorization. They suggested that individuals combine these three concepts into meaningful orientations toward success, and researchers should revisit the *value* concept partially accounted for *motivation* and *goal*. *Personality* research provides a framework that views consumers as possessing dispositional entities (Han, 2002; Sun, Horn, & Merritt, 2004). Accumulating evidence shows that personality traits are largely endogenous characteristics, while personal values are learned adaptations strongly influenced by the environment (Kropp, Lavack, & Silvera, 2005; Olver & Mooradian, 2003). Authors need to distinguish carefully among these concepts to preserve their discriminant validity.

Antecedents and Changes of Consumer Values

The English word *value* comes from the French verb *valoir*, which means "to be worth." *Value* originally was a philosophical concept about virtuous living and morality, and it evolved to imply valor and worthiness over time. Orthodox microeconomic theory assumes that consumer preferences are exogenous and constant (Friedman, 1976), while psychology and ethics deal with the formation and evaluation of preferences. Rokeach (1973) suggested the existence of values derived from Maslow's (1970) theory of needs. Maslowians viewed values as separately embedded rules, and they missed the dynamic nature of values system and environmental influence. For instance, Sawa and Sawa (1988) found that values confrontation could have dramatic influence on consumers' attitudes, satisfaction and enduring behaviors. Social adaptation theory (Kahle, 1996) holds that values are situational salient when people adapt to various life roles through values development and fulfillment. Most research on means-end chains (e.g., Homer & Kahle, 1988; Reynolds & Gutman, 1988; Reynolds & Olson, 2001) suggest that the ultimate reason for many consumer decisions relies on values. Thus, empirical studies of specific antecedents of value formation are largely underdeveloped. Kahle, Kau, Tambyah, Tan, and Jung (2005) found that religion and religiosity may provide one basis for the social identity and guide people to values-congruent choices. Most authors agree that the sources of values are complex and multidimensional (Joas, 2000).

Values change is another critical issue in consumer research but very limited in terms of the quantity of empirical studies (Barry & Wooton, 1977; Skelly, 1983). Witkowski (1998) identified some clusters of early American consumer values toward home designs—the search for authenticity, status presentation and ethic identification, nostalgia and tradition making, domesticity and feminism, and aesthetic conservatism. Kahle, Poulos and Sukhdial (1988) examined the changes in social values in the United States during the period from 1976 to 1986. The national survey results reveal relative stability in the importance placed on different values, but in 1986 more Americans were concerned with a sense of accomplishment and warm relationship with others, and fewer showed concern with security and self-fulfillment.

Values tend to change when the cultural, environmental, or social situations to which people must adapt, change. As people move into different life stages, social contexts, or situations, they reassess their core values. Rokeach (1973) showed that values can change with introduction of confrontation related to cognitive inconsistency. Consumer socialization research well documented the social perspective of values change in terms of social perspective taking and impression formation (John, 1999).

Concerns in Measuring Values

Any construct functionally is what researchers measure when they apply their instruments. Values have been measured in many different ways. Advertising agencies and research companies have their own techniques to measure something that is termed *values*. For example, the Yankelovich Monitor is frequently cited as providing evidence about society transitions in values and trends in North America. PRIZM classifies every U.S. zip code into one of 62 categories based on values and lifestyle. Global MOSAIC looks at lifestyles across 14 countries. The Paris organization Research Institute on Social Change looks at lifestyles and values in more than 40 countries. Many advertising organizations monitor lifestyle and value trends (Solomon, 2004).

VALS (Mitchell, 1978) and LOV (Kahle, 1983) have been used extensively in consumer studies (Beatty et al., 1985; Cummings & Ganderton, 1994; Dolfsma, 2004; Hayward, 1989; Henry, 1976; Kahle & Kennedy, 1989; Kahle et al., 1986; L. R. Kahle & Kennedy, 1988; Kamakura & Mazzon, 1991; McGregor, 2000; Reynolds, 1985; Swenson & Herche, 1994). With the development of technology and changes in consumer behaviors, it is crucial to reexamine the measurement accuracy on a regular basis to catch up with emerging trends and nuances. Updates have been done in both academe and industry. For instance, SRI (Winters, 1989) announced an improved version of VALS, named VALS 2, with fewer items and slightly different typology. Kahle (1996) proposed a revision of the LOV from its original methodology (Kahle 1983). Mostly the VALS system has been used in industry rather than academic studies because the secrecy that surrounds its methodology violates the scientific standard of public knowledge (Kahle, Kim, & Kambara, 1998).

One other widely used measure of values is the Rokeach Value Survey (RVS) (Rokeach, 1973). The LOV includes only 9 (terminal) values, to allow for ease of administration and to tie it more directly to Maslow's theory. The RVS includes 18 terminal values (desired end states) but also 18 instrumental values (codes of conduct). Using more items may tap into more complexity but may also excessively tax the short-term information processing capacities of survey respondents. Rokeach (1973) insists that the proper way to measure values is through ranking, whereas the LOV often employs a measurement strategy that uses both rating and ranking, thus allowing for higher level interval statistical analysis. The RVS has less relevance to daily life and lower test-retest reliability than the LOV (Beatty et al., 1985), but the longer list does provide more information about value choices.

In survey scale development and implementation, researchers ought to be aware of potential threats to measurement validity and reliability, such as social desirability biases. Fisher and Katz (2000) suggested that early control techniques could be helpful through adding statistical control, increasing response anonymity, and being sensitive to sample characteristics. On the other hand, it is equally important to avoid deliberate intervention to control for social desirability, because in essence, different socially desirable behaviors exhibit some values differences. The measure of values is in part a measure of what respondents find socially desirable. Qualitative approaches (e.g., Lastovicka, Murry, & Joachimsthaler, 1990) and content analysis (e.g., Spiggle, 1986) could also add some insights to consumer values by demonstrating deeper and more complex meanings.

Values-Attitude-Behavior Linkage

Theories about consumer values and behaviors often address a broad research question: "Why do we buy what we buy?" (Allan & Ng, 1999; Batra, Homer, & Kahle, 2001; Corfman et al., 1991; Gutman, 1982; Kim & Wyer, 2004; Lai,1995; McGregor, 2000; Pitts et al., 1985; Vriens & Hofstede, 2000). Gutman (1982) proposed a means-end model in which consumer values give consequences valence and importance. Consumer values structures were found to influence the importance of choice criteria for product categories and brands (Pitts & Woodside, 1984). Similarly, Sheth, Newman, and Gross (1991) found product choices and brand preferences between values and behaviors in tobacco uses. Batra et al. (2001) found that the casual relationship between values and susceptibility to normative influence (SNI) is strongest for external values, and that high SNI leads to greater importance for attributes that provide socially visible benefits. In another study, Corfman et al. (1991) suggested that values are an antecedent of perceived utility of product, and thus influence the purchase decisions. Further, Nelson (2004) examined values-confronting decisions and used image theory (Beach & Mitchell, 1990) to describe the decision process with respect to values, goals and strategies. Allan and Ng (1999) found that values would have a direct influence on product choices associated with symbolic meaning and make an affective judgment, and have an indirect influence via tangible attribute importance associated with utilitarian meaning and make a piecemeal judgment. When the marketplace is in a transaction stage, consumer behaviors are related with congruency between personal values and social values (McGregor, 2000). Ideally, theories and measurements of consumer values should account for the values systems, situational factors, and the environment (Kahle, 1996). This goal creates complications because of the large number of potential patterns of values, situational uncertainty, societal and cultural changes; however, some progress has been made with advanced statistical techniques that allow simultaneous considerations of value systems, situational and environmental factors (e.g., Kamakura & Novak, 1992; Madrigal & Kahle, 1994).

Cross-Cultural Studies

The impact of consumer values in the cross-geographic and cross-cultural contexts has been examined extensively during the past three decades (Al-Khatib, Vitell, & Rawwas, 1997; Briston & Amyx, 2001; Dutta-Bergman & Wells, 2002; Gregory & Much, 1997; Kilbourne, Grunhagen, & Foley, 2005; Kim, Forsythe, Gu, & Sook, 2002;. Kirby & Kirby, 1996; Kumar, Ganesh, & Echambadi,

1998; Lass & Hart, 2004; Lau-Gesk, 2003; Lu & Alon, 2004; McKinley-Floyd, 1998; Sung & Tinkham, 2005; Tan & Farley, 1987). While cross-national comparisons and contrasts of values are a major research stream, studies about subcultures have made significant progress in groups such as Afro-Americans (McKinley-Floyd, 1998), Anglo-American (Kumar & Thibodeaux, 1998), Navajos (Briston & Amyx, 2001), and even basketball fans in college (Kahle, Duncan, Dalakas, & Aiken, 2001). From a marketing standpoint, values in principle provide more information than mere demographics and nationality (Kahle, 1996). While past research focused on how values differ cross culturally, future research should also investigate different manifestations of similar values in different groups across regions and cultures. Further, studies on bicultural consumers' values can reveal significant insights about value systems and manifestations. For instance, Lau-Gesk (2003) examined how bicultural consumers respond to various types of persuasion appeals that promoted values unique to a particular culture, and the results show that bicultural consumers who tended to integrate both cultural dispositions were more likely to respond favorably than those who tended to compartmentalize each culture.

A number of challenges exist with cross-geographic and cross-cultural surveys. Researchers must convey the meaning of questions accurately and in a way respondents can grasp (Kahle, 1996). They must correctly incorporate subtleties and nuances of language, and select the most effective method of communication. Traditional mail surveys have been criticized for limited response rate and lack of depth, which could be threats in areas where the subtlety of value expressions is not adequately captured in the questionnaires. Thus, a combination of multiple approaches should be applied, such as interviews and formal surveys, depending on the economical, political, and cultural differences across regions. Further, construction of a representative sample is potentially far more complex for researchers in some countries than in others, because sources similar to the ones used to describe populations in some countries may not be available in others. Previous research primarily investigated regions where it was easier to access to a large number of respondents, such as major cities in North America, Europe, and East Asian. Researchers ought to carefully evaluate the representativeness of samples and penetrate to deeper levels of the subgroups. To understand the full complexity of values it is helpful to use samples that maximize the heterogeneity of variance in values. Finally, it is very important for researchers to be aware that certain questions to which some cultures are willing to respond may be considered sensitive or inappropriate by others (Kahle, 1996).

Applications of Consumer Values

Research on consumer values has provided meaningful insights to marketing practice (Kahle, 1996) in the areas of new product development, brand assessment and positioning, advertising strategies, and market segmentation (Vriens & Hofstede, 2000). Recent studies have applied consumer values in segmenting the global market by generational cohorts (Homer, 1993; Schewe & Meredith, 2004), consumer financial decisions (Vitt, 2004), music (Dolfsma, 2004), sports interests (Florenthal & Shoham, 2000), and retailing attributes (Erdem & Oumlil, 1999; Goldsmith, Freiden, & Kilsheimer, 1993; Rose, Shoham, Kahle, & Batra, 1994). The critical part is how to monitor the changes in consumer values accurately, and to apply the values appropriately in different contexts (Kassarjian, 1983; Martin, 1997; McQuarrie & Langmeyer, 1985). Fisher and Katz (2000) suggested that early control techniques could be helpful through adding statistical control, increasing response anonymity, and being sensitive to sample characteristics. Future monitoring of consumer values will probably prove more useful when applied thoughtfully and carefully to a specific product area in conjunction with other useful measures and with an understanding of the adaptive significance of the values in respondents' lives. With the development of technology and change, it is crucial to reexamine the measurement accuracy at regular intervals to catch up with emerging trends and nuances.

Postmodern Approach in Consumer Values Research

Another emerging stream is the post-modern approach to interpret consumer values (e.g.. Dolfsma, 2004; Hirschman, 1985; Thompson & Troester, 2002). In spite of the fact that postmodernists take an interpretative perspective on consumer values, they contribute to the field by adding detailed descriptions to the larger framework established by social scientists' continuous efforts. The richness of detail from some postmodern studies enhances our understanding of contextual issues that always loom large in value research. For instance, the studies of materialism integrated both qualitative interpretative approach and quantitative trait scale development (e.g., Belk, 1985; Richins & Dawson, 1992).

CONCLUSION

Values will continue to contribute to our understanding of human behavior in general and to consumer behavior in specific. We have learned a great deal about how to apply values to all elements of the marketing mix; but we still have many important factors to uncover, and the continued search will likely prove useful.

REFERENCES

Al-Khatib, J. A., Vitell, S. J., & Rawwas, M. Y. A. (1997). Consumer ethics: A cross-cultural investigation. *European Journal of Marketing, 31,* 750–767.

Alain, J., & Gary, B. (1997). Values, motivations, and personal goals: Revisited. *Psychology and Marketing, 14,* 675–688.

Allan, M. W., & Ng, S. H. (1999). The direct and indirect influences of human values on product ownership. *Journal of Economic Psychology, 20,* 5–39.

Alwitt, L. F., & Pitts, R. E. (1996). Predicting purchase intentions for an environmentally sensitive product, *Journal of Consumer Psychology, 5*(1), 49–64.

Barry, T. E., & Wooton, L. M. (1977). Forecasting consumer values. *European Journal of Marketing, 11,* 499–507.

Batra, R., Homer, P. M., & Kahle, L. R. (2001). Values, susceptibility to normative influence, and attribute importance weights: A nomological analysis. *Journal of Consumer Psychology, 11,* 115–128.

Beach, L. R., & Mitchell, T. R. (1990). Image theory: A behavioral theory of decisions in organizations. In B. M. Staw & L. L. Cummings (Eds.), *Research in organizational behavior* (Vol. 12, pp. 1–42). Greenwich, CT: JAI.

Beatty, S. E., Kahle, L. R., Homer, P., & Misra, S. (1985). Alternative measurement approaches to consumer values: The list of values and the Rokeach value survey. *Psychology & Marketing, 2,* 181.

Beldona, S., Kline, S. F., & Morrison, A. M. (2004). Utilitarian value in the Internet: Differences between broadband and narrowband users. *Journal of Travel & Tourism Marketing, 17,* 63–77.

Belk, R. W. (1985). Materialism: Trait aspects of living in the material world. *Journal of Consumer Research, 12,* 265–280.

Briston, D., & Amyx, D. (2001). A cross-cultural look at consumer values: A Navajo vs. Anglo comparison. *The Marketing Management Journal, 11,* 15–24.

Cho, B. J., Kwon, U., Gentry, J. W., Jun, S., & Kropp, F. (1999), Cultural values reflected in theme and execution: A comparative study of U. S. and Korean TV commercials," *Journal of Advertising, 4,* 59–73.

Corfman, K. P., Lehmann, D. R., & Narayanan, S. (1991). Values, utility, and ownership: Modeling the relationships for consumer durables. *Journal of Retailing, 67,* 184–204.

Cummings, R. G., & Ganderton, P. T. (1994). Substitution effects in CVM values. *American Journal of Agricultural Economics, 76*, 205–214.

Dibely, A., & Baker, S. (2001). Uncovering the links between brand choices and personal values among young British and Spanish girls. *Journal of Consumer Behavior, 1*, 77–93.

Dolfsma, W. (2004). Paradoxes of modernist consumption: Reading fashions. *Review of Social Economy, 62*, 351–364.

Dutta-Bergman, M. J., & Wells, W. D. (2002). The values and lifestyles of idiocentrics and allocentrics in an individualist culture: A descriptive approach. *Journal of Consumer Psychology, 12*, 231–242.

Erdem, O., & Oumlil, A. B. (1999). Consumer values and the importance of store attributes. *International Journal of Retail & Distribution Management, 27*, 137–144.

Fisher, R. J., & Katz, J. E. (2000). Social-desirability bias and the validity of self-reported values. *Psychology & Marketing, 172*, 105–120.

Florenthal, B., & Shoham, A. (2000), Value differences between risky sports participants and non-participants. *Sport Marketing Quarterly, 9*, 26–33.

Frank, H., Andreas, H., & Robert, E. M. (2001). Gaining competitive advantage through customer value oriented management. *Journal of Consumer Marketing, 18*, 41–53.

Friedman, M. (1976). *Price theory*. Chicago: Aldine.

Goldsmith, R. E., Freiden, J. B., & Kilsheimer, J. C. (1993). Social values and female fashion leadership: A cross-cultural study. *Psychology & Marketing, 10*, 399–412.

Gregory, G. D., & Much, J. M. (1997). Cultural values in international advertising: An examination of familial norms and roles in Mexico. *Psychology and Marketing, 14*, 99–119.

Grunert, S. C., & Scherhorn, G. (1990). Consumer values in West Germany underlying dimensions and cross-cultural comparison with North America. *Journal of Business Research, 20*, 97–107.

Gutman, J. (1982). A means-end chain model based on consumer categorization processes. *Journal of Marketing, 46*, 60–72.

Han, B. (2002). Toward a personology of the consumer. *Journal of Consumer Research, 29*, 286–292.

Hayward, S. (1989). The "mature" market. *Marketing Research, 1*, 84–86.

Henry, W. A. (1976). Cultural values do correlate with consumer behavior. *Journal of Marketing Research, 13*, 121–127.

Hilles, W. S., & Kahle, L. R. (1985), Social contract and social integration in adolescent development. *Journal of Personality and Social Psychology, 49*(October), 1114–1121.

Hirschman, E. C. (1985). Primitive aspects of consumption in modern American society. *Journal of Consumer Research, 12*, 142–154.

Hitlin, S., & Piliavin, J. A. (2004). Values: Reviving a dormant concept. *Annual Review of Sociology, 30*, 359–393.

Homer, P. M. (1993). Transmission of human values: A cross-cultural investigation of generational and reciprocal influence effects. *Genetic, Social, and General Psychology Monographs, 19*, 343–367.

Homer, P., M., &. Kahle, L. R. (1988), A structural equation test of the value-attitude-behavior hierarchy. *Journal of Personality and Social Psychology, 54*(April), 638–646.

John, D. R. (1999). Consumer socialization of children: A retrospective look at twenty-five years of research. *Journal of Consumer Research, 26*, 183–213.

Joas, H. (2000). *The genesis of values*. Cambridge: Polity.

Kahle, L. R. (Ed.) (1983), *Social values and social change: Adaptation to life in America*. New York: Praeger.

Kahle, L. R. (1996). Social values and consumer behavior: Research from the List of Values. In C. Seligman, J. M. Olson & M. P. Zanna (Eds.), *The psychology of values* (pp. 135–151). Mahwah, NJ: Erlbaum.

Kahle, L. R., Beatty, S. E., & Homer, P. (1986). Alternative measurement approaches to consumer values: The List of Values (LOV) and Values and Life Style (VALS). *Journal of Consumer Research, 13*, 405–409.

Kahle, L., Duncan, M., Dalakas, V., & Aiken, D. (2001). The social values of fans for men's versus women's university basketball. *Sport Marketing Quarterly, 10*, 156–162.

Kahle, L. R., P. M. Homer, R. M. O'Brien, & D. M. Boush (1997), Maslow's hierarchy and social adaptation as alternative accounts of value structures, In L. R. Kahle & L. Chiagouris (Eds.), *Values, lifestyles, and psychographics* (pp. 111–137). Mahwah, NJ: Erlbaum.

Kahle, L. R., K. M. Kambara, & G. M. Rose (1996). A functional model of fan attendance motivations for college football, *Sport Marketing Quarterly, 5*(Dec.), 51–60.

Kahle, L. R., Kau, K.A., Tambyah, S. K., Tan, S. J., & Jung, K. (2005). *Religion, religiosity, and values: Implications for consumer behavior.* Paper presented at International Research Conference, La Londe les Maure, France.

Kahle, L. R., & Kennedy, P. (1989). Using the List of Values (LOV) to understand consumers. *Journal of Consumer Marketing, 6,* 5–12.

Kahle, L. R., W. S. Kim, & K. Kambara (1998). The silence of the lambdas: Science, consulting, and public knowledge. In D. Grewal & C. Pechmann (Eds.), *Marketing theory and applications.* (pp. 217–218). Chicago, AMA. (Winter AMA Proceedings).

Kahle, L. R., R. A. Kulka & D. M. Klingel (1980), Low adolescent self-esteem leads to multiple interpersonal problems: A test of social adaptation theory. *Journal of Personality and Social Psychology, 39,* 492–502.

Kahle, L. R., Poulos, B., & Sukhdial, A. (1988). Changes in social values in the United States during the past decade. *Journal of Advertising Research, 28* (February-March), 35-41.

Kamakura, W. A., & Mazzon, J. A. (1991). Value segmentation: A model for the measurement of values and value systems. *Journal of Consumer Research, 18,* 208–218.

Kamakura, W. A., & Novak, T. P. (1992). Value-system segmentation: Exploring the meaning of LOV. *Journal of Consumer Research, 19,* 119–123.

Kassarjian, H. H. (1983). Social values and the Sunday comics: A content analysis. *Advances in Consumer Research, 10,* 434–438.

Kelman, H.C. (1974), Further thoughts on the processes of compliance, identification and internalization. In J. T. Tedeschi (Ed.), *Perspectives on Social Power* (pp. 125–171). Chicago: Aldine.

Kilbourne, W., Grunhagen, M., & Foley, J. (2005). A cross-cultural examination of the relationship between materialism and individual values. *Journal of Economic Psychology, 26,* 624–641.

Kim, J. O., Forsythe, S., Gu, Q. L ., & Sook, J. M. (2002). Cross-cultural consumer values, needs and purchase behavior. *Journal of Consumer Marketing, 19,* 481–502.

Kim, K., & Wyer Jr., R. S. (2004). The role of unconscious processes in consumer choice and decision making. *Advances in Consumer Research, 31,* 334–334.

Kim, W. S., Boush, D. M., Marquardt, A., & Kahle, L. R. (2006). Values, brands, and image. In L. R. Kahle & C. H. Kim (Eds.), *Creating images and the psychology of marketing communication* (pp. 279–290). Mahwah, NJ: Erlbaum.

Kirby, E. G., & Kirby, S. L. (1996). On the diffusion of international social values: Institutionalization and demographic transition. *Social Science Quarterly, 77,* 289–300.

Kropp, F., Lavack, A. M., Silvera, D. (2005) Values and collective self-esteem as predictors of consumer susceptibility to interpersonal influence among university students. *International Marketing Review, 22*(1), 7–33

Kumar, K., & Thibodeaux, M. S. (1998). Differences in value systems of Anglo-American and far Eastern students: Effects of American business education. *Journal of Business Ethics, 17,* 253–262.

Kumar, V., Ganesh, J., & Echambadi, R. (1998). Cross-national diffusion research: What do we know and how certain are we? *Journal of Product Innovation Management, 15,* 255–268.

Lai, A. W. (1995). Consumer values, product benefits and customer value: A consumption behavior approach. *Advances in Consumer Research, 22,* 381–388.

Lass, P., & Hart, S. (2004). National cultures, values and lifestyles influencing consumers' perception towards sexual imagery in alcohol advertising: An exploratory study in the UK, Germany and Italy. *Journal of Marketing Management, 20*(5–6), 607–623.

Lastovicka, J. L., Murry, J. P., Jr., & Joachimsthaler, E. (1990). Evaluating the measurement validity of lifestyle typologies with qualitative measures and multiplicative factoring. *Journal of Marketing Research, 27,* 11–23.

Lau-Gesk, L. G. (2003). Activating culture through persuasion appeals: An examination of the bicultural consumer. *Journal of Consumer Psychology, 13,* 301–315.

Lu, L., & Alon, H. (2004). Analysis of the changing trends in attitudes and values of the Chinese: The case of Shanghai's young and educated. *Journal of International and Area Studies, 11,* 67–88.

Madrigal, R., & Kahle, L. R. (1994). Predicting vacation activity preferences on the basis of value-system segmentation. *Journal of Travel Research, 32,* 22–28.

Maio, G. R., Olson, J. M., Bernard, M. M., & Luke, M. A. (2003). Ideoligies, values, attitudes, and behavior. In J. Delamater (Ed.), *Handbook of social psychology* (pp. 283–308). New York: Kluwer Academic/Plenum.

Martin, F. (1997). Justifying a high-speed rail project: social value vs. regional growth. *Annals of Regional Science, 31,* 155–174.

Maslow, A. H. (1970). *Motivation and personality* (2nd ed.). New York: Harper & Row.

McGregor, S. L. T. (2000). Using social and consumer values to predict market-place behavior: questions of congruency. *International Journal of Consumer Studies, 24,* 94–103.

McKinley-Floyd, L. A. (1998). The impact of values on the selection of Philanthropic clubs by elite African American women: An historical perspective. *Psychology & Marketing, 15,* 145–160.

McQuarrie, E. F., & Langmeyer, D. (1985). Using values to measure attitudes toward discontinuous innovation. *Psychology & Marketing, 2,* 239–252.

Murray, H. A. (1951). Some basic psychological assumptions and conceptions. *Dialectica, 5,* 266–292.

Nelson, K. A. (2004). Consumer decision making and image theory: Understanding value-laden decisions. *Journal of Consumer Psychology, 14*(1–2), 28–40.

Olver, J. M., & Mooradian, T. D. (2003). Personality traits and personal values: a conceptual and empirical integration. *Personality and Individual Differences, 35,* 109–125.

Piaget, J. (1952). *The origins of intelligence in children.* New York: International University Press.

Pitts, R. E., Canty, A. L., & Tsalikis, J. (1985). Exploring the impact of personal values on socially oriented communications. *Psychology & Marketing, 2,* 267–278.

Pitts, R. E., & Arch Woodside, A. (Eds.) (1984) *Personal values and consumer psychology,* Lexington, MA: Lexington Books

Raval, D., & Subramanian, B. (2004). Cultural values driven segmentation in social marketing. *Journal of Nonprofit & Public Sector Marketing, 12,* 73–85.

Reynolds, T. J. (1985). Implications for value research: A macro vs. micro perspective. *Psychology & Marketing, 2*(4), 297–305.

Reynolds, T. J., & Gutman, J. (1988). Laddering theory, method, analysis, and interpretation. *Journal of Advertising Research, 28*(1), 11–31.

Reynolds, T. J., & J. C. Olson (Eds.) (2001). *Understanding consumer decision making: The means-end approach to marketing and advertising strategy.* Mahwah, NJ: Erlbaum.

Richins, M. L. & Dawson S. (1992). A consumer values orientation for materialism and its measurement: Scale development and validation. *Journal of Consumer Research, 19,* 303–316

Rokeach, M. (1973). *The nature of human values.* New York: Free Press.

Rose, G. M., Shoham, A., Kahle, L. R., & Batra, R. (1994), Social values, conformity, and dress. *Journal of Applied Social Psychology, 24,* 1501–1519.

Sawa, S. L., & Sawa, G. H. (1988). The value confrontation approach to enduring behavior modification. *Journal of Social Psychology, 128*(2), 207–215.

Schwartz, S. H. (1996). Value priorities and behavior: Applying a theory of integrated value systems. In C. Seligman, J. M. Olson & M. P. Zanna (Eds.), *The psychology of values* (pp. 1–24). Mahwah, NJ: Erlbaum.

Schwartz, S. H., &, Bilsky, W. (1987). Toward a universal psychological structure of human values. *Journal of Personality and Social Psychology, 53*(3), 550–562.

Schewe, C. D., & Meredith, G. (2004). Segmenting global markets by generational cohorts: Determining motivations by age. *Journal of Consumer Behavior, 4,* 51–63.

Sheth, J. N., Newman, B., & Gross, B. (1991). Why we buy what we buy: A theory of consumption values. *Journal of Business Research, 22,* 159–170.

Sheth, J. N., Stern, B. I., & Gross, B. L. (1991). Consumption values and market choices: Theory and applications. Cincinnati: South-Western.Rokeach, M. (1973). *The nature of human values.* New York: Free Press.

Skelly, F. R. (1983). Using social trend data to shape marketing policy: Some do's and a don't. *Journal of Consumer Marketing, 1,* 14–17.

Spiggle, S. (1986). Measuring social values: A content analysis of Sunday comics and underground comix. *Journal of Consumer Research, 13,* 100–113.

Sun, T., Horn, M., & Merritt, D. (2004). Values and lifestyles of individualists and collectivists: a study on Chinese, Japanese, British and US consumers. *Journal of Consumer Marketing, 21,* 318–331.

Sung, Y., & Tinkham, S. F. (2005). Brand personality structures in the United States and Korea: Common and culture-specific factors. *Journal of Consumer Psychology, 15,* 334–350.

Swenson, M. J., & Herche, J. (1994). Social values and salesperson performance: An empirical examination. *Journal of the Academy of Marketing Science, 22,* 283–289.

Tan, C. T., & Farley, J. U. (1987). The impact of cultural patterns on cognition and intention in Singapore. *Journal of Consumer Research, 13*, 540–544.

Thompson, C. J., & Troester, M. (2002). Consumer value systems in the age of postmodern fragmentation: The case of the natural health microculture. *Journal of Consumer Research, 28*, 550–571.

Vitt, L. A. (2004). Consumers' financial decisions and the psychology of values. *Journal of Financial Service Professionals, 58*, 68–77.

Vriens, M., & Hofstede, F. T. (2000). Linking attribute, benefits, and consumer values. *Marketing Research, 12*, 4–10.

Winters, L. C. (1989). SRI announces VALS 2. *Marketing Research, 1*, 67–69.

Witkowski, T. H. (1998). The early American style: A history of marketing and consumer values. *Psychology & Marketing, 15*, 125–143.

V

BEHAVIORAL DECISION RESEARCH

23

Consumer Decision Making
A Choice Goals Approach

JAMES R. BETTMAN

MARY FRANCES LUCE

JOHN W. PAYNE

Duke University

Understanding the factors influencing consumers' choices is critical for the success of marketing and public policy initiatives and for helping consumers to maximize their satisfaction with their selections. Given the vast amounts of information about products on the Internet, the often dizzying array of options available (Schwartz, 2004), and the difficult tradeoffs consumers face in making such emotion-laden choices as decisions regarding medical care or retirement investments, the centrality of the study of consumer decision making is likely to continue.

Decades of decision research demonstrate that preferences are often highly dependent upon the particular features of the context in which a choice is made, such as the specific set of options available, the format and complexity of the information, and the difficulty of the tradeoffs involved. These effects suggest that preferences are often constructed during the process of decision making (Bettman, 1979; Bettman, Luce, & Payne, 1998; Slovic, 1995). That is, consumers often do not possess well-defined preferences but construct them on the spot as needed. Individuals may construct preferences because they lack the cognitive resources to generate well-defined preferences (March, 1978) or because they have multiple, conflicting goals. We believe that even when choices are constructed, and hence contingent on properties of the task and context, consumers' choices are often adaptive and intelligent, if not always optimal (Payne, Bettman, & Johnson, 1993). Note that not all preferences are constructive; consumers are likely to have stable preferences for some products, usually when they are familiar and experienced with the product. However, many consumer decisions are likely to involve constructive processes.

Consumer research has historically focused on relatively low-stakes decisions, as is reflected in most of the work we review below. We believe that the idea of constructive preferences has implications for higher-stakes consumer decisions as well, such as those involving health and safety, medical care, or insurance. High-stakes decisions often involve complicated information and difficult tradeoffs. They are also relatively infrequently made, with those with the most important uncertainties and consequences (e.g., automobile accidents, the need for catastrophic medical care) even less frequently resolved. Thus, consumer expertise and opportunity for feedback are likely to be limited. We believe that these factors pose particular challenges for frameworks for decision behavior, and in the final section of this chapter we focus on the implications of high stakes decision domains for our theoretical framework in particular.

Our framework for understanding constructive behavior starts with the assertion that choices are made to achieve goals, so it is critical to characterize the goals consumers have for specific choices in order to understand how task and context factors influence those choices. We believe that the most fruitful level of analysis for this explanatory framework is to examine consumers' metagoals for choice processing. We believe that four such metagoals are critical: maximizing the accuracy of a decision, minimizing the cognitive effort needed to reach a decision, minimizing the negative emotion experienced while making the decision, and maximizing the ease with which a decision can be justified. Although more specific goals may be relevant under some circumstances (e.g., valuing change for change's sake (Drolet, 2002)), we believe that these four metagoals can explain a wide range of findings in consumer decision making and capture many of the most important motivational aspects of consumer choice.

This choice goals framework has its roots in Simon's (1955) concept of bounded rationality, i.e., the notion that decision makers have important limits on their information processing capacity. The accuracy goal was the focus of the rational choice approach to decision making, with the goal being to maximize utility. However, limited working memory and computational abilities imply that decision makers must be concerned with effort as well as accuracy. Consumers must use simplifying strategies for making choices; consumers are not maximizers with complete knowledge who engage in complex calculations to maximize utility. Simon's (1955) notion of bounded rationality highlighted the importance of effort-related goals. Thus, it has long been argued that choice reflects effort-accuracy tradeoffs. More recently, it has been stressed that humans are also both emotional and social beings, so the choice goals framework includes dealing with the emotions involved in difficult tradeoffs and justifying decisions to others or to oneself as additional critical facets to consider.

Different goals may be relevant in different situations. If a decision is irreversible with potentially severe consequences, increased accuracy, decreased negative emotion, and increased ease of justification are likely to be most relevant, for example. Thus, for instance, high-stakes decision domains represent important, new application areas for our framework because the relevant decisions are characterized not only by a desire for decision accuracy, but also cognitive decision difficulty, emotion-laden tradeoffs, and the need to justify. Further, research addressing high-stakes decision making has argued that the relevant decision processes are often mediated by non-conscious processes, so that, for instance, the impact of negative affect on decision outcomes may be outside of the decision maker's control or introspection. Attempts to understand how these goal conflicts are reconciled in high-stakes domains therefore address the more general theoretical challenge of integrating our framework with the recent work in psychology arguing that nonconscious, automatic processes are involved in much of human behavior (Bargh & Chartrand, 1999). While our focus to date has been on more conscious, effortful, rule-based processes, we believe that there are opportunities to extend our theoretical view by integrating work on non-conscious processing.

An important condition for determining the weight placed on decision meta-goals is the ease and clarity of available feedback. The amount and timeliness of feedback present in the learning environment is crucial for the functioning of decision processes (e.g., Hogarth, 1987). In particular, it appears that non-conscious decision strategies are dependent on an environment with clear, consistent, and repeated feedback if these processes are to function most accurately (Hogarth, 2001; Stanovich, 2004). Effort and emotion feedback may be more readily available than accuracy feedback, for example, and what makes for a good justification may not always be clear. If effort and emotion feedback are often salient, then consumers may often choose to conserve effort and avoid difficult tradeoffs. For example, effort might even provide a justification in some situations, e.g., for choosing to indulge in luxuries as opposed to necessities as rewards from a customer frequency (loyalty) program (Kivetz & Simonson, 2002). Thus, both the mapping from specific decision strategies to attainment of each metagoal and the relationships among each of the four metagoals may depend on the task environment.

Finally, although we believe the four meta-goals described above are the most prominent, other metagoals may also be sought by consumers. For example, one possible metagoal is seeking positive experiences in decision making. We have not examined seeking positive emotion via buying and consumption experiences, but recent work provides a framework for conceptualizing the role of positive emotion in broadening thought-action repertoires and building resources for future coping (Fredrickson, 2001; Fredrickson & Branigan, 2005). Examining the effects of a metagoal for seeking positive emotions in decision making would be a promising area for future research. This goal could be integrated into our framework by extending the considered range of the negative emotion minimization goal. However, it is also possible that positive and negative emotion goals will operate independently, as positive and negative emotions often appear to operate independently and simultaneous experience of mixed positive and negative emotions is possible (Larsen, McGraw, & Cacioppo, 2001; Williams & Aaker, 2002).

In the remainder of this chapter, we review and extend the choice goals framework for understanding constructive, contingent consumer choices. Next, we briefly consider the nature of consumer decision tasks and decision strategies, and draw implications for consumers' adaptive strategy selection in response to task characteristics. We then apply the core principles of the choice goals framework to understanding accuracy-effort tradeoffs in consumer choice, analyzing emotion-laden decisions, and analyzing situations where the need to justify or provide reasons for a decision is relevant. We then apply our framework to high-stakes decision making.

ADAPTIVE SELECTION OF CONSUMER DECISION STRATEGIES

Decision Tasks

A typical consumer decision task involves a set of alternatives described by attributes or consequences. More formally, there is a set of m options where each option i is described by n attribute values $(x_{i1}, x_{i2}, ..., x_{in})$, where each attribute value x_{ij} reflects the extent to which the consumer values option i on attribute j. Many features of such a task can vary and influence consumers' choices. For example, the number of alternatives and attributes can differ, as can the number of different levels for the attributes across options. Consumers may be more or less certain about the values for some attributes for some options or they may not even have any information on some of these values. Some attributes, such as safety, may be more difficult for consumers to trade off with other attributes. Generally, choices will be more difficult to the extent that there is more information, more uncertainty about the attribute values, and more difficult tradeoffs.

Decision Strategies

There are many possible types of consumer decision strategies, or heuristics. We will review only a few such strategies here and discuss the overall properties of these strategies. For a more complete analysis of consumer strategies, see Bettman et al. (1998).

Three important types of strategies that provide exemplars for the different properties strategies may possess are weighted adding, lexicographic, and relational strategies such as compromise and asymmetric dominance (Simonson, 1989). Weighted adding is a classic decision making strategy that is often assumed by market researchers. Consumers are assumed to assess the importance weight of each attribute and then assign a subjective value to each attribute level for each option. In weighted adding, the consumer considers one alternative at a time. For each attribute, the consumer multiplies the weight times the subjective value; these products are then summed across all the attributes for that alternative to arrive at a total score for that alternative. This process is repeated across all the alternatives, and the alternative with the highest score is selected. Weighted adding considers all of the available information and involves explicit tradeoffs; it is considered to be more normatively accurate than strategies not possessing these characteristics (Frisch & Clemen, 1994).

The lexicographic strategy is simple to describe and execute. The individual selects the alternative with the best value on the most important attribute. If there are ties, the consumer considers the alternative with the best value on the second most important attribute, and so on. Note that only a portion of the available information is considered, and explicit tradeoffs are not made.

These two heuristics provide exemplars for considering four aspects characterizing choice strategies: the amount of information processed, the degree to which processing is selective, the pattern of processing (whether information is processed by alternative [brand] or by attribute), and whether the strategy is compensatory or noncompensatory.

The amount of information processed varies across strategies, with weighted adding processing all of the available information and the lexicographic strategy processing less of the available information. If different amounts of information are processed for each attribute or alternative, processing is said to be selective. Weighted adding is not selective, whereas the lexicographic strategy is highly selective across attributes but is not selective across alternatives (since one piece of information is examined for each alternative). Bounded rationality requires selective attention, and greater selectivity implies a stronger effect on choice of factors influencing the salience of information, such as how information is displayed.

Information can be processed in different patterns. In weighted adding, for example, information is processed by alternative, with multiple attributes of one option considered before another option is examined. In the lexicographic heuristic, on the other hand, information is processed one attribute at a time, examining the values of several options on an attribute.

Finally, strategies can be either compensatory or noncompensatory. In a compensatory strategy, such as weighted adding, a good value on one attribute can compensate for a bad value on another; this requires explicit tradeoffs among attributes. The lexicographic strategy, on the other hand, is noncompensatory; a good value on one attribute cannot make up for a poor value on another. If one decides safety is the most important attribute for a car and uses a lexicographic strategy to choose the safest car, then the value of that car on reliability or other attributes will not matter. Compensatory processing, the making of tradeoffs, is a core principle of rational choice.

Recent work in consumer research has focused on a different type of strategy in which the relationships of the values characterizing the choice options are the focus. For example, consider the simple options shown in Figure 23.1. One heuristic, asymmetric dominance, considers dominance relationships among the options. Dominance occurs if one alternative is better than or equal to another alternative on all attributes. According to asymmetric dominance, if a consumer were faced with a choice among options A, C, and D, the fact that option A dominates option D would make it more likely that the consumer would select option A (Huber, Payne, & Puto, 1982). Another heuristic, compromise, suggests that consumers might be more likely to select option B in a choice among options A, B, and C because B represents a compromise between the two more extreme options A and C (Simonson, 1989). Priester, Dholakia, and Fleming (2004) show that the

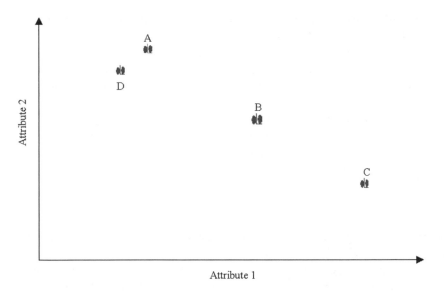

Figure 23.1   A set of alternatives showing possible asymmetric dominance (alternatives A, C, and D) and compromise (alternatives A, B, and C) effects.

degree to which the context of one choice influences later choices is increased by more thoughtful processing.

Tversky and Simonson (1993) propose a componential context model of choice that has such relational strategies as special cases. Their model has one term for the individual value of each option arrived at through a weighted additive process and another term reflecting the relative advantage of one option over another that considers the relationships among options. Relational strategies vary on the properties discussed above depending upon the particular strategy considered. The componential context model, for example, is compensatory, not selective, and has both alternative-based and attribute-based processing.

Note that because our focus is choice rather than judgment, the choice strategies we consider generally involve comparative processes. Although consumers can choose without making comparisons (see Posavac, Sanbonmatsu, Kardes, & Fitzsimons (2004) and Wang & Wyer (2002) for discussion of choice involving singular rather than comparative evaluation), we will focus on comparative evaluations.

The above section presented an overview of some typical strategies. We believe that individuals have a larger repertoire or toolbox of different strategies available for solving decision problems, acquired via experience or training (Payne, Bettman, & Johnson, 1993). Different consumers vary in terms of the range of strategies they possess. Next, we consider how properties of the decision task interact with consumers' important metagoals in order to shape decision strategy selection.

Adaptive Strategy Selection

In any given task situation, different strategies have varying advantages and disadvantages with respect to accomplishing the four goals outlined by the choice goals framework. For example, weighted adding generally may be more accurate, effortful, and more emotionally difficult (because it requires tradeoffs). Its extensive processing might aid justification, but use of subjective tradeoffs could hinder justification. Lexicographic choice, on the other hand, is less effortful, avoids emotional tradeoffs, and can be quite accurate in some environments (Payne, Bettman, & Johnson, 1988). Individual differences in computational skills and expertise can affect such advantages and disadvantages for a given strategy (Stanovich, 1999; Stanovich & West, 1998). For example, the ability to be selective of the most relevant information improves with expertise (Alba & Hutchinson, 1987).

A critical aspect of understanding adaptive strategy selection is that the relative advantages and disadvantages of each strategy may vary from one environment to another. A strategy that is more accurate in one environment may be less accurate in another (e.g., a lexicographic strategy will be more accurate when the important weights of attributes vary widely and less accurate when those weights are relatively uniform), and different information formats may make different strategies more or less effortful (Russo, 1977).

Given the toolbox of potential strategies and their relative advantages and disadvantages, we argue that the consumer selects a choice strategy that fits his or her goals for that situation. As a result, consumers will select different strategies as their goals, constraints, and characteristics of the task environment change. Note that much of our work to date has considered this to be a relatively conscious, controlled process. We examine how nonconscious, automatic processes may be integrated into our account within the context of high stakes decision making in the final sections of this chapter.

This outline of our approach is relatively general. We now examine three more specific examples of this approach. First we consider consumer accuracy-effort tradeoffs, followed by an analysis of emotion-laden decisions, and then an analysis of situations where ease of justification is important.

UNDERSTANDING CONSUMER ACCURACY-EFFORT TRADEOFFS

Analyzing Effects of Accuracy and Effort

Two major goals that characterize many decision situations are maximizing accuracy and minimizing effort (Beach & Mitchell, 1978; Hogarth, 1987; Payne et al., 1993; Shugan, 1980). We have examined how these goals interact in various environments by developing measures of cognitive effort and accuracy and simulating how various strategies perform in terms of effort and accuracy in different choice environments (Payne et al., 1993). To measure effort, we have modeled strategies according to the elementary information processes (EIPs) they require (e.g., reading information, comparing values, adding or multiplying values, eliminating options). We have successfully used the number of EIPs required to carry out a strategy as a measure of that strategy's effort (one can also weight different EIPs to model differences in effort across elementary operations (Bettman, Johnson, & Payne, 1990)). For accuracy, we have used the weighted adding strategy as a normative benchmark.

Using these measures of accuracy and effort, we have simulated the performance of various strategies in different environments and can draw general conclusions relative to accuracy-effort tradeoffs (Bettman, Johnson, Luce, & Payne, 1993; Creyer, Bettman, & Payne, 1990; Johnson & Payne, 1985; Payne et al., 1988). First, simplifying heuristics can often be highly accurate with substantial savings in effort. Thus, using simplifying strategies can be an adaptive response. Second, no single heuristic does well in accuracy across all environments. For example, lexicographic strategies do poorly if importance weights are relatively equal, and weighted adding does poorly under time pressure (because some options are not considered at all if time runs out). Thus, if a consumer wishes to achieve both reasonably high accuracy and low effort, he or she must use a repertoire of different strategies, with selection contingent upon task demands. We now turn to empirical research in consumer choice that is consistent with these principles.

Consumer Choice Research on Problem Difficulty

Many findings in consumer decision making can be accounted for using accuracy and effort goals, particularly work on factors influencing problem difficulty. In particular, we examine research related to amount of information, time pressure, attribute correlation, completeness of information, and information format. Decisions become more difficult as the amount of information increases, time pressure increases, conflict among attributes increases, missing information increases, and the information display format becomes less organized or more complex.

Amount of Information. As the number of alternatives available increases, consumers are more likely to use noncompensatory strategies that eliminate alternatives (Johnson & Meyer, 1984; Payne, 1976), whereas compensatory strategies are more common for few options. Changes in the number of attributes may increase selectivity but do not appear to lead to strategy changes as readily (Olshavsky, 1979; Payne, 1976). Gregan-Paxton and John (1997) extend this finding to children, finding that older childer (ages 10–11) adapt to problem size, but younger children often do not unless search costs are made salient. Recently, Lurie (2004) has argued that it is the amount of information (in an information-theoretic sense) that is critical, not merely the number of attributes and alternatives. He shows that an increase in the number of different attribute levels possible and a more even distribution of these possible values across options make decisions more difficult and increase selectivity. Our framework explains these findings by examining the way changes in the amount of information affect accuracy and effort in our simulation work. Payne et al. (1993, pp. 133–137) show that relative accuracy is fairly robust over changes in number of alternatives and that the effort required by strategies other than weighted adding increases much less rapidly than weighted adding as problem size increases. Thus, heuristics other than weighted adding will provide relatively more favorable accuracy-effort tradeoffs as problem size increases.

Whether consumers can be overloaded with information has been a long-time focus in consumer psychology. The answer to this question has obvious and important implications for both policy makers and consumers regarding whether to provide new information or whether to limit the amount of information available. Work on information load claiming that consumers could be overloaded and would make poorer decisions (Jacoby, Speller, & Kohn, 1974a, b) has been controversial, with several others disputing these conclusions (e.g., Keller & Staelin, 1987; Meyer & Johnson, 1989; Russo, 1974; Wilkie, 1974). Recent work argues that consumers may be faced with too many options from which to choose (Iyengar & Lepper, 2000; Schwartz, 2000; 2004). Iyengar and Lepper (2000) argue that having too many options may be demotivating, with individuals purchasing less often when faced with more extensive option sets than from a more limited array of choices. Schwartz et al. (2002) show that people can feel worse as the number of options increases, particularly if they are maximizers who wish to make the best possible choice. In a recent discussion of automatic decision behavior, Gladwell (2005) argues that the key to efficiently processing large amounts of information lies in the specific details on which one focuses. We believe that the essence of consumers' coping with large amounts of information is selectivity. If consumers can be selective in ways that are reflective of their values, then overload may be less harmful; if selectivity is based on irrelevant factors that increase salience but are not correlated with values, then overload will be more harmful.

Time Pressure. Individuals appear to engage in a hierarchy of responses to time pressure. Under moderate time pressure, individuals process each item more rapidly and become more selective. Under severe time pressure, people switch to more attribute-based processing. Quickly examining some information about each alternative is more effective than examining a limited set of options in more depth (Eisenhardt, 1989; Payne et al., 1988; Payne, Bettman, & Luce, 1996; Pieters, Warlop, & Hartog, 1997). Such shifts can be explained by our framework; effort is essentially fixed under time pressure, the accuracy of weighted adding degrades under time pressure, and the accuracy of attribute-based heuristics is relatively robust under time pressure.

Attribute Correlation. Interattribute correlation is related to both dominance and conflict: the more negative the correlations among attributes, the less likely there is to be dominance (occurring when one alternative is better than or equal to another on all attributes) and the more one has to give up of one attribute to get more of another. Bettman et al. (1993) show that simplifying heuristics become relatively less accurate than weighted adding under negative interattribute correlations; they found that individuals did shift toward more alternative-based and extensive processing when correlations became more negative for choices among gambles. Widing and Talarzyk (1993) show that a decision aid providing weighted adding scores resulted in the best accuracy in a negative correlation environment. Importantly, the relationship between negative interattribute correlation and alternative-based processing may not hold in all cases. Luce, Bettman, and Payne (1997) showed that processing became more attribute-based under negative correlation when decisions were *emotion-laden*, because the attribute-based processing enables individuals to avoid the negative emotion involved in difficult attribute tradeoffs.

Completeness of Information. Consumers may respond in many ways when information is missing, including inferring missing values based upon other values for that attribute in the set of options (other-brand information) or values for other attributes of the same option (same-brand information). Early work found that either other-brand (Huber & McCann, 1982; Meyer, 1981) or same-brand information (Ford & Smith, 1987; Johnson & Levin, 1985) was used in different situations. Several researchers have used Feldman and Lynch's (1988) accessibility-diagnosticity framework to argue that use of same-brand or other-brand information is contingent upon properties of the situation (Dick, Chakravarti, & Biehal, 1990; Ross & Creyer, 1992). The application of our framework to such results is relatively straightforward, with accessibility-diagnosticity goals being very similar to accuracy-effort tradeoffs in these situations. Other researchers have been cautious about the degree to which inferencing takes place (Broniarczyk & Alba, 1994; Simmons & Lynch, 1991). Kivetz and Simonson (2000) also argue that inferences cannot explain all of the effects of missing information. They demonstrate that buyers' interpretations of attribute values are biased so as to support the option which is better on an attribute with no missing information. Finally, Bradlow, Hu, and Ho (2004) model how respondents in a common marketing research task (conjoint analysis) may infer missing attribute values and how such inferences can affect the expressed preferences (see also Alba & Cooke, 2004).

Finally, Kardes, Posavac, and Cronley (2004) provide a thorough review of consumer inference, arguing that there are many possible responses to missing information, including failure to notice that information is indeed missing. They characterize inferences according to whether they are generated by induction vs. deduction, are stimulus-based vs. memory-based, or pertain to singular vs. comparative judgments. They also argue that spontaneous attitude formation only occurs when it is useful for consumers to possess attitudes.

Information Format. Several researchers have argued that making information easier to process can influence consumer choices (e.g., Russo's, 1977, classic illustration of increasing the effects of unit prices by providing lists with brands listed in order of unit price). Slovic (1972) postulated a related effect, a "concreteness principle," arguing that decision makers will tend to use information as it is displayed, without transforming it. This principle is supported by research by Bettman and Kakkar (1977) and Jarvenpaa (1989) showing that individuals process information in an order consistent with the form of a display. Similarly, sequential presentation of information leads to more significant pioneering effects (Kardes & Kalyanaram, 1992; Kardes et al., 1993). Concreteness does not always hold, however. If effort costs from following the given format are high, consumers may restructure the information (Coupey, 1994). Accuracy considerations can also override concreteness (Sethuraman, Cole, & Jain, 1994). These effects are easily explainable within our framework by examining the effects for format on effort costs of acquiring information and any effects of format on accuracy. Next, we turn to analyzing emotion-laden consumer choices.

ANALYZING EMOTION-LADEN CONSUMER CHOICES

Consumers often face choices that are emotion-laden and that pose very difficult and wrenching tradeoffs. A consumer may struggle to trade off safety versus environmental concerns in choosing a car (if large cars are safer but less environmentally friendly) or length of life versus quality of life in medical care decisions regarding a parent. Consumers may even refuse to think about tradeoffs such as the value versus the cost of a medical treatment for a family member. Tetlock (2002), and others have argued that such tradeoffs of sacred versus profane considerations are "taboo" (Baron & Spranca, 1997). Such difficult tradeoffs can lead to negative emotion due to the threats to attainment of valued goals (Lazarus, 1991). This emotion is related to the choice itself, particularly tradeoff difficulty, not unrelated affect such as mood attributable to noise at the decision site. We argue that individuals cope with such negative emotion and often have a goal to avoid such emotion. This goal of minimizing negative emotion experienced during choice can interact with the goals of accuracy and effort described above (see Mellers, Schwartz, & Ritov, 1999, for an account of decision affect theory, which also examines positive emotions associated with choice).

Two general types of strategies for coping with emotion are problem-focused coping (direct actions to improve the person-environment relationship leading to the emotion) and emotion-focused coping (indirect actions that minimize emotion by changing the amount or content of thought); these types of coping are typically both used simultaneously (Folkman & Lazarus, 1988). For decision making, we argue that problem-focused coping will lead to an emphasis on accuracy, especially extensive processing. Extensive processing is the most observable indicator to oneself and others that one is motivated to be accurate (Payne et al., 1988, p. 551, n. 4). We thus expect increased negative emotion due to tradeoff difficulty will lead to more extensive processing.

Emotion-focused coping often involves avoidant behaviors (Anderson, 2003), such as refusing to make a decision. The aspect of emotion-laden choices that is most troublesome is confronting the difficult tradeoffs required (Hogarth, 1987; Tetlock, 2002; Tversky & Shafir, 1992). Thus, consumers may cope with emotion-laden decisions by avoiding difficult tradeoffs, which can be done by using attribute-based, noncompensatory strategies. Thus, our framework argues than for negatively emotion-laden choices, consumers will both process more extensively and in a more attribute-based fashion. Note that this is opposite to typical findings for less emotion-laden decisions, where more extensive processing is associated with alternative-based processing (e.g., Bettman et al., 1993). This effect results from interactions among goals for accuracy, effort, and minimizing the experience of negative emotion.

Luce, Bettman, and Payne (2001) extend this theorizing by examining tradeoff difficulty and coping in consumer choice. They argue that two important antecedents of tradeoff difficulty are the type of attributes considered and attribute values, particularly the degree to which attributes conflict with one another and the degree to which the values involved are less favorable. Trade-off difficulty then affects the extensiveness of processing, the pattern of processing, and avoidant behavior as outlined above.

Next we turn to empirical research on emotion-laden consumer decisions within a choice goals framework. First, Luce (1998) showed that increases in negative emotion related to the choice led to increased avoidance in choice, i.e., increased tradeoff difficulty was associated with increased choice of the status quo option, increased choice of an asymmetrically dominating option, and greater tendency to prolong search. Choice of an avoidant option also led to less negative emotion following the choice. Luce et al. (1997) show the overall pattern of processing hypothesized above: increased negative emotion led to more extensive, more selective, and more attribute-based processing. Note that this is the opposite pattern from the Bettman et al. (1993) findings with non-emotional choices among gambles. Luce, Payne, and Bettman (1999, 2000) found that consumers were less willing to trade off higher values on a quality attribute for a lower price as the quality attribute increases in emotional tradeoff difficulty due to the type of attribute or the favorableness of its values, regardless of which attribute is perceived to be more important. Finally, Drolet and Luce (2004) show that increased cognitive load can paradoxically result in more normative decision behavior for emotion-laden choices by disrupting consumers' abilities to associate tradeoffs with goals and potential negative emotion. Dhar and Nowlis (1999), in a related finding, show that time pressure decreases choice deferral when choice conflict is high, but not when it is low.

These findings suggest some counterintuitive opportunities for decision support. First, helping decision makers cope with negative emotion may indirectly increase decision accuracy. For instance, Kahn and Luce (2003) find that women experiencing stressful false positive test results are more likely to maintain intentions to engage in normatively suggested mammography screening guidelines if they are given interventions to support either problem- or emotion-focused coping efforts. Second, accuracy could be increased through effort reduction in specific cases where lowered effort directly results in lowered emotion generation.

CHOICES WHEN EASE OF JUSTIFICATION IS RELEVANT

Consumers exist in a social environment, and they must often justify their choices to themselves or others (Tetlock, 2002). Providing justifications often involves being able to provide convincing reasons for a choice (Shafir, Simonson, & Tversky, 1993). Ease of justification has not been directly related to the choice goals approach in research to date, so our analysis is more speculative than in the previous sections. The most active area of research on justification and choice has involved the relational heuristics described earlier in this chapter, particularly the asymmetric dominance and compromise heuristics. Researchers have argued that relational heuristics can be easy to apply and can provide good reasons. For example, the fact that option A dominates option D in Figure 23.1 is a good reason for choosing option A based upon outcomes (A is clearly a better outcome than D). No process arguments based on tradeoffs or other concerns are required. Hamilton (2003) shows that consumers understand these principles and can design choice sets so as to influence others' choices based upon what relationships might provide good reasons. Relational heuristics, therefore, may often perform well with respect to ease of justification and effort goals. Relational heuristics may also, as Luce (1998) showed, allow avoidance of difficult tradeoffs and thus do well on minimizing negative emotions.

Such a complex interplay of several metagoals may characterize the analysis of choices involving relational heuristics and justification issues. For example, compromise effects may require a different analysis. Simonson (1989) shows that compromise options may not be seen as easier to justify, and developing reasons for compromise choices may actually require more effort and more negative emotion to deal with conflict. In addition, as noted above, increased effort may also serve as a justification (Kivetz & Simonson, 2002).

One of the classic findings regarding relational heuristics was Huber et al.'s (1982) demonstration of the asymmetric dominance effect. Adding an asymmetrically dominating option (e.g., D) to a choice set consisting of two nondominated options (e.g., A and C in Figure 23.1) increases the relative choice share of the dominating alternative A, violating the principle of regularity necessary for most probabilistic choice models (adding a new alternative cannot increase the probability of choosing a member of the original choice set) (see also Heath & Chatterjee, 1995; Huber & Puto, 1983; Simonson, 1989; Simonson & Tversky, 1992; Wedell, 1991; Wedell & Pettibone, 1996). Simonson (1989) was the first to propose that people can use the relationships among options as reasons for choice and showed that increased need for justification led to a greater asymmetric dominance effect.

Simonson also was the first to propose the compromise effect, i.e., that an option which is a compromise between two more extreme options may gain in choice share. He also showed that increased need for justification tended to result in stronger compromise effects. Simonson and Nowlis (2000) show that consumers with a high need for uniqueness are less likely to make compromise choices when asked to provide reasons. Briley, Morris, and Simonson (2000) argue that cultural differences between East Asian cultures and North American culture in terms of compromise will become salient when consumers are asked to provide reasons for their choices, and they show that differences in compromise effects across their Asian and American consumers only occurred when reasons for choice were elicited. Kivetz, Netzer, and Srinivasan (2004) have proposed several alternative models for capturing the compromise effect. Finally, Chernev (2005) argues that choice can be influenced not only by the relational properties among alternatives, but also by the distribution of attribute values within an option (e.g., whether an option has equal values across attributes, or what Chernev calls attribute balance).

Recent work has hinted at a fundamental difference between asymmetric dominance and compromise effects, namely that asymmetric dominance may be more perceptual and automatic, whereas compromise may be more cognitive and conscious in nature. Dhar and Simonson (2003), for example, show that adding a no choice option increases the asymmetric dominance effect and decreases the compromise effect. They argue that this shows that consumers consciously decide whether a compromise choice is appropriate but are unaware that dominance affects their preferences. In a provocative paper, Shafir, Waite, and Smith (2002) show that honeybees and gray jays show asymmetric dominance effects. This supports the argument that asymmetric dominance effects may be relatively more automatic and perceptual and less deliberative or cognitive.

It is apparent from the research reviewed above that much less work has been done on emotion-laden decisions that require justification. We believe the literature on high-stakes decision making is an important source for insight into these sorts of decisions. Investigating high-stakes decisions thus provides a major new direction for our choice goals approach. When considering such decisions, many researchers have argued that automatic, nonconscious reactions can play an important role. Our discussion above has focused almost exclusively on conscious, controlled processes and strategies. Thus, integrating automatic, nonconscious processes with more controlled and conscious processes provides a major challenge to the choice goals approach. We address these challenges next.

CHOICES WITH HIGH-STAKES DECISION OUTCOMES

Consumers often make decisions involving high-stakes, or extremely consequential, outcomes. High-stakes outcomes may follow from even seemingly routine decisions involving medical care (e.g., adherence to mammography or Prostrate-Specific Antigen (PSA) test screening guidelines), insurance (e.g., whether or not to buy government-subsidized flood insurance) and consumer products (e.g., whether to pay more for a car with side-impact airbags or an aspirin bottle with a child safety cap). These high-stakes outcomes are often associated with low probabilities, and it is low-probability high-consequence outcomes that seem to present some of the biggest challenges for individual consumers and policy makers. For instance, if drivers could routinely expect that an automobile would be in a life-threatening accident, then tradeoffs between price and safety measures would often be clear (but road trips would certainly be much less attractive). Thus, while acknowledging the importance of high-stakes, higher-probability decision outcomes (e.g., potentially those involving cancer treatments), we focus below on the problem of decision making involving low-probability high-consequence events. Examples include decisions regarding how much insurance to purchase, whether to purchase protective safety measures such as optional automobile airbags, or how often to engage in screening tests such as mammography or home radon testing. These decision contexts provide a potentially fruitful context for further integration of the four metagoals that have been the focus of our framework to date.

Low-probability high-consequence (LPHC) decision contexts present particular challenges for understanding how decision makers should, and do, resolve conflicts between our four metagoals. Decision accuracy is crucial in high-stakes decisions, almost by definition. Saying that the stakes of a decision are high is simply another way to say that the decision has potentially important implications for realized utility. Such decisions often involve complex and technical information with which the decision maker is relatively unfamiliar. Further, the relevant outcomes (e.g., automobile accidents, cancer diagnoses) are by definition infrequent; thus, consumers must often make these decisions without the benefit of feedback from previous decisions. These factors make bounded rationality particularly challenging (see Stanovich, 2004). Negative emotions are likely to follow from consideration of LPHC events, such as those involving life-threatening disease, terrorism, or natural disaster. Finally, these decisions often involve situations where others (e.g., family members, advisors) are both influenced and relied on for input. This social context is likely to bring justification considerations to the forefront. Thus, we believe that LPHC decisions are ones where all four of our commonly-considered metagoals are highly relevant, and potentially in conflict with one another.

Below, we briefly review prior findings on LPHC decision making, and we use this literature to extend the choice goals framework. We believe this extension is important for consumer decision making in part because it has important public policy implications. As we address further below, research within the LPHC domain points towards some complications with prescriptive efforts for improving decision making in these domains. In particular, one important variable moderating the effect of decision goals on decision outcomes may be whether the decision task itself is one more suited to controlled vs. automatic cognitive processing. Thus, one implication of the LPHC work reviewed below is that the choice goals framework should be extended to address the interaction of automatic and controlled cognitive processes.

Review of Selected LPHC Decision Research

The LPHC literature notes that laypersons are limited in terms of processing the information needed to make accurate decisions in many high-stakes domains. Much of this research documents decision biases or deviations from the decisions that would be expected to follow from a normative analysis of probabilities, costs, and benefits. Somewhat paradoxically, these deviations appear to include both over-reactions to risk and a neglect of risk.

There are several demonstrations of apparent overreaction to risks, specifically consumers demonstrating fear and avoidance of risks that experts judge to be negligible (e.g., the Alar apple scare or the subset of the population that eschews airplane travel in favor of objectively riskier automobile travel). This occurs at least in part because laypersons tend to stigmatize certain risks (e.g., radiation) such that perceptions of hazard are generalized beyond (often negligible) actual risks and overwhelm or reverse perceptions of the positive aspects of the relevant activities (e.g., alternative energy from nuclear power; see Flynn, Slovic, & Kunreuther, 2001). Such processes are often socially amplified due to the media (e.g., Kasperson et al., 2001). The net result of this stigmatization is avoidance of even largely beneficial activities involving the relevant risk.

Other research indicates under-reaction to or even avoidance of risk information, particularly of the probability component of risk, and associated neglect of protective measures that experts judge as valuable. Individuals fail to search for available probability data (Huber, Wider, & Huber, 1997) and show insensitivity to differences between low probabilities unless given extensive context information (Kunreuther, Novemsky, & Kahneman, 2001). A classic finding in this regard is consumers' apparent aversion to probabilistic insurance, whereby consumers are relatively insensitive to the value of reducing the probability of a loss unless the probability of that loss is reduced to zero (Kahneman & Tversky, 1979; Wakker, Thaler, & Tversky, 1997). Consideration of specific consequences, and associated emotional reactions, also appears to improperly drive probability judgments (Rottenstreich & Hsee, 2001). For instance, false positive test results causing consumers to temporarily experience a diagnosis inappropriately increase the perceived likelihood of a later, true positive diagnosis (Luce & Kahn, 1999). Thus, consumers appear sensitive to the presence or absence of some possible loss, yet relatively insensitive to variations in the probability of that loss. More generally, protective measures that appear to be utility-maximizing might be neglected if consumers are insensitive to changes in the probability of a risk.

In summary, the literature on high-stakes decision making documents many apparent errors in reactions to LPHC information. In his speech accepting the Distinguished Achievement Award from the society for risk analysis, Howard Kunreuther (2002) summarized the state of these empirical findings as follows: "More generally, in the case of low-probability events there are often two extreme reactions to risks: either 'it will happen to me' or 'it won't happen to me.'" Thus, decision makers often appear to inappropriately treat potential outcomes as dichotomous (having probabilities of 0 or 1), when in reality there is a gradient of risk. Researchers in this area are beginning to move beyond documenting these "decision errors" towards attempting to explain their origin. As we discuss next, we believe that these explanations are broadly consistent with the choice goals framework.

High-Stakes Decision Making From the Choice Goals Perspective

Researchers in the LPHC decision-making domain are beginning to consider emotion as an explanatory variable for understanding consumer reactions to risk and risk reduction methods. Hsee and Kunreuther (2000) demonstrate that decision makers will pay more to insure a vase described as one they "love" even though factors normatively relevant to the insurance loss (i.e., probability of loss, value of the vase) are held constant. Baron, Hershey, and Kunreuther (2000) document that subjective feelings of worry provide an explanation of individual differences in desire for risk reduction. Slovic et al. (2002) explain deviations from normative behavior in risk domains by proposing that decisions are made in accordance with the affect heuristic, whereby image-generated affect creates perception of negative risk/benefit correlation, minimizing perception of risk-benefit *tradeoffs* (i.e., if higher risk is associated with lower perceived benefits, there is no apparent tradeoff to be made).

This recent work on affect in the LPHC domain shares with the choice goals framework the view that negative emotion has an important impact on decision strategy selection. From this perspective, overreaction to risk and stigma is consistent with the general finding that avoidance of negative emotion results in more lexicographic treatment of emotion-laden decisions. If explicit consideration of a negative outcome will (or does) generate negative emotion, the consumer might react by refusing to consider actions that lead to acceptance or increase of the risk of that outcome. Thus, a "Safety first principle" may be employed for certain risks, leading to neglect of potentially beneficial actions based on a screening rule or some other method of avoiding the tradeoffs between risk and potential benefits.

Conversely, the neglect of risk information and protective measures is also consistent with our perspective that emotion-minimization leads to lexicographic behavior and that cognitive avoidance can be a popular coping strategy. That is, if a negative outcome cannot be feasibly reduced to a probability of zero, the consumer may prefer to ignore the risk rather than explicitly balancing various intermediate probabilities of it. Finally, note that explicit tradeoffs are often considered particularly hard to justify (Tetlock, 2002). This may, for instance, lead to "false security" effects, whereby decision makers ignore or deny risks rather than acknowledging that their own past behavior may have neglected risk-minimization in favor of other factors (Kahn & Luce, 2006). Thus, the emotional and justification costs of explicit, considered risk-relevant tradeoffs may explain the dual tendencies to minimize exposure to some risks whereas measures to mitigate other risks are neglected.

Although the choice goals framework is consistent with both over- and underreaction to risk, a deeper analysis brings up the question of whether and why decision makers would subvert accuracy in high-stakes domains in order to avoid seemingly minor emotional discomfort. Are decision makers really so averse to decision-related anxiety that they would eschew valuable protective measures simply to avoid considering risk? Perhaps sometimes they are. One important aspect of the LPHC decision domain is that all four decision metagoals are likely to be at stake, with multiple conflicts. Thus, desires for accuracy and justification are likely pitted squarely against desires to minimize negative emotion and minimize cognitive effort. For instance, increasing the decision maker's desire to justify may increase her willingness to work hard, but might also increase emotional threat, thereby exacerbating risk avoidance behaviors. In these demanding situations, it may be unclear how to improve decision performance. We also believe that emerging work within the LPHC domain provides a further explanation of this risky-choice behavior and that a consideration of this work suggests fruitful avenues for expanding the choice goals framework and its implications for decision aiding. Thus, although we argue above that the choice goals framework can enrich understanding of LPHC decision making, we also believe that work within the LPHC domain points to important challenges and necessary extensions for our framework.

Automatic and Controlled Processing and the Choice Goals Framework

Work on Slovic's affect heuristic (e.g., Slovic et al., 2002) points to a second important explanation for emotion-based neglect of risk tradeoffs, namely that some of these emotion-relevant processes may operate outside of conscious control. Slovic argues that processes inducing perception of negative risk-benefit correlations may operate automatically, and one cannot make risk/benefit tradeoffs if one doesn't perceive them. Slovic's view is consistent with an important trend in the decision making literature towards viewing decision processes as based on two separate, but interacting cognitive systems (e.g., see Kahneman, 2003). System 1 is postulated to be more automatic, basic, and intuitive, shaped by evolutionary pressures to trigger behavior optimized for the environment characterizing human evolution (Stanovich, 2004). Specific cognitive procedures within System 1 are believed to be "hard wired" by evolutionary pressures (e.g., a startle response to heights) in addition to being acquired through repetition (e.g., a driver hitting the brakes when other cars slow). System 2 is postulated to be evolutionarily newer and more flexible, allowing for rational reaction to current environmental characteristics in order to meet individual goals. Formal logic and problem solving activities are generally associated with this second system. System 1 processes are subject to neither conscious introspection (although System 1 outputs are present in consciousness) nor conscious control. While we will discuss System 1 as if it is a unitary set of processes below (mostly for contrast with System 2), note that System 1 is more appropriately conceptualized as many, independent, simultaneous routines. In fact, the power of System 1 processing lies at least in part in the fact that this simultaneity of multiple processes creates great efficiencies. Note that the theorizing and research paradigms of the choice goals framework are generally more relevant to controlled System 2 processes. For instance, prior work on the choice goals framework has used verbal protocols (and other self-report methodologies) to assess decision strategy selection, a paradigm that presupposes decision makers have conscious awareness of decision processes.

In order to extend the choice goals framework to incorporate System 1 processes, it is useful to postulate a model for interaction between the systems. Two such models exist. First, selection models suggest that there are two distinct modes of processing that are selected based on environmental factors, and that effective decision making results from matching tasks to systems appropriately. Thus, System 1 processes should be matched to "intuitive" tasks and System 2 processes to "analytical" tasks. These models suggest that decision errors can arise from a mis-match of type of task and type of processing. This model is implied when "working harder" by recruiting System 2 effort actually decreases task performance. For instance, May, Hasher, and Foong (2005) find that an increase in available System 2 cognitive resources associated with optimal times of day led to decrements in implicit memory tasks (see also Finger, 2002 on verbal overshadowing of recognition memory). Explicit justification instructions also seem to harm performance on intuitive tasks, presumably because they recruit ineffective System 2 processes where System 1 processes would be preferred (McMackin & Slovic, 2000; Wilson & Schooler, 1991).

Second, corrective models suggest that decision processing always begins with automatic inputs from System 1 processes that must be further refined by System 2. These models suggest that errors arise from a failure to engage System 2, for instance from decision makers failing to learn where intuition must be corrected (e.g., Hogarth, 2001). Kardes (2006) makes the related point that consumers should trust intuition only when there is high quality feedback and errors are easy to detect. Finally, note that under either model a potential source of error involves the use of biased System 1 output as a fundamental input for System 2 (e.g., either for analytical tasks or during correction; Stanovich, 2004).

The System 1 versus System 2 distinction has fundamental implications for how to use the choice goals framework to aid decision making. System 2 operates under cognitive control, but System 1 is not, by definition, subject to such control. Thus, the effect of altering the decision maker's choice goals (e.g., increasing the desire for accuracy or justification) is expected to be largely dependent on which cognitive system is the source of decision error. Below, we draw implications for using choice metagoals as a tool for decision aiding and policy.

Task Analysis: Implications for Decision Aiding and Policy

The discussion of System 1 inputs to decision making points to an aspect of decision task environments that has been relatively overlooked from the perspective of the choice goals framework. That is, it may be possible to distinguish between intuitive and analytic decision task environments. We believe that this distinction is a crucial moderator of the manner in which decision metagoals will interact to determine decision performance.

One way to define intuitive versus analytical tasks may be to consider the evolutionary environment under which hard-wired System 1 rules developed or alternatively the previous experiences under which the individual acquired automated System 1 procedures. In cases where there is a mis-match between these historical environments and current goals, some analytical override of System 1 by System 2 may be necessary. For instance, both evolutionary and experiential pressures might result in a very reasonable System 1 bias towards startle and flight at the sight of a snake. This bias would be perfectly acceptable to most individuals, but would have to be overridden if one's current environment as a zookeeper made the "overreaction" to the risk of being bitten interfere with one's job.

Another way to distinguish between types of tasks is to consider the computational limitations involved in each system. Although System 2 is smarter in terms of its flexibility and ability to acquire and conform to rules of formal logic, note that System 2 is also uniquely subject to the fundamental attentional constraints we associate with bounded rationality. Thus, System 1 may be advantaged for decisions that involve holistic or experiential outcomes based on numerous, interacting sensory inputs (McMackin & Slovic, 2000; Wilson & Schooler, 1991) or extremely fast action based on a large number of cues (Klein, 1998). The efficient pattern-matching abilities of System 1 processes may consistently out-perform the slower, more serial System 2 processes for such tasks (Gladwell, 2005).

In situations where System 1 processes are historically appropriate and computational demands are heavy due to time pressure or informational constraints, there are important implications for how to improve decision making. In these situations, increased cognitive processing should not help decision performance and in fact is likely to hurt it. Conversely, increased reliance on emotional reactions may help in these task environments, as one might expect emotional reactions to be evolutionarily-based shortcuts to (historically) appropriate action.

Conversely, in tasks characterized by a need to rely on formal logic or problem solving, increased cognitive effort and focus on accuracy may often improve decision performance. Emotion might interfere with decision performance if it causes avoidance of task information or tradeoffs and hence directs attention away from important task problems. On the other hand, emotion could improve performance if it signals the need for more System 2 effort to replace or correct the intuitions produced by System 1.

One important caveat to the above discussion is that cognitive processing can go awry even when an appropriate match between the task and the cognitive system is in place. The choice goals framework clearly notes that even with purely analytical tasks, maximal payoffs from cognitive processing rely on decision makers selecting information that is most diagnostic. Prior work has found that decision makers appear to make adaptive choices of information across task environments, but these processes of selectivity are by no means perfect, particularly when task environments are misleading (e.g., Bettman et al., 1993). Similarly, recent work on System 1 processes notes that the particular "thin slice" of behavior or information on which System 1 processes are focused has huge implications for the ultimate quality of the relevant decisions (Gladwell, 2005).

Our discussion of the interaction between task characteristics and metagoals for determining decision quality largely assumes appropriate selectivity by each cognitive system, and we view this appropriate selectivity as a crucial moderating factor.

In summary, relationships among decision metagoals appear to differ for intuitive versus analytical tasks. Analytical tasks have been the typical focus of the choice goals framework to date. These tasks are characterized by relatively straightforward effort-accuracy tradeoffs in decision strategy selection. Specifically, decision makers appear to approximate an efficient frontier where increased decision effort generally produces increased task accuracy. This is particularly true when attention is focused on appropriate or diagnostic inputs. In these situations, goals to minimize negative emotion often decrease decision performance because they reduce reliance on explicit decision tradeoffs. However, the impact of emotion depends on the particular direction of coping efforts. Emotion may often function as a signal generating increased effort consistent with problem-focused coping, but it often simultaneously causes avoidance of tradeoffs consistent with emotion-focused coping. These latter effects may decrease decision accuracy. Finally, accountability goals should generally increase effort allocation, and hence accuracy, unless special conditions are met (e.g., the person to whom the decision maker is accountable is anticipated to prefer a less accurate process or outcome).

Conversely, intuitive tasks appear to be characterized by a fundamental change in the relationships among decision metagoals. Intuitive tasks are defined as those tasks that are performed more accurately by System 1 (vs. System 2) processes. Thus, increased conscious effort (which must be System 2 by definition) should at best dilute the efforts of System 1. In this situation, increased effort should generally decrease decision accuracy. Thus, the fundamental relationship postulated and explored by the effort-accuracy paradigm will be reversed. In these cases, factors such as increased cognitive load or cognitive distraction may lead to more decision accuracy (Dijksterhuis, 2004). Similarly, these situations are often associated with reduced performance given accountability (McMackin & Slovic, 2000; Wilson & Schooler, 1991), presumably because accountability instructions recruit increased cognitive effort. In these situations, the effects of increased emotion are again likely to be moderated by the particular coping strategies available (and chosen).

CONCLUSIONS

This chapter reviews our choice goals framework for understanding constructive decision processing. We argue that decision strategy selection is shaped by goals to maximize accuracy, minimize effort, minimize negative emotion and maximize justifiability and that individuals adaptively respond to task characteristics in order to balance these four metagoals when selecting among available decision strategies. We extend our choice goals framework by considering high-stakes decision contexts, where the four choice goals are likely to be in substantial conflict. In these environments, it is difficult to generate prescriptions regarding increased decision performance, as intervention along the lines of one goal (increase justification) may cause difficulties with respect to another goal (increased emotional threat). This extension also points out the challenge of integrating nonconscious, automatic cognitive processes into our framework. Consideration of these processes further underscores the importance of a task analysis in general and a distinction between intuitive and analytical tasks in particular. This task distinction will determine how choice metagoals interact, for instance, whether increased effort or justification can in fact be expected to increase performance accuracy.

REFERENCES

Alba, J. W., & Cooke, A. D. J. (2004). When absence begets inference in conjoint analysis. *Journal of Marketing Research, 41,* 382–387.

Alba, J. W., & Hutchinson, J. W. (1987). Dimensions of consumer expertise. *Journal of Consumer Research, 13,* 411–454.

Anderson, C. J. (2003). The psychology of doing nothing: Forms of decision avoidance result from reason and emotion. *Psychological Bulletin, 129,* 139–167.

Bargh, J. A., & Chartrand, T. L. (1999). The unbearable automaticity of being. *American Psychologist, 54,* 462–479.

Baron, J., & Spranca, M. D. (1997). Protected values. *Organizational Behavior and Human Decision Processes, 70,* 1–16.

Baron, J., Hershey, J. C., & Kunreuther, H. (2000). Determinants of priority for risk reduction: The role of worry. *Risk Analysis, 20,* 413–427.

Beach, L. R., & Mitchell, T. R. (1978). A contingency model for the selection of decision strategies. *Academy of Management Review, 3,* 439–449.

Bettman, J. R. (1979). *An information processing theory of consumer choice.* Reading, MA: Addison-Wesley.

Bettman, J. R., Johnson, E. J., Luce, M. F., & Payne, J. W. (1993). Correlation, conflict, and choice. *Journal of Experimental Psychology: Learning, Memory, and Cognition, 19,* 931–951.

Bettman, J. R., Johnson, E. J., & Payne, J. W. (1990). A componential analysis of cognitive effort in choice. *Organizational Behavior and Human Decision Processes, 45,* 111–139.

Bettman, J. R., & Kakkar, P. (1977). Effects of information presentation format on consumer information acquisition strategies. *Journal of Consumer Research, 3,* 233–240.

Bettman, J. R., Luce, M. F., & Payne, J. W. (1998). Constructive consumer choice processes. *Journal of Consumer Research, 25,* 187–217.

Bradlow, E. T., Hu, Y., & Ho, T-H. (2004). A learning-based model for imputing missing levels in partial conjoint profiles. *Journal of Marketing Research, 41,* 369–381.

Briley, D. A., Morris, M. W., & Simonson, I. (2000). Reasons as carriers of culture: Dynamic versus dispositional models of cultural influence on decision making. *Journal of Consumer Research, 27,* 157–178.

Broniarczyk, S. M., & Alba, J. W. (1994). The role of consumers' intuitions in inference making. *Journal of Consumer Research, 21,* 393–407.

Chernev, A. (2005). Context effects without a context: Attribute balance as a reason for choice. *Journal of Consumer Research, 32,* 213–223.

Coupey, E. (1994). Restructuring: Constructive processing of information displays in consumer choice. *Journal of Consumer Research, 21,* 83–99.

Creyer, E. H., Bettman, J. R., & Payne, J. W. (1990). The impact of accuracy and effort feedback and goals on adaptive decision behavior. *Journal of Behavioral Decision Making, 3,* 1–16.

Dhar, R., & Nowlis, S. M. (1999). The effect of time pressure on consumer choice deferral. *Journal of Consumer Research, 25,* 369–384.

Dhar, R., & Simonson, I. (2003). The effect of forced choice on choice. *Journal of Marketing Research, 40,* 146–160.

Dick, A., Chakravarti, D., & Biehal, G. (1990). Memory-based inferences during consumer choice. *Journal of Consumer Research, 17,* 82–93.

Dijksterhuis, A. (2004). Think different: The merits of unconscious thought in preference development and decision making. *Journal of Personality and Social Psychology, 87,* 586–598.

Drolet, A. (2002). Inherent rule variability in consumer choice: Changing rules for change's sake. *Journal of Consumer Research, 29,* 293–305.

Drolet, A., & Luce, M. F. (2004). The rationalizing effects of cognitive load on emotion-based trade-off avoidance. *Journal of Consumer Research, 31,* 63–77.

Eisenhardt, K. M. (1989). Making fast strategic decisions in high-velocity environments. *Academy of Management Journal, 32,* 543–576.

Feldman, J. M., & Lynch, J. G. (1988). Self-generated validity and other effects of measurement on belief, attitude, intentions, and behavior. *Journal of Applied Psychology, 73,* 421–435.

Finger, K. (2002). Mazes and music: Using perceptual processing to release verbal overshadowing. *Applied Cognitive Psychology, 16,* 887–896.

Flynn, J., Slovic, P., & Kunreuther, H. (2001). *Risk, media and stigma*. London: Earthscan.

Folkman, S., & Lazarus, R. S. (1988). Coping as a mediator of emotion. *Journal of Personality and Social Psychology, 54*, 466–475.

Ford, G. T., & Smith, R. A. (1987). Inferential beliefs in consumer evaluations: An assessment of alternative processing strategies. *Journal of Consumer Research, 14*, 363–371.

Fredrickson, B. L. (2001). The role of positive emotions in positive psychology: The broaden-and-build theory of positive emotions. *American Psychologist, 56*, 218–226.

Fredrickson, B. L., & Branigan, C. (2005). Positive emotions broaden the scope of attention and thought-action repertoires. *Cognition and Emotion, 19*, 313–332.

Frisch, D., & Clemen, R. T. (1994). Beyond expected utility: Rethinking behavioral decision research. *Psychological Bulletin, 116*, 46–54.

Gladwell, M. (2005). *Blink: The power of thinking without thinking*. New York: Little, Brown and Company.

Gregan-Paxton, J., & John, D. R. (1997). The emergence of adaptive decision making in children. *Journal of Consumer Research, 24*, 43–56.

Hamilton, R. W. (2003). Why do people suggest what they do not want? Using context effects to influence others' choices. *Journal of Consumer Research, 29*, 492–506.

Heath, T. B., & Chatterjee, S. (1995). Asymmetric decoy effects on lower-quality versus higher-quality brands: Meta-analytic and experimental evidence. *Journal of Consumer Research, 22*, 268–284.

Hogarth, R. M. (1987). *Judgement and choice* (2nd ed.). New York: Wiley.

Hogarth, R. M. (2001). *Educating intuition*. Chicago: University of Chicago Press.

Hsee, C. K., & Kunreuther, H. (2000). The affection effect in insurance decisions. *Journal of Risk and Uncertainty, 20*, 141–159.

Huber, J., & McCann, J. M. (1982). The impact of inferential beliefs on product evaluations. *Journal of Marketing Research, 19*, 324–333.

Huber, J., Payne, J. W., & Puto, C. P. (1982). Adding asymmetrically dominated alternatives: Violations of regularity and the similarity hypothesis. *Journal of Consumer Research, 9*, 90–98.

Huber, J., & Puto, C. P. (1983). Market boundaries and product choice: Illustrating attraction and substitution effects. *Journal of Consumer Research, 10*, 31–44.

Huber, O., Wider, R., & Huber, O. W. (1997). Active information search and complete information presentation in naturalistic risky decision tasks. *Acta Psychologica, 95*, 15–29.

Iyengar, S. S., & Lepper, M. R. (2000). When choice is demotivating: Can one desire too much of a good thing? *Journal of Personality and Social Psychology, 79*, 995–1006.

Jacoby, J., Speller, D. E., & Kohn, C. A. (1974a). Brand choice behavior as a function of information load. *Journal of Marketing Research, 11*, 63–69.

Jacoby, J., Speller, D. E., & Kohn, C. A. (1974b). Brand choice behavior as a function of information load: Replication and extension. *Journal of Consumer Research, 1*, 33–42.

Jarvenpaa, S. L. (1989). The effect of task demands and graphical format on information processing strategies. *Management Science, 35*, 285–303.

Johnson, E. J., & Meyer, R. J. (1984). Compensatory choice models of noncompensatory choice processes: The effect of varying context. *Journal of Consumer Research, 11*, 528–541.

Johnson, E. J., & Payne, J. W. (1985). Effort and accuracy in choice. *Management Science, 31*, 394–414.

Johnson, R. D., & Levin, I. P. (1985). More than meets the eye: The effect of missing information on purchase evaluations. *Journal of Consumer Research, 12*, 169–177.

Kahn, B. E., & Luce, M.F. (2003). Understanding high-stakes consumer decisions: The Problem of mammography adherence following false alarm test results. *Marketing Science, 22*, 393–410.

Kahn, B. E., & Luce, M.F. (2006). Repeated-adherence protection model (RAP): I'm ok and it's a hassle. *Journal of Public Policy and Marketing, 25*, 79–89.

Kahneman, D. (2003). A perspective on judgment and choice: Mapping bounded rationality. *American Psychologist, 58*, 697–720.

Kahneman, D., & Tversky, T. (1979). Prospect theory: An analysis of decision under risk. *Econometrica, 47*, 263–292.

Kardes, F. R. (2006). When should consumers and managers trust their intuition? *Journal of Consumer Psychology, 16*, 20–24.

Kardes, F. R., & Kalyanaram, G. (1992). Order-of-entry effects on consumer memory and judgment: An information integration perspective. *Journal of Marketing Research, 29*, 343–357.

Kardes, F. R., Kalyanaram, G., Chandrashekaran, M., & Dornoff, R. J. (1993). Brand retrieval, consideration set composition, consumer choice, and the pioneering advantage. *Journal of Consumer Research, 20,* 62–75.

Kardes, F. R., Posavac, S. S., & Cronley, M. L. (2004). Consumer inference: A review of processes, bases, and judgment contexts. *Journal of Consumer Psychology, 14,* 230–256.

Kasperson, R., Jhaveri, N., & Kasperson, J. (2001). Stigma and the social amplification of risk: Toward a framework of analysis. In J. Flynn, P. Slovic & H. Kunreuther (Eds.), *Risk, Media and Stigma* (pp. 9–30). London: Earthscan.

Keller, K. L., & Staelin, R. (1987). Effects of quality and quantity of information on decision effectiveness. *Journal of Consumer Research, 14,* 200–213.

Kivetz, R., Netzer, O., & Srinivasan, V. (2004). Alternative models for capturing the compromise effect. *Journal of Marketing Research, 41,* 237–257.

Kivetz, R., & Simonson, I. (2000). The effects of incomplete information on consumer choice. *Journal of Marketing Research, 37,* 427–448.

Kivetz, R., & Simonson, I. (2002). Earning the right to indulge: Effort as a determinant of customer preferences toward frequency reward programs. *Journal of Marketing Research, 39,* 155–170.

Klein, G. A. (1998). *Sources of power: How people make decisions.* Cambridge, MA: MIT Press.

Kunreuther, H. (2002). Risk analysis and risk management in an uncertain world. *Risk Analysis, 22,* 655–664.

Kunreuther, H., Novemsky, N., & Kahneman, D. (2001). Making low probabilities useful. *Journal of Risk and Uncertainty, 23,* 103–120.

Larsen, J. T., McGraw, P. A., & Cacioppo, J. T. (2001). Can people feel happy and sad at the same time? *Journal of Personality and Social Psychology, 81,* 684–696.

Lazarus, R. S. (1991). Progress on a cognitive-motivational-relational theory of emotion. *American Psychologist, 46,* 819–834.

Luce, M. F. (1998). Choosing to avoid: Coping with negatively emotion-laden consumer decisions. *Journal of Consumer Research, 24,* 409–433.

Luce, M. F., Bettman, J. R., & Payne, J. W. (1997). Choice processing in emotionally difficult decisions. *Journal of Experimental Psychology: Learning, Memory, and Cognition, 23,* 384–405.

Luce, M. F., Bettman, J. R., & Payne, J. W. (2001). Emotional decisions: Tradeoff difficulty and coping in consumer choice. *Monographs of the Journal of Consumer Research, 1.* Chicago: University of Chicago Press.

Luce, M. F., & Kahn, B.E. (1999). Avoidance or vigilance? The psychology of false positive test result. *Journal of Consumer Research, 26,* 242–259.

Luce, M. F., Payne, J. W., & Bettman, J. R. (1999). Emotional trade-off difficulty and choice. *Journal of Marketing Research, 36,* 143–159.

Luce, M. F., Payne, J. W., & Bettman, J. R. (2000). Coping with unfavorable attribute values in choice. *Organizational Behavior and Human Decision Processes, 81,* 274–299.

Lurie, N. H. (2004). Decision making in information-rich environments: The role of information structure. *Journal of Consumer Research, 30,* 473–486.

March, J. G. (1978). Bounded rationality, ambiguity, and the engineering of choice. *Bell Journal of Economics, 9,* 587–608.

May, C. P., Hasher, L., & Foong, N. (2005). Implicit memory, age, and time of day: Paradoxical priming effects. *Psychological Science, 16,* 96–100.

McMackin, J., & Slovic, P. (2000). When does explicit justification impair decision making? *Applied Cognitive Psychology, 14,* 527–541.

Mellers, B., Schwartz, A., & Ritov, I. (1999). Emotion-based choice. *Journal of Experimental Psychology: General, 128,* 332–345.

Meyer, R. J. (1981). A model of multiattribute judgments under attribute uncertainty and information constraint. *Journal of Marketing Research, 18,* 428–441.

Meyer, R. J., & Johnson, E. J. (1989). Information overload and the nonrobustness of linear models: A comment on Keller and Staelin. *Journal of Consumer Research, 15,* 498–503.

Olshavsky, R. W. (1979). Task complexity and contingent processing in decision making: A replication and extension. *Organizational Behavior and Human Performance, 24,* 300–316.

Payne, J. W. (1976). Task complexity and contingent processing in decision making: An information search and protocol analysis. *Organizational Behavior and Human Performance, 16*, 366–387.

Payne, J. W., Bettman, J. R., & Johnson, E. J. (1988). Adaptive strategy selection in decision making. *Journal of Experimental Psychology: Learning, Memory, and Cognition, 14*, 534–552.

Payne, J. W., Bettman, J. R., & Johnson, E. J. (1993). *The adaptive decision maker.* Cambridge: Cambridge University Press.

Payne, J. W., Bettman, J. R., & Luce, M. F. (1996). When time is money: Decision behavior under opportunity-cost time pressure. *Organizational Behavior and Human Decision Processes, 66*, 131–152.

Pieters, R., Warlop, L., & Hartog, M. (1997). The effect of time pressure and task motivation on visual attention to brands. In M. Brucks & D. J. MacInnis (Eds.), *Advances in consumer research, Volume 24* (pp. 281–287). Provo, UT: Association for Consumer Research.

Posavac, S. S., Sanbonmatsu, D. M., Kardes, F. R., & Fitzsimons, G. J. (2004). The brand positivity effect: When evaluation confers preference. *Journal of Consumer Research, 31*, 643–651.

Priester, J. R., Dholakia, U., & Fleming, M. A. (2004). When and why the background contrast effect emerges: Thought engenders meaning by influencing the perception of applicability. *Journal of Consumer Research, 31*, 491–501.

Ross, W. T., & Creyer, E. H. (1992). Making inferences about missing information: The effects of existing information. *Journal of Consumer Research, 19*, 14–25.

Rottenstreich, Y., & Hsee, C.K. (2001). Money, kisses, and elextric shocks: On the affective psychology of risk. *Psychological Science, 12*, 185–190.

Russo, J. E. (1974). More information is better: A re-evaluation of Jacoby, Speller, and Kohn. *Journal of Consumer Research, 1*, 68–72.

Russo, J. E. (1977). The value of unit price information. *Journal of Marketing Research, 14*, 193–201.

Schwartz, B. (2000). Self-determination: The tyranny of freedom. *American Psychologist, 55*, 79–88.

Schwartz, B. (2004). *The paradox of choice: Why more is less.* New York: Ecco.

Schwartz, B., Ward, A., Monterosso, J., Lyubomirsky, S., White, K., & Lehman, D. R. (2002). Maximizing versus satisficing: Happiness is a matter of choice. *Journal of Personality and Social Psychology, 83*, 1178–1197.

Sethuraman, R., Cole, C., & Jain, D. (1994). Analyzing the effect of information format and task on cut-off search strategies. *Journal of Consumer Psychology, 3*, 103–136.

Shafir, E., Simonson, I., & Tversky, A. (1993). Reason-based choice. *Cognition, 49*, 11–36.

Shafir, S., Waite, T. A., & Smith, B. H. (2002). Context-dependent violations of rational choice in honeybees (*Apis millifera*) and gray jays (*Perisoreus Canadensis*). *Behavioral Ecology and Sociobiology, 51*, 180–187.

Shugan, S. M. (1980). The cost of thinking. *Journal of Consumer Research, 7*, 99–111.

Simmons, C. J., & Lynch, J. G. (1991). Inference effects without inference making? Effects of missing information on discounting and use of presented information. *Journal of Consumer Research, 17*, 477–491.

Simon, H. A. (1955). A behavioral model of rational choice. *Quarterly Journal of Economics, 69*, 99–118.

Simonson, I. (1989). Choice based on reasons: The case of attraction and compromise effects. *Journal of Consumer Research, 16*, 158–174.

Simonson, I., & Nowlis, S. M. (2000). The role of explanations and need for uniqueness in consumer decision making: Unconventional choices based on reasons. *Journal of Consumer Research, 27*, 49–68.

Simonson, I., & Tversky, A. (1992). Choice in context: Tradeoff contrast and extremeness aversion. *Journal of Marketing Research, 29*, 281–295.

Slovic, P. (1972). From Shakespeare to Simon: Speculation – and some evidence – about man's ability to process information. *Oregon Research Institute Bulletin, 12* (3).

Slovic, P. (1995). The construction of preference. *American Psychologist, 50*, 364–371.

Slovic, P., Finucane, M., Peters, E., & MacGregor, D.G. (2002). The affect heuristic. In T. Gilovich, D.Griffin, & D. Kahneman (Eds.), *Heuristics and biases: The psychology of intuitive judgment* (pp. 397–420). New York: Cambridge University Press.

Stanovich, K. E. (1999). *Who is rational? Studies of individual differences in reasoning.* Mahwah, NJ: Erlbaum.

Stanovich, K.E. (2004). *The robot's rebellion: Finding meaning in the age of Darwin.* Chicago: The University of Chicago Press.

Stanovich, K. E., & West, R. F. (1998). Individual differences in rational thought. *Journal of Experimental Psychology: General, 127,* 161–188.

Tetlock, P. E. (2002). Social functionalist frameworks for judgment and choice: Intuitive politicians, theologians, and prosecutors. *Psychological Review, 109,* 451–471.

Tversky, A., & Shafir, E. (1992). Choice under conflict: The dynamics of deferred decisions. *Psychological Science, 6,* 358–361.

Tversky, A., & Simonson, I. (1993). Context-dependent preferences. *Management Science, 39,* 1179–1189.

Wakker, P. P., Thaler, R. H., & Tversky, A. (1997). Probabilistic insurance. *Journal of Risk and Uncertainty, 15,* 7–28.

Wang, J., & Wyer, R. S. (2002). Comparative judgment processes: The effects of task objectives and time delay on product evaluations. *Journal of Consumer Psychology, 12,* 327–340.

Wedell, D. H. (1991). Distinguishing among models of contextually induced preferences. *Journal of Experimental Psychology: Learning, Memory, and Cognition, 17,* 767–778.

Wedell, D. H., & Pettibone, J. C. (1996). Using judgments to understand decoy effects in choice. *Organizational Behavior and Human Decision Processes, 67,* 326–344.

Widing, R. E., & Talarzyk, W. W. (1993). Electronic information systems for consumers: An evaluation of computer-assisted formats in multiple decision environments. *Journal of Marketing Research, 30,* 125–141.

Wilkie, W. L. (1974). Analysis of effects of information load. *Journal of Marketing Research, 11,* 462–466.

Williams, P., & Aaker, J. L. (2002). Can mixed emotions peacefully coexist? *Journal of Consumer Research, 28, 636–649.*

Wilson, T. D., & Schooler, J. W. (1991). Thinking too much: Introspection can reduce the quality of preferences and decisions. *Journal of Personality and Social Psychology, 60,* 181–192.

24

Dynamics of Goal-Based Choice
Toward an Understanding on How Goals Commit Versus Liberate Choice

Ayelet Fishbach

University of Chicago

Ravi Dhar

Yale University

INTRODUCTION

A major theme of research in psychology has been to identify the factors that influence consumer choice, and it has long been recognized that the pursuit of choice is driven by the consideration of various underlying goals (e.g., Aarts & Dijksterhuis, 2000; Carver & Scheier, 1998; Higgins, 1997; Kruglanski et al., 2002; Locke & Latham, 1990; Moskowitz, 2002). For example, consumers may wish to purchase a product that is reliable as well as inexpensive, to consume food that is tasty as well as healthy, and to attend a course that is interesting as well as useful; all of these are example of goals that might underlie the decision process (for review, see Baumgartner & Pieters, chapter 13, this volume). In contrast, much of behavioral decision research has looked at choice among a set of alternatives, regardless of underlying consumer motivation. A major finding from behavioral decision theory is that stated preferences are not stable but change with contextual factors that highlight different considerations and lead to potentially different preference assessments (see Bettman, Luce, & Payne, chapter 23, this volume, 1998; Payne, Bettman, & Johnson, 1992; Slovic, 1995). In traditional behavioral decision research, the focus is on the provided choice options and underlying goals are assumed but the manner in which they might influence choice is relatively ignored.

In addition, whereas a large proportion of behavioral decision research has focused on isolated choices, and the majority of goal research has focused on the pursuit of a single goal, people often make several potentially related choices and hold multiple goals at any given time. Thus, consumer research would benefit new insights by taking into account the pursuit of multiple goals and the opportunity to make a series of choices over time.

This chapter takes a goal-theoretic perspective to understand consumer choice and its underlying processes. It proposes a framework for understanding the interplay between multiple consumer goals that influence sequence of choices among available options. In what follows, we review prior research on the processes by which (a) a single goal influences a single choice and (b) multiple goals influence a single choice, and the consequences of these processes. This review leads to highlighting the limitation of prior goal and decision research with few notable exceptions. For example, unlike most goal research, individuals rarely pursue a single goal at a time and thus, an account of consumers' choices should take into consideration the pursuit of multiple and often inconsistent goals. Similarly, a limitation of research on decision making is that unlike many experimental studies, people rarely make their choices in isolation. It is thus necessary to address the influence of prior choices on subsequent ones. In order to address the effect of goals on choices, we describe our own theoretical framework on *dynamics of self-regulation*. We specifically address the patterns of these dynamics, the pre-conditions for each of these dynamics to take place, and the implications for choice.

SINGLE GOAL, SINGLE CHOICE

The process of self-regulation involves setting a goal, which then motivates actions toward the attainment of this desirable end-state and away from an existing, undesirable state (Carver & Scheier, 1998; Gollwitzer, 1999; Higgins, 1989). The main insights from a growing body of goal research are that goal representations can become momentarily accessible, and the activation of a specific goal construct would result in a more favorable evaluation of goal-related alternatives, which are further more likely to be selected and pursued.

The processes of goal setting are often conscious and involve explicit deliberation and planning (e.g., study for an "A," plan one's wedding). These goals in turn account for a large proportion of everyday choices that are meant to accomplish one's explicit goals, and which are often referred to as "goal striving" (e.g., selecting a textbook and a caterer for the academic and wedding goals, respectively). Explicit goals often take the form of specific performance standards that motivate congruent choice of actions until the standard is met (Bagozzi & Dholakia, 1999; Emmons, 1992; Heath, Larrick, & Wu, 1999; Kanfer, Ackerman, Murtha, Dugdale, et al., 1994; Locke & Latham, 2002). For example, previous research indicates that as a result of setting specific performance goals, loggers cut more trees (Latham & Locke, 1975), typists typed more pages per unit of time (Latham & Yukl, 1976), and students adhered to their academic tasks during the winter break (Gollwitzer & Brandstaetter, 1997).

On other occasions, goals may also operate implicitly. In their implicit form, goal representations become temporary accessible by the presence of contextual cues and are pursued without conscious awareness of the goal, deliberation on it, and a specific attainment plan. These goals elicit congruent choice, although a person is unaware of the motivation to make that particular choice or its relations to a mentally activated goal (Aarts & Dijksterhuis, 2000; Bargh, Gollwitzer, Lee-Chai, Barndollar, & Troetschel, 2001; Mandel & Johnson, 2002; Moskowitz, Gollwitzer, Wasel, & Schaal, 1999; Shah & Kruglanski, 2003). For instance, in a study that tested for implicit goal pursuit, a goal of cooperation was primed in a word puzzle that was administered at the beginning of the study and either had words related to cooperation (e.g., "fair" and "share") or not. Research participants who were primed with cooperation were subsequently more likely to choose a cooperative strategy in a commons-dilemma game than those in the no-prime condition, although they were unaware of their underlying goal (Bargh et al., 2001). This research suggests that social motives can be elicited by subtle, contextual cues, and they then influence players' strategy choice.

Recent research in marketing further demonstrates the effect of implicit goals on consumer choices. For example, Mandel and Johnson (2002) set an unconscious purchase goal by manipulating the background pattern of internet shopping websites, which were set to prime goal related to thrift versus quality. In one study, a goal of thrift was primed using a green background with dollar signs and a goal of safety was primed using a red flame-like background. Research participants who were primed with a thrift goal were subsequently more likely to choose an inexpensive but less safe car, whereas those who were primed with safety goal preferred a more expensive but safer car. Other researchers documented similar effects on consumer choice using other techniques of unobtrusive goal priming, such as background music. It was shown that French wine outsells German wine when French music is played in the background, whereas German wine outsells French wine when German music is played (North, Hargreaves, & McKendrick, 1997). Presumably, participants in these studies did not make explicit connections between the music and their choice.

Social interactions are another source of goal priming effects whenever individuals automatically adopt and adhere to another person's goals (Aarts, Gollwitzer, & Hassin, 2004; Chartrand & Bargh, 1999), or when they follow goals that another person holds for them (Fitzsimons & Bargh, 2003; Shah, 2003). For example, a person's decision to study can be influenced by the presence of an attentive student or by the presence of a parent, who would like that person to study. This pattern was recently illustrated in a study that subliminally primed concepts related to parenting (e.g., "father," "dad") and found a subsequent increased motivation to work on academic tasks that are associated with a goal parents hold for their children (Shah, 2003). This and similar studies documented a human tendency to choose actions that resemble others' actions or what others' would have liked to choose for a person.

The mechanism by which contextual goal-related cues such as semantic words, sensory (color or music) feedback and social interactions influence choice, involves changes in goal accessibility that lead to goal pursuit. It was often shown that whatever increases the temporary accessibility of goal constructs would subsequently increase the likelihood of making congruent choices that pursue these goals. More recent research further suggests that changes in goal accessibility leads to changes in the temporary valence of goal-related options relative to options that are unrelated to the goal or that directly interfere with it, and these changes in valence determine choice. What motivates people to pursue an accessible goal is therefore the positive evaluation of related options. We next describe the mechanism by which accessible goals affect evaluation and choice.

Goal-Based Evaluation

The notion that activated goals influence the value of related alternatives was originally presented in Kurt Lewin's (1935) seminal writing on self-regulation. According to Lewin, goals change the affective experience of choice alternatives that are related to their attainment. These early insights were supported by modern goal research, which shows that the manner in which people come to experience choice alternatives depends on their underlying goals (Brendl & Higgins, 1996; Ferguson & Bargh, 2004; Fishbach, Shah, & Kruglanski, 2004; Fiske, 1992). For example, a goal-based evaluation of a caffeinated beverage leads the person who wishes to stay awake to express a more favorable evaluation of the beverage (i.e., that person would associate it with positive concepts). However, another person who desires to sleep may express a negative evaluation of the beverage (i.e., that person would associate it with negative concepts).

The effect of goals on the evaluation and the affective experience of choice alternatives is explained in terms of the transfer of properties from goal attainment to the means of attainment. The cognitive organization of goals connects them to lower-level means of attainment in associative networks (Anderson, 1983; Anderson et al., 2004; Higgins, 1989). Along these networks, qualities such as activation and affective experience transfer from the higher-order goal to lower-order attainment means through spreading activation. Specifically, through a *transfer mechanism*, the quality and magnitude of positive feelings toward goal attainment become associated with goal-related means as a function of their association strength with the goal (Fishbach et al., 2004). As a result, the experience of choice alternatives or attributes (e.g., as relaxing or exciting) is influenced by the experience of accomplishing the underlying goal.

Importantly, a transfer mechanism does not require conscious awareness of the underlying goals that govern one's emotional response, and therefore, people are often unaware of the source of their positive and negative appraisals when making decisions. Moreover, people may not even be aware of the mere elicitation of appraisals when making decisions, although these evaluations influence the content of their decisions. Such implicit evaluations were demonstrated in studies that employed an evaluative priming procedure (cf., Fazio, Jackson, Dunton, & Williams, 1995) and they find an automatic positive evaluation of means to goal attainment. For example, thirsty individuals automatically associate objects related to drinking with positive evaluations, hence, among thirsty research participants concepts such as "water" or "juice" facilitated the categorization of positive attributes (e.g., "flower") and inhibited the categorization of negative attributes (e.g., "spider"). These implicit evaluations occur outside of conscious awareness as participants were not aware of the source and the content of their evaluations (Aarts, Dijksterhuis, & De Vries, 2001; Ferguson & Bargh, 2004).

There is also evidence for the transfer of negative affect, which is associated with goal failure, toward choice alternatives that hinder goal attainment. For example, dieters who were actively striving to lose weight expressed an implicit negative evaluation of concepts related to high-calorie foods (e.g., "cake" or "chocolate") that were presented in an evaluative priming task (Fishbach, Zhang, & Trope, 2007). Other studies find evidence for the implicit negative evaluation of objects that are neutral with respect to goal attainment, and hence distract one from the course of self-regulation toward a focal goal (Brendl, Markman, & Messner, 2003). For example, Brendl et al find a negative evaluation of nonfood consumer products around lunch time, when consumers are hungry and are pursuing an eating goal.

In sum, whereas the majority of choice research focuses on shifting preferences based on aspects of the task that are highlighted (e.g., Dhar & Sherman, 1996; Dhar & Simonson, 1992; Simonson & Tversky, 1992), goal research attests that evaluation and choice change based on changes in a person's underlying motivation. People's underlying motivations are, in turn, dynamic and subject to explicit processes of goal setting as well as implicit processes of goal activation and increased accessibility. In their implicit form, the accessibility of goals is often determined by contextual cues and these goals, in turn, influence the immediate evaluation and choice among alternatives that are goal-related to a various degree.

MULTIPLE GOALS, SINGLE CHOICE

The previous discussion concerns situations in which consumers hold a single, accessible goal that they wish to pursue through congruent choices. However, people are often motivated by the simultaneous consideration of several underlying goals that have implications for choice. For example, people wish to have food that is tasty, healthy, and inexpensive, or buy a car that is safe, trendy, and fuel efficient (Cantor & Langston, 1989; Emmons & King, 1988; Higgins, 1997; Markus & Ruvolo, 1989). On other occasions, people's explicit consideration refers to a single goal (e.g., getting a safe car) but other background goals (e.g., getting a trendy car) exert their influence outside of conscious awareness, and they lead to congruent choices. Choice research should therefore address the simultaneous influence of multiple goals.[1] Based on previous goal research, we have identified two principles that govern the effect of multiple goals on choice: *goal competition* and *multiple goal attainment*. In what follows, we address these principles and explain their implications for the content of choice and choice satisfaction.

Goal Competition

According to the principle of *goal competition,* simultaneously activated goals compete for limited motivational resources, which lead them to pull away resources from each other. In particular, goals compete for attention, commitment and effort (e.g., Anderson et al., 2004; Forster, Liberman, & Higgins, 2005; Shah, Friedman, & Kruglanski, 2002). Several predictions follow from the principle of goal competition, and they were demonstrated in recent goal research.

First, goal research shows that the activation of one goal leads to temporary inhibition of background goals that are unrelated to it and may compete with it on motivational resources. For example, the pursuit of academic objectives competes and therefore, inhibits the goal of keeping in shape. The mechanism of inter-goal inhibition was demonstrated in studies that tested for the accessibility of concepts related to a background goal after subliminally priming concepts related to a focal goal (Shah et al., 2002). These studies find, for example, that a subliminal presentation of a concept related to an academic goal (e.g., "study") leads to inhibition, as indicated by slower response time, of concepts related to a fitness goal (e.g., "jogging"). The degree of inhibition of alternatives in these studies was associated with maintaining the level of motivational strength to a focal goal and hence it was a functional mechanism of self-regulation.

Second, whereas in the course of self-regulation a focal goal inhibits the activation level of competing background goals, after a focal goal is accomplished it is inhibited. The inhibition of completed goals should then free the way for alternative goals to be selected and pursued (Forster et al., 2005). The mechanism of post-fulfillment inhibition was evident in studies that measured for the response time for recognizing concepts related to unaccomplished and accomplished goals, and they documented slower response times (above baseline) for recognizing concepts related to accomplished goals. For example, in the course of searching for an object (e.g., a pair of glasses) its accessibility increases; however, after the object is found, its accessibility drops down below baseline. Post-fulfillment inhibition as a self-regulatory mechanism reflects the principle of goal competition, as by inhibiting completed goals one eliminates the competition with completed goals and upcoming ones. For example, if the search for one's glasses is not inhibited when the glasses are found, it would interfere with the subsequent goal that required wearing eyeglasses.

This latter possibility was demonstrated in other studies that provide a third type of evidence for the principle of goal competition. These studies attest that an increase in the accessibility of background goals leads to a decrease in the performance on a focal goal (Shah & Kruglanski, 2002). Specifically, studies that presented contextual cues for some background goals (i.e., via subliminal priming of goal-related concepts) found that these cues pulled away motivational resources from a focal goal and, as a result, primed participants demonstrated poorer performance on the focal goal. Taken together, there is converging evidence from different lines of research for the principle of goal competition, which manifests itself through inhibition of background goals by a focal goal, inhibition of accomplished goals, and pulling of resources from a focal goal by background goals.

The principle of goal competition has important implications for consumer choice of actions that serve to accomplish multiple, distinctive goals. When people wish to bring together several goals into a single choice, normative choice theory (e.g., the multiattribute utility theory, MAUT) entails that they should integrate these different goals (or attributes) according to their predetermined importance weights. It is also assumed that the weight of a goal for the individual should be independent of the decision context (e.g., Baron, 2000; Keeney & Raiffa, 1976). However, research reviewed here attests that the relative weight of goals is dynamic and changes as a function of their status as focal or background goals, which is often the result of contextual variables. It follows that multiple goals are not usually integrated according to their predetermined weight. Rather, the goals that are brought into the decision process tend to inhibit each other and directly interfere with each other's attainment. The result of goal competition is that in any given choice situation, an individual may tend to overemphasize a subset of accessible goals, while overlooking some other, background goals that are temporarily inhibited. For example, when the context primes thrift, consumers may tend to overlook safety considerations, whereas when the context primes safety considerations, consumers may overlook price.

Moreover, since people are often unaware of the relative accessibility of certain goals, the change in the status of goals from focal and hence, inhibiting, to background and hence, inhibited, often goes unnoticed. The result is that consumers find it difficult to justify preference instability, mainly because they are unaware of the dynamic nature of their goals, and in particular, they are unaware of the goals that were accessible when they made their initial choice but are less accessible when they evaluate their choice at a later time. The changing status of goals that exert their influence outside of conscious awareness would therefore lead to regret and low choice satisfaction when consumers evaluate their past choices.

Multiple Goal Attainment

Another principle of multiple goal pursuit refers to the search for choice alternatives that maximize the attainment of several active goals. Given that resources are limited and the simultaneous activation of several goals, people seek to make choices that promote more than a single, focal goal. The problem of maximizing the attainment from several goals was addressed by normative decision theory such as MAUT. This theory offers a method of making tradeoff among features that map onto different goals (e.g., Baron, 2000; Keeney & Raiffa, 1976). However, as stated earlier, a normative theory does not typically take into account the dynamic nature of goals and their dependence on contextual cues.

Goal researchers addressed the problem of choice from a standpoint of a person who holds a set of preexisting accessible goals. When individuals are concerned with meeting multiple goals, any increase in the number of accessible goals negatively affects the number of satisfactory means, thus elevating the difficulty of the search (Kruglanski et al., 2002; Tversky, 1972). For example, while all jobs carry a paycheck by the end of the month, somewhat fewer are also interesting, fewer still have a reasonable commute, and fewer still please one's social needs. The result is that multiple consideration of different goals leads to greater selection of compromise options (Simonson, 1989), which are less effective at satisfy each goal.

The negative relationship between number of activated goals and number of satisfying choice alternatives has interesting implication for choice satisfaction. Since an increase in the number of goals leads to a decrease in the number of acceptable means, additional goals may further decrease choice satisfaction. Thus, for example, whenever a consumer wishes to consider all the possible goals that a single choice could potentially satisfy, that consumer would end up being less satisfied with his or her decision when compared to a consumer that did not consider a large array of possible goals. In a similar way, when contextual cues increase the number of accessible goals that a person considers, that person's choice satisfaction would most likely decline.

In general, the principles of goal competition and multiple goal attainment have several implications for choice satisfaction, defined as the extent to which choosers express a favorable evaluation of the chosen alternatives as well as the choice process. We have suggested that choice alternatives acquire the positive valence of goal attainment and the negative valence of failure to attain a goal (Brendl et al., 2003; Ferguson & Bargh, 2004; Fishbach et al., 2004). However, in the course of pursuing multiple goals, a means to one goal can potentially interfere with satisfying another goal. Hence, any chosen means can be a source of positive experience that is delivered from the goal it helps to attain and a source of negative affect that is delivered from the goal that it hinders. Consider, for example, the consumption of high-calorie food. This food can be associated with the positive experience of having a nice meal, but also with the negative experience of failing to have a slim figure, and these goals are often co-activated.

It follows that by simultaneously pursuing multiple goals, a person not only elevates the difficulty of the search, but further decreases the positive experience from finding adequate means. These means would then lead to ambivalent (positive and negative) feelings. Since choosers are generally motivated to maximize choice satisfaction (Bettman et al., 1998), the presence of multiple considerations should lead to choice deferral and decision aversion (Dhar, 1996, 1997; Iyengar & Lepper, 2000; Tversky & Shafir, 1992). Our analysis further implies that holding fewer goals increases choice satisfaction and promotes decision-seeking behavior. It implies, for example, that buyers who are mainly concerned with finding inexpensive products (a single goal) would enjoy the experience of going out shopping and be more likely to engage in shopping behavior compared to others, who hold multiple shopping goals, such as sharing equal concern with findings inexpensive and high quality products.

The presence of multiple underlying goals also affects the content of one's choice. Thus, it creates instability of choice of a means toward a focal goal, depending on the simultaneous activation of background goals. Research that tested for this possibility finds that a choice of a means to a focal goal changes systematically with the co-activation of some background goals to which a person is not necessarily consciously aware (Chun, Kruglanski, Sleeth-Keppler, & Friedman, 2006). For example, in a study that tested for a beverage choice, the focal goal of fulfilling one's thirst resulted in two different beverage selections (either Coke or Pepsi cola), depending on whether participants were also pursuing the goal of identifying or not identifying with the United States. Specifically, asking U.S. participants to consider the events of post-September 11, which presumably primes American pride, increased selection of Coke over Pepsi. The reason is that Coke is considered an "American drink." By a similar logic, considering an event which undermines American pride, the cases of anthrax around that time, was shown to increase selection of a "less American" Pepsi drink over Coke.

To summarize, research reviewed here identifies some principles that govern the effect of multiple goals on choice. First, the presence of simultaneous goals creates goal competition, which leads to inhibition of completing goals. Second, in response to multiple accessible goals, individuals seek choice options that satisfy more than a single, focal goal. It follows that having more accessible goals is negatively related to choice satisfaction and leads to choice deferral. This body of research, however, has also some limitation. In particular, it is limited to situations that involve a single choice that is made without considering previous or subsequent choices. In order to address this limitation, we have recently developed a novel theoretical framework that addresses the effect of multiple goals on choices that are made in a sequence, and this theory seeks to explain when initial choices commit versus liberate subsequent ones. In the rest of this chapter, we describe our theory, its main research findings and how it relates to previous goal research.

MULTIPLE GOALS, MULTIPLE CHOICES: DYNAMICS OF SELF-REGULATION

The research on goal-based choice provided important insights from exploring the basic effects of a single goal on a single choice. Based on that research, more recent goal research addressed the interplay between several (at least two) goals in predicting a single choice and we addressed this research in the previous section. In what follows, we describe our research program on goal-based choice. This research builds on past goal research while moving forward by exploring how several goals simultaneously influence choices in a sequence. In its most basic form, our research focuses on how two goals influence a sequence of two related choices. However, by exploring these patterns of self-regulation we wish to provide a more general framework that would account for the effect of holding any number of simultaneous goals on making any number of choices that are made in a sequence.

Our theoretical model focuses on two basic patterns of choice sequencing in regulating multiple goals: *highlighting* of a single, primary goal, and *balancing* among different goals of various importance. By *choice-highlighting* we refer to a dynamic of self-regulation that reflects commitment to a single focal goal and motivates multiple complementary choices that pursue the same goal. By *choice-balancing* we refer to a dynamic of self-regulation where pursuing one goal liberates the individual to pursue other, unrelated goals. This pattern of self-regulation balances among several unrelated goals of various importance and leads to seemingly incongruent choices that pursue these unrelated goals.

The basic dynamics of choice sequencing were originally demonstrated by Dhar and Simonson (1999), who studied the tradeoffs between consumption goals such as seeking pleasure (e.g., food consumption) and resource-maintaining goals (e.g., saving money). They found that when a resource goal such as saving money or time is viewed as a means to another overriding goal of seeking pleasure, people are willing spend the resource in order to ensure the attainment of the more important goal. For example, research participants were more likely to select an expensive entrée if they had already ordered an expensive (vs. less expensive) appetizer and hence stood a better chance to accomplish the overall pleasure-seeking goal. Choosing an unattractive second item would undermine that goal, hence it was avoided. The result was consistency or choice-highlighting. When however, the resource was seen as an equally important goal, there were two competing goals present and it was important for participants to attain both. That is where choice-balancing was likely to occur. For example, participants were more likely to select an expensive entrée if they already ordered a less (vs. more) expensive appetizer. Partitioning of the choice in such a way that both goals were partially attained (resource maintenance and pleasure experience) further meant that none of these goals were attained to the same degree of magnitude as might have been the case if there was only one superordinate goal.

Based on these initial demonstrations, our research program seeks to explore the antecedents and consequences of the two dynamics observed in goal-based choice. We propose that when an initial choice signals commitment to a goal, it establishes commitment to other choices that pursue the same underlying goal, which results in choice highlighting. Conversely, when an initial choice signals progress or partial goal attainment, it motivates choices that pursue other goals, which leads to choice balancing. The information from the initial choice, which refers to either goal commitment or progress, is therefore expected to elicit different patterns of self-regulation through subsequent choice when there are multiple goals. For example, with regard to career and social goals, an elevated sense of commitment following a career accomplishment increases the motivation to invest further in one's career, whereas a sense of goal attainment following a similar social accomplishment increases the motivation to move away from the attained goal and pursue social goals. Whether an action is seen as establishing commitment or progress (i.e., partial goal attainment) depends upon several factors and can be internally motivated or externally influenced.

The distinction between the two dynamics of self-regulation has further several implications for the study of goals and choice, and we explore these implications in our research. In addition, these different patterns of self-regulation can account for some inconsistencies in previous research that finds that initial choice leads to similar and dissimilar subsequent choices. In what follows, we first discuss our own research program on dynamics of self-regulation and then elaborate on the implications of this framework for previous findings in research on goals and choice.

DYNAMICS OF SELF-REGULATION: A CONCEPTUAL FRAMEWORK AND DATA

The basic premises of our theory are illustrated in Figure 24.1 (see also, Fishbach & Dhar, 2005; Fishbach, Dhar, & Zhang, 2006; Koo & Fishbach, in press, Zhang, Fishbach, & Dhar, 2007). As demonstrated, once a goal becomes accessible it leads to an initial congruent choice. Based on the initial goal-related choice, a person can then infer either greater goal-commitment or greater goal-progress. *Goal-commitment* refers to the strength of a preference (Atkinson & Raynor, 1978; Feather, 1990; Locke & Latham, 1990), Consistent with research on attitudes in social psychology, a choice that signals commitment is likely to increase the motivation toward similar actions (e.g., Aronson, 1997; Bem, 1972; Festinger, 1957). *Goal-progress* refers to reduction in the discrepancy to goal attainment (Carver & Scheier, 1998; Higgins, 1989; Soman & Shi, 2003) and in line with cybernetic model of self-regulation, moving toward goals provides a sense of partial goal attainment, and signals that less effort is needed to accomplish the goal (Carver & Scheier, 1998; Miller, Galanter, & Pribram, 1960; Powers, 1973).

The relative focus on goal-commitment versus goal-progress has, in turn, opposite implications for the direction of self-regulation through subsequent choice. That is, if a choice signals a generally high-level of commitment to a goal, it leads to a self-regulatory dynamic of choice-highlighting, which increases the motivation toward other goal-related actions and inhibits competing goals. If however, the same choice signals a high level of goal-progress, it leads to a self-regulatory dynamic of choice-balancing, which serves as a justification to move temporarily away from the focal goal that has been progressed or partially attained and choose actions that serve other goals. We further assume that goal progress and commitment are continuous variables and an action towards

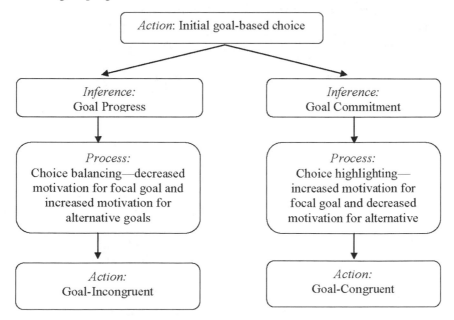

Figure 24.1   Dynamics of self-regulation

a certain goal is seen as increasing the progress along the goal or as increasing the commitment to the goal.

These dynamics of self-regulation characterize the pursuit of several underlying goals that a person wishes to attain simultaneously. In situations that involve multiple goals, a person is required to consider both the progress in moving towards the goal as well as the strength of the goal. If the progress is fast, a person feels that other background goals were relatively neglected, and the pursuit of a focal goal increases the motivation for subsequently pursuing these unrelated goals. Alternatively, if the goal is strong, a person may feel committed to pursue subsequent similar actions, and the pursuit of a focal goal increases the motivation for choosing related actions. What determines the relative focus on progress or commitment is the inference that is made based on goal pursuit (for further discussion of the role of inferences see Kardes, Posavac, Cronley, & Herr, chapter 6, this volume).

There are several self-regulatory phenomena to which these dynamics are applied. First, they explain the effect of expectations about future self-regulation on present choice of actions. Second, they are relevant for understanding the process of self-regulation through subgoals, and third, they can account for the resolution of self-control conflicts between important long-term goals (i.e., virtues) and interfering temptations (i.e., vices). In what follows we first outline our general findings on how goals liberate actions or increase the commitment to consistent actions. We then explore the implications of our theoretical framework for several phenomena in choice sequencing, including choosing present actions based on future expectations, choosing a sequence of several subgoals to an overall goal, and choosing between goal- and temptation-related actions based on previous success at exercising self-control.

Goals as Excuses Versus Guides in Choice Subsequence

We proposed that goals serve as guides when a goal-related choice signals commitment and a behavior toward the goal increases the likelihood of engaging in subsequent congruent action. Conversely, goals serve as "excuses" when a goal-related choice signals progress and a behavior towards one goal increases the likelihood of engaging in incongruent behavior and moving away from the goal.

Goals as Guides. There is some evidence that actions toward a goal motivate the choice of similar actions until the goal is accomplished. This pattern of self-regulation was observed in animal research, which documented an increase in the motivation to exert efforts to achieve a food prize after initial steps had been taken and the total distance to the food was reduced. For example, rats ran faster and pulled more weight the more they had progressed toward a food prize (Hull, 1935). More recently, a similar pattern was observed in marketing contexts and with humans (Kivetz et al., 2005). These researchers find that people work harder on a goal if they believe that progress had been made toward it. For example, Kivetz et al. handed coffee shoppers a coffee card that either required collecting 10 stamps (equal to 10 purchases) in order to earn one free coffee, or required collecting 12 stamps but had 2 pre-existing bonus stamps (also equal to 10 purchases). Although the required effort was identical, the 12-stamp card elicited greater motivation to collect stamps, presumably because it provided a greater sense of (illusionary) past goal accomplishment (2 out of 12 vs. 0 out of 10).

In another demonstration of this principle, an increase in the amount contributed to-date to a fund rising program (i.e., seed money) led to an increase in the rate of subsequent contributions (List & Lucking-Reiley, 2002). In addition, initial success on a goal was shown to increase the eagerness to maintain a high level of goal attainment by choosing risky, high-variance means that have greater potential for goal attainment, although they may potentially jeopardize previous success (Novemsky & Dhar, 2005). These studies also support the notion that when the focus is on a single goal, initial attainment increases commitment to exert more efforts.

Goals as Excuses. Other researchers find evidence for the undermining effect of initial goal pursuit on subsequent choice, in particular when individuals hold multiple goals. Under these conditions, an initial progress justifies subsequent disengagement and choice of actions that serve other, presumably neglected goals (e.g., Fishbach & Dhar, 2005; Monin & Miller, 2001). For example, in one study we found that an initial sense of successful weight loss increased dieters' tendency to indulge (Fishbach & Dhar, 2005). In this study, dieting participants were asked to draw a line that represented the distance between their current and ideal weight on a scale that either had –5 lbs. or –25 lbs. as its maximum discrepancy. Providing a scale with a wide range (–25 lbs.) created an illusion of smaller discrepancy (e.g., 4:% vs. 20%, for a person who would like to lose 1 lb.), which led to greater perceived goal progress. As a result, those who completed a wide (vs. narrow) scale were more likely to choose a chocolate bar over a low-calorie snack on a subsequent, supposedly unrelated, choice task.

In a follow up study that tested for a similar hypothesis we found that a subjective experience of goal progress mediated the liberating effect of initial goal-congruent choice on the subsequent decision to disengage with the goal. Participants in this study were college students who received feedback regarding their relative progress toward meeting their academic objectives. This feedback was delivered by asking them to list the amount of time that they spent on their coursework on a survey form that had been previously filled out, presumably by another participant, and partially erased. In this "partially filled-out" survey a fictitious participant listed either a small or a large amount of time spent studying and participants were asked to ignore that person's answer (e.g., Simonson, Nowlis, & Simonson, 1993). Comparing oneself to a low social standard (e.g., a person that listed a small amount of study time) was shown to increase participants' subjective sense of progress, which subsequently increased their interest in several nonacademic activities (e.g., going out, watching television). Importantly, the subjective reports of perceived goal progress significantly mediated the effect of social comparison standard (high vs. low) on interest in nonacademic activities (Fishbach & Dhar, 2005).

Guides Versus Excuses. The aforementioned research suggests that goals sometimes liberate the pursuit of incongruent actions and on other times they increase the commitment to congruent actions. Importantly, however, studies that find liberating effects concern the pursuit of multiple goals. Whether people choose to highlight a focal goal or balance between several goals may therefore depend on the number of co-activated goals: When a person is mainly concerned with the pursuit of a single objective (e.g., earning a free coffee), an initial amount of progress toward goal attainment increases the motivation for similar actions. However, when a person is concerned with the pursuit of several objectives (e.g., studying and socializing) an initial progress toward one goal signals that other goals have been neglected and increases the motivation for moving away from the focal goal. The number of accessible goals may thus influence the tendency to balance versus highlight, and by reminding people of alternative goals one could reverse the effect of initial pursuit. For example, an increase in the amount of money collected thus far by a charity campaign would increase subsequent donations if people only consider this specific charity cause, but it may decrease subsequent donations if people are also aware of other charity campaigns that have not been progressed to the same extent.

However, our theory suggests that even in the presence of multiple goals, pursuing a focal goal leads to moving away only if a person focuses on the progress from the action rather than on the commitment to the goal. When people infer goal-commitment, they tend to highlight the focal goal by choosing congruent actions and ignore other activated goals. Whether an initial goal-related choice would result in incongruent versus congruent choices would therefore depend on the presence of background goals and, provided that there are background goals, it depends on the framing of an initial action as indicating progress rather than commitment.

We tested for the opposite effects of commitment and progress focus in studies that manipulated the framing of an initial goal-based choice. For example, in one study we asked questions that either led respondents to focus on the commitment-to or progress-from their initial choices and they did it across several self-regulatory domains (i.e., studying for exams, saving money, and avoiding sun damage). In each domain, the relative focus on commitment versus progress had opposite consequences for subsequent choices. For example, with respect to the goal of avoiding sun damage, respondents were asked to reflect on the extent to which applying sunscreen (a goal-related means) makes them feel more committed versus makes them feel healthier. Those who focused on the commitment from their action were subsequently less likely to spend long hours in the sun (a goal-inhibiting means) than those who focused on the progress from their actions. Moreover, participants' ratings of commitment were negatively related to their choices of inhibiting means (e.g., spending time in the sun), such that greater commitment decreased interest in incongruent actions; whereas ratings of progress were positively related to inhibiting means, that is, greater progress increased interest in incongruent actions (Fishbach & Dhar, 2005).

These studies demonstrate the presence of two distinctive patterns of self-regulation in successive choice: highlighting of a focal goal whenever individuals focus on the commitment from their initial choice, and balancing between focal and background goals whenever individuals focus on the progress from their choice. In what follows, we test for the possibility that these patterns may be also activated by holding expectations about future goal pursuit. Future plans may impact present choice of actions whenever they establish a sense of goal commitment, or if they seem to secure the progress on a goal. As a result, holding future expectations affects the level of self-regulation in the present.

Future Expectations Effect on Present Choice

A sense of successful self-regulation can be based on actual past choices of actions congruent with the goal (Carver & Scheier, 1998; Dreze & Nunes, 2005; Kivetz, Urminsky, & Zheng, 2006; Miller et al., 1960). In addition, individuals obtain a sense of successful self-regulation from holding plans to make goal-congruent choices in the future (Bandura, 1997; Nowlis, Mandel, & McCabe, 2004; Oettingen & Mayer, 2002; Taylor & Brown, 1988). For example, whereas our research indicates that exercising and healthy eating are often viewed as two complementary means to the overall goal of leading a healthy lifestyle, it is possible that a choice of healthy food in the present is impacted by a person's planned future workouts or by actual past workouts. In our research, we addressed the question of whether future expectations affect immediate choice as much as past success was shown to influence this choice.

We propose that in choice sequences the order of an initial and subsequent choice should not matter much for highlighting and balancing considerations to take place. Thus, people can choose to pursue (or deter from) a goal in the present, either because they pursued it in the past or because they plan to pursue it in the future. However, for many goals, what distinguishes past from future self-regulation is an optimism bias, as people are unrealistically optimistic in predicting their future choices, believing that their expected goal pursuit will exceed past goal pursuits (Buehler, Griffin, & Ross, 2002; Weinstein, 1989; Zauberman & Lynch, 2005). For example, people tend to underestimate the obstacles that might prevent them from working out as much as they plan, meet their deadlines at work, controlling their food consumption, and more. Since people are generally optimistic, thinking about future choices can have greater influence on immediate choice because people believe that they will do more in the future. For instance, for a person who worked out moderately in the past but anticipates to work out more often in the future, focusing on the future will lead to a greater sense of means-attainment related to the goal, which in turn has a greater impact on the decision to pursue the goal in the present.

Based on our previous findings, we further assumed that the greater impact of future choices relative to similar past choices can result in both more goal-congruent actions as well as more goal disengagement, depending upon the framing of planned choice. When planned choices signal greater commitment, thinking about future success leads to greater persistence on the goal than thinking of actual (less successful) past choices. Conversely, when planned choices signal greater goal-progress, thinking about future success justifies disengagement from the focal goal more than actual past choices.

In support of this analysis, goal research finds evidence for the motivating and undermining effects of holding a plan for future self-regulation. First, studies that tested for self-regulation of a single goal often found that stating future intentions increases the likelihood of making congruent choices in the present (Fitzsimons & Williams, 2000; Sherman, 1980; Williams, Fitzsimons, & Block, 2004). For example, asking people whether they intended to choose a generally favorable brand in the future increased their actual choice of that brand in the present (Morwitz & Fitzsimons, 2004). Second, studies that tested for the self-regulation of multiple activated goals often found that elaborating on future fantasies substitutes for actual action (Oettingen & Mayer, 2002; Oettingen, Pak, & Schnetter, 2001; Taylor, Pham, Rivkin, & Armor, 1998). For example, Khan and Dhar (2006) found a tendency to anticipate choosing virtue options in the future (e.g., choosing a highbrow over a lowbrow magazine), which in turn justified choosing vice options at the present (e.g., a lowbrow over a highbrow magazine). Whereas the inconsistency in previous findings is predicted by our model and can be attributed to the consideration of a single goal that leads to highlighting, compared with multiple goals that promote balancing, our research program further identifies the conditions under which future plans lead to highlighting versus balancing in the present, in a multple goal environment. In addition, our model predicts that thinking of future plans would have greater impact on present choice than thinking of past actions, if a person did not experience successful self-regulation in the past but expects to succeed in the future.

Several studies confirmed our hypothesis that plans for successful self-regulation exert greater impact on present choice than thinking about past attempts and that the direction of the impact depends on the framing of future expectations. For example, in one study we asked gym members to evaluate the frequency of their workout last year or during the upcoming year. They then rated their agreements with statements that framed workout as either progress to a goal (e.g., "having worked out that much, I am closer to my workout objectives" or "planning to workout that much, I will be closer to my workout objectives") or commitment to a goal (e.g., "having worked out that much (vs. planning to workout that much), I am committed to my workout objectives"). The dependent measure referred to respondents' choice of a beverage that was given to them as a parting gift and which was either congruent with the overall goal of keeping-in-shape (spring water) or incongruent with it (sugar-containing soda). We found that gym members were indeed optimistic, such that on average they reported working out in the future more frequently than in the past. More importantly, under commitment frame, those who considered future workout were more likely to choose water (over sugary soda) than those who considered past workout. Under progress frame, those who considered in extensive future workout were less likely to choose water (over sugary soda) than those who considered the minimal past workout. Altogether, the framing of goal pursuits had greater impact on present choice when people consider future actions compared with past pursuits (Zhang, Fishbach, & Dhar, 2007).

We attributed the greater impact of considering future plans to people's optimistic expectations of successfully pursuing a goal in the future and therefore, the future seems more relevant for present choice. It follows that a debiasing intervention that decreases optimistic expectations should attenuate the effect of planned future pursuits on present choice. We tested for this possibility in another study that reduced the level of optimistic expectations by gym members to mentally simulate obstacles for successful future workout (e.g., Taylor et al., 1998). Specifically, participants in the study were asked to either mentally simulated obstacles to exercising or merely state their future plans to exercise. We found that those who simulated obstacles were equally interested in healthy food regardless of whether they focus on the commitment or progress from their planned exercise, hence, expectations did not affect present choice. The rest of the participants (in the unbiased condition) chose more healthy food if they considered their commitment and more unhealthy food if they considered their progress (Zhang et al., 2007).

In addition to experimental manipulations, the degree of optimism and people's action framing (commitment vs. progress) is also likely to vary across individuals. That is, individuals vary in the extent to which they are naturally optimistic and by the degree to which they tend to frame their self-regulatory attempts as signaling commitment or progress. These individual differences were explored in another study, which tested whether more optimistic individuals are more likely to make choices that are influenced by future plans. It found that gym members preferred to consume healthy (vs. unhealthy) foods to the extent that they tended to focus on the commitment from their planned workouts and they were generally optimistic (vs. less optimistic) that they will workout in the future. In addition, gym members preferred to choose less healthy foods if they focused on the progress from their planned workouts and were generally more (vs. less) optimistic that they will workout in the future. These results indicate that the tendency to focus on the commitment or progress from one's actions, and the degree of optimistic expectations are subject to individual differences and these two factors interact in predicting present choice.

In sum, our research indicates that due to optimistic expectations future plans to pursue a goal have greater impact on present choice than considering past choices. The direction of the influence, either increase or decrease in goal-congruent choices, depends on the framing of choice as signaling commitment to a goal or progress on that goal. This research further assumes that the framing of choice is subject to experimental manipulations as well as individuals' predispositions. We expected that the framing of choice can further be affected by the structure of the goal systems in memory and specifically, by the relative focus on the choice as an end in itself or a as a subgoal connected to an overall goal. We next consider whether the framing of choices as increasing commitment or progress may depend on the accessibility of an overall goal, which directs one's attention to the more abstract higher order goal that a choice serves versus the choice as an end in itself.

Choice of Subgoals to an Overall Goal

The process of self-regulation often involves breaking a goal into a series of goal-related choices that are spread over time, such that each choice comprises a separate subgoal to an overall goal. The question that arises is what are the implications of completing a subgoal for subsequent self-regulation and overall goal pursuit? Specifically, in our research we are interested in the factors that promote highlighting of the overall goal through several subgoals as opposed to disengagement as a result of breaking a goal into subgoals. Previous research illustrates the functionality of breaking an overall goal into separate subgoals that monitor action, and it was specifically shown that setting individual subgoals is often a necessary step in the accomplishment of complex goals (Carver & Scheier, 1990; Emmons, 1992; Gollwitzer, 1999; Gollwitzer & Brandstaetter, 1997; Locke & Latham, 1990; Vallacher & Wegner, 1987). However, this previous research did not address the effect of subgoal attainment on subsequent choice of additional subgoals and we predict that the effect of subgoals on subsequent choice may depend on the relative focus of one's attention on the specific subgoal attainment relative to the general goal that initiated it.

We propose that when subgoal attainment liberates the pursuit of incongruent actions it may interfere with the overall goal attainment. Under these conditions, breaking a goal into subgoals is sometimes maladaptive as the attainment of each subgoal is mistaken for overall goal attainment. Such *post completion errors* emerges, for example, when ATM users forget their card in the ATM machine as a result of mistaking getting cash (subgoal) to completing the transaction (overall goal; Anderson & Douglass, 2001; Byrne & Bovair, 1997). The result of post-completion errors is that people often disengage with an overall goal too soon, after receiving initial feedback on subgoal completion. According to our analysis, such errors are predicted whenever people focus on the completion of a subgoal and ignore the overall goal that initiated it. When the focus is on the sub-goal, progress along this subgoal signals that similar actions are redundant, but when the focus is on the overall goal, the same progress on the subgoal is perceived as relatively minor and a person is more likely to consider the commitment to the overall goal.

We specifically predict that when individuals consider the attainment of a subgoal itself, they experience some of the benefits associated with goal fulfillment, which motivates moving tempo-rarily away from the goal and pursuing other competing goals. But when the focus is on the overall goal, the same level of successful attainment highlights commitment to that overall goal more than it indicates goal progress, such that it motivates similar choices and inhibits the pursuit of compet-ing goals. What determines the effect of subgoal completion is therefore the relative focus on the abstract higher order goal versus the concrete subgoal in the associative goal network. For example, when the overall goal to save money is highly accessible, an initial success strengthens the commit-ment to this goal as well as related activities toward that end. When the goal is less accessible and a person focuses on the action itself, an initial success decreases the motivation for related activities and savers tend to increase their subsequent expenditure.

The relative accessibility of an overall goal may, however, have opposite consequences for fur-ther self-regulation if a person *failed* to complete an initial subgoal. Unlike success, failure on a subgoal can either signal that a person has failed to progress or that it undermines a person's com-mitment to the overall goal. These failure-based inferences have opposite implications for sub-sequent choice: if failure signals low commitment, it decreases the motivation to pursue similar actions to an overall goal (Soman & Cheema, 2004). However, when failure signals the absence of adequate progress toward a goal to which commitment remains intact, it increases the motivation to choose other complementary subgoals (Brunstein & Gollwitzer, 1996; Steele, 1988; Wicklund & Gollwitzer, 1982). For example, when a novice dancer demonstrates poor performance, she may feel less committed to her dancing career and forgo similar future attempts. Such a pattern of self-regulation is consistent with the dynamic of highlighting, as an initial low performance leads to subsequent disengagement. When however, a professional dancer, who is highly committed to her career, demonstrates poor performance, she experiences lack of progress and increases her subse-quent efforts. This pattern of self-regulation reflects a dynamic of balancing between an initial low performance and subsequent increased efforts. Since we expect goal accessibility to determine the relative focus on commitment versus progress, it is further assumed that failure is more motivating than success when the overall goal is inaccessible but it undermines the motivation relative to suc-cess when the goal is accessible.

We conducted a series of studies that tested for the effect of breaking a goal into subgoals on subsequent choice. These studies manipulated the success on an initial subgoal and the relative focus on the overall goal versus the subgoal itself. They demonstrate a tendency to disengage with a goal after successfully pursuing an initial subgoal toward this goal when the focus is on the subgoal itself, but to increase motivation for similar actions when the focus was on the overall goal (Fishbach, Dhar, & Zhang, 2006).

For example, in one study we tested for subgoal selection in three self-regulatory domains: preventing sun damage, doing well academically, and keeping in shape. In each domain, we first manipulated the accessibility of the overall goal by asking participants in the high accessibility condition to complete a scramble sentence task that included words related to the goal, while those in low accessibility condition completed a similar task with control words. For example, the sentences "most stores *honor* credit cards" versus "most stores *accept* credit cards" manipulated the high versus low accessibility of the goal of doing well academically. Next, in a supposedly unrelated study, participants rated their interest in pursuing a subgoal toward the overall goal as a function of whether they have already pursued an initial subgoal toward that aim or not. For instance, participants were asked to rate their interest in studying at night, after learning that they either studied or not during the morning. We found that in the absence of goal prime, those who already pursued (vs. not pursued) an initial subgoal were subsequently less interested in similar, congruent subgoals, which were seen as substitutable. However, in the presence of goal prime, those who already pursued (vs. not pursued) an initial subgoal were subsequently more interested in other subgoals, which were seen as complementary. Thus, those who studied during the day where subsequently less interested in studying at night when the focus was on the action by itself, and they more motivated to study at night when the focus was on the overall goal.

Another study replicated the effect of subgoal attainment by investigating the amount of efforts that people invest on a second subgoal. In this study we measured the amount of time that people persist on a test that had no correct solutions (e.g., Muraven, Tice, & Baumeister, 1998) as a function of their initial success or failure on a similar test of the same ability, and the accessibility of the overall achievement goal. As before, the accessibility of the overall achievement goal was manipulated in a scrambled sentence test that included words related to achievement (e.g., "succeed", "master" and "great") or not. This test was followed by success versus failure performance feedback, which indicated the level of performance on a subgoal. Having received success (vs. failure) feedback, participants were subsequently more likely to persist on the second unsolvable test if they were primed with the overall achievement goal, hence they were highlighting. However, having received success (vs. failure) feedback, participants were less likely to persist on the unsolvable test if they were not primed with the overall goal, hence they were balancing (Fishbach et al., 2006). Consistent with our model, we therefore find that success is motivating when the focus is on one's commitment to the overall goal as opposed to subgoal attainment, but failure is more motivating when one considers the lack of progress on the specific subgoal as opposed to low goal-commitment.

Another variable that influences the relative focus on the overall goal compared to the subgoal is the temporal distance from executing the subgoal. When actions are scheduled in the far (vs. near) future, they are framed in more global terms (Liberman & Trope, 1998; Trope & Liberman, 2003). In goal hierarchy, a more global framing leads to focus on the overall goal relative to the specific subgoals that serve its attainment. It follows that actions that are scheduled in the far future would promote a dynamic of "choice-highlighting" whereas the same actions, when they are scheduled in the near future, would promote a dynamic of "choice-balancing". This pattern was demonstrated in a study that tested for goal framing and goal-based choice in the domain of achieving academic success. It found that studying for a specific exam next month (vs. tomorrow) signaled greater commitment to the overall goal of academic success, as indicated by undergraduates' agreement with commitment framing statements (e.g., "by studying I express my commitment to doing well academically"). Performing the same activities (i.e., studying for an exam) tomorrow (vs. next month) signaled greater progress, as indicated by undergraduates' agreement with progress framing statements (e.g., "studying makes me closer to my academic objectives"). The ratings of agreement with framing statements in turn, influenced choice of subsequent actions, such that undergraduates who studied for one exam expressed an elevated interest studying for yet another exam only if it was scheduled in the far (vs. near) future (Fishbach et al., 2006).

Taken together, the research reviewed here suggests that whereas breaking a goal into subgoals is an adaptive means of self-regulation, by breaking a goal into subgoals individuals may also acquire feedback on their past progress, which decreases the likelihood of pursuing other subgoals unless the focus is on the commitment to the overall goal. This research further attests that the focus on a subgoal itself is motivating after initial failure, since it implies that a person has not made progress on a goal and it does not imply that this person is less committed. These opposite effects of initial failure and success as a function of the relative focus on the abstract goal versus specific subgoals have further implications for success at self-control. We suggest that people are more motivated to exercise self-control when they are aware of their previous success on what they consider to be an overall goal or their failure on what they consider to be a specific subgoal. We next address some of the implications of our analysis for success at self-control and overcoming temptation.

Sequencing Goals and Temptations

Our research addresses choice processes when there are multiple activated goals and naturally, the presence of multiple goals often poses a self-control dilemma. For example, a self-control dilemma is evoked when a person wishes to both eat healthy and flavorsome food, study and procrastinate, save and spend, etc. We define a self-control dilemma as a motivational conflict between two goals, one is of greater long-term importance than the other (Ainslie, 1992; Baumeister, Heatherton, & Tice, 1994; Dhar & Wertenbroch, 2000; Loewenstein, 1996; Metcalfe & Mischel, 1999; Rachlin, 1997; Thaler, 1991; Trope & Fishbach, 2000). A general insight from the self-control literature is that an abstract representation of the goal conflict helps maintain the commitment to an overall goal and discourages succumbing to immediate desires or temptations (Fujita, Trope, Liberman, & Levi-Sagi, 2005; Mischel, 1996; Mischel, Shoda, & Rodriguez, 1989; Rachlin, 1997, 2000). For example, an abstract representation of the conflict between smoking and quitting increases the motivation to withdraw from smoking, compared to a specific representation of any individual decision to smoke (Rachlin, 2000; Read, Loewenstein, & Rabin, 1999). In line with this insight, we also found that an abstract representation facilitates success at self-control, a pattern that we attributed to the greater focus on goal-commitment and the resulting dynamic of choice-highlighting following success. However, we further predicted and found that an abstract representation of self-control failure undermined the subsequent motivation to work on a goal since it signaled low goal-commitment.

Based on our theoretical framework we therefore propose that an abstract framing of goal conflict may not always facilitate success at exerting self-control and more specifically, the framing of succumbing to temptations would have opposite implications for subsequent choice than the framing of goal pursuits. When succumbing to temptation is framed more abstractly, it signals low goal-commitment, which undermines the motivation to work on a goal. Conversely, when succumbing to temptations is framed more concretely, it signals the absence of goal progress, which increases the subsequent motivation to work on a goal. In what follows, we consider the more direct implications of framing goal-pursuit versus succumbing-to-temptations in terms of commitment and progress for subsequent success at self-control.

First, when goal-related choices signal accumulating progress, they justify subsequently succumbing to temptation. This liberating effect of goals on choice received consistent support in our research and in research on moral licensing (e.g., Monin & Miller, 2001). Similar effects of initial success on subsequent disengagement are predicted by effort models of self-control, which share the assumption that an initial adherence to a goal results in depletion and subsequent succumbing to temptation (e.g., Baumeister, Bratslavsky, Muraven, & Tice, 1998; Muraven & Baumeister, 2000). The difference between these models and our analysis is that rather than assuming actual depletion of ego-resources, we focus on the information from an initial goal pursuit, and suggests that it is more legitimate to disengage from the goal after it appears to be progressed. Consistent with our analysis, recent research has documented a tendency to disengage with a self-control goal in anticipation of having to pursue the goal and "spend" resources at a later point in time (Shah, Brazy, & Jungbluth, 2005). In addition, the amount of depletion depends on people's lay belief that goals are indeed depleting and therefore that they justify succumbing to temptation on a subsequent task (Mukhopadhyay & Johar, 2005). In terms of our analysis, these results are congruent with the notion that when goal pursuit signals progress it justifies balancing between the goal and temptations even in the absence of actual psychological depletion.

Second, when goal-related choices signal commitment they guard against succumbing to temptation. Under commitment framing, an initial decision to pursue a goal establishes the commitment to the goal and steering away from temptations. Our research finds consistent support for the role of goal commitment in decreasing the likelihood of making incongruent choices that yield to temptations. Similar patterns were also documented in the literature on goal competition. Specifically, we reviewed research indicating that activated goals inhibit the motivational strength of alternative pursuits(e.g., temptations; Brendl et al., 2003; Forster et al., 2005; Shah et al., 2002).

There are relatively fewer studies that explore the effect of initial self-control failure on the subsequent motivation to disengage with the temptation and adhere to the overall goal (but see Cochran & Tessser, 1996; Soman & Cheema, 2004). In the absence of sufficient empirical evidence we can only conjecture: Our theory predicts that failure to pursue a goal and succumbing to temptations encourages overarching goal pursuits when it signals the absence of goal progress. In addition, temptations encourage moving away from the goal when they signal low goal-commitment. In support of these notions, research on counteractive mechanisms of self-control finds that tempting alternatives can increase the value of an overarching goal when they are seen as distracters or obstacles for making progress on a goal (e.g., Fishbach, Friedman, & Kruglanski, 2003; Fishbach & Trope, 2005; Trope & Fishbach, 2000). For example, in one study undergraduate students that mentally simulated leisure activities were subsequently more likely to study for an upcoming exam—a pattern that counteracts the effect of leisure interferences. On the other hand, temptations may interfere with adequate self-control when they signal low goal-commitment that undermines one's self-image as holding the overall goal. For example, research on the what-the-hell effect documented a tendency to give up on a dieting goal as a result of failing to pursue it and yielding to food temptations in the recent past (Cochran & Tessser, 1996; Polivy & Herman, 2002). Also congruent with this research, it was shown that people were less likely to adhere to their saving objectives after their saving goal was initially violated (Soman & Cheema, 2004).

Taken together, it appears that the focus on goal commitment (relative to goal progress) is adaptive for success in self-control when a person pursued the goal in the past or holds plans to pursue it in the future. As indicated earlier, such framing is more likely when people consider their actions in more abstract terms. By similar inferential logic, the relative focus on commitment (relative to progress) interferes with self-control if a person has already yielded to temptation. Under these conditions a concrete focus in terms of low goal-progress is more adaptive for self-control success.

The research reviewed in this section summarized the basic premises of our theoretical framework. It shows that when multiple goals are at stake and a person has the opportunity to make several related choices, a person can either highlight a single focal goal or balance between conflicting goals. When highlighting a single goal, an initial choice increases the motivation to choose congruent actions, but when balancing between goals, an initial choice increases the motivation to make conflicting subsequent choices that pursue other goals. These dynamics are elicited by considering past choices as well as future ones. In addition, these dynamics depend on the relative focus on an overall goal, which is associated with highlighting the commitment to a single goal, compared with focusing on a specific action, which is associated with balancing the progress on different goals. Finally, these dynamics have implications for the resolution of self-control conflicts between goals and temptations. We proposed that the focus on commitment from goal-related choices and the (lack of) progress from yielding to temptation facilitate success at self-control.

IMPLICATIONS FOR RESEARCH ON HUMAN MOTIVATION: SEARCHING FOR CONSISTENCY OR VARIETY?

Our research identifies the conditions under which initial choices increase or decrease the motivation to pursue congruent actions and thus, it has implications for understanding people's motivation to appear consistent or variety seeking. The question of whether people are driven by a general need for consistency or variety is fundamental for consumer research and research in social psychology. Accordingly, choice theories vary in terms of their basic underlying assumption: On the one hand, consistency theories attest that people wish to appear consistent in the eye of others and in their own eyes; therefore they express a general tendency to make similar successive choices (cf., Cialdini, Trost, & Newsom, 1995). This assumption underlies classical research in social psychology, including self-perception theory (Bem, 1972), cognitive dissonance (Festinger, 1957), and attribution theory (e.g., Gilbert & Malone, 1995; Jones & Harris, 1967). The common theme to these theoretical perspectives is the assumption that people wish to minimize the variance of the choice. On the other hand, a large proportion of choice research has been conducted under the assumption that people wish to maximize their choice variance and make divergent choices that pursue many different goals (Monin & Miller, 2001; Ratner, Kahn, & Kahneman, 1999; Simonson & Nowlis, 2000). Our theory can potentially reconcile this discrepancy between consistency and variety theories by addressing this question from the stand point of a person that can either highlight a single goal or balance between conflicting ones, depending on this person's accessible dynamic of self-regulation.

Consistency Versus Variety

A core assumption of attitude theories in social psychology is that people wish to pursue consistent behaviors over time (e.g., Aronson, 1997; Bem, 1972; Cialdini et al., 1995; Heider, 1958). This assumption was first introduced by cognitive dissonance theory, which documented a general discomfort when individuals' chosen actions or cognitions appeared inconsistent with each other. Therefore an initial action or verbal statement often led to congruent future choices that justified it (Cooper & Fazio, 1984; Festinger, 1957). A similar assumption was made by self-perception theory, which postulates that people learn about their preferences by watching themselves make particular choices. Once a person acknowledges the presence of a preference, s/he seeks to make further consistent choices that support this preference (Bem, 1972).

Persuasion research further emphasizes the importance that people assign to making congruent successive choices. For example, it was shown that if a person engages in an initial behavior such as agreeing to display a small sign to advocate driving safety, the person will feel later that s/he should engage in actions consistent with the underlying goal, such as displaying a large lawn sign to advocate the same cause (Freedman & Fraser, 1966). Communicators often rely on people's desire to appear consistent in their persuasion efforts. As indicated by the previous example, the foot-in-the-door technique involves a simple behavior that everyone agrees to perform, which is followed by a request to perform a more complex and costly actions that are consistent with the original effort (Cialdini, 2001). On a more intrapersonal level, a repetitive choice pattern was often associated with familiarity, security and generally positive feelings (e.g., Zajonc, 2001).

Furthermore, previous research indicates that people expect *others* to appear consistent by making similar consecutive choices. Thus, they readily infer a stable disposition based on a single choice and then expect the chooser to make future choices that conform to that stable disposition. By relying on dispositional inferences, people further undermine the possible effect of situational variables, satiation, and changing preferences and needs, which all create choice diversity (e.g., Gilbert & Malone, 1995; Jones & Harris, 1967).

In opposition to research on consistency, choice studies often postulate that choosers are motivated to maximize the variance within a choice set. According to this body of research, individuals believe they should incorporate variety into their choices even if one choice alternative clearly dominates others (e.g., McAlister & Pessemier, 1982; Read & Loewenstein, 1995; Simonson & Nowlis, 2000). A preference for variety was explained in terms of satiation, which follows from satisfying a need or a goal, and motivates a different choice that can potentially satisfy other needs or goals.

Importantly, whereas variety seeking behavior can result from real physical satiation (McAlister, 1982), it was also observed in choice situations where satiation is unlikely, for example, when research participants chose a different single snack per week for several consecutive weeks. Under these conditions, variety seeking behavior reflects a lay belief of what compromises a good choice (Read & Loewenstein, 1995; Simonson, 1990), or compliance with a perceived external standard (Kim & Drolet, 2003; Ratner & Kahn, 2002). In terms of our framework, when there is no real satiation, variety reflects the perception that a self-regulatory pattern of choice-balancing is appropriate.

Integration of Research on Consistency and Variety

According to our theory, a desire to appear consistent emerges when an initial choice signals commitment to an underlying goal. Conversely, a desire to seek variety is expected when the same initial choice signals progress or goal attainment. It is therefore the framing of choice, rather than its content (e.g., eating snacks vs. helping behavior), that determines whether a person is subsequently motivated to make choices that are different or similar to a previous one. The framing of choice further influences the perception of similar (vs. dissimilar) choices as socially desirable, and the tendency to predict these choices for others.

These notions are supported by our previous research, which demonstrates the effect of choice framing on the amount of variance that people incorporate to their choice. In addition, it was recently shown that when people choose high variety (e.g., several different snacks) they see each chosen item as increasing the progress toward satisfying this need or goal. However, when people choose low variety they see each chosen item as establishing the importance of this need or goal (Fishbach, Ratner, & Zhang, 2006). For example, in one study we asked research participants to read ambiguous information regarding a target person who engaged in a number of repetitive behaviors (e.g., always ate at the same place) and they were led to frame this target person's actions as either signaling loyalty or as boring. We assumed that a "loyal" (vs. "boring") framing hinders variety seeking and indeed, those who were primed with a positive framing of consistency chose less variety on a subsequent choice task than those who framed it as boringness. More importantly, those who were primed with loyalty (vs. boringness) framed their initial choice as indicating commitment (vs. progress) to the chosen alterative.

These and other findings undermine the universality of variety-seeking or consistency-seeking as the sole principle for successive choice. According to our research, a motivation for consistency is elicited when actions are framed as defining features of a person's self-concept, whereas a variety seeking motivation emerges when these actions signal progress along previously defined goals. Thus, our theory is consistent with previous research attesting that past choices influence future choices; however, the direction of the influence depends on individuals' framing of choice.

SUMMARY AND CONCLUSIONS

This chapter considers the effects of goals on choice. We reviewed research on the influence of single and multiple goals on single choice, which led to our research on the pursuit of multiple goals through repeated choices that are spread over time. We then introduced our theory of the dynamics of goal-based choice (e.g., Fishbach & Dhar, 2005; Fishbach et al., 2006; Zhang et al., 2006). This theory proposes two basic patterns of self-regulation in choice sequences: highlighting of a single goal and balancing among several goals (illustrated in Figure 24.1). It suggests that an initial choice evokes a dynamic of highlighting when it signals commitment to an overall goal. In addition, an initial choice evokes a dynamic of balancing when it signals progress on that goal.

Several predictions follow from our analysis and they received consistent support in our research. First, we proposed that in the course of pursuing multiple goals, the framing of an initial choice as indicating commitment promotes subsequent similar choices and inhibition of competing alternatives. Conversely, the framing of initial choice as indicating progress promotes subsequent different choices that pursue other goals. Second, as a result of optimistic expectations (e.g., Weinstein, 1989; Buehler, Griffin, & Ross, 1994), thinking about successful future goal attainment has greater impact on immediate actions than thinking about less successful past goal attainment. In particular, future plans (vs. past actions) motivate similar choices when they signal commitment and motivate incongruent choices when they signal progress. Third, these dynamics depend on the relative focus on the overall goal versus specific subgoal. When the focus is on the overall goal, an initial success signals commitment, which increases the likelihood of making complementary choices towards the same goal. But when the focus is on the subgoal itself, an initial success signals progress, which decreases likelihood of making complementary choices. Fourth, our theory has implications for the resolution of self-control conflicts between goals and temptations (e.g., Dhar & Wertenbroch, 2000; Loewenstein, 1996; Trope & Fishbach, 2000). It attests that success at self-control is attained when goal pursuits signal commitment and temptation pursuits signal lack of progress. Conversely, failures at self-control are more likely when temptation pursuits signal low commitment and goal pursuits signal progress. Finally, our findings are relevant to previous research on variety seeking versus research on the value of consistency, and we suggest that the apparent discrepancy between these two choice criteria may reflect the underlying dynamics of choice highlighting and balancing.

In general, the relative focus on commitment versus progress and the subsequent effect on choice may depend on many factors. These factors include for example, people's implicit theories

(Schwarz, 2004; Wyer, 2004), which influence the chronic activation of a certain dynamic of self-regulation (Zhang et al., 2007), or the temporal distance from an action, which is associated with increased commitment (vs. progress) action framing (Fishbach et al., 2006). Other variables that may affect the framing of action and the subsequent dynamic of self-regulation include the attribution of an action to personal versus external control, and personal attributions are more likely to lead to commitment framing, while external attributions are associated with progress framing. For example, we expect that a student who believes that her academic success is due to her talent (internal attribution) may infer commitment following success, whereas if she believes that her success is attributed to luck (external attribution), she may be more likely to infer progress after success. In addition, the relative focus on commitment versus progress may have implications for people's level of aspiration with regard to a single goal (Lewin, Dembo, Festinger, & Sears, 1944). That is, it is possible that individuals who focus on the commitment from their action set lower aspiration levels compared with those who focus on the progress from their action and wish to move on to a new level of performance. This and other implications of our theory of dynamic of goal-based choice are the focus of our future research.

NOTE

1. Our focus in on the goals that a decision is meant to accomplish (e.g., choosing a product that has high quality and low price), however other researchers addressed the goals of the decision process. In particular, Bettman and colleagues (in this volume) proposed that the focal goal of any decision process is to reach an *accurate decision*. However, the decision process further follows a combination of some other motives, such as *minimizing the cognitive efforts* required for the decision, *minimizing the negative affect* that may be associated with the decision process, and *maximizing the ease of justifying* one's decision to others and self (see also Bettman, 1979; Bettman et al., 1998).

REFERENCES

Aarts, H., & Dijksterhuis, A. (2000). Habits as knowledge structures: Automaticity in goal-directed behavior. *Journal of Personality and Social Psychology, 78*(1), 53–63.

Aarts, H., Dijksterhuis, A., & De Vries, P. (2001). On the psychology of drinking: Being thirsty and perceptually ready. *British Journal of Psychology, 92*(4), 631.

Aarts, H., Gollwitzer, P. M., & Hassin, R. R. (2004). Goal contagion: Perceiving is for pursuing. *Journal of Personality and Social Psychology, 87*(1), 23–37.

Ainslie, G. (1992). *Picoeconomics: The strategic interaction of successive motivational states within the person.* Cambridge: Cambridge University Press.

Anderson, J. R. (1983). *The architecture of cognition.* Cambridge, MA: Harvard University Press.

Anderson, J. R., Bothell, D., Byrne, M. D., Douglass, S., Lebiere, C., & Qin, Y. (2004). An integrated theory of the mind. *Psychological Review, 111*(4), 1036–1060.

Anderson, J. R., & Douglass, S. (2001). Tower of Hanoi: Evidence for the cost of goal retrieval. *Journal of Experimental Psychology: Learning, Memory, and Cognition, 27*(6), 1331–1346.

Aronson, E. (1997). The theory of cognitive dissonance: The evolution and vicissitudes of an idea. In C. McGarty & S. A. Haslam (Eds.), *The message of social psychology: Perspectives on mind in society* (pp. pp. 20–35). Cambridge, MA: Blackwell.

Atkinson, J. W., & Raynor, J. O. (1978). *Personality, motivation, and achievement.* New York: Halsted Press.

Bagozzi, R. P., & Dholakia, U. (1999). Goal setting and goal striving in consumer behavior. *Journal of Marketing, 63*(Special Issue), 19–32.

Bandura, A. (1997). *Self-efficacy: The exercise of control.* New York, NY: W. H. Freeman/Times Books/Henry Holt & Co.

Bargh, J. A., Gollwitzer, P. M., Lee-Chai, A., Barndollar, K., & Troetschel, R. (2001). The automated will: Nonconscious activation and pursuit of behavioral goals. *Journal of Personality and Social Psychology, 81*(6), 1014–1027.

Baron, J. (2000). *Thinking and deciding* (3rd ed.). Cambridge: Cambridge University Press.

Baumeister, R. F., Bratslavsky, E., Muraven, M., & Tice, D. M. (1998). Ego depletion: is the active self a limited resource? *Journal of Personality and Social Psychology, 74*(5), 1252–1265.

Baumeister, R. F., Heatherton, T. F., & Tice, D. M. (1994). *Losing control: How and why people fail at self-regulation*. San Diego: Academic.

Bem, D. J. (1972). Self-perception theory. In L. Berkowitz (Ed.), *Advances in experimental social psychology* (Vol. 6, pp. 1–62). New York: Academic Press.

Bettman, J. R. (1979). An Information Processing Theory of Consumer Choice. In *Reading* (pp. 107–111). Boston: Addison-Wesley.

Bettman, J. R., Luce, M. F., & Payne, J. W. (1998). Constructive consumer choice processes. *Journal of Consumer Research, 25*(3), 187–217.

Brendl, C., & Higgins, E. (1996). Principles of judging valence: What makes events positive or negative? In M. P. Zanna (Ed.), *Advances in experimental social psychology, Vol 28* (pp. 95–160). San Diego, CA: Academic Press.

Brendl, C., Markman, A. B., & Messner, C. (2003). The devaluation effect: Activating a need devalues unrelated objects. *Journal of Consumer Research, 29*(4), 463–473.

Brunstein, J. C., & Gollwitzer, P. M. (1996). Effects of failure on subsequent performance: The importance of self-defining goals. *Journal of Personality and Social Psychology, 70*(2), 395–407.

Buehler, R., Griffin, D., & Ross, M. (2002). Inside the planning fallacy: The causes and consequences of optimistic time predictions. In T. Gilovich, D. Griffin, et al. (Eds.), *Heuristics and biases: The psychology of intuitive judgment* (pp. 250–270). New York: Cambridge University Press.

Byrne, M. D., & Bovair, S. (1997). A working memory model of a common procedural error. *Cognitive Science, 21*(1), 31–61.

Cantor, N., & Langston, C. A. (1989). Ups and downs of life tasks in a life transition. In L. A. Pervin (Ed.), *Goal concepts in personality and social psychology* (pp. 127–167). Hillsdale: Erlbaum.

Carver, C. S., & Scheier, M. F. (1990). Principles of self-regulation: Action and emotion. In E. T. Higgins & R. M. Sorrentino (Eds.), *Handbook of motivation and cognition: Foundations of social behavior* (Vol. 2, pp. 3–52). New York: Guilford Press.

Carver, C. S., & Scheier, M. F. (1998). *On the self-regulation of behavior*. New York: Cambridge University Press.

Chartrand, T. L., & Bargh, J. A. (1999). The chameleon effect: The perception-behavior link and social interaction. *Journal of Personality and Social Psychology, 76*(6), 893–910.

Chun, W. Y., Kruglanski, A. W., Sleeth-Keppler, D., & Friedman, R. S. (2006). The multifinality principle in choice without awareness. Unpublished manuscript, University of Maryland.

Cialdini, R. B. (2001). *Influence: Science and practice* (4th ed.). New York: Allyn & Bacon.

Cialdini, R. B., Trost, M. R., & Newsom, J. T. (1995). Preference for consistency: The development of a valid measure and the discovery of surprising behavioral implications. *Journal of Personality and Social Psychology, 69*(2), 318–328.

Cochran, W., & Tessser, A. (1996). The "what the hell" effect: Some effects of goal proximity and goal framing on performance. In L. L. Martin & A. Tesser (Eds.), *Striving and feeling: interactions among goals, affect, and self-regulation* (pp. 99–120). Hillsdale, NJ: Erlbaum.

Cooper, J., & Fazio, R. H. (1984). A new look at dissonance theory. In L. Berkowitz (Ed.), *Advances in experimental social psychology* (Vol. 17, pp. 229–264). Orlando, FL: Academic Press.

Dhar, R. (1996). The effect of decision strategy on deciding to defer choice. *Journal of Behavioral Decision Making, 9*(4), 265–281.

Dhar, R. (1997). Consumer preference for a no-choice option. *Journal of Consumer Research, 24*(2), 215–231.

Dhar, R., & Sherman, S. J. (1996). The effect of common and unique features in consumer choice. *Journal of Consumer Research, 23*(3), 193–203.

Dhar, R., & Simonson, I. (1992). The effect of the focus of comparison on consumer preferences. *Journal of Marketing Research, 29*(4), 430–440.

Dhar, R., & Simonson, I. (1999). Making complementary choices in consumption episodes: Highlighting versus balancing. *Journal of Marketing Research, 36*(1), 29–44.

Dhar, R., & Wertenbroch, K. (2000). Consumer choice between hedonic and utilitarian goods. *Journal of Marketing Research, 37*(1), 60–71.

Emmons, R. A. (1992). Abstract versus concrete goals: Personal striving level, physical illness, and psychological well-being. *Journal of Personality and Social Psychology, 62*(2), 292–300.

Emmons, R. A., & King, L. A. (1988). Conflict among personal strivings: Immediate and long-term implications for psychological and physical well-being. *Journal of Personality and Social Psychology, 54*(6), 1040–1048.

Fazio, R. H., Jackson, J. R., Dunton, B. C., & Williams, C. J. (1995). Variability in automatic activation as an unobstrusive measure of racial attitudes: A bona fide pipeline? *Journal of Personality and Social Psychology, 69*(6), 1013–1027.

Feather, N. T. (1990). Bridging the gap between values and actions: Recent applications of the expectancy-value model. In E. T. Higgins & R. M. Sorrentino (Eds.), *Handbook of motivation and cognition: Foundations of social behavior* (Vol. 2, pp. 151–192). New York: Guilford.

Ferguson, M. J., & Bargh, J. A. (2004). Liking is for doing: The effects of goal pursuit on automatic evaluation. *Journal of Personality and Social Psychology, 87*(5), 557–572.

Festinger, L. (1957). *A theory of cognitive dissonance.* Evanston, IL: Row, Peterson.

Fishbach, A., & Dhar, R. (2005). Goals as excuses or guides: The liberating effect of perceived goal progress on choice. *Journal of Consumer Research, 32*, 370–377.

Fishbach, A., Dhar, R., & Zhang, Y. (2006). Subgoals as substitutes or complements: The role of goal accessibility. *Journal of Personality and Social Psychology, 91*(2), 232–242.

Fishbach, A., Friedman, R. S., & Kruglanski, A. W. (2003). Leading us not unto temptation: Momentary allurements elicit overriding goal activation. *Journal of Personality & Social Psychology, 84*(2), 296–309.

Fishbach, A., Shah, J. Y., & Kruglanski, A. W. (2004). Emotional transfer in goal systems. *Journal of Experimental Social Psychology, 40*, 723–738.

Fishbach, A., & Trope, Y. (2005). The substitutability of external control and self-control. *Journal of Experimental Social Psychology, 41*(3), 256–270.

Fishbach, A., Zhang, Y., & Trope, W. (2007). Asymmetric counteractive evaluation. Unpublished manuscript, University of Chicago.

Fiske, S. T. (1992). Thinking is for doing: Portraits of social cognition from Daguerreotype to laserphoto. *Journal of Personality and Social Psychology, 63*(6), 877–889.

Fitzsimons, G. J., & Williams, P. (2000). Asking questions can change choice behavior: Does it do so automatically or effortfully? *Journal of Experimental Psychology: Applied, 6*(3), 195–206.

Fitzsimons, G. M., & Bargh, J. A. (2003). Thinking of you: Nonconscious pursuit of interpersonal goals associated with relationship partners. *Journal of Personality and Social Psychology, 84*(1), 148–163.

Forster, J., Liberman, N., & Higgins, E. (2005). Accessibility from active and fulfilled goals. *Journal of Experimental Social Psychology, 41*(3), 220–239.

Freedman, J. L., & Fraser, C. C. (1966). Compliance without pressure: The foot-in-the-door technique. *Journal of Personality and Social Psychology, 4*(195–202).

Fujita, K., Trope, Y., Liberman, N., & Levi-Sagi, M. (2005). Construal levels and self-control. manuscript submitted for publication.

Gilbert, D. T., & Malone, P. S. (1995). The correspondence bias. *Psychological Bulletin, 117*(1), 21–38.

Gollwitzer, P. M. (1999). Implementation intentions: Strong effects of simple plans. *American Psychologist, 54*(7), 493–503.

Gollwitzer, P. M., & Brandstaetter, V. (1997). Implementation intentions and effective goal pursuit. *Journal of Personality and Social Psychology, 73*(1), 186–199.

Heath, C., Larrick, R. P., & Wu, G. (1999). Goals as reference points. *Cognitive Psychology, 38*(1), 79–109.

Heider, F. (1958). *The psychology of interpersonal relations.* New York: Wiley.

Higgins, T. E. (1989). Self-discrepancy theory: What patterns of self-beliefs cause people to suffer? In L. Berkowitz (Ed.), *Advances in experimental social psychology* (Vol. 22, pp. 93–136). San Diego CA: Academic Press.

Higgins, T. E. (1997). Beyond pleasure and pain. *American Psychologist, 52*(12), 1280–1300.

Iyengar, S. S., & Lepper, M. R. (2000). When choice is demotivating: Can one desire too much of a good thing? *Journal of Personality and Social Psychology, 79*(6), 995–1006.

Jones, E. E., & Harris, V. A. (1967). The attribution of attitudes. *Journal of Experimental Social Psychology, 3*, 1–24.

Kanfer, R., Ackerman, P. L., Murtha, T. C., Dugdale, B., & et al. (1994). Goal setting, conditions of practice, and task performance: A resource allocation perspective. *Journal of Applied Psychology, 79*(6), 826–835.

Keeney, R. L., & Raiffa, H. (1976). *Decisions with multiple objectives: Preferences and value tradeoffs.* New York: Wiley. (Reprinted 1993)

Khan, U., & Dhar, R. (2006). Effect of future choices on current preferences.

Kim, H. S., & Drolet, A. (2003). Choice and self-expression: A cultural analysis of variety-seeking. *Journal of Personality and Social Psychology, 85*(2), 373–382.

Kivetz, R., Urminsky, O., & Zheng, Y. (2006). The goal-gradient hypothesis resurrected: Purchase acceleration, illusionary goal progress, and customer retention. *Journal of Marketing Research, 43*(1), 39–58.

Koo, M., & Fishbach, A. (in press). Dynamics of self-regulation: How (un)accomplished goal actions affect motivation. *Journal of Personality and Social Psychology.*

Kruglanski, A. W., Shah, J. Y., Fishbach, A., Friedman, R., Chun, W. Y., & Sleeth-Keppler, D. (2002). A theory of goal systems. In M. P. Zanna (Ed.), *Advances in experimental social psychology* (Vol. 34, pp. 331–378). San Diego, CA: Academic Press.

Latham, G. P., & Locke, E. A. (1975). Increasing productivity and decreasing time limits: A field replication of Parkinson's law. *Journal of Applied Psychology, 60*(4), 524–526.

Latham, G. P., & Yukl, G. A. (1976). Effects of assigned and participative goal setting on performance and job satisfaction. *Journal of Applied Psychology, 61*(2), 166–171.

Lewin, K. (1935). *A dynamic theory of personality.* New York: McGraw Hill.

Lewin, K., Dembo, T., Festinger, L., & Sears, P. S. (1944). Level of aspiration. In J. M. Hunt (Ed.), *Personality and the Behavior Disorders* (Vol. 1, pp. 333–378). New York: Ronald Press.

Liberman, N., & Trope, Y. (1998). The role of feasibility and desirability considerations in near and distant future decisions: A test of temporal construal theory. *Journal of Personality and Social Psychology, 75*(1), 5–18.

List, J. A., & Lucking-Reiley, D. (2002). The effects of seed money and refunds on charitable giving: Experimental evidence from a university capital campaign. *Journal of Political Economy, 110*(1), 215–233.

Locke, E. A., & Latham, G. P. (1990). *A theory of goal setting and task performance.* Upper Saddle River, NJ: Prentice-Hall, Inc.

Locke, E. A., & Latham, G. P. (2002). Building a practically useful theory of goal setting and task motivation: A 35-year odyssey. *American Psychologist, 57*(9), 705–717.

Loewenstein, G. (1996). Out of control: Visceral influences on behavior. *Organizational Behavior & Human Decision Processes, 65*(3), 272–292.

Mandel, N., & Johnson, E. J. (2002). When web pages influence choice: Effects of visual primes on experts and novices. *Journal of Consumer Research, 29*(2), 235–245.

Markus, H., & Ruvolo, A. (1989). Possible selves: Personalized representations of goals. In L. A. Pervin (Ed.), *Goal concepts in personality and social psychology* (pp. 211–241). Hillsdale, NJ: Erlbaum.

McAlister, L. (1982). A dynamic attribute satiation model of variety-seeking behavior. *Journal of Consumer Research, 9*(2), 141–150.

McAlister, L., & Pessemier, E. (1982). Variety seeking behavior: An interdisciplinary review. *Journal of Consumer Research, 9*(3), 311–322.

Metcalfe, J., & Mischel, W. (1999). A hot/cool-system analysis of delay of gratification: Dynamics of willpower. *Psychological Review, 106*(1), 3–19.

Miller, G. A., Galanter, E., & Pribram, K. H. (1960). *Plans and the structure of behavior.* New York: Henry Holt.

Mischel, W. (1996). From good intentions to willpower. In P. M. Gollwitzer & J. A. Bargh (Eds.), *The psychology of action: Linking cognition and motivation to behavior* (pp. 197–218). New York: Guilford Press.

Mischel, W., Shoda, Y., & Rodriguez, M. L. (1989). Delay of gratification in children. *Science, 244*(4907), 933–938.

Monin, B., & Miller, D. T. (2001). Moral credentials and the expression of prejudice. *Journal of Personality & Social Psychology, 81*(1), 33–43.

Morwitz, V. G., & Fitzsimons, G. J. (2004). The mere-measurement effect: Why does measuring intentions change actual behavior? *Journal of Consumer Psychology, 14*(1-2), 64–74.

Moskowitz, G. B. (2002). Preconscious effects of temporary goals on attention. *Journal of Experimental Social Psychology, 38*(4), 397–404.

Moskowitz, G. B., Gollwitzer, P. M., Wasel, W., & Schaal, B. (1999). Preconscious control of stereotype activation through chronic egalitarian goals. *Journal of Personality and Social Psychology, 77*(1), 167–184.

Mukhopadhyay, A., & Johar, G. V. (2005). Where there is a will, is there a way? Effects of lay theories of self-control on setting and keeping resolutions. *Journal of Consumer Research, 31*(4), 779–786.

Muraven, M., & Baumeister, R. F. (2000). Self-regulation and depletion of limited resources: does self-control resemble a muscle? *Psychological Bulletin, 126*(2), 247–259.

Muraven, M., Tice, D. M., & Baumeister, R. F. (1998). Self-control as a limited resource: Regulatory depletion patterns. *Journal of Personality and Social Psychology, 74*(3), 774–789.

North, A. C., Hargreaves, D. J., & McKendrick, J. (1997). In-store music affects product choice. *Nature, 390*(6656), 132.

Nowlis, S. M., Mandel, N., & McCabe, D. B. (2004). The effect of a delay between choice and consumption on consumption enjoyment. *Journal of Consumer Research, 31*(3), 502–510.

Oettingen, G., & Mayer, D. (2002). The motivating function of thinking about the future: Expectations versus fantasies. *Journal of Personality and Social Psychology, 83*(5), 1198–1212.

Oettingen, G., Pak, H.-J., & Schnetter, K. (2001). Self-regulation of goal-setting: Turning free fantasies about the future into binding goals. *Journal of Personality and Social Psychology, 80*(5), 736–753.

Payne, J. W., Bettman, J. R., & Johnson, E. J. (1992). Behavioral decision research: A constructive processing perspective. *Annual Review of Psychology, 43*, 87–131

Polivy, J., & Herman, C. (2002). If at first you don't succeed: False hopes of self-change. *American Psychologist, 57*(9), 677–689.

Powers, W. T. (1973). *Behavior: The control of perception.* Oxford: Aldine.

Rachlin, H. (1997). Self and self-control. In J. G. Snodgrass & R. L. Thompson (Eds.), *The self across psychology: Self-recognition, self-awareness, and the self concept: Annals of the New York Academy of Sciences* (Vol. 818, pp. 85–97). New York: New York Academy of Sciences.

Rachlin, H. (2000). *The science of self-control.* Cambridge, MA: Harvard University Press.

Ratner, R. K., & Kahn, B. E. (2002). The impact of private versus public consumption on variety-seeking behavior. *Journal of Consumer Research, 29*(2), 246–257.

Ratner, R. K., Kahn, B. E., & Kahneman, D. (1999). Choosing less-preferred experiences for the sake of variety. *Journal of Consumer Research, 26*(1), 1–15.

Read, D., & Loewenstein, G. (1995). Diversification bias: Explaining the discrepancy in variety seeking between combined and separated choices. *Journal of Experimental Psychology: Applied, 1*(1), 34–49.

Read, D., Loewenstein, G., & Rabin, M. (1999). Choice bracketing. *Journal of Risk and Uncertainty, 19*(1), 171–197.

Schwarz, N. (2004). Metacognitive experiences in consumer judgment and decision making. *Journal of Consumer Psychology, 14*(4), 332–348.

Shah, J. (2003). The motivational looking glass: How significant others implicitly affect goal appraisals. *Journal of Personality and Social Psychology, 85*(3), 424–439.

Shah, J. Y., Brazy, P., & Jungbluth, N. (2005). SAVE it for later: Implicit effort regulation and the self-regulatory anticipation of volitional exertion. Unpublished manuscript, Duke University.

Shah, J. Y., Friedman, R., & Kruglanski, A. W. (2002). Forgetting all else: On the antecedents and consequences of goal shielding. *Journal of Personality and Social Psychology, 83*(6), 1261–1280.

Shah, J. Y., & Kruglanski, A. W. (2002). Priming against your will: How accessible alternatives affect goal pursuit. *Journal of Experimental Social Psychology, 38*(4), 368–383.

Shah, J. Y., & Kruglanski, A. W. (2003). When opportunity knocks: Bottom-up priming of goals by means and its effects on self-regulation. *Journal of Personality and Social Psychology, 84*(6), 1109–1122.

Sherman, S. J. (1980). On the self-erasing nature of errors of prediction. *Journal of Personality & Social Psychology, 39*(2), 211–221.

Simonson, I. (1989). Choice based on reasons: The case of attraction and compromise effects. *Journal of Consumer Research, 16*(2), 158–174.

Simonson, I. (1990). The effect of purchase quantity and timing on variety-seeking behavior. *Journal of Marketing Research, 27*(2), 150–162.

Simonson, I., & Nowlis, S. M. (2000). The role of explanations and need for uniqueness in consumer decision making: Unconventional choices based on reasons. *Journal of Consumer Research, 27*(1), 49–68.

Simonson, I., Nowlis, S. M., & Simonson, Y. (1993). The effect of irrelevant preference arguments on consumer choice. *Journal of Consumer Psychology, 2*(3), 287–306.

Simonson, I., & Tversky, A. (1992). Choice in context: Tradeoff contrast and extremeness aversion. *Journal of Marketing Research, 29*(3), 281–295.

Slovic, P. (1995). The construction of preference. *American Psychologist, 50*(5), 364–371.

Soman, D., & Cheema, A. (2004). When goals are counter-productive: The effects of violation of a behavioral goal on subsequent performance. *Journal of Consumer Research, 31*(1), 52–62.

Soman, D., & Shi, M. (2003). Virtual progress: The effect of path characteristics on perceptions of progress and choice behavior. *Management Science, 49*(9), 1229–1250.

Steele, C. M. (1988). The psychology of self-affirmation: Sustaining the integrity of the self. In L. Berkowitz (Ed.), *Advances in experimental social psychology* (Vol. 21, pp. 261–302). New York: Academic Press.

Taylor, S. E., & Brown, J. D. (1988). Illusion and well-being: A social psychological perspective on mental health. *Psychological Bulletin, 103*(2), 193–210.

Taylor, S. E., Pham, L. B., Rivkin, I. D., & Armor, D. A. (1998). Harnessing the imagination: Mental simulation, self-regulation, and coping. *American Psychologist, 53*(4), 429–439.

Thaler, R. H. (1991). *Quasi rational economics.* New York: Russel Sage Foundation.

Trope, Y., & Fishbach, A. (2000). Counteractive self-control in overcoming temptation. *Journal of Personality and Social Psychology, 79*(4), 493–506.

Trope, Y., & Liberman, N. (2003). Temporal construal. *Psychological Review, 110*(3), 403–421.

Tversky, A. (1972). Elimination by aspects: A theory of choice. *Psychological Review Vol 79(4) Jul 1972, 281–299 American Psychological Assn, US.*

Tversky, A., & Shafir, E. (1992). Choice under conflict: The dynamics of deferred decision. *Psychological Science, 3*(6), 358–361.

Vallacher, R. R., & Wegner, D. M. (1987). What do people think they're doing? Action identification and human behavior. *Psychological Review, 94*(1), 3–15.

Weinstein, N. D. (1989). Optimistic biases about personal risks. *Science, 246,* 1232–1233.

Wicklund, R. A., & Gollwitzer, P. M. (1982). *Symbolic self-completion.* Hillsdale, NJ: Erlbaum.

Williams, P., Fitzsimons, G. J., & Block, L. G. (2004). When consumers do not recognize "benign" intention questions as persuasion attempts. *Journal of Consumer Research, 31,* 540–550.

Wyer, R. S., Jr. (2004). *Social comprehension and judgment: The role of situation models, narratives, and implicit theories.* Mahwah, NJ: Erlbaum.

Zajonc, R. B. (2001). Mere exposure: A gateway to the subliminal. *Current Directions in Psychological Science, 10*(6), 224–228.

Zauberman, G., & Lynch, J. G., Jr. (2005). Resource slack and propensity to discount delayed investments of time versus money. *Journal of Experimental Psychology: General, 134*(1), 23–37.

Zhang, Y., Fishbach, A., & Dhar, R. (2007). When thinking beats doing: The role of optimistic expectations in goal-based choice. *Journal of Consumer Research.*

25

Hedonomics in Consumer Behavior

CHRISTOPHER K. HSEE

CLAIRE I. TSAI

University of Chicago

Virtually all consumers want to maximize the happiness that comes with consumption. In recent decades, consumer researchers, psychologists, and economists have accumulated empirical data and developed testable theories on happiness (e.g., Burroughs & Rindfleisch, 2002; Diener & Biswas-Diener, 2002; Easterlin, 2001; Frey & Stutzer, 2002a, 2002b; Kahneman, Diener & Schwarz, 1999; Kahneman & Sugden, 2005; Raghunathan & Irwin, 2001; Seligman, 2002).

There are at least two general ways to improve consumer's happiness. One is to enhance the magnitude of desired external stimuli (e.g., amount of income, size of home, number of shoes). The other is to find the optimal relationship between external stimuli and happiness. The following analogy illustrates the distinction between these approaches. Suppose that a child loves wooden blocks and possesses some. He has played with the ones he owns for a while and is bored with them. How can he increase his happiness? One approach is to obtain more blocks. The other approach is to find a better way to combine the existing pieces and build more enjoyable projects.

The first approach is embraced by most consumers in our society. It seeks to earn more money and buy more desired goods. Indeed, most consumers become increasingly wealthier and possess more goods now than ever before. The second approach is the focus of the present chapter. It seeks to optimize the relationship between external stimuli and happiness without having to increase the magnitude of the external stimuli per se. We refer to this approach as *hedonomics*, in contrast to economics. Obviously, economics is also concerned with the relationship between external stimuli, such as wealth, and subjective value or utility, and assumes not only that more wealth is better but that additional wealth has less additional utility for the rich than for the poor. Hedonomics goes beyond this simple diminishing-marginal-utility notion and examines more complex relationships.

Hedonomics would not be important if either of the following assumptions were true. First, happiness depends only or primarily on the magnitude of desired external stimuli (e.g., amount of income). Second, consumers fully understand the relationships between external stimuli and happiness and in making purchase or consumption decisions they are already maximizing their happiness. Nevertheless, as our review will show, neither of these assumptions is true. First, happiness depends not only on the magnitude of external stimuli, but also on how these stimuli are presented and evaluated, just as happiness associated with a set of wooden blocks depends not only on the quantity of blocks, but also on how these blocks are combined. Second, consumers commit systematic errors in their judgment of the relationship between external stimuli and happiness and often fail to maximize happiness, just as children do not always know how to combine the blocks they own to build the most enjoyable project,

In summary, our discussion about hedonomics revolves around two main topics: one concerning the relationship between external stimuli and happiness and the other concerning the relationship between choice and happiness. In the rest of the chapter we review existing research pertaining to these topics in turn. We wish to note that our review is illustrative rather than exhaustive and it examines primarily the behavioral decision theory literature. We focus on new developments rather than classic materials already familiar to the reader and we focus on research that considers happiness as momentary experience with specific stimuli rather than retrospective evaluation of a past consumption experience or overall satisfaction with life (see Kahneman & Riis, 2005; Kahneman et al., 2004a; Kahneman et al., 2004b; for a discussion of these two approaches). Likewise, when we say failure to maximize happiness, we mean failure to maximize momentary experience; it may not be a failure if other standards are used. Much of this chapter is based on an early version of Hsee and Hastie (in press). The words "happiness" and "experience" will be used interchangeably throughout the chapter.

EXTERNAL STIMULI AND HAPPINESS

In this section we review select literatures on relationships between external stimuli and experience. We examine five topics: (1) gains and losses, (2) evaluation mode and evaluability, (3) temporal factors, (4) option effect, and (5) cognition utilities.

Gain and Losses

Kahneman and Tversky's (1979) influential prospect theory was originally proposed to describe choice under risk. Nevertheless the theory also has important implications for consumption experience with riskless external stimuli. These implications can be briefly summarized as follows. First, one's experience with an external stimulus depends not on its absolute magnitude, but on the difference between the absolute magnitude and some reference point. A positive difference is a gain and evokes a positive experience, whereas a negative difference is a loss and evokes a negative experience. Second, the negative experience evoked by a loss is more intense than the positive experience evoked by a gain of the same magnitude—a principle termed *loss aversion*. Expressed in terms of a utility (value) function, where the x-axis denotes the external stimulus (gain or loss) and the y-axis denotes one's experience with the stimulus, loss aversion implies that the utility function is steeper in the loss domain than in the gain domain (see the solid curve in Figure 25.1). Finally, consumers are less sensitive to incremental changes in gains or losses as gains or losses accumulate. This principle implies that the utility function is concave on the gain side and convex on the loss side (see the solid curve in Figure 25.1).

Building on prospect theory and mental accounting (Thaler, 1980, 1985, 1999; Thaler & Johnson, 1990), Thaler (1985) proposed a set of happiness-maximizing strategies, which he termed "hedonic editing."

Strategy 1: If a consumer has two good events to enjoy (e.g., dining out with a charming friend and watching a favorite video), she should enjoy them on separate occasions, because multiple gains will yield greater total happiness if they are experienced separately than if they are experienced as one aggregate gain (due to concavity of the utility function in the gain domain).

Strategy 2: If a consumer has to experience two bad events (e.g., seeing a dentist and seeing a nagging aunt), it is better to experience them in close proximity, because multiple losses will yield less total pain if they are experienced as one integrated loss than if they are experienced separately (due to convexity of the utility function in the loss domain).

Strategy 3: If a consumer has a big bad event and a small good event to experience, she should experience them separately, because the utility function in the gain domain is concave and the utility of a separate small gain can exceed the utility of a reduction from a large loss.

Strategy 4: If a consumer has a small bad event and a big good event to experience, she should experience them in close proximity, because the utility function is convex in the loss domain, losses are experienced more intensely than gains. Thus, the negative utility of a separate small loss can exceed the negative utility of a reduction from a large gain.

Recent research has also identified important moderators for loss aversion. Novemsky and Kahneman (2005a, 2005b) propose that intentions to give up a good in exchange for another can moderate loss aversion for that good as intentions can determine the reference point against which outcomes are evaluated. If the exchange is intended to improve the status quo, people might focus on the benefits of the good they intend to acquire instead of obsessing about the good or money they intend to give up (Ariely, Huber, & Wertenbroch, 2005; Carmon & Ariely, 2000).

The intensions account can also explain the findings that when consumers have decided to sell an item, their asking price primarily depends on market price (which is usually lower than the asking price for sellers in classic endowment effect studies; Simonson & Drolet, 2004). Thus, consumers might be able to reduce anticipated negative experiences associated with losses if they focus on the benefits of the exchange.

Another plausible moderator of loss aversion is emotional attachment (Ariely et al., 2005; Ariely & Simonson, 2003; Carmon, Wertenbroch, & Zeelenberg, 2003; Strahilevitz & Loewenstein, 1998). Ariely and his colleagues (2005) propose that consumers become more reluctant to give up items increases as they anticipate negative utility associated with losses to increase. On the other hand, Novemsky and Kahneman (2005b) suggest that intentions can help break emotional attachment and reduce the discomfort of giving up items.

The emotional attachment account can explain the results in Dhar and Wertenbroch (2000). They show that consumers are less willing to give up hedonic than utilitarian items. The findings suggest that the intentions can more effectively reduce the loss associated with utilitarian items than hedonic items and perhaps the intentions to exchange are not sufficient to offset consumers' emotional attachment for hedonic items. On a related note, ambiguity of status quo might also reduce loss aversion given that the reference point is not as rigid and thus consumers are not as attached to such status quo.

Quantity and Value

Most utility theories assume that more of a desired stimulus is always better. For example, an airline passenger will always be happier if she receives 3000 bonus miles than if she receives 2000 bonus miles. Is this assumption true? Recent research (Hsee & Zhang, 2004; Hsee et al., 1999; Hsee, 1996) suggests that whether consumers are sensitive to the magnitude (for example, amount, quantity, duration, probability, or mileage) associated with a stimulus depends on at least two factors, evaluation mode and the evaluability of the relevant attribute.

What is evaluation mode? The evaluation of any stimuli proceeds in one or some combination of two modes: joint evaluation (JE) and single evaluation (SE). In JE, two or more stimuli are juxtaposed and evaluated comparatively. For example, if a passenger receives two sets of bonus miles from two airlines, she is in JE of these two sets of bonuses. Under SE, only one stimulus is present and evaluated in isolation, for example, a passenger receives only one set of bonus miles at a time.

Evaluation mode, JE or SE, can affect the utility function of the relevant attribute. Under JE, the utility function is relatively linear and steep, as depicted by the solid curve in Figure 25.1. In this case, consumers can directly compare different values on the attribute. As long as they know which direction is better, they will feel happier with the more desirable value.

In SE, however, the shape of the utility function will depend on another factor—evaluability. The evaluability of an attribute refers to the extent to which consumers can evaluate the desirability of any value on the attribute when the value is presented alone. The same attribute can be evaluable for one consumer but inevaluable for another. The more familiar a consumer is with the attribute in terms of its range, distribution, and other reference information, the more evaluable the attribute is to that consumer.

When evaluability is low, the utility function in SE will resemble a step function, steep around zero (or the neutral reference point) and flat elsewhere, as illustrated by dashed curve in Figure 25.1. For example, the number of bonus miles is a low-evaluability attribute for people who rarely receive bonus miles and do not know the range and distribution of such bonuses. They will be happy if they receive any, but will be relatively insensitive to how much they receive.

When evaluability is high, the utility function in SE will resemble the more linear JE function (the solid curve in Figure 25.1). For example, the number of bonus miles is a high-evaluability attribute for passengers who often receive such miles and know their range and distribution. They will be happier the more miles they receive.

In summary, in JE, the utility function is relatively linear regardless of evaluability of a relevant attribute. In SE, the shape of the utility function depends on the evaluability of the attribute. The less evaluable the attribute, the more the utility function resembles a step function. For recent stud-

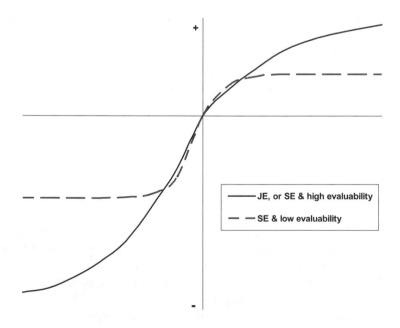

Figure 25.1   A conceptual illustration of utility functions of a relevant attribute in JE vs. SE.

ies on evaluability and related topics, see Hsee, Rottenstreich, & Xiao, 2005; Kunreuther, Novemsky, & Kahneman, 2001; Posavac et al., 2004, 2005; Yeung & Soman, 2005.

Life often presents itself in SE. For example, most passengers do not receive multiple sets of bonus miles at the same time. Furthermore, consumers do not have much information about the range and distribution of most product attributes. Thus, more of a good thing does not necessarily make consumers happier.

The analysis in this section provides a novel explanation for three common findings from the happiness literature. First, across generations where real income increases, people's happiness does not increase (e.g., Diener & Biswas-Diener, 2002; Easterlin, 1995). This finding is often attributed to hedonic adaptation, as we will review later. However, the phenomenon may arise simply because cross-generation comparison is a matter of SE, and absolute wealth is difficult to evaluate independently. As illustrated previously, passengers receiving 3,000 bonus miles are not going to be happier than passengers receiving 2,000 bonus miles if they do not compare the awards and if they are not familiar with the distribution or range of such promotions. Similarly, people in the 1980s with an annual income of $30,000 probably did not feel happier than people in the 1960s with an annual income of $20,000. It may not have anything to do with hedonic adaptation or treadmill effects. Although people in the 1980s may occasionally compare their wealth with that of their previous generations, so would people in the 1960s. Because each generation is wealthier than their previous generation, such comparisons would make both generations happy but not make them differentially happy.

Second, across income levels within a society at a given time, the wealthy are happier than the poor, although the correlation between wealth and happiness is not strong (e.g., Diener & Biswas-Diener, 2002; Frey & Stutzer, 2002a; Easterlin, 2001). Why? That may arise because within a society, people may sometimes, though not always, engage in JE, and therefore there is some, but not strong, correlation. Advertisements, "status exhibitions," rob people's noses in JE; differences in products, life style, remind everyone how relatively low they are (e.g., Frank, 2000; Frank & Cook, 1996).

Finally, people almost always prefer more money and believe they would be happier with greater amount of wealth (Campbell, 1981). That is because such preferences and beliefs are usually elicited in JE (comparing more wealth with less), and in JE the utility function is linear.

Time and Distribution

Many things consumers care about change over time. If a stimulus one cares about changes, for example, moving from a small apartment to larger unit, one will first experience a positive feeling and with the passage of time the elevated feeling will fade away. This is hedonic adaptation.

A landmark study by Brickman, Coates, and Janoff-Bulman (1978) suggests that people may even adapt to extreme changes in life such as permanent loss of limbs in a car accident and winning large sums of money from a state lottery (see similar results by Schulz & Decker, 1985). For more recent work on hedonic adaptation, see research on marriage by Lucas et al. (2003) and on health by Riis et al. (2005).

Hedonic adaptation occurs for multiple reasons. One is basic psychophysical adaptation (Helson, 1964): the longer we are exposed to a stimulus, the less sensitive we feel about it. For example, when a person first immerses her hand in 50 degree water, she will feel cold. After a while she will adapt to the temperature and no longer find the water cold. Another reason for hedonic adaptation is dilution of attention. For example, after a person moves to large apartment from a smaller place, she will first be overjoyed with the extra size, but before long, her attention will shift away from the house to many other things, such as her crying baby and her nagging husband. As a result, the size of her new apartment is just one of the myriad events that cause the ups and downs of her life. A third reason for hedonic adaptation is what Wilson, Meyers, and Gilbert (2003) refer to as "ordinization." Once an affective event happens, consumers have a tendency to rationalize it, make it seem ordinary, and thereby dampen its affective impact. This can happen to both positive and negative events. For example, if a bidder won an auction for a painting on eBay, he might think to himself, "It's no surprise. I bid a lot." If he was outbid, he might justify the loss by thinking, "It was not a very good painting anyway."

Hedonic adaptation occurs mostly when the new state remains stable, for example, when a person remains in the new apartment after moving or a person remains paralyzed after an accident. However, many events we care about constantly change over time, for example, gas price, stock price, or body weight. How do people react to such ongoing changes?

First, our momentary experience with such ongoing changes depends on the direction of the change, positive if the change is in the desirable direction and negative if the change is in the unwanted direction (e.g., Ariely & Zauberman, 2003; Diehl & Zauberman, 2005; Loewenstein & Prelec, 1993). Moreover, our momentary experience also depends on the rate of change, or velocity (Hsee & Abelson, 1991) in that we feel happier the faster a positive change, and feel less unhappy the slower a negative change. The velocity notion has received support from both lab experiments (e.g., Baumgartner, Sujan, & Padgett, 1997; Hsee & Abelson 1991) and field data (e.g., Clark, 1999). Finally, our momentary experience with an ongoing change may also depend on changes in velocity (Hsee, Salovey, & Abelson, 1994). In sum, consumers adapt to states and react to changes. They react more the faster the change, and they react not only to the rate of change, but also to changes in the rate.

Another factor that influences consumers' experience with a series of events over time is the distribution of the events. The distribution can be positively skewed, or negatively skewed. For example, suppose the quality of wines is proportional to their prices and there are two consumers. One drinks a $15 wine on most days and drinks a $30 wine occasionally, whereas the other drinks a $25 wine on most days and drinks a $10 wine occasionally. The average cost of the wines is $20 for both individuals. Here, the former situation is an example of a positively skewed distribution, and the latter an example of a negatively skewed distribution. Decades of research by Parducci and his coauthors (Parducci, 1965, 1995; Wedell & Parducci, 1988) suggests that the negatively-skewed distribution case creates a better consumption experience overall than the positively-skewed distribution case, because in the negative skewness condition the infrequent experiences of the $10 wine enhance his more frequent experiences of the $25 wine, whereas in the positive skewness condition the infrequent experiences of the $30 wine hurts his more frequent experiences of the $15 wine. The moral of this body of research is that consumers should arrange their consumption experiences in a negatively skewed distribution to maximize happiness (see Zhang & Hsee, 2006 for a different view on this topic.)

Choice and Options

Many believe that having a choice is always better than not having one and having more choices is always better than having fewer. In reality, neither of these beliefs is true (Schwartz, 2004). Research by Botti and Iyengar (2004) shows that if consumers have to experience one of several undesirable options, they will feel less unhappy if someone else makes the choice for them than if they have to make the choice themselves. For example, a consumer who is on diet and can only eat meals that are unappealing to her would feel better if someone else chooses the meal for her than if she has to make a choice herself, because making a choice among unappealing meals induces negative feelings.

Iyengar and Lepper (2000) demonstrate that if people make the choice themselves, they will be less satisfied with their choice if they have many options to choose from than if they have only a few options to choose from. Too many options can be demotivating because they are too complex and involve too many tradeoffs for consumers to manage. For example, shoppers were less happy with the chocolate they chose if they had 30 truffles to choose from than if they had only 6 options.

Actually, simply having more than one option can reduce happiness (Hsee & Leclerc, 1998). They show that if consumers are presented with one good option, they will be happy, but if they are presented with two good options, they will notice the disadvantages of each option relative to the other and will be less happy with either option. For example, if a consumer wins a free trip to Paris, she will be happy; if she wins a free trip to Hawaii, she will also be happy. But if the consumer wins a free trip and has to choose between Paris and Hawaii, she may be less happy, because each option contains shortcomings compared with the other: Paris does not have Waikiki Beach, and Hawaii does not have Louvre.

Finally, research by Carmon et al. (2003) shows that consumers will be less happy with their decision if they closely consider the options available to them than if they do not. In most cases a consumer can choose only one of the available options and has to forego the other options. Close deliberations can prompt consumers to form an emotional attachment to all the options, including those they have to forego. Thus, choosing one feels like losing the others to which they already have emotional attachment.

Cognition Utilities

Imagine that a person participated in a sweepstakes a month ago. She was just informed that she had won a 3-day vacation in Paris. What is the utility of this trip to her? Intuitively, one would say that the utility is the happiness she derives from the vacation. That can be referred to as *consumption utility*. But besides that, she experiences three other types of utilities: news utility—the feeling she experiences upon hearing the news that she won the vacation, anticipation utility—the feeling she experiences when anticipating for the trip, and memory utility—the feeling she experiences when recalling the trip after she is back home.

In a recent pilot study on news utility, students were prompted to report their momentary experiences five times during a class (Hsee). The first time was about 15 minutes into the class without any particular events (which established the baseline of happiness). The second time was immediately after the instructor announced that he would give each student a KitKat candy bar to eat later in the class; it measured news utility. The third time was about 10 minutes after the announcement of the news; it measured anticipation utility. The fourth time was right after the students had received the chocolate candy and were eating it; it measured consumption utility. The last time was some 10 minutes after the consumption; it measured memory utility. Compared with the baseline, the students reported the greatest happiness when they heard the news, followed by when they ate the chocolate candy, and lastly when they anticipated and recalled the consumption. We want to highlight two implications of the study. First, it shows the existence of news utility, besides consumption, anticipation, and memory utilities. Second, it shows the possibility for news to generate even greater happiness than consumption.

Compared with news utility, anticipation utility has been well documented in the literature (e.g., Bentham, 1789; Loewenstein, 1987; O'Curry & Strahilevitz, 2001; Prelec & Loewenstein, 1998; Shiv & Huber, 2000). In an ingenious study on anticipation utility (Loewenstein, 1987), respondents were asked to indicate how much they were willing to pay for receiving a kiss from their favorite movie star immediately, in three hours, or in three days. According to traditional discounted utility theory, people should be willing to pay more for the immediate kiss than for the delayed kisses, because experiences in the future are discounted and their appeal diminish. However, Loewenstein found that respondents were willing to pay more for receiving the kiss in three days than receiving it immediately or in three hours. Presumably, waiting for the kiss brings happiness.

Waiting, however, can also cause negative emotions such as anxiety and stress. The net effect of the anticipated pleasure and frustrations of waiting depends on the familiarity with the consumption event and the vividness of the imagined consumption experience (Nowlis, Mandel, & McCabe, 2004). If a consumer has never visited a restaurant, she will experience less anticipated pleasure than someone who has been or who actually sits in the restaurant and waits for her dinner to be served while watching other patrons enjoy their meal.

Memory utility is another important cognition utility. Memory of past events can influence happiness in two ways (Elster & Loewenstein, 1992). First, consumers may relive a positive (vs. negative) experience from their past and derive positive (versus negative) utility when recalling the past (consumption effect). For example, a person can derive pleasure by recalling the details about her last trip to Paris. Second, past experience can create a contrast effect or an assimilation effect on one's current experience. Which effect will dominate depends on the context (Tversky & Griffin, 1990). If the past event is similar to the current event (e.g., a fancy French dinner vs. a mediocre French dinner), the past experience will create a contrast effect. If the past event is dissimilar to the present event (e.g., a fancy French dinner vs. a mediocre movie), it will create an assimilation effect.

Intuitively, the primary source of happiness that a desirable stimulus (e.g., a chocolate bar or a vacation) brings is the consumption of the stimulus, whereas news, anticipation and memory are all secondary. In reality, cognition utilities may comprise a large portion of the happiness from the stimulus and sometimes even larger than that of consumption utility. This is especially true if one integrates these cognition utilities over time and compares the sum (temporal integral) with the sum (temporal integral) of the consumption utility. For example, the sum of the temporally-integrated happiness from hearing the news that one has won a free 3-day trip to Paris, from anticipating the visit and from recalling the visit for the rest of one's life may well exceed the temporally-integrated happiness from the 3-day trip per se. What our Kitkat example shows is that sometimes even momentary (not-integrated) news utility may exceed momentary consumption utility.

Consumption utility is like a light source, and cognition utility is like its halo. Without the light source, there will be no halo. But with the light source, the halo may be brighter than the source itself.

Summary

To build a good wooden block project, it requires sufficient blocks. But simply adding blocks is not sufficient; it also requires proper combinations. Similarly, to create happiness, it requires sufficient wealth. But simply increasing wealth is not sufficient; it also requires an understanding of the relationships between wealth and happiness. The literatures we just reviewed are about these relationships.

DECISION AND HAPPINESS

The first part of this chapter reviews select literatures on the relationships between external stimuli and happiness. The second part of this chapter reviews literatures on the ability of consumers to understand such relationships and make choices that maximize happiness.

Decades of behavioral decision research suggests that consumers often fail to maximize happiness. This failure can be attributed to one of two general reasons (Kahneman, 1994). First, consumers fail to accurately predict which option will bring them the best experience. Second, even if they could make accurate predictions, consumers may fail to base their choices on such predictions. In this section, we review eight specific reasons why consumers fail to maximize happiness: The first four are related to failure to make accurate predictions and the last four are related to failure to follow predictions about consumption experience.

Impact Bias

When asked to predict the experiential consequence of an event (e.g., moving to a larger apartment), consumers often ignore the power of adaptation and thereby overpredict the duration and the intensity of the experience (Buehler & McFarland, 2001; Wilson et al., 2000). Gilbert, Driver-Linn, and Wilson (2002) refer to this type of misprediction as impact bias (see also Wilson & Gilbert, 2003).

Impact bias can be attributed to two reasons. One is neglect of ordinization. As we reviewed earlier, when an emotion-triggering event happens, people will make sense of it and make the event seem ordinary (Wilson et al., 2003). Yet most people underestimate this ordinization effect.

Another reason for impact bias is focalism, that is, consumers pay too much attention to the focal event, overlook the dilution-of-attention effect (as we reviewed earlier), and thereby overestimate the affective impact of the focal event (e.g., Buehler & McFarland, 2001; Schkade & Kahneman, 1998; Wilson et al., 2000). For example, when predicting how much happier one will be if she moves from a smaller apartment to a larger one, she focuses her attention on the size dimension, but once she moves to the larger apartment, size is just one of many things that affect her life.

Distinction Bias

A recent graduate who currently lives in a 500-square-foot studio without indoor parking has found a job and has two options for housing, one a 1,250-square-foot apartment with indoor parking and the other a 1,500-square-foot apartment without indoor parking (rent is the same for both options). In comparison he notices the clear difference in size between the two options and predicts himself to be happier by living in the bigger apartment despite the lack of indoor parking so he chooses the bigger place. Is his choice the optimal decision? Probably not. In reality, he may well be happier if he rents the smaller apartment, because the difference between 1,250 and 1,500 square feet may make less of a difference in his day-to-day consumption (living) experience than the difference between having and having no indoor parking. As the example illustrates, when making a choice, the person overpredicts the difference in experience generated by two apparently distinct values on a particular dimension (in this case square footage). We refer to this prediction bias as the distinction bias.

The distinction bias arises because consumers are in different evaluation modes during prediction versus consumption. Predictions are often made in JE, and consumption often takes place in SE (Hsee & Zhang, 2004). For instance, prospective house buyers typically compare alternative homes in JE and predict their experiences. When they actually live in a home, they experience that place alone in SE. (Although people may occasionally think of the foregone alternatives, their predominant mode of evaluation during consumption is still SE.)

As we reviewed in the first part of this article, one's utility function of an attribute differs between JE and SE. In JE, the utility function is relatively linear and steep. In SE, the utility function is steep around the neutral reference point and flat elsewhere, and this tendency is more pronounced the less evaluable the attribute is (the dashed curve in Figure 25.1). Thus, during predictions consumers will generally follow the JE utility function (the solid curve in Figure 25.1) and be sensitive to variables in any part of the attribute range. But during consumption, consumers will follow the SE function (see Figure 25.1) and be sensitive to variations near zero (or the neutral reference point) on the attribute.

The analysis above leads to a simple theory about when consumers overpredict and when they don't. If two options differ near zero (or the neutral reference point) on the relevant attribute, they will not overpredict. If two options differ farther on the attribute, they will overpredict. For example, suppose that the person mentioned above uses his current apartment size—500 square feet—as his neutral reference point. Then he will be relatively accurate when predicting the difference in happiness between living in a 600-square-foot apartment and a 1,000-square-foot apartment, but less accurate when predicting the difference in happiness between living in a 1,250-square-foot apartment and living in a 1,500-square-foot apartment. In addition, he will be relatively accurate in predicting the difference in happiness between having no indoor parking (the status quo, which is usually one's reference point) and having indoor parking. If consumers do not realize the distinction bias, they may sacrifice things that are actually important to their consumption experience (e.g., the availability of indoor parking) for things that are not as important (e.g., the difference between 1,250 and 1,500 square feet).

Belief Bias

Mispredictions about consumption experience may also result from consumers' inaccurate lay theories concerning relationships between external stimuli and happiness (e.g., Kahneman & Snell, 1992; Novemsky & Ratner, 2003; Robinson & Clore, 2002; Snell, Gibbs, & Varey, 1995). Consumers may expect adaptation or satiation when it does not exist (e.g., Brickman, Coates, & Janoff-Bulman, 1978; Frederick & Loewenstein, 1999; Kahneman, 2000; Loewenstein & Schkade, 1999). For example, students believed that their liking for their favorite ice cream would decrease if they had it every day, but in reality their liking did not decrease as much as predicted (Kahneman & Snell, 1992).

Consumers may also overpredict contrast effect. For example, students believed that eating a tasty jellybean would reduce the enjoyment of a not-so-tasty jellybean. In fact, such contrast effects did not occur (Novemsky & Ratner, 2003). Consumers may also hold beliefs inconsistent with hedonomic editing. As we reviewed earlier, the diminishing-marginal-sensitivity notion suggests that people who have to experience multiple bad outcomes should experience them on one occasion, but most people prefer to experience them on separate occasions, believing that one bad outcome will make them more sensitive to another bad outcome if they are encountered together (Thaler, 1999).

Another common belief is that more options are always better. As we reviewed earlier, this belief is not true. Whether more options are better depends on the size of the choice set (Iyengar & Lepper, 2000), the mode of evaluation (Hsee & Leclerc, 1998), and the level of involvement (Carmon et al., 2003). A related common belief is that having the right to choose makes people happier than having someone else make the choice for them. Again, as we discussed earlier, this belief is not true for choosing among undesirable alternatives (Botti & Iyengar, 2004).

Projection Bias

Consumers often find themselves in different visceral (arousal) states (Loewenstein, 1996). Sometimes they are rested, satiated, or sexually unaroused; other times they are tired, hungry, or aroused. When consumers in one visceral state predict the experiences in another visceral state for themselves or others, they often commit a systematic error by projecting their current state into their predictions (Loewenstein, O'Donoghue, & Rabin, 2003; see also Loewenstein, 1996; Van Boven, Dunning, & Loewenstein, 2000; Van Boven & Loewenstein, 2003). For example, if a person is full now, she will underestimate how much she will enjoy her next meal when she is hungry again.

Projection bias can render important behavioral consequences. For example, hungry shoppers at a grocery store may buy more items than they need (Nisbett & Kanouse, 1969) and have planned to buy, unless they are reminded of their grocery list (Gilbert, Gill, & Wilson, 2002). A currently hungry person may choose a candy bar over an apple for a future consumption occasion on which she will be full, only to find that she actually prefers the apple when that moment comes (e.g., Read & van Leeuwen, 1998).

Rule-Based Choice

To choose the experientially optimal option, consumers not only need to accurately predict their future experience, but also need to base their choice on predicted experience. We have already discussed when consumers fail to accurately predict their future experiences. We will now discuss when they fail to follow predicted experience. In decision making consumers may base their choice on many other factors than predicted experience.

One such factor is decision rules (e.g., Prelec & Herrnstein, 1991; March, 1994; Simonson, 1989; Simonson & Nowlis, 2000). Decision rules come into being because they simplify decisions and they lead to optimal consequences under certain circumstances. Nevertheless, once these rules are internalized, people overapply these rules to circumstances that these rules do not lead to experientially optimal choices.

Examples of such decision rules include "seek variety or diversification" (e.g., Fox, Ratner, & Lieb, 2005; Simonson, 1990; Benartzi & Thaler, 2001; Ratner, Kahn, & Kahneman, 1999), "waste not" (e.g., Arkes & Ayton, 1999; Arkes & Blumer, 1985), "don't pay for delays" (Amir & Ariely, 2007), to name just a few.

For example, consumers may intuitively recognize the importance of anticipation utility and predict greater happiness from a concert that will take place in a week than a similar concert that will take place tonight, yet they are not willing to pay extra for the concert in a week, presumably because they want to adhere to the "don't pay for delays" rule (Amir & Ariely, in press).

Variety-seeking can also lead to an inconsistency between predicted experience and decision. In one of the original studies on variety-seeking, Simonson (1990) asked one group of students to make simultaneous choices of candies for future consumption occasions, and another group of students to make sequential choices of candies right before each consumption occasion. Most simultaneous choosers asked for a variety of snacks, but most sequential choosers asked only for their favorite snack repeatedly. What is more interesting about this study is that in a third group participants were in the same position as the simultaneous choosers and were asked to predict their future consumption experiences. They predicted better feelings with low variety than with high variety. This suggests that the simultaneous choosers were able to predict, if asked, that low variety would yield better experience, yet the rule of variety-seeking prevailed.

In another study on variety-seeking, Ratner and her coauthors (1999) asked participants to construct a song-sequence from one of two sets of songs. One set contains more songs than the other, but the additional songs were less enjoyable. They found that those who were given the larger set constructed sequences with greater variety but enjoyed them less. In a study on variety-seeking in a group context, Ariely and Levav (2000) found that diners tend to order different items than what their friends choose even though they will enjoy the items less.

Similarly, the "waste not" rule can also lead consumers to forego options that they predict more enjoyable and choose the less enjoyable one. Arkes and Blumer (1985) asked participants to imagine that they had purchased a $100 ticket for a weekend ski trip to Michigan and a $50 ticket for a weekend ski trip to Wisconsin. They later found out that the two trips were for the same weekend and had to pick one to use. Although the participants were told that the trip to Wisconsin was more enjoyable, the majority of them chose the more expensive trip to Michigan.

Lay Rationalism

Besides the specific rules we discussed above, consumers have a general tendency to resist immediate affective influence and base their choice on factors they consider "rational" (e.g., Hsee, 1999; Okada, 2005; Shafir, Simonson, & Tversky, 1993). This tendency is termed *lay rationalism* in Hsee et al. (2003b). Lay rationalism manifests itself in different forms. One is *lay economism*—the tendency to base decision on the financial aspects of the options and ignore other happiness-relevant factors. In a study by Hsee et al. (2003b), participants were given a choice between two sets of free dinners, four in each set. The dinners were to be consumed in the following four weeks. In one set, the dinners increased in value (original price) over the 4-week period and the total value was relatively lower. In the other set, the dinners decreased in value over the period and the total value was relatively higher. Participants predicted greater enjoyment from consuming the temporally-increasing set of dinners, yet they chose the set with the greater value in total.

Another manifestation of lay rationalism is *lay scientism*, a tendency to base decision on "hard" (objective and quantitative) attributes rather than "soft" (subjective and hard-to-quantify) attributes. In a study that tested lay scientism (Hsee et al., 2003b), participants were given a choice between two fictitious stereo systems, one having more power and the other having a richer sound. For half of the participants, power was described as an objective wattage rating and sound richness as a subjective experience. For the other half, power was described as a subjective experience and sound richness as an objective quantitative rating. When power was framed as objective, more participants chose the more-powerful stereo than they predicted they would enjoy it more. When sound richness was framed as objective, more participants chose the richer-sounding stereo than they predicted they would enjoy it more. In other words, the objectivity/subjectivity manipulation had a greater influence on choice than on predicted experience. This finding corroborates the notion that consumers base their choice not purely on predicted experience, but also on what they consider "rational," in this case, objective.

Impulsivity

We define an impulsive choice as choosing an option that yields a better short-term (immediate) experience over an option that yields a better long-term (immediate plus future) experience. For example, eating fatty food may produce better short-term enjoyment than eating healthy food, but it may cause obesity and other health-related problems in the long run. Thus, eating fatty food rather than healthy food can be considered an impulsive choice.

Consumers sometimes behave impulsively because they mispredict its consequences. For example, some people eat fatty foods, because they underpredict the negative consequences in the future. But more often than not, consumers commit impulsive behavior even though they are keenly aware of its aversive consequence, and they simply cannot resist the temptation (e.g., Kivetz & Simonson,

2002b; Loewenstein, 1996; Thaler & Shefrin, 1981). For example, many substance abusers are fully aware that drugs are ruining their lives and may even warn their friends to stay away from drugs, but they cannot resist the craving. In other words, impulsive choosers fail to base their choice on what they predict will bring them the best overall experience. Here, overall experience refers to long-term experience, i.e., the sum of immediate and future experiences.

Impulsive behavior is an extensively studied topic (e.g., Ainslie, 2001; Ariely & Wertenbroch, 2002; Baumeister & Heatherton, 1996; Baumeister & Vohs, 2004; Cheema & Soman, 2006; Kardes, Cronley, & Kim, 2006; Kivetz & Simonson, 2002a ; Prelec & Herrnsten, 1991; Schelling, 1980, 1984; Thaler, 1980; Thaler & Sherfrin, 1981; Trope & Liberman, 2003), and it is beyond the scope of this chapter to review this rich literature. However, we want to suggest a relationship between impulsive behavior and rule-based decisions.

So far we have reviewed impulsivity and rules-based-decisions as two unrelated topics. Yet they are inherently related. Most decision rules are antidotes to impulsivity and are self-control mechanisms. For example, consumers adopting the "waste not" rule may consciously or unconsciously want to preserve their savings so as not to suffer financially in the long run. In some cases, not wasting now can indeed serve that purpose and sometimes it cannot. The problem is that most consumers do not sufficiently distinguish these two types of cases and act too impulsively in the first case but overly apply the rule in the second.

For example, consider a college student who plans to travel in Europe for one week. She can travel within Europe either by train or by air. She thought traveling by air is more fun, so she paid $1,000 for a one-week air pass. Once in Europe, she realizes that traveling by train is more fun. She does not have much savings; if she spends more on the trip, she will not have enough money to go to school and finish college next semester. Consider two alternative scenarios. In Scenario 1, she does not have a train pass and to travel by train she will have to pay extra and cannot graduate next semester, an outcome that potentially lowers her well-being in the long run. In Scenario 2, she has a free train pass from a friend and traveling by train will not affect her graduation date. Normatively, she should travel by air in Scenario 1 and by train in Scenario 2. In reality she may not do differently in these scenarios; she may travel partially by train and partially by air in both scenarios. In Scenario 1, she travels partially by train because she wants to enjoy the train ride now even though doing so will deplete her savings for college and potentially lower her long-term well-being. This behavior can be considered impulsive. In Scenario 2, she travels partially by air because she does not want to waste the $1,000 air pass she already paid for. This behavior is an example of sunk cost fallacy, which is an overapplication of the "waste not" rule. This example illustrates that the same behavior, namely, traveling partially by train and partially by air, can be considered as either too impulsive or too rule-abiding, depending on the situation.

Medium Maximization

When people exert effort to obtain a desired outcome, the immediate reward they receive is usually not the outcome per se, but a medium—an instrument that they can trade for the desired outcome (e.g., Kivetz & Simonson, 2002a; van Osselaer, Alba, & Manchanda, 2004). For example, points for consumer loyalty programs and mileage for frequent flyer programs are both media.

In decisions involving a medium, consumers may maximize the medium rather than their predicted experiences with the ultimate outcomes (Hsee et al., 2003a). In an experiment designed to test the effect of media, respondents were given a choice between a shorter task which would award them 60 points or a larger task which would award them 100 points. Respondents were told that with 60 points they could get a serving of vanilla ice cream and with 100 points they could get the same amount of pistachio ice cream. Most respondents chose to work on the long task. However, when asked which type of ice cream they preferred or which type of task they preferred, most favored the vanilla ice cream and short task. It seems that the presence of a medium led the respondents to work more and enjoy less.

Normatively, when people exert effort to achieve a certain final outcome, they should ignore media and choose the option that yields the best consumption experience for every unit of effort they pay. In reality, people often choose the option that yields the greatest amount of media for every unit of effort they pay. According to Hsee et al. (2003a), people pursue media, because the media provide an illusion of certainty, an illusion of advantage or an illusion of a simple linear relationship between effort and reward.

Research on medium maximization has implications not only for consumer behavior, but for life in general. Besides survival, the ultimate objective of working is happiness. Yet when people work, the immediate reward is not happiness, but a medium, money. Instead of maximizing the work-to-happiness return, many people simply maximize the work-to-dollar return.

Decision rules, lay rationalism, impulses and media are only four examples of factors that can lead consumers to choose a different option than what has the best predicted future experience. Other than these factors, consumers may also base their choice on their gut feelings toward the options they face (e.g., Slovic et al., 2002) or on the inferences they make from their feelings (e.g., Pham, 2004). Like the other factors, gut feelings and feeling-inferred cognitions may differ from predicted future experience and may lead to experientially suboptimal choices.

Summary

To create a good wooden-block project, the child needs to accurately predict what a project will look like if he combines the blocks in a particular way and combine the blocks based on his predictions. Likewise, to pursue happiness, consumers need to accurately predict the affective consequences of their options and make their choices based on their predictions. The literatures we just reviewed examine when and why consumers fail to make accurate affective predictions or when and why they fail to act upon their predictions.

CONCLUSION

Hedonomics challenges two commonly held, often tacit assumptions in traditional economics—(1) that maximizing desired external stimuli (including goods and services) approximates maximizing consumer happiness and (2) that what consumers choose reflects what makes them happy. Correspondingly, hedonomics studies two topics—(1) how external stimuli actually affect consumers' happiness and (2) why and when consumers fail to maximize their happiness. A better understanding of these topics can potentially increase consumer happiness without expending more financial resources.

REFERENCES

Ainslie, G. (2001). *Breakdown of will.* New York: Cambridge University Press.

Amir, O., & Ariely, D. (2007). Decisions by rules: The case of unwillingness to pay for beneficial delays. *Journal of Marketing Research, 44,* 142–152.

Ariely, D., Huber, J., & Wertenbroch, K. (2005). When do losses loom larger than gains? *Journal of Marketing Research, 42,* 134–138.

Ariely, D., & Levav, J. (2000). Sequential choice in group settings: Taking the road less traveled and less enjoyed. *Journal of Consumer Research, 27,* 279–290.

Ariely, D., & Simonson, I. (2003). Buying, bidding, playing, or competing? Value assessment and decision dynamics in online auctions. *Journal of Consumer Psychology, 13*, 113–123.

Ariely, D., & Wertenbroch, K. (2002). Procrastination, deadlines, and performance: Self-control by precommitment. *Psychological Science, 13*, 219–224.

Ariely, D., & Zauberman, G. (2003). Differential partitioning of extended experiences. *Organizational Behavior and Human Decision Processes, 91*, 128–139.

Arkes, H. R., & Ayton, P. (1999). The sunk cost and Concorde effects: Are humans less rational than lower animals? *Psychological Bulletin, 125*, 591–600.

Arkes, H. R., & Blumer, C. (1985). The psychology of sunk cost. *Organizational Behavior and Human Decision Processes, 35*, 124–140.

Baumgartner, H., Sujan, M., & Padgett (1997). Patterns of affective reactions to advertisements: The integration of moment-to-moment responses. *Journal of Marketing Research, 34*, 219–232.

Baumeister, R. F., & Heatherton, T. F. (1996). Self-regulation failure: An overview. *Psychological Inquiry, 1*, 1–15.

Baumeister, R. F., & Vohs, K. D (Eds). (2004). *Handbook of self-regulation: Research, theory and applications.* New York: Guilford.

Benartzi, S., & Thaler, R.H. (2001). Naïve diversification strategies in defined contribution savings plans. *American Economic Review, 91*, 79–98.

Bentham, J. (1789; reprinted 1948). *An Introduction to the principles of morals and legislations.* Oxford: Blackwell.

Botti, S. & Iyengar, S. S. (2004). The psychological pleasure and pain of choosing: When people prefer choosing at the cost of subsequent outcome satisfaction. *Journal of Personality and Social Psychology, 87*, 312–326.

Brickman, P., Coates, D., & Janoff-Bulman, R. (1978). Lottery winners and accident victims: Is happiness relative? *Journal of Personality and Social Psychology, 36*, 917–927.

Buehler, R., & McFarland, C. (2001). Intensity bias in affective forecasting: The role of temporal focus. *Personality and Social Psychology Bulletin, 27*, 1480–1493.

Burroughs, J. E., & Rindfleisch, A. (2002). Materialism and well-being: A conflicting values perspective. *Journal of Consumer Research, 29*, 348–370.

Campbell, A. (1981). *The sense of well-being in America.* New York: McGraw-Hill.

Carmon, Z., & Ariely, D. (2000). Focusing on the forgone: How value can appear so different to buyers and sellers. *Journal of Consumer Research, 27*, 360–370.

Carmon, Z., Wertenbroch, K., & Zeelenberg M. (2003). Option attachment: When deliberating makes choosing feel like losing. *Journal of Consumer Research, 30*, 15–29.

Cheema, A., & Soman, D. (2006). Malleable mental accounting: The effect of flexibility on the justification of attractive spending and consumption decisions. *Journal of Consumer Psychology, 16*, 33–44.

Clark, A. E. (1999). Are wages habit-forming? Evidence from micro data. *Journal of Economic Behavior and Organization, 39*, 179–200.

Dhar, R., & Wertenbroch, K. (2000). Consumer choice between hedonic and utilitarian goods. *Journal of Marketing Research, 37*, 60–71.

Diehl, K., & Zauberman, G. (2005). Searching ordered sets: Evaluations from sequences under search. *Journal of Consumer Research, 31*, 824–832.

Diener, E., & Biswas-Diener, R. (2002). Will money increase subjective well-being? A literature review and guide to needed research. *Social Indicators Research, 57*, 119–169.

Easterlin, R. (1995). Will raising the incomes of all increase the happiness of all? *Journal of Economic Behavior and Organization, 27*, 35–48.

Easterlin, R. (2001). Income and happiness: Towards a unified theory. *Economic Journal, 111*, 465–484.

Elster, J., & Loewenstein, G. (1992). Utility from memory and anticipation. In G. Loewenstein & J. Elster (Eds.), *Choice over time* (pp. 213–234). New York: Russell Sage Foundation.

Fox, C. R., Ratner, R. K., & Lieb, D. S. (2005). How subjective grouping of options influences choice and allocation: Diversification bias and the phenomenon of partition dependence. *Journal of Experimental Psychology—General, 134*, 538–551.

Frank, R. H. (2000). *Luxury fever: Money and happiness in an era of excess.* New York: Free Press.

Frank, R. H., & Cook, P. J. (1996). *The winner-take-all society: Why the few at the top get so much more than the rest of us.* New York: Penguin Books.

Frederick, S., & Loewenstein, G. F. (1999). Hedonic adaptation. In D. Kahneman, E. Diener, & N. Schwarz (Eds.), *Well-being: The foundations of hedonic psychology* (pp. 302–329). New York: Russell Sage Foundation.

Frey, B. S., & Stutzer, A. (2002a). *Happiness and economics: How the economy and institutions affect human well-being.* Princeton, NJ: Princeton University Press.

Frey, B. & Stutzer, A. (2002b). What can economists learn from happiness research? *Journal of Economic Literature, 40,* 402–435.

Gilbert, D. T., Driver-Linn, E., & Wilson, T. D. (2002). The trouble with Vronsky: Impact bias in the forecasting of future affective states. In L. F. Barrett & P. Salovey (Eds.), *The wisdom in feeling: Psychological processes in emotional intelligence* (pp. 114–143). New York: Guilford.

Gilbert, D. T., Gill, M. J., & Wilson, T. D. (2002). The future is now: Temporal correction in affective forecasting. *Organizational Behavior and Human Decision Processes, 88,* 430–444.

Helson, H. (1964). *Adaptation-level theory: An experimental and systematic approach to behavior.* New York: Harper and Row.

Hsee, C. K. (1996). The evaluability hypothesis: An explanation for preference-reversal between joint and separate evaluations of alternatives. *Organizational Behavior and Human Decision Processes, 67,* 247–257.

Hsee, C. K. (1999). Value seeking and prediction-decision inconsistency: Why don't people take what they predict they'll like the most? *Psychonomic Bulletin and Review, 6,* 555–561.

Hsee, C. K. & Abelson, R. P. (1991). Velocity relation: Satisfaction as a function of the first derivative of outcome over time. *Journal of Personality and Social Psychology, 60,* 341–347.

Hsee, C. K. & Hastie, R. (forthcoming). Hedonomics: Bridging decision research with happiness research. *Perspectives on Psychological Science.*

Hsee, C. K. & Leclerc, F. (1998). Will products look more attractive when evaluated jointly or when evaluated separately? *Journal of Consumer Research, 25,* 175–186.

Hsee, C. K., Loewenstein, G. F., Blount, S., & Bazerman M. H. (1999). Preference-reversals between joint and separate evaluations of options: A review and theoretical analysis. *Psychological Bulletin, 125,* 576–591.

Hsee, C. K., Rottenstreich, U., & Xiao, Z. (2005). When is more better? On the relationship between magnitude and subjective value. *Current Directions in Psychological Science.*

Hsee, C. K., Salovey, P., & Abelson, R. P. (1994). The quasi-acceleration relation: Satisfaction as a function of the change of velocity of outcome over time. *Journal of Experimental Social Psychology, 30,* 96–111.

Hsee, C. K., Yu, F., Zhang, J., & Zhang, Y. (2003a). Medium maximization. *Journal of Consumer Research, 30,* 1–14.

Hsee, C. K. & Zhang, J. (2004). Distinction bias: Misprediction and mischoice due to joint evaluation. *Journal of Personality and Social Psychology, 86,* 680–695.

Hsee, C. K., Zhang, J., Yu, F., & Xi, Y. (2003b). Lay rationalism and inconsistency between predicted experience and decision. *Journal of Behavioral Decision Making, 16,* 257–272.

Iyengar, S. S., & Lepper, M. (2000). When choice is demotivating: Can one desire too much of a good thing? *Journal of Personality and Social Psychology, 76,* 995–1006.

Kahneman, D. (1994). New challenges to the rationality assumption. Journal of *Institutional and Theoretical Economics, 150,* 18–36.

Kahneman, D. (2000). Experienced utility and objective happiness: A moment-based approach. In D. Kahneman, & A. Tversky (Eds.), *Choices, values, and frames* (pp. 673–692). Cambridge: Cambridge University Press.

Kahneman, D., Diener., E., & Schwarz, N. (Eds.) (1999). Well-being: Foundations of hedonic psychology. New York: Russell Sage Foundation Press.

Kahneman, D., Krueger, A. B., Schkade, D. A., Schwarz, N., & Stone, A. A. (2004a). Toward national well-being accounts. *American Economic Review, 94,* 429–434.

Kahneman, D., Krueger, A. B., Schkade, D. A., Schwarz, N., & Stone, A. A. (2004b). A survey method for characterizing daily life experience: The day reconstruction method (DRM). *Science, 306,* 1776–1780.

Kahneman, D., & Riis, J. (2005). Living, and thinking about it: Two perspectives on life. In F. Huppert, B. Keverne, & N. Baylis (Eds.), *The science of well being* (pp. 285–304). Oxford: Oxford University Press.

Kahneman, D., & Snell, J. (1992). Predicting a changing taste: Do people know what they will like? *Journal of Behavioral Decision Making, 5,* 187–200.

Kahneman, D., & Sugden, R. (2005). Experienced utility as a standard of policy evaluation. *Environmental & Resource Economics, 32,* 161–181.

Kahneman, D., & Tversky, A. (1979). Prospect theory: An analysis of decisions under risk. *Econometrica, 47,* 313–327.

Kardes, F. R., Cronley, M. L., & Kim, J. (2006). Construal-level effects on preference stability, preference-behavior correspondence, and the suppression of competing brands. *Journal of Consumer Psychology, 16,* 135–144.

Kivetz, R., & Simonson, I. (2002a). Earning the right to indulge: Effort as a determinant of customer preferences toward frequency program rewards. *Journal of Marketing Research, 39,* 155–170.

Kivetz, R., & Simonson, I. (2002b). Self-control for the righteous: Towards a theory of pre-commitment to indulgence. *Journal of Consumer Research, 29,* 199–217.

Kunreuther, H., Novemsky, N., & Kahneman, D. (2001). Making low probabilities useful. *Journal of Risk and Uncertainty, 23,* 103–120.

Loewenstein, G. (1987). Anticipation and the valuation of delayed consumption. *The Economic Journal, 97,* 668–684.

Loewenstein, G. (1996). Out of control: visceral influences on behavior. *Organizational Behavior and Human Decision Processes, 65,* 272–292.

Loewenstein, G., O'Donoghue, T., & Rabin, M. (2003). Projection bias in predicting future utility. *Quarterly Journal of Economics, 118,* 1209–1248.

Loewenstein, G., & Prelec, D. (1993). Preferences for sequences of outcomes. *Psychological Review, 100,* 91–108.

Loewenstein, G., & Schkade, D. (1999). Wouldn't it be nice? Predicting future feelings. In D. Kahneman, E. Diener, & N. Schwarz. (Eds.), *Well-being: The foundations of hedonic psychology* (pp. 85–105). New York: Russell Sage Foundation.

Lucas, R. E., Clark, A. E., Georgellis, Y., & Diener, E. (2003). Reexamining adaptation and the set point model of happiness: Reactions to changes in marital status. *Journal of Personality and Social Psychology, 84,* 527–539.

March, J. (1994). *A primer on decision making: How decisions happen.* New York: Free Press.

Nisbett, R. E., & Kanouse, D. E. (1969). Obesity, hunger, and supermarket shopping behavior. *Journal of Personality and Social Psychology, 12,* 289–294.

Novemsky, N., & Kahneman, D. (2005a). The boundaries of loss aversion. *Journal of Marketing Research, 42,* 119–128.

Novemsky, N., & Kahneman, D. (2005b). How do intentions affect loss aversion? *Journal of Marketing Research, 42,* 119–128.

Novemsky, N., & Ratner, R.N. (2003). The time course and impact of consumers' erroneous beliefs about hedonic contrast effects. *Journal of Consumer Research, 29,* 507–516.

Nowlis, S. M., Mandel, N., & McCabe, D. B. (2004). The effect of a delay between choice and consumption on consumption enjoyment. *Journal of Consumer Research, 31,* 502–510.

O'Curry, S., & Strahilevitz, M. (2001). Probability and mode of acquisition effects on choices between hedonic and utilitarian options. *Marketing Letters, 12,* 37–49.

Okada, E. M. (2005). Justification effects on consumer choice of hedonic and utifitarian goods. *Journal of Marketing Research, 42,* 43–53.

Parducci, A. (1965). Category judgment: A range-frequency model. *Psychological Review, 72,* 407–418.

Parducci, A. (1995). *Happiness, pleasure, and judgment: The contextual theory and its applications.* Mahway, NJ: Erlbaum.

Pham, M. T. (2004). The logic of feelings. *Journal of Consumer Psychology, 14,* 360–369.

Posavac, S. S., Sanbonmatsu, D. M., Kardes, F. R., & Fitzsimons, G. J. (2004). The brand positivity effect: When evaluation confers preference. *Journal of Consumer Research, 31,* 643–651.

Posavac, S. S., Sanbonmatsu, D. M., Kardes, F. R., & Fitzsimons, G. J. (2005). Blissful insularity: When brands are judged in isolation from competitors. *Marketing Letters, 16,* 87–97.

Prelec, D., & Herrnstein, R. (1991). Preferences or principles: Alternative guidelines for choice. In R. J. Zeckhauser (Ed.), *Strategy and choice* (pp. 319–340). Cambridge, MA: MIT Press.

Prelec, D., & Loewenstein, G. (1998). The red and the black: Mental accounting of savings and debt. *Marketing Science, 17,* 4–27.

Raghunathan, R., & Irwin, J. R. (2001). Walking the hedonic product treadmill: Default contrast and mood-based assimilation in judgments of predicted happiness with a target product. *Journal of Consumer Research, 28,* 355–368.

Ratner, R. K., Kahn, B. E., & Kahneman, D. (1999). Choosing less-preferred experiences for the sake of variety. *Journal of Consumer Research, 26*, 1–15.

Read, D., & van Leeuwen, B. (1998). Predicting hunger: The effects of appetite and delay on choice. *Organizational Behavior and Human Decision Processes, 76*, 189–205.

Robinson, M. D., & Clore, G. L. (2002). Belief and feeling: Evidence for an accessibility model of emotional self-report. *Psychological Bulletin, 128*, 934–960.

Riis, J., Loewenstein, G., Baron, J., Jepson, C., Fagerlin, A., & Ubel, P. A. (2005). Ignorance of hedonic adaptation to Hemodialysis: A study using ecological momentary assessment. *Journal of Experimental Psychology: General, 134*, 3–9.

Schkade, D.A., & Kahneman, D. (1998). Does living in California make people happy? A focusing illusion in judgments of life satisfaction. *Psychological Science, 9*, 340–346.

Schelling, T. C. (1980). The intimate contest for self-command. *The Public Interest, 60*, 94–118.

Schelling, T. C. (1984). Self command in practice, in theory and in a theory of rational choice. *American Economic Review, 74*, 1–11.

Schulz, R., & Decker, S. (1985). Long-term adjustment to physical disability: The role of social support, perceived control, and self-blame. *Journal of Personality and Social Psychology, 48*, 1162–1172.

Schwartz, B. (2004). *The paradox of choice: Why more is less.* New York : ECCO.

Seligman, M. E. P. (2002). *Authentic happiness: Using the new positive psychology to realize your potential for lasting fulfillment.* New York: Free Press/Simon and Schuster.

Shafir, E., Simonson, I., & Tversky, A. (1993). Reason-based choice. *Cognition, 49*, 11–36.

Shiv, B., & Huber, J. (2000). The impact of anticipating satisfaction on consumer choice. *Journal of Consumer Research, 27*, 202–216.

Simonson, I. (1989). Choice based on reasons: The case of attraction and compromise effects. *Journal of Consumer Research, 16*, 158–174.

Simonson, I. (1990). The effect of purchase quantity and timing on variety-seeking behavior. *Journal of Marketing Research, 27*, 150–162.

Simonson, I., & Drolet, A. (2004). Anchoring effects on consumers' willingness-to-pay and willingness-to-accept. *Journal of Consumer Research, 31*, 681–690.

Simonson, I., & Nowlis, S. M. (2000). The role of explanations and need for uniqueness in consumer decision making: Unconventional choices based on reasons. *Journal of Consumer Research, 27*, 49–68.

Slovic, P., Finucane, M., Peters, E., & MacGregor, D. G. (2002). The affect heuristic. In T. Gilovich, D. Griffin, & D. Kahneman (Eds.), *Heuristics and biases: The psychology of intuitive judgment* (pp. 397–420). New York: Cambridge University Press.

Snell, J., Gibbs, B. J., & Varey, C. (1995). Intuitive hedonics: Consumer beliefs about the dynamics of liking. *Journal of Consumer Psychology, 4*, 33–60.

Strahilevitz, M. A., & Loewenstein, G. (1998). The effect of ownership history on the valuation of objects. *Journal of Consumer Research, 25*, 276–289.

Thaler, R. H. (1980). Toward a positive theory of consumer choice. *Journal of Economic Behavior and Organization, 1*, 39–60.

Thaler, R. H. (1985). Mental accounting and consumer choice. *Marketing Science, 4*, 199–214

Thaler, R. H. (1999). Mental accounting matters. *Journal of Behavioral Decision Making, 12*, 183–206.

Thaler, R. H. & Johnson, E. J. (1990). Gambling with the house money and trying to break even: the effects of prior outcomes on risky choice. *Management Science, 36*, 643–660.

Thaler, R. H., & Shefrin, H. M. (1981). An economic theory of self-control. *Journal of Political Economy, 89*, 392–406.

Trope, Y., & Liberman, N. (2003). Temporal construal. *Psychological Review, 110*, 403–421

Tversky, A., & Griffin, D.W. (1990). Endowment and contrast in judgments of wellbeing. In F. Strack, M. Argyle, & N. Schwarz (Eds.), *Subjective well-being* (pp. 101–118). New York: Pergamon.

Van Boven, L., Dunning, D., & Loewenstein, G. (2000). Egocentric empathy gaps between owners and buyers: misperceptions of the endowment effect. *Journal of Personality and Social Psychology, 79*, 66–76.

Van Boven, L., & Loewenstein, G. (2003). Projection of transient drive states. *Personality and Social Psychology Bulletin, 29*, 1159–1168.

van Osselaer, S. M. J, Alba, J. W., & Manchanda, P. (2004). Irrelevant information and mediated intertemporal choice. *Journal of Consumer Psychology, 14*, 257–270.

Wedell, D. H., & Parducci, A. (1988). The category effect in social judgment: Experimental ratings of happiness. *Journal of Personality and Social Psychology, 55,* 341–356.

Wilson, T. D., & Gilbert, D. (2003). Affective forecasting. *Advances in Experimental Social Psychology, 35,* 345–411.

Wilson, T. D., Meyers, J., & Gilbert, D. T. (2003). "How happy was I, anyway?" A retrospective impact bias. *Social Cognition, 21,* 407–432.

Wilson, T. D., Wheatley, T., Meyers, J., Gilbert, D. T., & Axsom, D. (2000). Focalism: a source of durability bias in affective forecasting. *Journal of Personality and Social Psychology, 78,* 821–836.

Yeung, C. W. M., & Soman, D. (2005). Attribute evaluability and the range effect. *Journal of Consumer Research, 32,* 363–369.

Zhang, J., & Hsee, C. K. (2006). Skewness and happiness. Working paper.

26

Behavioral Pricing

Maggie Wenjing Liu

Dilip Soman

University of Toronto

OVERVIEW

Imagine that you are getting ready to launch a new product and need to determine a price. What factors should you consider and how should you combine these factors in determining a final price? One standard approach to pricing prescribes that the manufacturer should take into account the demand curve, willingness to pay, economic value and costs of the products (Dolan & Simon, 1996). The thrust of much of the pricing work in marketing centers on the act of *determining* a price for the product or service, and makes the implicit assumption of description invariance (i.e., people are rational so that the manner in which the price is framed should not influence choice; Tversky & Kahneman, 1986).

However, the research reported in this chapter suggests that the manner in which the price is presented matters—and in some cases, might matter more than the dollar amount of the actual price itself. In particular, consider the following situations in which price presentation seems to influence consumers in ways which cannot be explained by traditional economic and choice theories.

> When credit cards were first introduced, consumers had to pay a surcharge to cover the costs of the transactions. This surcharge was strongly resisted by consumers. However, when retailers increased prices across the board and offered cash users a discount, the same differential between cash and credit purchases suddenly became a lot more acceptable to consumers.
>
> In her charity television appearances, Sally Struthers said that "Only 72 cents a day" we can feed a starving child, and a furniture retailer claimed that "if you can afford yoghurt for [$2/day], you can afford a living room set for [$1.69 a day]." Both Sally and the furniture retailer elicited a greater compliance than similar requests for an equivalent lump sum, even though they were really also asking for a lump sum.
>
> Flat-rate phone plans are more popular among customers than paying by the call, even though flat-rate plans may cost the consumer more overall.
>
> Supermarkets provide free air mile cards and encourage customers to collect air miles each time they make a purchase.
>
> A survey of prices in supermarkets and in department stores reveals that prices with odd endings [e.g., either $9 rather than $10, or $14.95 rather than $15] are significantly more prevalent than chance would suggest.

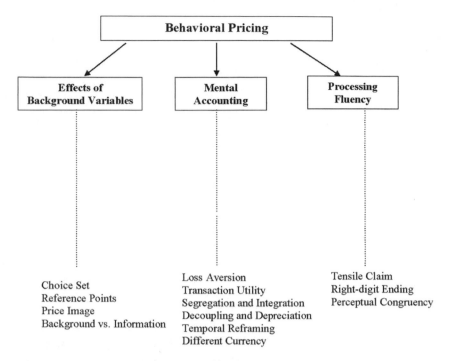

Figure 26.1 Overview of consumer psychology of pricing

The term "behavioral pricing" is used to capture aspects of how price presentation influences perceived value and consumer choice (rather than the actual act of price setting). This chapter reviews behavioral pricing and its impact on consumer value perception and consumption. Figure 26.1 depicts the three main areas and corresponding pricing phenomena and strategies. The next three sections (Section 2–4) give an overview of the three main areas of consumer psychology in pricing research, namely mental accounting, effects of background variables, and processing fluency. The last section (Section 5) emphasizes the common characteristics behind different perspectives, as well as outlines directions for future research.

MENTAL ACCOUNTING

Thaler (1985) proposed that individuals follow a cognitive version of cost accounting to organize and interpret transaction information as the basis for making a decision. Thaler dubbed this cognitive structure as a mental accounting system. Three ingredients of mental accounting are important here: (1) the manner in which the monetary outcome is framed and evaluated (using the prospect theory value function, Tversky & Kahneman, 1981), (2) the breadth of the mental account, including the bracket and time (Soman, 2004), and (3) the currency used in mental accounting. Mental accounts can be defined narrowly (e.g., a single transaction) or broadly (e.g., a spending category), can be defined with a fixed temporal life (e.g., monthly budgets), or extend over a period of time (e.g., one financial year). Six types of mental accounting effects in pricing are identified and relevant empirical research are reviewed in the rest of this section.

Loss Aversion

The Asian disease problem (from Tversky & Kahneman, 1981) is often used to illustrate the effect of framing information as gains vs. losses. In the example below, the numbers in parentheses against each option denote the percentage of subjects choosing that option.

Problem 1 (N = 152): Imagine that the U.S. is preparing for the outbreak of an unusual Asian disease, which is expected to kill 600 people. Two alternative programs to combat the disease have been proposed. Assume that the exact scientific estimates of the consequences of the programs are as follows:

> If program A is adopted, 200 people will be saved. [72%]
> If program B is adopted, there is a one-third probability that 600 people
>   will be saved and a two-thirds probability that no people will be saved. [28%]

It is clear that most of the respondents are risk averse in this frame of problem. That is, 72% of them prefer saving 200 lives over a gamble that offers a one-third chance of saving all the 600 lives. Now consider another problem in which the same cover story is followed by a different frame of the outcomes.

> **Problem 2 (N = 155):** If program C is adopted, 400 people will die. [22%]
> If program D is adopted, there is a one-third probability that nobody will
>   die and a two-thirds probability that 600 people will die. [78%]

It is easy to verify that programs A and B in Problem 1 are objectively identical with programs C and D in Problem 2, respectively. The results of Problem 2, however, indicate that the majority of respondents are risk seeking, rather than risk averse, in this frame of the decision problem. Namely, 78% of them prefer a gamble (program D) with two-thirds chance of losing all the 600 lives to a sure loss of 400 lives. Thus, different framing of the outcomes as losses or gains can shift people's choice from risk averse to risk seeking behavior.

The above analysis is a simple application of the loss aversion principle of prospect theory (Kahneman & Tversky, 1979), whose essential claim is that carriers of value are changes in wealth rather than the final state of welfare. Prospect theory distinguishes two phases in the choice process: an early phase of editing and a subsequent evaluating phase. The value function is (1) defined on deviations from the reference point; (2) generally concave for gains and convex for losses and both gains and losses functions display diminishing sensitivity; (3) steeper for losses than for gains, indicating loss aversion. The feature of diminishing sensitivity reflects the basic psychophysical principle that a price change from $10 to $20 seems bigger than a change from $100 to $110, irrespective of the sign. The S-shaped value function is steepest at the reference point and the value of each outcome is multiplied by a decision weight.

Replacing traditional utility function with the value function from prospect theory offers many insights to people's perception of pricing. Gains and losses are almost always defined relatively to a reference price. However, consumers may use multiple reference points when evaluating price in purchase decisions. Their reference prices can be either external or internal, affected by either framing of the offer or the expectation of consumers. According to Mayhew and Winer (1992), internal reference prices are memory-resident prices based on actual price or the "fair price," while external reference prices are observed stimuli, such as "regular prices" displayed by the stores. A change of reference point alters the coding of gains and losses and hence preference order for prospects.

As sellers, people usually will demand a higher selling price for an item they own than what they are willing to pay for the same item. Carmon and Ariely (2000) proposed that buying and selling price estimates reflect a focus on what the consumer forgoes in the potential exchange. Buyers and sellers differ in how they assess the value of the same item: Buyers tend to attend towards what they forgo (the expenditure); while by the same token sellers tend to focus on their sentiment to surrendering the item, thus selling prices are more heavily influenced by variables such as benefits of possessing the item. This phenomenon, dubbed as "endowment effect" by Thaler (1980), suggests that losses loom larger than gains.

The same notion that consumers react more strongly to negative deviations (losses) from the expected price than positive deviations (gains) was demonstrated by Kalwani et al.'s price expectation model (1990). Krishnamurthi, Mazumdar, and Raj (1992) also showed that consumers exhibited asymmetry in price sensitivity towards loss and gains, with switchers responding more strongly to a price loss than to a gain in their purchase quantity decisions.

Segregation, Integration, and Expense Categories

Consider a hypothetical consumer, Susan, who normally spends $50 each week on entertainment. If she got a $20 sports ticket for free, she might spend her entire $50 "budget" on entertainment this week. If she subsequently had to pay $20 for the ticket, she is more likely to spend only $30 on entertainment for the rest of the week. However, if she bought some cosmetics with the $20 instead of a sports ticket, Susan might still spend $50 in enjoying herself this week.

Susan underconsumes in her entertainment category after an unexpected purchase, and she is more likely to underconsume after buying something highly typical of the category than something untypical (Heath & Soll, 1996). Susan engages in mental accounting. Expenditures are grouped into different mental accounts (food, housing, "rainy day," etc.), and spending is often constrained by implicit or explicit budgets. Put differently, the assumption of fungibility of money (i.e., any dollar can be substituted by any other dollar) is violated once budgets are set by spending categories. An "entertainment dollar" is not the same as a "clothes and accessories dollar."

Heath and Soll (1996) described the mental accounting process of expenditure in two stages—booking and posting. First, expenses must be noticed; and second, the expense is assigned to its proper account. An expense will not affect mental budgets if either stage fails. Booking depends on attention and memory whereas posting depends on similarity judgments and categorization. Since money is not fungible across account boundaries, people may be especially likely to justify their expenses through various ingenious methods of hedonic posting—posting items in a way that satisfies short-term interests and skirts the budget. Stores and advertisers often attempt to aid potential consumers by suggesting alternative ways to post an expense.

When consumers evaluate purchases where combination of outcomes (cost vs. benefit, gains vs. losses) is involved, how do they code the outcomes, especially when the situation is structured in a neutral or ambiguous manner? Given the shape of the value function, four principles of hedonic posting in mental accounting are derived (Thaler, 1985, 1999):

1. Segregate gains: An increase in a gain should be segregated since the gain function is concave;
2. Integrate losses: An increase in the absolute value of a loss should be integrated because the loss function is convex;

3. Cancellation: A decrease in a gain should be integrated in order to offset loss aversion;
4. Silver lining: A small reduction in the absolute value of a loss should be segregated. Because the gain function is steepest near the reference point, the utility of a small gain can exceed the utility of slightly reducing a large loss.

Different pricing policies often encourage or facilitate people's engagement in such "hedonic editing," so that multiple outcomes from a purchase can be considered optimal. For instance, segregating gains are used at two levels in cable TV shopping. First, each of the product items is said to have multiple uses, which is demonstrated one by one; secondly several "bonus" items are included for free if you "call right now". The widespread use of rebates is also an example of the silver lining principle (Thaler, 1999). Three specific pricing strategies can be regarded as the application of segregation and integration principles.

Partitioned Pricing

Firms may choose to present separate prices for each component in a multi component product bundle rather than a single price. This fashion, called "partitioned pricing," produces results that are seemingly inconsistent with prospect theory. One typical means of two-part pricing is to divide the product's cost into two mandatory parts, such as the base price of a mail-order shirt and the surcharge for shipping. Previous research has suggested that with a consolidated tag, the total price is coded as a single loss but when the total price is partitioned with separate tags, each component price is coded as a separate loss and the total price could be evaluated more negatively when partitioned. Recent studies, however, have suggested that alternative method of the mental accounting may stem from price partitioning. Even if prices are partitioned by components, consumers can easily add them to determine a total price of the bundle and evaluate the loss. However, the generally incommensurate benefits of partitioned components are harder to combine directly. Hence the benefits (gains) are easier to be coded and evaluated separately. With a value function concave in gains, the component benefits would have a higher total perceived value when partitioned than consolidated.

Morwitz, Greenleaf, and Johnson (1998) tested how consumers processed partitioned prices and how partitioned pricing impacted consumers' processing of price information and their purchase intentions. Their results suggested that partitioned prices decreased consumers' recalled total costs and increased their demand. The manner in which the surcharge was presented and consumers' affect for the brand name also influenced how they reacted to partitioned prices. Chakravarti et al.'s experiments (2002) showed that consistent with a mental accounting analysis, a multicomponent product bundle was evaluated more favorably and chosen more often when its components were presented with partitioned (vs. consolidated) prices. The effects were, however, moderated by the way of components divided. In particular, it appeared that partitioning prices altered attention paid to the components partitioned and related product features, indicating a role of information processing effects.

Combined Currencies

The increasing popularity of loyalty programs and related marketing promotions has resulted in the abundance of new currencies (e.g., air miles, bonus points, store dollars) that consumers save, accumulate, budget, and spend much as they do with traditional paper money. Except retaining loyal customers, such "combined-currency pricing" has important implications in consumers' value perception. Utilizing the silver lining principle, the bonus points are segregated as a small gain against the major loss (product expense), therefore reducing the perceived cost of the purchase.

Nunes and Park (2003) proposed the concept of "incommensurate resources" as a way of understanding the use of multicurrency pricing. When two resources are delivered simultaneously, but in different currencies (e.g., receive 5 air miles with a purchase of $20 of groceries), the marginal value of the nonmonetary, incremental benefit may be difficult to evaluate in relation to the focal product or its price. Therefore, the value of the premium is less likely to be viewed in a relative sense and thus less likely to suffer from diminishing marginal returns. Dreze and Nunes (2004) explored how consumers evaluate transactions involving prices issued in multiple currencies with both formal mathematical proof and experimental support. Evidence shows that a price delivered in different currencies can be superior to a standard, single-currency price, either by lowering the psychological or perceived cost associated with the price, or by raising the amount of revenue collected given a particular perceived cost.

Multiple Discounts

When faced with multiple price changes instead of a single change of an equal amount, consumers are generally believed to segregate gains and integrate losses as indicated by the mental accounting principles. For instance, Büyükkurt (1986) stated that a large number of noticeable discounts could lead to a higher perceived value than a small number of extreme discounts. Mazumdar and Jun (1993) also found that multiple price decreases were evaluated more favorably than a single price decrease and multiple price increases were evaluated more unfavorably than a single price increase.

However, the effects of mental accounting principles are moderated by both price formulation and consumer factors. Mazumdar and Jun (1993) demonstrated that consumer price uncertainty and relative price magnitude can be potential moderators. Since price-uncertain consumers consider higher ranges of prices acceptable, they were less unfavorable to multiple price increases and more favorable to multiple price decreases than certain consumers. Moreover, when the magnitude of one price was very small relative to other prices, consumers' preference for multiple price decreases (relative to a single price decrease) was reduced.

The presence of both a promotion threshold and saturation point was illustrated in Gupta and Cooper's (1992) research. Whether consumers would discount the promotions depended on the discount level, store image, and whether the product advertised is a name brand or a store brand. They gathered empirical evidence that consumers did not change their intentions to buy unless the promotional discount was above a threshold level. This threshold point differed for name brands and store brands with the threshold for a name brand lower than that for a store brand. Their study also indicated the existence of a promotion saturation point above which the effect of discounts on consumers' purchase intention was minimal, confirming an S-shaped response to promotions for consumers.

Mental accounting principles generally prevail when the deviation from the reference price is in absolute dollar value (e.g., $10 dollar off the regular price). Consumers typically prefer segregating two discounts, segregating a price increase from a smaller discount (mixed loss), integrating a discount with a smaller price increase (mixed gain) and are indifferent between segregating and integrating two price increases. However, percentage-based frames (e.g., 30% off) are shown to alter certain principles by eliminating and reversing consumers' reactions to mixed gains and mixed losses (Heath & Chatterjee, 1995). When asked whether a $50 discount on a $1,300 couch was better than a $50 increase on a $1,000 couch together with a $100 discount on a $300 chair, subjects preferred the single outcome when absolute frames were used. However, when comparing a 3.8% couch discount with a 5% couch price increase and a 33% chair discount, subjects liked the multiple outcomes when relative frames of the same value were used.

Transaction Utility

Classical economics theory stresses the assumption that consumers are rational buyers who maximize the economic gains from a purchase transaction. However, utility maximization does not explain why some deals are too good to be missed, while certain products are rejected simply because they are in a lousy deal. Thaler (1985) proposed that consumers get both acquisition utility and transaction utility from a purchase. People evaluate transactions by total utility, which is the sum of acquisition utility (utility derived from the purchased good minus the price paid for the good) and transaction utility (internal reference price minus the purchase price).

A consumer's behavior depends not just on the value of goods and services comparing to their prices, but also on the consumers' perception of the financial quality of the deal. The new concept of transaction utility is modeled as the difference between the selling price and the reference price in consumer's mind, leading to the "fairness" idea. Its value equivalent is defined as the amount of cash the individual would need to make him indifferent to the choice between receiving the cash or the good z as a gift. The reference price is the amount of money a person expects to pay for z or an estimate of a fair or just price.

Acquisition utility represents the gain or loss from the transaction, capturing the usual results from traditional economic theory of consumer. Transaction utility represents the pleasure or displeasure associated with the financial terms of the deal per se. As indicated in equation (1), total utility is derived from acquisition utility (value of the purchased good $\bar{p}$ minus the price paid for the good p) and transaction utility (internal reference price p^* minus the purchase price p).

$$w(z, p, p^*) = v(\bar{p}, -p) + v(-p : -p^*) \tag{1}$$

The consumer will buy a good z at price p if $\dfrac{w(z, p, p^*)}{p} > k_i$, where k_{it} is the budget constraint for category i in time period t. Usually high k's are most likely to be observed for categories of goods that are particularly seductive or addictive in the short-run, like cigarettes and luxuries; and low k's are common for goods viewed to be beneficial in the long term, such as exercising or education (Thaler, 1985).

The addition of transaction utility to the purchase calculation leads to two kinds of effects in the marketplace. First, some goods are purchased primarily because they are especially good deals. In contrast, some purchases that could make the consumer better off might be avoided because of substantial transaction disutility. Simonson, Carmon, and O'Curry (1994) investigated the latter phenomena and proposed that consumers, who perceived a new feature or promotion as providing little or no value, would be less likely to purchase the enhanced brand even when the added feature clearly did not diminish the value of the brand. Their results suggested that when consumers were uncertain about the values of products and their preferences, such premiums provided reasons against buying the promoted brands and were seen as susceptible to criticism.

The concepts of acquisition utility and transaction utility have been widely adopted in marketing research to understand consumers' reaction to promotions. Grewal, Monroe, and Krishnan (1998) defined perceived acquisition value as buyer's net gain or tradeoff from acquiring the product or service, taking into consideration both price and quality; while perceived transaction value was regarded as the perception of psychological satisfaction or pleasure attained from taking advantage of the deal in financial terms. Lichtenstein, Netemeyer, and Burton (1990) applied acquisition utility and transaction utility to understanding value consciousness and deal proneness of different customers. Deal proneness is the increased propensity to respond to an offer because the form of the offer positively affects purchase evaluations; value consciousness is the concern for paying low prices, which is subject to some quality constraint. Individuals whose value perceptions are largely affected by acquisition utility (the inherent need-satisfying ability of the product) are more likely to be value conscious. On the other hand, people whose value perceptions are more dependent on transaction utility are likely to be coupon prone.

Transaction Decoupling and Payment Depreciation

Consider the following problem: Mr. A and Mr. B both have a ticket for a basketball game tonight. Mr. A paid a single price $40 for the ticket while Mr. B bought it as part of a bundled ticket ($200 for 5 games). Both men have equally anticipated the game and both tickets are nonrefundable and nonreusable if they miss the game. There is a snowstorm the night of the game and driving conditions are bad. Who is more likely to brave the storm and attend the game, Mr. A or Mr. B?

From an economic perspective, the pricing format of the ticket should have no impact on either man's consumption behavior. Both men would view the $40 payment as "sunk" and base their decision solely on the incremental costs and benefits of braving the storm. They should face identical costs and benefits and should be equal in likelihood of going for the game. Sunk cost literature, on the other hand, would suggest that each man will consider the sunk cost of his ticket, hence increasing his likelihood of going out on a snowstorm night. Having each paid an identical amount, the men face the same sunk cost and, again, should make the same decision.

However, Soman and Gourville (2001) suggested that the sunk cost effect is moderated by the ambiguity inherent in a bundled transaction. For unbundled transactions, costs and benefits are directly linked with each other, resulting in a strong sunk cost effect. But for products obtained with a bundled price, the association between costs and benefits is open to interpretation and could result in a much weaker sunk cost effect. In the above example, Mr. B who bought the ticket in a bundled price will have weaker sunk cost effect and is less likely to go to the game.

It is a widely held view that consumers consider historic, non-recoverable transaction costs (time, money, and effort) when deciding on a future course of action, a phenomenon called the "sunk cost effect." For a mechanism of tracking sunk costs, Thaler (1985, 1999) argued that a consumer creates a "mental account" upon entering a transaction (e.g., making payment) and closes that account upon completing the transaction (e.g., consuming the good or service). By establishing a transaction-specific mental account, the consumer creates a psychological link between the costs and the benefits of a given transaction.

However, recent research suggests that the identification and consideration of such costs may not be straightforward. For example, it is significantly more difficult to identify and consider the cost of a purchased product when that cost is incurred by credit card or check than by cash (Prelec & Loewenstein, 1998; Soman, 2001). Specifically, when consumers pay a bundled price for multiple products, the relationship between the costs and the benefits is one-to-many. In such a transaction, there is far greater ambiguity as to what costs are paying for what benefits. As a result, price bundling may lead to the psychological disassociation, or decoupling, of transaction costs and benefits so that the costs become less relevant to the consumption decision.

Such a disassociation between costs and benefits is labeled "transaction decoupling" and hypothesized to influence post-purchase consumption behaviors by reducing attention to sunk costs and decreasing a consumer's likelihood of consuming a paid-for service. In both lab and field studies, Soman and Gourville (2001) showed that multiperformance ticket holders were more likely to forgo a given theatrical performance than single-performance ticket holders, all else being equal. There was also evidence that the decreased attention to sunk costs brought about by price bundling can be either cognitively driven (i.e., difficulty in allocating a single payment across multiple benefits) or motivationally driven (i.e., an underlying desire to avoid consumption).

The dissociation between payment and benefit does not come solely from pricing formats. A temporal separation of costs from benefits will also make the mental account linkage weaker. In the case where payment occurs long before the actual consumption, a consumer might gradually adapt to a historic cost with the passage of time, thereby decreasing its sunk-cost impact on the consumption of a pending benefit. This process of gradual adaptation to costs is termed "payment depreciation" by Gourville and Soman (1998).

The concept of payment depreciation was best illustrated in a study of a health club, first reported by Gourville and Soman (1998), and then discussed in greater detail in Gourville and Soman (2002). They compare attendance rates of members across four pricing conditions. Across all conditions, members paid the same annualized membership fee, but differed in their timing. In the annual condition, members paid the full amount once a year, in the semi-annual condition, they paid two equal installments every six months, in the quarterly condition, they paid four equal installments every three months while in the monthly condition, they paid twelve equal installments each month. In the monthly condition, usage of facilities remains roughly constant on a month-by-month basis. For all other conditions, there was evidence of payment depreciation through falling usage rates over time, only to jump back up when another payment was made. As time passed, members adapted to the payment and were not as "pressurized" to use the facilities. In the annual condition, for instance, usage of the facilities is the highest in the month the payment is made, but them tapers off in an exponential fashion such that ten or eleven months later, the average usage rate is very low. However, this is precisely the point in time at which members make renewal decisions, and the low usage rate may prompt members to decide not to renew in subsequent years. Hence, while managers of subscription-based services may opt for annual pricing schemes to save costs, this may backfire at the level of lifetime value of the customer, as consumers do not use the service and hence do not see the need for renewal.

The mental accounting effects of decoupling are not necessarily associated with prepayment. In a vacation plan consumers often pay a fixed fee for a package deal including meals, lodging, and recreation. Such plans have two advantages. First, the extra cost of including the meals and recreation in the price will look relatively small when combined with the other costs. Second, under the alternative plan each of the small expenditures looks large by itself, and might cause transaction disutility compared with prices found elsewhere (Thaler, 1999). The piece-rate pricing policy makes the association between the payment and the specific consumption very salient, whereas the opposite is highly desirable. When the linkage between cost and benefit affects the actual experience of consumption, consumers don't like "watching the meter running." A decoupling between price and benefits could be viewed as one kind of "hedonic posting" willingly adopted by consumers, which explains the prevalence of flat-rate phone plans.

In contrast, a deliberate "coupling" between cost and benefit can serve as an instrument of consumer self-control. Wertenbroch (1998) used multiple empirical methods to show that consumers voluntarily and strategically paid a higher price to ration their purchase quantities of "vice" goods like cigarette and alcohol. For example, many regular smokers buy their cigarettes by the pack, even though they could easily afford the 10-pack cartons. These smokers knowingly forgo sizable per-unit savings from quantity discounts. Besides self-imposing additional transactions costs on marginal consumption, rationing purchase quantity can refresh a strong association between the high price and subsequent consumption, thereby enhancing their self-regulatory motivation to smoke less. In a similar vein, Soman and Gourville (2001) speculate that framing an annual price as a per use price may actually be used to boost the consumption of certain desirable services (e.g., healthcare, education).

Mental linkage between the cost and benefits not only occurs for single consumption experience, but also for durable goods. Gourville and Soman (1998) showed that when an upstream payment was sufficiently distant, consumers might fully adapt to the payment, resulting the pending benefit considered to be free. Okada (2001) proposed that during ownership of a product, a consumer mentally depreciated the initial purchase price, thus creating a "mental book value" for the product. The write-off of this mental book value is felt as the mental cost of a replacement purchase when facing the opportunity to upgrade to a new, higher-quality product. As a normative decision maker, the considers the purchase price of the new alternative, as well as the mental cost of retiring the old product. Based on the principles of mental accounting and mental depreciation, an individual's replacement decision may be more sensitive to the mental cost than the marginal cost, resulting in a misallocation of resources that does not add any value from the perspective of utility maximization (Okada, 2001).

Temporal Reframing

Marketers constantly search for ways to make products appear attractive and price affordable. For instance, which price is more desirable, "only 50 cents per day" for joining a gym or a $180 annual membership? Even though the wording is different, for either choice the physical payment remains aggregate and the same. This strategy of temporally reframing the cost of a product from an aggregate one-time cost to a series of small ongoing expenses is identified as "pennies-a-day" or PAD (Gourville, 1998).

According to standard economic theory, the reframing of a transaction from an aggregate to a PAD expense should not alter compliance unless there is a corresponding change in the physical cash flows. Some principles of prospect theory and hedonic editing would predict that consumers should prefer psychologically integrating a series of small losses into one large bundled cost, therefore the "pennies-a-day" strategy might actually backfire.

However, Gourville (1998) proposes that when faced with a single-alternative transaction, consumers often retrieve a category of comparable expenses for the purpose of providing comparison standards. If the target transaction is judged to be similar, assimilation occurs and the target transaction is accepted as a member of the retried category. The temporal framing of price for a single alternative transaction systematically affects the nature of the expenses that a consumer retrieves for the purpose of comparison. Framing the price as "pennies-a-day" is shown to foster retrieval and consideration of small, ongoing expenses, whereas an aggregate framing of the same amount might trigger the recall and consideration of large, infrequent expenses (Gourville, 1998). "Pennies-a-day" transactions take on the characteristics of coffee spending and lottery tickets, expenses typically thought of as trivial, affordable and out-of-pocket, therefore increasing consumer's likelihood of buying.

Temporal formulation is one example of price framing in marketing. Virtually all marketing elements can fall into the category of framing, with price being one of the most context-dependent variables. This might one important reason that classical economic theory does not receive good application in consumer research. Tversky and Kahneman (1981) displayed that choices often depended on the way a problem was posed as much as on its objective features. They used the term "decision frame" in reference to decision maker's conception of the acts, outcomes, and contingencies associated with a particular choice. The frame that a decision maker adopts is controlled partly by the formulation of the problem and partly by his/her norms, habits, and personal characteristics. For instance, judgment of gains is often risk averse while choice involving losses are often risk seeking.

In prospect theory the value of an uncertain outcome is multiplied by a decision weight $\pi(p)$, which is a monotonic function of p but not a probability. The weighting function has the following properties: first, impossible events are discarded so that $\pi(0) = (0)$, and $\pi(1) = 1$; second, low probabilities are overweighed, while moderate and high probabilities are underweighted, with the later effect more pronounced than the former; and third, for any fixed probability ratio q, the ratio of decision weights is closer to unity when the probabilities are low than when they are high. The major qualitative properties of decision weights can be extended to framing situations like tensile claiming, since under such cases the probabilities of outcomes are often subjectively assessed rather than explicitly given.

One of the most basic assumptions of the rational theory of choice is the principle of procedure invariance, requiring strategically equivalent methods of elicitation to yield identical preferences (Tversky, Slovic, & Sattath, 1988). However, at least two reasons can be used to account for why consumers fall for framings. First, instead of a well-defined choice set, most of real-world consumer problems only have a single-alternative, either to be rejected or accepted. This limits the width and depth of consumer information processing. Second, people generally adopt a minimal account in decision making which includes only the direct consequences of an action. It is because this mode of framing simplifies evaluation, reduces cognitive strain, reflects the cause-consequence intuition, and matches the properties of hedonic experience, which is more sensitive to desirable and undesirable changes than to steady states. Tversky and Kahneman (1981) suggested that individuals with a definite preference (1) might have a difference preference in another framing of the same problem, (2) are normally unaware of alternative frames and of their potential effects on option attractiveness, (3) would wish their preferences to be independent of framing, but (4) are often uncertain how to resolve detected inconsistencies. Empirically, Zeithaml (1982) revealed that the format of price information provision significantly affected subjects' cognitive, affective, and behavioral responses.

However, acting on the most readily available frame is not necessarily irrational when we follow Simon's theory of bounded rationality (1956). This is in reference to the mental effort required to explore alternative frames and avoid potential inconsistencies (Tversky & Kahneman, 1981). Psychology literature has illustrated that performing any act of decision making seems to deplete some crucial resource within the self, and that limited resource is then no longer available to help the person on subsequent decision-making or self-regulatory tasks (Baumeister, 2002). Therefore people often will adapt an available and reasonable frame instead of depleting their mental resources to get optimized results. Furthermore, sometimes the framing of an action affects the actual experience of its outcomes. Under such situations, deliberate manipulation of framing can serve as instruments of hedonic editing and self-control (Tversky & Kahneman, 1981).

Multiple Currencies

Another way of framing price is by scaling the numerical quantities in different currencies. It has been long noticed in economics that people focus on the nominal face value of a given amount of money, rather than its real value, when making economic decisions. Fisher (1928) coined the term "money illusion" to describe this phenomenon. Using experimental data, Shafir, Diamond, and Tversky (1997) showed that the face value of an amount of money (in dollars) exerts greater impact on consumer preferences than does its purchasing power (accounting for interest and inflation rates).

More recently, Wertenbroch, Soman, and Chattopadhyay (2006) invited subjects in Hong Kong to participate in a gamble in a fictitious foreign currency (PI$). Results showed that subjects who had PI$200 wagered an average amount equivalent to HK$12.06 as compared to HK$6.17 for subjects who had PI$2. When the exact same amount was framed as PI$200 rather than PI$2, individuals seemed to be more generous with the amount even when they are aware of the exchange rate.

There have been two explanations for this currency framing effect. In a recent paper, Raghubir and Srivastava (2002) propose an anchoring and adjustment process (Tversky & Kahneman, 1974) to explain why there is a systematic bias towards the nominal value of money. They argue that when facing a price in an unknown currency, consumers anchor on the nominal value, which is the most salient and accessible information. They then adjust using exchange rate to convert the unknown currency price into the home currency price. This adjustment process is cognitively consuming and therefore is often inadequate. A second explanation offered by Wertenbroch, Soman, and Chattopadhyay (2002) is based on the numerosity effect in making quantity judgments (Pelham, Sumarta, & Mayaskovsky, 1994). People use numerosity (i.e., the number of units in which the stimulus is divided, rather than their impact and hence the total size) as a heuristic to make judgments of quantity. They show that the currency framing effect has a number of real world implications, including the willingness to spend, price sensitivities, and the willingness to pay for a particular purchase.

On the other hand, pricing research has focused almost exclusively on money-based transactions and ignored other currencies (time, effort, etc.) people might pay for obtaining products. Okada and Hoch (2004) demonstrated systematic differences in the way that people spend time vs. money. People are willing to spend more time for higher risk, higher return options ex ante. However, this pattern is reversed when they spend money and show the more standard behavior of increasing risk aversion. Ex post, it is easier for people to accommodate negative outcomes by adjusting the value of their temporal inputs than monetary inputs.

Effect of Background Variables

Nowlis and Simonson (1997) claimed that product attributes differ in the degree to which they may be meaningfully evaluated in the absence of multiple alternatives. They argue that certain attributes such as brand quality are context independent, while others such as price are extremely context dependent. Evaluation of the price attribute is difficult and unreliable in absence of a context. Four streams of context effect literature are reviewed, including the choice set, reference points, price image, and consumer information vs. background.

Choice Set

Consider the following choice problem: A customer need to choose between two six-pack cola, product A is priced at $1.8 and has a quality rating of 50, and product B is priced at $2.6 with a 70 quality rating. The customer is having a hard time comparing the two products and making the price-quality tradeoff, so she delays the purchase and goes to another store. In this store she meets the same two products again, plus a new product C available with price $1.8 and quality rating 30. This time our customer happily bought product A.

The new product C is obviously worse than and dominated by product A, but not by product B. Therefore we would call C an asymmetrically dominated alternative. One prediction from a number of consumer choice models including Luce model of choice (1959) is that C would take disproportionally more market share from a similar product A rather than a dissimilar B, called similarity hypothesis. A second prediction of the Luce model would be that adding a new alternative cannot increase the probability of choosing a member of the original set, called regularity condition. Here both similarity hypothesis and regularity condition can be violated by addition of an asymmetrically dominated alternative C.

The story behind this problem is that the context of choice has been altered by adding of a new alternative. The addition of a low-quality product makes the 20 point quality difference between A and B less important, a manifestation of range strategy. A repetition of a low price $1.8 makes the price attribute more important, an instance of frequency strategy. Huber, Payne, and Puto (1982) had shown with their experiments that the range strategy could increase an average of 13% of market share for the target product, while a range-frequency strategy had a net gain of 8%. They suggested that (1) the range strategy can increase the range of the dimension on which the target is weakest, thereby decreasing the importance of a fixed difference on that dimension and making the competitor's advantage less extreme; (2) increasing the frequency of the dimension on which the target is superior might highlight the weight of that dimension. This is achieved by adding another price level thus drawing more attention to the price dimension. The addition of a new price might also spread the psychological distance of the price advantage the target has over its competitor.

In support of the range theory, Janiszewski and Lichtenstein (1999) showed that the range of prices a consumer evoked when evaluating a market price could have an independent influence on the judged attractiveness of the market price. Variance in the width of the evoked price range affected judgment of price-attractiveness in the absence of any variance in the internal preferential price. Niedrich, Sharma, and Wedell (2001) provided evidence that range-frequency theory accounted for reference price effects that the other theories could not, suggesting that consumers compared the target price against specific members of the category rather than the category prototype. Their experiment indicated that range and frequency effects can be moderated by the stimulus presentation condition. Consumers placed greater weight on extreme prices anchoring the range for internal reference prices than for external reference prices.

Simonson and Tversky (1992) proposed two hypotheses for context effect on consumer's choice problem—tradeoff contrast and extremeness aversion. Tradeoff contrast refers that the preference for an alternative is enhanced or hindered depending on whether the tradeoffs within the choice set are favorable or unfavorable to that option. Extremeness aversion claims that the attractiveness of an option is increased if it is an intermediate one in the choice set and is diminished if it is an extreme one. It is found that tradeoff contrasts are not limited to local context, or the context defined by the offered set itself. People also compare an option with relevant alternatives they have encountered in the past, or background contrast. For instance, subjects exposed to the background where the cost of computer memory is high would be more likely to select the computer with bigger memory. Both tradeoff contrast and extremeness aversion are expected to have less impact under situations where consumers have well-established preferences. Simonson and Tversky (1992) had further conducted a series of studies revealing that context effects were both common and robust.

Simonson and Tversky's reason-based choice model (1993) tried to explain the context effect from a reason analysis approach. It is argued that, when faced with the need to choose, decision makers often seek and construct reasons in order to resolve the conflict and justify their choice, either to themselves or to others. Framing effect and context effect, which are hard to interpret from the value maximization perspective, are easier to understand if we assume that various frames and contexts highlight certain aspects of the options, thus bringing forth different reasons to guide decision. Back to the three-product problem, the presence of C helps the decision maker to break the tie and builds up an argument for choosing A over B. Providing a context that presents compelling reasons for choosing an option apparently increases people's tendency to opt for that option, whereas lacking a good reason of choice often increase people's tendency to maintain the status quo or search for other alternatives.

Reference Points

Both internal and external reference prices can serve as context of evaluation. Liefeld and Heslop (1985) exposed consumers to five different price representations—regular price alone, sale price alone, regular price with Manufacturer's Suggested List Price (MSLP), sale price with regular price, or sale price with MSLP. Although perceptions of ordinary product prices were not affected by the presence or type of reference price, the subjects did have lower estimates of ordinary prices in the sale context. Adaval and Monroe (2002) showed that the context in which a product was seen influenced the internal standard that consumers used to judge both this and other products. Two of their experiments indicated that a product was judged as less expensive in a high-priced context than in a low-priced context, even though the product's actual price was recalled as higher in the first condition than the second. This effect of the initial context even carried over to a new product encountered two days later.

Existence of price promotion, either from the target brand itself or from competing brands, often provides reference points when consumer makes price estimation. Discounts can take the form of frequent but shallow discounts, or deep but infrequent discounts. Alba and Mela (1999) contrasted depth effect with frequency effect on consumer's estimation of price levels. Their experiment identified that frequency information was more influential when sets of interstore or interbrand comparative prices exhibited complex and overlapping distributions, hence creating processing difficulty; on the contrary, a depth bias occurred when prices had a simpler, dichotomous distribution. These results illustrated the importance of context in determining consumer price judgments in a promotional environment.

Research also suggests that the reference price provided by the context does not need to be a plausible one to influence consumer's judgments. Urbany, Bearden, and Weilbaker (1988) indicated that compared to an ad without a reference price, an ad with a plausible reference price raised subjects' estimates of the advertiser's regular price and perceived offer value. An exaggerated reference price had relatively the same positive effects on perception compared to a plausible one, even for the more skeptical subjects. Further, when subjects were presented with an advertised sale price above the lowest expected price, the exaggerated reference price increased the percentage of subjects who purchased the product from the advertiser without checking other stores' prices.

Prior research has demonstrated how unrelated numbers can influence decision making. The mechanism known as anchoring describes how random starting points systematically influence people's estimations (Tversky & Kahneman, 1974). More specifically, people often form estimates based on an initial but irrelevant anchor, and adjust from there to yield their final answer. Nunes and Boatwright (2004) explored the effect of incidental prices on the consumer's willingness to pay, and found that product prices that buyers encounter unintentionally (prices advertised, offered, paid for unrelated products) can serve as anchors, thus affecting willingness to pay for the product that they intend to buy.

Price Image

Store reputation and price image often provide a reference and context for the perceived price (un)fairness, an important variable for shopping intention. Bolton, Warlop, and Alba's study (2003) demonstrated consumers were inclined to believe that the selling price of a good or service was substantially higher than its fair price. They appeared sensitive to several reference points like past prices, competitor prices, and product costs, but underestimated impact from inflation, overattributed price differences to profits, and failed to take into account the full range of vending costs. Potential corrective interventions such as providing historical price information, explaining price differences, and cueing costs were only modestly effective. Campbell (1999) examined the influence of the inferred motive for price increase on perceptions of price unfairness and showed that the firm's reputation can influence the inferred motive of price increase, thereby altering perceptions of price unfairness. Specifically, participants would like to give a firm with a good reputation the benefit of the doubt when inferring its motive. The firm with a poor reputation, on the contrary, did not receive this benefit. Heyman and Mellers (2007, this volume) argue that industry norms and pricing structure transparency of the company also contribute to consumers' perception of pricing fairness.

Although low-price guarantee policies like price-matching refund are common in many retail environments, the impact of such policies on consumers are largely depending on consumer's reference price, search cost, and the store price image. Srivastava and Lurie (2003) exhibited that sometimes consumers perceived price-matching policies as signals of low store prices. The presence of a refund increased the likelihood of discontinuing price search when the search cost was high. Whereas when the search cost was low, presence of a price matching policy can even increase the number of stores searched. Biswas et al. (2002) suggested that the effect of a low price guarantee was likely to be moderated by other price cues such as reference prices and price image of the store. A low price guarantee resulted in higher value perception and shopping intention when reference prices were low or absent. Intention to search for a better price was lower when the low price guarantee was offered by a low price image store. For high price image stores, the low price guarantee can act as a double-edged sword, increasing both value perception and searching intentions.

Context also has an impact on the effectiveness of semantic cue used to communicate pricing image. Lichtenstein, Burton, and Karson (1991) examined the differential effects of two types of semantic cues. Their results suggested that, for manipulations of external reference prices with offering price held constant, semantic cues that connote high distinctiveness (vs. low consistency) of price discounts were more effective in influencing consumers' price-related evaluations. Grewal, Marmorstein, and Arun (1996) argued that the relative effectiveness of semantic cues depended on both consumers' decision context and the level of processing evoked by the discount size.

Information vs. Background

Research has shown that there is heterogeneity in consumer knowledge of prices and deals. Context effects are expected to be mitigated by consumers' knowledge of price and promotion. Buyers' purchase behavior can be influenced not only by the current price of a product, but also by what prices they expect in the future. Jacobson and Obermiller (1990) claimed that consumer's expected future price was very important among numerous potential reference prices, playing a crucial role in the decision to buy now or later. Hence the reference price should be characterized as a forward-looking concept. Krishna's model (1994) implied that normative purchase behavior was very different between consumers with and without knowledge of future deals. His model suggested that compared with less knowledgeable consumers, people with knowledge of future promotions could be more likely to purchase on low-value deals and discount on less preferred brands. Another implication of interest was that the relative quantity purchased by consumers who had deal knowledge depended on the time pattern of deals, comparing with no-knowledge consumers.

Herr's research (1989) illustrated that cognitive categories of price may be primed and become temporarily more accessible from memory, thus more likely to be used in subsequent information processing. Herr (1989) showed that an unfamiliar moderate quality product can be perceived as expensive or inexpensive depending on subtle contextual variables that influence what examples of a product category come to mind. When expensive examples come to mind, the unfamiliar product seems inexpensive. When inexpensive examples come to mind, the same product seems expensive. However, these effects were influenced by individual differences in consumer knowledge. Rao and Sieben (1992) assessed how differences in prior knowledge resulted in variability in price acceptability and information processing level. Acceptable price-range end-points were found to be lowest for low-knowledge subjects while more knowledge was accompanied by an increase in both limits of the acceptable price range. Moreover, the extent to which price and related extrinsic information was found to be lowest for moderately knowledgeable subjects.

On the other hand, pricing itself could serve as information in consumers' purchase decisions, as exhibited by price-quality inference and the effect of price discounts on brand loyalty. Cronley et al. (2005) suggest that consumers often rely heavily on price as a predictor of quality and typically overestimate the strength of this relation. Furthermore, the inferences of quality based on pricing can influence real purchase decisions. Their experiments concluded that quality inferences are more heavily influenced by price when individuals have a high need for cognitive closure and when the amount of information presented is high. Similarly, Kardes et al. (2004) suggest that consumers' quality inferences are less influenced by price when concern about closure is low (vs. high) and information is presented randomly (vs. ordered) or a small amount of information is presented. Regarding price's impact on brand loyalty, Dodson et al. (1978) believe that self-perception theory and economic utility theory provide complementary explanations for the effect of deals on brand switching. Ailawadi , Lehmann, and Neslin (2001) studied Procter and Gamble's (P&G's) value pricing strategy and found that, for the average brand, deals and coupons could increase market penetration and but surprisingly have little impact on customer retention.

PROCESSING FLUENCY

Processing fluency strategies refer to the pricing formats that exploit use of habits and cognitive constraints with which people perceive, encode, and process stimulus information. People are often "cognitive misers" who eschew any difficult intellectual activity, especially when involvement is low (Petty, Cacioppo, & Schumann, 1983). Processing fluency is different from framing. Framing strategies (like PAD) present the same price in another format to influence decision-maker's perspective, hence choice; while in processing fluency strategies like tensile claim and 9-ending prices, people mistakenly assumes or expect a different price from the actual price due to their information-processing habits and constraints. Such effects of processing fluency can occur either above or below conscious level.

Tensile Claims

When advertising discounts, retailers typically present price claims varying on two key dimensions. First, discounts may be specified either precisely (e.g., 40% off) or with nonspecific (tensile) information as in a range of discounts (e.g., up to 50% off). Second, discounts may be offered on an entire group (e.g., sale on "all" items) or on a subset of an advertised group of items (e.g., "Save 50–70% on selected items"). Such tensile price claims are found to have an impact on consumers' perceptions of offer value, information value, and price reduction.

Mobley, Bearden, and Teel's findings (1988) suggested that the use of tensile claims in conjunction with large advertised price reductions may result in decreased perceived offer value and substantial discounting of expected price reductions by the consumer. Dhar, González-Vallejo, and Soman (1995, 1999) proposed that consumers' valuation of an advertised offer depended on their subjective assessments about the probability with which they would find a desirable item at a discounted price (called subjective probability), the size of that discount (called subjective discount), and the probability of liking the sale item. Their results showed that when the fraction of stock specified to be on sale was low (high), consumers responding to a tensile claim were optimistic (pessimistic) about the discount they believed they would get, therefore expecting a greater (smaller) subjective discount than the midpoint of the tensile range. Correspondingly, in response to a precise claim, consumers expected a subjective discount equal to the advertised discount. Consequently, when the fraction of stock on sale was low (high), advertised deals with tensile claims were perceived to be more (less) attractive than with precise claims. Moreover, they found that there was a "threshold discount" level for each store above which tensile claims were more effective and below which precise claims were more effective, with the threshold level greater for a store with a higher price image.

Right-Digit Ending

Another preponderant pricing format is ending the price with the digit 9. Schindler and Kirby's analysis (1998) of the rightmost digits of selling prices confirmed the overrepresentation of the digits 0, 5, and 9 using a sample of retail price advertisements. The high cognitive accessibility of round numbers can account for the overrepresentation of 0- and 5- ending prices, suggesting two effects that could account for the overrepresentation of 9-ending prices: (1) a tendency of consumers to perceive a 9-ending price as a round-number price with a small amount given back, which is an application of the "silver lining" principle; and (2) a tendency of consumers to underestimate a 9-ending price by encoding it as the first round number evoked during incomplete left-to-right processing.

Similarly, Stiving, and Winer's model (1997) with scanner data provided support for both level effects (consumers may underestimate the value of a price) and image effects (consumers may infer meaning from the right-hand digits) in consumers' reaction to right-hand digits, showing that price format and the ensuing information processing level would have a joint impact.

Perceptual Congruency

Processing fluency does not have to occur above the consciousness threshold. An assumption of classical economic theory is that comparative price information is processed in a conscious, deliberate, and rational manner. However, recent studies have demonstrated that buyers do not always process pricing stimuli in a conscious, deliberate manner, but instead frequently rely on the nonconscious, automatic processes (Coulter & Coulter, 2005). When price information is processed at a nonconscious level, consumers typically demonstrate a lack of price awareness and are unable to recall the exact price of the product at a later time. Nonetheless those same consumers may still be able to judge the product as "expensive" or a "bargain." In other words, implicit estimates regarding the price and value of the product can still be made and hence impacts purchase decisions.

A key finding of Coulter and Coulter's study (2005) was that congruent and incongruent size dimensions impacted price assessments, value assessments, and purchase intentions. More specifically, presenting the lower sale prices in relatively small font resulted in more favorable value assessments and greater purchase likelihood than presenting the lower sale prices in relatively large font. This effect is similar to the concept of "perceptual fluency" in psychological literature where a stimulus' physical identity and form can influence the ease of information processing and consequently the liking of the stimulus (Schwarz, 2004). The use of distinctive color, movement, position, isolation, or contrast of price information can all serve as perceptually fluent ways to affect price information processing. Coulter and Coulter (2005) contemplated that presenting price information at the conscious and unconscious level may influence price evaluation simultaneously, perhaps in a manner analogous to the "central" vs. "peripheral" (Petty & Cacioppo, 1984) or "systematic" vs. "heuristic" (Chaiken, 1980) routes in persuasion literature.

CONCLUSIONS

Summary

Price is undoubtedly one of the most important market variables. Given the human complexity in psychological processes and limitation in cognitive capabilities, it is not surprising to see that traditional economic theory and normative choice models often fall short in explaining consumer choice and consumption. This is especially true because consumers never treat prices at their face value, but instead embed them in a broader context and attribute meaning above and beyond the notion of the monetary loss they create.

Drawing from theoretical and empirical research, we have summarized the effect of price presentation on consumer decision making in three main areas—mental accounting, effect of background variables, and processing fluency. Although a number of specific factors influence consumer judgment, two common themes emerge. First, people make pleasant decisions by engaging voluntarily or unconsciously in hedonic editing of information; second, people make satisfying (rather than optimizing) choices that are significantly influenced by the information processing level evoked during their evaluation process.

Future Research Directions

Finally, we hope to offer some insight into future pricing research by outlining several new directions. Delving into consumer psychology has greatly advanced our understanding of decision-making phenomena, biases, and processes. It is our belief that investigating price from various new approaches (e.g., implicit, emotional, and informational, etc.) could help us better comprehend the underlying mechanism of consumer choice.

Implicit Framing

Psychological literature has generally recognized the prevalence and powerfulness of automaticity and unconscious thinking (e.g., Bargh, 1994). Recent consumer research demonstrates that the standard people use to evaluate products can be below participants' perceptual and conceptual thresholds (e.g., Adaval & Monroe, 2002; Coulter & Coulter, 2005), raising the possibility of implicit framing of pricing information. Implicit framing refers to the price formulation manner which intends to appeal to people's liking without conscious awareness. In many everyday life scenarios, consumers pick up products from the shelf without extensive processing of price information.

One example of implicit framing occurs when different kinds of pricing policies try to meet various goals of consumers, thereby creating a regulatory focus fit (Higgins, 2002), or conceptual fluency. For instance, everyday-low-price might elicit more positive feelings from prevention-focused consumers while high-low pricing could meet goals of promotion-focused consumers. Whenever the pricing is congruent with our goals, the sense of "feeling right" might influence people's judgment and decision in an unconscious fashion. Under situations of low-level information processing, how to frame prices implicitly can be an interesting topic for future research.

Emotional Pricing

Recent decision-making research has put an increasingly interest in emotion relevant choice. Luce, Payne, and Bettman (1999) showed that in general, coping with potentially emotion-laden choice was one factor influencing consumer choice strategies, suggesting avoiding or otherwise coping with negative emotion as an important goal that guides decision behavior.

Unlike the economic belief regarding price as simply a representation of utility, consumers often get emotional with prices, with different emotion states leading to different behaviors intentions. For example, when a customer is delighted by a price, he is much more likely to preach about the brand to friends than if he feels merely satisfied. Contrary to common assumptions, Chernev's research (2003) demonstrated that consumers often preferred selecting rather than generating a price for the absence of a readily available reference price range.

When it is difficult for people to come up with a subjective value for an item, affect often plays a bigger role in evaluation, suggesting the significance of emotional pricing. Emotional pricing is more obvious when people are price generators, or in a more price-flexible environment such as online bidding/shopping. McGraw and Tetlock (2005) explored situations where people contemplated buying or selling objects endowed with special relational significance. They showed that pragmatic economic interests were balanced against the desire to be (or appear to be) a person honoring social-relational constraints, when the resources should be considered fungible in economics. Greenleaf (2004) showed that two emotions—anticipated regret and rejoicing—affected decision making in an online environment. His data from a simulated auction supported emotion's influence on seller's reserve prices.

Price, especially the "willingness to pay" information, is usually a motivation problem in essence. The central feature of affect is often not the feeling states associated with it, but its role in people's tendency to act. All affects address "go/no-go" questions which motivate approach or avoidance behaviors (Camerer, Loewenstein, & Prelec, 2004). Additional investigation into emotional pricing we could provide a better understanding of a consumer's decision-making process from a motivational approach.

Utility Blindness

The fundamental question in promotion research—why consumers respond to the deals— has always been a controversial one. Economic and game-theory research generally assumes that monetary savings from deals are what attract customers. Consumer research argues that people fall for the deals for their own demographic properties like deal proneness (e.g., Lichtenstein, Netemeyer, & Burton, 1990), for the customer value and positive experience, or for an array of both utilitarian and hedonic benefits the promotions may offer (Chandon, Wansink, & Laurent, 2000). The idea that consumers base their purchase decision on total utility (sum of acquisition utility plus transaction utility) has been widely accepted and applied to marketing research, especially in the sales promotions area (e.g., Thaler, 1985; Grewal, Monroe, & Krishnan, 1998; Lichtenstein, Netemeyer, & Burton, 1990). However, in real life consumers often seem to disobey the principle of total utility. As indicated by the phenomena that nearly everybody's house contains something we bought in a deal but seldom use, consumers might fall for an attractive deal even when the total utility from the purchase is negative.

It would be interesting to examine consumers' response to promotions from an information processing perspective. Utility blindness refers to the phenomena that under limited information processing consumers would base their purchase decision solely on the perceived gains from the deal (i.e., transaction utility) rather than total utility (Liu, 2005). When the deal is attractive enough, people would buy the product even though the total utility is negative; on the other hand, an unattractive deal would decrease people's purchase likelihood even when the total utility is not affected by the promotion.

REFERENCES

Adaval, R., & Monroe, K. B. (2002). Automatic construction and use of contextual information for product and price evaluations. *Journal of Consumer Research, 28*(4), 572–589.

Ailawadi, K. L., Lehmann, D. R., & Neslin, S. A. (2001). Market response to a major policy change in the marketing mix: Learning from Pro.cter and Gamble's value pricing strategy. *Journal of Marketing, 65*(1), 44–61.

Alba, J. W., & Mela, C. F. (1999). The effect of discount frequency and depth on consumer price judgments. *Journal of Consumer Research, 26*(92) 99–105.

Bargh, J. A. (1994). The four horsemen of Automaticity: Awareness, intention, efficiency and control in social cognition. In R. S. Wyer & T. K. Srull (Eds.), *Handbook of social cognition* (Vol. 1, pp. 1–40). Hillsdale, NJ: Erlbaum.

Baumeister, R. F. (2002). Yielding to temptation: Self-control failure, impulsive purchasing, and consumer behavior. *Journal of Consumer Research, 28*, 670–675.

Biswas, A., Pullig, C., Yagci, M. I., & Dean, D. H. (2002). Consumer evaluation of low price guarantees: The moderating role of reference price and store image. *Journal of Consumer Psychology, 12*(2), 107–119.

Bolton, L. E., Warlop, L., & Alba, J. W. (2003). Consumer perceptions of price (un)fairness. *Journal of Consumer Research, 29*(4), 474–492.

Büyükkurt, K. (1986). Integration of serially sampled price information: Modeling and some findings. *Journal of Consumer Research, 13*(3), 357–373.

Camerer, C., Loewenstein, G., & Drazen Prelec (2004). Neuroeconomics: How neuroscience can inform economics. Working paper.

Campbell, M. C. (1999). Perceptions of price unfairness: Antecedents and consequences. *Journal of Marketing Research, 36*(2), 187–200.

Chaiken, S. (1980). Heuristic versus systematic information-processing and the use of source versus messages cues in persuasion. *Journal of Personality and Social Psychology, 39*(5), 752–766.

Chakravarti, D., Krish, R., Paul, P., & Srivastava, J. (2002). Partitioned presentation of multicomponent bundle prices: Evaluation, choice and underlying processing effects. *Journal of Consumer Psychology, 12*(3), 215–230.

Chandon, P., Wansink, B., & Laurent, G. (2000). A Benefit Congruency Framework of Sales Promotion Effectiveness. *Journal of Marketing, 64*(4), 65–81.

Chernev, A. (2003). Reverse pricing and online price elicitation strategies in consumer choice. *Journal of Consumer Psychology, 13*(1/2), 51–63.

Coulter, K. S., & Coulter, R. A. (2005). Size does matter: The effects of magnitude representation congruency on price perceptions and purchase likelihood. *Journal of Consumer Psychology, 15*(1) 64–75.

Cronley, M. L., Posavac, S. S., Meyer, T, Kardes, F. R., & Kellaris, J. J. (2005). A selective hypothesis testing perspective on price-quality inference inference-based choice. *Journal of Consumer Psychology, 15*(2): 159–169

Dhar, S. K, González-Vallejo, C., & Soman, D. (1995). Brand promotions as a lottery. *Marketing Letters, 6*(3), 221–233.

Dhar, S. K, González-Vallejo, C., & Soman, D. (1999). Modeling the effects of advertised price claims: Tensile versus precise claims. *Marketing Science, 18*(2), 154–178.

Dodson, J. A., Tybout, A. M., & Sternthal, B. (1978) Impact of deals and deal retraction on brand switching. *Journal of Marketing Research, 15*(1), 72–82.

Dolan, R. J., & Simon, H. (1996), *Power pricing.* New York: The Free Press.

Dreze, X., & Nunes, J. C. (2004). Using Combined-Currency Prices to Lower Consumers' Perceived Cost. *Journal of Marketing Research, 41*(1), 59–73.

Fisher, I. (1928). *The money illusion.* New York: Adelphi.

Gourville, J. T. (1998). Pennies-a-day: The effect of temporal reframing on transaction evaluation. *Journal of Consumer Research, 24*(4), 395–409.

Gourville, J. T., & Soman, D. (1998). Payment depreciation: The behavioral effects of temporally separating payments from consumption. *Journal of Consumer Research, 25*(2), 160–175.

Gourville, J. T., & Soman, D. (2002). Pricing and the psychology of consumption. *Harvard Business Review,* (September), 90–96.

Greenleaf, E. A. (2004). Reserves, regret, and rejoicing in open English auctions. *Journal of Consumer Research, 31*(2), 264–274.

Grewal, D., Marmorstein, H., & Sharma, A. (1996). Communicating price information through semantic cues: The moderating effects of situation and discount size. *Journal of Consumer Research, 23*(2), 148–156.

Grewal, D., Monroe, K. B., & Krishnan, R. (1998). The effects of price-comparison advertising on buyers' perceptions of acquisition value, transaction value, and behavioral intentions. *Journal of Marketing, 62*(2), 45–60.

Gupta, S., & Cooper, L. G. (1992). The discounting of discounts and promotion thresholds. *Journal of Consumer Research, 19*(3), 401–412.

Heath, C., & Soll, J. B.(1996). Mental budgeting and consumer decision. *Journal of Consumer Research, 23*(1), 40–52.

Heath, T. B., & Chatterjee, S. (1995). Mental accounting and changes in price: The frame dependence of reference dependence. *Journal of Consumer Research, 22*(1), 90–97.

Herr, P. (1989). Priming price: Prior knowledge and context effects. *Journal of Consumer Research, 16*(1), 67–76.

Heyman, J. E., & Mellers, B. A. (2007). Perceptions of fair pricing. In C. P. Haugtvedt, P. M. Herr, & F. R. Kardes (Eds.), *Handbook of consumer psychology.* Mahwah, NJ: Erlbaum.

Higgins, E. T. (2002). How self-regulation creates distinct values: The case of promotion and prevention decision making. *Journal of Consumer Psychology, 12*(3), 177–191.

Huber, J., Payne, J. W., & Puto, C. (1982). Adding asymmetrically dominated alternatives: violations of regularity and similarity hypothesis. *Journal of Consumer Research, 9,* 90–98.

Jacobson, R., & Obermiller C. (1990). The Formation of Expected Future Price: A Reference Price for Forward-Looking Consumers. *Journal of Consumer Research, 16*(4) 420–433.

Janiszewski, C., & Lichtenstein, D. R. (1999). A range of theory account of price perception. *Journal of Consumer Research, 25*(4), 353–369.

Kahneman, D., & Tversky, A. (1979). Prospect theory: Analysis of decision under risk. *Econometrica, 47*(2), 263–291.

Kalwani, M. U., Yim, C. K., Rinne, H. J., & Sugita, Y. (1990). A price expectations model of customer brand choice. *Journal of Marketing Research, 27*(3), 251–263.

Kardes, F. R., Cronley, M. L., Kellaris, J. J., & Posavac, S. S. (2004). The role of selective information processing in price-quality inference *Journal of Consumer Research, 31*(2), 368–374.

Krishna, A. (1994). The effect of deal knowledge on consumer purchase behavior. *Journal of Marketing Research, 31*(1), 76–92.

Krishnamurthi, L., Mazumdar, T., & Raj, S. R. (1992). Asymmetric response to price in consumer brand choice and purchase quantity decisions. *Journal of Consumer Research, 19*(3), 387–403.

Lichtenstein, D. R., Netemeyer, R. G., & Burton, S. (1990). Distinguishing coupon proneness from value consciousness: An acquisition-transaction utility theory perspective. *Journal of Marketing, 54*(3), 54–68.

Lichtenstein, D. R., Burton, S., & Johnson, E. J.(1991). The effect of semantic cues on consumer perceptions of reference price aids. *Journal of Consumer Research, 18*(3), 380–392.

Liefeld, J., & Heslop, L. A. (1985). Reference prices and deception in newspaper advertising. *Journal of Consumer Research, 11*(4), 868–877.

Liu, W. (2005). Utility blindness: Why do we fall for the deal? Working Paper. University of Toronto.

Luce, D. R. (1959). *Individual choice behavior.* New York: Wiley.

Luce, M. F., Payne, J. W., & Bettman, J. R. (1999). Emotional trade-off difficulty and choice. *Journal of Marketing Research, 36*(2), 143–160.

Mazumdar, T., & Jun, S. Y. (1993). Consumer evaluations of multiple versus single price change. *Journal of Consumer Research, 20*(3), 441–450.

Mayhew, G. E., & Winer, R. S. (1992). An empirical analysis of internal and external reference prices using scanner data. *Journal of Consumer Research, 19*(1), 62–71.

McGraw, A. P., & Tetlock, P. E. (2005). Taboo trade-offs, relational framing, and the acceptability of xxchanges. *Journal of Consumer Psychology, 15*(1), 2–16.

Mobley, M. F., Bearden, W. O., & Teel, J. E. (1988).An investigation of individual responses to tensile price claims. *Journal of Consumer Research, 15*(2), 273–280.

Morwitz, V. G., Greenleaf, E. A., & Johnson, E. J. (1998). Divide and prosper: Consumers' reactions to partitioned prices. *Journal of Marketing Research, 35*(4), 453–464.

Niedrich, R. W., Sharma, S., & Wedell, D. H. (2001). Reference Price and Price Perceptions: A Comparison of Alternative Models. *Journal of Consumer Research, 28*(3) 339–355.

Nowlis, S. M., & Simonson, I. (2004). Attribute-task compatibility as a determinant of consumer preference reversals. *Journal of Marketing Research, 34*(2), 205–219.

Nunes, J. C., & Boatwright, P. (2004). Incidental prices and their effect on willingness to pay. *Journal of Marketing Research, 42*(4), 457–467.

Nunes, J. C., & Park, C. W. (2003). Incommensurate resources: Not just more of the aame. *Journal of Marketing Research, 40*(1), 26–38.

Okada, E. M. (2001). Trade-ins, mental accounting, and product replacement decisions. *Journal of Consumer Research, 27*(4), 433–447.

Okada, E. M. & Hoch, S. J. (2004). Spending time versus spending money. *Journal of Consumer Research, 31*(2), 313–324.

Pelham, B., Sumarta, T., & Myaskovsky, L. (1994). The easy path from many to much: The numerosity heuristic. *Cognitive Psychology, 26*, 103–133.

Petty, R. E., & Cacioppo, J. T. (1984). The effects of involvement on responses to argument quantity. *Journal of Personality and Social Psychology, 46*(1), 69–81.

Petty, R. E., Cacioppo, J. T., & Schumann, D. (1983). Central and peripheral routes to advertising effectiveness: The moderating role of involvement. *Journal of Consumer Research, 10*(2), 135–146.

Prelec, D., & Loewenstein, G. (1998). The red and the black: mental accounting of savings and debt. *Marketing Science, 17*(1), 4–29.

Rao, A. R., & Monroe, K. B. (1988). The moderating effect of prior knowledge on cue utilization in product evaluations. *Journal of Consumer Research, 15*(2), 253–265.

Rao, A. R., & Sieben, W. A. (1992).The effect of prior knowledge on price acceptability and the type of information examined. *Journal of Consumer Research, 19*(2), 256–271.

Raghubir, P., & Srivastava, J. (2002). Effect of face value on product valuation in foreign currencies. *Journal of Consumer Research, 29*(3), 335–348.

Schindler, R. M., & Kirby, P. N. (1997). Patterns of rightmost digits used in advertised prices: Implications for nine-ending effects. *Journal of Consumer Research, 24*(2), 192–202.

Schwarz, N. (2004). Meta-cognitive experiences in consumer judgment and decision-making. *Journal of Consumer Psychology, 14*, 332–348.

Shafir, E., Diamond, P., & Tversky, A. (1997). Money illusion. *Quarterly Journal of Economics, 112*, 342–374.

Simon, H. A. (1956).Rational choice and the structure of the environment. *Psychological Review, 63*(2), 129–138.

Simonson, I., Carmon, Z., & O'Curry, S. (1994). Experimental evidence on the negative effect of product features and sales promotion on brand choice. *Marketing Science, 13*(1), 23–41.

Simonson, I., & Tversky, A. (1992). Choice in context: Trade-off contrast and extremeness aversion. *Journal of Marketing Research, 29*, 281–295.

Simonson, S. E., & Tversky, A. (1993). Reason-based choice. *Cognition, 49*(1-2) 11–36.

Soman, D. (2001). Effects of payment mechanism on spending behavior: The role of rehearsal and immediacy of payments. *Journal of Consumer Research, 27*(4), 460–475

Soman, D. (2004). Framing, loss aversion and mental accounting. forthcoming In N. Harvey & D. Koehler (Eds.), *Blackwell handbook of judgment and decision Making Research*,

Soman, D., & Gourville, J. T. (2001). Transaction decoupling: How price bundling affects the decision to consume. *Journal of Marketing Research, 38*(1), 30–45.

Srivastava, J., & Lurie, N. (2001). A consumer perspective on price-matching refund policies: Effect on price perceptions and search eehavior. *Journal of Consumer Research, 28*(2), 296–308.

Stiving, M., & Winer, R. (1997). An empirical analysis of price endings with scanner data. *Journal of Consumer Research, 24*(1), 57–68.

Thaler, R. (1980). Toward a positive theory of consumer choice. *Journal of Economic Behavior and Organization, 1,* 39–60.

Thaler, R. (1985). Mental accounting and consumer choice. *Marketing Science, 4,* 199–204.

Thaler, R. (1999). Mental Accounting matters. *Journal of Behavioral Decision Making, 12*(3), 183–206.

Tversky, A., & Kahneman, D. (1974). Judgment under uncertainty—Heuristics and biases. *Science, 185*(4157), 1124–1131.

Tversky, A., & Kahneman, D. (1981). The framing of decisions and the psychology of choice. *Science, 211*(30), 453–458.

Tversky, A., Slovic, P., & Shmuel, S. (1988). Contingent weighting in judgment and choice. *Psychological Review, 95*(3), 371.

Urbany, J. E., Bearden, W. O., & Weilbaker, D. C. (1988). The effect of plausible and exaggerated reference prices on consumer perceptions and price dearch. *Journal of Consumer Research, 15*(1), 95–110.

Wertenbroch, K. (1998). Consumption self control by rationing purchase quantities of virtue and vice. *Marketing Science, 17*(4), 317–338.

Wertenbroch, K., Soman, D., & Chattopadhyay A. (in press). Currency numerosity effects on the perceived value of transactions. *Journal of Consumer Research.*

Zeithaml, V. A. (1982). Consumer response to in-store price information environments. *Journal of Consumer Research,* 8(4), 357–370.

27

Perceptions of Fair Pricing

James E. Heyman

University of St. Thomas

Barbara A. Mellers

University of California, Berkeley

INTRODUCTION

Economic theory predicts that market efficiencies are greatest when firms maximize their self-interests. Yet the actions of some firms seem contrary to this prediction. In 1982, Johnson & Johnson faced a public relations disaster. One of their products, Tylenol, had been laced with cyanide. Johnson & Johnson immediately took Tylenol off the shelves, designed a tamper-resistant bottle, and worked extensively with law-enforcement agencies to find and prosecute those responsible. When interviewed, Johnson & Johnson executives, far from taking their bows, simply said, "We believe our first responsibility is to the doctors, nurses, and patients, to the mothers and fathers, and to all others who use our products and services."

One could argue that Johnson & Johnson's actions were consistent with economic theory. Fair play and goodwill could be profitable long-term strategies. But an alternative explanation for Johnson & Johnson's behavior is a desire to be fair and "do the right thing," even in situations that preclude enforcement (Kahneman, Knetsch, & Thaler, 1986a).

What, exactly, does it mean to be fair? This chapter focuses on consumer perceptions of fair pricing. When is it fair for a firm to raise prices, to maintain prices, or to decrease prices? Before discussing when changes in prices are fair, it is useful to consider the processes involved in the initial assessments of prices. Consumer behavior researchers have shown that, when unfamiliar with a product, consumers gather information in the form of television ads, print ads, and conversations with family and friends. They form a reference price and compare it to actual prices. (For more on reference prices, see Liu & Soman, 2006.) Pre-purchase reference prices can be based on many factors including previous prices, firms' perceived profits, and the costs firms encounter in bringing products to market (Bolton, Warlop, & Alba, 2003). Even expected future prices have been shown to affect evaluations of current prices (Jacobson & Obermiller, 1990). Regardless of how the reference price is formed, actual prices below the reference price are usually perceived as fair, and those above are viewed as unfair.

If an exchange occurs, consumers compare their product expectations against their actual experiences (Levin & Gaeth, 1988; Heath, Warlop, & Wu, 1999). Product expectations arise from personal knowledge, store-based information, and other people's experiences. If the product falls short of expectations, consumers are likely to be dissatisfied and perceive the exchange as unfair (Hunt & Nevin, 1981). If the product lives up to expectations or even exceeds expectations, consumers will be satisfied and accept the exchange as fair. Furthermore, some consumers will purchase the product again. With repeat purchases, consumers evaluate fairness by comparing new prices to the earlier price or prices paid by others.

Dual Entitlement

Firms increase prices for several reasons. Economic theory says they raise prices when the cost of producing goods or services becomes higher. They also raise prices when they can benefit from either an excess of consumer demand or a shortage of product supply. Kahneman, Knetsch, and Thaler (1986) showed that not all of these reasons for increasing prices are viewed as fair. Based on responses to a national survey conducted in Canada, the researchers found that consumers believe it is fair for a firm to raise prices when costs increase. For example, it is fair for a firm to raise the price of a table if the cost of the raw materials is higher. Likewise, it is fair for a fancy hotel to charge more than a nearby grocery store for a cold beer. However, it is unfair for a firm to profit from excess demand. Consumers are unhappy when a hardware store raises the price of snow shovels from $15 to $20 after a large snowstorm. Moreover, it is unfair for a firm to profit from a shortage of supply by auctioning off the last of a popular toy to the highest bidder.

These assertions depend, of course, on the motives of the firm. If a hardware store increases the price of snow shovels after a large snowstorm and gives the funds to a local homeless shelter or if a department store auctions off the last of a popular toy and gives the proceeds to a worthy charity, increased prices are viewed as fair. Price increases associated with philanthropic motives are more readily accepted (Campbell, 1999).

Kahneman et al. argued that perceptions of fair prices could be described by the principle of dual entitlement. After an exchange has occurred, reference transactions are established. The customer feels entitled to a reference price and feels the firm is entitled to a reference profit. If firms have higher costs, they can maintain reference profits by raising prices. But if firms raise prices in response to excess demand or a shortage of supply, they are acting unfairly. Reference profits are higher at the consumers' expense. The dual entitlement principle has been supported in both surveys and experiments with financial incentives (Franciosi et al., 1995; Frey et al., 1984; Kachelmeier, Limburg, & Schadewald, 1991).

In 1999, the Coca-Cola Corporation violated the dual entitlement principle when they experimented with a vending machine that changed the price of a Coke based on the weather. Prices were higher on hotter days and lower on colder days. With this strategy, Coca Cola planned to increase profits in the absence of higher costs. One can imagine the company's logic: on a hot day people place greater value on a cold drink, so why don't we charge more? Feeling duly exploited, consumers reacted angrily. The Coca-Cola Corporation, surprised by the backlash, issued a press release saying there was a misunderstanding. They had no intention of using the vending machines either now or in the future.

Framing Effects

A well-established finding that pertains to fairness is called a framing effect (Kahneman & Tversky, 1986). Framing effects are changes in preferences due to a shift in the reference point (Kahneman, Knetsch, & Thaler, 1986a). They exert powerful effects on consumer choice. Johnson, Hershey, Meszaros, and Kunreuther (1993) described a framing effect in the insurance industry. In 1988, the standard auto policy in New Jersey did not allow drivers the right to sue for pain and suffering from minor injuries, although they could purchase the right with a higher-priced policy. Only 20% of New Jersey drivers bought the more expensive policy. In 1990, the standard auto policy in Pennsylvania included the right to sue, and 75% of Pennsylvania drivers purchased it. Johnson et al. (1993) estimated that Pennsylvanians spent $200 million more on auto insurance than they would have spent if the default had been the cheaper option.

Framing effects can also influence the perceived fairness of prices. Kimes and Wirtz (2003) examined framing effects in the golfing industry. Most golfers know that early weekend tee times are in greatest demand. Kimes and Wirtz (2003) showed that two identical pricing schemes produced different perceptions of fairness. Consumers believe it is fair if a golf course charges the regular price for early tee times and offers a 20% discount for later times. However, consumers believe it is unfair if a golf course adds a 20% premium to the price of early tee times and charges the regular price for later times.

Framing effects also occur in the airline industry. Northwest Airlines was one of the first airlines to charge different prices for the same ticket depending on where consumers purchased the ticket. Prices were $10 higher at the airport than they were online. The headline of a newspaper article covering the story read, "Why Fly? Get Charged $10 Just to Show Up!" Northwest executives pointed out that JetBlue had the same pricing structure. JetBlue executives replied by saying that Northwest was wrong. JetBlue charged regular prices for tickets bought at the airport, but gave customers a $10 discount if they purchased tickets electronically.

Perhaps Coca Cola should have considered framing effects when they began experimenting with temperature-sensitive vending machines. If the machines had charged regular prices on hotter days and offered discounts on colder days, customers might have been less angry, less outraged, and possibly even willing to go along with the new machines.

Another important use of framing effects involves opportunity costs versus out-of-pocket costs. People often underweight opportunity costs relative to out-of-pocket costs (Thaler, 1985). This tendency has implications for fairness. Most firms refer to price decreases as "discounts" or "sales" rather than reductions in list price. Why? The cancellation of a discount or the end of a sale is perceived as more fair and acceptable than an outright price increase (Liberman et al., 2005). Consumers will be less upset and less likely to resist the change.

The distinction between opportunity costs and out-of-pocket costs also applies when firms become more efficient. Kahneman, Knetsch, and Thaler (1986b) showed that, when firms reduce their costs, consumers believe it is fair for them to maintain their prices. Firms can increase reference profits in the absence of higher costs with no damage to their reputations. The increased efficiency gives firms the "right" to increased profits. Again, the absence of a price decrease is less painful than the presence of a price increase. What is out of sight is much easier to put out of mind. Consumers are less sensitive to information that is not presented and more sensitive to information that is presented, even when the available information is of limited diagnostic value (Sanbonmatsu, Kardes, Houghton, Ho, & Posavac, 2003).

Variable vs. Fixed Pricing

Much of the previous work on fairness has focused on markets with fixed prices of goods or services. Prices generally remain constant with the amount purchased, the timing of purchase, or the consumer who makes the purchase. Reference prices and reference profits are fairly stable, and perceptions of fair prices can be evaluated relative to these reference points.

In contrast, some markets have prices that vary on a monthly, weekly, or even daily basis. It is hard to apply the dual entitlement principle to these markets because both reference prices and reference profits are distributions rather than fixed points. Both sides of the exchange are more fluid, so a sense of entitlement is less likely to develop.

This more fluid pricing structure has a variety of names, including price discrimination, dynamic pricing, and revenue management. Hereafter, we will refer to it as variable pricing. Variable pricing uses technology and information to differentiate among consumers and charge each what the market will bear. The trick for firms is to discover the maximum amounts that consumers are willing to pay and ensure that they pay those amounts.

There are two major types of variable pricing. With the first type, firms charge consumers different prices for different units of a good or service. We refer to this practice as *variable unit pricing*. With the second type, firms charge different consumers different prices for similar units. We call this method of pricing *variable consumer pricing*. Variable consumer pricing is done with groups of consumers as well as individuals. Figure 27.1 presents a schema. We now explore perceptions of fairness when reference points vary.

To examine fairness with variable reference points, we asked 140 undergraduates at the University of California, Berkeley, to rate the fairness of 14 different scenarios. Respondents indicated whether the parties involved would find the situation to be "Fair," "Unfair," or "Neither." In situations where participants responded with "Neither," we assumed that the concept of fairness did not apply, and we removed those responses from the analyses.[1]

Variable Unit Pricing   Prices that vary per unit can differ either as function of when the purchase is made or by how many units are purchased. When time is the discriminating variable, prices depend on how far in advance the good or service was purchased. For example, lower-priced rental cars are often available to those who make early reservations. When quantity is the discriminating variable, prices vary according to the amount purchased. Larger quantities are typically sold at lower unit prices.

We tested the perceived fairness of variable unit pricing with quantity discounts using the following question:

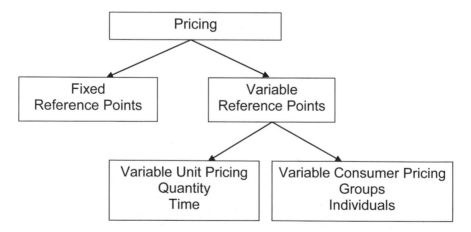

Figure 27.1   Schema for pricing. Prices can be fixed or variable. Variable prices can differ with quality or time (i.e., firms charge all customers different amounts for different units), or prices can differ across customers (i.e., firms charge different customers different amounts for the same units).

> Two neighbors, Mike and Jordan, are landscaping their backyards. Both need bricks. Mike needs 100 bricks and Jordan needs 500 bricks. When they arrive at the building supply store, they learn that the more bricks one purchases, the better the deal one can get. Mike pays $2 more per brick than Jordan pays.

The majority of participants thought that both Mike and Jordan would view the situation as fair. Most respondents (63%) said that Mike, who paid more per brick, would perceive the pricing as fair, and virtually all respondents (92%) thought Jordan would view it as fair ($\chi^2(1) = 7.7$, $N = 115$ for Mike and $\chi^2(1) = 92.4$, $N = 131$ for Jordan).

Airlines regularly use variable unit prices that differ with the timing of purchase. For many flights, consumers who book their tickets well in advance of the flight (e.g., vacationers) tend to pay less than those who book their tickets closer to the day of the flight (e.g., business executives) (Smith et al., 1992). There are several reasons for the general acceptance of this pricing scheme. First, it is a well-established industry norm. Second, on any given day, customers can choose whether or not to participate. Third, those who purchase early tickets usually accept restrictions on their tickets that reduce their value. Such tickets might not be refundable or costly to change. Those who purchase their tickets later often pay more for them in order to get the flexibility to change or cancel tickets at the last minute.[2]

The goal of most airlines is to sell enough advance tickets to ensure that seats are filled, while at the same time, keep enough seats available to serve the latecomers who are willing to pay full fare. Two things can go wrong. First, the airline may sell too many early restricted tickets and not have enough seats remaining to accommodate the full-fare passengers. Second, the airline may not sell enough restricted tickets and end up with too many full-fare seats available on the day of the flight. Airplane seats are a perishable good; any seats that are empty when the plane leaves are instantly worth nothing. To address this potential loss, some airlines drop the price of full-fare seats right before a flight when they are unlikely to capitalize on any more high-paying latecomers. These seats are typically the source of Web-based deals in which passengers buy on Friday to fly on Saturday.

This pricing strategy has implications for fairness. Passengers could find themselves sitting next to someone who paid significantly less for a ticket, but are eating the same peanuts, watching the same movie, and reaching the same location at the same time. Higher-paying passengers could easily be annoyed. But if it is common knowledge that earlier purchases are better deals and if passengers with lower fares purchased their tickets earlier, consumers may perceive this pricing structure as fair.

To examine people's perceptions of these pricing schemes, we introduced our survey participants to Mr. Thompson and Mr. Stone who meet on a flight from San Francisco to New York. We had four versions of the questionnaire. In all four versions, Mr. Thompson bought an unrestricted ticket one week prior to the flight and paid $400 more than Mr. Stone. Mr. Stone's bought his ticket either one month prior to the flight or the day of the flight, and his tickets were either restricted or unrestricted. One scenario read:

> Two airline passengers, Mr. Thompson and Mr. Stone, are both flying from San Francisco to New York City. They begin chatting and in the course of the conversation, they compare the prices they paid and when they purchased their tickets. Mr. Thompson bought his unrestricted ticket 1 week ago and paid $400 more than Mr. Stone who bought his restricted ticket 1 month ago.

Most participants (79%) thought Mr. Stone would perceive the situation as fair, and there was no effect of timing or restrictions. Reactions were more nuanced for Mr. Thompson. Logit analyses revealed that Mr. Thompson's perceptions depended on the timing of Mr. Stone's purchase, but not the restrictions on Mr Stone's ticket ($p = .05$).

When Mr. Stone purchased his ticket one month in advance, approximately half (54%) of participants thought Mr. Thompson would view the situation as unfair. But when Mr. Stone purchased his ticket the morning of the flight, there was a strong consensus. Virtually all respondents (84%) thought he would find the situation unfair ($\chi^2(1) = 24.9$, $N = 54$).

These questions show that variable unit pricing may be perceived as fair (e.g., bricks) or unfair (e.g., airlines). The brick question and the airlines questions differ in a host of ways. In the building supply industry, quantity discounts are a regular occurrence. In the airline industry, most passengers are aware that they can get lower fares with earlier purchases, but fewer are aware of the lower fares available at the last minute. Not only do fewer consumers know about this practice, it is also less common in the industry. Consistency of the variable pricing methods with industry norms may be at least one reason for the difference in the perceived fairness of the brick question versus the airline questions.

Another reason for the differences in perceptions may be the inconsistency in the firm's pricing strategies. With building supplies, there is a perfect correlation between amount purchased and price. Furthermore, two consumers who purchase the same number of bricks will be charged the same amount. But in the airline industry, the correlation between time of purchase and price is much lower and perhaps even nonexistent. Prices change all the time. Consumers might be more willing to accept variable pricing if prices were more predictable. If consumers knew they could get discounts for early purchases or discounts for last minute purchases, such prices might be more acceptable. But prices are both uncertain and contradictory. There are multiple rules that govern the actual prices at any given moment. Consumers simply don't know when to purchase their tickets to get the best deals, and the uncertainty may foster perceptions of unfairness. Being reminded of the inequality by sitting next to someone who got a better deal makes it even worse.

Variable Consumer Pricing   With variable consumer pricing, firms sell the same good or service to different consumers at different prices. The firm identifies differences in price sensitivity among consumers (either groups or individuals) and charges prices accordingly. Some firms segment consumers into groups based on an easily discernable trait (Carroll & Grimes, 1995). For example, many firms charge different prices based on age. Children and senior citizens often get discounts at the movies, on the subways, or in the amusement parks. Furthermore, such practices are readily accepted. Many people believe seniors and children are deserving of discounts. Another discriminating variable is gender. Some dry cleaners charge more to clean women's clothes than men's clothes. Similarly, many hair salons charge women more than men to cut and style their hair.

We explored some instances of variable consumer pricing among groups based on age. One question read:

> Carrie and her friends go to the movies. Carrie, who is 25 years old, pays $10 for her ticket. The man in front of her in line is 65 years old. He gets a senior discount and pays $6.

Most of the 61 participants (63%) thought that Carrie would perceive the situation as fair ($\chi^2(1) = 24.9$, $N = 115$), and a greater number of participants (92%) thought that the senior perceived it as fair ($\chi^2(1) = 90.7$). $N = 131$).

In the dry cleaning industry, the price of cleaning is based on the garment and what it costs to give it back to the consumer in a desired state. If women's clothes have more pleats, ruffles, or lace than men's clothes, if women expect better results than men, or if it costs more to press women's clothing than men's clothing because women's clothes don't fit the automatic press originally designed for men's clothes, dry cleaners are permitted to charge different prices based on gender.

We asked respondents what they thought about gender-based dry cleaning prices. Our question read:

> When Mrs. Simmon takes her blouse and her husband's dress shirt to the dry cleaners, she is told that prices differ for men's and women's shirts. Her blouse will cost $9, and her husband's dress shirt will cost $5.

Most (70%) believed Mrs. Simmon would perceive the situation as unfair ($\chi^2(1) = 9.6$, $N = 60$). Perhaps these views were based on uncertainty about whether Mrs. Simmon's blouse would truly take more work than Mr. Simmon's dress shirt. Alternatively, perceptions of unfairness may have been based on a general dislike for variable consumer pricing with gender as the discriminating variable.

Variable consumer pricing is widely accepted in today's marketplace, despite the fact that it is more likely than other forms of variable pricing to violate federal anti-discrimination laws. The two scenarios above show that variable consumer prices evoke a range of reactions. The senior citizen question and the dry cleaning question differ in many ways. Many people are familiar with senior discounts, and they may view this pricing method as a charitable gesture. People are generally less familiar with gender-based pricing in the dry cleaning industry, and they may view it as a form of sex discrimination.

Another important difference between the senior citizen question and the dry cleaning question is that prices were described as senior discounts rather than middle-aged premiums. When the higher price is the reference price, "discounts" may be more acceptable. Do perceptions of fairness change with the dry cleaning problem if men's prices are described as discounts? In another version of the question, we told respondents:

> When Mrs. Simmon takes her blouse and her husband's dress shirt to the dry cleaners, she is told that prices differ for men's and women's shirts. Her blouse will cost the regular price of $9. With the $4 discount for men's shirts, Mr. Simmon's dress shirt will cost $5.

Even when the higher price was the reference price and the lower price was described as a "discount" price, prices were still viewed as unfair. Roughly the same percentage of participants (71%) thought Mrs. Simmon would perceive the pricing as unfair ($\chi^2(1) = 4.9$, $N = 28$).

Firms apply variable consumer pricing to individuals as well as groups. Since individual consumers will pay different amounts for the same good or service, firms segment consumers into groups of size one and charge prices accordingly. This approach requires the firm to know each customer's demand function or at least have an accurate notion of the customer's tastes and spending habits. Variable consumer pricing at the individual level has been using in the airline industry with frequent flyer cards and in the supermarket industry with loyalty cards. But until recently, it has not been feasible for most industries (Carroll & Grimes, 1995). Now with the Internet, all of that has changed (Baker et al., 2001; Kambil et al., 2002).

Behavioral targeting is the term used to describe how firms come to marketing mix decisions based on the information that is collected about consumers. Stores can follow the movements of visitors online, keep track of what products they view, and keep records of their online purchases. Some firms secretly collect data about consumers' web activity and sell it to third-party marketing firms. Stores can supplement their databases with additional consumer information and score individuals based on characteristics, such as preferences for products. Based on this information, they offer different prices to different buyers for the same good or service.

It is legal for online stores to charge different prices to different consumers for the same good at the same time of the day. Some retailers now send out catalogs that contain the same items at different prices to different individuals. CDNow sends a Web site address to certain individuals so they can take advantage of lower prices. Amazon also charges different prices to different consumers for the same book, CD, or DVD.

We asked respondents how they perceived variable consumer pricing at the individual level. One question stated:

> Susan loves music and buys a CD online from Amazon for $21.99. The next day, she calls her friend, Marta, who also loves music, to tell her about the CD. Marta says that she already knows about the CD, and coincidentally, bought it from Amazon the same day as Susan bought hers. Marta paid $14.67.

Virtually everyone (89%, $\chi^2(1) = 80.3$, $N = 132$) believed that Susan would perceive the situation as unfair. Perhaps more interesting is the fact that, even though Marta was the beneficiary of the price difference, participants believed that Marta would also find the situation unfair (73%, $\chi^2(1) = 22.8$, $N = 108$).

Do people think variable consumer pricing among individuals is more acceptable if the individuals involved are aware that stores engage in such practices? To answer this question, we presented respondents with a similar scenario in which the characters knew about variable consumer pricing at the individual level. The question said:

> Kirstin and Julie spend a lot of time on the Internet. They know that companies keep track of their activities on Web sites and try to forecast individual price sensitivities. Both women go to the online store, Land's End. They buy the same cashmere sweater on the same day. The price offered to Kirstin is $99, while the price offered to Julie is $68.

Again, almost everyone (94%) thought Kirstin would perceive the situation as unfair, and the majority (69%) thought Julie would find it unfair ($\chi^2(1) = 100.7$, $N = 130$ for Kirstin and $\chi^2(1) = 16.0$, $N = 111$ for Julie). Apparently, even when consumers are aware of behavioral targeting, they believe such practices are unfair.

Capturing Perceived Fairness

There is no question that variable unit pricing and variable consumer pricing could, in principle, increase profits. The precise conditions under which these pricing methods are optimal are topics of much debate (e.g., Acquisti & Varian, 2003). But if these strategies reduce customer loyalty and patronage because consumers think they are unfair, firms might be well advised to avoid them. Consumers might "vote with their feet" and shop elsewhere, take actions to ensure that firms have no data on them (such as removing cookies), or voice their outrage in the form of protests, demonstrations, or litigation.

Our survey results tell us that, in some cases, variable unit pricing is perceived as fair (e.g., bricks), but in others, it is perceived as unfair (e.g., airline tickets). Similarly, in some cases, variable consumer pricing among groups is viewed as fair (e.g., senior citizens) and in others, it is unfair (e.g., dry cleaning). Among individuals, variable consumer pricing was perceived as unfair (e.g., CDs), regardless of whether the consumers are aware of such practices (e.g., cashmere sweater).

What are the underlying characteristics of variable prices that make one situation seem fair and another seem unfair? Four factors contribute to perceptions of fairness—industry norms, justification for price differences, consistency of prices, and transparency of the price structure.

Industry Norms   Industry norms go a long way toward making variable pricing seem fair. Lower fares for early purchases were perceived as fairer than lower fares for last minute purchases. One reason may have been because lower fares with early purchases are more common occurrences. Similarly, discounts for seniors were viewed as more fair than discounts for men's clothing, perhaps because senior discounts are the norm.

Many norms appear rather arbitrary. For example, it is unfair for restaurants to charge higher prices for seats with better views, but it is fine for a baseball stadium to do exactly that. New norms can be hard to establish. Changes in pricing often take time before they are accepted. Minnesota has recently started a program in which drivers can pay extra to drive in the carpool lane. Prices vary as a function of congestion. Drivers have accepted this variable pricing during rush hours but have loudly objected to the scheme during non-rush hours. Arbitrary or not, certain reference points become norms, even when those reference points vary.

Justification for Price Differences   Consumers will accept price differences when those differences seem reasonable and justified. Random price discrimination, for example, appears unacceptable to many people. In 2000, Amazon sold a set of DVDs at discounts of either 30% or 40%. Consumers discovered in an online chat room that Amazon had offered different prices to different customers. Amazon replied by telling consumers that the prices were determined on a random basis. But that did little to soothe their outrage. Amazon sent out additional 10% discounts to those who had been given the smaller discounts. One reporter said, "Imagine the outcry had Amazon actually raised them [the prices]" (Heun, 2001).

What if Amazon had awarded discounts based on the frequency of past purchases? If Amazon had given frequent customers an advantage over infrequent customers, would consumers view it as fair? What groups, besides seniors, can receive discounts with widespread acceptance? We gave our respondents the following scenario:

> For certain products, Amazon uses a customer's previous buying and shopping behavior to set prices. Amazon determines whether to discount the price of a product by either 30% or 40%. Specifically, they give a 40% discount to [frequent/infrequent] customers.

Virtually all respondents (94%) thought it was fair to give discounts to frequent customers ($\chi^2(1) = 25.6$, $N = 33$), but most rejected the idea when applied to infrequent customers. The majority (72%) viewed such discounts as unfair ($\chi^2(1) = 4.8$, $N = 25$). Although it is commonplace, discounts given to entice new customers to make purchases, at the expense of the loyal customers, is not a strategy that firms should adopt without careful consideration of the consequences.

In some cases, variable pricing based on gender is perceived as fair if the explanation seems reasonable. We examined explanations with our dry cleaning question and asked participants:

> Dry cleaners charge different amounts for different types of clothing. Women's clothes are often fancier with more pleats, ruffles, or sensitive fabric. These items require more time to clean and press. Mrs. Simmon takes her blouse and her husband's dress shirt to the local cleaners. Mr. Simmon's dress shirt costs $5 to clean, and Mrs. Simmon's blouse costs $8.

The majority of participants (81%) thought Mrs. Simmon's would view the situation as fair ($\chi^2(1) = 24.9$, $N = 52$). However, without apparent justification, the same pricing is unacceptable. Another question read:

> Dry cleaners charge different amounts for different types of clothing. Women are often willing to pay more than men. Mrs. Simmon takes her blouse and her husband's dress shirt to the local cleaners. Mr. Simmon's dress shirt costs $5 to clean, and Mrs. Simmon's blouse costs $8.

This time, the majority of respondents (59%) thought Mrs. Simmon would perceive the pricing as unfair. There is no reasonable basis for price differences in the mind of the consumer.

Some researchers distinguish between justifications and excuses (Scott & Lyman, 1968). Justifications are explanations in which the decision maker admits fault for the decision, but denies that the decision was inappropriate by appealing to a higher order concern that makes the decision seem morally defensible. Excuses are explanations in which the decision maker does not accept fault for the action, but admits that the decision was inappropriate. Blame is shifted to external causes that made the action unavoidable.

In a meta-analysis of explanations, Shaw, Wild, and Colquitt (2003) found that excuses were generally perceived as more fair than justifications. An excuse for a price increase might be that price increases are bad, but because of the higher costs of supplies and labor, such increases were inevitable. A justification for a price increase might be that the higher price might seem bad to customers, but actually, higher prices allow firms to maintain their competitive edge and attract the best possible employees. Justifications may invite customers to consider alternative goals, such as higher profits without higher costs.

Consistency of Prices   Although most consumers, if given a choice, would probably prefer fixed pricing to variable pricing, they eventually adapt to variable pricing if no other pricing schemes are available. Some indirect evidence for the claim that people would prefer fixed prices is the popularity of Southwest and JetBlue airlines. Not only do these companies have lower prices, they also have more consistent prices. These airlines are also doing extremely well, while traditional airline companies are losing profits. The predictability of price differences provides assurances to customers that they are getting the best deal now and in the future.

Transparency of Price Structure   Another critical factor in perceptions of fairness is transparency in the rules that govern price differences. Customers want transparency to check whether price differences actually follow a given pricing structure. Transparency can increase perceptions of fairness, especially if it gives customers some control over the price they pay or is the industry norm. But it can also decrease perceptions of fairness if it makes consumers aware of unjustified reasons for price differences or inconsistency of prices. When customers learned that Amazon was using random assignment of prices to customers, it led to customer outrage. Transparency increases the perceived fairness of a plan that, on the face of it, is perceived as fair and decreases the perceived fairness of a plan that is objectionable from the onset.

To what extent was there transparency in our survey questions? In the brick question, Mike and Jordan may not have known before they arrived at the store that they would pay different prices for the same brick if they purchased different amounts. However, most consumers are familiar with this type of pricing and understand the firm's incentives to encourage consumption. The reason for price differences was quite explicit.

In the airlines industry, consumers know they can often get better deals if they buy in advance, but such deals are, by no means, guaranteed. In fact, ticket prices may even decrease as the date of travel approaches, and many airlines drop their prices dramatically right before the flight. The lack of transparency across days prior to the flight may contribute to the mixed reactions and perceived unfairness in our airline questions.

Some airlines try to keep pricing rules hidden from their customers. But if customers find out, they view the attempted secrecy as yet another layer of unfairness (Kimes, 2002). The irony of the "we've got a secret" approach is that transparent rules might well generate the same amount of revenue with less consumer resistance. For example, an airline could differentiate the experience of the higher-paying passenger from that of the lower-paying passenger by giving the higher-paying passenger a seat with more leg room, free headphones, or complimentary food and drinks. Another possibility, and one that is commonly used, is to place significant restrictions on lower fares. A passenger who paid more for his or her ticket might view the price as more fair if the higher price permitted him or her to make last-minute changes in reservations at no additional cost.

In our variable consumer pricing questions, there were also different degrees of transparency. Most people know and accept the fact that seniors often get discounts. Furthermore, prices are clearly posted at most movie theaters, so consumers know before the exchange that prices vary with age. Finally, the clever selection of the reference price as the higher, middle-aged price goes even further in gaining public acceptance.

Price discrimination in the dry cleaning industry is more subjective and depends on the difficulty of cleaning (e.g., whether a particular garment has stains), as well as type of garment to be cleaned. Although there are exceptions, most dry cleaners do not post signs that give precise cost structures. This lack of transparency may contribute to perceptions of unfairness.

The Way of the Future

We believe that variable consumer pricing at the individual level will eventually become the norm. With access to vast amounts of information on and off the Internet, firms will continue to develop methods to estimate individual price sensitivities and cross their fingers that other firms will do the same. As this method becomes more acceptable, perceived fairness will depend on justification of price differences, consistency of prices, and transparency of the pricing structure. A study by Choi and Mattila (2004) examined peoples' reactions to hotels that quoted different room rates to different customers for comparable rooms. When customers are offered higher rates than those offered to others on the same occasion, they viewed the prices as unfair. Firms are increasing profits without higher costs. However, customers were not resistant to all price increases. They accept the fact that hotels change their rates over time. In fact, when the same customers are given higher room rates at a later date, they usually accept the price increase and attribute it to higher costs (Choi & Mattila, 2004).

Justification for price differences is a serious problem. In a national telephone survey, Turow, Feldman, and Meltzer (2005) found that 87% disagree with the statement, "It is OK if an online store I use charges different people different prices for the same products during the same hour." Even more (91%) disapprove of this practice in the supermarkets. Interestingly, most internet-using U.S. adults (80%) know that it is legal for firms to follow their behavior online, but they *do not* know that it is legal for online and offline stores to charge different people different prices (62%).

Variable consumer pricing at the individual level, at least at this point in time, is not publicly announced. In our survey, respondents thought it was unfair in the CD question and in the cashmere sweater question that specified consumer awareness. If firms made these pricing practices transparent, perceptions of fairness might drop even lower. If consumers with higher incomes were told explicitly that they were charged more than consumers with lower incomes for books or CDs, the higher-paying customers would likely become uncooperative to say the least.

Consumers might also feel indignation about the collection of their personal information and/ or the attempted secrecy of the practice. Not all uses of personal information are rejected. For example, Amazon uses terabytes worth of sales data to make recommendations about books and music its customers may like. We asked our respondents whether this practice was fair using the following question:

> Amazon uses their entire customer purchase database to make recommendations about what products a consumer might like.

A large proportion (77%) of the 107 respondents thought this practice was fair ($\chi^2(1)$ = 31.2). But firms also use individual information to determine a consumer's price sensitivity and set future prices for that consumer. Responses to the CD question and the cashmere sweater question tell us that these situations are perceived as unfair.

For firms to be given the benefit of the doubt when it comes to a price increase, they need to establish good reputations, and trust is a key component of a firm's reputation. When consumers visit a Web site, they trust that the descriptions of products and services are accurate. When they order and pay for a product, they trust the product will be delivered on time or that they can return something if they choose to do so. Violations of this trust mean that consumers will assume the worst whenever there is uncertainty about motives, prices, or policies.

Urban, Sultan, and Qualls (2000) found that consumers are more likely to trust online stores that provide complete, accurate, and unbiased information not only about their own products, but also about the competition. Consumers are also more likely to trust online stores that make searching, comparing, and purchasing easy. Finally, consumers are more likely to trust online stores that protect their privacy by keeping their personal data private. If security is breached, consumers expect online stores to inform them and be as helpful as possible if theft occurs.

Web sites that build trust often have customer communities that provide user feedback. eBay facilitates the exchange of billions of dollars worth of goods on an annual basis. To establish trust, eBay tracks and publishes the reputations of buyers and sellers on the basis of feedback from each transaction. In a controlled experiment of eBay transactions, buyers bid an average of 7.6% more for goods listed by repeat sellers who had good reputations (Resnick et al., 2004).

Some argue that trust depends on benevolence and competence (Ganesan & Hess, 1997; Sirdeshmukh, Singh, & Sabol, 2002). Benevolence is the feeling that the company will put the interests of the consumer ahead of profits. Competence is the belief that the company will reliably deliver promised goods or services. Fairness facilitates exchange, and trust, which depends on benevolence and competence, facilities long-term relationships.

CONCLUSION

Past research has found that price increases are generally perceived as fair if firms have increased costs (Kahneman et al., 1986) or if firms use the money for philanthropic purposes (Campbell, 1999). Price increases are unfair if firms exploit excess demand or shortage of supply (Kahneman et al., 1986). The dual entitlement principle captures these intuitions. Firms are entitled to a reference profit, and consumers are entitled to a reference price. With increased costs, a firm's profits will fall below the reference profits unless they raise prices. Price increases designed to cover these costs are viewed as fair. But price increases that purely exploit excess demand or monopoly power are viewed as unfair.

Perceptions of fairness depend on framing effects. Reference points establish the norm from which discounts and premiums are evaluated. Additional consumer costs can be framed as opportunity costs or out-of-pocket costs, and people are noticeably less sensitive to foregone costs than to costs they directly experience. This focus of attention helps explain why price decreases are usually called discounts or sales rather than reductions in list price. This tendency also helps explain why people accept variable consumer pricing among "deserving" groups; senior discounts are more palatable than middle-age surcharges. Finally, this result may also help explain the fact that consumers do not expect firms to decrease their prices when costs are reduced. The absence of a price decrease is less salient and annoying than the presence of a price increase.

Much of the past psychological work on perceptions of fair pricing has focused on fixed reference points—both prices and profits. These days, variable pricing methods are becoming more common. There are two general types: variable unit pricing and variable consumer pricing. With variable unit pricing, firms charge different prices for different units. With variable consumer pricing, firms charge different prices to different consumers for the same units. Variable pricing means that dual entitlement no longer applies. Consumers no longer are entitled to a reference price, and firms are no longer entitled to reference profits.

When are variable pricing structures perceived as fair? We believe that four factors are important predictors of the perceived fairness of variable pricing: (1) the extent to which variable pricing is the industry norm, (2) the apparent reasonableness of the price differences, (3) the consistency or predictability of prices over time, and (4) the degree to which price structures are made transparent.

Variable unit pricing and variable consumer pricing are more common in some industries than others. For example, variable unit pricing is often found in the clothing industry. A consumer who purchases 10 pairs of socks is likely to get a better price per pair than a consumer who buys 1 pair of socks. Variable unit pricing is also widespread in business-to-business exchanges.

But just because variable pricing is an industry norm doesn't guarantee its acceptance. For example, variable unit pricing is widely used in the airline, hotel, and rental car industries. In these cases, travelers who book their reservations earlier tend to get lower prices. But many people who imagine themselves seated beside someone who paid $400 less for their ticket are not necessarily pleased, especially if the cheaper ticket was purchased on the day of the flight.

Some forms of variable consumer pricing at the group level are also fairly widespread. Most people accept junior and senior discounts at the movies, on the airlines, or in the amusement parks. This type of pricing is more acceptable if there is a good reason for the price difference, and the higher price is treated as the reference price. The "deserving" group (e.g., children or senior citizens) receives the "discount."

Variable consumer pricing at the individual level occurs in the airlines and in the supermarkets with the use of frequent flyer cards and loyalty cards, respectively. With the Internet, it has become feasible for online industries to offer variable pricing without the use of such cards.. However, for most consumers, it is by no means the norm. In fact, many consumers are completely unaware of the current practices or the current trends in that direction.

Reasons for price differences are also important. Customers may accept different prices for dry cleaning men's and women's shirts if they feel those prices are due to increased labor. However, if they believe the price differences occur without increased cost for the firm, they view such differences as arbitrary and unfair. Predictability of price differences is also important. Perceptions of the airline industry suggest that people would prefer greater consistency, even if prices fluctuate.

Finally, transparency is also important. When variable prices are industry norms, consumers are more accepting of the practice when both the rules governing price differences and the reasons for those price differences are transparent and clear. That way, consumers may have some control over what price they pay. In addition, consumers don't trust firms that try to keep the rules governing price differences hidden. This lack of transparency adds yet another layer of unfairness on top of an already unfair situation.

Transparency is intimately tied to trust. Consumers are more accepting of variable pricing when they trust the firm and have confidence that the firm will give them accurate and complete information about goods and services, as well as meet their product expectations. Transparency can increase or decrease perceptions of fairness. When variable pricing is not the industry norm, transparency can make things even worse. For example, variable consumer pricing at the individual level is not only perceived as unusual, consumers who learn about the practice often feel betrayed. Firms that use such pricing strategies appear to be using consumers' data "against" them. Firms that try to cover their tracks, but end up getting caught, are perceived as even worse. It will take some major changes in the marketplace before variable consumer pricing among individuals is accepted. In the meantime, consumers are likely to put up a good fight.

The rise of the Internet has given consumers more power. It has increased their ability to collect and compare information about products, prices, and firms. But, at the same time that consumers are more powerful, firms are also more powerful. Firms have increased capability to collect consumer information, use it, and sell it to other firms. What we have is an information arms race, and we hope that both firms and consumers are winners.

NOTES

1. Out of the 1,960 questions answered by participants, 274 were rated "Neither." For these consumers, fairness seems to be a salient transaction attribute.
2. This pricing scheme has the somewhat awkward, albeit common, structure that frequent customers are charged more than infrequent customers.

REFERENCES

Acquisti, A., & Varian, H. (2003). *Conditioning prices on purchase history*. Unpublished manuscript.

Baker, W., Marn, M., et al. (2001). Price smarter on the net. *Harvard Business Review*, February, 122–127.

Bolton, L. E., Warlop, L., & Alba, J. W. (2003). Consumer perceptions of price (un)fairness. *Journal of Consumer Research, 29*, 474–491.

Campbell, M. C. (1999). Perceptions of price unfairness: Antecedents and Consequences. *Journal of Marketing Research, 36*(May), 187–199.

Carroll, W. J., & Grimes, R. C. (1995). Evolutionary change in product management: Experiences in the car rental industry. *Interfaces, 25*(5), 84–104.

Choi, S., & Mattila, A. S. (2004). Hotel revenue management and its impact on customers' perceptions of fairness. *Journal of Revenue and Pricing Management, 2*(4), 303–314.

Franciosi, R., Kugal, P., Michelitsch, R., Smith, V., & Dent, G. (1995). Fairness: Effect on temporary and equilibrium prices in posted-offer markets. *The Economic Journal, 105*, 938–950.

Frey, B. S., Pommerehne, W. W., Schneider, F., & Gilbert, G. (1984). Consensus and dissension among economists: An empirical inquiry, 74, 986–994.

Frey, B. S., & Pommerehne, W. W. (1993). On the fairness of pricing — An empirical survey among the general population. *Journal of Economic Behavior and Organization, 20*, 295–307.

Ganesan, S., & Hess, R. (1997). Dimensions and levels of trust: Implications for commitment to a relationship. *Marketing Letters, 63*, 70–87.

Heath, C., Larrick, R. P., & Wu, G. (1999). Goals as reference points. *Cognitive Psychology, 38*(1), 79–109.

Heun, C. T. (2001). Dynamic pricing boosts bottom line. *Information Week*. Available at: http://www.informationweek.com.

Hunt, S. D., & Nevin, J. R. (1981). Why consumers believe they are being ripped off. *Business Horizons, 24*(3), 48–52.

Jacobson, R., & Obermiller, C. (1990). The formation of expected future price: A reference price for forward-looking consumers. *Journal of Consumer Research, 16*, 420–432.

Johnson, E. J., Hershey, J., et al. (1993). Framing, probability distortions, and insurance decisions. *Journal of Risk and Uncertainty, 7*, 35–51.

Kachelmeier, S. J., Limberg, S. T., & Schadewald, M. S. (1991). A laboratory market examination of the consumer price response to information about producers' costs and profits. *The Accounting Review, 66,* 694–717.

Kahneman, D., Knetsch, J. L., & Thaler, R. (1986a). Fairness and the assumptions of economics. *Journal of Business, 59*(4), 285–300.

Kahneman, D., Knetsch, J. L., & Thaler, R. (1986b). Fairness as a constraint on profit seeking: Entitlements in the market. *American Economic Review, 76*(4), 728–741.

Kahneman, D., & Tversky, A. (1986). Rational choice and the framing of decisions. *Journal of Business, 59*(4), 251–278.

Kambil, A., Wilson III, H. J., et al. (2002). Are you leaving money on the table? *The Journal of Business Strategy, 23*(1), 40–43.

Kimes, S. E. (2002). Perceived fairness of yield management. *Cornell Hotel and Restaurant Administration Quarterly, 43*(1), 21–30.

Kimes, S. E., & Wirtz, J. (2003). Perceived fairness of revenue management in the US golf industry. *Journal of Revenue and Pricing Management, 1*(4), 332–344.

Levin, I. P., & Gaeth, G. J. (1988). How consumers are affected by the framing of attribute information before and after consuming the product. *Journal of Consumer Research, 15*(3), 374–378.

Liberman, N., Idson, L. C., et al. (2005). Predicting the intensity of losses vs. non-gains and non-losses vs gains in judging fairness and value: A test of the loss aversion explanation. *Journal of Experimental Social Psychology, 41*(5), 527–534.

Liu, M. W., & Soman, D. (2006). Behavioral Pricing. In C. P. Haugtvedt, P. M. Herr, & F. R. Kardes (Eds.), *Handbook of consumer psychology.*. Mahwah, NJ. Erlbaum.

Resnick, P., Zeckhauser, R., Swanson, J., & Lockwood, K. (2004). The value of reputation on eBay: A controlled experiment. *Experimental Economics, 9*(2), 79–101.

Scott, M. B., & Lyman, S. M. (1968). Accounts. *American Sociological Review, 33,* 46–62.

Shaw, J. C., Wild, E., & Colquitt, J. A. (2003). To justify or excuse? A meta-analytic review of the effects of explanations. *Journal of Applied Psychology, 88*(3), 444–458.

Sirdeshmukh, D., Singh, J., & Sabol, B. (2002). Consumer trust, value and loyalty in relational exchanges. *Journal of Marketing, 66,* 15–38.

Smith, B. A., Leimkuhler, J. F., et al. (1992). Yield Management at American Airlines. *Interfaces, 22*(1), 8–31.

Thaler, R. (1985). "ental accounting and consumer choice. *Marketing Science, 4*(3), 199–214.

Turow, J., Feldman, L., et al. (2005). *Open to exploitation: American shoppers online and offline.* Philadelphia, Annenberg Public Policy Center.

Urban, G. L., Sultan, F., et al. (2000). Placing trust at the center of your Internet strategy. *MIT Sloan Management Review, 42*(1), 39–48.

28

Associative Learning and Consumer Decisions

STIJN M. J. VAN OSSELAER

Erasmus University

When making decisions, consumers often depend heavily on what they have learned about the relations between concepts. Links between product cues (e.g., brand names, ingredients, other product attributes) and consumption benefits play an important role in consumers' evaluations of products. For example, a consumer who is trying to decide between different types of wine may rely on links in memory between grape varieties and taste quality. Given the crucial role these links play in consumer decisions, it is important to know how these links are formed and how they change over time. This is the domain of associative learning, or the learning of the ways in which concepts are related (see Shanks, 1994, for a similar definition).

I will provide an overview of associative learning theories that describe how human and nonhuman animals learn to predict outcomes. This overview starts with the original theories of Pavlovian or classical conditioning and ends with a proposal that consumers can use two distinct learning-and-memory processes to predict outcomes. I will conclude the chapter with some directions for future research.

ASSOCIATIVE LEARNING AND THE PREDICTION OF OUTCOMES

In the early 20th century, Ivan Pavlov (1927/1960) found that when a neutral stimulus such as a bell (the *conditioned stimulus*) was consistently followed by a biologically significant stimulus such as food (the *unconditioned stimulus*), dogs eventually started to salivate upon perceiving the initially neutral stimulus. This process was termed *classical* or *Pavlovian conditioning* and was interpreted in terms of the conditioned stimulus acquiring properties of the unconditioned stimulus. Thus, the learner responds to the conditioned stimulus as if it is the unconditioned stimulus. Many consumer learning studies, implicitly or explicitly, take this view of associative learning. For example, consumer researchers have investigated how affect toward a brand can be influenced by affect toward a picture in an advertisement (e.g., Stuart, Shimp, & Engle, 1987). In this case, a property of the unconditioned stimulus (i.e., the affect-evoking property of a picture) is taken on by a conditioned stimulus (i.e., the brand). The brand itself has become more attractive.

In the latter part of the 20th century, the interpretation of associative learning changed. As summarized in a seminal article by Rescorla (1988), the behavior of Pavlov's salivating dogs may be seen in a much more cognitive light, as the learning of predictive relationships between cues and motivationally relevant outcomes. Pavlov's dog learned to predict a motivationally relevant outcome (the unconditioned stimulus, i.e., food) on the basis of a previously unrelated cue (the conditioned stimulus, i.e., bell). Thus, instead of making the bell seem yummy, pairing the bell and the food taught the dog that the bell predicts food, making it salivate in anticipation of the food. In a consumer context, this implies that pairing a brand with a good outcome might lead to more positive brand evaluations, not because the brand name itself has acquired a positive halo, but because the brand predicts a good consumption experience. With few exceptions (e.g., Hutchinson & Alba, 1991; Meyer, 1987), consumer research has traditionally not adopted this cognitive perspective on associative learning. Consumer researchers have focused mostly on the transfer of affect between unconditioned and conditioned stimuli, so-called *evaluative conditioning* (e.g., C. T. Allen & Janiszewski, 1989; Bierley, McSweeney, & Vannieuwkerk, 1985; J. Kim, Allen, & Kardes, 1996; Shimp, Stuart, & Engle, 1991).[1] In this chapter, however, I will focus mostly on associative learning that allows consumers to predict outcomes such as product quality or more specific consumption benefits.

THE RESCORLA-WAGNER (1972) MODEL

The view of associative learning as a process geared at predicting outcomes based on cues is highly consistent with so-called *adaptive* or *error-driven learning models*. According to these models, humans and animals form associations from one or more cues to an outcome and adaptations to these associations depend on the extent to which predictions of the outcome diverge from the actual outcome. Thus, associative learning is geared at reducing prediction error.

Model

The most impactful adaptive model of associative learning was introduced by Rescorla and Wagner (1972) in the animal learning literature. Independently, an almost identical model was proposed in the engineering literature (Widrow & Hoff, 1960). The literature on *parallel distributed processing* (a.k.a. *connectionism* or *neural network models*) refers to the same rule as the *delta rule* or *Least Mean Squares rule* and borrowed it from engineering (e.g., Gluck & Bower, 1988; Rumelhart, Hinton, & McClelland, 1986). These models hold that there is an association (or connection; w_{ij}) between the representation of a cue i (e.g., the sounding of a bell) and an outcome j (e.g., the appearance of food). This association (w_{ij}) varies in its strength (or weight). The strength of an association is updated according to the discrepancy between a predicted outcome level (or activation of outcome node j; o_j) and a *teaching* signal representing the actual outcome level (d_j). More precisely (Gluck & Bower, 1988):

$$\Delta w_{ij} = \beta(d_j - o_j)a_i, \tag{1}$$

where (1) a_i is the activation of cue i, (2) a_i is usually assumed to be zero when cue i is absent and 1 when cue i is present, (3) β is a learning rate parameter, and (4) the predicted outcome level o_j is equal to

$$o_j = \Sigma_{i=1 \to n} w_{ij}a_i. \tag{2}$$

Process

Although it was not necessarily meant to describe a process as such, the Rescorla-Wagner model and its delta learning rule seem to reflect a specific psychological process that consumers could use to evaluate products (van Osselaer, Janiszewski, & Cunha, 2004).

First, the Rescorla-Wagner model assumes that a prediction is made during learning of a future outcome based on elements of information present in the environment. For example, Pavlov's dog makes a prediction about the imminent occurrence of food based on information about a bell. In many consumer situations, for example when choosing wine in a super market, consumers cannot directly assess future outcomes, such as the taste of wine. In those situations, consumers may make predictions of the future outcomes based on cues available in the store environment. For example, consumers may use the grape variety listed on a bottle of wine to predict its taste. This process of predicting *experience characteristics* on the basis of information about *search characteristics* (Nelson, 1970) may not be all that different from the dog's process involving a bell and food.

Second, the Rescorla-Wagner model suggests a process in which evaluations or predicted outcome levels depend on an additive combination of predictive values of cues. That is, when we make the common assumption that the activation of a cue is equal to one if present and zero when absent, then the predicted outcome level according to equation 2 is equal to the straight sum of the association strengths of all present cues. Thus, when Pavlov's dog perceives not just a bell but also a light, the intensity of the food expectation is equal to the expectation based on what the dog has learned about the bell as a predictor of food plus the expectation based on what the dog has learned about the light as a predictor of food. Translated to the consumer context, this type of additivity assumption is quite common. Whenever we use main-effect conjoint models or assume a weighted-additive decision rule as we do in multiattribute attitude models, we make the same assumption as the Rescorla-Wagner model. The predicted level of an outcome or evaluation is equal to the sum of the predictive values or part-worth utilities of that product's attributes.

Third, the Rescorla-Wagner model suggests that animals and humans receive feedback about the actual outcome level after making an outcome prediction and compare the actual with the predicted level. Thus, Pavlov's dog contrasts the prediction about the occurrence of food with the actual appearance of food. This process of predictions being contrasted with feedback is likely to occur in many consumer learning situations. For example when a consumer tastes a glass of wine, she can ask herself whether the wine is as good as she had expected. In fact, much of the literature on consumer satisfaction relies on the assumption of just such a comparison process (e.g., Oliver, 1980).

Fourth, the Rescorla-Wagner model suggests that the learner then updates the association strengths or predictive values by a percentage (β) of the positive or negative discrepancy between the predicted and actual outcome levels ($d_j - o_j$). This implies that the larger the discrepancy, or the more wrong the prediction, the larger the changes in association strengths and, hence, the faster the learning. This also implies that if the outcome is already correctly predicted, no new learning takes places. The learning process is lazy, but in a functional way. This is exactly what one would expect from an intelligent organism with constrained resources. Why change anything if your predictions of motivationally relevant outcomes are perfect? Thus, if Pavlov's dog correctly and confidently predicts the occurrence of food, it does not need to engage in additional learning. Similarly, if our consumer perfectly predicted the taste quality of the wine based on the brand name, she has reached her goal and does not need to engage in additional learning.

In sum, the Rescorla-Wagner model seems to describe an inherently adaptive and forward-looking learning process, in which a learner first makes a prediction of a future outcome based on currently present cues, then records feedback about the actual outcome, and then adapts the predictive values of the cues to reduce prediction error on the next occasion. I have argued that the characteristics of such a process match many situations in which consumers (learn to) evaluate products. Moreover, instead of just measuring part-worth utilities, I would like to argue that a Rescorla-Wagner-like model can help us predict how part-worth utilities change over time, in different situations, and under different consumer scenarios.

Phenomena Explained by the Rescorla-Wagner Model and Implications for Consumer Decisions

Together, the characteristics of the Rescorla-Wagner model outlined above have been used to explain and predict a large number of animal and human learning phenomena. Many of these are referred to as *cue interaction* phenomena and play a role in consumers' evaluations of products. Some of the phenomena were introduced to the consumer psychology literature by McSweeney and Bierley (1984), who discussed their implications for situations in which whole products or people are taken as cues. In the following subsections, I will outline implications for situations in which products are seen as constellations of multiple characteristics, such as brand names, features, ingredients, or other (search) attributes (e.g., Lancaster, 1966). Thus, in connectionist terms, the representation of a single product may be *distributed* among several cues. Table 28.1 summarizes the experimental designs for the cue interaction phenomena discussed in this chapter.

Blocking   Kamin (1969) discovered that when an animal is first conditioned to respond to a simple cue consisting of element A and is subsequently conditioned to respond to a compound of two cues consisting of element A plus element B, the second element (B) acquires little predictive value. In other words, learning of the second element will be, as it were, *blocked*. For example, Kamin (1969) repeatedly exposed one group of rats (the blocking group) to a noise (A) followed by an electric shock in a first learning phase and then repeatedly exposed the same rats to a compound of the same noise plus a light (B) followed by the same type of shock. After these two learning phases, he measured the suppression of baseline lever pressing activity, an indicator of rats' expectation of shock, as a result of the presentation of a light (B). Surprisingly, exposure to the light (B) hardly suppressed lever pressing activity at all, indicating that the acquisition of predictive value by the light (B) had been blocked by earlier learning about the noise (A). In addition, the response to the light (suppression) was significantly smaller than the response in a control condition with a single learning phase in which he had only exposed the rats to the compound of cues (i.e., the noise plus the light [AB] followed by shock, but without the initial phase of learning about the noise [A] only).

Table 28.1   Design Summary for Cue Interaction Phenomena

Phenomenon	Learning Phase 1	Learning Phase 2	Test Phase
Sequential Blocking	A+	AB+	A?, B?
Simultaneous Blocking	A+, AB+		A?, B?
Cue Competition	AB+		A?, B?
Summation	A+, B+		AB?, A?, B?
Overexpectation	A+, B+	AB+	A?, B?
Sequential Conditioned Inhibition	A+	AB0	A?, B?
Simultaneous Conditioned Inhibition	A+, AB0		A?, B?
Sequential Unblocking	A–	AB+	A?, B?
Simultaneous Unblocking	A0, AB+		A?, B?
Commoditization (simplified design)	A1B1+, A1B2+		A?, B?

Note.   A and B are cues. Subscripted numbers are used to indicate different versions of the same cue (e.g., different brand names). "+" indicates an outcome, "0" indicates no outcome, and "–" indicates inhibition of an outcome.

Later research by Wagner and Saavedra (Wagner, 1969), using shocks to rabbits' eyelids as the outcome to be predicted, found evidence for a *simultaneous* blocking effect, in which the A and AB learning trials were interspersed instead of presented in separate learning stages. In one of their experimental conditions, the rats received trials in which a light (A) was reinforced with shock interspersed with trials in which a compound of light plus tone (AB) was also reinforced. At test, they found that the amount of associative strength that had accrued to the tone was negligible. In other words, the acquisition of predictive value by the tone in the compound (AB) trials was blocked by the presence of the light-only (A) trials that were interspersed with the compound trial. Another experiment by Wagner and Saavedra (Wagner 1969) replicated the result when the unconditioned stimulus was a food reward instead of shock. Both the sequential and simultaneous blocking effect have been found in humans (e.g., Dickinson, Shanks, & Evenden, 1984; Shanks, 1991).

The sequential blocking effect in Kamin's experiment is easily explained by the Rescorla-Wagner model. During the first learning phase, only the noise (A) can be used to predict the outcome, shock. At the beginning of that first learning phase, rats have not established a non-zero association from noise to shock, and will initially not predict a shock when they hear the noise. This leads to underprediction—the prediction regarding shock is much weaker than the actual intensity of the shock—leading to strengthening of the noise-shock association. This continues until, after a number of learning trials, the prediction (almost) matches the actual. When the light (B) is added to the noise (A) in the second learning phase, the rats' prediction is a sum of their prediction based on the noise and their prediction based on the light. Because the light (B) is new and not yet associated with shock, the initial predictive value of the light is zero and the prediction is based entirely on the noise (A). Luckily, the rats have already learned to perfectly predict the shock based on the noise. As a result there is no discrepancy between predicted and actual outcome, and no updating of associations needs to take place. Thus, the light (B) does not develop a strong association with shock. It is blocked.

In a simultaneous blocking situation, predictive value accrues to the A cue on both the singular (A) and the compound (AB) trials. The predictive value of B only changes on the compound (AB) trials. When the predictive value of A, which is strengthened on each trial, becomes large, the AB compound will have a total predictive value ($w_{Aj} + w_{Bj}$) that is too large (i.e., $o_j > d_j$), leading to small decrements in the predictive values of both cues (A and B). Because the compound trials on which the predictive values of both cues go down are interspersed with A-only trials on which the predictive value of A still goes up; A ends up with all the predictive value in equilibrium.

The blocking effect may play an important role in consumers' product evaluations and in the value they attach to brand names and other product characteristics. For example, if consumers first learn to predict an outcome (e.g., taste quality or headache relief) based on a brand name (e.g., of a wine or headache medicine), subsequent learning of the importance of another characteristic (e.g., a grape variety or an active ingredient) may be blocked. This may happen despite the fact that a name inherently cannot directly cause most consumption outcomes whereas characteristics such as ingredients can (van Osselaer & Alba, 2000). It is not difficult to see that such a blocking effect of ingredients or other attributes by brand names reduces competition by (generic) competitors that share an established brand's attributes. This may have a negative effect on consumer welfare, by preventing consumers from learning which product characteristics really drive product performance. The failure to learn, in turn, leads consumers to continue paying extra for well-known brands that offer no better quality than cheaper alternatives that share the same critical ingredients.

A mixed, sequential and simultaneous, blocking effect may also occur in situations in which a well-known product that carries only a family brand name (e.g., Godiva chocolate) adds a subbranded product (e.g., L'Amour by Godiva chocolate truffles) with the same outcomes (e.g., identical levels of quality) to its product portfolio. In such situations, the sub-brand name will be blocked. It will not establish much predictive value, hence will develop little brand equity (Janiszewski & van Osselaer, 2000).

Cue Competition   Pavlov (1927/1960) presented dogs with two distinct but simultaneous tones (AB) followed by the appearance of food. He would do this repeatedly and, after a while, the dogs would start to salivate as soon as they heard the two tone-combination. Interestingly, if he then presented each of the tones separately the amount of salivation decreased dramatically. In addition, salivation in such test situations with a single tone (A or B) after training with two tones (AB) was much less than if he had tested *and* trained with a single tone. Thus, training with two tones prevented dogs from fully learning the predictive relationship between each of the two tones and the appearance of food. He also found that the effect was often not equally strong for each of the two tones. If the two cues differed in salience (e.g., loudness), the more salient cue suffered much less than the less salient cue. The more salient cue seemed to *overshadow* the less salient cue.

The Rescorla-Wagner model explains cue competition. To equalize predicted (o_j) and actual outcome (d_j), the sum of predictive values or association strengths ($w_{Aj} + w_{Bj}$) has to equal the actual outcome level (d_j) in the two-cue, cue competition situation. In a control condition with just one cue, equalization of predicted (o_j) and actual outcome (d_j) is achieved when the association strength of the single cue (w_{Aj}) is equal to the actual outcome level (d_j). Thus, with two cues instead of one cue, the same total amount of association strength or predictive value has to be divided among two cues instead of going entirely to one cue. If both cues have the same learning rates, that is, if the dogs learn equally fast about both tones, each tone's association with food will, at asymptote, be equally strong and half as strong as the association between the single tone and food in the control condition with one cue during the learning phase. However, if the two tones differ in salience, and, hence, in learning rate (β_i), the more salient tone will grab most of the available association strength at the expense of the less salient tone. Thus, the more salient cue overshadows the less salient cue.

It is easy to see how cue competition may affect consumers' evaluations of consumption outcomes. Cue competition implies that consistently pointing out specific product attributes (e.g., ingredients, features) to consumers along with a brand name will hurt the equity of the brand name. In fact, stressing product attributes may lead to a shift in the *locus of equity* from the brand to the attributes. That is, associations from brands to consumption outcomes are weakened relative to the situation in which specific attributes are not highlighted (van Osselaer & Alba, 2003). This shift in the locus of equity has two important implications. First, any difference in outcome predictions between the branded product and competing products that carry the same attributes is reduced, leading to more intense competition on price. Second, the branded product cannot easily extend its equity to product categories in which the attributes from the original category cannot be used. If equity is divided among brand name and attributes, then performance expectations are only marginally influenced by the brand name. This effect is exacerbated by the finding that if brand names and specific attributes are learned simultaneously, the attributes tend to acquire more equity than the brand names (van Osselaer & Alba, 2000). Thus, attributes tend to overshadow brands.

Cue competition may also occur between family brand names and sub-brand or ingredient brand names. For example, if a sub-brand name is consistently mentioned alongside a family brand name, predictive value or equity will be divided among the family and sub-brand names, weakening the family brand's equity. This can lead to problems if the family brand name is subsequently used to label new brand extension products that do not carry the sub-brand name. Due to cue competition in the category of origin, the family brand name has lost equity, which reduces initial outcome predictions (hence, product evaluations, and product trial) for the extension product relative to a situation in which no sub-brand was used in the original category.

Summation and Overexpectation   Originally discovered by Pavlov (1927/1960), the summation effect occurs when two cues are combined *after* both cues separately established a strong outcome association. In such situations, the additivity assumption underlying the Rescorla-Wagner model prescribes that responding to a combination of two cues that have previously been associated with an outcome is stronger than responding to either of the cues by itself. That is, as long as $w_{Aj} > 0$ and $w_{Bj} > 0$, $w_{Aj} + w_{Bj} > w_{Aj}$ and $w_{Aj} + w_{Bj} > w_{Bj}$. For example, Rescorla (1997) exposed rats to a light (A) followed by the appearance of a food pellet. In separate learning trials, he also exposed the same rats to a noise (B), equally followed by food. After this initial learning phase, he compared responding to the combination of the two cues (AB) with responding to each cue on its own (A or B). As expected, responding to the compound (AB) was stronger than to each of the cues (A or B) separately.

Implications of this summation effect for consumers are obvious. Adding good cues to a product makes it more attractive. For example, highlighting a specific product feature that consumers already associate with a good outcome will boost the predicted outcome level of that product beyond the prediction based on a brand name alone. In addition, combining two brand names (i.e., cues) that are both already associated with good taste (i.e., outcome) in a co-branded product will lead consumers to predict that the taste of the co-branded product will be better than if the new product had been introduced with either of the two brand names alone (Janiszewski & van Osselaer, 2000, Study 4).

One should not conclude from the summation phenomenon that highlighting known features or co-branding is always a good idea. Animal learning experiments show that if the enhanced outcome prediction based on the combination of cues (AB) is not followed by an enhanced actual outcome level in subsequent learning trials, the association between each cue (A or B) and the outcome may be weakened. For example, Rescorla (1970) first trained rats to predict shock based on a tone (A) and, separately, based on a flashing light (B). In a following learning phase, he exposed some of the rats to further learning trials in which the tone and light were presented simultaneously (AB) followed by the same level of shock. After this second learning phase, he measured responses to the tone and light separately (A and B) and compared those responses to responses by rats who had not been exposed to the second learning phase. He found that exposure to the AB compound of cues reduced responding to each of the cues by themselves.

The Rescorla-Wagner model explains this effect, which is commonly referred to as the *overconditioning* or *overexpectation* effect. If both cues have strong associations with an outcome, the sum of their association strengths will be so high that the predicted outcome level ($o_j = w_{Aj}a_A + w_{Bj}a_B = w_{Aj} * 1 + w_{Bj} * 1 = w_{Aj} + w_{Bj}$) is higher than the actual outcome level (d_j). Hence, there is a negative discrepancy between actual and predicted outcome. To reduce prediction error, the strength of both associations (w_{Aj} and w_{Bj}) has to be reduced.

The implication for consumers' evaluations is that initially beneficial summation effects can have negative consequences over time (Janiszewski & van Osselaer, 2000, Study 4). For example, if two brands have very strong associations with the same outcome, consumers will initially predict that a new co-branded product will do very well on that outcome, inducing them to try the new product. However, if the actual performance of the new, co-branded product on that outcome is not sufficiently higher than what the consumer would expect based on each of the brands separately, experience consuming the co-branded product will hurt both brands. That is, experience with the co-branded product leads to an overexpectation effect that weakens both brands' associations with the outcome. Thus, co-branding, or the addition of well-established features, can raise outcome expectations for a product, but consumption experiences can quickly bring down unrealistic expectations and produce a nasty by-product, a reduction in the association strengths of the brand(s) involved.

Conditioned Inhibition   Pavlov (1927/1960; see also Rescorla 1969 for an early review) introduced the phenomenon of conditioned inhibition. In a typical conditioned inhibition experiment, an animal is presented with two types of learning trials. In the first type of trials, a cue (A) is followed by a reward. In the second type of trials, the first cue is presented in compound with a second cue and this compound (AB) is not followed by a reward. Results indicate that the presence of the second cue (B) inhibits the response to the first cue (A), such that the animal only reacts to A when B is not also present. The second cue (B) is found to have acquired a strong predictive value of the opposite sign of that accrued to A.

Traditionally (Pavlov, 1927/1960), the A-only trials are presented in a first learning phase and the compound trials are presented in a second learning phase. However, conditioned inhibition has also been found when the two types of trials were not separated in time. For example, Rescorla and LoLordo (1965, Experiment 1) randomly interspersed the two types of classical conditioning trials and found a similar result. The conditioned inhibition effect has also been found in humans (e.g., Chapman & Robbins 1990).

The Rescorla-Wagner model accounts for sequential conditioned inhibition as follows: In the first learning phase, the animal learns to predict the reward solely based on the single presented cue (A). Thus, a strong positive association is formed. At the beginning of the second learning phase, the animal still predicts a positive reward based on the A cue when it is presented in a compound with another cue (AB). However, the compound (AB) is not followed by the reward. The prediction is too high. To achieve errorless prediction, both cues' associations have to become less positive. This leads to a positive but weakened association for the A cue. However, the B cue had a zero association and now needs to become negative (i.e., inhibitory). The animal does not learn that the B cue does not predict a reward, but actually learns that the B cue actively prevents a reward. In simultaneous conditioned inhibition the two types of trials are interspersed. In this type of situation, every compound trial (AB) leads both cues' associations to become less positive but each A-only trial makes the A cue become more positive again. Eventually, perfect prediction is reached when the A cue has a strong positive association and the B cue has acquired a strong negative association.

The conditioned inhibition phenomenon, which is also known as *feature negative discrimination*, has clear implications for consumers' responses to brand extensions. For example, suppose a company with a well-known brand (A) that has a strong positive association with an outcome wants to extend the brand to another product category. The extension product is given both the family brand name and a new sub-brand name (AB). Initial outcome predictions, hence inclination to try the new product, are highly positive based on the association between the family brand name (A) and the outcome. However, suppose the extension product's actual outcome performance is much worse than the original, as is often the case when companies in, for example the fashion industry, extend their brands downmarket. The conditioned inhibition findings suggest that the sub-brand (B) will acquire a negative association and will protect the family brand name's equity, reducing negative feedback effects in the original product category. Thus, sub-branding an extension product may provide much of the benefits of a straight brand extension, but may shield the original product and the family brand name from negative spillover effects if the extension product is not of the same quality as the original. Such a shielding effect was demonstrated by Janiszewski and van Osselaer (2000). It should be noted that a similar effect may also result from more inferential processes (Milberg, Park, & McCarthy, 1997).

Unblocking   Wagner and Saavedra (Wagner, 1969) discovered that when they interspersed learning trials on which a compound of light plus tone (AB) was followed by a shock with trials on which a light (A) was not followed by shock, the tone (B) acquired a very strong association with shock while the rats showed no fear reaction when the light (A) was presented. This phenomenon is referred to as simultaneous *unblocking*, because learning about the light-only (A) here increases the predictive value of the tone (B) instead of the blocking result in which learning about the light-only (A) decreases the predictive value that accrues to the tone (B). The results are interesting because the tone was equally often paired with shock in this condition as in a simultaneous blocking condition, but acquired little associative strength in the simultaneous blocking condition and a large amount of associative strength in this unblocking condition. It is also surprising that the light (A) did not yield any fear response notwithstanding the fact that the light was regularly followed by shock (in the AB trials). Rescorla (Rescorla & Wagner, 1972) showed a similar phenomenon, but using a sequential design in which he first taught rats that cue A inhibits an outcome before exposing the animals to a compound (AB) that was followed by the outcome. Shanks (1991) replicated the simultaneous unblocking effect with human participants.

In simultaneous unblocking, two types of trials, A-only trials not followed by the outcome and AB compounds followed by the outcome are interspersed. According to the Rescorla-Wagner model, both A and B will become more strongly associated with shock on the compound trials. That is, to make sure that the sum of associative strengths ($w_{Aj} + w_{Bj}$) adds up to a high actual outcome level (i.e., a substantial positive d_j) on AB trials, both weights become positive from an initial state of zero. However, this makes the outcome prediction on the A-only trial too high, because the actual outcome level on those trials is zero. Thus, a negative discrepancy between the actual and predicted outcome occurs (i.e., $d_j - o_j < 0$) on A-only trials, leading to negative updating of the association between A and the outcome. Hence, A loses predictive value on every A-only trial, whereas B only gains predictive value. In equilibrium, this leads to a situation in which B has all the predictive value and A does not possess any predictive value. Thus, the B cue's association strength is more positive and the A cue's association strength is less positive than in a cue competition situation (in which only AB trials are presented).

The sequential unblocking phenomenon is explained by the fact that during the first learning phase, the single cue (A) acquires a strong negative association. In the second learning phase, initial outcome predictions upon presentation of the compound (AB) are based on the negative association of the cue (A) that was presented in the first phase. However, the AB compound is followed by a positive outcome level (d_j). Thus, a large discrepancy ($d_j - o_j$) occurs between a positive actual outcome and a negative predicted outcome. This discrepancy is larger than if no first-phase learning had taken place. In that case, both cues (A and B) would have had a zero association leading to a zero prediction when the first AB compound was presented, leading to a smaller discrepancy. A larger discrepancy (i.e., prediction error) leaves more room for updating and leads to faster updating, allowing the B cue to be associated with a positive outcome level more strongly and more quickly in the unblocking scenario.

In general, the unblocking phenomenon, or *feature positive discrimination*, implies that if consumers learn that a product characteristic (A) is related to some level of product performance and that products that have that characteristic plus another characteristic (AB) perform better, the second characteristic (B) will acquire more positive predictive value as the quality level of the first characteristic-only product (A) decreases. In addition, the predictive value of the second characteristic (B) should be higher when the high quality compound product (AB) is accompanied by a low quality first characteristic-only product (A) than when the compound (AB) is alone on the market. For example, introducing a high quality (i.e., positive outcome) new product (B) in a downscale store (A) may lead to negative initial quality expectations and reduce trial, but in the long term may lead to more positive brand associations for the new product than if the product is introduced in an upscale store, where its associations may be blocked. Of course, the size of such effects would depend on the salience of the cues (e.g., the salience to the consumer of the store while choosing and consuming the product). Thus, the unblocking phenomenon is essentially a contrast effect--characteristics such as brand names may gain from negative expectations brought on by other characteristics.

Commoditization and Brand Enhancement   For reasons that I will not discuss in detail, the combination of additive prediction and error-driven learning gives a large precedence to the single best predictor of a consumption outcome in situations with multiple levels of an attribute or multiple brands. For example, van Osselaer and Alba (2000, Experiment 3) measured the impact of brand names on product quality predictions in two learning conditions. In one condition, there were two types of products. All high quality products had one brand name and one particular attribute level (e.g., a type of floor in a whitewater raft; $Attribute_1Brand_1 \rightarrow$ High Quality). All low quality products had another brand name and carried another level of the attribute ($A_2B_2 \rightarrow$ Low Quality). In the other condition, participants learned about four types of products. Two were high quality and carried one level of the attribute, but each had its own brand name (i.e., $A_1B_1 \rightarrow$ High Quality and $A_1B_3 \rightarrow$ High Quality). The two other product types were low quality and again shared an attribute level but not their brand name (i.e., $A_2B_2 \rightarrow$ Low Quality and $A_2B_4 \rightarrow$ Low Quality). As expected, the attribute had much more impact on quality predictions, and the brand names had much less impact on quality predictions, in the second condition. Thus, if an attribute is the single best predictor of quality, brand equities will go down and the attribute will become the main driver of consumer decisions, leading to commoditization among brands that carry the good level of that attribute. For example, if (1) several brands sell from-concentrate orange juice, (2) multiple other brands sell not-from-concentrate juice, (3) not-from-concentrate juice tastes better than from-concentrate juice, and (4) the (not-)from-concentrate attribute is highlighted, consumers will quickly learn to value the attribute at the expense of the brand names. In contrast, if each brand has its own attribute level, the situation is much less dramatic, as both brand and attribute will compete for associative strength. It is as if in that regular cue competition situation there is still much uncertainty as to which component drives product quality, the brand or the attribute.

The reverse scenario is also of interest. If a brand has a consistent quality level despite being paired with different attributes in different situations, consumers should quickly learn to predict quality based on brand name instead of attributes. This implies that as long as extension products provide the same consumption benefits as the original product, the introduction of family-branded extensions with different attributes can enhance brand equity at the expense of attribute equity. Although there is probably no causal reasoning involved in this associative process (van Osselaer & Alba, 2000), it is as if the extension products help relieve the ambiguity as to whether product quality is driven by brands or attributes.

Breaking Into the Black Box: Neuroscientific Support for the Rescorla-Wagner Model

Over the past decade, neuroscientists have made great strides in uncovering the neurophysiological bases of associative learning. One important finding is that different paradigms using different cues and outcomes seem to rely on different neural circuits (see, e.g., Fanselow & Poulos, 2005, for a review). For example, whereas the cerebellum is the primary substrate for associations between cues and outcomes in many classical conditioning paradigms (e.g., eyeblink conditioning; e.g., Thompson, 1990), the amygdala plays a primary role in associating cues with pain (i.e., in fear conditioning; e.g., LeDoux, 1995), and the basal ganglia play an important role in learning of associations involving rewards (e.g., many operant conditioning paradigms; e.g., Lauwereyns, Watanabe, Coe, & Hikosaka, 2002). Despite the differences in brain areas involved, evidence has been found for error-driven learning in all three groups of paradigms. For example, in an eyeblink conditioning paradigm, J. J. Kim, Krupa, and Thompson (1998) found evidence that when rabbits have learned to predict a puff of air to the eye (outcome) in a blocking experiment, the representation of that outcome is no longer activated in the cerebellum when the predicted outcome is presented. Because associative binding relies on activation of inputs representing a cue and an outcome, reducing the activation of the representation of the outcome prevents further learning. In fear conditioning, Fanselow (1998) reports a similar suppression of activation of predicted outcomes in the amygdala. Finally, in an operant conditioning of reward setting, Schultz and his colleagues (e.g., Montague, Dayan, & Sejnowski, 1996; Schultz, Dayan, & Montague, 1997) found a similar result of decreased responses upon presentation of the outcome. In addition, these authors found very specific evidence that dopamine neurons of the ventral tegmental area (VTA) and the substantia nigra code for error between predicted and actual reward. These midbrain (i.e., mesencephalic) dopamine neurons show increased phasic activity when a reward is better than predicted and decreased activity when a reward is worse than predicted. In sum, there is ample neuroscientific evidence for the type of error-driven learning proposed in the Rescorla-Wagner model (see also Schultz, 2005).

Conclusion: The Rescorla-Wagner Model

Both as a source of testable predictions and as an explanation of previously documented phenomena, the Rescorla-Wagner model has dominated research on associative learning in the latter quarter of the 20th century (see, e.g., Miller, Barnet, & Grahame, 1995; Siegel & Allan, 1996, for reviews). Outside the traditional realm of research on associative learning, the Rescorla-Wagner model has inspired associative theories in fields such as causality judgment (see, e.g., Young, 1995; Lober & Shanks, 2000; Shanks, Medin, & Holyoak, 1996), medical diagnosis (e.g., Gluck & Bower, 1988; Shanks, 1991), and categorization (e.g., Gluck & Bower, 1988; Shanks, 1991). Furthermore, the simple Rescorla-Wagner model has been successful at predicting consumers' evaluations of products or of specific consumption outcomes in different situations characterized by different branding strategies, different ways of presenting attribute information, and different competitive contexts (e.g., Janiszewski & van Osselaer, 2000; van Osselaer & Alba, 2000, 2003).

In addition to its empirical success and concrete implications, the Rescorla-Wagner model, aided by the rise of connectionism (e.g., Rumelhart & McClelland, 1986), inspired a change of perspective on human cognition. Relatively complex phenomena such as the overexpectation effect that one would expect to be caused by strategic, high-level reasoning can be explained by simple associative processes that are also found in rats and other animals (see, e.g., Lober & Shanks, 2000; van Osselaer & Alba, 2000; but see Cheng, 1997; Novick & Cheng, 2004). In fact, although implemented by a very simple learning process on a trial-by-trial basis, it can be shown that the Rescorla-Wagner model's learning rule essentially carries out the equivalent of a multiple linear regression of an outcome on a set of cues (Stone, 1986). Thus, humans are like rats, but rats are smarter than most of us are willing to admit.

With respect to consumers, the Rescorla-Wagner model suggests that consumers learn to predict consumption outcomes quickly and generally accurately through the combined work of several simple associations working in parallel. Consumers can be seen as arrays of simple, decentralized, prediction engines that build association strengths or part-worths, allowing quick construction of evaluations of new (or old) products. Specifically, consumers go through life making predictions about consumption outcomes based on information they receive about cues such as brand names, prices, features, ingredients, or other search characteristics. The predictions are then used to guide choices of products with the most attractive predicted levels of important consumption outcomes. Next, for example through consumption of the chosen product, consumers receive feedback regarding the consumption outcomes. Finally, based on the degree and direction of the gap between predicted and experienced consumption outcomes, consumers update their associations to reduce their prediction error on the next occasion.

The Rescorla-Wagner model maps on well to a constructive view of human decision making using a weighted-adding decision rule (see, e.g., Bettman, Luce, & Payne, 1998). Instead of merely measuring weights or part-worth utilities, the Rescorla-Wagner model tells us something about how these weights or part-worths are formed and change over time, as well as how they can be expected to change in the future under different informational and competitive scenarios. In addition, the Rescorla-Wagner model suggests that complicated decision rules such as weighted-adding can be implemented by a simple and rat-like associative process. Sophisticated and resource-intensive thought may not be needed to implement such a complex decision rule.

Finally, the Rescorla-Wagner model, and the *Rescorla revolution* of viewing associative learning in terms of prediction, highlight the role of brands (and attributes) as predictive cues. For example, instead of looking at associative learning as transferring affect and value to a brand name per se ("I love the brand"), associative learning also makes brands predictors of the consumption outcomes that consumers really care about. Thus, brand equity may have two bases. People may buy a brand because they love the brand, but they may also buy a brand because doing so is likely to provide them a good consumption experience.

CONFIGURALITY

XOR and Configural Representation

The Rescorla-Wagner model assumes *elemental representation* of cues. Elemental representation implies that stimuli are decomposed into their constituting elements and that only these elements are represented in memory. For example, the model assumes that the rats in Kamin's blocking experiments break down a noise-plus-light (AB) stimulus into its separate elements, noise (A) and light (B), and do not represent the combination, or *configuration*, of the two stimulus elements. Thus, there is no record that these two stimuli occurred together. If cues are represented elementally and combine linearly to determine a response, as in the Rescorla-Wagner model or in a main effects-only regression model, nonlinear discriminations cannot be learned. For example, no linear combination of association strengths from the elemental representations of noise (A) and light (B) can lead a rat to predict a shock (outcome) when noise (A) is present or light (B) is present, but not when both noise and light (AB) are present. Nevertheless, there is ample evidence that animals and humans can solve this type of nonlinear discrimination problem, known as *negative patterning discrimination* or the *exclusive-or* (XOR) problem (e.g., Bellingham, Gillette-Bellingham, & Kehoe, 1985; Pavlov, 1927/1960; Rescorla, 1972; Shanks, Charles, Darby, & Azmi, 1998; Shanks, Darby, & Charles, 1998; Young, Wasserman, Johnson, & Jones, 2000). Similarly, it seems safe to assume that consumers can learn that the value of an attribute depends on the level of another attribute. For example, consumers might learn that being of made of Chardonnay instead of Sauvignon Blanc grapes makes a bigger difference to the taste of a wine if it hails from Sonoma than from California's Central Valley. Thus, although some evidence indicates that learning models quickly become more powerful than the learning processes they are trying to model (e.g., Shanks, 1990), the Rescorla-Wagner model is simply too simple. Models of animal and human associative learning need to be able to represent combinations, or *configurations*, of cues, so that a combination's impact on outcome predictions can be more than a sum of the impacts of its elements. At the same time, these models should still be able to explain the cue interaction phenomena discussed in the previous section, such as blocking, unblocking, and summation.

Important attempts to simultaneously explain nonlinear discrimination and cue interaction phenomena such as blocking have relied on models that represent configurations of cues, but still rely on the same adaptive, error-minimizing learning rule used by Rescorla and Wagner (1972) to form associations between configurations and outcomes. For example, Pearce's (1994, 2002) configural model, with origins in the animal learning literature, and Kruschke's (1992) ALCOVE model, which is based on the human categorization model by Nosofsky (1986), assume that each stimulus, whether consisting of a single-element cue or of a compound of several cue elements, is represented as a configuration. The advantage of configural representation in these models is that single-element stimuli in an XOR scenario (e.g., A, B) can be represented separately from the compound stimulus (e.g., AB), allowing single elements to form strong positive associations to outcomes while the compound does not.

Stimulus Generalization and Lack of Catastrophic Interference

Adaptive learning models that assume delta-rule learning and configural stimulus representation can explain nonlinear discriminations, but an additional assumption about *stimulus generalization* must be made for these models to adequately account for cue interaction phenomena. In configural models, generalization occurs when the presentation of a stimulus (consisting of one or more cues) leads to activation of similar configural representations which, in turn, activate the outcome. Generalization plays an important role in cue interaction effects because it allows presentation of a compound of cues (e.g., AB) to activate the representations of elements of that compound (e.g., A). For example, blocking occurs when presentation of the AB compound stimulus activates the previously reinforced single-element configuration (A). Activation of the A configuration in memory leads to activation of the outcome, reduces the discrepancy between actual and desired outcome activations, and reduces the updating of the association strength between the AB configuration and the outcome. Thus, relatively broad generalization is required for configural models to explain cue interaction phenomena. For example, to obtain a strong blocking effect, the presentation of the AB stimulus in the second learning phase should lead to strong activation of the pre-exposed A cue. Similarly, to obtain a summation effect the presentation of the AB stimulus in the test phase should lead to strong activation of the previously exposed A and B cues.

The activation of related stimuli upon presentation of a stimulus implied by broad generalization should also lead to strong, sometimes catastrophic, interference effects. However, a number of recent experiments have found interference, hence, generalization, to be quite limited (e.g., Baeyens, Vansteenwegen, Hermans, Vervliet, & Eelen, 2001; Shanks, Charles, et al., 1998; Shanks, Darby, & Charles, 1998). For example, human participants in a study by Shanks, Darby, and Charles (1998) received, among other stimuli, AB → O(utcome) in a first learning phase followed by A → no O, and B → no O trials in a second learning phase before being tested with AB in a test phase. Broad generalization would imply that people would not predict the outcome when given the AB stimulus at test due to interference in the second learning phase. In the experiment, however, participants predicted the AB test stimulus to be followed by the outcome. These findings are problematic, especially for the Pearce (1994) model which has a fixed and relatively broad level of generalization. In contrast to Pearce's model, ALCOVE (Kruschke, 1992) has a free generalization parameter and can explain both narrow and broad generalization. It does not, however, predict when generalization will be narrow or broad.

In sum, generalization in human associative learning has to be both narrow and broad to account for seemingly contradictory empirical findings of cue interaction and lack of catastrophic interference.

TWO PROCESSES IN HUMAN ASSOCIATIVE LEARNING

Configural representation with a free generalization parameter is one possible way to account for broad and narrow generalization across a variety of learning tasks. However, an alternative solution to the generalization paradox might be that human associative learning relies on at least two separate processes, with separate representations in memory and characterized by different degrees of generalization (van Osselaer & Janiszewski, 2001; van Osselaer et al., 2004). According to the latter proposal, people can predict outcomes using two processes, an exemplar-based process characterized by configural stimulus representation with narrow generalization and an adaptive process characterized by broad generalization and cue interaction.

Exemplar-Based Process

The first, exemplar-based process is relatively unfocused and passive during learning. As long as a person pays sufficient attention, it automatically records whole experiences (i.e., exemplars or episodes), including cues and outcomes. Later, when the person has to make a prediction about an outcome based on the information about cues, she will make that prediction by retrieving experiences with identical or similar sets of cues and will base the prediction on the outcome levels stored as part of the configurations representing the retrieved experiences. Thus, representation in this process is configural. In addition, the process is backward-looking. At test, people look back to earlier, similar experiences. This process is also characterized by narrow generalization and little, if any, cue interaction. Finally, this process is still associative, in the sense that the different elements of an experience are all connected to each other, so that presenting parts of an experience helps retrieve the nonpresented parts of the same experience or similar experiences. For example, presenting a light and a tone (AB) helps retrieve the outcomes experienced during previous experiences with a light and a tone.

Adaptive Process

The second process is adaptive, in the sense that it adapts association strengths to minimize predictive error. This process may be described by the Rescorla-Wagner model and is characterized by a delta learning rule and elemental representation, hence broad generalization. As mentioned above when discussing the Rescorla-Wagner model, this is an inherently adaptive and forward-looking learning process, in which a learner first makes a prediction of a future outcome based on currently present cues, then records feedback about the actual outcome, and then updates the association strengths or predictive values of the cues to reduce prediction error on the next occasion. When a new stimulus is encountered, people do not have to look back and retrieve specific experiences or exemplars, but quickly construct a predicted outcome level by adding up the predictive value of the presented cues. This process makes a clear distinction between cues, which function as predictors, and outcomes, which are to be predicted. It does not merely store experiences, but is focused on prediction, with minimal error.

Empirical Evidence for Two Associative Learning Processes: Generalization

The dual-process proposal holds that recent findings of narrow and broad generalization are best explained by two separate processes. However, such a proposal has no competitive advantage over a single-process configural explanation with a free generalization parameter (e.g., Kruschke, 1992) unless it yields predictions, *a priori*, about the degree of generalization.

Summation Paradigm   Van Osselaer et al. (2004) empirically tested three such predictions of the dual process model using a summation paradigm (e.g., A → O, B → O, CD → O). During a single learning phase, all participants learned about a number of bottles of wine. For each bottle, information was given about one or more cues and an outcome. The outcome was a quality level (e.g., four stars), which was highly positive for all relevant bottles (A, B, and CD). For some bottles, only one cue was given (A or B). For other bottles, two cues were presented (CD). The A and C cues were countries of origin (e.g., A is California and C is France). The B and D cues represented, for example, that the wine had been aged in oak vats or came from a boutique vineyard. After the learning phase, participants were asked to judge the quality of two new wines based on two cues each. For one wine, participants had seen its two cues in the same combination (CD; e.g., a wine from a boutique vineyard in France). For the other wine, the cues represented a new combination of two cues that had previously been presented separately (AB; e.g., a wine from California that had been aged in oak vats).

In this paradigm, an adaptive process with broad generalization, as modeled by, for example, the Rescorla-Wagner learning rule, predicts that the new combination of previously separate cues (AB) would yield a higher prediction than the existing combination (CD). This occurs for two reasons. First, broad generalization implies that the associations that have been acquired by specific elements (A and B) should generalize to a combination of those elements (AB) if that combination is presented at test. Second, elements that have been learned alone should form stronger associations to an outcome than elements that have been learned in compound, due to cue competition (see the discussion of cue competition earlier in this chapter). That is, under broad generalization the associations from the A, B, C, and D cues to the outcome all generalize to their test compounds (AB and CD), but those associations are much stronger for the cues that were learned about separately (A and B) than for the cues that were presented together during learning (CD).

Under narrow generalization and configural representation, the opposite pattern of results obtains. Because the CD compound at test is identical to the CD compound of cues during learning, what has been learned about the CD compound during learning generalizes to the CD compound at test. Because the AB compound at test is not highly similar to the A and B stimuli during learning, there is only limited generalization of the A and B cues' associations to the AB test compound. Thus, participants judge the CD compound to be of higher quality than the AB compound.

Finally, if participants use a mixed strategy, the exemplar-based process to judge the CD test stimulus and the adaptive process to judge the AB test stimulus, quality predictions for the AB test stimulus should also be higher than for the CD test stimulus.

Prediction During Learning   If the adaptive process is inherently predictive, its influence on responses should be increased to the extent that people predict an outcome during learning. Thus, generalization should be broader if consumers are asked to make outcome predictions during learning. Van Osselaer et al. (2004) tested this prediction using the summation paradigm outlined above. The critical manipulation was that, during learning, half the participants were shown a bottle's cue or cues first, were then asked to predict its quality, and only then received feedback about that bottle's actual quality level. The other half of the sample were shown each bottle's cue and quality outcome information simultaneously and, hence, did not predict the outcome before receiving outcome feedback. As expected, participants who made predictions during learning expected the wine with the new combination of cues (AB) to be of higher quality than the wine with the previously encountered combination of cues (CD). Participants who did not make predictions during learning showed the opposite pattern. Purely configural models with a free generalization parameter such as ALCOVE (Kruschke, 1992) can fit this result post-hoc, but do not predict it *a priori*.

Looking Back at Test   More damaging for configural models with a free generalization parameter was a second experiment. In this experiment, all participants made predictions during learning in the same summation paradigm. However, at test, half the participants were asked to think back and recall the bottles of wine they had seen. Actively retrieving these exemplars should make them more accessible, increasing participants' reliance on the exemplar-based process at the expense of the adaptive process. As expected, participants who were asked to look back before making their judgments, but after learning, judged the wine with the previously encountered combination of cues (CD) to be of higher quality than the wine with cues that had previously been encountered separately (AB). When no such *look back* instruction was given, the opposite pattern obtained. Because the learning phase, and hence all learning, was the same for both groups, any learning model that relies on a single learning process involving a single set of outcome associations (e.g., from configural representations to outcomes or from elemental representations to outcomes, but not both) would not be able to explain this result. Thus, this result is not only problematic for models relying on associations from configural representations of (compounds of) cues such as ALCOVE (Kruschke, 1992) or RASHNL (Kruschke & Johansen, 1999), but also for recent *componential* versions of models relying on associations between elemental cue representations and outcomes (e.g., Brandon, Vogel, & Wagner, 2000; Wagner, 2003; Wagner & Brandon, 2001).

Very Similar Exemplars   The exemplar-based process should also have more impact on responses for test stimuli that are highly similar to exemplars experienced before. This might explain the lack of catastrophic interference found in recent studies of human associative learning. To test this assumption, van Osselaer et al. (2004) added a second learning phase to the learning phase used in the previous experiment, in a single-cell experiment. In the first learning phase, participants made predictions about A, B, and CD stimuli all followed by high quality feedback. In the second learning phase, participants made predictions about AB, C, and D stimuli that were all presented with low quality outcomes. After the second learning phase, participants were asked to judge the quality of AB and CD test stimuli. If participants' judgments are more strongly influenced by the exemplar-based process with narrow generalization when test stimuli are very similar to stimuli encountered earlier, then responses at test should rely mostly on experiences with the exact combination of cues tested (i.e., AB and CD) instead of being influenced heavily by generalization from the single-element experiences (i.e., A, B, C, and D). In this case, quality of the CD test stimulus, which had been paired with a positive outcome, should be judged higher than the AB test stimulus, which had been paired with a low quality outcome. Findings supported this prediction, and showed less-than-catastrophic interference of the low-quality C and D experiences in the second learning phase on test responses after that phase. Results also showed a replication of the effect found in the previous two experiments after the first learning phase. Pure reliance on either the adaptive or the exemplar-based process cannot explain this pattern of results.

Empirical Evidence for Two Associative Learning Processes: Cue Interaction

Despite myriad replications of basic cue interaction phenomena such as blocking, no evidence of cue interaction is found in some instances (e.g., Williams, Sagness, & McPhee, 1994). Discussing future research directions, McClelland (2000) suggests that human learning may rely on both error-driven learning, which is characterized by cue interaction phenomena, and Hebbian, non-error-driven learning, which is not. According to the dual-process proposal, cue interaction effects should obtain when the adaptive process drives responses but not when the exemplar-based process drives responses. Van Osselaer and Janiszewski (2001)[2] and van Osselaer and Alba (2003) tested whether the dual-process proposal could predict when cue interaction effects would obtain.

Prediction During Learning   Van Osselaer and Janiszewski (2001, Study 1) exposed human participants to the following trials: A → O-, AB → O+, C → O+, CD → O+, CD → O+. The stimuli they used were actual pieces of cake, where A, B, C, and D were (ingredient) brand names printed on the packaging of the pieces of cake, O+ was a strong chocolate flavor, and O- was a less attractive, mild chocolate flavor. In each learning trial, participants saw the brand name or names (cues), predicted an outcome, and received feedback by eating the cake. Half the participants predicted the chocolate flavor and half the participants predicted another outcome, moistness. At test, participants were asked to predict the chocolate flavor of two test stimuli, muffins identified by a new brand name combined with an ingredient brand name seen during the learning phase (i.e., EB and ED).

If an adaptive process drives responding, the EB muffin should be predicted to have a stronger chocolate flavor than the ED muffin. This would be the case because the B cue should develop a very strong association with the flavor outcome due to an unblocking effect and because the D cue should be blocked (see the discussion of blocking and unblocking earlier in this chapter). If an exemplar-based process drives responding, no cue interaction effects should occur and the strength of the associations between the ingredient brands and flavor should only depend on how often they were paired with the strong chocolate flavor outcome. Thus, although the difference would be small due to narrow generalization, the ED test stimulus would lead to stronger flavor predictions than the EB test stimulus, because the D ingredient brand was presented twice during learning whereas the B ingredient brand was presented only once.

The dual-process proposal holds that participants would engage in adaptive processing for the outcome they made predictions about during learning but not for the outcome they were not making predictions about during learning. As a result, flavor predictions at test should fit the adaptive process (EB > ED) when participants predicted flavor during learning. Flavor predictions should fit the exemplar-based process (ED > EB) when participants predicted the other outcome, moistness, during learning. Results supported these predictions.

A similar pattern of results was obtained when the hedonic relevance of the outcome was varied (van Osselaer & Janiszewski, 2001, Study 3). When outcomes are hedonically more relevant, people are more likely to make predictions about that outcome during learning instead of merely storing exemplars. Hence, the adaptive process is more likely to drive responses and cue-interaction phenomena are more likely to occur when an outcome is hedonically more relevant, such as when the outcome is a valenced consumption benefit (e.g., flavor) instead of a feature or attribute of the product (e.g., an ingredient name) that has no direct hedonic relevance.

Looking Back at Test   Similar to the generalization result, asking participants to retrieve exemplars after learning but before making test predictions should increase the impact of the exemplar-based process on test responses, hence, reduce cue interaction. Van Osselaer and Janiszewski (2001, Study 4) used essentially the same unblocking/blocking combination paradigm as in their Study 1. This time, all participants predicted the flavor outcome during learning. Half the participants were asked, right before indicating their taste predictions for the EB and ED test stimuli but after the learning phase, to recall the cakes (exemplars) they had tasted. The other half were not asked to retrieve any exemplars from memory. As expected, the data were consistent with exemplar-based processing that is not subject to cue interaction (i.e., ED > EB) when participants were asked to look back and retrieve exemplars, but were consistent with cue-interactive adaptive processing (i.e., EB > ED) when participants were not asked to retrospect.

Outcome Ambiguity   Adaptive learning, which relies on predicting outcomes, attending to feedback regarding these outcomes, and updating associations to improve the next prediction, should be less likely to occur if outcome feedback is perceived to be less diagnostic, for example when outcomes are clearly ambiguous. Thus, cue interaction phenomena such as blocking or cue competition should be less likely to occur when outcome information is very ambiguous. Van Osselaer and Alba (2003, Experiment 3) tested this hypothesis using a cue competition paradigm. As expected, they found cue competition when outcome information was unambiguous but not when outcome information was extremely ambiguous.

Breaking Into the Black Box: Support for Dual Processes From Neuroscience and Cognitive Modeling

Ample evidence indicates that the hippocampal region (i.e., the hippocampus proper, but also the subiculum, dentate gyrus, and entorhinal, perirhinal, and parahippocampal cortices) plays an important role in the encoding of exemplars or episodes (e.g., Cabeza & Nyberg, 2000; Eichenbaum, 2000; Jarrard, 1995). There is also evidence that the hippocampal region is involved in associative learning (e.g., Berger & Thompson, 1978). Interestingly, hippocampal damage does not completely prevent all associative learning and primarily affects associative learning requiring configural representation of stimuli (e.g., Alvarado & Rudy, 1995; Meeter, Myers, & Gluck, 2005; Thompson, 2005). Moreover, animals with lesions in the hippocampal region do not exhibit decreased responding when cues are presented in a different context or in combination with different cues than in learning (M. T. Allen, Padilla, Myers, & Gluck, 2002; Penick & Solomon, 1991). Decreased responding when cues are presented in combination with different (context) cues is an example of narrow generalization. Thus, narrow generalization, also referred to as high *specificity*, may require involvement of the hippocampal region. This is consistent with the hypothesis that exemplar-based memory, which relies heavily on the hippocampal region, is characterized by relatively narrow generalization (van Osselaer et al., 2004).

Based on these data, Meeter, Myers, and Gluck (2005) proposed that stimulus information is represented at different levels of configurality by three different brain structures. The neocortex codes individual features of experiences, including cue elements and features of the learning context. Presumably, representation at this level is completely elemental. The parahippocampal region, involving the perirhinal, entorhinal, and postrhinal-parahippocampal cortices, codes more integrated representations of stimuli and context. Finally, the hippocampus proper represents ensembles, or configurations of the whole experience. Interestingly, representations at each level are associated with outcomes in the structures responsible for associative learning (e.g., the cerebellum, the basal ganglia, or the amygdala, depending on the type of learning task). The authors assume that learning at each level is guided by the Rescorla-Wagner rule. Meeter et al. (2005) specified their theory in terms of a connectionist model awaiting empirical verification. Elements of the ideas that associations are learned at different levels, one between configural representations and outcomes and one between more elemental representations and outcomes, with the first type of representations heavily reliant on the hippocampus and the second heavily reliant on neocortical representations, are also found in other models (e.g., Sutherland & Rudy, 1989; Schmajuk & DiCarlo, 1992; Schmajuk, Lamoureux, & Holland, 1998; Squire, 1992).

Although more detailed simulation analyses would be required to assess if these models can fit the results obtained by van Osselaer and colleagues (van Osselaer et al., 2004; van Osselaer &

Janiszewski, 2001; van Osselaer & Alba, 2003), there is a high level of conceptual fit between these models and the adaptive and exemplar-based dual-process proposal.

In sum, recent neuroscientific evidence supports the idea that there are at least two types of associative learning processes. One relies heavily on the neocortex for the representation of simple, probably elemental, cue information that is associated, for example in the cerebellum, with outcome information using an error-driven learning rule such as the Rescorla-Wagner rule. These associations are not used for the other process. The other process relies on configural representations of exemplars or episodes encoded in the hippocampal region and involves a different associative learning process. The neuroscientific data are also consistent with the idea that the exemplar-based process is characterized by relatively narrow generalization.

Implications for Consumers' Evaluations of Products

The implication of a dual-process model for consumer psychology is that consumers have two learning-and-memory processes at their disposal to make predictions about consumption benefits. For example, a consumer considering the purchase of a wine can predict the taste quality of the wine in two different ways. If she relies on the adaptive process, she constructs a predicted quality level of the wine by adding up the predictive values of the characteristics listed on the bottle. These predictive values are based on association strengths. This process is very similar to what we assume when we use multiattribute attitude models, assume weighted-additive decision making, or use a traditional conjoint analysis.

Alternatively, the consumer may try to retrieve memory records of experiences with wines that listed similar characteristics on the bottle and predict the taste quality of the wine to be similar to the quality of the most similar wines. These two processes can lead to different predictions and, hence, product evaluations, decisions, and choices.

Cue Interaction   If decisions are made using the adaptive process, cue interaction phenomena are likely to occur. For example, due to blocking, learning about a brand name prevents consumers from learning the value of the ingredients, and vice versa. Similarly, sub-brands do not acquire much brand equity if the benefits of sub-branded extension products are the same as a parent product carrying only the family brand name. Due to cue competition, highlighting attribute information reduces the equity of a brand when brand and attribute information are learned about simultaneously. If decisions are made using the exemplar-based process, cue interaction phenomena do not occur. In those cases, cues' impact on evaluations, and hence their value, will depend much more on the mere frequency with which cues and outcomes co-occur. Thus, pre-exposure to a brand name will have little impact on learning of the importance of an ingredient, which mainly depends on how often that ingredient is accompanied by an outcome. Similarly, high quality brands are no longer hurt by simultaneous learning about an attribute.

Generalization   The adaptive process, due to its broad generalization, allows for much less product- and context-specificity of the value of product characteristics than the exemplar-based process. Although the Rescorla-Wagner model allows for competition between cues during learning, it does predict that the predictive value of a brand name or other attribute remains the same at test, regardless of what other characteristics it is combined with at that time. Thus, under adaptive processing, consumers' brand and attribute associations can be extended easily and widely to different products. Consumers just add up the association strengths of all present cues, regardless of whether these cues had or had not been experienced together in the past. The flipside of this broad generalizability is that experiences with one product can have a big impact on evaluations of other products. For example, if a company's product shares an important attribute with a competing product, damage to the attribute's associations due to a bad experience with the competing product will transfer easily to outcome predictions for the focal company's product. Similarly, if, perhaps due to cue competition, a product's positive evaluation is based mostly on an attribute's associations and not the brand's, any new competing product that incorporates that same attribute will freeride on the focal product's attribute associations and be evaluated almost as positively.

The narrow generalization and configural representation in the exemplar-based process make product evaluations much less dependent on previous experiences with products that share only some of their characteristics. In addition, effects of learning about some product on outcome expectations for other products depend much more on whether characteristics occur in the same combinations. For example, in the summation design discussed above (A → O, B → O, CD → O), evaluations at test of the product whose characteristics had been learned about in the same combination (CD) were more positive than evaluations of the product whose characteristics had been encountered separately (AB). This sensitivity to configuration, or the combinations in which product characteristics appear, also has implications for the measurement and prediction of consumers' attitudes and preferences. When decisions and responses to marketing research instruments are based on exemplar-based processing, *main effect* approaches such as orthogonal conjoint analyses and multiattribute attitude models are likely to be of little value. In exemplar-based situations, exemplar- and similarity-based models (e.g., Hintzman, 1986) may perform much better at predicting consumers' evaluations of products.

Predicting Which Process Drives Consumers' Behavior   If consumers can rely on two associative learning processes to evaluate products, it is important to know which process is most likely to drive evaluations in which type of situation. This requires an understanding of how the two processes interact. Problematically, there are many ways in which two psychological processes might interact to drive behavior and these many ways are difficult to identify empirically (Gilbert, 1999). The data discussed thus far suggest that the adaptive system is not always *on*. For example, when participants do not make predictions about an outcome during learning and instead make predictions about another outcome (van Osselaer & Janiszewski, 2001, Study 1) or merely evaluate stimuli consisting of cues and outcomes (van Osselaer et al., 2004, Study 1), no evidence of adaptive processing is found in participants' predictions at test. In contrast, the exemplar-based process, assuming sufficient attention is given to the learning stimuli, does seem to be encoding exemplars even when the participants' focus is not on recording these exemplars. For example, even when participants actively focus on predicting one outcome during learning, exemplar information is encoded. This encoding allows participants to make exemplar-based predictions about the other, nonfocal outcome later (e.g., van Osselaer & Janiszewski, 2001, Study 1). This is consistent with the idea that the exemplar-based system is relatively passive. It stores exemplars for potential future use without an indication of what that use might be. In contrast to the adaptive process, it does not actively divide stimuli into cues and outcomes and does not start to construct predictive values of individual cues for specific outcomes. The exemplar-based system merely records whatever is presented to it. This unstructured information can then flexibly be used to solve whatever problem is presented to the learner at test.

In sum, the data are consistent with the idea that adaptive learning is not always on but exemplar-based learning is. One possible reason adaptive learning is not always on might be that any adaptive learning system needs to know which parts of a stimulus function as predictors or cues, and which parts function as outcomes to be predicted. In many situations, it is completely unclear which elements of the stimulus should be predictors and which elements are to-be-predicted. Another reason that adaptive learning is not always on might be that it requires more resources during learning than the exemplar-based process. If this is true, one might speculate that the system that requires more resources tends to dominate responding when it is on. Another reason to suggest that the adaptive process often dominates responses when adaptive learning has taken place is that the exemplar-based system, due to narrow generalization, will only provide weak inputs to an evaluation unless the product to be evaluated is quite similar to products experienced in the past.

If the adaptive process tends to dominate when adaptive learning has taken place, it is important to know in what consumer learning situations the adaptive learning process is likely to be *on*. The most straightforward prediction is that the adaptive process will drive product evaluations when consumers have made predictions and attended to feedback during learning. This is very likely to be the case when consumers learn through their own consumption experiences. For example, a consumer in a store choosing a bottle of wine is likely to predict, consciously or unconsciously, how good a bottle will taste and is likely to compare, consciously or unconsciously, the actual taste of the wine with the expected taste when drinking the chosen bottle. In contrast, learning through communications such as word-of-mouth and advertising is much less likely to involve prediction. When presented with a TV commercial for a wine consumers may not make predictions about the wine's taste. Thus, a lot of learning from experience, by choosing, buying, and trying, may be fundamentally different from the learning involved in more passive processing of marketing communications.

Other factors might also influence the learner's opportunity or motivation to make outcome predictions and compare those predictions with outcome feedback. For example, more valenced stimulus elements, such as consumption benefits may be more likely to be predicted during learning (van Osselaer & Janiszewski, 2001, Study 3). In contrast, less valenced outcomes, such as grape information and other characteristics of the product and not so much of the consumption experience, are more likely to be used as cues. When predictions later have to be made about cues, only exemplar-based processing is available. In fact, several authors have failed to find cue interaction when people are asked to make judgments about cues (e.g., Matute, Arcediano, & Miller, 1996; Waldmann & Holyoak, 1992). Another factor might be the ambiguity of outcome information. When outcome information is absent or highly ambiguous, learning to predict that outcome is very difficult, reducing the effectiveness and perhaps also increasing the required resources of adaptive processing. This, in turn, might make it less likely that the adaptive learning process is used and more likely that consumers rely on an exemplar-based process (van Osselaer & Alba, 2003, Experiment 3). A similar increased reliance on exemplar-based processing with increased outcome ambiguity has been found in categorization and multiple-cue judgment tasks (Juslin, Jones, Olsson, & Winman, 2003; Juslin, Olsson, & Olsson, 2003).

When both adaptive and exemplar-based inputs are available for product evaluations, the exemplar-based process can be the primary driver of responses in some situations. This is likely to be the case when consumers are primed or otherwise encouraged to retrieve exemplars from memory (e.g., van Osselaer & Janiszewski, 2001, Study 4; van Osselaer et al., 2004, Study 2). For example, advertisements that encourage consumers to think about earlier experiences with the same or similar products may lead to exemplar-based evaluations. Most importantly, it is also likely that products that a consumer has consumed before, or products that are highly similar to recently experienced products, are evaluated using the exemplar-based system (van Osselaer et al., 2004, Study 3).

Conclusion: Two Associative Learning Processes

Based on experimental and neuroscientific data, a view emerges of associative learning as involving at least two qualitatively different processes that can lead to different product evaluations and decisions. These processes differ not just in the way they learn, but also in terms of representation in memory, neurological substrate, and evaluation or decision process.

The adaptive process is forward looking, using cues to predict outcomes, and updating associative strengths on an experience-by-experience basis to improve prediction during the next experience. It represents cues in memory as individual elements that have direct connections with outcomes. These connections are formed in different parts of the brain for different types of outcomes. For example, relationships between cues and positive outcomes may rely heavily on the cerebellum or the basal ganglia, whereas connections between cues and highly threatening outcomes rely more on the amygdala. Finally, evaluations and decisions are made by adding up the predictive values or association strengths of the individual cues present in the to-be-evaluated stimulus. These evaluations and decisions are subject to cue interaction phenomena and show broad generalization of learning about different products that share even few of their cues.

The exemplar-based process is more passive. During learning, all stimuli are stored in their entirety and parts of the stimulus are bound together merely by being presented as part of the same stimulus. Representation in memory is configural. That is, combinations of elements, presumably the whole stimulus, are represented as combinations that are different from a sum of their elements. These configural representations rely heavily on the hippocampal region. When consumers evaluate products using the exemplar-based process, they look back and retrieve similar exemplars they experienced before, inserting the outcomes from those experiences to evaluate the current product. These evaluations are not characterized by cue interaction and show relatively narrow generalization—extrapolation from previous experiences drops off relatively fast as products become less similar.

DISCUSSION

Situating Adaptive and Exemplar-Based Associative Learning in a Broader Theoretical Context

Because the adaptive and exemplar-based processes touch upon issues of learning, memory, and evaluation, it is important to discuss their similarities and differences with other theories in these areas.

Dual Processes in Decision Making and Social Cognition   There are striking similarities between the current dual-process proposal and dual-process theories in decision making and social cognition (see, e.g., Chaiken & Trope, 1999; Epstein, 1994; Kahneman & Frederick, 2002; Sloman, 1996). For example, Stanovich and West (2000), summarizing these theories, describe one system (System 1) that requires fewer resources and is more contextualized than the other (System 2). One might argue that this suggests that the exemplar-based system, which seems to require fewer resources and is more sensitive to contexts and specific combinations in which cues occur, maps on to one system (System 1). The adaptive system, perhaps requiring more resources and characterized by predictive values that do not depend on other cues at the time of decision, may be taken to map on to the other system (System 2). There are, however, strong arguments against such a mapping. System 2 is also described as rule-based, analytic, thoughtful, and based on explicit reasoning and learning. Because adaptive learning is a mainstay of psychological functioning in rats and pigeons that can presumably not reason consciously and logically, it is difficult to accept that adaptive learning should be classified under System 2. In addition, several authors have argued that adaptive learning, and especially cue interaction phenomena, are explained by an associative process and not a more elaborative reasoning process (e.g., Lober & Shanks, 2000; Shanks, Charles, Darby, & Dickinson, 1996; van Osselaer & Alba, 2000). Thus, the data do not support the assumption equating the adaptive learning process with System 2. Instead, the data suggest there are two qualitatively different types of associative, or System 1, processes.

The Use of Abstract Rules in Associative Learning   The idea that adaptive processing does not fit the rule-based System 2 in the decision making and social cognition literatures suggests that another, rule-based process might exist in associative learning tasks. Indeed, several authors have recently argued that humans sometimes use abstract rules in associative learning tasks (e.g., Lachnit & Lober, 2001; Lachnit, Lober, Reinhard, & Kinder, 2001; Shanks & Darby, 1998). For example, the XOR problem, in which one cue (A or B) is followed by an outcome but a configuration of two cues (AB) is not, may be solved by associations involving the specific elements and configuration (A, B, and AB), but also by using an abstract rule such as "single cues lead to the outcome but combined cues do not." It is possible that rule-based, System 2 processing relies on the same types of memory and learning as our exemplar-based process, but uses the retrieved exemplars as an input to a deliberative reasoning process to make judgments instead of judging by similarity.

Evaluative Conditioning   Product evaluations and consumer decisions are also influenced by a type of learning referred to as evaluative conditioning (e.g., De Houwer et al., 2001; Olson & Fazio, 2001, 2002). Thus far, this chapter has only discussed the role of associative learning in making predictions about an outcome. In evaluative conditioning, pairing a neutral element with a valenced element leads to a transfer of valence from one to the other element. As I already discussed briefly in the introduction to this chapter, there is a difference between choosing a product because one likes its search characteristics (as a result of evaluative conditioning) and choosing a product because its search characteristics allow one to predict a good consumption experience (as a result of the types of associative learning discussed in this chapter). An example may clarify the distinction.

Gorn (1982) showed participants a picture of one (e.g., blue) pen while playing a liked, pop song and a picture of another (e.g., beige) pen while playing disliked Indian classical music. In this design, the pens functioned as initially neutral conditioned stimuli and the music pieces functioned as unconditioned stimuli. After this learning phase, participants made a choice between the two pens. Presumably reflecting their evaluation of the conditioned stimuli, most participants chose the pen that had been paired with the liked music over the pen paired with the disliked music. This is an example of evaluative conditioning. The dependent variable is the evaluation of the conditioned stimulus (a pen). In the *signal* or *expectancy learning* experiments that form the main topic of this chapter, the dependent variable is a prediction of the unconditioned stimulus based on information about the conditioned stimulus. Thus, the signal learning equivalent of Gorn's experiment would be one in which participants at test were shown a pen and asked whether this pen would be followed by Indian classical music. Interestingly, most of the conditioning research in consumer psychology involves evaluative conditioning (e.g., C. T. Allen & Janiszewski, 1989; Bierley et al., 1985; J. Kim et al., 1996; Shimp et al., 1991; Stuart et al., 1987). In fact, one might say that consumer researchers have played a pioneering role in the evaluative conditioning literature.

Evaluative conditioning results often deviate from predictions made by the Rescorla-Wagner (1972) model. For example, several experiments have failed to find cue interaction phenomena (Baeyens, Crombez, De Houwer, & Eelen, 1996; Baeyens, Hendrickx, Crombez, & Hermans, 1998). Also, extinction, or the reduction of association strength when a conditioned stimulus is no longer paired with an unconditioned stimulus, is very slow in evaluative conditioning. Often, no significant extinction is found at all in evaluative conditioning studies (e.g., De Houwer, Baeyens, Vansteenwegen, & Eelen, 2000). In addition to these deviations from the Rescorla-Wagner model's predictions, several authors have argued that evaluative conditioning can take place incidentally, without conscious awareness of the contingency between conditioned and unconditioned stimulus (e.g., Olson & Fazio, 2001, 2002; De Houwer et al., 2001; but see Lovibond & Shanks, 2002). This suggests that evaluative conditioning requires few cognitive resources.

The evaluative conditioning results discussed in the previous paragraph seem consistent with an exemplar-based process, which is not subject to cue interaction and requires few cognitive resources during learning. It is unclear how fast extinction is in the exemplar-based process, but it is very well possible that extinction is relatively slow, more akin to the relatively slow forgetting of exemplars or episodes than to more active learning that a cue no longer predicts an outcome. On the other hand, evaluative conditioning does not seem to yield so-called *modulation* or *occasion setting* (Baeyens et al., 1996, 1998), a phenomenon that is often explained in terms of configural representation (see, e.g., Holland, 1992; Schmajuk & Holland, 1998; Schmajuk et al., 1998, for an introduction to this phenomenon). Thus, it is also possible that evaluative conditioning depends on a process that is simpler than both the adaptive and exemplar-based processes. Such a process may merely associate elements based on their co-occurrence (see De Houwer et al. 2001, for a description of such a *referential* account). In sum, it is possible that the psychological processes that drive evaluative conditioning and exemplar-based signal learning are different, but the similarities outlined above do raise the possibility that evaluative conditioning relies on the exemplar-based process.

If evaluative conditioning relies on the exemplar-based system, one would expect that the transfer of properties from the unconditioned stimulus to the conditioned stimulus could involve not only affect, but could also involve other properties. This is consistent with findings by J. Kim et al. (1996), who showed, for example, that properties such as the speediness of a pizza delivery company can be influenced by pairing the brand with pictures of a racecar.

There is also some evidence (van Osselaer & Alba, Experiment 3) that under exemplar-based processing, we may find transfer of associations between cues, not only between a cue and an outcome. Thus, evaluations of products with one cue that was co-presented with another cue, may be helped by associations acquired by the formerly co-presented cue. For example, presenting a brand name together with an attribute that has positive associations will boost the brand name's equity, instead of preventing the brand from acquiring it. However, narrow generalization and the indirect nature of such an effect imply that this effect will be relatively weak. That is, previous learning experiences involving an attribute but not involving a brand name have to generalize to experiences involving both brand name and attribute, which in turn have to generalize to a prediction situation involving only the brand name, which should yield a very weak effect under narrow generalization. Thus, consistent with empirical data (van Osselaer & Alba, 2003), these types of *affect referral* effects are expected to be small, or at least develop slowly, and are expected to be limited to exemplar-based decisions.

Questions for Future Research

In addition to discovering their role in consumer decision processes, particularly with respect to more and less deliberative decision processes, and their relationships to evaluative conditioning processes, there are many other unanswered questions regarding adaptive and exemplar-based learning-and-memory processes.

Specific Models of Adaptive and Exemplar-Based Processes   Many opportunities for future research exist in the cognitive modeling arena. Starting with the Rescorla-Wagner model and its connectionist implementations, there has been a growing interplay between experimental data and formal models of human and animal learning, with new data inspiring new models and vice versa.

With respect to modeling adaptive and exemplar-based processes, there are at least two families of candidate model architectures. First, cues may be represented both elementally and configurally, and both elements and configurations have associations to a representation of an outcome (e.g., Sutherland & Rudy, 1989). Several connectionist models exist that have an architecture of this type (e.g., Meeter et al., 2005; Schmajuk et al., 1998). The findings regarding adaptive versus exemplar-based processes discussed in this chapter suggest a number of characteristics that a model along these lines should have. For example, to account for results showing a lack of catastrophic interference, configural representations should be activated only by similar cue configurations (i.e., show narrow generalization) but should have a much stronger influence on outcome predictions than elemental associations if the configural representations are activated. In addition, to represent the idea that adaptive learning does not always take place, learning of associations from elements to outcomes should be much more dependent on attention than learning of associations from cue configurations to outcomes.

At least one characteristic inherent to models with element-to-outcome and configuration-to-outcome associations may be problematic. These models still require the learner to distinguish cues and outcomes during learning. However, in many situations, people seem to be able to make predictions about stimulus elements that were unlikely to be classified as outcomes instead of cues during learning. It is, of course, possible that during exemplar-based learning, all stimulus elements play multiple roles as cues and outcomes. This, however, seems very inefficient, because the number of associations that have to be learned is also multiplied. In addition, episodic or exemplar-based learning is often described explicitly as unstructured (e.g., Meeter et al., 2005). One modeling solution would be to assume that the two processes are more separate than assumed by the models that integrate element-to-outcome and configuration-to-outcome associations. That is, there may be one system relying on elemental cue to outcome associations that can be described by, for example, the Rescorla-Wagner model. This model may be largely separate from an exemplar-based system that is best described by models that do not differentiate cues and outcomes. Such a model of the exemplar-based process might be inspired by memory array models (e.g., Hintzman, 1986) or recurrent connectionist networks (e.g., McClelland & Rumelhart, 1986).

Neuroscience   The neuroscientific findings discussed earlier help to interpret the empirical results but also yield specific predictions. For example, whether or not people make predictions during learning (e.g., van Osselaer & Janiszewski, 2001; van Osselaer et al., 2004) should have little impact on activity in the hippocampal region but presenting new versus old stimuli should. In addition, neuroscientific data may help distinguish between the two families of models presented in the previous paragraphs. In learning situations in which only the exemplar-based system is active, the cerebellum, basal ganglia, or amygdala should be used if exemplar-based learning relies on associations between configural representations in the hippocampus and representations in the cerebellum, basal ganglia, or amygdala. However, if the exemplar-based process is more separate from the adaptive process and does not rely on distinct outcome representations, then exemplar-based learning should take place in the hippocampal region without heavy involvement of the cerebellum, basal ganglia, or amygdala.

Predictive Focus   The experimental data thus far provide little insight into the necessary conditions for adaptive learning. For example, in the experiments by van Osselaer and Janiszewski (2001; van Osselaer et al., 2004), participants were explicitly asked to focus on learning how to predict an outcome. Thus, it is possible that people need to actively try to learn something for adaptive learning to occur. However, it is also possible that it is sufficient that people merely make predictions during learning (e.g., ask themselves how good a bottle of wine will taste before buying the bottle) and attend to outcome feedback without actively trying to learn. Finally, it is possible that predictions during learning and recording feedback do not even have to be conscious. Because this issue has important implications as to the importance of adaptive learning in real-world consumer learning situations, further research is required in this area.

Multiple Goals   In many situations, consumers make decisions based on predicted levels of more than one consumption benefit or goal. Thus, many decisions involve multiple outcomes. Apart from van Osselaer and Janiszewski (2001), I am not aware of any empirical research or model in the associative learning literature that includes multiple outcomes. It is unclear if consumers ever learn adaptively about multiple goals and whether current models can accurately account for the data if consumers do learn adaptively about multiple goals.

Outcome Ambiguity   Recent findings suggest that people tend to switch to exemplar-based processing when outcome information is ambiguous or otherwise poor (Juslin, Jones, et al., 2003; Juslin, Olsson, et al. 2003; van Osselaer & Alba, 2003). However, in these experiments, participants had no strong expectations regarding the outcome prior to encountering the learning stimuli. In such a situation, consumers may avoid adaptive processing because poor feedback information reduces its effectiveness and efficiency. However, when consumers have strong prior expectations about an outcome and its relationship to a set of cues, ambiguous outcome information is less likely to clearly disconfirm the expected relationship, encouraging consumers to keep relying on an adaptive learning process and preventing them from updating, hence, learning. In this case, adaptive processing takes the shape of *confirmatory hypothesis testing*, leading to stronger perseverance of incorrect associations than one would if find the learner would rely on exemplar-based processing.

More Systems   There are indications that associative learning may involve more than two processes. As mentioned above, evaluative conditioning may be a different process and so may rule-based reasoning. In addition, there is some indication that there may be multiple learning systems with configural representation (McClelland, McNaughton, & O'Reilly, 1995). For example, there may be one fast-learning process for stimuli that are identical or highly similar to previously encountered stimuli (e.g., McClelland et al., 1995; see also Smith & Minda, 2000; but see Nosofsky, 2000) and another, slower-learning configural process for less similar stimuli.

Conclusion

Much of consumer judgment, evaluation, and choice rely on predictions of consumption outcomes or benefits. These predictions, in turn, have to rely on associations consumers learn between predictors of consumption benefits and those benefits as well as on how these associations are stored in memory. Despite the importance of associative learning and memory in consumer decisions, research linking associative learning and memory to consumer decision making remains sparse.

In this chapter, a proposal was put forward of consumer learning and memory as involving at least two qualitatively different processes on which consumers' decisions can be based. These processes, adaptive and exemplar-based, lead to different decision processes and different decisions, and each dominates decision making in different situations and for different decision options.

ACKNOWLEDGMENTS

The author would like to thank Chris Janiszewski, Vasily Klucharev, and Steven Sweldens for their helpful comments on a draft of this chapter.

NOTES

1. Most authors in the consumer psychology literature refer to the process in their experiments as classical conditioning. See De Houwer, Thomas, and Baeyens (2001) for a discussion of the differences and similarities between classical and evaluative conditioning.
2. Van Osselaer and Janiszewski (2001) referred to the exemplar-based process as Human Associative Memory (HAM) learning.

REFERENCES

Allen, C. T., & Janiszewski, C. A. (1989). Assessing the role of contingency awareness in attitudinal conditioning with implications for advertising research. *Journal of Marketing Research, 26*, 30–43.

Allen, M. T., Padilla, Y., Myers, C. E., & Gluck, M. A. (2002). Selective hippocampal lesions disrupt a novel cue effect but fail to eliminate blocking in rabbit eyeblink conditioning. *Cognitive, Affective, and Behavioral Neuroscience, 2*, 318–328.

Alvarado, M. C., & Rudy, J. W. (1995). A comparison of kainic acid plus colchicine and ibotenic acid-induced hippocampal formation damage in four configural tasks in rats. *Behavioral Neuroscience, 109*, 1052–1062.

Baeyens, F., Crombez, G., De Houwer, J., & Eelen, P. (1996). No evidence for modulation of evaluative flavor-flavor associations in humans. *Learning and Motivation, 27*, 200–241.

Baeyens, F., Hendrickx, H., Crombez, G., & Hermans, D. (1998). Neither extended sequential nor simultaneous feature positive training result in modulation of evaluative flavor-flavor conditioning in humans. *Appetite, 31*, 185–204.

Baeyens, F., Vansteenwegen, D., Hermans, D., Vervliet, B., & Eelen, P. (2001). Sequential and simultaneous feature positive discriminations: Occasion setting and configural learning in human Pavlovian conditioning. *Journal of Experimental Psychology: Animal Behavior Processes, 27*, 279–295.

Bellingham, W. P., Gillette-Bellingham, K., & Kehoe, E. J. (1985). Summation and configuration in patterning schedules with the rat and rabbit. *Animal Learning and Behavior, 13*, 152–164.

Berger, T. W., & Thompson, R. F. (1978). Neuronal plasticity in the limbic system during classical conditioning of the rabbit nicitating membrane response. I. The hippocampus. *Brain Research, 145*, 323–346.

Bettman, J. R., Luce, M. F., & Payne, J. W. (1998). Constructive consumer choice processes. *Journal of Consumer Research, 25*, 187–217.

Bierley, C., McSweeney, F. K., & Vannieuwkerk, R. (1985). Classical conditioning of preferences for stimuli. *Journal of Consumer Research, 12*, 316–323.

Brandon, S. E., Vogel, E. H., & Wagner, A. R. (2000). A componential view of configural cues in generalization and discrimination in Pavlovian conditioning. *Behavioural Brain Research, 110*, 67–72.

Cabeza, R., & Nyberg, L. (2000). Imaging cognition II: An empirical review of 275 PET and fMRI studies. *Journal of Cognitive Neuroscience, 12*, 1–47.

Chaiken, S., & Trope, Y. (Eds.). (1999). *Dual-process theories in social psychology.* New York: Guilford.

Chapman, G. B., & Robbins, S. J. (1990). Cue interaction in human contingency judgment. *Memory and Cognition, 18*, 537–545.

Cheng, P. W. (1997). From covariation to causation: A causal power theory. *Psychological Review, 104*, 367–405.

De Houwer, J., Baeyens, F., Vansteenwegen, D., & Eelen, P. (2000). Evaluative conditioning in the picture-picture paradigm with random assignment of conditioned stimuli to unconditioned stimuli. *Journal of Experimental Psychology: Animal Behavior Processes, 26*, 237–242.

De Houwer, J., Thomas, S., & Baeyens, F. (2001). Association learning of likes and dislikes: A review of 25 years of research on human evaluative conditioning. *Psychological Bulletin, 127*, 853–869.

Dickinson, A., Shanks, D., & Evenden, J. (1984). Judgement of act-outcome contingency: The role of selective attribution. *Quarterly Journal of Experimental Psychology, 36A*, 29–50.

Eichenbaum, H. (2000). Hippocampus: Mapping or memory? *Current Biology, 10*, R785–R787.

Epstein, S. (1994). Integration of the cognitive and the psychodynamic unconscious. *American Psychologist, 49*, 709–724.

Fanselow, M. S. (1998). Pavlovian conditioning, negative feedback, and blocking: Mechanisms that regulate association formation. *Neuron, 20*, 625–627.

Fanselow, M. S., & Poulos, A. M. (2005). The neuroscience of mammalian associative learning. *Annual Review of Psychology, 56,* 207–234.

Gilbert, D. T. (1999). What the mind's not. In S. Chaiken & Y. Trope (Eds.), *Dual-Process Theories in Social Psychology* (pp. 3–11). New York: Guilford.

Gluck, M. A., & Bower, G. H. (1988). From conditioning to category learning: An adaptive network model. *Journal of Experimental Psychology: General, 117,* 227–247.

Gorn, G. J. (1982). The effects of music in advertising on choice behavior: A classical conditioning approach. *Journal of Marketing, 46,* 94–101.

Hintzman, D. L. (1986). "Schema abstraction" in a multiple-trace memory model. *Psychological Review, 93,* 411–428.

Holland, P. C. (1992). Occasion setting in pavlovian conditioning. In D. L. Medin (Ed.), *The Psychology of Learning and Motivation* (Vol. 28, pp. 69–125). San Diego, CA: Academic Press.

Hutchinson, J. W., & Alba, J. W. (1991). Ignoring irrelevant information: Situational determinants of consumer learning. *Journal of Consumer Research, 18,* 325–345.

Janiszewski, C., & van Osselaer, S. M. J. (2000). A connectionist model of brand-quality associations. *Journal of Marketing Research, 37,* 331–350.

Jarrard, L. E. (1995). What does the hippocampus really do? *Behavioural Brain Research, 71,* 1–10.

Juslin, P., Jones, S., Olsson, H., & Winman, A. (2003). Cue abstraction and exemplar memory in categorization. *Journal of Experimental Psychology: Learning, Memory, and Cognition, 29,* 924–941.

Juslin, P., Olsson, H., & Olsson, A.-C. (2003). Exemplar effects in categorization and multiple-cue judgment. *Journal of Experimental Psychology: General, 132,* 133–156.

Kahneman, D., & Frederick, S. (2002). Representativeness revisited: Attribute substitution in intuitive judgment. In T. Gilovich, D. W. Griffin, & D. Kahneman (Eds.), *Heuristics and biases: The psychology of intuitive judgment* (pp. 49–81). New York: Cambridge University Press.

Kamin, L. J. (1969). Predictability, surprise, attention, and conditioning. In B. A. Campbell & R. M. Church (Eds.), *Punishment and aversive behavior* (pp. 279–296). New York: Appleton-Century-Crofts.

Kim, J., Allen, C. T., & Kardes, F. R. (1996). An investigation of the mediational mechanisms underlying attitudinal conditioning. *Journal of Marketing Research, 33,* 318–328.

Kim, J. J., Krupa, D. J., & Thompson, R. F. (1998). Inhibitory cerebello-olivary projections and blocking effect in classical conditioning. *Science, 279,* 570–573.

Kruschke, J. K. (1992). ALCOVE: An exemplar-based connectionist model of category learning. *Psychological Review, 99,* 22–44.

Kruschke, J. K., & Johansen, M. K. (1999). A model of probabilistic category learning. *Journal of Experimental Psychology: Learning, Memory, and Cognition, 25,* 1083–1119.

Lachnit, H., & Lober, K. (2001). What is learned in patterning discriminations? Further tests of configural accounts of associative learning in human electrodermal conditioning. *Biological Psychology, 56,* 45–61.

Lachnit, H., Lober, K., Reinhard, G., & Kinder, A. (2001). Evidence for the application of rules in Pavlovian electrodermal conditioning with humans. *Biological Psychology, 56,* 151–166.

Lancaster, K. J. (1966). A new approach to consumer theory. *Journal of Political Economy, 74,* 132–157.

Lauwereyns, J., Watanabe, K., Coe, B., & Hikosaka, O. (2002). A neural correlate of response bias in monkey caudate nucleus. *Nature, 418,* 413–417.

LeDoux, J. E. (1995). Emotion: Clues from the brain. *Annual Review of Psychology, 46,* 209–235.

Lober, K., & Shanks, D. R. (2000). Is causal induction based on causal power? Critique of Cheng (1997). *Psychological Review, 107,* 195–212.

Lovibond, P. F., & Shanks, D. R. (2002). The Role of awareness in pavlovian conditioning: Empirical evidence and theoretical implications. *Journal of Experimental Psychology: Animal Behavior Processes, 28,* 3–26.

Matute, H., Arcediano, F., & Miller, R. R. (1996). Test question modulates cue competition between causes and effects. *Journal of Experimental Psychology: Learning, Memory, and Cognition, 22,* 182–196.

McClelland, J. L. (2000). Connectionist models of memory. In E. Tulving & F. I. M. Craik (Eds.), *The oxford handbook of memory* (pp. 583–596). Oxford: Oxford University Press.

McClelland, J. L., McNaughton, B. L., & O'Reilly, R. C. (1995). Why there are complementary learning systems in the hippocampus and neocortex: Insights from the successes and failures of connectionist models of learning and memory. *Psychological Review, 102,* 419–457.

McClelland, J. L., & Rumelhart, D. E. (1986). A distributed model of human learning and memory. In J. L. McClelland & D. E. Rumelhart (Eds.), *Parallel distributed processing: Explorations in the microstructure of cognition: Vol. 2. Psychological and biological models* (pp. 170–215). Cambridge, MA: MIT Press.

McSweeney, F. K., & Bierley, C. (1984). Recent developments in classical conditioning. *Journal of Consumer Research, 11,* 619–631.

Meeter, M., Myers, C. E., & Gluck, M. A. (2005). Integrating incremental learning and episodic memory models of the hippocampal region. *Psychological Review, 112,* 560–585.

Meyer, R. J. (1987). The learning of multiattribute judgment policies. *Journal of Consumer Research, 14,* 155–173.

Milberg, S. J., Park, C. W., & McCarthy, M. S. (1997). Managing negative feedback effects associated with brand extensions: The impact of alternative branding strategies. *Journal of Consumer Psychology, 6,* 119–140.

Miller, R. R., Barnet, R. C., & Grahame, N. J. (1995). Assessment of the Rescorla-Wagner model. *Psychological Bulletin, 117,* 363–386.

Montague, P. R., Dayan, P., & Sejnowski, T. J. (1996). A framework for mesencephalic dopamine systems based on predictive hebbian learning. *Journal of Neuroscience, 16,* 1936–1947.

Nelson, P. (1970). Information and consumer behavior. *Journal of Political Economy, 78,* 311–329.

Nosofsky, R. M. (1986). Attention, similarity, and the identification-categorization relationship. *Journal of Experimental Psychology: General, 115,* 39–57.

Nosofsky, R. M. (2000). Exemplar representation without generalization? Comment on Smith and Minda's (2000) Thirty categorization results in search of a model. *Journal of Experimental Psychology: Learning, Memory, and Cognition, 26,* 1735–1743.

Novick, L. R., & Cheng, P. W. (2004). Assessing interactive causal influence. *Psychological Review, 111,* 455–485.

Oliver, R. L. (1980). A cognitive model of the antecedents and consequences of satisfaction decisions. *Journal of Marketing Research, 17,* 460–469.

Olson, M. A., & Fazio, R. H. (2001). Implicit attitude formation through classical conditioning. *Psychological Science, 12,* 413–417.

Olson, M. A., & Fazio, R. H. (2002). Implicit acquisition and manifestation of classically conditioned attitudes. *Social Cognition, 20,* 89–104.

Pavlov, I. P. (1960). *Conditioned reflexes: An investigation of the physiological activity of the cerebral cortex* (G. V. Anrep, Trans.). New York: Dover. (Original work published 1927).

Pearce, J. M. (1994). Similarity and discrimination: A selective review and a connectionist model. *Psychological Review, 101,* 587–607.

Pearce, J. M. (2002). Evaluation and development of a connectionist theory of configural learning. *Animal Learning and Behavior, 30,* 73–95.

Penick, S., & Solomon, P. R. (1991). Hippocampus, context, and conditioning. *Behavioral Neuroscience, 105,* 611–617.

Rescorla, R. A. (1969). Pavlovian conditioned inhibition. *Psychological Bulletin, 72,* 77–94.

Rescorla, R. A. (1970). Reduction in the effectiveness of reinforcement after prior excitatory conditioning. *Learning and Motivation, 1,* 372–381.

Rescorla, R. A. (1972). "Configural" conditioning in discrete-trial bar pressing. *Journal of Comparative and Physiological Psychology, 79,* 307–317.

Rescorla, R. A. (1988). Pavlovian conditioning: It's not what you think it is. *American Psychologist, 43,* 151–160.

Rescorla, R. A. (1997). Summation: Assessment of a configural theory. *Animal Learning and Behavior, 25,* 200–209.

Rescorla, R. A., & LoLordo, V. M. (1965). Inhibition of avoidance behavior. *Journal of Comparative and Physiological Psychology, 59,* 406–412.

Rescorla, R. A., & Wagner, A. R. (1972). A theory of pavlovian conditioning: Variations in the effectiveness of reinforcement and nonreinforcement. In A. H. Black & W. F. Prokasy (Eds.), *Classical conditioning II: Current research and theory* (pp. 64–99). New York: Appleton-Century-Crofts.

Rumelhart, D. E., Hinton, G. E., & McClelland, J. L. (1986). A general framework for parallel distributed processing. In D. E. Rumelhart & J. L. McClelland (Eds.), *Parallel distributed processing: Explorations in the microstructure of cognition: Vol. 1. Foundations* (pp. 45–76). Cambridge, MA: MIT Press.

Rumelhart, D. E., & McClelland, J. L. (Eds.). (1986). *Parallel distributed processing: Explorations in the microstructure of cognition: Vol. 1. Foundations.* Cambridge MA: MIT Press.

Schmajuk, N. A., & DiCarlo, J. J. (1992). Stimulus configuration, classical conditioning, and hippocampal function. *Psychological Review, 99,* 268–305.

Schmajuk, N. A., & Holland, P. C. (Eds.). (1998). *Occasion setting: Associative learning and cognition in animals.* Washington, DC: American Psychological Association.

Schmajuk, N. A., Lamoureux, J. A., & Holland, P. C. (1998). Occasion setting: A neural network approach. *Psychological Review, 105,* 3–32.

Schultz, W. (2005). Behavioral theories and the neurophysiology of reward. *Annual Review of Psychology, 57,* 87–115.

Schultz, W., Dayan, P., & Montague, P. R. (1997). A neural substrate of prediction and reward. *Science, 275,* 1593–1599.

Shanks, D. R. (1990). Connectionism and the learning of probabilistic concepts. *Quarterly Journal of Experimental Psychology, 42A,* 209–237.

Shanks, D. R. (1991). Categorization by a connectionist network. *Journal of Experimental Psychology: Learning, Memory, and Cognition, 17,* 433–443.

Shanks, D. R. (1994). Human associative learning. In N. J. Mackintosh (Ed.), *Animal learning and cognition* (pp. 335–374). San Diego, CA: Academic Press.

Shanks, D. R., Charles, D., Darby, R. J., & Azmi, A. (1998). Configural processes in human associative learning. *Journal of Experimental Psychology: Learning, Memory, and Cognition, 24,* 1353–1378.

Shanks, D. R., Charles, D., Darby, R. J., & Dickinson, A. (1996). Distinguishing associative and probabilistic contrast theories of human contingency judgment. In D. R. Shanks, D. L. Medin, & K. J. Holyoak (Eds.), *The psychology of learning and motivation: Vol. 34. Causal learning* (pp. 265–311). San Diego, CA: Academic Press.

Shanks, D. R., & Darby, R. J. (1998). Feature and rule-based generalization in human associative learning. *Journal of Experimental Psychology: Animal Behavior Processes, 24,* 405–415.

Shanks, D. R., Darby, R. J., & Charles, D. (1998). Resistance to interference in human associative learning: Evidence of configural processing. *Journal of Experimental Psychology: Animal Behavior Processes, 24,* 136–150.

Shanks, D. R., Medin, D. L., & Holyoak, K. J. (Eds.). (1996). *The psychology of learning and motivation: Vol. 34. Causal learning.* San Diego, CA: Academic Press.

Shimp, T. A., Stuart, E. W., & Engle, R. W. (1991). A program of classical conditioning experiments testing variations in the conditioned stimulus and context. *Journal of Consumer Research, 18,* 1–12.

Siegel, S., & Allan, L. G. (1996). The widespread influence of the Rescorla-Wagner model. *Psychonomic Bulletin and Review, 3,* 314–321.

Sloman, S. A. (1996). The empirical case for two systems of reasoning. *Psychological Bulletin, 119,* 3–22.

Smith, J. D., & Minda, J. P. (2000). Thirty categorization results in search of a model. *Journal of Experimental Psychology: Learning, Memory, and Cognition, 26,* 3–27.

Squire, L. R. (1992). Memory and the hippocampus: A synthesis from findings with rats, monkeys, and humans. *Psychological Review, 99,* 195–231.

Stanovich, K. E., & West, R. F. (2000). Individual differences in reasoning: Implications for the rationality debate? *Behavioral and Brain Sciences, 23,* 645–726.

Stone, G. O. (1986). An analysis of the delta rule and the learning of statistical association. In D. E. Rumelhart & J. L. McClelland (Eds.), *Parallel distributed processing: Explorations in the microstructure of cognition: Vol. 1. Foundations* (pp. 444–459). Cambridge, MA: MIT Press.

Stuart, E. W., Shimp, T. A., & Engle, R. W. (1987). Classical conditioning of consumer attitudes: Four experiments in an advertising context. *Journal of Consumer Research, 14,* 334–349.

Sutherland, R. J., & Rudy, J. W. (1989). Configural association theory: The role of the hippocampal formation in learning, memory, and amnesia. *Psychobiology, 17,* 129–144.

Thompson, R. F. (1990). Neural mechanisms of classical conditioning in mammals. *Philosophical Transactions of the Royal Society of London: Series B, 329,* 161–170.

Thompson, R. F. (2005). In search of memory traces. *Annual Review of Psychology, 56,* 1–23.

van Osselaer, S. M. J., & Alba, J. W. (2000). Consumer learning and brand equity. *Journal of Consumer Research, 27,* 1–16.

van Osselaer, S. M. J., & Alba, J. W. (2003). Locus of equity and brand extension. *Journal of Consumer Research, 29*, 539–550.

van Osselaer, S. M. J., & Janiszewski, C. (2001). Two ways of learning brand associations. *Journal of Consumer Research, 28*, 202–223.

van Osselaer, S. M. J., Janiszewski, C., & Cunha, M., Jr. (2004). Stimulus generalization in two associative learning processes. *Journal of Experimental Psychology: Learning, Memory, and Cognition, 30*, 626–638.

Wagner, A. R. (1969). Stimulus selection and a modified continuity theory. In G. H. Bower & J. T. Spence (Eds.), *The psychology of learning and motivation* (Vol. 3, pp. 1–41). New York: Academic Press.

Wagner, A. R., & Brandon, S. E. (2001). A componential theory of pavlovian conditioning. In R. R. Mowrer & S. B. Klein (Eds.), *Contemporary learning theories* (pp. 23–64). Mahwah, NJ: Erlbaum.

Wagner, A. R. (2003). Context-sensitive elemental theory. *Quarterly Journal of Experimental Psychology, 56B*, 7–29.

Waldmann, M. R., & Holyoak, K. J. (1992). Predictive and diagnostic learning within causal models: Asymmetries in cue competition. *Journal of ExperimentalPsychology: Learning, Memory, and Cognition, 121*, 222–236.

Widrow, G., & Hoff, M. E. (1960). *Adaptive Switching Circuits.* Paper presented at the Institute of Radio Engineers, Western Electronic Show and Convention, Convention Record.

Williams, D. A., Sagness, K. E., & McPhee, J. E. (1994). Configural and elemental strategies in associative learning. *Journal of Experimental Psychology: Learning, Memory, and Cognition, 20*, 694–709.

Young, M. E. (1995). On the origin of personal causal theories. *Psychonomic Bulletin and Review, 2*, 83–104.

Young, M. E., Wasserman, E. A., Johnson, J. L., & Jones, F. L. (2000). Positive and negative patterning in human causal learning. *Quarterly Journal of Experimental Psychology, 53B*, 121–138.

VI

PRODUCTS, PREFERENCES, PLACES, AND PEOPLE

29

A Role for Aesthetics in Consumer Psychology

JoAndrea Hoegg

University of British Columbia

Joseph W. Alba

University of Florida

Practitioners argue that product design is rapidly emerging as a determinant of marketplace success (Miller & Adler, 2003), in part because design can serve as a point of differentiation at a time when it is increasingly difficult to gain competitive advantage on the basis of price or reliability (Jordan, Thomas, & McClelland, 1996; Kalins, 2003). Design is also poised to become a topic of greater interest to consumer researchers due to a developing transformation in decision paradigms. Decision research historically has focused on salient verbal information at the expense of non-verbal cues. However, there is a growing belief that decisions are driven by "gut-level" reactions unrelated to the objective merits of the alternatives under consideration (see Loewenstein, 2001; Loewenstein, Weber, Hsee, & Welch, 2001). We argue that product design can provoke a variety of cognitive and noncognitive reactions that can guide decision making in ways not currently appreciated. Our intent is to describe some fundamental constructs, speculate about their implications for product preference, and map directions for future research.

Product design naturally encompasses many dimensions (Bloch, 1995; Creusen & Schoormans, 2005). Our focus is on the aesthetics of design. Most relevant research in philosophy, psychology, and marketing has centered on the question of what characteristics make an object seem more or less attractive (e.g., Berlyne, 1971, 1974; Martindale, 1988; Silvera, Josephs, & Giesler, 2002; Veryzer & Hutchinson, 1998)—a multifaceted question but one that only hints at the potential for rigorous inquiry. This chapter addresses the issue of attractiveness but primarily attempts to shed light on two fundamental issues: (1) how perceptual processing affects the evaluation of a product's design and (2) how the evaluation of a product's design can influence product choice.

Since Holbrook's (1980) call for a greater and more expansive emphasis on aesthetics in consumer research, the limited response has largely examined products that exist solely for an aesthetic purpose, such as music and art. To broaden the conversation, we focus on the visual processing of functional objects. Consequently, much of our review necessarily borrows from research conducted outside the domain of consumer research.

The chapter is organized as follows. The first section briefly presents some key findings from recent research on aesthetics. We then go beyond aesthetics, per se, to focus on the more fundamental issue of the visual processing of objects. Specifically, we examine the extent to which an object is perceived as a whole versus as a collection of components and review some of the conditions under which people are likely to process objects in one manner versus the other. We include a discussion of relevant findings in face perception because it is a domain that has been devoted to these issues. Borrowing from research on consumer learning and on the disruptive effects of verbalization, we consider how the manner in which a product is viewed can influence its evaluation.

The second half of the chapter refocuses on product appearance and on outcomes that stem from an affective response to product appearance. We discuss the social and cultural meanings of product design and how such elements of design can dramatically influence evaluation. We then consider more visceral responses to design. Inspired by research on motivated reasoning and the interplay of affect and cognition, we discuss how an automatic affective reaction to product appearance can shape a more cognitive or deliberative evaluation. In so doing, we also take up the issue of awareness. We conclude by briefly considering some managerial implications and directions for research.

BACKGROUND

Modern-day treatment of experimental aesthetics begins with Berlyne (1971), who argued that common criteria underlie aesthetic judgment. In particular, Berlyne generalized the Wundt curve to explain the experience of pleasure and displeasure in relation to the arousal potential of a stimulus. Berlyne's famous proposition that moderately complex aesthetic stimuli are preferred over very simple or very complex stimuli stems from the notion that the hedonic effects of stimulus patterns are due to their arousal potential. Simple stimuli are insufficiently arousing and complex stimuli are overly arousing.

According to Berlyne's theory, the arousal potential of a stimulus derives from four sources: (1) psychophysical properties such as intensity, pitch, and brightness; (2) ecological properties, i.e., the meaning or associations of the stimulus; (3) collative properties, i.e., aspects of the stimulus that create arousal, such as complexity, novelty, and surprise; and (4) the arousal potential of other non-focal stimuli. Berlyne hypothesized that the collative properties are the most important and that people have an affinity for the arousal that accompanies moderate levels of novelty and complexity.

Berlyne's predictions have received empirical support in numerous contexts, including that of product aesthetics (Cox & Cox, 2002). However, some studies have failed to conform. For example, Veryzer and Hutchinson (1998) investigated the concepts of unity and prototypicality, where unity referred to the congruity in a product's form and prototypicality referred the degree to which a product is representative of its category. Using familiar products such as telephones and refrigerators, Veryzer and Hutchinson found that not only was unity positively related to aesthetic response but so too was prototypicality. Insofar as products appear less complex with experience, this result suggests that greater familiarity with a design leads to greater preference rather than "wearout" and a decline in preference.

Preference for prototypical objects is consistent with literature on facial attractiveness, which shows that "averaged" or composite faces are rated as more attractive than individual faces (Rhodes et al., 2002; Rubenstein, Langlois, & Roggman, 2002). This averageness or prototype effect has also been found for objects as disparate as dogs, watches, and birds (Halberstadt & Rhodes, 2000).

Martindale (Martindale, 1984, 1988; Martindale & Moore, 1988; Martindale, Moore, & Borkum, 1990) similarly has demonstrated a consistent linear relationship between prototypicality and preference. Moreover, in tests of Berlyne's sources of arousal potential, he found that ecological properties (i.e., the meaningfulness of stimuli) explain more variance than the collative properties of complexity and novelty. In an effort to explain these conflicting findings, Martindale (1984, 1988) proposed a model of aesthetic response in which the pleasure someone receives from a work of art is posited to be a positive monotonic function of the extent to which the entire ensemble of cognitive units that code the stimulus are activated. As in perception, activation of cognitive units was deemed a function of (1) initial strength of the unit, (2) the strength of the stimulus, (3) the attention devoted to the stimulus, and (4) the extent to which lateral inhibition reduces activation. Because prototypical objects are coded by stronger cognitive units than unusual objects, they are preferred. Martindale was careful to note, however, that this view focuses only on disinterested aesthetic pleasure arising from the cognitive system; when the arousal and emotional systems are also activated, pleasure and displeasure might still be determined primarily by those systems rather than by the cognitive system.

Martindale's proposal is also consistent with a perceptual-fluency account of aesthetic response proposed by Reber and his colleagues (Reber, Schwarz, & Winkielman, 2004; Reber, Winkielman, and Schwarz, 1998; Winkielman, Schwarz, Fazendeiro, & Reber, 2003; Winkielman, Schwarz, Reber, & Fazendeiro, 2003), which argues that the positive "interpretation" of ease of processing—which may obtain from either repeated exposure or stimulus features such as symmetry or good figure-ground contrast—results in enhanced affect toward the object. Prototypical objects are, by definition, familiar as a category. Because familiarity leads to fluency and this fluency is positively valenced, prototypical objects are preferred.

To reconcile the prototypicality effect with Berlyne's inverted-U model of arousal, Whitfield (1983, 2000) proposed a "categorical-motivation model" of aesthetic response that borrows from Tversky's (1977) distinction between intensive and diagnostic feature salience. Stimuli high in diagnostic salience, or meaningfulness, favor prototypicality because aesthetic response is mediated by categorical processing, consistent with Martindale's contention of greater activation of cognitive units. Stimuli that are more abstract and therefore lower in diagnosticity but higher in intensive salience should possess high arousal potential and therefore lead to a pattern of preference consistent with Berlyne's predictions.

Each of these models of aesthetic response has some appeal. The role of stimulus salience is particularly noteworthy due to its potential to reconcile conflicting findings and its obvious relevance to consumer contexts. We devote much of the remainder of this chapter to consideration of a different aspect of salience, one that allows for a dynamic perspective. A product may alternatively be apprehended as a whole or as a collection of features. It has been argued that initial perception of a stimulus is relatively holistic or "gist-like" (Kimchi, 1992), i.e., that the whole is initially more salient than the individual components. Regardless of initial mode, it seems plausible that processing can switch between modes over time, making either the whole or the parts more salient under different conditions. If so, an important question concerns the implications for changes in aesthetic response. Consider an initial holistic perception that becomes more feature-based with exposure. Both Martindale's model and a perceptual-fluency account predict an increase in liking due to increased fluency or to an increase in the activation of cognitive units, respectively. However, it is not difficult to imagine cases in which increased activation or increased understanding could produce an opposite effect. To provide greater insight into aesthetic response, we first consider research on perceptual processing. We then consider the implications of processing mode for evaluative response.

THEORIES OF PERCEPTION

A processing distinction that carries important implications involves the scope and focus of the percept itself, portrayed here as a continuum that ranges from holistic to configural to featural. In this context it is useful to distinguish between the natural processing that occurs when a stimulus is first encountered and the subsequent impressions formed from the encounter. The latter can be influenced by a myriad of factors, most notably attention. These subsequent impressions are the focus of much cognitive research, as they are commonly invoked in the service of memory, concept formation, and categorization. Given the role of attention, it is unsurprising that the degree to which classifications are based on individual features versus overall similarity depends on time constraints, processing load, task objectives, discriminability of the stimuli, age of the respondent, and the salience of the diagnostic attributes (see Alba & Hutchinson, 1987; Hutchinson & Alba, 1991). Because these effects are more familiar to consumer researchers, we focus primarily on the natural mode of processing, examining whether the primary unit of perception is the whole or its individual features (Kimchi, 1992) and the extent to which the natural mode of processing is determined by the form of the stimulus itself (Kemler Nelson, 1984). Such issues may carry important implication for aesthetic response.

Holistic Processing

At the one extreme, the object is encoded in its entirety with no representation of individual parts (Tanaka & Farah, 1993). Such "holistic" processing goes by many names and, for present purposes, may be viewed as synonymous with "global" (e.g., Navon, 1977) or "nonanalytic" (Ward & Scott, 1987). The Gestalt school was the most prominent proponent of holistic processing and is most renown for the proposition that a perceived whole is different from the sum of its components (often misrepresented as "the whole is greater than the sum of its parts"). Although the Gestaltists did not deny the existence of parts, they did believe that elementary parts of an object interact in a nonlinear fashion in perception. The particular arrangement of the parts determines the appearance and identity of the object (Palmer, 1990).

More specifically, Gestalt psychology argued that when observing an object, people do not see individual visual elements but rather see configurations or patterns that depend on processes of perceptual organization that operate within the nervous system. Because some forms are better "organized" than others, the brain searches for the better forms. The Gestaltists attempted to specify the particular properties of a given percept—such as proximity, symmetry, closure, and good continuation—that cause it to be perceived as a whole rather than as a collection of parts (Koffka, 1935; see also Palmer, 1990).

The Gestalt view has been criticized for a lack of precision in its constructs and its treatment of features. For example, it was argued that the parts of an object become embedded within the whole and are hence unrecognizable. However, Gestalt theory does not address whether the parts are in fact perceived at some level or how they contribute to the process that ultimately generates the perceived whole (Lasaga, 1989). Parts clearly must play a role because otherwise people would have difficulty distinguishing between two objects with the same overall shape but different components.

Feature-Based Perception

The opposite end of the continuum consists of "featural" processing (Halberstadt, Goldstone, & Levine, 2003), also referred to as "analytic" (e.g., Kemler Nelson, 1989; Shepp, 1989), "local" (Navon, 1977), "part" (Latimer & Stevens, 1997), or "atomistic" (Veryzer & Hutchinson, 1998) processing. The common assumption is that individual stimulus dimensions are perceived and that evaluation, classification, and recognition are performed on the basis of dimensional properties.

Biederman's (1987) recognition-by-components (RBC) theory proposes that all objects in the world can be generalized into a set of approximately 36 components, or *geons*. Each geon is a component of a whole, and people automatically recognize geons as sections of objects through five properties of images: curvature, collinearity, symmetry, parallelism, and cotermination. These 36 geons can combine to form the overall shape of any object, and it is the perception of these components that drives recognition.

Treisman (1986) similarly argues that object recognition may be achieved through decomposition of objects into their components. She notes that if people applied a separate label to every occurrence of every possible object, the number of labels would be too large to process efficiently. Like Biederman, Treisman suggests that people classify based on various shared properties, which allows for different classifications based on different criteria. Before recognition can take place, the visual display must be organized into homogenous areas or elements, and figures must be separated from backgrounds.

Configural Percepts

Both Treisman and Biederman give a nod to the Gestalt perspective. In Treisman's view, early perceptual grouping is conducted through dimensional analysis, and it is during this early stage that Gestalt principles such as proximity, similarity, and good continuation are operative. Similarly, Biederman (1987) assumes that an object's components, or geons, are differentiated on the basis of Gestalt principles of perceptual organization such as good continuation, symmetry, and regularity or simplicity in shapes. That is, the principles of perceptual organization apply not to the entire object, as originally suggested by the Gestaltists, but rather to its individual components.

Some argue that attention is not paid to individual features but rather the spatial relations among the features. These interactions are sometimes referred to as relational features (Goldstone, Medin, & Gentner, 1991) or emergent features (Pomerantz, 1981). There is no assumption that features are not perceived, but instead that the feature interactions are more salient and may impair attention to the individual dimensions. Instead of the entire stimulus being processed holistically, these emergent features are processed as wholes, which therefore deflects attention from isolated features. This middle view does not argue that people fail to perceive parts. Rather, the claim is that the interrelationships and spatial locations of the parts too are important.

Contingent Models

Another class of models suggests that people have the ability to process stimuli as both wholes and parts, but the extent to which one attains greater prominence over the other varies as a function of numerous factors, including the duration of processing, the nature of the object, and the demands of the task (e.g., Cabeza & Kato, 2000; Garner, 1974; Kemler Nelson, 1989; Shepp, 1989). Research on such models has focused not only on which representation (the whole or its components) takes precedence but also on the extent to which particular types of stimuli are processed as wholes versus parts.

Global Precedence   The global precedence hypothesis claims that global properties of an object (i.e., the whole) have a temporal advantage over local properties (the features or components) in the development of the percept (Kimchi, 1992, 2003). Competing versions of this effect maintain that either (1) processing occurs sequentially from global to local or (2) global and local properties are processed in parallel but at different speeds.

To illustrate, consider Figure 29.1a and whether the large (global) letter is perceived prior to the small (local) letters. Navon (1977, 1981) argued for the primacy of global features in object perception, claiming that although both local and global elements are perceived in the final percept, the global representation has a temporal advantage. Thus, global properties, which are generally

Figure 29.1 Examples of global precedence research stimuli. Panel (a) shows typical compound letters used in most experiments. Panel (b) shows compound figures with equally salient local and global elements. (adapted from Love et al., 1999).

sufficient to identify the object, will be processed first and, if necessary, local properties will be processed subsequently.

A variety of claims against global precedence have been proposed since Navon's original formulation. Reversals of global precedence (i.e., local precedence) have been reported by a number of researchers who argue that the global precedence effect is due to experimental constraints of visual angle (e.g., Lamb & Robertson, 1990), spatial uncertainty (Lamb & Robertson, 1988), or the number of local elements in the stimulus (Martin, 1979). Hoffman (1980) presented an alternative explanation based on goodness of form and attentional allocation, essentially arguing that global precedence effects obtain because the typical paradigm (e.g., Figure 29.1a) is composed of global elements that are simply more conspicuous than the local elements (see also Lamb & Yund, 1993). When either the global or local level becomes more difficult to perceive through some deterioration of the features, the "easier" level becomes dominant. This account is consistent with research by Love, Rouder, and Wisniewski (1999), who controlled for stimulus property salience by using matrices of geometric shapes that were equally noticeable at the global and local levels (see Figure 29.1b). Their findings favor a parallel processing structure, in which both local and global identification occur in parallel but certain stimulus conditions determine which are identified faster. Love et al. suggest that people cluster local elements on the basis of proximity and/or similarity to other local elements. The spatial relationship between the clusters then defines the global pattern. Often, but not always, these clusters precede identification of the local elements; the order is simply a matter of the salience of information relevant to each mechanism.

In the global precedence paradigm the salience of the global versus local forms is controlled. In the marketplace, however, product or package designs vary dramatically in the salience of global and local elements. Assuming that the order in which global and local elements are perceived varies as a function of the composition of product features, so too will the psychological representation of the design and one's affective response to it.

Stimulus Effects and Classification The notion that physical properties of an object can determine the manner in which it is processed has support from Garner's (1974) assertion that the extent to which an object's properties are "integral" or "separable" influences its perception.

Garner defined integral stimuli as those for which the existence of one dimension depends on the existence of another dimension, with color saturation and brightness serving as a classic example. Separable stimuli were defined as those that have dimensions that can easily be perceived individually, such as the size and color of an object. Four criteria characterize integrality: (1) spontaneous classification of stimuli according to overall similarity rather than component dimensions, (2) interference from one dimension during selective attention to another, (3) a processing time

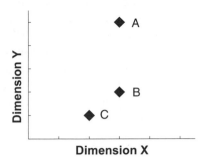

Figure 29.2   Example of classification task demonstrating classification by overall similarity (BC v. A) and dimensional similarity (AB v. C). (Smith, 1990)

redundancy gain when dimensions are correlated, and (4) a better fit of multidimensional similarity ratings to a Euclidean metric than to a city-block metric (Kemler Nelson, 1993).

Most empirical research has used Garner's criteria to classify stimuli. For example, in classification tasks, in which participants are presented with three objects and have to group the two that best go together, objects composed of integral dimensions tend to be classified by global similarity, whereas objects composed of separable dimensions tend to be grouped by dimensional similarity (e.g., Burns et al., 1978; Garner, 1974). Figure 29.2 is illustrative. If dimension X and dimension Y are separable, the adult perceiver will group A and B together due to their identical values on dimension X; if integral, the individual will group B and C together because they are more alike in terms of overall similarity.

In selective attention tasks, participants attempt to classify stimuli according to one dimension while another dimension is varied orthogonally from trial to trial. The typical dependent measure is processing speed. Integral dimensions display an increase in processing speed (facilitation) when the dimensions are correlated and a reduction in processing speed (interference) when the dimensions are orthogonal. Selective attention to integral dimensions is nearly impossible, and classification judgments map onto the Euclidean metric, i.e., overall similarity rather than dimensional similarity. In contrast, separable dimensions do not show any improvement with correlated dimensions or interference from orthogonal dimensions; selective attention is possible, and similarity judgments map onto the city block metric.

The integral-separable distinction has not gone unchallenged. Several studies have shown that people can and do perceive integral stimuli according to dimensions but that it is simply more difficult to do so (e.g., Garner & Felfoldy, 1970; Lockhead, 1972; Melara, Marks, & Potts, 1993b). Some argue that people naturally perceive all dimensions of a stimulus and that evidence to the contrary is due to artifacts inherent in the experimental manipulation. For example, Cheng and Pachella (1984) suggest that Garner-like interference obtains in many experiments because the experimenter-defined attributes do not correspond to the perceived psychological dimensions and, therefore, the participant fails the selective-attention task in the eyes of the experimenter even though perception of the dimensions did occur. Melara and his colleagues (e.g., Melara & Marks, 1990; Melara, Marks, & Potts, 1993a; Melara et al., 1993b) argue that even for seemingly integral stimuli, some dimensions are more prominent than others.

At this point it may be wise to view the integral-separable distinction as a continuum rather than a dichotomy (Kemler Nelson, 1993), which in turn would allow for shifts in perception along the continuum. For example, under certain circumstances, color can be decomposed into its dimensions of hue, saturation, and brightness (Garner, 1974; Melara et al., 1993b). In the consumer realm, a car is clearly composed of a number of separable components (Biederman, 1987), even though it is possible to perceive it in a more holistic manner and consider its overall styling or "personality." Garner and Felfoldy (1970) are cited for showing that reaction times are much longer when participants are asked to classify stimuli by dimensions rather than by overall similarity when stimuli are composed of integral dimensions. What is important to note is that despite differences in speed, people are able to classify integral stimuli according to dimensions.

Stimulus Effects and Memory   Much of the research reviewed thus far has employed classification tasks to reveal the nature of processing. However, evidence regarding the general questions of whether and when perception can be characterized as global versus featural can be gleaned from other paradigms, as well. For example, few would argue that faces are a collection of psychologically separable features. Nonetheless, an abundance of research on face recognition suggests that faces are processed in a Gestalt-like manner (e.g., Farah et al., 1998; Tanaka & Farah, 1993, 2003), with some investigators suggesting that the human face represents the quintessential whole or Gestalt (Pomerantz & Kubovy, 1986).

Support for configural face processing derives from a variety of studies on the inversion effect (e.g., Diamond & Carey, 1986; Farah, Tanaka, & Drain, 1995; Leder & Bruce, 2000; Tanaka & Farah, 1993). In the typical paradigm, participants are asked to learn faces, either upright or inverted, and then perform some kind of identification task of the face or a facial feature, again with the stimuli either upright or inverted (Leder & Bruce, 2000; Tanaka & Farah, 1993). The common finding is that recognition is impaired with inverted stimuli relative to upright stimuli. Moreover, this detrimental effect of inversion is not found for other objects such as houses or scrambled faces (Tanaka & Farah, 1993). Additional evidence for configural processing comes from experiments using composite faces (e.g., Young, Hellawell, & Hay, 1987). In these studies, stimuli are comprised of mismatched bottoms and tops of famous faces. In some cases the face halves are fused and in other cases they are misaligned. When fused, people take significantly longer to identify the person in the top half.

Although evidence for strictly holistic face processing is not compelling (Macho & Leder, 1998), a modified explanation of the inversion effect can be found in research on relational processing and emergent features (e.g., Pomerantz, 1981; Sergent, 1984), where it is argued that relational information among certain facial features drives face recognition. These relations create emergent features, which are more difficult to detect when inverted. For example, if people need only to attend to local features to identify a face and the relational information does not change, an inversion effect does not arise; performance does suffer, however, when the faces differ on relational attributes (Leder & Bruce, 2000).

It is plausible that although people do perceive the features in a face, relational information among features is important. However, there is no explanation regarding why this outcome is not true for all objects. Some researchers (e.g., Bruce & Humphreys, 1994; Diamond & Carey, 1986) believe that the inversion effect is not due to the uniqueness of facial processing, per se, but rather to the familiarity of facial stimuli. That is, the inversion effect and other evidence of configural processing is at least partially a result of expertise developed over years of encoding faces (but see Farah et al., 1998). This argument is supported by evidence that dog experts suffer an inversion effect for pictures of dogs (Diamond & Carey, 1986) and that people often suffer less of an inversion effect for other-race faces with which they presumably have less experience (Rhodes et al., 1989). Some have also found that young children are not susceptible to the face inversion effect (Diamond & Carey, 1986; Schwarzer, 2000; but see Carey & Diamond, 1994). Expertise therefore is purported to lead to configural processing, implying that people initially favor piecemeal processing but eventually develop a propensity to process interrelationships.

Facial stimuli have also been prominent in a different and currently popular memory paradigm—verbal overshadowing— that also speaks to the issue of a holistic-featural shift in processing. Verbal overshadowing refers to a reduction in recognition accuracy that occurs as a result of describing a stimulus (e.g., Melcher & Schooler, 1996; Schooler & Engstler-Schooler, 1990). In the typical paradigm, individuals encode a stimulus (e.g., colors, faces, wine) in a non-verbal manner. They then engage in a task that evokes verbal processing and later are asked to identify the original stimulus from a given set. Results show that generating a verbal description impairs recognition.

Various explanations have been offered to account for this phenomenon (Clare & Lewandowsky, 2004; Dodson, Johnson & Schooler, 1997; Macrae & Lewis, 2002; Schooler, 2002, Schooler, Fiore, & Brandimonte, 1997). The majority of evidence supports Schooler's (2002) hypothesis of a transfer-inappropriate shift in processing. Specifically, the initial nonverbal encoding of the stimulus occurs in a configural manner, but the verbalization task induces the individual to process in a featural manner. Subsequent attempts to identify the stimulus are impaired because the individual bases recognition of the object on its features although original encoding was configural. A recent investigation by Clare and Lewandowsky (2004) suggests that an increase in recognition threshold may also play a role.

Most of the verbal overshadowing literature employs self-generated descriptions of stimuli. However, Macrae and Lewis (2002) used manipulations from global precedence research (e.g., Kimchi, 1992; Navon, 1977) to induce holistic or featural processing. In an initial phase, they presented participants with a face. During an intermediate phase, rather than having participants describe the face, they had them look at compound letters (as in Figure 29.1a) and name either the large letter (a global/configural task) or the small letters (a local/featural task)—thereby inducing either global (configural) or local (featural) processing. Consistent with the task-inappropriate processing explanation, results showed that post-test recognition was impaired after insertion of the local task. Moreover, the global task actually enhanced recognition performance, presumably because it kept participants in a configural mode of processing.

Although the paradigm typically involves verbalizing a memory of a stimulus, there is some evidence that on-line description of a stimulus will also produce the overshadowing effect (Halberstadt, 1997). Thus, the phenomenon may reflect a more general separation between the *natural* encoding and the *verbal* encoding (i.e., the task induced encoding), regardless of the time of the verbalization. In Halberstadt's studies, processing was manipulated by having participants give either a name for a stimulus face or a description of the face. Overshadowing effects were found in the description conditions but not the naming conditions. Given the abundance of research suggesting that faces are naturally processed in a relatively holistic manner, it seems reasonable to conclude that the description task shifted participants to a feature-based processing mode, possibly altering the encoded representation of the stimulus.

Expertise has been shown to moderate the verbal overshadowing effect. Melcher and Schooler (1996) posit that wine experts are better equipped to distinguish particular features in wine and are thus less susceptible to overshadowing due to a featural description. On the other hand, Fallshore and Schooler (1995) show a detrimental effect of verbalization when people describe same-race faces (for which they are presumably experts) but not other-race faces. These findings might be reconciled by a clearer definition of expertise and consideration of the integral-separable dimension literature. Expertise in the verbal overshadowing context typically refers to verbal expertise rather than perceptual expertise. Verbal expertise refers to the ability to articulate features. Wine presumably resides on the integral side of the continuum and therefore may normally be encoded holistically. When an individual possesses verbal expertise, however, it may move the individual along the processing continuum to where the individual encodes integral stimuli in terms of features. This shift may change the perceptual representation, resulting in a reduced overshadowing effect.

IMPLICATIONS FOR PREFERENCE

The critical question for consumer psychology is whether a shift in processing (from holistic to featural or vice versa) can alter people's evaluation of an object. Oddly, the connection is not often made. Consider face processing. As discussed, a large body of research has investigated the extent to which faces are processed as wholes or as collections of features. An independent body of work has investigated the determinants of facial attractiveness and has shown that people tend to prefer prototypical or average faces (Light, Hollander, & Kayra-Stuart, 1981; Langlois, Roggman, & Musselman, 1994; Rhodes & Tremewan, 1996; Valentine, Darling, & Donnelly, 2004). Only recently has an effort been made to connect these dots. Halberstadt, Goldstone, and Levine (2003) attempted to understand whether people are primarily featural or holistic when making face preference judgments. In contrast to most of the face recognition literature, they found that people tended toward feature-based analysis in their evaluations. Of course, it is possible that the experimental task induced a greater level of analytic processing than typically associated with natural face processing.

This research provides a nice starting point but does not address whether the mode of processing influences preference. In a previous investigation, however, Levine, Halberstadt, and Goldstone (1996) asked participants to rate whether different facial features contributed to their liking or disliking of a face prior to making an overall rating. Although the focus was on understanding the effects of analyzing reasons on evaluation, the procedure had the flavor of a featural processing manipulation. Results suggest that reasoning about evaluations leads to greater variability in how attributes are weighted. In neither of these studies, however, was a direct attempt made to manipulate holistic and featural processing. Thus, the question of the extent to which holistic versus featural processing will influence evaluation is left largely unanswered.

The same question can be asked of product design: Can the way the product's design is processed impact the consumer's evaluation of it? As Shepp (1989) notes, altering the primary or most natural process that occurs upon exposure to a stimulus can have significant impact on performance. A reasonable hypothesis is that affective reactions may be influenced as well. This hypothesis has yet to be directly addressed; however, as we next discuss, indirect evidence is supportive.

Evidence From Consumer Learning and Evaluation

Evidence of the effects of processing style obtains from research designed to investigate exposure effects. Obermiller (1985) proposed that different processing styles might entail different levels of cognitive elaboration. Using melodies, Obermiller attempted to create three levels of encoding elaboration (minimal, limited, and elaborated) through five different processing styles: minimal, structural (limited), cognitive, affective, and associative (elaborated). Results showed that processing style influenced affective responses in an unexpected manner. Of particular interest for present purposes were differences between structural (i.e., a focus on the individual notes) and cognitive (i.e., devising names for the songs) processing: focusing on particular notes of the songs, which could be considered a featural processing mode, led to greater preference for the melodies than did naming them, which is more akin to holistic processing.

Consider, as well, the case of shifts between holistic and featural processing. For example, wine novices may taste a red wine and simply note whether they like it, a presumably holistic experience. However, with training, these consumers can learn to detect particular features of the wine, perhaps leading to a more positive (or negative) affective reaction. Of course, a socially induced learned appreciation for what constitutes superior features may play a role (see below), but it is also likely that feature detection increases a consumer's ability to identify preferred features. Indeed, West, Brown, and Hoch (1996) demonstrated that learning the vocabulary used to describe features of a product results in greater consistency of preference. Shapiro and Spence (2002) showed that the ambiguity in a sensory experience that has previously been found to be influenced by advertising (e.g., Braun, 1999; Hoch & Ha, 1986) can be reduced by learning the dimensions of the product. In the Shapiro and Spence study it is likely that natural processing mode was holistic, inasmuch as the stimulus involved sound quality, which can be difficult to process featurally (Kemler Nelson, 1993; Melara, Marks, & Potts, 1993b). In the West et al. (1996) study, however, participants presumably could see the individual features of the products (quilts) but may have been inclined to form an overall impression. In this instance, at least, it is unlikely that the provision of a consumption vocabulary altered perceptual processing; instead, the vocabulary may have heightened attention to specific features, thereby altering the manner in which the quilts were judged.

West et al. did not argue that a vocabulary affects product evaluations but rather that consumers simply become more adept at identifying their preferences and hence became more consistent in their stimuli evaluations. Nonetheless, an increase in consistency reflects changes in perception at the individual level, perhaps because a consumption vocabulary enhances consumers' sensitivity to individual features of the category. In both the West et al. (1996) and Shapiro and Spence (2002) studies, learning of dimensions was the key variable. However, the question remains as to whether simply altering the nature of processing, without learning, can influence evaluation. Some additional evidence outside the realm of consumer research provides support for the proposition.

Evidence From the Disruptive Effect of Verbalization

Verbalizing one's reasons for liking an object has been shown to disrupt attitudes and reduce attitude-behavior consistency (Wilson & Schooler, 1991; Wilson et al., 1984; Wilson, Hodges & LaFleur, 1995; Wilson, Kraft, & Dunn, 1989). The popular explanation is that verbalization causes people to focus on attributes that are accessible, plausible, and easy to verbalize at the expense of those attributes that drive evaluation under more normal circumstances. The result is that people become less consistent in how they weight stimulus attributes (Levine, Halberstadt, & Goldstone, 1996).

It has also been suggested that this verbalization effect is not orthogonal to verbal overshadowing (Wilson & Schooler, 1991). As noted, recent research has indicated that the verbal-overshadowing effect occurs as a result of a lack of correspondence between perceptual processing at encoding (which presumably is configural) and the perceptual memory that is elicited with verbalization (which presumably is featural). It seems plausible that a shift from configural processing to featural processing, perhaps induced through a verbalization manipulation, could alter the weights placed on design attributes and produce a subsequent change in preference.

Summary

Shifts in perceptual processing across the holistic, configural, and featural levels may alter the representation and evaluation of an object. Importance weights placed on features and feature interactions will be different, with configural processing leading to greater weight placed on feature interactions and featural processing leading to greater weight placed on individual design features. These altered weights will influence thoughts about the product and evaluation of its design. Extrapolating from Martindale (1988) and Reber et al. (2004), we can predict generally that a shift in processing from holistic to feature-based will increase liking, as more cognitive units are activated and people attend to the subtle details of the design. However, this directional shift in preference may not always hold. One processing mode may result in more consistent evaluation over the course of many product evaluations in a single category. There is some evidence that featural processing will result in more variance from judgment to judgment and therefore that configural processing will be more consistent. There is also evidence that over time people will focus on one or two features and become more consistent with featural evaluations than with overall evaluations. The ultimate outcome may depend on the integrality of the product category, the complexity of the stimulus, the attractiveness of the design, and the difficulty of differentiating among products.

REFLECTING ON DESIGN

Aside from changes resulting from increased exposure or an altered mode of processing, evaluation can change with greater understanding of the meaning of an object. Such understanding often enhances evaluation, such as when artwork that initially evokes a negative visceral reaction is appreciated upon learning of its symbolic significance. This "reflective" side of an aesthetic response focuses on the interpretation of a product's design or what it means to possess it, as influenced by knowledge and culture (Norman, 2004). Consider Norman's compelling example of art reproduction. One can purchase an original painting or a high quality reproduction. The objects may be aesthetically indistinguishable, but clearly there is some additional value in possessing the original. Reflective design is learned through time and differs from culture to culture.

Reflective processing is not addressed in most models of aesthetic response because such models tend to define the aesthetic experience as disinterested pleasure induced by a stimulus (Martindale, 1988) and tend to focus primarily on early stages of visual processing (Winkielman et al., 2003). Although there surely are times when meaning obtained from a stimulus is disinterested, it is more likely that the meaning carries with it an emotional component. The irony of some existing models of aesthetics is that they exploit stimulus meaning as an explanation for effects such as prototypicality bias yet they ignore the emotional content of the meaning. Whitfield (2000) addressed this issue in his revised model of aesthetic response, conceding that social significance may determine prototypicality in some cases.

Although most models do not address reflective appreciation of aesthetics, it is possible to consider the outcomes of reflective processing in terms of existing models. For example, reflective processing may alter the susceptibility of objects to typical exposure or wearout effects. In general, understanding the meaning of an object should push the perceiver further along the wearout curve, leading to a more rapidly achieved pinnacle of affective response. However, as a design is better understood, it should also be processed more deeply because it activates more cognitive units. Consistent with Martindale (1988), Whitfield (1983), and Reber et al. (2004), deeper processing should result in greater liking and may delay, if not eliminate, the wearout effect. For example, classical music is appreciated by those who understand it and rarely suffers wearout because the appreciation of the music requires understanding and skill on the part of the listener. Moreover, the semantics of a design may sustain an affective response beyond the effects of arousal and familiarity.

Socio-Cultural Meaning

The idea that objects can become more attractive when their meaning is understood is intuitive and consistent with models of aesthetic response. Associative effects may also enhance or reduce the pleasure experienced from an object, as illustrated in cross-cultural effects. Colors can have very distinct meanings in different cultures, as can certain patterns or geometric shapes. Even size can have a cultural association that alters evaluation. Research has demonstrated that people generally prefer large designs over small ones (Silvera et al., 2002), but it is unclear whether this would be the case in some eastern cultures where the western notion of "bigger is better" may be greeted unfavorably. Many symbols differ dramatically in the valence of the reactions they evoke in different cultures. The swastika, for example, is an auspicious and pleasing symbol in Hindu culture, yet in western society its mirror image is inescapably equated with Nazism.

In the marketplace, the most common type of reflective processing would be the social significance associated with owning particular products or brands. Marketers of luxury products diligently attempt to make their brand a symbol of prestige and status. Many consumers try to portray a certain image through the style of their car, clothing, or the furniture in their home (Twitchell, 2004; Wilson & MacKenzie, 2000). In these cases, evaluation of the design involves categorization and perhaps prototypicality (Whitfield, 2000). However, because social meaning can overwhelm a disinterested aesthetic reaction, it is unlikely that the standard prototypicality effect on preference will always obtain. A piece of furniture, for example, could be easily categorized as either modern and expensive or cold and harsh.

Ritterfeld (2002) advanced the notion of a "social heuristic," arguing that the social meaning of a product that is typical of a particular lifestyle is quickly and easily assessed because that lifestyle is highly accessible. Structural properties, on the other hand, are processed through a more systematic analysis. Ritterfeld reports that products typical of a social category (lifestyle) are evaluated faster than unusual products that are not prototypical of a particular lifestyle. Unfortunately, lifestyle typicality and overall familiarity may have been confounded in her research. Moreover, affective responses were not reported, so it is not possible to assess whether prototypical items were preferred or a negative social meaning overrode the prototypicality effect. Additional research is needed to determine the role of lifestyle typicality.

Although reflective preferences often conform to existing models of aesthetic response, there are clearly instances in which the models are too narrowly cast. The manner in which reflective processing interacts with other elements of aesthetic response represents a fertile research topic.

EVALUATIVE IMPLICATION OF MOTIVATION AND AWARENESS

Regardless of processing mode, consumers find some designs more appealing than others, even if those reactions are idiosyncratic. Current models of aesthetic response do not address how an aesthetic response, whatever its form, influences other processing and behavior. The question in this final section pertains to the influence of aesthetic response on processing of attribute information and overall product evaluation.

Self-Insight and Motivated Evaluation

The general view is that aesthetic appeal is important for almost every product category, whether defined functionally or otherwise (Holbrook, 1980; Holbrook & Zirlin, 1985; Kotler & Rath, 1984). A question of central concern is whether aesthetics has a greater influence than it should.

If consumers simply treat design as another attribute, there is little implication of bias, per se. Of course, people will idiosyncratically weight the aesthetic dimension but presumably will do so in accordance with their personal desires (Bloch, Brunel, & Arnold, 2003; Loewy, 1951). However, problems arise when consumers (1) place a weight on the aesthetic dimension that is inappropriate for the situation or (2) allow aesthetic reactions to color assessment of other attributes.

Attribute Weights   Research on the first problem is sparse, especially within the specific context of aesthetics. If one assumes that consumers can determine the appropriate weight, the issue is whether they consciously act in accordance with it. That is, in a multiattribute sense, do consumers understand the extent to which they have relied on the aesthetic dimension? The evidence is equivocal. It has long been argued that people lack insight into their decision weights (e.g., Slovic & Lichtenstein, 1971). However, Reilly and Doherty (1989) argued that self-insight may simply exceed a person's ability to articulate it. To our knowledge, only one study makes even tangential contact with this debate in a product context. Yamamoto and Lambert (1994) examined decision making in an industrial-products context, where aesthetics presumably should be least influential. They found that appearance exerted a nontrivial influence on choice, affecting managers across organizational areas and a range of technical orientations. Although the effect of aesthetics occurred at the margin, another result from the study is telling: the managers stated that appearance should not and did not influence product evaluation.

Biased Processing   Research on the second problem is copious. Social psychologists have amply demonstrated the impact of physical appearance on judgments of an individual's personality traits and capabilities (Dion, Berscheid, & Walster, 1972; Eagly et al., 1991; Landy & Sigall, 1974; Zebrowitz, 1997). For example, attractive people are viewed as having superior skills such as leadership, social ability, and job competence (Langlois et al., 2000).

Such results are striking because they occur in opposition to normative pressure to base judgments on the merits of the case exclusive of peripheral and unfair criteria. Hence, it has been persuasively argued that such biases are not consciously enacted. For example, research on halo and attractiveness effects suggests that people are not aware that they are being influenced (Nisbett & Wilson, 1977; Wilson & Nisbett, 1978). In a study on physical traits and personal characteristics, Hassin and Trope (2000) found that people are generally unable to avoid using physical characteristics in evaluating personality or ability traits, despite believing that they can do so (cf. Wilson & Brekke, 1994). Participants in this research were specifically instructed to ignore accompanying photographs of people when evaluating resumes of potential job candidates, and most (60%) indicated that they succeeded in doing so. Nonetheless, evidence showed that participants were influence by physical appearance, suggesting physical characteristics can play a role in evaluations beyond awareness and perhaps beyond attempts to correct for them.

Our obvious contention is that analogous effects may obtain in a product context, where product design reflects physical attractiveness (cf. Holbrook & Huber, 1979). However, the effect of aesthetics may not be limited to generalized halo. Insofar as aesthetic reaction is primary, it may "motivate" consumers, consciously and unconsciously, to interpret other product information in a biased fashion. Raghubir and Greenleaf (2006) demonstrated such an effect in an experiment that investigated aesthetic preference for the golden ratio of rectangles. Participants were presented with an invitation to a concert. The only difference between experimental conditions was that the invitation was printed on rectangular cards of one of two ratios: 1.38:1 or 1.62:1 (the golden ratio). Participants receiving the invitation conforming to the golden ratio rated the concert as more harmonious and indicated a higher likelihood of purchasing a CD of the performance than did participants receiving invitations with a 1.38:1 ratio.

The proposition that motivation can affect judgments has been studied and debated for decades. Kunda (1990; see also Kruglanski, 1996) argued that motivation and cognition interact to bias retrieval, belief formation, and evaluation. Nonetheless, as Kunda and others note, motivational biases are often constrained by the individual's desire to appear rational and objective (Boiney, Kennedy, & Nye, 1997). A plausible hypothesis, therefore, is that bias will be freest to emerge when the decision environment is ambiguous (cf. Darley & Gross, 1983).

In this regard, Hsee's notion of elastic justification (1995, 1996; Schweitzer & Hsee, 2002) suggests that if the decision criteria are ambiguous, people will use factors that they should otherwise ignore in order to achieve a motivated outcome. That is, when two options are presented, where one option is superior on a task-relevant (i.e., justifiable) factor and the other is inferior on the task-relevant factor but is superior on a factor that is irrelevant but personally appealing (i.e., an unjustifiable factor), choices will depend on the extent to which the task-relevant factor values are difficult to evaluate. When the values of the task-relevant factor are fixed and clear, people will choose the option that is superior on the justifiable factor; otherwise, they will be drawn to a personally attractive but potentially inferior option.

In a similar vein, research on predecisional distortion demonstrates how initial inclinations can bias subsequent interpretation of evidence (Russo, Medvec, & Meloy, 1996; Russo, Meloy, & Medvec, 1998). Although these results are often interpreted in terms of cognitively driven confirmation bias, a motivational component is difficult to rule out completely (see Brownstein, 2003).

Regardless of underlying process, aesthetic influence on elastic justification and predecisional distortion has large pragmatic import. Some have hinted that aesthetics influenced a $200 billion Pentagon decision that had no lack of objective attributes and decision criteria (Prasso, 2001). Although far from scientific, it seems not unreasonable that aesthetic design can represent a desirable but functionally irrelevant product feature, just as personal attractiveness can influence evaluations in situations where it clearly should not (Landy & Sigall, 1974). Such a result would go well beyond a ceteris parabus effect or one that could be rationalized in terms of overweighting attractiveness as an attribute. Rather, design could bias processing of functional attributes to the point that judgment of product quality becomes distorted.

Affect Versus Cognition

A product's design is easily perceived by an individual and may prompt an initial affective reaction prior to any cognitive appraisal. The affective reaction to the product's design may be consistent or inconsistent with a later more conscious or controlled evaluation, which may strengthen or weaken the initial reaction. The question of interest is the extent to which the affective reaction dominates or influences the cognitive evaluation.

Page and Herr (2002) argue that the *form* of a product produces an affective response associated with feeling-based, relatively automatic evaluative processes, whereas the *quality* of the product is based more on a higher-order cognitive evaluation. In support of their contention, they demonstrated that liking judgments occurred faster than quality judgments and, moreover, that product liking was driven by reaction to the product's design and was not influenced by brand name or functionality; in contrast, evaluation of the quality of the product seemed to integrate design, function, and brand information. Page and Herr also reported that when function and form were in conflict, participants used the strength of the brand name associated with the product to help them evaluate the product. Consistent with the present theme, the latter result suggests that aesthetics plays a role in the perception of quality (else participants would have been able to ignore the aesthetics of the product and focus solely on the functional information).

There is evidence to suggest that an affective reaction to a stimulus is resistant to change and may be a better predictor than cognitive evaluations of the type of thoughts people have about products. Edwards (1990) examined the resistance to change of both cognitively and affectively formed attitudes, looking specifically at how attitudes formed through affective means or through cognitive means could be altered using affective or cognitive persuasion. She demonstrated that the effectiveness of a rational (cognitive) or emotional (affective) persuasive message depends on the nature of the attitude's origin. Attitudes that are originally formed through an affective process are resistant to rational persuasive attempts but can be altered through affective means. Cognitive attitudes (those formed through rational means) on the other hand, can be altered through both cognitive and affective means of persuasion. Thus, a strong affective reaction to a product's appearance may override an evaluation made on the basis of other functional, and perhaps more appropriate, product characteristics.

Closer to the product context, Pham et al. (2001) similarly argued that affective reactions are better predictors of the number and valence of thoughts people have about products than are reason-based responses. Their data indicate that that feeling-based responses are generally faster than reason-based responses, suggesting that feeling-based evaluations are more natural and more consistent (see also Takahashi, 1995, on the psychology of aesthetics). Likewise, Shiv and Fedorikhin (1999) demonstrated how an affective reaction to a stimulus can dominate a cognitive evaluation when cognitive resources are constrained. They argue that, upon exposure to a choice, both affective and cognitive processes may be engendered; the affective reaction occurs relatively automatically, whereas the cognitive processes occur in a more controlled, resource-taxing manner. Due to the automatic nature of the affective reaction, only cognitive processing is impaired when processing resources are constrained.

Affect as Information   The affect-as-information model proposes that people use their feelings during judgment because they believe their feelings to be relevant to the judgment task (Schwarz & Clore, 1996). Such feelings can stem from the product itself. Norman (2004) has suggested that a product's design can act as a mood manipulation. A visually pleasing design can enhance mood, causing people to be more creative problem solvers and more willing to ignore details or small problems. An unattractive design can depress mood, leading people to be more analytical and heightening their tendency to expect and address problems. According to this logic, visually pleasing products may actually appear to work better.

CONCLUSIONS, FUTURE RESEARCH, AND MARKETING IMPLICATIONS

Most experimental research on the processing of product designs and aesthetics has centered on two topics: the extent to which certain properties of objects determine preference and the extent to which exposure or ease of processing increases preference. We maintain, however, that these questions represent only a subset of important issues in a domain that has been largely ignored by consumer psychologists. To this end, we have provided an overview of the existing literature and presented two general directions for future research. First, we extend the scope of research in design processing to include the mode of object perception. We propose that the mode of processing one employs when considering an object may influence aesthetic preference. Second, we encourage investigation into the unconscious influence of aesthetics on product evaluation. Specifically, we suggest that product design may bias the processing of more relevant functional attributes, potentially leading to non-normative decision making.

In addition to advancing our knowledge of the psychology of aesthetics and how consumers evaluate product designs, the study of consumer response to product design has implications for marketers and consumer welfare. Investigating the role of processing mode in design evaluation may improve a firm's understanding of how consumers process product designs. With particular regard to design testing, the extent to which preference is influenced by processing mode has nontrivial implications. Shiv and Fedorhikin (1999) demonstrated how the difference between pictorial representations of products versus the products themselves affected impulse behavior, presumably because the actual products provide more detailed sensory information. In a similar vein, we suggest that altered object processing may create different representations of the product and make it appear more or less attractive.

Although functional product attributes are important in product evaluation, many argue that other cues, sometimes called emotional cues (Berry, Carbone, & Haeckel, 2002), are equally important to consumers. In situations in which the product is difficult to evaluate, such as legal or medical services or technological products, an aesthetic reaction operates as a cue that can aid or bias evaluation (Arneill & Devlin, 2002; Berry & Bendapudi, 2003). "Anything that can be perceived or sensed…is an experience clue" (Berry et al., 2002, p. 86). Design is a powerful tool in this regard. A good product design may alter the way consumers process other product attributes. It may elevate mood levels, making consumers more willing to overlook functional flaws. During decision making, design may prompt motivated reasoning, such that functional attribute evaluation becomes biased in favor of the preferred design. If decisions with serious consequences are being biased by an affective reaction to product appearance, understanding the nature of this bias and how it can be avoided is of no small significance.

REFERENCES

Alba, J. W., & Hutchinson. J. W. (1987). Dimensions of consumer expertise. *Journal of Consumer Research*, 13, 411–454.

Arneill, A. B., & Sloan Devlin, A. (2002). Perceived quality of care: The influence of the waiting room environment. *Journal of Environmental Psychology*, 22, 345–360.

Berlyne, D. E. (1971). *Aesthetics and Psychobiology*, Meredith Corporation: New York.

Berlyne, D. E. (1974). Novelty, complexity and interestingness. In D. E. Berlyne (Ed.), *Studies in the new experimental aesthetics* (pp. 175–180). New York: Wiley.

Berry, L. L., & Bendapudi, N. (2003). Clueing in customers. *Harvard Business Review*, (February), 2–7.

Berry, L. L., Carbone, L. P., & Haeckel, S. H. (2002). Managing the total customer experience. *MIT Sloan Management Review*, (Spring), 85–89.

Biederman, I. (1987). Recognition-by-components: A theory of human image understanding. *Psychological Review*, 94, 115–147.

Bloch, P. H. (1995). Seeking the ideal form: Product design and consumer response. *Journal of Marketing*, 59, 16–29.

Bloch, P. H., Brunel, F. F., & Arnold, T. J. (2003). Individual differences in the centrality of visual product aesthetics: Concept and Measurement. *Journal of Consumer Research*, 29, 551–565.

Boiney, L. G., Kennedy, J., & Nye P. (1997). Instrumental bias in motivated reasoning: More when more is needed. *Organizational Behavior and Human Decision Processes*, 72, 1–24.

Braun, K. A. (1999). Postexperience advertising effects on consumer memory. *Journal of Consumer Research*, 25, 319–334.

Brownstein, A. L. (2003). Biased predecision processing. *Psychological Bulletin*, 129, 545–568.

Bruce, V. & Humphreys, G. W. (1994). Recognizing objects and faces. *Object and Face Recognition: Special Issue of Visual Cognition*, 1, 141–180.

Burns, B., Shepp, B. E., McDonough, D., & Weiner-Ehrlich, W. (1978). The relation between stimulus analyzability and perceived dimensional structure. In G. H. Bower (Ed.), *The psychology of learning and motivation: Advances in research and theory, Vol. 12* (pp. 77–115). New York: Academic Press.

Cabeza, R., & Kato, T. (2000). Features are also important: Contributions of featural and configural processing to face recognition. *Psychological Science*, 11, 429–433.

Carey, S., & Diamond, R. (1994). Are faces perceived as configurations more by adults than by children? *Object and Face Recognition: Special Issue of Visual Cognition, 1,* 253–274.

Cheng, P. W.,& Pachella, R. G. (1984). A psychophysical approach to dimensional separability. *Cognitive Psychology, 16,* 279–304.

Clare, J., & Lewandowsky, S. (2004). Verbalizing facial memory: Criterion effects in verbal overshadowing. *Journal of Experimental Psychology: Learning, Memory, and Cognition, 30,* 739–755.

Cox, D., & Cox, A. D. (2002). Beyond first impressions: The effects of repeated exposure on consumer liking of visually complex and simple product designs. *Journal of the Academy of Marketing Science, 30,* 119–130.

Creusen, M. E. H., & Schoormans, J. P. L. (2005). The different roles of product appearance in consumer choice. *Journal of Product Innovation Management, 22,* 63–81.

Darley, J. M., & Gross, P. H. (1983). A hypothesis-confirming bias in labeling effects. *Journal of Personality and Social Psychology, 44,* 20–33.

Diamond, R., & Carey, S. (1986). Why faces are and are not special: An effect of expertise. *Journal of Experimental Psychology: General, 115,* 107–117.

Dion, K. K., Berscheid, E., & Walster, E. (1972). What is beautiful is good. *Journal of Personality and Social Psychology, 24,* 285–290.

Dodson, C. S., Johnson, M. K., & Schooler, J.W. (1997). The verbal overshadowing effect: Why descriptions impair face recognition. *Memory & Cognition, 25,* 129–139.

Eagly, A. H., Ashmore, R. D., Makhijani, M. G., & Longo, L. C. (1991). What is beautiful is good, but…: A meta-analytic review of research on the physical attractiveness stereotype. *Psychological Bulletin, 110,* 109–128.

Edwards, K. (1990). The interplay of affect and cognition in attitude formation and change. *Journal of Personality and Social Psychology, 59,* 202–216.

Fallshore, M., & Schooler, J. W. (1995). Verbal vulnerability of perceptual expertise. *Journal of Experimental Psychology: Learning, Memory and Cognition, 21,* 1608–1623.

Farah, M., Wilson, K. D., Drain, H. M., & Tanaka, J. N. (1998). What is 'special' about face perception. *Psychological Review, 105,* 482–498.

Farah, M., Tanaka, J. N., & Drain, H. M. (1995). What causes the face inversion effect? *Journal of Experimental Psychology: Human Perception and Performance, 21,* 628–634.

Garner W. R. (1974). *The processing of information and structure.* Hillsdale, NJ: Erlbaum.

Garner W. R., & Felfoldy, G. L. (1970). Integrality of stimulus dimensions in various types of information processing. *Cognitive Psychology, 1,* 225–241.

Goldstone, R. L., Medin, D. L., & Gentner, D. (1991). Relational similarity and the nonindependence of features in similarity judgments. *Cognitive Psychology, 23,* 222–262.

Halberstadt, J. B. (1997). Effects of verbalization on configural and featural face recognition. Unpublished Dissertation, Indiana University.

Halberstadt, J., Goldstone, R. L., & Levine, G. M. (2003). Featural processing in face preferences. *Journal of Experimental Social Psychology, 39,* 270–278.

Halberstadt, J., & Rhodes, G. (2000). The attractiveness of nonface averages: Implications for an evolutionary explanation of the attractiveness of average faces. *Psychological Science, 11,* 285–289.

Hassin R., & Trope, Y. (2000). Facing faces: Studies on the cognitive aspects of physiognomy. *Journal of Personality and Social Psychology, 78,* 837–852.

Hoch, S. J., & Ha, Y. W. (1986). Consumer learning: Advertising and the ambiguity of product experience. *Journal of Consumer Research, 13,* 221–233.

Hoffman, J. E. (1980). Interaction between global and local levels of a form. *Journal of Experimental Psychology: Human Perception and Performance, 6,* 222–234.

Holbrook, M. B. (1980). Some preliminary notes on research in consumer esthetics. *Advances in Consumer Research, 7* 104–108.

Holbrook, M. B., & Huber, J. (1979). Separating perceptual dimensions from affective overtones: An application to consumer aesthetics. *Journal of Consumer Research, 5,* 272–283.

Holbrook, M. B., & Zirlin, R. B. (1985). Artistic creation, artworks, and aesthetic appreciation. *Advances in Non-Profit Marketing, 1,* 1–54.

Hsee, C. K. (1995). Elastic justification: How tempting but task-irrelevant factors influence decisions. *Organizational Behavior and Human Decision Processes, 62,* 330–129.

Hsee, C. K. (1996). Elastic justification: How unjustifiable factors influence judgments. *Organizational Behavior and Human Decision Processes, 66,* 122–129.

Hutchinson, J. W., & Alba, J. W. (1991). Ignoring irrelevant information: Situational determinants of consumer learning. *Journal of Consumer Research, 18,* 325–345.

Jordan, P. W., Thomas, B., & McClelland, I. L. (1996). Issues for usability evaluation in industry: Seminar discussions. In P. W. Jordan (Ed.), *Usability evaluation in industry* (pp. 237–243). London: Taylor and Francis.

Kalins, D. (2003). Design 2004: It's cool to be warm. *Newsweek,* October 27, 58–73.

Kemler Nelson, D. G. (1984). The effect of intention on what concepts are acquired. *Journal of Verbal Learning and Verbal Behavior, 23,* 734–759.

Kemler Nelson, D. G. (1989). The nature and occurrence of holistic processing. In B. E. Shepp & S. Ballesteros, (Eds.), *Object perception: Structure and process* (pp. 357–386). Hillsdale NJ: Erlbaum.

Kemler Nelson, D. G. (1993). Processing integral dimensions: The whole view. *Journal of Experimental Psychology: Human Perception and Performance, 19,* 1105–1113.

Kimchi, R. (1992). Primacy of wholistic processing and global/local paradigm: A critical review. *Psychological Bulletin, 112,* 24–38.

Kimchi, R. (2003). Relative dominance of holistic component properties in the perceptual organization of visual objects. In G. Rhodes & M. A. Peterson (Eds.), *Perception of faces, objects, and scenes: Analytic and holistic processes* (pp. 235–268). New York: Oxford University Press.

Koffka, K. (1935). *Principles of Gestalt psychology,* Harcourt Brace: New York.

Kotler, P., & Rath, G. A. (1984). Design: A powerful but neglected strategic tool. *Journal of Business Strategy, 5,* 16–21.

Kruglanski, A. W. (1996). Motivated social cognition: Principles of the interface. In E. T. Higgins & A. W. Kruglanski (Eds.), *Social psychology: Handbook of basic principles* (pp. 493–520). New York: Guilford.

Kunda, Z. (1990). The case for motivated reasoning. *Psychological Bulletin, 108,* 480–498.

Lamb, M. R., & Robertson, L. C. (1988). The processing of hierarchical stimuli: Effects of retinal locus, locational uncertainty, and stimulus identity. *Perception & Psychophysics, 44,* 172–181.

Lamb, M. R., & Robertson, L. C. (1990). The effect of visual angle on global and local reaction times depends on the set of visual angles presented. *Perception and Psychophysics, 47,* 489–496.

Lamb, M. R., & Yund, E. W. (1993). The role of spatial frequency in the processing of hierarchically organized stimuli. *Perception and Psychophysics, 54,* 773–784.

Landy, D., & Sigall, H. (1974). Beauty is talent: Task evaluation as a function of the performer's physical attractiveness. *Journal of Personality and Social Psychology, 29,* 299–304.

Langlois, J. H., Kalakanis, L. E., Rubenstein, A. J., Larson, A. D., Hallam M. J., & Smoot, M. T. (2000). Maxims or myths of beauty: A meta-analytic and theoretical review. *Psychological Bulletin, 126,* 390–423.

Lasaga, M. I. (1989). Gestalts and their components: Nature of information-precedence. In B. E. Shepp. & S. Ballesteros (Eds.), *Object perception: Structure and process* (pp. 165202). Hillsdale NJ: Erlbaum.

Latimer, C. & Stevens, C. (1997). Some remarks on wholes, parts and their perception. *Psycoloquy, 8,* 1–23.

Leder, H. & Bruce, V. (2000). When inverted faces are recognized: The role of configural information in face recognition. *The Quarterly Journal of Experimental Psychology, 53A,* 513–536.

Levine, G. M., Halberstadt, J. B., & Goldstone, R. L. (1996). Reasoning and the weighting of attributes in attitude judgments. *Journal of Personality and Social Psychology, 70,* 230–240.

Langlois, J. H., Roggman, L. A., & Musselman, L. (1994). What is average and not average about attractive faces? *Psychological Science, 5,* 214–220.

Light, L. L., Hollander, S., & Kayra-Stuart, F. (1981). Why attractive people are harder to remember. *Personality and Social Psychology Bulletin, 7,* 269–276.

Lockhead, G. R. (1972). Processing dimensional stimuli: A note. *Psychological* Review, 79, 410–419.

Loewenstein, G. F. (2001). The creative destruction of decision research. *Journal of Consumer Research, 28,* 499–505.

Loewenstein, G. F., Weber, E. U., Hsee, C. K., & Welch, N. (2001). Risk as feelings. *Psychological Bulletin, 127,* 267–286.

Loewy, R. (1951). *Never leave well enough alone,* New York: Simon & Schuster.

Love, B. C., Rouder, J. N., & Wisniewski, E. J. (1999). A structural account of global and local processing. *Cognitive Psychology, 38,* 291–316.

Macho, S. & Leder, H. (1998). Your eyes only? A test of interactive influence in the processing of facial features. *Journal of Experimental Psychology: Human Perception and Performance, 24,* 1486–1500.

Macrae, C. N., & Lewis, H. L. (2002). Do I know you? Processing orientation and face recognition. *Psychological Science, 13,* 194–196.

Martin, M. (1979). Local and global processing: The role of sparsity. *Memory and Cognition, 7,* 476–484.

Martindale, C. (1984). The pleasures of thought: A theory of cognitive hedonics. *The Journal of Mind and Behavior, 5,* 49–80.

Martindale, C. (1988). Aesthetics, psychobiology, and cognition. In F. Farley & R. Neperud (Eds.), *The foundations of aesthetics, art, and art education* (pp. 7–42). New York: Praeger.

Martindale, C., & Moore, K. (1988). Priming, prototypicality, and preference. *Journal of Experimental Psychology: Human Perception and Performance, 14,* 661–670.

Martindale, C. Moore, K., & Borkum, J. (1990). Aesthetic preference: Anomalous findings for Berlyne's psychobiological theory. *American Journal of Psychology, 103,* 53–80.

Melara, R. D., & Marks, L. E. (1990). Perceptual primacy of dimensions: Support for a model of dimensional interaction. *Journal of Experimental Psychology: Human Perception and Performance, 16,* 398–414.

Melara, R. D., Marks, L. E., & Potts, B. C. (1993a). Early-holistic processing or dimensional similarity? *Journal of Experimental Psychology: Human Perception and Performance, 91,* 1114–1120.

Melara, R. D., Marks, L. E., & Potts, B. C. (1993b). Primacy of dimensions in color perception. *Journal of Experimental Psychology: Human Perception and Performance, 19,* 1082–1104.

Melcher, J. M., & Schooler, J.W. (1996). The misremembrance of wines past: Verbal and perceptual expertise differentially mediate verbal overshadowing of taste memory. *Journal of Memory and Language, 35,* 231–245.

Miller, M., & Adler, J. (2003). Design 2004: Isaac hits his target. *Newsweek,* October 27, 2003, 74–77.

Navon, D. (1977). Forest before trees: The precedence of global features in visual perception. *Cognitive Psychology, 9,* 353–383.

Navon, D. (1981). The forest revisited: More on global precedence. *Psychological Research, 43,* 1–32.

Nisbett, R. E., & Wilson, T. D. (1977). The halo effect: Evidence for unconscious alteration of judgments. *Journal of Personality and Social Psychology, 35,* 250–256.

Norman, D. A. (2004). *Emotional design: Why we love (or hate) everyday things.* New York: Basic Books.

Obermiller, C. (1985). Varieties of mere exposure: The effects of processing style and repetition on affective response. *Journal of Consumer Research, 12,* 17–30.

Palmer, S. E. (1990). Modern theories of gestalt perception. *Mind and Language, 5,* 289–323.

Page, C., & Herr, P. M. (2002). An investigation of the processes by which product design and brand strength interact to determine initial affect and quality judgments. *Journal of Consumer Psychology, 12,* 133–147.

Pham, M. T., Cohen, J. B., Pracejus, J. W., & Hughes, G. D. (2001). Affect monitoring and the primacy of feelings in judgment. *Journal of Consumer Research, 28,* 167–188.

Pomerantz, J. R. (1981). Perceptual organization in information processing. In M. Kubovy, & J. R. Pomerantz (Eds.), *Perceptual organization.* Mahwah, NJ: Erlbaum.

Pomerantz, J. R., & Kubovy, M. (1986). Theoretical approaches to perceptual organization: Simplicity and likelihood principles. In K. R. Boff, L. Kaufman, & J. P. Thomas, (Eds.), *Handbook of perception and human performance: Cognitive process and performance* (pp. 3601–3646). New York: Wiley.

Prasso, S. (2001). Boeing gets beat. *Businessweek,* October 29, 12.

Raghubir, P., & Greenleaf, E. (2006). Ratios in proportion: What should the shape of the package be? *Journal of Marketing, 70,* 95–107.

Reber, R., Schwarz, N., & Winkielman, P. (2004). Processing fluency and aesthetic pleasure: Is beauty in the perceiver's processing experience? *Personality and Social Psychology Review, 8,* 364–382.

Reber, R., Winkielman, P., & Schwarz, N. (1998). Effects of perceptual fluency on affective judgments. *Psychological Science, 9,* 45–48.

Reilly, B. A., & Doherty, M. E. (1989). A note on the assessment of self-insight in judgment research. *Organizational Behavior and Human Decision Processes, 44,* 123–131.

Rhodes, G., Harwood, K., Yoshikawa, S., Nishitani, M., & McLean, I. (2002). The attractiveness of average faces: Cross-cultural evidence and possible biological basis. In G. Rhodes & L. A. Zebrowitz (Eds.), *Facial attractiveness* (pp. 35–58). Westport CT: Ablex Publishing.

Rhodes, G., Tan, S., Brake, S., & Taylor, K. (1989). Expertise and configural codeing in face recognition. *British Journal of Psychology, 80*, 313–331.

Rhodes, G., & Tremewan, T. (1996). Averageness, exaggeration, and facial attractiveness. *Psychological Science, 7*, 105–110.

Ritterfeld, U. (2002). Social heuristics in interior design preferences. *Journal of Environmental Psychology, 22*, 369–386.

Rubenstein, A. J., Langlois, J. H., & Roggman, L. A. (2002). What makes a face attractive and why: The role of averageness in defining facial beauty. In In G. Rhodes. & L. A. Zebrowitz (Eds.), *Facial attractiveness* (pp. 1–34). Westport CT: Ablex Publishing.

Russo, J. E., Medvec, V. H., & Meloy, M. G. (1996). The distortion of information during decisions. *Organizational and Human Decision Processes, 66*, 102–110.

Russo, J. E., Meloy, M. G., & Medvec, V. H. (1998). Predecisional distortion of product information. *Journal of Marketing Research, 35*, 438–452.

Schooler, J. W. (2002). Verbalization produces a transfer inappropriate processing shift. *Applied Cognitive Psychology, 16*, 989–997.

Schooler, J. W., & Engstler-Schooler, T. Y. (1990). Verbal overshadowing of visual memories: Some things are better left unsaid. *Cognitive Psychology, 22*, 36–71.

Schooler, J. W., Fiore, S. M., & Brandimonte, M. A. (1997). At a loss from words: Verbal overshadowing of perceptual memories. In Medin, D. (Ed.), *The psychology of learning and motivation: Advances in research and theory* (pp. 291–340). San Diego, CA: Academic Press.

Schwarz, N., & Clore, G. L. (1996). Feelings and phenomenal experiences. In E . T. Higgins & A. W. Kruglanski (Eds.), *Social psychology: Handbook of basic principles* (pp. 433–465). New York: Guilford.

Schwarzer, G. (2000). Development of face processing: The effect of face inversion. *Child Development, 71*, 391–401.

Schweitzer, M. E., & Hsee, C. K. (2002). Stretching the truth: Elastic justification and motivated communication of uncertain information. *The Journal of Risk and Uncertainty, 25*, 185–201.

Sergent, J. (1984). An investigation into component and configural processes underlying face recognition. *British Journal of Psychology, 75*, 221–242.

Shapiro, S., & Spence, M. T. (2002). Factors affecting encoding, retrieval, and alignment of sensory attributes in a memory-based brand choice task. *Journal of Consumer Research, 28*, 603–617.

Shepp, B. E. (1989). On perceiving objects: Holistic versus featural properties. In B. E. Shepp & S. Ballesteros (Eds.), *Object perception: Structure and process* (pp. 203–233). Mahwah, NJ: Erlbaum.

Shiv, B., & Fedorikhin, A. (1999). Heart and mind in conflict: The interplay of affect and cognition in consumer decision making. *Journal of Consumer Research, 26*, 278–292.

Silvera, D. H., Josephs, R. A., & Giesler, R. B. (2002). Bigger is better: The influence of physical size on aesthetic preference judgments. *Journal of Behavioral Decision Making, 15,* 189–202.

Slovic, P., & Lichtenstein, S. (1971). Comparison of bayesian and regression approaches to the study of information processing in judgment. *Organizational Behavior and Human Performance, 6*, 649–744.

Smith, L. B. (1990). A model of perceptual classification in children and adults. *Psychological Review, 96*, 125–144.

Takahashi, S. (1995). Aesthetic properties of pictorial perception. *Psychological Review, 102*, 671–683.

Tanaka, J. W. & Farah, M. J. (1993). Parts and wholes in face recognition. *The Quarterly Journal of Experimental Psychology, 46A*, 225–245.

Tanaka, J. W., & Farah, M. J. (2003). The holistic representation of faces. In G. Rhodes & M. A. Peterson, M. A. (Eds.), *Perception of faces, objects, and scenes: Analytic and holistic processes* (pp. 53–74). New York: Oxford University Press.

Treisman, A. (1986). Properties, parts and objects. In K. R. Boff, L. Kaufman, & J. P. Thomas, (Eds.), *Handbook of perception and human performance: Cognitive process and performance* (pp. 3501–3570). New York: Wiley.

Tversky, A. (1977). Features of similarity. *Psychological Review, 84*, 327–352.

Twitchell, J. B. (2004). An English teacher looks at branding. *Journal of Consumer Research, 31*, 484–489.

Valentine, T., Darling, S., & Donnelly, M. (2004). Why are average faces attractive? The effect of view and averageness on the attractiveness of female faces. *Psychonomic Bulletin & Review, 11*, 482–487.

Veryzer, R. W., Jr., & Hutchinson, J. W. (1998). The influence of unity and prototypicality on aesthetic response to new product designs. *Journal of Consumer Research, 24*, 374–394.

Ward, T. B., & Scott, J. (1987). Analytic and holistic modes of learning family-resemblance concepts. *Memory and Cognition, 15,* 42–54.

West, P. M., Brown, C. L., & Hoch, S. J. (1996). Consumption vocabulary and preference formation. *Journal of Consumer Research, 23,* 120–135.

Whitfield, T. W. A. (1983). Predicting preference for familiar, everyday objects: An experimental confrontation between two theories of aesthetic behavior. *Journal of Environmental Psychology, 3,* 221–237.

Whitfield, T. W. A. (2000). Beyond prototypicality: Toward a categorical-motivation model of aesthetics. *Empirical Studies of the Arts, 18,* 1–11.

Wilson, M. A., & MacKenzie, N. E. (2000). Social attributions based on domestic interiors. *Journal of Environmental Psychology, 20,* 343–354.

Wilson, T. D., & Brekke, N. (1994). Mental contamination and mental correction: Unwanted influences on judgments and evaluations. *Psychological Bulletin, 116,* 117–142.

Wilson, T. D., Dunn, D. S., Bybee, J. A., Hyman, D. B., & Rotondo, J. A. (1984). Effects of analyzing reasons on attitude-behavior consistency. *Journal of Personality and Social Psychology, 47,* 5–16.

Wilson, T. D., Hodges, S. D., & LaFleur, S. J. (1995). Effects of introspecting about reasons: Inferring attitudes from accessible thoughts. *Journal of Personality and Social Psychology, 69,* 16–28.

Wilson, T. D., Kraft, D., & Dunn, D. S. (1989). The disruptive effect of explaining attitudes: The moderating effect of knowledge about the attitude object. *Journal of Experimental Social Psychology, 25,* 379–400.

Wilson, T. D., & Nisbett, R. E. (1978). The accuracy of verbal reports about the effects of stimuli on evaluations and behavior. *Social Psychology, 41,* 118–131.

Wilson, T. D., & Schooler, J. W. (1991). Thinking too much: Introspection can reduce the quality of preferences and decisions. *Journal of Personality and Social Psychology, 60,* 181–192.

Winkielman, P., Schwarz, N., Fazendeiro, T. A., & Reber, R. (2003). The hedonic marking of processing fluency: Implications for evaluation judgment. In J. Musch & K. C. Klauer (Eds.), The *psychology of evaluation: Affective processes in cognition and emotion* (pp. 189–217). Mahwah, NJ: Erlbaum.

Winkielman, P., Schwarz, N., Reber, R., & Fazendeiro, T. A. (2003). Cognitive and affective consequences of visual fluency: When seeing is easy on the mind. In R. Batra & L. Scott (Eds.), *Visual persuasion* (pp. 75–89). Mahwah, NJ: Erlbaum.

Yamamoto, M., & Lambert, D. R. (1994). The impact of product aesthetics on the evaluation of industrial products. *Journal of Product Innovation Management, 11,* 309–324.

Young, A. W., Hellawell, D., & Hay, D. C. (1987). Configural information in face perception. *Perception, 16,* 747–759.

Zebrowitz, L. (1997). *Reading faces: Windows to the soul?* Boulder, CO: Westview Press.

30

Product Assortment

SUSAN M. BRONIARCZYK

University of Texas at Austin

Assortment is traditionally defined as the number of products offered within a single product category (Levy & Weitz, 2001). Considerable consumer research has examined the influence of the choice set on consumer decision making (see Payne, Bettman, & Johnson, 1993). These task and context effects though have typically been limited to small choice sets containing only three to six options. Yet, the size of product assortments confronting consumers has exploded in recent years with sprawling supermarkets, the entry of specialty category stores such as Best Buy electronics, and the advent of the Internet. For instance, the typical supermarket carries over 100 types of toothpastes varying on brand names (Colgate, Crest, Mentadent), benefits (tartar control, whitening, breath-freshening, sensitive), flavors (mint, cinnamon, citrus), and forms (gel, paste). Best Buy carries 183 televisions varying on brand names (Philips, RCA, Sony, Toshiba), display types (direct-view, flat panel, LCD, rear-projection, plasma), screen sizes (5"–50"), resolution (EDTV, HDTV, standard), and aspect ratio (16:9, 4:3). Increasing assortments are also evident in such consequential decisions as the 73 options for Medicare discount prescription cards (Salganik, 2004) and the 25% growth in options available in 401(k) plans over the past few years (Mottola & Utkus, 2003).

This chapter integrates the consumer behavior, marketing, and psychology literature to shed insight on how consumers make decisions in the face of such vast assortments. Webster's dictionary (2003) defines choice both as: (1) a sufficient number and variety to choose among and (2) the act of choosing. Consumer research has established that decision making from assortments is a hierarchical process with large product assortments attracting consumers in the first stage of choice and subsequently hindering the second-stage choice of selecting a final product (Kahn & Lehmann, 1991). The first part of the chapter will review the lure of assortments drawing on the retailing and variety-seeking literatures that broad assortments increase the probability that consumers will find their ideal product and offer flexibility for variety seekers. The next section examines how this lure though can backfire as vast assortments overload consumers, resulting in increased decision difficulty, lower choice accuracy, higher product regret, and a greater likelihood of purchase deferral. The chapter then reviews moderating conditions that may mitigate these negative consequences, enabling consumers to perceive the benefit of assortments without suffering the downsides of choosing from vast assortments. The chapter ends with a discussion of new assortment topics and future research opportunities and challenges.

THE LURE OF ASSORTMENTS

Consumers express a desire for assortments and are drawn to stores that offer wide product selection (Arnold, Oum, & Tigert, 1983). This lure isn't surprising as assortments offer significant process-related and choice-related benefits.

Process-Related Benefits

Large assortments afford several benefits to consumers engaged in the process of choosing. First, the complexity associated with numerous products and the novelty associated with unique items provides stimulation that is inherently satisfying (Berlyne, 1960). This stimulation is likely to be desirable for individuals with high optimal stimulation levels (Van Trijp, Hoyer, & Inman, 1996) or consumers who derive pleasure from the shopping experience (Babin, Darden, & Griffin, 1994). A plethora of options may also increase the anticipation of choosing. Savoring of the future choice and consumption experience may provide its own pleasure utility (Loewenstein, 1987).

Large assortments are also appealing for their perceived freedom (Reibstein, Youngblood, & Fromkin, 1975). Having a choice has been shown to increase intrinsic motivation and perceived control (Deci, 1981; Langer & Rodin, 1976) and predictions of satisfaction (Botti & Iyengar, 2004). Product choice is an opportunity to express one's individuality and such opportunities for self-determination contribute to the psychological well-being of individuals (Taylor & Brown, 1988).

Another advantage of assortments is that a comprehensive set of products provides full information to assist in developing one's preferences. Consumers can learn the relevant attributes, range of attributes, and attribute trade-offs for a category to make informed evaluations. Thus, a novice TV shopper may benefit from browsing Best Buy as the exposure to all products can be an educational experience enlightening consumers on the range of screen sizes, types of screen displays, and their associated prices. The proportion of the assortment devoted to each product type can also signal to consumers which options are the most popular or high market share products (Prelec, Wernerfelt, & Zettelmeyer, 1997).

Choice-Related Benefits

The foremost benefit of large assortments is an increase in the probability that a consumer will find a product matching his/her ideal point as the number of products increases (Baumol & Ide, 1956). For instance, a consumer who has researched a new TV purchase and decided their attribute preferences is more likely to find their optimal TV among Best Buy's 187 than the 30 televisions offered at Costco. Therefore, a key advantage of large assortments is they provide maximal opportunity to obtain the ideal product satisfying a consumer's preferences.

Another benefit of assortments is the provision of a diverse array of products for consumers to satisfy their needs across multiple contexts and multiple users. For instance, when purchasing toothpaste for the family, one may select a sensitive type for an elderly parent, a whitening type for a college-age daughter, a multicolor glitter toothpaste for a younger child, and a tartar control type for oneself all at a single location.

A desire to satisfy multiple tastes or variety-seek may also occur within a single consumer (see McAlister & Pessimeir, 1982 for a classic review of variety-seeking). Consumers' prior consumption experiences can lead them to become satiated on attributes and seek alternative products that offer high levels of another desirable attribute or attribute level (McAlister, 1982). Consumers are more inclined to variety-seek in low risk, hedonic product categories (Van Trijp et al., 1996) with attribute satiation more likely to occur for sensory attributes such as flavor than non-sensory attributes such as brand (Inman, 2001). Thus, broad assortments are appealing as they likely contain all of a consumer's desirable attribute options to accommodate variety seeking.

Large assortments also provide flexibility for consumers who are uncertain about their preferences and tastes (Kahn & Lehmann, 1991). When future preferences are unclear, consumers take actions to maintain their future options (March, 1978) and therefore prefer large assortments that provide flexibility (Kreps, 1979). As the time until consumption increases, the uncertainty associated with future tastes increases (March, 1978) and, consequently, assortments appear more attractive.

Simonson (1990) deftly illustrated how future preference uncertainty impacts variety-seeking by comparing consumers' simultaneous versus sequential purchase of snacks to be received at the end of three successive classes. The students in the sequential choice/sequential consumption condition made three separate choices, selecting one snack per class to be received that day. In contrast, the students in the simultaneous choice/sequential consumption condition selected all three snacks on Class 1 to be consumed that day and at the end of the next two classes. Results showed that students in the simultaneous choice condition were significantly more likely to select varied snacks than were students in the sequential choice condition, overestimating the likelihood that they would desire different snacks on future consumption occasions. This tendency to variety seek when choosing for multiple, future consumption occasions, termed the diversification bias (Read & Loewenstein, 1995), has been attributed to an incorrect expectation of attribute satiation, desire to reduce the risk associated with potentially changing future tastes, and a desire to simplify the decision (Simonson, 1990).

In summary, large assortments offer process-related benefits including stimulation, freedom of choice, and information about category attributes. Assortments also provide choice-related benefits including maximizing the likelihood of finding a single or multiple desired products and providing flexibility for variety seeking and uncertain preferences.

NEGATIVE CHOICE CONSEQUENCES OF ASSORTMENTS

However, this lure of assortment benefits is often a promise unfulfilled. While some choice is clearly beneficial, Schwartz (2000, 2004) persuasively argues that we have crossed the threshold on manageable choice and that the extreme selection of choices currently available instead presents a "tyranny of freedom." Assortments do indeed increase the probability that an ideal product is present on a store's shelf, but locating that product on the shelf now becomes a challenging endeavor. Kahn and Lehmann (1991) explicitly recognized this duality by modeling assortment utility as a hierarchical choice process. In their model, consumers first choose an assortment set that offers flexibility (i.e., choose between assortments offered by competing stores) and then in a subsequent stage confront the reality of choosing a single product from within the chosen assortment set (i.e., choose product at selected store).

This stepwise conflict of initial attraction to assortments followed by difficulty in product choice was powerfully demonstrated in a series of studies by Iyengar and Lepper (2000). They found that large assortments initially attracted consumers, but the decision difficulty they encountered upon trying to make a choice was demotivating, increasing regret and leading consumers to walk away without making a purchase.

Specifically, Iyengar and Lepper (2000) compared consumer reaction to 6 products (small assortment) versus 24 products (large assortment) of a gourmet jam brand in a field study at an upscale grocery. They showed that consumers were more attracted to a sampling station when it offered a greater assortment with 60% of shoppers sampling in the large 24 product condition compared to only 40% of shoppers sampling in the small 6 product condition. Thus, consistent with the benefits of assortments discussed, consumers were lured by greater assortment to approach the sampling display.

Consumers who visited the sampling station had the opportunity to sample the jams and received a $1 coupon for the gourmet jam brand. However, they needed to visit the regular shelf display containing all jam options to make a purchase. Purchase likelihood exhibited a strikingly different pattern with consumers more likely to purchase after sampling from the small (30% purchase) than large (3% purchase) assortment. That is, although consumers were initially more attracted to the larger relative to smaller sampling assortment, they were actually less inclined to buy. Notably, almost none of the consumers who approached the large assortment sampling station later made a product choice from the full shelf display.

In a follow-up laboratory study, Iyengar and Lepper (2000) compared subjects' reactions to a forced choice from either a small (6 products) or large (30 products) choice set of Godiva chocolates. Their results further corroborated an attraction/difficulty duality with subjects reporting that it was both more enjoyable and more difficult to choose from a large relative to small assortment. After consuming their chosen chocolate, subjects in the large compared to small assortment condition reported being less satisfied with their product choice and experiencing higher levels of regret that other foregone options might have been more preferable.

A final purchase phase further demonstrated the negative consequences of choosing from a large product selection. As compensation for participation, subjects could receive either $5 or a four-piece box of unspecified Godiva chocolates worth approximately $5. Almost half (48%) of subjects in the small assortment condition elected to receive a box of chocolate but only 12% of subjects in the large assortment condition elected to receive chocolate. Now, these chocolate purchase results may be viewed with some skepticism as the probability a subject's chosen chocolate was contained in the four-piece box was significantly lower in the large (4/30 = 13%) than small (4/6 = 67%) assortment condition. However, the fact that large assortment subjects reported lower satisfaction with their chosen chocolate does suggest that these subjects would be less inclined to purchase their chosen chocolate than more satisfied, small assortment subjects.

Chernev (2006) found that if the second stage of product choice was made salient, subjects' preference for large relative to small assortments was dampened but not reversed. In one study, subjects were asked to choose a pen from either Store A offering a small assortment of 12 options or Store B offering a large assortment of 60 options (12 options from small set plus 48 additional options). When subjects were told that final choice would occur at a later time, 97% selected Store B offering the large assortment. However, when subjects were told that they would need to make an immediate product choice, 81% selected Store B offering the large assortment. Other manipulations of product-choice focus including choice justification and prior experience choosing from a large assortment were similarly shown to dampen but not reverse subjects' preference for large relative to small assortments.

In summary, the two-stage process of consumer choice manifests a dual tension when consumers choose from large assortments. Large assortments are alluring and attract consumers. However, consumers appear to underestimate the decision difficulty they will encounter when they must choose a product from this vast array of options. Next, we review several research streams in consumer psychology to further illuminate three negative psychological consequences of selecting from large assortments: lower choice accuracy, lower satisfaction and higher regret, and higher choice avoidance. Table 30.1 summarizes the benefits and negative consequences of large assortments.

Table 30.1   Benefits and Negative Consequences of Assortment

Benefits of Assortment	
◆ Process-Related Benefits	• Stimulation and Shopping Pleasure • Positive Anticipation of Choosing • Freedom of Choice • Opportunity to Learn About Product Category • Attracts Consumers to Shelf Display
◆ Choice-Related Benefits	• Increases Probability of Finding Ideal Product • Increases Probability of Finding Multiple Products to Accommodate Multiple Users • Opportunity for Variety-Seeking • Flexibility for Uncertain Preferences
Negative Consequences of Assortment	

◆ Lower Choice Accuracy	• Increases Difficulty Locating Preferred Product on Shelf
	• Increases Cognitive Information Load, which is a positive function of:
	  ▫ Number of Alternatives
	  ▫ Similarity in Relative Attractiveness of Alternatives
	  ▫ Number of Attributes and Attribute Levels
	  ▫ Uniform Attribute Distribution and Low Attribute Importance
	• Increases Likelihood of Non-Compensatory Processing

◆ Lower Decision Satisfaction	• Increases Decision Difficulty and Consumer Confusion • Increases Decision Responsibility
◆ Lower Product Satisfaction	• Increases Product Expectations
◆ Greater Product Regret	• Increases Number of Foregone Alternatives
◆ Greater Choice Avoidance	• Increases Likelihood of Choosing Status Quo Option • Increases Likelihood of Deferring Choice

Lower Choice Accuracy

It is widely accepted that human beings have a limited capacity to process information (Simon, 1955). As the number of product alternatives increases, so does the cost of thinking (Shugan, 1980). Thus, the notion that too many product choices may be difficult and overwhelming to consumers is not novel. Consumer psychologists in the 1970s were cognizant of these limitations and attempted to ascertain when too much product packaging information would "overload" consumers.

A seminal study by Jacoby, Speller, and Kohn (1974) claimed to find evidence of information overload as the number of product alternatives increased. Information load was operationalized as a multiplicative function of the number of product alternatives (4, 8, or 12) X the number of product attributes (2, 4, or 6) per alternative. Information overload was operationalized as occurring when more information led to the negative consequence of decreased choice accuracy compared to a consumer's ideal based on stated attribute preferences.

Although few doubted the potential for information overload, a lively debate ensued as to the veracity of this overload claim given Jacoby et al.'s (1974) data (Wilkie, 1974; Summers, 1974; Jacoby, 1977). Reanalysis of the data showed that there was no evidence that a larger number of product alternatives led to information overload after choice accuracy was conditionalized on set size. That is, the finding of a larger number of product alternatives leading to lower choice accuracy was an artifact of failing to account for the higher chance probability of picking the best brand in small than large choice set sizes (Wilkie, 1974). However, later researchers such as Malholtra (1982) solidly demonstrated information overload when 10 or more alternatives were contained in the choice set.

Payne (1976) also provides evidence that increasing the information load (he referred to it as task complexity) leads consumers to resort to greater use of simplifying, choice heuristics. Using verbal protocols, he examined subject's decision strategies when the number of alternatives varied between 2 to 12 options and the number of attributes varied between 4 to 2 dimensions. His results showed that the number of alternatives had a greater impact on decision strategy than did the number of attributes. Specifically, with 2 alternatives, subjects exhibited compensatory processing with most subjects examining all the attributes for both alternatives. However, as the number of alternatives increased, subjects' decision strategies shifted to non-compensatory strategies of elimination by aspects and conjunctive models. Effectively, subjects reduced the information load by eliminating some of the alternatives on the basis of attribute criteria. Consistent with this premise, Payne et al. (1993) showed that the attractiveness of selective, attribute-based heuristics such as elimination by aspects increases as the number of product alternatives increase. Thus, when faced with greater assortments, consumers are more likely to engage in non-compensatory processing and selectively attend to a subset of the total information. This contingent processing in the face of high information loads contributes to lower levels of choice accuracy.

The Jacoby debate also pointed out that one needed to account for both the relative attractiveness of the alternatives in the choice set and information quality when determining the cognitive load (Wilkie, 1974; Summers, 1974). As Summers (1974, p. 467) states, "Clearly, the greater the variability in the 'attractiveness' of the alternatives, the easier it will be for the subject to select his 'best' brand." Malhotra (1982) found support for this assertion showing that as the variability of the relative attractiveness of the alternatives in the choice set increased, choice accuracy increased and subjects reported greater certainty, less confusion, and greater satisfaction with the task.

An inverted U relationship likely exists between the number of alternatives in the choice set and their variability in relative attractiveness. That is, when the product set is initially small, the addition of alternatives likely expands the attributes offered and/or the range of attributes offered. However, when more alternatives are added to an already large product set, the options are less likely to introduce new attributes and more likely to occur within the range offered by existing attributes, thereby increasing the similarity and relative attractiveness of the alternatives (Lehmann, 1998). Thus, we propose that the addition of product alternatives to a choice set initially increases a consumer's choice accuracy but the continued addition of product options results in a decrease in a consumer's choice accuracy.

Research on information quality is instructive to assortment researchers as it finds that the processing load for a constant number of product alternatives can vary substantially depending on the quality and type of attribute information presented. Three dimensions of attribute information that have been shown to affect the processing load of products in an assortment are attribute importance, the number of attribute levels, and the distribution of attribute levels across alternatives.

Keller and Staelin (1987) varied the number of product attributes (4, 8, 10 or 12) and the importance of the attributes (i.e., quality) holding constant the number of alternatives. For attribute quantity, they found an inverted U pattern such that more attributes per alternative initially increased but then decreased choice accuracy. However, when the quality of the attribute information increased, subjects responded by using more of the available information in their decision.

Thus, when deciding how much information to present for large assortments, this research suggests that marketers should limit and filter the availability of attribute information to only include the most important attributes.

Lurie (2004) advocates a comprehensive measure of cognitive information load that also incorporates the number of attribute levels and distribution of attribute levels. Drawing on Shannon's (1949) information theory, he finds that the processing load of product alternatives increases with the number of attribute levels and is greatest when attribute levels occur with uniform probability (i.e., symmetry). When attribute levels are uniformly distributed across alternatives (50% have attribute level 1 and 50% have attribute level 2), consumers are unable to guess the attribute level for a given alternative and have to engage in more processing than if the attribute levels are non-uniform (90% have attribute level 1 and 10% have attribute level 2). The rare events in non-uniform distributions are especially informative to consumers and therefore lighten the cognitive load.

Consistent with Payne (1976), he shows that the higher levels of information load associated with multiple, uniformly distributed attribute levels lead consumers to be more selective in their attribute information acquisition and this leads to lower choice accuracy. As large relative to small choice sets typically offer a greater number of attribute levels, these results imply that the cognitive load is likely even greater than previously thought. Yet, his results also suggest that an increasing assortment size does not necessarily mean an increasing cognitive load as the load can be mitigated if the attribute levels are non-uniformly distributed.

In conclusion, the information overload literature shows that the high cognitive load associated with large assortments decreases consumers' choice accuracy. As the number of product alternatives increases, consumers are more likely to resort to noncompensatory processing and selectively attend to information as a way to cope with the high information load. The exact point of information overload is arguably a calibration issue that will vary by product category, consumer, and situation. However, researchers can be guided by the knowledge that the cognitive processing load of assortments is a function of the number and relative attractiveness of product alternatives, the number and quality of attributes, and the number and dispersion of attribute levels.

The decision difficulty engendered by the high cognitive load of assortments also can lead to lower satisfaction. Next we review the negative consequences of large assortments leading to lower satisfaction with the choice process, lower satisfaction with product choice, and higher regret with product choice.

Lower Satisfaction and Higher Regret

Satisfaction with Choice Process The information overload research has also found that consumer satisfaction with the choice task decreases as the number of product alternatives increases (e.g., Maholtra, 1982). The complexity of a large assortment increased consumer confusion and contributed to lower satisfaction.

Huffman and Kahn (1998) examined consumer choice for 12 alternatives of sofas or hotels each described on 18 to 19 attributes in either an attribute-based or alternative-based information presentation format. Their findings showed that information format moderated the likelihood that a large assortment would lead to consumer confusion and lower satisfaction with the decision process. Specifically, subjects perceived less complexity with the choice set and were more satisfied with the decision process when assortment load was presented in an attribute-based format than an alternative-based format.

Apparently, when learning new information, it is easier for consumers to process information by attribute, comparing each alternative on a common feature. In contrast, presentation by alternative is more processing intensive as it requires consumers to integrate different attributes together to form an overall product assessment and then compare these overall assessments between different product alternatives. Thus, the cognitive load associated with processing assortments appears to be lighter when the information is presented in an attribute-based compared to alternative-based format and this positively impacts satisfaction with the choice process. This result implies that Internet retailers who possess the capability of attribute-based presentation have a distinct advantage in carrying broad assortments relative to brick-and-mortar retailers who are relegated to alternative-based presentation. Huffman and Kahn (1998) also found evidence that information format indirectly affected satisfaction with the choice through its influence on satisfaction with the process.

Satisfaction with Product Choice   Satisfaction with product choice is a comparison of the product's performance relative to expectations (Oliver, 1993). Thus, the reference point for satisfaction is internally generated (Tsiros & Mittal, 2000). For the same level of product performance, consumers may have different product satisfaction experiences depending on their expectations.

Schwartz et al. (2002) and Schwartz (2004) speculate that having a wide range of options increases consumer expectations about what constitutes an ideal product. As a consumer's ideal is composed of the best attributes of all product options considered, this ideal is likely to reach higher levels as more options are considered. Therefore, even if the chosen option is the best overall product amongst the choice set, it likely does not perform at the maximal performance level on all attributes. Consequently, the chosen product will fall short of a consumer's ideal expectations resulting in low satisfaction. If large relative to small assortments increase consumer expectations, then consumers will be less satisfied for an equivalent level of product experience.

Large assortments may also increase the perceived likelihood of success of finding the ideal product. That is, large assortments may create the impression that one can "have it all" in limitless choice sets and not have to trade-off product attributes. Schwartz et al. (2002) and Schwartz (2004) further conjecture that as a result, any performance deficiencies of the product will be felt acutely by the consumer. Having a wide selection of options discounts the situation as a source of blame and freedom of choice puts any attribution of product failure squarely on the shoulders of the chooser. The negative affect associated with poor attribute performance will thus be heightened for large assortments and further contribute to a consumer's lower satisfaction with product selection.

Regret with Product Choice   Regret is the result of comparing an outcome with a better outcome had a different alternative been selected (Tsiros & Mittal, 2000). That is, regret is a comparison between the chosen outcome and foregone options. As large assortments by definition denote a substantial number of product options, the potential for regret is high as there will be a substantial number of foregone options following choice.

Most regret research has examined situations where consumers know the outcome of the foregone alternatives. However, Tsiros and Mittal (2000) demonstrated that even if consumers do not know the outcome of these foregone alternatives, they may generate counterfactuals imagining how their outcome would have been different had they chosen differently. They found that subjects were more likely to generate counterfactuals when the chosen outcome was negative or not the status quo option. They conjecture that the reason switching from the status quo option results in regret is a subject's sense of decision responsibility.

If consumers do feel greater decision responsibility when choosing from a large assortment, one might predict that the likelihood of consumers generating counterfactuals and experiencing regret increases as the size of the assortment increases. Also, if large assortments entice motivated consumers to seriously consider more options, consumers may experience a greater post-choice discomfort and sense of loss for these foregone alternatives (Carmon, Wertenbroch, & Zeelenberg, 2003).

In summary, the higher cognitive load of large assortments is shown to lead to higher decision difficulty and consequently consumer dissatisfaction with the process of choosing from large assortments. Presenting the assortment information sequentially by attribute may facilitate processing and mitigate the negative effects on satisfaction. The large number of choice options associated with assortments may lead to lower satisfaction with the chosen outcome due to increased consumer expectations, greater self-blame, and higher regret that a foregone alternative would have been preferable to the chosen option. These negative consequences of large assortment may deter consumers from choosing at all.

Greater Choice Avoidance

Choice avoidance is a tendency to avoid making a product choice by seeking an easy way out that involves no change or postponing choice (for excellent review, see Anderson, 2003). Large assortments may trigger two choice avoidant behaviors, namely, a tendency to select the status quo option and a tendency to defer choice.

Status Quo Option   The status quo option is a preference for a product alternative that involves no change. For most consumer situations, the status quo option would entail selecting the same product previously purchased in the category or for new category purchases might entail selecting a brand previously purchased in another category. Hoyer (1984) finds that for frequently purchased, low involvement products, consumers use choice heuristics rather than engage in extended decision making. Specifically, observing laundry detergent purchases in grocery stores, he found that 72% of consumers looked at only one package during choice from the category shelf display. Assuming the prior choice experience was satisfactory, choice of a status quo option allows for a relatively quick and low effort decision. Choice of a status quo option is also highly justifiable to oneself and others and therefore may reduce the potential for regret (Simonson 1992; Inman & Zeelenberg, 2002). When faced with choosing from a large relative to small assortment, we would expect consumers to exhibit an even higher propensity of selecting a status quo option as a mechanism to cope with the choice complexity. The finding that availability of a favorite product was an important factor in consumer's perceptions of assortment is consistent with this premise (Broniarczyk, Hoyer, & McAlister, 1998).

Choice of a status quo option has also been shown to occur for high involvement decisions albeit via a very different processing route. Luce (1998) found that for decisions involving trade-offs on emotionally laden attributes (e.g., how high a price a consumer is willing to pay for auto safety), subjects who engaged in prolonged deliberation experienced negative emotion. These subjects consequently resorted to choosing an avoidant option as a mechanism to cope with the negative emotion generated from trade-off difficulty. If large assortments increase noncompensatory processing (Payne 1976), such trade-off difficulty may be alleviated if emotional-laden attributes are not the attribute criteria basis on which alternatives are eliminated.

Choice Deferral   Choice deferral encompasses postponing product choice either to search for more information or better alternatives or to simply choose not to purchase any of the available options. Greenleaf and Lehmann (1995) propose a typology of reasons why consumers defer product choice decisions. Reasons include perceived performance and financial risk, perceived social and psychological risk, being too busy to devote time to the decision, and needing to gather information or seek the advice of another. Large assortments exacerbate the likelihood of these deferral reasons occurring. A greater number of product alternatives makes it more difficult to determine the best performing product, increases one's concern that one is choosing the right product, increases the time needed to make a decision, and increases the likelihood that one may seek information to simplify one's task.

Iyengar, Jiang, and Huberman (2004) demonstrated the negative consequences of increasing option sizes on employee participation in retirement plans. Examining Vanguard 401(k) data, they found a 1.5% reduction in plan participation for every 10 fund options added. For instance, retirement plans that offered only 2 fund options had 75% employee participation whereas retirement plans that offered 59 fund options had only 60% employee participation. Thus, having a greater number of retirement fund options led to an increased incidence of choice deferral with employees electing not to participate at all in their retirement plans.

One reason large assortments may lead to choice deferral is if they increase the number of difficult attribute trade-offs consumers face (Luce 1998). Certainly, retirement fund plans that ask consumers to trade-off risk versus reward among fund options for their future financial security is an emotionally difficult decision.

Paralleling the prior discussion on choice accuracy, choice deferral has also been found to occur if the similarity between options increases, making consumers uncertain as to which is the single best alternative (Dhar, 1997). Extensive processing of an assortment set that contains options of relatively equally attractiveness exacerbates rather than resolves preference uncertainty and thereby increases the coping mechanism of choice deferral. However, choice deferral has been shown to be mitigated if assortments offer high attractive options or factors such as time pressure increase the extent of non-compensatory processing (Dhar & Nowlis, 1999). Dhar (1997) also showed that if consumers have the opportunity to select multiple alternatives, choice deferral decreased as consumers no longer had to choose between their uncertain preferences.

In conclusion, we have reviewed three potential negative consequences of large assortments on consumer decision making: lower choice accuracy, lower satisfaction and higher regret, and greater choice avoidant behavior. Higher cognitive loads generally associated with large assortments were shown to lead to non-compensatory processing and lower choice accuracy. The decision difficulty associated with choosing from a vast number of product options was shown to lead to lower satisfaction with the choice process, lower satisfaction with the chosen option, and higher regret that one of the foregone alternatives was preferable to the chosen option. Large assortments were shown to lead to a higher incidence of choice avoidant behavior due to their decision complexity, difficult attribute trade-offs, and similarity in relative attractiveness of options.

The above discussion paints a bleak picture of consumer choice from broad assortments. Although initially attracted to large assortments, consumers suffer a multitude of negative consequences when subsequently choosing from these sizeable choice sets. Next, we discuss several moderating factors that offer the possibility of a brighter picture whereby consumers may receive the benefits of assortments with limited negative consequences.

MODERATING ASSORTMENT FACTORS

Perceptions of Assortment

An assumption of early assortment research was that consumer perceptions of the assortment offered in a product category were a one-to-one function of the number of products offered in that category. The high processing load presented by broad assortments though makes it unlikely that consumers process all product information in extensive detail. Thus, more recent research has questioned this assumption and provided insight into the factors that affect how consumers actually perceive assortment including the composition of the product set and assortment display and organization.

Availability of Favorite Product and Shelf Display   Broniarczyk et al. (1998) found that in addition to the number of unique products offered, assortment perceptions were also a function of the heuristic cues of shelf space size and availability of favorite product. In a laboratory study, subjects shopped for microwavable popcorn in two mock stores, a base store containing 48 products, each receiving one shelf facing, and a test store and then made a surprise comparative rating of assortment. The test store varied the number of products offered (12, 24, 36, or 48) and the size of the shelf space (one shelf facing per product versus a constant 48 product facings). The smaller product sets contained the most attractive options and duplicate shelf facings in the constant shelf space condition. Results showed that if shelf space was held constant and a consumer's favorite was still available, subjects perceived no difference in the assortment offered by either the 24 or 36 product test stores relative to the 48 product base store. In fact, subjects actually perceived the 36 product store to offer more assortment than the 48 product base store if shelf space was held constant. This higher assortment perception was apparently due to the duplication of the most attractive products making it easier for consumers to find their favorite products.

A field study corroborated the findings that assortment perceptions were not a direct function of the number of products offered. Customers reported no change in assortment perceptions when the number of products offered in five high-selling categories in a convenience store were reduced by 50%. However, customers reported that it was now easier to shop. These findings led Broniarczyk et al. (1998) to suggest that assortment perceptions are a multidimensional construct comprised of both a cognitive dimension (total number of products offered, size of shelf space devoted to category) and an affective dimension (availability of favorite product, ease of shopping). Importantly, this research on assortment perceptions suggests the possibility of a win-win situation whereby a reduction in the number of products offered has the positive benefit of reducing consumers' processing load without altering the perceived assortment that consumers find alluring.

Product and Attribute Similarity   Consistent with the information load literature, research also finds that product and attribute similarity are important dimensions underlying consumer's perceptions of assortment. Hoch, Bradlow, and Wansink (1999) and Van Herpen and Pieters (2002) developed two mathematical models of assortment perception that they experimentally tested using hypothetical visual stimuli varying on color, shape, and name.[1]

Hoch et al. (1999) model the perceived assortment of a product category as the dissimilarity of product pairs and find that uniqueness of product pairs is critical with assortments containing duplicates severely penalized. Their results showed that attribute differences between products had a significant positive impact on assortment perceptions even when the number of products was held constant. However, adding a unique feature had diminishing returns if the products already differed on multiple attributes.

Attributes have also been shown to vary in their importance in affecting consumer perceptions of product assortment. In their visual task of hypothetical products, Hoch et al. (1999) found that the attributes of color and shape exerted the greatest influence on assortment perceptions. For actual grocery products where consumers have a priori preferences, brand name and flavor have been shown to be more important attributes than package size in affecting consumers' assortment reaction (Boatwright & Nunes, 2001, 2004). Therefore, one might hypothesize that consumers would perceive a small product set size that varies on important attributes as offering greater assortment than a larger product set size that offers minimal variation on important attributes.

Van Herpen and Pieters (2002) model the perceived assortment of a product category as a function of the dispersion of attribute levels across all products in the category and the correlation between product attributes. An assortment was perceived to be varied to the extent that multiple attribute levels were present and largest when all attribute levels occurred in equal proportions (i.e., symmetrical dispersion) and a low level of association existed between attribute pairs. Their results showed that although significant, product set size had a much smaller impact on assortment perceptions than attribute dispersion and disassociation, particularly if the initial assortment size was large.

Attribute dispersion may differentially affect the cognitive and affective dimensions of assortment perceptions. Van Herpen and Pieters'(2002) finding of higher perceived assortment for symmetrical attribute dispersions is consistent with Lurie's (2004) findings that symmetrical dispersions (e.g., 2 plasma TVs, 2 rear projection TVs) have a higher cognitive load than asymmetrical dispersions (e.g., 1 plasma TV, 3 rear projection TVs). Similarly, subjects in Kahn and Wansink's (2004) research rated symmetrical assortments as more complex and less fun to process than asymmetrical assortments. However, Kahn and Wansink (2004) speculate that the ease of processing associated with a rare option in an asymmetric dispersion will lead to greater perceived assortment than a symmetric dispersion. Direct measures of perceived assortment were not collected, but subjects were found to consume greater quantities from an asymmetrical than symmetrical assortment. Thus, the cumulative effect of attribute dispersion on the cognitive and affective dimensions of assortment perceptions remains open for future investigation.

The affective dimension of consumer satisfaction with the assortment was modeled in Kahn and Lehmann's (1991) previously discussed hierarchical choice model. Assortment utility was modeled as the sum of the utility of the most preferred product in the set and the utilities of the remaining acceptable products weighted by the amount of uniqueness they offer. Thus, consistent with Broniarczyk et al. (1998), the most preferred or favorite product exerts a disproportionately strong influence on consumer assortment judgments and consistent with Hoch et al. (1999) and Van Herpen and Pieters (2002), the uniqueness contributed by other products in the set is also an important element underlying consumer perceptions of assortment.

Assortment Organization   The information format of the assortment has also been shown to interact with the number of products offered in affecting consumer perceptions of assortment. An organized assortment (e.g., by brand or by flavor) provides a structure that facilitates consumer processing of the range of products offered. Thus, Kahn and Wansink (2004) found that for large assortments, perceived assortment is higher for organized displays that help consumers appreciate the broad range of options. However, for small product sets, organization facilitates consumer recognition that the number of products offered is limited and consequently perceived assortment was higher for disorganized relative to organized assortments.

Organization of an assortment display also increases the similarity of adjacent products. Consequently, Hoch et al. (1999) found that consumer's processing mode interacts with assortment organization in affecting consumers' perceptions of assortment. Specifically, consumers may evaluate the assortment display from two different processing orientations: a choice task versus a browsing task. When engaged in a choice task, consumers focus on specific attribute information to achieve their preferences. An organized assortment facilitates locating the portion of the display containing products that help achieve their attribute objectives and consequently leads to higher perceptions of assortment. In contrast, when engaged in a browsing task, consumers process the display holistically and a disorganized assortment is perceived as offering greater assortment.

However, not all organizations are equally effective at facilitating consumers processing of the assortment. Morales, Kahn, McAlister, and Broniarczyk (2005) show that the external structure of the assortment organization interacts with the internal representation of the category that the consumer brings to the decision situation. Specifically, Morales et al. (2005) show that when a consumer's internal structure for the category matches the external structure of the shelf display, the consumer is more likely to perceive greater assortment and be more satisfied with his/her choice. Thus, a consumer who is brand loyal when choosing a TV (e.g., Sony) will perceive a greater assortment when the display is organized by brand as the complete range of a brand's offering are now located in one section of the shelf display (e.g., direct-view, plasma, rear projection, HD, standard, all sizes). Conversely, a consumer who is most concerned about resolution will perceive a greater assortment when the product display is congruently organized by resolution (e.g., all HD TVs, all ED TVs, all direct view TVs).

Congruency between the external assortment organization and a consumer's internal structure on assortment perceptions was more important for consumers with high product category familiarity. For low familiarity consumers, their internal structures were less-well developed and consequently it was more important for the assortment organization to be congruent with their situational shopping goals (e.g., big-screen TV for entertainment room, small TV for kitchen).

In conclusion, perceived assortment extends beyond the number of products offered. Consumer assortment perceptions are also affected by the composition of products in the assortment, heuristic cues, and the format in which products are presented. Assortment perceptions are higher to the extent that the product set contains more unique alternatives, attributes and attribute levels, low levels of inter-attribute correlation, and preferred options. Thus, a product set containing a few, unique items may be perceived as offering greater assortment than a product set containing more, but similar items. Furthermore, holding the number of products and product set composition constant, products displays that occupy greater space and are organized to facilitate consumer processing of the assortment lead to higher perceptions of assortment. These findings offer prescriptions to marketers regarding conditions whereby consumers may reap the process and choice-related benefits of assortment without suffering detrimental processing loads.

Assortment Attribute Type

The assortment models of Hoch et al. (1999) and Van Herpen and Pieters (2002) showed that attribute dissimilarity increased assortment perceptions. This attribute dissimilarity can be further specified as either an alignable/nonalignable or a complementary/noncomplementary attribute difference. Markman and Medin (1995) define alignable attributes as different levels of the same attribute so consumers are making tradeoffs within an attribute. Nonalignable attributes, on the other hand, involve comparisons among different attributes so consumers are making tradeoffs between attributes. For instance, in computers, an alignable attribute would be processor speed that could vary from 1.60GHz, 2.40GHz, 2.80GHz, 3.00GHz. A nonalignable attribute would be computer peripherals that could range from monitor, printer, fax, to speakers.

Nonalignable attributes are more likely to increase perceived assortment than alignable attributes. However, Gourville and Soman (2005) showed that increasing brand assortments of nonalignable attributes had a negative impact on brand choice. They compared choice between two brands, Brand A offering a single product option and Brand B offering either a single product option or five product options. When Brand B increased its product assortment from one to five options and the attribute differences were nonalignable, its market share relative to Brand A *decreased* from 53% to 40%. However, when the attribute differences were alignable, the opposite pattern emerged. When Brand B increased its product assortment from one to five options and the attribute differences were alignable, its market share relative to Brand B *increased* from 53% to 73%.

Gourville and Soman (2005) examined two causal mechanisms underlying this differential effect of assortment type on product choice. First, nonalignable assortments place a heavier cognitive load on consumers than alignable assortments as comparisons between attributes are more difficult than comparisons across levels within an attribute. Thus, consumers may choose to simplify their decision by selecting the brand offering fewer options. Second, nonalignable assortments have been shown to lead to higher regret than alignable assortments. When choosing between nonalignable attributes, consumers with budget constraints must trade-off between attributes. These consumers are likely to experience a sense of regret about foregone options as a computer peripheral choice of a monitor means completely foregoing a printer, fax, or speakers. When choosing among alignable attributes, however, regret is minimized as the choice between levels of a common attribute (e.g., 1.6GHz vs. 2.0Ghz) still results in the consumer obtaining that attribute (e.g., a computer processor). Their experimental results supported both cognitive load and regret as causal mechanisms underlying the decreased choice likelihood for assortments differentiated on nonalignable attributes.

Chernev (2005) found similar moderating effects for the attribute type of complementarity on choice deferral from varying brand assortments. Complementary attributes were characterized as attributes whose utilities were additive increasing overall product attractiveness (e.g., tartar control + cavity protect for toothpaste) whereas noncomplementary attributes were characterized by their nonadditive utilities decreasing overall product attractiveness (e.g., mint flavor + banana flavor of toothpaste).

Chernev (2005) showed that choice deferral was higher when the options in the choice set were differentiated by complementary relative to noncomplementary attributes and that this effect was moderated by assortment size. Comparing choice sets comprised of two options versus five options, he found that when choosing among options differentiated on complementary attributes, 65% of subjects deferred choice in the larger choice set compared to 50% of subjects deferring choice in the smaller choice set. On the other hand, when choosing among options differentiated on noncomplementary features, an opposite pattern was observed such that subjects were less likely to defer choice for the larger (27%) compared to smaller (42%) choice sets.

Choice protocols in Chernev (2005) revealed that consumer expectations increased more for complementary than noncomplementary attributes. As assortment size increased, a subject's ideal product contained an aggregation of a larger number of attributes if the assortment was differentiated on complementary compared to noncomplementary attributes. As this increased ideal point is often unrealistic due to product or budget constraints, its unavailability led to a higher incidence of consumers deferring purchase.

Griffin and Broniarczyk (2007) find that this quest for the ideal product can lead consumers to continue searching for products even when it has diminishing returns on satisfaction. In an Internet search task, subjects searched more when options were nonalignable than alignable. Yet, this further search decreased subjects' satisfaction as the nonalignable options necessitated difficult trade-offs. These findings suggest that consumers may self-create large assortments of attractive options, and as a result, self-inflict negative decision-making consequences.

In summary, choice likelihood was shown to decrease as assortment size increased, particularly if the assortment was differentiated on nonalignable and complementary attributes. Three causal mechanisms of higher cognitive load, increased product expectations, and higher regret were shown to underlie the higher levels of choice avoidance associated with increasing assortments differentiated on nonalignable and complementary attributes. These findings are troublesome as the very attribute types (nonalignable, complementary) that positively impact assortment perceptions are the cause of subsequent choice difficulty. The constructs of attribute alignability and complementarity are conceptually very similar although inversely related. Most complementary attributes would be nonalignable (e.g., a computer would increase in attractiveness if it offered multiple peripherals of monitor, printer, and speakers). However, one could envision instances where complementary attributes have common, alignable levels (e.g., strawberry and banana make attractive combination flavor of strawberry-banana) and hence may increase the attraction of the assortment while limiting the deleterious effects on choice.

Preference Development

Consumer knowledge may also be helpful in offsetting the higher cognitive loads and increased product expectations of large assortments. A choice task though requires more than a mere knowledge of product attributes and product alternatives. In order to make a choice, the key is that consumers have developed preferences regarding attribute levels and formulated trade-offs on the relative importance of these attributes. Consumers with well-developed preferences have been shown to have an easier time processing large assortments, higher levels of satisfaction, and higher likelihood of choice from large assortments (Huffman & Kahn, 1998; Chernev, 2003a, 2003b).

In their study of consumer choice from large assortments, Huffman and Kahn (1998) examined the effects of preference development by varying three levels of a learning manipulation that occurred prior to choice. Specifically, they manipulated whether consumers had: (1) *attribute knowledge* where subjects were exposed to all attributes and attribute levels, (2) *attribute preference* where subjects expressed preference for attribute levels, or (3) *attribute importance* where subjects first rated relative importance between attributes and then expressed with-in attribute preferences.

Study 1 of Huffman and Kahn (1998) compared knowledge of attributes versus preferences for attributes (#1 vs. #2) on consumer choice of 12 alternatives of sofas or hotels each described on 18 to 19 attributes. Their results showed that subjects who had expressed attribute preferences perceived the choice set as less complex than consumers who merely had knowledge of the attributes. However, the learning manipulation of attribute knowledge versus attribute preference had no effect on the percentage of consumers who expressed a readiness to make a choice or satisfaction with choice.

A second study compared the two higher preference development levels of attribute preference versus attribute importance (#2 vs. #3). The choice context was 12 hotel alternatives each described on 25 attributes. Their results showed that subjects in the attribute preference condition perceived the choice set as less complex, were more satisfied with their chosen alternative, and more likely to believe they had made optimal choice than subjects in the attribute importance condition. That is, subjects who had expressed their attribute preferences had a more positive experience choosing from a large assortment than did subjects with more well-developed preferences that had also expressed relative attribute importance. This finding is likely attributable to the learning manipulation task being onerous for attribute importance subjects (trade-offs on 25 attributes) and their dissatisfaction carrying over to their later assortment choice. Thus, Huffman and Kahn (1998) recommend that if one is trying to assist novice consumers in choosing from a large assortment that developing attribute preferences strikes the correct balance between not being overwhelming in the learning phase and assisting in the product choice phase.

Chernev (2003a, 2003b) also posits that making a product choice from an assortment is a two-stage process of first deciding an ideal attribute combination and then locating the product in the assortment that best matches this ideal. He finds that consumers with well-developed preferences have an easier time choosing from assortments as their ideal product is already constructed. In contrast, consumers who do not possess well-developed product face the difficult two-stage process of first deciding their ideal attribute combination under a high cognitive load and then locating the product in the assortment that best matches this ideal.

In Chernev (2003a), subjects were asked to choose a product from either a small assortment containing 4 options or a large assortment containing 16 options (the 4 options from the small set and 12 additional options). The options were described on 4 attributes that could vary on 4 levels. Comparable to the attribute preference learning manipulation in Huffman and Kahn (1998), half of his subjects articulated their attribute preferences and half of subjects were simply exposed to the attribute information prior to choice (#2 vs. #1). His results showed that more subjects elected to choose a product from the large instead of the small assortment when they had articulated their preferences (96%) than when they had just received attribute information (72%). Thus, having more developed preferences increased the likelihood of consumers choosing a product from a large assortment. It is notable though that the majority of subjects in both conditions elected to choose from the large compared to small assortment set.

Chernev's (2003a) second study showed that consumers' initial search was more alternative-based (compared to attribute-based) when attribute preferences were expressed (92%) than when subjects merely had attribute knowledge (33%). Furthermore, subjects who had articulated their preferences examined only about half as many piece of information as subjects who only had attribute knowledge (13.4 vs. 22.1 information items). These process results support Chernev's proposed two-staged model as subjects who had expressed their attribute preferences prior to choice exhibited more selective, alternative-based processing trying to locate their ideal product. In contrast, subjects who had not articulated their preferences engaged in more attribute-based processing as they needed to complete the initial stage of determining their ideal product from the large assortment display prior to proceeding to second stage of product choice.

This differential processing of assortments as a result of preference development has also been shown to affect the strength of consumers' preference for their product choice from an assortment. Chernev (2003b) found that for large assortments, subjects had a lower propensity to switch their choice when preferences were articulated (13% switching) than when they were not articulated (38% switching). An opposite pattern was observed for small assortments whereby subjects who had articulated preferences had a higher propensity to switch from choice (27%) compared to subjects who had not formed their preferences (9% switching). For consumers with well-developed preferences, a large assortment increases the probability of finding a match with their ideal and thus they are less inclined to switch. However, these same consumers will not fare as well in finding a close match to their ideal in the small assortment set, and thus are more likely to switch.

In conclusion, having well-developed preferences facilitates consumers choosing from large assortments. Consumers who have well-developed preferences encounter less decision difficulty, are more likely to choose from large assortments, and have both stronger preferences for and are more confident in their chosen alternative than consumers who do not possess well-developed preferences. Consumers with well-developed preferences have already formed an ideal product and large assortments maximize the likelihood that the consumer's ideal product is available.

Maximizer-Satisficer

Individual difference variables will also affect how consumers deal with the challenge of choosing a product from a large assortment. In his seminal work that recognized the cognitive limitations of human ability, Simon (1956) suggested that for complex decisions, after one considered all the time, effort, and psychological cost involved in making a rational choice, satisficing or choosing an acceptable option rather than the best option was often an optimal strategy. Schwartz and colleagues (Schwartz et al., 2002) have developed an individual difference scale to measure an individual's propensity to be a Maximizer versus a Satisficer. Maximizers have the goal of choosing the absolute best product. Satisficers, on the other hand, have the goal of choosing a product that is good enough to meet their standards for acceptability.

The Maximizer-Satisficer scale of Schwartz et al. (2002) is comprised of 13 items that load on 3 factors. The first factor captures the extent to which an individual is on the look out for better options (e.g., imagine all possibilities, channel surf looking for better TV or radio shows). The second factor captures the extent to which an individual struggles to pick the best product (e.g., difficulty selecting best video, use of lists of recommended options). The third factor captures the extent to which an individual has high standards (e.g., never settle for second best).

In a series of studies, Schwartz and colleagues demonstrated that maximizers compared to satisficers have significantly lower levels of life satisfaction, happiness, optimism, and self-esteem and significantly higher levels of regret and depression. Additionally, maximizers were shown to engage in more product comparisons, social comparisons, and counterfactual comparisons but feel less satisfied with their decision. The higher incidence of comparisons and counterfactuals contributes to higher levels of product regret.

In the pursuit of obtaining the best product, maximizers have been found to achieve higher task performance but do worse subjectively than satisficers. Iyengar, Wells, and Schwartz (2006) compared the job search process of university graduates who were categorized on the basis of Schwartz et al.'s (2002) scales as maximizers or satisficers. Their research showed that maximizers obtained jobs with 20% higher starting salaries than satisficers. However, maximizers were less satisfied with the jobs they obtained and experienced greater negative affect through the job search process than satisficers. Apparently, the lower satisfaction and negative affect were driven by maximizers' pursuit of more job opportunities and greater social comparison to peers. Of particular relevance for assortment, they found that an increase in the number of options considered was associated with a steeper decrease in outcome satisfaction for maximizers compared to satisficers. That is, maximizers searched more job options, but the more options the searched, the less satisfied they were with their final option.

Thus, maximizers have a more difficult time selecting from a broad product assortment than satisficers. Maximizers are more likely to engage in compensatory processing and be overwhelmed with the cognitive load of large assortments. Conversely, satisficers are more likely to engage in non-compensatory processing to find an acceptable alternative that meets their minimal attribute cut-offs. As maximizers engage in more exhaustive product searches and consider more options, their product ideal becomes less obtainable in a single product than the ideal of a satisficer, and consequently they are less satisfied with their product choice. As assortment size increases, maximizers relative to satisficers are more likely to experience higher levels of regret due to their propensity to engage in social comparison and counterfactual reasoning.

Table 30.2 summarizes the four moderators of consumer choice from large assortments: assortment perceptions, assortment attribute type, consumer preference development, and the individual difference variable of maximizer-satisficier. Consumer assortment perceptions are shown to extend beyond the number of products offered and also be affected by the composition of products in the assortment, heuristic cues, and the format in which products are presented. Therefore, a smaller product set that is properly composed and organized can lead to higher assortment perceptions than a larger product set as well as facilitate choice. Assortments that were differentiated on nonalignable and complementary attributes though were shown to lead to a higher cognitive load,

TABLE 30.2   Assortment Moderating Factors

Assortment Perceptions

- Assortment perceptions are positively related to # of products offered. However, assortment perceptions are not one-to-one function of # of products offered. Smaller product sets may be perceived as offering greater assortment than larger product sets.
- Holding # of products constant, assortment perceptions can be increased by:
  - ◻ Offering more preferred products
  - ◻ Offering more unique attributes and alternatives
  - ◻ Offering more variability on important attributes
  - ◻ Increasing size of product display
  - ◻ Organizing product display congruent with consumers' internal category representations and/or shopping goals

Assortment Attribute Type

- Assortments differentiated on alignable (vs. non-alignable) attributes exhibit a lower incidence of choice avoidance.
- Assortments differentiated on non-complementary (vs. complementary) attributes exhibit a lower incidence of choice avoidance.

Consumer Preference Development

- When choosing from large assortments, consumers with well-developed (vs. less developed) preferences:
  - ◻ Encounter less decision difficulty
  - ◻ Engage in more alternative-based search for preferred alternative
  - ◻ Exhibit higher levels of decision satisfaction
  - ◻ Exhibit higher levels of product satisfaction and lower levels of product regret
  - ◻ Exhibit lower levels of choice deferral

Consumer Maximizer-Satisficer Tendency

- When choosing from large assortments, consumers who possess satisficer (vs. maximizer) tendencies:
  - ◻ Engage in less extensive decision-making
  - ◻ Exhibit higher levels of decision satisfaction
  - ◻ Exhibit lower levels of product regret

greater product expectations, and higher regret, and consequently, lower choice incidence. Two individual consumer factors were then shown to be capable of mitigating these negative decision-making consequences. Consumers with well-developed relative to less-developed preferences were shown to have less difficulty processing large assortments, higher levels of satisfaction with the choice process, higher incidence of choosing a large compared to small assortment, and greater preference with their chosen option. Secondly, consumers with exhibited satisficer relative to maximizer tendencies were shown to be less susceptible to the negative psychological consequences of large assortments experiencing higher satisfaction with the choice process and lower regret with product choice.

Next we discuss some new directions being explored in assortment research, the effects of assortment on consumption and well-being.

ASSORTMENT EFFECTS ON CONSUMPTION AND WELL-BEING

Assortment research has begun to move beyond examining product choice and address the later consumer decision-making stage of product consumption. The general finding is that individuals consume greater quantities as assortment size increases. Rolls et al. (1981) showed that the number of options in an assortment affected consumption quantity with subjects consuming more yogurt when presented with three than one flavor of yogurt.

Extending this research, Kahn and Wansink (2004) found that perceived assortment mediates the effect of actual assortment on consumption. As previously discussed, Kahn and Wansink (2004) showed that consumer perceptions of assortment are influenced by information structure variables. Specifically, they demonstrated that increasing the number of options increased perceived assortment more for organized and asymmetric assortment structures. In Study 2, subjects were ostensibly recruited for a study on television advertising and offered either 6 or 24 jelly bean options while they waited. The assortment structure varied whether the display was randomly disorganized or organized by flavor and color. Their results showed that as the assortment size increased from 6 to 24 options, consumption quantity increased for organized assortments (from 12.7 to 28.3) but not for disorganized assortments (22.2 and 22.6, respectively).

Increases in perceived assortment led subjects to anticipate higher enjoyment of the items to be consumed and this desire led them to consume greater quantities. When assortment size was made salient, subjects appeared to use the size of the assortment as consumption norm to gauge how many items to consume. Providing corroborating evidence in an experimental financial setting, Morrin, Imman, and Broniarczyk (2007) find that increases in the number of mutual funds offered in 401(k) plans led to increases in the number of funds investors placed in their investment portfolios.

The consequences of product assortments on consumer well-being is a topic of growing commentary. Kahn and Wansink (2004) suggest that health practitioners should be particularly cognizant of the effects of assortment size and structure on consumption in the mounting battle with obesity. Anecdotal evidence also suggests that increasing assortments may have negative consequences on consumer's mental health. Schwartz (2000, 2004) wonders if exploding product assortments are related to the rising depression rates in the United States. Although assortments offer the lure of control over product choice, the decision difficulty, lower satisfaction, and higher regret associated with choice from assortments may make the ultimate lack of control self-evident and contribute to depression.

Choice from a large assortment may also have a detrimental impact on subsequent consumer choices and behavior. Baumeister and Vohs (2003) demonstrate how product choice is ego-depleting and the energy expended in a current choice may leave a consumer with less willpower for a subsequent task. As choosing from large assortments is taxing, particularly for maximizers, this research suggests that maximizers may have less self-control for a subsequent product task. Mick, Broniarczyk, and Haidt (2004) speculate that choices from large assortments may cumulatively lead to a self-focus due to the repeated creation and activation of one's preferences. This self-focus may diminish the quality of subsequent other-focused activities such as later social interactions and altruistic behavior. In sum, initial evidence exists that broad assortments increase product consumption and thought-provoking reflections ponder their psychic toll.

SUMMARY AND FUTURE DIRECTIONS

Product assortments are a complex phenomenon, alluring but wrought with choice difficulty. Consumers find large assortments attractive for their process-related benefits of stimulation, choice freedom, and informative value and for their choice-related benefits of higher ideal product availability, ability to satisfy multiple needs in a single location, potential for variety-seeking, and flexibility for uncertain future preferences. However, the freedom and flexibility offered by assortments was shown to often backfire on consumers when then subsequently encounter difficulty choosing a product from within this assortment. Large relative to small assortments are associated with higher cognitive loads, difficult trade-offs, small differences in relative option attractiveness, and more foregone options upon choice. Consequently, large assortments were shown to lead to a greater incidence of failure to obtain the best product, dissatisfaction with the choice process and chosen product, higher regret with the chosen product, and a higher likelihood of choice avoidant behavior.

A key question is to what extent consumers recognize the downsides of large assortments for later choice. Even when product choice was made salient, the majority of subjects were shown to still be drawn to larger relative to smaller assortments (Chernev, 2006). The multi-dimensional nature of consumer assortment perceptions indicate that consumers have some implicit recognition of the dual tension between the attractiveness of assortments and subsequent difficulty of choosing a product from within the assortment. The cognitive dimension of assortment perceptions appears to capture the attractiveness of assortments being positively related to the number of unique options and size of assortment display. The affective dimension of consumer assortment perceptions appears to recognize the difficulty of choosing from large assortments being positively related to ease of shopping, ease of locating a favorite product, and congruency with shopping goals.

The pinnacle of assortment research is discovering how marketers can keep the gain and reduce the pain associated with choosing from large assortments. Research on consumer assortment perceptions suggests that product sets that are selectively comprised of favorite and unique products and appropriately organized and displayed can lead a choice set containing fewer products to be perceived as offering greater assortment than another choice set containing more products and simultaneously facilitate consumer choice.

Limiting the number of products though may prove difficult in product categories where consumer preferences are heterogeneous. In such cases, retailers should be cognizant that increasing product sets by adding options differentiated on nonalignable and complementary attributes will prove particularly taxing for consumer choice and may lead to lower choice incidence, particularly for consumers with ill-defined preferences and maximizer tendencies. Choosing from large assortments was shown to be easier if the assortments were differentiated on alignable or noncomplementary attributes and consumers possessed well-developed preferences or were willing to satisfice their product choice.

Research Challenges

Designing experiments to compare the effect of a small versus large number of product options would appear to be a straightforward task. However, there are a number of complexities that an assortment researcher needs to appreciate. First, one needs to determine the number of options that constitutes a small versus large assortment. As evidence suggests that having 10 or more options alters the complexity of the choice task (Maholtra, 1982), one might argue that 10 or more options constitutes a large assortment. Yet, by today's marketplace standards, ten options is a small choice set. Moreover, such an argument assumes that there is a threshold above which assortments become difficult to process without any further effects of additional increases in the number of options. That is, it assumes no difference between 10 versus 100 options. A serious limitation of assortment research is that much of it has been conducted comparing only two levels of option size. Future assortment research should consider manipulating at least three option size levels to rule out calibration issues and to test for non-linear effects.

A second challenge for assortment research is determining the composition of options within small versus large assortments. A researcher interested in isolating the effect of assortment size on a dependent variable of interest would need to control for or equate the option sets on a host of variables in order to rule out alternative explanations. The option sets would need to be equated on number of attributes, number of unique attributes, number of attribute levels, dispersion of attribute levels, and type of attribute differentiation. Additionally, the options sets would need to be equated in terms of attractiveness of options, trade-off difficulty, and relative difference in attractiveness between options. Quite a challenge! Other researchers may feel that assortment is interesting because of its natural correlation with many of these factors (i.e., large assortments offer more attributes and attribute levels) and prefer testing with higher ecological and lower internal validity. These researchers may determine the composition of the smaller option set by including only the most attractive options or by randomly drawing subsets of the options from the large option set to increase generalizability.

A third challenge of assortment research is the potential for option size to bias or impede hypothesis testing. As was demonstrated in the information overload debate, option size biased testing of choice accuracy, as the chance probability of selecting the best brand was higher for a smaller compared to large assortment. Therefore, an appropriate measure of choice accuracy is conditionalized on set size. Option size may also impede the testing of satisfaction as a dependent variable. Satisfaction is based on the difference between performance outcomes and expectations. But one can only equate outcomes for options that are common to both small and large assortments. If a subject is less satisfied with an option that is unique to the large assortment set, one will be uncertain whether this is due to the product performing poorly (outcome-driven) or because of high expectations.

Research Opportunities

Numerous assortment topics are avenues for future research. Decision aids that provide tools to help consumers with ill-defined preferences navigate the selection of product options from broad assortments would appear to be a commonsense intervention. But nascent research on filters and recommendations suggest that decision aids may be a double-edged sword. Morales et al. (2005) show that on-line mechanisms that filter the assortment do decrease consumer confusion and facilitate choice, but do so at the expense of lower assortment perceptions. Goodman, Broniarczyk, Griffin, and McAlister (2007) found that recommendation signage had the unexpected downside of heightening rather than alleviating the negative affect consumers experience during choice. As the number of product options increased, the likelihood that the recommendation was associated with a consumer's initial product inclination decreased, and the consumer now faced greater conflict trying to decide which one to buy.

Other decision aids may have similar unintended negative consequences. For instance, providing consumers with descriptions of product options to help determine the product that best meets their needs is likely to further contribute to cognitive overload. Additionally, product descriptions may cause a higher sense of attachment to foregone alternatives, thereby leading to a higher sense of loss and discomfort following product choice (Carmon et al., 2003). Additional research is warranted to identify decision aids that assist consumers through the complexity of choosing among a large number of options yet maintain high consumer perceptions of assortment.

Future research should also examine the generalizability and boundary conditions of extant assortment findings. Much of the assortment research to date has used hedonic product categories where consumers are likely to be promotion-focused and attracted to assortments. Limited research has examined the effect of assortment for prevention-focus choices such as medical and financial decision making. Botti and Iyengar (2006) suggest that for emotion-laden decisions among negative options (e.g., choosing the best cancer treatment), consumers are repelled, not attracted, by choice. They recommend the inclusion of a default option and option to delegate choice to assist consumers making prevention-focused choices.

Lastly, research examining the greater societal effects of vast assortments is a promising avenue for future research. Kahn and Wansink's (2004) result that perceived assortment is positively related to consumption quantity has far-reaching consequences for obesity, compulsive buying, and consumer debt. The intriguing effects of assortment on consumer future decision-making orientations and well-being are relatively untested and remain a fruitful area for inquiry and empirical validation.

CONCLUSION

Large assortments offer consumers numerous benefits, rendering them initially attractive, but ultimately causing a multitude of negative decision-making consequences when consumers face the daunting task of selecting a product from a vast array of options. Consumer research has only recently begun to examine the moderating factors and the extent of implications of product assortments. The challenge for consumer researchers is to decide which of the many worthwhile future assortment directions to pursue first.

ACKNOWLEDGMENTS

The helpful comments of Alex Chernev, Adam Duhachek, Joe Goodman, Jill Griffin, and Wayne Hoyer are greatly appreciated.

NOTES

1. The product dissimilarity model of Hoch et al. (1999) and the attribute based model of Van Herpen and Pieters (2002) have been shown to be mathematically similar if assortment size is accounted for (Hoch, Bradlow, & Wansink, 2002).

REFERENCES

Anderson, C. J. (2003). The psychology of doing nothing: Forms of decision avoidance result from reason and emotion. *Psychological Bulletin, 129*(1), 139–167.

Arnold, S. J., Oum, T. H. & Tigert, D. J. (1983). Determining attributes in retail patronage: Seasonal, yemporal, regional, and international comparisons. *Journal of Marketing Research*, 20(May), 149–157.

Babin, B. J., Darden, W. R., & Griffin, M. (1994). Work and/or fun: Measuring hedonic and utilitarian shopping value. *Journal of Consumer Research*, 20(March), 644–656.

Baumeister, R., & Vohs, K. (2003). Willpower, choice, and self-control In G. Loewenstein, D. Read, & R. Baumeister (Eds.), *Time and decision: Economic and psychological perspectives on intertemporal choice* (pp. 201–216). New York: Russell Sage Foundation,.

Baumol, W. J., & Ide, E. A. (1956). Variety in retailing. *Management Science, 3*(1), 93–101.

Berlyne, D. E. (1960). *Conflict, arousal, and curiosity.* New York: McGraw Hill.

Boatwright, P., & Nunes., J. C. (2001). Reducing assortment: An attribute-based approach. *Journal of Marketing, 65*(July), 50–63.

Boatwright, P., & Nunes, J. C. (2004). Correction to "Reducing assortment: An attribute-based approach," *Journal of Marketing, 68*(July), iv.

Botti, S., & Iyengar, S. S. (2004). The psychological pleasure and pain of choosing: when people prefer choosing at the cost of subsequent outcome satisfaction. *Journal of Personality and Social Psychology, 87*(3), 312–326.

Botti, S., & Iyengar, S. S. (2006). The dark side of choice: When choice impairs social welfare. *Journal of Public Policy and Marketing*, 25(Spring 2006), 24–38.

Broniarczyk, S., Hoyer, W. D., & McAlister, L. (1998). Consumers' perceptions of the assortment offered in a grocery category: The impact of item reduction. *Journal of Marketing Research*, 35(May), 166–176

Carmon, Z., Wertenbroch, K., & Zeelenberg, M. (2003). Option attachment: When deliberating makes choosing feel like losing. *Journal of Consumer Research*, 30(June), 15–29.

Chernev, A. (2003a). Product assortment and individual decision processes. *Journal of Personality and Social Psychology*, 85(July), 151–162.

Chernev, A. (2003b). When more is less and less is more: The role of ideal point availability and assortment in consumer choice. *Journal of Consumer Research*, 30(September), 170–183.

Chernev, A. (2005). Feature complementarity and assortment in choice. *Journal of Consumer Research*, 31(March), 748–759.

Chernev, A. (2006). Decision focus and consumer choice among assortments. *Journal of Consumer Research*, 33(June), 50–59.

Deci, E. L. (1981). *The psychology of self determination*. Lexington, MA: Heath.

Dhar, Ravi (1997). Consumer preference for a no-choice option. *Journal of Consumer Research*, 24(September), 215–231.

Dhar, R., & Nowlis, S. M. (1999. The effect of yime pressure on consumer choice deferral. *Journal of Consumer Research*, 25(March), 369–384.

Goodman, J. K., Broniarczyk, S. M., Griffin, J. G., & McAlister, L. (2007). Simplify or Intensify? The effect of best seller signage on consumer decision-making from large product assortments. Working paper, McCombs School of Business, The University of Texas at Austin.

Gourville, J., & Soman, D. (2005). Overchoice and assortment type: When and why variety backfires. *Marketing Science*, 24(Summer), 382–395.

Greenleaf, E. A., & Lehmann, D. R. (1995). Reasons for substantial delay in consumer decision making. *Journal of Consumer Research*, 22(September), 186–199.

Griffin, J. G., & Broniarczyk, S. M. (2007). The slippery slope: The impact of feature alignability on search and satisfaction. Working paper, McCombs School of Business, The University of Texas at Austin.

Hoch, S., Bradlow, E. T., & Wansink, B. (1999). The variety of an assortment. *Marketing Science*, 18(4), 527–546.

Hoch, S., Bradlow, E. T., & Wansink, B. (2002). Rejoinder to "The Variety of an Assortment: An Extension to the Attribute-Based Approach." *Marketing Science*, 21(3), 342–346.

Hoyer, W. D. (1984). An examination of consumer decision making for a common repeat purchase product. *Journal of Consumer Research*, 11(December), 822–829.

Huffman, C., & Kahn, B. E. (1998). Variety for sale: Mass customization or mass confusion. *Journal of Retailing*, 74(Winter), 491–513.

Inman, J. J. (2001). The role of sensory-specific satiety in attribute-level variety seeking. *Journal of Consumer Research*, 28, 105–120.

Inman, J. J., & Zeelenberg, M. (2002). Regret in repeat purchase versus switching decisions: The attenuating role of decision justifiability. *Journal of Consumer Research*, 29(June), 116–128.

Iyengar, S. S., & Lepper, M. R. (2000). When choice is demotivating: Can one desire too much of a good thing? *Journal of Personality and Social Psychology*, 79(December), 995–1006.

Iyengar, S. S. Iyengar, M. R., Wells, R. E., & Schwartz, B. (2006). Doing better but feeling worse: Looking for the "Best" job undermines satisfaction. *Psychological Science*, 17(February), 143–150.

Iyengar, S. S., Jiang, W., & Huberman, G. (2004). How much choice is too much: Determinants of individual contribution in 401K retirement plans. In O. S. Mitchell & S. Utkus (Eds.), *Pension design and structure: New lessons from behavioral finance* (pp. 83–97). Oxford: Oxford University Press.

Jacoby, J., Speller, D. E., & Kohn, C. A. (1974). Brand choice behavior as a function of information load. *Journal of Marketing Research*, 11(February), 63–69.

Jacoby, J. (1977). Information load and decision quality: Some contested issues. *Journal of Marketing Research*, 14(November), 569–573.

Kahn, B. E., & Lehmann, D. R. (1991). Modeling choice among assortments. *Journal of Retailing*, 67(Fall), 274–299.

Kahn, B. E., & Wansink, B. (2004). Assortment structure on perceived variety. *Journal of Consumer Research*, 30(March), 519–533.

Keller, K. L., & Staelin, R. (1987). Effects of quality and quantity of information on decision effectiveness. *Journal of Consumer Research, 14*(September), 200–213.

Kreps, D. M. (1979). A representation theorem for preference for flexibility. *Econometrica, 47*(May), 565–577.

Langer, E. J., & Rodin, J. (1976). The effects of choice and enhanced personal responsibility for the aged: A field experiment in an institutional setting. *Journal of Personality and Social Psychology, 34*(2), 191–198.

Lehmann, D. R. (1998). Consumer reactions to variety: Too much of a good yhing? *Journal of the Academy of Marketing Science, 26*(1), 62–65.

Levy, M., & Weitz, B. A. (2001). *Retailing management* (4th ed.). Boston: Irwin/McGraw Hill.

Loewenstein, G. (1987). Anticipation and the valuation of delayed consumption. *The Economic Journal, 97*(September), 666–684.

Luce, M. F. (1998). Choosing to avoid: Coping with negatively emotion-laden consumer decisions. *Journal of Consumer Research, 24*(March), 409–433.

Lurie, N. H. (2004). Decision making in information-rich environments: The role of information structure. *Journal of Consumer Research, 30*(March), 473–486.

Malholtra, N. K. (1982). Information load and consumer decision making. *Journal of Consumer Research, 8*(March), 419–430.

March, J. G. (1978). Bounded Rationality, Ambiguity, and the Engineering of Choice. *Bell Journal of Economics, 9*(2), 587–608.

Markman, A. B., & Medin, D. L. (1995). Similarity and alignment in choice. *Organization Behavior and Human Decision Processes, 63*(2), 117–130.

McAlister, L. (1982). A dynamic attribute satiation model of variety-seeking behavior. *Journal of Consumer Research, 9*(September), 141–150.

McAlister, L., & Pessemier, E. (1982). Variety-seeking behavior: An interdisciplinary review. *Journal of Consumer Research, 9*(December), 311–322.

Mick, D. G., Broniarczyk, S. M., & Haidt, J. (2004). Choose, choose, choose, choose, choose, choose, choose: Emerging and prospective research on the deleterious effects of living in consumer hyperxhoice. *Journal of Business Ethics, 52*, 207–211.

Morales, A., Kahn, B. E., McAlister, L., & Broniarczyk, S. M. (2005). Perceptions of assortment variety: The effects of congruency between consumers' internal and retailers' external organization. *Journal of Retailing, 81*(2), 159–169.

Morrin, M., Inman, J., & Broniarczyk, S. (2007). Decomposing the 1/n heuristic: The moderating effects of fund assortment size. Working paper, Marketing Department, Rutgers University at Camden.

Mottola, G. R., & Utkus, S. P. (2003). Can there be too much choice in a retirement savings plan. The Vanguard Center for Retirement Research, June 2003.

Oliver, R, L. (1993). Cognitive, affective, and attribute bases of the satisfaction response. *Journal of Consumer Research, 20*(December), 418–430.

Payne, J. W. (1976). Task complexity and contingent processing in decision making: An information search and protocol analysis. *Organizational Behavior and Human Performance, 16*, 366–387.

Payne, J. W., Bettman, J. R., & Johnson, E. J. (1993). *The adaptive decision maker,* New York: Cambridge University Press.

Prelec, D., Wernerfelt, B., & Zettelmeyer, F. (1997). The role of inference in context effects: Inferring what you want from what is available. *Journal of Consumer Research, 24*(June), 118–125.

Read, D., & Loewenstein, G. (1995). Diversification bias: Explaining the discrepancy in variety seeking between combined and separate choices. *Journal of Experimental Psychology: Applied,* 1(March), 34–49.

Reibstein, D. J., Youngblood, S. A., & Fromkin, H. L (1975). Number of choices and perceived decision freedom as a determinant of satisfaction and consumer behavior. *Journal of Applied Psychology, 60*(4), 434–437.

Rolls, B. J., Rowe, E. A.. Rolls, E. T., Kindston, B., Megson, A., & Gunary, R. (1981). Variety in a meal enhances food intake in man. *Physiology and Behavior, 26*(February), 215–221.

Salganik, M. W. (2004). Too many choices? *The Baltimore Sun,* June 27.

Schwartz, B. (2004). *The paradox of choice.* New York: Harper Collins.

Schwartz, B. (2000). Self-determination: The tyranny of Freedom. *American Psychologist, 55*(January), 79–88.

Schwartz, B., Ward, A., Monterosso, J., Lyubomirsky, S., White, K. & Lehman, D. R. (2002). Maximizing versus satisficing: Happiness is a matter of choice. *Journal of Personality and Social Psychology, 83*(November), 1178–1197.

Shannon, C. E. (1949). The mathematical theory of communication. In C. E. Shannon & W. Weaver (Eds.), *The mathematical theory of communication* (29–125), Urbana: University of Illinois Press.

Shugan, S. M. (1980). The cost of thinking. *Journal of Consumer Research, 7*(September), 99–111.

Simon, H. A. (1956). Rational choice and the structure of the environment. *Psychological Review, 63,* 129–138.

Simonson, I. (1990). The effect of purchase quantity and timing on variety seeking behavior. *Journal of Marketing Research, 27*(May), 150–162.

Simonson, I. (1992). The influence of anticipating regret and responsibility on purchase decisions. *Journal of Consumer Research, 19*(June), 1–14.

Summers, J. O. (1974). Less information is better? *Journal of Marketing Research, 11*(November), 467–468.

Taylor, S. E., & Brown, J. D. (1988). Illusion and well-being: A social-psychological perspective on mental health. *Psychological Bulletin, 103,* 193–210.

Tsiros, M., & Mittal, V. (2000). Regret: A model of its antecedents and consequences in consumer decision making. *Journal of Consumer Research, 26*(March), 401–417.

Van Herpen, E., & Pieters, R. (2002). The variety of an assortment: An extension to the attribute-based approach. *Marketing Science, 21*(3), 331–341.

Van Trijp, H., Wayne, C. M, Hoyer, D, & Inman, J. J. (1996). Why switch? Product category-level explanations for true variety-seeking behavior. *Journal of Marketing Research, 33*(August), 281–292.

Webster's New Collegiate Dictionary (2003). (11th ed.). Springfield, MA: Merriam-Webster.

Wilkie, W. L. (1974). Analysis of effects of information load. *Journal of Marketing Research, 11*(November), 462–466.

31

Brands and Their Meaning Makers

CHRIS T. ALLEN

University of Cincinnati

SUSAN FOURNIER

Boston University

FELICIA MILLER

Marquette University

INTRODUCTION

Just 25 years have passed since the publication of seminal works on the strategic power of the brand, yet, in this short time, branding has attained noted disciplinary status. Although only a handful of branding books were available a mere 15 years ago, and branding textbooks had yet been written, those interested in branding today can consult hundreds of books and articles, attend numerous conferences dedicated to building and leveraging brand assets, and hire a range of consultancies dedicated to specialized branding concerns. In the marketing academy, branding issues dominate the list of research priorities (Marketing Science Institute 2002, 2004), with particular attention to managerially directed topics including brand equity measurement, brand accountability, brand leverage and architecture, and internal branding. As recognition of the strategic value of branding has increased, the scope of application of branding insights has expanded in kind. Branding has extended beyond consumer goods and services to include business-to-business domains (Webster Jr. & Keller, 2004), countries (van Ham, 2001), and people (Schroeder, 2005a). Inside the firm, Chief Branding Officers have emerged, granting marketing a coveted boardroom voice (Davis & Dunn, 2002). With intangible assets now accounting, on average, for 75% of the value that investors place in firms (Knowles, 2003), we have entered what may be called the Golden Age of Brands.

Consumer psychologists have made significant contributions in shaping an interpretation of brands (e.g., Keller, 2003; Keller & Lehmann, 2005). Branding topics have been featured in a significant number of award-winning articles published in the *Journal of Marketing, Journal of Consumer Research*, and *Journal of Marketing Research* by consumer researchers: strategic brand management (Park, Jaworski, & MacInnis, 1986), brand knowledge (Keller, 1993), brand processing cues (Van Osselaer & Alba, 2000), and brand equity measurement (Ailawadi, Neslin, & Lehmann, 2003; Dillon et al., 2001) are exemplars. Moreover, these contributions have carried over to the practice of brand management. It is probably safe to say that no area of study in consumer psychology is more intertwined with management practice than branding.

But we are now also seeing indications that our understanding of brand is incomplete and sometimes even misaligned with revealed realities of the brand as experienced in today's consumer, corporate, and cultural worlds. By all counts, we are living in a different branding world than that operating in the heyday of mass marketing when the discipline was founded. As Stephen Brown (2006) notes, we have evolved to an intensely commercial world where TV shows feature stories about marketing and consumer psychology, stand-up comics perform skits about shopping routines and brand strategies, and mainstream magazines deconstruct retail redesigns and the persuasive intent of new advertising campaigns. Technology has intervened with capabilities for customization, addressability, and interactivity to create brand marketing opportunities and complexities never before imagined. In part enabled by these technologies, the marketplace has radically shifted its power base to consumers, where co-optation of brands is the norm. Marketing has also undergone a revolution wherein the paradigms of advertising and entertainment are increasingly merged, and mechanisms like coolhunting, buzz, and blogs are replacing mass media advertising as potent tools for building brands. Brands themselves have evolved to a new cultural platform where they serve not just as simplifying heuristics or risk reduction mechanisms for individual decision makers, but as sociopolitical ideology statements (O'Guinn & Muñiz, 2004). This same fusion of forces led Keller and Lehmann (2005) to conclude recently that "brand equity is increasingly built by activities outside the company's direct control" (p. 27).

Our branding theories need to probe the operation and implications of this new marketplace reality. As Keller (2003) concluded in his review: "The challenge and opportunity for consumer research…is fully appreciating the broad scope and complexity involved" (p. 599). Holt's (2005) critique is more pointed: "Psychological theories of branding have an Achilles heel they can no longer ignore." Lacking a proactive approach for accommodating this scope and complexity, where once consumer psychologists led the discussion of what brands mean to consumers, we now are in danger of falling behind.

If a brand is first and foremost a repository of meanings for consumers to use in living their own lives (Fournier, 1998; McCracken, 1986), then today's challenge is to understand more deeply the multiple sources and dynamic nature of that meaning. The goal for this chapter is to bring more of the complexity of the co-created experience of brands into our theories and research. In the sections below, we discuss three meaning makers that need to be considered for a full understanding of brands. The first two of these—cultures and consumers—are underrepresented in mainstream branding research. The third brand author is the familiar one: corporations that market brands. But even here our research fails in its accommodation of the new marketing models being leveraged to build strong brands. Our intent is to raise issues that will foster new theorizing to guide scholars in supplementing prevailing conceptions of branding and brands.

The chapter is organized as follows. First, we review briefly the dominant conception of branding in consumer psychology. We then provide an overview of an alternative paradigm that is often associated with interpretivist research. This alternative paradigm features the assumption that brands are repositories for meaning, and that brand meaning is effectively co-created by numerous and sometimes competing sources. After reviewing the relevant literatures on cultures and consumers as brand meaning co-creators, and discussing related implications for branding research, we then consider how trends in contemporary marketing practice also present new challenges for consumer psychologists with respect to our brand theories and research. The chapter concludes with a discussion of opportunities suggested by a synthesis of the traditional and alternative branding views.

THE RECEIVED VIEW

Over the past two decades a particular view of branding has coalesced. Core tenets and assumptions of this dominant perspective, as manifest in major U.S. journal articles, branding textbooks, and business books (cf. Aaker, 1991; 1996; Keller, 1993; 2003; Park, Jaworski, & MacInnis, 1986) can readily be articulated. These tenets are important and foundational as they have explicitly and implicitly shaped the course of mainstream brand theory and research.

The received view on branding is squarely grounded in the disciplines of psychology and information economics, and draws heavily upon the information processing theories of consumer behavior that were popular during the field's formative stages (Anderson, 1983). Within this frame, the brand holds ontological status expressly as a cognitive construal: the brand exists *in the mind of the consumer* (Ries & Trout, 2001) as a *knowledge structure* of brand-relevant *information* (Keller, 2003). The brand's semantic memory network contains a set of nodes of various levels of abstraction and links of varying strength, including: brand and product attributes and benefits; brand beliefs, judgments, attitudes, and perceptions; feelings and emotions; sensory images, and personal experiences connecting the consumer to the brand (Keller, 1993; 2003). Brand knowledge, retrieved through spreading activation (Loftus & Loftus, 1976), serves as a risk-reducing heuristic for the consumer: strong brands reduce ego risks, risks of making poor decisions, risks of wasting time (Maheswaran, Mackie, & Chaiken, 1992). Brand knowledge is assumed shared by all members of the target audience such that there exists one collectively held meaning for the brand.

Within both the information-economics and consumer psychology perspectives, managers are granted direction over brand image creation such that the shared knowledge that comes to reside in consumers' minds is the *intended* meaning for the brand. Brand positioning theory helps the manager select specific associations for emphasis in the knowledge web. The brand's associative web is assumed to be decompositional such that individual brand associations like perceived quality or connection to a particular celebrity endorser can be fruitfully highlighted and stressed. Positioning platforms are framed in the context of competitive product entries; uniqueness of a given brand association versus competition—the brand's points of difference—is cherished over all else (Aaker & Shansby, 1982; Keller, 1993; 2003; Keller, Sternthal, & Tybout, 2002; Ries & Trout, 2001). Tenets of simplicity, congruity, consistency, and coherence are encouraged when articulating the unique selling proposition (Reeves, 1961) or mantra (Keller, 1993; Keller, Sternthal, et al., 2002) for the brand. A preference exists for single-minded benefits or values assumed to remain stable and constant over time (Aaker, 1996).

The added value with which a brand is endowed—i.e., its brand equity—is then a direct result of these and other past marketing activities (Keller, 2001; Park et al., 1986). Successful implementation of the marketing program is gauged using metrics relevant to the psychological paradigm, most of which provide dimensions for distinguishing the strength and favorability of brand knowledge: brand awareness (strength of the brand trace in memory), brand beliefs (strength of a particular brand-attribute trace), accessibility and dominance of chosen attribute associations (salience of a particular attribute), clarity of brand perceptions (congruity among or shared content across brand associations), and the favorability and resistance of brand attitudes (valence and strength of attribute-based summary judgments of the brand) (Farquhar, Han, Herr, & Ijiri, 1992; Keller, 1993). A simple logic links brand knowledge selection to brand strength creation and, ultimately, to the capture of financial value in the brand (Hoeffler & Keller, 2003; Keller & Lehmann, 2005). The brand, as a company-owned and controlled asset, is thus built and leveraged for the creation and capture of incremental value to shareholders.

While the information-based conception of the brand, with its attendant focus on the creation and judicious management of brand equity, has been fruitfully applied in theory and research, it nonetheless represents only one perspective on the nature of brands and the process of branding. The distinction between *information* and *meaning* sheds light here (McCracken, 2005). Information concerns the disintegration and reduction of the complex into small, manageable bits, as per associative models that focus on decomposed, isolated, and product-centric attributes. Meaning, on the other hand, concerns the assembly of small bites into larger, more complex, and more abstract wholes; to derive meaning is to make larger sense out of many smaller units. An interesting paradox presents itself: in the search for meaning, context is everything; in the search for information, context is noise. Information and meaning thus work at cross purposes, such that a quest to maximize an information-based view will by definition compromise the quest for meaning. Anthropologist Clifford Geertz argues forcefully for the primacy of meaning over information in theory construction: "Explanation does not consist in the reduction of the complex to the simple. Rather it consists in a substitution of a complexity more intelligible for one which is less. Seek complexity and order it" (Geertz, 1973).

Knowledge-based conceptions of brand obscure the distinction between information and meaning: "brand associations are the information nodes linked to the brand node in memory and contain the meaning of the brand for consumers" (Keller, 1993, p. 3). Still, the conception of brand as information, and of brand managers as brand knowledge managers, dominates current thought (e.g., Keller, 2003; Keller & Lehmann, 2005). A concrete alternative is to focus not on the management of brand information by brand managers, but on the processes of brand meaning making that take place in the consumption world. This change in focus can provide many new directions for addressing the complexity that is part of today's branding landscape.

BRAND MEANING MAKING: AN ALTERNATIVE VIEW

A meaning-based view of branding is not new. Versions have been circulating in what is sometimes referred to as postmodern or interpretivist consumer research for many years, beginning with Belk's (1988) foundational article on possessions and the extended self and Hirschman and Holbrook's (1982) essay on symbolic consumer experiences. While consumer researchers working in the alternative paradigm operated with a plurality of theoretical and methodological approaches, these researchers converged on several foundational axioms and insights concerning consumer behavior and, accordingly, guiding tenets for brand-related consumer research. The paradigm shift at play favored attention to the under-explored and powerful experiential and symbolic aspects of consumption: the meanings that people value in real life. Consumer products were re-cast from simplifying informational vehicles to meaning-rich tools for personal and social identity construction. Consumers were re-conceptualized as active meaning makers rather than passive recipients of marketing products and communications. Founding interpretivists emphasized the need for consumer researchers to go beyond the study of individual consumers to consideration of consumers operating in cultures and social collectives. They embraced complexity, fragmentation, plurality, mutability, and the heterogeneous distribution of meanings in the marketplace. They favored tools, methods, and theoretical frameworks from anthropology, sociology, literature, history, gender and culture studies: sources capable of providing the complex socio-cultural contexts that were now considered critical in the assignment of meaning to consumption acts. Arnould and Thompson (2005) provide an extensive review of the knowledge produced through the stream of research they label as Consumer Culture Theory (CCT), much of which is relevant here.

Most early studies in this tradition were conducted in the broad context of products, not brands, as motivated by concerns about the ideology of materialism central to contemporary America at the time. Extensions to the branded world were soon revealed as legitimate and natural, and a thriving research tradition was spawned. Extended theoretical treatments of "cultural branding" are now beginning to appear (Holt, 2004; McCracken, 2005; Schroeder & Salzer-Mörling, 2006) such that the tenets of an alternative branding paradigm can be put forth.

At the heart of this emergent perspective on branding is the concept of co-creation. Co-creation has its roots in hermeneutic philosophy, which was applied in much early interpretivist research (Thompson, Pollio, & Locander, 1994). A foundational idea in hermeneutic philosophy is the hermeneutic circle, which, in the social science literature, concerns a general model for the process by which meaning is derived and understanding formed. This model contends that a person's understanding of a concept reflects broader (shared) cultural viewpoints, as interpreted through the lens of the individual's (unique) life experiences. Put differently, each person is the author of his/her own understandings, with the texts of these personal meanings written in culturally given terms (Gergen, 1990).

Refinements to this basic framework were introduced by McCracken (1986) in his model for the movement of meanings into consumer goods (see Figure 31.1). Culture is represented as the original source and location of the general categories of meanings from which brands ultimately draw. These categories represent fundamental coordinates of meanings: the basic distinctions that a culture uses to divide up and make sense of the phenomenal world. A central assumption of McCracken's model, and the anthropological theories that inform it (e.g., Douglas & Isherwood, 1978), is that shared understandings develop within a particular cultural meaning-making group concerning the major categories through which meaning is ascribed.

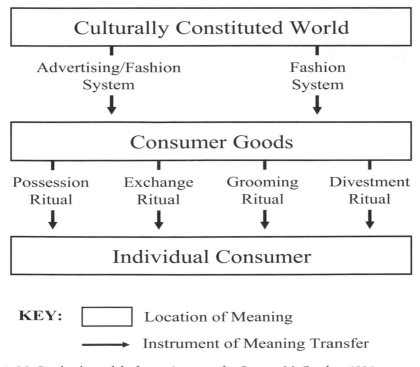

Figure 31.1 McCracken's model of meaning transfer. Source: McCracken 1986.

McCracken's model expressly considered the mechanisms through which shared cultural meanings were captured for and transferred to the product or brand. Two primary meaning making institutions or delivery mechanisms were offered. The first was the firm, whose marketing departments and creative directors create and capture brand meanings through the 4Ps (e.g., design of the product aesthetic, distribution, promotion, and price) and other marketing communications devices (e.g., public relations, product placements, sponsorships, endorsements). The second mechanism for the movement of meaning into the product/ brand lay outside the firm's control and concerned broad cultural production systems such as the mass media, the movie industry, writers and journalists, design agents in the fashion system, social critics, trend-setting opinion leaders, rebellious members of fringe social groups, and general historical events. Thus we obtain two brand authors within the cultural system of meaning co-creation: (1) the firm and (2) the broader cultural production systems that create, clarify, and sort these meanings over time. Subsequent research (Kozinets, 2001; Solomon, 1988a; Thompson & Haytko, 1997) reiterates the power and influence of these brand meaning makers.

McCracken's (1986) model specified a second system of meaning transfer whereby the culturally shared meanings resident in products and brands moved into the life of the consumer. *Consumer co-creation* concerned the adaptation of culturally shared meanings to the person's unique circumstance for purposes of individual communication and categorization. Reader response theory in the literature studies discipline emphasized a similar principle: the meanings derived from a given text depend upon the circumstances of the individual charged with making sense of that text (Mick & Buhl, 1992; Scott, 1994). A poignant example of the processes through which consumers adapted brand meanings to their individual life circumstances concerned product customization rituals through which people redefined consumption goods to make them uniquely their own (Schouten & McAlexander, 1995).

McCracken's model thus implied that the brand in essence possessed two distinct meanings. First was the shared meaning created through marketing systems and cultural traditions; second was the more personalized meaning constructed by the individual. Richins' (1994) concept of public (shared cultural) versus private (individual) meanings for possessions is also of relevance here. Exploratory research has suggested that the proportion of brand meaning that is widely shared may be as low as 50% (Hirschman 1981), with higher percentages contingent upon the interpreter's membership in a refined meaning-making community (Belk, Meyer, & Bahn, 1982; Belk, 1978). Elliott (1994) found that brands meant different things to different people, with shared meanings differing between genders and age groups; Holt (1998) revealed significant meaning distinctions across social capital (class) groups. The observation that localized interpretations of a brand varied greatly across social contexts and categories was also supported by Thompson and Haytko (1997). Still, the individual's reading of the brand was considered to be "bounded" (Hirschman, 1998). Although consumers exhibited a wide range of consumption meanings and practices, these were structured by general cultural and institutional forces such as the individual's own socio-demographic situation, and the articulations of sub-cultural members involved with the brand (Kozinets, 2001).

That consumers could interpret products differently, add localized meanings to them, and sometimes even redirect them from their original intentions derived from the postmodern realization that "products are only arbitrarily linked to their original functions and thus are infinitely open to diversion through the ordinary experiences of everyday life" (Cova, 1996, p. 18). In this sense, the product and brand meaning space was presented as "contestable terrain that consumers rework(ed) in terms of their localized knowledge and value systems" (Thompson & Haytko, 1997, p. 38). Culture provided meaning making *resources* for the consumer to use in definition and orientation, not a *blueprint* for the same (Holt, 2002).

Others have expanded upon McCracken's model by recognizing the reciprocating effects that consumer co-creation could have on the cultural meanings of products and brands (Fournier, 1998; Holt, 2002; Kozinets, 2001; Thompson & Haytko, 1997). While McCracken's model emphasized a one-directional flow of meanings from the culturally constituted product or brand to the consumer, these researchers emphasized that the interpretive activities of individual consumers could actually affect, shape, and reshape the cultural meanings of products and brands. Through social discourse, consumers reconfigured sponsored advertising messages for brands (Ritson & Elliott, 1999). Consumers even twisted brand meanings, diverting them in unintended directions and resignifying them in surprising ways (Firat & Venkatesh, 1995; Holt, 2002; Kozinets & Handelman, 2004; Thompson & Haytko, 1997). Shove and Pantzar (2005) note that what looks from the outside like the diffusion of a particular innovation is actually a sequential process of creative re-invention on the part of thousands of ordinary people involved in the meaning-making activity across time. This research stream supported a consumer-centric (vs. culture-driven) model for brand meaning making (Thompson & Haytko, 1997) and an expanded definition of the consumer as meaning maker that included this adaptation, manipulation, and revision of culturally shared meanings. Wipperfurth (2005), an advocate for the emergent paradigm, echoes this same conception: consumer co-creation happens when individuals enhance the original brand idea by creating new meanings, uses, or rituals for the brand/product and then translate that message to the mainstream. Through consumer co-creation, the individual becomes not only the author of his/her unique understandings, but also, through extension, a partial author of the brand.

Consumer co-creation figures prominently in contemporary marketing theory, where co-production has been offered as the cornerstone of a new dominant logic for marketing (Vargo & Lusch, 2004). Drawing from a services-marketing orientation (Gummesson, 1995), Vargo and Lusch emphasize the consumer's continuous and dynamic role in the use, maintenance, repair, and adaptation of products/services to his/her unique needs, usage situations, and behaviors. Vargo and Lusch call for proactive customer involvement in the design, production, marketing, and consumption of products and services, and a marketing function dedicated to doing things in interaction with consumers to create and capture more value from these collaborative roles. While different in its application and intention, co-creation as co-production calls for the same reconceptualization of the consumer that those in the interpretivist tradition support: namely, from consumer as operand resource (whereby consumers are acted upon to create transactions via marketing resources) to the consumer as operant resource (wherein the consumer is an active participant in relational exchanges and marketing co-productions). Participation also stands as a cornerstone of postmodern marketing theory (Brown, 2004; Cova, 1996; Salzer-Mörling & Strannegård, 2004). Within each of these theoretical paradigms, the concept of the participatory consumer rejects the notion of a static and constant brand in favor of one that is actively and dynamically renegotiated across both individuals and time.

Table 31.1 summarizes core tenets and axioms of the received versus emergent paradigms. In the alternative view, brands are conceived as socio-cultural creations shared in the marketplace, not psychological entities that exist solely in consumers' minds (O'Guinn & Muniz Jr., 2005). Ontologically, the emergent view accepts brands as dynamic, co-created entities, and brand meaning as neither inherent in the product nor constant across individuals, but rather derived from the "contexts" in which the brand "resides." As such, brands present themselves not as static, pre-formulated management construals—ideally guided with consistency tenets in mind—but as dynamic and actively co-created entities that evolve with consumers and cultures in kind. Multivocality in the brand voice is embraced and accepted in the emergent paradigm as consumers variously adapt and refine meanings as they fit brands into their lives.

Table 31.1   Central Tenets of the Received View vs. the Emergent Branding Paradigm

	Received View	Emergent Paradigm
Brands	Informational vehicles that support choice processes; Risk reduction tools and simplifying heuristics	Meaning rich tools that help people live their lives
Guiding Metaphor	Information	Meaning
Role of context in research	Context is noise	Context is everything
Central constructs of interest	Knowledge-based cognitions and attitudes	Experiential and symbolic aspects of consumption
Focal research domain	Purchase	Consumption
Guiding tenets	Simplification and control	Co-creation and complexity
Marketer's role	Owner and creator of brand assets	One of several brand meaning makers
Brand positioning assumptions	Consistency, constancy, simplicity	Complexity, mutability
Primary units of analysis	Individual consumers	Individuals, people in groups, consumers in cultures, cultural production mechanisms
Consumer's role	Passive recipient of marketer information	Active contributor to brand meaning making
Consumer's central activity	Realizing functional and emotional benefits	Meaning making

In this alternative paradigm the marketer stands as only one of many significant meaning makers, with consumers and broader cultural production systems playing notable and sometimes primary roles. Importantly, these are the sources and processes of brand meaning making that are generally overlooked by consumer psychologists in their models for managing brand equity. It is understandable that scholars trained in experimental design and theory falsification would not develop a natural appreciation for sociological and cultural matters such as these, but there can be no doubt that these disciplines are essential for developing a deep understanding of brands as symbolic creatures. In the sections to follow, we review academic literature and case histories pertinent to each of our three brand meaning makers. These are presented in order of their relative omission in classic theories of the brand: cultures, consumers, and the firm.

CULTURE AS A BRAND MEANING MAKER

Culture is one of the two …most complicated words in the English language.

Raymond Williams, 1983, p. 87

Williams doesn't tell us what the second most complicated word is, but brand may well be a contender.

Stephen Brown, 2006, p. 50

As Stephen Brown's (2006) recent essay emphasizes, "brand" and "culture" are both illusive terms, made even more complicated when one attempts to comprehend them together. Still, this section of our chapter aspires toward this rather grandiose goal: to make culture as it pertains to branding a bit more accessible and actionable for consumer psychologists. Our coverage of the question concerning what it means, exactly, when we say that "brands live in cultures" (Holt, 2004) is by necessity a selective treatment. For tractability, we also make artificial distinctions between what some would classify as "cultural forces" and what we later discuss as "consumer collaborators acting in groups." Indeed, in the natural setting, it may be ineffective to draw boundaries between cultures and consumers and companies in their co-creation activities for the brand. Qualifiers aside, we first reflect on some marketplace examples implicating the cultural context of the brand, to illuminate the "what" and "so what" of culture.

Harley-Davidson—a brand icon that stands unequivocally for rebellion, machismo, freedom, and America—provides a well-known case supporting our argument for culture as a dominant meaning maker for a brand. Culture's role in the making of Harley's meanings is perhaps most evident in the brand's status as the motorcycle of choice for the notorious Hell's Angels. These meaning makers did not constitute a target market for Harley-Davidson: in fact, there was a time when corporate strategies discouraged the attraction of this group. And yet, this community infused the brand with outlaw associations that derived from decades of highly visible brand consumption within the worlds of drugs, murder, and other illegal activities—associations that were more crude and real and authentic than anything corporate advertising could ever provide. Harley's outlaw meanings can be traced to an earlier cultural event, in what is now known as the 1957 Hollister riots. A pictorial essay in *Life* magazine revealed this shocking story of a band of drunken motorcyclists that rolled into an upstanding rural California town one weekend and literally took it over. The riot became the fodder for the cult film classic *The Wild One*, starring Hollywood's embodiment of raw masculinity, Marlon Brando. A notable scene from the film crystallizes the brand meaning making implications. Brando is drinking in the local bar; an innocent woman from the town circles him, fascinated by his presence. She reads Brando's jacket colors and asks: "Bay City Motorcycle Group Rebels…what are you rebelling against?" Brando's infamous response: "What've you got?" Through the ensuing decade, producers furthered the motorcycle-rebellion connection in countless movies concerning the dark underground, and through casting with quintessential rebels like James Dean.

As culture shifted and the counter-revolutionary 1960s took hold, Hollywood contributed a second round of meaning making through films like *The Escape* and *Easy Rider*. These iconic films added freedom and adventure to the rebellion base: freedom *from* the controlling "system" and freedom *to* pursue personal experiences and pleasures, however illegal these might be.

In 1985, culture intervened a third time to contribute core meanings for the brand as Harley-Davidson became the victim of a hostile takeover by the AMF Corporation. Here, culture provided the context in which to interpret this historical event. Harley had been taken over by a Japanese firm at a time when the press was peppered with confrontational stories of lazy Americans versus the inherently more efficient Japanese, and promises of the rise of Japan as the new world economic power. When Harley insiders leveraged a successful buy-back of their firm, even Richard Nixon celebrated the rescue of America's sole remaining motorcycle manufacturer from the clutches of "the enemy." More than any advertising campaign, these historical events and cultural circumstances defined the essence of the Harley-Davidson brand.

The $1.4 billion branding debacle involving Snapple offers another example of the ways that cultural meaning production systems define and ultimately govern the brand. In this case, management opted for a branding solution that unfortunately excised the brand from the cultural meaning making systems that give it life. Almost immediately upon acquisition of Snapple, Quaker jettisoned Howard Stern, Rush Limbaugh, and Long Island's own Wendy as uncontrollable, risky, irreconcilable spokespersons for the brand. Snapple's grassroots meaning-making partners in neighborhood Mom-and-Pop cold channels were exchanged for large format warm channel collaborators like Shaws that were capable of delivering growth for the brand. Quirky flavor variety was compromised as management sought more manageable expansion paths. Clearly, these marketing changes granted a "rationalized distribution network" for Snapple that made sense in the context of Quaker's successful acquisition of the Gatorade brand. But the strategy literally gutted the cultural meaning making mechanisms that had fueled Snapple's distinctive strength and value. Quaker management walked away from the brand's so-called secondary associations (Keller, 2005) and in the process negated the essence of their brand.

The Martha Stewart story similarly reinforces the power of cultural production mechanisms in dictating the fate of a brand (Fournier & Herman, 2005). After going public with Martha Stewart Living Omnimedia (MSLO) in 1999, the Stewart brand and person were propelled to a celebrity status that few brands can claim. "Martha Stewart" evolved to the more intimate "Martha," putting the person on par with other single-name celebrities like Madonna. An explosion of Martha Stewart copycats, made-for-TV movies, and unauthorized biographies further validated Stewart's iconic status. Parodies raged through email and chat rooms and received sanctioned commentary by respected gatekeepers on *60 Minutes*, CBS's *Sunday Morning* show, and *Saturday Night Live*. Stewart appeared in the public eye not simply as how-to presenter for MSLO but also as judge of the Miss America Beauty Pageant, host on public radio's *Car Talk*, and even trivia master on the *Jeopardy* game-show.

The meteoric rise of the Martha Stewart brand came to an abrupt halt in 2002 when Stewart was accused of illegal stock trading in her personal investment portfolio. An arduous 3 years in the media spotlight took their toll: advertising pages went down 55% in the flagship magazine, television shows were cancelled, staff in the television production unit was cut 65%, MSLO's Internet division was shut down. MSLO brand value declined 75% in the wake of the scandal that left Stewart convicted on four charges and sentenced to 6 months imprisonment and 6 months' house arrest.

Many contend that Stewart's conviction was as much an indictment against her gender and class as it was a judgment of legal rights or wrongs. It is difficult to argue that Stewart was not judged at least in part on the basis of the fundamental cultural categories defining her brand: a rich white woman made a mistake and that mistake landed her in jail. But "culture" damned Stewart in yet another way. This argument recognizes that the meanings of a celebrity are culturally constituted, and include in American society a ravenous appetite for the dark side, and sheer enjoyment in the predictable scandals that take celebrities at least temporarily out of play. Indeed, Stewart's attainment of celebrity brought with it the entry of a powerful player in the cultural brand meaning making game. These were the pundits who traded independently on Martha's currency: journalists and bloggers and biographers and television news critics whose job it was to dig up dirt on Martha, expose her weaknesses, and catch her in lies; in short, to find and sensationalize "breaks" in the managed image of the celebrity for profitable gain.

Stewart and MSLO never fully reckoned with these antagonistic meaning makers who transacted over the Martha Stewart brand equity for their own gain. They were ignored and sometimes publicly derided: "I don't have time for this C-R-A-P," Stewart said in a television interview on the subject of Oppenheimer's biography (*Larry King Live*, Sept 15, 2005). Attempts to quiet "uncontrolled" voices through political clout were even leveraged at times, as, for example, with attempts to halt publication of Byron's biography and a Harvard Business School case study of this nascent person-brand (Fournier et al., 2001). MSLO failed to realize that their brand meaning making process was socially negotiated—not only among creators and supporters, but also among those who profited from a critical view of the brand.

These diverse examples illustrate two important themes concerning cultures as brand meaning makers. First, per McCracken's (1986), is the overarching notion of culture as the original font from which all brand meanings flow. Second is the subject of cultural arbiters in the process of meaning making. Research relevant to these two themes is reviewed below.

CULTURE AS THE FOUNDATIONAL SOURCE OF BRAND MEANINGS

The case examples above reinforce a central premise in McCracken's (1986) original meaning making model (Figure 31.1): that culture stands as the original source and location of the general categories of meanings from which brands ultimately must draw. These categories provide the basic distinctions that a culture uses to divide up and make sense of the phenomenal world; they represent fundamental coordinates of meanings used to interpret the brand. Per McCracken (2005), central meaning categories about which shared understandings develop include gender meanings (Stewart and the roles of wife or mother), lifestyle meanings (Stewart's WASPY Connecticut style), age and cohort meanings (Snapple's Generation X), occupation meanings (Stewart's homemaking), class and status meanings (Stewart's aspiring upper class), decade meanings (Snapple and "the alternative 80s"), time and place meanings (Stewart's leisure vs. work time), value meanings (Harley's rebellion), and fad/fashion/trend meanings (the casual Pottery Barn taste expressions that supplant Martha Stewart today). Research by Thompson and Haytko (1997) and others (Brioschi, 2006; Elliott, 1994; Kozinets, 2001; Solomon, 1983) consistently reinforces the parameter-setting role of cultural codes in the process of brand meaning making. As Vince McMahon learned in his attempts to escape the exegesis of authentic sport (football) and spectacle (WWF wrestling), these cultural codes are robust and fundamental: they can not be conveniently discarded or willfully ignored.

Consumer Culture Theory research illuminates the context effects that determine interpretations of the cultural meanings claimed by a brand. The existence of distinct meaning-making communities defined along age, gender, and social class lines has been consistently validated (Belk, Meyer, & Bahn, 1982; Belk, 1978; Elliott, 1994; Holt, 1998; Thompson & Haytko, 1997). Recent research illuminates history as a basic yet underrepresented cultural code that constrains how brands produce meaning (Askegaard, 2006; Heilbrunn, 2006; Schultz & Hatch, 2006). Indeed, per the culturally constituted character of meaning, certain associations can be positive one day and negative the next as the broader cultural, political, legal, and market contexts change. The Martha Stewart case provides clear illustration of this meaning principle in action (Fournier & Herman, 2005). Stewart's perfectionism and controlling character, for example, were foundational strengths in the initial creation of the branded product portfolios, but a weakness when interpreted in light of the ImClone affair. In the context of the courtroom, Stewart's high style and cultured tastes were also translated into inferences that turned against her: "Martha may be above us all, but she is not above the law," jurors would later explain (Toobin, 2004, p. 65). While MSLO found that particular person meanings could perhaps for a time be sheltered (e.g., early charges against Stewart for recipe stealing), the cultural moments that made those hidden meanings relevant (i.e., the ImClone charges) were inevitable and strong.

Much has been written about the nature of the contemporary cultural landscape and the meanings that centrally define its contextual character for consumers today. Critiques by CCT researchers highlight themes of rebelliousness (Holt, 2004) and a hyper-savvy concerning marketing and consumer psychology that yields a tone of deep cynicism and informed skepticism (Brown, 2001; 2004; 2006). As expressed by Brown (2006), consumers "are cognizant that the customer is always right. They are aware that satisfaction and loyalty are the drivers of competitive strategy. They are fluent in Brandsperanto, Malltalk, Productpatter. They aren't as much Generation X, Y, or Z as Generation®" (p. 53). Brown (2001) further suggests that today's consumers have grown weary of marketers attending to their every desire; rather, they yearn for exclusivity, intrigue, and are always willing to be simply entertained.

Holt (2004) brought new energy to the theme of culture as a source of brand meanings by shifting from questions about cultural *content* and *context* to the *process* question of how exactly cultures create brands (see Figure 31.2). Holt's theory states that contradictions arise as an individual's experiences clash with the dominant cultural ideology, its moral imperatives, and the general vision to which the nation aspires, and that these contradictions make people feel anxious and isolated from the shared vision. These tensions then fuel a demand for myths that can "repair the culture when and where it is in particular need of mending" (Holt, 2003b, p. 48). Iconic brands step in to these culturally created myth markets to deliver those meanings that can assuage the feelings of isolation and distance of conflicted consumers. Thus, times of cultural anxiety and crisis provide windows of opportunity capable of birthing iconic brands.

Holt's theory is inspiring in that it offers a causal model whereby strong brands can be created out of cultural symbolism. His branding model also accommodates the dynamism that defines culture at its core, and touts change as a necessary brand condition, not a temptation destabilizing the brand. Per Holt, cultural contradictions are historically situated, and brands must be reincarnated as the cultural ideology ruptures, and veins of anxieties mutate in response. Holt offers a theory

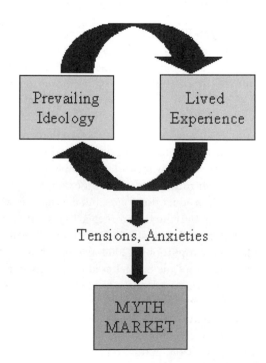

Figure 31.2   Holt's model for the creation of brand icons. Source: Holt 2004.

of the brand as an evolving story: a compelling dialogic device whereby iconic brands circulate as narratives encapsulating powerful myths defining the cultural world.

Dove's much-talked about Campaign for Real Beauty provides a contemporary case in support of Holt's thesis (Branch & Ball, 2005). Academic research on the psychology and sociology of beauty, as validated through Dove's worldwide consumer survey research, exposed intense anxieties and dysfunctionalities experienced by women as they compared themselves to the prevailing beauty ideology supported by fashion gatekeepers. While the dominant vision to which consumers were encouraged to aspire concerned perfection, youthfulness, and stereotypical "classic" looks, consumers' collective experiences stressed imperfection and individuality—a beauty that came in "many shapes and sizes" and a range of demographically defined forms. Building on this insight into veins of isolation and anxiety, Unilever adopted the ambitious mission of making more women feel beautiful by broadening the definition of beauty: something that, surprisingly, none in the industry had attempted before. As evidenced by extended discussion on *Oprah* and *Ellen*, unsolicited parodies on *Conan,* and literally thousands of pages of text on body size and age discrimination discussion forums, Dove's Campaign for Real Beauty has inarguably created social discourse around a resonant cultural issue. In the true spirit of the intention of cultural branding theory, the brand was not simply *on* the cultural agenda: the brand captured meanings that *comprised* the cultural agenda, thereby constituting fodder with which to build an iconic brand.

An interesting stream of research within the purview of cultural branding theory examines the flip side of the question concerning how cultures create brands. Indeed, Holt's theory (2004) suggests a mechanism through which brands not only mirror and mimic cultures, but also lead them by offering charismatic new visions of the world. Thompson and Haytko (1997) first offered evidence of the reciprocating effects between brands and cultures whereby localized changes in brand meanings inspired more widespread social changes that circled back to change the culture at play. Kozinets and Handelman (2004) provides evidence of the role of contemporary consumer movements that explicitly seek to transform consumer culture. Thompson and Arsel (2004) present the extreme form of this argument through their critical demonstration of the ways in which pro- and anti-Starbucks discourse can structure the entire competitive landscape by shaping people's ideas about the category and its operative values. Askegaard (2006) supports a similar thesis in his argument for the brand as a referent in a global ideoscape: a motivating idea that fundamentally reshapes the way consumers and producers view the world of goods. These studies collectively reinforce the central premise that brands can serve as a locus of meaningful social discourse, thereby shifting the level of inspired brand analysis from the psychological to the cultural plane.

CULTURAL PRODUCTION MECHANISMS THAT MAKE MEANINGS FOR THE BRAND

The brand examples used to open this section illuminate a second principle from McCracken's original (1986) process model. In the cases of Harley, Snapple, and Martha, brand meaning was significantly influenced by broad cultural production systems outside the firm's control, including media pundits, journalists, social critics, Hollywood producers, information gatekeepers and more. In fact, the cultural production systems that created, clarified, and sorted meanings for these brands arguably swamped the marketer-controlled messages receiving corporate funding and support.

Several researchers have attempted to broaden and deepen McCracken's specification of the cultural intermediaries (Featherstone, 1991) involved in making meanings for brands. Thompson and Haytko (1997) expand beyond McCracken's "fashion system" to identify an underdetermined force of "other cultural discourses" (e.g., folk theories on prevailing gender ideologies, or race/class relations) that contribute disparate meanings to the brand. Kozinets (2001) provides an expanded model of "media-based articulations in a mass media culture of consumption" such as that for the Star Trek brand. Kozinets highlights the contributions of certain cultural producers (e.g, Gene Roddenberry in the case of Star Trek) as offering encodings of a preferred reading for the brand, including canons whereby an object, image or ideology is declared as being officially part of the branded lexicon or not.

Using the Martha Stewart case as a point of departure, Fournier and Herman (2005) offer a process framework for person-brand meaning making that attempts a more comprehensive treatment of the cultural sources of brand co-creation that exist outside the formal structures of the firm. Their case analysis highlights meanings relevant to the dark side of Stewart's existence that become embedded in the cultural record: lawsuits filed by neighbors; altercations with limousine drivers and gardeners; anecdotal tales concerning explosive outbursts in the office or local marketplace; tales of exploitation at work; internal family feuds—all documented in unauthorized biographies, court records, spectacular television events, and chat registered at Internet sites like AmIAnnoying.com. The role of media pundits as cultural intermediaries that proved significant in the rise, fall, and resurgence of the Martha Stewart brand is also showcased in the research, as is the indirect but important meaning making roles played by the brand's business partners (e.g., Donald Trump's *Apprentice* and K-Mart). The issue of partner collaborations in brand meaning making is also considered in research by Bergvall (2006).

The discussion of the postmodern branding paradigm provided by Holt (2002) reminds us why marketer attention to uncultivated cultural sources of brand meaning making is critical to the stature of the brand. To succeed, marketers must grab authority and authenticity from the systems that can legitimately deliver this quality to a brand, and, as history has revealed, this no longer features the commercially driven systems of marketing. Holt identified several contemporary marketing techniques that have become quite popular toward this end, three of which explicitly strive to leverage cultural meaning production mechanisms. The first of these is what Holt calls coat-tailing on cultural epicenters. Through coat-tailing, the brand becomes part of a social movement or emergent meaning-making sub-culture such that it stands as a vested community member rather than a marketer who opportunistically appropriates authentic meanings for the brand (e.g., Red Bull's early sponsorship of the snowboard culture). A second tactic is lifeworld emplacement whereby street credentials are developed for the brand. Examples include Snapple's use of truck dispatcher Wendy as a primary spokesperson for their brand, or the signing of non-professional models for the Dove Real Beauty campaign. Last is stealth branding, wherein the brand shuns direct marketer communications in favor of the allegiance of tastemakers who use their influence to impart cultural capital credentials on the brand (e.g., James Dean and Dennis Hopper on a Harley).

BUILDING ON THE MOMENTUM: RESEARCH DIRECTIONS FOR CULTURAL MEANING MAKING

Research on cultural branding is in its nascent stages with much foundational work to be done. Clearly needed is a culturally sensitive coding scheme to catalogue the meanings claimed by a brand. Schemes in the received view are firm- and product-centric, and emphasize such meaning categories as product attributes, brand benefits, use occasions, and perhaps the emotions or values emanating from these (Aaker, 1991; Keller & Lehmann, 2005). McCracken's (2005) meaning categories offer a compelling alternative for codifying brand meanings along cultural lines. Zaltman's ZMET (Zaltman & Coulter, 1995) provides another option wherein brand concepts are coded in terms of eight deeply seated metaphors believed to structure cultural interpretations of experience and thought, including power, balance, and journey (Lakoff & Johnson, 1980). The ambitious project of codifying the iconography and symbolism contained in the cultural and brand meaning spaces can also prove instrumental to theory advancement. Valid methodologies that can elicit and structure this meaning space are critical and sorely needed: Englis and Solomon (2000) and Roedder-John, Loken, Kyeong-Heui, and Monga (2005) provide promising quantitative options toward this end. Meaning-based segmentation tools are also needed that derive not from the bottom-up perspective of objective brand attributes or benefits, but rather the top-down perspective of resonant socio-cultural meaning categories that add value more generally in people's lives.

While much has been written about the character of the contemporary cultural landscape as pertains to marketing and brands, these ideas have not yet figured prominently in our theories of the brand. Context in general is something that our branding theories and methods do not accommodate. Granted, it is accepted practice to provide context through specification of the brand's competitive set, or perhaps the advertising-program environment. But the contexts that give brands their meaning more often than not lie outside these manager-controlled domains and within the broader socio-cultural world. The meaning of Coke, for example, derived less from its taste profile versus the competition than from its historical time/place context: Coke's status as America's beverage during World War II; emplacements in the popular 1950s television show *The Eddie Fisher Hour*; the brand's starring role in the bucolic 1950s paintings of Norman Rockwell. A particular branding message interpreted in the context of today's marketing-savvy consumer will have a different effect than it might at another time. Indeed, the entire interpretive plane for marketing shifts when consumers' ingoing assumptions, frames, and attributions are shaped by cynicism, beliefs in customer superiority, and an insiders' knowledge of marketing operations and techniques. These interpretive frames clearly need to be accommodated in our research as something more than error variance or moderators of effects. Friestad and Wright's Persuasion Knowledge Model (1994) and their construal of cultural folk knowledge (1995) hold untapped promise in exploring these context effects in branding research.

Many particulars concerning marketers' operations within the contemporary cultural branding context also deserve research attention. Brown (2006) identifies three new branding twists popular in the current era of the marketing savvy-consumer: irony as a marketing voice (e.g., Sprite's Image is Nothing image, Death brand cigarettes, Aquafina's promise that there is no promise), anti-brand branding (e.g., Uniglos's claim "you are not what you wear!"), and the faux forthright format (e.g., Ronseal's "It does exactly what it says on the tin"). What drives the use and effectiveness of these branding formats? How are these provocative and ambiguous messages received? Per Brown (2006), are these messages flagrantly crude and naive, or the opposite? In the end, are attempts at "no marketing" interpreted as savvy marketing after all? Dedicated process models for Holt's culturally attuned branding strategies have also yet to be developed, and their effectiveness as contemporary brand building tools remains unexplored.

A general call for research on uncontrolled non-marketer meaning production systems can also be made. While CCT research consistently reinforces the significance of cultural brand meaning makers, and marketing practice reveals their use and support, considered treatment of particular mechanisms within the cultural production system is rarely attempted in the discipline. Meaning making groups involved in the production of celebrity remain unexplored in this era of entertainment marketing: media pundits who trade on celebrity value for profitable gain, informational gatekeepers at major news and entertainment agencies, the thriving worlds of sensationalist expose reports. Our lack of advance may reflect structural boundaries and biases operating within the marketing discipline. PR has long stood as the poor step child within the marketing mix family; media relations have been classified as the purview of those in communications fields. But these demarcations prove artificial (Jansson, 2002) if not intolerable in specifying a culturally driven production system for the brand.

Different research methodologies and skill sets will also be required in order to Braille cultures for their branding insights. Holt (2004) observes that true brand knowledge "comes from a cultural historian's understanding of ideology as it waxes and wanes, a sociologist's charting of the topography of contradictions the ideology produces, and a literary critic's expedition into the culture that engages these contradictions" (p. 49). Brand managers as possible authors of compelling stories have much to learn from the journalists, novelists, script writers, and cultural critics familiar with the optics of the narrative lens. As brand managers become trend managers—identifying and then capitalizing on cultural tensions and breaks—academicians may find more inspiration from industries such as movie making, music and fashion than the packaged goods and durables forums that have historically informed theories of the brand.

As our theories shift to the context of cultural meaning making, so too will our branding metrics need to respond in kind. While evaluations of attribute strength and dominance were useful in advancing associative network models, indicators of the socio-cultural qualities of claimed brand meanings will be needed to illuminate cultural theories of the brand. Measures of the authenticity of brand meanings (Grayson & Martinec, 2004), for example, could prove useful, as would indicators of the culturally resonant quality of claimed meanings for the brand (Fournier, Solomon, & Englis, 2007; McQuarrie & Mick, 1999). What constructs can we offer beyond credibility, expertise, and trustworthiness to help us understand the effectiveness of celebrities who acculturate the brand (McCracken, 1989)? The investigation of celebrity-infused brand meaning is long overdue.

CONSUMERS AS CO-CREATORS OF BRAND MEANING

It's not what you do. It's what they do with what you do.

John Grant, *The New Marketing Manifesto*

Our section on consumers as brand-meaning collaborators is again motivated by real world examples that capture the ways in which the meaning making activities of consumers and consumer collectives have determined the success or failure of the brand.

The story of Red Bull, pioneer of the now-thriving energy drinks category, presents a case of consumers adding so-called "unintended meanings" that not only established but propelled the status of the brand (see Kumar, Linguri, & Tavasssoli, 2004; Wipperfurth, 2003). Pre-launch marketing research for this vitamin-enriched, caffeinated beverage could not have been more damning. The color of the drink was unappetizing; the sticky mouth feel and taste were deemed disgusting; the price point, at eight times that for Coke, was considered unjustifiable. The overall product concept—to increase physical endurance, improve concentration and reaction speed, and to improve vigilance and stimulate the metabolism" (Kumar, Linguri, & Tavasssoli, 2004, p. 2)—was rated as irrelevant. The verdict by the market research firm was clear: "no other new product has ever failed this convincingly" (Wipperfurth, 2003). Red Bull's novel ingredient taurine also guaranteed a lengthy and risky product approval process, further discouraging launch. But founder Mateschitz was committed to the entrepreneurial venture for other reasons, and began the arduous process of attaining approval for Red Bull's ingredients and sale. It took 5 years to gain permission for product export from Germany; France and Denmark refused approval in light of potential health concerns. But, during the long wait period, consumer meaning making took off. Speculation circulated as to why the drink was illegal. It was rumored that taurine was made from bull's testicles, a known aphrodisiac. The brand developed street names: liquid cocaine, speed-in-a-can, liquid Viagra. Several deaths were rumored to be linked to product consumption. Munich became a thriving black market for the banned product. When Red Bull was finally granted approval in Germany, mothers boycotted the brand to have it banned again. Young Austrian clubbers began bringing Red Bull to the all-night raves that emerged on the cultural scene at that time, further adding cache to the brand's counter-cultural epicenter. The brand really took off when it became a mixer of choice for Snowboarders in Austrian ski resorts, where bartenders came up with the notorious *Stoli Bully* combination. Young adults could not get enough of the legendary cocktail rumored to have the power of Ecstacy with the kick of a pot of coffee.

This consumer-generated meaning making activity lent the brand an evolved in-market positioning as the ultimate edgy and dangerous anti-brand. Red Bull's marketing team was quick to recognize this consumer voice and engaged a host of stealth marketing campaigns to cultivate the revealed brand mythology. The company Web site fed content to the thriving rumor mill. The company leveraged the power of consumers as co-creators, and used them explicitly to build the brand. University students were hired as grassroots brand supporters; parties for product distribution received corporate funds. By 2003, the brand that was dubbed a hands-down market failure stood as one of Europe's top five brands; it now also dominates the energy drink category worldwide (Dolan, 2005).

The 1985 New Coke disaster provides a textbook example of the consumer-based realities of the brand (Fournier, 2002). In what is variously referred to as the Chernobyl of beverages and the Edsel of the marketing world, Coca-Cola management removed the company's flagship brand from store shelves and replaced it with what $4 million worth of consumer testing identified as a "newer, better tasting Coke." New Coke provided a sensible marketing resolution to an increasingly threatening competitive game. The Pepsi Challenge was storming across the country, demonstrating through on-camera taste tests what Coca-Cola management was later surprised to learn: people preferred the taste of Pepsi. But the research and its interpretation by management denied the contextual reality of consumers' relationships with the brand. Taste did not drive loyalty, the brand did, and the company's taste tests were all conducted blind. Vehement disapprovals of New Coke voiced in focus groups by loyal consumers were dismissed by management as a failure of qualitative methods to provide generalizable results. Customer calls placed in the aftermath of the product decision, and the media coverage of grassroots rebellion groups, were not recognized by management as "data." Eventually, the company gave in to consumer pressure and returned Old Coke to store shelves. Perhaps more vividly than any other, the New Coke case illustrated that consumers co-owned the brand, and exposed the fallacy of marketing decisions that ignored this collaborative fact.

The business press is replete with examples of the powerful ways in which consumers can augment, modify, and otherwise contribute to the process of brand meaning making. Brown (2004) observes that conscripting the consumer is one of the most striking marketing trends of recent years, often replacing paid corporate communications in light of the assumed benefits of credibility and authenticity that are obtained. In the discussion below, we review three consumer research streams aligned with the theme of consumers as brand co-creators: (1) individual consumers' uses of brands in identity management projects; (2) consumer collectives as brand meaning makers; and (3) consumers as contrary meaning makers for the brand.

INDIVIDUAL CONSUMERS' USE OF BRANDS IN IDENTITY MANAGEMENT TASKS

Research on individuals' uses of product and brand symbolism in identity management tasks has a long and respected tradition both within and outside the field of consumer psychology (see, for example, classic social science studies by Csikszentmihalyi and Rochberg-Halton (1981), Douglas and Isherwood (1978), and Sahlins (1972). Interestingly, this perspective on the symbolic self-completion functions of consumer goods harkened back to early branding theory, where these same arguments for the primacy of symbolic consumption were presented in published management works (Gardner & Levy, 1955; Levy, 1959).

Perhaps most well-known in the consumer behavior discipline is Belk's (1988) foundational article on possessions and their roles in defining an individual's sense of self. Belk's essay presented a compelling and comprehensive presentation of interdisciplinary evidence supporting the basic contention that individuals systematically appropriate possession meanings for purposes of self-definition. Belk's essay argued strongly for the consumer as active meaning creator. He provided a framework for understanding the many different ways in which consumers used their possessions not only to reflect but also to actively craft, shape, and maintain alternate views of the self across the lifespan. Belk's argument was compelling and provocative, and served to inspire significant critique (e.g., Cohen, 1989) and research.

Over the course of the next several years, researchers developed a deep appreciation of the many and varied ways in which consumers used the cultural meanings resident in products and brands to define and orient the individual. Consumers were shown to construct narratives of identity (Hill & Stamey, 1990; Holt, 2002) and fulfill goal-driven identity projects through brands (Fournier, 1998; Mick & Buhl, 1992; Thompson & Haytko, 1997). They created multiple self-representations in cyberspace (Schau & Gilly, 2003). They became brand reconstruction artists who used their nonconformist acts of consumption to express individuated identities that set them apart (Firat & Venkatesh, 1995; Holt, 2002; Kozinets & Handelman, 2004). Through these and other studies, consumers were shown to work and transform the meanings embedded in products and brands so as to fashion a coherent albeit fragmented and diversified sense of self (Arnould & Thompson, 2005; Elliott & Davies, 2006; Elliott & Wattanasuwan, 1998; Grayson & Martinec, 2004; Kozinets, 2001; Penaloza, 2000). The view of brands as cultural resources—useful components for the creation and management of the self concept—and of consumers as active identity makers who worked with marketer-generated materials to forge their identities became firmly established in the interpretivist tradition.

Much research on the self-brand identity connection pursued alternate definitions of the fragmented and multifaceted self. Solomon (1983), using symbolic interactionist theory (Mead, 1934), focused on the self as a role player in society, with a separate "me" for each assumed social role. Solomon's extensions (Solomon, 1988b; 1988c) expanded beyond consumers' use of individual products and brands as expressions of identity to the collective meanings of coherent bundles of brands and products assembled to express social roles. Empirical evidence revealed co-occurrence of products and brands in the inventories of select prototypical and socially defined roles such as yuppies (e.g., Rolex, Heinekin, Perrier, Barclay, BMW, *Esquire*, Brooks Brothers, and AMEX) and supported consensus across consumers regarding these role-based brand constellation gestalts. Wicklund and Gollwitzer (1982) also tested the degree to which individuals might use product and brand collectives to express desired role-based identities. They confirmed that MBA students who were insecure about future job prospects would adopt more of the consumption patterns of a stereotypical business person, thus actively engaging consumption constellations thought to bolster desired conceptions of the self.

Another interesting stream of research featured the undesired self: one of an individual's many possible selves that stood in opposition to the ideal self, essentially constituting the self the person lives in fear of becoming (Ogilvie, 1987). This research built upon Bourdieu's observation that tastes "are asserted purely negatively, by the refusal of other tastes" (Bourdieu, 1984, p. 56), and proposed that the consumer was defined as much by what s/he decided *not* to consume as they were by positively reinforcing consumption choices. Kleine, Kleine, and Allen (1995) explored possessions that were accepted or rejected as "me" or "not me." Wilk (1997) demonstrated that consumers had less difficulty articulating their dislikes than they did their desires, and were readily able to articulate negative consumption stereotypes associated with brand cues. Englis and Solomon (1995) and Freitas et al. (1997) showed that consumers eschewed the purchase and display of select products and brands because of a desire to distance themselves from particular associations. Hogg and Banister (2001) demonstrated negative self-incongruity; that is, the comparison between a negative product-image perception and a positive self-image belief, which resulted in avoidance purchase motivations. Thompson and Arsel (2004) revealed the power of distaste for a given brand to structure not just personal brand preferences but entire markets and competitive landscapes.

Elliot and Davies (2006) drew upon Featherstone's (1991) concept of the performing self: a consumption-centric self that places emphasis on appearance and the management of impressions. This ethnographic inquiry revealed a never-ending sequence of consumption-enabled in-between selves poised in transition from "who I am" to "who I want to become." The research emphasized that the self is never fixed nor coherent, and that what is observed as an actualized self is merely "one moment in time in a dynamic process of always becoming" (p. 263). The enactment of possible selves through consumption was also proposed in Goulding, Shankar, and Elliot's (2002) study of the working-week versus the rave-weekend selves.

Meaning making dynamics at the household level of identity-definition have also received research attention. Chang (2005) conducted a 16-month ethnographic investigation of so-called invisible brands that blend inconspicuously into the household environment. She suggests that the locus of meaning for such brands is not tied to individual identity but instead to a social identity process wherein the brand and the habits and patterns that surround it serve as a vital part of the household meaning-making system. Chang emphasized that consumers often purchased brands that were verbally judged as "not me" when those brands fit the larger context and logic of the household and the purchaser's role within that social system. This research reinforced that individual consumers do not always thoughtfully negotiate the assimilation of brands into their lives, nor are they always engaged in the negotiation of meanings toward self-identity refinement ends. Rather, consumers sometimes allowed their tacitly known household habits and systems to take over in the assignment of meaning to a brand.

Fournier (1998) took the self-brand connection argument to another plane in her phenomenological study of consumers and their brands. Fournier demonstrated that consumers formed relationships with brands when they considered the meanings of the brand as being useful in helping the person to live his/her life. In this interpretation, realized brand meanings were not inherent in the product, nor were they necessarily the meanings that had been reinforced and popularized through the firm's advertising and marketing campaigns. Rather, the brand's meanings were created by the individual as the brand intersected with important identity themes and life projects. Hence, one consumer might imbue a brand with "best in the category" associations to bolster a marginality versus significance tension in her life while another might invest a brand with the meanings of a significant other that once consumed the brand. In line with Consumer Culture Theory, Fournier argued that the active meaning creation processes stimulated by filtering the brand through the lens of the individual's identity projects created brand multivocality: the manifestation of different meanings for different persons for the same brand. A person's brand portfolio was highlighted as mutable and dynamic, with brands coming in and out as the person evolved and sought new (re)defining expressive meanings in response.

Others have followed in the tradition of exploring consumer-brand connections by accepting consumers and brands as active members of a relationship dyad. Fournier, Avery, and Wojnicki

(2004) examined longitudinal ethnographic and critical incident data to build on Fournier's (1998) insight that the reciprocating behaviors of consumers and brands resulted in different types or categories of relationships. These researchers showed how different rules and norms of behavior evolved over time through the signal-response mechanism of consumer and brand behaviors. The analysis revealed how the various rules at play in a given consumer-brand relationship cohered into a particular relationship template over time, with certain norms emerging as centrally defining. The partnership template, for example, was created by consumer and brand actions that were consistently true to a belief in mutual helping and sacrifice, accommodation, and optimistic investments in an imagined mutual future; the adversary template was grounded in prioritization of the self over the other, and expectations for inherent conflicts in interests and engagements. These alternative templates structured behavior by guiding future consumer actions and sense-making activities. Aggrawal (2004) focused on two dominant relationship templates in human psychology—communal and exchange—and demonstrated how these different framings differentially affected consumer relationship responses. This same process dynamic of a behaviorally driven relationship template was implicated in the findings of Aaker, Fournier, and Brasel (2004). Collectively, this line of research shows how consumer (and brand) actions help define the relationship, as interpreted within the blueprints offered by the culture at large.

CONSUMER COLLECTIVES AS BRAND MEANING COLLABORATORS

A second stream of research in the identity-making tradition extended beyond the traditional marketing view of consumers as individuals to recognize that consumers exist in webs of interpersonal interconnections and manifest themselves at least partly in groups (Muñiz & O'Guinn, 2005). Variously labeled as sub-cultures of consumption (Kates, 2002; Schouten & McAlexander, 1995), consumption microcultures (Thompson & Troester, 2002), cultures of consumption (Kozinets, 2001), tribes (Cova, 1997) and brand communities (Muñiz & O'Guinn, 2001), these micro-social consumption collectives comprise a network of heterogeneous persons linked by shared emotion and experience around a brand (Cova & Cova, 2002).

Studies in this tradition built on Boorstin's (1973) contention that one of the key ways of defining and expressing group membership in contemporary society was through shared consumption symbols that helped identify an individual's group membership and thereby express the social self. Per the pioneering work of Maffesoli (1996), consumption-based communities were thought to emerge when individuals attempted to assert a sense of local identity over what was perceived as the facelessness of globalization, as they sought to establish social connections in an era of radical individualism and isolation, or when they simply needed to fill the void of the contemporary empty self (Cova & Cova, 2002; Cushman, 1990; Goulding, Shankar, & Elliott, 2002). Cova and Cova (2002) described the movement to consumption collectives this way: "people who have finally managed to liberate themselves from social constraints are embarking on a reverse movement to recompose their social universes" (p. 596). In the contemporary consumption-based society, these restructurings were defined around the brands providing rich fodder for image (re)construction: that is, "Product symbolism creates a universe for the tribe" (Ostergaard & Jantzen, 2000). Branded products provided what Cova (1997) referred to as "linking value": the facilitation of the co-presence of individuals with common lifestyle interests. In this sense, products in branded communities offered consumers instrumental value versus terminal value-in-use, whether through temporary or more enduring connections.

Schouten and McAlexander (1995) introduced the concept of the consumption sub-culture to the consumer behavior discipline with their ethnographic research on Harley-Davidson rider groups. They emphasized the socio-cultural quality of this distinctive societal subgroup that self-selects based on a shared commitment to a particular product class, brand, or consumption activity. Social mechanisms identified at the heart of the sub-culture included: a shared ethos or set of brand-relevant values; a unique language system; signs and symbols as badges of membership; rituals; and mythic stories and heroes. The structure of the subculture was also identified as fundamental. Within the subculture, there existed an informal hierarchical social structure that reflected the status of group members within the collective. This was authenticated within the group through expressions of personal commitment and across groups per cultural capital claimed through acquired knowledge, skills, experiences, and social connections (see also Clay, 2003). A hard core group served as arbiters of core brand meanings while distinct subgroups allowed multiple interpretations of the ethos of the brand.

Subsequent empirical research (Algesheimer, Dholakia, & Herrmann, 2005; McAlexander, Schouten, & Koenig, 2002) demonstrated that identification with a branded sub-culture produced tangible benefits to marketers, including brand loyalty, price elasticity, word of mouth recommendation, and incremental dollars spent. Community attachment was also related to negative consequences such as normative community pressures, and, ultimately, reactance and resistance, especially for large collectives versus small.

Muñiz and O'Guinn (2001) followed with the broader concept of brand community, a form of social community defined as "a specialized, non-geographically bound community based on a structural set of social relations among admirers of a brand" (p. 412). Brand communities were identified as possessing three defining characteristics: (1) a consciousness of kind and sense of belonging to an in-group through shared product consumption; (2) rituals and traditions that reify the community and brand culture and help it to stay vital over time; and (3) publicly enacted morality and a shared (soft) sense of duty and obligation to other community members. Additional aspects of brand communities with a particular marketplace flavor included: oppositional brand loyalties (Aron & Muñiz, 2002); marketplace legitimacy, as reflected in whether the brand is "real" and the brand community members "legitimate" (Muñiz & O'Guinn, 2005); and desired marginality whereby community members tried to maintain cache as a core element of brand meaning by keeping community membership restricted and small.

A more temporary and unstable form of social grouping formed around shared identification with the brand was offered by Cova and Cova (2002) in the metaphor of the tribe. Like communities, neo-tribes thrived on shared experience and brand passion, but they were characterized by a "volatility of belonging" which meant that homogeneity of behavior and formal rules were eschewed. The temporary, time- or event-bound consumption community was also the subject of research by Goulding, Shankar, and Elliott (2002) on weekend rave cultures, McAlexander et al.'s Jeep brandfests (2002), Arnould and Price's extraordinary experience communities (1993), and McGrath, Sherry, and Heisley's (1991) periodic farmer's market communities. The notion of the hypercommunity was offered in Kozinets' (2002) study of the week-long anti-market Burning Man project to capture the notion of a temporary and short-lived but intensely well-organized and caring community form.

Research by Kozinets on the Star Trek culture of consumption (2001) and the Burning Man project (2002) has helped refine distinctions among sub-cultures and brand communities. Kozinets (2002) emphasized that communities form in response to an exploitative ethos that weakens social ties and dampens self-expressive practices. Thus a reconceptualization of the community of consumption was offered: as "re-gatherings of the collective force required to resist the atomizing and self-expression-crushing capabilities of large corporations…a banding together to assert agency and even ownership of the brand" (p. 33). In contrast with contemporary researchers who celebrate the non-geographically bound qualities of online or brand communities, Kozinets calls for the reinsertion of place into the community equation, noting that the time and space bound nature of select consumption collectives relates to primal conceptions of local communities of social actors who lived together.

Kozinets research on Star Trek also helped clarify the consumption collective's function as a meaning maker, and emphasized that these activities are still situated within a broader system of meaning making wherein the interplay of the community, individuals within the community, and the wider cultural production system was engaged. This research also reinforced how individuals within the culture acted as independent meaning makers ascribing divergent meanings to the brand in order to arrive at a personally appropriate definition of Star Trek consumption. These findings suggested further refinement of the community concept to exclude the assumed requirement for a commonly shared identity through the brand.

Moving beyond the collective as co-creator of brand meaning, Muñiz and Schau (2005) explored the case where the collective actually *became* the marketer, who through its actions, guides and sustains the brand over time. This research concerned the abandoned Apple Newton community, which, unlike the corporate-sponsored Harley-Davidson community, was supported exclusively through the grassroots efforts of involved consumers. Supernatural, religious, and magical motifs characterized members' community narratives, investing the brand with powerful meanings and perpetuating these through reinforcing rituals. The power of folklore, mythology and rumor in brand community maintenance was also stressed. This work reinforced the theory of the brand-as-narrative, wherein the brand was defined by the stories that took hold as the brand circulated through culture and consumption groups (Brown, 2003; Holt, 2004).

Recent community research has concerned specific mechanisms through which communities are formed and sustained. A vibrant research stream has developed around the concept of authenticity: the quest for the real, genuine, and irreplaceable that pioneering community researchers placed at the heart of brand community development, operation, and preservation (see also Elliott & Davies, 2006). Grayson and Martinec (2004) explored the concept of authenticity by drawing on semiotic theory. They suggest that authenticity can be explained: (1) in terms of the object's indexicality or its factual and spatio-temporal link with history; and (2) its iconic value in physically resembling or reproducing something that is authentic, as per the brand's essence. Work-in-progress by Leigh, Peters, and Shelton (2005) on the MGB brand community offers a three-pronged concept of authenticity when brand communities are operative that goes beyond the objective (i.e., verifiable product qualifications and originality) to involve constructive (i.e., subjective community-defined renegotiations concerning the definitions of the original or classic) and existential (i.e., activity-based experience in which the person feels they are in touch with the real world and their real self) facets. Recent research by Rose and Wood (2005) on reality television demonstrates how viewers can cope with and accept fantasy and simulation—obvious elements of inauthenticity and blatant violations of the genuine—through successful negotiation of the paradoxes presented in situations, characters, and production venues. This research reinforced authenticity as a co-production, an active discourse, an engaged and interactive process of viewer interpretation within the postmodern milieu. This insight parallels the work of Arnould and Price (2000), who argued that authenticity was created through the recital of authenticating acts revealing the true self and authoritative performances aimed at inventing or refashioning cultural traditions.

Recent community research also concerns the development of contingency theories that circumscribe community manifestations and qualify community forms. Cova and Cova (2002) offered a categorization scheme for the various roles that community members could adopt including: mere members, participants at select informal gatherings, practitioners who have quasi-daily involvement in tribal activities, and a large group of sympathizers or fellow travelers who are only virtually integrated into the tribe. Muñiz and O'Guinn (2005) specified the qualities of the brand that can facilitate community formation: distinctive brand meanings, a challenge that gives the community a reason to persevere, and the capacity for transformative consumption experiences. Research by Muñiz and Schau (2005) also offered qualifications for the types of products that legitimately foster community, suggesting that brands capable of providing transcendent magical or religious experiences foster community ties.

CONSUMERS AS CONTRARY BRAND MEANING MAKERS

As stressed in this section's introduction, consumer meaning making is an unruly process in which brands are sometimes refashioned in unanticipated and undesirable ways. Firat and Venkatesh (1995) were the first to expose the micro processes and practices through which postmodern consumers attempted to (re)gain control over marketer-dominated brands. Holt (2002) elaborated on consumers as unruly "bricoleurs" who never accepted marketer dictates and used brands for self-creation rather than allowing brands unequivocally to define them. Thompson and Haytko (1997) demonstrated the many specific ways in which clever consumers cobbled together, juxtaposed, and combined countervailing meanings in the fashion domain to create unique, personal meanings that often ran against the grain of existing social categories.

Research on the coffee culture by Thompson and Arsel (2004) provided evidence of consumer collectives hijacking particular brand meanings and expressions, as for example, with satires of the Starbucks logo (e.g., the addition of nipples to the brand icon) and plays on the Starbucks name (e.g., Frakenbucks, per the firm's use of genetically modified dairy products). The practice of "culture jamming" the signal of the broadcast marketing message—countering and otherwise undermining the continuous flow of marketing messages—has become especially prevalent (Lasn, 1999). Jamming activities aimed against advertising and the capitalist structure that supports it have been studied in the context of the quarterly magazine *Adbusters* (Rumbo, 2002), its sponsoring organization, *The Media Foundation* (Handelman, 1999), and *The Front for the Liberation from Advertising* (Kozinets & Handelman, 2004). Handelman (1999) provides numerous examples of the ways in which resistance against marketing is enacted, including changing ad copy and creating parodies of actual advertising campaigns (e.g., the Camel Joe Cool campaign becomes Joe Chemo), publishing content directly opposing and critiquing select and general marketing actions (e.g., *Adbusters* magazine), the production of so-called "un-commercials" (i.e., professionally produced 30-second ads touting anti-marketing ideology) and the generation of grassroots activities like the day-after-Thanksgiving "Buy Nothing Day."

Extensive research has shown that consumers' freedom to create new product and brand meanings through their own experiences is often levied for collective and individual resistance to and rebellion against the imposed meanings of marketers (Firat & Venkatesh, 1995; Holt, 2002; Klein, 1999; Kozinets, 2002; Kozinets & Handelman, 2004; Thompson, 2004; Thompson & Haytko, 1997; Thompson, Rindfleisch, & Arsel, 2006). Boycotts, especially of global brands, have received specific attention (Friedman, 1999; Garrett, 1987; Miller & Sturdivant, 1977). Brand community has been interpreted in terms of creative resistance whereby "consumers break down marketers' dominance by seeking out social spaces in which they produce their own cultures" (Holt, 2002, p. 72). Frank (1997) provides a detailed analysis of the use of brands in revolution. Arnould and Thompson (2005) provide a detailed review of CCT research on the practice of ideological reproduction and resistance in marketing. Vibrant debate rages concerning whether consumers can truly escape the hand of the market through their attempts to take control of the meanings of consumption and brands (Holt, 2002; Kozinets, 2002).

Enter O'Guinn and Muniz's (2004) conception of the polit-brand, wherein a community of users is at once centered on shared brand consumption *and* the furthering of a political goal. Unlike groups that fight perceived market dominance through boycotts or manipulation and avoidance of major branded products, these communities rebel through the community-sanctioned *consumption* of brands. Muniz and O'Guinn (2005) highlight the blurring of lines between brands and politics in the consumption of Ben & Jerry's, MAC, and SweatX clothes. Brand politics stands as the explicit agenda for BlackSpot sneakers, which positions itself squarely as the anti-brand brand.

Research on the resistance efforts of consumers has led some to argue that the entire domain of branded consumption is shifting to the political realm. The focus of "post postmodern" resistant consumers, it is argued, has turned from brand meanings and images to the morals and ethics of the organization behind the brand: its performance as a community stakeholder and civic institution and the social implications of its use (Holt, 2002). In this politically construed paradigm, emphasis shifts from surface-level brand image terms to a deeper integration between the actions of the company as manifest in the revealed values of the brand. Practitioner Marc Gobe (2002) embraces this shifting paradigm in his book, *Citizen Brand*.

SOME IMPLICATIONS OF CONSUMER CO-CREATION FOR BRANDING RESEARCH

As the review above attests, consumer co-creation has a rich and robust history within the consumer research field. Although it might be said that the elemental groundwork for the constructive use of brands in symbolic self completion tasks has been well laid, many interesting questions remain. Does there exist a consumer self: what is its nature and purpose, and how does this shape consumer relationships and responses? When does the political self supersede the personal self in identity expressions through brands? Is there a social patterning for brand-centric identity engagements? Does symbolic self completion activity spawn from crisis-induced triggers analogous to those Holt (2004) identifies for anxious cultures at large? How is self identity renegotiated in the face of transgressions and repositionings that present a new face for the brand (Avery, 2006)?

If there is a bias and therefore a gap in consumer identity-making research, it is a bias among consumer/social psychologists in favor of the micro processes of individuals and against explorations of consumers in collectives and groups. As O'Guinn and Muniz (2005) note, while norms and other social phenomena may be specified as moderating variables in our branding models, this is not the same thing as studying social brand behavior in the social context that gives it life. As the exception, we have developed a robust understanding of the functioning of brand communities and other related consumption collectives. Still, conceptual inconsistencies plague recent studies conducted under the "community" umbrella (Muñiz, O' Guinn, & Schau, 2006), and the social context of community remains under-defined (Luedicke & Giesler, 2006). Research is sorely needed on the fragmentation and sociological patterning of community groups over time, and the brand meaning arbitration that occurs within core and emergent (fringe) community subgroups. Moreover, community studies generally concern rather atypical and highly specialized consumer groups whose lifestyles are highly structured through brand interactions. Recent explorations of more time-bound or haphazard brand and marketplace communities are promising in their attempts to broaden the applicability of the community concept beyond the high cultural capital community pinnacle or core. Contingency theories that explore the dynamics of a range of community member types—from interlopers that receive benefits solely through community artifacts, to members-in-name-only, to the one-event-per-year "Plug and Players" who dip in and out of communities at will—hold great promise. Metrics for qualifying brand community participation are also needed, including operationalizations of core concepts such as social and cultural capital, distinctiveness and cohesiveness, group marginality, and the legitimacy or authenticity of consumers and the brand meanings that they claim.

Brand research is clearly called for in one natural domain wherein the influence of consumers as co-creators of brand meaning can only become more pronounced. This involves the increasingly popular Weblog or blog. Blogs are proliferating as a meaning-making venue, with 90,000 new blogs added to an estimated 9 million base every day (Baker & Green, 2005). Blogs that register complaints, reveal stories of victimization or unfair treatment, share "insider secrets" that derail company practices, or solicit participation in anti-brand campaigns, are thriving. The power of blogs as a meaning making mechanism is startling: within a two-week timeframe, for instance, the clamor on Weblogs felled CBS anchor Dan Rather and threatened the entire media establishment in his wake. Buzzophone.com provides downloadable versions of consumers' rants and tirades, further extending the reach of the blog space.

Two *Business Week* reporters offer this vision of where things go from here: "In a world chockfull of citizen publishers, we mainstream types control an ever-smaller chunk of human knowledge. Some of us will work to draw in more of what the bloggers know, vetting it, editing it, and packaging it into our closed productions. But here's betting that we also forge ahead in the open world. The measure of success in that world is not a finished product. The winners will be those who host the very best conversations" (Baker & Green, 2005, p. 64). The translation for brand meaning making is self evident: winning firms will be those that learn to embrace co-creation, with the preeminent goal of promoting open and honest conversations about their brands. This is unfamiliar territory for most brand managers trained in the received view.

Blogs do offer the type of authenticity which Holt (2002) argues today's consumers hunger for: information and opinion perceived as "invented and disseminated by parties without an instrumental economic agenda, by people who are intrinsically motivated by their inherent values" (p. 83). Yet such consumer co-creation presents a dilemma in contemporary branding: while it can bring a brand to life by providing vibrancy within the fabric of daily living (e.g., Red Bull), so too can the forces of consumer co-creation damage the brand through diversions that take meanings off course (e.g., Martha Stewart) or destroy it (e.g., Dan Rather). The parameters and dynamics of this delicate balancing act have yet to receive attention under the lens of brand research. Metrics that qualify and measure the risks that consumer co-creation inherently entails are sorely needed; Fournier and Herman (2005) provide promising ideas toward this end.

THE COMPANY AS BRAND MEANING MAKER

> Brands are like muscles: Exercise them, stretch them, and keep them moving and they'll have a longer, healthier life. Let them be couch potatoes and they'll atrophy.
>
> **Sergio Zyman,** *The End of Advertising As We Know It,* p. 61

Next, we turn to the "brand author" that is implicit in most consumer research: the companies that create and market brands. This has been an area where the work of consumer psychologists has significantly framed and influenced management practice and thought. The typical consumer psychology study on branding starts with assumptions about a brand's meaning (typically labeled brand equity) and then assesses things like how that meaning is altered via central or peripheral processing of ad messages and brand cues, or how new brand concepts fit with or extend the established equity of the brand. Earlier we referred to this as research following the received view, where the tenets and assumptions based in the field's information processing tradition play themselves out in service of the marketer's agenda for the brand.

But in today's marketplace we find sophisticated practitioners nearly in a scramble mode in search of new ideas and means to build their brands. It has become fashionable to contend that the old brand building model is broken and that a new one may now be emerging (Cappo, 2003; Gross, 2005; Heyer, 2003; Kiley, 2005; Neff & Sanders, 2004; Zyman, 2002). The result has been that media and methods that were once marginalized are now becoming commonplace (Muniz & O'Guinn, 2005). If one follows the money, it is clear that brand marketers are moving resources to new tools at unprecedented rates (Atkinson & Klaassen, 2005; Oser, 2005). What this means to academic researchers interested in brand is that our domain of inquiry is expanding rapidly. The critical question to consider is: are our theories and methods expanding to match the dynamic environment we are trying to comprehend? To develop a point of view regarding this question, we prime the pump with exemplars of what brand building actually looks like in the contemporary marketing age.

Full-Cycle Consumer Psychology

Any consumer psychologist intrigued by the possible meaning of brands should watch a NASCAR race, at least on television. (If you are already a NASCAR fan, skip this paragraph.) You are likely to be reminded of Robert Cialdini's day at Ohio Stadium which led him to declare to himself: "Cialdini, I think you're studying the *wrong* thing" (Cialdini, 1980, p. 22). While NASCAR is all about the drivers and the race, every race is also a colossal celebration of brands. There are the cars themselves, carrying the logos large and small of something like 800 NASCAR sponsors. TV announcers keep you informed throughout via the Old Spice Lap Leaders update and the Visa Race Break. We are told that Home Depot is the Official Home Improvement Warehouse of NASCAR and UPS is The Official Delivery Service of NASCAR. At commercial breaks there's the ever-present beer ads with Budweiser and Miller shouting at each other, and we rejoin the race following the Budweiser or Miller Lite car around the track. None of this should come as any surprise, because NASCAR openly and aggressively bills itself as the best marketing opportunity in sports (O'Keefe, Schlosser, Burke, & Mero, 2005). Yet something important seems to be going on here regarding the meaning of brands, and as consumer psychologists we should be embarrassed by our inability to explain what it is. Perhaps that's a little harsh, but the point is there is a richness and texture of branding activity in the marketplace that is understudied by consumer psychologists working in their labs.

If one is intrigued by the prospect of "full-cycle" consumer psychology (à la Cialdini, 1980), then there is much happening in the natural world of brand building to spark new constructs, theories and research methods. To paraphrase the classic line from Kurt Lewin: there is nothing so practical as a good theory, and there is nothing so stimulating of good theory as dynamic developments in one's natural domain (cf. Petty & Cacioppo, 1996). A few particularly important areas for such stimulation are considered below.

The Design Imperative

Some might contend that the hottest of the "hot topics" in the real world of brand building is *Design* (Neff, 2005; Nussbaum, Berner, & Brady, 2005; Reingold, 2005). Brands like Apple, BMW,

Target, Altoids, Starbucks, and L'Oreal certainly make design a primary element in their business strategies. However, what we now also see are champions of functional performance like Procter & Gamble and Whirlpool advocating the pre-eminence of design (Salter, 2005). At P&G, brands like Olay, Pampers, and Tampax have utilized new designs to create emotional connections with consumers (Neff, 2005). To formalize its commitment, P&G recently hired over 500 designers to staff its cross functional brand teams.

The design field is obviously many different things, drawing on disciplines such as ergonomics, human factors, engineering, industrial design, and marketing (Cagan & Vogel, 2002; Vogel, Cagan, & Boatwright, 2005). Designers provide beauty and enhance functionality. Often, they also create visual cues and identity systems in an effort to communicate desired meaning about brands. Design can be thought of as the outcome, but also can be represented as a systemic process for generating innovative outcomes, as championed by the highly regarded design firm IDEO (Brown, 2005; Kelley & Littman, 2001). When we consider all the things that design represents, it is hard to write it off as a fad or hot topic. Indeed, it is likely that any field interested in brands and how they acquire meaning will become increasingly irrelevant without a serious commitment to understanding design (cf. Schroeder, 2005b).

In the practical world of design one can point to many outcomes that could serve to inspire new directions in consumer research. For example, in the creation of visual identity systems, designers must anticipate multiple generations of brand extensions and provide a solution that is flexible enough so that extensions will have the symbolism and iconography that links them to the base brand, but at the same time signify that the extension is something innovative and new. The academic literature on brand extensions has overlooked the role of design cues in facilitating or inhibiting the viability of an extension. "Good identity systems" are intended to moderate fit issues and cannot be separated from the more abstract discussion now popular in our literature regarding brand architecture (Aaker & Joachimsthaler, 2000; DeFanti & Goodman, 2005). Our prolific literature on brand extensions (see Keller & Lehmann, 2005, for an overview) will remain an abstract, academic discussion without consideration of design's pivotal role in communicating and demarcating important meanings of the brand.

Another excellent opportunity for consumer psychologists is raised by what is a re-occurring theme among design practitioners. It merits emphasis that design is not simply a matter of maximizing aesthetic appeal at a single moment in time. Good design can also provide performance benefits that reinforce the value of the brand each and every time it is used, as in the OXO GoodGrips product line (Cagan & Vogel, 2002). Good design can yield re-occurring benefits through consistent pleasure in use (e.g., Bloch, 1995; Schmitt, 1999), especially in what Arnould and Thompson (2005) refer to as the management of servicescapes. It is this persistent benefit from good design that apparently accounts for the common observation that through design, one is able to foster meaningful emotional attachments to brands (Gobe, 2001; Reingold, 2005). To date, the connection between compelling design and emotional attachment to brands has been largely ignored (cf. Thomson, MacInnis, & Park, 2005).

Although the consumer psychology literature featuring design issues has been remarkably scant thus far (cf. Hoegg &Alba, chapter 29, this volume; Keller & Lehmann, 2005) some recent studies (Bloch, Brunel, & Arnold, 2003; Page & Herr, 2002; Veryzer & Hutchinson, 1998; Warlop, Ratneshwar, & van Osselaer, 2005) suggest important questions that the field could entertain if we wanted to get serious about design. In particular, Page and Herr (2002) model the interplay between aesthetic cues and product function in consumers' affective and cognitive judgments about brands. They show that simple product liking is most heavily influenced by aesthetic cues, in a process reminiscent of Zajonc's (1980) classic thesis about the automaticity of preference formation. Additionally,

Page and Herr show that quality judgments about brands are formed through a more effortful process that appears to combine information about design elements and functionality. In their 2003 article, Bloch, Brunel, and Arnold developed and validated an individual difference measure tapping design sensibility (the Centrality of Visual Product Aesthetics, CVPA) and showed that for consumers high in CVPA, product design is weighted more heavily in purchase intentions, and is important in more product categories than for low CVPA consumers. Given consumer psychologists' longstanding interest in questions concerning the interplay of affect and cognition and form versus function, Page and Herr open the door to many important questions, and measurement advances like the CVPA scale will benefit future empirical work.

More investigation is warranted on the issue of how aesthetic cues exploited by designers influence individuals' reactions to a brand. Research-in-progress investigates the link between design characteristics and brand personality perception (Brunel, 2003), and perceptions of novelty in product design elements as they relate to overall product evaluations (Brunel & Swain, 2005). Following Page and Herr (2002), it is reasonable to pursue this agenda where affective and cognitive judgments are treated as distinct entities. Other interesting questions are easily surfaced. For instance, when will a design-driven direct affect transfer process overwhelm more effortful (and cognitive) brand assessment? Are aesthetic cues best conceived as simple affect generators, or should they be treated as meaning makers that prompt inferences about the brand? If so, then when? Is it possible, as per the suggestion of Hoegg and Alba (chapter 29, this volume), that compelling design may even bias cognitive processing to yield sub-optimal decisions? Much like extant literature on the influence of visual elements in advertising (cf. McQuarrie & Phillips, 2005), our understanding of the "persuasiveness" of design elements in shaping all manner of product perceptions is lacking.

In acknowledging limitations, Page and Herr (2002) noted that their research concerned subjects' first impressions of a hypothetical new product. This is perhaps the most common limitation across branding studies: we study momentary responses to novel stimuli based on perfunctory assessments in a lab. It is hard to know from these instances whether we end up over- or underestimating the impact of design. If emotional attachments develop from repeated experiences with well-known brands, we will need more longitudinal studies with real brands in real consumption settings to better judge the impact of design.

Media Fragmentation and the Practice of Integrated Brand Promotion

If practice can ever be a valid point of reference for our theory building, then there can be little doubt that in the world of practice, integrated brand building is well established as a means by which sophisticated marketers attempt to shape and sharpen the meaning of their brands (Cappo, 2003; Keller & Lehmann, 2005; O'Guinn, Allen, & Semenik, 2006; Wellinghoff, 2003). For example, to introduce its new Blue card, American Express employed a diverse mix, starting with Blue-labeled water bottles given away at health clubs and Blue ads printed on millions of popcorn bags. They sponsored a Sheryl Crow concert in Central Park and transformed L.A.'s House of Blues jazz club into the "House of Blue," with performances by Elvis Costello, Stevie Wonder, and Counting Crows. Print ads and TV were also used to promote Blue, but following industry trends, spending in traditional media was cut over 50% compared to previous AmEx product launches. Making diverse components such as these work together in synergistic support of the brand is commonplace in today's world of practice.

By contrast, the lack of diversity and the univocal nature of studies by consumer researchers are disconcerting. One of the few "multi-media" studies in our literature used a TV ad in combination with the audio track from that ad to simulate radio (Edell & Keller, 1999), The authors concluded that coordinated TV and radio campaigns warrant consideration. Other published research on the virtues of integration indicates a possible synergy between TV and print (Naik & Raman, 2003). As a field, we have little to offer on the question of integrated brand promotion. Deighton (1995) extends our challenge by noting that sophisticated practitioners not only manage the synergy between media vehicles, but also coordinate messages targeted at multiple audiences (e.g., retail buyers vs. end users), and predetermine messaging to carry consumers through multiple stages in their relationship with a brand. Our research does not consider these and other levels on which integrated marketing programs are designed.

In this age of unbridled message clutter and increasing media fragmentation, "synergistic" and "integrated" continue to be the magic words for brand builders. However, there is belief in the power of integration with very little in the way of research that guides us with respect to how and why. Perhaps we will make more headway against integration issues if we acknowledge that marketers don't merely wish to communicate select messages: they spend huge sums of money on ads, events, signage, racecars, Web sites, product placements, and popcorn bags in order to build brands. Without an explicit focus on brand building, there will be very little integration. The challenge is to appropriately accommodate the complexity raised by the practice of brand builders in our academic research concerning the meaning of brands.

This is another area where research opportunities abound. First and foremost, consumer psychologists are challenged to put theories on the table that can help justify the perceived value of integration. Do multiple media generate the most value when they simply serve to reinforce a common message, or does real synergy emerge when different media carry distinct messages to allow consumers to accommodate their own desired meaning for a brand (cf. Keller & Lehmann, 2005)? And if stories are appropriate "constructs" for thinking about how consumers create and carry brand meaning (Holt, 2003a; Zaltman, 2003), then what media and messages prove most potent in shaping these holistic stories? Then of course there is the classic question of the meaning embedded in the medium per se. If the medium is the message, how do we think about the virtues of the implicit endorsement from a Sheryl Crow concert, versus explicit claims made in a print ad for a new credit card? At an even more basic level, we really don't know how communications and the products or services they support may interact to yield meaningful outcomes. For example, Apple's "Think Different" campaign was initially a disappointment (Gobe, 2001). But then along came the iMac and with this innovative and well designed product, the "Think Different" campaign worked synergistically to yield a remarkable turnaround for a struggling Apple (cf. O'Guinn, Allen, & Semenik, 2006). Synergy across many fronts has become the gospel for brand builders. If as consumer psychologists we want to contribute to an understanding of how brands acquire and maintain meaning, we will have to prioritize and learn how to investigate synergy in its many manifestations.

The New Persuasion

In the new form of persuasion commonly referred to as branded entertainment, we find celebrity and pop culture becoming totally intertwined with the meaning of brands. Branded entertainment entails embedding one's brand or brand icons as part of any entertainment property (e.g., a sporting event, TV show, theme park, short film, movie or videogame) in an effort to impress and connect with your consumer in a unique and compelling way (O'Guinn, Allen, & Semenik, 2006). Practitioners are increasing their investment in this form of brand building (Graser, Halliday, & Neff, 2005), yet it cannot be accommodated by the received view on branding, or mainstream theories of persuasion. For example, in his version of the "new marketing model" speech (Heyer, 2003),

Coca Cola's then Chief Operating Officer maintained that "The right associations with the right movies, artists, video games and events illustrates, enhances and accelerates the contemporization of core brand values. But that is no longer enough." In Heyer's view, the new persuasion entails alliances between Hollywood, Madison Avenue ad agencies, and brand marketers to deliver unique experiences to consumers. Product performance claims are absent in this new persuasion. Persuasion here is better conceived as co-creation where the meanings between brands and entertainment properties are intertwined.

We naturally use familiar theoretical frameworks in our first attempts to understand new forms of persuasion, as in research on product placements (Russell, 2002). But, for example, an elegant theoretical framework like the Elaboration Likelihood Model was never conceived with this kind of "persuasive activity" as its domain of application. In the domain of branded entertainment, everything must be considered a peripheral cue; there is no central processing of concrete message arguments or claims. The solitary ad processor assumed by the ELM is no longer relevant either, as consumers create and share their branded stories in co-authorship of the brand. Attitude change is not necessarily the point of all this, but rather some form of meaning transfer (à la McCracken, 1986). However, suggesting that meaning simply moves freely by association from any entity (e.g., a celebrity) to any brand (e.g., Keller, 2003) is not a coherent theoretical explanation. With messages and claims no longer a point of emphasis, we are challenged to reconsider the fundamental question of what it means to be persuaded.

If in branded entertainment we find celebrity and pop culture intertwined with brand meaning, we must also circle back to elemental questions concerning the meaning and process of celebrity as pertains to brands. We are not sure what celebrity is, how it develops, or how it operates to confer value upon a brand (cf. Fournier & Herman, 2005; McCracken, 1989). One thing is certain: notions of credibility, expertise, and trustworthiness (cf. Baker & Churchill Jr., 1977; Sternthal, Dholakia, & Leavitt, 1978) typically levied against the phenomenon are incomplete. Celebrities serve as vivid and provocative summary vessels of cultural meaning; their meaning making lives are much broader and more vibrant than their isolated applications to the brand. Here again the challenge to consumer psychologists is to bring new theory to the table that begins to address a new form of persuasion that is increasingly common.

Bottom-Up Branding—Managing the Buzz

The odd phrase "word of mouth" has been part of marketing vernacular for decades (e.g., Katz & Lazarsfeld, 1955), but it has never engendered the "buzz" that "buzz marketing" is receiving currently (Kahn & Wind, 2005). Perhaps this new buzz about an old idea can be partially attributed to Malcolm Gladwell and his best seller, *The Tipping Point* (2000), wherein the case is made that "mavens" and "connectors" are critically important in fostering social epidemics. To be sure, word-of-mouth advocacy is a more robust phenomenon when there exists a medium like the Internet that allows one to spread the word to thousands of one's close, personal friends with the simple click of a mouse. But not to be overlooked in the buzz about word of mouth is the proactive role that marketers now are playing. Sophisticated marketers are seeking not just to manage but also manufacturer buzz, especially on the Internet, and at an accelerating rate at that (Kahn & Wind, 2005; Neff, 2003; Steinberg, 2005).

These new word-of-mouth programs take many forms. One high profile exemplar has been a unit within Procter & Gamble branded as Tremor. P&G has assembled a panel of 250,000 teens with a special emphasis on signing up connectors/opinion leaders. These teens, 75% of whom are female, are then asked to spread the word about new products or product concepts that P&G sends their way. P&G asserts that panelists are not paid cash to make recommendations, but are rewarded with product samples and the enticement of being the "first to know" about new products and fashions. The dollars P&G invests in Tremor are miniscule compared to their investments in conventional media, but still they have generated much fanfare. In a perfect illustration of the uncontrollable nature of today's branding world, not all the fanfare has been flattering. Recent allegations that Tremor and other buzz marketing firms are acting to deceive consumers (Horovitz, 2005; Rodgers, 2005) reveal the dilemma inherent with these tactics.

Another related development is the emergence of "corporate blogs," once considered an oxymoron. Marketers are now moving proactively to harness the power of blogs for brand building. GM Vice Chairman Bob Lutz launched his own *FastLane Blog* to broker customer suggestions; Netflix streams information to respected blogger Mike Kaltschnee, who passes it on to movie fans. The contentious practice of paying bloggers for product support is also on the rise. Upstart Marqui paid 20 bloggers $800 a month to promote its Web marketing services; Republicans and Democrats sponsored three bloggers in recent election campaigns. Fake blogs (called flogs) are also emerging. McDonalds launched a fake blog to accompany its SuperBowl ad about a French fry shaped like Abe Lincoln; Captain Morgan created a fake blog to taut its rum drinks. Consumer research involving this unique meaning making venue is sorely needed if we are to maintain a leadership voice regarding the new dynamics of brand building.

As firms move to push the envelope on managing and sometimes concocting word of mouth, important questions about risks versus rewards are surfaced. Sony Ericcson's launch of their combination cell phone and digital camera stands as a notable case in point (see Brown, 2004). The $5 million campaign employed actors who pretended to be tourists at national landmark sites. Sony's fake tourists asked bystanders to take their pictures using their new Sony camera phones, and were quick to share relevant product information. The actors remained silent on their connection to the manufacturer unless explicitly queried. The campaign generated much word-of-mouth among potential consumers and was deemed a success by the firm. But it also caused outrage, generating attention from Ralph Nader's Commercial Alert. What are the effects of these "fabricated" co-creation strategies? Do they yield coveted authenticity for the brand? Are the benefits lasting or more fleeting and temporal? Importantly, what are the risks associated with the rewards, per effects on brand meaning, strength, and beyond? As firms scramble to harness the benefits of so-called buzz marketing, they are coming to realize the risks involved. Again, the robust natural phenomenon in play here presents tantalizing research opportunities for consumer psychologists.

Conclusions Concerning Companies as Co-Creators

To be clear, our argument is not that consumer psychologists should be doing more to serve the interests of sophisticated brand builders. But if we are to understand consumer-brand behavior, we must be able to account for the activities of brand builders in the theories we are testing. Per Cialdini (1980), "theory speaks only to the existence of the effects it predicts; it does not speak to the ecological importance of those effects" (p. 24). So, for example, while in theory a distinction between central and peripheral processing is important when studying persuasion, in today's marketplace the distinction may largely be irrelevant. There is reason to believe that our existing array of theories is behind the times for the study of branding and brands.

NEW DIRECTIONS

Given our review of today's brand building environment, it is sobering to consider an analysis like that of McQuarrie's (1998) concerning academic research on brand building, which for the most part has concerned advertising tests in lab experiments. McQuarrie conducted a content analysis of all advertising experiments published from 1942 to 1997 in the premier marketing journals. Over 400 experiments were coded for the presence of six reality factors: (1) was choice behavior accounted for, (2) were ads embedded in programming content, (3) were ad effects measured after a delay, (4) were competitive messages present, (5) was there repeated exposure to the messaging, and (6) did the ads promote familiar (versus fictitious) brands? Columns 1 and 2 in Table 31.2 summarize McQuarrie's results just for the *Journal of Consumer Research*; column 3 extends McQuarrie's analysis by including qualifying experiments from *Journal of Consumer Psychology* over the last 10 years. Conclusions from this analysis are straightforward: advertising experiments are common in consumer psychology; representing natural ad processing conditions in the lab has never been a high priority for consumer psychologists; and if anything, the trend is in the direction of less, not more, reality in the lab. McQuarrie refers to this trend as a growing detachment between advertising researchers and the goals of the advertiser. Our contention is that there exists a growing detachment between the research conducted by consumer psychologists and the goals of the brand builder as well. Certainly the complexity and dynamism of today's brand building environment, versus the simplicity and constancy of today's advertising experiment, appears as a contradiction; the realities of co-creation contrast starkly with the tenets of control that guide experimental design. As expressed in Cialdini's trapper metaphor (1980), "our finely-tuned traps allow us to capture phenomena without regard for their importance in the course of naturally occurring human behavior" (p. 23). There can be no doubt that we are proficient at laying finely-tuned traps. Conversely, applying the concept of representation (Shimp, 1994) and assessments of domain specificity (McQuarrie, 2004) remain low on the priority list.

Of course, the counterargument is long established (Berkowitz & Donnerstein, 1982; Calder, Phillips, & Tybout, 1981). Experiments are all about theory testing and it is our theories that allow us to generalize across domains of practitioner activity. We could never hope to capture the realities of the natural setting in our lab studies, nor should we even try. Let's keep working the current arsenal of theories to harness reliable generalizations.

But one has to wonder if testing and re-testing theories conceived at a different time and under simpler conditions is the right direction for the field. Even if ecological validity and mundane realism is not the right answer for consumer psychologists, we must push back and ask: what natural phenomenon did the theoretician have in mind when conceiving its constructs and axioms? It is likely for many of our theories that the original phenomenon did not include the complexities and qualities of today's brand building environment. Or as Peter Wright (2002) might contend, the marketplace metacognitions of consumers need to be considered, and our theories need to accommodate the dynamic nature of the phenomena we are trying to explain. To stay relevant as a field on the topic of brand, we will need new theory that accommodates and embraces a new level of complexity in the marketplace.

Beyond Brand Attitude

At the workbench level there are important implications to consider. Most centrally, we will likely need to reconsider our favorite dependent variable: brand attitude. Surely there is no more popular variable in consumer psychology, and for good reason. As Cohen (1990) observed, brand attitude was a logical focal point for researchers in search of "an intervening variable that would convincingly 'sum up' all the personal and marketplace influences at work and that would stand in direct line to behavior" (p. 153). This is a lot to ask of any single construct at any point in time, but in today's marketplace, maintaining attitude as a primary focal point in our theorizing may truly be insufficient. Consumer psychologists are thus challenged by the task of conceiving new constructs

Table 31.2   Reality Factors Common to Ad Experiments in JCR and JCP

	JCR 1974–1989 *(n=83)*	JCR 1990–1997 *(n=95)*	JCP 1995– 2005 *(n=65)*
Reality Factor			
(% of experiments)			
Choice	21%	12%	9%
Embedded exposure	19%	13%	6%
Measured after a delay	7%	4%	0%
Competitive message present	29%	26%	5%
Repeated exposure	26%	19%	8%
Familiar brand	41%	22%	43%
Number of factors addressed per study			
(% of experiments)			
Zero	29%	38%	37%
One	31%	38%	55%
Two	24%	15%	8%
Three	5%	10%	0%
Four	5%	0	0%
Five	6%	0	0%
Six	0%	0	0%
Average number of factors addressed			
(per experiment)	1.43	0.96	0.71

that accommodate the complexities of brand meaning and its making. There is no reason why the field cannot embrace this challenge.

One can legitimately argue that the brand-attitude construct is in need of fundamental reengineering in light of the observed branding "facts" we have reviewed. Brown (2006) argues persuasively that ambiguity and enigma are central to the magical aura that surrounds legendary brands. Holt (2004) identifies the creation and resolution of acute tensions as pivotal in the birth of the iconic brand. Muniz and Schau (2005) and others (Celsi, Rose, & Leigh, 1993) highlight the magical motifs and mystery and transcendence that enable loyalties and lasting brand community. These constructs—ambiguity, tension, mystery, transcendence—collectively characterize the conceptual domain not of an evaluative judgment, but of the narrative or story. Indeed, narrative is a frame that has many proponents in the interpretive branding paradigm (e.g., Holt, 2003b; Salzer-Morling & Strannegard, 2004; Zaltman, 2003). Within the frame of the story, the ambiguous, the equivocal, and the conflicted stand not as signals for the demise of the brand but rather, as necessary permissions for the involvement and individuated interpretations of text that create and enhance brand value. Conceiving brands as evolving texts or unfinished stories also accommodates the need for open brand meaning systems suggested in this review. Moreover, a reorientation from brand-as-attitude to brand-as-story can accommodate observed realities of brand multivocality, and our guiding tenet concerning multiple authorship for brands. Perhaps the single most important insight emanating from this review concerns the polymorphic nature of the brand: not only can brands mean dramatically different things to different people, they can mean multiple things to the same persons over contexts and time. One should expect this to be particularly true for mature brands (cf. Machieit, Allen, & Madden, 1993) that have acquired deep meanings for consumers through multiple interfaces. Implications for measurement are fairly straightforward: evaluating brands as narratives suggests promise not in simple evaluative judgments about the brand but in such constructs as ambiguity, resonance, and authenticity, which we have discussed throughout.

If attitude change no longer serves as a focal point for our branding research, then what process mechanism will fill the void? The obvious answer to this question is the process that we now can only vaguely refer to as "meaning transfer." Cultural theorists have argued for years that brands borrow important meanings from well defined cultural categories, such as celebrities, pop culture icons, and the contexts wherein brands are encountered. Can such meaning transfer be conceived as a spontaneous inference process per Kandes (see chapter 6, this volume), or do we need new process models to handle this phenomenon? In either case, there is no reason that consumer psychologists cannot contribute to our understanding of brand meaning and its making. Many interesting questions can be motivated here, including issues like the identification of contexts that facilitate or inhibit meaning transfer; brands that most benefit from meaning transfer; and consumer characteristics that govern receptivity to brand meaning making overall.

CONCLUDING THOUGHTS

As is true with all paradigmatic framings, both the associative network conception of brand and the meaning making view present certain limitations for our understanding of brands. As McCracken (2005) reminds us: "every theory trades certain kinds of knowledge at the expense of other kinds of knowledge; every piece of knowledge comes at the cost of a certain kind of blindness" (p. 169). We have not yet fully contemplated the implications of the streams of research reviewed above for the associative network conception of brand; the tenets of co-creation have yet to be fully rationalized with the dominant, received view. Keller recently echoed these same observations when he noted: "...there are multiple dimensions of brand knowledge as well as multiple potential sources or means to create that brand knowledge. It is essential that this multidimensionality be fully addressed in developing consumer behavior theory to explain branding phenomena. A potential danger with consumer research into branding is to adopt too narrow a perspective...The challenge and opportunity is fully appreciating the broad scope and complexity involved" (Keller, 2003, pp. 565, 596, 599).

By all counts we are living in a different branding world. Co-creation, collaboration, complexity, ambiguity, dynamism, loss of control, multivocality: such are the tenets of the new marketing world to which our brand theories must be held responsible. We have argued that on its own, the dominant branding paradigm cannot contend with the realities of this new branding world. The emerging branding paradigm embraces these tenets, and holds promise for realigning theory with today's marketplace. Consumer research has always aspired toward interdisciplinary status (e.g., Anderson, 1986), though this goal is seldom realized. In our studies of brands, there is an opportunity to fulfill this aspiration.

REFERENCES

Aaker, D. A. (1991). *Managing brand equity: Capitalizing on the value of a brand name.* New York: Free Press.

Aaker, D. A. (1996). Resisting temptations to change a brand position/execution: The power of consistency over time. *Journal of Brand Management, 4*(February), 251–258.

Aaker, D. A., & Joachimsthaler, E. (2000). The brand relationship spectrum: The key to the brand architecture challenge. *California Management Review, 42*(4), 8–23.

Aaker, D. A., & Shansby, G. J. (1982). Positioning your product. *Business Horizons, 25*(3), 56–62.

Aaker, J., Fournier, S., & Brasel, S. A. (2004). When good brands do bad. *Journal of Consumer Research, 31*(1), 1–16.

Aggarwal, P. (2004). The effects of brand relationship norms on consumer attitudes and behavior. *Journal of Consumer Research, 31*(1), 87–101.

Ailawadi, K. L., Neslin, S. A., & Lehmann, D. R. (2003). Revenue premium as an outcome measure of brand equity. *Journal of Marketing, 67*(4), 1–17.

Algesheimer, R., Dholakia, D. M., & Herrmann, A. (2005). The social influence of brand community: Evidence from European car clubs. *Journal of Marketing, 69*(3), 19–34.

Anderson, P. F. (1983). Marketing, scientific progress, and scientific method. *Journal of Marketing, 47*(Fall), 18–31.

Anderson, P. F. (1986). On method in consumer research: A critical relativist perspective. *Journal of Consumer Research, 13*(2), 155–173.

Arnould, E. J., & Price, L. L. (1993). River magic: Extraordinary experience and the extended service encounter. *Journal of Consumer Research, 20*(1), 24–45.

Arnould, E. J., & Price, L. L. (2000). Authenticating acts and authoritative performances: Questing for self and community. In S. Ratneshwar, D. G. Mick, & C. Huffman (Eds.), *The why of consumption: Contemporary perspectives on consumer motives, goals and desires.* London and New York: Routledge.

Arnould, E. J., & Thompson, C. J. (2005). Consumer culture theory (CCT): Twenty years of research. *Journal of Consumer Research, 31*(4), 868–882.

Aron, D., & Muñiz, A. M. (2002). Firing back: Consumer-created brand hate sites. Paper presented at the 105th annual convention of the American Psychological Association.

Askegaard, S. (2006). Brands as a global ideoscape. In J. Schroeder & M. Salzer-Mörling (Eds.), *Brand culture* (pp. 91–102). London: Routledge.

Atkinson, C., & Klaassen, A. (2005). P&G and GM slash TV spending. *Advertising Age* (June 13), 1, 46.

Avery, J. (2006). Intertwined identities: Consumer identity renegotitiation following brand meaning change. Working paper, Harvard University.

Baker, M. J., & Churchill Jr, G. A. (1977). The Impact of physically attractive models on advertising evaluations. *Journal of Marketing Research, 14*(4), 538–555.

Baker, S., & Green, H. (2005). Blogs will change your business. *Business Week* (May 2), 56–67.

Belk, R., Meyer, R., & Bahn, K. (1982). The eye of the beholder: Individual differences in perceptions of consumption symbolism. *Advances in Consumer Research, 9*(1), 523–530.

Belk, R. W. (1978). Assessing the effects of visible consumption on impression formation. *Advances in Consumer Research, 5*(1), 39–47.

Belk, R. W. (1988). Possessions and the extended self. *Journal of Consumer Research, 15*(2), 139-168.

Bergval, S. (2006). Brand ecosystems: Multilevel brand interaction. In J. Schroeder & M. Salzer-Mörling (Eds.), *Brand culture* (pp. 186–197). London: Routledge.

Berkowitz, L., & Donnerstein, E. (1982). External validity is more than skin deep. *American Psychologist, 37*(March), 245–257.

Bloch, P. H. (1995). Seeking the ideal form: Product design and consumer response. *Journal of Marketing, 59*(3), 16–29.

Bloch, P. H. , Brunel, F. F., & Arnold, T. J. (2003). Individual differences in the centrality of visual product aesthetics: Concept and measurement. *Journal of Consumer Research, 29*(4), 551–565.

Boorstin, D. (1973). *The Americans: The democratic experience.* New York: Random House.

Branch, S., & Ball, D. (2005). Does reality sell beauty? *Wall Street Journal* (June 5), B1–B8.

Brioschi, A. (2006). Selling dreams: The role of advertising in shaping luxury brands meaning. In J. Schroeder & M. Salzer-Mörling (Eds.), *Brand culture* (pp. 198–210). London: Routledge.

Brown, S. (2001). Torment your customers (they'll love it). *Harvard Business Review, 79*(9), 82–88.

Brown, S. (2003). Material girl or managerial girl? Charting Madonna's brand ambition. *Business Horizons, 46*(4), 2-10.

Brown, S. (2004). O customer, where art thou. *Business Horizons, 47*(4), 61–70.

Brown, S. (2006). Ambi-brand culture: On a wing and a swear with Ryannair. In J. Schroeder & M. Salzer-Mörling (Eds.), *Brand culture* (pp. 50–66). London: Routledge.

Brown, T. (2005).Strategy by design. *Fast Company* (95), 52–54.

Brunel, F. F. (2003). Linking visual product aesthetics to product personality. Working Paper Series, Boston University, School of Management Boston University, School of Management.

Brunel, F. F., & Swain, S. (2005). Advancing theoretical understanding for consumers' responses to product design. In B. A. Walker & M. B. Houston (Eds.), *American Marketing Association proceedings, Vol. 16*. San Francisco: American Marketing Association.

Cagan, J., & Vogel, C. M. (2002). *Creating breakthrough products*. Upper Saddle River, NJ: Prentice Hall.

Calder, B. J., Phillips, L. W., & Tybout, A. M. (1981). Designing research for application. *Journal of Consumer Research*, *8*(2), 197–207.

Cappo, J. (2003). *The future of advertising*. Chicago: Crain Communications.

Celsi, R. L., Rose, R. L., & Leigh, T. (1993). An exploration of high-risk leisure consumption through skydiving. *Journal of Consumer Research*, *20*(1), 1–23.

Chang, J. C. (2005). Invisible brands: An ethnography of households and the brands in their kitchen pantries. *Journal of Consumer Research*, *32*(June), 106–118.

Cialdini, R. B. (1980). Full-cycle social psychology. In L. Bickman (Ed.), Applied social psychology annual (pp. 21–47). Beverly Hills, CA: Sage.

Clay, A. (2003). Keepin' it real. *American Behavioral Scientist*, *46*(10), 1346–1358.

Cohen, J. B. (1989). An over-extended self? *Journal of Consumer Research*, *16*(1), 125–128.

Cohen, J. B. (1990), Attitude, Affect, and Consumer Behavior. In B. Moore & A. Isen (Eds.), *Affect and social behavior* (pp. 152–206). Cambridge: Cambridge University Press.

Cova, B. (1996). The postmodern explained to managers: Implications for marketing. *Business Horizons*, *39*(6), 15–23.

Cova, B. (1997). Community and consumption. *European Journal of Marketing*, 31(3/4), 297–316.

Cova, B., & Cova V. (2002), Tribal marketing: the tribilisation of society and its impact on the conduct of marketing. *European Journal of Marketing*, *36*(5/6), 595–620.

Csikszentmihalyi, M., & Rochberg-Halton, E. (1981). *The meaning of things: Domestic symbols and the self*. Cambridge: University Press.

Cushman, P. (1990). Why the self is empty. *American Psychologist, 45*(May), 599–611.

Davis, S. M., & Dunn, M. (2002). *Building the brand-driven business: Operationalize your brand to drive profitable growth*. San Francisco: Jossey-Bass.

DeFanti, M. P., & Goodman, J. K. (2005). Brand architecture and corporate reputation. *MSI Conference Summary, No. 05-303*, Cambridge, MA, Marketing Science Institute.

Deighton, J. (1995). The concept of integrated marketing communications. In J. P. Jones (Ed.), *Encyclopedia of advertising*.

Dillon, W. R., Madden, T. J., Kirmani, A., & Mukherjee, S. (2001). Understanding what's in a brand rating: A model for assessing brand and attribute effects and their relationship to brand equity. *Journal of Marketing Research*, *38*(4), 415–429.

Dolan, K. A. (2005). The soda with buzz. *Forbes*, *175*(6), 126–130.

Douglas, M., & Isherwood, B. (1978). *The world of goods: Towards an anthropology of consumption*. New York: W. W. Norton.

Edell, J. A., & Keller, K. L. (1999). The information processing of coordinated media campaigns. *Journal of Marketing Research*, *26*(2), 149–163.

Elliott, R. (1994). Exploring the symbolic meaning of brands. *British Journal of Management*, *5*(2), 13–19.

Elliott, R., & Davies, A. (2006). Symbolic brands and the authenticity of identity performance. In J. Schroeder & M. Salzer-Mörling (Eds.), *Brand culture* (pp. 155–170). London: Routledge.

Elliott, R., & Wattanasuwan, K. (1998). Brand as symbolic resources for the construction of identity. *International Journal of Advertising*, *17*(2), 131–144.

Englis, B. G., & Solomon, M. R. (1995). To be and not to be: Lifestyle imagery, reference groups, and the clustering of America. *Journal of Advertising*, *24*(1), 13–28.

Englis, B. G., & Solomon, M. R. (2000). Lifestyle onLine: A Web-based methodology for visually-oriented consumer research. *Journal of Interactive Marketing*, *14*(1), 2–14.

Farquhar, P. H., Han, J. Y., Herr, P. M., & Ijiri, Y. (1992). Strategies for leveraging master brands. *Marketing Research*, *4*(3), 32–43.

Featherstone, M. (1991). The body in consumer culture. In M. Featherstone, M. Hepworth, & B. Turner (Eds.), *The body: Social processes and cultural theory* (pp. 170–196) London: Sage.

Firat, A. F., & Venkatesh, A. (1995). Liberatory postmodernism and the reenchantment of consumption. *Journal of Consumer Research, 22*(3), 239–267.

Fournier, S. (1998). Consumers and their brands: Developing relationship theory in consumer research. *Journal of Consumer Research, 24*(4), 343–373.

Fournier, S. (2002). *Introducing New Coke.* Boston: Harvard Business School Publishing, No. 5-502-595.

Fournier, S., Avery, J, & Wojnicki, A. (2004). Contracting for relationships. Paper presented at the annual conference of the Association of Consumer Research.

Fournier, S., & Herman, K. (2005), Taking Stock in Martha Stewart: Insights into Person-Brand Building and the Cultural Management of Brands. Working paper at Boston University.

Fournier,.S., Solomon, M. R., &. Englis, B. G. (2007). Where brands resonate. In B. Schmitt (Ed.), *Handbook of brand and experience management.* Boston, MA: Elgar Publishing (in press).

Fournier, S., Winig, L., Herman, L., & Wojnicki, A. (2001). Martha Stewart Living Omnimedia (A). Boston: Harvard Business School Publishing, No. 9-501-080.

Frank, T. (1997). *The conquest of cool: Business culture, counterculture and the rise of hip consumerism.* Chicago: University of Chicago Press.

Freitas, A., Kaiser, S., Chandler, J., Hall, C., Jung-Won, K., & Hammidi, T. (1997). Appearance management as border construction: Least favorite clothing, group distancing, and identity ... not! *Sociological Inquiry, 67*(3), 323–335.

Friedman, M. (1999), *Consumer boycotts.* New York: Routledge.

Friestad, M., & Wright, P. (1994). The persuasion knowledge model: How people cope with persuasion attempts. *Journal of Consumer Research, 21*(June), 1–31.

Friestad, M., & Wright, P. (1995). Persuasion knowledge: Lay people's and researchers' beliefs about the psychology of advertising. *Journal of Consumer Research, 22*(June), 62–74.

Gardner, B. B., & Levy, S. J. (1955). The product and the brand. *Harvard Business Review, 33*(2), 33–39.

Garrett, D. E. (1987). The effectiveness of marketing policy boycotts: Environmental opposition to marketing. *Journal of Marketing, 51*(2), 46–57.

Geertz, C. (1973). *The interpretation of cultures.* New York: Basic Books.

Gergen, K. J. (1990). If person are texts. In S. Messer (Ed.), *Hermeneutics and psychological theory* (pp. 28–51). New Brunswick, NJ: Rutgers University Press.

Gladwell, M. (2000). *The tipping point.* Boston: Little, Brown and Company.

Gobe, M. (2001). *Emotional branding.* New York: Allworth Press.

Gobe, M. (2002). *Citizen brand: 10 commandments for transforming brand culture in a consumer democracy.* New York: Allworth Press.

Goulding, C., Shankar, A., & Elliott, R. (2002). Working weeks, rave weekends: Identity fragmentation and the emergence of new communities. *Consumption, Markets & Culture, 5*(4), 261–84.

Graser, M., Halliday, J., & Neff, J. (2005). P&G, GM lead parade to Mad & Vine. *Advertising Age, 76*(29), 8.

Grayson, K., & Martinec, R. (2004). Consumer perceptions of iconicity and indexicality and their influence on assessments of authentic market offerings. *Journal of Consumer Research, 31*(2), 296–312.

Gross, D. (2005). The scramble on Mad. Avenue. *Fortune, 152*(3), 63–64.

Gummesson, E. (1995). Relationship marketing: Its role in the service economy. In W. Glynn & J. Barnes (Eds.), *Understanding services management* (pp. 244–268). New York: Wiley.

Handelman, J. M. (1999). Culture jamming: Expanding the application of the critical research project. *Advances in Consumer Research, 26*(1), 399–404.

Heilbrunn, B. (2006). Brave new brands: Cultural branding between Utopia and A-topia. In J. Schroeder & M. Salzer-Mörling (Eds.), *Brand culture* (pp. 103–117). London: Routledge.

Heyer, S. J. (2003). Keynote remarks. *Advertising Age Madison + Vine Conference,* February 5.

Hill, R. P., & Stamey, M. (1990). The homeless in America: An examination of possessions and consumption behaviors. *Journal of Consumer Research, 17*(3), 303–322.

Hirschman, E. C. (1981). Community and idiosyncrasy in popular culture: An empirical examination of the layers of meaning concept. In E. C. Hirschman & M. B. Holbrook (Eds.), *Symbolic consumer behavior* (pp. 29–34). New York: Association for Consumer Research.

Hirschman, E. C. (1998). When expert consumers interpret textual products: Applying reader-response theory to television programs. *Consumption, Markets & Culture, 2*(3), 259–309.

Hirschman, E. C., & Holbrook, M. B. (1982). Hedonic consumption: Emerging concepts, methods and propositions. *Journal of Marketing, 46*(3), 92–101.

Hoeffler, S., & Keller, K. L. (2003). The marketing advantage of strong brands. *Journal of Brand Management, 10*(6), 421–445.

Hogg, M. K., &. Banister, E. N. (2001). Dislikes, distastes and the undesired self: Conceptualizing and exploring the role of the undesired end state in consumer experience. *Journal of Marketing Management, 17*(1/2), 73–104.

Holt, D. B. (1998). Does cultural capital structure American consumption? *Journal of Consumer Research, 25*(1), 1–24.

Holt, D. B. (2002). Why do brands cause trouble? A dialectical theory of consumer culture and branding. *Journal of Consumer Research, 29*(1), 70–90.

Holt, D. B. (2003a). *Brands and branding.* Boston: Harvard Business School Press, No. 9-503-045.

Holt, D. B. (2003b).What becomes an icon most? *Harvard Business Review, 81*(3), 43–49.

Holt, D. B. (2004). *How brands become icons: The principles of cultural branding.* Boston: Harvard Business School Press.

Holt, D. B. (2005). How societies desire brands. In D. G. Mick & S. Ratneshwar (Eds.), *Inside consumption.* London: Routledge.

Horovitz, B. (2005). P&G buzz marketing unit hit with complaint. Available at http://www.comercialalert.com (accessed 10/24/05).

Jansson, A. (2002). The mediatization of consumption: Toward an analytical framework of image culture. *Journal of Consumer Culture, 2*(1), 5–31.

Kahn, B., & Wind, J. (2005). What's the buzz about buzz marketing. Available at http://www.knowledge.wharton.upenn.edu (accessed 10/19/05).

Kates, S. M. (2002). The protean quality of subcultural consumption: An ethnographic account of gay consumers. *Journal of Consumer Research, 29*(3), 383–399.

Katz, E., & Lazarsfeld, P. F. (1955) *Personal influence.* Glencoe: IL: Free Press.

Keller, K. L. (1993). Conceptualizing, measuring, managing customer-based brand equity. *Journal of Marketing, 57*(1), 1–22.

Keller, K. L. (2001). Building customer-based brand equity: A blueprint for creating strong brands. In MSI Working Paper Series. Cambridge: Marketing Science Institute.

Keller, K. L. (2003). Brand synthesis: The multidimensionality of brand knowledge. *Journal of Consumer Research, 29*(4), 595–600.

Keller, K. L. (2005). Branding shortcuts. *Marketing Management, 14*(5), 18–23.

Keller, K. L., & Lehmann, D. R. (2003). How do brands create value? *Marketing Management, 12*(3), 26–31.

Keller, K. L., & Lehmann, D. R. (2005). Brands and branding: Research findings and future priorities. *MSI Special Report,* No. 05-200, Cambridge, MA, Marketing Science Institute.

Keller, K. L., Sternthal, B., & Tybout, A. M. (2002). Three questions you need to ask about your brand. *Harvard Business Review, 80*(9), 80–85.

Kelley, T., & Littman, J. (2001). *The art of innovation.* New York: Doubleday.

Kiley, D. (2005). Advertising of, by, and for the people. *Business Week* (July 25), 63–64.

Klein, N. (1999). *No logo: Taking aim at the brand bullies.* New York: Picador.

Kleine, S. S., Kleine III, R. E., & Allen, C. T. (1995). How is a possession 'me' or 'not me'? Characterizing types and an antecedent of material possession attachment. *Journal of Consumer Research, 22* (3), 327–343.

Knowles, J. (2003). Value based measurement and management. *Interactive Marketing, 5*(July-Sept), 40–50.

Kozinets, R. V. (2001). Utopian enterprise: Articulating the meanings of Star Trek's culture of consumption. *Journal of Consumer Research, 28*(1), 67–88.

Kozinets, R. V. (2002). Can consumers escape the market? Emancipatory illuminations from Burning Man. *Journal of Consumer Research, 29*(1), 20–38.

Kozinets, R. V., & Handelman, J. M. (2004). Adversaries of consumption: Consumer movements, activism, and ideology. *Journal of Consumer Research, 31*(3), 691–704.

Kumar, N., Linguri, S., & Tavasssoli, N. (2004). Red Bull: The anti-brand brand. Case LBS-CS-04-006, London, London Business School.

Lakoff, G., & Johnson, M. (1980). *Metaphors we live by.* Chicago: University of Chicago Press.

Lasn, K. (1999). *Culture jam.* New York: Harper Collins.

Leigh, T., Peters, C., & Shelton, J. (2005). The consumer quest for authenticity: An investigation of the multiplicity of meanings with the MGB Subculture. Working paper at Coca-Cola Center for Marketing, University of Georgia.

Levy, S. J. (1959). Symbols for sale. *Harvard Business Review, 37*(4), 117–124.

Loftus, E. F., &. Loftus, G. R. (1976). *Human memory: The processing of information.* Hillsdale, NJ: Erlbaum.

Luedicke, M., & Giesler, M. (2006). Beyond communalities: Conceptualizing brand community in context. Working paper at the Schulich School of Business.

Machieit, K. A., Allen, C. T., &. Madden, T. J. (1993). The mature brand and brand interest: An alternative consequence of ad-evoked affect. *Journal of Marketing, 57*(4), 72–82.

Maffesoli, M. (1996). *The time of the tribes.* Thousand Oaks, CA: Sage.

Maheswaran, D., Mackie, D. M., & Chaiken, S. (1992). Brand name as a heristic cue: The effects of task importance and expectancy confirmation on consumer judgment. *Journal of Consumer Psychology, 1*(4), 317–336.

McAlexander, J. H., Schouten, J. W, &. Koenig, H. F. (2002). Building brand community. *Journal of Marketing, 66*(1), 38–54.

McCracken, G. (1986). Culture and consumption: A theoretical account of the structure and movement of the cultural meaning of consumer goods. *Journal of Consumer Research, 13*(1), 71–84.

McCracken, G. (1989). Who is the celebrity endorser? Cultural foundations of the endorsement process. *Journal of Consumer Research, 16*(December), 310–321.

McCracken, G. (2005), *Culture and consumption II: Markets, meaning, and brand management.* Bloomington: Indiana University Press.

McGrath, M. A., Sherry, J. F., Jr., & Heisley, D. D. (1991). An ethnographic study of an urban periodic marketplace: Lessons from the Midville Farmers' Market. *Journal of Retailing, 69*(Fall), 280–319.

McQuarrie, E. F. (1998). Have laboratory experiments become detached from advertiser goals? A meta-analysis. *Journal of Advertising Research, 38*(6), 15–25.

McQuarrie, E. F. (2004). Integration of construct and external validity by means of proximal similarity: Implications for laboratory experiments in marketing. *Journal of Business Research, 57*(2), 142–153.

McQuarrie, E. F., & Mick, D. G. (1999). Visual rhetoric in advertising: Text-interpretive, experimental, and reader-response theory. *Journal of Consumer Research, 26*(June), 37–54.

McQuarrie, E. F., & Phillips, B. J. (2005). Indirect persuasion in advertising. *Journal of Advertising, 34*(2), 7–20.

Mead, G. H. (1934). *Mind, self and society.* Chicago: University of Chicago Press.

Mick, D. G., & Buhl, C. (1992). A meaning-based model of advertising experiences. *Journal of Consumer Research, 19*(3), 317–338.

Miller, K. E., & Sturdivant, F. D. (1977). Consumer responses to socially questionable corporate behavior: An empirical test. *Journal of Consumer Research, 4*(1), 1–7.

Muñiz, A. M., O' Guinn, T. C., & Schau, H. (2006). Preventing the death of the brand community construct. *Working paper at DePaul University.*

Muñiz, A. M., & O'Guinn, T. C. (2001). Brand community. *Journal of Consumer Research, 27*(March), 412–432.

Muñiz, A. M., & O'Guinn, T. C. (2005). Marketing communications in a world of consumption and brand communities. In A. J. Kimmel (Ed.), *Marketing communication: New approaches, technologies, and styles.* London: Oxford University Press.

Muñiz, A. M., & Jensen Schau, H. (2005). Religiosity in the abandoned Apple Newton brand community. *Journal of Consumer Research, 31*(4), 737–747.

Naik, Prasad A., & Raman, K. (2003). Understanding the impact of synergy in multimedia communications. *Journal of Marketing Research, 40*(4), 375–388.

Neff, J. (2003). P&G eyes the influencer. *Advertising Age, 74*(46), 3–43.

Neff, J. (2005). Why P&G won't win many Cannes lions. *Advertising Age, 76*(24), 3–45.

Neff, J., & Sanders, L. (2004). It's broken. *Advertising Age, 75*(7), 1–30.

Nussbaum, B., Berner, R., & Brady, D. (2005). GET CREATIVE! *Business Week* (August 2), 60–68.

Ogilvie, D. (1987). The undesired self: A neglected variable in personality research. *Journal of Personality and Social Psychology, 52*(2), 379–385.

O'Guinn, T. C., Allen, C. T., & Semenik, R. J. (2006). *Advertising and integrated brand promotion.* Mason, OH: Thomson South-Western.

O'Guinn, T. C., & Muñiz, A. M., Jr. (2004). The Polit-brand and blows against the empire: The collectively approved brands of the new-new left. *Advances in Consumer Research, 34*(1), 100.

O'Guinn, T. C., & Muñiz, A. M., Jr. (2005). Communal consumption and the brand. In D. G. Mick & S. Ratneshwar (Eds.), *Inside consumption: Frontiers of research on consumer motives, goals, and desires* (pp. 472–508). New York: Routledge.

O'Keefe, B. ,Schlosser, J. Burke, D., & Mero, J. (2005). America's fastest growing sport. *Fortune, 152*(5), 48–64.

Oser, K. (2005). Online crisis looms as ad demand surges. *Advertising Age, 76*(37), 1–53.

Ostergaard, P., & Jantzen, C. (2000). Shifting perspectives in consumer research: From buyer behaviour to consumption studies. In S. C. Beckmann & R. H. Elliott (Eds.), *Interpretive consumer research: Paradigms, methodologies and applications.* Copenhagen: Copenhagen Business School Press.

Page, C., & Herr, P. H. (2002). An investigation of the processes by which product design and brand strength interact to determine initial affect and quality judgments. *Journal of Consumer Psychology, 12*(2), 133–147.

Park, C. W., Jaworski, B. J., &. Maclnnis, D. J. (1986). Strategic brand concept-image management. *Journal of Marketing, 50*(October), 135–145.

Penaloza, L. (2000). The commodification of the American West: Marketers' production of cultural meanings at the trade show. *Journal of Marketing, 64*(4), 82–109.

Petty, R. E., & Cacioppo, J. T. (1996). Addressing disturbing and disturbed consumer behavior: Is it necessary to change the way we conduct behavioral science. *Journal of Marketing Research, 33*(1), 1–8.

Reeves, R. (1961). *Reality in advertising.* New York: Knopf.

Reingold, J. (2005). What P&G knows about the power of design. *Fast Company,* June (95), 56–57.

Richins, M. L. (1994). Valuing things: The public and private meanings of possessions. *Journal of Consumer Research, 21*(3), 504–521.

Ries, A., & Trout, J. (2001). *Positioning: The battle for your mind.* New York: McGraw-Hill.

Ritson, M., & Elliott, R. (1999). The social uses of advertising: An ethnographic study of adolescent advertising audiences. *Journal of Consumer Research, 26*(3), 260–77.

Rodgers, Z. (2005). Watchdog calls on FTC to investigate tremor. Available at http://www.clickz.com (accessed 10/24/05).

Roedder-John, D., Loken, B., Kyeong-Heui, K., & Monga A. B. (2005). Brand concepts maps: A methodology for identifying brand association networks. MSI Report No. 05-112, Cambridge, MA, Marketing Science Institute.

Rose, R. L., & Wood, S. L. (2005). Paradox and the consumption of authenticity through reality television. *Journal of Consumer Research, 32*(2), 284–296.

Rumbo, J. D. (2002). Consumer resistance in a world of advertising clutter: The case of adbusters. *Psychology & Marketing, 19*(2), 127–148.

Russell, C. A. (2002). Investigating the effectiveness of product placements in television shows: The role of modality and plot connection congruence on brand memory and attitude. *Journal of Consumer Research, 29*(December), 306–318.

Sahlins, M. (1972). *Stone age economics.* Chicago: Aldine.

Salzer-Mörling, M., & Strannegård, L. (2004). Silence of the brands. *European Journal of Marketing, 38*(1/2), 224–238.

Schau, H., & Gilly, M. (2003). We are what we post: Self-presentation in personal Web space. *Journal of Consumer Research, 30*(December), 385–404.

Schmitt, B. H. (1999). *Experiential marketing.* New York: Free Press.

Schouten, J. W., & McAlexander, J. H. (1995). Subcultures of consumption: An ethnography of the new bikers. *Journal of Consumer Research, 22*(1), 43–61.

Schroeder, J. E. (2005a). The artist and the brand. *European Journal of Marketing, 39*(11/12), 1291–1305.

Schroeder, J. E. (2005b). *Visual consumption.* London: Routledge.

Schultz, M., & Hatch, M. J. (2006). Corporate branding as strategy: The case of the LEGO company. In, J. Schroeder & M. Salzer-Mörling (Eds.), *Brand culture* (pp. 16–33). London: Routledge.

Scott, L. M. (1994). The bridge from text to mind: Adapting reader-response theory to consumer research. *Journal of Consumer Research, 21*(3), 461–479.

Shimp, T. A. (1994). Academic Appalachia and the discipline of consumer research. *Advances in Consumer Research, 21*(1), 1–7.

Shove, E., & Pantzar, M. (2005). Consumers, producers and practices. *Journal of Consumer Culture, 5*(1), 43–64.

Solomon, M. R. (1983). The role of products as social stimuli: A symbolic interactionism approach. *Journal of Consumer Research, 10*(December), 319–329.

Solomon, M. R. (1988a). Building up and breaking down: The impact of cultural sorting on symbolic consumption. *Research in Consumer Behavior, 3,* 325–351.

Solomon, M. R. (1988b). The forest or the trees? A Gestalt approach to symbolic consumption. In J. Umiker-Sebeok (Ed.), *Marketing and semiotics: New direction in the study of signs for sale* (pp. 189–218). Morton de Greyker.

Solomon, M. R. (1988c). Mapping product constellations: A social categorization approach to consumption symbolism. *Psychology & Marketing, 5*(3), 233–258.

Steinberg, B. (2005). Corporate blogging gets a chance. *Wall Street Journal* (May 8), B8.

Sternthal, B., Dholakia, R., & Leavitt, C. (1978). The persuasive effect of source credibility: Test of cognitive response. *Journal of Consumer Research, 4*(March), 252–260.

Thompson, C. J. (2004). Marketplace mythology and discourses of power. *Journal of Consumer Research, 31*(1), 162–180.

Thompson, C. J., & Arsel, Z. (2004). The Starbucks brandscape and consumers' (anticorporate) experiences of globalization. *Journal of Consumer Research, 31*(3), 631–642.

Thompson, C. J., &. Haytko, D. L. (1997). Speaking of fashion: Consumers' uses of fashion discourses and the appropriation of countervailing cultural meanings. *Journal of Consumer Research, 24*(1), 15–43.

Thompson, C. J., Pollio, H. R., & Locander, W. (1994). The spoken and the unspoken: A hermeneutic approach to understanding the cultural viewpoints that underlie consumers' expressed meanings. *Journal of Consumer Research, 21*(3), 432–452.

Thompson, C. J., Rindfleisch, A, & Arsel, Z. (2006). Emotional branding and the strategic value of Doppel-ganger brand image. *Journal of Marketing, 70*(January), 50–64.

Thompson, C. J., & Troester, M. (2002). Consumer value systems in the age of postmodern fragmentation: The case of the natural health microculture. *Journal of Consumer Research, 28*(4), 550–571.

Thomson, M. , MacInnis, D. J., & Park, C. W. (2005). The ties that bind: Measuring the strength of consumers' emotional attachments to brands. *Journal of Consumer Psychology, 15*(1), 77–91.

Toobin, J. (2004). A bad thing: Why did Martha Stewart lose. *The New Yorker* (March 22), 60–64.

van Ham, P. (2001). The rise of the brand state. *Foreign Affairs, 80*(5), 2-6.

Van Osselaer, S. M. J., & Alba, J. W. (2000). Consumer learning and brand equity. *Journal of Consumer Research, 27*(1), 1–16.

Vargo, S. L., &. Lusch, R. F. (2004). Evolving to a new dominant logic for marketing. *Journal of Marketing, 68*(1), 1–17.

Veryzer, R. W., & Hutchinson, J. W. (1998). The influence of unity and prototypicality on aesthetic responses to new product designs. *Journal of Consumer Research, 24*(4), 374–394.

Vogel, C. M., Cagan, J., & Boatwright, P. (2005). *The design of things to come.* Upper Saddle River, NJ: Wharton School of Publishing.

Warlop, L., Ratneshwar, S., &. van Osselaer, S. M. J. (2005). Distinctive brand cues and memory for product consumption experiences.*International Journal of Research in Marketing, 22*(1), 27–44.

Webster Jr, F. E., & Keller, K. L. (2004). A roadmap for branding in industrial markets. *Journal of Brand Management, 11*(May), 388–402.

Wellinghoff, L. (2003). Brand building in the 21st century. *ANA/The Advertiser,* October, 90–96.

Wicklund, R., & Gollwitzer, P. (1982). *Symbolic self completion.* Hillsdale, NJ: Erlbaum.

Wilk, R. (1997). A critique of desire: Distaste and dislike in consumer behavior. *Consumption, Markets & Culture, 1*(2), 175–196.

Wipperfurth, A. (2003). Speed-in-a-can: The Red Bull story. Available at http://www.plan-b.biz.

Wipperfurth, A. (2005), *Brand hijack: The marketing of no marketing.* San Francisco: Portfolio.

Wright, P. (2002). Marketplace metacognition and social intelligence. *Journal of Consumer Research, 28*(March), 677–682.

Zajonc, R. B. (1980). Feeling and thinking: Preferences need no inferences. *American Psychologist, 35*(February), 151–175.

Zaltman, G. (2003). *How customers think.* Boston: Harvard Business School Press.

Zaltman, G., & Coulter, R. H. (1995). Seeing the voice of the customer: Metaphor-based advertising research. *Journal of Advertising Research*, *35*(4), 35–51.

Zyman, S. (2002). *The end of advertising as we know it*. Hoboken, NJ: Wiley.

32

Theory in Consumer-Environment Research
Diagnosis and Prognosis

Sevgin A. Eroglu

Georgia State University

Karen A. Machleit

University of Cincinnati

INTRODUCTION

From Martineau's (1958) "store personality" and Kotler's (1974) "atmospherics" to Sherry and McGrath's (1989) "sense of place" and Bitner's (1992) "servicescapes," research on the built environment as a site of commercial and consumption domain continues to evolve as a critical influence on consumer and shopping behavior. At its core, this body of work has one common focus: to understand the person-environment relationship within the consumer-commercial domain context. In this chapter we examine selected literature in this area with the purpose of guiding future research where further inquiry is needed. A central conclusion from our review is that extant research can benefit from theory development and methodological diversity. Toward this end, we offer conceptual and methodological perspectives that invite research to enhance our understanding of environmental influences in commercial settings.

The focus of the chapter is on the physical *and* social characteristics of commercial environments, or "marketplaces and consumption sites" (Sherry, 1998, p. 1), as they impact various aspects of consumer behavior. Our emphasis is on built commercial environments and encompasses, but is not restricted to, their atmospheric elements alone. For the purpose of delimiting the plethora of environmental stimuli that operate inside and outside of commercial domains, we follow the frameworks conceptualized by Baker (1986) and Bitner (1992). The dimensions of environmental factors examined in this chapter are *internal* only and include ambient/design, space/function, signs/symbols/artifacts, and social dimensions. Our analysis is not limited to research on service domains alone, but includes all commercial settings where a marketing exchange takes place.

The purpose of the chapter is not to provide a comprehensive review of research in the area. An overview of the last 30 years of *experimental* research in the area has already been presented by Turley and Milliman (2000) and partly by Baker, Grewal, and Parasuraman (1994). Additionally, included in this book is a review (by Peck and Childers) of the research on the sensory factors in the environment. The purpose of this chapter is to examine the *theoretical* rigor in the field of environmental stimuli with the aim of identifying its challenges and promises.

The remainder of the chapter is organized in three sections. The first section focuses on the nature of environmental stimuli through which the commercial setting is communicated to its consumers. The second section presents an overview of the theoretical underpinnings of the area in marketing. The last section proposes a new conceptual approach to guide future research in the consumer-commercial setting context with the aim of advancing its frontiers.

THE COMMERCIAL ENVIRONMENT

At the outset, we need to specify what is meant by the term "commercial environment." Our focus here is on built (as opposed to natural), micro (as opposed to macro, such as countries), public (as opposed to primary and secondary, such as homes and neighborhoods, respectively), and commercial (as opposed to noncommercial) environments. Adapting from Barker's (1968) work on ecological psychology, we define the commercial environment as a "behavioral setting" which is characterized by specific spatial and temporal boundaries, where human and nonhuman components are designed to facilitate regularly occurring commercial activities. More specifically, our spotlight is on the retail environments where buyers and sellers interact for the exchange of goods and services. As such, our definition of the commercial environment transcends the spatial-physical qualities of a setting to incorporate its social and temporal dimensions. Any physical environment is a composite of the human (e.g., users and providers) and non-human (e.g., building, equipment, and fixtures) elements that are integrated to fulfill the purpose of all its users—in our context, they are the buyers and sellers.

All the physical and social stimuli in the environment help define the gestalt image that its inhabitants form about it and its usage. A stimulus "rouses or incites to action or increased action" (Sherman, Mathur, & Smith, 1997, p. 365). Several classifications have been offered in the marketing literature to categorize the stimuli originating in commercial domains where marketing exchanges of services and products take place. The most general classification identifies two groups: exterior and interior (Levy & Weitz, 2004). Exterior features include the architecture, marqués, frontage, parking areas and even the surrounding area of the site such as neighboring stores and landscape. The interior variables encompass all the design and spatial stimuli that aim the five senses. With a few exceptions (e.g., Kumar & Kirande, 2000; Ghosh & McLafferty, 1987; Rogers, 1992), most work in marketing has focused on the interior stimuli in commercial domains. The most dominant classifications in the area deal exclusively with the interior physical and social elements of commercial establishments.

Kotler's (1974) initial attempt at describing the physical features of commercial environments distinguishes between visual, aural, olfactory and tactile dimensions of a store and introduces the term "atmospherics" to capture the gestalt of these elements. Baker (1986) expands the definition to present a socio-physical classification which identifies four groups of stimuli: ambient (background elements such as music), design (such as color, style), functional/design (such as layout, signage), and social (customers and employees). Design is further divided into aesthetic (e.g., décor) and functional (e.g., layout, signage). Later, Bitner (1992) presents a tripartite conceptualization with ambient, space/function, and signs/symbols/artifacts as the three major categories. Ambient stimuli include background characteristics and, as a general rule, appeal to the five senses. Spatial/functional stimuli define the sizes and shapes of equipment and furnishings, the ways in which they are managed, the spatial relationships among them and their ability to facilitate performance.

Signs/symbols/artifacts are all the objects that implicitly or explicitly communicate information about the place to its users.

CONCEPTUAL BACKGROUND OF THE FIELD

Although Kotler (1974) is the first to introduce the term "atmospherics" into the marketing literature, research on consumer-environment interactions predates his work. Indeed, as early as the 1950s, marketing researchers were already examining physical qualities of retail outlets with respect to their "personalities" (Martineau, 1958).

Donovan and Rossiter (1982) applied Mehrabian and Russell's (1974) affect model (which posits that affect mediates the person-environment relationship) to a retail setting. Generally referred to as the Stimulus-Organism-Response (S-O-R) paradigm, this framework has found empirical support in both environmental psychology and marketing. Donovan and Rossiter's (1982) application of S-O-R in the retail context showed that two affect dimensions, arousal and pleasure, are good predictors of consumer responses to the shopping environment. Later studies in marketing have supported the basic tenets of the S-O-R paradigm applications in different retail contexts (e.g., Baker, Levy, & Grewal, 1992; Baker & Cameron, 1996; Wakefield & Blodgett, 1994; Russell & Pratt, 1980).

It is the work of Baker (1986) and Bitner (1992) that has pioneered the first comprehensive conceptualizations of environmental influences in marketing. Their early attempts at categorizing the environmental stimuli and developing theoretical frameworks inspired numerous contributions to the marketing literature. Baker's (1986) work has not only drawn attention to the role of environmental effects in marketing of services and products, but it has also fostered the field's theoretical development. Her identification of the social stimuli (customers and employees) as an essential part of commercial interiors has broadened the thinking in the area and inspired, for example, the integration of the personal selling and buyer-seller interaction research into the field (see for example, Bitner, 1990; Sharma & Stafford, 2000; Lam, Vandenbosch, & Pearce, 1998; Grewal, Baker, Levy, & Voss, 2003; Baker, Parasuraman, Grewal, & Voss, 2002).

Building on Baker's initial conceptualization and a vast inter-disciplinary literature, Bitner (1992) introduced the term "servicescapes" and called for research in "theory building, empirical testing, development of better measures and methods, and application/replication of findings from other fields" (p. 68). Her expanded framework has presented, to date, the most comprehensive approach to the environment-user relationships in commercial domains. Drawing mostly on environmental psychology, the framework focused on behavioral, emotional as well as physical influences of environmental stimuli on both customers and employees. Bitner's recognition of employees as another target of environmental impact expanded the theoretical realm of the research stream. Bitner's work continues to be a milestone in this research area, a departure point for numerous empirical, conceptual and managerial studies on consumer-environment research in marketing.

Sherry's (1998) edited collection on "markets as places" (p .1) is perhaps the last major conceptualization effort in this field. The volume contains works by an eclectic group of researchers who examine the role of place in consumer's encounter with the market. In the editor's own words, the volume has "an ambitious agenda (in which) the contributors are committed to a discovery-oriented, theory-building program of research into servicespaces" (p. 20). Notable for our purposes is a piece by Baker (1998) that examines the informational value of the store environment and proposes five theoretical frameworks (information processing, categorization, inference-making, semiotics and information integration) as potential bases for stimulating research on the cognitive role of environmental stimuli in consumer evaluations. Sherry's book makes at least two important contributions to the marketing literature in this area. First, it underscores the theoretical and managerial importance of place in contemporary markets and marketing. Second, it expands the theoretical and methodological possibilities, inspiring empirically and conceptually rigorous inquiry via conventional and, perhaps more importantly, unconventional thinking and methods in consumer-environment research.

PROBLEMS AND POTENTIAL IN CONSUMER-ENVIRONMENT THEORY

Based on the above background, we now present our assessment of the field by identifying (1) areas of theoretical challenges for consumer-environment research, and (2) issues of potential inquiry stemming from these limitations.

Theory Development and Use

Both theory development and theory use in the consumer-commercial environment research seem to be in infancy. With the exception of those contributions previously discussed, there have not been major conceptual developments in the past three decades of work in the area. As for theory use, the literature is equally limited. To date, a number of studies have resorted to S-O-R as their theoretical base, but even that is considered an approach rather than a full-fledged theory (Turley & Milliman, 2000). The predominant method in the field is to select one or more environmental stimuli and to examine their individual or joint effects on various consumer behavior variables. The Turley and Milliman (2000) review of the experimental studies in the area shows a visible concentration of research efforts on ambient stimuli (notably music and olfaction) as input variables, and three response groups (purchase, time in store and approach/avoidance) as output variables. Their review clearly underscores the need for theory development and concludes that in this research stream, "there has not been enough effort devoted to explaining, predicting and controlling the behavior of consumers" (p. 208). They also point out the necessity to go beyond the S-O-R and approach/avoidance paradigms in order to expand the scope of research in the area.

We find two major interrelated limitations in this research: (1) a tendency to view the commercial environment solely in discrete features and, (2) the overriding emphasis on causality, i.e., focus on finding direct cause-effect relationships between specific environmental stimuli and corresponding consumer responses (e.g., the impact of X on Y). We posit that both of these stem from the lack of a gestalt view of the environment, one that emphasizes the patterns of relationships between the environment and its inhabitants. The gestalt view is consistent with the notion of environment as a "place" (Sherry, 1998) with all of its interpersonal, sociocultural and physical qualities. It is also akin to the molecular vs. molar perspective of the environment, where the latter advocates a "holistic" approach to examining person-environment relationship (Werner & Altman, 2000; Wapner & Demick, 2000).

Generally referred to as the "transactional approach," this holistic philosophy is still considered to be the main theoretical foundation of environmental psychology (Saegert & Winkel, 1990; Stokols, 1987). Its unit of analysis is the person-in-environment and its focus the person's transactions (experience and actions) with the environment. Rather than emphasizing the antecedent-consequent or cause-effect relations, the attention is directed on understanding the whole transaction, the relationship between its aspects and how they work in combination. We posit that the transactional approach is a timely and fruitful perspective for examining consumer-commercial environment interactions; one that is appropriate for the inherently complex nature of the consumer-environment relationship. We further explore this perspective in the last section.

Almost eight years after the Turley and Milliman (2000) review, the dominant focus in the field still continues to be on the descriptive input/output models geared toward showing effects on various consumer behaviors. Yet, we must also note the research progress in the area. Prominent are the emerging efforts that aim to strengthen the conceptual basis of the field via applications of theories and constructs from the psychology, consumer behavior and environmental psychology literature. In this vein, Chebat and Dube (2000) recognize the "burgeoning pool of knowledge" (p. 89) in the field and the recent successful attempts to specify the underlying mechanisms of customer responses to shopping and service domains.

Environmental psychology, which focuses entirely on person-environment interactions, offers several conceptual frameworks that can enhance our understanding of consumer-environment interplay. Viewing the environment as a composite of physical, interpersonal, and socio-cultural dimensions, the environmental psychologists examine its physiological and psychological effects on its inhabitants. As such, the field offers a number of theoretical frameworks that can find application grounds in commercial settings.

As an example, we present one of the most established theoretical models used in environmental psychology, the *stimulus load theory,* and its potential application in the context of consumer-environment interactions. Rooted in information theory, the model is particularly appropriate for the consumer context since it encompasses all three domains (affective, behavioral and cognitive) of human behavior and can be applied to positive (enhancing) as well as negative (irritant) environmental stimuli. Essentially, the model is based on an inverted-U-shaped function between physical stimulation levels and human emotions, behavior and health. Too much stimulation (overload) or too little of it (understimulation) can both lead to environmental stress (Berlyne, 1960; Mehrabian & Russell, 1974; Wohlwill, 1974). In addition to physical factors, socio-cultural variables can also instigate stimulation overload (Scott & Howard, 1970).

Two dominant underlying mechanisms are believed to be responsible for the inverted-U shaped function between incoming stimuli and individuals' responses: *arousal and information overload.* Arousal plays an important role in several models of environmental psychology. For example, in examining the arousing effects of interpersonal distance and spatial confinement, Evans (1978) predicts that over-arousal increases individuals' efforts to minimize contact and lowers their task performance. Arousal is also linked to another central construct in person-environment research: emotion. Schachter and Singer (1962) contend that arousal is a necessary condition for emotion, however, the type of emotion experienced depends on the person's interpretation of the arousal state. Individuals in the aroused state will seek an explanation for their arousal (loud music, too many people, and so forth), which subsequently affects their attributions about and responses to the environment. This is closely related to the "scapegoating" theory advocated by Keating (1979) where people wrongly attribute their arousal induced by other reasons (such as unattained goals) to the most readily visible cause (such as too many people). Both over- and underarousal produce stress that may result in behavioral, psychological and physiological outcomes (Patterson, 1976).

Information overload is the second mechanism proposed to explain the inverted-U shaped function encountered in environmental influences. Milgram (1970) defines overload as a condition where the rate and amount of environmental stimuli exceed the capacity to cope with them. Rapoport (1976) expands the overload theory by proposing that there exists some optimal level of stimulation, which individuals strive to maintain. People generally avoid being in over- and understimulating conditions. On a similar note, Altman's (1975) privacy model proposes that individuals have a certain desired level of stimulation, which is shaped by their personal characteristics and situational factors. When over-stimulated, they resort to certain strategies such as withdrawing or limiting attention; conversely, when understimulated, they seek opportunities for interaction and information acquisition, exhibit friendly behaviors, and so forth.

The overload theory offers a solid theoretical basis for examining consumer-environmental effects in marketing domains. Saegert's (1973, 1974) applications of the concept to high density situations, for example, have shown that highly stimulating environments can lead to various cognitive and behavioral responses such as avoiding unfamiliar inputs, routinizing behaviors, and making decisions on smaller amount of information and analysis.

A number of research questions surface when we examine consumer-environment interactions from the arousal and overload perspectives. For example, what is the role of arousal in shaping consumers' responses to ambient stimuli in the retail context, such as music, olfaction, lighting, colors, merchandise density, and so forth? Perhaps arousal plays a mediating role between environmental stimuli and shoppers' reactions to them. The extent of over- or under-arousal experienced by the shoppers in the store influences their cognitive (e.g., store image), affective (e.g., shopping mood), and behavioral (e.g., time spent in store) responses. Similarly, what are the optimal levels for certain environmental stimuli (such as music, illumination, and consumer and merchandise density) that are shown to be influential in commercial domains? How do these levels vary across different retail/service environments? Is there an optimum level for social stimuli (e.g., service staff) in a servicescape? How do consumers cope with chronic overload conditions such as persistent loud music, noise or merchandise and customer density so common in certain commercial domains (e.g., mass merchandisers) or during particular situations (e.g., holiday shopping venues and crowded airports)? What is the relative importance of physical and social environmental stimuli in commercial domains? What impact do individual characteristics and cultural variables have in shaping optimum stimulation levels? What role do sociocultural and interpersonal qualities of a setting play in determining the optimum stimulation levels? How can the over- and undermanning theories contribute to our understanding of these dynamics? Which cognitive and behavioral mechanisms do consumers use while trying to restore their optimum stimulation levels in the shopping and service environments?

Intervening Factors

Much like beauty, the quality and amount of environmental impact seem to be in the eyes of its beholder. The perception and interpretation of environmental stimuli differ among individuals, as do their responses to them. For example, peoples' assessments of their own perceived control are found to mediate between consumer density and customers' evaluation of the service encounter (Hui & Bateson, 1991). Similarly, shoppers' tolerance for crowding (Eroglu, Machleit, & Barr, 2005) and their emotions (Sherman, Mathur, & Smith, 1997) are shown to mediate between certain store environmental stimuli and shopping behaviors.

Our review shows that, in general, there is need for more emphasis on the role of intervening variables in consumer-environment research in marketing. Research has to explicitly examine whether environmental influences on cognitive, affective and behavioral outcomes are direct or are partially or fully mediated by other variables. Going beyond the direct effects will enhance our understanding of the dynamics of environmental influences and improve predictions about both consumer and employee reactions to the commercial setting. There are a number of constructs that might serve as powerful mediators and moderators in this context.

Social Climate is one potential intervening factor that can enhance our understanding of environmental effects in commercial domains (Moos, 1973). Social climate refers to the interpersonal and socio-cultural qualities of a setting. Particularly in servicescapes, the social climate can play an important role in moderating customer reactions to environmental stimuli (Moos, 1973; Insel

& Moos, 1974; Kiretz & Moos, 1974). Environmental psychology literature identifies a number of dimensions that define the social climate of most organizations. At least three of these are relevant to marketing domains. The *relationship* dimension refers to the extent of individual's involvement with that setting and the extent of social support offered therein. It reflects, in part, a patron's identification with the shopping environment. Sirgy, Grewal, and Mangleburg (2000) posited that consumers whose actual, ideal and social self match their image of a store are more likely to patronize it.

System maintenance concerns the order, control and clarity in a setting. This dimension mirrors Bitner's (1990) findings on store and employee clutter and cleanliness and their effects on the customer. Similarly, work on consumers' way finding in stores (Titus & Everett, 1996) can be examined from a social climate perspective in terms of the degree of order and clarity in the store environment. The massive superstore and hypermarket formats are not only complex and hard to navigate, but they also rely heavily on self-service. Such low system-maintenance stores may affect store evaluations and behaviors of certain customer segments, such as the elderly and the harried shoppers.

The *personal development* dimension concerns the availability of personal growth and self-enhancement offered in the setting. It has implications for both consumers and employees. For example, in-store promotions, both physical (such as aisle banners and product signs) and social (e.g., cooking demos and food tasting), can enhance consumers' information base and, thus, their "personal development."

In sum, social climate variables are promising mediators for better understanding consumer-environment dynamic. The interaction of social climate variables with the environmental stimuli can be better predictors of consumer behavior than either of those variables alone.

Individual characteristics constitute another valuable set of intervening variables in this area. Despite Bitner's (1992) call, to date, very little research has been done to develop and test such constructs. Individual difference characteristics can help better explain and define the boundary conditions for responses to various commercial environments. Despite their consideration as being problematic factors in psychology and consumer behavior, individual variables can improve our understanding and predictions of consumer-commercial environment interactions. We believe it is particularly important to identify the critical individual characteristics and explain those that are systematic.

Baker (1998) suggests personality factors, such as sensation seeking, as plausible moderating variables. The list is long. Sensitivity to noise has been found to be predictive of a variety of responses including the level of disturbance that postoperative patients felt while recovering (Topf, 1985; Weinstein, 1978). Given that noise produces stress effects and annoyance (McLean & Tarnopolsky, 1977), it is likely that the level of noise in a service context (from individuals, music, and other sources) will affect the responses of patrons. Similarly, Baum et al. (1982) have shown that individuals who can screen out information are better able to cope with highly dense settings. Atmospheric responsiveness (Eroglu, Machleit, & Davis, 2003) and tolerance for crowding (Eroglu, Machleit, & Barr, 2005) are also found to have moderating effects on environmental influences on shoppers. Other potential individual variables include variety-seeking behavior (McAlister & Pessemier, 1982) and consumer need for uniqueness (Tian, Bearden, & Hunter, 2001), gender, and culture. For example, one interesting avenue of research is whether certain customer segments (such as the elderly, children, and women) are more/less susceptible to certain environmental cues and the types of coping mechanisms they may or may not have in place to deal with unfavorable environmental conditions, such as the overload. Haytko and Baker's (2004) examination of adolescent girls' mall shopping preference and behaviors with an eye on mall environment stimuli is a good example. In the case of older shoppers, challenges of wait-time due to customer density, hardships in way-finding and orientation as a result of signage and layout deficiencies, and unmet social needs due to under-staffing are issues with theoretical, managerial and, particularly, public policy implications.

Coping has been a major focus of research in environmental psychology for many years. For at least two reasons, coping can be a critical mediator between the negative store stimuli and consumer responses. First, the coping construct fits in well with the previously discussed arousal/ overload models, since it is "a process that unfolds in the context of a situation that is appraised as personally significant and taxing or exceeding the individual's resources for coping" (Folkman & Moskowitz, 2004, p. 747). Second, given that emotions and coping processes are inextricably linked (Lazarus, 1991) and that consumer-environment interactions are mediated by emotions, coping is a conceptually appropriate intervening variable in this context.

Research on coping is just beginning to proliferate in marketing (Duhachek, 2005; Duhachek & Iacobucci, 2005; Luce, 1998). Duhachek (2005) proposes a multi-dimensional model of consumer coping with the objective of accounting for the "multitude of strategies consumers enact" (p. 41). Many interesting issues can be addressed. Do different physical and social environmental cues instigate different coping strategies by shoppers? Put differently, are they "stimulus-specific" or do consumers have general coping strategies based on their past experiences in similar situations? For example, D'Astous (2000) has identified three major groups of irritants in the shopping context, ranging from bad smells, high temperatures and loud music to pressuring uncaring salespeople, crowded aisles and poor layout. Research on consumer-environment interaction, to date, has focused primarily on approach-avoidance means of coping with environmental stressors. Perhaps this orientation is too delimiting to capture the complex nature of consumer coping behaviors, as suggested by Duhachek (2005). Studies are needed to explain how various consumer experiences in irritating retailing domains are related to coping responses and how these strategies affect store evaluations and patronage behaviors.

In summary, we posit that mediator/moderator variables, which hitherto have not received their due attention in this research, have an important role in understanding consumer-environment interactions. Uncovering their potential contribution will help us better assess the underlying dynamics in the area.

A PROGNOSIS FOR THEORY IN CONSUMER-ENVIRONMENT RESEARCH: THE TRANSACTIONAL APPROACH

Perhaps the most significant developments in the consumer-environment research will come from those that improve and broaden the theoretical base of the field. Previously in the chapter we have mentioned several specific theories that can serve as potential frameworks for consumer-environment research. In this last section, we take a macro view and elaborate on an approach that might help further the theory-building and theory use in the area. Specifically, we posit that the *transactional approach* to consumer-environment studies can help re-shape the prevalent fragmented research tradition that characterizes this area in marketing and aid in developing some theoretical models to integrate and explain the empirical evidence to date. Our purpose here is not to claim one "correct" approach to guide theory in the consumer-environment research, but rather to introduce the basic tenets of an increasingly dominant view in environmental psychology and to explain our vision as to how it could enhance the theoretical rigor of our own area.

At the core of the transactional approach is the belief that phenomena should be studied as a gestalt system consisting of people, processes (psychological and social), the physical environment, and temporal qualities (Altman, Brown, Staples, & Werner, 1992; Werner, Altman, Oxley, & Haggard, 1987; Kaplan, 1987; Werner et al., 1992). Basically it advocates that: (1) Because people and psychological processes are inseparable from their physical and social context, the phenomena in these contexts should be treated as holistic units rather than combinations of separate elements; (2) Time and temporal qualities (in the form of change and continuity) are important aspects of these phenomena; and (3) Phenomena should be observed and understood from the view of different types of observers and participants, and the search should be for a formal cause (Altman et al., 1992). In the words of its leading proponent, Ittelson (1973), "Man is never encountered independent of the situation through which he acts, nor is the environment ever encountered independent of the encountering individual. It is meaningless to speak of either as existing apart from the situation in which it is encountered. The word "transaction" has been used to label such a situation…" (p. 18).

The emphasis on formal cause (rather than an "efficient" or forced cause) constitutes one of the guiding principles of the transactional approach (Altman et al., 1992; Werner, Brown, & Altman, 1997), one which we believe addresses a major weakness in the current consumer-environment research. Our review has shown that the predominant method in our field has been to isolate one or more environmental stimuli with the purpose of assessing their individual and joint effects on certain consumer behavior variables—namely, a focus on an antecedent-consequent relationship. For example, in store factors (such as music, illumination, crowding, scents, color, and so forth) are examined for their effects on selected shopping outcomes (such as the amount of purchase, time spent in store, satisfaction and re-patronage intentions). While this research approach has its advantages, an overarching reliance on such empirical focus comes at the expense of inadequate thought for theory building and use in the area. Such fragmented efforts also have a tendency to isolate one or a few environmental stimuli as the sole cause of outcomes that are far too complex to be explained by a single category (in this case, physical environmental) of determinants.

If the nature of the transactional approach is understood as above, what does it mean for the consumer-environment research? We posit that the shopping experience in a store consists of a sequence of events that make up the shopping routine with the events of this scenario unfolding in a coherent way. There is an unwritten but widely accepted shopping script, from the entrance to checkout register, where a choreography of actions develop continuously and in an interrelated fashion. In such a scenario, we would not expect any one event (e.g., a long wait time) or an environmental quality (e.g., music tempo or customer density) to be the sole "cause" for another event to occur, but that these actions would take place in an integrated fashion as congruent parts of a whole. Furthermore, this whole is not limited to physical environmental factors alone, but encompasses other elements such as the participants, processes and temporal qualities.

As an example of a transactional-based research in consumer-environment literature, we examine the crowding phenomenon. Let's assume that our study is stimulated by the desire to assess how a transactional approach might complement (or refute) the present findings that customer density in stores has both positive and negative shopping outcomes (Eroglu, Machleit, & Barr, 2005). In search of a formal cause, a key research question might be: How do the factors that create spatial and human density in a store fit together to instigate shoppers' crowding experience? Do they fit together in similar patterns regularly or do they change during special (e.g., holiday) and regular seasons? To address these questions, the transactional approach would advocate using multiple observers planted in the store to provide different perspectives and at multiple times to capture both regular and special seasons. These observations would be enhanced by numerous photographs, again taken at different times, and content-analyzed for the purpose of developing insights about the physical (e.g., shopping cart congestion in an aisle), psychological (e.g., via a discontented facial expression) and social (e.g., interaction with a cashier) processes taking place during the entire shopping episode. To expand the information base, researchers would conduct in-depth interviews with key informants such as the customer service staff and store manager as well as store designers and store prototype developers. This work, thus, would include a diverse number and composition of informants, observers and multiple methods and procedures at multiple time points. In sum, the research would be geared to expose the rich interconnectedness and the inherently holistic nature of the shopping scenario rather than a single snap shot. It would show how people (buyers and sellers), psychological and social processes, the physical qualities of the setting and temporal elements are coherent and inseparable—and how the recognition of this fact alone opens door for a greater understanding and prediction regarding crowding in commercial domains.

SUMMARY

To repeat our intent in this manuscript, we simply want to draw attention to the need and possibilities for theory building and use in consumer-environment research, and to introduce a new approach that might help guide the desirable development in this area. Clearly, progress will come from ever-broadening our vision regarding different theoretical and methodological possibilities. One such possibility is the transactional approach, not in lieu of, but as a complement to the existing deterministic view that dominates the current research orientation in this research stream. At the very least, we hope that this discussion will stimulate interest and advances in the theoretical rigor in consumer-environment research.

REFERENCES

Altman, I. (1975). *The environment and social behavior: Privacy, personal space, territory and crowding.* Monterey, CA: Brooks and Cole.

Altman, I., Brown, B. B., Staples, B., & Werner, C. M. (1992). A transactional approach to close relationships: Courtship, weddings, and placemaking. In B. Walsh, K. Craik, & R. Price (Eds.), *Person-environment psychology: Contemporary models and perspectives* (pp. 193–241). Hillsdale, NJ: Erlbaum.

Baker, J. (1986). The role of environment in marketing services: The consumer perspective. In J. A. Czpeil, C. Congram, & J. Shanaham (Eds.), *The services marketing challenge: Integrated for competitive advantage* (pp. 79–84). Chicago: American Marketing Association.

Baker, J., Levy, M., & Grewal, D. (1992). An experimental approach to making retail store environmental decisions. *Journal of Retailing, 68*(4), 445.

Baker, J. (1998). Examining the informational value of store environments. In J. F. Sherry (Ed.), *Servicescapes: The concept of place in contemporary markets.* Chicago: AMA, NTC Business Books.

Baker, J., Grewal, D., & Parasuraman, A. (1994). The influence of store environment on quality inferences and store image. *Journal of the Academy of Marketing Science, 22*(4), 328.

Baker, J., & Cameron, M. (1996). The effects of the service environment on affect and consumer perception of waiting time: An integrative review and research propositions. *Journal of the Academy of Marketing Science, 24*(4), 338.

Baker, J., Parasuraman, A., Grewal, D., & Voss, G. B. (2002). The influence of multiple store environment cues on perceived merchandise value and patronage intentions. *Journal of Marketing, 66*(2), 120.

Barker, R.G. (1968), *Ecological psychology: Concepts and methods for studying the environment of human behavior.* Stanford, CA: Stanford University Press.

Baum, A., Calesnick, L., Davis, G., & Gatchel, R. (1982). Individual differences in coping with crowding: Stimulus screening and social overload. *Journal of Personality and Social Psychology, 43*, 821–830.

Berlyne, D. E. (1960). *Conflict, arousal, and curiosity.* New York: McGraw Hill.

Bitner, M. J. (1990). Evaluating service encounters: The effects of physical Surroundings and employee responses. *Journal of Marketing, 54*(2), 69–82.

Bitner, M. J. (1992). Servicescapes: The impact of physical surroundings on customers and employees. *Journal of Marketing, 56*(2), 57–71.

Brehm, J. W. (1966). *A theory of psychological reactance.* New York: Academic Press.

Chebat, J.-C., & Dubé, L. (2000). Evolution and challenges facing retail atmospherics: The apprentice is dying. *Journal of Business Research, 49*(2), 89.

D'Astous, A. (2000). Irritating aspects of the shopping environment. *Journal of Business Research, 49*(2), 149.

Donovan, R. J., & Rossiter, J. R. (1982). Store atmosphere: An environmental psychology approach. *Journal of Retailing, 58*(1), 34.

Duhachek, A., & Iacobucci, D. (2005). Consumer personality and coping: Testing rival theories of process. *Journal of Consumer Psychology, 15*(1), 52–63.

Duhachek, A. (2005). Coping: A multidimensional, hierarchical framework of responses to stressful consumption episodes. *Journal of Consumer Research, 32*(1), 41.

Eroglu, S. A., & Machleit, K. A. (1990). An empirical study of retail crowding: Antecedents and consequences. *Journal of Retailing, 66*(2), 201.

Eroglu, S. A., Machleit, K. A., & Davis, L. M. (2003). Empirical testing of a model of online store atmospherics and shopper responses. *Psychology & Marketing, 20* (Special Issue on Behavioral Dimensions of e-Commerce), 139–150.

Eroglu, S. A., Machleit, K. A., & Barr, T. F. (2005). Perceived retail crowding and shopping satisfaction: The role of shopping value. *Journal of Business Research, 58* (Special Issue on Retail Consumer Decision Making), 143–150.

Evans, G. W. (1978). Human spatial behavior: The arousal model. In A. Baum & Y. Epstein (Eds.), *Human response to crowding* (283–303). Hillsdale, NJ: Erlbaum.

Folkman, S., & Moskowitz, J. T. (2004). Coping: Pitfalls and Promise. *Annual Review of Psychology, 55*(1), 745–774.

Ghosh, A., & McLafferty, S. L. (1987). Location strategies for retail and service firms. *CTS Accounting Software Survey.* .

Grewal, D., Baker, J., Levy, M., & Voss, G. B. (2003). The effects of wait expectations and store atmosphere evaluations on patronage intentions in service-intensive retail stores. *Journal of Retailing, 79*(4), 259.

Harrell, G. D., Hutt, M. D., & Anderson, J. C. (1980). Path analysis of buyer behavior under conditions of crowding. *Journal of Marketing Research, 17*(1), 45–51.

Haytko, D. L., & Baker, J. (2004). It's all at the mall: exploring adolescent girls' experiences. *Journal of Retailing, 80*(1), 67.

Hui, M. K., & Bateson, J. E .G. (1991). Perceived control and the effects of crowding and consumer choice on the service experience. *Journal of Consumer Research, 18,* 174–184.

Insel, P., & Moos, R.H. (1974). Psychological environments: Expanding the range of human ecology, *American Psychologist, 29,* 179–188.

Ittelson, W. H. (1973)., Environment perception and contemporary perceptual theory. *Environment and Cognition,* W.H. Ittelson, Seminar, New York.

Kaplan, R. (1987). Validity in environment/behavior research: Some cross-paradigm concerns,,*Environment and Behavior, 19*(4), 495–500.

Keating, J (1979), Environmental stressors: Misplaced emphasis. In I. Saranson & C. Speilberger (Eds.), Stress and anxiety (Vol. 6, 55–66). Washington, DC: Hemisphere.

Kiretz, S., & Moos, R. H. (1974). Physiological effects of social environments, *Psychosomatic Medicine, 36,* 96–114.

Kotler, P. (1973/1974). Atmospherics as a marketing tool. *Journal of Retailing, 49*(4), 48–64.

Kumar, V., & Karande, K. (2000). The effect of retail store environment on retailer performance. *Journal of Business Research, 49*(2), 167.

Lam, S., Vandenbosch, M., & Pearce, M. (1998). Retail sales force scheduling based on store traffic forecasting. *Journal of Retailing, 74*(1), 61–88.

Lazarus, R. S. (1991). Progress on a cognitive-motivational-relational theory of emotion. *American Psychologist, 46*(8), 819.

Levy, M., & Weitz, B.A., (2004). *Retailing management.* New York: McGraw Hill.

Luce, M. F. (1998). Choosing to avoid: Coping with negatively emotion-laden consumer decisions. *Journal of Consumer Research, 24*(4), 409.

Machleit, K. A., Kellaris, J. J., & Eroglu, S. A. (1994). Human versus spatial dimensions of crowding perceptions in retail environments: A note on their measurement and effect on shopper satisfaction. *Marketing Letters, 5*(2), 183–194.

Machleit, K. A., & Eroglu, S. A. (2000). Describing and measuring emotional response to shopping experience. *Journal of Business Research, 49*(2), 101–111.

Martineau, P. (1958). The personality of the retail wtore. *Harvard Business Review, 36*(1), 47–55.

McAlister, L., & Pessemier, E. (1982). Variety seeking behavior: An interdisciplinary review. *Journal of Consumer Research, 9*, 311–322.

McLean, E., & Tarnopolsky, A. (1977). Noise, discomfort, and mental health. *Psychological Medicine, 7*, 19–62.

Mehrabian, A., & Russell, J. A. (1974). *An approach to environmental psychology.* Cambridge, MA: MIT Press.

Milgram, S. (1970). The experience of living in cities. *Science, 167*, 1461–1468.

Moos, R. H. (1973). Conceptualizations of human environments. *American Psychologist, 28*, 652–665.

Patterson, M. L. (1976, May). *An intimacy-arousal model of crowding.* Paper presented at the Environmental Design Research Association, Vancouver, B.C., Canada.

Rapoport, A. (1976). Toward a redefinition of density. In S. C. Saegert (Ed.), *Crowding in real environments.* London: Sage.

Rogers, D. (1992). Review of sales forecasting models most commonly applied in retail site evaluation, *International Journal of Retail and Distribution Management, 4*, 3–11.

Russell, J. A., & Pratt, G. (1980). A description of the affective quality attributed to environments. *Journal of Personality and Social Psychology, 38*, 311–322.

Saegert, S. C. (1973). Crowding, cognitive overload and behavioral constraint. In N. Prieser (Ed.), *Environmental design and research* (pp.). PA: Dresden, Hutchinson and Ross.

Saegert, S. C. (1974). *Effects of spatial and social density on arousal, mood and social orientation.* Unpublished 7500793, University of Michigan.

Saegert, S.C. & Winkel, G. (1990). Environmental psychology., *Annual Review of Psychology, 41*, 441–447.

Schachter, S., & Singer, J. E. (1962). Cognitive, social and physiological determinants of emotional states. *Psychological Review, 69*, 379–399.

Scott, R., & Howard, A. (1970). Models of stress. In S. Levine & N. Scotch (Eds.), *Social Stress* (pp. 259–278). Chicago: Aldine.

Sharma, A., & Stafford, T. F. (2000). The effect of retail atmospherics on customers' perceptions of salespeople and customer persuasion: An empirical investigation. *Journal of Business Research, 49*(2), 183–191.

Sherman, E., Mathur, A., & Smith, R. B. (1997). Store environment and consumer purchase behavior: Mediating role of consumer emotions. *Psychology & Marketing, 14*(4), 361–378.

Sherry, J. F., Jr., & McGrath, M. A. (1989). *Unpacking the holiday presence: A comparative ethnography of two gift stores.* Paper presented at the Interpretive Consumer Research Conference, Provo, Utah.

Sherry, J. F., Jr. (1998). Understanding Markets as Places: An Introduction to Servicescapes. In J. F. Sherry, Jr. (Ed.), *Servicescapes. The concept of place in contemporary markets* (pp. 1–21.). Lincolnwood, IL: Nike Town Business Books.

Sirgy, M. J., Grewal, D., & Mangleburg, T. (2000). Retail environment, self-congruity, and retail patronage: An integrative model and a research agenda. *Journal of Business Research, 49*(2), 127–138.

Stokols, D. (1987). Conceptual strategies of environmental psychology. In D. Stokols & E. Altman (Eds.), *Handbook of environmental psychology.* New York: Wiley.

Tian, K. T., Bearden, W. O., & Hunter, G. L. (2001). Consumers' need for uniqueness: Scale development and validation. *Journal of Consumer Research, 28*, 50–66.

Titus, P. A., & Everett, P. B. (1996). Consumer wayfinding tasks, strategies, and errors: An exploratory field study. *Psychology & Marketing, 13*(3), 265–290.

Topf, M. (1985). Personal and environmental predictors of patient disturbance due to hospital noise. *Journal of Applied Psychology, 70*(1), 22–28.

Turley, L. W., & Milliman, R. E. (2000). Atmospheric effects on shopping behavior: A review of the experimental evidence. *Journal of Business Research, 49*(2), 193–211.

Wakefield, K. L., & Blodgett, J. G. (1994). The importance of servicescapes in leisure service settings. *The Journal of Services Marketing, 8*(3), 66–76.

Wapner, S., & Demick, J. (2000). Assumptions, methods and research problems of the holistic, developmental, systems-oriented perspective. In S. Wapner, J. Demick, T. Yamamato, & H. Minami (Eds.), *Theoretical perspectives in environment-behavior research: Underlying assumptions, research problems and methodologies.* New York: Kluver Academic/Plenum Press.

Weinstein, N. (1978). Individual differences in reactions to noise: A longitudinal study in a college dormitory. *Journal of Applied Psychology, 63*(4), 458–466.

Werner, C., & Altman, I. (2000). Humans and nature: Insights from a transactional view. In S. Wapner, J. Demick, T. Yamamato, & H. Minami (Eds.), *Theoretical perspectives in environment-behavior research: Underlying assumptions, research problems and methodologies.* New York: Kluver Academic/Plenum Press.

Werner, C. M. Altman, I., Brown, B. B., & Ginat, J. (1993). Celebrations in personal relationships: A transactional-dialectical perspective. In S. Duck (Ed.), Social context and relationships: Understanding relationship processes series (Vol. 3, pp. 109–138). Newbury Park, CA: Sage.

Werner, C. M., Altman, I., Oxley, D., & Haggard, L. (1987). People, place, and time: A transactional analysis of neighborhoods. In W. H. Jones & D. Perlman (Eds.), *Advances in personal relationships* (pp. 243–275). Greenwich, CT: JAI Press.

Werner, C. M., Brown, B. B., & Altman, I. (1997). Environmental psychology. In J. W. Berry, M. H. Segall, & C. Kagitcibasi (Eds.), *Handbook of cross-cultural psychology: Social behavior and applications* (Vol. 3, 2d ed., pp. 255–290). Needham Heights, MA: Allyn and Bacon.

Wohlwill, J. F. (1974). Human response to levels of environmental stimulation, *Human Ecology, 2,* 127–147.

33

Music and Consumers

James J. Kellaris

University of Cincinnati

Music touches the lives of consumers at many junctures (Kellaris & Kent, 1993; Rentfrow & Gosling, 2003). It is frequently used by sellers as a weapon of influence (Kellaris & Cox, 1989). A common feature of radio, television, and Internet advertisements, and a ubiquitous feature of retail environments, music is encountered by consumers as they attend to media, shop, wait for service, board flights, are placed on hold on the telephone, and in many other contexts (Blair & Kellaris, 1993). Music is also an object of consumption itself (Lacher & Mizerski, 1994), consumed both directly in the form of CDs, concerts, MP3 files, satellite radio, etc., and indirectly as a feature of other products (films, video games, sporting events, ceremonial occasions, religious services, etc).

Moreover, music provides a rich context for the study of basic, theoretical topics in consumer psychology, such as auditory perception, memory and recall, information processing, attitude formation, affect and emotion, behavioral conditioning, etc. Thus it is not surprising to find many studies investigating music's various influences on consumers. There are, however, some vexing challenges involved in compiling a review of this music-related work. First, much of the best music research in consumer psychology is not "about" music per se, but involves the use of musical stimuli in experimental investigations of ad processing, time perception, etc. Indeed the word "music" seldom appears in the title of non-applied studies that report music-related findings (e.g., Anand & Sternthal, 1990; Espinoza, Neto, & D'Angelo, 2004; Gorn, Goldberg, Chattopadhyay, & Litvack, 1991, 1993; Grewal Baker, Levy, & Voss 2003; Groenland & Schoormans, 1994; Mantel & Kellaris 2003; Miniard, Bhatla, & Sirdeshmukh, 1992; Muehling & Bozman, 1990; Olsen, 1997; Olsen & Pracejus, 2004; Roehm & Sternthal, 2001; and much of the work of Morris Holbrook). Thus there is a challenge of identifying relevant work that might be classified as "music research" in consumer psychology.

Second, much of the relevant research was conducted in other disciplines/contexts and applied to consumer psychology by analogy. The influence of music on human emotions, for example, is a central issue in the field of music therapy. Educational psychologists study how music influences the acquisition of information from educational television programs, instructional videos, and computer aided learning. Thus there is a challenge concerning where and how one draws boundaries around this vast topic. Are studies of background music's effects on vigilance performance in a radar screen monitoring task (e.g., Alikonis Warm, Matthews, Dember, Hitchcock, & Kellaris, 2002) sufficiently analogous to background music in commercials influencing consumers' attention to television advertisements to warrant inclusion in this review? Are studies of the therapeutic potential of music listening as a nursing intervention (Biley, 2000) sufficiently analogous to the use of environmental music to reduce shopper stress (Aylott & Mitchell, 1999)? Similar questions could be asked regarding studies in film communication that examine how music shapes the perception of information presented in the visual modality (Boltz, 2004). Scholars in many domains have examined how music influences the perception and remembering of other, concurrently or sequentially presented visual or auditory information.

Third, in consumer research studies, music is generally treated as an independent variable or stimulus. Research, however, tends to be organized by outcomes of interest, such as attention, perception, etc. Music influences a wide variety of cognitive, affective, and behavioral outcomes. Thus the literature on music and consumers crosses many theoretic boundaries and tends to reside in disparate areas identified with outcomes of interest.

A final challenge, and perhaps the greatest, stems from the fundamental question *what is music*? It is not my intent to open Pandora's box here. The practical problem is that the term *music* has been used broadly in consumer research to apply to background and foreground music, instrumental and vocal music, brashly commercial and sublimely artistic music, works of short duration (e.g., audio logos, ring tones, sonic branding) and long duration (e.g., a Mahler symphony), in diverse styles including commercial pop, classical masterpieces, jazz, and non-Western music. To add to the confusion, many effects attributed to "music" may actually stem from the verbal content of vocal music lyrics or song titles, or even the mere remembrance of such upon hearing an instrumental version of a piece strongly associated with textual material (e.g., Roehm, 2001). Additionally, music is frequently characterized in terms of subjective properties that are not constituent properties of music at all, but rather reactions resident within listeners (e.g., "pleasant music"). In summation, "music and consumers" is an important, exceedingly vast, yet poorly defined topic.

These challenges demand that some rather arbitrary limits be set on the scope of this chapter. With advance apologies for purposeful exclusions and unintentional sins of omission, this selective review will include a brief, historic overview of music research and critical summary of prior reviews by Bruner (1990) and Hargreaves and North (1997). The remainder of the review selectively examines empirical research in consumer psychology, marketing, and closely allied fields, pertaining to the influences of music on consumers, with special attention to music, time perception, and the "earworm" phenomenon. Related topics, such as the influences of music on employees and the consumption of musical products are not given full treatment in this review. The review offers directions for future research throughout. (The recent work of Charles Areni (2001, 2003a, 2003b, 2003c) on managers' implicit beliefs about music also provides an excellent source of ideas for future research, as some of the lay theories identified in this work have not been addressed in the literature.)

HISTORIC BACKGROUND ON MUSIC RESEARCH

Music figured prominently in the ancient world and was closely associated with philosophy, cosmology, mathematics, metaphysics, and healing (Sachs, 1943). The modern, scientific investigation of music traces its origins to Wundt (1874) and Helmholtz (1863), both of whom investigated objective properties of sound in relation to listeners' reactions. Helmholtz claimed that minor keys tend to induce feelings of sadness because the slight dissonance of the lowered third degree of the scale (which does not occur in the natural overtone series) provokes a peculiar nervous disturbance in listeners.

In the tradition of Helmholtz, Heinlein (1928), Gundlach (1932, 1935), Hevner (1935, 1936, 1937), and Rigg (1940) each conducted programs of experimentation to investigate how objective properties of music such as tempo and pitch influence subjective reactions, such as listeners' adjectival characterizations of music. They established a direct link between music's temporal and tonal attributes, and listeners' characterizations of musical mood. Henkin (1955, 1957) examined the interplay of multiple attributes of music in a series of factorial studies. This stimulus-response approach was more recently echoed in the work of Holbrook and Anand (1990), who examined the non-monotonic effects of tempo on listeners' responses to music, that of Kellaris and Kent (1991, 1993), who used digital technology to produce factorial manipulations, and that of Schubert (2004), which examined the emotional impact of multiple factors as they unfolded dynamically over time. From this research we may conclude that music can be characterized in terms of objective attributes stemming from the physical properties of sound, and that these properties (and their interactions) are partly responsible for listeners' reactions.

Cattell and Saunders (1954) developed the idea that musical preferences can reveal insights into personality. Recent work by Rentfrow and Gosling (2003, 2006) lends credence to this idea by documenting personality correlates of music listening preferences, and by showing that people use musical preferences to convey information about themselves and form accurate impressions of others. This may have implications for the emerging field of sonic branding—a point to which the review will return in a later section.

Early investigations of music effects also examined the potential of music to raise worker productivity. In 1915 Thomas Edison conducted experiments to ascertain the impact of recorded music on factory workers' productivity; however, he observed no effects, probably because the sound reproduction equipment was primitive and of low quality (Lundin, 1985). Wyatt and Langdon (1937) investigated the use of music to reduce fatigue and boredom among British factory workers. They found that playing phonograph records intermittently during the middle of a shift increased productivity among workers engaged in a monotonous, repetitive task. Interestingly, commercial services to distribute music to workplaces predate scientific verification of music's effectiveness in raising worker productivity – suggesting an implicit belief in beneficial effects of music. Whereas beneficial effects of music on employees may extend to their delivery of service to consumers, this could be an area for future research in the domain of consumer psychology.

Interest in musical influence on consumers increased during the second half of the 20th century with the proliferation in commercial applications, the advent of new media, and changes in popular culture (e.g., M-TV generation). This interest is reflected in work such as Smith and Curnow's (1966) study of the effects of music on purchasing behavior, Galizio and Hendrick's (1972) study on the effect of musical accompaniment on attitude, and Fried and Berkowitz (1979) study of music's role in enhancing compliance.

KEY LITERATURE REVIEWS

There have been two important literature reviews in recent history, including Bruner's (1990) seminal "Music, mood, & marketing" article in the *Journal of Marketing*, and Hargreaves and North's (1997) book *The Social Psychology of Music*, which contains a chapter on "music and consumer behaviour." Also worthy of mention is Turley and Milliman's (2000) review of experimental studies investigating atmospheric effects on shoppers, which includes those of environmental background music. The existence of prior reviews makes the current task much easier, as the present review is essentially an extension of Bruner (1990) and update of Hargreaves and North (1997).

Bruner

Bruner (1990) provides a useful overview of empirical studies of music's influences on listeners, with particular attention to effects on consumers' emotional and behavioral responses in commercial contexts. Perhaps the most important contribution of Bruner's review is that it reaffirmed that music is not a "unitary sonic mass," but rather a confluence of multiple stimulus properties. Bruner identified three primary dimensions underlying musical stimuli: time, pitch, and texture. The temporal dimension comprises variables such as speed ("tempo"), rhythm, and groupings ("meter" or time signature). The pitch dimension includes variables such as melody, harmony, and key. The textural dimension includes variables such as tone quality ("timbre"—the property that allows listeners to distinguish between, say, a violin and a trumpet playing the same pitch) and volume (loudness). Bruner proposes that listeners' reactions to music stem in part from the stimulus properties of sound.

The first part of Bruner's review is organized around the three dimensions of musical sound (time, pitch, texture). It establishes that the constituent properties of music can evoke predictable main and interactive effects. For example, music pitched in minor keys tends to be perceived as sad; music played at a fast tempo tends to be perceived as arousing. The second part of the review examines empirical findings in commercial contexts, documenting a number of behavioral and non-behavioral findings pertaining to music in ads and in stores. (No summary of these finds is offered here. Interested readers are referred to the source.) The review concludes with an inventory of research propositions and a discussion of methodological recommendations.

Significantly, Bruner's article raised the bar on the psychological sophistication of music-related studies that followed. Studies of the mere presence versus absence of music and studies of sung versus spoken messages virtually disappeared, because Bruner's review firmly established that music is not a "unitary sonic mass," and that its influences depend largely upon the constituent properties that evoke meanings and feelings.

With due respect for the welcome contribution this work represents, hindsight suggests several points of criticism. First, there is more to music than creating "moods." Certainly music is the par excellence nonverbal "language of emotion" and has profound potential to evoke feelings in listeners, so Bruner's emphasis on affect is both understandable and warranted. However, music can also affect cognitive outcomes, both directly (as auditory information that shapes perceptions and attitudes) and indirectly (by attracting attention, distracting, influencing cognitive load or resource availability). Second, by focusing on the properties of musical stimuli, Bruner's review ignores potentially important music by person interactions. On the basis of field theory (Lewin, 1951), one might argue that musical properties provide only half the picture. One man's Mozart is another man's Michael Jackson. Reactions to music should depend upon the joint interplay of the traits of the music and those of the individual listener. Third, although Bruner correctly points out that music is not literally a "unitary sonic mass," it may nonetheless convey a Gestalt impression and thus be perceived as such by listeners. As Scott (1990) argues, research has tended to treat music as a non-semantic, affective stimulus working independently of rhetorical meaning or context. Such an approach overlooks intended meanings consumers infer from the verbal and visual context within which music is heard. These criticisms notwithstanding, the Bruner article remains an important landmark in the history of music research in the fields of marketing and consumer behavior, succinctly summarizing the most important findings to date and defining a new state-of-the-art for future research.

Hargreaves and North

Hargreaves and North (1997) provide a useful review of studies documenting various influences of music on consumers. The review is organized by listening context and includes influences of music heard in advertisements, in retail shops, and consumed as entertainment. In advertising, music may serve as an unconditioned stimulus in a conditioning paradigm (Gorn, 1982; Blair & Shimp, 1992), such that audiences learn to associate feelings elicited by music with an advertised product. However, it appears that such conditioning occurs unreliably (Kellaris & Cox, 1989) and only under a limited set of circumstances (e.g., low involvement). The review also notes that when meanings conveyed by music are consistent with those conveyed by a brand message, music can be influential under conditions of high involvement (MacInnis & Park, 1991).

In retail settings, the loudness (Smith & Curnow, 1966) and speed (Milliman, 1982, 1986) of music can influence the pace of store traffic and duration of visit. The "fit" of music to products may influence purchasing directly (Areni & Kim 1993); the pleasure and arousal evoked by background music may influence approach behaviors such as the desire to affiliate (Dubé, Chebat, & Morin, 1995). Music has also been shown to influence perceptions of time in both laboratory (e.g., the work of Kellaris and colleagues) and field (e.g., the work of Chebat and colleagues) research.

Although the Hargreaves and North (1997) review identifies influential studies involving music and is faithful in reporting their findings, it is largely uncritical of these studies. For example, it does not recognize the possibility that some effects attributed to "music" may actually stem from the verbal content of musical lyrics. Additionally, the review ignores alternative explanations for findings and other possible roles of music in ads and stores, including audience-sorting and targeting, reinforcing brand images, attracting and maintaining attention, distraction, etc. Finally, as in any review (including the present one), there are some omissions. Hargreaves and North (1997) omit Anand and Sternthal (1990) and other studies that used musical stimuli, but which were not positioned as being "about" music (e.g., Holbrook & Huber, 1979; Holbrook & Gardner, 1993, 2000). Nevertheless, it provides a useful update to Bruner (1990).

Turley and Milliman

Turley and Milliman (2000) provide a review of experimental studies of atmospheric effects on shoppers, which includes effects of environmental music on shoppers. (Rieunier (1998) provides a similar review in French.) Most of the music studies cited were reviewed by Hargreaves and North (1997), with the notable exceptions of Andrus (1986), Brooker & Wheatley (1994); Gulas and Schewe (1994), Herrington and Capella (1996), and Hui, Dubé, and Chebat (1997). (To this list of exceptions I would also add a number of studies published in French, the most important of which are reviewed in Gallopel (2000) and in Ben Dahmane Mouelhi and Touzani (2003).) The authors call for theory development to move the state of research on atmospherics beyond the mere identification of effects, but they do not offer specific directions for doing so.

Theory development in the area of atmospheric music is constrained by the tendency of researchers to conduct field studies. It is difficult, impractical, often impossible, to measure intervening psychological processes in the field. This is a peculiar advantage of laboratory studies. Theory development is also constrained by the tendency to examine outcomes that are easily observed in stores, such as sales or time spent shopping. To understand the potential influences of music, researchers must get inside shoppers' heads and examine how music influences cognitive processes that shape evaluations, preferences, and choices. Research on music atmospherics should also benefit from thinking by analogy about music findings from other contexts. For example, studies of music in ads show that music can distract and thereby reduce cognitive resource availability (Anand & Sternthal, 1990). Might music heard in retail contexts shape time perceptions and decrease shoppers' sales resistance by a similar mechanism? If so, this could provide theoretic accounts for both shopping duration and sales effects.

WORK SINCE 1990

Music and Affect

Music is widely recognized as the par excellence language of human emotions and its role in shaping affective states of consumers in commercial contexts is well established (Alpert & Alpert, 1990; Bruner, 1990). It has been used as a mood induction in experimental research (e.g., Groenland & Schoormans, 1994; Miniard et al., 1992; Olsen & Pracejus, 2004; Roehm & Sternthal, 2001). Moreover, research has begun to identify specific attributes of music ("structural profiles") that are responsible for evoking particular affective reactions (Kellaris & Kent, 1993; Alpert, Alpert, & Maltz, 2005).

Clearly, music can elicit feelings of pleasure (Sweeney & Wyber, 2002) and convey intended emotions, such as anger, sadness, happiness, and fear (Juslin, 2000). It can mitigate stress and promote feelings of relaxation in a stressful waiting situation (Lee, Henderson, & Shum, 2004: Tansik & Routhieaux, 1999). Pleasant feelings induced by music can influence cognitive activity (Chebat Chebat, & Vaillant, 2001), product evaluations (Gorn, Goldberg, & Basu, 1993; Groenland & Schoormans, 1994) and encourage positive evaluations of overall experience in waiting situations (Cameron, Baker, Peterson, & Braunsberger, 2003), although reactions can vary significantly by gender (Kellaris & Rice, 1993) and may depended upon the "fit" of the music (MacInnis & Park, 1991; North MacKenzie, Law, & Hargreaves, 2004).

Brader (2005) used music in political ads to evoke emotions of enthusiasm or fear. Results of experimentation show that evoking feelings of enthusiasm during a positively framed message can motivate voter participation and activate party loyalties; evoking feelings of fear increased the persuasiveness of a negatively framed message. Hence using music that evokes message-congruent emotions appears to reinforce the message and effect desirable outcomes. Although many prior studies have shown that music can evoke positive or negative affect, this study demonstrates the ability of music to evoke very specific emotions. It also raises the chilling prospect that something as important as the democratic process can be manipulated via music in campaign ads.

Hughes and Lowis (2002) studied "spiritual-emotional responses" to Anglican hymn tunes as a function of their structural properties. The authors report that hymns in triple (vs. duple) meter evoked more positive scores. Because duple meters mimic natural biorhythms (such as heartbeats and respiration), music characterized by triple meters may have a "freeing" effect that facilitates religious sentiment.

There are many topics that could be explored vis-à-vis music and emotion. For example, when do people seek out music that is congruous with their current feelings versus seek out music to effect a favorable change in mood? Why do (some) people enjoy listening to sad music? How and when do negatively-valenced emotions convey positive utility? What are the personal and situational boundary conditions under which this happens? Might listening to sad music evoke a contrast effect, such that happy experiences seem by comparison happier? The ancient notion of *catharsis* has been used to explain the positive utility of exposure to negative stimulation, but consumer psychology potentially offers many alternative explanations that could be explored in future research with music (Matsumoto, 2002).

Another challenge for future research in this area is that there appears to be some confusion in the literature stemming from a failure to recognize the important distinction between consumers' affective reactions to music ("the music made me feel happy") and consumers' judgments of music's affective character ("the music sounds happy to me"). Exposure to music that is recognized as being happy in character does not necessarily instill feelings of happiness in the listener. Hence some observed effects attributed to music-induced affect may, in some instances, actually stem from thoughts evoked by music or thought processes influenced by music.

Music and Cognition

Recent studies of music and cognition have reported links between music and recall (Roehm, 2001; Stewart, Farmer, & Stannard, 1990; Stewart & Punj, 1998; Tom, 1990; Yalch, 1991), including auto-biographical memory (Baumgartner, 1992), message processing (Anand & Sternthal, 1990; Kellaris et al., 1993), evaluations (Dubé & Morin, 2001; Mattila & Wirtz, 2001), persuasion (Muehling & Bozman, 1990), willingness to spend and purchase intent (North & Hargreaves 1998; North et al., 2000).

On the basis of her studies of Appalachian ballads, Wallace (1991) proposed that sung (vs. spoken) messages may improve recall of advertisements under certain conditions. Indeed, several studies have shown recall effects of music. Tom (1990) found that ads with music scored especially for the ad were better remembered than ads using parody music or original versions of popular hit songs. This was explained in terms of stimulus congruity, the advantages of which are also demonstrated by Kellaris and Rice (1993).

The current trend in advertising, however, is to use popular music. There may be a recall advantage when instrumental (vs.vocal) versions of popular hits are used. Roehm (2001) speculated that instrumental versions of popular music may encourage audiences to generate lyrics—to "sing along" mentally. Generating lyrics rather than listening to them passively may increase message recall when the lyrics convey the ad message. Evidence from an experiment are consistent with this explanation, as only listeners familiar with the music recalled more when exposed to an ad containing an instrumental version of the music. Alternatively, however, the absence of verbal material in instrumental music may reduce cognitive load, freeing resources to process the spoken message without distraction.

When persuasion is the goal rather than recall, use of popular hits may increase message acceptance by drawing attention, reducing the capacity to counter-argue, and by encouraging a less critical mind-set. That is, ads featuring well-known popular music may seem more like entertainment than like an influence attempt. Hence, such ads may be processed less critically. This untested proposition poses a challenge for future research.

Although music has the potential to increase recall by drawing attention to an ad, it can also serve as a distraction that can reduce cognitive resources and thereby reduce recall. Olsen (1995) addressed this dilemma by examining continuous versus interrupted schedules of background music punctuated by silence. Recall increased when a radio ad cuts to silence just before presenting a crucial piece of information. Moreover, the effect depends upon the duration of the interstimulus interval and the resource demands of the (directed vs. incidental) listening task (Olsen, 1997).

In addition to influencing the acquisition and recollection of other (verbal, visual) information, music has been shown to influence message processing (Anand & Sternthal, 1990) and to convey meanings (Zhu & Meyers-Levy, 2005) that reinforce messages and shape perceptions and evaluations (Hung 2000, 2001; Zhu & Meyers-Levy, 2005). The work of Marilyn Boltz with film scores (e.g., Boltz 2001, 2004) demonstrates how music can shape viewers' perceptions and interpretations of visual information. Her findings should apply by analogy to background music in television and web advertisements. Muehling and Bozman, (1990) found music to interact with ad narratives, such that factual narratives were most persuasive in the presence of favorable (or no) music; evaluative narratives were most persuasive in the presence of neutral music.

Background music has also been found to influence willingness to spend and purchase intent (North & Hargreaves, 1998). For example, North et al. (2000) observed associations among the extent to which people like the style of music (e.g., classical, easy-listening, pop) played in a bar and in a bank, perceptions of the atmosphere, and willingness to spend. This study did not address the issue of the music's congruity with other elements of the environment or with listeners' expectations. (For an excellent treatment of these issues, see Baker, Parasuraman, Grewal, & Voss, 2002.) Dubé and Morin (2001) observed similar effects of music, with attitude toward the servicescape mediating the impact of pleasant background music on store evaluations.

In summary, the effect of music on cognitive responses depends largely on what is played and how it relates to other information (Baker et al., 2002). Many of the effects reported in the literature seem to stem from stimulus congruity and support the matching hypothesis. To the extent that the manner in which information is presented matches or is similar to the manner in which consumers prefer to represent information stored in memory, the presented information is easier to process and more influential on cognitive outcomes such as recall and evaluations. Support for the matching hypothesis has been found in persuasion research (Fabrigar & Petty, 1999; Petty & Wegener, 1998), memory research (transfer-appropriate processing theory; Roediger, 1990), and decision research (stimulus compatibility effects; Shafir, 1995).

Although the vast majority of the literature supports the matching hypothesis (Hahn & Hwang, 1999), support has also been found for a mismatching hypothesis in some circumstances (Millar & Millar, 1990). For example, when message arguments are weak, greater persuasion occurs when the presented information mismatches the functional basis of the attitude one is attempting to change (Petty & Wegener, 1998). A clearer understanding of the conditions under which matching versus mismatching is likely to occur and confer benefits could add much to the literature on the effects of music on cognitive outcomes.

The literature on music and cognition seems limited by its focus on a relatively small set of outcomes (recall, evaluation, willingness to spend, and buying intent). In practice, music is frequently used to draw and hold the attention of consumers; yet, studies of the influence of music on attention are rare (Hecker, 1984; Kellaris et al., 1993).

Music and Time Perception

One of the more fascinating findings involving music is the apparent ability of music to shrink or expand subjective time relative to objective, clock time. This has numerous applications in shaping the temporal experience of consumers while they shop, surf the web, wait for service, or wait in checkout lines and other queues.

Kellaris and colleagues have conducted a series of lab studies examining the influence of music on time perception (Kellaris & Altsech, 1992; Kellaris & Kent, 1992; Kellaris & Mantel, 1994a, 1994b, 1996, 2003; Kellaris et al., 1996; Mantel & Kellaris, 1993, 2003). Exposing participants to music varying in characteristics such as mode (major, minor, whole tone "keys"; Kellaris & Kent, 1992) and loudness (Kellaris et al., 1996) can influence the retrospective duration estimates of short intervals "filled" with music. Generally, time intervals seem longest when less arousing/distracting music is heard, subject to certain moderating conditions such as gender of listener (Kellaris & Altsech, 1992; Kellaris & Mantel, 1994; North et al., 1998), and the congruity of the music with other elements of a stimulus event (Kellaris & Mantel, 1996). The duration of past events seems longer in retrospect under conditions that permit reconstruction of the event from memory, such as when cognitive resource requirements "match" their availability (Mantel & Kellaris, 2003).

Chebat and colleagues have conducted numerous field studies examining influences of music on customers (e.g., Chebat et al., 2000, 2001; Chebat & Dubé, 2000), including perceptions of waiting times (e.g., Chebat & Gelinas-Chebat, 1993) in banks (e.g., Chebat et al., 1993) and in stores (Hui, Dube, & Chebat, 1997). Positively-valenced music was found to increase perceived waiting times, but this did not influence approach behaviors negatively. Thus it appears that the duration of a wait does not matter so much if the time is spent pleasantly. Similarly, Cameron et al. (2003) found that playing likeable music influenced wait length evaluations in a low cost waiting situation; however, wait length evaluations did not influence overall evaluations of the experience; and, Yalch and Spangenberg (2000) found that exposure to less familiar music decreased perceived times, increased actual time, but did not influence evaluations in a shopping simulation experiment.

Ironically, few studies have examined the influence of music's temporal aspects (e.g., tempo, rhythm) on time perception. An important exception is a field study by Steve Oakes (2003), which found time perceptions (perceived time–actual time) of students waiting in a registration queue to be positively related to the speed of the music to which they were exposed during the wait. One interpretation of this finding is that exposure to more musical information (music played at faster speeds contains more information per unit of time) evokes a numerosity heuristic. Further work by Oakes and Kellaris (in progress) is examining perceptions of event durations as a function of exposure to amount of musical information in the form of melodic information (i.e., fewer/more notes).

Resent work by Bailey and Areni shows that the number of songs to which listeners are exposed can serve as a basis for estimating time passage under conditions that encourage heuristic processing. Consistent with a segmentation-change theory of time perception, a numerosity effect was observed when participants in a lab study were engaged in a word puzzle task during exposure to music. In one study, those exposed to 8 short songs estimated a 20-minute interval to be longer than those exposed to 4 long songs during a 20-minute interval, irrespective of the type of music played (Bailey & Areni, 2006a).

In another study by Bailey and Areni (2006b), a 12-minute time interval seemed shorter to participants exposed to familiar/liked music (vs. unfamiliar music), when sitting idle (vs. engaged in a cognitive task). This effect was replicated in a follow-up experiment; moreover, familiar/liked music produced longer time estimates among individuals engaged in a memory task. These results are consistent with an attentional model under the low cognitive load condition and consistent with a discrete event model under the high cognitive load condition. Thus the effect of background music on the recollection of a past time interval appears to depend upon the availability of resources to monitor time passage.

Several studies have examined influences of music in the context of waiting on hold while on the telephone (Kellaris et al., 1999; North et al., 1999; Ramos, 1993). Ramos examined the effect of music formats on telephone waiting persistence on a Protective Services hotline. The greatest proportion of disconnects were observed under "relaxation music" format; the greatest persistence under a jazz condition. These results were explained in terms of the "*iso* matching principle." Callers presumably disconnected when music was incongruent with their current mood. (Given the nature of the hotline service, the author safely assumed callers to be distressed, agitated, in a state of high arousal.) Kellaris et al. (1999) proposed an alternative explanation for Ramos' findings, i.e., that relaxing music may have seemed boring, less distracting to distressed callers; ergo, the duration of the wait may have seemed longer. They tested this proposition in a simulation experiment. Participants were asked to imagine calling a technical service number and being placed on hold. They received 6-minute timed exposures to Alternative, Classical, Jazz, or Rock music. Retrospectively reported durations seemed longer than 6 minutes under all conditions, but were shortest, on average, under the Jazz music condition. This is consistent with the authors' speculation that time perceptions may have influenced subjects in Ramos' experiment. (A telephone persistence study by North et al. (1999) is reviewed in the section on music and behavior.)

Although shaping consumers' perceptions of waiting time is the par excellence application of music and time perception research, research in this area could be usefully extended to other contexts, such as web site visit duration (see Galan, 2002; Jacob & Guéguen, 2003). Streaming music that shrinks perceived time may encourage longer visits, which should increase opportunities for information acquisition, persuasion, and click-through. Another avenue for future research on music and time perception would be to explore different facets of subjective time, such as perceived duration (how long an event seemed to last) and perceived pace (how slowly/quickly an event seemed to have passed). Although Kellaris et al. (1996) introduced this distinction, it has not been fully explored. Finally, whereas several studies have found music that influences time perception does not influence evaluations, future research should investigate trade-offs and countervailing effects of music on different desirable outcomes. The effective use of music as a weapon of influence may best be approached as an optimization problem.

Music and Behavior

Although the theoretic accounts for observed effects vary widely, a number of studies report behavioral effects of music. For example, Kellaris (1992) reported a field study in which applause duration was found to be a quadratic (inverted U-shaped) function of the tempo of live Greek music (when controlling for other factors, such as the duration of each song performance). Applause behavior was interpreted as an indication of audience pleasure, which is maximized at an optimum stimulation level.

North and Hargreaves (1999) found people were willing to persist in waiting longer (for someone to return) when music was playing than under a no-music condition. The music might have disrupted participants' internal timers; or it may have reduced the stress of waiting. In a study of telephone callers placed on hold, callers exposed to liked music and music that was congruous with their expectations persisted longer on hold (North et al., 1999). These findings are consistent with the notion that pleasant stimuli encourage approach behaviors.

Caldwell and Hibbert (2002) found that exposure to preferred music increased the length of time spent in a restaurant. (Bailey & Areni, forthcoming b, may provide an alternative theoretic account for this field observation. That is, exposure to liked music may have diminished perceived time relative to clock time, such that patrons sat longer at table under the illusion that their stay was shorter.) Sullivan (2002) also found restaurant visits to be longer on average when patrons are exposed to music, and particularly when the music is popular and played at a low volume. Music played at soft volumes also had favorable effects on expenditures—an effect also observed by Lammers (2003).

The "wine shop study" of North et al. (1999) received international media attention as journalists interpreted the findings as evidence of "subliminal persuasion." Sales of French versus German wine increased when French music was playing in the store and vice versa. Upon questioning, less than 14% of shoppers attributed their product choice to the music; however, it is not clear whether shoppers were unaware of the music's influence (the "subliminal" effect sensationalized in the media) or if they were simply unwilling to admit it (social desirability bias). This study echoes an earlier study by Areni and Kim (1993), which found that wine shoppers exposed to classical (vs. Top-40) music spent more. Exposure to classical music did not increase the amount of wine purchased; rather consumers tended to by more expensive wine.

Exposure to fast music appears to provoke a faster pace of drinking (McElrea & Standing, 1992). Certain styles of music seem to encourage spending in a restaurant setting (Wilson, 2003), in a perfume and cosmetics shop (Ben Dahmane Mouelhi, & Touzani (2003), and in a supermarket

(Herrington, 1996). Theoretic accounts for these observations, however, are not fully developed. This represents an opportunity for future research.

Musical Preferences and Listening Behavior

Although it was not my intent to cover the consumption of music (Lacher & Mizerski, 1994) in this review, there are two streams of research that warrant mention by merit of their important implications for consumer psychology. The first is a series of studies by Rentfrow and Gosling (2003) exploring individual differences in musical preferences and the links between musical preferences and personality traits. The authors document the central role of music in the lives of consumers, provide evidence that people consider music to be important and that it is frequently consumed in a variety of contexts, identify the basic dimensions of music preferences, and show how preference structures relate to other aspects of personality, such as intelligence. In a follow-up study, the authors examined the role of music in interpersonal perception (Rentfrow & Gosling, 2006). They found that people use musical preferences to convey information about themselves and to form accurate impressions of others.

The second is work by Holbrook, Lacher, and LaTour (2006) on expert judgment versus popular appeal. They begin by noting the weak link between experts' judgments of aesthetic merit and those of non-expert consumers of "cultural products" (e.g., film, music, fine art, entertainment). In an empirical study involving listening to different recordings of the song "My Funny Valentine" performed by various artists in different styles, the impact of expert judgment on audience appeal was shown to be mediated by audience judgment, such that there are moderately positive associations between each link. This would seem to have major implications for understanding the phenomenon of "taste" (Holbrook & Schindler, 1989) and the role of critics in shaping the appeal and commercial success of cultural products.

The work of Rentfrow and Gosling and that of Holbrook and colleagues raises some intriguing questions regarding consumer tastes and preferences. How and to what extent are individual preferences—and by extension mass audience appeal—influenced by knowing what *should* be preferred (versus what *is* preferred)? Why do some consumers strive to develop "good taste" that is congruent with that of experts, while others are content to ignore the opinions of experts on matters of taste? What factors moderate the influence of experts' opinions on the formation and evolution of consumer preferences? The marketing concept suggests that customers' needs be served. Are needs better served by giving the customer what he thinks he wants or by teaching the customer to appreciate something that might confer more satisfaction? The issue of "should like" versus "do like" burns at the very heart of marketing and certainly warrants much more research.

Music and the "Earworm" Phenomenon

Igor Stravinsky is reputed to have said, "Too many pieces of music finish too long after the end." He may have been referring to what has come to be known as the "earworm" phenomenon. The term comes from the German *ohrwurm* and refers to a song, tune, or fragment of music that gets lodged in one's head, such that it seems to repeat itself involuntarily. This "song stuck in the head" phenomenon is also popularly called "repetunitis," "tune cooties," and by a variety of other names. It differs from *endomusia* (auditory hallucinations) in that the music is obsessively rehearsed mentally, but not actually heard as from an external source.

In reference to this phenomenon, Wanda Wallace wrote, "…consider how difficult it can be to get a jingle out of your head when you have heard it several times. Whether or not you like the jingle is irrelevant; you just can't seem to stop humming it. One well worn example is the Oscar Meyer song. Just saying the brand name is usually enough to start part of the jingle playing through your mind" (Wallace, 1991, p. 239).

Kellaris (2001) was the first to examine this phenomenon empirically in the field of consumer psychology. In a presentation to the Society for Consumer Psychology he presented a preliminary overview of the phenomenon, which generated world-wide media attention (e.g., Rivenburg, 2001). This study documented the existence and pervasiveness of the phenomenon, including the frequency and duration of episodes, and laid the groundwork for building a theoretic account and possible remediation strategies. This initial study also examined properties of songs that people report as have gotten stuck in their heads, strategies that people use to un-stick a stuck song, and lay explanations for why the phenomenon occurs. Whereas Kellaris believed that musical properties might prove key to explaining how and why songs become earworms, he provisionally outlined a theory of "cognitive itch."

> Just as certain bio-chemical agents (histamines) have physical properties that can cause the skin to itch, certain pieces of music may have properties that excite an abnormal reaction in the brain ("cognitive itch"). An itching sensation on the skin may motivate people to scratch to alleviate the discomfort. This, of course, only exacerbates the sensation, causing the familiar cycle of repeated itching and scratching.
>   By analogy… the only way to "scratch" a cognitive itch is to rehearse the responsible tune mentally. The process may start involuntarily, as the brain detects an incongruity or something "exceptional" in the musical stimulus. The ensuing mental repetition may exacerbate the "itch," such that the mental rehearsal becomes largely involuntary, and the individual feels trapped in a cycle or feedback loop. (Kellaris, 2001, p. 66)

In a follow-up study, Kellaris (2003) examined person traits and situations that might interact with musical properties to create an earworm experience. Surprisingly, there were no statistical associations between earworms (frequency, duration) and O-C scores. The frequency of earworm episodes were positively associated with neuroticism, with the "discomfort with ambiguity" dimension of need for cognitive closure, and with musical training and listening behaviors. Individuals characterized by low need for cognition are prone to longer earworm episodes. Findings regarding situational influences included primacy and recency effects, stress, and fatigue as contributory factors.

It appears that music characterized by simplicity, repetitiveness, and incongruous features such as odd meters or unexpected cadences is most likely to become an earworm. However, the earworm phenomenon cannot be explained by of the "stickiness" of musical properties alone. Person traits and situational factors also appear to play significant roles.

Work by Halpern and colleagues (e.g., Halpern, Zatorre, Bouffard, & Johnson 2004) has examined neural correlates of musical properties and found similar patterns of neural activation (fMRI evidence) for both perceived and imagined music. This may provide a clue to understanding the earworm phenomenon. It appears that the brain processes unheard (imagined) music similarly to heard (perceived) music. Moreover, a highly publicized study conducted by a team of researchers at Dartmouth (Kraemer, Macrae, Green, & Kelly, 2005) found that the brain tends to fill in missing information when a fragment of familiar music is interrupted. In fact, the tendency to do so is sufficiently strong that all subjects in the Dartmouth study reported subjectively hearing the (familiar) music during short gaps that were muted. Exposure to muted gaps in unfamiliar music did not produce this effect.

The theory of ironic processes of mental control (Wegner, 1994; Wenzlaff & Wegner, 2000) may provide a useful explanation for the fascinating earworm effect. According to the theory, mental control involves two processes: (1) an operating process that searches for mental contents consistent with one's goals (e.g., to not think of a particular tune), and (2) a monitoring process that searches for mental contents inconsistent with one's goals (e.g., how frequently one thinks about a tune about which one is trying not to think). The operating process requires greater cognitive effort and is more strongly influenced by cognitive load manipulations. Hence, under conditions of cognitive load, attempts to suppress an unwanted thought are ineffective. Furthermore, a post-suppression rebound effect is frequently observed. Thought suppression can be effective initially, but when one lets down one's guard and stops attempting to avoid thinking about an unwanted thought (tune), the unwanted thought occurs more frequently (compared to a no-suppression control condition).

Ironic processes theory has important implications for understanding substance abuse, PTDS, OCD, and offers counterintuitive implications for their treatment. People who suffer these challenges should abandon thought suppression in favor of other methods of mental control. Concentrating on attaining desirable goals rather than avoiding undesirable goals can be effective. Training on the use of more effective distracters can be effective. Paradoxically, even accepting and expressing unwanted thoughts can be effective under some circumstances. Wegner and Zanakos (1994) developed a self-report measure of the tendency to suppress thoughts, and this measure correlates positively with depression, obsession, dissociation, and anxiety. By analogy, earworms sufferers may be well advised to follow the prescriptions of ironic processes theory. As one research participant in a Kellaris study wrote, "never fight with an earworm—it will only make it angry!"

Music and Sonic Branding

Music is a nonverbal language that can convey abstract and concrete meanings (Zhu & Meyers-Levy, 2005) and cue memory (Stewart et al., 1990). As such, it may be particularly useful in cross-cultural communications when verbal languages impose a need for translation. The emerging field of "sonic branding" seeks to take advantage of music's ability to communicate nonverbally (Jackson, 2003).

The idea of sonic branding appears to have evolved from "audio logos," which have been in use for a long time. Older readers will recall examples such as the NBC television network's three note (*sol mi do*) chime motif and the ascending scale (*fa sol la ti do*) that accompanied the spelling of the word J-E-L-L-O. Yet, surprisingly, at the time of this writing, there are no academic studies of sonic branding known to the author. The work of Rentfrow and Gosling (2003, 2006), however, suggests the intriguing possibility of using music to convey brand personalities and to appeal to the idealized self of prospective consumers.

CONCLUSION

The question I am asked most frequently by business practitioners and journalists alike is "What is the best music to play in ___?" Fill in the blank with any context—an ad for shoe inserts, a store targeting adolescents, an upscale hotel lobby, a busy, downscale restaurant, a medical office waiting room, or a funeral home full of grieving relatives to be comforted and consoled. The answer is always the same and should be predictable to anyone in the field of consumer psychology: "It depends." It depends on the immediate and longer-term goals to be served, because music can elicit many different types of responses from consumers. A short list might include: evoke feelings, elevate or depress moods, calm or stimulate listeners, serve as an unconditioned stimulus in an associative learning paradigm, draw and hold attention, distract, reduce cognitive resource avail-ability, shape perceptions of visual stimuli, evoke imagery and meanings, enhance message learn-ing or acceptance, cue memories, reinforce store or brand images, target particular segments of consumers through their musical tastes and preferences (Sivadas Grewal, & Kellaris, 1998), shrink or expand perceived time relative to clock time, convey information about a product or organiza-tion non-verbally, reinforce verbal messages, reduce fatigue, stress, and boredom, boost employee morale and thereby enhance the delivery of service to customers, etc. Clearly, music can serve mul-tiple purposes (Dunbar, 1990; Morrison & Beverland, 2003). Moreover, sometimes these multiple purposes come in conflict with each other as music can have countervailing effects on different desirable outcomes (Chebat et al., 2001). Should a store play music that is preferred by customers or by employees? Should a restaurant play music that shrinks perceived waiting times or that aug-ments perceived time at table, such that table turn-over is greater without making customers feel rushed? There are simply no simple answers.

So what can we conclude from this brief overview of research on music and consumers? Research has come a long way from the foundational, 19th century work of Wundt and Helmholtz to studies such as Zhu and Meyers-Levy (2005). The literature of this subfield is scattered, intriguing, rapidly growing in volume, and evolving in terms of psychological sophistication. This review provides an opportunity to reflect on the current state of the subfield and offers suggestions for future research on this fascinating topic.

ACKNOWLEDGMENTS

The author gratefully acknowledges the indispensable assistance of doctoral student and fellow musician "PK" Vijaykumar Krishnan Palghat, and that of Jennifer "Kat" Bechkoff. He would also like to thank editor Frank Kardes for his helpful suggestions.

REFERENCES

Alikonis, C. R., Warm, J. S., Matthews, G., Dember, W. N., Hitchcock, E. M., & Kellaris, J. J. (2002). *Vigilance, workload, and boredom: Two competing models.* Presented at the Human Factors and Ergonomics Soci-ety, 46th annual meeting, September 2002, Baltimore, MD .

Alpert, J. I., & Alpert, M. I. (1990). Music influences on mood and purchase intentions. *Psychology & Market-ing, 7*(2), 109.

Alpert, M. I., Alpert, J. I., & Maltz, E. N. (2005). Purchase occasion influence on the role of music in advertis-ing. *Journal of Business Research, 58*(3), 369–376.

Anand, P., & Sternthal, B. (1990). Ease of message processing as a moderator of repetition effects in advertis-ing. *Journal of Marketing Research, 27*, 345–353.

Andrus, D. (1986). Office atmospherics and dental service satisfaction. *Journal of Professional Services Mar-keting, 1*, 77–85.

Areni, C. (2001). Examining the use and selection of atmospheric music in the hospitality industry: Are man-agers tuned into academic research? *Australian Journal of Hospitality Management, 8*(1), 27–40.

Areni, C. S. (2003a). Examining managers' theories of how atmospheric music effects perception, behavior and financial performance. *Journal of Retailing and Consumer Services, 10*(5), 263–274.

Areni, C. S. (2003b). Exploring managers' implicit theories of atmospheric music: Comparing academic anal-ysis to industry insight. *The Journal of Services Marketing, 17*(2/3), 161–184.

Areni, C. S. (2003c). Positioning strategy influences managers' beliefs about the effects of atmospheric music on financial performance. *Journal of Hospitality and Tourism Management, 10*(1), 13–22.

Areni, C. S., & Kim, D. (1993). The influence of background music on shopping behavior: Classical versus top-forty music in a wine store. *Advances in Consumer Research, 20*(1), 336–340.

Aylott, R., & Mitchell, V.-W. (1999). An exploratory study of grocery shopping stressors. *British Food Journal, 101*(9), 683–700.

Bailey, N., & Areni, C. S. (2006a). Keeping time to the tune: Background music as a quasi clock in retrospective duration judgments. *Perceptual and Motor Skills, 102*, 435–444.

Bailey, N., & Areni, C. S. (2006b). When a few minutes sound like a lifetime: Does atmospheric expand or contract perceived time? *Journal of Retailing, 82*, 189–202.

Baker, J., Parasuraman, A., Grewal, D., & Voss, G.B. (2002). The influence of multiple store environment cues on perceived merchandise value and patronage intentions. *Journal of Marketing, 66*(2), 120–141.

Baumgartner, H. (1992). Remembrance of things past — Music, autobiographical memory, and emotion. *Advances in Consumer Research, 19*, 613–620.

Ben Dahmane Mouelhi, N., & Touzani, M. (2003). Les réactions des acheteurs aux modalités de la musique d'ambiance: Cas de la notoriété et du style. *Revue Français du Marketing, 194*(4/5), 66–81.

Biley, F. C. (2000). The effects on patient well-being of music listening as a nursing intervention: A review of the literature. *Journal of Clinical Nursing, 9*(5), 668–677.

Blair, M. E., & Kellaris, J. J. (1993). Music in ads, stores, and homes. In L. McAlister, & M. L. Rothschild (Eds.), *Advances in consumer research* (Vol. 20, pp. 558). Provo, UT: Association for Consumer Research.

Blair, M. E., & Shimp, T. A. (1992). Consequences of an unpleasant experience with music: A second-order negative conditioning perspective. *Journal of Advertising, 21*(1), 35.

Boltz, M. G. (2001). Musical soundtracks as a schematic influence on the cognitive processing of filmed events. *Music Perception, 18*, 427–454.

Boltz, M. G. (2004). The cognitive processing of film and musical soundtracks. *Memory & Cognition, 32*(7):1194–1205

Brader, T. (2005). Striking a responsive chord: How political ads motivate and persuade voters by appealing to emotions. *American Journal of Political Science, 49*(2), 388.

Brooker, G., & Wheatley, J.J. (1994). Music and radio advertising: Effect of tempo and placement. In C. T. Allen & D. R. John (Eds.), *Advances in consumer research* (Vol. 21, pp. 286–290). Provo, UT: Association for Consumer Research.

Bruner, G. C., II (1990). Music, mood, and marketing. *Journal of Marketing, 54*(4), 94.

Caldwell, C., & Hibbert, S.A. (2002). The influence of music tempo and musical preference on restaurant patrons' behavior. *Psychology & Marketing, 19*(11), 895.

Cameron, M. A., Baker, J., Peterson, M., & Braunsberger, K. (2003). The effects of music, wait-length evaluation, and mood on a low-cost wait experience. *Journal of Business Research, 56*(6), 421.

Cattell, R. B., & Saunders, D. R. (1954). Musical preferences and personality diagnosis: A factorization of one hundred and twenty themes. *Journal of Social Psychology, 39*, 3–24.

Chebat, J. C., Chebat, C. G., & Vaillant, D. (2001). Environmental background music and in-store selling. *Journal of Business Research, 54*(2), 115–123.

Chebat, J. C., & Dube, L. (2000). Evolution and Challenges Facing Retail Atmospherics: The Apprentice Sorcerer Is Dying. *Journal of Business Research, 49*(2), 89–90.

Chebat, J. C., & Gelinas-Chebat, C. (1993a). Interactive effects of musical and visual cues on time perception: An application to waiting. *Perceptual and Motor Skills, 77*, 995.

Chebat, J. C., Gelinaschebat, C., & Filiatrault, P. (1993b). Interactive effects of musical and visual cues on time perception — An application to waiting lines in banks. *Perceptual and Motor Skills, 77*(3), 995–1020.

Chebat, J. C., Vaillant, D., & Gelinas-Chebat, C. (2000). Does background music in a store enhance salespersons' persuasiveness? *Perceptual and Motor Skills, 91*(2), 405–424.

Dube, L., Chebat, J.-C., & Morin, S. (1995). The effects of background music on consumers' desire to affiliate in buyer-seller interactions. *Psychology & Marketing, 12*(4), 305.

Dube, L., & Morin, S. (2001). Background music pleasure and store evaluation: Intensity effects and psychological mechanisms. *Journal of Business Research, 54*(2), 107.

Dunbar, D. S. (1990). Music, and advertising. *International Journal of Advertising, 9*(3), 197.

Espinoza, F., Neto, G. L., & D'Angelo, A. C. (2004). Testing the influence of retail atmosphere on store choice criteria, perceived value, and patronage intentions. *American Marketing Association. Conference Proceedings, 15*, 120.

Fabrigar, L. R., & Petty, R. E. (1999). The role of the affective and cognitive bases of attitudes in susceptibility to affectively and cognitively based persuasion. *Personality and Social Psychology Bulletin, 25*(3), 363–381.

Fried, R., & Berkowitz, L. (1979). Music hath charms… And can influence helpfulness. *Journal of Applied Social Psychology, 9*(3), 199–208.

Galizio, M., & Hendrick, C. (1972). Effect of musical accompaniment on attitude: The guitar as a prop for persuasion. *Journal of Applied Social Psychology, 2*(4), 350–359.

Galan, J.-Ph. (2002). L'analyse des fichiers log pour étudier l'impact de la musique sur le comportement des visiteurs d'un site Web culturel. *18eme Congrès International d l'Association Française de Marketing*, Lille.

Gallopel, K. (2000). Contributions affective et symbolique de la musique publicitaire : Une étude empirique. *Recherche et Applications en Marketing, 15*(1), 3–19.

Gorn, G. J. (1982). The effect of music in advertising on choice behavior: a classical conditioning approach. *Journal of Marketing, 46*, 94–101.

Gorn, G. J., Goldberg, M. E., & Basu, K. (1993). Mood, Awareness, and Product Evaluation. *Journal of Consumer Psychology, 2*, 237.

Gorn, G. J., Goldberg, M. E., Chattopadhyay, A., & Litvack, D. (1991). Music and information in commercials: Their effects with an. *Journal of Advertising Research, 31*(5), 23.

Grewal, D., Baker, J., Levy, M., & Voss, G. B. (2003). The effects of wait expectations and store atmosphere evaluations on patronage intentions in service-intensive retail stores. *Journal of Retailing, 79*, 259.

Groenland, E. A., & Schoormans, J. P. (1994). Comparing mood-induction and affective conditioning as mechanisms influencing product evaluation and product choice. *Psychology & Marketing (1986–1998), 11*(2), 183.

Gulas C. S., & Schewe, C. D. (1994). Atmospheric segmentation: Managing store image with background music. In R. Acrol & A. Mitchell (Eds.), *Enhancing knowledge development in marketing* (pp. 325–330). American Marketing Association, Chicago, IL.

Gundlach, R. H. (1932). A quantitative analysis of Indian music. *American Journal of Psychology, 44*, 133–145.

Gundlach, R. H. (1935). Factors determining the characterization of musical phrases. *American Journal of Psychology, 47*, 624–643.

Hahn, M., & Hwang, I. (1999). Effects of tempo and familiarity of background music on message processing in tv advertising: A resource-matching perspective. *Psychology & Marketing, 16*(8), 659–675.

Halpern, A. R., Zatorre, R. J., Bouffard, M., & Johnson, J. A. (2004). Behavioral and neurological correlates of perceived and imagined musical timbre. *Neuropsychologia, 42*, 1281–1292.

Hargreaves, D. J., & North, A. C. (1997). *The social psychology of music*. Oxford University Press.

Hecker, S. (1984). Music for advertising effect. *Psychology & Marketing, 1*, 3–8.

Heinlein, C. P. (1928). The affective characters of the major and minor modes in music. *Comparative Psychology, 8*(2), 101–142.

Helmholtz, H. (1883). *Die Lehre von den Tonempfindungen*. Verlag vo Fr. Vieweg u. Sohn, Braunschweig.

Henkin, R. I. (1955). A factorial study of the components of music. *Journal of Psychology, 39*, 161–181.

Henkin, R. I. (1957). A reevaluation of factorial study of the components of music. *Journal of Psychology, 43*, 301–306.

Herrington, J.D., & Capella, L. M. (1996). Effects of music in service environments: A field study. *Journal of Services Marketing, 10*, 26–41.

Hevner, K. (1935a). The affective character of the major and minor modes in music. *American Journal of Psychology, 47*, 103–118.

Hevner, K. (1935b). Expression in music: A discussion of experimental studies and Theories. *Psychological Review, 42*, 186–203.

Hevner, K. (1936). Experimental studies of the elements of expression in music. *American Journal of Psychology, 48*, 246–268.

Hevner, K. (1937). The affective value of pitch and tempo in music. *American Journal of Psychology, 49*, 621–630.

Holbrook, M. B., & Anand, P. (1990). Effects of tempo and situational arousal on the listener's perceptual and affective responses to music. *Psychology of Music, 18*, 150–162.

Holbrook, M. B., & Gardner., M. P. (1993). An approach to investigating the emotional determinants of consumption durations: Why do people consume what they consume for as long as they consume it? *Journal of Consumer Psychology, 2*(2), 123–142.

Holbrook, M. B., & Gardner, M. P. (2000). Illustrating a dynamic model of the mood-updating process in consumer behavior. *Psychology & Marketing, 17*(3), 165–194.

Holbrook, M. B., & Huber, J. (1979). Separating perceptual dimensions from affective overtones: An application to consumer aesthetics. *Journal of Consumer Research, 5*, 272–283.

Holbrook, M. B., Lacher, K. T., & LaTour, M. S. (2006). Audience judgments as the potential missing link between expert judgments and audience appeal: An illustration based on musical recordings of "My Funny Valentine." *Journal of the Academy of Marketing Science, 34*(1), 8–18.

Holbrook, M. B., & Schindler, R. M. (1989). Some exploratory findings on the development of musical tastes. *Journal of Consumer Research, 16*, 119–124.

Hughes, A. G., & Lowis, M. J. (2002). The role of rhythm and mode in emotional responses to hymn tunes. *Mankind Quarterly, 42*(4), 441–454.

Hui, M. K., Dube, L., & Chebat, J. C. (1997). The impact of music on consumers' reactions to waiting for services. *Journal of Retailing, 73*(1), 87–104.

Hung, K. (2000). Narrative music in congruent and incongruent tv advertising. *Journal of Advertising, 29*(1), 25–34.

Hung, K. (2001). Framing meaning perceptions with music: The case of teaser ads. *Journal of Advertising, 30*(3), 39–49.

Jackson, D. M. (2003). *Sonic Branding: An essential guide to the art and science of sonic branding.* Ebbu Vale, UK: Palgrave/MacMillan.

Jacob, C., &.Guéguen, N. (2003). L'impact d'une musique d'ambience online sur la perception temporelle, la mémorisation et l'appréciation d'un site web. *Deuxième Workshop de Marsouin, 4&5*(décembre 2003), ENST Bretagne, Brest.

Juslin, P. N. (2000). Cue utilization in communication of emotion in music performance: Relating performance to perception. *Journal of Experimental Psychology-Human Perception and Performance, 26*(6), 1797–1812.

Kellaris, J. J. (1992). Consumer aesthetics outside the lab — Preliminary-report on a musical field-study. *Advances in Consumer Research, 19*, 730–734.

Kellaris, J .J. (2003). Dissecting earworms: Further evidence on the "song-stuck-in-your-head" phenomenon. In Christine Page & Steve Posavac (Eds.), *Proceedings of the Society for Consumer Psychology Winter 2003 Conference* (pp. 220–222). Presented American Psychological Society, New Orleans., Louisiana.

Kellaris, J. J. (2001). Identifying properties of tunes that get "stuck in your head": Toward a theory of cognitive itch. In S. E. Heckler & S. Shapiro (Eds.), *Proceedings of the Society for Consumer Psychology Winter 2001 Conference*, Scottsdale, AZ, American Psychological Society.

Kellaris, J. J., & Altsech, M.B. (1992). The experience of time as a function of musical loudness and gender of listener. *Advances in Consumer Research, 19*, 725–729.

Kellaris, J. J., & Cox, A. D. (1989). The effects of background music in advertising: A reassessment. *Journal of Consumer Research, 16*(1), 113.

Kellaris, J. J., Cox, A. D., & Cox, D. (1993). The effect of background music on ad processing - a contingency explanation. *Journal of Marketing, 57*(4), 114–125.

Kellaris, J. J., & Kent, R. J. (1993). An exploratory investigation of responses elicited by music varying in tempo, tonality, and texture. *Journal of Consumer Psychology, 2*(4), 381–401.

Kellaris, J. J., & Kent, R. J. (1991). Exploring tempo and modality effects, on consumer responses to music. *Advances in Consumer Research, 18*, 243–248.

Kellaris, J. J., & Kent, R.J . (1992). The influence of music on consumers' temporal perceptions: Does time fly when you're having fun? *Journal of Consumer Psychology, 1*(4), 365–376.

Kellaris, J. J., & Mantel, S. P. (1996). Shaping time perceptions with background music: The effect of congruity and arousal on estimates of ad durations. *Psychology & Marketing, 13*(5), 501.

Kellaris, J. J., & Mantel, S. P. (2003). The impact of motivation on judgmental accuracy in easy versus difficult time estimation tasks. In C. Page & S. Posavac (Eds.), *Proceedings of the Society for Consumer Psychology Winter 2003 Conference* (pp. 128–129). New Orleans, LA: American Psychological Society.

Kellaris, J. J., & Mantel, S. P. (1994a). The influence of music-induced stimulus congruity and internal states on perceptions of event durations. In W. Hutchinson & K. L. Keller (Eds.), *Proceedings of the Society for Consumer Psychology 1994 winter conference* (pp. 29–30). St. Petersburg, FL: American Psychological Association.

Kellaris, J. J., & Mantel, S. P. (1994b). The influence of mood and gender on consumers' time perceptions. In C. T. Allen & D. Roedder John (Eds.), *Advances in consumer research* (Vol. 21, pp. 514–518). Provo, UT: Association for Consumer Research.

Kellaris, J. J., Mantel, S. P., & Altsech, M. B. (1996). Decibels, disposition, and duration: The impact of musical loudness and internal states on time perceptions. In K. Corfman & J. Lynch (Eds.), *Advances in consumer research* (Vol. 23, pp. 498–503). Provo, UT: Association for Consumer Research,.

Kellaris, J. J., & Rice, R. C. (1993). The influence of tempo, loudness, and gender of listener on responses to music. *Psychology & Marketing, 10*(1), 15.

Kellaris, J. J., Winter, F., & O'Brien, M. (1999). Waiting on musical hold: Insights from an applied study. In M. Viswanathan, L. Compeau, & M. Hastak (Eds.), *Proceedings of the Society for Consumer Psychology 1999 Winter Conference* (pp. 91–93). St. Petersburg, FL: American Psychological Association.

Kraemer, D. J. M., Macrae, C. N., Green, A. E., & Kelly, W. M. (2005). Sound of silence activates auditory cortex. *Nature, 434,* 158.

Lacher, K. T., & Mizerski, R. (1994). An exploratory-study of the responses and relationships involved in the evaluation of, and in the intention to purchase new rock-music. *Journal of Consumer Research, 21*(2), 366–380.

Lammers, H. (2003). An oceanside field experiment on background music effects on the restaurant tab. *Perceptual and Motor Skills, 96*(3), 1025–1026.

Lee, D., Henderson, A., & Shum, D. (2004). The effect of music on preprocedure anxiety in Hong Kong Chinese day patients., *Journal of Clinical Nursing, 13,* 297–303

Lemoine, J.-F. (2003). Vers une approche globale de l'atmosphère du point de vente. *Revue Française du Marketing, 194*(4), 83.

Lewin, K. (1951). *Field theory insSocial science,* New York: Harper.

Lundin, R. W. (1985). *An objective psychology of music.* Krieger Publishing.

MacInnis, D. J., & Park, C.W. (1991). The differential role of characteristics of music on high- and low-involvement consumers' processing of ads. *Journal of Consumer Research, 18,* 161–173.

Mantel, S. P., & Kellaris, J. J. (1993). The influence of arousal and stimulus congruity on consumers' time perceptions: A test of competing explanations. In B. Varadarajan & B. Jaworski (Eds.), *Marketing theory and applications* (Vol. 4, pp. 347). Chicago: American Marketing Association.

Mantel, S. P., & Kellaris, J. J. (2003). Exploring determinants of psychological time: The impact of cognitive resources required and available on the estimation of lapsed time. *Journal of Consumer Research, 29*(4), 531–538.

Matsumoto, J. (2002). Why people listen to sad music: Effects of music on sad moods. *Japanese Journal of Educational Psychology, 50*(1), 23–32.

Mattila, A. S., & Wirtz, J. (2001). Congruency of scent and music as a driver of in-store evaluations and behavior. *Journal of Retailing, 77*(2), 273.

McElrea, H., & Standing, L. (1992). Fast music causes fast drinking. *Perceptual and Motor Skills, 75*(2), 362.

Millar, M. G., & Millar, K. U. (1990). Attitude change as a function of attitude type and argument type. *Journal of Personality and Social Psychology, 59*(2), 217–228.

Milliman, R. E. (1982). Using background music to affect the behavior of supermarket shoppers. *Journal of Marketing, 46,* 86–91.

Milliman, R. E. (1986). The influence of background music on the behavior of restaurant patrons. *Journal of Consumer Research, 13,* 286–289.

Miniard, P. W., Bhatla, S., & Sirdeshmukh, D. (1992). Mood as a determinant of post-consumption product evaluations: Mood effects and their dependency on the affective intensity of the consumption experience. *Journal of Consumer Psychology, 1*(2), 173–195.

Morrison, M., & Beverland, M. (2003). In search of the right in-store music. *Business Horizons, 46*(6), 77.

Mouelhi, N. B. D., & Touzani, M. (2003). Les réactions des acheteurs aux modalités de la musique d'ambiance: Cas de la notoriété et du style. *Revue Française du Marketing, 194*(4), 65.

Muehling, D. D., & Bozman, C. S. (1990). An examination of factors influencing effectiveness of 15-second advertisements. *International Journal of Advertising, 9*(4), 331.

North, A. C., & Hargreaves, D. J. (1996). Situational influences on reported musical preference. *Psychomusicology, 15*(1-2), 30–45.

North, A. C., & Hargreaves, D. J. (1997). Music and consumer behavior. In North, A. C., & Hargreaves, D. J. (Eds.), *The social psychology of music* (pp. 268–289).Oxford University Press.

North, A. C., Hargreaves, D. J., & McKendrick, J. (1999). Music and on-hold waiting time. *British Journal of Psychology, 90*(1), 161–164.

North, A. C., Hargreaves, D. J., & McKendrick, J. (2000). The effects of music on atmosphere in a bank and a bar. *Journal of Applied Social Psychology, 30*(7), 1504–1522.

North, A. C. & Hargreaves, D. J. (1998). The effect of music on atmosphere and purchase intentions in a cafeteria. *Journal of Applied Social Psychology, 28*(24), 2254–2273.

North, A. C., Hargreaves, D. J., & McKendrick, J. (1999). The influence of in-store music on wine selections. *Journal of Applied Psychology, 84*(2), 271.

North, A. C., & Hargreaves, D. J. (1999). Can music move people? The effects of musical complexity and silence on waiting time. *Environment and Behavior, 31*(1), 136.

North, A. C., Shilcock, A., & Hargreaves, D. J. (2003). The effect of musical style on restaurant customers' spending. *Environment and Behavior, 35*(5), 712.

North, A. C., MacKenzie, L. C., Law, R. M., & Hargreaves, D. J. (2004). The effects of musical and voice "fit" on responses to advertisements. *Journal of Applied Social Psychology, 34*(8), 1675–1708.

Oakes, S. (2000). The influence of the musicscape within service environments. *Journal of Services Marketing, 14*(7), 539.

Oakes, S. (2003). Musical tempo and waiting perceptions. *Psychology & Marketing, 20*(8), 685–705.

Olsen, G. D. (1995). Creating the contrast: The influence of silence and background music on recall and attribute importance. *Journal of Advertising, 24*(4), 29.

Olsen, G. D. (1997). The impact of interstimulus interval and background silence on recall. *Journal of Consumer Research, 23*(4), 295.

Olsen, G. D., & Pracejus, J. W. (2004). Integration of positive and negative affective stimuli. *Journal of Consumer Psychology, 14*(4), 374–384.

Petty, R. E., & Wegener, D. T. (1998). Matching versus mismatching attitude functions: Implications for scrutiny of persuasive messages. *Personality & Social Psychology Bulletin, 24*(3), 227–240.

Ramos, L.-V. (1993). The effects of on-hold telephone music on the number of premature disconnections to a statewide protective services abuse hotline. *Journal of Music Therapy, 30,* 119–129.

Rentfrow, P. J., & Gosling, S. D. (2003). The *do re mi's* of everyday life: Examining the structures and personality correlates of music preferences. *Journal of Personality and Social Psychology, 84,* 1236–1256.

Rentfrow, P. J., & Gosling, S. D. (2006). Message in a ballad — The role of music preferences in interpersonal perception. *Psychological Science, 17*(3), 236–242.

Rieunier, S. (1998). L'influence de la musique d'ambiance sur le comportement du client: Revue de littérature, défis méthodologiques et voies de recherches. *Recherche et Applications en Marketing, 13* (3), 57–77.

Rigg, M. G. (1940). Speed as a dterminer of musical mood. *Journal of Experimental Psychology, 27,* 566–571.

Rivenburg, R. (2001). The science behind the song stuck in your head. *Los Angeles Times,* October 7, 2001, p. E1.

Roediger, H. L. (1990). Implicit memory. *American Psychologist, 45*(9), 1043–1056.

Roehm, M. L. (2001). Instrumental vs. Vocal versions of popular music in advertising. *Journal of Advertising Research, 41*(3), 49.

Roehm, M. L., & Sternthal, B. (2001). The moderating effect of knowledge and resources on the persuasive impact of analogies. *Journal of Consumer Research, 28*(2), 257–272.

Sachs, C. (1943). *The rise of music in the ancient world.* W. W. Norton.

Schubert, E. (2004). Modeling perceived emotion with continuous musical features. *Music Perception, 21*(4), 561–585.

Scott, L. M. (1990). Understanding jingles and needledrop: A rhetorical approach to music in advertising. *Journal of Consumer Research, 17,* 223–236.

Shafir, E. (1995). Compatibility in cognition and decision. In J. Busemeyer, R. Hastie, & D. L. Medin (Eds.), *Decision making from a cognitive perspective: The psychology of learning and motivation* (Vol. 32, pp. 247–274). San Diego: Academic Press.

Sivadas, E., Grewal, R., & Kellaris, J. J. (1998). The internet as a micro marketing tool: Targeting consumers through preferences revealed in music newsgroup usage. *Journal of Business Research, 41*(3), 179–186.

Smith, P., & Curnow, R. (1966). Arousal hypothesis and the effects of music on purchasing behavior. *Journal of Applied Psychology, 50,* 255–256.

Stewart, D. W., Farmer, K. M., & Stannard, C. I. (1990). Music as a recognition cue in advertising-tracking studies. *Journal of Advertising Research, 30*(4), 39.

Stewart, D. W., & Punj, G. N. (1998). Effects of using a nonverbal (musical) cue on recall and playback of television advertising: Implications for advertising tracking. *Journal of Business Research, 42*(1), 39.

Sullivan, M. (2002). The impact of pitch, volume and tempo on the atmospheric effects of music. *International Journal of Retail & Distribution Management, 30*(6/7), 323.

Sweeney, J. C., & Wyber, F. (2002). The role of cognitions and emotions in the music-approach-avoidance behavior relationship. *The Journal of Services Marketing, 16*(1), 51.

Tansik, D. A., & Routhieaux, R. (1999). Customer stress-relaxation: the impact of music in a hospital waiting room. *International Journal of Service Industry Management, 10*(1), 68.

Tom, G. (1990). Marketing with music. *The Journal of Consumer Marketing, 7*(2), 49.

Tom, G. (1990). Exploratory study: Marketing with music. *The Journal of Consumer Marketing, 7*(2), 49.

Tom, G. (1995). Classical conditioning of unattended stimuli. *Psychology & Marketing, 12*(1), 79.

Turley, L. W., & Milliman, R. E. (2000). Atmospheric effects on shopping behavior: A review of the experimental evidence. *Journal of Business Research, 49*(2), 193–211.

Tybout, A. M., & Artz, N. (1994). Consumer psychology. *Annual Review of Psychology, 45*, 131–169.

Wallace, W. T. (1991). Jingles in advertising: Can they improve recall? In R. H. Holman, & M. R. Solomon (Eds.), *Advances in consumer research* (Vol. 18, pp. 239–242). Provo, UT: Association for Consumer Research.

Wegner, D. M. (1994). Ironic processes of mental control. *Psychological Review 101*(1), 34–52.

Wegner, D. M., & Zanakos, S. (1994). Chronic thought suppression. *Journal of Personality, 62*(4), 615–640.

Wenzlaff, R .M., & Wegner, D. M. (2000). Thought suppression. In S. T. Fiske, D. L. Schacter, & C. Zahn-Waxler (Eds.), *Annual Review of Psychology* (Vol. 51, pp. 59–91). Palo Alto, CA: Annual Reviews.

Wilson, S. (2003). The effect of music on perceived atmosphere and purchase intentions in a restaurant. *Psychology of Music, 31*(1), 93–109.

Wirtz, J., Mattila, A. S., & Tan, R.L.P. (2000). The moderating role of target-arousal on the impact of affect on satisfaction — An examination in the context of service experiences. *Journal of Retailing, 76*(3), 347–365.

Wundt, W. M. (1874). *Grundzuge der Physiologischen Psychology.* Leipzig, Engleman.

Wyatt, S., & Langdon, J. N. (1937). *Fatigue and boredom in repetitive work.* Industrial Health Research Board Report No. 77, Great Britain Medical Research Council, London.

Yalch, R. F. (1991). Memory in a jingle jungle: Music as a mnemonic device in com. *Journal of Applied Psychology, 76*(2), 268.

Yalch, R., & Spangenberg, E. (1990). Effects of store music on shopping behavior. *The Journal of Consumer Marketing, 7*(2), 55.

Yalch, R., & Spangenberg, E. (1993). Using store music for retail zoning: A field experiment. *Advances in Consumer Research, 20*, 632.

Yalch, R. F., & Spangenberg, E. R. (2000). The effects of music in a retail setting on real and perceived shopping times. *Journal of Business Research, 49*(2), 139.

Zhu, R., & Meyers-Levy, J. (2005). Distinguishing between the meanings of music: When background music affects product perceptions. *Journal of Marketing Research, 42*, 333–345.

34

Consumer Psychology of Sport
More Than Just a Game

ROBERT MADRIGAL

University of Oregon

VASSILIS DALAKAS

Northern Kentucky University

Hedonic psychology has been referred to as "the study of what makes experiences and life pleasant or unpleasant" (Kahneman, Diener, & Schwarz, 1999, p. ix). It encompasses those activities from which people derive enjoyment (see also Hirschman & Holbrook, 1982). Of interest here is one very specific type of hedonic activity that contributes to the pleasure (and often pain) people feel in their daily lives: the vicarious consumption of competitive sporting events. According to Kubovy (1999), sports spectatorship is a pleasure of the mind because its enjoyment derives from a process whereby emotions and cognitions are blended in such a way as to give meaning to the overall experience. Watching a sporting event is an emotional rollercoaster, fraught with hopes and fears about what may befall a favorite team.[1] The intensity of the experience can not be overstated for those whose avidity is most fanatical because, for these fans, feelings of self worth are often tied directly to a favorite team's fortunes.

Fanatic consumer behavior has been described as the pursuit of "consumption activities with a level of passion grossly out of proportion to that experienced by other more temperate consumers of the same product category" (Holbrook, 1987, pp. 144–145). It represents an extreme form of enduring involvement that is characterized by an ongoing commitment of resources over time (Scammon, 1987) and an intense devotion which leans toward excessive or uncritical (Holbrook, 1987). As with other forms of consumer fanaticism, sports is no different. Sports fans develop long-term relationships with a favorite team or athlete and typically exhibit an enthusiastic devotion that is often overwhelming and uncritical.

The importance of sports fanaticism as a predominant cultural force is nothing new. Beginning with a focus on the beauty and reverence for athletic prowess on display at the ancient Olympic Games (776 B.C.–A.D. 393), fans' attention later turned to the "blood-sports" of the Roman Empire which were noted for drawing over 40,000 paid attendees to witness the gladiatorial events held in the Coliseum (Harris, 1972). Spectator sports were also widely popular in ancient China and Japan (Midwinter, 1986). In the United States, baseball emerged as a national game after the Civil War with the first professional baseball teams appearing in 1869 (McChesney, 1989). A new middle class emerged following the Industrial Revolution with more leisure time and disposable income to spend on spectator sports in the late 19th century. Also, during this period, spectator sports made their appearance for the first time in colleges and universities.

Spectator sports today remain as popular, if not more popular, as ever with an appeal that cuts across nationalities, social status, race, and education level. Sporting events may be consumed either directly (e.g., attendance) or indirectly (e.g., media). For example, consumers in the United States spent nearly $16 billion on sports admissions in 2005 (Bureau of Economic Analysis, 2006). Arguably the most popular sport in the United States, football, routinely averages higher ratings than prime-time programming (Marchland, 2006) with prices for a :30 second television ad averaging $2.5 million during the first half of the 2006 Super Bowl (Klaasen & Frazier, 2006). The popularity of spectator sports is not limited to just the United States. The 2002 World Cup was televised in 213 countries and broadcast over 41,100 hours of programming. The 20 most viewed matches had an average share of almost 85% which suggests that in almost every location throughout the world people were watching soccer almost exclusively (Fédération Internationale de Football Association, 2005).

The preceding begs a simple question: What makes spectator sports such a compelling form of consumer entertainment? The remainder of this chapter attempts to answer this question. The review offered here is the first to systematically categorize research on sports fans from a consumer behavior perspective. Although some of the discussion is peripherally relevant to other forms of entertainment, our primary focus is on explaining the psychological processes engaged by fans within the context of competitive sporting events. We begin by describing the unique nature of sporting events and how it affects spectators differently than other forms of mass entertainment. We then turn our attention to why people care about the outcomes of sporting events. The focus in this section is on the affective consequences of sporting event outcomes. Next, the prejudiced judgments and biased processing displayed by highly allegiant sports fans are examined. Our final section discusses the fan experience. In particular, we consider fan motives and the ways in which fans consume the sporting event. Implications for future research are discussed.

THE UNIQUE NATURE OF SPORTING EVENTS

Deighton (1992) created a typology of strategies for emphasizing the drama exhibited in performance that varies along the dimensions of observation/participation and realism/fantasy. Of interest here are skill performances such as sporting events or jury trials which are staged displays of competence occurring in naturalistic settings that emphasize the event's realism. This differs from a show performance (e.g., theater) that is contrived for the audience's benefit, occurs in an artificial setting and emphasizes elements of fantasy. Although the role of the observer in both types of performance is as a witness to the action rather than as a direct participant, the outcome of a show performance is usually predictable or ritualistic. Conversely, skill performance is characterized by tension and uncertainty about the eventual outcome. Competitive sporting events represent a type of contested skill performance (Barthes, 1972). Although ties do occur in a number of sports, competitive sporting events are contested so as to result in one of two outcomes, each in direct opposition to the other: one competitor wins and the other loses. The competitive nature of sports distinguishes it from many other forms of entertainment performances.

It is the experience of suspense arising from the possibility of alternative outcomes to a competitive sporting event that makes this form of entertainment so compelling to spectators. Uncertainty increases as the subjective probability of an event's occurrence gets closer to its nonoccurrence and is at a maximum when the odds for one outcome are approximately equal to that of another (i.e., 50/50). However, uncertainty over the outcome is not enough to generate feelings of suspense.

For example, being uncertain about whether a taxi will appear at a given intersection at a particular time is not especially suspenseful—unless, of course, the consequences of such an event are sufficiently compelling. It is, then, concern over the desirability or undesirability of the consequences associated with alternative outcomes that constitutes the other necessary requirement of suspense.

According to Zillmann (1996), concern over the outcome is more critical to the experience of suspense than uncertainty. Suspense depends on a bottom-up process in which appraisals of the action occurring during the contest and the associated implications of those actions on the desirability of the eventual outcome vacillate from one moment to the next. Changing appraisals lead to feelings of (a) fear that a desirable outcome may not befall a preferred competitor, (b) fear that an undesirable outcome may befall a preferred competitor, (c) hope that a desirable outcome will befall a preferred competitor, (d) hope that an undesirable outcome will not befall a preferred competitor, and (e) any possible combination of these hopes and fears (Carroll, 1996). According to Zillmann (1996), "hopes and fears are inseparably intertwined in the apprehensions that produce suspense" (p. 202). It is therefore not surprising that appraisal theorists Ortony, Clore, and Collins (1988) view suspense as "involving a Hope emotion and a Fear emotion coupled with the cognitive state of uncertainty" (capitalized in the original, p. 130; see also Kubovy, 1999).

That viewers watch competitive sports for purposes of pleasure seems at first to be counterintuitive given the noxious state of apprehension that often accompanies high levels of suspense. Yet, it is the tension arising from vacillating feelings of hope and fear that people seek from the experience. In fact, research has shown that the entertainment value derived from this form of skill performance increases at greater levels of suspense (Gan, Tuggle, Mitrook, Coussement, & Zillmann, 1997). Interestingly, entertainment value may be greater under conditions of high suspense regardless of the outcome. Madrigal, Bee, and LaBarge (2005) reported in multiple studies that viewers of simulated races derived greater enjoyment following high-suspense races in which their preferred competitor lost than did those whose competitor won a low-suspense race. It should be noted, however, that the competitors used in these studies evoked relatively low levels of fan allegiance.

Section Summary

Sporting events represent a unique form of consumer entertainment that emphasizes the skill of the actors which are, in this case, athletes or teams. The purpose of such performances is to produce an unequivocal winner. Given that winning is available to only one competitor, sporting events represent a type of competitive contest in which the action is unscripted and unfolds naturally with outcomes seldom known until the very end of the experience. Uncertainty about how things will turn out coupled with a strong preference for one outcome over another creates feelings of suspense. It is these feelings of suspense which are characterized by intertwined feelings of hope and fear over the possibility of alternative outcomes that constitute the value proposition derived from the fan experience.

THE AFFECTIVE CONSEQUENCES OF CARING ABOUT WHO WINS

Viewers' concern over potential alternative outcomes depends on their affective dispositions toward the team. According to Zillmann, Bryant, and Sapolsky (1989), two propositions underlie disposition theory. First, in the case of a win, enjoyment is hypothesized to increase when the spectator has a positive affective disposition toward the team and to decrease in the presence of a negative affective disposition. A corollary proposition suggests that enjoyment also increases when a disliked competitor loses and decreases when a liked competitor loses. The latter proposition is consistent with the notion of *schadenfreude*, a German word that describes the pleasure that one party experiences at the misfortunes of another; a response that is heightened when feelings of antagonism exist among the concerned parties (Heider, 1958; see Leach Spears, Branscombe, & Doosje, 2003). Thus, based on disposition theory, two options exist for a desirable (undesirable) outcome: a liked competitor wins (loses) or a disliked competitor loses (wins).

According to Ortony et al. (1988), the moment-to-moment hope and fear that is felt during suspense immediately give rise to the disconfirmation emotions of relief and disappointment once the outcome becomes known. In the case of relief pleasure is felt when the prospect of an undesirable outcome has been eliminated or changed for the better (i.e., disconfirmed), whereas disappointment occurs when the prospect for a desirable outcome has been disconfirmed (see also Lazarus, 1991). In a test of disposition theory, Bee and Madrigal (2003) manipulated viewer empathy toward the athlete. In one condition, an unknown target athlete was described in favorable terms so as to create a positive affective disposition toward the target and his competitor was described in neutral terms. In another condition, the athlete was described in unfavorable terms in order to create a negative affective disposition and, again, his competitor was described in neutral terms. The results indicated that empathy toward the athlete moderated viewers' feelings of relief and disappointment over the outcome. Specifically, a hedonic reversal was evidenced in the Empathy (liked vs. disliked) × Outcome (win vs. loss) disordinal interaction for both emotions. The expected differences in each emotion were found between liked and disliked athletes within each outcome condition (e.g., greater relief was felt when a liked athlete won compared to when a disliked athlete won). However, consistent with a *schadenfreude* effect, no emotion difference was found between liked and disliked athletes across outcome conditions. For example, feelings of relief (disappointment) were equivalent following a winning (losing) effort by a liked competitor and a losing (winning) effort by a disliked competitor.

Relief has also been featured prominently in the literature on suspense. Specifically, the intensity of relief is thought to vary proportionately with the level of distress that is experienced during the suspenseful episode. Zillmann (1996) has gone so far as to note that spectators endure the noxiousness associated with suspense specifically because of the extraordinary relief they feel once a desirable outcome is realized. A conceptual rationale for this effect is provided by excitation transfer theory (Zillmann, 1978, 1983). The theory posits that in contrast to spectators' cognitive adjustment to a contest's outcome which occurs quickly, the heightened levels of arousal due to increased sympathetic activity decay more slowly. This creates residual excitation from the preceding distressing emotional state that is transferred into subsequent affective reactions based on the desirability of the outcome. Feelings of relief following a desirable outcome are therefore accentuated due to excitation transfer and these feelings compensate spectators for their willingness to put up with the unpleasant feelings experienced during suspense (see Cantor, Zillmann, & Bryant, 1975; Reisenzein, 1983; Sparks, 1991; Zillmann, 1978, for examples in the context of suspenseful media). Recently, Madrigal et al. (2005) provided evidence that relief mediates the effect of game outcome (i.e., win vs. loss) on the entertainment value derived by spectators from a competitive event under conditions of high suspense, but not under conditions of low suspense.

In addition to relief and disappointment, other specific emotions arising as a result of caring about game outcomes have also been investigated (Bizman & Yinon, 2002; Sloan, 1989; Wann & Branscombe, 1992; Wann, Dolan, McGeorge, & Allison, 1994). For example, Madrigal (2003) examined the antecedents and consequences of attribution-dependent emotions during a series of basketball games as they were being played. Attribution-dependent emotions (Ortony et al., 1988) were defined as the specific types of emotions arising from the praiseworthy (e.g., pride, respect, admiration) or blameworthy (e.g., irritation, frustration, anger) actions of the preferred team during each game. Madrigal (2003) found that the importance of seeing a favorite team win a particular game was positively related both to praiseworthy and blameworthy emotions. In effect, those fans wanting to see a victory most reported more emotion, regardless of valence. The results also indicated a positive (negative) relationship between praiseworthy (blameworthy) emotions and satisfaction with the team's performance. Interestingly, the impact of outcome importance on blameworthy emotions was greater at the end of the game than at the beginning. This suggests that the frequency of emotions arising in fans caring most deeply about the outcome become increasingly dependent on an attribution of blame rather than praise at the later stages of a game.

Another affective consequence arising from a contest's outcome that has received some attention over the years is basking in reflected glory (BIRG). BIRGing refers to an individual's inclination to "share in the glory of a successful other with whom they are in some way associated" (Cialdini et al., 1976, p. 366; see Dalakas, Madrigal, & Anderson, 2004, for a review). Consistent with balance theory (Heider, 1958) fans BIRG by increasing their association with a successful team in order to increase their own self-esteem in the eyes of others, even though the connection is relatively trivial or seemingly incidental. A complementary tendency of BIRG is cutting off reflected failure (CORF; Snyder, Lassegard, & Ford, 1986) which is an ego-protection technique that fans use to distance themselves from an unsuccessful team.

Wann and Branscombe (1990) found that die-hard fans tended to BIRG more and CORF less than fans with moderate or low levels of team commitment. The authors argued that the inability of die-hard fans to CORF was due to their psychological commitment to the team. Bizman and Yinon (2002) examined BIRG/CORF behavior from a temporal perspective. They found that self-esteem is implicated following an outcome but its effect is only temporary. Their data indicated that highly allegiant fans appear to CORF for a short while following a loss in order to preserve their self-esteem but the carryover of this effect is relatively brief and they soon regain their former level of fan allegiance to the team. Madrigal (1995) also considered team allegiance effects as they relate to the BIRG phenomenon using a temporal perspective. He reported that pre-game disposition toward the team (i.e., team identification) and the quality of the team's opponent were each positively related to post-game BIRG. Moreover, BIRG was a positive predictor of fans' overall satisfaction with attending the game.

A study considering both the affective and behavioral consequences of BIRG was reported by Hirt, Zillmann, Erickson, and Kennedy (1992). They found that for those most favorably disposed, a team's success or failure was perceived as a personal success or failure. Their results indicated that not only was fans' mood improved following a win, so too were fans' estimates of both the team's chances in the future and their own ability to perform on an unrelated set of physical, mental and social tasks. In contrast, a loss led to a reduced mood and decreased confidence in performing these tasks. Consistent with the BIRG hypothesis, self-esteem and not mood was found to mediate the influence of future estimates on both team and their own future performance.

In addition to BIRG and CORF, a third technique of indirect self-presentation used by fans is the public blasting of one's rivals. The idea behind blasting is that if fans try to increase their esteem in the eyes of others by associating with a successful team (i.e., BIRG), they might also seek to increase their esteem by denigrating the perceived value of an opponent's achievements. Thus, blasting refers to derogatory comments made by fans toward an opponent following a defeat as a way of restoring their own damaged sense of identity and self-esteem (Cialdini & Richardson, 1980; Branscombe & Wann, 1994). Branscombe and Wann (1992a) found that highly allegiant fans that were unable to distance themselves (i.e., CORF) from their preferred team following a loss resorted to blasting behavior directed at players and fans of the opposing team. In an unexpected finding,

End (2001) reported that blasting actually increased following victories than losses which would suggest that blasting may operate as an extended form of BIRG.

Section Summary

The preceding section described how disposition theory explains fans' reactions to game outcomes. A desirable outcome is one in which either a liked competitor wins or a disliked competitor loses, and an undesirable outcome is one in which either a liked competitor loses or a disliked competitor wins. Central to disposition theory is that a game outcome is in itself objectively neutral except for the fan's disposition toward the teams. Moreover, it is the fan's disposition toward the team that influences the type of subsequent emotions that are felt once a contest is over. The initial emotions experienced after a game outcome are either relief or disappointment, depending on fans' dispositions toward each of the competing teams. Relief is an especially important reaction to desirable outcomes, particularly under conditions of high suspense. In fact, relief is thought to contribute directly to the enjoyment of suspenseful contests. Finally, other affective consequences (e.g., attribution emotions, BIRGing) of game outcomes that are linked to team liking were also discussed.

Research Implications

Hedonic products such as sporting events are consumed primarily for their emotional content. A sporting event may be viewed as a series of episodes that collectively comprise the experience. Pleasure is derived not just from the overall outcome, but also from the instant utility of the moment which may be defined as "the strength of the disposition to continue or to interrupt the current experience" (Kahneman, 1999, p. 4). Research suggests that the retrospective evaluations of temporal experiences depend on a simple peak-end rule. That is, consumers' evaluations are predicted by an average of the peak affective response recorded during the experience and the ratings that are recorded immediately before the experience terminates (Fredrickson & Kahneman, 1993; Varey & Kahneman, 1992; Woltman-Elpers, Mukherjee, & Hoyer, 2004). The latter would suggest that fans' retrospective evaluation of a sporting event in which the favorite team loses in the final minutes of the contest would generate a negative judgment. Yet, under conditions of relatively low allegiance, enjoyment appears to be moderated by suspense such that a highly suspenseful contest with a negative outcome was evaluated more favorably than a less suspenseful one with a positive outcome (Madrigal et al., 2005). Thus, it would appear that the enjoyment of a sporting event is a multifaceted phenomenon and further research is needed to understand the variables that contribute to fan enjoyment.

In general, the importance of the temporal domain on fans' enjoyment of the sporting event experience has received little attention. As noted, the instant utility of the moment underlies the consumption experience. Although the peak-end rule appears to be predictive of summary judgments of most experiences, sporting events represent a unique context. A better understanding is needed of the contribution of momentary experiences and events to retrospective evaluations and fans' interest in re-engaging in consumption in the future. Various methods may be used to capture momentary experiences (see Larsen & Fredrickson, 1999, for a review). Respondents can provide continuous self-reports of emotion or cognition variables using rating dials. The approach allows respondents to provide real-time ratings as an experience unfolds. Unfortunately, respondents are constrained in how much information they can provide on a momentary basis and are usually limited to providing data on just a single bipolar or unipolar scale at a time. This shortcoming can be addressed by collecting moment-to-moment self-reports to the same experimental stimuli (e.g., video clip of a game) via multiple iterations of collection wherein different groups of respondents provide data on different moment-to-moment variables during each iteration (see Woltman-Elpers et al., 2004). Another option is the use of cued reviews which is a video recall technique in which respondents are asked to stop the video replay at moments when they remember having felt an emotion or experienced a relevant cognition such as an attribution during the original viewing. Experience sampling is another option available to researchers interested in collecting real-time data (see Stone, Shiffman, & DeVries, 1999, for a review). Experience sampling attempts to sample randomly during an experience. Respondents typically carry beepers and are asked to provide data upon receiving a signal.

Another area of future research pertaining to in-situ emotions and retrospective evaluations of sporting events is the examination of how environmental stimuli external to the consumer may moderate the fan experience. Despite the social nature of many sporting event experiences, only Holt's (1995) ethnography has considered social interaction effects during consumption. In other research, interaction among consumers of a hedonic product has been shown to enhance summary evaluations (Arnould & Price, 1993; Celsi Rose, & Leigh, 1993) and Deighton (1992) has posited that spectators play a crucial role in producing the experience that is collectively consumed. Consistent with these points, a theoretical framework for studying how other fans involved in the collective consumption of a sporting event influence a fan's perceptions of the experience would be emotional contagion. Emotional contagion refers to "the tendency to automatically mimic and synchronize movements, expressions, postures, and vocalizations with those of another person and, consequently, to converge emotionally" (Hatfield, Caccioppo, & Rapson, 1992, pp. 153–154). To date, research considering emotional contagion within groups has been limited (George, 1990; George & James, 1993; Totterdell Kellett, & Teuchmann, 1998; Yammarino & Markham, 1992). Thus, consideration of emotional contagion on fans' moment-to-moment experience during consumption and its subsequent effect on summary evaluations would appear to be a fruitful area of future research.

Another outside stimulus that could potentially affect the consumption experience is the use of techniques aimed at heightening fans' arousal. For example, teams often show video highlights on the Jumbotron or play rock music before the start of a game in order to increase fans' sense of excitement. Theoretical frameworks for addressing related effects include excitation transfer theory (Zillmann, 1978, 1983) and prior work on affective expectations (Wilson, Lisle, Kraft, & Wetzel, 1989; see also Madrigal, 2003, for an example involving sports fans).

PREJUDICED JUDGMENTS AND THE BIASED PROCESSING OF SPORTS FANS

The expression "love is blind" appears to apply just as appropriately to sports fans as it does to romantic partners. Fans' positive affective dispositions toward a team lead them to process information about that team in a consistently biased manner (Hastorf & Cantril, 1954; Mann, 1974). In particular, despite the presence of "objective" information, fans have a tendency to distort reality so as to hold the team in a favorable light. For example, Canadian fans of Ben Johnson—a Canadian— were reluctant to blame him for taking steroids prior to the 1988 Olympics in spite of mounting evidence to the contrary (Tanner, Sev'er, & Ungar, 1989). Similarly, fans of basketball star Kobe Bryant maintained their loyalty to him despite his admission of immoral behavior and the legal charges facing him (Johnson, 2005). In a similar fashion, Hastorf and Cantril (1954) found that perceptions about the violent play in a college football game led fans from both schools to recognize that "rough and dirty" play occurred, but each side was reluctant to blame their own players for it. Thus, in spite of having access to the same objective information, each group saw a markedly different game.

An explanation for the biased processing of sports fans may be found in social identity theory which posits that people define themselves in part by their memberships and affiliations to various social groups (Hogg & Abrams, 1988; Tajfel & Turner, 1979; Turner, 1982). Increased levels of identification with a group lead to a greater sense of oneness or connectedness to that group. A person's sense of self is comprised of many self-identities, each varying along a continuum that ranges from individual characteristics at the personal extreme to social categorical characteristics at the social extreme (Turner, 1982). Sports teams represent one form of social group attachment from which great meaning is derived by many fans (see Madrigal, 2004, for a detailed review). According to social identity theory, an individual's social identification is clarified through social comparisons by which ingroup members are evaluated against others belonging to an outgroup on dimensions generally considered to have social value or importance to the ingroup (Abrams & Hogg, 1990). In an effort to maintain or enhance self-esteem in the eyes of others (Heider, 1958), members accentuate intergroup differences on those dimensions that favor the ingroup. Such favoritism is frequently displayed as an ingroup bias.

Whereas earlier studies found biases simply as a result of fans' positive affective dispositions toward a team (Hastorf & Cantril, 1954; Mann, 1974), more recent work has characterized disposition in terms of team identification. Research in this area has clearly demonstrated an ingroup bias that is reflected in the tendency of highly identified fans to: attribute a team's victories to internal causes and losses to external causes (Lau & Russell, 1980; Wann & Dolan, 1994a; Wann & Schrader, 2000); generate a greater number of self-serving attributions following a game (Wann & Wilson, 2001); and favorably evaluate fellow fans of the same team and unfavorably evaluate fans of an opposing team (Wann & Dolan, 1994b). Research examining the effect of team identification on fans' perceptions of a favorite team's corporate sponsors has also consistently demonstrated an ingroup bias. For example, highly identified fans are more aware of a team's sponsors (Dalakas & Levin, 2005), have more favorable attitudes toward the team's sponsors (Dalakas & Levin, 2005; Madrigal, 2000, 2001), and are more favorably inclined to purchase the sponsor's products (Madrigal, 2000, 2001).

A recent study involving NASCAR fans found that an ingroup bias may also have negative consequences for sponsors of opposing teams. Dalakas and Levin (2005) reported that highly identified fans of a particular driver actually had negative attitudes toward the sponsors of opposing drivers that they disliked. For example, Jeff Gordon elicited strong feelings that were both pro and con. Fans positively disposed toward Gordon had a very favorable attitude toward his primary sponsor, DuPont (9.4 on a 10-point scale). In contrast, those fans who indicated that Gordon was their least favorite driver had very unfavorable attitudes toward DuPont (3.9). Similarly, among Gordon fans, Rusty Wallace was rated as the most disliked driver and fans' attitude toward Wallace's primary sponsor (Miller Lite) was also unfavorable (3.6).

An area that has also received some empirical attention is the manner in which ingroup favoritism contributes to between-group differentiation. LaLonde et al. (1987) reported data from four separate hockey games that considered differences in fans' perceptions between an ingroup (home team) and an outgroup (opponent) over the course of each game. Fans provided ratings of each team prior to the start of the game and after each period on a variety of positive (e.g., aggressive-clean) and negative (e.g., aggressive-dirty) team characteristics. Not unexpectedly, main effects were observed that demonstrated an ingroup favorability bias on each characteristic. However, of greater interest was the finding that ingroup favoritism and outgroup discrimination appear to operate separately. For certain positive characteristics (cohesive, speedy, hard-working and intelligent), between-group differentiation occurred toward the end of the game and was due to higher ratings of the home team (i.e., ingroup favoritism) as the game progressed rather than lower ratings of the opponent (i.e., outgroup discrimination). Moreover, ratings of the home team on these characteristics followed a positive linear path as the game progressed whereas ratings of the opponent varied little. Wann and Dolan (1994b) also considered how ingroup favoritism contributes to between-group differentiation. Similar to results found by LaLonde, Moghaddam, and Taylor. (1987), they found that between-group differentiation among highly identified fans was not due to negative evaluations of outgroup members but was instead due to more favorable evaluations of fellow ingroup members.

Another example of the prejudiced processing exhibited by sports fans is that of hindsight bias and counterfactual arguments. Hindsight bias is fans' post-facto exaggerated certainty in the probability of a contest's outcome, a feeling that they knew it all along, even though their certainty was actually much lower prior to the outcome. Roese and Maniar (1997) found a strong hindsight bias among Northwestern football fans for three big victories by the team. For fans asked before the game, the mean probability given to the possibility that the team would win by more than 10 points was 14%. However, the estimate jumped to 45% among fans who were asked after the game to indicate their pre-game certainty for a win of this magnitude. In addition, the results indicated that fans asked to generate counterfactual (i.e., thoughts of what might have been) and causal thoughts about the outcome after the game generated greater hindsight bias than a control group. Thus, contrary to previous work suggesting a negative correlation between the two classes of cognitions, counterfactual thinking and the hindsight bias coexist for sports fans. Another study by Tykocinski, Pick, and Kedmi (2002) provides an alternative explanation for the hindsight bias among sports fans, especially after a favorite team's defeat. They propose that fans may appear as if they were essentially expecting the loss, thus making the defeat less disappointing and easier to cope with.

In addition to hindsight bias, fans' allegiance toward a team and their desire to see it do well also appear to bias fans' estimates of how well the team will do in the future. Hirt et al. (1992) noted that predictions of future performance among highly allegiant fans were moderated by the team's current performance. Following a win, fans that were most favorably disposed (as opposed to less favorably disposed) toward a team were more hopeful about the team's future performance. However, following a loss, highly allegiant fans were more pessimistic about future performance. In a later study, Wann and Dolan (1994c) reported a main effect for team identification such that highly identified fans compared to lowly identified fans were more optimistic about the team's performance in the future (and also in their recall of their favorite team's past performance). They attributed this bias to social identity effects. However, Hirt and Ryalls (1994) challenged this claim based on Hirt et al.'s (1992) findings that the effect of team allegiance on future performance expectations was moderated by game outcome. Also noted was that self-esteem mediated the effect of outcome on future expectations for highly allegiant fans. Higher levels of self-esteem after a win led to predictions of greater team success in the future, whereas lower levels of self-esteem after a loss led to predictions of poorer future performance. Consequently, Hirt and Ryalls (1994) argued that the positivity bias reported by Wann and Dolan (1994c) was due to changes in self-esteem coinciding with the favorite team's successful performance in conference play that season and not due to identification effects. Wann (1994) responded by reporting the results of a separate study involving an unsuccessful team. The findings were consistent with those reported for a successful team by Wann and Dolan (1994c), thus indicating a positivity bias among highly identified fans regardless of team success. Wann (1994) concluded that the key difference between the two articles was that Wann and Dolan (1994c) assessed optimism days after the game had been completed whereas Hirt, Zillmann, Erickson, and Kennedy (1992) manipulated self-esteem by including game outcomes. Moreover, Wann (1994) conceded that a similar effect as that found by Hirt et al. (1992) would have probably been found had game outcome been considered.

More recently, across six different games (five losses and one victory), Madrigal (2003) found that optimism about the team's chances in future games following a win was not significantly different than that following a narrow loss and only differed when the preferred team lost by a large margin. No identification measure was taken. However, an interesting contribution of this study was an explicit test of a hierarchical model of the in-situ fan experience in which an unexpected positive effect of goal relevance on optimism was found. He concluded that "regardless of the frequency of attribution-dependent emotion felt during a game and satisfaction with the quality of a preferred team's performance in any one game, spectators' desire to see their team do well is positively related to future expectations" (p. 42). In effect, regardless of the events transpiring during a given game, fans who were most committed to seeing the team do well had the greatest optimism about the team's chances in future games. These results are similar to others who found a bias among sports fans and bettors in predicting game outcomes which indicated that wishful thinking perseveres in spite of objective information to the contrary (Babad, 1987; Babad & Katz, 1991).

Section Summary

Research has consistently found a positivity bias for fans when it comes to interpreting information about a favorite team. Such an effect appears to be consistent with a social identification perspective in which the team is seen as an extension of self. Fans' social identification is clarified by making social comparisons by which the actions of ingroup members (e.g., fellow fans, the team itself) are evaluated against the actions of outgroup members. In general, these comparisons are made on dimensions considered important to the ingroup. For the most part, fans show an ingroup bias favoring their own team and fellow fans in order to maintain or enhance their own self-esteem. Research has found a positivity bias for fans' evaluations of past performance, judgments about current performance, and expectations about future performance. Moreover, evidence suggests that this bias is only minimally affected by current or past team performance.

Research Implications

The preceding makes clear how sports fanaticism impacts fans' lives by influencing their perceptions of events and other people. Consideration of attitudinal and behavioral differences related to variance in fans' avidity toward a team has been widely recognized in recent years. Disposition toward a favorite team has been conceptualized in terms of social identity theory and operationalized using a variety of instruments including the Sport Spectator Identification Scale (Wann & Branscombe, 1993) and variants of the organizational identification measure designed by Mael and Ashforth (1992). One aspect of team identification that has received limited attention pertains to whether identification changes over time. Although Wann (1996) reported that levels of team identification remain fairly constant across different levels of fan avidity during a single season, future research should consider whether team identification remains constant during the off season. An assumption would be that in-season competition reinforces salience and thus identification levels should be higher during these periods than when the team is not competing. Future insight in this area has implications for the sales of licensed merchandise, timing of corporate sponsorships, and when data assessing team identification should be collected.

The importance of self-esteem in affecting fans' attitudes and behavior has been widely documented (Branscombe & Wann, 1992b; Cialdini et al., 1976; Hirt et al., 1992; Hirt & Ryalls, 1994). Self-esteem has been hypothesized to play a prominent role in achievement theories of fan psychology (Sloan, 1989; Zillmann & Paulus, 1993) as well as in social identification theory (Abrams

& Hogg, 1990; Tajfel & Turner, 1979). Yet, the degree to which fans' positivity bias is the result of increased self-esteem due to team performance versus enduring identification with the team remains a point of contention (Hirt & Ryalls, 1994; Wann, 1994). A somewhat different perspective by Fisher and Wakefield (1998) suggests that fans of unsuccessful teams identify with a team on the basis of their involvement with the game itself and the desirability of the personality traits displayed by the team's players rather than with team success, whereas identification with successful teams is premised on self-esteem benefits. Clearly, more research is needed on the multiple ways that self-esteem affects fans' attitudes and behavior.

There are also behavioral implications associated with the favoritism associated with an ingroup bias. In addition to engaging in socially acceptable behaviors that show support for the team (Fisher & Wakefield, 1998), the ingroup bias favoring a particular team also contributes to negative behaviors such as when college boosters give illegal gifts to student athletes or when fans commit acts of violence (Russell & Arms, 1998; see Wann & Wilson, 2001 for a review of the spectator aggression literature). For example, research by Wann, Hunter, Ryan, and Wright (2001) examined the moderating influence of team identification on fans' willingness to consider illegally assisting their team. They found that while it was only a small minority of student fans that admitted they would be willing to commit anti-social acts of cheating to help their favorite team if their anonymity was guaranteed, there was a positive correlation between team identification and reports of willingness to engage in such behavior. Future research should look more closely at the "dark side" of team identification, both in terms of antecedents and consequences.

Establishing conditions in which fans' biases might be observed empirically presents a number of methodological challenges. For example, Roese and Maniar (1997) selected three games to include in their study in order to capture pre-game expectation data for outcomes ending in at least one win and one loss; but, as things turned out, the target team with which fans were identified won each game. Similarly, Madrigal (1995) collected data from four games that were all won by the target team and in a later study (Madrigal, 2003) reported the results of six different games—five of which the previously undefeated target team lost and one which the team won. One way to overcome this obstacle is through the use of taped games where the researchers have advanced knowledge of the outcome but the participants do not. Although this approach may be problematic if it involves unknown competitors for whom respondents have little allegiance, it may nevertheless be possible to generate feelings of empathy and caring for competitors based on pre-event information presented to study participants (see Bee & Madrigal, 2003). A tactic that might also be used is to present respondents with edited games that combine different portions of an actual game but manipulate the sequence in which plays appear (see Madrigal & Bee, 2002). Another methodological problem that exists in this area of research is the possibility of ceiling effects in the measures used to assess fan avidity. The extremity of fans' allegiance toward a team may be so strong that it reduces measure variance to the point where effects can not be statistically observed. Much more work is needed in developing reliable and valid measures of fan avidity that guarantee a full range of responses.

An applied area of research that has emerged in recent years demonstrating biased effects due to fan allegiance is that of corporate sponsorship (Dalakas & Levin, 2005; Madrigal, 2000; 2001). Following Cialdini et al.'s (1976) suggestion that the underlying mechanism explaining positivity bias in such instances is balance theory (Heider, 1958), it has been suggested that fans feel indebted to reciprocate or repay a corporate sponsor for their support of a favorite team (Crimmins & Horn, 1996; Pracejus, 2004). The need to reciprocate an agent for past favors is a strong moral norm (Gouldner, 1960). Its application in the context of sponsorship would seem especially appropriate. However, no research has appeared that has explicitly tested reciprocity effects in the context of corporate sponsorship. The need to reciprocate could be examined as an individual difference variable or reciprocity could be treated as a mediator. For example, to what extent is the effect of fan avidity on purchase intentions mediated by feelings of reciprocity? Future research examining the effects of fan allegiance on attitudes and intentions toward corporate sponsors should include process measures such as reciprocity that more carefully explore what fans think about when considering a company that is aligned with their favorite team.

UNDERLYING MOTIVES AND FACETS OF SPORTING EVENT CONSUMPTION

Sports fanaticism has also been investigated from the perspective of the underlying motives that cause fans to watch competitive sports and the ways in which spectators consume sporting events. In a conceptual overview, Sloan (1989) discussed a number of theories that might apply to fans' motives for watching sports, including those related to recreation and entertainment, catharsis and aggression, achievement seeking, and stress and stimulation. Kahle, Kambara, and Rose (1996) offered a more focused perspective of motives based on Kelman's (1974) functional theory of attitudinal motivation. Based on fans' attachment to a particular team, they reported that fans are motivated by a desire for a unique, self-expressive experience; camaraderie (desire for group affiliation); and internalization (an overall attachment to and love of the game). Motives that were antecedent to a unique, self-expressive experience were identification with winning and a desire for a self-expressive experience. Camaraderie was predicted by obligation and compliance.

In an empirical study investigating more specifically defined motives for sports viewing, Gantz and Wenner (1991) found that a person's sex was an important individual difference variable. Compared to men, women were more likely to be motivated to watch sports for social reasons. In contrast, men were more likely to watch sports to get psyched up, relax, let off steam, and drink alcohol. Men were also motivated to watch because they enjoyed the tension and drama of a competitive contest and because it gave them something to talk about. The results of more recent research by Wann (1995) and his associates (Wann, Schrader, & Wilson, 1999; see Wann, Melnick, Russell, & Pease, 2001, for a review) using the Sport Fan Motivation Scale (SFMS) also implicate the differential effect of spectator sex on motives for watching sports. Compared to women, men reported higher levels of eustress (i.e., pleasant stress), self-esteem, escape, and aesthetics (James & Ridinger, 2002, found a similar effect for the aesthetics motive). Women, on the other hand, reported higher levels of family motivation (see also Dietz-Uhler, Harrick, End, & Jacquemotte, 2000).

The actual consumption experience of fans during a sporting event has also received empirical attention. In these studies, sporting event consumption has been viewed as being related to, but distinct from, fans' motives for watching sports. Rather, the focus in these studies is on the nature of the consumption experience itself. In an ethnographic study of spectators at Chicago Cubs games, Holt (1995) identified four metaphors to explain fans' consumption of a baseball game. The first, consuming as experience, considers on how spectators make sense of baseball, evaluate player performance and respond emotionally to the game. The second metaphor, consuming as integration, focuses on how fans assimilate and personalize aspects of the game so as to create the impression that they are part of the team. Consuming as play, the third metaphor, addresses a metacommunicational dimension incorporating how fans commune and socialize with other fans. The final metaphor, consuming as classification, refers to the behaviors that fans engage in to identify and present themselves as fans of the team. Kelley and Tian (2004) extend the work of Holt (1995) by not restricting the consumption experience to just in-stadium activities. Using the daily journals of avid sports fans, the researchers identified six broad themes of fan consumption: game participation, social events surrounding the game, fan contests, role conflicts ensuing from fan identity, social connectedness ensuing from fan identity, and life lessons and decisions related to fan identity.

Rather than using an ethnographic or journal approach to studying the consumption experience, Madrigal (2006) created a scale called FANDIM to assess the dimensions along which fans consume a sporting event. Conceptualized as a multifaceted concept, FANDIM is comprised of two higher-order factors, each of which is represented by three unidimensional scales. The first higher-order dimension is Autotelism (c.f. Csikszentmihalyi, 1975; Holt, 1995) and refers to those elements of consumption that have a purpose in and not apart from themselves. The multiple-item scales of flow (i.e., a psychological state characterized by intense absorption in the moment), fantasy (i.e., imagining that you are part of the action) and evaluation (i.e., critically judging both the quality of the action and athletes' performance) are considered to be autotelic because each is an element of the consumption experience that is an end unto itself and reflects the consumer's immersion in the event. The second dimension is Appreciation (c.f. Holt, 1995) and is comprised of aesthetics (i.e., attending to the grace and beauty of the game), personalities (i.e., focusing attention on specific athletes while consuming the game) and physical attraction (i.e., attending to the sensual appeal of individual competitors during consumption). Each of the scales comprising this dimension involves an appreciation or estimation of the qualities inherent in the athlete and the sport. In a series of five studies, Madrigal established the FANDIM's reliability, as well as its convergent, concurrent and discriminant validity. In addition, differences across the FANDIM dimensions were found according to the functional nature of the sport (i.e., aesthetic vs. purposive[2]) and by respondent sex.

Section Summary

The motives of sports fans have been investigated from a number of different perspectives. Beginning with Sloan's (1989) conceptual overview of fans' motives for watching sports, the preceding section then presented the results of a number of empirical studies investigating the needs satisfied by watching competitive sporting events. Also discussed was the importance of considering sex differences in fans' motivations. Finally, the section presented the results of qualitative and quantitative research investigating the ways in which sporting events are consumed by fans.

Research Implications

Motives induce people to behave in certain ways. Therefore, understanding fans' motives for watching sports represents a promising area of inquiry. Most of the research on the topic has focused on fans' general interest in sports rather than their interest in specific sports. This presents an opportunity for research exploring the differential motives driving the consumption of various types of sporting events. However, there are acknowledged difficulties in collecting data on specific sports. For example, a challenge often faced by researchers gathering information on multiple sports is that of sample size. There may simply not be enough individuals in a given sample for each sport to be adequately represented in the analysis if each respondent selects his or her favorite sport. If a sufficiently large sample is not available, one alternative is to ask respondents to provide information on multiple sports. The advantage of this approach is that it yields data that can be compared on a within-subjects basis. A disadvantage of this approach is that it may lead to respondent fatigue and boredom if the surveys include multiple measures.

Another tactic to incorporate multiple sports is one used by Madrigal (2006) in which four groups of three sports each were created based on Best's (1978) functional classification of sport.

The four groups were aesthetic sports performed by (1) women or (2) men, and purposive sports performed by (3) women or (4) men. Each respondent was presented with a list of three sports that represented one of the four groups and asked to select his or her favorite from that list. All scale items were then completed in reference to the selected sport. Only those individuals indicating at least a casual interest in the sport were included in the analyses. This approach allowed for random assignment, varied performer sex, and also gave respondents enough flexibility to select a sport that they had some interest in. Between-group differences could then be assessed on the dimensions comprising a particular motivation scale. Ultimately, it may be that different patterns of individual motives emerge for different sports.

Regarding the act of sporting event consumption, the use of ethnographies (Holt, 1995) and daily journals (Kelley & Tian, 2004) represent excellent means for collecting rich and varied data on fan behavior. However, these approaches tend to be limited in the number of observations that are collected, are time consuming, and require a great deal of researcher expertise to produce accurate interpretations. Although allowing for easier use in a field setting, the use of Madrigal's (2006) FANDIM scale also has its limitations. The retrospective nature of the scale may be problematic in collecting accurate data for certain dimensions (e.g., flow) and it assumes that respondents can provide accurate data on thoughts they had while consuming an activity that has occurred in the past. It may be fruitful for researchers to construct a study in which data on each of the dimensions are collected during an actual sporting event. This could be done by first dividing a recorded sporting event into multiple segments (see Madrigal, 2003). After each segment, respondents could be asked to indicate the extent to which they attended to each of the dimensions during the preceding game segment. Similarly, cued reviews of videotaped games could be used. Either of these approaches provides a more accurate representation of fans' thoughts during an actual sporting event than that provided by a post hoc data collection. Again, as described in the previous paragraph, this information could then be used as a basis for describing various fan segments.

Recently, Raney (2003) commented that a contest's outcome may be less relevant to some fans than the performance of a favorite athlete. That is, a retrospective evaluation of a particular contest may be favorable in spite of a loss if the fan's favorite player has an outstanding game. Raney noted that such an effect is deserving of study because of "the growing cult of personality in professional sports" (p. 410). If such a cult is in fact emerging in sports, future research may do well to consider potential moderating effects attributable to the personalities dimension of the FANDIM instrument during consumption. It would also be interesting to examine how team loyalty is affected following the departure of a favorite player through free agency or trade. To date, no research has considered this question at either the aggregate or individual levels of analysis.

CONCLUSION

The information presented in this chapter clearly demonstrates that sporting events represent a pleasure of the mind (Kubovy, 1999). Enjoyment is derived from a process that incorporates both cognitive and affective elements that are dependent on the instant utility of the moment (Kahneman, 1999). It is the sequencing of different emotions during and immediately following a sporting event that gives meaning to the experience. Hope and fear emotions during consumption vacillate according to appraisals about the consequences of specific actions on the contest's eventual outcome and serve as the basis for the type and intensity of subsequent disconfirmation emotions (i.e., relief, disappointment) and summary evaluations of the experience. However, it is the dispositions held by the fan toward the team that determine how real-time action is interpreted and how outcomes are judged. Thus, cognitive processes are essential in determining which specific emotion is aroused in response to a given action. Consistent with appraisal theory (Lazarus, 1991; Ortony et al., 1988), fans' preexisting expectations and prejudices provide the context for understanding the intra-individual variations in the emotions aroused by a particular action (Kubovy, 1999).

Fans develop a close psychological relationship with a team and this alignment often provides significant meaning to their lives. Fans frequently use this relationship tactically to either enhance or protect their self-esteem. As suggested by balance theory (Heider, 1958), observers perceive two objects as being similar when they are in close proximity. Thus, when a fan is associated with a team, he or she may be judged by others either positively or negatively depending on how the team is evaluated. A fan's self-esteem is enhanced in the eyes of others following a win because the team is evaluated favorably, whereas it is threatened following a loss due to an unfavorable evaluation. Consequently, fans are able to manage their public image by the distance they put between themselves and the team. Interestingly, Wann and Branscombe (1990) noted that highly committed fans were unable to distance themselves. In contrast, Bizman and Yinon (2002) argued that these fans were in fact able to cut off reflected failure but the carryover of this reaction was short lived. In either case, the evidence presented throughout the chapter suggests that affective disposition toward a team is an important moderating variable that affects fans' reactions to sporting events.

The chapter also addressed the underlying motives that draw fans to watch sporting events, as well as the ways in which sporting events are consumed. Although the outcome of a sporting event is important for fans' enjoyment of the experience, its significance may vary according to the motives that drive the fan to the event. For certain motives such as achievement-seeking (Sloan, 1989) or economic value (i.e., financial gains derived from wagering; Wann, 1995) the outcome is critical for overall enjoyment, whereas it may be of secondary importance for other motives like eustress or aesthetics (Sloan, 1989). We also provided an overview of the elements to which fans attend to during an event. Whereas research in recent years has begun to empirically examine fans' underlying motives for watching sports, relatively little is known about their in-situ cognitions and consumption behaviors during sporting events.

In closing, it is our hope that this chapter stimulates further research into the psychology of sports fans. Competitive sporting events represent a unique context for studying human behavior that can not be easily duplicated by other forms of entertainment. The action exhibited in a sporting event unfolds naturally with each competitor seeking to gain the same ultimate prize—victory. In most cases, spectators are psychologically aligned with just one of the competitors and even if they are not will often select one to pin their hopes on simply to enhance the quality of the experience. In our opinion, these are the defining characteristics that make watching sports so compelling. The only form of entertainment that approaches this dynamic is reality television. In both, the competitive nature of the event and the tendency for spectators to choose sides contributes to the drama of the moment. However, in contrast to reality television, sports represent an important part of the culture in virtually every society on the planet. As suggested in the Olympic ideal, sports have the potential to bring humanity together in a spirit of fellowship and fair play to celebrate the thrill of competition. Simply put, sports matter and understanding why they matter to so many people represents an important area of consumer inquiry.

NOTES

1. Although we recognize that fans form affective dispositions toward athletes as well as teams, we will refer to the phenomenon using the latter term for purposes of presentation. However, the terms may be used interchangeably.

2. Best (1978) classified the function of a sport as being either purposive or aesthetic. Purposive sports are those in which the purpose of the action is independent of the manner in which it is achieved. For example, the purpose of playing soccer is to score more goals than the opponent. This may be achieved in a variety of ways. Although the action may be aesthetically pleasing to watch, it is incidental to the primary purpose. In contrast, the purpose of aesthetic sports can't be separated from the means by which it is achieved and are explicitly judged on aesthetic norms. A springboard diver does not merely jump from the board to the water. Instead, divers are rewarded for the way appropriate skills are executed while they are falling toward the water. Demonstration of the aesthetic is not incidental but vital to how the performance is scored.

REFERENCES

Abrams, D., & Hogg, M. A. (1990). An introduction to the social identity approach. In D. Abrams & M. A. Hogg (Eds.), *Social identity theory: Constructive and critical advances* (pp. 1–27). New York Springer-Verlag.

Arnould, E. J., & Price, L. L. (1993). River magic: Extraordinary experience and the extended service encounter. *Journal of Consumer Research, 20,* 24–45.

Babad, E. (1987). Wishful thinking and objectivity among sports fans. *Social Behaviour, 2,* 231–240.

Babad, E., & Katz, Y. (1991). Wishful thinking—against all odds. *Journal of Applied Social Psychology, 21,* 1921–1938.

Barthes, R. (1972). *Mythologies.* New York: Hill and Wang.

Bee, C., & Madrigal, R. (2003). Empathy toward the character as a moderator of relief and disappointment reactions following exposure to suspenseful drama. In C. Page & S. S. Posavac (Eds.), *Proceedings of the Society for Consumer Psychology winter conference* (pp. 157–166).

Best, D. (1978). The aesthetic in sport. In D. Best (Ed.), *Philosophy and human movement* (pp. 99–122). London, UK: Allen and Unwin.

Bizman, A., & Yinon, Y. (2002). Engaging in distancing tactics among sport fans: Effects on self-esteem and emotional responses. *Journal of Social Psychology, 142,* 381–392.

Branscombe, N. R., & Wann, D. L. (1992a). Physiological arousal and reactions to outgroup members during competitions that implicate an important social identity. *Aggressive Behavior, 18,* 85–93.

Branscombe, N. R., & Wann, D. L. (1992b). Role of identification with a group, arousal categorization processes, and self-esteem in sport spectator aggression. *Human Relations, 45,* 1013–1033.

Branscombe, N. R., & Wann, D. L. (1994). Collective self-esteem consequences of outgroup derogation when a valued social identity is on trial. *European Journal of Social Psychology, 24,* 641–657.

Bureau of Economic Analysis (2006). National Economic Accounts: Table 2.4.5U. Personal Expenditures by Type of Product. Retrieved September 26, 2006 from https://bea.gov/beahome.html.

Cantor, J. R., Zillmann, D., & Bryant, J. (1975). Enhancement of experienced sexual arousal in response to erotic stimuli through misattribution of unrelated residual excitation. *Journal of Personality & Social Psychology, 32,* 69–75.

Carroll, N. (1996). The paradox of suspense. In P. Vorderer, H. J. Wulff, & M. Friedrichsen (Eds.), *Suspense: Conceptualizations, theoretical analyses, and empirical explorations* (pp. 71–91). Mahwah, NJ: Erlbaum.

Celsi, R. L., Rose, R. L., & Leigh, T. W. (1993). An exploration of high-risk leisure consumption through skydiving. *Journal of Consumer Research, 20,* 1–23.

Cialdini, R. B., & Richardson, K. D. (1980). Two indirect tactics of image management: Basking and blasting. *Journal of Personality & Social Psychology, 39,* 406–415.

Cialdini, R. B., Borden, R. J., Thorne, A., Walker, M. R., Freeman, S., & Sloan, L. R. (1976). Basking in reflected glory: Three (football) field studies. *Journal of Personality & Social Psychology, 34,* 366–375.

Crimmins, J., & Horn, M. (1996). Sponsorship: From management ego trip to marketing success. *Journal of Advertising Research, 36,* 11–21.

Csikszentmihalyi, M. (1975). *Flow: The psychology of optimal experience.* New York: Harper and Row.

Dalakas, V., & Levin, A. M. (2005). The balance theory domino: How sponsorships may elicit negative consumer attitudes. In G. Menon & A. Rao (Eds.), *Advances in consumer research* (Vol. 32, pp. 91–97).

Dalakas, V., Madrigal, R., & Anderson, K. L. (2004). "We are number one!" The phenomenon of Basking-in-Reflected-Glory and its implications for sports marketing. In L. R. Kahle & C. Riley (Eds.), *Sports marketing and the psychology of marketing communication* (pp. 67–79). Mahwah, NJ: Erlbaum.

Deighton, J. (1992). The consumption of performance. *Journal of Consumer Research, 19*, 362–372.

Dietz-Uhler, B., Harrick, E. A., End, C., & Jacquemotte, L. (2000). Sex differences in sport fan behavior and reasons for being a sport fan. *Journal of Sport Behavior, 23*, 219–231.

End, C. M. (2001). An examination of NFL fans' computer mediated BIRGing. *Journal of Sport Behavior, 24*, 162–181.

Fédération Internationale de Football Association (2005). 2002 FIFA World Cup TV coverage. Retrieved July 8, 2005 from http://www.fifa.com/en/marketing/newmedia/index/0,3509,10,00.html.

Fisher, R. J., & Wakefield, K. (1998). Factors leading to group identification: A field study of winners and losers. *Psychology & Marketing, 15*, 23–40.

Fredrickson, B. L., & Kahneman, D. (1993). Duration neglect in retrospective evaluations of affective episodes. *Journal of Personality & Social Psychology, 65*, 45–55.

Gan, S. L., Tuggle, C. A., Mitrook, M. A., Coussement, S. H., & Zillmann, D. (1997). The thrill of a close game: Who enjoys it and who doesn't? *Journal of Sport and Social Issues, 21*, 53–64.

Gantz, W., & Wenner, L. A. (1991). Men, women, and sports: Audience experiences and effects. *Journal of Broadcasting & Electronic Media, 35*, 233–243.

George, J. M. (1990). Personality, affect, and behavior in groups. *Journal of Applied Psychology, 75*, 107–116.

George, J. M., & James, L. R. (1993). Personality, affect, and behavior in groups revisited: Comment on aggregation, levels of analysis, and a recent application of within and between analysis. *Journal of Applied Psychology, 78*, 798–804.

Gouldner, A. W. (1960). The norm of reciprocity. *American Sociological Review, 25*, 161–178.

Harris, H. A. (1972). *Aspects of Greek and Roman life: Sport in Greece and Rome.* Ithaca, NY: Cornell University Press.

Hastorf, A., & Cantril, H. (1954). They saw a game: A case study. *Journal of Abnormal and Social Psychology, 49*, 129–134.

Hatfield, E., Cacioppo, J. T., & Rapson, R. L. (1992). Primitive emotional contagion. In M. S. Clark (Ed.), *Emotion and social behavior* (pp. 151–177). Newbury Park, CA: Sage.

Heider, F. (1958). *The psychology of interpersonal relations.* New York: Wiley.

Hirschman, E. C., & Holbrook, M. B. (1982). Hedonic consumption: Emerging concepts, methods and propositions. *Journal of Marketing, 46*, 92–101.

Hirt, E. R., Zillmann, D., Erickson, G. A., & Kennedy, C. (1992). Costs and benefits of allegiance: Changes in fans' self-ascribed competencies after team victory versus defeat. *Journal of Personality & Social Psychology, 63*, 724–738.

Hirt, E. R., & Ryalls, K. R. (1994). Highly allegiant fans and sports team evaluation: The mediating role of self-esteem. *Perceptual & Motor Skills, 79*, 24–26.

Hogg, M. A., & Abrams, D. (1988). *Social identifications: A social psychology of intergroup relations and group processes.* London, UK: Routledge.

Holbrook, M. B. (1987). An audiovisual inventory of some fanatic consumer behavior. In M. Wallendorf & P. Anderson (Eds.), *Advances in consumer research* (Vol. 14, pp. 144–149). Provo, UT: Association for Consumer Research.

Holt, D. B. (1995). How consumers consume: A typology of consumption practices. *Journal of Consumer Research, 22*, 1–16.

James, J. D., & Ridinger, L. L. (2002). Female and male sport fans: A comparison of sport consumption motives. *Journal of Sport Behavior, 25*, 260–278.

Johnson, A. R. (2005). When celebrity identity is tied to immoral behavior: Consumer reactions to Michael Jackson and Kobe Bryant. In G. Menon & A. Rao (Eds.), *Advances in consumer research* (Vol. 32, pp. 100–101).

Kahle, L. R., Kambara, K. M., & Rose, G. M. (1996). A functional model of fan attendance motivations for college football. *Sport Marketing Quarterly, 5*, 51–60.

Klaasen, A., & Frazier, M. (2006, January 9). Fourth and goal: Eight spots left in Super Bowl. *Advertising Age, 77*, 3, 33.

Kahneman, D. (1999). Objective happiness. In D. Kahneman, E. Diener, & N. Schwarz (Eds.), *Well-being: The foundations of hedonic psychology* (pp. 3–25). New York: Russell Sage Foundation.

Kelman, H. C. (1974). Further thoughts on the processes of compliance, identification, an internalization. In J. T. Tedeschi (Ed.), *Perspectives on social power* (pp. 125–171). Chicago, IL: Aldine.

Kelley, S. W., & Tian, K. (2004). Fanatical consumption: An investigation of the behavior of sports fans through textual data. In L. R. Kahle & C. Riley (Eds.), *Sports marketing and the psychology of marketing communication* (pp. 27–65). Mahwah, NJ: Erlbaum.

Kubovy, M. (1999). On the pleasures of the mind. In D. Kahneman, E. Diener, & N. Schwarz (Eds.), *Well-being: The foundations of hedonic psychology* (pp. 134–54). New York: Russell Sage Foundation.

LaLonde, R. N., Moghaddam, F. M., & Taylor, D. M. (1987). The process of group differentiation in a dynamic intergroup setting. *Journal of Social Psychology, 127*, 273–287.

Larsen, R. J., & Fredrickson, B. L. (1999). Measurement issues in emotion research. In D. Kahneman, E. Diener, & N. Schwarz (Eds.), *Well-being: The foundations of hedonic psychology* (pp. 40–60). New York: Russell Sage Foundation.

Lau, R. R., & Russell, D. (1980). Attributions in the sports pages. *Journal of Personality & Social Psychology, 39*, 29–38.

Lazarus, R. S. (1991). *Emotion and adaptation.* New York: Oxford Press.

Leach, C. W., Spears, R., Branscombe, N. R., & Doosje, B. (2003). Malicious pleasure: Schadenfreude at the suffering of another group. *Journal of Personality & Social Psychology, 84*, 932–943.

Madrigal, R. (1995). Cognitive and affective determinants of fan satisfaction. *Journal of Leisure Research, 27*, 205–227.

Madrigal, R. (2000). The influence of social alliances with sports teams on intentions to purchase corporate sponsors' products. *Journal of Advertising, 29*, 13–24.

Madrigal, R. (2001). Social identity effects in a beliefs—attitude—intentions hierarchy: Implications for corporate sponsorship. *Psychology & Marketing, 18*, 145–165.

Madrigal, R. (2003). Investigating an evolving leisure experience: Antecedents and consequences of spectator affect during a live sporting event. *Journal of Leisure Research, 35*, 23–48.

Madrigal, R. (2004). A review of team identification and its influence on consumers' responses toward corporate sponsors. In L. R. Kahle & C. Riley (Eds.), *Sports marketing and the psychology of marketing communication* (pp. 241–255). Mahwah, NJ: Erlbaum.

Madrigal, R. (2006). Measuring the multidimensional nature of sporting event performance consumption. *Journal of Leisure Research, 38*, 267–292.

Madrigal, R., & Bee, C. C. (2002). Effects of moment-to-moment emotions and outcome involvement on relief and enjoyment following exposure to suspenseful drama. In J. A. Edell & R. C. Goodstein (Eds.), *Proceedings of the Society for Consumer Psychology winter conference* (pp. 66–75).

Madrigal, R., Bee, C., & LaBarge, M. (2005). The thrill of victory and agony of defeat: An affective sequence describing the experience of suspense. Working paper. Eugene, OR: R. Madrigal.

Mael, F., & Ashforth, B. E. (1992). Alumni and their alma mater: A partial test of the reformulated model of organizational identification. *Journal of Organizational Behavior, 13*, 103–123.

Mann, L. (1974). On being a sore loser: How fans react to their team's failure. *Australian Journal of Psychology, 26*, 37–47.

Marchland, A. (2006, August 21). Can the NFL push NBC's prime-time lineup from worst to first? *Sports Business Journal, 9*, 1, 8–10.

McChesney, R. W. (1989). Media made sport: A history of sports coverage in the United States. In L. A. Wenner (Ed.), *Media, sports and society* (pp. 49–69). Newbury Park, CA: Sage.

Midwinter, E. C. (1986). *Fair game: Myth and reality in sport.* Boston: Allen.

Ortony, A., Clore, G. L., & Collins, A. (1988). *The cognitive structure of emotions.* New York: Cambridge University Press.

Pracejus, J. W. (2004). Seven psychological mechanisms through which sponsorship can influence consumers. In L. R. Kahle & C. Riley (Eds.), *Sports marketing and the psychology of marketing communication* (pp. 175–189). Mahwah, NJ: Erlbaum.

Raney, A. A. (2003). Enjoyment of sport spectatorship. In J. Bryant & D. Roskos-Ewoldsen (Eds.), *Communication and emotion: Essays in honor of Dolf Zillmann* (pp. 397–416). Mahwah, NJ: Erlbaum.

Reisenzein, R. (1983). The Schachter theory of emotion: Two decades later. *Psychological Bulletin, 94*, 239–264.

Roese, N. J., & Maniar, S. D. (1997). Perceptions of purple: Counterfactual and hindsight judgments at Northwestern Wildcats football games. *Personality and Social Psychology Bulletin, 23*, 1245–1253.

Russell, G. W., & Arms, R. L. (1998). Toward a social psychological profile of would-be rioters. *Aggressive Behavior, 24*, 219–226.

Scammon, D. L. (1987). Breeding, training, and riding: The serious side of horsing around. In M. Wallendorf & P. Anderson (Eds.), *Advances in consumer research* (Vol. 14, pp. 125–128). Provo, UT: Association for Consumer Research.

Sloan, L. R. (1989). The motives of sports fans. In J. H. Goldstein (Ed.), *Sports, games and play: Social and psychological viewpoints* (pp. 175–240). Hillsdale, NJ: Erlbaum.

Snyder, C. R., Lassegard, M. A., & Ford, C. E. (1986). Distancing after group success and failure: Basking in reflected glory and cutting off reflected failure. *Journal of Personality and Social Psychology, 51,* 382–388.

Sparks, G. G. (1991). The relationship between distress and delight in males' and females' reactions to frightening films. *Human Communication Research, 17,* 625–637.

Stone, A. A., Shiffman, S. S., & DeVries, M. W. (1999). Ecological momentary assessment. In D. Kahneman, E. Diener, & N. Schwarz (Eds.), *Well-being: The foundations of hedonic psychology* (pp. 26–39). New York: Russell Sage Foundation.

Tajfel, H., & Turner, J. C. (1979). An integrative theory of intergroup conflict. In W. G. Austin & S. Worchel (Eds.), *The social psychology of intergroup relations* (pp. 33–47). Monterey, CA: Brooks Cole.

Tanner, J., Sev'er, A., & Ungar, S. (1989). Explaining the "steroid scandal": How Toronto students interpret the Ben Johnson case. *International Journal of Sport Psychology, 20,* 297–308.

Totterdell, P., Kellett, S., & Teuchmann, K. (1998). Evidence of mood linkage in work groups. *Journal of Personality & Social Psychology, 74,* 1504–1515.

Turner, J. C. (1982). Towards a cognitive redefinition of the social group. In H. Tajfel (Ed.), *Social identity and intergroup relations* (pp. 15–40). New York: Cambridge.

Turner, J. C., Hogg, M. A., Oakes, P. J., Reicher, S. D., & Wetherell, M. S. (1982). *Rediscovering the social group: A self-categorization theory.* Cambridge, MA: Blackwell.

Tykocinski, O. T., Pick, D., & Kedmi, D. (2002). Retroactive pessimism: A different kind of hindsight bias. *European Journal of Social Psychology, 32,* 577–588.

Varey, C. A., & Kahneman, D. (1992). Experiences extended across time: Evaluation of moments and episodes. *Journal of Behavioral Decision Making, 5,* 169–185.

Wann, D. L. (1994). Biased evaluations of highly identified sport spectators: A response to Hirt and Ryalls. *Perceptual & Motor Skills, 79,* 105–106.

Wann, D. L. (1995). Preliminary validation of the sport fan motivation scale. *Journal of Sport and Social Issues, 19,* 377–396.

Wann, D. L. (1996). Seasonal changes in spectators' identification and involvement with and evaluations of college basketball and football teams. *Psychological Record, 46,* 201–215.

Wann, D. L., & Branscombe, N. R. (1990). Die-hard and fair-weather fans: Effects of identification on BIRGing and CORFing tendencies. *Journal of Sport and Social Issues, 14,* 103–117.

Wann, D. L., & Branscombe, N. R. (1992). Emotional responses to the sports page. *Journal of Sport and Social Issues, 16,* 49–64.

Wann, D. L., & Branscombe, N. R. (1993). Sports fans: Measuring degree of identification with their team. *International Journal of Sport Psychology, 24,* 1–17.

Wann, D. L., & Dolan, T. J. (1994a). Attributions of highly identified sports spectators. *Journal of Social Psychology, 134,* 783–792.

Wann, D. L., & Dolan, T. J. (1994b). Influence of spectators' identification on evaluation of the past, present, and future performance of a sports team. *Perceptual & Motor Skills, 78,* 547–552.

Wann, D. L., & Dolan, T. J. (1994c). Spectators' evaluations of fellow and rival fans. *Psychological Record, 44,* 351–358.

Wann, D. L., & Schrader, M. P. (2000). Controllability and stability in the self-serving attributions of sport spectators. *Journal of Social Psychology, 140,* 160–168.

Wann, D. L., & Wilson, A. M. (2001). The relationship between the sport team identification of basketball spectators and the number of attributions they generate to explain their team's performance. *International Sports Journal, 5,* 43–50.

Wann, D. L., Schrader, M. P., & Wilson, A. M. (1999). Sport fan motivation: Questionnaire validation, comparisons by sport, and relationship to athletic motivation. *Journal of Sport Behavior, 22,* 114–139.

Wann, D. L., Dolan, T. J., McGeorge, K. K., & Allison, J. A. (1994). Relationships between spectator identification and spectators' perceptions of influence, spectators' emotions, and competition outcome. *Journal of Sport & Exercise Psychology, 16,* 347–364.

Wann, D. L., Hunter, J. L., Ryan, J. A., & Wright L. A. (2001). The relationship between team identification and willingness of sport fans to consider illegally assisting their team. *Social Behavior and Personality, 29,* 531–536.

Wilson, T. D., Lisle, D. J., Kraft, D., & Wetzel, C. G. (1989). Preferences as expectation-driven inferences: Effects of affective expectations on affective experiences. *Journal of Personality & Social Psychology, 56,* 519–530.

Wann, D. L., Melnick, M. J., Russell, G. W., & Pease, D. G. (2001). *Sports fans: The psychology and social impact of spectators.* New York: Routledge.

Woltman-Elpers, J. L. C. M., Mukherjee, A., & Hoyer, W. D. (2004). Humor in television advertising: A moment-to-moment analysis. *Journal of Consumer Research, 31,* 592–598.

Yammarino, F. J., & Markham, S. E. (1992). On the application of within and between analysis: Are absence and affect really group-based phenomena? *Journal of Applied Psychology, 77,* 168–176.

Zillmann, D. (1978). Attribution and misattribution of excitatory reaction. In J. H. Harvey, W. J. Ickes, & R. F. Kidd (Eds.), *New directions in attribution research, Vol. 2* (pp.335–368). Hillsdale, NJ: Erlbaum.

Zillmann, D. (1983). Transfer of excitation in emotional behavior. In J. T. Cacioppo & R. E. Petty (Eds.), *Social psychophysiology: A sourcebook* (pp. 221–240). New York: Guilford.

Zillmann, D. (1991). Television viewing and physiological arousal. In B. Jennings & D. Zillmann (Eds.), *Responding to the screen: Reception and reaction processes* (pp. 103–133). Hillsdale, NJ: Erlbaum.

Zillmann, D. (1996). The psychology of suspense in dramatic exposition. In P. Vorderer, H. J. Wulff, & M. Friedrichsen (Eds.), *Suspense: Conceptualizations, theoretical analyses, and empirical explorations* (pp. 199–231). Mahwah, NJ: Erlbaum.

Zillmann, D., & Paulus, P. B. (1993). Spectators: Reactions to sports events and effects on athletic performance. In R. N. Singer, M. Murphey, & L. K. Tennant (Eds.), *Handbook of research on sport psychology* (pp. 600–619). New York: Macmillan.

Zillmann, D., Bryant, J., & Sapolsky, B. S. (1989). Enjoyment from sports spectatorship. In J. H. Goldstein (Ed.), *Sports, games and play: Social and psychological viewpoints* (pp. 241–278). Hillsdale, NJ: Erlbaum.

35

Diversity Issues in Consumer Psychology

JEROME D. WILLIAMS

WEI-NA LEE

Universitiy of Texas at Austin

GERALDINE R. HENDERSON

Northwestern University

As the population of the United States grows ever more diverse, the body of research from the field of consumer psychology faces some of the same challenges faced in other fields such as educational or counseling psychology, social psychology, and psychiatry (Markus, 2005; Helms, 2005). That is, our knowledge base reflects what we know about White, European Americans, with very few studies providing an understanding of people from diverse populations. For example, in the field of psychiatry, researchers reviewed the best available studies of psychiatric drugs for various disorders and found that just 8% of the patients studied were minorities, with many studies having no representation of minorities at all. For those that did, generally the numbers were too small to tell doctors anything meaningful (Vedantam, 2005). Such a dearth in research can be deadly given the proven differences in impact of certain drugs on certain populations. There are even drugs that have been introduced and targeted to particular populations. Similarly for consumer psychology, for the most part, our knowledge is mainly about White, Anglo European, heterosexual, middle income and above, fairly educated, males. What Pollay (1986) has argued about advertising also is reflective of consumer psychology, namely, "while it may be true that advertising reflects cultural values, it does so on a very selective basis, echoing and reinforcing certain attitudes, behaviors, and values far more frequently than others" (p. 33). A similar expression that further drives home this point is from the book *Race and Ethnicity in Research Methods* (Stanfield & Dennis, 1993): "Too many studies are published claiming to be 'American studies' that are rooted in white populations and samples, with, perhaps, short notes explaining the reasons for excluding people of color, whose presence would just complicate the analysis" (p. 27).

Over the years there have been several efforts designed to identify the extent of research in psychology and specifically marketing and consumer psychology that is devoted to increasing our understanding of diverse populations. For example, in psychology, Graham (1992) conducted a content analysis of over 14,000 articles published in American Psychological Association journals from 1970 to 1989 and found the number of articles dealing with African Americans abysmally low. In a literature search of the major academic marketing journals (i.e., *Journal of Marketing, Journal of Marketing Research,* and *Journal of Consumer Research*) from 1987–1992, Gilly (1993) found that minority issues received virtually no attention. Only one article could be found in the *Journal of Consumer Research* that examined Hispanics and none could be found that addressed the needs of African Americans or Asian Americans. Narrowing in on the field of consumer psychology, Williams (1995) conducted a content analysis of journals emphasizing consumer research (i.e., *Journal of Consumer Research, Journal of Consumer Psychology,* and *Psychology and Marketing*) for all issues until 1994 and found that only 3.4% of the total number of articles had a racial or ethnic minority focus; only 2.3% of the total number of subjects were identified as racial or ethnic minorities.

In preparing the chapter for this volume, we conducted a content analysis to update Williams' (1995) findings, following the same methodology employed in his content analysis. We especially wanted to see if there had been any significant change in the more recent literature. In other words, we wanted to see if the consumer psychology body of knowledge had become more inclusive of diverse populations. Similar to Williams' study, our content analysis focused on the *Journal of Consumer Psychology,* the *Journal of Consumer Research,* and *Psychology & Marketing.* Since Williams' analysis ended with 1994, we examined the 10-year period from 1995 to 2004 and reached conclusions similar to Williams' (1995) analysis of consumer research studies in the earlier period. Our more recent analysis shows that still little attention is being paid to race/ethnicity in consumer research. In fact, the numbers from our analysis are slightly lower than the earlier time period. As indicated in Table 35.1, we found that only 2.5% of the total number of articles had a racial or ethnic minority focus, compared to 3.4% in the earlier period, and only 2.0% of the total number of subjects were identified as racial or ethnic minorities, compared to 2.3% in the earlier period.

With an increasingly diverse population, it becomes questionable whether theories developed and tested for, by, and of the dominant consumer group (i.e., White, European Americans) can be appropriately applied to ethnic minority consumer groups (e.g., African Americans, Hispanics, Asian-Americans, etc.), who perhaps differ in terms of household compositions, values, lifestyles, self-perceptions, and aspirations (Gilly, 1993; cf. Riche, 1990). Different racial and ethnic groups have different cultural histories and, for a variety of reasons, may respond differently to marketplace questions and attempts by researchers to measure various consumer psychological constructs (Baker, Motley, & Henderson, 2004; Motley, Henderson, & Baker 2003). In fact, a recent *Yankelovich Monitor* indicates that Hispanic and African American consumers share many points of view that White consumers do not. For instance, they differed in terms of perceptions about participation in activities that celebrate culture and heritage, preserving family-cultural traditions, and in the important attribute they considered in deciding where to shop (Common Ground, 2004; Markus, 2005; Briley & Aaker, 2006).

Since methodological problems with respect to race and ethnicity can occur at all levels of the research process, a significant challenge facing consumer researchers will be to adapt the methods and approaches that have been successful with nonminority populations to the special circumstances of racial/ethnic minorities. Unfortunately, many researchers naively assume that research methods can be transferred wholesale among racial and ethnic populations without taking into consideration these differences (Adams & Adams-Esquivel, 1981; Dauten & Menendez, 1984; Williams, 1995; Garcia & Gerdes, 2004). As noted by Marin and Marin (1991) in analyzing research methods with Hispanic populations, ignoring such differences can lead to findings based on methodology so faulty that it renders the results uninterpretable or misleading.

Darley and Williams (2006) acknowledge that conducting research among and across race and ethnic groups is fraught with many problems, including practical, strategic, ethical, and epistemological issues. They address a number of methodological problems associated with consumer

Table 35.1 Racial and Ethnic Minority Consumer Research: A Content Analysis of Consumer Psychology Journals 1995–2004

Journal	1995	1996	1997	1998	1999	2000	2001	2002	2003	2004	Total
Journal of Consumer Psychology											
# Articles	36	27	33	26	24	36	43	47	45	77	394
# Min. Articles	0	0	0	0	1	0	0	2	0	2	5
# Subjects	13,529	4,220	46,908	8,800	7,285	14,053	11,883	13,707	20,018	37,933	178,336
# Minority Subjects	8	6	10	33	7	74	268	349	0	1,714	2469
Psychology & Marketing											
# Articles	46	44	43	49	42	47	57	50	53	52	483
# Min. Articles	0	0	2	3	2	4	1	4	1	1	18
# Subjects	11,362	123,403	7,804	12,146	20,332	11,422	11,031	7,450	19,374	13,972	238,296
# Minority Subjects	0	165	811	173	1,781	1,412	284	103	383	676	5,788
Journal of Consumer Research											
# Articles	17	17	23	15	19	21	28	31	48	31	250
# Min. Articles	1	1	0	0	1	0	0	1	1	0	5
# Subjects	4,304	4,750	4,584	4,613	2,815	9,129	5,881	12,157	12236	6498	66967
# Minority Subjects	220	0	0	0	838	89	0	160	82	64	1453
Total for all Journals											
# Articles	99	88	99	90	85	104	128	128	146	160	1127
# Min. Articles	1	1	2	3	4	4	1	7	2	3	28
% Minority Articles	1.01%	1.14%	2.02%	3.33%	4.71%	3.85%	0.78%	5.47%	1.37%	1.88%	2.48%
# Subjects	29,195	132,373	59,296	25,559	30,432	34,604	28,795	33,314	51,628	58,403	483,599
# Minority Subjects	228	171	821	206	2626	1575	552	612	465	2454	9710
% Minority Subjects	0.78%	0.13%	1.38%	0.81%	8.63%	4.55%	1.92%	1.84%	0.90%	4.20%	2.01%

research of ethnic minority populations that can arise, and provide a number of recommendations. Attention to these methodological issues will lead to better consumer research on diverse populations and result in advancing our knowledge concerning consumer psychology beyond the dominant population that forms the basis of what we presently know.

In addition to being critical about issues such as functional, conceptual, measurement, sampling equivalence, data collection procedures when researching minority consumers, a more pressing need is for researchers to make a conscious effort to include race, ethnic, and cultural variables in marketing and consumer research. This will help to establish the boundaries and limitations of our marketing and consumer psychology knowledge. One of the first places to start is to define precisely what constitutes a minority consumer and to clearly identify when being a minority versus non-minority makes a difference (Williams, 1995). Thus, in the next section we address issues related to the construction of racial and ethnic categories.

CATEGORY CONSTRUCTION: RACE AND ETHNICITY

Race and ethnicity have been used interchangeably to classify and identify people (Betancourt & Lopez, 1993). Although related, race and ethnicity are nonetheless different concepts. Race is, in essence, based on socially constructed definitions of physical differences. In contrast, ethnicity is usually defined as membership in a cultural group on the basis of country of origin, language, religion or cultural traditions (Banton, 1987; Baxter & Sansom, 1972; Hutchison, 1988). To be more precise, Hispanics can be Asian, Black, or White, or some combination of any or all of them. Therefore race signifies biological differences whereas ethnicity refers primarily to social and cultural forms of identification or self-identification. Consider the instance of Pedro, one of our former students, who was Peruvian (by culture), Japanese (by biology), and American (via immigration). From just looking at him, one might simply conclude that he was Asian; after just hearing him speak, one might simply conclude that he was Hispanic; and after just observing his behavior, one might simply conclude that he was American. Thus, not only are ethnicity, race, and nationality different classifications, they each may suggest different behaviors and perceptions. And even though racial groups may appear to be mutually exclusive, they often have overlaps. Consider CNN reporter Soledad O'Brien who actively identifies with all aspects of her Australian/Irish (father) and Afro-Cuban (mother) heritage. In response to these classification complexities, the 2000 Census, for the first time ever, allowed individuals to claim multiple racial affiliations. In addition, these racial affiliations are repeated for both Hispanics and non-Hispanics, thus doubling the number of categories from which a respondent may choose. As a form of identification, ethnicity permits the possibility that an individual may belong to more than one group.

Ethnic identification may range from passive acquiescence to active participation and from denial to passionate commitment. Smith (1980) and Weinreich and Mason (1986) suggest that we should understand ethnic identification from three domains: the *natal domain* such as birthplace of self, natural parents and siblings; the *subjective domain* such as self-identification of preferred ethnic group, preferred reference group and real and aspired self-image; and the *behavioral domain* such as language use, participation in cultural and religious activities, and music and food preferences. Collectively, they provide a composite of an individual's ethnic identity. Some researchers have gone further to suggest subjective self-labeling as the only valid measure of ethnicity because it represents an individual's internal beliefs and, therefore, reflects one's cultural reality (Cohen, 1978; Hirschman, 1981).

Even among racial and ethnic group members, there is disagreement as to what is more appropriate when self-selecting a category (Williams, 1995). It is likely that the primary cultural identification may be different from the self-perceived ethnicity. In Jewell's 1985 study, African American college students were found to identify themselves using eight different categories: Black, Black American, Negro, Afro American, Black-Negro, Mixed, Colored and Negro-Indian. Many Blacks find the term *African American* to be problematic since technically, the term could also describe Charlize Theron (native of South Africa) or Theresa Heinz-Kerry (native of Mozambique). In a similar vein, Hispanic and Asian Americans are far from being homogeneous. About three quarters of Hispanics are of Mexican, Puerto Rican, and/or Cuban ancestry. Each country of origin carries an accompanying set of unique traditions and way of thinking. Depending on where they reside in the United States, the term *Latinos* is sometimes preferred as a group label. Many Texans and Californians, for instance, prefer the term *Chicano*/a which they believe better reflects their Mexican heritage. Hispanics may further define themselves, in part, through language preference: English-dominant, Spanish-dominant, or bilingual (Vence, 2004). Similarly complex, Asian Americans include individuals from China, India, Japan, Korea, the Philippines, etc. Not only do they have physical differences, their language, religion, and cultural traditions, although similar, are not at all the same. Therefore, for a valid identification of any ethnicity, it is essential to employ a combination of multiple indicators.

Other researchers have suggested that, in addition to the multiple indicator approach, intensity of affiliation should be taken into consideration when measuring ethnic identification. Characteristically, those with a weak identification could be different from those with a very strong identification. Failure to include the intensity of affiliation would render the classification and understanding of an individual's identity invalid. Research on Jews (Hirschman, 1981), Hispanics (Valencia, 1985; Deshpande, Hoyer, & Donthu, 1986), Chinese (Tan & McCullough, 1985) and Blacks (Williams, 1989) has taken this approach with insightful findings. Stayman and Deshpande (1989) further suggest that the self-selection of ethnicity can also be situation dependent, thus adding to the classification framework another dimension for consideration. Asian Americans seem to possess less ethnic identification relative to Blacks and Hispanics but instead respond favorably to an advertiser's cultural sensitivity (Karande, 2005).

Hirschman (1981) measured Jewish ethnicity with a single item such as: "How strongly do you identify with your racial/ethnic group?" Along a different path, Valencia (1985) developed a scale to measure an individual's "Hispanicness." However, this approach presents a problem since the mean level and associated variance differ from group to group. As an improvement, Phinney (1992) proposed the Multigroup Ethnic Identity Measure based on elements of ethnic identity that are common across groups. Since the focus here is on elements that are common across groups, variations within each cultural group are therefore not accounted for and valuable insights could have been lost. A possible solution for this dilemma might be for researchers to start with an etic construct and then seek emic operationalization via multi-item measures. Such an approach will allow for within group accuracy and between group comparability. Meanwhile, the nature of multi-item measures allows the inclusion of elements along different comparison dimensions with varying levels of intensity.

There are two basic approaches researchers in consumer psychology can take in applying theories to diverse populations to expand our knowledge to be more inclusive of these diverse populations. One approach is to take standard theories and constructs that have been applied to the dominant population and see what differences emerge when applied to diverse populations. Typically, this can be done by making sure the study has an adequate sample of subjects from diverse populations so that valid comparisons can be made. As Table 35.1 indicates, consumer psychologists have not had diversity in their research subject samples, have not captured information on race/ethnicity/nationality, or both. Of all of the articles published in the *Journal of Consumer Research*, the *Journal of Consumer Psychology*, and *Psychology & Marketing* from 1995 through 2004, only 2% of research participants were persons of color (of African, Asian, or Hispanic Heritage). Given that these groups represent nearly a third of the U.S. Population (and even greater numbers worldwide), it is highly unusual to find research so heavily skewed toward only one group in the population. In our opinion, capturing and analyzing rac /ethnicity/nationality as part of a research program is the single most important action that should be taken by researchers who want to insure both the validity and relevance of their research for future generations. That is, most researchers normally include age and gender as at least covariates in their experimental designs to rule out effects that could arise due to these factors but not accounted for otherwise in their research studies. We suggest that it is well past the time for race/ethnicity/nationality to be included in these background factors, as well. In the second approach, researchers can examine typical marketplace response behavior to standard marketing mix variables, i.e., produce, place, price, and promotion, and see if there are differences between the mainstream population and diverse populations. Subsequently, the researcher then can identify and suggest which theories can account for and explain these differences.

EXTENDING DOMINANT POPULATION BASED THEORIES TO DIVERSE POPULATIONS

In this section of the chapter, we identify and summarize a number of the major theories that have been used in consumer research on the dominant population and that have been extended to diverse populations.

Distinctiveness Theory

Appiah (2004) notes that distinctiveness theory maintains that that people define themselves on traits that are numerically rare in their local environment. In other words, a person's distinctive traits (e.g., African American, redhead) are more salient to him/her than more prevalent traits (e.g., Caucasian, brunette) possessed by other people in the environment (McGuire, 1984; McGuire, McGuire, Child, & Fujioka, 1978). This is particularly true for people who belong to a racial group that is part of a numeric minority. African Americans, for instance, would be highly aware and mindful of their race in personal and mediated situations as a result of being a numeric minority in the United States. In addition to relatively low numbers of African Americans in the United States, there are also relatively few African Americans in the media, thus contributing to African Americans audiences being more sensitive to their presence in the media.

Applications of distinctiveness theory to consumer behavior have provided a wealth of insights into how social context and individual characteristics jointly influence consumer responses to advertising (Grier & Brumbaugh, 2004). Prior research has shown that members of distinctive groups attend more to targeted advertisements, process and interpret targeted messages differently, and favor targeted ads more strongly relative to non-distinctive consumers (Aaker, Brumbaugh, & Grier, 2000; Deshpandé & Stayman, 1994; Forehand & Deshpandé, 2001; Forehand, Deshpandé, & Reed, 2002; Grier & Brumbaugh, 1999; Grier & Deshpandé, 2001; cf. Wooten, 1995). More specifically, for example, Deshpande and Stayman (1994) found that Hispanic Americans living in Austin (where they are an ethnic minority) were more likely to believe that a Hispanic spokesperson was trustworthy than those Hispanics living in San Antonio (where they are an ethnic majority). Similarly, Aaker, Brumbaugh, and Grier (2000) found that Blacks (a minority group) had more favorable attitudes toward an advertisement featuring Black characters than Whites (a majority group) had toward an advertisement featuring White characters. These are consistent with a larger body of consumer research on spokesperson ethnicity effects in advertising (Whittler, 1991, 1989; Whittler & DiMeo, 1991; Williams & Qualls, 1989, Williams, Qualls, & Grier, 1995).

Grier and Brumbaugh (2004) further observe that incorporating the distinctiveness construct into research exploring ethnicity, culture, and advertising provides a much-needed theoretical boost to understanding how advertising targeting culturally diverse audiences works, when it is most effective, and why it occasionally fails to have its desired effects. Given these efforts, we now know that ethnic similarity between the viewer and sources depicted in advertising enhances ad responses among targeted ethnic minorities because similarity judgments are more readily made among these numerically distinctive individuals (Deshpandé & Stayman, 1994) and impact the effectiveness of targeting efforts (Aaker et al., 2000). Furthermore, it has been suggested that the meanings associated with ethnic and other cultural group membership impact ad attitudes favorably among targeted individuals, but unfavorably among non-target majority consumers (Aaker et al., 2000; Forehand & Deshpandé, 2001). Brumbaugh (2002) explains this phenomenon by distinguishing between membership in the dominant culture versus a subculture. In particular, she posits that those of a subculture within the dominant culture possess knowledge about both cultures and may be more positively predisposed to messages from sources of either culture. However, those of the dominant culture only possess knowledge of the dominant culture and will thus only respond favorably to messages from dominant culture sources.

However, Grier, and Brumbaugh (2004) also caution that cultural group membership alone is not sufficient to induce the target market effects advertisers desire, as cultural group membership and distinctiveness are two different entities that act in concert to induce felt distinctiveness that subsequently impacts advertising responses (Forehand & Deshpandé, 2001; Forehand et al., 2002). Notably, the relationships between groups emerge as important in determining when and which group membership is salient and important in drawing on aspects of one's self identity to create ad meanings (Grier & Deshpandé, 2001). Grier and Brumbaugh (2004) conclude that although integrating distinctiveness theory into advertising research in a multicultural context has yielded these important insights, much work remains to be done and ample opportunities abound for future research.

Categorization Theory and Identification Theory

Spira and Whittler (2004) discuss how categorization theory can be applied to research on diverse consumer populations. They note that an intuitive way to explain the race effect in advertising is that people favor those who are similar to versus different from them. Extending this line of thought, they suggest that it seems logical that this increased liking could lead to more favorable dispositions toward the product endorsed by a similar (vs. different) spokesperson. They then make the connection by noting that these intuitive explanations are aligned with predictions derived from social categorization theory (for a discussion see Fiske & Taylor, 1991). The basic premise of the theory is that individuals assign objects to groups and may apply any affect or beliefs associated with the group to the individual object by virtue of its group membership. The basis for classification may be any important feature that differentiates one group from another, such as race.

In a similar way, identification theory (Kelman, 1961) maintains that people automatically assess their level of similarity with a source during an interaction and make similarity judgments (Hovland & Weis, 1951; Kelman, 1961). This process drives individuals to connect with spokespersons in advertising based on perceived similarities between themselves and the spokesperson (Kelman, 1961; Basow & Howe, 1980). When viewers perceive that the source possesses characteristics similar to their own such as race, they begin to infer that the source will also share other characteristics, all of which lead to greater identification (Brock, 1965; Feick & Higie, 1992). Studies have shown that individuals who are more likely to identify with television characters are more affected by the media content in which those characters are engaged (Huesman, Eron, Klein, Brice & Fischer, 1983).

Identification theory is closely connected to and can have a strong impact on racial identification. For example, Appiah (2004) observes that among Blacks who maintain strong racial identities, awareness of and preference for Black spokespersons is heightened. Racial and ethnic identity is a person's knowledge of membership in a social group and the value and emotional significance attached to that membership (Phinney, 1992). On the other hand, among Whites, strength of racial identity may play little if any role in how they respond to advertising. Phinney (1992) shows that minority group members consistently place higher importance on their racial and ethnic identity than Whites do. However, when "Whites are the minority, they show traits like ethnic minorities in society" (Appiah, 2004, p. 170). Since majority White viewers are less concerned about and less conscious of race, the spokesperson's race in an ad does not seem to matter to Whites (Whittler, 1989). What may be more important to White audiences is their ability to understand, relate to, and perceive similarities with Black models in advertising in areas that are not just skin deep.

Appiah (2004) also discusses how identification theory takes into account different types of characteristics that may be the main driver in determining what the basis of identification is by the consumer. For example, Appiah (2004) notes that viewers who do not identify with television models based on race (i.e., skin color) may identify with other characteristics that the models possess. For instance, White viewers may use occupational status or social class cues rather than racial cues to determine perceived similarity between themselves and a source. In fact, many researchers (Coleman, Jussim, & Kelley, 1995; Insko, Nacoste, & Moe, 1983; Locksley, Hepburn, & Ortiz, 1982) argue that characteristics such as personal appearance, dialect style, and socioeconomic status have a greater impact on Whites' evaluations of a source than does the race of a source. In support, studies on race-class stereotypes reveal that the dominant criterion used by White subjects to evaluate people is occupational (Feldman, 1972) or social-class status (Smedley & Bayton, 1978) and not race. Smedley and Bayton discovered that White subjects rated middle-class Blacks and Whites equally favorably and rate lower-class Whites and Blacks equally less favorably. Similarly, Jackson, Hymes, and Sullivan (1987) found that when evaluating law-school applicants, White subjects evaluated both White and Black applicants equally favorably.

According to Appiah (2004), identification often occurs when individuals infer that their tastes and preferences are similar to those of the source (Eagly, Wood, & Chaiken, 1978). For instance, White adolescents may not perceive themselves as racially similar to Black models but may infer that they have other characteristics in common with Black models, and thereby find Black models appealing. For White youth, the simple presence of Blacks in ads may invoke certain race-based stereotypes that characterize Blacks as cool, hip, musical, athletic, and fashionable, many of which are highly desirable among White youth. Additionally, White youth are likely to identify with and imitate attitudes or behaviors of Black models simply because the models are in a particular social group (e.g., professional athlete, actor, and musician) to which they aspire (see reference group theory, Siegel & Siegel, 1957). It is likely that Black viewers also have affinity toward certain models in the media when they observe some commonalities, other than physical attribute such as skin color, with these models.

In-Group Bias Theory

Spira and Whittler (2004) further point out that an important consequence of social categorization is a phenomenon known as in-group favoritism (for a discussion see Fiske & Taylor, 1991). Individuals have a tendency to evaluate people who are members of their own group (the "in-group") more favorably than those who belong to other groups (the "out-group"). Results from many advertising studies are consistent with this effect: consumers respond more favorably to a spokesperson classified as a member of their in-group than one who is classified as a member of an out-group due to similarities or differences in racial background, respectively.

However, Spira and Whittler (2004) point out that the manifestation of in-group favoritism relies on the perceiver classifying others into in- and out-groups. With respect to a spokesperson's race, this means that the viewer of the advertisement must use race as a basis for categorizing the spokesperson. A number of variables that influence the salience or importance of race may influence whether and when it is used as a basis for categorization. One individual difference variable that some marketers have focused on relates to an individual's connection with his or her own ethnic or racial group. The notion is that spokesperson's race may be more meaningful to individuals who feel a strong (instead of weak) affiliation with their own racial group.

Qualls and Moore (1990) suggest that in-group bias occurs is because members of the in-group are perceived to be less different than the evaluator and that the social distance between an individual and the affiliated in-group is less than the social distance between that individual and members of out-groups. As a result of such favoritism towards one's own group, one would expect that White (Black) observers would evaluate White (Black) actors more favorably than Black (White) actors. Worth noting here is that, in the absence of other information, in-group bias theory would argue that, people will rely on their knowledge of members of their own group and on preconceived assumptions and biases regarding out-group members in making comparisons and evaluations of other people. As suggested by the categorization theory described above, of particular importance here then is to understand the role of race in how minority individuals see themselves relative to others.

Elaboration Likelihood Model (ELM)

The Elaboration Likelihood Model (ELM) is discussed extensively elsewhere in this volume, where a "multiple roles for variables" perspective is taken. In this sense, it is very possible and indeed likely, that the role a particular spokesperson plays for one group is likely to be different for another group. Because of differences in source perception being driven by the ethnic background of the recipient or the source (or the interaction of a variety of factors), source can be an additional argument, an inducement to process, a biasing factor, or a cue.

Specifically, the ELM posits yet another role for variables in the persuasion setting: they may bias processing of the message's arguments (for a discussion see Petty & Wegener, 1998). Spira and Whittler (2004) offer results that suggest that a spokesperson's race may bias viewers' message processing (Whittler & Spira, 2002). They found that Blacks who identified strongly with Black culture rated an advertisement as stronger and more persuasive when it featured a Black versus a White spokesperson. On the other hand, Blacks who had a weak identification with Black culture rated the advertisement as equally strong and persuasive given a Black or White spokesperson. It seems as though the Black spokesperson's race may have positively biased high identification Blacks' perception of the advertisement.

Spira and Whittler (2004) reason that race might also function as a peripheral cue. However, they also note that ELM holds that variables may have multiple roles in persuasion (for a discussion see Petty & Wegener, 1998), and suggest that race effects do not occur simply through cue processing. Consistent with this postulate, White and Harkins (1994) concluded that source's race affects the extent of message elaboration. Petty, Fleming, and White (1999) further report findings similar to those of White and Harkins (1994).

Polarized Appraisal Theory

Polarized appraisal theory (PAT) (Linville, 1982, Linville, & Jones, 1980) states that because in-group members are evaluated on the basis of a greater number of dimensions than out-group members, out-group members would be evaluated more extremely than in-group members. Such a theory would lead to the prediction that ads featuring Black actors with positive characteristics will be viewed more positively than ads with White actors with similar characteristics by Whites.

Conversely, Black actors who are perceived to have negative characteristics (e.g., Amos and Andy) will be viewed more unfavorably. This theory implies that under certain conditions the use of minority actors would lead to a more favorable evaluation of the advertisement and product.

PAT is based on the premise that because individuals have more complex cognitive schemas for in-group members (i.e., identifying characteristics), it is harder for in-group members to fit such schemas when being categorized and evaluated, resulting in less extreme evaluations of these in-group members. For example, one of the most credible sources in advertising to White consumers in the 1980s was Black actor Bill Cosby. PAT suggests that because Cosby portrays positive characteristics, these characteristics are exaggerated by White consumers so that they evaluate him more favorably than they would a White actor with similar characteristics.

As a cognitive-based theory of stereotyping, two aspects of the PAT proposed by Linville and Jones (1980) and Linville (1982) are essential if the basic underlying premise regarding extreme evaluations of out-group members is to hold true. First is the contention that people have a more complex cognitive schema regarding in-group than out-group members. Linville and Jones (1980) found that White subjects demonstrated greater cognitive complexity regarding Whites than they did Blacks, which resulted in more moderate evaluations of their own group. Second, this conceptualization implies that the lower cognitive complexity for out-group members will increase the variability (i.e., extremity) of their evaluation. This is because people process new information selectively as filtered by their current cognitive schema, which causes an individual's initial conceptualizations of in-group and out-group members to remain relatively stable over time. This also suggests that, people's evaluations and categorization of other people are determined by their initial cognitive structures. As a result of having more information and experience with one's own in-group, evaluations will tend to be more extreme (positive or negative) with respect to out-group members, where less information is available. When Whites are members of the in-group and, thus, have less information and experience with Blacks (members of the out-group), they will evaluate Blacks more extremely (positively or negatively) than they will Whites.

Qualls and Moore (1990) conducted a study using polarized appraisal theory (PAT) as a theoretical framework. The major finding of the Qualls and Moore (1990) study is that in-group bias theory explains the effect of race in consumers' evaluation of advertising more accurately than does polarized appraisal theory. This suggests that, although a single theory may hold promise by itself, issues related to race and ethnicity in the marketplace are complex and may require the application of multiple theories simultaneously to understand their relative impact.

Other-Race-Effect (ORE)

The other-race-effect (ORE) is pertinent for consumer psychologists to understand because it has significant implications for not only multiethnic celebrity facial recognition in advertising, but also for other marketing-related issues, including customer service, direct marketing, and personal selling. In a strict sense, the other-race-effect occurs when people display a differential ability to recognize faces of their *own* race compared to those of another race (Chance, Goldstein, & McBride, 1975; Bothwell, Brigham, & Malpass, 1989). Researchers have been interested in the phenomenon of differential face recognition for a long time. Other than few exceptions (e.g., Henderson, Williams, Grantham, & Lwin, 1999), little attention has been given to applying this concept to the phenomenon in the marketing literature.

The closest other-race-effect research in marketing was demonstrated in the context of convenience stores (Brigham, Maass, Snyder, & Spaulding, 1982; Platz & Hosch, 1988). Here, if a store clerk does not recognize a repeat customer and therefore fails to establish or maintain some type of ongoing service provider/customer relationship with him or her, it reduces the level of service provided to the customer. As a result, the nature of the overall exchange may be diminished. The repeat customer may spend a great deal of money in the store, but if he is treated as if each time is his first time in the store, then it may lead to feelings of alienation and an increase in customer dissatisfaction.

There have been some recent attempts to examine how the other-race-effect varies across cultures and countries. Henderson, Ostrom, Barnett, Dillon, and Lynch (1997) analyzed differences in the recognition of Black and White faces in the United States and South Africa and found a main effect for subject race as well as race of face. Interestingly enough, in their study they found that Whites were better at recognizing all faces, regardless of the race of face. This finding was contrary to existing research that found just the opposite: Blacks were generally better at the facial recognition task. In addition, they also found that all subjects were better at recognizing Black faces than White faces. Again, this finding was a complete reversal of earlier findings in which White faces were generally better recognized. Also, Henderson et al. (1999) analyzed the expanded other-race-effect concept by examining the differential ability of the majority racial/ethnic group in two different countries/cultures (Chinese Asians in Singapore and Whites in the United States) to recognize Black and White faces. It is worth noting that the application of other-race-effect in cross-country research should inspire the need to apply it in research within the United States, across diverse consumer populations.

Accommodation Theory and Intercultural Accommodation

Green's (1999) application of Accommodation Theory to ethnic evaluations of advertising is another area of potentially fruitful research. In essence, accommodation theory provides a framework for understanding how individuals react to communication attempts by persons who differ from themselves. It suggests that as A becomes more similar to B, the likelihood that B will favorably evaluate A is increased (Koslow, Shamdasani, & Touchstone, 1994). Holland and Gentry (1999) introduce the concept of intercultural accommodation in evaluating the impact of cultural symbols (i.e., language, music, art, attire, spokesperson of a similar ethnic background) on advertising effectiveness. The term *intercultural* refers to the notion that communication occurs between two different cultural groups (e.g., the advertiser, representing the dominant culture, and the African American culture), and the targeted group is expected to react most favorably to advertisements that are culturally accommodating (i.e., featuring models of similar ethnic background or placed in culturally congruent media).

Accommodation theory is applicable to studies examining target marketing and a few researchers have used it in an advertising context (e.g., Holland & Gentry, 1999; Koslow, Shamdasani, & Touchstone, 1994). Koslow and his colleagues (1994) examined the effects of using Spanish versus English in ads targeted to Hispanics. They hypothesized that "because more effortful accommodation results in a more favorable response, increasing the amount of Spanish in an advertisement should increase the positive effects" (p. 576).

The concept can also be applied also to media placement. Hence, placing ads with White models or with Black models in minor or background roles in racially targeted media should be perceived as less accommodating than placing these ads in nontargeted media, resulting in less favorable evaluations. Along the same lines, placing ads with Black models or with Black models in major or dominant roles (as opposed to White models) in racially targeted media should be perceived as more accommodating than placing such ads in nontargeted media, resulting in more positive evaluations. Given the strong African American culture embedded in racially targeted media (e.g., Black models and role models, culturally relevant symbols, language, culturally specific products, etc.) a large proportion of African Americans seem likely to embrace and identify with certain types of media (e.g., *Ebony, Essence*) and to view being targeted through those media as effortful accommodation on the part of the advertiser. Strength of ethnic identification can be expected to interact with the type of media in which ads are placed.

Persuasion Knowledge Model (PKM)

According to Friestad and Wright (1994), "one of a consumer's primary tasks is to interpret and cope with marketers' sales presentations and advertising" (p. 1). PKM suggests that people's knowledge of persuasion attempts influences their response to the attempt. Within the model, targets are people whom the persuasion attempt is meant to reach, and agents refer to whomever the target perceives is responsible for making the persuasion attempt.

Williams, Qualls, and Ferguson (2007) apply PKM to better understanding subsistence consumes in the United States. As they note, when identifying subsistence U. S. consumers, it becomes difficult to disentangle this from a discussion of racial/ethnic minority consumers, particularly African Americans and Hispanics. This is because the demographic characteristics of subsistence consumers are highly correlated with the demographic characteristics of these consumer segments in terms of lower household incomes and the likelihood of having finished fewer years of school.

A key question that Williams, Qualls, and Ferguson (2007) assess is: How vulnerable are U.S. subsistence consumers to the persuasiveness of marketing communications? They suggest that the PKM framework offers one approach to assessing the ability of "cognitively vulnerable" consumers, who live at a subsistence level, to cope with persuasive marketing communications. As such, they attempt to identify if low-literate consumers more vulnerable in the marketplace because their cognitive capacity is sufficiently low to preclude their use of persuasion knowledge to draw higher-order inferences about possible ulterior motives of salespeople or to correct invalid inferences. Along with the PKM framework, they provide insight into the coping processes of these consumers by offering several propositions incorporating the select cognitive constructs of self-esteem, locus of control, and powerlessness. Future research should explore other ways in which there may be racial differences with respect to PKM.

THEORETICAL EXPLANATIONS OF DIFFERENT RESPONSES TO MARKETING MIX ELEMENTS AND STRATEGIES

In the previous section, we discussed various theories, such as distinctiveness theory, in-group-bias theory, and polarized appraisal theory that typically have been used to conduct research on the dominant White, Anglo European population and highlighted different studies where these theories have been applied to diverse populations. In this section, we focus on marketing mix elements and strategies and how consumer psychology researchers can apply theories to broaden our knowledge base of how diverse consumers respond in the marketplace.

One approach is to consider a typical marketing planning and strategy model and adapt it to emphasize race/ethnic considerations. Figure 35.1 offers such a model. While the major components and flow are essentially what one would find in a typical model focusing on the dominant population, this model has been adapted to specifically consider race/ethnic marketing planning and strategy such as social and ethical dimensions of products targeted to minority consumers (e.g., alcohol, tobacco, certain foods/beverages that exacerbate health disparities, etc.), ethnic product considerations (e.g., cosmetics for different skin tones), pricing consideration (e.g., price responsiveness and brand loyalty), distribution considerations (e.g., emotional responses to retail discrimination), and promotion considerations (e.g., appeal of ethnic spokespersons).

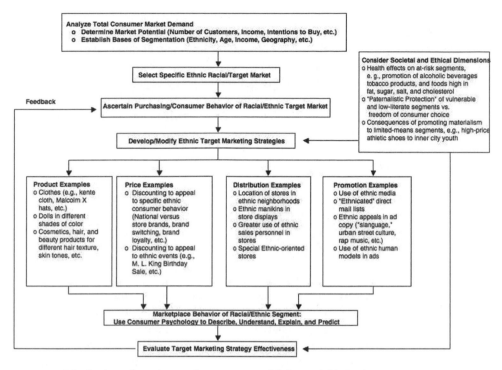

Figure 35.1   Marketing planning and strategy model for racial/ethnic consumer segments.

Consumer psychologists can contribute to broadening our knowledge base to be more inclusive of diverse populations by examining the various steps in the marketing planning and strategy process, as illustrated in Figure 35.1, and seeking opportunities to apply theories that have been used to explain mainstream marketplace behavior to understanding marketplace behavior by diverse populations. In this section, we examine several of the steps in Figures 35.1 to suggest how this can be done and highlight some examples of research to support this effort. While there are opportunities for consumer psychologists to contribute to any of the steps in Figure 35.1, in the following discussion we will focus on just a few, namely, selecting specific ethnic target markets, social and ethical dimensions, and each of the traditional four Ps of marketing.

Selecting Specific Ethnic Target Markets

Early in the planning process, one of the first steps a marketer must take is to select the specific target market. Earlier in this chapter, we discussed some of the methodological challenges facing researchers in racial/ethnic category construction and measuring levels of ethnic identity. In ethnic market segmentation, it's important for the marketer to know precisely who is in the selected segment.

Williams and Qualls (1989) point out that marketing research has been historically deficient in recognizing the diversity among ethnic market segments. For example, they note that models to capture the diversity within the Black consumer segment have received little attention. Williams (1989) reviewed over 50 marketing journal studies covering the period from 1960 to 1987 and concluded that researchers concentrated primarily on low-income Blacks, generally women, in urban areas, and then often generalized results to all Black consumers. In similar studies, Robinson and Rao (1986) and Reid, Stagmaier, and Reagan (1986) reached the same conclusions. While minority consumers, particularly African Americans and Hispanics, are overrepresented at the lower socioeconomic levels, there are opportunities for researchers to focus on the heterogeneity among diverse populations, such as the study of middle-class Blacks as opposed to lower-socioeconomic status Blacks (Williams and Qualls 1989).

Ethnic identity is one of those areas where consumer psychologists can pursue research to provide marketers with richer bases for segmenting markets. For example, earlier we mentioned Phinney's (1992) Multigroup Ethnic Identity Measure based on elements of ethnic identity that are common across groups. Also, Williams and Qualls (1989) highlight several of the intensity of ethnic identification measures that have been used in previous research to demonstrate the potential for a much greater degree of heterogeneity in segmenting African Americans. These include various psychological measures, such as Psychological "Nigrescence" Scales, the Developmental Inventory of Black Consciousness, Racial Identity Attitude Scale, African Self-Consciousness Scale, and Ethnic Minority Identification Scale. We will further discuss ethnic identity in the context of strength of ethnic identity later in this section under "Promotion."

Social and Ethical Dimensions

On the one hand, marketers have observed that multicultural purchasing power has continued to expand rapidly, and more and more consumers from diverse backgrounds are moving into the middle and upper income class categories. On the other hand, consumers from diverse populations still are overrepresented in the lower income categories. For example, in 2004, the median income for Black households was about $30,000, which was 62% of the median for non-Hispanic White households (about $48,000), compared to $33,000 for Hispanic households and $50,000+ for Asian American households (DeNavas-Walt, Proctor, & Mills, 2005). We also know that functionally illiterate consumers are disproportionately more highly represented among the poor, and that subsistence market consumers are likely to have finished fewer years of school, be more functionally illiterate, be geographically limited in their consumer experiences, and have fewer opportunities for a variety of shopping experiences (Williams, Qualls, & Ferguson 2007). All of these factors combined limit their opportunities as consumers and often results in their being labeled as being more "vulnerable" as consumers.

Andreasen (1993) has noted that past contributions by the academic community have been limited in attempting to understand issues related to the disadvantaged consumer and there has been a lack of persistence in researching problems that do not lend themselves to easy solutions. Typically, past research on disadvantaged consumers has focused on a number of personal, socioeconomic, and demographic factors that would tend to hamper them in the marketplace, e.g., income, education, occupational status, family size, age, female heads of houses. However, there also has been a long-standing call for a research agenda that also would include internal cognitive factors, such as values, goals, attitudes, etc. (Andreasen, 1982), and this is where consumer psychology researchers likely could make their greatest contributions (Reed, Wooten, & Bolton, 2002).

Getting a better understanding of what constitutes a "vulnerable" consumer is one area for consumer psychologists to consider. Baker, Gentry, and Rittenburg (2005) note that the field lacks consensus as to what exactly consumer vulnerability refers, and it is the misconception of what constitutes real vulnerability that muddies the waters. They observe that consumer vulnerability is a sometimes misunderstood or misused concept that is equated erroneously with demographic characteristics, stigmatization, consumer protection, unmet needs, discrimination, or disadvantage. They attempt to bring some clarity to our understanding of vulnerability by suggesting that multiple and simultaneous internal and external factors contribute to consumer experiences of vulnerability.

One factor that has received attention in recent years is the susceptibility of vulnerable consumer to persuasive communication (Wooten & Reed, 2004), particularly targeted communication about products many consider as having harmful effects, e.g., alcohol, tobacco, low-nutrient/high calorie foods (Lee & Callout, 1994). However, there has been little empirical evidence to demonstrate one way or the other whether targeted disadvantaged consumers are less capable than the general population to cope with persuasive communications (see earlier discussion of PKM as an example of a theoretical framework to examine this issue). In fact, there is some evidence to suggest that low income shoppers are in fact quite sophisticated in their interactions in the marketplace and quite capable of coping with the persuasive efforts of marketers. For example, Williams, Qualls, and Ferguson (2007) observe that it is possible that poor people may have acquired excellent skills to cope with certain kinds of marketing communications, and are sophisticated in their awareness of several persuasive communication tactics. They may be very sensitive to the value received for their more scarce resources, and because of this orientation, may be more motivated to cope effectively with persuasive marketing communications.

However, regardless of the inconclusiveness concerning the susceptibility of certain segments of consumers to persuasive communication, there is no escaping the reality that the disproportionate consumption of certain products, such as alcohol, tobacco, low-nutrient/high calorie foods, can have deleterious effects. Consumer psychologists may be able to contribute to our understanding of what drives the disproportionate consumption of certain products. For example, the percentage of Blacks who smoke tends to vary by age group, with younger Blacks smoking at a lower rate than Whites, and older Blacks smoking at a higher rate. While it is not at all clear as to what accounts for this differential crossover in smoking rates, Moore, Williams, and Qualls (1996) allude to some psychological factors by suggesting that differential coping habits between Blacks and Whites in dealing with day-to-day life circumstances could partially account for the difference. In other words, older Blacks may have to cope with greater effects and stress in society due to greater awareness or at least perceptions of racism, discrimination, and prejudice.

Similarly, in the food and beverage areas, consumer psychologists also can make contributions. Obesity is a huge population health challenge in the United States, and there are differences among racial/ethnic groups, with certain ethnic groups having a significantly higher prevalence of obesity. As a result, the health status of people of color in the United States remains unconscionably low when contrasted with that of the majority population in the United States (Williams & Kumanyika, 2002). Given that the disproportionate consumption of foods that are high in calories, fats, and sugars, along with fast foods and soft drinks, play a key contributing role in obesity, consumer psychologists can explore social marketing interventions to determine which can be most effective in modifying the behavior of consumers from diverse backgrounds.

Because people's habits and lifestyles, attitudes, and their knowledge regarding health issues are significantly influenced by their cultural background, consumer psychologists will need to view health, dietary, and physical activity behavior through a cultural lens before aiding social marketers to develop more effective programs that are culturally relevant for each market segment. For example, Williams and Kumanyika (2002) discuss how programs to change African Americans' dietary behavior should recognize that food may be a particularly salient ethnic symbol for people who have experienced severe forms of oppression such as slavery and that making certain types of dietary changes could be particularly difficult for African Americans because of the central place of certain foods that are high in fat or saturated fat or high in salt in their dietary practices. In addition, they indicate that due to the apparent importance of fellowship and sense of community as a part of the eating experience, where and with whom food is eaten may be of equivalent importance to attitudes about specific foods. Behavior change approaches that fail to account for this interpersonal context aspect of eating might fall short of the mark.

The cultural lens concept also applies to specific challenges in changing weight control and physical activity behavior. There are significant differences in body image norms among African Americans, Asians, Hispanics, and Whites. For example, norms that are associated with generally less negative attitudes about overweight women are more prevalent in the Black community (Kumanyika, 2001), although these obesity-tolerant attitudes may co-exist with dominant values for leanness and thinness. Weight management issues are, therefore, potentially more complicated for Black women than for White women and more challenging for social marketers attempting to reach Black women, as there may be greater ambivalence or uncertainty about the trade-offs involved in losing weight.

Finally, there also are mixed attitudes about physical activity in the Black community that may complicate the efforts by social marketers. There is a substantial amount of data suggesting that usual physical activity levels are lower for Blacks than Whites (Kumanyika, 2001) which may reflect attitudes that discourage physical activity in leisure time. Such attitudes may be shaped by images of Black people doing hard physical labor under conditions of slavery or low paying jobs. For example, Airhihenbuwa, Kumanyika, Agurs,and Lowe (1995), in a focus group study among African Americans, found evidence of a common perception that rest is as or more important to health than exercise. The focus group data also suggested that beliefs about harmful effects of exercise (e.g., as a stressor that raises blood pressure) were common among African Americans. In addition, the concerns about safety in some predominantly, lower-income Black communities may discourage outdoor, early morning, and/or late evening exercise.

Product and Brand Issues

Consumer research has documented numerous differences in products and brand consumption between consumers from diverse populations and the dominant population. However, it is not always clear as to what drives these differences. Consumer psychologists may be able to contribute to a better understanding of issues such as brand loyalty and brand switching as drivers of product and brand consumption

Although African Americans and Hispanics make up approximately 25% of the United States population, they account for a significant portion of consumers in many product categories, in some cases as much as 50%–70%, while spending considerably less in other product categories. For example, *The 2003 Annual Consumer Expenditure Survey* data (United States Department of Labor, 2005) indicated that the average Black household spends a higher proportion of their money on certain items (e.g., telephone services, shoes, children's apparel, TVs, radio, sound equipment, personal care products and services, women's and girl's apparel, and major appliances), and a significantly smaller proportion of their total expenditures on other items (e.g., entertainment, health care, reading materials, household textiles, and small appliances).

An examination of the food and beverage product categories typifies the challenges for consumer researchers. These are excellent product categories to consider because they also relate to the discussion on social and ethical issues above, given that research suggests that products such as carbonated beverages and fast foods are some of the prime contributors to the disparity in obesity rates between minorities and non-minorities (Block, Scribner, & DeSalvo, 2004). Based on usage index data for selected brands in the soft drink and fast food categories, African Americans and Hispanics tend to overindex in these product categories generally but usage can vary significantly by specific brands.

Consumer psychologists will be able to contribute to a better understanding of such product and brand behavior by examining the factors driving these differences, such as cognitive factors that go beyond the income differences that for decades have been the focus of much of the traditional research. Some of the earliest work on Black-White consumption and spending patterns was conducted by Alexis (1962). While recognizing that Blacks spent their incomes differently from comparable income Whites, Alexis (1962) attributed this alleged difference in spending behavior to economic and social discrimination. Feldman and Star (1968) compared Black and White consumers with respect to race, income, and eleven aspects of nonfood shopping behavior, and found that substantial differences tended to disappear when income was considered, thus concluding that differences in the consumer behavior of Blacks and Whites are a by-product of socioeconomic factors and not race per se. However, Cicarelli (1974), using the same data, but a different assumption (i.e., he based his analysis on the relative income hypothesis instead of using Black absolute income), indicated that his results revealed that Black-White differences do not tend to vanish as relative income changes. Adding to the debate, Akers (1968) compared Blacks and Whites on ownership of automobiles and concluded that the differences he found could not be explained by the relative income hypothesis. Other consumer behavior theorists have argued that Blacks strive for at least partial cultural assimilation with Whites (Bullock, 1961; Bauer & Cunningham, 1970) and that this effort increases with socioeconomic status (Karon, 1958; Williams, 1985). Consistent with this reasoning, Feldman and Star (1968) found that Black-White differences in shopping behavior were greater among the lower classes. Building on this theoretical and empirical work, Moschis (1985) proposed that "Black/white differences in consumer behaviors are greater among lower-class than higher-class adults" (p. 257).

Another fertile area for consumer psychologists to contribute is in better understanding the concepts of brand loyalty and brand switching as it applies to consumers from diverse backgrounds, especially from a cognitive perspective. Brand loyalty is not a simple concept. There are many different views as to the definition and measurement of brand loyalty. A basic issue among consumer researchers is whether to define the concept in terms of consumer behavior or consumer attitudes.

Most studies of brand loyalty and brand switching among consumers from diverse backgrounds stem from self-report measures. There are studies that show Hispanics are less willing to buy new brands (Saegert, Hoover, & Hilger, 1985), have strong brand preferences (Deshpande, Hoyer, & Donthu, 1986) and have high scores on brand loyalty scales (Webster, 1987). However, other studies find that Hispanics are not particularly brand loyal, which has caused some researchers to express skepticism about the brand loyalty of Hispanics. For example, Mulhern and Williams (1995) found evidence based on scanner data of actual purchasing behavior, as opposed to the self reports of other studies, that suggests little difference in brand substitution behavior between Hispanics and non-Hispanics, thus challenging the generally accepted notion of Hispanic brand loyalty. Given the conflicting evidence that exists for brand loyalty among diverse consumers, this may be a prime area to apply consumer psychology theory to advance our understanding of diverse population consumer behavior.

Understanding product and brand issues such as the ones raised above is imperative for consumer psychologists not only because of the growing prevalence of consumers of color in the marketplace, but as Grier, Brumbaugh, and Thornton (2006) point out, originally ethnically-oriented products are crossing over in the mainstream at an increasing rate. In the section below, we discuss pricing issues as they relate to consumers of color.

Pricing Issues

The racial/ethnic characteristics of consumers in a retail market area can dramatically affect purchase behavior in response to pricing. Much of the literature in marketing on ethnicity maintains that consumers from diverse backgrounds are more price sensitive than other consumers (Mulhern, Williams, & Leone, 1998). A review of marketing and consumer behavior textbooks, and the business press, almost universally espouses this assertion. However, empirical evidence is scant and equivocal. Consumer psychologists may be able to advance our understanding of price response behavior of diverse consumers by exploring the cognitive factors that drive this behavior.

For African Americans, there are many characteristics associated with their shopping orientation. Store attribute preference profiles suggest that they should be more price sensitive than the general population. For example, Wilkes and Valencia (1986) found that African Americans indicate a greater tendency to embrace bargaining as part of their shopping lifestyle than Whites. A study by Deloitte and Touche and Impact Resources, Inc. (1990) found that African American women are primarily motivated by price and selection when shopping. Wilkes and Valencia (1986) found that African Americans spend relatively more money on generic grocery purchases than Whites.

Several studies have found that Hispanic consumers are very price sensitive. Gillette and Scott (1974) found that Hispanics, in response to direct questioning, place more importance on price and promotion than non-Hispanics. Similarly, Saegert, Hoover, and Hilger (1985) reported that, relative to non-Hispanics, Hispanics rate price as more important in shopping decisions. Hoyer and Deshpande (1982) found that Hispanics are more likely to say they buy the lowest priced brand in a category. Saegert and Yokum (1986) found that the reported price paid for several items is lower among Hispanic shoppers. Similarly, Mulhern, and Williams (1994) found price sensitivity is greater in stores located in Hispanic market areas than in those located in non-Hispanic areas.

One of the difficulties in studying ethnic group price response behavior is the interaction between ethnicity and other demographic characteristics, particularly income. As indicated above, both African American and Hispanic households, on average, tend to have lower socioeconomic status and incomes when compared to Anglo households. As a result, the price sensitivity often attributed to African Americans and Hispanics could be a function of income rather than ethnicity. Although a somewhat difficult task, research by consumer psychologists may be able to play a role in teasing out the differences between ethnic groups in price responsiveness due to cognitive factors versus non-cognitive factors such as income. This is similar to the challenge faced by researchers studying tipping behavior and alternative explanations such as price sensitivity. Although there is documented evidence of Black-White differences in tipping behavior, it is not totally clear whether these differences should be attributed to income or other factors (e.g., see Lynn & Thomas-Haysbert, 2003).

In fact, consumer researchers already have made some attempts to tease out income from ethnicity in price responsiveness behavior. For example, Mulhern, Williams, and Leone (1998) investigated the effect of income versus ethnicity on price sensitivity by examining the purchase behavior for groups of consumers that have different levels of income based on demographics surrounding each store. In an attempt to isolate the effect of income on price sensitivity from ethnic effects, they included in their analysis retail stores located in market areas that feature a variety of income levels for different ethnic populations, with varying percentages of ethnic representation in the various market areas. Their results showed that the magnitude of brand price elasticity was directly related to the household income in a market area and inversely related to the proportion of residents in a market area who were African-American.

As opposed to the Mulhern, Williams, and Leone's (1998) study at the brand level, Hoch, Kim, Montgomery, and Rossi (1995) conducted a similar analysis at the product category level and Hoch et al. (1995) incorporated ethnicity into their analysis by aggregating African Americans and Hispanics into a single composite ethnic group, while Mulhern, Williams, and Leone (1998) separately evaluated how price responsiveness relates to the portion of residents in a market area that are African American and Hispanic. Hoch et al. (1995) found no relationship between income and price sensitivity at the product category level. Thus, Mulhern, Williams, and Leone (1998) suggested that an income effect may be more likely at the brand level. This is due to the fact that several close substitutes are available, and higher income consumers can better afford higher price brands, and therefore may be less sensitive to price. On the other hand, lower income consumers constrained by a smaller budget may be more inclined to be thrifty and price sensitive. Research by consumer psychologists has the potential to bring greater clarity to understanding price responsiveness by diverse consumers and to assist in resolving some of the conflicting studies.

Distribution Issues

For retailers, demographic changes and growth in multicultural purchasing power is particularly important. For example, according to the 2003 National Shopping Behavior Study from Meridian, a Troy, Michigan-based strategic marketing communications agency, ethnic minority consumers are becoming more important to department store retailers (Henderson, 2004). In the most recent Meridian study, 15% of Hispanics and 18% of African Americans reported spending the most at a department store compared to only 11% of Caucasians. Data from the 2003 study indicates that the African American and Hispanic consumer groups accounted for 25%–30% of department store sales. According to the report, the significant changes in the shopping behavior of these consumer groups and their purchasing motivations require department store management to make meaningful changes to their strategies to effectively accommodate their new customers.

One area in the distribution domain that is receiving increased research attention is consumer racial profiling and marketplace discrimination (Harris, Henderson, & Williams, 2005). This area also offers some significant research opportunities for consumer psychologists. Some of the approaches, methodologies, and theories that are being applied to this domain of research are Implicit Association Test, Power-Responsibility Equilibrium Model, Marketplace Testing Protocols, Aversive Racism, Modern Racism Scale, Social Identity Theory, and Theory of Social Justice (Harris, Henderson, & Williams, 2004). The remaining discussion in this section will focus on consumer racial profiling and marketplace discrimination and how consumer psychologists can contribute to the research base in this area.

For many researchers, "consumer racial profiling" is analogized to law enforcement racial profiling; hence, it would involve suspicion of criminal activity, such as shoplifting in a retail setting. However, Williams, Harris, and Henderson (2006) emphasize that it is important to recognize that in a retail context, many types of marketplace discrimination do not involve suspecting customers of engaging in criminal activity. Hence, they use "marketplace discrimination" as a broader term to capture not only Consumer Racial Profiling (CRP), but other types of discriminatory marketplace situations where consumers do not receive equal treatment for equal dollars. An analysis of federal cases by Harris, Henderson, and Williams (2005) demonstrates that marketplace discrimination can occur in a broad array of places of public accommodation such as hotels, restaurants, gas stations, and service providers, as well as retail establishments including grocery/food stores, clothing stores, department stores, home improvement and office equipment stores. Furthermore, their analysis shows marketplace discrimination impacts members of minority groups beyond those classified as Black/African American, such as Hispanics, Asians, Native, and Arab Americans.

There is mounting evidence that retailers oftentimes fail to provide a "welcoming" shopping environment for consumers from diverse backgrounds. For example, Williams and Snuggs (1997) conducted a mail survey of 1,000 households and found that 86% of African Americans felt that they were treated differently in retail stores based on their race, compared to 34% of Whites. Also, according to a Gallup Poll Social Audit Series on Black/White Relations in the United States (Henderson, 2001), 35% of Blacks say they are treated less fairly than Whites in neighborhood shops,

46% say they are treated less fairly in stores downtown or in malls, and 39% say they are treated unfairly in restaurants, bars, and theaters. This poll also indicated that 27% of all Black respondents, and 41% of Black males between 18 and 34 years of age, felt that they were treated unfairly in the last 30 days in a store where they shop.

Unfortunately, very little research has been conducted on marketplace discrimination to help retailers better understand how they can effectively respond to the changing multicultural marketplace climate, and particularly to issues related to marketplace discrimination. Because so little research has been done in this area, and because retailers are now beginning to pay more attention to this topic, it represents an opportunity for consumer psychology researchers to make a contribution in this developing field. There are only a few published studies on marketplace discrimination. Below is an overview of the major ones

Gabbidon (2003) reviewed the recent literature on Shopping While Black (SWB) and examined legal cases where retailers have been accused of engaging in racial profiling in retail establishments. He concluded that, like racial profiling in automobiles, the concept of Shopping While Black requires serious scholarly attention. Harris, Henderson, and Williams (2005) analyzed 81 federal court decisions made between 1990 and 2002 involving customers' allegations of race and/or ethnic discrimination in the marketplace and found that as many as 40% of the cases they examined involved allegations that customers were treated as criminals. Two thirds of the cases they examined contained allegations of degradation of goods and/or services. Those cases were almost evenly divided between subtle degradation (28 cases or 35% of all cases) and overt degradation (26 cases or 32% of all cases). Although the cases arose in many different types of retail establishments, a significant number took place in large retail stores. Among the cases (one third of all cases) involving a denial of goods and/or services, 78% contained allegations of overt denial and only 22% were subtle denials. More than one third of these cases (37%) arose in bars and/or restaurants.

Using a similar framework, Williams, Harris, and Henderson (2006a) analyzed federal court decisions involving consumer racial profiling and other marketplace discrimination solely in the State of Illinois, along with state court decisions and complaints brought before the Illinois Human Rights Commission. This "drill-down" approach allowed them to focus on a particular geographic location (i.e., Illinois) and gain some insight as to how the courts and the Human Rights Commission in this location have dealt with marketplace discrimination, and to compare the results to the broader, national Harris, Henderson, and Williams (2005) study. Using the three themes of alleged discrimination (subtle or overt), the level of service (degradation or denial), and the existence of criminal suspicion (present or absent), they concluded that real and perceived consumer discrimination remains a problem in the American marketplace, and specifically Illinois. They also called for further research in order for researchers, marketers, public policy makers, and the law enforcement community to effectively address the issue.

In addition, there have been several studies that have taken a more psychological perspective. For example, Davidson and Schumann (2005) have developed a model of perceived discrimination and have tested it empirically. They use the Cognitive-Emotive Model of Consumer Complaint Behavior (CEMCCB) developed by Stephens and Gwinner (1998) as a useful framework for organizing the constructs and variables involved in perceptions of discrimination in retail settings. In the CEMCCB, the dissatisfying marketplace experience serves as the trigger that activates the appraisal process (Stephens & Gwinner, 1998). In the Davidson and Schumann (2005) model, perceived discrimination is the cognitive appraisal that is triggered by a combination of the target personal factors, situational factors and agent personal factors.

Also, Williams, Lwin, Harris, and Gooding (2007) have developed a conceptual model to measure marketplace discrimination concern among consumers from various multicultural backgrounds using a power-responsibility equilibrium framework. Their model allows the integration of the hitherto unstudied triad of (1) retailer/marketer business policies and actions toward marketplace discrimination, (2) government regulation and public policies toward marketplace discrimination, and (3) consumer responses to marketplace discrimination. In the Williams, Lwin, Harris, and Gooding model, discrimination concern is measured using a validated psychological scale, the Perceived Ethnic Discrimination Questionnaire (Brondolo et al., 2005).

Finally, Carter, Forsyth, Mazzula, and Williams (2005) explored the psychological and emotional effects of racism for people of color through a phenomenologically based qualitative investigation. Although their study did not focus specifically on a retail setting, the results have implications for retailing. Their analysis attempts to deconstruct racism through a differentiation between two types of racism, and to argue for a distinction that does not currently exist in the literature. They offer a new paradigm for understanding race-based traumatic stress that involves unpacking racism and distinguishing between racial discrimination and harassment. The results of their exploratory investigation support the contention of numerous scholars who claim that racial discrimination and harassment can result in race-related stress reactions. Crockett and Wallendorf (2004) go a step further by suggesting that normative political ideology (which arises, in part, as a response to racism) forms and informs shopping behavior particularly among African American consumers.

Promotion Issues

As our society becomes more multicultural, one would expect to see an increasing representation of people from diverse backgrounds in advertising. However, evidence suggests that people from diverse backgrounds are still underrepresented in mainstream mass-targeted magazines and prime-time television (Green, 1991, 1992; Williams, Qualls & Grier, 1995; Wilkes & Valencia, 1989). Thus, the often-used depiction of America as a "melting pot" may not be accurately portrayed in American advertising and may still support Pollay's (1986) observation that advertising reflects cultural values on a very selective basis. During the sixties and seventies, as the United States made significant strides in civil rights for people from diverse backgrounds, a number of researchers and advertisers were concerned about "White backlash" (Schlinger & Plummer; 1972; Tolley & Goett, 1971; Stafford, Birdwell, & Van Tassel, 1970). That is, would including more people of color in advertising cause White consumers to react negatively to these efforts? There is evidence that concerns about race in advertising still prevail in the 21st century (Sanders, 2006, Dingle & Harris, 2006).

Spira and Whittler (2004) note that these may be legitimate concerns given the mounting evidence that various source characteristics may influence an individual's reactions to a persuasive message. For instance, sources that are perceived as more attractive, credible, and similar to the message recipient are more persuasive than their counterparts in delivering the same message (for a review see Eagly & Chaiken, 1993). A spokesperson's race or ethnicity is often one of the most readily apparent physical traits, thus it may likely influence persuasion. In this section of the chapter, we discuss some of the research that has examined individuals' responses to race or ethnicity in persuasive messages. We consider three areas where consumer psychologists may be able to contribute in advancing our knowledge base in this area, namely, what effect does spokesperson's race have on viewers' responses, ethnic importance or identity, and racial prejudice.

Effect of Spokesperson's Race on Viewers' Responses   Spira and Whittler (2004) note that most of the research examining race effects in advertising has led to the same general conclusion: viewers respond more favorably to messages presented by a similar- versus different-race spokesperson (for a review see Whittler, 1991, and Snuggs & Qualls, 1987). However, Williams, Qualls, and Grier (1995) point out that responses to a spokesperson's race may not be as straightforward as many researchers have argued. For example, the findings of most studies suggest that generally when

Black actors are included in advertisements, Black consumers are better able to recall the advertisement content, and have more positive affect toward the advertisement and the actors (Tolley & Goett, 1971; Schlinger & Plummer, 1972; Szybillo & Jacoby, 1974; Kerin, 1979; Whittler, 1989; Whittler & DiMeo, 1991). However, Williams, Qualls, and Grier (1995) point out that several studies on racial inclusion do not support these general findings (e.g., Petrof, 1968; Orpen, 1975; Solomon, Bush, & Hair 1976). When it comes to White respondents, the findings also may not be as straightforward as the general assumption made by researchers. For example, some studies find that White respondents evaluate ads with White models more favorably than ads with Black models (Cagley & Cardozo, 1970; Schlinger & Plummer, 1972; Kerin, 1979, Whittler, 1989; Whittler & DiMeo, 1991), while other studies find that White respondents evaluate ads with Black models *as favorably* as ads with Anglo models (Guest, 1970; Stafford, Birdwell, & Van Tassel, 1970; Muse, 1971; Tolley & Goett, 1971; Solomon, Bush, & Hair, 1976; Bush, Hair, & Solomon, 1979). Further research by consumer psychologists may increase our understanding of the role of race in advertising by shedding additional light on who is likely to respond to spokesperson's race, how it is manifested, and when this response is likely to occur.

One specific area where the role of race is likely to influence the response of viewers is the use of celebrities in advertising. Research suggests that this special class of Black models is particularly effective in stimulating attention and recall (Williams, 1987). Henderson and Williams (2004) explored the implications of the other-race-effect (see earlier discussion in this chapter) and celebrity advertising. They point out that very few studies have addressed the issue of race/ethnicity with respect to celebrity spokespersons (Drugas, 1985). Williams and Qualls (1989) found that the intensity of Black consumers' ethnic identification was positively related to their responses to ads featuring African American celebrities. DelVecchio and Goodstein (2004) found that matching viewers and endorsers' ethnicity and other-group orientation adds significantly to the explained variance in ratings of endorsers, thus highlighting the need to consider the perceived ethnic-identity of both endorsers and audiences in future research. Marketing News reported that celebrity athletes and celebrity entertainers were the most likely advertising spokespersons that would cause Black consumers to buy a product (Survey Measures, 1981). One study indicated that Black consumers were at least twice as likely as Whites to rate celebrities as being more believable than noncelebrity endorsers (Hume, 1983). This area may offer further opportunity for study by consumer psychologists.

Ethnic Importance or Identity   Appiah (2001) points out that strength of ethnic identity may have a significant effect on consumers' evaluations of advertisements, yet this is a concept that is often overlooked by researchers. (see earlier related discussions in this chapter on ethnic identity and strength of ethnic affiliation). Ethnic identity is defined as a person's knowledge of his or her membership in a social group and the value and emotional significance attached to that membership (Phinney, 1992; Reed, 2004). Strong or high ethnic identifiers should display attitudes and behaviors that are consistent with the core cultural values (e.g., customs, language, dress, foods, religion, product use, and media use) of their ethnic group, which should thereby lead to a preference for advertisements and other media that depict these cultural values. In contrast, consumers who maintain weak or low ethnic identities should display attitudes and behaviors that are less consistent with traditional cultural values and closer to those of the dominant culture. Compared to strong ethnic identifiers, weak ethnic identifiers should demonstrate less of a preference for advertisements and other media that depict their cultural values.

Williams and Tharp (2002) point out that when individuals identify as members of a particular ethnic group, they typically practice and retain the customs, language, and social views of the group. Still, not all individuals within a particular minority culture share all its values and expressions of behaviors. As a result, there may be different degrees of affiliation within the minority culture. For instance, some consumers from diverse backgrounds may feel a strong identification with being African American, Hispanic, Asian, etc., while others may feel a lesser affiliation with those cultures and may in fact feel more at home with mainstream Euro-American values and beliefs.

Researchers believe that advertisements targeting minorities appeal to the target audience more when race-specific cultural cues are used in the advertisements (Pitts, Whalen, O'Keefe, & Murray, 1989). This may be particularly true for minorities with strong ethnic identities. For example, Williams and Qualls (1989) found that for certain advertising appeals, the responses of middle-class African Americans were closer to those of middle-class Whites than to lower socioeconomic status African Americans. However, they also found that middle class Blacks with high levels of strength of ethnic identification were influenced in their behavior on other dimensions that made them closer to lower socioeconomic Blacks with high levels of ethnic identification.

In another study on ethnic identity, Whittler and Spira (2002) exposed Black consumers to a print ad that featured either a Black or a White spokesperson and contained either strong or weak product claims (Whittler & Spira, 2002). Their results showed that Blacks responded more favorably to an advertisement featuring a Black rather than a White spokesperson, and these effects were moderated by identification with Black culture: high identification of product and spokesperson evaluations were more favorable given the Black versus White spokesperson, whereas low identification evaluations did not differ by the spokesperson's race. This result indicates that the effect of race is not the same for all ad viewers.

Forehand and Deshpande (2001) investigated ethnic self-awareness instead of ethnic identification in their examination of consumer responses to targeted advertising. They differentiated ethnic self-awareness from ethnic identification by noting that the former is a relatively temporary state that may be elicited by external factors (i.e., ethnic primes) while the latter represents a more enduring association. The distinction is important because elements of advertisements (e.g., cultural symbols) may serve as ethnic primes that influence ethnic self-awareness. Forehand and Deshpande's (2001) results indicated that exposure to an ethnic prime increased Asian consumers' ethnic self-awareness and thereby positively influenced their responses to an Asian spokesperson and the advertisement in which the individual was featured.

Racial Prejudice   Spira and Whittler (2004) suggest that a related individual difference variable that may moderate the influence of the spokesperson's race is racial prejudice. In this case, it is the viewer's feelings toward the spokesperson's racial group in general that may influence the viewer's reactions to both the spokesperson and the advertised product. For instance, Spira and Whittler (2004) believe that not all Whites will react negatively or less favorably to a Black rather than a White spokesperson. For Whites, who may not feel a similar sense of connection to being "White" as Blacks may to being "Black," the propensity to exhibiting such reactions may be linked to feelings of prejudice toward Blacks rather than to feelings of affiliation toward Whites. They tested this notion by exposing White consumers to an advertisement that featured either a White or a Black spokesperson (Whittler & DiMeo, 1991). Ten items from The Subtle Derogatory Belief Scale of the Multifactor Racial Inventory (Woodmansee & Cook, 1967) were used to measure the racial prejudice of Whites toward Blacks. They found that prejudice did moderate White evaluations of the spokesperson. Low prejudice Whites perceived similarity to the spokesperson and their ability to identify with her was unchanged whether the spokesperson was Black or White, whereas high prejudice Whites perceived themselves as less similar to the Black than White spokesperson and were less able to identify with her.

Other issues related to racial prejudice are discussed elsewhere in this volume, where reference is made to some of the current work in psychology involving prejudice, discrimination, modern racism scale, aversive racism, etc., that can be applied to consumer research. Much of this work is applicable for advertising. For example, Sargent (2004) considers how the Implicit Association Test (IAT) can be used to help resolve some of the inconsistencies in studies examining the impact of White racial prejudice on their evaluations of advertisements featuring Black or White individuals. He concludes that the effects of stigmatized sources in persuasive appeals may be more complex than previous analyses suggest. Whereas explicit, self-report measures of racial attitudes might appear to account for little variance in responses to advertisements featuring Blacks, Sargent (2004) argues that implicit measures may prove more useful and calls for future studies that should address these issues so that a comprehensive understanding of the effects of stigmatized sources can be developed. Also, Livingston (2004) explores the issue of nonconscious bias and unintentional discrimination in advertising. He suggests that because a firm's primary objective is typically profit generation rather than social reform, advertisers may consciously depict minorities in stereotypic roles simply because it sells. He further observes that stereotypic portrayals of musical, happy-go-lucky African Americans enjoying chicken wings may serve the added psychological function of providing comfort and security to "traditional" audiences by affirming their cultural worldviews as opposed to challenging them (Solomon, Greenberg, & Pyszczynski, 1991).

DIVERSITY IN CONSUMER PSYCHOLOGY—MOVING BEYOND RACE AND ETHNICITY

This chapter has focused primarily on diversity issues related to race and ethnicity, mainly because in the past this is where most of the attention has been focused and where most of the research has been conducted. However, we argue that any definition of diversity must be one that incorporates all types of consumers and should extend beyond just race and ethnicity. Therefore, diversity issues in consumer psychology should not only focus on consumers who are White, Black, Hispanic, Asian, Native American, Asian-Indian Americans, etc., but also should include consumers who are old, young, Christian, Muslim, the gay and lesbian community, both male and female single-parent households and families, religious groups, the mobility-disabled segment, biracial and multiracial consumers, selected age segments such as mature consumers, Gen X, Gen Y, etc. Also, in addition to issues related to racial and ethnic discrimination, prejudice, and bias, the issue of sexism should be considered.

Historically, these "other" diverse segments have not been primary target segments for marketers and advertisers due to size and purchasing power. However, just as more and more attention has been given to racial and ethnic segments due to their significant growth in size and purchasing power, similar trends are occurring among these other diverse segments. In the 1960s, we saw the beginning of a consistent stream of research assessing African Americans, followed in the 1980s by research examining Hispanic Americans, and then in the 1990s studies focusing on the representation of Asian Americans. More recently we are beginning to see an expansion of research to include these other diverse segments. We feel that this is necessary if we are to understand the changing face of the contemporary consumer and to really come to understand what diversity means in the 21st century.

We advocate that consumer psychologists should be in the forefront of examining issues related to our more inclusive consumer society and should recognize that diversity includes "everyone." In the remaining part of this section of the chapter, we briefly highlight research that is being conducted in each of the following "other" diverse areas: gender, sexism, sexual orientation, disability, and religion. Due to space considerations, we do not consider research in the cross-cultural area, i.e., those studies looking at consumers and cultures beyond the United States

Gender-Related Research

Wolin (2003) undertook a comprehensive oversight synthesis of three decades of gender-related advertising research from 1970 to 2002. She found that the spokesperson gender effects research indicates that controversy exists, and that the gender advertising response research shows that gender differences in advertising responses exist. She further asserts that while it is clear that levels of masculinity and femininity exist, typically in advertising research it is not necessary to evaluate gender or gender role attitudes as a self-assessed continuous variable because the results are generally identical whether gender is operationalized as a binary or continuous construct.

Meyers-Levy and Maheswaran (1991) explored differences in male and female message processing strategies. Their findings suggest that whether gender differences in processing occur depends on the nature of the response task and the level of cue incongruity contained in the message. They note that differences in the accessibility of message cues and in the genders' likelihood of using alternative processing strategies seem likely to account for these findings.

Stout and Villegas (2004) use the selectivity hypothesis (Meyers-Levy, 1989) to provide an explanatory framework for understanding gender differences in communication design. This model proposes that the main source of differences between cognitive abilities of males and females is the different configuration and use of the brain's cortical hemispheres. They use this framework to investigate hypotheses about gender differences in information processing of Web-based messages, with particular attention to interactivity, networkability, sensory vividness, and modifiability.

Sexism-Related Research

Livingston (2004) reports on studies of the systematic bias in the way in which women are spatially depicted, referred to as "face-ism," or the level of facial prominence by computing the ratio between the distance from the top of the head to the lower point of the chin, over the distance between the top of the head and the lowest part of the body that is depicted in the frame or photograph (Goffman, 1976). The more the frame is occupied by the face, the higher the level of face-ism. He notes that differences in face-ism between men and women were attenuated in more "feminist" outlets such as *Ms.* and *Working Women*, compared to more traditional periodic publications such as *Time* and *Newsweek*. Based on such findings, Zuckerman and Kieffer (1994) reason that differences in face-ism are determined to some extent by individual differences in creators' attitudes toward the targets that are being depicted, but, nevertheless, maintain that differences in face-ism are the result of nonconscious rather than conscious bias. They argue that, "in all likelihood, the values one holds can affect the level of face-ism in the picture one produces without awareness or intention" (Zuckerman & Kieffer, 1994; p. 91). Livingston supports this reasoning and observes that while individual differences in stereotyping or prejudice toward women may affect face-ism, it does not seem to be the case that photographers or camera people consciously produce these facial prominence effects. However, notwithstanding, Livingston (2004) also notes that differences in face-ism can have an insidious effect on social perception, i.e., faces high or low in face-ism actually *cause* members the social groups to be perceived more or less stereotypically. Specifically, high face-ism reinforces judgments of power and dominance. Livingston (2004) also reports on studies by Zuckerman and Kieffer (1994) that empirically demonstrate this effect of face-ism.

Livingston (2004) also reports on research evidence that exposure to bias in advertising can lead to increased stereotyping and discrimination. For example, Rudman and Borgida (1995) found that exposing men to sexist advertising caused them to perceive female job candidates more stereotypically (Rudman & Borgida, 1995). Their results were consistent with Glick and Fiske's (1996) model of benevolent sexism which posits that sexist attitudes may be characterized by positive affect toward women mixed with negative beliefs toward the competence of women. In other words, sexist men *like* women (usually more than they like men), but they don't necessarily *respect* women. In addition to sexist perceptions, research by Rudman and Borgida (1995) showed that exposure to sexist ads actually increased the incidence of sexist behavior toward women.

Finally, there is evidence that exposure to sexist advertising can impair women's academic performance. For example, research by Davies, Spencer, Quinn, and Gehardstein (2002) found that exposure to sexist television commercials made women more susceptible to "stereotype threat" effects (Steele & Aronson, 1995), which occur when activation of negative stereotypes about one's group disrupts performance on tasks that are behaviorally relevant to the stereotype (see Steele, 1997; Steele & Aronson 1995 for discussion). The stereotype examined in this study was the belief that women are not good at math. These researchers found that women exposed to sexist ads did worse in math compared to women exposed to counterstereotypic ads. They also showed less interest in careers involving math compared with women shown stereotypic ads.

Vargas, Sekaquaptewa, and von Hippel (2004) investigate *how* people think about outgroup members and assess the stereotypic biases that people show when they process information about these groups. They use two examples of stereotypic biases to assess how prejudice might be manifested as biased information processing, namely, the Linguistic Intergroup Bias (LIB) and the Stereotypic Explanatory Bias (SEB). These measures do not, like traditional prejudice measures, require respondents to indicate what they think about the outgroup; rather, these measures operationalize prejudice in terms of encoding processes, or the proclivity of an individual to think in stereotype-congruent ways. Using these types of measures, they design and conduct a series of studies to predict prejudice towards women, or sexism. Their results suggest that implicit prejudice/sexism measures reliably predict cognitive and behavioral responses to outgroup members, while more explicit measures, such as the Attitudes Towards Women Scale (ATWS), do not.

Sexual Orientation-Related Research

Greenlee (2004) focuses on the communications strategies available to mainstream marketers targeting the gay and lesbian community via gay- and lesbian-oriented print media. He provides a research agenda designed to provide insight for mainstream marketers as they attempt to secure a portion of the gay and lesbian consumer market. Greenlee (2004) also presents a five-stage hierarchical advertising strategy model for targeting the gay and lesbian market through gay- and lesbian-oriented print media. The model suggests various strategies marketers can use to communicate varying degrees of marketer commitment and openness toward gay and lesbian issues.

Oakenfull (2004) examines the advertising strategies that are available to advertisers in pursuit of the gay market, and reflects on the issues that advertisers must consider to carefully balance gay goodwill with the potential stigma attached to courting the gay market. A framework based on sexual orientation, gay identity, and attitude toward homosexuality within which advertisers may identify the appropriate message and medium for their target market is presented. Drawing from subculture research, advertising strategies that may allow marketers to target gay and "gay-friendly" consumers without risk of alienating heterosexual consumers who may disapprove of such a strategy are considered. Oakenfull (2004) also presents a framework to aid advertisers in identifying the most effective strategies in terms of content and media placement for reaching gay and lesbian consumers.

Disability-Related Research

Baker and her colleagues have written much in this area (Baker, 2006; Baker & Kaufman-Scarborough, 2001; Baker, Stephens, & Hill, 2001). In addition, Sargent (2004) reports on studies that show that people often act on socially unacceptable motives (e.g., prejudice) under conditions of attributional ambiguity (Gaertner & Dovidio, 1977; Snyder, Kleck, Strenta, & Mentzer, 1979). In other words, when a socially unacceptable motive is but one of a number of plausible explanations for a particular behavior, people are more likely to act on that motive. For example, Sargent (2004) describes the Snyder et al. (1979) study that presented individuals with a choice between two seating areas, in either of which they could view a film while seated near another person. In one area, the potential seating partner appeared to have a physical disability (implied by leg braces and Canadian crutches). The person in the other area did not. Snyder et al. (1979) found that participants who believed that different movies would be shown in the two seating areas were more likely to choose the nondisabled partner than participants who believed that the same movie would be showing in each area. Snyder et al. (1979) assumed that many participants were motivated to avoid sitting near the disabled person, but they deemed this avoidance motive socially unacceptable, and only acted on it when their choice could be attributed to a preference for one movie over another. Put differently, the existence of attributional ambiguity (in the different movies condition) may have lowered participants' concern with appearing prejudiced against the disabled. In contrast, low ambiguity (in the same movie condition) maintained or heightened their concerns with appearing prejudiced.

Religion-Related Research

Vargas, Sekaquaptewa, and von Hippel (2004) report on a series of studies they conducted where they developed an implicit attitude measure that relied on the tendency for people's attitudes to color the way they perceive events. The measures consisted of a series of brief vignettes, each of which described a different individual engaging in ambiguous, or inconsistent behaviors. One of the vignettes was used to assess attitudes toward religion, describing a woman who didn't go to church once the whole time she was in college, but who claimed that she was still a very religious person. Participants were asked to indicate the extent to which the target was religious. According to the logic behind this measure, these behaviors should fall in latitudes of rejection for both religious and atheistic people, alike. As such, the targets should be perceived as relatively atheistic by religious people, and as relatively religious by atheistic people. Vargas, Sekaquaptewa, and von Hippel (2004) found this to be the case, as perceived religiosity reliably predicted self-reported behavior.

RECOMMENDATIONS FOR FUTURE RESEARCH ON DIVERSITY ISSUES IN CONSUMER PSYCHOLOGY

In this final section of the chapter, we list a number of recommendations to consider in broadening our knowledge base so we truly can say that what we know about consumer psychology is not just about White, Anglo European, middle-income and above, straight, males. To a certain extent, scholars in the related fields of anthropology, sociology, and the nonconsumer domains of psychology, such as cognitive psychology, developmental psychology, social psychology, etc., have a much longer and richer tradition of research that takes into consideration issues related of diversity (Henderson & Motley, 2004). The following list of recommendations, drawn largely from Lee, Williams, and La Ferle (2004) and Williams (1995), are designed to assist consumer psychology researchers to close that gap. The reader is referred to these sources for a more in-depth discussion of these recommendations.

Recognize Within-Group Variations/Avoid Fallacy of Assuming Group Homogeneity

Researchers need to go beyond broad categories of African American, Hispanic, Asian American, etc., and begin to recognize the richness of within-group segmentation. Rather than treating racial/ethnic segments as one homogeneous, monolithic group, it behooves researchers to pay close attention to how these within-group differences manifest themselves in marketplace behavior. Researchers need to be aware that generally there are more within-group differences than between-group differences. Based on the characteristics used to define race, which is nothing more than a socially constructed category (Williams & Tharp, 2002), there actually are more similarities than differences (Betancourt & Lopez, 1993).

Consider Multicultural Individuals

The Census Bureau in 2000 recognized the increasing racial/ethnic diversity of the American population and for the first time allowed people to identify with more than one race (Williams & Tharp, 2001). As more people of mixed racial and ethnic backgrounds start giving equal weight to each of their respective racial and ethnic heritages, it becomes increasingly difficult to place people into discrete racial/ethnic cells. Some research already has suggested that individuals can be "multicultural" in the sense of exhibiting behavior and attitudes from extensive life experiences in two or more cultures (Williams & Qualls, 1989; Luna & Peracchio, 2002, 2005). Future research should recognize that individuals can simultaneously belong to more than one group and reflect the complexity of their psychological dispositions and behaviors.

Conduct Research That Is More Inclusive

Future research on diversity should study not only people with different ethnic origins but also should expand to include those with different value systems, conduct historical and sociological analysis to provide a better understanding of how various groups emerge as target markets, and broaden traditional theories which were developed based on limited populations (Brumbaugh & Grier, 2006).

Expand Acculturation Research

For years, research on diversity issues has employed acculturation as a theoretical framework. In considering one perspective of acculturation that refers to the process by which aspects of two cultures mingle and merge, the notion of what gets changed in what situation and how forms the basic premise for acculturation studies in disciplines such as anthropology, sociology, psychology, communication, and marketing. To be thorough in the scope of our investigation and to be relevant, future acculturation research needs to expand beyond simply studying immigrant groups. The traditional notions of a culture's powerful force and the dominant paradigm of assimilation may need to be reconsidered (Luna & Gupta, 2001). Factors such as country of origin, generations, life stages, and even sexual orientations will all impact on how the process of acculturation takes place and evolves.

Expand Policy Implications Research

Future research needs to examine diversity issues within the context of socio and political environments in order to fully assess the impact of public policies on citizens belonging to different groups in the United States.

More Precise Category Construction and Measurement

There is significant research needed on precisely defining the nature of consumers from diverse backgrounds to clearly identify when being a minority versus being a non-minority makes a difference.

New Paradigm for Comparative Studies

It has been common for research on consumers from diverse backgrounds to be criticized for excluding a comparative White sample. The implicit assumption is that diverse consumers are not relevant enough to stand on their own in analysis unless they are compared with Whites. Instead of comparing ethnic minorities to Whites, Jackson (1991) postulates that the comparative research framework needs to be applied more vigorously to the heterogeneity among ethnic minorities themselves. Currently, journal editors and manuscript reviewers are not receptive to such comparisons, but with changing consumer demographics it is our hope that the new paradigm of comparative studies will allow researchers to conduct studies to examine within group differences of a specific diverse consumer segment, and that such studies will receive the same intellectual respect as traditional comparative studies.

REFERENCES

Aaker, J. L., Brumbaugh, A. M., & Grier, S. A. (2000). Nontarget markets and viewer distinctiveness: The impact of target marketing on advertising attitudes. *Journal of Consumer Psychology, 9*(3), 127–140.

Adams, L. H., & Adams-Esquivel, H. (1981). Experts dispel myths, provide tips on conducting hispanic market research. *Marketing News, 14*, 16.

Airhihenbuwa, C. O., Kumanyika, S., Agurs, T. D., & Lowe, A. (1995). Perceptions and beliefs about exercise, rest, and health among African-Americans. *American Journal of Health Promotion, 9*(6), 426–429.

Akers, F. C. (1968). Negro and White automobile-buying behavior: New evidence. *Journal of Marketing Research, 5*(3), 283–289.

Alexis, M. (1962). Some Negro-White differences in consumption. *American Journal of Economics & Sociology, 21*(1), 11–28.

Andreasen, A. R. (1982). Disadvantaged Hispanic consumers: a research perspective and agenda. *Journal of Consumer Affairs, 16*(1), 46–61.

Andreasen, A. R. (1993). Revisiting the disadvantaged: old lessons and new problems. *Journal of Public Policy & Marketing, 12*(2), 270–275.

Appiah, O. (2001). Ethnic identification on adolescents' evaluations of advertisements. *Journal of Advertising Research, 41*(5), 7–22.

Appiah, O. (2004). Effects of ethnic identification on Web browsers' attitudes toward and navigational patterns on race-targeted sites. *Communication Research, 31*(3), 312–337.

Baker, S. M. (2006). Consumer normalcy: Understanding the value of shopping through narratives of consumers with visual impairments. *Journal of Retailing, 82*(1), 37–50.

Baker, S. M., Gentry, J. W., & Rittenburg, T. L. (2005). Building understanding of the domain of consumer vulnerability. *Journal of Macromarketing, 25*(2), 128–139.

Baker, S. M., & Kaufman-Scarborough, C. (2001). Marketing and public accommodation: A retrospective on Title III of the Americans with Disabilities Act. *Journal of Public Policy & Marketing, 20*(2), 297–304.

Baker, S. M., Motley, C. M., & Henderson, G. R. (2004). From despicable to collectible — The evolution of collective memories for and the value of black advertising memorabilia. *Journal of Advertising, 33*(3), 37–50.

Baker, S. M., Stephens, D. L., & Hill, R. P. (2001). Marketplace experiences of consumers with visual impairments: Beyond the Americans with disabilities act. *Journal of Public Policy & Marketing, 20*(2), 215–224.

Banton, M. P. (1987). *Racial theories.* New York: Cambridge University Press.

Basow, S. A., & Howe, K. G. (1980). Role-model influence: effects of sex and sex-role attitude in college students. *Psychology of Women Quarterly, 4*(4), 558–572.

Bauer, R. A., & Cunningham, S. M. (1970). The Negro market. *Journal of Advertising Research, 10*(2), 3–13.

Baxter, P., & Sansom, B. (Eds.). (1972). *Race and social difference: Selected readings.* Baltimore: Penguin.

Betancourt, H., & Lopez, S. R. (1993). The study of culture, ethnicity, and race in American psychology. *American Psychologist, 48*(6), 629–637.

Block, J. P., Scribner, R. A., and DeSalvo, K. B. (2004). Fast food, race/ethnicity, and income: A geographic analysis. *American Journal of Preventive Medicine, 27*(3), 211–217.

Bothwell, R. K., Brigham, J. C., & Malpass, R. S. (1989). Cross-racial identification. *Personality and Social Psychology Bulletin, 15*(1), 19–25.

Brigham, J. C., Maass, A., Snyder, L. D., & Spaulding, K. (1982). Accuracy of eyewitness identifications in a field setting. *Journal of Personality and Social Psychology, 42*(4), 673–681.

Briley, D. A., & Aaker, J. L. (2006). When does culture matter? Effects of personal knowledge on the correction of culture-based judgments. *Journal of Marketing Research, 43*(3), 395–408.

Brock, T. C. (1965). Communicator-recipient similarity and decision change. *Journal of Personality and Social Psychology, 1*(6), 650–654.

Brondolo, E., Kelly, K. P., Coakley, V., Gordon, T., Thompson, S., Levy, E., et al. (2005). The perceived ethnic discrimination questionnaire: Development and preliminary validation of a community version. *Journal of Applied Social Psychology, 35*(2), 335–365.

Brumbaugh, A. M. (2002). Source and nonsource cues in advertising and their effects on the activation of cultural and subcultural knowledge on the route to persuasion. *Journal of Consumer Research, 29*(2), 258–269.

Brumbaugh, A. M., & Grier, S. A. (2006). Insights from a "failed" experiment — Directions for pluralistic, multiethnic advertising research. *Journal of Advertising, 35*(3), 35–46.

Bullock, H. A. (1961). Consumer motivations in Black and White, part I. *Harvard Business Review, 39,* 102.

Bush, R. F., Hair, J. F., & Solomon, P. J. (1979). Consumers level of prejudice and response to black models in advertisements. *Journal of Marketing Research, 16*(3), 341–345.

Cagley, J. W., & Cardozo, R. N. (1970). White response to integrated advertising. *Journal of Advertising Research, 10*(2), 35–39.

Carter, R. T., Forsyth, J. M., Mazzula, S. L., & Williams, B. (2005). Racial discrimination and race-based traumatic stress: An exploratory investigation. In R. T. Carter (Ed.), *Handbook of racial-cultural psychology and counseling: Training and practice* (Vol. 2, pp. 447–476). Hoboken, NJ: Wiley.

Chance, J., Goldstein, A. G., & McBride, L. (1975). Differential experience and recognition memory for faces. *Journal of Social Psychology, 97*(2), 243–253.

Cicarelli, J. (1974). On Income, Race, and Consumer Behavior. *The American Journal of Economics and Sociology, 33*(3), 5.

Cohen, R. (1978). Ethnicity: problem and focus in anthropology. *Annual Review of Anthropology, 7,* 379–403.

Coleman, L. M., Jussim, L., & Kelley, S. H. (1995). A study of stereotyping: Testing three models with a sample of Blacks. *Journal of Black Psychology, 21*(4), 322–356.

Common Ground: Hispanic and African-American Consumers Share Many Points of View that White Consumers Don't (Yankelovich Monitor, Yankelovich Partners, Inc.). (2004). *Marketing News,* 3.

Crockett, D., & Wallendorf, M. (2004). The Role of Normative Political Ideology in Consumer Behavior. *Journal of Consumer Research, 31*(3), 511–528.

Darley, W., & Williams, J. D. (2006). Methodological issues in ethnic consumer survey research: Changing consumer demographics and implications. In C. P. Rao (Ed.), Marketing and multicultural diversity (pp. 93–118). Hampshire: Ashgate.

Dauten, D., & Menendez, T. (1984). Hispanic research is comparable to general research-provided differences are respected. *Marketing News, 18,* 18.

Davidson, E. F., & Schumann, D. (2005). Shopping while Black: An examination of perceived discrimination in retail settings. Knoxville, TN: The University of Tennessee, Department of Marketing, Logistics, and Transportation.

Davies, P. G., Spencer, S. J., Quinn, D. M., & Gerhardstein, R. (2002). Consuming images: How television commercials that elicit stereotype threat can restrain women academically and professionally. *Personality and Social Psychology Bulletin, 28*(12), 1615–1628.

Deloitte and Touche. (1990). *Market opportunities: Insight into Black American consumers' buying habits.* Columbus, OH: Impact Resources, Inc.

DelVecchio, D., & Goodstein, R. C. (2004). Moving beyond race: The role of ethnic identity in evaluating celebrity endorsers. In J. D. Williams, W.-N. Lee, & C. P. Haugtvedt (Eds.), *Diversity in advertising: Broadening the scope of research* (pp. 259–277). Hillsdale, NJ: Erlbaum.

DeNavas-Walt, C., Proctor, B. D., & Lee, C. H. (2005). *Income, poverty, and health insurance coverage in the United States: 2004 U.S. Census Bureau* (pp. 60–229). Washington, DC: United States Printing Office.

Deshpande, R., Hoyer, W. D., & Donthu, N. (1986). The intensity of ethnic affiliation: a study of the sociology of Hispanic consumption. *Journal of Consumer Research, 13*(2), 214–220.

Deshpande, R., & Stayman, D. M. (1994). A tale of 2 cities - distinctiveness theory and advertising effectiveness. *Journal of Marketing Research, 31*(1), 57–64.

Dingle, D. T., & Harris, W. (2006). Advertising agencies. *Black Enterprise, 36*(11), 163–168.

Drugas, C. (1985). Marketers find celebrity endorsers sell En Espano. *Ad Forum,* 13–16.

Eagly, A. H., & Chaiken, S. (1993). *The psychology of attitudes.* Harcourt Brace Jovanovich College Publishers.

Eagly, A. H., Wood, W., & Chaiken, S. (1978). Causal inferences about communicators and their effect on opinion change. *Journal of Personality and Social Psychology, 36*(4), 424–435.

Feick, L., & Higie, R. A. (1992). The effects of preference heterogeneity and source characteristics on ad processing and judgments about endorsers. *Journal of Advertising, 21*(2), 9–24.

Feldman, J. M. (1972). Stimulus characteristics and subject prejudice as determinants of stereotype attribution. *Journal of Personality and Social Psychology, 21*(3), 333–340.

Feldman, L. P., & Star, A. D. (1968, June). *Racial factors in shopping behavior, in a new measure of responsibility for marketing.* Paper presented at the American Marketing Association Educator's Meeting, Chicago, IL.

Fiske, S. T., & Taylor, S. E. (1991). *Social cognition* (2nd ed.). New York: McGraw-Hill.

Forehand, M. R., & Deshpande, R. (2001). What we see makes us who we are: Priming ethnic self-awareness and advertising response. *Journal of Marketing Research, 38*(3), 336–348.

Forehand, M. R., Deshpande, R., & Reed, A. (2002). Identity salience and the influence of differential activation of the social self-schema on advertising response. *Journal of Applied Psychology, 87*(6), 1086–1099.

Friestad, M., & Wright, P. (1994). The Persuasion Knowledge Model: How People Cope with Persuasion Attempts. *Journal of Consumer Research, 21*(6), 1–31.

Gabbidon, S. L. (2003). Racial Profiling by Store Clerks and Security Personnel in Retail Establishments. *Journal of Contemporary Criminal Justice, 19*(3), 345.

Gaertner, S. L., & Dovidio, J. F. (1977). The subtlety of White racism, arousal, and helping behavior. *Journal of Personality and Social Psychology, 35*(10), 691–707.

Garcia, J., & Gerdes, R. (2004). To win Latino market, know pitfalls, learn rewards. *Marketing News, 38*(4), 14–19.

Gillette, P. L., & Scott, R. A. (1974). *Shopping opinions of Mexican-American consumers: A comparative analysis.* Paper presented at the Educators' Conference.

Gilly, M. (1993). Studies of women and minorities in marketing research. Paper presented at the American Marketing Association Winter Educators' Conference.

Glick, P., & Fiske, S. T. (1996). The Ambivalent Sexism Inventory: Differentiating hostile and benevolent sexism. *Journal of Personality and Social Psychology, 70*(3), 491–512.

Goffman, E. (1976). *Gender advertisements.* New York: Harper Row.

Graham, S. (1992). Most of the subjects were white and middle-class: Trends in published research on African-Americans in selected apa journals, 1970–1989. *American Psychologist, 47*(5), 629–639.

Green, C. L. (1999). Ethnic evaluations of advertising: Interaction effects of strength of ethnic identification, media placement, and degree of racial composition. *Journal of Advertising, 28*(1), 49–64.

Green, M. (1991). *Invisible people: The depiction of minorities in magazine ads and catalogs.* New York: City of New York Department of Consumer Affairs.

Green, M. (1992). *Still invisible: The depiction of minorities in magazine ads one year after the consumer affairs department study.* New York: City of New York Department of Consumer Affairs.

Greenlee, T. B. (2004). Mainstream marketers advertise to gays and lesbians: Strategic issues and research agenda. In J. D. Williams, W.-N. Lee, & C. P. Haugtvedt (Eds.), *Diversity in advertising: Broadening the scope of research directions* (pp. 357–368). Mahwah, NJ: Erlbaum.

Grier, S. A., & Brumbaugh, A. M. (1999). Noticing cultural differences: Ad meanings created by target and non-target markets. *Journal of Advertising, 28*(1), 79–93.

Grier, S. A., & Brumbaugh, A. M. (2004). Consumer Distinctiveness and Advertising Persuasion. In J. D. Williams, W.-N. Lee, & C. P. Haugtvedt (Eds.), *Diversity in advertising: Broadening the scope of research directions* (pp. 217–236). Hillsdale, NJ: Erlbaum.

Grier, S. A., Brumbaugh, A. M., & Thornton, C. G. (2006). Crossover dreams: Consumer responses to ethnic-oriented products. *Journal of Marketing, 70*(2), 35–51.

Grier, S. A., & Deshpande, R. (2001). Social dimensions of consumer distinctiveness: The influence of social status on group identity and advertising persuasion. *Journal of Marketing Research, 38*(2), 216–224.

Guest, L. (1970). How Negro models affect company image. *Journal of Advertising Research, 10*(2), 29–33.

Harris, A. M. G., Henderson, G. R., & Williams, J. D. (2005). Courting customers: Assessing consumer racial profiling and other marketplace discrimination. *Journal of Public Policy & Marketing, 24*(1), 163–171.

Helms, J. (2005, February). Keynote speech. Paper presented at the Society for Consumer Psychology Winter Conference, St. Pete Beach, FL.

Henderson, G. R., & Motley, C. A. (2004). Is it worth it? If so, research it: Exploring the place of diversity research in marketing. In *Advances in consumer research, Volume Xxxi* (Vol. 31, pp. 225–225).

Henderson, G. R., Ostrom, A., Barnett, T. D., Dillon, K. D., & Lynch, J. G. (1997). Confusing Consumers: The Impact of the Other-Race Effect on Customer Service. CIBER Working Paper, Duke University Fuqua School of Business.

Henderson, G. R., Williams, J. D., Grantham, K. D., & Lwin, M. (1999). The commodification of race in Singapore: The customer service implications of the other-race. *Asia Pacific Journal of Management, 16*(2), 213.

Henderson, G. R., & Williams, J. D. (2004). Michael Jordan who? The impact of other-race contact in celebrity endorser recognition. In J. D. Williams, W.-N. Lee & C. P. Haugtvedt (Eds.), *Diversity in advertising: Broadening the scope of research directions.* (pp. 279–297). Hillsdale, NJ: Erlbaum.

Henderson, T. P. (2001). Perception that some merchants practice racial profiling generates debate. *Stores, 83*(6), 26–32.

Henderson, T. P. (2004). Another Potential Solution. *Stores, 86*(2), 8.

Hirschman, E. C. (1981). American Jewish ethnicity — Its relationship to some selected aspects of consumer-behavior. *Journal of Marketing, 45*(3), 102–110.

Hoch, S. J., Kim, B. D., Montgomery, A. L., & Rossi, P. E. (1995). Determinants of store-level price elasticity. *Journal of Marketing Research, 32*(1), 17–29.

Holland, J., & Gentry, J. W. (1999). Ethnic consumer reaction to targeted marketing: A theory of intercultural accommodation. *Journal of Advertising, 28*(1), 65–77.

Hovland, C., & Weis, W. (1951). The influence of source credibility on communication effectiveness. *Public Opinion Quarterly*, 635–660.

Hoyer, W. D., & Deshpande, R. (1982). Cross-cultural influences on buyer behavior: The impact of Hispanic ethnicity. Paper presented at the Assessment of Marketing Thought and Practice: 1982 Educators' Conference, Chicago.

Huesman, L. R., Eron, L. D., Klein, R., Brice, P., & Fischer, P. (1983). Mitigating the imitation of aggressive behaviors by changing children's attitudes about medial violence. *Journal of Personality and Social Psychology, 44*, 899–910.

Hume, S. (1983). Stars are lacking luster as ad presenters. *Advertising Age*, 3.

Hutchison, R. (1988). A critique of race, ethnicity, and social-class in recent leisure-recreation research. *Journal of Leisure Research, 20*(1), 10–30.

Insko, C. A., Nacoste, R. W., & Moe, J. L. (1983). Belief congruence and racial-discrimination — Review of the evidence and critical-evaluation. *European Journal of Social Psychology, 13*(2), 153–174.

Jackson, J. S. (1991). Black American life course. In J. S. Jackson (Ed.), *Life in Black America* (pp. 264–273). Newbury Park, CA: Sage.

Jackson, L. A., Hymes, R. W., & Sullivan, L. A. (1987). The effects of positive information on evaluations of black-and-white targets by black-and-white subjects. *Journal of Social Psychology, 127*(3), 309–316.

Jewell, K. S. (1985). Will the real black, AfroAmerican, mixed, colored, negor please stand up: Impact of the black social movement, 20 years later. *Journal of Black Studies, 16*(1), 57–75.

Karande, K. (2005). Minority response to ethnically similar models in advertisements: an application of accommodation theory. *Journal of Business Research, 58*(11), 1573–1580.

Karon, B. P. (1958). *The Negro personality: A rigorous investigation of the effects of culture.* New York: Springer.

Kaufman-Scarborough, C., & Baker, S. M. (2005). Do people with disabilities believe the ADA has served their consumer interests? *Journal of Consumer Affairs, 39*(1), 1–26.

Kelman, H. C. (1961). Processes of opinion change. *Public Opinion Quarterly, 25*(1), 57–78.

Kerin, R. (1979). Black model appearance and production evaluation. *Journal of Communication, 29*, 123–128.

Koslow, S., Shamdasani, P. N., & Touchstone, E. E. (1994). Exploring language effects in ethnic advertising: A sociolinguistic perspective. *Journal of Consumer Research, 20*(4), 575–585.

Kumanyika, S. K. (2001). Minisymposium on obesity: Overview and some strategic considerations. *Annual Review of Public Health, 22*(1), 293.

Lee, W.-N., & Callcott, M. (1994). Billboard Advertising: A comparision of vice products across ethnic groups. *Journal of Business Research, 30*(1), 85–94.

Lee, W.-N., Williams, J. D., & La Ferle, C. (2004). Diversity in advertising: A summary and research agenda. In J. D. Williams, W.-N. Lee, & C. P. Haugtvedt (Eds.), *Diversity in advertising: Broadening the scope of research directions* (pp. 3–20). Mahwah, NJ: Erlbaum.

Linville, P. W. (1982). The complexity-extremity effect and age-based stereotyping. *Journal of Personality and Social Psychology, 42*(2), 193–211.

Linville, P. W., & Jones, E. E. (1980). Polarized appraisals of out-group members. *Journal of Personality and Social Psychology, 38*(5), 689–703.

Livingston, R. W. (2004). Demystifying the Nonconscious: Unintentional discrimination in society and the media. In J. D. Williams, W.-N. Lee, & C. P. Haugtvedt (Eds.), *Diversity in advertising: Broadening the scope of research directions* (pp. 59–74). Mahwah, NJ: Erlbaum.

Locksley, A., Hepburn, C., & Ortiz, V. (1982). On the effects of social stereotypes on judgments of individuals — Comment. *Social Psychology Quarterly, 45*(4), 270–273.

Luna, D., & Gupta, S. F. (2001). An integrative framework for cross-cultural consumer behavior. *International Marketing Review, 18*(1), 45–69.

Luna, D., & Peracchio, L. A. (2002). "Where there is a will ...": Motivation as a moderator of language processing by bilingual consumers. *Psychology & Marketing, 19*(7–8), 573–593.

Luna, D., & Peracchio, L. A. (2005). Sociolinguistic effects on code-switched ads targeting bilingual consumers. *Journal of Advertising, 34*(2), 43–56.

Lynn, M. & Thomas-Haysbert, C. (2003). Ethnic differences in tipping: Evidence, explanations, and implications. *Journal of Applied Social Psychology, 33*(8), 1747–1772.

Marin, G., & Marin, B. V. (1991). *Research with Hispanic populations* (Vol. 23). Newbury Park, CA: Sage.

Markus, H. (2005, February). Keynote speech. Paper presented at the Society for Consumer Psychology Winter Conference, St. Pete Beach, FL.

Meyers-Levy, J. (1989). Gender differences in information processing: A selectivity interpretation. In P. Cafferata & A. M. Tybout, (Eds.), Cognitive and affective responses to advertising (pp. 219–260). Lexington, MA: Lexington Books.

Meyers-Levy, J., & Maheswaran, D. (1991). Exploring differences in males' and females' processing strategies. *Journal of Consumer Research, 18*(June), 63–70.

McGuire, W. J. (1984). Search for the self: Going beyond self-esteem and the reactive self. In J. A. R. A. Zucker & A. I. Rabin (Ed.), *Personality and the prediction of behavior* (pp. 73–120). New York: Academic Press.

McGuire, W. J., McGuire, C. V., Child, P., & Fujioka, T. (1978). Salience of ethnicity in the spontaneous self-concept as a function of one's ethnic distinctiveness in the social environment. *Journal of Personality and Social Psychology, 36*(5), 511–520.

Moore, D. J., Williams, J. D., & Qualls, W. J. (1996). Target marketing of tobacco and alcohol-related products to ethnic minority groups in the U.S. *Ethnicity and Disease, 6*(1 and 2), 83–98.

Moschis, G. P. (1987). *Consumer socialization.* Lexington, MA: Lexington Books.

Motley, C. M., Henderson, G. R., & Baker, S. M. (2003). Exploring collective memories associated with African-American advertising memorabilia — The good, the bad, and the ugly. *Journal of Advertising, 32*(1), 47–57.

Mulhern, F. J., & Williams, J. D. (1995). Understanding Hispanic shopping behavior using retail scanner data. *Stores Magazine, 77*(4), RR3.

Mulhern, F. J., & Williams, J. D. (1994). A comparative analysis of shopping behavior in Hispanic and non-Hispanic market areas. *Journal of Retailing, 70*(3), 231–251.

Mulhern, F. J., Williams, J. D., & Leone, R. P. (1998). Variability of brand price elasticities across retail stores: Ethnic, income, and brand determinants. *Journal of Retailing, 74*(3), 427–446.

Muse, W. V. (1971). Product-related response to use of Black models in advertising. *Journal of Marketing Research, 8*(1), 107–109.

Oakenfull, G. K. (2004). Targeting consumer segments based on sexual orientation: Can advertisers swing both ways? In J. D. Williams, W.-N. Lee, & C. P. Haugtvedt (Eds.), *Diversity in advertising: Broadening the scope of research directions* (pp. 369–382). Mahwah, NJ: Erlbaum.

Orpen, C. (1975). Reactions to Black and white models. *Journal of Advertising Research, 15*(5), 75–79.

Petrof, J. V. (1968). Reaching the Negro market: A segregated vs. a general newspaper. *Journal of Advertising Research, 8*(2), 40–43.

Petty, R. E., Fleming, M. A., & White, P. H. (1999). Stigmatized sources and persuasion: Prejudice as a determinant of argument scrutiny. *Journal of Personality and Social Psychology, 76*(1), 19–34.

Petty, R. E., & Wegner, D. T. (1998). Attitude change: Multiple roles for persuasion variables. In S. F. D. Gilbert & G. Lindzey (Ed.), *Handbook of social psychology* (4th ed., Vol. 1, pp. 322–390). New York: McGraw-Hill.

Phinney, J. S. (1992). The multigroup ethnic identity measure: A new scale for use with diverse groups. *Journal of Adolescent Research, 7*(2), 156–176.

Pitts, R. E., Whalen, D. J., O'Keefe, R., & Murray, V. (1989). Black and White response to culturally targeted television commercials: A value-based approach. *Psychology & Marketing, 6*(4), 311–328.

Platz, S. J., & Hosch, H. M. (1988). Cross-racial ethnic eyewitness identification: a field study. *Journal of Applied Social Psychology, 18*(11), 972–984.

Pollay, R. W. (1986). The distorted mirror —Reflections on the unintended consequences of advertising. *Journal of Marketing, 50*(2), 18–36.

Qualls, W. J., & Moore, D. J. (1990). Stereotyping effects on consumers evaluation of advertising: Impact of racial differences between actors and viewers. *Psychology & Marketing, 7*(2), 135–151.

Reed, A. (2004). Activating the self-importance of consumer selves: Exploring identity salience effects on judgments. *Journal of Consumer Research, 31*(2), 286–295.

Reed, A., Wooten, D. B., & Bolton, L. E. (2002). The temporary construction of consumer attitudes. *Journal of Consumer Psychology, 12*(4), 375–388.

Reid, I. D., Stagmaier, J., & Reagan, C. C. (1986). Research design use to describe and explain Black consumer behavior. Paper presented at the Cultural and Subcultural Influences in Consumer Behavior in Marketing Conference, Chicago.

Riche, M. F. (1990). Demographic change and its implications for marketing research. *Applied Marketing Research, 30*(3), 23–27.

Robinson, P. A., & Rao, C. P. (1986). *A critical review and reassessment of Black consumer behavioral research.* Paper presented at the Southwestern Marketing Association Conference.

Rudman, L. A., & Borgida, E. (1995). The afterglow of construct accessibility: The behavioral consequences of priming men to view women as sexual objects. *Journal of Experimental Social Psychology, 31*(6), 493–517.

Saegert, J., Hoover, R. J., & Hilger, M. T. (1985). Characteristics of Mexican-American consumers. *Journal of Consumer Research, 12*(1), 104–109.

Saegert, J., & Yokum, T. (1986). Characteristics of Hispanic consumers in the Los Angeles Times data base. Paper presented at the Workshop on Cultural and Subcultural Influences in Consumer Behavior, Chicago, IL.

Sanders, L. (2006). NYC slaps subpoena on ad chiefs. *Advertising Age, 77*(24), 1–39.

Sargent, M. J. (2004). On the predictive utility of the implicit association test: Current research and future directions. In J. D. Williams, W.-N. Lee, & C. P. Haugtvedt (Eds.), *Diversity in advertising: Broadening the scope of research directions* (pp. 43–58). Hillsdale, NJ: Erlbaum.

Schlinger, M. J., & Plummer, J. T. (1972). Advertising in Black and White. *Journal of Marketing Research, 9*(2), 149–153.

Siegel, A. E., & Siegel, S. (1957). Reference groups, membership groups, and attitude change. *Journal of Abnormal & Social Psychology, 55*(3), 360–364.

Smedley, J. W., & Bayton, J. A. (1978). Evaluative race-class stereotypes by race and perceived class of subjects. *Journal of Personality and Social Psychology, 36*(5), 530–535.

Smith, T. W. (1980). Ethnic measurement and identification. *Ethnicity, 7*(1), 78–95.

Snuggs, T. L., & Qualls, W. J. (1987). Portrayal of Blacks in advertising: A critical review of the literature. Paper presented at the Minority Marketing: Issues and Prospects: Proceedings of the Academy of Marketing Science Conference, Charleston, SC.

Snyder, M. L., Kleck, R. E., Strenta, A., & Mentzer, S. J. (1979). Avoidance of the handicapped - attributional ambiguity analysis. *Journal of Personality and Social Psychology, 37*(12), 2297–2306.

Solomon, P. J., Bush, R. F., & Hair, J. F. (1976). White and black consumer sales response to black models. *Journal of Marketing Research, 13*(4), 431–434.

Solomon, S., Greenberg, J., & Pyszczynski, T. (1991). A terror management theory or social behavior: The psychological function of self-esteem and cultural worldviews. In M. Zanna (Ed.), *Advances in experimental social psychology* (Vol. 24, pp. 93–159). San Diego: Academic Press.

Spira, J. S., & Whittler, T. E. (2004). Style or substance? Viewers' reactions to spokesperson's race in advertising. In J. D. Williams, W.-N. Lee, & C. P. Haugtvedt (Eds.), *Diversity in advertising: Broadening the scope of research directions* (pp. 247–257). Hillsdale, NJ: Erlbaum.

Stafford, J. E., Birdwell, A. E., & Van Tassel, C. E. (1970). Integrated advertising — White backlash. *Journal of Advertising Research, 10*(2), 15–20.

Stanfield, J. H., II, & Dennis, R. M. (1993). *Race and ethnicity in research methods.* Thousand Oaks, CA: Sage.

Stayman, D. M., & Deshpande, R. (1980). Situational ethnicity and consumer behavior. *Journal of Consumer Research, 16*(December), 361–371.

Steele, C. M. (1997). A threat in the air - How stereotypes shape intellectual identity and performance. *American Psychologist, 52*(6), 613–629.

Steele, C. M., & Aronson, J. (1995). Stereotype threat and the intellectual test-performance of African-Americans. *Journal of Personality and Social Psychology, 69*(5), 797–811.

Stephens, N., & Gwinner, K. P. (1998). Why don't some people complain? A cognitive-emotive process model of consumer complaint behavior. *Journal of the Academy of Marketing Science, 26*(3), 172–189.

Stout, P. A., & Villegas, J. (2004). HealthpPromotion and interactive technology: Do gender differences matter in message design? In J. D. Williams, W.-N. Lee, & C. P. Haugtvedt (Eds.), *Diversity in advertising: Broadening the scope of research directions* (pp. 383–399). Hillsdale, NJ: Erlbaum.

Survey Measures Blacks' Media, Product, Ad Preferences. (1981). *Marketing News,* 6.

Szybillo, G. J., & Jacoby, J. (1974). Effect of different levels of integration on advertising preference and intention to purchase. *Journal of Applied Psychology, 59*(3), 274–280.

Tan, C. T., & McCollough, J. (1985). Relating ethnic attitudes and consumption values in an Asian context. *Advances in Consumer Research, 12*, 122–125.

Tolley, B. S., & Goett, J. J. (1971). Reactions to Blacks in newspaper ads. *Journal of Advertising Research, 11*(2), 11–17.

U.S. Department of Labor (2005). *Consumer expenditures in 2003, Report 986.* Washington, DC: U.S. Bureau of Labor Statistics, U.S. Department of Labor.

Valencia, H. (1985). Developing an index to measure "hispanicness." *Advances in Consumer Research, 12*(1), 118–121.

Vargas, P. T., Sekaquaptewa, D., & Von Hippel, W. (2004). It's not just what you think, it's also how you think: Prejudice as biased information processing. In J. D. Williams, W.-N. Lee, & C. P. Haugtvedt (Eds.), *Diversity in advertising: Broadening the scope of research* (pp. 93–120). Hillsdale, NJ: Erlbaum.

Vedantam, S. (2005). *Patients' diversity is often discounted, alternatives to mainstream medical treatment call for recognizing ethnic, social differences* (pp. 01): The Washington Post.

Vence, D. L. (2004). You talkin' to me? *Marketing News, 38*(4), 1–11.

Webster, C. (1987). Strong-weak Hispanic identification shopping and media behavior differences. *Proceedings: Workshop on Cultural and Subcultural Influences in Consumer Behavior in Marketing II.* Chicago, IL: American Marketing Association.

Weinreich, P., Rex, J., & Mason, D. (1986). The operationalism of identity theory in racial and ethnic relations. In *Theories of race and ethnic relations* (pp. 299–320): Cambridge University Press.

White, P. H., & Harkins, S. G. (1994). Race of source effects in the elaboration likelihood model. *Journal of Personality and Social Psychology, 67*(5), 790–870.

Whittler, T. E. (1989). Viewers' processing of actor's race and message claims in advertising stimuli. *Psychology & Marketing, 6*(4), 287–309.

Whittler, T. E. (1991). The effects of actors race in commercial advertising - review and extension. *Journal of Advertising, 20*(1), 54–60.

Whittler, T. E., & Dimeo, J. (1991). Viewers reactions to racial cues in advertising stimuli. *Journal of Advertising Research, 31*(6), 37–46.

Whittler, T. E., & Spira, J. S. (2002). Model's race: A peripheral cue in advertising messages? *Journal of Consumer Psychology, 12*(4), 291–301.

Wilkes, R. E., & Valencia, H. (1986). Shopping-related characteristics of Mexican-Americans and Blacks. *Psychology & Marketing, 3*(4), 247–259.

Williams, J. D. (1985). African and European roots of multi-culturalism in the consumer behavior of American Blacks. Paper presented at the Historical Perspectives in Consumer Research: National and International Perspectives: Proceedings of the Association for Consumer Research International Meeting, Singapore.

Williams, J. D. (1987). Examining the effectiveness of celebrity advertising to minorities: Entertainers vs. athletes. Paper presented at the Minority Marketing: Issues adn Prospects: Proceedings of the Academy of Marketing Science Conference, Charleston, SC.

Williams, J. D. (1989). Black consumer segmentation and ethnic identification: A critical review and pilot study. Paper presented at the Proceedings of the Division of Consumer Psychology: American Psychological Association 1988 Annual Convention, Atlanta, GA.

Williams, J. D. (1995). Book review of race and ethnicity in research methods. *Journal of Marketing Research, 32*(2), 239–243.

Williams, J. D., Harris, A.-M. G., & Henderson, G. R. (2006a). Equal treatment for equal dollars in Illinois: Assessing consumer racial profiling and other marketplace discrimination. *The Law Enforcement Executive Forum, 5*(7), 83–104.

Williams, J. D., Harris, A.-M. G., & Henderson, G. R. (2006b). States of denial and degradation both subtle and overt: Marketplace discrimination across America. Paper presented at the The Proceedings of the Marketing and Public Policy Conference, Long Beach, CA.

Williams, J. D., Henderson, G. R., & Harris, A.-M. (2001). Consumer racial profiling: Bigotry goes to market. *New Crisis (15591603), 108*(6), 22.

Williams, J. D., & Kumanyika, S. K. (2002). Is social marketing an effective tool to reduce health disparities? *Social Marketing Quarterly, 8*(4), 14–31.

Williams, J. D., Lwin, M. O., Harris, A.-M. G., & Gooding, V. A. (forthcoming 2007). Developing a power-responsibility equilibrium model to assess "brick & mortar" retail discrimination: Balancing consumer, corporate, and government interests. In T. M. Lowrey (Ed.), *Brick and mortar shopping in the 21st century*. Mahwah, NJ: Erlbaum.

Williams, J. D., & Qualls, W. J. (1989). Middle-class Black consumers and intensity of ethnic identification. *Psychology & Marketing, 6*(4), 263–286.

Williams, J. D., Qualls, W. J., & Ferguson, N. (forthcoming 2007). Potential vulnerabilities of U.S. subsistence consumers to persuasive marketing communications. In J. A. Rosa & M. Viswanathan (Eds.), *Product and market development for subsistence marketplaces: Consumption and entrepreneurship beyond literacy and resource barriers*. UK: Elesevier.

Williams, J. D., Qualls, W. J., & Grier, S. A. (1995). Racially exclusive real estate advertising: Public policy implications for fair housing practices. *Journal of Public Policy & Marketing, 14*(2), 225–244.

Williams, J. D., & Snuggs, T. L. (1997). Survey of attitudes toward customer ethnocentrism and shopping in retail stores: The role of race. Paper presented at the Society for Consumer Psychology 1997 Winter Conference, Potsdam, NY.

Williams, J. D., & Tharp, M. C. (2002). African Americans: Ethnic roots, cultural diversity. In M. Tharp (Ed.), *Marketing and consumer identity in multicultural America* (pp. 165–211). Thousand Oaks, CA: Sage.

Wolin, L. D. (2003). Gender issues in advertising — An oversight synthesis of research: 1970–2002. *Journal of Advertising Research, 43*(1), 111–129.

Woodmansee, J. J., & Cook, S. W. (1967). Dimensions of verbal racial attitudes: their identification and measurement. *Journal of Personality and Social Psychology, 7*(3), 240–250.

Wooten, D. B. (1995). One-of-a-kind in a full house: Some consequences of ethnic and gender distinctiveness. *Journal of Consumer Psychology, 4*(3), 205–224.

Wooten, D. B. (2006). From labeling possessions to possessing labels: Ridicule and socialization among adolescents. *Journal of Consumer Research, 33*(2), 188–198.

Wooten, D. B., & Reed, A. (2004). Playing it safe: Susceptibility to normative influence and protective self-presentation. *Journal of Consumer Research, 31*(3), 551–556.

Zuckerman, M., & Kieffer, S. C. (1994). Race differences in face-ism — Does facial prominence imply dominance. *Journal of Personality and Social Psychology, 66*(1), 86–92.

VII

CONSUMER WELL-BEING

36

Consumers and the Allure of "Safer" Tobacco Products
Scientific and Policy Issues

Eugene Borgida

Anita Kim

Emily N. Stark

Christopher Miller

University of Minnesota

According to the U.S. Surgeon General (2004), cigarette smoking is the leading preventable cause of death and disease in the United States, causing more than 440,000 premature deaths a year. Given these health risks, the development and marketing of products designed to reduce the harmful effects of tobacco use should come as no surprise (Kozlowski, 1984). The Institute of Medicine (IDM; 2001) groups these products under the term "potentially reduced-exposure products" (PREPs). PREPs are "tobacco products that have been modified or designed in some way to reduce users' exposure to tobacco toxins. As a marketing tactic, some manufacturers claim that reduced exposure to tobacco toxins may lead to reduced risk of cancer or other health conditions" (Hatsukami & Hecht, 2005, p. 5).

In this chapter, we examine the scientific and policy issues associated with reduced harm products. We begin with a primer on PREPs and the set of issues and health claims associated with them, including some epidemiological and clinical research on tobacco toxin exposure suggesting that product labels claiming reduced risk in fact may pose a health threat to consumers. We then examine divergences and convergences of opinion and perception of PREPs held by public health experts and tobacco control advocates, on the one hand, and the public at large, on the other hand. Next, our focus shifts to a discussion of theory and research from the psychology of attitudes in social psychology for a more nuanced and psychological understanding of the bases of *public* attitudes toward harm reduction and PREPs. One of our central claims in this chapter is that the psychology of attitudes can indeed make such a contribution. Finally, in the last section of the chapter, we discuss one approach to the "psychology of harm reduction" (MacCoun, 1998) as it has been applied to the development of policies aimed at the effective control of illicit drug use in the United States. We discuss the extent to which the psychology of harm reduction analogously pertains to the on-going regulatory debate about the marketing of PREPs. Harm reduction, in this context, represents one of a few strategies that policy makers should consider integrating in the development of effective science-based regulatory policies on PREPs.

A PRIMER ON PREPS

PREPs generally fall into one of two categories: variants of traditional tobacco cigarettes or pharmaceutical agents that are meant to aid in smoking cessation. Inherent in the IOM definition of PREPs are two significant issues. First, there is a wide variety of different kinds of PREPs. Although the use of PREPs serve to meet a primary objective (to reduce exposure to harm), they are a very broad category with new products being introduced into the marketplace (Shiffman, Gitchell, Warner, Slade, Henningfield, & Pinney, 2002). The second issue is related to the breadth of the product category: what is known about their benefits and risks is as broad as the product category itself. Some PREPs have a longer history, and more is known about them. However, some products have been introduced relatively recently; these products may reduce exposure to known toxins but may introduce or increase others. Importantly, "there is no evidence to suggest that there is enough of a reduction in tobacco toxin exposure with any of the existing PREPs to expect a significant reduction in disease risk, nor do we know the extent of toxin exposure reduction that is necessary to result in reduction of disease" (Hatsukami & Hecht, 2005, p. 5).

The first broad category of PREPs comprises cigarette-like or other tobacco products that, while still containing tobacco, are meant to reduce exposure to other potential toxins. It is this category of PREPs that we focus on in this chapter. These products include traditional smokeless tobacco (i.e., chew), new cigarettes that heat rather than burn tobacco, and even "light" cigarettes that use special filters to allegedly expose the user to less tar. The toxicology of smokeless tobacco and "light" cigarettes is relatively well known because they have been on the market longer (Shiffman et al., 2002). Using traditional smokeless tobacco reduces the risk for some diseases associated with traditional cigarettes and presumably reduces harm to non-smokers because there is no second-hand smoke. However, smokeless tobacco is definitively linked to other kinds of diseases, most notably oral cancer (Shiffman et al., 2002), although in Sweden, the link between oral cancer and oral snuff or snus has been weak, perhaps due to the lower levels of tobacco-specific nitrosamines found in the products manufactured in Sweden. Similarly, the research on "light" cigarettes has led many to conclude that they offer no health benefits to the smoker (Shiffman et al., 2002; U.S. Department of Health and Human Services, 2004). In contrast, toxicology results on new cigarettes that heat rather than burn tobacco are mixed. Because the tobacco is not burned, users are not exposed to some of the carcinogens that result from tobacco combustion. However, there is some evidence that users are exposed to the same (or even increased) levels of *other* toxins. Furthermore, the changed form of delivery introduces the possibility of new risks, like the inhalation of glass fibers that have been associated with some of these products (Shiffman et al., 2002).

The second category of PREPs includes pharmaceutical agents like nicotine replacement products (e.g., nicotine gum, lozenges, and nicotine patch) that are meant to aid in smoking cessation. With respect to these PREPs, scientific evidence for long-term use is limited, although the public health community perceives these products as significantly less toxic than cigarettes and oral smokeless tobacco products. Available evidence suggests these products are safe to use over a short period of time, that they stave off cravings for traditional cigarettes, and that they pose no health risks to nonusers (with the possible exception of use during pregnancy). However, because these products are generally used short-term, more research needs to be conducted to better understand their toxicology, especially regarding long-term use (Shiffman et al., 2002).

The focus of the present chapter, however, is on another type of health risk associated with PREPs that is less obvious than their direct health effects. Consumer perception of the safety of these products and the potential for these perceptions to influence consumer behavior represents a potentially significant public health threat. PREPs have largely been developed in response to an increased understanding of the danger of regular cigarette smoking and they are often marketed with claims that indirectly imply safety (Hatsukami & Zeller, 2004). Thus, some consumers are likely to turn to these products believing that they reduce their exposure to toxic ingredients (see MacCoun (2004) for an interesting analysis of how emerging "vaccines" against tobacco addiction might be perceived as a cure for addiction and potentially increase tobacco initiation rates). Unfortunately, these product marketing claims are rarely scientifically verified or regulated by an independent organization. Although the FDA regulates those nicotine replacement products that make health claims (*FDA v. Brown & Williamson Tobacco Corp*, 2000), tobacco-based PREPs are not regulated (Hatsukami & Zeller, 2004).

Furthermore, PREPs may be safer in some ways but they may also be more dangerous in ways that are unknown to consumers. As just discussed, the toxicology of tobacco-based PREPs in particular is mixed. As reviewed by Hatsukami and Zeller (2004), there are five major conclusions about the effects of using PREPs that can be drawn from the research to date. First, the use of machine-derived measurements to determine the levels of toxins from smoking light cigarettes is not accurate and therefore not sufficient. Smokers do not smoke like machines and therefore the machine-determined yields are inadequate in reflecting actual smoking behavior. Second, there is wide variation in the level of exposure to toxins across smokers when examining a PREP, which means that using mean levels of reduction is not useful. Third, although exposure to some toxins is reduced, exposure to other toxins may, in fact, increase. As an example, Hatsukami and Zeller cite the finding that use of Eclipse brand cigarettes (R.J. Reynolds' brand of cigarette that involves heating rather than burning the tobacco) resulted in lower levels of some toxins, but increased exposure to carbon monoxide. Fourth, to date, there is no evidence showing that reduced exposure to toxins actually reduces harm to the user in any meaningful way. In other words, even if data suggest that using a particular PREP results in lower levels of all toxins, there is no proof that the user benefits from a lower risk for disease or mortality.

Last, Hatsukami and Zeller argue that if a reduction of toxins is achievable, then we should consider making this reduction the standard across all similar products, meaning there would be no need to market reduced harm claims in the first place. The marketing claims for PREPs are an important part of this discussion because the misperception of the safety of PREPs is problematic in many ways. Public health experts express concern that smokers who do not want to (or cannot) quit smoking may turn to using PREPs instead of quitting in the future, and non-smokers may initiate use of PREPs because they believe they are a safer alternative to traditional cigarettes (e.g., Hatsukami & Zeller, 2004; Warner, 2002). This is a frightening prospect with respect to adolescents, who may be especially prone to perceive PREPs as a safer way to adopt the smoking habits to which they may already be drawn (see chapter 37, this volume). Not only are adolescents at a time in life when long-term health risks are discounted more than immediate benefits, but a preference for less systematic or deliberative information processing strategies (also a characteristic of adult consumer inferencing) may further reinforce these perceptions and choices (Shavitt & Wanke, 2001). Newer forms of smokeless tobacco like Exalt and Revel that do not involve spitting (tobacco juices) are good examples of products that may hold a special appeal to adolescents. Although some studies in Sweden suggest that the adoption of these products lead to reduced rates of lung cancer, some experts feel the confectionary-like presentation of some of these products may appeal to youth (Shiffman et al., 2002).

Understanding how adult (and adolescents, for that matter) consumers think about reduced exposure products and their perceived risks and benefits represents one approach to the consumer health controversy surrounding PREPs. Epidemiological studies and biomarkers research (research that examines if reduced exposure, toxicity, and disease risk claims about reduced exposure products are well founded) represent different approaches to PREPs that are not based on assessing subjective perceptions.

Epidemiological studies, for example, have compared regular, light, and ultra-light cigarettes, and have not found any significant reductions in lung cancer rates. In fact, they have found an increase in adenocarcinoma, a cancer that strikes peripheral tissues of the lung, which may be a result of deeper inhalation of smoke (Harris, Thun, Mondul, & Calle 2004). To the disappointment of many in the public health community, the promise of a "reduced harm" cigarette has not been fulfilled (Thun & Burns, 2001). As Shiffman, Pillitteri, Burton, and Di Marino (2004) and others have shown, most of the public remains unaware.

More recently, researchers have sought to move beyond epidemiological studies in their analysis of tobacco products. Epidemiological studies require very large samples measured over a number of years, often decades. They also require large effect sizes to find significant results. As noted before, they are unable to measure or control for most compensatory behaviors in smoking. For these reasons, researchers also use methods that measure the immediate biological exposure of tobacco toxins to individuals.

An example is the assessment of individual exposure to carcinogens through measurement of biological by-products found in their urine. While individuals differ in their absorption and metabolism of carcinogens, with an adequate sample size, this method can deliver an accurate picture of carcinogen exposure. It can be used to test products that are about to or have just been introduced to a market, and the method does not require waiting until they are used by people for a number of years.

Findings of epidemiologists about "light" cigarettes were confirmed using these methods. A study comparing the by-products of carcinogen exposure in regular, light, and ultra-light cigarette smokers found no significant differences in the level of exposure to two major carcinogens, NNK, a known tobacco-specific lung carcinogen, and pyrene, an indicator of polycylic aromatic hydrocarbons (PAH). The cotinine (a by-product or metabolite of nicotine) levels were not significantly different among the three groups. The absence of significant differences in nicotine exposure is further evidence that smokers are modifying their smoking behavior to achieve a certain dose of nicotine (Hecht, Murphy, Camella, Li, Jensen, Le, Joseph, & Hatsukami, 2005).

As various modified tobacco PREPs have been tested and produced, researchers have been able to subject marketing claims to immediate scientific scrutiny. One such product, the now discontinued Omni cigarette, performed very well on the FTC testing protocol, showing a 53% reduction in NNK and a 20% reduction in PAH. Biomarker studies, however, demonstrated the reductions in NNK and PAH were less than half what was claimed. NNK was reduced by only 21% and PAH reduction (5%) was nonsignificant (Hatsukami, Henningfield, & Kotlyar, 2004). Another study of Omni, conducted by Hughes, Hecht, Carmella, Murphy, and Callas (2004), showed a smaller, nonsignificant reduction in NNK (17%) and a larger, but still non-significant reduction in PAH (10%).

Cigarette-like delivery devices, such as Eclipse and Accord, have also been subjected to the rigors of biomarkers testing. Eclipse has shown a reduction in urine metagenicity (genes damaged by carcinogen exposure), 72%–79% in one experiment (Smith et al., 1996) and 70%–77% in another (Bowman et al., 2002). The Eclipse cigarette also maintained nicotine levels. Although no marketing claims have to date been made about Accord, Accord has shown a reduction of urine metagenicity between 53% and 66% in one experiment (Roethig et al., 2005). Further, several studies have shown a reduction in carbon monoxide, by as much as 70% (Buchhalter, Schrinel, & Eissenberg, 2001); however, this research also reported a significant reduction in nicotine levels as well. Studies have found Accord was ineffective at reducing nicotine cravings (Buchalter & Eissenberg, 2000).

In sum, the evidence based on the biomarkers approach suggests that the claims of reduced exposure or disease risk are not well supported. Some data demonstrate less reduction in exposure than FTC testing, other data show reduction in some biomarkers but increases in others, and still others show reduction. In fact, the implications of this work suggest that such reduced exposure or disease risk claims may well mislead consumers and (a) undermine smoking cessation efforts and/or (b) increase the probability that PREPs, whose reduced harm is unclear at best, will be increasingly used by individuals who otherwise might not be inclined to smoke. As the concluding section of this chapter suggests, it is crucial that independent researchers (i.e., those without conflict of interest with the tobacco industry) continue to scrutinize the marketing claims associated with PREPs and make available any of the scientific-based evidence pertinent to these claims (Hatsukami & Hecht, 2005, p. 5; Hatsukami et al., in press).

PUBLIC PERCEPTIONS AND MISPERCEPTIONS

The issues surrounding PREPs are complex and involve risks that go beyond obvious health effects. As reviewed by Fairchild and Colgrove (2004), the complexity of these reduced harm issues is exemplified by the history of the "light" cigarette in the United States, perhaps the first PREP. The debate around light cigarettes has encompassed concerns as broad as their questionable health risks and benefits as well as their social impact, and has fueled an enormous amount of litigation (see Johnston & Warner, 2006).

In response to concerns about the hazards of cigarette smoking, many tobacco companies began introducing "safer" ("light") cigarettes) in the 1950s and 1960s. Marketing claimed light cigarettes reduce harm to the smoker by reducing exposure to toxins like tar, nicotine, and carbon monoxide, most commonly through the use of a filter. Adoption of light cigarettes was quick, indicating both public interest in safer cigarettes and the widespread perception that the products were safer. As we shall later discuss, this misperception regarding the safety of light cigarettes has had deleterious effects on public health.

At first, the public health community and even the Surgeon General were optimistic and supportive of such efforts to develop a "safer" cigarette, fueling consumer misperception of the safety of these products. Fairchild and Colgrove argue that this support was largely a function of the fact that the tobacco industry's deceptions had not yet been revealed. It is also important to note that the list of diseases associated with cigarette smoking was significantly shorter in the 1950s and 1960s than it is now (U.S. Department of Health and Human Services, 2004), so people believed that the health risks of smoking were much more limited than is appreciated today. Therefore, since people's beliefs about cigarette smoking were not yet influenced by the knowledge of health risks and the tobacco companies' deception, the prevailing attitude toward safer cigarettes was positive.

Upon the introduction of light cigarettes to the marketplace, the typical consumer and even some health experts were supportive of, these products (Fairchild & Colgrove, 2004). What has been surprising, however, is the *continuing* consumer perception that light cigarettes are safer than traditional cigarettes, despite the marked critical shift among health experts (e.g., Fairchild & Colgrove, 2004; Warner, 2002).

Unfortunately, the evidence-based beliefs of the public health and tobacco control communities have not been adopted by the average consumer. Kozlowski, Goldberg, Yost, White, Sweeney, and Pillitteri (1998), for example, found that less than 10%–14% of smokers knew that light cigarettes could yield similar levels of tar as regular cigarettes. In a random digit dial (RDD) survey of 2,120 daily smokers, Shiffman, Pillitteri, Burton, Rohay, and Gitchell (2001a) assessed beliefs about the tar and nicotine delivery, related health benefits, and perceived harshness of light cigarettes. In their sample, 46% reported smoking regular cigarettes, 39% light cigarettes, and 15% reported smoking ultra-light cigarettes; the sample was weighted to reflect the U.S. smoker population with respect to age, sex, and ethnicity. Their study revealed that most smokers believe light and ultra-light cigarettes deliver less tar and nicotine than regular cigarettes. Smokers of these lighter cigarettes also reported feeling the products were less harsh. Although most smokers believe that smoking safer cigarettes is riskier than not smoking at all, they still believe that smoking safer cigarettes offers between a 25%–33% reduction in risk compared to smoking regular cigarettes. This misperception about the health benefits of light cigarettes—that reduced toxicant levels as measured by machines meant reduced risk—is especially alarming due to additional evidence suggesting that these beliefs detract smokers from intentions to quit. Shiffman, Pillitteri, Burton, Rohay, and Gitchell (2001b) found that smokers of light and ultra-light cigarettes who believed their products were safer and delivered less tar and nicotine exhibited significantly lower levels of interest in quitting. (The relationship between perceptions of harshness and quitting intent was marginally significant.) Kozlowski et al. (1998) found that roughly one third of light and ultra-light cigarette smokers said they would be more likely to quit if they learned that the tar levels of light cigarettes were comparable to regular cigarettes.

In terms of social impact, there is some evidence that the misperception of light cigarettes as a safer product may have resulted in more smoking than would have occurred if they had never been introduced (Warner, 2002). Smokers and non-smokers alike seem to regard smoking light cigarettes as less hazardous a behavior, so they are less likely to quit and may be more likely to start smoking, respectively. Again, this raises the possibility that adolescents may initiate smoking under the misguided belief that they are being careful when in fact they may be exposing themselves to a known health risk (U.S. Department of Health and Human Services, 1989).

In sum, the issues surrounding PREPs are varied and complex. As a category, PREPs are so broad that it is difficult to make generalizations about what is known and not known (see Shiffman et al., 2002). With respect to health and safety issues, some PREPs are directly or indirectly marketed as safer alternatives though the actual risks and benefits are mixed and vary depending on the product. Generally, the products that solely deliver nicotine are considered to be safer than tobacco products. However, other or non-combustible tobacco products bear greater scientific evaluation. In terms of societal impact, there is some evidence to suggest that the introduction of the newer PREPs may perpetuate the market for tobacco products because consumers believe that PREPs are a safer product. Obviously, public health experts are more sophisticated with respect to the issues surrounding PREPs, their history, and empirical evidence. But there is evidence that this knowledge does not trickle down to the public to the extent that it should, as is the case with light cigarettes, though marketing approaches can be constructed to inform consumers about the risks of lights (Kozlowski, Goldberg, Sweeney, Palmer, Pillitteri, White, & Stine, 1999; Kozlowski et al., 2000)

SCIENTIFIC ISSUES

Expert and Public Opinion on PREPs

One of the issues surrounding PREPs is the disparity between what public health experts and the general public think about PREPs, especially light cigarettes. The public is vulnerable to believing that reduced exposure to toxins (associated with PREPs) means a reduced risk of disease. Consumer perceptions, however, may be quite different than the views of public health experts or tobacco control advocates who should be more scientifically informed and less susceptible to holding this belief. The effects of PREPs and their marketing strategies on experts should be quite different from the effects on consumer perceptions.

Warner and Martin (2003) and Joseph, Hennrikus, Thoele, Krueger, and Hatsukami (2004), for example, conducted studies examining tobacco control leaders' attitudes toward harm reduction approaches, including PREPs. Joseph and her colleagues conducted nine focus groups of 48 local tobacco control leaders in Minnesota. Participants were classified as public policy experts, clinicians, and youth development/education specialists. Joseph et al.'s groups identified any strategy designed to reduce tobacco use or health risks associated with using tobacco.

Among the strategies these participants listed are PREPs (both modified traditional tobacco products and nicotine replacement therapy), smoking fewer cigarettes, and public policies designed to reduce smoking in the population at large (e.g., smoking bans, increased taxes). While discussing the risks of the various tobacco strategies, focus group participants expressed concern that endorsement of tobacco exposure reduction products sends a confusing message to society. They argued that since *any* level of tobacco is *not* safe, smokers might be lulled into a false sense of security. Another related concern they discussed was the possibility that the strategy of tobacco exposure reduction would increase tobacco use through the use of modified tobacco PREPs, and other kinds of "closet smoking." Other risks they discussed were: lack of evidence that the strategies offer any benefit to the user, the cost of diverting energy to researching the efficacy of tobacco harm reduction, inadvertently benefitting the tobacco industry, and the risks of chemoprevention. In light of these concerns, Joseph and colleagues found that tobacco control leaders were most supportive of regulatory policy as the best tobacco exposure reduction strategy. Participants considered FDA regulation of tobacco products, taxes and pricing, restrictions on youth access, and clean indoor air legislation as examples of these policies. Generally, participants felt regulatory policy had the greatest potential for having the largest impact on society and sending the most consistent and clear message about tobacco use, and anticipated policy change would be more cost effective and produce the most sustainable results.

Warner and Martin's (2003) Internet-based survey research study captured similar attitudes toward tobacco exposure reduction as Joseph et al.'s (2004) focus groups. Warner and Martin conducted an Internet survey (and follow up telephone interviews to some non-respondents) of a total of 2,833 U.S. tobacco control leaders. Participants were selected on the basis of their registration for the 2001 National Conference on Tobacco or Health. Overall, Warner and Martin's sample was skeptical of tobacco exposure reduction. Of those who reported being aware of tobacco exposure reduction as a strategy ($N = 1,473$), almost half (49%) agreed that such an approach would actually reduce the numbers of those who would otherwise quit smoking completely (a concern also raised by a number of the focus group participants). Also, a majority (63%) felt that there would be unintended negative health effects on PREP users.

Recall that Kozlowski et al. (1998) and the smokers in Shiffman's (2001a) survey rated smoking light and ultra-light cigarettes as significantly less risky than smoking regular cigarettes. In stark contrast, nearly 21% of Warner and Martin's participants reported thinking that these "safer" cigarettes actually *increased* the smokers' health risks (and only 10% reported believing the opposite). It is not surprising, then, that 40% answered that the collective health of Americans would be better now if light cigarettes had never been introduced to the market.

Similar to the discussion in Joseph et al.'s (2004) focus groups, the attitudes expressed by Warner and Martin's sample (2003) illustrate the complexity of issues surrounding PREPs. The focus group members of Joseph et al.'s (2004) study explicitly acknowledged that an exposure reduction approach might reduce harm and help smokers who can or will not quit. However, in both samples it was found that a tobacco exposure reduction approach was perceived as an obstacle to some smokers who otherwise might have tried to quit altogether. In addition to these negative attitudes toward tobacco harm reduction, Warner and Martin (2003) reported that their sample was also supportive of regulatory policy. Warner and Martin (2003) assessed support for various policies designed to regulate the production and marketing of PREPs; agreement was assessed by aggregating responses across "agree" and "strongly agree." Respondents were most supportive of the surveillance and banning of products found to cause unacceptable health risks or to attract children (93% agreed), a requirement for pre-marketing approval of health claims (91% agreement), and the regulation of marketing techniques (90% agreement). However, respondents were significantly less supportive of a tax based on the level of risk to the consumer (65% agreement).

This discussion of tobacco control leaders' attitudes toward tobacco exposure reduction (including PREPs) raises the question of what the average consumer thinks. Accordingly, Kim, Borgida, and Stark (2007) conducted a mail survey in the Fall of 2003 with the Minnesota Center for Survey Research. Surveys were mailed to a random sample of households in the five-state Upper Midwest region of the United States (Minnesota, Iowa, North Dakota, South Dakota, and Wisconsin); 438 adult participants (38%) returned the survey, and 21.9% of these respondents reported that they had smoked in the past 30 days. All respondents first read the IOM (2001) definition of harm reduction. The survey then assessed participants' opinions about PREPs and measured their beliefs about government and regulation of these products.

First, Kim, Borgida, and Stark (2007) found that most of their sample (68%) had not heard of (or were unsure whether they had heard of) tobacco harm reduction and PREPs, and rated their knowledge of this approach very low. Furthermore, participants agreed that people should be made more aware of PREPs. Nevertheless, the average consumer surveyed had ambivalent feelings about PREPs as did Warner and Martin's (2003) and Joseph et al.'s (2004) tobacco control leaders (see Table 36.1). For instance, respondents agreed that PREPs are as addictive as smoking regular cigarettes and expressed pessimism that PREPs will change anything. They also expressed anger that some people use PREPs instead of simply quitting their tobacco use entirely. However, they expressed optimism about the development of PREPs (they were pleased that PREPs are being developed), and felt that PREPs give hope for smokers who want to quit.

Table 36.1   Participants' Feelings and Opinions About PREPs

	M*	SD
People should be made more aware of reduced harm products	2.6	1.6
I am happy that reduced harm products are being developed	3.2	1.8
Reduced harm products are just as addictive as smoking	3.0	1.6
I feel pessimistic that reduced harm products won't really change anything	3.2	1.7
Reduced harm gives me hope for smokers who want to quit	3.7	1.8
It makes me mad to think people use reduced harm products instead of quitting entirely	3.6	2.0
Reduced harm products are a good compromise for people trying to quit	4.0	1.7
Reduced harm products increase the probability of someone quitting smoking	4.0	1.8
Reduced harm products provide a safer way to get nicotine	4.3	1.8
Reduced harm products are not effective	3.8	1.4
Reduced harm balances addictions and desires to quit	4.2	1.6
Only people who want to quit smoking should use reduced harm products	4.8	1.9

*Based on a 7-point Likert scale in which 1 corresponded with "Strongly Agree" and 7 corresponded with "Strongly Disagree" (From: Kim, Borgida, & Stark, 2007).

Table 36.2   Comparison of Attitudes Toward Regulation of PREPs for Warner and Martin's (2003) Tobacco Control Leader Sample and the Average Consumer

	Tobacco control leaders	Average consumer		
	% Agree*	% Agree*	M	SD
Watched and banned as necessary	93	61	2.7	2.0
Subject to approval based on health evidence	91	74	2.1	1.6
Subject to government regulation of marketing techniques	90	60	2.7	1.9
Subject to taxes based on level of risk to user	65	49	3.4	2.2

*Agreement for tobacco advocates was calculated with answers of 1-2 on a 5-point scale, whereas agreement for the Kim, Borgida, and Stark (20067) sample was calculated using 1-3 on a 7-point scale.

Similar to tobacco leaders' views about PREPs, respondents in the Kim et al. (2006) study also supported the federal regulation of PREPs. Table 36.2 presents a comparison of the Warner and Martin (2003) sample with the Kim, Borgida, and Stark sample on agreement with regulatory policy. Although they were less enthusiastic than Warner and Martin's sample (as can be seen by their lower levels of agreement), the average consumer was still very supportive of regulating PREPs. In particular, they were most supportive of subjecting PREPs to approval based on health evidence (74% agreement). Results from the lay sample were also similar to Warner and Martin's sample in that they were least supportive of regulatory policies involving user taxes. As was stated earlier, 65% of Warner and Martin's sample supported taxation of PREPs, which is a great reduction in support compared to the other proposed regulatory policies (see Table36.2; at least 90% of the Warner and Martin sample supported the other regulatory policies). Similarly, slightly less than half of average consumers (49%) supported differential taxation.

Consumers' opinions towards PREPs and their selective support for their regulation (i.e., not supporting taxation in particular) underscores the need for a better understanding of the *psychological* bases of these attitudes. As we shall discuss in the next section, the psychology of attitudes can contribute to an understanding of the structural and functional bases of consumers' views of these products, and also suggest ways in which these attitudes may be modified by targeted persuasion efforts.

THE PSYCHOLOGY OF ATTITUDES

One of the central claims in this chapter is that the psychology of attitudes can contribute to our understanding of public attitudes toward exposure reduction and PREPs. Several studies have been conducted examining public attitudes toward varying types of tobacco products, including reduced exposure products. These give us insight both into what the public believes about tobacco products, and also what may be influencing or informing their attitudes toward these products and issues related to exposure reduction.

In the Shiffman et al. (2001a) study, for example, most smokers believed light and ultra-light cigarettes were less harsh and delivered less tar and nicotine (also see Kozlowski et al., 1999). More importantly, these beliefs each independently contributed to the belief that these cigarettes were safer than regular cigarettes. Over half of participants rated the claims made in advertisements for light and ultra-light cigarettes as delivering less tar and being milder as credible, and 15.9% of smokers found claims made that these types of cigarettes were safer as credible. On average, smokers believed that smoking light cigarettes carried a 25% reduction in risk, and smoking ultra-light cigarettes carried a 33% reduction in risk compared to smoking regular cigarettes.

These data show that many smokers harbor misconceptions about light and ultra-light cigarettes, based on their experience with these cigarettes and exposure to advertising claims about these cigarettes. Their beliefs that light and ultra-light cigarettes are milder, and deliver less tar and nicotine, lead to beliefs that these cigarettes are safer to smoke. Shiffman et al. attributes these misconceptions to deliberate advertising by tobacco companies to promote light and ultra-light cigarettes as safer and milder, an attribution based on the marketing strategies uncovered in tobacco industry documents obtained in the tobacco master settlement (e.g., Pauly, Mepani, Lesses, Cummings, & Streck, 2002). These beliefs combine with sensory impressions of light and ultra-light cigarettes as milder to reinforce the perception of safety and reduced risk (see Kozlowski et al., 1999). Shiffman et al. also suggest that scientific data may not be as persuasive as these sensory impressions and beliefs, making it difficult to change smokers' beliefs about these products.

Hamilton, Ouellette, Rhodes, Kling, and Connolly (2004) replicated the above effect by showing participants advertisements for regular, light, and reduced-harm cigarettes, and obtaining ratings of safety and other perceptions of these ads. These participants also believed that light and reduced-harm cigarettes posed fewer health risks than regular cigarettes, despite the absence of independently verifiable scientific evidence that these products are lower in risk. This study also shows the power of advertisements for new products: only 7.7% of participants said they had previously seen the advertisement for the reduced-harm product, but most participants perceived a health and safety advertising message associated with these products, and ascribed lower risk to these products (also see Kozlowski et al., 2000). Shiffman et al. (2004) extended this work to reduced exposure products. Smokers ($N = 1,000$) and ex-smokers ($N = 499$) completed a telephone survey regarding their smoking history and their perceptions of the reduced exposure product Eclipse, a modified cigarette. The interviewer described Eclipse to the participants using language based on the manufacturer's descriptions. Participants then answered questions about their perceptions of Eclipse.

Almost all current smokers (91.7%) and ex-smokers (81.3%) thought Eclipse was safer than regular cigarettes, and many also perceived Eclipse as safer than light or ultra-light cigarettes. Almost a quarter of all smokers perceived Eclipse as completely safe—as carrying the same risk as not smoking at all. Also, many current smokers (57.4%) replied that they were somewhat or very likely to purchase Eclipse in the coming months. It seems clear that participants in this study overestimated claims of "reduced risk" by the manufacturers of Eclipse, with many taking this to mean "no risk." It may be the case that this perception would lead non-smokers to take up smoking if they thought they could use a tobacco product that did not carry any risks. Participants were not only being influenced by the manufacturer's claims about Eclipse, but they were overextending these claims and forming impressions of this new product as completely safe to use.

The key public health issue is that the attitudes of consumers toward these reduced harm products may well be shaped by advertising of these products (see chapter 37, this volume). However, it is our contention that *the psychological basis of the attitude* also may influence the way consumers respond to these messages. Many psychological studies of attitudes have examined the relationship between attitudes and their structural components, focusing primarily on cognitive and affective bases of attitudes (Eagly & Chaiken, 1993; Crites, Fabrigar, & Petty, 1994; Haddock & Zanna, 1998). The cognitive component of an attitude refers to a person's thoughts and beliefs about a certain attitude object, whereas the affective component reflects a person's feelings about that attitude object.

Previous research (e.g., Edwards, 1990; Millar & Millar, 1990; Fabrigar & Petty, 1999) has identified that attitudes toward an object, and the success of persuasion attempts, are connected to whether that attitude is based on feelings or thoughts about the object. This research has also suggested that these different bases of attitudes (thoughts vs. feelings) have different implications for persuasion and other communications: people may read and understand information about an issue or product differently as a function of whether their attitude towards this issue or product is based primarily on their thoughts or their feelings.

Consistent with this structural approach to understanding attitudes, our research (Stark, Borgida, Kim, & Pickens, in press) examined how a person's thoughts and/or feelings about tobacco harm reduction are related to their overall attitude towards harm reduction products, in the context of the same mail survey described above (Kim et al., 2007). The ratings of thoughts and feelings about harm reduction, as well as predictors such as knowledge about tobacco products, and experience with smoking, were regressed onto overall attitudes toward harm reduction products in order to understand the primary predictors of overall attitudes. It was found that, for smokers, their feelings about harm reduction were the primary predictor of their overall attitudes toward harm reduction, but for non-smokers, neither their thoughts nor their feelings about tobacco exposure reduction predicted their overall attitudes.

This suggests that one way of understanding consumer attitudes towards these products lies in understanding the structural basis of their attitudes; whether their attitudes are primarily derived from their feelings or primarily from their thoughts about the products. Also, a consumer's *experience* with tobacco products may influence the base of their attitudes toward harm reduction, so experience in the form of personal smoking history also needs to be taken into account. Therefore, the concern that Shiffman et al. raise in their 2001 papers—that sensory impressions of light cigarettes as milder lead to difficult-to-change beliefs that these cigarettes are safer—may be true. The feelings associated with smoking—taste, reduction of cravings, relaxation—may create positive attitudes that are difficult to counter through merely providing relatively abstract data on the health risks of these products (also see Kozlowski et al., 1999). A smoker's feelings about tobacco products must be taken into account in order to understand and predict his or her attitude towards other issues related to tobacco consumption, such as regulation or responses to marketing of new products.

In addition to differentiating the cognitive and affective base, a second approach involves examining whether the attitude reflects different *functional* qualities—the satisfaction of value expressiveness (symbolic beliefs) or instrumental needs (self-interest). Kim, Borgida, and Stark (2007) examined three potential predictors of support for federal regulation of harm reduction products: product knowledge, self-interest, and symbolic beliefs about the role of government in society. Symbolic beliefs are value-laden, emotionally driven, stable beliefs that are learned early in life, and that have a strong influence on a range of social policy preferences. For example, Sears, Lau, Tyler, and Allen (1979) showed that attitudes of Whites toward busing Black students into predominantly White schools districts were more strongly influenced by their values and affect about race than whether they lived in a district in which busing would occur. Similarly, political ideology (liberalism vs. conservatism) is a stronger predictor for a variety of policies including preference for government-provided health insurance or privatized health care (even among those who do not have health care) and agreement that the government should guarantee jobs for everyone (even among those who were personally affected by unemployment).

Kim et al. (2007) chose these three predictors because the messages about potential reduced exposure products are often constructed in terms of educating the public about the risks associated with traditional tobacco (i.e., improving their knowledge), or emphasizing how these products affect people's direct interests (i.e., appealing to their self-interests). However, symbolic beliefs have been shown to have a stronger influence on policy preferences than self-interest, unless the self-interest component of the policy is very clear (e.g., Chong, Citrin, & Conley, 2001; Young, Thompson, Borgida, Sullivan, & Aldrich, 1991).

Kim et al. (2007) found that attitudes regarding the federal regulation of conventional tobacco and exposure reduction products are in line with predictions based on theory and research on symbolic politics: as with other social policy issues, when confronted with the overall issue of regulation, consumers tend to evaluate issues on the basis of pre-established symbolic beliefs and values. If, however, the costs of the policy are clear and cognitively accessible to the consumer, as is the case with issues involving taxation, then they are more likely to evaluate issues on the basis of their self-interest (not supporting increased taxation of these products). Also, knowledge about potentially reduced exposure products did not play a role in influencing attitudes toward regulation of these products. Again, personal experience played a role, with people identifying as current smokers basing their attitude towards regulation more in terms of their self-interest (not supporting taxation), and non-smokers basing their attitude more in terms of their symbolic beliefs and values about government. So attitudes toward federal regulation of these products may be driven either by symbolic beliefs and values about the role of government and regulation, or consumer's self-interest in avoiding increased taxation. Message content (i.e., whether it triggers a response in terms of self-interest or symbolic beliefs) will play an important role in activating different attitude bases, and perhaps even different attitudes.

In general, the question posed in this section is: on what basis do consumers think about these messages and marketing claims about reduced harm? The research reviewed suggests that the psychology of attitudes can generate some new insights into understanding how consumers react to messages about products claiming reduced harm, and how their attitudes toward these products may shape their reaction to and processing of these messages, not to mention their consumer behavior and public health, more generally. Also, experience with these reduced exposure products plays an important role in shaping attitudes, whether attitudes are based more on affect than cognition, or on motives like self-interest or symbolic beliefs that suggest a functional perspective on the attitudes held. Future research will need to take these different types of attitude structures and functions into account when examining how people respond to and process messages about these products. If these are the bases on which consumers process product advertisements, then (consistent with the psychology of attitudes) these are the very processes that must be considered when developing and implementing effective interventions to persuade consumers about the risks and benefits of these products.

POLICY IMPLICATIONS

"A popular reduced-exposure cigarette," suggests Gertner (2005), "is the kind of earthquake that many in the public health field have anticipated, like a team of worried geologists, for several years. According to a number of scientists and tobacco policy makers, PREPs are the single most ethically agonizing and professionally confusing issue they have ever encountered" (p. 46). Based on the scientific issues reviewed in this chapter, there are substantive reasons to be concerned about the extent to which PREPs pose a public health threat to consumers. Moreover, as our chapter highlights, the implications of several biomarkers studies investigating the reduced exposure claims associated with PREPs suggest that these claims may well lead adolescent and adult consumers down very counterproductive pathways.

Underlying the idea that the marketing of PREPs may "send the wrong message" to the public and potentially mislead consumers is the "psychology of harm reduction" (MacCoun, 1998). The concept of *harm reduction* was developed during the 1980s as an approach to addressing the risks that illicit drugs pose to public health in the United States. Although this approach has been especially pertinent to the development and implementation of various harm reduction interventions in the context of drug control (e.g., needle and syringe exchanges, low-threshold methadone maintenance), the issues at the abstract level are remarkably similar to the issues associated with other policy domains such as PREPs. Each policy domain discussed by MacCoun (1998), for example, from needle exchange programs to school condom programs to welfare programs, "raises the question about the relative efficacy of policies that aim to reduce the harmful consequences of a risky behavior (harm reduction) versus policies designed to discourage the behavior itself ..." (pp. 1200–1201).

We suggest that the issues associated with PREPs and in particular the controversy surrounding the regulation of PREPs exemplify the psychology of harm reduction, according to MacCoun's (1998) analysis. For example, the goal of U.S. drug policy, has been *prevalence reduction* or "to reduce the total number of users by discouraging initiation on the part of nonusers, and by promoting abstinence for current users" (MacCoun, 1998, p.1199). But discouraging people from engaging in risky behavior is not the only goal in the development of an effective drug policy. MacCoun argues persuasively that there are other strategic options available for consideration when developing an effective national drug policy. Besides *prevalence reduction*, *quantity reduction* (encouraging people to reduce the frequency of the risky behavior) and *harm reduction* (reduce the harmful consequences of the behavior when it occurs) represent other, non-mutually exclusive goals for establishing an effective drug control policy.

Based on our discussion of the scientific issues associated with the marketing and promotion of PREPs, an extension of MacCoun's (1998) analysis would suggest that smoking cessation (or, rather, prevalence reduction) may represent only one strategy for tobacco control policy makers to consider. Reduced harm approaches may not lead to cessation, but cessation as an *exclusive* goal may not be as effective as its proponents claim (MacCoun, 1998). Thus, harm reduction and quantity reduction both represent important strategies that, in the PREPs context as well, are not mutually exclusive with a prevalence reduction strategy. However, as MacCoun discusses in his theoretical analysis of these three strategies in the drug policy domain, risk-benefit trade-offs must be systematically evaluated with scientific data before these three strategies can be successfully integrated into some sort of overall drug control or tobacco use policy (also see Kozlowski, Strasser, Giovino, Erickson, & Terza [2001] on their risk/use equilibrium for determining the most effective harm reduction strategy for current smokers). MacCoun (1998) offers several interesting hypotheses for thinking about how to integrate harm reduction and quantity reduction strategies with the more influential prevalence reduction strategy into a national drug control strategy. Perhaps the most pertinent of MacCoun's hypotheses with regard to developing tobacco control policies for PREPs is the following: "Harm-reduction interventions should have the greatest political viability when they can demonstrate a reduction in average harm—especially harms that affect nonusers—without increasing drug use levels" (MacCoun, 1998, p.1207). As reviewed in this chapter, reducing harm to nonusers and not increasing overall tobacco use levels are certainly central to the scientific and policy issues associated with PREPs: "An appealing product could have substantial population effects, by persuading smokers that cessation is unnecessary, persuading ex-smokers that it is now safe to resume smoking, and/or persuading potential initiates that smoking could be adopted without endangering themselves" (Shiffman, Gitchell, Warner, Slade, Henningfield, & Pinney, 2002, p. S121; also see Kozlowski et al., 2001). Therefore, as in the drug policy debate, it becomes important in the domain of regulatory policies pertaining to PREPs to develop a rigorous scientific database to be able to evaluate these different types of outcome effects: whether smokers perceive or have been persuaded that cessation is unnecessary; whether ex-smokers perceive or have been persuaded that it is now safe to resume smoking; and/or whether potential initiates perceive or have been persuaded that smoking could be adopted without endangering themselves.

The availability of scientific studies that shed credible light on these different types of consumer outcomes in the context of PREPs has become crucial. Many policy scholars and federal legislators are now calling for a change in the regulatory environment surrounding PREPs. U.S. Senators DeWine and Kennedy introduced legislation in 2004, for example, that called for FDA authority to regulate the sale, distribution, and advertising of cigarettes and smokeless tobacco, and to require manufacturers to disclose the contents and health consequences of products with new, stronger warning labels. However, these features never made it out of the joint Congressional conference committee and were not included in the legislation that subsequently passed (Hulse, 2004). The proposed legislation attracted considerable attention (Shatenstein, 2004) and certainly was not without its critics (Siegel, 2004). But others also argued that, overall, the pros associated with the proposed legislation outweighed the cons (Myers, 2004).

Well-known policy advocates like Matthew Myers, who directs the National Center for Tobacco-Free Kids, have argued for quite some time for strict testing standards and limits on the marketing claims that tobacco companies and pharmaceutical companies now affix to a variety of reduced exposure products. For example, Myers (2000) challenged the lack of health regulation over reduced exposure tobacco products, argued that tobacco companies cannot be the only source of scientific information about their products, and strongly advocated "full authority over tobacco for the FDA" as the only meaningful approach to effective government regulation of tobacco products. "Regulation of tobacco products by the FDA is not a panacea, but it is an essential component of the effort to reduce the death toll from tobacco use. To be effective, the FDA must be given formal authority over tobacco products, similar to the authority it currently has over drugs and drug-delivery devices. It must have the power to compel the tobacco companies to make public the full truth and to require changes in its products and marketing tactics in order to protect the public health" (p. 1809).

Myers is by no means alone in calling for federal regulation. The Institute of Medicine (2001) proffered several criteria for the regulation of PREPs, including the requirement that manufacturers disclose all ingredients to an appropriate regulatory authority, and the requirement of scientific proof before authorizing marketing claims about reduced harm, and mandating that labels and ads and market promotions not be "false or misleading." Hodge and Eber (2004) in their review and analysis of federal interventions to achieve tobacco control, suggested that federal regulation and oversight of tobacco industry marketing claims about the alleged safety of reduced exposure products is crucial to ensure the accuracy of information conveyed to consumers. "Lacking accurate data, people cannot make rational health decisions" (p. 4). Consumers, as Kozlowski and Edwards (2005) argue, have the right to consider scientifically-sound, health relevant information, including information about the comparative risks associated with different products.

More generally, Hodge and Eber (2004), like Warner and Martin (2003) and MacCoun (1998), argue that the development of any comprehensive tobacco control policy must at its core be science-based, and not based on conjecture or vested interests: "In areas where the prevalence of tobacco use in the population is unknown, or the public health effects in specific populations are unmeasured, policy makers and anti-tobacco advocates need to study the impact of tobacco use on the public's health" (p. 7).

Gilhooley (2002) also suggests that the legislative process is perhaps the most appropriate approach to establishing a regulatory scheme for tobacco control, especially if the goal is to involve FDA oversight. She points out that the IOM (2001) report that examined PREPs suggested that such products could be beneficial to consumers if there was an "adequate" regulatory scheme in place. In fact, Gilhooley argues even without *new* legislation the FDA's extant authority (as framed in the U.S. Supreme Court decision in *FDA v. Brown & Williamson Tobacco Corp.*, 2000) may already permit regulatory authority over reduced exposure products based on the rationale that such reduced-risk products are *intended* to prevent disease and may benefit those consumers who would like to stop smoking. Like Myers (2000) and the IOM report (2001), Gilhooley argues for less misleading testing and marketing procedures and a role for the FDA in ensuring that PREPs have an adequate scientific foundation. Her view is that a regulatory role for the FDA in this area is currently unresolved, but crucial, because of new products being introduced to consumers.

Based on the research reviewed in this chapter, calls for a change in the regulatory environment that would create strict testing standards and place limits on marketing claims seem justified on consumer health grounds. As this chapter has suggested, reduced exposure claims may well be misleading consumers and either undermining smoking cessation efforts or increasing the odds that PREPs, which in some instances have been shown to be as harmful as regular cigarettes, will be used by individuals who otherwise are not inclined to smoke. The latter claims are central to understanding the scope of the health threat to consumers, and, as MacCoun (1998) has suggested, these claims about outcomes are quite amenable to rigorous scientific assessment.

What role science-based regulatory policies will play remains to be seen, however. The history of developing, enacting, and enforcing legislative interventions in this arena, as Hodge and Eber (2004) discuss, reflects a complex set of considerations above and beyond just the need for accurate data and sound science. MacCoun (1998), for example, suggests that the development of an effective, integrated drug control policy also must contend with various instrumental (e.g., do reduced harm interventions reduce harm without increasing overall use?) and symbolic (e.g., biased beliefs about other people's ability to control their behavior, unresolved value conflicts, hostility toward *any* form of drug use) concerns: "The tone of the harm-reduction debate suggests that attitudes toward drug policies—on both sides—are influenced by deeply rooted and strongly felt symbolic factors that are largely independent of concerns about policy effectiveness per se" (p.1202). In addition, any underappreciation of the value of science-based policy recommendations must also take into consideration the extent to which policy makers may hold different views of scientific disciplines, and some disciplines, like psychological science, may be held in less regard by policy makers than others (Arkes, 2003). In other words, for legislators and other policy makers to appreciate, pay attention to, and commit to a scientific foundation for policy recommendations and legislation in the tobacco control arena will require an approach that incorporates more complex political and legal considerations as well as quality science.

ACKNOWLEDGMENTS

Preparation of this chapter was in part supported by pilot grant funding to Eugene Borgida from the Minnesota Transdisciplinary Tobacco Use Research Center, NCI/NIDA P50 DA-13333, 2002-2004. The authors wish to thank Mary Rumsey for her research assistance, and Dorothy Hatsukami, Anne M. Joseph, Lynn T. Kozlowski, Robert MacCoun, and Alex Rothman for their insightful comments on an earlier version of this chapter.

REFERENCES

Arkes, H. R. (2003). The nonuse of psychological research at two federal agencies. *Psychological Science, 14,* 1–6.

Bowman, D. L., Smith, C. J., Bombbick, B. R., Avalos, J. T., Davis, R. A., Morgan, W. T., & Doolittle, D.J.. (2002). Relationship between FTC 'tar' and urine mutagenicity in smokers of tobacco-burning or Eclipse cigarettes. *Mutation Research, 361,* 1–9.

Buchalter, A. R., & Eissenberg, T. (2000) Preliminary evidence of a novel smoking system: effects of subjective and psychological measures and on smoking behavior. *Nicotine and Tobacco Research, 2*(1), 39 –43.

Buchalter, A. R., Schrinel, L., & Eissenberg, T. (2001) Withdrawal-suppressing effects of a novel smoking system: comparison with own brand, not own brand, and de-nicotinized cigarettes. *Nicotine and Tobacco Research, 3*(2), 111 –8.

Chong, D., Citrin, J., & Conley, P. (2001). When self-interest matters. *Political Psychology, 22*, 541–570.

Crites Jr., S.; Fabrigar, L. & Petty, R. (1994). Measuring the affective and cognitive properties of attitudes: Conceptual and methodological issues. *Personality and Social Psychology Bulletin, 20*, 619–634.

Eagly, A. H., & Chaiken, S. (1993). *The psychology of attitudes.* Fort Worth, TX: Harcourt, Brace, Jovanovich.

Edwards, K. (1990). The interplay of affect and cognition in attitude formation. *Journal of Personality and Social Psychology, 59*, 202–216.

Fabrigar, L., & Petty, R. (1999). The role of the affective and cognitive bases of attitudes in susceptibility to affectively and cognitively based persuasion. *Personality and Social Psychology Bulletin, 25*, 363–381.

Fairchild, A., & Colgrove, J. (2004). Out of the ashes: The life, death and rebirth of the "safer" cigarette in the United States. *American Journal of Public Health, 94*, 192–204.

FDA v. Brown & Williamson Tobacco Corp., 529 U.S. 120 (2000). Petitioner's Reply Brief.

Gertner, J. (June 12, 2005). Incendiary device. The *New York Times Magazine*, 45–51.

Gilhooley, M. (2002). Tobacco unregulated: Why the FDA failed, and what to do now. *Yale Law Journal, 111*, 1179–1209.

Haddock, G., & Zanna, M. (1998). Assessing the impact of affective and cognitive information in predicting attitudes toward capital punishment. *Law and Human Behavior, 22*, 325–339.

Hamilton, W., Norton, G., Ouellette, T., Rhodes, W., Kling, R., & Connolly, G. (2004). Smokers' responses to advertisements for regular and light cigarettes and potential reduced-exposure products. *Nicotine & Tobacco Research, 6*, S353–S362.

Harris, J. E., Thun, M. J., Mondul, A. M., & Calle, E. E. (2004). Cigarette tar yield in relation to mortality from lung cancer in the cancer prevention study II prospective cohort, 1982–88. *British Medical Journal, 328*, 72–76.

Hatsukami, D., & Hecht, S. (2005). *Hope or hazard? What research tells us about "potentially reduced-exposure" tobacco products.* Report issued by the University of Minnesota Transdisciplinary Tobacco Use Research Center.

Hatsukami, D. K., Joseph, A. M., LeSage, M., Murphy, S. E., Pentel, P., Kotlvar, M., Borgida, E., Le, Chap, & Hecht, S. S. (in press). The science base for reducing tobacco harm. *Nicotine and Tobacco Research.*

Hatsukami, D. K., & Zeller, M. (2004). Tobacco harm reduction: The need for research to inform policy. *Psychological Science Agenda, 18*, 5–8.

Hatsukami, D. K., Henningfield, J. E., & Kotlyar, M. (2004). Harm reduction approaches to reducing tobacco-related mortality. *Annual Review of Public Health, 25*, 377–85.

Hecht, S. S., Murphy, S. E., Carmella, S. G., Li, S., Jensen, J., Le, C., Joseph, A. M., & Hatsukami, D. K. (2005). Similar uptake of lung carcinogens by smokers of regular, light and ultralight cigarettes. *Cancer Epidemiol Biomarkers Prevention, 14*, 693–698.

Hodge, J. G., Jr., & Eber, G. B. (2004). Tobacco control legislation: Tools for public health improvement. *Journal of Law, Medicine, and Ethics, 32*, 516–523.

Hughes, J. R., Hecht, S. S., Carmella, S. G., Murphy, S. E., & Callas, P. (2004). Smoking behavior and toxin exposure during six weeks use of a potential reduced exposure product: Omni. *Tobacco Control, 13*(2), 175–179.

Hulse, C. (July 16, 2004). Senate approves tobacco buyout and new curbs. The *New York Times*, p.A1, A20.

Institute of Medicine (2001). Clearing the smoke: Assessing the science base for tobacco harm reduction. Washington, DC: Author.

Johnston, D. C., & Warner, M. (September 26, 2006). Tobacco makers lose key ruling on latest suits: Light cigarettes at issue. *New York Times*, pp. A1 & C4.

Joseph, A. M., Hennrikus, D., Thoele, M. J., Krueger, R., & Hatsukami, D. (2004). Community tobacco control leaders' perceptions of harm reduction. *Tobacco Control, 13*, 108–113.

Kim, A., Borgida, E., & Stark, E. (2007). Symbolic politics and attitudes toward the regulation of reduced-exposure tobacco products. Unpublished manuscript, University of Minnesota.

Kozlowski, L. T. (1984). Less-hazardous tobacco use as a treatment for the "smoking and health" problem. In R. J. Smart, H. D. Cappell, F. Glaser, Y. Israel, H. Kalant, W. Schmitt, & E. M. Sellers (Eds.), *Research advances in drug and alcohol problems* (Vol. 8, 309–328). New York: Plenum.

Kozlowski, L.T., & Edwards, B.Q. (2005). "Not safe" is not enough: Smokers have a right to know more than there is no safe tobacco product. *Tobacco Control, 14*, ii3–ii7.

Kozlowski, L. T., Goldberg, M. E., Yost, B. A., White, E. L., Sweeney, C. S., & Pillitteri, J. L. (1998). Smokers' misperceptions of light and ultra light cigarettes may keep them smoking. *American Journal of Preventive Medicine, 15*, 9–16.

Kozlowski, L. T., Goldberg, M. E., Sweeney, C. T., Palmer, R.F., Pillitteri, J. L., White, E. L., & Stine, M. M.(1999). Smoker reactions to a radio message that light cigarettes are as dangerous as regulars. *Nicotine and Tobacco Research, 1*, 67–76.

Kozlowski, L.T., Berwood, Y., Stine, M. M., & Celebucki, C. (2000). Massachusetts' advertising against Light cigarettes appears to change beliefs and behavior. *American Journal of Preventive Medicine, 18*(4), 339–342.

Kozlowski, L. T., Strasser, A. A., Giovino, G. A., Erickson, P. A., & Terza, J. V. (2001). Applying the risk/use equilibrium: Use medicinal nicotine now for harm reduction. *Tobacco Control, 10*, 201–203.

MacCoun, R. J. (1998). Toward a psychology of harm reduction. *American Psychologist, 53*, 1199–1208.

MacCoun, R. J. (2004). Anticipating unintended consequences of vaccine-like immunotherapies for addictive drug use. In H. R. Harwood & T. G. Myers (Eds.), *New treatments for addiction: Behavioral, ethical, legal, and social questions.* National Research Council and the Institute of Medicine. Washington, DC: National Academy Press.

Millar, M., & Millar, K. (1990). Attitude change as a function of attitude type and argument type. *Journal of Personality and Social Psychology, 59*, 217–228.

Myers, M. L. (2000). Protecting the public health by strengthening the Food and Drug Administration's authority over tobacco products. *The New England Journal of Medicine, 343*(24), 1806–1809.

Myers, M. L. (2004). Opposition in search of a rationale: The case for Food and Drug Administration regulation. *Tobacco Control, 13*, 441–443.

Pauly, J. L., Mepani, A. B., Lesses, J. D., Cummings, K. M., & Streck, R. J. (2002). Cigarettes with defective filters marketed for 40 years: What Philip Morris never told smokers. *Tobacco Control, 11*, i51–i61.

Roethig, H. J., Kinser, R. D., Lau, R. W., Walk, R. A., & Wang, N.. (2005). Short-term exposure evaluation of adult smokers switching from conventional to first-generation electrically heated cigarettes during controlled smoking. *Journal of Clinical Pharmacology, 45(2)*, 133–145.

Sears, D.O., Lau, R. R., Tyler, T. R., Allen, H. M. (1979). Self-interest vs. symbolic politics in policy attitudes in presidential voting. *The American Political Science Review, 74*, 670–684.

Shatenstein, S. (2004). Food and Drug Administration regulation of tobacco products: introduction. *Tobacco Control, 13*, 438.

Shavitt, S., & Wanke, M. (2001). Consumer behavior. In A. Tesser & N. Schwarz (Eds.), *Blackwell handbook of social psychology: Intraindividual processes* (pp. 569–590). Oxford: Blackwell Publishers.

Shiffman, S., Gitchell, J. G., Warner, K. E., Slade, J., Henningfield, J. E., & Pinney, J. M. (2002). Tobacco harm reduction: Conceptual structure and nomenclature for analysis and research. *Nicotine & Tobacco Research, 4*, S113–S127.

Shiffman, S. et al. (2004). Smoker and ex-smoker responses to cigarettes claiming reduced risk. *Tobacco Control, 13*, 78–84.

Shiffman, S., Pillitteri, J. L., Burton, S. L., Rohay, J. M., & Gitchell, J. G. (2001a). Smoker's beliefs about "Light" and "Ultra Light" cigarettes. *Tobacco Control, 10*, i17–i23.

Shiffman, S., Pillitteri, J. L., Burton, S. L. Rohay, J. M., & Gitchell, J. G. (2001b). Effect of health messages about "Light" and "Ultra Light" cigarettes on beliefs and quitting intent. *Tobacco Control, 10*, i24–i32.

Siegel, M. (2004). Food and Drug Administration regulation of tobacco: Snatching defeat from the jaws of victory. *Tobacco Control, 13*, 439–440.

Smith, C. J., McKarns, S. C., Davis, R. A., Livingston, S. D., Bombick, B. R., Avalos, J. T., Morgan, W. T., & Doolittle, D. J. (1996). Human urine mutagenicity study comparing cigarettes which burn or primarily heat tobacco. *Mutation Research, 361*(1), 1–9.

Stark, E., Borgida, E., Kim, A., & Pickens, B. (in press). Understanding public attitudes toward tobacco harm reduction: The role of attitude structure. *Journal of Applied Social Psychology.*

Thun, M. J., & Burns, D. M. (2001). Health impact of "reduced yield" cigarettes: A critical assessment of the epidemiological evidence. *Tobacco Control, 10*, i4–i11.

U.S. Department of Health and Human Services. (1989). Reducing the health consequences of smoking: 25 years of progress: A report of the Surgeon General. (DHHS Publication No. (CDC) 89-8411). Washington, DC: Center for Chronic Disease Prevention and Health Promotion, Office on Smoking and Health.

U.S. Department of Health and Human Services. (2004). The health consequences of smoking: A report of the Surgeon General. Retrieved June 15, 2005, from http://www.cdc.gov/tobacco/sgr/sgr_2004/index.htm.

Warner, K. E. (2002). Tobacco harm reduction: Promise and perils. *Nicotine & Tobacco Research, 4*, S89-S101.

Warner, K. E., & Martin, E.G. (2003). The US tobacco control community's view of the future of harm reduction. *Tobacco Control, 12*, 383–390.

Young, J., Thompson, C. J., Borgida, E., Sullivan, J. L., & Aldrich, J. H. (1991). When self-interest makes a difference: The role of construct accessibility in political reasoning. *Journal of Experimental Social Psychology, 27*, 271–296.

37

Assessing the Relationship Between Tobacco Advertising and Promotion and Adolescent Smoking Behavior
Convergent Evidence

Marvin E. Goldberg

Pennsylvania State University

Society's concern for the manner in which adolescents negotiate the critical teenage years is evident. At the very broadest of levels, there are discussion forums and studies considering how our materialistic society is shaping youths at an increasingly younger age with values that give precedence to the quest for material things over other more time enduring values (Achenreiner, 1997; Kasser et al., 1995; Goldberg et al., 2003). Of more immediate concern are the risky behaviors that teens engage in including drug usage, underage alcohol consumption (National Research Council and Institute of Medicine, 2003); and smoking cigarettes (USDHHS, 1994). Inevitably, this leads to a consideration of what/who the critical influencers are and how to offset/counter these influences.

This chapter is concerned with the specific question: does the advertising and promotion of tobacco products influence the smoking behavior of youth? The choice of research methods in addressing issues such as the impact of advertising on youth typically involves a set of trade-offs and it is for this reason that researchers have argued for "triangulating" the results of multiple studies using a diversity of methods in the establishment of validity (Campbell & Fiske, 1959). Because each study has its own unique strengths and weaknesses, the convergence in findings that results from different methodological approaches "…enhances our belief that the results are valid and not a methodological artifact" (Bouchard, 1976, p. 268). It is the triangulation of data resulting from different measurement approaches that allow for the elimination of alternative explanations to the hypothesis at hand (Webb, Campbell, Schwartz, & Sechrest, 1966).

Most typically, it is the survey method and laboratory experiment that are juxtaposed. The strength of the former lies in its ability to assess the degree of covariation among naturally occurring phenomenon. Its weakness lies in its inability to permit the interpretation of causality. By contrast, laboratory experiments facilitate the interpretation of causal direction but fall short in their ability to assess the form of the relationship between predictor and dependent measures. Relatedly, a typical strength of the correlational study is its generalizability, while the strength of the experiment is its precision.

The evidence drawn upon in this chapter includes both studies using the survey method and laboratory experiment. More fully, the sections below review evidence drawn from: (1) longitudinal or prospective studies (using survey methods); (2) controlled, laboratory experiments; (3) econometric or time series analyses; (4) studies illustrating the effects of "shock" changes in tobacco advertising and promotion over time; (5) economic analysis; (6) evidence, drawn largely from tobacco industry documents, as to the goals of the industry regarding adolescents in their advertising and promotion efforts; (7) self-reports, in particular, by smokers.

Evidence of a relationship between tobacco advertising and adolescent smoking behavior would be strengthened to the extent there is evidence of a relationship between tobacco advertising and mediators that serve to heighten the risk of adolescent smoking. These mediators/risk factors include the degree to which advertising and promotion lead adolescents to develop: (1) positive imagery of smoking and smokers; (2) the perception of smoking as normative; (3) a "friendly familiarity" with tobacco and smoking as a valid/legitimate activity; (4) the high levels of tobacco brand identification on the part of even young children; evidence, in part of "friendly familiarity," and (5) evidence of advertising priming adolescents in ways that facilitate interpersonal (peer) influence.

Lastly, also examined in this chapter are the "enabling" conditions for tobacco advertising to be able to influence adolescents. These include: (1) the extent to which the key motives and goals adolescents have at their stage of development are reflected in tobacco advertising; (2) the degree to which adolescents' incomplete and immature understanding of the health risks of smoking and unrealistic expectations of how difficult it is to quit, makes them more vulnerable to tobacco advertising; (3) the degree to which adolescents are actually exposed to tobacco advertising and promotion; this includes both the nature and extent of tobacco advertising and promotion, and the degree to which these efforts have reached/captured adolescent audiences.

EMPIRICAL EVIDENCE OF THE EFFECTS OF TOBACCO ADVERTISING AND PROMOTION ON ADOLESCENTS

Longitudinal or Prospective Studies

Three longitudinal or prospective studies offer evidence regarding the relationship between cigarette advertising and cigarette uptake by youths (Aitken, Eadie, Hastings, & Haywood, 1991; Biener & Siegel, 2000; Pierce et al., 1998). These studies identify youths who initially do not smoke and express a disinclination to smoke, and then follow them over a period of time. When re-interviewed between 1 and 4 years later, significant numbers of these initially confirmed non-smokers had progressed towards smoking. In some cases they expressed the intention to smoke, in other cases they actually had begun to smoke. In all three studies, those who earlier had greater familiarity with or appreciation of tobacco advertising and/or those who had received or were willing to receive promotional materials from the tobacco companies, were more likely to have progressed towards smoking or to have begun smoking. Each study went to great lengths to rule out potential alternative influences that might have accounted for these results. These included the youth's socio-economic status, whether their family members or peers smoked and whether they were rebellious-type adolescents.

Pierce et al. (1998); California Study   From a considerably larger sample, 1,752 California adolescents were identified who had never smoked and were negatively predisposed towards smoking. These "nonsusceptible" teenagers indicated that they would "definitely not" (1) try a cigarette soon, (2) take a cigarette if offered by one of their best friends, (3) smoke a cigarette any time in the next year (note that even those who hesitated and indicated they would "probably not" smoke were not included in this category). These "nonsusceptible" teens were interviewed via telephone and then re-interviewed 3 years later. Among these youths, those who initially had been able to name a favorite cigarette ad and/or owned or were willing to consider owning a tobacco promotional item were more likely to have progressed towards smoking uptake 3 years later. The analyses indicated that tobacco advertising and promotion played an independent role, separate from factors such as peer or familial smoking. Those most receptive to both the advertising and promotions were almost three times more likely to have progressed towards smoking 3 years later.

Aitken et al. (1991); Scottish Study   In this study, 640 Glasgow youths, aged 11–14, were interviewed twice with a 1-year interval. Among those who initially claimed they would not smoke, those who were initially more aware of and/or more appreciative of cigarette advertising were more likely to have positive intentions to smoke 1 year later. Both of these factors were significant contributors towards the youths' intentions to smoke even after statistically accounting for the potential influence of a host of other factors that might represent competing explanations for the results (including socio-economic status and whether or not friends, parents, and siblings smoked).

Biener and Siegel (2000); Massachusetts Study   Over 500 adolescents ($n = 529$) who initially were disinclined to smoke were interviewed 4 years later. Those who initially had owned a tobacco promotional item and named a cigarette brand that attracted their attention were more than twice as likely to become established smokers, relative to adolescents who did neither. Statistical procedures were used to control for an extensive list of potentially confounding variables that might be responsible for the observed relationship. These included family and peer smoking, rebelliousness, and income.

Controlled, Causal Experiments

Two experiments complement the longitudinal studies considered above. As part of one larger study, a movie replete with cigarette smoking scenes (*Reality Bites* with Ethan Hawke and Winona Ryder; 1994) was used to create two experimental versions: in one a professional editor eliminated all smoking-related scenes, the other left the smoking scenes intact. Non-smoking ninth graders were then shown either the version of the movie with or without the smoking scenes. Those who saw the movie with the smoking scenes were: (1) more likely to indicate that they intended to smoke, and (2) more likely to regard those who smoke (including themselves, if they were to smoke) as smarter, more successful, more fit, and athletic (Pechmann & Shih, 1999). The conclusion drawn was that exposure to smoking by attractive actors is the cause of the youths' intentions to smoke and of their more positive image of smokers.[1]

An experiment conducted by Pechmann and Knight (2002) provides additional insight into how exposure to smoking stimuli works both directly and through peers to influence youths (Pechmann & Knight, 2002). As part of this study, over 700 California ninth graders were shown a 12-minute "reality" video that featured five ninth grade actors (ranging in appearance from attractive to unattractive). In a 2×2 design, four versions of the video were created. In the earlier part of each version, the teenagers in the video (the actors) were shown gathering ads, ostensibly for a communications class. In two of the versions, cigarette ads were among those gathered and displayed; in two others, they were not. In the latter part of each version, the teenage actors were shown sitting outdoors relaxing and having lunch. In two versions they smoked during the lunch; in two they did not.

After viewing the particular version of the videotape associated with the condition they were in, the subjects were then asked about their image of a smoker and whether they themselves intended to smoke. The results indicated a main effect for exposure to the cigarette advertising in the course of the video: the ninth graders who saw the cigarette ads being gathered and displayed held a more positive image of teenagers who smoke. This main effect was conditioned by an advertising by exposure to peer smoking interaction: relative to the three other conditions, those who were first exposed to tobacco advertising on the video and then saw the peers (actors) smoking over lunch had a relatively more positive image of smokers and heightened intentions to smoke.

The researchers in the two experiments reported above were ethically prohibited from actually offering cigarettes to youths in an effort to assess the effects of the stimuli to which they are exposed. Results were limited to the youths' expressed intentions. This restriction does not apply in the case of food advertising. Here, experiments have shown a direct link between exposure to advertising and children's actual consumption behavior. In one study set in a summer camp, every day for 2 weeks, children were exposed to TV commercials for either candy or fruit and either Kool-Aid or orange juice in the course of a cartoon program. When subsequently offered choices between fruit or candy and between the two beverages for daily afternoon snacks, their selections reflected the advertising to which they had been exposed (Goldberg & Gorn, 1982). To the extent that this reflects what might occur in tobacco experiments were cigarettes offered to youths, these results offer further evidence of the potential for tobacco advertising to impact actual smoking behavior by youths.

Econometric Studies

Econometric or time-series studies have assessed the relationship between the level of tobacco advertising expenditures and the level of tobacco consumption over time, factoring out other possible influences. A meta-analysis that combined 50 different econometric studies (about half domestic and half foreign, including 24 with estimates of advertising elasticities) concluded that advertising for cigarettes does build aggregate demand over time; the greater the level of advertising expenditures, the greater the level of tobacco consumption (Andrews & Franke, 1991).

Very few adults begin to smoke in their adult years, and most smokers have developed smoking habits/levels that are typically not subject to radical change. As a result, econometric studies that focus on the broad (adult) population are limited in the extent to which they can show year-to-year changes in the level of tobacco consumption as a result of changes in levels of advertising expenditures. By contrast, Lewit, Coate, and Grossman (1981) examined the relationship between level of advertising over a number of years and tobacco usage for 12- to 17-year-olds, who are in their formative period with regard to tobacco consumption and so, less "anchored" by habit.

Lewit et al. used data from the U.S. Health Examination Survey (HES III) with a total sample of over 5,000 youths, aged 12–17, collected annually from 1966–70. The study focused on TV, the medium emphasized by the industry during this period; (in 1970, just prior to the ban on TV advertising, that medium accounted for well over half—57.4%—of all tobacco advertising and promotion expenditures; FTC, 2005). Time series analyses were conducted using the sample of youths. The researchers used data as to the number of cigarette commercials aired on TV for the 12 months prior to each annual measurement period; they then used each youth's report as to how much TV he or she watched during that period to develop an estimate of actual exposure to cigarette commercials. Beyond these two key measures, several additional measures were also obtained and controlled for in the analyses. These included: the price of cigarettes for each time period in each locality in which the respondent lived; level of smoking by siblings/friends; parental smoking and demographic factors, including income.

The analyses revealed a significant relationship between level of exposure to tobacco advertising on TV for the 12 months prior to measurement and the likelihood of the teen being a current smoker at that point. Holding all other factors constant, for every 10 hours per week they watched TV in the previous year, they were 11% more likely to be a current smoker.

At the brand level, separate econometric analyses of adolescent and adult cigarette purchases/preferences indicate that adolescent smokers' brand preferences are much more closely related to the levels of cigarette advertising expenditures over time (Pollay et al., 1996). Teen's brand preference elasticities (sensitivity to advertising levels) are 3 times that of adults. Given that this refers in considerable measure to starter smokers, these results likely reflect more than a fight for market share, but are indicative of advertising's power to stimulate aggregate demand by inducing additional adolescents to begin to smoke.

The brand preferences of teenagers (far more than adults) converge around the three most heavily advertised brands (Pierce et al., 1991; Pollay et al., 1996). During the recession of the early 1990s as many as 40% of adults shifted to nonadvertised cheaper generic brands. This was not true for teenagers, who, despite their limited level of discretionary dollars, continued to purchase the more expensive, heavily advertised brands (Cavin & Pierce, 1996).

STUDIES ILLUSTRATING THE EFFECTS OF "SHOCK" CHANGES IN THE TOBACCO ENVIRONMENT OVER TIME

Econometric studies tend to measure small and gradual increases in tobacco advertising from year to year and so are limited in the degree to which they can show a relationship between tobacco advertising and consumption. By contrast, alternative studies have been able to measure larger, more dramatic year-to-year changes in the level of exposure to tobacco advertising. The discussion below points to an assessment of levels of tobacco consumption where tobacco advertising was either rapidly introduced or withdrawn from various markets.

In the mid-to-late 1980s, significant increases in advertising expenditures for American cigarettes were associated with the elimination of trade barriers for American cigarettes in four southeast Asian countries—South Korea, Thailand, Japan, and Taiwan. This resulted in: (1) an increased share of market for American cigarettes, and (2) an estimated increase of 10% in total cigarette consumption above and beyond the secular trend. The increases were proportionately lower in South Korea and Thailand where relatively more restrictions were placed on the nature and amount of advertising and proportionately greater in Japan where fewer restrictions were put in place (Chaloupka & Laixuthai, 1996).

Evidence from broad studies of sharp reductions in the level of tobacco advertising due to advertising bans reveals reductions in cigarette consumption. A study of 102 countries from 1981 to 1991 documents that countries with *comprehensive* ad bans saw an average decrease in per capita cigarette consumption of about 8%. Countries without comprehensive ad bans saw a decrease in consumption of about 1% (Saffer, 2000). A related study reanalyzed a wide set of time series, cross-sectional and tobacco advertising ban studies. These included data pertaining to countries with no, limited or comprehensive ad bans and the corresponding levels of cigarette consumption. The researchers concluded that while a comprehensive ad ban would result in a lowering of cigarette consumption by about 8%, *partial* ad bans aren't effective because of circumvention strategies on the part of the tobacco industry. In essence, there is considerable substitutability among the various advertising and promotion vehicles the tobacco industry can and has used to reach its market (Saffer & Chaloupka, 2000)

Considering 22 OECD countries from 1960 to 1986, Laugesen and Meads (1991) arrived at a similar conclusion: "If those countries without a complete tobacco advertising ban had introduced such a total ban in early 1986 consumption in the year would have ... [decreased by] 6.8%" (Laugesen & Meads, 1991, p. 1351). The findings of a 1989 New Zealand government study of tobacco promotion and tobacco consumption in 33 countries converges with the studies cited above. Across these various countries, to the extent advertising and promotion were constrained, aggregate consumption of tobacco was reduced; where they were not, aggregate consumption increased. In countries like Norway, there was a significant decline in tobacco consumption. In countries where advertising and promotion were partially curtailed, there was a more modest reduction in tobacco consumption and where tobacco companies had full access to all media, there was an increase in tobacco consumption over time. In Norway, where advertising and promotion were completely eliminated, there was a decline of 7% among 15- to 16-year-old boys and 11% among 15- to 16-year-old girls from before to after the enactment of the regulations (New Zealand Toxic Substance Board, 1989).

Historical evidence in the United States indicates that advertising campaigns for a particular brand with appeal for young audiences have been successful not only in stimulating demand for that particular brand, but for all brands with that same target audience. These campaigns were not simply a battle for market share—one brand's success did not come at the expense of other brands. As an example, the R.J. Reynolds' "Joe Camel" campaign succeeded in increasing demand for the Camel brand among (mainly male) adolescents from below 4% in 1987 to 13% by 1993 (Food and Drug Administration, 1996). During the same period, the percentage of 12th-grade boys who smoked rose from 27% to 31% (Johnston, O'Malley, & Bachman, 2001). This "larger pie" meant that Camel's increased share did not, in itself, contribute to a reduction in the number of smokers of other brands. (In fact, the total percentage of males who smoked increased sharply to 37% by 1997 and only then, coincident with the termination of the Joe Camel campaign, did the rate start to decline).

Economic Analysis

An economic analysis suggests that given the very high degree of brand loyalty of smokers, it would be quite maladaptive to spend the considerable amounts of money on advertising and promotion (as described below) in an effort to simply win greater market share (Davis, 1996; Siegel et al., 1996; see also Phillip Morris, 1990). Less than 10% of smokers switch brands in any given year and only 7% switch from one company's brands to another's. The bottom line value of these smokers to a tobacco firm is miniscule compared to the money expended on advertising and promotion. With nine in ten smokers starting by the time they are 18 and over half of these smoking daily by that age (USDHHS, 1994), it would be unusual if youths were not of considerable interest to the tobacco companies. As evidence of this perspective, consider the following analysis by an R.J. Reynolds executive, expressing the view that the value of young starter smokers who commit to a particular brand is of considerable financial importance to the tobacco firms:

> Strong performance among younger adult smokers [defined in Appendix B as 14–24] is critical to generating sustained growth momentum for brands/companies....Younger adult gains have been a long term leading indicator of the brand's market share gains....A "first brand" strategy (which necessarily targets younger adult smokers) provides an opportunity for unique long term benefits.... (R.J. Reynolds, 1984, pp. 27–28)

> Therefore, RJR should make a substantial long term commitment of manpower and money dedicated to younger adult smoker programs. (R.J. Reynolds, 1984, p, iii)

Evidence From Internal Corporate Documents

Over the past 10 to 15 years, extensive internal corporate documents have been made available as a function of litigation (see for example, *State of Minnesota et al. v. Philip Morris et al.,* 1998). The documents are most readily accessible through http://www.tobaccodocuments.org. Using these documents, the strategic focus of the tobacco industry on adolescents as a key target market has been well documented (Cummings, Morley, Horan, Steger, Leavell, 2002). The document cited above support this perspective. In the section below, we draw on a broader set of these documents to paint a more comprehensive picture of the goals and tactics of the tobacco industry with regard to youths.

A 1981 Philip Morris report entitled "Young Smokers: Prevalence, Trends, Implications, and Related Demographic Trends" is emphatic in the criticality of underage smokers to Philip Morris:

> It is important to know as much as possible about teenage smoking patterns and attitudes. Today's teenager is tomorrow's potential regular customer, and the overwhelming majority of smokers first begin to smoke while still in their teens.... The smoking patterns of teenagers are particularly important to Philip Morris.... Furthermore, it is during the teenage years that the initial brand choice is made: At least a part of the success of Marlboro Red during its most rapid growth period was because it became the brand of choice among teenagers who then stuck with it as they grew older.... Because of our high share of the market among the youngest smokers, Philip Morris will suffer more than the other companies from the decline in the number of teenage smokers. (pp. 1–2; emphasis added)

An earlier Philip Morris document indicated that Philip Morris strategically sought to attract young starters: "we also should win more young non-smokers with mildness" (Philip Morris, 1959).

A 1978 Lorillard document was straightforward in its interest in underage high school smokers. In a memo to the then CEO of Lorillard, Curtis Judge, T.L. Achey noted: "The success of NEW-PORT has been fantastic during the past few years....*the base of our business is the high school student*" (emphasis added).

All firms in the tobacco industry had similar interests in the youth market, as competitively, they would have to. An American Tobacco company document entitled "The American Tobacco Company Lucky Filters" (Jan. 5, 1968), begins by stating that it's immediate marketing objective was: "To obtain trial on a broad scale for Lucky Strike Filters (either 100mm or 85mm) with current filter cigarette smokers, *particularly the younger smoker and the new smoker entering the market*" (emphasis added). Similarly, their long term objective was: "To establish Lucky Strike Filters as a primary brand with enough filter smokers, *particularly younger smokers and new smokers entering the market,* to enable Lucky Strike Filters to at least offset the decline of Lucky Strike Regulars" (emphasis added).

A 1973 report offered detailed directions as to how R.J. Reynolds should strategically focus on the "youth market," defined as "those in the approximately twenty-one and under group."

> *Realistically, if our company is to survive and prosper, over the long term we must get our share of the youth market.* In my opinion this will require new brands tailored to the youth market.... Brands tailored for the *beginning smoker* should emphasize the desirable psychological effects of smoking.... Happily, then, it should be possible to aim a cigarette promotion at the beginning smoker at the same time making it attractive to the confirmed smoker. (R. J. Reynolds, 1973, pp 1, 4; emphasis added)

> If we are to attract the nonsmoker or the pre-smoker [typically those under 18], there is nothing in this type of product that he would currently understand or desire...Instead, we somehow must convince him with wholly irrational reasons that he should try smoking. (R.J. Reynolds 1973)

A 1980 R.J. Reynolds internal memorandum expressed concern that the company was losing market share among 14- to 17-year-olds and concluded "Hopefully, our various planned activities that will be implemented this fall will aid in some way in reducing or correcting these trends." (R.J. Reynolds, 1980).

A 1974 document entitled "Domestic Operating Goals" was presented to the R.J. Reynolds board of directors. The first goal listed was to: "Increase our Young Adult Franchise." "Young adult" was defined in the document as 14- to 24-year-olds. A subsequent statement makes R.J. Reynolds' strategy clear: "*We will direct advertising appeal to this young adult group....*" (emphasis added; R.J. Reynolds, 1974).

A 1972 R.J. Reynolds memorandum commented on the need for a new product that appealed to youths:

> Competitive brands, e.g. Marlboro and Kool, have exhibited exceptional strength in the under 35 age group, especially the 14–24 group. RJR Brands do not generally skew toward the younger socio-economic groups, and *a product strategically targeted at this group would complement our current product line.* (emphasis added; R.J. Reynolds, 1972)

Insofar as the marketers at these firms did not consider it a waste of their time, energy or money to target youths via their promotional and advertising efforts, their working assumption would have to be that these efforts and expenditures would pay off by generating new young smokers— that there was/is a causal relationship between their efforts and the outcomes they sought/seek.

Self-Reports

When asked to select the most important 13 reasons that led them to start smoking, few youths chose advertising (Boddewyn, 1987). However, as Pollay (1993) points out, for these results to be taken at face value would require that youths both understand and admit to advertising's impact upon them. An extensive body of research suggests that not just children, but adults tend to be inaccurate in understanding and reporting on the causes of their own behavior. In a wide series of experiments "...factors that had a pronounced effect on behavior were denied to have had any effect... and ... factors that had no detectable effect were asserted to be influential" (Nisbett & Ross, 1980)

As an example, one experiment (Weiss & Brown, 1977) illustrated that people cannot accurately report on the causes of their own happiness or unhappiness. Women were asked to keep a diary for 2 months, recording their mood each day and several possible causes of that mood including: the amount of sleep they had the night before, day of the week, the weather etc. At the end of the 2 months of diary keeping, the women were asked for their perceptions as to how important each factor was in determining their mood. There were great discrepancies between the day-to-day factors that actually predicted their daily mood and what the women *felt* were important predictors of their mood. For example, across the sample, using the daily data, "day of the week" tended to be fairly significant, while sleep was not. When asked, the women generally felt that the opposite was true.

In the same way, Pechmann and Knight (2002) report that "self-reported reasons for smoking may be misleading " (p. 15). Smokers tend to attribute their smoking uptake to the influence of their peers who smoke(d), given how proximate and obvious these peers are, yet fail to recognize the more distal and subtle, yet powerful influence of tobacco advertising (Pechmann & Knight, 2002).

MEDIATORS OF THE RELATIONSHIP BETWEEN ADVERTISING AND PROMOTION AND ADOLESCENT SMOKING BEHAVIOR

Positive Imagery of Smoking and Smokers

Youths as young as 12 years of age understand and can play back the main advertising themes associated with cigarette smoking, including success, romance, and independence (Aitken, Leather, &

O'Hagan, 1985). Through repetitive exposure to tobacco advertising campaigns, a subset of adolescents learn to associate smoking with specific (stereotypic) attributes of smokers; in particular, being cool or macho ("cool," "tough," and "brave") and being social: ("being popular," "likes dating," and "likes to be with a group"). This represents an important part of a process inducing adolescents to smoke: across a 1-year span, when an adolescent's actual or desired self-image was more closely aligned with the stereotypic image of a smoker, the adolescent was almost twice as likely to become a smoker, compared to the adolescent whose self-image was more disparate with that of a smoker (Aloise-Young, Hennigan, & Graham, 1996). In a parallel study, adolescents whose self-concept and that of their "ideal date" were more closely aligned with the smoker stereotype, were more likely to be smokers; if non-smokers, they were more likely to indicate they intended to smoke (Chassin, Presson, Sherman, Corty, & Oshavsky, 1981).

Perception of Smoking as Normative

Heavy exposure to cigarette advertising creates a perception that smoking is more prevalent than it actually is. In effect, adolescents develop the belief that the pervasiveness of cigarette marketing and advertising is, itself, an accurate barometer of how many people smoke. Research supports this perspective: adolescents who are more exposed to magazine advertising for cigarettes estimate a higher prevalence of cigarette smoking (Botvin, Goldberg, Botvin, & Dusenbury, 1993). Overestimation of the number of peers who smoke is a strong risk factor leading to smoking: adolescents who believe that many of their peers smoke, are likely to see it as a more acceptable behavior (Chassin et al., 1984; Leventhal, Glynn, & Fleming, 1987).

"Friendly Familiarity" With Tobacco and Smoking and the "Truth Effect"

The heavy advertising expenditures by tobacco advertisers detailed below leads to multiple exposures on the part of the consumer, resulting in a "friendly familiarity" with tobacco and smoking, with the resulting "truth effect." Advertising claims that are made familiar by virtue of repeated exposure to the claim are perceived as more truthful than they would be in the absence of such repetition—regardless of the underlying truth or falsity of the claims at issue (Hawkins & Hoch, 1992). Psychologists call this "the truth effect" (Hasher, Goldstein, & Toppino, 1977). Advertising executives have labeled it "friendly familiarity" (Burnett, 1961, p. 217, cited in USDHHS, 1994, p. 172). Just as people react to the unknown with some level of discomfort, they find comfort in the familiar. Moreover, such familiarity-induced comfort can lead people to believe that what is familiar is also true, regardless of whether it actually is true or false. When consumers recognize that they have come across an advertising claim or message before, they are more likely to believe it is true. This is especially the case under the very common condition in which advertising is processed under low involvement conditions—as a background phenomenon, as we catch the ad out of the corner of our eye.

High Levels of Tobacco Brand Identification as Evidence of "Friendly Familiarity"

Extensive tobacco advertising campaigns over many decades has led many youths to have a high level of name and logo recognition. During the time the R.J. Reynolds Joe Camel campaign ran, the cartoon camel, Joe, was as recognizable to children as young as pre-schooler age as was Mickey Mouse (Fischer et al., 1991). Inasmuch as Joe Camel was prohibited from appearing on TV, the high level of recognition among these preschoolers is evidence of the character's omnipresence in other media, from in-store signage to billboards to magazine ads.

The extensive level of worldwide advertising and promotion for American cigarettes is evident in recognition studies among 8- to 13-year-olds in Hong Kong and Turkey. In Hong Kong, when the Marlboro red chevron logo was inserted among five other logos representing different product categories, 76% of the children were able to identify the chevron as representing a brand of cigarettes. When the Marlboro name, as produced in Chinese characters was (separately) presented to the children it was correctly classified as a cigarette by 95% of them (Peters et al., 1995). Similarly in Turkey, brand name and logo recognition rates for Camel was 84% and 91% respectively and for Marlboro was 92% and 70% respectively (Emri, Tülay, Karakoca, & Baris, 1998). It is evident that heavy advertising leads to a familiarity with brand names for even the very young.

Advertising Primes Adolescents, Facilitating Interpersonal (Peer) Influence

As the Pechmann and Knight (2002) experiment reviewed above suggests, by glamorizing tobacco smoking and tobacco smokers, the tobacco advertising helps sensitize, shape, or "prime" how adolescents view their peers who smoke. Those who have been exposed to the tobacco advertising will tend to see the featured, glamorized traits in their smoking peers, who in the absence of the advertising would be seen as quite average (ranging, as they do in the Pechmann and Knight 2002 experiment, from attractive to unattractive). The last step in this process is when those who have been exposed to the tobacco advertising come to regard the peers as role models and are influenced by them to smoke (Pechmann & Knight, 2002).

It has also been observed that to the extent studies document a relationship between having friends who smoke and smoking, this is reflective of peer *selection* and not peer *pressure*. Susceptible teens peruse their environment in a radar-like fashion and identify peers with whom they would like to "hang out." As noted in the Pechmann and Knight (2002) study above, for a significant subset of these youths, the images shaped by tobacco advertising serve to enhance their views of smokers and so they gravitate to these peers. Note that this is *not*, as cigarette companies would describe, a situation in which a set of smoking teenagers approach a lone peer and pressure him/her to begin smoking. (Leventhal & Keeshan, 1993; Urberg, Shiang-Jeou, & Liang, 1990).

The conjunction of advertising and promotion with interpersonal influence among youths is readily modeled by the "multi-step" flow of influence (Assael, 2004). This process refers to the fact that those around us can and do influence us, but this influence comes as a consequence of the media messages to which we are all exposed (Assael, 2004).

More recently, this process has been referred to as viral marketing (Godin, 2001):

> …the future belongs to marketers who establish a foundation and process where interested people can market to *each other*. Ignite consumer networks and then get out of the way and let them talk" (Godin, 2001, p. 15; emphasis in the original).

Advertising serves to initiate discussion by both "opinion leaders" and their "followers" who touch base with one another to assess the merits of what they have seen/heard. As Godin further notes:

> …the advertiser creates an environment in which the idea can replicate and spread. It's the virus that does the work, not the marketer (Godin, 1995, p. 26)

An analysis of the six most popular brands of the mid-20th century uses the term "bandwagon effect" to capture something parallel to the multi-step flow or viral marketing: an R.J. Reynolds report (R.J. Reynolds, 1984) identifies a "bandwagon effect" that accrues to a "first brand" which achieves a 30% share among underage smokers (p. 28). It is the widespread exposure of this segment to the advertising in question that creates the initial level of focus on the brand by youths and from that point, the bandwagon or viral effect, ensures the brand's eventual dominance (Burrows, 1984; pp. 27–28).

ENABLING CONDITIONS

Adolescents' Motives/Goals Render Them Uniquely Vulnerable to Tobacco Advertising. Tobacco Advertising Reflects These Motives/Goals

Individuation   As part of a natural maturation process, young adolescents want and need to separate from their parents and develop separate identities even as they seek approval from their peers (Steinberg, 1993). One aspect of individuation is that the adolescent is motivated to take increasing responsibility for his/her actions—to make independent decisions (Steinberg, 1993). Research funded by tobacco companies has given these firms an understanding of this process and enabled them to exploit it. A Canadian industry report describes young male smokers as "going through a stage where they are seeking to *express their independence and individuality… [smoking] … appeals to their rebellious nature….*" (Imperial Tobacco, 1982, p. 119; emphasis added)

By positioning Marlboro as it has, Philip Morris has fully capitalized on the adolescent motive to individuate:

> Smoking a cigarette for the beginner is a symbolic act. The smoker is telling his world, 'This is the kind of person I am.' Surely there are many variants of the theme, 'I am no longer my mother's child,' 'I am tough' 'I am adventurous' 'I'm not a square.' (Philip Morris document, 1969, p. 3)

> … the Marlboro cowboy symbolizes the ability to make your own decisions…he represents the ability to make a choice and a decision. (Morgan in Thames Broadcasting Co. interview, 1976, p. 3)

Similarly, in *State of Minnesota et al. vs. Philip Morris et al.* Morgan was asked: "Well does the Marlboro Man project self-reliance, independence?" He responded: "I'd say those are values I—I would associate with Marlboro, yes" (Morgan, 1998).

Growing Up   In a presentation to the Philip Morris Board of Governors, a senior Philip Morris executive, states: "The 16 to 20 year old begins smoking for psychosocial reasons. The act of smoking is symbolic; it signifies adulthood…." (Wakeham, 1969, p. 8). The tobacco firms understand that there is nothing a 17-year-old would rather be than 21; nothing a 15-year-old would rather be than 18. This dynamic cannot be captured by "hanging out" with other 15-year-olds; hence the power of using young, attractive models in cigarette advertising. Adolescents look up to and aspire to be like the young, attractive models in cigarette ads. While tobacco advertisers are restricted by their own code to using models who are 25 years of age or older, research has documented that the models they select are perceived by a significant portion of the population to be younger than that (Mazis, Ringold, Perry, & Denman, 1992).

Industry documents make it clear that the tobacco firms understood this dynamic: "As a group, younger smokers probably emulate the smoking habits in the next oldest group, the 18–24 year olds…" (R.J. Reynolds, 1977). In fact, in targeting 15-year-olds, it is *more* powerful and effective to use 25-year-olds who look like 21 than it would be to use 15-year-olds. In court testimony, A. Schindler, CEO of R.J. Reynolds, acknowledged the influence of older teens upon younger teens (*State of Minnesota et al. v. Philip Morris et al.*, 1998, p. 6438–6439):

> *Question:* Do you think 18-year-olds influence 17-year-olds?
> *Schindler:* I imagine they do.
> *Question:* Do you think 19-year-olds influence 17-year-olds?
> *Schindler:* I imagine they might, yes.
> *Question:* They're called peers; aren't they?
> *Schindler:* You—could call them peers.

In its 1967 report to Congress, the FTC recognized that the Cigarette Advertising Code's prohibition of the use of young models had failed to protect young people:

> The most startling example of an advertisement that does not violate any of the specific prohibitions of the Cigarette Code is the Lucky Strike jingle that states: "Lucky Strike separates the men from the boys—but not from the girls." In which category—with "the men" or with "the boys"—would any normal teenage male want to place himself? (FTC 1967 Report to Congress; p. 27)

Equally, when Philip Morris advertised that it "…doesn't Want Kids to Smoke"; but then portrayed the decision to smoke as "forbidden fruit" saying, "we believe smoking is an *adult* decision" (Philip Morris, undated advertisement, emphasis added), that could readily stimulate an adolescent's interest in smoking.

Acceptance by Peers   As discussed above, advertising effects are likely to be mediated (facilitated or transmitted) by social agents—among others—peers. Peers are an important part of the teenager's environment. Together, peers experience the influence of the culture around them, including the heavy levels of cigarette advertising. They gather together to communicate and validate their understanding of their culture and in so doing, create shared meaning for themselves. Cigarettes and smoking are part of this shared meaning, helping to cement group members' ties to one another and separating them from those not sharing this activity—including their parents.

With a relatively weak sense of self and correspondingly shaky self-confidence, adolescents feel they are on stage and their every move is being closely examined (Lynch & Bonnie, 1994, p. 119]. They seek the approval and support of peers and, in this relatively vulnerable state, they are open to suggested "props" that will help them portray a desired image so as to be accepted by others. Tobacco firms have recognized adolescents' vulnerabilities by creating advertising that skillfully associates positive images with tobacco products and in so doing provides youths with some of these props. Consider the following comment in an R.J. Reynolds planning document for Camels:

> …CAMEL advertising will be directed toward using peer acceptance/ influence to provide the motivation for target smokers to select CAMEL. Specifically, advertising will be developed with the objective of convincing target smokers that by selecting CAMEL as their usual brand they will project an image that will enhance their acceptance among their peers. (R.J. Reynolds, 1986)

There is little question that the above comment is made with adolescents in mind. Since sensitivity to peers has been found to peak at the 9th grade (14- to 15-year-olds; Berndt, 1996) it is adolescents that are the most vulnerable to this type of campaign. Indeed, it makes no sense to contemplate anyone other than a teenager trying to gain "peer acceptance/influence" by virtue of which brand of cigarettes they were smoking.

ADOLESCENT VULNERABILITY IS MANIFESTED IN THEIR INCOMPLETE AND IMMATURE UNDERSTANDING OF THE HEALTH RISKS OF SMOKING AND UNREALISTIC EXPECTATIONS OF HOW DIFFICULT IT IS TO QUIT

While almost all youths agree that smoking a package a day will eventually harm a person's health, 40% of those who smoke believe that "…the very next cigarette…will probably not cause any harm." Half of those who smoke believe that "harmful effects of smoking rarely occur until a person has smoked steadily for many years" (Slovic, 2000). These views are likely to encourage adolescents to start smoking.

Relatedly, smoking initiation by youths is also encouraged by their failure to appreciate the difficulty smokers have in stopping smoking once one has started. Well over half (56%) of youths who smoke indicate that they "probably" or "definitely" will not be smoking in 5 years time. Nevertheless, 5–6 years later, over two thirds (68%) were still smoking; the vast majority (87%) at the same level or higher (Monitoring the Future Project, Institute for Social Research, University of Michigan, unpublished data as reported in Lynch & Bonnie, 1994, pp. 50–55). This relatively high level of continued smoking results not from a lack of efforts by the young to quit. Almost three quarters (74%) of 12- to 18-year-old smokers in a national survey indicated they had seriously thought about quitting and almost half (49%) indicated they had tried to quit within the previous 6 months (Lynch & Bonnie, 1994).

More recently, a parallel analysis, based on a 1995 follow up survey, showed similar results. "Nearly two-thirds (63%) of those who had been daily smokers in the twelfth grade were still daily smokers 7 to 9 years later, although in high school only 3% of them had thought they would 'definitely' be smoking five years hence." (Johnston, O'Malley, & Bachman, 2002, p. 26). Evidently, even at this early age, quitting is not an easy task. In fact, girls can become nicotine dependent within weeks, and boys within months (DiFranza et al., 2002).

In sum, this evidence suggests that adolescents tend to see little risk from smoking in the near future and that they underestimate the difficulties they are likely to have in stopping smoking. As such they can be viewed as a relatively vulnerable audience. Not surprisingly, it is largely in the teenage years that smokers indicate they started to smoke. Nearly 9 in 10 adults (89%) aged 30–39 who smoke indicate they started before age 18; more than 6 in 10 (62%) were smoking before age 16. Over half (53%) were smoking daily by age 18, and over three quarters (77%) by age 20 (Lynch & Bonnie, 1994; USDHHS, 1994). In effect, if one doesn't start smoking as an adolescent, one is unlikely to start smoking at all.

THE NATURE AND EXTENT OF TOBACCO INDUSTRY ADVERTISING AND PROMOTION ENSURES ADOLESCENT EXPOSURE

What is the evidence that adolescents are, in fact, exposed to tobacco advertising?

From 1940 to 2006, the tobacco industry spent over $250 billion on advertising and promotion—averaging about $10 million per day. (data drawn from Federal Trade Commission; FTP, 2007; figures for years prior to 1970, 1971 through 1974, and 2006 are estimates; all expenditures reported are adjusted to 2006 dollars). In 2005, the last year for which figures are available, the industry spent over $13.5 billion—about $37 million per day (FTC, 2007).

As indicated in Table 37.1, total expenditures climbed from $1.9 billion in 1970 to $13.5 billion in 2005 (FTC, 2007). Across the same time period, the percentage of total marketing expenditures shifted dramatically: from 82% allocated for advertising and just 18% for promotion in 1970 to almost 100% for promotion and 0% for advertising in 2005 (FTC, 2007). This shift to promotion

Table 37.1   Cigarette Advertising and Promotional Expenditures in the United States, 1970–2005
Relative Emphasis on Advertising vs Promotion (in hundreds of millions of dollars*)

	Advertising Expenditures in Measured Media†	Promotional Expenditures & "Others"‡	Total
1970	$1,526 (82%)	$332 (18%)	$1,858
1975	$1,228 (67%)	$596 (33%)	$1,824
1980	$1,915 (64%)	$1,096 (36%)	$3,011
1985	$1,730 (38%)	$2,867 (62%)	$4,597
1990	$1,276 (21%)	$4,823 (79%)	$6,099
1995	$740 (12%)	$5,674 (88%)	$6,414
2000	$413 (4%)	$10,711 (96%)	$11,124
2005	$58 (0%)	$13,475 (100%)	$13,533

Source of data: Federal Trade Commission (FTC, 2007)
*Adjusted to 2006 dollars using the consumer price index (all items).
†Advertising expenditures include newspapers, magazines, outdoor, and transit.
‡Promotional expenditures include point of sale, promotional allowances, Sampling distribution, specialty item distribution, public entertainment, direct mail, endorsements/testimonials, Internet, coupons, retail value added, and all others.

reflects, in part, the constraints placed upon the industry with regard to the use of mass (measured) media. In 1971, TV and radio were no longer permitted as advertising vehicles for the tobacco industry. As of the "Master Settlement Agreement (MSA)" of 1998 (National Association of Attorneys General 1998), billboard advertising was no longer permitted, and some constraints were imposed upon advertising in magazines to the extent they attracted a substantial adolescent readership. The focus of the industry shifted to in-store (largely convenience store) promotional strategies.

Table 37.2 documents the extremely steep climb in overall advertising and promotion expenditures from $8.3 billion in 1998, the year the MSA took effect, doubling to a peak of $16.6 billion in 2003 and then the first noted decline, to $13.5 billion in 2005 (FTC, 2007). Reasons for the recent decline are not clear. It may be that the industry sees far more growth opportunities in the rest of the world than in the United States and has adjusted its promotional efforts accordingly. In addition, the industry's current focus on in-store promotion may result in a ceiling on promotional expenditures: while spending on measured media, the industry's earlier focus, may be expanded without much limit, in-store expenditures may be constrained by the relatively finite number of outlets.

Also as noted in Table 37.2, *Price Discounts* now account for the overwhelming percentage of promotional expenditures; $10.1 billion or 74.4% in 2005. Since this category was not previously broken out separately, it is difficult to determine its rate of growth relative to previous years. Once the *Price Discounts* category is extracted, the two categories that earlier accounted for the bulk of promotional spending are now considerably diminished: (1) in 2005, just under $1 billion, or 7% of total promotional expenditures, was spent on *Promotional Allowances* (primarily payments to retailers, typically for displaying and merchandising brands); (2) until 1997 the FTC cigarette reports had listed *Coupons* together with the *Retail Value added* category (the costs associated with offers such as "buy 3 packs, get a free T-shirt") and so, in Table 37.2 we have done the same for comparative purposes. Expenditures on this category in 2005 were just under $1.7 billion, or 12% of total promotional dollars. The trend in annual expenditures, from 1970 to 2005, is represented in Figure 37.1.

Table 37.2 Cigarette Advertising and Promotional Expenditures in the United States, 1995–2005 (in billions of dollars*)

	Total Advertising and Promotional Expenditures	Expenditures on Promotional Allowances**	Expenditures on Coupons & Retail Value Added**	Expenditures on Price Discounts***
1995	6.414	2.444 (38%)	1.766 (28%)	
1996	6.501	2.737 (42%)	1.666 (26%)	
1997	7.042	3.034 (43%)	1.894 (27%)	
1998 (MSA)	8.249	3.527 (43%)	2.670 (32%)	
1999	9.873	4.247 (43%)	3.704 (38%)	
2000	11.124	4.539 (41%)	4.823 (43%)	
2001	12.647	5.020 (40%)	6.048 (48%)	
2002	14.000	1.997 (14%)	1.806 (13%)	8.627 (63%)
2003	16.594	2.098 (13%)	1.477 (9%)	11.842 (71%)
2004	15.101	1.060 (7%)	1.497 (10%)	11.665 (77%)
2005	13.534	0.907 (7%)	1.654 (12%)	10.095 (75%)

Source of data: Federal Trade Commission (FTC, 2007)
*Adjusted to 2006 dollars using the consumer price index (all items). Figures rounded to nearest million.
**Percentages represent the share of total expenditures devoted to the category listed.
***Price discounts were itemized separately beginning for 2002.

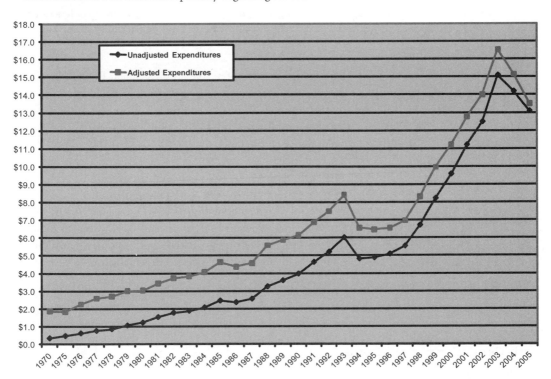

Figure 37.1 Total spending on tobacco advertising and promotion 1970–2005 (in billions of dollars; adjusted to 2006 dollars). Source: FTC, 2005.

Youths' Exposure to Tobacco Advertising in Measured Media   Does this extensive level of advertising and promotion actually reach adolescents? The tobacco industry argues strenuously that it does not target youths. Thus James Morgan (who rose to the level of CEO) of Philip Morris argued:

> Philip Morris does not market or sell [to youth or non-smokers] and has nointention to do so, does not do so, and actually takes many affirmative steps to make sure that it doesn't happen, sell to either nonsmokers or to minors. (Morgan in *Engle v R.J. Reynolds*, 1999, 34763)

When pressed in court, however, Morgan did admit that "…if you're asking me to swear that [our marketing efforts were] not seen by people under 18, I will not say that because I don't know that … It['s] an uncalculated outcome of the effort that Marlboro makes on the 18–24 age group" (Morgan in *State of Minnesota et al. v. Philip Morris et al.*, 1998).

Three different government-related reports across three decades have come to the view that adolescents cannot have escaped the tobacco industry's omnipresent advertising:

> So pervasive is cigarette advertising that it is virtually impossible for Americans of almost any age to avoid cigarette advertising. (FTC Trade Regulation Rule as cited in FTC Report to Congress, 1967, p. 12)

> Children are not isolated from tobacco advertising's attractiveness or inducements. *There is no "magic curtain" around children and teenagers…* (FDA, 1996, p. 44494; emphasis added)

> The sheer amount of expenditures for advertising and promotion assures that young people will be exposed to these messages on a massive scale. (Institute of Medicine report cited in Lynch & Bonnie, 1994, p. 131)

These conclusions reflect data from studies that trace across four decades. In the 1960s and 1970s television was the dominant means of delivering tobacco advertising. A study of the television schedule in 1963 indicated that the tobacco industry bought television schedules with a disproportionate (28%–30%) share of teenagers and children in their audiences (Pollay, 1994). The more teenagers (but not adults) in the audience, the greater the likelihood that the tobacco firms would sponsor the program (Pollay & Compton, 1992).

Most recently, the "Master Settlement Agreement" of 1998 between the National Association of Attorneys General and the tobacco industry sought in part to reduce adolescents' exposure to tobacco advertising (National Association of Attorneys General, 1998). One aspect of the agreement states: "[n]o Participating Manufacturer may take any action, directly or indirectly, to target Youth." In reviewing a broad set of magazines both before and after the 1998 settlement, King & Siegel (2001) came to the conclusion that the industry had not heeded this restriction.

> …both before and after the 1998 Master Settlement Agreement, tobacco companies consistently allocated to youth-oriented magazines a higher proportion of their expenditures for the advertising of youth brands than of expenditures for the advertising of adult brands and consistently maintained higher levels of exposure among young people to advertising for youth brands than to advertising for adult brands. (King & Sieger, 2001, p. 509)

Relatedly in *People of the State of CA vs. R.J. Reynolds* (2002) Judge R. S. Prager concluded:

> …an examination of the data RJR had available to it would have shown that in 1999 its advertising reached 97.1 percent of Youth 68.1 times; that in 2001 it reached 85.5 percent of Youth 16.3 times on

average…. …a substantial portion of RJR's advertisement appeared in publications where Youth comprise a disproportionately higher share of readers than adult smokers…RJR succeeded in exposing Youth at essentially the same levels as it targeted young adult smokers and violated the provisions of the MSA…." (Prager, 2002, p. 15–17)

It seems fairly clear that youth's have been exposed tobacco advertising.

Youths' Exposure to In-Store Tobacco Advertising   The data on expenditures presented above demonstrates the shift over the last 15 years or so to a strong focus on in-store promotions, in particular to promotions focusing on convenience stores. Close to 60% of all cigarettes are sold in convenience stores. In 2000, cigarettes were the leading category in sales for convenience stores. Cigarettes accounted for 37% of gross sales at convenience stores and represent the second most significant source of gross profits for convenience stores (National Association of Convenience Stores, as reported in DiPasquale, 2002).

The shift to in-store promotion, in particular since the MSA in 1998, is evidenced not only in the gross expenditure figures reported annually by the industry to the FTC, but also in empirical/observational studies of retail outlets. In 1999, the presence of tobacco point-of-purchase advertising was examined in a national U.S. study covering 3000 retail outlets. Almost all stores (92%) had some form of tobacco point-of-purchase advertising. Four of five (80%) had interior tobacco point-of-purchase advertising. Over two thirds (69%) had at least one tobacco-branded functional object. Over one third (36%) had self-service cigarette pack placement and one-quarter (25%) had multi-pack discounts (*Morbidity and Mortality Weekly Report; MMWR*, 2002).

Significant increases in tobacco promotion were noted from the period just prior to the implementation of the billboard ban (part of the Master Settlement Agreement) to the period just after the settlement These included: (1) the percentage of stores carrying interior store advertising for tobacco products and the extent of that advertising, (2) the percentage of stores carrying exterior advertising for tobacco products and the extent of that advertising, (3) the percentage of stores carrying a range of promotions, including gift-with-purchase, cents-off promotions, and multi-pack discounts, and (4) the percentage of stores carrying tobacco-related functional objects and the extent to which these objects were in the store (Wakefield et al., 2000).

In 2001, a cross-section of 586 California retailers was found to have an average of over 17 tobacco point-of-purchase (POP) ads in or around the store. More than four-fifths of these (85%) were located within four feet of the counter; one in ten (11%) had large exterior signs—in violation of the MSA; about 50% had ads below child level (3 feet); just under a quarter (23%) had cigarette product displays next to candy (Feighery, Ribisl, Shleicher, & Halvorson, 2000).

The specific nature of in-store cigarette product and ad placement as well as promotion is of particular relevance to this discussion given the frequency of youth shopping at convenience stores: nationally, three out of four teenagers shop at a convenience store at least once a week, staying an average of 10 minutes per visit—twice as long as adults; one third of both adults and teenagers stop in at least two or three times a week (Chanil 2002). According to a Channel One Network study, the 23 million U.S. teenagers visit convenience stores nearly 100 million times per month (Channel One Network 2000 as cited in Henriksen, Flora, Feighery, & Fortmann, 2002).

Tobacco's Current Emphasis on In-Store Promotion   As discussed above, the preponderance of moneys spent by the tobacco industry over the past 15 years or so, especially in the years since the MSA, has been spent on in-store promotion. Does this focus on in-store advertising and promotional efforts influence the cigarette purchasing behavior of youths? A national study of over 17,000 9th- through 12th-grade-students at 202 schools in 1996 assessed the brand preferences of the 3,282 students who smoked. The study sought to determine the relationship between the youths' smoking behavior and the extent of cigarette advertising in their retail environment. To that end, information was gathered from 302 convenience stores within a 1-mile radius of participating schools. The findings indicated that where the stores featured Marlboro in their advertising and promotions, students in the nearby schools tended to prefer Marlboro. Where the stores featured Camels, the students preferred Camels (Wakefield et al., 2001).

A study employing an experimental design exposed eighth and ninth graders to photos of a convenience store that was either dominated by or devoid of tobacco advertising. Youths who were exposed to the store full of tobacco POP perceived significantly easier access to cigarettes both in the pictured store and others in their neighborhood relative to the youths who saw the store without tobacco POP. Importantly, the perceived prevalence of smoking by peers—a key risk factor leading to smoking experimentation—was higher for the youths exposed to the store full of tobacco POP. Lastly, exposure to in-store tobacco advertising led the youths to be weaker in their support of tobacco control measures such as restricting tobacco marketing and increasing tobacco prices (Henriksen et al., 2002).

Presumably laws restricting access to tobacco products by minors would obviate the influence of in-store advertising and promotions. However, there is considerable evidence, based on national surveys of youths, that such laws have not been effective. In the 1993 national Teenage Attitudes and Practices Surveys of 12- to 17-year-olds (TAPS II), almost half (45%) of 12- to 17-year-olds who smoked reported never having been asked to show proof of age when buying or trying to buy cigarettes. Among those who had never smoked, 45% believed it would be easy for them to buy cigarettes (*MMWR*, February 1996). In the 1995 national CDC Youth Risk Behavior Survey of 9th- through 12th graders, 78% of those who were current smokers reported never being asked for proof of age when buying cigarettes in a store during the 30 days preceding the survey (*MMWR*, May 1996). More recently, the Monitoring the Future study results suggest that cigarettes are almost universally available to teens. About two thirds (68%) of eighth graders and nearly nine tenths (86%) of tenth graders say that cigarettes are "fairly easy" or "very easy" for them to get, if they want them (Johnston, O'Malley, & Bachman, 2002).

Three separate studies show that cigarette promotions, not necessarily limited to in-store distribution, are associated with cigarette uptake by adolescents. One study used Monitoring the Future data (Johnston et al., 2001) pertaining to almost 100,000 high school students from 1978 through 1995. In a time series analysis, the study concluded: "Large promotional pushes by cigarette marketers in the 1980s and 1990s appear to be linked with increased levels of daily smoking initiation among ninth graders" (Redmond, 1999, p. 243).

A Vermont study followed 480 4th- to 11th-grade-students for 21 months. Those who initially had never smoked and were judged non-susceptible to smoking at time period one, but owned or were willing to use a cigarette promotional item, were more than twice as likely to have progressed towards smoking 21 months later. This remained true after controlling for a series of other factors including whether friends and/or family members smoked, gender, school performance and level of parents education (Sargent et al., 2000).

A third study (also referenced earlier) focused on California adolescents. When first telephoned in 1993, 1,752 of those approached had never smoked and indicated that they were not susceptible to smoking. When these adolescents were re-interviewed 3 years later, those who either initially possessed or were willing to possess a tobacco promotional item (such as a lighter or t-shirt) were almost three times more likely to indicate that they had started to smoke or intended to start, relative to those who did not own or were not interested in promotional items (Pierce et al., 1998).

The Increased Importance of Packaging   In a sense, the ultimate promotional device is the cigarette package, both because it represents a key element of the in-store display and is used repeatedly, coincident with product use. A 1963 Liggett & Myers report states: "The primary job of the package is to create a desire to purchase and try. To do this it must look new and different enough to attract the attention of the consumer" (Liggett & Myers, 1963). More recently, referring to an innovative package introduced for Kool cigarettes, a senior B&W executive commented: "The response from consumers is 'this is a pack to be seen with.'" (Cremers as cited in Ives, 2004, p.C11).

With the retail outlet more and more becoming the focus of the tobacco industry's marketing efforts, the cigarette pack itself, given it's visibility has become a significant in-store promotional vehicle. As a senior vice president for Brown & Williamson has noted: "The...cigarette pack...is being used to deliver a message that would usually have been relegated to advertising" (Bexon as cited in Pollack, 1999, p. 12). The cigarette display in effect can and has become an in-store "advertisement" As noted in an American Tobacco Company memo: "An integrated package design can provide for a greater in-store presence....[T]he arrangement of packs at the point of purchase themselves become ad advertisement for the brand family" (Bogie, 1991).

Such is the importance of the package that constraining its design is likely to challenge the viability of the brand itself. An extensive Canadian government report examining the potential impact of mandating plain (white) packaging found that the brand identity of even well established brands would be at risk in the absence of the supportive imagery on the package (Health Canada, 1995).

Research suggests that packaging is of critical importance to teenagers. In one survey close to 9 in 10 teens interviewed, felt that packaging was "very important." Just under 8 in 10 indicated that they frequently purchase products because they are influenced by the way they are packaged (Rand, 1981).

For young teens starting to smoke, a distinct cigarette package that reinforces a distinct brand image is critical for both purposes of self-definition and presentation to others. Teenagers who point to a brand favored by themselves and their peers typically feel that the "badge value" created by the distinct packaging helps them make the case that "this is the brand I smoke and my friends smoke."

CONSENSUS REPORTS

Reviewing evidence such as that discussed above, three government "consensus" reports: (1) the Food and Drug Administration (FDA 1996), (2) the Surgeon General of the United States (USDHSS 1994), and (3) the Institute of Medicine (Lynch & Bonnie, 1994) have concluded that there is a consensus regarding the body of scientific knowledge relating tobacco advertising and promotion to youth tobacco consumption. Each concluded that advertising plays a significant role in influencing youth to smoke:

> ...the substantial convergent evidence that advertising and promotion increases tobacco use by youths is impressive....Does the preponderance of evidence suggest that features of advertising and promotion tend to encourage youths to smoke? The answer is yes. (Institute of Medicine cited in Lynch & Bonnie, 1994, pp. 130, 131)

> A substantial and growing body of scientific literature...offer(s) a compelling argument for the mediated relationship of cigarette advertising and adolescent smoking. (Surgeon General, USDHHS, 1994, p. 188)

> ...the agency, like the 1994 SGR (Surgeon General) and the IOM (Institute of Medicine) Report, finds that an adequate basis does exist to conclude that advertising plays a "mediated relationship" to adolescent tobacco use....Does FDA have a solid body of evidence establishing that advertising encourages young people's tobacco use... The answer to this question is "yes." (FDA, 1996, p. 44488)

Considerably, earlier, in 1962, commenting on the steep increase in teenage smoking, the Chairman of the National Association of Broadcasters (NAB), LeRoy Collins, came to the same conclusion:

> ...this condition [teenage smoking] is being made continually worse under the promotional impact of advertising designed primarily to influence young people. Certainly the moral responsibility rests first on the tobacco manufacturers. Certainly it also rests on the advertising agencies. (Collins, cited in Hill & Knowlton internal memo, Nov. 20, 1962)

As the Surgeon General's report (1994) indicates, this broad consensus is generated, *despite* the absence of a study that would generate proof positive. As they note:

> To date...no longitudinal study of the direct relationship of cigarette advertising to smoking initiation has been reported in the literature. This lack of definitive literature does not imply that a causal relationship does not exist; rather, better quantification of exposure, effect and etiology is needed. (USDHHS, 1994, p. 188)

It is worthwhile considering why the Surgeon General's Report refers, on the one hand, to a longitudinal study as some sort of ideal, but concludes nevertheless, that even without such a study, a causal relationship exists. In fact, the ideal, longitudinal experiment is, in effect, unthinkable in a free and open society. It might call for randomized groups of 2-year-olds to be placed in communities where, during their formative years, they would be either exposed or not exposed to the type of heavy tobacco advertising that has existed over the decades. At 18 years of age, cigarettes would be made readily available to both groups and we would see how many of each group chose to smoke. Obviously this is not feasible—not only for the degree of intrusion and control into people's lives, but for the potential harm. But even in the absence of this unattainable and unacceptable "ideal" experiment, after thorough consideration of the available evidence, three government bodies (as well as the National Association of Broadcasters) have concluded that exposure to tobacco advertising does contribute to adolescents' smoking behavior.

This chapter has examined the convergent, triangulated evidence that led to the common conclusion reached in each of the consensus reports cited above. The results of longitudinal (prospective) studies and those of controlled, causal experiments converge to suggest a causal relationship between tobacco advertising and adolescent smoking behavior. Econometric studies and relatedly, studies examining shock changes in levels of tobacco advertising over time, support the same conclusion. Economic analyses of brand loyalty and brand shifting point away from the targeting of existing smokers as a rationale for the enormous sums spent on advertising and promotion. Internal tobacco industry documents make it evident that industry executives were aware of the importance of persuading youngsters to start smoking, that they commissioned and reviewed studies of youth smoking and devoted considerable effort to persuade youths to smoke.

Exposure to tobacco advertising is related to various mediating variables which heighten the risk of adolescent smoking. These mediators include the development of: positive imagery of smoking and smokers, the perception of smoking as normative, a "friendly familiarity" with tobacco and smoking as a valid/legitimate activity, the high levels of tobacco brand identification, and tobacco advertising's priming of adolescents, such that peer influence is facilitated.

Lastly, a set of "enabling" factors were reviewed. These include the unique vulnerability of adolescents to tobacco advertising and promotion and its extent—over $13.5 billion in 2005 or about $37 million per day (FTC, 2007)—which ensures that adolescents (and everyone else) are exposed to it.

The convergent evidence derived from the multiple approaches and the multiple variables considered in this chapter heightens confidence in the validity of the relationship in question. While any single study or methodological approach can be challenged as a function of its limitations, when the results of as broad an array of approaches as were considered in this chapter converge, confidence in the relationship is high; it is in this way that science extends a body of knowledge.

NOTES

1. Several content analyses have established that cigarettes have appeared in American movies over the last four decades—on average every 10–15 minutes—and typically are presented in a positive light. (Terre, Drabman, & Speer, 1991; Hazan & Glantz, 1994; Stockwell & Glantz, 1997; Ng & Dakake, 2002). More directly supportive of the Pechmann and Knight experimental results is a correlational study by Distefan, Gilpin, Sargent, and Pierce (1999) indicating that adolescents whose favorite movie stars smoke on or off the screen are more likely to have smoked than those whose favorite movie stars do not smoke. Among adolescents who have never smoked, those whose favorite movie stars do smoke are more susceptible to starting to smoke relative to those whose favorite stars don't smoke (Distefan et al., 1999).

REFERENCES

Achenreiner, G. B. (1997). Materialistic values and susceptibility to influence in children. *Advances in Consumer Research, 24,* 82–88.

Assael, H. (2004). *Consumer behavior: A strategic approach.* Boston: Houghton Mifflin.

Aitken, P. P., Leather, D. S., & F.J. O'Hagan, F. J. (1985). Children's perceptions of advertisements for cigarettes. *Social Science Medical, 21*(7), 785-797.

Aitken, P. P., D. R. Eadie, G. B. Hastings, & A. J. Haywood (1991), Predisposing effects of cigarette advertising on children's intentions to smoke when older. *British Journal of Addiction, 86,* 383–390.

Aloise-Young, P. A., Hennigan, K. M., & Graham, J. W. (1996). Role of the self-image and smoker stereotype in smoking onset during early adolescence: A longitudinal study. *Health Psychology, 15*(6), 494–497.

American Tobacco Company. (1968). Document: "The American Tobacco Company; Lucky Filters" (January 5).

Andrews, R. L., & Franke, G. R. (1991). The determinants of cigarette consumption: A meta-analysis. *Journal of Public Policy & Marketing, 10*(1), 3–27.

Berndt, T. (1979). Developmental changes in conformity to peers and parents *Developmental Psychology, 15*(6), 608–616.

Biener, L., & Siegel, M. (2000). Tobacco marketing and adolescent smoking: More support for a causal inference. *American Journal of Public Health, 98*(3), 407–411.

Boddewyn, J. J. (Ed.). (1987), *Why do juveniles start smoking?* (2nd ed., pp. 1–33). New York: International Advertising Association.

Bogie, J. C. (1991). Approval recommendation—Lucky Strike Package Design Exploratory, Memo to R. E. Smith, January 7. American Tobacco Company. Bates No. 970530514-970530521. As cited in Wakefield, M. C. Morley, J. K. Horan, K. M. Cummings, The cigarette pack as image: new evidence from tobacco industry documents. *Tobacco Control* 2002, *11* (Suppl. 1): i73–i80.

Botvin, G. J., Goldberg, C. J., Botvin, E. M., & Dusenbury, L. (1993). Smoking behavior of adolescents exposed to cigarette advertising, *108*(2), 217–224.

Bouchard, T. J., Jr. (1976). Unobtrusive measures. *Sociological Methods & Research, 4*(3) 267–300.

Burnett (1961). *Communications of an advertising man,* cited in USDHHS (1994), *Preventing tobacco use among young people: A report of the surgeon general.* Altanta, GA: U.S. Department of Health and Human Services.

Campbell, D. T., & Fiske, D. W. (1959). Convergent and discriminant validation by the multitrait-multimethod matrix. *Psychologicial Bulletin, 56*(2) 81–105

Cavin, S. W., & Pierce, J. P. (1996). Low-cost cigarettes and smoking behavior in California, 1990–1993. *American Journal of Preventive Medicine, 12*(1), 17–21.

Chaloupka, F., & Laixuthai, A. (1996). U.S. trade policy and cigarette smoking in Asia. *NBER Working Paper Series* (5543), 1–20.

Chanil, D. (2002). Profile of the convenience store customer. *Convenience Store News, 11* (February), 54–70.

Channel One Network (2000). *Teen fact book 2000.* New York.

Chassin, L., Presson, C., Sherman, S. J., Corty, E., & Oshavsky, R. W. (1981). Self-images and cigarette smoking in adolescence. *Personality and Social Psychology Bulletin, 7*(4), 670–676.

Chassin, L., Presson, C. C., Sherman, S. J., Corty, E., & Olshavsky, R. W. (1984). Predicting the onset of cigarette smoking in adolescents: A longitudinal study. *Journal of Applied Social Psychology, 14*(3), 224–243.

Cigarette Advertising Code. 1964; Bates No. 503813713-503813721. Retrieved July 9, 2004, from http://tobaccodocuments.org/youth/AmToMUL19640000.co.html.

Collins, L. (1962). *Information memorandum* (re: Cigarette Advertising Code). Rereprinted in Hill & Knowlton Document Nov. 20, 1962. (p. 22).

Cummings, K. M., Morley, C. P. , Horan, J. K. , Steger, C., Leavell, N-R. (2002) Marketing to America's youth: Evidence from corporate documents. *Tobacco Control, 11*(Suppl. 1), 5–17.

Davis, R. (1996). The effects of tobacco advertising: Brand loyalty, brand switching, or market expansion?" Guest Editorial; *American Journal of Preventive Medicine, 12*(1) 2–3.

DiFranza, J. R., Savageau, J. A., Rigotti, N. A., Fletcher, K., Ockene, J. K., McNeill, A. D., Coleman, M., & Wood, C. (2002). *Tobacco Control, 11,* 228–235.

Dipasquale, C. (2002). Store wars: With advertising options dwindling, tobacco marketers take the battle to convenience stores. *Advertising Age,* (14), January 4–8.

Distefan, J. M., Gilpin, E. A., Sargent, J. D., & Pierce, J. P. (1999). Do movie stars encourage adolescents to start smoking? Evidence from California. *Preventive Medicine, 28,* 1–11.

Emri, S., Tülay Bagci, T., Karakoca, Y., & Baris, E. (1998). Recognition of cigarette brand names and logos by primary schoolchildren in Ankara, Turkey. *Tobacco Control, 7,* 386–392.

Federal Trade Commission (1967). Report to Congress (June 30).

Federal Trade Commission. (2005), Federal Trade Commission Cigarette Report for 2003. Retrieved July 7, 2005, from http://www.ftc.gov/

Feighery, E., Ribisl, K., Shleicher, N., & Halvorson, S. (2001). igarette advertising and promotional strategies in retail outlets: Results of a statewide survey in California *Tobacco Contro._10*(1) 184–188.

Fischer, .P. M., Schwartz, M. P., Richards, J. W., Goldstein, A. O., & Rojas, T. (1991). Brand logo recognition by children aged 3 to 6 Years. *JAMA, 266*(22), 3145–3148.

Food and Drug Administration (1996). Regulations restricting the sale and distribution of cigarettes and smokeless tobacco to protect children and adolescents; final rule. *Federal Register, 168*(61), 44396–44618.

Godin, S. (2001). *Unleashing the ideavirus,* New York: Hyperion.

Goldberg, M. E., &. Gorn, G. L. (1982). Behavioral evidence of the effects of televised food messages on children. Journal of Consumer Research, (September), 200–205.

Goldberg, M. E., Gorn, G. J., Perrachio. L., & Bamossey, G. (2003). Understanding materialism among youth. *Journal of Consumer Psychology,_13*(3), 278–288.

Hasher, L,, & Goldstein, D. (1977). Frequency and the conference of referential validity. *Journal of Verbal Learning and Verbal Behavior, 16,* 107–112.

Hawkins, S. A., & Hoch, S. J. (1992). Low-involvement learning: Memory without evaluation. *Journal of Consumer Research, 19*(September), 212–225.

Health Canada (1995). When packages can't speak; possible impacts of plain and generic packaging of tobacco products. (March), Ottawa: Government of Canada.

Henriksen L., Flora, J. A., Feighery, E., & Fortmann, S. P. (2002). Effects on youth of exposure to retail tobacco advertising. *Journal of Applied Social Psychology 32*(9) 1771–1789.

Imperial Tobacco. (1982). Export family strategy document (March 22). In B. S. & R. J. Bonnie (1994), *Growing up tobacco free: Preventing nicotine addiction in children and youths.* Washington, DC: National Academy Press.

Ives, N. (2004). Kool cigarettes in new flavors draw criticism. *New York Times* (March 9), C-1.

Johnston, L. D., O'Malley, P. M., & Bachman, J. G. (2001), *Monitoring the future; national results on adolescent drug use: Overview of key findings, 2000,* NIH Publication No. 01-4923. Betheseda, MD: National Institute on Drug Abuse.

Johnston, L. D., O'Malley, P. M., & Bachman, J. G. (2002). *National survey on drug use, 1975–2001; Volume 1: Secondary school students.* NIH Publication No. 02-5106. Bethesda, MD: National Institute on Drug Abuse.

Kasser, T., Ryan, R. M., Zax, M., & Sameroff, A. (1995). The relations of maternal and social environments to late adolescents' materialistic and prosocial values. *Developmental Psychology, 31*(6), 907–914.

King, C., III, & Siegel, M. (2001). The master settlement agreement with the tobacco industry and cigarette advertising in magazines. *New England Journal of Medicine, 345* (7), 504–511.

Laugesen, M., & Meads, C. (1991). Tobacco advertising restrictions, price, income and tobacco consumption in OECD countries. *British Journal of Addiction, 86*, 1343–1354.

Leventhal, H., Glynn, K., & Fleming, R. (1987). Is the smoking decision an "Informed Choice." *Journal of the American Medical Association, 257*(24), 3373–3376.

Leventhal, H., & Keeshan, P. (1993). Promoting healthy alternatives to substance abuse. In S. G. Millstein, A. C. Petersen, & E. O. Nightingale (Eds.), *Promoting healthy alternatives to substance abuse* (pp. 260–284). New York: Oxford University Press.

Lewit, E. M., Coate, D., & Grossman, M. (1981). The effects of government regulation on teenage smoking. *Journal of Law and Economics, 24*(Dec.), 545–569.

Liggett & Myers (1963). Development of cigarette packaging #194. A Miner, p. 19.

Lorillard (1978). Scientific research liason committee should re-convene. Handwritten notes of Curtis Judge, CEO (April 21).

Lynch, B. S., & Bonnie, R. J. (1994). *Growing up tobacco free: Preventing nicotine addiction in children and youths.* Washington, DC: National Academy Press.

Mazis, M. B., Debra J. Ringold, D. J., Perry, E. S., & Denman, D. W. (1992). Perceived age and attractiveness of models in cigarette advertisements. *Journal of Marketing, 56*(1), 22–37.

Morbidity and Mortality Weekly Report (*MMWR*; 2002). Point-of-purchase tobacco environments and variation by store type—United States, 1999, *51*(9), 184–186.

Morbidity And Mortality Weekly Report (*MMWR*; 1994). Changes in the cigarette brand preferences of adolescent smokers — United States, 189–1993. *The New England Journal of Medicine, 43*(32), 586–582.

Morgan, J. J. (1998), Testimony in *State of Minnesota and Blue Cross and Blue Shield of Minnesota, Plaintiffs, V. Philip Morris Inc. et. al.* Trial transcript; Docket-Number C1-94-8565; Minnesota District Court, Second Judicial District, Ramsey, April 23–24, 1998.

Morgan, J. (1976). This week: Philip Morris. Interview with P. Taylor. Thames Broadcasting Co. (Aug. 16).

National Association of Attorneys General. (1998). *Master settlement agreement (MSA).* Retrieved July 25, 2004, from http://www.naag.org/upload/1032468605_cigmsa.pdf.

New Zealand Toxic Substance Board (1989). *Health or tobacco: An end to tobacco advertising promotion.* Wellington, New Zealand: Publications Division, Government Printing Office.

Ng, C., & Dakake, B. (2002). Tobacco at the movies: Tobacco use in PG-13 films. Boston, MA Masspirg Education Funds, 1–12.

Nisbett, R., & Ross, L. (1980). The lay scientist self examined. In *Human inference: Strategies and shortcomings of social judgment.* Englewood Cliffs, NJ: Prentice-Hall.

Opatow, L. (1984). Packaging is most effective when it works in harmony with the positioning of a brand. *Marketing News, 18*(February), 3–4.

Pechmann, C., & Shih, C-H. (1999). Smoking scenes in movies and antismoking advertisements before movies: Effects on youth. *Journal of Marketing,* (63), 1–26.

Pechmann, C., &. Knight, S. J. (2002). An experimental investigation of the joint effects of advertising and peers on adolescents' beliefs and intentions about cigarette consumption. *Journal of Consumer Research,* 29 (June) 5–19.

Peters, J., Betson, C. L., Hedley, A. J., Liam, T-H., Ong, S-G., Wong , C-M., & Fielding, R. (1995). Recognition of cigarette brand names and logos by young children in Hong Kong. *Tobacco Control, 4*, 150–155.

Philip Morris (1959). Roper attitude study of January 195., Memo from W.H. Danker to Dr. R. N. DuPuis (May 28, 1959).

Philip Morris (1969). Smoker psychology research. Presentation by H. Wakeham to the Philip Morris Board of Directors (Nov. 26).

Philip Morris (1980). High nicotine, low TPM cigarettes. Memo from W. L. Dunn to R. B. Seligman (March 24).

Philip Morris (1981). Young smokers, prevalence, trends implication and relased demographic trends. Report M.E. Johnston (March 31).

Philip Morris (1990). Marlboro 1990 Marketing Pla. (Sept. 17) 20449770856.

Pierce, J. P., Gilpin, E., Burns, D. M., Whalen, E., Rosbrook, B., Shopland, D., & Johnson, M. (1991). Does tobacco advertising target young people to start smoking? *Journal of the American Medical Association, 266*(22), 3154–3158.

Pierce, J. P.,. Choi, W. S., Gilpin, E. A., Farkas, A. J., & Berry, C. C. (1998). Tobacco industry promotion of cigarettes and adolescent smoking. *Journal of the American Medical Association, 279*(7), 511–515.

Pollack, J. (1999). B&W's Carlton relaunch first since new ad rules: No outdoor for ultralow-tar brank, which will 'do things differently.' *Advertising Age,* (March 01), 12.

Pollay (1994). Exposure of US youth to cigarette television advertising in the 1960s. *Tobacco Control, 3*(2), 130–133.

Pollay, & Compton, D. L. (1992). Cigarette exposure to youth: TV use under self-regulation [1963]. Working Paper, University of British Columbia (June).

Pollay, & Compton, D. L. (1993). Guest editorial: Cigarette advertising; pertinent research and impertinent opinions: Our contributions to the cigarette advertising policy debate. *Journal of Advertising, 22*(4) 110–117.

Pollay , &. Compton, D. L. , Siddarth, S., Siegel, M., Haddix, A., Robert K. Merritt, R. K., et al. (1996). The last straw? Cigarette advertising and realized market shares among youths and adults, 1979–1993. *Journal of Marketing,* 60(April) 1–16.

Rand, L. (1981). Testing the teens. In Walter Stern (Ed.), *Handbook of package design research* (pp. 377–386). New York: Wiley.

Redmond, W. H. (1999). Effects of sales promotion on smoking among U.S. ninth graders. *Preventive Medicine, 28,* 243–250.

R. J. Reynolds (1973). *Research planning memorandum on some thoughts about new brands of cigarettes for the youth market.* Report by Claude Teague, Jr.

R. J. Reynolds (1977, Oct. 31). Share of smokers by age group. Memo by T. L. Ogburn, Jr.

R. J. Reynolds (1980, Jult 22) *MDD report on teenage smokers* (14–17). G .H. Long (July 22).

R. J. Reynolds (1984, Feb. 29), *Strategic research report,* D.S. Burrows.

R. J. Reynolds (1986, March 12). Camel new advertising campaign development. Memo from R.T. Caufield to D. N. Iauco..

Roper, E. (1959). Highlights of the Survey; p. 7 as cited in a defendant legal review of the survey; Bates No. 2024941033).

Roper Research Associates (1970, July). A study of public attitudes toward cigarette smoking and the tobacco industry. *The Tobacco Institute.*

Saffer, H. (2000). Tobacco advertising and promotion. In J. Prabhart & F. J. Chaloupka (Eds.), *Tobacco control in developing countries.* New York: Oxford University Press.

Saffer, H., & Chaloupka F. (2000). The effect of tobacco advertising bans on tobacco consumption. *Journal of Health Economic,*19 1117–1137.

Sargent, J., Dalton, M., Beach, M., et al. (2000). Effect of cigarette promotions on smoking uptake among adolescents. *Preventive Medicine,* (30) 320–327.

Schindler A. (1998). *Testimony in State of Minnesota and Blue Cross and Blue Shield of Minnesota, Plaintiffs, vs. Philip Morris et al.*; C1-94-8565

Siegel, M., & Nelson, D. E., Peddicord, J. P., Merritt, R. K., Giovino, G. A., & Eriksen, M. (1996). The extent of cigarette brand and company switching: Results from the adult use-of-tobacco survey. *American Journal of Preventative Medicine, 12*(1), 14–15.

Slovic, P. (2000). What does it mean to know a cumulative risk? Adolescents' perceptions of short-term and long-term consequences of smoking. *Journal of Behavioral Decision Making,* 13, 259–266.

Steinberg, .L. (1993). *Adolescence* (3rd ed., pp. 286–304). New York: McGraw-Hill.

Stockwell, T., & Glantz, S. (1997). Tobacco use increasing in popular films. *Tobacco Control, 6,* 282–284.

Terre, L., Drabman, R. S., & Speer, P. (1991). Health-relevant behaviors in media. *Journal of Applied Social Psychology, 21*(16) 1303–1319.

Urberg, K. A., Shyu, S-J., & Liang, J. (1990). Peer influence in adolescent cigarette smoking. *Addictive Behaviors, 15,* 247–255.

U.S. Congress, Committee on Government Reform and Oversight; Minority Staff Report (1997, June 12). Secret attorney-client documents are evidence of potential crimes or fraud by the tobacco industry report.

U.S. Department of Health and Human Services (1994). *Preventing tobacco use among young people: A report of the surgeon general.* Washington, DC: U.S Department of Health and Human Services. Centers for Disease Control and Prevention. National Center for Chronic Disease Prevention and Health Promotion. Office on Smoking and Health.

Wakefield, M., Yvonne Terry, Y., Chaloupka, F., Barker, D., Slater, S., Clark, P., & Giovino, G. (2000). Changes at the point-of-sale for tobacco following the 1999 tobacco billboard advertising ban. *ImpacTeen*, July(4), 1–18.

Wakefield, M., Ruel, E. E., Chaloupka, F. J., Slater, S., & Kaufman, N. J. (2002). Association of point-of-purchase tobacco advertising and promotions with choice of usual brand among teenage smokers. *Journal of Health Communication, 7*, 113–121.

Webb, E. J., Campbell, D. T., Schwartz, R. D., & Sechrest, L. (1966). *Unobtrusive measures: Nonobtrusive measures: Nonreactive research in the social sciences.* Chicago: Rand McNally.

Weiss, J., &. Brown, P. (1977). *Self-insight error in the explanation of mood.* Unpublished manuscript, Harvard University, 1977.

38

The Social Marketing of Volunteerism
A Functional Approach

Arthur A. Stukas

La Trobe University

Mark Snyder

University of Minnesota

E. Gil Clary

College of St. Catherine

From every corner of society, voices have been raised to urge people to volunteer their time and effort for the common good. People can get involved through a variety of organizations, from religious institutions to youth groups to workplaces to schools. Communities often thrive on contributions from within, as do the arts and the environment, as well as sports and recreational activities of every variety. Those in need find solace and support for problems associated with poverty, ill health, loneliness, hunger, and strife. Indeed, in the United States, for example, people who have long been taught that idle hands do the devil's work have also learned to put those hands to good use, devoting ample amounts of their leisure or discretionary time to volunteerism.

Whether cause or effect of this volunteer work ethic, successive governments have sought to channel the efforts of a growing number of Americans toward good ends, weighing in with a series of policies and initiatives to promote volunteer work, from the Peace Corps and Volunteers in Service to America (VISTA) to the current plethora of programs for student volunteers (AmeriCorps and Learn and Serve America), and elder volunteers (Retired and Senior Volunteer Program; RSVP). Moreover, it appears that the efforts of government and non-government sectors have been successful, as the monetary value of volunteerism in the United States has been calculated to be some \$239.2 billion dollars for 2001 alone (Snyder, Omoto, & Lindsay, 2004). The same holds true for other countries as well; for example, the comparable figure for Australia is AU\$41.7 billion dollars in 1997 alone (Ironmonger, 2000; see also Salamon, 1999, 2004). Whereas some might suggest that such policies may simply mean that some services formerly supplied by the government may now be provided for "free" by community members, others might point out that volunteerism provides benefits to all concerned. In this chapter, we will examine, from the perspective of theoretical and empirical work in the social and behavioral sciences, the role of volunteerism in the lives of "all concerned"—those who volunteer, the recipients of their services, their communities, and society at large. In addition, we will examine the strategies that can be employed to encourage, promote, and "market" sustained volunteerism.

BENEFITS OF VOLUNTEERISM

To Society

At the societal level, volunteerism has been identified as a form of civic participation that is very likely to lead to *social capital*, the connections between individuals that are thought to foster feelings of trust and generalized norms of reciprocity (e.g., Putnam, 2000). In turn, social capital has been suggested as a contributor to lower crime rates, less alienation, less poverty, and the amelioration of social problems, generally (Putnam, 2000; but see Portes, 1998). Although any kind of associational membership is thought to produce social capital, recent evidence suggests that different types of participation in different types of organizations may result in varying contributions to societal levels of social capital (e.g., Stolle & Rochon, 1998).

Volunteerism for organizations that are community or "public-serving" as opposed to "member-serving" (Lyons, 2002) may be more likely to increase bonds of trust and reciprocity across previously delineated group lines in society. Indeed, in Stolle and Rochon's (1998) survey of Swedish, German, and American associations, members of more diverse community organizations (as well as members of cultural associations and personal interest groups) showed high rates of social capital relative to members of other less diverse organizations and different types of organizations. Thus, policies and programs which aim to increase volunteerism may also serve consequently to reduce the types of social ills which result from a lack of broad social connections in society. (However, the mechanisms by which increased social capital results in decreases in social problems have yet to be clearly elucidated.)

To the Community

At the community level, volunteers may provide services that help the day-to-day "life" of the community to run more smoothly. Neighborhood watch groups, community taskforces, meals-on-wheels programs, school crossing guard arrangements, and other community-serving volunteer activities provide services that fill in the gaps between government and family provided support. Some community volunteers donate time and energy to causes that benefit the entire community (rather than only those currently in need), for example, by working at animal shelters, engaging in litter clean-up days, participating in events that provide money to charities (like read-a-thons, walk-a-thons, and even triathlons; in Australia, people dye their hair or shave it off for the Leukemia foundation).

Of course, aside from the practical functions that community-based volunteer activities serve, it is likely too that such volunteer work contributes to community-building or social capital. As such, the community may serve as both a context for volunteerism, drawing in people who are concerned with the fate of their communities to give time and energy, and as an outcome of volunteerism, providing those who do serve with a strengthened psychological sense of community (Omoto & Snyder, 2002). Indeed, a feedback loop may be created if this stronger sense of community subsequently encourages further volunteerism by a growing network of community members.

To Recipients

At the recipient level, volunteers can and do provide necessary services to the sick (e.g., in programs that sponsor visits to sick children by "candy stripers," clowns and others, or that provide companions to persons living with HIV disease, or through donations of blood, marrow, and organs), to the lonely or housebound (e.g., by delivering meals on wheels or Thanksgiving dinners, or in programs that match young and old), to disadvantaged youth (e.g., in Big Brothers/Big Sisters and other mentoring programs, in school-based tutoring programs, or by offering leadership in scouting and 4H programs), and to the poor and the homeless (e.g., by lending a hand at soup kitchens, homeless shelters, or toy drives). Few systematic studies of recipient outcomes from volunteerism exist; however, Snyder et al. (2004) reported improvements in psychological and physical functioning of those persons with AIDS who were assigned a volunteer companion or "buddy." Although recipients may vary in the amount and duration of services required, it seems clear that acts of generosity are not forgotten when they are no longer needed; survey data from Independent Sector (1988) suggests that former recipients often return the favor by volunteering themselves when they are able. Thus, again, volunteerism may influence further volunteerism.

To Volunteers

Finally, at the level of the individual volunteer, there is mounting evidence that volunteers themselves receive benefits from their activities. Volunteers routinely report higher levels of well-being than non-volunteers (e.g., Thoits & Hewitt, 2001) and greater amounts of participation are related to better mental health (e.g., Piliavin, 2005) and better physical health, especially among the elderly (although there may be limits to the amount of service that is helpful; Musick, Herzog, & House, 1999). Research that takes a functional approach to the study of volunteerism (e.g., Clary, Snyder, Ridge, Copeland, Stukas, Haugen, & Miene, 1998; Snyder, Clary, & Stukas, 2000) has demonstrated that volunteers often engage in their activities for a number of different reasons or functions. Thus, volunteers may seek to gain career benefits by making new contacts or adding a new line to their résumé. They may hope to learn more about their community and the people in it, perhaps especially people with whom they might not ordinarily come into contact. Volunteers may seek to express their own deeply held values or moral principles or they may wish to live up to the ideals of others. They may use volunteer work to make themselves feel better or to divert their attention away from things that make them feel worse. All told, volunteers seek and receive a wide array of personal benefits, at the same time as they contribute to increasing the well-being of others and their community and society.

The Problem of Inaction

Yet, despite these potential benefits to society, the community, recipients, and volunteers, rates of volunteerism are still outstripped by the positive attitudes held about such activities. That is, formal volunteer programs suffer from what has been called the "problem of inaction" (e.g., Snyder, 1993; Snyder & Clary, 1990): although a large number of people are willing to say that volunteerism is worthwhile, fewer actually engage in service (see also Snyder, Omoto, & Smith, in press). In the last Independent Sector survey to assess the issue, Americans agreed by a 3 to 1 margin that volunteerism is important but only 38.5% reported that they had volunteered in the previous month (Independent Sector, 1988). More recent data indicate that currently only 28% of Americans over the age of 21 volunteer monthly or more frequently (a somewhat different statistic; Independent Sector, 2001). The trick for organizations seeking volunteers, then, is to turn good intentions into good behavior, to overcome the "problem of inaction." Research on the promotion of volunteerism offers many parallels to the methods used by a growing number of practitioners engaged in social marketing. A comparison of the two approaches reveals how social scientific research can inform, and provide empirical grounding and refinement to, the social marketing of volunteerism.

EFFORTS TO INCREASE RATES OF VOLUNTEERISM

We began our discussion by noting that successive American governments (and governments in other countries, as well; e.g., Ontario Ministry of Education, 1999) have implemented programs designed to increase volunteerism as a form of civic participation. Such initiatives (and other efforts to promote volunteerism) may be understood as falling along a continuum of persuasive techniques designed to increase the likelihood of behavior, techniques varying in the "strength" of the measures that they employ or the "freedom" that is available to targeted individuals to make their own decisions about how to behave (e.g., Kelman & Warwick, 1978). As Maibach (2002) has recently noted, targets of persuasion attempts (i.e., efforts to change attitudes or behavior) may vary in their receptiveness toward the message and their willingness to change their behavior. Maibach argued that targets could be grouped according to whether they were "prone to behave as desired", "open to good offers", or "resistant to behave as desired". Such a framework echoes Kelman's (1961) classic work on social influence; he suggested that people behave according to group norms because they have "internalized" the norms, or because they "identify" with others who follow the norms, or because they seek only to "comply" with norms to avoid punishments or receive rewards.

Maibach (2002) theorized that different types of persuasive efforts would be needed to ensure that those who fall at different spots on the "readiness" continuum change their behavior in line with the aims of the persuader (i.e., organization, community, or society). For example, those who are already prone to behave as desired may need only to be told where, when, and how to engage in the behavior; thus educational campaigns of the kind commonly seen on TV in public service announcements may be enough to motivate this group.

At the other end of the spectrum, those who are resistant to changing their behavior may require more pressure to be applied in order to get them to change. Thus, the most extreme persuasion attempts can carry with them the weight of the law (and its associated fines and penalties), such as when seat belt use became mandatory. Such efforts often require continued surveillance (as Kelman, 1961, pointed out), but manipulating people to comply with behaviors to which they are resistant was always likely to be an uphill battle.

In the middle of the spectrum lie those individuals who are neither prone nor resistant. Like independent voters, these individuals are open to influence, ready to take the best offer, and as such may be tempted by benefits and incentives, including both financial incentives (such as tuition breaks or loan waivers for students) and nonfinancial incentives (such as opportunities to identify with sports stars, leaders, and other esteemed people). Persuasive campaigns with these varying degrees of pressure, presumably aimed at prone, resistant, and open individuals respectively, have all been constructed to promote volunteerism.

Targeting Those Prone to Volunteer

People who are already prone to volunteer but not currently doing so might be encouraged to begin simply by providing them with information or "education" about how to do so. As an example of this kind of strategy, consider the national "Give Five" campaign, initiated by Independent Sector in 1987, to encourage people to contribute 5 hours per week of their time to volunteering, and 5% of their income to charitable organizations. This appeal was disseminated through public service announcements on radio and television, in magazine and newspaper ads, and on billboard displays. Although the campaign remained silent about where, when, and how people could get involved (while still being very specific about "how much"), its major focus would seem to have been to remind people of their positive attitudes toward volunteering and to encourage the prone to get (up and) involved.

On a smaller scale, at the local level where specifics can be offered, many volunteer service organizations publish notices in community newspapers or distribute brochures in community gathering places announcing their need for volunteers and informing prospective volunteers of how and where to sign up. Similarly, "event volunteerism," focused on one-time only or circumscribed participation activities such as toy-drives or litter clean-ups, may find favor because these events provide those who are ready to volunteer with a clear message about when, where, and how to do so. Special events, such as annual walk-a-thons, may also serve as fundraising opportunities, at the same time as they are high profile advertisements that can draw new volunteers into organizations. By offering information and opportunities, such educational campaigns can and do attract those already prone or willing to volunteer, who simply need to be mobilized; such efforts seem unlikely to work on those who are waiting for a good offer (because often they offer no explicit incentives) or especially those who are disinclined to volunteer.

Targeting Those Resistant to Volunteering

Indeed, those who are resistant to volunteering (or generally disinclined) may require the most pressure to be applied to generate behavior change. Although other countries often use laws to mandate participation in service (e.g., Israel, Germany, Taiwan, and many other countries require military or community service of young men), such has not been the case in the United States—at least not at the national level. Recently, however, there has been a growth in the United States in required community service programs, usually associated with educational institutions, that make participation in activities similar to those engaged in by actual volunteers a contingency of the successful completion of a course or degree (see Sobus, 1995; Stukas, Clary, & Snyder, 1999; Stukas & Dunlap, 2002). For example, the state of Maryland requires its high school students to engage in 40 hours of community service in order to graduate and a similar requirement exists in the province of Ontario, Canada. In addition, a multitude of individual schools (public, private, and religious) and school districts across the United States have included community service as a condition of graduation. Other states (e.g., Florida, Michigan) make community service a condition for eligibility for academic awards and scholarships. Even the U. S. Department of Housing and Urban Development has gotten into the act, recently requiring all residents of public housing to contribute 8 hours of community service a month.

Such requirements to volunteer, while certainly engaging people in community service (the prone, the open, and the resistant together), may also have other unanticipated and potentially negative outcomes. For example, Stukas, Snyder, and Clary (1999) assessed participants in a required university-level community service program for business students and found that those who felt most controlled by the requirement indicated that they were less likely to volunteer again in the future (as compared to those who felt less controlled) and this effect was larger for those who had greater past volunteer experience. Such results suggest that requirements (or heavy-handed persuasion efforts) that target those already prone to volunteer in addition to those resistant to volunteering may potentially do more harm to past volunteers than good. Conversely, it seems likely that those who are resistant to volunteering may find requirements more controlling than those already prone to volunteering, suggesting that requirements may not be able to increase volunteer behavior beyond the required amount for those who have never volunteered (despite the hopes of requirement proponents that even such forced activities will make the benefits of volunteerism known to all). A consideration of the ethics of required programs also suggests that the types of volunteer work promoted and the particular beneficiaries of this work need to be carefully evaluated (e.g., Clary & Snyder, 2002; Kelman & Warwick, 1978).

Targeting Those Open to Good Offers

Perhaps then, educational campaigns merely mobilize those who have internalized the value of volunteerism whereas requirements and laws merely force those who have not to comply temporarily. How, then, can the potentially larger middle group, those "open to a good offer" as Maibach (2002) put it, be influenced to volunteer? What sorts of "offers" might be constructed to persuade people to incorporate volunteer action into their regular schedules? Given that the very word "offer" constitutes an element of a formal exchange and reminds us of a marketplace where trades are bartered and deals are negotiated, it should come as no surprise that Maibach (2002) and others (e.g., Kotler, Roberto, & Lee, 2002) see marketing techniques and strategies as the best tools to use to increase behavior, including prosocial behavior as well as consumer behavior. When positive social behaviors are the focus, such techniques are properly known as "social marketing." For Maibach (2002):

> Social marketing is a process that attempts to create voluntary exchange between a marketing organization and members of a target market based on mutual fulfillment of self-interest. The marketing organization uses its resources to understand the perceived interests of target market members, to enhance and deliver the package of benefits associated with a product, service or idea, and to reduce barriers that interfere with its adoption or maintenance. Target market members, in turn, expend their resources (e.g., money, time, effort) in exchange for the offer when it provides clear advantages over alternative behaviors. Success of the social marketing program is defined primarily in terms of its contribution to the well-being of target market members, or to society as a whole. (p. 9)

We know of no attempts yet to use an explicit social marketing campaign to increase rates of volunteerism. However, we think that the premises and principles of the functional approach to promoting and understanding volunteerism (e.g., Clary et al., 1998; Snyder, Clary, & Stukas, 2000) bear a strong family resemblance to the premises and principles of many social marketing campaigns (e.g., Andreason, 1995; Donovan & Henley, 2003; Fine, 1990; Kotler et al., 2002). As such, we feel that a discussion of the similarities and dissimilarities of the two approaches may serve to better organize research and applied campaigns aimed at understanding or encouraging volunteerism.

SOCIAL MARKETING AND FUNCTIONAL APPROACHES

Social marketing campaigns place the consumer center stage, believing that "an understanding of the consumer and what makes her or him act is the essential first step in any strategic planning process" (Andreason, 2002, p. 42). This focus on individual motivation ("what makes her or him act") is also a key element of functional approaches to the study of human behavior (see Snyder & Cantor, 1998). In keeping with earlier functional theories of attitudes (e.g., Katz, 1960; Smith, Bruner, & White, 1959), functional approaches to the study of behavior propose that different people may engage in the same behavior to serve different functions (i.e., for different reasons and purposes) or to serve more than one function. Understanding why people act the way that they do is key to developing ways to alter their behavior while still allowing them freedom to choose.

Thus, when Maibach (2002) argued that some people might be open to a good offer, he was suggesting that by highlighting or offering incentives and by reducing or eliminating costs, people themselves might willfully choose to engage in the behavior. It's worth noting that one prominent definition of social marketing suggests that the goal of such programs is to "influence the *voluntary* behavior of target audiences in order to improve their personal welfare and that of their society" (Andreason, 1995, p. 7, italics added). This effort to encourage voluntary choice is the hallmark of a consumer orientation that takes as sacrosanct the belief that any exchange should benefit both the consumer and the marketer (i.e., business or society), thus making for a sustainable and (presumably) equitable arrangement.

It should also not go unsaid that allowing target audiences greater freedom to make choices about how to behave is associated with greater ethicality of social intervention strategies by some (e.g., Kelman & Warwick, 1978). Indeed, volunteerism itself is typically defined with explicit reference to the freedom of choice surrounding decisions to serve (e.g., Clary & Snyder, 1999; Cordingley, 2000). Thus, allowing an audience the freedom to make their own decisions means that influence strategies must rely on the art and science of persuasion (without crossing the line into manipulation or propaganda; Kelman & Warwick, 1978). Knowing which benefits are desirable to the target audience is the key to successful commercial marketing; knowing how to alert target audiences to benefits that may not be immediately apparent (or available in the short-term) is often the key to successful social marketing. In psychology, functional approaches also begin with an assessment of the benefits to be gained from acting, the reasons why the behavior is enacted.

THE MOTIVATIONS TO VOLUNTEER

Research applying a functional approach to the study of volunteerism therefore began by enumerating the reasons why people engage in volunteer activities and the types of personal benefits that might be gained by doing so. Drawing upon both classic theories (e.g., Katz, 1960; Smith et al., 1956) and existing empirical research (e.g., Clary & Miller, 1986; Gidron, 1978; Jenner, 1982) to guide their thinking about motivation, Clary et al. (1998) developed a 30-item instrument, the Volunteer Functions Inventory (VFI), to assess the different reasons that people may have for volunteering. Unlike other approaches to the study of helping behavior that have emphasized altruism (e.g., Batson, 1991) or egoism (e.g., Maner et al., 2002) predominantly, the functional approach allows for the possibility that volunteers may have both other-focused and self-focused motives for helping. The VFI has been demonstrated to have satisfactory psychometric properties in samples of both volunteers and non-volunteers (e.g., Clary et al., 1998; Okun, Barr, & Herzog, 1998). Thus, volunteerism has been found to allow people to meet the following six goals:

- *Values*: to express humanitarian and prosocial values through action;
- *Career*: to explore career options and increase the likelihood that a particular career path can be pursued;
- *Understanding*: to gain greater understanding of the world, the diverse people in it, and ultimately oneself;
- *Enhancement*: to boost self-esteem, to feel important and needed by others, and to form new friendships;
- *Protective*: to distract oneself from personal problems or to work through problems in the context of service;
- *Social*: to satisfy the expectations of friends and close others.

Omoto and Snyder (1995) have also designed an inventory to assess the reasons why people volunteer to provide services for people living with AIDS. Scales that assess motives that are particular to the specific type of volunteerism under consideration may be necessary to capture goals not assessed by the VFI. Omoto and Snyder's measure contains similar, though more specifically focused, scales to the VFI, but notably adds a motive reflecting identification with the community of people particularly influenced by AIDS:

- *Community Concern*: to demonstrate one's interest in, and commitment to, one's community.

Research using the VFI begins by assessing the extent to which potential volunteers feel that the six functions are important or accurate reasons for them to volunteer. Such research efforts are equivalent to the types of consumer research conducted by marketers to determine whether different people are attracted to different products or the different aspects of products which might be appealing to different types of people. Social marketing, like other forms of marketing, operates by creating different persuasive appeals and marketing campaigns for different segments of the target audience. The search for appropriate dimensions by which to segment the target audience, that are clearly related to the types of benefits or barriers they may see associated with the target behavior, is a key task for social marketers (e.g., Kotler et al., 2002).

The functional approach to volunteerism provides a ready scheme by which to segment the market for volunteer activities. Indeed, Kotler et al. (2002) and Donovan and Henley (2003) both suggest that motivational variables—or psychographics—may be useful for market segmentation. If we assume that potential volunteers motivated by volunteerism's ability to help them with career goals differ from potential volunteers motivated by volunteerism's ability to afford a way to express their prosocial or humanitarian values, then it follows that different persuasive messages and perhaps different volunteer activities may appeal to these two groups. The tailoring of message—and product—to the audience is essential to the concept of the marketing mix discussed shortly.

THE MATCHING OF MOTIVATIONS TO AFFORDANCES

According to the functional approach, particular types of volunteer work are expected to attract individuals with different motives, because particular types of volunteer activities offer different "affordances" for volunteers to meet their goals or motives (Clary, Snyder, & Stukas, 1996; Clary, Snyder, & Worth, 2003). Indeed, a key premise of functional approaches revolves around the extent to which volunteers are able to fulfill their motivations through their activities. This is known as the "matching principle" and it suggests that volunteers who receive benefits matched to their motives will be more satisfied, more inclined to continue volunteering, and perhaps more effective in their volunteer efforts (e.g., Snyder et al., 2000).

Recruiting Volunteers

Thus, just as social marketers seek to tailor their persuasive messages to the audience, adherents of the functional approach to volunteerism match their messages to the motives thought to underlie volunteer activity (e.g., Clary & Snyder, 1993). Research studies support this practice. For example, Clary, Snyder, Ridge, Miene, and Haugen (1994) presented university students with video advertisements based on volunteer motives that were either matched to the viewer's primary motive for volunteering (assessed prior to the study) or were mismatched; viewers preferred matched ads to mismatched ads, feeling that the former would be more likely to get them to volunteer. Similarly, Clary et al. (1998) asked research participants to assess the appeal of a set of brochures that encouraged students to participate in a volunteer fair (one technique often used to advertise opportunities to potential university student volunteers). Each brochure systematically appealed to one of the various motives measured by the VFI. They found that the relevant VFI scale scores best predicted ratings of each brochure.

Two field studies focused on AIDS volunteers have also found that matched advertisements were perceived to be better recruiting tools than mismatched advertisements. Using a sample of current AIDS volunteers, Omoto, Snyder, and Smith (1999) found that pre-measured assessments of motivations to volunteer (using the Omoto & Snyder, 1995, inventory of motivations for AIDS volunteerism) predicted the relative appeal of three types of newspaper advertisements, designed to highlight self-focused reasons for service, other-focused reasons for service, or no motivational content. Thus, the volunteers' other-focused motivation scores (such as community concern and value expression) significantly predicted ratings of the other-focused ad whereas self-focused motivation scores did not. A similar matching effect occurred for ratings of the self-focused ad, which were significantly predicted by self-focused motivation scores (such as understanding, career, and enhancement) but not by other-focused motivation scores. Smith, Omoto, and Snyder (2001) subsequently placed newspaper advertisements promoting AIDS volunteerism in student newspapers in two states, varying whether the ads focused on other-focused reasons for volunteering or self-focused reasons for volunteering. Respondents to each ad then completed the AIDS volunteerism questionnaire. Results demonstrated that those who responded to the other-focused ad had higher other-focused motivation than those who responded to the self-focused ad (or a control ad). These studies provide further evidence to support the underlying theoretical premises of the functional approach as well as to suggest that segmenting the target audience according to their motivations for volunteerism and then specifically tailoring messages to those motivations is likely to be a successful strategy for social marketers and volunteer recruitment professionals.

Sustaining Volunteers

Volunteers who find activities that offer benefits related to their primary motivations, perhaps by responding to a targeted advertisement, are also predicted to feel more satisfied by these activities than volunteers who wind up in activities that offer benefits related to less important motivations (e.g., Snyder et al., 2000). Finding an activity that affords benefits related to one's own important motives and goals is also likely to promote sustained volunteerism, perhaps as a result of the increased satisfaction available from the task (e.g., Omoto & Snyder, 1995). Research by Clary et al. (1998; Study 5 with elder volunteers, and Study 6 with university student volunteers) examined the influence of each motive on volunteer outcomes separately, demonstrating that both importance of a motive (assessed with the VFI) and the availability of matched or functionally-relevant benefits received from volunteer activities (assessed at a future point) were necessary for greater satisfaction and heightened intentions to volunteer in the future. Thus, for example, volunteers who had strong understanding motivation and found that they were able to learn more about the world and themselves through their service were more satisfied and more likely to continue their volunteer activities (in both the short and long term future) than volunteers who either did not have strong understanding motivation (for whom understanding benefits, if received, had less relevance) or those who had strong understanding motivation but were not able to learn through their activities.

Also relevant to the goal of sustaining volunteer participation, O'Brien, Crain, Omoto, and Snyder (2000) found that AIDS volunteers, categorized as either relatively self-focused or relatively other-focused in their reasons for volunteering, who later reported that their reasons for volunteering were satisfied by being a buddy to a person with AIDS were more committed to the organization. In this study, commitment was operationalized as a linear combination of measures tapping volunteer satisfaction, length of service, and perceived cost of volunteering. The effect of matching on commitment was demonstrated by a significant interaction term in a 2 (motive: self vs. other) × 2 (benefits: self vs. other) analysis of variance, where matched volunteers were significantly more committed than mismatched volunteers.

More recently, Worth, Snyder, and Clary (2005) and Stukas, Daly, and Cowling (2005) have examined the six motives for volunteering (assessed by the VFI) as a set, demonstrating in separate cross-sectional field studies with community volunteers in America and Australia, that the *number* of important motives (operationalized as above the median) matched by available benefits is a strong predictor of satisfaction and future intentions as well as (in Worth et al., 2005) positive emotion experienced during service and (in Stukas et al., 2005) two indicators of social capital, psychological sense of community and generalized trust. Such results suggest that the experience of having one's goals met by a volunteer activity may be essential for volunteer retention—and having more goals met is better than having fewer goals met (see also Tschirhart, Mesch, Perry, Miller, & Lee, 2001).

Focusing on benefits available to volunteers is central to the functional approach (e.g., Snyder et al., 2000), and there is some evidence to suggest that volunteers who seek and receive benefits for themselves may sustain their service longer than volunteers who seek only to help others. In their original study of AIDS volunteers, Omoto and Snyder (1995) found that the more volunteers reported being motivated by self-focused benefits (such as esteem enhancement), the longer they sustained their participation; by contrast, the extent to which volunteers reported being motivated by other-focused benefits (such as community concern) did not predict length of service.

These findings fit well with the social marketing conception of volunteerism as an exchange between the volunteer and the community (or recipient) from which both receive benefits, in this case with volunteers receiving benefits such as new skills and enhanced self-esteem and the recipients receiving the benefits of the help and services provided by volunteers. Such findings have implications for the way in which volunteerism is often discussed as an intrinsically altruistic or purely self-less activity, suggesting that reframing community service in terms of its benefits to all (the volunteers themselves, the recipients of volunteer services, the community at large) might work toward improving commitment to volunteerism in the community. Moreover, an individual's contribution to the community promises to provide some sort of return to the individual as a member of the community.

VOLUNTEERISM AND THE MARKETING MIX

For social marketers, then, the goal is to guide people to make voluntary choices by alerting them to the targeted benefits they can receive from their behavior. The functional approach also suggests that persuasive messages can play a crucial role in alerting volunteers to activities that allow them to satisfy their motivations. However, both approaches also require that actual benefits be received from the behavioral choice. For the functional approach, this means ensuring that features of the volunteer environment actually provide affordances for motivations to be met. Social marketers, in turn, focus on the "marketing mix" (Kotler et al., 2000; Maibach, 2003), paying attention to the *product* offered (e.g., the behavior itself and its associated benefits), the *price* it extols from the actor, and the *place* it can be enacted, as well as the messages designed for *promotion* of the behavior.

The Product

When it comes to the marketing of volunteer activities, the product in question is among the most diverse around. A large number of organizations worldwide offer a wide array of activities, from hands-on labor to boardroom politics and everything in between. For this reason, it is imperative that organizations find their niche and promote their product vigorously to their segment of the market. In terms of the functional approach, this means describing the volunteer activities with regard to the benefits they can offer. Clary, Snyder, and Worth (2003) recently surveyed 1,388 volunteers from 83 affiliates of the Volunteer Resource Center, a regional volunteer placement agency in Minneapolis-St. Paul, Minnesota. Volunteers working for organizations in such varied areas as education, human services, health, public benefit, arts and culture, environment, and youth development scored differently on the motivations assessed by the six scales of the VFI, particularly on the values, understanding, and career motives, suggesting that those with different goals are attracted to different areas of service (see also Clary et al., 1996, for results from an earlier Gallup Poll). Volunteers from different types of organizations also reported that they were able to satisfy different needs in their volunteer work (i.e., received different functionally-relevant benefits). For example, from the total sample, 82 volunteers reported working in the area of youth development (for organizations such as Boy and Girl Scouts, Camp Fire Groups, 4-H Clubs, youth groups with religious affiliations, and Little Leagues or other athletic groups). As compared to volunteers working for other types of organizations, youth development volunteers were generally higher in VFI-assessed values, career, and understanding motivation. Youth development volunteers also reported having more opportunities to act on and to express their values than other volunteers and fewer opportunities to meet the social expectations of their friends and family. (For more in depth treatment of volunteerism to youth, see Stukas, Daly, & Clary, 2006.)

Data from an organization's own volunteers may help to identify both the goals sought by typical volunteers and the affordances provided by the types of tasks available in the organization. Such information can allow volunteer positions to be properly advertised to attract volunteers who seek the benefits available from an organization's activities (as in Smith et al., 2001). However, this does not preclude an alternate strategy based on an assessment of the motivations possessed by the potential volunteer pool in a community. With this strategy, volunteer activities can be modified by organizations to provide functionally-relevant benefits (geared to the primary motives of likely volunteers in a community) where previously they did not. For example, providing seminars or retreats for volunteers to learn more about the cause or the recipients of their services may go a long way toward helping them to meet goals related to the understanding function. Showing volunteers their worth by holding "thank you" dinners or bestowing awards may help to boost self-esteem in volunteers motivated by the enhancement function. Even framing identical tasks in different ways in order to highlight the ways in which the task can be construed as matching a primary motivation has been shown to have effects on willingness to volunteer (e.g., O'Brien et al., 2000). Attention to the affordances provided by the product may provide both the essential ingredients by which volunteerism can be marketed to an audience segmented according to their primary motivations and a guarantee that such motivations may be satisfied by the product, thereby potentially sustaining volunteers over the long haul.

The Price

Of course, volunteerism also takes time, emotion, and effort and such costs must be factored into the price of the product when a social marketing strategy is being developed (e.g., Kotler et al., 2002). Such costs vary from activity to activity and organizations may need to balance carefully the benefits available to volunteers and the commitment expected of volunteers. Being upfront about the costs of volunteering—and assisting potential volunteers to overcome cost-related barriers to volunteering—is another part of the social marketer's task. Any advertisement of benefits in a persuasive message might be counterbalanced with an honest report of potential challenges (see Snyder, 1993). This simple strategy, ensuring that volunteers who sign up have carefully weighed the pros and cons of the activity for themselves, may ward off later disenchantment (see also Omoto, Gunn, & Crain, 1998, for a discussion of volunteers' often impossibly high expectations for the effects of their labors on clients or social issues).

Indeed, some forms of volunteerism may entail significant costs (i.e., the price for participation is high) and organizations may need to alert potential volunteers to these costs or suffer unsustainable levels of turnover. For example, many AIDS volunteers report experiences of stigmatization (i.e., having been made to feel embarrassed, uncomfortable, or otherwise devalued) as a result of their volunteer work (e.g., Snyder, Omoto, & Crain, 1999). Such feelings may function as barriers and deterrents to volunteering. Moreover, even among those who do become volunteers, feelings of stigmatization seem to function as barriers and deterrents to continuing and effective service. In one longitudinal study of AIDS volunteers, for example, Omoto, Snyder, and Crain (2001) found that feelings of stigmatization were associated with early termination of volunteer service and, among those who continued to serve, with feelings of stress and demoralization related to one's volunteer work. The potential for stigmatization could be raised and discussed with volunteers who sign up to work with people with AIDS during an orientation or training session along with appropriate coping strategies. Similarly, those who volunteer to mentor youth may need to be alerted to the difficulties inherent in forming relationships with "at risk" children and may need to have organization support and counseling to help them with their tasks (see Stukas & Tanti, 2005). These costs must be calculated into the price of volunteer work, to allow potential participants a fair chance to make a voluntary choice about how to behave, an important factor in the social marketer's rule book (e.g., Andreason, 2002). From a functionalist point of view, it is important to ensure that any costs of volunteering for the volunteer do not undermine or eliminate the functionally-relevant benefits that he or she can receive.

However, even when costs are not as extreme as in the case of AIDS volunteerism or of mentoring at-risk youth, volunteering can still entail significant monetary and non-monetary costs when adopted as a new behavior. Worth, Clary, and Snyder (2004) asked their sample of 1,388 volunteers (described earlier) to assess the volunteer environment surrounding their service, both in terms of facilitators of, and barriers to, the receipt of functionally-relevant benefits. Volunteers also provided ratings of the emotions, positive and negative, that they experienced during service. Analyses demonstrated that the extent of perceived facilitators in the environment predicted volunteers' intentions to continue volunteering at the same organization and this effect was mediated by the experience of positive emotions. The extent of perceived barriers in the environment predicted volunteers' intentions to volunteer at a different organization in the future; this effect was mediated by the experience of negative emotions.

With regard to the price of volunteering, these findings suggest that volunteers are sensitive to the factors that help or hinder their goals for volunteering and that such factors have direct impacts on their day-to-day emotional experiences in volunteerism. Indeed, barriers and facilitators to goal achievement in the volunteer environment and the resultant emotions they elicit from volunteers may determine whether volunteers remain at an organization or not. Decisions to volunteer or to remain in a volunteer position may be best understood not only as a cost-benefit analysis, but as a cost-benefit analysis relative to cost-benefit analyses for other "competing" behaviors (see Kotler et al., 2002). In this study, volunteers who saw more barriers at one organization could foresee themselves shifting to a new volunteer organization in the future.

The Place

The third element of the marketing mix, place, refers to the location at which the activity takes place, or the "distribution channel" by which "the product is made available to members of the target market at a time and place when it will be of most value to them" (Maibach, 2003, p. 11). For volunteerism, "place" may be synonymous with "price", in that distance to travel and ease of access may be important factors in choosing an activity or organization for many volunteers. However, identifying where potential volunteers are located and bringing volunteer tasks to them, if possible, is one lesson that can be learned from the social marketing approach.

This point about place was not lost on the Red Cross when they introduced the bloodmobile as a way to increase donations. Thus, making it possible for people to volunteer to help in their own communities, schools, or even workplaces, may increase rates of volunteerism and potentially the functionally-relevant benefits that volunteers may receive (e.g., the ability to meet the expectations of one's social network seems more likely when volunteering in one's own community). Indeed, school-based youth mentoring programs may provide a safe, familiar, and accessible location for volunteers to interact with challenging kids, reducing costs for volunteers, parents, and students themselves (e.g., Stukas & Tanti, 2005). Allowing volunteers to do some tasks from home (for example, fund-raising, preparation of mailings) may increase the ease of doing volunteer work, reducing time spent in travel to an organization's headquarters while also extending the hours and days of the week during which activities may occur (e.g., Kotler et al., 2002).

Corporate volunteerism programs make it easier for employees to engage in service, by reducing the price, facilitating the place, and potentially choosing a product that fits with the goals and interests of employees. Marketing volunteerism to corporations rather than directly to individual volunteers represents distribution channel marketing (e.g., Kotler et al., 2002). By use of an appeal targeted carefully to a corporation's mission statement or the primary motivations of their employees, volunteerism by a large number of people may be facilitated, taking advantage of a corporation's own internal structure to promote and encourage service. The contribution of community service by a corporation is often seen to boost its public image (and perhaps its profit margin), thereby cementing the exchange nature of the relationship that underscores the social marketing approach. Wooing customers by making contributions of time or money to charities and other community groups (i.e., "cause related marketing") has the potential to aid both the community and big business (though perhaps only when the approach does not seem overly cynical; Endacott, 2004).

The development of mutually-beneficial relationships between volunteer organizations and other institutions (schools, corporations, religious institutions) in the community reminds us again that the "place" for volunteerism is often the geographical community itself. Omoto and Snyder's (2002) analysis of the community as the context for service suggests that the promotion of volunteer work needs to be true to the community's social and cultural norms (as well as varying legal contexts). Indeed, many volunteer organizations began with a focus on their own geographical community and their efforts focused on making that community better. When volunteer agencies maintain a focus on the local community and work to improve a psychological sense of community, they may also increase the appeal of volunteering in that "place" (e.g., Omoto & Snyder, 2002). Of course, it goes without saying that communities may be both geographically and relationally defined (i.e., based on interests or skills; see Stukas & Dunlap, 2002) and that service to relational communities may also occur from a distance (perhaps in a cyber-place).

Promotion

Although we have already discussed ways of tailoring persuasive messages to audiences segmented by their motivations to volunteer, the concept of the marketing mix also advises that one pay careful attention to the channels through which messages are delivered. Therefore, when deciding how to promote volunteerism, social marketers might do well to take into account not only the demographic or psychographic characteristics of the target audience but also the places where audience members congregate, the other activities in which they engage, and the interests they maintain. Indeed, a careful assessment of the social and physical contexts in which potential volunteers are found may be necessary to make sure that messages are received. Although the traditional marketing tools of television and print advertising may capture a large audience (and may be amenable to utilizing the functional approach; Clary et al., 1994, 1998; Smith et al., 2001), other tools and channels may work better for specific segments of the target audience.

Both Omoto and Snyder (2002) and Stukas and Tanti (2005) suggest that recruitment of new volunteers by existing volunteers from their own social networks is likely to be successful. Such initiatives, if formalized in practices such as "recruitment evenings" when volunteers bring interested friends to the organization, may take advantage of social ties and expectations, as well as provide an opportunity to discuss the real benefits and costs of volunteering with new recruits in terms of their own goals and from the perspective of an actual volunteer. Relying on social connections to promote volunteerism is a reminder that persuasion and marketing often occur on a one-to-one basis, and not always in large scale campaigns. Moreover, the power of social connections to promote volunteerism is another example of how social capital may both be built by volunteerism and result in greater levels of volunteerism; indeed, Omoto and Snyder (2002) reported that a large percentage of AIDS volunteers both made new friends with other current volunteers and recruited their existing friends to become new volunteers.

VOLUNTEERISM IN CONTEXT

In addition to providing insight into where and when promotional messages can be delivered to encourage volunteerism, an analysis of the social and physical contexts inhabited by potential volunteers can also show how volunteer activity could fit into a volunteer's life. Just as motivations and preferences for certain types of volunteer activities can vary among the target audience, so too can barriers to volunteering. Potential volunteers differ in their family and work commitments, they differ in their modes of transportation, and they differ in their needs for accommodation and assistance in carrying out their volunteer service activities. Knowing how to adjust aspects of volunteer activities to reduce potential barriers requires recruiters to examine the decision to volunteer (and to keep volunteering) as made by individuals both in the context of their decision to choose one volunteer opportunity over another and in the context of the other decisions they make about how to use their time and lives. That is, volunteering must be seen in the context of its potential competition with other opportunities in the social environment.

Competition From Other Volunteer Opportunities

As Andreason (2002) pointed out, although it may appear "unseemly" for community and social service organizations to compete against each other for the pool of volunteers, this is exactly what must be done. Such competition may help to ensure that the tasks available to volunteers really do offer important benefits, allowing volunteers to behave like consumers and choose between opportunities based on the benefits available from them. Thus, competition may help to make volunteering, as a product, an even better one.

But achieving "competitive superiority" (Kotler et al., 2002, p. 176) over other volunteer organizations, while potentially productive, may not be the main focus of those organizations. After all, many volunteers serve more than one organization (sometimes simultaneously), and, given that different tasks offer different benefits, the competition may only be fierce between very similar organizations or tasks. Indeed, the very fact that different types of volunteerism may offer different benefits may be useful to volunteer coordinators who seek to recruit and to retain volunteers, allowing them to attract the segment of the target audience that is most likely to be seeking the benefits they can offer or to position their opportunity against other opportunities that offer different benefits. Organizations within a community may even choose to work together. For example, to the extent that a volunteer's motives may change over time (a possibility according to the functional approach; Snyder et al., 2000), then re-orienting that volunteer to a new competing task or organization may provide for a new way to meet an old motivation or a way to meet a newly important motivation.

Competition From Other Life Tasks

Moreover, the competition that volunteerism faces may not be limited to competition among potential volunteer opportunities, but also may stem from the competition between volunteering and other activities that compete for the potential volunteer's time and energy. After all, volunteering may take time away from work, from friends and family, and from leisure time and recreational activities. That is, by choosing to volunteer, people are suffering "opportunity costs" in addition to any other costs; the social marketer must try to beat out this form of competition, making a good offer to those potentially interested that tops other offers and opportunities that must be foregone. With respect to matters of competition, Kotler et al. (2002) have suggested that "competitive superiority" may be achieved by a number of different strategies, including by focusing on highlighting or increasing the benefits of volunteering relative to other leisure time activities (benefit-to-benefit superiority); by focusing on the low costs of volunteering and at the same time undermining the perceived benefits of other activities (cost-to-benefit superiority); by focusing on both the benefits of volunteerism and the costs of alternate activities (benefit-to-cost superiority); or by focusing on decreasing the costs of volunteering relative to the costs of other activities (cost-to-cost superiority).

To date, research on volunteerism generated by the functional approach has focused on how volunteer work may allow people to satisfy important personal motivations. The extent to which volunteer activities are better than other activities at providing benefits matched to these motivations has not yet been determined. Nevertheless, we believe that a focus on benefits (i.e., a benefit-to-benefit superiority strategy), in combination with careful attention to maximizing the other elements of the marketing mix, that involves both increasing the facilitators of such benefits and decreasing any barriers to achieving such benefits (e.g., Clary et al., 2003), is likely to result in competitive superiority over other discretionary time activities.

Yet, as successful as a benefit-to-benefit comparison may be for promoting volunteerism above other competing activities, it may not be enough to retain some volunteers. Research suggests that the factors that predict recruitment to volunteer activities and the factors that predict attrition from volunteer activities may be different (e.g., Gidron, 1985). Although volunteer satisfaction has been identified as one predictor of sustained volunteerism (e.g., Penner & Finkelstein, 1998), and the provision of matched benefits has been related to volunteer satisfaction (e.g., Clary et al., 1998; Tschirhart et al., 2001), the reasons that people provide for leaving a volunteer activity are often unrelated to satisfaction or dissatisfaction with their service (e.g., Davis, Hall, & Meyer, 2003). Thus, volunteer satisfaction may be a necessary, though not a sufficient, condition for ensuring longevity and warding off attrition. Instead, a focus on minimizing *barriers* that make volunteerism difficult to perform (as well as barriers that make benefits difficult to obtain) may also be required for greater retention of volunteers.

Such barriers may include a lack of time or some degree of trouble in reaching the volunteer site. Community volunteers who ceased their activities in Davis's (2005) study cited "time conflicts" (48%) as the number one reason for discontinuing volunteerism, with "change in residence" a distant second (at 15%). Only 12 out of 101 departing volunteers mentioned dissatisfaction as a reason for quitting. Such results point to the potential for ensuring retention of volunteers by minimizing these costs of volunteerism for the volunteer relative to the costs of other leisure time activities (i.e., a cost-to-cost superiority strategy; Kotler et al., 2002).

Competition From Other Norms and Values

Although deciding to volunteer is likely to reflect a personal choice based on a number of factors (including a comparison of benefits and costs), volunteer action is also responsive to the social expectations of other people. Social expectations can serve to increase a volunteer's tendency to initiate volunteering (e.g., Clary et al., 1998). Moreover, social expectations also may influence a volunteer to continue volunteering, as the social role of volunteer may become a core component of his or her identity (e.g., Grube & Piliavin, 2000). Finally, many people initiate their volunteer service because they have been contacted by a friend or acquaintance and asked to do so (e.g., Independent Sector, 2001) or because they belong to an organization that includes volunteer service as part of its mission (e.g., Penner, 2002). In this way, some volunteers may engage in service because such helpful action is normative for their social group.

Social norms, it should be recognized, may be either *descriptive*, reflecting the typical behaviors of a social group, or *injunctive*, reflecting behaviors that are strongly encouraged or discouraged by social groups (e.g., Cialdini & Trost, 1998). In this sense, volunteer service may be primarily influenced by descriptive norms—many people may volunteer because such behavior is typical of their friends and neighbors. However, Omoto and Snyder (2002) have suggested that volunteer work can reflect a psychological sense of community and this may be especially true when that community is made up of people who often engage in service. In this sense, volunteering for one's community may reflect the community's values and preferences, and thus be guided by injunctive norms.

Furthermore, Okun (2002) has reported that the perception that important others either favored or disfavored volunteering was a significant predictor of students' intentions to enroll in a college volunteer program. At the societal level, the norm of social responsibility (e.g., Berkowitz, 1972) that suggests that people should help those in need may also influence volunteer behavior. However, the power of these injunctive norms may not be particularly strong. Research suggests that whereas prosocial behavior may be encouraged by social groups, these groups often impose few penalties for failing to engage in prosocial behavior (e.g., White, 1984).

In certain situations, or for people who belong to a number of different social groups, competing norms may be available to guide behavior. Scales (2003) has suggested that norms to provide support and guidance to children in a community may compete with norms to mind one's own business or to avoid potential accusations of improper interactions between adults and children, and has recommended ways to increase the salience or importance of certain norms over others as a way of resolving norm conflict (see also Cialdini & Trost, 1998). More generally, there may be competing norms at play in determining whether individuals volunteer or not, and the strength of competing norms may create ambiguity about how or even whether to act. The political discourse surrounding volunteerism and its role in society has highlighted concerns that some types of service could be detrimental to society (though not going so far as to suggest that helpfulness itself should be avoided). From the perspective of some social observers and commentators, volunteerism may provide little more than temporary solutions that maintain the *status quo* and prevent the emergence of long term social change and permanent solutions to society's problems (e.g., Onyx & Leonard, 2000). From the perspective of others, however, volunteerism and the nonprofit sector as a whole, often contain associations of individuals that challenge the status quo and thereby offer society the potential for social change through social movements (for a fuller consideration of these tensions, see Van Til, 1988).

In other cases, norms that suggest that one should not get involved appear to represent another form of concern for others. For example, Skinner (1978) has reminded us that in helping another, we may actually be doing a disservice to the recipient and illustrates this with the example of tying the shoelace of a child who is in the process of learning to tie his or her shoes. Moreover, whereas recipients of the help offered by volunteers can benefit in many ways from that help, the help given can carry a message that is unflattering to the recipient of help. Research on recipients' reactions to aid (e.g., Nadler, 1991; Nadler & Fisher, 1986) has found that help suggests that the recipient is inferior to and of lower status than the help-giver, and longer-term may contribute to self-perceptions of helplessness and dependent actions. People may see receiving help as threatening and those people who are most competent and efficacious may be especially likely to feel threatened by the prospect of being in the role of recipient (see Nadler & Fisher, 1986). Thus, those people who may be in the best position to offer help (i.e., those who are themselves most competent and efficacious) may be the very people who are most sensitive to the negative connotations of receiving help. As a result, social norms that suggest that those low in power should be empowered and treated with respect may therefore compete with (or cloud the importance of) norms that suggest that the fortunate should intervene in the lives of the less fortunate.

CONCLUSION

A comparison of the strategies, goals, and techniques of social marketers and of those who seek to promote and encourage volunteerism reveals a considerable degree of overlap between the approaches. Importantly, there is the shared central focus on the "social good" and attempts at encouraging involvement in activities that benefit the community (which can be defined narrowly or broadly). Social marketing and the functional approach to volunteerism also share an explicit concern with exchanges, both between the desires of the consumer or potential volunteer and the opportunities afforded by the product, service or idea, and between the volunteer and the recipient or organization. Additionally, there are the similar goals of initially attracting consumers and potential volunteers to a particular action or activity, and then of sustaining or retaining them in those actions and activities over time. Finally, both the social marketing approach and the functional approach rely on consumer satisfaction as a key barometer of whether the strategy has been successful.

Our application of the principles of social marketing to the promotion of volunteerism offers lessons to both researchers and practitioners.

First, a focus on the target audience of potential volunteers, their needs, goals, and the potential benefits they may reap from volunteerism, is likely to offer an attractive selling point for many volunteer activities. Research on the functional approach to volunteerism supports the social marketing principle that persuasive messages targeted to an audience's characteristics, in this case, the reasons and benefits that motivate audience members to volunteer, is likely to increase recruitment of volunteers.

Second, a focus on the costs of volunteerism for volunteers, understood in terms of the marketing mix (product, price, place, promotion), may help efforts to retain volunteers, as well as to recruit them. For social marketers, satisfaction is the key to sustained activity and reducing costs increases it. Research on the functional approach suggests that as barriers to the receipt of benefits that match a volunteer's motivations increase, so too do the negative emotions experienced and the likelihood that a volunteer will move to another organization. Minimizing other costs related to the price of volunteering (e.g., time commitment, travel distance) may serve to reduce attrition in those satisfied.

Third, a focus on the context in which volunteerism occurs can help to increase the success of promotion efforts, as well as allow for an examination of the benefits and costs of particular volunteer activities for particular volunteers. Social marketing principles direct us to be aware of how decisions to volunteer compete with decisions to engage in other activities and how competitive superiority can be achieved by maximizing benefits and minimizing costs relative to other activities. Understanding volunteerism in the context of competing social norms may also yield insights into why decisions to volunteer may not always be easy to make.

In conclusion, we see that there is much to be gained from the adoption of social marketing principles for the promotion of volunteerism, particularly when such techniques include segmentation of the potential volunteer audience based on their motivations to volunteer. Careful consideration of principles identified by social marketers, as well as the evidence provided by research on volunteerism itself, should result in both greater insights into the volunteer process and more successful promotion efforts.

REFERENCES

Andreason, A. R. (1995). *Marketing social change: Changing behavior to promote health, social development, and the environment*. San Francisco: Jossey-Bass.

Andreason, A. R. (2002). Commercial marketing and social change. *Social Marketing Quarterly, 8*(2), 41–45.

Batson, C. D. (1991). *The altruism question: Toward a social psychological answer*. Hillsdale, NJ: Erlbaum.

Berkowitz, L. (1972). Social norms, feelings, and other factors affecting helping and altruism. In L. Berkowitz (Ed.), *Advances in experimental social psychology* (Vol. 6, pp. 63–108). New York: Academic Press.

Cialdini, R. B., & Trost, M. R. (1998). Social influence: Social norms, conformity, and compliance. In D. Gilbert, S. Fiske, & G. Lindzey (Eds.), *The handbook of social psychology* (4th ed., Vol. 2, pp. 151–192). New York: McGraw-Hill.

Clary, E. G., & Miller, J. (1986). Socialization and situational influences on sustained altruism. *Child Development, 57*, 1358–1369.

Clary, E. G., & Snyder, M. (1993). Persuasive communications strategies for recruiting volunteers. In D. R. Young, R. M. Hollister, & V. A. Hodgkinson (Eds.), *Governing, leading and managing nonprofit organizations* (pp. 121–137). San Francisco: Jossey-Bass.

Clary, E. G., & Snyder, M. (2002). Community involvement: Opportunities and challenges in socializing adults to participate in society. *Journal of Social Issues, 58*(3), 581–591.

Clary, E. G., Snyder, M., Ridge, R. D., Copeland, J., Stukas, A. A., Haugen, J., & Miene, P. (1998). Understanding and assessing the motivations of volunteers: A functional approach. *Journal of Personality and Social Psychology, 74*(6), 1516–1530.

Clary, E. G., Snyder, M., Ridge, R. D., Miene, P., & Haugen, J. (1994). Matching messages to motives in persuasion: A functional approach to promoting volunteerism. *Journal of Applied Social Psychology, 24*, 1129–1149.

Clary, E. G., Snyder, M., & Stukas, A. A. (1996). Volunteers' motivations: Findings from a national survey. *Nonprofit and Voluntary Sector Quarterly, 25*, 485–505.

Clary, E. G., Snyder, M., & Worth, K. (2003). *The volunteer organization environment: Key dimensions and distinctions*. Report to the Aspen Institute Nonprofit Sector Research Fund.

Cordingley, S. (2000). The definition and principles of volunteering: A framework for public policy. In J. Warburton & M. Oppenheimer (Eds.), *Volunteers and volunteering* (pp. 73–82). Sydney, NSW: Federation.

Davis, M. H. (2005). Becoming (and remaining) a community volunteer: Does personality matter? In A. M. Omoto (Ed.), *Processes of community change and social action* (pp. 67–82). Mahwah, NJ: Erlbaum.

Davis, M. H., Hall, J. A., & Meyer, M. (2003). The first year: Influences on the satisfaction, involvement, and persistence of new community volunteers. *Personality and Social Psychology Bulletin, 29*(2), 248–260.

Donovan, R. J., & Henley, N. (2003). *Social marketing: Principles and practice*. East Hawthorn, VIC, Australia: IP Communications.

Endacott, R. W. J. (2004). Consumers and CRM: A national and global perspective. *The Journal of Consumer Marketing, 21*, 183–189.

Fine, S. H. (1990). *Social marketing: Promoting the causes of public and nonprofit agencies*. Boston, MA: Allyn and Bacon.

Gidron, B. (1978). Volunteer work and its rewards. *Volunteer Administration, 11*, 18–32.

Gidron, B. (1985). Predictors of retention and turnover among service volunteer workers. *Journal of Social Service Research, 8*(1), 1–16.

Grube, J. A. & Piliavin, J. A. (2000). Role identity, organizational experiences, and volunteer performance. *Personality and Social Psychology Bulletin*, *26*, 1108–1120.

Independent Sector (1988). *Giving and volunteering in the United States*. Washington, DC: Author.

Independent Sector (2001). *Giving and volunteering in the United States*. Washington, DC: Author.

Ironmonger, D. (2000). Measuring volunteering in economic terms: 2,200 million hours worth $42 billion a year. In J. Warburton & M. Oppenheimer (Eds.), *Volunteers and volunteering* (pp. 56–72). Sydney, NSW: Federation.

Jenner, J. R. (1982). Participation, leadership, and the role of volunteerism among selected women volunteers. *Journal of Voluntary Action Research*, *11*, 27–38.

Kelman, H. C. (1961). Processes of opinion change. *Public Opinion Quarterly*, *25*, 57–78.

Kelman, H. C., & Warwick, D. P. (1978). The ethics of social intervention: Goals, means, and consequences. In G. Bermant, H. C. Kelman, & D. P. Warwick (Eds.), *The ethics of social intervention* (pp. 3–33). Washington, DC: Hemisphere.

Kotler, P., Roberto, N., & Lee, N. (2002). *Social marketing: Improving the quality of life*. Thousand Oaks, CA: Sage.

Lyons, M. (2002, May). Volunteering, active membership, and voluntary associations. In A.A. Stukas & M. Foddy (chairs), *Working for the common good*. Workshop sponsored by the Academy of Social Sciences in Australia at La Trobe University, Melbourne.

Maibach, E. W. (2003). Explicating social marketing: What is it, and what isn't it? *Social Marketing Quarterly*, *8*(4), 7–13.

Maner, J. K., Luce, C. L., Neuberg, S. L., Cialdini, R. B., Brown, S., & Sagarin, B. J. (2002). The effects of perspective-taking on motivations for helping: Still no evidence for altruism. *Personality and Social Psychology Bulletin*, *28*(11), 1601–1610.

Musick, M. A., Herzog, A. R., & House, J. S. (1999). Volunteering and mortality among older adults: Findings from a national sample. *The Journals of Gerontology: Psychological Sciences and Social Sciences*, *54B*, S173–S180.

Nadler, A. (1991). Help-seeking behavior: Psychological costs and instrumental benefits. In M. S. Clark (Ed.), *Prosocial behavior* (pp. 290–311). Thousand Oaks, CA: Sage.

Nadler, A., & Fisher, J. D. (1986). The role of threat to self-esteem and perceived control in recipient reactions to aid: Theory development and empirical validation. In L. Berkowitz (Ed.), *Advances in experimental social psychology* (Vol. 19, pp. 81–123). New York: Academic Press.

O'Brien, L. T., Crain, A. L., Omoto, A. M., & Snyder, M. (2000, May). *Matching motivations to outcomes: Implications for persistence in service*. Paper presented at the annual meetings of the Midwestern Psychological Association, Chicago, IL.

Okun, M. (2002). Application of planned behavior theory to predicting volunteer enrollment by college students in a campus-based program. *Social Behavior and Personality*, *30*(3), 243–250.

Okun, M. A., Barr, A., & Herzog, A. R. (1998). Motivation to volunteer by older adults: A test of competing measurement models. *Psychology and Aging*, *13*, 608–621.

Omoto, A. M., Gunn, D. O., & Crain, A. L. (1998). Helping in hard times: Relationship closeness and the AIDS volunteer experience. In V. J. Derlega & A. P. Barbee (Eds.), *HIV & social interaction* (pp. 106–128). Thousand Oaks, CA: Sage.

Omoto, A. M., & Snyder, M. (1995). Sustained helping without obligation: Motivation, longevity of service, and perceived attitude change among AIDS volunteers. *Journal of Personality and Social Psychology*, *68*(4), 671–686.

Omoto, A. M., & Snyder, M. (2002). Considerations of community: The context and process of volunteerism. *American Behavioral Scientist*, *45*(5), 846–867.

Omoto, A. M., Snyder, M., & Crain, A. L. (2001). *On the stigmatization of people who do good work: The case of AIDS volunteers*. Manuscript in preparation, Claremont Graduate University, and University of Minnesota.

Omoto, A. M., Snyder, M., & Smith, D. M. (1999). [Unpublished Data]. Lawrence, KS: University of Kansas.

Ontario Ministry of Education (1999). Ontario secondary schools, grades 9 to 12: Program and diploma requirements 1999. Retrieved on July 8, 2005, from http://www.edu.gov.on.ca/eng/document/curricul/secondary/oss/oss.html

Onyx, J., & Leonard, R. (2000). Women, volunteering, and social capital. In J. Warburton & M. Oppenheimer (Eds.), *Volunteers and volunteering* (pp. 113–124). Sydney, NSW: Federation.

Penner, L. A. (2002). Dispositional and organizational influences on sustained volunteerism: An interactionist perspective. *Journal of Social Issues, 58,* 447–467.

Penner, L. A. & Finkelstein, M. A. (1998). Dispositional and structural determinants of volunteerism. *Journal of Personality and Social Psychology, 74*(2), 525–537.

Piliavin, J. A. (2005). Feeling good by doing good: Health consequences of social service. In A. M. Omoto (Ed.), *Processes of community change and social action* (pp. 29–50). Mahwah, NJ: Erlbaum.

Portes, A. (1998). Social capital: Its origins and applications in modern sociology. *Annual Review of Sociology, 24,* 1–24.

Putnam, R. D. (2000). *Bowling alone: The collapse and revival of American community.* New York: Simon & Schuster.

Salamon, L. M. (Ed.) (1999). *Global civil society: Dimensions of the nonprofit sector* (Vol. 1). Bloomfield, CT: Kumarian.

Salamon, L. M. (Ed.) (2004). *Global civil society: Dimensions of the nonprofit sector* (Vol. 2). Bloomfield, CT: Kumarian.

Scales, P. C. (2003). *Other people's kids: Social expectations and American adults' involvement with children and adolescents.* New York: Kluwer Academic/Plenum.

Skinner, B. F. (1978). The ethics of helping people. In L. Wispé (Ed.), *Altruism, sympathy, and helping: Psychological and sociological principles* (pp. 249–262). New York: Academic Press.

Smith, D. M., Omoto, A. M., & Snyder, M. (2001, June). Motivation matching and recruitment of volunteers: A field study. Presented at the annual meetings of the American Psychological Society, Toronto, Canada.

Snyder, M. (1993). Basic research and practical problems: The promise of a "functional" personality and social psychology. *Personality and Social Psychology Bulletin, 19,* 251–264.

Snyder, M., & Cantor, N. (1998). Understanding personality and social behavior: A functionalist strategy. In D. Gilbert, S. Fiske, & G. Lindzey (Eds.), *The handbook of social psychology* (4th ed., Vol. 1, pp. 635–679). New York: McGraw-Hill.

Snyder, M., & Clary, E. G. (1990, August). Social activism and the problem of inaction: A functional perspective. Presented at the annual meetings of the American Psychological Association, Boston, MA.

Snyder, M., Clary, E. G., & Stukas, A. A. (2000). The functional approach to volunteerism. In G. R. Maio & J. M. Olson (Eds.), *Why we evaluate: Functions of attitudes* (pp. 365–393). Hillsdale, NJ: Erlbaum.

Snyder, M., Omoto, A. M., & Crain, A. L. (1999). Punished for their good deeds: Stigmatization of AIDS volunteers. *American Behavioral Scientist, 42,* 1175–1192.

Snyder, M., Omoto, A. M., & Lindsay, J. J. (2004). Sacrificing time and effort for the good of others: The benefits and costs of volunteerism. In A. Miller (Ed.), *The social psychology of good and evil* (pp. 444–468). New York: Guilford.

Snyder, M., Omoto, A. M., & Smith, D. M. (in press). The role of persuasion strategies in motivating individual and collective action. In E. Borgida, J. Sullivan, & E. Reidel (Eds.), *The political psychology of democratic citizenship.* New York: Cambridge University Press.

Sobus (1995). Mandating community service: Psychological implications of requiring prosocial behavior. *Law and Psychology Review, 19,* 153–182.

Stolle, D., & Rochon, T. R. (1998). Are all associations alike? Member diversity, associational type, and the creation of social capital. *American Behavioral Scientist, 42,* 47–65.

Stukas, A. A., Clary, E. G., & Snyder, M. (1999). Service learning: Who benefits and why. *Social Policy Report: Society for Research on Child Development, 13,* 1–19.

Stukas, A. A., Daly, M., & Clary, E. G. (2006). Lessons from research on volunteering for mobilizing adults to volunteer for positive youth development. In E. G. Clary & J. E. Rhodes (Eds.), *Mobilizing adults for positive youth development: Strategies for closing the gap between beliefs and behaviors* (pp. 65–82). New York, NY: Springer.

Stukas, A. A., Daly, M., & Cowling, M. J. (2005). Volunteerism and social capital: A functional approach. *Australian Journal on Volunteering, 10*(2), 35–44.

Stukas, A. A., & Dunlap, M. R. (2002). Community involvement: Theoretical approaches and educational initiatives. *Journal of Social Issues, 58*(3), 411–427.

Stukas, A. A., Snyder, M., & Clary, E. G. (1999). The effects of "mandatory volunteerism" on intentions to volunteer. *Psychological Science, 10*(1), 59–64.

Stukas, A. A., & Tanti, C. (2005). Recruiting and sustaining volunteer mentors. In D. L. DuBois & M. J. Karcher (Eds.), *Handbook of youth mentoring* (pp. 235–250). Newbury Park, CA: Sage.

Thoits, P. A., & Hewitt, L. N. (2001). Volunteer work and well-being. *Journal of Health and Social Behavior, 42*, 115–131.

Tschirhart, M., Mesch, D. J., Perry, J. L., Miller, T. K., & Lee, G. (2001). Stipended volunteers: Their goals, experiences, satisfaction, and likelihood of future service. *Nonprofit and Voluntary Sector Quarterly, 30*(3), 422–443.

Van Til, J. (1988). *Mapping the third sector: Voluntarism in a changing social economy.* New York: The Foundation Center.

White, M. J. (1984). Social expectations for prosocial behavior and altruism. *Academic Psychology Bulletin, 6*, 71–93.

Worth, K. A., Clary, E. G., & Snyder, M. (2004, January). The role of facilitators and barriers in understanding the processes of volunteerism. Presented at the annual meeting of the Society for Personality and Social Psychology, Austin, TX.

Worth, K. A., Snyder, M., & Clary, E. G. (2005, January). New approaches to investigating the matching of motives to experiences in the volunteer process. Presented at the annual meeting of the Society for Personality and Social Psychology, New Orleans, LA.

39

Health Risk Perceptions and Consumer Psychology

GEETA MENON

New York University

PRIYA RAGHUBIR

University of Carlifornia, Berkeley

NIDHI AGRAWAL

Northwestern University

WHAT IS RISK?

Risk, according to the Miriam Webster Online dictionary,[1] is defined as the possibility of loss or injury. In any task that involves action, people typically assess the probability of such loss or injury. If the probability falls with the "acceptable" range, people engage in the risky behavior (see chapters in Fischhoff et al., 1984). Otherwise, they refrain. This assessment of what qualifies as acceptable risk can vary depending on the context.

Risk has been studied from many different perspectives: economic, psychological, and consumption. Economists and insurers define risk in terms of a company, country, or instrument defaulting (i.e., not following through on a promised or expected return; see McFadden, 1999). Finance defines risk in terms of the volatility of price around a mean (Shefrin, 2005). Statisticians think of risk in terms of uncertainty, or a probabilistic assessment of the likelihood of an event occurring versus not occurring with this usage common in the behavioral decision theory literature as well (Tversky & Kahneman, 1974). Because of the multidimensional nature of risk, methods for studying and observing its effects have varied within and across paradigms and disciplines.

In this chapter, we define risk as a *negatively-valenced likelihood assessment that an unfavorable event will occur*. Risk, as defined by us, differs from an uncertainty judgment in three different ways. First, uncertainty judgments can be positively valenced (e.g., winning a sweepstake) or negatively-valenced (e.g., having an accident), whereas we define risk as always being in a negatively-valenced domain. Second, events that occur with a probability of 0.50 are more uncertain than those that occur with a probability closer to either 0 or 1, whereas, risk increases as a probability approaches 1. Third, less controllable events are more uncertain, while they may be no more or less risky.

In summary, we define health risk as the perception of the subjective likelihood of the occurrence of a *negative* event related to health for a person or group of people over a specified time period.

IMPORTANCE OF STUDYING HEALTH RISK PERCEPTIONS

Health risk perceptions are important to study because they are theoretically interesting, managerially relevant, and have consumer welfare and public policy implications. The domain of health provides a rich set of constructs that allow a consumer researcher to examine larger theoretical questions such as: What is the interplay of the cognitive and affective systems (in the construction of risk estimates)? What factors moderate the link between judgments (like risk perceptions) and (health related) behavior? How is memory-based information used along with context-based information to make (risk) judgments? Do individuals differ in the manner in which they process information and make judgments? This chapter focuses on the theoretical antecedents of risk perceptions, the behavioral consequences of accepting risk, and the factors that moderate the link between the two.

Beyond theoretical reasons, however, the antecedents and consequences of health risk perceptions are of increasing managerial importance given the rise in direct-to-consumer advertising which relies on consumers' ability to self- or proxy-diagnose.[2] From a consumer welfare perspective, the almost epidemic rise in health conditions ranging from depression, anxiety, and bi-polar disorder, to obesity, autism, alcoholism, pre-menstrual disorder (PMDD), erectile dysfunction (ED), and attention deficit disorder (ADD), added to preexisting health conditions like cholesterol, blood pressure, heart disease, cancer, hepatitis, and AIDS suggests that a better understanding of a person's level of risk will allow them to make better informed life choices for themselves and others.[3] Finally, an unhealthy workforce has public policy implications as preventing, identifying, and treating physical and mental disorders can reduce the number of lost working days and health care costs in the country.

The rest of this chapter is organized as follows: We integrate several extant approaches to studying health risk and propose a conceptual model of the antecedents and consequences of health risk perceptions. We place the extant research in the health domain in our proposed framework, with the antecedents, consequences, and factors moderating their link described in detail. We conclude with open questions for future research that emerge from this synthesis.

EXTANT APPROACHES AND A PROPOSED MODEL OF HEALTH RISK PERCEPTIONS

The psychology of health is a large and growing area (see Taylor, 1990, 2003 for reviews). One of the earliest models proposed was the Health Belief Model (Becker, 1974; Rosenstock, 1974) which proposes that increasing risk perceptions should lead to precautionary behavior. The primary critique against this model is the increasing evidence that accepting risk is a necessary but not a sufficient condition to engage in health related behaviors in domains ranging from AIDS (Gerrard, Gibbons, & Bushman, 1996) to depression (Raghubir & Menon, 2005a).

One of the widest used models to examine health risk is the Theory of Reasoned Action (Ajzen & Fishbein, 1975). This theory has the following key features: (a) Behavior is predicted to follow a behavioral intention, which in turn is based on an overall attitude. (b) The overall attitude is constructed using a weighted average of the belief that a particular attitude object has a given level of an attribute, weighted by the importance of that attribute; as well as subjective norms which are based on perceptions of the preferences of others, weighted by the importance of these others. (c) The model is predominantly a cognitive, rational one, where beliefs, and importance weights for aspects intrinsic to the attitude object, as well as extrinsic to it, together are integrated into an attitude. (d) The model is a compensatory one (i.e., is additive) where lower levels of performance on one attribute can compensate for higher levels of performance on another attribute.

The model has been widely tested in the health domain (e.g., Fishbein & Middlestadt, 1989; Albarracin, Johnson, Fishbein, & Muellerleile, 2001; Fishbein, Middlestadt, & Hitchcock, 1994).

A meta-analysis by Albarracin et al. (2001) of 96 data sets from 42 articles (n = 22,594) using this paradigm to examine condom use shows that condom use was related to intentions (r = .45), which, themselves, were based on attitudes (r = .58) and subjective norms (r = .39), with attitudes based on behavioral beliefs related to condom use (r = .56), and subjective norms related to normative beliefs (r = .46). However, just as the health belief model was critiqued on the grounds that risk perceptions do not always translate into behavior, the theory of reasoned action is critiqued on the grounds that intentions do not necessarily translate into behavior. There is, accordingly, a need to identify: (a) antecedents other than cognitive belief based ones; (b) factors that moderate the cognitive, motivational, and affective antecedents of risk perceptions; and (c) factors that moderate the judgment-intention-behavior link.

The Theory of Planned Behavior (Ajzen, 1991) suggests that perceived control is an independent construct that affects both intentions as well as future behavior: the higher the perceived controllability of a symptom, the higher the intention to engage in precautionary or preventive behavior, and the greater the likelihood of engaging in the behavior. Perceived controllability has also been shown to affect people's perceptions of risk and intentions to seek assistance (Lin, Lin, & Raghubir, 2003a; Raghubir & Menon, 2005a; Taylor, Lichtman, & Wood, 1984; Taylor, Helgeson, Reed, & Skokan, 1991), though its role for automatic or habitual behaviors has been contended (Eagly & Chaiken, 1993). In fact, current research on these theories has suggested that "past behavior" may be another important construct that affects actual behavior, intentions, perceived control, attitudes, norms, as well as beliefs (Figure 3 in Albarracin et al., 2001).

A different approach to understanding health risk and the risk-behavior link is the Cognitive Adaptation theory (Taylor, 1983). Given that psychological well-being may be necessary to achieve physiological well-being, those who do not fully accept their risk may have better mental health, and so may, counter-intuitively be better able to accept and cope with physiological risk (Taylor & Brown, 1988, see also Taylor, 2003; Taylor et al., 2003). The basic argument put forward is that accepting physiological risk may be potentially harmful to psychological risk. Therefore, being unrealistically optimistic in the domain of a health risk, such as cancer, may encourage people to seek diagnosis, which would assist prevention and early cure (Taylor, 1983). For example, Taylor et al. (1992) found that HIV positive men who inaccurately, but optimistically, believed that they could halt the progression of AIDS, practiced better health habits than those who were pessimistic (see also Reed, Kemeny, Taylor, Wang, & Visscher, 1994).

Taylor, Kemeny, Reed, Bower, & Gruenewald (2000) reviewed a decade of research on the relationship between optimism and perceived control with mental and physical health. They find that unrealistically optimistic beliefs, that are associated with mental well-being, may also be health protective, as they act as resources which allow consumers to cope with negative life events. This theory explicitly recognizes the role that emotions and affect play in assessing risk and deciding on behavioral actions. Newer additions to the theory allow for the positive effect of mental simulation where people can imagine possible positive scenarios and, therefore, regulate their behavior to work towards bringing them about (Taylor & Schneider, 1989; Taylor, Pham, Rivkin, & Armor., 1998; for a review see Taylor, 1998), as well as mindset (Taylor & Gollwitzer, 1995). Their body of work suggests that individual differences moderate the effect of motivational effects on risk perceptions. While coping is one example, albeit an important one, of the factor moderating the risk perception-diagnostic behavior link, we propose that it is only one of a genre that includes other aspects of risk.

Each of the above models makes interesting and unique predictions. However, their individual scope is limited in laying out the growing array of effects, factors, and processes being documented in the area of health risks. We propose a theoretical model that combines the lessons from the above models with other health research and more general consumer research to provide a broader road-map to studying the psychology of health risk perceptions. Our model categorizes the antecedents of health risk perceptions into five broad categories: motivational, cognitive, affective, contextual, and individual differences. Individually and interactively, these factors are integrated to form a judgment of health risk. We further propose that there are several primary behavioral consequences of forming such a judgment. These are categorized as awareness, interest, trial, adoption, repeat-behavior, and word-of-mouth, based on the consumer diffusion of product innovations (Rogers, 1962; 1987). Finally, we propose that four related risk perceptions—financial, performance, psycho-social, and physiological risk—moderate the likelihood that a health risk perception will translate to a behavioral consequence. Our conceptual model is depicted in Figure 39.1.

The key aspects of our model that differentiate it from others are: (a) A broader incorporation of cognitive, motivational, and affective factors; (b) Individual factors proposed both as antecedents of health risk perceptions and moderators of the motivational antecedents of risk; (c) Contextual factors proposed both as antecedents of health risk perceptions and moderators of the cognitive antecedents of risk; (d) The consideration of a variety of behavioral consequences; and (e) The conceptualization of four other perceived risks that moderate the risk perception-behavior link that incorporate prior proposed constructs (such as perceived control and coping), but also suggest new ones.

One of the primary contributions of our approach is to examine the contextual antecedents of risk perceptions, whose direct and moderating effect suggest that eliciting health risk perceptions may serve a persuasive role besides a measurement role. Given that the measurement of risk perceptions are prone to a variety of context effects, one way of thinking about this malleable quality of health risk is to categorize changes in risk perceptions as measurement *errors*. Thus, one could attempt to increase the reliability of the data collected. Another way to think about the malleability of health risk is as a measurement *effect*. For example, Morwitz and her colleagues have examined how the mere measurement of a construct changes the likelihood that an event will occur in the future (e.g., Dholakia & Morwitz, 2002; Fitzsimons & Morwitz, 1996; Morwitz & Schmittlein, 1992; Morwitz, Johnson, & Schmittlein, 1993). By thinking of it as a measurement effect, one can view the risk measuring instrument as a persuasive device that can be strategically used to make people's risk estimates more in line with reality, less biased, and more likely to be used to make a judgment regarding preventative or diagnostic behavior. Thus, one could leverage the context effects to change risk perceptions, and get consumers to take action. Intertwined in the examination of the different antecedents of risk perceptions, we also review the different ways in which risk has been measured and the pros and cons of these techniques.

ANTECEDENTS OF CONSUMER PERCEPTIONS OF RISK

The antecedents of health risk perceptions in the existing literature can be classified into five major types of psychological factors: motivational, cognitive, affective, contextual, and individual differences (see left side of Figure 39.1). Table 39.1 summarizes some of the key findings in the literature pertaining to these antecedents, together with their implications for theory and practice, and some open questions that may be addressed through future research. We elaborate on each of the antecedents in greater detail in the sections below.

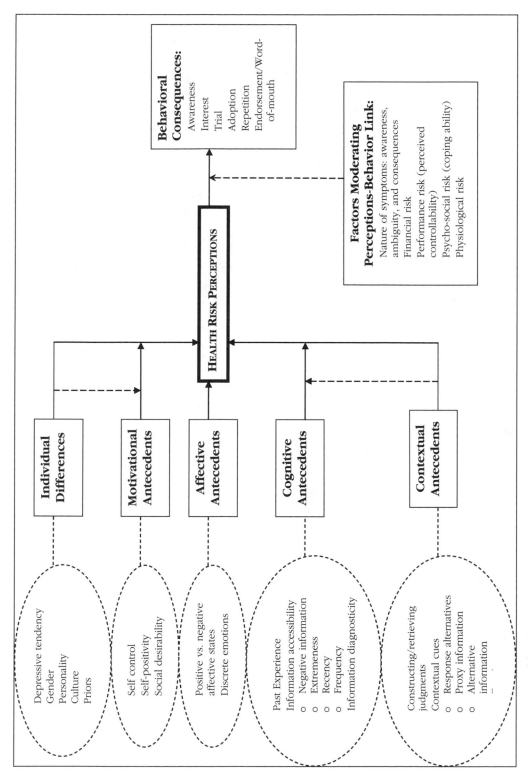

Figure 39.1   Health risk perceptions — antecedents of risk

Table 39.1   Health Risk Perceptions — Antecedents of Risk

Antecedents of Risk	Key findings	Implications	Some prescriptions for theory	Selected prescriptions for practice	Some open questions for future research
Motivational	Short-term rather than long-term goals often lead to under-estimation of risk.	Encourage consumers to focus on long-term goals like self-efficacy and improvement rather than immediate goals like mood and self enhancement.	Consider the goals that might get activated while considering risk.	Make consumers feel good and focus on benefits when health messages may trigger mood or image management.	What factors influence what type of goals are activated? Are there short term goals that encourage risk acceptance?
	Self-Positivity Bias: People estimate they are less at risk than others, especially known and similar others.	Absolute measures of risk may be over or under stated compared to actual rates, but relative measures best show whether a person believes they are less likely to get a disease than a target reference group.	Elicit relative measures of risk: self, average person. Counterbalance the order of elicitation. Increase the accessibility of own causal behaviors to encourage accuracy in risk estimation.	Goal should be to bring self-perceptions in line with perceptions of the risk of others, rather than increase or decrease absolute levels of perceived risk. Highlight that issues that people feel could only happen to others could also happen to them.	Which estimates are more tensile: self or others? Which would be easier to change? And what would be the effect of a change in either on behavioral intentions and actions?
	Social Desirability Bias: People under- (over-) report the extent they engage in a risky (preventative) behavior.	Self-reports need to be adjusted.	Identify occurrence of a problem or symptom through different methods.	Improve accuracy through use of counter-biasing, indirect questioning, camouflaging and the randomized response technique.	Examine if improving accuracy would follow through to behavior.
Cognitive	Greater accessibility of • Negative information • Extreme information • Recent information • Frequent behavior.	Negative, extreme, recent, and frequent behaviors are likely to be given more weight in aggregate risk judgments, even though they may be no more diagnostic of risk.	Risk perceptions are tensile and can be changed depending on prior questions.	Ask consumers to recall few vs. more symptoms; provide common symptoms on list (rather than unusual or extreme ones); Increase awareness of symptoms.	Are the four constructs distinct, or do they have interactive effects? Are constructs perceived to be correlated? Can their effects be disentangled?

	A behavior will be incorporated into risk estimated to the extent to which a behavior is perceived to be diagnostic.	Increasing perceptions of diagnosticity increase the likelihood that if a symptom is identified it will enter through to risk judgments.		Increase communication about the diagnosticity of various symptoms and behaviors for a disease.	Can providing information about diagnosticity lead to long term belief change? What is the best way to frame such information for it to have maximum impact?
Affective	Positive vs. Negative Affect	The level of fear follows an inverted-U shaped curve, with low and high levels of fear backfiring. Consumers in a negative affective state are more likely to update risk estimates.	Control and measure affective states.	All communication should include elements of hope to counteract fear and anxiety.	Identify roles of fear, hope, regret and others in the decision calculus that consumer used to trade off a current affective state over a future affective/physiological state.
	Discrete emotions	Emotions such as hope are savored, while those such as anxiety are not.	Emotions of the same valence do not lead to the same effects.		Examine the interplay between affective and cognitive and physical and mental health.
Contextual	Alternative information	Consumers construct rather than retrieve judgments using contextual cues making their risk judgments tensile and easily changed. While survey methodologists can use this information to improve response accuracy, social marketers can use this information to increase estimates of risk so as to encourage behavior change..	Test order effects and counter-balance.	Increase the salience of alternate information that consumers could use to make risk judgments (such as the accessibility of their own behavior).	Does measuring risk increase likelihood of performing a desirable behavior?
	Response alternatives		Measure subjective symptoms using subjective response scales.	Define ambiguous behaviors and symptoms carefully.	Can changing response alternatives formats increase perceptions of risk?
	Proxy information		Proxy information is typically based on self-estimates.	It may be easier to frame communication in terms of a "close other" to reduce defensive tendencies.	Are proxy reports subject to the same biases as self reports?
	Framing		Consider the frame surrounding estimates.	Frame base-rates, actual risks in ways that make them real and personal.	What kind of frames affects base-rate estimates?

(Continued)

Table 39.1 Continued

Antecedents of Risk	Key findings	Implications	Some prescriptions for theory	Selected prescriptions for practice	Some open questions for future research
Individual Differences	Demographic variables (*e.g.*, gender, culture)	Men have a greater sense of controllability and are more prone to self-positivity; Collectivistic cultures are less prone to self-positivity in some domains.	Measure individual difference variables.	Separate analyses by individual difference variables and identify different methods to increase compliance towards a desirable behavior for different segments.	Identifying other individual difference variables that moderate the extent of self-positivity and those that moderate the risk perception–behavior link.
	Personality (*e.g.*, depressive tendency)	Depressives are less prone to self-positivity; optimists are less likely to update risk estimates.			
Factors affecting the risk perception-behavior link	Perceptions of controllability of disease	More controllable events are more prone to self-positivity and have a higher likelihood of risk judgments translating into behavior.			Identifying other moderators and mediating mechanisms, as well as identifying ways of mitigating or exacerbating these. These could include contextual cues, advertising, framing effects and other methods.
	Awareness of symptoms	Increasing awareness of symptoms, increases risk perceptions.			
	Ambiguity of symptoms	The more ambiguous the symptom, the less likely it will be incorporated into judgments, and the more likely it will be prone to context effects.			
	Extremity of consequence of symptoms	Consumers may use the presence of an extreme symptom on an inventory to categorize themselves as "not at risk."			
	Risk: Financial, social, performance, psychological and physiological	The higher the risk, the lower the likelihood of risk judgments translating into behavior.			

Motivational Factors

A variety of factors and biases in the domain of health risks may be attributed to motivational factors. Motivational factors are inherently intertwined with perceptions of health risk. Three primary phenomena highlight the motivational factors affecting health risk perceptions: self-positivity (or unrealistic optimism), social desirability, and self-control.

Self-Positivity Bias To accommodate a need for mental well-being and self-enhancement, people might be unrealistically optimistic in their own risk perceptions (Taylor & Brown, 1988). This motivationally driven bias, referred to as the self-positivity bias (Ragubir & Menon, 1998), is widely documented in the health literature and can affect risk perceptions in several ways (for a review see Taylor, 2003; Taylor et al., 2000). Stemming from a desire to self-enhance, the self-positivity bias is people's tendency to believe that bad things are less likely to happen to them than to the average person—an "It cannot happen to me" syndrome (Taylor & Brown, 1988; Weinstein, 1980). The self-positivity effect was first tested in the domain of health risk perceptions by Perloff and Fetzer (1986) and has since become a topic of mainstream interest in consumer psychology (Chandran & Menon, 2004; Keller, Lipkus, & Rimer, 2003; Lin, Lin, & Raghubir, 2003b; Luce & Kahn, 1999; Menon, Block, & Ramanathan, 2002; Raghubir & Menon, 1998, 2001). It has been shown for a number of different diseases, including HIV and AIDS (e.g., Raghubir & Menon, 1998; Schneider, Taylor, Kemeny, & Hammen, 1991; Bauman & Siegel, 1987; Joseph et al., 1987), mononucleosis and heart problems (e.g., Chandran & Menon, 2004; Lee, 1989; Dolinski, Gromski, & Zawisza, 1987; Weinstein & Lachendro, 1982), flu (Larwood, 1978), hepatitis (Menon et al., 2002), cancer (Lin et al., 2003a, 2003b; Perloff & Fetzer, 1986), and mental illness, including depression and suicide (e.g., Drake, 1987; Kuiper & MacDonald, 1982; Perloff & Fetzer, 1986). Shepperd, Helweg-Larsen, and Ortega (2003) found that self-positivity manifests regardless of time, as well as whether or not one has experienced related event.

Self-positivity leads people to perceive themselves as being less risk-prone than known or similar others in the same risk group (e.g., their best friend). Self-positivity effects may be due to an overall desire to feel happy (Raghubir & Menon, 1998) and to maintain or enhance self-esteem (Lin et al., 2003b; Weinstein, 1980). Lin et al. (2003b) showed that self-positivity effects are greater for events perceived to be controllable (see also Burger & Palmer, 1992; see Harris, 1996, for a review on the effects on controllability on self-positivity effects), and therefore, counter-intuitively, information highlighting an individual's lack of control in contracting a disease can increase the likelihood that they go for screening. They argued that if people can attribute a lower risk of a negative event to their own actions, which is more likely to be true for controllable (vs. less controllable) events, the belief that they are less at risk than others should improve their self-esteem.

If consumers assume that they are less at risk than others, they may tune out preventative advertising directed to them (Diclemente & Peterson, 1994; Fisher & Fisher, 1992). Raghubir and Menon (1998) showed that people believe they are less at risk of contracting AIDS than are others. Self-positivity could also promote complacency (Skinner, 1995) rather than effective goal-relevant behavior (Weinstein 1989). On the one hand, self-positivity motivated by self-enhancement may have negative effects on health outcomes through a lack of attention or defensiveness towards another wise relevant risk. Self-enhancement motives operating through the same self-positivity effect could create an illusion of positivity that might provide a stress-buffering resource to deal with information that conveys a relevant risk (Taylor et al., 2003). Taylor and Brown (1988) argue that self-positivity may carry benefits such as goal attainment and positive mental health. On the other hand, self-positivity could also have a positive effect on health behaviors if people thought a treatment would more likely work for them than for others; that is, the efficacy of a treatment was higher for themselves than others. Self-positivity could provide a buffer for people to deal with the negative impact of considering risk and help them process information. While extant research recognizes both the positive and the negative consequences of self-enhancement motives, often manifesting in self-positivity, there is little research on how and when self-enhancement motives will affect risk perceptions such that people are more willing to accept risk, and affect behaviors in a healthy way. Future research is needed to understand clearly the conditions when self-positivity could play a positive rather than a negative role in motivating healthy cognition and behavior.

One of the implications of the self-positivity bias pertains to its measurement. Given that the bias is a relative one, it implies that changing the absolute level of risk may not be either necessary or sufficient to de-bias risk estimates. The use of a relative difference in the perceived likelihood of an event occurring has the advantage of measuring the extent of "bias" (difference from an objective reality), as well as a few pleasing psychonomic properties: (a) The perception of the risk of another person serves as a within-subjects control. Relative measures are less dependent on individual heterogeneity in reading and responding to scale measures, leading to lower variance in the actual estimates of risk. (b) The variance in actual self-estimates bring in statistical noise that is reduced when a relative measure is used (because people are likely to use the scale in a similar way for both themselves and another person). (c) The use of absolute estimates could lead to erroneous conclusions (e.g., that people believe they are more at risk of getting AIDS than they actually are even though they believe that they are less at risk than another person, and therefore, they should be educated into believing that they are less at risk).

Overall, the self-positivity bias is weaker between one's self and a close friend or a parent or siblings than it is for a less specific target such as the average undergraduate or average person (Chandran & Menon, 2004; Helweg-Larsen & Shepperd, 2001; Menon et al., 2002; Perloff & Fetzer, 1986; Raghubir & Menon, 1998). Perloff and Fetzer (1986) argued that while predicting the risk level of a vague target (i.e., the average person), respondents may have chosen a person who fit their stereotype of someone to whom the event would occur, leading to the bias being stronger when an unknown target is used as a comparison other.

The self-positivity bias is also a function of the manner of elicitation of the risk estimate. Otten and van der Pligt (1996) showed that the self-positivity bias was greater when respondents were asked a directly comparative estimate (e.g., "How much are you at risk compared to an average person?") rather than when these were inferred from two separate responses indirectly. They found that direct relative estimates were the least prone to order effects as well, as respondents appeared to base them on actual behavioral data using themselves as a standard.

One of the open questions of research in this area is to examine whether, when, and why self estimates or other estimates are more tensile and prone to being affected by contextual cues. Most prior research suggests that it is self estimates that change. For example, Raghubir and Menon (1998) showed that self-perceptions of the risk of AIDS were more tensile and affected by the number of AIDS-related behaviors that people recalled. Menon et al. (2002) showed that self-perceptions of hepatitis C were tensile and were affected by the type of behaviors listed in an ad. Lin et al. (2003b) showed that self-estimates were more likely to change as a function of the order in which estimates were elicited as compared to others' estimates.

Social Desirability Bias   The social desirability bias is motivated by social goals and the concern among consumers about the impression they make (Fenigstein, Scheier, & Buss, 1975). Ajzen and Fishbien (1980) also recognized the role played by social goals (through normative beliefs: what one should do, and through subjective norms: whether it is socially or interpersonally desirable to perform a behavior) in determining behavioral intentions and behavioral change. They argue that if an individual, who would like others to think of him/herself in a positive way, believes these relevant others would see a certain behavior as positive (i.e., subjective norms surrounding the behavior are positive), the individual will have higher behavioral intentions and is more likely to perform the behavior. If a subjective norm surrounding a behavior is negative (e.g., my friends think smoking is bad), then an individual is less likely to perform that behavior. Argo, Dahl, and Manchanda (2005), for example, demonstrated that people's shopping habits undergo a change when there is a sales person around (see also Dahl, Manchanda, & Argo, 2001). Thus, social desirability effects are likely to manifest more when there is an outsider present that may have an opportunity to observe and hear how consumers might react to health messages. For topics such as sex, drugs, alcohol, religion and voting, where social desirability has been most examined (see Schwarz & Sudman, 1994), there tends to be a strong consensus of what is socially desirable or acceptable. To the extent that a consumer wishes to portray that they are not promiscuous, they are less likely admit to engaging in behaviors that are central to how some diseases are contracted.

While behavioral reports for socially desirable behaviors, such as practicing safe sex, are typically biased upwards, those for socially undesirable behaviors such as marijuana and cocaine consumption, are typically under-reported (Fendrich & Vaughn, 1994). Overall, the more sensitive the question, the greater the likelihood that respondents will tailor their responses towards what they believe is socially acceptable (Maccoby & Maccoby, 1954). The bias is robust across measures, behaviors, and disciplines (Fisher, 1993; Levy, 1981; Peltier & Walsh, 1990; Robinette, 1991; Simon & Simon, 1975; Zerbe & Palhaus, 1987). One of the primary problems associated with the social desirability bias is that it can lead to misleading results, not only in terms of the mean likelihood of an event occurring (Peterson & Kerin, 1981), but also the strength of the relationship between interventions, attitudes and behavior (Zerbe & Paulhus, 1987).

Understanding the precise social motive that may drive the bias (e.g., privacy vs. image management concerns) can help identify relevant ways to reduce the bias. Given that this bias may be a measurement artifact, the suggested ways of decreasing the bias are discussed below.

Indirect questioning is an inquiry made of a respondent, in a structured or unstructured format, on behalf of another person, rather than for themselves (Fisher, 1993). Indirect questioning is hypothesized to be successful as the respondent projects their own unconscious biases into ambiguous situations which end up revealing their own attitudes, without the embarrassment of revealing their own private attitudes. Fisher (1993) found that using structured projective techniques reduced social desirability biases for behaviors that were subject to social influence rooted in both privacy as well self-presentation.

The *Shopping List technique* was originally used by Haire (1950) to measure attitudes to instant coffee. In this technique, respondents are given a shopping list with a target item (or a control item), and asked to describe the personality of the person shopping. This indirect method allows the researcher to examine the implications of a product on the shopping list from the point of view of the inferences people draw about the person buying it. In a recent application of this technique to the domain of safe sex, Dahl, Darke, Gorn, & Weinberg (2005) found that one of the reasons people were reticent about carrying condoms was that they believed it signaled overconfidence and promiscuity, rather than responsibility. This, added to the fact that there is embarrassment associated with the purchase of condoms (Dahl, Gorn, & Weinberg, 1998, 1999) is a major obstacle to the practice of safe sex

Mode of administration may also affect risk assessments. Aquilino (1994) showed that that self-administered questionnaires were more successful in getting people to admit that they consumed illicit drugs compared to personal face-to-face-interviews, that worked better than telephone interviews due to the ability of the interviewer to assuage confidentiality concerns, and build rapport (see Aquilino & LoSciuto, 1990, for a discussion of success of this technique by race).

Randomized response technique also satiates privacy concerns (Warner, 1965). In this technique, based on a random event (e.g., coin flip), respondents are asked to "yes" or "no" to one of two questions one of which is the sensitive question and the other an innocuous question with a known population probability. The aggregate probability of the group responding to the sensitive question can then be calculated given the known probabilities of the random event and the innocuous question.[4]

Camouflaging sensitivity may also help reducing biases in the measurement of risk. Hiding the sensitive question among a group of more innocuous questions is another recommended technique (Bradburn, Sudman, Blair, Stocking, 1978; Sudman & Bradburn, 1974). When a behavior is one on a list of many behaviors, it is less threatening and increases the chances that a respondent will answer it truthfully.

Counterbiasing techniques involve introducing the target socially undesirable behavior as a "normal" one by suggesting how common it is in the population, and therefore, reducing the embarrassment associated with admitting to it (Barton, 1958; Bradburn et al., 1978; Sudman & Bradburn, 1974). Applying the technique to reports of safe sex, Raghubir and Menon (1996) found that providing counter-biasing information as a base-rate (a population average) rather than in term of individuating information (an average member of the population) was more effective, presumably because it carried more information, being based on a large sample size.

Self-Control   Most messages that highlight health risks convey information that is emotionally aversive but beneficial to long-term well-being. That is, an effective health message should enable a person to recognize risks and act on it to get tested or change behaviors in the long run, but in the short run recognizing risk might lead to unpleasant trade-offs. Sometimes short term goals (e.g., participating in a sex encounter even in the absence of protection) are in conflict with long term goals (e.g., staying healthy), presenting a self-control problem (Loewenstein, 1996). Thus, in the short run, consumers are motivated to lower the immediate intangible costs (e.g., time, effort, emotion) of recognizing risk perceptions (Agrawal, Menon, & Aaker, 2007; Raghunathan & Trope, 2002; Keller et al., 2003). On the other hand, consumers could be motivated to seek the long-term benefits of recognizing risk such as preventing a disease or detecting it in early stages or seeking early treatment. Thus, depending on whether a consumer is focused on long-term or immediate motives, they may be more open to health risk consideration. These long-term or short-term motives may not only influence risk perceptions and behavioral intentions, but may also influence the likelihood of practicing a healthy lifestyle. For instance, the short-term motive of self-enhancement may lead to a lower risk perception of contracting AIDS (Raghubir & Menon, 1998), but even if risk were recognized, the short-term motive of gratification might lead one to still have unsafe sex. Interventions that highlight long-term benefits of processing health risks could help people recognize risk and practice healthy behaviors (Raghunathan & Trope, 2002).

In summary, self-positivity, social desirability and self control are three motivational factors that affect the perceptions and report of a person's own health risk. Our model proposes that the extent to which they exist is a function of individual and contextual differences (both of which are discussed later in this section). We now discuss affective factors impacting health risk judgments.

Affective Factors

Affective factors play a role in terms of people's ability to deal with negative events or information. People might anticipate and experience the negative affective consequence of considering health risks. In the context of processing health message information in the domains of skin cancer and sexually transmitted diseases, Block and Keller (1995) demonstrated that information that highlights negative consequences of contracting a disease is more persuasive when there are cues in the message that induce in-depth processing. On the other hand, when the information is being processed only in a shallow manner, the valence of the information presented did not affect persuasion. For example, highlighting negative consequences may lead to feelings of fear, which may decrease the persuasiveness of an appeal (Keller & Block, 1996; Roger & Mewborn, 1976). Furthermore, while positive affect fosters the processing of negative information, negative affect hinders this processing because people are in a mood repair mode and negative information does not contribute to this goal (Keller et al., 2003; Raghunathan & Trope, 2002; Salovey et al., 1991).Thus, if consumers are asked their perceptions of risk of health hazards when in a positive affective state, they may be more open with dealing with the reality, and may estimate risk perceptions that reflect less of the self-positivity bias. On the other hand, if consumers are in a negative affective state, they are less likely to be willing to process negative information, and the self-positivity bias may be enhanced. Taking this one step further, Agrawal et al. (2007) examine the role of discrete emotions in enhancing health message persuasiveness. They theorize that discrete emotions play a dual role in influencing the effectiveness of health-related messages: as a provider of resources and of information. While the valence of the emotion provides resources as demonstrated by Raghunathan and Trope (2002), other appraisal dimensions of the emotions (e.g., self/other-relatedness, uncertainty) provide information that people use to decipher information provided in a health message.

Given the strong inter-connections between the health domain and emotions, this is an important antecedent of health risk perception, albeit under-researched, and therefore, and a future avenue for rich theoretical research.

Cognitive Factors

Feldman and Lynch's (1988) accessibility-diagnosticity framework help us understand how the different pieces of information that are salient to a consumer at a given time might influence the kind of risk related cues that come to mind. They predict that "(a given piece of information)…will be used as an input to a subsequent response if the former is accessible and if it is perceived to be more diagnostic than other accessible inputs" (p. 431). *Accessibility* is defined as the ease of retrieving an input from memory. *Diagnosticity* is defined in terms of how complete the input is to make a judgment. The greater the accessibility and diagnosticity of an input for a judgment relative to alternate inputs, the greater the likelihood that it will be used (Simmons, Bickart, & Lynch 1993). The interplay of accessibility and diagnosticity in the domain of risk judgments is now discussed.

Accessibility of Information in Memory   Accessibility is a direct function of the frequency and recency of activation of information in memory (Higgins, 1989). The higher the information accessibility, the more easily should information come to mind, and to the extent this information is diagnostic of making a risk judgment, the lower should be the self-positivity bias. Raghubir and Menon (1998) showed that increasing the accessibility of causal information reduced the self-positivity bias, and potentially increasing the accessibility of preventive behaviors enhances the self-positivity bias. This was because the accessibility of information was more diagnostic of, and accordingly, affected perceptions of own risk more than it affected perceptions of others' risk. There are four different aspects of accessibility of information in memory: valence (negativity or positivity), extremity, recency, and frequency. These are elaborated on below.

Negative information comes to mind more easily than positive information (Higgins, 1989) and so may be more likely to influence a risk judgment. This implies that framing could affect the efficacy of health messages (Block & Keller, 1995; Keller et al., 2003; Maheswaran & Meyers-Levy, 1990; Meyerowitz & Chaiken, 1987). Furthermore, if the retrieval of negative information puts the person in a negative mood, they are less likely to process a health message that touts the negatives associated with a disease and the potential of the person having the disease (Agrawal et al., 2007; Keller et al., 2003).

Extreme information is likely to make other equally accessible information less diagnostic. For example, Raghubir and Menon (2005a) showed that while risk estimates are affected by the presence or absence of suicide in a self-diagnosis inventory for depression, intentions to seek assistance are only marginally so. They also showed that including an extreme behavior in a behavioral checklist, decreases the diagnosticity of the other behavioral symptoms included in the battery, in the absence of information about the diagnosticity of the behaviors. However, the same behavior, "thoughts of suicide or death" also led to other behavioral symptoms being perceived to be more controllable. They conclude that this symptom may act as a double-edged sword, its presence at the same time depressing estimates of risk but increasing perception of control over those symptoms. If this is the case, then including the behavior in the self-diagnosis inventory brings substantial benefits, especially if one can control or limit the informative value (or perceived diagnosticity) of the behavior for the remaining symptoms of depression. Thus, the information value of response alternatives can be leveraged to limit the perceived diagnosticity of any extreme behavioral symptom in a risk inventory.

Recently engaged-in behaviors are likely to be more accessible than behaviors engaged in further back in time (Higgins, 1989). Therefore, if recent behaviors are recalled as they are diagnostic of the health hazard in question, risk perceptions are likely to be inflated. On the other hand, if the behaviors that lead to the disease are recalled but are less accessible because they occurred further back in time, they may be (wrongly) judged to be less diagnostic of the disease, and discounted when arriving at risk perceptions, even though a single encounter of unprotected sex with a person with AIDS might result in a person becoming HIV positive (see Raghubir & Menon, 2005b, for when the recency of information recalled undercuts the diagnosticity of recalling more numerous pieces of information on judgments related to the content of this information).

Another factor that affects information accessibility, and hence risk perceptions based on this information, is the *frequency* with which people engage in behaviors or are exposed to information about these behaviors. Furthermore, the regularity of the frequent behavior is also key in how this information is represented in memory and whether this information is going to more or less accessible and in what form. For example, Menon (1993, 1997) demonstrated that people tend to have a rate-of-occurrence easily accessible in memory that is used in subsequent frequency, and potential risk estimation, tasks. On the other hand, for irregular behaviors which occur at less periodic time intervals, people have to resort to specific episodes, and less frequent behaviors then are more highly accessible than frequent ones. Depending on the domain of risk estimation, then, the regularity and the frequency of the behaviors will impact final risk perceptions (see also Albarracin et al., 2001 for evidence regarding the importance of past experience as an antecedent of risk judgments and the risk-intention-behavior link).

Diagnosticity of information cues to make judgments   Consumers could use the diagnosticity of cues either retrieved from memory or provided in the context to infer risk perceptions (Feldman & Lynch, 1988). The mere accessibility of the information provided could also in and of itself be used as a diagnostic cue (Menon & Raghubir, 2003), implying that if risky behaviors are easily retrieved from memory, risk perceptions would be higher than if they were difficult to recall. Further, the presence of a single extreme factor could overshadow the diagnosticity of less extreme factors that should be normatively used to estimate risk (Raghubir & Menon, 2005a, for this demonstration in the domain of depression with the presence of the symptom: "thoughts of suicide/ death"). To summarize, the accessibility and diagnosticity of information in memory can affect people's perceptions of health risk.

However, judgments may be memory-based, context-based, or a combination of these. Thus, contextual factors moderate the extent to which cognitive, memory based factors are used to estimate risk (see Menon, Raghubir, & Schwarz, 1995a, 1997; Sudman, Bradburn, and Schwarz, 1995 for the interplay between these two sets of factors). These contextual cues are discussed next.

Contextual Factors

One of the better studied contextual sources of information to make responses is the questionnaire itself (Bickart, 1993), including the manner in which questions are framed, the order in which they are asked, the response alternatives used to elicit their responses and other incidental information in the questionnaire that ends up serving an informative function rather than the pure recording function for which it was intended. The cognitive aspects of survey methodology literature shows that the manner of construction of a questionnaire affects the reports elicited, and can, in turn, affect later responses (see Sudman et al., 1995, for a review). These contextual factors as they pertain to health judgments are discussed below.

Response Alternatives   The range of response alternatives used may be informative if respondents believe that the set constructed by the researcher reflects a population's frequency distribution, leading to their inferring how often an average person behaves, and then categorizing themselves with respect to this average person (e.g., Menon et al., 1995b, 1997; Schwarz et al., 1985). The use of response alternatives increases when reports are made for another person for whom memory-based information is even less accessible than for oneself (Schwarz & Bienias, 1990), and as the task complexity increases (Bless, Bohner, Hild, & Schwarz, 1992). Given the number and types of scales used to elicit behavioral and other symptoms for conditions ranging from depression to diabetes, the manner of construction of these scales could affect risk judgments. Other contextual factors that have been examined include the enhanced accessibility of responses to earlier questions (Menon et al., 1995a), the effects of question framing (Raghubir & Johar, 1999), and the presence of middle and explicit "don't know" options (see Schuman & Presser, 1996 for a review of question form, wording and context effects). All these factors will also affect risk perceptions. Future research needs to be conducted to examine the effects of response scales on behavior identification and the likelihood of using the behavior to construct a risk judgment.

Proxy Information   Proxy-diagnosis is when you ask a person whether they believe someone they know is at risk of a disease. A common practice, it has many of the advantages of indirect questioning, as motivational antecedents are less important in assessing others' risk versus own risk. When judgments relate to another person whom one knows, such as a significant other, people are more likely to project their own attitudes and behaviors to the other person (Davis, Hoch, & Ragsdale, 1986). People tend to assume that those similar to themselves, share their attitudes and behaviors. For example, Menon et al. (1995b) showed that respondents based their reports of their spouse's behavioral frequencies on their own behavioral frequencies (see also Bickart Menon, Schwarz, & Blair, 1994). Menon et al. (1995b) found that proxy-reports are frequently based on self-reports, as self-reports are an easily accessible source of information to use to make judgments about others.

Assessing whether proxy-reports are subject to the same contextual cues that self-reports are is an area for future research. Prior research has found mixed results. Raghubir and Menon (1998) found that self-reports changes more than other-reports when AIDS related behaviors were made contextually accessible, while Menon et al. (2002) found that when an advertiser listed two ways that Hepatitis C could be contracted, people assume that there were fewer ways for the average person to contract the disease than when eight ways were listed.

Availability of Alternative Sources of Information   Given that an over-arching goal of health-marketers is to bring risk perceptions in line with reality (and objective data), a legitimate question is whether providing simply base-rates of an event can achieve this goal. If people are prone to self-positivity because they do not have sufficient information about others or fail to consider other people's circumstances (Regan, Snyder, & Kassin, 1995), then providing them base-rates should reduce the self-positivity bias. For example, Weinstein and Lachendro (1982) were able to reduce the self-positivity bias by providing detailed, personalized information about the risk status of five other students or asking participants to imagine that they were the typical same-sex student. However, it is plausible that base-rates may not eliminate the self-positivity bias as consumers are notorious for ignoring base-rate information (Tversky & Kahneman, 1974).

Framing   A topic of recent interest is how the manner in which risk information is provided could itself bias people's perceptions of risk. For example, respondents have been shown to ignore the format in which numerical information is provided and make judgments based on the absolute magnitudes of the number provided (Halpern, Blackman, & Salzman, 1989). This led to people perceiving "100% greater" to mean "twice" as large, and "200% greater" to also mean "twice" as large! Halpern et al. (1989) also showed that "4.15 times greater" was perceived to be equivalent to "415% times greater" rather than the normatively correct "315% times greater." Interestingly, presenting information as a percentage or as number of times (i.e., actual frequency), also affected risk perceptions: though people perceived "4.15 times" to be the same as "415%" they judged 415% to be a greater risk of death than 4.15 times. Applying these findings to framing counter-biasing information to reduce under-reports of undesirable behaviors, Raghubir and Menon (1996) found that presenting information as "1 out of 5" (people performed the undesirable behavior) was less effective than presenting the same information as "20%."

In a recent paper, Chandran and Menon (2004) demonstrated the differential effects of framing a health hazard as occurring every day versus every year (called "temporal framing"), two reference periods that objectively refer to the present, but are subjectively perceived as different. Drawing on Construal Level Theory (Trope & Liberman, 2000), they showed that temporal framing mimics the effects of temporal distance such that an "every day" framing makes risks seem more proximal and concrete than a "every year" framing, resulting in higher perceptions of self-risk, more concerned attitudes, higher intentions to behave in a precautionary manner, greater anxiety about the hazard, and enhanced effectiveness of risk communication. For example, they reported that perceptions of self-risk, measured on a 101-point probability scale went from 4.86 in the "every year" condition to 22.00 in the "every day" condition. Furthermore, an "every day" attenuated the self-positivity bias was mitigated, but the "every year" framing enhanced it. Finally, these results were reversed when the health message was framed as "averting" a health hazard as opposed to "succumbing" to one, such that the "every day" frame increased the probability of avoiding the disease in the "avert" condition compared to the "every year" frame.

Framing effects can be constructed at the geographical level, the psychological level, other demographic level, or at a mere aggregate statistical level. That is, suggesting that a million Americans have a problem would be less effective than suggesting that 100,000 Californians have the same problem (given California accounts for approximately 10% of the U.S. population), which would be less effective than suggesting that 25,000 residents of the Bay area have the problem (given that a quarter of Californians, approximately 6 million people, reside in the Bay area), which would be less effective than suggesting that over 400 people in the city of Berkeley suffer from that problem (given that Berkeley has a population of approximately 100,000). Examining these predictions as well as other forms and effects of framing are be interesting areas of future research.

Individual Differences

There are many individual difference variables that may also account for systematic differences in risk perceptions between groups of individuals.

Depressive Tendency One of the few groups of people who have been shown to *not* have the self-positivity bias are depressives. Their risk estimates are more realistic than the average population, a term referred to as "depressive realism" (cf. Alloy & Abramson, 1979; Keller, Lipkus, & Rimer, 2002; see Ackermann & DeRubeis, 1991, for a review). Depressives are less prone to self-positivity as they view their life and future in negative terms (Beck, 1967, 1976), have low self-esteem (Gerrard, Gibbons, Reis-Bergan, & Russell, 2000), with their risk estimates reflecting pessimism (versus an absolute risk level) and self-negativity (versus another person; Keller, Lipkus, & Rimer, 2002). Lin et al. (2003a) showed that optimists are less likely to update self-estimates of controllable events when provided with base-rates, while pessimists incorporate base-rates into their judgments for all events.

Depressives appear to view their life and future in negative terms (Beck, 1967, 1976), relying more on chronically accessible negative self-constructs (e.g., Gotlib & McCann, 1984; for a review of the automaticity of cognitive processes in depression see Moretti and Shaw, 1989). Information processing in depressives has been shown to be context-dependent with a controlled decision to engage in (negative) self-referential thoughts preceding the automatic activation of self-related constructs (Bargh & Tota, 1988), which reflects a tendency to interpret a behavior as consistent with a chronically accessible construct (Higgins & King, 1981).

Gender Women have been found to be more prone to depression, though this may simply reflect their higher likelihood of seeking assistance and diagnosis. In fact, the psychosocial implications of being depressed may be worse for men due to the greater stigma attached to depression for this category (Russell, 2000). Gender differences have also been documented in the self-positivity bias (Lin & Raghubir, 2005). Several biases and factors affecting risk may have gender specific effects.

Personality At the individual personality level, there is evidence that controllability attenuates the self-positivity bias (Darvill & Johnson, 1991), with optimists less likely to update their beliefs about themselves even when provided base-rate information (Lin et al., 2003b).

Culture Cross-cultural variations in self-positivity have also been noted in the literature. Heine and Lehman (1995) showed that the belief that positive events are more likely to happen to ones self (relative to one's peer) was significantly reduced for Japanese individuals relative to Canadian individuals. Similarly, Chang (1996) found that across multiple measures, Chinese individuals were more pessimistic than were their American peers. There are also cross-cultural differences between U.K. and U.S. populations in the size of the self-positivity bias in the context of cancer that reflect differences in the perception of control of cancer (Fontaine & Smith, 1995). However, Sedikides, Gaertner, and Toguchi (2003) have recently suggested that self-positivity may be a universal phenomenon, but the domain in which it is seen may differ for those from individualistic versus collectivistic cultures. Overall, those from a country with a "collectivist" versus "individualistic" orientation (cf. Hofstede, 1990) have been shown to have a smaller magnitude of the bias, though it remains significant. In addition, to self-positivity, Eastern cultures may be more susceptible to social desirability biases than western culture (Lalwani, Shavitt, & Johnson, 2006).

Priors   In addition to the above effects, individuals may also vary in their beliefs or lay theories about health concerns, which may themselves play a role in the construction of risk perceptions (Kelly et al., 2005; Leventhal, Cameron, Leventhal, & Ozakinci, 2005). For instance, if individuals believed that a family history of cancer is a good predictor of cancer risk, then those who have a family history of cancer are likely to report higher risk estimated than those who do not. Note here that not all health related beliefs are true and could be systematically mislead risk perceptions.

To summarize, we have delineated five separate antecedents of risk perceptions: motivational, cognitive, affective, contextual, and individual differences. While Figure 39.1 presents these graphically in a conceptual model, Table 39.1 summarizes the key findings and potential areas for future research.

Consequences of Risk Perceptions

Risk perceptions can play two major roles: On the one hand, they can be highly correlated with behavior, such that when one believes that one is at risk, and then engages in more preventative, precautionary, and healthy behavior. This is the role of risk perceptions as a mediator to behavior. Relatedly, there are several factors that guide when risk mediates behaviors and when this link between risk and behavior breaks down. On the other hand, there could be other factors that interact with risk perceptions, and determine what kind of behaviors might be affected by the risk perceptions. This is the role of risk perceptions as a moderator. Our model emphasizes the need to understand the persuasive consequences of risk elicitation. Hence, it is important to understand when risk would mediate health behaviors and what kind of behaviors would be influenced. Both of these roles of risk perceptions are described below and are depicted graphically on the right side of Figure 39.1.

Risk as a Mediator to Behavioral Consequences

The extant literature has focused on reducing self-positivity in risk estimates with the idea of encouraging preventive behaviors (Chandran & Menon, 2004; Menon et al., 2002; Raghubir & Menon, 1998; Perloff & Fetzer, 1986; Weinstein, 1980). The focus has thus been to enhance self-risk perceptions, with the hope that doing so will reduce the distance between perceptions of risk between self and other (e.g., average person), and thus enhance people's vigilance of the health hazard. Another potential future research idea then is to systematically examine situations in which the risk perceptions associated with the average person may increase or decrease and affect the self-positivity bias. This may also affect the commitment to more preventive behaviors on the part of the target audience.

Factors Affecting When Risk Mediates Behavior   Whereas for most health hazards, increasing risk perceptions to bring them in line with reality may be adequate at encouraging action, this may not always be the case. There are several instances and reasons for when risk might not mediate behavior. Perceiving a very high risk may for instance turn away or "shut down" processing of health information (Keller & Block, 1996). For example, persuading potential depressives that they could be at risk may be relatively easy (due to "depressive realism" Keller et al., 2002), but inadequate to persuade them to seek medical advice. They must also believe depression is controllable if they are to seek treatment. Interventions that can simultaneously bring self-perceptions of risk in line with behavioral symptoms, and increase beliefs in the controllability of those symptoms (Ajzen, 1991; Ajzen & Fishbien, 1980), should have a positive persuasive effect on seeking assistance and practicing health behaviors.

Recent work by Agrawal and Menon (2005) suggests that sometimes incidental emotions can moderate the risk-perception-behavior relationship as well. For example, the emotion being experienced at the time of processing a health message can have undercurrents of uncertainty, and could be positive (e.g., hope) or negative (e.g., anxiety). Therefore, if people are hopeful about a situation (e.g., they will not test positive for HIV), this hope may lead to people wanting to savor the feeling, and hence not implementing behavioral changes (e.g., get tested) for fear that the result may turn out to be negative. On the other hand, if people are anxious about the outcome, this anxiety may lead people to find closure to the negative uncertain emotion, and lead to behavioral change (e.g., they may want to get tested).

One reason why people might avoid processing of beneficial health information or performing healthy behaviors when they feel at risk might be that the thought of being at high risk is psychologically taxing. In this case, coping research might suggest ways of alleviating the psychological burden, and hence strengthening the risk and behavior link. Different coping mechanisms might be amenable to different types of information or behaviors. For instance, if people are more likely to cope by withdrawing, it is best not to actively try and persuade them. On the other hand, some people might cope by talking about their concerns and expressing their emotions, in which case it would be great to give them the opportunity of doing so. Some other situations or people might cope by looking for information and hence it would be best to provide comprehensive information (Duhachek, 2006; Kahn & Luce, 2003).

In addition to risk affecting behavior such that perceiving a high risk may lead to protective action, there are at least two other relationships between risk and behavior (Brewer, Weinstein, Cuite, & Herrington, 2004). For instance, one might reappraise risk after performing a risky or healthy behavior. Or that risk perceptions themselves might be an accurate reflection of risky behavior. That is, people who more likely perform risky behaviors are likely to think they are at higher risk. Various factors may affect which relationship between risk and behaviors holds at a given point in time or given context. Future research is needed to address these relationships.

Risk as a Moderator of Behavioral Consequences

The link between risk and behavior can also be analyzed from the perspective of the different forms that the risk might take for the consumer. We defined risk as *negatively-valenced likelihood assessment that an unfavorable event will occur* in an abstract way. From a consumer standpoint, this risk could manifest in many different domains or forms. For instance, the risk could be related to *performance* of a test or treatment or health product, or it could be *financial*, *physiological*, or *psycho-social*. The form the risk takes for the consumer can govern how it influences decisions or behaviors, and what interventions may be effective in eliciting healthy behavioral patterns. These forms of risk may be associated with the health problem itself or with preventive/corrective behaviors. The extent to which judgments of risk translate into corrective behavioral consequences depends on both, the risks associated with the health problem, as well as the risk related to the corrective behavior(s). Most existing models of health psychology discussed earlier endorse the importance of studying the risk-behavior link. However, their conceptualization of risk is mostly unidimensional. Our model recognizes that risk may manifest in several forms and these different forms of risk may lead to distinct behavioral outcomes. Related to the notion of distinct behavioral outcomes, the existing models of health psychology do not discriminate between various types of behavioral outcomes that may result from risk evaluation. In our model, we rely on previous marketing research (Rogers, 1962, 1987) to identify a variety of different consumer decisions or behaviors that may occur due to risk evaluation. In the following section, we discuss the effects of different types of risks and how they affect a variety of consumer decisions.

Using Risk to Influence Behavior: Strategies From a Decision-Making Perspective

Consumer adoption of new products has been modeled in the literature on consumer diffusion of product innovations (e.g., Rogers, 1962, 1987, 1995). For example, this literature suggests that consumers go through multiple stages of decision-making before they adopt a new product. In this section, we adapt the diffusion of innovation paradigm to examine changes in a person's behavior when faced with a health hazard.

The steps that a person may go through when facing a health hazard may be: *awareness, interest, trial, adoption, repetition,* and *endorsement* for medical diagnosis, treatment, and following healthy behaviors. Awareness may mean identifying symptoms or causes of a health problem (e.g., knowing that smoking may cause lung cancer). Interest or desire might lead a consumer to follow-up on a symptom or behavior, or seek diagnosis or to acquire more information to take preventive action (e.g., young adults seeking information about sexually transmitted diseases, or wanting to find out about the correct testing procedures for HIV). Trial relates to getting a consumer to go to their doctor for a diagnosis. Adoption may mean starting a course of treatment if one has a disease (*e.g.,* starting on anti-cholesterol drugs), or starting a course of preventive action to prevent getting or exacerbating a disease (*e.g.,* starting a regimen of heart-healthy food and daily exercise to bring the cholesterol ratios to acceptable levels). Repetition might translate to continuing a course of medication rather than stopping it and being regular in habits that are preventative in nature (e.g., practicing safe sex, eliminating irregular social smoking or drug use, going to the gym, etc.). Endorsement emphasizes word-of-mouth that suggests to others to take preventative action, or seek diagnosis and treatment.

Next, we discuss how different forms of risk could affect the consumer decision-making in different situations and how interventions can be designed to strategically influence the risk behavior link in specific situations. This conceptual model is presented as Table 39.2 and includes some examples of how understanding the link between antecedents of risk perception can affect the manner in which we can improve the link between specific forms of risk and behavior.

Performance risk is the likelihood that the treatment will not perform as per prior consumer expectations, or that another alternative treatment may perform better than the chosen one. This construct has been explicitly referred to as "control" in prior work in the health field. Ajzen and Fishbein (1980) argued that beliefs about the how effective a behavior is in achieving a desired outcome may predict intentions and actual behavior. In a health domain, Block and Keller (1995) found that consumers uncertain about efficacy of taking preventive action against skin cancer, processed persuasive messages in greater depth, and were more likely to engage in preventive behaviors as compared to others. As many diagnostic procedures carry a performance risk (e.g., indicating a "false positive" for a test; Luce & Kahn, 1999), and the efficacy and side-effects of treatments are also relatively ambiguous, the manner in which each of these are communicated to consumers could play a role in getting consumers to appropriately recognize their risk levels and take action (Block & Keller, 1995, 1997). Table 39.2 summarizes various actions that will help consumers make

Table 39.2   Types of Consumer Decisions and Strategies to Enhance Health

Types of Consumer health Decisions/Behaviors	Awareness	Interest/ Desire	Trial	Adoption	Repeat Behavior	Endorsement/ Word-of-Mouth
Characteristics of different types of decisions	*Examples in the Health-Cycle domain*	*Identification of symptoms or behaviors that are related to the disease (and diagnostic means of identifying them).*	*Using presence of symptoms to make diagnostic judgment regarding risk level, whether to seek diagnosis, engage in prevention*	*Decision to go to a doctor/undergo a test to seek diagnosis or to try out new regimens for healthy living.*	*Starting preventative action/starting a course of medication*	*Continuing prevention strategies and/or medication*	*Increasing awareness, identifying those at risk, persuading others to engage in desirable behaviors (prevention, diagnosis, medication etc.).*

Performance Risk	The risk that a test, medication, or behavior will not be as effective as expected, be difficult to use, and have false-positives or missed diagnoses.	Increase the awareness of the link between a symptom/ behavior and a disease/ consequence (*E.g.*, "*Supersize Me*" highlights the link between fast food and obesity.)	Increase the perceptions of the controllability with appropriate courses of action (*E.g.*, "The risk of pregnancy with the use of a condom is less than 1%.")	Specify the hit-rate of a diagnostic course of action (*E.g.*, "Depression is curable in 80% of the cases with medication and therapy.")	Highlighting the risks associated with taking versus not taking a particular course of action (*E.g.*, the ease of use and effectiveness of blood sugar monitors for diabetics to regulate intake).	Reminder advertising and communication from health practitioners (*E.g*, the use of "You are Due" postcards from the dentists for regular dental check ups).	Using existing consumers who suffer from a problem and are committed to a course of action as a missionary force to convince others who are at different stages of recognizing their symptoms; identifying their risk level; and choosing to take action using methods like: • Testimonials to reduce performance risk
Financial Risk	The cost of tests/ medication	Increase insurance coverage and encourage low-cost options. Identify different price framing methods to equate the costs of treatment with other consumer expenses allowing for a cost/ benefit analysis.					
Physiological Risk	Fear of side-effects.	Identify beliefs that are spurious versus accurate and estimate and communicate the risk of side-effects (*E.g.*, identify whether the nicotine patch is not used because it is perceived to cause skin irritation, and then document the incidence of this problem.)		Allow the product to be scalable (*E.g.*, Use of samples to allow trial and measure side-effects.)	Highlight ways to reduce the risk of side-effects (*E.g.*, liver checks ups for those taking cholesterol medications.)	Encourage repurchase through use of reminders, price promotions and other marketing methods.	• Proxy Reports ("Do you or someone you know suffer from ...") • Support groups such as Alcoholics Anonymous and WeightWatchers.

(Continued)

Table 39.2   Continued

Types of Consumer health Decisions/Behaviors	Awareness	Interest/Desire	Trial	Adoption	Repeat Behavior	Endorsement/ Word-of-Mouth
Psycho-Social Risk	Fear of stigma, embarrassment associated with a problem or using a corrective course of action.	Reduce the fuzzy boundaries between socially acceptable behaviors and problems (*E.g.*, define irregular "social smoking" as unhealthy).	Reframing (*E.g.*, "Depression is not a weakness, it is an illness.") and highlighting risks (*E.g.*, different impact levels at 35mph vs. 42 mph).	Legislate and highlights costs associated with not following a course of action (*E.g.*, penalties for not wearing a bicycle helmet).	Reminder advertising highlighting costs associated with a single error (*E.g.*, penalties for drunk driving for a one-time offender).	Testimonials through celebrities and others.

different types of decisions about a corrective course of action by reducing their perception of performance risk.

Financial risk is the perceived likelihood associated with not getting the expected return (financial, utilitarian, or hedonic) on a financial outlay (e.g., the price of the treatment). Typically, the higher the initial cost of a treatment, the greater the financial risk and the lower the likelihood of trying, adopting or repeating the treatment. The high cost of medications and the high percentage of the under-insured or uninsured in the United States and other countries make it pertinent for consumer researchers to examine the extent to which financial risk considerations in seeking diagnosis and treatment are a factor that inhibit consumer from wishing to recognize their actual level of risk. In other words, if one cannot afford the treatment for AIDS, then one may prefer to not be diagnosed and may strategically underestimate the risk of contracting AIDS to maintain positive mental health as argued by Taylor and Brown (1988).

Physiological risk is the set of beliefs that undertaking a product or service may cause harm (e.g., many consumers believed that microwaves could lead to cancer and were hesitant about buying them when microwave ovens were introduced to them). Given that health risk almost always has a physiological aspect, and its testing can frequently be invasive (e.g., blood tests, x-rays, mammograms, etc.), as can its treatment (e.g., side effects of medications) understanding the factors that inhibit people from being tested, starting treatment, and continuing treatment is key to understanding the psychology of health risk. Highlighting actual risks, and debunking common myths, as well as highlighting benefits will allow consumers to make informed health related choices.

Psycho-social risk is the belief that using a product or service will cause a reduction in the psychological well being or the social status of the consumer. Psychological risk can lead consumers to shut-down, deny risk, or delay taking preventive action. For example, consumers might find treatments that involve trading off between two important attributes (e.g., trade-off involving safety, Luce, 1998) emotionally difficult and this might discourage them from taking preventive action. Risk perceptions involving self-positivity highlight the importance of mental well-being and usually have a psycho-social component. The most common psycho-social risk that has been studied is that of coping and social support mechanisms (e.g., Dunkell-Schetter, Feinstein, Taylor, & Falke, 1992; Taylor et al., 1986; Wood, Taylor, & Lichtman, 1985). Psycho-social risk exists in many health domains, albeit it comes in a full range of flavors. Our discussion on social desirability bias also highlights the importance of social risk posed by health risk considerations. For example, many people believe that depression is a weakness of the mind rather than an illness, and this inhibits them from seeking diagnosis and treatment (Jamison, 1999). Others are embarrassed about purchasing condoms and carrying them as it may signal promiscuity rather than being careful (Dahl et al., forthcoming). Yet others are socially embarrassed about refusing alcohol, drugs, or cigarettes in a social setting. Reframing these behaviors as safe rather than wimpy, intelligent rather than unfashionable, may effectively reduce psycho-social risks in the health domain.

A systematic bias in perceptions of absolute or relative levels of any of these forms of risk can lead to non-optimal purchases, decisions, and behaviors. In this chapter, we focus on one type of risk perception: *health risks*. Health-risk perceptions embody physiological, performance, psycho-social, and financial risk in a single construct (see Table 39.2). Thus, not only are they interesting to examine from the point of view of public policy and social welfare, they also provide a theoretically interesting construct incorporating the many facets of consumers' risk perceptions.

Most of the extant work in marketing has examined how risk perceptions are formed, and how these can assist in getting consumers to try preventive courses of action. The links to the other later behaviors in the various stages of consumer decision-making chain are a rich future source of enquiry. For example: What strategies are effective to get people to stay on a course of action?

What are the primary reasons for their dropping out—is it fear of failure or fear of success? What is needed to get consumers to encourage others? How does a health movement get momentum? How can health messages be best framed to make goals achievable?

CONCLUSIONS

The objective of this chapter was to review the extant literature on health risk perceptions with the aim of: (a) deriving a conceptual framework that addresses how the different antecedents and consequences of risk perceptions identified in the literature tie together, and (b) examining the importance for more research in this area. In Table 39.1, we summarize some of the key findings and implications of these findings for both academicians and social marketers, and list a few areas for future research.

While we made an effort to include most of the current research in health risk perceptions that is pertinent to consumer psychologists, we do not claim that this is chapter is comprehensive by any means. We hope that our conceptualization will foster more directed research in the area of health perceptions as this domain is quickly becoming a mainstream one which speaks to both social and commercial marketers and those who examine questions from the consumer welfare as well as the public policy point of view. One of our goals was to demonstrate that health risk perceptions and decisions have a lot in common with other mainstream consumer decisions that are well studied but are arguably of less consequence for a consumer, and conceptualizing them as such will assist not only a systematic investigation into health perception, but will also draw bridges between what have heretofore been distinct streams of academic research.

NOTES

1. http://www.m-w.com/cgi-bin/dictionary?book=Dictionaryandva=risk
2. National Health Council Statement, *Direct-To-Consumer Prescription Drug Advertising,* January 2002, http://www.nationalhealthcouncil.org/advocacy/dtc.htm
3. http://www.nimh.nih.gov
4. P(Yes) = [P(Answering 1st question) x P(Answer to 1st question is yes)] + [P(Answering 2nd question) x P(Drug Use)] → P(Yes) = [(0.5 x 0.5)] + [.5 x P(Drug Use)] → P (Drug Use) = [P("Yes" responses) – 0.25) / 0.5]

REFERENCES

Ackermann, R. E., & DeRubies, R. J. (1991). Is depressive realism real? *Clinical Psychology Review, 11*, 565–584.

Agrawal, N., Menon, G., & Aaker, J. (2007). Getting emotional about health. *Journal of Marketing Research, 34*(February), 100–113.

Agrawal, N., & Menon, G. (2005). Using discrete emotions to judge health risk. Working paper, New York University.

Ajzen, I. (1991). The theory of planned behavior. *Organizational Behavior and Human Decision Processes, 50*(December), 179–211.

Ajzen, Icek, & Fishbein, M. (1975). A Bayesian analysis of attribution processes. *Psychological Bulletin, 82*(March), 261–277.

Ajzen, Icek, & Fishbein, M. (1980). *Understanding attitudes and predicting social behavior.* Prentice-Hall, NJ: Englewood Cliffs.

Albarracin, D., Johnson, B. T., Fishbein, M., & Muellerleile, P. (2001). Theories of reasoned action and planned behavior as models of condom use: A meta-analysis. *Psychological Bulletin, 127*(January), 142–161.

Alloy, L. .B. , & Abramson, L. Y. (1979). Judgment of contingency in depressed and nondepressed students: sadder but wiser." *Journal of Experimental Psychology: General, 108*(December), 441–485.

Aquilino, W. S. (1994). Interview mode effects in surveys of drug and alcohol use: A field experiment. *Public Opinion Quarterly*, *58*(Summer), 210–240.

Aquilino, W., & LoSciuto, L. A. (1990). Effects of interview mode on self-reported drug use. *Public Opinion Quarterly*, *54*(Fall), 362–395

Argo, J. J., Dahl, D. W., & Manchanda, R. V. (2005). The influence of a mere social presence in a retail context. *Journal of Consumer Research*, *32*(September), 207–212.

Bargh, J. A., & Tota, M. E. (1988). Context-dependent automatic processing in depression: Accessibility of negative constructs with regard to self but not other. *Journal of Personality and Social Psychology*, *54*(June), 925–939.

Barton, A. H. (1958). Asking the embarrassing question. *Public Opinion Quarterly*, *22*, 67–68.

Bauman, L. J., & Siegel, K. (1987). Misperception among gay men of the risk of AIDS associated with their sexual behavior. *Journal of Applied Social Psychology*, *17*(March), 329–350.

Beck, A. T. (1967). *Depression: Clinical, experimental, and theoretical aspects*. New York: Harper and Row.

Beck, A. T. (1976). *Cognitive therapy and emotional disorders*. New York: International Universities Press.

Becker M. H (1974). The health belief model and personal health behavior. *Health Education Monographs*, *2*(4), 409–419.

Bickart, B. (1993). Carryover and backfire effects in marketing research. *Journal of Marketing Research*, *30*(February), 52–62.

Bickart, B., Menon, G., Schwarz, N., & Blair, J. (1994). The use of anchoring strategies in the construction of proxy reports of attitudes. *International Journal of Public Opinion Research*, *6*(4), 375–379.

Bless, H., Bohner, G., Hild, T., & Schwarz, N. (1992). Asking difficult questions: Task complexity increases the impact of response alternatives. *European Journal of Social Psychology*, *22*, 309–312.

Block, L. G., & Keller, P. A. (1995). When to accentuate the negative: The effects of perceived efficacy and message framing on intentions to perform a health related behavior. *Journal of Marketing Research*, *32*(May), 192–203.

Block, L. G., & Keller, P. A.(1997), "Effects of Self-Efficacy and Vividness on the Persuasiveness of Health Communications," *Journal of Consumer Psychology*, *6*(1), 31–54.

Bradburn, N. M; Seymour Sudman, S., Blair, Stocking, C. (1978). Question threat and response bias. *Public Opinion Quarterly*, *42*(Summer), 221–234.

Brewer, N. T., Weinstein, N., Cuite, C., & Herrington, J. (2004). Risk perceptions and their relation to risk behavior. *Annals of Behavioral Medicine*, *27*(2), 124–130.

Burger, J. M., & Palmer, M. L. (1992). Changes in and generalization of unrealistic optimism following experiences with stressful events: Reactions to the 1989 California earthquake. *Personality and Social Psychology Bulletin*, *18*(February), 39–43.

Chandran, S., & Menon, G. (2004). When a day means more than a year: Effects of temporal framing on judgments of health risk. *Journal of Consumer Research*, *31*(September), 375–389.

Chang, E. C. (1996). Evidence for the cultural specificity of pessimism in Asians and Caucasians: A test of the general negativity hypothesis. *Personality and Individual Differences, 21,* 819–822.

Dahl, D. W., Manchanda, R. V., & Argo, J. J. (2001). Embarrassment in consumer purchase: The roles of social presence and purchase familiarity. *Journal of Consumer Research*, *28*(December), 473–481.

Dahl, D. W., Darke, P., Gorn, G. J., & Weinberg, C. B. (2005). Promiscuous or confident?: Attitudinal ambivalence towards condom purchase. *Journal of Applied Social Psychology, 35*(4), 869–887.

Dahl, D. W., Gorn, G. J., & Weinberg, C. B. (1998). The impact of embarrassment on condom purchase behavior. *Canadian Journal of Public Health*, *89*(6), 368–370.

Dahl, D. W., Gorn, G. J., & Weinberg, C. B. (1999). Encouraging use of coupons to stimulate condom purchase. *American Journal of Public Health*, *89*(12), 1866–1869.

Darvill, T. J., & Johnson, R. C. (1991). Optimism and perceived control of life events as related to personality. *Personality & Individual Differences*, *12*(9), 951–954.

Davis, H. L., Hoch, S. J., & Ragsdale, E. K. (1986). An anchoring and adjustment model of spousal predictions. *Journal of Consumer Research*, *13*(June), 25–37.

Dholakia, U. M., & Morwitz, V. G. (2002). The scope and persistence of mere-measurement effects: Evidence from a field-study of customer satisfaction measurement. *Journal of Consumer Research*, *29*(September), 159–167.

DiClemente, R. J., & Peterson, J. L. (1994). *Preventing aids*. New York: Plenum Press.

Dolinski, D., Gromski, W., & Zawisza, E. (1987). Unrealistic pessimism. *Journal of Social Psychology,* *127*(October), 511–516.

Drake, R. A. (1987). Conceptions of own versus others' outcomes: Manipulation by monaural attentional orientation. *European Journal of Social Psychology, 17*(July–September), 373–375.

Dunkel-Schetter, C., Feinstein, L. G., Taylor, S. E., & Falke, R. L. (1992). Patterns of coping with cancer. *Health Psychology, 11*(2) 79–87.

Eagly, A. H., & Chaiken, S. (1993). *The psychology of attitudes,* Orlando, FL: Harcourt Brace Jovanovich College Publishers.

Feldman, J. M., & Lynch, Jr., J. G. (1988). Self-generated validity and other effects of measurement on belief, attitude, intention and behavior. *Journal of Applied Psychology, 73*(August), 421–435.

Fendrich, M., & Vaughn, C. M. (1994). Diminished lifetime substance use over time: An inquiry into differential underreporting. *Public Opinion Quarterly, 58*(Spring), 96–123.

Fenigstein, A., Scheier, M., & Buss, A. (1975). Public and private consciousness: Assessment and theory. *Journal of Consulting and Clinical Psychology, 43*(August), 522–527.

Fishbein, M., & Middlestadt, S. E. (1989). Using the theory of reasoned action as a framework for understanding and changing AIDS-related behaviors. In V. Mays, G. Albee, & S. F. Schneider (Eds.), *Primary prevention of AIDS: Psychological approaches* (pp. 93–110). Thousand Oaks, CA: Sage.

Fishbein, M., Middlestadt, S. E., &. Hitchcock, P. J. (1994). Using information to change sexually transmitted diseased related behaviors: An analysis based on the theory of reasoned action. In R. J. DiClemente & J. L. Peterson (Eds.), Preventing AIDS: Theories and methods of behavioral interventions (61–78). New York: Plenum.

Fischhoff, B., Lichtenstein, S., Slovic, P., Derby, S., & Keeney, R. (1984). *Acceptable risk,* New York: Cambridge University Press.

Fisher, J. D., & Fisher, W. A. (1992). Changing AIDS-risk behavior. *Psychological Bulletin, 111*(3), 455–474.

Fisher, R. J. (1993). Social desirability bias and the validity of indirect questioning. *Journal of Consumer Research, 20*(September), 303–315.

Fitzsimons, G., & Morwitz, V. G. (1996). The effect of measuring intent on brand level purchase behavior. *Journal of Consumer Research, 23*(June), 1–11.

Fontaine, K.. R., & Smith, S. (1995). Optimistic bias in cancer risk perception: A cross-national study. *Psychological Reports, 77*(August), 143–146.

Gerrard, M., Gibbons, F. X., & Bushman, B. J. (1996). Relation between perceived vulnerability to HIV and precautionary sexual behavior. *Psychological Bulletin, 119*(May) 390–409.

Gerrard, Meg, Gibbons, F. X., Reis-Bergan, M., & Russell, D. W. (2000). Self-esteem, self-serving cognitions, and health risk behavior. *Journal of Personality, 68*(December), 1177–1201.

Gotlib, I. H., & McCann, C. D. (1984). Construct accessibility and depression: An examination of cognitive and affective factors. *Journal of Personality and Social Psychology, 93*(August), 19–30.

Haire, M. (1950). Projective techniques in marketing research. *Journal of Marketing Research, 4*(5), 649–656.

Halpern D. F., Blackman, S. & Salzman, B. (1989). Using statistical risk information to assess oral contraceptive safety. *Applied Cognitive Psychology, 3*(3), 251–260.

Harris, P. (1996). Sufficient grounds for optimism? The relationship between perceived controllability and optimistic bias. *Journal of Social and Clinical Psychology, 15*, 9–52.

Heine, S. J., & Lehman, D. R. (1995). Cultural variation in unrealistic optimism: Does the West feel more invulnerable than the East? *Journal of Personality and Social Psychology, 68*(April), 595–607.

Helweg-Larsen, M., & Shepperd, J. A. (2001). Do moderators of the optimistic bias affect personal or target risk estimates? A Review of the literature. *Personality and Social Psychology Review, 5*(1), 74–95.

Higgins, E. T. (1989). Knowledge accessibility and activation: Subjectivity and suffering from unconscious sources. In James S. Uleman & John A. Bargh (Eds.), *Unintended thought* (pp. 75–123). New York: Guilford.

Higgins, E. T., & King. G. A. (1981). Accessibility of social constructs: Information processing consequences of individual and contextual variability. In *Personality, Cognition, and Social Interaction* (pp. 68–121). Hillsdale, NJ: Erlbaum, 69–121.

Hofstede, G. H. (1990). *Cultures and organizations: Software of the mind.* London: McGraw-Hill.

Jamison, K. R. (1999). *Night falls fast: Understanding suicide* (pp. 21–25). New York: Alfred A. Knopf.

Joseph, J. G., Montgomery, S. A., Emmons, C-A., Kirscht, J. P., Kessler, R. C., Ostrow, D. G., et al. (1987). Perceived risk of AIDS: Assessing the behavioral and psychosocial consequences in a cohort of gay men. *Journal of Applied Social Psychology, 1*(March), 231–250.

Kahn, B. E., & Luce, M. F. (2003). Understanding high-stakes consumer decisions: Mammography adherence Following false alarm test results. *Marketing Science, 22*(3), 393–410.

Keller, A., Lipkus, I. M., & Rimer, B. K. (2002). Depressive realism and health risk accuracy: The negative consequences of positive mood. *Journal of Consumer Research, 29*(June), 57–69.

Keller, P. A., Lipkus, I. M., & Rimer, B. K. (2003). Affect, framing, and persuasion. *Journal of Marketing Research, 40*(February), 54–65.

Kelly, K., Leventhal, H., Andrykowski, M., Toppmeyer, D., Much, J., Dermody, J., et al. (2005). Using the common sense model to understand perceived cancer risk in individuals testing for BRCA1/2 Mutations. *Psycho-Oncology, 14*(January), 34–48.

Keller, P. A., & Block, L. G. (1996). Increasing the persuasiveness of fear appeals: The effect of arousal and elaboration. *Journal of Consumer Research, 22*(March), 448–459.

Kuiper, N. A., & MacDonald, M. R. (1982). Self and other perception in mild depressives. *Social Cognition, 1*(3), 223–239.

Lalwani, A., Shavitt, S., & Johnson, T. (2006). What is the relation between cultural orientation and socially desirable responding? *Journal of Personality and Social Psychology, 90*(1), 165–178.

Larwood, L. (1978). Swine flu: A field study of self-serving bias. *Journal of Applied Social Psychology, 17*, 231–250.

Lee, C. (1989). Perceptions of immunity to disease in an adult smoker. *Journal of Behavioral Medicine, 12*, 267–277.

Leventhal, H., Cameron, L., Leventhal, E., & Ozakinci, G. (2005). Do messages from your body, your friends, your doctor, or the media shape your health behavior? T. C. Brock & M. C. Green (Eds.), *Persuasion: Psychological insights and perspectives* (2nd ed., pp. 195–223). Thousand Oaks, CA: Sage.

Levy, S. J. (1981). Interpreting consumer mythology: A structural approach to consumer behavior. *Journal of Marketing, 45*(Summer), 49–61.

Lin, C-H, Lin, Y. C., & Raghubir, P. (2003a). The interaction between order effects and perceived controllability on the self-positivity bias: Implications for self-esteem. In B. Kahn & M. F. Luce (Eds.), *Advances in onsumer Research* (Vol. 31, pp. 523–529). Provo, UT: Association for Consumer Research.

Lin, C-H, Lin, Y. C., & Raghubir, P. (2003b). Avoiding anxiety, being in denial or simply stroking self-esteem: Why self-positivity?" *Journal of Consumer Psychology, 13*, 464–477.

Lin, Y. C., & Raghubir, P. (2005). Gender differences in unrealistic optimism about marriage and divorce: Are men more optimistic and women more realistic?" *Personality and Social Psychology Bulletin, 31*(2), 1–10.

Loewenstein, G. F. (1996). Out of control: Visceral influences on behavior. *Organizational Behavior and Human Decision Processes, 65*(March), 272–292.

Luce, M. F. (1998). Choosing to avoid: Coping with negatively emotion-laden consumer decisions. *Journal of Consumer Research, 24*(March), 409–433.

Luce, M. F., & Kahn, B. E. (1999). Avoidance or vigilance? The psychology of false positive test results. *Journal of Consumer Research, 26*(December), 242–259.

Maheswaran, D., & Meyers-Levy, J. (1990). The influence of message framing and issue involvement. *Journal of Marketing Research, 27*(August), 361–367.

Maccoby, E. E., & Maccoby, N. (1954). The interview: A tool of social science. In G. Lindzey (Ed.), *Handbook of social psychology* (Vol. 1, pp. 449–487). Cambridge, MA: Addison-Wesley,

McFadden, D. (1999). Rationality for economists? *Journal of Risk and Uncertainty, 19*(1-3), 73–105.

Menon, G. (1993). The effects of accessibility of information in memory on judgments of behavioral frequencies. *Journal of Consumer Research, 20*(December), 431–440.

Menon, G. (1997). Are the parts better than the whole? The effect of decompositional questions on judgments of frequent behaviors," *Journal of Marketing Research, 34*(August), 335–346.

Menon, G., & Raghubir, P. (2003). Ease-of-retrieval as an automatic input in judgments: A mere accessibility framework? *Journal of Consumer Research, 30*(September), 230–243.

Menon, G., Block, L., & Ramanathan, S. (2002). We're at as much risk as we're led to believe: Effects of message cues on judgments of health risk. *Journal of Consumer Research, 28*(March), 533–549.

Menon, G., Raghubir, P., & Schwarz, N. (1995a). Behavioral frequency judgments: An accessibility-diagnosticity framework. *Journal of Consumer Research, 22*(September), 212–228.

Menon, G., Raghubir, P., & Schwarz, N. (1997). How much will I spend? Factors affecting consumers' estimates of future expenses." *Journal of Consumer Psychology, 6*(2), 141–164.

Menon, G., Bickart, B., Sudman, S., & Blair, J. (1995b). How well do you know your partner? Strategies for formulating proxy-reports and their effects on convergence to self-reports. *Journal of Marketing Research, 32*(February), 75–84.

Meyerowitz, B. E., & Chaiken, S. (1987). The effect of message framing on breast self-examination attitudes, intentions, and behavior. *Journal of Personality and Social Psychology, 52*(March), 500–510.

Moretti, M, M., & Shaw, B. F. (1989). Automatic and dysfunctional cognitive processes in depression. In J. S. Uleman & J. A. Bargh (Eds.), *Unintended thought* (pp. 383–421). New York: Guilford.

Morwitz, V. G., & Schmittlein, D. C. (1992). Using segmentation to improve sales forecasts based on purchase intent: Which 'intenders' actually buy? *Journal of Marketing Research, 29*(November), 391–405.

Morwitz, V. G., Johnson, E., & Schmittlein, D. C. (1993). Does measuring intent change behavior? *Journal of Consumer Research, 20*(June), 46–61.

Otten, W., & van der Pligt, J. (1996). Context effects in the measurement of comparative optimism in probability judgments. *Journal of Social and Clinical Psychology, 15*(Spring), 80–101.

Peltier, B. D., & Walsh, J. A. (1990). An investigation into response bias in the Chapman scales. *Educational and Psychological Measurement, 50*(4), 803–815.

Perloff, L. S. , & Fetzer, B. K. (1986). Self-other judgments and perceived vulnerability to victimization. *Journal of Personality and Social Psychology, 50*(March), 502–510.

Peterson, R. A., & Kerin, R. A (1981). The quality of self-report data: Review and synthesis. In B. M. Enis & K. J. Roering (Eds.), *Review of marketing* (pp. 5–20). Chicago: American Marketing Association.

Raghubir, P., & Menon, G. (1996). Asking sensitive questions: The effects of type of referent and frequency wording in counterbiasing methods. *Psychology and Marketing, 13*(October), 1–20.

Raghubir, P., & Menon, G. (1998). AIDS and me, never the twain shall meet: Factors affecting judgments of risk. *Journal of Consumer Research, 25*(June), 52–63.

Raghubir, P., & Johar, G. V. (1999). Hong Kong 1991 in Context. *Public Opinion Quarterly, 63*(4), 543–565.

Raghubir, P., & Menon, G. (2001), "Framing Effects in Risk Perceptions Of AIDS," *Marketing Letters,* 12 (May), 145–156.

Raghubir, P., & Menon, G. (2005a). Depressed or just blue? The persuasive effects of a self-diagnosis inventory. *Journal of Applied Social Psychology, 35*(12), 2535–2559.

Raghubir, P., & Menon, G. (2005b). When and why is ease of retrieval informative? *Memory & Cognition, 33*(July) 5, 821–832.

Raghunathan, R., & Trope, Y. (2002). Walking the tightrope between feeling good and being accurate: Mood as a resource in processing persuasive messages. *Journal of Personality and Social Psychology, 83*(3), 510–525.

Regan, P. C., Snyder, M., & Kassin, S. M. (1995). Unrealistic optimism: Self-enhancement or person positivity? *Personality and Social Psychology Bulletin, 21*(October), 1073–1082.

Reed, G. M., Kemeny, M. E.,. Taylor, S. E., Wang, H-Y, & Visscher, B. R. (1994). "Realistic acceptance" as a predictor of decreased survival time in gay men with AIDS. *Health Psychology, 13*(July), 299–307.

Robinette, R. L. (1991). The relationship between the Marlowe-Crowne form C and the validity scales of MMPI, *Journal of Clinical Psychology, 47*(May), 396–399.

Rogers, E. M. (1962). *Diffusion of innovation.* New York: Free Press.

Rogers, E. M. (1987). The diffusion of innovations perspective. In N. Weinstein (Ed.),*Taking care: Understanding and encouraging self-protective behavior.* New York: Cambridge University Press.

Rogers, E. M. (1995). *Diffusion of innovations* (4th ed.). New York: The Free Press.

Roger, R. W., & Mewborn, C. R. (1976). Fear appeals and attitude change: Effects of a threat's noxiousness, probablity of occurrence, and the efficacy of coping resources. *Journal of Personality and Social Psychology, 34,* 54–61.

Rosenstock, I. M. (1974). Historical origins of the health belief model. *Health Education Monographs, 2,* 328–335.

Russell, S. (2000). Sad men. *San Francisco Chronicle,* October 1, 2000.

Salovey, P., O'Leary, A., Stretton, M. S., Fishkin, S. A., & A. Drake, C. A. (1991). Influence of mood on judgments about health and illness. In J. P. Forgas (Ed.), *Emotion and social judgments* (pp. 241–262). Elmsford, NY: Pergamon.

Schneider, S. G., Taylor, S. E., Kemeny, M. E., & Hammen, C. (1991). AIDS-related factors predictive of suicidal ideation of low and high intent among gay and bisexual men. *Suicide & Life-Threatening Behavior, 21,* 313–328.

Schuman, H., & Presser, S. (1996). *Questions and answers in attitude surveys: Experiments on question form, wording, and context.* San Diego: Sage.

Schwarz, N., & Bienias, J. L. (1990). What mediates the impact of response alternatives on frequency reports of mundane behaviors? *Applied Cognitive Psychology, 4,* 61–72.

Schwarz, N., & Sudman, S. (1994). *Autobiographical memory and the validity of retrospective reports.* New York: Springer-Verlag.

Schwarz, N Hippler, H. J., Deutsch, B., & Strack, F. (1985). Response scales: Effects of category range on reported behavior and subsequent judgments. *Public Opinion Quarterly, 49,* 388–395.

Sedikides, C., Gaertner, L., & Toguchi, Y. (2003). Pancultural self-enhancement. *Journal of Personality and Social Psychology, 84*(January), 60–79.

Shefrin, H. (2005). *A behavioral approach to asset pricing,* New York: Academic Press.

Shepperd, J. A., Helweg-Larsen, M., & Ortega, L. (2003). Are comparative risk judgments consistent over time and events. *Personality and Social Psychology Bulletin, 29*(September), 1169–1180.

Simon, J., & Simon, R. (1975). The effect of money incentives on family size: A hypothetical-question study. *Public Opinion Quarterly, 38,* 585–595.

Simmons, C. J., Bickart, E. J., & Lynch, Jr., J. G. (1993). Capturing and creating public opinion in survey research. *Journal of Consumer Research, 20*(September), 316–329.

Skinner, E. A. (1995). *Perceived control, motivation, and coping.* Thousand Oaks, CA: Sage.

Sudman, S., & Bradburn, N. A. (1974). *Asking questions: A practical guide to questionnaire design,* New York: Jossey Bass.

Sudman, S., Bradburn, N. M., & Schwarz, N. (1995). *Thinking about answers: The application of cognitive processes to survey methodology,* New York: Jossey-Bass.

Taylor, S. E. (1983). Adjustment to threatening events: A theory of cognitive adaptation. *American Psychologist, 38*(11), 1161–1173.

Taylor, S. E. (1990). Health psychology: The science and the field. *American Psychologist, 45*(1), 40–50.

Taylor, S. E. (1998). The social being in social psychology. In D. Gilbert, S. Fiske, & G. Lindsey (Eds.), *The handbook of social psychology* (pp. 54–98). New York: McGraw-Hill,

Taylor, S. E. (2003). *Health psychology,* New York: McGraw Hill.

Taylor, S. E., & Brown, J. D. (1988). Illusion and well-being: A social psychological perspective on mental health. *Psychological Bulletin, 103*(2), 193–210.

Taylor, S. E., & Gollwitzer, P. M. (1995). The effects of mindset on positive illusions. *Journal of Personality and Social Psychology, 69*(August), 213–226.

Taylor, S. E., & Schneider, S. K. (1989). Coping and the simulation of events. *Social Cognition, 7*(Summer), 176–196.

Taylor, S. E., Lichtman, R. R., & Wood, J. V. (1984). Attributions, beliefs about control, and adjustment to breast cancer. *Journal of Personality and Social Psychology, 46*(March), 489–502.

Taylor, S. E., Falke, R. L., Shoptaw, S. J., & Lichtman, R. R. (1986). Social support, support groups, and the cancer patient. *Journal of Consulting and Clinical Psychology, 54*(October), 608–615.

Taylor, S. E., Helgeson, V. S., Reed, G. M., & Skokan, L. A. (1991). Self-generated feelings of control and adjustment to physical iillness. *Journal of Social Issues, 47*(Winter), 91–109.

Taylor, S. E., Pham, L. B., Rivkin, I., & Armor, D. (1998). Harnessing the imagination: Mental simulation and self-regulation of behavior. *American Psychologist, 53*(April), 429–439.

Taylor, S. E., Kemeny, M., Reed, G. M., Bower J. E., & Gruenewald, T. L. (2000). Psychological resources, positive illusions, and health. *American Psychologist, 55*(January), 99–109.

Taylor, S. E., Lerner, J. S., Sherman, D. K., Sage, R. M., McDowell, N. K. (2003). Are self-enhancing cognitions associated with healthy or unhealthy biological profiles? *Journal of Personality and Social Psychology, 85*(October), 605–615.

Taylor, S. E., Kemeny, M., Aspinwall, L. G., Schneider, S. G., Rodriguez, R., & Herbert, M. (1992). Optimism, coping, psychological distress, and high-risk sexual behavior among men at risk for AIDS. *Journal of Personality and Social Psychology, 63*(September), 460–473.

Trope, Y., & Liberman, N. (2000). Temporal construal and time-dependent changes in rreference. *Journal of Personality and Social Psychology, 79*(December), 876–889.

Tversky, A., & Kahneman, D. (1974). Judgment under uncertainty: Heuristics and biases. *Science, 185*(September), 1124–1131.

Warner, S. L. (1965). Randomized response: A survey technique for estimating error answer bias. *Journal of the American Statistical Association, 60*(309), 63–69.

Weinstein, N. D. (1980). Unrealistic optimism about future life events. *Journal of Personality and Social Psychology, 39*(October), 806–820.

Weinstein, N. D. (1989). Effects of personal experience on self-protective behavior. *Psychological Bulletin, 105*(January), 31–50

Weinstein, N. D., & Lachendro, E. (1982). Egocentrism as a source of unrealistic optimism. *Personality and Social Psychology Bulletin, 8*(June), 195–200.

Wood, J. V., Taylor, S. E., & Lichtman, R. R. (1985). Social comparison in adjustment to breast cancer. *Journal of Personality and Social Psychology, 49*(November), 1169–1183.

Zerbe, W. J., & Palhaus, D. L. (1987). Socially desirable responding in organizational behavior: A reconception. *Academy of Management Review, 12*(April), 250–264.

40

Toward a Psychology of Consumer Creativity

James E. Burroughs

University of Virginia

C. Page Moreau

University of Colorado

David Glen Mick

University of Virginia

Understanding creativity has been one of the most vexing challenges facing psychologists over the past 50 years. Michelangelo's sculpture of *David*, Einstein's Theory of Relativity, and Mozart's piano concertos inspire awe as to their creativity. But more mundanely, creativity is also evident in the toil of an individual working to customize their pickup truck, or the clever way a mother uses hair spray to remove an ink stain. These examples are so disparate, what connects them? What defines something as creative? Creativity is difficult to make sense of, but essential to human functioning.

Creativity is ubiquitous in consumer behavior. In everything from vehicles and homes to clothing and a mundane fix for a stain, creativity permeates the consumption realm. Yet few attempts have been made to translate basic observation into theoretical treatise, and even fewer attempts have been made to empirically document the role of creativity in the consumer behavior literature. The purpose of this chapter is to outline a psychology of consumer creativity. Our discussion will integrate considerations of creativity from the perspectives of the product, the process, the person, and the environment, and will consider the implications of each within the consumption realm. The topic of creativity remains an open frontier in consumer psychology.

CONCEPTUAL BACKGROUND

Creativity is often defined as an outcome (a work, a product, an idea) that is both novel and appropriate to the given context or circumstance from which it arises. As basic as this definition appears, a modern understanding of creativity has been long in coming, and at various points emphasis has been on the creative person, the creative process, and the creative environment. To appreciate the modern conceptualization of creativity and how its various facets interrelate, it is useful to trace a brief history of creativity research.

Some of the earliest descriptions of creativity equated it with genius and a gift of divine providence. By the late 18th century a great deal of effort had been expended trying to decipher the source and nature of creative genius. This interest in creativity coincided with a time of great debate over the indemnity of individual freedom versus the need for social strictures and the rule of law. Even casual observation confirmed that creative individuals often flout convention and disdain rules, which are personality characteristics that would later become hallmarks of the creative person. The question was how to encourage creativity while maintaining a semblance of order. If the Renaissance demonstrated one thing, it was that creativity could not flourish in repressive societies. The inherent tension between creative expression and social prescription would ultimately culminate in the doctrine of individualism, if not the French Revolution itself (see Albert & Runco, 1999).

The debate about creativity intensified with the onset of the Industrial Revolution. Intellectuals of the day hastened to point out that individuals were increasingly being subjugated to rote tasks and undifferentiated, sprawling urban areas that stripped all manner of creativity from daily life. It is notable that these early considerations of creativity made little attempt to distinguish between its individual and social aspects, seeing them as parts of an indivisible whole. As the discussions of creativity progressed, however, the social aspects of creativity were largely lost. For the most part, the modern study of creativity has been a study of the internal workings of the individual, stripped of social context. When today's postmodern researchers describe consumers' reclamation of creativity from a mass-produced world, there is a tendency to view these accounts as paradigmatically incompatible with psychological perspectives of creativity that focus on knowledge, aptitude, motivation, and other individual aspects. This was not always the case, and a number of prominent psychologists have recently commented on the need to put more of the social back into the psychology of creativity (Csikszentmihalyi, 1999; Hennessey, 2003).

The treatment of creativity as a formal topic of scientific investigation is a 20th century development. The first half the 20th century can be characterized as the psychodynamic period of creativity research (Sternberg & Lubart, 1999). Consistent with Freud's popular views of the time, the psychodynamic perspective held creativity to be the byproduct of a struggle to reconcile unconscious drives with conscious inhibitions. Great paintings, epic literature, monumental structures, all were displaced attempts to quell this inveterate conflict. Interestingly, and despite the fact that this psychodynamic tension should apply to anyone, creativity continued to be largely viewed as a unique ability possessed by a gifted few (the notion that it was somehow divinely imparted did, however, fall into decline). The psychodynamic period was characterized by case studies of eminent individuals in order to try and glimpse the wellspring of creative inspiration.[1]

Paul Guilford's (1950) Presidential Address to the *American Psychological Association* represented a watershed moment in creativity research. In his speech, Guilford asserted the incontrovertible importance of creativity to psychology (and all aspects of human functioning) and beseeched the field to do better in investigating this crucial phenomenon. Though it would be many years before the creativity research revolution Guilford envisioned would be realized, there is no doubt his speech gave creativity research a major boost. Many consider Guilford's speech to be the defining moment that brought creativity research into its modern age.

Guilford's call for more rigorous research on creativity coincided with a time of rapid developments in psychological measurement. Thus, the 1950s and 1960s can be broadly characterized as the psychometric period of creativity research (Plucker & Renzulli, 1999; Sternberg & Lubart, 1999). During this time a number of creative batteries were developed, perhaps the best known of which were the *Torrance Tests of Creative Thinking* (1966). The development of pencil-and-paper tests that could be administered to a wide swath of the population brought the study of creativity from the domain of rarified genius to the realm of ordinary individuals. Increasingly, creativity came to be seen as the product of ordinary cognitive processes as opposed to some exceptional or mystical gift (Ward, Smith, & Finke, 1999). Viewing creativity as a normal cognitive process made it accessible to mainstream methods of cognitive science (Hershman & Leib, 1988). Coincidentally, the psychometric period saw the development of other psychological tests, particularly intelligence tests, so it is not surprising that considerable effort went into investigating the empirical connection between creativity and intelligence. What were unexpected were the results. Though some level of intelligence is necessary for creativity, it proved of surprisingly limited explanatory power (Albert & Runco, 1999). As a result, those scholars who had equated creativity with intelligence were forced to cast a wider nomological net.

Analogical reasoning and metaphorical thinking emerged as possible critical links to creative insight, and the 1970s and 1980s would witness a number of important discussions on the role of figurative language in creative thought (see e.g., Barron, 1988; Ward, Smith, & Finke, 1999 also provide an excellent overview of this cognitive perspective on creativity). During this time period social psychologists began to consider motivational aspects of creativity, finding intrinsic motivation to be particularly crucial (see, e.g., Amabile, 1983).

As the study of creativity branched into different areas, not surprisingly the literature became fragmented. Social psychologists focused on motivation and personality traits, cognitive psychologists on the process of creative thought, educational psychologists on the efficacy of creative education programs, and so forth. The field of psychology lacked a unifying perspective and research was accused of being atheoretical and descriptive. Moreover, despite important progress, creativity still remained an underdeveloped topic in psychology.

Sternberg and Lubart (1999) suggest that part of the reason for creativity's continued obscurity was attributable to the rise of the experiment as psychology's preeminent methodology. This presents the obvious challenge of studying a phenomenon that is fluid and emergent using a methodology predicated on structure and control. Within the domain of consumer psychology, creativity was basically persona non grata to this point, save for a few pioneering researchers (Hirschman, 1980; Price & Ridgeway, 1982).

The 1990s witnessed the creative revolution Guilford envisioned. In 1988, the first academic journal dedicated to empirical research on creativity was launched, the *Creativity Research Journal*. More than a dozen edited books on creativity were also issued in this general time period (see, e.g., Boden, 1996; Dartnall, 2002; Glover, Ronning, & Reynolds, 1989; Houtz, 2003; Isaksen et al., 1993; Runco, 1997, 2003; Smith, Ward, & Finke, 1995; Smith, Ward, & Vaid, 1997; Shaw & Runco, 1994; Sternberg, 1988a, 1999a; Sternberg, Grigorenko, & Singer, 2004). What was once an obscure topic in psychology became a required chapter (if not a dedicated book) in nearly any compendium of psychological research, including research on problem solving (Lubart & Mouchiroud, 2003), motivation (Hennessey, 2000), group dynamics (Paulus & Nijstad, 2003), artificial intelligence (McDonough, 2002), and positive psychology (Nakamura & Csikszentmihalyi, 2003), and now consumer psychology.

This "golden age" (Plucker & Renzulli, 1999) of creativity research produced valuable advances in the experimental procedures used to study creativity, and some of the most influential studies to date have been of the experimental variety (see Runco & Sakamoto, 1999, for a review). Ironically, advances in the experimental procedures used to study creativity have highlighted the value of other methodologies, particularly when used in tandem with experiments.

Perhaps the most important development in the creativity revolution has been the development of confluence models of creativity which unify creativity's diverse aspects (see, e.g., Csikszentmihalyi, 1999; Woodman & Schoenfeldt, 1990). The confluence perspective holds that creativity is a product of multiple, simultaneous, often interactive influences. In other words, to truly understand how creativity comes about, one must consider not only cognitive abilities such as intelligence and analogical reasoning, but also personality characteristics such as tolerance for ambiguity, risk taking, and novelty seeking, motivational factors such as intrinsic interest and involvement, as well as the role of the environment (at both the situational and sociocultural levels).

Though researchers still tend to focus on one area of creativity (e.g., creative cognition), they acknowledge their findings to be part of a broader theoretical framework (Ward et al., 1999). Moreover, some studies have begun to incorporate variables from multiple domains in order to gauge relative effects on creativity in a given context. For example, Burroughs and Mick (2004) examined the interactive effects of time (an environmental constraint) with locus of control (a personality variable) and with situational involvement (a motivational variable) on creative outcomes. Though the value of a confluence perspective may seem somewhat self evident, it is important to keep in mind that for most of its history the study of creativity was a search for the "magic bullet" or all-encompassing mechanism to explain it (Mumford, 2003).

The potential for applying a confluence perspective to research on creativity in consumer behavior is high. Consumption is a social phenomenon exemplified by strong personal, situational, and cultural forces, often acting in unison. Both motivational and ability factors are crucial to a wide variety of consumption activities. Consumer behavior also ranges from immediate and localized problem solving to enduring and complex social exchange. It is difficult to envision a better contemporary setting for studying the spectrum of creative behaviors than consumption. This is not an idle opportunity, as researchers have repeatedly pointed out the lack of studies of creativity in real-world settings (see e.g., Lubart, 1994).

The creativity revolution has started to make its way into consumer psychology. There have been several recent special sessions on creativity at national consumer research conferences (see, e.g., Burroughs & Moreau, 2004; Burroughs & Otnes, 2001), some of which have included leading creativity scholars from other fields. Even more encouraging, articles explicitly dedicated to the topic of creativity have begun to appear in the leading marketing and consumer research journals (see, e.g., Burroughs & Mick, 2004; Dahl & Moreau, 2002; Goldenberg, Mazursky, & Solomon, 1999; Moreau & Dahl, 2005). The rest of this chapter will be dedicated to building a confluence model of consumer creativity and highlighting opportunities for further research in this area. We begin with creativity's epicenter, the creative product.

AN INTEGRATIVE FRAMEWORK OF CONSUMER CREATIVITY

The Creative Product

MacKinnon (1978, p. 187) argued that, "the starting point, indeed the bedrock of all studies of creativity, is an analysis of creative products." By product, MacKinnon meant some type of creative *outcome*. Thus, while researchers may focus on the creative individual or the creative process, it always comes back to the outcome produced. However, determining what constitutes a creative product is itself challenging.

Guilford (1964) equated creativity with problem-solving. A creative outcome is one that provides a unique solution to a practical problem, and a huge portion of research on creativity has been conducted under the auspices of problem solving. However, many creative acts, such as painting, do not solve any specific problem. This led researchers to specify the dimensions of creativity more broadly (and develop techniques for assessing these dimensions).

The Novelty and Functionality Dimensions of Creativity   It is universally accepted that, to be creative, an outcome must be novel. Novelty goes to the heart of what sets a creative outcome apart from any other. Novelty is usually gauged in terms the extent to which the outcome departs from what is typical or conventional in a given situation, problem, or context. In consumer behavior, novelty can bee seen in the application of a product to a purpose other than that for which it was originally intended, the alteration of a product to enhance its performance or appearance, or the combination of two or more products in a new way, perhaps to achieve functional synergies. This broaches the second dimension of creativity, functionality. Being novel simply by being bizarre is not creative (Lubart, 1994). To be creative, an outcome must also serve some useful purpose. In other words, the change must be constructive.

While the functionality of an outcome is relatively easy to determine in the context of problem solving, this notion is less applicable to expressive and artistic forms of creativity. An artistic product can be functional, but this is clearly not what sets it apart as creative.

The Aesthetic Dimension   When acts of creativity are enacted for more artistic and expressive purposes, creativity's second dimension is more closely associated with aesthetics. Here creativity is derived from an outcome that is not only unusual, but exhibits a certain beauty, elegance, or attractiveness. Because researchers have historically tended to focus on one domain of creativity (problem solving/scientific) or the other (artistic), the question of what to label this second dimension has not been at issue. However, many acts of creative consumption contain both functional and aesthetic aspects. Changes in the appearance of a product can, and often do, arise from practical considerations, while a very practical problem can be solved in an elegant way. This led Burroughs and Mick (2004) to propose the possibility of a three-dimensional conceptualization of creativity, where the most creative acts of consumption are high in novelty, functionality, and aesthetics.

Two examples help illustrate the usefulness of moving to a three-dimensional conceptualization of creative consumption. The examples come from consumer interviews conducted by Burroughs (1998). The first example highlights how creativity driven by a practical need can also have an aesthetic quality. The second example highlights how an act of consumer creativity that is aesthetically motivated can still revolve around a practical problem.

Example one involves a retiree who lives in New Jersey but winters in Florida. An ever-present concern of such individuals is that if the heat in their northern home fails while they are away, the pipes may freeze and burst. A product specifically designed to address this problem is the *Winter Watchman*. The device is very similar to a light timer, but works on temperature. If the temperature in the house ever falls below a preset limit (e.g., 50 degrees), the *Watchman* senses this and activates an electrical receptacle embedded in the unit. Users are instructed to plug a lamp into the *Watchman*, place the lamp in a window, and tell a neighbor that if they ever see this light go on to call the local utility company immediately because the heat has failed. The obvious limitation of this product is that it relies on the vigilance of a neighbor. What our informant did was plug his answering machine into the *Watchman* instead. Then he would call home once a day. As long as the answering machine did not pick up, he knew the heat was functioning normally and he was not charged for the call. If, however, the answering machine ever did pick up, he knew he had a problem. This bit of ingenuity allowed our retiree to remotely monitor his home, solving a common problem in a practical yet elegant way.

The second example revolves around household furnishings and is predicated on the very practical problem of a lack of money. It happened that the interviewee needed a new coffee table but could not afford one. So, she removed the legs from her current table, went to the hardware store and purchased copper tubing and threaded dowels, and then attached the tubing to the table in place of the wooden legs. This simple substitution modernized the look of her décor with minimal investment.

Numerous other examples of creative consumption with a more aesthetic bent can be found in the consumer behavior literature (e.g., Holt, 1997; Kates, 2002; Thompson & Haytko, 1997).

The Consensual Assessment Technique for Creative Products   Even settling the issue of creativity's dimensions still leaves open the issue of assessment. How is one to determine the extent to which an outcome is "novel," "functional," or "aesthetic"? For example, the paintings of Monet were initially rejected by the Parisian art establishment as heretical. Today, of course, they are recognized as creative masterpieces. And this problem is not limited to art. The brilliant scientist Thomas Young (who gave us the wave theory of light) was so far ahead of his time that, "a mass of his most important thoughts remained buried and forgotten in the *Transactions of the Royal Society* until a later generation by slow degrees arrived at the rediscoveries, and came to appreciate the force of his arguments and the accuracy of his conclusions" (Helmholtz, 1873, as appeared in Martindale, 2001, p. 343). Thus it is creativity's paradox that something may be so novel, and so ahead of its time, as to be beyond immediate comprehension.

Fortunately, such extreme instances are of creativity are rare (particularly in consumer behavior) and Amabile (1982) has developed a very useful technique for assessing creativity in most situations. Her *Consensual Assessment Technique* is predicated on two basic premises. First, the dimensions of creativity are relative and reside on a continuum. Take, for instance, the issue of novelty. Any outcome is at least unique to its own time and circumstance, but is also based in part on that which came before it. Watson and Crick's double-helix model of DNA is sometimes perceived as miraculously inspired when, in fact, it is partly predicated on the work of Linus Pauling, who had not long before proposed the structure of the protein alpha-keratin to be helical (Weisburg, 1999). Similarly, Picasso's paintings, *Les demoiselles d'Avignon* and *Guernica*, were based on initial sketches that built upon earlier works by both himself and other artists (Dasgupta, 2004; Weisburg, 1999). Therefore, it is not a question of novel versus not novel, but rather how novel. Creativity's other two dimensions are similarly a matter of degree.

The second premise of the *Consensual Assessment Technique* is that even if the dimensions of creativity are almost impossible to establish in an absolute sense, individuals usually have little difficulty recognizing and evaluating creativity when they see it. Thus, the creativity of an outcome can be ascertained through consensus of independent judges. Individuals implicitly factor in issues such as relative distinctiveness and social context (e.g., evaluating a child's art vs. that of a trained painter) in making their creative evaluations. The consensual assessment approach has been combined with psychometric scales that tap the specific dimensions of creative outcomes (see, e.g., O'Quin & Besemer, 1989) to arrive at a final creative determination.

Opportunities for Studying Creative Products in Consumer Psychology   To date, no research has attempted to create a typology of the creative changes consumers make to products. However, research by Goldenberg et al. (1999) documented how changes in product form over time often follow certain templates, which can be useful for predicting future product innovations. A template specifies certain generalized relationships that allow individuals to export a logical sequence of changes in one product and apply them to different product categories. For example, a consumer's attribute dependency template between color and temperature (i.e., red equals hot) can be applied to a wide variety of otherwise unrelated product concepts including washing machines, pizza delivery services, infant bottle warmers, and so forth. As such, templates help efficiently guide the new product creation process.

It is also worth noting that manufacturers are increasingly reliant on consumers as a source of creative new product ideas, as well as to serve as co-producers of products already commercially available. Home Depot, Ikea, and Michaels are all highly successful marketing franchises that rely heavily on consumer creativity as a key component of their commercial success. Consumers' growing appetite for do-it-yourself projects around the home and in their leisure time opens a plethora of research opportunities in the area of understanding consumers' frustrations, elations, and overall satisfaction with the creative use of products. Such expanded understanding is critical not only to a broadened perspective on consumer behavior, but also as a way of designing more consumer-centered products. It is somewhat contrary to prevailing wisdom, but some consumers seem to derive great satisfaction from having a portion of the marketing burden shifted to them (e.g., product assembly, product alteration) as opposed to just having marketers provide ready-made solutions in final form. It is clear that these consumers gain a sense of efficacy and pleasure from such creative interaction with products.

Additionally, researchers need to gain a better understanding of the antecedents of creative consumption outcomes. These might include further investigations of the role of time (Burroughs & Mick, 2004, Moreau & Dahl, 2005), analogical reasoning (Dahl & Moreau, 2002), and consumer knowledge, issues we will take up in greater detail later in the chapter.

The Creative Process

How do creative products come about? In its most basic terms, the creative process involves the retrieval and novel combination of fragments of knowledge from disparate locations in memory, such that it constructively addresses a given issue (Smith, 1995). The creative process is thought to involve four stages: exploration, fixation, incubation, and insight (Ward et al., 1999). The basic cognitive processes studied extensively in psychology (e.g., access, retrieval, analogical reasoning, and knowledge transfer) describe mental activities that occur at each of these stages (Ward et al., 1999). It should be noted that some researchers add a stage to either end of the the creative process. They include a preparatory stage, in which a foundation for creativity is laid before specific deliberative effort is expended, and/or an evaluation stage, in which a creative insight is further scrutinized, refined, or expanded (Martindale, 1999).

Exploration   In response to a specific problem or creative task, individuals enter an exploratory phase in which they search for known solutions or access inputs relevant for constructing an appropriate response. During this phase, the formation of associations is open ended, though usually guided by existing knowledge structures, environmental cues and primes, and external constraints (Ward et al., 1999). The process of combining ideas is typically an incremental one that begins with examination of closely related conceptual linkages and moves concentrically outward (though highly creative individuals often jump to more divergent associations). Perkins (1997) discusses this process as a search through the "possibility space" of solutions, acknowledging that different mental typographies can make solutions (or their relevant inputs) either very accessible or extremely hard to find. As various new mental linkages are formed, discarded, and expanded, pre-inventive structures emerge (Ward et al., 1999). Pre-inventive structures are symbolic patterns, exemplars, mental models, or unique verbal combinations that are precursors to creative thought.

Fixation   An interim stage of the creative process is fixation. Given the natural progression of the exploratory phase, it is unusual that someone immediately comes to a remote, decisive insight. As often as not, cognitive roadblocks impede progress. This is because individuals begin with a bias towards existing knowledge structures and known solutions to similar problems that they are reluctant to abandon when they fail. The brain is hardwired for efficiency, to quickly apply existing solutions to like problems (hence the reason that the creative thought process is mentally taxing). Ward (1994) calls this tendency one of "following the path-of-least-resistance" (the POLR strategy).

Breaking free of existing mental frames is a struggle and, even when successful, creative insight may still remain beyond reach. As ever-more remote conceptual combinations are explored, some pathways will appear promising, but illusory. Sensing a breakthrough is close, the individual presses even harder down the errant path, struggling to make the proverbial square peg fit the round hole (Smith, 1995). Ironically, the closer the inadequate solution to an adequate one, the more likely it is to block successful creative insight. The individual becomes fixated.

This stage of the creative process is informed by a very important realization; in many instances, the framing of the problem itself is responsible for the fixation. Thus, creative insight is often not only about "problem solving," but also realigning the representation of the problem itself or seeing the problem in an entirely new way. This process is referred to as "problem finding" (Segal, 2004).

Contextual factors such as incidental environmental cues may also complicate the creative task at this stage by biasing the individuals toward a particular mindset (Smith, 1995). For example, Dahl and Moreau (2002) found that subjects who were asked to design a new product to facilitate eating while driving, came up with less original ideas if they were first shown a sketch of a proto-typical design concept. It appears that the mere exposure to such a preformed concept was sufficient to inhibit individuals' from freely generating new ideas. Because such environmental influences are often beyond conscious awareness, their influence can be difficult to recognize.

Incubation   After a period of fixation, the activated mental models that impede creative progress will begin to destabilize. Though new environmental influences or conscious effort can sometimes hasten their demise, a major factor is often simply time. The individual becomes exhausted and loses focus. Interestingly, this allows the creative process to again move forward. A withdrawal of attention away from the problem allows activated models to decompose and new linkages to form (Segal, 2004). This period of destabilization and reorientation is known as the incubation stage of creativity. Freed of inhibiting mental modes produced from past experience or early promise, the creative breakthrough again becomes possible (Smith, 1995).

Insight   The final phase of the creative process is insight. Because a period of incubation is typically necessary in order to nurture creative insight, creative breakthroughs often occur after a problem is no longer being actively considered. At a preconscious level, the mind continues to mull over the problem and abruptly thrusts the solution through to conscious awareness. These moments represent some of the most emotionally charged in the human experience. It is one of the remarkable capabilities of the mind to encounter new information and, without deliberate effort, connect this information back to previously activated problems and issues in new ways.

Opportunities for Studying the Creative Process in Consumer Psychology   To our knowledge, no research in consumer behavior has attempted to document, start-to-finish, the creative thought processes individuals go through as they engage in consumption tasks. While the creative cognition approach holds that the same mental processes are involved in everything from eminent creative accomplishment to mundane problem solving, it remains to be seen if some processing strategies are more effective at devising creative solutions to consumption problems than others, and if these strategies vary by consumption instance (e.g., consumer problem solving versus more socioculturally rooted acts of consumption). Moreau and Dahl (2005) did conduct several studies in which subjects were charged with designing a new type of toy using a predetermined set of shapes or components. They then examined how specific contingencies and external influences affected participants' tendencies to deviate from the POLR; however, their research did not examine the distinct stages of the creative process described above. Given that creativity involves a great deal of trial and error, it would be valuable to document subjects thought processes and strategies as they work through consumption problems.

Additionally, it is well known that consumers often alter their dress, domicile, or vehicle as part of cultural discourse. Creative changes build upon prior changes made by others (see, e.g., Kates, 2002; Thompson & Haytko, 1997). However, while this research acknowledges the crucial role of creativity in social discourse, it does not generally concern itself with the more internal aspects of the process, opting instead to try and understand the social arrangements structured by creative acts. Since the basic creative processes described above in the context of problem solving are also most certainly active during more expressive acts of creative consumption, it would be interesting to examine how and at which stages various sociocultural cues enter the creative process. How do social exchanges contribute to issues such as fixation and insight?

Finally, since no consumer research has tried to dissect the creative process, there is little understanding how cognitive activities at each stage might differentially impact the dimensions of creativity. Perhaps the exploratory stage has the largest influence on the novelty dimension but contributes little to the functionality of the solution. Conversely, functionality would seem likely to be determined during the incubation and insight stages of the creative process. These assertions are clearly speculative at this point and worthy of further theoretical and empirical work.

The Creative Person

Factors within the individual will affect the creative process. These factors fall into three categories: ability factors, motivational factors, and affective states. In considering ability factors, three are critical: intelligence, analogical reasoning (metaphoric thinking), and knowledge.

Ability Factors

Intelligence   As briefly touched upon earlier, a great deal of scholarly effort has been expended trying to understand the connection between intelligence and creativity. Is creativity a unique ability, different from intelligence? Is creativity a type of intelligence? Does intelligence inform creativity? These questions have been at the forefront of research in this area.

Early research often presumed that creativity and intelligence were synonymous, or at least highly correlated. The rationale is that if creativity involves the formation of new cognitive connections via the manipulation of knowledge structures, then those with the highest IQs should be most effective at this mentally intensive task. One of the earliest empirical investigations of creativity in a consumer context focused on intelligence. Hirschman (1983) found a moderate correlation (r =.37, p <.01) between intelligence and creativity among a group of consumers. Hirschman's findings are largely consistent with other researchers working in the area at the time. In general, the correlation between intelligence and creativity ranges from weak to moderate, depending on how each construct is assessed (see Sternberg, 1999b, Sternberg & O'Hara, 1999). There also appears to be a threshold effect. Some minimum level of intelligence is necessary for creativity, after which they become largely unrelated (an IQ of around 115 is the cutoff, though it is much higher in some sciences; Schubert, 1972; Sternberg, 1999b). Sternberg even goes on to suggest intelligence could interfere with creativity if high IQ individuals are so praised for their intellect that they fail to work at developing the creative potential within.

A number of more complex theories of the relationship between creativity and intelligence have been proposed. These theories can be classified as those that treat creativity as a subcomponent of intelligence and those that treat intelligence as a subcomponent of creativity (Sternberg, 1999b).

Two prominent theories that view creativity as a subset of intelligence are Guilford's *Structure-of-Intellect Model* (SOI) and Gardner's *Multiple Intelligences Theory* (MIT). According to the SOI model, three basic dimensions of intelligence form a conceptual cube: *operations* such as convergent thinking, memory, and divergent thinking; *content* such as visual images, symbols, and semantic meanings; and *products* such as units, transformations, and implications (Guilford, 1985). By crossing these three facets, 120 specific intelligence factors are possible (which Guilford later expanded to 150; Bachelor & Michael, 1997). Thus, Guilford did not believe in a general intelligence factor, but rather diverse forms based on these dimensions. Among the varied factors, Guilford believed divergent production to be most crucial to creativity. Divergent production involves the broad search for information and the generation of multiple, novel answers to problems. Guilford further believed cognitive orientations such as sensitivity, fluency, flexibility, and originality to be important to creative thinking. Guilford's ideas provided the basis for his own *Unusual Uses Test,* as well as the *Torrence Tests of Creative Thinking*. Recent empirical evidence suggests Guilford's dimensions of intelligence do not factor out as he intended, and the *Unusual Uses Test* often fails to converge with other creativity assessments (Sternberg, 1999b).

Like Guilford's theory, Gardner's *Multiple-Intelligences Theory* suggests people can be intelligent in a variety of ways (Gardner, 1983, Feldman with Gardner, 2003). Specifically, Gardner conceived of eight different types of intelligence (or separate areas of cognitive functioning), including linguistic, logical-mathematical, spatial, kinesthetic, musical, interpersonal, intrapersonal, and naturalist. Today, most intelligence tests are actually multiple tests directed at these various areas (e.g., verbal ability, visual-spatial reasoning, etc.). In studying eminent creative individuals, Gardner found one characteristic they shared was that, even though their creative contributions tended to be in one area (such as music), they usually excelled in more than one type of intelligence. Highly creative individuals are able to productively combine the different types of intelligences synergistically. Interestingly, Gardner noted that while eminent creative individuals tend to excel in more than one type of intelligence, they were often notably deficient in others (e.g., a brilliant mathematician who lacks basic social skills).

In contrast to the views of Guilford and Gardner, Sternberg views intelligence as a subcomponent of creativity. Sternberg's initial ideas were outlined in his *Triarchic Model of Intelligence*, a model he later folded into his *Investment Theory of Creativity*. Sternberg considers intelligence to be one of six sociocognitive elements that converge to produce creative outcomes (the others being, knowledge, thinking styles, personality, motivation and the environment). We discuss the *Triarchic Model* here, and take up *Investment Theory* in a subsequent section.

According to the *Triarchic Model of Intelligence*, three aspects of intelligence are central to creativity: synthetic abilities, analytic abilities, and practical abilities (Sternberg, 1988b, 1999b; Sternberg & Lubart 2003). Synthetic abilities reflect the ability to integrate information and are predicated on two broad components: a metacomponent and a knowledge-acquisition component. A metacomponent is a, "higher-order executive process used in planning, monitoring, and evaluating task performance" (Sternberg, 1999b, p. 84). It helps individuals recognize problems more quickly but also creatively redefine these problems in new ways that make them more soluble. Sternberg devised a way to assess an individual's ability to redefine problems in new ways. Modeled on Nelson Goodman's new riddle of induction, participants are taught a novel concept, such as the notion of grue (green until 2050, blue thereafter) or bleen (blue until 2050, green thereafter), and then made to utilize this concept. Not only did creative thinkers appear more facile in adapting to these concepts but, more important, were more flexible in their ability to switch back and forth between conceptual systems (i.e., grue and bleen versus blue and green). The metacomponential aspect of intelligence also guides the formulation of a strategy for solving a problem once redefined (Sternberg & Lubart, 2003).

The other half of synthesis is the knowledge-acquisition function. Specifically, creative individuals use their intelligence to selectively:

a) *encode* information (i.e., distinguish relevant from irrelevant information). Sternberg offers as a famous example Alexander Fleming's discovery of penicillin. Fleming was doing a laboratory experiment on the growth of bacteria when one of his Petri dishes got infiltrated by mold which killed the subjects. Sternberg notes that when their experiments go awry most scientists, "curse their luck, label the experiment a 'pilot experiment' and keep doing pilot experiments until they get the thing to work, at which point they label it a real experiment." (Sternberg & Lubart, 2003, p. 165)

b) *combine* information (i.e., integrate disparate pieces of information into a unified whole that may not be apparent by its component parts). Sternberg offers Charles Darwin's *Theory of Evolution* as a famous example. The constituent pieces of Darwin's theory were drawn from information readily available to anyone in the scientific community of the time. Darwin's contribution was to combine these pieces into a unified account of how life evolves on Earth. (Sternberg & Lubart, 2003, p. 166)

c) *compare* information (i.e., recognize how information from the past can be brought to bear on a present problem). Selective comparisons usually involve analogical thinking in the sense that the person recognizes how an experience from the past is analogous to the present situation. Sternberg offers Niels Bohr's model of the atom as an example of comparative insight. Bohr recognized that the solar system could provide a visual metaphor for the structure of the atom. (Sternberg, 1999b, pp. 84–5)

The second aspect of intelligence crucial to creativity, according to the *Triarchic Model*, is analytic ability. Analytic ability refers to the ability to critically evaluate information, including the merits and limitations of one's own ideas. Analytic abilities would appear particularly useful during the exploratory stage of the creative process (in determining which paths or ideas are best to pursue) as well as the evaluation stage. The third pillar of Sternberg's *Triarchic Model of Intelligence* is the ability to practically apply one's skills in everyday contexts. Because creative ideas are, by definition, out of the ordinary, a certain level of salesmanship is necessary for creativity. One must be able to show others the value of ones ideas, new ways of thinking, or novel products. This practical aspect of the *Triarchic Model* starts to take it beyond a purely intellect-based account of creativity, and into the socila realm.

Opportunities for Studying Intelligence and Creativity in Consumer Psychology It can be pointed out that intelligence is a neglected area in consumer research in general (Alba, 2000). One question is whether different types or aspects of intelligence differentially relate to varied forms of creative consumption. Gardner's *Multiple Intelligences Theory* seems particularly applicable here. Given that expressive acts of creative consumption are socioculturally based, it might be suggested that higher social intelligence should be related to more expressive acts of creative consumption or more strongly related to the aesthetic dimension of creative consumption. However, staying true to Gardner's thesis would suggest some additional form(s) of intelligence would also be necessary, though it is not immediately clear which form(s) these may be. Conversely, do consumers who exhibit high creative problem solving abilities (presumably due to strong logical-mathematical and spatial abilities) struggle in consumer settings predicated on social interaction? Gardner's *MIT* would seem to suggest that consumers who would be quite creative in one context may not be in another.

Analogical Reasoning/Metaphoric Thinking Perhaps no construct elicits more intrigue and trepidation in creativity research circles than metaphorical thinking and analogical reasoning. If creativity has an all-important mechanism, this is widely believed to be it (Hummel & Holyoak, 2002). Creativity involves making new internal cognitive connections and representations of the external world, and this goes to the heart of metaphor. We previously alluded to the importance of metaphors and analogies to creativity, and a greater appreciation for their potential role can be gained by returning to the insight stage of the creative process. When the mind transcends the conceptual void and connects two disparate ideas in a flash of insight, this connection is nearly always metaphorically described, be it Einstein's "trains" for the theory of relativity, Keukle's "snakes" for the structure of benzene, or Watson and Crick's "staircase" to describe DNA.

If metaphors were merely a vehicle for expressing creative discoveries derived by other cognitive means, this would not be impressive. But metaphors are much more fundamental. They are, quite directly, the way creative insights are formed. They are creativity's glue. Einstein said he could only envision his theory of relativity through metaphors, after which he considered the complex formulas associated with this theory rather pedestrian. Other eminent creative individuals similarly describe their reliance on metaphors in order to derive and comprehend their own creative insights (see Driestadt, 1968; Martindale, 2001).

To illustrate the essential nature of metaphors in creative thought, it is necessary to consider how things would differ if thoughts could only be literal. This requires a brief digression into lower order animals. Carpenter ants burrow their nests into decaying or weakened wood, a response that is rote, automatic, and almost certainly lacking in any semantic understanding of the concept of wood. Carpenter ants are only capable of interacting with wood in one way. At this point, figurative understanding is unnecessary and creativity impossible. Humans, on the other hand, have a more fluid conception of wood. Metaphors and analogies allow humans to see wood as furniture, a weapon, a home, fuel, or most anything else. Our ability to process information figuratively allows us to compare and transform the conception of wood in relation to other things. At this point, a whole host of creativity opportunities opens up and, indeed, humans have used wood in an imponderable variety of ways.

So how does the mind utilize metaphors in the creative process? This is obviously a difficult question to answer, but perhaps the most compelling answer comes from neural-network theory and the notion of semantic schemas (Hummel & Holyoak, 2002, Martindale, 1995). According to neural network theory, concepts are arranged in memory in associative hierarchies. Concepts that share a steep associative gradient have a strong level of connectedness, whereas those more weakly or distally related have a flatter associative gradient. To make a creative connection, the mind must move out along the associative plane, mapping distal concepts to proximate ones such that there is a correspondence between the two ideas. Metaphors are the mechanism of this connection. They bridge the conceptual divide to reveal a connectedness that was before unrecognized. The greater the divide between source and target concept, the more novel and creative the resulting insight (Hummel & Holyoak, 2002).

As previously noted, the act of focusing intensively on a problem (i.e., fixation) appears to inhibit its creative resolution, at least initially. From the perspective of neural-network theory, as attention becomes focused concepts that share a steep associative gradient (i.e., are closely related) become more strongly activated, whereas those that are more weakly connected (more diffusely associated) become blocked, a phenomenon known as lateral inhibition (Martindale, 1995). The brain focuses on those conceptual connections closely linked to the focal problem or issue. As attention wanes, the connection among associative links begins to weaken and diffuse. The associative network becomes characterized by a relatively wider set of partially activated nodes (i.e., the associations connect farther back into long-term memory and transcend a wider array of semantic concepts); this signals entry into the incubation stage of the creative process.

Thus far the discussion has focused on state level aspects of associative networks and the role of metaphor and analogy in producing creative insights (i.e., anyone is capable of making a creative connection). But to understand creativity one must also consider trait aspects of how different individuals form and maintain these networks. Most individuals have a propensity to operate from a relatively limited set of concepts that share steep associative gradients. Thus, they do not tend to exhibit a great deal of creativity (Martindale, 1995). Conversely, some individuals are more inclined to utilize flatter associative networks (i.e. maintain many linkages weakly activated).[2] As such, they are more likely fan out across the conceptual plane and make the metaphorical connections that result in creative insight. This is not to say such individuals lack the ability for intensive focus, but their propensity towards working from broad associative network structures makes them less prone to fixation-related blockages.

Empirical data have been collected on both enduring and situational aspects of neural network theory, metaphorical thinking, and creativity. On the latter issue, anything that increases states of arousal tends to decrease creativity (Martindale, 1990). Arousal is associated with intensity of focus and a constricting of the associative network. Related empirical research finds that creative individuals are able to maintain lower and more diffuse levels of arousal when completing creativity-related tasks than individuals who are less creative (Martindale, 1990). However, Csikszentmihalyi's (1996) *Flow* theory of creativity stands somewhat in contrast to Martindale's findings. *Flow* theory describes how individuals become so immersed in creative endeavors that they actually lose connection with the outside world. The mind becomes fused with the task. So, how to reconcile Martindale's and Csikszentmihalyi's observations? Part of the explanation may lie in an individual's affective state at the time. Individuals who become frustrated with a lack of progress (i.e., negative affective state) are likely to bear down even further and be less creative. By contrast, individuals in a flow condition are experiencing a state of positive psychological rhythm, which may allow them to move their focus about as necessary to leverage distal connection and directed effort. It is also known that highly passive, lethargic states (highly decentralized cortical activation) are not conducive to creativity either.

Other research has examined the guiding role of metaphors and analogies in creative problem solving. Among the better known of these studies is Gick and Holyoak's (1980) investigation of remote analogies and creativity. Gick and Holyoak demonstrated that the provision of certain metaphors can increase the association gradient between otherwise distal concepts leading to more creative solutions to problems. In one study, subjects were told that a patient has an inoperable stomach tumor and direct radiation will destroy too much healthy tissue. They were then asked to come up with creative ways to save the patient. Subjects who first read a story about a general attacking a fort by having his army converge on it from multiple sides were more likely to propose irradiating the tumor with small doses of radiation from multiple angles.[3] Similarly, if subjects first read about the general discovering a hidden supply route into the fort and sending his army through it, they were more likely to propose inserting a tube down the esophagus and sending radiation through the tube.

Though Gick and Holyoak's (1980) findings came in a laboratory setting, the environment is replete with stimuli that could incidentally cue creative solutions to consumption problems. For example, in another consumer interview conducted by the first author, an informant recounted the time he had a problem flying his kite on a windy day because the kite string kept becoming entangled. His solution was to attach a fishing swivel between the string and the kite (a fishing swivel is a piece of hardware that allows a hooked fish to turn and thrash without twisting the fishing line). The fact that this bit of insight came to him in a park on the shores of Lake Michigan with fishermen milling about appears beyond chance.

In addition to manipulating metaphors in different situations, metaphorical thinking has also been approached as an individual differences variable in creativity research. Burroughs and Mick (2004) developed the *Metaphoric Thinking Ability-Sentence Completion* task (MTA-SC), to test an individuals' propensity and ability to think metaphorically. Individuals are given sentence stems of abstract concepts (e.g., "Helping someone is…") and asked to complete the sentence in such as way as to "capture the essence of each concept as succinctly as possible." Individuals who completed the test using more immediate, literal associations (e.g., "Helping someone gives you a good feeling.") demonstrated less creativity on a subsequent problem-solving task than individuals who completed the sentences using more remote, metaphorical associations (e.g., "Helping someone is to make a deposit in the bank of Karma."). The problem-solving task confronted subjects with a pair of scuffed shoes just prior to a social engagement, in which they discover they are also out of shoe polish. High MTA individuals appeared to recognize color, consistency, and parallel use analogies with other substances that could serve as a substitute for polish and came up with more creative solutions as a result. For example, one high MTA individual combined eye mascara with petroleum jelly to produce an impromptu polish that would restore both color and luster to the shoes.

Knowledge   A third major factor that affects an individual's ability to be creative is knowledge. On one level, knowledge is an axiom in the creative process. If creativity involves the formation of new conceptual linkages, then a corpus of knowledge concepts is, by definition, required. However, the exact role and nature of knowledge in the creative process has been a topic of debate, with some scholars arguing greater knowledge universally benefits creativity and others advocating that knowledge plays a much more limited role or can even be detrimental. These varied perspectives are reflected in the foundational and the tension views of creativity, respectively (Weisberg, 1999).

The tension view holds that because creativity must fundamentally represent an outcome that goes beyond existing knowledge, a tension exists between what is known and what we can discover. At some point, creativity necessarily involves breaking free of past ways of thinking and viewing the world, and in this respect existing knowledge represents an impediment to creativity.

An extreme derivative of the tension view is what has come to be known as evolutionary epistemology (Dasgupta, 2004). Initially proposed by Campbell (1960), and later expanded by Simonton (1999), this perspective advances that creative outcomes are quasi-random products of a nearly blind process, with little, if any, connection to the past (i.e., existing knowledge) (Hausman, 1984). In other words, a process of essentially free and random associations will occasionally produce extraordinary results. In making his initial case for the evolutionary view of creativity, Campbell (1960) pointed out that a monkey randomly pecking keys will eventually type *Hamlet*. The fact that the insight stage of creativity is often removed from conscious deliberation does support an element of randomness to the process.

Though the evolutionary epistemology of knowledge creation has attracted some powerful adherents, including philosophy of science giant Karl Popper, it has also had its share of critics. Two specific rebuttals are worth mentioning. In a 1986 project, Richard Dawkins took up Campbell's challenge that even a monkey could eventually write *Hamlet*. He wrote a computer program to randomly generate letters targeted to a single line of the play, "Methinks it is like a weasel." He found the chances of a monkey randomly producing just this one statement to be 1/28.[27] At this rate the monkey would, quite literally, evolve into a human faster than it would randomly reproduce the entire play by Shakespeare. By contrast, if each random trial that came successively closer to the end target were retained moving forward (a condition that would clearly implicate a knowledge component in the creative process), the line from *Hamlet* will be reproduced in only 10 to 50 generations.

The other critique of evolutionary epistemology is supplied by Dasgupta (2004) in his historical analysis of Picasso and his painting of *Guernica*. Picasso's chaotic style of painting makes him a popular subject when it comes to the argument that creativity is a stochastic process (Picasso himself recounted how his vision for a painting almost seemed to come in a fit). And yet Dasgupta's careful reconstruction of the chronology of the painting of *Guernica* would suggest it was anything but random. A series of precursory sketches (linked to his own works as well as those of other artists) betray a highly deliberative process that unfolded over a period of weeks if not longer. Creative insights may appear to come in an instant, but are nurtured over a protracted period and it is difficult to deny the role of prior knowledge and experience.

For this reason, most adherents of the tension view adopt a more tempered perspective on the role of knowledge in the creative process. These individuals subscribe to what is known as the inverted-U hypothesis of knowledge and creativity. This hypothesis maintains that some basic level of knowledge and understanding is necessary for creativity, but beyond this point knowledge starts to work against the creative process by encouraging entrenched ways of thinking. Deep knowledge of an area lends a certain comfort and dependency on particular models and modes of thinking that the individual may be reluctant to abandon (Frensch & Sternberg, 1989). The inverted-U helps explain why relative novices occasionally produce extraordinary creative breakthroughs in a given area. These novices are not wedded to traditional viewpoints and dominant paradigms of thought. Empirical support for the inverted-U hypothesis was supplied by Simonton (1984). He studied more than 300 individuals of eminent creative importance from the 15th to 19th centuries (e.g., Mozart, Galileo, Rembrandt) and found the highest levels of creative eminence to be associated with only moderate levels of formal education.

Yet even a tempered version of the tension view has its opponents. Weisburg (1999), for example, is quick to point out that while relative novices may occasionally produce eminent creative works, it is their very rarity that makes them so noteworthy. In studying eminent creative contributions across a wide variety of disciplines, including literature, the visual arts, science, and music, Weisburg consistently finds that the vast bulk of eminent creative contributions come from individuals with substantial time in task. Because creative contributions build upon prior creative work, Weisburg argues, an individual needs time to develop sufficient foundation in an area before a creative contribution can be made.

In further building his case for the foundational perspective, Weisburg (1999) comments on Simonton's (1984) historical eminence study. Weisburg aptly points out that formal education is not equivalent to knowledge, and that educational standards varied widely across the period Simonton studied. Moreover, during this time many individuals were self taught. For example, Thomas Jefferson, one of Simonton's subjects, was a statesman, philosopher, architect, horticulturist, naturalist, author, and inventor. Yet he had little or no formal training in any of these areas. This is an important distinction because most creative individuals exhibit not only depth of knowledge in a given area, but breadth of knowledge across many areas—an obvious asset when attempting to draw together concepts from disparate conceptual planes. Not surprisingly, it is adherents to the foundational view of knowledge and creativity that add a preparatory stage to the creative process.

An emerging view takes a hybrid approach to the knowledge-creativity question. Gruber's *Evolving Systems Approach* (ESA) is one account that draws elements from both the evolutionary and foundational perspectives (see Gruber and Wallace 2001). ESA grew out of Gruber's prolonged interest in the creative works of Charles Darwin and Jean Piaget. ESA notes that, at a minimum the environment in which the individual finds themselves in is, to some degree, random (the fact individuals cannot produce creative works at will further supports that the process is not entirely deterministic). And yet, Gruber's studies strongly indicate that it is remiss to simply treat creative breakthroughs as random occurrences. Creative individuals go through an evolution in their thinking about an issue in which their knowledge (and the system of metaphors used to develop this knowledge) is expanded and revised. Gruber and Wallace (2001, p. 346) even suggest the moment of insight in creativity may be overstated:

> The common idée fixe is that a single, sudden transformative illumination is the essence of creativity. But Gruber's immersion in Darwin's notebooks demonstrates that Darwin had many insights, perhaps hundreds. Having the experience of insight does not inevitably represent a break with the past, but rather may reflect the fluctuating but steady state of a cognitive system at work. Needless to say, some insights are wrong, others reflect ideas previously encountered and then forgotten, and some very occasionally reveal the romantic revelations that are the grist for the mill of storybook psychology. Thus, Darwin's celebrated insight on Malthus had many forerunners and foreshadowings.[4]

In sum, it appears knowledge is necessary for, but no guarantee of, creative insight.

Opportunities for Studying Knowledge and Creativity in Consumer Psychology A number of studies in consumer behavior have incorporated knowledge considerations into research on creativity, and additional opportunities exist. For example, Burroughs and Mick (2004) found formal education to be negatively related to creativity on an everyday problem solving task. On the one hand, this finding would seem to support the tension view of creativity (i.e., that knowledge can be detrimental). On the other hand, it is possible a lack of formal education forced these individuals to learn to be resourceful. In other words, their lack of schooled knowledge was more than offset by the knowledge they accumulated through life experiences. Clearly, further research is needed before any definitive assertions can be made.

As another possible avenue of further investigation in this area, Alba and Hutchinson (1987) proposed that product category structure is more veridical, complex, and less stereotyped in consumers who possess high levels of knowledge about a product category than novices. Alba and Hutchinson also suggested that greater knowledge allows more abstract levels of comprehension in products, facilitating comparison of dissimilar product types. To the extent these two assertions are true, they would support that use innovativeness—the creative application of products to uses for which they were not initially intended—should benefit from higher levels of product knowledge (i.e., a position consistent with the foundational view).

Alba and Hutchinson (1987) go on to suggest that individuals with high levels of product knowledge engage in selective encoding of new information. To the extent selective encoding helps the consumer move more quickly to a state of convergent thinking (i.e., the selective focus on those cognitive connections most relevant solving a problem), this would also be consistent with the foundational view and benefit creativity.[5] In other words, consumers who are experts may be more creative not only because they have more information available to them, but because they are better able to determine which information is most useful.

On the other hand, if high levels of product knowledge lead consumers to engage in selective encoding of new information, this could potentially work against creativity by limiting the amount of additional information available for novel conceptual combination (a position more consistent with the tension view). In any case, more work is needed in identifying the conditions under which knowledge enhances consumer creativity and those in which it inhibits it.

Motivational Factors

While ability factors provide the mechanism of creativity, they alone are not sufficient to guarantee a creative outcome. The personality of the individual is also important, particularly as it relates to their motivation. Two motivational constructs relevant to creativity are risk taking and intrinsic motivation.

Risk Taking   Risk taking and the closely related issues of novelty seeking and tolerance for ambiguity are integral to creativity. To be creative, individuals must be willing to step outside their comfort zone and to undertake initiatives where the outcome is uncertain and potentially erroneous. Also, because the creative process usually involves a period of conceptual abyss, an individual must be able to endure ambiguity in order to see the process through. In fact, not only must the individual be able to tolerate risk and ambiguity, they must exhibit a certain affinity for it. Creative individuals break their own path (Sternberg & Lubart, 1995) and research by Bagozzi and Foxall (1996) confirms this to be as true of consumer behavior as any area. Specifically, Bagozzi and Foxall found consumer innovators like to go their own way, exhibit a disdain for rule governance, and flout convention. They also found consumer innovators were willing to propose many solutions to a problem, even if impracticable. Given the relatively dispersed associative networks associated with creative thinking, a certain level of inefficiency and ambiguity is an inherent part of the creative process.

Among the more systematic theories to address the risk taking aspect of creativity is Sternberg and Lubart's (1996) *Investment Theory of Creativity*. Sternberg and Lubart employ a finance metaphor to highlight the characteristics of successful creative individuals:

1. Successful financial investors have to be willing to take risks, and ready to act contrary to the behavior of other investors. Creative individuals must take risks, even at the prospect of going against the crowd.
2. A key to successful investing is to buy low and sell high. Creative individuals must vest themselves in ideas that are currently out of favor but that have great potential for influence at a later point.
3. Successful investors must adopt a long-term horizon and be willing to weather periods of tumult and uncertainty in the marketplace. Creative individuals must persevere through periods of ambiguity and uncertainty in order to see their undertaking through to its ultimate success.

However, Sternberg and Lubart add that creative individuals also differ from financial investors in some key respects. Namely, creative individuals must not only buy into ideas that are out of favor, but shoulder the added burden of having to "sell" the worth of these ideas to others. For this reason, verbal ability is also an important component of *Investment Theory*.

Intrinsic Motivation   Early perspectives on creativity adapted a psychodynamic perspective which held that creativity resulted from the inherent tension between unconscious desires and conscious constraints, a somewhat dark view of motivation. However, the tenability of this position is challenged by the undeniable observation that humans often pursue and persevere in creative endeavors out of sheer enjoyment (Nakamura & Csikszentmihalyi, 2003). This aspect of creativity is captured in the concept of intrinsic motivation.

The role of intrinsic motivation in creativity can be traced back to studies of children and the seminal work of White (1959). Play is critical to early childhood development and studies unequivocally point to the value of play in the creative process (see, e.g., Howard-Jones, Taylor, & Sutton, 2002; Russ, 2003; Trevlas, Matsouka, & Zachopoulou, 2003). Because it is essential to development, children are capable of engaging in sustained periods of creative play, a capacity that carries into adulthood.

Probably no scholar has studied the relationship between intrinsic motivation and creativity more extensively than Teresa Amabile. Like most contemporary creativity researchers, Amabile takes a confluence view of creativity, but her central focus has always been intrinsic motivation (Amabile, 1996). Over the span of 25 years, Amabile has conducted empirical research on the role of intrinsic motivation in creativity across education, the arts, and the workplace (see Collins & Amabile, 1999, for a summary of this program of research). The general finding from this research is that intrinsic motivation is an essential and positive contributor to creative performance.

However, the nature and role of intrinsic motivation in the creative process has been pulled into a broader debate on the interaction between intrinsic motivation and extrinsic influences on performance (see Hennessey, 2000, for a review). A fairly robust finding in the creativity literature is that extrinsic factors (including rewards) can undermine creativity by reducing intrinsic motivation. External rewards divert attention away from inherent interest in the task and toward the unrelated reward (Deci & Ryan, 1985). Hennessey (2000) expands this position and offers that the interaction of intrinsic and extrinsic factors can be explained by the well-known discount principle in psychology. When humans perform a task that could be driven by both internal and external motives, individuals tend to discount internal motives in favor of external ones. For example, if a child is at home coloring and asked why she is coloring, she will usually respond that it is because she likes to color. However, if this same question is posed to a child while at school, she will often respond that she is coloring because she will get a good participant sticker. Since enjoyment must ultimately come from within, the result is de-motivation and diminished creativity.

However, there appear to be boundary conditions on the negative role of extrinsic factors on creative outcomes. A number of studies have found that under certain conditions extrinsic rewards can even be beneficial (Collins & Amabile, 1999; Shalley & Perrry-Smith, 2001). Noteworthy among these were the "immunization" studies conducted by Hennessey and colleagues (e.g., Hennessey, Amabile, & Martinage, 1989; Hennessey & Zbikowski, 1993). They wondered if it might be possible to immunize individuals against the adverse effects of extrinsic influences on intrinsic motivation. What they found was that when subjects were specifically trained to focus on the aspects of a task they found intrinsically interesting, the provision of an extrinsic reward had no adverse effect on creative performance. In fact, the provision of the reward had an additive effect by reinforcing the positive reasons the individual engaged in the task to begin with. By contrast, when the presence of an extrinsic factor is interpreted as a competing reason for undertaking an activity, it undermines intrinsic interest in the manner described earlier. Thus, it appears an individual's interpretations as to the reasons they are engaged in a task plays an important role in how extrinsic factors influence creative performance.

Opportunities for Studying Motivation and Creativity in Consumer Psychology   Given that both extrinsic factors and intrinsic interest are present in many consumer settings, this may provide a good venue for researching the influence of motivation on creativity. One distinction that has been made in past consumer research is between mundane problem solving and more expressive or artistic forms of consumer creativity. From our observations, individuals solve many routine consumption problems simply to get on with the business of life. In these externally driven situations, we would expect intrinsic motivation to be relatively unimportant. With almost no intrinsic motivation to be undermined, extrinsic motivators should directly and positively impact creative problem solving. By contrast, in endeavors where the individual seeks out opportunities to engage in creative acts of consumption (e.g., fashion), intrinsic motivation will be high and extrinsic factors would seem likely to impinge on task enjoyment and creativity in a manner similar to other areas of creativity. Of course, individuals' interpretations as to the reasons for the presence of an extrinsic factor would represent an important moderator.

Another interesting research avenue would be to investigate if intrinsic and extrinsic factors differentially affect the various dimensions of creativity. Perhaps extrinsic factors encourage novel thinking, but not necessarily any more effective thinking, while intrinsic motivation helps sustain the individual through to achieving the most effective solution.

A final research possibility would be to introduce other personality variables into the intrinsic/extrinsic equation. Creativity researchers have called for the inclusion of additional personality variables in the study of intrinsic motivation, but this call has gone largely unheeded.[6] Perhaps individuals high in self-monitoring exhibit more positive creative responses to extrinsic reinforcements than individuals low in self-monitoring because high self-monitors are attracted to this type of stimulus. Again, the nature of consumption (transcending both mundane and enduring social activities) would provide an interesting context to investigate an issue such as this.

Affect

A fairly robust finding in the creativity literature is that positive moods foster creative thinking. Studies have found that individuals in a good mood perform better on a number of creativity tests including Dunker's candle problem and Mednick's remote associates test (Isen, 1999). Why do positive moods lead to more creative thinking? The answer, it is believed, is because positive associations are more fluid, diverse, extensive, and interconnected than neutral or negative associations (Isen, 1999). Additionally, positive moods appear to predispose individuals toward over-inclusion and loose conceptual boundaries (Bowden, 1994). In short, they expand the associative network.

Interestingly, Lubart and Getz (1997) propose that positive moods and affect may also enhance creativity vis-à-vis metaphorical thought processing. They note that certain emotions are idiosyncratic and tied to specific past experiences (e.g., emotions tied to a wedding or vacation). Metaphors connect these emotional "endocepts" to episodic memory as well as other endocepts in the cognitive system. The process begins when some element in the environment is analogous to a prior experience, metaphorically transporting the individual back to an earlier time and place. In other words, because emotions can only be understood metaphorically, metaphors are generated to tie these events together. This spreading emotional activation causes two temporally distal experiences to appear related, setting up fertile conditions for creativity. Thus, metaphors not only link distal semantic concepts, but also emotional ones. In partial support of their theory, Lubart and Getz had students describe the emotions associated with an elevator. One student found elevators to be "cold," which elicited thoughts of caged animals in a zoo. This metaphorical connection prompted the suggestion that elevators be equipped with softer furnishings and displays to make them appear less cage-like.[7]

There may also be a physiological basis for affect's association with creativity. Ashby, Isen, and Turken (1997) note that positive mood states involve the release of the neurotransmitter dopamine, a chemical that has been correlated with cognitive flexibility in humans. This may not only have cognitive benefits for creativity, but behavioral ones as well. Kahn and Isen (1993) found individuals who are in a good mood are more likely to engage in variety seeking behavior. Thus, not only might a good mood benefit immediate problem solving though increased cognitive flexibility, it might also help build an individual's repertoire of experiences for future creative problem solving.

Some recent research qualifies the mood-creativity relation. Weisberg (1994) suggests that positive mood states may result in increased creative productivity, but not necessarily increased creative quality. Additionally, Kaufman and Vosburg (2002) found that while positive moods facilitated early-stage idea production, neutral and negative moods were actually more strongly associated with late-stage creative production (when time constraints begin to set in). During late-stage creative production, individuals in a negative mood exhibited the relatively flat association gradients characteristic of creativity, whereas individuals in positive moods exhibited steeper, non-creative response gradients. This led Kaufman to later suggest that the influence of mood may depend on what stage of the creative process one is in (Kaufman, 2003). Finally, research by George and Zhou (2002) suggests that extrinsic motivators may moderate the mood—creativity relation. They found that a negative mood actually enhanced creativity when perceived recognition and extrinsic rewards were high.

The Creative Environment

The role of the environment has received only limited consideration in creativity research, with discussions often directed at the macro-social level (e.g., the characteristics of society that produce an atmosphere of creativity such as tolerance for others, safeguards for freedom of expression, and so forth; see, e.g., Csikszentmihalyi, 1999). When more proximate aspects of the environment have been the focus of research, the following general conclusions have emerged. The environment plays a critically important role in determining creative acts, particularly in the case of more mundane consumer problem solving. Elements of the environment can compel creativity by constraining resources normally available for routine problem solving such as a lack of time (Burroughs & Mick, 2004) or materials (Moreau & Dahl, 2005). Though there is a tendency among consumer researchers to presume that the resources and products necessary for consumption are available, many (perhaps even most) instances of consumer behavior are constrained. Stores close, products are out of stock, and money is tight. The consumer must navigate a difficult consumption environment and creativity helps make this possible.

As the focus moves from mundane and immediate problem solving to more social and expressive forms of creative consumption, it appears that the role of the environment diminishes and individual characteristics, particularly intrinsic motivation, become increasingly important drivers of creative behavior. The environment is still important, but instead of reacting to the environment, consumers now seek out situations and places in which to exhibit creativity.

The Creative Experience

An earlier section considered how affect influences creative outcomes. However, it is just as important to consider how acting creativity influences emotional and psychological outcomes. Creativity is incredibly important to self-construction and positive affect. Yet, the consumer psychology literature has almost nothing to say about how creatively interacting with products enhances the consumption experience, including an individual's overall level of satisfaction (for an exception see Burroughs and Mick (2004) who found that acting creatively elevated positive affect and satisfaction with the consumption experience). The satisfaction and sense of efficacy individuals derive from acting creatively is likely to be a powerful driver of future consumption behaviors.

We also know individuals enter into creative "flow" states in conjunction with some consumption activities (particularly those that are experiential or playful in nature; Mathwick and Rigdon, 2004), but we have little understanding of what produces these flow states or how the consumption process may be altered as a result (Kowal & Fortier, 1999). Given that consumers undertake many consumption activities of their own volition, researchers need to do more to understand when and how creativity may impel consumers to seek out certain consumption opportunities or engage the consumption process in particular ways.

FURTHER DISCUSSION

Opportunities to research creativity in consumer psychology extend beyond the topics covered here and entire areas of consumer research can be opened up to the issue of creativity. As but a few brief examples, consider the topics of shopping, gift giving, and rhetoric. At a recent conference, Guiry and Lutz (2001) presented research to suggest that consumers can be highly creative in their approach to shopping, utilizing their creative skills to find the best deals, most efficiently cover the retail space, and maximize their enjoyment of the shopping experience. They suggest some consumers may even define themselves, in part, based on their creative shopping prowess.

In another conference presentation, Otnes, Kacen, and Lowrey (2001) focused on the role of creativity in Christmas gift giving. In addition to external constraints such as budgets, Otnes et al. suggest that creativity in gift giving may be motivated by internal constraints, such as a felt need to do something special for the recipient besides just giving a store-bought item. It is not a great stretch to suggest that gifts that include a creative touch produce more powerful interpersonal connections than those that are simply purchased. Once again, however, context and interpretation are likely to come into play. If the gift recipient interprets the creativity on the part of the giver as a way to avoid spending money instead of as a genuine personal gesture, the relationship may actually be weakened. We have little understanding of creativity's impact on the interpersonal dynamics of gift exchange.

Finally, a series of studies by McQuarrie and Mick (e.g., 1999, 2003) on advertising rhetoric documented the powerful role of figurative language in ad processing. Specifically, they found that advertisements that use figurative language (e.g., rhyme, antithesis, metaphor, puns) are more likely to elicit attention, produce greater message elaboration, be more memorable, and result in more favorable reactions, than ads that are primarily literal. It is quite possible that creativity represents an important link that helps explain this phenomenon. Gruber and Wallace (2001) outlined how figurative language plays an important role in the creative process (see, e.g., Gruber & Wallace, 2001), and this includes not only metaphor, but other tropes as well, including irony and hyperbole. Rhetorical figures force a message recipient to create a conceptual connection as opposed to having the connection literally provided to him or her. It is this creative connection that makes two otherwise disparate concepts ironic, humorous, or entertaining. In this sense, rhetorical figures force the recipient to be a co-producer of message meaning. It is not surprising then to find that the individual elaborates more or finds the message to be more interesting and memorable. Considerations of creativity may offer an interesting opportunity to extend McQuarrie and Mick's work.

New Product Development

We previously alluded to the fact that consumer creativity may have marketing benefits, particularly in the area of new product development. This is an area of such potential import that it merits its own consideration. No issue in new product development (NPD) is more critical than consumer acceptance. Most new product failures are ultimately a failure to adequately understand and meet the needs of some customer base. It is therefore somewhat perplexing that consumer creativity has received limited attention as a possible source of new product ideas (for exceptions see Dahl & Moreau, 2002; Prahalad & Ramaswamy, 2000; von Hippel, Thomke, & Sonnack, 1999).

However, rather than speculate on why consumer creativity is not sourced more heavily in the new product development process and make normative suggestions for increasing consumer involvement in NPD, we take a slightly different tact. We consider some of the major challenges facing the new product development process and relate these to issues discussed earlier in conjunction with consumer creativity. Hopefully, this discussion will provide new vantage points on the role and application of consumer creativity to the new product development process.

Lead Users   VonHippel (1986) discusses the importance of lead users in the product development process. Lead users are consumers who face a need ahead of the mainstream market, and in so doing, they often create their own solutions. These instances of creative consumption regularly occur well before there is any commercial product available to address the given need (e.g., the secretary, tired of retyping entire pages, would ultimately be the one to come up with idea for liquid paper). For this reason, lead users are often an invaluable source of new product ideas and improvements. But beyond their first-hand knowledge, are there other reasons lead users are so valuable to NPD?

Their value may also stem from the exploration and incubation stages of the creative process. Recall that individuals must often struggle with multiple potential approaches to a problem or issue, and that a period of apparent idle time often precedes creative insight. The very nature of lead users puts them in a position to benefit the most from the way the creative process unfolds. When lead users encounter a problem with a particular product, they are likely to struggle with it repeatedly over multiple instances and settings. As with any creative breakthrough, the moment of insight is likely to reflect a prolonged period of exposure to the product and its problems. Conversely, individuals who have only occasional contact with a product (including, perhaps, product developers) are going to be less cognizant of a product's deficiencies and frustrations, and the ways the product could be improved.

Another interesting issue related to lead users revolves around the question of intrinsic motivation. We have previously reviewed the benefits of intrinsic motivation to the creative process, but it is interesting to consider this issue in the context of lead users. Lead users' contact with a given product often occurs through their jobs. Individuals hold jobs for any number of reasons, with some people deriving great personal satisfaction from their work and others seeing a job as little more than a paycheck. This range of work orientations is likely to have a pronounced effect on the creativity of lead users. Individuals who interact with products because they must in order to do their job are likely to be less creative then individuals whose interaction with products is derived from an inherent interest in their work. While a great deal of research effort has been expended in marketing and management to understand the impact work orientations on job performance, these findings have not been extended to the issue of creativity, lead users, or new product development.

Affect   New product development (and the workplace more generally) may provide an interesting context to examine the role of affect on creativity. We previously discussed the benefits of positive affect for the creative process. In support of this premise, Amabile and Conti (1999) describe how positive workplace environments foster creativity, whereas workplace creativity declines during periods of downsizing. But many creative innovations are as driven by tension and apprehension as by interest and enjoyment (sometimes at the same time). This raises the interesting question as to when stress (a negative affective state) is actually conducive to creativity. Amabile et al. (1996) suggested that an individual's interpretation of pressures may impact their creative responses. When stressors are interpreted as challenges they tend to enhance creativity while those that are interpreted as excess burdens tend to impede it (Amaible et al., found support for the former condition but not the latter one). Aside from this research, the issue of how negative affective states impact workplace creativity, particularly in the creation of new products, remains largely unexamined.

Metaphor   The potential of incorporating metaphor into new product design is not something most researchers consider. Most new product design processes begin by asking how a product functions rather than why consumers use them. Yet, what a product symbolizes is often more important than what it actually does, and there are opportunities to incorporate metaphorical considerations into design concepts (see Mick, Burroughs, Hetzel, & Brannen, 2004). Producers of successful new products not only incorporate performance considerations into their designs, they also consider what the product will symbolize to others. All aspects of a product (lines, shapes, colors, textures, materials) create the metaphorical basis of a product's meaning and, by extension, a metaphor of its user. Products tell a story of how its owner is unique, or how he or she fits in. For this reason, the moment a product enters the marketplace its form is not static. Consumers change it, add to it, and combine it with other products to create new personal and social meanings. This transformative process has been documented in the areas of antiquities (Holt, 1997), gay subculture (Kates, 2002), and consumer rebellion (Hebdidge, 1977). Though marketers may be primarily responsible for the initial meanings in a product, consumers appropriate these meanings, change them, and force marketers to respond with new product offerings and meanings. This entire interaction is metaphorical in nature. By adopting a model of the product as metaphor, designers put themselves in a unique position to design products in truly innovative ways.

Closing

Consumer creativity is a complex process that reflects a confluence of factors. At its most elemental level, creativity combines remote concepts in new and appropriate ways. The creative process encompasses a series of stages where metaphorical thinking fuses semantic concepts during a period of incubation (diffused neural network activation) that results in novel insights in the marketplace. Individuals higher in certain types of intelligence are able to activate more concepts in the neural network, and those with higher levels of knowledge have a wider repertoire of concepts and domains to draw from in formulating creative responses. Moreover, the creative process will be moderated by other aspects of the individual consumer including the propensity for risk, the level of intrinsic motivation, and affective states. Overlaid on all this, the environment will compel and facilitate (or discourage and preclude) specific types of creative responses.

The topic of creativity is essential yet neglected in consumer psychology. We have tried to provide an integrative review of creativity's most central elements, and identify opportunities to extend this research into the realm of consumer behavior. We feel we have only scratched the surface and that creativity remains a truly open frontier. Perhaps 10 years hence this volume will be updated. It will be interesting at that point to see whether creativity has become an essential part of mainstream consumer psychology, or remains an area of unrealized promise.

NOTES

1. While useful to separate the study of creativity into different eras, the evolution of creativity research is hardly linear. Psychodynamic studies of creativity that characterized the early 20th century continued well beyond their halcyon days, even becoming popular again in the 1970s (and case study method originally associated with the psychodynamic perspective is still an important methodology in creativity research). The same can be said of other eras. For example, studies of intelligence and creativity

popular during the psychometric period of the 1950s and 1960s were actually undertaken as early as the 1920s, and psychometric approaches also remain an important subcomponent of creativity research to this day.

2. Interestingly, individuals afflicted with psychoses (e.g., schizophrenia and related disorders) as well as borderline psychotics exhibit a flattening and widening of the associative gradient. Their thinking becomes over-inclusive and they have difficulty deciphering rational boundaries. Psychotic individuals also appear to produce a disproportionate number of extraordinary creative insights. For a more academic treatment of psychosis and creativity see Eysenck (1997).

3. The inoperable tumor described above is a variant of Dunker's (1945) radiation problem and is widely used in research on creativity and metaphor.

4. Weisberg and Alba (1981) similarly suggest that the moment of "insight" may be overemphasized in creativity research. In their work on creative problem solving, they find that, as often as not, people simply, "apply their knowledge to new problems, and if their knowledge is not directly useful, they try to produce something new that will solve the problem through a straightforward extension of what they know" (p. 189). In other words, through an arduous process the person either works out a creative solution to their problem or fails in the attempt. However, from a phenomenological perspective at least, the moment of insight remains a powerful component of the creative experience and one that is not easily dismissed.

5. Though not as frequently discussed as its divergent counterpart, convergent thinking is just as important to the creative process. Individuals must be able to identify and eliminate superfluous information if they are to be creatively productive (Runco, 2003).

6. Cheek and Stahl (1986) did find introverts to be particularly susceptible to the negative effects of external evaluation on creative performance.

7. Within the marketing and consumer behavior literature the *Zaltman Metaphor Elicitation Technique* (ZMET) appears to tap into very similar cognitive structures as those uncovered by Lubart and Getz. The ZMET technique is predicated on the understanding that consumers' desires often reside below the surface of consciousness and cannot always be verbally expressed. Researchers can, however, tap into these hidden emotional states through metaphors (Zaltman, 2003).

REFERENCES

Alba, J. W. (2000). Dimensions of consumer expertise…or lack thereof. In S. J. Hoch & R. J. Meyer (Eds.), *Advances in consumer research* (Vol. 27, pp. 109). Provo, UT: Association for Consumer Research.

Alba, J. W., & Hutchinson, J. W. (1987). Dimensions of consumer expertise. *Journal of Consumer Research, 13*(March), 411–454.

Albert, R. S., & Runco. M. A. (1999). A history of research on creativity. In R. J. Sternberg (Ed.), *Handbook of creativity* (pp. 16–34). Cambridge: Cambridge University Press.

Amabile, T. M. (1982). Social psychology of creativity: A consensual assessment technique. *Journal of Personality and Social Psychology, 43*(5), 997–1013.

Amabile, T. M. (1983). *The social psychology of creativity.* New York: Springer-Verlag.

Amabile, T. M. (1996). *Creativity in context.* New York: Westview Press.

Amabile, T. M., Conti, R., Coon, H., Lazenby, J., & Herron, M. (1996). Assessing the work environment for creativity. *Academy of Management Journal, 39*(October), 1154–1184.

Amabile, T. M., & Conti, R. (1999). Changes in the work environment for creativity during downsizing. *Academy of Management Journal, 42*(December), 630–640.

Ashby, F. G., Isen, A. M., & Turken, A. U. (1997). A neuropsychological theory of positive affect and its influence on cognition. *Psychological Review, 106*(3), 529–550.

Bachelor, P. A., & Michael, W. B. (1997). The structure-of-intellect model revisited. In M. A. Runco (Ed.), *The creativity research handbook* (pp. 155–182). Cresskill, NJ: Hampton Press.

Bagozzi, R. P., & Foxall, G. R. (1996). Construct validation of a measure of adaptive-innovative cognitive styles in consumption. *International Journal of Research in Marketing, 13*, 201–213.

Barron, F. (1988). Putting creativity to work. In R. J. Sternberg (Ed.), *The nature of creativity: Contemporary psychological perspectives* (pp. 76–98). Cambridge: Cambridge University Press.

Boden, M. A. (Ed.). (1996). *Dimensions of creativity.* Cambridge, MA: MIT Press.

Bowden, C. L. (1994). Bipolar disorder and creativity. In M. P. Shaw & M. A. Runco (Eds.), *Creativity and affect* (pp. 73–86). Norwood, NJ: Ablex.

Burroughs, J. E. (1998). Creative consumption in an everyday problem solving context: Theory, practice, and evidence. Unpublished doctoral dissertation, University of Wisconsin, Madison.

Burroughs, J. E., & Mick, D. G. (2004). Exploring antecedents and consequences of consumer creativity in a problem-solving context. *Journal of Consumer Research, 31*(3), 402–411.

Burroughs, J. E. & Moreau, P. (2004). Advances in the study of creative cognition in consumer behavior. In B. E. Kahn & M. F. Luce (Eds.), *Advances in consumer research* (Vol. 31, pp. 403–404). Valdosta, GA: Association for Consumer Research.

Burroughs, J. E., & Otnes, C. (2001). New explorations in consumer creativity. In R. Krishnan & M. Viswanathan (Eds.), *AMA winter educators' conference: Marketing theory and applications* (Vol. 12, pp. 54–55). Chicago: American Marketing Association.

Campbell, D. T. (1960). Blind variation and selective retention in creative thought as in other knowledge processes. *Psychological Review, 67*, 380–400.

Cheek, J. M., & Stahl, S. (1986). Shyness and verbal creativity. *Journal of Research in Personality, 20*, 51–61.

Collins, M. A.. & Amabile, T. (1999). Motivation and creativity. In R. J. Sternberg (Ed.), *Handbook of creativity* (pp. 297–312).New York: Cambridge University Press.

Csikszentmihalyi, M. (1996). *Creativity: Flow and the psychology of discovery and invention.* New York: Harper Collins.

Csikszentmihalyi, M. (1999). Implications of a systems perspective for the study of creativity. In R. J. Sternberg (Ed.), *Handbook of creativity* (313–338). Cambridge, UK: Cambridge University Press.

Dahl, D. W., & Moreau, P. (2002). The influence and value of analogical thinking during new product ideation. *Journal of Marketing Research, 39*(February), 47–60.

Dartnall, T. (Ed.). (2002). *Creativity, cognition, and knowledge: An interaction*, Westport, CT: Praeger.

Dasgupta, S. (2004). Is creativity a Darwinian process? *Creativity Research Journal, 16*(4), 403–413.

Dawkins, R. (1986). *The blind watchmaker.* New York: Norton.

Deci, E. L., & Ryan, R. W. (1985). *Intrinsic motivation and self-determination in human behavior.* New York: Plenum.

Driestadt, R. (1968). An analysis of the use of analogies and metaphors in science. *The Journal of Psychology, 68*, 97–116.

Duncker, K. (1945). On problem solving. *Psychological Monographs, 58*, no. 270.

Eysenck, H. J. (1997). Creativity and personality. In M. A. Runco (Ed.), *The creativity research handbook* (pp. 42–66). Creskill, NJ: Hampton Press,.

Feldman, D. H. with Gardner, H. (2003). The creation of multiple intelligences theory: A study in high-level thinking. In R. K. Sawyer (Ed.), *Creativity and development* (pp. 139–185). New York: Oxford University Press.

Frensch, P. A., & Sternberg, R. J. (1989). Expertise and intelligent thinking: When is it worse to know better? In R. J. Sternberg (Ed.), *Advances in the psychology of human intelligence* (Vol. 5., pp. 157–188). Hillsdale, NJ: Erlbaum.

Gardner, H. (1983). *Frames of mind.* New York: Basic Books.

George, J. M., & Zhou, J. (2002). Understanding when bad moods foster creativity and good ones don't: The role of context and clarity of feelings. *Journal of Applied Psychology, 87*(4), 687–697.

Gick, M. L., Holyoak, K. J. (1980). Analogical problem solving. *Cognitive Psychology, 12*, 306–355.

Glover, J. A., Ronning, R. R., & Reynolds, C. R. (Eds.). (1989). *Handbook of creativity: Perspectives on individual differences.* New York: Plenum Press.

Goldenberg, J., Mazursky, D., & Solomon, S. (1999). Toward identifying the inventive templates of new products: A channeled ideation approach. *Journal of Marketing Research, 36*(May), 200–210.

Guilford, J. P. (1950). Creativity. *American Psychologist, 5*, 444–454.

Guilford, J. P. (1964). Creative thinking and problem solving. *Education Digest, 13*, 21–31.

Guilford, J. P. (1985). The structure-of-intellect model. In B. B. Wolman (Ed.), *Handbook of intelligence* (pp. 225–266). New York: Wiley.

Guiry, M., & Lutz, R. J. (2001). Shopping to create the self: Creativity and the recreational shopper. Presentation made at the AMA Winter Educator's Conference.

Gruber, H. E., & Wallace, D. B. (2001). Creative work: The case of Charles Darwin. *American Psychologist, 56*(4), 346–349.

Hausman, C. R. (1984). *Discourse on novelty and creation.* Albany, NY: SUNY Press.

Hebdidge, D. (1977). *Subculture: The meaning of style.* New York: Routledge.

Hennessey, B. A. (2000). Rewards and creativity. In C. Sansone & J. H. Harackiewicz (Eds.), *Intrinsic and extrinsic motivation: The search for optimal human performance* (pp. 55–78). New York: Academic Press.

Hennessey, B. A. (2003). The social psychology of creativity. *Scandinavian Journal of Educational Research,* 47(3), 253–271.

Hennessey, B. A., Amabile, T. M., & Martinage, M. (1989). Immunizing children against the negative effects of reward. *Contemporary Educational Psychology, 14,* 212–227.

Hennessey, B. A., & Zbikowski, S. M. (1993). Immunizing children against the negative effects of reward: A further examination of intrinsic motivation training techniques. *Creativity Research Journal, 6,* 297–307.

Hershman, D. L., & Leib, J. (1988). *The key to genius.* Buffalo, NY: Prometheus.

Hirschman, E. C. (1980). Innovativeness, novelty seeking, and consumer creativity. *Journal of Consumer Research, 7*(December), 283–295.

Hirschman, E. C. (1983). Consumer intelligence, creativity, and consciousness: Implications for consumer protection and education. *Journal of Public Policy and Marketing, 2,* 153–170.

Holt, D. B. (1997). Poststructuralist lifestyle analysis: Conceptualizing the social patterning of consumption in postmodernity. *Journal of Consumer Research, 23*(March), 326–350.

Houtz, J. C. (Ed.). (2003). *The educational psychology of creativity.* Creskill, NJ: Hampton Press.

Howard-Jones, P. A., Taylor, J. R., & Sutton, L. (2002). The effect of play on the creativity of young children during subsequent activity. *Early Child Development and Care, 172*(4), 323–328.

Hummel, J. E., & Holyoak, K. J. (2002). Analogy and creativity: Schema induction in a structure-sensitive connectionist model. In T. Dartnall (Ed.), *Creativity, cognition and knowledge: An interaction* (pp. 181–210). Westport, CT: Praeger.

Isaksen, S. G., Murdock, M. C., Firestien, R. L., & Treffinger, D. J. (Eds.). (1993). *Understanding and recognizing creativity: The emergence of a discipline.* Norwood, NJ: Ablex Publishing.

Isen, A. M. (1999). Positive affect. In T. Dagleisch & M. Power (Eds.), *Handbook of cognition and emotion* (pp. 521–539). New York: Wiley.

Kahn, B., & Isen, A. (1993). The influence of positive affect on variety seeking among safe, enjoyable products. *Journal of Consumer Research, 20*(September), 257–270.

Kates, S. M. (2002). The protean quality of subcultural consumption: An ethnographic account of gay consumers. *Journal of Consumer Research, 29*(December), 383–399.

Kaufman, G. (2003). Expanding the mood-creativity equation. *Creativity Research Journal, 15*(2&3), 131–135.

Kaufman, G., & Vosburg, S. K. (2002). The effects of mood on early and late idea production. *Creativity Research Journal, 14*(3&4), 317–330.

Kowal, J., & Fortier, M. S. (1999). Motivational determinants of flow: Contributions from self-determination thoery. *The Journal of Social Psychology, 139*(3), 355–368.

Lubart, T. I. (1994). Creativity. In R. J. Sternberg (Ed.), *Handbook of perception and cognition: Thinking and problem solving* (pp. 289–332). New York: Academic Press.

Lubart, T. I., & Getz, I. (1997). Emotion, metaphor, and the creative process. *Creativity Research Journal, 10*(4), 285–301.

Lubart, T. I., & Mouchiroud, C. (2003). Creativity: A source of difficulty in problem solving. In J. E. Davidson & R. J. Sternberg (Eds.), *The psychology of problem solving* (127–148). Cambridge: Cambridge University Press.

MacKinnon, D. W. (1978). *In search of human effectiveness: Identifying and developing creativity.* Buffalo, NY: Creative Education Foundation.

Martindale, C. (1990). Creative imagination and neural activity. In R. Kunzendorf & A. Sheikh (Eds.), *Psychophysiology of mental imagery: Theory, research, and application* (pp. 89–108). Amityville, NY: Baywood Books.

Martindale, C. (1995). Creativity and connectionism. In S. M. Smith, T. B. Ward, & R. A. Finke (Eds.), *The creative cognition approach* (pp. 249–268). Cambridge, MA: MIT Press.

Martindale, C. (1999). Biological bases of creativity. In R. J. Sternberg (Ed.), *Handbook of creativity* (137–152). Cambridge: Cambridge University Press.

Martindale, C. (2001). Oscillations and analogies: Thomas Young, MD, FRS, genius. *American Psychologist*, 56(4), 342–345.

Mathwick, C., & Rigdon, E. (2004). Play, flow and the online search experience. *Journal of Consumer Research*, 31(September), 324–332.

McDonough, R. (2002). Emergence and creativity: Five degrees of freedom. In T. Dartnall (Ed.), *Creativity, cognition, and knowledge: An interaction* (pp. 283–320). Westport, CT: Praeger.

McQuarrie, E. F., & Mick, D. G. (1999). Visual rhetoric in advertising: Text interpretive, experimental, and reader response analyses. *Journal of Consumer Research*, 26(June), 37–54.

McQuarrie, E. F., & Mick, D. G. (2003). Visual and verbal rhetorical figures under directed processing versus incidental exposure to advertising. *Journal of Consumer Research*, 29(March), 579–587.

Mick, D. G., Burroughs, J. E., Hetzel, P., & Brannen, M. Y. (2004). Pursuing the meaning of meaning in the commercial world: An international review of marketing and consumer research founded on semiotics. *Semiotica*, 152(1/4), 1–74.

Moreau, C. P., & Dahl, D. W. (2005). Designing the solution: The impact of constraints on consumer creativity. *Journal of Consumer Research*, 32(June), 13–22.

Mumford, M. D. (2003). Where have we been, where are we going? Taking stock of creativity research. *Creativity Research Journal*, 15(2&3), 107–120.

Nakamura, J., & Csikszentmihalyi, M. (2003). The motivational sources of creativity as viewed from the paradigm of positive psychology. In L. G. Aspinwall & U. M. Staudinger (Eds.), *A psychology of human strengths: Fundamental questions and future directions for a positive psychology* (pp. 257–269). Washington, DC: American Psychological Association.

O'Quin, K., & Besemer, S. (1989). The development, reliability and validity of the revised creative product semantic scale. *Creativity Ressearch Journal*, 2(4), 267–278.

Otnes, C., Kacen, J., & Lowrey, T. M. (2001). Consumer innovativeness and Christmas gift giving. Presentation made at the *AMA Winter Educator's Conference*.

Paulus, P. B., & Nijstad, B. A. (Eds.). (2003). *Group creativity: Innovation through collaboration*. New York: Oxford University Press.

Perkins, D. N. (1997). Creativity's camel: The role of analogy in invention. In T. B. Ward, S. M. Smith, & J. Vaid (Eds.), *Creative thought: An investigation of conceptual structures and processes* (pp. 523–538). Washington, DC: American Psychological Association.

Plucker, J. A., & Renzulli, J. S. (1999). Psychometric approaches to the study of human creativity. In R. Sternberg (Ed.), *Handbook of creativity* (pp. 35–61). New York: Cambridge University Press.

Prahalad, C. K., & Ramaswamy, V. (2000). Co-opting customer competence. *Harvard Business Review*, January–February, 79–87.

Price, L. L., & Ridgeway, N. M. (1982). Use innovativeness, vicarious exploration and purchase exploration: Three facets of consumer varied behavior. In B. J. Walker (Ed.), *AMA National Educators' Conference Proceedings* (pp. 56–60). Chicago: American Marketing Association.

Runco, M. A. (Ed.). (1997). *The creativity research handbook*, Vol. 1. Cresskill, NJ: Hampton Press.

Runco, M. A. (Ed.). (2003). *Critical creative processes*. Cresskill, NJ: Hampton Press.

Runco, M. A., & Sakamoto, S. O. (1999). Experimental studies of creativity. In R. Sternberg (Ed.), *Handbook of creativity* (pp. 62–92). New York: Cambridge University Press.

Russ, S. W. (2003). Play and creativity: Developmental issues. *Scandinavian Journal of Psychology*, 47(3), 291–303.

Schubert, D. S. P. (1973). Intelligence as necessary but not sufficient for creativity. *The Journal of Genetic Psychology*, 122, 45–47.

Segal, E. (2004). Incubation and insight in problem solving. *Creativity Research Journal*, 16(1), 141–148.

Shalley, C. E., & Perry-Smith, J. E. (2001). Effects of social-psychological factors on creative performance: The role of informational and controlling expected evaluation and modeling experience. *Organizational Behavior and Human Decision Processes*, 84(1), 1–22.

Shaw, M. P., & Runco, M. A. (Ed.). (1994). *Creativity and affect*, Norwood, NJ: Ablex.

Simonton, D. K. (1984). *Genius, creativity, and leadership*. Cambridge: Cambridge University Press.

Simonton, D. K. (1999). *Origins of genius: Darwinian perspectives of creativity*. New York: Oxford University Press.

Smith, S. M. (1995). Fixation, incubation and insight in memory and creative thinking. In S. M. Smith, T. B. Ward, & R. A. Finke (Eds.), *The creative cognition approach* (pp. 135–156). Cambridge, MA: MIT Press.

Smith, S. M., Ward, T. B., & Finke, R. A. (Eds.). (1995). *The creative cognition approach*. Cambridge, MA: MIT Press.

Smith, S. M., Ward, T. B., & Vaid, J. (Eds.). (1997). *Creative thought: An investigation of conceptual structures and processes*. Washington, DC: American Psychological Association.

Sternberg, R. J. (Ed.). (1988a). *The nature of creativity: Contemporary psychological perspectives*. Cambridge: Cambridge University Press.

Sternberg, R. J. (1988b). A three-facet model of creativity. In R. J. Sternberg (Ed.), *The nature of creativity: Contemporary psychological perspectives* (pp. 125–147). Cambridge: Cambridge University Press.

Sternberg, R. J. (Ed.). (1999a). *Handbook of creativity*. (pp. 3–15). Cambridge: Cambridge University Press.

Sternberg, R. J. (1999b). Intelligence. In M. A. Runco & S. R. Pritzker (Eds.), *Encyclopedia of creativity* (Vol. 2, pp. 81–87). New York: Academic Press.

Sternberg, R. J., Grigorenko, E. L., & Singer, J. L. (Ed.). (2004). *Creativity: From potential to realization*. Washington, DC: American Psychological Association.

Sternberg, R. J., & Lubart, T. I. (1995). *Defying the crowd: Cultivating creativity in a culture of conformity*. New York: Free Press.

Sternberg, R. J., & Lubart, T. I. (1996). Investing in creativity. *American Psychologist*, 51(7), 677–688.

Sternberg, R. J., & Lubart, T. I. (1999). The concept of creativity: Prospects and paradigms. In R. Sternberg (Ed.), *Handbook of creativity* (pp. 5–15). Cambridge: Cambridge University Press.

Sternberg, R. J., & Lubart, T. I. (2003). The role of intelligence in creativity. In M. A. Runco (Ed.), *Critical creative processes: Perspectives in creativity research* (pp. 153–187). Cresskill, NJ: Hampton Press.

Sternberg, R. J., & O'Hara, L. A. (1999). Creativity and intelligence. In R. Sternberg (Ed.), *Handbook of creativity* (pp. 251–272). Cambridge: Cambridge University Press.

Thompson, C. J., & Haytko, D. L. (1997). Speaking of fashion: Consumers' uses of fashion discourses and the appropriation of countervailing cultural meanings. *Journal of Consumer Research, 24*(June), 15–42.

Torrance, P. (1966). *The Torrance tests of creative thinking: Technical-norms manual* (research ed.). Princeton, NJ: Personnel Press.

Trevlas, E., Matsouka, O., & Zachopoulou, E. (2003). Relationship between playfulness and motor creativity in preschool children. *Early Child Development and Care, 173*(5), 535–543.

vonHippel, E. (1986). Lead users: A source of novel product concepts. *Management Science, 32*(July), 791–805.

von Hippel, E., Thomke, S., & Sonnack, M. (1999). Creating breakthroughs at 3M. *Harvard Business Review, 77*(September-October), 47–57.

Ward, T. B. (1994). Structured imagination: The role of category structure in exemplar generation. *Cognitive Psychology, 27*(1), 1–40.

Ward, T. B., Smith, S. M., & Finke, R. A. (1999). Creative cognition. In R. Sternberg (Ed.), *Handbook of creativity* (pp. 189–212). New York: Cambridge University Press.

Weisburg, R. W. (1994). Genius and madness? A quasi-experimental test of the hypothesis that manic-depression increases creativity. *Psychological Science, 5*, 361–367.

Weisberg, R. W. (1999). Creativity and knowledge: A challenge to theories. In R. J. Sternberg (Ed.), *Handbook of creativity* (pp. 226–250). New York: Cambridge University Press.

Weisberg, R. W., & Alba, J. W. (1981). An examination of the alleged role of "Fixation" in the solution of several "Insight" problems. *Journal of Experimental Psychology: General*, 110, 169–192.

White, R. W. (1959). Motivation reconsidered: The concept of competence. *Psychological Review, 66*(5), 297–333.

Woodman, R. W., & Schoenfeldt, L. F. (1990). An interactionist model of creative behavior. *Journal of Creative Behavior, 24*(1), 10–20.

Zaltman, G. (2003). *How customers think: Essential insights into the mind of the market*. Boston: HBS Press.

41

Compulsive Buying
Review and Reflection

RONALD J. FABER

University of Minnesota

THOMAS C. O'GUINN

University of Wisconsin

Over the past 20 years compulsive buying has moved from relative obscurity to a frequently mentioned topic in many of our leading institutions ranging from the mass media to the courts. Its progression has gone from a derisive topic of humor (usually at the expense of women) in comic strips and talk show monologues to serious discussions on television, in newspapers and magazines, to serving as a mitigating circumstance in criminal trials, to a research topic at first tier medical schools and universities. In fact, compulsive buying is now commonly recognized and addressed by clinical practice, and is being considered as a disorder for inclusion in the *DSM* (the *Diagnostic and Statistical Manual of Mental Disorders* published by the American Psychiatric Association). There have now been several score of academic papers written on this topic in fields as diverse as finance, accounting, law, medicine, psychology, sociology, psychiatry, and economics. This is a great distance traveled from where we began our research on compulsive buying almost 20 years ago.

While prior to the mid-1980s, there was virtually nothing written about compulsive buying, its existence was not completely unknown. Indeed, it (or something like it) was reported in psychiatric textbooks as early as 1915 under the term *oniomania* or buying mania (Kraepelin, 1915). It was discussed in the psychiatric literature for about 10 years and then largely disappeared until we and a small number of others began researching it anew in the mid 1980's.

The first mention of compulsive buying in the early 1900s occurs during the period that historians have located the decisive institutionalization of U.S. consumer culture and the tipping point between Victorian and modernist views of consumption, self-control, hedonism, and therapy (Marchand, 1985; Lasch, 1991). It is surely not a coincidence that it was in this environment that appropriate, inappropriate, and excessive modes of consumption would be discussed and placed in a therapeutic context (Lears, 1983; Schudson, 1984).

In the early 20th century, compulsive buying was seen as being one of a number of monomanias or impulse disorders which also included kleptomania, pyromania and extreme collecting. Oniomania was initially defined as being impulsively driven buying that resulted in a senseless amount of debt (Kraepelin, 1915). Of course, in 1915 readily available consumer credit was still five decades away, and what constituted "senseless debt" was in all likelihood small in comparison to contemporary standards of household debt load. Patients with oniomania were said to be unable to control their behavior or even to recognize the senseless consequences of their actions (Bleuler, 1924). We should note that even very early on, a consequence of the condition, debt and its life disruption was a defining indicator. It still is today.

Despite the early recognition and diagnosis of a severe buying problem, there was virtually no further mention of compulsive buying until the mid 1980s when the formation of self-help groups began to gain media attention (Holstrom, 1985; Mundis, 1986). Again, it is interesting that the topic re-emerges during a period in which discussions of consumption and its excesses were common. A few years later, articles on compulsive buying began to appear in the academic literature in psychotherapy (Krueger, 1988), addiction (Glatt & Cook, 1987), and consumer behavior (Faber, O'Guinn, & Krych, 1987; O'Guinn & Faber, 1989). Since that time we have begun to develop a better understanding of this problem; its complexity, varying contributory causes, the severity of its effects, and the size of the problem. Of course, there is still much to understand. This chapter attempts to report on our current knowledge of compulsive buying and address key facets of its social circumstance and construction. We have also now had the advantage of history in that we can see the critical role played by social forces when it comes to how this disorder has been conceived and viewed.

DEFINING CRITERIA

Compulsive buying has been defined as chronic, repetitive purchasing that becomes a primary response to negative feelings and that provides immediate short-term gratification, but which ultimately causes harm to the individual and/or others (O'Guinn & Faber, 1989). Similarly, Edwards (1992) labeled it a chronic, abnormal form of shopping and spending, characterized by overpowering uncontrollable and repetitive urges to buy. Thoughts of shopping are intrusive and accompanied by powerful urges. It also is experienced as a continual and repetitive problem.

Defining criteria for this disorder also include the fact that the urges are perceived as undesirable and that the behavior interferes with the individuals life functioning. For example, Goldsmith and McElroy (2000) propose three criteria for someone to be diagnosed as having compulsive buying disorder. These include:

1. Frequent preoccupations with buying, or actual buying, that is viewed as excessive, intrusive, or senseless
2. These impulses or behaviors cause marked distress and significantly interfere with social or occupational functioning and/or result in serious financial problems.
3. The buying or shopping does not only occur during periods of hyomania or mania.

AREAS OF CONFUSION REGARDING COMPULSIVE BUYING

Compulsive buying has been the subject of a great deal of confusion in the consumer behavior literature. Some of this confusion stems from the name itself. When we originally began to study this phenomenon, the self-help groups and the press were referring to people with this problem as "shopaholics." We felt that this term trivialized the disorder to some degree and would make it more difficult for the problem to be taken seriously. Additionally, some authors in psychology and medicine distinguish between addictions, which involve consuming substances like alcohol or drugs, and excessive behaviors that do not.

In trying to match our findings to what appeared to be similar in the psychiatric literature, the closest disorder seemed to be what was then called "compulsive gambling". Borrowing from this nomenclature, we labeled the phenomenon we were studying "compulsive buying". Unfortunately, what we did not know is that around that point in time, psychiatry would change the term "compulsive gambling" to "pathological gambling" because of confusion about whether it was symptomatic of obsessive-compulsive disorder, or was an impulse control disorder centered on gambling. A similar confusion has also occurred with "compulsive buying."

In hindsight, it probably would have been better if we had chosen to label this phenomenon "pathological buying." However, even changing the name would not have completely alleviated the problem. There is a question in the psychiatric literature to this day about whether compulsive buying is a form of obsessive-compulsive disorder (OCD). Some authors believe that compulsive buying may be related to OCD (Frost, Kim, Bloss, Murrey-Close, & Steketee, 1998; McElroy et al., 1994; Schlosser, Black, Repertinger, & Freet, 1994). Others argue that it should more properly be classified as an Impulse Control Disorder (Christenson et al. 1994; Koran, Bullock, Hartson, Elliott & D'Andrea, 2002; Kraepelin, 1915). Most clinicians currently diagnose it under the "Impulse Control Disorder – Not otherwise Specified" category in the *DSM-IV* (Swan-Kremeier, Mitchell, & Faber, 2005). However, this is subject to change, and as several authors point out, it is likely that compulsive buying has some characteristics of both disorders (Schlosser et al., 1994; Swan-Kemeier et al., 2005). Indeed, some consider both OCD and impulse control disorders to be subsumed under a broader classification called "affect spectrum disorder" (McElroy, Keck, & Phillips, 1995).

Partly due to its possible classification as an impulse control disorder and partly due to some potential behavioral similarities, people sometimes confuse compulsive buying with impulse buying. Some extreme examples of impulse buying can resemble descriptions of compulsive buyers (see Rook, 1987, for example). However, these two constructs differ in several important ways, and we maintain that they should be considered separately.

First, impulse buying is generally seen as externally generated through a reaction to a specific item or environment, while compulsive buying urges are internally generated. Even though mood states may influence impulse buying, the focus of the desire is on a specific item and desire for that item will, at least temporarily, outweigh the willpower to resist it (Hock & Lowenstein, 1991). Compulsive buying, however, is typically more about the desire to buy than about the actual item bought (O'Guinn & Faber, 1989). In compulsive buying an urge or tension to buy is experienced as mounting pressure and can be relieved only after a purchase is made (Christenson et al., 1994). This urge often begins well before the individual is even in a buying environment and is often weakly related to typical retail environmental cues or brand features. In somewhat overly simplified terms: compulsive buying is more about buying; impulse buying is more about what is bought.

Second, impulse buying is a behavior that is engaged in by a large percentage of the population at relatively infrequent intervals. Compulsive buying however, affects only a small percentage of the population that experiences these urges frequently. Typically, compulsive buyers engage in this behavior at least several times a week (Christenson et al., 1994; Schlosser et al., 1994).

Third, the consequences of compulsive buying are significantly more severe than that of impulse buying.

Finally, while self-regulatory failure has been linked to both impulse buying and compulsive buying (Faber & Vohs, 2004), they involve different types of failure. Impulse buying is viewed as involving individual instances of self-regulatory failure. After this temporary lapse, people re-establish control over their purchasing behavior. With impulse buying, the specific failure is frequently due to a depletion of regulatory resources that leads to underregulation of the behavior.

On the other hand, compulsive buying is seen as a chronic and complete breakdown of the self-regulatory process. This occurs because of conflicting goals—the need to maintain emotional stability overwhelms efforts to maintain purchasing and economic goals. This explanation is consistent with other work that finds that when there is a need to regulate affect and a behavior, priority will be given to the affective needs (Tice, Bratslavsky, & Baumeister, 2001). Additionally, compulsive buying can result in cognitive narrowing that prohibits one from monitoring one's behavior. This can be seen in the quasidissociative states some compulsive buyers experience where they feel they are outside of their body watching someone else act, or even experience difficulty recalling having bought items they purchased. Thus, compulsive buying is due more to what is called misregulation rather than underregulation (Baumeister, Heatherton, & Tice, 1994).

Another major area of confusion in the consumer research literature regarding compulsive buying is whether it is a psychological disorder or simply represents one end of a continuum that can be used to assess all consumers. This type of debate is common among a number of related disorders including eating disorders and alcoholism. In fact, this is a common theme in the history of clinical psychology: Is a certain behavior merely an extreme manifestation of something more modal, or is it something altogether different? The answer has historically been significantly formed just as much by social and political forces as scientific or empirical ones. For example, when factor analytic and other tools for classification emerged, there was a tendency to lean toward discreet categories. At other times political and social forces have dictated the boundaries of "normality" broadened. Thus the degree of deviation vs. the discreet disorder debate is often socio-political. At the moment, a growing number of researchers believe that advances in biological psychology will ultimately resolve these controversies. (Personally, we think it unlikely that the politics of difference/sameness will ever be absent from this domain). Until that time, however, clinical experience and non-biological empirical research will have to guide science in the area.

While acknowledging these debates, we have long held that compulsive buying is a disorder that one either experiences or does not. This view corresponds with the one that exists in the medical literature and is consistent with its early roots (Bleuler, 1924; Kraepelin, 1915). It is also consistent with literature that suggests that compulsive buying has a biological or genetic component (Black, 1996; Faber 1992; Schlosser et al., 1994). Evidence for its biological component comes both from reports that compulsive buyers have a family history of related psychiatric disorders (Black, 1996; McElroy et al., 1994) and from studies that have reported some success in treating compulsive buyers with medications such as fluvoxamine and citalopram (Black, Monahan, & Gabel 1997; Koran et al., 2002; McElroy et al., 1994). For these reasons, we believe that compulsive buyers should be treated as a distinct population from general consumers.

We developed the Compulsive Buying Scale (CBS) as an attempt to specifically identify items that distinguished members of these two populations: compulsive buyers and the general population (Faber & O'Guinn, 1992).The assessment of the validity of the CBS was done by showing that members of the general population who were identified by the scale as being compulsive buyers scored very similarly to a self-identified group of compulsive buyers and very differently from other general consumers on a number of behavioral and economic items.

Subsequent research has used the CBS to identify or screen compulsive buyers and then used psychiatric interviews to further validate that people meet diagnostic criteria for being a compulsive buyer (Miltenberger, Redlin, Crosby, Stickney, Mitchell, Wonderlich, 2003; Schlosser et al., 1994). These and other studies have shown that the CBS performs exceptionally well at identifying compulsive buyers and distinguishing them from noncompulsive buyers (Black, 2000). For example, a validation study for the CBS compared its classification of self-identified compulsive buyers and matched control subjects with those of trained clinicians using semi-structured interviews to classify subjects (Faber & O'Guinn, 1992). The results found that the CBS correctly classified 87.5% of the people.

More recent studies using the CBS have found that people identified as compulsive buyers by this instrument possess other criteria related to being a compulsive buyer. For example, in one study all 24 people who were identified as compulsive buyers by this scale also reported that their buying behaviors caused personal distress and financial, marital, family, social and/or occupational problems (Christenson et al., 1994). In another study, all 33 people who were classified as compulsive buyers by the CBS also meet clinical diagnostic criteria for compulsive buying (Black, Repertinger, Gaffney, & Gabel, 1998). The reverse has also been shown to be true. Among people identified by psychiatrists has meeting criteria for compulsive buying, 87% received scores that would classify them as compulsive buyers on the CBS. Thus, this instrument seems to be very successful at identifying people who psychiatrists would classify as compulsive buyers.

While our instrument was designed to identify people who meet clinical criteria for compulsive buying, a number of consumer behavior researchers have used the CBS and other instruments with general populations of consumers (typically undergraduates). They treat scores on these scales as continuous measures and compared those scoring high versus low on these instruments (d'Astous, 1990; Haney & Smith, 1996; Mowen & Spears, 1999; Roberts, 1998). In literature reviews, the results from both of these types of studies are often combined as if they were from the same population. While in a number of cases the findings converge, we strongly believe that it is a mistake to do this. Evidence suggests that these are two very different populations. This can perhaps best be seen in a plot from the Faber and O'Guinn (1992) scale development study (see Figure 41.1). The two distributions are highly skewed in opposite directions. Thus, very few people in a general sample who score highly on the CBS would have scored similarly to our compulsive buyers. In fact, the CBS cut-point for classifying compulsive buyers places them two standard deviations beyond the algorithmic mean score from the general population. Therefore, combining results from these two types of studies confounds excessive buying with what we label as compulsive buying or pathological buying.

We are not arguing that one approach is right and the other wrong, but simply that these two types of studies tell us about different things. Studies comparing people who buy more excessively with those who do not are definitely valuable and should be studied in consumer behavior. It is

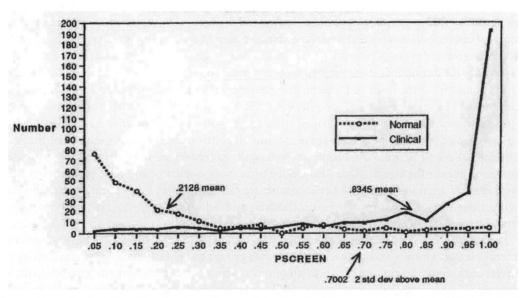

Figure 41.1   Probability distribution of compulsive buying (Source: Faber, R. J. & O'Guinn, T. C., 1992, p. 463).

also important to compare results from these two types of studies (i.e., consumers who just buy excessively vs. truly compulsive buyers) to see what overlaps exist and what common antecedents may emerge. For example, both types of studies have reported that compulsive buyers have low self-esteem (Dittmar, 2000; O'Guinn & Faber, 1989; Roberts, 1998; Schlosser et al., 1994). Thus, self-esteem may play a role in both excessive and compulsive buying. However, it is equally important to recognize where differences exist.

For example, studies of pathological compulsive buyers have generally reported that possessiveness is not a motivation for this behavior. Compulsive buyers have been found to be no more materialistic than other consumers, or if they are more materialistic, it is due to differences in the interpersonal dimension of materialism and not in the desire for goods themselves (O'Guinn & Faber, 1989; Scherhorn, Reich, & Raab, 1990). On the other hand, studies looking at continuous scores from non-clinical populations have tended to report that compulsive buyers are more materialistic and more concerned about possessions than other consumers (Dittmar, Beattie, & Friese 1996; Mowen & Spears, 1999; Yurchisin & Johnson, 2004). Given these findings, it would appear that the gratifications from purchasing may be very different for these two groups. Pathological compulsive buyers frequently do not use the things they buy (O'Guinn & Faber, 1989), while excessive buyers gain considerable meaning and pleasure from using the goods they acquire (Dittmar et al. 1996; Yurchisin & Johnson, 2004). We should also note that we are not entirely convinced of the validity of measures of materialisim. It is a highly politicized, cultural, dynamic, and very subject construct, in our view.

Another distinction between excessive buyers and pathological compulsive buyers is the role of negative affect and mood state. Compulsive buyers' are often triggered to buy by negative cues (Faber, Ristvedt, Mackenzie, & Christenson (1996) and are more likely to buy when in negative mood states (Faber, O'Guinn, & Krych, 1987; Faber & Christenson, 1996). Excessive buyers may be more similar to impulse buyers who are more likely to purchase things when they are in a positive mood state (Beatty & Ferrell, 1998; Rook & Gardner, 1993).

Finally, biological differences and the comorbidity of other disorders are likely to distinguish pathological compulsive buyers from those labeled as compulsive buyers in studies using continuous measures from a general population. As a result, the feeling of mounting, uncontrollable tension that compulsive buyers feel when they haven't bought something are likely to be absent in excessive buyers.

Another indication that there are two separate groups of people who are labeled as compulsive buyers comes from the work of DeSarbo and Edwards (1996). They identified compulsive buyers both by use of a scale and by self-identification. They found these compulsive buyers formed two separate clusters. The first cluster seemed to be more motivated by internal feelings such as low self-esteem and having a short-term sense of power or control. This group appears most similar to pathological compulsive buyers. People in the second cluster seemed to be driven more by materialism and a desire for objects. They also tended to be more impulsive and have poor coping skills. These clusters seem to distinguish between what we call compulsive buyers and people who score high on continuous measures. However, DeSarbo and Edwards (1996) found that how subjects were identified did not predict group membership in their study.

More research needs to be done to clearly distinguish pathological compulsive buyers from more general excessive buyers and to compare these two groups to help us identify the similarities and differences among these populations. In all of our research, and in the remainder of this chapter, when we refer to compulsive buyers we are talking about just those people whose behavior can be viewed as pathological and would meet the definitional criteria previously discussed.

INCIDENCE OF COMPULSIVE BUYING

An initial indication of the prevalence of compulsive buying came from the scale development work of Faber and O'Guinn (1992). This scale has become a standard instrument for both epidemiological and diagnostic evaluation (Black, 2000). They applied the CBS to a sample selected to approximate the general population of Illinois. The Illinois population did not deviate markedly from the U.S. population on any dimension where an a priori confound was theorized.

Using a measure shown to have good validity, and a very conservative cut-point criterion, a .05 Maximum-Likelihood Probability, Faber and O'Guinn (1992) estimated the prevalence of compulsive buying at 1.8% of the population. Significantly, the 1.8% estimate is in-line with incidence estimates for a wide variety of other impulse related disorders. Given the relatively high comorbidity between many of these disorders, there is an empirical suspicion that this population may over the course of their lives experience more than one of these pathologies. Indeed, studies of the lifetime occurrence of various other disorders among compulsive buyers have shown this to be true (Black, 1996; Christenson et al., 1994; Schlosser et al., 1994). However, one must remember that statistically based cut-points are undeniably arbitrary. Using a less conservative but very defendable cut-point of 2 standard deviations above the mean for normal consumers would yield a prevalence estimate of 8.1%.

More recently, the first nationwide epidemiological study of the prevalence of compulsive buying was conducted (Koran, Farber, Aboujaoude, Large, & Serpe, 2006). They administered the CBS to respondents from a random sample national household telephone survey. Using the more moderate 2 standard deviation cut-point from Faber and O'Guinn (1992), they estimated prevalence at 5.8%. The more conservative cut-point yielded a prevalence estimate of 1.4%.

It is helpful to put these estimates in context. In 2005, the Surgeon General of the United States put the 1-year incidence of some sort of mental disease at one in four U.S. adults (U.S. Surgeon General, 2005). So, what might at first blush seem like a relatively high estimate is probably (especially given the high comorbidity with other related disorders differing primarily in the object of one's behavior) a fairly reasonable one.

ONSET, PROGRESSION, AND GENDER

The onset of this disorder has generally been estimated to occur in the late teens or twenties (Black, 1996; Christenson et al., 1994; Schlosser et al., 1994). Typically it occurs a point when people start to live on their own and are able to financially support themselves, although an age-related biological onset dynamic can not been ruled out. The fact that most compulsive buyers don't recognize or admit that they have a problem until well after on-set makes the development of this disorder difficult to assess. However, given that credit is available to people at younger and younger ages, and that consumption and shopping are among the set of defining youth experiences, it is possible that onset may become even younger.

Initially, it was thought that people with less income might be more prone to becoming compulsive buyers. The idea was that fewer financial resources would make buying loom larger for the relatively deprived and would be more disruptive. However, research has generally found this is not to be the case. Instead, people at widely varying income levels have been shown equally susceptible to becoming compulsive buyers (Christenson et al., 1992; O'Guinn & Faber, 1989; Scherhorn et al., 1990). People with limited income manifest this behavior by buying at thrift shops and garage sales, while those with very large incomes may be more likely to buy in exclusive boutiques, or excessively spend on large ticket items such as cars and real estate. It is, however, conceivable that among the very rich disruption of normal life functioning might be significantly delayed. However, while financial resources may not run out, other problems such as family conflicts are likely to occur. Domestic violence against women and financial stress over secreted buying behavior are not strangers.

Although most of the research on compulsive buying comes from the United States, this disorder appears to exist in a wide range of developed and developing countries. Studies of compulsive buyers have been conducted in numerous countries including England, Sweden, Germany, Australia, France, Spain, Mexico, and South Korea. While these are primarily industrialized and generally prosperous nations, we believe that this disorder can, and does, exist in societies with less affluence. Our reasons for this belief should become clear as we move forward.

By far the most frequently mentioned demographic characteristic among compulsive buyers is gender; compulsive buying appears to be much more prevalent among women than men. Most studies report that between 80 and 95% of compulsive buyers are women (Black, 2001). Some of this imbalance may be due to the fact that most research has relied on volunteers or people who have sought treatment. Both volunteering and seeking help for ailments are more common among women. A more therapeutic culture among women probably leads to a significant reporting error among men. Nonetheless, the size of the disparity was thought to suggest a true gender difference. Particularly given the fact that in modern times buying is itself heavily gendered. However, the only large scale epidemiological study (Koran et al., 2006) reporst that men are about equally likely to be compulsive buyers as women. They caution that additional research is needed to determine if a true gender difference exists.

Gender inequity has been found for a number of other impulse control disorders. For example, women have historically been more likely to develop eating disorders such as anorexia and bulimia, or to suffer from kleptomania, while men have been more likely to develop alcohol and substance abuse problems and pathological gambling. It should be noted that the gender differences in all of these disorders are currently experiencing some degree of change. This suggests that gender differences among impulse control disorders most likely occur, in part, because of socialization and shifting social norms.

CORE COMMONALITIES AMONG COMPULSIVE BUYERS

There is some variety in the way in which different compulsive buyers experience the disorder. Some report that they experience urges to buy every day while others report the behavior as more episodic. On average, compulsive buyers report engaging in this behavior 2–3 times a week, although reported frequencies of binge buying range from once a month to several times a day (Christenson et al., 1994; O'Guinn & Faber, 1989; Schlosser et al., 1994). These differences could be attributable to all sorts of factors from idiosyncratic variations to severity of the disorder or etiological ones. In general, the extant data do support the idea of a progressive disorder. The types of items purchased also vary, although clothing and shoes are most commonly mentioned items, especially for women (Christenson et al., 1994; Schlosser et al., 1994). Most compulsive buyers report buying primarily for themselves, although a few report buying almost exclusively for others (O'Guinn & Faber, 1989).

The excessive nature of compulsive buying can be seen in a number of different ways. These include the number of shopping trips compulsive buyers make, the time spent buying or shopping, the total amount spent, the amount of debt amassed and even the number of credit cards held. For example, Schlosser et al. report that the average number of shopping trips per month among the compulsive buyers they studied was 12.9 and ranged as high as 60. The average amount spent on each of these trips was just under $100. Many compulsive buyers also report that they buy multiples of the same item (e.g., 3 raincoats or 10 shirts). This may be indicative of a quintessential compulsive behavior, set completion: the need to complete through buying all the items in a set of consumer offerings.

Compulsive buying typically leads to large debt. O'Guinn and Faber (1989) found that compulsive buyers had an average of 3.7 major credit cards compared to an average of 2.2 for general consumers. Additionally, the compulsive consumers had significantly fewer cards paid in full each month and significantly more cards within $100 of their maximum. Schlosser et al. (1994) reported that compulsive buyers had an average of 3.8 credit cards with an outstanding balance each month. This leads compulsive consumers to use a large portion of their income every month just to pay off existing debts. Christenson et al. (1994) found that compulsive buyers use approximately 50% of their household income to pay off debts. O'Guinn and Faber (1989) similarly found that compulsive buyers reported 46% of their income went to pay non-mortgage related debts each month compared to just 22% of the income for non-compulsive buyers.

One of the most interesting and possibly significant aspects of compulsive buying involves the role of the purchased items themselves. Although compulsive buyers acquire a lot of things, they frequently report that they never use these items once they are purchased (Boundy, 2000; O'Guinn & Faber, 1989). Items may instead remain in their original boxes and bags long after they are purchased. One explanation for this is that these items are seen as object reminders and concrete evidence of the presence of a problematic behavior. If left unopened and out of sight, then they are less ego threatening. Another explanation is that the objects are being hidden in the way an alcoholic hides or disposes of evidence of the secreted behavior. While both of these explanations probably play some role, the explanation to which we give most credence is that compulsive buying is not about acquisitions; it is more about the act of buying rather than possessing. This is one reason we chose to term the phenomenon compulsive buying as opposed to compulsive consumption. Some researchers takes this even further and believe that compulsive shopping without buying should be included as part of this syndrome (Goldsmith & McElroy, 2000; McElroy et al., 1994). In our research, however, we have found that for most compulsive buyers purchasing is necessary to stop the feelings of mounting tension.

Several of the compulsive buyers we have interviewed spoke of their relationships with shopping clerks, UPS delivery people, and home shopping sales staff. These interactions with stores and clerks were important to them. If one is looking for affirmation regarding one's various qualities and roles (e.g., mother, wife, girlfriend), shopping is a good place to look. Clerks, usually self-interested but not necessarily insincere, will tell these women how good they look, what a good shopper they are, or that they are pretty, sexy, and desirable, that they are good mothers, wives, daughters, and friends. They treat the consumer as an important person. This is sometimes something compulsive buyers do not experience enough in other areas of their lives. However, once they leave the buying environment the positive feelings stop. This may be why the purchased items do not satisfy. Instead, it is in the feelings of self-worth and value where the gratification lies. This is not an altogether irrational economic behavior.

In the 3 years of field work leading up to our initial attempts at measurement and scale development, it became clear to us that our a priori beliefs about compulsive buyers being highly materialistic were simply wrong. Instead, we found consumers who really gave no evidence that the objects were particularly important to them at all; in fact, it was just the opposite. The desire to possess objects did not appear to be the motivation for this behavior. Years of subsequent work, both quantitative and qualitative, have done nothing but further confirm this. Compulsive buyers do not score higher on measures of possessiveness or object attachment than other consumers (Edwards,

1992; O'Guinn & Faber, 1989; Scherhorn et al., 1990). They are not demonstrably more materialistic. Rather, the object of the compulsive buyer's gratification is the purchasing experience itself and the positive feelings of self-worth that it can engender.

ETIOLOGY OF COMPULSIVE BUYING

There is no single cause to explain compulsive buying, or to precisely map its course. Some have use a biopsychosocial model to explain this behavior (Faber, 1992). As the compound name suggests, this model posits that there are biological, psychological, and sociological factors that can all contribute to the development of compulsive buying. This model has been found to operate with a number of different excessive and addictive behaviors (Donovan, 1988).

The possibility of biological factors is suggested by research examining lifetime comorbidity and family history as well as more direct evidence from drug studies. Some researchers have speculated that there may be a genetic element that makes people from families with one type of impulse control disorder more at risk for this and other disorders (Donovan, 1988). For example, studies of alcoholism have found that sons of alcoholic fathers are four times more likely than other males to become alcoholics, even when reared apart from their fathers (Collins, 1985; Goodwin, 1984). Other studies have found that people with impulse control problems are significantly more likely to have relatives with other impulse control disorders than the public at large (McElroy, Pope, Hudson, Keck & White, 1991).

McElroy et al. (1994) reported that 17 of 18 compulsive buyers studied had a relative with a mood disorder. Additionally, 61% had a close relative diagnosed with alcoholism or substance abuse and 17% had a relative with an anxiety disorder. In another study of a small sample of compulsive buyers, half reported having a first-degree relative with alcoholism or substance abuse, 50% with a mood disorder and 40% had a relative who had a compulsive buying problem (Black, 1996).

Research has also found that compulsive buyers themselves have frequently had a history of having substance abuse, mood disorders and anxiety disorders (Christenson et al., 1994; McElroy et al., 1994; Schlosser et al., 1994). Additionally, several studies have reported co-morbidity between compulsive buying and eating disorders (Faber, Christenson, deZwaan, & Mitchell, 1995; McElroy, 1994), as well as with other impulse control disorders (Christenson et al., 1994; Goldsmith & McElroy, 2000; McElroy et al., 1994). While comorbidity can occur for a number of reasons other than biological causes, some theories suggest that common biological or genetic issues underlie all of these problems (Goldsmith & McElroy, 2000; Jacobs, 1989).

The most widely examined biological cause involves levels of neurotransmitters that can affect mood states. Several medical studies have attempted to use drugs to alter brain chemistry and determine if this reduces compulsive buying urges and behaviors. Some very small-scale studies reported that the use of anti-depressants reduced both the urges to shop and buying behaviors (McElroy et al., 1991; Lejoyeux, Hourtane, & Ades, 1995). Lejoyeux, Tassain, Solomon, and Ades (1997) have suggested that depression is what directly causes compulsive buying and that drug treatment simply reduces depression. However, other research has found that patients who are not suffering from depression also report that drug treatment significantly reduces buying thoughts and urges (Black, Monahan, & Gabel, 1997). This suggests that the relationship between brain chemistry and buying urges and behavior is not fully mediated by depression. More recent studies have continued to find that compulsive buyers have fewer buying episodes, buy less and have fewer desires to buy when treated with drugs (Koran et al., 2002, 2003).

Probably the most studied aspects of compulsive buying are the psychological factors associated with this disorder. Numerous studies have found that compulsive buyers score high on measures of depression and anxiety (Christenson et al., 1994; O'Guinn & Faber, 1989; Scherhorn et al., 1990). Clinical studies show that between one-quarter and one-half of all compulsive buyers have histories of major depressive disorder (Black, 1996; McElroy et al., 1994; Schlosser et al., 1994).

Compulsive buyers have also been found to have low self-esteem (Elliott, 1994; Friese & Koenig, 1993; O'Guinn & Faber, 1989; Scherhorn et al., 1990). This is particularly apparent in interviews with compulsive buyers when they compare themselves to siblings (Faber, 2004; Faber & O'Guinn, 1988). A reason why compulsive buyers may experience these negative feelings is that they tend to be perfectionist (DeSarbo & Edwards, 1996; O'Guinn & Faber, 1989). They often try to please others, especially parents, but frequently feel as if they have failed (Faber, 2004; Faber & O'Guinn, 1988). Such failures may contribute to the development and reinforcement of their low self-esteem. Of course, low self-esteem in clinical populations always presents a classic cause and effect question. Compulsive buying is no different. It seems most likely to us that the best model of compulsive buying would be recursive with respect to self-esteem.

The negative affect common among compulsive buyers plays a prominent role in each of three theories that have been proposed to explain this behavior. The first theory comes from Jacobs' (1989) *General Theory of Addictions*. He proposed that people who are prone to addictions have experienced a childhood and adolescence marked by feelings of inadequacy and low self-esteem. Another critical component in Jacobs' theory is that people who are predisposed to becoming addicted have a baseline level of arousal that they experience as aversive. As a result, they are prone to develop problems with behaviors that both alter their level of arousal in a direction that makes it more pleasurable to them and that allow them to temporarily escape their feelings of low self-esteem through fantasy.

Anecdotal evidence at least suggests that compulsive buyers seek higher levels of arousal (Faber, 2000) and that they experience heightened levels of arousal from both the buying experience and its aftermath (Faber, 1992; Faber & Christenson, 1996; McElroy et al., 1991). Research also suggests that compulsive buyers may have a high propensity to fantasize (Edwards, 1992; Goldman, 2000; O'Guinn & Faber, 1989). This ability to fantasize may allow them to temporarily imagine themselves differently or to imagine that others will see them in a different light, especially when buying (Goldman, 2000). This provides a temporary escape from their negative self-image. This ability to fantasize may also result in the clinical concept of grandiosity. This is a stage compulsive buyers and others with addictive disorders typically go through where they recognize that they have a potential problem, but believe, that unlike others, they can control it.

A more basic theory to explain compulsive buying is that it serves as a form of mood management (Faber & Christenson ,1996). Researchers in a wide variety of disciplines, including psychology, communications, and consumer behavior, have noted that people engage in specific behaviors to alleviate negative moods states or extend positive ones (Bryant & Zillmann, 1984; Isen, Clark & Schwartz, 1976; Rook, 1987). Research with compulsive buyers has consistently found that negative mood states precede buying episodes (Elliott, 1994; Faber & Christenson, 1996; Faber, O'Guinn, & Krych, 1987).

One study asked compulsive buyers to indicate which of a list of over 400 items worsened their compulsive buying urges or behaviors (Faber et al., 1996). The items on the list represented a wide range of activities, feeling states, places, objects and circumstances. Twenty-three of these items were selected by at least one-third of the compulsive buyers. One item, Christmas, was selected by virtually everyone. While there are several reasons why Christmas may heighten compulsive buying problems, one may be that it is a time that is associated with stressful feelings and negative mood states. The other items selected by the compulsive buyers formed two factors. One was items associated with shopping and buying. These include places like shopping malls and department stores, as well as buying motives (wanting something, item on sale) and payment symbols (money, credit cards). The second factor was a negative affect factor that included items like feeling bored, stressed, overweight, angry, hurt, depressed, etc.). This again indicates that buying may be triggered by negative mood states.

It has also been found that buying provides a temporary improvement in mood either by reducing the negative mood states or increasing positive ones (Elliott, 1994; Faber & Christenson, 1996; Friese & Koenig, 1993). One study examined mood changes as a result of buying among both compulsive buyers and a matched control sample (Faber & Christenson, 1996). Only about one-fourth of the control group stated that their moods changed as a result of buying. However, virtually all of the compulsive buyers (95.8%) indicated that their moods changed immediately after making a purchase. Additionally, the vast majority (over 80%) of the compulsive buyers indicated that their mood change was in a positive direction. Although the majority of the control group who said they experienced a change also indicated that this was in a positive direction, the percentage was significantly smaller than for the compulsive buyers. This suggests that mood manipulation may be a motive for compulsive buying and that in the short run it successfully achieves this goal (although this is not true in the long run).

The final, and perhaps most complete, theory that may explain why people engage in compulsive buying is escape theory (Faber & Vohs, 2004). Escape theory was developed to explain why people may engage in self-destructive actions and has been applied to behaviors such as eating disorders and suicide (Baumeister, 1991; Heatherton & Vohs, 1998). This theory proposes that self-awareness can be very painful for some people (Baumeister, 1991). To temporarily avoid these painful feelings, people narrow their attention by focusing exclusively on immediate, concrete tasks (such as buying). While this cognitive narrowing may block out painful thoughts, it also creates disinhibition and prevents considerations of the long-term consequences of the action (Heatherton & Vohs, 1998). Additionally, it can give rise to magical or fanciful thinking (grandiosity).

All of the characteristics of escape theory can be seen in compulsive buyers. Research cited above has shown that compulsive buyers often experience low self-esteem, feelings of failure and depression. Indeed, particular episodes of these negative feelings often trigger compulsive buying episodes. Thus, buying may serve to diminish the negative feelings when they become extremely painful.

Descriptions of compulsive buying episodes are often characterized by heightened focus on the immediate buying environment (Faber, Peterson, & Christenson, 1994; O'Guinn & Faber, 1989; Schlosser et al., 1994). Additionally, compulsive buyers dislike anything that will interfere with their focus when shopping. This is one reason why most do not like to go shopping with others (Elliott, 1994; Schlosser et al., 1994). This intense focus on buying may serve to block out negative self-awareness. Stores are information and sensory rich environments providing sights, textures, sounds and smells to engage the consumer. Thus, stores offer an excellent environment to promote cognitive narrowing. Some compulsive buyers talk about how they are enveloped by the store atmosphere and the stimuli there and those items just seem to beckon them. The cognitive narrowing that occurs may cause them to temporarily fail to recognize the long-term negative consequences of their buying.

Finally, escape theory states that during these periods of narrowing people will experience irrational and magical thinking. Compulsive buyers report that during buying episodes they view themselves as being more powerful or admired (Krueger, 2000, Scherhorn et al., 1990). These feelings of grandiosity may also allow them to think they will be able to handle the debt or expenses they are incurring. While the notion of grandiosity has a long clinical tradition, it has been a rather under-theorized one. Employing the idea of cognitive narrowing, we can see why and how grandiosity, as well as personal immunity myths, might occur. When grandiosity is present, we would predict personal risk assessments and judgments to be affected. Thus, narrowing leads to grandiosity, grandiosity to diminished risk assessments and ultimately to riskier judgments. This is an area where judgment theory and research with clinical populations might yield some very useful findings.

SOCIAL AND CULTURAL ASPECTS

Compulsive buying lies at the intersection of some very culturally charged notions. Self-control is a central idea in canonical social thought, and norms and expectations regarding self-control are as culturally determined as anything we know. Social control is a definitional function of societies; philosophies, codes, and structures. Ideas of self-control sit at the very center of moral systems, laws and religions. The regulation of pleasure, acquisition, possession and money are central concerns of society's institutions and informed a great deal of fundamental modern social theory. In fact, they still do. We should, therefore, expect compulsive buying to be heavily constructed by social forces. Indeed, discourse regarding compulsive buying is heavily seasoned with platitudes, snickers, moral cautionary tales, talk of sin, notions of social justice, and assessments of (in)-appropriateness. These take many forms, but often involve the idea that it is wrong to compulsively spend one's money, even if one has the resources to do so. While the "well, it's their money" pronouncement is common, it is often followed quickly by the requisite, "but…." The objection to follow is typically about the moral failure associated with poor self-control. The fact that the lack of control involves money, material things, and is primarily engaged in by women drives much of our social views about this disorder.

One of the problems we initially faced is to what extent this problem should be taken seriously. Should we view compulsive buying as a serious problem? Should academic researchers be studying it? While these questions have generally abated, we still face them occasionally and they reveal some of the biases and factors that produce this ambivalence.

First, is gender. Compulsive buying is most often about women and women's lives, and this has a great deal to do with its occasional trivialization. This bias has a long cultural history (c.f. Freidan, 1963; Faludi, 1988; Bordo, 1993; Briens, 1992; Marchand, 1985) and that there has long been a belief in the inherent irrationality of women with respect to purchases (Marchand, 1985). Early advertisers openly discussed the idea of an overly emotional female buying public who could be taught the value of buying as an appropriate response to trying life events and negative feelings (Marchand, 1985). For most of the last century it was a cultural truism that women should and do use shopping and buying as a perfectly acceptable form of emotional succor. If a woman bought a lot, she was just foolish and caught up in buying, but didn't have a serious problem. When it became clear she was buying too much, then she had poor self-control and needed to exert greater discipline. It was (and often still is) hard to accept that she could be suffering from a true psychiatric disorder.

The popularization of compulsive buying also came in the form of women's popular discourse: *The Oprah Winfrey Show, Glamour Magazine, Self Magazine*, the section of the newspaper devoted to advice columns and household information, etc. The message was clear that any problem associated with shopping was a woman's problem. It had the added strike against it by cultural elites of being popularized through the mass media: *if it was discussed on Oprah, how serious could it be?* Both sexism (and elitism) were operating to foster an early ambivalence about this topic.

Independent of gender is the problem that this is a disorder regarding things and money. Western and particularly American views of the appropriate role of things in people's lives is hardly resolved. Indeed, it is a topic of considerable renown. One unfortunate result of this is that compulsive buying is often treated as symptomatic of an overly materialistic society. This is clearly seen in the pop-press notion of *affluenza*, a fictitious disease of wealthy commercial cultures. We are led to believe that compulsive buying could only occur in an overly materialistic society. We do not subscribe to this point of view. The actual research on compulsive buying indicates it has very little to do with materialism and, therefore, is not simply a symptom of a materialistic culture. We have tried to distance our selves from a view that is a-historic, disconnected from anthropology and material culture, and transparently polemic. Compulsive buying is not simply a symptom of an overly materialistic culture.

We ourselves began our investigation of compulsive buying with the belief that compulsive buying might have resulted from viewing TV programs and other media portrayals that were populated by people with lots of nice possessions and no financial concerns. We thought that this view of the mediated world may have lead compulsive buyers to feel that they too deserved these things. However, after observing just one self-help group and having an initial discussion with them, we realized that compulsive buying was a very different phenomenon from what we originally conceived. These several years of work were also an object lesson in the value of lengthy engagement fieldwork.

When we directly asked compulsive buyers about the role of advertising and media in this problem we were consistently met with a blank stare and the question, "What does that have to do with this problem?" When asked to talk about an item they purchased and really liked, compulsive buyers would frequently be unable to think of anything or they would tell us about something that was given to them by someone else rather than something they had purchased. We rapidly learned from listening to our informants that compulsive buying is really about coping with aversive self-awareness and self-worth. It is about interpersonal and intrapersonal relations, not about object attachment. In fact, in our first large-scale study we found that general consumers scored higher on a measure of object attachment than did compulsive buyers (O'Guinn & Faber, 1989). It is because of these findings that we reject the idea that materialism causes compulsive buying.

The causal elements of compulsive buying, along with other impulse control disorders, are likely to be primarily physiological and psychological. Why people choose buying (as opposed to substances or other activities such as sexual behavior, gambling, or food), and how they think about them and further construct them is, however, socio-cultural. Nonetheless, we believe compulsive buying could exist in some form in many human societies not just wealthy ones. Research has found that compulsive buying is unrelated to income (O'Guinn & Faber, 1989; Sherhorn et al., 1990). People with money often spend it on large ticket items (e.g., cars, designer clothes, land) and may eventually encounter negative consequences from their buying. Those with little money buy at thrift shops, garage sales, or do whatever is necessary to gain money or incur large levels of debt. Thus, if buying is possible and people find it can temporarily relieve the emotional distress they otherwise feel, then compulsive buying can occur.

But what is the role of the object, the material good that is purchased? There are two different answers to this question. On the one hand, compulsive buyers do tend to buy specific types of items. Women frequently report buying clothes, shoes, and jewelry, while men typically buy clothes, car related items, and electronic goods. On the other hand, compulsive buyers frequently report that they never use their purchases, often leaving them in their original packaging or with the tags still on them (Faber et al., 1987; Scherhorn et al.,1990). It appears that the preference for buying specific types of products may be primarily the result of gender roles and places where buyers can best receive positive feedback from store personal and others.

WHY BUYING?

Our general belief is that there are a number of biological and psychological factors that may predispose someone to suffer from some type of impulse control disorder. These people may by matter of circumstance, and sociology, end up with a problem with substances, or any number of activities, including buying. Chance encounters with activities that provide a temporary relief from negative self-feelings will motivate a person prone to an impulse control disorder to repetitively engage in this behavior. Over time, this becomes their primary response to negative events and feelings.

Cultural norms direct people to different activities when they are depressed and can thereby alter the probabilities that one will develop a problem with a specific behavior or substance. Additionally, some activities are more socially sanctioned than others. If an individual finds that multiple activities can provide a temporary release for them, those activities that are socially viewed as beneficial, or at least benign, may be particularly likely to be selected and become problematic. Behaviors such as eating, drinking, exercise, work, and sex are all examples of behaviors that were once seen as socially approved activities and means of escape, but are now recognized to have significant abuse potential for people with impulse control problems. The same is true for buying.

Since its inception, modern consumer societies (Marchand, 1985) have relied on women to do a disproportional amount of shopping and buying. Most advertising has been directed at women, and still is. Buying is often not only seen as okay, but even encouraged as a social activity and a form of escape. Women use shopping as a mode for care-giving, parenting, and social bonding. The act of buying for self and others is intertwined with the enactment of all sorts of women's social roles and functions. Even more significantly, there is a long-standing tradition of linking consumption with emotional therapy for women (Friedan, 1963; Marchand, 1985). Put simply, society says "when feeling bad, buy something." So, it is not surprising that women predisposed to impulse control disorders are particularly likely to develop problems with this behavior. As previously noted, the consequences of compulsive buying for women are not trivial.

CONCLUDING THOUGHTS

When we first informally discussed the idea of examining compulsive buying back in the mid-1980s, we thought that the topic was both interesting and important. However, we were concerned about how it might be received by the field of consumer research. Indeed, the first time we presented our work at an *Association for Consumer Research* conference, one of the first questions we received was from a very well known and esteemed colleague who said, "You're studying crazy people. Why should we care about crazy people?" While we would reject the idea that compulsive buyers are "crazy," this question did reflect the concern we feared regarding how compulsive buying would fit into the larger realm of consumer behavior. As it turned out, compulsive buying became one of a small set of phenomena that opened up what has since become known as the "dark side" of consumer behavior. This area has grown since then, and we are honored to be associated with some outstanding research that has been done in this subfield. We certainly encountered those (and still do from time to time) who believe that consumer research should be reserved for those studies that promote a narrow view of the marketer's agenda. Of course, we dissent.

While our knowledge of the psychological and physiological factors that influence compulsive buying has been increasing, our understanding of the socio-cultural factors has been progressing at a slower rate. Part of the reason for this may be that academics have viewed the sociological factors as they imagined them to be, not as they really are. An understanding of compulsive buying suggests that there are important sociological questions to examine. For example, we might want to look at the location of rewards and compliments in society. These may now be less frequently found in the workplace and more frequently in the mall. Changing social dynamics have had an impact on feelings of loneliness, alienation and depression. All of these factors may be important in the development of impulse control disorders. Additionally, changes in gender roles and norms are likely to play an important role in altering both the prevalence of specific impulse control disorders and the proportion of men and women experiencing and reporting each of these. In recent years, gambling has become more of a problem for women while males have been experiencing more eating disorders. As social expectations and values regarding buying change we should expect similar changes in the proportion of men and women who become compulsive buyers.

As we look back, we are amazed at the long way compulsive buying has come since our initial investigation: from a disorder that was getting a few brief mentions in the trade press as a curiosity to a legitimate topic of research in medical schools. When we first started our research, compulsive buyers would tell us in interviews that they wished they were an alcoholic or a drug addict, because at least those diseases had names and people did not think they were crazy when they said they couldn't stop buying. When these (mostly women) people went to psychologists for treatment they were told, *"oh that isn't your real problem."* Their concern was often trivialized. Now, efforts are underway to try to get compulsive buying listed in the *DSM*. Treatment programs are being developed using cognitive behavioral therapy as well as drug therapy. Even some courts have begun to recognize this may be a contributing factor in some criminal actions. The cultural view of compulsive buying has begun to change and we are pleased to have played a role in fostering this.

REFERENCES

Baumeister, R. F. (1991). The self against itself: Escape or defeat? In R. C. Curtis (Ed.), *The rational self: Theoretical convergence in psychoanalysis and social psychology* (pp. 238–256). New York: Guilford.

Beatty, S. E., & Ferrell, M. E. (1998). Impulse buying: Modeling its precursors. *Journal of Retailing, 74*, 169–191.

Black, D. W. (2001). Compulsive buying disorder: Definition, assessment, epidemiology and clinical management. *CNS Drugs, 15*, 17-27.

Black, D. W. (1996). Compulsive buying: A review. *Journal of Clinical Psychiatry, 57*(Suppl. 8), 50–54.

Black, D. W., Monahan, P., & Gabel, J. (1997). Fluvoxamine in the treatment of compulsive buying. *Journal of Clinical Psychiatry, 58*(4), 159–163.

Bleuler, E. (1924). *Textbook of psychiatry*. New York: McMillan.

Bordo, S. (1993). Hunger as ideology. In J. B. Schor & D. B. Holt (Eds.), *The consumer society reader* (pp. 99–114). New York: New Press..

Bryant, J., & Zillmann, D. (1984). Using television to alleviate boredom and stress: Selective exposure as a function of induced excitational states. *Journal of Broadcasting, 28*, 1–20.

Christenson, G. A., Faber, R. J., de Zwaan, M., Raymond, N., Specker, S., Eckert, M.D., et al. (1994). Compulsive buying: Descriptive characteristics and psychiatric comorbidity. *Journal of Clinical Psychiatry, 55*, 5–11.

Collins, A. C. (1985). Inheriting addictions: A genetic perspective with emphasis on alcohol and nicotine. In H. B. Milkman & H. J. Shaffer (Eds.), *The addictions: Multidisciplinary perspectives and treatment* (pp. 3–10). Lexington, MA: D.C. Heath.

DeSarbo, W. S., & Edwards, E. A. (1996). Typologies of compulsive buying behavior: A constrained clusterwise regression approach. *Journal of Consumer Psychology, 5*(3), 231-262.

Dittmar, H., Beattie, J., & Friese, S. (1996). Objects, decision considerations and self-image in men's and women's impulse purchases. *Acta Psychologica, 93*, 187–206.

Donovan, D. M. (1988). Assessment of addictive behaviors: Implications of an emerging biopsychosocial model. In D. M. Donovan & G. A. Marlatt (Eds.), *Assessment of addiction behaviors* (pp. 3–48). New York: Guilford.

Edwards, E. A. (1992). The measurement and modeling of compulsive buying behavior. *Dissertation Abstracts International, 53*(11-A).

Elliott, R. (1994). Addictive consumption: Function and fragmentation in postmodernity. *Journal of Consumer Policy, 17,* 159–179.

Faber, R. J. (2003). Self-control and compulsive buying. In T. Kasser & A. Kanner (Eds.), *Psychology and the Culture of Consumption* (pp. 169–187). Washington, DC: American Psychological Association.

Faber, R. J. (2000). A systematic investigation into compulsive buying. In A. L. Benson (Ed.), *I shop, therefore I am: Compulsive buying and the search for self* (pp. 27–54). Northvale, NJ: Aronson Press.

Faber, R. J. (1992). Money changes everything: Compulsive buying from a biopsychosocial perspective. *American Behavioral Scientist, 35,* 809–819.

Faber, R. J., & Christenson, G. A. (1996). In the mood to buy: Differences in the mood states experienced by compulsive buyers and other consumers. *Psychology and Marketing, 13,* 803–820.

Faber, R. J., Christenson, G. A., de Zwaan, M., & Mitchell, J. E. (1995). Two forms of compulsive consumption: Comorbidity of compulsive buying and binge eating. *Journal of Consumer Research, 22,* 296–304.

Faber, R. J., & O'Guinn, T. C. (1988). Dysfunctional consumer socialization: A search for the roots of compulsive buying. In P. Vanden Abeele (Ed.), *Psychology in micro and macro economics* (Vol. 1, pp. 1–15). Leuven, Belgium: International Association for Research in Economic Psychology.

Faber, R. J., & O'Guinn, T. C. (1992). A clinical screener for compulsive buying. *Journal of Consumer Research, 19,* 459–469.

Faber, R. J., O'Guinn, T. C., & Krych, R. (1987). Compulsive consumption. In M. Wallendorf and P. Anderson (Ed.), *Advances in consumer research* (pp. 132–135). Provo, UT: Association for Consumer Research.

Faber, R. J., Peterson, C., & Christenson, G. A. (1994). Characteristics of compulsive buyers: An examination of stress reaction and absorption. Paper presented at the American Psychological Association Conference, Los Angeles.

Faber, R. J., Ristvedt, S. L., Mackenzie, T. B., & Christenson, G. A. (1996). Cues that trigger compulsive buying. Paper presented at the Association for Consumer Research Conference, Tucsun, AZ.

Faber, R. J., & Vohs, K. (2004). To buy or not to buy?: Self-control and self-regulatory failure in purchase behavior. In R. Baumeister & K. Vohs (Eds.), *The handbook of self-regulation* (pp. 509–524). New York: Guilford.

Friedan, B. (1963). The sexual sell. In *The feminine mystique* (pp. 206–232). New York: Norton.

Friese, S., & Koenig, H. (1993). Shopping for trouble. *Advancing the consumer interest, 5*(1), 24–29.

Glatt, M. M., & Cook, C. C. (1987). Pathological spending as a form of psychological dependence. *British Journal of Addiction, 82,* 1257–1258.

Goldman, R. (2000). Compulsive buying as an addiction. In A. L. Benson (Ed.), *I shop, therefore I am: Compulsive buying and the search for self* (pp. 245–267). Northvale, NJ: Aronson Press.

Goldsmith, T., & McElroy, S. (2000). Compulsive buying: Associated disorders and Drug Treatment. In A. L. Benson (Ed.), *I shop, therefore I am: Compulsive buying and the search for self* (pp. 217–242). Northvale, NJ: Aronson Press.

Goodwin, D. W. (1984). Studies of familial alcoholism: A review. *Journal of Clinical Psychiatry, 45,* 14–17.

Heatherton, T. F., & Vohs, K. D. (1998). Why is it so difficult to inhibit behavior? *Psychological Inquiry, 9,* 212–215.

Holmstrom, D. (1985). Controlling compulsive spending. *American Way, 18*(Oct. 15), 67–69.

Isen, A. M., Clark, M., & Schwartz, M. F. (1976). Duration of the effect of good mood on helping: Footprints on the sands of time. *Journal of Personality and Social Psychology, 34*(3), 385–393.

Jacobs, D. F. (1989). A general theory of addictions: Rationale for and evidence supporting a new approach for understanding and treating addictive behaviors. In H. J. Shaffer, S. A. Stein, B. Gambino, & T. N. Cummings (Eds.), *Compulsive gambling: Theory, research and practice* (pp. 35–64). Lexington, MA: D.C. Heath.

Koran, L. M., Bullock, K. D., Hartston H. J., Elliott, M. A., & D'Andrea, V. (2002) Citalopram treatment of compulsive shopping: An open-label study. *Journal of Clinical Psychiatry, 63,* 704–708.

Koran, L. M., Chuong, H. W., Bullock, K. D., & Smith, S. C.(2003) Citalopram for compulsive shopping disorder: An open-label study followed by double-blind discontinuation. *Journal of Clinical Psychiatry, 64,* 793–798.

Korrin, L. M., Faber, R. J., Aboujaoude, E., Large, M. D., & Serpe, R. T. (2006). Estimated prevalence of compulsive buying in the United States. *American Journal of Psychiatry, 163*(10), 1806–1812.

Kraeplin, E. (1915) *Psychiatrie* (8th ed.). Leipzig: Verlag Von Johann Ambrosius Barth.

Krueger, D. (2000). The use of money as an action symptom. In A. L. Benson (Ed.), *I shop, therefore I am: Compulsive buying and the search for self.* Northvale, NJ: Aronson Press.

Krueger, D. (1988). On compulsive shopping and spending: A psychodynamic inquiry. *American Journal of Psychotherapy, 42*, 574–585.

Lasch, C. (1991). *The true and only heaven: Progress and its critics.* New York: Norton.

Lears, T. J. (1983). From salvation to self-realization: Advertising and the therapeutic roots of the consumer culture, 1880–1930. In T. J. Jackson Lears & R. Wightman (Eds.), *The culture of consumption: Critical essays in American history: 1880–1980* (pp. 1–38). New York: Pantheon.

Lejoyeux, M., Hourtane, M., & Ades, J. (1995). Compulsive buying and depression (letter). *Journal of Clinical Psychiatry, 56*(1), 38.

Lejoyeux, M., Tassain, V., Solomon, J,. & Ades, J. (1997). Study of compulsive buying in depressed patients. *Journal of Clinical Psychiatry, 58*(4), 169–173.

Marchand, R. (1985). *Advertising: The American dream*, Berkeley: University of California Press.

McElroy, S. L., Keck Jr., P. E., Pope Jr., H. J., Smith, J. M., & Strakowski, S. M. (1994). Compulsive buying: A report of 20 cases. *Journal of Clinical Psychiatry, 55*(June), 242–248.

McElroy, S. L., Satlin, A., Pope, H .G., Keck, P. E., & Hudson, J. I. (1991). Treatment of compulsive shopping with antidepressants: A report of three cases. *Annals of Clinical Psychiatry, 3*, 199–204.

Mowen, J. C., & Spears, N. (1999). Understanding compulsive buying among college students: A hierarchical approach. *Journal of Consumer Psychology, 8*(4), 407–430.

Mundis, J. (1986). A way back from deep debt. *New York Times Magazine*, Jan. 5, 22–26.

O'Guinn, T. C., & Faber, R. J. (1989). Compulsive buying: A phenomenological exploration. *Journal of Consumer Research, 16*, 147–157.

Rook, D. (1987). The buying impulse. *Journal of Consumer Research, 14*, 189–199.

Rook, D. W., & Gardner, M. P. (1993). In the mood: Impulse buying's attractive antecedents. *Research in Consumer Behavior, 6*, 1–28.

Scherhorn, G., Reisch, L. A., & Raab, G. (1990). Addictive buying in West Germany: An empirical study. *Journal of Consumer Policy, 13*, 355–387.

Schlosser, S., Black, D. W., Repertinger, S., & Freet, D. (1994). Compulsive buying: Demography, phenomenology, and comorbidity in 46 subjects. *General Hospital Psychiatry, 16*, 205–212.

Schulman, B. J. (2001c). Conclusion: End of the seventies, end of the century. In *The Seventies: The Great Shift in American Culture, Society, and Politics* (pp. 253–257). Cambridge, MA: Da Capo.

Schudson, M. (1984). *Advertising, the uneasy persuasion: Its dubious impact on American society.* New York: Basic Books.

Swan-Kremeir, L. A., Mitchell, J. E., & Faber, R. J. (2005). Compulsive buying: A disorder of compulsivity or impulsivity. In J. S. Abramowitz & A. D. Houts (Eds.), *Concepts and controversies in obsessive-compulsive disorder* (pp. 185–190). New York: Springer-Verlag.

United States Surgeon General (2005). Mental health: A report of the Surgeon General: Epidemiology of mental illness. Retrieved from http://www.surgeongeneral.gov/library/mentalhealth/chapter2/sec2_1.html#table2_6

Yurchisin, J., & Johnson, K. K. P. (2004). Compulsive buying behavior and its relationship to perceived social status associated with buying, materialism, self-esteem, and apparel-product involvement. *Family and Consumer Science Research Journal, 32*(3), 291–314.

42

Summing Up the State of Coping Research
Prospects and Prescriptions for Consumer Research

ADAM DUHACHEK

Indiana University

The contemporary consumer faces a multitude of stressors. Some stressors originate from attempts to purchase products and services, some originate from attempts to process marketing messaging, and some consumers cope with life's stresses by consuming. Consider the consumer reacting to poor quality service, failing or underperforming products, pushy salespeople or annoying sales calls. It seems that all too often consumption and the need to cope go hand in hand. Phenomenologically speaking, most anyone can point to a particular experience they have faced and recount how they "coped" with stress and negative emotion in their lives and, for many of us, these instances relate to consumption-based events. Despite (or perhaps because of) the seemingly everyday presence of coping phenomena, consumer researchers have only recently begun to investigate the processes at work when consumers confront stresses.

Recently, the domain of coping scholarship has experienced a significant growth in interest. Originally rooted in the early psychoanalytical work of Freud and others (Freud, 1946; Selye, 1956), coping research today exists as a diverse body of literature spanning several related, yet distinct disciplines, including social, clinical, counseling and developmental psychology, sociology and anthropology. In addition to the abundance of research entering the literature in recent years (cf. Aldwin, 1999; Folkman & Moskowitz, 2004; Schwarzer & Schwarzer, 1996, for reviews), consumer research has begun to build on these findings expanding coping theoretical frameworks to include new variables and address pertinent consumer behavior phenomena (cf. Luce, Bettman, & Payne, 2001). Despite these noteworthy developments in recent years, many important implications of coping research have remained relatively unexplored. The goal of this chapter is to profile the existing body of coping research and to highlight several areas of consumer research that would benefit from a more rigorous examination of coping theory. The chapter focuses on several streams of nascent consumer coping research and makes prescriptive recommendations for progress within these areas.

The remainder of this chapter proceeds as follows: First, a brief history of coping scholarship and the predominant theoretical model of coping are reviewed. Next, the broad coping literature is summarized, parsing this diverse body of research into two distinct streams closely applicable to consumer behavioral research. Within each stream, connections are drawn to existing consumer research and additional opportunities for research are developed. The chapter concludes by outlining some basic prescriptions for future research related to these areas.

A HISTORICAL CONTEXT FOR MODERN COPING SCHOLARSHIP

One area from which coping scholarship originated exists in the influential writings of early psychoanalysts, perhaps none more important than Freud (1894). Freud conceived a broader process of adaptation and motivation, subsuming latent subconscious phenomena later termed defense mechanisms (Freud, 1946). Although many of these subconscious processes resemble modern day "coping strategies", these early writings did not consider these processes to be volitionally enacted, nor did Freud postulate an emotional-cognitive appraisal network—the keystone of contemporary coping theories. However, despite these rather rudimentary beginnings, the psychoanalytic approach has exerted significant influence on the development of coping scholarship (Vaillant, 1977).

A different classical perspective on coping originated from a humanistic psychological perspective, most cogently expressed by Maslow (1987). Maslow distinguished between two broad classes of human behavior—coping and expressive. Coping behaviors encompass all purposive, motivated behaviors enacted in response to external environmental and cultural variables, whereas expressive behaviors are unmotivated, noninstrumental, and enacted to reflect internal states. According to Maslow, the same behavior can be viewed as either coping or expressive depending upon the motivations of the individual. For instance, a consumer could shop for new clothes to fulfill some need state, such as to look nice at work or to impress others. Alternatively, the same consumer's shopping could be classified as expressive if they found such experiences intrinsically rewarding.

Maslow's definition of coping actually shares many conceptual similarities with the modern day coping theories to be reviewed shortly. Like the modern day transactional model (Lazarus & Folkman, 1984), Maslow's view of coping behaviors holds that such behaviors characteristically emerge in order to change need states and are effortful, conscious and learned. He characterized coping behaviors as attempts to change the world; automated responses enacted by individuals in order to control their environment. In contrast, he believed that expressive behaviors revealed something deeper about the psychology of the individual expressing them. For Maslow, expressive behaviors allow for the detection of primarily psychological phenomena, whereas coping behaviors incorporate worldly phenomena. He believed that expressive behaviors more closely revealed the nature of an individual's character and psychology (Maslow, 1987). Maslow desired more theory and research into expressive behaviors, although his writings on coping have been quite influential.

A second classic approach that has greatly influenced modern day coping research stemmed from clinical psychological work on adaptation. According to this view, adaptive behavior in response to environmental stress was observable among all living organisms (Selye, 1956). This definition of stress was quite broad and encompassed all environmental changes affecting the organism. These adaptive processes were characterized by promoting two basic stress orientations: one directed at impelling the organism toward a perceived cause of stress (a vigilance or approach orientation) and an aversive orientation impelling the organism away from a perceived source of stress. Remnants of this classic motivational distinction still exist within modern coping theories, and more will be said of this distinction subsequently.

THE TRANSACTIONAL MODEL OF APPRAISAL AND COPING

First, a brief introduction of the predominant theoretical view of the coping process found in the literature is discussed. Among the most widely cited coping theories, the influential model developed by Richard Lazarus and Susan Folkman has contributed greatly to coping's conceptual and theoretical development. In fact, a review of the coping literature determined that the coping inventory developed by Lazarus and Folkman based on their conceptual model is the most frequently used empirical coping measure (Schwarzer & Schwarzer, 1996). Their conception of coping emphasizes the conscious set of adaptive strategies individuals use to overcome stress, and they define coping as the set of constantly changing cognitive and behavioral efforts to manage specific external and/ or internal demands that are appraised as taxing with the goal of reducing stress (Lazarus & Folkman, 1984, p. 141). According to this perspective, coping is a highly diverse activity encompassing a multitude of potential adaptive phenomena. Another key tenet of this view of coping relates to the conceptualization of coping as a process. The process-based view of coping is noteworthy because it distinguishes coping from related concepts, such as personality. They coined the term *transactional model* to represent their belief that coping processes reflect an interaction between personality and situational influences. Also apparent from the definition is the fact that coping is distinguished from its consequences by referring to coping processes as the efforts to reduce stress and negative emotion—the key consequences of coping behaviors.

Using this basic construct definition, Lazarus and Folkman developed an appraisal-based model postulating both situational (state) and dispositional (trait) influences. Lazarus and Folkman's transactional model (see Figure 42.1) bears strong similarity to the set of cognitive theories of emotion. The transactional model, like cognitive-emotional models, hinges on the core notion of cognitive appraisal (Roseman, Antoniou, & Jose, 1996; Roseman, Spindel, & Jose, 1990; Smith & Ellsworth, 1985). According to their model, an individual's decision to engage in one or more specific ways of coping is driven by a set of cognitive appraisals (Lazarus & Folkman, 1984).

As shown in Figure 42.1, these appraisals influence coping both directly and indirectly, through their effects on stress-related emotions (Chang, 1998). The *primary appraisal* involves key assessments of whether a perceived stimulus has motivational implications or "goal relevance" for an individual (e.g., "Does this situation affect me?"). Positive and negative implications are differentiated in an assessment of "goal congruence" (e.g., "Is this situation helpful or harmful?"). Primary appraisals give rise to threat and challenge appraisals, respectively. When a focal stressor is perceived negatively, a threat appraisal is generated. Threat appraisals are characterized by the onset of fear, worry and other anxiety-related emotions (Skinner & Brewer, 2002). When a focal stressor

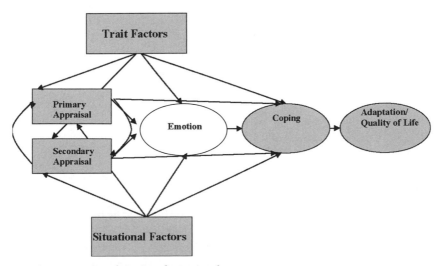

Figure 42.1   A transactional coping framework.

is perceived positively, a challenge appraisal is generated (Skinner & Brewer, 2002). Challenge appraisals are characterized by hopefulness, eagerness and confidence in one's ability to cope with an impending stressor. Whether a primary appraisal results in perceptions of threat or challenge fundamentally impacts the nature of secondary appraisal.

Secondary appraisals are undertaken to assess one's potential behavioral response to an observed stimulus. This set of appraisals includes blame attributions (self vs. other), assessments of one's ability to cope with a stimulus (coping potential), and future expectations regarding the stimulus. Lazarus and Folkman stress the extemporaneous, reflexive nature of this process, whereby multiple appraisals (both primary and secondary) may occur nearly simultaneously and may often be codetermined by changing environmental conditions. That is to say, primary appraisals need not temporally precede secondary appraisals in practice, but the distinction between the two remains an important one in conceptualizing the cognitive processes preceding emotion and coping.

In this model, the appraisal process (both primary and secondary appraisals) determines an individual's emotional response to potentially stressing stimuli, a key premise of cognitive theories of emotion (cf. Johnson & Stewart, 2005; Frijda, 1987). According to these theories, appraisal processes give rise to the full range of human emotions, by implicating a unique action tendency (i.e., coping strategy). Lazarus formalized this linkage between stress appraisal and emotion, arguing that the two phenomena were inextricably linked (Lazarus, 1991). A growing body of research has begun to investigate these linkages, finding support for reliable associations between appraisal and emotion (Ellsworth & Smith, 1988; Folkman & Lazarus, 1988). The final stage in the transactional view links emotions and coping strategies. The determination to employ a particular coping strategy is driven by an interaction of cognitive appraisal and emotional perceptions (Duhachek, 2005). Research has begun to establish these links, offering support for the existence of reliable associations between emotions and coping (Yi & Baumgartner, 2004).

The structural properties of the coping process have been represented multiple ways in the coping literature. Researchers have conceptualized coping using several distinct competing conceptual frames (more will be said of this subsequently). In its simplest, most widely accepted form, the conceptualization of coping strategies contrasts problem-focused and emotion-focused means of coping. Problem-focused coping subsumes all attempts to fundamentally change the nature of a stressor directly. For instance, a consumer may cope with the stress imposed by a pushy or rude sales clerk by reporting such behavior to a store manager. Subsumed under problem-focused coping are a variety of related, active attempts to cope. Engaging in rational thinking, enlisting the instrumental support of social resources and information seeking are all dimensions of problem-focused coping. Conversely, emotion-focused strategies do not involve an attempt to alter the source of stress directly, but rather, they are initiated to regulate one's emotional response to a stress event. For example, the same consumer may choose to vent their emotions aloud in order to "let off steam" or "cool down." Several different emotion-focused coping strategies exist, including seeking emotional support, relying on positive thinking, and engaging in avoidance and distancing behaviors. However, the structure of coping issue is still unsettled and numerous views exist in the literature.

Transactional Influences on the Appraisal Process

Another key premise of the transactional model relates to the set of factors that influence the conceptual system depicted in Figure 42.1. Personality researchers working in the coping area have identified a range of trait factors that relate to coping dispositions. Many of these associations have proven quite robust, such as the relationship between neuroticism and the use of maladaptive coping strategies. Such findings have caused some to advocate a personality-driven model of coping. According to the transactional approach, this view oversimplifies the coping process. The transactional model acknowledges links between traits and coping and argues for a more systematic trait influence throughout the coping process (Bolger, 1990; Bolger & Zuckerman, 1995). In this view, trait influences impact primary and secondary appraisal, emotions and coping simultaneously, and higher order interactions (e.g., trait x appraisal x emotion factors) are possible.

In addition to hypothesizing a more integrative role for personality factors, the transactional model also accounts for situational variability that impacts coping. These state influences include a variety of contextual factors that impact the appraisal, emotion and coping process. For example, the level of ambiguity has been shown to be one such factor. Research has identified multiple forms of ambiguity. One type is defined as the degree to which the outcome of a stress situation is apparent. Ambiguity of this type has been to impact the nature of consumers' cognitive appraisals, the emotions experienced and the strategies undertaken for coping. Another form of ambiguity relates to the uncertainty of meaning of environmental stimuli (i.e., "What is the source of stress?"). This situational uncertainty can contribute to stress and be interpreted in multiple ways by consumers, leading to differential coping responses. Another key ambiguity dimension is temporally based. Temporal uncertainty, an example of which is experienced by the consumer who knows that their old car is unreliable and likely to break down soon although the timing of that event is uncertain, presents unique challenges in coping. In these instances, consumers must contend with both the eventuality that coping resources will be needed to address their future transportation issues as well as heightened anxiety in knowing that these resources could be required at any moment. This temporal uncertainty usually requires heightened vigilance and usually demands greater resources.

A general finding from the ambiguity literature on coping is that ambiguity leads to more stressful conditions and therefore heightened (more effortful) coping responses. One key finding from the ambiguity and coping literature is that under high ambiguity conditions, individuals' coping processes are determined to a greater extent by personality than under low ambiguity conditions. In such instances, trait factors shape one's interpretation of ambiguous stimuli due to the lack of clarity over exact meanings.

Several other situational factors have been identified in the literature. One such factor is the level of personal commitment or involvement related to the domain in which the stressor falls. Research has shown that these domain distinctions directly impact the appraisal process (Kobasa, 1982). Another factor identified as exerting significant influence on appraisal is temporally-based. A common finding is that the appraisal process is fundamentally changed as stressors draw near. Early findings note that the intensity and diversity of coping strategies increase as anticipated stressors draw nearer in time. Each of these situational factors exerts influence on the appraisal process, and, as is true of the personality factors influencing coping, higher order interactions between situation factor x appraisal x emotion factors are possible.

The transactional model accounts for all of these effects by theorizing consumers' coping reactions are influenced by the transaction between their inherent personality influences and the relevant situational factors exigent in the stress context. Only by understanding and modeling both trait and state influences can a full understanding of coping effects be reached. Despite the predominance of the transactional model as a conceptual framework, coping research in practice has often focused on either state or trait effects in isolation.

Although the transactional model reviewed has had profound impact in shaping the thinking of scholars by providing a useful theoretical lens for viewing coping phenomena, many empirical questions related to this model remain. These gaps and opportunities for future research will be examined as they relate to a few focal streams of research within the larger coping literature. The

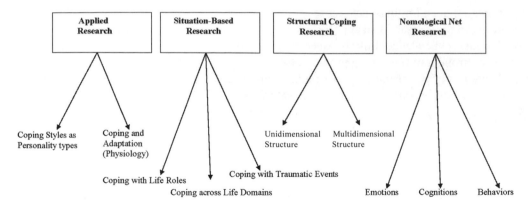

Figure 42.2 A summary of the modern era of coping scholarship.

emphasis on a subset of the voluminous coping literature is necessarily reductive. Several comprehensive reviews of this literature have been published in recent years, (cf. Skinner, Edge, Altman, & Sherwood, 2003; Schwarzer & Schwarzer, 1996) and the goal of the current chapter is more pointed, focusing specifically on the intersection between coping and consumer research.

Figure 42.2 classifies the sizeable coping literature into four key areas of emphasis. This chapter hones in on two of these areas most promising for consumer research, and the remainder of the chapter addresses opportunities for such research within the transactional model framework. The two key areas reviewed are: (1) applied coping research focusing on coping's relationship to long-term health and adaptation, and (2) situation-based approaches to coping.

PERSONALITY, COPING, AND HEALTH PSYCHOLOGY

One central area within coping research focuses on coping's role as a mediator of stress and health. Research investigating the role of coping in determining clinical health outcomes and many important advances have stemmed from this body of research in recent years. One important objective of this stream of research has involved identifying individual difference factors that relate to coping styles, as well as coping consequences, such as stress levels, subjective well-being, and life satisfaction. Research in this area has centered on distinguishing coping strategies linked to clinical diagnoses for disorders from coping strategies that are correlated with prosocial behaviors and those that promote healthy psychological functioning and adaptation (Thoits, 1995). Through this research, scholars have uncovered consistent links between specific personality types, choice of adaptive mechanisms and various long-term individual health outcomes. This section provides a brief overview of this stream of research and draws connections to the consumer health literature, revealing several opportunities for future research within this area.

Personality and clinical coping researchers have long investigated associations between personality, stress and coping processes and health outcomes. Because these researchers view the choices individuals make in coping as being guided by inflexible "styles" as opposed to "states," personality-based coping studies frequently attempt to correlate broad measures of psychological health with specific coping styles, assuming a relatively high level of consistency across stressful episodes and over time.

This literature has indeed found support for the hypothesized link between personality, coping and health, linking specific personality styles, choice of specific coping responses and clinical health outcomes (Florian, Mikulincer, & Taubman, 1995). These researchers, many of whom aver a personality-driven approach to coping, emphasize the significant empirical correlation between many coping behaviors and stable personality traits (cf. McCrae & Costa, 1986). In this view, coping strategies resemble personality types and individuals tend to exhibit highly invariant coping choices over time. Coping in any particular instance, is a process largely determined by the psychological orientation of the individual. Two predominant personality dispositions this research has examined include anxiety-related and depressive-related personality traits.

Neuroticism, Anxiety-Related Disorders, and Coping

The global trait of neuroticism has received significant attention in the personality and coping literature. Neuroticism, defined by propensities to experience negative affect and exhibit less affective stability, has been shown to exert significant influence on the stress and coping process (Brown & Moskowitz, 1997; Schimmack, Olshi, Furr, & Funder, 2004). Individuals high in neuroticism are more likely to appraise transient events as stressful, therefore resulting in more exposures to stress and the initiation of more coping behaviors (Bolger & Zuckerman, 1995). In another study, individuals high and low in neuroticism were contrasted with respect to the type and severity of stressors they report, as well as the coping behaviors toward which they gravitate. The efficacy of selected coping behaviors in reducing subsequent distress has also been shown to vary as a function of neuroticism, with problem-focused coping behaviors being less effective ameliorators of stress for high neuroticism individuals (Gunthert, Cohen, & Armeli, 1999). Individuals high in neuroticism have also been shown to rely more heavily on less adaptive emotion-focused coping behaviors, such as hostility and venting (Gunthert et al., 1999).

Another key variable examined by personality coping researchers is trait-based anxiety. Trait anxiety and other anxiety-related personality variables have also been investigated extensively by coping researchers. These effects are among the most widely reported in the literature, with consistent support for the negative influence of these factors on adaptation. Trait anxiety has been shown to result in more threat appraisals as well as more negative emotional responses (Gunthert et al., 1999; Raffety, Smith, & Ptacek, 1997). Thus, it has been suggested that trait anxiety and neuroticism may deleteriously affect long-term health.

These studies seem to support the notion that not only do anxious and neurotic dispositions exert a direct effect on long-term health consequences, but that this effect is mediated by coping. A consistent finding is that trait anxiety reduces reliance on active or problem-focused coping behaviors and increase reliance on avoidant or disengagement coping behaviors. For some stressors, anxiety has been linked to use of social support seeking strategies.

As is the case for individuals high in neuroticism, individuals high in trait anxiety have reported higher levels of chronic stress and are more likely to report stress in multiple life domains (e.g., financial, interpersonal, etc.). The effects of high levels of chronic stress on these individuals are not yet widely understood, but as more research is conducted, a clearer picture of the pervasive negative impact of stress on psychological and physical health is forming. For instance, high anxiety individuals are more likely to suffer acute cardiac failure (Penley, Tomaka, & Wiebe, 2002) and other physiological conditions. Therefore, these effects extend beyond purely psychological consequences and appear to have serious implications for long-term health and subjective well-being.

Depression and Coping

Another major personality trait frequently studied in this literature relates to personality variables associated with depression. One key finding from this area of study is that, similar to anxiety-related dispositions, the patterns of coping among depressed individuals do systematically differ.

For instance, depressed persons are less likely to rely on problem-focused coping strategies and are more likely to rely on emotional venting and avoidance strategies (Rohde Lewinsohn, Tilson, & Seeley, 1990). This research has also shown that coping by means of avoidant strategies are associated with more severe cases of depression, indicating the possible operation of negative feedback loops, where ineffective coping choices negatively impact well-being which in turn negatively impacts coping choices in subsequent coping episodes.

Unlike high anxiety individuals, depressive personalities are unlikely to reach out to others using social support coping. These findings are particularly meaningful because multiple studies have found that among depressed populations, the use of problem-focused and emotion suppressing coping behaviors promote healthful adaptation to stress and are associated with less severe forms of dysfunction stemming from stressful episodes (Billings & Moos, 1984). Thus, it appears that pessimistic and depressive personality traits not only reduce the ability to employ several key coping strategies, but that these deficiencies or personality-related biases result in severe detrimental health consequences. While the salutary benefits of problem-focused coping have also been observed in nondepressed populations, these effects are particularly pronounced among those that suffer from depression.

Subjective Well-Being and Positive Coping

The recent groundswell of research related to positive emotions and positive psychology has coincided with an interest among coping researchers in identifying factors positively associated with long-term psychological and physical health. Just as researchers have identified traits associated with maladaptive coping and negative health consequences, coping researchers have also identified traits associated with more positive adaptation, quality of life and subjective well-being. This stream of research seeks to identify personality characteristics that seem to inoculate or severely attenuate certain individuals from stressful experiences. Traits such as optimism (Florian, Mikulincer, & Taubman., 1995), hardiness (Florian et al., 1995), and mastery (Ben-Zur, 2002) have been found to greatly improve an individual's ability to counter stress. These traits appear to impact health by providing a high tolerance for stressful experiences and a strong sense of efficacy regarding one's chances to rebound from stress (even severely traumatic stress episodes). These traits also operate through the coping process by increasing reliance on problem-focused coping means. In addition to impacting health through appraisal and coping, these traits also impact emotions and appear to also impact subjective well-being. Empirical research has just begun to test these proposed linkages, although notable coping theorists have raised speculation that increased research attention is needed in this area (Folkman & Moskowitz, 2000). Particularly, the role of positive emotions in the coping process has not been sufficiently explored, with the bulk of research focusing on the role of negative emotions. Positive emotions, through their ability to promote flexible and creative thinking may effectively buffer consumers from negative outcomes (Isen, Daubman, & Nowicki, 1987).

To summarize the health and personality coping literature, several strong associations between personality, appraisal, coping and health outcomes have been identified (Bolger, 1990). Certain personality traits, such as neuroticism, trait anxiety and depression seem to exert a negative overall influence on both appraisal, choice of coping strategy and psychological health. Other traits, such as mastery, seem to facilitate adaptive outcomes in the face of stressful experiences. A summary of these effects are displayed in Table 42.1. Not only do preexisting personal factors influence coping and stress outcomes, but the choice of particular coping strategies does seem to significantly affect the consequences of stress on psychological well-being. For instance, those individuals who tend to employ problem-focused coping strategies seem to suffer from less intense manifestations of stress,

Table 42.1 A Summary of Key Trait Effects on Stress, Appraisal, Emotions, Coping, and Adjustment

Trait	Stress effect	Appraisal efect	Emotion effect	Coping effect	Adaptive effect on subjective well-being (SWB)
Neuroticism	Elevated stress	Increase negative primary appraisal Increase negative secondary appraisal	Increase threat	Increase avoidant Increase social support	Decrease SWB
Anxiety	Elevated stress	Increase negative primary appraisal Increase negative secondary appraisal	Increase threat	Increase social support Increase rumination	Decrease SWB
Depression	Elevated stress	Increase negative primary appraisal Increase negative secondary appraisal	Increase loss	Decrease problem-focused Increase venting Increase avoidance	Decrease SWB
Optimism	Diminished stress	Increase positive primary appraisal Increase positive secondary appraisal	Increase challenge	Increase problem-focused Increase social support	Increase SWB
Hardiness	Diminished stress	Increase positive primary appraisa Increase positive secondary appraisal	Increase challenge	Increase problem-focused	Increase SWB
Mastery	Diminished stress	Increase positive primary appraisal Increase positive secondary appraisal	Increase challenge	Increase problem-focused	Increase SWB

become stressed less frequently than those that cope by other means (Aldwin & Revenson, 1987). Conversely, emotion-focused coping behaviors are often found to be maladaptive (Raffety, Smith, & Ptacek, 1997). Additionally, social support coping can also promote healthful adaptation, although maladaptive social support also has been observed in certain contexts. These contingent findings suggest that many moderators influence the relationships between personality, coping, and health outcomes. Although extant research has produced significant progress on these dimensions, the contingent and sometimes discrepant findings suggest that the nuances of the nexus between personality, the use of specific coping strategies and adaptation is in need of further study.

Situational Influences on Health

Apart from the growing set of findings linking various personality variables to health outcomes, the coping literature has revealed insights into the effectiveness of particular strategies in promoting healthy adjustment and adaptation, controlling for trait effects. Research suggests that problem-focused coping behaviors are effective promoters of adaptive responses to stress. Social support coping strategies have also been implicated in dampening the psychological impact of traumatic stress episodes and buffering individuals from experiencing stress (Drach-Zahavy, 2004). Among individuals with a well-established support system and among those that frequently draw from this support system when faced with adversity, stress experiences are less severe and these individuals report being happier (Thoits, 1986).

Some important contingencies of the main effect findings of problem-focused and social support coping and adaptation have been noted. In low controllability stress conditions, reliance on problem-focused coping may increase short-term stress and negative emotion, whereas in high controllability conditions, problem-focused coping reduces stress and negative emotion (Park, Folkman, & Bostrom, 2001). Thus, the ability to directly manipulate the stress-inducing factors in the environment appears to moderate the impact of problem-focused coping on adaptation. Similarly, social support also has the potential to produce adverse reactions to stress, particularly when the support is unsolicited or stems from an obligatory (as opposed to discretionary) network source (Bolger & Eckenrode, 1991).

Consumer Health Research

Although consumer researchers have begun to integrate coping theory into a range of different research contexts, several extremely promising areas relate to the emerging consumer health literature (see chapter 39, this volume for additional discussion of these issues). The extant consumer health literature has focused on determining how consumers process health-related messaging, with an emphasis on the self-positivity bias—the tendency of consumers to underestimate their own individual susceptibility to illness (Lin, Lin, & Raghubir, 2003; Menon, Block, & Ramanathan, 2002). This research has revealed a fairly robust finding—a general tendency of consumers to believe they are much less at risk for illness or disease when compared to the average individual. Subsequent research in this area has shown that several factors moderate this process, including both contextual and personality variables.

One key contextual factor involves the perceived controllability of the undesired outcome. The self-positivity bias is stronger for more controllable (i.e., avoiding unsafe sex to prevent contracting HIV) as compared to less controllable (contracting cancer) events (Menon, Block, & Ramanathan, 2002). The assessment of perceived controllability presents obvious linkages to secondary appraisal within the transactional model of coping. No research has, as of yet, examined long-term coping and appraisal differences between optimists and pessimists.

One key personality distinction moderating the self-positivity bias on risk perceptions is between optimists and pessimists (Keller, Lipkus, & Rimer, 2003). Whereas optimists exude heightened self-positivity bias, as evidenced by a dispositional tendency to underestimate their own susceptibility to illness, pessimists display a self-negativity bias, evidenced by an overestimation of their own likelihood to contract an illness or experience a negative outcome.

Another main area of consumer health research has involved various tests of protection motivation theory (Keller, Lipkus, & Rimer, 2002; Luce & Kahn, 1999; Block & Keller, 1995). Protection motivation theory provides a framework accounting for consumer reactions to fear-based marketing appeals. The theory states that consumers make appraisals regarding their own vulnerability along four key dimensions. For example, a consumer viewing an advertisement warning about the dangers of smoking will experience threat and will first consider the perceived severity of the threatening event, in this case perhaps cancer or other debilitating or potentially fatal afflictions. Second, consumers will assess the likely probability such an outcome will occur based on their own perceived vulnerability. Next, consumers will assess the perceived efficacy of some recommended preventative behavior, in the smoking example, the likelihood that a smoking cessation program would effectively assist them in kicking their habit. Finally, consumers assess their own perceived self-efficacy in being able to undertake the recommended preventative behavior. Empirical consumer health research has examined vulnerability perceptions resulting from false positive medical test results, finding that false positives do increase consumers' vulnerability perceptions and that increases in perceived vulnerability impact future compliance (Luce & Kahn, 1999). Other research examining protection motivation theory has studied the effects of high versus low efficacy appraisals, depth of message processing and message framing (Keller, Lipkus, & Rimer, 2003). This research found that situations of low efficacy give rise to deeper levels of processing and more elaborated responses than high efficacy conditions. Other research has shown that message framing interacts with the type of emotional appeal used to produce differential processing of health-related messaging (Agrawal, Menon, & Aaker, 2007).

The recent interest in consumer emotions research has also shed light on the ways consumers cope. A great deal of research in the health area has shed light on how motivations to repair negative moods (e.g., coping) drives processing and impacts the persuasive power of health-related messaging (Keller, Lipkus, & Rimer, 2003; Block & Keller, 1995). This research has shown that consumers in a negative mood are motivated to cope with their mood by selectively processing information that will enhance their mood (i.e., positive, uplifting information), while those in a positive mood are motivated by mood-maintenance goals. Thus, for different reasons, consumers are more persuaded by gain frames to repair or maintain their affective state. Research is needed to move beyond mood-based valence effects to consider the potential of differential processing effects of discrete negative emotions that are prevalent in health-contexts, such as anger, anxiety, shame and guilt. Additionally, research is needed to consider additional framing effects beyond gain and loss, such as the way negative consequences of health actions are framed (Agrawal, Menon & Aaker, 2007; Duhachek & Agrawal, 2007).

Opportunities for Consumer Coping and Health Research

The consumer health literature has just begun to scratch the surface in examining the role of coping in health-related contexts (see Moorman, 2002, for a discussion). Within this literature, a few key theoretical frameworks have steered the course of research. Given the influential role of a few predominant theoretical frameworks in both the consumer health and general psychology literature, future research should attempt to conjoin these frameworks.

Specifically, future research should integrate the self-positivity framework with the transactional approach (Agrawal & Duhachek, 2007). Extant research has revealed several contextual factors that reduce the degree of positivity bias in consumer risk assessments, yet some of these factors may interact with coping. For instance, higher controllability perceptions may impact consumers' self-risk estimates, but the downstream effects on appraisal and coping have not been explored. By integrating self-positivity and the transactional framework, competing predictions emerge. Self-positivity would predict that the increased perception of risk would lead to increased compliance with health-related messaging, yet the transactional model suggests a different possibility. According to this view, increased risk perceptions are likely to impact threat appraisals which would predict increased use of avoidant coping. Research is needed to reconcile these opposing predictions and determine the long-term effects of risk perceptions on compliance and adaptation.

Such research should also seek to understand how personality impacts consumer health. Research should address how chronically depressed and anxious consumers process health-related messaging. It is likely that these consumers process health messaging uniquely, creating significant differences in how consumers cope with fear-based appeals, affecting appraisal and coping. Both laboratory and longitudinal studies are needed to provide a more complete picture of these processes, covering both immediate effects of personality on appraisal in addition to long-term differences.

Another personality-related research stream with high impact potential relates to revealing the effects of dispositional coping styles on the processing of health-related messaging. Research has shown that consumers differ in their relative propensities to engage in problem-focused versus emotion-focused coping. Such differences suggest significant differences in how these groups' process stress-related stimuli, evaluate their options for coping and adapt to stress. Individuals high in problem-focused coping could engage in more systematic processing and individuals high in emotion-focused coping could be influenced more by emotionally-based messaging (Williams & Drolet, 2005). Research is needed to examine the role of coping disposition on processing and evaluation and identify moderators of these relationships.

Specifically, the influential protection motivation framework should be examined in the context of the transactional model. Protection motivation research thus far has been primarily focused toward revealing effects on judgments and behavioral intentions, and has not yet explored long-term health consequences. The transactional model posits long-term adaptive consequences, yet unexplored in consumer research.

Also, the subjective well-being and quality of life literature should be examined more closely. Currently, the consumer health literature has not examined how consumer differences in message processing translate into meaningful differences in consumer quality of life. Some general frameworks for such questions have been raised, incorporating the ideas of psychoimmunology and consumer behavior (Moorman, 2002), yet great opportunity in this area remains.

SITUATION-BASED COPING RESEARCH

In contrast to personality-based coping researchers who focus on the relative stability of coping strategies as evidenced by an individual's propensity to gravitate toward similar coping strategies over time, situation-based ("state") coping researchers emphasize the low to moderate correlation between dispositional coping and reported coping behavior in any particular stressful episode. Empirically, the correlations between dispositional measures of coping and coping in the context of a single stress experience have been found to be quite low, suggesting the significance of situational factors. Rather than correlating personality types with long-term outcomes longitudinally, the method of inquiry for situational-based coping investigations differs both in focus and in method. For example, one longitudinal study comparing personality-based coping styles with situational coping reports at different temporal frames across the duration of a stress episode showed correlations ranging from .13 to .70 (Carver & Scheier, 1994). These results are congenial with the view that a consumer's propensity to cope in a particular manner is highly variable and depends upon a variety of situation-based factors. Some examples include the consumer's relevant coping resources available during the stress episode and situational appraisals and emotions among other factors.

In situation-based studies, respondents are often asked to recall a particularly stressful episode experienced within a recent, standard period of time (e.g., the past week or month) and answer questions relating to how they attempted to cope with this episode. The most frequently investigated stress context pertains to students coping with the stress associated with impending exams (Smith & Ellsworth, 1987). Rather than asking respondents questions to determine dispositional levels of relevant variables, such as anxiety or optimism, most situation-specific studies seek to learn how contextual variables impact appraisal and coping, such as momentary perceptions of control, ambiguity and emotional experience (Carver & Scheier, 1994; Carver, Scheier & Weintraub, 1989; Parkes, 1984; Tomaka et al., 1997). Many of the coping studies in consumer behavior to be reviewed subsequently are situationally oriented.

Situational perceptions of control directly impact stress, appraisal, emotions and coping (Folkman, 1984). Significant empirical evidence has demonstrated the effect of high controllability on stress and adaptation. These high controllability perceptions promote less threatening appraisal, less severe negative emotions, as well as the use of proactive coping strategies (Parkes, 1984). An additional situational determinant relating to coping is consumers' personal efficacy (Bandura, 1977). Distinct from trait efficacy, stress scenarios also produce situation-based perceptions of efficacy. High efficacy perceptions promote more positive appraisal responses, less threatening emotional responses and positive coping and adaptation. Interestingly, research has begun to investigate the simultaneous effect of both control and efficacy perceptions. One key finding demonstrates that stress and negative emotion is significantly elevated in scenarios where control perceptions are high and efficacy perceptions are low (Schaubroeck & Merritt, 1997).

In general, the body of situation-based coping research is primarily concerned with identifying appraisal distinctions across episodes that differentially impact coping. Rather than present a comprehensive review, the remainder of this section details some key approaches within this literature that may hold the greatest promise for further integration with consumer research.

Coping With Major Trauma

A classic situational approach examines coping responses to singular traumatic stress episodes. Some of the earliest coping studies were conducted using populations of severely traumatized individuals, such as soldiers returning from battle and victims of catastrophe. More recently, this research has examined coping episodes in response to stressful life events such as coping with abortion (Major et al., 1998), heart failure (Holahan, Moos, Holahan, & Brennan, 1997), or life threatening illness such as cancer and HIV (Park, Folkman, & Bostrom, 2001). Findings from this area have included the observation that individuals exhibit a great deal of variability across stress episodes and as a function of stage in the stress event. Also, coping scholars have observed that the use of individual coping strategies is differentially effective at reducing stress depending upon which stage in the stress event it occurs. For instance, it may be ameliorative to engage in avoidance coping strategies, particularly in instances when the individual cannot directly influence the outcome (Park, Folkman, & Bostrom, 2001; Terry & Hynes, 1998). This finding seems to reinforce the dynamic, process view of coping and provokes several additional research questions, suggesting that the decision of when to employ a particular coping strategy may be as important as the nature of the strategy itself.

Coping and Life Roles

One means of examining across forms of stress involves examining coping episodes not by phenomenological experience, but by the life role in which they occur (Mattlin, Wethington, & Kessler, 1990). The hypothesis among coping researchers using this distinction is that one key influence on coping is environmentally determined. Specifically, different life roles are accompanied by different types of stress, thereby implicating unique patterns of coping. One robust method for revealing these patterns is to analyze coping responses across major life domains and life roles. Within this literature, coping strategy differences have been explored across both life role and life domain.

One classic study conducted by Pearlin and Schooler (1978) studied coping variability in 4 different life roles: spouse, parent, personal finance manager and employee. This research found that each of the four life roles under study not only varied in the degree of reliance on particular strategies, but each role instantiated use of coping strategies particular to that role. For example, their data revealed that a selective ignoring strategy was used across all four life roles. In contrast, the role of personal finance manager demonstrated the use of faith as an adaptive strategy unique to that role. These findings suggest life role is an important moderator, and point to the context-dependent nature of many coping strategies.

Situational Coping Studies in Consumer Behavior

Situational coping research in consumer behavior has burgeoned in recent years and most of this research involves identifying the nature of context-dependent coping strategies in particular episodes. Among the first applications of coping theory in marketing is the research of Luce and her colleagues (Luce, 1998; Luce, Bettman, & Payne, 1999, 2000). This research models choice conflict resulting from difficult, emotionally-taxing attribute tradeoffs in choice scenarios. Luce et al. (2000) delineate conditions under which consumers will engage in problem-focused coping (e.g., manifest as increased vigilance or commitment to the choice task) or will opt for a status quo option (i.e., indicative of avoidant coping behavior). They find that consumers rely on avoidant strategies to reduce negative emotions when trade-off difficulty is high. They conclude that coping with emotion-laden choice contexts is an important factor determining consumer choice patterns.

Another application of coping theory can be found in a set of studies using ethnographic methods. The research of Mick and Fournier (1999) outlines the set of strategies consumers use for coping with a particular kind of stress, that associated with technology and ownership and the use of technological products. Their research highlights four general strategies for coping in this context, pre-acquisition avoidance and pre-acquisition confrontive and consumption avoidance and consumption confrontive. These overarching strategies subsume more nuanced coping facets. For example, they found evidence of several pre-acquisition avoidance strategies, such as ignoring information about products equipped with better technology. Other ethnographic consumer research has also found evidence for the important role of stage of coping as a critical determinant of coping strategies (Pavia & Mason, 2004). This research examined consumption as a means of coping with life-threatening illness. This research identified several different consumption-oriented coping strategies employed by seriously ill consumers as a means of confronting their illness, including an important difference across temporal stages of coping, noting differences in how consumers use consumption as a coping mechanism. Planning for vacations, buying durable goods, and even saving for future consumption opportunities all represent consumption-oriented consumer coping strategies.

Another cognate consumer literature that has important implications for coping is the literature investigating the antecedents of materialism (Arndt, Solomon, Kasser, & Sheldon, 2004; Burroughs & Rindfleisch, 2002). Recently, scholars have theorized that materialism, defined as the placement of value on the acquisition and possession of material objects, may serve a critical stress-ameliorating role for some individuals (Rindfleisch & Burroughs, 2004). This notion has profound implications for those residing in many contemporary consumption-rich societies. In this view, some individuals may seek to reduce stress through the acquisition of material possessions. The gaining of material possessions accords status which may be transferred to perceptions of self-worth and well-being, thereby fulfilling a key coping function. There has been relatively scant empirical research to test this notion, although preliminary findings offer mixed support for the thesis that materialism offers an effective means of reducing stress. It is possible that materialistic pursuits do offer some stress-reducing benefits for some at-risk populations in the short-term, such as children coping with family disruption (Roberts, Tanner, & Manolis, 2004). However, more research is needed to determine how, and under what conditions, consumption-related activities provide an effective means of coping for consumers.

Most coping studies found in the consumer literature have identified a single coping context, with few studies even theorizing about the nature of coping outside of the focal context. One study where multiple coping contexts were considered was conducted by Sujan, Sujan, Verhallen, and Bettman (1999). This research contrasts coping behaviors in two stressing consumer contexts: choice-related stressors and ambient store stressors encountered during shopping experiences. Relying on consumers' narrative descriptions of their own coping behaviors, these findings confirm more general findings from the coping literature in psychology and indicate that self-efficacy is a critical determinant of consumer coping. Specifically, confident consumers engaged in more varied, elaborate coping behaviors. The study was limited to two specific stress types and did not find evidence for a range of coping behaviors widely observed outside consumer behavior. Additionally, Sujan et al. also relied on a qualitative design, thus their data did not allow for a structural assessment of the coping construct.

Another interesting study that examined more general forms of coping was conducted by Kirmani & Campbell (2004). Their study articulated a key coping difference related to how consumers responded to interpersonal persuasion attempts by salespeople. Using qualitative data, they developed two distinct consumer coping strategies. The first, goal-seeking strategy is used by consumers to attain their goals and mitigate stress. The second, persuasion-sentry strategy is used by consumers in a defensive footing to combat the aggressive and persuasive effects of salespeople. Their research theorizes that the relationship between consumer-sales agent and persuasion experience interactively influence whether seeker or sentry strategies are enacted.

Opportunities for Situational Consumer Coping Research

The current literature in consumer behavior has revealed important differences across the problem-focus versus emotion-focus coping distinction. Within this framework, one primary research focus has been toward identifying consequences of emotion-focused coping strategies. Of this research, a predominant emotion-focus coping behavior frequently studied has been avoidance. In addition to the emotion-focused coping findings increasing understanding of the factors that give rise to avoidance coping, there remain several promising research avenues within the domain of emotion-focused coping. Comparatively, the situational antecedents giving rise to other forms of emotion-focused coping are relatively underresearched. The factors that lead to the use of emotional venting, emotional suppression and positive thinking are less understood. Future research should attempt to determine how use of these coping strategies differs from the factors leading to avoidance coping.

One promising area relates to the set of coping behaviors used in deriving positive meaning in the face of stress. Meaning formation is critically important in adapting to some of the most severe forms of stress, such as bereavement (Davis, Nolen-Hoeksma, & Larson, 1998). This severe form of stress may have analogous consumption-related manifestations, such as loss of valued possessions. To date, meaning formation as a means of consumer coping has not been explored. The coping literature has found that this form of emotion-focus coping can be a useful means of ameliorating stress, particularly in low control scenarios. This research has revealed two distinct forms of meaning-based coping. The first, sense-making, is primarily concerned with the cognitive reorganization of loss events to make sense of them without changing their existing fundamental schemas. This form of meaning-based coping differs from benefit-finding, a second form of meaning-oriented coping which is primarily concerned with deriving positive implications or benefits in the face of loss events. Research has shown that these forms of coping operate differentially across the stress process, with sense-making being associated with lower distress immediately following a loss and benefit finding being associated with lower distress over time (Davis et al., 1998). Because these processes have been shown to result in effective adaptation, they may be of particular interest to marketers and consumer researchers.

A final area of opportunity in the situational research domain pertains to the nexus between role, identity, and coping behaviors. The coping literature demonstrating situational differences as a function of life roles suggests that this may be an important moderating factor in determining coping responses. Key differences in appraisal and coping emerge as consumers shift across roles as "parents," "spouses," or "employees." These differences raise the possibility that social identities may impact coping decisions more generally as a function of the salience of group and social identities (Reed, 2004). The salience of a specific social identity may implicate various aspects of appraisal, such as the degree to which consumers feel in control of a situation as well as the degree of efficacy they perceive over the stress situation. Research has shown that when a salient identity is threatened, coping options are similarly influenced by the nature of the identity (Matheson & Cole, 2004). Research is needed to examine how these identity effects alter consumer behavior, such as the degree to engage in problem and emotion-focused coping behaviors. These identity-based appraisal differences should be investigated in terms of the transactional coping model.

PRESCRIPTIONS FOR FUTURE CONSUMER COPING RESEARCH

As consumer research interest in coping continues to flourish, future research programs should attempt to fill in some of the gaps identified in the present review. In this section, seven strategies for producing new coping related insights are articulated. The list, presented in random order, outlines broad prescriptions for building theory related to several promising avenues:

1. *Study the Downstream Effect of Stress and Coping.* The consumer coping literature has focused predominantly on the immediate and short-term psychological consequences of stress. Little is known about how appraisal and coping differences impact other important areas of consumer behavior. One possibility is that individual consumer differences in coping styles extend beyond the transactional framework. Research should emphasize

these downstream effects to explore information processing differences, susceptibility to persuasion, and possible biases in judgment and choice related to coping style. Such research would further cement the import of coping research to consumer theory.

2. *Look Past Context-Dependent Models of Coping.* Because the consumer literature has emphasized context-dependent models of coping, relatively less is known about how stable coping styles impact long-term consumer well-being. These long-term effects may reveal dispositional differences in how consumers interact with firms, adjust to market-related stressors as well as their degree of loyalty to specific firms. Although there is significant benefit in examining coping within circumscribed contextual boundaries, as important is the ability to see how coping styles operate across contexts.

3. *Examine the Role of Positive Emotions.* The impact of positive emotions within the transactional framework has been largely ignored by both consumer coping researchers and by coping researchers in psychology. Positive emotions are often experienced coincident with negative emotions (Folkman & Moskowitz, 2004), and these phenomena merit further scholarly attention. It is possible that the presence of positive emotions moderates many of the observed relationships within the transactional framework.

4. *Address fundamental questions related to coping's structure.* The coping literature has experienced significant debate regarding the structure of coping. This polemic bears similarity to ontological debates waged by emotions and personality researchers in recent years. This discourse has shed light on the possibility that several competing structural views of coping are possible. In consumer behavior, research to date has not moved beyond the problem-focused/emotion-focused typology. However, consumer researchers should be aware that several alternative structural theories exist and future consumer research should test these alternative views.

5. *Make praxis a priority.* It is perhaps somewhat surprising given the enormous potential of consumer researchers to affect change among marketers and policy makers that coping research to date has not had more to say regarding critical coping-related issues, such as consumer health. Additionally, the problem of soaring levels of consumer credit debt is considered to be at a near crisis point, and millions of consumers are struggling with record levels of debt. As of yet, consumer research has been agnostic as to how consumers and marketers can address these critical societal problems and assist consumers in coping with these issues. Consumer coping research has the potential to influence regulatory policy and assist consumer advocacy programs to better deal with important consumer stressors, such as health-related issues and financial strife. These aims should be of central importance to coping researchers in the coming years.

6. *Examine the role of consumption as coping.* As emerging consumer research into topics such as materialism and impulsive shopping has helped to articulate, in many instances, consumers consume as a pathway to feeling better about environmental pressures or life's stresses. The presence of consumption-related aphorisms such as "retail therapy" and "when the going gets tough, the tough go shopping" in the consumer vernacular demonstrate that many consumers derive quality of life-related benefits from their acts of consumption. Research is needed to understand these phenomena. A fuller understanding of specific motivations for consumption-based coping mechanisms is needed.

7. *Study Coping in the Long Run.* To date, consumer coping research has largely neglected temporal effects. While collecting longitudinal data offers unique challenges, existing research has not studied short-term versus long-term coping consequences. Many consumer behaviors that may provide coping relief in the short run have deleterious long-

term consequences, such as addictions (e.g., drugs, alcohol, food, shopping, etc.) and vices. Research is needed to better understand the tradeoffs consumers make emphasizing short-term pleasures at the expense of long-term outcomes. Beyond actually measuring long-term outcomes, research investigating consumers' perceptions of the long-term consequences of consumption decisions would contribute greatly to our knowledge of several coping strategies, such as rationalization and denial. Understanding the ways consumers respond to the marketing of products and services in these domains is essential to building theories of consumer welfare.

The future of consumer coping research looks bright. The goal of this chapter was to identify key avenues for the advancing theory. Several such avenues were developed, and it appears that the transactional coping framework presents a promising conduit for dialogue with other more ensconced consumer research paradigms, such as information processing, persuasion and decision-making. Drawing connections between coping and these paradigms, as well as addressing practical coping issues should be high priorities for researchers in the field.

ACKNOWLEDGMENTS

The author gratefully acknowledges the assistance of his dissertation advisor, Dawn Iacobucci and James E. Burroughs for their helpful comments regarding this chapter.

REFERENCES

Agrawal, N., & Duhachek, A. (2007). Coping tendencies and the effectiveness of emotional appeals in public service advertising. Working paper.

Agrawal, N., Menon, G., & Aaker, J. L. (2007). Getting emotional about health. *Journal of Marketing Research, 44,* 100–113.

Aldwin, C. M. (1999). *Stress, coping and development: An integrative approach.* New York: Guilford.

Aldwin, C. M., & Revenson, (1987). Does coping help? A reexamination of the relation between coping and mental health. *Journal of Personality and Social Psychology, 53*(2), 337–348.

Arndt, J., Solomon, S., Kasser, T., & Sheldon, K. (2004). The urge to splurge: A terror management account of materialism and consumer behavior. *Journal of Consumer Psychology, 14,* 198–212.

Bandura, A. (1977). Self-efficacy: Toward a unifying theory of behavioral change. *Psychological Review, 84*(2) 191–215.

Ben-Zur, H. (2002). Coping, affect and aging: The roles of mastery and self-esteem. *Personality and Individual Differences, 32*(2), 357–352.

Billings, A. G., & Moos, R. G. (1984). Coping stress and social resources among adults with unipolar depression. *Journal of Personality and Social Psychology, 46,* 877–891.

Block, L. G., & Keller, P. A. (1995). When to accentuate the negative: The effects of perceived efficacy and message framing on intentions to perform a health-related behavior. *Journal of Marketing Research, 32,* 192–203.

Bolger, N. (1990). Coping as a personality process: A prospective study. *Journal of Personality and Social Psychology, 59,* 525–537.

Bolger, N., & Eckenrode, J. (1991). Social relationships, personality, and anxiety during a major stressful event. *Journal of Personality and Social Psychology, 61,* 440–449.

Bolger, N., & Zuckerman, A. (1995). A framework for studying personality in the stress process. *Journal of Personality and Social Psychology, 69,* 890–902.

Brown, K. W., & Moskowitz, D. S. (1997). Does unhappiness make you sick? The role of affect and neuroticism in the experience of common physical symptoms. *Journal of Personality and Social Psychology, 72*(4), 907–917.

Burroughs, J. E., & Rindfleisch, A. (2002). Materialism and well-being: A conflicting values perspective. *Journal of Consumer Research, 29,* 348–370.

Carver, C. S., & Scheier, M. F. (1994). Situational coping and coping dispositions in a stressful transaction. *Journal of Personality and Social Psychology, 66*(1), 184–195.

Carver, C. S., Scheier, M. F., & Weintraub, J. K. (1989). Assessing coping strategies: A theoretically based approach. *Journal of Personality and Social Psychology, 56*, 267–283.

Chandran, S. & Menon, G. (2004). When a day means more than a year: Effects of temporal framing on judgments of health risk. *Journal of Consumer Research, 31*(3), 375–389.

Chang, E. (1998). Dispositional optimism and primary and secondary appraisal of a stressor: Controlling for confounding influences and relations to coping and psychological and physical adjustment. *Journal of Personality and Social Psychology, 74*(4), 1109–1120.

Davis, C. G., & Nolen-Hoeksema, S., & Larson, J. (1998). Making sense of loss and benefiting from the experience: Two construals of meaning. *Journal of Personality and Social Pscyhology,* 561–574.

Drach-Zahavy, A. (2004). Toward a multidimensional construct of social support: Implications of provider's self-reliance and request characteristics. *Journal of Applied Social Psychology, 34*, 1395–1420.

Drach-Zahavy, A., & Erez, M. (2002). Challenge versus threat effects on the goal-performance relationship. *Organizational Behavior and Human Decision Processes, 88*, 667–682.

Duhachek, A. (2005). A multidimensional, hierarchical model of coping: Examining emotional antecedents and consequences. *Journal of Consumer Research, 32*, 41–54.

Duhachek, A., & Agrawal, N. (2007). Consumed by shame and guilt: Ad framing and negative emotion in public service advertising. Working paper.

Ellsworth, P., & Smith, C. A. (1988). From appraisal to emotion: Differences among unpleasant feelings. *Motivation and Emotion, 12*, 271–302.

Florian, V., Mikulincer, M., & Taubman, O. (1995). Does hardiness contribute to mental health during a stressful real-life situation? The roles of appraisal and coping. *Journal of Personality and Social Psychology, 68*, 687–695.

Folkman, S. (1984). Personal control and stress and coping processes: A theoretical analysis. *Journal of Personality and Social Psychology, 46*(4), 839–852.

Folkman, S., & Lazarus, R. S. (1985). If it changes it must be a process: A study of emotion and coping during three stages of a college examination. *Journal of Personality and Social Psychology, 48*(1), 150–170.

Folkman, S., & Lazarus, R. S. (1988). Coping as a mediator of emotion. *Journal of Personality and Social Psychology, 54*(3), 466–475.

Folkman, S., & Moskowitz, J. (2004). Coping: Pitfalls and promise. *Annual Review of Psychology, 55,* 745–774.

Folkman S., & Moskowitz, J. (2000). Positive affect and the other side of coping. *American Psychologist, 55,* 655–662.

Freud, A. (1946). *The ego and mechanisms and defence.* New York: International University Press.

Freud, S. (1894). The neuro-psychoses of defence. *Standard Edition, 3,* 45–61.

Frijda, N. H. (1987). Emotion, cognitive structure, and action tendency. *Cognition and Emotion, 1,* 115–143.

Gunthert, K. C., Cohen, L. H., & Armeli, S. (1999). The role of neuroticism in daily stress and coping. *Journal of Personality and Social Psychology, 77*(5), 1087–1100.

Holahan, C. J. & Moos, R. H. (1987). Personal and contextual determinants of coping strategies. *Journal of Personality and Social Psychology, 52*(5), 946–955.

Holahan, C. J., Moos, R. H., Holahan, C. K., & Brennan, P. L. (1997). Psychosocial adjustment in patients with cardiac illness. *Psychology and Health, 12,* 345–360.

Isen, A. M., Daubman, K. A., & Nowicki, G. P. (1987). Positive affect facilitates creative problem solving. *Journal of Personality and Social Psychology, 52,* 1122–1131.

Johnson, A. R., & Stewart, D. (2005). A re-appraisal of the role of emotion in consumer behavior: Traditional and contemporary approaches. In N. Malhotra (Ed.), *Review of marketing research* (Vol. 1). Armonk NJ: M. E. Sharpe.

Keller, P., Lipkus, I., & Rimer, B. K. (2003), Affect, framing and persuasion. *Journal of Marketing Research, 40*(1), 54–64

Keller, P., Lipkus, I., & Rimer, B. K. (2002). Depressive realism and health risk accuracy: The negative consequences of positive mood. *Journal of Consumer Research, 29,* 57–69.

Kirmani, A., & Campbell, M. (2004). Goal seeker and persuasion sentry: How consumer targets respond to interpersonal marketing persuasion. *Journal of Consumer Research, 31,* 573–582.

Kobasa, S. C. (1982). Commitment and coping in stress resistance among lawyers. *Journal of Personality and Social Psychology, 42*, 707–717.

Lazarus, R. S. (1991). *Emotion and adaptation.* New York: Oxford University Press.

Lazarus, R. S., & Folkman, S. (1984). *Stress, appraisal, and coping.* New York: Springer.

Lin, Y. C., Lin, C. H., & Raghubir, P. (2003). Avoiding anxiety, being in denial, or simply stroking self-esteem: Why self-positivity? *Journal of Consumer Psychology, 13*(4) 464–477.

Luce, M. F. (1998). Choosing to avoid: Coping with negatively emotion-laden consumer decisions. *Journal of Consumer Research, 24*(4), 409–433.

Luce, M. F., Bettman, J. R. & Payne, J. W. (2001). *Emotional decisions: Tradeoff difficulty in consumer choice.* Monographs of the *Journal of Consumer Research.* University of Chicago Press.

Luce, M. F., & Kahn, B. E. (1999). Avoidance or vigilance: The psychology of false-positive test results. *Journal of Consumer Research, 26*(3) 242–259.

Luce, M. F., Payne, J. W., & Bettman, J. R. (1999). Emotional trade-off difficulty and choice. *Journal of Marketing Research, 36*(2), 143–159.

Major, B., Richards, C., Cooper, M. L., Cozzarelli, C., & Zubek, J. (1998). Personal resilience, cognitive appraisals, and coping: An integrative model of adjustment to abortion. *Journal of Personality and Social Psychology, 74*(3), 735–752.

Maslow, A. H. (1987). *Motivation and personality* (3d ed.). New York: HarperCollins..

Matheson, K., & Cole, B. M. (2004). Coping with a threatened identity: Psychological and neuroendocrine responses. *Journal of Experimental Social Psychology, 40*, 777–786.

Mattlin, J. A., Wethington, E., & Kessler, R. C. (1990). Situational determinants of coping and coping effectiveness. *Journal of Health and Social Behavior, 31*(1), 103–122.

Menon, G., Block, L. G., & Ramanathan, S. (2002). We're at as much risk as we are led to believe: Effects of message cues on judgments of health. *Journal of Consumer Research, 28*(4) 533–549.

Menon, G., Raghubir, P., & Agrawal, N. (2006). Health risk perceptions and consumer psychology. forthcoming in *Handbook of Consumer Psychology.*

McCrae, R., & Costa, P. T. (1986). Personality, coping and coping effectiveness in an adult sample. *Journal of Personality, 54*, 384–405.

Mick, D. G., & Fournier, S. (1998). Paradoxes of technology: Consumer cognizance, emotions, and coping strategies. *Journal of Consumer Research, 25*(2), 123–43.

Moorman, C. (2002). Consumer health under the scope. *Journal of Consumer Research, 29*(June), 152–158.

Park, C. L., Folkman, S., & Bostrom, A. (2001). Appraisals of controllability and coping in caregivers and HIV+ men: Testing the goodness-of-fit hypothesis. *Journal of Consulting and Clinical Psychology, 69*(3), 481–488.

Parkes, K. R. (1984). Locus of control, cognitive appraisal, and coping in stressful episodes. *Journal of Personality & Social Psychology, 46*(3), 655–668.

Pavia, T. M., & Mason, M. J. (2004). The reflexive relationship between consumer behavior and adaptive coping. *Journal of Consumer Research, 31*(3), 441–454.

Pearlin, L. I., & Schooler, C. (1978). The structure of coping. *Journal of Health and Social Behavior, 19*, 2–21.

Penley, J., Tomaka, J., & Wiebe, J. (2002). The association of coping to physical and psychological health outcomes: A meta-analytic review. *Journal of Behavioral Medicine, 25*(6), 551–603.

Raffety, B. D., Smith, R., & Ptacek, J. (1997). Facilitating and debilitating trait anxiety, situational anxiety and coping with an anticipated stressor: A process analysis. *Journal of Personality and Social Psychology, 72*(4), 892–906.

Rindfleisch, A., & Burroughs, J. E., (2004). Terrifying thoughts, terrible materialism? Contemplations on a terror management account of materialism and consumer behavior. *Journal of Consumer Psychology, 14*, 219–224.

Roberts, J. A., Tanner, Jr., J. F., & Manolis, C. (2004). Materialism and the family structure-stress relation. *Journal of Consumer Psychology, 15*, 183–190.

Rohde, P., Lewinsohn, P., Tilson, M., & Seeley, J. R. (1990). The dimensionality of coping and its relation to depression. *Journal of Personality and Social Psychology, 58*, 499–511.

Roseman, I., Antoniou, A. A., & Jose, P. E. (1996). Appraisal determinants of emotions: Constructing a more accurate and comprehensive theory. *Cognition and Emotion, 10*(3), 241–277.

Roseman, I., Spindel, M., & Jose, P. E. Appraisal of emotion-eliciting events: Testing a theory of discrete emotions. *Journal of Personality and Social Psychology, 59*, 899–915.

Schaubroeck, J., & Merritt, D. M. (1997). Divergent effects of job control on coping with work stressors: The key role of self-efficacy. *Journal of Applied Psychology, 40,* 738–754.

Schimmack, U., Olshi, S., Furr, R. M., & Funder, D. C., (2004). Personality and life satisfaction: A facet-level analysis. *Journal of Personality and Social Psychology, 30*(8), 1062–1075.

Schwarzer, R., & Schwarzer, C. (1996). A critical survey of coping instruments. In M. Zeidner & N. S. Endler (Eds.), *Handbook of coping: Theory, research and applications* (pp. 107–132). New York: Wiley.

Selye, H. (1956). *The stress of life,* New York: McGraw-Hill.

Skinner, E., Edge, K., Altman, J., & Sherwood, H. (2003). Searching for the structure of coping: A review and critique of category systems for classifying ways of coping. *Psychological Bulletin, 129*(2), 216–269.

Skinner, N., & Brewer, E. (2002). The dynamics of threat and challenge appraisals prior to stressful achievement events. *Journal of Personality and Social Psychology, 83,* 678–692.

Smith, C. A., & Ellsworth, P. E. (1985). Patterns of cognitive appraisal in emotion. *Journal of Personality and Social Psychology, 48*(4), 813–838.

Smith, C. A., & Ellsworth, P. E. (1987). Patterns of appraisal and emotion related to taking an exam. *Journal of Personality and Social Psychology, 52,* 475–488.

Sujan, M., Sujan, H., Bettman, J. R., & Verhallen, T. (1999). Sources of consumers' stress and their coping strategies. in Proceedings of *European Advances in Consumer Research, 4,* 182–187.

Terry, D., & Hynes, T. (1998). Adjustment to a low-control situation: Reexamining the role of coping responses. *Journal of Personality and Social Psychology, 74,* 1078–1092.

Thoits, P. A. (1986). Social support as coping assistance. *Journal of Consulting and Clinical Psychology, 54*(4), 416–423.

Thoits, P. A. (1995). Stress, coping and social support processes: Where are we? What next? *Journal of Health and Social Behaivor,* 53–79.

Tomaka, J., Blascovich, J., Kibler, J., & Ernst, J. (1997). Cognitive and physiological antecedents of threat and challenge appraisal. *Journal of Personality and Social Psychology, 73*(1), 63–72.

Vaillant, G. (1977). *Adaptation to life.* Boston: Little Brown.

Williams, P., & Drolet, A. (2005). Age-related differences in responses to emotional advertisements. forthcoming in *Journal of Consumer Research.*

Wooten, D. B., & Reed II, A. (2004). Playing it safe: Susceptibility to normative influence and protective self-presenatation. *Journal of Consumer Research, 31,* 551–556.

Yi, S., & Baumgartner, H. (2004). Coping with negative emotions in purchase-related situations.*Journal of Consumer Psychology, 14,* 303–317.

VIII

ADVANCES IN RESEARCH METHODS

43

Self-Reports in Consumer Research

KIMBERLEE WEAVER

NORBERT SCHWARZ

University of Michigan

A central goal of marketing research is to systematically gather information from consumers in order to adequately understand and fulfill their needs. In pursuit of this goal, researchers ask consumers to express their attitudes toward products (e.g., Do you feel that organic food tastes better than conventional food?), estimate their support for new products (e.g., If there was a service that allowed you to organize all your financial information under one roof, would you use it?), and report their behaviors (e.g., How frequently have you visited the local mall in the past month?). Marketing managers use this survey information to make strategic decisions including forecasting demand and return-on-investment, identifying new areas for growth, gauging customer satisfaction, and segmenting the market.

Unfortunately, the results of marketing surveys—and the decisions based on them—are only as meaningful as the answers respondents provide. These answers are highly context dependent and profoundly influenced by the specific wording and format of the questions asked, the content of preceding questions, and similar variables. While rigorous methods have been applied to address practical problems of question form, wording, and context (e.g., Payne, 1951; Schuman & Presser, 1981), a coherent conceptual framework has long been missing. This changed over the last two decades, as psychologists, survey methodologists and consumer behavior researchers focused the research spotlight on the cognitive and communicative processes underlying the question answering process (for comprehensive reviews see Sudman, Bradburn, & Schwarz, 1996; Tourangeau, Rips, & Rasinski, 2000). In this chapter, we summarize what has been learned and analyze the implications for the attitudinal and behavioral reports relied upon by marketing researchers.

RESPONDENTS' TASKS

Answering a survey question involves several tasks. First, respondents have to understand the question asked to determine what they are to report on. If the question is an opinion question, they may either retrieve a previously formed opinion from memory or they may form an opinion on the spot. While researchers typically hope for the former, the latter is far more likely. Even when respondents have a previously formed opinion accessible in memory, it is unlikely to match the specifics of the question asked, forcing respondents to compute a new judgment. To do so, they need to retrieve relevant information from memory to form a mental representation of the target that they are to evaluate. In most cases, respondents will also need to retrieve or construct some standard against which the target is evaluated. Once a "private" judgment is formed in their mind, respondents have to communicate it to the researcher. In most cases, they will not be allowed to report it in their own words but instead will need to format their judgment to fit the response alternatives provided by the researcher. Finally, respondents may wish to edit their response before they communicate it, due to influences of social desirability and situational adequacy.

Similar considerations apply to behavioral frequency questions. Again, respondents first need to understand what the question refers to, that is, which behavior they are supposed to report on. Next, they must recall or reconstruct relevant instances of this behavior from memory. If the question specifies a reference period, they must determine if the recalled instances occurred during this time frame or not. Similarly, if the question refers to their "usual" behavior, respondents have to determine if the recalled or reconstructed instances are reasonably representative, or if they reflect a deviation from their usual behavior. In many cases, relevant behavioral information will not be readily accessible in memory and respondents will need to rely on a variety of estimation and inference strategies to arrive at a plausible answer. Finally, respondents need to communicate their estimate to the researcher. They may need to map their estimate onto a response scale provided to them, and they may want to edit it for reasons of social desirability.

Accordingly, interpreting the question, generating an opinion or a representation of the relevant behavior, formatting the response, and editing the answer are the main psychological components of a process that starts with respondents' exposure to a survey question and ends with their overt report (Strack & Martin, 1987; Tourangeau, 1984). We first consider issues of question comprehension and subsequently return to respondents' other tasks in the context of attitude and behavior questions.

MAKING SENSE OF QUESTIONS: COGNITIVE AND CONVERSATIONAL PROCESSES

When a consumer answers a market research question, does her understanding of it match what the researcher has in mind? The answer to this question is crucial and involves two intertwined processes: respondents' comprehension of the question's literal meaning as well as their comprehension of its pragmatic meaning (Clark & Schober, 1992; Strack & Schwarz, 1992). *Literal meaning* refers to whether consumers understand the words. To facilitate literal understanding researchers are usually admonished to design survey items with the target population in mind, to use simple sentences and to avoid ambiguous or unfamiliar terms (see Bradburn, Sudman, & Wansink, 2004, for good hands-on advice). However, understanding the literal meaning is not sufficient to provide a meaningful answer. For example, if a consumer is asked, "How frequently do you go online to get news?" she is likely to understand the literal meaning of the words. Even so, she now needs to decide what exactly the researcher means by "getting news." Should she include brief web searches for the local weather and glances at the day's headlines? Or only occasions where she reads news stories in some depth? *Pragmatic meaning* signifies this leap between hearing what a marketing researcher *says* and deciding what the researcher actually *means*. A listener who is asked a question in the course of a regular conversation can ask for clarification. However, such opportunities are usually unavailable in survey contexts, where a well-trained interviewer may merely repeat the question or where nobody may be available to ask for clarification, as is the case for self-administered questionnaires or internet surveys. Hence, respondents are likely to look to the context surrounding the question and apparently "formal" features of the questionnaire itself to infer the question's intended meaning.

To understand how consumers infer the pragmatic meaning of survey items, we first need to consider the norms and expectations that people have about conversations in everyday settings, norms and expectations that respondents also bring to the research situation. Paul Grice (1975), a philosopher of language, observed that conversations proceed according to a cooperativeness principle. People discern meaning in conversations, he argued, by following a series of tacit assumptions or "conversational norms." In a nutshell, these norms hold that speakers should be informative, truthful, relevant, and clear when speaking to one another (Grice, 1975). More important, listeners interpret a speaker's utterances by assuming that speakers are trying to live up to these ideals, unless the listener's understanding of the social situation implies that the speaker may not be fully cooperative. Because research participants rarely assume that the researcher is not a cooperative communicator, they consider all contributions of the researcher relevant to the ongoing conversation (Schwarz, 1996). As a consequence, features of the survey context itself such as preceding survey items as well as apparently formal characteristics of the questionnaire itself serve as information to respondents, as subsequent examples will illustrate.

RESPONSE ALTERNATIVES

Open Versus Closed Question Formats

Most survey questions follow a *closed response* format by presenting respondents with a set of predetermined response alternatives. The choice of response alternatives can profoundly affect respondents' answers, when compared to an *open response* format that allows respondents to answer in their own words (see Schuman & Presser, 1981). As an example, consider a Pew Research Institute survey conducted a few weeks after the 2004 Presidential election (Pew Research Center, 2004). Voters were first asked, "What one issue mattered most to you in deciding how you voted for President?" In an open-ended format, only 14% of respondents spontaneously mentioned an issue that could be classified as "moral values" as the decisive factor in their vote. In contrast, 27% of respondents picked "moral values" as the most important factor when presented with the following list: "Iraq; Economy/Jobs; Terrorism; Healthcare; Moral values; Education; Taxes; Other." Thus, researchers may draw quite different conclusions about respondents' priorities depending on the type of question response format they use.

In general, respondents assume that the response alternatives indicate what the researcher is interested in and they work within the constraints of the response alternatives provided to them (Schuman & Presser, 1981; Schwarz, 1996). In addition to imposing constraints, the response alternatives offered may remind respondents of options that might otherwise not come to mind. These two question formats have unique advantages and drawbacks. On the positive side, open-ended questions capture what is on consumers' minds; on the negative side, the answers are limited to what is most accessible, e.g., the products or services of well-known brands that come to mind most easily. Conversely, closed-ended response formats have the advantage of gathering information about a larger range of issues, products, and services, but have the disadvantage of reminding consumers of products and services that may otherwise not have come to mind.

Numeric Values of Frequency Scales

Respondents also look to more subtle aspects of survey questions for question clarification. Suppose that a consumer is asked how frequently she follows news about the stock market. To answer this question, she first needs to determine what "follow the news" means in this context. Does the question refer to how frequently she watches the recap of the rise or fall in the major U.S. stock indices on the nightly news? Or to how frequently she reads the financial pages of the *Wall Street Journal* in depth? To clarify the intended meaning of the question, respondents may consult the frequency values provided as part of the response scales. If the scale presents low frequency categories, e.g., ranging from "less than once a year" to "one or two times a week," respondents may infer that the researcher is interested in relatively rare events rather than in the nightly news reports watched by most Americans. But if the scale presents high frequency categories, like "several times a week" or "every day," respondents may infer that the researcher is interested in frequent events, such as the nightly financial report. Supporting this assumption, Schwarz, Strack, Müller, and Chassein (1988) found that the range of frequencies given in a rating scale influenced respondents' interpretation of an ambiguous question (e.g., how often respondents felt "really annoyed"). When the scale provided low frequency ranges, respondents inferred that the question pertained to strong emotions—ones that are *not* experienced frequently. In contrast, when high frequency ranges were presented, respondents inferred that the question was asking about more minor everyday annoyances. As a result, respondents deliberately report on substantively different behaviors and experiences when the same question stem is accompanied by different frequency scales.

Reference Periods

The same logic applies to reference periods (e.g., Winkielman, Knäuper, & Schwarz, 1998). Suppose a consumer is asked, "How often did you go shopping last week?" versus "How often did you go shopping during the last 3 months (that is, since...)?" What does the term "shopping" refer to? A recent experiment with undergraduate consumers indicates that "shopping" is assumed to include minor shopping activity when the reference period is short (like one week), but to refer to major shopping activity when the reference period is long (like 3 months). Accordingly, only 13% of the respondents reported spending more than $50 on a "typical" shopping occasion when the question pertained to last week, whereas 59% reported doing so when the question pertained to the last 3 months (Schwarz, unpublished data). In short, the same question stem can acquire different meaning when combined with a different reference period.

Numeric Values of Rating Scales

The numerical values of rating scales can also influence respondents' inferences about the intended meaning of a question. Suppose a researcher asks, "How successful would you say you have been in life?", accompanied by a rating scale from "not at all successful" to "extremely successful" (Schwarz, Knäuper, Hippler, Noelle-Neumann, & Clark, 1991). What does "not at all successful" mean? Does it refer to the absence of great success or to the presence of failure? The numeric values of the rating scale can provide relevant clues. When the scale ranges from 0 = "not at all successful" to 11 = "extremely successful" it suggests a unipolar dimension that represents different degrees of success. However, a formally equivalent range of –5 = "not at all successful" to +5 = "extremely successful" suggests a bipolar dimension that spans the range from failure to success. As a result, 34% of respondents endorsed a value below the midpoint of the 0 to 10 scale, whereas only 13% endorsed a value below the midpoint of the –5 to +5 scale—after all, there are more people who merely lack great accomplishments in life than there are people who have explicitly failed.

Similarly, Haddock and Carrick (1999) observed that UK citizens rated the British Prime Minister Tony Blair as more honest, intelligent, caring, and friendly when the numeric values of the rating scale ranged from –5 to +5 rather than from 0 to 10. These shifts again indicate that the scale anchor "not at all honest" refers to an absence of great honesty in a unipolar format, but to the presence of dishonesty in a bipolar format. Importantly, once respondents made these trait ratings, they used them as input into the next judgment. Those making initial judgments along the –5 to +5 scale subsequently arrived at a more favorable overall assessment of Tony Blair. Accordingly, the numeric values of rating scales may not only influence respondents' interpretation of a specific question, with corresponding shifts in ratings, but may also affect subsequent judgments to which those ratings are relevant.

QUESTION CONTEXT

In addition to drawing on the "formal" characteristics that accompany each individual question to determine its intended meaning, respondents also attend to the larger survey context itself for insight. As a particularly informative example, consider research in which respondents are asked to report their opinion about a highly obscure, or even completely fictitious, issue, such as the "Agricultural Trade Act of 1978" (e.g., Bishop, Tuchfarber, & Oldendick 1986; Schuman & Presser, 1981). Apparently confirming researchers' nightmares, about 30% of respondents are willing to report an opinion on such topics, presumably in the absence of any knowledge about them. Yet, their answers to such questions may be more meaningful than has typically been assumed.

From a conversational point of view, the sheer fact that a question about some issue is asked presupposes that this issue exists—respondents have no reason to assume that the researcher would ask a meaningless question (or get funded for doing so). Hence, they try to make sense of the question by drawing on contextual information, unless a "Don't Know" alternative provides an easy way out (e.g., Schuman & Presser, 1981). One way to do so is by attending to the content of preceding questions to interpret the meaning of subsequent ones. Once respondents have used the survey context to assign a plausible meaning to an unknown or little known issue, they have no difficulty reporting a subjectively meaningful opinion. Supporting this assumption, Strack, Schwarz, and Wänke (1991) observed that German university students reported different attitudes towards the introduction of a fictitious "educational contribution," depending on the content of a preceding question. Some students were first asked to estimate the average tuition fees that students have to pay at U.S. universities (in contrast to Germany, where university education is free), whereas others first estimated the amount of money that the Swedish government pays every student as financial support. As expected, respondents inferred that the fictitious "educational contribution" pertained to students having to pay money when it followed the U.S. tuition question, but to students receiving money when it followed the Swedish financial support question. Accordingly, respondents reported a more favorable attitude toward the introduction of an "educational contribution" in the former than in the latter case—hardly a meaningless response. In fact, opinions on fictitious issues are often meaningfully related to respondents' background characteristics (Schuman & Kalton, 1985).

Respondents are more likely to draw on contextual information the more ambiguous the question is or the less they know about the topic. Unfortunately, variables that increase the response rate of a survey, such as paying respondents to answer questionnaires and multiple follow up contacts, may also increase the percentage of uninformed responses (Hawkins & Coney, 1981) and hence the impact of contextual information. Offering respondents an easy way out, e.g., in form of a "Don't Know" response alternative (Hawkins & Coney, 1981; Schuman & Presser, 1981), can reduce the percentage of answers based on contextual inferences.

Finally, it is worth noting that the influence of question context depends on the mode of data collection. In all cases, earlier questions can influence how respondents interpret later ones. Under self-administered questionnaire conditions, however, respondents can read ahead and can return to earlier ambiguous questions once they determined a plausible interpretation in light of later questions (e.g., Schwarz & Hippler, 1995). We return to the emergence of question order effects in our discussion of attitude questions.

RESEARCHER'S AFFILIATION

In natural conversations, we take our knowledge about the speaker into account when we interpret his or her utterances. The same logic becomes extended to research situations, where the researcher's affiliation may provide important clues. For example, Norenzayan and Schwarz (1999) asked respondents to explain a case of mass murder, described in a newspaper clipping. The questionnaire was either printed on the letterhead of an "Institute for Personality Research" or on the letterhead of an "Institute for Social Research." As expected, respondents' explanations showed more attention to personality variables or to social-contextual variables, depending on whether they thought the researcher was a personality psychologist or a social scientist. As requested by the norms of conversational conduct, they took the researcher's affiliation into account to determine which information would be most relevant to the researcher's likely epistemic interest.

CONCLUSIONS

As our selective review indicates, question comprehension is not only about words – it is also about speaker meaning. To intuit the speaker's intended meaning, respondents pay close attention to contextual information, bringing the tacit assumptions that govern conversations in daily life to the research situation (Grice, 1975; Schwarz, 1996). That their responses are systematically affected by minor features of the research instrument highlights how closely respondents attend to the specifics at hand in their quest to provide informative answers. Unfortunately, these efforts are rarely appreciated by the researcher, who considers such features substantively irrelevant and treats their influence as an undesirable artifact. Nor are researchers likely to note these influences in regular surveys, where control conditions with different question formats are missing, or in regular field pretests, where problems can only be identified when respondents give obviously meaningless answers or complain about the questions asked.

To reduce question comprehension problems, researchers are well advised to use cognitive interviewing procedures at the questionnaire development stage (see Sudman et al., 1996, chapter 2, and the contributions in Schwarz & Sudman, 1996, for reviews). Most widely used are verbal protocols, in the form of concurrent or retrospective think-aloud procedures. In addition, respondents are often asked to paraphrase the question, thus providing insight into their interpretation of question meaning (see DeMaio & Rothgeb, 1996, for commonly employed combinations of methods). Cognitive pretests that illuminate respondents' understanding of a question within its intended context can be conducted with a relatively small number of respondents and provide the best available safeguard against later surprises.

ASKING QUESTIONS ABOUT ATTITUDES

Assessment of consumer attitudes—whether toward current products and services, competitor products and services, or future offerings still in the pipeline—is an integral component of almost all market research surveys. Attitudes have traditionally been defined as "an enduring organization of motivational, emotional, perceptual, and cognitive processes with respect to some aspect of the individual's world" (Krech & Crutchfield, 1948, p. 152), although in subsequent decades, the attitude concept has been largely reduced to its evaluative component (i.e., Bem, 1970). Most important for survey contexts is the fact that people's attitudinal reports are highly context dependent. The fact that attitudes change with the context has led many researchers to conclude that all we assess in attitude measurement are evaluative judgments that respondents construct on the spot, based on whatever information is accessible at that time (for a review see Schwarz & Bohner, 2001). Next, we address the processes underlying context effects in attitude measurement, with special attention to the conditions that give rise to assimilation (or "carry-over") and contrast (or "backfire") effects.

QUESTION ORDER EFFECTS IN ATTITUDE MEASUREMENT

Not only can the order of survey questions influence respondents' interpretation of the meaning of a given question, question order can also affect the information that comes to mind and the inference rules respondents' apply when thinking about and answering attitude questions. Adding further complexity, consumers can draw on a range of different information when evaluating an attitude object, such as a product or brand. This information includes accessible features of the target (discussed below), respondents' metacognitive experiences while thinking about the target (for a review see Schwarz, 2004), and their apparent affective response to it (for reviews see Pham, 2004; Schwarz & Clore, 1996). Here, we focus on the processes involved in feature-based attitude judgments, which are at the heart of question order effects in survey research. Our discussion follows the logic of the inclusion/exclusion model (Schwarz & Bless, 1992a, in press), which conceptualizes the emergence, direction, and size of context effects in feature-based judgment.

Mental Construal

Feature-based evaluations require two mental representations: a representation of the target itself (i.e., the to-be-evaluated object) and a representation of a standard against which the target is evaluated. Both representations are context dependent and include information that is chronically accessible as well as information that is only temporarily accessible, for example, because that piece of information was recently brought to mind when answering a preceding question. People rarely retrieve all information that may be relevant to a judgment and instead truncate the search process as soon as "enough" information has come to mind to form a judgment with sufficient certainty (Bodenhausen & Wyer, 1987; Higgins, 1996). Hence, information that is the most accessible or "top of mind" exerts a disproportionate influence. How accessible information influences the judgment depends on whether it is used in forming a representation of the target itself or whether it is used when forming a representation of the standard.

Assimilation Effects

Information that is included in respondents' temporary representation of the target itself results in *assimilation effects*. That is, respondents' judgments will be more positive (negative) when positive (negative) information comes to mind. The size of assimilation effects increases with the amount and extremity of temporarily accessible information and decreases with the amount and extremity of chronically accessible information included in the representation of the target (see Bless, Schwarz, & Wänke, 2003), provided that the information is diagnostic for the judgment at hand (Feldman & Lynch, 1988).

For example, Schwarz, Strack, and Mai (1991) asked respondents to report their marital satisfaction and their general life-satisfaction in different question orders. The obtained answers correlated $r = .32$ in the life-marriage order, but $r = .67$ in the marriage-life order. This pattern reflects that respondents can draw on a wide range of information to evaluate their general lives and are more likely to consider their marriage if it has just been brought to mind by the preceding question. Accordingly, happily married respondents reported higher, and unhappily married respondents lower, mean life-satisfaction in the marriage-life than in the life-marriage order. This increase in correlation was attenuated, $r = .43$, when questions about three different life-domains (job, leisure time, and marriage) preceded the general question, thus bringing a more diverse range of information to mind.

Similarly, Schul and Schiff (1993) observed in a customer satisfaction survey that specific features of a telephone company's service exerted more influence on customers' overall service satisfaction when the evaluation of the features preceded rather than followed the overall satisfaction question (see also DeMoranville & Bienstock, 2003). Importantly, however, this order effect was more pronounced for positive than for negative features. Presumably, unfavorable features of the company's service were more likely to be on consumers' minds independent of question order, whereas favorable features were taken for granted, unless attention was drawn to them by the preceding questions.

Contrast Effects

The same piece of accessible information that may elicit an assimilation effect in one case may also elicit a *contrast effect* in another; i.e., a more negative (positive) judgment when positive (negative) information is brought to mind. This is the case when the information is excluded from, rather than included in, the cognitive representation formed of the target.

As a first possibility, suppose that a given piece of information with positive (negative) implications is excluded from the representation of the target category. If so, the representation will contain less positive (negative) information, resulting in less positive (negative) judgments. This possibility is referred to as a *subtraction-based contrast effect* (Schwarz & Bless, 1992a). For example, rules of conversational conduct request speakers to provide information that is new to the recipient, rather than to reiterate information that has already been given (Grice, 1975). Applying this rule to the survey interview, respondents may interpret a subsequent question as a request for new information, thus inducing them to disregard information that they have already provided. In the above study of marital satisfaction and life-satisfaction (Schwarz et al., 1991), both questions correlated $r = .67$ in the marriage-life order. However, this correlation dropped to $r = .18$ in the same question order when both questions were introduced by a joint lead-in that read, "We now have two questions about your life. The first pertains to your marriage and the second to your life as a whole." Increasing the conversational relatedness of the questions in this way induced respondents to interpret the general life-satisfaction question as if it were worded, "Aside from your marriage, which you already told us about, how satisfied are you with other aspects of your life?" Consistent with this assumption, a condition in which this reworded general question was presented resulted in a correlation of $r = .20$. Once respondents disregarded their marriage, happily married respondents reported lower, and unhappily married respondents higher, general life-satisfaction than without the lead-in. Such subtraction-based contrast effects are limited to the specific target (here, "my life") from whose representation a given piece of information is subtracted. The size of subtraction-based contrast effects increases with the amount and extremity of the temporarily accessible information that is excluded from the representation of the target, and decreases with the amount and extremity of the information that remains in the representation of the target (Schwarz & Bless, 1992a).

Contrast effects may also arise when temporarily accessible information is used to construct a standard of comparison. To the degree that a more positive (negative) standard is constructed, the target will be evaluated less positively (negatively). The size of *comparison-based contrast effects* increases with the extremity and amount of temporarily accessible information used in constructing the standard, and decreases with the extremity and amount of chronically accessible information used when constructing the standard. While subtraction-based contrast effects are limited to a specific target, comparison-based contrast effects generalize to all targets to which the standard is applicable (Schwarz & Bless, 1992a).

To illustrate this principle, consider the impact of political scandals on assessments of the trust-worthiness of politicians. Not surprisingly, bringing to mind a politician who was embroiled in a scandal, say Richard Nixon, decreases people's judgments of the trustworthiness of politicians in general. In theoretical terms, the exemplar (Nixon) is included in the representation formed of the superordinate category (American politicians), which is now unduly affected by a highly accessible untrustworthy exemplar. On the other hand, if the trustworthiness question pertains to a specific other politician, say George W. Bush, the primed exemplar cannot be included in the representa-tion formed of the target—after all, Bush is not Nixon. Instead, Nixon serves as a standard of com-parison, and Bush appears more trustworthy by virtue of this comparison than would otherwise be the case. An experiment with German exemplars confirmed these predictions: Thinking about a politician who was involved in a scandal decreased the trustworthiness of politicians in general, but increased the trustworthiness of all specific individual politicians assessed (Schwarz & Bless, 1992b).

Determinants of Information Use

Numerous variables can influence whether information is used in forming a representation of the target, resulting in assimilation effects, or in forming a representation of the standard, resulting in contrast effects. The variables that influence information use can be organized by assuming that respondents tacitly ask themselves three questions, which serve as filters that channel information use.

The first filter pertains to awareness of an undue influence: "Am I only thinking of this informa-tion because it was brought to mind by some irrelevant influence?" If respondents' answer to this question is yes, they will not use the accessible information to form a representation of the target. Accordingly, awareness of the priming episode (e.g., Lombardi, Higgins, & Bargh, 1987; Martin, 1986; Strack, Schwarz, Bless, Kübler, & Wänke, 1993) reliably undermines use of the primed infor-mation, resulting in contrast effects. This type of contrast effect, however, is more likely to occur in experiments, where the priming task and the judgment task are usually presented as unrelated, than in survey interviews, where respondents are more likely to assume that adjacent questions are meaningfully related to one another and thus are less likely to correct for the influence of earlier questions (Schwarz, 1996).

When the information passes this first test, the second filter is: "Does this information repre-sent a feature of the target?" This decision is driven by the numerous variables known to influ-ence the categorization of information (Smith, 1995), including the information's extremity and typicality (e.g., Herr, 1986), salient category boundaries (e.g., Strack, Schwarz, & Gschneidinger, 1985; Wänke, Bless, & Schwarz, 1998), sequential versus simultaneous presentation formats (e.g., Wedell, Parducci, & Geiselman, 1987), and related context variables (for reviews see Schwarz & Bless, 1992a, in press).

The third and final filter pertains to the norms of conversational conduct that govern informa-tion use in conversations: "Is it conversationally appropriate to use this information?" As previ-ously noted, conversational norms prohibit redundancy and invite speakers to provide information that is new to the recipient, rather than information that the recipient already has (for a review see Schwarz, 1996). Hence, when highly accessible information violates the conversational norm of redundancy, it will not be used and instead will result in a contrast effect. As an example, recall that the correlation between marital satisfaction and life-satisfaction dropped from $r = .67$ to $r = .18$

when the conversational context induced respondents to consider the two questions separately (Schwarz et al., 1991; see also Strack, Martin, & Schwarz, 1988).

Information that passes all three tests is included in the representation formed of the target and results in assimilation effects. Information that fails any one of these tests is excluded from the representation formed of the target, but may be used in forming a representation of the standard, resulting in contrast effects. Schwarz and Bless (in press) provide a more detailed discussion of the underlying processes and Sudman et al. (1996, chapter 5) highlight the implications for questionnaire design.

RESPONSE ORDER EFFECTS

Many consumer surveys ask respondents which of several opinion statements comes closest to their own position, or which of several products they prefer. For example, respondents may be asked, "Where would you rather spend a weekend: In Washington, D.C., or in New York City?" A respondent who first thinks about Washington, D.C., may quickly come up with a few good reasons for a visit, truncating the consideration of the other alternative. Yet, had the same respondent first thought about New York City, some good reasons for this destination would have come to mind as well. As a result, respondents' answers often depend on which alternative they think about first (see Krosnick & Alwin, 1987; Sudman et al., 1996, for related conceptualizations).

When the response alternatives are presented in a visual format (e.g., a self-administered questionnaire), respondents are likely to proceed through the list in the order in which the alternatives are presented, elaborating more on the initial than on the subsequent ones. When the response alternatives are read to respondents (e.g., in a telephone interview), respondents are likely to begin with what is still "in their ears," elaborating more on the last item read to them (Krosnick & Alwin, 1987). As a result, the same alternative is more likely to be endorsed when presented first rather than last in a visual format (resulting in a *primacy effect*), and when presented last rather than first in an auditory format (resulting in a *recency effect*).

AGE AND CULTURE RELATED DIFFERENCES

Further complicating consumer researchers' task is the fact that context effects in attitude measurement are influenced by age-related changes in cognitive functioning as well as cultural differences in cognition and communication. This makes comparisons across age groups and cultures fraught with uncertainty, presenting a formidable challenge for consumer research in an increasingly global market place that is populated by an ever larger number of older consumers.

Age-Related Differences

Normal human aging is associated with decreasing cognitive capacity and memory function (for a review see Park, 2000). Accordingly, information brought to mind by preceding questions fades more quickly from older respondents' memory, attenuating or eliminating the question order effects observed for younger respondents (for a review see Schwarz & Knäuper, 2004). At the same time, however, older respondents find it more difficult to keep multiple response alternatives in mind and elaborate on their implications and relative advantages. Accordingly, response order effects increase with increasing age (for a meta-analysis see Knäuper, 1999). In both cases, the size of age-sensitive context effects can be sufficiently large to reverse the ordinal placement of cohorts.

For example, Schwarz and Knäuper (2004) asked younger (age 20 to 40) and older (age 65+) adults, which of four cities they find most attractive. Washington, D.C., was read to them as either the first or last choice. Twenty-nine percent of the younger adults chose Washington, D.C. when presented first, whereas 37% did so when presented last, for a recency effect of 8 percentage points. In contrast, 17% of the older adults chose Washington, D.C., when presented first, whereas 41% did so when presented last, for a recency effect of 24 percentage points. Note that younger adults' preference for the capital exceeds older adults' preference by 12 percentage points when Washington, D.C., is presented first, whereas older adults' preference exceeds younger adults' preference by 4 percentage point when it is presented last. Such reversals have been repeatedly observed (Knäuper, 1999) and can severely compromise comparisons across age groups, suggesting misleading conclusions about cohort differences or changes in preference across the life-span.

Culture-Related Differences

In addition to age-related differences, a still small body of research suggests that cultural differences in cognition and communication may give rise to culture-sensitive context effects (for a review see Schwarz, 2003). For example, interdependent Asian cultures value more indirect forms of communication, which require a higher amount of "reading between the lines," based on close attention to the conversational context. We may therefore expect that interdependent respondents are more sensitive to the common ground established by their previous answers, with important implications for the nature of question order effects.

Recall that speakers are supposed to provide new information rather than to reiterate information that the recipient already has (Grice, 1975). As reviewed above, Schwarz et al. (1991) observed that the correlation of marital satisfaction and general life-satisfaction dropped from $r = .67$ in the marriage-life order to $r = .18$ when the same questions were introduced by a joint lead-in that evoked the conversational norm of nonredundancy. In a follow-up study, Haberstroh and colleagues (2002) asked German and Chinese students to report on their general life-satisfaction as well as their academic satisfaction. Replicating earlier results, the answers of German students correlated $r = .53$ in the life-academic order, and this correlation increased to $r = .78$ in the academic-life order. The answers of the Chinese students showed a nearly identical correlation of $r = .50$ in the life-academic order, yet this correlation dropped to $r = .36$ in the academic-life order. In short, the Chinese students spontaneously disregarded previously provided information and responded as if the general question were worded, "Aside from what you already told me about...?" Subsequent experiments with German participants (Haberstroh, Oyserman, Schwarz, Kuhnen, & Ji., 2002) tested the causal role of independence/interdependence through priming procedures, resulting in parallel effects.

This differential sensitivity to conversational norms may produce many surprises in cross-cultural consumer studies. Suppose, for example, that a researcher first inquires about consumers' satisfaction with a specific product feature, followed by overall satisfaction with the product experience. Whereas Western consumers are likely to draw on the features brought to mind by the earlier question, Asian consumers may deliberately disregard them, paralleling the above pattern. Hence, the researcher may erroneously conclude that the product feature makes a profound contribution to overall satisfaction for American consumers, but not for Chinese consumers. Note also that these findings highlight the limits of question translation. No matter how well we equate the literal meaning of a given question through careful backtranslations, its pragmatic meaning in the context of other questions will differ across cultures when respondents are differentially likely to bring contextual information to bear on it.

A NOTE ON ATTITUDE STRENGTH

From the perspective of traditional attitude theories, context effects indicate that consumers have not yet formed a "strong" or "crystallized" attitude and are hence susceptible to temporary influences (e.g., Converse, 1964). Empirically, however, the widely shared hypothesis that context effects in attitude measurement "are greater in the case of weaker attitudes has clearly been disconfirmed," as Krosnick and Abelson (1992, p. 193) concluded after an extensive review of the literature (see also Krosnick & Schuman, 1988). This observation stands in stark contrast to the reliable finding that strong attitudes are more resistant to explicit persuasion attempts than weak attitudes (Krosnick & Abelson, 1992). However, both influence situations differ in an important respect: Explicit persuasion attempts are transparent and likely to elicit counterarguing; in contrast, questions are just perceived as questions and the thoughts they bring to mind are experienced as one's own thoughts. Hence, survey respondents are less likely to perceive an influence attempt to begin with, leaving them more susceptible to contextual influences. From the perspective of construal models, the attitude judgment is based on the current mental construal of the attitude object in both cases. However, this representation includes counterarguments in the case of explicit persuasion attempts, but not in the case of question answering, resulting in the observed asymmetries.

CONCLUSIONS

As our selective review illustrates, attitude judgments are highly context dependent. Throughout, the available findings are in accordance with the assumption that attitude judgments are constructed on the spot, based on information that is accessible at the time the attitude question is asked. In addition, construal models specify when attitude judgments will likely be stable over time (see Schwarz & Bohner, 2001, for a more detailed discussion). First, attitude judgments should be stable when the context of the attitude judgment remains the same because the same information will be temporarily accessible at t1 and t2. Second, attitude judgments should be stable when the judgment is based solely on chronically accessible information which comes to mind at both points in time, a situation that may arise when the context does not provide relevant information (e.g., Sia, Lord, Blessum, Ratcliff, & Lepper, 1997). Third, attitude judgments should be stable even when the mental representations formed at both times include a considerable amount of different information, as long as the information brought to mind at t1 and t2 has equivalent evaluative implications. That is, simply replacing one piece of information with a different one of similar valence will not change the evaluative judgment (e.g., Sia et al., 1997). Finally, attitude judgments will be similar at different points in time when the size of context effects is small, as reviewed in our discussion of the size of assimilation and contrast effects.

Construal models also specify the conditions under which we can expect attitudes to predict behaviors. In general, high attitude-behavior consistency will be observed when the representation of the attitude object formed at the time of judgment matches the representation formed at the time of the behavioral decision. Most variables known to influence attitude-behavior consistency, from previous experience with the attitude object (for a review see Fazio & Zanna, 1981) to the measurement procedures recommended by Fishbein and Ajzen (1975), can be conceptualized in these terms (see Schwarz & Bohner, 2001, for a detailed review).

ASKING QUESTIONS ABOUT BEHAVIORS

Market researchers are often interested in behavioral frequency reports. Depending on the product or service in which they are interested, market researchers may ask consumers how many fast food restaurants they have visited in the past week, how many airplane flights they have taken over the past year, or how many stock trades they have made in the past 6 months. Marketing managers need accurate frequency information for a variety of reasons. Usage estimates can be used to monitor marketing performance and improve products and services for current customers. Knowing how many times a customer uses a service, for instance, can allow a firm to retain profitable customers and increase those customers' product satisfaction through targeted promotional offers. Frequency-of-use information is also important for many marketing segmentation decisions. Targeting high and low usage segments separately, for instance, can help a firm more effectively leverage advertising campaigns. Finally, usage information is important before embarking on a new product offering because it allows companies to make market-size estimates as well as return-on–investment projections. Costly errors can be avoided by obtaining accurate information about the target market in advance.

When market researchers ask behavioral frequency questions, they would ideally like the consumer to accurately identify the behavior of interest, think back carefully over the specified period of time, recall all the times she engaged in the activity, and count them accurately. Unfortunately, autobiographical memory does not easily lend itself to this strategy. Next, we review key aspects of autobiographical memory and subsequently address the strategies respondents are likely to use when answering behavioral frequency questions.

AUTOBIOGRAPHICAL MEMORY

Not surprisingly, people forget events in their lives as time goes by, even when the event is relatively important and distinct. For example, Cannell, Fisher, and Bakker (1965) observed that only 3% of their respondents failed to report an episode of hospitalization when interviewed within ten weeks of the event, yet a full 42% did so when interviewed 1 year after the event. Moreover, when a question pertains to a frequent behavior, such as brushing one's teeth or grocery shopping, respondents are unlikely to have detailed representations of individual episodes stored in memory. Instead, the various instances of closely-related behaviors blend into one global, knowledge-like representation that lacks specific time or location markers (Linton, 1982; Strube, 1987). As a result, individual episodes of frequent behaviors become indistinguishable and irretrievable. Throughout, the available research suggests that the recall of individual behavioral episodes is largely limited to rare and unique behaviors of considerable importance, and poor even under these conditions.

Complicating things further, our autobiographical knowledge is not organized by categories of behavior (e.g., "drinking alcohol") that map easily onto survey questions. Instead, the structure of autobiographical memory can be thought of as a hierarchical network that includes extended periods (e.g., "the years I lived in New York") at the highest level of the hierarchy. Nested within this high-order period are lower-level extended events pertaining to this time, like "my first job" or "the time I was married to Bob." Further down the hierarchy are summarized events, which correspond to the knowledge-like representations of repeated behaviors noted above (e.g., "During that time, Bob and I went out to eat nearly every evening."). Specific events, like a particular episode of eating out, are represented at the lowest level of the hierarchy. To be represented at this level of specificity, however, the event has to be very unique and meaningful. As these examples illustrate, autobiographical memory is primarily organized by time ("the years in New York") and relatively global themes ("first job;" "first marriage") in a hierarchical network (see Belli, 1998, for a review). The search for any specific event in this network takes considerable time and the outcome is somewhat haphazard, depending on the entry point into the network at which the respondent begins the memory search. Hence, using multiple entry points and forming connections across different periods and themes improves recall.

FACILITATING RECALL

Drawing on basic research into the structure of autobiographical memory, researchers have developed a number of strategies to facilitate autobiographical recall (for reviews see Schwarz & Oyserman, 2001; Sudman et al., 1996; Schwarz & Sudman, 1994; Tourangeau et al., 2000).

To some extent, researchers can improve the likelihood of accurate recall by restricting the recall task to a *short and recent reference period*. This strategy, however, has its drawbacks. It may result in many "zero" answers from respondents who rarely engage in the behavior, thus limiting analyses to respondents with high behavioral frequencies. As a second strategy, researchers can provide appropriate *recall cues*. In general, the date of an event is the poorest cue, whereas cues pertaining to what happened, where it happened, and who was involved are more effective (e.g., Wagenaar, 1986). Note, however, that recall cues share many of the characteristics of closed response formats and accordingly can constrain the inferred question meaning. It is therefore important to ensure that the recall cues are relatively exhaustive and compatible with the intended interpretation of the question.

Closely related to the use of recall cues is the *decomposition* of a complex task into several more specific ones. For example, instead of asking respondents how often they ate out last month, one might ask them how often they ate at an Italian restaurant, a fast food restaurant, and so on, with the type of restaurant serving as a recall cue (e.g., Sudman & Schwarz, 1989). This strategy reliably results in higher frequency reports (e.g., Blair & Burton, 1987; Sudman & Schwarz, 1989), which initially led many researchers to conclude that it counteracts forgetting. But unfortunately, "more" is not always "better" and decomposition does not necessarily increase the *accuracy* of the obtained reports (e.g., Belli, Schwarz, Singer, & Talarico, 2000). As many studies documented, frequency estimates are regressive and people commonly overestimate low frequencies, but underestimate high frequencies (e.g., Lee, Hu, & Toh, 2000; see Belli et al., 2000 for a review). Hence, decomposing a frequent activity ("eating out") into several less frequent ones ("eating out at specific types of restaurants") appears to merely replace one error (underestimation) with another (overestimation).

In addition, autobiographical recall will improve when respondents are given sufficient *time* to search memory. Recalling specific events may take up to several seconds and repeated attempts to recall may result in the retrieval of additional material, even after a considerable number of previous trials (e.g., Williams & Hollan, 1981). Unfortunately, respondents are unlikely to have sufficient time (or motivation) to engage in repeated retrieval attempts in most research situations. Accordingly, explicitly instructing respondents that the next question is really important, and that they should do their best and take all the time they may need, has been found to improve recall (e.g., Cannell, Miller, & Oksenberg, 1981). Note, however, that this technique needs to be employed sparingly as it may lose its credibility when used for too many questions within an interview.

Although the above strategies improve recall to some extent, they fail to take full advantage of what has been learned about the hierarchical structure of autobiographical memory. A promising alternative approach is offered by the *event history calendar* (see Belli, 1998, for a review), which takes advantage of the hierarchically nested structure of autobiographical memory to facilitate recall. To help respondents recall their alcohol consumption during the last week, for example, they may be given a calendar grid that provides a column for each day of the week, cross-cut by rows that pertain to relevant contexts. They may be asked to enter for each day what they did, who they were with, if they ate out, and so on. Reconstructing the last week in this way provides a rich set of contextual cues for recalling specific episodes, in this case of alcohol consumption.

SELF-REPORTS IN CONSUMER RESEARCH

ESTIMATION STRATEGIES

Given the impediments to accurate autobiographical recall, it is not surprising that respondents resort to a variety of inference strategies to arrive at plausible estimates of their past behaviors (for a review see Sudman et al., 1996, chapter 9). When the behavior is highly regular, respondents can make frequency estimates by using *rate information* (Menon, 1993, 1994). Respondents who go to church every Sunday, or wash their hair every day, face little difficulty in computing a weekly or monthly estimate. Unfortunately, exceptions are likely to be missed and the obtained answers are only accurate when the behavior does indeed conform to the assumed rate. A related estimation strategy relies on *extrapolation* from partial recall (e.g., Blair & Burton, 1987). When asked how often she bought gasoline during the last month, for example, a respondent may reason, "I got gas once this week, so probably four times a month is about right." The accuracy of this estimate will again depend on the accuracy of the underlying assumptions.

In other cases, respondents may draw on *subjective theories* that bear on the behavior in question (for a review see Ross, 1989). When asked about past behavior, for example, respondents may ask themselves if there is reason to assume that their past behavior was different from their present behavior—if not, they may use their present behavior as an approximation. Brown (2002) and Schwarz and Oyserman (2001) review these and related strategies.

Frequency Scales

Another strategy respondents can use to estimate their behavior is consulting the formal characteristics of the questionnaire, namely frequency scales. In most studies, respondents are asked to report how frequently they engage in behaviors by checking a value on a numeric frequency scale. Consistent with the pragmatic assumptions discussed above, they assume that the researcher constructed a meaningful scale that reflects the distribution of the behavior in the "real world." Specifically, respondents assume that values in the middle range of the scale reflect the "average" or "usual" behavioral frequency, whereas values at the extremes of the scale correspond to the extremes of the distribution. Since respondents use the frequency range of the scale as a frame of reference, a respondent who considers himself to be "average" on the behavior may select an option in the middle of the scale whereas one who considers himself on the high end of the distribution will select an option on the scale extreme. This results in higher estimates when the scale presents high rather than low frequency values.

For example, only 16.2% of a sample of German consumers reported watching TV for more than 2 1/2 hours a day when presented with the low frequency scale shown in Table 43.1, whereas

Table 43.1 Reported Daily TV Consumption as a Function of Response Alternatives

Reported Daily TV Consumption			
Low Frequency Alternatives		**High Frequency Alternatives**	
Up to ½ hour	7.4%	Up to 2½ hours	62.5%
½ hour to 1 hour	17.7%	2½ hours to 3 hours	23.4%
1 hour to 1½ hours	26.5%	3 hours to 3½ hours	7.8%
1½ hours to 2 hours	14.7%	3½ hours to 4 hours	4.7%
2 hours to 2½ hours	17.7%	4 hours to 4½ hours	1.6%
More than 2½ hours	16.2%	More than 4½ hours	0.0%

Note: N = 132. Adapted from Schwarz, Hippler, Deutsch, & Strack, 1985, p. 388–395. Reprinted by permission.

37.5% did so when presented with the high frequency scale (Schwarz, Hippler, Deutsch, & Strack, 1985). Similar results have been obtained for a wide range of different behaviors, including health behaviors (e.g., Schwarz & Scheuring, 1992), sexual behaviors (e.g., Tourangeau & Smith, 1996), and consumer behaviors (e.g., Menon, Raghubir, & Schwarz, 1995). More demanding estimation tasks increase the degree to which scale anchors affect people's personal frequency estimates (e.g., Bless, Bohner, Hild, & Schwarz, 1992) and the less concrete information people have in memory, the more they rely on the scale when making their judgments (e.g., Schwarz & Bienias, 1990). In contrast, the impact of response alternatives is weak or absent when the question pertains to highly regular behaviors, for which respondents can draw on rate-of-occurrence information (e.g., "once a week"; Menon, 1994; Menon et al., 1995).

Because respondents infer information about the "average" or "usual" behavioral frequency from the scale, the scale may also influence subsequent related judgments. For example, the low frequency scale shown in Table 43.1 suggests that a TV consumption of "2 1/2 h a day" is above average, whereas the high frequency scale suggests that it is below average. Drawing on this comparison information, respondents who had reported their TV consumption on the low frequency scale also reported being less satisfied with the variety of things they do in their leisure time when compared with respondents who had reported their behavior on the high frequency scale (Schwarz et al., 1985). Such comparison effects have even been obtained under conditions where the behavioral report itself is not influenced by the response alternatives (e.g., Menon et al., 1995).

To avoid these problems, it is usually advisable to ask frequency questions in an open response format, such as, "How many times a week do you …? ___ times a week." While the answers will not be accurate, the open response format will at least avoid the systematic biases introduced by frequency scales.

Age- and Culture-Related Differences in Estimation

Given age-related declines in memory, we may expect that the impact of response alternatives is more pronounced for older than for younger respondents. The available data support this prediction with some qualifications. For example, Knäuper, Schwarz, and Park (2004) observed that the frequency range of the response scale affected older respondents more than younger respondents when the question pertained to mundane behaviors, such as buying a birthday present. On the other hand, older respondents were less affected than younger respondents when the question pertained to the frequency of physical symptoms, which older people more closely monitor and thus have more accurate memory representations.

In addition to age-related differences, studies have also observed pronounced cultural differences in respondents' everyday need to estimate, which in turn affect their behavioral frequency judgments (Ji, Schwarz, & Nisbett, 2000). In general, collectivist cultures put a higher premium on "fitting in" than individualist cultures (Oyserman, Coon, & Kemmelmeier, 2002). To "fit in," people need to monitor their own publicly observable behavior as well as the behavior of others to note undesirable deviations. On the other hand, such monitoring is not required for private, unobservable behaviors. We may therefore expect that public behaviors are better represented in memory for people living in collectivistic rather than individualistic cultures, whereas private behaviors may be equally poorly represented in both cultures. To test these conjectures, Ji and colleagues (2000) asked students in China and the United States to make frequency estimates for public and private behaviors along high or low frequency scales, or in an open response format. Replicating earlier findings, American students reported higher frequencies when presented with a high rather than low frequency scale, independent of whether the behavior was private or public. Chinese students' reports were similarly influenced by the frequency scale when the behavior was private, confirming that they relied on the same estimation strategy. In contrast, Chinese students' reports were unaffected by the response format when the behavior was public and hence needed to be monitored to ensure social fit.

As these examples illustrate, social groups differ in the extent to which they pay close attention to a given behavior. These differences in behavioral monitoring, in turn, influence the extent to which respondents need to rely on estimation strategies in reporting on their behaviors, rendering them differentially susceptible to contextual influences. Importantly, such differences in respondents' strategies can result in misleading substantive conclusions about behavioral differences across cultures and cohorts.

VAGUE QUANTIFIERS

Given the low accuracy of numeric frequency reports, researchers are often tempted to simplify respondents' task by using vague quantifiers, such as "sometimes," "frequently," and so on. Little is gained by this attempt. In general, vague quantifiers do not reflect absolute frequencies, but frequencies relative to the respondent's (usually unknown) expectations (see Pepper, 1981, for an extensive review). Accordingly, identical terms can imply vastly different frequencies in different content domains. For example, "frequently" buying a new car is quite different from "frequently" having a snack, and what counts as "frequent" car problems depends in part on how old one's car is. Importantly, different market segments may use the identical term to convey different absolute frequencies of the same behavior. For example, eating out "often" is likely to reflect higher frequencies for affluent consumers than for less affluent ones and so on. As a result, the reports are not comparable across different behaviors and market segments, rendering it unadvisable to use vague quantifiers as response alternatives.

PROXY-REPORTS: ANSWERING QUESTIONS ABOUT OTHER HOUSEHOLD MEMBERS

The difficulties associated with retrospective autobiographical behavioral reports are compounded when the questions pertain to the behavior of other household members rather than to the respondent's own behavior. Such *proxy-reports* are accepted in many surveys when the other household members are not available for an interview, thus eliminating the need for return visits or repeated calls to same household. But how much do people living in the same household really know about each other's consumption habits? Do the reports of proxy reporters actually map on to the self-reports of the targets for whom they are providing responses?

Experimental studies, based on the collection of self- and proxy-reports from two members of the same household, obtained moderate degrees of agreement between self- and proxy-respondents (e.g., Mingay, Shevell, Bradburn, & Ramirez, 1994; Skowronski, Betz, Thompson, Walker, & Shannon, 1994; Sudman, Bickart, Blair, & Menon, 1994). Not surprisingly, agreement is highest for behaviors in which both household members participated (reaching $r = .8$ for frequency reports in some cases) and lowest for individual behaviors that are rarely discussed in the household (with r's hovering around .4). Frequently discussed individual behaviors fall in between these extremes (with r's around .6). In general, proxy-respondents tend to underreport behaviors of other household members (e.g., Bickart, Blair, Sudman, & Menon, 1991; Bose & Giesbrecht, 2005).

Note that self-reports are reports of an actor about his or her own behavior, whereas proxy-reports are reports of an observer about a (well-known) other's behavior. Accordingly, we may bring basic research on actor-observer differences in social perception (Jones & Nisbett, 1971) to bear on these tasks. As experimental research in social psychology demonstrated (see Watson, 1982, for a review), observers are more likely to draw on the actor's disposition in explaining his or her behavior than is the actor him- or herself. Hence, proxy-respondents may derive their reports to a larger degree from their assumptions about the actor's disposition, a tendency that is further facilitated by their lack of situational knowledge when they did not themselves participate in the respective behavior. Consistent with this assumption, several experiments indicated that proxy-reports are more likely to be derived from dispositional information than self-reports, which are more likely to be based on episodic information (Schwarz & Wellens, 1997).

As a result of these different inferential strategies, proxy-reports on issues that are related to one another show a higher internal consistency than do self-reports for the same issues, since proxy respondents base their judgments on the same dispositional information. Hence, the internal consistency of proxy-reports should not be taken as evidence for their accuracy. Moreover, proxy-respondents underestimate the variability of the actor's behavior over time. Accordingly, proxy-reports and self-reports of behavioral frequencies show low convergence for short and recent reference periods, periods for which the actor can actually draw on episodic information in providing a self-report. As the actor's access to episodic information decreases due to longer or more distant reference periods, however, the actor has to rely on dispositional information as well. As a result, the convergence of self- and proxy-reports increases, although this increase presumably reflects reliance on the same inference strategies rather than higher accuracy (Schwarz & Wellens, 1997).

CONCLUDING REMARKS

After two decades of research at the interface of psychology and survey methodology, the general processes underlying self-reports are reasonably well understood (see Schwarz, 1999; Sudman et al., 1996; Tourangeau et al., 2000, for reviews). The accumulating evidence highlights that every questionnaire design decision involves complex trade-offs, requiring researchers to think through the issues at hand for every particular study (for guidelines see Sudman et al., 1996; Schwarz & Oyserman, 2001). Some obvious precautions include the use of cognitive pretests (see the contributions in Schwarz & Sudman, 1996) that explore potential differences in question interpretation with a small number of respondents from all target populations. In doing so, it is important to test questions in the context in which they are to be presented in the final questionnaire otherwise contextual influences on question interpretation will be missed. Moreover, the order in which response alternatives, or substantively related questions, are presented should be varied to alert researchers to the potential influence of order effects. Theoretically, such context effects reflect the constructive nature of consumer preferences and are an integral part of consumer judgment. To the extent possible, the context created in the questionnaire should therefore resemble the context in which consumers are likely to make the respective decision in daily life, discovery of which usually requires exploratory studies. Admittedly, this recommendation is more easily offered than heeded in practice.

Unfortunately, it is usually impossible to optimize all features of questionnaire design at the same time and the researcher faces complex trade-offs (Schwarz & Oyserman, 2001; Sudman et al., 1996) that require an understanding of the psychology of self-reports. At present, the standard training of consumer researchers does little to equip them for this task. Although they are likely to learn about the contextualized nature of human cognition and judgment in their consumer behavior courses, the material is often not linked to the question answering process that is at the heart of data collection, while methods training is frequently limited to advanced statistics. Given the current state of knowledge, this is hard to justify. Unless the context dependency of self-reports receives more attention in consumer research, theory tests and managerial decisions may often be at the mercy of haphazard decisions at the data collection stage. No statistical magic can compensate for the resulting problems after the fact.

REFERENCES

Belli, R. F. (1998). The structure of autobiographical memory and the event history calendar: Potential improvements in the quality of retrospective reports in surveys. *Memory, 6,* 383–406.

Belli, R. F., Schwarz, N., Singer, E., & Talarico, J. (2000). Decomposition can harm the accuracy of behavioral frequency reports. *Applied Cognitive Psychology, 14,* 295–308.

Bem, D. J., (1970). *Beliefs, attitudes and human affairs.* Belmont, CA: Brooks/Cole.

Bickart, B., Blair, J., Sudman, S., & Menon, G. (1991). An experimental study of the effects of level of participation on proxy reports of vacation planning. *Proceedings of the Survey Research Methods Section, American Statistical Association,* 397–401.

Bishop, G. F., Tuchfarber, A. J. & Oldendick, R. W. (1986). Opinions on fictitious issues: The pressure to answer survey questions. *Public Opinion Quarterly, 50,* 240–250.

Blair, E., & Burton, S. (1987). Cognitive processes used by survey respondents to answer behavioral frequency questions. *Journal of Consumer Research, 14,* 280 – 288.

Bless, H., Bohner, G., Hild, T., & Schwarz, N. (1992). Asking difficult questions: Task complexity increases the impact of response alternatives. *European Journal of Social Psychology, 22,* 309–312.

Bless, H., Schwarz, N., & Wänke, M. (2003). The size of context effects in social judgment. In J. P. Forgas, K. D. Williams, & W. Von Hippel (Eds.), *Social judgments: Implicit and explicit processes* (pp. 180–197). Cambridge: Cambridge University Press.

Bodenhausen, G. V., & Wyer, R. S. (1987). Social cognition and social reality: Information acquisition and use in the laboratory and the real world. In H. J. Hippler, N. Schwarz, & S. Sudman (Eds.), *Social information processing and survey methodology* (pp. 6–41). New York: Springer Verlag.

Bose, J., & Giesbrecht, L. (2005). *Patterns of proxy usage in the 2001 National Household Travel Survey.* Bureau of Transportation Statistics 10th Transportation Planning Applications Conference. Portland, Oregon.

Bradburn, N., Sudman, S., & Wansink, B. (2004). *Asking questions: The definitive guide to questionnaire design.* San Francisco: Jossey-Bass.

Brown, N. R. (2002). Encoding, representing, and estimating event frequencies: Multiple strategy perspectives. In P. Sedlmeier & T. Betsch (Eds.), *Etc.: Frequency processing and cognition* (pp. 37–54). New York: Oxford University Press.

Cannell, C. F., Fisher, G., & Bakker, T. (1965). Reporting on hospitalization in the Health Interview Survey. *Vital and health statistics* (PHS Publication No. 1000, Series 2, No. 6). Washington, DC: U.S. Government Printing Office.

Cannell, C. F., Miller, P. V., & Oksenberg, L. (1981). Research on interviewing techniques. In S. Leinhardt (Ed.), *Sociological Methodology* (pp. 389–437). San Francisco: Jossey-Bass.

Clark, H. H., & Schober, M. F. (1992). Asking questions and influencing answers. In J. M. Tanur (Ed.), *Questions about questions: Inquiries into the cognitive bases of surveys* (pp. 15–48). New York: Russell Sage.

Converse, P. E. (1964). The nature of belief systems in the mass public. In D. E. Apter (Ed.), *Ideology and discontent* (pp. 206–261). New York: Free Press.

Demaio, T. J., & Rothgeb, J. M. (1996). Cognitive Interviewing Techniques: In the Lab and in the Field, in N. Schwarz and S. Sudman (Eds.), *Answering questions: Methodology for determining cognitive and communicative processes in survey research* (pp. 177–195). San Francisco: Jossey-Bass Publishers.

DeMoranville, C. W., & Bienstock, C. C. (2003). Question order effects in measuring service quality. *International Journal of Research in Marketing, 20,* 217–231.

Fazio, R. H., & Zanna, M. P. (1981). Direct experience and attitude-behavior consistency. In L. Berkowitz (Ed.), *Advances in experimental social psychology* (Vol. 14, pp. 161–202). New York: Academic Press.

Feldman, J. M., & Lynch, J. G. (1988). Self-generated validity and other effects of measurement on belief, attitude, intention, and behavior. *Journal of Applied Psychology, 73,* 421–435.

Fishbein, M., & Ajzen, I. (1975). *Belief, attitude, intention, and behavior: An introduction to theory and research*. Reading, MA: Addison-Wesley.

Grice, H. P. (1975). Logic and conversation. In P. Cole, & J. L. Morgan (Eds.), *Syntax and semantics, Vol.3: Speech acts* (pp. 41–58). New York: Academic Press.

Haberstroh, S., Oyserman, D., Schwarz, N., Kuhnen, U., & Ji, L. (2002) Is the interdependent self more sensitive to the question context than the independent self? Self-construal and the observation of the conversational norms. *Journal of Experimental Social Psychology, 38*, 323–329.

Haddock, G., & Carrick, R. (1999). How to make a politician more likeable and effective: Framing political judgments through the numeric values of a rating scale. *Social Cognition, 17*, 298–311.

Hawkins, D. I., & Coney, K. A. (1981). Uninformed response error in survey research. *Journal of Marketing Research, 18*, 370–374.

Herr, P. M. (1986). Consequences of priming: Judgment and behavior. *Journal of Personality and Social Psychology, 51*, 1106–1115.

Higgins, E. T. (1996). Knowledge activation: Accessibility, applicability, and salience. In E. T. Higgins & A. W. Kruglanski (Eds.), *Social psychology: Handbook of basic principles* (pp. 133–168). New York: Guilford.

Ji, L., Schwarz, N., & Nisbett, R. E. (2000). Culture, autobiographical memory, and behavioral frequency reports: Measurement issues in cross-cultural studies. *Personality and Social Psychology Bulletin, 26*, 586–594.

Jones, E. E., & Nisbett, R. E. (1971). The actor and the observer: Divergent Perceptions of the Causes of Behavior. In E. E. Jones, D. E. Kanouse, H. H. Kelley, R. E. Nisbett, S. Valins, & B. Weiner (Eds.), *Attribution: Perceiving the causes of behavior* (pp. 79–94). Morristown, NJ: General Learning Press.

Knäuper, B. (1999). The impact of age and education on response order effects in attitude measurement. *Public Opinion Quarterly, 63*, 347–370.

Knäuper, B., Schwarz, N., & Park, D. C. (2004). Frequency reports across age groups: Differential effects of frequency scales. *Journal of Official Statistics, 20*, 91–96.

Krech, D., & Crutchfield R. S. (1948). *Theory and problems of social psychology*. New York: McGraw-Hill.

Krosnick, J. A., & Abelson, R. P. (1992). The case for measuring attitude strength in surveys. In J. M. Tanur (Ed.), *Questions about questions: Inquiries into the cognitive bases of surveys* (pp. 177–203). New York: Russell-Sage.

Krosnick, J. A., & Alwin, D. F. (1987). An evaluation of a cognitive theory of response order effects in survey measurement. *Public Opinion Quarterly, 51*, 201–219.

Krosnick, J. A., & Schuman, H. (1988). Attitude intensity, importance, and centrality, and susceptibility to response effects. *Journal of Personality and Social Psychology, 54*, 940–952.

Lee, E., Hu, M. Y., & Toh, R. S. (2000). Are consumer survey results distorted? Systematic impact of behavioral frequency and duration on survey response errors. *Journal of Marketing Research, 37*, 125–133.

Linton, M. (1982). Transformations of memory in everyday life. In U. Neisser (Ed.), *Memory observed: Remembering in natural contexts* (pp. 77–91). San Francisco: Freeman.

Lombardi, W. J., Higgins, E. T., & Bargh, J. A. (1987). The role of consciousness in priming effects on categorization: Assimilation and contrast as a function of awareness of the priming task. *Personality and Social Psychology Bulletin, 13*, 411–429.

Martin, L. L. (1986). Set/reset: use and disuse of concepts in impression formation. *Journal of Personality and Social Psychology, 51*, 493–504.

Menon, G. (1993). The effects of accessibility of information in memory on judgments of behavioral frequencies. *Journal of Consumer Research, 20*, 431–440.

Menon, G. (1994). Judgments of behavioral frequencies: Memory search and retrieval strategies. In N. Schwarz & S. Sudman, S. (Eds.) (1994). *Autobiographical memory and the validity of retrospective reports* (pp. 161–172). New York: Springer Verlag.

Menon, G., Raghubir, P., & Schwarz, N. (1995). Behavioral frequency judgments: An accessibility-diagnosticity framework. *Journal of Consumer Research, 22*, 212–228.

Mingay, D. J., Shevell, S. K., Bradburn, N. M., & Ramirez, C. (1994). Self and proxy reports of everyday events. In N. Schwarz & S. Sudman (Eds.), *Autobiographical memory and the validity of retrospective reports* (pp. 235–250). New York: Springer Verlag.

Norenzayan, A., & Schwarz, N. (1999) Telling what they want to know: Participants tailor causal attributions to researchers' interests. *European Journal of Social Psychology, 29*, 1011–1020.

Oyserman, D., Coon, H., & Kemmelmeier, M. (2002). Rethinking individualism and collectivism: Evaluation of theoretical assumptions and meta-analyses. *Psychological Bulletin, 128*, 3–73.

Park, D. C. (2000). The basic mechanisms accounting for age-related decline in cognitive function. In D. C. Park & N. Schwarz (Eds.), *Cognitive aging: A primer* (pp. 3–22). Philadelphia: Psychology Press.

Payne, S. L. (1951). *The art of asking questions*. Princeton, NJ: Princeton University Press.

Pepper, S. C. (1981). Problems in the quantification of frequency expressions. In D. W. Fiske (Ed.), *Problems with language imprecision: New directions for methodology of social and behavioral science* (Vol. 9). San Francisco: Jossey-Bass.

Pew Research Center (2004). Moral values: How important? Voters liked campaign 2004 But too much 'mud slinging.' *The Pew Research Center Survey Reports, November 11, 2004.*

Pham, M. T. (2004). The logic of feeling. *Journal of Consumer Psychology, 14*, 360–369.

Ross, M. (1989). The relation of implicit theories to the construction of personal histories. *Psychological Review, 96*, 341–357.

Schul, Y., & Schiff, M. (1993). Measuring satisfaction with organizations: Predictions from information accessibility. *Public Opinion Quarterly, 57*, 536–551.

Schuman, H., & Kalton, G. (1985). Survey methods. In G. Lindzey, & E. Aronson (Eds.), *Handbook of social psychology* (Vol. 1, pp. 635–697). New York: Random House.

Schuman, H., & Presser, S. (1981). *Questions and answers in attitude surveys*. New York: Academic Press.

Schwarz, N. (1996). Survey research: Collecting data by asking questions. In G. Semin & K. Fiedler (Eds.), *Applied social psychology* (pp. 65–90). Thousand Oaks, CA: Sage.

Schwarz, N. (1999). Self-reports: How the questions shape the answers. *American Psychologist, 54*, 93–105.

Schwarz, N. (2003). Culture-sensitive context effects: A challenge for cross-cultural surveys. In J. Harkness, F. van de Vijver, & P. Ph. Mohler (Eds.), *Cross-cultural survey methods* (pp. 93–100). New York: Wiley.

Schwarz, N. (2004). Meta-cognitive experiences in consumer judgment and decision making. *Journal of Consumer Psychology, 14*, 332–348.

Schwarz, N. (2007). The meaning of shopping. Unpublished raw data.

Schwarz, N., & Bienias, J. (1990). What mediates the impact of response alternatives on frequency reports of mundane behaviors? *Applied Cognitive Psychology, 4*, 61–72.

Schwarz, N., & Bless, H. (1992a). Assimilation and contrast effects in attitude measurement: An inclusion/exclusion model. *Advances in consumer research, 19*, 72–77.

Schwarz, N., & Bless, H. (1992b). Scandals and the public's trust in politicians: Assimilation and contrast effects. *Personality and social psychology bulletin, 18*, 574–579.

Schwarz, N., & Bless, H. (in press). Mental construal processes: The inclusion/exclusion model. In D. A. Stapel & J. Suls (Eds.), *Assimilation and contrast in social psychology*. Philadelphia: Psychology Press.

Schwarz, N., & Bohner, G. (2001). The construction of attitudes. In A. Tesser & N. Schwarz (Eds.), *Intraindividual processes (Blackwell handbook of psychology, Vol. 1)*. Oxford: Blackwell.

Schwarz, N., & Clore, G. L. (1996). Feelings and phenomenal experiences. In E. T. Higgins & A. Kruglanski (Eds.) *Social psychology: Handbook of basic principles* (pp. 433–465). New York: Guilford.

Schwarz, N., & Hippler, H. J. (1995). Subsequent questions may influence answers to preceding questions in mail surveys. *Public Opinion Quarterly, 59*, 93–97

Schwarz, N., Hippler, H. J., Deutsch, B., & Strack, F. (1985). Response categories: Effects on behavioral reports and comparative judgments. *Public Opinion Quarterly, 49*, 388–395.

Schwarz, N., & Knäuper, B. (2004). Kognitionspsychologie und Umfrageforschung: Altersabhängige Kontexteffekte. [Cognitive psychology and survey research: Age-sensitive context effects.] *Kölner Zeitschrift für Soziologie und Sozialpsychologie.*

Schwarz, N., Knäuper, B., Hippler, H. J., Noelle-Neumann, E., & Clark, F. (1991). Rating scales: Numeric values may change the meaning of scale labels. *Public Opinion Quarterly, 55*, 570–582.

Schwarz, N., & Oyserman, D. (2001). Asking questions about behavior: Cognition, communication and questionnaire construction. *American Journal of Evaluation, 22*, 127–160.

Schwarz, N., & Scheuring, B. (1992). Selbstberichtete Verhaltens- und Symptomhäufigkeiten: Was Befragte aus Anwortvorgaben des Fragebogens lernen. [Frequency-reports of psychosomatic symptoms: What respondents learn from response alternatives.] *Zeitschrift für Klinische Psychologie, 22*, 197–208.

Schwarz, N., Strack, F., & Mai, H. P. (1991). Assimilation and contrast effects in part-whole question sequences: A conversational logic analysis. *Public Opinion Quarterly, 55*, 3–23.

Schwarz, N., Strack, F., Müller, G., & Chassein, B. (1988). The range of response alternatives may determine the meaning of the question: Further evidence on informative functions of response alternatives. *Social Cognition, 6*, 107–117.

Schwarz, N., & Sudman, S. (1994). *Autobiographical memory and the validity of retrospective reports.* New York: Springer Verlag.

Schwarz, N., & Sudman, S. (1996). *Answering questions: Methodology for determining cognitive and communicative processes in survey research.* San Francisco: Jossey-Bass.

Schwarz, N., & Wellens, T. (1997). Cognitive dynamics of proxy responding: The diverging perspectives of actors and observers. *Journal of Official Statistics, 13,* 159–179.

Sia, T. L., Lord, C. G., Blessum, K. A., Ratcliff, C. D., & Lepper, M. R. (1997). Is a rose always a rose? The role of social category exemplar change in attitude stability and attitude-behavior consistency. *Journal of Personality and Social Psychology, 72,* 501–514.

Skowronski, J. J., Betz, A. D., Thompson, C. P., Walker, W. R., & Shannon, L. (1994). The impact of differing memory domains on event dating processes in self and proxy reports. In S. Sudman, & N. Schwarz, (Eds.), *Autobiographical memory and the validity of retrospective reports* (pp. 217–234). New York: Springer-Verlag.

Smith, E. E. (1995). Concepts and categorization. In E. E. Smith & D. N. Osherson (Eds.), *Thinking: An invitation to cognitive science* (2nd ed., Vol. 3, pp. 3–32). Cambridge, MA: MIT Press.

Strack, F., & Martin, L. L. (1987). Thinking, judging, and communicating: A process account of context effects in attitude surveys. In H. J. Hippler, N. Schwarz, & S. Sudman (Eds.), *Social information processing and survey methodology* (pp. 123–148). New York: Springer Verlag.

Strack, F., Martin, L. L., & Schwarz, N. (1988). Priming and communication: The social determinants of information use in judgments of life-satisfaction. *European Journal of Social Psychology, 18,* 429–442.

Strack, F., & Schwarz, N. (1992). Implicit cooperation: The case of standardized questioning. In G. Semin & F. Fiedler (Eds.), *Social cognition and language* (pp. 173–193). Beverly Hills: Sage.

Strack, F., Schwarz, N., Bless, H., Kübler, A., & Wänke, M. (1993). Awareness of the influence as a determinant of assimilation versus contrast. *European Journal of Social Psychology, 23,* 53–62.

Strack, F., Schwarz, N., & Gschneidinger, E. (1985). Happiness and reminiscing: The role of time perspective, mood, and mode of thinking. *Journal of Personality and Social Psychology, 49,* 1460–1469.

Strack, F., Schwarz, N., & Wänke, M. (1991). Semantic and pragmatic aspects of context effects in social and psychological research. *Social Cognition, 9,* 111–125.

Strube, G. (1987). Answering survey questions: The role of memory. In H. J. Hippler, N. Schwarz, & S. Sudman (Eds.), *Social information processing and survey methodology* (pp. 86–101). New York: Springer Verlag.

Sudman, S., Bickart, B. A., Blair, J., & Menon, G. (1994). The effect of level of participation on reports of behavior and attitudes by proxy reporters. In N. Schwarz & S. Sudman (Eds.) *Autobiographical memory and the validity of retrospective reports* (pp. 161–172). New York: Springer Verlag.

Sudman, S., Bradburn, N. M., & Schwarz, N. (1996). *Thinking about answers: The application of cognitive processes to survey methodology.* San Francisco, CA: Jossey-Bass.

Sudman, S., & Schwarz, N. (1989). Contributions of cognitive psychology to advertising research. *Journal of Advertising Research, 29,* 43–53.

Tourangeau, R. (1984). Cognitive science and survey methods: A cognitive perspective. In T. Jabine, M. Straf, J. Tanur, & R. Tourangeau (Eds.), *Cognitive aspects of survey methodology: Building a bridge between disciplines* (pp. 73–100). Washington, DC: National Academy Press.

Tourangeau, R., Rips, L. J., & Rasinski, K. (2000). *The psychology of survey response.* Cambridge: Cambridge University Press.

Tourangeau, R., & Smith, T. (1996). Asking sensitive questions: The impact of data collection, question format, and question context. *Public Opinion Quarterly, 60,* 275–304.

Wagenaar, W. A. (1986). My memory: A study of autobiographical memory over six years. *Cognitive Psychology, 18,* 225–252.

Wänke, M., Bless, H., & Schwarz, N. (1998). Context effects in product line extensions. *Journal of Consumer Psychology, 7,* 299–322.

Watson, D. (1982). The actor and the observer: How are their perceptions of causality divergent? *Psychological Bulletin, 92,* 682–700.

Wedell, D. H., Parducci, A., & Geiselman, R. E. (1987). A formal analysis of ratings of physical attractiveness: Successive contrast and simultaneous assimilation. *Journal of Experimental Social Psychology, 23,* 230–249.

Williams, M. D., & Hollan, J. D. (1981). The process of retrieval from very long term memory. *Cognitive Science, 5,* 87–119.

44

Cross-Cultural Consumer Psychology

Sharon Shavitt

University of Illinois at Urbana-Champaign

Angela Y. Lee

Northwestern University

Timothy P. Johnson

University of Illinois at Chicago

OVERVIEW

Every year, multinational companies spend billions of dollars in marketing their products around the world. Some of this money is wasted or, worse, actually damages the marketer's reputation through cultural or linguistic *faux pas* (e.g., Ricks, 1983). As new global markets emerge, and existing markets become increasingly segmented along ethnic or subcultural lines, the need to market effectively to consumers who have different cultural values has never been more acute. Thus, it is no surprise that in the last ten to 15 to 20 years, culture has rapidly emerged as a central focus of research in consumer psychology.

What Is Culture?

Culture is a crucial concept for the understanding of consumer behavior because it is the lens through which people view marketing messages and products. Culture consists of shared elements that provide the standards for perceiving, believing, evaluating, communicating, and acting among those who share a language, a historical period, and a geographic location. As a psychological construct, culture can be studied in multiple ways—across nations, across ethnic groups within nations, across individuals within nations (focusing on cultural orientation), and even within individuals through the priming of cultural values. As will be discussed presently, regardless of how culture is studied, cultural distinctions have been demonstrated to have important implications for advertising content, persuasiveness of appeals, consumer motivation, consumer judgment processes, and consumer response styles.

Chapter Organization and Scope

In this chapter, numerous studies on these topics are reviewed and discussed. Because reviewing the rapidly growing area of cross-cultural psychology could fill several handbook chapters, we are by necessity selective in our coverage. We focus more heavily on findings specific to the consumer domain rather than a more general review of cultural differences. The content is organized around both the theoretical and the methodological implications of cultural differences in consumer judgments. The individualism/collectivism cultural construct and independent/interdependent self-construal construct are given special attention because extensive research has demonstrated the implications of these variables for outcomes relevant to consumer behavior. Because the study of culture requires the cross-cultural equivalence of measurement, the second half of this chapter addresses in detail specific measurement issues and culturally based response biases likely to be of interest to consumer psychologists. We close with a review of issues and methods for addressing measurement equivalence and cultural variability in response styles.

CULTURAL VARIATION: STRUCTURAL ISSUES

What Are the Key Cultural Constructs or Dimensions?

The constructs of *individualism* and *collectivism* represent the most broadly used dimensions of cultural variability for cross-cultural comparison (Gudykunst & Ting-Toomey, 1988). In individualistic (IND) cultures, people tend to prefer independent relationships to others and to subordinate the goals of their ingroups to their own personal goals. In collectivistic (COL) cultures, in contrast, individuals tend to prefer interdependent relationships to others and to subordinate their personal goals to those of their ingroups (Hofstede, 1980, 2001; Triandis, 1989). The key distinction involves the extent to which one defines the self in relation to others. The focus is on whether the self is defined as autonomous and unique or seen as inextricably and fundamentally embedded within a larger social network. This distinction has also been referred to as egocentric versus sociocentric selves (Shweder & Bourne, 1982), or independent vs. interdependent self-construal (Markus & Kitayama, 1991).

The independent self-construal defines the individual in terms of unique attributes and characteristics that distinguish him or her from others, whereas the interdependent self-construal defines the individual in terms of social roles and relationships with others. National cultures that celebrate the values of independence, as in the United States, Canada, Germany, and Denmark, are typically categorized as individualistic societies in which an independent self-construal is common. In contrast, cultures that nurture the values of fulfilling one's obligations and responsibilities over one's own personal wishes or desires, including most East Asian and Latin American countries, such as China, Korea, Japan, and Mexico, are categorized as collectivistic societies in which an interdependent self-construal is common (Hofstede, 1980, 2001; Markus & Kitayama, 1991; Triandis, 1989).

A very large body of research in psychology has demonstrated the many implications of individualism/collectivism and independent/interdependent self-construals for social perception and social behavior (see Markus & Kitayama, 1991; Triandis, 1989, 1995). In consumer-relevant domains, several comparisons between individualistic and collectivistic societies have pointed to important differences in the content of advertising appeals (e.g., Alden, Hoyer, & Lee, 1993; S. M. Choi, Lee, & Kim, 2005; Han & Shavitt, 1994; Hong, Muderrisoglu, & Zinkhan, 1987; Kim & Markus, 1999; Lin, 2001), the processing and persuasiveness of advertising appeals (Aaker & Maheswaran, 1997; Aaker & Williams, 1998; Han & Shavitt, 1994; Zhang & Gelb, 1996), and the determinants of consumers' purchase intentions (C. Lee & Green, 1991).

Recent developments suggest that these two distinct culturally determined self-schemas may co-exist in memory, such that contextual factors can temporarily activate either the independent or the interdependent self-construal. It is relatively easy to activate distinct independent versus interdependent self-views (e.g., by asking people to circle singular vs. plural first-person pronouns in a 1-paragraph essay, Brewer & Gardner, 1996). Indeed, people in general, and especially bicultural people, can readily switch back and forth between these independent and interdependent cultural frames in response to their contexts (Fu, Chiu, Morris, & Young, 2006; Lau-Gesk, 2003). When activated, these situationally accessible self-views appear to alter social perception and consumer judgments in ways that are highly consistent with cross-cultural findings (e.g., Brewer & Gardner, 1996; Gardner, Gabriel, & Lee, 1999; Hong, Ip, Chiu, Morris, & Menon, 2001; Lee, Aaker, & Gardner, 2000; Mandel, 2003; Torelli, 2006; Trafimow, Triandis, & Goto, 1991). For instance, Lau-Gesk (2003) found that independent (interdependent) self-construals were temporarily activated when bicultural consumers were exposed to individually-focused (interpersonally focused) appeals.

In sum, the distinctions between IND and COL societies, and independent and interdependent self-construals, are crucial to the cross-cultural understanding of consumer behavior. Indeed, whereas the 1980s were labeled the decade of individualism/collectivism in cross-cultural psychology (Kagitcibasi, 1994), similar distinctions represent the dominant structural approach in cross-cultural consumer research in 1990s and 2000s. The studies to be reviewed in this chapter offer a wealth of evidence that these cultural classifications have fundamental implications for consumption-related outcomes.

Emergent Topics: Expanding the Set of Cultural Dimensions

The conceptualizations of IND and COL, and independence/interdependence, have historically been broad and multidimensional, summarizing a host of differences in focus of attention, self-definitions, motivations, emotional connections to ingroups, as well as belief systems and behavioral patterns (M. H. Bond, 2002; Ho & Chiu, 1994; Hofstede, 1980; Oyserman, Coon, & Kemmelmeier, 2002; Triandis, 1995; Triandis, Bontempo, Villareal, Asai, & Lucca, 1988; Triandis, Leung, Villareal, & Clack, 1985). Nevertheless, recent studies have proposed useful refinements to the broader INDCOL or independent/interdependent cultural categories. For instance, Rhee, Uleman, and Lee (1996) distinguished between kin and nonkin versions of IND and COL and showed that Asians and European Americans manifested distinct patterns of relations between kin and nonkin IND. Gelfand, Bhawuk, Nishii, and Bechtold (2004) distinguished between institutional and ingroup collectivism, and showed that there can be substantial differences in the degree to which a society encourages institutional collective action versus interpersonal interdependence (e.g., Scandinavian societies emphasize the former but not the latter).

Gaines et al. (1997) distinguished between IND, COL, and *familism* (orientation toward the welfare of one's family), and showed that this delineation better captured the cultural orientations observed in racial minority respondents in the United States. IND, COL, and familism proved to be separate dimensions that differed in their ability to account for race/ethnicity differences in cultural values. Cross, Bacon, and Morris (2000) demonstrated that a more relational version of interdependence applies in Western compared to Eastern societies, and provided a scale for its measurement (see also Kemmelmeier & Oyserman, 2001). Gabriel and Gardner (1999) examined this distinction in relational (dyadic) versus more group-oriented interdependence and reported gender differences indicating that women are more relational but less group-oriented than men in their patterns of interdependent judgments and behaviors. Theirs are among several studies pointing to gender differences in specific cultural orientations (see Cross & Madson, 1997; Kashima et al., 1995).

In sum, the nature and meaning of IND and COL (or of independent and interdependent self-construals) appear to vary across cultural, institutional, gender, and ethnic lines. Although the breadth of the INDCOL constructs lends integrative strengths, further refinement of these categories holds the potential to enhance prediction of consumer behavior.

The Horizontal/Vertical Distinction   Which additional cultural categories offer value in the prediction of cross-cultural consumer behavior? Within the INDCOL framework, Triandis and his colleagues (Singelis, Triandis, Bhawuk, & Gelfand, 1995; Triandis, 1995; Triandis & Gelfand, 1998) have recently introduced a further distinction between societies that are *horizontal* (valuing equality) and those that are *vertical* (emphasizing hierarchy). The horizontal/vertical distinction emerges from the observation that American or British individualism differs from, say, Norwegian or Danish individualism in much the same way that Japanese or Korean collectivism differs from the collectivism of the Israeli kibbutz. Specifically, in vertical individualist societies (VI; e.g., U.S., Great Britain, France), people tend to be concerned with improving their individual status and distinguishing themselves from others via competition. In contrast, in horizontal individualist societies (HI; e.g., Sweden, Norway, Australia), where people prefer to view themselves as equal to others in status, the focus is on expressing one's uniqueness, capability, and self-reliance. In vertical collectivist societies (VC; e.g., Japan, Korea, India), people focus on fulfilling obligations to others, and on enhancing the status of their ingroups in competition with outgroups, even when that entails sacrificing their own personal goals. In horizontal collectivist societies (HC; exemplified historically by the Israeli kibbutz), the focus is on sociability, benevolence, and interdependence with others in an egalitarian context (Erez & Earley, 1987).

When such distinctions are taken into account, however, it becomes apparent that the societies chosen to represent IND and COL cultural syndromes in consumer research have almost exclusively been vertically oriented. Specifically, the modal comparisons are between the United States (VI) and any of a number of Pacific Rim countries (VC). It may be argued, therefore, that much of what is known about consumer behavior in individualistic and collectivistic societies reflects vertical forms of these syndromes and may not generalize, for example, to comparisons between Sweden (HI) and Israel (HC) or other sets of horizontal cultures. As an example, conformity in product choice, as examined by Kim and Markus (1999), may be a tendency specific to VC cultures, in which deference to authority and to ingroup wishes is stressed. Much lower levels of conformity may be observed in HC cultures, which emphasize sociability but not deference (Triandis & Gelfand, 1998). Thus, it may be inappropriate to ascribe differences in consumers' conformity between Korea (VC) and the United States (VI) solely to the role of IND/COL or independence/interdependence, because such conformity might not be prevalent in horizontal societies. That is, levels of product conformity in HC contexts might not exceed those in HI contexts.

Indeed, several recent studies examining the implications of this horizontal/vertical cultural distinction have provided evidence for its value as a predictor of new consumer psychology phenomena and as a basis for refining the understanding of known phenomena (Shavitt, Lalwani, Zhang, & Torelli, 2006). For instance, Gürhan-Canli and Maheswaran (2000) demonstrated that the tendency to favor products from one's own country over foreign products (a country-of-origin effect) emerged more strongly in Japan (a VC culture) than in the United States (a VI culture). This fits well with a conceptualization of collectivists as being oriented toward their ingroups. However, mediational analyses using individual consumers' self-rated cultural values indicated that only the vertical dimension of IND and COL accounted for the country-of-origin effects in Japan. In other words, the collectivistic tendency to favor one's own country's products appeared to be driven by cultural values that stress hierarchy, competition, and deference to ingroup wishes, not by values that stress interdependence more generally.

In line with this, research suggests that advertising messages with themes that emphasize status, prestige, hierarchy, and distinction may be more prevalent and persuasive in vertical cultural contexts (Shavitt, Lalwani et al., 2006). Such advertisements also appear to be generally more persuasive for those with a vertical cultural orientation, and may be inappropriate for those with a horizontal one. Shavitt, Zhang, and Johnson (2006) asked U.S. respondents to write advertisements that they personally would find persuasive. The extent to which the ad appeals that they wrote emphasized status themes was positively correlated with respondents' vertical cultural orientation (and negatively correlated with their horizontal cultural orientation). Moreover, content analyses of magazine advertisements in several countries suggested that status-oriented themes of hierarchy, luxury, prominence, and distinction were generally more prevalent in societies presumed to have vertical cultural profiles (e.g., Korea, Russia) than a horizontal cultural profile (Denmark).

Lalwani, Shavitt, and Johnson (2006) showed that the horizontal/vertical distinction provides a basis for refining our understanding of individualism/collectivism effects. Their studies showed that individualism/collectivism differences in socially desirable responding appear to be mediated at the individual level by horizontal (but not vertical) IND and COL values. These findings shed light on the motivational drivers linking culture with socially desirable response styles. Specifically, the response styles that were observed appeared to reflect distinct self-presentational goals—goals of being seen as sociable and benevolent (HC) versus self-reliant and capable (HI).

Additional Dimensions Numerous other cultural dimensions deserve further attention in consumer research. A focus upon these relatively under-researched dimensions as antecedents may allow for broadening the range of cultural differences beyond those currently investigated. For instance, Schwartz's extensive research (e.g., Schwartz, 1992; Schwartz & Bilsky, 1987, 1990) has validated 10 motivationally distinct types of values. The quasi-circumplex structure of values that has emerged cross-nationally (Schwartz & Boehnke, 2004) appears largely consistent with the HI, VI, HC, VC typology. Data from two independent sets of 23 samples drawn from 27 countries ($N = 10,857$) supported the assumption of contradiction between values such as power and achievement (corresponding to a vertical orientation) and benevolence and universalism (corresponding to a horizontal orientation), which were hypothesized to be structurally oppositional (Schwartz & Boehnke, 2004). Although few if any consumer psychology studies have employed Schwartz's value typology, it does offer a particularly detailed and comprehensive basis for classification.

In his large-scale studies of work values, Hofstede (1980, 2001) derived three other dimensions of cultural variation in addition to individualism: *power distance* (acceptance of power inequality in organizations, a dimension conceptually relevant to the vertical/horizontal distinction), *uncertainty avoidance* (the degree of tolerance for ambiguity or uncertainty about the future), and *masculinity/femininity* (preference for achievement and assertiveness versus modesty and nurturing relationships). A few marketing-oriented studies have employed these nation-level classifications (e.g., Blodgett, Lu, Rose, & Vitell, 2001; e.g., Dwyer, Mesak, & Hsu, 2005; Earley, 1999; Johnson, Kulesa, Cho, & Shavitt, 2005; Spencer-Oatey, 1997), but more potential remains for identifying consequences for consumer judgments and behaviors. For instance, uncertainty avoidance has been conceptualized as a syndrome related to anxiety, rule orientation, need for security, and deference to experts (Hofstede, 1980). As such, one might speculate that the level of uncertainty avoidance in a culture will predict the tendency for advertisements to use fear appeals or appeals to safety and security, and the tendency for advertisements to employ expert spokespersons. Differences along this cultural dimension may also predict the level of public support for stricter regulation of marketers and advertisers. Moreover, patterns in the diffusion of product innovations, particularly innovations whose purchase entails a degree of risk, may vary with the level of uncertainty avoidance in a society.

The main point here is that these relatively unexplored dimensions of cultural comparison have multiple implications for advertising and marketing processes. Attention to a broader set of cultural dimensions will not only expand the range of independent variables in our research, but will also prompt consideration of cultural consequences hitherto unexamined in cross-cultural studies.

CULTURE AND THE SELF: SELF-REGULATORY FOCUS

Regardless of whether they are chronically or temporarily made accessible, alternative self-construals are thought to reflect different psychological goals. More specifically, the independent goal of distinguishing oneself from others through success and achievement and the interdependent goal of maintaining harmony with respect to others through the fulfillment of obligations and responsibilities serve as self-regulatory guides that direct consumers' attention, attitudes, and behaviors (Higgins, 1997).

The independent goal of being positively distinct, with its emphasis on achievement and autonomy, is more consistent with a promotion focus; whereas the interdependent goal of harmoniously fitting in with others, with its emphasis on fulfilling social roles and maintaining connections with others, is more consistent with a prevention focus. People with a promotion focus regulate their attitudes and behaviors toward the pursuit of growth and the achievement of hopes and aspirations to satisfy their needs for nurturance. They pursue their goals with eagerness and are sensitive to the absence and presence of positive outcomes. In contrast, those with a prevention focus regulate their attitudes and behaviors toward the pursuit of safety and the fulfillment of duties and obligations to satisfy their needs for security. They pursue their goal with vigilance and are sensitive to the absence and presence of negative outcomes.

The notion that people from Western cultures (whose independent self-construal is more accessible) tend to be promotion focused and people from Eastern cultures (whose interdependent self-construal is more accessible) tend to be prevention focused is consistent with the pattern of results found in self-enhancement studies. For example, as will be discussed shortly, it has been shown that Americans are more likely to engage in self-enhancement that focuses on the positive features of the self, whereas Japanese are more likely to engage in self-criticism that focuses on the negative aspects of the self in order to avoid future mishaps (Heine, Lehman, Peng, & Greenholtz, 2002; Kitayama, Markus, Matsumoto, & Norasakkunkit, 1997).

That distinct self-construals are associated with distinct types of self-regulatory focus has important implications for consumer research. First, consumers consider information that is compatible with the dominant self view to be more important (Lee et al., 2000). Specifically, promotion (prevention) focused information that addresses the concerns of growth and achievement (safety and security) is more relevant and hence deemed more important to those individuals with a dominant independent (interdependent) self-construal (Aaker & Lee, 2001; Lee et al., 2000). Using different operationalizations of self-construal that include cultural orientation (North American vs. East Asian), individual disposition (Singelis, 1994), and situational prime, Lee and her colleagues (Lee et al., 2000) demonstrate that individuals with a more accessible independent self view perceive a scenario that emphasizes gains or nongains to be more important than one that emphasizes losses or nonlosses. They also experience more intense promotion-focused emotions such as cheerfulness and dejection. In contrast, those with a more dominant interdependent self view perceive a scenario that emphasizes losses or nonlosses to be more important than one that emphasizes gains or nongains. They also experience more intense prevention-focused emotions such as peacefulness and agitation. Thus, consumers with distinct self-construals are more persuaded by information that addresses their regulatory concerns when argument quality is strong (Aaker & Lee, 2001; Agrawal & Maheswaran, 2005; J. Wang & Lee, 2006), but less persuaded when the argument quality is weak. Chen, Ng, and Rao (2005) also find that consumers with a dominant independent self-construal are more willing to pay for expedited delivery when presented with a promotion framed message (i.e., to enjoy a product early), whereas those with a dominant interdependent self-construal are more willing to pay for expedited delivery when presented with a prevention framed message (i.e., avoid delay in receiving a product). These matching effects between self-construal and regulatory focus are observed regardless of whether self-construal is situationally made more accessible or culturally nurtured (Aaker & Lee, 2001; Agrawal & Maheswaran, 2005; Chen et al., 2005). Interestingly, brand commitment (defined as consumers' public attachment or pledging to the brand) seems to moderate the effectiveness of the chronic versus situational regulatory relevance effects (Agrawal & Maheswaran, 2005). In particular, Agrawal and Maheswaran (2005) find that appeals consistent with the chronic self-construal are more persuasive under high brand commitment, whereas appeals consistent with the primed (independent or interdependent) self-construal are more effective under low brand commitment. According to the authors, consumers who are committed to the brand have a readily accessible knowledge structure related to the brand. To these consumers, not only is brand information highly accessible, it is also linked to other chronically accessible cognition in memory. Hence exposure to brand information such as an advertising appeal is likely to activate their chronic self-construal. Thus, appeals consistent with their chronic self-construal are more persuasive. However, for the low commitment consumers, brand information is not linked to any chronic knowledge base. Thus, appeals that are consistent with their more accessible self-construal at any one time (i.e., their primed self-construal) are more persuasive.

More recent research suggests that regulatory relevance effects may be moderated by involvement such that people are more likely to rely on their regulatory focus as a filter to selectively process information when they are not expending cognitive resources to process information (Briley & Aaker, 2006; Wang & Lee, 2006). For example, Briley and Aaker (2006) demonstrate that participants who are culturally inclined to have a promotion or prevention focus hold more favorable attitudes toward those products that address their regulatory concerns—but only when they are asked to provide their initial reactions or when their evaluation is made under cognitive load or under time pressure. The culturally induced regulatory relevance effects disappear when participants are asked to make deliberated evaluations or when they are able to expend cognitive resources on the task.

Distinct self-construals with their corresponding regulatory goals also appear to be the basis of different temporal perspectives across members of different cultures such that those with a dominant independent self-construal are more likely to construe events at a more distant future than those with a dominant interdependent self-construal. For the independents, their regulatory goal that emphasizes growth and achievement takes time to attain. Further, their sensitivity to gains and nongains prompts them to focus on positives (vs. negatives), which are more salient in the distant future (Eyal, Liberman, Trope, & Walther, 2004). In contrast, for the interdependents, their regulatory orientation that emphasizes safety and security necessitates their keeping a close watch on their surrounding environment and on the immediate future. Further, their sensitivity to losses and nonlosses prompts them to focus on negatives (vs. positives), which are more salient in the near future. Interdependents' close attention to the self in relationship with others also requires their construing the self and others in contexts that are concrete and specific (vs. abstract and general, Choi, Dalal, Kim-Prieto, & Park, 2003), which are more characteristic of near versus far temporal distance. Indeed, Lee and Lee (2005) observe that those with a dominant interdependent self-construal (e.g., Koreans) are likely to construe a future event to be temporally more proximal than those with a dominant independent self-construal (e.g., Americans); interdependents also respond more positively to events scheduled in the near future than do independents. The implication is that appeals that make salient the temporal distance that corresponds with consumers' self view would be more persuasive than appeals that make salient a mismatched temporal distance.

It is important to note that temporal perspective in terms of event construal (i.e., temporal construal) is different from temporal perspective in terms of how far reaching are the consequences of an event (i.e., the "ripple effect," Maddux & Yuki, 2006). The ability of those with a dominant interdependent self-construal to recognize the interrelationships between people, objects, and situations should prompt them to perceive events to have far-reaching consequences, even though they are more likely to have a proximal temporal perspective. In contrast, the perception by those with an accessible independent self-construal of people, objects and situations as being discrete rather than intertwined should prompt people to think that the consequences of events are relatively short-lived, even though they are more likely to have a distant temporal perspective (Lee & Lee, 2005).

This section highlights the importance of understanding the regulatory orientation of the two distinct self views. However, efforts to generalize this relationship should proceed with caution. As discussed earlier, cultures differ not only in their levels of individualism and collectivism, but also in the extent to which they are vertical (emphasizing hierarchy) or horizontal (emphasizing equality or openness, Triandis, 1995; Triandis & Gelfand, 1998). It is possible that construal-induced shifts in regulatory focus are limited to cultures that are vertical in structure. To the extent that competing to distinguish oneself positively is more prevalent in vertical than horizontal individualist cultures, an independent promotion focus is more likely among members of a vertical individualist culture (e.g., United States) than a horizontal individualist culture (e.g., Norway, Sweden). And to the extent that obligations and responsibilities are better defined in a vertical collectivist culture with its roles and norms than in a horizontal collectivist culture, an interdependent prevention focus should be more prevalent among members of a vertical collectivist culture (e.g., Japan, Korea) than a horizontal collectivist culture (e.g., an Israeli kibbutz). More research is thus needed to investigate whether the relationship between self-construal and regulatory focus may be generalized across both horizontal and vertical types of individualism and collectivism.

CULTURE AND THE SELF: MAKING RISKY CHOICES AND SELF-REGULATION

Another area of interest related to self-regulation is how culture influences people's attitudes toward risk and the way they make risky choices. Based on the literature reviewed in the previous section, one would expect that members of collectivist cultures who tend to be prevention-focused would be more risk averse than members of individualist cultures who tend to be promotion-focused (Lee et al., 2000). In particular, individuals who are promotion focused are inclined to adopt an eagerness strategy, which translates into greater openness to risk, whereas those who are prevention focused are inclined to adopt a vigilant strategy, which usually translates into more conservative behaviors (Crowe & Higgins, 1997). Further, options that have greater potential upsides are likely to also come with greater potential downsides, whereas options with smaller potential downsides are often those with smaller potential upsides. Thus, when choosing between a risky alternative with greater upsides and downsides and a conservative alternative with smaller downsides and upsides, individuals who pay more attention to positive outcomes would favor the risky option, whereas those who focus more on negative outcomes would favor the conservative option. These different attitudes toward risk are consistent with findings that promotion-focused participants emphasize speed at the expense of accuracy in different drawing and proofreading tasks and that the reverse is true for those with a prevention focus (Förster, Higgins, & Bianco, 2003).

However, empirical investigations examining the difference between people with distinct cultural self-construals have produced mixed results. For instance, Briley and Wyer (2002) found that those primed with an interdependent versus independent self-construal were more likely to choose a compromise alternative (i.e., an option with moderate values on two different attributes) over more extreme options (i.e., options with a high value on one attribute and a low value along a second attribute) when choosing between such products as cameras, stereo sets, or computers. When presented with the task of picking two pieces of candy, interdependence-primed participants were also more likely to pick two different candies than two pieces of the same candy. To the extent that choosing the compromise alternative or picking one of each candy reduces the risk of social embarrassment and post-choice regret, these results provide support that those with a dominant interdependent self-construal are indeed more risk averse. Similarly, Mandel (2003) observed that participants primed with an interdependent versus independent self-construal were more likely to choose a safe versus a risky option when choosing a shirt to wear to a family gathering or when playing truth or dare. However, these same participants were more likely to choose the risky option when making a decision regarding a lottery ticket or a parking ticket. Along similar lines, Hsee and Weber (1999) presented Chinese and Americans with safe versus risky options in three decision domains—financial (to invest money in a savings account or in stocks), academic (to write a term paper on a conservative topic so that the grade would be predictable or to write the paper on a provocative topic so the grade could vary), and medical (to take a pain reliever with a moderate but sure effectiveness or one with a high variance of effectiveness). They found that Chinese were more risk-seeking in the financial domain than their American counterparts, but not in the academic and medical domains. Taken together, these results suggest that while individuals with a dominant interdependent self-construal are more risk averse than those with a dominant independent self-construal in general, they are less risk averse when their decision involves financial risks.

To account for these findings in the financial domain, Weber and Hsee (Weber & Hsee, 1998, 2000) proposed that members of collectivist cultures can afford to take greater financial risks because their social network buffers them from financial downfalls. That is, individuals' social networks serve as a cushion which could protect them should they take risks and fall; and the wider is their social network, the larger is the cushion. Because people in collectivist cultures have larger social networks to fall back on relative to those in individualist cultures, they are more likely to choose seemingly riskier options because their perceived risks for those options are smaller than they are for people in individualist cultures. In one study, Weber and Hsee (1998) surveyed American, German, Polish, and Chinese respondents about their perception of the riskiness of a set of financial investment options and their willingness to pay for these options and found that their Chinese respondents thought the risks were the lowest and paid the highest prices for the investments, and the opposite was true for Americans. Once risk perception was accounted for, the cross-cultural difference in risk aversion disappeared. Mandel (2003) also found that the difference between independent and interdependent participants' risky financial choices is mediated by the size of the participants' social network.

Hamilton and Biehal (2005) suggest that this social network cushioning effect may be moderated by people's self-regulatory goals. They find that those primed with an independent self-construal tend to prefer mutual funds that are more risky (i.e., more volatile) than those primed with an interdependent self-construal; and this difference is mediated by the strength of their regulatory goal in that risky preferences are fostered by promotion goals and discouraged by prevention goals. They further show that interdependent participants' preferences for the less risky options may be moderated by their bias toward maintaining the status quo. That is, when interdependent primed participants were told that they had previously chosen a more volatile mutual fund, they were more likely to choose the high-risk versus the safer options. In contrast, the preference of those primed with an independent self-construal was not affected by status quo information.

It is interesting to note that both Mandel (2003) and Hamilton and Biehal (2005) manipulated self-construal but found opposite effects of self-construal on risky financial decisions. Hamilton and Biehal (2005) suggest that perhaps Mandel's (2003) interdependence prime, which implied that "you depend on others," prompted a stronger promotion orientation than Hamilton and Biehal's interdependence induction, which emphasized the notion that "others depend on you." Hence, Mandel's interdependent participants were more risk-seeking. This "you depend on others" mind-set may have also characterized Weber and Hsee's (1998) risk-seeking Chinese participants who were university students, especially in light of their likelihood of being the only child in the family.[1] More systematic investigations of how culture and self-construal affect consumers' risky decision making are warranted.

Besides having an influence on the individual's self-regulatory focus and attitude toward risks, culture also plays an important role in the individual's self-regulation of emotions and behaviors. Because the maintenance of harmony within the group may hinge on members' ability to manage their emotions and behaviors, collectivist cultures tend to emphasize the control and moderation of one's feelings and actions more so than do individualistic cultures (Potter, 1988; Russell & Yik, 1996; Tsai & Levenson, 1997). Indeed, it has been reported that members of collectivist cultures often control their negative emotions and only display positive emotions to acquaintances (Gudykunst, 1993). Children in these societies are also socialized to control their impulses at an early age (Ho, 1994).

It follows that culture would play an important role in consumers' purchase behavior by imposing norms on the appropriateness of impulse buying activities (Kacen & Lee, 2002). When consumers believe that impulse buying is socially unacceptable, they are more likely to refrain from acting on their impulsive tendencies (Rook & Fisher, 1995). Whereas members of individualist cultures are more motivated by their own preferences and personal goals, members of collectivist cultures are often motivated by norms and duties imposed by society. Thus, people with a dominant interdependent self-construal who tend to focus on relationship harmony and group preferences should be better at monitoring and adjusting their behavior based on "what is right" rather than on "what I want." Consistent with this notion, Kacen and Lee (2002) surveyed respondents from Australia, the U. S. Midwest, Singapore, Malaysia, and Hong Kong, and found that the relationship between trait buying impulsiveness and actual impulsive buying behavior is stronger for individualists (respondents from Australia, and the United States) than for collectivists (respondents from Hong Kong, Malaysia, and Singapore). Further, this relationship is observed to be positively correlated with respondents' independent self-construal among the individualists, but not among the collectivists. These results are consistent with findings that attitude-behavior correlations are weaker in collectivist than individualist cultures (Bagozzi, Wong, Abe, & Bergami, 2000; Kashima, Siegal, Tanaka, & Kashima, 1992; Lee, 2000). Along similar lines, Chen, Ng, and Rao (2005) also find that consumers with a dominant independent self-construal are less patient in that they are willing to pay more to expedite the delivery of an online book purchase than those with a dominant interdependent self-construal.

However, there are also reasons to believe that those with a dominant independent self-construal may have better self-control than those whose interdependent self-construal is more dominant. Recent research by Dholakia and his colleagues (Dholakia, Gopinath, Bagozzi, & Nataraajan, 2006) suggests that although prevention-focused consumers report lower desires for tempting objects, it is the promotion-focused consumers who are more successful in resisting temptation. More specifically, their participants were asked to imagine that they were on a tight budget shopping for socks, and were tempted with an expensive sweater. The approach to the self-control strategies of the promotion-primed participants, which tended to focus on achieving their goal (e.g., "socks are more important right now"), were more effective than the avoidance strategies employed by the prevention-primed participants, which tended to focus on the temptation (e.g., "I don't need this sweater"). Future research is warranted to investigate the role that culture and self-construal play in self-regulation and impulse purchase behavior. In particular, investigations into the interplay between chronic and situationally induced self-views and regulatory foci may offer important insights to help consumers make better choices.

CULTURE AND CONSUMER PERSUASION

Most research on cultural influences on judgment and persuasion has examined the implications of individualism/collectivism or independent/interdependent self-construals. Initial research on these questions examined the degree to which the prevalence or the persuasiveness of appeals matches the cultural value orientation of the society. Several of these studies sought evidence for "cultural matching" in the nature of appeals that tend to be found in a society's advertising media. Others examined whether culturally matched message appeals have a greater persuasive impact than mismatched messages. We review these studies presently.

Content Analyses: Cultural Differences in the Prevalence of Appeals

What can be learned about culture by analyzing a society's advertisements? Through content analyses of advertisements, researchers can infer changes in consumption and cultural values from changes in advertising appeals (Pollay, 1986). Cross-cultural comparisons can also yield evidence for distinctions between cultures.

For instance, U. S. advertisers are often exhorted to focus on the advertised brand's attributes and advantages (e.g., Ogilvy, 1985), based on the assumption that consumer learning about the brand precedes other marketing effects, such as liking and buying the brand (Lavidge & Steiner, 1961), at least under high involvement conditions (Vaughn, 1980). Thus, advertisements that attempt to "teach" the consumer about the advertised brand are typical in the United States, although other types of advertisements are also used.

In contrast, as Miracle (1987) has suggested, the typical goal of advertisements in Japan appears very different. There, advertisements tend to focus on "making friends" with the audience and showing that the company understands their feelings (Javalgi, Cutler, & Malhotra, 1995). The assumption is that consumers will buy once they feel familiar with and have a sense of trust in the company. Because Japan, Korea, and other Pacific Rim countries are collectivist, "high context" cultures that tend toward implicit and indirect communication practices (Hall, 1976), Miracle suggested that the mood and tone of commercials in these countries will be particularly important in establishing good feelings about the advertiser (see also Taylor, Miracle, & Wilson, 1997). Indeed, studies have shown that advertisements in Japan and Korea rely more on symbolism, mood, and aesthetics and less on direct approaches such as brand comparisons than do advertisements in the United States (Cho, Kwon, Gentry, Jun, & Kropp, 1999; di Benedetto, Tamate, & Chandran, 1992; Hong et al., 1987; Javalgi et al., 1995).

This is not to argue that advertisements in collectivist societies use more of a "soft sell" approach in contrast to a "hard sell," information-driven approach in the West. Information content in the advertisements of collectivist cultures can be very high (Tse, Belk, & Zhou, 1989), sometimes higher than that of U.S. advertisements (Hong et al., 1987; Rice & Lu, 1988; for a review see Taylor et al., 1997). It is generally more an issue of the type of appeal that the information is supporting.

For instance, a content analysis of magazine advertisements revealed that in Korea, as compared to the United States, advertisements are more focused on family well-being, interdependence, group goals, and harmony, whereas they are less focused on self-improvement, ambition, personal goals, independence, and individuality (Han & Shavitt, 1994). However, as one might expect, the nature of the advertised product moderated these effects. Cultural differences emerged strongly only for products that tend to be purchased and used along with other persons (e.g., groceries, cars). Products that do not tend to be shared (e.g., health and beauty aids, clothing) are promoted more in terms of personal, individualistic benefits in both countries.

Paralleling the overall cross-national differences, a content analysis by Kim and Markus (1999) indicated that Korean advertisements, compared to U.S. advertisements, were characterized by more conformity themes (e.g., respect for collective values and beliefs) and fewer uniqueness themes (e.g., rebelling against collective values and beliefs). (See also Cho et al., 1999; Choi et al., 2005; Javalgi et al., 1995; Tak, Kaid, & Lee, 1997, for other ad comparisons relevant to individualism/collectivism).

Recently, studies have extended these cultural conclusions into analyses of website content (Cho & Cheon, 2005; Singh & Matsuo, 2004). For instance, Cho and Cheon (2005) found that corporate Web sites in the United States and the United Kingdom tend to emphasize consumer-message and consumer-marketer interactivity. In contrast, those in Japan and Korea tend to emphasize consumer-consumer interactivity, a pattern consistent with cultural values stressing collectivistic activities that foster interdependence and sociability.

Finally, in studying humorous appeals, Alden, Hoyer, and Lee (1993) found that advertisements from both Korea and Thailand contain more group-oriented situations than do those from Germany and the United States. However, it is worth noting that in these studies, evidence also emerged for the value of the vertical/horizontal distinction previously discussed. Specifically, relationships between the central characters in advertisements that used humor were more often unequal in cultures that were characterized as having higher power distance (i.e., relatively vertical cultures, such as Korea) than in those labeled as lower in power distance (such as Germany), in which these relationships were more often equal. Such unequal relationships portrayed in the advertisements may reflect the hierarchical interpersonal relationships that are more likely to exist in vertical societies.

Cultural Differences in Judgment and Persuasion

The persuasiveness of appeals appears to mirror the cultural differences in their prevalence. An experiment by Han and Shavitt (1994) showed that appeals to individualistic values (e.g., "Solo cleans with a softness that you will love") are more persuasive in the United States and appeals to collectivistic values (e.g., "Solo cleans with a softness that your family will love") are more persuasive in Korea. Again, however, this effect was much more evident for products that are shared (laundry detergent, clothes iron) than for those that are not (chewing gum, running shoes).

Zhang and Gelb (1996) found a similar pattern in the persuasiveness of individualistic versus collectivistic appeals in an experiment conducted in the United States and China. Moreover, this effect appeared to be moderated by whether the advertised product is socially visible (camera) versus privately used (toothbrush). Finally, Wang and Mowen (1997) showed in a U.S. sample that individual differences in separateness/connectedness self-schema (i.e., the degree to which one views the self as independent of or interconnected with important others) predicts attitudes toward individualistic versus collectivistic ad appeals for a credit card. Thus, cultural orientation as well as national culture have implications for the effectiveness of appeals. However, such cultural differences are only anticipated for those products or uses that are relevant to both personal and group goals.

Wang, Bristol, Mowen, and Chakraborty (2000) further demonstrated that individual differences in separateness/connectedness self-schema mediate both the effects of culture and of gender on the persuasiveness of individualistic versus collectivistic appeals. However, their dimensional analysis demonstrates that this mediating role is played by distinct dimensions of separateness/connectedness self-schema for cultural as opposed to gender-based effects.

Less is known regarding the impact of culture on the cognitive processing of persuasive messages. Some studies attest that existing models of cognitive processing and cognitive responding serve as useful frameworks across cultures (Aaker & Maheswaran, 1997; Aaker & Williams, 1998; Alden, Stayman, & Hoyer, 1994; Leong, Ang, & Tham, 1996).

Cultural differences in persuasion are also revealed in the diagnosticity of certain types of information. For instance, Aaker and Maheswaran (1997) showed that consensus information regarding other consumers' opinions is not treated as a heuristic cue by Hong Kong Chinese (as it is in the United States, Maheswaran & Chaiken, 1991) but is instead perceived and processed as diagnostic information. Thus, collectivists resolve incongruity in favor of consensus information, not brand attributes. This would be expected in a culture that stresses conformity and responsiveness to others' views. On the other hand, cues whose (low) diagnosticity is not expected to vary cross-culturally (e.g., number of attributes presented) elicit similar heuristic processing in the United States and Hong Kong.

Further research indicates that, whereas members of both U.S. and Chinese cultures resolve incongruities in the product information they receive, they tend to do so in different ways (Aaker & Sengupta, 2000). Specifically, U.S. consumers tend to resolve incongruity with an "attenuation strategy" in which one piece of information is favored over another, inconsistent piece of information. In contrast, Hong Kong Chinese consumers tend to follow an additive strategy in which both pieces of information are combined to influence judgments. This is consistent with a view of East Asian individuals as thinking *holistically*, and taking more information into account when making judgments (Choi et al., 2003; Nisbett, Peng, Choi, & Norenzayan, 2001).

Finally, although numerous studies on culture and consumer persuasion have pointed to cultural-congruity effects, suggesting that culturally matched ad appeals are more prevalent and/or persuasive than culturally mismatched appeals, a growing number of studies have suggested that the situation in rapidly transitioning economies may be more complex. For example, Westernized appeals, such as appeals to youth/modernity, individuality/independence, and technology are rather salient in Chinese advertisements (Zhang & Shavitt, 2003) as well as frequently employed by current Taiwanese advertising agencies (Shao, Raymond, & Taylor, 1999). These cultural-incongruity findings may be driven by government policies guiding internal development and modernization, by public exposure to Western media, and by demographic and geographic contact zones.

In addition, consumers in developing countries tend to respond favorably to markedly Western products. For instance, in one study of Indian consumers (Batra, Ramaswamy, Alden, Steenkamp, & Ramachander, 2000), brands perceived as having a nonlocal (Western) country of origin were favored over brands perceived to be local. This effect was stronger for consumers with a greater admiration for the lifestyle in economically developed countries. These cultural-incongruity findings are meaningful because they suggest the important role that advertising can play in reshaping cultural values in countries experiencing rapid economic growth (Zhang & Shavitt, 2003). Rather than reflecting existing cultural values, advertising content in those countries promotes new aspirational values, such as individuality and modernity, hence these new values become acceptable and desirable among consumers.

MEASUREMENT AND METHODOLOGY: OVERVIEW

We turn now to a consideration of the measurement issues and challenges facing consumer psychologists who seek to compare distinct cultural groups. It is now generally understood that substance and measurement artifacts can become confounded if care is not taken when conducting cross-cultural research (Harkness, van de Vijver, & Mohler, 2003; Singh, 1995), and that such issues complicate cross-cultural marketing research (Malhotra, Agarwal, & Peterson, 1996). These measurement artifacts may take several forms. Cultural conditioning, for example, can mediate how individuals comprehend or interpret survey questions. Recognized for years as a problem in achievement testing (Flaugher, 1978; Hambleton, Merenda, & Spielberger, 2005; Williams, 1977), the uncritical adoption of measures developed within one cultural context for use with persons of differing cultural backgrounds may misrepresent the thoughts, feelings, and behaviors of those individuals, leading to erroneous conclusions (Johnson et al., 1997; Marin & Marin, 1989; Rogler, 1989). Similarly, culture-based variations in perceptions of social desirability and concerns about social presentation may also be mistaken for substantive group differences, or mask real differences (Johnson & van de Vijver, 2003; Keillor, Owens, & Pettijohn, 2001; Middleton & Jones, 2000). Communication norms are also influenced by culture (Gudykunst & Kim, 1992; Kochman, 1981) and may contribute to differences in response patterns to survey questionnaires and interviews that reflect cultural, as well as substantive, concerns. Research to be reviewed later in this chapter has documented race, national and ethnicity-based variability in several survey response behaviors, including acquiescent response behavior (Grimm & Church, 1999; Smith, 2004; van Herk, Poortinga, & Verhallen, 2004) and preferences for or against extreme response options (Bachman & O'Malley, 1984; Clarke, 2000; Marin & Marin, 1989). These cultural artifacts threaten the comparability of survey data collected across nations and across cultural subgroups within countries.

The potential effects of cultural influences on survey data collection have not always been recognized. For example, the highly regarded cross-national study of civic behavior conducted in the early 1960s by Almond and Verba (1963) compared and analyzed survey data collected in five nations (Germany, Great Britain, Italy, Mexico, the United States) without considering potential culture-based differences in question processing, communication norms or response behaviors. During that same decade, several other studies began documenting the presence of culture-driven measurement artifacts in survey measures. Dohrenwend (1966) identified differences in perceptions of the desirability of various psychological symptoms across samples of four ethnic groups residing in New York City. These differences were related to the prevalence of each symptom type within each cultural group such that less stigma was associated with the more common symptoms found within each group. This work inspired a series of subsequent studies concerned with the potential bias introduced by race/ethnic variability in response styles (Carr, 1971; Cunningham, Cunningham, & Green, 1977; Zax & Takahashi, 1967). Around the same time, a landmark study reported by Hofstede (1980) examined survey data collected from IBM employees in 40 countries between 1967 and 1973. Among the numerous important findings reported by Hofstede was the fact that measures of response acquiescence varied across these nations. To address this potential confound, Hofstede reported a method of score standardization that was designed to eliminate the differential effects of acquiescence.

During these same years, research contributed by a variety of disciplines also began pointing to differences in how questions and concepts were being interpreted across race and ethnic groups

(Mirowsky & Ross, 1980; Zola, 1966). Collaborations between survey methodologists and cognitive psychologists in the early 1980s led to the development of formal models of the survey response process (Jabine, Straf, Tanur, & Tourangeau, 1984). This work integrated question interpretation, recall, judgment formation and mapping, and response editing processes into a unified conceptual model of respondent processing of survey questions. Subsequent work has identified evidence that race & ethnicity may influence the processes in this model at multiple points (Johnson et al., 1997; Warnecke et al., 1997).

In the late 1950s, concern was also being expressed that quantitative measures were being systematically contaminated by social desirability, or the need for social approval (Crowne & Marlowe, 1960; Edwards, 1957). Interestingly, one of the first field reports of this phenomenon described a communication pattern among East Asian survey respondents that was labeled a "courtesy bias" (Jones, 1963). This cultural norm, it was reported, emphasized the importance of establishing and maintaining polite and cordial interactions with visitors, even at the cost of providing inaccurate information. Indeed, it is now understood that this norm can complicate the interpretation of market research data because consumers in some societies hesitate to express the critical product perceptions they hold (Douglas & Craig, 1983; Witkowski, Ma, & Zheng, 2003). Numerous studies have also investigated the potential effects of this and similar social desirability biases on race & ethnic group comparisons (Crandall, Crandall, & Katkovsky, 1965; Edwards & Riordan, 1994; Ross & Mirowsky, 1984).

More recent research, to be reviewed in the next section, has moved beyond the documentation of race/ethnic/national differences in culturally based measurement bias towards understanding the processes by which culture influences survey error, as well as strategies for developing and testing measures that are more equivalent across cultural groups. It is to this latter problem that we next turn our attention.

CONSTRUCTING EQUIVALENT MEASURES

Measurement theory traditionally emphasizes the fundamental importance of reliability and validity considerations when constructing survey and other quantitative measures (Nunnally, 1978). In conducting cross-cultural research, the equivalence of measures is also an important consideration, one that has been all-too-often overlooked. As van de Vijver and Leung (2000) wrote in a special "Millennium" issue of the *Journal of Cross-Cultural Psychology*, the "uncritical acceptance of observed differences in the social domain as reflecting valid cross-cultural differences (p. 35)" is a serious barrier to continued progress in cross-cultural research. Recent research has in fact documented numerous examples of cultural variability in the performance of measures initially developed in mono-cultural settings that may raise questions of cross-group applicability. Wong, Rindfleisch, and Burroughs (2003) have demonstrated that the use of scales that employ both positive and reverse-worded items may be seriously problematic in some cultures, but not others, thus limiting the cross-cultural usefulness of this common measurement strategy. There is also evidence that culture may differentially influence the use of response scale end-points (van Herk et al., 2004), the reporting of behavior frequencies (Ji, Schwarz, & Nisbett, 2000; Schwarz, 2003) and the reporting of sensitive information (Johnson & van de Vijver, 2003).

Although there is growing recognition of the need to address the equivalence of measures, there is little consensus regarding the dimensionality and assessment of that equivalence. For example, more than 100 types of equivalence have been referenced in the research literature (Brown, 2000) and numerous equivalence typologies have been proposed (J. Singh, 1995; Steenkamp & Baumgartner, 1998; Stewart & Napoles-Springer, 2000; van de Vijver, 1998). Two very general classes of equivalence tend to dominate these discussions: those that are primarily concerned with the psychometric comparability of measures across cultural groups—what Johnson (1998) has referred to as forms of procedural equivalence—and those that emphasize shared meaning of the construct being measured—interpretive equivalence. Interpretive equivalence is a necessary precondition for procedural equivalence and it is important to recognize that some constructs may not have the cross-cultural equivalents necessary to develop comparable measures. We also note that anthropologists and cross-cultural psychologists distinguish between etic and emic concepts (Triandis, 1972). Etics are those concepts that are believed to be shared across multiple cultures, and emics are those that have important meaning within one or more cultures, but no equivalent within others. As an example, love for one's children would seem to be a universal value, and hence, an etic concept. Various cultures, however, may have differing norms for expressing it, a situation that might require an emic, or culture-specific, measurement strategy.

Prior to developing measures for cross-cultural applications, it is thus necessary to evaluate the degree to which the constructs to be measured are etic or emic across the cultures of interest. Although numerous strategies have been proposed, there is as of yet no consensus regarding best practices for evaluating and constructing equivalent measures across cultural groups. Several procedures are now being successfully employed to address the equivalency of survey measures. These include cognitive interviewing (Johnson et al., 1997), group translation procedures (Harkness, 2003; Harkness, Pennell, & Schoua-Glusberg, 2004), assessments of differential item functioning using Rasch and item response theory methods (Ewing, Salzberger, & Sinkovics, 2005; Teresi, Holmes, Ramirez, Gurland, & Lantigua, 2001) and covariance structure modeling (Devins, Beiser, Dion, Pelletier, & Edwards, 1997; Scholderer, Grunert, & Brunso, 2005; Steenkamp & Baumgartner, 1998). Below, we describe recent innovative approaches to addressing this problem.

One promising methodology involves the use of anchoring vignettes to confront the challenge of group differences in question interpretations by directly assessing and calibrating survey response categories across cultures. This method, recently introduced by King, Murray, Salomon, and Tandon (2004), measures individual responses to a series of vignettes, which are then used to standardize survey responses across groups that employ varying frames of reference. King et al. present both parametric and nonparametric methods for making cross-cultural adjustments. A recent application of this technique is described by Salomon, Tandon, and Murray (2005), who use it to assess the equivalence of health self-ratings across six under-developed nations.

Behavior coding, a technique originally developed to evaluate interviewer and respondent behaviors (Cannell, Fowler, & Marquis, 1968), has also been recently applied to assessments of cultural variability in question comprehension. Johnson and colleagues (2006) coded and analyzed more than 13,000 answers to survey questions provided by 345 African American, Mexican American, Puerto Rican, and non-Hispanic white respondents. They identified respondent behaviors that were indicative of comprehension difficulties (e.g., asking for question clarification, indicating uncertainty about a question, rephrasing a question before answering) and examined variability in these response patterns across respondent and question characteristics using hierarchical linear (HLM) models. These analyses suggested that respondent culture was independently associated with general variability in comprehension difficulty, and also with differences that were linked to specific questionnaire design features.

In sum, although advancements have been made in exploring potential techniques for assessing and establishing the equivalence of survey measures across cultural groups, there remains no agreement regarding best practices in this area. Decisions regarding which approaches to employ are often dictated by time constraints, budget restrictions, and the technical skills of the researcher. There is also no consensus regarding how to organize and define conceptualizations of equivalence.

Resolution of this latter problem will be a necessary prerequisite to further progress towards the former.

CULTURE AND RESPONSE STYLES

Response styles are of central interest in the study of cross-cultural consumer psychology because of their potential to complicate measurement and interpretation of cultural differences. Vogt (1999, p. 248) describes response styles as "a tendency ... to give the same type of answer to all questions rather than answering questions based solely on their content." In other words, response styles represent systematic sources of variation in respondent answers that are determined by factors other than the content of the survey questions. Several common types of response styles include the tendency to provide socially desirable answers, the tendency to provide acquiescent answers, and the tendency to select the most extreme response options when answering questions. Each of these response styles have been linked with the cultural background of survey respondents and may pose an obstacle to cross-cultural measurement.

Social Desirability

Respondent reporting of information that projects a favorable image of themselves, sometimes at the expense of accuracy, is commonly known as social desirability bias (Nederhof, 1985). This reporting style reflects the human propensity to emphasize, and occasionally overstate, positive qualities and behaviors, while de-emphasizing/understating negative ones. Survey validation studies generally support this presumption, as socially desirable behaviors such as voting (Sigelman, 1982), church attendance (Hadaway, Marler, & Chaves, 1993), and physical exercise (Adams et al., 2005) are often overreported, whereas undesirable behaviors such as drug use (Fendrich, Johnson, Sudman, Wislar, & Spiehler, 1999) and a history of sexually transmitted diseases (Clark, Brasseux, Richmond, Getson, & D'angelo, 1997) are sometimes underreported.

Several self-report measures have been developed to assess socially desirable response tendencies (Crowne & Marlowe, 1964; Edwards, 1957; Eysenck & Eysenck, 1964; Paulhus, 1998a). Persons scoring highly on such measures as the Crowne-Marlowe scale that taps impression management have been found less likely to report dark side consumer behaviors and values, such as alcohol consumption, intoxication, and marijuana use (Bradburn & Sudman, 1979) as well as materialism (Mick, 1996).

As noted earlier, mean scores on these socially desirable responding measures have also been found to vary across nations and across ethnic and racial groups within nations (Johnson & van de Vijver, 2003; Keillor et al., 2001; Lalwani et al., 2006), and more recent research is beginning to identify the underlying cultural orientations and values that may account for these differences. Middleton and Jones (2000), for example, have suggested that variability across each of Hofstede's (2001) cultural dimensions may underlie higher impression management scores for East Asian compared to North American survey respondents. At the national level, van Hemert et al. (2002) reported significant negative correlations between one of these orientations—individualism scores—and mean scores on the Lie scale of the Eysenck Personality Inventory (Eysenck & Eysenck, 1964). Other research has identified greater tendencies among collectivists towards conformity (R. Bond & Smith, 1996) and unwillingness to self-disclose (P. B. Smith & Bond, 1998), characteristics also likely to be associated with socially desirable reporting. One might also expect that socially desirable response styles would be more common in "tight" cultures, a characteristic closely associated with collectivism (Triandis, 1995), in which prescribed norms of behavior would be most explicit.

However, the nature of the relation between cultural variables and this response style is also dependent on the type of socially desirable responding in question. As indicated earlier, Lalwani, Shavitt, and Johnson (2006) argued that two distinct response patterns should emerge as a function of cultural orientations or backgrounds—Impression Management (IM) and Self-Deceptive Enhancement (SDE) (Gur & Sackeim, 1979; Paulhus, 1991; Sackeim & Gur, 1979). Each of these response styles corresponds to different culturally relevant goals. Subscales measuring these dimensions compose the Paulhus Deception Scales (Paulhus, 1984, 1991, 1998b). As implied earlier, IM reflects the traditional definition of socially desirable responding. It refers to an attempt to present one's self-reported actions in the most positive manner to convey a favorable image (Paulhus, 1998a; Schlenker & Britt, 1999; Schlenker, Britt, & Pennington, 1996). This construct is often associated with dissimulation or deception (Mick, 1996), and is tapped by such items as, "I have never dropped litter on the street" and "I sometimes drive faster than the speed limit" (reverse scored; Paulhus, 1998a). SDE refers to the tendency to describe oneself in inflated and overconfident terms. It is a predisposition to see one's skills in a positive light, and has been described as a form of "rigid overconfidence" (Paulhus, 1998a). SDE is assessed by such items as, "My first impressions of people usually turn out to be right" and "I am very confident of my judgments."

Lalwani et al. (2006) showed that U.S. respondents (IND), compared to those from Singapore (COL), scored higher in self-deceptive enhancement and lower in impression management. Similarly, European American respondents (IND), compared to Korean American respondents (COL), scored higher in self-deceptive enhancement and lower in impression management.

Moreover, data in the United States as a function of cultural orientation, incorporating the horizontal/vertical cultural distinction described earlier, shed light on the specific cultural goals served by these response styles. Specifically, people with an HC cultural orientation, who emphasize sociability, benevolence, and cooperation, tended to engage in IM. On the other hand, people with an HI orientation, who emphasize self-competence, self-direction, and independence, tended to engage in SDE. The observed response styles thus appear to reflect distinct self-presentational goals—to be seen as sociable and benevolent (HC orientation) versus self-reliant and capable (HI orientation).

In the consumer context, such findings offer implications for understanding how cultural background and orientation influences the way consumers respond to marketing surveys, as well as the way they view and present themselves to consumers and marketers more generally. These patterns of self-presentational styles may lead those with an HI cultural orientation to express relatively inflated levels of confidence in their own consumer skills and to view themselves as unrealistically capable of making good choices in the marketplace. On the other hand, those with an HC cultural orientation may be more likely to distort their previous purchases and marketplace behaviors in a manner designed to appear normatively appropriate and sociable.

Acquiescent Response Style

A second response style, known as acquiescent behavior or "yea-saying," was first recognized prior to World War II (Lentz, 1938). Acquiescence is defined as the tendency of some respondents to agree with survey statements, regardless of content. Stricker (1963) distinguished acquiescent from socially desirable responding by suggesting that the latter represented conformity on items for which clear and unambiguous social norms existed, whereas acquiescence represented conformity on items for which social norms were unclear or did not exist. Hence, social desirability represents a response style motivated by conformity to specific social or cultural norms, in contrast to acquiescent responding, which represents a more general pattern of conformity that is less dependent on question content. Recognition of this phenomenon led to early recommendations that multi-item scales should balance the numbers of positive and reverse-worded items as a method of addressing this bias (Lentz, 1938). However, as noted earlier, recent research has pointed to cross-national equivalence problems associated with the use of reverse-worded items (Wong et al., 2003).

Unlike the social desirability construct, there are no multi-purpose measures of acquiescence available. Rather, it tends to be measured on an ad hoc basis from study-to-study via total agreement with heterogeneous sets of survey items (Bachman & O'Malley, 1984), the extent of agreement with pairs of oppositely worded items (Johnson et al., 2005), agreement with general sets of items worded in positive and negative directions (Watson, 1992), or by combining two or more of these indices (Baumgartner & Steenkamp, 2001).

Variability in propensity to acquiesce has been identified both within racial and ethnic subgroups within nations and also across countries (Aday, Chiu, & Andersen, 1980; Javeline, 1999; Johnson et al., 1997; Ross & Mirowsky, 1984; van Herk et al., 2004). Research has also begun to identify cultural dimensions that may underlie cross-group variability. Acquiescence may be more common in cultures that value deference, politeness and hospitality (Javeline, 1999). Mounting evidence also suggests that acquiescent response styles may be more common within more collectivistic cultures (Grimm & Church, 1999; Hofstede, 2001; Johnson et al., 2005; Smith, 2004; Smith & Fisher, 2006; van de Vijver, Ploubidis, & van Hemert, 2004).

In addition, acquiescence has been linked with uncertainty avoidance. Smith (2004) found that nations scoring high in uncertainty avoidance also scored higher across several measures of acquiescence. He hypothesized that uncertainty avoidant cultures are more anxiety prone and have less tolerance for ambiguity, and that these traits may be associated with this response style. Similar national level findings have been reported by van de Vijver et al. (2004). In contrast, hierarchical analyses have found acquiescent responding to be higher within cultures that score *low* in uncertainty avoidance (Johnson et al., 2005), a finding that supports the view that acquiescence is more common in social environments with greater tolerance for ambiguity and uncertainty.

Extreme Response Style

It has also been recognized for many years that some respondents prefer selecting the extreme endpoints of response scales (Cronbach, 1946). Systematic preferences for either extreme or middle responses can produce considerable variance in scale scores that are attributable to this response style, independent of the construct being assessed. There are several approaches to measuring extreme responding. Most commonly, it is assessed as the proportion of survey items for which a respondent selects an extreme response option (Bachman & O'Malley, 1984). Other approaches include evaluating the variance around mean responses (Kiesler & Sproull, 1986) and use of a measure developed by Greenleaf (1992) that has good psychometric properties (i.e., the items are uncorrelated and have equal proportions of positive and negative extreme response proportions).

As with the other response styles evaluated, extreme responding is known to vary across race/ethnic groups within the United States (Bachman & O'Malley, 1984; Hui & Triandis, 1989), and considerable evidence exists of cross-national differences (Chun, Campbell, & Yoo, 1974; Clarke, 2000; C. Lee & Green, 1991; van Herk et al., 2004). Additional evidence of a linkage between culture and extreme responding comes from findings that this construct is inversely associated with level of acculturation among Latinos in the United States (Marin, Gamba, & Marin, 1992), and that English-Spanish bilinguals show a greater preference for extreme responses when interviewed in Spanish as compared to English (Gibbons, Zellner, & Rudek, 1999).

Significantly, several of Hofstede's (2001) cultural dimensions have also been associated with this response style, including individualism (Chen, Lee, & Stevenson, 1995; Smith & Fisher, 2006), power distance and masculinity (Johnson et al., 2005) and uncertainty avoidance (van de Vijver et al., 2004). Taken together, these findings suggest that extreme responding is characteristic of cultures that value distinctive, competitive, assertive, decisive and sincere behavior, and that have a low tolerance for ambiguity (Hamilton, 1968; Marin et al., 1992). Conversely, preference for middling response options may be more common within cultures that value modesty, interpersonal harmony and subtlety.

Addressing Cultural Variability in Response Styles

Multiple approaches have been proposed to deal with the potentially contaminating effects of cultural variability in survey response styles. These include strategies that emphasize construction of items and scales that are less susceptible to these measurement artifacts and analytic approaches to assessing and adjusting for response style differences across groups. Some specific questionnaire design recommendations include the avoidance of agree-disagree question response formats (Converse & Presser, 1986) and the use of measurement scales that contain balanced sets of positively and negatively worded questions to eliminate or minimize the effects of acquiescence (Cloud & Vaughan, 1970; Javeline, 1999; Knowles & Nathan, 1997; Mirowsky & Ross, 1991; Ray, 1979). Others have attempted to avoid acquiescence and extreme responding effects by developing ipsative (i.e., ranking) measures that are believed to be less susceptible to these forms of bias (Schuman & Presser, 1981; Toner, 1987). Smith (2003) discusses several additional approaches to designing survey questions that may minimize these response effects across groups.

Analytic strategies that have been recommended include the use of ipsative rescaling of items to address acquiescence and/or extreme responding (Cunningham et al., 1977) and statistical adjustments using standardized measures of social desirability (Paulhus, 1991; Pleck, Sonenstein, & Ku, 1996). Hofstede, Ten Berge, and Hendriks (1998) review several alternative procedures for scoring questionnaires to correct for acquiescence and extreme responding. Multiple group confirmatory factor analysis, structural equation modeling and latent class factor strategies have also been proposed to identify and adjust for cultural differences in these response styles (Billiet & McClendon, 2000; Cheung & Rensvold, 2000; Moors, 2003; Watson, 1992). Numerous additional methods have also been proposed for addressing social desirability bias in mono-cultural research (King & Bruner, 2000; Nederhof, 1985) and some of these may be adaptable for use in cross-cultural contexts. As Cheung and Rensvold (2000) observe, however, there is no single procedure that is generally applicable to addressing this issue. Rather, confronting the effects of cultural differences in response styles will require both careful attention to the design of survey questionnaires and careful analyses of the data obtained, using some combination of the procedures currently available for addressing these phenomena.

CONCLUSIONS

As marketing efforts have become increasingly globalized, understanding cross-cultural consumer psychology has become a mainstream goal of consumer research. In recent years, a rapidly expanding volume of research has addressed a broadening set of cross-cultural issues and dimensions. Significant progress has come on several fronts, including an enhanced understanding of the relations between culture and self-construal, motivation, self-regulation, and consumer persuasion. However, with the expansion of research activity comes a greater awareness of the unique challenges posed by cross-cultural measurement. Our review has addressed some of the ways in which culture influences respondents' comprehension or interpretation of measures, as well as the ways culture influences the respondents' styles in answering questions. Ongoing progress in cross-cultural consumer research will require careful attention to both the methodological and the conceptual issues that remain to be addressed.

NOTE

1. China introduced the one-child policy in 1979. As a result, Chinese people who were born after 1979 tend to have a more accessible independent self-construal (Lee & Gardner, 2005).

REFERENCES

Aaker, J. L., & Lee, A. Y. (2001). "I" seek pleasures and "we" avoid pains: The role of self-regulatory goals in information processing and persuasion. *Journal of Consumer Research, 28*(1), 33–49.

Aaker, J. L., & Maheswaran, D. (1997). The effect of cultural orientation on persuasion. *Journal of Consumer Research, 24*(3), 315–328.

Aaker, J. L., & Sengupta, J. (2000). Addivity versus attenuation: The role of culture in the resolution of information incongruity. *Journal of Consumer Psychology, 9*(2), 67–82.

Aaker, J. L., & Williams, P. (1998). Empathy versus pride: The influence of emotional appeals across cultures. *Journal of Consumer Research, 25*(3), 241–261.

Adams, S. A., Matthews, C. E., Ebbeling, C. B., Moore, C. G., Cunningham, J. E., Fulton, J., et al. (2005). The effect of social desirability and social approval on self-reports of physical activity. *American Journal of Epidemiology, 161*(4), 389–398.

Aday, L. A., Chiu, G. Y., & Andersen, R. (1980). Methodological issues in health care surveys of the Spanish heritage population. *American Journal of Public Health, 70*(4), 367–374.

Agrawal, N., & Maheswaran, D. (2005). The effects of self-construal and commitment on persuasion. *Journal of Consumer Research, 31*(March), 841–849.

Alden, D. L., Hoyer, W. D., & Lee, C. (1993). Identifying global and culture-specific dimensions of humor in advertising: A multinational analysis. *Journal of Marketing, 57*(2), 64–75.

Alden, D. L., Stayman, D. M., & Hoyer, W. D. (1994). Evaluation strategies of American and Thai consumers. *Psychology & Marketing, 11*(2), 145–161.

Almond, G. A., & Verba, S. (1963). *The civic culture: Political attitudes and democracy in five nations.* Princeton, NJ: Princeton University Press.

Bachman, J. G., & O'Malley, P. M. (1984). Yea-saying, nay-saying, and going to extremes: Black-White differences in response style. *Public Opinion Quarterly, 48*(2), 491–509.

Bagozzi, R. P., Wong, N., Abe, S., & Bergami, M. (2000). Cultural and situational contingencies and the theory of reasoned action: Application to fast food restaurant consumption. *Journal of Consumer Psychology, 9*(2), 97–106.

Batra, R., Ramaswamy, V., Alden, D. L., Steenkamp, J.-B. E. M., & Ramachander, S. (2000). Effects of brand local and nonlocal origin on consumer attitudes in developing countries. *Journal of Consumer Psychology, 9*(2), 83–95.

Baumgartner, H., & Steenkamp, J.-B. E. M. (2001). Response styles in marketing research: A cross-national investigation. *Journal of Marketing Research, 38*(2), 143–156.

Billiet, J. B., & McClendon, M. J. (2000). Modeling acquiescence in measurement models for two balanced sets of items. *Structural Equation Modeling, 7*(4), 608–628.

Blodgett, J. G., Lu, L.-C., Rose, G. M., & Vitell, S. J. (2001). Ethical sensitivity to stakeholder interests: A cross-cultural comparison. *Journal of the Academy of Marketing Science, 29*(2), 190–202.

Bond, M. H. (2002). Reclaiming the individual from Hofstede's ecological analysis—A 20-year odyssey: Comment on Oyserman et al. (2002). *Psychological Bulletin, 128*(1), 73–77.

Bond, R., & Smith, P. B. (1996). Culture and conformity: A meta-analysis of studies using Asch's (1952b, 1956) line judgment task. *Psychological Bulletin, 119*(1), 111–137.

Bradburn, N. M., & Sudman, S. (1979). Reinterpreting the Marlowe-Crowne scale. In N. M. Bradburn & S. Sudman (Eds.), *Improving interview method and questionnaire design* (pp. 85–106). San Francisco: Jossey-Bass.

Brewer, M. B., & Gardner, W. (1996). Who is this "We"? Levels of collective identity and self representations. *Journal of Personality & Social Psychology, 71*(1), 83–93.

Briley, D. A., & Aaker, J. L. (2006). When does culture matter? Effects of personal knowledge on the correction of culture-based judgments. *Journal of Marketing Research, 43,* 395–408.

Briley, D. A., & Wyer, R. S., Jr. (2002). The effect of group membership salience on the avoidance of negative outcomes: Implications for social and consumer decisions. *Journal of Consumer Research, 29*(3), 400–415.

Brown, K. F. (2000). *A critical ethnography of the cross-cultural adaptation of HRQoL instruments.* Unpublished doctoral dissertation, Burwood, Australia: Deakin University.

Cannell, C. F., Fowler, F. J., & Marquis, K. H. (1968). The influence of interviewer and respondent psychological and behavioral variables on the reporting in household interviews. *Vital Health and Statistics, 2*(26). Washington, DC: Government Printing Office.

Carr, L. G. (1971). The Srole items and acquiescence. *American Sociological Review, 36*(2), 287–293.

Chen, C., Lee, S.-y., & Stevenson, H. W. (1995). Response style and cross-cultural comparisons of rating scales among East Asian and North American students. *Psychological Science, 6*(3), 170–175.

Chen, H., Ng, S., & Rao, A. R. (2005). Cultural differences in consumer impatience. *Journal of Marketing Research, 42*(3), 291–301.

Cheung, G. W., & Rensvold, R. B. (2000). Assessing extreme and acquiescence response sets in cross-cultural research using structural equations modeling. *Journal of Cross-Cultural Psychology, 31*(2), 187–212.

Cho, B., Kwon, U., Gentry, J. W., Jun, S., & Kropp, F. (1999). Cultural values reflected in theme and execution: A comparative dtudy of U.S. and Korean Television Commercials. *Journal of Advertising, 28*(4), 59–73.

Cho, C.-H., & Cheon, H. J. (2005). Cross-cultural comparisons of interactivity on corporate websites. *Journal of Advertising, 34*(2), 99–115.

Choi, I., Dalal, R., Kim-Prieto, C., & Park, H. (2003). Culture and judgement of causal relevance. *Journal of Personality and Social Psychology, 84*(1), 46–59.

Choi, S. M., Lee, W.-N., & Kim, H.-J. (2005). Lessons from the rich and famous: A cross-cultural comparison of celebrity endorsement in advertising. *Journal of Advertising, 34*(2), 85–98.

Chun, K.-T., Campbell, J. B., & Yoo, J. H. (1974). Extreme response style in cross-cultural research: A reminder. *Journal of Cross-Cultural Psychology, 5*(4), 465–480.

Clark, L. R., Brasseux, C., Richmond, D., Getson, P., & D'angelo, L. J. (1997). Are adolescents accurate in self-report of frequencies of sexually transmitted diseases and pregnancies? *Journal of Adolescent Health, 21*(2), 91–96.

Clarke, I., III. (2000). Extreme response style in cross-cultural research: An empirical investigation. *Journal of Social Behavior & Personality, 15*(1), 137–152.

Cloud, J., & Vaughan, G. M. (1970). Using balanced scales to control acquiescence. *Sociometry, 33*(2), 193–202.

Converse, J. M., & Presser, S. (1986). *Survey questions: Handcrafting the standardized questionnaire.* Thousand Oaks: Sage.

Crandall, V. C., Crandall, V. J., & Katkovsky, W. (1965). A children's social desirability questionnaire. *Journal of Consulting Psychology, 29*(1), 27–36.

Cronbach, L. J. (1946). Response sets and test validity. *Educational and Psychological Measurement, 6,* 475–494.

Cross, S. E., Bacon, P. L., & Morris, M. L. (2000). The relational-interdependent self-construal and relationships. *Journal of Personality and Social Psychology, 78*(4), 791–808.

Cross, S. E., & Madson, L. (1997). Models of the self: Self-construals and gender. *Psychological Bulletin, 122*(1), 5–37.

Crowe, E., & Higgins, E. (1997). Regulatory focus and strategic inclinations: Promotion and prevention in decision-making. *Organizational Behavior and Human Decision Processes, 69*(2), 117–132.

Crowne, D. P., & Marlowe, D. (1960). A new scale of social desirability independent of pathology. *Journal of Consulting Psychology, 24*(4), 349–354.

Crowne, D. P., & Marlowe, D. (1964). *The approval motive.* New York: Wiley.

Cunningham, W., Cunningham, I. C., & Green, R. T. (1977). The ipastive process to reduce response set bias. *Public Opinion Quarterly, 41,* 379–394.

Devins, G. M., Beiser, M., Dion, R., Pelletier, L. G., & Edwards, R. (1997). Cross-cultural measurements of psychological well-being: The psychometric equivalence of Cantonese, Vietnamese, and Laotian translations of the Affect Balance Scale. *American Journal of Public Health, 87*(5), 794–799.

Dholakia, U. M., Gopinath, M., Bagozzi, R. P., & Nataraajan, R. (2006). The role of regulatory focus in the experience and self-control of desire for temptations. *Journal of Consumer Psychology, 16*(2), 163–175.

di Benedetto, C. A., Tamate, M., & Chandran, R. (1992). Developing creative advertising strategy for the Japanese marketplace. *Journal of Advertising Research, 32*, 39–48.

Dohrenwend, B. (1966). Social status and psychological disorder: An issue of substance and an issue of method. *American Sociological Review, 31*, 14–34.

Douglas, S. P., & Craig, S. C. (1983). *International marketing research.* Englewood Cliffs, NJ: Prentice-Hall.

Dwyer, S., Mesak, H., & Hsu, M. (2005). An exploratory examination of the influence of national culture on cross-national product diffusion. *Journal of International Marketing, 13*(2), 1–27.

Earley, P. C. (1999). Playing follow the leader: Status-determining traits in relation to collective efficacy across cultures. *Organizational Behavior and Human Decision Processes, 80*(3), 192–212.

Edwards, A. L. (1957). *The social desirability variable in personality assessment and research.* NY: Druiden Press.

Edwards, D., & Riordan, S. (1994). Learned resourcefulness in Black and White South African university students. *Journal of Social Psychology, 134*(5), 665–675.

Erez, M., & Earley, P. (1987). Comparative analysis of goal-setting strategies across cultures. *Journal of Applied Psychology, 72*(4), 658–665.

Ewing, M. T., Salzberger, T., & Sinkovics, R. R. (2005). An alternate approach to assessing cross-cultural measurement equivalence in advertising research. *Journal of Advertising, 34*(1), 17–36.

Eyal, T., Liberman, N., Trope, Y., & Walther, E. (2004). The pros and cons of temporally near and distant action. *Journal of Personality & Social Psychology, 86*(6), 781–795.

Eysenck, H. J., & Eysenck, S. B. G. (1964). *The manual of the Eysenck personality inventory.* London: University of London Press.

Fendrich, M., Johnson, T. P., Sudman, S., Wislar, J. S., & Spiehler, V. (1999). Validity of drug use reporting in a high-risk community sample: A comparison of cocaine and heroin survey reports with hair tests. *American Journal of Epidemiology, 149*(10), 955–962.

Flaugher, R. L. (1978). The many definitions of test bias. *American Psychologist, 33*(7), 671–679.

Förster, J., Higgins, T. E., & Bianco, A. T. (2003). Speed/accuracy decisions in task performance: Built-in trade-off or separate strategic concerns? *Organizational Behavior and Human Decision Processes, 90*(1), 148–164.

Fu, J. H., Chiu, C., Morris, M. W., & Young, M. Y. (2007). Spontaneous inferences from cultural cues: Varying responses of cultural insiders, and outsiders. *Journal of Cross-Cultural Psychology, 38*, 58–75.

Gabriel, S., & Gardner, W. L. (1999). Are there "his" and "hers" types of interdependence? The implications of gender differences in collective versus relational interdependence for affect, behavior, and cognition. *Journal of Personality and Social Psychology, 77*(3), 642–655.

Gaines, S. O., Jr., Marelich, W. D., Bledsoe, K. L., Steers, W., Henderson, M. C., Granrose, C. S., et al. (1997). Links between race/ethnicity and cultural values as mediated by racial/ethnic identity and moderated by gender. *Journal of Personality and Social Psychology, 72*(6), 1460–1476.

Gardner, W. L., Gabriel, S., & Lee, A. Y. (1999). "I" value freedom, but "we" value relationships: Self-construal priming mirrors cultural differences in judgment. *Psychological Science, 10*(4), 321–326.

Gelfand, M. J., Bhawuk, D., Nishii, L. H., & Bechtold, D. J. (2004). Individualism and Collectivism. In R. J. House, P. J. Hanges, M. Javidan, P. W. Dorfman, & V. Gupta (Eds.), *Culture, leadership, and organizations: The GLOBE study of 62 societies* (pp. 437–512). Thousand Oaks, CA: Sage.

Gibbons, J. L., Zellner, J. A., & Rudek, D. J. (1999). Effects of language and meaningfulness on the use of extreme response style by Spanish-English bilinguals. *Cross-Cultural Research: The Journal of Comparative Social Science, 33*(4), 369–381.

Greenleaf, E. A. (1992). Measuring extreme response style. *Public Opinion Quarterly, 56*(3), 328–351.

Grimm, S. D., & Church, A. (1999). A cross-cultural study of response biases in personality measures. *Journal of Research in Personality, 33*(4), 415–441.

Gudykunst, W. B. (1993). *Communication in Japan and the United States.* Albany: State University of New York Press.

Gudykunst, W. B., & Kim, Y. Y. (1992). *Communicating with strangers: an approach to intercultural communication* (2nd ed.). New York: McGraw-Hill.

Gudykunst, W. B., & Ting-Toomey, S. (1988). *Culture and interpersonal communication.* Newbury Park, CA: Sage.

Gur, R. C., & Sackeim, H. A. (1979). Self-deception: A concept in search of a phenomenon. *Journal of Personality and Social Psychology, 37*(2), 147–169.

Gürhan-Canli, Z., & Maheswaran, D. (2000). Cultural Variations in Country of Origin Effects. *Journal of Marketing Research, 37*(3), 309–317.

Hadaway, K., Marler, P., & Chaves, M. (1993). What the polls don't show: A closer look at U.S. church attendance. *American Sociological Review, 58*(6), 741–752.

Hall, E. T. (1976). *Beyond culture*. Oxford: Anchor.

Hambleton, R. K., Merenda, P. F., & Spielberger, C. D. (2005). *Adapting educational and psychological tests for cross-cultural assessment*. Mahwah, NJ: Erlbaum.

Hamilton, D. L. (1968). Personality attributes associated with extreme response style. *Psychological Bulletin, 69*(3), 192–203.

Hamilton, R. W., & Biehal, G. J. (2005). Achieving your goals or protecting their future? The effects of self-view on goals and choices. *Journal of Consumer Research, 32*(2), 277–283.

Han, S.-P., & Shavitt, S. (1994). Persuasion and culture: Advertising appeals in individualistic and collectivistic societies. *Journal of Experimental Social Psychology, 30*(4), 326.

Harkness, J. A. (2003). Questionnaire translation. In J. A. Harkness, F. J. van de Vijver, & P. P. Mohler (Eds.), *Cross-cultural survey methods*. Hoboken, NJ: Wiley.

Harkness, J. A., Pennell, B., & Schoua-Glusberg. (2004). Questionnaire translation and assessment. In S. Presser, J. M. Rothgeb, M. P. Couper, J. T. Lessler, E. Martin & E. Singer (Eds.), *Methods for testing and evaluating survey questionnaires*. Hoboken, NJ: Wiley.

Harkness, J. A., van de Vijver, F. J., & Mohler, P. P. (2003). *Cross-cultural survey methods*. New York: Wiley.

Heine, S. J., Lehman, D. R., Peng, K., & Greenholtz, J. (2002). What's wrong with cross-cultural comparisons of subjective Likert scales: The reference-group problem. *Journal of Personality and Social Psychology, 82*(6), 903–918.

Higgins, E. T. (1997). Beyond pleasure and pain. *American Psychologist, 52*(12), 1280.

Ho, D. Y.-F. (1994). Cognitive socialization in Confucian heritage cultures. In P. M. Greenfield & R. R. Cocking (Eds.), *Cross-cultural roots of minority child development* (pp. 285–313). Mahwah, NJ: Erlbaum.

Ho, D. Y.-F., & Chiu, C.-Y. (1994). Component ideas of individualism, collectivism, and social organization: An application in the study of Chinese culture. In U. Kim, H. C. Triandis, C. Kagitcibasi, S.-C. Choi & G. Yoon (Eds.), *Individualism and collectivism: Theory and applications* (pp. 137–156). Thousand Oaks, CA.: Sage Publications, Inc.

Hofstede, G. H. (1980). *Culture's consequences: International differences in work-related values*. Newbury Park: Sage.

Hofstede, G. H. (2001). *Culture's consequences: Comparing values, behaviors, institutions and organizations across nations*. Thousand Oaks, Calif.: Sage.

Hofstee, W., Ten Berge, J., & Hendriks, A. (1998). How to score questionnaires. *Personality and Individual Differences, 25*(5), 897–909.

Hong, J. W., Muderrisoglu, A., & Zinkhan, G. M. (1987). Cultural differences and advertising expression: A comparative content analysis of Japanese and U.S. magazine advertising. *Journal of Advertising, 16*(1), 55–62.

Hong, Y.-y., Ip, G., Chiu, C.-y., Morris, M. W., & Menon, T. (2001). Cultural identity and dynamic construction of the self: collective duties and individual rights in Chinese and American cultures. *Social Cognition, 19*(3), 251–268.

Hsee, C. K., & Weber, E. U. (1999). Cross-national differences in risk preference and lay predictions. *Journal of Behavioral Decision Making, 12*(2), 165–179.

Hui, C., & Triandis, H. C. (1989). Effects of culture and response format on extreme response style. *Journal of Cross-Cultural Psychology, 20*(3), 296–309.

Jabine, T. B., Straf, M. L., Tanur, J. M., & Tourangeau, R. (1984). *Cognitive aspects of survey methodology: Building a bridge between disciplines. Report of the Advanced Research Seminar on Cognitive Aspects of Survey Methodology*. Washington, DC: National Academy Press.

Javalgi, R. G., Cutler, B. D., & Malhotra, N. K. (1995). Print advertising at the component level: A cross-cultural comparison of the United States and Japan. *Journal of Business Research, 34*(2), 117–124.

Javeline, D. (1999). Response effects in polite cultures. *Public Opinion Quarterly, 63*(1), 1–28.

Ji, L.-J., Schwarz, N., & Nisbett, R. E. (2000). Culture, autobiographical memory, and behavioral frequency reports: Measurement issues in cross-cultural studies. *Personality and Social Psychology Bulletin, 26*(5), 585–593.

Johnson, T. P. (1998). Approaches to equivalence in cross-cultural and cross-national survey research. *Zuma Nachrichten Spezial, 3*, 1–40.

Johnson, T. P., Cho, Y. I., Holbrook, A. L., O'Rourke, D., Warnecke, R., & Chavez, N. (2006). Cultural variability in the effects of question design features on respondent comprehension of health surveys. *Annals of Epidemiology, 15*, 661–668.

Johnson, T. P., Kulesa, P., Cho, Y. I., & Shavitt, S. (2005). The relation between culture and response styles: Evidence from 19 Countries. *Journal of Cross-Cultural Psychology, 36*(2), 264–277.

Johnson, T. P., O'Rourke, D., Chavez, N., Sudman, S., Warnecke, R., Lacey, L., et al. (1997). Social cognition and responses to survey questions among culturally diverse populations. In L. Lyberg, P. Biemer, M. Collins, E. de Leeuw, C. Dippo, N. Schwarz, & D. Trewin (Eds.), *Survey measurement and process quality* (pp. 87–113). New York: Wiley..

Johnson, T. P., & van de Vijver, F. J. (2003). Social desirability in cross-cultural research. In J. A. Harkness, F. J. van de Vijver & P. P. Mohler (Eds.), *Cross-cultural survey methods* (pp. 193–209). New York: Wiley.

Jones, E. L. (1963). The courtesy bias in South-East Asian surveys. *International Social Science Journal, 15*, 70–76.

Kacen, J. J., & Lee, J. A. (2002). The influence of culture on consumer impulsive buying behavior. *Journal of Consumer Psychology, 12*(2), 163–176.

Kagitcibasi, C. (1994). A critical appraisal of individualism and collectivism: Toward a new formulation. In U. Kim, H. C. Triandis, C. Kagitcibasi, S.-C. Choi & G. Yoon (Eds.), *Individualism and collectivism: Theory, method, and applications* (pp. 52–65). Thousand Oaks: Sage.

Kashima, Y., Siegal, M., Tanaka, K., & Kashima, E. S. (1992). Do people believe behaviours are consistent with attitudes? Towards a cultural psychology of attribution processes. *British Journal of Social Psychology, 31*(2), 111–124.

Kashima, Y., Yamaguchi, S., Kim, U., Choi, S.-C., Gelfand, M. J., & Yuki, M. (1995). Culture, gender, and self: A perspective from individualism-collectivism research. *Journal of Personality and Social Psychology, 69*(5), 925–937.

Keillor, B., Owens, D., & Pettijohn, C. (2001). A cross-cultural/cross-national study of influencing factors and socially desirable response biases. *International Journal of Market Research, 43*(1), 63–84.

Kemmelmeier, M., & Oyserman, D. (2001). The ups and downs of thinking about a successful other: Self-construals and the consequences of social comparisons. *European Journal of Social Psychology, 31*(3), 311–320.

Kiesler, S., & Sproull, L. S. (1986). Response effects in the electronic survey. *Public Opinion Quarterly, 50*(3), 402–413.

Kim, H. S., & Markus, H. R. (1999). Deviance or uniqueness, harmony or conformity? A cultural analysis. *Journal of Personality & Social Psychology, 77*(4), 785–800.

King, G., Murray, C. J. L., Salomon, J. A., & Tandon, A. (2004). Enhancing the validity and cross-cultural comparability of measurement in survey research. *American Political Science Review, 98*, 191–207.

King, M. F., & Bruner, G. C. (2000). Social desirability bias: A neglected aspect of validity testing. *Psychology & Marketing, 17*(2), 79–103.

Kitayama, S., Markus, H. R., Matsumoto, H., & Norasakkunkit, V. (1997). Individual and collective processes in the construction of the self: Self-enhancement in the United States and self-criticism in Japan. *Journal of Personality and Social Psychology, 72*(6), 1245–1267.

Knowles, E. S., & Nathan, K. T. (1997). Acquiescent responding in self-reports: Cognitive style or social concern? *Journal of Research in Personality, 31*(2), 293–301.

Kochman, T. (1981). *Black and White styles in conflict.* Chicago: University of Chicago Press.

Lalwani, A. K., Shavitt, S., & Johnson, T. (2006). What is the relation between cultural orientation and socially desirable responding? *Journal of Personality and Social Psychology, 90*(1), 165–178.

Lau-Gesk, L. G. (2003). Activating culture through persuasion appeals: An examination of the bicultural consumer. *Journal of Consumer Psychology, 13*(3), 301–315.

Lavidge, R. J., & Steiner, G. A. (1961). A Model for Predictive Measurements of Advertising Effectiveness. *Journal of Marketing, 25*(6), 59–62.

Lee, A. Y., Aaker, J. L., & Gardner, W. L. (2000). The pleasures and pains of distinct self-construals: The role of interdependence in regulatory focus. *Journal of Personality and Social Psychology, 78*(6), 1122–1134.

Lee, A. Y., & Lee, S. (2005). The far and near of self views: Self-construal and temporal perspective. Working paper, Northwestern University.

Lee, C., & Green, R. T. (1991). Cross-cultural examination of the fishbein behavioral intentions model. *Journal of International Business Studies, 22*(2), 289–305.

Lee, J. A. (2000). Adapting Triandis's model of subjective culture and social behavior relations to consumer behavior. *Journal of Consumer Psychology, 9*(2), 117–126.

Lentz, T. (1938). Acquiescence as a factor in the measurement of personality. *Psychological Bulletin, 35*, 659.

Leong, S. M., Ang, S. H., & Tham, L. L. (1996). Increasing brand name recall in print advertising among Asian consumers. *Journal of Advertising, 25*(2), 65–81.

Lin, C. A. (2001). Cultural values reflected in Chinese and American Television Advertising. *Journal of Advertising, 30*(4), 83–94.

Maddux, W. W., & Yuki, M. (2006). The 'Ripple Effect': Cultural differences in perceptions of the consequences of events. *Personality and Social Psychology Bulletin, 32*(5), 669–683.

Maheswaran, D., & Chaiken, S. (1991). Promoting systematic processing in low-motivation settings: Effect of incongruent information on processing and judgment. *Journal of Personality & Social Psychology, 61*(1), 13–25.

Malhotra, N. K., Agarwal, J., & Peterson, M. (1996). Methodological issues in cross-cultural marketing research: A state-of-the-art review. *International Marketing Review, 13*(5), 7–43.

Mandel, N. (2003). Shifting selves and decision making: The effects of self-construal priming on consumer risk-taking. *Journal of Consumer Research, 30*(1), 30–40.

Marin, G., Gamba, R. J., & Marin, B. V. (1992). Extreme response style and acquiescence among Hispanics: The role of acculturation and education. *Journal of Cross-Cultural Psychology, 23*(4), 498–509.

Marin, G., & Marin, B. V. (1989). *Research with Hispanic populations*. Newbury Park, CA: Sage.

Markus, H. R., & Kitayama, S. (1991). Culture and the self: Implications for cognition, emotion, and motivation. *Psychological Review, 98*(2), 224–253.

Mick, D. G. (1996). Are studies of dark side variables confounded by socially desirable responding? The case of materialism. *Journal of Consumer Research, 23*(September), 106–119.

Middleton, K. L., & Jones, J. L. (2000). Socially desirable response sets: The impact of country culture. *Psychology & Marketing, 17*(2), 149–163.

Miracle, G. E. (1987). Feel-Do-Learn: An alternative sequence underlying Japanese consumer response to television commercials. In F. G. Feasley (Ed.), Proceedings of the L.A. Conference of the American Academy of Advertising. Columbia, S.C.: The University of South Carolina.

Mirowsky, J., & Ross, C. E. (1980). Minority status, ethnic culture, and distress: A comparison of Blacks, Whites, Mexicans, and Mexican Americans. *American Journal of Sociology, 86*, 479–495.

Mirowsky, J., & Ross, C. E. (1991). Eliminating defense and agreement bias from measures of the sense of control: A 2 × 2 index. *Social Psychology Quarterly, 54*(2), 127–145.

Moors, G. (2003). Diagnosing response style behavior by means of a latent-class factor approach. Socio-demographic correlates of gender role attitudes and perceptions of ethnic discrimination reexamined. *Quality & Quantity: International Journal of Methodology, 37*(3), 277–302.

Nederhof, A. J. (1985). Methods of coping with social desirability bias: A review. *European Journal of Social Psychology, 15*(3), 263–280.

Nisbett, R. E., Peng, K., Choi, I., & Norenzayan, A. (2001). Culture and systems of thought: Holistic versus analytic cognition. *Psychological Review, 108*(2), 291–310.

Nunnally, J. C. (1978). *Psychometric theory*. New York: McGraw-Hill.

Ogilvy, D. (1985). *Ogilvy on advertising*. New York: Vintage Books.

Oyserman, D., Coon, H. M., & Kemmelmeier, M. (2002). Rethinking individualism and collectivism: Evaluation of theoretical assumptions and meta-analyses. *Psychological Bulletin, 128*(1), 3–72.

Paulhus, D. L. (1984). Two-component models of socially desirable responding. *Journal of Personality and Social Psychology, 46*(3), 598–609.

Paulhus, D. L. (1991). Measurement and control of response bias. In J. P. Robinson & P. R. Shaver (Eds.), *Measures of personality and social psychological attitudes* (pp. 17–59). San Diego: Academic Press.

Paulhus, D. L. (1998a). Interpersonal and intrapsychic adaptiveness of trait self-enhancement: A mixed blessing? *Journal of Personality and Social Psychology, 74*(5), 1197–1208.

Paulhus, D. L. (1998b). *Paulhus deception scales: User's manual*. North Tonawanda, NY: Multi-Health Systems.

Pleck, J. H., Sonenstein, F. L., & Ku, L. (1996). Black-white differences in adolescent males' substance use: Are they explained by underreporting by Blacks? *Journal of Gender, Culture, and Health, 1*, 247–265.

Pollay, R. W. (1986). The distorted mirror: Reflections on the unintended consequences of advertising. *Journal of Marketing, 50*(2), 18–36.

Potter, S. H. (1988). The cultural construction of emotion in rural Chinese social life. *Ethos, 16*(2), 181–208.

Ray, J. (1979). Is the acquiescent response style problem not so mythical after all? Some results from a successful balanced F scale. *Journal of Personality Assessment, 43*(6), 638–643.

Rhee, E., Uleman, J. S., & Lee, H. K. (1996). Variations in collectivism and individualism by ingroup and culture: Confirmatory factor analysis. *Journal of Personality and Social Psychology, 71*(5), 1037–1054.

Rice, M. D., & Lu, Z. (1988). A content analysis of Chinese magazine advertisements. *Journal of Advertising, 17*(4), 43–48.

Ricks, D. (1983). *Big business blunders: Mistakes in multi-national marketing*. Homewood, IL: Dow Jones-Irwin.

Rogler, L. H. (1989). The meaning of culturally sensitive research in mental health. *American Journal of Psychiatry, 146*(3), 296–303.

Rook, D. W., & Fisher, R. J. (1995). Normative influences on impulsive buying behavior. *Journal of Consumer Research, 22*(3), 305–313.

Ross, C. E., & Mirowsky, J. (1984). Socially-desirable response and acquiescence in a cross-cultural survey of mental health. *Journal of Health and Social Behavior, 25*(2), 189–197.

Russell, J. A., & Yik, M. S. (1996). Emotion among the Chinese. In M. H. Bond (Ed.), *The handbook of Chinese psychology* (pp. 166–188). Hong Kong, China: Oxford University Press.

Sackeim, H. A., & Gur, R. C. (1979). Self-deception, other-deception, and self-reported psychopathology. *Journal of Consulting and Clinical Psychology, 47*(1), 213–215.

Salomon, J. A., Tandon, A., & Murray, C. J. L. (2005). Comparability of self rated health: Cross sectional multi-country survey using anchoring vignettes. *British Medical Journal, 328*, 258–261.

Schlenker, B. R., & Britt, T. W. (1999). Beneficial impression management: Strategically controlling information to help friends. *Journal of Personality and Social Psychology, 76*(4), 559–573.

Schlenker, B. R., Britt, T. W., & Pennington, J. (1996). Impression regulation and management: Highlights of a theory of self-identification. In R. M. Sorrentino & E. T. Higgins (Eds.), *Handbook of motivation and cognition, Vol. 3: The interpersonal context* (pp. 118–147). New York: Guilford.

Scholderer, J., Grunert, K. G., & Brunso, K. (2005). A procedure for eliminating additive bias from cross-cultural survey data. *Journal of Business Research, 58*(1), 72–78.

Schuman, H., & Presser, S. (1981). *Questions and answers in attitude surveys: Experiments in question form, wording, and context*. New York: Academic Press.

Schwartz, S. H. (1992). Universals in the content and structure of values: Theoretical advances and empirical tests in 20 countries. In M. P. Zanna (Ed.), *Advances in experimental social psychology* (Vol. 25, pp. 1–65). New York: Academic Press.

Schwartz, S. H., & Bilsky, W. (1987). Toward a universal psychological structure of human values. *Journal of Personality and Social Psychology, 53*(3), 550–562.

Schwartz, S. H., & Bilsky, W. (1990). Toward a theory of the universal content and structure of values: Extensions and cross-cultural replications. *Journal of Personality and Social Psychology, 58*(5), 878–891.

Schwartz, S. H., & Boehnke, K. (2004). Evaluating the structure of human values with confirmatory factor analysis. *Journal of Research in Personality, 38*(3), 230–255.

Schwarz, N. (2003). Self-reports in consumer research: The challenge of comparing cohorts and cultures. *Journal of Consumer Research, 29*(4), 588–594.

Shao, A. T., Raymond, M. A., & Taylor, C. (1999). Shifting Advertising Appeals in Taiwan. *Journal of Advertising Research, 39*(6), 61–69.

Shavitt, S., Lalwani, A. K., Zhang, J., & Torelli, C. J. (2006). The horizontal/vertical distinction in cross-cultural consumer research. *Journal of Consumer Psychology, 16*(4), 325–342.

Shavitt, S., Zhang, J., & Johnson, T. P. (2006). Horizontal and vertical cultural differences in advertising and consumer persuasion. Unpublished data, University of Illinois.

Shweder, R. A., & Bourne, E. J. (1982). Does the concept of person vary cross-culturally? In A. J. Marsella & G. M. White (Eds.), *Cultural conceptions of mental health and therapy* (pp. 130–204). London: Reidel.

Sigelman, L. (1982). The nonvoting voter in voting research. *Public Opinion Quarterly, 26,* 47–56.

Singelis, T. M. (1994). The measurement of independent and interdependent self-construals. *Personality and Social Psychology Bulletin, 20*(5), 580–591.

Singelis, T. M., Triandis, H. C., Bhawuk, D., & Gelfand, M. J. (1995). Horizontal and vertical dimensions of individualism and collectivism: A theoretical and measurement refinement. *Cross-Cultural Research: The Journal of Comparative Social Science, 29*(3), 240–275.

Singh, J. (1995). Measurement issues in cross-national research. *Journal of International Business Studies, 26*(3), 597–619.

Singh, N., & Matsuo, H. (2004). Measuring cultural adaptation on the Web: a content analytic study of U.S. and Japanese Web sites. *Journal of Business Research, 57*(8), 864–872.

Smith, P. B. (2004). Acquiescent response bias as an aspect of cultural communication Style. *Journal of Cross-Cultural Psychology, 35*(1), 50–61.

Smith, P. B., & Bond, M. H. (1998). *Social psychology across cultures* (2nd ed.). Hemel Hempstead: Harvester Wheatsheaf.

Smith, P. B., & Fischer, R. J. (2006). Acquiescence, extreme response bias and culture: A multi-level analysis. In F. J. van de Vijver, D. A. van Hemert, & Y. H. Poortinga (Eds.), *Individuals and cultures in multi-level analysis*: Mahwah, NJ: Erlbaum, in press.

Smith, T. W. (2003). Developing comparable questions in cross-national surveys. In J. A. Harkness, F. J. van de Vijver, & P. P. Mohler (Eds.), *Cross-cultural survey methods* (pp. 69–91). New York: Wiley.

Spencer-Oatey, H. (1997). Unequal relationships in high and low power distance societies: A comparative study of tutor-student role relations in Britain and China. *Journal of Cross-Cultural Psychology, 28*(3), 284–302.

Steenkamp, J.-B. E. M., & Baumgartner, H. (1998). Assessing measurement invariance in cross-national consumer research. *Journal of Consumer Research, 25*(1), 78–90.

Stewart, A. L., & Napoles-Springer, A. (2000). Health-related quality-of-life assessments in diverse population groups in the United States. *Medical Care, 38*(Suppl9), II102–II124.

Stricker, L. J. (1963). Acquiescence and social desirability response styles, item characteristics, and conformity. *Psychological Reports, 12*(2), 319–341.

Tak, J., Kaid, L. L., & Lee, S. (1997). A cross-cultural study of political advertising in the United States and Korea. *Communication Research, 24,* 413–430.

Taylor, C. R., Miracle, G. E., & Wilson, R. D. (1997). The impact of information level on the effectiveness of U.S. and Korean television commercials. *Journal of Advertising, 26*(1), 1–18.

Teresi, J. A., Holmes, D., Ramirez, M., Gurland, B. J., & Lantigua, R. (2001). Performance of cognitive tests among different racial/ethnic and education groups: Findings of differential item functioning and possible item bias. *Journal of Mental Health and Aging, 7*(1), 79–89.

Toner, B. (1987). The impact of agreement bias on the ranking of questionnaire response. *Journal of Social Psychology, 127*(2), 221–222.

Torelli, C. J. (2006). Individuality or conformity? The effect of independent and interdependent self-concepts on public judgments. *Journal of Consumer Psychology, 16*(3), 240–248.

Trafimow, D., Triandis, H. C., & Goto, S. G. (1991). Some tests of the distinction between the private self and the collective self. *Journal of Personality & Social Psychology, 60*(5), 649–655.

Triandis, H. C. (1972). *The analysis of subjective culture.* New York: Wiley-Interscience.

Triandis, H. C. (1989). The self and social behavior in differing cultural contexts. *Psychological Review, 96*(3), 506–520.

Triandis, H. C. (1995). *Individualism & collectivism.* Boulder, CO: Westview Press.

Triandis, H. C., Bontempo, R., Villareal, M. J., Asai, M., & Lucca, N. (1988). Individualism and collectivism: Cross-cultural perspectives on self-group relationships. *Journal of Personality and Social Psychology, 54*(2), 323–338.

Triandis, H. C., & Gelfand, M. J. (1998). Converging measurement of horizontal and vertical individualism and collectivism. *Journal of Personality and Social Psychology, 74*(1), 118–128.

Triandis, H. C., Leung, K., Villareal, M. J., & Clack, F. L. (1985). Allocentric versus idiocentric tendencies: Convergent and discriminant validation. *Journal of Research in Personality, 19*(4), 395–415.

Tsai, J. L., & Levenson, R. W. (1997). Cultural influences of emotional responding: Chinese American and European American dating couples during interpersonal conflict. *Journal of Cross-Cultural Psychology, 28*(5), 600–625.

Tse, D. K., Belk, R. W., & Zhou, N. (1989). Becoming a consumer society: A longitudinal and cross-cultural content analysis of print ads from Hong Kong, the People's Republic of China, and Taiwan. *Journal of Consumer Research, 15*(4), 457–472.

van de Vijver, F. J. (1998). Towards a theory of bias and equivalence. *Zuma Nachrichten Spezial, 3*, 41–65.

van de Vijver, F. J., & Leung, K. (2000). Methodological issues in psychological research on culture. *Journal of Cross-Cultural Psychology, 31*(1), 33–51.

van de Vijver, F. J., Ploubidis, G., & van Hemert, D. A. (2004). *Toward an understanding of cross-cultural differences in acquiescence and extremity scoring.* Paper presented at the Sheth/Sudman Symposium on Cross-Cultural Survey Research Methodology, Urbana, IL.

van Hemert, D. A., van de Vijver, F. J., Poortinga, Y. H., & Georgas, J. (2002). Structural and functional equivalence of the Eysenck personality questionnaire within and between countries. *Personality and Individual Differences, 33*(8), 1229–1249.

van Herk, H., Poortinga, Y. H., & Verhallen, T. M. (2004). Response styles in rating scales: Evidence of method bias in data from six EU countries. *Journal of Cross-Cultural Psychology, 35*(3), 346–360.

Vaughn, R. (1980). How advertising works: A planning model. *Journal of Advertising Research, 20*(5), 27–33.

Vogt, W. P. (1999). *Dictionary of statistics & methodology* (2nd ed.). Thousand Oaks, CA: Sage.

Wang, C. L., Bristol, T., Mowen, J. C., & Chakraborty, G. (2000). Alternative modes of self-construal: Dimensions of connectedness-separateness and advertising appeals to the cultural and gender-specific self. *Journal of Consumer Psychology, 9*(2), 107–115.

Wang, C. L., & Mowen, J. C. (1997). The separateness-connectedness self-schema: Scale development and application to message construction. *Psychology & Marketing, 14*(2), 185–207.

Wang, J., & Lee, A. Y. (2006). The role of regulatory fit on information search and persuasion. *Journal of Marketing Research, 43*(1), 28–38.

Warnecke, R. B., Johnson, T. P., Chavez, N., Sudman, S., O'Rourke, D., Lacey, L., et al. (1997). Improving question wording in surveys of culturally diverse populations. *Annals of Epidemiology, 7*, 334–342.

Watson, D. (1992). Correcting for acquiescent response bias in the absence of a balanced scale: An application to class consciousness. *Sociological Methods & Research, 21*, 52–88.

Weber, E. U., & Hsee, C. K. (1998). Cross-cultural differences in risk perception, but cross-cultural similarities in attitudes towards perceived risk. *Management Science, 44*(9), 1205–1217.

Weber, E. U., & Hsee, C. K. (2000). Culture and individual judgment and decision making. *Applied Psychology: An International Review, 49*(1), 32–61.

Williams, R. L. (1977). Critical issues in achievement testing for children from diverse ethnic packgrounds. In M. J. Wargo & D. R. Green (Eds.), *Achievement testing of disadvantaged and minority students for educational program evaluation* (pp. 41–72). Monterey, CA: CTB/McGraw Hill.

Witkowski, T. H., Ma, Y., & Zheng, D. (2003). Cross-cultural influences on brand identity impressions: KFC in China and the United States. *Asia Pacific Journal of Marketing and Logistics, 15*(1/2), 74–88.

Wong, N., Rindfleisch, A., & Burroughs, J. E. (2003). Do reverse-worded items confound measures in cross-cultural consumer research? The case of the material values scale. *Journal of Consumer Research, 30*(1), 72–91.

Zax, M., & Takahashi, S. (1967). Cultural influences on response style: Comparisons of Japanese and American college students. *Journal of Social Psychology, 71*(1), 3–10.

Zhang, J., & Shavitt, S. (2003). Cultural values in advertisements to the Chinese X-generation: Promoting modernity and individualism. *Journal of Advertising, 32*(1), 23–33.

Zhang, Y., & Gelb, B. D. (1996). Matching advertising appeals to culture: The influence of products' use conditions. *Journal of Advertising, 25*(3), 29–46.

Zola, I. K. (1966). Culture and symptoms: An analysis of patients' presenting complaints. *American Sociological Review, 31*(5), 615–630.

45

Measurement Error in Experimental Designs in Consumer Psychology

Madhu Viswanathan

University of Illinois at Urbana-Champaign

What is measurement error and why does it matter for experimental research in consumer psychology, which involves manipulations? An apparent reason is that dependent variables and covariates need to be measured. But a subtler reason is that measurement of an individual construct versus its manipulation can be viewed as two sides of the same coin. Understanding measurement error is central to any research design including experimental designs used in consumer psychology. The premise of this chapter is that understanding the measurement of one thing is central to understanding the measurement and manipulation of many things and, in fact, the entire research design. Measurement error is as germane to experimental design as it is to survey design. It manifests in different ways but is essentially the same.

There is much to be learnt across different paradigms in research that often develop in relative independence, such as between research traditions in measurement, experimental designs and survey designs. Along these lines, the purpose of this chapter is to highlight the central importance of measurement in experimental research in consumer psychology. The topics of measurement and experimental design have been written about extensively (Nunnally, 1978; Cook & Campbell, 1979; Aronson, Carlsmith, Ellsworth, & Gonzales., 1990). This chapter offers a different perspective on merging insights from both perspectives to gain new insights on experimental designs. The chapter aims to provide depth of understanding of issues of measurement in experimental design in consumer psychology. Although survey designs are common in consumer psychology, measurement issues in survey design in consumer psychology are not in focus here. Moreover, the discussion of experimental designs also covers the measurement of the dependent variables.

The chapter is written assuming basic knowledge of measurement and experimental designs. It borrows heavily from a recent book on measurement error and research design (Viswanathan, 2005). The first section provides an overview of experimental research designs. The second section uses issues in measure development, assessment and usage to derive implications for designing experiments in consumer psychology. The third section translates a finer taxonomy of types of measurement error to errors in an experimental context. The fourth section draws some broader parallels between measurement and research designs. These three sections are, therefore, at three different levels of analysis, beginning with a translation of measure development, assessment, and usage to issues experimental designs, then using a formal taxonomy of measurement errors to draw parallels between measurement and experimental design, and finally using types of reliability and validity to draw broader parallels between measurement and research designs. A concluding discussion summarizes the key points.

EXPERIMENTAL RESEARCH DESIGNS

Experimental Designs in Consumer Psychology

A cursory examination of articles in the *Journal of Consumer Psychology* and the *Journal of Consumer Research* provides many examples of innovative designs. As an example, in a study of time constraints and price judgments (Suri & Monroe, 2003), a series of pretests were used to decide on product categories, brand names, and high and low price levels. The time pressure manipulation was designed by first determining average time to process information. Then, different time pressure conditions were created based on absolute time using average time as a baseline. Respondents were assigned to different conditions and shown a monitor with the average time to complete the task and the time allotted to them. Each time pressure condition was assessed through determining responses to items tapping into subjective time pressure. In a study of gender typed ads and impression formation (Johar Moreau, & Schwarz, 2003), respondents completed a scale on tendency to gender stereotype in a first session. Two weeks later, in a second session of seemingly unrelated tasks, respondents rated ads, which were then followed by the experimenter leaving the room and a different experimenter administering the second task, and rating a woman based on an ambiguous description. Ads were selected from 2 weeks of television programming, identifying ads that showed women as homemakers and ads as controls in similar product categories. A large set of ads were pretested to identify a smaller set in both conditions that was similar on variables such as familiarity and liking.

A number of elements of experimental designs are reflected in these and other examples. There are many elements to an experiment including a cover story, relevant stimuli for the sample in question, the experimental task and instructions, the setting, levels of manipulations, and dependent variables. There are several procedures, such as series of pretests and pilot tests, often beginning with a larger set of stimuli. Testing of one element of a design requires assumptions about other elements. Many variables are controlled, one or more manipulated. Often, the sample is the first convenient starting point, based on which relevant stimuli such as product categories are chosen. The experimental task is another important decision, including the choice of the context, whether it is evaluating an ad or reading a magazine and so forth. All these elements have to work synchronously for a successful design. Elements of the design have to be pretested, such as whether the cover story and stimuli achieve control on specific variables and whether the manipulation is successful on the construct of interest without confounding other constructs. Sometimes, there is a "chicken and egg" problem in deciding where to begin.

Overview of Research Designs

A brief overview of research designs is provided as background to subsequent discussion of experimental designs. A method comprises of the choice of a type of design (e.g., a lab experiment vs. a survey), operationalization of key variables (whether measured or manipulated), samples and settings, and procedures. In other words, the method includes who provides the data (sample), where they provide the data (setting), on what they provide the data (measures and manipulations), and how they provide the data (administration procedures). The method is essentially everything that is done to collect the data. This is one of those statements that may be obvious, yet its implications are often not reflected in the practice of research. The significance of this statement is in understanding that a variety of factors, such as the setting and the nature of administration, may cause error, whereas most of the effort on the part of the researcher may be on designing a manipulation and developing valid measures. These manipulations and measures have to be valid in the actual usage conditions of the study. For example, the choice of setting and the use of individual versus group administrations can have important consequences. Yet, casual observation suggests that these issues sometimes do not receive sufficient consideration. For instances, large classroom administrations can cause distractions among participants whereas smaller groups maintain some of the efficiencies while gaining control over the administration. After the "difficult" task of designing manipulations and measures is completed, considerable weight may be placed on practical considerations of efficiency, sometimes jeopardizing the manipulation and the basic design.

Methods range from correlational designs, where all variables are continuous and measured, to experimental designs, where at least one independent variable is manipulated and categorical in nature. Pure experiments are defined by the manipulation of levels of a variable and random assignment of respondents to various conditions (either multiple treatment conditions or treatment and control conditions). Experimental variables may also be manipulated either between-subjects (where each respondent is assigned to one level of the experimental variable or treatment) or within-subjects (where each respondent is assigned to several or all levels of the treatment) (Greenwald, 1976). Whereas independent variables may be manipulated in pure experiments, they may be "naturally occurring" in quasi-experiments. Moreover, a correlational design could be analyzed as an experimental design by categorizing a continuous variable. Researchers may also examine differences in means across different levels of a measured variable or study a variable such as family size and examine data as a quasi-experiment. The distinction between experiments and surveys may be blurred. Experiments versus surveys or correlational designs can be viewed as a continuum.

The view of experiments and surveys as a continuum also lends itself to another important issue. The aim in research is usually to make causal inferences from data; therefore, experimental and survey paradigms can benefit from each other. Experimental designs devote considerable attention to clean inferences of causality covering issues that are relevant in developing sequencing of measures in surveys to minimize error due to sources such as hypothesis guessing. Similarly, survey research has devoted considerable attention to question wording and related issues, as well as the measurement of a specific construct; issues that are important for the measurement of dependent variables in experiments. Different paradigms emphasize different aspects of a design, implicitly prioritizing specific aspects.

Issues in Experimental Research Designs

A number of issues of relevance in experimental research designs are covered here as background for the rest of the chapter.

Manipulation Checks and Confounding Checks

Manipulations involve *creating* levels of an independent variable rather than measuring it. Manipulation checks are used to measure manipulations to assess whether levels of an independent variable have been achieved (Figure 45.1). The convergence between a manipulation of a variable and its measurement is examined through a manipulation check. Divergence between a manipulation and measures of variables that it is not supposed to manipulate needs to be assessed as well through confounding checks (Figure 45.1). For example, the manipulation of argument strength

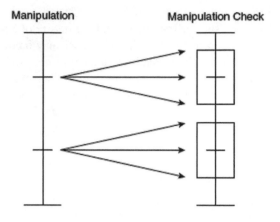

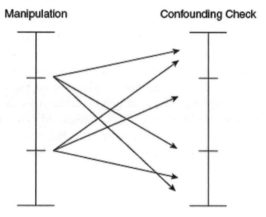

Figure 45.1   Manipulation and confounding checks. (Source: Viswanathan, M, *Measurement Error and Research Design*, p. 317, Figure 10.3. Copyright © 2005. Reprinted by permission of Sage Publications.)

should not lead to a manipulation of distinctly different constructs, say, the amount of information presented.

Pretesting and Pilot Testing

Experimental studies are usually preceded by preliminary testing to adjust aspects of the design. Pretests (used here to refer to tests of some aspect of the experiment) and pilot tests (used here to refer to tests of the entire experiment) typically precede experimental studies. They ensure that investment in large-scale data collection for an experiment is judicious and provide a basis to make design choices about all aspects of the operationalization. In this regard, along the lines of learning across paradigms, open-ended approaches can be used in pretesting and pilot testing to assess what the experimental procedures mean to respondents as well as the adequacy of various procedures, and instructions. Such approaches are used in survey design to assess and improve question wording. Such open-ended procedures can follow data collection on more structured scales. Another issue in pretesting is the use of a within-subjects design to evaluate manipulations, whereas the main experiment may involve a between-subjects design (e.g., the same respondents in a pretest rating three brands of high, medium, and low quality versus different respondents rating different brands in the main experiment).[1] Therefore, the manipulations rated in pretests within the context provided by other brands may not be valid in an experiment without such context.

In experiments, levels of the independent variable should allow for sufficient variation in the dependent variables to enable tests of hypotheses. The dependent variables ideally should be in the middle of the effective range (usually but not always the middle of the actual range; for example, in a true/false recognition test where pure guessing can lead to 50% accuracy). The method should be calibrated to allow sufficient variation to test hypotheses. For example, in memory research, the number of items used as stimuli should be calibrated to enable variation in recall, recognition, or other memory tests.

Sequencing Variables

Another key issue in experimental design is to prioritize the sequencing of variables to enable a manipulation of the independent variable(s) and collection of data on the central dependent variable(s). Independent variables and central dependent variables should ideally be sequenced ahead of other variables to enable a clean inference of causality. If data on individual differences is collected in an experimental context, it may be preferable to sequence such measures after the central dependent variable. This is not to preclude disguising the independent and dependent variables, such as by using fillers and distracter tasks consistently across all respondents. However, when a relevant variable precedes the independent variable or the central dependent variable, it provides an alternative explanation for differences in the dependent variable across conditions by systematically influencing the outcome (i.e., $X \rightarrow Y \rightarrow Z$ instead of $X \rightarrow$ Fillers$\rightarrow Z$ where the specific response on Y may directly or through an interaction with X influence response on Z, whereas filler tasks picked from unrelated domains are less likely to do so).

Strength of Manipulations

A key element of experimental design is the trade-off in designing manipulations between making tests too strong (i.e., loading the dice against) versus too weak. Manipulations should be designed to generate levels of the independent variable while not generating levels of confounding variables. For the sake of discussion, ways of manipulating a variable range from a direct statement of a manipulation level to a weak or subtle manipulation. Strong manipulations may lead to confounding variables, such as hypothesis guessing. Consider a scenario where the status connoted by a product is to be manipulated. A strong manipulation could directly state that a product is of high or low status, whereas a subtler manipulation could couch the claim in other information. Whereas the strong manipulation runs the risk of causing hypothesis guessing, the subtler manipulation runs the risk of being too weak. Pretests should be used to ascertain whether subtler manipulations evoke status considerations without confounding other variables. This is the constant trade-off between strong and subtle manipulations.

Hypothetically, the most direct form of testing is to ask respondents about a hypothesis (i.e., the relationship between two constructs). Relative to this extreme, indirect testing would involve obtaining data on individual constructs and assessing or computing the association between them. Respondents may be (1) aware of the relationships being tested, (2) aware of the constructs on which data are being collected but not aware of the relationships being assessed, or (3) not aware of either the individual constructs being measured or the relationship being tested. Awareness of a construct being measured or of the relationship being measured could be decreased through administration procedures as well, such as interspersion of items from different measures or separation of measures and manipulations. Administration factors, such as cover stories, separation of focal variables, and interspersion of items from different variables, would serve to disguise relationships being examined and constructs being measured. For example, a study of product preferences and environmental concerns (Nelson, 2004) started out with measurement of a broad range of values followed by product choice scenarios and specific attitudes and behaviors pertaining to the environment. The aim here was to disguise the purpose of the study in terms of the relationship between product preferences and specific environmental concerns. A study manipulating self-importance (Reed, 2004) asked respondents for handwriting samples on sentiments about relationships with parents emphasizing interconnectedness versus independence (low vs. high self-importance, respectively). After a 10-minute delay, a different experimenter administered a product evaluation that appeared to be unrelated to the first task. These procedures serve to disguise the purpose of the study.

Successful manipulations usually elicit certain levels of a construct without respondents' awareness of constructs and/or relationships between constructs or without such awareness affecting subsequent responses. Alternatively, if respondents are aware of elicited constructs, their responses should be unaffected by this awareness. Whether responses are affected by awareness of constructs being manipulated needs to be determined in pretests or pilot tests. Think alouds and other open-ended procedures during pretesting and pilot testing may be very useful in this regard. If responses are affected, their effects have to be interpreted in light of the nature of the results and the direction of the effects. An uninformed parallel can be drawn with Heisenberg's uncertainty principle that both the location and energy of an electron cannot be specified simultaneously, because location requires the use of energy that displaces the electron. The goal of a successful treatment is to elicit levels of a construct without focusing attention on it.

The "stereotype threat" in ability tests provides an interesting example of the very process of measurement altering the phenomenon being measured. Steele (1997) assigned African American and Caucasian students to two conditions; one where they were told their intellectual ability was being measured and another where they were told the test was unrelated to ability. On a test consisting of difficult verbal items from the GRE, Caucasian students scored higher than the African American students in the former (threat) condition, but differences were not found in the latter (nonthreat) condition. These results were consistent with the rationale that informing past victims of stereotyping that their ability is being measured affects their performance.

Another example (Dehaene, 1997) relates to a horse, who could "count." In Germany in the early 1900s, the horse, Hans, was "taught" to count by his trainer (Dehaene, 1997). When given a simple arithmetic problem, Hans tapped his hoof the correct number of times, presumably to provide a response. The public posed a problem to the trainer (e.g., 5 + 3) during demonstrations. The trainer then placed five objects and three objects, respectively, on different tables and Hans would tap his hoof eight times. He also appeared to add fractions and find divisors. Although a team of experts concluded that the feat was authentic, one psychology student probed further. The student presented a problem to the trainer and the horse, however, the problem was altered slightly so that the trainer saw 6 + 2, but Hans saw 6 + 3. Hans made errors, providing responses that were correct for the problem posed to the trainer. It appeared that Hans was sensing minor involuntary movements of the trainer's head or eyebrows when the correct number of knocks was reached.

These examples highlight the insidious nature of demand characteristics in interfering with the measurement process and highlights the Heisenberg uncertainty principle in social science measurement. The very act of measuring a construct affects its measurement. When respondents are made aware of the "construct" being measured, their awareness influences responses in several ways.

Experimental designs isolate the dimension to be manipulated and generate levels of the dimension in question. Ideally, the design should avoid making respondents aware of such elicitation. Initially, pretests should aim to assess whether levels of the construct being manipulated are achieved through a multiple item measure or manipulation check. Open-ended responses to pointed questions about the stimuli along specific dimensions can also be used in pretests to gain insight. Manipulation checks can also be embedded among other measures of potentially confounding variables as a way of gaining initial insight into a potential lack of discriminant validity.[2] Subsequent pretests could fine-tune the stimuli with the aim of manipulating the focal construct without confounding such attempts with other variables. The notion that successful measurement and manipulation are achieved by respondents being unaware applies to hypothesis testing but is, of course, not universally the case. Transparent measurement may be preferable in many situations, for, say, measuring liking for a product or person. Noteworthy, though, is that the aim here is not to test hypotheses but to measure a specific variable. If the relationship between liking and purchasing, for example, is to be assessed, it may be necessary to disguise the purpose of the study through separation or other means. To summarize, human beings have complex motivations and, when aware of the purpose of a study, may react differently and in unpredictable ways. Variables could be measured or manipulated in a disguised way or the relationship under study could be disguised. Such disguising could be achieved through several means. Separating variables whose relationships are being tested is one such approach. Alternatively, one or more constructs being measured or manipulated could be disguised.[3]

Strength of Tests

Any research design should be evaluated in terms of its effect on the strength of a test. A weak manipulation can lead to a strong test. Student samples are often associated with lack of involvement but such samples could provide strong tests if hypothesized results are obtained, despite low involvement and "light" attention counteracting predicted effects. However, if light attention in a student sample affects the meaning that respondents assign to an experimental task and therefore, the degree to which underlying constructs are captured, it undermines the construct validity of the design. The problem occurs when hypothesized results for strong tests are not obtained, an issue that should be addressed in pretests and pilot tests while calibrating procedures to achieve manipulation effects with the sample in question. Several procedural details—such as administration in small numbers, computer-based administration, the use of short experimental sessions, provision of incentives, and adjustment of manipulations—warrant attention. The key point to note is that any sample characteristic is not, per se, a positive or a negative. In fact, a seemingly negative characteristic could well lead to strong tests. Thus, any sample characteristic—or, more broadly, any characteristic of the method—has to be viewed in light of the entire design in terms of its effects (Lynch, 1982; Calder, Phillips, & Tybout, 1981).

Brevity and weakness have been argued to be two characteristics of lab experiments (Ellsworth, 1977). Higher levels of a construct may be qualitatively different than lower levels studied in the lab, thus confounding a construct with levels of a construct. For example, high levels of arousal may be qualitatively different from milder arousal that is studied in a lab experiment. Field studies with varying levels of a construct need to be conducted to assess generalizability to higher levels of a construct.

In an artificial setting it is possible to show what *can* happen (such as Milgram's studies where participants complied in administering electric shocks) (Mook, 1983). The key here is to ensure that the study captures the essence of the theory being tested through conveying appropriate meaning to participants. The meaning that respondents assign to an experimental situation is more important to the generalizability of an experiment than surface-level similarities with reality (Berkowitz

& Donnerstein, 1982). Is the construct in question being manipulated? Based on the combination of sample, stimulus, and other characteristics—essentially, everything done to collect the data—is the appropriate level of the intended construct being manipulated?

TRANSLATING ISSUES IN MEASURE DEVELOPMENT, VALIDATION, AND USAGE TO EXPERIMENTAL DESIGN

A number of issues usually associated with measure development, assessment, and usage are briefly discussed for the purpose of examining implications for experimental designs in consumer psychology.

Conceptual Definition, Domain Delineation, and Item Generation

An important distinction in measurement is between conceptual and operational definitions of constructs (Kerlinger, 1986). The level of abstraction of a construct is an important consideration; constructs that are too concrete may not be as useful for theoretical generalization, whereas constructs that are too abstract may be difficult to measure directly. Discussions of conceptual relationships between constructs and hypotheses about these relationships may confound constructs with their operationalizations, essentially mixing two different levels of analysis. These two levels of analysis need to be kept separate while iterating between them in terms of issues, such as conceptual definitions of constructs and rationale for conceptual relationships between constructs. Measures of a specific construct may assess a related construct. Constructs may also be multidimensional, with each dimension having a different relationship with other constructs.

All of these issues are just as germane in conceptual and operational definitions of variables manipulated in experimental design. These issues cannot be underemphasized for experimental designs that involve creating, or generating levels of a variable rather than measuring levels. For instance, the underlying dimensionality of the construct needs to be explicated before it can be operationalized through manipulation. In addition, levels at which a construct will be operationalized need to be discussed as well. Whereas very abstract constructs are difficult to manipulate, concrete constructs may not be sufficient for the purpose of theoretical generalization.

An important step in measure development is domain delineation (Churchill, 1979; DeVellis, 1991), which involves explicating what the construct is and is not. This step involves understanding what is being measured by elaborating on the concept, before the measure is designed and items in the measure are generated. Issues considered here include using past literature and relating the construct to other constructs, placing the construct in the context of existing knowledge, and describing the construct in different ways, in terms of what is included and what is *not* included by the domain.

A clear understanding of the domain of a construct versus related constructs is also essential in experimental designs in moving from the conceptual to the operational domain and manipulating a construct in experimental design. Such delineation is important even if the construct is "self-evident." Moreover, such delineation also is subsequently useful in assessing the operationalization through manipulation and confounding checks (Figure 45.1). Often, researchers are not sure what confounding checks to employ to assess a manipulation. A full understanding of the domain of the construct would be useful in subsequent assessment of the operationalization through manipulation and confounding checks. Delineation is also useful in developing a measure or using an existing measure as a manipulation check.

A key point worth reemphasizing in the context of experimental design is the need to explicate the construct and its domain *before* developing and assessing manipulations. Careful construct definition and domain delineation are just as important when developing manipulations as when developing measures. The operationalization to construct link needs to be made carefully when developing manipulations just as it is when developing measures. The sizable effort that is invested in developing measures in a measure development effort is noteworthy. Such effort is just as warranted when developing manipulations. Often, the step from construct to manipulation is made without sufficient understanding of the domain and the variety of ways of manipulating a construct. Essentially, whereas measurement involves rules for assigning numbers based on responses on some continuum, manipulation involves *creating* levels of a construct on a continuum. In measure development, there are no direct empirical measures of content validity, and assessment is based on whether (1) a representative set of items was developed, and (2) acceptable procedures were employed in developing items (Nunnally, 1978). Similarly, appropriate procedures are necessary to design manipulations in experiments to enable content validity, including pretesting of a range of stimuli.

Measure design and item generation follows domain delineation in measure development. Before specific items can be generated, the design of the measure needs to be determined and can range from observational data to behavioral inventories. Measure design is followed by item generation, a stage where redundancy is a virtue and the actual effects of minor wording differences are put to empirical test. Large pools of items as well as procedures to develop large pools are important. Such procedures include asking experts to generate items, and asking experts or respondents to evaluate items in the degree to which they capture defined constructs (Haynes, Richard, & Kubany, 1995).

In place of measure design and item generation, designing manipulations involves developing the experimental task. Manipulations can range from artificial scenarios to lab studies involving confederates and role-playing to actual interventions in field research. For example, in a study on consumer disclosure in marketing relationships (White, 2004), scenarios about a fictitious service were used to manipulate deep versus shallow relationships; for instance, the deep relationship was manipulated by asking respondents to imagine that they had an ongoing relationship and by describing some characteristics of the service provider. In contrast, a field experiment can be designed where prespecified scenarios are enacted by service providers. Procedures for assessing content validity of measures can be applied for assessing manipulations during their development, including evaluation by experts.

A variety of approaches to manipulating a construct need to be considered before deciding on a subset. For example, in manipulating arousal, a number of approaches (akin to measure design) need to be considered, such as manipulation through physical exercise or through music. Though it may not be practical to test each and every possible approach, different approaches should be considered in light of the literature to decide on an existing approach or design a new one. The point to note here is that an approach cannot be taken to be valid because of its use in past research just as the psychometric properties of a measure from past research should be assessed when using it. In fact, this point applies to a greater degree to manipulations than to measures, because measures are more likely to have been developed and validated for use in different situations or across different samples.

Once an approach has been chosen, an often under-appreciated aspect is the need to assess a number of stimuli as well as variations in the experimental task. Manipulations are not administered in isolation but in the larger context of a cover story and experimental instructions as well as specific stimuli. Important here in preparing materials for pretesting, which is akin to item generation, is the need to start with a sizable, even a redundant set of stimuli to test. For example, Escalas, Moore, and Britton, (2004) used 10 stimulus ads in a study of responses to ads that were based on ratings of a larger set of 38 television ads by independent coders on attributes such as quality.

Similarly, in manipulating arousal, a number of pieces of music may need to be tested in a series of pretests for varying lengths of time before deciding on a few options. A key issue here is the need for the manipulation to work in light of various methodological choices. Also akin to item editing is the need to examine and redesign manipulations before the fact that appear to capture related constructs, or that confound multiple constructs between levels of the manipulation. For instance, when using manipulations involving detailed scenarios, it is important to manipulate only the construct under study and not other constructs. In a sense, measure development is generic in that a measure is expected to be used in a variety of settings across different samples, whereas a manipulation tends to be designed relatively idiosyncratic to a study.[4] Successful manipulations are, of course, often used and reused. While recognizing the differences between relatively generic measures and relatively idiosyncratic manipulations, the point here is that there is much to be learnt from generic measurement for designing manipulations.

Assessment of Reliability and Validity

Measures are assessed for reliability and validity. Measures relatively free of random error are considered *reliable* (Nunnally, 1978). Whether a measure is accurate or not is the realm of *validity*, the degree to which a measure is free of random and systematic error (Nunnally, 1978). Random error may reduce correlations between a measure and other variables, whereas systematic error may increase or reduce correlations between two variables. Types of reliability include internal consistency reliability and stability reliability; internal consistency assesses whether items within a set are consistent with each other, that is, covary with each other; stability reliability relates to whether consistent responses would be obtained for the same measure across time. Types of validity include content validity discussed earlier, convergent validity (does the measure correlate or converge with another measure of the *same* construct?), discriminant validity (is the measure of a construct not correlated with measures of constructs to which it is not expected to be related?), nomological validity (does the measure of a construct relate to measures of other constructs with which it is theoretically expected to be correlated; that is, considering a nomological or theoretical network of constructs, does the measure behave in theoretically expected ways?), and construct validity (does a measure measure what it aims to measure; does a measure or operationalization correspond to the underlying construct it is aiming to measure?)

Measurement is central to developing reliable and valid manipulations (Perdue & Summers, 1986). Manipulations need to be reliable and valid. Reliable manipulations produce a consistent effect on respondents (Figure 45.2). Valid manipulations manipulate the intended construct and do not manipulate other constructs. As discussed, convergence between a manipulation of a variable and its measurement is examined through a manipulation check and divergence between a manipulation and measures of variables that it is not supposed to manipulate is assessed through confounding checks (Figure 45.1). For example, the manipulation of, say, argument strength should not lead to a manipulation of distinctly different constructs, say, amount of information presented. A study of humor in ads (Krishnan & Chakravarti, 2003) used product categories relevant to students and fictitious brand names chosen from a standardized word list that were similar on characteristics such as memorability. Humor strength was manipulated using puns, a format that was argued to allow for control of confounding variables such as length, rather than a cartoon format, which may confound pictorial processing with humor. Manipulation and confounding checks for assessing manipulations parallel convergent and discriminant validity in assessing measures. Though ruling out all possible confounding variables when manipulating an abstract construct may not be feasible, plausible alternatives need to be ruled out. In fact, this is another parallel with

Reliable Manipulation   Unreliable Manipulation

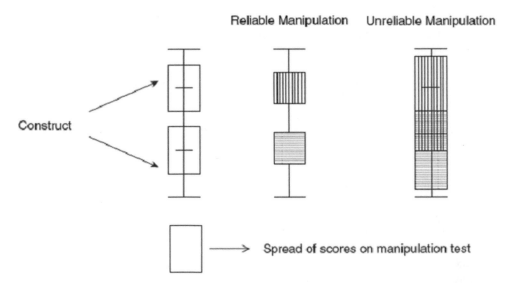

Figure 45.2   Reliability of manipulations. (Source: Viswanathan, M., *Measurement Error and Research Design*, p. 317, Figure 10.2. Copyright © 2005. Reprinted by permission of Sage Publications.)

measurement; strong tests of discriminant validity of a measure of a construct should distinguish it from measures of constructs that may be plausibly related, as distinct from weak tests that could potentially distinguish the measure from numerous measures of unrelated constructs. In this regard, domain delineation is useful for both developing manipulation checks and for identifying confounding checks to use and constructs to distinguish the focal construct from.

Usage of Existing Measures

A common situation that researchers face is the need to use previously developed measures in research designs. A careful methodological review of the literature, as distinct from a substantive review, should precede the use of a specific existing measure. A methodological review would cover conceptual definitions of constructs rooted in relevant literature and distinguished from related constructs through delineation of domains. Current definitions may need to be modified if they have not been properly defined in past research. Available measures need to be examined in light of the conceptual definition of a construct, whether the entire domain of a construct as defined is captured, and the sample and usage conditions of previous psychometric work.

Modifying individual items of previously validated measures requires extensive conceptual and empirical support. Rationale as well as empirical evidence is needed for using measures in different populations, such as student, nonstudent, or cross-cultural samples, or for making changes in procedures or method of administration. When using previously validated scales without modification, psychometric properties should be reported. Measures need to be assessed in usage conditions

A similar set of issues are pertinent in using existing manipulations. A careful review of the literature should precede the choice of an existing manipulation or the decision to design a new manipulation. Changes in existing manipulations are more likely to be required than changes to validated measures, presumably because measures have been validated for use in a variety of setting whereas manipulations are more circumscribed to the context of specific experiments. As discussed, this is, in fact, one key difference; whereas measures are often designed for enduring traits or for attitudes, manipulations are designed idiosyncratic to a study or a research stream. Manipulations would need to be modified to fit specific settings, samples, and administration procedures. However, they need to be assessed in terms of reliably and validly creating levels of the underlying construct. Often, manipulations that worked in past research may not work in a different context or may need to be modified to be effective. If anything, this distinction between measures developed and validated for generic usage and manipulations developed idiosyncratic to a study emphasizes the need to carefully assess manipulations from past research before using them.

Designing Collection of Data on Multiple Measures

When using surveys to collect data on a variety of measures of constructs, the sequencing and administration of these variables has bearing on the nature of error that is likely to result. Plausible sources of error, such as hypothesis guessing, halo effects, and common method factors, require explanation in such situations. Strong tests can be designed or strong evidence can be inferred from results by assessing the separation or grouping of central variables in light of hypothesized relationships between them. By separating (grouping) measures of distinct constructs in a variety of ways, strong tests of hypotheses of sizable (small or nonsignificant) relationships can be created and strong evidence can be interpreted.

Careful sequencing and execution of manipulations with a view to making clean inferences of causality is a strength of experimental designs. But this same rationale needs to be carried through when using multiple dependent variables. For instance, when using a covariate such as an individual difference variable, it has to be sequenced with some separation from the manipulation and the dependent variable. Placing the individual difference variable at the beginning may prime it for subsequent manipulations. Important here is the appropriate sequencing of manipulations and central dependent variables to make clean inferences of causality. Therefore, measurement of covariates either in a previous session or after the central dependent variables preferably with the use of fillers, may be preferable. Similarly, manipulation checks in the main study, if at all employed, need to be placed after all dependent variables. In general, manipulations must be assessed before investing in the main study. Moreover, manipulations may be dissipated in the main study when manipulation checks are employed after a delay to allow for the central dependent variables to precede them.

In this regard, perhaps the most effective and efficient step in methodological design is pretesting or pilot testing prior to investing in a substantive study. This key step may often be short-changed in light of pragmatic concerns such as time pressure or the lack of easy access to samples. This is often a significant problem, particularly when respondents are not conveniently accessible for a variety of reasons (e.g., managers in organizations). The payoff from a sound methodological basis established through pretesting and pilot testing can extend to several studies in a program of research. Several pilot studies are usually needed to calibrate stimuli and purify measures. Ideally, the manipulations employed in a study should have been demonstrated to be reliable and valid. Lacking this, there is considerable uncertainty on multiple fronts, making it difficult, perhaps impossible, to draw meaningful conclusions.

Choosing Measured Dependent Variables in Experimental Designs

All of the issues relating to measure development, validation, and usage apply to measured dependent variables in experimental designs. This is where the degrees of freedom associated with specific paradigms may come into play. Whereas sufficient effort may be invested in the design of manipulations in experiments, it may sometimes be at the expense of the choice and sequencing of dependent variables.

FROM MEASUREMENT ERROR TO MEASUREMENT/ MANIPULATION ERROR IN EXPERIMENTAL DESIGNS

This section starts out with a discussion of types of measurement errors followed by a translation of these errors to an experimental setting. Most of the discussion in this section is reprinted from Viswanathan (2005).

Types of Random and Systematic Error

This brief discussion provides a taxonomy of types of measurement error. Measurement error has been categorized as either random or systematic error (e.g., Churchill, 1979).

Random Error   Random error is any type of error that is inconsistent or does not repeat in the same magnitude or direction except by chance. Random error occurs when inconsistent responses are provided over time or across items. A distinction can be made between idiosyncratic random error, which affects a small proportion of individuals in an administration—such as those that result from mood or language difficulties—and generic random error, which has a broad-based effect across a sizable proportion of respondents in an administration, such as those that result from item-wording effects. Such a distinction is useful in understanding the relationship between certain sources of random error commonly discussed in the literature, such as mood, and likely outcomes in terms of error. Typically, such generic random error is likely to be caused by factors with pervasive effects, such as item wording (e.g., ambiguous wording) or the nature of the setting (e.g., a noisy setting). Random error in measures attenuates observed relationships (Nunnally, 1978).[5] Whereas the effect of idiosyncratic random error can be minimized through larger sample sizes, generic random error in the measurement of a construct attenuates relationships.

Systematic Error   Systematic error is reflected in consistent but inaccurate responses.

Additive systematic error   is consistent error that deviates by a constant magnitude from the true score (Figure 45.3). Such error is reflected in extreme means. It influences observed relationships only when it reduces item variance to the point of inhibiting covariation with other items. *Correlational systematic error* occurs when responses vary consistently by different degrees over and above true differences in the construct being measured. For example, different individuals may interpret and use response categories, such as "very good" to "very bad," in consistent but different ways so that "very good" is more or less positive for different respondents. Correlational systematic error can strengthen or weaken observed relationships (Nunnally, 1978).[6]

Within-measure correlational systematic error occurs between different items of the same measure. For example, inflated relationships may be observed between items of a measure due to the use of the same response format or similar word-stems, or the completion of items in close proximity. Additive systematic error is likely to have no effect or to attenuate relationships due to decreased variance.[7] Correlational systematic error can strengthen or weaken observed relationships (Nunnally, 1978).

Whereas within-measure correlational systematic error occurs between items of a measure, across-measure correlational systematic error occurs across measures of different constructs (Figure 45.4). A common method factor that affects both measures is a source of across-measure correlational systematic error. For example, the use of the same paper-and-pencil method (that taps, for example, say, a response style of using certain parts of the scale) is likely to inflate correlations.

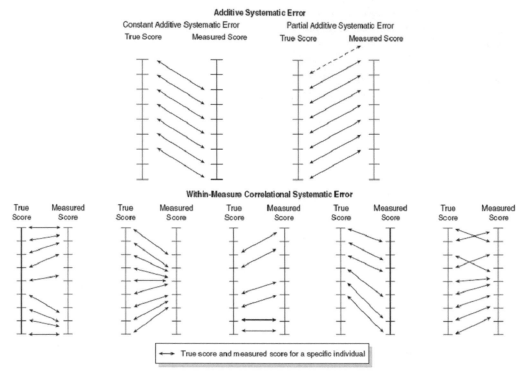

Figure 45.3　Types of systematic error. (Source: Viswanathan, M., *Measurement Error and Research Design*, p. 107. Copyright © 2005. Reprinted by permission of Sage Publications.)

Likewise, if subsequent measures are influenced by earlier ones, then the scales completed first may introduce systematic error in later measures. For example, hypothesis guessing may result from responses to the first measure influencing responses to the second measure.[8]

Measurement and Manipulation Error in Experimental Design

In translating measurement error to an experimental context, the similarities and dissimilarities with a correlational context are noteworthy. Consider an experiment with one independent variable manipulated at two levels and one measured dependent variable. Systematic error within measures versus across measures is blurred in an experimental context. In a correlational design, within-measure correlational systematic error could occur wherein responses reflect differences across individuals over and above the construct in question. On the other hand, across-measure systematic error occurs between measures of different constructs. In experimental designs, the manipulation is not measured but created at specific levels of the independent variable. Therefore, random error, additive systematic error, and within-measure (i.e., within-manipulation) correlational systematic error are germane only when a manipulation is being assessed in pretesting through manipulation checks (i.e., in the measurement of the levels of manipulations achieved). In an experimental context, error is reflected in the measurement of the dependent variable; therefore, errors due to the manipulation are across manipulation/measure, paralleling across-measure systematic error. If there are multiple dependent variables, across-measure systematic error occurs between these dependent variables.

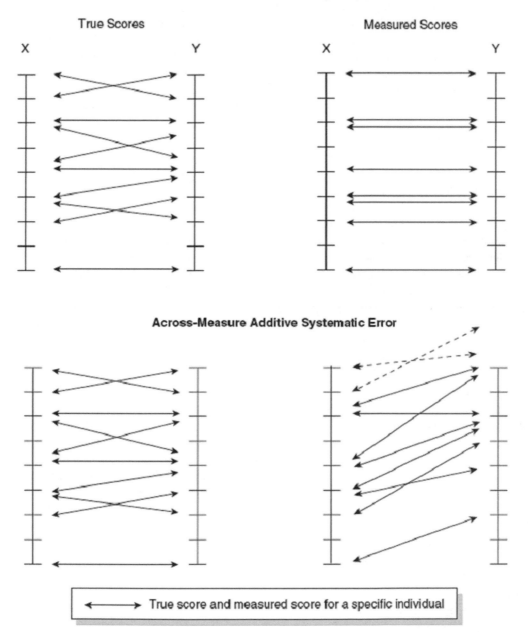

Figure 45.4   Across-measure systematic error. (Source: Viswanathan, M., *Measurement Error and Research Design*, p. 112. Copyright © 2005. Reprinted by permission of Sage Publications.)

A second way in which experiments are different is in the central importance of differences between groups of individuals representing treatment conditions. Individual differences within a condition are germane in adding to error variance in tests of differences. Differences across conditions are compared to differences within in statistical tests. Therefore, correlational systematic error, in the sense of differences across individuals over and above the construct in question, can influence error variance while also affecting mean differences between conditions. However, additive systematic error can only affect mean differences across conditions. It is useful, in this regard, to treat conditions as the unit of analysis rather than individuals, and to consider additive and correlational systematic error for this unit of analysis. Figure 45.5 illustrates this translation of measurement error to an experimental setting. From this perspective, variations within a condition among individuals would be categorized as random error. With these two distinctions, experimental designs are discussed below from the perspective of measurement error. A manipulation is considered first in isolation from the context of pretesting and measuring achieved manipulation levels. Then, the discussion focuses on the effects of the manipulation on dependent variables.

Random error is of concern in the manipulation of independent variables (Figure 45.2). Random error could result from inconsistent manipulations, deflating the relationship between independent and dependent variables. Whereas idiosyncratic random error in manipulations can be accounted for through large samples, generic random error has similar effects as generic random error in correlational designs. Consider a variable that needs to be manipulated at two levels. Random error is introduced because of dispersions in ratings of specific levels of dimensions. For example, in the manipulation of message credibility in a distracting setting, random error would blur the statistical difference between levels of a manipulated variable. The use of a heterogeneous sample may cause random error in treatments.

If two levels of a manipulation are inflated upward (downward) as measured by the manipulation check, this is akin to constant additive systematic error (e.g., if two levels of a credibility manipulation intended to be high versus low are very high and medium; see Figure 45.6). If such inflation is affected by finite ends of the scale, this is akin to partial additive systematic error, as indicated by ratings on manipulation checks being at the high (low) end of the scale (Figure 45.6). In addition to the manipulation, control variables and all other aspects of the design, including the sample and settings, can contribute to such error. Error occurs when the intended levels of the manipulation are not achieved. The aim here is not to measure the true score of a respondent on a construct, but to create certain levels of a construct. The term, *error,* is used in the context of an experimental design to refer to deviation from the intended level of a construct, with the measure used as a manipulation check assumed to have been validated, i.e., shown to be reliable and valid. In many scenarios, constant additive systematic error may not be noticed or even relevant because the focus is on achieving differences across levels of manipulation. However, noteworthy here is the potential problem of confounding levels of a construct with the construct (Cook & Campbell, 1979). For instance, a construct manipulated at two specific levels may not lead to a significant difference on the dependent variable, yet a stronger manipulation (i.e., a larger difference between the two levels) may lead to significant differences. This is not just in terms of main effects but also in terms of interactions with other constructs. Correlational systematic error would be reflected in differences across levels over and above the intended levels of differences (Figure 45.6). For instance, such error would occur if the difference between two levels of a manipulation is much larger than intended. This may be particularly problematic when a factor in an experiment is manipulated within subjects, wherein strong manipulations may lead to a carry-over effect. This is within-manipulation correlational systematic error; differences over and above the construct being manipulated.

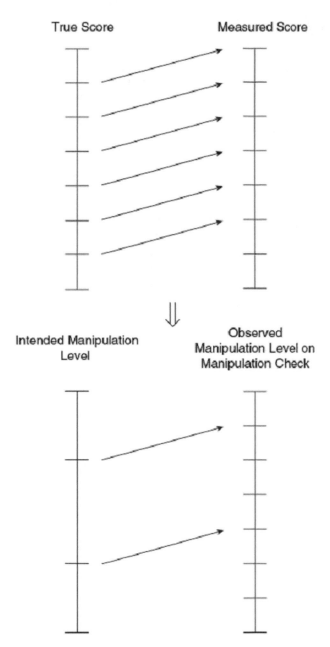

Figure 45.5 Translating measurement error to experimental design. (Source: Viswanathan, M., *Measurement Error and Research Design*, p. 324. Copyright © 2005. Reprinted by permission of Sage Publications.)

The actual calibration of differences may be critical; otherwise, as discussed above, a construct may be confounded with levels of the construct (Cook & Campbell, 1979). When manipulations generate levels of unintended constructs (e.g.., a manipulation of product status that leads to a manipulation of product quality or price perception), this is similar to within-measure (across-treatment) correlational systematic error, except that the error is across treatment levels (i.e., generated

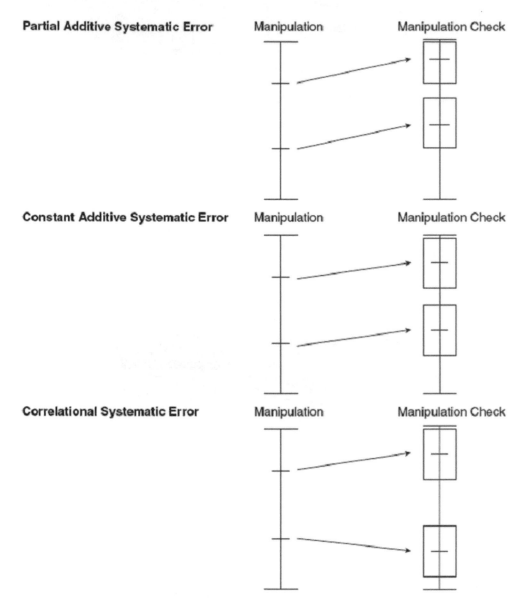

Figure 45.6   Measurement error in manipulating variables. (Source: Viswanathan, M., *Measurement Error and Research Design*, p. 325. Copyright © 2005. Reprinted by permission of Sage Publications.)

levels of the intended construct). With strong manipulations, multiple constructs may be unintentionally manipulated, leading to within-manipulation (across-treatment) systematic error. Weak manipulations may not capture sufficient differences in the construct of interest, whereas strong manipulations may lead to demand artifacts. Strong manipulations can lead to across-manipulation/measure systematic error by evoking confounding variables (e.g., hypothesis guessing) (see Figure 45.7). When a manipulation affects responses to dependent variables, this is akin to across-measure correlational systematic error. However, it could be additive or correlational depending on the nature of the effect across individuals; hence, it is referred to here as across-manipulation/

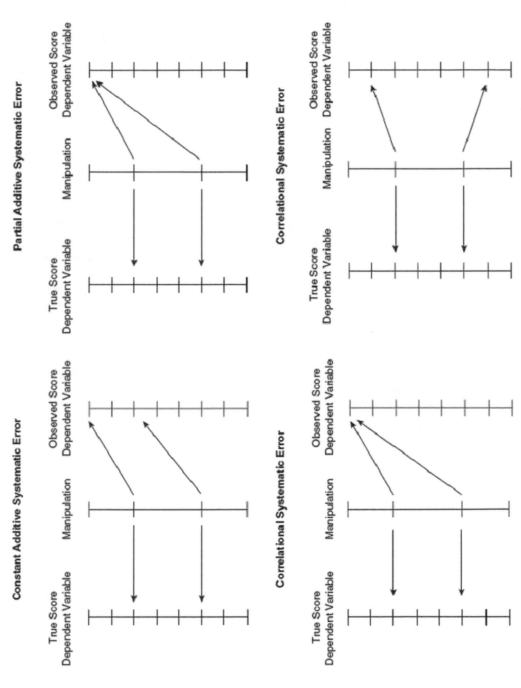

Figure 45.7   Across manipulation/measure systematic error. (Source: Adapted from *Viswanathan, M., Measurement Error and Research Design*, p. 327. Copyright © 2005. Reprinted by permission of Sage Publications.)

measure systematic error. In this regard, issues relating to separation or grouping of measures for validation are germane to sequencing manipulations and dependent variables.

A number of examples of across-manipulation/measure systematic error are available in the literature, such as in the use of response times as dependent variables. Fazio (1990), in a discussion of the use of response times in social psychology, describes a study relating to spontaneous attitude formation in which one of the treatment conditions involved a cue of future questioning about the attitude objects. Faster response times could be hypothesized for questions about attitudes toward focal objects when such a cue is provided, due to previous attitude formation. However, an opposite effect could also occur if the cue also changed decision criteria in the speeded task toward being more accurate in anticipation of future questioning. This issue was addressed by using filler objects and response times on questions about these objects as comparison points.

In considering the effects of manipulations on dependent variables (i.e., across manipulation/measure systematic error that is either correlational or additive in nature), several issues are noteworthy. Across-manipulation/measure systematic error occurs when a manipulation leads to ceiling or floor effects in the dependent variables. Thus, stimuli should be calibrated to minimize such effects. The choice of stimuli should minimize ceiling or floor effects. Here, the design has to be calibrated subtly to avoid too weak or too strong a manipulation. Consider a control variable, such as the amount of information to be presented or the number of pieces of information to employ in a memory task. A choice should be made that enables sufficient variation on the measure of memory by achieving means near 50% through pretests. Similarly, measures of other constructs, such as attitudes, ideally, should provide sufficient room for variation and be ascertained through pretests and pilot tests. Amounts that are too high or too low may lead to ceiling and floor effects, respectively, minimizing variance in dependent variables. With constant additive systematic error, variance will not be affected. But with partial additive systematic error due to finite end points of scales, variance will be affected.

In essence, any methodological design involves certain control variables, and experiments involve manipulated variables as well. Control variables provide the context for the methodological design. For example, if an experiment requires knowledgeable respondents, knowledge may be a control variable. Similarly, if respondents are presented with information, then the amount of information is a control variable. Thus, methodological design involves many control variables. The choice of setting (e.g., classroom or lab), sample, and administration are, in effect, all control variables. The choice of a sample of respondents (such as individuals, companies, industries) should allow for sufficient variation. Experiments often involve a cover story, again aimed at establishing one or more control variables at specific levels. For example, a cover story about sources of product information, such as *Consumer Reports,* may serve to set levels of specific control variables, such as credibility of information. Control variables may also be set based on the choice of settings and samples. Sufficient variance among variables is necessary to provide tests of hypotheses. Independent variables need to be designed to achieve sufficient variation in dependent variables in an experimental design. All of the elements of the design, such as the cover story, need to be tested to assess whether they achieve objectives, including allowing sufficient variation and controlling for specific variables.

As discussed, pilot tests involve the complete procedure used to test hypotheses with a view toward gauging the entire methodology on issues such as hypothesis guessing and ceiling or floor effects. Pilot tests should also evaluate across-measure systematic error among dependent variables and across-manipulation/measure systematic error between independent and dependent variables. If there are multiple dependent variables, several sources can cause across-measure systematic error just as is the case with surveys.

The terminology of within-treatments random error, within-manipulation (across-treatment) systematic error, and across–manipulation/measure systematic error provides a means of understanding experimental design from a measurement perspective. Pretests should be used to examine such errors. Hypothesis guessing is the result of across-manipulation/measure or within-manipulation (across-treatment) systematic error, thus suggesting changes in the treatments or in some other aspect of the design, such as the use of filler tasks. Exclusive focus on treatment levels as requiring calibration neglects the context of the entire design. Pretests can be employed to elicit treatment levels, whereas pilot tests can assess the entire design.

A small holdout sample could be employed to assess factors, such as hypothesis guessing, through open-ended, think-aloud responses, self-reports on rating scales, and open-ended responses to pointed questions. Think-aloud procedures are employed in survey research to evaluate specific questions. However, such procedures could also be employed to assess entire research designs.

BROADER PARALLELS BETWEEN MEASUREMENT AND EXPERIMENTAL RESEARCH DESIGN

Some broader parallels between measurement and research design in general, and experimental research designs in particular are discussed here. This discussion serves to further show the similarities between these two methodological paradigms.

Types of Validity of Research Designs

A brief detour into the validity of research designs is warranted here to distinguish this term from its use in measurement. The level of analysis here needs to be distinguished when interpreting the usage of the term, validity, for individual measures versus the entire research design. The literature on the validity of research designs has developed mainly within an experimental context. Borrowing from the classic writings of Cook and Campbell (1979), four types of validity of research designs have been discussed.

Statistical conclusion validity, as the name suggests, deals with drawing accurate or valid statistical conclusions about covariations, i.e., whether a study will detect an effect and its magnitude accurately. Threats to this form of validity relate to purely statistical issues (such as violation of assumptions, statistical power, and fishing and error rate problems) as well as measurement issues that bear on statistical error (such as reliability, randomness in experimental settings, and random heterogeneity in respondents). Internal validity relates to *causal* relationships between operations *irrespective of what these operations represent in terms of underlying constructs* (Figure 45.8). Threats to internal validity relate to events that may *co-occur* with operations that may lead to alternative causal explanations (such as history, maturation, selection, testing, and mortality). Using control groups and randomization rules out several, but not all, of these threats.

Construct validity relates to the extent to which it is possible to generalize from the relationship between two variables at the operational level to the relationship between two constructs at the conceptual level (Figure 45.8). A set of threats to construct validity relates to the construct validity of individual measures of constructs—such as lack of explication of constructs, and mono-operation bias, or the use of a single operationalization—whereas other threats relate to the construct validity of *relationships*—such as using a single method, hypothesis guessing, evaluative apprehension (respondents being apprehensive and presenting themselves in positive light), experimenter expectancies, and improper calibration.

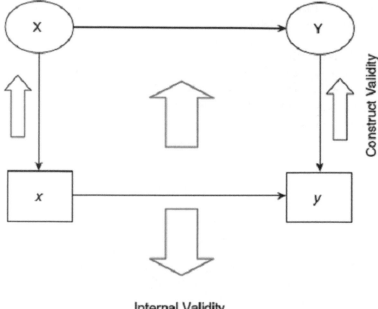

Figure 45.8 Validity of research designs. (Source: Viswanathan, M., *Measurement Error and Research Design*, p. 344. Copyright © 2005. Reprinted by permission of Sage Publications.)

For purposes of internal validity analyses, the operationalization is taken as capturing the intended construct, and all other variables are considered threats to internal validity. In experimental terms, any effect due to a variable other than the treatment is a threat to internal validity. Construct validity issues relate to what the operationalization purports to capture in terms of underlying constructs. Hence, threats to construct validity arise because of problems either in the operationalization of individual constructs or in generalizing from the relationship between measures and manipulations as operationalized to the relationship between constructs (Figure 45.8).[9] Construct validity asks the question, can the relationship between variables as operationalized be generalized to the relationship between constructs? Hence, multiple operationalizations of a single construct and multiple methods provide support for the construct validity of a relationship. Multiple, divergent methods that suggest a relationship provide strong evidence of construct validity.

External validity has been used to refer to the validity of conclusions "drawn about the generalizability of a causal relationship to and across populations, of persons, settings, and times" (Cook & Campbell, 1979, p. 39). External validity asks the question, does a theoretical relationship generalize to a variety of settings and samples? Hence, a variety of background factors come into play and moderate a relationship. The meaning of external validity has been much debated elsewhere (Berkowitz & Donnerstein, 1982; Calder, Phillips, & Tybout, 1981; Lynch, 1982; Mook, 1983). Researchers have noted that the meaning that respondents assign to an experimental task is central to external validity (Berkowitz & Donnerstein, 1982) and that what generalizes from a study is not so much the findings but the theoretical understanding (Mook, 1983; Calder et al., 1981; Lynch, 1982). Therefore, both construct validity and external validity ultimately pertain to the generalizability of theoretical understanding. Whereas construct validity relates to generalizability from operational results to theoretical relationships, external validity relates to the generalizability of theoretical understanding.

Parallels Between Measurement and Research Design

Internal consistency translates to the extent to which results in the context of a single study are consistent. For example, if multiple replications of the manipulation of a construct were used, internal consistency would parallel the results being replicable or consistent within the study. Strict replications of construct relationships are akin to test-retest reliability. A design is replicated exactly in all respects. Are the results consistent without significant changes in operationalizations? Conceptual replications use different operationalizations to test the same conceptual relationships. Such replications are similar to convergent validity; whether the measure of a construct correlates or converges with another measure of the *same* construct? Do different operationalizations of constructs lead to similar results? This is a matter of degree and often, variations in result are explained by differences in levels of moderating variables or of aspects of methods employed. With the use of dependent variables that have not been evaluated psychometrically, such as those often-employed in experimental designs, the use of conceptual replications takes on added significance. Whether a pattern of results across studies can be uniquely explained by a theory is the aim of such studies. Nevertheless, lacking psychometric assessment of the reliability and validity of operationalizations, a pattern of results is susceptible to a variety of alternative explanations. Preexperimental procedures should strive to establish evidence of the construct validity of operationalizations.

Similarly, multiple operationalizations of specific constructs and multiple studies using different methods are recommended to establish construct validity when generalizing from the relationship between specific operationalizations of constructs to constructs. The more divergent the method, the stronger the evidence, somewhat like hearing a surprising piece of information (such as an assassination) from relatively independent sources. Multiple operationalizations enable tests of convergent validity. Multiple manipulations are similar and enable tests of replications, although the unit of analysis here is not specific constructs but relationships between constructs.

Nomological validity for individual measures, in a broad sense, places measures of constructs in a nomological network. Similarly, relationships between constructs in different studies can be interpreted in light of a larger nomological network and theoretical coherence. Thus, are results of association between constructs and interrelationships with other constructs interpretable with plausible theoretical explanations? Are the results amenable to the larger theoretical knowledge in an area? Are the results interpretable in light of what is known?

Discriminant validity is provided by the degree to which a measure is discriminating, i.e., the degree to which a measure is not related to constructs to which it is not supposed to be related. One aspect of discriminant validity is that a measure is unrelated to other constructs to which it is supposed to be unrelated. Another sense of discriminant validity is in measures having small relationships with measures of related constructs. Moving the unit of analysis up to the level of relationships between constructs, the question of discriminant validity in the sense of nonrelationships is an interesting one. Are patterns of relationships between variables unaffected by certain alternative variables? For example, the moderating effect of a covariate, such as social desirability, should be minimal. Rather than explain the relationships between focal constructs, variables such as hypothesis guessing (i.e., alternative explanations) should be accounted for conceptually and operationally in the design of methodology. Discriminant validity at the level of construct relationships asks whether relationships between measures can be uniquely attributed to constructs, thus making threats to construct validity relevant.

In viewing parallels between measure validation and research design, interitem issues translate to intermeasure issues. Random error in item response translates to random error in relationships. Within-measure correlational systematic error translates to across-measure correlational systematic error. Consistency in measuring one thing across items or time translates to consistency in relationships, say, through strict replications. Convergent validity translates to conceptual replications of relationships—the more different the method, the greater the credence. Construct validity here is at the level of the relationship. Thus, at the core, what is essential is (1) consistency or replicability, (2) convergence across multiple operationalizations, (3) compatibility with existing knowledge, and (4) ability to distinguish alternative explanations of relationships. Strict and conceptual replications, theoretical consistency, and discriminability are at the center of validity. Is the result replicable across time? Across operationalizations? Is the result theoretically consistent? Is the result uniquely attributable to underlying constructs? The framework of measurement of a single construct generalizes to the entire research design. Show consistency or replicability, show convergence across different methods, place results in the context of knowledge to date, and distinguish explanations from plausible alternative explanations. That's it. It's very simple.

DISCUSSION

Limitations of Experimental Research Designs

Some limitations of experimental designs are noteworthy to place this method in perspective. Experimental research involves a basic assumption that constructs can be isolated and measured or manipulated just as the basis for psychometric measurement is that a single construct is being measured. Controlled experiments aim for such isolation. Natural experiments are quasi-experiments in that constructs are not strictly isolated. Yet, alternative explanations could be accounted for at a conceptual level. In experimental studies, conceptual arguments need to be made to isolate constructs and understand interrelationships. For instance, manipulations of constructs such as product status may involve potential confounds, requiring conceptual arguments in addition to empirical evidence against alternative explanations. In designing high, medium, or low levels of status of, say, a restaurant, several other variables, such as price or quality perceptions, may be manipulated. Are results then due to status levels or price or quality differences? Some constructs may be difficult to isolate for manipulation. Others may be impossible to manipulate (or measure) because of their level of abstraction. In such scenarios, conceptual arguments have to be made against possible alternative explanations for findings. For instance, in the example above, alternative explanations in terms of quality or price differences rather than status differences have to be countered. Conceptual arguments have to be used to argue against plausible alternative explanations for findings in experimental research. In this regard, researchers have argued for a comparative rather than a confirmatory approach to theory testing (Sternthal, Tybout, & Calder, 1987); the former emphasizes showing the superiority of one explanation over rival explanations, whereas the latter emphasizes using validated measures and multiple operationalizations. A series of studies may need to be designed to show that the results can be uniquely explained by a variable, such as status, and by ruling out alternative explanations (Sternthal et al., 1987). For instance, the effect of status on a number of variables could be studied, or the effect of a number of variables on status could be studied.

The assumption in experimental research that a single construct can be isolated and measured or manipulated has important implications for conceptual and methodological issues. Qualitative research is a viable approach for studying a number of interrelated constructs that cannot be isolated but must be studied as complex relationships. Conceptualizations in qualitative research can be more organic in nature rather than of a strict linear, causal form.

Summary

A brief summary of the key points is provided here. Understanding the measurement of one thing is central to understanding the measurement and manipulation of many things and to the entire design. Measurement of an individual construct versus its manipulation can be viewed as two sides of the same coin. The method is essentially everything that is done to collect the data, therefore, all aspects of the method require careful attention. The distinction between experiments and surveys can be blurred. A correlational design could be analyzed as an experimental design by categorizing a continuous variable. Moreover, experimental and survey design paradigms can benefit from each other. A number of issues usually associated with measure development, validation, and usage are central to the design of manipulations in experimental designs; defining the construct being measured (manipulated) conceptually, delineating its domain (which can facilitate the choice of manipulation and confounding checks), and designing measures and generating items (manipulation), assessing reliability and validity of measures (manipulations), using existing measures (manipulations), collecting data on multiple measures (sequencing manipulations, filler tasks, and measures), and choosing measured dependent variables. The language of measurement error in terms of a detailed typology of errors can be translated to an experimental setting. The framework of measurement of a single construct generalizes to the entire research design. Strict and conceptual replications, theoretical consistency, and discriminability are at the core of construct validity of research designs and parallel reliability, convergent validity, nomological validity, and discriminant validity, respectively, in the construct validity of measures. And finally, experimental research involves a basic assumption that constructs can be isolated and measured or manipulated just as the basis for psychometric measurement is that a single construct is being measured.

ACKNOWLEDGMENT

Much of the material in this chapter is reprinted or adapted from chapters of *Measurement Error and Research Design* (Viswanathan, 2005). Copyright 2005, by permission of Sage Publications.

NOTES

1. I am thankful to an anonymous reviewer for making this important point.
2. Discriminant validity in a measurement context relates to the degree to which a measure is discriminating, i.e., the degree to which a measure is not related to constructs to which it is not supposed to be related.
3. Exceptions to every rule are what make research design in the social sciences interesting. For example, consider manipulating awareness itself, such as awareness of one's affective state in order to enable, say, attribution to it. Participants may need to have their attention drawn to the affective state, even by completing a "manipulation check" of their affective state. Nevertheless, such a design should be executed without participants being aware of the hypothesis under study. In other words, the awareness manipulation needs to be strong enough to elicit the intended manipulation, but subtle enough to avoid hypothesis guessing.
4. This characterization of measures as being validated for a variety of usage settings is only in contrast to manipulations. In fact, there are many examples of usage of measures in conditions they have not been previously validated in.
5. Random error can inflate observed relationships in multivariate analysis (Bollen, 1989).
6. Though additive and correlational errors are distinguished here, nonlinear errors such as multiplicative errors may also occur (Bagozzi & Yi, 1991; Campbell & O'Connell, 1967; Bagozzi, 1993; Bagozzi & Yi, 1992).

7. It should be noted that any constant additive error, by definition, cannot affect correlations. The point here, however, is that if there is an additive effect and finite endpoints to a scale, then responses are all biased upward (or downward) toward the end of the scale, thus reducing its variance and its ability to covary. Here, it is referred to as partial additive systematic error and is subsumed under additive systematic error (Figure 45.3).

8. Although hypothesis guessing is used throughout this chapter, several conditions have to be fulfilled before it affects responses; demand cues that suggest a hypothesis have to be encoded, the hypothesis has to be discerned accurately, and the respondent has to act on the hypothesis (Shimp, Hyatt, & Snyder, 1991). Moreover, hypothesis guessing can result in random or systematic errors (Shimp et al., 1991).

9. In this regard, internal validity and construct validity of research designs may be traded off when placing fillers between the independent and dependent variables in an experiment. Such fillers may disguise the purpose of the study and minimize hypothesis guessing, a threat to construct validity, but may be at the expense of internal validity in terms of the causal link between the independent variable as operationalized and the dependent variable as operationalized.

REFERENCES

Aronson, E., Carlsmith, J. M., Ellsworth, P. C., & Gonzales, M. H. (1990). *Methods of research in social psychology* (2nd ed.). New York: McGraw-Hill.

Berkowitz, L., & Donnerstein, E. (1982). External validity is more than skin deep: Some answers to criticisms of laboratory experiments. *American Psychologist, 37*(3), 245–257.

Calder, B. J., Phillips, L. W., & Tybout, A. M. (1981). Designing research for application. *Journal of Consumer Research, 8*(2), 197–207.

Churchill, G. A. (1979). A paradigm for developing better measures of marketing constructs. *Journal of Marketing Research, 16*(1), 64–73.

Cook, T. D., & Campbell, D. T. (1979). *Quasi-experimentation: Design and analysis issues for field settings.* Chicago: Rand McNally.

Dehaene, S. (1997). *The number sense: How the mind creates mathematics.* New York: Oxford University Press.

DeVellis, R. F. (1991). *Scale development: Theory and applications.* Thousand Oaks, CA: Sage.

Ellsworth, P. C. (1977). From abstract ideas to concrete instances: Some guidelines for choosing natural research settings. *American Psychologist, 32*(8), 604–615.

Escalas, J. E., Moore, M.C., & Britton, J.E. (2004). Fishing for feelings? Hooking viewers helps! Journal of Consumer Psychology, 14 (1 & 2), 105–114.

Fazio, R. H. (1990). A Practical guide to the use of response latency in social psychological research. In C. Hendrick & M. S. Clark (Eds.), *Research Methods in Personality and Social Psychology* (pp. 74–97). Newbury Park, CA: Sage.

Greenwald, A. G. (1976). Within subjects designs: To use or not to use? *Psychological Bulletin, 83*(2), 314–320.

Haynes, S. N., Richard, D. C. S., & Kubany, E. S. (1995). Content validity in psychological assessment: A functional approach to concepts and methods. *Psychological Assessment, 7*(3), 238–247.

Johar, G. V., Moreau, P., & Schwarz, N. (2003). Gender typed advertisements and impression formation: The role of chronic and temporary accessibility. *Journal of Consumer Psychology, 13*(3), 220–229.

Kerlinger, F. N. (1986). Constructs, variables, and definitions. In F. N. Kerlinger (Ed.), *Foundations of behavioral research* (3rd. ed., pp. 26–44). New York: Holt, Rinehart and Winston.

Krishnan, H. S., & Chakravarti, D. (2003). A process analysis of the effects of humorous advertising executions on brand claims memory. *Journal of Consumer Psychology, 13*(3), 230–245.

Lynch, J. G. (1982). On the external validity of experiments in consumer research. *Journal of Consumer Research, 9*(3), 225–239.

Mook, D. G. (1983). In defense of external invalidity. *American Psychologist, 38*(4), 379–387.

Nelson, K. A. (2004). Consumer decision making and image theory: Understanding value-laden decisions. *Journal of Consumer Psychology, 14*(1/2), 28–40.

Nunnally, J. C. (1978). *Psychometric theory.* New York: McGraw-Hill.

Perdue, B. C., & Summers, J. O. (1986). Checking the success of manipulations in marketing experiments. *Journal of Marketing Research, 23*(4), 317–326.

Reed, A. (2004). Activating the self-importance of consumer selves: Exploring identity salience effects on judgments. *Journal of Consumer Research, 31*(2), 286–295.

Shimp, T. A., Hyatt, E. M., & Snyder, D. J. (1991). A critical appraisal of demand artifacts in consumer research. *Journal of Consumer Research, 18*, 273–283.

Steele, C. M. (1997). A threat in the air: How stereotypes shape intellectual identity and performance. *American Psychologist, 52*(6), 613–629.

Sternthal, B., Tybout, A. M., & Calder, B. J. (1987). Confirmatory versus comparative approaches to judging theory tests. *Journal of Consumer Research, 14*(1), 114–125.

Suri, R., & Monroe, K. B., (2003). The effects of time constraints on consumers' judgments of prices and products. *Journal of Consumer Research, 30*(1), 92–104.

Viswanathan, M. (2005). *Measurement error and research design.* Thousand Oaks, CA: Sage.

White, T. B. (2004). Consumer disclosure and disclosure avoidance: A motivational framework. *Journal of Consumer Psychology, 14*(1/2), 41–51.

46

Individual Differences
Tools for Theory Testing and Understanding in Consumer Psychology Research

Curtis P. Haugtvedt

Kaiya Liu

Ohio State University

Kyeong Sam Min

University of South Dakota

As illustrated by the studies described in the chapters of this volume, consumer researchers have been very creative in designing situational manipulations to induce specified psychological conditions in order to better understand processes underlying attitude change, memory, perception, decisions and/or phenomena of theoretical or practical interest. Many of the research methods in consumer psychology studies parallel the research methods used in psychology. Nevertheless, one of the research methods underutilized in consumer psychology studies is that of using individual difference or personality measures as part of research projects designed to better understand underlying processes. An overriding goal of this chapter is to advocate greater and more appropriate use of individual difference variables in experimental consumer research.

The usefulness of personality and individual difference measures in behavioral research has faced various challenges over the years. Debates about contributions of the person versus situation determining behavior have a rich history in psychology (see Swann & Seyle, 2005). Likewise, what researchers can and should expect from personality or individual differences measures has been a source of considerable theoretical and empirical debate (e.g., Funder & Colvin, 1991; Mischel, 1968).

Early reviews appearing in the consumer literature focused on measurement issues and discussed possible reasons for the failure of personality measures to predict behavior. For example, Kassarjian (1971) noted that many of the individual difference measures used by consumer researchers were reduced scales from broad measures in clinical and other areas of psychology. He advocated the creation and testing of relevant individual difference measures in consumer contexts. Subsequent general reviews by Kassarjian and colleagues in the following two decades (Kassarjian & Sheffet, 1981; 1991) showed continued concerns about the utility of personality variables in consumer research. Much of the early work focused on using personality variables as predictors of attitudes or behaviors.

There are many different approaches for the use of personality or individual difference variables in consumer research. Baumgartner (2002) advocates the development of research on the "personology of the consumer." Baumgartner's goal is to understand the "individual person in his or her role as a consumer" (p. 286). Such a perspective is consistent with classic and recent theoretical and empirical work in psychology (e.g., McAdams, 1996; 2001). In another approach, Snyder and his colleagues focus on how individuals might create or put themselves in situations that best match their personalities (e.g., Snyder & Cantor, 1998).

We concur that these types of research are important and of value to the discipline of consumer psychology. Such research often involves longitudinal observational research in natural settings. Taking an approach different than those just described, our purpose in this chapter is to briefly describe how consumer researchers can use personality and individual difference measures as one of the tools to better understand basic processes. Rather than rely on broad multidimensional personality measures, the approaches we advocate rely on relatively short questionnaires designed to tap (ideally) a single dominant factor. These individual difference measures are often meant to capture the essence of a theoretical construct thought to be central to the particular process of interest. Our perspective is that individual differences variables make certain psychological processes more or less likely, and it is the process-level understanding (in the context of appropriate theoretical formulations) that will allow researchers greater abilities to predict attitudes and behaviors.

Consider the following example. Researchers are interested in studying how situational variables influence the motivation of participants to think about an issue or product. A common manipulation used in such experimental work is a situational manipulation of the personal relevance of the issue or product (e.g., Petty, Cacioppo, & Goldman, 1981; Petty, Cacioppo, & Schumann, 1983). In this kind of work, persons who are randomly assigned to the high personal relevance condition tend to think about the product in different ways (e.g., they elaborate more in developing their attitude) than persons randomly assigned to a low personal relevance condition (e.g., they tend to rely on factors other than elaboration of attributes, such as the celebrity status of the endorser in the development of their attitude). However, as with any study, there was error variance to be accounted for. For example, some of the persons assigned to the low motivation condition tended to elaborate about the product to a degree similar to those randomly assigned to the high motivation manipulation condition.

There are numerous individual difference measures that we feel are worthy of additional attention by consumer researchers. In the following sections, we selectively discuss a few as examples. In addition, we recommend the development of specific individual difference measures for use in relevant research.

NEED FOR COGNITION

Cacioppo and Petty (1982) reasoned that just as there are situational factors that induce people to think more or less, so should there be reliable individual differences in this regard. Cacioppo and Petty (1982) developed and refined a measure on an individual's intrinsic enjoyment of thinking. In our review of the literature, Need for Cognition (NFC) was one of the most frequently used individual difference variables. In most contemporary research, an 18-item scale is used (Cacioppo, Petty, & Kao, 1984). In a persuasion context, research by Cacioppo, Petty, and Morris (1983) showed that variation in argument quality (using lengthy articles on topics like tuition increases) had a greater influence on the final attitudes of persons scoring high in need for cognition (HNC) than persons scoring low in need for cognition (LNC). Additional analyses showed greater elaboration of message content by HNC individuals. Studies by Haugtvedt, Petty, and Cacioppo (1992) (using short advertising messages) also showed greater elaboration of message content by HNC individuals and greater reliance on source and other factors by LNC individuals. In discussing the personality research, Haugtvedt et al. (1992) noted that the usefulness of personality variables in consumer research is enhanced by their fit as operationalizations of constructs in broader theoretical frameworks used by the researchers to guide their work.

NFC serves as a way to operationalize motivation in persuasion research and it fits into the overall framework of the Elaboration Likelihood Model and other models that postulate important roles for moderators of the extent of thinking. As such, studies that focus on understanding issues like the role of elaboration in the development of strong attitudes have been able to use the NFC variable as a tool, much in the same way standardized situational manipulations have been used in other research (see chapter 15, this volume). The availability of an individual difference or dispositional measure that can serve to operationalize the same kind of construct as a situational manipulation is able to operationalize is especially important in programmatic research approaches where one is interested in mapping out the boundary conditions of various phenomena and processes.

NEED FOR EVALUATION

Some situations call for persons to derive judgments about the positivity or negativity of stimuli they encounter at the time they encounter the material whereas other situations make it more likely that persons will simply encode information without engaging in much evaluative activity. Indeed, some theorists have argued that persons do not form judgments until they are asked to do so, whereas others have argued that evaluation is pervasive. Classic work on attitude change and persuasion suggests that factors like the situational personal relevance of a topic influence the way in which persons approach a message. Participants randomly assigned to the high personal relevance condition are hypothesized to engage in more evaluative responding at the time of exposure to a message whereas participants in the low personal relevance condition might not engage in evaluative responding until asked to do so later on. Jarvis and Petty (1996) reasoned that just as there are situations that make it more or less likely for persons to engage in evaluative responding, so too should there be individual differences in the degree to which persons spontaneously engage in evaluative responding.

In a series of studies, Jarvis and Petty (1996) developed and validated a 16-item individual difference measure of Need to Evaluate (NE). In one study, using a 29-item political questionnaire, they were able to show that persons scoring high in need for evaluation (HNE) reported having attitudes toward a wider array of issues than persons scoring low in need for evaluations (LNE). In another study, Jarvis and Petty (1996) found a positive relationship between NE scores and evaluative responding in a situation where they were not cued to the evaluative nature of a task (simply viewing pictures from a library database). In a final study, Jarvis and Petty (1996) found that even though the total amount of daily thoughts were similar from persons for both groups, HNE individuals provided more evaluative narratives than LNE individuals. Individual differences in NE may be used as a tool to understand survey research question response behavior (Petty & Jarvis, 1996). NE may also be an important tool for use in research on topics like consumer satisfaction, dissatisfaction, and complaining behavior (Haugtvedt, Kasmer, Samuelsen, Hansen, & Lorentzen, 2004).

NEED FOR UNIQUENESS

A significant body of research in general shows that people view a scarce product as more attractive and valuable (cf. Brock, 1968). There are a variety of reasons as to why the item might be seen as more attractive and valuable when it is scarce. As discussed in economic, psychological, and sociological literature, the possession of a scarce item (e.g., Pablo Picasso's painting, Lamborghini car) can be a source of power, or status, and also enhance the owner's self-image (Lynn, 1992). Most important for our discussion is the idea that just as the situational perception of scarcity can influence perceptions of value, there are differences among persons with regard to uniqueness seeking motives.

Need for uniqueness (Snyder & Fromkin, 1980) refers to an individual's motive to be independent and different from other people. As conceptualized in theories in social psychology, uniqueness is one of the key dimensions that individuals want to seek and maintain (Brewer, 1991; Snyder, 1992). To capture the individual difference in uniqueness motives, Snyder and Fromkin (1977) developed and validated a 32-item Need for Uniqueness scale (NFU). The scale represents several aspects of an individual's desire to appear unique, including desires to openly defend their own opinions, as well as individuals' motivation not to conform to other people's expectations and other social actions.

A typical study that addresses how people pursue a sense of self-distinctiveness explores the influence of an individual's uniqueness motive when a situational variable like product scarcity is manipulated (e.g., Lynn, 1991; Lynn & Snyder, 2002; Snyder, 1992). As shown in Lynn's (1991) meta-analytic review on scarcity effects, researchers often find that individuals high in NFU view a scarce product as more attractive and valuable than an abundant product, compared to individuals low in NFU. The interaction between NFU and preferences for a scarce product seems to result mainly from the fact that individuals who seek uniqueness are able to establish and maintain a sense of specialness by possessing a scarce product. It is important to note that understanding the role of need for uniqueness not only helps researchers identify a boundary condition for scarcity effects (e.g., some persons will react more and some less), such findings might also offer marketers insights into how and with whom they should highlight scarcity.

Another stream of research that investigates how people seek a sense of uniqueness investigates the influence of a uniqueness motive when a contextual variable such as a decision frame or a presence of a particular alternative in a choice set is manipulated. In this research paradigm, researchers examine how individuals make a choice in the presence of contextual information (e.g., Drolet, 2002; Kim & Drolet, 2003; Simonson & Nowlis, 2000). In their work on reasons-based choice, Simonson and Nowlis (2000) studied the role of need for uniqueness in consumer decision making when background information was varied. They find that consumer choice is primarily influenced by an interactive effect between need for uniqueness and the availability of an external audience to explain an individual's choice. Specifically, they observe that high NFU consumers are less likely to be influenced by price promotion, are less susceptible to decision framing, and are less likely to choose a conventional and popular alternative, like a compromise option, only when they have to make a public choice, These findings indicate that, when accountable, individuals high in NFU are more likely to make rational and independent decisions and be less influenced by contextual information.

In reviewing the studies, we found that that some researchers manipulate an individual's uniqueness motive by directly priming participants with products or advertisements that elicit this motive (e.g., Ames & Iyengar, 2005; Kim & Drolet, 2003) while others measured dispositional need for uniqueness either before (e.g., Ames & Iyengar, 2005; Lynn, 1989) or after (e.g., Drolet, 2002; Simonson & Nowlis, 2000) they manipulated key situational factors. When the individual difference was measured, researchers used Snyder and Fromkin's original need for uniqueness scale (NFU) or more domain specific scales such as Lynn and Harris' (1997) desire for unique consumer products (DUCP) scale and Tian, Bearden, and Hunter's (2001) consumers' need for uniqueness

(CNFU) scale. In analyzing the data, most of the researchers used median splits to create high versus low need for uniqueness conditions (e.g., Lynn, 1989; Simonson & Nowlis, 2000; Drolet, 2002) even though some adopted a regression approach that treated the measure as a continuous variable (e.g., Ames & Iyengar, 2005). In general, consumer studies included need for uniqueness measures at the end of a study while psychology studies tended to measure it before participants were exposed to the main stimuli.

In conclusion, several studies have used an individual's need for uniqueness to gain a better understanding of various social phenomena. Evidence exists that need for uniqueness serves as an important moderator when situational variables such as scarcity and choice contexts are manipulated. Future studies should consider more situational factors that can interact with need for uniqueness so that our understanding of the underlying process of interest can be enhanced. Just as general manipulations of choice context and scarcity can influence choice behavior, other manipulations might enhance or diminish the extent to which an individual's uniqueness motive might influence the processes underlying perception and choice (cf. Ames & Iyengar, 2005). These things might include manipulations to consider self-values, social validation, cultural norms, and other situational factors.

NEED FOR CLOSURE

There are situations in which persons need to make quick judgments or decisions because of time pressure or other factors. Academic job interviewers, for example, need to make a quick judgment about which final candidate to select from a large group of candidates in a short period of time. Consumers may use heuristics to simplify their decisions if a store carries too many similar brands. While individuals are often motivated to make fast judgments or decisions due to situational influences, some individuals are chronically more susceptible to these external influences than other people.

Need for closure (Kruglanski & Freund, 1983; Webster & Kruglanski, 1994) refers to an individual's desire for definite, certain, or unambiguous knowledge. When an individual perceives that having closure is beneficial or lacking it is costly, need for closure is more likely to be enhanced. An individual high in need for closure tends to be motivated to seize on closure immediately (i.e., an "urgency" tendency) while freezing on obtained knowledge permanently (i.e., a "permanence" tendency). To tap the chronic accessibility of an individual's need for closure, Webster and Kruglanski (1994) developed and validated a 42-item Need for Closure Scale (NFCS). This scale includes five dimensions: an individual's preference for order, preference for predictability, decisiveness, discomfort with ambiguity, and close-mindedness.

A growing body of research has supported the idea that need for closure impacts a variety of intrapersonal and interpersonal situations (Kruglanski & Chun, in press). One notable area that addresses the impact of need for closure is research on selective information processing. Selective information processing can often result in heuristic-based judgments such as primary effects, anchoring effects, and price-quality inferences. In this research paradigm, researchers study the influence of need for closure when a situational variable like information presentation order is manipulated (e.g., Kruglanski & Freund, 1983; Webster & Kruglanski, 1994).

A common procedure employed in this research program is to ask people to evaluate a target when the information about the target is presented in different orders. What researchers often find is that high NFCS individuals are more motivated to seize on the early information quickly and then freeze on the judgments than are low NFCS individuals. This results in stronger primacy or anchoring effects. Similarly, in their heuristic judgment studies, Kardes, Cronley, Kellaris, and

Posavac (2004) examined the role of need for closure when the information load or organization was manipulated. Kardes and his colleagues asked individuals to predict quality of each product after presenting them the information about various product attributes, including price. They find that high NFCS individuals are more selective in processing the information and thus exhibit stronger price-quality inferences than low NFCS individuals. Such a result implies that high NFCS consumers are more motivated to use belief-consistent information (e.g., "price is closely related to quality") in order to possess closure quickly, compared to low NFCS consumers. These studies demonstrate that a difference in dispositional need for closure is a critical boundary condition for selective information processing.

Some other studies have also provided evidence that need for closure affects persuasion and attitude change. For example, Klein and Webster (2000) investigated how need for closure influences the way individuals process information. Their study included a manipulation of argument quality (e.g., strong vs. weak arguments) and a variable that could serve as a heuristic cue in message (e.g., small vs. large number of arguments). Klein and Webster (2000) found that high NFCS individuals were more likely to rely on a heuristic cue while low NFCS individuals relied more on argument quality. They suggest that the presence of a heuristic cue allowed high NFCS individuals to come to a quick decision.

In terms of methodological issues, some researchers manipulated an individual's concern for closure by inducing a sense of urgency in judgment (e.g., Kruglanski & Freund, 1983; Webster, 1993; Webster, Richter, & Kruglanski, 1996) while others measured it by employing the dispositional need for closure scale either before (e.g., De Grada, Kruglanski, Mannetti, & Pierro, 1999; Webster & Kruglanski, 1994) or after (e.g., Kardes et al., 2004; Silvera, Kardes, & Harvey, 2005) the main task was introduced. When the individual difference was measured, most of the researchers adopted the original NFCS but some used two different latent structures in the NFCS separately: preference for simple knowledge structures (e.g., need for structure) and preference for immediate answers (e.g., decisiveness) (e.g., Hirt, Kardes, & Markman, 2004; Roets, Van Hiel, & Cornelis, 2006).

When the dispositional need for closure was used in the analysis of data, researchers categorized participants into high and low need for closure people on the basis of various criteria. Common criteria were median splits (e.g., De Grada et al., 1999; Kardes et al., 2004; Silvera et al., 2005), top 25% versus bottom 25% (e.g., Klein & Webster, 2000; Webster & Kruglanski, 1994), or top third versus bottom third of the need for closure distribution (e.g., Webster & Kruglanski, 1994). Depending on the nature of the study, some researchers grouped participants into high, medium, and low need for closure conditions based on top 25%, middle 50%, and bottom 25% of the distribution (e.g., Webster & Kruglanski, 1994) and others treated the need for closure measure as a continuous variable (e.g., Klein & Webster, 2000). We also noticed that consumer researchers tended to measure need for closure in the conclusion of the study and applied median splits while psychologists measured it before the main study and often invited only the participants who exhibited extreme levels of need for closure for the main study. While a majority of the participants were college students, they represented diverse cultural backgrounds because many researchers conducted their studies outside of the United States and used one of the 12 different language versions of the need for closure scale (Kruglanski & Chun, in press).

In conclusion, we limited our review to two topic areas that dealt with an individual's urgency and permanence tendency. As discussed above, much research consistently shows that need for closure serves as a moderator when various situational factors in judgment and persuasion contexts or messages are varied. Future studies should examine new situational factors that would lead to the same process as an individual's chronic concern for closure. We might consider using more promotion-oriented situational factors (e.g., Webster, 1993) that can highlight the perceived benefits of seizing on closure (e.g., interesting task, recognition, incentives). A majority of researchers have used the prevention-oriented situational factors that focus on the perceived costs of lacking closure (e.g., time pressure, noise, fatigue) even though the theory predicts that need for closure can be elevated when people perceive either the benefits of possessing closure or the costs of not having closure.

INTEGRATIVE COMPLEXITY

There are situations and times in which all individuals will tend to think about issues or materials in more complex manners. Ideally, jurors thoroughly and critically examine the all evidence because their decisions can influence an individual's life. While people are often forced to think in a complex manner in stressful situations, there may be stable cognitive styles among people in terms of the degree to which they can think in multifaceted and integrative ways when situations are not as strong.

Integrative complexity (Suedfeld, Tetlock, & Streufert, 1992; Tetlock, 1983) refers to an individual's tendency to think various perspectives of an issue in an integratively complex manner. Integrative complexity has two cognitive properties: differentiation and integration Individuals high in integrative complexity acknowledge the presence of different perspectives (i.e., differentiation) and synthesize them using a sophisticated cognitive system (i.e., integration). In their early work, Tetlock and his colleagues examined the effect of the situational variable of accountability (e.g., Tetlock, 1983; Tetlock & Boettger, 1989; Tetlock, Lerner, & Boettger, 1996). In a typical study, research participants are situationally induced to believe that they need to justify their decisions to other people and then asked to make a final judgment. Using the same procedure, Tetlock and Boettger (1989) explored why accountable individuals would be more likely to rely on nondiagnostic information in making a final judgment (i.e., dilution effects), compared to nonaccountable individuals. What they find is that accountable individuals are more motivated to process the information in an integratively complex manner than nonaccountable individuals. Tetlock et al. (1996) further studied the role of integrative complexity and found that integrative complexity served as a mediator in judgment.

Even though it is beneficial to use integrative complexity, consumer psychologists have not yet widely adopted it with only a few exceptions (e.g., Lee, Herr, Kardes, & Kim, 1999; Schlosser, 2005). In her film review study, Schlosser (2005) explored the role of integrative complexity when a situational determinant like a film review writing task was manipulated. What she finds is that individuals who expect to write a film review for an audience on the Internet ("posters") are more likely to process the information in an integratively complex fashion than those who privately write a film review ("lurkers"). In addition, there was some evidence that integrative complexity was responsible for magnifying negativity bias, a tendency to rely more on negative, rather than positive, information in evaluation. Integrative complexity helps us not only improve our knowledge on the process in which consumers assess information, but also capture domain-specific consumer reaction.

With respect to analytical issues, we found that researchers measured integrative complexity using an open-ended response mode after introducing key manipulations of their studies (e.g., Schlosser 2005; Tetlock, 1983; Tetlock et al., 1996). Independent judges coded this individual difference measure on a scale that ranges from 1 (low differentiation-low integration) to 7 (high differentiation-high integration) (Tetlock, Skitka, & Boettger, 1989). Researchers usually treated the integrative complexity measure as a continuous variable and used the whole range of the distribution of the scale for the analysis. As in other studies using individual difference measures, researchers mostly relied on student participants in studying the impact of integrative complexity

In conclusion, our review suggests that while integrative complexity is more difficult to assess than some other individual difference measures, it has several merits. Integrative complexity can be used as a tool to directly test the underlying process and also address domain-specific issues. We need additional research that employs integrative complexity in consumer psychology settings while finding a way to simplify the coding procedure in the future. Future research should examine integrative complexity as a stable individual difference variable that can be measured prior to use in a study.

REGULATORY FOCUS

A large literature in psychology and behavioral decision making in particular has established that consumer preferences are often constructed, instead of simply being recalled from memory (Payne, Bettman, & Johnson, 1992). This constructive process is sensitive to changes in the contextual factors as well as motivational states of the decision maker, such as need for cognition and need for cognitive closure as discussed previously. Consistent with this approach, regulatory focus theory suggests that judgmental processes can also be affected by individual's regulatory goals salient at the time of evaluation.

According to regulatory focus theory (Higgins, 1997), self-regulation operates differently when it serves fundamentally different survival needs of the individual, such as nurturance (obtaining nourishing food) and security (protection). The theory assumes that self-regulation that directs at nurturance needs involves a promotion focus, which is concerned with the presence or absence of positive outcomes and underlies higher level motivations of accomplishment and achievement. In contrast, self-regulation that directs at security needs involves a prevention focus, which is concerned with the presence or absence of negative outcomes and underlies higher level concerns of safety and responsibility. Regulatory focus theory also proposes that self-regulatory goals may be achieved with eagerness or approach-related means or with vigilance or avoidance related means. Most importantly, the theory proposes that people prefer using eagerness-related means when they strive for promotion focused goals and prefer using vigilance-related means when they try to achieve prevention focused goals. The fit between regulatory focus and goal striving means creates value beyond the basic hedonic value of the goal itself.

Regulatory focus has been studied both as a situationally manipulated variable and as a chronic and stable individual difference variable. Regulatory focus as individual difference has been assessed using the Self-Guide Strength Measure (Higgins, Shah, & Friedman, 1997; Shah & Higgins, 1997) and, more recently, the Regulatory Focus Questionnaire (Higgins et al., 2001).

The Self-Guide Strength questionnaire measures the chronic accessibility of people's ideals and oughts using response time collected when participants list and rate attributes that they would ideally like to have and attributes that they think they ought to have. Strong ideal self-guides, as measured by short response time to the ideal items, signals greater accessibility of aspirations and indicates a strong promotion focus. Strong ought self-guides, as measured by short response time to the ought items, reveals greater accessibility of responsibilities and obligations, which indicates strong prevention focus.

The Regulatory Focus Questionnaire (RFQ) measures people's subjective history of promotion versus prevention success. The RFQ distinguishes between promotion pride and prevention pride, which are conceptualized as "orientations (i.e., anticipatory goal reactions) to new task goals that derive from a subjective history of past success in promotion and prevention goal attainment, respectively" (Higgins et al., 2001, p. 6). Higgins et al. (2001) shows that people high in promotion pride are more likely to use approach eagerness means in goal attainment than people high in prevention pride and vice versa. The effect of regulatory focus as well as regulatory fit on judgmental processes has recently been reviewed elsewhere (Avnet & Higgins, 2006; Higgins & Spiegel, 2004), and we will only use one example from message framing research to illustrate how regulatory focus can be used to understand complex processes.

Efforts in persuasion research on message framing have been focused on understanding whether framing a message in terms of gains if a recommended action is adopted is more effective in persuading people than framing a message as losses if the action is not adopted. For example, is a sunscreen lotion ad more effective if it emphasizes the benefits of healthier skin by its use or more effective if it emphasizes the risk of skin cancer if it is not used? Research in this tradition has failed to produce consistent findings (Levin, Schneider, & Gaeth, 1998; O'Keefe & Jensen, 2006). Recent developments in this literature suggest that the compatibility between goal attainment strategy and people's regulatory focus may be an important moderating variable.

Regulatory focus theory predicts that promotion focused people are sensitive to the presence and absence of positive outcomes (gain and nongain) while prevention focused people are more sensitive to the presence or absence of negative outcomes (loss and nonloss). People may interpret the same information in different ways. For example, a positively valenced outcome may be interpreted as a gain by promotion focused people but as a nonloss by prevention focused people. For example, promotion focused people may interpret the claim that "use sunscreen and it will bring you healthier skin" as a gain if they use sunscreen, but prevention focused people may see it as a nonloss. Since maximizing gains is more consistent with the regulatory orientation of promotion focused people, regulatory focus theory predicts that gain framed messages would be more persuasive for them than for prevention focused people. In contrast, a negatively valenced outcome may be interpreted as a loss by prevention focused people and simply as a nongain by promotion focused people. Objectively, skin cancer is a negative outcome, but a claim that "if you don't use sunscreen regularly you risk of developing skin cancer" may be construed as a loss by prevention focused people if they don't use sunscreen, but as a nongain by promotion focused people. In this case, the message fits better with the regulatory orientation of prevention focused people than with promotion focused people, and it should be more effective for prevention focused people.

These propositions were tested and supported in several studies (Cesario, Grant, & Higgins, 2004; Keller, 2006; Lee & Aaker, 2004; Wang & Lee, 2006). Using a variety of situational manipulations of regulatory focus, these studies also show that multiple processes may be causing the increased persuasion effect, such as perceptual salience of information that fits with regulatory focus, transfer of "feeling right" to value assessment when means of goal pursuit sustains existing regulatory orientation, higher confidence, and increased strength of engagement. Similar processes should be active when individual differences measures are used in place of the situational manipulations.

One of the studies reported in Cesario, Grant, and Higgins (2004; study 2) took a step in this direction. In this study, participants first filled out the RFQ and then read a message with a positively framed outcome (tax support for an after school program) which could be achieved through either eagerness means (e.g., advance education and support success) or vigilance means (e.g., secure education and prevent failure). It was found that promotion focused people are more persuaded when the eagerness means was used than when the vigilance means was used, and vice versa for prevention focused people. The results from Cesario et al. (2004) not only complement other studies that used situational manipulations of regulatory focus, but are also consistent with a study by Sherman, Mann, and Updegraff (2006) who used the conceptually analogous behavior inhibition/activation measure (Carver & White, 1994). Future research should more systematically examine process level differences across individuals with different regulatory orientations.

PROPENSITY TO SELF-REFERENCE

How prior experiences and knowledge influence processes of attitude change and persuasion is a central theme throughout much theorizing in social psychology. Indeed, the cognitive response perspective posits that idiosyncratic thoughts are better predictors of attitude change and maintenance than is recall of message arguments. Consistent with this idea, Shavitt and Brock (1986) found that coding for self-originated thoughts improved predictions of attitude above traditional cognitive response polarity measures.

The Shavitt and Brock (1986) work focused on coding of cognitive responses naturally elicited by persuasive messages. In research on the topic of self-referencing, variables designed to increase or decrease the likelihood of self-related thoughts have been manipulated. For example, Burnkrant and Unnava (1989) presented college students with advertisements for a razor (see Petty et al., 1983) that addressed the reader directly (e.g., you) or indirectly (e.g., people). In addition, the quality of the product attributes was manipulated to be relatively strong and convincing or weak (see Petty et al., 1983). As discussed in other chapters in this volume, a manipulation of attribute or argument quality can provide insights as to the degree to which participants are elaborating on message content. Consistent with their predictions, Burnkrant and Unnava (1989) found that advertisements that addressed participants directly (e.g., you; high self-referencing) led to more extensive elaboration. Participants receiving the strong argument version liked the product significantly more than participants receiving the weak argument version. However, this was not the case for participants who were exposed to an advertisement that addressed the participants indirectly (e.g., people; low self-referencing). Burnkrant and Unnava (1989, 1995) suggest that the difference in the extent of elaboration may not be due to differences in participant motivation. Rather, they argue that participants are more likely to use self-knowledge structures and prior personal experiences as a basis for elaborating on the advertising content to a greater degree when they are addressed directly.

While Burnkrant and Unnava's (1989) research suggests that higher levels of self-referencing should enhance message-relevant elaboration, research by Baumgartner, Bettman, and Sujan (1992) and Sujan, Bettman, and Baumgartner (1993) suggests that high levels of self-referencing might lead to lesser degrees of message-relevant elaboration. In a study employing an argument quality manipulation for wine, Sujan et al. (1993) found support for this idea. In their high self-referencing condition participants were asked to form an impression of the advertised brand in the context of an autobiographical memory; in the low self-referencing conditions no specific encouragement was provided. Consistent with their predictions, they found the greatest differentiation in argument quality for the low self-referencing condition.

These results appear to be inconsistent with the work of Burnkrant and Unnava (1989). One possible explanation of this inconsistency relates to the idea that some individuals might be so focused on their own prior experiences that processing of the stimulus material is reduced. Indeed, Sujan et al.'s (1993) preferred explanation for their findings is that participants in their high self-referencing condition were overwhelmed by the influence of emotions associated with past experiences, and were thus unable or unwilling to focus on the stimulus materials.

Haugtvedt (1994) was interested in developing a measure that would assess the degree to which individuals might differ in their natural propensity to think about one's own prior experiences when exposed to persuasive materials. The starting point for this individual difference measure was the manipulation check items used in the Burnkrant and Unnava (1989) and Sujan et al. (1993)

studies. Additional items were generated, and a pool of 28 potential items was included in a questionnaire containing other individual difference measures and general questions focusing on attitudes toward a variety of products and issues. From the initial set of 28 items, 8 items loaded on a single factor thought to capture the extent to which persons draw on and integrate their own experiences when encountering persuasive messages. While we will not go into detail here, further scale development testing was conducted in which the contents of thoughts were examined for greater degrees of self-related experiences.

Of most interest for our current discussion is a study (Haugtvedt, Shakarchi, & Jarvis, 2002) in which students were exposed to advertisements for a calculator. The stimulus materials used the indirect method of addressing participants (i.e., "people," as in Burnkrant & Unnava, 1989). Strong- and weak-argument versions of the calculator advertisement were also created and pretested. The Propensity to Self-Reference (PSR) measure was completed by students in a separate session. Consistent with the interest in gaining an understanding of the attitude change processes for low and high self-referencing, participants were categorized as low, moderate, or high in PSR based on a tercile split their scores from the questionnaire.

Interestingly, the data comparing low to moderate PSR appear to mirror the data reported by Burnkrant and Unnava (1989), such that those moderate in PSR were more influenced by argument strength than are those low in PSR. On the other hand, the comparison of the moderate to high PSR groups mirrors the data reported by Sujan et al. (1993), such that those moderate in PSR are more influenced by argument strength than are those high in PSR. Taken together, this study (Haugtvedt et al., 2002) found that individuals characterized as moderate in self-referencing engaged in the greatest degree of message-relevant elaboration (as indicated by the degree of difference in attitudes as a function of message strength). Such results are thus suggestive of an optimal level of self-referencing that will maximize the persuasive effect of a strategic communication. With low levels of self-referencing, individuals may not see the cogency or weaknesses in message arguments, but with high levels of self-referencing, individuals may be too focused on their own past experiences to fully appreciate the information contained in the persuasive materials.

The PSR individual difference measure may also have some important implications for other areas of persuasion and compliance. As was noted earlier, the individual difference measure was developed to capture the processes activated by words used in advertising copy that might prompt thinking about personal experiences. It is also likely that various interpersonal compliance-gaining strategies prompt greater or lesser degrees of self-referencing.

Along the same lines, an intriguing study by Gregory, Cialdini, and Carpenter (1982) showed that requests asking persons to "imagine the benefits" of cable television were significantly more likely to subscribe one month later than persons simply told the "benefits of cable television." One possible explanation for these findings is that people were more likely to feel as if they had come up with the idea and/or benefits of cable television if they were successful in imagining themselves enjoying the benefits. Part of the ability to imagine such benefits might be related to the extent to which persons are prompted to think about their own prior experiences at the time of the information presentation. Alternatively, some persons, (e.g., those high in PSR) may naturally reflect on their own prior experiences and thus be more susceptible to forgetting the source of the information. Even more interesting than the possibility that such individuals would be more likely to forget source information is the possibility that such individuals might be more likely to see themselves as the source of the information after some delay. If this kind of process is activated, it may have implications for understanding the sleeper effect as well. In a related way, salespeople and other compliance practitioners often face an attribution problem because they are seen as benefiting when a consumer complies and purchases a product or service (Friestad & Wright, 1995). Because of this, consumers might discount the information presented by the salesperson as biased in some way. The use of factors that increase the likelihood of self-referencing might reduce the extent to which consumers discount salesperson information because the person will think that they generated the information him/herself. Of course, there are likely situations in which seeing one's self as the source of information will lead to greater or lesser confidence on one's attitude. In any case, there appear to be many interesting avenues for future research as we continue in our quest to better understand the antecedents and consequences of attitude changes.

INDIVIDUAL DIFFERENCES IN CONSUMER PSYCHOLOGY RESEARCH: PRACTICAL MATTERS

In the preceding pages, we briefly reviewed how individual difference variables have been used in consumer psychology studies. Many individual difference measures are available for use and many more are in the process of development. As stated at the beginning of this chapter, we suggest that the choice of a specific individual difference variable for use in a particular project depends on the nature of the constructs specified by theory.

In serving as reviewers of work on this topic, we often see papers that report the inclusion of an individual difference variable without theoretical or methodological justification. Perhaps not surprisingly, the researchers often fail to find significant effects associated with the measure. Just as with situational manipulations, the use of an individual difference measure requires many considerations. One must understand how the individual difference construct is likely to be influenced by other factors in the study (e.g., strong or weak situational manipulations). In addition, studies often do not have a sufficient range of scores on the individual difference variable or sufficient power (see Iacobucci, 2001; MacCallum, Zhang, Preacher, & Rucker, 2000). While researchers may improve statistical power in follow-up tests and find more distinctive results by focusing on individuals who have extreme scores on a continuous scale, there is a concern about using extreme data only. As discussed in Preacher, Rucker, MacCallum, and Nicewander (2005), this extreme grouping method can produce biased results because it does not use a full range of the continuous data. In particular, if a true relationship of the individual difference variable and some process is curvilinear, researchers may draw conclusions by relying only on extreme data. For discussions regarding analytical techniques, readers are referred to Preacher et al. (2005).

Ideally, in our view, individual difference variables will be used in a program of research in which the processes of interest are examined in many ways. This may include a series of related situational manipulations, the use of relevant individual difference variables, or a combination of individual difference variables and situational manipulations to operationalize theoretical constructs of interest. For example, in research examining the endpoints of an elaboration continuum, one might have a low motivation situational manipulation with individuals who score in the bottom 25% of the Need for Cognition scale contrasted with a high situational motivation manipulation and individuals who score in the top 25% of Need for Cognition. Of course, the researchers would also need to verify that initial knowledge and attitudes as well as other characteristics of the persons at the low and high end of the Need for Cognition scale did not differ prior to the study. One might also imagine research in which one recruits participants possessing desired combinations of scores on more than one individual difference measure.

It is important to emphasize that we believe that initial research in attempting to understand a particular process underlying consumer behavior can be conducted with situational manipulations of variables of interest or by employing relevant individual difference variables. For a complete understanding, a program of research using both individual difference and situational operationalizations adds to our confidence that the individual difference measures and situational manipulations are converging on a particular construct.

In writing this chapter, we examined the content of articles appearing in the *Journal of Consumer Research* (*JCR*) from 1995 to 2005. Overall, studies employing measures of individual differences account for about 15% of all the studies published in the *JCR* in this time frame. We hope that in a future revision and extension of this chapter, we can report even higher numbers of studies in which individual differences have been used by consumer researchers.

REFERENCES

Ames, D. R., & Iyengar, S. S. (2005). Appraising the unusual: Framing effects and moderators of uniqueness-seeking and social projection. *Journal of Experimental Social Psychology, 41*, 271–282.

Avnet, T., & Higgins, E. T. (2006). How regulatory fit affects value in consumer choices and opinions. *Journal of Marketing Research, 43*, 1-10.

Baumgartner, H. (2002). Toward a personology of the consumer. *Journal of Consumer Research, 29*, 286–292.

Baumgartner, H., Bettman, J. R., & Sujan, M. (1992). Autobiographical memories, affect, and consumer information processing. *Journal of Consumer Psychology, 1*, 53–82.

Brewer, M. B. (1991). The social self: On being the same and different at the same time. *Personality and Social Psychology Bulletin, 17*, 475–482.

Brock, T. C. (1968). Implications of commodity theory for value change. In A. G. Greenwald, T. C. Brock, & T. M. Ostrom (Eds.). *Psychological foundations of attitudes* (pp. 243–275). New York: Academic Press.

Burnkrant, R. E., & Unnava, H. R. (1989). Self-referencing: A strategy for increasing processing of message content. *Personality and Social Psychology Bulletin, 15*, 628–638.

Burnkrant, R. E., & Unnava, H. R. (1995). Effects of self-referencing on persuasion. *Journal of Consumer Research, 22*, 17–26.

Cacioppo, J. T., & Petty, R. E. (1982). The need for cognition. *Journal of Personality and Social Psychology, 42*, 116–131.

Cacioppo, J. T., Petty, R. E., & Kao, C. F. (1984). The efficient assessment of need for cognition. *Journal of Personality Assessment, 48*, 306–307.

Cacioppo, J. T., Petty, R. E., & Morris, K. (1983). Effects of need for cognition on message evaluation, recall, and persuasion. *Journal of Personality and Social Psychology, 51*, 1032–1043.

Carver, C. S., & White, T. L. (1994). Behavioral inhibition, behavioral activation, and affective responses to impending reward and punishment: The BIS/BAS Scales. *Journal of Personality and Social Psychology, 67*, 319–333.

Cesario, J., Grant, H., & Higgins, E. T. (2004). Regulatory fit and persuasion: Transfer from 'feeling right.'" *Journal of Personality and Social Psychology, 86*, 388–404.

De Grada, E., Kruglanski, A. W., Mannetti, L., & Pierro, A. (1999). Motivated cognition and group interaction: need for closure affects the contents and processes of collective negotiations. *Journal of Experimental Social Psychology, 35*, 346–365.

Drolet, A. (2002). Inherent rule variability in consumer choice: Changing rules for change's sake. *Journal of Consumer Research, 29*, 293–305.

Friestad, M., & Wright, P. (1995). Persuasion knowledge — Lay peoples and researchers beliefs about the psychology of advertising. *Journal of Consumer Research, 22*, 62–74.

Funder, D. C., & Colvin, C. R. (1991). Explorations in behavioral consistency: Properties of persons, situations, and behaviors. *Journal of Personality and Social Psychology, 60*, 773–794.

Gregory, W. L., Cialdini, R. B., & Carpenter, K. M. (1982). Self-relevant scenarios as mediators of likelihood estimates and compliance: Does imagining make it so? *Journal of Personality and Social Psychology, 43*, 89–99.

Haugtvedt, C. P. (1994, February). Individual differences in propensity to self-reference: Implications for attitude change processes. Paper presented at the 1st Winter Meeting of the Society for Consumer Psychology, St. Petersburg, FL.

Haugtvedt, C. P., Kasmer, J. A.,Samuelsen, B., Hansen, H., & Lorentzen, B. (2004, July). An elaboration likelihood model analysis of consumer satisfaction and dissatisfaction. Paper presented at the Annual Meeting of the American Psychological Association, Honolulu, Hawaii.

Haugtvedt, C. P., Petty, R. E., & Cacioppo, J. T. (1992). Need for cognition and advertising: Understanding the role of personality variables in consumer behavior. *Journal of Consumer Psychology, 1*, 239–260.

Haugtvedt, C. P., Shakarchi, R, & Jarvis, B. (2002). *Propensity to self-reference and attitude change processes.* Working paper, Fisher College of Business, Ohio State University.

Higgins, E. T. (1997). Beyond pleasure and pain. *American Psychologists, 53,* 1280–1300.

Higgins, E. T., Friedman, R. S., Harlow, R. E., Idson, L. C., Ayduk, O. N., & Taylor, A. (2001). Achievement orientations from subjective histories of success: Promotion pride versus prevention pride. *European Journal of Social Psychology, 31*, 3–23.

Higgins, E. T., Shah, J., & Friedman, R. (1997). Emotional responses to goal attainment: Strength of regulatory focus as moderator. *Journal of Personality and Social Psychology, 72*, 515–525.

Higgins, E. T., & Spiegel, S. (2004). Promotion and prevention strategies for self-regulation: A motivated cognition perspective. In R. F. Baumeister & K. D. Vohs (Eds.). *Handbook of self-regulation* (pp. 171–187). New York: Guilford.

Hirt, E. R., Kardes, F. R., & Markman, K. D. (2004). Activating a mental simulation mind-set through generation of alternatives: Implications for debiasing in related and unrelated domains. *Journal of Experimental Social Psychology, 40*, 374–383.

Iacobucci, D. (Ed.). (2001). Special issue: Methodological and statistical concerns of the experimental behavioral researcher. *Journal of Consumer Psychology, 10*, 48–53.

Jarvis, B., & Petty, R. E. (1996). The need to evaluate. *Journal of Personality and Social Psychology, 70*, 172–194.

Kardes, F. R., Cronley, M. L., Kellaris, J. J., & Posavac, S. S. (2004). Selective information processing. *Journal of Consumer Research, 31*, 368–374.

Kassarjian, H. (1971). Personality and consumer behavior: A review. *Journal of Marketing Research, 8*, 409–418.

Kassarjian, H., & Sheffet, M. J. (1981). Personality and consumer behavior: An update. In H. Kassarjian & T. Robertson (Eds.), *Perspectives on consumer behavior* (pp. 160–180). Glenview, IL: Scott, Foresman.

Kassarjian, H., & Sheffet, M. J. (1991). Personality and consumer behavior: An update. In H. Kassarjian & T. Robertson (Eds.), *Perspectives on consumer behavior* (pp. 281–303). Englewood Cliffs, NJ: Prentice Hall.

Keller, P. A. (2006). Regulatory focus and efficacy of health messages. *Journal of Consumer Research, 33*(1), 109–114.

Kim, H., & Drolet, A. (2003). Choice and self-expression: A cultural analysis of variety-seeking. *Journal of Personality and Social Psychology, 85*, 373–382.

Klein, C. T. F., & Webster, D. M. (2000). Individual differences in argument scrutiny as motivated by need for cognitive closure. *Basic and Applied Social Psychology, 22*, 119–129.

Kruglanski, A. W., & Chun, W. Y. (in press). Motivated closed mindedness and its social consequences. In J. Shah & W. Gardner (Eds.). *Handbook of motivation science.* New York: Guilford.

Kruglanski, A. W., & Freund, T. (1983). The freezing and unfreezing of lay inferences: Effects of impressional primacy, ethnic stereotyping, and numerical anchoring. *Journal of Experimental Social Psychology, 19*, 448–468.

Lee, A. Y., & Aaker, J. L. (2004). Bringing the frame into focus: The influence of regulatory fit on processing fluency and persuasion. *Journal of Personality and Social Psychology, 86*, 205–218.

Lee, H., Herr, P. M., Kardes, F. R., & Kim, C. (1999). Motivated search: Effects of choice, accountability, issue involvement, and prior knowledge on information acquisition and use. *Journal of Business Research, 45*, 75–88.

Levin, I. P., Schneider, S. L., & Gaeth, G. J. (1998). All frames are not created equal: A typology and critical analysis of framing effects. *Organizational Behavior and Human Decision Processes, 76*, 149–188.

Lynn, M. (1991). Scarcity effects on value: A quantitative review of the commodity theory literature. *Psychology and Marketing, 8*, 43–57.

Lynn, M. (1992). The psychology of unavailability: Explaining scarcity and cost effects on value. *Basic and Applied Social Psychology, 13*, 3–7.

Lynn, M., & Harris, J. (1997). The desire for unique consumer products: A new individual differences scale. *Psychology and Marketing, 14*, 601–616.

Lynn, M., & Snyder, C. R. (2002). Uniqueness seeking. In L. Michael & C. R. Snyder (Eds.), *Handbook of positive psychology* (pp. 395–410). New York: Oxford University Press.

MacCallum, R. C., Zhang, S., Preacher, K. J., & Rucker, D. D. (2000). On the practice of dichotomization of quantitative variables. *Psychological Methods, 7*, 19–40.

McAdams, D. P. (1996). *The stories we live by: Personal myths and the making of the self.* New York: Guilford.

McAdams, D. P. (2001). *The person: An integrated introduction to personality psychology.* Fort Worth: TX: Hartcourt College Publishers.

Mischel, W. (1968). *Personality and assessment.* New York: Wiley.

O'Keefe, D. J., & Jensen, J. D. (2006). The advantages of compliance or the disadvantage of noncompliance? A meta-analytic review of the relative persuasive effectiveness of gain-framed and loss-framed messages. *Communication Yearbook, 30*, 1–43.

Payne, J. W., Bettman, J. R., & Johnson, E. J. (1992). Behavioral decision research: A constructive processing perspective. *Annual Review of Psychology, 43*, 87–131.

Petty, R. E., Cacioppo, J. T., & Goldman, R. (1981). Personal involvement as a determinant of argument-based persuasion. *Journal of Personality and Social Psychology, 41*, 847–855.

Petty, R. E., Cacioppo, J. T., & Schumann, D. (1983). Central and peripheral routes to advertising effectiveness: The moderating role of involvement. *Journal of Consumer Research, 10*, 135–146.

Petty, R. E., & Jarvis, B. G. (1996). An individual differences perspective on assessing cognitive processes. In N. Schwarz & S. Sudman (Eds.), *Answering questions: Methodology for determining cognitive and communicative processes in survey research* (pp. 221–257). San Francisco: Jossey-Bass.

Preacher, K. J., Rucker, D. D., MacCallum, R. C., & Nicewander, W. A. (2005). Use of the extreme groups approach: A critical reexamination and new recommendations. *Psychological Methods, 10*, 178–192.

Roets, A. Van Hiel, A., & Cornelis, I. (2006). The dimensional structure of the need for cognitive closure scale: Relationships with "seizing" and "freezing" processes. *Social Cognition, 24*, 22–45.

Schlosser, A. E. (2005). Posting versus lurking: Communicating in a multiple audience context, *Journal of Consumer Research, 32*, 260–265.

Shavitt, S., & Brock, T. C. (1986). Self-relevant responses to commercial persuasion: Field and experimental tests. In K. Sentis & J. Olson (Eds.), *Advertising and consumer psychology* (Vol. 3, pp. 149–171). New York: Praeger.

Shah, J., & Higgins, E. T. (1997). Expectancy * value effects: Regulatory focus as determinant of magnitude and direction. *Journal of Personality and Social Psychology, 73*, 447–458.

Sherman, D. K., Mann, T., & Updegraff, J. A. (2006). Approach/avoidance motivation, message framing, and health behavior: Understanding the congruency effect. *Motivation and Emotion, 30*, 165–169.

Silvera, D. H., Kardes, F. R., & Harvey, N. (2005). Contextual influences on omission neglect in the fault tree paradigm. *Journal of Consumer Psychology, 15*, 117–126.

Simonson, I., & Nowlis, S. M. (2000). The role of explanations and need for uniqueness in consumer decision making: Unconventional choices based on reasons. *Journal of Consumer Research, 27*, 49–68.

Snyder, C. R. (1992). Product scarcity by need for uniqueness interaction: A consumer catch-22 carousel? *Basic and Applied Social Psychology, 13*, 9–24.

Snyder, C. R., & Fromkin, H. L. (1977). Abnormality as a positive characteristic: The development and validation of a scale measuring need for uniqueness. *Journal of Abnormal Psychology, 86*, 518–527.

Snyder, C. R., & Fromkin, H. L. (1980). *Uniqueness: The human pursuit of difference.* New York: Plenum.

Snyder, M., & Cantor, N. (1998). Understanding personality and social behavior: A functionalist strategy. In D. T. Gilbert, S. T. Fiske, & G. Lindzey (Eds.), *The handbook of social psychology: Vol. 1.* (4th ed., pp. 635–679). Boston: McGraw-Hill.

Suedfeld, P., Tetlock, P. E., & Streufert, S. (1992). Conceptual/integrative complexity. In C. P. Smith (Ed.), *Motivation and personality: Handbook of thematic content analysis* (pp. 393–400). Cambridge: Cambridge University Press.

Sujan, M., Bettman, J. R., & Baumgartner, H. (1993). Influencing consumer judgments via autobiographical memories: A self-referencing perspective. *Journal of Marketing Research, 30*, 422–436.

Swann, W. B., & Seyle, C. (2005). Personality psychology's comeback and its emerging symbiosis with social psychology. *Personality and Social Psychology Bulletin, 31*, 155–165.

Tetlock, P. E. (1983). Accountability and complexity of thought. *Journal of Personality and Social Psychology, 45*, 74–83.

Tetlock, P. E., & Boettger, R. (1989). Accountability: A social magnifier of the dilution effect. *Journal of Personality and Social Psychology, 57*, 388–398.

Tetlock, P. E., Lerner, J. S., & Boettger, R. (1996). The dilution effect: Judgmental bias, conversational convention, or a bit of both? *European Journal of Social Psychology, 26*, 915–934.

Tetlock, P. E., Skitka, L., & Boettger, R. (1989). Social and cognitive strategies for coping with accountability: Conformity, complexity, and bolstering. *Journal of Personality and Social Psychology, 57*, 632–640.

Tian, K. T., Bearden, W. O., & Hunter, G. L. (2001). Consumers' need for uniqueness: Scale development and validation. *Journal of Consumer Research, 28*, 50–66.

Wang, J., & Lee, A. Y. (2006). The role of regulatory focus in preference construction. *Journal of Marketing Research, 43*(1), 28–38.

Webster, D. M. (1993). Motivated augmentation and reduction of the overattribution bias. *Journal of Personality and Social Psychology, 65*, 261–271.

Webster, D. M., & Kruglanski, A. W. (1994). Individual differences in need for cognitive closure. *Journal of Personality and Social Psychology, 67*, 1049–1062.

Webster, D. M., Richter, L., & Kruglanski, A. W. (1996). On leaping to conclusions when feeling tired: Mental fatigue effects on impressional primacy. *Journal of Experimental Social Psychology, 32*, 181–195.

47

Neuroeconomics
Foundational Issues and Consumer Relevance

Giovanna Egidi

Howard C. Nusbaum

John T. Cacioppo

University of Chicago

Two cornerstones of classic economic theory are the assumptions that individuals are rational decision makers and have purely self-regarding preferences (Camerer & Fehr, 2006). These assumptions fly in the face of most theories of consumer behavior, where individuals are depicted as characterized by bounded rationality and bounded self-interests.

In the 1950s, a popular television show called *The Millionaire* was based on the premise that an unseen multimillionaire would dispatch his associate carrying a tax-free cashier's check for $1,000,000 made out to "random" individuals on condition that they never attempt to discover who sent it, or reveal where the money came from, except to their husband or wife. The new millionaires would accept the check and experience a series of dramatic events, the details of which would vary with each episode. There was no drama in whether they would accept $1,000,000 from a stranger without context or explanation and who demanded total secrecy. Classic economic theory tells us that a rational person would accept the offer, and the intuition of the television audience was in agreement. However, if a complete stranger were to actually approach you on the street and offer you $1,000,000, with no explanation or preamble, would you or the average person truly just accept the offer without some kind of deliberation or consideration of the situation? You might consider the norm of reciprocity and what future obligations to this person you were incurring, or you might hesitate remembering the aphorism that "if it looks too good to be true, it usually is." In fact, work in psychology and behavioral economics suggests that most people would respond with a kind of bounded rationality (cf. Gigerenzer & Selten, 2002; Kahneman, 2003; Simon, 1982) reflecting a greater knowledge of people and behavior. Perhaps even a strictly Bayesian response might be modulated by the highly improbable nature of this event, which in this case makes this kind of out-of-the-blue offer extremely suspicious.

Imagine a more likely scenario: Someone approaches you to offer $100 that was money you had already spent. Perhaps spending this money was not even originally your choice—you had to spend the money for a tax or a fee or being overcharged. Imagine the person approaching you is a known public figure. Under these circumstances, who would not accept the return of their own money?

Just as in the case of *The Millionaire*, it appears intuitive that no one would be so irrational as to reject the money.

Certainly Bill Frist, the Senate Republican Majority Leader in 2006, thought that taxpayers would readily accept a $100 "rebate," given the soaring price of gas. This was an offer to return $100 to taxpayers with no strings attached. The response was completely unexpected: Senators received direct feedback from taxpayers rejecting the offer. Constituents were angry and insulted by the offer of $100. How can an offer of $100 with no immediate or apparent quid pro quo be viewed as insulting? Perhaps the average taxpayer considered the broader and longer term nature of the energy price problem that this proposal could not truly address and was insulted.

In some sense, the failed Senate Republican proposal has the structure of a simple game that is used in behavioral economics research, the ultimatum game (e.g., Guth, Schmittberger, & Schwartze, 1982; see Thaler, 1988). In this game, two players are apprised of the size of a pot of money. One player (the Allocator) makes an offer about how to split the pot. The other player (the Responder) decides whether to reject or accept the offer. If the offer is accepted, both players get their respective parts of the pot. If the offer is rejected, neither player gets anything. From the perspective of a rationalist economist (e.g., Rubenstein, 1982), the best offer for the Allocator is a penny (or the smallest offer possible) regardless of the size of the pot, and the Responder should accept this offer. Why give up a penny and get nothing when you can keep a penny? However, people do not usually act in this fashion. In general, most Allocators make much larger (and therefore irrational) offers than predicted (see Thaler, 1988), and Responders reject offers that seem insulting relative to some standard of fairness (e.g., Sanfey, Rilling, Aronson, Nystrom, & Cohen, 2003). Furthermore, brain imaging studies indicate that the brain system involved in reward is activated when Responders (in a similar game) spend money to punish unfair partners (de Quervain et al., 2004). This finding has been interpreted as signifying "altruistic punishment," meaning that people are deriving personal pleasure from foregoing their rational self-interests and pursuing what is in the interest of the collective. That is, the behavioral and neuroimaging evidence suggest the operation of bounded rationality and bounded self-interests.

The use of brain imaging to investigate processes of economic decision illustrates a new approach to the study of economic behavior termed "neuroeconomics." Neuroeconomics is an interdisciplinary field with the goal of building a neural model of decision making in economic environments. To achieve this goal, investigators typically examine brain function when individuals formulate or express preferences, evaluate decisions, categorize risks and rewards, or make choices to test economic hypotheses. Our goal in the present chapter is to review foundational issues in neuroeconomics to permit readers to better understand and evaluate the burgeoning literature in this field and its possible relevance to consumer behavior. We will draw from the literature on neuroeconomics to illustrate specific points, but space precludes a complete review of neuroeconomic models per se.

EXPLAINING ECONOMIC DECISIONS

The apparent irrationality of the average economic decision maker has been well studied and documented as contrary to the assumptions of standard economics (e.g., Tversky & Kahneman, 1981). Rational choice theorists have continued to hew to the coldly rationalist model of the individual decision maker in part by questioning the generalizability of those results to actual economical decision settings, in part by reasoning that what appears to be irrational behavior is in fact coldly rational but reflective of utility functions that were incorrectly or incompletely specified, and in part by noting that economic theory makes predictions about aggregate, not individual behavior, and irrationality does not have an impact on aggregate human behavior. For instance, if the irrationality describing individual behavior is unsystematic, then the departure from rationality will sum to zero as one aggregates over individuals, leaving the rational choice theory of economic behavior intact.

Behavioral economists, psychologists, and consumer behaviorists have contested each of these defenses of rational choice theory. Federal Reserve Chairman Alan Greenspan's use of the term "irrational exuberance" in 1996 to describe what he viewed as an overvalued U.S. stock market was an acknowledgement that irrationality was not confined to university experiments. The suggestion that incompletely specified utility functions accounted for what appeared to be irrational decision making, although plausible, is not falsifiable. And the notion that irrationality is haphazard and, therefore, sums to zero when aggregated is not supported by the extant data. A half century ago, McGuire (1960) proposed a theory of belief, which addresses how a change in one belief can impact inferential changes in beliefs and preferences, on which deviations from rationality are systematic and predictable. In McGuire's (1960, 1981) theory, beliefs are conceptualized as having a syllogistic structure, with a major premise ("*Time* magazine has the best movie reviews of any weekly publication"), a minor premise ("Weekly movie reviews are very valuable"), and a conclusion ("*Time* magazine is valuable"). McGuire reasoned that an individual's belief in a premise or conclusion is not necessarily all or none, so a probability or confidence statement can be assigned to each premise and conclusion. The probability of the conclusion can be designated as p(B), the probability of the minor premise can be designated as p(A), and the major premise can be designated as p(B/A). Bayes theorem provides the probability that the conclusion will be held, based on pure logic, given an individual's other beliefs (Wyer & Goldberg, 1970). By a simple extension, changes in beliefs about the major or minor premises produce point predictions about the resulting changes in an individual's endorsement of the conclusion (i.e., preferences).

Empirical research on McGuire's theory has produced evidence for bounded rationality. Evidence for rationality, termed "logical consistency" in the model, refers to the finding that people's endorsement of conclusions is in general accord with predictions derived by Bayes theorem. However, there are also significant discrepancies between predicted and observed conclusions, and the discrepancies are systematic. Specifically, the desirability of the conclusion to an individual influences the likelihood the individual will endorse the belief. This effect, variously termed "wishful thinking" and "hedonic consistency," is especially evident in the behavior of individuals who are less educated (Watts & Holt, 1970).

If individual choice is characterized by bounded rationality and bounded self-interest, and if deviations from these bounded conditions are systematic rather than random, then aggregate prediction of economic behavior, including aggregate consumer behavior, can benefit from a better understanding of the individual decision process.

Although behavioral economists and psychologists have worked to better characterize the psychological process of economic decision making, there are limitations to relying on single behavioral outcomes (i.e., expressed decision) when trying to break down the process into subcomponents (component processes). Of course, additional information can be measured or collected, such as how quickly the decision is made, or how confident or valuable the decision is, or an introspective report of the decision process using a talk-aloud protocol (Waterman & Newell, 1971). But the decision itself reflects the pinnacle of a set of processes and these ancillary measures cannot be parsed into the partial influences of the component processes or mechanisms (cf. Small & Nusbaum, 2004). Simply asking participants about the nature of their decision process is not a reliable means of investigating decision making: The conscious introspective parsing of such processes by participants often deviates significantly from objective measures of processing (e.g., Nisbett &

Wilson, 1977) and is more influenced by folk psychology and biases than the actual processing that takes place. Additive factors methods (Sternberg, 1969) offered some hope for decomposing from a response time measure the component processes underlying the response, but the componential analysis of response times is not without its own limitations and drawbacks (e.g., McClelland, 1979).

Although behavioral measures play an important role, any reliable and valid data that bears directly on the component processes as they unfold contributes to the generation of better theories and better means of falsifying theories. It is partly for this reason that neuroeconomics has quickly gained traction.

Within the last decade, the development of neuroimaging methods has offered a new and more powerful extension of an old approach to understanding the mechanisms that underlie behavior (cf. Petty & Cacioppo, 1986; Coles, Donchin, & Porges, 1986). As we learn about the functional properties of different parts of the brain, this knowledge can guide understanding of other psychological processes. Of course, it is important to note that neuroimaging data are only correlational with behavior and not necessarily the causal basis for behavior (Uttal, 2001). However, there is some reliability across studies of human neuroimaging in terms of the patterns of brain activity, particularly those that correspond to lower level sensory processing (e.g., vision, touch; cf. Gazzaniga, 2004). There is no simple one-to-one mapping between activity in a neural region and psychological function (one region is associated with many functions and one function is distributed across several regions), but there is consistency in the patterns of activity across studies suggesting that distributed networks can be associated with psychological processes. Therefore, although behaviorally a decision itself is realized generally as a single output (e.g., taking money) with few dimensions of analysis (e.g., vigor and speed of response), neurally the decision is accompanied by a spatial and temporal distribution of activity within the brain (Cacioppo & Nusbaum, 2003). This neuroanatomical distribution of brain activity can be related by careful analysis to the specific nature of psychological processing thereby offering a different kind of window into understanding decision making or any psychological function (cf. Small & Nusbaum, 2004).

In addition, it is possible to intervene in the neural processing of specific brain regions thereby testing causal hypotheses about the function of those locations. Of course, each such intervention has its own set of caveats and the localizationist assumptions about the specificity of any intervention may be overly optimistic. However, the lesion model has been used for decades to study the effects of brain damage on neural and psychological processes. Today, it is possible to damage focal areas in animal's brains and evaluate the resulting effects. In addition, it is possible to excite or inhibit neural processes by applying electrical stimulation directly to human cortical tissue (e.g., Penfield & Roberts, 1959; Ojemann, 1991) or to animal brains (e.g., Bliss & Lomo, 1973) or through transcranial magnetic stimulation of human brains (Fadiga et al., 1999). It is also possible to directly change the neural communication that takes place in the brain through the use of drugs, hormones, and other steroids. Thus, bringing the brain into scientific consideration goes beyond just providing a broader picture of the processing underlying economic decision making and offers a new means of testing hypotheses.

FINDING YOUR WAY AROUND THE BRAIN—
ANATOMY, PHYSIOLOGY, AND FUNCTION

A basic assumption of neuroeconomics—as in cognitive and social neuroscience—is that the ability to make judgments and decisions depends on the integrated functioning of the nervous system (Camerer, Loewenstein, & Prelec, 2004). Research in this discipline attempts to identify both the neural systems in which activity is associated with decision-making and the role of these systems in the process. This research is based on a diverse body of research in neural functioning that has examined domains such as motivation, avoidance, drives, and reward among others. To understand this literature, it is important to have at least some basic knowledge of the nervous system. Therefore, we begin here with a very brief description of neural structure and function, from the cellular level to the most complex level of central neural systems. For those with some background and understanding of very general neuroanatomy and physiology, it is safe to skip over this section; for those without this background (see Kandel, Schwartz, & Jessel, 2000), this brief section will lay some foundation for understanding any review of neuroeconomics research.

Neural Communication—Neurons and Circuits, Neurotransmitters

Although the majority of research in neuroeconomics depends on understanding gross brain anatomy and function, we will start with a brief description and review of neural communication, the underlying basis for all neural processes. The basic building blocks of the brain are neurons, whose function is to process, store, and transmit information across the nervous system. The term "information" is used here in a loose way, since the representation of neural information is not understood well. However, it is clear that neurons have internal states that perseverate, that they are modified by inputs from other neurons and from the local chemical and electrical environment in the brain, and that these inputs affect the outputs sent to other neurons (Black, 1994).

Very briefly, the primary process by which neurons interact unfolds as follows: each neuron receives input from thousands of other neurons via terminals, called *synapses*, connected to those neurons. Specific synaptic input provided to the neuron may bias it towards or against sending signals through the use of *neurotransmitters*. These neurotransmitters, as inputs to neurons, change the electrical state of the neuron either by exciting or inhibiting it. The sum of all inputs (both excitatory and inhibitory) therefore determines whether the neuron fires (produces an output). If the input is sufficiently positive to surpass a certain threshold, an electric *action potential* is generated inside the neuron body, which causes it to release neurotransmitter.

Neurons consist of a main body as well as input and output extensions (*dendrites* and *axons*) that provide the means for communication with other cells. Both body and extensions are protected by a membrane, which consists of channels that allow sodium, potassium, and chlorine ions to enter and exit the cell. The permeability of the membrane is variable, that is, in certain conditions (detailed later) the membrane will allow ions to enter and in certain cases it will not. The cell body (or *soma*) contains its nucleus, where the chromosomes with the cell's genetic code are stored and where protein biosynthesis occurs to produce neurotransmitters to stimulate or inhibit other neurons. The nucleus also provides for basic maintenance of the cell as well as structural modifications due to experience (e.g., Kandel, Schwartz, & Jessel, 2000). Dendrites continuously grow and transform throughout life: intellectual activity promotes their growth, but diseases that bring about mental retardation or senility are usually characterized by reduced dendritic length. Drugs such as cocaine and amphetamine can also lead to an increase in dendritic branching in regions associated with high level cognitive functioning. Such increased branching can in turn lead to long-term behavioral effects and can result from changes in experience (e.g., Withers & Greenough, 1989). The terminal endings of the dendrites contain chemical *receptors*, providing the basis for receiving input from other neurons.

In absence of stimulation, the electric potential inside the membrane is negative with respect to environment outside the cell (at approximately –70 mV, called *resting potential*) due to a concentration of negatively charged sodium ions inside the cell and positively charged potassium ions outside the cell. When a neurotransmitter binds at a receptor, ions either enter or exit via the membrane: positively charged sodium ions or negatively charged chlorine ions pass the membrane inward and positively charged potassium ions pass the membrane outward. When positive sodium ions pass the membrane inward, the membrane is depolarized, i.e., its voltage tends to zero. When positive potassium ions pass the membrane outward or negative chlorine ions pass the membrane inward, the internal negative voltage of the membrane increases so that it is hyperpolarized. When the membrane depolarizes to about −50mV, it becomes completely permeable to positive sodium ions until the voltage reverses to about +40 or 50 mV. At the same time, the membrane lets out positively charged potassium ions, thus balancing the inflow of positive sodium ions. This process occurs within half a millisecond, after which the membrane again becomes impermeable to positive sodium ions and its resting potential is restored.

This sudden reversal of polarity and the restoration of the resting potential is the action potential. When the sum of the stimulation received at the dendritic level exceeds the threshold, the action potential is initiated at the cell body and it travels on the axon to the synapses to transmit a signal to other neurons (and the neuron is said to fire or discharge). Action potentials are an all-or-none phenomenon and do not vary in amplitude or intensity, but can vary in frequency. Thus neurons fire an action potential each time the electric potential internal to the membrane reaches threshold. Most neurons fire fewer than 100 times per second, but they can reach a maximum of 1,000 times per second.

For neuroscientists, having the ability to detect the changes in electrical activity caused by action potentials (either via single cell recordings or recording of field potentials) is one of the main tools for studying brain function. The primary means of communication among neurons is generally taken as the firing rate of the neuron. Electrodes inserted into the brain can record these electrical impulses from single neurons, groups of neurons, or from entire population responses. These aggregate population responses can also be recorded from electrodes placed on the scalp and are the basis for electroencephalography (EEG) and the measurement of *event-related potentials* (ERPs). The detection of these population responses at the scalp in ERP experiments is limited to neurons whose axons are oriented perpendicularly to the surface of the cortex. In addition, magnetoencephalography (MEG) can detect changes in the magnetic fields induced by fluctuation in voltage. Moreover, just as electrodes can record brain electrical activity, electrodes can also deliver electrical stimulation to neurons simulating aspects of neural firing. More recently, transcranial magnetic stimulation (TMS) has been used induce electrical current in neural tissue to excite or inhibit neural population responses. These latter two approaches make it possible to test causal hypotheses about neural function by changing the inputs to neural tissue without damaging the brain.

The ability to rapidly generate action potentials within the neuron body is matched by a mechanism that assures rapid propagation of the electrical impulse through the axon so that neurotransmitters are released quickly after generation of an action potential. The axons of most neurons are coated with myelin sheaths, lipidic insulating shells that leave the axon exposed in only specific areas (called *nodes of Ranvier*) thus speeding the axon's electrical conduction. In fact, since the electrical impulse can only travel on the exposed part of the axon's membrane, it "jumps" from one node of Ranvier to the next. These myelinated lengths of axon form the basis for tissue that is detected in diffusion tensor imaging (DTI) which allows the tracing of connections within the brain.

Since axons terminals and dendrites are not in direct contact, when a neuron fires it releases its neurotransmitters in the *synaptic cleft*, a thin break between the cells about 20 nm wide. After the neurotransmitters bind to the receptors on the dendrites they are removed from the cleft by digestion by an enzyme, by being taken back into the neuron (*reuptake*), or by being broken down and rendered inactive (or the combination of the last two). The receptors that come in contact with the neurotransmitters are responsible for the change in the membrane's permeability to the ions. Some receptors also initiate a sequence of chemical changes within the cell, which may further regulate ion inflow. The chemicals involved in this process are called *secondary messengers*. Ligand binding studies allow researchers to radioactively tag neurotransmitter receptors and detect, using positron emission tomography (PET), the distribution of these receptors that form the basis for neural communication. Moreover, iontophoretic application of neurotransmitter agonist or antagonists can increase or decrease specific neurotransmitter effects in particular brain areas (Williams & Goldman-Rakic, 1995) allowing causal tests of hypotheses about neurotransmitter effects (e.g., the role of dopamine in working memory). Similarly, the oral administration of precursors to neurotransmitters, selective serotonin reuptake inhibitors (SSRIs), transmitter agonists and antagonists, and other pharmacologic agents (e.g., amphetamine) can change neurotransmitter function in the brain (Cooper, Bloom, & Roth, 2003), which allows testing for specific cognitive or social effects (e.g., Luciana & Collins, 1997).

When studying how neural activity is associated with behavior, social and cognitive neuroscientists typically study groups, or populations of neurons. These populations are typically determined by anatomical criteria (e.g., cytoarchitectonic criteria), such as being formed of the same cell types with similar connectivity. Neighboring neurons tend to respond to the same or similar stimuli and to connect to the similar neurons or sets of neurons forming networks. When these groups are interconnected or have convergent or divergent connections, they are said to form *neural circuits*.

Brain atlases such as the Talairach and Tournoux (1988) standard allow neuroscientists to use gross anatomical landmarks (such as bumps and turns in gyri or sulci—ridges and valleys) to identify specific anatomical regions. Such anatomical regions have been traditionally assumed to have specific functions. For example, damage to the frontal gyrus (inferior frontal) was identified by Broca (1861) as producing a loss of expressive language function or aphasia. While many such function-region identifications have been made over the years (e.g., see Gazzaniga, 1987), there is now a greater appreciation of the many-to-many mapping between psychological functions and brain regions and the need to consider broader networks in the brain (e.g., Haxby et al., 2001; Nyberg & McIntosh, 2001). However, in recent years there has also been an attempt to identify "functional" regions of the brain (e.g., Kanwisher, McDermott, & Chun, 1997) under the assumption that anatomical criteria may not be as good a demarcation of anatomical specialization as the function itself. Functional regions are identified by using a neuroimaging method that registers changes in neural processing during a specific task. The metabolic activity that accompanies neural processing is detected as functional neural activity in PET (see Posner & Raichle, 1994), and changes in blood oxygenation level resulting from this metabolic activity (see Logothetis, Pauls, Augath, Trinath, & Oeltermann, 2001) are detected as functional neural activity in functional magnetic resonance imaging (fMRI). So called "localizer tasks" can identify brain regions that respond to a particular kind of stimulus or psychological process such as preferential responses to faces relative to other body parts or objects (e.g., Kanwisher, 2000). This functionally defined region can serve as the basis for subsequent study.

A major advance in cognitive and social neuroscience comes from being able to identify patterns of brain activity with anatomical regions whether these regions are defined by purely anatomical criteria or functional criteria. At the same time, there has been a substantial shift in research from studying single brain regions associated with specific psychological functions to identifying complex networks associated with these processes (e.g., Haxby et al., 2001; Nyberg & McIntosh, 2001). In order to understand these networks it is necessary to understand the general structure of the brain. Although it is the neural processes associated with small neuron populations that provide the physical and physiological basis for measuring brain responses, in human neuroscience, the majority of studies focus on the grosser organization of these units into anatomical and functional regions. Understanding how these regions are organized is important to understanding the results of cognitive and social neuroscience research. The next section provides a thumbnail sketch of the overall organization of the anatomical regions of the brain most relevant to understanding neuro-economics research.

The Big Brain Picture—Cortical and Subcortical Parts

There are a number of different ways that neuroscience research describes the landscape of the brain. Given the assumption of some relationship between function and structure, it is important to be able to identify which parts of the brain are involved (active) during different kinds of psychological processing. In order to refer to different parts of the brain, a number of different taxonomic schemes are used in research, with different strengths and weaknesses. However, it is important to be able to recognize which scheme is being used and to have some idea of how to interpret the intended reference.

Brodmann (1909) numbered brain areas according to cellular composition (cytoarchitecture) and this numbering scheme is still widely used to identify different brain regions, although there have been criticisms raised of this work (e.g., von Bonin & Bailey, 1925). Brain regions are numbered from 1 to 52 with subareas identified with letters. For example, Brodmann area 4 refers to primary motor cortex and 22 to a part of the superior temporal gyrus.

A different approach is provided in the stereotactic coordinate system described by Talairach and Tournoux (1988). In many studies, brain areas are referred to by a set of x, y, z coordinates that specify position in the left-right dimension, the anterior-posterior dimension, and the ventral-dorsal dimension (down vs. up). These coordinates are relative to an anatomical landmark called the anterior commissure or AC. Software such as the Talairach Daemon (http://ric.uthscsa.edu/projects/tdc/) maps between this coordinate system and more conventional anatomic designations such as the caudate or superior frontal gyrus. For example, entering Talairach coordinates such as 38, 40, 33 will identify this as the right superior frontal gyrus and Brodmann area 9. In neuroimaging studies, results are often identified by tables of Talairach coordinates that specify the center of mass of brain activity.

Beyond these taxonomic conventions for referring to specific parts of the brain, it is useful to think of the brain in terms of overall structural organization. The more central (medial) parts of the brain are generally viewed as important for regulation of the most basic and essential bodily functions, whereas more lateral parts of the brain, including the cerebral cortex, are mainly involved in higher-level mental functions. Following this general distinction, the brain can be partitioned into subcortical and cortical regions. In terms of evolutionary history, the subcortical systems, physically located underneath the cerebral cortex, developed earlier than the cortex. In what follows, we describe the subcortical areas according to their location in the brain, following a path that begins at the base of the head, where it connects to the spinal cord, and that ends at the cortex. At the same time, we also trace the path of the subcortical systems main functions from the most basic ones to the gradually more complex ones.

Attached to the spinal cord is the *hindbrain*, a system responsible for regulating involuntary musculature and basic bodily functions such as digestion, breathing, heart rate, and blood pressure. Posterior and lateral to the hindbrain is the *cerebellum*, responsible for the ability to coordinate functionally related muscles, execute smooth movements, and integrate motor commands with sensory feedback, although it has been viewed more recently as being important for certain cognitive functions (e.g., Bischoff-Grethe, Ivry, & Grafton, 2002; Justus, Ravizza, Fiez, & Ivry, 2005).

Superior to the brainstem is the *midbrain*, which receives projections from the retina and the ear and therefore contributes to the initial processing of visual and auditory stimuli and the control of visually and auditorily related behaviors. Additionally, neurons in the midbrain that utilize the neurotransmitter *dopamine* (called *dopaminergic neurons*) have been shown to play a pivotal role in processing motivations and rewards (Wise, 1982; Montague, Dayan, & Sejnowski, 1996).

Superior to the midbrain is the *diencephalon*, a system that includes two structures that play an important role in behavior and perception: the *hypothalamus* and the *thalamus*. The hypothalamus regulates body growth, body temperature, hunger, thirst, sexual activity, and endocrine functions (i.e., the production and circulation of hormones in the body). The thalamus, a bulb located centrally superior to the hypothalamus, allows the passage of sensory information (excluding smell) from the sensory organs to the cortical regions and is important for the attentional control of sensory information processing (e.g., Shipp, 2004). Both systems are involved in almost all aspects of behavior and higher functions.

Superior to the diencephalon, located centrally, are the *basal ganglia*, structures associated with the initiation and termination of action and with learning. Finally, wrapped around the thalamus and approximately in the center of the brain, is the *limbic system*, a ring-shaped set of structures that perform several related functions. The most frontal parts of the limbic system include the *amygdala*, a structure that has a main role in the regulation of emotional responses and memory for emotional events. More posterior, structures such as the *hippocampus* and the *mamillary bodies* are pivotal to our ability to form new memories. These structures are immediately adjacent to the cortical areas, or cortex.

The cortex is the part of the brain that has most expanded during evolution and now comprises about 80% of the human brain. The surface has grown in volume and has become more and more convoluted with evolutionary development. Now it covers a surface of about 2500 cm^2, about 1.5 to 3 mm thick. Its folded structure is necessary to fit such a high area in a proportionally small skull. The external surfaces of these convolutions are called *gyri*, and the dips are called *sulci*. Particularly large sulci are called *fissures*. More than two thirds of the cortex is in the sulci.

The cortex consists of layers of neuronal bodies, arranged in groups of different cell types. The density of the neurons' distribution varies depending on the region and the layer of the cortex. The cortex, particularly the regions responsible for the processing of sensory information, has a vertical organization, in that groups of cells at different levels form neural circuits with vertical afferent and efferent connections to groups of cells in other layers. The activity in cortical regions is influenced by their reciprocal connectivity with other regions (called *reentry*) and by feedback loops with subcortical regions as well.

Within the cortex the two largest anatomical structures are the two hemispheres—left and right—which are roughly symmetrical and separated in all their length by a fissure, called *longitudinal fissure*. However, they are connected inferiorly, near the limbic system, by a large band of fibers called *corpus callosum* by which most inter-hemispheric communication occurs. The thalamus, the basal ganglia, and the limbic system are also connected with both hemispheres, thus allowing passage of information as well, though less directly. Due to its high connectivity, the cortex is well designed to process properties of stimuli across different sensory modalities and can perform higher-level processing than the subcortical parts.

The Cortical Terrain of the Mind

Each cortical hemisphere is considered as divided in four lobes: the *occipital* lobe in the inferior and posterior part of the head, the *parietal* lobe in the superior and posterior part, the *temporal* lobe on the lateral sides, at the level of the temples, and the *frontal* lobe, in the superior and frontal part, behind the eyes and forehead.

The occipital, parietal, and temporal lobes contain regions that have direct interactions with thalamic regions and therefore perform the primary and more basic processing of sensory information. These areas are called *primary sensory cortex*. In these areas, sensory information is organized in maps that preserve the initial organization in the sensory organs. For example, the occipital lobes host the primary visual cortex, a fissure located inferiorly near the cerebellum (called *calcarine fissure*), where there are different neurons that respond—among other things—to the orientation, the length, and the movement of visual stimuli. These neural groups preserve the spatial organization of an image initially projected by the light on the eyes' retina in a *retinotopic map*. This kind of topographic representation is typical of representation in many parts of the brain from somatosensory cortex (e.g., Buonomano & Merzenich, 1998) to motor cortex (e.g., Penfield & Jasper, 1954).

The temporal lobes are the location of the primary auditory cortex, a gyrus on the superior convolution, neighboring to the frontal lobe (called *transverse temporal gyrus*), in which neurons are sensitive to different sound frequencies. The parietal lobes host the somatosensory cortex, a superior gyrus bordering the frontal lobe (called *postcentral gyrus*), which is the main receptive area of basic somatic sensations and perceptions. The frontal lobe hosts the *primary motor cortex*, a superior gyrus adjacent to the primary somatosensory area in the parietal lobe and the upper section of the connected sulcus (called *precentral gyrus* and *anterior central sulcus*), whose neurons are responsible for the movement of the body parts.

Adjacent to the primary sensory and motor cortices are areas that perform higher level processing of sensory stimuli, called *association cortex*. Some of these regions receive projections from the primary regions and perform subsequent and more specialized processing the stimuli coming from them (these regions are called *secondary cortex*). For example, in the occipital lobe, the secondary visual cortex (also extrastriate cortex), located around the primary, consists of different neurons that process—among other things—color, form, and movement of objects.

Association cortices include regions connected to both primary and secondary areas, as well as to other lobes. These regions combine information from more than one system when performing complex functions. For example, the *parietal-temporal-occipital association area* includes parts of the parietal, the temporal, and the occipital lobes. It integrates visual information with sensory and auditory information for higher-level functions such as multimodal language comprehension and spatial orientation. Indeed, a number of areas such as the superior temporal sulcus integrate information from different modalities and are active in during a wide range of psychological processes from understanding biological motion (Pelphey, Morris, Michelich, Allison, & McCarthy, 2005; Thompson, Clarke, Stewart, & Puce, 2005) to spoken language (Belin, Zatorre, Lafaille, Ahad, & Pike, 2000; Binder, 2000).

Among the more complex functions that the brain performs are psychological operations sometimes referred to as *executive functions* that involve reasoning, planning, and making judgments and decisions. Performing these functions widely involves the *prefrontal cortex*, the anterior regions of the frontal lobes. These areas play a major role in evaluating future consequences of current actions, monitoring current behavior, choosing more preferable actions over less preferable ones, controlling impulses and socially unacceptable behaviors, pursuing goals, evaluating options, general problem solving and socialization skills. Damage to these areas can result in impulsive behavior, can impair the ability to plan complex sequences of actions, and can inhibit the ability to make a behavior change following changes in the social environment.

Perhaps the most often cited and notable example of the effects of damage to the prefrontal regions is the case of Phineas Gage, a railroad worker who in a dynamite blast was hit by a metal rod. The rod entered his skull and damaged parts of his left prefrontal cortex. Gage survived the accident and healed from the wound, but his behavior radically changed from before the accident. He became careless, unreliable, inappropriately disinhibited, impatient, stubborn, yet capricious, unable to hold on to any plan of future action and unable to keep a job (Harlow, 1868; Damasio, 1994).

Though there is some controversy on which areas of Gage's prefrontal cortex were exactly damaged, it is generally acknowledged that the orbitofrontal cortex (the region of the prefrontal cortex behind the eyes orbits) and sections of the ventromedial cortex (the inferior and central region of the prefrontal cortex) were severely injured (Damasio, 1994; Macmillan, 2000). In experimental settings, neurological patients with similar damages have shown similar impairments in planning (e.g., Bechara, Damasio, Tranel, & Damasio, 1997; Goel, Grafman, Tajik, Gana, & Danto, 1997). Moreover, patients with behavior control problems such as intermittent explosive disorder—a problem of controlling aggressive responses—show behavioral deficits consistent with neurological damage to this region of the brain (Best, Williams, & Coccaro, 2002). Such findings have led to models of self-regulation problems (Davidson, Putnam, & Larson, 2000) and emotional dysregulation as in depression (Davidson, Pizzagalli, Nitschke, & Putnam, 2002) that suggest an important interdependence between prefrontal brain networks and the limbic system. These models suggest that immediate affective responses may be related to specific patterns of activity in the limbic system whereas prefrontal activity may be important in controlling or regulating acting on these affective states.

This interaction among brain systems spans a wide range of psychological situations and includes the failure to restrain aggressive impulses to affective disorders such as depression. However, it also suggests that for complex psychological processes that involve cognition, emotion, and social interaction, a broad set of cortical and subcortical areas will be involved. Historically, much of the research on such complex psychological processing depended on natural "experiments" in which brain trauma adversely affected brain function in particular regions. Such trauma comes from a wide range of sources including accidents such as Gage's, but also including diseases such as herpes simplex encephalitis and stroke, as well as surgical resection in cases of extreme epilepsy. Unfortunately, in these cases damage is seldom restricted to specific anatomical regions. Damage may span large regions of the brain, such as in the case of Broca's patient Leborgne (Dronkers, 2000; Dronkers & Larsen, 2001). Although such cases have been used to draw specific conclusions about the function of particular brain areas (e.g., inferior frontal gyrus and Broca's aphasia, Geschwind, 1970), a damaged brain is not easily compared to an intact brain simply on the grounds of lost brain region or regions. It is reasonable to say that even focal brain damage has effects beyond the local tissue damage including modification of cortical blood flow and neural communication. Thus while much has been learned from patients with brain damage (e.g., Farah, 2004; Farah & Feinberg, 2000), it is also important to be able to measure brain responses during complex psychological processes. Over the past 15 to 20 years, there has been a revolution in neuroscience that has taken place by the development of neuroimaging methods that allow just this kind of measurement (Cabeza & Kingstone, 2001; Posner & Raichle, 1994).

NEUROPHYSIOLOGICAL MEASUREMENTS

Systems neuroscience has contributed a substantial body of knowledge about brain function. Much of our understanding of many cortical and subcortical systems is grounded in neurophysiological research using nonhuman animals. One major contribution of this work has been to map out the relative sensitivities of specific brain areas to different kinds of stimuli and the participation of those areas in particular psychological functions such as vision, learning, and motor control (e.g., Kandel et al., 2000). These studies have been done using a broad array of research methods that includes recording electrical activity from individual neurons and groups, ablation, stimulation, and pharmacologic intervention in neural processing. Prior to the development of functional neuroimaging methods, human neuroscience had few methods for measuring brain activity in ways that could be directly related to this foundational research. However, the development of a variety of new technologies makes it possible to measure neurophysiological activity without the kind of invasive procedures that have been used on nonhuman animals.

These technologies make it possible to study the neural activity that accompanies complex cognitive, affective, and social processes in humans. At present however, each neurophysiological method has specific strengths and weaknesses that make it more suitable for addressing some research questions and less suitable for others. For example, some of the current methods enable measurement of the timing of neural activity with very high accuracy (on the order of milliseconds); these methods measure changes in the electric or magnetic field on the surface of the head, which directly results from patterns of neural firing in the brain. However, when these electrical and magnetic fields are measured from the scalp, it is difficult to determine accurately the sources or generators of these fields. Thus, these measures are said to have good temporal resolution, but relatively poor spatial resolution (on the order of centimeters). In contrast, other technologies have been developed to measure metabolic changes in blood flow or molecular motion, and these enable researchers to assess the location at which neural activity takes place with good spatial precision (on the order of millimeters). However, because these methods depend on metabolic changes that occur on the time scale of many seconds—a scale that is much slower than that of neural firing— they do not offer good temporal resolution.

In this section, we review the major neuroimaging methods used in current cognitive and social neuroscience and neuroeconomics. We describe first those that have good temporal accuracy: *event-related brain potential* (ERP) and *magnetoencephalography* (MEG), and then those that have good spatial resolution: *positron emission tomography* (PET), *functional magnetic resonance imaging* (fMRI) and *diffusion tensor imaging* (DTI).

The ERP method is sensitive to voltage fluctuations (potentials) on the scalp that occur as a consequence of repeated experimental events such as a stimulus presentation (see Fabiani, Gratton, & Federmeier, 2007, for a more extensive introduction to ERP). These voltage changes are attributed to neural population responses resulting from changes in firing rate of neurons organized perpendicular to the lateral surface of the cortex. Where axons are not organized in coherent parallel structures (e.g., cerebellum), these potentials cannot be recorded. As a consequence, only a specific set of neurons are contributing to the measurement of ERPs. ERPs are generally interpreted as reflecting the neurophysiological activity associated with psychological processes involved in performing an experimental task. ERPs are measured by amplifying small voltages recorded by electrodes placed on the scalp of the participant using the same kind of apparatus used for elecroencephalography (EEG). The electroencephalograph takes a continuous readout of the voltage changes measured at the scalp. These EEGs are then averaged across many discrete experimental trials to establish an ERP associated with the event types specific to different trials. The electroencephalograph records electrical activity simultaneously at several locations (Fabiani et al., 2007) ranging from just a few electrodes to as many as 256 with increasing numbers of electrodes providing more reliable information about the cortical location of possible neural generators contributing to the ERPs.

Different procedures can be used to extract ERPs from the continuous EEG measurements, but the most common is averaging those time-locked (or related to a certain time frame) portions of the EEG that correspond to repeated occurrences of the experimental events. In practice, the time periods immediately following the presentation of each type of stimuli are pooled together and averaged to improve the signal to noise ratio. This averaging establishes the typical ERP response to that type of stimulus. The averaging produces a reduction of the noise, because it is assumed that the EEG recordings that are independent of the stimulus presentation vary randomly (Fabiani et al., 2007).

The resulting ERP waveforms are informative of the polarity, latency, and location of the neural activity recorded. Polarity is expressed by positive or negative peaks, and it is assumed to reflect positive or negative activity of neuronal populations. Latency is expressed by the time at which peaks and troughs in the signal appear following the presentation of a stimulus, and has a temporal resolution on the order of few milliseconds. These changes in voltage are thought to reflect the time at which activation or deactivation occurs in postsynaptic sites. Location is expressed by the position of the electrodes on the scalp and reflects the projection of neural activity on the scalp. However, even though the recording is made on the scalp, mathematical methods are necessary to specify in more detail the location of the neural generators of the signal. For such methods the higher the number of electrodes used, the better the spatial resolution of the source of the signal. However, since the brain is a volume conductor of electricity but the head is not a homogeneous medium (the skull distorts the electric field) and many neural structures can generate the same signal, source localization with ERP may not be very accurate (Fabiani et al., 2007), typically localizing signal much more coarsely than other neuroimaging methods.

Magnetoencephalography (MEG) is a method that provides substantially better spatial resolution than ERP, while preserving the same level of temporal accuracy (in milliseconds). However, this technique has other limitations with respect to ERP. MEG is based on the fact that the electrical activity of neural firing produces magnetic fields perpendicular to the electric flow. Sensors that detect extracranial magnetic fields (magnetometers) are placed around participants' heads and record neural activity on the cortical surface.

A drawback of this method is that since only electrical activity tangential and parallel to the head surface gives rise to an extracranial magnetic field and dendrites extend mostly perpendicular to the cortex surface, magnetometers record mainly the activity of the cortical fissures (Hari, Levänen, & Raij, 2000; Hari, 1998). An advantage of MEG over ERP for source localization is that magnetic fields are less sensitive than electrical fields to variations of the conductivity of the medium. Since magnetic fields fade off proportionally with the distance from the source, this localization is mostly effective for the most lateral cortical areas and localization of the signal generator loses accuracy with cortical depth of the generator (Fabiani et al., 2007; Hari et al., 2000).

In order to accurately localize neural activity in deeper and midline brain structures, a different approach is needed. Electrical signals and the magnetic fields resulting from their fluctuations are relatively weak and difficult to localize. Although electrical signals are most closely related to the basis for neural communication, there are other neurophysiological processes closely tied to neuro-electric signals that can be used for more robust measures of the spatial distribution of neural activity. Increases in neural firing rate are related to changes in neural metabolism and the consumption of glucose, oxygen, and water and blood flow. By measuring metabolic and blood oxygenation changes respectively, PET and fMRI measure neural activity indirectly (see Logothetis et al., 2001) allowing researchers to make inferences about the localization of such activity (see Wager, Hernandez, Jonides, & Lindquist, 2007 for a more extensive introduction to both PET and fMRI).

PET measures glucose metabolism, oxygen consumption, and neurotransmitter binding. Protons emitted by radioactive isotopes collide with the electrons in the environment, thus producing measurable electromagnetic radiation. In a PET study, participants first ingest or are injected with a tracer, an infusion that contains a radioactive isotope of carbon, nitrogen, oxygen, or fluorine that diffuses in the brain (and the whole body). As the radioactivity of the tracer decays, it emits positrons that collide with the nearby electrons in the blood. Such collision produces a release of photons that travel in opposite directions and are detected by the photoreceptive cells of the PET scans. These detectors measure the energy resulting from the protons' and electrons' collision from many different angles, thus allowing the reconstruction of a visual image of the density of the radioactive substance in each brain region. The image thus reconstructed reflects the rate of water or glucose intake into a tissue or the binding rate of dopamine, factors that are assumed to depend on the activity of the brain region (Wager et al., 2007; see also Posner & Raichle, 1994). Areas of the brain that have greater neural activity have higher metabolic activity leading to greater uptake of radioactive tracer. The distribution of the tracer (as measured by spatially distributed detectors around the skull) can be related to the amount of neural activity within those tissue areas. Statistical comparison of these measures across different experimental conditions has been used to draw inferences about the activity that might be attributed to the difference in psychological processes across the conditions (e.g., Peterson et al., 1988; Raichle, 2001).

By comparison, fMRI has several advantages with respect to PET. First, it has higher spatial resolution allowing more accurate localization of neural activity. Second, it allows measurements without the ingestion of a radioactive tracer or contrast agent, thus being less invasive and allowing repeated observations and easier application in a research setting. Third, fMRI allows more flexibility in experimental design. PET tracer uptake requires a relatively long period of time and experiment designs take into account longer times (~40 s for PET vs. less than a second for fMRI—although there are physiological limits on hemodynamic response not reflected in this number for fMRI).

These differences are a result of the use of an exogenous radioactive contrast agent in PET compared to a measurement of a natural contrast in the brain using fMRI. In fMRI, local changes in blood flow across brain regions can be assessed by measuring the oxygenation levels of the hemoglobin contained in the blood. It is based on the fact that oxygenated and deoxygenated hemoglobin emit different magnetic signals that can be detected by a magnetic resonance imaging (MRI) scanner. Such a scanner applies a strong magnetic field around a participant's heads so that the protons present in the biological tissues change the direction of their rotation axis (precession) and align it with that of the magnetic field. The MRI signal is created by applying a second pulsating magnetic field perpendicular to the first one. When this field is on, it perturbs the precession equilibrium the first magnetic field had created. When it is off, the protons are free to align again to the first magnetic field. This process of realignment (called relaxation) can take different amounts of time depending on the density of the microscopic medium of the measured protons (Jezzard & Clare, 2001; Wager et al., 2007).

Magnetic resonance images reflect a contrast: either between structurally different brain tissues (using MRI), or between functionally different tissues (using fMRI). To construct structural images of the brain (i.e., structural images of the types used for medical purposes), the magnet measures the relaxation rates of mostly hydrogen protons contained in water molecules, because they have the strongest sensitivity to the magnetic field (compared to other biological important atoms) and are ubiquitous in cerebral tissues. Because different structures have different water concentration, the relaxation rates of hydrogen protons vary across different brain structures. Consequently, the resulting signals reflect structural differences (Jezzard & Clare, 2001; Wager et al., 2007).

To construct functional images—or images of brain functioning—scanners measure variations of relaxation rates caused by variations in the magnetic susceptibility of blood hemoglobin. Because of metabolic processes, hemoglobin may contain more or less oxygen. When brain cells increase their activity, they consume oxygen. This is reflected in increased levels of deoxygenated hemoglobin. However, this temporary increase in de-oxygenation is quickly followed by a more long-lasting increase in blood flow to the region, which brings with it oxygenated hemoglobin. Thus areas that are involved in the neural functioning will be associated with a change in the local concentration of oxygen in the blood. Since oxygenated and deoxygenated hemoglobin have different relaxation rates, such blood oxygenation level dependent changes (BOLD signal) in the magnetic resonance signal reflect brain regions' consumption of oxygen, which is taken to reflect their differential activation (Jezzard & Clare, 2001; Wager et al., 2007).

Magnetic resonance imaging is used in different ways to capture both the structure and the function of neural tissue. Recent advances suggest that this approach will be useful for measuring additional aspects of brain structure and function. These differences can be realized by changing the pulse sequence by which the scanner generates signals. For example, *diffusion tensor imaging* (DTI) is carried out using the same kind of scanner as is used for MRI and fMRI with a different kind of programming. This technique does not measure brain function, but images the connectivity between different regions. It is based on the fact that in cerebral tissue the motion of water molecules, or water diffusion, is restricted by the myelin sheaths on the neurons' membrane (see Zhang, Kindlmann, & Laidlaw, 2005 for a more extensive introduction to DTI). In absence of restrictions, water molecules tend to move randomly in all directions (Brownian motion), but the properties of the medium in which they move can constrain the direction of this motion. For example, in pure liquids such as water, Brownian motion is unconstrained and it is said to be isotropic. However, cell membranes and large protein molecules present in biological tissues often restrict this motion of water molecules (Cooper, Chang, Young, Martin, & Ancker-Johnson, 1974). In the brain, the myelin coating on the axons membrane and the architecture of the axons in parallel bundles restrict the movement of the water molecules in directions perpendicular to the axons, favoring only their diffusion along the axons. This movement with preferential direction is called anisotropic movement, and it is what DTI measures and images (Le Bihan, 1991).

In DTI, water diffusion in brain tissue is described by using the concept of tensor, an array of three-dimensional vectors. A tensor describing diffusion in all spatial directions is calculated for each volume unit of the brain. This is accomplished by collecting data from six encoding directions. In an anisotropic diffusion, the highest value of the tensor matrix reflects the direction of maximum diffusion, and the lowest value the direction of minimum diffusion. In an isotropic diffusion, the three values of the tensor matrix are equal. Thus, the differences in anisotropy between different brain regions allow researchers using DTI to map the tracts that have best conductivity in the brain, thus indirectly measuring brain connectivity (Peled, Gudbjartsson, Westin, Kikinis, & Jolesz, 1998; Wager et al., 2007) and to study the disruption of fiber tracts in patient populations (e.g., Johansen-Berg et al., 2004).

The development of modern neuroimaging methods makes it possible to relate statistically specific aspects of psychological processing with neural activity in different parts of the brain. Although a lot of research is carried out by assessing how the magnitude of neural activity changes with psychological processing, many theories of brain function are quite simple. For example, the notion that face perception is carried out by a single brain region (fusiform face area, Kanwisher et al., 1997) has given way to the notion that a broad network of brain areas work together during face perception (e.g., Haxby et al., 2001). This change from an emphasis on single region-single function theory to distributed neural networks (e.g., Nyberg & McIntosh, 2001) carries with it a need to understand both the distribution of neural activity as well as the nature of the connectivity among areas in the brain. DTI and fMRI therefore provide very different views that can converge on the types of neural network descriptions that will be needed for the most complex psychological processes such as those studied in neuroeconomics.

ISSUES IN STUDYING THE BRAIN TO UNDERSTAND THE MIND

The development of new neuroimaging methods has produced a significant change in the field of psychology with the emergence of cognitive neuroscience (Gazzaniga, 2004) and more recently social neuroscience (Cacioppo & Berntson, 2005). These methods make it possible to measure neural activity in healthy intact human brains carrying out complex psychological processing. For many researchers, neuroimaging is taken simply as a new dependent measure of psychological processing that can be applied to test hypotheses about the difference in neural responses in two different conditions. While this is true in one respect, this overlooks the fact that neuroimaging is a qualitatively different method (e.g., Small & Nusbaum, 2004) measuring different properties in a different way. In addition, there is a tendency to attribute greater validity to neurophysiological measurements compared to behavioral measurements because the former are perceived as being direct and unmediated (see Cacioppo & Nusbaum, 2003). It is therefore important to understand what neuroimaging measures can tell us about psychology and the brain and what the limitations of these measures are.

Behavioral research on judgment and decision making has produced a wealth of evidence showing that people do not always behave in the most rational and utility-maximizing way (see Gilovich, Griffin, & Kahnemann, 2002, for a review). One of the benefits in applying neuroimaging techniques to the study of decision making is the promise of being able to spatially and anatomically decompose some of the systems and processes involved in producing decisions and choices. Of course, this research method relies on the assumption that there is a systematic relationship between psychological functions and behavior and brain activity. However, it is always important to remember that neuroimaging measures—indeed all neurophysiological measures—are simply correlative (associated) with behavior and mental activity (see Uttal, 2001). There is a temptation to view measures of brain activity as the cause of a behavior or mental process under investigation but the reality is that these measures are only statistically associated with the processes of interest. For example, there could always be unmeasured activity that is directly causally responsible.

Behavioral measures such as overt responses and reaction times are informative of processing outputs and of the time it takes to perform a task, but they offer limited insight on the mental operations taking place during each stage of processing. Neuroscience methods provide independent information as to the components of processing underlying different behaviors by offering an indirect but canonical observation into the activity going on inside the "black box" of the brain. Specifically, measuring correlates of neural activity offers two main advantages for developing theories of decision making and neuroeconomics. First, these methods make it possible to identify brain regions associated with the performance of psychological functions. This is best seen in technologies that offer good spatial resolution of cerebral activity (PET, fMRI). For example, analyses of fMRI data can reveal what brain regions are activated in a statistically reliable way during a given cognitive task and which brain regions are differentially active during the performance of two different tasks. Second, measures of neural activity permit the identification of rapid changes in neural activity during the performance of a task. This is best achieved by technologies that offer good temporal resolution (ERP, MEG). For example, the different peaks and troughs of an ERP waveform reflect the continuous changes that take place in neural activity of neuron populations during the performance of specific tasks. Such measurements are acquired without the need for overt behavioral responses (although such responses are often required at some points during the experiments to make sure participants actually do the tasks as asked). This is not simply a practical advantage, because behavioral responses during a cognitive task can change how the task is performed. Overt responses can affect neural activity in the systems of interest (Hasson, Nusbaum, & Small, 2006; Small & Nusbaum, 2004).

In what follows, we describe in greater detail some of the primary advantages offered by measuring brain activity in terms of localization of function and detection of changes in neural activity over time. Concurrently, we discuss the theoretical assumptions on the relationship between psychological processes and their neural implementation, which are the working assumptions at the basis of brain imaging techniques.

Prior to the advent of neuroimaging, patients with brain lesions, such as Phineas Gage, were used as evidence that damage to relatively circumscribed areas of the brain can result in the loss of relatively specific functions—even though these cases seldom had truly anatomically circumscribed damage. As a consequence, over time researchers have generally accepted the claim that circumscribed brain regions can be associated with specific mental functions (e.g., see Farah & Feinberg, 2000; Gazzaniga, 1987; Geschwind, 1970). Certainly acceptance of this position was not without controversy, with some arguing that brain activity should instead be regarded as a distributed or holistic process (e.g., Ivry & Robertson, 1997). This tension between the localistic and distributed approaches to brain functions is still evident in current imaging research.

In the case of some "simple" psychological functions, the localistic assumption is often taken to be reasonable (e.g., face perception in the fusiform; Kanwisher et al., 1997). In these cases, neuroimaging techniques have contributed to the understanding of what neural substrates underlie psychological functions by allowing for localization of neural activity in specific areas associated with those psychological functions. Studies that examine localized activity in specific brain regions are perhaps most informative when examining whether structures already known to be involved in specific functions are also involved in others. For example, after identifying the amygdala as a structure that plays an important role in emotional responses, researchers have shown that activity in the amygdala shows differential activity for more and less racist people (Phelps et al., 2000). However, even for such simple cases, the evidence supporting the claim of simple function-anatomy relationships is weak. For example, is the fusiform gyrus specialized for face perception (Kanwisher, 2000) or is it specialized for a kind of general learned visual expertise (Gauthier, Skudlarski, Gore, & Anderson, 2000)? Although the fusiform is one of a small number of areas argued to be specialized for a particular psychological function, other research has shown convincingly that the same kind of information available in the fusiform face area is available widely throughout the brain (Haxby et al., 2001). The difference in findings can be attributed in large part to the difference in methods. By restricting data analyses to functionally defined localized regions, and requiring activation to meet a very stringent criterion, it is easy to overlook more complex patterns of information encoded in population and network responses.

When it comes to more complex functions that engage cognitive, affective, and social processes, understanding neural mechanisms is considerably more complicated. Such functions are most likely a result of modulated conjoint activity distributed across several different networks rather than the result of activity in one particular network of brain regions. When a number of neural networks are associated with a certain complex phenomenon, there are at least two ways to understand how their joint activity is associated with the cognitive function. One approach is to regard each network activated or modulated during the performance of a particular cognitive function as a component network that contributes to an identifiable part of the entire process. For example, a component network can be responsible for an early or late stage of a complex process that is composed of a set of psychological functions (cf. Cacioppo et al., 2003; Passingham, Stephan, & Kötter, 2002). For example, Cacioppo and Nusbaum (2003) discussed the set of apparently disjoint brain regions active in different conditions of a simple neuroeconomics experiment. Rather than view these as very different areas active in each of four cells of a design, it may be more informative to view all four cells of the design as involving a motor network (each cell involved a response), a utility or valuation network (as outcome evaluation was involved), and a calculation network (as odds were calculated). What might appear to be separate and unrelated brain areas can often be related to differential modulation of networks that subserve identifiable psychological functions. Such functions might include working memory (see Smith & Jonides, 1998), motor planning and control (see Bizzi & Clarac, 1999), action understanding (see Rizzolatti & Craighero, 2004), attention (see Shipp, 2004), and theory of mind (e.g., Saxe & Kanwisher, 2003), and many other cognitive and affective functions. Each of these psychological functions plays an important role in a wide range of daily activities but their role and importance may be modulated by the specific demands and nature of the activity or task. Thus what might appear to be a strange collection of unrelated brain areas may be more interpretable if viewed as modulate fragments of a set of neural networks representing coordinate psychological functions.

A different approach to understanding joint activity of multiple regions is to posit that the psychological function is a result of synchronization in the activity of several brain areas. For example, research has shown that even during rest, neural activity is distributed into functional networks characterized by synchronized activity within the network (Fox et al., 2005). Thus, on this approach, the activity in the network of brain regions is not a sum of a parts but an emergent feature of synchronized activity in the network (cf. Gabrieli, Poldrack, & Desmond, 1998).

The message from these findings is that patterns of detected neural activity should be interpreted while keeping in mind that behaviorally defined psychological constructs do not map isomorphically on brain activity (Cacioppo et al., 2003; Sarter, Berntson, & Cacioppo, 1996). In other words, psychological functions such as memory, emotion, or decision making, that have been originally defined in contexts of behavioral performance, are theoretical constructs that do not bear a unitary correspondence with neural activity in certain brain regions (e.g., Gabrieli et al., 1998).

Complicating matters even further, finding regional brain activity that is associated with a specific function does not allow for drawing the inference that this area actually contributed to the task, because its activation could instead depend on cognitive or physiological contextual factors (e.g., the attention devoted to the task, the strategy adopted, specific features of the task; Cacioppo & Tassinary, 1990). These modulations can affect even brain regions thought to perform relatively low-level perceptual operations (Hopfinger, Buonocore, & Mangun, 2000). Additionally, since the brain is to a certain extent able to complete the same functions using different mechanisms, contextual factors can influence which structures and systems are employed to perform a certain function.

Furthermore, interpreting the lack of differences in neural activity between two conditions cannot allow for drawing the conclusion that the area is not a neural substrate for the operation in this specific instance (assuming that the technique used was sensitive enough to measure it). For example, Phelps et al. (2000) presented participants with faces of white and black people and examined amygdala activity. They found no difference in activity between the conditions, which could have been erroneously interpreted as suggesting that the structure does not mediate emotional responses. However, the reason for the null effect was that the more racist participants showed more activity to black faces in this region, whereas the less racist participants showed the opposite pattern. Perhaps more important still, Phelps et al. (2000) subsequently showed that this apparent difference could be due to differential familiarity with the faces for the different groups. Hence, even null results do not rule out the involvement of a region in a cognitive function. Furthermore, the standard notion of activation (BOLD response) that exceeds a statistical threshold overlooks other models of detecting neural population response. Besides regressing behavioral measures onto brain activity to look for a relationship (instead of an absolute effect) as Phelps and others have in various ways (e.g., Hasson et al., 2004), it is possible to look for relationships in the patterns of activity across areas (e.g., Nyberg & McIntosh, 2001).

In some cases, activation of diffusely organized systems does not yield a strong enough signal to differentiate it from noise, or can be overestimated if only a region within a larger network of activation is detected. Finally, localization can be underestimated if overlapping systems are activated in performing multiple functions (Cacioppo, Tassinary, & Berntson, 2007). Thus simply seeking "active areas" may not be as effective a research strategy as modeling the activation relationships among areas or between neural and behavioral response patterns.

The interpretation of rapid changes in indexes of neural activity using ERP and MEG should also be done with caution. Whereas behavioral reaction times consist of a single measure that includes the entire processing span to that point, measuring the neural activity during task performance is done on a temporally continuous scale and intrinsically offers insight into different stages of the processing. ERP waveforms, for example, describe the continuous varying of neural activity over time during the performance of a task.

Here too, the interpretation of the characteristic properties of ERP waveforms is subject to certain important assumptions. Processing times are often interpreted as a linear summation of cognitive processing stages (e.g., Sternberg, 1969; Treisman & Souther, 1985), but this type of inference is more difficult for ERP waveforms. Peaks and troughs may have some degree of correspondence with the different stages of processing as defined cognitively (much research assumes that there is, and tried identifying components that map onto theoretical processes), but some have argued that there is not an isomorphic relationship between ERP peaks and troughs (components) and cognitive components (Cacioppo et al., 2003; Sarter et al., 1996). A cognitive processing stage can affect more than one ERP component at a time and several cognitive stages can affect a single ERP component. Furthermore, even when certain components do map onto recognized cognitive functions, such components can be generated in parallel and as a result sum together or cancel each other out in the waveform.

The logic underlying this argument applies also to subtractive analysis, a strategy often used in experiments that measure neural activation (Raichle, 2001; Friston et al., 1996). Subtractive analysis refers to a method of data analysis in which scientists compare neural activity during a task that utilizes a certain component process to that occurring during a baseline control task that does not include that component. For example, the activity of reading words (experimental condition) could be compared to that of viewing a cross (baseline condition). Since both conditions involve basic visual processing but only the experimental condition involves word recognition, the subtractive method should allow for canceling out the basic visual processing, thus detecting the neural activity involved in word recognition (Petersen et al., 1989). The assumption behind this logic is that inserting a cognitive component to a task evokes additional physiological activation in a way that does not affect earlier ones in the sequence (pure insertion; Friston et al., 1996). In other words, it is assumed that there is not dependency between how earlier stages of processing are performed and the nature of later processing stages. However, this assumption of independence between the stages is invalid if the relationship between psychological functions and brain activity is nonlinear, and this issue is, in itself, a topic of ongoing research. A better way to design experiments is to integrate subtraction methods with factorial and parametric designs abandoning the assumption of pure insertion (Friston et al., 1996; Cacioppo et al., 2003).

However, with the application of independent components analysis (e.g., Calhoun, Adali, Kraut, & Pearlson, 2001), structural equation modeling (Buchel & Friston, 1997; Horwitz, Tagamets, & McIntosh, 1999; McIntosh & Gonzalez-Lima, 1994), and other covariance based approaches, it becomes easier to begin to understand patterns of neural activity in complex psychological processes. These techniques have been applied across several different neuroimaging and neurophysiological methods as there is a greater trend towards understanding brain responses in terms of distributed representations across neural populations interacting over time. Since Nyberg and Mcintosh (2001) introduced the concept of the "neural context of processing," it becomes more important to consider that functional networks may be dynamically assembled by the demands of any particular task. While this complexity may seem discouraging given the initial optimism and apparent simplicity inherent in the notion of noninvasively measuring a person's brain activity while engaged in a complex psychological process from making moral decisions (Greene, Sommerville, Nystrom, Darley, & Cohen, 2001; Greene, Nystrom, Engell, Darley, & Cohen, 2004) to religious experience (Azari et al., 2001), it really should serve to remind us that we do not understand the brain any better than we understand the mind. However, with appropriate caveats and concerns it may be possible to study mind and brain together in real psychological settings.

THE NEUROSCIENCE OF UTILITY

How do we decide to buy something? When framed in the abstract, the problem is simple and economists generally consider such problems as abstractions. Given a goal of buying, with a set of options, we try to evaluate the options in some fashion and pick the best one. The concept of *homo economicus* is the basis for most economists' views of economic decision making. This is a rational agent who operates by a very idealized set of decision principles, perhaps best characterized by a Bayesian process that takes into account past outcomes and sets the determination of a decision in the context of the alternatives. However, there are a number of known findings in behavioral economics that argue against the strictest form of this model. Framing effects, temporal discounting, and a wide range of context effects all indicate that a decision is not made solely on the merits of costs and benefits but can be shaped by influences such as wishful thinking (Maguire, 1990). While such apparent deviations from homo economicus seem to be appalling human frailty, in fact, these may reflect much broader cognitive mechanisms found across a wide evolutionary swath of species (e.g., Chen & Hauser, 2005; Marsh & Kacelnik, 2002; Padoa-Schioppa & Assad, 2004).

In economic terms, the value of a choice, also called utility (or expected utility), is a subjective property that can be thought of as gratification or satisfaction associated with the outcome of a choice (Fellows, 2004). Expected utility has two fundamental components: one is the magnitude of the reward that the chosen option would provide (e.g., the amount of money a person could gain) and the other is the probability that the choice would lead to obtaining the reward (e.g., the likelihood that that specific option would really yield that amount of money; Bernoulli, 1954). Thus, according to the standard economics model, assessing the value of an option involves calculating the magnitude of the reward and estimating the probability to gain it. While simple to state, both of these are not easy to do in practice. For example, the same choice received immediately has a different reward value than when it is received at some point in the future. This phenomenon of temporal discounting is well known and described (e.g., Laibson, 1997; McClure, Laibson, Loewenstein, & Cohen, 2004a) but it is not understood. For short time delays, for example, people tend to choose more immediate and smaller rewards. Thus, if offered $50 in an hour or $55 in a month, most people would choose $50 in an hour. When the delay is long, people tend to choose a later and greater reward, thus maximizing utility. Thus, if offered to choose to obtain $50 in 12 or $55 in 13 months, most people would choose to wait 13 months for the $55 (see Rachlin, 2000, for a review).

While temporal discounting can be determined behaviorally by measuring the value a person puts on immediate vs. delayed rewards (perhaps by asking a participant to set a price for goods received immediately and at different delays) this pattern of response cannot explain the source of discounting. For example, even if told that someone will receive a reward with 100% probability in five minutes or in five weeks, the Bayesian prior certainly drops for receiving something the longer you wait. As an event occurrence recedes into the future, the chances of it actually occurring drop. Thus, given a simple two-stage model of assigning value and probability of receiving the value, it is possible that the estimate of the probability of gaining a reward drops with increasing delay. On the other hand, it is possible that the hedonic value of an object recedes with anticipated delay. This cannot be determined easily in the paradigm of behavioral economics. However, neuroimaging and some knowledge of functional neuroanatomy can shed light on this kind of question.

If participants are presented with choices, differing in face value (e.g., gift certificates of varying denominations) and differing in amount of delay from no delay to weeks, it is possible to give pairs in which the immediate reward has a lower face value than the delayed reward or vice versa. At some face value differences, a smaller but immediate reward will typically be preferred—this is the basis of temporal discounting. However, pairs can be constructed for which both rewards differ in face value but can be received in the near term, or with some delay for the soonest. In this way it is possible to separately assess the impact of the face value of the rewards, the impact of the soonest one could receive a reward, and the impact of the delay between them.

If these choices are made in an fMRI scanner, it is possible to assess both the behavioral choice and the corresponding patterns of brain activity (McClure et al., 2004a). In one study, McClure and colleagues postulated the existence of two different brain systems implicated in the behavior of temporal discounting. The first set of structures are regions of the limbic system that serve as part of the brain's reward system, and these structures should respond strongly to the prospect of immediate rewards. The second set of structures consists of the lateral prefrontal areas implicated in cognitive decision making. This second set would be associated with the more "rational" decision making about the long term rewards, for which the limbic system should be less active.

The neuroimaging results indeed implicated two different sets of brain regions. One set was most active when one of the choices was immediately available and included a set of medial brain structures closely associated with the limbic system including ventral striatum, medial orbitofrontal, medial prefrontal, posterior cingulate, and left posterior hippocampus. The second set of structures were active independent of the delay and included right dorsolateral prefrontal cortex, right ventrolateral prefrontal cortex, right lateral orbitofrontal cortex, intraparietal cortex, regions of visual cortex, and areas in the motor system. The areas affected by the magnitude of the delay were the prefrontal and orbitofrontal regions. Thus McClure et al. (2004a) found activity in a visual network (for perceiving stimuli), motor areas (for responding), and areas involved in numerical calculation (e.g., intraparietal cortex). From this study, one could draw the conclusion that the hedonic evaluation of utility is carried out by the limbic structures that are most active in the near term reward conditions whereas the probability of reward and rational assessment of utility is carried out in these prefrontal structures. This division seems to partition the notion of utility in ways that are not anticipated in the standard economic view and is not be available from behavioral data alone.

Other studies have also provided evidence that the mechanisms underlying expected utility may not be as simple as conceived from behavioral studies. Indeed, it appears that the evaluation of utility is associated with activity in a neural network involving subcortical regions projecting to the frontal cortical areas (see Sanfey, 2004; Knutson & Peterson, 2005, for reviews). The subcortical regions of this network involve part of the basal ganglia and limbic system. In particular, the striatum (part of the limbic system) contains the nucleus accumbens (located ventrally) which is a region that has been found to play an important role in decision making processes (detailed later;

Knutson, Adams, Fong, & Hommer, 2001a; Knutson, Fong, Adams, Varner, & Hommer, 2001b; Knutson, Taylor, Kaufman, Peterson, & Glover, 2005). These areas are related to the ventral striatum identified by McClure et al. (2004a) as involved in a neural "hedonic" response to immediate rewards. The cortical areas include mostly the medial prefrontal cortex (Knutson et al., 2005; Knuston & Peterson, 2005) and are also are active in the neural response to immediate rewards. This supports the notion that utility has a strong limbic component as suggested by McClure et al. (2004a).

Research that directly examines the neural processing of utility have mostly focused on expected utility, which is operationalized as anticipation of gains and losses (Knutson et al., 2001a, 2001b, 2005), although without consideration of the temporal discounting process. Using fMRI, Knutson and colleagues demonstrated that when participants were anticipating a near-term gain, neural activity in subcortical areas (the thalamus and the striate) correlated with the magnitude of this gain (Knutson et al., 2001a). The thalamus and the dorsal striatum showed increased activation when participants expected both gains and losses, indicating that activity in these regions is not sensitive to the valence of the outcome. In contrast, the nucleus accumbens (the ventral striatum) showed activation only when participants expected gains (Knutson et al., 2001a). This suggests that distinct neural systems are involved in anticipating gains and losses. Furthermore, the activation of the nucleus accumbens decreased once participants obtained the reward, suggesting that activity in this brain structure is more related to anticipating the expected value of a reward rather than to experiencing the reward itself (this has been referred to as a dissociation between expected value and actual value; Knutson et al., 2001b).

The economical notions of value and monetary reward are clearly linked to basic aspects such as reward drive. It is therefore important to note that the striate is innervated by the dopamine system: dopamine neurons have been found to be sensitive to the magnitude of the reward (e.g., Tobler, Fiorillo, & Schultz, 2005) and there is a positive correlation between dopaminergic release in the ventral striatum and self-reports of positive affective states (Drevets et al., 2001; Volkow et al., 2002). In Knutson and colleagues' studies, participants reported higher positive affect (as measured by arousal) when expecting greater gains (Knutson et al., 2001a, 2005). Thus, one hypothesis is that both the increased activation of the ventral striatum and the positive mood ratings might depend on dopamine release. In these studies it was also found that failure to obtain expected rewards was associated with deactivation in medial prefrontal cortex. This has been taken to suggest that the region is involved in providing feedback when rewards are different than expected (Knutson et al., 2001b; 2005). Thus, the regions sensitive to expected value and obtained value are different.

Of course, the expectation and experience of a particular outcome or reward is only part of the notion of utility. It is also important to be able to determine the probability of any particular outcome. Some of these studies have also begun to address this question as well. Activity in participants' medial prefrontal cortex has been shown to correlate with the probability of obtaining a reward (Knutson et al., 2005). This region was not activated when the probability to gain a reward was constant, suggesting that it is a region sensitive to changes in outcome probability (Knutson et al., 2001b). It is also important to note that this region was active in the McClure et al. (2004a) study for immediate rewards but it was not independent of delay. If this area is involved in calculation of probability of an outcome, it is different from the kind of numerical calculation that is explicit in the precuneus, paracentral region, and parietal cortex (Zago et al., 2001) and from odds calculation in other economic decision research (see Cacioppo & Nusbaum, 2003). An alternative interpretation of the medial prefrontal activity is that it is related to relative risk assessment in cases of anticipated reward (e.g., Cacioppo & Nusbaum, 2003).

Studies examining the neural mechanisms involved in the assessment of value reveal activity in large parts of the prefrontal cortex and limbic system: these regions include the orbitofrontal cortex (e.g., Arana et al., 2003; Baxter et al., 2000; Padoa-Schioppa & Assad, 2006) the anterior cingulate cortex (e.g., Carter et al., 1998; Paulus & Frank, 2003), and the amygdala (e.g., Arana et al., 2003; Baxter et al., 2000). The differences in results among these studies appear to depend on a combination of several factors: how reward and value have been operationalized (e.g., incentive for action, hedonic properties, guide for learning), task features (e.g. presence or absence of a choice, preference judgments), the measures used (e.g., more invasive and reliable cell recordings on animals, or noninvasive imaging studies on humans; see Fellows, 2004, for a review).

The involvement of the amygdala, the dopamine system, and their relation to positive arousal discussed up to this point suggests that brain regions involved in affect significantly impact economic decision making. Making a decision in a risky situation, where there are chances of both gains and losses, is very likely to elicit emotions. In this situation, two types of emotions have been individuated: anticipatory emotions and anticipated emotions. Anticipatory emotions are those triggered by risk and uncertainty themselves, include fear and anxiety (Loewenstein et al., 2001), and have been shown to lead to cautious and risk aversive decisions (Lerner & Keltner, 2001). Anticipated emotions are those expected to be experienced once the choice is made and are thus integral part of the expected consequences of the decision (Loewenstein et al., 2001). These emotions may induce a person to misrepresent probabilities (Loewenstein et al., 2001; Maguire, 1990). For example, people in a negative affective state judge deaths by floods and strange diseases as more likely than people in a positive state (Johnson & Tversky, 1983). Moreover, such emotions may desensitize a person to changes in probability (Loewenstein et al., 2001). For example, people's anxiety, as measured by physiological changes in anticipation of an imminent shock, is the same regardless of the stated likelihood of the shock (unless this probability is said to be zero; Bankart & Elliott, 1974).

Understanding the neural mechanisms underlying emotion has grown to be a substantial research enterprise on its own (see Damasio, 2000; Panksepp, 1998; Rolls, 1999). However, it has become clear from the study of neural mechanisms in decision making, personality, and even depression (Damasio, 1994; Davidson et al., 2002) that an overlapping set of complex neural networks is involved in all of these. According to these studies, the dopaminergic system connecting amygdala, hippocampus, anterior cingulate cortex, and prefrontal cortex constitute a unitary network involved in both the representation and the regulation of affect, and this is proving to be more important in understanding economic decision making than would be suggested by the standard view of homo economicus.

One view of the medial prefrontal cortex (e.g., Knutson & Peterson, 2005) is that it is involved in calculating the probability of a positive reward. Indeed, research has indicated that prefrontal structures can be activated even in cases of evaluating abstract or symbolic gains or losses (e.g., O'Doherty et al., 2001). This seems a slightly different interpretation than McClure et al.'s (2004a) view that these structures are part of the impulsive-passionate affective response system that drives the utility valuation of immediate rewards. The difference between the formation of an expectation or probability of an outcome seems different from the impulsive limbic drive for immediate reward. Indeed, the notion of expectation of a reward may be very different from a simple probability. Patients with damage to these brain structures do not simply fail to anticipate a negative outcome in their choice behavior based on past probabilities—they also fail to show physiological evidence of an affective reaction (Bechara et al., 1997). As a result, Bechara and colleagues argued that these prefrontal structures can serve a regulatory role in behavior. By recording past affective experiences along with the context of their occurrence, ventromedial prefrontal cortex can bias cognitive determinations in other cortical regions through projections of various types.

Clearly, the connection between the ventral striatum and prefrontal areas that are active in the McClure and colleagues' (2004a) study in response to near-term reward is an important part of understanding the concept of utility. However, the role of the prefrontal regions may not be in the affective appreciation of an anticipated reward but rather in biasing action in service of receiving that reward. At the present time, there are thus several views about the function of prefrontal regions including direct participation in the hedonic value of reward, estimation of the probability of reward, and a biasing signal anticipating reward in response to choice

Beyond their implication in monetary reward in neuroeconomics studies, the striatum and its midbrain dopaminergic interactions are clearly an important part of the neural reward system (Schultz, 2000). The striatum responds to sexual arousal (Karama et al., 2002), humor (Mobbs, Greicius, Abdel-Azim,Menon, & Reiss, 2003), drug hedonic value (Wise & Hoffman, 1992; Robinson & Berridge, 1993) and is generally viewed as part of a complex system that includes prediction of reward and the reinforcing outcome of reward. As a result it is clear why it would be a target system for understanding the neural mechanisms underlying the concept of utility in economics. It should also be clear that there are more components to the system than would be postulated by a model that only takes into account probability and value. For example, the dorsal striatum may be more involved with the prediction of reward while the ventral striatum may be more involved with maintenance of outcome information to aid in biasing choices (e.g., O'Doherty et al., 2004). In this case, prediction of rewards and biasing selection are very different operations from appraising value and estimating probability of outcome as a more standard economic view might suggest. Moreover, there is neural evidence that the attributed utility of a reward (money earned) is different depending on whether the reward is contingent on behavior or not (earned vs. simply received)— the striatum is more active for an earned reward (Zink, Pagnoni, Martin-Skurski, Chappelow, & Berns, 2004) suggesting that it is less responsive to the face value of a choice than all the anticipated and integrated hedonic dimensions. However, at this point it seems plausible that there will be no single part of the brain that is simply registering utility and no single part registering probability.

THE NEUROSCIENCE OF CHOICE

From an economic perspective, understanding utility should be sufficient to explain choice behavior. This would suggest a relatively straightforward neural model of consumer decisions. Items that produce greater levels of activity within the limbic areas identified with utility evaluation should be selected in a choice. Indeed, Prelec, Knutson, Loewenstein, Rick, and Wimmer (2006) reported that activation of the nucleus accumbens correlated positively with participants' willingness to spend money on a purchase and activation of the insula correlated negatively with it.. These patterns of activity predicted purchases independently from self-report variables. As noted previously, the nucleus accumbens is usually active for anticipation of rewards whereas the insula is active for anticipation of pain. Thus two different hedonic valuation systems play off against each other in making purchasing decisions.

However, the neural networks involved in choice go well beyond evaluation of the pain and pleasure of a purchase. For example, consider the basic consumer choice among different sodas. Presumably a consumer will choose the soda that produces the highest activity within those areas of the limbic system identified as relevant to utility. To test this, a group of consumers participated in a blind tasting of decarbonated Pepsi and Coke while being scanned using fMRI (McClure et al., 2004b). The participants' preference for a particular soda was associated with increasing activity in the ventromedial prefrontal cortex. This is one area that has been identified with determination of the probability of an outcome (e.g., Knutson et al., 2005) but not the evaluation of the magnitude of a reward, which would seem to be associated more with activity in the ventral striatum (e.g., Knutson et al., 2005; Schultz, 2000). However this study did not report any striatum activity associated with tasting the soda when participants did not know which soda was being tasted, nor was there any striatum activity related to preferences expressed before the scanning session. One could, in principle, correlate activity in the ventromedial prefrontal cortex with hemodynamic measurements made in the ventral striatum to assess whether the variation in striatum activity was associated with prefrontal activity even if the striatal activity did not exceed threshold. The ventromedial prefrontal activity is consistent with Bechara et al.'s (1997) suggestion that this area may bias choices.

In real life, consumer choices are often affected as much by culturally induced expectations and advertisement as by the actual taste of a product. For example, McClure and colleagues (2004b) found that people prefer Coke more often when they are comparing it to a soda that could be either Pepsi or Coke (but which is actually Coke), than when they are blindly tasting and comparing Pepsi and Coke. Participants' experience of the beverage in the taste test was affected by their knowledge and expectations about the brand. Previous knowledge about a product can clearly override the sensory information people received from the stimulus.

This kind of knowledge and expectation may influence decision making by modulating activity in reward-sensitive brain regions (Erk, Spitzer, Wunderlich, Galley, & Walter, 2002). More interestingly, a second neural network seems to be involved in shaping these kinds of consumer choices compared with the apparent solitary activation of ventromedial prefrontal cortex in blind tasting of sodas. The relative engagement of these two systems depends on whether the type of information available to the person is only sensory (such as when people are blindly tasting Pepsi and Coke) or it is accompanied by brand name information (such as when people know that one of the drinks is Coke). McClure et al. showed that when brand information was available the second system was active, including the dorsolateral prefrontal cortex and the hippocampus. Given the important role of the hippocampus in memory, it is possible that it is involved in recalling the information associated to the brand name (McClure et al., 2004b).

Dorsolateral prefrontal cortex is implicated in a number of cognitive processes such as working memory and selective attention. The hippocampus is implicated in cognitive processes such as episodic memory. While both of these areas are implicated in other kinds of functions as well, these cognitive functions seem well suited to the use of past knowledge and experience in shaping attention and expectations about the taste of a soda. However, these are not areas that are typically implicated in the research on utility as we have discussed it previously. This suggests that it is important to broaden our consideration of the neural mechanisms involved in consumer decisions.

At present there are no models proposed that purport to integrate the diverse set of brain areas active in neuroeconomics. Indeed there are few models of complex psychological processing at all. However there is one exception which is a model of the interaction of affective responses, cognitive processes, and choice processing that involves many of the brain regions we have discussed so far. Davidson and his colleagues (Davidson et al., 2000; Davidson et al., 2002) have discussed a view of affective and behavioral control that involves three sets of brain regions: (1) the limbic structures such as the striatum and amygdala, (2) the dorsolateral prefrontal cortex and the anterior cingulate and hippocampus, and (3) the ventromedial and orbitofrontal cortex. In their discussions, the primary concern is with serotonergic systems that are implicated in aggression and depression, but in neuroeconomics, it appears that dopaminergic systems are more relevant.

Nonetheless the sets of brain structures involved in economic choice and depression and aggression seem closely related.

In an overly simple caricature of these brain areas, we can think about them as related to (1) the expectation and evaluation of utility in structures like the striatum, (2) the biasing and regulation of choice, and (3) expectations, attention, and memory. Each of these systems is complex and multipartite and none is truly independent. But in considering how expectations and past experience and expected utility can bias choices, this model has the functional elements that are needed to develop a neural model of choice behavior. One prediction of such a model might be that focal brain damage in limbic regions might potentiate a more rationalist basis for making economic decisions. Shiv, Lowenstein, Bechara, Damasio, and Damasio (2006) found that winning or losing money led to changes in investment strategy that were more conservative for normal participants than for patients with damage to the limbic system. These patients were less affected by the outcome of previous trials. As a result, patients with limbic system damage actually made better investment decisions over the course of the experiment than normal control participants. While a very simple model of utility-in-the-limbic-system might predict a failure of investment performance given a reduction in functionality in the limbic system, a more complex model positing that affective responses and cognitive responses interact, puts the role of limbic system activity in a different perspective. Indeed, such a model can also account for tradeoffs that occur when cognitive information (e.g., brand information) is ambiguous or noninformative, thus allowing for an increase of affective responses versus activation of prefrontal areas (Plassmann, 2006).

This model reflects a substantial amount of research in affective neuroscience on the one hand and cognitive neuroscience on the other. As a model of economic choice, this model grounds decision making in two disciplines that have longer histories and considerably more research than neuroeconomics itself. By treating utility, choice, and expectation within this framework, it is possible to make predictions about neural processing during economic decisions in a way that extends beyond the relatively simple prediction that the limbic system will be involved in utility-relevant decisions. It should be possible to make predictions about the modulation of brain activity in one region (e.g., limbic areas) based on activation in other areas (e.g., dorsolateral prefrontal cortex) that can be tested using structural equation models and covariance analysis (e.g., Buchel & Friston, 1997; Nyberg & McIntosh, 2001). Moreover, by using repeated transcranial magnetic stimulation (rTMS), it is now possible to directly change the neural activity in a brain area and, guided by this kind of model, test how this affects economic decisions. In a recent study (Knoch, Pascual-Leone, Meyer, Treyer, & Fehr, 2006) rTMS was applied to either the right or left dorsolateral prefrontal cortex (DLPFC) to affect decisions about unfair offers. The results showed that rTMS to right but not left DLPFC increased the rate of accepting unfair offers. Changing activation in one part of the network can actually change the speed and probability of accepting unfair offers, even though the offers are still considered unfair. Thus using a model of economic decision making, the functional role of different brain areas can be directly tested by causal intervention in the processing of those areas. Although this model provides a richer theoretical framework for investigating and understanding the neural processing of consumer behavior, it may not be sufficient to account for the breadth of situations in which consumers actually make economic decisions.

THE SOCIAL NEUROSCIENCE OF ECONOMIC EXCHANGE

In the ultimatum game, discussed previously as used by behavioral economists, decisions to accept or reject an offer seem relatively straightforward. For economists (and homo economicus in general), if the offer exceeds zero, there is a benefit, so the offer should be accepted. For everyone else, if the offer seems fair, the offer should be accepted. Of course, this begs the question of what defines fair and the behavioral economists have provided the empirical answer (e.g., see Thaler, 1988): A fair offer is a little under half of the pool, letting the offerer keep a little more than half for the effort of making the offer.

How do participants in the game come to that determination? There is no answer at this point, but one could infer a highly rational computational process that reasons about the role of the offerer and recipient and estimates reasonable portions based on a purely logico-deductive process. This would appeal to traditional economists and behavioral economists since it is a rational process that assigns utility differently than postulated by traditional economists. Within the context of the neural framework for a decision-making model we have just discussed, there are elements that are entirely consistent with this explanation. The recipient's goals of earning money and being fairly treated (using lateral frontal brain regions involved in attention and working memory for holding goals in mind) may bias some responses over others (using orbitofrontal and ventromedial prefrontal regions) depending on the assessed utility of the alternative (through limbic areas such as the midbrain dopaminergic system including the striatum).

In the three different views of playing the recipient in the ultimatum game—traditional economist's, behavioral economist's, and neuroeconomist's—there are certainly similarities but there are also important differences. The emphasis shifts from monetary value (offer above zero) to contextualized value (offer deemed "fair") to an interaction of goals, hedonic states and estimates, and response biases. The neural model actually makes explicit—because it is part of the measured responses—aspects of the economic decision that no economist would deny, but also that no economist would consider. It is this kind of perspective shift (e.g., Kuhn, 1963) that is at the foundation of conceptual advances in a field.

However, there is still something missing from the neuroeconomic model we have been discussing. In all three perspectives, utility is critical to selection of a choice. In the neuroeconomics model, expectation can play a role in modulating choice behavior, through an attentional-memory network involving dorsolateral cortex. But it is not clear why choice behavior should change if expectations are constant, the face value of a reward is constant, and other aspects of the received value are constant. Utility should not change. In the neuroeconomic model, the definition of a fair offer in the ultimatum game should be relatively invariant.

In a recent study, Sanfey et al. (2003) had participants play the ultimatum game as recipients with one small change: Sometimes offers were made by a human partner and sometimes offers were made by a computer partner. Brain activity was measured using fMRI to assess the neural activity accompanying the economic decisions. Sanfey and colleagues reported increased activation in three brain regions when participants were presented with unfair offers compared to fair ones. The first, the anterior insula, is a region whose activation has often been found to correlate with negative emotions (e.g., Calder & Lawrence, 2001) such as anger and disgust. Its activity here suggests that emotions are playing a role in guiding participants' choice in an area not typically associated with utility. Activity in the insula was proportional to the unfairness of the offers. Across participants, it showed higher activation for the unfair offers that were rejected. Additionally, participants who had rejected the highest number of unfair offers showed higher insula activation (Sanfey et al., 2003).

Rejections of unfair offers can be seen as the result of a conflict between satisfaction of two goals: cognitive goals that push the player to accept the even small gain, and emotional goals that push the player to reject the insulting offer (Sanfey et al., 2003). Consistent with this hypothesis, the second region showing more activation for unfair offers was the dorsolateral prefrontal cortex, an area known to be involved in goal maintenance and cognitive control (Miller & Cohen, 2001). The third region was the anterior cingulate cortex, an area involved in the detection of cognitive conflict (Fehr & Schmidt, 1999; Greene et al., 2004). The activity in these two latter regions, while greater for unfair offers, did not vary with the degree of unfairness, in contrast to the pattern found in the insula (Sanfey et al., 2003). These areas are consistent with the "cognitive" regions described in the neuroeconomic model of choice, whereas the insula represents a different kind of affective activity pattern (related to social affective responses directed at a partner) than is represented by the limbic activity related to utility.

Moreover it is important to note that these results held only when participants were offered unfair shares by human partners. When the offers were made by a computer, not only did participants accept unfair offers more often, but the activity in the insula, dorsolateral prefrontal cortex, and anterior cingulate was not significantly increased for unfair offers (Sanfey et al., 2003). Clearly a decision made in a social setting can strongly depend on attributions made about the participants. The notion of fairness and the emotional consequences people experience when they are offered unfair options depend on being able to attribute a theory of mind to the agent making the offer (e.g., McCabe, Houser, Ryan, Smith, & Trouard, 2001). Only once such attributions are made can expectations come into play. Notice that the social setting need not be complex or realistic. A simple and structured interaction such as the one offered by the ultimatum game suffices.

This adds another kind of dimension to the neuroeconomic model. Economic decisions are often made in social settings (including both cooperation and competition, Decety, Jackson, Sommerville, Chaminade, & Meltzoff, 2004; Rilling et al., 2002) and this suggests that we need to consider social neuroscience mechanisms (Lieberman, 2006) in addition to affective and cognitive neuroscience when thinking about the full scope of a neuroeconomic model. In particular, we need to consider the possibility that social emotions are involved, sensitivity to acceptance and rejection (see Eisenberger & Lieberman, 2004), the use of theory of mind (e.g., Rilling et al., 2004; Saxe & Kanwisher, 2003), perspective taking (Decety & Sommerville, 2003; Jackson, Meltzoff, & Decety, 2006) and empathy (Jackson et al., 2006; Decety & Jackson, 2006).

When an offer is rejected in the ultimatum game neither of the players receives money. Therefore, rejecting unfair offers is a (costly) way to punish a player who made an unfair offer. This kind of behavior has been termed "altruistic punishment" (de Quervain et al., 2004) because it is costly for the punisher and it is useful for the punished, since it decreases the chances that this person will adopt that behavior again. However, a PET study showed that the desire people have to punish a perpetrator of a misdeed is less altruistic than it seems and it actually has a hedonistic component (de Quervain et al., 2004).

In this experiment, two players were engaged in a game of trust. In order to make money, participants had to entrust money to their partner. If they did, the amount of money quadrupled in the partner's hands. The partner had then the choice of keeping all of the money or giving half back. Thus the payoff for the participants depended on trusting the partner and on the partner being trustworthy. If the partner was not trustworthy, participants could decide to punish him by reducing his payoff (de Quervain et al., 2004).

Participants were scanned while they were deciding whether to punish traitors. The areas that showed activation during this operation were the caudate, the thalamus, ventromedial and orbitofrontal cortices. The caudate, a dorsal part of the striatum, showed increased activation when participants had a strong desire to punish traitors, independent of whether this punishment would be costly or not for the participants. But when the betrayal was nonintentional, the caudate was deactivated. The activation in this area correlated with the strength of selected punishment: it is possible that higher expected satisfaction from the punishment led participants to inflict higher punishments (de Quervain et al., 2004). Additionally, the thalamus also showed increased activation when participants inflicted real punishments (vs. symbolic). Finally, frontal regions (ventromedial and orbitofrontal) showed higher activation when the punishments were costly for the participants (de Quervain et al., 2004).

Interestingly, as in Sanfey et al.'s (2003) study, an attribution of intentionality was necessary for first players to rate traitors as unfair and to feel the desire to punish them. When the betrayal was not intentional, partners were perceived as much less unfair and deserving punishment. Additionally, the punishments first players imposed on their partners were higher when the betrayal was intentional than when it was unintentional (de Quervain et al., 2004).

Trust and betrayal are certainly important elements of social interaction that takes place in economic exchanges. In one study, social cooperation resulted in activity in the ventral striatum, and the medial prefrontal cortices (Rilling et al., 2002) consistent with increasing utility and bias for cooperation. As two people play a cooperative economic game, and trust between them grows, there is increasing activity within the caudate nucleus, related to increasing expectation of utility (King-Casas et al., 2005). However, with strong prior positive or negative expectations about a potential economic partner, successive interactions have little impact on the ventral striatum or the caudate (Delgado, Frank, & Phelps, 2005a).

These studies suggest that patterns of brain activity are sensitive to participants' moment-by-moment experiences. Activity in areas involved in affective learning such as the caudate or ventral striatum is greater with increasing trust. Similarly, activity in the anterior insula seems to increase with violations of trust. Other brain areas such as medial prefrontal cortex, posterior cingulate, and angular gyrus (Greene et al., 2001) as well as posterior superior temporal sulcus (Rilling et al., 2004) may reflect aspects of processing specific to reasoning about other people's thinking (or theory of mind). Other areas in the cingulate seem to reflect aspects of cognitive control (Delgado et al., 2005a; King-Casas et al., 2005).

Areas related to theory of mind and empathy have not figured in neuroeconomics studies that seem to mainly find brain networks involved in the reward system, the motor system, and a system relevant to calculation (Cacioppo & Nusbaum, 2003). In part, this may be due to the relative importance of the social interaction that, in the participant's mind, is occurring in the economic task. This suggests that the participants' expectations about the study (i.e., the task and social interactions) are critical to the way the brain processes information. For example, although the same adjectives can be used to describe people or products (e.g., reliable, effective), these adjectives mean different things in those two cases. Yoon, Gutchess, Feinberg, and Polk (2006) examined brain activity to judgments about the relevance of an adjective as a description of a person or a product brand. The person could either be the participant (self-relevant condition) or a famous person; the product brand could either be relevant to the participant (self-relevant) or not. When the adjectives were judged in relation to people, activity was found in the medial prefrontal cortex but when the adjectives were judged in relation to brands, activity was found in the dorsolateral prefrontal region—an area that has been implicated previously in making economic decisions. This might suggest that expectations about the nature of a judgment (applied to a person or a product) may lead to different kinds of neural activity, thus showing a separation of neural networks involved in reasoning about people and reasoning about products. However, this result may be specific to the kind of judgments used in this study, which are based on the different kind of expectations we have about people and brands. If the expectations about people were more focused on the economic implications of the judgments, a different kind of coupling among brain areas might be observed.

Delgado, Frank, and Phelps (2005) reported that when participants were given clear information about the moral character of their partner before playing a game together, these expectations dramatically reduced the sensitivity of the caudate to moment-by-moment interactions during the game. Participants read a biography of their partners in an economic game. These biographies depicted partners as morally good, bad, or neutral. Once participants had formed opinions, they played a trust game similar to the one described above. Although the behavior of the "good partners" was not consistent with prior expectations and many violations occurred, participants kept sharing more money with good partners than with bad. This was mirrored by altered neural striatal activity.

Delgado et al. interpret this result as suggesting that the caudate activity in other studies that examine the development of trust may have reflected the accrual of information about partners. With prior expectations, this system does not play a large role in the social interaction. Delgado et al. monitored neural activity in two phases of the experiment: when participants received responses from their partners and when they decided to share or keep their money on the following trial. During the first phase, the caudate showed differential activation only for collaborative and defective responses from neutral partners. However, no increased activation was found for responses given by good or bad partners. During the following phase, the ventral striatum showed differential activation for decisions to share or keep but only when interacting with bad or neutral partners thus showing that the activation of this region is also sensitive to expectations. In this phase, cortical areas associated with cognitive control (cingulate cortex and insular cortex) showed increased activation as well. However, this activation was limited to those choices that were inconsistent with the bias created by the initial biography (i.e., keeping the money when playing with the good partner and sharing with the bad one). This suggests that, although top-down information influences subcortical regions, it may not alter the functioning of the cortical ones (Delgado et al., 2005).

These findings indicate that social interaction systematically modifies aspects of cognitive and affective mechanisms. While some aspects of these interactions can be viewed as simply modifying utility, other aspects (such as unexpected unfair offers) appear to invoke affective systems associated with feelings of anger or disgust. In this way, neuroscience has broadened our understanding of economic decisions both by making more explicit the kinds of processes involved and by changing the way we think about longstanding theoretical concepts such as utility.

TOWARDS A SOCIAL NEUROSCIENCE OF CONSUMER BEHAVIOR

Behavioral economics has provided a different perspective on consumer behavior than the traditional approach of economics. By introducing and emphasizing the role of heuristics and a variety of cognitive effects such as framing that are not apparent from the surface of strict rationality—but are not irrational—our understanding of consumer behavior has changed. Neuroeconomics is beginning to have the same effect. Utility, as conceived by economists, has been demonstrated in many studies now to depend on a complex set of neural structures that are important in reward assessment and behavioral control.

Moreover, there are no clear models that can provide a framework that integrates the operation of neural networks subserving "simpler" functions such as working memory or affective states as seen in economic decision making and exchange. Davidson and his colleagues (2000, 2002) have described one kind of model that seems to combine three separable systems—a cognitive memory-attention system, a behavioral control system, and an affective reward system. Although an intriguing start, it is likely that this model is too simple even to account for the pathologies they were directed at. Although one can conceive of depression in mostly affective and cognitive terms, additional networks involved in theory of mind and perspective taking (see Cacioppo, Visser, & Pickett, 2005) will need to be incorporated. Of course, this will be true for any neural model of economic decision making.

Models of economic decision making will need to take into account two fundamental principles of human neural systems discussed by Berntson and Cacioppo (in press). First, rather than conceive of neural networks in a strictly hierarchical arrangement of interactions where simpler sensory systems feed up to associative systems, it is important to recognize the heterarchical nature of neural systems. Although there may be clear anatomical connections between systems that suggest a kind of organization by which information may feedforward and feedback, it is better to consider the notion that there are long-distance connections in the brain, ascending and descending subcortical connections, and adjacent connections that together can dynamically assemble functional neural networks to meet the moment-by-moment demands of any particular psychological process.

Second, there is substantial re-representation in the brain for many different kinds of processes. Although much neuroscience work is concerned with the kind of population codes and topographical representations that map differences in function to spatial location in the brain (e.g., retinotopic representation or the homunculus in the premotor region), these representations occur at many different levels over and over again for different purposes. Thus, there may be any number of different representations of "utility" for different reasons from biasing an immediate response or choice to forming an expectation that will operate in the future. From the research published to date, there is good reason to think that the concept of utility should be broadened and should be informed by the differences in these functional mechanisms.

However, as long as neuroeconomics continues to analyze patterns of brain activity simply by searching for the most reliable peak of activity, it will be difficult to realize the benefits that neuroeconomics can bring to understanding economic decision making. Rather than look for disjoint active spots in the brain, researchers need to begin to use more sophisticated techniques to assess the functional assembly of neural networks. While some studies have begun to regress behavioral data onto brain activity (e.g., McClure et al., 2004b) and others have examined the interaction between activity in one brain and activity in another brain (King-Casas et al., 2005) to understand joint neural changes in social interaction, it will be necessary to develop more sophisticated analytic models in neuroeconomics that consider the covariance among brain regions rather than simple magnitude of activity.

To date, the research in neuroeconomics has focused on nomothetic analyses, emphasizing the regions of activation in the brain observed in judgment and decision making in economic contexts. Results are in accord with work in consumer behavior indicating that individuals are characterized by bounded rationality, and points to specific component processes that promote systematic deviations from rationality which summate rather than cancel when aggregated across individuals. Consumer researchers have long focused also on individual differences in judgment and decision making. We believe individual as well as situational differences in the nature and extent of irrational information processing in economic judgment and decision making will similarly be a fertile area for future research in neuroeconomics.

ACKNOWLEDGMENTS

We thank Barnaby Marsh, Derek Neal, Ashley Swanson, and John Henly for discussions on issues regarding economics and neuroeconomics. Funding was provided by the National Institute of Mental Health Grant No. P50 MH72850 and the John Templeton Foundation.

REFERENCES

Arana, F. S., Parkinson, J. A., Hinton, E., Holland, A. J., Owen, A. M., & Roberts, A. C. (2003). Dissociable contributions of the human amygdala and orbitofrontal cortex to incentive motivation and goal selection. *Journal of Neuroscience, 23,* 9632.

Azari, N. P., Nickel, J., Wunderlich, G., Niedeggen, M., Hefter, H., Tellmann, L., Herzog, H., Stoerig, P., Birnbacher, D., & Seitz, R. J. (2001). Neural correlates of religious experience. *European Journal of Neuroscience, 13,* 1649–1652.

Bankart, C. P., & Elliott, R. (1974). Heart rate and skin conductance in anticipation of shocks with varying probability of occurrence. *Psychophysiology, 11,* 160–174.

Baxter, M. G., Parker, A., Lindner, C. C., Izquierdo, A. D., & Murray, E. A. (2000). Control of response selection by reinforcer value requires interaction of amygdala and orbital prefrontal cortex. *Journal of Neuroscience, 20,* 4311–4319.

Bechara, A., Damasio, H., Tranel, D., & Damasio, A. R. (1997). Deciding advantageously before knowing the advantageous strategy. *Science, 275,* 1293–1295.

Belin, P., Zatorre, R. J., Lafaille, P., Ahad, P., & Pike, B. (2000). Voice-selective areas in human auditory cortex. *Nature, 403,* 309–312.

Bernoulli, D. (1954). Exposition of a new theory on the measurement of risk. *Econometrica, 22,* 23–36.

Berntson, G. G., & Cacioppo, J. T. (in press). The neuroevolution of motivation. In J. Shah & W. Gardner (Eds.), *Handbook of motivation science.* New York: Guilford.

Best, M., Williams, J. M., & Coccaro, E. F. (2002). Evidence for a dysfunctional prefrontal circuit in patients with an impulsive aggressive disorder. *Proceedings of the National Academy of Sciences, 99,* 8448–8453.

Binder, J. (2000). The new neuroanatomy of speech perception. *Brain, 123,* 2371–2372.

Bischoff-Grethe, A., Ivry, R. B., & Grafton, S. T. (2002). Cerebellar involvement in response reassignment rather than attention. *Journal of Neuroscience, 22,* 546–553.

Bizzi, E., & Clarac, F. (1999) Motor systems. *Current Opinion in Neurobiology, 9,* 659–662.

Black, I. B. (1994). *Information in the brain.* Cambridge: The MIT Press.

Bliss, T. V., & Lomo, T. (1973). Long-lasting potentiation of synaptic transmission in the dentate area of the anaesthetized rabbit following stimulation of the perforant path. *Journal of Physiology, 2,* 331–356.

Broca, P. (1861). Perte de la parole, ramollissement chronique et destruction partielle du lobe antérieur gauche du cerveau. *Bulletin de la Société de Anthropologie (Paris), 2,* 235–238.

Brodmann, K. (1909). *Brodmann's "localisation in the cerebral cortex."* London: Smith-Gordon. (Original work published 1909).

Buchel, C., & Friston, K. J. (1997). Modulation of connectivity in visual pathways by attention: cortical interactions evaluated with structural equation modelling and fMRI. *Cerebral Cortex, 7,* 768–778.

Buonomano, D. V., & Merzenich, M. M. (1998). Cortical plasticity: From synapses to maps. *Annual Review of Neuroscience, 21,* 149–186.

Cabeza, R., & Kingstone, A. (Eds). (2001). *Handbook of functional neuroimaging of cognition.* MIT Press: Cambridge, 49–72.

Cacioppo, J. T., Berntson, G. G., Lorig, T. S., Norris, C. J., Rickett, E., & Nusbaum, H. (2003). Just because you're imaging the brain doesn't mean you can stop using your head: A primer and set of first principles. *Journal of Personality and Social Psychology, 85,* 650–661.

Cacioppo, J. T., & Berntson, G. G. (2005). *Social neuroscience.* New York: Psychology Press.

Cacioppo J. T., & Nusbaum, H. C. (2003). Component processes underlying choice. *Proceedings of the National Academy of Sciences, 100,* 3016–3017.

Cacioppo, J. T., Visser, P. S., & Pickett, C. L. (2005). *Social neuroscience: People thinking about thinking people.* Cambridge, MIT Press.

Cacioppo, J. T., & Tassinary, L. G. (1990). Inferring psychological significance from physiological signals. *American Psychologist, 45,* 16–28.

Cacioppo, J. T., Tassinary, L. G., & Berntson, G. G. (2007). Psychophysiological science: Interdisciplinary approaches to classic questions about the mind. In J. T. Cacioppo, L. G. Tassinary, & G. G. Berntson (Eds.), *Handbook of psychophysiology* (3rd ed., pp. 1–5). New York Cambridge University Press.

Calder, A. J., Lawrence, A. D., & Young, A. W. (2001). Neuropsychology of fear and loathing. *Nature Reviews Neuroscience, 2,* 352–363.

Calhoun, V. D., Adali, T., Kraut, M., & Pearlson, G. (2001). Spatial versus temporal independent component analysis of functional MRI data containing a pair of task-related waveforms. *Human Brain Mapping, 13*, 43–53.

Camerer, C. F., Loewenstein, G., & Prelec, D. (2004). Neuroeconomics: Why economics needs brains. *Scandinavian Journal of Economics, 106*, 555–579.

Camerer, C. F., & Fehr, E. (2006). When does "economic man" dominate social behavior? *Science, 311*, 47–52.

Carter, C. S., Braver, T. S., Barch, D. M., Botvinick, M. M., Noll, D., & Cohen, J. D. (1998). Anterior cingulate cortex, error detection, and the online monitoring of performance. *Science, 280*, 747–749.

Chen, M. K., & Hauser, M. (2005). Modeling reciprocation and cooperation in primates: Evidence for a punishing strategy. *Journal of Theoretical Biology, 235*, 5–12.

Coles, M. G. H., Donchin, E., & Porges, S. W. (1986). *Psychophysiology: Systems, Processes & Applications.* New York: Guilford.

Cooper, J. R., Bloom, R. E., & Roth, R. H. (2003). *The biochemical basis of neuropharmacology.* Oxford: New York.

Cooper, R. L., Chang, D. B., Young, A. C., Martin, C. J., & Ancker-Johnson, D. (1974). Restricted diffusion in biophysical systems. *Biophysical Journal, 14*, 161–177.

Damasio, A. R. (1994). *Descartes' error: Emotion, rationality and the human brain.* New York: Putnam.

Damasio, A. (2000). *The feeling of what happens.* Harcourt: New York.

Davidson, R. J., Pizzagalli, D., Nitschke, J. B., & Putnam, K. (2002). Depression: Perspectives from affective neuroscience. *Annual Review of Psychology, 53*, 545–577.

Davidson, R. J., Putnam, K. M., & Larson, C. L. (2000). Dysfunction in the neural circuitry of emotion regulation—A possible prelude to violence. *Science, 289*, 591–594.

de Quervain, D. J.-F., Fischbacher, U., Treyer, V., Schellhammer, M., Schnyder, U., Buck, A., & Fehr, E. (2004). The neural basis of altruistic punishment. *Science, 305*, 1254–1258.

Decety, J., & Jackson, P.L. (2006). A social neuroscience perspective on empathy. *Current Directions in Psychological Science, 15*, 54–58.

Decety, J., Jackson, P. L., Sommerville, J. A., Chaminade, T., & Meltzoff, A. N. (2004). The neural bases of cooperation and competition: An fMRI investigation. *NeuroImage, 23*, 744–751.

Decety, J., & Sommerville, J.A. (2003). Shared representations between self and others: A social cognitive neuroscience view. *Trends in Cognitive Science, 7*, 527–533.

Delgado, M. R., Frank, R. H., & Phelps, E. A. (2005). Perceptions of moral character modulate the neural systems of reward during the trust game. *Nature Neuroscience, 8*, 1611.

Donchin, E., Coles, M. G. H., & Porges, S. W. (1986). *Psychophysiology: Systems, processes, and applications.* New York: Guilford.

Drevets, W. C., Gautier, C., Price, J. C., Kupfer, D. J., Kinahan, P. E., Grace, A. A., et al. (2001). Amphetamine-induced dopamine release in human ventral striatum correlates with euphoria. *Biological Psychiatry, 49*, 81–96.

Dronkers, N. F. (2000). The gratuitous relationship between Broca's aphasia and Broca's area, *Behavioral and Brain Sciences*, 30–31.

Dronkers, N. F., & Larsen, J. L. (2001). Neuroanatomy of the classical syndromes of aphasia. In F. Boller & J. Grafman (Eds.) *Handbook of neuropsychology* (2nd ed., pp. 19–30). New York: Elsevier Science.

Eisenberger, N. I., & Lieberman, M. D. (2004). Why rejection hurts: a common neural alarm system for physical and social pain. *Trends in Cognitive Sciences, 8*, 294–300.

Erk, S., Spitzer, M., Wunderlich, A. P., Galley, L., & Walter, H. (2002). Cultural objects modulate reward circuitry. *Neuroreport, 13*, 2499–2503.

Fabiani, M., Gratton, G., & Federmeier, K. D. (2007). Event-related brain potentials: Methods, theory, and applications. In J. T. Cacioppo, L. G. Tassinary, & G. G. Berntson (Eds.), *Handbook of psychophysiology* (3rd ed., pp. 85–119). New York: Cambridge University Press.

Fadiga L., Buccino G., Craighero L., Fogassi L., Gallese V., & Pavesi G. (1999). Corticospinal excitability is specifically modulated by motor imagery: a magnetic stimulation study. *Neuropsychologia, 37*, 147–158.

Farah, M. J. (2004). *Visual agnosia.* New York: Bradford Book.

Farah, M. J., & Feinberg, T. E. (2000). *Patient-based approaches to cognitive neuroscience.* MIT Press: Cambridge.

Fehr, E., & Schmidt, K.M. (1999). A theory of fairness, competition and cooperation. *Quarterly Journal of Economics, 114*, 817–868.

Fellows, L. K. (2004). The cognitive neuroscience of human decision making: A review and conceptual framework. *Behavioral and Cognitive Neuroscience Reviews, 3*, 159–172.

Fisher, I. (1911). *The purchasing power of money.* Macmillan: New York.

Fox, M. D., Snyder, A. Z., Vincent, J. L., Corbetta, M., Van Essen, D. C., & Raichle, M. E. (2005). The human brain is intrinsically organized into dynamic, anticorrelated functional networks. *Proceedings of the National Academy of Sciences, 102*, 9673–9678.

Friston, K. J., Price, C. J., Fletcher, P., Moore, C., Frackowiak, R. S. J., & Dolan, R. J. (1996). The trouble with cognitive subtraction. *NeuroImage, 4*, 97–104.

Gabrieli, J. D., Poldrack, R. A., & Desmond, J. E. (1998). The role of left prefrontal cortex in language and memory. *Proceedings of the National Academy of Sciences, 95*, 906–913.

Gauthier, I., Skudlarski, P., Gore, J.C., & Anderson, A. W. (2000). Expertise for cars and birds recruits brain areas involved in face recognition. *Nature Neuroscience, 3*, 191–197.

Gazzaniga, M. S., Ed. (2004). *The cognitive neurosciences III.* MIT Press: Cambridge.

Gazzaniga, M. S. (1987). *The social brain: Discovering the networks of the mind.* New York: Basic Books.

Geschwind, N. (1970). The organization of language and the brain. *Science, 170*, 940–944.

Gigerenzer, G., & Selten, R. (2002). *Bounded rationality.* Cambridge: The MIT Press.

Gilovich, T., Griffin, D., & Kahneman, D. (2002). *Heuristics and biases: The psychology of intuitive judgment*: Cambridge University Press.

Goel, V., Grafman, J., Tajik, J., Gana, S., & Danto, D. (1997). A study of the performance of patients with frontal lobe lesions in a financial planning task. *Brain, 120*, 1805–1822.

Greene, J. D., Sommerville, R. B., Nystrom, L. E., Darley, J. M., & Cohen, J. D. (2001). An fMRI investigation of emotional engagement in moral judgment. *Science, 293*, 2105–2108.

Greene, J. D., Nystrom, L. E., Engell, A. D., Darley, J. M., & Cohen, J. D. (2004). The neural bases of cognitive conflict and control in moral judgment. *Neuron, 44*, 389–400.

Guth, W., Schmittberger, R., & Schwartze, B. (1982). An experimental analysis of ultimatum bargaining. *Journal of Economic Behavior and Organization, 3*, 367–388.

Hari, R. (1998). Megnetoencephalography as a tool of clinical neurophysiology. In E. Niedermeyer & F. Lopes da Silva (Eds.), *Electroencephalography: Basic principles clinical applications, and related fields* (pp. 1107–1134). Baltimore: Williams & Wilkins.

Hari, R., Levanen, S., & Raij, T. (2000). Timing of human cortical functions during cognition: role of MEG. *Trends in Cognitive Science, 4*, 455–462.

Harlow, J. M. (1868). Recovery from the passage of an iron bar through the head. *Publications of the Massachusetts Medical Society, 2*, 327–347.

Hasson, U., Nir, Y., Levy, I., Fuhrmann, G., & Malach, R. (2004). Intersubject synchronization of cortical activity during natural vision. *Science, 303*, 1634–1640.

Hasson U., Nusbaum H.C., & Small S.L. (2006). Repetition suppression for spoken sentences and the effect of task demands. *Journal of Cognitive Neuroscience. 18*, 2013–2029.

Haxby, J. V., Gobbini, M. I., Furey, M. L., Ishai, A., Schouten, J. L., & Pietrini, P. (2001). Distributed and overlapping representations of faces and objects in ventral temporal cortex. *Science, 293*, 2425– 430.

Hopfinger, J. B., Buonocore, M. H., & Mangun, G. R. (2000). The neural mechanisms of top-down attentional control. *Nature Neuroscience, 3*, 284–291.

Horwitz, B., Tagamets, M. A. & McIntosh, A. R. (1999). Neural modeling, functional brain imaging, and cognition. *Trends in Cognitive Science, 3*, 91–98.

Ivry, R. B., & Robertson, L. C. (1998). *The two sides of perception.* New York: Bradford Book.

Jackson, P. L., Brunet, E., Meltzoff, A. N., & Decety, J. (2006). Empathy examined through the neural mechanisms involved in imagining how I feel versus how you feel pain. *Neuropsychologia, 44*, 752–761.

Jackson, P. L., Meltzoff, A. N., & Decety, J. (2006). Neural circuits involved in imitation and perspective-taking. *NeuroImage, 31*, 429–439.

Jezzard, P., & Clare, S. (2001). Principles of nuclear magnetic resonance and MRI. In P. Jezzard, P. M. Matthews & S. M. Smith (Eds.), *Functional MRI: an introduction to methods* (pp. 67–93). Oxford: Oxford University Press.

Johansen-Berg, H., Behrens, T. E., Robson, M. D., Drobnjak, I., Rushworth, M. F., Brady, J. M., et al. (2004). Changes in connectivity profiles define functionally distinct regions in human medial frontal cortex. *Proceedings of the National Academy of Science, 101*, 13335–13340.

Johnson, E. J., & Tversky, A. (1983). Affect, generalization, and the perception of risk. *Journal of Personality and Social Psychology, 45*, 20–31.

Justus, T., Ravizza, S. M., Fiez, J. A., & Ivry, R. B. (2005). Reduced phonological similarity effects in patients with damage to the cerebellum. *Brain and Language, 95*, 304–318.

Kahneman, D. (2003). Maps of bounded rationality: Psychology for behavioral economics. *The American Economic Review, 93*, 1449–1475.

Kandel, E. R., Schwartz, J. H., & Jessel, T. M. (2000). *Principles of neural science.* New York: McGraw Hill.

Kanwisher, N. (2000). Domain specificity in face perception. *Nature Neuroscience, 3,*759–763.

Kanwisher, N., McDermott, J., & Chun, M. M. (1997). The fusiform face area: a module in human extrastriate cortex specialized for face perception. *Journal of Neuroscience, 17,* 4302–4311.

King-Casas, B., Tomlin, D., Anen, C., Camerer, C. F., Quartz, S. R., & Montague, P. R. (2005). Getting to know you: Reputation and trust in a two-person economic exchange. *Science, 308,* 78–83.

Karama, S., Lecours, A. R., Leroux, J.-M., Bourgouin, P., Beaudoin, G., Joubert, S., & Beauregard, M. (2002). Areas of brain activation in males and females during viewing of erotic film excerpts. *Human Brain Mapping, 16,* 1–13.

Knoch, D., Pascual-Leone, A., Meyer, K., Treyer, V., & Fehr, E. (2006). Diminishing reciprocal fairness by disrupting the right prefrontal cortex. *Science, 314,* 829–832.

Knutson, B., Adams, C. M., Fong, G. W., & Hommer, D. (2001a). Anticipation of increasing monetary reward selectivity recruits nucleus accumbens. *The Journal of Neuroscience, 21,* 1–5.

Knutson, B., Fong, G. W., Adams, C. M., Varner, J. L., Hommer, D. (2001b). Dissociation of reward anticipation and outcome with event-related fMRI. *NeuroReport, 12,* 3683–3687

Knutson, B., & Peterson, R. (2005). Neurally reconstructing expected utility. *Games and Economic Behavior, 52,* 305–315.

Knutson, B., Taylor, J., Kaufman, M., Peterson, R., & Glover, G. (2005). Distributed neural representation of expected value. *Journal of Neuroscience, 25,* 4806–4812.

Kuhn, T. S. (1963). *The structure of scientific revolutions.* Chicago: The Univeristy of Chicago Press.

Laibson, D. I. (1997) Golden eggs and hyperbolic discounting. *Quarterly Journal of Economics, 62,* 443–478.

Le Bihan, D. (1991). Molecular diffusion nuclear magnetic resonance imaging. *Magnetic Resonance Quant, 17,* 1–30.

Lerner, J. S., & Keltner, D. (2001). Fear, anger, and risk. *Journal of Personality and Social Psychology, 81,* 146–159.

Lieberman, M. D. (2006). Social cognitive neuroscience: A review of core processes. *Annual Review of Psychology, 58.*

Loewenstein, G. F., Weber, E. U., Hsee, C. K., & Welch, N. (2001). Risk as feelings. *Psychological Bulletin, 127,* 267–286.

Logothetis, N. K., Pauls, J., Augath, M. A., Trinath, T., & Oeltermann, A. (2001). Neurophysiological investigation of the basis of the fMRI signal. *Nature, 412,* 150–157.

Luciana, M., & Collins, P. (1997). Dopaminergic modulation of working memory for spatial but not object cues in normal humans. *Journal of Cognitive Neuroscience, 9,* 330–347.

MacMillan, M. (2002). *An odd kind of fame: Stories of Phineas Gage.* Cambridge: The MIT Press.

Maguire, W. F. (1990). Dynamic operations of thought systems. *American Psychologist, 45,* 504–512.

Marsh, B., & Kacelnik, A. (2002). Framing effects and risky decisions in starlings. *Proceedings of the National Academy of Sciences, 99,* 3352–3355.

McCabe, K., Houser, D., Ryan, L., Smith, V., & Trouard, T. (2001). A functional imaging study of cooperation in two-person reciprocal exchange. *Proceedings of the National Academy of Sciences, 98,* 11832–11835.

McClelland, J. L. (1979). On the time relations of mental processes: An examination of systems of processes in cascade. *Psychological Review, 86,* 287–330.

McClure, S. M., Laibson, D. I., Loewenstein, G., & Cohen, J. D. (2004a). Separate neural systems value immediate and delayed monetary rewards. *Science, 306*(5695), 503–507.

McClure, S. M., Li, J., Tomlin, D., Cypert, K. S., Montague, L. M., & Montague, P. R. (2004b). Neural correlates of behavioral preference for culturally familiar drinks. *Neuron, 44,* 379–387.

McGuire, W. J. (1960). A syllogistic analysis of cognitive relationships. In M. J. Rosenberg, C. I. Hovland, W. J. McGuire, R. P. Abelson, & J. W. Brehm (Eds.), *Attitude organization and change: An analysis of consistency among attitude components* (pp. 65–111). New Haven: Yale University Press.

McGuire,W.J. (1981). The probabilogical model of cognitive structure and attitude change. In R. E. Petty, T. M. Ostrom, & T. C. Brock (Eds.), *Cognitive responses in persuasion* (pp. 291–307). Hillsdale, NJ: Erlbaum.

McIntosh, A. R., & Gonzalez-Lima, F. (1994). Structural equation modelling and its application to network analysis in functional brain imaging. *Human Brain Mapping, 2,* 2–22.

Miller E. K., & Cohen J. D. (2001). An integrative theory of prefrontal cortex function. *Annual Review of Neuroscience,* 24, 167–202.

Montague, P. R., Dayan, P., & Sejnowski, T. J. (1996). A framework for mesencephalic dopamine systems based on predictive Hebbian learning. *Journal of Neuroscience, 16,* 1936–1947.

Mobbs, D., Greicius, M. D., Abdel-Azim, E., Menon, V., & Reiss, A. L. (2003). Humor modulates the mesolimbic reward centers. *Neuron, 40,* 1041–1048.

Nisbett, R., & Wilson, T. (1977). Telling more than we can know: Verbal reports on mental processes. *Psychological Review, 84,* 231–259.

Nyberg, L., & McIntosh, A. R., (2001). Functional neuroimaging: Network analyses. In R. Cabeza & A. Kingstone (Eds). *Handbook of functional neuroimaging of cognition* (pp. 49–72). MIT Press: Cambridge.

O'Doherty, J., Dayan, P., Schultz, J., Deichmann, R., Friston, K., & Dolan, R. J. (2004). Dissociable roles of ventral and dorsal striatum in instrumental conditioning. *Science, 304,* 452–454.

O'Doherty, J., Kringelbach, M. L., Rolls, E. T., Hornak, J., & Andrews, C. (2001). *Nature Neuroscience, 4,* 95–102.

Ojemann, G. A. (1991). Cortical organization of language. *Journal of Neuroscience, 11,* 2281–2287.

Padoa-Schioppa, C., & Assad, J. A. (2004). Neurons in the orbitofrontal cortex encode economic value. *Nature, 44,* 223–226.

Panksepp, J. (1998). *Affective neuroscience.* Oxford Univiversity Press: New York.

Passingham, R. E., Stephan, K. E., & Kotter, R. (2002). The anatomical basis of functional localization in the cortex. *Nature Reviews Neuroscience, 3,* 606–616.

Paulus, M. P., & Frank, L. R. (2003). Ventromedial prefrontal cortex activation is critical for preference judgments. *NeuroReport, 14,* 1311–1315.

Peled, S., Gudbjartsson, H., Westin, C. F., Kikinis, R., & Jolesz, F. A. (1998). Magnetic resonance imaging shows orientation and asymmetry of white matter fiber tracts. *Brain Research, 780,* 27– 33.

Pelphrey, K. A., Morris, J. P., Michelich, C. R., Allison, T., & McCarthy, G. (2005). Functional anatomy of biological motion perception in posterior temporal cortex: An fMRI study of eye, mouth and hand movements. *Cerebral Cortex, 15,*1866–1876.

Petersen, S. E., Fox, P. T., Snyder, A. Z., & Raichle, M. E. Activation of extrastriate and frontal cortical areas by visual words and word-like stimuli. *Science, 249,* 1041–1044.

Phelps, E. A., O'Connor, K. J., Cunningham, W. A., Funayama, E. S., Gatenby, J. C., Gore, J. C., et al. (2000). Performance on indirect measures of race evaluation predicts amygdala activation. *Journal of Cognitive Neuroscience, 12,* 729–738. .

Penfield, W. G., & Jasper, H. H. (1954).*Epilepsy and the functional anatomy of the human brain.* Boston: Little Brown.

Penfield, W. G., & Roberts, L. (1959). *Speech and brain mechanisms.* Princeton, NJ: Princeton University Press.

Peterson, S. E., Fox, P. T., Posner, M. I., Mintun, M., & Raichle, M. E. (1988). Positron emission tomographic studies of the cortical anatomy of single-word processing. *Nature, 331,* 585–589.

Petty, R. E., & Cacioppo, J. T. (1986). The elaboration likelihood model of persuasion. In L. Berkovitz (Ed.), *Advances in experimental social psychology* (Vol. 19, pp. 123–205). New York: Academic Press.

Plassmann, H. (2006). The influence of brand name decisions on decisions under ambiguity: First evidence from neuroeconomic research. Paper presented at the 2006 Association for Consumer Research Preconference, Orlando, FL.

Posner, M. I., & Raichle, M. E. (1994). *Images of mind.* New York: Scientific American Library.

Prelec, D., Knutson, B., Lowenstein, G., Rick, S., & Wimmer, G. E. (2006). Neural predictors of purchases. Paper presented at the 2006 Association for Consumer Research Preconference, Orlando, FL.

Rachlin, H. (2000). *The science of self-control.* Cambridge: Harvard University Press.

Raichle, M. E. (2001). Functional neuroimaging: A historical and physiological perspective. In R. Cabeza, & A. Kingstone (Eds.), *Handbook of functional neuroimaging of cognition* (pp. 3–27). Cambridge: The MIT Press.

Rilling, J. K., Gutman, D. A., Zeh, T. R., Pagnoni, G., Berns, G. S., Kitts, C. D. (2002). A neural basis for social cooperation. *Neuron, 35*, 395–405.

Rilling, J. K., Sanfey, A. G., Aronson, J. A., Nystrom, L. E., & Cohen, J. D. (2004). The neural correlates of theory of mind within interpersonal interactions. *NeuroImage, 22*, 1694–1703.

Rizzolatti G., & Craighero L. (2004).The mirror-neuron system. *Annual Review Neuroscience, 27*, 69–92.

Robinson, T. E., & Berridge, K. C. (1993). The neural basis for drug craving: an incentive-sensitization theory of addiction. *Brain Research Review, 18*, 247–291.

Rolls, E. T. (1999). *Brain and emotion.* Oxford: Oxford Univiversity Press.

Rubenstein, A. (1982). Perfect equilibrium in a bargaining model. *Econometrica, 50*, 97–110.

Sanfey, A. G. (2004). Neural computations of decision utility. *Trends in cognitive sciences, 8*, 519–521.

Sanfey, A. G., Loewenstein, G., McClure, S. M., & Cohen, J. D. (2006). Neuroeconomics: cross-currents in research on decision-making. *Trends in Cognitive Sciences, 10*, 108–116.

Sanfey, A. G., Rilling, J. K., Aronson, J. A., Nystrom, L. E., & Cohen, J. D. (2003). The neural basis of economic decision-making in the ultimatum game. *Science, 300*, 1755–1758.

Sarter, M., Berntson, G. G., & Cacioppo, J. T. (1996). Brain imaging and cognitive neuroscience: Toward strong inference in attributing function to structure. *American Psychologist, 51*, 13–21.

Saxe, R., & Kanwisher, N. (2003). People thinking about thinking people: The role of the temporo-parietal junction in theory of mind. *NeuroImage, 19*, 1835–1842.

Schultz, W. (2000). Multiple reward signals in the brain. *Nature Reviews Neuroscience, 1*, 199–207.

Shipp, S. (2004). The brain circuitry of attention. *Trends in Cognitive Sciences, 8*, 223–230.

Shiv, B., Lowenstein, G., Bechara, A., Damasio, H., & Damasio, A. (2006). Investment behavior and the negative side of emotion. Paper presented at the 2006 Association for Consumer Research Preconference, Orlando, FL.

Simon, H. A. (1982). *Models of bounded rationality.* Cambridge: The MIT Press.

Small, S. L., & Nusbaum, H. C. (2004). On the neurobiological investigation of language understanding in context. *Brain and Language, 89*, 300–311.

Smith, E. E., & Jonides, J. (1998). Neuroimaging analyses of human working memory. *Proceedings of the National Academy of Sciences, 95*, 12061–12068.

Sternberg, S. (1969). The discovery of processing stages: extensions of Donders' method. *Acta Psychologica, 30*, 276–315.

Talairach, J., & Tournoux, P. (1988). *Co-planar Stereotaxic Atlas of the Human Brain: 3-Dimensional Proportional System — An Approach to Cerebral Imaging.* New York: Thieme Medical Publishers.

Thaler, R. (1988). Anomalies: The ultimatum game. *The Journal of Economic Perspectives, 2*, 195–206.

Thompson, J. C., Clarke, M., Stewart T., & Puce, A. (2005). Configural processing of biological motion in human superior temporal sulcus. *Journal of Neuroscience, 25*, 9059–9066.

Tobler, P. N., Fiorillo, C. D. & Schultz, W. (2005). Adaptive coding of reward value by dopamine neurons. *Science, 307*, 1642–1645.

Treisman, A., & Souther, J. (1985). Search asymmetry: A diagnostic for preattentive processing of separable features. *Journal of Experimental Psychology: General, 114*, 285–310.

Tversky, A., & Kahneman, D. (1974). Judgment under uncertainty: heuristics and biases. *Science, 185*, 453–458.

Tversky, A., & Kahneman, D. (1981). The framing of decisions and the psychology of choice. *Science, 211*, 1124–1131.

Uttal, W. R. (2001). *The new phrenology: The limits of localizing cognitive processes in the brain.* Cambridge: The MIT Press.

Volkow, N. D., Wang, G. J., Fowler, J. S., Logan, J., Gatley, S. J., Wong, C., et al. (1999). Reinforcing ffects of psychostimulants in humans are associated with increases in brain dopamine and occupancy of D2 receptors. *Journal of Pharmacology and Experimental Therapeutics, 291*, 409–415.

von Bonin, G., & Bailey, P. (1925). *The neocortex of Macaca Mulatta.* Urbana: The University of Illinois Press.

Wager, T. D., Hernandez, L., Jonides, J., & Lindquist, M. (2007). Elements of functional neuroimaging. In J. T. Cacioppo, L. G. Tassinary, & Berntson (Eds.), *Handbook of Psychophysiology* (pp. 19–56). New York Cambridge University Press.

Waterman, D. A., & Newell, A. (1971). Protocol analysis as a task for artificial intelligence. *Artificial Intelligence, 2*, 285–318.

Watts, W.A., & Holt, L.E. (1970). Logical relationships among beliefs and timing as factors in persuasion. *Journal of Personality and Social Psychology, 16*, 571–582.

Williams, G. V., & Goldman-Rakic, P. S. (1995). Modulation of memory fields by dopamine D1 receptors in prefrontal cortex. *Nature, 376*, 572–575.

Wise, P. M. (1982). Norepinephrine and dopamine activity in microdissected brain areas of the middle-aged and young rat on proestrus. *Biology of Reproduction, 27*, 562–574.

Wise, R. A. & Hoffman, D. C. (1992). Localization of drug reward mechanisms by intracranial injections. *Synapse, 10*, 247–263.

Withers, G. S., & Greenough, W. T. (1989). Reach training selectively alters dendritic branching in subpopulations of layer II-III pyramids in rat motor-somatosensory forelimb cortex. *Neuropsychologia, 27*, 61–69.

Wyer, R. S., & Goldberg, L. (1970). A probabilistic analysis of relationships among beliefs and attitudes. *Psychological Review, 77*, 100–120.

Yoon, C., Gutchess, A. H., Feinberg, F., & Polk, T. (2006). A functional magnetic resonance imaging study of neural dissociations between brand and person judgments. *Journal of Consumer Research, 33*, 31–40.

Zago, L., Pesenti, M., Mellet, E., Crivello, F., Mazoyer, B. & Tzouri-Mazoyer, N. (2001). *NeuroImage, 13*, 314–327.

Zhang, S., Kindlmann, G., & Laidlaw, D. (2004). Diffusion tensor MRI visualization. In C. D. Hansen & C. R. Johnson (Eds.), *The visualization handbook* (pp. 327–341). New York: Elsevier.

Zink, C. F., Pagnoni, G., Martin-Skurski, M. E., Chappelow, J. C., & Berns, G. S. (2004). Human striatal responses to monetary reward depend on saliency. *Neuron, 42*, 509–517.

Author Index

Subject Index